EMPLOYMENT, HOURS, AND EARNINGS

STATES AND AREAS

Third Edition
2008

Edited by Mary Meghan Ryan

Bernan Press

Published in the United States of America
by Bernan Press, a wholly owned subsidary of
The Rowman & Littlefield Publishing Group, Inc.
4501 Forbes Boulevard, Suite 200
Lanham, Maryland 20706

Bernan Press
800-865-3457
info@bernan.com
www.bernan.com

ISBN-13: 978-1-59888-267-4
ISBN-10: 1-59888-267-8
eISBN-13: 978-1-59888-289-6
eISBN-10: 1-59888-289-9

⊗™ The paper used in this publication meets the minimum requirements of American National
Standard for Information Sciences—Permanence of Paper for Printed Library Materials, ANSI/NISO
Z39.48-1992.
Manufactured in the United States of America.

CONTENTS

PART A: STATE DATA—*Continued*

PART B: METROPOLITAN STATISTICAL AREA (MSA) DATA

PART B: METROPOLITAN STATISTICAL AREA DATA—*Continued*

PREFACE

Bernan Press is proud to present the third edition of *Employment, Hours, and Earnings: States and Areas, 2008*. This reference is a special edition of Bernan Press's *Handbook of U.S. Labor Statistics: Employment, Earnings, Prices, Productivity, and Other Labor Data*. It brings together a wealth of employment data compiled by the Bureau of Labor Statistics (BLS) and includes new types of data not presented in the previous editions.

Features of this publication include:

- Nearly 300 tables with data on employment for each state, the District of Columbia, and the nation's 100 largest metropolitan statistical areas (MSAs), which is double the amount that appeared in the second edition

- Detailed industry data organized by month and on a non-seasonally adjusted basis

- Hours and earnings data are provided, where available, by industry for each state

- An introduction page for each state and the District of Columbia that emphasizes salient data and note-worthy trends, including data from the Local Area Unemployment Statistics (LAUS) program as well as an updated figure detailing employment by industry

- Concise technical notes that explain pertinent facts about the data, including sources, definitions, and significant changes; this section also provides references for further guidance on the subject

- An appendix that details the geographical components of the MSAs

The employment, hours, and earnings data in this publication provide a detailed and timely picture of the 50 states, the District of Columbia, and the nation's largest MSAs.

They can be used to analyze key factors affecting state and local economies and to compare national cyclical trends to local-level economic activity.

This reference is an excellent source of information for analysts in both the public and private sectors. Readers who are involved in public policy can use the data to determine the health of the economy, to clearly identify which sectors are growing and which are declining, and to determine the need for federal assistance. State and local jurisdictions can use the data to determine the need for services, including training and unemployment assistance, and for planning and budgetary purposes. In private industry, the data can be used by business owners to compare their company to the economy as a whole. In addition, the data can be used to identify suitable locations when making decisions about plant locations and wholesale and retail trade outlets and for locating a particular sector base.

Mary Meghan Ryan, a research editor with Bernan Press, edited this edition. She received her bachelor's degree in economics from the University of Maryland and is a former economist with the American Economics Group. Additionally, Ms. Ryan has worked as a research assistant for FRANDATA. She has also served as the associate editor of the *Handbook of U.S. Handbook of Labor Statistics: Employment, Earnings, Prices, Productivity, and Other Labor Data*; *Business Statistics of the United States: Patterns of Economic Change*; *The Almanac of American Education*; *United States Foreign Trade Highlights: Trends in the Global Market* and *Vital Statistics of the United States: Births, Life Expectancy, Deaths, and Selected Health Data*; all published by Bernan Press.

As always, special thanks are due to the many federal agency personnel who assisted the editor in obtaining the data, provided excellent resource on their Web sites, and patiently answered questions.

TECHNICAL NOTES

OVERVIEW

This publication presents monthly and annual average data on employment for each state, the District of Columbia, and the nation's 100 largest metropolitan statistical areas (MSAs). In addition, hours and earnings data are provided, where available, for each state. The industry data is based on the North American Industry Classification System (NAICS), which is discussed in greater detail later in these notes. The employment data are presented on a monthly and annual basis from 2000 to 2007, while the hours and earnings data are only available from 2001.

The Bureau of Labor Statistics (BLS), the statistical agency within the U.S. Department of Labor, conducts the Current Employment Statistics (CES) survey to provide national, state, and local nonfarm employment data by industry and hours and earnings data for nonfarm workers in the private sector. The unemployment data, as well as the estimates for the civilian labor force and the employment-population ratio on each state introduction page are from the Local Area Unemployment Statistics (LAUS) Program, which provides monthly employment and unemployment data for approximately 7,200 geographic areas.

The data from both the CES and LAUS data are derived from federal-state cooperative collection efforts in which state employment security agencies prepare data using concepts, definitions, and technical procedures prescribed by the BLS. Although the estimation of the two data sets are based on differing methodologies (described in more detail later in this section), their inclusion together in this reference is intended to provide a broad overview of state and local labor market conditions.

THE CURRENT EMPLOYMENT STATISTICS (CES) SURVEY–EMPLOYMENT, HOURS, AND EARNINGS DATA

The CES survey is commonly referred to as the establishment or payroll survey. Its estimates are derived from a sample of about 150,000 private nonfarm businesses (such as factories, offices, and stores) and federal, state, and local government entities, which cover approximately 390,000 individual worksites in all 50 states, the District of Columbia, Puerto Rico, the U.S. Virgin Islands, and more than 300 metropolitan areas and divisions. These establishments are classified on the basis of their primary activity by major industry groupings in accordance with NAICS. For an establishment engaging in more than one activity, the entire establishment is included under the industry indicated as the principal activity.

All establishments with 1,000 employees or more are asked to participate in the survey, along with a representative sample of smaller businesses. Every month, the BLS Regional Data Collection Centers gathers the data. Each firm is initially enrolled by telephone and the data is then collected for several months by Computer Assisted Telephone Interviewing (CATI). Whenever possible, respondents are transferred to a self-reporting mode such as Touchtone Data Entry (TDE), fax, or Internet collection. Gathering data via the Internet is one of the fastest growing forms of data collection but still remains a relatively small percentage of the total data collected each month. Electronic Data Interchange (EDI), in which each firm provides the BLS with an electronic file in a prescribed format, remains the most popular method of collecting the data.

State estimation procedures are designed to produce accurate data for each individual state. The BLS independently develops the national series and does not force state estimates to sum to the national total. Because each state series is subject to larger sampling and nonsampling errors than the national series, summing them cumulates individual state level errors and can cause significant distortions at an aggregate level. As a result of these statistical limitations, the BLS does not compile a "sum of states" employment series, and cautions users that doing so may result in a series with a relatively large and volatile error structure.

More information on the exact methodology used to obtain data for employment, hours, and earnings was originally detailed in the *BLS Handbook of Methods*. The *Handbook* was updated in 2004 and can be found online at <http://www.bls.gov/opub/hom>. Information on the CES survey can also be found on the BLS Web site at <http://www.bls.gov/sae>.

CONCEPTS

Industries

Nonfarm employment includes employment in all goods-producing and service-providing industries. The goods-producing sector includes natural resources and mining, construction, and manufacturing, the last of which is made up of durable and non-durable goods (these breakdowns are not provided in this publication). The service-providing sector includes both private service-providing and government employment. Private service-sector employment includes trade, transportation, and utilities, which is comprised of wholesale trade, retail trade, and transportation and utilities; information; financial activities; professional and business services; educational and health services; leisure and hospitality; and other services. Government employment encompasses federal-, state-, and local-level civilian employees. Subcategories of these industries are available on the BLS Web site at <http://www.bls.gov/sae>.

Employment

Employment is the total number of persons employed either full or part-time in nonfarm business establishments during a specific payroll period. Temporary employees are included. Unpaid family members working in a family-owned business, domestic workers in private homes, and self-employed persons are all excluded from the CES. In addition, employees on layoff, on leave without pay, on strike for the entire pay period, or who had been hired but did not start work during the pay period are also excluded.

The reference period includes all persons who worked during, or received pay, for any part of the pay period that includes the 12th of the month, a standard for all federal agencies collecting employment data from business establishments. Workers who are on paid sick leave (when pay is received directly from the employer) or paid holiday or vacation, or who worked during only part of the specified pay period (because of unemployment or strike during the rest of the pay period) are counted as employed by the establishment survey. Employees on the payroll of more than one establishment during the pay period are counted in each establishment that reports them, whether the duplication is due to turnover or dual jobholding.

CES government employment statistics refer only to civilian government employees. Employees of the Central Intelligence Agency, the National Security Agency, the National Imagery and Mapping Agency, and the Defense Intelligence Agency are excluded.

Hours and Earnings

The hours and earnings data series for states are based on reports from industry payrolls and the corresponding hours paid for construction workers, production workers, and nonsupervisory workers. It includes workers who received pay for any part of the pay period that includes the 12th day of the month. Since not all sample respondents report production worker hours and earnings data, insufficient sample sizes preclude hours and earnings data from many sectors in many states. Therefore, the data available and thus published vary from state to state.

The payroll for these workers is reported *before deductions of any kind* including Social Security, unemployment insurance, group health insurance, withholding taxes, retirement plans, or union dues.

Included in the payroll report of earnings is pay for all hours worked, including overtime, shift premiums, vacations, holiday, and sick-leave pay. Bonuses and commissions excluded unless they are earned and paid regularly each pay period. Benefits, such as health insurance and contribution to a retirement fund are also excluded.

Hours include all hours worked (including overtime hours) and hours paid for holidays, vacations, and sick leave during the pay period that includes the 12th of the month. Average weekly hours differs from the concept of scheduled hours worked due to factors such as unpaid absenteeism, labor turnover, part-time work, and strikes, as well as fluctuations in work schedules. Average weekly hours are typically lower than scheduled hours of work.

Average hourly earnings are derived by dividing gross payrolls by total hours, reflecting the actual earnings of workers (including premium pay). They differ from wage rates, which are the amounts stipulated for a given unit of work or time. Average hourly earnings do not represent total labor costs per hour because they exclude retroac-

tive payments and irregular bonuses, employee benefits, and the employer's share of payroll taxes. Earnings for employees not included in the production worker or non-supervisory categories are not reflected in the estimates in this publication.

Average weekly earnings are derived by multiplying average weekly hours by average hourly earnings.

Users should note that in the context of historical data, long-term trends in hours and earnings data also reflect structural changes, such as the changing mixes of full-time and part-time employees and highly paid and lower-wage workers within businesses and across industries.

In March 2008, beginning with the release of the January 2008 data, the BLS discontinued the publication of all metropolitan hours and earnings data. In addition, it eliminated the employment data for 65 small metropolitan areas. This is result of a reduction in funding to the BLS from the 2008 Consolidated Appropriations Act enacted on December 26, 2007. More information on this can be found on the BLS Web site at <http://www.bls.gov/bls/budgetimpact.htm>.

Metropolitan Statistical Areas (MSAs) and New England City and Town Areas (NECTAs)

A metropolitan statistical area (MSA) is a core area with a large population nucleus, combined with adjacent communities that have high degrees of economic and social integration with the core area. The standard definition of a MSA is determined by the Office of Management and Budget (OMB), which updates the definition based on the decennial census and updated information provided by the Census Bureau between the censuses.

New England city and town areas (NECTAs) are similar to MSAs, but are defined using cities and towns instead of counties in the six New England states. The NECTAs included in this publication are Boston-Cambridge-Quincy, MA-NH; Providence-Fall River-Warwick, RI-MA; Hartford-West Hartford-East Hartford, CT; Bridgeport-Stamford-Norwalk-CT; Springfield, MA-CT; New Haven, CT; and Worcester, MA-CT. All other areas are MSAs.

The appendix that follows the tables detail the geographic components for each MSA and NECTA.

REVISIONS TO THE DATA

North American Industry Classification System (NAICS)

The most far-reaching revision of the CES data occurred when the industrial classification system was changed from the 60-year-old Standard Industrial Classification (SIC) system to the North American Industry Classification System (NAICS) in January 2003. This changed how establishments were classified into industries in order to more accurately reflect the current composition of U.S. businesses. In March 2008, the CES state and area non-farm payroll series was converted to the 2007 NAICS series. This resulted in relatively minor changes. NAICS was adopted as the standard measure of industry classification by statistical agencies in the United States, Canada, and Mexico in order to enhance the comparability of economic data across the North American Free Trade Association (NAFTA) trade area. The revisions in 2003 were so profound as to preclude comparison between the present NAICS and the old SIC. The BLS has thus not updated the SIC data nor (for the most part) linked the historical SIC data with the current NAICS data. The employment data in this edition begin with 2000 and are fully consistent for all subsequent years. Data from 1990 to 2003 are available in the first edition and data from 1995 to 2006 are available in the second edition of *Employment, Hours and Earnings: States and Areas.*

Benchmark Revisions

Employment estimates are adjusted annually to a complete count of jobs—called benchmarks—which are primarily derived from tax reports submitted by employers covered by state unemployment laws (which cover most establishments). In this re-anchoring of sample-based employment estimates to full population counts, the original sample-based estimates are replaced with the benchmark data from the previous year. The benchmark information is used to adjust monthly estimates between the new benchmark and the preceding benchmark, thereby preserving the continuity of the series and establishing the level of employment for the new benchmark month.

Seasonal Adjustment

Over the course of a year, the size of a state's employment level undergoes sharp fluctuations because of changes in the weather, reduced or expanded production, harvests, major holidays, and the like. Because these seasonal events follow a more or less regular pattern each year, adjusting the data on a month-to-month basis may eliminate their influence on data trends. These adjustments make it easier for users to observe the cyclical and other nonseasonal movements in the data series, but it must be noted that the seasonally adjusted series are only an approximation based on past experience. The seasonally adjusted data have a broader margin of error than the unadjusted data because they are subject to both sampling and other errors

and the seasonal adjustment process. The data presented in this publication are not seasonally adjusted; therefore, the month-to-month variations in the data contain seasonal variations that may distort month-to-month comparisons. Data for MSAs are also not seasonally adjusted, as the sample sizes do not allow for reliable estimates for seasonal adjustment factors.

THE LOCAL AREA UNEMPLOYMENT STATISTICS (LAUS) PROGRAM

The Local Area Unemployment Statistics (LAUS) program provides monthly and annual estimates for unemployment rates as well as labor force, employment, and unemployment totals for the states and many local areas. As mentioned previously, the unemployment data as well as the civilian labor force estimates and the employment-population ratio are from the LAUS program. The unemployment rate is shown for each state in 2000 and 2007 along with the rank for each state. The states are ranked by unemployment in ascending order. Unemployment data are not available by industry.

The concepts and definitions underlying the LAUS program come from the Current Population Survey (CPS), the household survey conducted by the Census Bureau for the BLS. The LAUS models combine current and historical data from the CPS, the CES, and the State Unemployment Insurance (UI) Systems. There are numerous conceptual and technical differences between the household and establishment surveys, and estimates of monthly employment changes from these two surveys usually do not match in size or even direction. As a result, the unemployment data along with the civilian labor force estimates and the employment-population ratios on each state header page presented in this edition are not directly comparable to the employment data. However, this publication includes this information to provide complementary information on labor market conditions in each state and the District of Columbia. Monthly and annual data are available from the BLS on their Web site at <http://www.bls.gov/lau/>. A full description of the differences between the different surveys, as well as guidance on the complex methods used to obtain the LAUS data, is provided by the BLS online at <http://www.bls.gov/lau/laufaq.htm>.

PART A

STATE DATA

Population
    2000 census: 4,447,100
    2007 estimate: 4,627,851
    Percent change, 2000–2007: 4.1%

Percent change in total nonfarm employment, 2000–2007: 3.9%

Industry with the largest growth in employment, 2000–2007 (thousands)
    Professional and business services, 35.3

Industry with the largest decline in employment, 2000–2007 (thousands)
    Manufacturing, -54.7

Civilian labor force
    2000: 2,154,545
    2007: 2,182,779

Employment-population ratio
    2000: 61.2%
    2007: 59.2%

Unemployment rate and rank among states
    2000: 4.1%, 32nd
    2007: 3.5%, 11th

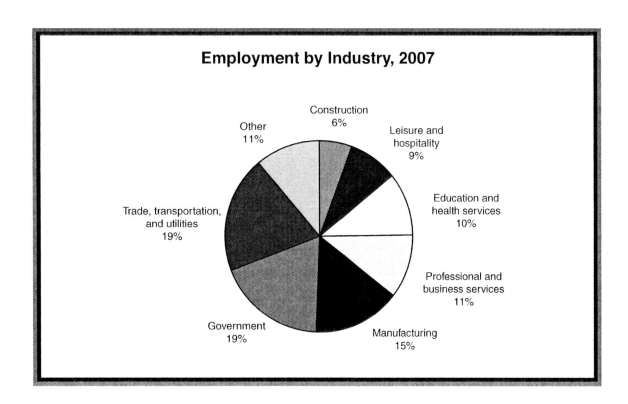

Employment by Industry, 2007

Construction 6%
Other 11%
Leisure and hospitality 9%
Trade, transportation, and utilities 19%
Education and health services 10%
Professional and business services 11%
Government 19%
Manufacturing 15%

Employment by Industry: Alabama, 2000–2007

(Numbers in thousands, not seasonally adjusted.)

Industry and year	January	February	March	April	May	June	July	August	September	October	November	December	Annual Average
Total Nonfarm													
2000	1,903.3	1,910.4	1,929.1	1,931.3	1,945.0	1,941.0	1,922.4	1,928.7	1,941.2	1,936.3	1,941.9	1,943.7	1,931.2
2001	1,894.4	1,903.9	1,914.8	1,919.6	1,921.2	1,918.6	1,897.5	1,905.2	1,910.2	1,903.5	1,908.1	1,907.9	1,908.7
2002	1,859.7	1,868.4	1,882.6	1,888.3	1,891.6	1,886.1	1,872.4	1,879.8	1,888.3	1,889.9	1,897.0	1,894.8	1,883.2
2003	1,857.0	1,864.0	1,875.0	1,879.1	1,882.2	1,875.8	1,862.1	1,869.3	1,877.1	1,883.7	1,889.6	1,891.8	1,875.5
2004	1,862.6	1,872.4	1,886.5	1,899.3	1,903.8	1,908.8	1,900.9	1,903.9	1,908.4	1,915.6	1,926.2	1,932.4	1,901.7
2005	1,899.8	1,910.5	1,925.1	1,943.1	1,948.2	1,951.4	1,939.6	1,947.9	1,958.2	1,961.9	1,974.2	1,979.2	1,944.9
2006	1,944.9	1,956.1	1,974.5	1,978.5	1,984.2	1,994.6	1,972.0	1,981.0	1,990.4	1,984.2	1,994.6	2,000.1	1,979.6
2007	1,974.9	1,987.3	2,004.4	2,002.8	2,010.6	2,019.8	1,996.3	2,005.0	2,013.6	2,014.2	2,023.2	2,025.1	2,006.4
Total Private													
2000	1,551.7	1,556.0	1,570.8	1,574.7	1,580.3	1,592.6	1,583.9	1,592.0	1,590.8	1,583.0	1,588.0	1,589.8	1,579.5
2001	1,542.9	1,548.5	1,559.6	1,564.4	1,566.0	1,570.1	1,557.7	1,563.8	1,557.7	1,547.8	1,551.5	1,551.3	1,556.8
2002	1,507.2	1,512.5	1,526.0	1,530.0	1,534.1	1,534.8	1,531.1	1,537.2	1,532.0	1,529.7	1,535.4	1,533.4	1,528.6
2003	1,498.7	1,502.0	1,512.1	1,515.7	1,518.9	1,521.4	1,517.7	1,522.9	1,517.7	1,521.1	1,526.5	1,530.3	1,517.0
2004	1,503.9	1,510.7	1,524.6	1,536.5	1,541.9	1,550.0	1,552.1	1,553.3	1,548.4	1,553.9	1,563.1	1,569.2	1,542.3
2005	1,539.7	1,547.5	1,561.6	1,578.3	1,582.7	1,587.2	1,587.2	1,592.8	1,595.3	1,594.5	1,606.1	1,611.4	1,582.0
2006	1,578.2	1,587.1	1,603.9	1,606.4	1,611.2	1,622.4	1,612.0	1,618.4	1,618.8	1,610.3	1,619.8	1,624.8	1,609.4
2007	1,600.7	1,610.7	1,626.5	1,624.2	1,631.1	1,640.5	1,632.1	1,637.1	1,636.4	1,634.4	1,641.9	1,644.8	1,630.0
Goods-Producing													
2000	469.5	469.5	472.3	472.2	472.5	476.7	471.9	475.0	473.3	467.6	465.7	464.6	470.9
2001	448.8	448.8	451.4	450.3	449.4	447.6	441.8	443.9	443.0	436.6	434.4	431.7	444.0
2002	420.1	419.9	422.5	422.3	423.5	422.2	418.9	421.9	421.4	420.1	418.3	415.7	420.6
2003	408.4	408.2	409.7	407.8	407.6	406.4	402.6	404.7	404.1	405.6	403.9	404.3	406.1
2004	398.3	400.1	402.7	404.5	405.9	407.0	409.0	408.3	409.2	412.1	412.1	412.4	406.8
2005	405.6	406.8	411.0	416.8	417.5	417.5	418.0	419.6	421.3	422.2	424.6	425.4	417.2
2006	421.6	423.7	427.6	427.9	428.0	430.5	427.7	427.2	426.6	423.3	422.3	422.6	425.8
2007	420.1	421.6	423.9	421.5	422.0	424.6	422.6	422.2	423.8	422.5	422.0	421.5	422.4
Natural Resources and Mining													
2000	14.6	14.4	14.4	13.8	13.7	13.8	13.7	13.7	13.7	13.7	13.7	13.6	13.9
2001	13.4	13.5	13.5	13.6	13.5	13.5	13.5	13.5	13.5	13.4	13.3	13.3	13.5
2002	13.2	13.1	13.2	13.0	13.0	13.0	12.9	13.0	12.9	12.6	12.5	12.5	12.9
2003	12.5	12.4	12.5	12.5	12.5	12.5	12.4	12.5	12.6	12.5	12.5	12.5	12.4
2004	12.2	12.2	12.2	12.2	12.3	12.4	12.4	12.5	12.6	12.7	12.6	12.7	12.4
2005	12.7	12.7	12.7	12.8	13.0	13.0	13.1	13.0	13.2	13.0	13.1	13.1	13.0
2006	13.0	13.1	13.1	13.0	13.0	13.2	13.1	13.1	13.2	12.9	13.0	13.1	13.1
2007	12.9	13.0	13.1	12.8	12.9	12.9	12.8	12.9	12.8	12.7	12.8	12.8	12.9
Construction													
2000	101.1	101.7	103.6	104.6	105.0	106.8	107.3	108.3	109.4	107.2	106.6	105.9	105.6
2001	101.6	102.7	104.8	106.6	107.7	107.9	106.3	106.2	105.8	104.7	104.4	102.1	105.1
2002	96.8	98.3	100.5	99.7	100.9	100.0	100.3	101.4	102.1	102.7	101.1	99.2	100.3
2003	97.3	97.6	99.3	98.4	98.8	98.9	99.0	100.1	100.7	103.2	102.4	101.7	99.7
2004	99.6	101.2	103.0	102.4	102.6	102.6	104.1	103.1	103.2	104.9	104.0	103.3	102.8
2005	100.6	101.6	104.2	106.2	105.4	105.2	105.2	106.2	107.0	108.6	108.6	107.5	105.5
2006	105.1	106.2	109.5	110.2	110.2	111.1	110.4	111.0	111.7	111.1	111.0	110.2	109.8
2007	109.4	110.7	113.2	112.1	112.6	113.4	112.5	112.7	114.5	114.6	114.2	113.7	112.8
Manufacturing													
2000	353.8	353.4	354.3	353.8	353.8	356.1	350.9	353.0	350.2	346.7	345.4	345.1	351.4
2001	333.8	332.6	333.1	330.1	328.2	326.2	322.0	324.2	323.7	318.5	316.7	316.3	325.5
2002	310.1	308.5	308.8	309.6	309.6	309.2	305.7	307.5	306.4	304.8	304.7	304.0	307.4
2003	298.6	298.2	297.9	296.9	296.3	295.0	291.2	292.1	290.8	289.9	289.0	290.1	293.8
2004	286.5	286.7	287.5	289.9	291.0	292.0	292.5	292.7	293.4	294.5	295.5	296.4	291.6
2005	292.3	292.5	294.1	297.8	299.1	299.3	299.7	300.4	301.1	300.6	302.9	304.8	298.7
2006	303.5	304.4	305.0	304.7	304.8	306.2	304.2	303.1	301.7	299.3	298.3	299.3	302.9
2007	297.8	297.9	297.6	296.6	296.5	298.3	297.3	296.6	296.5	295.2	295.0	295.0	296.7
Service-Providing													
2000	1,433.8	1,440.9	1,456.8	1,459.1	1,472.5	1,464.3	1,450.5	1,453.7	1,467.9	1,468.7	1,476.2	1,479.1	1,460.3
2001	1,445.6	1,455.1	1,463.4	1,469.3	1,471.8	1,471.0	1,455.7	1,461.3	1,467.2	1,466.9	1,473.7	1,476.2	1,464.8
2002	1,439.6	1,448.5	1,460.1	1,466.0	1,468.1	1,463.9	1,453.5	1,457.9	1,466.9	1,469.8	1,478.7	1,479.1	1,462.7
2003	1,448.6	1,455.8	1,465.3	1,471.3	1,474.6	1,469.4	1,459.5	1,464.6	1,473.0	1,478.1	1,485.7	1,487.5	1,469.4
2004	1,464.3	1,472.3	1,483.8	1,494.8	1,497.9	1,501.8	1,491.9	1,495.6	1,499.2	1,503.5	1,514.1	1,520.0	1,494.9
2005	1,494.2	1,503.7	1,514.1	1,526.3	1,530.7	1,533.9	1,521.6	1,528.3	1,536.9	1,539.7	1,549.6	1,553.8	1,527.7
2006	1,523.3	1,532.4	1,546.9	1,550.6	1,556.2	1,564.1	1,544.3	1,553.8	1,563.8	1,560.9	1,572.3	1,577.5	1,553.8
2007	1,554.8	1,565.7	1,580.5	1,581.3	1,588.6	1,595.2	1,573.7	1,582.8	1,589.8	1,591.7	1,601.2	1,603.6	1,584.1
Trade, Transportation, and Utilities													
2000	381.6	379.9	382.0	380.9	384.4	386.4	383.4	384.5	385.2	386.4	393.0	396.6	385.4
2001	379.9	377.7	379.9	379.4	380.8	382.3	378.5	379.0	377.3	378.3	384.8	387.6	380.5
2002	371.1	369.3	372.0	370.1	371.0	370.5	371.0	370.0	368.6	370.2	377.0	380.9	371.8
2003	366.0	364.2	367.1	368.1	369.2	370.7	372.2	372.9	371.9	374.4	379.5	383.5	371.6
2004	371.3	370.8	374.5	375.0	375.9	377.0	376.4	376.0	374.4	377.3	384.1	389.6	376.9
2005	376.6	376.0	378.3	380.5	381.6	382.9	382.4	382.8	382.5	383.3	391.2	396.3	382.9
2006	382.6	381.5	385.4	384.1	385.2	387.4	386.3	387.3	388.1	388.9	396.8	401.7	387.9
2007	387.8	387.5	391.8	391.4	394.8	397.1	396.1	395.8	396.3	397.6	403.8	407.9	395.7
Wholesale Trade													
2000	83.4	83.6	84.1	83.6	84.1	84.5	84.3	84.6	84.6	84.7	84.9	85.1	84.3
2001	84.1	84.4	84.2	84.0	83.9	83.8	83.3	83.2	82.8	82.4	81.8	81.7	83.3
2002	79.9	79.5	79.5	78.7	78.6	78.6	78.5	78.5	78.4	78.0	78.2	78.4	78.7
2003	76.8	76.8	77.0	76.6	77.1	77.2	77.3	77.3	77.4	77.9	77.9	78.1	77.3
2004	76.9	77.0	77.6	78.1	78.3	78.6	78.7	78.7	78.5	79.0	78.8	79.1	78.3
2005	78.1	78.4	78.8	79.3	79.3	79.5	79.8	79.7	80.0	79.9	80.0	80.5	79.4
2006	79.9	80.3	81.0	81.0	81.5	81.9	81.9	82.0	82.1	81.9	82.1	82.5	81.5
2007	81.3	81.6	82.1	82.1	82.4	83.2	82.5	82.4	82.9	83.2	83.3	83.7	82.6

Employment by Industry: Alabama, 2000–2007—*Continued*

(Numbers in thousands, not seasonally adjusted.)

Industry and year	January	February	March	April	May	June	July	August	September	October	November	December	Annual Average
Retail Trade													
2000	231.1	229.0	230.6	230.4	232.6	233.8	231.2	231.9	232.9	234.0	240.3	243.8	233.5
2001	229.2	226.0	227.9	227.4	228.6	229.7	227.0	227.4	226.5	228.1	235.5	238.2	229.3
2002	226.4	225.0	227.3	225.5	225.8	225.2	225.3	224.1	223.0	225.3	231.9	235.7	226.7
2003	223.5	222.2	224.8	226.6	226.6	227.7	228.7	229.6	228.7	230.7	236.0	239.7	228.7
2004	229.5	228.8	231.0	231.2	231.5	231.8	231.1	230.7	229.6	231.9	238.7	243.4	232.4
2005	232.7	231.5	233.1	234.3	234.9	235.4	234.6	235.2	234.3	234.7	242.4	246.3	235.8
2006	234.2	232.7	235.2	233.6	233.9	234.9	234.0	234.6	234.9	236.2	243.5	247.1	236.2
2007	236.4	235.7	238.9	238.8	241.1	242.1	242.1	241.9	241.8	242.6	248.5	251.7	241.8
Transportation and Utilities													
2000	67.1	67.3	67.3	66.9	67.7	68.1	67.9	68.0	67.7	67.7	67.8	67.7	67.6
2001	66.6	67.3	67.8	68.0	68.3	68.8	68.2	68.4	68.0	67.8	67.5	67.7	67.9
2002	64.8	64.8	65.2	65.9	66.6	66.7	67.2	67.4	67.2	66.9	66.9	66.8	66.4
2003	65.7	65.2	65.3	64.9	65.5	65.8	66.2	66.0	65.8	65.8	65.6	65.7	65.6
2004	64.9	65.0	65.9	65.7	66.1	66.6	66.6	66.6	66.3	66.4	66.6	67.1	66.2
2005	65.8	66.1	66.4	66.9	67.4	68.0	68.0	67.9	68.2	68.7	68.8	69.5	67.6
2006	68.5	68.5	69.2	69.5	69.8	70.6	70.4	70.7	71.1	70.8	71.2	72.1	70.2
2007	70.1	70.2	70.8	70.5	71.3	71.8	71.5	71.5	71.6	71.8	72.0	72.5	71.3
Information													
2000	32.4	32.5	33.0	32.9	33.2	33.7	34.2	34.5	34.4	34.6	34.8	35.2	33.8
2001	35.0	34.9	35.0	34.5	34.6	34.5	34.0	33.8	33.3	33.1	33.2	33.2	34.1
2002	32.9	32.6	32.8	32.5	32.4	32.4	32.3	31.9	31.4	31.4	31.4	31.3	32.1
2003	30.7	30.8	30.8	29.8	29.9	30.0	30.0	29.7	29.3	29.5	29.8	29.9	30.0
2004	29.5	29.4	29.5	29.6	29.6	29.7	29.7	29.5	29.3	29.3	29.5	29.6	29.5
2005	29.3	29.3	29.3	29.4	29.3	29.3	29.3	29.3	29.0	28.9	29.0	29.1	29.2
2006	28.7	28.7	28.8	28.7	28.8	28.8	28.5	28.4	28.2	28.1	28.2	28.3	28.5
2007	27.9	28.1	28.2	28.3	28.5	28.5	28.2	28.1	27.9	28.3	28.6	28.8	28.3
Financial Activities													
2000	97.3	97.3	98.0	98.5	98.7	99.3	100.0	100.0	99.4	99.4	99.4	99.8	98.9
2001	96.9	97.0	97.4	97.9	98.3	99.0	99.0	98.9	98.3	97.7	97.5	98.0	98.0
2002	96.8	96.4	96.7	97.3	97.6	97.8	97.9	97.8	97.0	97.0	96.8	97.2	97.2
2003	95.9	95.5	95.7	96.0	96.2	96.8	97.3	97.2	96.4	96.3	96.4	96.7	96.3
2004	95.6	95.9	96.2	96.5	96.8	97.7	97.7	97.8	97.2	97.7	97.7	97.9	97.1
2005	96.2	96.8	97.3	97.6	97.6	98.2	98.4	98.1	98.5	101.2	99.9	100.1	98.3
2006	97.1	98.3	98.5	98.4	98.8	99.4	99.1	99.1	98.9	98.8	99.1	99.7	98.8
2007	99.0	99.1	99.7	99.7	99.7	100.7	100.7	100.4	100.5	100.7	100.6	101.0	100.2
Professional and Business Services													
2000	177.9	180.0	183.0	184.9	183.6	186.2	185.6	188.2	189.2	188.5	187.9	187.2	185.2
2001	183.2	185.3	187.7	187.7	186.6	188.3	187.5	190.0	189.0	187.4	185.4	184.8	186.9
2002	178.9	180.6	184.6	185.9	185.6	187.2	187.5	190.6	189.8	190.1	189.1	187.7	186.5
2003	184.1	185.8	187.4	188.2	188.2	188.7	187.9	189.5	189.3	189.5	190.3	190.3	188.3
2004	188.9	190.2	192.7	196.5	197.6	200.0	201.0	202.5	201.3	202.1	201.4	202.4	198.1
2005	200.1	202.9	204.2	206.8	206.3	207.8	209.7	212.0	213.5	214.7	215.4	214.9	209.0
2006	208.8	211.4	213.5	213.7	213.7	216.7	214.2	217.1	217.8	216.7	217.0	217.1	214.8
2007	215.4	218.1	221.1	219.8	219.8	221.2	219.0	222.0	221.9	222.4	222.8	222.7	220.5
Education and Health Services													
2000	172.1	173.4	174.1	175.1	175.0	175.0	175.3	175.9	177.4	177.3	178.6	178.1	175.6
2001	171.8	174.8	174.9	176.9	176.3	175.8	175.9	176.8	179.1	179.8	182.5	182.4	177.3
2002	177.1	180.9	181.2	183.2	182.5	182.2	181.0	182.7	185.0	185.9	188.3	187.1	183.1
2003	184.4	186.2	186.5	187.7	187.4	185.7	185.6	185.8	186.6	188.1	190.0	189.3	186.9
2004	188.0	189.4	190.0	192.3	191.7	191.7	191.9	192.9	194.3	195.1	197.7	197.7	192.7
2005	196.0	197.3	198.2	199.4	200.1	199.1	199.2	200.3	202.6	200.7	202.2	201.8	199.7
2006	199.6	200.4	202.1	203.2	203.8	203.1	202.0	203.9	205.3	205.5	207.5	206.5	203.6
2007	204.8	206.6	207.5	207.8	208.3	207.9	207.1	209.5	209.7	210.4	211.8	211.1	208.5
Leisure and Hospitality													
2000	141.8	143.5	147.3	149.1	151.7	153.6	151.8	152.4	150.5	147.8	147.3	146.7	148.6
2001	143.1	145.3	148.8	152.6	154.8	157.1	155.4	155.5	152.2	149.8	148.9	149.0	151.0
2002	144.3	146.2	149.2	151.9	154.6	155.9	156.3	156.2	153.5	150.3	150.1	149.6	151.5
2003	146.1	148.0	151.5	154.5	156.4	158.6	158.3	159.3	157.1	154.9	154.4	154.3	154.4
2004	151.2	153.5	157.2	160.2	162.2	164.1	164.1	164.2	161.3	159.1	159.4	158.4	159.6
2005	155.1	157.5	162.0	166.4	168.5	170.4	168.7	169.6	167.2	163.6	163.9	163.6	164.7
2006	160.3	163.3	167.6	170.1	172.6	174.9	173.5	174.8	173.4	169.0	168.8	168.7	169.8
2007	165.8	169.2	172.9	174.5	176.6	178.8	177.4	178.4	175.7	172.4	172.1	171.6	173.8
Other Services													
2000	79.1	79.9	81.1	81.1	81.2	81.7	81.7	81.5	81.4	81.4	81.3	81.6	81.1
2001	84.2	84.7	84.5	85.1	85.2	85.5	85.6	85.9	85.5	85.1	84.8	84.6	85.1
2002	86.0	86.6	87.0	86.8	86.9	86.6	86.2	86.1	85.3	84.7	84.4	83.9	85.9
2003	83.1	83.3	83.4	83.6	84.0	84.5	83.8	83.8	83.0	82.8	82.2	82.0	83.2
2004	81.1	81.4	81.8	81.9	82.2	82.8	82.3	82.1	81.4	81.2	81.2	81.2	81.7
2005	80.8	80.9	81.3	81.4	81.8	82.0	81.5	81.1	80.7	79.9	79.9	80.2	81.0
2006	79.5	79.8	80.4	80.3	80.3	81.6	80.7	80.6	80.5	80.0	80.1	80.2	80.3
2007	79.9	80.5	81.4	81.2	81.4	81.7	81.0	80.7	80.6	80.1	80.2	80.2	80.7
Government													
2000	351.6	354.4	358.3	356.6	364.7	348.4	338.5	336.7	350.4	353.3	353.9	353.9	351.7
2001	351.5	355.4	355.2	355.2	355.2	348.5	339.8	341.4	352.5	355.7	356.6	356.6	352.0
2002	352.5	355.9	356.6	358.3	357.5	351.3	341.3	342.6	356.3	360.2	361.6	361.4	354.6
2003	358.3	362.0	362.9	363.4	363.3	354.4	344.4	346.4	359.4	362.6	363.1	361.5	358.4
2004	358.7	361.7	361.9	362.8	361.9	358.8	348.8	350.6	360.0	361.7	363.1	363.2	359.4
2005	360.1	363.0	363.5	364.8	365.5	364.2	352.4	355.1	362.9	367.4	368.1	367.8	362.9
2006	366.7	369.0	370.6	372.1	373.0	372.2	360.0	362.6	371.6	373.9	374.8	375.3	370.2
2007	374.2	376.6	377.9	378.6	379.5	379.3	364.2	367.9	377.2	379.8	381.3	380.3	376.4

Average Weekly Hours by Selected Industry: Alabama, 2001–2007

(Not seasonally adjusted.)

Industry and year	January	February	March	April	May	June	July	August	September	October	November	December	Annual Average
Manufacturing													
2001	40.9	39.9	40.6	40.6	40.8	41.1	41.1	41.6	41.5	41.2	41.1	41.1	41.0
2002	40.7	40.6	40.9	41.8	42.1	41.5	41.5	41.8	42.0	41.1	41.2	41.7	41.4
2003	41.7	41.6	41.3	41.4	41.6	41.1	40.4	40.8	40.9	40.3	40.5	40.6	41.0
2004	40.9	40.0	40.4	41.1	41.9	41.3	41.0	41.0	38.7	41.2	40.7	41.9	40.8
2005	42.1	41.5	40.9	40.4	40.9	41.2	39.6	41.4	40.6	39.1	40.7	41.6	40.8
2006	40.4	40.8	40.6	40.1	41.4	42.6	41.4	41.0	41.1	40.8	40.6	40.5	40.9
2007	40.1	40.1	40.1	40.1	40.2	40.3	40.3	40.3	40.2	40.2	40.3	40.4	40.2

Average Hourly Earnings by Selected Industry: Alabama, 2001–2007

(Dollars, not seasonally adjusted.)

Industry and year	January	February	March	April	May	June	July	August	September	October	November	December	Annual Average
Manufacturing													
2001	12.56	12.45	12.57	12.67	12.80	12.82	12.81	12.89	12.90	12.84	12.85	13.00	12.76
2002	12.87	12.88	12.94	13.01	13.12	13.14	13.19	13.19	13.23	13.16	13.15	13.34	13.10
2003	13.28	13.19	13.44	13.45	13.44	13.46	13.39	13.59	13.86	14.01	13.82	13.83	13.56
2004	13.61	13.53	13.83	14.17	14.26	14.50	14.58	14.62	14.68	14.56	14.61	14.99	14.33
2005	14.73	14.70	14.62	14.50	14.59	14.53	14.78	14.98	15.22	15.46	15.49	15.56	14.93
2006	15.51	15.57	15.26	15.19	15.25	15.70	15.53	15.55	15.75	15.72	15.78	15.90	15.56
2007	15.79	15.77	15.71	15.71	15.77	15.75	15.70	15.75	15.75	15.72	15.76	15.81	15.75

Average Weekly Earnings by Selected Industry: Alabama, 2001–2007

(Dollars, not seasonally adjusted.)

Industry and year	January	February	March	April	May	June	July	August	September	October	November	December	Annual Average
Manufacturing													
2001	513.70	496.76	510.34	514.40	522.24	526.90	526.49	536.22	535.35	529.01	528.14	534.30	523.16
2002	523.81	522.93	529.25	543.82	552.35	545.31	547.39	551.34	555.66	540.88	541.78	556.28	542.34
2003	553.78	548.70	555.07	556.83	559.10	553.21	540.96	554.47	566.87	564.60	559.71	561.50	555.96
2004	556.65	541.20	558.73	582.39	597.49	598.85	597.78	599.42	568.12	599.87	594.63	628.08	584.66
2005	620.13	610.05	597.96	585.80	596.73	598.64	585.29	620.17	617.93	604.49	630.44	647.30	609.14
2006	626.60	635.26	619.56	609.12	631.35	668.82	642.94	637.55	647.33	641.38	640.67	643.95	636.40
2007	633.18	632.38	629.97	629.97	633.95	634.73	632.71	634.73	633.15	631.94	635.13	638.72	633.15

Population
    2000 census: 626,932
    2007 estimate: 683,478
    Percent change, 2000–2007: 9.0%

Percent change in total nonfarm employment, 2000–2007: 11.9%

Industry with the largest growth in employment, 2000–2007 (thousands)
    Education and health services, 11.1

Industry with the largest decline in employment, 2000–2007 (thousands)
    Information, -0.6

Civilian labor force
    2000: 319,002
    2007: 352,304

Employment-population ratio
    2000: 68.6%
    2007: 66.2%

Unemployment rate and rank among states
    2000: 6.2%, 51st
    2007: 6.2%, 49th

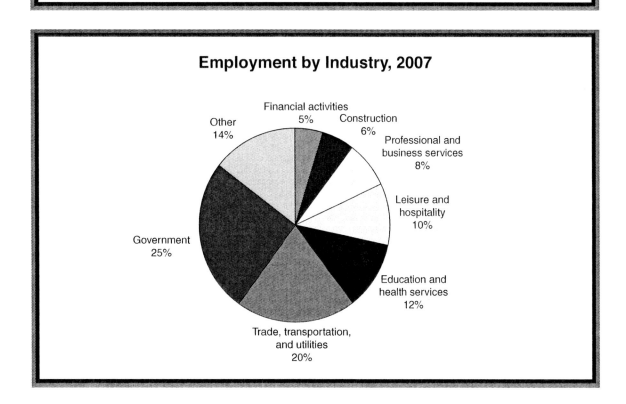

Employment by Industry, 2007

Financial activities 5%
Other 14%
Construction 6%
Professional and business services 8%
Leisure and hospitality 10%
Government 25%
Education and health services 12%
Trade, transportation, and utilities 20%

Employment by Industry: Alaska, 2000–2007

(Numbers in thousands, not seasonally adjusted.)

Industry and year	January	February	March	April	May	June	July	August	September	October	November	December	Annual Average
Total Nonfarm													
2000	260.9	268.2	271.7	276.0	288.5	298.5	305.4	304.8	297.5	284.3	275.7	274.4	283.8
2001	264.8	274.2	276.8	281.9	293.4	303.8	311.7	312.4	305.1	290.4	280.2	277.3	289.3
2002	271.1	280.3	283.5	287.0	297.7	308.5	315.1	315.8	309.8	297.3	287.9	286.0	295.0
2003	278.2	284.5	287.5	290.2	303.8	314.7	319.9	320.5	314.7	299.6	290.5	288.5	299.4
2004	283.3	286.8	291.2	295.2	306.3	318.9	327.1	325.9	320.6	305.6	296.0	294.3	304.3
2005	288.6	293.0	296.3	301.3	313.5	325.4	333.4	333.1	325.5	308.7	301.2	297.1	309.8
2006	291.4	298.0	302.4	307.3	319.8	336.9	337.8	337.6	330.3	311.4	305.0	301.8	315.0
2007	296.3	303.0	305.8	309.8	322.4	336.5	339.5	340.2	332.2	314.6	307.3	303.5	317.6
Total Private													
2000	188.2	193.7	195.8	200.0	210.9	225.0	234.0	233.4	223.1	208.7	200.3	198.9	209.3
2001	189.1	195.9	197.6	201.6	212.1	225.7	236.1	236.3	225.1	209.5	199.7	197.1	210.5
2002	193.4	199.8	202.2	204.9	215.6	228.2	239.3	238.4	227.8	215.1	205.7	202.9	214.4
2003	198.2	202.4	204.5	206.9	220.0	233.0	243.0	242.7	232.0	216.9	208.2	206.1	217.8
2004	202.4	205.0	208.2	212.1	223.6	238.5	250.4	248.6	239.0	223.0	213.7	211.6	223.0
2005	208.3	211.0	213.8	218.0	230.2	245.1	257.2	255.9	243.8	226.1	218.7	215.0	228.6
2006	212.4	215.9	219.6	223.7	236.1	254.5	261.4	259.9	247.8	228.8	222.7	219.7	233.5
2007	216.9	220.5	222.6	226.0	238.6	255.3	263.1	262.7	249.4	231.0	224.0	220.4	235.9
Goods-Producing													
2000	28.5	32.1	32.5	34.2	36.5	41.4	49.0	48.2	43.4	37.7	32.5	30.2	37.1
2001	29.9	35.0	35.5	35.6	37.2	41.7	49.9	49.4	44.6	38.4	32.4	29.8	38.3
2002	30.9	35.0	35.3	34.5	36.2	40.9	48.9	47.9	43.6	39.2	33.8	31.0	38.1
2003	31.1	34.7	35.3	33.8	37.2	43.3	50.9	49.5	44.7	39.8	34.0	31.0	38.8
2004	33.7	35.0	35.6	35.6	38.3	44.8	53.2	50.8	46.0	40.6	35.2	32.3	40.1
2005	35.3	36.6	37.6	37.7	39.8	46.1	54.7	53.5	47.9	42.1	37.4	34.1	41.9
2006	36.3	38.2	39.3	40.0	41.7	50.6	56.6	54.9	49.3	43.6	39.2	35.8	43.8
2007	38.0	39.7	40.0	40.5	42.1	50.0	57.0	56.1	50.3	44.6	39.8	36.1	44.5
Natural Resources and Mining													
2000	8.9	10.1	10.3	10.4	10.9	11.2	11.7	12.1	12.8	11.8	11.4	11.5	11.0
2001	10.5	11.5	11.6	11.8	12.0	12.3	12.2	12.1	12.0	11.8	11.2	10.7	11.6
2002	10.5	10.7	10.8	11.1	10.9	11.1	11.6	11.5	11.2	11.1	10.8	10.5	11.0
2003	10.0	10.2	10.3	10.2	10.4	10.3	10.4	10.4	10.3	10.0	9.8	9.7	10.2
2004	9.4	9.7	9.9	10.2	10.3	10.4	10.5	10.6	10.3	10.1	10.0	10.1	10.1
2005	9.9	10.3	10.5	10.4	10.5	10.8	11.1	11.2	11.2	11.3	11.3	11.3	10.8
2006	11.0	11.4	11.5	12.1	12.4	12.8	12.7	12.9	12.9	12.8	12.8	12.9	12.4
2007	12.9	13.2	13.3	13.5	13.6	14.1	14.1	14.4	14.4	14.5	14.4	14.2	13.9
Construction													
2000	11.1	11.5	11.8	12.5	14.3	16.6	17.0	17.7	16.6	15.8	13.3	12.5	14.2
2001	10.9	11.5	12.1	13.3	14.9	17.2	18.2	19.0	18.1	16.8	14.1	13.1	14.9
2002	12.2	12.4	12.8	13.4	15.8	18.1	19.0	19.6	18.9	17.7	15.5	14.3	15.8
2003	12.5	12.7	13.1	14.6	17.4	19.3	20.4	21.0	20.5	19.2	16.8	15.5	16.9
2004	13.7	13.8	14.1	15.3	17.7	20.1	21.4	21.7	21.0	19.6	17.5	16.2	17.7
2005	14.6	14.7	15.3	17.1	19.0	21.1	22.3	22.8	21.7	20.2	17.6	16.3	18.6
2006	14.5	14.7	15.3	16.6	18.8	21.0	21.4	21.5	21.0	19.8	17.4	16.1	18.2
2007	14.3	14.8	14.9	16.0	18.0	20.2	20.7	21.1	20.2	18.9	16.4	15.1	17.6
Manufacturing													
2000	8.5	10.5	10.4	11.3	11.3	13.6	20.3	18.4	14.0	10.1	7.8	6.2	11.8
2001	8.5	12.0	11.8	10.5	10.3	12.2	19.5	18.3	14.5	9.8	7.1	6.0	11.7
2002	8.2	11.9	11.7	10.0	9.5	11.7	18.3	16.8	13.5	10.4	7.5	6.2	11.3
2003	8.6	11.8	11.9	9.0	9.4	13.7	20.1	18.1	13.9	10.6	7.4	5.8	11.7
2004	10.6	11.5	11.6	10.1	10.3	14.3	21.3	18.5	14.7	10.9	7.7	6.0	12.3
2005	10.8	11.6	11.8	10.2	10.3	14.2	21.3	19.5	15.0	10.6	8.5	6.5	12.5
2006	10.8	12.1	12.5	11.3	10.5	16.8	22.5	20.5	15.4	11.0	9.0	6.8	13.3
2007	10.8	11.7	11.8	11.0	10.5	15.7	22.2	20.6	15.7	11.2	9.0	6.8	13.1
Service-Providing													
2000	232.4	236.1	239.2	241.8	252.0	257.1	256.4	256.6	254.1	246.6	243.2	244.2	246.6
2001	234.9	239.2	241.3	246.3	256.2	262.1	261.8	263.0	260.5	252.0	247.8	247.5	251.1
2002	240.2	245.3	248.2	252.5	261.5	267.6	266.2	267.9	266.2	258.1	254.1	255.0	256.9
2003	247.1	249.8	252.2	256.4	266.6	271.4	269.0	271.0	270.0	259.8	256.5	257.5	260.6
2004	249.6	251.8	255.6	259.6	268.0	274.1	273.9	275.1	274.6	265.0	260.8	262.0	264.2
2005	253.3	256.4	258.7	263.6	273.7	279.3	278.7	279.6	277.6	266.6	263.8	263.0	267.9
2006	255.1	259.8	263.1	267.3	278.1	286.3	281.2	282.7	281.0	267.8	265.8	266.0	271.2
2007	258.3	263.3	265.8	269.3	280.3	286.5	282.5	284.1	281.9	270.0	267.5	267.4	273.1
Trade, Transportation, and Utilities													
2000	56.5	56.6	57.1	57.8	61.3	63.9	64.7	65.2	63.3	60.1	59.0	59.1	60.3
2001	55.6	55.3	55.7	57.8	61.2	64.0	65.6	65.5	63.4	60.5	58.8	58.7	60.2
2002	56.6	57.0	57.9	58.8	62.4	64.9	66.3	66.4	64.1	61.2	59.4	59.3	61.2
2003	57.1	56.8	57.2	58.5	62.2	64.4	65.3	65.6	63.8	60.0	59.2	59.6	60.8
2004	57.0	57.0	58.0	59.5	63.6	65.8	67.5	67.4	65.7	62.0	60.7	60.7	62.1
2005	58.3	58.4	59.0	60.7	64.8	66.9	68.5	68.5	66.3	62.6	61.4	61.0	63.0
2006	59.4	58.9	60.0	61.6	65.8	68.6	69.0	69.0	66.5	62.2	61.8	61.9	63.7
2007	59.9	59.8	60.4	61.7	65.9	68.6	69.0	69.2	66.9	62.5	62.2	62.0	64.0
Wholesale Trade													
2000	6.0	6.1	6.2	6.1	6.2	6.4	6.8	6.8	6.5	6.1	6.0	6.0	6.2
2001	5.9	5.9	5.9	6.0	6.2	6.4	7.0	6.9	6.4	6.0	5.9	5.9	6.2
2002	5.7	5.7	5.8	6.1	6.2	6.5	7.0	6.9	6.4	6.0	5.9	5.9	6.2
2003	5.9	5.8	5.8	5.9	6.1	6.4	6.5	6.5	6.4	6.1	6.0	6.0	6.1
2004	5.9	6.0	6.1	6.1	6.2	6.4	6.6	6.6	6.4	6.2	6.0	6.1	6.2
2005	5.9	6.0	6.0	6.1	6.4	6.5	6.8	6.7	6.5	6.3	6.2	6.2	6.3
2006	6.2	6.2	6.3	6.3	6.6	6.8	7.0	7.0	6.8	6.5	6.3	6.4	6.5
2007	6.3	6.3	6.4	6.5	6.6	6.8	6.9	7.0	6.7	6.4	6.1	6.3	6.5

Employment by Industry: Alaska, 2000–2007—*Continued*

(Numbers in thousands, not seasonally adjusted.)

Industry and year	January	February	March	April	May	June	July	August	September	October	November	December	Annual Average
Retail Trade													
2000	32.1	31.7	32.0	32.4	33.9	35.1	35.2	35.1	34.4	33.5	33.6	33.8	33.5
2001	31.5	31.0	31.1	32.0	33.4	34.9	35.1	35.1	34.3	33.5	33.4	33.4	33.2
2002	32.0	31.9	32.2	32.6	34.2	35.4	35.8	35.6	34.9	34.3	34.0	34.2	33.9
2003	32.3	32.1	32.2	32.8	34.3	35.6	35.8	35.7	35.1	34.1	33.9	34.3	34.0
2004	32.4	32.2	32.8	33.7	35.4	36.9	37.3	37.2	36.3	35.3	35.4	35.5	35.0
2005	33.8	33.7	33.9	34.8	36.3	37.7	38.0	37.9	37.0	35.8	35.7	35.8	35.9
2006	34.3	33.6	34.0	34.9	36.5	37.9	37.8	37.5	36.5	35.4	35.5	35.7	35.8
2007	34.3	33.8	34.2	34.8	36.5	37.8	38.1	37.8	36.7	35.6	35.9	35.9	36.0
Transportation and Utilities													
2000	18.4	18.8	18.9	19.3	21.2	22.4	22.7	23.3	22.4	20.5	19.4	19.3	20.5
2001	18.2	18.4	18.7	19.8	21.6	22.7	23.5	23.5	22.7	21.0	19.5	19.4	20.8
2002	18.9	19.4	19.9	20.1	22.0	23.0	23.5	23.9	22.8	20.9	19.5	19.2	21.1
2003	18.9	18.9	19.2	19.8	21.8	22.4	23.0	23.4	22.3	19.8	19.3	19.3	20.7
2004	18.7	18.8	19.1	19.7	22.0	22.5	23.6	23.6	23.0	20.5	19.3	19.1	20.8
2005	18.6	18.7	19.1	19.8	22.1	22.7	23.7	23.9	22.8	20.5	19.5	19.0	20.9
2006	18.9	19.1	19.7	20.4	22.7	23.9	24.2	24.5	23.2	20.3	20.0	19.8	21.4
2007	19.3	19.7	19.8	20.4	22.8	24.0	24.0	24.4	23.5	20.5	20.2	19.8	21.5
Information													
2000	7.5	7.5	7.5	7.5	7.5	7.7	7.7	7.6	7.5	7.4	7.4	7.5	7.5
2001	7.3	7.4	7.4	7.2	7.4	7.5	7.5	7.5	7.3	7.3	7.3	7.2	7.4
2002	6.9	6.8	6.9	7.1	7.1	7.2	7.4	7.2	7.2	7.1	7.0	7.1	7.1
2003	6.8	6.8	6.8	6.9	7.0	7.1	7.1	7.0	7.0	6.9	6.9	6.9	6.9
2004	6.8	6.8	6.8	6.8	6.9	6.9	6.9	6.9	6.9	6.9	6.9	7.0	6.9
2005	6.8	6.9	6.9	6.9	7.0	7.0	7.0	7.0	7.0	6.9	7.0	7.0	7.0
2006	6.9	7.0	7.0	6.9	7.0	7.1	7.0	7.1	7.0	7.0	7.0	7.0	7.0
2007	6.9	6.9	6.9	6.8	6.9	7.0	7.0	7.0	6.9	7.0	6.9	6.9	6.9
Financial Activities													
2000	13.5	13.5	13.6	13.6	13.8	14.5	14.5	14.6	14.2	14.0	13.7	13.8	13.9
2001	13.4	13.4	13.4	13.6	14.0	14.5	14.3	14.5	14.0	13.7	13.5	13.5	13.8
2002	13.2	13.1	13.4	13.3	13.7	14.2	14.3	14.4	14.2	14.0	13.9	13.8	13.8
2003	13.6	13.6	13.9	14.0	14.4	14.8	15.0	15.1	14.8	14.6	14.3	14.4	14.4
2004	13.9	14.0	14.1	14.5	14.6	15.0	15.0	15.2	14.9	14.7	14.6	14.7	14.6
2005	14.3	14.2	14.2	14.4	14.7	15.1	15.3	15.3	15.2	15.1	14.9	14.8	14.8
2006	14.5	14.5	14.6	14.7	15.0	15.4	15.5	15.6	15.2	14.8	14.7	14.7	14.9
2007	14.4	14.6	14.7	14.8	15.2	15.5	15.5	15.7	15.1	14.9	14.6	14.7	15.0
Professional and Business Services													
2000	22.2	22.7	23.0	23.6	24.6	26.1	26.1	26.0	25.3	24.7	23.8	24.0	24.3
2001	21.2	21.8	22.0	22.2	23.1	24.2	24.5	24.7	23.6	22.4	21.7	21.7	22.8
2002	21.2	21.8	22.0	22.2	23.1	24.0	23.9	24.2	23.2	22.6	22.0	21.9	22.7
2003	21.7	21.7	21.9	22.5	23.9	24.7	24.5	24.9	23.8	22.7	22.2	22.3	23.1
2004	21.7	21.9	22.4	22.6	23.2	24.4	24.9	25.0	24.7	23.4	22.8	22.9	23.3
2005	21.9	22.4	22.3	23.0	24.2	25.6	25.7	25.9	25.0	23.4	23.1	23.0	23.8
2006	22.2	22.9	23.3	23.8	25.0	26.1	25.9	25.9	25.6	24.1	23.6	23.8	24.4
2007	23.2	23.7	23.9	24.3	25.7	26.6	26.5	26.6	26.1	24.6	24.2	24.1	25.0
Education and Health Services													
2000	25.2	25.8	25.8	25.7	26.0	26.0	25.6	25.8	26.0	26.0	26.1	26.4	25.8
2001	26.5	27.0	27.2	27.4	27.7	28.0	28.1	28.3	28.4	28.6	28.9	29.0	27.9
2002	29.0	29.4	29.7	30.1	30.5	30.8	30.8	31.0	30.8	31.2	31.5	31.9	30.6
2003	31.2	32.0	32.2	32.8	33.1	33.2	33.3	33.5	33.4	33.6	33.8	34.2	33.0
2004	33.8	34.2	34.5	34.8	35.0	34.9	34.6	34.4	34.7	34.9	35.1	35.5	34.7
2005	35.1	35.4	35.9	35.8	36.1	36.4	36.0	36.1	36.1	36.2	36.4	36.7	36.0
2006	36.4	36.9	37.0	37.2	37.5	37.6	37.2	37.2	37.1	36.7	36.9	37.0	37.1
2007	36.6	37.1	37.3	37.3	37.3	37.1	36.7	36.9	36.5	36.5	36.5	36.7	36.9
Leisure and Hospitality													
2000	23.1	23.6	24.2	25.5	28.9	32.9	34.1	33.9	31.2	26.6	25.5	25.5	27.9
2001	23.8	24.5	24.7	26.0	29.3	33.5	34.1	34.2	31.7	26.7	25.3	25.4	28.3
2002	24.0	24.9	25.0	26.9	30.5	34.3	35.7	35.4	33.0	28.3	26.7	26.6	29.3
2003	25.7	25.7	26.0	27.1	30.8	34.1	35.6	35.8	33.4	28.1	26.7	26.6	29.6
2004	24.9	25.3	25.9	27.1	30.5	35.0	37.1	37.5	34.8	29.2	27.2	27.4	30.2
2005	25.8	26.1	26.8	28.3	32.4	36.7	38.6	38.3	35.1	28.6	27.3	27.3	30.9
2006	25.8	26.5	27.2	28.5	32.9	37.9	38.8	38.9	35.7	29.0	28.1	28.2	31.5
2007	26.8	27.3	27.9	29.2	33.7	38.8	39.7	39.4	35.8	29.2	28.4	28.5	32.1
Other Services													
2000	11.7	11.9	12.1	12.1	12.3	12.5	12.3	12.1	12.2	12.2	12.3	12.4	12.1
2001	11.4	11.5	11.7	11.8	12.2	12.3	12.1	12.2	12.1	11.9	11.8	11.8	11.9
2002	11.6	11.8	12.0	12.0	12.1	11.9	12.0	11.9	11.7	11.5	11.4	11.3	11.8
2003	11.0	11.1	11.2	11.3	11.4	11.4	11.3	11.3	11.1	11.2	11.1	11.1	11.2
2004	10.6	10.8	10.9	11.2	11.5	11.7	11.2	11.4	11.3	11.3	11.2	11.1	11.2
2005	10.8	11.0	11.1	11.2	11.2	11.3	11.4	11.3	11.2	11.2	11.1	11.1	11.2
2006	10.9	11.0	11.2	11.0	11.2	11.2	11.4	11.3	11.4	11.4	11.4	11.3	11.2
2007	11.1	11.4	11.5	11.4	11.8	11.7	11.7	11.8	11.8	11.7	11.4	11.4	11.6
Government													
2000	72.7	74.5	75.9	76.0	77.6	73.5	71.4	71.4	74.4	75.6	75.4	75.5	74.4
2001	75.7	78.3	79.2	80.3	81.3	78.1	75.6	76.1	80.0	80.9	80.5	80.2	78.9
2002	77.7	80.5	81.3	82.1	82.1	80.3	75.8	77.4	82.0	82.2	82.2	83.1	80.6
2003	80.0	82.1	83.0	83.3	83.8	81.7	76.9	77.8	82.7	82.7	82.3	82.4	81.6
2004	80.9	81.8	83.0	83.1	82.7	80.4	76.7	77.3	81.6	82.6	82.3	82.7	81.3
2005	80.3	82.0	82.5	83.3	83.3	80.3	76.2	77.2	81.7	82.6	82.5	82.1	81.2
2006	79.0	82.1	82.8	83.6	83.7	82.4	76.4	77.7	82.5	82.6	82.3	82.1	81.4
2007	79.4	82.5	83.2	83.8	83.8	81.2	76.4	77.5	82.8	83.6	83.3	83.1	81.7

Average Weekly Hours by Selected Industry: Alaska, 2001–2007

(Not seasonally adjusted.)

Industry and year	January	February	March	April	May	June	July	August	September	October	November	December	Annual Average
Natural Resources and Mining													
2001	47.5	44.6	46.4	48.0	46.9	48.6	47.4	48.8	45.9	48.4	47.3	45.6	47.1
2002	45.8	47.1	48.1	48.9	47.5	49.5	49.1	48.4	46.3	41.9	41.9	41.5	46.4
2003	41.0	41.7	44.6	43.9	42.5	41.7	41.6	42.2	44.8	43.6	45.5	40.4	42.8
2004	42.5	44.6	45.5	40.1	41.2	43.1	41.4	41.1	42.4	41.7	50.8	45.6	43.2
2005	46.6	45.6	44.3	46.6	48.4	49.7	51.6	53.3	49.2	46.2	46.9	47.0	48.0
2006	44.1	46.6	46.6	46.5	48.4	49.5	49.2	48.2	49.4	50.8	49.6	50.4	48.3
2007	47.3	45.3	47.3	48.4	42.5	44.9	47.1	47.6	48.0	47.6	48.6	45.9	46.7
Construction													
2001	37.5	36.9	38.5	38.1	45.8	43.3	44.7	48.5	44.8	43.9	37.2	38.6	42.2
2002	38.0	40.4	39.9	38.7	40.7	43.2	42.8	44.0	44.5	41.2	38.4	39.7	41.3
2003	39.8	39.6	39.2	40.0	44.4	43.3	44.5	45.6	44.8	43.5	37.6	38.3	42.2
2004	37.8	37.2	39.7	38.8	41.7	43.6	44.1	43.9	42.1	43.2	38.5	39.8	41.3
2005	39.1	39.2	38.6	40.7	43.9	44.3	44.5	46.2	44.0	43.3	40.9	39.1	42.4
2006	40.4	40.4	42.6	41.8	44.7	47.4	45.7	47.6	50.3	45.6	38.1	39.5	44.2
2007	38.8	39.3	39.3	38.1	41.4	43.3	46.3	48.7	48.4	47.1	42.1	40.7	43.5
Manufacturing													
2001	31.2	47.1	52.0	33.8	32.0	37.6	49.1	50.9	44.6	43.8	33.8	34.3	43.1
2002	32.8	45.4	46.3	36.9	34.8	29.2	40.0	44.3	33.5	31.3	29.8	30.2	37.4
2003	22.2	47.5	39.9	38.7	44.0	39.7	51.5	49.1	46.2	39.5	38.0	39.0	43.0
2004	35.9	47.7	41.0	28.3	34.5	30.8	47.3	49.0	48.4	38.1	34.0	36.0	40.6
2005	28.0	30.7	35.0	25.3	29.3	28.3	41.8	38.8	35.3	33.6	23.6	26.6	32.9
2006	26.4	29.0	34.6	32.9	34.0	40.1	50.5	49.1	44.4	41.5	42.4	43.5	40.6
2007	40.0	43.4	47.2	46.4	48.6	51.2	45.2	46.7	47.3	41.7	41.7	36.5	45.4
Trade, Transportation, and Utilities													
2001	32.8	34.6	35.3	34.7	33.9	35.7	36.1	36.6	35.6	34.3	33.3	34.0	34.8
2002	32.5	33.6	33.5	32.3	32.3	35.6	34.1	34.4	34.8	33.6	33.4	33.6	33.7
2003	32.7	34.2	34.3	34.3	34.5	36.2	35.4	35.6	35.1	34.0	35.0	33.7	34.6
2004	33.7	34.2	32.5	33.1	34.3	35.1	35.2	35.4	34.0	32.5	33.0	32.5	33.8
2005	31.6	30.7	31.5	31.4	33.8	35.2	34.4	33.7	33.8	34.3	33.6	33.6	33.2
2006	32.9	33.1	33.0	32.0	32.3	33.0	39.5	33.6	32.8	33.3	33.8	35.7	33.8
2007	34.5	33.4	33.2	34.0	33.1	36.2	36.2	35.6	34.7	33.5	34.1	34.3	34.4
Wholesale Trade													
2001	34.9	34.5	37.0	40.2	37.9	39.2	40.0	37.9	39.0	36.8	37.3	39.2	37.9
2002	36.7	39.5	38.8	39.9	40.3	42.5	40.7	39.6	40.6	37.9	38.3	38.1	39.5
2003	36.4	37.7	37.4	38.8	38.5	39.6	38.8	39.2	38.3	37.9	38.8	36.9	38.2
2004	39.7	39.3	38.9	39.9	40.5	39.9	38.8	40.8	39.6	38.2	38.9	37.4	39.3
2005	38.0	37.3	36.6	37.5	37.5	37.9	37.0	38.7	32.7	37.8	38.9	33.7	37.0
2006	38.7	35.0	34.0	35.2	35.9	36.6	37.7	36.5	36.6	40.2	35.8	41.6	37.0
2007	39.3	38.5	38.9	38.7	39.3	40.6	42.4	41.0	33.9	36.7	41.7	40.5	39.3
Retail Trade													
2001	33.2	36.0	36.6	34.6	34.5	36.5	35.8	37.7	36.4	34.9	34.2	34.3	35.4
2002	33.1	34.1	34.0	31.9	32.0	32.8	32.8	33.4	33.3	32.4	32.8	32.5	32.9
2003	32.5	33.8	32.8	33.2	34.0	35.0	34.5	35.0	34.0	33.5	33.7	32.4	33.7
2004	31.9	32.1	30.9	31.8	32.3	32.6	32.3	32.7	32.1	31.2	31.5	31.1	31.9
2005	29.8	29.0	28.8	29.0	30.3	30.9	30.1	29.6	29.6	29.2	28.7	29.7	29.6
2006	28.0	29.0	29.3	29.2	29.2	30.1	41.4	31.2	31.6	31.7	31.9	32.3	31.3
2007	32.0	31.8	32.2	32.0	30.0	31.1	31.1	30.5	31.0	29.8	30.1	29.9	30.9
Transportation and Utilities													
2001	31.3	32.1	32.6	33.2	31.7	33.4	35.4	34.4	33.3	32.3	30.4	31.7	32.7
2002	29.9	30.8	31.1	30.7	30.7	38.7	34.3	34.5	35.7	34.7	33.0	34.6	33.4
2003	31.9	33.8	36.2	35.1	34.4	37.5	35.9	35.6	36.2	33.8	36.3	35.3	35.2
2004	35.3	36.9	33.5	33.6	36.3	38.4	39.4	38.5	35.8	33.1	34.1	33.8	35.9
2005	33.2	31.9	35.4	34.3	39.2	42.5	41.0	39.3	41.8	43.3	41.9	41.9	39.0
2006	40.6	40.4	39.8	36.6	36.9	37.2	36.8	36.8	33.7	33.9	37.0	41.1	37.4
2007	37.9	34.8	33.0	36.4	36.8	44.0	43.4	42.6	41.6	39.8	39.8	41.6	39.6
Financial Activities													
2001	35.8	35.0	35.4	35.6	35.7	34.8	35.8	35.6	34.0	35.5	33.8	33.5	35.1
2002	34.0	33.0	33.2	34.2	32.8	34.3	31.8	34.0	36.8	32.9	34.6	37.9	34.1
2003	35.7	38.4	39.1	36.8	36.9	38.2	35.4	37.6	36.8	37.8	35.9	34.6	36.9
2004	35.2	36.2	34.5	35.8	38.3	35.0	34.9	36.8	34.4	35.2	34.5	35.5	35.5
2005	38.0	35.6	36.4	37.0	38.5	35.9	36.2	36.6	36.5	39.0	37.0	41.0	37.3
2006	39.1	37.0	35.2	38.7	35.6	37.0	39.2	38.2	37.3	39.8	37.7	37.0	37.7
2007	39.5	38.5	35.9	37.9	34.7	35.4	37.4	35.2	37.1	35.7	35.5	36.2	36.6

Average Hourly Earnings by Selected Industry: Alaska, 2001–2007

(Dollars, not seasonally adjusted.)

Industry and year	January	February	March	April	May	June	July	August	September	October	November	December	Annual Average
Natural Resources and Mining													
2001	26.71	27.83	27.73	27.60	27.88	27.69	27.33	26.88	27.24	27.46	27.46	27.66	27.46
2002	27.75	28.12	27.63	27.73	27.60	27.66	27.96	27.79	27.62	26.84	29.72	29.22	27.94
2003	29.59	30.63	30.56	30.19	30.04	31.10	30.76	29.99	29.03	28.85	30.35	29.69	30.07
2004	30.52	30.61	30.39	29.67	29.36	31.25	30.96	30.63	31.95	30.21	27.59	29.68	30.23
2005	27.54	26.87	27.28	27.98	27.74	28.20	28.57	29.00	29.65	29.70	32.34	31.10	28.89
2006	31.02	31.19	31.02	32.35	32.11	32.26	32.68	31.83	33.58	34.24	34.40	32.91	32.53
2007	33.47	31.28	33.77	32.63	36.40	32.49	32.46	32.89	34.70	33.47	32.69	33.56	33.31
Construction													
2001	25.10	25.59	26.90	26.22	25.41	27.87	27.56	27.15	28.23	27.18	24.91	24.71	26.66
2002	24.96	24.96	25.71	25.82	26.64	26.13	26.50	26.81	28.38	27.08	26.84	28.11	26.64
2003	27.23	26.69	27.07	29.72	29.83	29.47	29.96	30.02	29.45	29.20	29.05	28.28	29.07
2004	27.61	26.63	26.64	28.20	28.13	28.73	28.71	29.04	28.90	29.06	28.43	29.75	28.48
2005	29.59	29.84	28.47	28.30	29.41	29.55	31.95	31.80	32.41	32.00	30.85	30.39	30.60
2006	30.46	30.53	31.03	32.86	30.96	32.52	32.20	33.91	33.53	32.44	31.11	31.75	32.16
2007	31.25	30.98	33.31	31.12	32.17	33.69	33.42	33.89	34.83	34.11	33.59	34.60	33.27
Manufacturing													
2001	15.30	11.36	10.39	12.31	13.46	12.21	10.36	11.14	11.09	11.55	15.13	16.13	11.70
2002	15.50	11.75	11.78	13.54	14.54	14.40	13.16	12.85	13.01	13.21	14.69	15.20	13.24
2003	14.48	12.32	11.74	12.05	12.25	12.73	11.90	11.64	11.41	12.11	13.51	13.82	12.18
2004	11.49	11.85	11.40	14.02	15.14	13.98	11.43	11.17	10.45	11.73	12.74	13.69	12.01
2005	11.68	12.19	12.04	16.11	16.24	14.40	14.57	15.34	14.07	14.65	14.62	15.14	14.22
2006	13.10	14.65	15.06	15.16	15.01	14.54	12.47	12.41	15.87	16.66	16.64	16.10	14.31
2007	15.70	13.64	13.96	15.14	17.52	14.20	14.75	15.30	15.53	17.48	21.57	23.64	15.77
Trade, Transportation, and Utilities													
2001	14.64	14.30	14.28	14.88	15.15	15.24	15.28	15.19	15.63	15.54	15.96	15.98	15.19
2002	15.59	15.67	16.17	16.27	16.18	16.09	16.01	16.08	16.34	16.09	15.78	15.64	16.00
2003	15.67	15.84	15.41	15.63	15.69	15.12	15.79	16.11	15.97	15.55	15.67	15.65	15.68
2004	15.84	15.58	15.53	15.65	15.51	15.08	15.28	15.36	16.13	15.81	15.56	15.30	15.54
2005	16.07	15.51	15.29	15.41	14.93	15.13	15.71	15.67	15.04	14.87	14.59	14.57	15.23
2006	14.43	14.35	14.12	13.97	14.38	14.46	15.52	15.07	15.51	15.47	15.70	15.67	14.92
2007	15.91	16.50	16.72	16.64	16.93	16.29	16.76	16.58	16.94	18.20	17.73	17.83	16.91
Wholesale Trade													
2001	17.56	17.49	18.57	17.98	17.41	18.23	18.11	18.16	19.74	18.34	18.33	19.10	18.26
2002	17.52	17.14	18.02	18.40	18.12	17.91	17.07	17.93	18.39	17.71	17.88	17.42	17.79
2003	18.15	19.37	18.21	18.02	18.01	17.34	18.04	18.10	18.06	17.32	16.72	16.45	17.80
2004	16.62	16.92	16.80	17.79	17.27	16.24	17.98	18.23	18.24	17.34	16.74	16.96	17.28
2005	18.08	17.28	17.30	18.62	18.14	17.00	18.75	18.60	18.80	18.36	17.33	18.50	18.07
2006	17.20	17.62	17.04	17.31	18.15	18.22	18.66	20.18	21.41	20.33	20.72	21.02	19.06
2007	21.72	22.13	23.00	22.02	21.84	20.64	22.20	22.01	22.37	23.59	21.76	22.04	22.08
Retail Trade													
2001	12.97	12.38	12.07	12.94	13.70	13.28	13.13	13.10	13.45	13.66	14.22	14.03	13.25
2002	13.94	14.07	14.36	14.58	14.93	14.96	14.60	14.47	14.46	14.44	14.08	14.03	14.41
2003	13.93	13.93	13.56	13.65	13.64	13.21	13.03	13.43	13.75	13.28	13.24	13.50	13.50
2004	13.29	13.70	13.70	13.47	13.49	13.74	13.44	13.36	13.72	13.61	13.55	13.31	13.53
2005	13.99	13.67	13.73	13.91	13.37	13.56	13.26	13.01	13.33	13.06	12.99	12.85	13.39
2006	12.67	12.85	13.01	12.45	12.39	12.55	14.01	13.27	13.71	13.63	14.12	13.93	13.27
2007	14.42	14.48	14.57	15.30	15.65	15.25	15.06	15.06	15.23	15.13	14.56	14.71	14.96
Transportation and Utilities													
2001	16.86	17.16	17.30	17.32	17.07	17.90	17.95	18.04	18.32	18.29	18.87	18.93	17.85
2002	18.39	18.43	19.19	18.72	17.78	17.21	17.97	18.13	18.78	18.55	18.48	18.21	18.28
2003	18.37	18.46	17.82	18.37	18.54	17.65	19.69	19.97	19.03	19.42	19.93	19.46	18.91
2004	20.24	18.45	18.47	19.00	18.23	16.83	17.18	17.50	19.24	19.34	19.00	18.53	18.40
2005	19.20	18.20	17.23	16.84	16.26	16.76	18.01	18.24	16.32	16.26	15.96	16.01	17.06
2006	15.95	15.45	14.84	15.30	16.11	16.13	17.48	16.10	16.45	16.84	16.81	16.66	16.18
2007	16.26	17.94	18.26	16.93	17.14	16.32	17.26	16.81	17.79	21.09	21.26	21.16	18.11
Financial Activities													
2001	18.28	18.45	18.43	18.86	19.02	19.37	19.26	18.47	21.76	19.89	22.47	20.86	19.57
2002	21.21	21.38	21.24	21.48	21.71	20.71	20.45	19.66	19.79	19.31	19.37	18.85	20.39
2003	19.52	20.49	18.69	18.53	18.18	18.22	18.64	20.52	19.84	19.61	21.37	20.85	19.51
2004	21.57	21.76	19.28	19.90	19.43	20.20	20.02	20.21	20.59	21.19	20.35	19.91	20.36
2005	20.71	20.97	19.74	19.53	19.08	21.00	21.90	20.91	20.61	20.60	20.66	19.97	20.45
2006	23.58	22.73	22.76	22.86	24.03	28.45	28.05	26.78	26.42	26.43	25.42	25.10	25.27
2007	24.66	23.70	23.70	23.12	25.23	25.29	24.02	23.85	23.76	21.11	22.75	22.39	23.64

Average Weekly Earnings by Selected Industry: Alaska, 2001–2007

(Dollars, not seasonally adjusted.)

Industry and year	January	February	March	April	May	June	July	August	September	October	November	December	Annual Average
Natural Resources and Mining													
2001	1,268.73	1,241.22	1,286.67	1,324.80	1,307.57	1,345.73	1,295.44	1,311.74	1,250.32	1,329.06	1,298.86	1,261.30	1,293.37
2002	1,270.95	1,324.45	1,329.00	1,356.00	1,311.00	1,369.17	1,372.84	1,345.04	1,278.81	1,124.60	1,245.27	1,212.63	1,296.42
2003	1,213.19	1,277.27	1,362.98	1,325.34	1,276.70	1,296.87	1,279.62	1,265.58	1,300.54	1,257.86	1,380.93	1,199.48	1,287.00
2004	1,297.10	1,365.21	1,382.75	1,189.77	1,209.63	1,346.88	1,281.74	1,258.89	1,354.68	1,259.76	1,401.57	1,353.41	1,305.94
2005	1,283.36	1,225.27	1,208.50	1,303.87	1,342.62	1,401.54	1,474.21	1,545.70	1,458.78	1,372.14	1,516.75	1,461.70	1,386.72
2006	1,367.98	1,453.45	1,445.53	1,504.28	1,554.12	1,596.87	1,607.86	1,534.21	1,658.85	1,739.39	1,706.24	1,658.66	1,571.20
2007	1,583.13	1,416.98	1,597.32	1,579.29	1,547.00	1,458.80	1,528.87	1,565.56	1,665.60	1,593.17	1,588.73	1,540.40	1,555.58
Construction													
2001	941.25	944.27	1,035.65	998.98	1,163.78	1,206.77	1,231.93	1,316.78	1,264.70	1,193.20	926.65	953.81	1,125.05
2002	948.48	1,008.38	1,025.83	999.23	1,084.25	1,128.82	1,134.20	1,179.64	1,262.91	1,115.70	1,030.66	1,115.97	1,100.23
2003	1,083.75	1,056.92	1,061.14	1,188.80	1,324.45	1,276.05	1,333.22	1,368.91	1,319.36	1,270.20	1,092.28	1,083.12	1,226.75
2004	1,043.66	990.64	1,057.61	1,094.16	1,173.02	1,252.63	1,266.11	1,274.86	1,216.69	1,255.39	1,094.56	1,184.05	1,176.22
2005	1,156.97	1,169.73	1,098.94	1,151.81	1,291.10	1,309.07	1,421.78	1,469.16	1,426.04	1,385.60	1,261.77	1,188.25	1,297.44
2006	1,230.58	1,233.41	1,321.88	1,373.55	1,383.91	1,541.45	1,471.54	1,614.12	1,686.56	1,479.26	1,185.29	1,254.13	1,421.47
2007	1,212.50	1,217.51	1,309.08	1,185.67	1,331.84	1,458.78	1,547.35	1,650.44	1,685.77	1,606.58	1,414.14	1,408.22	1,447.25
Manufacturing													
2001	477.36	535.06	540.28	416.08	430.72	459.10	508.68	567.03	494.61	505.89	511.39	553.26	504.27
2002	508.40	533.45	545.41	499.63	505.99	420.48	526.40	569.26	435.84	413.47	437.76	459.04	495.18
2003	321.46	585.20	468.43	466.34	539.00	505.38	612.85	571.52	527.14	478.35	513.38	538.98	523.74
2004	412.49	565.25	467.40	396.77	522.33	430.58	540.64	547.33	505.78	446.91	433.16	492.84	487.61
2005	327.04	374.23	421.40	407.58	475.83	407.52	609.03	595.19	496.67	492.24	345.03	402.72	467.84
2006	345.84	424.85	521.08	498.76	510.34	583.05	629.74	609.33	704.63	691.39	705.54	700.35	580.99
2007	628.00	591.98	658.91	702.50	851.47	727.04	666.70	714.51	734.57	728.92	899.47	862.86	715.96
Trade, Transportation, and Utilities													
2001	480.19	494.78	504.08	516.34	513.59	544.07	551.61	555.95	556.43	533.02	531.47	543.32	528.61
2002	506.68	526.51	541.70	525.52	522.61	572.80	545.94	553.15	568.63	540.62	527.05	525.50	539.20
2003	512.41	541.73	528.56	536.11	541.31	547.34	558.97	573.52	560.55	528.70	548.45	527.41	542.53
2004	533.81	532.84	504.73	518.02	531.99	529.31	537.86	543.74	548.42	513.83	513.48	497.25	525.25
2005	507.81	476.16	481.64	483.87	504.63	532.58	540.42	528.08	508.35	510.04	490.22	489.55	505.64
2006	474.75	474.99	465.96	447.04	464.47	477.18	613.04	506.35	508.73	515.15	530.66	559.42	504.30
2007	548.90	551.10	555.10	565.76	560.38	589.70	606.71	590.25	587.82	609.70	604.59	611.57	581.70
Wholesale Trade													
2001	612.84	603.41	687.09	722.80	659.84	714.62	724.40	688.26	769.86	674.91	683.71	748.72	692.05
2002	642.98	677.03	699.18	734.16	730.24	761.18	694.75	710.03	746.63	671.21	684.80	663.70	702.71
2003	660.66	730.25	681.05	699.18	693.39	686.66	699.95	709.52	691.70	656.43	648.74	607.01	679.96
2004	659.81	664.96	653.52	709.82	699.44	647.98	697.62	743.78	722.30	662.39	651.19	634.30	679.10
2005	687.04	644.54	633.18	698.25	680.25	644.30	693.75	719.82	614.76	694.01	674.14	623.45	668.59
2006	665.64	616.70	579.36	609.31	651.59	666.85	703.48	736.57	783.61	817.27	741.78	874.43	705.22
2007	853.60	852.01	894.70	852.17	858.31	837.98	941.28	902.41	758.34	865.75	907.39	892.62	867.74
Retail Trade													
2001	430.60	445.68	441.76	447.72	472.65	484.72	470.05	493.87	489.58	476.73	486.32	481.23	469.05
2002	461.41	479.79	488.24	465.10	477.76	490.69	478.88	483.30	481.52	467.86	461.82	455.98	474.09
2003	452.73	470.83	444.77	453.18	463.76	462.35	449.54	470.05	467.50	444.88	446.19	437.40	454.95
2004	423.95	439.77	423.33	428.35	435.73	447.92	434.11	436.87	440.41	424.63	426.83	413.94	431.61
2005	416.90	396.43	395.42	403.39	405.11	419.00	399.13	385.10	394.57	381.35	372.81	381.65	396.34
2006	354.76	372.65	381.19	363.54	361.79	377.76	580.01	414.02	433.24	432.07	450.43	449.94	415.35
2007	461.44	460.46	469.15	489.60	469.50	474.28	468.37	459.33	472.13	450.87	438.26	439.83	462.26
Transportation and Utilities													
2001	527.72	550.84	563.98	575.02	541.12	597.86	635.43	620.58	610.06	590.77	573.65	600.08	583.70
2002	549.86	567.64	596.81	574.70	545.85	666.03	616.37	625.49	670.45	643.69	609.84	630.07	610.55
2003	586.00	623.95	645.08	644.79	637.78	661.88	706.87	710.93	688.89	656.40	723.46	686.94	665.63
2004	714.47	680.81	618.75	638.40	661.75	646.27	676.89	673.75	688.79	640.15	647.90	626.31	660.56
2005	637.44	580.58	609.94	577.61	637.39	712.30	738.41	716.83	682.18	704.06	668.72	670.82	665.34
2006	647.57	624.18	590.63	559.98	594.46	600.04	643.26	592.48	554.37	570.88	621.97	684.73	605.13
2007	616.25	624.31	602.58	616.25	630.75	718.08	749.08	716.11	740.06	839.38	846.15	880.26	717.16
Financial Activities													
2001	654.42	645.75	652.42	671.42	679.01	674.08	689.51	657.53	739.84	706.10	759.49	698.81	686.91
2002	721.14	705.54	705.17	734.62	712.09	710.35	650.31	668.44	728.27	635.30	670.20	714.42	695.30
2003	696.86	786.82	730.78	681.90	671.58	696.00	659.86	771.55	730.11	741.26	767.18	721.41	719.92
2004	759.26	787.71	665.16	712.42	744.17	707.00	698.70	743.73	708.30	745.89	702.08	706.81	722.78
2005	786.98	746.53	718.54	722.61	734.58	753.90	792.78	765.31	752.27	803.40	764.42	818.77	762.79
2006	921.98	841.01	801.15	884.68	855.47	1,052.65	1,099.56	1,023.00	985.47	1,051.91	958.33	928.70	952.68
2007	974.07	912.45	850.83	876.25	875.48	895.27	898.35	839.52	881.50	753.63	807.63	810.52	865.22

Population
    2000 census: 5,130,632
    2007 estimate: 6,338,755
    Percent change, 2000–2007: 23.5%

Percent change in total nonfarm employment, 2000–2007: 18.9%

Industry with the largest growth in employment, 2000–2007 (thousands)
    Education and health services, 91.5

Industry with the largest decline in employment, 2000–2007 (thousands)
    Manufacturing, -28.2

Civilian labor force
    2000: 2,505,306
    2007: 3,029,090

Employment-population ratio
    2000: 62.5%
    2007: 61.2%

Unemployment rate and rank among states
    2000: 4.0%, 28th
    2007: 3.8%, 15th

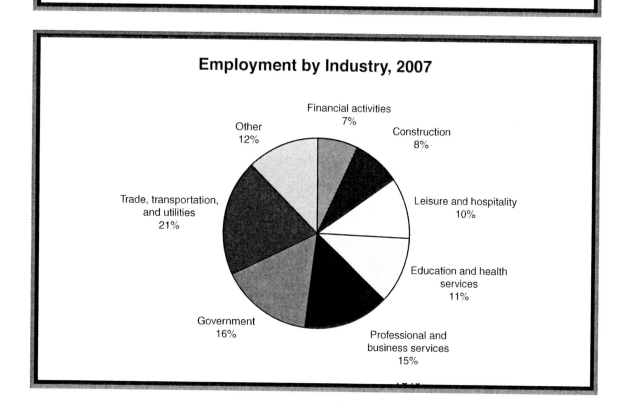

Employment by Industry, 2007

Financial activities 7%
Construction 8%
Leisure and hospitality 10%
Education and health services 11%
Professional and business services 15%
Government 16%
Trade, transportation, and utilities 21%
Other 12%

Employment by Industry: Arizona, 2000–2007

(Numbers in thousands, not seasonally adjusted.)

Industry and year	January	February	March	April	May	June	July	August	September	October	November	December	Annual Average
Total Nonfarm													
2000	2,184.1	2,220.3	2,239.7	2,240.3	2,253.5	2,224.9	2,192.9	2,218.5	2,259.3	2,274.6	2,293.1	2,311.5	2,242.7
2001	2,239.4	2,275.4	2,291.5	2,287.0	2,279.8	2,251.8	2,216.2	2,243.8	2,266.6	2,269.7	2,276.8	2,281.5	2,265.0
2002	2,228.2	2,251.8	2,268.3	2,279.9	2,276.0	2,250.9	2,209.5	2,245.4	2,265.9	2,282.2	2,310.9	2,311.9	2,265.1
2003	2,253.0	2,279.4	2,292.3	2,297.7	2,300.0	2,271.3	2,239.4	2,279.5	2,302.9	2,330.7	2,347.1	2,363.2	2,296.4
2004	2,308.5	2,339.1	2,357.8	2,375.8	2,377.2	2,352.9	2,331.7	2,368.3	2,396.8	2,435.9	2,455.8	2,475.8	2,381.3
2005	2,413.1	2,454.6	2,473.7	2,506.0	2,507.8	2,481.1	2,468.1	2,507.4	2,545.7	2,558.1	2,585.5	2,604.6	2,508.8
2006	2,562.0	2,606.5	2,629.1	2,634.7	2,643.5	2,615.9	2,586.9	2,624.2	2,655.8	2,669.2	2,687.4	2,698.6	2,634.5
2007	2,630.7	2,668.5	2,686.3	2,676.0	2,680.6	2,647.1	2,612.3	2,653.4	2,670.4	2,679.8	2,692.8	2,693.5	2,666.0
Total Private													
2000	1,825.5	1,848.7	1,863.0	1,862.1	1,870.4	1,880.7	1,860.5	1,876.2	1,886.5	1,895.6	1,913.0	1,930.5	1,876.1
2001	1,873.9	1,891.5	1,906.4	1,900.3	1,896.2	1,898.2	1,875.5	1,882.9	1,879.2	1,876.1	1,880.1	1,886.0	1,887.2
2002	1,845.9	1,856.5	1,871.6	1,879.4	1,881.3	1,879.7	1,859.0	1,871.4	1,869.2	1,877.2	1,898.5	1,906.2	1,874.7
2003	1,864.2	1,875.4	1,888.5	1,894.4	1,898.1	1,896.6	1,886.8	1,901.4	1,906.0	1,924.8	1,941.4	1,956.9	1,902.9
2004	1,918.1	1,933.0	1,951.1	1,967.7	1,971.4	1,975.9	1,974.7	1,983.9	1,988.0	2,020.1	2,040.1	2,059.1	1,981.9
2005	2,017.5	2,040.0	2,061.8	2,093.5	2,098.0	2,102.5	2,102.7	2,118.4	2,134.6	2,143.2	2,169.1	2,189.3	2,105.9
2006	2,161.6	2,190.2	2,212.8	2,218.5	2,225.8	2,233.4	2,216.4	2,230.1	2,239.1	2,244.3	2,261.9	2,277.5	2,226.0
2007	2,220.9	2,242.9	2,259.4	2,249.5	2,254.7	2,255.5	2,225.0	2,235.8	2,234.3	2,239.0	2,249.6	2,252.1	2,243.2
Goods-Producing													
2000	375.6	378.6	380.7	382.1	384.5	391.2	390.5	393.6	394.4	393.7	393.6	395.5	387.8
2001	384.7	386.4	389.8	387.9	388.6	390.5	389.3	389.6	384.9	379.8	375.1	371.4	384.8
2002	363.5	363.5	365.1	364.8	365.6	367.4	367.0	368.4	365.1	362.7	361.2	359.4	364.5
2003	353.9	353.2	354.5	356.0	358.1	360.8	360.7	362.9	362.5	363.6	363.8	365.1	359.5
2004	360.6	363.7	366.6	368.9	371.6	377.1	380.5	381.7	383.2	388.4	389.9	393.1	377.1
2005	386.4	391.6	396.7	403.2	406.3	413.0	415.5	418.0	419.7	420.5	423.9	428.2	410.3
2006	423.7	430.4	435.0	437.9	440.4	445.0	443.5	442.6	439.8	434.6	430.1	428.5	436.0
2007	418.8	421.9	422.7	419.1	420.2	424.7	419.9	420.9	416.8	412.9	407.2	404.4	417.5
Natural Resources and Mining													
2000	9.6	9.7	9.7	9.7	9.8	10.0	9.9	9.9	9.8	9.7	9.6	9.7	9.7
2001	9.6	9.6	9.6	9.6	9.7	9.7	9.6	9.6	9.5	9.5	9.4	9.2	9.6
2002	8.9	8.9	8.9	9.0	8.8	8.9	8.7	8.7	8.7	8.6	8.4	8.4	8.7
2003	8.2	8.0	7.9	8.0	8.0	8.1	8.1	8.1	8.0	8.0	8.0	8.0	8.0
2004	7.8	7.9	7.9	8.1	8.3	8.4	8.4	8.5	8.5	8.7	8.7	8.7	8.3
2005	8.6	8.7	8.8	9.0	9.1	9.3	8.1	8.0	8.0	8.0	8.4	9.0	8.6
2006	9.0	9.1	9.2	9.5	9.7	10.1	10.2	10.3	10.4	10.4	10.5	10.5	9.9
2007	10.5	10.5	10.7	10.7	10.9	11.2	11.4	11.7	11.9	12.1	12.1	12.2	11.3
Construction													
2000	159.6	161.2	162.9	164.3	166.7	170.3	169.9	171.9	172.5	172.9	172.1	173.4	168.1
2001	166.5	168.8	172.4	172.1	173.6	176.7	177.5	179.6	177.3	174.9	172.9	170.4	173.6
2002	167.0	167.4	169.7	170.1	172.0	174.0	174.1	176.6	174.8	174.3	173.9	172.4	172.2
2003	168.7	169.0	170.5	172.0	174.7	177.1	177.7	179.8	180.1	181.6	181.5	181.7	176.2
2004	178.3	180.6	183.0	185.8	187.9	191.4	194.3	195.7	197.1	201.0	201.8	203.8	191.7
2005	199.2	203.3	207.9	213.7	215.9	220.8	224.1	226.0	228.2	228.8	231.6	233.3	219.4
2006	229.7	234.4	238.7	241.1	244.0	247.5	246.1	245.6	243.8	240.0	237.8	235.4	240.3
2007	226.7	227.6	228.5	226.3	227.3	231.1	226.9	227.3	224.3	220.5	215.1	211.6	224.4
Manufacturing													
2000	206.4	207.7	208.1	208.1	208.0	210.9	210.7	211.8	212.1	211.1	211.9	212.4	209.9
2001	208.6	208.0	207.8	206.2	205.3	204.1	202.2	200.4	198.1	195.4	192.8	191.8	201.7
2002	187.6	187.2	186.5	185.7	184.8	184.5	184.2	183.1	181.6	179.8	178.9	178.6	183.5
2003	177.0	176.2	176.1	176.0	175.4	175.6	174.9	175.0	174.4	174.0	174.3	175.4	175.3
2004	174.5	175.2	175.7	175.0	175.4	177.3	177.8	177.5	177.6	178.7	179.4	180.6	177.1
2005	178.6	179.6	180.0	180.5	181.3	182.9	183.3	184.0	183.5	183.7	183.9	185.9	182.3
2006	185.0	186.9	187.1	187.3	186.7	187.4	187.2	186.7	185.6	184.2	181.8	182.6	185.7
2007	181.6	183.8	183.5	182.1	182.0	182.4	181.6	181.9	180.6	180.3	180.0	180.6	181.7
Service-Providing													
2000	1,808.5	1,841.7	1,859.0	1,858.2	1,869.0	1,833.7	1,802.4	1,824.9	1,864.9	1,880.9	1,899.5	1,916.0	1,854.9
2001	1,854.7	1,889.0	1,901.7	1,899.1	1,891.2	1,861.3	1,826.9	1,854.2	1,881.7	1,889.9	1,901.7	1,910.1	1,880.1
2002	1,864.7	1,888.3	1,903.2	1,915.1	1,910.4	1,883.5	1,842.5	1,877.0	1,900.8	1,919.5	1,949.7	1,952.5	1,900.6
2003	1,899.1	1,926.2	1,937.8	1,941.7	1,941.9	1,910.5	1,878.7	1,916.6	1,940.4	1,967.1	1,983.3	1,998.1	1,936.8
2004	1,947.9	1,975.4	1,991.2	2,006.9	2,005.6	1,975.8	1,951.2	1,986.6	2,013.6	2,047.5	2,065.9	2,082.7	2,004.2
2005	2,026.7	2,063.0	2,077.0	2,102.8	2,101.5	2,068.1	2,052.6	2,089.4	2,126.0	2,137.6	2,161.6	2,176.4	2,098.6
2006	2,138.3	2,176.1	2,194.1	2,196.8	2,203.1	2,170.9	2,143.4	2,181.6	2,216.0	2,234.6	2,257.3	2,270.1	2,198.5
2007	2,211.9	2,246.6	2,263.6	2,256.9	2,260.4	2,222.4	2,192.4	2,232.5	2,253.6	2,266.9	2,285.6	2,289.1	2,248.5
Trade, Transportation, and Utilities													
2000	432.5	433.1	432.2	429.5	430.5	433.6	430.6	433.7	436.4	442.2	455.7	464.0	437.8
2001	444.1	441.9	440.9	439.7	438.4	438.5	434.8	434.9	434.7	439.1	447.2	452.5	440.6
2002	437.2	434.0	436.7	437.4	439.1	439.9	435.3	436.8	438.1	442.1	452.9	460.9	440.9
2003	442.6	441.7	442.7	440.7	441.1	440.5	439.5	441.4	441.9	450.3	461.3	469.0	446.0
2004	453.6	453.1	455.0	456.8	458.4	458.8	459.1	460.5	459.0	468.4	481.0	488.8	462.7
2005	476.8	477.8	479.9	481.8	482.3	482.3	485.8	487.2	490.1	494.4	507.7	516.8	488.6
2006	502.1	501.6	505.9	505.7	506.4	506.4	507.8	509.8	510.9	517.9	531.3	540.4	512.2
2007	522.0	520.8	523.2	522.6	524.0	523.6	519.7	520.3	520.1	524.6	535.0	538.2	524.5
Wholesale Trade													
2000	94.4	95.3	95.8	93.6	93.7	94.3	93.9	93.9	94.4	95.4	97.1	98.7	95.0
2001	97.6	98.3	98.5	97.3	96.3	95.8	94.8	94.6	94.0	94.0	94.3	95.2	95.9
2002	94.2	94.4	95.0	93.5	94.3	94.0	93.4	93.4	93.3	94.0	94.6	95.4	94.1
2003	94.3	94.6	94.4	93.2	93.3	92.9	91.8	91.7	91.6	91.9	92.7	94.1	93.0
2004	94.3	94.5	94.8	94.5	94.9	95.3	95.8	95.8	94.5	96.4	97.0	98.5	95.5
2005	97.6	98.6	99.2	99.3	99.3	99.6	100.0	99.9	100.2	100.9	102.2	104.1	100.1
2006	103.5	104.3	104.8	104.6	104.7	105.3	105.6	105.8	106.2	106.8	107.9	109.4	105.7
2007	107.7	108.3	108.9	108.1	108.3	109.1	108.0	107.4	107.1	107.8	108.5	109.2	108.2

Employment by Industry: Arizona, 2000–2007—*Continued*

(Numbers in thousands, not seasonally adjusted.)

Industry and year	January	February	March	April	May	June	July	August	September	October	November	December	Annual Average
Retail Trade													
2000	264.3	264.2	263.5	263.2	263.9	265.7	262.8	265.2	267.1	271.4	282.3	288.4	268.5
2001	270.0	266.8	265.7	265.6	264.7	265.1	262.9	263.3	264.2	269.0	277.4	282.4	268.1
2002	268.9	265.6	267.0	268.6	269.2	269.4	265.8	266.8	268.4	270.6	280.7	287.8	270.7
2003	271.5	270.3	271.4	270.9	271.2	271.3	271.7	273.5	273.9	281.1	291.2	297.0	276.2
2004	282.4	281.8	282.7	284.5	285.5	285.5	285.1	286.4	286.6	292.0	303.9	309.9	288.9
2005	299.5	299.1	300.6	302.7	302.3	302.0	305.0	305.8	307.8	311.5	322.4	328.1	307.2
2006	316.0	314.8	318.2	317.8	318.2	317.6	318.2	319.2	319.1	325.7	337.4	343.1	322.1
2007	328.5	326.6	328.5	328.5	329.1	327.9	326.5	327.4	328.0	331.7	340.9	342.6	330.5
Transportation and Utilities													
2000	73.8	73.6	72.9	72.7	72.9	73.6	73.9	74.6	74.9	75.4	76.3	76.9	74.2
2001	76.5	76.8	76.7	76.8	77.4	77.6	77.1	77.0	76.5	76.1	75.5	74.9	76.6
2002	74.1	74.0	74.7	75.3	75.6	76.5	76.1	76.6	76.4	77.5	77.6	77.7	76.0
2003	76.8	76.8	76.9	76.6	76.6	76.3	76.0	76.2	76.4	77.3	77.4	77.9	76.7
2004	76.9	76.8	77.5	77.8	78.0	78.0	78.2	78.3	77.9	80.0	80.1	80.4	78.3
2005	79.7	80.1	80.1	79.8	80.7	80.7	80.8	81.5	82.1	82.0	83.1	84.6	81.3
2006	82.6	82.5	82.9	83.3	83.5	83.5	84.0	84.8	85.6	85.4	86.0	87.9	84.3
2007	85.8	85.9	85.8	86.0	86.6	86.6	85.2	85.5	85.0	85.1	85.6	86.4	85.8
Information													
2000	51.6	52.6	54.8	55.1	55.6	55.6	55.1	55.1	54.5	53.6	54.1	54.6	54.3
2001	53.7	54.9	54.4	54.4	53.8	54.2	53.7	53.8	53.2	53.0	54.0	53.2	53.9
2002	53.2	53.2	52.7	52.7	52.3	51.7	51.6	51.4	50.6	49.9	50.7	50.8	51.7
2003	49.6	49.9	50.1	50.1	50.0	50.1	49.5	49.3	48.6	48.7	49.7	49.5	49.5
2004	48.5	48.5	48.8	48.7	48.0	47.7	46.8	45.9	44.6	44.8	45.3	44.9	46.9
2005	44.2	44.8	45.1	45.9	46.1	45.7	45.3	45.0	44.6	44.9	45.5	46.1	45.3
2006	45.4	45.5	45.5	44.5	44.7	44.6	43.8	43.7	42.9	42.5	43.1	43.3	44.1
2007	41.5	42.4	42.3	42.7	43.5	43.4	43.1	42.6	42.5	42.4	42.8	42.8	42.7
Financial Activities													
2000	147.2	149.9	149.9	149.2	150.1	151.6	150.5	151.4	152.0	152.7	153.0	154.4	150.9
2001	149.2	150.8	152.3	152.4	152.8	153.5	154.4	154.6	154.7	154.6	155.3	156.3	153.4
2002	153.2	154.7	154.2	155.2	154.6	154.5	154.2	154.4	154.5	155.7	157.7	158.6	155.1
2003	156.5	157.4	158.9	158.7	159.5	160.0	160.8	162.0	161.3	161.2	161.5	162.4	160.0
2004	160.3	161.2	162.2	164.3	164.0	164.2	165.1	165.5	165.2	167.4	168.0	169.2	164.7
2005	167.3	168.8	169.4	172.1	172.5	173.5	174.9	176.6	177.6	179.0	179.8	181.2	174.4
2006	178.5	179.9	180.9	181.4	182.2	182.7	182.8	183.5	184.0	185.1	185.3	187.2	182.8
2007	184.3	185.9	186.5	186.5	186.2	185.7	184.0	181.8	180.8	180.6	180.3	180.7	183.6
Professional and Business Services													
2000	309.5	316.1	321.9	324.6	328.2	329.2	325.4	329.8	330.6	331.6	332.5	335.2	326.2
2001	319.1	324.5	328.7	326.4	324.1	324.7	318.1	318.4	317.3	314.5	310.6	312.2	319.9
2002	303.6	307.7	313.1	316.9	315.9	316.7	313.7	317.2	315.5	314.8	317.2	317.2	314.1
2003	308.8	313.2	317.3	319.7	320.6	321.6	318.2	321.1	322.7	326.0	326.3	329.3	320.4
2004	319.0	322.7	327.5	335.2	335.1	338.3	340.4	341.7	343.9	351.3	352.6	356.1	338.7
2005	346.0	351.5	356.1	363.6	363.2	366.5	367.7	371.5	374.8	374.2	377.2	379.7	366.0
2006	374.0	382.7	386.6	389.6	391.8	396.5	394.7	398.9	402.3	403.5	404.9	407.2	394.4
2007	394.5	399.3	403.9	401.9	402.5	405.3	400.1	403.2	401.6	401.0	403.1	403.4	401.7
Education and Health Services													
2000	208.7	211.4	212.1	211.1	211.3	210.6	208.1	211.2	213.7	214.8	215.8	217.7	212.2
2001	214.5	216.8	218.6	218.5	218.2	218.5	215.3	220.1	221.8	223.5	225.3	227.6	219.9
2002	227.3	229.4	230.7	230.0	231.6	231.0	226.9	232.0	233.9	237.5	239.9	240.7	232.6
2003	239.8	242.5	243.1	245.7	246.2	245.1	243.2	247.9	250.3	251.3	252.8	254.2	246.8
2004	253.6	255.2	256.5	258.8	259.4	258.8	256.1	260.9	263.3	267.2	268.6	270.4	260.7
2005	266.2	268.4	271.4	275.6	276.7	273.7	271.5	277.0	279.6	281.0	282.9	284.3	275.7
2006	282.5	286.3	288.8	289.3	290.3	289.0	286.6	292.5	295.1	297.3	299.4	302.4	291.6
2007	296.6	301.1	302.8	301.5	302.9	301.7	298.6	304.0	306.4	308.2	309.6	311.1	303.7
Leisure and Hospitality													
2000	224.1	229.3	233.2	233.2	232.4	230.1	222.6	224.1	227.6	229.4	230.3	230.6	228.9
2001	226.7	232.8	236.9	236.9	235.4	231.7	224.4	225.6	226.5	227.4	227.9	228.0	230.0
2002	223.0	228.4	232.5	235.7	235.2	230.8	224.3	225.1	225.3	228.3	232.6	232.2	229.5
2003	228.0	232.2	235.8	238.0	236.8	232.4	227.5	228.5	230.2	234.6	236.4	237.7	233.1
2004	234.7	239.5	244.9	246.2	246.0	241.8	237.2	238.1	239.4	242.4	244.5	246.0	241.7
2005	242.5	248.1	252.9	259.9	259.0	255.7	250.6	251.8	256.1	256.6	258.8	259.4	254.3
2006	258.1	264.2	268.9	271.6	270.1	267.6	261.3	262.6	266.6	267.5	271.0	271.1	266.7
2007	266.8	272.9	278.4	278.0	277.7	272.6	263.8	267.8	269.9	273.1	275.3	275.5	272.7
Other Services													
2000	76.3	77.7	78.2	77.3	77.8	78.8	77.7	77.3	77.3	77.6	78.0	78.5	77.7
2001	81.9	83.4	84.8	84.1	84.9	86.6	85.5	85.9	86.1	84.2	84.7	84.8	84.7
2002	84.9	85.6	86.6	86.7	87.0	87.7	86.0	86.1	86.2	86.2	86.3	86.4	86.3
2003	85.0	85.3	86.1	85.5	85.8	86.1	87.4	88.3	88.5	89.1	89.6	89.7	87.2
2004	87.8	89.1	89.6	88.8	88.9	89.2	89.5	89.6	89.4	90.2	90.2	90.6	89.4
2005	88.1	89.0	90.3	91.4	91.9	92.1	91.4	91.3	92.1	92.6	93.3	93.6	91.4
2006	97.3	99.6	101.2	98.5	99.9	101.6	95.9	96.5	97.5	95.9	96.8	97.4	98.2
2007	96.4	98.6	99.6	97.2	97.7	98.5	95.8	95.2	96.2	96.2	96.3	96.0	97.0
Government													
2000	358.6	371.6	376.7	378.2	383.1	344.2	332.4	342.3	372.8	379.0	380.1	381.0	366.6
2001	365.5	383.9	385.1	386.7	383.6	353.6	340.7	360.9	387.4	393.6	396.7	395.5	377.8
2002	382.3	395.3	396.7	400.5	394.7	371.2	350.5	374.0	396.7	405.0	412.4	405.7	390.4
2003	388.8	404.0	403.8	403.3	401.9	374.7	352.6	378.1	396.9	405.9	405.7	406.3	393.5
2004	390.4	406.1	406.7	408.1	405.8	377.0	357.0	384.4	408.8	415.8	415.7	416.7	399.4
2005	395.6	414.6	411.9	412.5	409.8	378.6	365.4	389.0	411.1	414.9	416.4	415.3	402.9
2006	400.4	416.3	416.3	416.2	417.7	382.5	370.5	394.1	416.7	424.9	425.5	421.1	408.5
2007	409.8	425.6	426.9	426.5	425.9	391.6	387.3	417.6	436.1	440.8	443.2	441.4	422.7

Average Weekly Hours by Selected Industry: Arizona, 2001–2007

(Not seasonally adjusted.)

Industry and year	January	February	March	April	May	June	July	August	September	October	November	December	Annual Average
Construction													
2001	35.6	36.7	37.4	36.9	37.8	38.2	37.9	37.6	37.5	37.2	36.5	36.2	37.1
2002	37.0	37.1	37.7	37.5	37.8	37.3	36.9	37.9	37.0	37.9	37.5	38.0	37.5
2003	37.4	36.3	37.3	37.9	37.7	38.3	37.5	38.0	37.3	37.7	36.9	37.6	37.5
2004	37.4	37.3	37.6	37.8	38.0	37.9	37.3	37.3	37.6	38.2	37.9	37.6	37.7
2005	37.5	36.6	37.3	36.7	36.7	37.2	36.9	37.6	37.8	37.6	37.5	37.5	37.3
2006	36.8	36.6	36.7	36.4	36.5	37.0	36.9	37.0	36.9	37.1	37.7	37.7	36.9
2007	37.3	37.1	37.3	37.8	38.4	38.1	37.8	37.5	37.4	37.6	37.8	37.6	37.6
Manufacturing													
2001	40.6	40.1	40.4	39.5	39.4	39.8	39.9	40.8	40.9	40.7	40.4	40.5	40.3
2002	40.1	39.9	40.3	40.4	40.0	40.2	40.3	39.9	39.8	39.7	39.8	39.9	40.0
2003	40.4	39.2	40.0	40.4	40.6	40.7	39.8	40.2	40.5	40.6	41.3	41.3	40.4
2004	40.8	40.5	39.6	39.8	39.5	39.5	40.5	40.5	40.6	41.1	41.3	42.0	40.5
2005	41.3	41.3	41.5	41.0	40.7	40.8	40.0	40.1	40.0	40.9	40.9	40.5	40.7
2006	39.9	40.5	40.8	40.4	40.4	40.5	40.8	41.0	40.7	40.5	40.9	41.1	40.6
2007	41.1	41.1	41.3	40.9	40.8	40.4	40.6	41.3	41.5	40.9	40.8	41.5	41.0
Trade, Transportation, and Utilities													
2001	33.1	32.9	33.1	33.5	32.6	32.8	33.4	33.1	33.0	33.0	32.7	33.5	33.1
2002	33.1	33.3	33.5	33.3	33.4	33.6	33.5	33.6	33.6	33.6	33.3	34.1	33.5
2003	33.9	33.9	33.9	33.9	34.1	34.6	34.6	34.7	34.2	34.7	34.5	34.7	34.3
2004	34.3	34.6	34.1	34.2	34.5	34.3	34.5	34.9	34.9	34.4	33.9	34.3	34.4
2005	34.1	34.4	34.5	34.1	34.4	34.4	34.4	34.4	34.8	34.2	34.5	34.7	34.4
2006	33.7	33.7	33.6	33.5	33.7	33.9	33.6	33.3	33.8	33.2	33.8	33.6	33.6
2007	33.4	33.4	33.6	33.4	32.6	33.3	33.5	33.3	33.4	33.1	33.8	34.0	33.4
Wholesale Trade													
2001	38.2	38.6	38.5	39.2	38.1	38.7	39.9	38.7	39.1	39.9	39.3	39.7	39.0
2002	39.9	41.1	39.9	39.9	38.9	37.9	36.8	37.8	38.9	39.0	38.4	39.6	39.0
2003	40.2	39.3	39.6	38.9	39.3	39.3	39.6	39.6	38.9	38.3	39.2	40.3	39.4
2004	40.6	40.9	39.7	39.9	40.3	40.3	40.0	41.2	40.1	39.8	40.0	39.6	40.2
2005	39.8	39.8	39.6	38.8	39.0	38.8	38.8	39.3	39.2	38.7	38.0	38.7	39.0
2006	39.0	37.9	38.3	38.7	39.0	38.8	38.7	38.5	37.7	37.6	37.6	37.2	38.2
2007	38.3	38.7	38.6	38.7	38.4	39.0	39.6	38.8	39.0	38.2	38.5	39.6	38.8
Retail Trade													
2001	30.5	30.5	30.5	30.6	30.3	30.6	30.9	30.9	30.4	30.1	30.4	31.3	30.6
2002	30.6	30.9	31.2	31.1	31.4	31.7	31.9	31.6	31.3	31.4	31.0	31.9	31.3
2003	30.9	31.4	31.0	31.4	31.3	32.1	32.0	32.1	31.6	32.3	31.6	32.0	31.6
2004	31.1	31.3	31.0	31.0	31.5	31.3	31.7	31.7	32.3	31.7	30.9	31.8	31.4
2005	31.4	31.5	31.8	31.5	31.7	31.9	31.9	31.8	32.5	31.6	32.1	32.4	31.8
2006	31.8	32.1	31.8	31.5	31.7	32.0	31.6	31.6	32.2	31.5	32.3	32.3	31.8
2007	31.5	31.3	31.6	31.3	30.4	31.0	31.1	31.1	31.2	31.2	32.0	32.0	31.3

Average Hourly Earnings by Selected Industry: Arizona, 2001–2007

(Dollars, not seasonally adjusted.)

Industry and year	January	February	March	April	May	June	July	August	September	October	November	December	Annual Average
Construction													
2001	15.45	15.46	15.56	15.56	15.18	14.80	14.75	14.40	14.50	14.46	14.46	14.76	14.94
2002	14.42	14.28	14.22	14.31	14.25	14.21	14.32	14.37	14.53	14.59	14.78	14.82	14.43
2003	14.89	14.87	14.98	15.03	15.13	15.40	15.34	15.24	15.39	15.16	15.23	15.38	15.18
2004	15.42	15.29	15.29	15.24	15.33	15.29	15.25	15.29	15.27	15.34	15.52	15.58	15.34
2005	15.34	15.55	15.57	15.58	15.93	16.03	16.04	16.00	16.00	15.93	16.00	16.14	15.85
2006	16.18	16.29	16.35	16.37	16.54	16.59	16.74	16.81	17.03	17.07	16.94	16.98	16.66
2007	16.90	17.24	17.27	17.61	17.49	17.75	18.07	18.17	18.00	18.08	18.28	18.56	17.78
Manufacturing													
2001	13.48	13.50	13.70	13.71	13.72	13.73	13.89	13.76	14.01	13.94	14.09	14.11	13.80
2002	14.06	14.10	14.14	14.04	14.16	14.22	14.18	14.09	14.13	14.16	14.16	14.50	14.16
2003	14.41	14.26	14.28	14.24	14.33	14.34	14.45	14.49	14.35	14.46	14.62	14.33	14.38
2004	14.24	14.17	14.27	14.28	14.13	14.08	13.96	14.21	14.29	14.19	14.40	14.22	14.20
2005	14.41	14.54	14.43	14.73	15.01	14.94	14.89	14.67	14.31	14.18	14.33	14.15	14.55
2006	14.52	14.42	14.57	14.70	14.99	15.14	14.95	15.34	15.32	15.14	14.76	14.63	14.88
2007	14.95	15.25	15.15	15.31	15.66	15.76	15.97	15.76	15.69	16.00	15.96	15.87	15.61
Trade, Transportation, and Utilities													
2001	12.90	13.05	13.11	13.03	12.96	12.94	12.76	12.97	13.18	12.99	13.08	13.14	13.01
2002	12.97	13.07	13.12	13.11	13.13	13.17	13.10	13.07	13.38	13.26	13.29	13.09	13.15
2003	13.40	13.42	13.53	13.34	13.46	13.51	13.49	13.41	13.58	13.43	13.82	13.44	13.49
2004	13.90	14.07	13.87	13.94	14.12	14.17	14.28	14.34	14.48	14.59	14.49	14.37	14.22
2005	14.76	14.87	14.74	14.76	14.74	14.76	14.97	14.92	14.98	15.10	14.98	14.89	14.87
2006	14.33	14.16	14.04	14.28	14.19	14.13	14.42	14.53	14.20	14.26	14.12	14.08	14.23
2007	14.48	14.46	14.69	14.84	14.87	14.89	14.84	14.79	14.70	14.65	14.58	14.43	14.68
Wholesale Trade													
2001	15.44	15.90	15.62	15.52	15.05	15.32	14.97	15.38	15.59	15.12	14.92	15.24	15.34
2002	15.06	14.85	14.93	15.38	15.65	16.12	16.58	16.19	16.49	16.22	16.37	16.51	15.85
2003	16.01	16.00	16.48	16.32	16.65	17.15	17.11	17.25	17.66	17.50	18.03	17.49	16.97
2004	17.94	18.09	17.99	18.24	18.79	18.85	18.91	18.82	18.65	18.17	17.62	17.98	18.34
2005	18.42	18.67	18.59	18.75	18.94	18.71	18.95	18.38	18.72	18.47	18.65	18.46	18.64
2006	18.25	17.70	17.48	17.87	18.15	17.98	18.27	18.65	18.69	18.63	18.96	19.47	18.34
2007	19.19	18.77	19.20	19.24	19.50	19.47	19.58	19.88	19.53	19.58	20.08	19.48	19.46
Retail Trade													
2001	11.08	11.25	11.46	11.38	11.27	11.30	10.96	11.29	11.44	11.21	11.55	11.36	11.30
2002	11.17	11.35	11.35	11.27	11.25	11.27	11.11	11.17	11.41	11.34	11.33	11.12	11.26
2003	11.41	11.47	11.55	11.52	11.58	11.56	11.53	11.32	11.47	11.47	11.77	11.42	11.51
2004	11.73	11.86	11.65	11.56	11.57	11.54	11.58	11.56	11.91	12.08	11.96	11.68	11.73
2005	11.94	12.08	12.05	12.13	12.13	12.13	12.31	12.26	12.21	12.27	12.19	12.01	12.14
2006	12.37	12.38	12.27	12.37	12.13	12.09	12.35	12.35	11.98	12.05	11.85	11.70	12.15
2007	12.00	12.12	12.28	12.42	12.35	12.36	12.17	12.10	12.16	12.17	12.00	11.91	12.17

Average Weekly Earnings by Selected Industry: Arizona, 2001–2007

(Dollars, not seasonally adjusted.)

Industry and year	January	February	March	April	May	June	July	August	September	October	November	December	Annual Average
Construction													
2001	550.02	567.38	581.94	574.16	573.80	565.36	559.03	541.44	543.75	537.91	527.79	534.31	554.27
2002	533.54	529.79	536.09	536.63	538.65	530.03	528.41	544.62	537.61	552.96	554.25	563.16	541.13
2003	556.89	539.78	558.75	569.64	570.40	589.82	575.25	579.12	574.05	571.53	561.99	578.29	569.25
2004	576.71	570.32	574.90	576.07	582.54	579.49	568.83	570.32	574.15	585.99	588.21	585.81	578.32
2005	575.25	569.13	580.76	571.79	584.63	596.32	591.88	601.60	604.80	598.97	600.00	605.25	591.21
2006	595.42	596.21	600.05	595.87	603.71	613.83	617.71	621.97	628.41	633.30	638.64	640.15	614.75
2007	630.37	639.60	644.17	665.66	671.62	676.28	683.05	681.38	673.20	679.81	690.98	697.86	668.53
Manufacturing													
2001	547.29	541.35	553.48	541.55	540.57	546.45	554.21	561.41	573.01	567.36	569.24	571.46	556.14
2002	563.81	562.59	569.84	567.22	566.40	571.64	571.45	562.19	562.37	562.15	563.57	578.55	566.40
2003	582.16	558.99	571.20	575.30	581.80	583.64	575.11	582.50	581.18	587.08	603.81	591.83	580.95
2004	580.99	573.89	565.09	568.34	558.14	556.16	565.38	575.51	575.51	580.17	583.21	594.72	597.24	575.10
2005	595.13	600.50	598.85	603.93	610.91	609.55	595.60	588.27	572.40	579.96	586.10	573.08	592.19
2006	579.35	584.01	594.46	593.88	605.60	613.17	609.96	628.94	623.52	613.17	603.68	601.29	604.13
2007	614.45	626.78	625.70	626.18	638.93	636.70	648.38	650.89	651.14	654.40	651.17	658.61	640.01
Trade, Transportation, and Utilities													
2001	426.99	429.35	433.94	436.51	422.50	424.43	426.18	429.31	434.94	428.67	427.72	440.19	430.63
2002	429.31	435.23	439.52	436.56	438.54	442.51	438.85	439.15	449.57	445.54	442.56	446.37	440.53
2003	454.26	454.94	458.67	452.23	458.99	467.45	466.75	465.33	464.44	466.02	476.79	466.37	462.71
2004	476.77	486.82	472.97	476.75	487.14	486.03	492.66	500.47	505.35	501.90	491.21	492.89	489.17
2005	503.32	511.53	508.53	503.32	507.06	507.74	514.97	513.25	521.30	516.42	516.81	516.68	511.53
2006	482.92	477.19	471.74	478.38	478.20	479.01	484.51	483.85	479.96	473.43	477.26	473.09	478.13
2007	483.63	482.96	493.58	495.66	484.76	495.84	497.14	492.51	490.98	484.92	492.80	490.62	490.31
Wholesale Trade													
2001	589.81	613.74	601.37	608.38	573.41	592.88	597.30	595.21	609.57	603.29	586.36	605.03	598.26
2002	600.89	610.34	595.71	613.66	608.79	610.95	610.14	611.98	641.46	632.58	628.61	653.80	618.15
2003	643.60	628.80	652.61	634.85	654.35	674.00	677.56	683.10	686.97	670.25	706.78	704.85	668.62
2004	728.36	739.88	714.20	727.78	757.24	759.66	756.40	775.38	747.87	723.17	704.80	712.01	737.27
2005	733.12	743.07	736.16	727.50	738.66	725.95	735.26	722.33	733.82	714.79	708.70	714.40	726.96
2006	711.75	670.83	669.48	691.57	707.85	697.62	707.05	718.03	704.61	700.49	712.90	724.28	700.59
2007	734.98	726.40	741.12	744.59	748.80	759.33	775.37	771.34	761.67	747.96	773.08	771.41	755.05
Retail Trade													
2001	337.94	343.13	349.53	348.23	341.48	345.78	338.66	348.86	347.78	337.42	351.12	355.57	345.78
2002	341.80	350.72	354.12	350.50	353.25	357.26	354.41	352.97	357.13	356.08	351.23	354.73	352.44
2003	352.57	360.16	358.05	361.73	362.45	371.08	368.96	363.37	362.45	370.48	371.93	365.44	363.72
2004	364.80	371.22	361.15	358.36	364.46	361.20	367.09	366.45	384.69	382.94	369.56	371.42	368.32
2005	374.92	380.52	383.19	382.10	384.52	386.95	392.69	389.87	396.83	387.73	391.30	389.12	386.05
2006	393.37	397.40	390.19	389.66	384.52	386.88	390.26	386.56	385.76	379.58	382.76	377.91	386.37
2007	378.00	379.36	388.05	388.75	375.44	383.16	378.49	376.31	379.39	379.70	384.00	381.12	380.92

Population
    2000 census: 2,673,400
    2007 estimate: 2,834,797
    Percent change, 2000–2007: 6.0%

Percent change in total nonfarm employment, 2000–2007: 3.9%

Industry with the largest growth in employment, 2000–2007 (thousands)
    Education and health services, 27.0

Industry with the largest decline in employment, 2000–2007 (thousands)
    Manufacturing, -51.1

Civilian labor force
    2000: 1,260,256
    2007: 1,367,801

Employment-population ratio
    2000: 59.6%
    2007: 59.8%

Unemployment rate and rank among states
    2000: 4.2%, 33rd
    2007: 5.4%, 43rd

Employment by Industry, 2007

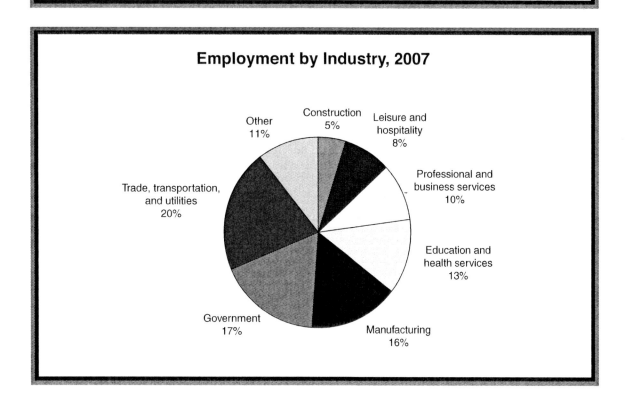

Employment by Industry: Arkansas, 2000–2007

(Numbers in thousands, not seasonally adjusted.)

Industry and year	January	February	March	April	May	June	July	August	September	October	November	December	Annual Average
Total Nonfarm													
2000	1,135.6	1,143.8	1,158.4	1,158.7	1,166.5	1,168.3	1,148.2	1,156.6	1,168.4	1,168.1	1,167.4	1,163.1	1,158.6
2001	1,139.8	1,147.3	1,157.0	1,160.8	1,162.8	1,161.3	1,143.9	1,151.5	1,159.6	1,155.5	1,154.2	1,151.0	1,153.7
2002	1,125.3	1,132.8	1,144.1	1,148.4	1,155.3	1,155.0	1,138.2	1,143.2	1,157.2	1,151.7	1,151.8	1,152.4	1,146.3
2003	1,128.7	1,133.1	1,140.4	1,142.6	1,149.2	1,146.0	1,131.1	1,141.2	1,155.5	1,159.1	1,156.3	1,158.4	1,145.1
2004	1,135.2	1,142.5	1,152.9	1,157.7	1,162.2	1,161.1	1,146.8	1,155.4	1,169.0	1,168.7	1,172.0	1,173.6	1,158.1
2005	1,151.0	1,162.1	1,173.0	1,178.4	1,182.2	1,180.9	1,165.3	1,172.0	1,192.7	1,189.1	1,193.1	1,194.7	1,177.9
2006	1,178.2	1,186.6	1,198.5	1,203.8	1,206.7	1,205.3	1,184.1	1,193.2	1,208.6	1,205.5	1,205.7	1,207.3	1,198.6
2007	1,184.9	1,193.3	1,207.8	1,208.0	1,211.5	1,210.0	1,187.5	1,197.9	1,211.3	1,211.9	1,211.9	1,212.1	1,204.0
Total Private													
2000	947.1	952.0	964.0	965.3	969.2	977.9	971.9	975.2	977.1	973.6	972.2	968.7	967.9
2001	948.5	951.8	960.5	963.7	966.4	970.3	965.1	969.1	963.8	956.5	954.0	951.2	960.1
2002	930.4	933.8	944.1	949.6	956.8	962.1	957.7	959.7	961.0	952.6	951.3	952.1	950.9
2003	932.0	932.8	939.0	941.7	948.7	950.3	945.8	952.7	954.7	955.4	951.8	954.6	946.6
2004	935.7	939.3	948.9	954.8	959.7	964.4	962.5	964.6	966.1	963.4	965.2	968.0	957.7
2005	950.1	956.1	966.6	970.5	975.6	979.5	976.9	979.4	985.2	980.2	983.7	986.3	974.2
2006	972.6	976.6	987.3	992.0	996.1	1,001.2	992.3	996.2	997.8	993.2	992.1	995.0	991.0
2007	976.8	979.7	993.2	993.6	998.6	1,001.8	994.5	999.9	998.1	996.1	995.6	996.6	993.7
Goods-Producing													
2000	297.2	297.7	301.0	300.0	301.3	303.5	302.5	302.4	302.1	299.8	298.1	297.0	300.2
2001	291.1	288.9	290.7	290.0	289.9	290.7	289.0	289.8	287.3	283.7	280.4	279.0	287.5
2002	273.3	273.4	274.6	274.9	276.7	278.9	277.8	277.3	276.7	273.1	270.9	270.1	274.8
2003	265.2	263.5	263.9	263.0	263.9	264.4	263.3	264.4	264.6	264.1	261.1	261.7	263.6
2004	257.5	257.4	259.5	261.9	263.4	264.9	264.3	264.5	264.3	262.0	261.0	260.2	261.7
2005	258.1	258.6	260.7	261.3	263.3	264.5	263.7	264.7	265.9	264.4	264.7	264.8	262.9
2006	261.9	262.8	262.7	264.5	265.3	267.7	265.1	265.9	264.8	261.4	258.1	258.8	263.3
2007	255.0	253.9	256.9	256.3	257.0	257.2	256.3	256.3	254.7	253.4	251.3	250.9	254.9
Natural Resources and Mining													
2000	6.7	6.6	6.6	6.5	6.7	6.9	6.9	7.0	7.0	6.9	6.7	6.8	6.7
2001	6.5	6.6	6.7	6.9	7.1	7.2	7.3	7.3	7.2	7.1	7.0	6.8	7.0
2002	6.5	6.5	6.6	6.6	6.8	6.9	6.9	7.0	7.0	6.9	6.9	6.8	6.8
2003	6.5	6.6	6.6	6.8	7.0	7.1	7.0	7.2	7.2	7.2	7.2	7.2	7.0
2004	7.0	6.9	6.9	6.9	7.0	7.0	7.0	7.2	7.2	7.0	6.8	6.8	7.0
2005	6.5	6.6	6.7	6.9	7.0	7.2	7.2	7.3	7.3	7.2	7.2	7.3	7.0
2006	6.8	6.8	6.9	7.4	7.6	7.8	7.7	7.8	8.1	8.0	8.1	8.2	7.6
2007	8.4	8.7	9.0	9.0	9.2	9.5	9.8	10.0	10.0	10.1	10.2	10.1	9.5
Construction													
2000	50.3	50.7	53.0	52.5	53.4	54.5	54.1	54.5	55.0	53.9	52.8	52.0	53.0
2001	49.6	49.9	52.2	52.9	54.4	55.3	56.1	56.6	55.7	54.4	53.9	53.3	53.7
2002	51.3	51.7	53.2	54.0	55.2	56.6	57.1	57.1	56.0	54.2	53.0	52.2	54.3
2003	49.3	48.7	49.5	50.1	51.3	51.7	51.9	52.4	52.2	51.9	50.5	50.2	50.8
2004	47.8	47.8	49.7	51.3	52.4	53.3	53.3	53.4	53.3	52.1	51.6	51.2	51.4
2005	50.3	50.9	52.5	53.8	55.3	55.7	56.0	56.5	56.8	55.9	55.9	56.2	54.7
2006	54.0	55.0	54.8	56.6	57.9	58.9	57.8	58.4	59.0	57.3	56.1	56.4	56.9
2007	53.9	53.6	56.4	56.8	57.5	58.1	57.3	57.7	57.4	56.3	55.3	54.8	56.3
Manufacturing													
2000	240.2	240.4	241.4	241.0	241.2	242.1	241.5	240.9	240.1	239.0	238.6	238.2	240.3
2001	235.0	232.4	231.8	230.2	228.4	228.2	225.6	225.9	224.4	222.2	219.5	218.9	226.9
2002	215.5	215.2	214.8	214.3	214.7	215.4	213.8	213.2	213.7	212.0	211.0	211.1	213.7
2003	209.4	208.2	207.8	206.1	205.6	205.6	204.4	204.8	205.2	205.0	203.4	204.3	205.8
2004	202.7	202.7	202.9	203.7	204.0	204.6	204.0	203.9	203.8	202.9	202.6	202.2	203.3
2005	201.3	201.1	201.5	200.6	201.0	201.6	200.5	200.9	201.8	201.3	201.6	201.3	201.2
2006	201.1	201.0	201.0	200.5	199.8	201.0	199.6	199.7	197.7	196.1	193.9	194.2	198.8
2007	192.7	191.6	191.5	190.5	190.3	189.6	189.2	188.6	187.3	187.0	185.8	186.0	189.2
Service-Providing													
2000	838.4	846.1	857.4	858.7	865.2	864.8	845.7	854.2	866.3	868.3	869.3	866.1	858.4
2001	848.7	858.4	866.3	870.8	872.9	870.6	854.9	861.7	872.3	871.8	873.8	872.0	866.2
2002	852.0	859.4	869.5	873.5	878.6	876.1	860.4	865.9	880.5	878.6	880.9	882.3	871.5
2003	863.5	869.6	876.5	879.6	885.3	881.6	867.8	876.8	890.9	895.0	895.2	896.7	881.5
2004	877.7	885.1	893.4	895.8	898.8	896.2	882.5	890.9	904.7	906.7	911.0	913.4	896.4
2005	892.9	903.5	912.3	917.1	918.9	916.4	901.6	907.3	926.8	924.7	928.4	929.9	915.0
2006	916.3	923.8	935.8	939.3	941.4	937.6	919.0	927.3	943.8	944.1	947.6	948.5	935.4
2007	929.9	939.4	950.9	951.7	954.5	952.8	931.2	941.6	956.6	958.5	960.6	961.2	949.1
Trade, Transportation, and Utilities													
2000	237.8	237.8	239.9	240.5	241.3	243.1	241.3	242.2	242.6	243.5	245.8	247.6	241.9
2001	238.6	237.5	240.4	241.5	242.5	243.2	241.4	241.7	240.9	241.2	243.7	244.6	241.4
2002	236.9	236.9	239.8	240.4	242.0	242.5	241.6	241.4	241.8	240.4	243.0	244.4	240.9
2003	236.2	235.3	236.7	237.3	238.2	238.7	238.5	239.7	240.9	242.4	244.1	246.3	239.5
2004	237.6	237.6	239.3	240.1	241.4	242.2	242.1	242.4	243.2	243.2	245.8	248.7	242.0
2005	241.1	240.6	242.7	244.2	244.9	246.0	245.7	245.4	247.2	246.4	249.7	252.0	245.5
2006	244.8	244.4	247.8	247.3	248.8	248.8	247.7	248.3	249.2	249.6	252.5	254.6	248.7
2007	246.2	245.9	250.3	248.2	250.0	250.7	249.3	249.9	249.8	250.0	252.6	254.4	249.8
Wholesale Trade													
2000	44.6	44.9	45.6	45.6	45.9	46.7	46.4	46.2	46.2	45.9	45.6	45.6	45.7
2001	45.1	45.3	45.8	45.8	45.9	46.3	46.1	45.9	45.5	45.3	45.0	44.9	45.6
2002	44.2	44.2	44.8	44.9	45.1	45.6	45.3	45.2	45.3	44.9	44.6	44.6	44.9
2003	43.9	44.1	44.4	44.4	44.9	45.4	45.1	45.2	45.4	45.3	45.1	45.2	44.9
2004	44.6	44.8	45.4	46.0	46.5	46.8	46.9	46.5	46.6	46.5	46.6	47.1	46.2
2005	46.5	46.8	47.3	47.5	47.8	48.0	47.8	47.6	47.6	47.2	47.1	47.5	47.4
2006	46.9	47.1	47.5	47.9	48.2	48.5	48.1	48.1	48.2	47.9	47.9	48.2	47.9
2007	47.2	47.4	48.0	48.1	48.3	48.6	48.3	48.3	48.2	47.9	47.7	48.0	48.0

Employment by Industry: Arkansas, 2000–2007—*Continued*

(Numbers in thousands, not seasonally adjusted.)

Industry and year	January	February	March	April	May	June	July	August	September	October	November	December	Annual Average
Retail Trade													
2000	130.2	130.2	131.2	131.6	132.3	132.9	131.7	132.6	132.5	133.1	135.9	137.4	132.6
2001	130.5	129.0	130.9	131.5	132.4	132.5	130.9	130.8	130.3	130.3	133.5	134.6	131.4
2002	128.6	127.5	129.1	129.7	130.8	130.7	130.1	129.5	129.4	128.8	131.8	133.5	130.0
2003	127.1	126.0	126.8	127.3	127.8	127.9	127.9	128.7	129.3	130.2	132.4	134.6	128.8
2004	128.5	128.1	129.4	129.8	130.5	130.7	130.3	130.6	130.6	131.1	134.0	135.6	130.8
2005	129.9	128.8	130.2	131.3	131.5	132.1	131.6	131.4	131.9	132.2	135.5	136.9	131.9
2006	131.8	130.9	133.5	132.6	133.6	132.9	132.2	132.7	132.6	133.2	136.0	137.5	133.3
2007	132.3	131.4	134.6	132.9	134.0	134.2	133.6	133.6	133.6	134.1	137.2	138.3	134.2
Transportation and Utilities													
2000	63.0	62.7	63.1	63.3	63.1	63.5	63.2	63.4	63.9	64.5	64.3	64.6	63.5
2001	63.0	63.2	63.7	64.2	64.2	64.4	64.4	65.0	65.1	65.6	65.2	65.1	64.4
2002	64.1	65.2	65.9	65.8	66.1	66.2	66.2	66.7	67.1	66.7	66.6	66.3	66.1
2003	65.2	65.2	65.5	65.6	65.5	65.4	65.5	65.8	66.2	66.9	66.6	66.5	65.8
2004	64.5	64.7	64.5	64.3	64.4	64.7	64.9	65.3	66.0	65.6	65.2	66.0	65.0
2005	64.7	65.0	65.2	65.4	65.6	65.9	66.3	66.4	67.7	67.0	67.1	67.6	66.2
2006	66.1	66.4	66.8	66.8	67.0	67.4	67.4	67.5	68.4	68.5	68.6	68.9	67.5
2007	66.7	67.1	67.7	67.2	67.7	67.9	67.4	68.0	68.0	68.0	67.7	68.1	67.6
Information													
2000	19.9	19.9	20.1	19.8	20.1	20.4	20.6	21.0	21.1	21.2	21.4	21.5	20.5
2001	21.2	21.2	21.0	20.8	20.8	20.9	21.1	21.1	21.0	20.8	20.9	20.8	21.0
2002	20.8	20.5	20.2	20.2	20.2	20.5	20.4	20.3	20.2	20.2	20.4	20.3	20.4
2003	20.1	20.1	20.1	20.0	20.1	20.3	20.5	20.5	20.3	20.4	20.5	20.6	20.3
2004	20.4	20.3	20.3	20.2	20.2	20.3	20.1	20.2	20.1	20.0	20.2	20.3	20.2
2005	20.2	20.4	20.3	20.0	20.1	20.0	19.9	20.0	19.8	19.8	19.8	19.8	20.0
2006	19.7	19.7	19.7	19.7	19.7	19.6	19.6	19.7	19.7	19.4	19.4	19.4	19.6
2007	19.6	19.6	19.6	19.7	19.8	19.8	19.8	19.9	19.9	19.9	19.9	20.0	19.8
Financial Activities													
2000	49.1	49.1	49.4	49.6	49.5	50.1	49.6	49.4	49.2	49.1	49.1	49.4	49.3
2001	48.7	48.9	49.0	49.1	49.4	49.8	49.8	49.7	49.6	49.2	49.4	49.9	49.4
2002	49.4	49.2	49.5	49.5	49.7	50.0	50.0	49.9	49.8	49.3	49.4	49.8	49.6
2003	49.4	49.4	49.6	49.9	50.2	50.7	50.9	50.9	50.7	50.6	50.8	51.3	50.4
2004	50.2	50.3	50.5	50.7	50.9	51.3	51.2	51.1	51.1	50.8	50.9	51.4	50.9
2005	50.8	50.7	50.9	50.7	51.0	51.6	51.8	51.8	51.8	51.7	51.8	52.5	51.4
2006	51.8	51.8	52.0	52.2	52.5	52.9	52.9	53.1	53.0	52.7	52.9	53.2	52.6
2007	52.4	52.4	52.6	53.1	53.4	53.8	53.8	53.8	53.6	53.5	53.6	54.1	53.3
Professional and Business Services													
2000	98.3	99.4	101.4	100.2	100.9	102.4	101.9	103.9	104.2	103.2	102.6	100.5	101.6
2001	100.9	102.4	102.6	102.1	102.4	103.0	102.3	104.0	102.7	100.7	99.6	98.3	101.8
2002	96.4	96.9	99.1	100.4	101.2	102.4	102.3	103.3	104.5	103.7	102.6	102.9	101.3
2003	101.0	101.5	102.0	103.0	104.2	104.4	102.6	105.5	105.7	107.2	105.8	105.3	104.0
2004	105.2	105.2	106.5	107.1	107.1	107.9	109.0	109.7	109.3	110.4	110.7	110.7	108.2
2005	107.1	108.8	110.5	110.6	110.7	111.5	111.8	112.8	113.2	113.1	113.1	113.3	111.4
2006	111.5	112.9	115.1	114.5	114.9	115.6	114.0	114.6	115.6	115.1	114.7	114.6	114.4
2007	114.0	115.1	116.6	116.6	116.8	117.4	115.6	118.0	118.3	118.8	118.4	117.9	117.0
Education and Health Services													
2000	125.5	126.9	127.7	127.7	127.0	126.0	124.9	125.4	128.9	129.3	129.6	129.1	127.3
2001	127.8	130.0	130.4	131.0	130.5	129.6	129.3	130.8	132.9	134.0	134.4	134.5	131.3
2002	133.0	133.8	135.0	135.4	135.3	134.1	133.2	134.9	137.4	137.9	138.6	138.7	135.6
2003	137.3	138.6	139.6	139.8	140.0	137.9	136.7	138.4	141.4	142.2	142.0	142.4	139.7
2004	140.1	141.4	142.3	142.7	142.3	141.2	140.2	141.1	143.9	144.9	145.3	145.2	142.6
2005	144.1	145.4	145.8	146.0	146.0	144.1	143.6	144.9	148.1	149.1	148.9	148.6	146.2
2006	148.4	149.7	150.7	151.2	150.9	150.0	148.2	149.8	152.5	152.7	152.8	153.0	150.8
2007	150.8	153.0	153.9	154.3	154.5	153.6	151.9	153.9	155.6	156.5	156.8	156.8	154.3
Leisure and Hospitality													
2000	78.9	80.6	83.5	86.5	87.8	90.4	89.4	89.4	87.8	86.5	84.8	82.9	85.7
2001	79.7	82.3	85.3	88.3	89.8	91.3	90.7	90.6	88.5	86.4	85.2	83.7	86.8
2002	80.5	82.8	85.2	88.0	90.6	92.0	91.0	91.3	89.6	87.5	85.9	85.3	87.5
2003	82.6	84.3	86.6	88.0	91.0	92.2	92.0	92.1	90.2	87.7	86.7	86.1	88.3
2004	84.2	86.4	89.5	90.8	92.9	94.4	93.8	94.1	92.9	91.1	90.1	90.0	90.9
2005	87.5	90.1	93.5	94.9	96.6	98.3	97.1	96.8	96.2	93.4	93.3	92.7	94.2
2006	92.0	92.7	96.2	99.0	99.8	101.7	99.8	99.7	98.0	97.5	96.7	96.1	97.4
2007	94.0	94.9	97.8	100.1	101.6	103.2	102.2	102.6	100.9	99.0	97.9	97.3	99.3
Other Services													
2000	40.4	40.6	41.0	41.0	41.3	42.0	41.7	41.5	41.2	41.0	40.8	40.7	41.1
2001	40.5	40.6	41.1	40.9	41.1	41.8	41.5	41.4	40.9	40.5	40.4	40.4	40.9
2002	40.1	40.3	40.7	40.8	41.1	41.7	41.4	41.3	41.0	40.5	40.5	40.6	40.8
2003	40.2	40.1	40.5	40.7	41.1	41.7	41.3	41.2	40.9	40.8	40.8	40.9	40.9
2004	40.5	40.7	41.0	41.3	41.5	42.2	41.8	41.5	41.3	41.0	41.2	41.5	41.3
2005	41.2	41.5	42.2	42.8	43.0	43.5	43.3	43.0	43.0	42.3	42.4	42.6	42.6
2006	42.5	42.6	43.1	43.6	44.2	44.9	45.0	45.1	45.0	44.8	45.0	45.3	44.3
2007	44.8	44.9	45.5	45.3	45.5	46.1	45.6	45.5	45.3	45.0	45.1	45.2	45.3
Government													
2000	188.5	191.8	194.4	193.4	197.3	190.4	176.3	181.4	191.3	194.5	195.2	194.4	190.7
2001	191.3	195.5	196.5	197.1	196.4	191.0	178.8	182.4	195.8	199.0	200.2	199.8	193.7
2002	194.9	199.0	200.0	198.8	198.5	192.9	180.5	183.5	196.2	199.1	200.5	200.3	195.4
2003	196.7	200.3	201.4	200.9	200.5	195.7	185.3	188.5	200.8	203.7	204.5	203.8	198.5
2004	199.5	203.2	204.0	202.9	202.5	196.7	184.3	190.8	202.9	205.3	206.8	205.6	200.4
2005	200.9	206.0	206.4	207.9	206.6	201.4	188.4	192.6	207.5	208.9	209.4	208.4	203.7
2006	205.6	210.0	211.2	211.8	210.6	204.1	191.8	197.0	210.8	212.3	213.6	212.3	207.6
2007	208.1	213.6	214.6	214.4	212.9	208.2	193.0	198.0	213.2	215.8	216.3	215.5	210.3

Average Weekly Hours by Selected Industry: Arkansas, 2001–2007

(Not seasonally adjusted.)

Industry and year	January	February	March	April	May	June	July	August	September	October	November	December	Annual Average
Manufacturing													
2001	40.7	39.7	39.7	39.2	40.0	40.1	39.9	40.2	40.3	39.8	39.0	39.9	39.9
2002	39.6	39.3	39.8	39.5	40.3	39.7	39.3	40.1	40.3	39.6	38.7	40.2	39.7
2003	39.7	39.0	39.1	39.5	39.3	39.8	39.1	40.2	40.5	39.7	39.3	40.4	39.6
2004	39.7	39.4	39.4	40.1	40.4	40.6	40.4	40.3	39.6	40.0	39.5	39.6	39.9
2005	39.4	38.7	39.0	39.1	39.7	40.3	40.1	40.2	41.0	40.2	40.8	40.1	39.9
2006	39.7	39.5	39.9	41.0	41.8	42.1	41.6	41.4	41.6	41.3	40.8	40.9	41.0
2007	40.8	40.2	39.5	38.9	39.2	40.3	39.1	39.1	40.2	39.9	39.9	39.8	39.7

Average Hourly Earnings by Selected Industry: Arkansas, 2001–2007

(Dollars, not seasonally adjusted.)

Industry and year	January	February	March	April	May	June	July	August	September	October	November	December	Annual Average
Manufacturing													
2001	12.79	12.71	12.73	12.80	12.74	12.87	13.02	12.96	12.97	12.97	13.04	13.20	12.90
2002	13.12	13.09	13.13	13.26	13.25	13.39	13.52	13.38	13.34	13.34	13.42	13.41	13.30
2003	13.39	13.54	13.69	13.79	13.71	13.68	13.75	13.58	13.48	13.33	13.35	13.38	13.55
2004	13.40	13.45	13.56	13.61	13.49	13.58	13.49	13.55	13.48	13.45	13.68	13.50	13.49
2005	13.69	13.68	13.78	13.62	13.79	13.81	13.82	13.84	13.72	13.61	13.68	13.53	13.71
2006	13.36	13.50	13.29	13.21	13.15	13.24	13.32	13.30	13.40	13.36	13.46	13.60	13.35
2007	13.77	13.92	13.95	13.99	14.04	14.12	14.11	14.10	14.07	14.22	14.24	14.21	14.06

Average Weekly Earnings by Selected Industry: Arkansas, 2001–2007

(Dollars, not seasonally adjusted.)

Industry and year	January	February	March	April	May	June	July	August	September	October	November	December	Annual Average
Manufacturing													
2001	520.55	504.59	505.38	501.76	509.60	516.09	519.50	520.99	522.69	516.21	508.56	526.68	514.71
2002	519.55	514.44	522.57	523.77	533.98	531.58	531.34	536.54	537.60	528.26	519.35	539.08	528.01
2003	531.58	528.06	535.28	544.71	538.80	544.46	537.63	545.92	545.94	529.20	524.66	540.55	536.58
2004	531.98	529.93	534.26	545.76	545.00	551.35	545.00	546.07	533.81	538.00	525.75	534.60	538.25
2005	539.39	529.42	537.42	532.54	547.46	556.54	554.18	556.37	562.52	547.12	558.14	542.55	547.03
2006	530.39	533.25	530.27	541.61	549.67	557.40	554.11	550.62	557.44	551.77	549.17	556.24	547.35
2007	561.82	559.58	551.03	544.21	550.37	569.04	551.70	551.31	565.61	567.38	568.18	565.56	558.18

Population
    2000 census: 33,871,648
    2007 estimate: 36,553,215
    Percent change, 2000–2007: 7.9%

Percent change in total nonfarm employment, 2000–2007: 4.7%

Industry with the largest growth in employment, 2000–2007 (thousands)
    Education and health services, 263.3

Industry with the largest decline in employment, 2000–2007 (thousands)
    Manufacturing, -389.5

Civilian labor force
    2000: 16,857,578
    2007: 18,188,055

Employment-population ratio
    2000: 63.8%
    2007: 62.1%

Unemployment rate and rank among states
    2000: 4.9%, 43rd
    2007: 5.4%, 43rd

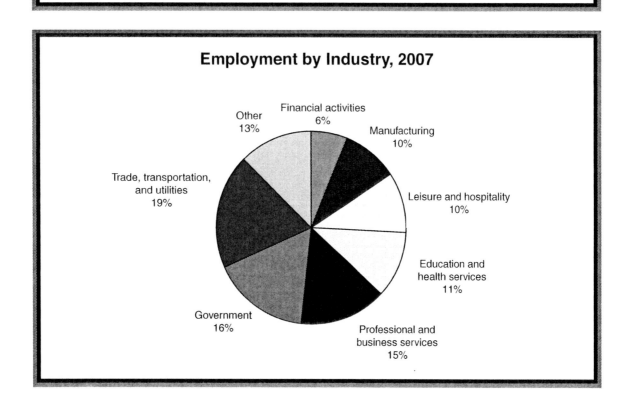

Employment by Industry, 2007

- Other 13%
- Financial activities 6%
- Manufacturing 10%
- Leisure and hospitality 10%
- Education and health services 11%
- Professional and business services 15%
- Government 16%
- Trade, transportation, and utilities 19%

Employment by Industry: California, 2000–2007

(Numbers in thousands, not seasonally adjusted.)

Industry and year	January	February	March	April	May	June	July	August	September	October	November	December	Annual Average
Total Nonfarm													
2000	14,030.7	14,170.1	14,323.4	14,354.0	14,493.4	14,599.8	14,450.0	14,521.9	14,645.0	14,649.8	14,760.9	14,859.0	14,488.2
2001	14,513.5	14,598.0	14,713.1	14,650.1	14,697.5	14,752.3	14,494.8	14,534.8	14,551.8	14,549.5	14,569.2	14,598.9	14,602.0
2002	14,237.6	14,328.0	14,459.1	14,448.7	14,531.1	14,581.6	14,352.9	14,404.4	14,465.9	14,505.6	14,575.1	14,604.0	14,457.8
2003	14,240.1	14,302.1	14,380.3	14,379.4	14,439.0	14,493.8	14,282.8	14,328.7	14,386.9	14,452.7	14,488.3	14,539.7	14,392.8
2004	14,232.6	14,328.5	14,441.7	14,462.2	14,544.8	14,605.6	14,497.8	14,504.4	14,575.3	14,670.2	14,744.5	14,783.3	14,532.6
2005	14,455.2	14,571.6	14,674.5	14,729.3	14,783.9	14,852.2	14,738.0	14,794.5	14,906.3	14,952.4	15,043.2	15,114.9	14,801.3
2006	14,759.7	14,885.2	14,969.2	14,971.6	15,082.6	15,170.5	14,999.8	15,052.2	15,139.2	15,173.8	15,238.1	15,281.6	15,060.3
2007	14,938.0	15,047.2	15,151.5	15,111.8	15,200.0	15,269.2	15,129.4	15,132.2	15,193.2	15,228.6	15,266.6	15,290.5	15,163.2
Total Private													
2000	11,748.4	11,859.0	11,982.0	12,004.4	12,093.9	12,239.6	12,224.0	12,312.7	12,365.6	12,313.6	12,398.9	12,499.4	12,170.1
2001	12,170.6	12,231.5	12,329.3	12,242.4	12,279.4	12,332.9	12,201.4	12,249.8	12,192.7	12,128.7	12,122.1	12,158.0	12,219.9
2002	11,815.0	11,878.2	11,979.9	11,958.2	12,034.1	12,089.5	11,993.9	12,062.3	12,057.9	12,038.7	12,091.9	12,129.3	12,010.7
2003	11,789.2	11,839.2	11,900.2	11,904.7	11,965.3	12,023.5	11,937.3	12,012.6	12,016.0	12,033.8	12,055.3	12,123.9	11,966.8
2004	11,835.3	11,916.2	12,011.5	12,026.7	12,106.7	12,167.1	12,184.7	12,215.5	12,219.4	12,258.3	12,313.2	12,363.8	12,134.9
2005	12,051.5	12,141.8	12,228.4	12,277.4	12,324.6	12,398.5	12,406.1	12,467.7	12,515.8	12,512.6	12,584.1	12,665.5	12,381.2
2006	12,328.5	12,428.3	12,495.8	12,494.7	12,597.0	12,686.4	12,632.3	12,698.5	12,717.4	12,692.5	12,735.9	12,789.2	12,608.0
2007	12,462.9	12,548.4	12,630.3	12,586.9	12,664.6	12,734.7	12,721.9	12,738.7	12,730.6	12,702.7	12,719.7	12,748.3	12,665.8
Goods-Producing													
2000	2,511.0	2,525.7	2,552.8	2,563.7	2,587.9	2,635.9	2,646.7	2,671.9	2,679.0	2,655.2	2,655.6	2,666.1	2,612.6
2001	2,600.9	2,609.0	2,629.6	2,606.1	2,613.6	2,626.3	2,602.7	2,615.8	2,586.0	2,542.2	2,503.1	2,479.7	2,584.6
2002	2,400.1	2,409.9	2,427.3	2,420.7	2,439.2	2,453.3	2,441.2	2,467.1	2,457.7	2,430.7	2,408.8	2,391.7	2,429.3
2003	2,332.5	2,329.9	2,343.2	2,337.9	2,355.5	2,377.6	2,368.8	2,398.7	2,397.8	2,376.0	2,359.9	2,359.3	2,361.4
2004	2,316.3	2,329.3	2,351.1	2,369.8	2,390.1	2,416.0	2,439.8	2,450.8	2,447.6	2,425.4	2,402.9	2,395.0	2,394.5
2005	2,334.2	2,361.3	2,382.5	2,401.4	2,417.5	2,446.8	2,470.5	2,488.4	2,491.3	2,471.0	2,458.1	2,454.4	2,431.5
2006	2,402.7	2,425.2	2,428.5	2,415.1	2,454.5	2,481.7	2,477.4	2,494.0	2,492.0	2,455.2	2,426.6	2,407.6	2,446.7
2007	2,354.1	2,366.0	2,383.0	2,373.7	2,391.2	2,415.5	2,422.3	2,424.9	2,408.3	2,370.8	2,343.5	2,322.3	2,381.3
Natural Resources and Mining													
2000	24.2	24.0	24.0	25.1	26.7	27.5	27.9	28.3	28.1	27.7	27.3	26.7	26.5
2001	24.6	24.1	24.2	25.1	26.4	26.8	26.4	26.7	26.6	26.2	25.6	24.2	25.5
2002	22.5	22.4	22.1	22.1	23.0	23.6	23.6	23.9	23.9	23.8	23.6	22.7	23.1
2003	20.8	21.0	21.0	21.0	21.8	22.7	23.2	23.2	22.9	23.5	23.0	22.7	22.2
2004	21.5	21.6	21.7	22.2	23.0	23.4	23.4	23.5	23.5	23.8	23.3	22.9	22.8
2005	21.7	21.9	22.0	22.4	23.0	23.8	24.5	24.7	24.8	24.9	24.6	24.3	23.6
2006	23.0	23.4	23.3	23.4	24.8	25.7	26.2	26.6	26.7	26.4	25.9	25.2	25.1
2007	24.6	24.8	24.6	25.2	25.9	26.4	26.8	27.0	26.8	26.6	26.2	25.6	25.9
Construction													
2000	678.1	678.9	691.4	705.8	721.7	745.2	750.1	762.9	769.8	764.6	765.1	767.5	733.4
2001	738.7	742.9	760.1	766.7	783.0	798.1	800.2	814.7	804.7	797.1	785.0	773.4	780.4
2002	736.1	742.5	753.0	756.6	770.8	783.3	783.4	801.8	798.1	795.9	790.3	780.9	774.4
2003	755.0	752.3	764.9	770.1	788.6	805.9	810.9	827.0	826.6	825.4	819.3	815.7	796.8
2004	792.8	798.3	811.6	830.0	842.5	861.3	875.2	884.1	886.9	884.1	871.5	866.4	850.4
2005	823.8	844.8	862.3	880.4	895.0	915.7	931.5	942.8	947.4	944.2	940.1	935.6	905.3
2006	903.9	916.0	914.6	908.8	940.9	959.0	957.9	966.3	962.7	941.3	923.8	908.8	933.7
2007	874.6	879.9	894.0	890.5	903.4	917.1	919.6	921.3	906.8	884.0	866.4	849.7	892.3
Manufacturing													
2000	1,808.7	1,822.8	1,837.4	1,832.8	1,839.5	1,863.2	1,868.7	1,880.7	1,881.1	1,862.9	1,863.2	1,871.9	1,852.7
2001	1,837.6	1,842.0	1,845.3	1,814.3	1,804.2	1,801.4	1,776.1	1,774.4	1,754.7	1,718.9	1,692.5	1,682.1	1,778.6
2002	1,641.5	1,645.0	1,652.2	1,642.0	1,645.4	1,650.4	1,634.2	1,641.4	1,635.7	1,611.0	1,594.9	1,588.1	1,631.8
2003	1,556.7	1,556.6	1,557.3	1,546.8	1,545.1	1,549.0	1,534.7	1,548.5	1,548.3	1,527.1	1,517.6	1,520.9	1,542.4
2004	1,502.0	1,509.4	1,517.8	1,517.6	1,524.6	1,531.3	1,541.2	1,543.2	1,537.2	1,517.5	1,508.1	1,505.7	1,521.3
2005	1,488.7	1,494.6	1,498.2	1,498.6	1,499.5	1,507.3	1,514.5	1,520.9	1,519.1	1,501.9	1,493.4	1,494.5	1,502.6
2006	1,475.8	1,485.8	1,490.6	1,482.9	1,488.8	1,497.0	1,493.3	1,501.1	1,502.6	1,487.5	1,476.9	1,473.6	1,488.0
2007	1,454.9	1,461.3	1,464.4	1,458.0	1,461.9	1,472.0	1,475.9	1,476.6	1,474.7	1,460.2	1,450.9	1,447.0	1,463.2
Service-Providing													
2000	11,519.7	11,644.4	11,770.6	11,790.3	11,905.5	11,963.9	11,803.3	11,850.0	11,966.0	11,994.6	12,105.3	12,192.9	11,875.5
2001	11,912.6	11,989.0	12,083.5	12,044.0	12,083.9	12,126.0	11,892.1	11,919.0	11,965.8	12,007.3	12,066.1	12,119.2	12,017.4
2002	11,837.5	11,918.1	12,031.8	12,028.0	12,091.9	12,124.3	11,911.7	11,937.3	12,008.2	12,074.9	12,166.3	12,212.3	12,028.5
2003	11,907.6	11,972.2	12,037.1	12,041.5	12,083.5	12,116.2	11,914.0	11,930.0	11,989.1	12,076.7	12,128.4	12,180.4	12,031.4
2004	11,916.3	11,999.2	12,090.6	12,092.4	12,154.7	12,189.6	12,058.0	12,053.6	12,127.7	12,244.8	12,341.6	12,388.3	12,138.1
2005	12,121.0	12,210.3	12,292.0	12,327.9	12,366.4	12,405.4	12,267.5	12,306.1	12,415.0	12,481.4	12,585.1	12,660.5	12,369.9
2006	12,357.0	12,460.0	12,540.7	12,556.5	12,628.1	12,688.8	12,522.4	12,558.2	12,647.2	12,718.6	12,811.5	12,874.0	12,613.6
2007	12,583.9	12,681.2	12,768.5	12,738.1	12,808.8	12,853.7	12,707.1	12,707.3	12,784.9	12,857.8	12,923.1	12,968.2	12,781.9
Trade, Transportation, and Utilities													
2000	2,674.5	2,668.1	2,679.6	2,674.7	2,692.7	2,720.0	2,722.1	2,733.5	2,740.9	2,749.5	2,810.2	2,868.7	2,727.9
2001	2,756.1	2,734.5	2,745.4	2,729.6	2,735.6	2,754.5	2,735.9	2,738.7	2,738.8	2,735.0	2,772.6	2,809.4	2,748.8
2002	2,698.0	2,680.5	2,694.9	2,691.5	2,707.3	2,726.8	2,712.6	2,719.9	2,728.0	2,730.7	2,782.2	2,830.4	2,725.2
2003	2,700.2	2,683.2	2,686.9	2,681.2	2,694.2	2,710.5	2,695.6	2,704.2	2,714.0	2,748.8	2,778.1	2,823.8	2,718.4
2004	2,702.6	2,692.4	2,707.3	2,710.0	2,729.2	2,748.9	2,747.0	2,751.8	2,758.1	2,788.7	2,848.2	2,883.5	2,755.6
2005	2,778.9	2,762.0	2,769.0	2,770.1	2,785.0	2,799.0	2,810.1	2,823.0	2,837.6	2,852.1	2,911.9	2,966.5	2,822.1
2006	2,832.0	2,816.4	2,829.4	2,828.9	2,848.6	2,868.6	2,868.4	2,882.1	2,890.7	2,901.9	2,967.0	3,009.1	2,878.6
2007	2,895.7	2,871.3	2,878.1	2,871.2	2,887.4	2,898.7	2,906.9	2,912.5	2,915.6	2,922.2	2,970.0	3,001.2	2,910.9
Wholesale Trade													
2000	630.4	636.2	640.6	640.4	643.8	650.3	649.0	651.2	652.8	650.6	651.6	657.1	646.2
2001	656.2	662.1	665.2	661.5	661.1	665.6	659.3	658.6	656.6	655.5	652.3	652.5	658.9
2002	644.0	647.4	651.5	651.4	653.8	656.4	652.7	654.7	654.9	651.8	652.3	653.8	652.1
2003	644.5	646.6	649.7	650.8	652.7	655.2	649.2	651.0	650.7	647.9	646.4	648.9	649.5
2004	641.6	645.0	648.4	650.5	654.0	659.4	658.1	658.2	658.1	661.8	662.9	663.7	655.1
2005	660.1	662.7	666.4	671.8	675.1	677.8	678.7	680.0	681.7	683.7	684.4	686.9	675.8
2006	683.6	690.2	694.4	697.2	701.3	707.1	706.4	707.9	710.5	708.8	709.6	712.4	702.5
2007	704.7	709.1	713.7	712.9	716.7	720.0	720.3	720.1	721.5	721.7	720.9	721.1	716.9

Employment by Industry: California, 2000–2007—*Continued*

(Numbers in thousands, not seasonally adjusted.)

Industry and year	January	February	March	April	May	June	July	August	September	October	November	December	Annual Average
Retail Trade													
2000	1,534.4	1,522.4	1,527.5	1,520.4	1,533.0	1,549.4	1,551.9	1,560.1	1,565.8	1,577.1	1,635.8	1,683.5	1,563.4
2001	1,582.5	1,558.7	1,562.8	1,550.7	1,556.8	1,570.1	1,560.5	1,564.0	1,566.9	1,566.0	1,616.3	1,655.7	1,575.9
2002	1,568.2	1,545.6	1,558.0	1,551.9	1,561.8	1,575.8	1,567.1	1,570.8	1,579.3	1,585.7	1,637.9	1,684.2	1,582.2
2003	1,577.0	1,558.5	1,558.7	1,553.4	1,561.7	1,572.3	1,566.8	1,573.7	1,579.7	1,615.9	1,648.8	1,693.7	1,588.4
2004	1,589.5	1,575.6	1,584.0	1,584.3	1,597.1	1,607.9	1,604.7	1,609.3	1,611.3	1,631.1	1,689.9	1,728.3	1,617.8
2005	1,638.6	1,618.0	1,622.0	1,615.6	1,624.5	1,634.8	1,643.5	1,654.7	1,664.1	1,676.5	1,735.0	1,783.8	1,659.3
2006	1,663.6	1,640.6	1,646.5	1,644.3	1,654.1	1,663.5	1,666.2	1,676.0	1,677.0	1,690.6	1,752.6	1,785.9	1,680.1
2007	1,695.5	1,666.1	1,669.7	1,660.6	1,669.1	1,674.3	1,678.8	1,684.7	1,681.8	1,688.4	1,734.4	1,762.7	1,688.8
Transportation and Utilities													
2000	509.7	509.5	511.5	513.9	515.9	520.3	521.2	522.2	522.3	521.8	522.8	528.1	518.3
2001	517.4	513.7	517.4	517.4	517.7	518.8	516.1	516.1	515.3	513.5	504.0	501.2	514.1
2002	485.8	487.5	485.4	488.2	491.7	494.6	492.8	494.4	493.8	493.2	492.0	492.4	491.0
2003	478.7	478.1	478.5	477.0	479.8	483.0	479.6	479.5	483.6	485.0	482.9	481.2	480.6
2004	471.5	471.8	474.9	475.2	478.1	481.6	484.2	484.3	488.7	495.8	495.4	491.5	482.8
2005	480.2	481.3	480.6	482.7	485.4	486.4	487.9	488.3	491.8	491.9	492.5	495.8	487.1
2006	484.8	485.6	488.5	487.4	493.2	498.0	495.8	498.2	503.2	502.5	504.8	510.8	496.1
2007	495.5	496.1	494.7	497.7	501.6	504.4	507.8	507.7	512.3	512.1	514.7	517.4	505.2
Information													
2000	537.8	550.5	560.5	562.9	572.8	580.2	580.3	590.4	588.2	592.7	603.0	601.0	576.7
2001	587.3	588.8	590.2	571.4	557.8	554.8	537.6	534.7	529.4	524.2	523.7	522.8	551.9
2002	510.2	511.4	519.9	502.6	503.3	501.6	484.6	490.5	481.4	487.8	495.8	479.4	497.3
2003	480.3	487.1	481.7	470.7	475.2	467.9	467.1	478.4	466.3	476.9	483.7	477.8	476.1
2004	485.6	490.7	487.8	477.6	483.5	474.0	478.8	479.4	470.6	483.4	492.5	484.3	482.4
2005	473.1	477.0	480.7	470.3	469.9	470.3	466.9	473.2	472.5	471.4	480.2	477.9	473.6
2006	468.2	476.3	475.5	467.7	468.6	470.7	464.8	464.9	459.4	456.0	456.5	463.4	466.0
2007	463.3	471.2	473.5	464.8	471.5	475.5	472.7	479.7	481.7	473.4	471.2	475.0	472.8
Financial Activities													
2000	797.0	802.5	806.5	800.5	803.8	810.8	805.1	809.7	809.0	808.5	809.8	819.5	806.9
2001	818.5	826.5	834.1	831.7	834.8	841.1	834.7	838.4	837.1	841.0	843.9	850.6	836.0
2002	835.1	840.7	844.0	845.0	848.7	853.7	852.5	857.8	858.1	860.2	866.5	873.9	853.0
2003	866.0	871.2	876.2	881.5	887.4	891.8	890.2	894.4	892.9	890.7	890.8	895.2	885.7
2004	886.9	890.5	894.9	896.4	899.0	902.1	907.3	908.7	907.2	907.7	910.2	915.2	902.2
2005	908.6	912.7	917.6	918.7	922.1	926.0	930.5	933.9	934.8	937.5	938.3	945.2	927.2
2006	934.3	937.1	940.2	939.3	943.1	942.3	935.7	935.3	932.6	927.8	926.1	928.5	935.2
2007	914.4	920.6	922.3	914.1	913.0	912.5	908.4	905.3	896.5	894.6	889.0	888.4	906.6
Professional and Business Services													
2000	2,109.5	2,140.0	2,171.4	2,193.6	2,203.3	2,240.6	2,237.3	2,264.3	2,272.3	2,264.0	2,273.8	2,291.2	2,221.8
2001	2,203.0	2,216.0	2,233.7	2,202.9	2,206.3	2,212.5	2,177.9	2,183.6	2,167.5	2,149.3	2,138.5	2,144.5	2,186.3
2002	2,095.2	2,108.4	2,131.3	2,114.0	2,116.8	2,124.5	2,111.3	2,126.6	2,122.8	2,120.0	2,126.9	2,129.9	2,119.0
2003	2,064.4	2,077.8	2,095.7	2,090.7	2,088.8	2,096.1	2,074.5	2,089.0	2,085.1	2,079.8	2,081.5	2,089.9	2,084.4
2004	2,032.8	2,054.6	2,078.0	2,078.0	2,085.7	2,101.7	2,101.8	2,115.1	2,112.0	2,125.4	2,132.8	2,144.8	2,096.9
2005	2,095.0	2,121.7	2,137.2	2,142.8	2,139.6	2,156.7	2,162.1	2,178.6	2,188.9	2,187.1	2,197.2	2,210.1	2,159.8
2006	2,164.5	2,192.2	2,209.1	2,215.2	2,225.2	2,250.8	2,247.8	2,267.0	2,272.7	2,279.9	2,283.7	2,289.5	2,241.5
2007	2,212.5	2,240.2	2,255.9	2,243.7	2,250.9	2,269.4	2,271.7	2,279.5	2,276.9	2,281.7	2,286.3	2,291.2	2,263.3
Education and Health Services													
2000	1,378.2	1,403.2	1,413.1	1,402.2	1,404.6	1,395.1	1,375.0	1,377.1	1,414.5	1,414.4	1,421.2	1,413.5	1,401.0
2001	1,406.7	1,431.0	1,444.8	1,442.0	1,451.1	1,441.8	1,414.6	1,435.0	1,454.4	1,474.4	1,487.1	1,492.3	1,447.9
2002	1,465.6	1,491.8	1,503.1	1,496.2	1,504.4	1,491.2	1,474.3	1,477.0	1,500.2	1,518.7	1,531.0	1,532.7	1,498.9
2003	1,502.3	1,524.1	1,534.5	1,547.5	1,550.6	1,540.3	1,513.8	1,512.9	1,536.8	1,550.6	1,557.7	1,564.4	1,536.3
2004	1,535.8	1,558.3	1,569.7	1,565.2	1,565.0	1,554.8	1,532.6	1,531.6	1,556.1	1,579.3	1,585.4	1,586.7	1,560.0
2005	1,557.4	1,580.2	1,588.1	1,596.2	1,597.1	1,583.8	1,556.2	1,557.0	1,586.8	1,605.9	1,614.7	1,614.5	1,586.5
2006	1,582.8	1,609.0	1,618.8	1,618.1	1,620.2	1,609.5	1,582.8	1,587.2	1,617.4	1,634.6	1,642.4	1,645.1	1,614.0
2007	1,626.1	1,657.7	1,672.0	1,662.2	1,668.2	1,654.3	1,637.3	1,636.5	1,668.5	1,689.7	1,698.4	1,700.1	1,664.3
Leisure and Hospitality													
2000	1,267.1	1,289.6	1,311.7	1,320.3	1,339.6	1,361.6	1,368.3	1,375.2	1,368.3	1,340.9	1,336.4	1,347.6	1,335.6
2001	1,313.8	1,333.9	1,352.8	1,360.7	1,378.0	1,394.5	1,396.9	1,401.4	1,377.3	1,361.3	1,352.7	1,358.1	1,365.1
2002	1,318.3	1,335.5	1,355.6	1,382.3	1,403.3	1,419.2	1,410.0	1,417.2	1,402.9	1,384.1	1,375.0	1,385.6	1,382.4
2003	1,345.9	1,362.7	1,376.5	1,388.7	1,404.4	1,425.8	1,425.3	1,432.5	1,418.7	1,406.9	1,401.8	1,411.7	1,400.1
2004	1,380.9	1,400.7	1,418.0	1,425.4	1,447.2	1,460.7	1,471.1	1,474.1	1,461.4	1,444.3	1,438.5	1,450.5	1,439.4
2005	1,408.5	1,424.5	1,446.1	1,468.6	1,483.0	1,502.3	1,504.9	1,509.6	1,497.4	1,483.1	1,480.9	1,492.9	1,475.2
2006	1,451.1	1,472.8	1,491.8	1,506.5	1,526.6	1,548.3	1,548.4	1,556.2	1,540.4	1,526.8	1,523.6	1,535.9	1,519.0
2007	1,496.8	1,514.2	1,534.7	1,548.3	1,569.2	1,589.8	1,585.0	1,582.7	1,565.4	1,552.7	1,544.9	1,553.0	1,553.1
Other Services													
2000	473.3	479.4	486.4	486.5	489.2	495.4	489.2	490.6	493.4	488.4	488.9	491.8	487.7
2001	484.3	491.8	498.7	498.0	502.2	507.4	501.1	502.2	502.2	501.3	500.5	500.6	499.2
2002	492.5	500.0	503.8	505.9	512.1	515.2	507.4	506.2	506.8	506.5	505.7	505.7	505.7
2003	497.6	503.2	505.5	506.5	509.2	513.5	502.0	502.5	504.4	504.1	501.8	501.8	504.3
2004	494.4	499.7	504.7	504.3	507.0	508.9	506.3	504.0	506.4	504.1	502.7	503.8	503.9
2005	495.8	502.4	507.2	509.3	510.4	513.6	504.9	504.0	506.5	504.5	502.8	504.0	505.5
2006	492.9	499.3	502.5	503.9	510.2	514.5	507.0	511.8	512.2	510.3	510.0	510.1	507.1
2007	500.0	507.2	510.8	508.9	513.2	519.0	517.6	517.6	517.7	517.6	516.4	517.1	513.6
Government													
2000	2,282.3	2,311.1	2,341.4	2,349.6	2,399.5	2,360.2	2,226.0	2,209.2	2,279.4	2,336.2	2,362.0	2,359.7	2,318.1
2001	2,342.9	2,366.5	2,383.8	2,407.7	2,418.1	2,419.4	2,293.4	2,285.0	2,359.1	2,420.8	2,447.1	2,440.9	2,382.0
2002	2,422.6	2,449.8	2,479.2	2,490.5	2,497.0	2,492.1	2,359.0	2,342.1	2,408.0	2,466.9	2,483.2	2,474.7	2,447.1
2003	2,450.9	2,462.9	2,480.1	2,474.7	2,473.7	2,470.3	2,345.5	2,316.1	2,370.9	2,418.9	2,433.0	2,415.8	2,426.1
2004	2,397.3	2,412.3	2,430.2	2,435.5	2,438.1	2,438.5	2,313.1	2,288.9	2,355.9	2,411.9	2,431.3	2,419.5	2,397.7
2005	2,403.7	2,429.8	2,446.1	2,451.9	2,459.3	2,453.7	2,331.9	2,326.8	2,390.5	2,439.8	2,459.1	2,449.4	2,420.2
2006	2,431.2	2,456.9	2,473.4	2,476.9	2,485.6	2,484.1	2,367.5	2,353.7	2,421.8	2,481.3	2,502.2	2,492.4	2,452.3
2007	2,475.1	2,498.8	2,521.2	2,524.9	2,535.4	2,534.5	2,407.5	2,393.5	2,462.6	2,525.9	2,546.9	2,542.2	2,497.4

Average Weekly Hours by Selected Industry: California, 2001–2007

(Not seasonally adjusted.)

Industry and year	January	February	March	April	May	June	July	August	September	October	November	December	Annual Average
Manufacturing													
2001	39.4	39.8	39.8	39.2	39.5	39.4	39.2	39.7	39.9	39.6	39.4	40.0	39.6
2002	38.5	39.1	39.8	39.6	39.5	40.0	39.0	39.9	40.2	39.8	40.0	40.4	39.6
2003	39.1	39.5	39.6	39.4	39.7	40.0	39.2	39.7	39.8	39.8	40.5	40.1	39.7
2004	39.5	39.9	40.1	39.7	40.3	40.0	39.9	40.3	39.6	39.9	40.1	40.3	40.0
2005	39.7	39.7	39.9	39.8	39.9	39.7	39.6	40.1	40.3	40.6	40.1	39.8	39.9
2006	39.8	40.0	40.0	40.0	40.1	40.5	40.2	40.3	40.4	40.6	40.4	41.2	40.3
2007	40.1	40.0	40.2	40.4	40.4	40.7	40.6	40.9	40.9	40.7	40.7	40.8	40.5

Average Hourly Earnings by Selected Industry: California, 2001–2007

(Dollars, not seasonally adjusted.)

Industry and year	January	February	March	April	May	June	July	August	September	October	November	December	Annual Average
Manufacturing													
2001	14.50	14.47	14.48	14.56	14.59	14.72	14.85	14.76	14.80	14.78	14.84	14.99	14.69
2002	15.02	14.94	14.87	14.89	14.85	14.89	14.86	14.76	14.80	14.79	14.93	15.12	14.89
2003	15.01	14.96	14.97	14.92	14.94	15.02	15.09	15.04	15.06	15.05	15.14	15.26	15.04
2004	15.26	15.22	15.23	15.32	15.35	15.38	15.37	15.30	15.42	15.43	15.49	15.60	15.36
2005	15.59	15.62	15.61	15.63	15.69	15.72	15.76	15.72	15.72	15.75	15.72	15.87	15.70
2006	15.67	15.67	15.64	15.67	15.69	15.74	15.80	15.78	15.80	15.89	15.90	16.00	15.77
2007	16.07	16.07	16.12	16.16	16.21	16.18	16.19	16.22	16.29	16.37	16.39	16.41	16.22

Average Weekly Earnings by Selected Industry: California, 2001–2007

(Dollars, not seasonally adjusted.)

Industry and year	January	February	March	April	May	June	July	August	September	October	November	December	Annual Average
Manufacturing													
2001	571.30	575.91	576.30	570.75	576.31	579.97	582.12	585.97	590.52	585.29	584.70	599.60	581.72
2002	578.27	584.15	591.83	589.64	586.58	595.60	579.54	588.92	594.96	588.64	597.20	610.85	589.64
2003	586.89	590.92	592.81	587.85	593.12	600.80	591.53	597.09	599.39	598.99	613.17	611.93	597.09
2004	602.77	607.28	610.72	608.20	618.61	615.20	613.26	616.59	610.63	615.66	621.15	628.68	614.40
2005	618.92	620.11	622.84	622.07	626.03	624.08	624.10	630.37	633.52	639.45	630.37	631.63	626.43
2006	623.67	626.80	625.60	626.80	629.17	637.47	635.16	635.93	638.32	645.13	642.36	659.20	635.53
2007	644.41	642.80	648.02	652.86	654.88	658.53	657.31	663.40	666.26	666.26	667.07	669.53	656.91

COLORADO
At a Glance

Population
   2000 census: 4,301,261
   2007 estimate: 4,861,515
   Percent change, 2000–2007: 13.0%

Percent change in total nonfarm employment, 2000–2007: 5.3%

Industry with the largest growth in employment, 2000–2007 (thousands)
   Education and health services, 47.2

Industry with the largest decline in employment, 2000–2007 (thousands)
   Manufacturing, -42.5

Civilian labor force
   2000: 2,364,990
   2007: 2,705,557

Employment-population ratio
   2000: 70.5%
   2007: 70.0%

Unemployment rate and rank among states
   2000: 2.7%, 3rd
   2007: 3.8%, 15th

Employment by Industry, 2007

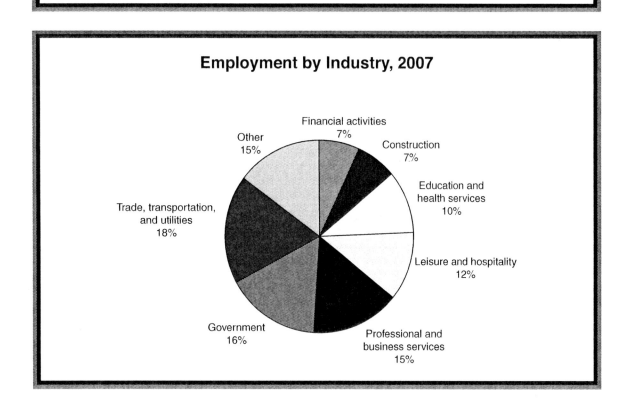

Employment by Industry: Colorado, 2000–2007

(Numbers in thousands, not seasonally adjusted.)

Industry and year	January	February	March	April	May	June	July	August	September	October	November	December	Annual Average
Total Nonfarm													
2000	2,134.4	2,156.2	2,181.4	2,188.0	2,202.3	2,234.0	2,227.4	2,239.1	2,239.6	2,237.5	2,251.4	2,274.6	2,213.8
2001	2,210.5	2,222.7	2,236.5	2,230.5	2,232.1	2,261.9	2,240.1	2,240.2	2,225.5	2,206.4	2,203.7	2,212.1	2,226.9
2002	2,148.8	2,159.6	2,172.9	2,181.8	2,191.1	2,214.2	2,193.6	2,199.7	2,189.0	2,178.8	2,183.0	2,197.7	2,184.2
2003	2,131.3	2,135.4	2,139.3	2,138.4	2,147.2	2,169.2	2,156.1	2,163.8	2,158.1	2,159.4	2,158.0	2,177.4	2,152.8
2004	2,123.5	2,132.9	2,151.7	2,168.0	2,174.1	2,201.8	2,190.0	2,196.3	2,197.2	2,195.9	2,199.6	2,224.4	2,179.6
2005	2,163.5	2,181.9	2,199.1	2,207.3	2,215.8	2,244.7	2,238.4	2,241.5	2,247.8	2,244.0	2,251.3	2,276.6	2,226.0
2006	2,220.1	2,235.1	2,254.9	2,259.9	2,274.4	2,307.5	2,286.3	2,294.1	2,295.1	2,293.2	2,302.9	2,325.8	2,279.1
2007	2,262.6	2,280.5	2,306.3	2,313.7	2,328.0	2,357.9	2,342.2	2,350.6	2,352.2	2,348.5	2,353.0	2,367.4	2,330.2
Total Private													
2000	1,810.6	1,820.8	1,840.7	1,846.5	1,853.2	1,896.4	1,906.2	1,916.5	1,901.8	1,893.6	1,906.1	1,929.3	1,876.8
2001	1,878.4	1,878.6	1,891.5	1,885.2	1,883.5	1,917.8	1,911.9	1,910.0	1,878.0	1,853.0	1,847.9	1,857.0	1,882.7
2002	1,804.7	1,804.7	1,814.7	1,823.6	1,828.8	1,858.5	1,854.9	1,859.2	1,832.5	1,814.0	1,817.1	1,833.0	1,828.8
2003	1,780.8	1,774.9	1,776.8	1,778.0	1,781.0	1,813.4	1,818.1	1,825.1	1,801.9	1,797.0	1,795.7	1,816.8	1,796.6
2004	1,773.9	1,773.5	1,789.5	1,804.4	1,807.8	1,842.7	1,851.4	1,855.0	1,836.8	1,828.9	1,831.8	1,857.9	1,821.1
2005	1,810.7	1,817.2	1,833.2	1,839.8	1,845.1	1,881.7	1,893.2	1,896.4	1,882.8	1,873.1	1,880.6	1,906.9	1,863.4
2006	1,863.3	1,866.7	1,883.3	1,889.1	1,899.9	1,939.4	1,937.5	1,942.7	1,925.3	1,918.0	1,926.9	1,950.5	1,911.9
2007	1,902.3	1,905.8	1,928.3	1,935.2	1,946.0	1,983.4	1,986.7	1,991.4	1,972.8	1,963.5	1,966.7	1,982.9	1,955.4
Goods-Producing													
2000	345.8	349.0	354.8	357.0	363.6	372.0	373.6	374.9	373.2	372.8	369.9	369.5	364.7
2001	356.8	356.6	360.4	360.7	365.0	370.5	369.2	367.9	362.6	356.7	350.5	344.1	360.1
2002	330.2	329.3	332.8	336.5	342.3	346.7	346.0	345.8	340.0	336.8	331.9	327.1	337.1
2003	314.4	311.6	311.0	313.1	317.8	323.3	323.2	323.0	319.2	319.4	315.4	312.6	317.0
2004	303.3	302.2	306.8	312.8	316.8	323.9	326.3	326.5	324.5	324.9	322.0	319.7	317.5
2005	309.5	312.1	316.4	319.4	324.2	332.6	337.4	338.7	337.0	335.9	335.0	333.3	327.6
2006	325.1	326.2	330.7	333.4	339.3	347.0	346.1	346.4	343.9	342.1	338.7	336.6	338.0
2007	323.1	323.6	330.5	334.2	341.4	348.7	350.0	349.9	345.9	343.6	339.5	334.2	338.7
Natural Resources and Mining													
2000	11.9	11.9	12.0	12.0	12.2	12.3	12.5	12.5	12.5	12.3	12.2	12.2	12.2
2001	11.9	12.1	12.4	12.5	12.8	13.2	13.5	13.4	13.4	13.3	13.4	13.3	12.9
2002	12.9	12.8	12.9	12.8	12.9	13.1	13.2	13.1	13.1	13.0	12.8	12.7	12.9
2003	12.5	12.6	12.7	12.8	13.1	13.3	13.4	13.5	13.4	13.6	13.6	13.5	13.2
2004	13.2	13.4	13.6	13.9	14.2	14.5	14.9	15.1	15.0	15.0	15.2	15.3	14.4
2005	15.4	15.8	16.1	16.2	16.5	17.2	17.7	18.1	18.1	18.2	18.5	18.7	17.2
2006	18.7	19.1	19.6	19.7	20.3	21.1	21.6	22.2	22.2	22.7	22.8	23.3	21.1
2007	23.1	23.6	23.9	24.5	25.1	25.8	25.9	26.2	25.7	25.9	26.0	26.2	25.2
Construction													
2000	146.5	149.6	154.8	157.7	163.9	170.4	171.5	172.8	171.2	170.6	167.7	165.9	163.6
2001	159.1	159.4	163.1	165.3	169.7	175.2	175.7	176.1	172.9	169.6	165.4	160.3	167.7
2002	150.5	151.3	154.5	158.8	164.3	168.4	168.5	168.8	164.5	162.2	158.5	154.3	160.4
2003	145.2	143.1	143.4	145.6	150.3	155.3	156.1	155.9	153.4	153.7	149.8	147.2	149.9
2004	140.1	138.7	142.7	147.7	151.1	156.3	158.3	158.2	157.0	157.4	154.8	152.7	151.3
2005	144.7	146.3	150.1	153.3	157.7	164.6	168.1	169.3	168.3	167.2	166.0	164.2	160.0
2006	157.7	158.3	161.9	164.7	169.7	175.7	174.6	174.4	172.6	170.7	167.6	165.3	167.8
2007	154.0	154.4	160.5	164.1	169.9	175.6	176.9	176.7	173.1	171.6	167.7	161.9	167.2
Manufacturing													
2000	187.4	187.5	188.0	187.3	187.5	189.3	189.6	189.6	189.5	189.9	190.0	191.4	188.9
2001	185.8	185.1	184.9	182.9	182.5	182.1	180.0	178.4	176.3	173.8	171.7	170.5	179.5
2002	166.8	165.2	165.4	164.9	165.1	165.2	164.3	163.9	162.4	161.6	160.6	160.1	163.8
2003	156.7	155.9	154.9	154.7	154.4	154.7	153.7	153.6	152.4	152.1	152.0	151.9	153.9
2004	150.0	150.1	150.5	151.2	151.5	153.1	153.1	153.2	152.5	152.5	152.0	151.7	151.8
2005	149.4	150.0	150.2	149.9	150.0	150.8	151.6	151.3	150.6	150.5	150.5	150.4	150.4
2006	148.7	148.8	149.2	149.0	149.3	150.2	149.9	149.8	149.1	148.7	148.3	148.0	149.1
2007	146.0	145.6	146.1	145.6	146.4	147.3	147.2	147.0	147.1	146.1	145.8	146.1	146.4
Service-Providing													
2000	1,788.6	1,807.2	1,826.6	1,831.0	1,838.7	1,862.0	1,853.8	1,864.2	1,866.4	1,864.7	1,881.5	1,905.1	1,849.2
2001	1,853.7	1,866.1	1,876.1	1,869.8	1,867.1	1,891.4	1,870.9	1,872.3	1,862.9	1,849.7	1,853.2	1,868.0	1,866.8
2002	1,818.6	1,830.3	1,840.1	1,845.3	1,848.8	1,867.5	1,847.6	1,853.9	1,849.0	1,842.0	1,851.1	1,870.6	1,847.1
2003	1,816.9	1,823.8	1,828.3	1,825.3	1,829.4	1,845.9	1,832.9	1,840.8	1,838.9	1,840.0	1,842.6	1,864.8	1,835.8
2004	1,820.2	1,830.7	1,844.9	1,855.2	1,857.3	1,877.9	1,863.7	1,869.8	1,872.7	1,871.0	1,877.6	1,904.7	1,862.1
2005	1,854.0	1,869.8	1,882.7	1,887.9	1,891.6	1,912.1	1,901.0	1,902.8	1,910.8	1,908.1	1,916.3	1,943.3	1,898.4
2006	1,895.0	1,908.9	1,924.2	1,926.5	1,935.1	1,960.5	1,940.2	1,947.7	1,951.2	1,951.1	1,964.2	1,989.2	1,941.2
2007	1,939.5	1,956.9	1,975.8	1,979.5	1,986.6	2,009.2	1,992.2	2,000.7	2,006.3	2,004.9	2,013.5	2,033.2	1,991.5
Trade, Transportation, and Utilities													
2000	410.1	409.1	409.3	411.2	412.1	416.8	416.5	420.6	419.7	423.7	435.1	443.0	418.9
2001	425.2	420.3	421.4	420.2	420.7	425.2	423.8	423.6	420.7	419.8	425.4	429.3	423.0
2002	409.0	405.3	406.4	408.1	410.3	415.0	413.7	413.6	410.6	409.8	418.3	424.6	412.1
2003	405.6	401.6	400.8	399.2	399.3	402.0	402.5	404.1	402.6	405.4	412.2	418.3	404.5
2004	401.7	397.7	399.3	401.5	403.2	406.9	407.9	408.6	406.3	408.2	415.6	422.8	406.6
2005	405.8	403.7	406.1	405.9	407.4	411.7	413.7	413.3	414.3	416.7	425.1	431.8	413.0
2006	414.2	409.5	411.9	413.3	414.8	419.6	418.9	419.6	418.7	421.9	431.2	438.3	419.3
2007	424.2	419.7	422.3	422.9	424.7	429.4	431.0	431.5	430.4	432.2	441.4	447.1	429.7
Wholesale Trade													
2000	96.9	97.5	98.4	98.9	99.8	100.6	99.3	99.6	99.4	100.2	100.5	101.1	99.4
2001	100.0	100.8	101.0	100.5	100.4	100.7	100.1	100.0	99.2	98.5	98.1	98.0	99.8
2002	95.7	95.7	95.7	95.6	95.7	95.8	95.6	95.1	94.5	93.9	93.7	94.0	95.1
2003	92.8	92.3	92.4	92.2	92.2	92.5	92.2	91.9	91.5	91.9	91.5	91.8	92.1
2004	90.6	90.7	91.2	91.6	91.8	92.5	92.3	92.4	92.3	92.4	92.6	92.8	91.9
2005	91.7	92.1	92.6	92.9	93.2	93.7	94.2	94.4	94.4	94.2	94.3	94.7	93.5
2006	93.9	94.3	94.9	95.4	96.1	97.2	97.0	97.4	97.2	97.5	97.9	98.5	96.4
2007	97.2	97.7	98.4	98.7	99.3	100.1	100.0	100.2	99.7	100.0	100.0	100.2	99.3

Employment by Industry: Colorado, 2000–2007—*Continued*

(Numbers in thousands, not seasonally adjusted.)

Industry and year	January	February	March	April	May	June	July	August	September	October	November	December	Annual Average
Retail Trade													
2000	240.5	238.6	238.1	238.6	239.1	242.6	242.7	246.1	245.6	248.5	257.9	264.6	245.2
2001	247.0	242.0	242.8	242.3	243.1	246.7	245.6	244.9	243.6	244.0	250.9	255.3	245.7
2002	240.2	236.4	237.6	239.1	240.8	244.9	243.5	243.5	241.3	241.3	249.1	254.5	242.7
2003	238.7	235.4	234.6	234.5	235.5	238.0	238.3	239.9	239.0	240.9	247.2	252.2	239.5
2004	238.8	234.7	235.6	236.9	238.3	240.7	241.4	242.2	240.4	242.4	249.5	254.7	241.3
2005	240.9	238.3	240.3	240.1	241.9	244.8	245.7	245.1	246.2	248.4	256.4	261.0	245.8
2006	246.3	241.4	243.0	244.2	245.0	247.4	247.3	247.5	246.8	250.0	258.4	262.5	248.3
2007	251.1	246.7	248.4	248.4	249.7	252.8	254.5	254.6	254.0	255.2	263.6	267.7	253.9
Transportation and Utilities													
2000	72.7	73.0	72.8	73.7	73.2	73.6	74.5	74.9	74.7	75.0	76.7	77.3	74.3
2001	78.2	77.5	77.6	77.4	77.2	77.8	78.1	78.7	77.9	77.3	76.4	76.0	77.5
2002	73.1	73.2	73.1	73.4	73.8	74.3	74.6	75.0	74.8	74.6	75.5	76.1	74.3
2003	74.1	73.9	73.8	72.5	71.6	71.5	72.0	72.3	72.1	72.6	73.5	74.3	72.9
2004	72.3	72.3	72.5	73.0	73.1	73.7	74.2	74.0	73.6	73.4	73.5	75.3	73.4
2005	73.2	73.3	73.2	72.9	72.3	73.2	73.8	73.8	73.7	74.1	74.4	76.1	73.7
2006	74.0	73.8	74.0	73.7	73.7	75.0	74.6	74.7	74.7	74.7	74.4	74.9	74.6
2007	75.9	75.3	75.5	75.8	75.7	76.5	76.5	76.7	76.7	77.0	77.8	79.2	76.6
Information													
2000	102.1	103.7	105.0	106.0	107.1	108.8	110.3	111.0	111.2	111.3	112.0	112.8	108.4
2001	113.2	112.8	112.0	110.3	109.3	109.3	106.6	105.5	103.8	102.2	101.7	100.5	107.3
2002	98.1	97.0	96.2	95.2	94.1	93.7	91.7	91.0	89.9	89.3	89.4	88.6	92.9
2003	86.5	86.1	85.7	84.9	84.8	84.8	84.5	84.2	83.3	83.1	83.6	83.7	84.6
2004	82.7	82.8	82.6	81.9	81.9	81.9	81.2	80.9	79.5	79.3	79.6	79.6	81.2
2005	78.3	77.9	77.8	77.1	77.1	77.1	76.8	76.4	76.0	75.8	76.0	76.2	76.9
2006	75.8	75.6	75.8	75.4	75.7	75.7	75.3	75.2	74.7	75.0	75.4	75.5	75.4
2007	74.9	75.0	75.0	75.8	76.2	76.9	76.6	76.7	76.2	76.9	77.2	76.8	76.2
Financial Activities													
2000	146.3	147.1	147.7	146.5	145.8	147.3	147.1	147.3	146.3	146.2	147.0	149.6	147.0
2001	147.0	147.7	149.0	148.7	148.1	149.7	149.4	148.9	147.4	147.3	147.5	149.2	148.3
2002	147.7	148.3	148.7	147.8	147.6	149.0	149.3	150.2	149.6	150.3	151.8	154.1	149.5
2003	152.4	152.8	153.2	153.3	153.2	154.6	155.5	156.0	154.6	154.2	153.8	155.9	154.1
2004	153.5	153.8	154.2	154.0	153.3	154.7	155.2	155.2	154.6	154.6	154.8	157.1	154.6
2005	155.2	156.0	157.0	157.2	157.1	158.7	159.6	160.0	159.9	159.3	159.9	162.4	158.5
2006	159.3	159.8	160.2	160.0	160.0	161.3	161.0	161.1	160.3	159.8	160.1	162.3	160.4
2007	159.6	160.1	160.4	160.0	159.2	160.5	160.4	160.1	158.8	158.3	158.2	159.4	159.6
Professional and Business Services													
2000	302.2	303.1	308.2	313.1	316.6	322.8	325.9	328.2	327.9	326.6	325.1	325.8	318.8
2001	311.3	313.1	315.4	316.6	317.4	320.1	318.1	317.1	310.6	306.3	301.2	300.4	312.3
2002	288.6	291.0	292.8	297.4	300.0	301.7	299.6	302.7	298.7	295.8	293.4	293.0	296.2
2003	282.6	283.7	284.4	288.4	290.7	295.7	296.2	299.0	295.8	297.0	294.0	296.2	292.0
2004	287.2	289.8	293.7	301.9	303.8	309.2	311.7	312.5	310.4	310.0	308.2	310.9	304.1
2005	302.6	303.7	306.4	314.1	315.9	320.7	322.9	324.1	322.9	322.5	321.6	324.6	316.8
2006	314.7	318.4	321.6	327.4	331.9	338.6	337.8	340.0	338.1	337.5	337.0	339.1	331.8
2007	332.0	334.0	338.8	344.3	349.0	355.1	354.6	356.6	355.3	354.3	350.7	351.5	348.0
Education and Health Services													
2000	187.4	189.3	190.1	191.3	191.8	193.0	192.1	193.4	194.6	195.2	196.9	198.0	192.8
2001	196.1	198.0	198.7	199.1	200.0	200.5	199.7	201.5	201.3	203.8	204.9	206.2	200.8
2002	204.2	205.7	206.4	208.0	208.7	208.4	207.7	209.1	209.7	210.2	211.4	212.0	208.5
2003	209.8	211.1	211.7	212.4	212.9	213.1	212.3	213.1	213.5	214.5	215.2	216.1	213.0
2004	214.7	216.0	217.1	217.6	218.2	218.3	217.0	218.1	219.5	220.5	221.6	223.1	218.5
2005	220.3	223.0	223.5	224.0	225.0	225.3	223.6	224.6	225.2	225.5	226.9	228.0	224.6
2006	225.9	228.5	229.3	230.0	231.1	231.2	229.4	230.8	232.1	233.9	235.3	236.5	231.2
2007	233.7	236.8	238.4	238.9	239.9	239.9	238.6	240.3	241.4	243.2	244.2	245.1	240.0
Leisure and Hospitality													
2000	237.5	240.5	245.6	242.3	236.6	254.0	258.9	259.5	248.5	238.0	240.5	250.1	246.0
2001	246.2	247.4	251.2	246.3	239.4	257.0	259.9	260.3	247.9	233.8	233.7	243.6	247.2
2002	242.2	243.4	246.1	245.2	240.3	256.9	259.6	260.0	248.7	237.2	236.0	248.5	247.0
2003	243.8	242.8	244.8	241.2	236.6	252.5	256.6	258.8	247.6	238.2	236.1	247.9	245.6
2004	244.8	245.5	249.7	248.2	244.0	259.6	263.5	264.5	253.9	243.3	242.2	256.1	251.3
2005	250.8	252.7	257.5	253.7	250.0	266.0	269.7	270.0	259.1	249.5	248.6	262.5	257.5
2006	258.5	259.0	263.3	259.2	256.5	273.7	277.2	277.9	266.7	257.4	258.7	271.0	264.9
2007	263.4	264.7	270.0	266.6	263.0	278.7	281.9	282.6	271.6	262.6	263.1	275.5	270.3
Other Services													
2000	79.2	79.0	80.0	79.1	79.6	81.7	81.8	81.6	80.4	79.8	79.6	80.5	80.2
2001	82.6	82.7	83.4	83.3	83.6	85.5	85.2	85.2	83.7	83.1	83.0	83.7	83.8
2002	84.7	84.7	85.3	85.4	85.5	87.1	87.3	86.8	85.3	84.6	84.9	85.1	85.6
2003	85.7	85.2	85.2	85.5	85.7	87.4	87.3	86.9	85.3	85.2	85.4	86.1	85.9
2004	86.0	85.7	86.1	86.5	86.6	88.2	88.6	88.7	88.1	88.1	87.8	88.6	87.4
2005	88.2	88.1	88.5	88.4	88.4	89.6	89.5	89.3	88.4	87.9	87.5	88.1	88.5
2006	89.8	89.7	90.5	90.4	90.6	92.3	91.8	91.7	90.8	90.4	90.5	91.2	90.8
2007	91.4	91.9	92.9	92.5	92.6	94.2	93.6	93.7	93.2	92.4	92.4	93.3	92.8
Government													
2000	323.8	335.4	340.7	341.5	349.1	337.6	321.2	322.6	337.8	343.9	345.3	345.3	337.0
2001	332.1	344.1	345.0	345.3	348.6	344.1	328.2	330.2	347.5	353.4	355.8	355.1	344.1
2002	344.1	354.9	358.2	358.2	362.3	355.7	338.7	340.5	356.5	364.8	365.9	364.7	355.4
2003	350.5	360.5	362.5	360.4	366.2	355.8	338.0	338.7	356.2	362.4	362.3	360.6	356.2
2004	349.6	359.4	362.3	363.6	366.3	359.1	338.6	341.3	360.4	367.0	367.8	366.5	358.5
2005	352.8	364.7	365.9	367.5	370.7	363.0	345.2	345.1	365.0	370.9	370.7	369.7	362.6
2006	356.8	368.4	371.6	370.8	374.5	368.1	348.8	351.4	369.8	375.2	376.0	375.3	367.2
2007	360.3	374.7	378.0	378.5	382.0	374.5	355.5	359.2	379.4	385.0	386.3	384.5	374.8

Average Weekly Hours by Selected Industry: Colorado, 2001–2007

(Not seasonally adjusted.)

Industry and year	January	February	March	April	May	June	July	August	September	October	November	December	Annual Average
Construction													
2001	39.2	37.6	38.1	36.0	41.1	41.3	41.4	41.5	42.2	41.8	41.6	40.7	40.3
2002	40.0	40.4	38.7	41.2	41.1	41.5	41.5	42.2	40.6	41.3	39.9	39.7	40.7
2003	39.5	38.0	39.1	40.0	40.1	40.9	39.9	39.4	38.1	38.1	38.6	37.1	39.1
2004	38.1	37.1	37.6	37.7	38.2	39.5	39.0	38.2	37.2	37.4	37.5	37.5	37.9
2005	35.8	36.9	38.1	36.5	38.6	39.6	39.2	39.0	39.5	38.7	39.5	38.0	38.3
2006	38.4	37.8	38.5	40.2	40.1	40.0	39.8	39.5	39.3	39.6	38.9	38.7	39.3
2007	36.7	37.1	38.9	39.1	39.6	39.9	39.8	39.8	39.2	39.1	38.8	37.7	38.9
Manufacturing													
2001	40.6	40.7	40.9	39.7	40.4	41.5	41.3	41.0	41.8	41.0	40.0	39.9	40.7
2002	39.9	40.1	39.9	39.5	40.7	41.4	41.2	40.4	39.8	41.2	42.0	41.3	40.6
2003	39.6	41.1	40.2	39.4	39.8	39.1	40.3	40.9	40.9	41.2	40.9	40.7	40.4
2004	40.5	41.3	40.6	39.8	39.4	40.4	40.6	40.7	40.3	40.5	39.4	40.9	40.4
2005	38.4	37.4	37.8	37.9	38.1	38.2	38.1	39.0	39.4	39.7	38.9	39.4	38.5
2006	38.6	38.6	39.1	39.8	39.5	39.5	39.5	39.6	39.1	39.3	39.0	38.6	39.2
2007	38.3	38.9	39.7	39.9	40.0	40.5	40.2	40.3	39.9	40.4	40.0	40.4	39.9

Average Hourly Earnings by Selected Industry: Colorado, 2001–2007

(Dollars, not seasonally adjusted.)

Industry and year	January	February	March	April	May	June	July	August	September	October	November	December	Annual Average
Construction													
2001	17.32	17.39	17.32	17.35	17.33	17.29	17.11	17.29	17.33	17.29	17.38	17.45	17.32
2002	17.65	17.71	17.66	17.61	17.49	17.58	17.48	17.92	18.24	17.83	18.25	18.37	17.81
2003	18.18	18.58	18.36	18.33	18.55	18.40	18.44	18.68	18.72	18.57	18.91	18.90	18.55
2004	18.94	18.94	18.93	19.04	18.89	18.49	18.65	18.91	19.29	19.07	18.65	19.31	18.92
2005	19.01	19.20	19.55	19.49	19.46	19.15	19.37	19.58	19.79	19.60	20.09	20.08	19.55
2006	19.97	19.87	19.79	19.95	20.13	20.20	20.28	20.45	20.67	20.61	20.55	20.62	20.27
2007	20.41	20.53	20.57	20.73	20.74	20.72	20.80	20.77	20.79	20.59	20.83	20.85	20.70
Manufacturing													
2001	14.45	14.62	14.65	14.56	14.66	14.43	14.66	14.74	14.69	14.93	15.00	15.41	14.72
2002	15.32	15.30	15.42	15.40	15.61	15.48	15.44	15.30	15.43	15.29	15.29	16.02	15.44
2003	16.09	16.04	16.30	17.24	17.11	17.14	17.45	17.34	17.26	16.88	16.83	16.86	16.89
2004	16.73	16.70	16.58	16.45	16.72	16.38	16.42	16.25	16.79	16.28	16.09	16.14	16.46
2005	15.95	15.82	16.03	15.91	15.97	15.87	15.89	15.91	15.64	15.88	15.93	16.12	15.91
2006	16.14	15.79	16.13	16.26	16.37	16.37	16.48	16.82	16.84	17.31	17.25	17.22	16.59
2007	17.06	16.79	17.17	17.36	17.48	17.63	17.97	17.99	18.11	18.33	18.96	18.26	17.76

Average Weekly Earnings by Selected Industry: Colorado, 2001–2007

(Dollars, not seasonally adjusted.)

Industry and year	January	February	March	April	May	June	July	August	September	October	November	December	Annual Average
Construction													
2001	678.94	653.86	659.89	624.60	712.26	714.08	708.35	717.54	731.33	722.72	723.01	710.22	698.00
2002	706.00	715.48	683.44	725.53	718.84	729.57	725.42	756.22	740.54	736.38	728.18	729.29	724.87
2003	718.11	706.04	717.88	733.20	743.86	752.56	735.76	735.99	713.23	707.52	729.93	701.19	725.31
2004	721.61	702.67	711.77	717.81	721.60	730.36	727.35	722.36	717.59	713.22	699.38	724.13	717.07
2005	680.56	708.48	744.86	711.39	751.16	758.34	759.30	763.62	781.71	758.52	793.56	763.04	748.77
2006	766.85	751.09	761.92	801.99	807.21	808.00	807.14	807.78	812.33	816.16	799.40	797.99	796.61
2007	749.05	761.66	800.17	810.54	821.30	826.73	827.84	826.65	814.97	805.07	808.20	786.05	805.23
Manufacturing													
2001	586.67	595.03	599.19	578.03	592.26	598.85	605.46	604.34	614.04	612.13	600.00	614.86	599.10
2002	611.27	613.53	615.26	608.30	635.33	640.87	636.13	618.12	614.11	629.95	642.18	661.63	626.86
2003	637.16	659.24	655.26	679.26	680.98	670.17	703.24	709.21	705.93	695.46	688.35	686.20	682.36
2004	677.57	689.71	673.15	654.71	658.77	661.75	666.65	661.38	676.64	659.34	633.95	660.13	664.98
2005	612.48	591.67	605.93	602.99	608.46	606.23	605.41	620.49	616.22	630.44	619.68	635.13	612.54
2006	623.00	609.49	630.68	647.15	646.62	646.62	650.96	666.07	658.44	680.28	672.75	664.69	650.33
2007	653.40	653.13	681.65	692.66	699.20	714.02	722.39	725.00	722.59	740.53	758.40	737.70	708.62

CONNECTICUT
At a Glance

Population
   2000 census: 3,405,565
   2007 estimate: 3,502,309
   Percent change, 2000–2007: 2.8%

Percent change in total nonfarm employment, 2000–2007: 0.3%

Industry with the largest growth in employment, 2000–2007 (thousands)
   Education and health services, 42.5

Industry with the largest decline in employment, 2000–2007 (thousands)
   Manufacturing, -44.3

Civilian labor force
   2000: 1,736,831
   2007: 1,865,483

Employment-population ratio
   2000: 65.4%
   2007: 65.4%

Unemployment rate and rank among states
   2000: 2.3%, 1st
   2007: 4.6%, 31st

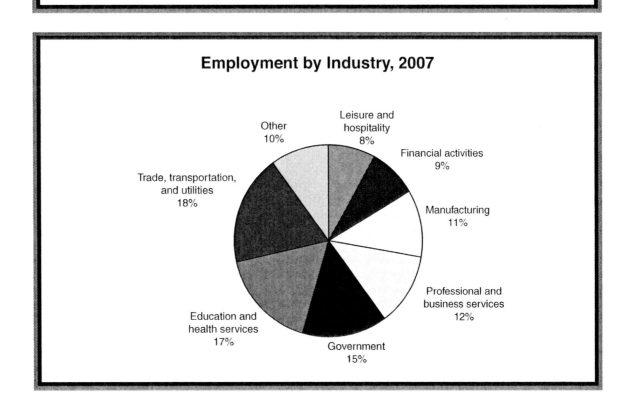

Employment by Industry, 2007

Other 10%
Leisure and hospitality 8%
Financial activities 9%
Manufacturing 11%
Professional and business services 12%
Government 15%
Education and health services 17%
Trade, transportation, and utilities 18%

Employment by Industry: Connecticut, 2000–2007

(Numbers in thousands, not seasonally adjusted.)

Industry and year	January	February	March	April	May	June	July	August	September	October	November	December	Annual Average
Total Nonfarm													
2000	1,655.0	1,661.5	1,675.9	1,687.0	1,700.9	1,713.0	1,695.5	1,685.8	1,703.4	1,704.2	1,712.1	1,723.8	1,693.2
2001	1,665.2	1,661.0	1,667.3	1,677.0	1,690.4	1,699.4	1,676.5	1,669.7	1,683.4	1,687.9	1,694.2	1,701.2	1,681.1
2002	1,648.1	1,648.7	1,657.5	1,670.2	1,679.9	1,687.0	1,655.0	1,652.0	1,663.3	1,665.2	1,673.1	1,678.2	1,664.9
2003	1,630.9	1,626.0	1,630.8	1,641.6	1,653.8	1,659.7	1,633.2	1,630.5	1,642.6	1,655.7	1,663.3	1,665.7	1,644.5
2004	1,616.6	1,618.6	1,627.7	1,646.3	1,658.3	1,667.0	1,644.2	1,642.0	1,655.7	1,664.6	1,675.4	1,681.3	1,649.8
2005	1,630.3	1,636.0	1,639.6	1,663.5	1,670.4	1,681.7	1,653.9	1,651.0	1,668.0	1,673.3	1,683.9	1,692.8	1,662.0
2006	1,648.5	1,650.7	1,656.0	1,678.4	1,687.3	1,698.5	1,672.5	1,673.7	1,685.3	1,694.5	1,704.9	1,716.6	1,680.6
2007	1,666.5	1,668.4	1,671.9	1,689.4	1,705.7	1,719.9	1,691.3	1,689.8	1,704.0	1,712.5	1,722.0	1,729.3	1,697.6
Total Private													
2000	1,417.6	1,417.2	1,428.6	1,439.8	1,450.2	1,470.4	1,466.4	1,460.6	1,463.3	1,459.3	1,465.5	1,477.1	1,451.3
2001	1,423.4	1,414.3	1,420.0	1,429.8	1,443.3	1,456.8	1,449.0	1,443.1	1,438.9	1,436.7	1,438.7	1,446.0	1,436.7
2002	1,399.4	1,393.8	1,401.7	1,415.6	1,425.7	1,436.9	1,423.9	1,418.1	1,416.5	1,413.6	1,417.8	1,423.7	1,415.6
2003	1,380.6	1,373.4	1,377.6	1,390.1	1,402.6	1,413.6	1,405.0	1,400.4	1,400.4	1,408.2	1,413.0	1,417.0	1,398.5
2004	1,374.3	1,371.2	1,378.9	1,398.2	1,411.4	1,425.0	1,419.2	1,413.7	1,416.3	1,417.5	1,425.3	1,432.6	1,407.0
2005	1,388.8	1,389.1	1,393.2	1,414.9	1,422.6	1,437.1	1,428.8	1,422.6	1,424.8	1,424.1	1,432.1	1,440.9	1,418.3
2006	1,402.9	1,401.3	1,406.8	1,428.2	1,437.5	1,453.7	1,444.4	1,440.9	1,441.4	1,444.3	1,451.8	1,463.1	1,434.7
2007	1,419.0	1,416.0	1,420.1	1,437.1	1,453.8	1,471.4	1,460.6	1,456.0	1,455.6	1,457.2	1,464.1	1,471.5	1,448.5
Goods-Producing													
2000	293.9	292.7	295.6	298.8	300.7	304.4	304.0	304.9	306.2	304.1	303.8	303.4	301.0
2001	293.5	291.3	292.5	295.4	296.7	298.5	295.1	294.7	292.8	289.6	287.3	285.8	292.8
2002	277.2	274.5	275.5	277.7	278.8	280.2	276.3	276.6	275.2	272.7	270.9	268.5	275.3
2003	261.0	257.3	257.9	261.5	264.1	266.2	264.3	265.1	264.4	264.2	264.0	262.4	262.7
2004	255.1	253.4	256.5	262.2	264.8	268.1	267.6	268.2	267.8	267.2	266.8	265.5	263.6
2005	258.0	255.9	257.1	261.7	263.8	267.0	265.6	265.2	263.6	262.4	261.9	260.2	261.9
2006	255.4	254.8	253.5	261.0	262.8	266.5	265.8	265.7	263.9	262.9	262.3	261.7	261.4
2007	255.1	253.0	254.8	258.5	261.2	265.5	264.8	265.1	263.4	263.0	262.4	260.3	260.6
Natural Resources and Mining													
2000	0.7	0.6	0.7	0.8	0.8	0.8	0.9	0.8	0.8	0.8	0.8	0.8	0.7
2001	0.7	0.6	0.7	0.7	0.8	0.8	0.8	0.8	0.8	0.7	0.7	0.7	0.7
2002	0.7	0.6	0.7	0.7	0.8	0.8	0.8	0.8	0.8	0.8	0.8	0.8	0.8
2003	0.7	0.6	0.6	0.7	0.8	0.8	0.8	0.8	0.8	0.8	0.8	0.7	0.7
2004	0.6	0.6	0.7	0.7	0.8	0.8	0.8	0.8	0.8	0.8	0.8	0.7	0.7
2005	0.7	0.6	0.6	0.7	0.8	0.8	0.8	0.8	0.8	0.8	0.8	0.7	0.7
2006	0.7	0.7	0.7	0.8	0.8	0.8	0.8	0.8	0.8	0.8	0.8	0.7	0.8
2007	0.7	0.6	0.6	0.7	0.7	0.8	0.8	0.8	0.8	0.8	0.8	0.7	0.7
Construction													
2000	58.1	57.1	59.9	62.9	65.0	67.0	68.0	68.5	68.0	67.3	67.1	66.0	64.5
2001	59.1	58.3	59.6	64.2	66.7	68.5	69.8	70.0	68.8	67.6	66.6	65.1	65.4
2002	59.4	58.5	59.9	63.3	65.0	66.4	66.8	66.7	65.5	64.5	63.7	61.3	63.4
2003	56.2	54.3	55.2	59.1	62.4	64.0	65.9	66.4	65.6	65.5	65.3	63.3	61.9
2004	57.5	56.4	58.6	64.3	66.9	68.7	69.9	70.5	69.9	69.5	68.8	67.1	65.7
2005	60.9	59.6	60.5	65.2	67.1	69.0	70.0	70.1	68.9	67.7	67.2	65.1	65.9
2006	60.9	60.4	61.9	66.0	67.8	69.8	70.9	71.3	70.2	69.8	68.9	67.6	67.1
2007	62.6	60.7	62.4	67.1	69.6	71.8	72.6	72.8	71.8	71.4	70.5	68.2	68.5
Manufacturing													
2000	235.1	235.0	235.0	235.1	234.9	236.6	235.1	235.6	237.4	236.0	235.9	236.6	235.7
2001	233.7	232.4	232.2	230.5	229.2	229.2	224.5	223.9	223.2	221.3	220.0	220.0	226.7
2002	217.1	215.4	214.9	213.7	213.0	213.0	208.7	209.1	208.9	207.4	206.4	206.4	211.2
2003	204.1	202.4	202.1	201.7	200.9	201.4	197.6	197.9	198.0	197.9	197.9	198.4	200.0
2004	197.0	196.4	197.2	197.2	197.1	198.6	196.9	196.9	197.1	196.9	197.2	197.7	197.2
2005	196.4	195.7	196.0	195.8	195.9	197.2	194.8	194.3	193.9	193.9	193.9	194.4	195.2
2006	193.8	193.7	190.9	194.2	194.2	195.9	194.1	193.6	192.9	192.3	192.6	193.4	193.5
2007	191.8	191.7	191.8	190.7	190.9	192.9	191.4	191.5	190.8	190.8	191.1	191.4	191.4
Service-Providing													
2000	1,361.1	1,368.8	1,380.3	1,388.2	1,400.2	1,408.6	1,391.5	1,380.9	1,397.2	1,400.1	1,408.3	1,420.4	1,392.1
2001	1,371.7	1,369.7	1,374.8	1,381.6	1,393.7	1,400.9	1,381.4	1,375.0	1,390.6	1,398.3	1,406.9	1,415.4	1,388.3
2002	1,370.9	1,374.2	1,382.0	1,392.5	1,401.1	1,406.8	1,378.7	1,375.4	1,388.1	1,392.5	1,402.2	1,409.7	1,389.5
2003	1,369.9	1,368.7	1,372.9	1,380.1	1,389.7	1,393.5	1,368.9	1,365.4	1,378.2	1,391.5	1,399.3	1,403.3	1,381.8
2004	1,361.5	1,365.2	1,371.2	1,384.1	1,393.5	1,398.9	1,376.6	1,373.8	1,387.9	1,397.4	1,408.6	1,415.8	1,386.2
2005	1,372.3	1,380.1	1,382.5	1,401.8	1,406.6	1,414.7	1,388.3	1,385.8	1,404.4	1,410.9	1,422.0	1,432.6	1,400.2
2006	1,393.1	1,395.9	1,402.5	1,417.4	1,424.5	1,432.0	1,406.7	1,408.0	1,421.4	1,431.6	1,442.6	1,454.9	1,419.2
2007	1,411.4	1,415.4	1,417.1	1,430.9	1,444.5	1,454.4	1,426.5	1,424.7	1,440.6	1,449.5	1,459.6	1,469.0	1,437.0
Trade, Transportation, and Utilities													
2000	314.8	311.6	313.0	314.5	316.1	318.4	313.1	312.2	316.9	319.5	326.7	333.2	317.5
2001	314.2	306.4	307.0	308.8	311.5	313.6	309.5	307.8	310.0	313.6	318.9	324.7	312.2
2002	309.4	303.8	305.4	307.7	309.7	312.7	305.9	304.3	308.6	308.2	314.3	320.4	309.2
2003	306.3	300.9	302.5	301.4	304.0	306.9	300.5	299.4	303.9	308.5	313.6	318.1	305.5
2004	304.9	301.0	302.3	303.7	306.4	309.3	304.4	302.6	307.2	310.5	318.3	324.2	307.9
2005	310.2	306.3	306.6	308.4	310.0	312.4	306.2	304.9	309.2	310.2	317.5	324.5	310.5
2006	311.7	305.4	307.3	308.6	310.3	313.2	306.2	305.0	308.4	311.2	318.8	325.1	310.9
2007	311.2	305.3	306.6	306.1	311.3	314.6	308.2	306.6	310.1	312.0	319.4	325.8	311.4
Wholesale Trade													
2000	66.9	67.0	67.3	68.1	68.5	68.7	68.4	68.2	68.5	68.4	68.9	69.3	68.1
2001	67.0	67.1	67.3	67.9	68.1	68.2	67.7	67.2	66.9	67.2	66.8	67.2	67.4
2002	65.9	65.5	65.7	66.1	66.3	66.4	66.3	66.2	66.0	65.8	65.8	66.2	66.0
2003	65.3	65.0	65.4	65.4	65.5	66.0	65.5	65.4	65.2	65.5	65.6	65.7	65.5
2004	64.8	64.9	65.4	65.9	66.2	66.7	66.0	66.0	65.8	65.4	65.8	66.2	65.8
2005	65.7	65.4	65.6	65.9	66.3	66.7	66.8	66.8	66.9	66.9	67.1	67.5	66.5
2006	66.9	66.8	67.1	67.5	67.7	68.1	67.7	67.6	67.3	67.7	67.7	67.9	67.5
2007	67.5	67.5	67.5	67.5	67.8	68.2	68.2	68.2	68.1	68.4	68.3	68.6	68.0

Employment by Industry: Connecticut, 2000–2007—*Continued*

(Numbers in thousands, not seasonally adjusted.)

Industry and year	January	February	March	April	May	June	July	August	September	October	November	December	Annual Average
Retail Trade													
2000	196.4	192.9	194.4	194.5	195.7	197.8	194.8	195.0	195.7	197.3	204.2	210.6	197.4
2001	195.6	188.6	189.4	190.0	192.3	194.6	193.6	193.8	193.0	195.3	201.4	206.8	194.5
2002	194.9	189.5	191.1	192.0	193.7	196.5	193.2	192.9	192.8	192.0	198.2	204.0	194.2
2003	192.1	187.3	188.2	187.5	189.6	191.6	189.3	189.3	189.3	192.2	197.3	201.7	191.3
2004	191.1	187.2	188.0	188.0	189.9	191.9	191.4	190.4	190.3	192.2	199.2	204.6	192.0
2005	193.0	189.3	189.1	190.1	191.0	192.4	190.2	189.8	189.2	190.4	196.7	202.2	192.0
2006	192.3	186.4	187.8	188.7	189.8	191.9	189.6	189.4	188.4	190.5	197.8	202.4	191.3
2007	191.1	185.5	186.7	186.4	190.6	193.0	190.7	190.3	188.9	190.2	197.5	202.1	191.1
Transportation and Utilities													
2000	51.5	51.7	51.3	51.9	51.9	51.9	49.9	49.0	52.7	53.8	53.6	53.3	51.8
2001	51.6	50.7	50.3	50.9	51.1	50.8	48.2	46.8	50.1	51.1	50.7	50.7	50.3
2002	48.6	48.8	48.6	49.6	49.7	49.8	46.4	45.2	49.8	50.4	50.3	50.2	49.0
2003	48.9	48.6	48.9	48.5	48.9	49.3	45.7	44.7	49.4	50.8	50.7	50.7	48.8
2004	49.0	48.9	48.9	49.8	50.3	50.7	47.0	46.2	51.1	52.9	53.3	53.4	50.1
2005	51.5	51.6	51.9	52.4	52.7	53.3	49.2	48.3	53.1	52.9	53.7	54.8	52.1
2006	52.5	52.2	52.4	52.4	52.8	53.2	48.9	48.0	52.7	53.0	53.3	54.8	52.2
2007	52.6	52.3	52.4	52.2	52.9	53.4	49.3	48.1	53.1	53.4	53.6	55.1	52.4
Information													
2000	45.2	45.4	45.7	45.5	45.8	46.5	46.9	47.0	47.0	47.1	47.4	47.6	46.4
2001	46.3	46.4	46.0	45.3	45.1	45.1	44.2	44.2	43.6	43.2	43.3	43.3	44.7
2002	42.2	41.9	41.8	41.5	41.4	41.5	41.0	40.7	40.2	40.0	39.9	40.0	41.0
2003	40.1	39.9	39.8	39.6	39.5	39.8	39.6	39.5	39.1	39.2	39.4	39.5	39.6
2004	39.2	38.8	38.9	38.9	39.0	39.4	39.3	39.3	39.3	38.8	38.6	38.9	39.0
2005	38.5	38.6	38.3	38.2	38.2	38.5	38.2	38.0	37.6	37.5	37.7	37.8	38.1
2006	37.9	37.9	37.9	37.7	37.8	37.9	38.0	38.0	37.7	37.8	38.1	38.3	37.9
2007	37.5	37.9	37.7	38.0	38.9	38.5	38.6	38.6	38.8	38.8	39.1	39.3	38.5
Financial Activities													
2000	141.2	141.2	141.8	141.5	142.1	144.2	145.1	145.3	143.9	143.0	143.0	144.1	143.0
2001	142.1	141.8	142.1	142.0	142.5	144.1	144.8	144.9	143.1	142.3	142.4	143.2	142.9
2002	142.8	142.1	142.1	141.4	142.1	143.4	143.9	143.8	142.5	141.8	142.5	143.1	142.6
2003	142.4	141.7	141.7	142.6	143.3	144.7	144.3	144.0	142.4	141.5	141.4	142.0	142.7
2004	140.1	139.6	139.8	139.7	140.1	141.6	142.0	142.1	140.7	140.3	140.7	141.1	140.7
2005	140.5	140.5	140.5	141.6	141.5	143.4	144.2	144.0	142.7	142.4	142.6	143.5	142.3
2006	143.0	142.7	142.9	142.9	143.4	145.1	145.6	145.8	144.5	144.6	145.1	145.6	144.3
2007	144.9	144.4	144.1	144.1	144.5	146.3	146.2	145.9	144.2	143.5	143.4	143.4	144.6
Professional and Business Services													
2000	207.7	208.9	211.6	214.4	216.1	220.9	219.7	219.5	219.4	217.6	217.2	218.0	215.9
2001	207.3	204.7	206.6	209.6	214.4	215.2	212.4	212.1	211.7	209.3	207.8	207.4	209.9
2002	197.7	197.7	200.7	203.2	203.9	206.2	203.3	204.1	203.4	201.6	201.2	201.0	202.0
2003	193.5	193.4	194.4	196.9	197.1	198.5	196.6	197.7	197.8	198.1	198.7	198.3	196.8
2004	191.2	191.3	193.4	196.7	197.7	200.7	199.3	199.6	199.4	197.2	198.5	199.6	197.1
2005	191.9	193.2	195.3	199.1	199.2	203.1	202.4	202.3	203.3	202.2	203.1	204.0	199.9
2006	196.0	198.5	200.8	204.6	204.7	208.8	205.0	206.2	206.8	205.7	206.3	208.3	204.3
2007	199.4	200.4	201.6	206.0	207.6	211.2	207.3	208.0	207.6	206.4	207.1	208.0	205.9
Education and Health Services													
2000	243.4	245.6	246.7	246.3	245.7	244.5	244.2	240.6	244.6	245.7	247.0	248.8	245.2
2001	248.3	252.0	252.0	251.7	248.5	249.8	249.4	247.5	254.7	257.5	259.6	260.8	252.7
2002	255.1	258.9	258.9	260.3	259.6	257.1	255.9	253.7	259.4	264.4	266.5	266.9	259.7
2003	261.1	264.3	263.0	265.1	264.6	261.4	260.0	257.0	262.4	268.5	270.0	270.3	264.0
2004	264.4	268.2	267.0	270.3	270.3	266.6	264.3	261.3	268.3	274.0	275.0	274.8	268.7
2005	269.0	273.4	271.8	275.6	274.0	270.1	268.6	265.9	273.1	278.3	279.7	279.8	273.3
2006	274.7	278.4	277.2	280.9	279.5	276.1	275.8	273.7	280.6	284.8	286.4	287.2	279.6
2007	282.1	286.6	285.2	289.2	287.5	285.7	283.9	281.3	288.3	292.9	294.4	294.8	287.7
Leisure and Hospitality													
2000	111.9	112.1	114.2	118.2	122.9	129.6	130.9	129.3	124.1	120.9	119.0	120.3	121.1
2001	111.0	111.0	112.7	115.8	122.9	127.7	129.7	128.6	121.2	118.9	116.9	118.0	119.5
2002	112.9	113.0	115.0	120.8	126.4	131.4	133.5	131.6	125.2	122.9	120.2	121.0	122.8
2003	114.7	114.6	116.4	121.3	127.8	132.9	136.1	134.7	128.7	126.2	123.9	124.1	125.1
2004	117.9	117.5	119.2	124.4	130.5	136.0	138.3	137.0	131.8	127.5	124.8	126.0	127.6
2005	119.1	119.5	121.5	127.6	133.0	138.5	139.5	138.8	132.8	128.6	126.9	127.7	129.5
2006	122.1	121.8	124.8	129.3	135.2	141.6	142.8	141.7	135.7	133.1	130.6	132.3	132.6
2007	125.4	125.2	126.5	131.3	138.6	144.3	146.1	145.5	139.1	136.3	134.0	135.2	135.6
Other Services													
2000	59.5	59.7	60.0	60.6	60.8	61.9	62.5	61.8	61.2	61.4	61.4	61.7	61.0
2001	60.7	60.7	61.1	61.2	61.7	62.8	63.9	63.3	61.8	62.3	62.5	62.8	62.1
2002	62.1	61.9	62.3	63.0	63.8	64.4	64.1	63.3	62.0	62.0	62.3	62.8	62.8
2003	61.5	61.3	61.9	61.7	62.2	63.2	63.6	63.0	61.7	62.0	62.0	62.3	62.2
2004	61.5	61.4	61.8	62.3	62.6	63.3	64.0	63.6	62.3	62.2	62.3	62.6	62.5
2005	61.6	61.7	62.1	62.7	62.9	64.1	64.1	63.5	62.5	62.5	62.7	63.4	62.8
2006	62.1	61.8	62.4	63.2	63.8	64.5	65.2	64.8	63.8	64.2	64.2	64.6	63.7
2007	63.4	63.2	63.6	63.9	64.2	65.3	65.5	65.0	64.1	64.3	64.3	64.7	64.3
Government													
2000	237.4	244.3	247.3	247.2	250.7	242.6	229.1	225.2	240.1	244.9	246.6	246.7	241.8
2001	241.8	246.7	247.3	247.2	247.1	242.6	227.5	226.6	244.5	251.2	255.5	255.2	244.4
2002	248.7	254.9	255.8	254.6	254.2	250.1	231.1	233.9	246.8	251.6	255.3	254.5	249.3
2003	250.3	252.6	253.2	251.5	251.2	246.1	228.2	230.1	242.2	247.5	250.3	248.7	246.0
2004	242.3	247.4	248.8	248.1	246.9	242.0	225.0	228.3	239.4	247.1	250.1	248.7	242.8
2005	241.5	246.9	246.4	248.6	247.8	244.6	225.1	228.4	243.2	249.2	251.8	251.9	243.8
2006	245.6	249.4	249.2	250.2	249.8	244.8	228.1	232.8	243.9	250.2	253.1	253.5	245.9
2007	247.5	252.4	251.8	252.3	251.9	248.5	230.7	233.8	248.4	255.3	257.9	257.8	249.0

Average Weekly Hours by Selected Industry: Connecticut, 2001–2007

(Not seasonally adjusted.)

Industry and year	January	February	March	April	May	June	July	August	September	October	November	December	Annual Average
Construction													
2001	39.0	39.1	39.0	38.4	40.4	40.4	40.1	40.2	39.7	40.1	39.2	38.7	39.6
2002	38.4	39.0	39.6	40.0	40.0	40.4	40.9	40.8	40.1	40.2	39.2	39.7	39.9
2003	39.2	38.8	39.7	38.4	40.3	39.7	40.3	40.4	40.1	40.0	39.0	39.4	39.6
2004	38.8	38.7	38.8	38.2	39.7	39.7	39.1	38.9	37.7	39.0	38.5	38.1	38.8
2005	37.2	38.3	38.1	38.8	39.6	40.0	39.1	39.5	38.9	38.7	39.0	38.1	38.8
2006	38.6	38.4	38.8	38.3	38.2	39.2	38.7	39.4	38.8	38.7	38.5	39.0	38.7
2007	38.8	38.6	39.0	38.4	38.7	38.9	39.2	39.3	38.5	38.9	38.2	38.1	38.7
Manufacturing													
2001	42.1	41.6	42.0	40.9	41.7	41.7	41.5	41.5	42.1	42.3	41.9	40.9	41.7
2002	41.8	41.3	41.5	41.6	41.4	42.1	41.0	41.4	42.0	41.8	41.9	41.9	41.6
2003	41.6	41.1	41.3	41.3	41.2	41.1	40.5	40.8	41.9	41.8	42.3	42.5	41.4
2004	41.8	41.5	41.7	41.5	42.1	42.0	41.4	41.3	41.5	42.1	42.4	42.6	41.8
2005	42.0	41.9	42.0	42.3	42.2	42.5	42.1	41.8	42.0	42.1	42.3	42.7	42.2
2006	42.5	42.3	42.0	41.6	42.0	42.2	42.4	41.9	42.4	42.1	42.0	42.7	42.2
2007	42.1	42.4	42.4	42.4	42.2	42.2	42.3	42.1	42.6	42.4	42.4	42.6	42.3

Average Hourly Earnings by Selected Industry: Connecticut, 2001–2007

(Dollars, not seasonally adjusted.)

Industry and year	January	February	March	April	May	June	July	August	September	October	November	December	Annual Average
Construction													
2001	21.59	21.38	21.68	21.82	22.03	22.11	21.96	22.18	22.26	22.30	21.90	22.12	21.96
2002	22.35	22.00	22.00	21.93	22.01	22.19	22.38	22.65	22.31	22.26	22.22	22.15	22.21
2003	22.54	22.52	22.52	22.54	22.57	22.59	22.82	22.96	22.50	22.85	22.72	22.92	22.84	22.71
2004	22.93	23.10	23.17	22.99	22.52	22.71	23.29	23.07	23.08	22.65	22.76	22.45	22.89
2005	21.96	22.61	22.80	23.37	23.83	23.74	23.84	23.43	23.44	22.43	22.84	22.57	23.11
2006	22.43	22.81	23.05	23.60	23.15	23.26	23.33	23.76	23.55	23.67	23.76	23.40	23.34
2007	23.18	23.29	23.81	23.77	23.87	23.46	23.83	24.00	24.47	24.65	24.49	24.78	23.98
Manufacturing													
2001	16.05	16.16	16.31	16.40	16.30	16.34	16.54	16.50	16.56	16.68	16.75	16.46	16.42
2002	16.99	16.91	17.14	17.21	17.09	17.18	17.26	17.22	17.44	17.45	17.37	17.67	17.24
2003	17.25	17.42	17.73	17.58	17.68	17.74	17.89	17.79	17.97	17.95	17.93	18.01	17.74
2004	17.99	17.99	18.11	18.24	18.07	18.09	18.26	18.36	18.69	18.69	18.77	18.90	18.35
2005	18.85	18.82	18.93	18.67	18.69	18.68	18.76	18.92	19.21	19.25	19.30	19.48	18.96
2006	19.47	19.52	19.58	19.56	19.51	19.73	19.60	19.86	19.96	20.10	20.21	20.25	19.78
2007	20.26	20.29	20.26	20.32	20.29	20.57	20.68	20.75	20.91	20.89	21.01	21.24	20.62

Average Weekly Earnings by Selected Industry: Connecticut, 2001–2007

(Dollars, not seasonally adjusted.)

Industry and year	January	February	March	April	May	June	July	August	September	October	November	December	Annual Average
Construction													
2001	842.01	835.96	845.52	837.89	890.01	893.24	880.60	891.64	883.72	894.23	858.48	856.04	869.62
2002	858.24	858.00	871.20	877.20	880.40	896.48	915.34	924.12	894.63	894.85	871.02	879.36	886.18
2003	883.57	873.78	894.84	866.69	910.38	905.95	925.29	909.00	916.29	908.80	893.88	899.90	899.32
2004	889.68	893.97	899.00	878.22	894.04	901.59	910.64	897.42	870.12	883.35	876.26	855.35	888.13
2005	816.91	865.96	868.68	906.76	943.67	949.60	932.14	925.49	911.82	868.04	890.76	859.92	896.67
2006	865.80	875.90	894.34	903.88	884.33	911.79	902.87	936.14	913.74	916.03	914.76	912.60	903.26
2007	899.38	898.99	928.59	912.77	923.77	912.59	934.14	943.20	942.10	958.89	935.52	944.12	928.03
Manufacturing													
2001	675.71	672.26	685.02	670.76	679.71	681.38	686.41	684.75	697.18	705.56	701.83	673.21	684.71
2002	710.18	698.38	711.31	715.94	707.53	723.28	707.66	712.91	732.48	729.41	727.80	740.37	717.18
2003	717.60	715.96	732.25	726.05	728.42	729.11	724.55	725.83	752.94	750.31	758.44	765.43	734.44
2004	751.98	746.59	755.19	756.96	760.75	759.78	755.96	758.27	775.64	786.85	795.85	805.14	767.03
2005	791.70	788.56	795.06	789.74	788.72	793.90	789.80	790.86	806.82	810.43	816.39	831.80	800.11
2006	827.48	825.70	822.36	813.70	819.42	832.61	831.04	832.13	846.30	846.21	848.82	864.68	834.72
2007	852.95	860.30	859.02	861.57	856.24	868.05	874.76	873.58	890.77	885.74	890.82	904.82	872.23

DELAWARE
At a Glance

Population
    2000 census: 783,600
    2007 estimate: 864,764
    Percent change, 2000–2007: 10.4%

Percent change in total nonfarm employment, 2000–2007: 4.0%

Industry with the largest growth in employment, 2000–2007 (thousands)
    Education and health services, 12.5

Industry with the largest decline in employment, 2000–2007 (thousands)
    Manufacturing, -8.1

Civilian labor force
    2000: 416,503
    2007: 442,692

Employment-population ratio
    2000: 67.4%
    2007: 64.0%

Unemployment rate and rank among states
    2000: 3.3%, 14th
    2007: 3.4%, 10th

Employment by Industry, 2007

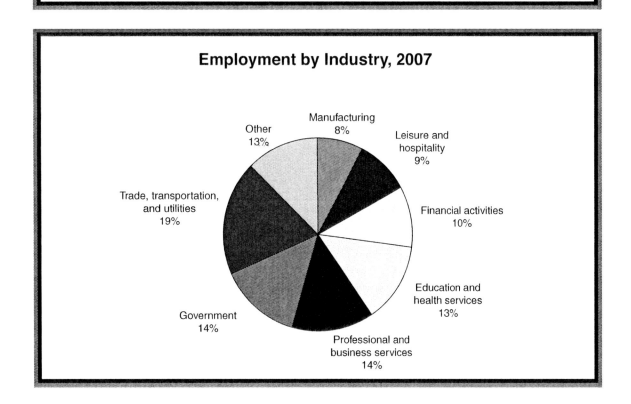

Other 13%
Manufacturing 8%
Leisure and hospitality 9%
Trade, transportation, and utilities 19%
Financial activities 10%
Education and health services 13%
Government 14%
Professional and business services 14%

Employment by Industry: Delaware, 2000–2007

(Numbers in thousands, not seasonally adjusted.)

Industry and year	January	February	March	April	May	June	July	August	September	October	November	December	Annual Average
Total Nonfarm													
2000	407.0	408.9	415.2	417.8	421.2	426.6	425.8	423.5	422.4	421.8	424.1	425.9	420.0
2001	410.9	412.3	419.7	419.8	422.9	427.2	422.9	421.5	417.9	417.8	419.9	419.8	419.4
2002	403.5	405.1	407.9	411.6	417.3	419.3	418.6	417.9	419.5	415.8	418.3	418.9	414.5
2003	403.1	400.4	404.6	409.9	416.1	421.4	418.1	418.0	419.0	419.7	421.2	422.9	414.5
2004	410.7	412.6	417.4	418.1	424.6	430.0	426.9	426.5	427.2	428.8	431.1	430.8	423.7
2005	416.8	417.9	422.8	428.7	433.2	434.5	434.3	434.4	435.5	435.7	440.4	439.2	431.1
2006	425.6	425.9	430.5	434.3	438.9	442.6	437.6	437.4	437.9	438.6	440.3	442.0	436.0
2007	425.8	425.1	430.4	434.1	440.0	445.0	440.2	439.5	437.8	438.4	442.3	443.3	436.8
Total Private													
2000	352.7	353.2	357.7	360.0	362.9	369.4	368.9	368.8	367.2	365.3	366.4	368.1	363.3
2001	354.7	355.3	361.5	361.3	364.8	370.3	366.4	366.8	363.2	361.2	362.4	362.1	362.5
2002	347.8	348.1	350.2	353.7	359.6	363.1	363.8	364.5	362.0	357.2	359.0	359.9	357.4
2003	346.4	343.1	346.9	351.7	357.5	364.2	363.2	364.2	361.8	361.3	362.9	364.4	357.3
2004	353.6	354.8	358.6	360.0	366.0	372.7	371.7	371.8	369.0	370.3	372.4	372.0	366.1
2005	359.1	359.1	362.8	368.5	372.6	376.6	376.9	378.2	375.9	374.3	378.9	378.0	371.7
2006	365.9	365.2	368.4	372.1	376.5	382.9	379.4	380.3	377.7	377.0	378.4	380.4	375.4
2007	366.2	364.0	368.0	371.6	377.2	383.8	380.4	381.0	377.2	377.1	380.3	380.9	375.6
Goods-Producing													
2000	64.3	64.8	66.1	66.3	67.0	68.3	66.5	66.7	66.4	66.8	65.8	65.4	66.2
2001	60.9	61.3	64.1	64.4	64.8	66.1	64.8	64.8	64.5	63.7	63.8	63.3	63.9
2002	60.5	61.1	61.2	59.7	61.8	62.2	62.3	62.2	61.9	61.1	60.8	60.8	61.3
2003	57.5	57.1	57.9	58.7	60.2	61.8	60.5	61.2	61.4	62.0	61.8	60.5	60.1
2004	58.7	59.1	60.1	60.8	61.2	62.2	62.2	62.1	61.2	61.7	61.6	61.0	61.0
2005	58.1	59.0	60.0	61.2	61.9	61.1	61.1	62.4	62.3	61.9	64.2	61.2	61.2
2006	61.7	61.3	62.0	62.7	63.1	64.1	63.0	63.7	63.8	63.7	63.2	62.8	62.9
2007	60.3	59.0	60.1	60.6	61.5	62.1	60.9	61.5	60.7	61.2	62.8	62.7	61.1
Natural Resources, Mining, and Construction													
2000	24.1	23.2	24.5	24.9	24.8	25.5	25.1	25.1	24.9	25.5	24.5	24.2	24.6
2001	23.0	23.1	23.6	23.9	24.4	25.4	24.8	25.2	25.1	25.0	25.5	24.9	24.5
2002	23.4	23.1	23.2	24.0	24.4	24.9	25.3	25.1	24.6	24.1	24.0	24.2	24.2
2003	23.0	21.6	22.2	23.4	24.3	24.9	25.5	25.5	25.2	25.7	25.8	25.6	24.4
2004	24.4	24.1	25.1	25.8	26.1	27.0	27.4	27.5	27.3	27.7	27.6	26.8	26.4
2005	25.9	25.5	26.3	27.5	27.9	28.5	28.7	28.5	28.4	29.6	30.4	28.9	28.0
2006	28.0	27.8	28.3	29.3	29.6	30.5	30.5	30.2	30.1	30.1	29.5	29.1	29.4
2007	27.2	26.0	26.8	27.4	28.0	28.3	28.2	28.1	28.2	28.2	28.3	28.3	27.8
Manufacturing													
2000	40.2	41.6	41.6	41.4	42.2	42.8	41.4	41.6	41.5	41.3	41.3	41.2	41.5
2001	37.9	38.2	40.5	40.5	40.4	40.7	40.0	39.6	39.4	38.7	38.3	38.4	39.4
2002	37.1	38.0	38.0	35.7	37.4	37.3	37.0	37.1	37.3	37.0	36.8	36.6	37.1
2003	34.5	35.5	35.7	35.3	35.9	36.9	35.0	35.7	36.2	36.3	36.0	34.9	35.7
2004	34.3	35.0	35.0	35.0	35.1	35.2	34.8	34.6	33.9	34.0	34.0	34.2	34.6
2005	32.2	33.5	33.7	33.7	34.0	32.6	32.4	33.9	33.9	32.3	33.8	32.3	33.2
2006	33.7	33.5	33.7	33.4	33.5	33.6	32.9	33.5	33.7	33.6	33.7	33.7	33.5
2007	33.1	33.0	33.3	33.2	33.5	33.8	32.7	33.4	32.5	33.0	34.5	34.4	33.4
Service-Providing													
2000	342.7	344.1	349.1	351.5	354.2	358.3	359.3	356.8	356.0	355.0	358.3	360.5	353.8
2001	350.0	351.0	355.6	355.4	358.1	361.1	358.1	356.7	353.4	354.1	356.1	356.5	355.5
2002	343.0	344.0	346.7	351.9	355.5	357.1	356.3	355.7	357.6	354.7	357.5	358.1	353.2
2003	345.6	343.3	346.7	351.2	355.9	359.6	357.6	356.8	357.6	357.7	359.4	362.4	354.5
2004	352.0	353.5	357.3	357.3	363.4	367.8	364.7	364.4	366.0	367.1	369.5	369.8	362.7
2005	358.7	358.9	362.8	367.5	371.3	373.4	373.2	372.0	373.2	373.8	376.2	378.0	369.9
2006	363.9	364.6	368.5	371.6	375.8	378.5	374.6	373.7	374.1	374.9	377.1	379.2	373.0
2007	365.5	366.1	370.3	373.5	378.5	382.9	379.3	378.0	377.1	377.2	379.5	380.6	375.7
Trade, Transportation, and Utilities													
2000	77.4	76.6	76.7	77.9	78.5	79.7	79.6	79.4	79.5	79.4	80.9	83.0	79.0
2001	76.7	76.0	76.6	75.3	75.7	77.0	76.3	76.2	76.1	77.2	78.3	79.4	76.7
2002	74.9	74.2	75.1	75.4	76.9	77.8	77.8	77.7	77.9	77.3	79.0	80.4	77.0
2003	76.1	75.1	76.2	77.0	78.3	79.4	78.9	79.4	79.1	79.8	81.3	83.3	78.7
2004	78.6	78.1	78.7	79.4	80.2	81.8	81.3	81.0	80.8	81.5	83.6	84.5	80.8
2005	79.9	78.9	79.8	80.3	81.1	81.8	82.1	82.1	81.7	82.5	84.5	86.1	81.7
2006	81.1	80.1	80.9	81.7	82.8	83.5	83.0	82.4	81.9	82.5	84.7	85.6	82.5
2007	81.9	80.6	81.1	81.3	83.0	84.1	83.8	83.7	83.3	84.1	85.7	86.0	83.2
Wholesale Trade													
2000	12.7	12.8	12.9	13.3	13.2	13.3	13.4	13.5	13.5	13.6	13.6	13.7	13.2
2001	13.4	13.5	13.6	13.3	13.3	13.4	13.3	13.3	13.3	13.4	13.3	13.4	13.4
2002	13.3	13.2	13.6	13.5	13.7	13.8	13.8	13.9	13.8	13.7	13.6	13.7	13.6
2003	13.6	13.6	13.9	14.0	14.3	14.2	14.4	14.5	14.4	14.3	14.3	14.4	14.2
2004	14.3	14.3	14.4	14.7	14.8	14.9	15.0	14.9	14.8	15.0	14.9	14.9	14.7
2005	14.8	14.8	14.9	14.9	14.9	14.8	14.8	14.8	14.8	15.0	15.1	15.3	14.9
2006	14.9	15.0	15.0	15.2	15.3	15.3	15.3	15.2	15.1	15.0	14.9	15.2	15.1
2007	14.8	14.7	14.7	14.9	15.0	15.1	15.1	15.1	14.9	15.0	14.8	14.8	14.9
Retail Trade													
2000	50.3	49.4	49.4	50.2	50.9	52.2	52.2	51.9	51.7	51.5	53.1	55.0	51.4
2001	50.4	49.7	50.1	49.1	49.6	50.7	50.4	50.6	50.2	50.7	52.1	53.3	50.6
2002	49.6	48.7	49.3	49.7	50.7	51.7	51.9	51.9	51.6	51.0	52.8	54.2	51.1
2003	50.0	49.0	49.8	50.5	51.3	52.4	52.4	52.8	51.8	52.4	53.8	55.1	51.8
2004	51.0	50.3	50.7	51.1	51.9	53.2	53.1	53.2	52.4	52.8	54.9	55.7	52.5
2005	52.0	51.1	51.6	52.3	53.1	53.8	54.4	54.4	53.4	53.7	55.6	57.0	53.5
2006	52.9	51.7	52.4	52.9	53.6	54.2	54.3	53.9	52.8	53.2	55.7	56.1	53.6
2007	53.1	52.1	52.7	52.8	53.9	55.0	55.1	54.9	54.2	54.7	56.4	56.8	54.3

Employment by Industry: Delaware, 2000–2007—*Continued*

(Numbers in thousands, not seasonally adjusted.)

Industry and year	January	February	March	April	May	June	July	August	September	October	November	December	Annual Average
Transportation and Utilities													
2000	14.4	14.4	14.4	14.4	14.4	14.2	14.0	14.0	14.3	14.3	14.2	14.3	14.2
2001	12.9	12.8	12.9	12.9	12.8	12.9	12.6	12.3	12.6	13.1	12.9	12.7	12.8
2002	12.0	12.3	12.2	12.2	12.5	12.3	12.1	11.9	12.5	12.6	12.6	12.5	12.3
2003	12.5	12.5	12.5	12.5	12.7	12.8	12.1	12.1	12.9	13.1	13.2	13.8	12.7
2004	13.3	13.5	13.6	13.6	13.5	13.7	13.2	12.9	13.6	13.7	13.8	13.9	13.5
2005	13.1	13.0	13.3	13.1	13.1	13.2	12.9	12.8	13.5	13.8	13.8	13.8	13.3
2006	13.3	13.4	13.5	13.6	13.9	14.0	13.4	13.3	14.0	14.3	14.1	14.3	13.8
2007	14.0	13.8	13.7	13.6	14.1	14.0	13.6	13.7	14.2	14.4	14.5	14.4	14.0
Information													
2000	8.1	8.3	8.4	8.0	8.1	8.1	8.3	7.6	8.3	8.1	8.2	8.2	8.1
2001	8.0	8.0	8.1	8.1	8.1	8.2	8.2	8.2	8.1	7.9	8.0	8.0	8.1
2002	7.8	7.8	7.8	7.7	7.7	7.8	7.8	7.9	7.7	7.6	7.7	7.6	7.7
2003	7.5	7.5	7.5	7.4	7.4	7.4	7.4	7.4	7.3	7.1	7.2	7.2	7.4
2004	7.3	7.2	7.3	7.0	7.0	7.0	7.0	7.0	6.9	7.0	7.0	7.0	7.1
2005	6.4	6.4	6.5	6.7	6.8	6.8	6.8	6.7	6.7	6.8	6.8	6.8	6.7
2006	6.7	6.7	6.6	6.6	6.6	6.7	6.7	6.8	6.7	6.7	6.8	6.8	6.7
2007	6.8	6.8	6.8	6.9	7.0	7.0	6.9	7.0	6.9	6.8	6.9	6.8	6.9
Financial Activities													
2000	46.2	46.4	46.3	46.0	46.1	46.6	46.7	46.9	46.4	46.2	46.5	46.8	46.4
2001	46.6	46.7	46.9	47.0	47.1	47.3	47.3	47.2	46.8	46.3	46.0	45.8	46.8
2002	46.7	46.6	46.6	46.3	46.5	46.7	47.1	46.9	46.2	45.8	45.8	45.8	46.4
2003	45.5	45.3	45.2	45.6	45.6	45.7	46.5	46.0	45.3	44.2	44.2	44.2	45.3
2004	44.1	44.1	44.3	44.3	44.6	45.0	45.6	45.7	45.0	44.4	44.6	44.5	44.7
2005	45.1	45.1	44.9	44.8	45.0	45.3	45.9	45.8	45.3	45.1	45.2	45.2	45.2
2006	44.5	44.4	44.2	44.5	44.4	44.6	44.7	45.3	45.0	44.9	45.0	45.2	44.7
2007	44.8	44.9	44.9	45.1	45.3	45.8	46.1	45.8	45.5	45.5	45.6	45.8	45.4
Professional and Business Services													
2000	64.9	64.8	65.9	65.6	65.2	66.2	66.7	67.0	67.0	66.7	67.2	67.3	66.2
2001	66.6	66.6	67.3	66.2	66.3	66.5	65.3	66.0	65.1	64.7	65.6	65.2	66.0
2002	61.0	60.6	60.3	61.2	61.0	60.1	60.5	60.9	60.9	60.5	60.8	61.3	60.8
2003	59.1	57.9	58.2	58.3	58.7	58.9	58.5	58.5	58.8	59.6	59.8	60.8	58.9
2004	59.8	61.2	61.8	60.1	61.5	62.2	61.4	61.7	61.5	62.4	63.0	63.5	61.7
2005	60.8	60.7	61.2	62.6	62.7	63.1	62.7	62.7	62.7	62.7	63.3	64.3	62.5
2006	60.8	61.0	61.5	61.3	61.4	61.2	60.7	61.0	60.7	60.7	60.9	62.6	61.2
2007	58.3	58.5	59.4	60.1	60.5	60.9	60.1	60.1	60.0	60.2	60.4	61.1	60.0
Education and Health Services													
2000	44.5	44.9	45.3	45.4	45.2	45.3	45.4	45.6	46.1	46.0	46.4	46.6	45.5
2001	46.4	46.9	47.3	47.3	47.4	47.4	46.7	47.0	47.6	48.3	48.3	48.3	47.4
2002	47.6	48.0	48.2	48.6	48.8	48.6	48.1	48.7	49.2	49.3	49.6	49.7	48.7
2003	49.7	49.6	50.0	50.2	50.3	50.3	49.7	49.9	50.7	51.1	51.4	51.7	50.4
2004	51.0	51.1	51.4	51.6	51.9	51.9	51.2	51.3	52.2	53.5	53.4	53.6	52.0
2005	53.2	53.4	53.8	54.1	54.3	54.3	53.4	53.5	54.3	54.5	54.7	54.9	54.0
2006	54.8	55.0	55.3	55.7	55.9	56.1	56.2	56.1	56.5	56.8	57.2	57.3	56.1
2007	57.0	57.1	57.4	57.6	57.9	57.9	57.6	57.7	58.4	58.8	59.0	59.2	58.0
Leisure and Hospitality													
2000	31.8	31.9	33.3	35.0	37.0	39.1	39.7	39.5	37.6	35.6	34.9	34.4	35.8
2001	32.4	32.7	33.9	35.8	38.1	39.9	40.4	40.0	37.8	35.8	35.1	34.7	36.4
2002	32.4	32.6	33.7	37.0	38.9	41.5	42.0	42.0	40.4	37.3	37.1	36.0	37.6
2003	33.3	33.0	34.2	36.6	38.9	42.1	43.1	43.1	40.8	38.9	38.4	37.9	38.4
2004	35.5	35.3	36.1	38.2	40.9	43.6	44.1	44.1	42.7	40.6	40.0	38.7	40.0
2005	36.3	36.3	37.2	39.2	41.2	44.4	45.0	45.0	43.1	40.7	40.0	39.2	40.6
2006	36.3	36.6	37.6	39.3	42.0	46.1	44.6	44.7	43.1	41.3	40.1	39.3	40.9
2007	36.8	37.0	38.0	39.7	41.7	45.3	44.6	44.9	42.3	40.1	39.2	38.8	40.7
Other Services													
2000	15.5	15.5	15.7	15.8	15.8	16.1	16.0	16.1	15.9	16.5	16.5	16.4	15.9
2001	17.1	17.1	17.3	17.2	17.3	17.9	17.4	17.4	17.2	17.3	17.3	17.4	17.3
2002	16.9	17.2	17.3	17.8	18.0	18.4	18.2	18.2	17.8	18.3	18.2	18.3	17.9
2003	17.7	17.6	17.7	17.9	18.1	18.6	18.6	18.7	18.4	18.6	18.8	18.8	18.3
2004	18.6	18.7	18.9	18.6	18.7	19.0	18.9	18.9	18.7	19.2	19.2	19.2	18.9
2005	19.3	19.3	19.4	19.6	19.6	19.8	19.9	20.0	19.8	20.1	20.2	20.3	19.8
2006	20.0	20.1	20.3	20.3	20.3	20.6	20.5	20.3	20.0	20.4	20.5	20.8	20.3
2007	20.3	20.1	20.3	20.3	20.3	20.7	20.4	20.3	20.1	20.4	20.7	20.5	20.4
Government													
2000	54.3	55.7	57.5	57.8	58.3	57.2	56.9	54.7	55.2	56.5	57.7	57.8	56.6
2001	56.2	57.0	58.2	58.5	58.1	56.9	56.5	54.7	54.7	56.6	57.5	57.7	56.9
2002	55.7	57.0	57.7	57.9	57.7	56.2	54.8	53.4	57.5	58.6	59.3	59.0	57.1
2003	56.7	57.3	57.7	58.2	58.6	57.2	54.9	53.8	57.2	58.4	58.3	58.5	57.2
2004	57.1	57.8	58.8	58.1	58.6	57.3	55.2	54.7	58.2	58.5	58.7	58.8	57.7
2005	57.7	58.8	60.0	60.2	60.6	57.9	57.4	56.2	59.6	61.4	61.5	61.2	59.4
2006	59.7	60.7	62.1	62.2	62.4	59.7	58.2	57.1	60.2	61.6	61.9	61.6	60.6
2007	59.6	61.1	62.4	62.5	62.8	61.2	59.8	58.5	60.6	61.3	62.0	62.4	61.2

Average Weekly Hours by Selected Industry: Delaware, 2001–2007

(Not seasonally adjusted.)

Industry and year	January	February	March	April	May	June	July	August	September	October	November	December	Annual Average
Manufacturing													
2001	39.5	39.3	38.6	38.1	39.2	40.2	40.8	40.5	39.9	40.5	39.2	40.9	39.7
2002	38.5	38.5	39.3	39.2	40.5	41.3	41.1	41.5	40.5	39.3	40.1	40.4	40.0
2003	39.4	40.0	39.8	39.5	39.8	41.4	40.7	40.8	40.5	40.6	40.4	40.4	40.3
2004	40.2	39.7	39.8	39.8	41.0	40.3	41.0	40.4	40.8	40.0	38.9	38.8	40.1
2005	39.9	39.4	39.3	39.9	39.5	39.4	39.6	40.4	39.3	39.6	40.2	40.2	39.7
2006	40.1	40.5	40.0	39.1	40.2	39.9	39.9	39.8	39.9	39.5	39.6	39.7	39.9
2007	38.5	38.1	39.1	39.8	39.2	40.2	39.1	40.7	39.9	40.1	38.7	39.5	39.4

Average Hourly Earnings by Selected Industry: Delaware, 2001–2007

(Dollars, not seasonally adjusted.)

Industry and year	January	February	March	April	May	June	July	August	September	October	November	December	Annual Average
Manufacturing													
2001	16.02	16.13	17.02	16.88	16.38	16.71	16.89	16.86	16.89	16.35	16.37	16.17	16.56
2002	16.01	16.38	16.40	16.68	16.26	16.29	16.47	16.76	16.84	16.87	17.07	17.22	16.60
2003	16.83	16.74	16.85	16.51	16.41	16.64	16.99	17.05	17.20	17.35	17.24	17.09	16.91
2004	17.39	17.64	17.63	17.83	17.36	17.43	17.54	17.55	17.81	17.83	17.82	18.09	17.66
2005	17.34	17.91	17.67	17.69	18.12	17.56	17.55	17.88	17.80	17.79	17.98	17.48	17.74
2006	18.09	18.08	18.32	18.33	18.07	17.88	18.00	18.00	18.28	18.14	18.04	18.08	18.11
2007	17.69	17.82	17.60	17.98	17.92	18.11	17.28	17.93	17.66	18.42	17.88	17.66	17.83

Average Weekly Earnings by Selected Industry: Delaware, 2001–2007

(Dollars, not seasonally adjusted.)

Industry and year	January	February	March	April	May	June	July	August	September	October	November	December	Annual Average
Manufacturing													
2001	632.79	633.91	656.97	643.13	642.10	671.74	689.11	682.83	673.91	662.18	641.70	661.35	657.43
2002	616.39	630.63	644.52	653.86	658.53	672.78	676.92	695.54	682.02	662.99	684.51	695.69	664.00
2003	663.10	669.60	670.63	652.15	653.12	688.90	691.49	695.64	696.60	704.41	696.50	690.44	681.47
2004	699.08	700.31	701.67	709.63	711.76	702.43	719.14	709.02	726.65	713.20	693.20	701.89	708.17
2005	691.87	705.65	694.43	705.83	715.74	691.86	694.98	722.35	699.54	704.48	722.80	702.70	704.28
2006	725.41	732.24	732.80	716.70	726.41	713.41	718.20	716.40	729.37	716.53	714.38	717.78	722.59
2007	681.07	678.94	688.16	715.60	702.46	728.02	675.65	729.75	704.63	738.64	691.96	697.57	702.50

Population:
    2000 census: 572,059
    2007 estimate: 588,292
    Percent change, 2000–2007: 2.8%

Percent change in total nonfarm employment, 2000–2007: 6.9%

Industry with the largest growth in employment, 2000–2007 (thousands)
    Professional and business services, 20.5

Industry with the largest decline in employment, 2000–2007 (thousands)
    Information, -3.6

Civilian labor force
    2000: 309,421
    2007: 325,562

Employment-population ratio
    2000: 63.7%
    2007: 64.3%

Unemployment rate and rank among states
    2000: 5.7%, 49th
    2007: 5.7%, 47th

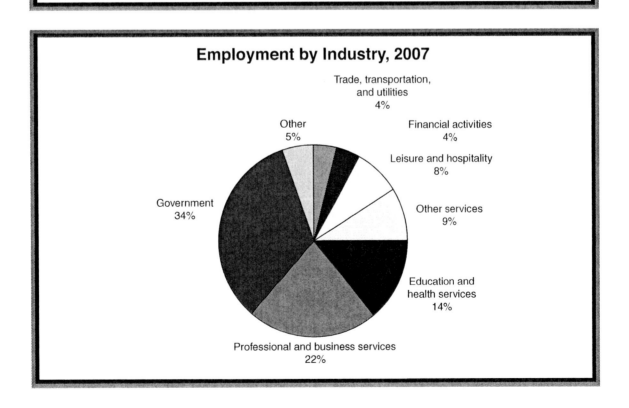

Employment by Industry, 2007

Trade, transportation, and utilities 4%
Financial activities 4%
Leisure and hospitality 8%
Other services 9%
Education and health services 14%
Professional and business services 22%
Government 34%
Other 5%

Employment by Industry: District of Columbia, 2000–2007

(Numbers in thousands, not seasonally adjusted.)

Industry and year	January	February	March	April	May	June	July	August	September	October	November	December	Annual Average
Total Nonfarm													
2000	628.8	634.5	638.9	643.9	644.0	652.1	661.5	656.6	654.0	659.0	662.9	667.2	650.2
2001	640.7	641.9	647.1	647.2	649.9	654.6	662.6	662.9	656.7	661.1	659.3	659.8	653.7
2002	648.3	653.3	660.3	662.6	660.9	664.8	674.4	669.9	666.9	667.4	670.9	671.1	664.2
2003	656.9	659.0	665.2	666.3	665.7	666.5	672.6	663.7	665.8	667.0	668.0	669.5	665.5
2004	657.9	665.1	670.7	673.8	673.9	676.6	680.0	679.0	675.0	678.8	680.8	678.6	674.2
2005	670.3	676.0	679.3	681.9	681.6	683.3	688.1	684.8	679.7	684.2	688.5	688.7	682.2
2006	675.4	681.8	686.2	685.3	684.6	689.4	695.5	689.8	685.3	691.4	693.6	693.4	687.6
2007	681.8	690.3	693.1	693.1	691.0	693.2	701.9	696.3	690.7	699.5	702.5	704.6	694.8
Total Private													
2000	407.1	413.1	417.4	422.3	420.1	426.3	428.8	427.3	430.6	438.2	441.2	443.5	426.3
2001	419.7	423.3	427.2	427.2	428.6	428.8	427.8	428.1	427.4	431.4	430.8	429.9	427.5
2002	418.0	424.2	430.5	433.8	431.4	432.3	434.3	432.3	435.0	438.2	440.5	439.9	432.5
2003	427.3	429.4	434.2	435.9	435.2	434.3	435.5	432.2	435.6	438.1	439.8	441.0	434.9
2004	429.0	436.5	441.3	444.5	445.4	445.7	443.8	441.4	445.0	447.8	448.6	446.0	442.9
2005	438.6	444.8	448.1	450.1	449.7	448.6	446.1	443.4	448.8	452.0	455.5	456.1	448.5
2006	443.6	450.4	454.8	455.3	453.9	455.9	452.7	449.4	454.6	460.2	462.4	462.0	454.6
2007	453.8	461.4	464.9	465.1	462.6	462.0	459.2	456.4	460.8	467.3	470.2	471.3	462.9
Goods-Producing													
2000	13.8	13.7	14.5	14.6	14.8	15.0	15.3	15.5	15.5	15.4	15.7	15.8	15.0
2001	14.9	14.7	14.8	15.0	15.4	15.6	15.2	15.4	15.0	14.8	14.6	14.4	15.0
2002	14.3	14.4	14.6	14.4	14.9	15.3	15.9	16.2	16.3	16.5	16.4	16.3	15.5
2003	15.6	15.4	15.8	15.4	15.2	15.4	15.7	15.7	15.7	15.4	15.2	14.9	15.5
2004	14.3	14.4	14.7	14.9	15.1	14.7	15.0	14.8	14.8	15.0	15.0	14.8	14.8
2005	14.5	14.8	14.8	15.1	15.2	15.2	14.8	14.9	14.5	14.3	14.4	14.4	14.7
2006	13.7	14.0	14.2	14.1	14.3	14.5	14.7	14.8	14.6	14.2	14.0	13.8	14.2
2007	13.9	13.7	13.8	13.9	14.3	14.4	14.5	14.9	14.7	14.5	14.5	14.2	14.3
Natural Resources, Mining, and Construction													
2000	10.1	10.1	10.8	10.9	11.1	11.3	11.6	11.8	11.8	11.7	12.0	12.0	11.3
2001	11.4	11.2	11.2	11.5	11.9	12.1	11.8	12.0	11.7	11.6	11.4	11.3	11.6
2002	11.1	11.3	11.4	11.5	12.0	12.4	12.8	13.1	13.2	13.4	13.3	13.3	12.4
2003	13.0	12.8	13.2	12.8	12.7	12.9	13.2	13.2	13.2	12.9	12.7	12.4	12.9
2004	11.9	11.9	12.2	12.5	12.7	12.3	12.5	12.3	12.3	12.6	12.6	12.5	12.4
2005	12.3	12.6	12.6	12.9	13.0	13.0	12.7	12.8	12.5	12.4	12.5	12.4	12.6
2006	11.9	12.2	12.4	12.3	12.5	12.7	13.0	13.1	12.9	12.5	12.3	12.1	12.5
2007	12.2	12.0	12.1	12.2	12.6	12.7	12.8	13.2	13.0	12.8	12.8	12.6	12.6
Manufacturing													
2000	3.7	3.6	3.7	3.7	3.7	3.7	3.7	3.7	3.7	3.7	3.7	3.8	3.7
2001	3.5	3.5	3.6	3.5	3.5	3.5	3.4	3.4	3.3	3.2	3.2	3.1	3.4
2002	3.2	3.1	3.2	2.9	2.9	2.9	3.1	3.1	3.1	3.1	3.1	3.0	3.1
2003	2.6	2.6	2.6	2.6	2.5	2.5	2.5	2.5	2.5	2.5	2.5	2.5	2.5
2004	2.4	2.5	2.5	2.4	2.4	2.4	2.5	2.5	2.5	2.4	2.4	2.3	2.4
2005	2.2	2.2	2.2	2.2	2.2	2.2	2.1	2.1	2.0	1.9	1.9	2.0	2.1
2006	1.8	1.8	1.8	1.8	1.8	1.8	1.7	1.7	1.7	1.7	1.7	1.7	1.8
2007	1.7	1.7	1.7	1.7	1.7	1.7	1.7	1.7	1.7	1.7	1.7	1.6	1.7
Service-Providing													
2000	615.0	620.8	624.4	629.3	629.2	637.1	646.2	641.1	638.5	643.6	647.2	651.4	635.3
2001	625.8	627.2	632.3	632.2	634.5	639.0	647.4	647.5	641.7	646.3	644.7	645.4	638.7
2002	634.0	638.9	645.7	648.2	646.0	649.5	658.5	653.7	650.6	650.9	654.5	654.8	648.8
2003	641.3	643.6	649.4	650.9	650.5	651.1	656.9	648.0	650.1	651.6	652.8	654.6	650.1
2004	643.6	650.7	656.0	658.9	658.8	661.9	665.0	664.2	660.2	663.8	665.8	663.8	659.4
2005	655.8	661.2	664.5	666.8	666.4	668.1	673.3	669.9	665.2	669.9	674.1	674.3	667.5
2006	661.7	667.8	672.0	671.2	670.3	674.9	680.8	675.0	670.7	677.2	679.6	679.6	673.4
2007	667.9	676.6	679.3	679.2	676.7	678.8	687.4	681.4	676.0	685.0	688.0	690.4	680.6
Trade, Transportation, and Utilities													
2000	29.3	29.4	29.4	29.2	29.2	29.8	29.1	29.0	29.4	29.7	30.5	31.3	29.6
2001	28.2	27.8	28.0	27.7	27.9	28.3	27.7	28.0	28.1	28.3	28.5	28.8	28.1
2002	27.5	27.7	27.4	27.6	27.7	28.0	27.9	27.6	27.7	27.9	28.4	29.0	27.9
2003	27.5	27.3	27.7	27.5	27.6	28.1	27.9	27.9	27.9	28.3	28.7	29.2	28.0
2004	27.8	27.7	28.1	27.9	28.1	28.3	27.8	27.4	27.6	27.6	28.0	28.4	27.9
2005	27.3	27.1	27.6	27.4	27.5	27.6	27.8	27.5	27.6	28.2	28.4	29.3	27.8
2006	28.1	27.9	27.8	27.5	27.6	27.9	27.7	27.6	27.8	27.9	28.2	28.6	27.9
2007	27.5	27.2	27.4	27.8	27.9	28.0	27.5	27.3	27.4	27.5	27.8	28.2	27.6
Wholesale Trade													
2000	4.5	4.5	4.5	4.4	4.4	4.4	4.3	4.3	4.3	4.4	4.4	4.5	4.4
2001	4.3	4.3	4.3	4.3	4.3	4.4	4.5	4.5	4.5	4.4	4.3	4.4	4.4
2002	4.1	4.2	4.2	4.2	4.2	4.3	4.5	4.4	4.5	4.5	4.5	4.6	4.4
2003	4.5	4.5	4.5	4.4	4.5	4.5	4.6	4.5	4.5	4.6	4.6	4.6	4.5
2004	4.5	4.6	4.5	4.6	4.6	4.6	4.6	4.5	4.6	4.5	4.6	4.6	4.6
2005	4.6	4.6	4.6	4.6	4.6	4.7	4.6	4.6	4.6	4.5	4.6	4.6	4.6
2006	4.7	4.7	4.6	4.6	4.6	4.6	4.7	4.7	4.7	4.7	4.7	4.8	4.7
2007	4.8	4.8	4.8	4.8	4.9	4.9	4.8	4.8	4.8	4.8	4.7	4.7	4.8
Retail Trade													
2000	17.1	17.0	17.2	16.9	17.0	17.4	17.1	17.1	17.6	17.8	18.5	18.9	17.5
2001	17.3	17.0	17.1	16.7	16.9	17.0	16.6	16.9	17.0	17.5	17.9	18.1	17.2
2002	17.3	17.2	17.0	17.0	17.1	17.2	17.0	16.8	16.9	17.0	17.5	18.0	17.2
2003	16.7	16.6	16.7	16.8	16.8	17.3	17.0	17.1	17.2	17.5	17.9	18.5	17.2
2004	17.2	17.1	17.3	17.4	17.6	17.9	17.6	17.4	17.5	17.6	17.9	18.4	17.6
2005	17.4	17.1	17.5	17.3	17.4	17.4	17.6	17.4	17.5	17.9	18.2	18.9	17.6
2006	18.0	17.9	17.8	17.5	17.5	17.9	17.8	17.7	18.0	18.2	18.5	18.8	18.0
2007	18.0	17.8	17.8	18.2	18.1	18.3	17.9	17.7	17.8	18.0	18.3	18.7	18.1

Employment by Industry: District of Columbia, 2000–2007—*Continued*

(Numbers in thousands, not seasonally adjusted.)

Industry and year	January	February	March	April	May	June	July	August	September	October	November	December	Annual Average
Transportation and Utilities													
2000	7.7	7.9	7.7	7.9	7.8	8.0	7.7	7.6	7.5	7.5	7.6	7.9	7.7
2001	6.6	6.5	6.6	6.7	6.7	6.9	6.6	6.6	6.6	6.4	6.3	6.3	6.6
2002	6.1	6.3	6.2	6.4	6.4	6.5	6.4	6.4	6.3	6.4	6.4	6.4	6.4
2003	6.3	6.2	6.5	6.3	6.3	6.3	6.3	6.3	6.2	6.2	6.2	6.1	6.3
2004	6.1	6.0	6.3	5.9	5.9	5.8	5.6	5.5	5.5	5.5	5.5	5.4	5.8
2005	5.3	5.4	5.5	5.5	5.5	5.5	5.6	5.5	5.5	5.7	5.7	5.8	5.5
2006	5.4	5.3	5.4	5.4	5.5	5.4	5.2	5.2	5.1	5.0	5.0	5.0	5.2
2007	4.7	4.6	4.8	4.8	4.9	4.8	4.8	4.8	4.8	4.7	4.8	4.8	4.8
Information													
2000	24.3	24.5	24.7	24.8	24.7	25.6	25.9	26.1	26.2	26.0	26.2	26.5	25.5
2001	25.3	25.5	25.5	25.8	25.8	25.8	25.5	26.3	26.0	26.0	26.0	26.1	25.8
2002	25.7	25.6	26.0	25.7	25.7	25.8	25.3	25.3	25.1	24.6	24.7	24.7	25.4
2003	25.0	25.3	25.4	24.5	24.6	24.4	24.5	24.4	24.4	23.9	24.0	23.8	24.5
2004	24.3	24.1	24.2	24.0	24.1	24.1	24.4	24.4	24.0	22.9	22.8	22.7	23.8
2005	22.8	23.0	22.8	22.6	22.4	22.6	22.7	22.5	22.4	22.2	22.3	22.3	22.6
2006	22.0	21.9	22.2	22.1	22.1	22.4	22.4	22.2	22.3	22.0	22.1	22.1	22.2
2007	22.4	22.5	22.4	21.9	21.8	22.2	22.3	22.2	21.3	21.2	21.3	21.4	21.9
Financial Activities													
2000	29.4	29.6	29.9	29.5	29.2	29.6	30.1	30.3	30.3	30.5	30.7	31.4	30.0
2001	30.4	30.4	30.5	31.0	31.0	31.1	31.5	31.5	31.2	31.3	31.2	31.5	31.1
2002	30.4	30.6	30.9	30.3	30.3	30.6	31.0	31.2	31.0	31.2	31.3	31.3	30.8
2003	30.8	30.8	30.8	30.9	31.0	31.0	31.1	30.9	30.7	30.4	30.3	30.5	30.8
2004	30.0	30.1	30.2	30.8	31.0	31.2	30.6	30.5	30.5	30.6	30.7	30.7	30.6
2005	29.9	30.1	29.8	30.6	30.7	30.5	30.3	30.2	30.3	30.1	30.0	30.4	30.2
2006	29.5	29.7	29.9	29.2	29.3	29.4	29.6	29.6	29.5	29.3	29.1	29.2	29.4
2007	29.5	29.7	29.7	29.4	29.1	29.2	29.0	28.8	28.7	28.7	28.8	29.0	29.1
Professional and Business Services													
2000	126.4	128.5	128.8	130.5	131.0	133.9	135.6	134.8	135.1	139.3	140.1	141.4	133.8
2001	135.9	137.3	138.4	137.6	138.0	140.8	140.2	139.5	137.4	139.9	139.9	140.1	138.8
2002	135.2	136.2	137.5	139.3	139.1	141.1	141.2	140.2	139.5	139.6	140.0	140.5	139.1
2003	137.7	137.9	138.8	142.3	143.0	144.2	143.4	142.4	142.3	142.2	142.3	143.3	141.7
2004	137.7	139.5	140.9	142.9	144.0	146.8	146.2	145.5	145.1	146.0	145.5	146.1	143.9
2005	144.2	145.5	147.0	147.4	147.8	150.3	150.3	149.5	149.4	149.5	149.6	150.1	148.4
2006	147.4	149.2	150.5	151.4	152.1	155.8	153.7	152.5	152.3	153.4	153.5	153.5	152.1
2007	150.7	152.3	152.8	153.3	154.7	157.0	155.3	154.9	153.7	155.4	155.5	156.2	154.3
Education and Health Services													
2000	84.2	86.0	86.7	87.9	85.3	85.5	86.6	86.7	87.6	89.9	91.0	90.8	87.4
2001	84.5	85.5	86.2	86.6	86.1	81.5	83.0	83.3	86.3	87.7	86.8	85.7	85.3
2002	86.9	89.7	92.1	92.1	88.5	85.6	86.3	86.5	89.5	92.2	93.5	92.4	89.6
2003	88.3	89.7	90.7	89.1	86.8	84.1	86.4	85.5	88.8	90.8	91.8	91.4	88.6
2004	89.7	94.2	94.9	94.7	92.2	89.0	88.8	88.2	92.1	94.5	95.1	93.5	92.2
2005	91.6	94.7	94.6	93.8	91.5	87.4	86.5	86.0	91.3	94.6	97.4	96.4	92.2
2006	92.6	96.0	96.4	96.6	93.1	88.8	88.3	87.5	92.6	97.1	99.4	98.8	93.9
2007	97.3	101.6	102.4	101.2	96.8	92.1	91.8	91.1	97.0	101.4	103.7	103.2	98.3
Leisure and Hospitality													
2000	43.5	44.7	46.2	48.4	48.7	49.3	48.6	47.7	49.0	50.2	50.6	50.3	48.1
2001	45.9	47.6	48.6	48.0	48.6	49.1	48.9	48.3	47.7	46.7	47.0	46.2	47.7
2002	43.4	44.9	46.7	48.3	49.2	49.5	49.6	48.5	49.3	49.9	49.9	49.3	48.2
2003	47.4	47.7	49.2	50.3	50.8	50.5	49.6	48.9	49.4	50.5	50.6	50.4	49.6
2004	48.0	49.0	50.3	50.9	52.1	52.1	51.3	51.0	51.6	52.1	51.9	51.0	50.9
2005	50.5	51.5	52.8	54.2	55.4	55.1	54.1	53.4	54.4	54.4	54.3	53.8	53.7
2006	51.7	52.7	54.3	54.6	55.3	55.8	54.5	53.9	54.5	54.9	54.3	53.6	54.2
2007	51.5	52.8	54.5	55.4	55.5	55.5	55.4	54.7	55.5	55.7	55.3	54.7	54.7
Other services													
2000	56.2	56.7	57.2	57.4	57.2	57.6	57.6	57.2	57.5	57.2	56.4	56.0	57.0
2001	54.6	54.5	55.2	55.5	55.8	56.6	55.8	55.8	55.7	56.7	56.8	57.1	55.8
2002	54.6	55.1	55.3	56.1	56.0	56.4	57.1	56.8	56.6	56.3	56.3	56.4	56.1
2003	55.0	55.3	55.8	55.9	56.2	56.6	56.9	56.5	56.4	56.6	56.9	57.5	56.3
2004	57.2	57.5	58.0	58.4	58.8	59.5	59.7	59.6	59.3	59.1	59.6	58.8	58.8
2005	57.8	58.1	58.7	59.0	59.2	59.9	59.9	59.6	59.4	58.9	58.7	59.1	59.4	59.0
2006	58.6	59.0	59.5	59.8	60.1	61.3	61.8	61.3	61.0	61.4	61.8	62.4	60.7
2007	61.0	61.6	61.9	62.2	62.5	63.6	63.4	62.5	62.5	62.9	63.3	64.4	62.7
Government													
2000	221.7	221.4	221.5	221.6	223.9	225.8	232.7	229.3	223.4	220.8	221.7	223.7	223.9
2001	221.0	218.6	219.9	220.0	221.3	225.8	234.8	234.8	229.3	229.7	228.5	229.9	226.1
2002	230.3	229.1	229.8	228.8	229.5	232.5	240.1	237.6	231.9	229.2	230.4	231.2	231.7
2003	229.6	229.6	231.0	230.4	230.5	232.2	237.1	231.5	230.2	228.9	228.2	228.5	230.6
2004	228.9	228.6	229.4	229.3	228.5	230.9	236.2	237.6	230.0	231.0	232.2	232.6	231.3
2005	231.7	231.2	231.2	231.8	231.9	234.7	242.0	241.4	230.9	232.2	233.0	232.6	233.7
2006	231.8	231.4	231.4	230.0	230.7	233.5	242.8	240.4	230.7	231.2	231.2	231.4	233.0
2007	228.0	228.9	228.2	228.0	228.4	231.2	242.7	239.9	229.9	232.2	232.3	233.3	231.9

Population
   2000 census: 15,982,378
   2007 estimate: 18,251,243
   Percent change, 2000–2007: 14.2%

Percent change in total nonfarm employment, 2000–2007: 13.7%

Industry with the largest growth in employment, 2000–2007 (thousands)
   Professional and business services, 249.7

Industry with the largest decline in employment, 2000–2007 (thousands)
   Manufacturing, -77.3

Civilian labor force
   2000: 7,869,690
   2007: 9,147,797

Employment-population ratio
   2000: 60.6%
   2007: 61.2%

Unemployment rate and rank among states
   2000: 3.8%, 25th
   2007: 4.0%, 20th

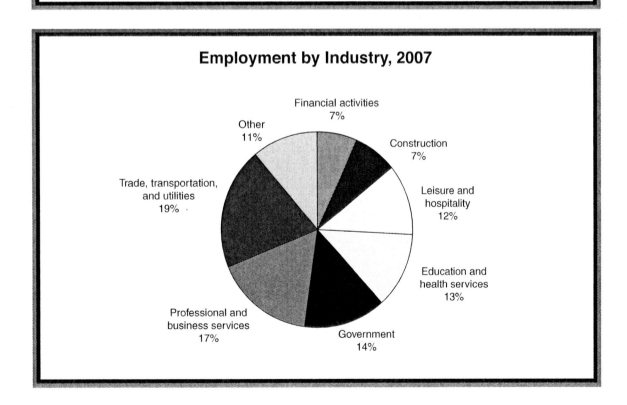

Employment by Industry, 2007

Financial activities 7%
Other 11%
Construction 7%
Trade, transportation, and utilities 19%
Leisure and hospitality 12%
Education and health services 13%
Professional and business services 17%
Government 14%

Employment by Industry: Florida, 2000–2007

(Numbers in thousands, not seasonally adjusted.)

Industry and year	January	February	March	April	May	June	July	August	September	October	November	December	Annual Average
Total Nonfarm													
2000	6,919.5	6,981.9	7,061.4	7,045.6	7,079.3	7,029.7	6,963.8	7,069.9	7,104.9	7,118.3	7,197.1	7,262.5	7,069.5
2001	7,096.7	7,167.7	7,229.5	7,194.7	7,198.5	7,135.1	7,046.0	7,147.1	7,147.8	7,138.8	7,187.0	7,228.0	7,159.7
2002	7,089.1	7,144.9	7,206.4	7,186.4	7,198.3	7,116.4	7,037.0	7,143.5	7,154.3	7,184.2	7,253.2	7,310.5	7,168.7
2003	7,176.8	7,232.3	7,287.6	7,262.3	7,266.8	7,184.5	7,116.9	7,217.7	7,238.0	7,283.2	7,331.2	7,403.3	7,250.1
2004	7,332.7	7,404.7	7,470.8	7,507.1	7,511.6	7,444.1	7,405.6	7,493.2	7,471.0	7,555.0	7,657.0	7,736.5	7,499.1
2005	7,621.9	7,704.9	7,751.6	7,794.2	7,812.4	7,718.4	7,698.1	7,815.0	7,860.0	7,866.8	7,941.2	8,014.6	7,799.9
2006	7,882.6	7,957.3	8,037.8	8,018.1	8,035.9	7,951.3	7,878.1	7,994.8	8,011.0	8,012.8	8,096.3	8,153.2	8,002.4
2007	8,010.9	8,077.4	8,141.6	8,099.3	8,096.0	7,988.2	7,885.1	7,992.9	7,984.7	8,022.4	8,074.4	8,124.4	8,041.4
Total Private													
2000	5,927.9	5,980.4	6,051.7	6,031.0	6,045.2	6,081.4	6,031.1	6,064.2	6,095.0	6,100.1	6,171.7	6,233.4	6,067.8
2001	6,082.0	6,139.5	6,195.2	6,159.5	6,161.9	6,166.3	6,093.1	6,113.9	6,108.6	6,097.1	6,139.2	6,178.8	6,136.3
2002	6,055.2	6,100.7	6,157.6	6,137.1	6,144.6	6,138.5	6,073.0	6,095.3	6,097.7	6,122.2	6,188.4	6,243.0	6,129.4
2003	6,124.1	6,168.8	6,220.5	6,196.7	6,194.8	6,190.6	6,135.9	6,160.7	6,175.1	6,212.2	6,257.4	6,327.6	6,197.0
2004	6,268.1	6,326.9	6,390.2	6,427.6	6,432.1	6,440.6	6,413.4	6,421.7	6,394.9	6,471.1	6,565.1	6,643.2	6,432.9
2005	6,540.8	6,611.4	6,655.8	6,698.7	6,713.7	6,719.2	6,697.4	6,731.9	6,762.1	6,758.7	6,830.3	6,905.0	6,718.8
2006	6,782.3	6,846.4	6,923.1	6,906.7	6,928.0	6,937.2	6,863.5	6,891.9	6,895.9	6,883.9	6,959.6	7,019.8	6,903.2
2007	6,887.1	6,942.3	7,001.0	6,960.4	6,960.0	6,946.9	6,844.0	6,860.7	6,844.1	6,871.6	6,918.2	6,968.4	6,917.1
Goods-Producing													
2000	910.1	917.7	926.0	919.5	924.5	934.2	930.7	934.0	939.6	933.3	935.3	938.0	928.6
2001	923.6	925.7	928.5	921.2	922.2	926.3	918.3	921.2	918.2	916.3	915.5	915.1	921.0
2002	896.4	897.4	900.5	895.8	898.4	899.9	891.2	898.2	897.6	901.4	904.5	905.3	898.9
2003	891.3	894.9	898.1	890.6	896.1	900.8	894.8	900.9	903.8	905.7	906.4	914.2	899.8
2004	912.0	921.6	933.1	939.1	943.6	951.6	954.5	957.5	956.8	966.4	974.5	983.3	949.5
2005	972.7	983.4	991.4	1,002.3	1,011.1	1,020.5	1,025.0	1,031.8	1,040.4	1,041.5	1,048.6	1,057.7	1,018.9
2006	1,044.6	1,058.1	1,070.5	1,069.1	1,076.2	1,082.5	1,069.1	1,070.9	1,068.4	1,057.2	1,052.6	1,050.3	1,064.1
2007	1,022.2	1,023.7	1,027.5	1,010.1	1,007.1	1,007.6	984.1	982.8	974.2	969.7	957.1	954.5	993.4
Natural Resources and Mining													
2002	7.3	7.4	7.3	7.3	7.3	7.3	7.2	7.2	7.1	7.0	7.0	7.0	7.2
2003	7.1	7.0	7.0	6.9	7.1	7.1	7.1	7.2	7.2	7.2	7.2	7.2	7.1
2004	7.2	7.2	7.2	7.2	7.1	7.1	7.1	7.1	7.1	7.0	7.1	7.1	7.1
2005	7.1	7.1	7.1	7.2	7.2	7.2	7.2	7.2	7.0	6.8	6.8	6.9	7.1
2006	6.6	6.6	6.7	6.7	6.7	6.8	6.6	6.4	6.5	6.5	6.6	6.6	6.6
2007	6.7	6.8	6.7	6.8	6.7	6.8	6.5	6.5	6.4	6.5	6.5	6.4	6.6
Construction													
2000	439.4	443.9	449.5	445.0	448.8	455.9	455.3	458.5	463.2	460.4	462.1	464.0	453.8
2001	458.7	461.5	464.9	462.2	464.9	471.0	471.0	474.7	474.7	476.9	477.8	477.2	469.6
2002	466.1	467.2	470.0	468.7	472.2	473.9	470.5	477.1	477.8	483.7	486.3	487.0	475.0
2003	477.8	482.2	485.6	483.5	489.3	494.4	494.2	499.4	501.7	504.4	505.8	511.7	494.2
2004	510.9	518.4	527.3	532.1	535.4	542.6	547.1	549.8	550.6	560.7	567.3	573.9	543.0
2005	567.5	576.0	582.5	592.1	599.3	607.1	613.4	619.3	627.0	629.2	635.9	642.5	607.7
2006	631.9	643.6	654.5	655.3	661.1	666.3	658.1	660.2	658.3	650.6	646.5	642.8	652.4
2007	620.2	621.2	625.3	609.6	606.9	607.8	592.2	591.0	584.1	583.0	569.7	566.2	598.1
Manufacturing													
2000	461.9	465.0	467.6	465.9	467.0	469.5	466.8	466.9	467.7	464.1	464.6	465.4	466.0
2001	456.6	455.9	455.3	450.8	449.0	447.1	439.2	438.6	435.6	431.7	430.1	430.3	443.4
2002	423.0	422.8	423.2	419.8	418.9	418.7	413.5	413.9	412.7	410.7	411.2	411.3	416.6
2003	406.4	405.7	405.5	400.2	399.7	399.3	393.5	394.3	394.9	394.1	393.4	395.3	398.5
2004	393.9	396.0	398.6	399.8	401.1	401.9	400.3	400.6	399.1	398.7	400.1	402.3	399.4
2005	398.1	400.3	401.8	403.0	404.6	406.2	404.4	405.3	406.4	405.5	405.9	408.3	404.2
2006	406.1	407.9	409.3	407.1	408.4	409.4	404.4	404.3	403.6	400.1	399.5	400.9	405.1
2007	395.3	395.7	395.5	393.7	393.5	393.0	385.4	385.3	383.7	380.2	380.9	381.9	388.7
Service-Providing													
2000	6,009.4	6,064.2	6,135.4	6,126.1	6,154.8	6,095.5	6,033.1	6,135.9	6,165.3	6,185.0	6,261.8	6,324.5	6,140.9
2001	6,173.1	6,242.0	6,301.0	6,273.5	6,276.3	6,208.8	6,127.7	6,225.9	6,229.6	6,222.5	6,271.5	6,312.9	6,238.7
2002	6,192.7	6,247.5	6,305.9	6,290.6	6,299.9	6,216.5	6,145.8	6,245.3	6,256.7	6,282.8	6,348.7	6,405.2	6,269.8
2003	6,285.5	6,337.4	6,389.5	6,371.7	6,370.7	6,283.7	6,222.1	6,316.8	6,334.2	6,377.5	6,424.8	6,489.1	6,350.3
2004	6,420.7	6,483.1	6,537.7	6,568.0	6,568.0	6,492.5	6,451.1	6,535.7	6,514.2	6,588.6	6,682.5	6,753.2	6,549.6
2005	6,649.2	6,721.5	6,760.2	6,791.9	6,801.3	6,697.9	6,673.1	6,783.2	6,819.6	6,825.3	6,892.6	6,956.9	6,781.1
2006	6,838.0	6,899.2	6,967.3	6,949.0	6,959.7	6,868.8	6,809.0	6,923.9	6,942.6	6,955.6	7,043.7	7,102.9	6,938.3
2007	6,988.7	7,053.7	7,114.1	7,089.2	7,088.9	6,980.6	6,901.0	7,010.1	7,010.5	7,052.7	7,117.3	7,169.9	7,048.1
Trade, Transportation, and Utilities													
2000	1,484.1	1,483.0	1,491.2	1,483.4	1,488.1	1,495.1	1,479.5	1,490.2	1,494.5	1,500.1	1,537.4	1,568.5	1,499.6
2001	1,498.0	1,493.6	1,503.5	1,492.8	1,490.3	1,486.5	1,474.0	1,479.0	1,478.8	1,481.4	1,508.0	1,530.8	1,493.1
2002	1,478.6	1,469.5	1,476.7	1,469.4	1,470.5	1,465.0	1,453.4	1,459.7	1,460.6	1,467.6	1,494.6	1,523.5	1,474.1
2003	1,464.3	1,456.7	1,459.2	1,454.6	1,455.1	1,450.8	1,446.4	1,452.0	1,456.3	1,470.0	1,497.0	1,527.3	1,465.8
2004	1,484.5	1,482.3	1,489.1	1,493.7	1,496.6	1,494.9	1,493.5	1,495.2	1,489.4	1,511.5	1,551.6	1,582.8	1,505.4
2005	1,534.6	1,537.8	1,544.6	1,555.2	1,560.4	1,559.0	1,559.6	1,565.3	1,569.2	1,576.7	1,605.4	1,636.9	1,567.1
2006	1,587.1	1,586.3	1,597.6	1,593.8	1,596.7	1,594.6	1,583.8	1,588.3	1,587.9	1,595.1	1,632.1	1,661.7	1,600.4
2007	1,607.2	1,603.8	1,612.6	1,606.8	1,611.6	1,606.2	1,591.6	1,593.8	1,593.1	1,605.1	1,637.7	1,666.7	1,611.4
Wholesale Trade													
2000	311.5	312.7	315.8	314.6	316.2	318.1	316.6	317.7	320.0	319.1	320.4	323.0	317.1
2001	315.5	317.3	319.1	318.2	318.2	317.2	314.5	314.9	315.1	314.8	314.9	316.4	316.3
2002	313.9	315.2	316.0	314.0	315.5	315.1	313.7	314.6	315.3	316.4	318.3	320.2	315.7
2003	315.4	316.3	316.8	316.3	316.4	316.1	315.8	316.6	317.6	318.1	319.6	322.7	317.3
2004	321.4	323.8	325.5	326.3	327.8	328.4	327.3	327.9	327.3	330.5	333.6	336.0	328.0
2005	333.7	336.0	336.8	339.9	341.9	341.9	341.6	342.4	343.6	343.9	345.5	349.1	341.4
2006	344.8	347.5	349.5	350.4	352.1	352.6	350.7	351.6	352.1	352.9	354.5	357.3	351.3
2007	354.4	356.8	357.7	357.5	358.6	358.1	354.9	355.2	355.1	357.2	358.3	361.3	357.1

Employment by Industry: Florida, 2000–2007—*Continued*

(Numbers in thousands, not seasonally adjusted.)

Industry and year	January	February	March	April	May	June	July	August	September	October	November	December	Annual Average
Retail Trade													
2000	928.7	926.1	930.3	924.0	927.0	932.1	918.4	927.5	928.2	935.3	968.9	991.4	936.5
2001	939.1	932.8	939.9	929.3	927.8	925.5	916.1	920.4	920.3	924.6	951.6	968.3	933.0
2002	927.6	917.6	922.2	917.1	917.6	913.5	903.7	909.3	910.1	916.3	940.4	963.8	921.6
2003	917.1	909.7	911.6	907.3	909.2	907.3	904.0	908.2	911.5	924.4	949.3	972.3	919.3
2004	934.2	928.9	933.1	936.0	938.4	937.0	935.6	934.7	929.7	945.6	979.5	1,002.9	944.6
2005	963.4	963.2	968.0	974.0	976.2	976.7	977.7	982.2	983.5	990.9	1,014.6	1,037.0	984.0
2006	998.3	994.6	1,002.3	998.0	999.0	997.4	991.2	992.8	991.1	998.4	1,031.3	1,050.5	1,003.7
2007	1,008.7	1,003.3	1,009.9	1,003.1	1,007.5	1,003.1	993.7	995.0	994.3	1,002.3	1,031.4	1,049.9	1,008.5
Transportation and Utilities													
2000	243.9	244.2	245.1	244.8	244.9	244.9	244.5	245.0	246.3	245.7	248.1	254.1	246.0
2001	243.4	243.5	244.5	245.3	244.3	243.8	243.4	243.7	243.4	242.0	241.5	246.1	243.7
2002	237.1	236.7	238.5	238.3	237.4	236.4	236.0	235.8	235.2	234.9	235.9	239.5	236.8
2003	231.8	230.7	230.8	231.0	229.5	227.4	226.6	227.2	227.2	227.5	228.1	232.3	229.2
2004	228.9	229.6	230.5	231.4	230.4	229.5	230.6	232.6	232.4	235.4	238.5	243.9	232.8
2005	237.5	238.6	239.8	241.3	242.3	240.4	240.3	240.7	242.1	241.9	245.3	250.8	241.8
2006	244.0	244.2	245.8	245.4	245.6	244.6	241.9	243.9	244.7	243.8	246.3	253.9	245.3
2007	244.1	243.7	245.0	246.2	245.5	245.0	243.0	243.6	243.7	245.6	248.0	255.5	245.7
Information													
2000	175.9	177.1	180.5	177.3	178.9	182.4	184.0	185.5	187.2	187.0	188.6	190.5	182.9
2001	186.1	187.1	187.7	185.9	185.8	185.5	183.3	182.2	180.3	178.4	178.4	179.1	183.3
2002	176.1	175.6	175.8	173.6	173.9	173.4	171.9	171.3	170.4	169.8	170.4	171.0	172.8
2003	167.3	167.6	168.0	165.7	166.7	166.3	166.1	166.1	165.1	164.9	165.6	166.3	166.3
2004	163.1	162.5	163.6	162.4	163.1	163.5	162.4	162.5	161.3	162.3	163.6	164.2	162.9
2005	161.9	162.7	162.9	162.1	163.8	163.9	163.5	163.5	164.0	162.6	163.6	164.0	163.2
2006	160.5	161.3	161.5	161.2	162.3	163.0	162.7	162.0	161.0	160.8	161.8	162.6	161.7
2007	160.2	161.2	161.8	162.1	162.8	163.2	161.7	161.6	160.3	160.4	161.2	160.7	161.4
Financial Activities													
2000	454.0	455.7	460.1	459.6	461.8	467.9	463.7	464.9	465.6	465.4	466.9	470.1	463.0
2001	460.1	463.4	467.2	468.8	469.5	472.9	471.4	472.7	471.2	470.6	471.3	473.1	469.4
2002	469.5	471.7	473.3	471.8	472.7	474.9	475.5	476.8	475.5	476.5	479.3	481.7	474.9
2003	475.9	477.7	479.7	481.7	483.6	486.3	487.6	489.9	489.4	490.3	490.3	494.9	485.6
2004	490.5	493.5	496.9	501.2	502.5	504.5	506.8	507.6	505.8	510.6	512.6	517.6	504.2
2005	512.1	516.0	517.9	523.4	526.1	530.0	532.4	534.1	535.3	538.3	541.8	548.0	529.6
2006	538.1	542.3	545.8	546.5	548.5	550.0	546.7	547.4	545.4	546.7	547.7	552.1	546.4
2007	540.5	544.1	546.1	543.1	543.6	544.8	541.9	540.2	537.4	539.5	539.7	541.2	541.8
Professional and Business Services													
2000	1,040.2	1,054.7	1,074.0	1,069.7	1,074.1	1,082.1	1,072.7	1,085.1	1,096.4	1,092.5	1,102.4	1,110.5	1,079.5
2001	1,090.6	1,114.3	1,126.6	1,117.3	1,117.6	1,119.3	1,104.0	1,109.5	1,108.0	1,104.7	1,106.2	1,106.8	1,110.4
2002	1,084.4	1,105.8	1,120.0	1,121.0	1,122.1	1,119.6	1,108.5	1,103.9	1,105.3	1,109.8	1,121.8	1,128.7	1,112.6
2003	1,110.5	1,128.8	1,145.6	1,143.0	1,133.7	1,130.2	1,111.4	1,114.3	1,114.4	1,132.4	1,133.1	1,138.9	1,128.0
2004	1,133.2	1,152.8	1,169.3	1,188.7	1,186.9	1,192.2	1,185.7	1,186.8	1,182.9	1,206.4	1,223.0	1,239.8	1,187.3
2005	1,222.7	1,244.1	1,250.9	1,260.5	1,260.4	1,261.9	1,259.6	1,269.5	1,278.8	1,271.2	1,285.1	1,295.6	1,263.4
2006	1,275.0	1,290.1	1,310.2	1,306.8	1,313.2	1,319.9	1,306.7	1,316.4	1,321.7	1,313.6	1,326.6	1,337.8	1,311.5
2007	1,319.3	1,334.7	1,345.8	1,337.7	1,334.8	1,332.3	1,313.3	1,319.1	1,314.5	1,324.1	1,333.4	1,341.3	1,329.2
Education and Health Services													
2000	801.0	808.7	815.6	812.3	814.5	815.3	810.8	817.6	827.0	830.3	835.6	840.8	819.1
2001	823.9	832.6	837.6	838.7	842.0	844.2	834.7	842.4	851.0	856.0	860.7	866.8	844.2
2002	850.0	857.8	865.4	862.3	865.6	864.3	854.4	863.8	872.1	878.4	884.5	888.8	867.3
2003	880.3	890.6	896.4	895.3	898.7	896.8	889.8	898.6	908.5	911.2	913.8	919.2	899.9
2004	912.7	920.8	925.0	927.9	930.6	926.6	918.6	924.0	925.4	932.8	938.7	941.7	927.1
2005	932.7	941.5	944.6	949.3	950.7	945.3	940.7	949.8	957.5	959.4	962.8	968.3	950.2
2006	957.0	965.4	972.0	972.2	976.1	973.5	964.5	975.3	982.7	984.6	991.2	997.0	976.0
2007	986.9	997.9	1,003.2	1,004.7	1,007.4	1,005.6	992.1	1,004.0	1,012.9	1,020.3	1,022.8	1,026.0	1,007.0
Leisure and Hospitality													
2000	775.9	794.4	812.0	816.8	809.2	808.1	794.8	792.9	789.3	794.7	808.7	817.3	801.2
2001	805.8	826.4	845.0	837.2	835.3	829.3	807.9	807.0	800.9	790.1	797.4	803.6	815.5
2002	796.0	816.1	835.4	835.8	832.5	830.8	809.5	811.9	806.2	805.8	818.0	827.5	818.8
2003	819.0	834.0	852.0	845.4	840.2	837.9	824.2	824.9	822.8	824.1	837.6	850.6	834.4
2004	853.3	872.1	890.7	890.6	883.5	878.9	866.3	863.2	849.0	857.8	874.6	887.1	872.3
2005	877.1	896.6	913.0	914.4	909.1	906.4	886.9	889.0	886.1	881.7	894.6	904.7	896.6
2006	894.5	913.8	933.0	925.8	921.5	917.3	898.3	899.7	895.1	891.8	910.9	919.6	910.1
2007	912.2	934.6	957.2	952.7	947.5	939.3	917.6	917.0	908.7	909.9	923.2	932.1	929.3
Other Services													
2000	286.7	289.1	292.3	292.4	294.1	296.3	294.9	294.0	295.4	296.8	296.8	297.7	293.9
2001	293.9	296.4	299.1	297.6	299.2	302.3	299.5	299.9	300.2	299.6	301.7	303.5	299.4
2002	304.2	306.8	310.5	307.4	308.9	310.6	308.6	309.7	310.0	312.9	315.3	316.5	310.1
2003	315.5	318.5	321.5	320.4	320.7	321.5	315.6	314.0	314.8	313.6	313.6	316.2	317.2
2004	318.8	321.3	322.5	324.0	325.3	328.4	325.6	324.9	324.3	323.3	326.5	326.7	324.3
2005	327.0	329.3	330.5	331.5	332.1	332.2	329.7	328.9	330.8	327.3	328.4	329.8	329.8
2006	325.5	329.1	332.5	331.3	333.5	336.4	331.5	331.9	333.7	334.1	336.7	338.7	332.9
2007	338.6	342.3	346.8	343.2	345.2	347.9	341.7	342.2	343.0	342.6	343.1	345.9	343.5
Government													
2000	991.6	1,001.5	1,009.7	1,014.6	1,034.1	948.3	932.7	1,005.7	1,009.9	1,018.2	1,025.4	1,029.1	1,001.7
2001	1,014.7	1,028.2	1,034.3	1,035.2	1,036.6	968.8	952.9	1,033.2	1,039.2	1,041.7	1,047.8	1,049.2	1,023.4
2002	1,033.9	1,044.2	1,048.8	1,049.3	1,053.7	977.9	964.0	1,048.2	1,056.6	1,062.0	1,064.8	1,067.5	1,039.2
2003	1,052.7	1,063.5	1,067.1	1,065.6	1,072.0	993.9	981.0	1,057.0	1,062.9	1,071.0	1,073.8	1,075.7	1,053.0
2004	1,064.6	1,077.8	1,080.6	1,079.5	1,079.5	1,003.5	992.2	1,071.5	1,076.1	1,083.9	1,091.9	1,093.3	1,066.2
2005	1,081.1	1,093.5	1,095.8	1,095.5	1,098.7	999.2	1,000.7	1,083.1	1,097.9	1,108.1	1,110.9	1,109.6	1,081.2
2006	1,100.3	1,110.9	1,114.7	1,111.4	1,107.9	1,014.1	1,014.8	1,102.9	1,115.1	1,128.9	1,136.7	1,133.4	1,099.3
2007	1,123.8	1,135.1	1,140.6	1,138.9	1,136.0	1,041.3	1,041.1	1,132.2	1,140.6	1,150.8	1,156.2	1,156.0	1,124.4

Average Weekly Hours by Selected Industry: Florida, 2001–2007

(Not seasonally adjusted.)

Industry and year	January	February	March	April	May	June	July	August	September	October	November	December	Annual Average
Manufacturing													
2001	40.9	40.5	40.4	39.3	39.9	40.6	40.3	40.7	39.9	40.8	41.6	42.7	40.6
2002	41.9	41.2	42.5	42.2	41.9	41.7	41.3	42.0	42.1	41.4	43.5	43.2	42.1
2003	42.3	41.8	41.6	41.3	40.0	40.5	39.7	40.7	41.5	40.5	41.2	40.8	41.0
2004	41.1	42.0	41.4	41.2	42.4	41.5	41.4	39.4	39.2	41.1	41.0	41.3	41.1
2005	41.6	42.7	41.7	41.8	42.0	41.6	40.9	41.0	41.5	41.6	42.0	41.7	41.7
2006	41.1	41.3	41.3	40.6	41.6	41.4	40.5	41.4	42.4	42.1	42.5	42.2	41.5
2007	41.9	41.1	40.3	40.6	40.5	41.6	41.8	41.4	41.3	41.1	41.1	41.0	41.2

Average Hourly Earnings by Selected Industry: Florida, 2001–2007

(Dollars, not seasonally adjusted.)

Industry and year	January	February	March	April	May	June	July	August	September	October	November	December	Annual Average
Manufacturing													
2001	12.57	12.58	12.60	12.59	12.55	12.68	12.63	12.71	12.61	12.68	12.91	13.08	12.68
2002	13.03	13.07	13.01	13.02	13.14	13.15	13.18	13.41	13.48	13.54	13.65	13.90	13.30
2003	14.15	14.01	14.07	13.89	14.14	14.13	14.33	13.98	13.96	14.14	14.06	14.29	14.09
2004	14.17	14.42	14.35	13.93	13.83	13.84	13.89	13.15	13.62	13.26	13.54	13.91	13.84
2005	13.86	13.21	13.33	13.27	13.67	13.72	13.77	14.15	14.34	14.30	14.42	14.51	13.89
2006	14.22	14.44	14.56	14.47	14.64	14.93	14.94	14.62	14.78	15.15	15.13	15.07	14.75
2007	15.30	15.38	15.54	15.72	15.86	16.07	16.25	16.40	16.47	16.72	16.81	16.97	16.12

Average Weekly Earnings by Selected Industry: Florida, 2001–2007

(Dollars, not seasonally adjusted.)

Industry and year	January	February	March	April	May	June	July	August	September	October	November	December	Annual Average
Manufacturing													
2001	514.11	509.49	509.04	494.79	500.75	514.81	508.99	517.30	503.14	517.34	537.06	558.52	514.81
2002	545.96	538.48	552.93	549.44	550.57	548.36	544.33	563.22	567.51	560.56	593.78	600.48	559.93
2003	598.55	585.62	585.31	573.66	565.60	572.27	568.90	568.99	579.34	572.67	579.27	583.03	577.69
2004	582.39	605.64	594.09	573.92	586.39	574.36	575.05	518.11	533.90	544.99	555.14	574.48	568.82
2005	576.58	564.07	555.86	554.69	574.14	570.75	563.19	580.15	595.11	594.88	605.64	605.07	579.21
2006	584.44	596.37	601.33	587.48	609.02	618.10	605.07	605.27	626.67	637.82	643.03	635.95	612.13
2007	641.07	632.12	626.26	638.23	642.33	668.51	679.25	678.96	680.21	687.19	690.89	695.77	664.14

Population
    2000 census: 8,186,453
    2007 estimate: 9,544,750
    Percent change, 1995–2006: 16.6%

Percent change in total nonfarm employment, 2000–2007: 5.0%

Industry with the largest growth in employment, 2000–2007 (thousands)
    Education and health services, 103.1

Industry with the largest decline in employment, 2000–2007 (thousands)
    Manufacturing, -107.2

Civilian labor force
    2000: 4,242,889
    2007: 4,814,831

Employment-population ratio
    2000: 67.2%
    2007: 64.9%

Unemployment rate and rank among states
    2000: 3.5%, 19th
    2007: 4.4%, 25th

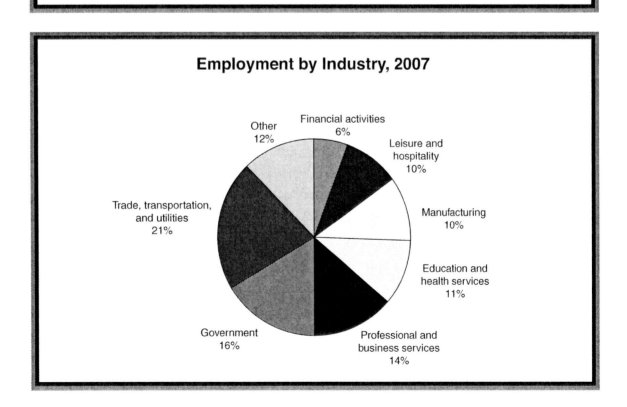

Employment by Industry, 2007

Other 12%
Financial activities 6%
Leisure and hospitality 10%
Trade, transportation, and utilities 21%
Manufacturing 10%
Education and health services 11%
Government 16%
Professional and business services 14%

Employment by Industry: Georgia, 2000–2007

(Numbers in thousands, not seasonally adjusted.)

Industry and year	January	February	March	April	May	June	July	August	September	October	November	December	Annual Average
Total Nonfarm													
2000	3,851.6	3,880.3	3,922.3	3,925.6	3,958.4	3,971.6	3,944.4	3,970.6	3,978.7	3,982.0	3,994.0	4,012.1	3,949.3
2001	3,931.3	3,945.2	3,971.8	3,951.7	3,958.3	3,962.4	3,915.3	3,947.1	3,939.0	3,929.7	3,933.0	3,934.7	3,943.2
2002	3,816.3	3,833.3	3,860.3	3,870.6	3,885.1	3,895.3	3,841.1	3,875.6	3,874.5	3,881.8	3,896.8	3,903.3	3,869.5
2003	3,797.4	3,809.7	3,832.0	3,836.4	3,847.1	3,842.0	3,819.9	3,858.1	3,865.3	3,861.1	3,878.0	3,892.1	3,844.9
2004	3,816.2	3,836.1	3,864.9	3,888.9	3,898.9	3,892.0	3,883.7	3,920.8	3,907.9	3,943.5	3,961.9	3,967.3	3,898.5
2005	3,908.8	3,929.5	3,937.0	3,993.3	4,011.1	3,996.2	3,982.7	4,032.3	4,031.3	4,044.6	4,071.8	4,076.0	4,001.2
2006	4,016.0	4,037.5	4,056.5	4,082.6	4,098.5	4,091.0	4,057.9	4,099.9	4,096.7	4,128.1	4,150.7	4,153.6	4,089.1
2007	4,094.3	4,114.8	4,130.9	4,140.4	4,158.9	4,147.4	4,115.9	4,160.0	4,154.3	4,171.4	4,186.0	4,189.8	4,147.0
Total Private													
2000	3,259.3	3,283.4	3,321.2	3,324.5	3,346.0	3,374.3	3,367.0	3,385.3	3,383.8	3,381.4	3,391.1	3,407.8	3,352.1
2001	3,330.6	3,338.6	3,362.4	3,342.1	3,346.7	3,355.4	3,329.1	3,339.9	3,322.8	3,308.0	3,308.2	3,311.3	3,332.9
2002	3,199.1	3,213.6	3,234.6	3,243.9	3,256.8	3,275.9	3,242.2	3,253.9	3,241.1	3,246.8	3,259.3	3,268.8	3,244.7
2003	3,164.4	3,171.7	3,192.5	3,197.6	3,210.7	3,218.6	3,215.2	3,235.1	3,231.4	3,222.1	3,237.5	3,253.0	3,212.5
2004	3,186.4	3,199.3	3,226.8	3,244.6	3,257.5	3,265.5	3,275.4	3,286.6	3,264.0	3,297.1	3,312.1	3,320.9	3,261.4
2005	3,266.3	3,279.6	3,285.6	3,341.8	3,359.9	3,357.9	3,363.3	3,382.1	3,374.5	3,384.5	3,409.4	3,414.5	3,351.6
2006	3,359.7	3,373.5	3,390.4	3,418.4	3,434.7	3,435.9	3,427.2	3,441.2	3,427.8	3,454.1	3,472.8	3,476.6	3,426.0
2007	3,423.7	3,435.3	3,449.7	3,461.2	3,479.7	3,479.6	3,472.6	3,490.3	3,474.4	3,486.4	3,498.3	3,502.4	3,471.1
Goods-Producing													
2000	752.0	755.8	762.8	761.5	764.2	769.3	762.0	764.7	762.5	755.7	751.8	752.4	759.6
2001	741.9	742.8	743.3	735.7	733.5	733.9	722.9	723.6	717.8	707.3	700.4	699.3	725.2
2002	678.4	684.1	686.8	685.7	686.3	687.6	684.3	684.0	680.5	675.5	672.7	670.2	681.3
2003	658.4	661.6	661.2	658.9	661.0	661.6	656.5	658.8	659.4	658.3	656.6	658.9	659.3
2004	648.2	651.5	655.3	656.1	656.7	661.5	664.8	666.3	662.7	667.2	666.5	666.7	660.3
2005	657.2	659.5	658.8	668.0	672.1	673.5	673.9	678.3	678.0	674.2	678.1	677.2	670.7
2006	672.0	674.8	676.1	679.0	681.9	685.0	681.7	684.7	682.0	678.8	674.4	671.7	678.5
2007	667.6	668.5	667.8	667.2	668.8	669.0	665.9	666.9	661.7	657.9	656.1	656.0	664.5
Natural Resources and Mining													
2000	14.0	14.2	14.2	13.8	13.9	13.9	14.0	14.0	13.9	13.8	13.8	13.8	13.9
2001	13.6	13.5	13.5	13.2	13.2	13.2	13.1	13.2	13.0	12.9	12.9	12.8	13.2
2002	12.7	12.7	12.8	12.6	12.6	12.6	12.1	12.3	12.2	11.9	11.8	12.0	12.4
2003	12.1	12.1	12.1	12.2	12.4	12.4	12.3	12.4	12.4	12.3	12.4	12.4	12.3
2004	12.3	12.2	12.2	12.1	12.1	12.2	12.3	12.3	12.2	12.1	12.1	12.2	12.2
2005	11.8	11.9	11.9	12.1	12.2	12.2	12.3	12.3	12.2	12.1	12.1	12.1	12.1
2006	12.4	12.1	12.1	12.3	12.3	12.3	12.3	12.3	12.1	12.2	12.1	12.1	12.2
2007	12.1	12.1	12.1	12.0	12.0	12.0	11.9	12.0	11.8	11.8	11.8	11.9	12.0
Construction													
2000	198.1	200.6	205.8	205.5	207.5	211.8	211.2	211.4	211.4	209.9	207.6	207.9	207.4
2001	201.9	203.6	205.3	207.1	209.1	211.3	211.0	211.0	208.7	207.3	204.9	203.7	207.1
2002	195.2	197.8	199.1	198.3	199.0	200.0	199.3	199.5	198.2	196.5	195.8	194.3	197.8
2003	188.5	190.0	191.7	191.2	193.1	194.7	196.9	197.9	198.9	199.0	198.6	199.1	195.0
2004	193.7	193.3	196.0	196.8	197.2	200.4	203.7	203.6	200.9	204.4	204.0	203.7	199.8
2005	199.8	200.6	200.0	206.3	209.1	210.0	212.2	213.9	213.4	213.4	214.6	212.7	208.8
2006	209.2	211.0	212.5	215.4	217.9	220.6	223.0	224.5	223.7	223.6	222.9	221.4	218.8
2007	218.6	220.2	221.3	221.7	223.1	224.1	223.0	224.0	221.6	221.2	219.2	219.6	221.5
Manufacturing													
2000	539.9	541.0	542.8	542.2	542.8	543.6	536.8	539.3	537.2	532.0	530.4	530.7	538.2
2001	526.4	525.7	524.5	515.4	511.2	509.4	498.8	499.4	496.1	487.1	482.6	482.8	505.0
2002	470.5	473.6	474.9	474.8	474.7	475.0	472.9	472.2	470.1	467.1	465.1	463.9	471.2
2003	457.8	459.5	457.4	455.5	455.5	454.5	447.3	448.5	448.1	447.0	445.6	447.4	452.0
2004	442.2	446.0	447.1	447.2	447.4	448.9	448.8	450.4	449.6	450.7	450.4	450.8	448.3
2005	445.6	447.0	446.9	449.6	450.8	451.3	449.4	452.1	452.4	448.7	451.4	452.4	449.8
2006	450.4	451.7	451.5	451.3	451.7	452.1	446.4	447.9	446.2	443.0	439.4	438.2	447.5
2007	436.9	436.2	434.4	433.5	433.7	432.9	431.0	430.9	428.3	424.9	425.1	424.5	431.0
Service-Providing													
2000	3,099.6	3,124.5	3,159.5	3,164.1	3,194.2	3,202.3	3,182.4	3,205.9	3,216.2	3,226.3	3,242.2	3,259.7	3,189.7
2001	3,189.4	3,202.4	3,228.5	3,216.0	3,224.8	3,228.5	3,192.4	3,223.5	3,221.2	3,222.4	3,232.6	3,235.4	3,218.1
2002	3,137.9	3,149.2	3,173.5	3,184.9	3,198.8	3,207.7	3,156.8	3,191.6	3,194.0	3,206.3	3,224.1	3,233.1	3,188.2
2003	3,139.0	3,148.1	3,170.8	3,177.5	3,186.1	3,180.4	3,163.4	3,199.3	3,205.9	3,202.8	3,221.4	3,233.2	3,185.7
2004	3,168.0	3,184.6	3,209.6	3,232.8	3,242.2	3,230.5	3,218.9	3,254.5	3,245.2	3,276.3	3,295.4	3,300.6	3,238.2
2005	3,251.6	3,270.0	3,278.2	3,325.3	3,339.0	3,322.7	3,308.8	3,354.0	3,353.3	3,370.4	3,393.7	3,398.8	3,330.5
2006	3,344.0	3,362.7	3,380.4	3,403.6	3,416.6	3,406.0	3,376.2	3,415.2	3,414.7	3,449.3	3,476.3	3,481.9	3,410.6
2007	3,426.7	3,446.3	3,463.1	3,473.2	3,490.1	3,478.4	3,450.0	3,493.1	3,492.6	3,513.5	3,529.9	3,533.8	3,482.6
Trade, Transportation, and Utilities													
2000	851.3	853.1	861.7	863.2	867.0	870.9	865.2	871.2	871.2	877.6	890.8	902.5	870.5
2001	872.0	866.0	870.9	856.2	857.6	858.9	858.5	859.1	858.1	857.0	867.5	873.7	863.0
2002	835.1	830.5	834.0	833.7	837.1	840.5	832.8	834.1	833.4	844.5	858.4	871.0	840.4
2003	819.0	814.2	818.2	814.4	818.6	819.5	820.2	823.9	824.7	828.5	842.1	851.4	824.6
2004	817.4	813.9	820.0	820.9	825.7	826.3	829.5	830.8	826.6	837.8	852.4	860.6	830.2
2005	832.8	831.4	833.1	846.2	850.1	848.4	856.3	855.2	853.3	861.4	878.8	887.7	852.9
2006	856.2	853.2	857.4	865.0	870.4	869.0	865.2	867.3	866.9	880.1	898.6	906.2	871.3
2007	880.7	874.8	877.1	878.7	884.5	885.2	885.7	886.4	886.0	895.7	907.4	915.1	888.1
Wholesale Trade													
2000	209.2	210.7	212.5	213.2	214.1	215.4	214.3	215.1	214.8	215.5	214.8	215.0	213.7
2001	215.5	215.7	216.4	212.5	212.2	213.1	214.4	213.7	212.8	211.7	210.2	209.1	213.1
2002	206.0	206.1	207.4	207.2	207.2	207.7	206.3	205.9	205.0	207.6	206.7	206.7	206.7
2003	204.0	204.3	205.3	204.6	205.1	205.0	205.3	205.3	205.4	204.9	205.4	206.2	205.1
2004	202.8	202.9	204.2	205.7	206.8	207.2	207.7	208.3	207.2	209.1	209.2	209.6	206.7
2005	207.9	209.0	209.1	211.5	211.8	211.8	212.7	213.4	213.6	213.5	213.7	214.2	211.9
2006	211.8	212.6	213.0	214.2	215.8	215.4	216.2	216.3	216.5	219.2	218.2	218.4	215.6
2007	216.7	217.4	217.5	219.0	219.5	219.4	220.2	220.6	220.3	220.7	219.1	219.7	219.2

Employment by Industry: Georgia, 2000–2007—*Continued*

(Numbers in thousands, not seasonally adjusted.)

Industry and year	January	February	March	April	May	June	July	August	September	October	November	December	Annual Average
Retail Trade													
2000	462.1	462.5	467.9	466.3	469.2	471.3	466.9	470.9	470.9	474.0	488.2	499.6	472.5
2001	473.0	467.3	471.6	461.4	462.7	463.0	459.7	461.4	462.0	460.4	475.0	482.3	466.7
2002	453.9	449.3	452.2	449.9	452.4	453.9	449.9	451.3	452.6	453.4	467.3	479.0	455.4
2003	440.7	436.1	438.6	437.6	440.5	441.1	440.8	443.7	443.9	446.9	459.2	467.8	444.7
2004	439.8	436.3	440.1	439.1	441.8	442.3	443.4	443.6	441.2	449.2	462.7	470.9	445.9
2005	447.5	443.6	444.8	454.9	457.7	456.6	460.8	459.5	456.4	464.3	479.3	486.1	459.3
2006	464.3	460.3	462.9	468.0	470.6	468.6	464.0	465.4	463.6	474.1	492.9	497.5	471.0
2007	479.3	472.3	474.0	473.5	476.6	475.0	476.2	475.6	474.5	482.8	495.7	501.4	479.7
Transportation and Utilities													
2000	180.0	179.9	181.3	183.7	183.7	184.2	184.0	185.2	185.5	188.1	187.8	187.9	184.3
2001	183.5	183.0	182.9	182.3	182.7	182.8	184.4	184.0	183.3	184.9	182.3	182.3	183.2
2002	175.2	175.1	174.4	176.6	177.5	178.9	176.6	176.9	175.8	183.5	184.4	185.3	178.4
2003	174.3	173.8	174.3	172.2	173.0	173.4	174.1	174.9	175.4	176.7	177.5	177.4	174.8
2004	174.8	174.7	175.7	176.1	177.1	176.8	178.4	178.9	178.2	179.5	180.5	180.1	177.6
2005	177.4	178.8	179.2	179.8	180.6	180.0	182.8	182.3	183.3	183.6	185.8	187.4	181.8
2006	180.1	180.3	181.5	182.8	184.0	185.0	185.0	185.6	186.8	186.8	187.5	190.3	184.6
2007	184.7	185.1	185.6	186.2	188.4	190.8	189.3	190.2	191.2	192.2	192.6	194.0	189.2
Information													
2000	140.1	140.5	140.2	139.3	140.5	143.1	143.5	144.9	144.8	146.0	146.9	148.3	143.2
2001	145.0	145.7	146.3	144.5	144.4	145.0	143.0	142.3	141.2	140.7	141.2	140.9	143.4
2002	134.0	133.8	132.4	131.5	131.4	130.9	130.5	130.0	128.7	129.7	127.7	127.7	130.7
2003	127.9	127.0	124.9	122.9	121.8	121.3	119.6	119.0	116.7	116.4	117.3	117.1	121.0
2004	116.0	115.7	116.0	117.0	116.7	117.3	116.5	116.0	115.2	113.9	114.8	114.8	115.8
2005	113.8	114.1	114.5	114.4	113.6	115.0	114.5	113.1	113.2	113.7	114.6	115.1	114.1
2006	113.5	113.8	114.5	113.6	114.1	113.7	112.3	112.4	112.4	113.0	114.0	114.5	113.5
2007	115.0	114.7	114.8	113.4	114.1	114.3	113.9	114.2	114.3	115.0	115.2	115.5	114.5
Financial Activities													
2000	208.9	209.6	210.3	213.1	213.8	215.6	213.9	213.9	212.3	211.7	211.9	213.5	212.4
2001	210.5	210.8	211.8	213.3	213.5	214.2	216.7	217.1	215.8	215.5	215.5	215.9	214.2
2002	214.4	213.7	213.5	213.6	214.4	215.2	214.8	215.5	214.1	215.8	216.0	217.3	214.9
2003	213.1	213.0	214.6	214.8	216.3	217.7	218.8	219.6	219.3	219.3	216.4	217.2	216.4
2004	214.9	215.9	216.4	217.7	218.0	218.0	219.5	219.7	218.5	221.9	221.8	222.7	218.8
2005	222.3	223.3	223.0	223.9	225.1	225.3	224.7	225.7	225.3	228.0	228.2	229.6	225.4
2006	226.0	227.4	227.8	229.6	230.7	230.6	231.2	232.3	231.7	233.5	233.5	234.1	230.7
2007	230.5	232.1	232.0	231.6	231.9	231.8	232.5	232.4	230.7	229.9	229.1	228.4	231.1
Professional and Business Services													
2000	511.7	518.3	525.0	517.3	520.9	529.0	527.5	531.8	533.5	528.6	527.8	529.9	525.1
2001	516.1	517.7	520.9	516.3	514.9	515.5	513.8	518.8	514.4	512.2	507.9	508.0	514.7
2002	489.5	495.2	497.9	502.5	503.7	505.2	505.0	509.1	506.2	505.0	505.4	503.7	502.4
2003	481.0	485.6	488.4	489.7	487.8	490.6	494.1	499.5	498.9	497.8	498.5	500.9	492.7
2004	493.6	498.7	505.2	507.7	508.0	509.0	514.3	516.1	511.9	522.0	521.3	521.4	510.8
2005	517.2	522.3	522.6	529.1	530.5	531.8	534.4	542.5	543.7	545.5	546.3	544.4	534.2
2006	537.8	541.5	544.2	549.2	547.9	551.2	551.7	554.6	551.6	553.8	554.1	555.3	549.4
2007	547.7	552.9	558.3	556.4	558.9	560.3	559.0	565.9	563.5	566.5	566.8	566.3	560.2
Education and Health Services													
2000	341.7	346.0	347.7	349.8	350.7	350.7	349.6	352.9	356.5	360.4	361.4	360.9	352.4
2001	355.7	358.8	362.0	361.5	362.0	362.6	359.8	364.0	367.8	370.6	372.1	372.4	364.1
2002	365.6	369.4	373.5	373.8	374.7	374.0	371.8	377.1	379.1	381.2	383.3	383.2	375.6
2003	383.5	385.7	390.4	394.2	396.5	394.7	392.5	397.7	399.7	399.9	401.8	402.9	395.0
2004	400.8	404.1	405.4	407.0	408.2	404.2	406.0	410.8	410.0	417.5	418.9	418.3	409.3
2005	415.8	417.8	414.8	423.5	424.9	419.6	421.6	426.1	427.4	431.6	432.9	432.3	424.0
2006	433.1	435.8	435.2	437.4	438.6	432.7	434.1	438.1	438.5	449.3	450.2	449.3	439.4
2007	445.9	450.0	449.1	453.6	454.4	449.8	450.1	457.1	459.5	464.6	466.0	465.3	455.5
Leisure and Hospitality													
2000	319.6	323.1	333.2	336.0	341.4	344.9	348.4	347.9	343.1	338.9	337.1	334.3	337.3
2001	323.5	328.0	335.3	342.2	347.6	350.9	345.1	346.3	340.4	338.4	337.4	335.3	339.2
2002	321.3	325.5	334.4	343.0	348.4	361.0	346.8	347.7	343.0	338.5	338.3	339.1	340.6
2003	328.5	331.4	340.3	348.4	353.1	356.2	356.6	359.6	356.0	349.2	348.9	348.9	348.1
2004	340.6	344.6	352.0	361.2	366.9	370.7	366.9	369.5	363.6	361.8	361.2	361.6	360.1
2005	352.3	355.4	362.9	378.5	384.4	384.9	377.6	380.0	374.6	371.9	371.9	369.9	372.0
2006	364.2	369.6	377.7	385.3	390.6	392.6	389.7	391.3	385.6	386.3	388.5	387.0	384.0
2007	378.2	383.7	391.6	399.7	405.4	406.6	402.8	404.9	398.0	396.0	396.3	394.9	396.5
Other Services													
2000	134.0	137.0	140.3	144.3	147.5	150.8	156.9	158.0	159.9	162.5	163.4	166.0	151.7
2001	165.9	168.8	171.9	172.4	173.2	174.4	169.3	168.7	167.3	166.3	166.2	165.8	169.2
2002	160.8	161.4	162.1	160.1	160.8	161.5	156.2	156.4	156.1	156.6	157.5	156.6	158.8
2003	153.0	153.2	154.5	154.3	155.6	157.0	156.9	157.0	156.7	155.7	155.9	155.7	155.5
2004	154.9	154.9	156.5	157.0	157.3	158.5	157.9	157.4	155.5	155.0	155.2	154.8	156.2
2005	154.9	155.8	155.9	158.2	159.2	159.4	160.3	161.2	159.0	158.2	158.6	158.3	158.3
2006	156.9	157.4	157.5	159.3	160.5	161.1	161.3	160.5	159.1	159.3	159.5	158.5	159.2
2007	158.1	158.6	159.0	160.6	161.7	162.6	162.7	162.5	160.7	160.8	161.4	160.9	160.8
Government													
2000	592.3	596.9	601.1	601.1	612.4	597.3	577.4	585.3	594.9	600.6	602.9	604.3	597.2
2001	600.7	606.6	609.4	609.6	611.6	607.0	586.2	607.2	616.2	621.7	624.8	623.4	610.3
2002	617.2	619.7	625.7	626.7	628.3	619.4	598.9	621.7	633.4	635.0	637.5	634.5	624.8
2003	633.0	638.0	639.5	638.8	636.4	623.4	604.7	623.0	633.9	639.0	640.5	639.1	632.4
2004	629.8	636.8	638.1	644.3	641.4	626.5	608.3	634.2	643.9	646.4	649.8	646.4	637.2
2005	642.5	649.9	651.4	651.5	651.2	638.3	619.4	650.2	656.8	660.1	662.4	661.5	649.6
2006	656.3	664.0	666.1	664.2	663.8	655.1	630.7	658.7	668.9	674.0	677.9	677.0	663.1
2007	670.6	679.5	681.2	679.2	679.2	667.8	643.3	669.7	679.9	685.0	687.7	687.4	675.9

Average Weekly Hours by Selected Industry: Georgia, 2001–2007

(Not seasonally adjusted.)

Industry and year	January	February	March	April	May	June	July	August	September	October	November	December	Annual Average
Manufacturing													
2001	39.8	38.9	40.3	39.2	40.0	40.4	40.7	41.5	41.6	41.2	40.5	40.8	40.4
2002	41.0	40.0	41.1	40.6	40.8	41.3	39.9	41.0	41.4	41.2	41.1	41.4	40.9
2003	39.9	40.2	40.3	39.8	40.1	40.6	39.9	38.9	39.3	38.9	39.6	39.8	39.8
2004	39.1	39.2	38.4	38.4	39.2	40.0	39.7	38.9	38.6	39.1	39.8	39.5	39.2
2005	39.3	38.5	38.9	38.7	38.9	39.2	39.0	39.5	38.6	39.3	39.1	39.3	39.0
2006	39.6	39.4	40.9	39.0	39.1	39.0	39.1	39.1	38.5	38.5	40.2	41.4	39.5
2007	38.6	39.5	40.0	38.6	39.0	39.4	39.8	39.8	39.7	39.7	39.0	39.0	39.3

Average Hourly Earnings by Selected Industry: Georgia, 2001–2007

(Dollars, not seasonally adjusted.)

Industry and year	January	February	March	April	May	June	July	August	September	October	November	December	Annual Average
Manufacturing													
2001	11.98	12.16	12.05	12.08	12.22	12.49	12.57	12.76	12.82	12.77	12.77	13.42	12.50
2002	13.24	13.50	13.21	13.11	13.16	13.22	12.92	12.94	13.45	13.64	13.88	14.34	13.38
2003	13.88	13.95	13.87	13.83	14.20	14.10	14.02	13.79	13.85	14.57	14.25	14.66	14.08
2004	14.21	14.61	15.00	14.98	14.76	14.68	14.54	14.28	14.54	14.34	14.19	14.36	14.54
2005	14.31	14.31	14.49	14.82	14.70	14.65	14.55	14.53	14.43	14.82	14.49	14.59	14.56
2006	14.32	14.05	14.38	14.93	14.80	14.85	14.92	14.61	14.46	14.98	14.93	15.61	14.74
2007	15.20	14.43	14.68	14.79	14.76	14.97	14.97	15.03	15.02	14.90	14.98	14.84	14.88

Average Weekly Earnings by Selected Industry: Georgia 2001–2007

(Dollars, not seasonally adjusted.)

Industry and year	January	February	March	April	May	June	July	August	September	October	November	December	Annual Average
Manufacturing													
2001	476.80	473.02	485.62	473.54	488.80	504.60	511.60	529.54	533.31	526.12	517.19	547.54	505.00
2002	542.84	540.00	542.93	532.27	536.93	545.99	515.51	530.54	556.83	561.97	570.47	593.68	547.24
2003	553.81	560.79	558.96	550.43	569.42	572.46	559.40	536.43	544.31	566.77	564.30	583.47	560.38
2004	555.61	572.71	576.00	575.23	578.59	587.20	577.24	555.49	561.24	560.69	564.76	567.22	569.97
2005	562.38	550.94	563.66	573.53	571.83	574.28	567.45	573.94	557.00	582.43	566.56	573.39	567.84
2006	567.07	553.57	588.14	582.27	578.68	579.15	583.37	571.25	556.71	576.73	600.19	646.25	582.23
2007	586.72	569.99	587.20	570.89	575.64	589.82	595.81	598.19	596.29	591.53	584.22	578.76	584.78

Population
    2000 census: 1,211,537
    2007 estimate: 1,283,388
    Percent change, 2000–2007: 5.9%

Percent change in total nonfarm employment, 2000–2007: 13.1%

Industry with the largest growth in employment, 2000–2007 (thousands)
    Professional and business services, 14.6

Industry with the largest decline in employment, 2000–2007 (thousands)
    Information, -1.6

Civilian labor force
    2000: 609,018
    2007: 649,080

Employment-population ratio
    2000: 64.9%
    2007: 63.9%

Unemployment rate and rank among states
    2000: 4.0%, 28th
    2007: 2.6%, 1st

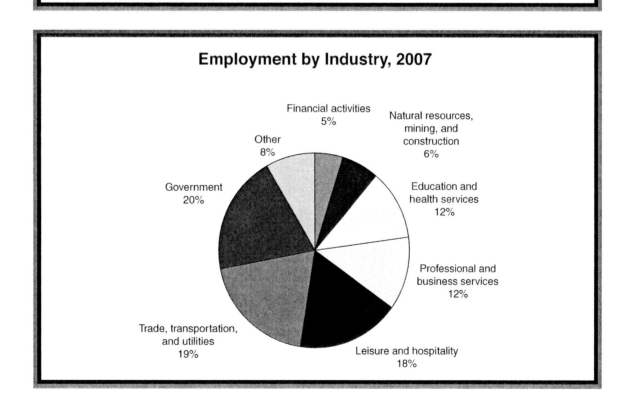

Employment by Industry, 2007

Financial activities 5%
Natural resources, mining, and construction 6%
Other 8%
Government 20%
Education and health services 12%
Professional and business services 12%
Trade, transportation, and utilities 19%
Leisure and hospitality 18%

Employment by Industry: Hawaii, 2000–2007

(Numbers in thousands, not seasonally adjusted.)

Industry and year	January	February	March	April	May	June	July	August	September	October	November	December	Annual Average
Total Nonfarm													
2000	535.1	542.9	548.8	548.3	552.2	556.3	547.6	548.2	552.3	555.3	561.9	567.4	551.4
2001	546.9	557.4	561.2	556.1	557.5	562.9	552.5	554.6	555.5	548.1	551.9	555.5	555.0
2002	541.9	549.4	554.0	547.9	558.0	564.7	553.2	554.2	557.3	560.7	566.9	573.4	556.8
2003	559.6	564.5	567.8	562.7	568.2	568.9	562.3	563.4	566.1	570.0	576.2	581.9	567.6
2004	568.9	574.5	578.0	578.6	582.4	584.2	578.9	580.5	584.1	589.8	599.2	601.8	583.4
2005	585.0	593.1	597.4	598.5	602.0	604.4	597.3	601.3	604.2	605.8	611.8	618.9	601.6
2006	600.2	611.0	615.2	612.5	617.9	621.0	610.6	615.7	620.4	618.2	630.3	632.3	617.1
2007	614.9	623.0	626.6	618.2	626.7	630.0	615.7	617.5	622.4	623.4	629.6	635.2	623.6
Total Private													
2000	424.5	427.8	431.4	431.2	432.6	438.6	437.9	439.1	442.0	441.2	445.3	449.3	436.7
2001	438.8	441.3	444.1	440.9	442.7	445.6	443.7	444.8	443.5	432.6	432.8	435.5	440.5
2002	427.3	430.3	433.4	433.4	436.5	440.7	441.2	441.9	443.0	441.9	446.0	450.9	438.9
2003	440.7	442.9	445.4	443.7	445.8	447.8	448.4	450.3	451.8	450.3	454.9	460.0	448.5
2004	450.5	453.6	455.5	456.9	459.2	463.3	464.7	465.9	467.4	469.4	474.6	478.9	463.3
2005	468.8	472.1	475.2	477.1	479.3	482.9	483.3	485.6	487.7	485.7	490.0	496.3	482.0
2006	484.5	489.1	492.3	490.3	494.0	498.7	496.1	499.7	500.4	495.9	502.1	507.0	495.8
2007	495.0	498.8	501.7	498.3	501.4	506.5	500.3	502.1	501.5	499.9	504.5	509.0	501.6
Goods-Producing													
2000	39.1	39.1	39.9	40.2	40.6	41.3	42.0	42.5	42.7	42.3	42.3	42.6	41.2
2001	41.4	41.3	41.4	40.9	41.2	41.2	41.3	41.6	41.5	40.5	40.6	40.7	41.1
2002	40.0	39.9	40.6	40.2	40.6	41.6	41.8	42.1	41.7	41.8	42.1	42.2	41.2
2003	41.4	41.5	41.8	42.4	42.8	43.1	43.4	43.7	43.8	43.9	43.9	43.8	43.0
2004	42.9	43.3	42.7	43.8	44.3	45.1	45.4	45.5	45.8	45.9	46.3	46.7	44.8
2005	45.9	46.3	47.0	47.5	48.1	48.7	49.1	49.7	50.2	49.9	50.1	50.6	48.6
2006	49.5	49.8	50.1	50.1	50.9	51.7	52.0	52.8	53.5	53.1	53.9	54.6	51.8
2007	52.7	53.3	53.5	53.3	53.9	54.8	54.3	54.8	55.0	54.7	55.0	55.4	54.2
Natural Resources, Mining, and Construction													
2000	23.0	23.1	23.7	24.0	24.4	24.8	25.5	25.8	26.0	25.6	25.6	25.9	24.8
2001	24.8	24.7	24.8	24.4	24.6	24.6	24.8	25.0	25.0	24.5	24.6	24.7	24.7
2002	24.4	24.3	24.9	25.1	25.4	26.2	26.6	27.0	26.8	26.9	27.1	27.2	26.0
2003	26.7	26.8	27.1	27.5	27.9	28.1	28.4	28.7	28.7	28.6	28.5	28.3	27.9
2004	27.6	27.9	27.4	28.4	28.9	29.5	30.0	30.1	30.4	30.6	30.9	31.3	29.4
2005	30.8	31.1	31.8	32.4	33.0	33.6	34.0	34.4	34.9	34.7	34.9	35.3	33.4
2006	34.5	34.7	34.9	35.0	35.7	36.4	36.7	37.3	37.9	37.8	38.4	39.0	36.5
2007	37.5	37.9	38.1	38.2	38.6	39.4	39.2	39.6	39.8	39.7	39.9	40.2	39.0
Manufacturing													
2000	16.1	16.0	16.2	16.2	16.2	16.5	16.5	16.7	16.7	16.7	16.7	16.7	16.4
2001	16.6	16.6	16.6	16.5	16.6	16.6	16.5	16.6	16.5	16.0	16.0	16.0	16.4
2002	15.6	15.6	15.7	15.1	15.2	15.4	15.2	15.1	14.9	14.9	15.0	15.0	15.2
2003	14.7	14.7	14.7	14.9	14.9	15.0	15.0	15.0	15.1	15.3	15.4	15.5	15.0
2004	15.3	15.4	15.3	15.4	15.4	15.6	15.4	15.4	15.4	15.3	15.4	15.4	15.4
2005	15.1	15.2	15.2	15.1	15.1	15.1	15.1	15.3	15.3	15.2	15.2	15.3	15.2
2006	15.0	15.1	15.2	15.1	15.2	15.3	15.3	15.5	15.6	15.3	15.5	15.6	15.3
2007	15.2	15.4	15.4	15.1	15.3	15.4	15.1	15.2	15.2	15.0	15.1	15.2	15.2
Service-Providing													
2000	496.0	503.8	508.9	508.1	511.6	515.0	505.6	505.7	509.6	513.0	519.6	524.8	510.1
2001	505.5	516.1	519.8	515.2	516.3	521.7	511.2	513.0	514.0	507.6	511.3	514.8	513.9
2002	501.9	509.5	513.4	507.7	517.4	523.1	511.4	512.1	515.6	518.9	524.8	531.2	515.6
2003	518.2	523.0	526.0	520.3	525.4	525.8	518.9	519.7	522.3	526.1	532.3	538.1	524.7
2004	526.0	531.2	535.3	534.8	538.1	539.1	533.5	535.0	538.3	543.9	552.9	555.1	538.6
2005	539.1	546.8	550.4	551.0	553.9	555.7	548.2	551.6	554.0	555.9	561.7	568.3	553.1
2006	550.7	561.2	565.1	562.4	567.0	569.3	558.6	562.9	566.9	565.1	576.4	577.7	565.3
2007	562.2	569.7	573.1	564.9	572.8	575.2	561.4	562.7	567.4	568.7	574.6	579.8	569.4
Trade, Transportation, and Utilities													
2000	109.5	109.3	109.3	108.6	108.9	110.4	110.4	110.9	111.4	111.6	114.1	115.4	110.8
2001	112.3	111.7	111.9	111.2	111.5	112.2	111.8	112.0	111.6	108.9	107.6	109.2	111.0
2002	105.5	104.8	104.9	105.0	105.5	106.5	107.0	107.3	107.1	107.5	109.0	111.0	106.8
2003	107.4	107.0	106.8	106.2	106.4	106.9	107.6	107.9	108.0	108.2	110.1	112.2	107.9
2004	109.3	108.8	109.1	110.1	110.8	111.9	112.1	112.6	113.0	114.5	116.8	118.4	112.3
2005	114.9	114.9	115.2	115.5	116.4	117.3	118.2	118.7	119.1	118.9	120.7	122.9	117.7
2006	119.2	118.9	119.8	119.5	120.0	121.3	120.7	121.7	121.7	120.6	123.2	125.0	121.0
2007	121.6	120.3	121.4	120.3	120.7	121.4	120.8	120.8	120.5	120.6	122.8	124.7	121.3
Wholesale Trade													
2000	16.0	16.0	16.1	16.0	16.0	16.3	16.3	16.4	16.4	16.4	16.5	16.5	16.2
2001	16.4	16.4	16.4	16.4	16.5	16.6	16.5	16.6	16.5	16.3	16.2	16.4	16.4
2002	16.1	16.1	16.2	16.2	16.3	16.4	16.5	16.5	16.5	16.6	16.7	16.9	16.4
2003	16.5	16.5	16.6	16.6	16.7	16.7	16.8	16.8	16.8	16.8	16.8	16.9	16.7
2004	16.7	16.8	16.8	16.9	17.0	17.1	17.1	17.1	17.1	17.2	17.3	17.4	17.0
2005	17.1	17.3	17.4	17.4	17.5	17.6	17.7	17.8	17.9	17.9	17.9	18.1	17.6
2006	17.7	17.7	17.7	17.8	17.9	18.1	18.0	18.2	18.2	18.2	18.4	18.5	18.0
2007	18.2	18.2	18.4	18.3	18.3	18.4	18.4	18.5	18.5	18.5	18.6	18.7	18.4
Retail Trade													
2000	66.0	65.5	65.3	64.7	65.0	65.7	65.9	66.3	66.4	66.7	68.8	70.0	66.4
2001	67.2	66.5	66.5	65.9	65.9	66.3	66.1	66.3	66.0	64.9	65.3	66.7	66.1
2002	63.8	63.0	62.9	62.8	63.0	63.7	64.1	64.1	63.9	64.1	65.3	67.1	64.0
2003	64.0	63.4	63.1	62.8	63.0	63.7	64.3	64.4	64.3	64.6	66.4	68.4	64.4
2004	65.8	65.1	65.2	65.1	65.6	66.3	66.6	66.9	67.0	68.1	70.1	71.8	67.0
2005	68.5	68.1	68.2	67.8	68.0	68.3	69.1	69.3	69.3	69.7	71.3	73.3	69.2
2006	70.0	69.5	69.8	69.1	69.2	69.8	69.4	69.7	69.4	69.5	71.7	73.1	70.0
2007	70.4	69.4	70.1	69.3	69.5	70.0	69.6	69.4	69.2	69.5	71.7	73.0	70.1

Employment by Industry: Hawaii, 2000–2007—*Continued*

(Numbers in thousands, not seasonally adjusted.)

Industry and year	January	February	March	April	May	June	July	August	September	October	November	December	Annual Average
Transportation and Utilities													
2000	27.5	27.8	27.9	27.9	27.9	28.4	28.2	28.2	28.6	28.5	28.8	28.9	28.2
2001	28.7	28.8	29.0	28.9	29.1	29.3	29.2	29.1	29.1	27.7	26.1	26.1	28.4
2002	25.6	25.7	25.8	26.0	26.2	26.4	26.4	26.7	26.7	26.8	27.0	27.0	26.4
2003	26.9	27.1	27.1	26.8	26.7	26.5	26.5	26.7	26.9	26.8	26.9	26.9	26.8
2004	26.8	26.9	27.1	28.1	28.2	28.5	28.4	28.6	28.9	29.2	29.4	29.2	28.3
2005	29.3	29.5	29.6	30.3	30.9	31.4	31.4	31.6	31.9	31.3	31.5	31.5	30.9
2006	31.5	31.7	32.3	32.6	32.9	33.4	33.3	33.8	34.1	32.9	33.1	33.4	32.9
2007	33.0	32.7	32.9	32.7	32.9	33.0	32.8	32.9	32.8	32.6	32.5	33.0	32.8
Information													
2000	11.5	11.5	11.7	12.4	12.3	12.7	12.0	12.5	13.3	12.9	12.4	12.1	12.3
2001	12.1	12.1	12.4	11.8	12.1	11.9	11.7	11.9	11.5	11.5	11.7	11.6	11.9
2002	11.7	11.7	11.6	11.5	11.5	11.3	11.2	11.3	12.0	11.1	11.1	11.7	11.5
2003	10.8	10.9	10.9	10.5	11.1	10.9	10.1	10.0	9.9	9.9	10.0	10.1	10.4
2004	10.2	10.1	10.4	10.2	10.5	10.6	11.1	11.0	11.1	11.1	11.6	11.5	10.8
2005	10.4	10.6	10.4	10.7	10.9	10.5	10.5	10.9	11.0	10.9	11.1	11.6	10.8
2006	10.8	11.1	10.9	10.2	11.0	10.8	10.3	10.5	11.0	10.3	10.8	10.9	10.7
2007	10.4	11.0	10.9	10.5	11.2	11.1	10.4	10.9	10.5	10.6	10.7	10.7	10.7
Financial Activities													
2000	28.4	28.6	28.6	28.4	28.4	28.6	28.7	28.7	28.5	28.5	28.4	28.9	28.6
2001	28.1	28.2	28.4	28.2	28.2	28.3	28.1	28.1	28.0	27.6	27.6	27.7	28.0
2002	27.2	27.3	27.6	27.4	27.6	27.8	27.8	27.8	27.8	27.9	28.1	28.4	27.7
2003	27.7	27.9	28.1	28.0	28.2	28.5	28.6	28.8	28.6	28.6	28.5	28.8	28.4
2004	28.5	28.5	28.6	28.7	28.7	28.9	28.9	28.8	28.7	29.0	29.1	29.3	28.8
2005	28.7	29.0	29.0	28.9	29.1	29.2	29.4	29.5	29.5	29.5	29.7	29.9	29.3
2006	29.5	29.6	29.9	29.9	30.0	30.2	30.1	30.2	30.0	29.9	30.1	30.3	30.0
2007	29.9	30.0	30.2	29.9	30.0	30.2	30.2	30.1	29.9	29.9	30.0	30.2	30.0
Professional and Business Services													
2000	59.3	59.8	60.6	60.7	60.7	61.4	61.6	61.7	62.4	62.5	63.0	63.7	61.5
2001	62.3	63.1	63.9	63.3	63.8	64.7	64.4	64.9	64.8	63.5	64.1	64.4	63.9
2002	63.5	64.9	65.4	65.9	66.5	67.5	67.8	68.6	68.8	68.8	68.6	70.6	67.2
2003	69.0	68.6	69.2	68.9	68.8	69.6	69.4	70.3	70.8	69.6	70.6	71.1	69.7
2004	69.4	70.1	70.6	70.2	69.5	70.2	70.6	71.4	71.2	71.3	71.7	72.7	70.7
2005	71.9	72.5	73.1	73.6	73.0	74.0	74.2	74.9	74.8	75.1	76.1	77.3	74.2
2006	75.3	76.8	77.2	76.7	76.6	77.6	77.5	77.7	77.2	75.6	76.1	77.2	76.8
2007	75.1	75.7	76.0	75.0	75.2	77.1	75.9	76.1	76.3	76.0	76.7	77.8	76.1
Education and Health Services													
2000	58.2	59.4	59.9	59.4	59.7	60.7	60.0	59.1	60.0	60.0	60.9	61.5	59.9
2001	59.9	61.0	61.4	61.4	61.8	62.2	62.1	61.5	62.0	62.0	63.0	63.2	61.8
2002	61.5	62.6	62.9	63.0	63.4	63.5	63.5	62.5	63.7	63.8	65.0	64.4	63.3
2003	63.1	64.6	65.1	65.0	65.2	64.9	65.2	64.7	66.0	66.0	66.8	67.2	65.3
2004	65.5	66.6	67.1	66.9	67.7	67.7	67.4	67.0	68.3	68.5	69.4	69.9	67.7
2005	68.7	69.5	69.9	69.9	70.2	70.3	69.5	69.0	70.2	69.9	70.4	70.8	69.9
2006	68.9	70.1	70.7	70.7	71.4	71.8	70.6	71.2	71.7	71.8	72.6	73.0	71.2
2007	71.1	72.7	72.9	72.9	73.2	73.6	72.3	72.1	73.0	72.6	73.4	73.6	72.8
Leisure and Hospitality													
2000	96.7	97.7	98.8	98.8	99.2	100.5	100.3	100.6	100.7	100.2	100.6	101.5	99.6
2001	99.5	100.5	101.0	100.4	100.5	101.1	100.4	101.1	100.4	95.3	94.9	95.3	99.2
2002	94.7	95.8	96.8	96.8	97.7	98.7	98.3	98.5	98.0	97.2	98.2	98.6	97.4
2003	97.8	98.5	99.5	98.5	99.0	99.5	99.9	100.6	100.4	99.9	100.5	102.2	99.7
2004	100.9	102.1	102.6	102.7	103.1	104.2	104.7	105.1	104.9	104.4	105.0	105.5	103.8
2005	103.8	104.7	105.9	105.9	106.2	107.5	107.2	107.5	107.4	106.1	106.4	107.4	106.3
2006	105.9	107.1	107.8	107.3	107.9	109.1	108.9	109.3	109.0	108.2	108.9	109.5	108.2
2007	108.4	109.6	110.4	110.1	110.7	111.7	110.0	110.6	109.5	108.6	108.9	109.7	109.9
Other Services													
2000	21.8	22.4	22.6	22.7	22.8	23.0	22.9	23.1	23.0	23.2	23.6	23.6	22.9
2001	23.2	23.4	23.7	23.7	23.6	24.0	23.9	23.7	23.7	23.3	23.3	23.4	23.6
2002	23.2	23.3	23.6	23.6	23.7	23.8	23.8	23.8	23.9	23.8	23.9	24.0	23.7
2003	23.5	23.9	24.0	24.2	24.3	24.4	24.2	24.3	24.3	24.2	24.5	24.6	24.2
2004	23.8	24.1	24.4	24.3	24.6	24.7	24.5	24.5	24.4	24.7	24.7	24.9	24.5
2005	24.5	24.6	24.7	25.1	25.4	25.4	25.2	25.4	25.5	25.4	25.5	25.8	25.2
2006	25.4	25.7	25.9	25.9	26.2	26.2	26.0	26.3	26.3	26.4	26.5	26.5	26.1
2007	25.8	26.2	26.4	26.3	26.5	26.6	26.4	26.7	26.8	26.9	27.0	26.9	26.5
Government													
2000	110.6	115.1	117.4	117.1	119.6	117.7	109.7	109.1	110.3	114.1	116.6	118.1	114.6
2001	108.1	116.1	117.1	115.2	114.8	117.3	108.8	109.8	112.0	115.5	119.1	120.0	114.5
2002	114.6	119.1	120.6	114.5	121.5	124.0	112.0	112.3	114.3	118.8	120.9	122.5	117.9
2003	118.9	121.6	122.4	119.0	122.4	121.1	113.9	113.1	114.3	119.7	121.3	121.9	119.1
2004	118.4	120.9	122.5	121.7	123.2	120.9	114.2	114.6	116.7	120.4	124.6	122.9	120.1
2005	116.2	121.0	122.2	121.4	122.7	121.5	114.0	115.7	116.5	120.1	121.8	122.6	119.6
2006	115.7	121.9	122.9	122.2	123.9	122.3	114.5	116.0	120.0	122.3	128.2	125.3	121.3
2007	119.9	124.2	124.9	119.9	125.3	123.5	115.4	115.4	120.9	123.5	125.1	126.2	122.0

Average Weekly Hours by Selected Industry: Hawaii, 2001–2007

(Not seasonally adjusted.)

Industry and year	January	February	March	April	May	June	July	August	September	October	November	December	Annual Average
Natural Resources, Mining, and Construction													
2001	37.7	35.7	38.7	36.1	38.8	33.9	37.4	36.3	35.4	32.5	32.9	34.1	35.8
2002	36.1	36.7	38.9	39.2	36.4	35.1	38.6	37.1	39.1	38.2	34.3	39.1	37.4
2003	38.2	36.7	37.9	37.6	37.9	33.3	37.0	35.2	35.7	33.6	33.4	35.8	36.0
2004	34.7	36.2	37.3	36.1	38.7	34.8	38.3	38.5	37.4	34.8	35.0	36.8	36.6
2005	37.6	37.7	38.8	40.9	40.8	39.8	39.9	40.3	39.8	36.0	36.3	39.6	39.0
2006	39.9	38.8	37.6	38.5	39.1	34.6	38.2	39.0	38.7	34.4	36.9	37.1	37.7
2007	36.1	37.5	36.3	37.2	36.1	32.3	37.3	35.4	37.4	33.9	34.3	35.0	35.7
Manufacturing													
2001	34.5	36.0	35.9	37.0	36.1	35.6	36.6	36.4	35.3	35.7	36.5	36.8	36.0
2002	35.0	36.0	35.6	35.6	34.5	36.0	34.3	34.9	36.9	35.5	35.6	37.7	35.6
2003	34.8	36.4	35.8	35.4	36.8	36.9	36.2	37.9	37.4	38.9	40.7	38.9	37.2
2004	37.1	38.8	39.1	36.2	37.2	36.1	36.6	37.7	38.0	38.6	39.5	39.7	37.9
2005	38.4	38.2	36.1	37.0	38.3	37.7	38.6	39.6	38.8	39.7	38.6	40.0	38.4
2006	39.0	38.6	38.6	40.3	39.6	39.1	39.2	38.3	36.9	38.4	37.3	38.2	38.6
2007	36.7	36.1	35.9	38.7	38.2	38.7	37.6	36.4	36.7	36.7	37.7	37.7	37.3
Trade, Transportation, and Utilities													
2001	32.0	32.2	31.9	31.8	32.3	32.4	32.4	32.2	32.4	31.3	31.4	32.7	32.1
2002	31.9	32.5	32.2	32.0	32.4	32.9	32.5	32.1	32.6	31.4	31.4	32.5	32.2
2003	31.1	32.1	32.1	31.5	31.6	33.5	32.6	32.9	32.4	32.2	32.9	32.1	32.2
2004	31.2	31.8	32.0	31.7	32.8	32.5	33.0	33.9	33.6	33.0	32.9	34.3	32.8
2005	34.3	33.6	33.6	33.3	34.0	33.6	33.3	33.0	33.3	33.2	32.4	32.2	33.3
2006	32.9	32.0	31.8	33.4	32.8	33.5	35.0	33.5	33.6	34.4	33.5	32.8	33.3
2007	32.3	33.0	32.6	33.9	32.9	33.8	34.1	33.4	34.7	33.3	33.8	34.0	33.5
Wholesale Trade													
2001	35.2	35.6	35.3	36.6	35.5	34.4	35.6	33.8	35.2	33.8	34.1	35.9	35.1
2002	35.9	35.7	36.2	36.2	35.4	36.4	36.5	35.1	36.6	34.8	34.7	37.2	35.9
2003	34.1	35.8	35.6	33.7	33.8	35.0	36.3	35.1	36.4	37.0	38.2	36.0	35.6
2004	36.2	36.8	37.9	37.1	38.3	35.9	38.7	38.7	35.9	36.6	35.1	35.7	36.9
2005	35.9	35.2	36.7	35.4	35.7	36.5	36.1	36.7	35.6	34.3	34.2	35.2	35.6
2006	35.2	34.4	35.4	36.7	35.5	36.8	37.9	37.1	37.4	38.6	38.1	36.9	36.7
2007	34.3	37.0	36.2	38.4	36.2	36.6	40.1	38.8	41.4	39.7	36.7	39.6	37.9
Retail Trade													
2001	30.3	30.7	30.4	30.6	30.4	31.0	30.7	30.1	30.4	29.2	29.4	30.7	30.3
2002	30.1	30.5	30.4	30.1	30.6	31.4	31.2	31.0	31.4	30.1	29.8	31.0	30.6
2003	30.5	31.2	31.3	31.0	30.9	32.6	31.2	31.7	31.3	30.8	31.1	30.9	31.2
2004	29.7	30.5	30.5	30.3	30.7	30.6	30.7	31.1	31.0	30.0	30.0	30.9	30.5
2005	30.3	29.9	29.6	29.6	30.3	30.1	30.4	30.0	30.1	30.2	29.4	29.3	29.9
2006	29.5	29.0	29.4	30.2	29.5	30.0	31.1	30.0	30.0	29.5	29.2	29.2	29.7
2007	29.1	29.9	29.7	30.5	29.9	30.6	31.2	30.2	31.4	30.0	30.6	29.9	30.2
Financial Activities													
2001	35.7	36.1	36.9	35.8	33.6	33.9	34.9	33.0	34.7	33.6	34.2	36.3	34.9
2002	34.6	34.7	32.7	33.1	33.0	34.3	33.1	33.6	34.0	32.3	31.9	34.8	33.5
2003	33.9	35.2	34.5	33.2	33.2	35.0	33.4	36.0	33.5	34.3	35.4	33.1	34.2
2004	33.7	36.5	34.1	34.1	35.4	34.4	34.1	37.3	35.2	35.9	37.3	36.4	35.4
2005	38.5	36.2	36.3	37.1	38.4	35.3	35.1	34.8	34.9	35.3	36.3	36.2	36.2
2006	37.0	35.9	34.3	35.6	34.8	33.7	34.3	33.8	33.2	33.8	32.7	33.1	34.3
2007	33.8	33.8	33.9	34.9	34.1	34.4	33.8	34.9	34.9	33.0	33.1	33.9	34.0

Average Hourly Earnings by Selected Industry: Hawaii, 2001–2007

(Dollars, not seasonally adjusted.)

Industry and year	January	February	March	April	May	June	July	August	September	October	November	December	Annual Average
Natural Resources, Mining, and Construction													
2001	27.37	27.61	27.61	27.46	27.33	27.88	27.86	27.52	27.58	27.54	27.69	27.28	27.56
2002	26.83	26.48	27.17	26.78	26.75	27.07	27.61	27.66	28.60	28.30	27.47	28.17	27.45
2003	28.23	28.20	28.41	27.21	27.56	27.91	28.73	28.81	28.47	28.85	29.05	29.01	28.36
2004	29.65	28.89	29.36	29.11	28.70	28.60	28.36	27.80	28.11	27.20	27.81	28.12	28.44
2005	27.38	27.60	27.30	26.90	27.42	27.47	27.28	27.71	28.06	27.32	28.60	28.25	27.61
2006	28.64	28.56	28.47	28.40	28.44	28.70	28.79	28.31	28.71	28.50	29.14	29.42	28.68
2007	29.96	29.49	29.96	29.68	30.35	30.36	30.14	30.54	30.59	30.13	31.08	31.81	30.34
Manufacturing													
2001	12.83	12.78	12.87	12.96	12.98	13.17	13.49	13.19	13.23	13.44	13.65	13.61	13.18
2002	13.61	13.53	13.20	13.33	13.13	12.90	13.20	12.87	12.98	12.79	12.63	12.68	13.07
2003	12.50	12.38	12.49	12.63	13.36	13.08	13.37	13.05	13.15	12.83	12.77	13.16	12.90
2004	13.27	13.36	13.56	13.30	13.43	13.52	13.85	13.78	13.60	13.31	13.56	13.42	13.50
2005	13.62	13.53	13.66	13.69	14.15	14.11	14.29	14.45	14.63	15.10	15.49	15.17	14.34
2006	15.45	15.24	15.53	15.26	15.28	15.86	15.75	16.25	16.82	16.31	16.66	16.39	15.89
2007	16.25	16.85	16.25	16.74	17.07	17.33	17.47	16.96	16.96	17.05	17.88	17.86	17.06
Trade, Transportation, and Utilities													
2001	12.78	12.73	12.73	12.71	12.36	12.37	12.45	12.35	12.43	12.56	12.69	12.72	12.57
2002	12.94	12.83	12.83	12.74	12.79	12.98	13.01	13.03	13.06	13.15	13.35	13.35	13.01
2003	13.45	13.59	13.45	13.37	13.21	13.32	13.51	13.67	13.84	13.89	14.03	13.85	13.60
2004	14.24	14.33	14.04	13.97	14.00	14.06	13.93	13.73	14.01	13.88	13.73	13.61	13.95
2005	13.80	13.84	13.92	14.10	14.21	14.08	14.03	14.14	14.23	14.63	14.44	14.47	14.16
2006	14.73	14.56	14.59	14.80	14.78	14.91	14.61	14.83	14.95	14.88	14.68	14.69	14.75
2007	15.14	14.82	15.02	14.83	14.69	15.15	14.74	14.91	15.31	15.46	15.41	15.75	15.11
Wholesale Trade													
2001	13.21	13.17	13.14	13.46	13.27	13.52	13.52	13.39	13.72	13.71	14.06	13.76	13.49
2002	13.73	13.79	13.78	13.12	13.24	13.51	13.51	13.60	13.78	13.65	14.43	14.43	13.72
2003	14.68	14.86	15.10	15.13	14.84	15.16	15.53	15.87	15.93	15.77	16.43	16.54	15.50
2004	16.34	16.44	16.21	16.15	16.51	15.99	15.43	15.00	15.62	15.59	15.10	15.99	15.86
2005	16.04	15.99	15.45	16.25	16.10	15.40	15.06	14.67	15.05	15.28	14.81	14.77	15.40
2006	15.05	14.68	14.80	14.96	15.15	15.35	15.62	15.98	16.46	16.67	16.91	17.46	15.79
2007	18.23	18.90	18.41	18.88	17.63	18.22	18.13	18.17	18.06	18.36	18.60	18.58	18.35
Retail Trade													
2001	10.91	10.74	10.93	10.91	10.74	10.82	10.87	10.78	10.94	10.93	10.94	10.77	10.86
2002	11.15	11.02	10.97	10.95	10.92	10.97	10.85	10.86	10.86	10.92	11.00	11.03	10.96
2003	11.09	11.37	11.20	11.07	11.03	11.03	11.06	10.91	11.18	11.26	11.09	11.06	11.11
2004	11.44	11.57	11.28	11.37	11.40	11.66	11.53	11.49	11.57	11.70	11.73	11.52	11.52
2005	11.81	11.67	11.58	11.64	11.74	11.60	11.73	11.90	12.06	12.58	12.27	12.59	11.94
2006	12.71	12.35	12.58	12.81	12.64	12.77	12.42	12.43	12.54	12.69	12.55	12.73	12.60
2007	13.29	12.64	13.44	12.84	12.89	13.09	12.99	13.02	13.56	13.70	13.59	14.01	13.26
Financial Activities													
2001	14.88	14.81	14.86	15.41	15.11	15.00	15.47	15.19	15.19	15.38	15.33	16.02	15.22
2002	15.57	15.54	16.01	15.73	16.17	15.95	15.72	15.75	16.07	15.49	15.70	16.11	15.82
2003	15.95	16.47	16.54	16.30	16.49	16.42	15.81	16.10	16.20	16.02	16.00	15.87	16.18
2004	15.68	15.99	15.41	15.34	16.10	15.72	16.17	16.69	16.67	16.51	16.72	17.17	16.20
2005	17.16	17.19	16.90	16.95	16.47	16.86	16.44	16.85	16.30	16.30	16.00	16.13	16.63
2006	16.47	16.61	16.62	16.61	17.01	17.27	17.43	17.65	18.16	18.27	18.49	18.55	17.42
2007	18.47	18.61	18.77	18.94	19.21	19.09	19.82	20.12	19.81	20.19	20.04	20.59	19.47

Average Weekly Earnings by Selected Industry: Hawaii, 2001–2007

(Dollars, not seasonally adjusted.)

Industry and year	January	February	March	April	May	June	July	August	September	October	November	December	Annual Average
Natural Resources, Mining, and Construction													
2001	1,031.85	985.68	1,068.51	991.31	1,060.40	945.13	1,041.96	998.98	976.33	895.05	911.00	930.25	986.65
2002	968.56	971.82	1,056.91	1,049.78	973.70	950.16	1,065.75	1,026.19	1,118.26	1,081.06	942.22	1,101.45	1,026.63
2003	1,078.39	1,034.94	1,076.74	1,023.10	1,044.52	929.40	1,063.01	1,014.11	1,016.38	969.36	970.27	1,038.56	1,020.96
2004	1,028.86	1,045.82	1,095.13	1,050.87	1,110.69	995.28	1,086.19	1,070.30	1,051.31	946.56	973.35	1,034.82	1,040.90
2005	1,029.49	1,040.52	1,059.24	1,100.21	1,118.74	1,093.31	1,088.47	1,116.71	1,116.79	983.52	1,038.18	1,118.70	1,076.79
2006	1,142.74	1,108.13	1,070.47	1,093.40	1,112.00	993.02	1,099.78	1,104.09	1,111.08	980.40	1,075.27	1,091.48	1,081.24
2007	1,081.56	1,105.88	1,087.55	1,104.10	1,095.64	980.63	1,124.22	1,081.12	1,144.07	1,021.41	1,066.04	1,113.35	1,083.14
Manufacturing													
2001	442.64	460.08	462.03	479.52	468.58	468.85	493.73	480.12	467.02	479.81	498.23	500.85	474.48
2002	476.35	487.08	469.92	474.55	452.99	464.40	452.76	449.16	478.96	454.05	449.63	478.04	465.29
2003	435.00	450.63	447.14	447.10	491.65	482.65	483.99	494.60	491.81	499.09	519.74	511.92	479.88
2004	492.32	518.37	530.20	481.46	499.60	488.07	506.91	519.51	516.80	513.77	535.62	532.77	511.65
2005	523.01	516.85	493.13	506.53	541.95	531.95	551.59	572.22	567.64	599.47	597.91	606.80	550.66
2006	602.55	588.26	599.46	614.98	605.09	620.13	617.40	622.38	620.66	626.30	621.42	626.10	613.35
2007	596.38	608.29	583.38	647.84	652.07	670.67	656.87	617.34	622.43	625.74	674.08	673.32	636.34
Trade, Transportation, and Utilities													
2001	408.96	409.91	406.09	404.18	399.23	400.79	403.38	397.67	402.73	393.13	398.47	415.94	403.50
2002	412.79	416.98	413.13	407.68	414.40	427.04	422.83	418.26	425.76	412.91	419.19	433.88	418.92
2003	418.30	436.24	431.75	421.16	417.44	446.22	440.43	449.74	448.42	447.26	461.59	444.59	437.92
2004	444.29	455.69	449.28	442.85	459.20	456.95	459.69	465.45	470.74	458.04	451.72	466.82	457.56
2005	473.34	465.02	467.71	469.53	483.14	473.09	467.20	466.62	473.86	485.72	467.86	465.93	471.53
2006	484.62	465.92	463.96	494.32	484.78	499.49	511.35	496.81	502.32	511.87	491.78	481.83	491.18
2007	489.02	489.06	489.65	502.74	483.30	512.07	502.63	497.99	531.26	514.82	520.86	535.50	506.19
Wholesale Trade													
2001	464.99	468.85	463.84	492.64	471.09	465.09	481.31	452.58	482.94	463.40	479.45	493.98	473.50
2002	492.91	492.30	498.84	474.94	468.70	491.76	493.12	477.36	504.35	475.02	500.72	536.80	492.55
2003	500.59	531.99	537.56	509.88	501.59	530.60	563.74	557.04	579.85	583.49	627.63	595.44	551.80
2004	591.51	604.99	614.36	599.17	632.33	574.04	597.14	580.50	560.76	570.59	530.01	570.84	585.23
2005	575.84	562.85	567.02	575.25	574.77	562.10	543.67	538.39	535.78	524.10	506.50	519.90	548.24
2006	529.76	504.99	523.92	549.03	537.83	564.88	592.00	592.86	615.60	643.46	644.27	644.27	579.49
2007	625.29	699.30	666.44	724.99	638.21	666.85	727.01	705.00	747.68	728.89	682.62	735.77	695.47
Retail Trade													
2001	330.57	329.72	332.27	333.85	326.50	335.42	333.71	324.48	332.58	319.16	321.64	330.64	329.06
2002	335.62	336.11	333.49	329.60	334.15	344.46	338.52	336.66	341.00	328.69	327.80	341.93	335.38
2003	338.25	354.74	350.56	343.17	340.83	359.58	345.07	345.85	349.93	346.81	344.90	341.75	346.63
2004	339.77	352.89	344.04	344.51	349.98	356.80	353.97	357.34	358.67	351.00	351.90	355.97	351.36
2005	357.84	348.93	342.77	344.54	355.72	349.16	356.59	357.00	363.01	379.92	360.74	368.89	357.01
2006	374.95	358.15	369.85	386.86	372.88	383.10	386.26	372.90	376.20	374.36	366.46	371.72	374.22
2007	386.74	377.94	399.17	391.62	385.41	400.55	405.29	393.20	425.78	411.00	415.85	418.90	400.45
Financial Activities													
2001	531.22	534.64	548.33	551.68	507.70	508.50	539.90	501.27	527.09	516.77	524.29	581.53	531.18
2002	538.72	539.24	523.53	520.66	533.61	547.09	520.33	529.20	546.38	500.33	500.83	560.63	529.97
2003	540.71	579.74	570.63	541.16	547.47	574.70	528.05	579.60	542.70	549.49	566.40	525.30	553.36
2004	528.42	583.64	525.48	523.09	569.94	540.77	551.40	622.54	586.78	592.71	623.66	624.99	573.48
2005	660.66	622.28	613.47	628.85	632.45	595.16	577.04	586.38	568.87	575.39	580.80	583.91	602.01
2006	609.39	596.30	570.07	591.32	591.95	582.00	597.85	596.57	602.91	617.53	604.62	614.01	597.51
2007	624.29	629.02	636.30	661.01	655.06	656.70	669.92	702.19	691.37	666.27	663.32	698.00	661.98

Population
    2000 census: 1,293,953
    2007 estimate: 1,499,402
    Percent change, 2000–2007: 15.9%

Percent change in total nonfarm employment, 2000–2007: 17.2%

Industry with the largest growth in employment, 2000–2007 (thousands)
    Professional and business services, 22.4

Industry with the largest decline in employment, 2000–2007 (thousands)
    Manufacturing, -4.0

Civilian labor force
    2000: 662,958
    2007: 754,136

Employment-population ratio
    2000: 66.5%
    2007: 66.0%

Unemployment rate and rank among states
    2000: 4.6%, 41st
    2007: 2.7%, 2nd

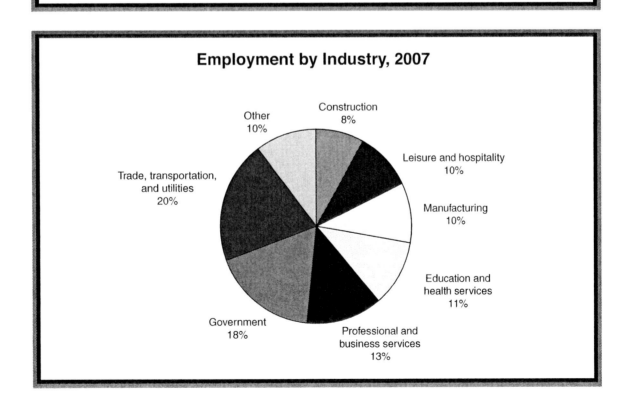

Employment by Industry, 2007

Construction 8%
Other 10%
Leisure and hospitality 10%
Trade, transportation, and utilities 20%
Manufacturing 10%
Education and health services 11%
Government 18%
Professional and business services 13%

Employment by Industry: Idaho, 2000–2007

(Numbers in thousands, not seasonally adjusted.)

Industry and year	January	February	March	April	May	June	July	August	September	October	November	December	Annual Average
Total Nonfarm													
2000	533.0	537.1	543.9	552.9	562.0	569.2	564.6	569.0	574.0	570.2	570.7	568.5	559.6
2001	549.3	553.7	561.0	565.2	571.1	578.9	572.3	576.3	578.0	572.5	568.7	565.6	567.7
2002	545.8	548.2	553.8	562.1	569.4	578.4	574.2	575.9	579.7	579.1	577.2	575.0	568.2
2003	555.3	556.5	561.2	564.8	571.5	580.4	574.9	578.2	583.1	581.0	578.6	578.2	572.0
2004	558.3	564.1	571.9	581.7	589.1	597.5	594.6	596.9	601.3	600.2	599.8	598.9	587.9
2005	581.5	588.5	594.4	603.2	609.5	617.9	617.5	621.1	628.4	624.0	624.6	625.0	611.3
2006	607.9	615.0	622.6	631.7	640.4	649.7	645.7	649.2	654.0	649.0	648.6	647.4	638.4
2007	628.2	635.5	642.3	650.0	660.0	669.5	662.5	666.4	667.5	664.5	662.6	658.0	655.6
Total Private													
2000	428.0	429.3	435.2	441.8	447.0	458.3	460.5	465.8	465.8	459.4	460.1	458.6	450.8
2001	443.7	444.0	450.2	453.9	458.6	468.2	467.1	471.8	466.8	458.6	455.3	453.0	457.6
2002	436.4	436.2	440.6	448.8	454.9	464.1	467.4	470.3	467.7	464.6	462.5	461.1	456.2
2003	444.7	443.9	447.1	451.5	456.0	465.3	467.1	471.4	469.2	465.1	463.2	463.6	459.0
2004	447.9	450.0	457.0	465.6	472.3	482.7	485.7	488.3	485.8	482.8	482.6	483.0	473.7
2005	469.4	472.6	477.8	486.4	492.1	501.8	508.4	512.3	511.7	505.9	506.8	508.5	496.1
2006	493.9	497.6	504.8	513.1	521.1	532.4	535.7	539.6	537.6	530.6	530.8	530.9	522.3
2007	515.1	518.7	525.1	531.8	540.7	551.5	551.6	554.2	548.0	542.5	541.1	537.3	538.1
Goods-Producing													
2000	105.0	104.8	106.0	107.9	110.5	114.5	115.3	116.3	115.8	114.4	114.0	111.7	111.4
2001	107.7	107.2	108.6	109.5	112.0	115.6	115.7	116.6	114.5	111.6	108.0	104.8	111.0
2002	100.0	98.8	99.6	101.8	105.5	108.8	110.5	111.0	110.0	109.2	107.8	105.7	105.7
2003	99.6	98.6	98.0	99.5	101.8	104.9	105.7	106.4	106.0	106.2	104.0	102.1	102.7
2004	97.9	97.9	99.8	103.1	105.5	108.8	110.4	111.4	110.4	110.6	109.1	107.7	106.1
2005	103.1	103.7	105.7	108.5	110.9	114.5	116.9	118.3	118.5	118.2	117.2	116.9	112.7
2006	112.4	113.5	115.9	118.8	122.4	127.1	128.1	128.4	127.8	126.0	124.5	122.6	122.3
2007	117.3	118.0	119.4	121.6	125.0	127.9	128.4	128.0	125.6	124.2	122.6	120.4	123.2
Natural Resources and Mining													
2000	4.6	4.5	3.9	3.7	4.2	4.9	5.2	5.2	5.2	5.0	4.8	4.6	4.7
2001	4.2	4.1	3.6	3.1	3.4	4.2	4.6	4.7	4.6	4.4	4.1	3.9	4.0
2002	3.7	3.6	3.2	2.7	3.1	4.0	4.3	4.3	4.3	4.2	4.0	3.7	3.7
2003	3.5	3.2	2.9	2.7	3.1	3.7	4.1	4.2	4.2	4.1	3.9	3.6	3.6
2004	3.6	3.5	3.2	3.1	3.7	4.2	4.5	4.5	4.6	4.4	4.2	4.0	4.0
2005	3.8	3.6	3.5	3.4	3.8	4.3	4.5	4.7	4.7	4.6	4.3	4.2	4.1
2006	3.8	3.7	3.7	3.5	4.0	4.6	4.7	4.7	4.8	4.5	4.3	4.3	4.2
2007	4.0	4.0	3.8	3.6	4.3	4.8	4.9	5.0	4.9	4.7	4.6	4.6	4.4
Construction													
2000	31.4	31.2	32.6	34.9	36.5	38.7	39.3	40.1	39.7	38.5	37.6	36.0	36.4
2001	33.2	32.8	34.6	36.8	38.9	41.0	41.5	42.3	41.1	39.6	37.8	35.2	37.9
2002	31.5	31.0	31.9	34.4	37.3	38.6	40.0	40.1	39.4	39.0	38.0	36.8	36.5
2003	32.3	32.0	32.7	34.5	36.7	38.4	39.6	40.2	39.8	39.6	38.4	37.1	36.8
2004	33.6	33.5	35.4	38.3	40.1	41.8	43.0	43.7	43.0	42.8	42.1	41.1	39.9
2005	37.7	38.2	40.0	42.8	44.3	46.9	48.4	49.1	49.0	48.3	48.5	47.2	45.0
2006	44.4	45.4	47.4	50.1	52.8	55.9	56.2	56.5	55.6	54.3	53.5	51.4	52.0
2007	47.4	47.8	49.4	51.6	53.9	55.8	56.1	56.5	54.7	53.8	52.5	50.4	52.5
Manufacturing													
2000	69.0	69.1	69.5	69.3	69.8	70.9	70.8	71.0	70.9	70.9	71.6	71.1	70.3
2001	70.3	70.3	70.4	69.6	69.7	70.4	69.6	69.6	68.8	67.6	66.1	65.7	69.0
2002	64.8	64.2	64.5	64.7	65.1	66.2	66.2	66.6	66.3	66.0	65.8	65.2	65.5
2003	63.8	63.4	62.4	62.3	62.0	62.8	62.0	62.0	62.0	62.5	61.7	61.4	62.4
2004	60.7	60.9	61.2	61.7	61.7	62.8	62.9	63.2	62.8	63.4	62.8	62.6	62.2
2005	61.6	61.9	62.2	62.3	62.8	63.3	64.0	64.5	64.8	65.3	64.4	65.5	63.6
2006	64.2	64.4	64.8	65.2	65.6	66.6	67.2	67.2	67.4	67.2	66.7	66.9	66.1
2007	65.9	66.2	66.2	66.4	66.8	67.3	67.4	66.5	66.0	65.7	65.5	65.4	66.3
Service-Providing													
2000	428.0	432.3	437.9	445.0	451.5	454.7	449.3	452.7	458.2	455.8	456.7	456.8	448.2
2001	441.6	446.5	452.4	455.7	459.1	463.3	456.6	459.7	463.5	460.9	460.7	460.8	456.7
2002	445.8	449.4	454.2	460.3	463.9	469.6	463.7	464.9	469.7	469.9	469.4	469.3	462.5
2003	455.7	457.9	463.2	465.3	469.7	475.5	469.2	471.8	477.1	474.8	474.6	476.1	469.2
2004	460.4	466.2	472.1	478.6	483.6	488.7	484.2	485.5	490.9	489.6	490.7	491.2	481.8
2005	478.4	484.8	488.7	494.7	498.6	503.4	500.6	502.8	509.9	505.8	507.4	508.1	498.6
2006	495.5	501.5	506.7	512.9	518.0	522.6	517.6	520.8	526.2	523.0	524.1	524.8	516.1
2007	510.9	517.5	522.9	528.4	535.0	541.6	534.1	538.4	541.9	540.3	540.0	537.6	532.4
Trade, Transportation, and Utilities													
2000	116.3	115.6	116.8	118.4	119.7	121.5	121.9	123.8	123.8	123.5	124.8	124.6	120.9
2001	115.5	114.6	115.4	115.7	116.7	117.6	115.9	116.3	116.5	116.0	117.3	117.7	116.3
2002	113.0	112.1	112.8	114.1	115.3	116.1	115.9	116.4	116.5	116.2	117.9	118.4	115.4
2003	113.3	112.5	113.4	113.8	114.5	115.6	115.7	116.5	116.5	116.2	118.0	118.8	115.4
2004	113.4	113.0	114.2	115.9	117.4	118.4	118.8	118.8	118.6	119.2	121.1	122.2	117.6
2005	117.7	117.7	118.9	120.3	121.3	122.7	123.8	124.5	124.8	124.5	126.7	127.8	122.6
2006	122.9	122.6	123.7	125.3	126.6	128.3	128.1	129.1	129.5	129.6	131.9	132.9	127.5
2007	128.8	128.6	130.1	130.4	131.6	133.4	133.0	133.7	133.3	133.7	135.3	135.1	132.3
Wholesale Trade													
2000	24.7	24.7	25.0	25.3	25.4	25.6	25.5	25.4	25.7	25.4	25.4	25.4	25.3
2001	24.8	24.8	25.1	25.1	25.2	25.2	24.6	24.3	24.6	24.6	24.6	24.4	24.8
2002	23.9	24.1	24.3	24.5	24.7	24.8	24.6	24.4	24.7	24.5	24.7	24.4	24.5
2003	23.8	23.9	23.9	24.4	24.5	24.5	24.6	24.4	24.6	24.0	24.2	24.3	24.3
2004	23.8	24.0	24.4	24.7	24.9	25.1	25.4	25.4	25.5	25.4	25.5	25.4	25.0
2005	25.7	25.9	26.4	26.6	26.6	26.6	26.8	26.7	27.0	26.7	26.8	26.8	26.6
2006	26.1	26.4	26.7	27.0	27.1	27.3	27.1	27.1	27.3	27.1	27.4	27.4	27.0
2007	27.2	27.5	27.7	27.8	28.1	28.4	28.3	28.4	28.5	28.5	28.5	28.5	28.1

Employment by Industry: Idaho, 2000–2007—*Continued*

(Numbers in thousands, not seasonally adjusted.)

Industry and year	January	February	March	April	May	June	July	August	September	October	November	December	Annual Average
Retail Trade													
2000	73.4	72.7	73.7	74.9	76.1	77.1	77.6	79.1	78.9	78.8	80.3	79.6	76.9
2001	71.8	71.1	71.5	71.8	72.6	73.3	72.4	72.8	72.6	72.3	73.8	74.5	72.5
2002	70.9	69.7	70.3	71.3	72.2	72.7	72.9	73.1	72.8	72.5	74.2	75.0	72.3
2003	70.8	70.1	70.9	71.2	71.8	72.6	72.5	73.2	72.9	73.1	74.8	75.4	72.4
2004	71.0	70.5	71.1	72.5	73.7	74.2	74.4	74.4	74.0	74.6	76.4	77.4	73.7
2005	73.4	73.0	73.8	74.9	75.9	76.9	77.5	78.1	78.0	77.9	80.0	80.8	76.7
2006	77.3	76.6	77.5	78.5	79.7	80.7	80.9	81.6	81.7	82.0	83.9	84.5	80.4
2007	81.1	80.6	82.1	82.1	82.9	84.2	84.0	84.2	83.6	83.9	85.6	85.6	83.3
Transportation and Utilities													
2000	18.2	18.2	18.1	18.2	18.2	18.8	18.8	19.3	19.2	19.3	19.1	19.6	18.8
2001	18.9	18.7	18.8	18.8	18.9	19.1	18.9	19.2	19.3	19.1	18.9	18.8	18.9
2002	18.2	18.3	18.2	18.3	18.4	18.6	18.4	18.9	19.0	19.2	19.0	19.0	18.6
2003	18.7	18.5	18.6	18.2	18.2	18.5	18.6	18.9	19.0	19.1	19.0	19.1	18.7
2004	18.6	18.5	18.7	18.7	18.8	19.1	19.0	19.0	19.1	19.2	19.2	19.4	18.9
2005	18.6	18.8	18.7	18.8	18.8	19.2	19.5	19.7	19.8	19.9	19.9	20.2	19.3
2006	19.5	19.6	19.5	19.8	19.8	20.3	20.1	20.4	20.5	20.5	20.6	21.0	20.1
2007	20.5	20.5	20.3	20.5	20.6	20.8	20.7	21.1	21.2	21.3	21.2	21.0	20.8
Information													
2000	9.3	9.4	9.7	9.4	9.6	9.8	9.8	9.8	9.8	9.7	9.7	9.8	9.7
2001	9.6	9.7	9.7	9.6	9.6	9.8	9.7	9.8	9.5	9.4	9.4	9.4	9.6
2002	9.2	9.1	9.1	9.2	9.3	9.3	9.1	9.1	9.1	9.1	9.3	9.3	9.2
2003	9.1	9.1	9.1	9.2	9.2	9.2	9.1	9.1	9.1	9.1	9.3	9.3	9.2
2004	9.2	9.2	9.3	9.4	9.7	10.0	10.0	10.1	9.9	9.9	9.9	9.9	9.7
2005	10.0	10.1	10.1	10.3	10.4	10.4	10.5	10.3	10.3	10.5	10.4	10.6	10.3
2006	10.3	10.3	10.3	10.5	10.6	10.8	10.8	10.8	10.7	10.6	10.7	10.8	10.6
2007	10.6	10.6	10.7	10.8	10.9	11.1	11.0	11.0	10.9	10.9	10.9	10.9	10.9
Financial Activities													
2000	24.9	24.9	24.9	25.1	25.2	25.4	25.3	25.4	25.4	25.1	25.2	25.1	25.2
2001	24.2	24.2	24.5	24.8	24.9	25.2	25.4	25.7	25.2	25.1	25.1	25.4	25.0
2002	25.1	25.2	25.3	25.3	25.7	25.8	26.3	26.3	26.1	26.1	26.2	26.4	25.8
2003	26.1	26.1	26.3	26.5	26.8	27.2	27.5	27.6	27.4	27.4	27.3	27.6	27.0
2004	26.9	27.0	27.4	27.6	27.7	28.0	28.3	28.3	28.4	28.5	28.5	28.8	28.0
2005	28.3	28.5	28.4	28.8	29.1	29.6	30.2	30.4	30.5	30.5	30.7	30.8	29.7
2006	30.5	30.7	31.1	31.4	31.6	31.9	32.2	32.4	32.3	32.0	32.0	32.3	31.7
2007	31.8	31.9	32.0	32.5	32.9	33.0	33.0	32.8	32.4	32.6	32.6	31.9	32.5
Professional and Business Services													
2000	55.6	56.2	57.9	58.9	60.3	62.1	61.7	62.7	63.4	63.1	63.4	62.6	60.7
2001	64.0	63.9	65.8	66.7	68.2	69.4	69.1	71.1	69.6	68.5	68.1	67.1	67.6
2002	63.7	64.5	65.5	68.5	69.1	70.8	70.8	71.9	71.2	71.7	70.8	69.9	69.0
2003	66.2	67.0	68.2	69.3	69.9	71.5	70.7	72.1	71.9	70.9	70.5	70.3	69.9
2004	67.1	68.1	69.8	72.0	73.5	75.4	75.3	76.1	75.7	75.1	74.9	74.8	73.2
2005	71.5	73.3	74.5	77.0	78.0	79.1	79.8	80.7	80.6	78.9	79.3	78.8	77.6
2006	76.0	77.3	78.8	80.9	82.6	83.9	83.3	84.3	83.8	81.9	81.9	81.0	81.3
2007	77.5	78.8	80.2	82.9	84.0	85.6	85.3	86.4	85.6	84.5	83.7	82.5	83.1
Education and Health Services													
2000	51.3	51.9	52.2	52.3	51.4	51.8	51.7	52.3	53.9	54.3	54.7	55.3	52.8
2001	54.9	55.8	56.2	57.0	55.7	56.1	56.0	56.6	58.1	58.5	59.1	59.6	56.9
2002	58.6	58.9	59.4	59.8	58.9	59.1	59.0	59.1	60.4	60.8	61.3	61.6	59.7
2003	61.3	61.4	61.7	62.3	61.6	61.8	61.6	61.8	63.2	63.4	64.0	64.1	62.4
2004	63.2	64.0	64.6	65.2	64.4	65.0	64.4	64.6	66.3	67.0	67.6	67.3	65.3
2005	66.9	67.5	67.4	67.8	67.0	67.1	66.6	67.1	68.4	68.3	68.6	68.6	67.6
2006	67.8	68.5	69.2	69.2	68.8	68.8	69.9	70.4	71.8	72.1	72.7	72.7	70.2
2007	71.7	72.5	72.8	72.9	73.4	73.8	73.2	73.8	74.4	74.3	74.9	74.9	73.6
Leisure and Hospitality													
2000	48.5	49.2	50.2	52.1	52.2	55.1	56.7	57.3	55.8	51.6	50.6	51.4	52.6
2001	50.0	50.6	51.7	52.3	53.2	55.9	56.8	57.2	55.3	51.7	50.6	51.3	53.0
2002	49.5	50.0	50.8	52.1	53.1	56.0	57.2	57.8	56.3	53.4	51.2	51.9	53.2
2003	51.4	51.4	52.4	52.8	54.1	56.8	58.3	59.2	56.9	53.9	52.1	53.4	54.4
2004	52.5	53.0	53.8	54.0	55.7	58.7	59.6	60.1	58.2	54.4	53.4	54.2	55.6
2005	54.0	53.7	54.7	55.4	57.0	59.8	61.5	62.0	60.1	56.5	55.4	56.6	57.2
2006	55.7	56.2	57.2	58.2	59.6	62.3	63.6	64.5	62.5	59.4	58.2	59.6	59.8
2007	58.7	59.4	60.7	61.4	63.4	66.9	67.7	68.4	66.2	63.0	61.8	62.3	63.3
Other Services													
2000	17.1	17.3	17.5	17.7	18.1	18.1	18.1	18.2	17.9	17.7	17.7	18.1	17.8
2001	17.8	18.0	18.3	18.3	18.3	18.6	18.5	18.5	18.1	17.8	17.7	17.7	18.1
2002	17.3	17.6	18.1	18.0	18.0	18.2	18.6	18.7	18.1	18.1	18.0	17.9	18.1
2003	17.7	17.8	18.0	18.1	18.1	18.3	18.5	18.7	18.2	18.0	18.0	18.0	18.1
2004	17.7	17.8	18.1	18.4	18.4	18.6	18.9	18.9	18.3	18.1	18.1	18.1	18.3
2005	17.9	18.1	18.1	18.3	18.4	18.6	19.1	19.0	18.5	18.5	18.5	18.4	18.5
2006	18.3	18.5	18.6	18.8	18.9	19.3	19.7	19.7	19.2	19.0	18.9	19.0	19.0
2007	18.7	18.9	19.2	19.3	19.5	19.8	20.0	20.1	19.6	19.3	19.3	19.3	19.4
Government													
2000	105.0	107.8	108.7	111.1	115.0	110.9	104.1	103.2	108.2	110.8	110.6	109.9	108.8
2001	105.6	109.7	110.8	111.3	112.5	110.7	105.2	104.5	111.2	113.9	113.4	112.6	110.1
2002	109.4	112.0	113.2	113.3	114.5	114.3	106.8	105.6	112.0	114.5	114.7	113.9	112.0
2003	110.6	112.6	114.1	113.3	115.5	115.1	107.8	106.8	113.9	115.9	115.4	114.6	113.0
2004	110.4	114.1	114.9	116.1	116.8	114.6	108.9	108.6	115.5	117.4	117.2	115.9	114.2
2005	112.1	115.9	116.6	116.8	117.4	116.1	109.1	108.8	116.7	118.1	117.8	116.5	115.2
2006	114.0	117.4	117.8	118.6	119.3	117.3	110.0	109.6	116.4	118.4	117.8	116.5	116.1
2007	113.1	116.8	117.2	118.2	119.3	118.0	110.9	112.2	119.5	122.0	121.5	120.7	117.5

Average Weekly Hours by Selected Industry: Idaho, 2001–2007

(Not seasonally adjusted.)

Industry and year	January	February	March	April	May	June	July	August	September	October	November	December	Annual Average
Manufacturing													
2001	39.2	39.2	39.4	39.1	39.0	38.6	38.5	38.5	39.7	39.3	39.0	39.6	39.1
2002	38.4	37.8	38.8	38.8	39.4	39.6	38.4	37.9	42.0	40.6	40.6	42.3	39.6
2003	39.1	38.8	40.9	40.5	42.4	43.6	42.1	42.1	41.5	41.0	41.7	41.5	41.3
2004	41.2	40.3	40.6	40.8	41.3	40.5	39.8	40.2	40.5	40.9	40.5	39.6	40.5
2005	38.6	38.4	38.4	39.6	40.7	41.1	40.4	40.5	41.2	43.0	40.8	40.4	40.3
2006	39.1	38.9	40.6	41.2	40.8	42.9	41.5	40.7	41.6	42.2	44.1	46.1	41.7
2007	42.2	42.2	41.6	39.8	42.4	42.3	40.5	41.1	41.5	40.6	41.1	41.1	41.4

Average Hourly Earnings by Selected Industry: Idaho, 2001–2007

(Dollars, not seasonally adjusted.)

Industry and year	January	February	March	April	May	June	July	August	September	October	November	December	Annual Average
Manufacturing													
2001	13.72	13.78	13.42	13.63	13.78	13.58	13.83	13.93	14.20	14.13	14.29	14.00	13.85
2002	14.14	14.06	13.77	13.84	13.87	13.90	13.84	13.79	13.83	13.58	13.48	13.53	13.80
2003	13.56	13.78	13.78	13.58	13.74	13.79	13.84	13.94	13.94	13.72	13.50	13.70	13.72
2004	13.75	13.97	13.84	14.12	13.92	14.17	14.35	14.35	14.47	14.16	14.31	14.34	14.15
2005	14.22	14.36	14.43	14.49	14.59	14.40	14.79	15.02	15.13	15.32	16.08	16.44	14.96
2006	16.62	16.77	16.20	16.36	16.33	16.37	17.08	17.51	17.24	17.29	16.90	17.76	16.89
2007	18.55	18.31	18.46	19.71	18.39	18.75	19.04	19.31	19.47	19.49	19.30	19.55	19.02

Average Weekly Earnings by Selected Industry: Idaho, 2001–2007

(Dollars, not seasonally adjusted.)

Industry and year	January	February	March	April	May	June	July	August	September	October	November	December	Annual Average
Manufacturing													
2001	537.82	540.18	528.75	532.93	537.42	524.19	532.46	536.31	563.74	555.31	557.31	554.40	541.54
2002	542.98	531.47	534.28	536.99	546.48	550.44	531.46	522.64	580.86	551.35	547.29	572.32	546.48
2003	530.20	534.66	555.42	547.16	582.58	601.24	582.66	586.87	578.51	562.52	562.95	568.55	566.64
2004	566.50	562.99	561.90	576.10	574.90	573.89	571.13	576.87	586.04	579.14	579.56	567.86	573.08
2005	548.89	551.42	554.11	573.80	593.81	591.84	597.52	608.31	623.36	658.76	656.06	664.18	602.89
2006	649.84	652.35	657.72	674.03	666.26	702.27	708.82	712.66	717.18	729.64	745.29	818.74	704.31
2007	782.81	772.68	767.94	784.46	779.74	793.13	771.12	793.64	808.01	791.29	793.23	803.51	787.43

Population
 2000 census: 12,419,293
 2007 estimate: 12,852,548
 Percent change, 2000–2007: 3.5%

Percent change in total nonfarm employment, 2000–2007: -1.0%

Industry with the largest growth in employment, 2000–2007 (thousands)
 Education and health services, 98.2

Industry with the largest decline in employment, 2000–2007 (thousands)
 Manufacturing, -194.6

Civilian labor force
 2000: 6,467,692
 2007: 6,697,382

Employment-population ratio
 2000: 66.1%
 2007: 64.8%

Unemployment rate and rank among states
 2000: 4.5%, 38th
 2007: 5.0%, 39th

Employment by Industry, 2007

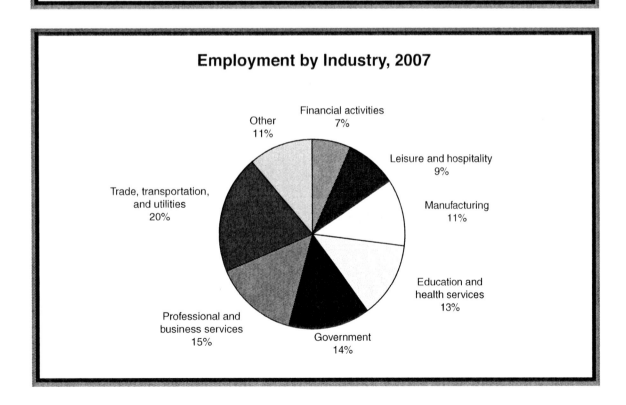

Other 11%

Financial activities 7%

Leisure and hospitality 9%

Trade, transportation, and utilities 20%

Manufacturing 11%

Education and health services 13%

Professional and business services 15%

Government 14%

Employment by Industry: Illinois, 2000–2007

(Numbers in thousands, not seasonally adjusted.)

Industry and year	January	February	March	April	May	June	July	August	September	October	November	December	Annual Average
Total Nonfarm													
2000	5,874.4	5,906.8	5,973.3	6,025.9	6,078.8	6,124.8	6,061.6	6,080.5	6,095.3	6,092.5	6,115.2	6,108.5	6,044.8
2001	5,906.2	5,930.3	5,977.0	6,016.0	6,060.4	6,093.1	6,013.3	6,012.8	6,006.1	5,976.1	5,977.2	5,974.4	5,995.2
2002	5,778.6	5,781.4	5,819.3	5,875.3	5,921.8	5,948.7	5,897.0	5,910.8	5,914.5	5,914.1	5,926.8	5,918.3	5,883.9
2003	5,713.0	5,712.1	5,742.5	5,797.6	5,843.1	5,869.6	5,829.7	5,839.2	5,843.1	5,845.7	5,842.4	5,851.7	5,810.8
2004	5,666.8	5,673.3	5,723.9	5,789.2	5,842.7	5,877.9	5,855.2	5,855.0	5,854.9	5,872.1	5,882.2	5,897.6	5,815.9
2005	5,700.8	5,716.3	5,756.8	5,844.9	5,886.3	5,904.9	5,905.1	5,907.1	5,921.3	5,922.6	5,938.7	5,938.4	5,861.9
2006	5,774.8	5,798.4	5,845.0	5,904.9	5,953.7	6,003.7	5,966.3	5,972.5	5,982.5	5,987.1	6,002.3	6,001.7	5,932.7
2007	5,843.2	5,845.5	5,903.2	5,960.7	6,018.2	6,052.5	6,011.5	6,013.6	6,024.3	6,029.2	6,042.1	6,033.1	5,981.4
Total Private													
2000	5,057.8	5,065.8	5,123.3	5,178.3	5,216.7	5,278.9	5,251.7	5,274.2	5,261.9	5,243.1	5,258.7	5,251.9	5,205.2
2001	5,079.7	5,077.5	5,120.1	5,159.7	5,196.0	5,242.0	5,188.1	5,194.2	5,158.0	5,111.7	5,108.2	5,103.3	5,144.9
2002	4,932.8	4,915.3	4,946.8	4,999.5	5,040.3	5,083.5	5,069.0	5,088.1	5,064.3	5,042.3	5,049.9	5,043.0	5,022.9
2003	4,865.9	4,846.5	4,874.2	4,927.0	4,972.7	5,013.4	5,001.6	5,019.4	5,002.8	4,988.6	4,983.8	4,995.5	4,957.6
2004	4,829.6	4,821.1	4,867.3	4,934.3	4,988.1	5,036.6	5,034.4	5,039.2	5,021.2	5,016.1	5,022.6	5,044.8	4,971.3
2005	4,867.8	4,865.2	4,900.7	4,990.7	5,029.1	5,067.8	5,078.7	5,085.9	5,076.4	5,067.1	5,079.2	5,084.0	5,016.1
2006	4,942.5	4,945.0	4,988.3	5,050.2	5,095.7	5,158.7	5,146.2	5,157.4	5,136.8	5,133.3	5,144.4	5,148.9	5,087.3
2007	5,008.2	4,988.7	5,043.8	5,099.9	5,156.6	5,207.5	5,189.4	5,196.3	5,168.8	5,162.4	5,175.6	5,172.9	5,130.8
Goods-Producing													
2000	1,112.9	1,115.9	1,132.6	1,150.3	1,160.8	1,174.3	1,169.7	1,170.9	1,166.6	1,159.9	1,154.2	1,134.0	1,150.1
2001	1,091.1	1,093.2	1,102.0	1,113.9	1,122.0	1,131.3	1,114.4	1,114.7	1,106.3	1,092.2	1,082.5	1,068.2	1,102.7
2002	1,020.9	1,015.9	1,023.0	1,037.9	1,047.3	1,060.2	1,055.9	1,059.7	1,055.8	1,048.5	1,041.8	1,026.8	1,041.1
2003	982.6	975.7	982.6	999.2	1,009.1	1,018.3	1,013.7	1,016.3	1,010.5	999.8	990.7	981.5	998.3
2004	939.1	934.1	948.0	967.5	982.5	996.7	996.6	997.1	996.3	992.4	987.8	980.7	976.6
2005	931.9	931.2	940.0	963.7	974.0	984.9	984.1	985.2	984.0	980.1	976.5	963.5	966.6
2006	935.7	935.2	942.7	964.8	973.9	991.2	987.9	988.5	985.5	981.3	975.7	964.0	968.9
2007	931.2	918.6	936.6	953.5	967.0	980.4	974.8	974.4	969.3	963.5	962.1	951.5	956.9
Natural Resources and Mining													
2000	9.7	9.5	9.7	9.8	9.8	9.9	10.0	10.0	10.0	10.1	10.1	9.9	9.8
2001	9.4	9.4	9.8	10.0	10.1	10.2	10.4	10.2	10.2	10.1	10.1	10.0	10.0
2002	9.6	9.5	9.7	9.6	9.6	9.8	9.7	9.7	9.7	9.8	9.7	9.7	9.7
2003	9.1	9.1	9.3	9.6	9.6	9.8	9.4	9.5	9.5	9.5	9.5	9.3	9.4
2004	8.6	8.6	9.0	9.3	9.5	9.7	9.7	9.7	9.8	9.5	9.6	9.5	9.4
2005	8.8	8.9	9.2	9.6	9.8	10.1	10.2	10.2	10.3	10.4	10.4	10.4	9.9
2006	10.0	9.9	10.0	10.1	10.4	10.6	10.5	10.3	10.3	10.4	10.3	10.2	10.3
2007	9.7	9.7	10.0	10.1	10.4	10.6	10.4	10.2	9.9	9.9	9.9	9.7	10.0
Construction													
2000	234.8	234.6	248.2	266.1	276.3	285.2	287.1	289.7	286.6	284.7	279.6	263.8	269.7
2001	239.0	241.5	252.3	272.0	284.5	293.0	295.5	297.6	292.8	291.1	289.4	278.9	277.3
2002	246.4	244.1	251.4	268.3	278.9	289.5	295.2	298.3	296.4	295.4	289.9	276.9	277.6
2003	246.8	240.8	248.2	268.1	280.1	289.4	295.1	297.7	294.0	287.4	280.1	270.1	274.8
2004	238.8	233.7	245.1	263.4	274.8	283.7	287.7	287.4	286.0	285.6	281.2	273.4	270.1
2005	236.7	235.7	243.1	263.5	273.8	281.6	285.0	285.8	285.6	284.8	280.5	266.4	268.5
2006	245.2	244.7	252.9	272.5	281.8	292.3	292.1	293.6	289.9	287.9	281.7	269.0	275.3
2007	244.5	233.6	249.8	266.5	279.3	288.1	288.3	288.4	285.2	283.3	278.8	266.4	271.0
Manufacturing													
2000	868.4	871.8	874.7	874.4	874.7	879.2	872.6	871.2	870.0	865.1	864.5	860.3	870.5
2001	842.7	842.3	839.9	831.9	827.4	828.1	808.5	806.9	803.3	791.0	783.0	779.3	815.4
2002	764.9	762.3	761.9	760.0	758.8	760.9	751.0	751.7	749.7	743.3	742.2	740.2	753.9
2003	726.7	725.8	725.1	721.5	719.4	719.1	709.2	709.1	707.0	702.9	701.1	702.1	714.1
2004	691.7	691.8	693.9	694.8	698.2	703.3	699.2	700.0	700.5	697.3	697.0	697.8	697.1
2005	686.4	686.6	687.7	690.6	690.4	693.2	688.9	689.2	688.1	684.9	685.6	686.7	688.2
2006	680.5	680.6	679.8	682.2	681.7	688.3	685.3	684.6	685.3	683.0	683.7	684.8	683.3
2007	677.0	675.3	676.8	676.9	677.3	681.7	676.1	675.8	674.2	670.3	673.4	675.4	675.9
Service-Providing													
2000	4,761.5	4,790.9	4,840.7	4,875.6	4,918.0	4,950.5	4,891.9	4,909.6	4,928.7	4,932.6	4,961.0	4,974.5	4,894.6
2001	4,815.1	4,837.1	4,875.0	4,902.1	4,938.4	4,961.8	4,898.9	4,898.1	4,899.8	4,883.9	4,894.7	4,906.2	4,892.6
2002	4,757.7	4,765.5	4,796.3	4,837.4	4,874.5	4,888.5	4,841.1	4,851.1	4,858.7	4,865.6	4,885.0	4,891.5	4,842.7
2003	4,730.4	4,736.4	4,759.9	4,798.4	4,834.0	4,851.3	4,816.0	4,822.9	4,832.6	4,845.9	4,851.7	4,870.2	4,812.5
2004	4,727.7	4,739.2	4,775.9	4,821.7	4,860.2	4,881.2	4,858.6	4,857.9	4,858.6	4,879.7	4,894.4	4,916.9	4,839.3
2005	4,768.9	4,785.1	4,816.8	4,881.2	4,912.3	4,920.0	4,921.0	4,921.9	4,937.3	4,942.5	4,962.2	4,974.9	4,895.3
2006	4,839.1	4,863.2	4,902.3	4,940.1	4,979.8	5,012.5	4,978.4	4,984.0	4,997.0	5,005.8	5,026.6	5,037.7	4,963.9
2007	4,912.0	4,926.9	4,966.6	5,007.2	5,051.2	5,072.1	5,036.7	5,039.2	5,055.0	5,065.7	5,080.0	5,081.6	5,024.5
Trade, Transportation, and Utilities													
2000	1,232.7	1,220.7	1,226.6	1,231.2	1,238.7	1,246.8	1,242.8	1,249.5	1,249.3	1,256.9	1,280.0	1,295.7	1,247.6
2001	1,241.9	1,225.7	1,230.2	1,233.2	1,236.7	1,242.1	1,225.1	1,224.0	1,221.6	1,217.0	1,234.9	1,246.2	1,231.6
2002	1,194.2	1,176.7	1,182.1	1,186.3	1,193.8	1,198.7	1,192.2	1,195.6	1,196.6	1,200.7	1,220.0	1,235.1	1,197.8
2003	1,180.2	1,168.0	1,171.1	1,173.2	1,181.7	1,186.2	1,173.0	1,177.0	1,178.7	1,185.8	1,201.8	1,217.3	1,182.8
2004	1,164.7	1,153.2	1,159.7	1,167.1	1,179.1	1,184.7	1,176.7	1,178.6	1,180.0	1,188.3	1,206.5	1,222.3	1,180.1
2005	1,170.9	1,159.2	1,166.4	1,176.0	1,184.5	1,188.6	1,184.2	1,187.0	1,188.4	1,193.0	1,213.1	1,230.2	1,186.8
2006	1,182.0	1,171.7	1,179.7	1,185.1	1,195.2	1,203.4	1,195.6	1,197.5	1,197.8	1,203.0	1,226.4	1,242.2	1,198.3
2007	1,201.3	1,185.7	1,196.3	1,196.2	1,210.3	1,218.2	1,211.0	1,211.3	1,212.2	1,213.5	1,235.0	1,250.1	1,211.8
Wholesale Trade													
2000	315.9	316.3	318.2	319.5	321.0	323.6	322.9	322.5	321.9	322.6	322.2	323.2	320.8
2001	316.8	316.5	317.6	319.8	319.8	320.7	318.2	317.4	315.9	312.7	312.1	311.8	316.6
2002	305.7	305.0	305.9	307.0	307.9	310.4	308.1	307.8	307.3	307.3	307.7	307.7	307.3
2003	303.6	303.2	304.2	304.2	305.0	305.6	303.9	302.4	301.2	300.8	300.8	301.0	303.0
2004	296.0	295.4	297.1	298.9	301.0	302.6	301.6	301.0	300.3	301.5	301.6	302.4	300.0
2005	296.7	296.9	299.5	302.0	303.1	305.2	305.2	304.7	304.7	304.7	305.4	306.6	302.9
2006	303.2	303.3	305.2	306.7	308.4	311.2	309.7	308.9	308.3	308.8	308.8	310.0	307.7
2007	305.9	305.5	307.6	309.2	311.1	314.2	312.8	312.1	311.8	311.5	311.0	312.1	310.4

Employment by Industry: Illinois, 2000–2007—*Continued*

(Numbers in thousands, not seasonally adjusted.)

Industry and year	January	February	March	April	May	June	July	August	September	October	November	December	Annual Average
Retail Trade													
2000	644.4	632.8	636.2	637.2	642.2	648.6	645.7	650.4	648.3	654.0	676.8	690.7	650.6
2001	650.5	636.2	638.6	638.1	640.9	647.5	637.0	637.4	633.9	634.2	655.4	669.4	643.3
2002	630.4	615.4	620.3	620.9	626.9	632.2	628.2	629.8	628.2	630.9	651.4	665.7	631.7
2003	621.0	611.1	613.4	614.7	621.0	626.4	620.3	623.5	622.1	627.5	643.7	658.8	625.3
2004	618.1	608.0	611.4	614.5	622.3	628.9	622.4	624.2	621.8	626.0	644.5	659.5	625.1
2005	619.9	608.1	611.4	617.0	623.2	626.6	625.8	627.4	624.1	627.3	645.4	659.3	626.3
2006	622.6	611.8	615.8	618.2	624.2	630.8	627.3	628.5	622.8	628.5	650.8	661.7	628.6
2007	632.8	618.0	624.5	623.4	633.0	638.8	636.4	635.6	631.9	634.3	655.4	666.9	635.9
Transportation and Utilities													
2000	272.4	271.6	272.2	274.5	275.5	274.6	274.2	276.6	279.1	280.3	281.0	281.8	276.1
2001	274.6	273.0	274.0	275.3	276.0	273.9	269.9	269.2	271.8	270.1	267.4	265.0	271.7
2002	258.1	256.3	255.9	258.4	259.0	256.1	255.9	258.0	261.1	262.5	261.9	261.7	258.7
2003	255.6	253.7	253.5	254.3	255.7	254.2	248.8	251.1	255.4	257.5	257.3	257.5	254.6
2004	250.6	249.8	251.2	253.7	255.8	253.2	252.7	253.4	257.9	260.8	260.4	260.4	255.0
2005	254.3	254.2	255.5	257.0	258.2	256.8	253.2	254.9	259.6	261.0	262.3	264.3	257.6
2006	256.2	256.6	258.7	260.2	262.6	261.4	258.6	260.1	266.7	265.7	266.8	270.5	262.0
2007	262.6	262.2	264.2	263.6	266.2	265.2	261.8	263.6	268.5	267.7	268.6	271.1	265.4
Information													
2000	143.9	144.4	145.8	145.8	147.0	148.5	148.9	149.5	147.8	148.7	150.0	150.8	147.6
2001	148.0	148.4	148.8	148.6	149.0	150.4	148.3	147.8	145.7	143.7	143.9	144.4	147.3
2002	141.3	140.6	140.4	140.3	140.0	139.6	136.7	136.2	133.5	133.0	132.5	132.0	137.2
2003	129.0	128.9	127.8	128.0	128.1	128.4	128.1	127.4	126.3	126.0	126.1	126.2	127.5
2004	122.2	122.1	121.8	121.6	121.7	121.8	121.1	120.4	118.9	119.2	119.3	120.0	120.8
2005	118.8	118.3	118.4	119.0	119.0	119.4	119.3	118.4	117.3	116.6	116.7	117.0	118.2
2006	116.4	116.0	116.2	116.9	117.1	117.4	117.1	116.3	115.1	115.3	115.3	115.9	116.3
2007	115.3	115.7	115.7	116.0	116.6	117.4	117.2	117.3	116.3	116.6	116.4	116.8	116.4
Financial Activities													
2000	403.0	402.8	402.6	402.1	402.7	407.4	406.2	406.8	402.1	402.8	403.1	407.6	404.1
2001	400.4	401.1	403.5	404.3	404.3	408.7	407.6	406.7	402.0	400.7	401.8	403.7	403.6
2002	398.7	398.3	399.1	398.2	399.4	403.3	402.7	402.9	400.1	400.2	401.3	403.7	400.7
2003	398.9	398.1	399.3	400.1	402.1	406.3	406.1	406.5	403.0	399.4	399.7	401.7	401.8
2004	396.7	396.2	398.0	397.0	398.6	402.5	403.0	403.0	399.1	398.7	398.8	401.7	399.4
2005	396.2	395.9	396.6	399.6	400.9	403.9	406.4	406.3	403.8	403.7	403.6	406.2	401.9
2006	401.0	401.1	402.4	403.2	404.5	408.1	408.6	408.7	405.6	406.0	405.7	407.3	405.2
2007	403.3	402.8	402.8	403.6	404.9	408.1	407.7	406.3	402.2	403.2	403.9	405.2	404.5
Professional and Business Services													
2000	799.5	807.1	822.3	839.0	843.5	859.3	855.3	865.2	863.3	856.3	853.7	848.0	842.7
2001	812.2	810.9	816.3	823.7	828.2	837.2	828.8	832.7	824.4	818.0	807.9	804.0	820.4
2002	771.2	769.7	773.2	789.7	792.8	799.3	802.8	810.9	806.4	799.3	795.5	786.8	791.5
2003	754.9	753.7	757.2	769.9	774.7	779.2	781.8	789.9	793.4	795.3	789.2	789.2	777.4
2004	758.5	762.3	771.0	791.9	798.3	810.7	813.5	817.1	815.8	815.5	811.8	817.8	798.7
2005	786.6	790.8	797.8	820.0	821.6	832.1	838.5	843.2	845.1	850.4	848.7	844.4	826.6
2006	815.2	819.1	830.0	847.3	852.4	866.4	866.5	873.1	870.6	874.9	870.2	865.2	854.2
2007	835.2	837.5	847.2	867.6	873.5	883.9	882.3	887.1	882.2	883.7	880.0	873.0	869.4
Education and Health Services													
2000	671.6	676.6	680.0	681.5	682.9	684.2	673.8	675.4	683.8	684.3	689.0	690.4	681.1
2001	682.2	688.5	694.9	696.8	698.0	697.7	692.0	695.5	702.4	703.2	706.7	707.9	697.2
2002	699.8	706.1	709.9	711.1	713.9	710.3	703.0	705.0	712.8	716.0	719.4	720.5	710.7
2003	709.0	712.2	716.0	715.6	717.9	716.7	712.7	715.1	720.5	724.8	727.2	728.7	718.0
2004	719.7	723.9	727.3	729.7	730.9	727.4	723.6	724.7	731.3	736.9	740.0	743.5	729.9
2005	734.6	738.3	740.1	745.5	746.9	741.7	740.8	740.8	748.8	752.4	755.1	757.2	745.2
2006	748.0	755.2	758.7	759.3	762.0	760.5	756.2	759.3	767.5	770.6	774.6	775.2	762.3
2007	765.9	773.8	777.4	777.7	779.0	777.3	772.9	774.3	782.4	789.8	790.4	790.5	779.3
Leisure and Hospitality													
2000	454.1	457.1	469.7	483.6	496.1	509.4	506.9	508.6	501.5	489.5	483.5	479.5	486.6
2001	459.6	463.5	475.1	490.5	506.3	518.3	514.4	516.1	504.0	488.0	480.2	477.9	491.2
2002	459.7	460.6	469.9	486.1	502.6	515.0	515.6	517.6	508.1	494.9	488.0	486.7	492.1
2003	464.7	463.5	471.5	492.3	509.2	522.0	520.8	521.7	513.7	501.0	493.6	494.0	497.3
2004	473.9	473.3	483.5	501.5	518.3	528.8	531.4	531.4	522.4	507.8	501.5	499.5	506.1
2005	476.4	478.5	487.0	511.0	525.4	534.8	537.8	537.7	530.9	514.3	508.4	506.4	512.4
2006	487.5	491.0	500.7	517.9	533.4	548.1	547.9	547.4	537.1	524.3	518.6	518.9	522.7
2007	500.7	499.2	509.4	527.2	545.0	556.2	553.7	555.7	544.0	531.4	524.5	521.0	530.7
Other Services													
2000	240.1	241.2	243.7	244.8	245.0	249.0	248.1	248.3	247.5	244.7	245.2	245.9	245.2
2001	244.3	246.2	249.3	250.1	251.5	256.3	257.5	256.7	251.6	248.9	250.3	251.0	251.1
2002	247.0	247.4	249.2	249.9	250.5	257.1	260.1	260.2	251.0	249.7	250.4	251.4	252.0
2003	246.6	246.4	248.7	248.7	249.9	256.3	265.4	265.5	256.7	256.5	255.5	256.9	254.4
2004	254.8	256.0	258.0	258.0	258.7	264.0	268.5	266.9	257.4	257.3	256.9	259.3	259.7
2005	252.4	253.0	254.4	255.9	256.8	262.4	267.6	267.3	258.1	256.6	257.1	259.1	258.4
2006	256.7	255.7	257.9	255.7	257.2	263.6	266.4	266.6	257.6	257.9	257.9	260.2	259.5
2007	255.3	255.4	258.4	258.1	260.3	266.0	269.8	269.9	260.2	260.7	263.3	264.8	261.9
Government													
2000	816.6	841.0	850.0	847.6	862.1	845.9	809.9	806.3	833.4	849.4	856.5	856.6	839.6
2001	826.5	852.8	856.9	856.3	864.4	851.1	825.2	818.6	848.1	864.4	869.0	871.1	850.4
2002	845.8	866.1	872.5	875.8	881.5	865.2	828.0	822.7	850.2	871.8	876.9	875.3	861.0
2003	847.1	865.6	868.3	870.6	870.4	856.2	828.1	819.8	840.3	857.1	858.6	856.2	853.2
2004	837.2	852.2	856.6	854.9	854.6	841.3	820.8	815.8	833.7	856.0	859.6	852.8	844.6
2005	833.0	851.1	856.1	854.2	857.2	837.1	826.4	821.2	844.9	855.5	859.5	854.4	845.9
2006	832.3	853.4	856.7	854.7	858.0	845.0	820.1	815.1	845.7	853.8	857.9	852.8	845.5
2007	835.0	856.8	859.4	860.8	861.6	845.0	822.1	817.3	855.5	866.8	866.5	860.2	850.6

Average Weekly Hours by Selected Industry: Illinois, 2001–2007

(Not seasonally adjusted.)

Industry and year	January	February	March	April	May	June	July	August	September	October	November	December	Annual Average
Construction													
2001	37.2	37.0	35.7	36.6	37.8	38.4	39.1	37.7	38.3	36.6	38.0	37.4	37.5
2002	36.3	36.4	36.8	35.9	36.3	36.8	38.1	37.5	38.9	38.9	38.2	37.9	37.4
2003	36.7	35.2	36.1	36.4	37.2	37.2	37.3	38.2	38.6	37.3	37.9	35.5	37.0
2004	36.5	36.4	36.4	37.8	36.4	36.5	38.2	38.3	37.0	38.2	38.4	36.2	37.2
2005	36.1	36.2	37.3	37.2	36.1	38.2	36.8	36.4	37.0	38.6	37.7	36.6	37.0
2006	35.9	36.3	36.7	37.3	37.1	38.0	37.6	38.4	37.9	39.2	39.1	39.1	37.8
2007	39.0	37.3	39.9	39.8	41.6	42.1	41.5	41.4	41.5	41.4	41.1	41.1	40.8
Manufacturing													
2001	41.2	40.9	40.7	39.3	41.0	41.2	40.8	41.2	41.7	41.0	41.2	41.7	41.0
2002	40.5	40.8	41.1	41.1	41.3	41.7	41.1	41.6	41.8	41.7	42.0	42.1	41.4
2003	40.6	40.5	40.4	40.1	40.5	40.6	39.6	40.6	41.0	40.7	41.1	41.6	40.6
2004	40.3	40.6	40.9	40.8	41.3	41.2	40.9	41.4	40.9	41.2	41.3	41.7	41.0
2005	41.1	40.5	40.7	40.5	40.5	40.8	40.6	40.8	41.1	41.2	41.0	41.1	40.8
2006	40.8	40.9	41.0	40.8	41.1	41.3	41.1	41.3	41.2	41.2	41.4	41.5	41.1
2007	41.0	40.8	41.1	40.8	41.2	41.3	40.8	41.0	41.1	41.1	41.1	41.2	41.0
Wholesale Trade													
2001	38.5	38.4	38.5	38.9	38.7	38.4	38.4	39.0	38.7	38.3	38.8	38.8	38.6
2002	38.2	38.3	38.6	38.6	39.4	39.8	39.1	39.1	39.7	39.6	39.0	39.5	39.1
2003	38.2	39.6	39.0	38.7	39.3	39.4	39.2	38.8	39.5	39.5	40.0	39.0	39.2
2004	38.6	39.2	39.4	39.8	39.9	39.1	39.0	39.8	40.3	39.4	39.7	39.6	39.5
2005	39.4	39.1	39.1	39.6	40.1	39.7	39.2	39.5	39.8	39.9	39.9	39.8	39.6
2006	40.0	39.8	39.6	39.8	39.6	39.8	39.7	39.5	39.6	39.6	39.6	39.6	39.7
2007	39.0	39.0	39.4	40.0	39.7	40.2	40.4	40.4	40.5	40.1	40.1	40.2	39.9
Retail Trade													
2001	28.3	28.1	28.2	28.6	28.8	29.1	29.7	30.5	30.4	29.6	29.8	30.6	29.3
2002	29.0	29.7	30.0	30.2	30.4	31.2	31.3	30.6	30.4	29.9	29.6	30.7	30.3
2003	28.7	29.1	29.3	29.4	29.8	30.3	30.3	30.2	29.8	29.6	29.6	30.3	29.7
2004	29.0	29.4	29.3	29.3	29.7	29.9	29.6	29.9	30.4	29.9	29.2	30.1	29.6
2005	29.4	29.6	29.7	30.0	30.1	30.3	30.6	30.1	30.6	30.0	30.4	30.8	30.1
2006	30.3	30.5	30.2	30.1	29.6	30.1	30.3	30.2	30.6	30.5	30.6	31.0	30.3
2007	29.1	28.7	29.1	28.9	28.9	29.5	29.4	29.6	29.8	29.7	30.2	30.2	29.4
Information													
2001	39.5	40.1	39.4	39.3	38.9	39.2	39.4	39.6	39.5	39.6	39.7	39.9	39.5
2002	39.7	40.1	39.7	39.6	39.4	39.1	39.2	38.6	37.6	37.8	37.6	37.1	38.8
2003	36.6	35.8	35.6	36.5	36.0	36.5	36.1	36.0	35.5	35.5	37.6	36.3	36.2
2004	36.7	36.8	36.0	36.2	36.9	36.6	37.2	36.8	36.1	36.5	36.7	35.5	36.5
2005	36.5	35.9	36.8	37.3	37.4	36.9	37.5	36.3	36.9	37.0	37.5	37.3	36.9
2006	37.6	36.9	37.2	37.5	37.3	37.5	37.2	37.1	37.6	37.7	37.5	37.4	37.4
2007	36.9	36.4	36.5	35.8	35.7	35.9	36.3	36.0	36.3	36.1	35.9	36.0	36.1
Financial Activities													
2001	34.4	34.9	34.9	35.8	35.3	35.8	35.7	35.0	35.6	35.0	34.9	36.1	35.3
2002	34.6	35.0	35.1	35.0	35.3	36.0	35.1	35.4	35.9	35.8	35.3	36.2	35.4
2003	36.1	36.9	36.9	36.0	36.0	37.1	36.1	36.0	35.7	35.8	36.9	36.0	36.3
2004	35.7	36.1	35.7	35.9	36.7	35.8	35.5	36.0	35.8	36.0	35.9	35.6	35.9
2005	36.5	36.1	36.0	36.2	36.8	35.8	35.6	35.5	36.0	35.9	35.8	35.9	36.0
2006	36.2	35.5	35.5	35.8	35.5	35.7	35.8	35.4	35.9	36.4	36.6	36.5	35.9
2007	36.6	36.9	36.6	37.5	37.2	37.1	38.0	37.9	38.0	37.7	37.7	37.8	37.4
Education and Health Services													
2001	33.1	32.9	33.0	33.2	33.4	33.2	33.5	33.2	33.7	33.1	33.3	33.9	33.3
2002	33.5	33.4	33.6	33.5	33.6	34.2	33.3	33.1	34.0	33.1	33.2	33.4	33.5
2003	32.8	33.3	33.2	32.8	32.7	33.0	32.7	32.4	32.3	32.0	32.8	32.2	32.7
2004	32.3	32.6	32.1	32.1	32.5	32.1	32.2	32.4	32.0	31.9	32.1	32.3	32.2
2005	32.9	32.4	32.5	32.2	32.5	32.2	32.9	32.7	33.1	32.9	33.2	33.2	32.7
2006	33.5	33.0	32.9	33.5	33.1	33.2	33.1	32.9	32.9	32.9	32.9	32.8	33.1
2007	32.7	32.5	32.7	33.2	33.0	33.0	33.6	33.7	33.8	33.9	34.1	34.0	33.3
Other Services													
2001	31.7	31.5	32.0	31.8	31.7	31.6	31.9	31.9	32.1	31.7	31.7	32.3	31.8
2002	31.4	31.1	31.3	31.4	32.1	32.9	31.5	31.6	32.2	31.4	31.2	32.0	31.7
2003	31.0	31.5	30.8	29.8	30.3	30.7	30.2	30.2	29.9	30.0	30.6	29.6	30.4
2004	29.6	30.5	30.1	30.6	31.2	30.7	30.7	31.0	30.6	31.1	30.8	30.3	30.6
2005	30.6	30.3	30.7	30.4	30.9	30.7	30.4	30.5	30.6	30.7	30.9	30.9	30.6
2006	31.3	31.0	31.0	31.5	31.0	31.9	31.9	32.0	32.1	32.6	32.5	32.6	31.8
2007	32.2	31.8	32.2	31.9	31.6	32.7	33.4	33.4	33.5	33.4	33.2	33.3	32.7

Average Hourly Earnings by Selected Industry: Illinois, 2001–2007

(Dollars, not seasonally adjusted.)

Industry and year	January	February	March	April	May	June	July	August	September	October	November	December	Annual Average
Construction													
2001	25.00	25.43	24.88	24.72	25.15	25.09	25.16	25.31	25.53	25.50	25.58	25.86	25.28
2002	25.61	26.09	25.86	26.08	25.85	26.06	26.21	26.43	26.54	26.49	26.33	26.24	26.17
2003	25.82	25.94	26.20	26.07	26.14	26.39	26.60	26.69	26.80	26.94	26.90	26.83	26.47
2004	26.68	26.87	27.14	27.16	26.85	26.97	27.14	27.37	27.41	27.51	27.68	27.75	27.23
2005	27.64	27.81	27.73	27.68	27.53	27.75	27.98	27.95	28.06	28.12	27.99	28.07	27.87
2006	28.14	28.27	28.52	28.50	28.47	28.55	28.64	28.83	28.96	29.01	29.06	29.08	28.69
2007	28.90	29.10	29.38	29.46	29.63	29.80	29.80	29.89	29.90	30.09	30.09	29.95	29.70
Manufacturing													
2001	14.39	14.37	14.36	14.52	14.56	14.69	14.79	14.75	14.90	14.81	14.86	14.94	14.66
2002	14.91	14.77	14.81	14.84	14.90	14.98	15.04	14.99	15.18	15.11	15.13	15.17	14.99
2003	15.18	15.07	15.07	15.10	15.16	15.21	15.12	15.20	15.35	15.21	15.34	15.41	15.20
2004	15.39	15.38	15.54	15.64	15.56	15.65	15.69	15.68	15.73	15.66	15.68	15.71	15.61
2005	15.74	15.71	15.74	15.68	15.87	15.91	16.01	15.88	15.91	15.91	15.84	15.92	15.84
2006	15.92	15.94	15.91	15.97	15.93	16.00	16.06	16.09	16.08	16.12	16.16	16.20	16.03
2007	16.29	16.18	16.31	16.38	16.37	16.52	16.57	16.66	16.67	16.68	16.54	16.49	16.47
Wholesale Trade													
2001	15.80	15.81	15.82	15.92	15.81	15.58	15.79	15.75	15.79	16.08	16.02	16.07	15.85
2002	16.12	16.11	16.18	16.13	16.21	16.14	15.87	15.94	15.78	15.85	15.72	15.88	15.99
2003	15.73	15.74	15.59	15.50	15.48	15.54	15.41	15.52	15.61	15.69	15.65	15.64	15.59
2004	15.81	16.12	15.99	15.93	16.20	16.06	16.06	16.23	16.24	16.29	16.23	16.31	16.12
2005	16.39	16.40	16.29	16.55	16.54	16.35	16.52	16.44	16.42	16.45	16.50	16.54	16.45
2006	16.52	16.64	16.48	16.54	16.47	16.55	16.63	16.68	16.70	16.77	16.85	16.90	16.65
2007	16.91	16.90	16.78	17.02	16.96	16.95	16.90	17.03	17.14	17.15	17.19	17.26	17.02
Retail Trade													
2001	10.73	10.97	11.07	10.99	10.88	10.86	10.84	10.95	11.10	11.10	11.17	11.06	10.97
2002	11.13	11.18	11.20	11.27	11.17	11.16	11.11	11.31	11.19	11.28	11.28	11.29	11.22
2003	11.35	11.35	11.28	11.26	11.20	11.21	11.16	11.21	11.18	11.08	11.13	10.98	11.19
2004	11.03	11.24	11.22	11.24	11.07	11.10	10.89	11.05	11.09	11.13	11.09	11.01	11.10
2005	11.08	11.16	11.19	11.29	11.33	11.41	11.40	11.42	11.51	11.45	11.43	11.42	11.34
2006	11.41	11.49	11.48	11.57	11.62	11.79	11.86	11.86	11.90	11.77	11.65	11.70	11.68
2007	11.80	11.81	12.06	12.04	12.15	12.10	12.20	12.07	12.16	12.15	11.93	11.98	12.04
Information													
2001	18.26	18.20	18.45	18.57	18.65	18.70	18.72	18.83	19.04	19.19	19.01	19.07	18.72
2002	19.22	19.25	19.12	19.25	19.27	19.20	19.20	18.76	18.93	18.57	19.04	18.66	19.05
2003	18.71	18.94	19.10	19.09	19.30	19.30	19.30	19.16	19.42	19.45	19.48	19.50	19.23
2004	19.60	19.85	20.00	19.86	20.09	20.13	20.30	20.51	20.55	20.59	20.45	20.55	20.21
2005	20.75	20.98	21.12	20.92	20.65	20.43	20.50	20.56	20.41	20.52	20.55	20.57	20.66
2006	20.52	20.42	20.58	20.79	20.70	20.53	20.61	20.70	20.48	20.50	20.77	20.80	20.62
2007	20.78	21.00	21.11	20.80	21.00	20.80	21.00	20.87	20.78	20.73	20.40	20.52	20.82
Financial Activities													
2001	15.82	15.95	15.95	15.99	15.95	15.87	15.97	15.98	16.09	16.14	16.22	16.26	16.02
2002	16.23	16.44	16.40	16.38	16.46	16.48	16.64	16.68	16.83	16.91	16.92	16.98	16.62
2003	17.11	17.34	17.28	17.17	16.99	17.14	17.27	17.34	17.34	17.37	17.32	17.36	17.25
2004	17.55	17.69	17.54	17.40	17.63	17.29	17.40	17.44	17.40	17.36	17.28	17.19	17.43
2005	17.19	17.10	17.15	17.18	17.39	17.25	17.29	17.30	17.35	17.36	17.37	17.34	17.27
2006	17.41	17.33	17.46	17.56	17.67	17.71	17.78	17.64	17.80	17.87	17.94	18.08	17.69
2007	18.18	18.38	18.61	18.77	18.59	18.77	18.94	19.17	19.30	19.37	19.55	19.60	18.94
Education and Health Services													
2001	13.93	13.94	13.92	14.05	13.94	14.00	14.17	14.18	14.34	14.34	14.36	14.33	14.13
2002	14.38	14.39	14.44	14.43	14.46	14.50	14.50	14.62	14.65	14.79	14.81	14.86	14.92	14.60
2003	14.86	14.94	14.93	14.96	14.99	15.03	15.12	15.13	15.16	15.21	15.23	15.25	15.07
2004	15.32	15.42	15.51	15.52	15.56	15.59	15.72	15.77	15.82	15.88	15.83	15.86	15.65
2005	15.78	15.78	15.83	15.86	15.82	15.89	15.96	15.95	16.16	16.20	16.20	16.18	15.97
2006	16.14	16.26	16.37	16.34	16.37	16.44	16.49	16.58	16.65	16.60	16.70	16.76	16.48
2007	16.66	16.70	16.78	16.78	16.85	16.90	16.89	16.87	16.92	16.92	16.95	16.92	16.85
Other Services													
2001	13.31	13.41	13.40	13.42	13.52	13.43	13.63	13.67	13.66	13.72	13.55	13.65	13.53
2002	13.65	13.49	13.52	13.40	13.51	13.59	13.61	13.75	13.88	13.85	14.02	13.92	13.69
2003	13.88	13.97	14.17	14.12	14.12	14.22	14.19	14.22	14.16	14.14	14.22	14.21	14.14
2004	14.36	14.36	14.13	14.19	14.37	14.19	14.29	14.39	14.33	14.35	14.36	14.37	14.31
2005	14.37	14.38	14.45	14.43	14.55	14.54	14.58	14.57	14.64	14.72	14.69	14.66	14.55
2006	14.71	14.37	14.55	14.57	14.52	14.58	14.62	14.54	14.62	14.69	14.75	14.79	14.61
2007	14.68	14.86	14.85	14.90	14.98	14.93	15.14	15.19	15.14	15.31	15.29	15.37	15.06

Average Weekly Earnings by Selected Industry: Illinois, 2001–2007

(Dollars, not seasonally adjusted.)

Industry and year	January	February	March	April	May	June	July	August	September	October	November	December	Annual Average
Construction													
2001	930.00	940.91	888.22	904.75	950.67	963.46	983.76	954.19	977.80	933.30	972.04	967.16	948.00
2002	929.64	949.68	951.65	936.27	938.36	959.01	998.60	991.13	1,032.41	1,030.46	1,005.81	994.50	978.76
2003	947.59	913.09	945.82	948.95	972.41	981.71	992.18	1,019.56	1,034.48	1,004.86	1,019.51	952.47	979.39
2004	973.82	978.07	987.90	1,026.65	977.34	984.41	1,036.75	1,048.27	1,014.17	1,050.88	1,062.91	1,004.55	1,012.96
2005	997.80	1,006.72	1,034.33	1,029.70	993.83	1,060.05	1,029.66	1,017.38	1,038.22	1,085.43	1,055.22	1,027.36	1,031.19
2006	1,010.23	1,026.20	1,046.68	1,063.05	1,056.24	1,084.90	1,076.86	1,107.07	1,097.58	1,137.19	1,136.25	1,137.03	1,084.48
2007	1,127.10	1,085.43	1,172.26	1,172.51	1,232.61	1,254.58	1,236.70	1,237.45	1,240.85	1,245.73	1,236.70	1,230.95	1,211.76
Manufacturing													
2001	592.87	587.73	584.45	570.64	596.96	605.23	603.43	607.70	621.33	607.21	612.23	623.00	601.06
2002	603.86	602.62	608.69	609.92	615.37	624.67	618.14	623.58	634.52	630.09	635.46	638.66	620.59
2003	616.31	610.34	608.83	605.51	613.98	617.53	598.75	617.12	629.35	619.05	630.47	641.06	617.12
2004	620.22	624.43	635.59	638.11	642.63	644.78	641.72	649.15	643.36	645.19	647.58	655.11	640.01
2005	646.91	636.26	640.62	635.04	642.74	649.13	650.01	647.90	653.90	655.49	649.44	654.31	646.27
2006	649.54	651.95	652.31	651.58	654.72	660.80	660.07	664.52	662.50	664.14	669.02	672.30	658.83
2007	667.89	660.14	670.34	668.30	674.44	682.28	676.06	683.06	685.14	685.55	679.79	679.39	675.00
Wholesale Trade													
2001	608.30	607.10	609.07	619.29	611.85	598.27	606.34	614.25	611.07	615.86	621.58	623.52	611.81
2002	615.78	617.01	624.55	622.62	638.67	642.37	620.52	623.25	626.47	627.66	613.08	627.26	625.21
2003	600.89	623.30	608.01	599.85	608.36	612.28	604.07	602.18	616.60	619.76	626.00	609.96	611.13
2004	610.27	631.90	630.01	634.01	646.38	627.95	626.34	645.95	654.47	641.83	644.33	645.88	636.74
2005	645.77	641.24	636.94	655.38	663.25	649.10	647.58	649.38	653.52	656.36	658.35	658.29	651.42
2006	660.80	662.27	652.61	658.29	652.21	658.69	660.21	658.86	661.32	664.09	667.26	669.24	661.01
2007	659.49	659.10	661.13	680.80	673.31	681.39	682.76	688.01	694.17	687.72	689.32	693.85	679.10
Retail Trade													
2001	303.66	308.26	312.17	314.31	313.34	316.03	321.95	333.98	337.44	328.56	332.87	338.44	321.42
2002	322.77	332.05	336.00	340.35	339.57	348.19	347.74	346.09	340.18	337.27	333.89	346.60	339.97
2003	325.75	330.29	330.50	331.04	333.76	339.66	338.15	338.54	333.16	327.97	329.45	332.69	332.34
2004	319.87	330.46	328.75	329.33	328.78	322.34	330.40	348.84	337.14	332.79	323.83	331.40	328.56
2005	325.75	330.34	332.34	338.70	341.03	345.72	348.84	343.74	352.21	343.50	347.47	351.74	341.33
2006	345.72	350.45	346.70	348.26	343.95	354.88	359.36	358.17	364.14	358.99	356.49	362.70	353.90
2007	343.38	338.95	350.95	347.96	351.14	356.95	358.68	357.27	362.37	360.86	360.29	361.80	353.98
Information													
2001	721.27	729.82	726.93	729.80	725.49	733.04	737.57	745.67	752.08	759.92	754.70	760.89	739.44
2002	763.03	771.93	759.06	762.30	759.24	750.72	752.64	724.14	711.77	701.95	715.90	692.29	739.14
2003	684.79	678.05	679.96	696.79	694.80	704.45	696.73	689.76	689.41	690.48	732.45	707.85	696.13
2004	719.32	730.48	720.00	718.93	741.32	736.76	755.16	754.77	741.86	751.54	750.52	729.53	737.67
2005	757.38	753.18	777.22	780.32	772.31	753.87	768.75	746.33	753.13	759.24	770.63	767.26	762.35
2006	771.55	753.50	765.58	779.63	772.11	769.88	766.69	767.97	770.05	772.85	778.88	777.92	771.19
2007	766.78	764.40	770.52	744.64	749.70	746.72	762.30	751.32	754.31	748.35	732.36	738.72	751.60
Financial Activities													
2001	544.21	556.66	556.66	572.44	563.04	568.15	570.13	559.30	572.80	564.90	566.08	586.99	565.51
2002	561.56	575.40	575.64	581.04	573.30	593.28	584.06	590.47	604.20	605.38	597.28	614.68	588.35
2003	617.67	639.85	637.63	618.12	611.64	635.89	623.45	624.24	619.04	621.85	639.11	624.96	626.18
2004	626.54	638.61	626.18	624.66	647.02	618.98	617.70	627.84	622.92	624.96	620.35	611.96	625.74
2005	627.44	617.31	617.31	621.92	639.95	617.55	615.52	614.15	624.60	623.22	621.85	622.51	621.72
2006	630.24	615.22	619.83	628.65	627.29	632.25	636.52	624.46	639.02	650.47	656.60	659.92	635.07
2007	665.39	678.22	681.13	703.88	691.55	696.37	719.72	726.54	733.40	730.25	737.04	740.88	708.36
Education and Health Services													
2001	461.08	458.63	459.36	466.46	465.60	464.80	474.70	470.78	483.26	474.65	478.19	485.79	470.53
2002	481.73	480.63	485.18	483.41	485.86	495.90	486.85	484.92	502.86	490.21	493.35	498.33	489.10
2003	487.41	497.50	495.68	490.69	490.17	495.99	494.42	490.21	489.67	486.72	499.54	491.05	492.79
2004	494.84	502.69	497.87	498.19	505.70	500.44	506.18	510.95	506.24	506.57	508.14	512.28	503.93
2005	519.16	511.27	514.48	510.69	514.15	511.66	525.08	521.57	534.90	532.98	537.84	537.18	522.22
2006	540.69	536.58	538.57	547.39	541.85	545.81	545.82	545.48	547.79	546.14	549.43	549.73	545.49
2007	544.78	542.75	548.71	557.10	556.05	557.70	567.50	568.52	571.90	573.59	578.00	575.28	561.11
Other Services													
2001	421.93	422.42	428.80	426.76	428.58	424.39	434.80	436.07	438.49	434.92	429.54	440.90	430.25
2002	428.61	419.54	423.18	420.76	433.67	447.11	428.72	434.50	446.94	434.89	437.42	445.44	433.97
2003	430.28	440.06	436.44	420.78	427.84	436.55	428.54	429.44	423.38	424.20	435.13	420.62	429.86
2004	425.06	437.98	425.31	434.21	448.34	435.63	438.70	446.09	438.50	446.29	442.29	435.41	437.89
2005	439.72	435.71	443.62	438.67	449.60	446.38	443.23	444.39	447.98	451.90	453.92	452.99	445.23
2006	460.42	445.47	451.05	458.96	450.12	465.10	466.38	465.28	469.30	478.89	479.38	482.15	464.60
2007	472.70	472.55	478.17	475.31	473.37	488.21	505.68	507.35	507.19	511.35	507.63	511.82	492.46

Population
    2000 census: 6,080,485
    2007 estimate: 6,345,289
    Percent change, 2000–2007: 4.4%

Percent change in total nonfarm employment, 2000–2007: -0.4%

Industry with the largest growth in employment, 2000–2007 (thousands)
    Education and health services, 65.6

Industry with the largest decline in employment, 2000–2007 (thousands)
    Manufacturing, -114.4

Civilian labor force
    2000: 3,144,379
    2007: 3,211,461

Employment-population ratio
    2000: 66.3%
    2007: 63.3%

Unemployment rate and rank among states
    2000: 2.9%, 10th
    2007: 4.5%, 27th

Employment by Industry, 2007

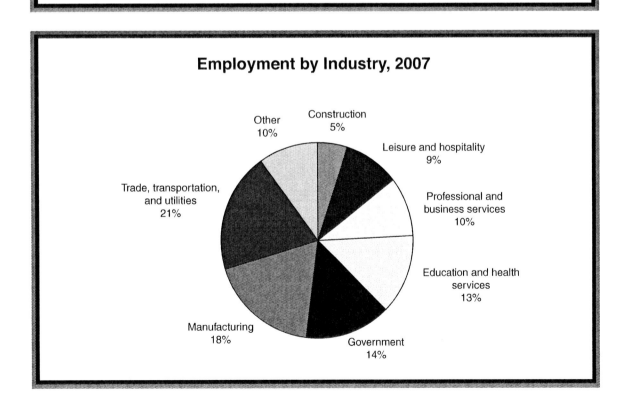

Other 10%
Construction 5%
Leisure and hospitality 9%
Professional and business services 10%
Trade, transportation, and utilities 21%
Education and health services 13%
Manufacturing 18%
Government 14%

Employment by Industry: Indiana, 2000–2007

(Numbers in thousands, not seasonally adjusted.)

Industry and year	January	February	March	April	May	June	July	August	September	October	November	December	Annual Average
Total Nonfarm													
2000	2,947.2	2,957.5	2,989.7	3,016.3	3,046.3	3,024.0	2,971.9	2,986.0	3,030.8	3,014.3	3,011.7	3,005.0	3,000.0
2001	2,901.7	2,915.7	2,937.1	2,959.2	2,969.7	2,949.5	2,892.6	2,918.5	2,953.7	2,938.8	2,935.3	2,928.8	2,933.4
2002	2,833.3	2,847.0	2,865.1	2,893.0	2,921.6	2,907.8	2,885.3	2,912.7	2,940.0	2,932.8	2,938.9	2,933.2	2,900.9
2003	2,846.3	2,849.6	2,868.9	2,894.4	2,919.4	2,896.1	2,854.0	2,887.2	2,922.5	2,936.4	2,935.7	2,933.2	2,895.3
2004	2,851.2	2,857.3	2,891.0	2,934.1	2,951.5	2,935.8	2,910.0	2,923.1	2,971.4	2,974.5	2,979.0	2,967.9	2,928.9
2005	2,882.2	2,900.6	2,923.1	2,963.7	2,974.5	2,956.2	2,925.3	2,940.6	2,997.9	3,000.0	3,003.7	2,994.0	2,955.2
2006	2,911.1	2,927.8	2,957.9	2,979.2	2,993.2	2,984.2	2,934.0	2,958.2	3,006.1	3,009.4	3,012.3	3,011.3	2,973.7
2007	2,921.6	2,924.6	2,965.4	2,989.2	3,010.1	3,000.1	2,955.8	2,992.3	3,021.1	3,025.9	3,030.6	3,020.8	2,988.1
Total Private													
2000	2,540.9	2,544.1	2,572.8	2,598.0	2,620.9	2,633.1	2,606.8	2,618.1	2,613.4	2,602.1	2,598.9	2,593.9	2,595.3
2001	2,492.4	2,492.9	2,511.4	2,534.7	2,549.6	2,559.3	2,532.2	2,543.9	2,534.1	2,514.2	2,510.6	2,505.3	2,523.4
2002	2,423.8	2,423.0	2,441.2	2,466.4	2,496.5	2,514.7	2,508.5	2,521.3	2,512.2	2,498.3	2,503.0	2,498.0	2,483.9
2003	2,427.7	2,418.6	2,435.1	2,462.9	2,486.4	2,493.0	2,475.3	2,495.2	2,490.8	2,497.4	2,496.8	2,493.7	2,472.7
2004	2,424.5	2,422.7	2,452.7	2,496.9	2,516.5	2,530.5	2,527.5	2,533.8	2,534.2	2,532.9	2,537.7	2,530.9	2,503.4
2005	2,453.4	2,461.4	2,484.1	2,524.7	2,538.5	2,553.3	2,545.3	2,553.8	2,558.8	2,557.1	2,562.9	2,556.3	2,529.1
2006	2,485.4	2,490.3	2,519.3	2,542.1	2,557.1	2,580.0	2,558.0	2,567.5	2,567.6	2,566.7	2,568.7	2,567.4	2,547.5
2007	2,493.6	2,484.0	2,521.4	2,548.0	2,572.4	2,590.1	2,572.9	2,579.9	2,578.1	2,577.8	2,583.2	2,574.9	2,556.4
Goods-Producing													
2000	810.7	811.4	818.8	825.7	831.5	838.2	831.8	834.3	827.6	817.1	809.6	800.3	821.4
2001	770.4	770.9	773.1	779.1	783.4	786.6	777.0	778.7	770.7	759.6	753.7	746.6	770.8
2002	723.6	724.0	729.0	735.7	744.1	754.3	753.2	757.8	752.9	745.6	742.7	734.6	741.5
2003	716.2	712.4	715.9	720.9	728.5	732.8	724.3	736.2	729.8	729.7	724.9	721.0	724.4
2004	703.2	701.6	710.5	723.6	732.6	740.0	735.2	741.7	738.8	734.2	730.4	726.6	726.5
2005	707.5	707.2	713.2	725.7	729.8	736.0	731.4	737.1	735.3	733.3	730.9	726.8	726.2
2006	710.2	707.8	715.8	723.6	728.1	738.2	729.9	734.1	727.9	724.3	718.9	716.1	722.9
2007	695.2	688.2	700.4	705.9	714.0	721.3	717.6	718.6	714.4	711.7	708.1	702.2	708.1
Natural Resources and Mining													
2000	6.5	6.5	6.6	6.8	6.9	6.9	6.9	6.9	6.9	6.8	6.8	6.7	6.7
2001	6.4	6.5	6.7	7.1	7.2	7.3	7.4	7.4	7.4	7.4	7.3	7.1	7.1
2002	6.8	6.9	7.0	7.2	7.2	7.3	7.2	7.2	7.2	7.1	7.0	7.0	7.1
2003	6.6	6.7	6.7	7.0	7.0	7.1	7.1	7.1	7.2	7.1	7.1	7.0	7.0
2004	6.8	6.7	7.0	7.3	7.4	7.4	7.3	7.3	7.2	6.9	6.9	6.8	7.1
2005	6.7	6.7	6.8	7.0	7.0	7.1	7.0	7.0	6.9	6.9	6.9	6.8	6.9
2006	6.5	6.5	6.6	7.0	7.1	7.2	7.2	7.1	7.1	7.1	7.0	7.0	7.0
2007	6.8	6.7	6.9	7.0	7.1	7.2	7.2	7.3	7.3	7.2	7.2	7.0	7.1
Construction													
2000	138.0	136.8	144.3	151.1	155.3	159.1	159.2	159.3	156.4	151.7	148.5	142.7	150.2
2001	130.6	132.1	138.2	146.3	152.2	156.7	157.3	158.5	154.8	153.0	152.4	147.5	148.3
2002	134.4	133.5	137.0	142.9	147.9	152.3	155.2	155.1	152.6	149.5	148.1	143.6	146.0
2003	131.7	128.5	133.0	141.8	148.0	149.9	153.0	154.2	151.3	152.4	148.6	144.7	144.8
2004	131.4	129.6	136.5	146.7	152.6	155.6	158.9	156.8	155.0	153.5	151.1	146.5	147.9
2005	132.4	132.1	136.8	147.7	150.2	154.1	156.6	156.8	155.5	155.1	153.2	148.2	148.2
2006	136.9	136.1	140.9	148.0	153.4	157.1	157.3	157.8	156.2	156.4	154.3	152.0	150.5
2007	138.9	132.4	142.1	148.9	155.5	159.0	159.1	159.1	157.3	156.9	154.0	148.3	151.0
Manufacturing													
2000	666.2	668.1	667.9	667.8	669.3	672.2	665.7	668.1	664.3	658.6	654.3	650.9	664.5
2001	633.4	632.3	628.2	625.7	624.0	622.6	612.3	612.8	608.5	599.2	594.0	592.0	615.4
2002	582.4	583.6	585.0	585.6	589.0	594.7	590.8	595.5	593.1	589.0	587.6	584.0	588.4
2003	577.9	577.2	576.2	572.1	573.5	575.8	564.2	574.9	571.3	570.2	569.2	569.3	572.7
2004	565.0	565.3	567.0	569.6	572.6	577.0	569.0	577.6	576.6	573.8	572.4	573.3	571.6
2005	568.4	568.4	569.6	571.0	572.6	574.8	567.8	573.3	572.9	571.3	570.8	571.8	571.1
2006	566.8	565.2	568.3	568.6	567.6	573.9	565.4	569.2	564.6	560.8	557.6	557.1	565.4
2007	549.5	549.1	551.4	550.0	551.4	555.1	551.3	552.2	549.8	547.6	546.9	546.9	550.1
Service-Providing													
2000	2,136.5	2,146.1	2,170.9	2,190.6	2,214.8	2,185.8	2,140.1	2,151.7	2,203.2	2,197.2	2,202.1	2,204.7	2,178.6
2001	2,131.3	2,144.8	2,164.0	2,180.1	2,186.3	2,162.9	2,115.6	2,139.8	2,183.0	2,179.2	2,181.6	2,182.2	2,162.6
2002	2,109.7	2,123.0	2,136.1	2,157.3	2,177.5	2,153.5	2,132.1	2,154.9	2,187.1	2,187.2	2,196.2	2,198.6	2,159.4
2003	2,130.1	2,137.2	2,153.0	2,173.5	2,190.9	2,163.3	2,129.7	2,151.0	2,192.7	2,206.7	2,210.8	2,212.2	2,170.9
2004	2,148.0	2,155.7	2,180.5	2,210.5	2,218.9	2,195.8	2,174.8	2,181.4	2,232.6	2,240.3	2,248.6	2,241.3	2,202.4
2005	2,174.7	2,193.4	2,209.9	2,238.0	2,244.7	2,220.2	2,193.9	2,203.5	2,262.6	2,266.7	2,272.8	2,267.2	2,229.0
2006	2,200.9	2,220.0	2,242.1	2,255.6	2,265.1	2,246.0	2,204.1	2,224.1	2,278.2	2,285.1	2,293.4	2,295.2	2,250.8
2007	2,226.4	2,236.4	2,265.0	2,283.3	2,296.1	2,278.8	2,238.2	2,273.7	2,306.7	2,314.2	2,322.5	2,318.6	2,280.0
Trade, Transportation, and Utilities													
2000	607.2	602.1	607.9	611.1	615.8	617.9	616.0	617.0	615.3	622.2	632.1	639.5	617.0
2001	602.0	594.3	596.1	599.2	602.4	604.6	599.0	599.4	596.2	595.6	604.0	608.0	600.1
2002	579.0	572.6	574.5	575.9	581.1	584.0	582.7	583.2	580.7	579.3	590.8	595.6	581.6
2003	568.8	561.7	564.6	570.2	573.7	575.1	572.5	574.0	572.7	576.9	586.4	591.1	574.0
2004	566.6	561.1	565.9	572.2	576.9	579.4	579.9	580.5	576.5	581.4	591.2	596.1	577.3
2005	570.1	567.6	571.7	578.4	583.6	584.0	585.2	585.4	585.0	588.0	597.7	600.9	583.1
2006	576.9	572.6	577.4	579.2	584.4	587.0	584.8	585.7	584.5	587.8	598.6	602.8	585.1
2007	578.8	572.5	579.9	582.1	588.2	592.1	588.5	587.5	585.7	589.4	602.0	604.1	587.6
Wholesale Trade													
2000	123.8	124.2	125.5	125.7	126.4	127.2	126.9	126.8	126.2	126.2	126.0	125.8	125.9
2001	123.7	123.6	124.1	123.8	124.1	124.5	123.8	123.4	122.8	122.4	121.8	121.7	123.3
2002	119.7	119.3	119.3	120.0	120.6	121.1	120.5	119.9	119.2	118.5	118.3	118.3	119.6
2003	117.6	117.3	117.4	117.6	118.1	118.5	118.0	117.5	116.8	116.9	116.9	117.1	117.5
2004	116.1	116.3	117.5	118.9	119.8	120.6	121.2	120.8	119.8	120.5	120.5	120.6	119.4
2005	119.0	119.2	119.8	121.1	121.8	122.5	122.9	122.5	121.8	122.0	122.1	122.3	121.4
2006	121.1	121.2	122.0	122.8	123.8	125.0	124.4	123.8	123.4	123.6	123.5	123.9	123.2
2007	122.8	122.9	124.0	124.6	125.5	126.5	127.6	126.5	125.7	125.9	126.1	126.2	125.4

Employment by Industry: Indiana, 2000–2007—*Continued*

(Numbers in thousands, not seasonally adjusted.)

Industry and year	January	February	March	April	May	June	July	August	September	October	November	December	Annual Average
Retail Trade													
2000	354.0	348.6	352.1	353.9	357.8	358.9	355.7	356.2	355.5	360.2	372.6	379.4	358.7
2001	351.8	344.9	345.4	346.5	349.4	350.8	346.0	345.8	344.6	346.1	355.7	358.8	348.8
2002	338.8	333.7	335.8	336.3	340.5	342.8	340.7	340.6	339.1	337.7	348.4	353.8	340.7
2003	331.1	325.4	327.8	331.0	334.3	335.8	333.0	334.4	333.4	335.2	345.0	349.5	334.7
2004	329.7	323.8	326.1	328.3	332.0	333.8	332.0	332.3	329.3	332.3	341.9	346.3	332.3
2005	325.4	321.8	324.5	328.1	332.0	331.5	332.5	331.9	331.3	333.7	342.4	345.7	331.7
2006	326.9	322.0	325.0	325.9	329.0	329.8	328.5	329.3	327.6	330.5	340.3	343.4	329.9
2007	325.6	319.5	324.0	324.9	329.2	330.9	328.1	327.4	325.9	328.8	340.3	343.7	329.0
Transportation and Utilities													
2000	129.4	129.3	130.3	131.5	131.6	131.8	133.4	134.0	133.6	135.8	133.5	134.3	132.4
2001	126.5	125.8	126.6	128.9	128.9	129.3	129.2	130.2	128.8	127.1	126.5	127.5	127.9
2002	120.5	119.6	119.4	119.6	120.0	120.1	121.5	122.7	122.4	123.1	124.1	123.5	121.4
2003	120.1	119.0	119.4	121.6	121.3	120.8	121.5	122.1	122.5	124.8	124.5	124.5	121.8
2004	120.8	121.0	122.3	125.0	125.1	125.0	126.7	127.4	127.4	128.6	128.8	129.2	125.6
2005	125.7	126.6	127.4	129.2	129.8	130.0	129.8	131.0	131.9	132.3	133.2	132.9	130.0
2006	128.9	129.4	130.4	130.5	131.6	132.2	131.9	132.6	133.5	133.7	134.8	135.5	132.1
2007	130.4	130.1	131.9	132.6	133.5	134.7	132.8	133.6	134.1	134.7	135.6	134.2	133.2
Information													
2000	45.7	45.9	46.4	45.4	46.0	46.7	46.1	46.4	46.1	45.7	46.2	46.3	46.1
2001	45.5	45.3	45.6	45.0	45.2	45.3	45.0	44.6	44.0	43.6	43.8	43.9	44.7
2002	42.9	42.6	42.9	42.5	42.8	43.1	42.8	42.8	42.1	41.7	41.9	41.8	42.5
2003	41.0	40.7	41.1	40.8	41.4	42.0	41.9	42.1	41.4	41.0	41.2	41.3	41.3
2004	40.8	40.4	40.9	40.8	41.3	41.8	41.4	41.1	40.3	40.5	40.6	40.8	40.9
2005	40.0	40.1	40.1	40.2	40.7	41.0	40.8	40.7	40.0	39.7	40.0	40.4	40.3
2006	39.5	39.8	39.8	39.9	40.2	40.6	40.3	40.1	39.5	39.3	39.6	39.8	39.9
2007	39.5	39.6	39.5	39.6	40.1	40.6	40.8	40.8	40.2	40.3	41.1	41.0	40.3
Financial Activities													
2000	144.4	144.1	144.5	144.7	145.7	147.1	146.3	146.0	144.7	143.9	143.9	144.9	145.0
2001	142.0	142.2	142.8	143.6	144.3	146.0	144.6	144.0	141.8	140.8	140.8	141.5	142.9
2002	139.2	138.9	138.9	138.8	139.8	141.1	141.5	141.6	140.3	139.8	140.1	140.8	140.1
2003	139.5	139.5	140.2	140.5	141.9	143.1	143.2	143.3	141.8	141.0	140.4	140.9	141.3
2004	138.6	138.6	138.9	139.2	140.3	141.6	141.7	141.6	139.8	139.5	139.3	140.0	139.9
2005	137.2	137.2	137.2	138.0	138.7	139.9	140.4	140.7	139.6	139.0	138.8	139.4	138.8
2006	138.4	138.6	138.8	139.1	139.9	141.2	140.6	140.5	139.2	138.8	138.5	139.3	139.4
2007	137.5	137.8	138.1	138.6	139.4	140.6	140.3	139.9	138.7	138.4	138.1	138.4	138.8
Professional and Business Services													
2000	249.1	250.4	255.3	261.0	263.4	266.1	261.5	263.8	264.5	260.9	259.4	256.4	259.3
2001	241.6	242.2	246.1	250.3	251.7	253.8	252.1	256.2	252.7	251.9	249.6	247.6	249.7
2002	239.4	240.8	244.8	251.4	255.8	258.2	259.1	261.7	260.2	258.9	257.9	256.3	253.7
2003	246.5	246.5	248.2	251.2	254.4	255.4	254.4	257.8	257.8	259.7	260.1	257.4	254.1
2004	248.9	251.7	256.7	264.8	266.9	269.7	272.2	274.3	273.1	273.7	274.1	270.6	266.4
2005	260.5	264.1	266.8	273.1	274.2	276.2	276.2	279.8	280.4	281.2	280.5	278.2	274.3
2006	266.5	269.5	274.7	280.0	282.6	285.5	282.8	288.9	288.2	286.5	285.8	285.0	281.3
2007	275.8	276.8	283.5	289.8	292.6	294.3	290.2	295.6	295.4	295.9	294.7	290.1	289.6
Education and Health Services													
2000	327.0	330.6	332.4	333.6	333.7	326.9	321.5	324.1	332.9	334.8	335.5	336.4	330.8
2001	335.6	338.4	340.0	341.8	337.0	330.0	327.7	330.2	346.3	346.7	348.3	349.1	339.3
2002	345.2	347.3	348.4	349.4	348.6	344.1	342.7	344.5	353.5	355.7	357.2	357.8	349.5
2003	357.5	359.6	360.8	362.7	359.2	351.5	350.3	349.0	362.0	367.7	367.6	367.8	359.6
2004	365.3	367.3	369.5	372.7	365.0	359.0	360.3	356.3	373.7	378.1	379.7	376.8	368.6
2005	371.6	375.7	377.5	380.6	373.1	371.3	369.8	366.6	382.9	388.5	390.1	387.0	377.9
2006	381.7	386.7	389.5	389.8	382.4	380.8	377.6	374.0	390.5	396.7	397.2	394.5	386.8
2007	389.2	391.4	393.6	396.6	392.2	389.8	390.1	388.7	403.4	406.6	407.0	408.6	396.4
Leisure and Hospitality													
2000	250.0	251.9	258.4	266.8	274.6	279.2	274.2	276.9	273.0	269.1	264.0	261.7	266.7
2001	249.0	252.5	259.5	267.1	276.0	282.0	277.6	281.9	275.2	269.7	264.2	262.2	268.1
2002	250.5	252.1	257.1	266.2	276.3	280.9	278.7	282.1	276.1	271.2	266.5	265.0	268.6
2003	253.9	253.2	258.4	270.0	279.6	284.1	280.2	284.3	277.5	273.8	269.0	266.5	270.9
2004	255.0	255.3	262.5	274.4	283.6	287.7	285.6	287.2	281.8	275.1	272.4	269.9	274.2
2005	257.5	260.0	266.9	277.2	286.2	292.0	289.2	291.4	284.4	276.8	274.6	273.0	277.4
2006	263.2	266.0	272.6	279.2	287.2	293.3	289.8	292.2	286.4	282.5	279.9	279.1	281.0
2007	268.1	268.1	275.1	283.2	292.7	297.2	291.9	296.0	288.4	283.7	280.6	278.6	283.6
Other Services													
2000	106.8	107.7	109.1	109.7	110.2	111.0	109.4	109.6	109.3	108.4	108.2	108.4	109.0
2001	106.3	107.1	108.2	108.6	109.6	111.0	109.2	108.9	107.2	106.3	106.2	106.4	107.9
2002	104.0	104.7	105.6	106.5	108.0	109.0	107.8	107.6	106.4	106.1	105.9	106.1	106.5
2003	104.3	105.0	105.9	106.6	107.7	109.0	108.5	108.5	107.8	107.6	107.2	107.7	107.2
2004	106.1	106.7	107.8	109.2	109.9	111.3	111.2	111.1	110.2	110.4	110.0	110.1	109.5
2005	109.0	109.5	110.7	111.5	112.2	112.9	112.3	112.1	111.2	110.6	110.3	110.6	111.1
2006	109.0	109.3	110.7	111.3	112.3	113.4	112.2	112.0	111.4	110.8	110.2	110.8	111.1
2007	109.5	109.6	111.3	112.2	113.2	114.2	113.5	112.8	111.9	111.8	111.6	111.9	112.0
Government													
2000	406.3	413.4	416.9	418.3	425.4	390.9	365.1	367.9	417.4	412.2	412.8	411.1	404.8
2001	409.3	422.8	425.7	424.5	420.1	390.2	360.4	374.6	419.6	424.6	424.7	423.5	410.0
2002	409.5	424.0	423.9	426.6	425.1	393.1	376.8	391.4	427.8	434.5	435.9	435.2	417.0
2003	418.6	431.0	433.8	431.5	433.0	403.1	378.7	392.0	431.7	439.0	438.9	439.5	422.6
2004	426.7	434.6	438.3	437.2	435.0	405.3	382.5	389.3	437.2	441.6	441.3	437.0	425.5
2005	428.8	439.2	439.0	439.0	436.0	402.9	380.0	386.8	439.1	442.9	440.8	437.7	426.0
2006	425.7	437.5	438.6	437.1	436.1	404.2	376.0	390.7	438.5	442.7	443.6	443.9	426.2
2007	428.0	440.6	444.0	441.2	437.7	410.0	382.9	412.4	443.0	448.1	447.4	445.9	431.8

Average Weekly Hours by Selected Industry: Indiana, 2001–2007

(Not seasonally adjusted.)

Industry and year	January	February	March	April	May	June	July	August	September	October	November	December	Annual Average
Construction													
2001	37.4	36.1	36.1	37.5	38.7	39.3	40.4	40.3	39.7	36.6	40.1	36.4	38.3
2002	37.0	37.8	38.1	37.1	36.8	40.7	41.1	40.0	40.4	39.8	38.5	38.6	38.9
2003	37.4	36.0	37.0	36.5	37.6	37.6	38.0	39.2	39.5	36.7	37.2	36.0	37.4
2004	38.1	38.2	39.0	39.1	38.9	38.0	38.8	40.1	38.1	37.5	37.8	38.1	38.5
2005	36.4	36.5	38.6	39.3	38.8	39.0	38.1	38.6	37.9	39.3	39.6	39.4	38.5
2006	38.2	39.0	38.8	39.1	38.3	39.7	37.7	39.0	38.7	40.0	38.4	37.3	38.7
2007	38.8	36.1	39.1	37.7	40.1	40.7	40.8	40.4	41.0	41.3	40.0	40.0	39.8
Manufacturing													
2001	40.9	40.6	40.6	39.5	41.1	41.1	40.5	41.5	41.5	41.3	41.5	42.2	41.0
2002	41.9	41.7	42.8	42.6	42.6	42.5	41.5	42.8	43.0	42.4	42.5	43.0	42.4
2003	42.3	42.0	41.9	41.7	41.7	41.7	40.9	42.0	42.9	42.1	42.4	42.9	42.1
2004	42.3	42.0	42.3	42.1	42.2	42.1	41.4	42.2	41.8	42.2	42.1	42.6	42.1
2005	42.3	41.9	41.9	41.4	41.3	41.5	41.2	42.0	42.3	42.5	42.3	42.3	41.9
2006	42.1	41.8	42.2	41.3	42.2	41.9	41.2	42.3	41.2	41.4	40.8	41.6	41.7
2007	40.8	40.0	41.8	41.2	42.1	42.0	41.3	42.0	42.6	41.6	42.2	42.4	41.7
Retail Trade													
2003	29.0	29.6	29.9	30.0	30.6	30.7	30.9	30.9	30.7	30.5	30.5	31.2	30.4
2004	30.2	30.5	30.7	30.9	31.0	30.9	31.2	31.0	31.3	30.6	30.1	30.4	30.7
2005	29.6	29.9	30.1	30.7	30.9	31.2	31.2	31.5	31.6	30.9	32.1	31.1	30.9
2006	30.7	31.3	30.6	31.0	31.7	31.3	32.1	32.2	32.0	31.6	32.3	32.3	31.6
2007	30.8	30.6	30.5	30.6	31.5	31.6	31.2	31.5	31.9	32.1	32.9	32.7	31.5
Financial Activities													
2001	36.7	35.9	35.8	36.2	36.3	36.6	37.0	36.8	36.6	36.3	36.4	36.7	36.5
2002	36.3	36.3	36.2	35.9	36.8	36.1	35.8	35.9	36.0	35.8	35.5	35.7	36.0
2003	35.5	35.4	35.5	35.2	35.7	35.9	35.8	35.7	35.7	35.7	35.6	35.7	35.6
2004	35.6	35.8	35.7	36.0	35.8	35.5	35.5	35.5	35.5	35.5	35.5	35.5	35.6
2005	35.4	35.5	35.5	35.5	35.5	35.5	35.4	35.5	35.4	35.5	35.4	35.4	35.5
2006	35.4	35.4	35.3	35.4	35.3	35.3	35.3	35.3	35.3	35.4	35.3	35.3	35.3
2007	35.3	35.3	35.3	35.3	35.3	35.2	35.3	35.3	35.3	35.4	35.4	35.4	35.3

Average Hourly Earnings by Selected Industry: Indiana, 2001–2007

(Dollars, not seasonally adjusted.)

Industry and year	January	February	March	April	May	June	July	August	September	October	November	December	Annual Average
Construction													
2001	19.70	19.95	19.86	20.14	20.23	20.49	20.83	20.77	21.06	20.43	20.43	19.69	20.34
2002	19.63	19.65	19.71	19.50	19.69	19.78	19.64	19.20	19.52	20.03	20.08	20.51	19.74
2003	20.41	20.73	21.14	21.34	20.44	20.24	20.06	20.02	20.37	19.81	19.55	19.43	20.27
2004	20.48	20.14	20.20	20.34	20.42	20.18	20.14	20.38	20.49	20.87	21.02	20.68	20.45
2005	20.59	20.93	20.97	21.88	21.10	21.01	21.23	20.99	20.72	21.07	21.08	20.56	21.02
2006	20.89	20.62	20.59	20.97	20.95	21.07	21.75	21.42	21.44	21.72	21.92	22.16	21.31
2007	22.30	22.47	22.29	22.18	22.33	22.23	22.56	22.31	22.85	22.31	22.95	22.50	22.44
Manufacturing													
2001	16.09	16.16	16.05	16.34	16.23	16.37	16.40	16.54	16.58	16.71	16.80	16.90	16.42
2002	17.00	17.01	17.02	16.95	17.01	17.07	17.04	17.16	17.15	17.21	17.47	17.69	17.15
2003	17.66	17.78	17.74	17.74	17.84	17.86	17.67	17.90	17.86	17.89	18.00	18.15	17.84
2004	17.93	17.96	17.82	17.91	17.86	18.06	17.72	17.93	18.17	17.79	17.88	18.03	17.92
2005	17.83	17.92	17.88	17.88	18.14	18.24	18.02	18.29	18.21	18.21	18.32	18.70	18.14
2006	18.66	18.53	18.49	18.34	18.46	18.62	18.69	18.43	18.66	18.58	18.87	18.56	18.57
2007	18.81	18.98	18.73	18.93	18.62	18.75	18.66	18.90	18.48	18.45	18.52	18.56	18.70
Retail Trade													
2003	10.54	10.52	10.57	10.20	10.25	10.40	10.50	10.63	10.63	10.71	10.54	10.71	10.52
2004	10.73	10.82	10.92	10.62	10.73	10.91	10.77	10.79	10.91	10.89	10.90	11.00	10.83
2005	11.16	11.15	11.07	10.80	10.83	10.79	10.93	11.16	11.07	11.12	11.19	11.02	11.02
2006	11.19	11.07	11.16	11.30	11.16	11.09	10.79	10.67	10.79	10.77	10.51	10.61	10.92
2007	10.81	10.86	11.07	11.09	11.13	11.27	11.07	10.83	11.07	11.05	11.01	11.00	11.02
Financial Activities													
2001	12.58	13.16	13.34	13.27	13.33	13.23	13.26	13.27	13.38	13.44	13.54	13.50	13.27
2002	13.61	13.65	13.64	13.76	13.64	13.60	13.55	13.55	13.55	13.46	13.54	13.63	13.60
2003	13.75	13.68	13.75	13.79	13.80	13.67	13.69	13.73	13.70	13.68	13.69	13.69	13.72
2004	13.71	13.71	13.71	13.57	13.54	13.56	13.57	13.57	13.58	13.56	13.58	13.53	13.60
2005	13.56	13.51	13.53	13.49	13.49	13.48	13.46	13.44	13.48	13.48	13.42	13.40	13.48
2006	13.44	13.41	13.44	13.43	13.46	13.43	13.44	13.44	13.46	13.49	13.51	13.47	13.45
2007	13.51	13.51	13.48	13.46	13.45	13.42	13.45	13.45	13.50	13.53	13.57	13.59	13.49

Average Weekly Earnings by Selected Industry: Indiana, 2001–2007

(Dollars, not seasonally adjusted.)

Industry and year	January	February	March	April	May	June	July	August	September	October	November	December	Annual Average
Construction													
2001	736.78	720.20	716.95	755.25	782.90	805.26	841.53	837.03	836.08	747.74	819.24	716.72	779.02
2002	726.31	742.77	750.95	723.45	724.59	805.05	807.20	768.00	788.61	797.19	773.08	791.69	767.89
2003	763.33	746.28	782.18	778.91	768.54	761.02	762.28	784.78	804.62	727.03	727.26	699.48	758.10
2004	780.29	769.35	787.80	795.29	794.34	766.84	781.43	817.24	780.67	782.63	794.56	787.91	787.33
2005	749.48	763.95	809.44	859.88	818.68	819.39	808.86	810.21	785.29	828.05	834.77	810.06	809.27
2006	798.00	804.18	798.89	819.93	802.39	836.48	819.98	835.38	829.73	868.80	841.73	826.57	824.70
2007	865.24	811.17	871.54	836.19	895.43	904.76	920.45	901.32	936.85	921.40	918.00	900.00	893.11
Manufacturing													
2001	658.08	656.10	651.63	645.43	667.05	672.81	664.20	686.41	688.07	690.12	697.20	713.18	673.22
2002	712.30	709.32	728.46	722.07	724.63	725.48	707.16	734.45	737.45	729.70	742.48	760.67	727.16
2003	747.02	746.76	743.31	739.76	743.93	744.76	722.70	751.80	766.19	753.17	763.20	778.64	751.06
2004	758.44	754.32	753.79	754.01	753.69	760.33	733.61	756.65	759.51	750.74	752.75	768.08	754.43
2005	754.21	750.85	749.17	740.23	749.18	756.96	742.42	768.18	770.28	773.93	774.94	791.01	760.07
2006	785.59	774.55	780.28	757.44	779.01	780.18	770.03	779.59	768.79	769.21	769.90	772.10	774.37
2007	767.45	759.20	782.91	779.92	783.90	787.50	770.66	793.80	787.25	767.52	781.54	786.94	779.79
Retail Trade													
2003	305.66	311.39	316.04	306.00	313.65	319.28	324.45	328.47	326.34	326.66	321.47	334.15	319.81
2004	324.05	330.01	335.24	328.16	332.63	337.12	336.02	334.49	341.48	333.23	328.09	334.40	332.48
2005	330.34	333.39	333.21	331.56	334.65	336.65	341.02	351.54	349.81	343.61	359.20	342.72	340.52
2006	343.53	346.49	341.50	350.30	353.77	347.12	346.36	343.57	345.28	340.33	339.47	342.70	345.07
2007	332.95	332.32	337.64	339.35	350.60	356.13	345.38	341.15	353.13	354.71	362.23	359.70	347.13
Financial Activities													
2001	461.69	472.44	477.57	480.37	483.88	484.22	490.62	488.34	489.71	487.87	492.86	495.45	484.36
2002	494.04	495.50	493.77	493.98	501.95	490.96	485.09	486.45	487.80	481.87	480.67	486.59	489.60
2003	488.13	484.27	488.13	485.41	492.66	490.75	490.10	490.16	489.09	488.38	487.36	488.73	488.43
2004	488.08	490.82	489.45	488.52	484.73	481.38	481.74	481.74	482.09	481.38	482.09	480.32	484.16
2005	480.02	479.61	480.32	478.90	478.90	478.54	476.48	477.12	477.19	478.54	475.07	474.36	478.54
2006	475.78	474.71	474.43	475.42	475.14	474.08	474.43	474.43	475.14	477.55	476.90	475.49	474.79
2007	476.90	476.90	475.84	475.14	474.79	472.38	474.79	474.79	476.55	478.96	480.38	481.09	476.20

Population
  2000 census: 2,926,324
  2007 estimate: 2,988,046
  Percent change, 2000–2007: 2.1%

Percent change in total nonfarm employment, 2000–2007: 2.6%

Industry with the largest growth in employment, 2000–2007 (thousands)
  Education and health services, 20.7

Industry with the largest decline in employment, 2000–2007 (thousands)
  Manufacturing, -21.9

Civilian labor force
  2000: 1,601,920
  2007: 1,660,979

Employment-population ratio
  2000: 69.7%
  2007: 69.1%

Unemployment rate and rank among states
  2000: 2.8%, 8th
  2007: 3.8%, 15th

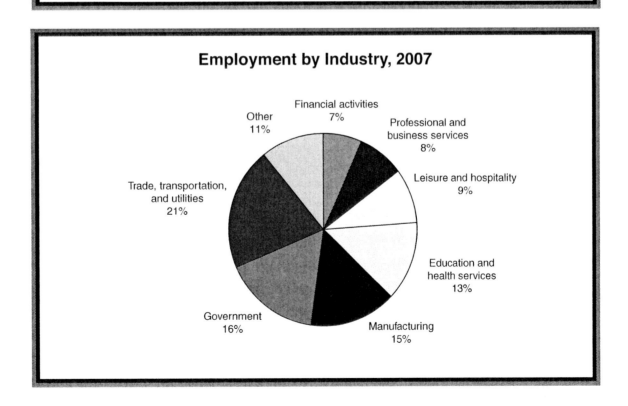

Employment by Industry, 2007

Financial activities 7%

Other 11%

Professional and business services 8%

Trade, transportation, and utilities 21%

Leisure and hospitality 9%

Education and health services 13%

Government 16%

Manufacturing 15%

Employment by Industry: Iowa, 2000–2007

(Numbers in thousands, not seasonally adjusted.)

Industry and year	January	February	March	April	May	June	July	August	September	October	November	December	Annual Average
Total Nonfarm													
2000	1,443.6	1,446.8	1,465.5	1,479.2	1,493.0	1,495.9	1,474.0	1,473.8	1,487.2	1,494.5	1,497.3	1,490.7	1,478.4
2001	1,446.7	1,444.5	1,455.0	1,475.3	1,488.0	1,490.3	1,457.6	1,458.1	1,469.9	1,468.0	1,468.7	1,464.8	1,465.6
2002	1,422.6	1,420.8	1,429.7	1,453.1	1,466.4	1,469.6	1,437.7	1,435.6	1,454.4	1,457.5	1,462.0	1,458.6	1,447.3
2003	1,411.9	1,411.4	1,420.5	1,440.2	1,453.7	1,455.2	1,427.0	1,430.3	1,450.8	1,460.6	1,462.4	1,461.3	1,440.4
2004	1,417.8	1,419.7	1,433.0	1,460.0	1,469.2	1,476.6	1,450.7	1,449.9	1,467.6	1,477.3	1,482.5	1,482.7	1,457.3
2005	1,434.2	1,442.3	1,459.1	1,483.4	1,494.3	1,499.3	1,473.1	1,472.6	1,496.0	1,501.7	1,505.7	1,504.3	1,480.5
2006	1,462.9	1,471.0	1,484.8	1,506.6	1,519.6	1,527.0	1,492.6	1,492.5	1,515.6	1,523.4	1,527.6	1,527.2	1,504.2
2007	1,482.6	1,485.7	1,496.4	1,516.7	1,533.2	1,541.6	1,507.6	1,507.5	1,527.3	1,534.5	1,536.9	1,534.2	1,517.0
Total Private													
2000	1,202.1	1,201.1	1,217.5	1,230.7	1,240.2	1,249.6	1,248.4	1,249.6	1,245.9	1,246.7	1,248.1	1,241.6	1,235.1
2001	1,202.1	1,196.3	1,205.9	1,225.1	1,236.7	1,241.8	1,230.7	1,232.9	1,225.4	1,217.6	1,216.4	1,214.1	1,220.4
2002	1,177.4	1,172.5	1,180.5	1,203.4	1,214.7	1,221.6	1,214.3	1,214.0	1,212.7	1,209.2	1,211.7	1,208.3	1,203.4
2003	1,168.9	1,162.7	1,170.7	1,190.1	1,201.7	1,207.5	1,203.1	1,207.5	1,206.7	1,209.8	1,210.1	1,208.4	1,195.6
2004	1,174.5	1,171.3	1,184.0	1,209.4	1,217.7	1,226.9	1,227.1	1,226.8	1,224.3	1,227.1	1,230.7	1,232.0	1,212.7
2005	1,191.8	1,194.3	1,209.7	1,233.2	1,241.8	1,250.8	1,248.9	1,248.2	1,250.5	1,249.9	1,252.6	1,251.9	1,235.3
2006	1,219.1	1,220.3	1,233.5	1,254.8	1,265.9	1,275.4	1,266.9	1,266.9	1,267.8	1,269.9	1,272.7	1,272.8	1,257.2
2007	1,235.0	1,232.0	1,242.8	1,262.6	1,276.6	1,288.0	1,278.9	1,278.9	1,276.9	1,277.8	1,279.1	1,276.9	1,267.1
Goods-Producing													
2000	304.9	303.4	310.2	316.1	321.0	327.2	327.9	326.7	322.8	320.9	318.0	311.3	317.5
2001	300.6	298.7	300.7	307.8	312.8	317.1	316.0	314.9	309.7	302.6	299.9	296.7	306.5
2002	284.3	281.7	284.2	293.4	298.8	303.3	302.3	300.8	297.3	295.2	293.9	289.1	293.7
2003	277.2	273.3	275.7	283.0	288.2	292.9	292.7	294.3	292.5	293.4	292.1	288.6	287.0
2004	277.9	275.7	280.8	291.4	295.3	302.0	303.8	301.4	300.5	300.4	300.1	297.9	293.9
2005	285.5	284.9	290.8	300.0	304.3	311.0	312.6	312.0	309.7	308.6	307.9	303.6	302.6
2006	295.7	295.0	298.8	306.2	310.4	316.3	316.1	315.6	313.0	310.8	309.0	305.5	307.7
2007	293.6	289.3	292.9	299.6	305.2	311.4	312.7	312.9	310.5	309.6	307.9	303.5	304.1
Natural Resources and Mining													
2000	1.8	1.8	2.0	2.1	2.2	2.3	2.3	2.3	2.3	2.3	2.2	1.9	2.1
2001	1.6	1.7	1.8	2.1	2.2	2.2	2.2	2.2	2.1	2.0	2.0	2.0	2.0
2002	1.7	1.7	1.9	2.0	2.1	2.1	1.9	2.1	2.0	2.0	2.0	1.9	2.0
2003	1.5	1.5	1.6	1.9	2.0	2.1	2.0	2.2	2.2	2.1	2.1	2.0	1.9
2004	1.6	1.6	1.9	2.2	2.3	2.3	2.2	2.2	2.2	2.2	2.1	2.0	2.1
2005	1.7	1.7	2.0	2.1	2.2	2.3	2.3	2.3	2.2	2.2	2.2	2.0	2.1
2006	1.8	1.8	1.9	2.2	2.3	2.4	2.4	2.4	2.3	2.2	2.2	2.1	2.2
2007	1.8	1.7	2.0	2.2	2.3	2.3	2.3	2.3	2.3	2.3	2.2	2.0	2.1
Construction													
2000	54.5	53.4	58.2	62.8	66.4	69.9	70.9	70.8	68.2	67.0	65.0	60.0	63.9
2001	53.4	52.6	54.1	61.0	66.6	70.4	71.5	71.9	69.4	68.5	67.4	63.7	64.2
2002	54.8	53.1	55.4	62.9	67.1	70.2	71.2	70.9	68.6	68.2	67.1	63.4	64.4
2003	55.2	52.5	54.6	62.0	66.9	69.8	71.2	72.2	70.7	70.9	69.2	66.0	65.1
2004	57.5	55.6	59.7	67.9	70.8	74.3	75.4	75.2	73.5	72.3	71.7	69.2	68.6
2005	59.0	58.4	62.3	69.9	72.7	76.6	78.5	78.8	77.0	76.4	75.9	71.3	71.4
2006	64.9	64.6	67.1	72.8	76.3	79.7	80.8	80.7	79.7	77.8	76.2	72.4	74.4
2007	64.0	60.7	63.4	69.5	74.5	78.3	78.8	79.1	77.7	77.0	75.4	71.1	72.5
Manufacturing													
2000	248.6	248.2	250.0	251.2	252.4	255.0	254.7	253.6	252.3	251.6	250.8	249.4	251.4
2001	245.6	244.4	244.8	244.7	244.0	244.5	242.3	240.8	238.2	232.1	230.5	231.0	240.2
2002	227.8	226.9	226.9	228.5	229.6	231.0	229.2	227.8	226.7	225.0	224.8	223.8	227.3
2003	220.5	219.3	219.5	219.1	219.3	221.0	219.5	219.9	219.6	220.4	220.8	220.6	220.0
2004	218.8	218.5	219.2	221.3	222.2	225.4	226.2	224.0	224.8	225.9	226.3	226.7	223.3
2005	224.8	224.8	226.5	228.0	229.4	232.1	231.8	230.9	230.5	230.0	229.8	230.3	229.1
2006	229.0	228.6	229.8	231.2	231.8	234.2	232.9	232.5	231.0	230.8	230.6	231.0	231.1
2007	227.8	226.9	227.5	227.9	228.4	230.8	231.6	231.5	230.5	230.3	230.3	230.4	229.5
Service-Providing													
2000	1,138.7	1,143.4	1,155.3	1,163.1	1,172.0	1,168.7	1,146.1	1,147.1	1,164.4	1,173.6	1,179.3	1,179.4	1,160.9
2001	1,146.1	1,145.8	1,154.3	1,167.5	1,175.2	1,173.2	1,141.6	1,143.2	1,160.2	1,165.4	1,168.8	1,168.1	1,159.1
2002	1,138.3	1,139.1	1,145.5	1,159.7	1,167.6	1,166.3	1,135.4	1,134.8	1,157.1	1,162.3	1,168.1	1,169.5	1,153.6
2003	1,134.7	1,138.1	1,144.8	1,157.2	1,165.5	1,162.3	1,134.3	1,136.0	1,158.3	1,167.2	1,170.3	1,172.7	1,153.5
2004	1,139.9	1,144.0	1,152.2	1,168.6	1,173.9	1,174.6	1,146.9	1,148.5	1,167.1	1,176.9	1,182.4	1,184.8	1,163.3
2005	1,148.7	1,157.4	1,168.3	1,183.4	1,190.0	1,188.3	1,160.5	1,160.6	1,186.3	1,193.1	1,197.8	1,200.7	1,177.9
2006	1,167.2	1,176.0	1,186.0	1,200.4	1,209.2	1,210.7	1,176.5	1,176.9	1,202.6	1,212.6	1,218.6	1,221.7	1,196.5
2007	1,189.0	1,196.4	1,203.5	1,217.1	1,228.0	1,230.2	1,194.9	1,194.6	1,216.8	1,224.9	1,229.0	1,230.7	1,212.9
Trade, Transportation, and Utilities													
2000	310.4	308.4	310.6	313.7	315.1	317.0	317.0	316.9	315.9	317.9	322.6	324.2	315.8
2001	310.8	306.3	306.9	310.3	312.6	313.2	311.9	312.8	310.5	309.7	314.7	315.4	311.3
2002	303.6	299.1	300.3	304.2	305.6	307.9	307.2	307.4	306.0	306.4	310.9	312.3	305.9
2003	299.5	295.7	297.6	301.1	304.0	304.1	304.6	304.5	303.1	304.9	308.8	310.0	303.2
2004	299.5	296.8	298.6	302.7	304.0	305.4	307.1	307.1	304.8	306.0	310.7	313.0	304.6
2005	300.1	298.2	301.1	305.4	306.9	307.8	308.3	307.5	306.7	307.5	312.3	314.9	306.4
2006	303.8	301.5	303.6	308.0	309.9	311.1	309.3	308.6	307.6	309.5	314.3	316.5	308.6
2007	305.5	302.5	304.1	306.9	310.6	312.2	310.3	309.0	308.0	308.9	313.4	315.8	308.9
Wholesale Trade													
2000	66.4	66.3	67.5	68.8	68.7	69.2	70.6	69.2	68.8	68.5	67.7	67.4	68.2
2001	66.7	66.3	67.0	68.4	68.9	69.0	70.2	70.1	69.4	68.1	67.6	67.0	68.2
2002	65.8	65.4	65.5	66.9	66.8	67.3	68.8	68.0	67.3	67.0	66.5	66.0	66.8
2003	64.1	63.7	64.2	65.4	65.7	65.9	67.0	66.6	65.7	65.7	65.2	64.7	65.3
2004	63.9	63.7	64.4	66.2	66.1	66.6	67.8	67.4	66.6	67.0	67.0	66.8	66.1
2005	65.3	65.3	66.2	67.8	67.9	68.1	68.7	68.1	67.9	68.1	67.7	67.3	67.4
2006	66.6	66.3	66.8	68.0	68.1	68.3	68.4	67.9	67.7	67.5	67.7	67.1	67.5
2007	66.2	65.9	66.5	67.7	68.3	68.6	68.9	68.3	68.5	68.5	68.2	67.9	67.8

Employment by Industry: Iowa, 2000–2007—*Continued*

(Numbers in thousands, not seasonally adjusted.)

Industry and year	January	February	March	April	May	June	July	August	September	October	November	December	Annual Average
Retail Trade													
2000	187.2	185.3	185.7	187.0	188.5	189.8	188.6	189.4	189.1	191.0	196.5	198.7	189.7
2001	187.7	183.6	183.3	185.1	186.6	186.8	185.0	185.6	184.4	184.8	190.1	191.5	186.2
2002	182.4	178.5	179.2	181.2	182.3	183.6	181.1	181.5	181.2	181.3	185.9	187.7	182.2
2003	179.0	175.8	176.6	178.7	180.8	181.0	180.1	180.0	179.7	180.9	185.3	186.9	180.4
2004	178.5	176.1	176.6	178.2	179.5	180.3	180.7	181.0	179.6	180.2	185.3	187.9	180.3
2005	177.6	175.6	176.8	179.0	180.2	180.8	180.4	180.1	179.1	179.5	184.3	186.7	180.0
2006	177.8	176.0	176.9	179.4	180.7	181.2	179.8	178.9	177.8	179.5	183.9	186.1	179.8
2007	178.0	175.3	175.7	177.1	179.5	180.5	179.4	178.4	177.1	177.9	182.4	184.7	178.8
Transportation and Utilities													
2000	56.8	56.8	57.4	57.9	57.9	58.0	57.8	58.3	58.0	58.4	58.4	58.1	57.8
2001	56.4	56.4	56.6	56.8	57.1	57.4	56.7	57.1	56.7	56.8	57.0	56.9	56.8
2002	55.4	55.2	55.6	56.1	56.5	57.0	57.3	57.9	57.5	58.1	58.5	58.6	57.0
2003	56.4	56.2	56.8	57.0	57.5	57.2	57.5	57.9	57.7	58.3	58.3	58.4	57.4
2004	57.1	57.0	57.6	58.3	58.4	58.5	58.6	58.7	58.6	58.8	58.4	58.3	58.2
2005	57.2	57.3	58.1	58.6	58.6	58.8	58.9	59.2	59.3	59.7	59.9	60.3	59.0
2006	59.4	59.2	59.9	60.6	61.1	61.6	61.1	61.8	62.1	62.5	62.7	63.3	61.3
2007	61.3	61.3	61.9	62.1	62.8	63.1	62.0	62.3	62.4	62.5	62.8	63.2	62.3
Information													
2000	39.8	39.7	40.2	40.6	40.8	41.3	40.5	40.0	39.7	39.9	40.6	41.2	40.3
2001	38.5	38.5	39.0	38.1	37.8	37.8	37.7	36.8	36.5	36.5	36.3	36.0	37.5
2002	35.6	35.6	35.4	35.5	35.6	35.6	34.8	34.7	34.4	34.4	34.7	34.5	35.1
2003	33.6	33.9	33.7	33.4	33.6	33.6	33.7	33.9	33.5	33.5	33.6	33.7	33.6
2004	33.3	33.3	33.4	33.6	33.6	33.7	33.7	34.0	34.0	33.7	33.7	34.0	33.7
2005	33.4	33.3	33.5	33.3	33.2	33.1	33.1	32.6	32.5	32.4	32.5	32.7	33.0
2006	32.2	32.4	32.6	32.9	33.0	33.2	33.1	33.0	33.0	33.1	33.4	33.7	33.0
2007	33.0	33.5	33.7	34.1	34.3	34.4	33.6	33.3	33.2	33.1	33.2	33.0	33.5
Financial Activities													
2000	88.8	88.7	88.5	89.1	89.5	90.6	90.5	90.7	90.0	89.6	89.8	90.3	89.6
2001	90.0	89.8	90.4	90.8	91.5	93.0	93.2	93.1	92.6	92.6	93.1	94.1	92.0
2002	93.0	93.0	93.3	93.7	93.7	94.7	95.0	94.7	93.8	93.8	93.7	94.2	93.9
2003	94.2	94.2	94.2	94.4	95.0	95.8	95.9	96.0	95.4	95.4	95.6	95.9	95.2
2004	95.3	95.4	95.4	96.3	96.7	97.6	98.1	98.3	97.3	97.3	97.3	98.1	96.9
2005	97.3	97.4	97.5	97.6	98.0	98.9	99.0	99.0	98.6	98.4	98.5	99.4	98.3
2006	98.8	99.0	99.7	99.8	100.4	101.6	101.5	101.3	101.2	101.1	100.9	101.8	100.6
2007	101.1	101.2	101.6	102.0	102.5	104.0	104.0	103.7	103.1	103.0	102.7	103.4	102.7
Professional and Business Services													
2000	103.9	103.9	106.4	107.3	107.1	108.6	109.1	109.2	108.5	109.7	109.2	108.7	107.6
2001	107.3	106.2	106.7	108.8	109.1	109.1	106.9	108.3	106.8	107.4	105.6	105.4	107.3
2002	102.4	102.6	103.7	105.5	105.5	107.5	107.4	107.0	107.0	106.1	106.9	106.1	105.6
2003	102.3	102.2	102.5	105.6	104.8	106.2	106.6	107.9	107.2	107.8	107.0	107.1	105.6
2004	104.1	104.3	105.3	108.8	108.3	109.2	110.0	110.2	108.7	110.9	110.8	110.7	108.4
2005	107.0	108.4	109.8	112.6	112.5	113.9	114.6	115.1	116.1	116.7	116.3	116.2	113.3
2006	111.7	112.6	114.3	116.8	117.2	118.7	118.5	118.8	118.7	120.0	120.4	119.4	117.3
2007	116.1	117.1	117.7	121.3	120.8	123.2	122.8	123.6	122.1	122.4	122.1	121.7	120.9
Education and Health Services													
2000	180.3	182.2	184.0	183.6	182.5	177.9	173.3	174.4	181.5	187.0	187.9	187.7	181.8
2001	183.8	185.5	187.9	188.9	187.3	182.0	176.4	177.5	184.9	190.0	190.4	190.7	185.4
2002	187.0	188.7	189.6	190.4	189.5	183.6	178.7	179.4	187.9	192.6	193.8	194.3	188.0
2003	189.9	191.9	193.1	191.9	190.4	185.3	180.3	180.6	188.7	193.7	194.6	194.5	189.6
2004	191.2	193.0	194.3	194.1	192.7	187.6	182.5	182.6	190.5	195.5	196.5	197.2	191.5
2005	193.1	195.5	196.7	197.2	196.0	191.1	186.7	186.8	195.5	199.9	200.9	201.5	195.1
2006	197.5	199.8	201.0	201.6	200.3	195.2	190.4	190.6	198.6	203.5	204.8	205.3	199.1
2007	201.2	204.1	205.5	204.5	203.1	198.4	193.1	194.0	202.1	207.1	208.2	208.1	202.5
Leisure and Hospitality													
2000	118.0	118.7	121.2	123.7	127.4	129.6	132.6	134.5	130.7	124.9	123.0	121.5	125.4
2001	115.3	115.5	118.1	123.9	129.0	132.2	131.7	132.8	128.4	122.7	120.4	119.6	124.1
2002	115.7	115.9	117.7	123.9	129.1	131.6	131.7	132.9	129.8	124.0	121.2	121.5	124.6
2003	116.6	116.0	118.0	124.4	129.4	132.8	132.6	134.2	130.1	124.8	122.3	122.2	125.3
2004	117.3	117.3	120.3	126.2	130.7	134.3	134.5	136.5	132.4	126.8	125.1	124.7	127.2
2005	120.1	121.1	124.3	130.7	134.6	137.7	137.6	138.6	135.2	130.3	128.1	127.3	130.5
2006	123.5	124.3	127.3	132.9	137.8	141.5	140.6	141.9	138.9	135.1	132.9	133.3	134.2
2007	127.9	127.9	130.2	136.6	142.0	145.2	144.0	144.5	140.3	135.9	133.7	133.4	136.8
Other Services													
2000	56.0	56.1	56.4	56.6	56.8	57.4	57.5	57.2	56.8	56.8	57.0	56.7	56.7
2001	55.8	55.8	56.2	56.5	56.6	57.4	56.9	56.7	56.0	56.1	56.0	56.2	56.4
2002	55.8	55.9	56.3	56.8	56.9	57.4	57.2	57.1	56.5	56.7	56.6	56.3	56.6
2003	55.6	55.5	55.9	56.3	56.3	56.7	56.5	56.5	56.2	56.3	56.1	56.4	56.2
2004	55.9	55.5	55.9	56.3	56.4	57.1	57.1	56.7	56.4	56.5	56.3	56.4	56.4
2005	55.3	55.5	56.0	56.4	56.3	57.3	57.0	56.6	56.2	56.1	56.1	56.3	56.3
2006	55.9	55.7	56.2	56.6	56.9	57.8	57.4	57.1	56.8	56.8	57.0	57.3	56.8
2007	56.6	56.4	57.1	57.6	58.1	59.2	58.4	57.9	57.6	57.8	57.9	58.0	57.7
Government													
2000	241.5	245.7	248.0	248.5	252.8	246.3	225.6	224.2	241.3	247.8	249.2	249.1	243.3
2001	244.6	248.2	249.1	250.2	251.3	248.5	226.9	225.2	244.5	250.4	252.3	250.7	245.2
2002	245.2	248.3	249.2	249.7	251.7	248.0	223.4	221.6	241.7	248.3	250.3	250.3	244.0
2003	243.0	248.7	249.8	250.1	252.0	247.7	223.9	222.8	244.1	250.8	252.3	252.9	244.8
2004	243.3	248.4	249.0	250.6	251.5	249.7	223.6	223.1	243.3	250.2	251.8	250.7	244.6
2005	242.4	248.0	249.4	250.2	252.5	248.5	224.2	224.4	245.5	251.8	253.1	252.4	245.2
2006	243.8	250.7	251.3	251.8	253.7	251.6	225.7	225.6	247.8	253.5	254.9	254.4	247.1
2007	247.6	253.7	253.6	254.1	256.6	253.6	228.7	228.6	250.4	256.7	257.8	257.3	249.9

Average Weekly Hours by Selected Industry: Iowa, 2001–2007

(Not seasonally adjusted.)

Industry and year	January	February	March	April	May	June	July	August	September	October	November	December	Annual Average
Goods-Producing													
2001	40.5	40.1	40.1	39.1	40.2	40.6	41.1	40.5	41.4	41.0	41.0	41.0	40.5
2002	40.2	40.4	40.3	40.4	40.4	40.8	40.3	40.7	41.2	41.2	41.2	41.0	40.7
2003	40.1	39.3	40.1	40.0	41.1	41.8	40.7	42.7	42.1	41.9	42.5	41.4	41.2
2004	41.3	40.9	41.1	42.1	41.8	41.8	41.4	41.6	40.9	41.3	41.6	41.5	41.5
2005	40.2	39.9	40.6	40.5	40.2	41.7	41.2	40.4	41.8	42.5	42.0	41.7	41.1
2006	41.1	40.1	39.6	39.7	40.8	42.6	40.8	41.4	41.1	41.6	40.9	40.8	40.9
2007	39.8	39.9	40.5	40.7	41.7	42.1	43.6	42.4	43.3	42.8	42.9	40.3	41.7
Natural Resources and Mining													
2001	40.0	40.3	41.0	44.6	45.4	45.1	47.4	41.9	44.5	43.3	43.5	41.0	44.1
2002	41.7	43.4	38.3	43.5	45.6	46.4	47.7	47.6	48.8	48.9	46.3	44.2	45.4
2003	42.9	42.1	44.4	45.5	50.8	51.8	50.1	51.3	49.7	50.9	49.8	41.6	48.0
2004	36.5	37.0	44.4	48.6	48.7	49.9	51.2	52.1	50.1	52.1	50.6	47.7	48.1
2005	42.2	44.3	47.4	51.4	50.1	51.4	52.5	51.5	51.9	51.5	51.1	43.7	49.5
2006	41.5	43.2	48.8	47.4	52.3	51.8	51.1	51.5	49.9	50.6	48.4	47.8	49.0
2007	42.3	40.7	44.5	46.0	49.6	49.8	50.1	49.2	49.3	50.5	51.6	42.7	47.5
Construction													
2001	37.7	36.5	36.6	37.9	39.5	39.4	42.9	40.5	41.1	39.7	38.9	36.9	39.2
2002	36.7	36.5	36.3	36.7	39.3	38.6	38.2	38.6	40.5	41.3	40.4	38.6	38.6
2003	37.6	36.0	37.9	38.5	40.0	41.0	39.5	42.3	40.2	41.3	39.9	36.4	39.4
2004	38.4	36.9	37.2	39.2	37.2	38.8	40.6	40.6	39.2	40.1	40.7	38.4	39.1
2005	36.4	36.7	37.4	37.9	36.9	40.4	40.7	38.4	40.7	42.4	41.1	39.7	39.2
2006	40.4	37.9	38.5	40.4	40.7	42.4	41.7	41.2	40.6	42.4	42.4	41.0	40.9
2007	39.0	39.7	41.4	40.1	44.5	45.7	44.8	43.2	43.7	43.9	44.5	39.8	42.7
Manufacturing													
2001	41.1	40.9	40.9	39.3	40.3	41.0	40.5	40.5	41.4	41.4	41.6	42.2	40.9
2002	41.0	41.4	41.3	41.5	40.7	41.5	41.0	41.4	41.4	41.1	41.5	41.7	41.3
2003	40.7	40.1	40.6	40.4	41.4	42.1	41.1	42.8	42.7	42.1	43.3	43.0	41.7
2004	42.1	42.0	42.2	42.9	43.3	42.8	41.6	41.8	41.4	41.7	41.8	42.5	42.2
2005	41.3	40.8	41.4	41.3	41.3	42.0	41.2	41.1	42.1	42.4	42.2	42.4	41.6
2006	41.4	40.7	39.9	39.4	40.7	42.6	40.3	41.4	41.1	41.2	40.3	40.7	40.8
2007	40.1	39.9	40.2	40.8	40.7	40.8	43.2	42.0	43.1	42.3	42.3	40.5	41.3
Wholesale Trade													
2001	37.3	37.1	37.1	37.4	38.5	37.9	37.5	37.7	37.9	39.5	39.3	36.8	37.8
2002	37.1	37.9	37.4	38.7	38.6	40.2	38.4	38.4	38.4	38.1	38.6	37.9	38.3
2003	37.5	36.9	37.7	36.8	37.8	38.2	37.2	36.9	37.8	38.9	38.4	37.1	37.6
2004	36.9	37.2	37.5	39.6	36.6	36.6	36.0	36.0	35.5	37.1	37.2	36.0	36.8
2005	37.0	36.9	37.0	37.5	38.0	37.7	37.2	37.3	37.8	38.8	37.7	37.9	37.6
2006	36.6	35.0	35.5	37.1	36.1	36.0	36.3	36.6	36.2	37.5	36.8	36.9	36.4
2007	36.1	36.6	36.2	37.6	37.1	36.0	37.3	37.2	37.6	37.3	38.6	37.5	37.1
Retail Trade													
2001	26.6	26.2	26.6	27.4	28.0	28.6	28.8	29.3	27.9	27.2	27.4	27.9	27.7
2002	26.3	27.0	26.8	26.9	27.9	28.4	28.5	28.1	27.3	26.9	26.9	27.8	27.4
2003	26.2	26.7	26.7	26.8	27.4	28.3	28.2	28.2	27.4	27.2	27.4	27.1	27.3
2004	26.3	27.1	26.6	27.5	28.6	29.3	29.4	29.2	29.1	27.9	27.9	28.6	28.1
2005	27.2	27.4	27.5	27.8	28.2	28.8	28.5	28.6	29.1	27.8	28.5	28.3	28.1
2006	27.5	27.3	27.2	27.8	31.3	31.0	30.7	30.6	30.2	29.1	29.6	29.7	29.3
2007	28.5	28.4	28.5	28.0	28.1	28.9	28.9	28.6	28.6	27.9	29.0	28.6	28.5
Financial Activities													
2001	34.9	36.3	35.3	36.2	34.5	40.0	40.9	40.3	41.0	39.5	40.4	41.5	38.4
2002	40.1	39.8	39.8	38.7	40.0	40.0	38.6	38.6	38.6	37.8	36.7	37.4	38.8
2003	36.9	37.5	36.8	36.0	36.2	36.9	36.4	36.7	36.0	36.5	36.4	35.0	36.4
2004	37.1	36.2	36.0	36.1	36.5	35.9	35.3	36.2	35.7	35.3	35.4	35.9	35.9
2005	37.5	36.7	35.8	36.3	36.5	36.4	36.4	35.0	36.7	36.8	36.4	36.2	36.4
2006	37.5	37.1	36.9	37.2	36.6	37.3	37.7	37.6	37.5	38.8	38.0	38.1	37.5
2007	38.1	37.6	36.8	37.7	36.4	37.2	38.0	36.7	37.2	36.5	36.3	38.0	37.2

Average Hourly Earnings by Selected Industry: Iowa, 2001–2007

(Dollars, not seasonally adjusted.)

Industry and year	January	February	March	April	May	June	July	August	September	October	November	December	Annual Average
Goods-Producing													
2001	14.88	14.72	14.84	15.05	15.00	14.98	15.41	15.24	15.30	15.20	15.57	15.52	15.15
2002	15.54	15.44	15.69	15.64	15.87	15.83	15.92	15.97	16.11	16.06	16.20	16.42	15.90
2003	15.89	15.73	15.98	16.12	16.20	15.96	16.07	16.13	16.25	16.07	16.48	16.46	16.12
2004	16.36	16.31	16.58	16.43	16.22	16.46	16.30	16.43	16.95	16.71	16.72	16.73	16.52
2005	16.54	16.63	16.54	16.53	16.57	16.63	16.97	16.79	16.84	16.87	16.77	17.27	16.75
2006	17.05	16.69	16.88	16.75	17.07	17.31	17.40	17.16	17.54	17.13	17.69	18.23	17.25
2007	17.23	17.45	17.59	17.72	17.86	17.84	17.86	18.09	18.21	17.87	17.82	17.90	17.80
Natural Resources and Mining													
2001	12.75	12.52	12.10	12.72	13.11	13.12	13.84	14.13	15.29	14.25	14.00	14.06	13.58
2002	14.70	15.02	13.79	13.19	13.95	14.03	14.46	14.05	14.17	14.28	14.13	14.16	14.14
2003	13.91	14.14	14.46	14.54	15.21	15.10	14.94	15.13	15.22	15.21	15.09	14.77	14.90
2004	15.15	15.10	15.20	15.03	15.32	15.29	15.62	15.74	15.71	16.05	16.00	15.91	15.55
2005	15.90	15.83	16.54	15.91	16.13	16.11	16.08	16.27	16.39	16.46	16.16	15.86	16.16
2006	16.33	16.37	16.33	16.09	16.85	16.39	16.32	16.54	16.62	16.81	16.54	17.01	16.53
2007	16.77	16.13	16.45	16.91	17.37	17.20	17.50	17.78	17.45	17.81	17.99	17.26	17.29
Construction													
2001	16.46	16.50	16.47	16.72	16.69	16.54	16.84	16.73	17.25	16.85	17.58	17.89	16.89
2002	17.85	17.95	18.18	18.00	17.88	17.89	17.48	17.91	18.23	18.24	18.08	18.13	17.98
2003	18.09	18.23	18.40	17.62	17.69	17.09	16.95	17.34	17.61	17.44	17.53	17.37	17.56
2004	17.47	17.59	17.41	17.65	17.31	16.92	17.25	17.77	17.92	18.24	18.41	18.36	17.70
2005	18.46	18.24	17.93	17.67	17.92	17.93	18.59	18.37	18.50	18.47	18.54	19.29	18.34
2006	19.35	18.57	18.93	18.65	19.51	20.00	20.14	19.78	20.46	20.12	20.00	20.64	19.73
2007	20.19	20.35	20.97	20.53	20.39	20.24	20.27	21.08	21.33	20.51	20.71	20.82	20.62
Manufacturing													
2001	14.56	14.37	14.52	14.65	14.52	14.52	14.93	14.75	14.68	14.69	14.98	14.92	14.67
2002	15.02	14.90	15.15	15.05	15.28	15.22	15.44	15.37	15.44	15.36	15.62	15.96	15.32
2003	15.38	15.18	15.42	15.70	15.73	15.58	15.78	15.71	15.81	15.61	16.17	16.23	15.70
2004	16.10	16.02	16.39	16.08	15.90	16.33	15.97	15.96	16.64	16.21	16.16	16.26	16.17
2005	16.08	16.25	16.18	16.20	16.15	16.17	16.39	16.24	16.25	16.29	16.15	16.66	16.25
2006	16.39	16.17	16.28	16.09	16.21	16.35	16.35	16.18	16.47	16.00	16.84	17.44	16.40
2007	16.41	16.69	16.62	16.85	16.91	16.88	16.95	16.96	17.08	16.90	16.78	16.99	16.84
Wholesale Trade													
2001	13.27	13.44	13.57	13.59	13.25	13.52	13.38	13.31	13.44	13.53	13.30	13.62	13.43
2002	12.79	12.95	13.13	13.13	13.57	13.92	13.56	13.87	13.83	14.02	14.92	14.73	13.72
2003	13.89	14.12	14.25	14.44	14.21	14.79	15.10	15.36	15.04	14.79	14.86	15.04	14.66
2004	14.95	15.02	14.86	14.94	14.94	14.79	14.78	14.78	14.73	14.54	14.65	14.99	14.83
2005	15.80	15.17	15.36	15.28	15.24	15.26	15.35	15.75	15.53	16.53	17.08	16.85	15.78
2006	17.58	17.88	18.22	18.46	18.00	17.69	17.56	17.33	18.26	18.40	17.63	17.54	17.88
2007	17.66	17.67	17.36	17.48	17.48	17.64	17.83	18.02	17.79	18.08	17.35	17.95	17.69
Retail Trade													
2001	10.21	10.25	10.34	10.38	10.27	10.36	10.31	9.97	10.44	10.56	10.58	10.41	10.34
2002	10.53	10.56	10.80	10.60	10.52	10.44	10.43	10.47	10.64	10.51	10.46	10.42	10.53
2003	10.52	10.58	10.62	10.68	10.49	10.47	10.47	10.56	10.56	10.53	10.55	10.67	10.56
2004	10.80	10.70	10.87	10.86	10.86	10.91	10.85	10.94	11.12	11.12	11.02	10.99	10.92
2005	11.18	11.21	11.26	11.24	11.17	11.21	11.16	11.22	11.43	11.48	11.42	11.38	11.28
2006	11.54	11.56	11.85	11.46	10.55	10.71	11.06	11.19	11.33	10.96	10.84	11.07	11.16
2007	11.22	11.26	11.38	11.35	11.29	11.40	11.50	11.39	11.61	11.50	11.45	11.72	11.42
Financial Activities													
2001	14.18	13.93	14.18	14.59	14.46	14.69	14.96	14.69	15.10	15.29	15.07	14.89	14.70
2002	15.25	15.22	15.40	15.55	15.41	15.02	15.10	15.06	15.74	15.49	15.48	14.65	15.28
2003	14.57	15.05	15.25	15.14	15.18	14.83	14.96	15.22	15.17	15.17	15.18	15.07	15.06
2004	14.61	14.62	14.69	14.94	15.03	14.76	15.33	15.37	15.68	15.73	15.77	15.97	15.20
2005	16.13	15.70	16.74	15.84	15.94	16.04	16.23	16.17	15.65	15.95	15.76	16.10	16.02
2006	16.37	16.16	16.11	16.04	16.18	16.01	16.21	16.15	16.27	16.27	16.32	16.48	16.21
2007	16.26	17.12	16.57	16.81	16.82	16.74	16.63	16.80	16.90	17.09	17.16	17.50	16.86

Average Weekly Earnings by Selected Industry: Iowa, 2001–2007

(Dollars, not seasonally adjusted.)

Industry and year	January	February	March	April	May	June	July	August	September	October	November	December	Annual Average
Goods-Producing													
2001	602.64	590.27	595.08	588.46	603.00	608.19	633.35	617.22	633.42	623.20	638.37	636.32	613.58
2002	624.71	623.78	632.31	631.86	641.15	645.86	641.58	649.98	663.73	661.67	667.44	673.22	647.13
2003	637.19	618.19	640.80	644.80	665.82	667.13	654.05	688.75	684.13	673.33	700.40	681.44	664.14
2004	675.67	667.08	681.44	691.70	678.00	688.03	674.82	683.49	693.26	690.12	695.55	694.30	685.58
2005	664.91	663.54	671.52	669.47	666.11	693.47	699.16	678.32	703.91	716.98	704.34	720.16	688.43
2006	700.76	669.27	668.45	664.98	696.46	737.41	709.92	710.42	720.89	712.61	723.52	743.78	705.53
2007	685.75	696.26	712.40	721.20	744.76	751.06	778.70	767.02	788.49	764.84	764.48	721.37	742.26
Natural Resources and Mining													
2001	510.00	504.56	496.10	567.31	595.19	591.71	656.02	592.05	680.41	617.03	609.00	576.46	598.88
2002	612.99	651.87	528.16	573.77	636.12	650.99	689.74	668.78	691.50	698.29	654.22	625.87	641.96
2003	596.74	595.29	642.02	661.57	772.67	782.18	748.49	776.17	756.43	774.19	751.48	614.43	715.20
2004	552.98	558.70	674.88	730.46	746.08	762.97	799.74	820.05	787.07	836.21	809.60	758.91	747.96
2005	670.98	701.27	784.00	817.77	808.11	828.05	844.20	837.91	850.64	847.69	825.78	693.08	799.92
2006	677.70	707.18	796.90	762.67	881.26	849.00	833.95	851.81	829.34	850.59	800.54	813.08	809.97
2007	709.37	656.49	732.03	777.86	861.55	856.56	876.75	874.78	860.29	899.41	928.28	737.00	821.28
Construction													
2001	620.54	602.25	602.80	633.69	659.26	651.68	722.44	677.57	708.98	668.95	683.86	660.14	662.09
2002	655.10	655.18	659.93	660.60	702.68	690.55	667.74	691.33	738.32	753.31	730.43	699.82	694.03
2003	680.18	656.28	697.36	678.37	707.60	700.69	669.53	733.48	707.92	720.27	699.45	632.27	691.86
2004	670.85	649.07	647.65	691.88	643.93	656.50	700.35	721.46	702.46	731.42	749.29	705.02	692.07
2005	671.94	669.41	670.58	669.69	661.25	724.37	756.61	705.41	752.95	783.13	761.99	765.81	718.93
2006	781.74	703.80	728.81	753.46	794.06	848.00	839.84	814.94	830.68	853.09	848.00	846.24	806.96
2007	787.41	807.90	868.16	823.25	907.36	924.97	908.10	910.66	932.12	900.39	921.60	828.64	880.47
Manufacturing													
2001	598.42	587.73	593.87	575.75	585.16	595.32	604.67	597.38	607.75	608.17	623.17	629.62	600.00
2002	615.82	616.86	625.70	624.58	621.90	631.63	633.04	636.32	639.22	631.30	648.23	665.53	632.72
2003	625.97	608.72	626.05	634.28	651.22	655.92	648.56	672.39	675.09	657.18	700.16	697.89	654.69
2004	677.81	672.84	691.66	689.83	688.47	698.92	664.35	667.13	688.90	675.96	675.49	691.05	682.37
2005	664.10	663.00	669.85	669.06	667.00	679.14	675.27	667.46	684.13	690.70	681.53	706.38	676.00
2006	678.55	658.12	649.57	633.95	659.75	696.51	658.91	669.85	676.92	659.20	678.65	709.81	669.12
2007	658.04	665.93	668.12	687.48	688.24	688.70	732.24	712.32	736.15	714.87	709.79	688.10	695.49
Wholesale Trade													
2001	494.97	498.62	503.45	508.27	510.13	512.41	501.75	501.79	509.38	534.44	522.69	501.22	507.65
2002	474.51	490.81	491.06	508.13	523.80	559.58	520.70	532.61	531.07	534.16	575.91	558.27	525.48
2003	520.88	521.03	537.23	531.39	537.14	564.98	561.72	566.78	568.51	575.33	570.62	557.98	551.22
2004	551.66	558.74	557.25	591.62	546.80	541.31	532.08	532.08	522.92	539.43	544.98	539.64	545.74
2005	584.60	559.77	568.32	573.00	579.12	575.30	571.02	587.48	587.03	641.36	643.92	638.62	593.33
2006	643.43	625.80	646.81	684.87	649.80	636.84	637.43	634.28	661.01	690.00	648.78	647.23	650.83
2007	637.53	646.72	628.43	657.25	648.51	635.04	665.06	670.34	668.90	674.38	669.71	673.13	656.30
Retail Trade													
2001	271.59	268.55	275.04	284.41	287.56	296.30	296.93	292.12	291.28	287.23	289.89	290.44	286.42
2002	276.94	285.12	289.44	285.14	293.51	296.50	297.26	294.21	290.47	282.72	281.37	289.68	288.52
2003	275.62	282.49	283.55	286.22	287.43	296.30	295.25	297.79	289.34	286.42	289.07	289.16	288.29
2004	284.04	289.97	289.14	298.65	310.60	319.66	318.99	319.45	323.59	310.25	307.46	314.31	306.85
2005	304.10	307.15	309.65	312.47	314.99	322.85	318.06	320.89	332.61	319.14	325.47	322.05	316.97
2006	317.35	315.59	322.32	318.59	330.22	332.01	339.54	342.41	342.17	318.94	320.86	328.78	326.99
2007	319.77	319.78	324.33	317.80	317.25	329.46	332.35	325.75	332.05	320.85	332.05	335.19	325.47
Financial Activities													
2001	494.88	505.66	500.55	528.16	498.87	587.60	611.86	592.01	619.10	603.96	608.83	617.94	564.48
2002	611.53	605.76	612.92	601.79	616.40	600.80	582.86	581.32	607.56	585.52	568.12	547.91	592.86
2003	537.63	564.38	561.20	545.04	549.52	547.23	544.54	558.57	546.12	553.71	552.55	527.45	548.18
2004	542.03	529.24	528.84	539.33	548.60	529.88	541.15	553.32	553.50	561.56	558.26	573.32	545.68
2005	604.88	576.19	599.29	574.99	581.81	583.86	590.77	565.95	574.36	586.96	573.66	582.82	583.13
2006	613.88	599.54	594.46	596.69	592.19	597.17	611.12	607.24	610.13	631.28	620.16	627.89	607.88
2007	619.51	643.71	609.78	633.74	612.25	622.73	631.94	616.56	628.68	623.79	622.91	665.00	627.19

Population
    2000 census: 2,688,418
    2007 estimate: 2,775,997
    Percent change, 2000–2007: 3.3%

Percent change in total nonfarm employment, 2000–2007: 2.4%

Industry with the largest growth in employment, 2000–2007 (thousands)
    Education and health services, 23.0

Industry with the largest decline in employment, 2000–2007 (thousands)
    Manufacturing, -15.1

Civilian labor force
    2000: 1,405,104
    2007: 1,478,781

Employment-population ratio
    2000: 67.5%
    2007: 67.5%

Unemployment rate and rank among states
    2000: 3.8%, 25th
    2007: 4.1%, 21st

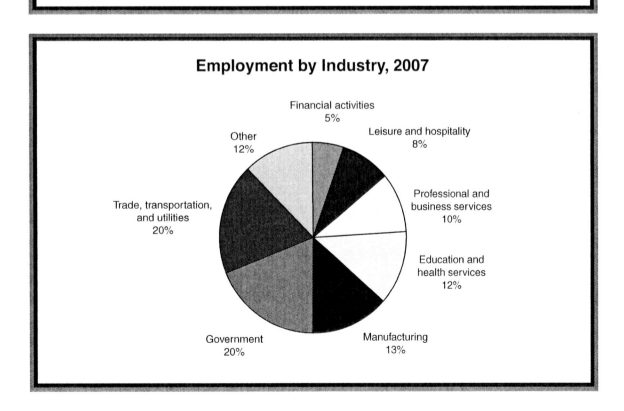

Employment by Industry, 2007

Financial activities 5%
Leisure and hospitality 8%
Other 12%
Professional and business services 10%
Trade, transportation, and utilities 20%
Education and health services 12%
Government 20%
Manufacturing 13%

Employment by Industry: Kansas, 2000–2007

(Numbers in thousands, not seasonally adjusted.)

Industry and year	January	February	March	April	May	June	July	August	September	October	November	December	Annual Average
Total Nonfarm													
2000	1,317.3	1,320.0	1,334.4	1,350.8	1,360.1	1,365.4	1,333.8	1,332.6	1,350.9	1,359.4	1,364.8	1,363.7	1,346.1
2001	1,330.1	1,333.1	1,346.9	1,356.7	1,363.0	1,365.5	1,337.9	1,333.7	1,351.6	1,355.2	1,356.1	1,356.2	1,348.8
2002	1,320.9	1,319.7	1,331.7	1,345.5	1,352.0	1,354.7	1,326.0	1,324.7	1,339.7	1,335.9	1,341.7	1,340.7	1,336.1
2003	1,301.0	1,301.9	1,307.9	1,316.4	1,325.4	1,324.7	1,297.5	1,295.8	1,315.5	1,320.7	1,324.9	1,326.2	1,313.2
2004	1,290.3	1,291.1	1,308.0	1,327.9	1,336.2	1,339.9	1,316.0	1,312.8	1,339.6	1,342.1	1,346.2	1,349.3	1,325.0
2005	1,302.6	1,315.3	1,329.3	1,338.2	1,344.3	1,349.4	1,311.8	1,312.2	1,341.4	1,344.7	1,352.3	1,355.9	1,333.1
2006	1,317.9	1,333.2	1,345.9	1,351.5	1,361.3	1,369.7	1,330.3	1,335.8	1,369.9	1,371.8	1,374.5	1,384.0	1,353.8
2007	1,341.2	1,351.9	1,372.9	1,378.0	1,387.2	1,398.0	1,369.6	1,367.9	1,391.0	1,393.7	1,399.6	1,396.8	1,379.0
Total Private													
2000	1,078.0	1,077.4	1,086.7	1,098.8	1,103.8	1,113.8	1,107.7	1,109.2	1,110.5	1,108.2	1,110.7	1,110.1	1,101.2
2001	1,085.0	1,084.3	1,094.2	1,102.6	1,108.1	1,117.4	1,108.9	1,108.4	1,103.8	1,099.4	1,098.7	1,098.6	1,100.8
2002	1,070.4	1,067.6	1,075.7	1,088.9	1,093.1	1,099.0	1,093.4	1,093.9	1,090.7	1,081.6	1,085.3	1,084.2	1,085.3
2003	1,050.4	1,049.3	1,052.2	1,060.7	1,066.9	1,069.6	1,066.0	1,067.7	1,068.0	1,066.1	1,068.1	1,068.5	1,062.8
2004	1,040.9	1,039.1	1,053.0	1,070.1	1,076.5	1,083.0	1,085.9	1,085.4	1,087.9	1,085.3	1,087.7	1,090.1	1,073.7
2005	1,057.2	1,061.1	1,071.3	1,079.5	1,084.7	1,092.5	1,089.7	1,089.7	1,089.8	1,086.2	1,091.9	1,094.7	1,082.4
2006	1,069.8	1,075.0	1,084.7	1,091.7	1,097.8	1,109.2	1,104.6	1,108.3	1,112.4	1,109.1	1,110.4	1,118.8	1,099.3
2007	1,090.0	1,091.8	1,109.5	1,115.8	1,122.7	1,132.7	1,134.0	1,134.0	1,132.6	1,129.3	1,133.1	1,130.8	1,121.4
Goods-Producing													
2000	267.6	267.5	269.8	273.2	274.6	278.7	277.1	276.2	275.4	273.8	271.9	268.1	272.8
2001	262.1	260.4	264.3	268.3	269.5	272.5	271.5	270.9	268.1	265.8	264.3	260.5	266.5
2002	251.6	250.0	251.8	254.1	255.6	258.5	257.1	258.0	255.9	251.3	249.9	248.2	253.5
2003	239.9	241.1	242.2	242.6	245.6	245.2	245.9	246.5	245.4	245.2	244.1	242.2	243.8
2004	237.0	235.0	240.5	245.4	246.9	249.4	253.2	252.2	251.7	251.7	250.5	250.2	247.0
2005	240.4	241.7	245.9	248.5	251.0	254.8	255.7	255.3	253.2	252.6	252.6	251.5	250.3
2006	247.0	248.8	251.1	252.7	254.7	259.9	260.5	260.6	259.2	257.8	256.4	257.1	255.5
2007	251.9	250.2	256.2	256.6	258.6	263.3	264.8	265.0	264.0	262.9	262.5	259.8	259.7
Natural Resources and Mining													
2000	6.2	6.2	6.4	6.6	6.6	6.8	6.6	6.7	6.7	6.9	7.0	6.9	6.6
2001	6.6	6.6	6.7	6.8	7.0	7.1	7.1	7.3	7.3	7.1	7.0	7.0	7.0
2002	6.6	6.5	6.5	6.6	6.6	6.7	6.6	6.5	6.5	6.4	6.4	6.4	6.5
2003	6.2	6.2	6.3	6.4	6.5	6.6	6.6	6.7	6.7	6.7	6.8	6.8	6.5
2004	6.6	6.5	6.7	6.8	6.9	7.0	7.3	7.5	7.6	7.4	7.3	7.3	7.1
2005	7.2	7.3	7.3	7.4	7.5	7.6	7.6	7.7	7.7	7.9	7.9	8.0	7.6
2006	8.0	8.2	8.4	8.3	8.5	8.7	8.7	8.8	8.9	8.9	9.0	9.1	8.6
2007	8.9	8.9	9.0	9.2	9.2	9.1	9.1	9.2	9.2	9.1	9.1	9.2	9.1
Construction													
2000	60.5	60.3	62.2	65.9	67.1	69.7	69.8	69.8	68.7	67.0	64.6	61.4	65.6
2001	57.9	57.5	60.7	64.9	66.6	68.9	68.3	68.0	65.9	65.1	64.5	62.2	64.2
2002	58.2	57.6	59.5	62.4	64.1	66.4	67.2	66.7	65.2	64.3	63.5	62.4	63.1
2003	58.0	58.1	59.7	62.4	63.9	65.6	65.8	65.8	64.7	64.3	63.1	60.7	62.7
2004	57.4	54.7	59.0	63.3	64.1	66.5	67.6	66.8	65.8	65.3	64.1	63.0	63.1
2005	55.1	56.0	59.3	61.7	63.3	65.6	66.7	66.6	65.3	64.5	63.6	61.6	62.4
2006	59.2	59.8	61.7	63.2	64.4	67.2	67.7	67.4	66.3	64.6	63.9	63.6	64.1
2007	60.6	57.8	62.5	63.5	64.8	67.9	69.0	69.1	68.3	67.2	66.5	63.8	65.1
Manufacturing													
2000	200.9	201.0	201.2	200.7	200.9	202.2	200.7	199.7	200.0	199.9	200.3	199.8	200.6
2001	197.6	196.3	196.9	196.6	195.9	196.5	196.1	195.6	194.9	193.6	192.8	191.3	195.3
2002	186.8	185.9	185.8	185.1	184.9	185.4	183.3	184.8	184.2	180.6	180.0	179.4	183.9
2003	175.7	176.8	176.2	173.8	175.2	173.0	173.5	174.0	174.0	174.2	174.2	174.7	174.6
2004	173.0	173.8	174.8	175.3	175.9	175.9	178.3	177.9	178.3	179.0	179.1	179.9	176.8
2005	178.1	178.4	179.3	179.4	180.2	181.6	181.4	181.0	180.2	180.2	181.1	181.9	180.2
2006	179.8	180.8	181.0	181.2	181.8	184.0	184.0	184.3	184.0	184.3	183.5	184.4	182.8
2007	182.4	183.5	184.7	183.9	184.6	186.3	186.6	186.7	186.6	186.6	186.8	186.8	185.5
Service-Providing													
2000	1,049.7	1,052.5	1,064.6	1,077.6	1,085.5	1,086.7	1,056.7	1,056.4	1,075.5	1,085.6	1,092.9	1,095.6	1,073.3
2001	1,068.0	1,072.7	1,082.6	1,088.4	1,093.5	1,093.0	1,066.4	1,062.8	1,083.5	1,089.4	1,091.8	1,095.7	1,082.3
2002	1,069.3	1,069.7	1,079.9	1,091.4	1,096.4	1,096.2	1,068.9	1,066.7	1,083.8	1,084.6	1,091.8	1,092.5	1,082.6
2003	1,061.1	1,060.8	1,065.7	1,073.8	1,079.8	1,079.5	1,051.6	1,049.3	1,070.1	1,075.5	1,080.8	1,084.0	1,069.3
2004	1,053.3	1,056.1	1,067.5	1,082.5	1,089.3	1,090.5	1,062.8	1,060.6	1,087.9	1,090.4	1,095.7	1,099.1	1,078.0
2005	1,062.2	1,073.6	1,083.4	1,089.7	1,093.3	1,094.6	1,056.1	1,056.9	1,088.2	1,092.1	1,099.7	1,104.4	1,082.9
2006	1,070.9	1,084.4	1,094.8	1,098.8	1,106.6	1,109.8	1,069.8	1,075.2	1,110.7	1,114.0	1,118.1	1,126.9	1,098.3
2007	1,089.3	1,101.7	1,116.7	1,121.4	1,128.6	1,134.7	1,104.8	1,102.9	1,127.0	1,130.8	1,137.1	1,137.0	1,119.3
Trade, Transportation, and Utilities													
2000	273.6	271.4	272.3	273.8	274.5	276.8	273.8	274.8	274.7	275.8	280.5	282.6	275.4
2001	272.5	269.2	269.2	270.4	271.9	272.5	271.3	271.8	270.5	271.6	274.1	276.5	271.8
2002	266.6	262.8	263.1	266.4	267.4	268.7	266.0	266.0	265.6	265.9	269.4	271.0	266.6
2003	260.2	258.0	258.3	260.0	261.2	261.3	260.9	261.8	262.5	263.0	266.5	268.7	261.9
2004	258.7	256.6	257.6	260.3	262.5	263.7	261.8	261.7	263.6	263.2	267.2	268.7	262.1
2005	258.6	257.5	258.5	259.7	261.0	261.7	260.4	260.8	260.4	260.4	264.8	267.4	260.9
2006	257.3	256.1	257.7	258.0	259.1	260.4	258.8	260.2	260.9	260.6	264.2	267.9	260.1
2007	258.9	257.7	261.5	261.2	263.0	264.2	264.5	264.7	264.1	264.4	268.4	269.3	263.5
Wholesale Trade													
2000	61.6	61.6	61.9	61.6	61.9	63.2	62.6	62.0	61.7	61.6	61.3	61.4	61.9
2001	61.4	61.2	61.3	61.5	61.9	62.8	62.5	61.7	61.1	61.3	60.9	61.1	61.6
2002	60.6	60.5	60.7	61.2	61.1	61.9	61.9	61.3	60.8	60.3	60.1	60.1	60.9
2003	58.8	58.6	58.6	58.5	58.7	59.6	59.7	59.2	58.7	58.7	58.7	59.0	58.9
2004	57.5	57.5	57.9	58.3	58.8	60.1	60.2	59.7	59.3	59.3	59.2	59.0	58.9
2005	58.5	58.6	58.9	59.7	59.9	61.2	60.8	60.4	60.1	59.2	59.3	59.6	59.7
2006	58.9	59.1	59.3	58.3	58.7	60.2	60.1	59.8	59.7	59.3	59.2	59.8	59.4
2007	59.3	59.3	60.0	59.7	60.0	61.4	61.5	60.8	60.6	60.2	60.1	60.0	60.2

Employment by Industry: Kansas, 2000–2007—*Continued*

(Numbers in thousands, not seasonally adjusted.)

Industry and year	January	February	March	April	May	June	July	August	September	October	November	December	Annual Average
Retail Trade													
2000	157.9	155.9	156.4	156.7	157.3	158.5	156.6	157.8	157.8	158.2	163.5	165.5	158.5
2001	156.7	154.0	154.1	155.0	156.0	156.6	155.8	156.3	155.4	155.7	159.2	161.8	156.4
2002	153.9	150.7	150.9	152.6	153.5	154.1	152.1	152.2	152.2	152.6	156.3	158.0	153.3
2003	149.5	147.5	147.9	148.8	149.7	150.0	149.7	150.7	151.0	151.4	155.0	157.0	150.7
2004	150.3	148.2	149.0	150.1	151.5	151.5	149.6	149.2	151.3	150.4	154.5	156.3	151.0
2005	148.1	146.8	147.3	147.9	148.9	148.8	147.7	147.3	147.1	148.2	152.1	153.7	148.7
2006	146.3	145.0	146.3	147.0	147.8	147.7	146.8	147.2	147.6	147.7	151.2	153.3	147.8
2007	146.3	145.3	147.8	147.3	148.6	148.3	149.1	149.0	148.3	148.8	152.9	153.9	148.8
Transportation and Utilities													
2000	54.1	53.9	54.0	55.5	55.3	55.1	54.6	55.0	55.2	56.0	55.7	55.7	55.0
2001	54.4	54.0	53.8	53.9	54.0	53.1	53.0	53.8	54.0	54.6	54.0	53.6	53.9
2002	52.1	51.6	51.5	52.6	52.8	52.7	52.0	52.5	52.6	53.0	53.0	52.9	52.4
2003	51.9	51.9	51.8	52.7	52.8	51.7	51.5	51.9	52.8	52.9	52.8	52.7	52.3
2004	50.9	50.9	50.7	51.9	52.2	52.1	52.0	52.8	53.0	53.5	53.5	53.4	52.2
2005	52.0	52.1	52.3	52.1	52.2	51.7	51.9	53.1	53.2	53.0	53.4	54.1	52.6
2006	52.1	52.0	52.1	52.7	52.6	52.5	51.9	53.2	53.6	53.6	53.8	54.8	52.9
2007	53.3	53.1	53.7	54.2	54.4	54.5	53.9	54.9	55.2	55.4	55.4	55.4	54.5
Information													
2000	44.7	44.7	45.1	46.8	46.9	47.6	48.5	48.5	48.8	47.8	48.7	48.9	47.3
2001	51.0	51.3	51.4	50.9	50.9	50.5	51.4	50.7	50.2	49.5	49.7	50.0	50.6
2002	50.0	49.8	49.9	50.0	49.5	49.3	48.9	48.4	47.6	46.8	47.2	47.2	48.7
2003	46.7	46.0	45.7	45.1	44.7	44.9	44.3	43.6	43.3	42.9	42.9	42.9	44.4
2004	42.9	42.7	42.5	42.5	42.6	42.6	42.3	41.8	41.2	40.0	40.1	40.5	41.8
2005	40.2	40.3	40.0	40.3	40.2	40.1	40.0	39.4	39.2	38.2	38.6	38.9	39.6
2006	38.6	38.6	39.0	40.1	40.1	40.5	40.4	40.2	40.1	40.5	40.7	40.9	40.0
2007	41.2	41.2	41.3	41.3	41.4	41.4	41.4	41.0	40.5	40.1	40.5	40.8	41.0
Financial Activities													
2000	64.7	64.7	64.5	65.0	65.5	66.1	66.3	66.4	65.9	65.8	65.6	66.6	65.6
2001	66.0	66.0	66.3	66.5	67.0	67.8	68.4	68.3	67.6	67.7	67.9	68.4	67.3
2002	68.2	68.4	68.8	68.4	68.7	69.0	69.5	69.3	68.8	69.0	69.3	69.6	68.9
2003	68.5	68.5	69.0	69.5	69.6	70.0	70.1	70.5	69.7	69.6	69.4	69.7	69.5
2004	68.8	69.0	69.6	69.9	70.0	70.6	71.0	70.8	70.0	69.8	69.7	70.3	70.0
2005	69.3	69.4	69.6	70.0	70.1	70.7	71.1	71.0	70.8	71.0	71.1	71.8	70.5
2006	70.9	70.8	71.0	71.6	72.1	72.5	73.3	73.2	73.0	72.9	73.3	74.2	72.4
2007	73.2	73.3	73.9	73.7	74.2	74.7	75.1	74.9	74.4	74.4	74.3	74.3	74.2
Professional and Business Services													
2000	128.3	127.5	130.7	130.9	131.2	133.1	130.5	131.5	131.4	132.3	132.2	132.5	131.0
2001	128.8	130.3	132.3	131.2	131.2	133.6	131.1	130.6	130.7	129.1	127.6	127.5	130.3
2002	124.5	125.4	127.4	130.2	129.5	130.7	131.2	130.8	130.2	127.2	128.0	127.7	128.6
2003	123.5	123.1	122.9	126.0	125.5	127.7	124.9	125.3	124.6	124.6	124.7	126.2	124.9
2004	121.0	122.1	125.1	127.8	127.8	129.7	130.1	131.6	132.0	131.6	131.9	132.7	128.6
2005	127.8	128.7	130.5	131.8	131.3	133.0	133.9	135.2	135.3	135.8	136.8	137.7	133.2
2006	133.5	135.5	137.5	138.0	137.2	139.2	138.0	138.6	140.2	140.5	140.5	142.0	138.4
2007	138.1	139.5	141.3	143.4	143.4	144.8	146.1	147.1	147.4	147.0	146.4	147.1	144.3
Education and Health Services													
2000	144.8	145.5	146.2	146.9	147.3	146.4	147.3	147.8	150.4	150.6	151.3	151.7	148.0
2001	150.0	151.6	152.3	153.4	153.8	153.4	151.7	152.2	154.3	153.3	154.2	155.4	153.0
2002	154.2	155.1	155.9	157.8	158.4	157.1	155.8	156.3	158.7	159.0	159.5	159.6	157.3
2003	156.0	156.2	155.9	158.2	157.8	155.6	155.4	155.7	158.2	158.5	158.8	158.8	157.1
2004	157.4	158.2	159.3	160.4	160.6	159.6	160.4	160.5	162.9	162.4	164.6	164.2	161.0
2005	163.3	163.9	164.2	165.1	165.1	164.4	161.7	161.8	164.6	163.8	164.4	165.0	163.9
2006	163.1	164.3	165.1	165.6	166.3	166.3	164.3	164.9	168.5	169.0	169.1	169.9	166.4
2007	167.6	168.8	170.1	170.6	171.0	171.4	170.2	170.7	173.4	172.7	172.9	172.6	171.0
Leisure and Hospitality													
2000	103.1	104.5	106.4	110.8	112.1	113.3	112.2	112.0	111.6	109.8	108.4	107.5	109.3
2001	102.9	103.7	106.1	109.5	111.7	113.5	111.6	111.6	110.0	109.4	108.2	107.3	108.8
2002	103.0	103.7	106.0	108.9	110.9	111.8	111.8	112.3	110.6	109.5	109.2	108.0	108.8
2003	103.4	103.9	105.5	106.9	109.4	111.7	111.5	111.5	111.3	109.4	108.7	106.8	108.3
2004	103.0	103.2	105.7	110.2	112.8	113.9	114.0	113.9	113.1	111.6	110.6	110.3	110.2
2005	105.5	106.8	109.2	111.3	113.3	115.2	114.8	114.5	113.9	111.7	111.1	110.3	111.5
2006	107.6	108.7	110.7	114.1	116.4	118.4	117.9	118.9	118.2	116.2	114.7	114.9	114.7
2007	108.3	109.8	113.0	116.4	118.8	120.4	119.5	118.0	116.1	115.3	115.6	114.5	115.5
Other Services													
2000	51.2	51.6	51.7	51.4	51.7	51.8	52.0	52.0	52.3	52.3	52.1	52.2	51.9
2001	51.7	51.8	52.3	52.4	52.5	52.7	52.6	52.3	52.4	53.0	52.7	53.0	52.5
2002	52.3	52.4	52.8	53.1	53.1	53.9	53.1	52.8	53.3	52.9	52.8	52.9	53.0
2003	52.2	52.5	52.7	52.4	53.1	53.2	53.0	52.8	53.0	52.9	53.0	53.2	52.8
2004	52.1	52.3	52.7	53.6	53.3	53.5	53.1	52.9	53.4	53.2	53.1	53.2	53.0
2005	52.1	52.8	53.4	52.8	52.7	52.6	52.1	51.7	52.4	52.7	52.5	52.1	52.5
2006	51.8	52.2	52.6	51.6	51.9	52.0	51.4	51.7	52.3	51.6	51.5	51.9	51.9
2007	50.8	51.3	52.2	52.6	52.3	52.5	52.4	52.6	52.7	52.5	52.5	52.4	52.2
Government													
2000	239.3	242.6	247.7	252.0	256.3	251.6	226.1	223.4	240.4	251.2	254.1	253.6	244.9
2001	245.1	248.8	252.7	254.1	254.9	248.1	229.0	225.3	247.8	255.8	257.4	257.6	248.1
2002	250.5	252.1	256.0	256.6	258.9	255.7	232.6	230.8	249.0	254.3	256.4	256.5	250.8
2003	250.6	252.6	255.7	255.7	258.5	255.1	231.5	228.1	247.5	254.6	256.8	257.7	250.4
2004	249.4	252.0	255.0	257.8	259.7	256.9	230.1	227.4	251.7	256.8	258.5	259.2	251.2
2005	245.4	254.2	258.0	258.7	259.6	256.9	222.1	222.5	251.6	258.5	260.4	261.2	250.8
2006	248.1	258.2	261.2	259.8	263.5	260.5	225.7	227.5	257.5	262.7	264.1	265.2	254.5
2007	251.2	260.1	263.4	262.2	264.5	265.3	235.6	233.9	258.4	264.4	266.5	266.0	257.6

Average Weekly Hours by Selected Industry: Kansas, 2001–2007

(Not seasonally adjusted.)

Industry and year	January	February	March	April	May	June	July	August	September	October	November	December	Annual Average
Manufacturing													
2001	40.8	40.8	40.6	39.8	40.4	40.9	40.0	40.8	41.4	41.0	40.7	40.8	40.7
2002	40.3	40.5	40.3	40.8	40.8	40.6	40.6	40.9	41.6	41.2	40.4	41.0	40.8
2003	40.7	40.6	40.5	40.3	40.5	40.0	39.9	40.0	40.4	40.8	41.2	41.3	40.5
2004	41.5	41.6	41.2	40.9	41.1	40.8	40.7	40.3	40.4	41.0	40.7	41.3	41.0
2005	40.6	40.5	40.8	40.9	41.3	41.5	41.5	41.5	42.1	42.0	39.2	40.8	41.1
2006	41.0	40.8	42.7	41.7	42.2	42.4	42.8	44.5	44.6	44.2	43.9	45.1	43.0
2007	43.1	44.9	45.2	44.7	43.8	45.7	45.4	44.2	45.4	44.2	43.6	44.0	44.5

Average Hourly Earnings by Selected Industry: Kansas, 2001–2007

(Dollars, not seasonally adjusted.)

Industry and year	January	February	March	April	May	June	July	August	September	October	November	December	Annual Average
Manufacturing													
2001	15.48	15.37	15.29	15.27	15.33	15.37	15.51	15.53	15.57	15.67	15.62	15.71	15.48
2002	15.79	15.97	15.95	16.00	15.97	15.93	15.75	16.29	16.44	16.03	15.96	15.71	15.98
2003	15.83	15.82	15.70	15.57	15.57	15.61	15.68	15.85	15.88	16.10	16.13	16.14	15.83
2004	16.32	16.29	16.23	16.46	16.47	16.49	16.57	16.66	16.75	16.79	16.82	17.01	16.57
2005	16.78	16.93	16.99	16.96	16.98	16.98	17.06	17.19	17.05	17.50	17.87	17.46	17.14
2006	17.43	17.61	17.59	17.58	17.71	17.75	17.04	17.67	17.88	17.80	17.80	18.30	17.69
2007	18.12	18.14	18.03	18.47	18.14	18.05	17.52	17.99	17.95	17.93	18.20	18.36	18.07

Average Weekly Earnings by Selected Industry: Kansas, 2001–2007

(Dollars, not seasonally adjusted.)

Industry and year	January	February	March	April	May	June	July	August	September	October	November	December	Annual Average
Manufacturing													
2001	631.58	627.10	620.77	607.75	619.33	628.63	620.40	633.62	644.60	642.47	635.73	640.97	630.04
2002	636.34	646.79	642.79	652.80	651.58	646.76	644.18	666.26	683.90	660.44	644.78	644.11	651.98
2003	644.28	642.29	635.85	627.47	630.59	624.40	625.63	634.00	641.55	656.88	664.56	666.58	641.12
2004	677.28	677.66	668.68	673.21	676.92	672.79	674.40	671.40	676.70	688.39	684.57	702.51	679.37
2005	681.27	685.67	693.19	693.66	701.27	708.07	707.99	713.39	717.81	735.00	700.50	712.37	704.45
2006	714.63	718.49	751.09	733.09	747.36	752.60	729.31	786.32	797.45	786.76	781.42	825.33	760.67
2007	780.97	814.49	814.96	825.61	794.53	824.89	795.41	795.16	814.93	792.51	793.52	807.84	804.12

Population
    2000 census: 4,041,769
    2007 estimate: 4,241,474
    Percent change, 2000–2007: 4.9%

Percent change in total nonfarm employment, 2000–2007: 2.3%

Industry with the largest growth in employment, 2000–2007 (thousands)
    Education and health services, 32.3

Industry with the largest decline in employment, 2000–2007 (thousands)
    Manufacturing, -54.7

Civilian labor force
    2000: 1,949,013
    2007: 2,043,770

Employment-population ratio
    2000: 60.5%
    2007: 59.1%

Unemployment rate and rank among states
    2000: 4.2%, 33rd
    2007: 5.5%, 45th

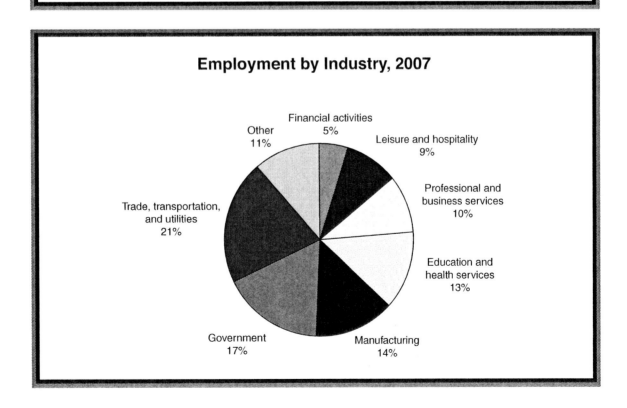

Employment by Industry, 2007

Financial activities 5%
Other 11%
Leisure and hospitality 9%
Professional and business services 10%
Trade, transportation, and utilities 21%
Education and health services 13%
Government 17%
Manufacturing 14%

Employment by Industry: Kentucky, 2000–2007

(Numbers in thousands, not seasonally adjusted.)

Industry and year	January	February	March	April	May	June	July	August	September	October	November	December	Annual Average
Total Nonfarm													
2000	1,781.5	1,793.4	1,817.0	1,827.7	1,842.9	1,840.2	1,821.5	1,830.2	1,837.8	1,842.7	1,844.7	1,845.0	1,827.1
2001	1,791.5	1,796.6	1,800.6	1,813.4	1,821.5	1,824.7	1,800.3	1,807.0	1,803.6	1,801.4	1,804.6	1,799.8	1,805.4
2002	1,759.5	1,762.0	1,774.7	1,787.6	1,800.6	1,801.8	1,783.5	1,790.8	1,796.1	1,799.6	1,806.6	1,803.0	1,788.8
2003	1,754.8	1,752.5	1,767.8	1,780.4	1,793.8	1,793.0	1,770.4	1,785.0	1,794.8	1,798.5	1,802.5	1,806.6	1,783.3
2004	1,760.8	1,763.1	1,779.0	1,796.9	1,803.7	1,808.8	1,789.1	1,803.3	1,811.9	1,817.1	1,824.1	1,825.4	1,798.6
2005	1,778.9	1,787.2	1,801.4	1,822.9	1,833.2	1,838.3	1,818.2	1,834.8	1,841.5	1,840.1	1,849.5	1,848.2	1,824.5
2006	1,810.2	1,814.1	1,836.0	1,845.6	1,857.1	1,859.5	1,833.9	1,850.7	1,856.4	1,855.4	1,865.8	1,876.7	1,846.8
2007	1,830.8	1,830.9	1,849.8	1,865.0	1,881.6	1,886.5	1,860.8	1,871.5	1,877.9	1,885.3	1,893.7	1,893.9	1,869.0
Total Private													
2000	1,484.1	1,484.8	1,503.6	1,513.5	1,525.5	1,530.8	1,526.2	1,533.2	1,532.3	1,532.6	1,533.1	1,533.5	1,519.4
2001	1,482.9	1,483.4	1,486.5	1,499.0	1,505.4	1,511.6	1,498.9	1,503.1	1,489.9	1,486.2	1,488.4	1,484.1	1,493.3
2002	1,447.2	1,445.6	1,456.5	1,468.2	1,480.9	1,486.9	1,480.8	1,489.3	1,480.3	1,481.2	1,486.9	1,485.0	1,474.1
2003	1,442.1	1,435.4	1,450.0	1,461.9	1,473.5	1,479.7	1,471.2	1,484.1	1,482.7	1,485.5	1,489.0	1,495.0	1,470.8
2004	1,451.5	1,450.4	1,464.7	1,481.3	1,489.9	1,499.7	1,490.7	1,504.1	1,501.4	1,504.8	1,510.8	1,513.8	1,488.6
2005	1,469.3	1,473.3	1,486.2	1,505.6	1,514.9	1,525.0	1,515.3	1,526.8	1,525.9	1,522.5	1,530.7	1,530.5	1,510.5
2006	1,496.3	1,496.0	1,516.4	1,524.1	1,534.5	1,544.3	1,527.2	1,538.0	1,535.9	1,533.1	1,542.5	1,553.9	1,528.5
2007	1,513.0	1,508.9	1,526.2	1,539.1	1,554.3	1,564.4	1,547.4	1,552.2	1,550.8	1,553.9	1,561.1	1,561.5	1,544.4
Goods-Producing													
2000	411.3	409.9	415.3	417.6	420.3	421.3	418.7	420.6	420.6	418.8	417.1	417.4	417.4
2001	400.6	401.1	400.1	404.0	405.4	407.3	401.1	402.0	398.8	395.1	393.5	390.2	399.9
2002	378.6	377.0	378.2	379.3	380.2	382.0	378.1	381.3	379.0	378.9	377.2	375.0	378.7
2003	364.4	360.6	363.4	365.1	367.5	369.1	367.7	370.3	370.7	371.1	369.4	370.4	367.5
2004	361.0	358.9	361.4	365.0	368.0	370.2	363.4	371.5	371.3	370.1	370.1	369.3	366.7
2005	358.9	359.1	362.2	366.8	369.4	372.3	365.4	372.0	372.3	371.8	372.5	370.6	367.8
2006	364.3	362.6	365.6	366.7	368.6	371.3	364.4	371.1	369.8	364.1	363.8	367.7	366.7
2007	358.7	356.1	358.5	363.4	365.9	369.4	362.4	364.1	366.5	365.5	364.9	360.9	363.0
Natural Resources and Mining													
2000	20.1	19.8	20.2	19.5	19.5	19.6	19.2	19.2	19.2	18.8	18.8	18.6	19.4
2001	18.7	19.0	19.2	19.8	20.2	20.6	20.8	21.2	21.3	21.5	21.8	21.8	20.5
2002	21.2	21.0	20.8	20.4	20.4	20.5	20.2	20.2	20.2	19.8	19.8	19.7	20.4
2003	19.4	19.3	19.3	18.7	18.6	18.8	18.7	18.9	19.1	19.0	19.0	19.5	19.0
2004	19.1	18.9	19.2	19.6	19.6	19.8	19.7	19.8	19.7	20.1	20.1	20.3	19.7
2005	20.1	20.1	20.5	20.9	21.2	21.5	21.6	21.8	22.2	22.3	22.6	22.7	21.5
2006	22.3	22.3	22.7	22.9	23.0	23.2	23.2	23.1	23.1	22.9	22.9	22.9	22.9
2007	22.2	22.2	22.4	22.1	22.0	22.2	22.1	22.2	22.2	22.2	22.2	22.2	22.2
Construction													
2000	81.8	81.8	86.1	87.3	88.9	89.9	90.1	89.2	89.3	89.8	88.8	88.6	87.6
2001	79.9	81.4	82.3	87.9	89.8	92.2	92.5	92.0	90.8	89.2	88.4	85.4	87.7
2002	77.9	78.2	79.7	82.0	83.4	85.1	85.7	86.7	86.2	86.1	85.3	83.3	83.3
2003	76.6	74.2	78.4	82.4	84.4	85.5	86.5	86.3	86.0	87.1	85.4	83.8	83.1
2004	77.5	76.5	78.8	82.6	84.5	86.0	87.5	86.9	86.7	85.8	85.2	83.7	83.5
2005	76.2	77.4	79.5	83.2	85.6	87.6	89.1	88.0	87.2	87.0	86.0	84.0	84.2
2006	78.8	78.2	80.2	82.1	84.3	85.5	85.8	86.0	85.2	84.4	84.0	83.1	83.1
2007	77.4	75.5	80.9	84.2	86.4	88.2	88.5	88.9	88.7	88.4	88.0	86.7	85.2
Manufacturing													
2000	309.4	308.3	309.0	310.8	311.9	311.8	309.4	312.2	312.1	310.2	309.5	310.2	310.4
2001	302.0	300.7	298.6	296.3	295.4	294.5	287.8	288.8	286.7	284.4	283.3	283.0	291.8
2002	279.5	277.8	277.7	276.9	276.4	276.4	272.2	274.4	272.6	273.0	272.1	272.0	275.1
2003	268.4	267.1	265.7	264.0	264.5	264.8	262.5	265.1	265.6	265.0	265.0	267.1	265.4
2004	264.4	263.5	263.4	262.8	263.9	264.4	256.2	264.8	264.9	264.2	264.8	265.3	263.6
2005	262.6	261.6	262.2	262.7	262.6	263.2	254.7	262.2	262.9	262.5	263.9	263.9	262.1
2006	263.2	262.1	262.7	261.7	261.3	262.6	255.4	262.0	261.5	256.8	256.9	261.7	260.7
2007	259.1	258.4	255.2	257.1	257.5	259.0	251.8	253.0	255.6	254.9	254.7	252.0	255.7
Service-Providing													
2000	1,370.2	1,383.5	1,401.7	1,410.1	1,422.6	1,418.9	1,402.8	1,409.6	1,417.2	1,423.9	1,427.6	1,427.6	1,409.6
2001	1,390.9	1,395.5	1,400.5	1,409.4	1,416.1	1,417.4	1,399.2	1,405.0	1,404.8	1,406.3	1,411.1	1,409.6	1,405.5
2002	1,380.9	1,385.0	1,396.5	1,408.3	1,420.4	1,419.8	1,405.4	1,409.5	1,417.1	1,420.7	1,429.4	1,428.0	1,410.1
2003	1,390.4	1,391.9	1,404.4	1,415.3	1,426.3	1,423.9	1,402.7	1,414.7	1,424.1	1,427.4	1,433.1	1,436.2	1,415.9
2004	1,399.8	1,404.2	1,417.6	1,431.9	1,435.7	1,438.6	1,425.7	1,431.8	1,440.6	1,447.0	1,454.0	1,456.1	1,431.9
2005	1,420.0	1,428.1	1,439.2	1,456.1	1,463.8	1,466.0	1,452.8	1,462.8	1,469.2	1,468.3	1,477.0	1,477.6	1,456.7
2006	1,445.9	1,451.5	1,470.4	1,478.9	1,488.5	1,488.2	1,469.5	1,479.6	1,486.6	1,491.3	1,502.0	1,509.0	1,480.1
2007	1,472.1	1,474.8	1,491.3	1,501.6	1,515.7	1,517.1	1,498.4	1,507.4	1,511.4	1,519.8	1,528.8	1,533.0	1,506.0
Trade, Transportation, and Utilities													
2000	383.6	381.0	384.7	387.3	390.3	391.4	392.0	392.9	392.3	394.6	400.0	402.1	391.0
2001	383.0	379.4	378.9	379.5	379.8	380.0	377.9	378.2	375.8	378.2	383.2	384.3	379.9
2002	370.1	367.1	369.5	369.1	371.7	372.1	371.7	372.3	370.6	372.1	378.9	382.8	372.3
2003	366.0	362.9	365.9	366.8	369.7	370.2	369.0	372.2	371.5	373.9	379.2	383.5	370.9
2004	367.9	365.3	368.1	370.0	372.2	373.6	371.7	373.5	373.5	377.0	383.1	386.5	373.5
2005	372.4	370.1	372.7	375.1	377.5	378.5	378.3	379.0	377.8	377.9	385.5	388.7	377.8
2006	374.7	371.6	376.5	377.1	380.2	381.9	378.5	379.4	379.1	381.9	389.2	394.2	380.4
2007	381.1	378.2	383.2	383.1	386.7	388.7	385.2	385.2	385.6	388.9	395.3	399.0	386.7
Wholesale Trade													
2000	72.7	72.6	73.1	73.3	73.5	73.5	73.0	73.1	73.1	74.5	75.3	75.1	73.6
2001	73.7	73.5	73.3	72.9	73.1	73.3	72.8	72.8	72.1	72.4	72.5	72.8	72.9
2002	72.2	72.1	71.5	71.8	72.3	72.2	71.9	72.1	71.8	72.3	72.8	73.2	72.2
2003	72.8	72.6	72.4	72.7	73.2	73.4	73.0	73.5	73.3	73.2	73.7	74.3	73.2
2004	73.7	73.5	73.6	73.9	73.9	74.1	74.3	74.2	73.9	74.2	74.8	75.2	74.1
2005	74.3	74.0	74.1	74.4	74.6	74.6	74.5	74.6	74.5	74.5	74.8	75.2	74.5
2006	74.7	74.7	75.4	75.8	76.2	76.5	75.9	76.0	75.9	76.5	76.7	77.3	76.0
2007	76.6	76.6	77.2	77.3	77.4	77.8	77.4	77.4	77.6	77.8	78.1	78.4	77.5

Employment by Industry: Kentucky, 2000–2007—*Continued*

(Numbers in thousands, not seasonally adjusted.)

Industry and year	January	February	March	April	May	June	July	August	September	October	November	December	Annual Average
Retail Trade													
2000	220.6	218.6	221.1	221.1	223.8	225.1	224.8	226.0	225.8	224.6	229.7	232.1	224.4
2001	217.0	214.1	214.6	214.8	216.4	216.6	213.5	214.1	213.0	214.0	219.3	220.6	215.7
2002	209.6	207.5	210.6	211.4	213.3	213.8	211.2	211.4	210.8	210.9	217.3	220.6	212.4
2003	207.3	204.3	206.4	207.5	209.8	210.2	209.7	211.3	211.2	212.3	217.6	221.0	210.7
2004	208.4	206.1	208.1	209.2	210.8	211.6	209.4	210.6	211.0	212.4	218.0	220.8	211.4
2005	210.0	207.7	209.5	210.6	212.5	212.7	212.2	212.0	210.9	211.1	217.5	220.3	212.3
2006	209.8	207.4	210.5	210.5	212.3	212.2	210.2	210.5	209.2	211.2	217.4	220.0	211.8
2007	211.0	208.5	212.3	212.2	215.0	215.2	213.9	213.1	212.5	214.5	219.8	221.6	214.1
Transportation and Utilities													
2000	90.3	89.8	90.5	92.9	93.0	92.8	94.2	93.8	93.4	95.5	95.0	94.9	93.0
2001	92.3	91.8	91.0	91.8	90.3	90.1	91.6	91.3	90.7	91.8	91.4	90.9	91.3
2002	88.3	87.5	87.4	85.9	86.1	86.1	88.6	88.8	88.0	88.9	88.8	89.0	87.8
2003	85.9	86.0	87.1	86.6	86.7	86.6	86.3	87.4	87.0	88.4	87.9	88.2	87.0
2004	85.8	85.7	86.4	86.9	87.5	87.9	88.0	88.7	88.6	90.4	90.3	90.5	88.1
2005	88.1	88.4	89.1	90.1	90.4	91.2	91.6	92.4	92.4	92.3	93.2	93.2	91.0
2006	90.2	89.5	90.6	90.8	91.7	93.2	92.4	92.9	94.0	94.2	95.1	96.9	92.6
2007	93.5	93.1	93.7	93.6	94.3	95.7	93.9	94.7	95.5	96.6	97.4	99.0	95.1
Information													
2000	31.9	32.2	32.8	32.8	33.2	33.4	33.5	33.7	33.7	33.4	33.4	33.5	33.1
2001	33.3	33.4	33.6	33.3	33.4	33.4	33.0	32.7	32.2	31.9	31.8	31.9	32.8
2002	32.3	32.2	32.2	31.6	31.5	31.6	31.3	31.2	30.9	30.5	30.7	30.8	31.4
2003	30.5	30.6	30.8	30.1	30.2	29.9	29.5	29.3	28.8	29.0	29.0	29.1	29.7
2004	28.9	29.0	29.0	29.0	29.1	29.4	29.3	29.1	28.7	28.9	29.1	29.4	29.1
2005	28.6	28.7	29.0	29.0	29.4	29.6	29.6	29.6	29.3	29.2	29.5	29.7	29.3
2006	29.4	29.5	29.5	29.4	29.6	29.7	29.5	29.4	29.2	29.5	29.6	29.7	29.5
2007	29.6	29.5	29.6	29.9	30.3	30.5	30.3	30.3	30.1	30.2	30.4	30.5	30.1
Financial Activities													
2000	84.7	84.8	84.4	84.2	84.7	85.7	83.0	83.1	82.6	82.8	83.0	82.9	83.8
2001	83.3	83.1	83.5	84.1	84.5	85.3	85.1	85.3	84.6	84.0	84.2	84.9	84.3
2002	83.6	83.9	84.1	84.5	85.1	85.6	85.3	85.4	84.9	84.8	85.0	85.4	84.8
2003	84.8	84.7	85.2	85.8	86.4	87.1	87.0	87.8	87.4	87.4	87.5	87.9	86.6
2004	86.5	86.5	87.0	87.3	87.4	87.5	87.4	87.6	86.8	86.5	86.6	87.2	87.0
2005	86.4	86.5	86.6	87.3	87.5	88.4	88.2	88.4	88.2	88.4	88.6	89.2	87.8
2006	89.0	89.3	90.1	90.4	91.0	91.6	91.1	91.3	91.6	91.9	92.3	93.1	91.1
2007	92.3	92.3	92.4	92.9	93.2	93.9	93.9	93.8	93.3	93.9	93.8	94.4	93.3
Professional and Business Services													
2000	152.4	152.8	156.6	155.6	156.4	157.2	158.8	160.9	161.8	162.8	163.0	161.8	158.3
2001	156.3	156.4	157.1	156.5	156.1	157.2	154.9	156.8	155.4	154.4	153.8	153.0	155.7
2002	149.2	149.2	151.1	152.7	154.6	156.3	155.8	159.5	158.1	158.0	158.7	157.5	155.1
2003	151.0	149.7	151.6	153.5	154.4	154.2	153.1	156.4	156.8	160.1	161.4	162.7	155.4
2004	153.7	154.8	156.5	159.3	159.9	161.3	162.8	165.6	166.9	169.7	170.7	171.1	162.7
2005	164.1	165.7	167.5	170.0	169.9	171.7	170.4	173.7	175.7	177.4	179.0	179.0	172.0
2006	172.1	172.4	177.0	177.1	177.4	179.6	178.0	180.9	181.4	182.6	185.0	187.4	179.2
2007	177.0	177.0	179.6	180.4	181.8	182.6	180.6	182.5	182.2	183.2	184.9	186.8	181.6
Education and Health Services													
2000	204.7	206.8	207.7	208.0	208.4	208.1	207.8	209.4	209.9	210.4	210.6	210.4	208.5
2001	209.1	210.4	211.2	211.8	212.1	212.4	213.3	214.2	214.7	216.6	217.1	217.2	213.3
2002	217.3	218.2	218.7	221.5	222.0	222.2	222.3	223.4	224.6	226.1	227.3	227.5	222.6
2003	225.8	226.6	227.5	227.2	227.8	227.6	224.9	226.4	229.0	229.5	229.4	229.4	227.6
2004	227.7	229.2	230.1	230.3	230.1	230.2	230.4	231.2	232.0	233.4	234.0	234.3	231.1
2005	231.4	233.7	233.5	234.7	235.5	235.2	235.4	236.0	237.0	236.6	236.2	236.9	235.2
2006	235.1	236.3	237.3	237.7	237.6	238.1	236.7	236.8	238.0	239.3	239.3	240.1	237.7
2007	238.8	239.5	240.5	239.7	240.8	241.5	240.5	241.0	241.5	241.7	242.2	241.8	240.8
Leisure and Hospitality													
2000	140.9	142.1	146.5	152.3	156.1	157.3	157.6	157.7	156.7	155.2	151.1	150.3	152.0
2001	143.2	145.2	147.4	155.0	159.0	160.0	159.0	159.3	154.6	152.3	151.1	148.3	152.9
2002	141.8	143.5	147.8	153.7	159.7	160.2	160.2	160.3	156.7	155.0	153.1	150.0	153.5
2003	144.1	144.7	149.4	156.7	160.3	163.6	162.6	163.7	160.8	156.7	155.6	154.2	156.0
2004	149.0	149.7	155.0	161.8	164.5	168.1	168.0	167.9	164.8	162.6	160.8	159.3	161.0
2005	152.1	153.6	158.4	166.5	169.1	172.6	171.9	172.0	169.6	165.4	163.5	160.4	164.6
2006	156.6	158.8	163.9	169.8	174.0	175.5	173.3	173.9	171.7	168.8	168.4	166.4	168.4
2007	160.9	161.7	166.9	173.8	179.1	180.6	178.4	179.0	175.3	174.0	173.2	171.6	172.9
Other Services													
2000	74.6	75.2	75.6	75.7	76.1	76.4	74.8	74.9	74.7	74.6	74.9	75.1	75.2
2001	74.1	74.4	74.7	74.8	75.1	76.0	74.6	74.6	73.8	73.7	73.7	74.3	74.5
2002	74.3	74.5	74.9	75.8	76.1	76.9	76.1	75.9	75.5	75.8	76.0	76.0	75.7
2003	75.5	75.6	76.2	76.7	77.2	78.0	77.4	78.0	77.7	77.8	77.5	77.8	77.1
2004	76.8	77.0	77.6	78.6	78.7	79.4	77.7	77.7	77.4	76.6	76.4	76.7	77.6
2005	75.4	75.9	76.3	76.2	76.6	76.7	76.1	76.1	76.0	75.8	75.9	76.0	76.1
2006	75.1	75.5	76.5	75.9	76.1	76.6	75.7	75.2	75.1	75.0	74.9	75.3	75.6
2007	74.6	74.6	75.5	75.9	76.5	77.2	76.1	76.3	76.3	76.5	76.4	76.5	76.0
Government													
2000	297.4	308.6	313.4	314.2	317.4	309.4	295.3	297.0	305.5	310.1	311.6	311.5	307.6
2001	308.6	313.2	314.1	314.4	316.1	313.1	301.4	303.9	313.7	315.2	316.2	315.7	312.1
2002	312.3	316.4	318.2	319.4	319.7	314.9	302.7	301.5	315.8	318.4	319.7	318.0	314.8
2003	312.7	317.1	317.8	318.5	320.3	313.3	299.2	300.9	312.1	313.0	313.5	311.6	312.5
2004	309.3	312.7	314.3	315.6	313.8	309.1	298.4	299.2	310.5	312.3	313.3	311.6	310.0
2005	309.6	313.9	315.2	317.3	318.3	313.3	302.9	308.0	315.6	317.6	318.8	317.7	314.0
2006	313.9	318.1	319.6	321.5	322.6	315.2	306.7	312.7	320.5	322.3	323.3	322.8	318.3
2007	317.8	322.0	323.6	325.9	327.3	322.1	313.4	319.3	327.1	331.4	332.6	332.4	324.6

Average Weekly Hours by Selected Industry: Kentucky, 2001–2007

(Not seasonally adjusted.)

Industry and year	January	February	March	April	May	June	July	August	September	October	November	December	Annual Average
Natural Resources and Mining													
2001	51.3	50.5	50.6	49.9	49.8	49.2	49.4	49.6	49.8	49.2	48.6	50.1	49.8
2002	49.1	48.6	48.3	47.9	49.2	49.3	49.7	49.1	49.9	49.6	48.7	49.5	49.1
2003	48.3	47.1	49.0	48.8	49.3	48.4	48.4	48.3	48.3	48.8	49.4	48.2	48.5
2004	48.9	49.3	49.5	49.3	49.2	49.5	49.2	49.5	49.5	50.0	49.1	49.4	49.4
2005	49.3	49.7	49.8	49.6	49.4	49.1	49.2	49.4	49.6	49.6	49.7	49.8	49.5
2006	49.8	49.6	49.5	49.5	49.3	49.5	49.3	49.4	49.5	49.6	49.5	49.6	49.5
2007	49.7	49.8	49.9	49.7	49.8	49.9	50.0	50.1	50.2	50.1	50.0	50.1	49.9
Manufacturing													
2001	41.6	41.0	41.3	40.7	41.6	41.9	41.5	41.7	41.5	41.5	41.5	42.1	41.5
2002	41.9	41.8	42.0	41.9	41.8	42.5	42.2	42.4	42.6	42.3	42.3	42.9	42.2
2003	41.9	41.8	41.8	41.7	41.6	41.5	41.4	42.1	41.9	41.6	41.8	41.7	41.7
2004	41.2	41.2	41.1	41.2	41.0	40.9	40.8	40.8	40.7	40.2	40.4	40.5	40.8
2005	40.3	40.1	40.4	40.3	40.3	40.6	40.6	40.7	41.0	41.1	41.1	41.2	40.6
2006	41.0	41.0	41.2	41.1	41.0	41.0	41.1	41.1	41.3	41.3	41.2	41.3	41.1
2007	41.2	41.3	41.4	41.2	41.3	41.3	41.2	41.2	41.2	41.2	41.3	41.4	41.3

Average Hourly Earnings by Selected Industry: Kentucky, 2001–2007

(Dollars, not seasonally adjusted.)

Industry and year	January	February	March	April	May	June	July	August	September	October	November	December	Annual Average
Natural Resources and Mining													
2001	14.67	14.65	14.64	14.51	14.67	14.85	14.79	14.79	14.87	14.74	14.81	14.70	14.73
2002	14.66	14.58	14.58	14.49	14.50	14.84	14.79	14.72	14.83	14.84	14.87	15.08	14.73
2003	15.33	15.47	15.69	15.41	15.34	15.19	15.28	15.45	15.40	15.54	15.87	16.58	15.55
2004	16.85	17.21	17.98	18.01	18.56	18.45	17.95	17.51	17.10	17.42	16.99	17.68	17.64
2005	17.67	17.62	17.85	17.79	17.95	18.04	17.91	18.00	17.97	17.66	17.69	17.62	17.81
2006	17.60	17.61	17.56	17.55	17.59	17.78	17.71	17.82	17.92	17.95	17.92	17.90	17.74
2007	17.97	17.81	17.83	17.82	17.53	17.50	17.80	17.91	17.93	17.93	17.97	17.83	17.82
Manufacturing													
2001	15.14	15.17	15.22	15.37	15.51	15.54	15.43	15.57	15.61	15.46	15.55	15.70	15.44
2002	15.54	15.61	15.59	15.76	15.72	15.80	15.39	15.76	15.87	15.95	15.80	15.96	15.73
2003	16.09	15.81	15.70	15.86	15.64	15.88	16.12	16.09	16.06	16.15	16.30	16.47	16.01
2004	16.37	16.49	16.51	16.57	16.53	16.75	16.60	16.53	16.42	16.35	16.51	16.40	16.50
2005	16.42	16.38	16.44	16.66	16.67	16.87	16.48	16.81	16.76	16.82	16.72	16.72	16.65
2006	16.87	16.95	17.02	16.93	17.02	16.94	16.66	16.85	17.19	16.97	16.80	16.86	16.92
2007	16.80	16.97	16.92	16.88	16.88	17.09	16.88	16.78	16.76	16.94	17.09	17.04	16.92

Average Weekly Earnings by Selected Industry: Kentucky, 2001–2007

(Dollars, not seasonally adjusted.)

Industry and year	January	February	March	April	May	June	July	August	September	October	November	December	Annual Average
Natural Resources and Mining													
2001	752.57	739.83	740.78	724.05	730.57	730.62	730.63	733.58	740.53	725.21	719.77	736.47	733.55
2002	719.81	708.59	704.21	694.07	713.40	731.61	735.06	722.75	740.02	736.06	724.17	746.46	723.24
2003	740.44	728.64	768.81	752.01	756.26	735.20	739.55	746.24	743.82	758.35	783.98	799.16	754.18
2004	823.97	848.45	890.01	887.89	913.15	913.28	883.14	866.75	846.45	871.00	834.21	873.39	871.42
2005	871.13	875.71	888.93	882.38	886.73	885.76	881.17	889.20	891.31	875.94	879.19	877.48	881.60
2006	876.48	873.46	869.22	868.73	867.19	880.11	873.10	880.31	887.04	890.32	887.04	887.84	878.13
2007	893.11	886.94	889.72	885.65	872.99	873.25	890.00	897.29	900.09	898.29	898.50	893.28	889.22
Manufacturing													
2001	629.82	621.97	628.59	625.56	645.22	651.13	640.35	649.27	647.82	641.59	645.33	660.97	640.76
2002	651.13	652.50	654.78	660.34	657.10	671.50	649.46	668.22	676.06	674.69	668.34	684.68	663.81
2003	674.17	660.86	656.26	661.36	650.62	659.02	667.37	677.39	672.91	671.84	681.34	686.80	667.62
2004	674.44	679.39	678.56	682.68	677.73	685.08	677.28	674.42	668.29	657.27	667.00	664.20	673.20
2005	661.73	656.84	664.18	671.40	671.80	684.92	669.09	684.17	687.16	691.30	687.19	688.86	675.99
2006	691.67	694.95	701.22	695.82	697.82	694.54	684.73	692.54	709.95	700.86	692.16	696.32	695.41
2007	692.16	700.86	700.49	695.46	697.14	705.82	695.46	691.34	690.51	697.93	705.82	705.46	698.80

LOUISIANA
At a Glance

Population
  2000 census: 4,468,976
  2007 estimate: 4,293,204
  Percent change, 2000–2007: -3.9%

Percent change in total nonfarm employment, 2000–2007: 0.2%

Industry with the largest growth in employment, 2000–2007 (thousands)
  Education and health services, 23.2

Industry with the largest decline in employment, 2000–2007 (thousands)
  Manufacturing, -19.2

Civilian labor force
  2000: 2,031,292
  2007: 1,997,873

Employment-population ratio
  2000: 58.7%
  2007: 59.3%

Unemployment rate and rank among states
  2000: 5.0%, 44th
  2007: 3.8%, 15th

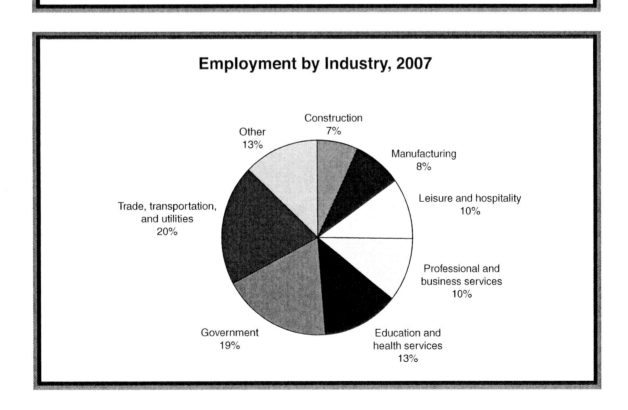

Employment by Industry, 2007

Construction 7%
Other 13%
Manufacturing 8%
Leisure and hospitality 10%
Trade, transportation, and utilities 20%
Professional and business services 10%
Government 19%
Education and health services 13%

Employment by Industry: Louisiana, 2000–2007

(Numbers in thousands, not seasonally adjusted.)

Industry and year	January	February	March	April	May	June	July	August	September	October	November	December	Annual Average
Total Nonfarm													
2000	1,887.8	1,901.7	1,916.5	1,922.1	1,938.3	1,929.5	1,904.4	1,907.6	1,922.4	1,921.7	1,925.8	1,935.0	1,917.7
2001	1,897.3	1,908.9	1,923.1	1,924.4	1,930.8	1,930.7	1,900.6	1,906.5	1,918.5	1,911.7	1,915.8	1,916.1	1,915.4
2002	1,872.2	1,880.1	1,890.9	1,903.1	1,907.1	1,907.5	1,883.9	1,888.2	1,899.8	1,897.6	1,908.7	1,908.4	1,895.6
2003	1,882.8	1,893.1	1,899.4	1,906.4	1,913.2	1,911.5	1,890.8	1,895.0	1,908.7	1,916.9	1,923.4	1,925.2	1,905.5
2004	1,891.4	1,902.7	1,919.7	1,924.7	1,923.0	1,924.5	1,905.9	1,908.5	1,913.3	1,922.0	1,935.8	1,939.0	1,917.5
2005	1,904.9	1,913.9	1,930.8	1,948.5	1,951.8	1,953.3	1,937.6	1,941.1	1,823.8	1,776.0	1,801.9	1,817.6	1,891.8
2006	1,789.8	1,813.1	1,839.8	1,841.5	1,854.3	1,859.4	1,835.0	1,852.4	1,874.9	1,880.5	1,892.9	1,904.6	1,853.2
2007	1,876.5	1,895.4	1,915.5	1,912.0	1,920.2	1,926.1	1,904.9	1,924.6	1,933.1	1,941.2	1,948.7	1,949.5	1,920.6
Total Private													
2000	1,517.2	1,525.1	1,537.0	1,542.9	1,553.3	1,555.6	1,539.6	1,547.9	1,550.8	1,547.9	1,552.1	1,562.0	1,544.3
2001	1,525.2	1,530.8	1,544.0	1,547.0	1,553.8	1,556.2	1,537.9	1,545.8	1,545.5	1,535.7	1,538.2	1,539.1	1,541.6
2002	1,502.2	1,504.6	1,513.8	1,525.6	1,529.5	1,531.1	1,517.2	1,523.7	1,524.7	1,518.9	1,527.5	1,529.5	1,520.7
2003	1,508.3	1,511.4	1,516.3	1,523.4	1,531.1	1,531.3	1,519.4	1,527.5	1,529.5	1,534.3	1,539.0	1,543.8	1,526.3
2004	1,514.1	1,518.6	1,533.8	1,539.3	1,539.2	1,542.6	1,532.2	1,536.7	1,530.3	1,535.9	1,548.9	1,553.4	1,535.4
2005	1,528.4	1,530.6	1,547.7	1,564.3	1,569.6	1,573.6	1,567.8	1,570.9	1,445.7	1,415.8	1,441.1	1,458.7	1,517.9
2006	1,446.8	1,463.6	1,488.7	1,492.2	1,504.4	1,517.8	1,501.0	1,513.2	1,522.0	1,526.8	1,536.9	1,549.0	1,505.2
2007	1,527.8	1,538.2	1,556.0	1,553.2	1,561.4	1,569.9	1,557.9	1,572.7	1,569.4	1,574.0	1,580.0	1,582.2	1,561.9
Goods-Producing													
2000	348.8	349.9	353.1	354.8	359.0	360.0	353.3	355.6	354.0	352.6	349.8	349.4	353.4
2001	343.7	345.5	350.7	350.2	354.6	355.6	351.2	352.4	350.0	345.2	341.3	337.2	348.1
2002	328.4	326.6	327.4	328.7	330.6	330.4	327.2	329.0	328.0	329.4	326.4	324.3	328.0
2003	321.1	320.1	320.4	319.3	324.8	325.6	321.6	322.8	322.9	324.5	320.9	319.1	321.9
2004	313.2	312.9	317.2	315.7	314.3	315.8	314.7	312.6	312.3	314.5	315.1	314.9	314.4
2005	308.9	310.5	314.4	319.9	321.9	323.5	321.6	323.0	307.5	311.6	315.1	317.7	316.3
2006	320.4	322.8	327.9	329.7	331.9	336.2	328.0	332.4	336.5	338.0	338.1	341.0	331.9
2007	332.2	335.5	338.7	340.2	343.1	345.7	343.4	346.9	346.9	348.7	347.9	347.8	343.1
Natural Resources and Mining													
2000	44.9	45.0	44.8	46.0	46.8	47.8	48.0	48.6	49.0	48.4	48.4	49.1	47.2
2001	50.0	51.1	51.9	52.1	52.9	53.7	53.0	53.4	53.1	51.8	50.2	50.2	52.0
2002	49.5	48.8	48.5	48.2	48.6	48.9	48.7	48.8	48.7	47.5	47.4	47.4	48.4
2003	47.3	47.3	47.4	47.2	47.4	48.2	47.3	47.5	47.0	46.8	46.5	45.8	47.1
2004	44.9	44.9	45.4	45.2	44.7	45.0	44.3	44.4	43.9	44.6	44.5	44.5	44.7
2005	44.0	44.2	44.8	45.2	45.5	46.0	45.8	46.0	45.7	45.4	45.1	45.3	45.3
2006	46.4	46.9	47.3	47.2	47.6	48.6	49.1	49.7	50.5	50.1	49.9	50.1	48.6
2007	49.6	49.8	50.0	50.8	51.1	51.4	51.2	51.5	51.7	51.6	51.4	51.6	51.0
Construction													
2000	126.8	128.8	131.9	132.1	133.9	134.1	128.3	129.5	127.8	126.1	124.3	123.2	128.9
2001	118.9	120.5	124.5	124.6	127.3	127.2	126.4	127.6	126.5	125.3	124.4	121.7	124.6
2002	119.2	117.8	118.4	119.9	120.8	119.1	118.3	119.4	118.9	120.8	118.6	116.9	119.0
2003	117.2	117.3	117.0	118.1	120.9	120.3	119.6	119.9	120.1	121.5	118.7	117.6	119.0
2004	116.8	116.6	120.1	117.9	116.4	116.3	116.7	114.2	114.1	115.7	116.6	115.7	116.4
2005	112.2	113.9	116.2	120.7	121.4	121.6	120.9	121.2	114.5	118.5	121.8	122.8	118.8
2006	125.7	127.3	130.8	132.4	133.3	134.9	127.3	129.0	130.3	131.8	131.6	133.3	130.6
2007	129.1	130.5	132.7	132.5	134.2	135.1	133.6	136.6	135.8	137.2	136.5	136.0	134.2
Manufacturing													
2000	177.1	176.1	176.4	176.7	178.3	178.1	177.0	177.5	177.2	178.1	177.1	177.1	177.2
2001	174.8	173.9	174.3	173.5	174.4	174.7	171.8	171.4	170.4	168.1	166.7	165.3	171.6
2002	159.7	160.0	160.5	160.6	161.2	162.4	160.2	160.8	160.4	161.1	160.4	160.0	160.6
2003	156.6	155.5	156.0	154.0	156.5	157.1	154.7	155.4	155.8	156.2	155.7	155.7	155.8
2004	151.5	151.4	151.7	152.6	153.2	154.5	153.7	154.0	154.3	154.2	154.0	154.7	153.3
2005	152.7	152.4	153.4	154.0	155.0	155.9	154.9	155.8	147.3	147.7	148.2	149.6	152.2
2006	148.3	148.6	149.8	150.1	151.0	152.7	151.6	153.7	155.7	156.1	156.6	157.6	152.7
2007	153.5	155.2	156.0	156.9	157.8	159.2	158.6	158.8	159.4	159.9	160.0	160.2	158.0
Service-Providing													
2000	1,539.0	1,551.8	1,563.4	1,567.3	1,579.3	1,569.5	1,551.1	1,552.0	1,568.4	1,569.1	1,576.0	1,585.6	1,564.4
2001	1,553.6	1,563.4	1,572.4	1,574.2	1,576.2	1,575.1	1,549.4	1,554.1	1,568.5	1,566.5	1,574.5	1,578.9	1,567.2
2002	1,543.8	1,553.5	1,563.5	1,574.4	1,576.5	1,577.1	1,556.7	1,559.2	1,571.8	1,568.2	1,582.3	1,584.1	1,567.6
2003	1,561.7	1,573.0	1,579.0	1,587.1	1,588.4	1,585.9	1,569.2	1,572.2	1,585.8	1,592.4	1,602.5	1,606.1	1,583.6
2004	1,578.2	1,589.8	1,602.5	1,609.0	1,608.7	1,608.7	1,591.2	1,595.9	1,601.0	1,607.5	1,620.7	1,624.1	1,603.1
2005	1,596.0	1,603.4	1,616.4	1,628.6	1,629.9	1,629.8	1,616.0	1,618.1	1,516.3	1,464.4	1,486.8	1,499.9	1,575.5
2006	1,469.4	1,490.3	1,511.9	1,511.8	1,522.4	1,523.2	1,507.0	1,520.0	1,538.4	1,542.5	1,554.8	1,563.6	1,521.3
2007	1,544.3	1,559.9	1,576.8	1,571.8	1,577.1	1,580.4	1,561.5	1,577.7	1,586.2	1,592.5	1,600.8	1,601.7	1,577.6
Trade, Transportation, and Utilities													
2000	384.1	385.3	388.3	387.2	390.1	391.8	387.7	390.8	391.6	390.3	396.5	402.5	390.5
2001	386.0	384.9	387.9	387.8	388.3	389.8	386.8	389.2	388.2	386.5	391.9	395.3	388.6
2002	379.9	378.4	381.6	383.6	384.8	386.6	383.8	384.3	383.8	381.8	388.2	393.0	384.2
2003	379.1	377.9	379.4	379.5	379.8	380.8	378.0	379.6	378.9	380.7	386.1	390.2	380.8
2004	376.6	376.0	379.1	379.6	380.7	381.3	377.8	377.9	376.0	378.7	383.6	388.5	379.7
2005	375.8	375.1	378.2	381.3	382.9	384.2	385.1	385.1	353.2	348.5	361.8	369.9	373.4
2006	361.1	362.9	369.6	368.9	371.4	374.4	373.2	374.6	375.2	377.0	382.4	388.6	373.3
2007	378.9	377.9	382.4	379.3	381.1	382.0	380.9	383.2	383.1	383.4	389.6	391.3	382.8
Wholesale Trade													
2000	76.2	76.4	77.2	77.8	78.4	78.6	78.4	78.6	78.4	77.3	77.3	77.8	77.7
2001	76.7	77.0	77.5	78.0	78.1	78.9	77.7	78.0	78.0	77.6	77.6	77.9	77.8
2002	76.5	76.6	76.9	77.6	78.0	78.2	77.4	77.4	77.2	76.6	76.7	76.7	77.2
2003	76.2	76.1	76.3	75.5	75.7	76.1	75.5	75.6	75.5	75.4	75.3	74.9	75.7
2004	75.1	75.1	75.6	75.9	75.9	75.7	75.3	75.4	75.3	74.3	74.4	74.4	75.2
2005	73.6	73.8	74.1	75.0	75.3	75.4	76.3	76.3	71.6	71.0	71.4	71.8	73.8
2006	70.5	71.1	71.8	72.1	72.7	73.5	73.2	73.5	73.5	73.4	73.7	74.1	72.8
2007	74.9	75.2	75.8	75.0	75.5	76.0	75.8	76.3	76.2	76.0	76.4	76.3	75.8

Employment by Industry: Louisiana, 2000–2007—*Continued*

(Numbers in thousands, not seasonally adjusted.)

Industry and year	January	February	March	April	May	June	July	August	September	October	November	December	Annual Average
Retail Trade													
2000	229.1	229.3	231.6	230.1	232.0	232.8	228.9	230.7	231.4	231.3	237.5	242.3	232.3
2001	228.6	226.3	228.2	226.8	227.2	227.3	226.1	227.7	226.7	224.9	231.4	234.5	228.0
2002	223.0	221.6	224.3	225.0	225.1	226.5	224.0	224.2	223.7	221.8	227.9	232.4	225.0
2003	221.6	220.5	222.2	222.1	221.9	222.5	221.0	222.3	221.9	223.4	228.3	232.7	223.4
2004	222.1	221.2	223.1	223.8	224.3	225.0	222.5	222.2	220.6	223.3	228.2	232.2	224.0
2005	222.1	220.9	223.1	224.9	225.8	226.7	226.5	226.6	204.2	201.7	213.4	219.6	219.6
2006	213.8	214.7	219.2	218.1	219.3	220.4	219.3	219.9	219.8	222.1	226.7	230.3	220.3
2007	222.3	221.2	224.8	222.6	223.6	223.6	223.3	224.3	224.4	225.2	230.8	232.6	224.9
Transportation and Utilities													
2000	78.8	79.6	79.5	79.3	79.7	80.4	80.4	81.5	81.8	81.7	81.7	82.4	80.5
2001	80.7	81.6	82.2	83.0	83.0	83.6	83.0	83.5	83.5	84.0	82.9	82.9	82.8
2002	80.4	80.2	80.4	81.0	81.7	81.9	82.4	82.7	82.9	83.4	83.6	83.9	82.0
2003	81.3	81.3	80.9	81.9	82.2	82.2	81.5	81.7	81.5	81.9	82.5	82.6	81.8
2004	79.4	79.7	80.4	79.9	80.5	80.6	80.0	80.3	80.1	81.1	81.0	81.9	80.4
2005	80.1	80.4	81.0	81.4	81.8	82.1	82.3	82.2	77.4	75.8	77.0	78.5	80.0
2006	76.8	77.1	78.6	78.7	79.4	80.5	80.7	81.2	81.9	81.5	82.0	84.2	80.2
2007	81.7	81.5	81.8	81.7	82.0	82.4	81.8	82.6	82.5	82.2	82.4	82.4	82.1
Information													
2000	28.9	28.5	28.8	29.1	29.2	29.9	30.7	30.9	30.5	30.3	30.5	31.0	29.8
2001	30.0	30.2	30.4	30.2	30.6	30.6	30.3	30.1	29.7	30.0	30.1	29.8	30.1
2002	29.3	29.3	29.5	29.0	28.9	29.3	29.0	29.0	28.9	28.5	28.8	28.9	29.0
2003	29.2	28.9	29.1	29.0	29.4	29.8	28.4	28.9	28.8	28.7	28.9	29.0	29.0
2004	29.1	29.4	29.3	30.3	30.0	30.7	29.6	31.1	29.9	30.9	33.0	31.5	30.4
2005	31.2	30.3	30.3	29.5	29.3	29.6	30.0	30.4	28.6	26.4	26.9	27.0	29.1
2006	27.2	27.3	29.2	28.2	28.3	27.6	25.9	25.8	25.7	25.8	26.4	26.6	27.0
2007	26.5	27.5	29.6	28.8	28.7	29.2	28.0	27.4	26.4	26.3	26.2	26.6	27.6
Financial Activities													
2000	97.2	97.4	97.7	96.8	97.6	97.6	97.7	97.8	97.7	97.3	97.5	98.3	97.6
2001	96.6	97.2	97.0	97.1	97.0	97.6	97.7	97.8	97.1	96.8	96.8	96.9	97.1
2002	96.7	96.6	96.8	97.8	97.9	98.0	98.0	97.8	98.1	97.7	98.0	98.4	97.7
2003	98.6	98.8	98.6	98.8	98.9	99.2	99.5	99.8	99.5	99.8	99.5	100.2	99.3
2004	99.5	99.6	100.0	100.3	100.2	100.6	100.8	100.8	100.1	100.1	99.9	100.4	100.2
2005	98.6	98.9	99.1	98.8	98.9	99.6	100.5	100.7	95.3	96.2	96.8	97.0	98.4
2006	95.2	95.2	95.4	94.8	95.1	95.4	94.8	95.1	95.1	95.6	95.6	96.2	95.3
2007	97.7	98.0	97.1	96.6	96.6	96.8	96.9	97.2	96.7	97.0	97.0	96.9	97.0
Professional and Business Services													
2000	178.4	179.3	181.1	184.7	184.1	183.4	182.5	184.1	185.3	184.6	185.1	186.6	183.3
2001	183.7	183.5	183.6	183.4	183.1	184.1	181.1	182.2	182.8	182.0	182.3	183.9	183.0
2002	181.7	182.1	183.3	183.7	182.0	182.3	179.3	180.2	179.3	177.7	177.4	177.3	180.5
2003	177.8	178.8	179.7	181.5	180.3	180.2	179.4	180.9	180.4	182.2	183.5	185.3	180.8
2004	181.8	182.9	185.0	186.5	184.8	185.9	183.2	184.2	182.9	184.1	186.1	187.1	184.5
2005	187.0	187.4	189.8	194.1	192.1	191.6	191.8	192.7	175.7	181.0	185.8	188.2	188.1
2006	185.7	188.5	191.4	192.4	193.8	195.6	193.3	195.5	196.8	197.1	197.1	198.1	193.8
2007	197.8	199.7	201.7	200.8	201.1	202.2	200.3	203.1	202.2	202.8	202.3	202.5	201.4
Education and Health Services													
2000	220.6	223.4	223.9	224.6	223.6	220.6	219.5	220.0	224.4	227.9	227.9	228.4	223.7
2001	225.9	227.8	228.3	229.6	229.2	226.6	223.0	225.4	230.9	231.9	234.2	234.4	228.9
2002	230.1	232.5	232.8	235.5	234.8	232.3	230.7	233.8	240.1	240.5	243.5	242.6	235.8
2003	242.2	243.2	242.7	244.7	244.9	241.0	240.2	242.2	247.7	249.2	251.8	250.7	245.0
2004	248.7	249.8	250.5	252.3	251.7	247.6	247.9	251.4	252.7	253.0	254.7	253.5	251.2
2005	254.9	254.9	256.2	258.1	257.1	254.9	252.3	252.6	239.8	222.7	222.3	223.2	245.8
2006	225.1	226.8	228.8	232.0	233.6	233.0	232.2	234.9	238.4	240.0	242.1	241.2	234.0
2007	241.2	243.1	244.6	246.0	245.6	245.6	243.9	248.7	249.8	250.9	252.2	250.9	246.9
Leisure and Hospitality													
2000	189.3	191.0	193.2	195.0	198.6	201.0	197.4	197.3	195.9	194.1	194.5	195.3	195.2
2001	190.4	192.5	196.3	197.4	199.4	200.1	197.1	197.6	195.7	192.7	191.3	191.6	195.2
2002	186.8	189.4	192.1	196.2	198.9	200.3	198.4	198.2	195.7	192.1	193.6	193.1	194.6
2003	190.0	193.3	195.5	199.5	201.5	202.9	202.1	203.0	200.9	198.3	197.6	198.6	198.6
2004	195.1	197.6	201.7	203.5	206.1	208.9	206.7	207.3	205.2	204.0	205.9	206.8	204.1
2005	202.0	203.3	208.3	211.0	215.6	218.0	214.3	214.3	180.4	167.3	168.9	171.9	198.0
2006	169.7	176.6	181.8	181.6	184.8	189.5	188.0	189.0	187.6	186.5	188.2	189.9	184.4
2007	186.4	188.7	193.2	193.0	196.0	198.6	196.1	196.8	195.0	195.9	196.0	197.1	194.4
Other Services													
2000	69.9	70.3	70.9	70.7	71.1	71.3	70.8	71.4	71.4	70.8	70.3	70.5	70.8
2001	68.9	69.2	69.8	71.3	71.6	71.8	70.7	71.1	71.1	70.6	70.3	70.0	70.5
2002	69.3	69.7	70.3	71.1	71.6	71.9	71.0	71.1	71.2	70.9	71.2	71.6	70.9
2003	70.3	70.4	70.9	71.1	71.5	71.8	70.2	70.3	70.4	70.9	70.7	70.7	70.8
2004	70.1	70.4	71.0	71.1	71.4	71.8	71.5	71.4	71.2	70.6	70.6	70.7	71.0
2005	70.0	70.2	71.4	71.6	71.8	72.2	72.2	72.1	65.2	62.1	62.6	63.8	68.8
2006	62.4	63.5	64.6	64.6	65.5	66.1	65.6	65.9	66.7	66.8	67.0	67.4	65.5
2007	67.1	67.8	68.7	68.5	69.2	69.8	68.4	69.4	69.3	69.0	68.8	69.1	68.8
Government													
2000	370.6	376.6	379.5	379.2	385.0	373.9	364.8	359.7	371.6	373.8	373.7	373.0	373.4
2001	372.1	378.1	379.1	377.4	377.0	374.5	362.7	360.7	373.0	376.0	377.6	377.0	373.7
2002	370.0	375.5	377.1	377.5	377.6	376.4	366.7	364.5	375.1	378.7	381.2	378.9	374.9
2003	374.5	381.7	383.1	383.0	382.1	380.2	371.4	367.5	379.2	382.6	384.4	381.4	379.3
2004	377.3	384.1	385.9	385.4	383.8	381.9	373.7	371.8	383.0	386.1	386.9	385.6	382.1
2005	376.5	383.3	383.1	384.2	382.2	379.7	369.8	370.2	378.1	360.2	360.8	358.9	373.9
2006	343.0	349.5	351.1	349.3	349.9	341.6	334.0	339.2	352.9	353.7	356.0	355.6	348.0
2007	348.7	357.2	359.5	358.8	358.8	356.2	347.0	351.9	363.7	367.2	368.7	367.3	358.8

Average Weekly Hours by Selected Industry: Louisiana, 2001–2007

(Not seasonally adjusted.)

Industry and year	January	February	March	April	May	June	July	August	September	October	November	December	Annual Average
Natural Resources and Mining													
2004	47.1	45.0	52.5	50.1	48.0	52.3	48.6	52.0	49.7	50.6	50.0	49.4	49.6
2005	51.5	50.1	48.8	46.7	47.8	46.7	45.5	49.2	48.7	49.8	49.2	47.8	48.5
2006	45.9	44.4	42.8	44.6	40.9	42.8	41.8	49.3	51.0	48.4	48.2	44.9	45.5
2007	49.1	44.6	42.8	40.3	42.4	41.1	40.5	40.9	40.4	40.1	43.8	40.7	42.2
Manufacturing													
2001	40.9	42.5	42.5	41.4	43.4	43.9	43.3	43.6	43.4	43.8	44.1	44.0	43.1
2002	42.2	40.7	43.9	43.2	43.7	45.1	44.4	44.6	45.3	43.7	44.9	44.5	43.9
2003	43.0	42.8	42.3	43.7	44.7	44.5	43.6	44.2	45.4	45.2	45.0	44.5	44.1
2004	43.3	44.0	44.2	44.2	43.8	43.6	42.7	43.2	41.4	45.3	45.5	46.2	43.9
2005	43.4	41.6	42.9	42.5	42.2	42.8	42.0	43.0	38.9	40.6	41.6	42.2	42.0
2006	42.5	40.8	42.5	41.5	43.5	43.9	43.5	43.7	42.2	44.7	43.7	43.8	43.0
2007	41.5	41.9	41.7	41.5	41.7	42.4	43.0	43.8	42.1	41.6	42.1	41.9	42.1

Average Hourly Earnings by Selected Industry: Louisiana, 2001–2007

(Dollars, not seasonally adjusted.)

Industry and year	January	February	March	April	May	June	July	August	September	October	November	December	Annual Average
Natural Resources and Mining													
2004	17.58	18.47	19.49	19.00	18.87	19.02	19.83	19.14	19.22	19.48	19.87	20.34	19.21
2005	20.39	20.25	20.04	20.58	20.41	20.41	19.63	19.67	21.62	21.84	20.27	22.95	20.67
2006	22.26	22.03	22.99	21.90	23.10	21.61	22.30	21.99	21.70	22.30	21.96	22.74	22.22
2007	22.38	21.75	22.65	22.40	22.35	22.38	22.59	22.39	21.54	22.31	22.58	22.36	22.31
Manufacturing													
2001	15.84	15.82	15.84	16.21	16.16	16.11	16.19	16.05	16.31	16.27	16.51	16.81	16.18
2002	16.53	16.95	16.94	17.16	17.09	17.15	17.03	16.93	16.90	16.93	17.20	17.56	17.03
2003	17.10	17.58	17.21	17.03	17.08	17.21	16.78	16.55	16.78	16.35	16.08	16.78	16.86
2004	16.47	16.69	16.35	16.17	16.14	16.42	16.87	16.56	16.99	16.12	15.93	16.18	16.40
2005	16.98	16.93	16.90	16.98	17.62	17.48	16.84	17.23	17.43	17.77	17.47	18.02	17.30
2006	18.30	18.34	18.18	19.14	17.32	17.48	17.64	17.22	18.45	17.58	17.76	17.99	17.94
2007	18.53	18.90	18.80	19.38	19.12	19.22	19.45	19.54	19.65	19.56	20.09	19.69	19.33

Average Weekly Earnings by Selected Industry: Louisiana, 2001–2007

(Dollars, not seasonally adjusted.)

Industry and year	January	February	March	April	May	June	July	August	September	October	November	December	Annual Average
Natural Resources and Mining													
2004	828.02	831.15	1,023.23	951.90	905.76	994.75	963.74	995.28	955.23	985.69	993.50	1,004.80	952.82
2005	1,050.09	1,014.53	977.95	961.09	975.60	953.15	893.17	967.76	1,052.89	1,087.63	997.28	1,097.01	1,002.50
2006	1,021.73	978.13	983.97	976.74	944.79	924.91	932.14	1,084.11	1,106.70	1,079.32	1,058.47	1,021.03	1,011.01
2007	1,098.86	970.05	969.42	902.72	947.64	919.82	914.90	915.75	870.22	894.63	989.00	910.05	941.48
Manufacturing													
2001	647.86	672.35	673.20	671.09	701.34	707.23	701.03	699.78	707.85	712.63	728.09	739.64	697.36
2002	697.57	689.87	743.67	741.31	746.83	773.47	756.13	755.08	765.57	739.84	772.28	781.42	747.62
2003	735.30	752.42	727.98	744.21	763.48	765.85	731.61	731.51	757.27	739.02	723.60	746.71	743.53
2004	713.15	734.36	722.67	714.71	706.93	715.91	720.35	715.39	703.39	730.24	724.82	747.52	719.96
2005	736.93	704.29	725.01	721.65	743.56	748.14	707.28	740.89	678.03	721.46	726.75	760.44	726.60
2006	777.75	748.27	772.65	794.31	753.42	767.37	767.34	752.51	778.59	785.83	776.11	787.96	771.42
2007	769.00	791.91	783.96	804.27	797.30	814.93	836.35	855.85	827.27	813.70	845.79	825.01	813.79

Population
    2000 census: 1,274,923
    2007 estimate: 1,317,207
    Percent change, 2000–2007: 3.3%

Percent change in total nonfarm employment, 2000–2007: 2.3%

Industry with the largest growth in employment, 2000–2007 (thousands)
    Education and health services, 18.6

Industry with the largest decline in employment, 2000–2007 (thousands)
    Manufacturing, -20.4

Civilian labor force
    2000: 672,440
    2007: 704,693

Employment-population ratio
    2000: 65.4%
    2007: 63.4%

Unemployment rate and rank among states
    2000: 3.3%, 14th
    2007: 4.7%, 34th

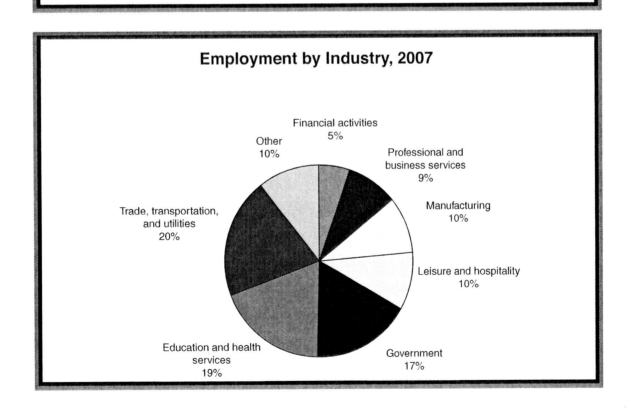

Employment by Industry, 2007

Financial activities 5%
Other 10%
Professional and business services 9%
Manufacturing 10%
Trade, transportation, and utilities 20%
Leisure and hospitality 10%
Education and health services 19%
Government 17%

Employment by Industry: Maine, 2000–2007

(Numbers in thousands, not seasonally adjusted.)

Industry and year	January	February	March	April	May	June	July	August	September	October	November	December	Annual Average
Total Nonfarm													
2000	576.1	580.2	586.0	593.8	606.9	617.8	615.8	614.4	614.7	611.5	612.8	611.7	603.5
2001	588.5	590.3	592.6	601.5	613.1	625.2	618.0	618.4	618.0	614.6	610.4	607.1	608.1
2002	583.7	585.5	588.9	598.3	610.4	622.3	618.5	618.2	617.1	614.2	610.5	609.9	606.5
2003	584.0	585.2	587.8	595.2	608.2	618.7	617.3	619.2	618.8	617.5	615.5	614.0	606.8
2004	588.4	591.6	594.0	601.9	614.0	625.4	622.8	623.5	622.8	620.0	619.6	616.7	611.7
2005	589.5	591.3	592.1	603.0	614.6	625.6	623.2	623.2	623.1	619.2	618.2	617.8	611.7
2006	592.1	592.6	596.1	606.5	617.4	629.9	624.1	626.6	625.1	622.9	621.1	621.4	614.7
2007	596.1	596.2	599.1	604.5	618.3	632.5	628.8	629.5	628.8	626.3	625.0	624.2	617.4
Total Private													
2000	478.7	479.0	482.2	491.5	502.7	517.0	528.3	528.4	515.0	508.7	508.4	507.0	503.9
2001	488.0	486.4	488.3	496.8	508.0	522.1	528.1	528.7	515.5	508.4	503.5	499.4	506.1
2002	481.8	480.3	482.7	492.8	504.1	517.6	526.8	527.6	514.5	508.1	502.7	501.9	503.4
2003	481.1	478.7	480.8	488.5	501.5	514.2	525.6	527.8	515.5	510.4	507.1	505.3	503.0
2004	484.8	484.3	486.2	494.0	506.3	519.6	529.7	531.0	518.3	511.9	510.2	507.6	507.0
2005	485.5	483.7	484.5	495.4	506.7	519.3	530.2	530.6	518.0	511.5	509.2	508.9	507.0
2006	487.8	485.9	488.8	499.3	509.7	525.3	532.1	533.4	520.7	514.8	512.2	512.7	510.2
2007	492.4	489.9	492.1	498.0	510.6	527.4	536.6	538.1	524.1	518.1	515.7	515.3	513.2
Goods-Producing													
2000	108.3	108.4	108.8	110.9	113.0	114.5	114.4	116.2	109.9	109.3	112.6	111.1	111.5
2001	106.7	105.3	105.8	106.2	108.7	110.9	109.1	110.1	108.3	106.0	105.4	102.8	107.1
2002	98.0	96.5	96.3	98.5	100.5	102.7	101.5	103.3	101.8	101.3	101.2	99.3	100.1
2003	93.9	92.1	92.6	94.0	97.2	99.2	99.2	100.9	99.8	99.4	99.5	97.6	97.1
2004	93.1	91.7	92.3	93.4	96.4	98.6	99.0	100.2	98.9	97.8	98.3	96.5	96.4
2005	91.3	90.5	90.5	92.8	95.0	97.2	97.6	98.1	96.6	95.6	96.3	94.8	94.7
2006	90.7	89.8	90.3	92.3	94.7	96.8	96.8	97.1	97.8	96.1	95.1	94.5	94.0
2007	89.3	87.7	88.5	89.7	92.3	95.7	96.0	96.6	95.1	94.0	93.7	92.4	92.6
Natural Resources and Mining													
2000	2.9	3.0	2.8	1.9	1.9	2.5	2.8	2.9	2.9	2.9	2.9	3.0	2.7
2001	2.9	2.9	2.8	2.0	1.9	2.5	2.8	2.8	2.9	2.8	2.8	2.8	2.7
2002	2.8	2.8	2.7	2.0	1.9	2.4	2.7	2.8	2.8	2.8	2.8	2.8	2.6
2003	2.7	2.7	2.6	2.0	1.8	2.4	2.7	2.8	2.7	2.7	2.7	2.7	2.5
2004	2.7	2.7	2.7	2.1	2.0	2.4	2.6	2.7	2.7	2.8	2.9	2.9	2.6
2005	2.9	2.9	2.8	2.2	2.0	2.5	2.8	2.8	2.8	2.8	2.9	2.9	2.7
2006	2.9	2.9	2.8	2.1	2.1	2.6	2.9	2.9	2.9	2.9	3.0	2.8	2.7
2007	2.9	2.9	2.9	2.0	1.9	2.5	2.8	2.8	2.8	2.9	2.8	2.9	2.7
Construction													
2000	25.7	25.4	25.8	28.4	30.2	30.8	31.7	31.7	31.2	31.0	29.9	28.8	29.2
2001	26.6	26.1	26.7	28.3	30.8	32.0	32.5	32.2	31.7	31.3	30.6	29.0	29.8
2002	26.4	25.5	25.6	28.0	30.1	31.2	31.7	31.8	31.3	31.4	30.8	29.5	29.4
2003	27.0	26.0	26.5	28.5	31.3	32.5	33.2	33.2	32.8	32.8	31.8	30.3	30.5
2004	28.0	27.5	28.3	29.4	31.7	32.6	33.3	33.0	32.3	31.9	31.2	29.9	30.8
2005	27.0	26.5	26.7	29.2	31.4	32.8	33.6	33.2	32.7	32.4	31.9	30.4	30.7
2006	28.3	27.5	28.0	30.3	32.3	33.7	33.9	33.9	33.1	32.6	31.6	30.6	31.3
2007	28.1	26.9	27.4	29.1	31.4	33.0	33.3	33.3	32.8	32.3	31.4	30.3	30.8
Manufacturing													
2000	79.7	80.0	80.2	80.6	80.9	81.2	79.9	81.6	75.8	75.4	79.8	79.3	79.5
2001	77.2	76.3	76.3	75.9	76.0	76.4	73.8	75.1	73.7	71.9	72.0	71.0	74.6
2002	68.8	68.2	68.0	68.5	68.5	69.1	67.1	68.7	67.7	67.1	67.6	67.0	68.0
2003	64.2	63.4	63.5	63.5	64.1	64.3	63.3	64.9	64.3	63.9	65.0	64.6	64.1
2004	62.4	61.5	61.3	61.9	62.7	63.6	63.1	64.5	63.9	63.1	64.2	63.7	63.0
2005	61.4	61.1	61.0	61.4	61.6	61.9	61.2	62.1	61.1	60.4	61.5	61.5	61.4
2006	59.5	59.4	59.5	59.9	60.3	60.5	60.3	61.0	60.1	59.5	60.1	59.8	60.0
2007	58.3	57.9	58.2	58.6	59.0	60.2	59.9	60.5	59.5	58.8	59.5	59.2	59.1
Service-Providing													
2000	467.8	471.8	477.2	482.9	493.9	503.3	501.4	498.2	504.8	502.2	500.2	500.6	492.0
2001	481.8	485.0	486.8	495.3	504.4	514.3	508.9	508.3	509.7	508.6	505.0	504.3	501.0
2002	485.7	489.0	492.6	499.8	509.9	519.6	517.0	514.9	515.3	512.9	509.3	510.6	506.4
2003	490.1	493.1	495.2	501.2	511.0	519.5	518.1	518.3	519.0	518.1	516.0	516.4	509.7
2004	495.3	499.9	501.7	508.5	517.6	526.8	523.8	523.3	523.9	522.2	521.3	520.2	515.4
2005	498.2	500.8	501.6	510.2	519.6	528.4	525.6	525.1	526.5	523.6	521.9	523.0	517.0
2006	501.4	502.8	505.8	514.2	522.7	533.1	527.0	528.8	529.0	527.8	526.6	528.1	520.6
2007	506.8	508.5	510.6	514.8	526.0	536.8	532.8	532.9	533.7	532.3	531.3	531.8	524.9
Trade, Transportation, and Utilities													
2000	118.4	116.1	116.3	117.4	119.4	123.8	126.1	126.1	125.2	126.1	128.8	128.7	122.7
2001	120.9	118.2	117.7	119.3	121.8	125.4	126.7	126.6	124.7	126.0	127.9	128.1	123.6
2002	120.3	118.1	118.1	119.6	121.7	125.2	127.1	127.0	124.5	124.0	125.7	127.4	123.2
2003	119.5	116.9	116.8	118.1	120.9	124.2	126.2	127.0	124.7	125.7	128.6	129.4	123.2
2004	121.3	119.8	119.7	120.8	123.4	126.4	128.2	128.3	126.0	127.2	130.0	131.5	125.2
2005	123.1	120.7	119.8	121.3	123.0	126.1	127.7	127.9	126.1	126.4	129.4	130.8	125.2
2006	123.4	119.9	120.3	121.7	123.3	126.7	127.7	128.0	126.2	127.2	131.1	132.2	125.6
2007	123.9	120.7	121.1	121.2	123.8	127.4	129.3	129.4	126.7	127.8	132.0	133.1	126.4
Wholesale Trade													
2000	18.9	18.8	18.9	19.2	19.3	19.6	19.9	20.0	19.9	20.0	19.9	20.0	19.5
2001	20.0	19.8	19.8	20.1	20.1	20.5	20.7	20.6	20.3	20.4	20.2	20.3	20.2
2002	19.8	19.7	19.7	20.0	20.1	20.4	20.9	20.9	20.8	20.8	20.8	20.8	20.4
2003	20.4	20.2	20.3	20.6	20.9	21.3	21.5	21.6	21.5	21.4	21.5	21.5	21.1
2004	20.9	20.9	21.0	21.2	21.4	21.6	21.9	21.9	21.5	21.5	21.3	21.3	21.4
2005	20.9	20.9	20.9	21.1	21.4	21.7	21.9	21.9	21.7	21.6	21.5	21.6	21.4
2006	21.1	21.0	21.1	21.4	21.5	22.0	22.0	21.9	21.6	21.5	21.3	21.3	21.5
2007	20.8	20.7	20.9	21.0	21.2	21.5	21.8	21.7	21.4	21.3	21.2	21.3	21.2

Employment by Industry: Maine, 2000–2007—*Continued*

(Numbers in thousands, not seasonally adjusted.)

Industry and year	January	February	March	April	May	June	July	August	September	October	November	December	Annual Average
Retail Trade													
2000	82.2	80.3	80.4	81.3	82.9	86.1	87.8	88.3	87.5	88.3	90.7	91.1	85.6
2001	83.9	81.6	81.1	82.5	84.9	87.4	88.5	88.5	87.0	88.1	90.4	90.4	86.2
2002	83.8	81.8	81.9	83.0	84.7	87.5	88.8	88.8	86.4	85.9	88.0	89.6	85.9
2003	82.7	80.5	80.4	81.6	83.7	86.2	87.8	88.5	86.3	87.2	90.3	91.2	85.5
2004	84.2	82.7	82.6	83.5	85.5	87.8	89.4	89.5	87.7	88.7	91.7	93.2	87.2
2005	85.6	83.3	82.7	84.1	85.3	87.5	88.9	89.0	87.4	87.8	91.1	92.1	87.1
2006	85.7	82.3	82.8	84.0	85.2	87.5	88.5	89.0	87.4	88.4	92.6	93.4	87.2
2007	86.1	83.1	83.4	83.6	85.8	88.4	90.0	90.1	87.7	88.8	93.3	94.0	87.9
Transportation and Utilities													
2000	17.3	17.0	17.0	16.9	17.2	18.1	18.4	17.8	17.8	17.8	18.2	17.6	17.6
2001	17.0	16.8	16.8	16.7	16.8	17.5	17.5	17.5	17.4	17.5	17.3	17.4	17.2
2002	16.7	16.6	16.5	16.6	16.9	17.3	17.4	17.3	17.3	17.3	16.9	17.0	17.0
2003	16.4	16.2	16.1	15.9	16.3	16.7	16.9	16.9	16.9	17.1	16.8	16.7	16.6
2004	16.2	16.2	16.1	16.1	16.5	17.0	16.9	16.9	16.8	17.0	17.0	17.0	16.6
2005	16.6	16.5	16.2	16.1	16.3	16.9	16.9	17.0	17.0	17.0	16.8	17.1	16.7
2006	16.6	16.6	16.4	16.3	16.6	17.2	17.2	17.1	17.2	17.3	17.2	17.5	16.9
2007	17.0	16.9	16.8	16.6	16.8	17.5	17.5	17.6	17.6	17.7	17.5	17.8	17.3
Information													
2000	12.1	12.1	12.2	12.3	12.3	12.2	12.3	11.0	12.2	12.2	12.3	12.3	12.1
2001	12.3	12.4	12.3	12.3	12.3	12.3	12.2	12.1	12.0	11.8	11.9	11.9	12.2
2002	11.8	11.7	11.6	11.6	11.7	11.7	11.6	11.5	11.4	11.3	11.5	11.6	11.6
2003	11.3	11.4	11.3	11.3	11.2	11.3	11.3	11.3	11.2	11.5	11.5	11.6	11.4
2004	11.6	11.4	11.4	11.0	10.9	11.1	11.3	11.2	11.0	11.1	11.3	11.3	11.2
2005	11.2	11.1	11.2	11.1	11.2	11.1	11.2	11.2	11.1	11.1	11.1	11.3	11.2
2006	11.2	11.2	11.1	11.1	11.1	11.3	11.3	11.3	11.1	11.3	11.3	11.4	11.2
2007	11.2	11.4	11.4	11.5	11.4	11.4	11.3	11.3	11.1	11.2	11.2	11.3	11.3
Financial Activities													
2000	33.4	33.3	33.5	33.7	33.8	34.3	34.9	34.9	34.4	34.2	34.1	34.6	34.1
2001	34.2	34.5	34.7	35.0	35.0	35.4	35.9	35.9	35.2	35.1	35.1	35.4	35.1
2002	34.6	34.6	34.8	34.7	34.9	35.5	35.7	35.7	35.6	35.2	35.2	35.4	35.1
2003	34.8	34.8	34.9	35.0	35.0	35.2	35.7	35.5	35.0	34.9	34.9	35.3	35.1
2004	34.9	35.0	34.9	34.8	35.0	35.3	35.5	35.4	34.6	34.5	34.3	34.4	34.9
2005	34.0	33.9	34.0	33.9	34.1	34.3	34.8	34.6	34.0	34.2	34.0	34.1	34.2
2006	33.7	33.6	33.5	33.5	33.5	34.1	34.0	34.1	33.4	33.5	33.2	33.5	33.6
2007	33.0	33.0	33.0	33.1	33.3	33.7	33.9	33.8	33.2	33.1	33.0	33.1	33.3
Professional and Business Services													
2000	49.0	49.1	49.8	51.2	52.0	53.3	53.7	53.7	53.1	52.4	52.0	52.6	51.8
2001	50.8	51.0	51.4	52.7	53.2	53.8	52.8	52.5	51.4	51.1	50.6	50.4	51.8
2002	49.4	49.4	50.0	51.4	52.0	53.1	52.9	52.8	51.7	51.7	51.3	50.8	51.4
2003	49.2	49.1	49.3	50.1	50.5	51.1	51.4	51.8	51.1	50.5	49.9	49.5	50.3
2004	47.8	48.2	48.4	49.5	50.2	50.7	50.7	50.7	49.7	49.7	49.9	49.3	49.6
2005	47.8	47.8	48.2	49.7	50.6	51.2	51.9	52.1	51.3	51.2	50.9	51.0	50.3
2006	48.9	49.4	49.7	52.3	53.0	54.0	53.5	53.6	52.8	52.3	52.4	52.6	52.0
2007	51.1	51.0	51.3	52.9	53.8	55.2	55.4	55.6	54.6	54.4	54.2	53.9	53.6
Education and Health Services													
2000	94.2	96.5	96.9	97.2	97.2	95.8	96.8	96.7	98.8	99.5	100.0	100.0	97.5
2001	97.7	100.1	100.5	100.5	100.5	99.7	99.7	99.9	101.3	102.8	102.9	103.2	100.7
2002	101.9	104.2	104.8	105.5	105.3	104.0	104.4	104.0	105.2	106.4	106.8	106.6	104.9
2003	104.3	106.3	107.0	107.2	106.9	106.0	106.7	106.3	108.0	109.5	109.6	109.9	107.3
2004	108.4	110.3	111.0	111.4	110.9	109.9	110.1	110.0	111.2	112.5	113.1	112.1	110.9
2005	110.0	111.6	111.9	112.7	112.8	111.5	111.5	111.3	112.3	113.6	114.1	113.5	112.2
2006	111.6	113.6	114.2	114.4	114.1	113.0	112.9	113.3	114.4	115.5	115.9	115.9	114.1
2007	114.2	116.5	116.6	116.3	116.4	115.1	114.9	115.2	116.0	117.2	117.4	117.4	116.1
Leisure and Hospitality													
2000	45.5	45.7	46.8	50.6	56.6	64.4	71.1	70.9	62.9	56.7	50.4	49.4	55.9
2001	46.7	46.2	47.0	51.9	57.4	65.2	71.9	72.1	63.5	56.6	50.7	48.7	56.5
2002	46.7	46.7	47.9	51.9	58.2	65.4	73.0	72.8	64.6	58.5	51.3	51.1	57.3
2003	48.0	48.0	48.7	52.5	59.3	66.4	74.3	74.4	65.5	59.0	53.3	52.2	58.5
2004	48.1	48.3	48.9	53.2	59.4	67.4	74.2	74.5	66.6	59.1	53.4	52.6	58.8
2005	48.6	48.6	49.2	53.9	59.8	67.6	74.9	75.0	66.4	59.5	53.6	53.5	59.2
2006	48.9	49.0	50.2	54.5	60.3	69.4	75.3	75.2	67.1	60.2	54.1	54.0	59.9
2007	50.3	50.3	50.8	53.6	59.6	68.6	75.3	75.8	67.4	60.4	54.3	54.2	60.1
Other Services													
2000	17.8	17.8	17.9	18.2	18.4	18.7	19.0	18.9	18.5	18.3	18.2	18.3	18.3
2001	18.7	18.7	18.9	18.9	19.1	19.4	19.8	19.5	19.1	19.0	19.0	18.9	19.1
2002	19.1	19.1	19.2	19.6	19.8	20.0	20.6	20.6	20.1	19.7	19.7	19.7	19.8
2003	20.1	20.1	20.2	20.3	20.5	20.8	20.8	20.6	20.2	19.9	19.8	19.8	20.3
2004	19.6	19.6	19.6	19.9	20.1	20.2	20.7	20.7	20.3	20.0	19.9	19.9	20.0
2005	19.5	19.5	19.7	20.0	20.2	20.3	20.6	20.4	20.2	19.9	19.8	19.9	20.0
2006	19.4	19.4	19.5	19.5	19.7	20.0	20.3	20.3	20.1	19.6	19.7	19.8	19.7
2007	19.4	19.3	19.4	19.7	20.0	20.3	20.5	20.4	20.0	20.0	19.9	19.9	19.9
Government													
2000	97.4	101.2	103.8	102.3	104.2	100.8	87.5	86.0	99.7	102.8	104.4	104.7	99.6
2001	100.5	103.9	104.3	104.7	105.1	103.1	89.9	89.7	102.5	106.2	106.9	107.7	102.0
2002	101.9	105.2	106.2	105.5	106.3	104.7	91.7	90.6	102.6	106.1	107.8	108.0	103.1
2003	102.9	106.5	107.0	106.7	106.7	104.5	91.7	91.4	103.3	107.1	108.4	108.7	103.7
2004	103.6	107.3	107.8	107.9	107.9	105.8	93.1	92.5	104.5	108.1	109.4	109.1	104.7
2005	104.0	107.6	107.6	107.6	107.9	106.3	93.0	92.6	105.1	107.7	109.0	108.9	104.8
2006	104.3	106.7	107.3	107.2	107.7	104.6	92.0	93.2	104.4	108.1	108.9	108.7	104.4
2007	103.7	106.3	107.0	106.5	107.7	105.1	92.2	91.4	104.7	108.2	109.3	108.9	104.3

Average Weekly Hours by Selected Industry: Maine, 2001–2007

(Not seasonally adjusted.)

Industry and year	January	February	March	April	May	June	July	August	September	October	November	December	Annual Average
Manufacturing													
2001	40.1	39.9	39.6	39.5	39.8	39.4	40.0	39.1	39.3	39.9	40.2	40.4	39.8
2002	39.5	39.5	40.0	39.8	39.6	39.9	39.3	39.0	40.5	40.3	40.3	40.8	39.9
2003	40.0	39.4	40.0	40.3	39.8	39.7	40.0	39.8	40.6	40.2	40.1	40.7	40.0
2004	39.5	39.4	39.8	39.1	39.2	39.4	38.9	39.9	39.7	40.1	39.6	40.7	39.6
2005	38.9	38.1	38.3	39.5	40.0	39.8	39.0	39.4	40.4	41.3	40.5	40.2	39.6
2006	40.5	40.8	40.6	40.7	41.2	41.2	41.9	41.4	42.1	42.2	41.8	42.3	41.4
2007	41.9	41.0	41.8	41.6	41.2	41.3	41.6	41.8	42.8	42.4	42.5	42.6	41.9

Average Hourly Earnings by Selected Industry: Maine, 2001–2007

(Dollars, not seasonally adjusted.)

Industry and year	January	February	March	April	May	June	July	August	September	October	November	December	Annual Average
Manufacturing													
2001	14.26	14.39	14.47	14.56	14.55	14.66	15.05	14.77	14.88	14.93	14.99	15.09	14.71
2002	15.21	15.33	15.02	15.23	15.33	15.36	15.93	15.65	15.71	15.82	15.85	16.13	15.55
2003	16.11	16.16	16.05	16.03	16.23	16.16	16.22	16.29	16.41	16.54	16.59	16.52	16.28
2004	16.73	16.72	16.66	16.85	16.83	16.79	17.15	17.13	17.58	17.48	16.59	17.04	16.97
2005	16.94	17.21	16.78	17.05	16.93	17.11	17.57	17.60	17.59	17.48	17.44	17.58	17.28
2006	17.64	17.84	17.93	18.08	18.45	18.40	19.00	19.02	19.24	19.18	19.02	18.97	18.58
2007	19.03	18.98	19.04	19.21	19.01	19.04	19.13	19.30	19.39	19.38	19.39	19.37	19.19

Average Weekly Earnings by Selected Industry: Maine, 2001–2007

(Dollars, not seasonally adjusted.)

Industry and year	January	February	March	April	May	June	July	August	September	October	November	December	Annual Average
Manufacturing													
2001	571.83	574.16	573.01	575.12	579.09	577.60	602.00	577.51	584.78	595.71	602.60	609.64	585.46
2002	600.80	605.54	600.80	606.15	607.07	612.86	626.05	610.35	636.26	637.55	638.76	658.10	620.45
2003	644.40	636.70	642.00	646.01	645.95	641.55	648.80	648.34	666.25	664.91	665.26	672.36	651.20
2004	660.84	658.77	663.07	658.84	659.74	661.53	667.14	683.49	697.93	700.95	656.96	693.53	672.01
2005	658.97	655.70	642.67	673.48	677.20	680.98	685.23	693.44	710.64	721.92	706.32	706.72	684.29
2006	714.42	727.87	727.96	735.86	760.14	758.08	796.10	787.43	810.00	809.40	795.04	802.43	769.21
2007	797.36	778.18	795.87	799.14	783.21	786.35	795.81	806.74	829.89	821.71	824.08	825.16	804.06

Population
    2000 census: 5,296,486
    2007 estimate: 5,618,344
    Percent change, 2000–2007: 6.1%

Percent change in total nonfarm employment, 2000–2007: 6.3%

Industry with the largest growth in employment, 2000–2007 (thousands)
    Education and health services, 64.9

Industry with the largest decline in employment, 2000–2007 (thousands)
    Manufacturing, -40.2

Civilian labor force
    2000: 2,811,657
    2007: 2,980,353

Employment-population ratio
    2000: 67.9%
    2007: 66.4%

Unemployment rate and rank among states
    2000: 3.6%, 20th
    2007: 3.6%, 13th

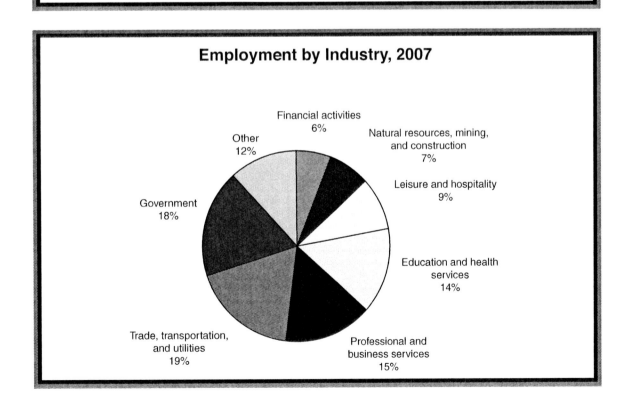

Employment by Industry, 2007

Financial activities 6%
Other 12%
Natural resources, mining, and construction 7%
Government 18%
Leisure and hospitality 9%
Education and health services 14%
Trade, transportation, and utilities 19%
Professional and business services 15%

Employment by Industry: Maryland, 2000–2007

(Numbers in thousands, not seasonally adjusted.)

Industry and year	January	February	March	April	May	June	July	August	September	October	November	December	Annual Average
Total Nonfarm													
2000	2,369.5	2,377.8	2,419.0	2,439.9	2,456.8	2,485.8	2,472.4	2,468.9	2,481.1	2,483.8	2,495.9	2,509.8	2,455.1
2001	2,415.0	2,429.3	2,450.9	2,462.7	2,482.8	2,506.4	2,481.2	2,481.6	2,475.0	2,481.9	2,493.2	2,500.7	2,471.7
2002	2,421.1	2,436.6	2,462.2	2,472.8	2,494.5	2,513.4	2,491.1	2,490.3	2,490.9	2,490.0	2,499.6	2,501.6	2,480.3
2003	2,429.3	2,426.9	2,452.7	2,477.4	2,499.9	2,519.4	2,498.7	2,495.5	2,503.8	2,505.8	2,513.3	2,519.8	2,486.9
2004	2,448.7	2,451.5	2,485.1	2,501.8	2,525.6	2,547.0	2,532.9	2,532.2	2,531.9	2,543.7	2,551.4	2,560.6	2,517.9
2005	2,482.0	2,494.1	2,513.8	2,544.2	2,565.7	2,581.1	2,572.0	2,571.0	2,580.7	2,577.4	2,589.4	2,597.1	2,555.7
2006	2,523.7	2,535.9	2,568.2	2,583.6	2,602.4	2,619.4	2,598.4	2,596.4	2,600.5	2,604.4	2,613.9	2,626.2	2,589.4
2007	2,550.8	2,552.7	2,586.3	2,597.6	2,621.9	2,635.7	2,623.1	2,620.7	2,618.6	2,627.9	2,638.9	2,645.4	2,610.0
Total Private													
2000	1,927.6	1,931.0	1,962.5	1,984.5	2,001.5	2,034.9	2,035.8	2,036.5	2,033.5	2,027.0	2,036.6	2,050.2	2,005.1
2001	1,966.8	1,971.7	1,990.1	2,000.9	2,021.6	2,052.1	2,041.4	2,042.4	2,020.2	2,017.1	2,024.2	2,031.7	2,015.0
2002	1,963.7	1,969.2	1,990.3	2,004.4	2,025.2	2,049.6	2,043.3	2,043.2	2,027.4	2,017.5	2,025.6	2,028.9	2,015.7
2003	1,970.1	1,958.5	1,981.3	2,007.1	2,029.8	2,056.6	2,054.2	2,057.6	2,042.9	2,038.5	2,045.1	2,052.4	2,024.5
2004	1,989.5	1,986.9	2,015.8	2,033.9	2,055.5	2,086.6	2,089.4	2,089.1	2,075.4	2,073.3	2,078.1	2,089.1	2,055.2
2005	2,024.8	2,027.9	2,045.8	2,074.5	2,093.1	2,119.8	2,122.6	2,122.0	2,115.0	2,102.2	2,109.7	2,119.2	2,089.7
2006	2,063.8	2,064.0	2,091.5	2,106.0	2,123.8	2,153.3	2,144.7	2,144.2	2,131.2	2,123.5	2,130.7	2,142.4	2,118.3
2007	2,083.4	2,074.2	2,102.1	2,114.1	2,135.5	2,161.5	2,158.1	2,157.1	2,142.5	2,140.8	2,147.7	2,154.5	2,131.0
Goods-Producing													
2000	320.4	318.4	326.6	329.7	332.3	338.1	339.4	340.4	339.8	338.3	336.9	336.1	333.0
2001	324.0	326.0	330.4	332.8	334.7	339.7	338.6	338.9	335.7	333.1	331.1	329.7	332.9
2002	316.6	317.4	320.9	323.2	325.1	328.6	326.4	326.9	324.1	320.2	319.6	316.8	322.2
2003	309.1	305.8	309.5	312.3	315.7	318.8	318.5	319.7	317.8	317.0	316.5	315.5	314.7
2004	306.5	305.1	311.3	315.9	319.2	323.7	325.9	326.3	324.9	323.6	322.7	323.2	319.0
2005	314.6	312.7	315.7	322.4	325.1	328.9	329.7	331.0	330.6	327.2	328.4	327.9	324.5
2006	318.6	317.9	323.1	325.0	326.5	331.2	330.9	331.0	329.2	326.5	325.2	324.9	325.8
2007	316.1	312.0	318.1	320.7	323.6	327.8	327.9	328.2	325.5	324.5	323.0	322.0	322.5
Natural Resources, Mining, and Construction													
2000	150.1	148.0	154.9	157.9	160.1	164.0	166.1	167.6	166.9	165.7	165.2	164.0	160.9
2001	155.5	157.2	161.7	164.7	167.6	171.6	171.6	172.7	170.4	169.5	168.6	167.3	166.5
2002	159.2	160.2	163.8	166.2	168.3	171.4	171.9	172.5	170.5	169.0	168.8	166.4	167.4
2003	160.8	158.3	161.7	165.1	168.8	171.7	173.8	175.5	174.5	174.5	174.0	173.3	169.3
2004	166.1	164.8	170.6	174.7	177.7	181.5	183.4	184.1	183.5	182.4	181.7	181.8	177.7
2005	174.7	173.0	175.8	182.5	185.4	189.0	190.5	191.5	191.7	189.4	190.3	189.7	185.3
2006	183.1	182.6	187.3	189.5	191.2	195.0	195.0	195.2	194.3	192.4	191.4	190.9	190.7
2007	183.9	180.2	186.0	188.9	191.5	195.1	195.4	195.9	194.1	193.0	191.4	190.5	190.5
Manufacturing													
2000	170.3	170.4	171.7	171.8	172.2	174.1	173.3	172.8	172.9	172.6	171.7	172.1	172.2
2001	168.5	168.8	168.7	168.1	167.1	168.1	167.0	166.2	165.3	163.6	162.5	162.4	166.4
2002	157.4	157.2	157.1	157.0	156.8	157.2	154.5	154.4	153.6	151.2	150.8	150.4	154.8
2003	148.3	147.5	147.8	147.2	146.9	147.1	144.7	144.2	143.3	142.5	142.5	142.2	145.4
2004	140.4	140.3	140.7	141.2	141.5	142.2	142.5	142.2	141.4	141.2	141.0	141.4	141.3
2005	139.9	139.7	139.9	139.9	139.7	139.9	139.2	139.5	138.9	137.8	138.1	138.2	139.2
2006	135.5	135.3	135.8	135.5	135.3	136.2	135.9	135.8	134.9	134.1	133.8	134.0	135.2
2007	132.2	131.8	132.1	131.8	132.1	132.7	132.5	132.3	131.4	131.5	131.6	131.5	132.0
Service-Providing													
2000	2,049.1	2,059.4	2,092.4	2,110.2	2,124.5	2,147.7	2,133.0	2,128.5	2,141.3	2,145.5	2,159.0	2,173.7	2,122.0
2001	2,091.0	2,103.3	2,120.5	2,129.9	2,148.1	2,166.7	2,142.6	2,142.7	2,139.3	2,148.8	2,162.1	2,171.0	2,138.8
2002	2,104.5	2,119.2	2,141.3	2,149.6	2,169.4	2,184.8	2,164.7	2,163.4	2,166.8	2,169.8	2,180.0	2,184.8	2,158.2
2003	2,120.2	2,121.1	2,143.2	2,165.1	2,184.2	2,200.6	2,180.2	2,175.8	2,186.0	2,188.8	2,196.8	2,204.3	2,172.2
2004	2,142.2	2,146.4	2,173.8	2,185.9	2,206.4	2,223.3	2,207.0	2,205.9	2,207.0	2,220.1	2,228.7	2,237.4	2,198.7
2005	2,167.4	2,181.4	2,198.1	2,221.8	2,240.6	2,252.2	2,242.3	2,240.0	2,250.1	2,250.2	2,261.0	2,269.2	2,231.2
2006	2,205.1	2,218.0	2,245.1	2,258.6	2,275.9	2,288.2	2,267.5	2,265.4	2,271.3	2,277.9	2,288.7	2,301.3	2,263.5
2007	2,234.7	2,240.7	2,268.2	2,276.9	2,298.3	2,307.9	2,295.2	2,292.5	2,293.1	2,303.4	2,315.9	2,323.4	2,287.5
Trade, Transportation, and Utilities													
2000	459.9	456.5	460.1	463.1	466.3	471.9	469.3	471.8	472.7	477.1	488.2	498.5	471.3
2001	469.0	462.1	463.3	461.9	465.6	469.4	464.6	465.4	465.8	467.7	476.5	483.3	467.9
2002	460.5	455.0	459.4	460.4	463.9	468.6	463.7	463.1	463.4	465.3	472.7	480.0	464.7
2003	455.3	449.4	452.7	454.9	459.2	463.7	460.4	462.3	462.8	466.0	475.9	482.9	462.1
2004	459.8	455.2	459.0	460.4	464.4	471.4	466.3	466.5	466.6	470.6	479.4	487.6	467.3
2005	462.1	459.4	461.7	464.0	467.9	471.8	472.6	472.0	471.8	473.4	482.0	491.8	470.9
2006	470.6	465.1	468.9	469.8	473.5	477.6	473.9	473.7	472.6	476.4	487.5	496.0	475.5
2007	474.8	467.3	471.8	470.3	475.9	479.7	477.4	475.8	474.9	477.1	486.1	493.4	477.0
Wholesale Trade													
2000	89.7	90.5	91.7	91.9	92.2	93.3	93.5	94.0	93.6	94.1	94.3	94.8	92.8
2001	93.3	93.7	94.4	94.8	94.9	95.0	94.5	94.5	94.3	94.1	94.1	94.2	94.3
2002	93.3	93.2	93.5	93.0	93.2	93.5	93.1	93.2	92.7	92.9	92.9	92.9	93.1
2003	91.1	90.7	91.3	91.0	91.5	91.8	91.4	91.3	91.1	91.1	91.3	91.4	91.3
2004	89.9	90.2	90.9	91.6	91.9	92.8	93.1	92.9	92.8	93.2	93.4	93.6	92.2
2005	92.6	92.9	93.1	93.8	94.4	95.0	95.2	95.1	94.6	94.4	94.4	95.0	94.2
2006	93.7	94.1	94.6	95.3	95.6	96.2	95.7	95.6	95.2	95.3	95.1	95.6	95.2
2007	94.0	94.3	94.7	95.2	95.6	96.0	95.6	95.5	95.4	95.7	95.8	95.9	95.3
Retail Trade													
2000	291.5	287.7	289.7	292.3	295.1	299.0	297.6	299.0	298.7	300.7	312.0	321.0	298.7
2001	297.9	291.3	291.8	289.5	292.6	296.3	294.3	295.0	294.4	295.1	304.3	311.0	296.1
2002	292.1	287.0	290.8	290.3	292.7	297.2	295.0	294.2	294.0	294.5	302.4	309.6	295.0
2003	289.7	284.5	286.3	289.0	291.7	295.3	293.9	295.3	294.2	295.7	305.5	311.6	294.4
2004	292.1	287.6	289.9	290.2	293.2	298.3	295.4	296.1	294.8	298.4	306.9	313.8	296.4
2005	291.9	288.5	289.9	292.6	295.2	297.7	299.7	299.3	297.7	299.2	307.2	314.4	297.8
2006	298.2	291.8	294.5	294.8	297.5	300.1	298.8	298.5	296.2	299.9	310.7	316.2	299.8
2007	300.2	292.5	295.9	295.2	299.3	301.9	301.9	300.9	298.9	300.6	309.0	315.1	301.0

Employment by Industry: Maryland, 2000–2007—*Continued*

(Numbers in thousands, not seasonally adjusted.)

Industry and year	January	February	March	April	May	June	July	August	September	October	November	December	Annual Average
Transportation and Utilities													
2000	78.4	78.0	78.4	78.8	78.8	79.4	78.1	78.8	80.4	82.3	81.9	82.5	79.7
2001	77.8	77.3	77.1	77.7	78.2	78.4	76.2	76.2	77.4	78.6	78.1	78.1	77.6
2002	75.2	74.8	75.1	77.2	78.1	78.0	75.6	75.7	76.7	77.9	77.4	77.5	76.6
2003	74.5	74.2	75.1	75.0	76.0	76.6	75.1	75.5	77.2	79.1	79.2	79.9	76.5
2004	77.7	77.5	78.2	78.5	79.2	80.1	77.6	77.3	78.8	78.9	79.0	80.2	78.6
2005	77.6	78.0	78.7	77.6	78.3	79.1	77.7	77.6	79.5	79.8	80.4	82.4	78.9
2006	78.7	79.2	79.8	79.7	80.4	81.3	79.4	79.6	81.2	81.2	81.7	84.2	80.5
2007	80.6	80.5	81.2	79.9	81.0	81.8	79.9	79.4	80.6	80.8	81.3	82.4	80.8
Information													
2000	56.3	56.6	57.3	57.7	58.2	59.1	59.4	54.2	60.0	60.3	60.8	62.1	58.5
2001	59.7	60.1	60.1	59.3	59.4	59.5	58.4	58.1	57.0	56.8	56.7	56.6	58.5
2002	55.2	54.9	54.8	54.4	54.4	54.0	53.3	53.0	52.2	50.7	51.4	51.1	53.3
2003	50.4	50.5	50.6	51.1	51.7	51.6	51.4	51.1	50.7	50.7	51.4	51.5	51.1
2004	50.3	49.6	50.5	50.2	50.6	51.1	49.9	50.1	49.5	49.3	49.6	49.6	50.0
2005	48.8	49.0	49.1	49.3	49.8	50.1	51.3	51.7	51.6	51.9	51.8	51.9	50.5
2006	50.5	50.8	51.2	50.6	50.9	50.9	50.2	50.2	49.9	49.6	50.2	50.5	50.5
2007	49.3	49.7	50.5	50.4	50.9	51.6	51.1	51.6	51.0	51.1	51.4	51.6	50.9
Financial Activities													
2000	144.0	144.2	145.2	145.4	146.1	148.4	148.7	148.7	147.8	147.1	147.9	149.2	146.9
2001	145.1	146.0	147.0	147.2	148.0	150.0	150.3	150.5	149.2	149.0	149.7	150.5	148.5
2002	148.7	149.2	149.3	149.8	150.6	152.2	152.5	152.8	152.1	152.0	152.6	153.7	151.3
2003	153.1	153.2	154.2	154.7	156.0	157.6	158.5	158.7	157.5	155.5	155.9	156.3	155.9
2004	153.6	153.7	154.7	154.8	155.4	156.1	157.4	157.7	156.4	157.2	157.1	157.8	156.0
2005	156.2	156.6	156.6	157.7	158.2	160.0	160.8	160.9	160.4	159.3	159.3	160.0	158.8
2006	158.5	159.0	159.6	159.6	159.9	161.6	161.2	161.0	159.8	159.1	159.1	160.1	159.9
2007	157.9	158.0	158.3	157.7	158.1	158.9	158.6	157.7	156.4	155.9	156.2	156.8	157.5
Professional and Business Services													
2000	352.8	357.4	365.4	367.5	369.5	374.6	373.9	377.9	375.4	372.8	373.0	373.1	369.4
2001	363.1	365.5	369.2	372.1	374.6	376.9	376.9	377.9	371.8	370.6	371.7	371.7	371.8
2002	357.3	360.1	364.2	367.2	370.0	372.5	371.9	374.4	371.0	369.4	369.9	369.8	368.1
2003	358.4	356.6	361.6	368.5	370.8	374.5	373.1	375.5	373.7	375.3	374.4	375.8	369.9
2004	364.5	366.6	373.7	375.2	378.4	382.7	383.8	384.3	382.5	384.4	383.3	384.8	378.7
2005	373.9	377.0	382.6	388.4	390.6	393.9	393.5	394.6	394.3	392.8	391.6	391.4	388.7
2006	383.4	386.3	392.7	396.3	397.4	400.9	400.2	400.9	398.5	396.7	395.5	396.1	395.4
2007	384.8	386.2	391.8	395.7	396.9	400.5	400.0	401.7	399.4	401.2	401.2	401.6	396.8
Education and Health Services													
2000	299.1	302.0	303.9	308.5	308.2	308.2	308.7	308.0	311.9	313.9	315.8	317.6	308.8
2001	310.8	314.4	316.4	318.0	319.1	321.2	317.5	316.7	319.4	323.6	326.3	328.3	319.3
2002	324.1	329.0	330.0	328.9	330.0	329.5	327.9	326.8	329.6	334.2	337.0	337.6	330.4
2003	333.4	335.0	337.3	338.8	339.7	340.5	340.0	340.3	340.5	342.2	343.8	344.6	339.7
2004	342.9	343.4	345.5	345.4	346.5	347.6	349.6	348.2	347.8	350.2	351.9	352.1	347.6
2005	347.5	350.2	351.4	353.5	353.9	353.0	352.0	351.1	354.7	358.8	360.3	361.4	354.0
2006	356.7	359.5	362.4	362.7	363.8	363.7	360.9	360.2	364.5	368.1	370.0	371.7	363.7
2007	367.6	370.1	372.8	372.6	373.4	373.5	371.3	370.7	374.5	378.0	379.7	380.5	373.7
Leisure and Hospitality													
2000	184.8	184.7	191.0	198.7	206.1	217.9	220.7	219.9	210.5	202.8	199.2	198.2	202.9
2001	186.2	187.6	192.8	199.3	208.3	221.3	221.9	222.1	210.7	205.6	201.5	200.1	204.8
2002	191.4	192.5	199.1	207.1	216.9	228.0	230.1	230.1	220.6	211.8	208.2	205.1	211.7
2003	197.5	194.7	200.3	210.7	220.1	230.9	233.2	233.1	224.6	216.8	212.7	210.5	215.4
2004	200.5	201.0	207.8	215.7	224.2	236.1	238.4	238.9	231.0	222.0	218.0	217.4	220.9
2005	206.8	207.3	212.1	222.6	230.6	244.0	245.5	243.8	235.4	223.6	220.7	218.8	225.9
2006	210.7	210.2	217.4	225.3	234.6	248.8	249.2	249.3	239.5	230.5	226.4	225.6	230.6
2007	216.7	214.7	221.4	229.7	238.9	250.2	252.4	252.9	242.8	234.7	231.6	229.7	234.6
Other Services													
2000	110.3	111.2	113.0	113.9	114.8	116.7	115.7	115.6	115.4	114.7	114.8	115.4	114.3
2001	108.9	110.0	110.9	110.3	111.9	114.1	113.2	112.8	110.6	110.7	110.7	111.5	111.3
2002	109.9	111.1	112.6	113.4	114.3	116.2	117.5	116.1	114.4	113.9	114.2	114.8	114.0
2003	112.9	113.3	115.1	116.1	116.6	119.0	119.1	116.9	115.3	115.0	114.5	115.3	115.8
2004	111.4	112.3	113.3	116.3	116.8	117.9	118.1	117.1	116.7	116.0	116.1	116.6	115.7
2005	114.9	115.7	116.6	116.6	117.0	118.1	117.2	116.9	116.2	115.2	115.6	116.0	116.3
2006	114.8	115.2	116.2	116.7	117.2	118.6	118.2	117.9	117.2	116.6	116.8	117.5	116.9
2007	116.2	116.2	117.4	117.0	117.8	119.3	119.4	118.5	118.0	118.3	118.5	118.9	118.0
Government													
2000	441.9	446.8	456.5	455.4	455.3	450.9	436.6	432.4	447.6	456.8	459.3	459.6	449.9
2001	448.2	457.6	460.8	461.8	461.2	454.3	439.8	439.2	454.8	464.8	469.0	469.0	456.7
2002	457.4	467.4	471.9	468.4	469.3	463.8	447.8	447.1	463.5	472.5	474.0	472.7	464.7
2003	459.2	468.4	471.4	470.3	470.1	462.8	444.5	437.9	460.9	467.3	468.2	467.4	462.4
2004	459.2	464.6	469.3	467.9	470.1	460.4	443.5	443.1	456.5	470.4	473.3	471.5	462.7
2005	457.2	466.2	468.0	469.7	472.6	461.3	449.4	449.0	465.7	475.2	479.7	477.9	466.0
2006	459.9	471.9	476.7	477.6	478.6	466.1	453.7	452.2	469.3	480.9	483.2	483.8	471.1
2007	467.4	478.5	484.2	483.5	486.4	474.2	465.0	463.6	476.1	487.1	491.2	490.9	479.0

Average Weekly Hours by Selected Industry: Maryland, 2003–2007

(Not seasonally adjusted.)

Industry and year	January	February	March	April	May	June	July	August	September	October	November	December	Annual Average
Manufacturing													
2003	39.0	38.0	39.2	39.5	40.1	40.1	39.4	39.3	39.3	39.9	40.3	40.5	39.5
2004	40.5	40.3	39.9	40.0	40.0	40.1	40.1	40.0	39.2	40.6	40.4	40.7	40.1
2005	41.2	40.0	40.3	39.9	39.8	39.8	39.6	40.4	40.0	40.0	40.3	40.4	40.1
2006	40.4	40.2	40.3	40.3	40.7	40.4	40.7	40.6	40.7	40.9	40.7	40.7	40.6
2007	40.5	39.9	40.7	40.0	40.3	40.5	40.5	40.2	40.6	40.4	40.4	40.4	40.4

Average Hourly Earnings by Selected Industry: Maryland, 2003–2007

(Dollars, not seasonally adjusted.)

Industry and year	January	February	March	April	May	June	July	August	September	October	November	December	Annual Average
Manufacturing													
2003	15.43	15.43	15.16	15.62	15.79	15.67	16.04	15.96	15.84	15.81	16.00	16.21	15.74
2004	16.51	16.31	16.45	16.32	16.25	16.42	16.46	16.43	16.76	16.34	16.64	16.79	16.47
2005	16.62	16.43	16.38	16.47	17.10	17.22	17.14	17.23	17.19	17.13	17.64	17.24	16.98
2006	17.57	17.72	17.56	17.79	18.02	18.24	18.06	17.91	17.97	17.78	18.01	17.93	17.88
2007	17.78	17.83	17.55	17.75	17.53	17.80	17.44	17.41	17.61	17.48	17.50	18.18	17.65

Average Weekly Earnings by Selected Industry: Maryland, 2003–2007

(Dollars, not seasonally adjusted.)

Industry and year	January	February	March	April	May	June	July	August	September	October	November	December	Annual Average
Manufacturing													
2003	601.77	586.34	594.27	616.99	633.18	628.37	631.98	627.23	622.51	630.82	644.80	656.51	621.73
2004	668.66	657.29	656.36	652.80	650.00	658.44	660.05	657.20	656.99	663.40	672.26	683.35	660.45
2005	684.74	657.20	660.11	657.15	680.58	685.36	678.74	696.09	687.60	685.20	710.89	696.50	680.90
2006	709.83	712.34	707.67	716.94	733.41	736.90	735.04	727.15	731.38	727.20	733.01	729.75	725.93
2007	720.09	711.42	714.29	710.00	706.46	720.90	706.32	699.88	714.97	706.19	707.00	734.47	713.06

Population
    2000 census: 6,349,097
    2007 estimate: 6,449,755
    Percent change, 2000–2007: 1.6%

Percent change in total nonfarm employment, 2000–2007: -1.6%

Industry with the largest growth in employment, 2000–2007 (thousands)
    Education and health services, 78.0

Industry with the largest decline in employment, 2000–2007 (thousands)
    Manufacturing, -107.8

Civilian labor force
    2000: 3,365,573
    2007: 3,408,197

Employment-population ratio
    2000: 66.4%
    2007: 63.8%

Unemployment rate and rank among states
    2000: 2.7%, 3rd
    2007: 4.5%, 27th

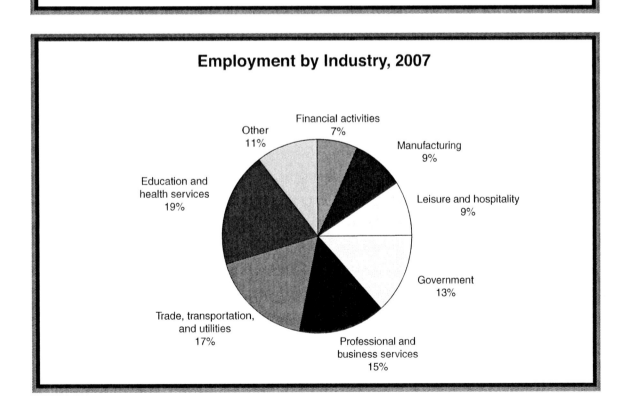

Employment by Industry, 2007

Financial activities 7%

Other 11%

Manufacturing 9%

Education and health services 19%

Leisure and hospitality 9%

Government 13%

Trade, transportation, and utilities 17%

Professional and business services 15%

Employment by Industry: Massachusetts, 2000–2007

(Numbers in thousands, not seasonally adjusted.)

Industry and year	January	February	March	April	May	June	July	August	September	October	November	December	Annual Average
Total Nonfarm													
2000	3,221.4	3,240.7	3,263.5	3,308.1	3,332.3	3,362.9	3,334.5	3,325.1	3,365.2	3,385.2	3,398.3	3,413.9	3,329.3
2001	3,317.0	3,326.5	3,335.4	3,356.2	3,373.9	3,390.0	3,330.3	3,322.3	3,335.7	3,331.8	3,325.8	3,326.2	3,339.3
2002	3,217.6	3,216.2	3,235.5	3,261.5	3,284.1	3,298.0	3,258.0	3,249.2	3,272.3	3,272.6	3,274.2	3,272.1	3,259.3
2003	3,158.8	3,148.5	3,161.2	3,195.7	3,222.1	3,233.5	3,198.0	3,188.4	3,218.1	3,219.2	3,221.2	3,215.9	3,198.4
2004	3,113.0	3,123.0	3,145.8	3,188.7	3,212.0	3,232.6	3,207.8	3,194.9	3,222.4	3,230.3	3,233.0	3,235.8	3,194.9
2005	3,125.8	3,142.6	3,150.7	3,204.9	3,227.3	3,248.4	3,224.3	3,214.9	3,243.0	3,243.9	3,254.6	3,258.3	3,211.6
2006	3,158.0	3,169.0	3,189.5	3,233.2	3,256.1	3,286.0	3,258.0	3,249.7	3,274.1	3,285.3	3,290.8	3,295.8	3,245.5
2007	3,198.5	3,206.1	3,221.1	3,262.9	3,296.7	3,326.7	3,290.3	3,283.2	3,299.9	3,310.0	3,314.7	3,315.8	3,277.2
Total Private													
2000	2,789.9	2,799.9	2,823.0	2,863.3	2,879.6	2,923.9	2,927.7	2,925.9	2,929.1	2,942.6	2,952.7	2,969.4	2,893.9
2001	2,877.9	2,878.5	2,886.9	2,906.5	2,922.3	2,949.1	2,921.4	2,917.8	2,893.2	2,883.0	2,875.7	2,875.3	2,899.0
2002	2,776.2	2,767.3	2,785.9	2,814.2	2,836.3	2,860.5	2,851.1	2,847.4	2,834.7	2,835.9	2,834.4	2,834.2	2,823.2
2003	2,729.1	2,712.0	2,724.6	2,759.1	2,785.1	2,805.4	2,800.8	2,797.3	2,787.8	2,790.6	2,791.7	2,786.9	2,772.5
2004	2,693.9	2,694.0	2,715.6	2,756.9	2,779.9	2,808.4	2,816.8	2,811.1	2,798.1	2,800.9	2,801.1	2,804.8	2,773.5
2005	2,704.5	2,709.2	2,717.4	2,770.4	2,791.3	2,821.4	2,829.3	2,827.1	2,817.0	2,809.9	2,817.9	2,823.6	2,786.6
2006	2,732.9	2,733.2	2,752.6	2,795.2	2,816.2	2,853.7	2,858.4	2,857.9	2,844.1	2,847.3	2,850.0	2,856.6	2,816.5
2007	2,768.6	2,766.4	2,780.3	2,820.9	2,852.0	2,890.8	2,888.9	2,888.2	2,866.5	2,869.4	2,870.1	2,872.4	2,844.5
Goods-Producing													
2000	512.6	510.6	517.4	527.6	532.5	543.0	541.1	545.4	541.3	544.8	545.0	543.7	533.8
2001	533.6	531.0	530.4	536.1	539.5	542.3	530.5	531.8	527.2	522.2	515.3	509.7	529.1
2002	490.0	483.7	485.9	491.6	497.4	501.2	494.2	496.1	493.4	491.5	488.7	481.3	491.3
2003	462.9	453.4	454.4	463.5	469.5	472.7	467.0	468.6	465.4	462.5	461.1	454.1	462.9
2004	436.7	433.5	439.5	450.5	457.8	464.3	462.6	465.0	461.9	457.9	456.7	452.4	453.2
2005	433.9	430.1	430.6	443.3	450.4	456.4	456.0	457.1	455.4	451.2	450.7	446.7	446.8
2006	431.1	428.3	430.8	441.4	446.1	452.5	451.1	451.9	449.0	445.9	442.7	439.8	442.6
2007	425.0	419.4	421.0	428.3	437.5	445.3	442.7	443.9	441.1	438.0	436.2	432.1	434.2
Natural Resources and Mining													
2000	1.2	1.2	1.3	1.5	1.5	1.5	1.5	1.5	1.5	1.5	1.5	1.4	1.4
2001	1.3	1.3	1.3	1.5	1.6	1.6	1.6	1.6	1.6	1.6	1.6	1.6	1.5
2002	1.3	1.3	1.4	1.6	1.7	1.7	1.7	1.7	1.8	1.8	1.8	1.7	1.6
2003	1.5	1.5	1.5	1.7	1.8	1.9	1.9	1.9	2.0	2.0	2.0	1.9	1.8
2004	1.7	1.6	1.6	1.9	2.0	2.0	2.1	2.1	2.0	2.0	2.0	2.0	1.9
2005	1.8	1.7	1.7	2.0	2.1	2.1	2.1	2.1	2.1	2.0	2.0	1.8	2.0
2006	1.6	1.6	1.7	1.8	1.9	1.9	2.0	1.9	1.9	1.9	1.9	1.7	1.8
2007	1.4	1.3	1.4	1.5	1.7	1.8	1.7	1.7	1.7	1.6	1.6	1.6	1.6
Construction													
2000	112.5	110.1	115.6	124.5	129.0	134.6	138.3	139.4	137.7	137.6	136.9	134.0	129.1
2001	124.5	123.3	125.4	135.6	142.1	146.4	147.9	148.4	146.1	145.5	143.5	139.9	139.1
2002	128.4	125.8	128.8	137.8	144.3	147.0	148.6	149.4	146.6	147.5	145.9	139.3	140.8
2003	126.9	120.6	122.7	133.2	140.5	143.5	145.5	146.0	143.7	142.2	141.0	135.8	136.8
2004	122.5	120.1	124.8	134.6	141.8	146.3	148.6	148.8	146.5	144.6	143.4	139.2	138.4
2005	124.5	120.7	122.3	135.3	141.9	146.4	150.3	150.7	149.3	145.8	145.8	141.4	139.5
2006	129.2	126.6	129.3	140.1	144.4	148.3	150.2	150.4	147.7	145.4	142.5	138.7	141.1
2007	126.7	121.5	123.8	131.8	140.1	145.3	146.7	146.7	144.8	142.6	140.8	136.7	137.3
Manufacturing													
2000	398.9	399.3	400.5	401.6	402.0	406.9	401.3	404.5	402.1	405.7	406.6	408.3	403.1
2001	407.8	406.4	403.7	399.0	395.8	394.3	381.0	381.8	379.5	375.1	370.2	368.2	388.6
2002	360.3	356.6	355.7	352.2	351.4	352.5	343.9	345.0	345.0	342.2	341.0	340.3	348.8
2003	334.5	331.3	330.2	328.6	327.2	327.3	319.6	320.7	319.7	318.3	318.1	316.4	324.3
2004	312.5	311.8	313.1	314.0	314.0	316.0	311.9	314.1	313.4	311.3	311.3	311.2	312.9
2005	307.6	307.7	306.6	306.0	306.4	307.9	303.6	304.3	304.0	303.4	302.9	303.5	305.3
2006	300.3	300.1	299.8	299.5	299.8	302.3	298.9	299.6	299.4	298.6	298.3	299.4	299.7
2007	296.9	296.6	295.8	295.0	295.7	298.2	294.3	295.5	294.6	293.8	293.8	293.8	295.3
Service-Providing													
2000	2,708.8	2,730.1	2,746.1	2,780.5	2,799.8	2,819.9	2,793.4	2,779.7	2,823.9	2,840.4	2,853.3	2,870.2	2,795.5
2001	2,783.4	2,795.5	2,805.0	2,820.1	2,834.4	2,847.7	2,799.8	2,790.5	2,808.5	2,809.6	2,810.5	2,816.5	2,810.1
2002	2,727.6	2,732.5	2,749.6	2,769.9	2,786.7	2,796.8	2,763.8	2,753.1	2,778.9	2,781.1	2,785.5	2,790.8	2,768.0
2003	2,695.9	2,695.1	2,706.8	2,732.2	2,752.6	2,760.8	2,731.0	2,719.8	2,752.7	2,756.7	2,760.1	2,761.8	2,735.5
2004	2,676.3	2,689.5	2,706.3	2,738.2	2,754.2	2,768.3	2,745.2	2,729.9	2,760.5	2,772.4	2,776.3	2,783.4	2,741.7
2005	2,691.9	2,712.5	2,720.1	2,761.6	2,776.9	2,792.0	2,768.3	2,757.8	2,787.6	2,792.7	2,803.9	2,811.6	2,764.7
2006	2,726.9	2,740.7	2,758.7	2,791.8	2,810.0	2,833.5	2,806.9	2,797.8	2,825.1	2,839.4	2,848.1	2,856.0	2,802.9
2007	2,773.5	2,786.7	2,800.1	2,834.6	2,859.2	2,881.4	2,847.6	2,839.3	2,858.8	2,872.0	2,878.5	2,883.7	2,843.0
Trade, Transportation, and Utilities													
2000	591.3	584.4	585.5	587.1	590.5	599.2	592.1	592.1	595.6	602.0	613.9	627.6	596.7
2001	595.1	584.9	585.4	587.4	591.1	600.3	589.7	588.3	588.2	589.7	599.9	607.0	592.3
2002	577.4	567.4	569.5	572.3	577.4	586.5	580.5	578.1	579.6	581.0	589.3	598.8	579.8
2003	568.8	560.2	562.2	566.2	571.6	579.6	572.6	571.7	574.2	578.2	587.2	593.5	573.8
2004	568.2	561.4	563.0	564.4	569.4	577.2	571.4	569.1	568.7	575.6	584.2	593.0	572.1
2005	565.2	559.8	559.0	563.7	568.2	575.4	569.6	569.4	568.5	570.9	579.9	590.5	570.0
2006	566.5	555.3	558.0	562.6	566.8	575.1	569.4	569.8	570.4	573.9	584.1	593.3	570.4
2007	567.3	557.2	558.8	561.0	568.9	578.1	571.4	570.2	569.9	573.5	581.6	590.1	570.7
Wholesale Trade													
2000	137.1	137.1	137.9	138.4	138.9	140.7	139.6	139.6	139.7	140.7	141.3	143.0	139.5
2001	141.5	141.6	142.0	142.5	142.3	143.3	142.4	142.0	140.8	140.1	139.8	139.9	141.5
2002	136.4	135.7	136.2	136.0	136.5	137.7	136.9	136.6	135.8	135.4	135.5	136.3	136.3
2003	135.0	134.5	134.6	134.6	134.9	135.7	135.8	135.5	135.1	134.7	135.3	135.8	135.1
2004	133.6	133.6	134.7	134.3	134.1	135.0	134.4	133.9	132.7	132.6	132.5	132.7	133.7
2005	131.4	131.2	131.1	132.1	133.1	134.2	134.6	135.0	134.6	135.3	136.1	136.8	133.8
2006	134.9	134.5	135.0	136.2	136.6	138.1	138.3	138.7	137.9	138.1	138.2	138.8	137.1
2007	136.7	136.4	136.9	137.0	137.7	139.3	139.4	139.3	138.2	138.6	139.0	140.0	138.2

Employment by Industry: Massachusetts, 2000–2007—Continued

(Numbers in thousands, not seasonally adjusted.)

Industry and year	January	February	March	April	May	June	July	August	September	October	November	December	Annual Average
Retail Trade													
2000	361.8	354.9	355.4	354.0	356.4	362.3	360.0	360.2	359.7	364.2	376.4	387.9	362.7
2001	360.9	350.7	351.0	351.7	354.9	361.9	357.2	357.2	354.1	357.2	369.7	378.0	358.7
2002	354.8	346.0	347.8	349.5	353.2	360.1	359.3	358.0	355.5	356.6	365.9	375.4	356.8
2003	348.4	341.1	342.7	346.5	350.7	357.3	354.9	355.1	353.3	357.4	366.2	372.4	353.8
2004	352.2	345.8	346.1	346.7	350.9	357.1	356.2	355.4	352.2	357.7	367.1	376.1	355.3
2005	352.3	347.2	346.5	349.5	352.2	357.3	355.1	355.4	351.0	353.4	361.7	370.3	354.3
2006	351.1	340.5	342.3	344.9	347.4	352.5	350.4	350.6	346.5	350.4	360.8	368.1	350.5
2007	347.3	338.1	338.8	340.4	346.4	352.3	350.2	349.5	345.1	348.8	356.9	363.2	348.1
Transportation and Utilities													
2000	92.4	92.4	92.2	94.7	95.2	96.2	92.5	92.3	96.2	97.1	96.2	96.7	94.5
2001	92.7	92.6	92.4	93.2	93.9	95.1	90.1	89.1	93.3	92.4	90.4	89.1	92.0
2002	86.2	85.7	85.5	86.8	87.7	88.7	84.3	83.5	88.3	89.0	87.9	87.1	86.7
2003	85.4	84.6	84.9	85.1	86.0	86.6	81.9	81.1	86.3	86.1	85.7	85.3	84.9
2004	82.4	82.0	82.2	83.4	84.4	85.1	80.8	79.8	83.8	85.3	84.6	84.2	83.2
2005	81.5	81.4	81.4	82.1	82.9	83.9	79.9	79.0	82.9	82.2	82.1	83.4	81.9
2006	80.5	80.3	80.7	81.5	82.8	84.5	80.7	80.5	86.0	85.4	85.1	86.4	82.9
2007	83.3	82.7	83.1	83.6	84.8	86.5	81.8	81.4	86.6	86.1	85.7	86.9	84.4
Information													
2000	104.1	105.2	106.8	108.6	110.4	112.7	115.4	107.3	115.1	115.0	115.9	116.7	111.1
2001	116.4	116.2	115.8	115.0	113.8	113.4	111.6	110.5	108.0	106.1	105.4	104.7	111.4
2002	103.5	102.7	102.5	100.4	100.0	99.9	99.5	98.8	96.9	96.9	96.7	96.9	99.6
2003	93.7	93.1	93.0	91.9	91.7	92.4	91.0	90.9	89.7	89.3	89.2	89.2	91.3
2004	87.4	86.8	87.5	86.8	87.2	87.8	87.8	87.7	86.9	87.0	87.6	87.7	87.4
2005	86.5	86.7	86.7	86.4	86.6	87.3	88.0	87.6	86.9	86.2	86.6	87.1	86.9
2006	86.5	86.5	86.5	85.9	86.4	87.3	87.1	87.5	86.5	87.0	87.4	88.0	86.9
2007	86.4	86.7	87.6	88.0	87.5	88.3	89.1	88.9	88.7	89.2	89.7	90.2	88.4
Financial Activities													
2000	224.7	224.0	224.6	225.7	226.0	230.0	230.3	230.6	229.0	229.5	230.0	232.4	228.0
2001	228.4	228.7	229.9	229.7	229.7	233.1	234.1	233.7	230.5	229.4	229.7	230.6	230.6
2002	230.2	228.9	228.3	226.8	227.2	229.7	230.8	230.3	226.9	226.4	225.6	226.4	228.1
2003	224.7	223.2	223.5	223.5	224.0	226.2	226.5	226.4	222.5	221.1	221.0	221.6	223.7
2004	218.8	218.6	218.9	219.3	219.6	222.2	223.3	222.6	219.8	217.9	217.4	218.5	219.7
2005	217.5	217.1	217.6	218.2	219.6	222.9	225.6	225.9	223.7	222.0	222.7	224.4	221.4
2006	220.6	220.4	220.8	221.5	222.8	225.8	227.9	227.4	225.0	224.2	224.3	225.9	223.9
2007	223.9	223.8	223.8	224.0	224.8	227.5	227.9	227.7	224.0	223.3	223.1	224.4	224.9
Professional and Business Services													
2000	464.8	468.5	475.2	485.3	487.0	499.4	504.1	508.0	505.5	504.3	506.0	507.8	492.9
2001	494.3	492.1	493.3	493.1	493.4	496.5	487.0	485.9	479.5	472.3	468.0	466.6	485.2
2002	448.6	445.3	448.4	455.8	456.9	460.7	458.9	458.5	455.0	453.5	452.2	449.8	453.6
2003	433.5	428.3	429.5	438.9	441.0	444.8	446.3	446.0	443.4	444.6	445.5	445.4	440.6
2004	431.7	431.6	435.6	448.4	450.8	457.7	460.4	461.2	459.3	458.5	458.7	459.3	451.1
2005	443.1	443.3	445.4	459.5	460.8	467.9	468.8	469.5	468.3	466.5	468.5	467.8	460.8
2006	453.0	454.7	458.4	469.1	471.8	480.4	479.3	481.0	477.5	478.2	479.0	478.2	471.7
2007	461.9	463.8	467.2	480.0	484.4	492.0	489.6	491.4	486.1	487.1	487.7	486.4	481.5
Education and Health Services													
2000	537.9	549.8	551.0	552.4	544.5	532.1	530.0	529.6	543.4	555.2	560.0	560.8	545.5
2001	543.4	556.3	557.2	560.0	553.5	541.5	541.6	541.5	553.0	566.9	571.1	572.5	554.9
2002	558.0	569.3	573.1	575.3	568.5	555.9	553.2	551.6	566.6	578.5	584.9	585.7	568.4
2003	568.3	578.1	581.5	583.3	575.5	561.9	560.8	558.1	573.9	585.3	589.9	589.4	575.5
2004	573.5	584.8	588.0	589.4	581.4	568.6	569.1	566.1	580.4	592.4	596.5	596.2	582.2
2005	578.9	591.7	593.4	596.8	589.2	576.4	576.8	574.6	588.8	601.5	606.9	606.7	590.1
2006	591.8	604.6	609.0	610.3	604.0	593.3	593.2	590.5	605.8	618.0	622.6	623.0	605.5
2007	612.0	623.1	624.7	630.3	623.6	610.4	612.8	610.7	622.9	634.7	638.9	638.4	623.5
Leisure and Hospitality													
2000	246.9	249.0	253.4	266.8	277.8	294.8	301.1	299.6	287.6	280.1	270.1	267.8	274.5
2001	254.3	256.3	260.9	271.0	285.8	303.4	306.3	305.7	291.0	280.6	270.4	267.7	279.5
2002	254.1	255.4	262.0	275.6	291.3	306.8	312.4	312.7	299.5	291.1	279.9	278.0	284.9
2003	262.2	260.9	264.5	275.6	294.4	308.3	315.6	315.8	302.1	293.6	281.4	277.2	287.6
2004	263.4	262.8	267.5	282.2	296.8	311.6	321.4	319.1	305.1	295.4	283.9	280.9	290.8
2005	265.2	265.9	269.2	285.3	298.8	314.1	322.0	321.3	307.2	294.6	285.3	282.2	292.6
2006	267.6	267.9	272.1	286.7	299.7	317.2	326.8	326.6	311.3	302.0	292.1	289.9	296.7
2007	276.2	276.0	279.8	291.1	305.6	325.4	330.3	330.9	314.2	304.9	294.8	292.3	301.8
Other Services													
2000	107.6	108.4	109.1	109.8	110.9	112.7	113.6	113.3	111.6	111.7	111.8	112.6	111.0
2001	112.4	113.0	114.0	114.2	115.5	118.6	120.6	120.4	115.8	115.8	115.9	116.5	116.1
2002	114.4	114.6	116.2	116.4	117.6	119.8	121.6	121.3	116.8	117.0	117.1	117.3	117.5
2003	115.0	114.8	116.0	116.2	117.4	119.5	121.0	119.8	116.6	116.0	116.4	116.5	117.1
2004	114.2	114.5	115.6	115.9	116.9	119.0	120.8	120.3	116.0	116.2	116.1	116.8	116.9
2005	114.2	114.6	115.5	117.2	117.7	121.0	122.5	121.7	118.2	117.0	117.3	118.2	117.9
2006	115.8	115.5	117.0	117.7	118.6	122.1	123.6	123.2	118.6	118.1	117.8	118.5	118.9
2007	115.9	116.4	117.4	118.2	119.7	123.8	125.1	124.5	119.6	118.7	118.1	118.5	119.7
Government													
2000	431.5	440.8	440.5	444.8	452.7	439.0	406.8	399.2	436.1	442.6	445.6	444.5	435.3
2001	439.1	448.0	448.5	449.7	451.6	440.9	408.9	404.5	442.5	448.8	450.1	450.9	440.3
2002	441.4	448.9	449.6	447.3	447.8	437.5	406.9	401.8	437.6	436.7	439.8	437.9	436.1
2003	429.7	436.5	436.6	436.6	437.0	428.1	397.2	391.1	430.3	428.6	429.5	429.0	425.9
2004	419.1	429.0	430.2	431.8	432.1	424.2	391.0	383.8	424.3	429.4	431.9	431.0	421.5
2005	421.3	433.4	433.3	434.5	436.0	427.0	395.0	387.8	426.0	434.0	436.7	434.7	425.0
2006	425.1	435.8	436.9	438.0	439.9	432.3	399.6	391.8	430.0	438.0	440.8	439.2	429.0
2007	429.9	439.7	440.8	442.0	444.7	435.9	401.4	395.0	433.4	440.6	444.6	443.4	432.6

Average Weekly Hours by Selected Industry: Massachusetts, 2001–2007

(Not seasonally adjusted.)

Industry and year	January	February	March	April	May	June	July	August	September	October	November	December	Annual Average
Manufacturing													
2001	40.7	40.4	40.9	39.6	40.4	40.7	39.3	39.8	40.4	39.8	40.3	41.3	40.3
2002	40.2	40.5	40.9	40.8	41.0	41.6	39.5	40.9	41.1	40.4	40.5	41.6	40.8
2003	40.3	40.5	41.0	40.3	40.4	40.7	39.8	40.3	40.8	40.2	40.9	41.4	40.6
2004	40.8	41.3	40.8	41.0	40.9	41.6	40.9	41.1	40.8	40.8	41.7	41.9	41.1
2005	41.0	41.2	41.5	41.4	41.5	41.5	41.2	41.8	42.3	41.7	41.3	41.3	41.5
2006	40.6	40.4	40.7	40.7	40.7	41.2	40.5	40.4	40.8	40.8	40.9	40.6	40.7
2007	39.9	40.3	41.3	40.8	40.5	41.3	40.5	40.9	40.9	40.6	40.6	40.3	40.7

Average Hourly Earnings by Selected Industry: Massachusetts 2001–2007

(Dollars, not seasonally adjusted.)

Industry and year	January	February	March	April	May	June	July	August	September	October	November	December	Annual Average
Manufacturing													
2001	15.34	15.42	15.49	15.56	15.52	15.75	16.01	15.88	15.91	16.04	16.06	16.17	15.75
2002	16.00	15.96	16.04	16.06	16.09	16.19	16.49	16.47	16.43	16.26	16.38	16.67	16.25
2003	16.48	16.37	16.44	16.54	16.49	16.55	16.49	16.51	16.54	16.60	16.70	16.71	16.53
2004	16.58	16.62	16.70	16.73	16.64	16.51	16.66	16.84	17.22	17.27	17.47	17.37	16.89
2005	17.54	17.47	17.52	17.49	17.66	17.54	17.71	17.72	17.67	17.89	17.88	17.88	17.66
2006	17.87	17.91	17.96	18.05	18.06	18.24	18.34	18.39	18.53	18.59	18.56	18.64	18.26
2007	18.68	18.80	18.92	18.93	19.01	19.11	19.16	19.21	19.42	19.96	19.81	20.16	19.26

Average Weekly Earnings by Selected Industry: Massachusetts, 2001–2007

(Dollars, not seasonally adjusted.)

Industry and year	January	February	March	April	May	June	July	August	September	October	November	December	Annual Average
Manufacturing													
2001	624.34	622.97	633.54	616.18	627.01	641.03	629.19	632.02	642.76	638.39	647.22	667.82	634.73
2002	643.20	646.38	656.04	655.25	659.69	673.50	651.36	673.62	675.27	656.90	663.39	693.47	663.00
2003	664.14	662.99	674.04	666.56	666.20	673.59	656.30	665.35	674.83	667.32	683.03	691.79	671.12
2004	676.46	686.41	681.36	685.93	680.58	686.82	681.39	692.12	702.58	704.62	728.50	727.80	694.18
2005	719.14	719.76	727.08	724.09	732.89	727.91	729.65	740.70	747.44	746.01	738.44	738.44	732.89
2006	725.52	723.56	730.97	734.64	735.04	751.49	742.77	742.96	756.02	758.47	759.10	756.78	743.18
2007	745.33	757.64	781.40	772.34	769.91	789.24	775.98	785.69	794.28	810.38	804.29	812.45	783.88

Population
    2000 census: 9,938,444
    2007 estimate: 10,071,822
    Percent change, 2000–2007: 1.3%

Percent change in total nonfarm employment, 2000–2007: -8.9%

Industry with the largest growth in employment, 2000–2007 (thousands)
    Education and health services, 92.9

Industry with the largest decline in employment, 2000–2007 (thousands)
    Manufacturing, -281.6

Civilian labor force
    2000: 5,143,916
    2007: 5,019,984

Employment-population ratio
    2000: 65.9%
    2007: 59.7%

Unemployment rate and rank among states
    2000: 3.7%, 22nd
    2007: 7.2%, 51st

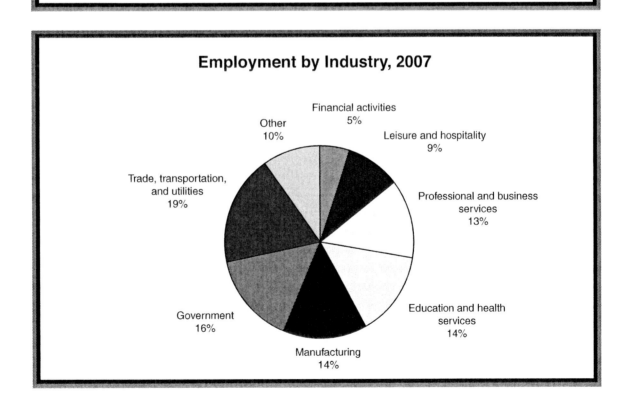

Employment by Industry, 2007

Financial activities 5%
Other 10%
Leisure and hospitality 9%
Trade, transportation, and utilities 19%
Professional and business services 13%
Government 16%
Education and health services 14%
Manufacturing 14%

Employment by Industry: Michigan, 2000–2007

(Numbers in thousands, not seasonally adjusted.)

Industry and year	January	February	March	April	May	June	July	August	September	October	November	December	Annual Average
Total Nonfarm													
2000	4,562.0	4,585.1	4,621.9	4,673.2	4,730.0	4,745.6	4,641.2	4,668.5	4,711.1	4,729.6	4,730.4	4,723.8	4,676.9
2001	4,511.7	4,535.6	4,558.1	4,584.6	4,629.6	4,641.2	4,519.5	4,548.8	4,573.3	4,562.2	4,555.6	4,549.8	4,564.2
2002	4,389.0	4,410.0	4,436.7	4,469.7	4,533.1	4,547.9	4,446.7	4,485.1	4,527.4	4,537.0	4,539.1	4,527.7	4,487.5
2003	4,353.5	4,356.8	4,370.3	4,396.1	4,469.1	4,476.2	4,340.3	4,393.4	4,445.3	4,468.4	4,465.8	4,462.3	4,416.5
2004	4,303.4	4,313.5	4,339.4	4,397.9	4,451.6	4,450.2	4,325.6	4,382.7	4,448.8	4,460.2	4,463.9	4,457.1	4,399.5
2005	4,289.9	4,323.6	4,339.7	4,398.4	4,449.5	4,441.0	4,325.7	4,366.7	4,444.7	4,433.8	4,443.6	4,427.2	4,390.3
2006	4,266.0	4,280.4	4,303.7	4,341.6	4,385.9	4,394.7	4,249.9	4,295.4	4,362.3	4,345.1	4,354.6	4,345.7	4,327.1
2007	4,186.2	4,213.0	4,234.0	4,262.5	4,325.9	4,328.6	4,204.4	4,246.7	4,297.2	4,282.8	4,285.9	4,276.4	4,262.0
Total Private													
2000	3,889.6	3,889.7	3,917.1	3,973.0	4,029.9	4,072.8	4,022.4	4,056.5	4,030.2	4,026.2	4,020.4	4,018.1	3,995.5
2001	3,830.1	3,835.0	3,850.9	3,880.8	3,930.0	3,960.4	3,896.7	3,928.1	3,893.3	3,857.1	3,845.3	3,842.6	3,879.2
2002	3,700.2	3,704.2	3,727.5	3,772.6	3,838.5	3,873.1	3,827.9	3,865.4	3,842.5	3,822.2	3,821.2	3,815.0	3,800.9
2003	3,663.4	3,647.6	3,662.1	3,692.0	3,768.3	3,802.7	3,726.3	3,782.8	3,768.2	3,753.5	3,751.9	3,753.8	3,731.1
2004	3,617.2	3,612.3	3,635.3	3,696.7	3,755.5	3,781.6	3,720.0	3,779.4	3,770.0	3,756.9	3,757.2	3,755.6	3,719.8
2005	3,612.4	3,626.2	3,640.8	3,700.8	3,757.6	3,777.7	3,728.3	3,767.5	3,766.9	3,738.5	3,743.6	3,734.3	3,716.2
2006	3,594.3	3,590.0	3,608.4	3,653.9	3,705.3	3,740.8	3,656.5	3,705.5	3,697.4	3,660.2	3,665.9	3,663.3	3,661.8
2007	3,526.0	3,535.1	3,551.0	3,586.5	3,651.8	3,680.3	3,617.0	3,654.5	3,640.9	3,605.6	3,605.6	3,603.4	3,604.8
Goods-Producing													
2000	1,085.4	1,085.6	1,092.6	1,117.7	1,134.5	1,148.2	1,125.1	1,141.0	1,128.6	1,127.8	1,117.3	1,105.7	1,117.5
2001	1,037.6	1,043.0	1,043.7	1,047.7	1,057.5	1,063.7	1,035.7	1,049.3	1,042.0	1,023.9	1,011.8	1,005.9	1,038.5
2002	949.4	956.1	958.4	965.3	982.0	993.6	975.2	991.4	982.9	976.8	970.1	958.9	971.7
2003	912.2	902.1	903.9	906.6	930.8	944.1	897.4	936.5	930.2	922.8	920.4	914.1	918.4
2004	876.3	871.1	879.1	897.2	912.4	919.2	877.7	922.3	920.0	914.3	910.9	902.9	900.3
2005	854.8	862.0	860.8	873.8	891.7	897.2	863.7	890.2	891.8	887.4	885.7	871.4	877.5
2006	830.5	826.2	828.7	845.7	856.3	865.0	816.1	850.0	844.9	830.7	829.3	818.8	836.9
2007	774.0	782.3	785.0	792.3	806.2	816.3	783.6	807.6	800.6	782.1	781.5	775.0	790.5
Natural Resources and Mining													
2000	8.8	8.6	8.7	9.2	9.4	9.7	10.1	10.1	9.8	10.1	10.0	9.6	9.5
2001	8.8	8.9	9.1	9.2	9.6	9.7	9.6	9.6	9.5	9.5	9.3	9.1	9.3
2002	8.0	8.0	8.1	8.4	8.9	9.0	9.0	8.8	8.9	8.9	8.8	8.5	8.6
2003	7.6	7.6	7.6	7.9	8.6	8.9	8.3	8.3	8.3	8.4	8.2	7.9	8.1
2004	7.4	7.4	7.6	8.0	8.4	8.4	8.6	8.7	8.7	8.5	8.3	7.9	8.2
2005	7.7	7.7	7.7	8.4	8.8	9.0	9.0	8.9	8.6	8.6	8.4	8.0	8.4
2006	7.4	7.5	7.5	7.9	8.2	8.5	8.5	8.5	8.3	8.3	8.1	7.6	8.0
2007	7.2	7.2	7.0	7.3	7.8	8.2	8.2	8.1	7.8	7.7	7.5	7.2	7.6
Construction													
2000	182.3	180.4	188.3	205.6	216.6	224.8	227.7	227.1	224.2	220.6	213.9	203.2	209.6
2001	182.5	180.8	185.6	198.3	211.8	218.7	222.6	223.1	219.2	215.7	210.7	203.9	206.1
2002	182.3	177.8	180.4	192.3	206.9	213.0	216.0	215.8	210.7	207.6	201.5	190.6	199.6
2003	168.8	163.0	164.5	178.6	196.4	204.5	208.5	208.0	204.5	202.8	197.5	190.2	190.6
2004	166.8	163.4	167.4	183.2	195.7	203.9	208.6	207.8	205.2	203.9	200.5	191.2	191.5
2005	168.0	164.6	167.4	183.1	195.2	203.2	206.7	204.9	201.5	198.7	193.9	182.4	189.1
2006	162.5	158.7	161.7	174.5	185.4	192.5	192.5	191.2	187.7	183.5	177.0	168.7	178.0
2007	150.7	145.2	149.7	158.1	171.6	178.9	180.5	180.5	178.0	174.2	168.0	158.7	166.2
Manufacturing													
2000	894.3	896.6	895.6	902.9	908.5	913.7	887.3	903.8	894.6	897.1	893.4	892.9	898.4
2001	846.3	853.3	849.0	840.2	836.1	835.3	803.5	816.6	813.3	798.7	791.8	792.9	823.1
2002	759.1	770.3	769.9	764.6	766.2	771.6	750.2	766.8	763.3	760.3	759.8	759.8	763.5
2003	735.8	731.5	731.8	720.1	725.8	730.7	680.6	720.2	717.4	711.6	714.7	716.0	719.7
2004	702.1	700.3	704.1	706.0	708.3	706.9	660.5	705.8	706.1	701.9	702.1	703.8	700.7
2005	679.1	689.7	685.7	682.3	687.7	685.0	648.0	676.4	681.7	680.1	683.4	681.0	680.0
2006	660.6	660.0	659.5	663.3	662.7	664.0	615.1	650.3	648.9	638.9	644.2	642.5	650.8
2007	616.1	629.9	628.3	626.9	626.8	629.2	594.9	619.0	614.8	600.2	606.0	609.1	616.8
Service-Providing													
2000	3,476.6	3,499.5	3,529.3	3,555.5	3,595.5	3,597.4	3,516.1	3,527.5	3,582.5	3,601.8	3,613.1	3,618.1	3,559.4
2001	3,474.1	3,492.6	3,514.4	3,536.9	3,572.1	3,577.5	3,483.8	3,499.5	3,531.3	3,538.3	3,543.8	3,543.9	3,525.7
2002	3,439.6	3,453.9	3,478.3	3,504.4	3,551.1	3,554.3	3,471.5	3,493.7	3,544.5	3,560.2	3,569.0	3,568.8	3,515.8
2003	3,441.3	3,454.7	3,466.4	3,489.5	3,538.3	3,532.1	3,442.9	3,456.9	3,515.1	3,545.6	3,545.4	3,548.2	3,498.0
2004	3,427.1	3,442.4	3,460.3	3,500.7	3,539.2	3,531.0	3,447.9	3,460.4	3,528.8	3,545.9	3,553.0	3,554.2	3,499.2
2005	3,435.1	3,461.6	3,478.9	3,524.6	3,557.8	3,543.8	3,462.0	3,476.5	3,552.9	3,546.4	3,557.9	3,555.8	3,512.8
2006	3,435.5	3,454.2	3,475.0	3,495.9	3,529.6	3,529.7	3,433.8	3,445.4	3,517.4	3,514.4	3,525.3	3,526.9	3,490.3
2007	3,412.2	3,430.7	3,449.0	3,470.2	3,519.7	3,512.3	3,420.8	3,439.1	3,496.6	3,500.7	3,504.4	3,501.4	3,471.4
Trade, Transportation, and Utilities													
2000	866.5	858.9	864.7	869.5	881.2	886.7	874.0	879.9	878.4	889.3	905.2	919.7	881.2
2001	865.3	854.8	855.5	859.5	867.4	870.6	857.1	860.2	853.7	853.6	865.3	871.7	861.2
2002	826.1	814.9	820.4	825.6	838.6	843.5	834.7	838.3	836.8	832.8	845.8	854.0	834.3
2003	807.8	798.8	800.7	803.8	816.9	822.8	814.9	820.3	819.5	823.8	833.4	841.8	817.0
2004	796.9	789.9	792.0	800.7	812.7	817.1	811.5	814.1	808.1	813.7	826.4	834.3	809.8
2005	791.0	785.3	788.1	796.9	807.8	811.9	811.0	811.7	806.8	806.1	818.8	825.7	805.1
2006	784.5	776.1	780.3	787.3	797.5	803.6	796.4	798.8	795.0	795.4	809.1	816.0	795.0
2007	779.2	770.1	772.1	777.4	790.0	795.0	792.6	792.1	788.0	790.6	800.8	806.5	787.9
Wholesale Trade													
2000	184.0	184.8	185.8	185.8	187.1	188.0	187.0	186.7	185.2	185.8	185.3	186.4	186.0
2001	180.3	180.8	181.2	183.2	183.4	183.0	181.1	180.7	178.9	177.9	176.9	177.1	180.4
2002	173.0	173.0	173.6	175.0	177.1	177.8	176.5	176.7	175.4	175.3	175.5	175.9	175.4
2003	171.7	171.7	172.2	172.6	173.5	174.1	173.1	173.2	172.3	172.4	171.8	172.1	172.6
2004	167.2	167.4	168.8	170.2	171.6	172.6	172.3	172.0	171.0	171.1	171.0	171.3	170.5
2005	167.8	168.2	169.1	170.3	172.0	172.5	172.4	172.2	171.1	171.2	170.9	171.2	170.7
2006	167.9	168.1	169.0	171.1	172.2	173.7	172.8	172.0	170.7	170.0	169.5	169.8	170.6
2007	167.2	166.8	167.2	169.3	170.8	171.6	170.9	170.7	169.5	168.9	168.2	168.5	169.1

Employment by Industry: Michigan, 2000–2007—*Continued*

(Numbers in thousands, not seasonally adjusted.)

Industry and year	January	February	March	April	May	June	July	August	September	October	November	December	Annual Average
Retail Trade													
2000	550.0	541.8	546.3	549.1	558.5	562.1	552.8	557.5	557.9	564.6	581.7	595.5	559.8
2001	553.8	544.2	544.9	544.2	550.8	553.0	543.8	546.0	542.5	542.4	556.8	563.5	548.8
2002	526.7	515.8	519.5	522.8	531.8	534.9	530.1	532.2	532.6	528.2	542.1	551.1	530.7
2003	511.0	503.1	503.9	505.8	516.4	521.0	517.0	520.8	521.2	524.5	535.6	543.7	518.7
2004	507.6	500.1	500.9	506.2	515.6	518.0	513.7	515.4	510.5	513.5	526.9	534.5	513.6
2005	499.0	492.2	493.5	500.1	507.5	509.7	510.5	508.8	505.5	504.9	517.4	523.3	506.0
2006	490.1	481.9	484.6	488.8	496.1	499.4	497.4	497.2	494.9	496.7	510.5	514.8	496.0
2007	486.6	476.7	478.6	480.5	489.6	492.1	494.5	490.4	487.8	491.4	502.0	506.0	489.7
Transportation and Utilities													
2000	132.5	132.3	132.6	134.6	135.6	136.6	134.2	135.7	135.3	138.9	138.2	137.8	135.4
2001	131.2	129.8	129.4	132.1	133.2	134.6	132.2	133.5	132.3	133.3	131.6	131.1	132.0
2002	126.4	126.1	127.3	127.8	129.7	130.8	128.1	129.4	128.8	129.3	128.2	127.0	128.2
2003	125.1	124.0	124.6	125.4	127.0	127.7	124.8	126.3	126.0	126.9	126.0	126.0	125.8
2004	122.1	122.4	122.3	124.3	125.5	126.5	125.5	126.7	126.6	129.1	128.5	128.5	125.7
2005	124.2	124.9	125.5	126.5	128.3	129.7	128.1	130.7	130.2	130.0	130.5	131.2	128.3
2006	126.5	126.1	126.7	127.4	129.2	130.5	126.6	129.6	129.4	128.7	129.1	131.4	128.4
2007	125.4	126.6	126.3	127.6	129.6	131.3	127.2	131.0	130.7	130.3	130.6	132.0	129.1
Information													
2000	76.1	75.8	76.7	76.0	76.7	77.2	77.0	77.1	77.7	75.8	76.5	77.2	76.7
2001	75.5	75.7	76.1	75.5	76.2	76.6	76.3	76.2	75.6	75.6	76.7	76.3	76.0
2002	76.1	75.9	75.8	74.4	74.7	74.7	73.1	72.7	71.7	71.7	72.3	72.6	73.8
2003	71.0	70.8	71.1	70.9	71.1	71.1	70.0	69.9	69.2	69.1	69.6	69.9	70.3
2004	68.8	68.3	68.5	68.3	68.7	69.1	69.1	68.8	67.9	68.1	68.6	68.9	68.6
2005	68.0	67.4	67.5	67.5	67.9	68.1	67.7	67.4	66.6	66.2	66.8	67.0	67.3
2006	66.6	66.7	66.3	66.4	66.9	67.3	66.0	65.8	65.0	65.1	65.4	65.5	66.1
2007	65.6	65.6	65.3	65.3	66.2	66.2	66.1	66.0	65.2	64.9	65.2	65.4	65.6
Financial Activities													
2000	206.7	206.4	206.4	208.7	209.9	212.3	212.2	211.4	209.3	209.3	209.3	210.9	209.4
2001	205.1	206.1	207.3	208.8	212.1	214.3	213.1	213.4	210.5	210.4	210.7	212.4	210.4
2002	212.0	212.2	212.2	213.7	215.6	216.6	216.8	217.6	215.2	214.8	215.3	216.5	214.9
2003	214.7	214.7	215.0	218.0	220.3	222.1	222.0	222.2	219.1	217.6	216.6	217.4	218.3
2004	214.5	214.0	215.1	217.1	218.7	220.4	220.7	220.2	217.9	216.2	216.4	217.8	217.4
2005	216.3	216.3	216.3	217.3	218.7	220.7	220.3	220.3	218.1	216.9	216.9	217.1	217.9
2006	215.3	215.2	214.9	215.5	217.2	219.3	218.0	217.9	215.2	213.6	213.2	214.0	215.8
2007	211.1	211.1	210.9	211.6	213.3	214.9	214.4	213.3	209.9	208.6	208.5	209.0	211.4
Professional and Business Services													
2000	621.9	619.8	626.2	634.5	641.8	648.3	638.5	649.2	644.6	636.9	632.6	628.7	635.3
2001	601.8	602.1	604.0	610.1	613.0	617.4	604.5	614.3	607.5	596.7	590.7	587.1	604.1
2002	572.4	573.4	576.7	588.3	598.0	603.5	596.7	609.4	605.0	602.6	601.4	599.0	593.9
2003	573.3	571.7	573.9	584.0	592.3	595.3	580.1	590.7	587.1	582.6	583.3	580.7	582.9
2004	559.8	559.8	561.6	577.9	585.3	590.7	582.8	593.8	592.4	592.3	590.4	588.1	581.2
2005	569.0	570.0	571.5	587.4	592.1	595.0	590.1	599.8	602.2	596.6	595.6	592.7	588.5
2006	570.8	568.1	568.4	577.3	582.6	590.9	579.3	590.3	590.1	587.0	588.0	586.9	581.6
2007	560.5	563.2	563.6	572.6	579.8	583.9	568.5	580.0	579.9	577.9	576.0	573.6	573.3
Education and Health Services													
2000	492.6	499.1	500.0	501.5	501.5	502.1	498.0	499.1	504.1	507.0	511.0	509.3	502.1
2001	504.0	509.1	512.2	516.0	518.0	520.3	515.1	516.6	520.2	524.7	528.9	529.0	517.8
2002	522.4	528.0	531.0	536.4	538.1	538.0	528.9	530.2	536.2	541.7	546.0	544.3	535.1
2003	538.5	541.1	544.8	544.7	546.5	544.7	540.0	540.8	547.9	554.2	558.3	558.2	546.9
2004	548.8	555.2	558.5	562.0	562.1	556.6	553.2	553.4	564.1	569.6	574.0	573.3	560.9
2005	564.1	572.8	576.0	576.1	577.1	570.1	566.4	566.9	579.7	583.8	588.6	588.1	575.8
2006	575.2	580.6	585.4	583.0	586.0	580.6	573.7	573.6	587.6	588.4	592.6	593.2	583.3
2007	584.9	591.3	594.2	595.4	598.2	592.0	586.1	586.4	598.6	601.7	605.7	605.2	595.0
Leisure and Hospitality													
2000	369.7	371.5	376.2	389.7	408.4	420.6	420.5	421.4	411.8	404.7	393.1	390.7	398.2
2001	368.0	369.5	375.5	386.2	407.1	417.0	416.9	419.3	407.6	396.5	384.7	382.8	394.3
2002	367.2	367.8	375.6	390.1	411.0	421.1	421.3	424.0	414.3	402.1	391.1	389.3	397.9
2003	369.0	368.0	373.5	387.1	412.2	423.6	421.4	421.3	415.3	403.7	390.9	391.0	398.1
2004	375.3	375.9	381.3	395.1	415.5	426.7	424.8	426.3	419.1	402.6	391.3	390.5	402.0
2005	373.1	375.4	382.1	401.6	420.6	431.0	427.8	430.6	422.0	403.1	393.0	393.1	404.5
2006	376.6	381.2	386.9	401.1	419.8	433.0	428.2	430.3	421.7	403.8	392.2	391.9	405.6
2007	377.9	377.8	384.6	396.5	420.7	432.1	427.0	429.9	420.8	403.5	391.7	391.7	404.5
Other Services													
2000	170.7	172.6	174.3	175.4	175.9	177.4	177.1	177.4	175.7	175.4	175.4	175.9	175.3
2001	172.8	174.7	176.6	177.0	178.7	180.5	178.0	178.8	176.2	175.7	176.5	177.4	176.9
2002	174.6	175.9	177.4	178.8	180.5	182.1	181.2	181.8	180.4	179.7	179.2	180.4	179.3
2003	176.9	177.4	179.2	176.9	178.2	179.0	180.5	181.1	179.9	179.7	179.4	180.7	179.1
2004	176.8	178.1	179.2	178.4	180.1	181.8	180.2	180.5	180.5	180.1	179.2	179.8	179.6
2005	176.1	177.0	178.5	180.2	181.7	183.7	181.3	180.8	179.7	178.4	178.2	179.2	179.6
2006	174.8	175.9	177.5	177.6	179.0	181.1	178.4	178.8	177.9	176.2	176.1	177.0	177.5
2007	172.8	173.7	175.3	175.4	177.4	179.9	178.7	179.2	177.9	176.3	176.2	177.0	176.7
Government													
2000	672.4	695.4	704.8	700.2	700.1	672.8	618.8	612.0	680.9	703.4	710.0	705.7	681.4
2001	681.6	700.6	707.2	703.8	699.6	680.8	622.8	620.7	680.0	705.1	710.3	707.2	685.0
2002	688.8	705.8	709.2	697.1	694.6	674.8	618.8	619.7	684.9	714.8	717.9	712.7	686.6
2003	690.1	709.2	708.2	704.1	700.8	673.5	614.0	610.6	677.1	714.9	713.9	708.5	685.4
2004	686.2	701.2	704.1	701.2	696.1	668.6	605.6	603.3	678.8	703.3	706.7	701.5	679.7
2005	677.5	697.4	698.9	697.6	691.9	663.3	597.4	599.0	677.8	695.3	700.0	692.9	674.1
2006	671.7	690.4	695.3	687.7	680.6	653.9	593.4	589.9	664.9	684.9	688.7	682.4	665.3
2007	660.2	677.9	683.0	676.0	674.1	648.3	587.4	592.2	656.3	677.2	680.3	673.0	657.2

Average Weekly Hours by Selected Industry: Michigan, 2003–2007

(Not seasonally adjusted.)

Industry and year	January	February	March	April	May	June	July	August	September	October	November	December	Annual Average
Construction													
2003	37.9	37.0	37.5	37.8	38.6	39.2	38.3	38.9	40.1	39.7	37.7	37.0	38.4
2004	36.3	36.6	36.5	38.0	38.0	38.2	39.2	39.7	38.2	39.0	38.8	37.0	38.1
2005	36.4	36.6	36.6	38.0	37.8	38.8	39.5	39.4	38.9	39.4	38.9	37.4	38.3
2006	37.3	37.0	36.9	38.2	37.7	40.0	39.5	39.5	38.3	38.0	36.4	37.2	38.1
2007	36.1	34.8	35.9	36.7	37.1	37.6	37.5	37.3	37.2	36.9	35.8	35.4	36.6
Manufacturing													
2003	43.1	41.8	41.8	42.0	42.2	42.3	40.2	39.1	42.8	42.5	43.0	44.0	42.1
2004	42.6	42.5	42.9	42.3	42.5	42.5	39.8	42.1	42.7	42.4	42.9	43.2	42.4
2005	41.8	41.3	41.0	41.3	41.3	41.6	39.5	42.0	42.6	42.2	42.9	41.7
2006	40.8	41.3	41.7	40.7	42.9	43.4	40.9	43.3	43.6	42.8	41.9	42.7	42.2
2007	40.7	41.8	42.3	42.0	42.9	43.3	40.4	43.2	43.4	43.6	42.3	43.6	42.5
Wholesale Trade													
2003	35.8	35.9	35.4	35.1	36.4	35.9	36.1	35.1	36.2	36.4	37.3	36.5	36.0
2004	37.7	37.9	37.1	37.8	38.2	37.4	36.6	36.1	35.9	36.6	36.7	37.2	37.1
2005	36.6	36.6	35.7	35.2	36.2	36.5	36.7	37.8	37.7	38.3	38.6	38.6	37.1
2006	38.2	37.9	38.0	38.1	38.7	39.7	39.7	39.7	39.9	39.9	39.8	39.5	39.1
2007	38.9	38.6	39.2	39.5	39.5	39.6	39.1	39.3	39.7	39.1	38.8	39.1	39.2
Retail Trade													
2003	28.1	28.6	28.7	28.6	29.0	29.6	29.9	29.2	29.3	29.0	28.9	29.7	29.1
2004	28.4	29.2	29.0	29.2	29.5	29.8	30.3	30.4	30.1	29.6	29.2	30.1	29.6
2005	28.6	28.9	29.0	28.9	29.4	30.0	30.4	29.9	29.9	29.2	29.3	29.7	29.4
2006	28.6	28.8	29.0	29.2	29.1	29.7	30.1	29.9	30.3	30.0	30.6	30.8	29.7
2007	30.0	30.2	30.3	30.5	30.6	31.1	31.3	31.4	31.5	30.9	31.8	31.6	30.9
Information													
2003	31.8	32.2	31.8	32.0	31.5	31.7	33.0	31.7	31.5	31.7	32.9	32.5	32.0
2004	32.7	33.8	33.8	33.2	32.4	37.1	36.9	37.7	36.5	36.1	35.8	36.6	35.2
2005	36.1	35.9	35.6	37.3	37.4	37.0	36.3	35.9	35.4	35.8	35.3	35.1	36.1
2006	34.8	35.8	34.3	34.8	34.1	34.5	34.3	35.4	35.3	35.6	35.2	34.3	34.9
2007	33.4	34.2	33.9	34.3	34.1	34.4	34.3	34.2	34.5	34.3	34.6	34.2	34.2
Financial Activities													
2003	37.2	37.1	37.2	36.6	36.3	36.7	36.0	36.0	35.8	35.1	35.2	34.3	36.1
2004	34.8	34.8	34.6	34.4	34.4	34.1	33.6	34.0	33.6	33.0	33.0	33.6	34.0
2005	33.5	33.3	33.4	33.2	34.0	33.3	34.5	33.5	33.7	34.2	34.0	34.4	33.7
2006	34.2	33.6	33.4	33.8	33.8	34.2	34.0	33.7	33.5	33.8	33.5	34.1	33.8
2007	34.2	34.3	34.2	34.5	34.3	34.4	34.7	34.3	34.4	34.6	34.6	35.3	34.5
Professional and Business Services													
2003	33.2	33.7	33.4	32.9	34.8	35.1	33.9	33.9	34.2	34.5	34.8	34.0	34.0
2004	33.0	35.1	34.9	35.0	36.1	35.0	35.0	35.6	35.1	35.2	34.8	34.2	34.9
2005	34.0	34.3	34.2	34.7	34.9	34.6	34.6	34.5	34.0	34.5	34.1	33.6	34.3
2006	33.9	33.6	34.3	34.1	34.8	35.5	34.6	34.4	35.1	34.9	35.0	34.9	34.6
2007	34.5	34.7	34.8	34.3	35.0	34.8	34.9	35.0	35.2	34.9	34.5	34.5	34.8
Leisure and Hospitality													
2003	21.4	21.6	21.8	21.7	22.6	23.5	23.9	23.9	23.2	22.9	22.4	22.6	22.7
2004	21.8	22.2	22.4	22.5	22.9	23.1	23.7	23.9	23.1	23.1	22.7	22.6	22.9
2005	22.2	22.4	22.3	22.7	23.0	23.4	24.2	24.2	23.4	23.0	22.6	22.6	23.0
2006	22.7	22.6	22.5	22.2	22.7	23.6	24.1	24.3	22.9	22.8	22.5	22.4	23.0
2007	21.7	21.8	21.9	21.9	22.4	22.7	23.1	23.6	22.5	22.4	22.3	22.4	22.4

Average Hourly Earnings by Selected Industry: Michigan, 2003–2007

(Dollars, not seasonally adjusted.)

Industry and year	January	February	March	April	May	June	July	August	September	October	November	December	Annual Average
Construction													
2003	22.13	22.18	22.04	22.13	21.41	21.56	21.77	21.35	21.94	21.65	21.93	21.81	21.80
2004	21.90	21.96	21.94	21.63	21.59	21.71	22.10	21.93	21.85	22.08	22.07	22.12	21.91
2005	22.01	22.37	22.09	22.10	21.96	22.01	22.12	22.12	22.11	22.36	22.30	22.19	22.14
2006	21.83	22.03	21.70	21.78	21.65	21.71	21.90	21.41	21.58	21.74	21.85	21.97	21.75
2007	21.95	21.87	21.90	22.03	21.79	21.86	21.59	21.75	21.97	22.12	22.11	22.15	21.92
Manufacturing													
2003	21.02	20.99	20.89	20.96	21.00	21.13	20.37	21.18	21.62	21.45	21.64	21.98	21.20
2004	21.70	21.68	21.57	21.38	21.33	21.40	20.61	21.47	21.85	21.48	21.67	21.86	21.51
2005	21.74	21.72	21.32	21.39	21.29	21.51	20.65	21.35	21.67	21.56	21.78	21.89	21.50
2006	21.56	21.77	21.89	21.85	21.90	22.12	20.53	21.78	22.17	21.71	22.15	22.50	21.84
2007	22.08	21.76	21.87	22.17	22.00	22.25	21.46	22.03	22.05	21.89	22.39	22.83	22.07
Wholesale Trade													
2003	18.77	18.62	18.61	17.99	17.77	18.43	18.12	18.51	18.49	18.20	18.46	18.04	18.33
2004	19.00	18.87	18.81	18.83	18.97	19.36	19.41	19.18	18.70	19.01	19.00	19.25	19.03
2005	19.35	19.30	18.94	18.97	18.84	18.84	18.93	18.90	18.93	19.16	18.85	19.06	19.00
2006	18.71	19.07	18.87	18.87	18.91	19.10	18.93	19.04	19.31	18.93	19.53	19.10	19.03
2007	19.40	19.69	19.49	19.46	19.38	19.31	19.98	19.45	19.37	19.50	19.58	19.44	19.50
Retail Trade													
2003	10.94	11.08	11.02	10.98	11.04	11.07	11.01	10.97	10.99	11.07	11.13	11.03	11.03
2004	11.25	11.18	11.29	11.44	11.52	11.49	11.31	11.36	11.47	11.40	11.30	11.39	11.37
2005	11.99	11.94	11.77	11.84	11.76	11.74	11.81	11.84	11.75	11.84	11.98	12.12	11.87
2006	12.41	12.54	12.26	12.54	12.51	12.45	12.60	12.21	12.30	12.33	12.14	12.03	12.35
2007	12.13	12.16	12.20	12.23	12.22	12.18	12.28	12.41	12.23	12.24	12.32	12.08	12.22
Information													
2003	15.96	15.43	15.69	16.63	15.98	16.34	16.35	15.95	16.38	16.48	16.51	16.26	16.16
2004	15.98	16.54	15.99	16.83	17.07	17.35	16.67	16.94	17.90	17.05	17.24	17.15	16.91
2005	17.30	17.33	17.94	17.37	17.96	18.26	18.49	18.53	18.99	19.65	19.51	19.87	18.42
2006	20.42	18.89	19.76	20.37	19.66	20.33	20.68	20.16	19.90	20.56	20.62	21.32	20.22
2007	21.56	20.78	20.89	21.30	21.21	21.12	21.87	21.19	21.97	21.45	21.43	21.47	21.35
Financial Activities													
2003	14.93	15.51	15.62	15.67	15.64	15.65	15.48	16.05	15.94	15.87	15.85	15.90	15.68
2004	15.75	15.37	15.21	15.31	15.50	15.54	15.74	16.31	15.99	15.94	16.49	16.60	15.82
2005	16.63	16.95	17.47	17.44	17.61	17.41	17.28	17.61	17.44	17.71	17.44	17.85	17.41
2006	17.96	17.74	17.76	17.77	17.49	17.44	17.53	17.44	17.64	17.87	17.96	18.61	17.77
2007	18.44	18.27	18.43	18.60	18.74	18.03	18.37	18.61	18.92	19.01	18.84	19.10	18.62
Professional and Business Services													
2003	16.73	16.73	16.60	16.88	16.47	16.37	16.19	15.76	15.96	16.10	16.32	16.46	16.37
2004	16.61	16.70	16.50	16.62	16.66	16.56	16.82	16.77	17.70	17.31	17.49	17.92	16.99
2005	17.86	17.71	17.60	17.56	17.57	17.37	17.44	16.98	17.62	17.95	18.10	18.31	17.67
2006	18.67	18.92	18.47	18.76	18.51	18.37	18.80	18.63	18.75	19.15	19.14	19.33	18.79
2007	19.61	19.98	19.58	19.84	19.56	19.45	19.67	19.37	19.66	19.37	19.57	19.85	19.62
Leisure and Hospitality													
2003	8.00	8.11	8.07	8.20	8.28	8.18	8.14	8.07	8.16	8.14	8.15	8.29	8.15
2004	8.22	8.13	8.18	8.10	8.17	8.08	8.16	8.10	8.21	8.04	8.09	8.05	8.13
2005	8.06	8.04	8.01	8.14	8.16	8.10	8.04	8.16	8.36	8.32	8.32	8.38	8.17
2006	8.20	8.25	8.26	8.26	8.32	8.29	8.35	8.46	8.59	8.94	8.95	9.13	8.50
2007	8.96	8.97	8.95	8.99	9.05	8.98	9.04	9.08	9.23	9.23	9.20	9.38	9.09

Average Weekly Earnings by Selected Industry: Michigan, 2003–2007

(Dollars, not seasonally adjusted.)

Industry and year	January	February	March	April	May	June	July	August	September	October	November	December	Annual Average
Construction													
2003	838.73	820.66	826.50	836.51	826.43	845.15	833.79	830.52	879.79	859.51	826.76	806.97	837.12
2004	794.97	803.74	800.81	821.94	820.42	829.32	866.32	870.62	834.67	861.12	856.32	818.44	834.77
2005	801.16	818.74	808.49	839.80	830.09	853.99	873.74	871.53	860.08	880.98	867.47	829.91	847.96
2006	814.26	815.11	800.73	832.00	816.21	868.40	865.05	845.70	826.51	826.12	795.34	817.28	828.68
2007	792.40	761.08	786.21	808.50	808.41	821.94	809.63	811.28	817.28	816.23	791.54	784.11	802.27
Manufacturing													
2003	905.96	877.38	873.20	880.32	886.20	893.80	818.87	828.14	925.34	911.63	930.52	967.12	892.52
2004	924.42	921.40	925.35	904.37	906.53	909.50	820.28	903.89	933.00	910.75	929.64	944.35	912.02
2005	908.73	897.04	874.12	883.41	879.28	894.82	815.68	896.70	923.14	918.46	919.12	939.08	896.55
2006	879.65	899.10	912.81	889.30	939.51	960.01	839.68	943.07	966.61	929.19	928.09	960.75	921.65
2007	898.66	909.57	925.10	931.14	943.80	963.43	866.98	951.70	956.97	954.40	947.10	995.39	937.98
Wholesale Trade													
2003	671.97	668.46	658.79	631.45	646.83	661.64	654.13	649.70	669.34	662.48	688.56	658.46	659.88
2004	716.30	715.17	697.85	711.77	724.65	724.06	710.41	692.40	671.33	695.77	697.30	716.10	706.01
2005	708.21	706.38	676.16	667.74	682.01	687.66	694.73	714.42	713.66	733.83	727.61	735.72	704.90
2006	714.72	722.75	717.06	718.95	731.82	758.27	751.52	755.89	770.47	755.31	777.29	754.45	744.07
2007	754.66	760.03	764.01	768.67	765.51	764.68	781.22	764.39	768.99	762.45	759.70	760.10	764.40
Retail Trade													
2003	307.41	316.89	316.27	314.03	320.16	327.67	329.20	320.32	322.01	321.03	321.66	327.59	320.97
2004	319.50	326.46	327.41	334.05	339.84	342.40	342.69	345.34	345.25	337.44	329.96	342.84	336.55
2005	342.91	345.07	341.33	342.18	345.74	352.20	359.02	354.02	351.33	345.73	351.01	359.96	348.98
2006	354.93	361.15	355.54	366.17	364.04	369.77	379.26	365.08	372.69	369.90	371.48	370.52	366.80
2007	363.90	367.23	369.66	373.02	373.93	378.80	384.36	389.67	385.25	378.22	391.78	381.73	377.60
Information													
2003	507.53	496.85	498.94	532.16	503.37	517.98	539.55	505.62	515.97	522.42	543.18	528.45	517.12
2004	522.55	559.05	540.46	558.76	553.07	643.69	615.12	638.64	653.35	615.51	617.19	627.69	595.23
2005	624.53	622.15	638.66	647.90	671.70	675.62	671.19	665.23	672.25	703.47	688.70	697.44	664.96
2006	710.62	676.26	677.77	708.88	670.41	701.39	709.32	713.66	702.47	731.94	725.82	731.28	705.68
2007	720.10	710.68	708.17	730.59	723.26	726.53	750.14	724.70	757.97	735.74	741.48	734.27	730.17
Financial Activities													
2003	555.40	575.42	581.06	573.52	567.73	574.36	557.28	577.80	570.65	557.04	557.92	545.37	566.05
2004	548.10	534.88	526.27	526.66	533.20	535.03	528.86	554.54	537.26	526.02	544.17	557.76	537.88
2005	557.11	564.44	583.50	579.01	598.74	579.75	596.16	589.94	587.73	605.68	592.96	614.04	586.72
2006	614.23	596.06	593.18	600.63	591.16	596.45	596.02	587.73	590.94	604.01	601.66	634.60	600.63
2007	630.65	626.66	630.31	641.70	642.78	620.23	637.44	638.32	650.85	657.75	651.86	674.23	642.39
Professional and Business Services													
2003	555.44	563.80	554.44	555.35	573.16	574.59	548.84	534.26	545.83	555.45	567.94	559.64	556.58
2004	548.13	586.17	575.85	581.70	601.43	579.60	588.70	597.01	621.27	609.31	608.65	612.86	592.95
2005	607.24	607.45	601.92	609.33	613.19	601.00	603.42	585.81	599.08	619.28	617.21	615.22	606.08
2006	632.91	635.71	633.52	639.72	644.15	652.14	650.48	640.87	658.13	668.34	669.90	674.62	650.13
2007	676.55	693.31	681.38	680.51	684.60	676.86	686.48	677.95	692.03	676.01	675.17	684.83	682.78
Leisure and Hospitality													
2003	171.20	175.18	175.93	177.94	187.13	192.23	194.55	192.87	189.31	186.41	182.56	187.35	185.01
2004	179.20	180.49	183.23	182.25	187.09	186.65	193.39	193.59	189.65	185.72	183.64	181.93	186.18
2005	178.93	180.10	178.62	184.78	187.68	189.54	194.57	197.47	195.62	191.36	188.03	189.39	187.91
2006	186.14	186.45	185.85	183.37	188.86	195.64	201.24	205.58	196.71	203.83	201.38	204.51	195.50
2007	194.43	195.55	196.01	196.88	202.72	203.85	208.82	214.29	207.68	206.75	205.16	210.11	203.62

Population
   2000 census: 4,919,479
   2007 estimate: 5,197,621
   Percent change, 2000–2007: 5.7%

Percent change in total nonfarm employment, 2000–2007: 3.2%

Industry with the largest growth in employment, 2000–2007 (thousands)
   Education and health services, 103.5

Industry with the largest decline in employment, 2000–2007 (thousands)
   Manufacturing, -55.4

Civilian labor force
   2000: 2,807,668
   2007: 2,930,553

Employment-population ratio
   2000: 72.9%
   2007: 69.6%

Unemployment rate and rank among states
   2000: 3.1%, 12th
   2007: 4.6%, 31st

Employment by Industry, 2007

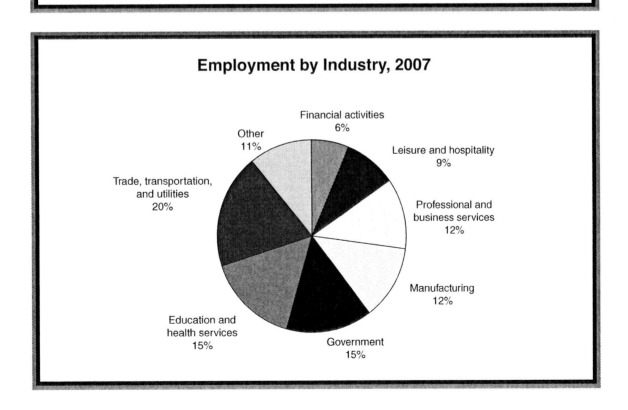

Employment by Industry: Minnesota, 2000–2007

(Numbers in thousands, not seasonally adjusted.)

Industry and year	January	February	March	April	May	June	July	August	September	October	November	December	Annual Average
Total Nonfarm													
2000	2,600.1	2,613.2	2,633.4	2,665.8	2,700.3	2,727.8	2,690.8	2,698.9	2,713.0	2,723.5	2,727.4	2,725.0	2,684.9
2001	2,648.8	2,654.2	2,664.9	2,681.6	2,716.0	2,735.7	2,690.0	2,688.6	2,699.3	2,704.0	2,700.8	2,689.5	2,689.5
2002	2,612.2	2,610.2	2,617.1	2,641.5	2,681.6	2,706.2	2,673.8	2,673.3	2,690.0	2,690.2	2,693.5	2,684.0	2,664.5
2003	2,605.4	2,607.4	2,613.4	2,646.1	2,685.6	2,703.0	2,663.6	2,671.3	2,681.5	2,686.9	2,680.3	2,679.1	2,660.2
2004	2,598.2	2,601.3	2,612.8	2,668.0	2,705.2	2,727.4	2,690.3	2,693.1	2,707.5	2,724.7	2,720.9	2,722.9	2,681.0
2005	2,629.3	2,634.4	2,648.3	2,705.1	2,746.5	2,768.3	2,737.9	2,743.8	2,757.5	2,769.6	2,769.8	2,768.9	2,723.3
2006	2,701.9	2,700.9	2,715.7	2,737.9	2,775.2	2,810.0	2,766.1	2,767.7	2,775.9	2,781.5	2,783.9	2,781.2	2,758.2
2007	2,711.4	2,711.9	2,722.2	2,744.3	2,793.8	2,821.9	2,784.6	2,787.0	2,787.9	2,796.9	2,799.8	2,787.5	2,770.8
Total Private													
2000	2,198.8	2,201.6	2,218.7	2,246.8	2,276.2	2,312.7	2,311.0	2,322.7	2,312.5	2,311.1	2,308.3	2,307.3	2,277.3
2001	2,243.9	2,237.8	2,247.7	2,263.6	2,295.9	2,318.8	2,308.5	2,314.8	2,295.1	2,286.9	2,280.4	2,268.2	2,280.1
2002	2,197.9	2,189.8	2,197.1	2,223.3	2,261.5	2,285.3	2,282.4	2,293.5	2,279.6	2,270.3	2,266.1	2,259.0	2,250.5
2003	2,192.6	2,185.8	2,192.0	2,223.5	2,263.4	2,285.0	2,278.8	2,288.5	2,277.0	2,269.5	2,260.6	2,257.4	2,247.8
2004	2,186.6	2,182.4	2,193.9	2,247.5	2,282.8	2,312.6	2,306.6	2,313.9	2,300.4	2,305.5	2,297.5	2,298.0	2,269.0
2005	2,212.9	2,212.3	2,225.4	2,280.5	2,321.6	2,348.3	2,346.8	2,359.1	2,348.8	2,349.0	2,349.6	2,346.7	2,308.4
2006	2,286.7	2,279.4	2,293.2	2,314.9	2,351.7	2,388.3	2,374.9	2,381.3	2,365.0	2,359.1	2,358.1	2,354.2	2,342.2
2007	2,297.2	2,291.4	2,302.6	2,323.4	2,369.5	2,400.0	2,394.8	2,402.5	2,379.0	2,375.5	2,374.7	2,362.6	2,356.1
Goods-Producing													
2000	496.0	495.2	501.1	513.6	525.5	540.1	542.8	547.2	540.4	534.5	526.9	519.2	523.5
2001	500.5	496.7	497.3	501.3	511.8	520.9	523.2	524.8	519.5	511.1	502.3	490.7	508.3
2002	470.1	464.8	466.9	474.5	489.1	501.5	503.6	508.2	501.7	494.4	486.5	474.4	486.3
2003	455.7	450.3	451.6	461.9	477.3	489.6	491.1	494.8	489.1	485.2	477.3	467.4	474.3
2004	446.5	443.6	446.4	465.0	477.9	492.1	496.4	500.1	496.0	495.6	487.4	479.5	477.2
2005	454.7	452.5	455.7	470.7	487.2	499.4	502.9	506.4	500.7	494.2	488.6	477.6	482.6
2006	461.5	457.6	460.7	469.3	482.6	497.6	496.8	498.5	492.1	487.4	477.0	467.7	479.1
2007	452.0	446.6	449.4	455.0	472.1	485.7	485.9	487.9	479.8	474.6	466.8	455.9	467.6
Natural Resources and Mining													
2000	7.8	7.7	7.7	7.8	8.2	8.3	8.5	8.5	8.4	8.4	8.1	7.8	8.1
2001	7.5	6.9	6.6	6.3	6.7	6.9	6.3	7.0	6.9	6.9	6.3	6.2	6.7
2002	6.2	5.6	6.2	6.1	6.4	6.7	6.7	6.8	6.7	6.7	6.6	6.3	6.4
2003	6.1	6.0	6.0	5.9	6.3	6.4	6.5	6.1	5.9	6.0	5.8	5.6	6.0
2004	5.6	5.6	5.6	5.8	6.1	6.3	6.4	6.5	6.4	6.2	6.1	6.0	6.1
2005	5.6	5.7	5.7	5.8	6.1	6.3	6.3	6.3	6.2	6.1	6.0	5.7	6.0
2006	5.7	5.8	5.8	5.8	5.9	6.3	6.4	6.4	6.2	6.2	6.0	5.8	6.0
2007	5.6	5.6	5.6	5.6	5.9	6.1	6.3	6.4	6.2	6.2	6.0	5.8	5.9
Construction													
2000	97.3	97.0	101.2	112.4	122.6	130.7	132.7	134.2	131.1	129.0	122.9	115.1	118.8
2001	104.0	102.6	104.9	112.5	123.9	134.0	138.1	139.3	135.0	133.6	129.2	120.0	123.1
2002	106.1	103.2	104.1	113.0	126.5	134.5	139.6	141.2	138.1	134.5	128.6	119.3	124.1
2003	106.0	102.6	103.6	113.3	127.2	136.1	140.2	141.9	138.9	137.1	130.7	121.4	124.9
2004	105.5	103.5	105.8	120.3	131.4	138.7	143.3	144.0	141.5	140.7	136.5	127.3	128.2
2005	108.3	106.5	108.5	120.6	132.7	140.9	145.5	146.1	143.2	139.0	135.1	126.4	129.4
2006	114.6	112.8	114.2	120.8	131.6	139.7	139.7	139.3	136.7	133.7	127.7	118.8	127.5
2007	108.0	104.0	106.5	110.7	125.3	133.0	133.5	134.2	129.9	127.4	121.6	112.4	120.5
Manufacturing													
2000	390.9	390.5	392.2	393.4	394.7	401.1	401.6	404.5	400.9	397.1	395.9	396.3	396.6
2001	389.0	387.2	385.8	382.5	381.2	380.0	378.8	378.5	377.6	370.6	366.8	364.5	378.5
2002	357.8	356.0	356.6	355.4	356.2	360.3	357.3	360.2	356.9	353.2	351.3	348.8	355.8
2003	343.6	341.7	342.0	342.7	343.8	347.1	344.4	346.8	344.3	342.1	340.8	340.4	343.3
2004	335.4	334.5	335.0	338.9	340.4	347.1	346.7	349.6	348.1	348.7	344.8	346.2	343.0
2005	340.8	340.3	341.5	344.3	348.4	352.2	351.1	354.0	351.3	349.1	347.5	345.5	347.2
2006	341.2	339.0	340.7	342.7	345.1	351.6	350.7	352.8	349.2	347.5	343.3	343.1	345.6
2007	338.4	337.0	337.3	338.7	340.9	346.6	346.1	347.3	343.7	341.0	339.2	337.7	341.2
Service-Providing													
2000	2,104.1	2,118.0	2,132.3	2,152.2	2,174.8	2,187.7	2,148.0	2,151.7	2,172.6	2,189.0	2,200.5	2,205.8	2,161.4
2001	2,148.3	2,157.5	2,167.6	2,180.3	2,204.2	2,214.8	2,166.8	2,163.8	2,179.8	2,192.9	2,198.5	2,198.8	2,181.1
2002	2,142.1	2,145.4	2,150.2	2,167.0	2,192.5	2,204.7	2,170.2	2,165.1	2,188.3	2,195.8	2,207.0	2,209.6	2,178.2
2003	2,149.7	2,157.1	2,161.8	2,184.2	2,208.3	2,213.4	2,172.5	2,176.5	2,192.4	2,201.7	2,203.0	2,211.7	2,186.0
2004	2,151.7	2,157.7	2,166.4	2,203.0	2,227.3	2,235.3	2,193.9	2,193.0	2,211.5	2,229.1	2,233.5	2,243.4	2,203.8
2005	2,174.6	2,181.9	2,192.6	2,234.4	2,259.3	2,268.9	2,235.0	2,237.4	2,256.8	2,275.4	2,281.2	2,291.3	2,240.7
2006	2,240.4	2,243.3	2,255.0	2,268.6	2,292.6	2,312.4	2,269.3	2,269.2	2,283.8	2,294.1	2,306.9	2,313.5	2,279.1
2007	2,259.4	2,265.3	2,272.8	2,289.3	2,321.7	2,336.2	2,298.7	2,299.1	2,308.1	2,322.3	2,333.0	2,331.6	2,303.1
Trade, Transportation, and Utilities													
2000	532.2	527.9	529.0	531.8	536.8	541.1	538.3	540.0	539.1	544.9	553.9	559.9	539.6
2001	540.6	533.4	534.3	536.0	542.4	544.2	540.1	539.3	534.9	538.4	544.9	547.1	539.6
2002	525.2	516.0	516.8	521.8	527.7	529.1	523.4	523.1	521.7	524.5	534.3	538.9	525.2
2003	518.6	511.2	511.4	517.4	523.9	524.8	518.4	520.2	518.9	522.9	528.9	532.2	520.7
2004	511.5	506.0	507.0	517.3	524.6	528.9	525.4	526.0	524.6	530.0	537.8	542.6	523.5
2005	517.6	512.7	514.4	522.6	528.3	531.1	527.6	528.7	526.9	531.9	540.0	545.0	527.2
2006	525.7	519.4	520.5	523.7	529.4	534.1	527.1	527.0	526.2	527.8	538.3	541.1	528.4
2007	523.6	518.8	519.3	523.3	531.1	534.8	529.3	529.7	528.1	532.9	542.2	544.7	529.8
Wholesale Trade													
2000	126.6	126.5	127.3	128.2	129.0	131.2	130.0	130.5	129.0	129.6	130.0	130.4	129.0
2001	130.3	129.8	130.3	131.1	131.9	132.1	132.0	131.2	129.6	129.3	129.0	128.6	130.4
2002	126.6	126.4	126.2	127.4	128.1	128.6	128.7	128.1	126.5	127.0	126.6	126.3	127.2
2003	126.6	126.7	126.7	128.1	128.8	129.6	129.6	129.2	127.8	127.8	127.2	127.1	127.9
2004	125.0	125.0	125.5	129.1	130.0	131.3	131.3	131.1	129.3	129.8	129.8	129.9	128.9
2005	127.3	127.4	127.5	131.1	131.4	133.3	132.8	133.1	132.0	132.2	132.3	132.4	131.1
2006	131.3	131.4	132.2	133.1	134.0	135.1	134.6	134.5	133.1	133.0	133.0	132.7	133.2
2007	131.0	131.0	131.6	132.8	134.4	135.4	135.0	135.0	133.0	133.6	133.7	133.3	133.3

Employment by Industry: Minnesota, 2000–2007—*Continued*

(Numbers in thousands, not seasonally adjusted.)

Industry and year	January	February	March	April	May	June	July	August	September	October	November	December	Annual Average
Retail Trade													
2000	303.8	299.5	299.4	300.7	304.2	306.9	306.0	307.2	305.3	309.7	318.8	324.5	307.2
2001	307.6	301.6	301.6	301.7	306.5	309.0	306.8	307.7	303.2	307.4	316.2	319.9	307.4
2002	302.5	294.6	295.8	298.4	302.6	304.8	302.7	303.4	300.7	301.4	311.7	317.5	303.0
2003	299.0	292.2	292.5	296.7	302.1	303.7	299.5	302.0	299.2	301.4	308.4	312.3	300.8
2004	296.1	290.7	291.1	295.8	301.1	304.5	302.4	303.0	299.5	302.0	309.8	314.5	300.9
2005	296.0	290.7	291.9	296.0	300.7	303.2	300.3	301.8	299.8	303.8	311.9	316.5	301.1
2006	300.3	294.7	294.8	297.4	301.4	305.2	301.5	302.2	298.5	300.0	309.0	312.5	301.5
2007	299.2	293.7	294.4	296.7	302.1	305.5	302.4	302.7	299.3	302.4	311.2	314.3	302.0
Transportation and Utilities													
2000	101.8	101.9	102.3	102.9	103.6	103.0	102.3	102.3	104.8	105.6	105.1	105.0	103.3
2001	102.7	102.0	102.4	103.2	104.0	103.1	101.3	100.4	102.1	101.7	99.7	98.6	101.8
2002	96.1	95.0	94.8	96.0	97.0	95.7	92.0	91.6	94.5	96.1	96.0	95.1	95.0
2003	93.0	92.3	92.2	92.6	93.0	91.5	89.3	89.0	91.9	93.7	93.3	92.8	92.1
2004	90.4	90.3	90.4	92.4	93.5	93.1	91.7	91.9	95.8	98.2	98.2	98.2	93.7
2005	94.3	94.6	95.0	95.5	96.2	94.6	94.5	93.8	95.1	95.9	95.8	96.1	95.1
2006	94.1	93.3	93.5	93.2	94.0	93.8	91.0	90.3	94.6	94.8	96.3	95.9	93.7
2007	93.4	94.1	93.3	93.8	94.6	93.9	91.9	92.0	95.8	96.9	97.3	97.1	94.5
Information													
2000	66.7	67.3	67.5	68.2	68.7	70.3	70.7	70.8	69.8	70.0	70.5	70.6	69.2
2001	70.6	70.6	70.6	69.8	70.6	71.5	70.3	69.7	68.5	68.9	69.1	69.0	69.9
2002	67.5	67.2	67.2	67.4	67.3	67.7	67.2	66.1	64.9	64.4	64.5	64.3	66.3
2003	62.5	62.3	62.3	62.7	62.9	62.6	62.0	61.7	60.8	60.6	61.1	61.4	61.9
2004	60.6	60.5	60.7	61.1	61.3	61.0	60.1	59.5	58.8	58.6	59.2	59.2	60.1
2005	58.7	58.6	58.7	59.7	59.8	60.0	59.6	59.0	58.5	58.4	58.7	59.0	59.1
2006	58.3	58.1	58.4	57.8	58.3	58.7	58.2	58.2	58.3	57.5	57.3	57.7	58.0
2007	57.9	57.9	58.2	58.0	58.4	58.6	58.2	58.4	57.7	57.7	57.7	58.3	58.1
Financial Activities													
2000	162.0	161.9	162.5	163.1	163.6	166.0	166.4	166.7	165.6	166.3	166.3	167.7	164.8
2001	166.2	166.9	167.6	168.0	168.7	170.7	170.6	170.7	168.8	168.2	168.7	169.4	168.7
2002	168.3	168.6	168.6	169.6	170.4	171.5	173.3	173.9	173.1	173.0	173.8	174.8	171.6
2003	172.0	172.6	173.2	174.9	176.1	178.1	178.3	178.7	177.3	175.3	175.1	175.9	175.6
2004	174.9	174.6	174.6	176.6	177.0	178.8	177.7	177.9	176.4	176.4	176.5	177.3	176.6
2005	175.2	175.1	175.7	179.9	180.6	182.5	181.5	182.1	180.8	180.0	180.2	181.2	179.6
2006	179.8	179.7	180.2	179.5	180.7	182.4	181.7	181.5	180.0	179.8	180.1	181.0	180.5
2007	178.6	179.2	179.3	178.2	178.7	181.0	180.9	180.7	178.7	178.0	178.0	179.0	179.2
Professional and Business Services													
2000	308.6	307.9	311.6	316.3	317.8	325.0	323.6	325.5	323.7	325.0	324.0	322.1	319.2
2001	312.2	309.5	310.4	314.0	314.4	317.5	313.2	312.6	309.6	307.9	305.0	302.6	310.7
2002	290.1	289.8	290.4	292.7	295.5	299.7	301.3	304.4	302.2	302.9	300.3	297.7	297.3
2003	287.8	288.1	288.9	292.3	294.5	298.0	298.1	299.8	299.4	301.2	299.7	300.6	295.7
2004	288.7	290.6	292.8	299.7	302.2	306.6	306.2	307.3	304.7	306.9	305.4	304.1	301.3
2005	291.1	292.0	294.8	304.1	307.3	311.6	310.5	314.5	315.1	319.5	319.2	319.0	308.2
2006	313.2	313.6	315.3	319.8	322.9	329.0	327.0	329.5	328.1	329.6	329.5	328.6	323.8
2007	319.9	321.1	323.2	324.8	329.0	332.6	333.5	336.7	332.3	333.1	331.6	329.9	329.0
Education and Health Services													
2000	315.7	321.3	323.5	324.6	324.7	320.4	318.5	317.4	325.8	332.3	334.5	335.6	324.5
2001	328.1	332.9	335.8	337.5	339.4	334.3	332.0	332.7	339.5	348.1	350.4	350.6	338.4
2002	346.3	353.1	355.2	357.1	359.4	352.9	349.9	351.0	356.7	363.2	365.5	365.9	356.4
2003	361.7	368.3	369.8	370.1	371.5	365.7	364.0	363.3	369.0	373.3	374.8	374.0	368.8
2004	369.6	374.1	375.7	377.9	379.0	374.4	372.3	371.8	375.6	381.9	383.3	385.7	376.8
2005	377.6	384.1	385.9	388.3	392.1	387.1	388.8	389.8	394.8	399.8	402.2	403.8	391.2
2006	399.2	402.1	404.4	407.0	408.3	406.3	407.7	407.9	411.4	415.2	419.0	420.6	409.1
2007	418.0	421.1	422.9	425.9	427.9	426.2	426.0	426.3	429.8	435.8	439.4	436.4	428.0
Leisure and Hospitality													
2000	204.8	206.4	208.8	215.1	225.1	235.0	236.6	240.4	234.0	222.1	216.3	215.3	221.6
2001	209.7	211.5	214.2	219.2	230.4	241.0	242.4	248.0	237.9	226.5	220.5	220.0	226.8
2002	213.8	213.6	215.0	222.3	233.9	243.6	244.2	246.9	240.1	228.7	221.7	222.8	228.9
2003	216.6	215.1	216.4	225.8	238.5	246.5	246.4	249.4	242.4	232.0	224.6	226.1	231.7
2004	217.8	216.9	219.4	231.0	242.2	251.0	250.5	252.6	246.5	238.1	230.3	231.2	235.6
2005	223.0	222.3	224.6	237.0	247.3	256.9	256.8	259.0	252.7	246.0	241.7	241.3	242.4
2006	233.5	233.5	236.4	239.8	250.9	260.3	257.7	259.8	251.4	243.4	237.7	238.1	245.2
2007	232.1	231.9	234.0	241.5	254.8	263.0	263.4	265.4	256.5	247.2	242.4	241.8	247.8
Other Services													
2000	112.8	113.7	114.7	114.1	114.0	114.8	114.1	114.7	114.1	116.0	115.9	116.9	114.6
2001	116.0	116.3	117.5	117.8	118.2	118.7	116.7	117.0	116.4	117.8	119.5	118.8	117.6
2002	116.6	116.7	117.0	117.9	118.2	119.3	119.5	119.9	119.9	119.2	119.5	120.2	118.6
2003	117.7	117.9	118.4	118.4	118.7	119.7	120.5	120.6	120.1	119.0	119.1	119.8	119.2
2004	117.0	116.1	117.3	118.9	118.6	119.8	118.0	118.7	117.8	118.0	117.6	118.4	118.0
2005	115.0	115.0	115.6	118.2	119.0	119.7	119.1	119.6	119.3	119.2	119.0	119.8	118.2
2006	115.5	115.4	117.3	118.0	118.6	119.9	118.7	118.8	118.3	118.6	118.8	119.3	118.1
2007	115.1	114.8	116.3	116.7	117.5	118.1	117.6	117.4	116.1	116.2	116.1	116.6	116.5
Government													
2000	401.3	411.6	414.7	419.0	424.1	415.1	379.8	376.2	400.5	412.4	419.1	417.7	407.6
2001	404.9	416.4	417.2	418.0	420.1	416.9	381.5	373.8	404.2	417.1	420.4	421.3	409.3
2002	414.3	420.4	420.0	418.2	420.1	420.9	391.4	379.8	410.4	419.9	427.4	425.0	414.0
2003	412.8	421.6	421.4	422.6	422.2	418.0	384.8	382.8	404.5	417.4	419.7	421.7	412.5
2004	411.6	418.9	418.9	420.5	422.4	414.8	383.7	379.2	407.1	419.2	423.4	424.9	412.1
2005	416.4	422.1	422.9	424.6	424.9	420.0	391.1	384.7	408.7	420.6	420.2	422.2	414.9
2006	415.2	421.5	422.5	423.0	423.5	421.7	391.2	386.4	410.9	422.4	425.8	427.0	415.9
2007	414.2	420.5	419.6	420.9	424.3	421.9	389.8	384.5	408.9	421.4	425.1	424.9	414.7

Average Weekly Hours by Selected Industry: Minnesota, 2001–2007

(Not seasonally adjusted.)

Industry and year	January	February	March	April	May	June	July	August	September	October	November	December	Annual Average
Manufacturing													
2001	39.8	39.6	40.1	39.8	39.6	39.3	38.8	39.3	40.4	39.5	39.3	40.0	39.6
2002	39.0	39.4	38.6	39.1	39.0	40.0	39.4	40.1	40.2	40.0	40.6	41.2	39.7
2003	39.2	39.5	39.9	39.2	39.4	40.3	39.4	40.7	41.5	40.6	41.8	40.3	40.2
2004	41.1	40.7	40.8	41.0	40.8	40.4	40.1	41.1	40.7	41.9	41.4	41.3	40.9
2005	40.5	40.3	40.3	40.2	40.2	40.3	40.9	40.9	41.6	42.0	42.0	42.0	40.9
2006	41.5	41.9	40.9	40.6	42.3	41.4	40.6	41.0	41.5	40.2	40.1	40.1	41.0
2007	41.1	41.5	41.9	41.7	41.3	41.7	40.6	40.6	40.2	40.1	40.5	40.6	41.0
Wholesale Trade													
2001	37.4	37.5	37.4	37.7	38.0	38.1	37.2	36.5	38.3	38.4	37.9	37.7	37.7
2002	36.7	36.5	37.6	36.6	37.9	38.4	36.9	37.2	37.9	37.4	37.5	36.7	37.3
2003	35.7	38.3	38.5	37.4	38.9	39.1	38.6	39.6	39.1	40.2	39.4	38.5	38.6
2004	39.0	39.6	39.1	39.3	39.3	40.3	39.5	38.6	38.3	38.8	37.9	38.0	38.9
2005	38.3	37.9	37.9	37.9	39.0	38.8	38.4	38.8	39.0	40.1	39.6	38.7	38.7
2006	37.5	37.6	37.8	39.2	38.3	39.3	38.3	38.0	37.6	37.7	38.0	38.2	38.1
2007	38.3	38.6	38.2	39.2	39.5	39.0	38.9	40.2	39.5	39.7	39.2	39.1	39.1
Retail Trade													
2001	26.7	26.5	26.9	27.2	27.1	28.0	28.2	28.4	27.6	27.3	26.4	27.8	27.3
2002	25.6	25.7	25.2	25.4	26.0	27.0	27.5	27.0	26.8	25.7	26.3	28.3	26.4
2003	26.0	26.2	26.2	26.5	27.1	27.8	27.8	26.9	26.1	26.3	25.8	26.4	26.6
2004	25.7	26.1	25.8	25.9	26.2	26.8	27.3	28.1	27.7	26.8	26.4	27.3	26.7
2005	26.0	25.9	25.7	25.9	26.5	27.2	27.1	27.0	27.2	26.3	26.6	27.6	26.6
2006	27.0	26.6	26.1	26.9	26.9	27.4	27.9	27.9	28.1	28.3	29.0	29.4	27.6
2007	27.1	27.8	27.7	27.7	27.4	28.6	29.1	29.0	29.6	28.7	29.7	30.2	28.6
Information													
2001	38.1	37.1	37.9	38.6	37.7	37.5	38.0	36.6	38.3	37.7	37.2	38.1	37.7
2002	36.4	36.4	37.0	36.5	37.3	38.5	38.1	39.4	40.2	38.0	37.9	39.3	38.0
2003	37.4	38.8	39.1	38.1	38.5	39.6	39.2	40.1	39.4	37.9	37.2	36.6	38.5
2004	37.1	39.2	40.0	40.6	40.7	40.7	40.7	38.9	38.9	39.5	39.2	38.6	39.5
2005	40.0	39.8	39.7	40.6	40.4	41.2	42.6	40.5	41.9	42.3	41.7	39.9	40.9
2006	40.5	38.6	40.1	39.0	37.7	39.2	38.3	39.4	39.0	38.8	36.9	36.7	38.7
2007	36.4	36.2	37.0	36.9	36.3	36.0	36.9	38.7	37.4	37.7	36.9	37.4	37.0

Average Hourly Earnings by Selected Industry: Minnesota, 2001–2007

(Dollars, not seasonally adjusted.)

Industry and year	January	February	March	April	May	June	July	August	September	October	November	December	Annual Average
Manufacturing													
2001	14.66	14.56	14.54	14.72	14.65	14.65	14.71	14.74	14.85	14.99	15.00	15.07	14.76
2002	14.94	14.89	14.91	15.12	15.07	14.98	14.94	15.18	15.19	15.14	15.13	15.24	15.06
2003	15.35	15.34	15.35	15.49	15.47	15.56	15.33	15.30	15.39	15.27	15.47	15.81	15.43
2004	15.96	15.85	15.97	16.13	16.02	16.15	16.17	15.89	16.17	16.12	16.01	15.99	16.04
2005	16.32	16.25	16.48	16.46	16.45	16.45	16.45	16.50	16.87	16.95	16.97	17.36	16.63
2006	17.30	17.23	17.18	17.24	17.38	17.38	17.18	17.21	17.18	17.31	16.88	17.36	17.24
2007	17.69	17.29	17.52	17.36	17.32	17.22	17.05	17.20	17.37	17.53	17.49	17.74	17.40
Wholesale Trade													
2001	18.60	18.47	18.79	18.99	18.40	18.68	18.32	18.39	18.51	18.25	18.54	18.56	18.54
2002	18.54	18.88	18.27	18.94	19.26	19.96	19.63	19.55	19.56	19.12	19.52	19.19	19.21
2003	18.92	19.56	19.92	19.60	18.24	18.21	18.80	18.53	18.80	18.74	18.60	18.45	18.85
2004	18.41	17.86	18.18	17.91	17.70	18.13	18.68	18.75	18.75	18.77	18.58	18.57	18.35
2005	18.91	19.14	18.71	19.19	19.03	18.64	19.31	19.11	19.05	19.63	19.68	19.14	19.14
2006	20.44	20.02	20.07	20.69	21.30	20.31	20.67	20.47	21.34	21.68	21.13	21.01	20.76
2007	20.86	21.08	20.70	21.51	20.89	20.31	20.87	20.90	20.97	20.49	20.55	21.02	20.84
Retail Trade													
2001	11.53	11.75	11.74	11.74	11.74	11.57	11.57	11.71	11.84	11.88	12.04	12.02	11.76
2002	12.00	12.04	12.24	12.10	12.23	11.92	11.81	11.93	11.96	12.01	12.05	12.00	12.02
2003	11.83	12.08	11.85	11.86	11.87	11.86	11.78	11.85	11.90	11.64	11.64	11.52	11.80
2004	11.67	11.67	11.90	11.84	11.96	11.77	11.71	11.62	11.72	11.76	11.58	11.58	11.73
2005	11.96	11.92	12.01	12.15	12.16	12.02	12.13	12.22	12.55	12.44	12.28	12.11	12.16
2006	12.76	12.15	12.32	12.80	13.00	12.92	12.78	12.74	13.11	12.99	12.40	12.18	12.68
2007	12.32	12.26	12.40	12.52	12.94	12.83	12.81	12.51	12.77	12.57	12.15	11.98	12.50
Information													
2001	18.80	17.81	17.61	18.24	18.25	18.33	18.43	18.72	18.89	19.24	19.56	19.47	18.61
2002	19.75	18.57	18.39	19.71	18.75	18.53	19.58	19.16	20.39	20.87	21.55	21.45	19.77
2003	21.47	21.23	20.99	20.83	20.44	20.54	20.34	20.12	19.59	19.91	19.22	19.32	20.31
2004	19.11	19.66	19.15	19.48	19.63	20.12	20.06	20.95	21.63	21.67	21.68	21.57	20.38
2005	21.06	20.99	22.11	22.34	21.65	20.80	21.69	20.97	21.31	20.83	19.59	21.09	21.21
2006	22.25	21.55	21.78	22.51	21.62	20.07	20.48	18.85	19.62	19.40	19.76	19.56	20.63
2007	20.18	20.15	19.94	20.22	19.80	19.91	20.35	20.67	21.90	21.70	22.09	22.34	20.77

Average Weekly Earnings by Selected Industry: Minnesota, 2001–2007

(Dollars, not seasonally adjusted.)

Industry and year	January	February	March	April	May	June	July	August	September	October	November	December	Annual Average
Manufacturing													
2001	583.47	576.58	583.05	585.86	580.14	575.75	570.75	579.28	599.94	592.11	589.50	602.80	584.50
2002	582.66	586.67	575.53	591.19	587.73	599.20	588.64	608.72	610.64	605.60	614.28	627.89	597.88
2003	601.72	605.93	612.47	607.21	609.52	627.07	604.00	622.71	638.69	619.96	646.65	637.14	620.29
2004	655.96	645.10	651.58	661.33	653.62	652.46	648.42	653.08	658.12	675.43	662.81	660.39	656.04
2005	660.96	654.88	664.14	661.69	661.29	662.94	672.81	674.85	701.79	711.90	712.74	729.12	680.17
2006	717.95	721.94	702.66	699.94	735.17	719.53	697.51	705.61	712.97	695.86	676.89	696.14	706.84
2007	727.06	717.54	734.09	723.91	715.32	718.07	692.23	698.32	698.27	702.95	708.35	720.24	713.40
Wholesale Trade													
2001	695.64	692.63	702.75	715.92	699.20	711.71	681.50	671.24	708.93	700.80	702.67	699.71	698.96
2002	680.42	689.12	686.95	693.20	729.95	766.46	724.35	727.26	741.32	715.09	732.00	704.27	716.53
2003	675.44	749.15	766.92	733.04	709.54	712.01	725.68	733.79	735.08	753.35	732.84	710.33	727.61
2004	717.99	707.26	710.84	703.86	713.31	716.14	721.05	729.38	718.13	728.28	704.18	705.66	713.82
2005	724.25	725.41	709.11	727.30	742.17	723.23	741.50	741.47	742.95	787.16	760.32	761.62	740.72
2006	766.50	752.75	758.65	811.05	815.79	798.18	791.66	777.86	802.38	817.34	802.94	802.58	790.96
2007	798.94	813.69	790.74	843.19	825.16	792.09	811.84	840.18	828.32	813.45	805.56	821.88	814.84
Retail Trade													
2001	307.85	311.38	315.81	319.33	318.15	323.96	326.27	332.56	326.78	324.32	317.86	334.16	321.05
2002	307.20	309.43	308.45	307.34	317.98	321.84	324.78	322.11	320.53	308.66	316.92	339.60	317.33
2003	307.58	316.50	310.47	314.29	321.68	329.71	327.48	318.77	310.59	306.13	300.31	304.13	313.88
2004	299.92	304.59	307.02	306.66	313.35	315.44	319.68	326.52	324.64	315.17	305.71	316.13	313.19
2005	310.96	308.73	308.66	314.69	322.24	326.94	328.72	329.94	341.36	327.17	326.65	334.24	323.46
2006	344.52	323.19	321.55	344.32	349.70	354.01	356.56	355.45	368.39	367.62	359.60	358.09	349.97
2007	333.87	340.83	343.48	346.80	354.56	366.94	372.77	362.79	377.99	360.76	360.86	361.80	357.50
Information													
2001	716.28	660.75	667.42	704.06	688.03	687.38	700.34	685.15	723.49	725.35	727.63	741.81	701.60
2002	718.90	675.95	680.43	719.42	699.38	713.41	746.00	754.90	819.68	793.06	816.75	842.99	751.26
2003	802.98	823.72	820.71	793.62	786.94	813.38	797.33	806.81	771.85	754.59	714.98	707.11	781.94
2004	708.98	770.67	766.00	790.89	798.94	818.88	816.44	814.96	841.41	855.97	849.86	832.60	805.01
2005	842.40	835.40	877.77	907.00	874.66	856.96	923.99	849.29	892.89	881.11	816.90	841.49	867.49
2006	901.13	831.83	873.38	877.89	815.07	786.74	784.38	742.69	765.18	752.72	729.14	717.85	798.38
2007	734.55	729.43	737.78	746.12	718.74	716.76	750.92	799.93	819.06	818.09	815.12	835.52	768.49

Population
    2000 census: 2,844,658
    2007 estimate: 2,918,785
    Percent change, 2000–2007: 2.6%

Percent change in total nonfarm employment, 2000–2007: -0.1%

Industry with the largest growth in employment, 2000–2007 (thousands)
    Education and health services, 20.7

Industry with the largest decline in employment, 2000–2007 (thousands)
    Manufacturing, -52.8

Civilian labor force
    2000: 1,314,154
    2007: 1,314,811

Employment-population ratio
    2000: 59.1%
    2007: 56.7%

Unemployment rate and rank among states
    2000: 5.7%, 49th
    2007: 6.3%, 50th

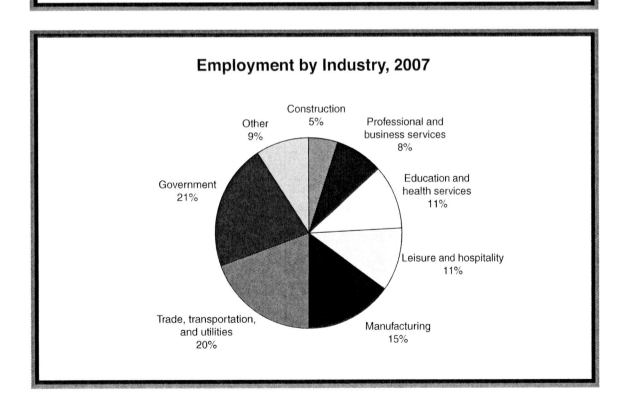

Employment by Industry, 2007

Construction 5%
Professional and business services 8%
Education and health services 11%
Leisure and hospitality 11%
Manufacturing 15%
Trade, transportation, and utilities 20%
Government 21%
Other 9%

Employment by Industry: Mississippi, 2000–2007

(Numbers in thousands, not seasonally adjusted.)

Industry and year	January	February	March	April	May	June	July	August	September	October	November	December	Annual Average
Total Nonfarm													
2000	1,144.1	1,145.0	1,153.8	1,158.3	1,166.7	1,164.0	1,147.2	1,157.0	1,155.3	1,149.8	1,150.7	1,150.7	1,153.5
2001	1,128.8	1,128.8	1,131.1	1,136.3	1,138.2	1,135.1	1,120.8	1,131.7	1,130.9	1,124.9	1,126.6	1,126.1	1,129.9
2002	1,111.0	1,113.8	1,120.3	1,127.8	1,131.7	1,133.2	1,119.6	1,128.3	1,130.6	1,122.1	1,121.5	1,123.2	1,123.6
2003	1,107.2	1,108.7	1,112.1	1,116.4	1,116.6	1,110.8	1,104.4	1,111.7	1,119.4	1,123.1	1,124.7	1,123.2	1,114.9
2004	1,108.3	1,113.3	1,120.9	1,129.8	1,129.4	1,125.6	1,114.7	1,124.1	1,132.1	1,130.3	1,132.9	1,133.1	1,124.5
2005	1,118.4	1,126.1	1,134.2	1,139.0	1,138.7	1,133.6	1,123.4	1,134.3	1,120.1	1,125.0	1,137.7	1,132.0	1,130.2
2006	1,116.2	1,126.0	1,137.1	1,141.0	1,144.8	1,143.9	1,125.2	1,143.8	1,153.0	1,149.0	1,155.9	1,156.0	1,141.0
2007	1,138.4	1,144.5	1,148.3	1,153.8	1,156.3	1,152.6	1,136.4	1,152.5	1,160.1	1,159.0	1,162.2	1,161.3	1,152.1
Total Private													
2000	913.9	913.8	920.3	923.9	927.5	931.6	920.1	924.3	920.2	914.0	913.8	913.6	919.7
2001	891.6	890.5	892.6	897.2	899.0	898.8	890.4	895.5	892.3	885.9	887.8	887.3	892.4
2002	872.8	874.5	880.7	887.1	890.6	893.7	886.0	889.4	888.4	879.4	878.7	880.4	883.5
2003	865.9	866.5	869.0	873.0	875.3	873.7	871.9	875.9	876.3	878.8	880.3	882.4	874.1
2004	867.6	869.7	875.9	884.0	885.5	885.9	882.8	886.3	887.6	884.8	887.3	891.7	882.4
2005	878.0	881.9	889.6	894.4	895.2	893.6	891.6	896.8	878.8	883.6	895.6	893.9	889.4
2006	878.3	885.0	896.0	900.0	904.9	906.3	897.8	907.2	909.7	905.9	912.1	915.7	901.6
2007	897.6	899.9	903.5	908.0	911.1	910.8	903.6	911.4	913.1	911.7	914.8	915.1	908.4
Goods-Producing													
2000	289.9	289.2	290.3	290.2	290.7	291.2	286.8	286.0	283.4	282.2	279.3	277.3	286.4
2001	269.0	266.8	264.3	265.9	265.0	264.9	260.1	260.9	259.8	258.3	257.6	255.1	262.3
2002	252.8	253.2	254.0	253.0	253.7	255.0	251.5	251.2	250.3	246.6	244.3	243.1	250.7
2003	239.8	239.6	239.3	239.2	239.1	238.2	236.6	236.4	237.2	238.6	237.9	237.5	238.3
2004	233.7	233.9	235.6	238.1	238.3	240.1	237.6	239.1	238.9	238.2	238.7	238.7	237.6
2005	235.9	235.8	238.0	239.7	240.2	240.7	239.4	239.8	236.0	239.8	241.9	243.7	239.2
2006	239.5	239.5	241.7	242.8	244.6	247.1	244.0	244.0	242.8	242.3	243.0	243.1	242.9
2007	239.0	238.2	235.0	239.3	238.9	238.7	236.1	237.2	237.6	236.7	236.5	235.9	237.4
Natural Resources and Mining													
2000	9.2	9.3	9.4	9.2	9.3	9.4	9.4	9.3	9.4	9.6	9.5	9.5	9.3
2001	9.3	9.3	9.6	9.7	9.6	9.7	9.7	9.8	9.8	9.6	9.6	9.6	9.6
2002	8.9	8.9	9.0	8.9	9.0	9.0	9.0	9.0	9.0	8.8	8.7	8.5	8.9
2003	8.3	8.3	8.5	8.7	8.8	8.8	8.9	9.0	9.1	8.9	8.9	8.9	8.8
2004	8.6	8.5	8.8	8.7	8.8	8.9	9.0	9.0	8.8	8.9	9.0	8.9	8.8
2005	8.5	8.4	8.6	8.8	8.8	8.8	8.8	8.9	8.8	8.9	8.9	8.9	8.8
2006	8.9	9.0	9.2	9.6	9.6	9.5	9.5	9.7	9.6	9.7	9.8	9.6	9.5
2007	9.2	9.3	9.4	9.6	9.7	9.5	9.5	9.6	9.6	9.6	9.7	9.7	9.5
Construction													
2000	53.4	54.1	55.0	54.5	55.3	56.4	55.9	55.6	54.4	53.9	52.9	52.3	54.5
2001	48.6	49.6	49.9	51.3	51.7	52.4	52.2	53.2	53.0	53.4	54.2	53.7	51.9
2002	53.3	53.2	53.9	53.6	54.3	55.7	54.8	54.9	54.7	53.3	52.7	52.4	53.9
2003	51.0	51.1	50.8	51.1	50.9	50.9	50.6	50.6	50.7	50.4	49.6	49.2	50.6
2004	47.2	47.0	47.7	48.9	49.2	50.1	50.0	50.3	50.6	49.8	49.7	49.0	49.1
2005	47.4	47.5	49.0	50.5	51.5	52.1	52.3	52.6	54.5	55.6	56.4	57.3	52.2
2006	54.7	54.3	55.6	56.8	58.6	60.7	58.9	59.1	58.9	58.3	58.3	58.3	57.7
2007	56.9	56.6	58.4	58.0	58.2	58.7	58.2	58.8	59.1	59.0	58.5	58.1	58.2
Manufacturing													
2000	227.3	225.8	225.9	226.5	226.1	225.4	221.5	221.1	219.6	218.7	216.9	215.5	222.5
2001	211.1	207.9	204.8	204.9	203.7	202.8	198.2	197.9	197.0	195.3	193.8	191.8	200.8
2002	190.6	191.1	191.1	190.5	190.4	190.3	187.7	187.3	186.6	184.5	182.9	182.2	187.9
2003	180.5	180.2	180.0	179.4	179.4	178.5	177.1	176.8	177.4	179.3	179.4	179.4	179.0
2004	177.9	178.4	179.1	180.5	180.3	181.1	178.6	179.8	179.5	179.5	180.0	180.8	179.6
2005	180.0	179.9	180.4	180.4	179.9	179.8	178.3	178.3	172.7	175.3	176.6	177.5	178.3
2006	175.9	176.2	176.9	176.4	176.4	176.9	175.6	175.2	174.3	174.3	174.9	175.2	175.7
2007	172.9	172.3	167.2	171.7	171.0	170.5	168.4	168.8	168.9	168.1	168.3	168.1	169.7
Service-Providing													
2000	854.2	855.8	863.5	868.1	876.0	872.8	860.4	871.0	871.9	867.6	871.4	873.4	867.2
2001	859.8	862.0	866.8	870.4	873.2	870.2	860.7	870.8	871.1	866.6	869.0	871.0	867.6
2002	858.2	860.6	866.3	874.8	878.0	878.2	868.1	877.1	880.3	875.5	877.2	880.1	872.9
2003	867.4	869.1	872.8	877.2	877.5	872.6	867.8	875.3	882.2	884.5	886.8	885.7	876.6
2004	874.6	879.4	885.3	891.7	891.1	885.5	877.1	885.0	893.2	892.1	894.2	894.4	887.0
2005	882.5	890.3	896.2	899.3	898.5	892.9	884.0	894.5	884.1	885.2	895.8	888.3	891.0
2006	876.7	886.5	895.4	898.2	900.2	896.8	881.2	899.8	910.2	906.7	912.9	912.9	898.1
2007	899.4	906.3	913.3	914.5	917.4	913.9	900.3	915.3	922.5	922.3	925.7	925.4	914.7
Trade, Transportation, and Utilities													
2000	225.1	224.5	225.7	226.1	227.8	228.5	226.1	227.4	227.3	226.5	229.1	231.4	227.1
2001	223.2	221.4	223.0	222.7	223.5	224.1	221.2	222.2	221.7	222.1	225.2	226.8	223.1
2002	217.9	217.1	218.1	219.7	220.9	222.6	221.2	221.6	221.7	220.6	223.1	225.6	220.8
2003	217.3	216.7	216.5	216.3	217.8	218.3	218.1	218.9	218.8	220.0	222.6	224.7	218.8
2004	217.2	216.4	218.0	218.7	219.9	220.2	219.2	219.7	219.4	220.6	223.1	226.4	219.9
2005	218.1	217.3	219.4	220.1	220.3	220.5	220.8	222.4	217.1	218.3	224.0	228.2	220.5
2006	221.3	221.5	224.7	224.7	225.8	226.1	224.8	226.1	226.2	225.7	228.7	231.8	225.6
2007	224.2	223.3	226.1	225.7	227.3	227.8	225.7	226.7	227.1	227.4	230.7	231.5	227.0
Wholesale Trade													
2000	36.9	37.0	37.0	36.9	36.9	37.2	37.0	37.4	37.2	36.7	36.5	36.6	36.9
2001	35.9	35.4	35.5	35.2	35.1	35.4	35.4	35.7	35.5	35.0	34.8	35.2	35.3
2002	34.9	34.9	34.9	34.9	34.8	35.1	35.1	35.5	35.4	35.0	34.8	35.1	35.0
2003	34.7	34.6	34.5	34.6	34.8	35.2	34.9	35.1	35.0	34.9	34.9	35.1	34.9
2004	34.8	34.7	34.7	34.9	34.8	35.0	35.1	35.2	35.1	34.9	34.9	35.2	34.9
2005	34.6	34.7	34.9	35.2	35.4	35.5	35.6	35.9	35.3	35.2	35.3	35.8	35.3
2006	35.7	35.9	36.1	35.9	36.2	36.5	36.4	37.0	36.7	36.6	36.6	37.1	36.4
2007	36.6	36.6	36.6	36.6	36.7	36.9	36.9	37.3	37.1	37.2	37.0	37.2	36.9

Employment by Industry: Mississippi, 2000–2007—*Continued*

(Numbers in thousands, not seasonally adjusted.)

Industry and year	January	February	March	April	May	June	July	August	September	October	November	December	Annual Average
Retail Trade													
2000	143.7	142.9	144.0	144.2	145.5	145.8	143.9	144.6	144.7	144.6	147.6	150.0	145.1
2001	141.9	140.7	142.1	141.6	142.3	142.7	140.1	140.6	140.4	141.0	144.6	145.9	142.0
2002	138.3	137.5	138.7	139.8	140.4	141.5	140.3	139.7	139.9	139.0	141.8	144.3	140.1
2003	137.1	136.4	136.7	136.2	137.2	137.2	137.4	138.0	137.9	139.1	141.6	143.7	138.2
2004	136.8	136.0	137.2	137.5	138.2	138.3	137.6	137.4	137.2	138.3	140.9	143.3	138.2
2005	137.0	136.1	137.4	137.8	137.8	137.9	138.1	138.9	134.8	136.4	141.7	144.9	138.2
2006	139.1	138.8	141.5	141.5	142.0	142.0	141.2	141.4	141.3	141.0	143.9	145.9	141.6
2007	139.9	139.2	141.5	141.0	142.1	142.5	140.6	140.7	141.1	141.3	144.7	145.2	141.7
Transportation and Utilities													
2000	44.5	44.6	44.7	45.0	45.4	45.5	45.2	45.4	45.4	45.2	45.0	44.8	45.1
2001	45.4	45.3	45.4	45.9	46.1	46.0	45.7	45.9	45.8	46.1	45.8	45.7	45.8
2002	44.7	44.7	44.5	45.0	45.7	46.0	45.8	46.4	46.4	46.6	46.5	46.2	45.7
2003	45.5	45.7	45.3	45.5	45.8	45.9	45.8	45.8	45.9	46.0	46.1	45.9	45.8
2004	45.6	45.7	46.1	46.3	46.9	46.9	46.5	47.1	47.1	47.4	47.3	47.9	46.7
2005	46.5	46.5	47.1	47.1	47.1	47.1	47.1	47.6	47.0	46.7	47.0	47.5	47.0
2006	46.5	46.8	47.1	47.3	47.6	47.6	47.2	47.7	48.2	48.1	48.2	48.8	47.6
2007	47.7	47.5	48.0	48.1	48.5	48.4	48.2	48.7	48.9	48.9	49.0	49.1	48.4
Information													
2000	16.8	16.8	17.0	16.9	17.1	17.5	17.7	17.7	17.6	17.6	17.8	17.9	17.4
2001	17.6	17.5	17.4	17.1	17.1	17.3	17.0	16.7	16.5	16.4	16.5	16.5	17.0
2002	16.5	16.4	16.3	16.3	16.3	16.2	16.1	16.0	15.8	15.7	15.8	15.7	16.1
2003	15.5	15.3	15.3	15.1	15.1	15.0	15.0	15.0	14.9	14.9	15.0	15.1	15.1
2004	14.9	14.8	14.8	14.6	14.6	14.7	14.6	14.5	14.4	14.3	14.5	14.5	14.6
2005	14.5	14.5	14.5	14.4	14.4	14.6	14.3	14.3	14.0	14.0	14.0	14.1	14.3
2006	14.0	13.9	13.9	13.8	13.8	13.9	13.7	13.6	13.4	13.3	13.3	13.4	13.7
2007	13.2	13.3	13.3	13.3	13.3	13.5	13.6	13.4	13.3	13.3	13.3	13.3	13.3
Financial Activities													
2000	45.8	45.8	45.9	45.9	46.0	46.5	46.1	45.9	46.0	45.6	45.7	46.0	45.9
2001	45.3	45.5	45.5	45.6	45.8	46.2	46.1	46.3	46.0	45.8	45.8	46.1	45.8
2002	45.6	45.4	45.5	45.7	45.7	46.1	45.8	45.8	45.6	45.7	46.0	46.0	45.7
2003	45.8	45.7	45.8	45.7	46.0	46.1	46.2	46.1	46.0	45.7	45.7	46.0	45.9
2004	45.5	45.4	45.6	45.9	45.9	46.3	46.3	46.3	46.1	46.1	46.1	46.5	46.0
2005	45.9	45.9	46.1	46.0	46.2	46.3	46.7	46.6	45.8	46.6	46.8	46.9	46.3
2006	45.6	46.3	46.3	46.2	46.3	46.7	46.8	46.8	46.7	46.5	46.8	47.1	46.5
2007	46.5	46.7	46.8	47.0	47.2	47.3	47.1	47.2	47.0	46.6	46.6	46.9	46.9
Professional and Business Services													
2000	78.5	78.7	79.4	79.9	80.0	80.5	79.0	80.6	80.3	78.3	78.7	78.2	79.3
2001	76.2	77.1	76.9	77.2	76.9	76.8	77.1	77.7	77.2	76.1	76.0	76.6	76.8
2002	76.0	76.7	77.3	78.7	78.2	79.3	78.6	79.7	78.9	77.5	76.8	77.4	77.9
2003	77.3	77.5	77.4	79.1	78.7	78.8	79.0	79.9	80.2	81.0	81.1	81.8	79.3
2004	80.7	81.5	82.0	83.6	83.0	83.4	83.5	83.4	84.0	83.4	83.5	85.0	83.1
2005	85.3	87.4	87.8	87.9	86.6	86.8	87.2	88.2	88.6	91.1	92.8	92.6	88.5
2006	91.4	93.4	95.2	95.7	96.0	95.2	93.2	94.5	94.5	93.8	94.7	94.5	94.3
2007	93.0	94.3	95.4	94.5	94.3	94.3	93.8	95.1	95.9	96.3	96.0	96.0	94.9
Education and Health Services													
2000	104.0	104.3	104.8	105.1	105.3	103.1	102.6	104.3	106.2	106.8	107.1	107.5	105.1
2001	108.0	108.7	109.3	109.8	110.2	107.6	107.6	110.0	111.4	111.8	112.2	112.6	109.9
2002	111.6	111.9	112.6	113.5	113.6	110.6	109.9	111.8	114.2	114.6	114.9	115.2	112.9
2003	114.3	114.7	115.2	116.1	116.2	113.6	112.9	115.2	116.7	118.0	118.4	118.3	115.8
2004	118.3	118.9	119.2	119.5	119.4	115.9	116.2	117.6	120.8	120.7	121.1	121.3	119.1
2005	120.6	121.3	121.5	121.8	121.5	117.9	117.6	119.8	121.0	120.8	121.1	121.8	120.6
2006	120.6	121.5	122.3	122.5	122.8	119.0	118.7	121.8	124.6	124.6	125.2	125.5	122.4
2007	124.5	125.1	125.9	125.9	126.2	123.3	122.5	126.2	127.5	127.6	127.7	127.7	125.8
Leisure and Hospitality													
2000	118.9	119.3	121.6	124.1	124.8	127.9	125.8	126.6	123.6	121.6	120.7	119.8	122.9
2001	116.2	117.3	119.8	122.3	123.6	124.4	124.1	124.5	122.5	118.5	117.6	116.6	120.6
2002	115.6	116.9	119.6	122.7	124.6	125.9	125.4	126.0	124.6	121.6	120.7	120.3	122.0
2003	118.7	119.7	121.5	123.6	124.6	125.7	126.2	126.8	124.9	123.2	122.4	121.7	123.3
2004	119.8	121.0	123.0	125.6	126.5	127.2	127.8	128.3	126.6	124.4	123.3	122.3	124.7
2005	120.7	122.1	124.8	126.7	128.2	129.0	128.2	128.2	128.4	119.8	116.6	110.1	122.8
2006	109.6	111.9	114.9	117.3	118.6	120.8	119.4	123.3	124.6	123.1	123.9	123.8	119.3
2007	120.4	121.9	123.6	125.2	126.7	128.4	127.6	128.5	127.6	127.1	126.9	126.3	125.9
Other Services													
2000	34.9	35.2	35.6	35.7	35.8	36.4	36.0	35.8	35.8	35.4	35.4	35.5	35.6
2001	36.1	36.2	36.4	36.6	36.9	37.5	37.2	37.2	37.2	36.9	36.9	37.0	36.8
2002	36.8	36.9	37.3	37.5	37.6	38.0	37.5	37.3	37.3	37.1	37.1	37.1	37.3
2003	37.2	37.3	38.0	37.9	37.8	38.0	37.9	37.6	37.5	37.4	37.3	37.4	37.6
2004	37.5	37.8	37.7	38.0	37.9	38.1	37.6	37.4	37.4	37.1	37.0	37.0	37.5
2005	37.0	37.6	37.5	37.5	37.8	37.8	37.4	37.3	36.5	36.4	36.5	36.5	37.2
2006	36.3	37.0	37.0	37.0	37.0	37.5	37.2	37.1	36.9	36.6	36.5	36.5	36.9
2007	36.8	37.1	37.4	37.1	37.2	37.5	37.2	37.1	37.1	36.7	37.1	37.5	37.2
Government													
2000	230.2	231.2	233.5	234.4	239.2	232.4	227.1	232.7	235.1	235.8	236.9	237.1	233.8
2001	237.2	238.3	238.5	239.1	239.2	236.3	230.4	236.2	238.6	239.0	238.8	238.8	237.5
2002	238.2	239.3	239.6	240.7	241.1	239.5	233.6	238.9	242.2	242.7	242.8	242.8	240.1
2003	241.3	242.2	243.1	243.4	241.3	237.1	232.5	235.8	243.1	244.3	244.4	240.8	240.8
2004	240.7	243.6	245.0	245.8	243.9	239.7	231.9	237.8	244.5	245.5	245.6	241.4	242.1
2005	240.4	244.2	244.6	244.6	243.5	240.0	231.8	237.5	241.3	241.4	242.1	238.1	240.8
2006	237.9	241.0	241.1	241.0	239.9	237.6	227.4	236.6	243.3	243.1	243.8	240.3	239.4
2007	240.8	244.6	244.8	245.8	245.2	241.8	232.8	241.1	247.0	247.3	247.4	246.2	243.7

Average Weekly Hours by Selected Industry: Mississippi, 2001–2007

(Numbers in thousands, not seasonally adjusted.)

Industry and year	January	February	March	April	May	June	July	August	September	October	November	December	Annual Average
Manufacturing													
2001	40.1	39.4	39.5	38.3	39.3	39.4	39.7	39.9	40.2	39.4	39.7	41.8	39.7
2002	41.1	41.1	41.3	40.8	41.0	41.2	40.1	40.5	40.7	39.3	39.2	41.5	40.6
2003	40.3	40.2	39.6	38.2	38.5	39.5	39.2	40.2	40.5	40.5	40.6	41.1	39.9
2004	40.6	39.8	40.3	39.9	39.9	39.4	39.5	40.6	40.1	39.7	40.3	41.5	40.1
2005	40.7	40.4	40.6	40.1	39.3	39.2	39.1	40.5	40.3	39.2	40.0	41.2	40.1
2006	40.1	39.5	39.7	37.6	39.2	39.3	39.2	39.7	39.4	38.8	39.5	40.6	39.4
2007	39.9	39.5	39.8	39.8	40.4	40.8	41.4	41.7	41.6	40.3	40.4	41.2	40.6

Average Hourly Earnings by Selected Industry: Mississippi, 2001–2007

(Dollars, not seasonally adjusted.)

Industry and year	January	February	March	April	May	June	July	August	September	October	November	December	Annual Average
Manufacturing													
2001	11.93	11.85	11.80	11.87	11.87	11.86	11.88	11.94	11.92	11.96	12.06	12.28	11.93
2002	12.16	12.30	12.24	12.30	12.21	12.26	12.14	12.31	12.39	12.41	12.48	12.62	12.32
2003	12.72	12.83	12.77	12.73	12.77	12.83	12.79	12.88	12.98	13.04	13.09	13.21	12.89
2004	12.92	12.91	12.97	13.00	13.03	13.08	13.11	13.31	13.31	13.21	13.24	13.34	13.12
2005	13.47	13.34	13.48	13.51	13.37	13.25	13.48	13.84	13.77	13.49	13.67	13.71	13.53
2006	13.65	13.62	13.71	13.73	13.68	13.73	13.74	13.76	13.88	13.94	13.95	13.95	13.78
2007	13.99	13.84	13.74	13.95	13.86	13.73	13.77	13.71	13.76	13.73	13.75	13.72	13.79

Average Weekly Earnings by Selected Industry: Mississippi, 2001–2007

(Dollars, not seasonally adjusted.)

Industry and year	January	February	March	April	May	June	July	August	September	October	November	December	Annual Average
Manufacturing													
2001	478.39	466.89	466.10	454.62	466.49	467.28	471.64	476.41	479.18	471.22	478.78	513.30	473.62
2002	499.78	505.53	505.51	501.84	500.61	505.11	486.81	498.56	504.27	487.71	489.22	523.73	500.19
2003	512.62	515.77	505.69	486.29	491.65	506.79	501.37	517.78	525.69	528.12	531.45	542.93	514.31
2004	524.55	513.82	522.69	518.70	519.90	515.35	517.85	540.39	533.73	524.44	533.57	553.61	526.11
2005	548.23	538.94	547.29	541.75	525.44	519.40	527.07	560.52	554.93	528.81	546.80	564.85	542.55
2006	547.37	537.99	544.29	516.25	536.26	539.59	538.61	546.27	546.87	540.87	551.03	566.37	542.93
2007	558.20	546.68	546.85	555.21	559.94	560.18	570.08	571.71	572.42	553.32	555.50	565.26	559.87

Population
    2000 census: 5,595,211
    2007 estimate: 5,878,415
    Percent change, 2000–2007: 5.1%

Percent change in total nonfarm employment, 2000–2007: 1.7%

Industry with the largest growth in employment, 2000–2007 (thousands)
    Education and health services, 50.0

Industry with the largest decline in employment, 2000–2007 (thousands)
    Manufacturing, -65.3

Civilian labor force
    2000: 2,973,092
    2007: 3,031,187

Employment-population ratio
    2000: 67.9%
    2007: 63.8%

Unemployment rate and rank among states
    2000: 3.3%, 14th
    2007: 5.0%, 39th

Employment by Industry, 2007

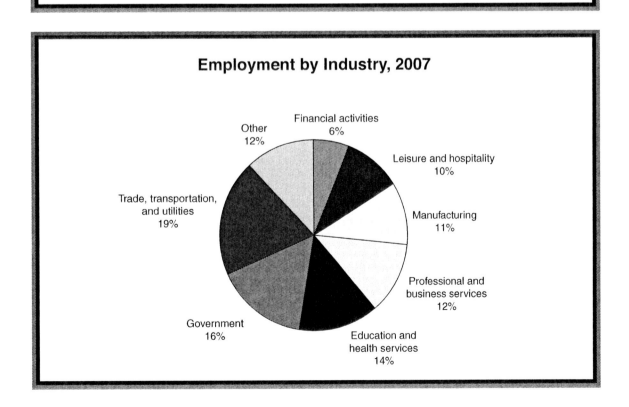

Employment by Industry: Missouri, 2000–2007

(Numbers in thousands, not seasonally adjusted.)

Industry and year	January	February	March	April	May	June	July	August	September	October	November	December	Annual Average
Total Nonfarm													
2000	2,691.1	2,701.1	2,735.0	2,758.5	2,774.3	2,786.0	2,729.8	2,733.4	2,763.1	2,771.8	2,774.5	2,766.2	2,748.7
2001	2,688.3	2,700.8	2,727.1	2,751.7	2,765.9	2,775.1	2,708.4	2,717.0	2,738.2	2,730.3	2,731.9	2,730.4	2,730.4
2002	2,660.5	2,667.2	2,690.7	2,705.7	2,720.2	2,727.9	2,661.1	2,677.6	2,719.1	2,716.1	2,720.5	2,720.0	2,698.9
2003	2,640.4	2,643.1	2,664.8	2,690.0	2,703.5	2,709.6	2,654.6	2,662.6	2,695.0	2,704.2	2,699.1	2,698.5	2,680.5
2004	2,629.6	2,630.8	2,666.9	2,702.5	2,713.1	2,724.1	2,673.1	2,684.3	2,717.9	2,730.2	2,730.2	2,730.9	2,694.5
2005	2,656.0	2,671.5	2,703.3	2,749.3	2,758.2	2,764.0	2,721.5	2,735.7	2,761.0	2,763.2	2,768.9	2,771.5	2,735.3
2006	2,706.5	2,722.9	2,755.6	2,784.7	2,798.2	2,804.6	2,751.6	2,760.9	2,793.4	2,797.3	2,805.4	2,809.4	2,774.2
2007	2,729.0	2,741.7	2,785.3	2,804.4	2,825.6	2,826.1	2,771.7	2,788.9	2,817.4	2,819.1	2,822.9	2,815.3	2,795.6
Total Private													
2000	2,265.6	2,267.4	2,294.5	2,325.0	2,336.2	2,355.5	2,336.2	2,340.1	2,338.6	2,342.4	2,338.6	2,330.9	2,322.6
2001	2,260.2	2,265.4	2,290.2	2,314.3	2,327.4	2,341.0	2,317.3	2,324.5	2,305.8	2,293.7	2,292.5	2,287.9	2,301.7
2002	2,224.6	2,228.1	2,250.0	2,264.7	2,277.2	2,294.2	2,271.2	2,287.0	2,287.6	2,275.9	2,277.3	2,275.9	2,267.8
2003	2,203.0	2,200.5	2,221.4	2,242.8	2,255.0	2,269.0	2,265.0	2,273.0	2,263.0	2,266.2	2,260.2	2,260.4	2,248.3
2004	2,198.3	2,193.4	2,226.1	2,260.4	2,273.6	2,294.8	2,282.5	2,291.6	2,285.8	2,292.4	2,289.9	2,292.0	2,265.1
2005	2,228.2	2,235.0	2,264.3	2,309.0	2,318.9	2,335.1	2,324.9	2,335.0	2,331.5	2,327.3	2,329.7	2,331.9	2,305.9
2006	2,274.8	2,281.4	2,311.0	2,339.8	2,352.2	2,373.7	2,356.0	2,361.9	2,357.4	2,353.9	2,358.8	2,363.2	2,340.3
2007	2,292.4	2,295.3	2,336.2	2,353.8	2,373.1	2,387.8	2,371.8	2,383.2	2,373.9	2,369.6	2,371.0	2,363.6	2,356.0
Goods-Producing													
2000	501.8	500.9	505.3	509.6	513.7	520.5	510.0	511.4	508.3	512.7	509.6	503.9	509.0
2001	488.3	489.9	494.7	499.1	500.8	502.8	488.5	495.2	489.2	481.0	480.7	477.2	490.6
2002	461.9	462.5	465.8	464.5	465.6	470.8	458.1	471.2	469.8	465.5	462.9	461.2	465.0
2003	447.8	444.8	448.9	451.1	454.5	458.6	452.4	459.3	456.3	457.9	454.8	452.1	453.2
2004	439.9	435.9	445.7	453.2	456.0	462.4	453.6	462.8	460.3	458.0	455.6	454.4	453.2
2005	440.0	441.4	448.6	457.5	461.4	465.6	456.0	466.0	464.0	463.6	462.2	460.5	457.2
2006	449.7	451.0	457.6	462.0	463.4	470.3	464.1	465.4	462.5	459.8	458.8	457.4	460.2
2007	443.4	440.4	451.7	453.5	458.3	462.1	455.2	459.7	457.2	454.3	453.1	447.6	453.0
Natural Resources and Mining													
2000	5.5	5.5	5.6	6.0	6.0	6.0	5.5	5.5	5.4	5.4	5.3	5.1	5.6
2001	4.8	4.9	5.0	5.2	5.1	5.2	5.1	5.2	5.0	4.8	4.7	4.6	5.0
2002	4.5	4.5	4.5	4.5	4.6	4.7	4.7	4.7	4.7	4.6	4.6	4.5	4.6
2003	4.4	4.4	4.4	4.5	4.6	4.7	4.6	4.7	4.6	4.6	4.5	4.5	4.5
2004	4.6	4.5	4.6	4.8	4.8	4.9	5.0	5.0	5.0	4.9	4.8	4.7	4.8
2005	4.9	4.9	5.1	5.3	5.4	5.5	5.5	5.5	5.4	5.4	5.4	5.4	5.3
2006	5.3	5.3	5.4	5.4	5.5	5.6	5.6	5.5	5.5	5.4	5.3	5.2	5.4
2007	5.1	5.0	5.2	5.2	5.3	5.5	5.9	6.3	6.3	6.3	6.2	6.1	5.7
Construction													
2000	129.0	128.6	133.0	136.8	139.7	144.2	143.7	144.9	144.1	142.9	140.1	135.1	138.5
2001	128.2	129.2	134.8	140.6	144.0	149.0	148.1	148.1	144.7	143.0	141.1	138.3	140.8
2002	129.8	129.0	132.1	131.8	134.0	138.9	141.7	141.0	138.8	137.4	135.1	133.8	135.3
2003	125.3	123.1	126.4	131.7	134.9	138.5	141.2	141.0	139.1	139.4	136.6	133.3	134.2
2004	126.2	122.3	130.3	136.5	139.0	142.7	145.2	144.2	142.3	141.3	139.1	137.7	137.2
2005	126.5	127.6	133.9	142.0	145.6	148.6	150.9	151.1	149.9	148.8	147.0	144.8	143.1
2006	139.1	139.5	143.6	147.8	149.2	153.9	153.6	153.4	151.1	149.3	146.9	145.1	147.7
2007	138.2	133.1	143.4	146.1	150.4	154.8	154.7	154.8	151.9	151.7	149.1	144.2	147.7
Manufacturing													
2000	367.3	366.8	366.7	366.8	368.0	370.3	360.8	361.0	358.8	364.4	364.2	363.7	364.9
2001	355.3	355.8	354.9	353.3	351.7	348.6	335.3	341.9	339.5	333.2	334.9	334.3	344.9
2002	327.6	329.0	329.2	328.2	327.0	327.2	311.7	325.5	326.3	323.5	323.2	322.9	325.1
2003	318.1	317.3	318.1	314.9	315.0	315.4	306.6	313.6	312.6	313.9	313.7	314.3	314.5
2004	309.1	309.1	310.8	311.9	312.2	314.8	303.4	313.6	313.0	311.8	311.7	312.0	311.1
2005	308.6	308.9	309.6	310.2	310.4	311.5	299.6	309.4	308.7	309.4	309.8	310.3	308.9
2006	305.3	306.2	308.6	308.8	308.7	310.8	304.9	306.5	305.9	305.1	306.6	307.1	307.0
2007	300.1	302.3	303.1	302.2	302.6	301.8	294.6	298.6	299.0	296.3	297.8	297.3	299.6
Service-Providing													
2000	2,189.3	2,200.2	2,229.7	2,248.9	2,260.6	2,265.5	2,219.8	2,222.0	2,254.8	2,259.1	2,264.9	2,262.3	2,239.8
2001	2,200.0	2,210.9	2,232.4	2,252.6	2,265.1	2,272.3	2,219.9	2,221.8	2,249.0	2,249.3	2,251.2	2,253.2	2,239.8
2002	2,198.6	2,204.7	2,224.9	2,241.2	2,254.6	2,257.1	2,203.0	2,206.4	2,249.3	2,250.6	2,257.6	2,258.8	2,233.9
2003	2,192.6	2,198.3	2,215.9	2,238.9	2,249.0	2,251.0	2,202.2	2,203.3	2,238.7	2,246.3	2,244.3	2,246.4	2,227.2
2004	2,189.7	2,194.9	2,221.2	2,249.3	2,257.1	2,261.7	2,219.5	2,221.5	2,257.6	2,272.2	2,274.6	2,276.5	2,241.3
2005	2,216.0	2,230.1	2,254.7	2,291.8	2,296.8	2,298.4	2,265.5	2,269.7	2,297.0	2,299.6	2,306.7	2,311.0	2,278.1
2006	2,256.8	2,271.9	2,298.0	2,322.7	2,334.8	2,334.3	2,287.5	2,295.5	2,330.9	2,337.5	2,346.6	2,352.0	2,314.0
2007	2,285.6	2,301.3	2,333.6	2,350.9	2,367.3	2,364.0	2,316.5	2,329.2	2,360.2	2,364.8	2,369.8	2,367.7	2,342.6
Trade, Transportation, and Utilities													
2000	550.9	548.0	552.9	555.0	557.1	556.2	553.7	553.4	558.9	561.6	571.0	576.8	558.0
2001	544.1	538.8	541.3	542.4	544.6	545.7	541.8	541.5	542.7	544.8	553.4	556.2	544.8
2002	535.9	530.9	535.1	533.6	537.9	539.1	537.6	537.1	542.3	540.7	549.8	554.0	539.5
2003	529.4	524.8	527.6	528.8	530.7	530.4	529.1	530.1	530.4	538.0	543.8	547.3	532.5
2004	525.1	519.7	524.7	527.6	531.6	533.2	530.0	530.1	532.2	537.2	545.8	551.0	532.4
2005	530.4	526.0	531.2	538.0	540.8	541.5	540.4	541.2	541.0	542.8	551.9	556.3	540.1
2006	538.3	534.1	538.8	541.2	544.4	545.7	541.3	543.3	544.7	547.1	555.6	561.0	544.6
2007	542.1	538.4	546.0	546.7	550.6	550.4	546.0	546.2	548.1	550.2	558.6	563.1	548.9
Wholesale Trade													
2000	120.5	121.1	122.1	121.6	121.6	122.2	121.6	121.3	122.1	122.1	122.6	123.2	121.8
2001	120.8	121.0	121.2	121.1	121.1	121.6	121.1	120.6	120.3	119.6	118.9	119.2	120.5
2002	119.3	119.2	119.8	119.4	119.5	120.2	120.4	119.4	119.5	118.8	118.8	118.7	119.4
2003	117.8	117.9	118.1	118.4	118.6	118.9	119.1	119.2	118.2	118.3	118.4	118.6	118.5
2004	117.7	117.6	118.6	119.6	119.8	121.2	120.9	120.1	121.0	120.4	120.4	121.1	119.9
2005	121.7	120.9	121.5	121.6	121.7	122.6	122.5	122.4	121.3	120.9	121.3	121.8	121.7
2006	120.7	120.5	121.5	122.3	123.0	124.0	123.1	123.4	123.3	123.5	123.8	124.8	122.8
2007	123.0	123.7	124.8	124.6	125.0	126.0	125.6	125.6	125.3	125.1	125.5	126.2	125.0

Employment by Industry: Missouri, 2000–2007—*Continued*

(Numbers in thousands, not seasonally adjusted.)

Industry and year	January	February	March	April	May	June	July	August	September	October	November	December	Annual Average
Retail Trade													
2000	310.0	306.0	309.1	310.9	312.4	312.6	310.9	310.8	312.5	314.9	324.2	329.8	313.7
2001	310.6	305.1	306.7	308.0	310.0	311.9	308.9	308.4	309.3	312.3	321.5	325.0	311.5
2002	308.6	304.1	307.3	306.0	309.2	310.8	308.5	308.8	312.9	311.5	320.9	326.4	311.3
2003	305.3	300.7	303.7	305.3	307.3	308.0	307.2	308.6	309.1	315.8	322.6	326.1	310.0
2004	306.7	301.4	304.6	305.8	309.1	310.7	308.9	308.8	308.9	313.6	322.0	326.1	310.6
2005	309.2	305.7	309.5	313.8	316.0	316.3	316.8	316.4	315.3	317.5	325.8	328.7	315.9
2006	313.3	309.3	312.7	314.1	316.0	316.7	314.5	314.6	314.4	316.8	324.8	328.0	316.3
2007	312.9	308.6	314.0	315.4	318.0	318.4	315.5	314.3	314.5	316.9	324.7	327.7	316.7
Transportation and Utilities													
2000	120.3	120.7	121.7	122.4	123.0	121.2	120.9	121.0	123.9	124.6	124.2	123.8	122.3
2001	112.7	112.7	113.4	113.3	113.5	112.2	111.8	112.5	113.1	112.9	113.0	112.0	112.8
2002	108.0	107.6	108.0	108.2	109.2	108.3	109.0	109.2	110.1	110.4	110.1	108.9	108.9
2003	106.3	106.2	105.8	105.1	104.8	103.5	102.8	102.3	103.1	103.9	102.8	102.6	104.1
2004	100.7	100.7	101.5	102.2	102.7	101.3	100.2	101.2	102.3	103.2	103.4	103.8	101.9
2005	99.5	99.4	100.2	102.6	103.1	102.6	101.1	102.4	104.4	104.4	104.8	105.8	102.5
2006	104.3	104.3	104.6	104.8	105.4	105.0	103.7	105.3	107.0	106.8	107.0	108.2	105.5
2007	106.2	106.1	107.2	106.7	107.6	106.0	104.9	106.3	108.3	108.2	108.4	109.2	107.1
Information													
2000	77.0	76.9	76.8	76.8	76.6	76.6	76.3	76.2	76.0	75.9	75.9	75.7	76.4
2001	74.8	75.3	75.6	75.1	74.9	75.4	74.9	74.6	74.1	73.1	73.1	71.9	74.4
2002	72.8	72.8	72.4	70.9	71.1	71.1	69.2	69.1	68.7	66.9	67.4	67.6	70.0
2003	68.0	68.5	68.6	67.1	66.6	67.0	66.0	65.5	65.0	64.5	64.6	65.0	66.4
2004	65.1	65.2	65.3	64.8	64.6	64.7	63.9	63.2	62.8	63.6	64.1	63.6	64.2
2005	62.8	62.9	63.2	64.2	64.3	64.5	64.4	64.0	63.8	63.9	64.0	63.8	63.8
2006	63.0	63.0	63.2	62.9	63.0	63.4	62.9	62.8	62.8	62.7	63.1	63.5	63.0
2007	62.2	62.4	62.9	62.6	63.1	63.7	63.4	63.6	63.7	64.0	64.3	64.3	63.4
Financial Activities													
2000	155.3	155.6	156.4	157.8	158.0	159.9	160.2	159.8	158.8	159.3	159.7	160.6	158.5
2001	158.2	158.3	159.0	159.8	161.0	162.4	162.4	162.3	160.6	159.6	159.7	160.2	160.3
2002	158.5	158.4	160.7	160.3	160.8	161.5	161.3	161.6	160.8	160.8	161.1	162.0	160.7
2003	160.5	160.4	160.8	161.8	162.5	163.9	165.4	165.7	164.1	163.4	162.7	162.9	162.8
2004	160.1	159.8	160.4	161.8	162.2	164.1	164.5	164.8	163.1	163.2	162.7	163.1	162.5
2005	160.8	161.6	162.2	162.7	162.7	164.1	165.4	165.0	164.3	163.9	163.9	164.3	163.4
2006	162.1	162.5	163.3	164.5	165.6	167.0	166.9	167.2	166.4	165.1	165.0	165.6	165.1
2007	164.5	164.9	165.6	166.2	166.9	168.2	169.8	169.4	168.4	167.7	167.5	167.1	167.2
Professional and Business Services													
2000	307.9	309.1	313.8	319.6	317.6	323.7	320.5	321.6	320.5	318.3	317.3	315.0	317.1
2001	312.8	314.8	318.3	318.9	317.1	318.7	313.7	315.1	311.8	310.1	307.8	308.7	314.0
2002	299.4	302.5	304.7	306.3	304.8	305.9	303.7	305.2	305.5	307.0	307.5	306.7	304.9
2003	296.5	297.0	299.7	301.2	299.9	302.4	301.4	303.2	303.2	303.2	301.4	302.8	301.0
2004	296.5	296.8	302.4	306.5	305.3	310.5	310.0	311.7	310.8	312.3	311.8	313.6	307.4
2005	309.4	311.9	316.0	321.8	319.2	322.8	323.2	323.1	324.7	323.5	324.1	325.4	320.4
2006	318.7	322.2	327.2	331.6	330.5	335.4	332.7	334.4	334.2	336.6	336.8	339.1	331.6
2007	327.6	328.9	334.8	337.6	337.5	341.2	340.3	343.2	340.8	341.1	340.1	339.6	337.7
Education and Health Services													
2000	328.5	331.4	332.7	335.2	333.7	332.5	332.1	332.1	336.0	337.2	338.2	338.0	334.0
2001	336.4	339.1	340.8	342.8	342.9	342.7	342.8	343.0	345.2	346.7	348.3	348.4	343.3
2002	345.6	348.4	348.8	349.7	350.5	349.8	348.1	348.7	353.4	352.8	354.1	354.4	350.4
2003	349.7	352.0	353.1	353.2	352.3	351.3	352.2	352.1	354.8	355.5	356.1	356.7	353.3
2004	352.2	355.9	356.9	358.1	358.0	357.2	357.4	357.1	360.4	363.5	363.8	364.2	358.7
2005	359.6	363.1	364.4	368.7	368.1	367.2	367.2	367.4	371.7	374.6	375.4	376.2	368.6
2006	369.6	374.0	375.3	377.2	377.0	375.5	373.9	374.1	379.6	382.1	384.9	384.1	377.3
2007	376.3	381.2	383.2	384.2	384.2	382.5	381.7	382.7	386.6	388.2	388.7	388.0	384.0
Leisure and Hospitality													
2000	231.3	232.1	242.1	256.0	264.1	270.1	267.8	269.7	263.9	261.0	250.6	244.2	254.4
2001	230.2	233.3	243.0	258.0	267.0	272.8	273.7	273.3	264.0	260.8	251.8	247.5	256.3
2002	234.9	236.5	245.6	261.8	268.6	276.8	274.9	276.0	269.4	264.6	257.2	252.7	259.9
2003	235.5	237.0	245.8	262.1	270.6	276.4	277.6	276.7	270.4	265.0	258.5	255.0	260.9
2004	242.6	243.0	252.5	268.7	276.1	281.7	282.1	281.3	276.0	274.2	266.3	262.6	267.3
2005	247.2	249.7	259.9	276.2	282.6	288.3	287.6	288.0	282.5	276.0	269.8	266.2	272.8
2006	254.3	256.5	266.6	280.2	288.0	294.6	292.9	293.8	286.9	280.4	274.4	272.2	278.4
2007	257.7	260.1	271.7	282.5	291.3	297.8	293.7	297.0	288.6	283.7	278.5	273.9	281.4
Other Services													
2000	112.9	113.4	114.5	115.0	115.4	116.0	115.6	115.9	116.2	116.4	116.3	116.7	115.4
2001	115.4	115.9	117.5	118.2	119.1	120.5	119.5	119.5	118.2	117.6	117.7	117.8	118.1
2002	115.6	116.1	116.9	117.6	117.9	119.2	118.3	118.1	117.7	117.6	117.3	117.3	117.5
2003	115.6	116.0	116.9	117.5	117.9	119.0	120.9	120.4	118.8	118.7	118.3	118.6	118.2
2004	116.8	117.1	118.2	119.7	119.8	121.0	121.0	120.6	120.2	120.4	119.8	119.5	119.5
2005	118.0	118.4	118.8	119.9	119.8	121.1	120.7	120.3	119.5	119.0	118.5	119.0	119.4
2006	119.1	118.1	119.0	120.2	120.3	121.8	121.3	120.9	120.3	120.1	120.2	120.3	120.1
2007	118.6	119.0	120.3	120.5	121.2	121.9	121.7	121.4	120.5	120.4	120.2	120.0	120.5
Government													
2000	425.5	433.7	440.5	433.5	438.1	430.5	393.6	393.3	424.5	429.4	435.9	435.3	426.2
2001	428.1	435.4	436.9	437.4	438.5	434.1	391.1	392.5	432.4	436.6	439.4	442.5	428.7
2002	435.9	439.1	440.7	441.0	443.0	433.7	389.9	390.6	431.5	440.2	443.2	444.1	431.1
2003	437.4	442.6	443.4	447.2	448.5	440.6	389.6	389.6	432.0	438.0	438.9	438.1	432.2
2004	431.3	437.4	440.8	442.1	439.5	429.3	390.6	392.7	432.1	437.8	440.3	438.9	429.4
2005	427.8	436.5	439.0	440.3	439.3	428.9	396.6	400.7	429.5	435.9	439.2	439.6	429.4
2006	431.7	441.5	444.6	444.9	446.0	430.9	395.6	399.0	436.0	443.4	446.6	446.2	433.9
2007	436.6	446.4	449.1	450.6	452.5	438.3	399.9	405.7	443.5	449.5	451.9	451.7	439.6

Average Weekly Hours by Selected Industry: Missouri, 2001–2007
(Not seasonally adjusted.)

Industry and year	January	February	March	April	May	June	July	August	September	October	November	December	Annual Average
Construction													
2001	36.2	33.3	35.2	35.0	36.4	37.8	36.2	37.6	38.0	35.2	34.0	34.1	35.8
2002	35.4	34.5	35.7	35.0	33.4	34.5	34.9	34.5	36.3	36.0	34.1	35.2	35.0
2003	34.2	34.0	36.6	36.8	37.1	37.3	38.6	38.6	36.1	36.1	34.8	33.7	36.2
2004	36.6	36.6	37.8	37.7	35.0	36.3	37.0	38.2	37.9	32.9	33.9	37.3	36.4
2005	32.0	34.2	35.5	35.7	36.7	37.1	37.6	36.3	35.9	37.9	34.4	35.9	35.9
2006	34.7	35.2	36.0	37.2	35.9	37.8	35.2	36.7	35.5	36.7	35.3	35.0	36.0
2007	34.7	33.1	37.5	36.1	37.5	38.9	37.8	38.5	38.4	37.6	37.3	37.9	37.2
Manufacturing													
2001	40.0	40.0	39.9	39.0	40.6	40.1	38.7	40.5	41.4	40.6	40.9	41.2	40.3
2002	40.3	40.3	40.1	40.5	40.3	39.6	38.3	38.2	37.9	36.2	39.0	40.2	39.3
2003	40.4	41.4	41.1	38.9	39.3	40.5	40.0	40.8	40.9	41.1	41.0	40.7	40.5
2004	39.3	39.5	38.9	40.4	40.7	40.7	40.6	40.6	40.5	40.1	40.3	41.0	40.2
2005	39.4	39.4	40.7	40.1	39.4	39.8	38.9	39.7	40.3	38.7	38.5	39.8	39.6
2006	37.8	37.3	38.2	39.0	39.8	39.7	38.6	40.5	41.0	40.2	39.9	39.4	39.3
2007	39.2	40.3	40.2	40.4	40.6	41.8	40.0	41.2	40.4	39.9	40.0	40.1	40.3
Wholesale Trade													
2001	39.8	40.6	40.6	40.7	40.2	39.9	40.0	40.4	40.7	39.5	40.4	40.8	40.3
2002	39.0	39.5	40.8	40.3	41.6	41.2	40.1	41.6	41.2	39.4	38.5	39.7	40.2
2003	37.9	39.3	39.1	39.4	38.4	39.5	39.6	40.4	40.0	41.7	40.0	39.6
2004	39.6	38.8	36.3	37.5	38.1	37.9	37.9	39.0	38.2	38.2	36.3	38.0	38.0
2005	39.5	38.9	38.5	40.4	39.6	37.9	37.6	38.1	38.3	39.5	36.9	37.0	38.5
2006	38.9	38.3	38.8	38.6	36.2	38.1	39.0	39.6	38.8	38.1	37.2	36.5	38.2
2007	36.8	37.1	37.6	37.7	36.8	36.8	37.2	37.0	37.1	36.9	37.3	37.4	37.1
Retail Trade													
2001	29.7	29.2	29.8	29.8	30.0	30.6	30.9	30.1	30.3	34.1	33.7	35.0	31.1
2002	37.2	33.6	34.5	34.5	34.2	35.6	35.5	34.3	34.2	32.8	32.7	33.2	34.3
2003	31.1	31.8	31.7	31.6	32.0	32.7	32.8	32.8	32.7	32.3	31.6	32.4	32.1
2004	31.2	32.0	31.7	31.9	32.1	32.4	32.5	32.6	33.2	32.2	32.6	33.1	32.3
2005	31.8	32.3	32.0	32.7	32.4	32.3	32.5	32.4	33.3	32.1	33.1	32.9	32.5
2006	31.7	31.5	32.0	31.8	32.0	32.3	32.4	32.1	33.2	32.5	32.8	32.3	32.2
2007	30.5	31.1	31.5	31.0	31.3	31.7	31.7	31.4	32.4	31.8	32.0	31.2	31.5
Information													
2003	39.0	39.6	38.5	38.6	40.0	39.9	39.4	39.2	38.3	37.3	38.4	37.1	38.8
2004	37.2	37.3	36.6	37.6	38.9	39.6	38.6	39.4	39.3	39.4	39.0	39.4	38.5
2005	40.2	38.9	38.4	37.7	38.4	38.0	37.2	37.5	39.1	39.8	38.3	38.3	38.5
2006	38.3	37.2	38.0	37.5	37.3	37.0	36.2	38.1	37.9	38.5	38.1	38.1	37.7
2007	38.3	37.7	36.9	38.4	36.9	36.3	35.7	36.8	37.1	36.8	36.9	36.9	37.1
Financial Activities													
2001	36.8	35.8	35.5	38.4	35.6	35.9	38.2	36.9	36.3	37.0	36.3	37.6	36.7
2002	38.8	37.2	36.8	37.7	36.1	37.9	37.4	37.7	37.8	37.2	37.4	37.8	37.5
2003	37.1	38.1	38.2	37.0	37.0	38.6	37.5	36.7	36.5	36.2	36.6	35.6	37.1
2004	35.6	35.8	35.1	35.6	35.2	34.3	34.6	35.2	34.8	36.2	36.1	36.5	35.4
2005	36.8	36.8	36.2	36.4	37.0	35.5	35.5	35.2	37.5	38.0	36.6	36.0	36.5
2006	36.7	36.8	36.4	37.0	35.5	38.1	37.6	37.8	37.2	37.2	36.8	37.8	37.1
2007	37.6	37.3	36.7	37.5	36.6	38.4	36.9	36.3	36.8	36.7	36.7	37.0	37.0

Average Hourly Earnings by Selected Industry: Missouri, 2001–2007

(Dollars, not seasonally adjusted.)

Industry and year	January	February	March	April	May	June	July	August	September	October	November	December	Annual Average
Construction													
2001	22.42	22.04	22.28	22.01	22.12	22.78	22.97	22.65	22.17	22.70	22.41	22.65	22.45
2002	22.18	22.21	22.26	22.86	22.06	22.84	23.15	23.01	23.14	22.94	22.66	22.95	22.70
2003	22.26	21.84	21.87	22.09	22.40	22.55	22.96	22.57	21.99	21.94	22.75	22.39	22.32
2004	22.04	22.06	22.21	21.80	22.32	22.24	21.96	22.00	21.63	22.79	22.39	22.14	22.12
2005	22.08	22.45	21.88	21.59	21.94	22.08	21.56	21.69	21.91	21.88	21.93	21.69	21.88
2006	21.67	21.90	21.66	21.56	21.71	21.47	21.45	21.53	21.89	21.62	21.67	21.35	21.62
2007	21.83	22.14	21.99	21.90	22.31	21.99	21.86	22.06	22.09	22.28	22.09	22.37	22.08
Manufacturing													
2001	15.44	15.68	15.97	16.23	16.14	15.72	15.69	16.53	16.56	16.14	16.61	16.56	16.11
2002	16.71	16.50	16.62	17.09	16.99	17.06	16.16	15.92	15.93	16.56	17.95	18.07	16.80
2003	18.50	18.43	18.16	18.03	18.11	18.42	17.68	18.26	18.14	18.20	18.26	18.39	18.22
2004	18.12	18.37	18.07	18.05	17.93	17.91	17.26	17.85	18.07	17.95	17.63	17.93	17.92
2005	17.51	17.67	17.89	17.69	17.53	17.56	16.40	17.08	17.71	17.43	17.29	17.19	17.42
2006	17.20	17.17	17.29	17.13	17.06	16.98	16.47	17.34	17.35	17.23	17.41	17.30	17.16
2007	16.30	16.80	16.89	16.64	16.95	16.86	16.40	17.37	17.54	17.08	17.41	17.74	17.00
Wholesale Trade													
2001	15.88	17.84	17.87	18.84	19.43	18.67	20.28	20.89	20.94	19.73	18.07	17.49	18.83
2002	17.59	17.66	18.24	18.55	18.47	16.34	18.06	17.89	17.94	18.45	18.42	17.73	17.94
2003	18.66	18.10	17.39	18.06	18.16	19.20	20.61	19.84	20.08	17.82	18.75	18.62	18.78
2004	19.09	19.06	18.00	17.99	17.62	17.80	18.39	17.94	18.62	19.22	18.45	17.54	18.31
2005	18.07	18.35	18.44	18.05	17.81	18.27	19.29	19.17	19.06	18.93	19.77	19.73	18.73
2006	19.62	19.82	19.89	19.54	19.87	19.66	19.62	18.29	18.51	19.05	19.34	19.68	19.40
2007	19.75	19.40	19.70	19.69	20.69	20.55	20.60	20.92	21.27	21.08	20.81	21.05	20.46
Retail Trade													
2001	9.75	9.76	9.69	9.91	9.88	9.92	10.04	9.99	10.00	11.06	11.10	11.01	10.21
2002	12.20	13.70	14.24	13.52	13.50	13.69	13.31	13.26	13.06	12.87	12.85	11.81	13.16
2003	11.20	11.81	11.86	11.73	11.55	11.41	11.33	11.24	11.13	11.05	10.81	10.68	11.31
2004	10.87	10.95	10.86	10.84	10.87	10.90	11.07	11.15	11.28	11.34	11.63	11.60	11.12
2005	11.43	11.77	11.33	11.52	11.58	11.67	11.83	11.90	11.69	11.53	11.39	11.44	11.59
2006	11.68	11.45	11.71	11.62	11.44	11.63	11.64	12.10	11.75	11.89	11.54	11.59	11.67
2007	11.80	11.99	11.57	11.66	11.77	11.66	11.56	11.56	11.51	11.46	11.39	11.01	11.57
Information													
2003	20.94	22.47	20.42	20.42	21.43	22.58	22.90	22.39	22.36	20.34	21.03	20.74	21.52
2004	20.30	18.74	18.95	18.32	18.81	18.77	18.76	18.82	18.61	18.57	19.85	20.20	19.05
2005	19.79	18.28	19.68	19.69	18.53	19.07	19.10	19.23	19.18	19.18	19.17	19.78	19.22
2006	19.64	19.58	19.74	19.70	19.53	19.97	19.35	19.52	19.56	19.82	19.49	19.44	19.61
2007	19.41	19.57	19.55	19.98	19.86	19.05	19.28	18.83	19.16	18.90	18.33	18.55	19.21
Financial Activities													
2001	13.00	13.94	13.24	12.77	13.32	13.05	12.76	12.45	12.75	12.82	13.20	13.29	13.04
2002	12.91	13.49	13.49	13.70	13.72	13.36	13.45	13.63	13.69	13.76	13.79	14.02	13.59
2003	13.56	13.62	13.54	13.97	14.16	13.86	14.07	14.07	14.42	14.37	14.44	14.47	14.04
2004	14.58	15.08	15.19	15.36	15.45	15.52	15.97	16.05	16.34	16.20	16.49	16.47	15.73
2005	16.55	16.82	17.04	17.24	16.67	17.01	17.18	17.42	17.95	18.36	18.11	18.48	17.41
2006	18.45	18.56	18.30	18.32	17.94	18.13	17.76	17.69	17.53	17.81	17.85	17.43	17.97
2007	17.58	17.69	17.57	18.24	17.07	17.56	17.11	16.82	16.59	16.43	16.82	16.84	17.19

Average Weekly Earnings by Selected Industry: Missouri, 2001–2007

(Dollars, not seasonally adjusted.)

Industry and year	January	February	March	April	May	June	July	August	September	October	November	December	Annual Average
Construction													
2001	811.60	733.93	784.26	770.35	805.17	861.08	831.51	851.64	842.46	799.04	761.94	772.37	803.71
2002	785.17	766.25	794.68	800.10	736.80	787.98	807.94	793.85	839.98	825.84	772.71	807.84	794.50
2003	761.29	742.56	800.44	812.91	831.04	841.12	886.26	871.20	793.84	792.03	791.70	754.54	807.98
2004	806.66	807.40	839.54	821.86	781.20	807.31	812.52	840.40	819.78	749.79	759.02	825.82	805.17
2005	706.56	767.79	776.74	770.76	805.20	819.17	810.66	787.35	786.57	829.25	754.39	778.67	785.49
2006	751.95	770.88	779.76	802.03	779.39	811.57	755.04	790.15	777.10	793.45	764.95	747.25	778.32
2007	757.50	732.83	824.63	790.59	836.63	855.41	826.31	849.31	848.26	837.73	823.96	847.82	821.38
Manufacturing													
2001	617.60	627.20	637.20	632.97	655.28	630.37	607.20	669.47	685.58	655.28	679.35	682.27	649.23
2002	673.41	664.95	666.46	692.15	684.70	675.58	618.93	608.14	603.75	599.47	700.05	726.41	660.24
2003	747.40	763.00	746.38	701.37	711.72	746.01	707.20	745.01	741.93	748.02	748.66	748.47	737.91
2004	712.12	725.62	702.92	729.22	729.75	728.94	700.76	724.71	731.84	719.80	710.49	735.13	720.38
2005	689.89	696.20	728.12	709.37	690.68	698.89	637.96	678.08	713.71	674.54	665.67	684.16	689.83
2006	650.16	640.44	660.48	668.07	678.99	674.11	635.74	702.27	711.35	692.65	694.66	681.62	674.39
2007	638.96	677.04	678.98	672.26	688.17	704.75	656.00	715.64	708.62	681.49	696.40	711.37	685.10
Wholesale Trade													
2001	632.02	724.30	725.52	766.79	781.09	744.93	811.20	843.96	852.26	779.34	730.03	713.59	758.85
2002	686.01	697.57	744.19	747.57	768.35	673.21	724.21	744.22	739.13	726.93	709.17	703.88	721.19
2003	707.21	711.33	679.95	711.56	697.34	758.40	816.16	801.54	803.20	712.80	781.88	744.80	743.69
2004	755.96	739.53	653.40	674.63	671.32	674.62	696.98	699.66	711.28	734.20	669.74	666.52	695.78
2005	713.77	713.82	709.94	729.22	705.28	692.43	725.30	730.38	730.00	747.74	729.51	730.01	721.11
2006	763.22	759.11	771.73	754.24	719.29	749.05	765.18	724.28	718.19	725.81	719.45	718.32	741.08
2007	726.80	719.74	740.72	742.31	761.39	756.24	766.32	774.04	789.12	777.85	776.21	787.27	759.07
Retail Trade													
2001	289.58	284.99	288.76	295.32	296.40	303.55	310.24	300.70	303.00	377.15	374.07	385.35	317.53
2002	453.84	460.32	491.28	466.44	461.70	487.36	472.51	454.82	446.65	422.14	420.20	392.09	451.39
2003	348.32	375.56	375.96	370.67	369.60	373.11	371.62	368.67	363.95	356.92	341.60	346.03	363.05
2004	339.14	350.40	344.26	345.80	348.93	353.16	359.78	363.49	374.50	365.15	379.14	383.96	359.18
2005	363.47	380.17	362.56	376.70	375.19	376.94	384.48	385.56	389.28	370.11	377.01	376.38	376.68
2006	370.26	360.68	374.72	369.52	366.08	375.65	377.14	388.41	390.10	386.43	378.51	374.36	375.77
2007	359.90	372.89	364.46	361.46	368.40	369.62	366.45	362.98	372.92	364.43	364.48	343.51	364.46
Information													
2003	816.66	889.81	786.17	788.21	857.20	900.94	902.26	877.69	856.39	758.68	807.55	769.45	834.98
2004	755.16	699.00	693.57	688.83	731.71	743.29	724.14	741.51	731.37	731.66	774.15	795.88	733.43
2005	795.56	711.09	755.71	742.31	711.55	724.66	710.52	721.13	749.94	763.36	734.21	757.57	739.97
2006	752.21	728.38	750.12	738.75	728.47	738.89	700.47	743.71	741.32	763.07	742.57	740.66	739.30
2007	743.40	737.79	721.40	767.23	732.83	691.52	688.30	692.94	710.84	695.52	676.38	684.50	712.69
Financial Activities													
2001	478.40	499.05	470.02	490.37	474.19	468.50	487.43	459.41	462.83	474.34	479.16	499.70	478.57
2002	500.91	501.83	496.43	516.49	495.29	506.34	503.03	513.85	517.48	511.87	515.75	529.96	509.63
2003	503.08	518.92	517.23	516.89	523.92	535.00	527.63	516.37	526.33	520.19	528.50	515.13	520.88
2004	519.05	539.86	533.17	546.82	532.34	552.56	564.96	568.63	586.44	595.29	601.16	665.28	556.84
2005	609.04	618.98	616.85	627.54	616.79	603.86	609.89	613.18	673.13	697.68	662.83	656.88	635.47
2006	677.12	683.01	666.12	677.84	636.87	690.75	667.78	668.68	652.12	662.53	656.88	658.85	666.69
2007	661.01	659.84	644.82	684.00	624.76	674.30	631.36	610.57	610.51	602.98	617.29	623.08	636.03

Population
    2000 census: 902,195
    2007 estimate: 957,861
    Percent change, 2000–2007: 6.2%

Percent change in total nonfarm employment, 2000–2007: 13.2%

Industry with the largest growth in employment, 2000–2007 (thousands)
    Construction, 12.1

Industry with the largest decline in employment, 2000–2007 (thousands)
    Manufacturing, -2.1

Civilian labor force
    2000: 468,865
    2007: 501,349

Employment-population ratio
    2000: 65.0%
    2007: 64.8%

Unemployment rate and rank among states
    2000: 4.8%, 42nd
    2007: 3.1%, 8th

Employment by Industry, 2007

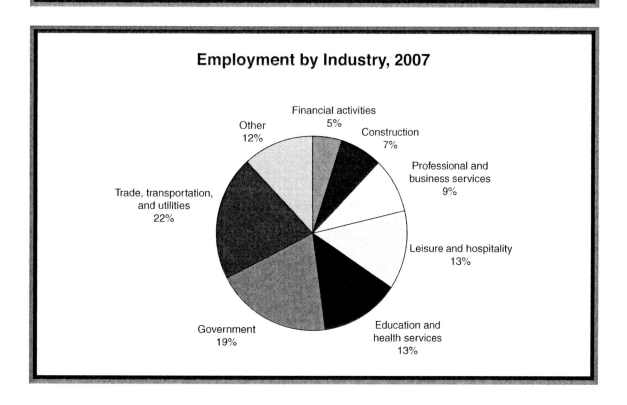

125

Employment by Industry: Montana, 2000–2007

(Numbers in thousands, not seasonally adjusted.)

Industry and year	January	February	March	April	May	June	July	August	September	October	November	December	Annual Average
Total Nonfarm													
2000	376.5	378.4	385.5	387.4	396.2	398.8	395.7	398.3	399.9	395.2	393.6	390.5	391.3
2001	379.8	381.1	385.1	388.0	396.1	400.6	395.3	397.3	397.4	395.3	392.7	391.1	391.7
2002	381.7	383.3	385.6	390.7	398.9	404.7	400.4	402.0	404.1	401.5	399.7	399.7	396.0
2003	386.4	388.7	390.4	397.1	404.1	407.1	404.5	407.7	408.3	407.1	403.6	403.9	400.7
2004	390.5	394.3	399.4	409.1	414.4	421.3	419.0	418.4	419.2	417.7	416.2	416.6	411.3
2005	400.7	405.9	410.6	414.7	421.3	428.4	428.2	428.5	429.7	428.8	427.6	426.8	420.9
2006	414.6	419.1	423.9	429.7	437.6	447.2	446.6	443.0	440.6	439.2	437.7	439.2	432.5
2007	427.0	430.2	436.4	440.0	447.8	454.1	454.7	455.4	450.5	449.2	447.8	447.6	443.0
Total Private													
2000	294.0	294.3	298.8	301.5	308.0	316.8	318.0	319.4	314.9	308.5	307.1	305.5	307.2
2001	295.7	295.8	299.1	302.3	308.6	316.5	317.3	319.0	313.5	309.5	307.3	306.2	307.6
2002	298.1	298.2	299.9	304.9	311.3	319.6	321.1	322.9	318.6	315.2	312.3	312.0	311.2
2003	303.3	303.0	304.4	309.0	315.0	322.4	324.3	326.3	321.2	318.7	315.4	315.9	314.9
2004	306.4	307.3	311.8	320.5	325.0	333.6	337.0	337.3	332.2	329.1	326.8	328.0	324.6
2005	315.9	318.7	323.0	327.1	333.0	342.2	346.9	348.3	343.6	340.5	338.6	338.4	334.7
2006	329.8	331.5	335.5	340.9	347.3	358.1	358.3	359.7	354.1	350.4	348.0	350.7	347.0
2007	341.3	342.2	347.4	351.9	358.6	367.1	369.5	370.9	365.0	361.9	359.9	359.8	358.0
Goods-Producing													
2000	45.1	44.9	46.1	47.7	49.4	51.3	51.5	52.0	51.2	51.4	49.9	47.9	49.0
2001	45.3	45.0	45.6	47.0	49.1	50.9	51.8	52.3	51.4	51.0	49.3	47.5	48.9
2002	44.0	43.5	43.4	45.3	47.8	50.1	50.9	51.6	50.6	50.5	49.0	47.5	47.9
2003	44.3	43.7	43.9	46.6	49.0	50.8	51.2	51.2	50.6	50.9	48.9	47.6	48.2
2004	45.0	45.0	46.4	50.0	51.2	53.4	54.7	54.8	53.9	54.3	53.2	52.2	51.2
2005	48.0	49.4	50.6	52.8	54.7	56.6	58.4	59.2	58.1	58.7	57.5	55.1	54.9
2006	52.7	52.8	53.8	55.8	58.9	62.0	62.4	62.5	61.5	61.4	60.1	59.2	58.6
2007	56.1	55.9	57.7	59.8	62.4	64.4	64.3	64.9	63.4	63.7	62.5	60.6	61.3
Natural Resources and Mining													
2000	5.9	5.8	5.8	5.6	5.9	6.3	6.1	6.2	6.0	6.3	6.3	6.1	6.0
2001	6.0	6.0	5.8	5.7	6.0	6.4	6.5	6.5	6.5	6.7	6.5	6.3	6.2
2002	5.9	5.9	5.8	5.8	6.0	6.3	6.4	6.5	6.4	6.5	6.3	6.3	6.2
2003	6.0	5.9	5.7	5.4	5.8	6.2	6.3	6.3	6.3	6.6	6.7	6.7	6.2
2004	6.6	6.5	6.6	6.8	7.0	7.3	7.6	7.5	7.4	7.4	7.5	7.4	7.1
2005	7.3	7.5	7.4	7.2	7.5	7.9	8.1	8.2	8.0	8.0	7.9	7.9	7.7
2006	7.8	7.8	7.9	7.8	8.2	8.6	8.7	8.6	8.4	8.4	8.4	8.3	8.2
2007	8.1	8.1	8.3	8.1	8.2	8.6	8.7	8.7	8.5	8.5	8.5	8.5	8.4
Construction													
2000	17.0	16.9	18.0	19.9	21.1	22.4	22.7	23.0	22.3	22.2	20.7	19.4	20.4
2001	17.7	17.4	18.4	20.2	21.9	23.1	23.7	24.0	23.4	22.8	21.9	20.4	21.2
2002	18.2	18.0	18.1	19.9	21.9	23.5	24.1	24.5	24.0	23.7	22.7	21.5	21.7
2003	19.2	19.0	19.4	22.4	24.1	25.4	25.7	25.9	25.5	25.4	23.3	21.9	23.1
2004	19.8	19.9	21.1	24.4	25.2	26.8	27.6	27.8	27.1	27.4	26.2	25.2	24.9
2005	21.7	22.8	24.0	26.3	27.8	29.0	30.5	31.1	30.6	30.7	29.6	27.2	27.6
2006	25.3	25.3	26.2	28.2	30.6	32.9	33.2	33.5	32.8	32.5	31.1	30.2	30.2
2007	27.8	27.6	29.1	31.5	33.8	35.1	35.0	35.6	34.6	34.7	33.5	31.6	32.5
Manufacturing													
2000	22.2	22.2	22.3	22.2	22.4	22.6	22.7	22.8	22.9	22.9	22.9	22.4	22.5
2001	21.6	21.6	21.4	21.1	21.2	21.4	21.6	21.8	21.5	21.5	20.9	20.8	21.4
2002	19.9	19.6	19.5	19.6	19.9	20.3	20.4	20.6	20.2	20.3	20.0	19.7	20.0
2003	19.1	18.8	18.8	18.8	19.1	19.2	19.2	19.0	18.8	18.9	18.9	19.0	19.0
2004	18.6	18.6	18.7	18.8	19.0	19.3	19.5	19.5	19.4	19.5	19.5	19.6	19.2
2005	19.0	19.1	19.2	19.3	19.4	19.7	19.8	19.9	19.5	20.0	20.0	20.0	19.6
2006	19.6	19.7	19.7	19.8	20.1	20.5	20.5	20.4	20.3	20.5	20.6	20.7	20.2
2007	20.2	20.2	20.3	20.2	20.4	20.7	20.6	20.6	20.3	20.5	20.5	20.5	20.4
Service-Providing													
2000	331.4	333.5	339.4	339.7	346.8	347.5	344.2	346.3	348.7	343.8	343.7	342.6	342.3
2001	334.5	336.1	339.5	341.0	347.0	349.7	343.5	345.0	346.0	344.3	343.4	343.6	342.8
2002	337.7	339.8	342.2	345.4	351.1	354.6	349.5	350.4	353.5	351.0	350.7	352.2	348.2
2003	342.1	345.0	346.5	350.5	355.1	356.3	353.3	356.5	357.7	356.2	354.7	356.3	352.5
2004	345.5	349.3	353.0	359.1	363.2	367.9	364.3	363.6	365.3	363.4	363.0	364.4	360.2
2005	352.7	356.5	360.0	361.9	366.6	371.8	369.8	369.3	371.6	370.1	370.1	371.7	366.0
2006	361.9	366.3	370.1	373.9	378.7	385.2	384.2	380.5	379.1	377.8	377.6	380.0	373.9
2007	370.9	374.3	378.7	380.2	385.4	389.7	390.4	390.5	387.1	385.5	385.3	387.0	381.7
Trade, Transportation, and Utilities													
2000	84.5	83.9	84.4	85.3	86.6	88.0	87.7	88.2	87.1	86.1	86.9	87.5	86.3
2001	83.9	83.0	83.5	84.6	85.9	86.5	86.2	86.3	85.2	85.0	85.6	85.9	85.1
2002	82.6	82.1	82.6	83.9	85.2	86.0	86.3	86.1	85.4	85.3	85.8	86.4	84.8
2003	82.5	81.8	82.2	82.8	84.4	85.2	85.0	85.5	85.3	85.6	86.5	87.0	84.5
2004	83.9	83.6	84.3	85.5	86.7	87.4	87.3	87.0	86.2	86.7	87.8	88.5	86.2
2005	85.0	84.6	85.5	86.3	87.4	88.5	88.9	88.9	88.2	88.3	89.0	90.2	87.6
2006	86.7	86.5	87.1	88.1	89.4	90.6	90.2	90.4	89.9	90.1	91.4	92.5	89.4
2007	89.6	89.4	90.2	90.6	92.2	92.8	93.7	93.3	93.1	93.1	94.0	94.9	92.2
Wholesale Trade													
2000	15.5	15.5	15.6	15.9	16.0	16.1	15.9	15.8	15.7	15.4	15.3	15.4	15.6
2001	15.2	15.0	15.2	15.5	15.7	15.8	15.6	15.6	15.3	15.3	15.3	15.2	15.4
2002	14.9	14.8	14.9	15.3	15.5	15.6	15.7	15.6	15.4	15.4	15.4	15.5	15.3
2003	15.0	14.9	15.0	15.4	15.6	15.7	15.6	15.6	15.5	15.5	15.6	15.7	15.4
2004	15.5	15.5	15.7	16.0	16.1	16.3	16.5	16.4	16.2	16.1	16.3	16.3	16.1
2005	15.8	15.9	16.1	16.3	16.5	16.6	16.6	16.5	16.3	16.2	16.2	16.4	16.3
2006	16.0	16.1	16.3	16.3	16.6	16.8	16.8	16.8	16.7	16.7	16.8	16.8	16.6
2007	16.4	16.6	16.7	16.8	17.1	17.1	17.3	17.1	17.1	17.0	17.1	17.2	17.0

Employment by Industry: Montana, 2000–2007—*Continued*

(Numbers in thousands, not seasonally adjusted.)

Industry and year	January	February	March	April	May	June	July	August	September	October	November	December	Annual Average
Retail Trade													
2000	52.4	51.8	52.2	52.6	53.5	54.9	55.0	55.4	54.5	53.6	54.6	55.1	53.8
2001	52.6	51.9	52.0	52.6	53.5	54.2	54.6	54.8	53.9	53.5	54.3	54.6	53.5
2002	52.0	51.6	51.9	52.8	53.7	54.4	54.7	54.6	54.1	53.9	54.7	55.1	53.6
2003	52.2	51.7	52.0	52.3	53.4	54.1	54.3	54.6	54.1	54.3	55.2	55.7	53.7
2004	53.2	53.0	53.4	54.1	55.1	55.6	55.6	55.3	54.5	54.7	55.6	56.2	54.7
2005	53.6	53.1	53.7	54.3	55.1	56.0	56.4	56.4	55.7	55.8	56.5	57.2	55.3
2006	54.5	54.1	54.4	55.2	56.1	57.0	57.0	57.1	56.2	56.5	57.8	58.6	56.2
2007	56.5	56.0	56.7	56.9	58.0	58.8	59.5	59.4	58.9	58.8	59.6	60.2	58.3
Transportation and Utilities													
2000	16.6	16.6	16.6	16.8	17.1	17.0	16.8	17.0	16.9	17.1	17.0	17.0	16.8
2001	16.1	16.1	16.3	16.5	16.7	16.5	16.0	15.9	16.0	16.2	16.0	16.1	16.2
2002	15.7	15.7	15.8	15.8	16.0	16.0	15.9	15.9	15.9	16.0	15.7	15.8	15.9
2003	15.3	15.2	15.2	15.1	15.4	15.4	15.1	15.3	15.7	15.8	15.7	15.6	15.4
2004	15.2	15.1	15.2	15.4	15.5	15.5	15.2	15.3	15.5	15.9	15.9	16.0	15.5
2005	15.6	15.6	15.7	15.7	15.8	15.9	15.9	16.0	16.2	16.3	16.3	16.6	16.0
2006	16.2	16.3	16.4	16.6	16.7	16.8	16.4	16.5	17.0	16.9	16.8	17.1	16.6
2007	16.7	16.8	16.8	16.9	17.1	16.9	16.9	16.8	17.1	17.3	17.3	17.5	17.0
Information													
2000	7.9	7.9	8.0	8.0	8.1	8.1	7.8	7.8	7.8	8.0	8.0	8.0	7.9
2001	7.9	8.0	7.9	7.8	7.9	8.0	7.9	8.0	7.8	7.9	8.0	7.8	7.9
2002	7.8	7.8	7.8	7.8	7.9	7.9	8.0	7.9	7.8	7.7	7.8	7.8	7.8
2003	7.7	7.8	7.7	7.6	7.6	7.6	7.6	7.6	7.7	7.7	7.7	7.6	7.7
2004	7.6	7.6	7.7	7.7	7.8	7.9	8.0	8.1	7.8	7.7	7.8	7.8	7.8
2005	7.7	7.8	7.8	7.7	7.8	7.9	7.9	7.9	7.7	7.7	7.7	7.8	7.8
2006	7.7	7.8	7.7	7.7	7.8	7.9	7.8	7.8	7.7	7.6	7.6	7.7	7.7
2007	7.4	7.5	7.5	7.6	7.6	7.6	7.7	7.7	7.8	7.7	7.7	7.8	7.6
Financial Activities													
2000	18.1	18.2	18.3	18.5	18.7	19.0	19.0	19.0	18.7	18.4	18.4	18.6	18.5
2001	18.4	18.3	18.4	18.5	18.8	19.1	19.3	19.2	19.1	18.8	18.8	19.0	18.8
2002	18.8	18.9	19.0	19.2	19.4	19.6	19.3	19.3	19.1	19.6	19.6	19.9	19.3
2003	19.9	19.9	20.0	19.9	20.0	20.4	20.6	20.8	20.5	20.5	20.5	20.7	20.3
2004	20.7	20.7	20.8	20.8	21.0	21.3	21.5	21.5	21.2	21.1	21.0	21.3	21.1
2005	20.8	20.8	20.8	21.0	21.2	21.5	21.8	21.8	21.7	21.8	21.9	22.2	21.4
2006	21.7	21.8	21.9	22.0	21.9	22.3	22.3	22.2	21.9	21.8	21.7	21.9	22.0
2007	21.4	21.4	21.6	21.5	21.7	21.9	22.0	22.1	21.8	21.8	21.9	22.0	21.8
Professional and Business Services													
2000	28.6	29.1	29.9	30.2	30.7	31.7	31.9	31.9	31.6	31.6	31.8	31.3	30.8
2001	30.4	31.0	31.4	31.7	32.1	32.8	32.4	32.6	32.0	31.8	31.6	31.7	31.8
2002	31.3	31.6	31.7	31.9	32.0	32.8	33.0	33.4	33.3	32.9	32.3	31.7	32.3
2003	31.2	31.3	31.7	32.6	32.9	33.4	33.6	33.8	32.9	32.9	32.1	32.0	32.5
2004	30.4	31.0	31.6	33.2	33.8	34.7	34.9	34.9	34.3	34.2	33.9	33.3	33.4
2005	32.1	32.7	33.3	34.4	34.7	35.8	36.6	36.8	36.2	36.4	36.5	36.2	35.1
2006	35.5	35.9	36.6	37.5	38.2	39.6	39.4	40.2	39.2	39.0	38.5	38.6	38.2
2007	38.1	38.5	39.3	40.3	41.1	42.1	42.1	42.6	41.4	41.4	41.1	40.7	40.7
Education and Health Services													
2000	48.6	49.0	49.2	48.9	49.2	48.9	48.2	48.6	49.2	49.1	49.5	49.6	49.0
2001	48.4	48.7	49.3	49.5	49.6	49.4	48.7	49.3	50.0	50.4	51.1	51.4	49.7
2002	51.4	51.6	51.9	52.2	52.4	51.9	50.6	50.9	51.8	52.8	53.3	53.3	52.0
2003	53.2	53.6	53.5	53.3	53.4	52.6	51.5	52.2	52.6	53.5	53.9	54.1	53.1
2004	53.5	53.7	54.3	54.5	54.5	54.4	54.0	53.1	53.3	54.6	55.1	55.7	56.1	54.4
2005	55.5	55.7	56.1	55.5	55.7	55.8	54.9	55.0	56.1	56.5	56.9	56.9	55.9
2006	56.4	56.9	57.3	57.7	57.6	57.2	56.4	56.8	57.9	58.0	58.4	58.7	57.4
2007	58.2	58.7	59.0	58.9	58.9	58.4	57.6	58.0	59.2	59.8	60.3	60.4	59.0
Leisure and Hospitality													
2000	46.2	46.2	47.5	47.4	49.7	54.2	56.4	56.6	53.8	48.7	47.3	47.4	50.1
2001	45.9	46.2	47.1	47.1	48.9	53.3	54.9	55.3	51.9	48.7	47.0	46.9	49.4
2002	46.7	47.1	47.8	48.7	50.5	55.0	56.7	57.4	54.3	50.2	48.3	49.1	51.0
2003	48.6	49.0	49.4	49.8	51.3	56.0	58.4	58.8	55.2	51.0	49.3	50.2	52.3
2004	49.0	49.3	50.1	52.1	53.3	58.0	60.5	60.6	57.2	53.1	50.6	51.9	53.8
2005	50.4	51.1	52.2	52.7	54.7	59.1	61.7	61.9	58.8	54.5	52.5	53.2	55.2
2006	52.6	53.2	54.2	55.1	56.4	61.2	62.7	62.7	58.9	55.4	53.3	55.0	56.7
2007	53.7	54.0	54.9	55.9	57.5	62.3	65.0	65.1	61.3	57.4	55.4	56.2	58.2
Other Services													
2000	15.0	15.1	15.4	15.5	15.6	15.6	15.5	15.3	15.5	15.2	15.3	15.2	15.3
2001	15.5	15.6	15.9	16.1	16.3	16.5	16.1	16.0	16.1	15.9	15.9	16.0	16.0
2002	15.5	15.6	15.7	15.9	16.1	16.3	16.3	16.3	16.3	16.2	16.2	16.3	16.1
2003	15.9	15.9	16.0	16.4	16.4	16.4	16.4	16.3	16.5	16.6	16.5	16.7	16.3
2004	16.3	16.4	16.6	16.7	16.8	16.9	17.0	17.1	17.0	16.9	16.8	16.9	16.8
2005	16.4	16.6	16.7	16.7	16.8	17.0	16.7	16.8	16.8	16.6	16.6	16.8	16.7
2006	16.5	16.6	16.9	17.0	17.1	17.3	17.1	17.1	17.1	17.1	17.0	17.1	17.0
2007	16.8	16.8	17.2	17.3	17.2	17.5	17.1	17.1	17.1	17.0	17.0	17.2	17.1
Government													
2000	82.5	84.1	86.7	85.9	88.2	82.0	77.7	78.9	85.0	86.7	86.5	85.0	84.1
2001	84.1	85.3	86.0	85.7	87.5	84.1	78.0	78.3	83.9	85.8	85.4	84.9	84.1
2002	83.6	85.1	85.7	85.8	87.6	85.1	79.3	79.1	85.5	86.3	87.4	87.7	84.9
2003	83.1	85.7	86.0	88.1	89.1	84.7	80.2	81.4	87.1	88.4	88.2	88.0	85.8
2004	84.1	87.0	87.6	88.6	89.4	87.7	82.0	81.1	87.0	88.6	89.4	88.6	86.8
2005	84.8	87.2	87.6	87.6	88.3	86.2	81.3	80.2	86.1	88.3	89.0	88.4	86.3
2006	84.8	87.6	88.4	88.8	90.3	89.1	88.3	83.3	86.5	88.8	89.7	88.5	85.5
2007	85.7	88.0	89.0	88.1	89.2	87.0	85.2	84.5	85.5	87.3	87.9	87.8	85.1

Average Weekly Hours by Selected Industry: Montana, 2001–2007

(Not seasonally adjusted.)

Industry and year	January	February	March	April	May	June	July	August	September	October	November	December	Annual Average
Manufacturing													
2001	38.6	38.7	38.3	37.8	38.3	39.5	38.1	39.1	38.8	38.3	39.9	39.2	38.8
2002	37.1	37.1	37.7	38.3	38.1	39.3	36.0	38.4	38.6	39.0	39.5	39.5	38.2
2003	39.1	38.4	37.9	38.7	38.5	39.1	37.4	38.3	38.2	38.3	38.3	38.4	38.4
2004	38.0	37.7	37.5	38.5	37.4	37.9	37.3	39.9	38.4	39.1	38.6	39.4	38.3
2005	40.2	38.6	40.2	40.3	40.7	40.3	39.0	39.1	39.9	41.7	40.6	41.3	40.1
2006	40.5	39.8	40.2	41.1	40.0	40.6	37.4	40.5	40.2	40.0	39.4	39.7	39.9
2007	39.0	39.8	40.2	40.4	40.7	38.9	40.5	39.6	40.4	41.0	39.0	39.3	39.9

Average Hourly Earnings by Selected Industry: Montana, 2001–2007

(Dollars, not seasonally adjusted.)

Industry and year	January	February	March	April	May	June	July	August	September	October	November	December	Annual Average
Manufacturing													
2001	13.81	13.73	14.00	13.88	13.80	13.88	14.18	13.95	14.13	14.43	14.20	14.41	14.03
2002	14.54	14.45	14.61	14.53	14.46	14.42	14.45	14.35	14.33	14.30	14.44	14.31	14.43
2003	14.20	14.07	14.21	14.14	13.73	13.75	13.87	14.05	13.94	14.05	14.16	14.15	14.02
2004	14.46	14.62	14.68	14.79	14.74	14.92	14.91	15.22	15.38	14.89	14.76	14.98	14.87
2005	15.18	14.98	15.16	15.24	15.42	15.40	15.72	15.80	16.01	16.29	15.94	16.13	15.62
2006	16.19	16.45	16.26	15.75	15.96	15.75	15.71	15.88	15.85	16.23	15.47	15.24	15.90
2007	15.79	15.42	15.52	15.59	15.67	15.86	15.95	16.41	15.87	15.93	16.57	15.87	15.88

Average Weekly Earnings by Selected Industry: Montana, 2001–2007

(Dollars, not seasonally adjusted.)

Industry and year	January	February	March	April	May	June	July	August	September	October	November	December	Annual Average
Manufacturing													
2001	533.07	531.35	536.20	524.66	528.54	548.26	540.26	545.45	548.24	552.67	566.58	564.87	544.36
2002	539.43	536.10	550.80	556.50	550.93	566.71	520.20	551.04	553.14	557.70	570.38	565.25	551.23
2003	555.22	540.29	538.56	547.22	528.61	537.63	518.74	538.12	532.51	538.12	542.33	543.36	538.37
2004	549.48	551.17	550.50	569.42	551.28	565.47	556.14	607.28	590.59	582.20	569.74	590.21	569.52
2005	610.24	578.23	609.43	614.17	627.59	620.62	613.08	617.78	638.80	679.29	647.16	666.17	626.36
2006	655.70	654.71	653.65	647.33	638.40	639.45	587.55	643.14	637.17	649.20	609.52	605.03	634.41
2007	615.81	613.72	623.90	629.84	637.77	616.95	645.98	649.84	641.15	653.13	646.23	623.69	633.61

Population
    2000 census: 1,711,263
    2007 estimate: 1,774,571
    Percent change, 2000–2007: 3.7%

Percent change in total nonfarm employment, 2000–2007: 5.3%

Industry with the largest growth in employment, 2000–2007 (thousands)
    Education and health services, 21.7

Industry with the largest decline in employment, 2000–2007 (thousands)
    Manufacturing, -12.6

Civilian labor force
    2000: 949,762
    2007: 983,438

Employment-population ratio
    2000: 71.9%
    2007: 70.7%

Unemployment rate and rank among states
    2000: 2.8%, 8th
    2007: 3.0%, 4th

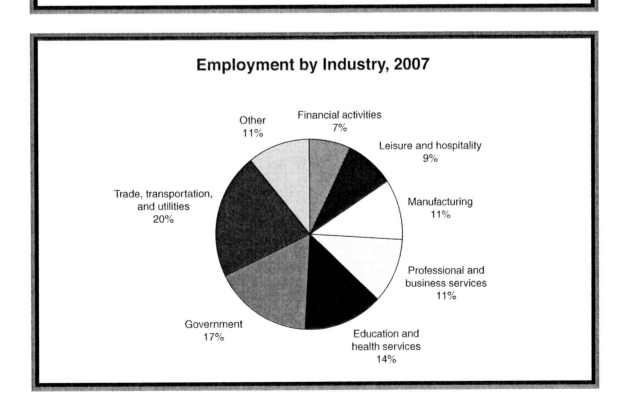

Employment by Industry, 2007

Other
11%

Financial activities
7%

Leisure and hospitality
9%

Trade, transportation,
and utilities
20%

Manufacturing
11%

Professional and
business services
11%

Government
17%

Education and
health services
14%

Employment by Industry: Nebraska, 2000–2007

(Numbers in thousands, not seasonally adjusted.)

Industry and year	January	February	March	April	May	June	July	August	September	October	November	December	Annual Average
Total Nonfarm													
2000	891.9	895.4	905.0	911.8	920.1	929.2	914.8	916.4	918.0	919.1	922.7	923.2	914.0
2001	901.3	902.6	909.3	918.5	928.7	933.8	918.3	921.5	922.4	923.4	929.3	927.2	919.7
2002	894.3	898.2	905.2	913.8	919.3	922.5	907.5	908.0	916.3	915.8	918.1	918.5	911.5
2003	899.7	899.8	903.6	915.3	920.4	924.2	908.7	913.8	916.7	921.7	922.6	923.6	914.2
2004	901.2	898.6	907.8	920.1	929.9	935.3	924.6	925.3	928.8	930.1	932.7	933.7	922.3
2005	911.1	915.0	923.7	933.1	941.5	947.3	936.0	935.7	940.1	943.7	947.1	945.6	935.0
2006	924.4	928.9	935.8	942.5	952.4	959.5	945.4	945.8	952.0	954.5	959.1	959.2	946.6
2007	938.1	940.7	947.4	957.8	968.6	974.6	964.0	967.3	969.2	972.1	975.1	976.0	962.6
Total Private													
2000	739.1	741.4	748.5	756.0	760.7	771.0	766.3	768.1	764.7	764.9	766.8	767.3	759.6
2001	748.5	747.3	752.7	760.8	768.0	773.6	768.2	770.2	765.2	764.9	768.3	767.1	762.9
2002	737.9	738.7	745.0	753.3	756.5	760.8	755.9	757.1	758.4	754.2	755.9	756.9	752.6
2003	740.0	739.1	742.7	751.8	755.4	760.2	757.0	763.9	760.1	759.9	760.8	762.0	754.4
2004	742.4	738.6	746.9	758.1	766.0	772.5	771.2	772.4	768.7	768.3	770.4	771.4	762.2
2005	751.3	754.1	761.8	770.3	776.7	783.6	782.1	782.6	779.0	779.6	782.4	781.9	773.8
2006	763.5	766.3	772.3	778.3	786.0	794.0	791.4	791.9	789.6	789.6	793.5	794.5	784.2
2007	775.1	776.8	783.2	792.1	800.1	807.1	808.3	810.9	805.6	804.9	808.2	809.3	798.5
Goods-Producing													
2000	153.0	153.3	156.2	158.4	160.4	163.7	162.4	162.1	160.5	160.3	159.0	157.3	158.9
2001	152.8	152.1	152.9	156.2	158.5	160.5	159.8	159.4	156.9	156.3	155.3	153.9	156.2
2002	148.2	147.4	148.5	151.1	153.2	155.6	155.9	155.6	154.3	153.4	152.2	151.0	152.2
2003	145.7	144.5	145.1	148.4	150.8	152.9	153.2	153.4	151.6	151.8	150.7	149.8	149.8
2004	144.6	143.2	145.8	148.6	150.9	153.2	153.6	153.0	151.0	150.5	149.8	148.9	149.4
2005	142.7	143.2	145.7	148.3	150.0	152.7	153.3	152.8	151.5	150.9	150.3	148.3	149.1
2006	144.9	145.2	146.6	148.9	150.2	153.0	153.1	152.7	152.1	151.5	150.5	149.2	149.8
2007	144.7	144.4	146.6	149.7	151.9	154.7	156.2	156.2	154.8	154.5	153.9	153.1	151.7
Natural Resources, Mining, and Construction													
2000	40.5	40.4	42.3	44.7	46.4	48.4	48.0	48.2	47.0	46.4	44.7	42.9	45.0
2001	39.7	39.4	40.6	44.1	46.7	48.5	48.6	48.9	47.4	47.2	46.6	45.3	45.3
2002	41.2	40.8	42.4	45.3	47.2	48.8	49.3	49.1	48.3	47.9	46.9	45.8	46.1
2003	42.7	41.8	42.7	46.0	48.3	50.2	51.0	51.2	49.8	49.6	48.6	47.3	47.4
2004	43.6	42.4	44.9	48.3	50.1	51.8	52.2	51.7	50.2	49.7	48.7	47.3	48.4
2005	43.0	42.7	44.7	47.1	49.0	50.9	51.4	51.1	50.1	49.2	48.5	46.2	47.8
2006	43.4	43.5	44.9	47.4	49.2	51.2	51.3	51.1	50.8	50.1	49.4	48.0	48.4
2007	44.7	44.0	46.2	49.1	50.8	53.0	54.4	54.7	53.6	52.6	51.8	50.7	50.5
Manufacturing													
2000	112.5	112.9	113.9	113.7	114.0	115.3	114.4	113.9	113.5	113.9	114.3	114.4	113.9
2001	113.1	112.7	112.3	112.1	111.8	112.0	111.2	110.5	109.5	109.1	108.7	108.6	111.0
2002	107.0	106.6	106.1	105.8	106.0	106.8	106.6	106.5	106.0	105.5	105.3	105.2	106.1
2003	103.0	102.7	102.4	102.4	102.5	102.7	102.2	102.2	101.8	102.2	102.1	102.5	102.4
2004	101.0	100.8	100.9	100.3	100.8	101.4	101.4	101.3	100.8	100.8	101.1	101.6	101.0
2005	99.7	100.5	101.0	101.2	101.0	101.8	101.9	101.7	101.4	101.7	101.8	102.1	101.3
2006	101.5	101.7	101.7	101.5	101.0	101.8	101.8	101.6	101.3	101.4	101.1	101.2	101.5
2007	100.0	100.4	100.4	100.6	101.1	101.7	101.8	101.5	101.2	101.9	102.1	102.4	101.3
Service-Providing													
2000	738.9	742.1	748.8	753.4	759.7	765.5	752.4	754.3	757.5	758.8	763.7	765.9	755.1
2001	748.5	750.5	756.4	762.3	770.2	773.3	758.5	762.1	765.5	767.1	774.0	773.3	763.5
2002	746.1	750.8	756.7	762.7	766.1	766.9	751.6	752.4	762.0	762.4	765.9	767.5	759.3
2003	754.0	755.3	758.5	766.9	769.6	771.3	755.5	760.4	765.1	769.9	771.9	773.8	764.4
2004	756.6	755.4	762.0	771.5	779.0	782.1	771.0	772.3	777.8	779.6	782.9	784.8	772.9
2005	768.4	771.8	778.0	784.8	791.5	794.6	782.7	782.9	788.6	792.8	796.8	797.3	785.9
2006	779.5	783.7	789.2	793.6	802.2	806.5	792.3	793.1	799.9	803.0	808.6	810.0	796.8
2007	793.4	796.3	800.8	808.1	816.7	819.9	807.8	811.1	814.4	817.6	821.2	822.9	810.9
Trade, Transportation, and Utilities													
2000	195.8	194.4	195.1	196.2	197.1	199.0	197.4	197.7	196.9	198.6	201.5	203.6	197.8
2001	197.0	195.0	195.6	197.2	199.2	199.4	198.0	198.0	197.4	197.7	201.2	202.7	198.2
2002	194.9	192.4	193.1	194.3	196.0	196.1	194.8	194.8	195.1	194.4	198.1	200.1	195.3
2003	193.0	191.5	192.5	193.6	194.8	195.2	193.4	194.1	194.1	195.4	197.9	199.9	194.6
2004	192.8	190.3	191.7	194.3	196.6	197.5	196.8	197.7	197.8	199.2	201.6	203.7	196.7
2005	197.1	196.5	198.1	198.6	200.9	201.0	200.1	200.1	199.7	200.4	203.4	205.1	200.1
2006	196.8	196.0	197.1	197.9	200.3	200.7	200.0	200.5	200.8	202.1	206.0	208.1	200.5
2007	200.9	199.9	201.1	202.4	205.0	205.3	204.7	205.0	204.7	206.0	208.9	210.5	204.5
Wholesale Trade													
2000	41.7	41.8	41.9	41.6	41.7	42.0	42.1	42.1	41.6	41.4	41.3	41.2	41.7
2001	42.1	42.1	42.3	42.6	43.1	43.3	43.2	42.8	42.3	42.2	42.0	41.9	42.5
2002	41.1	40.9	41.3	41.6	42.0	42.2	42.5	42.0	41.6	41.0	41.0	41.1	41.5
2003	40.4	40.3	40.5	41.0	41.3	41.6	41.5	41.4	41.2	41.2	40.8	41.0	41.0
2004	40.0	39.9	40.3	41.0	41.2	41.3	41.6	41.1	40.8	40.9	40.7	40.7	40.8
2005	40.0	40.0	40.4	40.5	40.9	41.0	41.3	40.8	40.4	40.5	40.4	40.5	40.6
2006	40.2	40.2	40.4	40.8	41.2	41.4	41.3	40.9	40.7	40.6	40.6	40.9	40.8
2007	39.9	39.8	40.2	40.8	41.2	41.6	41.5	41.0	40.9	40.7	40.6	40.6	40.7
Retail Trade													
2000	109.9	108.5	108.9	109.7	110.8	112.3	110.3	110.4	110.0	111.8	114.7	116.9	111.2
2001	110.1	108.0	108.2	109.1	110.6	110.8	109.5	110.0	109.8	110.4	113.9	115.3	110.5
2002	108.5	106.3	106.6	107.4	108.7	108.8	107.8	108.0	108.9	109.0	112.3	114.2	108.9
2003	106.7	104.9	105.6	106.2	106.8	106.9	105.9	106.2	106.3	107.7	110.7	112.3	107.2
2004	106.3	104.2	104.5	105.3	106.7	107.1	106.1	106.5	106.1	107.5	110.6	112.4	106.9
2005	106.0	105.0	105.9	106.5	107.7	107.4	106.8	106.8	106.3	107.2	109.8	111.1	107.2
2006	105.0	103.8	104.4	104.8	106.1	106.1	105.7	105.9	105.7	107.0	110.5	111.9	106.4
2007	105.6	104.5	105.2	106.2	108.0	107.8	107.4	107.7	107.7	107.1	108.2	111.4	113.2	107.7

Employment by Industry: Nebraska, 2000–2007—*Continued*

(Numbers in thousands, not seasonally adjusted.)

Industry and year	January	February	March	April	May	June	July	August	September	October	November	December	Annual Average
Transportation and Utilities													
2000	44.2	44.1	44.3	44.9	44.6	44.7	45.0	45.2	45.3	45.4	45.5	45.5	44.9
2001	44.8	44.9	45.1	45.5	45.5	45.3	45.3	45.2	45.3	45.1	45.3	45.5	45.2
2002	45.3	45.2	45.2	45.3	45.3	45.1	44.5	44.8	44.6	44.4	44.8	44.8	44.9
2003	45.9	46.3	46.4	46.4	46.7	46.7	46.0	46.5	46.6	46.5	46.4	46.6	46.4
2004	46.5	46.2	46.9	48.0	48.7	49.1	49.1	50.1	50.9	50.8	50.3	50.6	48.9
2005	51.1	51.5	51.8	51.6	52.3	52.6	52.0	52.5	53.0	52.7	53.2	53.5	52.3
2006	51.6	52.0	52.3	52.3	53.0	53.2	53.0	53.7	54.4	54.5	54.9	55.3	53.4
2007	55.4	55.6	55.7	55.4	55.8	55.9	55.8	56.3	56.7	57.1	56.9	56.7	56.1
Information													
2000	27.5	27.1	26.7	27.2	26.8	27.0	27.0	26.7	26.4	26.4	26.6	26.6	26.8
2001	26.3	26.2	26.3	26.5	26.2	26.3	25.8	25.4	25.2	25.2	25.2	25.3	25.8
2002	24.5	24.3	24.0	23.8	23.5	23.3	23.0	22.8	22.5	22.3	22.0	21.8	23.2
2003	21.5	21.5	21.5	21.4	21.4	21.6	21.6	21.3	21.2	21.4	21.5	21.7	21.5
2004	21.3	21.3	21.3	21.2	21.1	21.2	21.2	21.0	20.9	20.8	20.9	20.7	21.1
2005	20.4	20.5	20.4	20.3	20.0	20.3	20.2	20.2	20.0	20.0	20.0	20.1	20.2
2006	19.7	19.6	19.6	19.6	19.5	19.7	19.6	19.5	19.3	19.1	19.2	19.3	19.5
2007	19.1	19.1	19.1	19.2	19.2	19.5	19.6	19.7	19.5	19.4	19.2	19.3	19.3
Financial Activities													
2000	60.4	60.2	60.1	60.3	60.4	60.9	60.3	60.3	60.1	59.9	60.1	60.4	60.3
2001	59.1	59.2	59.3	59.7	60.1	61.0	60.8	60.8	60.5	60.3	60.5	61.0	60.2
2002	60.6	60.7	60.9	61.0	61.3	61.9	61.9	61.8	61.4	61.6	61.7	62.2	61.4
2003	61.8	61.9	62.0	62.0	62.3	62.9	63.0	62.9	62.3	62.3	62.3	62.8	62.4
2004	62.2	62.1	62.6	62.8	63.1	63.6	63.7	63.8	63.4	63.5	63.8	64.2	63.2
2005	63.5	63.8	63.9	64.1	64.5	64.9	64.9	65.0	64.7	64.8	64.7	65.0	64.5
2006	64.6	64.9	65.2	65.7	66.4	67.2	67.4	67.6	67.2	67.4	67.8	68.5	66.7
2007	67.7	68.2	68.4	68.7	69.4	69.8	70.0	69.7	69.2	68.8	68.9	69.3	69.0
Professional and Business Services													
2000	92.0	92.5	93.6	95.4	95.7	97.8	97.5	97.7	97.3	97.9	98.4	98.8	96.2
2001	95.8	96.1	96.7	97.2	97.9	99.2	98.2	98.8	97.4	96.4	96.7	95.8	97.2
2002	89.0	89.8	91.4	92.9	92.7	93.1	91.3	91.2	90.8	90.9	90.9	90.5	91.2
2003	88.3	89.0	89.7	92.0	91.8	92.9	92.9	93.8	94.4	94.2	93.7	93.8	92.2
2004	91.1	91.1	92.3	94.7	94.8	96.0	95.2	95.7	94.7	95.3	95.4	95.1	94.3
2005	93.9	94.5	95.7	97.3	97.5	98.5	98.5	99.0	98.9	100.3	100.5	100.5	97.9
2006	97.9	98.7	100.4	101.2	102.3	104.4	103.8	103.4	102.9	102.5	102.5	102.1	101.8
2007	100.5	101.2	102.0	103.4	104.0	105.8	105.9	106.1	105.6	105.7	106.2	106.6	104.4
Education and Health Services													
2000	107.4	109.7	110.5	109.5	109.0	109.6	109.7	110.9	112.4	112.7	113.3	113.6	110.7
2001	112.7	113.5	114.7	114.4	113.8	113.6	112.8	114.3	117.2	120.3	121.5	120.9	115.8
2002	116.7	119.0	120.8	119.9	117.6	116.4	115.1	115.9	121.7	121.4	122.0	122.2	119.1
2003	122.2	123.0	122.6	122.8	120.5	119.8	119.3	124.0	124.1	124.3	125.2	125.3	122.8
2004	124.1	124.4	125.0	125.6	125.5	125.7	125.6	125.9	126.7	126.6	127.3	127.3	125.8
2005	126.0	126.9	127.3	127.9	127.6	128.1	127.7	127.8	128.7	129.5	130.5	130.5	128.2
2006	128.8	129.9	130.2	129.9	130.3	130.6	129.7	130.6	131.4	131.5	133.0	132.5	130.7
2007	130.3	131.9	132.1	131.7	131.0	131.1	132.0	133.6	133.2	133.3	134.7	134.4	132.4
Leisure and Hospitality													
2000	71.5	72.4	74.2	76.9	79.0	80.5	79.8	80.5	79.1	77.0	75.9	75.1	76.8
2001	72.6	72.8	74.5	77.0	79.4	80.6	79.7	80.5	78.0	75.9	75.1	74.8	76.7
2002	71.9	72.6	73.8	76.8	78.7	80.8	80.2	81.6	79.4	77.0	76.0	76.0	77.1
2003	73.9	74.0	75.3	77.5	79.7	80.6	79.7	80.6	78.7	76.9	75.9	75.2	77.3
2004	72.9	72.7	74.5	77.0	79.9	80.9	80.6	80.9	79.7	77.8	77.0	76.6	77.5
2005	73.9	74.4	76.3	79.3	81.5	83.2	82.5	83.1	81.1	79.4	78.8	78.2	79.3
2006	76.8	77.8	78.7	80.5	82.5	83.6	83.0	83.3	81.6	80.9	80.0	80.4	80.8
2007	77.7	77.8	79.2	82.1	84.4	85.7	84.9	85.8	83.8	82.1	81.3	81.2	82.2
Other Services													
2000	31.5	31.8	32.1	32.1	32.3	32.5	32.2	32.2	32.0	32.1	32.0	31.9	32.1
2001	32.2	32.4	32.7	32.6	32.9	33.0	33.1	33.0	32.6	32.8	32.8	32.7	32.7
2002	32.1	32.5	32.5	33.5	33.5	33.6	33.7	33.4	33.2	33.2	33.0	33.1	33.1
2003	33.6	33.7	34.0	34.1	34.1	34.3	34.0	33.8	33.7	33.6	33.6	33.5	33.8
2004	33.4	33.5	33.7	33.9	34.1	34.4	34.5	34.4	34.5	34.6	34.6	34.9	34.2
2005	33.8	34.3	34.4	34.5	34.7	34.9	34.9	34.6	34.4	34.3	34.2	34.2	34.4
2006	34.0	34.2	34.5	34.6	34.5	34.8	34.8	34.3	34.3	34.6	34.5	34.4	34.5
2007	34.2	34.3	34.7	34.9	35.2	35.2	35.0	34.8	34.8	35.1	35.1	34.9	34.9
Government													
2000	152.8	154.0	156.5	155.8	159.4	158.2	148.5	148.3	153.3	154.2	155.9	155.9	154.4
2001	152.8	155.3	156.6	157.7	160.7	160.2	150.1	151.3	157.2	158.5	161.0	160.1	156.8
2002	156.4	159.5	160.2	160.5	162.8	161.7	151.6	150.9	157.9	161.6	162.2	161.6	158.9
2003	159.7	160.7	160.9	163.5	165.0	164.0	151.7	149.9	156.6	161.8	161.8	161.6	159.8
2004	158.8	160.0	160.9	162.0	163.9	162.8	153.4	152.9	160.1	161.8	162.3	162.3	160.1
2005	159.8	160.9	161.9	162.8	164.8	163.7	153.9	153.1	161.1	164.1	164.7	163.7	161.2
2006	160.9	162.6	163.5	164.2	166.4	165.5	154.0	153.9	162.4	164.9	165.6	164.7	162.4
2007	163.0	163.9	164.2	165.7	168.5	167.5	155.7	156.4	163.6	167.2	166.9	166.7	164.1

Average Weekly Hours by Selected Industry: Nebraska, 2001–2007

(Not seasonally adjusted.)

Industry and year	January	February	March	April	May	June	July	August	September	October	November	December	Annual Average
Manufacturing													
2001	40.6	39.8	40.9	39.3	41.6	40.7	41.3	42.1	42.0	41.6	41.8	43.2	41.2
2002	41.8	41.5	42.1	41.8	41.9	43.2	42.5	42.6	41.9	40.8	41.4	41.7	41.9
2003	41.3	41.4	41.8	40.9	40.9	42.1	41.8	42.0	41.8	41.7	42.0	41.6	41.6
2004	42.1	41.7	41.5	40.9	41.9	42.2	40.5	42.1	41.4	41.3	41.5	42.2	41.6
2005	40.6	39.3	39.4	40.4	40.8	41.2	41.3	40.4	39.3	39.1	38.8	39.5	40.0
2006	38.8	40.2	40.5	40.0	41.1	42.4	41.2	41.1	40.6	41.4	41.1	42.0	40.9
2007	42.4	42.3	43.2	43.2	43.0	42.9	42.8	42.7	42.8	42.5	41.9	41.3	42.6
Professional and Business Services													
2001	34.0	33.9	34.7	35.1	35.5	36.1	36.4	35.5	35.4	35.3	35.6	35.7	35.3
2002	35.0	35.2	35.0	35.3	35.1	36.3	34.6	35.1	35.3	34.4	35.3	35.9	35.2
2003	33.7	34.6	34.3	32.8	33.2	34.4	33.4	33.5	32.4	32.7	32.5	31.9	33.3
2004	32.9	33.0	32.0	31.9	32.3	33.0	33.3	33.9	33.2	33.0	33.0	32.8	32.9
2005	32.2	32.0	32.1	32.7	33.7	32.7	33.2	33.2	33.4	34.0	32.6	33.1	32.9
2006	33.9	33.5	33.3	33.7	33.3	33.8	35.0	33.9	33.5	34.0	32.5	32.2	33.5
2007	32.0	32.6	32.7	33.0	32.6	33.2	33.3	33.2	33.6	32.4	32.7	33.3	32.9

Average Hourly Earnings by Selected Industry: Nebraska, 2001–2007

(Dollars, not seasonally adjusted.)

Industry and year	January	February	March	April	May	June	July	August	September	October	November	December	Annual Average
Manufacturing													
2001	13.59	13.52	13.33	13.48	13.46	13.58	13.50	13.50	13.68	14.02	14.09	13.84	13.64
2002	13.78	13.72	13.74	14.03	13.99	14.08	14.26	14.13	14.06	14.17	14.13	14.50	14.05
2003	14.61	14.49	14.61	14.70	14.65	14.63	14.94	14.84	14.87	15.29	15.09	15.60	14.86
2004	15.48	15.26	15.17	14.99	15.00	15.16	15.34	15.17	15.31	15.12	15.08	15.16	15.19
2005	15.42	15.34	15.42	15.17	15.24	15.40	15.83	15.44	15.85	15.45	15.54	15.15	15.44
2006	15.15	14.84	14.87	14.76	14.60	14.97	14.84	15.11	15.18	15.56	15.51	15.13	15.04
2007	15.11	15.17	15.27	15.18	15.35	15.22	15.18	15.02	15.10	15.12	15.15	15.42	15.19
Professional and Business Services													
2001	14.99	15.09	15.16	15.53	15.58	15.40	15.50	15.59	15.95	15.94	16.36	16.69	15.65
2002	17.01	17.07	17.16	17.23	17.32	16.78	16.74	16.57	16.51	16.16	16.38	16.54	16.79
2003	16.68	16.49	16.45	16.54	16.43	16.29	16.24	15.97	16.12	15.86	16.00	15.84	16.24
2004	16.39	16.20	16.08	16.11	16.22	16.40	16.76	16.74	16.60	16.54	16.37	16.36	16.40
2005	17.32	16.47	16.51	16.62	16.42	16.20	16.05	16.13	15.88	16.10	15.84	16.74	16.35
2006	17.28	17.00	17.36	17.39	17.35	16.35	16.28	16.16	16.44	16.43	17.13	17.17	16.85
2007	17.49	17.72	18.63	17.86	18.19	18.08	17.67	17.70	17.48	17.55	17.15	17.44	17.74

Average Weekly Earnings by Selected Industry: Nebraska, 2001–2007

(Dollars, not seasonally adjusted.)

Industry and year	January	February	March	April	May	June	July	August	September	October	November	December	Annual Average
Manufacturing													
2001	551.75	538.10	545.20	529.76	559.94	552.71	557.55	568.35	574.56	583.23	588.96	597.89	561.97
2002	576.00	569.38	578.45	586.45	586.18	608.26	606.05	601.94	589.11	578.14	584.98	604.65	588.70
2003	603.39	599.89	610.70	601.23	599.19	615.92	624.49	623.28	621.57	637.59	633.78	648.96	618.18
2004	651.71	636.34	629.56	613.09	628.50	639.75	621.27	638.66	633.83	624.46	625.82	639.75	631.90
2005	626.05	602.86	607.55	612.87	621.79	634.48	653.78	623.78	622.91	604.10	602.95	598.43	617.60
2006	587.82	596.57	602.24	590.40	600.06	634.73	611.41	621.02	616.31	644.18	637.46	635.46	615.14
2007	640.66	641.69	659.66	655.78	660.05	652.94	649.70	641.35	646.28	642.60	634.79	636.85	647.09
Professional and Business Services													
2001	509.66	511.55	526.05	545.10	553.09	555.94	564.20	553.45	564.63	562.68	582.42	595.83	552.45
2002	595.35	600.86	600.60	608.22	607.93	609.11	579.20	581.61	582.80	555.90	578.21	593.79	591.01
2003	562.12	570.55	564.24	542.51	545.48	560.38	542.42	535.00	522.29	518.62	520.00	505.30	540.79
2004	539.23	534.60	514.56	513.91	523.91	541.20	558.11	567.49	551.12	545.82	540.21	536.61	539.56
2005	557.70	527.04	529.97	543.47	553.35	529.74	532.86	535.52	530.39	547.40	516.38	554.09	537.92
2006	585.79	569.50	578.09	586.04	577.76	552.63	569.80	547.82	550.74	558.62	556.73	552.87	564.48
2007	559.68	577.67	609.20	589.38	592.99	600.26	588.41	587.64	587.33	568.62	560.81	580.75	583.65

Population
    2000 census: 1,998,257
    2007 estimate: 2,565,382
    Percent change, 2000–2007: 28.4%

Percent change in total nonfarm employment, 2000–2007: 25.8%

Industry with the largest growth in employment, 2000–2007 (thousands)
    Professional and business services, 47.7

Industry with the largest decline in employment, 2000–2007 (thousands)
    Information, -3.5

Civilian labor force
    2000: 1,062,845
    2007: 1,335,852

Employment-population ratio
    2000: 66.6%
    2007: 65.4%

Unemployment rate and rank among states
    2000: 4.5%, 38th
    2007: 4.8%, 37th

Employment by Industry, 2007

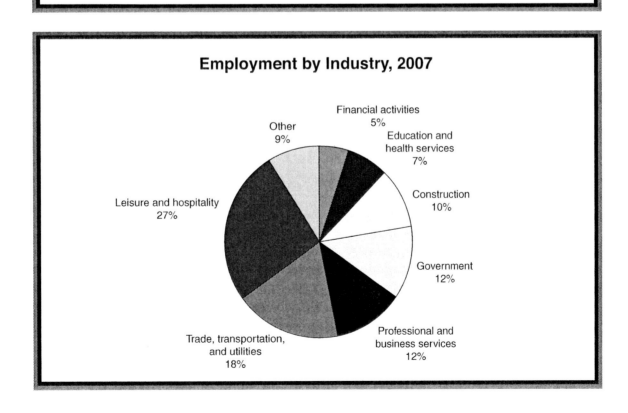

Financial activities 5%
Education and health services 7%
Construction 10%
Government 12%
Professional and business services 12%
Trade, transportation, and utilities 18%
Leisure and hospitality 27%
Other 9%

Employment by Industry: Nevada, 2000–2007

(Numbers in thousands, not seasonally adjusted.)

Industry and year	January	February	March	April	May	June	July	August	September	October	November	December	Annual Average
Total Nonfarm													
2000	991.6	997.5	1,007.4	1,014.8	1,028.0	1,027.7	1,024.8	1,038.3	1,043.6	1,046.7	1,051.1	1,051.3	1,026.9
2001	1,033.8	1,043.2	1,051.7	1,053.1	1,060.2	1,062.4	1,052.3	1,058.6	1,063.1	1,048.0	1,047.0	1,043.4	1,051.4
2002	1,019.1	1,025.9	1,037.4	1,046.2	1,055.6	1,053.6	1,049.2	1,057.5	1,063.6	1,070.5	1,072.2	1,072.7	1,052.0
2003	1,053.5	1,062.9	1,071.8	1,074.1	1,084.1	1,083.6	1,083.2	1,093.2	1,103.9	1,114.3	1,115.2	1,119.9	1,088.3
2004	1,101.5	1,108.3	1,122.0	1,140.2	1,148.3	1,153.7	1,153.6	1,158.8	1,174.0	1,189.2	1,189.4	1,193.0	1,152.7
2005	1,166.7	1,179.5	1,195.0	1,216.5	1,221.8	1,226.7	1,225.7	1,229.5	1,246.4	1,250.3	1,256.3	1,261.5	1,223.0
2006	1,239.8	1,255.0	1,268.3	1,276.3	1,286.3	1,291.2	1,279.8	1,282.9	1,292.6	1,292.0	1,294.8	1,295.6	1,279.6
2007	1,268.2	1,283.1	1,290.7	1,294.1	1,303.9	1,302.3	1,286.7	1,287.9	1,291.7	1,294.1	1,299.5	1,301.0	1,291.9
Total Private													
2000	874.0	876.6	884.7	891.7	900.8	910.5	910.2	920.1	922.2	920.9	925.1	925.4	905.1
2001	911.0	915.9	923.6	923.5	931.5	936.9	933.5	939.3	934.4	917.9	916.3	912.0	924.7
2002	893.2	895.0	905.4	914.4	922.9	924.3	926.5	934.5	932.5	934.3	935.4	935.5	921.2
2003	922.1	926.4	934.5	937.0	946.1	949.9	956.5	966.7	969.0	976.0	976.6	980.7	953.5
2004	967.8	970.3	981.7	999.9	1,006.9	1,017.2	1,023.7	1,029.4	1,034.2	1,045.0	1,044.8	1,048.1	1,014.1
2005	1,027.6	1,035.3	1,048.7	1,070.3	1,074.7	1,084.2	1,089.8	1,094.7	1,101.9	1,101.1	1,106.0	1,110.9	1,078.8
2006	1,095.6	1,104.9	1,117.3	1,124.0	1,133.5	1,143.0	1,138.6	1,142.2	1,142.0	1,135.9	1,137.5	1,138.2	1,129.4
2007	1,116.8	1,125.2	1,132.2	1,134.0	1,143.4	1,146.7	1,138.7	1,141.2	1,135.5	1,132.7	1,137.4	1,138.2	1,135.2
Goods-Producing													
2000	137.3	137.9	140.4	141.1	142.9	145.9	145.8	146.7	145.1	144.2	144.0	143.9	142.9
2001	139.4	140.2	142.0	143.0	145.5	148.4	148.4	150.0	148.2	147.0	144.5	140.9	144.8
2002	136.1	136.6	139.0	141.9	144.1	144.7	147.1	149.6	148.2	148.2	147.0	145.6	144.0
2003	142.4	144.0	146.7	148.0	150.9	153.3	155.3	157.9	157.9	160.3	158.9	159.0	152.9
2004	155.8	158.8	161.6	168.2	170.8	174.7	178.5	180.6	182.5	185.4	183.8	183.9	173.7
2005	176.8	181.1	185.5	190.0	191.0	193.7	197.8	199.7	201.9	201.2	200.5	201.1	193.4
2006	196.3	200.1	202.5	205.6	208.7	211.5	210.0	210.5	208.5	204.4	201.3	198.9	204.9
2007	191.9	193.5	196.9	197.0	200.3	200.9	199.8	200.8	197.4	195.5	193.3	191.2	196.5
Natural Resources and Mining													
2000	10.9	11.2	11.2	10.6	10.7	10.8	10.8	10.7	10.6	10.6	10.5	10.4	10.7
2001	9.9	9.9	9.8	9.6	9.8	9.7	9.7	9.6	9.4	9.4	9.3	9.2	9.6
2002	9.0	8.9	8.8	8.8	8.8	8.9	8.9	8.9	8.8	8.8	8.6	8.7	8.8
2003	8.2	8.6	8.7	8.6	8.7	8.9	9.1	9.1	8.9	9.1	9.1	9.2	8.9
2004	9.0	9.1	9.2	9.2	9.3	9.5	9.9	10.0	10.0	9.9	9.8	9.8	9.6
2005	9.8	9.8	10.1	10.5	10.4	10.8	11.1	11.2	11.1	11.2	11.0	11.0	10.7
2006	11.0	10.9	11.1	11.3	11.5	11.7	11.9	12.0	11.9	11.8	11.8	11.8	11.6
2007	11.8	11.7	11.9	11.9	12.1	12.4	12.4	12.4	12.2	12.3	12.2	12.3	12.1
Construction													
2000	84.7	84.8	87.0	88.4	89.9	92.3	92.1	93.0	91.5	90.1	89.8	89.5	89.4
2001	85.7	86.4	88.0	89.3	91.5	94.0	94.2	95.9	94.7	94.0	92.0	88.7	91.2
2002	85.0	85.6	88.1	90.8	92.6	92.9	94.8	97.3	96.1	95.7	94.7	93.3	92.2
2003	91.2	92.4	94.9	96.3	98.7	100.8	102.3	104.6	105.0	106.8	105.4	105.4	100.3
2004	102.8	105.2	107.5	113.6	115.6	118.9	122.2	123.9	126.1	128.8	127.1	127.3	118.3
2005	120.2	124.3	128.1	131.8	132.9	134.8	138.4	140.3	142.2	141.4	141.0	141.5	134.7
2006	136.9	140.2	141.9	144.2	146.7	148.8	146.9	147.3	145.3	141.9	138.8	136.3	142.9
2007	130.3	132.0	134.7	134.6	137.5	137.5	136.6	137.5	134.6	132.6	130.5	128.3	133.9
Manufacturing													
2000	41.7	41.9	42.2	42.1	42.3	42.8	42.9	43.0	43.0	43.5	43.7	44.0	42.7
2001	43.8	43.9	44.2	44.1	44.2	44.7	44.5	44.5	44.1	43.6	43.2	43.0	44.0
2002	42.1	42.1	42.1	42.3	42.7	42.9	43.4	43.4	43.3	43.7	43.7	43.6	42.9
2003	43.0	43.0	43.1	43.1	43.5	43.6	43.9	44.2	44.0	44.4	44.4	44.4	43.7
2004	44.0	44.5	44.9	45.4	45.9	46.3	46.4	46.7	46.4	46.7	46.9	46.8	45.9
2005	46.8	47.0	47.3	47.7	47.7	48.1	48.3	48.2	48.6	48.6	48.5	48.6	48.0
2006	48.4	49.0	49.5	50.1	50.5	51.0	51.2	51.2	51.3	50.7	50.7	50.8	50.4
2007	49.8	49.8	50.3	50.5	50.7	51.0	50.8	50.9	50.6	50.6	50.6	50.6	50.5
Service-Providing													
2000	854.3	859.6	867.0	873.7	885.1	881.8	879.0	891.6	898.5	902.5	907.1	907.4	883.9
2001	894.4	903.0	909.7	910.1	914.7	914.0	903.9	908.6	914.9	901.0	902.5	902.5	906.6
2002	883.0	889.3	898.4	904.3	911.5	908.9	902.1	907.9	915.4	922.3	925.2	927.1	908.0
2003	911.1	918.9	925.1	926.1	933.2	930.3	927.9	935.3	946.0	954.0	956.3	960.9	935.4
2004	945.7	949.5	960.4	972.0	977.5	979.0	975.1	978.2	991.5	1,003.8	1,005.6	1,009.1	979.0
2005	989.9	998.4	1,009.5	1,026.5	1,030.8	1,033.0	1,027.9	1,029.8	1,044.5	1,049.1	1,055.8	1,060.4	1,029.6
2006	1,043.5	1,054.9	1,065.8	1,070.7	1,077.6	1,079.7	1,069.8	1,072.4	1,084.1	1,087.6	1,093.5	1,096.7	1,074.7
2007	1,076.3	1,089.6	1,093.8	1,097.1	1,103.6	1,101.4	1,086.9	1,087.1	1,094.3	1,098.6	1,106.2	1,109.8	1,095.4
Trade, Transportation, and Utilities													
2000	179.4	178.7	178.9	180.8	181.9	183.4	184.1	186.6	188.2	189.6	193.7	197.1	185.2
2001	188.2	186.5	186.8	188.1	189.6	191.0	191.3	191.9	191.7	191.8	193.8	194.9	190.5
2002	187.5	185.6	186.4	188.9	190.1	190.7	191.4	191.4	192.0	194.6	197.0	199.3	191.2
2003	190.2	189.7	191.3	190.5	191.8	193.0	193.7	195.9	197.6	201.3	204.8	207.9	195.6
2004	197.9	197.5	199.1	200.7	202.0	204.2	204.7	205.3	205.8	209.2	213.1	215.6	204.6
2005	207.6	207.5	208.9	211.0	211.9	213.5	215.1	215.8	217.9	219.4	223.6	226.2	214.9
2006	220.4	220.2	222.6	223.0	224.2	225.4	225.1	226.1	226.9	228.6	233.1	235.9	226.0
2007	228.6	227.5	228.8	229.5	231.0	232.0	231.5	232.6	232.7	234.2	239.2	241.4	232.4
Wholesale Trade													
2000	32.6	32.8	33.1	33.4	33.8	34.1	34.2	34.4	34.5	34.5	35.0	35.3	33.9
2001	34.5	34.7	34.8	35.0	35.2	35.5	35.3	35.3	35.2	35.1	34.9	34.9	35.0
2002	34.4	34.6	35.0	35.0	35.0	35.1	34.9	34.9	34.7	34.7	34.6	34.7	34.8
2003	34.0	34.2	34.2	34.1	34.1	34.2	34.4	34.3	34.3	34.6	34.6	34.7	34.3
2004	34.4	34.5	34.7	34.9	35.1	35.4	35.9	35.8	35.9	36.2	36.1	36.3	35.4
2005	36.1	36.5	36.7	37.0	37.2	37.4	37.6	37.6	37.8	37.7	37.8	38.0	37.3
2006	37.8	38.1	38.4	38.5	38.7	38.9	38.9	39.0	39.1	39.1	39.1	39.3	38.7
2007	38.9	39.1	39.3	39.3	39.4	39.7	39.6	39.7	39.6	39.7	39.7	39.8	39.5

Employment by Industry: Nevada, 2000–2007—*Continued*

(Numbers in thousands, not seasonally adjusted.)

Industry and year	January	February	March	April	May	June	July	August	September	October	November	December	Annual Average
Retail Trade													
2000	106.8	105.8	105.3	106.4	107.3	108.0	108.3	110.2	111.3	112.0	115.3	118.3	109.5
2001	112.3	110.4	110.3	111.0	111.9	113.0	113.3	114.0	114.1	114.5	117.1	118.3	113.4
2002	112.3	110.6	111.1	112.5	113.7	114.3	114.3	114.1	114.9	117.0	120.7	123.2	114.9
2003	115.4	114.5	115.8	115.2	116.4	117.4	118.0	120.0	121.2	123.9	127.3	129.9	119.6
2004	120.9	120.4	121.4	122.9	123.9	125.5	125.1	125.7	126.1	128.2	132.2	134.6	125.6
2005	127.3	126.5	127.3	128.1	128.5	129.5	130.8	131.2	132.5	134.0	137.5	139.3	131.0
2006	134.1	133.6	135.2	135.2	135.8	136.1	135.7	136.2	136.6	138.1	141.7	143.5	136.8
2007	137.5	136.3	137.0	137.7	138.8	139.0	139.0	139.4	139.2	140.6	145.2	147.0	139.7
Transportation and Utilities													
2000	40.0	40.1	40.5	41.0	40.8	41.3	41.6	42.0	42.4	43.1	43.4	43.5	41.6
2001	41.4	41.4	41.7	42.1	42.5	42.5	42.7	42.6	42.4	42.2	41.8	41.7	42.1
2002	40.8	40.4	40.3	41.4	41.4	41.3	42.2	42.4	42.4	42.9	41.7	41.4	41.6
2003	40.8	41.0	41.3	41.2	41.3	41.4	41.3	41.6	42.1	42.8	42.9	43.3	41.8
2004	42.6	42.6	43.0	42.9	43.0	43.3	43.7	43.8	43.8	44.8	44.8	44.7	43.6
2005	44.2	44.5	44.9	45.9	46.2	46.6	46.7	47.0	47.6	47.7	48.3	48.9	46.5
2006	48.5	48.5	49.0	49.3	49.7	50.4	50.5	50.9	51.2	51.4	52.3	53.1	50.4
2007	52.2	52.1	52.5	52.5	52.8	53.3	52.9	53.5	53.9	53.9	54.3	54.6	53.2
Information													
2000	19.1	18.6	19.0	18.7	19.5	19.4	19.1	19.5	19.3	19.7	19.8	19.2	19.2
2001	19.9	21.5	21.3	19.8	19.7	19.0	18.0	17.7	17.3	17.7	18.0	17.6	19.0
2002	17.5	17.3	17.1	17.1	17.3	16.9	16.7	16.8	16.7	16.4	16.5	16.5	16.9
2003	16.1	16.0	15.8	15.8	15.9	15.8	15.4	15.2	15.1	15.0	15.1	15.2	15.5
2004	14.9	14.6	14.5	15.7	15.0	14.9	14.8	14.6	14.5	14.8	14.8	14.6	14.8
2005	15.0	14.4	14.4	15.0	15.4	14.7	14.5	14.4	14.2	14.7	14.6	14.5	14.7
2006	14.8	15.2	14.7	15.1	15.2	15.2	15.6	15.7	15.2	15.2	15.1	15.0	15.2
2007	15.3	15.8	15.6	15.8	16.1	16.1	15.5	16.0	15.7	15.4	15.5	15.4	15.7
Financial Activities													
2000	51.0	51.2	51.6	51.8	52.1	52.7	53.1	53.3	53.2	53.0	53.6	54.1	52.5
2001	53.9	54.3	54.8	54.7	54.8	55.4	55.3	55.8	55.9	55.4	55.2	55.8	55.1
2002	54.4	55.1	55.4	55.5	55.6	55.8	55.9	56.3	56.0	56.5	57.0	57.2	55.9
2003	56.6	56.9	57.0	57.6	58.4	58.5	59.2	59.3	59.6	59.7	59.6	60.0	58.5
2004	59.5	59.7	60.1	60.5	60.7	61.4	62.0	62.2	62.3	63.1	63.2	64.0	61.6
2005	63.0	63.0	63.6	63.7	64.0	64.5	64.3	64.8	65.0	64.8	65.0	65.3	64.3
2006	64.2	64.2	64.8	64.8	65.2	65.7	65.7	65.8	66.1	65.5	65.8	66.2	65.3
2007	65.0	65.1	65.5	65.0	65.4	65.5	64.9	64.7	64.4	64.2	64.1	64.5	64.9
Professional and Business Services													
2000	104.5	105.4	106.3	108.3	110.2	111.2	108.7	111.5	115.1	114.4	115.0	113.3	110.3
2001	113.4	115.1	116.1	114.3	115.1	114.8	111.8	113.9	112.6	111.0	111.6	109.6	113.3
2002	110.7	110.7	112.6	112.5	113.5	112.6	112.5	116.3	116.8	116.5	117.5	116.2	114.0
2003	117.4	117.8	118.1	118.7	119.2	118.2	120.2	123.8	124.2	126.7	126.4	126.3	121.4
2004	128.0	126.4	127.8	130.5	131.4	132.3	132.7	134.9	136.2	140.9	139.1	138.2	133.2
2005	139.4	140.1	141.9	144.4	144.4	145.4	145.5	147.8	148.9	150.9	153.4	154.3	146.4
2006	153.6	154.8	157.3	157.8	158.8	159.8	157.4	159.0	158.6	158.9	159.8	159.1	157.9
2007	158.4	161.1	159.4	159.7	159.9	159.1	156.2	157.9	156.0	156.1	156.9	154.9	158.0
Education and Health Services													
2000	60.6	61.4	62.3	62.1	62.3	63.0	62.9	63.2	64.1	64.8	65.3	66.0	63.1
2001	66.1	66.7	67.4	67.2	67.9	68.3	67.8	68.7	69.0	69.2	69.6	70.0	68.2
2002	69.1	70.0	70.7	71.5	72.1	72.0	71.6	72.3	72.6	73.4	73.8	74.0	71.9
2003	73.5	74.4	74.7	74.9	75.3	75.1	74.9	75.4	76.3	76.6	77.3	77.5	75.5
2004	77.2	78.0	78.9	79.4	79.3	79.4	80.0	80.1	81.5	81.8	82.1	82.6	80.0
2005	81.9	82.9	83.7	84.5	84.6	84.8	84.2	84.2	84.8	84.6	85.1	85.9	84.3
2006	85.0	86.1	86.8	86.7	87.1	87.7	86.8	87.4	88.6	89.3	90.0	90.6	87.7
2007	89.7	91.2	91.6	91.2	92.0	92.2	91.8	92.3	92.9	93.4	94.1	94.5	92.2
Leisure and Hospitality													
2000	296.2	297.2	299.5	302.1	304.8	307.4	309.0	311.7	309.6	307.8	306.4	304.4	304.6
2001	302.2	303.4	306.5	307.1	309.1	309.5	311.0	311.2	309.6	296.3	294.5	294.0	304.5
2002	288.9	290.3	294.3	297.1	300.0	301.1	301.6	302.0	300.8	299.4	297.4	297.6	297.5
2003	296.5	298.0	300.9	301.8	304.6	305.3	307.1	308.4	307.6	305.8	303.7	303.7	303.6
2004	303.1	303.2	306.5	311.4	313.7	315.5	317.3	318.0	317.6	315.4	314.7	315.1	312.6
2005	311.5	313.6	317.5	328.5	329.9	333.5	334.2	333.6	334.6	331.0	329.1	328.5	327.1
2006	327.4	330.0	333.6	336.0	338.8	341.8	342.0	341.4	341.7	337.9	336.4	336.6	337.0
2007	332.7	335.7	338.4	339.4	341.9	343.5	341.8	339.6	339.1	337.0	337.5	339.6	338.9
Other Services													
2000	25.9	26.2	26.7	26.8	27.1	27.5	27.5	27.6	27.6	27.4	27.3	27.4	27.0
2001	27.9	28.2	28.7	29.3	29.8	30.5	29.9	30.1	30.1	29.5	29.1	29.2	29.4
2002	29.0	29.4	29.9	29.9	30.2	30.5	29.7	29.8	29.4	29.3	29.2	29.1	29.6
2003	29.4	29.6	30.0	29.7	30.0	30.7	30.7	30.8	30.7	30.6	30.8	31.1	30.3
2004	31.4	32.1	33.2	33.5	34.0	34.8	33.7	33.7	33.8	34.4	34.0	34.1	33.6
2005	32.4	32.7	33.2	33.2	33.5	34.1	34.2	34.4	34.6	34.5	34.7	35.1	33.9
2006	33.9	34.3	35.0	35.0	35.5	35.9	36.0	36.3	36.4	36.1	36.0	35.9	35.5
2007	35.2	35.3	36.0	36.4	36.8	37.4	37.2	37.3	37.3	36.9	36.8	36.7	36.6
Government													
2000	117.6	120.9	122.7	123.1	127.2	117.2	114.6	118.2	121.4	125.8	126.0	125.9	121.7
2001	122.8	127.3	128.1	129.6	128.7	125.5	118.8	119.3	128.7	130.1	130.7	131.4	126.8
2002	125.9	130.9	132.0	131.8	132.7	129.3	122.7	123.0	131.1	136.2	136.8	137.2	130.8
2003	131.4	136.5	137.3	137.1	138.0	133.7	126.7	126.5	134.9	138.3	138.6	139.2	134.9
2004	133.7	138.0	140.3	140.3	141.4	136.5	129.9	129.4	139.8	144.2	144.6	144.9	138.6
2005	139.1	144.2	146.3	146.2	147.1	142.5	135.9	134.8	144.5	149.2	150.3	150.6	144.2
2006	144.2	150.1	151.0	152.3	152.8	148.2	141.2	140.7	150.6	156.1	157.3	157.4	150.2
2007	151.4	157.9	158.5	160.1	160.5	155.6	148.0	146.7	156.2	161.4	162.1	162.8	156.8

Average Weekly Hours by Selected Industry: Nevada, 2001–2007

(Not seasonally adjusted.)

Industry and year	January	February	March	April	May	June	July	August	September	October	November	December	Annual Average
Construction													
2001	34.9	36.3	38.0	38.5	38.3	38.1	38.3	39.2	38.3	38.4	36.7	37.4	37.7
2002	37.1	38.1	37.9	38.2	38.6	39.7	38.8	40.1	39.3	39.4	37.6	38.7	38.7
2003	37.6	36.0	37.7	38.8	38.4	38.9	38.6	39.6	38.4	37.4	36.2	35.9	37.8
2004	35.5	35.1	36.7	38.1	38.0	38.6	39.6	39.5	38.9	38.5	37.6	36.9	37.8
2005	36.1	36.0	36.9	37.3	37.5	38.0	38.8	39.2	38.8	38.6	38.2	37.7	37.8
2006	36.7	36.3	36.9	37.1	37.6	38.1	38.1	38.2	37.6	37.5	38.2	38.2	37.5
2007	38.0	38.1	37.9	37.6	37.8	37.8	37.5	37.3	37.6	37.5	37.3	37.4	37.7
Manufacturing													
2001	38.5	39.1	39.0	38.1	39.4	39.4	38.3	38.8	38.6	38.4	38.2	38.1	38.7
2002	37.9	39.5	39.8	39.6	39.8	39.5	38.5	39.7	37.9	37.4	38.3	38.1	38.8
2003	38.0	37.5	38.7	38.3	39.0	39.4	40.0	40.3	39.8	39.3	39.3	38.7	39.0
2004	39.3	39.1	39.2	39.6	40.1	39.7	40.3	40.6	40.4	40.2	41.1	41.0	40.1
2005	40.5	40.3	39.9	39.6	39.8	39.4	39.6	39.6	39.9	39.7	39.8	39.5	39.8
2006	39.1	39.2	39.3	39.8	39.9	39.9	39.2	39.4	39.2	39.3	39.2	39.3	39.4
2007	39.1	39.4	39.5	39.5	39.6	39.7	39.1	39.1	39.3	39.1	39.0	39.1	39.3
Wholesale Trade													
2001	38.9	38.2	38.8	40.5	40.3	41.3	42.8	41.1	42.4	39.8	41.3	40.1	40.5
2002	38.3	38.0	37.5	37.9	36.9	37.9	38.1	39.0	38.4	38.5	37.2	38.2	38.0
2003	38.5	37.7	36.5	37.1	37.1	36.8	37.4	35.4	36.1	36.9	36.7	36.4	36.9
2004	35.2	35.8	35.6	36.1	36.8	36.7	37.2	37.3	36.7	37.0	36.5	36.2	36.4
2005	35.6	35.5	35.8	36.3	36.2	35.4	35.7	35.8	36.0	36.2	36.0	35.8	35.9
2006	35.3	35.4	35.7	36.0	36.1	36.0	36.1	35.7	36.1	35.9	36.2	36.1	35.9
2007	35.6	35.7	36.0	35.8	35.7	35.9	36.2	36.4	36.2	35.9	36.1	36.2	36.0
Retail Trade													
2001	28.9	28.1	27.6	27.5	27.6	28.4	28.8	29.2	30.6	30.6	31.5	31.7	29.2
2002	30.7	30.8	31.3	32.0	31.6	32.6	32.8	32.0	31.6	31.3	31.0	31.7	31.6
2003	31.2	32.1	32.4	32.4	32.2	33.4	32.5	33.0	33.3	34.6	35.3	36.4	33.3
2004	34.8	33.1	32.3	33.5	34.9	35.1	35.0	35.8	36.2	36.8	37.0	36.7	35.1
2005	35.1	33.7	34.1	34.2	33.9	34.1	34.1	34.3	34.5	34.9	35.6	36.1	34.6
2006	35.3	34.1	34.2	34.3	34.1	34.1	34.3	34.1	34.5	34.3	34.3	34.2	34.3
2007	33.9	34.1	34.1	34.2	34.2	34.3	34.4	34.3	34.6	34.3	34.7	34.6	34.3

Average Hourly Earnings by Selected Industry: Nevada, 2001–2007

(Dollars, not seasonally adjusted.)

Industry and year	January	February	March	April	May	June	July	August	September	October	November	December	Annual Average
Construction													
2001	21.07	20.76	20.87	20.84	20.84	20.59	20.51	20.88	21.02	20.86	20.52	20.53	20.77
2002	20.56	20.55	20.91	21.02	21.36	21.15	21.45	21.29	21.39	21.38	20.98	21.48	21.14
2003	21.09	21.40	21.69	21.77	21.98	22.17	21.89	22.03	21.57	21.02	20.91	21.06	21.55
2004	21.34	21.10	21.36	21.20	21.30	21.55	21.67	21.71	21.67	21.52	21.44	21.65	21.47
2005	21.73	21.55	21.45	21.78	21.49	21.39	21.57	21.28	21.43	21.38	21.55	21.88	21.54
2006	21.94	21.89	21.81	21.87	21.95	21.94	22.47	22.16	22.28	22.18	21.91	21.95	22.03
2007	22.09	21.97	21.86	21.84	21.77	21.81	22.02	22.13	22.27	22.20	22.23	22.26	22.03
Manufacturing													
2001	13.85	13.77	13.99	14.08	13.94	13.97	13.55	13.38	13.44	13.65	13.81	14.12	13.79
2002	14.42	14.30	14.35	14.46	14.67	14.36	14.85	15.07	14.80	14.93	14.73	14.53	14.62
2003	14.65	14.46	14.28	14.50	14.68	14.46	14.70	14.93	14.99	14.86	14.58	14.38	14.63
2004	14.20	14.28	14.32	14.33	14.39	14.74	14.62	14.50	14.75	15.02	14.97	15.01	14.60
2005	14.95	15.04	14.96	14.93	14.83	14.94	14.97	14.97	14.92	15.01	15.05	15.19	14.98
2006	15.26	15.31	15.34	15.55	15.43	15.49	15.55	15.44	15.55	15.56	15.55	15.52	15.46
2007	15.60	15.49	15.47	15.49	15.42	15.47	15.57	15.59	15.60	15.61	15.56	15.56	15.54
Wholesale Trade													
2001	15.98	16.12	15.75	16.05	15.32	14.92	15.11	14.93	15.26	15.36	14.75	15.08	15.37
2002	14.80	14.83	14.62	14.52	14.76	14.91	15.35	15.77	15.54	15.65	15.76	15.96	15.21
2003	16.54	17.09	17.48	17.05	17.43	17.86	17.95	17.64	17.13	16.86	16.70	16.77	17.20
2004	16.43	16.30	16.22	16.18	16.15	16.13	16.60	16.95	17.20	17.10	17.06	17.20	16.65
2005	16.90	16.86	16.49	16.51	16.58	16.76	16.82	16.72	16.67	16.60	16.65	16.75	16.69
2006	16.58	16.55	16.60	16.70	16.78	16.88	17.25	17.25	17.23	17.26	16.89	16.94	16.91
2007	16.84	16.80	16.87	16.78	16.77	16.82	17.01	16.91	16.98	17.05	17.05	17.03	16.91
Retail Trade													
2001	11.23	11.55	11.43	11.50	11.50	11.52	11.43	11.76	11.76	11.55	11.59	11.57	11.54
2002	11.74	11.58	11.79	12.10	11.99	11.88	12.03	12.03	12.24	12.16	12.19	12.37	12.02
2003	12.52	12.79	12.40	12.70	12.81	12.92	12.78	12.62	12.44	12.17	12.03	11.83	12.48
2004	11.98	12.00	11.82	12.08	11.92	12.30	12.26	12.40	12.45	12.30	12.23	12.25	12.18
2005	12.64	12.54	12.58	12.42	12.38	12.59	12.62	12.55	12.44	12.52	12.47	12.35	12.51
2006	12.66	12.61	12.72	12.69	12.70	12.90	12.93	12.85	12.85	12.75	12.75	12.78	12.76
2007	12.88	12.85	12.87	12.82	12.83	12.89	12.85	12.90	12.79	12.75	12.65	12.66	12.81

Average Weekly Earnings by Selected Industry: Nevada, 2001–2007

(Dollars, not seasonally adjusted.)

Industry and year	January	February	March	April	May	June	July	August	September	October	November	December	Annual Average
Construction													
2001	735.34	753.59	793.06	802.34	798.17	784.48	785.53	818.50	805.07	801.02	753.08	767.82	783.03
2002	762.78	782.96	792.49	802.96	824.50	839.66	832.26	853.73	840.63	842.37	788.85	831.28	818.12
2003	792.98	770.40	817.71	844.68	844.03	862.41	844.95	872.39	828.29	786.15	756.94	756.05	814.59
2004	757.57	740.61	783.91	807.72	809.40	831.83	858.13	857.55	842.96	828.52	806.14	798.89	811.57
2005	784.45	775.80	791.51	812.39	805.88	812.82	836.92	834.18	831.48	825.27	823.21	824.88	814.21
2006	805.20	794.61	804.79	811.38	825.32	835.91	856.11	846.51	837.73	831.75	836.96	838.49	826.13
2007	839.42	837.06	828.49	821.18	822.91	824.42	825.75	825.45	837.35	832.50	829.18	832.52	830.53
Manufacturing													
2001	533.23	538.41	545.61	536.45	549.24	550.42	518.97	519.14	518.78	524.16	527.54	537.97	533.67
2002	546.52	564.85	571.13	572.62	583.87	567.22	571.73	598.28	560.92	558.38	564.16	553.59	567.26
2003	556.70	542.25	552.64	555.35	572.52	569.72	588.00	601.68	596.60	584.00	572.99	556.51	570.57
2004	558.06	558.35	561.34	567.47	577.04	585.18	589.19	588.70	595.90	603.80	615.27	615.41	585.46
2005	605.48	606.11	596.90	591.23	590.23	588.64	592.81	592.81	595.31	595.90	598.99	600.01	596.20
2006	596.67	600.15	602.86	618.89	615.66	618.05	609.56	608.34	609.56	611.51	609.56	609.94	609.12
2007	609.96	610.31	611.07	611.86	610.63	614.16	608.79	609.57	613.08	610.35	606.84	608.40	610.72
Wholesale Trade													
2001	621.62	615.78	611.10	650.03	617.40	616.20	646.71	613.62	647.02	611.33	609.18	604.71	622.49
2002	566.84	563.54	548.25	550.31	544.64	565.09	584.84	615.03	596.74	602.53	586.27	609.67	577.98
2003	636.79	644.29	638.02	632.56	646.65	657.25	671.33	624.46	618.39	622.13	612.89	610.43	634.68
2004	578.34	583.54	577.43	584.10	594.32	591.97	617.52	632.24	631.24	632.70	622.69	622.64	606.06
2005	601.64	598.53	590.34	599.31	600.20	593.30	600.47	598.58	600.12	600.92	599.40	599.65	599.17
2006	585.27	585.87	592.62	601.20	605.76	607.68	622.73	615.83	622.00	619.63	611.42	611.53	607.07
2007	599.50	599.76	607.32	600.72	598.69	603.84	615.76	615.52	614.68	612.10	615.51	616.49	608.76
Retail Trade													
2001	324.55	324.56	315.47	316.25	317.40	327.17	329.18	343.39	359.86	353.43	365.09	366.77	336.97
2002	360.42	356.66	369.03	387.20	378.88	387.29	394.58	384.96	386.78	380.61	377.89	392.13	379.83
2003	390.62	410.56	401.76	411.48	412.48	431.53	415.35	416.46	414.25	421.08	424.66	430.61	415.58
2004	416.90	397.20	381.79	404.68	416.01	431.73	429.10	443.92	450.69	452.64	452.51	449.58	427.52
2005	443.66	422.60	428.98	424.76	419.68	429.32	430.34	430.47	429.18	436.95	443.93	445.84	432.85
2006	446.90	430.00	435.02	435.27	433.07	439.89	443.50	438.19	439.88	437.33	437.33	437.08	437.67
2007	436.63	438.19	w438.87	438.44	438.79	442.13	442.04	442.47	442.53	437.33	438.96	438.04	439.38

Population
    2000 census: 1,235,786
    2007 estimate: 1,315,828
    Percent change, 2000–2007: 6.5%

Percent change in total nonfarm employment, 2000–2007: 4.3%

Industry with the largest growth in employment, 2000–2007 (thousands)
    Education and health services, 19.5

Industry with the largest decline in employment, 2000–2007 (thousands)
    Manufacturing, -24.6

Civilian labor force
    2000: 694,254
    2007: 738,314

Employment-population ratio
    2000: 71.1%
    2007: 68.4%

Unemployment rate and rank among states
    2000: 2.7%, 3rd
    2007: 3.6%, 13th

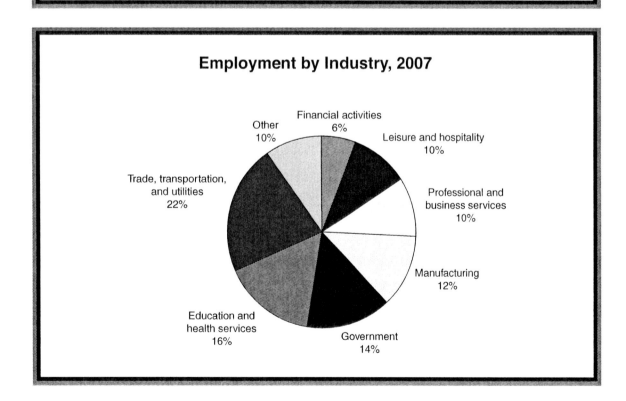

Employment by Industry, 2007

Other 10%
Financial activities 6%
Leisure and hospitality 10%
Trade, transportation, and utilities 22%
Professional and business services 10%
Manufacturing 12%
Education and health services 16%
Government 14%

Employment by Industry: New Hampshire, 2000–2007

(Numbers in thousands, not seasonally adjusted.)

Industry and year	January	February	March	April	May	June	July	August	September	October	November	December	Annual Average
Total Nonfarm													
2000	603.3	605.6	609.6	615.8	623.4	631.4	625.1	624.6	628.9	628.6	631.5	637.1	622.0
2001	622.1	622.8	623.6	625.3	633.4	638.4	627.4	627.4	628.3	626.0	624.6	627.4	627.2
2002	608.3	607.7	610.7	613.9	620.7	626.9	621.1	621.9	623.7	621.0	620.4	624.2	618.4
2003	603.5	602.7	605.1	608.9	617.4	625.4	621.1	624.3	624.6	625.8	626.0	629.4	617.9
2004	608.0	609.2	615.4	621.4	630.1	635.4	632.3	632.2	635.9	635.7	634.8	638.2	627.4
2005	621.4	620.2	622.0	630.7	638.1	643.9	640.8	639.5	645.1	642.2	643.2	648.2	636.3
2006	625.2	626.9	630.3	638.2	643.4	651.2	646.2	644.8	649.4	647.8	647.2	652.5	641.9
2007	632.0	633.9	635.8	638.7	648.9	656.1	652.8	653.5	659.7	658.1	656.7	660.5	648.9
Total Private													
2000	520.7	519.7	522.9	529.4	536.2	549.3	550.7	551.7	544.9	542.6	544.3	550.5	538.5
2001	537.4	535.0	535.2	537.7	545.1	554.2	552.8	553.2	540.8	535.7	533.5	536.1	541.4
2002	521.4	517.4	519.6	523.9	531.6	540.2	541.9	543.7	535.1	528.7	526.8	530.5	530.1
2003	514.8	510.5	512.4	516.4	526.3	536.3	540.1	544.4	534.5	531.8	531.3	534.2	527.8
2004	518.9	517.4	521.8	528.3	536.9	547.6	552.4	553.6	545.0	541.1	539.9	543.1	537.2
2005	528.5	526.1	527.1	536.6	543.2	555.5	560.8	560.6	552.3	547.6	547.6	552.4	544.9
2006	535.0	532.1	534.9	542.8	548.1	562.2	564.7	565.1	554.8	551.4	550.7	555.2	549.8
2007	539.9	537.5	539.1	542.2	552.8	565.7	570.3	571.8	564.3	559.9	558.6	562.0	555.3
Goods-Producing													
2000	124.8	124.2	125.2	127.1	128.4	130.0	129.3	130.8	129.9	130.4	131.0	131.3	128.5
2001	128.4	128.0	127.6	128.4	129.3	129.1	126.1	126.4	123.7	122.0	119.8	118.7	125.6
2002	114.5	113.2	113.2	114.4	115.5	115.5	114.4	114.9	113.7	112.8	111.6	112.2	113.8
2003	108.3	106.7	107.3	108.9	110.9	112.2	111.0	112.7	111.6	111.7	111.3	110.5	110.3
2004	106.7	105.8	106.7	109.6	111.3	112.9	113.2	113.4	112.6	111.7	110.8	110.3	110.4
2005	107.1	106.6	106.9	110.1	111.4	112.9	112.2	112.9	111.9	112.0	112.2	111.3	110.6
2006	106.5	105.4	106.2	108.8	109.8	111.0	110.0	111.1	110.2	109.8	108.6	107.4	108.7
2007	104.1	102.9	103.4	105.0	107.4	108.5	109.0	110.3	109.7	109.1	108.4	107.8	107.1
Natural Resources and Mining													
2000	1.0	1.0	1.0	0.9	1.0	1.1	1.1	1.1	1.1	1.1	1.1	1.1	1.0
2001	1.0	1.0	1.0	0.9	1.0	1.0	1.0	1.0	1.0	1.0	1.0	1.0	1.0
2002	0.9	0.9	0.9	0.9	0.9	1.0	1.0	1.0	1.0	1.0	0.9	0.9	0.9
2003	0.9	0.8	0.9	0.9	0.9	1.0	1.0	1.0	1.0	1.0	1.0	0.9	0.9
2004	0.8	0.9	0.9	0.9	1.0	1.0	1.0	1.0	1.1	1.1	1.0	1.0	1.0
2005	0.9	0.9	1.0	1.0	1.0	1.1	1.1	1.1	1.1	1.1	1.1	1.1	1.0
2006	0.9	0.9	1.0	1.0	1.1	1.1	1.2	1.2	1.2	1.2	1.1	1.1	1.1
2007	1.0	1.0	1.0	1.1	1.1	1.2	1.2	1.2	1.2	1.2	1.1	1.1	1.1
Construction													
2000	22.4	21.8	22.5	24.0	25.1	26.3	26.7	26.8	26.2	26.1	26.0	25.5	24.9
2001	23.8	23.5	23.8	25.8	27.7	28.8	29.6	29.7	28.8	28.7	28.3	28.1	27.2
2002	26.2	25.4	25.7	27.4	28.9	29.0	28.8	29.4	28.8	28.9	28.2	28.0	27.9
2003	25.7	24.9	25.2	27.4	29.4	30.5	31.2	31.4	30.8	30.9	30.2	29.4	28.9
2004	26.4	25.7	26.2	28.8	30.3	31.2	31.8	31.6	31.0	30.5	29.7	29.0	29.4
2005	26.3	25.8	26.0	28.9	30.1	31.0	31.5	31.5	30.9	30.7	30.7	29.8	29.4
2006	27.2	26.5	27.1	29.2	30.2	31.3	31.3	31.3	30.9	30.3	29.2	28.0	29.4
2007	25.6	24.6	24.8	26.3	28.6	29.2	29.9	30.8	30.3	29.8	29.1	28.4	28.1
Manufacturing													
2000	101.4	101.4	101.7	102.2	102.3	102.6	101.5	102.9	102.6	103.2	103.9	104.7	102.5
2001	103.6	103.5	102.8	101.7	100.6	99.3	95.5	95.7	93.9	92.3	90.5	89.6	97.4
2002	87.4	86.9	86.6	86.1	85.7	85.5	84.6	84.5	83.9	82.9	82.5	83.3	85.0
2003	81.7	81.0	81.2	80.6	80.6	80.7	78.8	80.3	79.8	79.8	80.1	80.2	80.4
2004	79.5	79.2	79.6	79.9	80.0	80.7	80.4	80.8	80.5	80.1	80.1	80.3	80.1
2005	79.9	79.9	79.9	80.2	80.3	80.8	79.6	80.3	79.9	80.2	80.4	80.4	80.2
2006	78.4	78.0	78.1	78.6	78.5	78.6	77.5	78.6	78.1	78.3	78.3	78.3	78.3
2007	77.5	77.3	77.6	77.6	77.7	78.1	77.9	78.3	78.2	78.1	78.2	78.3	77.9
Service-Providing													
2000	478.5	481.4	484.4	488.7	495.0	501.4	495.8	493.8	499.0	498.2	500.5	505.8	493.5
2001	493.7	494.8	496.0	496.9	504.1	509.3	501.3	501.0	504.6	504.0	504.8	508.7	501.6
2002	493.8	494.5	497.5	499.5	505.2	511.4	506.7	507.0	510.0	508.2	508.8	512.0	504.6
2003	495.2	496.0	497.8	500.0	506.5	513.2	510.1	511.6	513.0	514.1	514.7	518.9	507.6
2004	501.3	503.4	508.7	511.8	518.8	522.5	519.1	518.8	523.3	524.0	524.0	527.9	517.0
2005	514.3	513.6	515.1	520.6	526.7	531.0	528.6	526.6	533.2	530.2	531.0	536.9	525.7
2006	518.7	521.5	524.1	529.4	533.6	540.2	536.2	533.7	539.2	538.0	538.6	545.1	533.2
2007	527.9	531.0	532.4	533.7	541.5	547.6	543.8	543.2	550.0	549.0	548.3	552.7	541.8
Trade, Transportation, and Utilities													
2000	135.6	133.0	133.3	134.8	136.3	138.6	137.0	137.1	136.3	137.4	141.0	144.8	137.1
2001	137.3	134.2	133.7	134.8	136.7	138.6	137.4	137.6	136.4	137.7	140.6	143.1	137.3
2002	137.1	133.6	134.3	135.9	137.3	139.5	138.6	139.2	138.9	138.7	141.0	144.6	138.2
2003	136.0	133.3	134.3	135.2	136.9	139.2	139.2	140.0	138.9	140.3	142.9	144.7	138.4
2004	137.1	135.2	136.3	137.5	139.2	140.9	140.5	140.1	139.5	140.6	143.0	145.7	139.6
2005	139.2	136.7	136.6	137.8	139.5	141.8	141.5	141.5	141.7	140.2	141.7	144.2	140.6
2006	140.2	137.5	138.3	140.1	141.1	143.0	142.2	142.3	140.7	141.5	144.9	147.7	141.6
2007	141.5	138.1	138.6	139.1	141.1	143.2	142.8	143.0	141.8	142.8	145.4	148.0	142.1
Wholesale Trade													
2000	24.5	24.6	24.8	24.9	25.8	26.2	26.3	26.4	26.2	26.3	26.4	26.7	25.7
2001	26.3	26.3	26.3	26.5	26.6	26.9	27.0	26.9	26.7	26.9	26.6	26.8	26.7
2002	26.5	26.4	26.5	26.4	26.4	26.7	26.7	26.7	26.6	26.8	26.6	26.8	26.6
2003	26.2	26.1	26.0	26.4	26.6	27.0	27.2	27.3	26.9	26.9	26.9	26.9	26.7
2004	26.6	26.6	26.9	27.2	27.3	27.5	27.7	27.8	27.4	27.3	27.1	27.2	27.2
2005	27.1	26.9	27.0	27.4	27.6	27.7	27.8	27.7	27.4	27.8	27.7	27.7	27.5
2006	27.5	27.4	27.6	27.9	28.2	28.4	28.3	28.4	28.2	28.2	28.1	28.3	28.0
2007	28.2	28.0	28.2	28.4	28.5	28.7	28.8	29.0	28.6	28.5	28.4	28.5	28.5

Employment by Industry: New Hampshire, 2000–2007—*Continued*

(Numbers in thousands, not seasonally adjusted.)

Industry and year	January	February	March	April	May	June	July	August	September	October	November	December	Annual Average
Retail Trade													
2000	94.2	91.7	91.9	93.1	93.7	95.2	94.6	94.6	93.3	94.0	97.8	101.2	94.6
2001	95.4	92.2	91.9	92.5	94.0	95.5	95.0	95.4	93.7	94.8	98.2	100.5	94.9
2002	95.3	92.0	92.5	93.7	94.9	96.6	96.2	96.2	96.9	96.3	95.8	98.4	101.6	95.9
2003	94.1	91.8	92.7	93.2	94.4	96.2	96.5	97.4	96.0	97.2	99.9	101.7	95.9
2004	95.1	93.4	94.2	95.0	96.3	97.6	97.8	97.6	96.4	97.3	100.2	102.8	97.0
2005	96.6	94.4	94.2	95.0	96.3	98.1	98.3	98.6	96.9	98.1	100.7	103.0	97.5
2006	97.5	94.9	95.4	96.7	97.2	98.6	98.5	98.6	96.6	97.6	101.1	103.2	98.0
2007	98.0	94.9	95.1	95.3	97.0	98.6	98.8	98.9	97.5	98.4	101.3	103.7	98.1
Transportation and Utilities													
2000	16.9	16.7	16.6	16.8	16.8	17.2	16.1	16.1	16.8	17.1	16.8	16.9	16.7
2001	15.6	15.7	15.5	15.8	16.1	16.2	15.4	15.3	16.0	16.0	15.8	15.8	15.8
2002	15.3	15.2	15.3	15.8	16.0	16.2	15.7	15.6	16.0	16.1	16.0	16.2	15.8
2003	15.7	15.4	15.6	15.6	15.9	16.0	15.5	15.3	16.0	16.2	16.1	16.1	15.8
2004	15.4	15.2	15.2	15.3	15.6	15.8	15.0	14.7	15.7	16.0	15.7	15.7	15.4
2005	15.5	15.4	15.4	15.4	15.6	16.0	15.4	15.4	15.9	15.8	15.8	16.1	15.6
2006	15.2	15.2	15.3	15.5	15.7	16.0	15.4	15.3	15.9	15.7	15.7	16.2	15.6
2007	15.3	15.2	15.3	15.4	15.6	15.9	15.2	15.1	15.7	15.9	15.7	15.8	15.5
Information													
2000	13.3	13.3	13.4	13.7	14.0	14.2	14.2	13.6	14.1	14.5	14.6	14.6	13.9
2001	14.3	14.2	14.1	13.8	13.7	13.8	13.7	13.6	13.5	13.4	13.4	13.4	13.7
2002	13.4	13.3	13.1	13.0	12.9	12.9	12.8	12.7	12.7	12.7	12.7	12.6	12.9
2003	12.4	12.2	12.2	12.1	12.1	12.2	12.2	12.1	11.9	12.0	12.2	12.3	12.2
2004	12.1	12.3	12.4	12.6	12.6	12.6	12.7	12.7	12.5	12.6	12.7	12.8	12.6
2005	12.5	12.5	12.5	12.7	12.8	12.8	12.9	12.9	12.7	12.7	12.9	12.9	12.7
2006	12.8	12.6	12.7	12.7	12.7	12.6	12.7	12.6	12.5	12.3	12.1	12.1	12.2	12.5
2007	12.3	12.2	12.1	12.2	12.3	12.5	12.4	12.3	12.2	12.2	12.4	12.4	12.3
Financial Activities													
2000	34.1	33.9	33.8	33.7	33.8	34.3	34.3	34.4	34.1	34.1	34.4	34.8	34.1
2001	34.9	35.1	35.3	35.4	35.7	36.1	36.1	36.3	35.8	35.6	35.8	36.3	35.7
2002	36.3	36.2	36.2	36.1	36.3	36.7	36.8	37.0	36.8	36.7	36.7	36.8	36.6
2003	36.8	36.8	36.7	37.1	37.3	37.5	37.5	37.5	36.8	36.6	36.6	36.8	37.0
2004	36.7	36.7	37.1	37.1	37.3	37.7	37.8	38.0	37.4	37.6	37.6	38.0	37.4
2005	38.2	38.1	38.3	38.9	39.1	39.8	40.3	40.4	40.0	39.7	39.6	40.0	39.4
2006	39.1	39.2	39.3	39.3	39.2	39.8	40.0	39.7	39.3	39.2	39.0	39.2	39.4
2007	38.1	38.1	38.2	38.1	38.2	38.7	38.9	39.0	38.6	38.6	38.5	38.6	38.5
Professional and Business Services													
2000	55.4	56.1	57.1	58.1	58.4	59.8	59.4	60.0	59.3	59.5	60.0	60.3	58.6
2001	57.4	56.9	57.1	57.3	58.0	58.5	57.7	57.9	56.6	55.6	55.2	55.2	57.0
2002	53.0	52.8	53.1	53.9	54.7	55.0	55.4	55.7	55.0	54.5	54.6	53.9	54.3
2003	52.5	52.3	52.3	54.0	54.5	55.5	55.6	56.3	55.7	55.7	56.0	56.0	54.7
2004	54.3	54.6	55.6	57.2	57.6	58.0	58.2	59.2	58.0	58.3	58.5	58.5	57.3
2005	56.6	56.7	56.9	58.9	59.0	60.0	60.4	60.6	60.1	60.0	60.4	60.3	59.2
2006	58.3	58.8	58.8	61.6	61.7	63.4	63.2	63.4	63.0	63.2	63.1	63.4	61.8
2007	62.4	63.2	63.1	64.9	65.8	66.7	66.7	67.4	66.8	66.7	66.6	66.6	65.6
Education and Health Services													
2000	81.8	82.8	83.3	84.3	84.1	84.2	83.2	83.4	85.1	84.8	85.4	85.5	83.9
2001	86.9	88.3	88.4	88.3	88.2	88.4	88.3	88.6	89.6	90.2	91.0	91.5	89.0
2002	90.4	91.5	92.2	92.1	92.4	92.1	91.0	91.0	92.4	91.8	92.4	92.3	91.8
2003	92.1	92.9	93.2	92.8	92.9	92.8	91.9	92.3	93.4	93.7	94.4	94.3	93.1
2004	93.6	94.5	94.9	95.1	95.0	94.8	94.0	94.0	95.4	96.0	96.5	96.2	95.0
2005	95.7	96.6	96.9	97.8	97.7	97.6	97.4	97.2	98.9	98.8	99.1	99.7	97.8
2006	98.7	99.4	99.8	99.9	99.9	100.2	99.6	99.5	100.7	101.2	101.8	102.5	100.3
2007	101.0	102.5	102.9	102.7	102.8	103.4	102.8	102.8	104.6	104.7	105.2	105.5	103.4
Leisure and Hospitality													
2000	52.3	52.9	53.2	53.9	57.2	63.8	68.8	68.3	61.8	57.9	53.8	55.1	58.2
2001	54.4	54.6	54.5	55.4	59.1	65.4	69.5	69.4	62.3	58.7	55.1	55.6	59.5
2002	54.8	54.9	55.7	56.6	60.4	66.3	70.9	71.1	64.1	60.6	57.1	57.5	60.8
2003	56.3	56.0	55.9	55.9	61.1	66.2	71.4	72.2	65.4	61.3	57.3	58.9	61.5
2004	57.8	57.9	58.2	58.5	62.9	69.3	74.3	74.6	68.2	63.3	59.7	60.5	63.8
2005	58.5	58.2	58.1	59.0	62.3	69.0	74.3	73.1	67.0	61.6	58.1	60.1	63.3
2006	58.5	58.3	58.8	59.1	62.3	70.1	74.8	74.3	67.0	62.9	59.6	61.2	63.9
2007	59.2	59.1	59.2	58.7	63.4	70.2	75.1	74.4	68.2	63.7	60.1	61.0	64.4
Other Services													
2000	23.4	23.5	23.6	23.8	24.0	24.4	24.5	24.1	24.3	24.0	24.1	24.1	23.9
2001	23.8	23.7	24.5	24.3	24.4	24.3	24.0	23.4	22.9	22.5	22.6	22.3	23.6
2002	21.9	21.9	21.8	21.9	22.1	22.2	22.0	22.1	21.5	20.9	20.7	20.6	21.6
2003	20.4	20.3	20.5	20.4	20.6	20.7	21.3	21.3	20.8	20.5	20.6	20.7	20.7
2004	20.6	20.4	20.6	20.7	21.0	21.4	21.7	21.6	21.4	21.0	21.1	21.1	21.1
2005	20.7	20.7	20.9	21.4	21.4	21.6	21.8	21.8	21.5	21.1	21.1	21.3	21.3
2006	20.9	20.9	21.0	21.3	21.5	22.0	22.3	22.3	21.6	21.5	21.6	21.6	21.5
2007	21.3	21.4	21.6	21.5	21.8	22.5	22.6	22.6	22.4	22.1	22.0	22.1	22.0
Government													
2000	82.6	85.9	86.7	86.4	87.2	82.1	74.4	72.9	84.0	86.0	87.2	86.6	83.5
2001	84.7	87.8	88.4	87.6	88.3	84.2	74.6	74.2	87.5	90.3	91.1	91.3	85.8
2002	86.9	90.3	91.1	90.0	89.1	86.7	79.2	78.2	88.6	92.3	93.6	93.7	88.3
2003	88.7	92.2	92.7	92.5	91.1	89.1	81.0	79.9	90.1	94.0	94.7	95.2	90.1
2004	89.1	91.8	93.6	93.1	93.2	87.8	79.9	78.6	90.9	94.6	94.9	95.1	90.2
2005	92.9	94.1	94.9	94.1	94.9	88.4	80.0	78.9	92.8	94.6	95.6	95.8	91.4
2006	90.2	94.8	95.4	95.4	95.3	89.0	81.5	79.7	94.6	96.4	96.5	97.3	92.2
2007	92.1	96.4	96.7	96.5	96.1	90.4	82.5	81.7	95.4	98.2	98.1	98.5	93.6

Average Weekly Hours by Selected Industry: New Hampshire, 2001–2007

(Not seasonally adjusted.)

Industry and year	January	February	March	April	May	June	July	August	September	October	November	December	Annual Average
Manufacturing													
2001	41.7	41.7	41.9	40.1	40.0	40.0	39.8	40.4	40.6	40.3	40.2	40.5	40.6
2002	39.7	40.1	40.6	39.8	39.3	39.8	39.1	39.0	40.0	39.7	40.0	40.5	39.8
2003	40.0	40.4	40.5	39.9	39.8	40.0	39.4	39.4	40.2	39.6	40.5	40.6	40.0
2004	40.6	40.4	40.3	40.0	39.7	39.5	39.3	39.2	40.3	40.0	40.4	40.3	40.0
2005	39.9	40.3	40.1	40.3	40.3	40.8	40.6	41.3	41.9	42.5	42.9	42.8	41.2
2006	42.4	41.8	41.7	41.2	42.1	42.5	40.7	39.7	40.0	40.1	40.7	41.3	41.2
2007	41.2	40.5	40.3	40.0	39.5	40.0	39.3	40.1	40.7	40.3	40.7	40.5	40.3

Average Hourly Earnings by Selected Industry: New Hampshire, 2001–2007

(Dollars, not seasonally adjusted.)

Industry and year	January	February	March	April	May	June	July	August	September	October	November	December	Annual Average
Manufacturing													
2001	13.87	13.87	13.86	14.01	14.06	14.09	14.02	14.02	14.00	13.95	14.07	13.97	13.98
2002	13.94	13.91	13.84	13.98	13.96	14.02	14.01	14.27	14.60	14.53	14.59	14.87	14.21
2003	14.94	14.71	14.89	14.94	14.87	14.83	14.95	14.63	14.65	14.79	14.89	15.11	14.85
2004	15.29	15.18	15.34	15.48	15.40	15.42	15.73	15.74	15.52	15.59	15.53	15.54	15.48
2005	15.61	15.60	15.80	15.86	15.76	15.76	15.89	15.83	16.00	16.13	15.99	16.16	15.87
2006	16.07	16.08	16.21	16.32	16.28	16.49	16.75	16.80	16.80	16.80	16.94	17.04	17.07	16.57
2007	16.90	17.14	17.06	17.09	17.17	17.06	17.15	17.20	17.04	17.01	17.10	17.23	17.10

Average Weekly Earnings by Selected Industry: New Hampshire, 2001–2007

(Dollars, not seasonally adjusted.)

Industry and year	January	February	March	April	May	June	July	August	September	October	November	December	Annual Average
Manufacturing													
2001	578.38	578.38	580.73	561.80	562.40	563.60	558.00	566.41	568.40	562.19	565.61	565.79	567.59
2002	553.42	557.79	561.90	556.40	548.63	558.00	547.79	556.53	584.00	576.84	583.60	602.24	565.56
2003	597.60	594.28	603.05	596.11	591.83	593.20	589.03	576.42	588.93	585.68	603.05	613.47	594.00
2004	620.77	613.27	618.20	619.20	611.38	609.09	618.19	617.01	625.46	623.60	627.41	626.26	619.20
2005	622.84	628.68	633.58	639.16	635.13	643.01	645.13	653.78	670.40	685.53	685.97	691.65	653.84
2006	681.37	672.14	675.96	672.38	685.39	700.83	681.73	666.96	672.00	679.29	693.53	704.99	682.68
2007	696.28	694.17	687.52	683.60	678.22	682.40	674.00	689.72	693.53	685.50	695.97	697.82	689.13

Population
    2000 census: 8,414,350
    2007 estimate: 8,685,920
    Percent change, 2000–2007: 3.2%

Percent change in total nonfarm employment, 2000–2007: 2.0%

Industry with the largest growth in employment, 2000–2007 (thousands)
    Manufacturing, -108.6

Industry with the largest decline in employment, 2000–2007 (thousands)
    Education and health services, 83.8

Civilian labor force
    2000: 4,287,783
    2007: 4,466,275

Employment-population ratio
    2000: 64.1%
    2007: 63.4%

Unemployment rate and rank among states
    2000: 3.7%, 22nd
    2007: 4.2%, 22nd

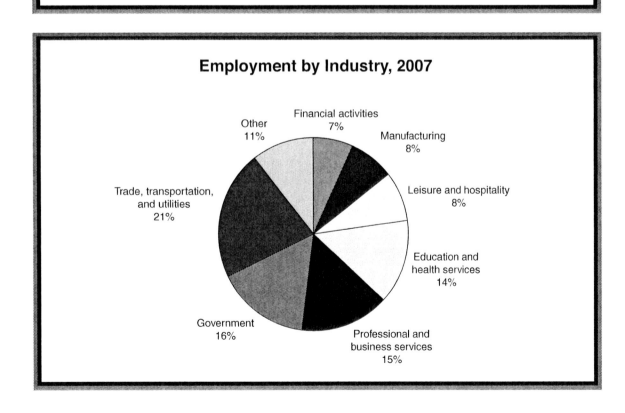

Employment by Industry, 2007

Financial activities 7%

Other 11%

Manufacturing 8%

Leisure and hospitality 8%

Trade, transportation, and utilities 21%

Education and health services 14%

Government 16%

Professional and business services 15%

Employment by Industry: New Jersey, 2000–2007

(Numbers in thousands, not seasonally adjusted.)

Industry and year	January	February	March	April	May	June	July	August	September	October	November	December	Annual Average
Total Nonfarm													
2000	3,887.9	3,896.4	3,942.9	3,975.9	4,006.9	4,060.6	4,020.0	4,002.5	4,014.9	4,017.6	4,042.4	4,066.5	3,994.5
2001	3,922.5	3,931.9	3,957.0	3,994.2	4,026.2	4,073.3	4,008.6	3,990.9	3,995.1	4,010.2	4,023.7	4,032.5	3,997.1
2002	3,932.8	3,940.2	3,968.8	3,982.7	4,007.4	4,042.7	3,982.8	3,970.8	3,974.7	3,983.2	4,006.5	4,014.6	3,983.9
2003	3,908.0	3,898.5	3,922.2	3,956.5	3,993.1	4,032.1	4,003.2	3,986.4	3,991.5	4,006.7	4,019.9	4,027.9	3,978.8
2004	3,905.8	3,907.6	3,944.2	3,969.9	4,014.9	4,063.0	4,023.0	4,005.1	4,014.9	4,026.9	4,050.2	4,064.0	3,999.1
2005	3,946.0	3,951.3	3,975.3	4,024.8	4,057.6	4,111.9	4,066.0	4,048.7	4,054.4	4,059.1	4,082.2	4,091.9	4,039.1
2006	3,984.6	3,992.5	4,028.4	4,050.8	4,090.9	4,143.4	4,091.5	4,076.5	4,075.3	4,088.1	4,107.4	4,122.3	4,071.0
2007	3,993.6	3,989.4	4,020.6	4,050.1	4,100.6	4,157.0	4,098.7	4,079.4	4,073.3	4,093.7	4,108.5	4,121.2	4,073.8
Total Private													
2000	3,307.4	3,306.1	3,346.9	3,379.8	3,406.3	3,463.7	3,451.2	3,444.9	3,439.0	3,421.2	3,439.2	3,462.4	3,405.6
2001	3,330.1	3,326.5	3,350.1	3,385.9	3,419.5	3,465.1	3,431.4	3,421.9	3,400.4	3,394.7	3,400.8	3,408.4	3,394.5
2002	3,320.8	3,317.8	3,343.0	3,358.9	3,384.4	3,421.7	3,397.7	3,395.3	3,376.2	3,362.9	3,378.7	3,387.5	3,370.4
2003	3,291.6	3,271.1	3,291.4	3,325.1	3,362.4	3,402.2	3,403.9	3,401.0	3,383.6	3,375.9	3,382.9	3,391.8	3,356.9
2004	3,281.0	3,271.3	3,303.1	3,329.6	3,375.4	3,422.0	3,414.1	3,406.7	3,391.5	3,381.9	3,399.4	3,412.6	3,365.7
2005	3,309.8	3,302.7	3,325.3	3,373.0	3,409.0	3,461.0	3,450.0	3,443.0	3,426.1	3,409.3	3,425.5	3,435.4	3,397.5
2006	3,340.7	3,336.1	3,370.0	3,392.0	3,435.5	3,486.1	3,469.4	3,465.5	3,445.1	3,433.0	3,447.6	3,462.8	3,423.7
2007	3,348.4	3,332.8	3,360.8	3,390.9	3,442.8	3,496.7	3,476.2	3,468.0	3,442.6	3,438.9	3,447.9	3,460.9	3,425.6
Goods-Producing													
2000	556.8	555.3	565.1	573.8	577.5	583.6	574.7	577.5	578.0	578.5	578.6	577.6	573.1
2001	554.7	556.1	560.5	566.4	571.3	574.5	564.2	566.0	563.4	559.2	554.6	549.9	561.7
2002	527.3	526.6	529.5	534.1	537.7	540.0	532.7	535.9	533.9	530.2	528.0	523.7	531.6
2003	503.7	498.3	501.0	511.0	517.3	521.4	518.6	520.3	519.0	515.6	513.2	509.9	512.4
2004	490.6	487.4	495.3	501.6	508.7	514.5	513.9	514.9	514.8	511.2	509.0	506.9	505.7
2005	487.8	484.1	488.5	498.4	504.7	509.5	507.4	509.4	510.2	507.7	506.6	502.7	501.3
2006	489.5	488.7	494.8	502.0	506.1	509.5	506.8	507.3	505.6	501.4	499.0	496.3	500.6
2007	477.3	470.4	475.8	484.1	490.4	495.9	492.9	493.6	491.4	489.0	487.4	484.0	486.0
Natural Resources and Mining													
2000	1.9	1.7	1.8	2.0	2.0	2.0	2.0	2.0	2.1	2.0	2.0	1.9	1.9
2001	1.6	1.5	1.6	1.8	1.8	1.9	1.9	1.9	1.9	1.8	1.8	1.8	1.7
2002	1.6	1.6	1.7	1.5	1.5	1.6	1.5	1.5	1.5	1.6	1.7	1.7	1.6
2003	1.4	1.4	1.5	1.5	1.6	1.6	1.6	1.6	1.6	1.6	1.6	1.6	1.6
2004	1.5	1.4	1.5	1.6	1.7	1.7	1.7	1.7	1.7	1.7	1.7	1.7	1.6
2005	1.6	1.5	1.6	1.7	1.8	1.8	1.8	1.8	1.8	1.8	1.8	1.8	1.7
2006	1.6	1.6	1.7	1.8	1.8	1.8	1.8	1.7	1.7	1.7	1.7	1.6	1.7
2007	1.6	1.5	1.6	1.6	1.7	1.7	1.7	1.7	1.7	1.7	1.6	1.6	1.6
Construction													
2000	138.2	135.3	143.2	148.7	151.6	154.7	153.9	155.1	154.8	153.6	153.6	152.0	149.5
2001	141.8	142.6	147.0	155.2	160.5	163.7	164.5	166.4	165.1	167.7	166.2	164.4	158.7
2002	153.0	152.2	155.2	160.7	164.1	166.9	167.5	169.2	167.5	166.9	165.7	161.8	162.6
2003	149.1	144.3	147.1	157.1	162.9	165.8	168.2	169.1	167.8	167.1	165.3	162.0	160.5
2004	151.0	148.0	154.9	162.4	167.8	171.4	173.4	174.7	173.9	173.0	171.2	169.0	165.9
2005	155.4	151.4	154.7	166.0	171.6	174.8	176.6	178.0	178.5	174.7	176.0	172.0	169.1
2006	161.5	161.2	166.5	175.4	178.8	181.0	181.1	182.3	181.2	178.4	176.8	175.3	175.0
2007	161.2	155.4	160.7	169.7	175.5	179.2	178.2	179.3	177.4	175.9	174.4	171.4	171.5
Manufacturing													
2000	416.7	418.3	420.1	423.1	423.9	426.9	418.8	420.4	421.1	422.9	423.0	423.7	421.5
2001	411.3	412.0	411.9	409.4	409.0	408.9	397.8	397.7	396.4	389.7	386.6	383.7	401.2
2002	372.7	372.8	372.6	371.9	372.1	371.5	363.7	365.2	364.9	361.7	360.6	360.2	367.5
2003	353.2	352.6	352.4	352.4	352.8	354.0	348.8	349.6	349.6	346.9	346.3	346.3	350.4
2004	338.1	338.0	338.9	337.6	339.2	341.4	338.8	338.5	339.2	336.5	336.1	336.2	338.2
2005	330.8	331.2	332.2	330.7	331.3	332.9	329.0	329.6	329.9	329.2	328.8	328.9	330.4
2006	326.4	325.9	326.6	324.8	325.5	326.7	323.9	323.3	322.7	321.3	320.5	319.4	323.9
2007	314.5	313.5	313.5	312.8	313.2	315.0	313.0	312.6	312.3	311.4	311.4	311.0	312.9
Service-Providing													
2000	3,331.1	3,341.1	3,377.8	3,402.1	3,429.4	3,477.0	3,445.3	3,425.0	3,436.9	3,439.1	3,463.8	3,488.9	3,421.4
2001	3,367.8	3,375.8	3,396.5	3,427.8	3,454.9	3,498.8	3,444.4	3,424.9	3,431.7	3,451.0	3,469.1	3,482.6	3,435.4
2002	3,405.5	3,413.6	3,439.3	3,448.6	3,469.7	3,502.7	3,450.1	3,434.9	3,440.8	3,453.0	3,478.5	3,490.9	3,452.3
2003	3,404.3	3,400.2	3,421.2	3,445.5	3,475.8	3,510.7	3,484.6	3,466.1	3,472.5	3,491.1	3,506.7	3,518.0	3,466.4
2004	3,415.2	3,420.2	3,448.9	3,468.3	3,506.2	3,548.5	3,509.1	3,490.2	3,500.1	3,515.7	3,541.2	3,557.1	3,493.4
2005	3,458.2	3,467.2	3,486.8	3,526.4	3,552.9	3,602.4	3,558.6	3,539.3	3,544.2	3,553.4	3,575.6	3,589.2	3,537.9
2006	3,495.1	3,503.8	3,533.6	3,548.8	3,584.8	3,633.9	3,584.7	3,569.2	3,569.7	3,586.7	3,608.4	3,626.0	3,570.4
2007	3,516.3	3,519.0	3,544.8	3,566.0	3,610.2	3,661.1	3,605.8	3,585.8	3,581.9	3,604.7	3,621.1	3,637.2	3,587.8
Trade, Transportation, and Utilities													
2000	885.2	876.5	882.5	887.9	892.7	899.8	896.9	896.5	900.5	905.8	922.7	941.1	899.0
2001	895.2	881.3	883.1	887.5	891.9	899.7	886.1	883.0	883.5	886.0	899.6	911.3	890.6
2002	879.3	869.5	874.8	873.0	877.3	887.4	875.0	873.2	877.8	882.3	896.1	910.7	881.4
2003	873.8	863.9	865.2	867.1	873.7	881.0	871.0	869.0	873.5	880.1	891.5	904.4	876.2
2004	866.8	859.3	863.2	860.7	872.4	882.2	871.0	869.5	872.0	879.7	893.2	906.5	874.7
2005	870.8	862.3	864.9	868.4	875.7	885.6	876.7	873.6	875.4	877.1	890.8	906.2	877.3
2006	871.2	859.3	863.8	863.3	872.8	881.7	872.8	870.3	871.9	878.8	895.6	910.5	876.0
2007	871.2	857.7	860.6	861.6	874.5	886.2	875.9	872.6	873.6	879.5	894.1	908.2	876.3
Wholesale Trade													
2000	237.3	237.7	239.0	240.9	242.5	241.2	244.1	243.2	243.6	242.8	242.9	245.2	241.7
2001	241.7	242.1	242.7	243.5	243.3	244.1	242.7	242.1	241.7	239.5	239.4	239.5	241.8
2002	238.5	238.2	239.3	237.8	237.7	238.1	235.5	234.8	234.4	234.8	234.5	234.9	236.5
2003	232.3	232.0	232.1	233.5	233.6	234.4	234.0	232.6	233.4	233.7	231.6	232.1	232.7
2004	228.7	228.9	230.5	230.1	231.2	232.5	232.9	233.4	233.0	233.7	233.5	234.3	231.9
2005	232.7	233.2	233.2	233.8	234.3	236.0	234.7	234.9	234.1	232.9	232.9	233.3	233.8
2006	230.7	230.9	231.5	231.9	233.5	234.9	234.5	233.9	233.2	233.0	233.6	234.6	233.0
2007	230.8	230.3	230.8	231.2	232.3	234.4	233.8	233.5	232.4	232.6	232.6	233.2	232.3

Employment by Industry: New Jersey, 2000–2007—*Continued*

(Numbers in thousands, not seasonally adjusted.)

Industry and year	January	February	March	April	May	June	July	August	September	October	November	December	Annual Average
Retail Trade													
2000	457.9	448.7	452.7	453.8	457.5	464.8	463.2	465.2	462.0	463.8	479.9	495.4	463.7
2001	465.5	451.0	452.4	455.3	459.3	466.9	460.2	460.2	454.9	459.1	475.2	487.5	462.2
2002	461.2	451.7	455.7	455.1	459.4	468.1	464.3	464.4	461.9	462.8	477.1	491.9	464.5
2003	461.9	453.3	454.1	456.5	462.3	468.5	465.3	466.1	462.7	467.9	479.6	491.1	465.8
2004	461.5	453.8	455.3	455.1	463.3	471.1	468.5	468.2	463.0	468.7	481.9	494.2	467.1
2005	466.1	457.3	457.7	460.8	466.7	473.3	472.5	470.7	465.1	467.2	479.7	492.3	469.1
2006	465.9	453.5	457.1	456.7	462.5	469.7	467.3	466.3	460.1	466.4	481.5	492.3	466.6
2007	464.8	452.7	454.2	456.0	464.4	472.5	471.0	469.0	462.6	467.4	481.5	491.8	467.3
Transportation and Utilities													
2000	190.0	190.1	190.8	193.2	192.7	193.8	189.6	188.1	194.9	199.2	199.9	200.5	193.5
2001	188.0	188.2	188.0	188.7	189.3	188.7	183.2	180.7	186.9	187.4	185.0	184.3	186.5
2002	179.6	179.6	179.8	180.1	180.2	181.2	175.2	174.0	181.5	184.7	184.5	183.9	180.4
2003	179.6	178.6	179.0	177.1	177.8	178.1	171.7	170.3	178.7	180.6	180.3	181.2	177.8
2004	176.6	176.6	177.4	175.5	177.9	178.6	169.6	167.9	176.0	177.3	177.8	178.0	175.8
2005	172.0	171.8	174.0	173.8	174.7	176.3	169.5	168.0	176.2	177.0	178.2	180.6	174.3
2006	174.6	174.9	175.2	174.7	176.8	177.1	171.0	170.1	178.6	179.4	180.5	183.6	176.4
2007	175.6	174.7	175.6	174.4	177.8	179.3	171.1	170.1	178.6	179.5	180.0	183.2	176.7
Information													
2000	126.6	126.3	127.4	126.2	126.8	128.5	128.0	123.7	127.4	126.2	127.4	128.6	126.9
2001	127.2	127.8	128.4	127.0	127.3	128.1	126.1	123.5	126.3	124.5	125.3	125.3	126.4
2002	121.0	120.3	120.3	116.3	116.5	115.7	111.4	111.0	109.4	104.6	106.1	105.6	113.2
2003	102.8	102.4	102.8	102.0	102.1	102.5	102.3	102.9	101.0	101.1	101.4	101.2	102.0
2004	100.1	98.7	99.6	98.2	98.0	97.9	97.3	97.1	96.2	96.9	97.5	97.9	98.0
2005	96.7	96.4	97.0	96.2	96.6	97.8	97.4	97.2	96.7	96.9	97.8	98.3	97.1
2006	97.4	98.1	98.2	97.0	97.4	98.3	97.7	98.1	97.9	96.4	96.2	96.5	97.4
2007	96.3	97.1	97.5	97.1	97.4	98.1	98.1	99.2	97.7	98.0	98.6	99.1	97.9
Financial Activities													
2000	262.5	263.0	264.1	264.9	266.1	271.1	272.4	271.6	268.8	265.8	265.4	266.7	266.8
2001	262.0	261.9	262.2	265.5	267.1	271.1	270.0	269.1	266.8	280.9	279.9	281.3	269.8
2002	277.3	276.2	275.1	275.7	276.1	277.7	279.4	278.9	276.6	275.1	275.8	276.4	276.7
2003	274.5	273.8	274.3	274.0	275.0	278.2	279.5	279.6	276.9	276.3	276.1	275.8	276.2
2004	273.1	272.7	273.6	275.6	276.9	279.5	280.9	280.4	277.0	277.2	277.7	278.1	276.9
2005	275.8	275.1	275.9	277.5	278.7	281.8	284.0	284.4	281.7	279.6	280.8	281.0	279.7
2006	276.8	276.5	277.4	278.4	279.7	282.0	283.7	283.1	279.3	278.6	278.4	278.6	279.4
2007	274.9	274.3	274.3	274.8	276.0	278.7	279.0	277.9	273.7	271.4	270.6	270.5	274.7
Professional and Business Services													
2000	575.8	579.3	591.6	595.6	597.6	610.9	608.7	610.3	608.5	598.7	601.0	604.3	598.5
2001	580.7	582.0	590.9	597.3	599.8	607.5	599.2	599.6	595.0	588.9	586.3	582.4	592.4
2002	569.0	570.8	581.0	584.2	583.6	588.2	584.9	587.8	582.2	580.1	581.9	579.9	581.1
2003	562.2	559.0	565.2	572.0	575.1	581.0	585.4	589.1	587.6	586.8	586.8	587.6	578.2
2004	564.0	562.7	572.1	582.0	585.3	592.1	592.1	593.0	591.5	592.3	593.9	592.8	584.5
2005	570.0	571.5	577.0	593.0	594.2	604.3	600.3	601.6	599.8	600.7	600.3	597.4	592.5
2006	577.5	582.6	591.5	597.0	602.4	611.9	609.8	613.7	610.5	611.3	612.4	611.6	602.7
2007	584.4	585.3	594.0	604.8	610.6	620.1	617.2	620.2	615.8	615.3	615.3	614.5	608.1
Education and Health Services													
2000	484.3	488.2	490.7	494.2	494.7	496.8	493.6	491.0	497.9	503.1	506.2	509.2	495.8
2001	492.6	496.4	499.3	504.4	507.8	511.1	503.6	501.6	505.8	510.3	514.3	517.1	505.3
2002	517.6	522.9	524.4	526.2	528.8	529.4	524.7	522.0	526.6	531.3	535.6	536.2	527.1
2003	532.3	532.5	536.2	537.3	540.9	540.2	536.5	531.8	537.3	541.6	544.1	544.8	538.0
2004	537.4	539.9	543.6	544.5	548.9	549.6	543.2	540.1	545.6	552.5	554.7	556.4	546.4
2005	549.3	552.9	555.3	556.9	561.3	561.0	555.3	551.2	557.1	565.0	567.6	568.1	558.4
2006	560.8	563.2	567.1	566.2	571.3	571.5	563.9	562.2	567.8	573.2	576.4	579.7	568.6
2007	571.6	575.6	580.1	577.3	583.5	581.6	574.5	570.4	577.3	585.4	588.3	589.8	579.6
Leisure and Hospitality													
2000	278.0	278.5	285.1	295.4	308.3	328.1	330.8	329.3	315.5	301.5	296.3	292.6	303.2
2001	278.9	281.6	285.4	296.0	310.6	327.2	334.2	332.4	315.6	299.1	294.6	294.2	304.1
2002	283.3	285.0	290.8	302.2	316.0	333.2	338.8	336.5	322.4	310.8	306.8	306.0	311.0
2003	293.7	292.7	297.3	310.3	325.8	342.8	354.8	352.9	334.9	321.0	316.2	314.0	321.4
2004	298.1	299.2	303.5	314.0	330.3	349.5	358.5	355.3	340.5	318.1	319.3	319.5	325.5
2005	305.1	305.3	311.3	324.2	338.8	359.8	367.5	364.9	348.2	327.7	324.5	323.9	333.4
2006	310.7	310.8	319.0	327.5	343.7	366.5	371.6	368.9	353.0	333.5	329.5	328.4	338.6
2007	313.2	312.8	318.2	327.8	345.4	367.7	371.4	368.3	350.3	337.3	330.6	330.6	339.5
Other Services													
2000	138.2	139.0	140.4	141.8	142.6	144.9	146.4	145.0	142.4	141.6	141.6	142.3	142.1
2001	138.8	139.4	140.3	141.8	143.7	145.9	148.0	146.7	144.0	145.8	146.2	146.9	143.9
2002	146.0	146.5	147.1	147.2	148.4	150.1	150.8	150.0	147.3	148.5	148.4	149.0	148.3
2003	148.6	148.5	149.4	151.4	152.5	155.1	155.1	155.8	155.4	153.4	153.6	154.1	152.6
2004	150.9	151.4	152.2	153.0	154.9	156.7	157.2	156.4	153.9	154.0	154.1	154.5	154.1
2005	154.3	155.1	155.4	158.4	159.0	161.2	161.4	160.7	157.0	156.6	157.1	157.8	157.8
2006	156.8	156.9	158.2	160.6	162.1	164.7	163.1	161.9	159.1	159.8	160.1	161.2	160.4
2007	159.5	159.6	160.3	163.4	165.0	168.4	167.2	165.8	162.8	163.0	163.0	164.2	163.5
Government													
2000	580.5	590.3	596.0	596.1	600.6	596.9	568.8	557.6	575.9	596.4	603.2	604.1	588.8
2001	592.4	605.4	606.9	608.3	606.7	608.2	577.2	569.0	594.7	615.5	622.9	624.1	602.6
2002	612.0	622.4	625.8	623.8	623.0	621.0	585.1	575.5	598.5	620.3	627.8	627.1	613.5
2003	616.4	627.4	630.8	631.4	630.7	629.9	599.3	585.4	607.9	630.8	637.0	636.1	621.9
2004	624.8	636.3	641.1	640.3	639.5	641.0	608.9	598.4	623.4	645.0	650.8	651.4	633.4
2005	636.2	648.6	650.0	651.8	648.6	650.9	616.0	605.7	628.3	649.8	656.7	656.5	641.6
2006	643.9	656.4	658.4	658.8	655.4	657.3	622.1	611.0	630.2	655.1	659.8	659.5	647.3
2007	645.2	656.6	659.8	659.2	657.8	660.3	622.5	611.4	630.7	654.8	660.6	660.3	648.3

Average Weekly Hours by Selected Industry: New Jersey, 2001–2007

(Not seasonally adjusted.)

Industry and year	January	February	March	April	May	June	July	August	September	October	November	December	Annual Average
Manufacturing													
2001	40.2	40.5	40.6	40.1	40.7	40.9	40.6	41.0	40.5	40.8	40.6	41.3	40.6
2002	40.3	40.3	40.9	40.5	40.7	41.4	40.7	41.1	41.1	41.3	41.3	41.5	40.9
2003	40.2	39.9	40.6	40.7	41.1	41.3	40.9	40.9	41.1	41.3	41.4	42.4	41.0
2004	40.6	40.8	41.3	41.4	42.2	42.4	42.8	42.7	42.9	42.4	42.9	42.6	42.1
2005	41.5	41.5	41.6	41.7	41.8	41.8	41.7	42.3	42.7	42.5	42.8	42.5	42.0
2006	42.0	41.7	42.0	41.8	42.4	42.6	42.4	42.3	42.4	41.8	41.9	42.0	42.1
2007	41.6	41.1	41.1	41.0	41.1	41.8	41.4	40.0	40.4	40.6	41.8	42.2	41.2
Information													
2002	36.0	35.7	36.0	35.6	35.0	37.9	35.6	37.8	38.3	37.6	37.6	38.2	36.8
2003	37.5	37.5	37.4	37.2	37.4	38.2	37.7	37.7	37.5	37.4	37.9	36.7	37.5
2004	37.2	37.6	37.4	37.5	37.8	36.5	35.5	36.0	36.5	37.4	37.1	37.6	37.0
2005	37.0	37.3	37.8	37.2	37.9	37.0	36.5	37.1	37.6	37.7	37.6	36.8	37.3
2006	36.3	36.3	36.2	36.9	36.4	36.1	36.0	35.9	35.8	36.0	35.4	35.1	36.0
2007	35.6	36.0	35.8	35.9	35.7	35.9	36.3	35.7	35.7	34.8	34.2	34.7	35.5

Average Hourly Earnings by Selected Industry: New Jersey, 2001–2007

(Dollars, not seasonally adjusted.)

Industry and year	January	February	March	April	May	June	July	August	September	October	November	December	Annual Average
Manufacturing													
2001	14.48	14.67	14.68	14.78	14.80	14.49	14.58	14.66	14.82	14.82	14.88	15.22	14.74
2002	14.99	15.02	14.95	15.12	15.10	15.02	15.29	15.12	15.22	15.52	15.49	15.48	15.19
2003	15.09	15.02	15.13	15.25	15.47	15.56	15.69	15.61	15.74	15.58	15.69	15.60	15.45
2004	15.53	15.55	15.67	15.76	15.86	15.86	16.05	16.09	16.01	16.04	16.05	16.12	15.89
2005	16.05	16.18	16.25	16.31	16.31	16.27	16.30	16.41	16.52	16.41	16.49	16.44	16.33
2006	16.36	16.30	16.45	16.50	16.54	16.52	16.49	16.53	16.54	16.68	16.75	17.09	16.56
2007	16.82	16.78	16.84	17.02	17.14	17.01	17.37	17.49	17.50	17.47	17.45	17.64	17.21
Information													
2002	20.13	20.58	20.57	20.32	20.81	21.12	23.01	24.87	25.49	25.58	27.29	27.96	23.20
2003	27.11	27.31	26.97	26.79	27.30	28.42	27.23	29.02	29.04	28.66	28.81	28.49	27.96
2004	28.94	29.29	29.89	31.19	30.55	29.28	28.49	29.21	29.47	29.12	28.64	28.64	29.37
2005	28.81	29.88	30.14	30.02	30.26	29.80	29.03	29.38	30.22	30.67	30.65	30.37	29.95
2006	31.29	31.03	30.98	31.13	30.92	31.29	31.35	31.63	31.68	32.34	32.40	33.20	31.59
2007	32.82	32.52	33.35	33.19	33.76	32.89	31.56	31.62	32.00	32.29	32.49	32.33	32.56

Average Weekly Earnings by Selected Industry: New Jersey, 2001–2007

(Dollars, not seasonally adjusted.)

Industry and year	January	February	March	April	May	June	July	August	September	October	November	December	Annual Average
Manufacturing													
2001	582.10	594.14	596.01	592.68	602.36	592.64	591.95	601.06	600.21	604.66	604.13	628.59	598.44
2002	604.10	605.31	611.46	612.36	614.57	621.83	622.30	621.43	625.54	640.98	639.74	642.42	621.27
2003	606.62	599.30	614.28	620.68	635.82	642.63	641.72	638.45	646.91	643.45	649.57	661.44	633.45
2004	630.52	634.44	647.17	652.46	669.29	672.46	686.94	687.04	686.83	680.10	688.55	686.71	668.97
2005	666.08	671.47	676.00	680.13	681.76	680.09	679.71	694.14	705.40	697.43	705.77	698.70	685.86
2006	687.12	679.71	690.90	689.70	701.30	703.75	699.18	699.22	701.30	697.22	701.83	717.78	697.18
2007	699.71	689.66	692.12	697.82	704.45	711.02	719.12	699.60	707.00	709.28	729.41	744.41	709.05
Information													
2002	724.68	734.71	740.52	723.39	728.35	800.45	819.16	940.09	976.27	961.81	1,026.10	1,068.07	853.76
2003	1,016.63	1,024.13	1,008.68	996.59	1,021.02	1,085.64	1,026.57	1,094.05	1,089.00	1,071.88	1,091.90	1,045.58	1,048.50
2004	1,076.57	1,101.30	1,117.89	1,169.63	1,154.79	1,068.72	1,011.40	1,051.56	1,075.66	1,089.09	1,062.54	1,076.86	1,086.69
2005	1,065.97	1,114.52	1,139.29	1,116.74	1,146.85	1,102.60	1,059.60	1,090.00	1,136.27	1,156.26	1,152.44	1,117.62	1,117.14
2006	1,135.83	1,126.39	1,121.48	1,148.70	1,125.49	1,129.57	1,128.60	1,135.52	1,134.14	1,164.24	1,146.96	1,165.32	1,137.24
2007	1,168.39	1,170.72	1,193.93	1,191.52	1,205.23	1,180.75	1,145.63	1,128.83	1,142.40	1,123.69	1,111.16	1,121.85	1,155.88

Population
    2000 census: 1,819,046
    2007 estimate: 1,969,915
    Percent change, 2000–2007: 8.3%

Percent change in total nonfarm employment, 2000–2007: 13.2%

Industry with the largest growth in employment, 2000–2007 (thousands)
    Education and health services, 29.3

Industry with the largest decline in employment, 2000–2007 (thousands)
    Manufacturing, -4.6

Civilian labor force
    2000: 852,293
    2007: 943,062

Employment-population ratio
    2000: 60.3%
    2007: 60.9%

Unemployment rate and rank among states
    2000: 5.0%, 44th
    2007: 3.5%, 11th

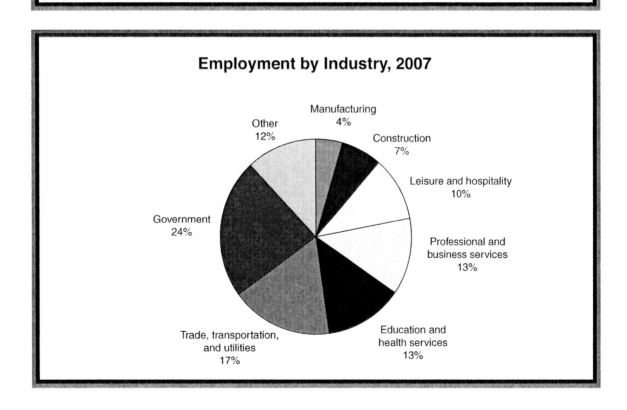

Employment by Industry, 2007

Manufacturing 4%
Other 12%
Construction 7%
Leisure and hospitality 10%
Government 24%
Professional and business services 13%
Trade, transportation, and utilities 17%
Education and health services 13%

Employment by Industry: New Mexico, 2000–2007

(Numbers in thousands, not seasonally adjusted.)

Industry and year	January	February	March	April	May	June	July	August	September	October	November	December	Annual Average
Total Nonfarm													
2000	722.5	730.2	738.0	741.0	747.3	746.2	742.3	748.3	754.9	752.3	755.5	759.1	744.8
2001	739.8	748.1	755.1	756.4	762.3	762.5	754.7	759.6	763.9	759.9	761.1	762.6	757.2
2002	748.5	754.1	760.9	764.2	770.0	769.4	763.7	768.3	774.1	770.6	773.7	776.2	766.1
2003	759.5	765.2	769.9	772.6	777.2	776.5	772.1	776.7	781.4	783.8	784.8	787.4	775.6
2004	769.8	778.0	783.8	788.7	792.6	791.1	787.0	789.5	795.3	801.5	802.5	805.2	790.4
2005	786.5	793.6	799.1	806.9	810.1	808.6	805.2	809.7	818.8	818.5	822.3	824.5	808.7
2006	809.2	819.7	827.1	828.6	835.2	837.3	828.0	832.0	842.5	839.5	842.9	844.3	832.2
2007	824.4	833.9	842.3	840.5	845.8	846.3	838.8	844.3	850.4	849.9	850.3	851.1	843.2
Total Private													
2000	543.8	546.3	551.4	554.5	559.3	566.9	565.1	570.8	570.8	567.6	570.8	573.5	561.7
2001	560.5	562.5	567.7	568.8	574.2	578.4	576.2	579.6	574.6	571.6	572.6	573.8	571.7
2002	563.4	563.4	568.8	572.1	576.9	579.1	579.2	582.5	580.3	576.7	579.0	581.0	575.2
2003	569.0	569.9	573.4	575.3	580.6	582.8	583.8	587.4	584.6	584.6	585.8	588.3	580.5
2004	576.8	578.5	583.1	587.9	592.3	594.5	596.3	597.5	595.9	599.3	599.7	602.8	592.1
2005	590.3	591.5	595.7	603.2	606.0	609.1	611.4	614.9	615.4	613.9	617.3	620.1	607.4
2006	610.4	614.1	620.8	623.2	629.3	645.7	642.5	645.1	647.0	642.8	645.9	647.4	634.5
2007	633.8	637.9	644.6	643.7	649.1	653.6	651.9	655.8	654.3	651.7	651.5	652.3	648.4
Goods-Producing													
2000	95.4	96.2	97.6	98.7	100.4	102.4	103.4	105.9	105.7	104.7	104.0	103.9	101.5
2001	101.6	101.7	103.3	103.8	105.2	106.4	105.9	107.1	105.3	103.6	102.3	100.9	103.9
2002	97.6	96.6	97.5	98.0	98.8	99.2	99.4	100.5	98.9	98.5	97.2	96.3	98.2
2003	94.4	94.1	94.9	95.9	97.4	99.0	99.7	100.9	99.6	100.1	99.2	98.4	97.8
2004	96.1	96.0	97.2	99.0	100.6	102.1	104.2	104.4	103.9	104.8	103.6	104.1	101.3
2005	101.4	101.4	103.0	104.5	105.7	107.4	109.8	110.7	111.2	111.3	111.6	111.4	107.5
2006	110.1	111.7	113.1	113.8	115.3	117.2	117.5	118.3	118.4	118.3	116.5	115.7	115.5
2007	112.5	113.1	114.4	114.6	116.0	117.7	117.4	118.1	117.1	116.8	114.6	113.8	115.5
Natural Resources and Mining													
2000	13.9	14.2	14.3	14.6	14.8	14.8	14.9	15.3	15.4	15.2	15.3	15.6	14.8
2001	15.6	15.7	15.8	15.8	16.0	15.8	16.0	16.1	15.8	15.3	14.9	14.9	15.6
2002	14.6	14.4	14.3	14.0	14.0	13.9	13.8	13.9	13.7	13.9	13.8	13.8	14.0
2003	13.8	13.9	14.0	14.1	14.3	14.4	14.4	14.4	14.4	14.6	14.7	14.8	14.3
2004	14.4	14.3	14.5	14.7	14.8	15.0	15.1	15.4	15.4	15.6	15.7	16.1	15.1
2005	15.9	15.9	16.1	16.2	16.4	16.6	17.2	17.4	17.8	17.8	17.7	17.7	16.9
2006	17.8	18.0	18.1	18.3	18.5	18.8	18.8	19.1	19.1	19.2	19.1	19.2	18.7
2007	19.3	19.0	19.1	19.2	19.4	19.6	19.8	19.8	19.4	19.6	19.5	19.5	19.4
Construction													
2000	41.1	41.4	42.5	43.4	44.4	45.7	46.4	47.2	47.0	46.7	46.5	46.3	44.8
2001	44.5	44.7	45.9	46.7	47.9	49.4	49.1	49.4	48.2	47.6	48.0	46.9	47.4
2002	44.7	44.3	45.1	45.8	46.3	46.5	46.1	46.8	45.8	46.2	46.0	45.6	45.8
2003	44.4	44.2	44.9	46.0	47.1	48.0	48.4	48.9	47.8	48.4	48.0	47.7	47.0
2004	46.7	46.8	47.7	48.9	50.0	50.9	52.6	52.1	51.5	52.3	51.7	51.9	50.3
2005	50.2	50.3	51.6	52.8	53.7	55.0	56.5	56.6	56.5	56.4	56.9	56.8	54.4
2006	55.9	56.8	58.1	58.5	59.8	60.9	60.4	60.4	60.4	60.4	59.4	58.7	59.1
2007	56.0	56.8	58.1	58.6	59.6	60.8	60.3	60.5	60.0	59.9	58.7	58.0	58.9
Manufacturing													
2000	40.4	40.6	40.8	40.7	41.2	41.9	42.1	43.4	43.3	42.8	42.2	42.0	41.7
2001	41.5	41.3	41.6	41.3	41.3	41.2	40.8	41.6	41.3	40.7	39.4	39.1	40.9
2002	38.3	37.9	38.1	38.2	38.5	38.8	39.5	39.8	39.4	38.4	37.4	36.9	38.4
2003	36.2	36.0	36.0	35.8	36.0	36.6	36.9	37.6	37.4	37.1	36.5	35.9	36.5
2004	35.0	34.9	35.0	35.4	35.8	36.2	36.5	36.9	37.0	36.9	36.2	36.1	36.0
2005	35.3	35.2	35.3	35.5	35.6	35.8	36.1	36.7	36.9	37.1	37.0	36.9	36.1
2006	36.4	36.9	36.9	37.0	37.0	37.5	38.3	38.8	38.9	38.7	38.0	37.8	37.7
2007	37.2	37.3	37.2	36.8	37.0	37.3	37.3	37.8	37.7	37.3	36.4	36.3	37.1
Service-Providing													
2000	627.1	634.0	640.4	642.3	646.9	643.8	638.9	642.4	649.2	647.6	651.5	655.2	643.2
2001	638.2	646.4	651.8	652.6	657.1	656.1	648.8	652.5	658.6	656.3	658.8	661.7	653.2
2002	650.9	657.5	663.4	666.2	671.2	670.2	664.3	667.8	675.2	672.1	676.5	679.9	667.9
2003	665.1	671.1	675.0	676.7	679.8	677.5	672.4	675.8	681.8	683.7	685.6	689.0	677.8
2004	673.7	682.0	686.6	689.7	692.0	689.0	682.8	685.1	691.4	696.7	698.9	701.1	689.1
2005	685.1	692.2	696.1	702.4	704.4	701.2	695.4	699.0	707.6	707.2	710.7	713.1	701.2
2006	699.1	708.0	714.0	714.8	719.9	720.1	710.5	713.7	724.1	721.2	726.4	728.6	716.7
2007	711.9	720.8	727.9	725.9	729.8	728.6	721.4	726.2	733.3	733.1	735.7	737.3	727.7
Trade, Transportation, and Utilities													
2000	134.8	134.0	134.4	135.5	137.1	137.7	136.3	137.6	137.8	138.4	141.2	142.3	137.2
2001	136.4	134.4	134.7	134.3	135.5	135.4	135.0	135.8	134.8	134.7	137.0	138.5	135.5
2002	133.9	132.7	133.1	133.7	135.3	135.7	135.0	136.0	135.8	135.9	138.2	139.9	135.4
2003	134.1	133.3	134.1	134.1	135.2	134.8	134.7	135.9	135.8	136.9	139.0	140.6	135.7
2004	135.9	135.4	136.2	136.5	137.4	137.2	137.1	137.3	136.9	138.5	140.7	142.2	137.6
2005	137.5	136.9	137.4	138.0	139.2	138.9	139.5	140.4	140.0	140.5	143.0	144.5	128.2
2006	139.6	138.5	139.8	140.0	141.3	141.4	141.6	142.3	142.0	142.0	144.9	146.3	141.6
2007	142.3	141.8	143.2	142.4	144.0	143.9	144.1	145.0	144.7	145.3	147.6	148.8	144.4
Wholesale Trade													
2000	21.9	22.0	22.3	22.6	22.9	23.0	22.8	22.9	22.9	22.9	22.8	22.8	22.6
2001	22.7	22.7	22.8	22.7	22.9	23.1	23.0	23.0	23.0	22.7	22.7	22.7	22.8
2002	22.5	22.5	22.5	22.5	22.6	22.8	22.9	22.8	22.5	22.5	22.5	22.5	22.6
2003	21.9	21.9	22.2	22.2	22.1	22.2	22.2	22.2	22.0	22.0	21.9	22.0	22.1
2004	21.7	21.8	22.1	22.3	22.3	22.4	22.5	22.3	22.2	22.3	22.2	22.4	22.2
2005	22.2	22.4	22.5	22.6	22.8	22.9	23.0	22.9	22.8	22.8	22.9	23.0	22.7
2006	22.6	22.7	22.9	23.1	23.3	23.6	23.7	23.7	23.6	23.5	23.5	23.5	23.3
2007	23.4	23.4	23.4	23.5	23.6	23.9	24.1	24.0	23.9	24.0	24.1	24.1	23.8

Employment by Industry: New Mexico, 2000–2007—*Continued*

(Numbers in thousands, not seasonally adjusted.)

Industry and year	January	February	March	April	May	June	July	August	September	October	November	December	Annual Average
Retail Trade													
2000	89.7	88.7	88.9	89.2	90.2	91.2	90.6	91.1	90.7	91.2	94.1	95.2	90.9
2001	90.2	88.7	88.8	88.7	89.6	90.1	90.0	90.1	88.7	88.8	91.3	92.7	89.8
2002	88.7	87.6	88.2	88.5	89.9	90.8	90.1	90.4	90.2	90.1	92.4	94.1	90.1
2003	89.5	88.7	89.2	89.2	90.3	90.4	90.4	91.1	90.7	91.6	93.9	95.3	90.9
2004	90.9	90.4	90.8	91.1	91.9	92.2	92.1	92.0	91.4	92.7	95.1	96.3	92.2
2005	92.3	91.5	91.6	92.2	93.1	93.4	93.9	94.2	93.6	94.1	96.4	97.3	93.6
2006	93.1	91.9	93.1	93.1	94.0	94.2	94.3	94.6	94.1	94.3	97.0	97.8	94.3
2007	94.2	93.6	95.0	94.2	95.5	95.7	96.0	96.1	95.5	96.0	98.0	98.9	95.7
Transportation and Utilities													
2000	23.2	23.3	23.2	23.7	24.0	23.5	22.9	23.6	24.2	24.3	24.3	24.3	23.7
2001	23.5	23.0	23.1	22.9	23.0	22.2	22.0	22.7	23.1	23.2	23.0	23.1	22.9
2002	22.7	22.6	22.4	22.7	22.8	22.1	22.0	22.8	23.1	23.3	23.3	23.3	22.8
2003	22.7	22.7	22.7	22.7	22.8	22.2	22.1	22.6	23.1	23.3	23.2	23.3	22.8
2004	23.3	23.2	23.3	23.1	23.2	22.6	22.5	23.0	23.3	23.5	23.4	23.5	23.2
2005	23.0	23.0	23.3	23.2	23.3	22.6	22.6	23.3	23.6	23.6	23.7	24.2	23.3
2006	23.9	23.9	23.8	23.8	24.0	23.6	23.6	24.0	24.3	24.2	24.4	25.0	24.0
2007	24.7	24.8	24.8	24.7	24.9	24.3	24.0	24.9	25.3	25.3	25.5	25.8	24.9
Information													
2000	16.3	16.3	16.4	16.3	16.4	16.7	16.9	17.2	17.3	16.7	16.7	17.2	16.7
2001	17.3	17.6	17.5	16.9	17.1	17.0	16.8	16.9	17.0	16.9	17.0	17.0	17.1
2002	16.8	17.1	17.2	17.0	17.0	16.8	17.0	16.8	16.6	16.4	16.8	16.8	16.9
2003	16.3	16.1	16.3	15.8	16.0	16.0	15.7	15.5	15.5	15.2	15.3	15.3	15.8
2004	14.9	15.2	15.0	14.7	15.0	14.9	14.7	14.7	14.3	14.9	15.1	15.0	14.9
2005	13.9	14.1	14.1	15.3	15.1	14.7	14.8	14.8	14.5	14.9	15.0	15.4	14.7
2006	14.5	15.4	15.9	15.0	15.6	17.4	15.1	15.9	17.1	14.9	15.9	16.9	15.8
2007	14.5	15.5	15.8	14.4	14.8	16.4	15.3	16.5	17.3	16.2	16.3	16.6	15.8
Financial Activities													
2000	33.5	33.5	33.6	33.3	33.4	33.5	33.4	33.3	33.2	33.3	33.5	33.8	33.4
2001	33.1	33.3	33.4	33.3	33.3	33.5	33.5	33.4	33.1	33.1	33.5	33.8	33.3
2002	33.4	33.3	33.4	33.3	33.3	33.4	33.7	33.9	33.6	33.4	33.5	33.8	33.5
2003	33.3	33.4	33.4	33.5	33.8	34.0	34.2	34.5	34.2	34.1	34.0	34.4	33.9
2004	34.3	34.1	34.4	34.1	34.1	34.4	34.5	34.4	34.4	34.5	34.5	34.9	34.4
2005	34.7	34.6	34.6	34.7	34.8	35.1	35.2	35.1	35.0	34.9	35.0	35.6	34.9
2006	35.2	35.2	35.2	35.1	35.2	35.3	35.2	35.1	35.0	34.9	34.9	35.3	35.1
2007	34.9	35.0	35.3	35.2	35.2	35.4	35.5	35.4	35.2	35.2	35.2	35.7	35.3
Professional and Business Services													
2000	82.7	83.4	84.1	85.4	85.3	86.7	86.5	87.0	87.7	87.6	88.6	89.0	86.1
2001	86.4	87.4	88.4	88.7	88.9	89.7	89.3	89.4	88.3	89.1	88.4	88.6	88.6
2002	87.7	87.8	88.9	88.6	89.0	89.2	90.1	90.0	89.9	89.3	89.7	90.2	89.2
2003	87.7	88.6	88.8	88.6	88.6	88.4	88.5	88.8	88.2	88.6	88.2	88.7	88.5
2004	87.0	87.6	88.6	89.6	90.0	90.2	90.2	90.5	90.8	91.0	92.1	91.3	90.0
2005	90.2	90.5	90.7	92.8	92.4	93.3	93.2	93.6	94.0	93.5	94.3	94.3	92.7
2006	93.6	94.5	95.2	96.0	96.6	108.1	107.3	107.6	107.5	107.7	107.6	107.9	102.5
2007	106.3	107.6	108.3	108.3	108.7	109.3	109.6	110.4	109.2	109.0	108.6	108.3	108.6
Education and Health Services													
2000	81.2	82.3	82.8	82.4	82.2	80.5	78.8	79.7	83.1	83.5	84.4	84.6	82.1
2001	85.1	86.6	87.2	87.5	88.0	85.3	84.9	86.1	89.5	89.8	91.0	91.2	87.7
2002	91.7	92.6	93.5	94.6	94.6	91.3	90.4	91.7	95.9	96.4	97.6	97.3	94.0
2003	97.7	98.5	98.6	99.2	99.2	95.8	95.9	96.7	100.5	100.8	101.9	102.0	98.9
2004	101.6	102.4	102.4	103.1	103.0	99.7	99.0	100.0	103.5	104.1	105.4	104.8	102.4
2005	104.0	104.6	105.1	105.4	105.6	102.0	101.5	102.7	106.7	107.1	107.6	107.6	105.0
2006	106.9	107.4	108.4	108.3	108.7	105.6	104.5	105.2	109.4	109.7	110.8	110.6	108.0
2007	110.1	110.9	111.8	112.5	112.9	109.3	108.0	108.7	112.3	112.9	113.8	113.7	111.4
Leisure and Hospitality													
2000	73.4	73.8	75.7	76.1	77.3	80.2	80.6	81.1	79.4	77.0	75.9	76.2	77.2
2001	74.8	75.3	76.8	77.9	79.5	81.9	81.5	82.1	79.7	77.8	77.1	77.3	78.5
2002	75.7	76.3	78.0	79.6	81.3	83.6	83.6	83.9	81.9	79.1	78.4	79.1	80.0
2003	78.0	78.3	79.6	80.7	82.5	84.6	84.7	85.0	82.6	80.8	80.1	80.7	81.5
2004	79.1	79.7	81.1	82.8	83.8	85.3	85.4	85.3	83.4	82.0	80.8	81.8	82.5
2005	80.6	81.1	82.5	84.1	84.6	86.7	86.3	86.7	85.2	83.3	82.3	82.7	83.8
2006	82.6	83.0	84.6	86.3	87.6	89.3	89.9	89.7	88.4	86.3	86.3	86.0	86.7
2007	84.9	85.3	86.9	87.6	88.4	90.2	90.5	90.8	89.3	87.3	86.4	86.7	87.9
Other Services													
2000	26.5	26.8	26.8	26.8	27.2	29.2	29.2	29.0	26.6	26.4	26.5	26.5	27.2
2001	25.8	26.2	26.4	26.4	26.7	29.2	29.3	28.8	26.9	26.6	26.7	26.8	27.2
2002	26.6	27.0	27.2	27.3	27.6	29.9	30.0	29.7	27.7	27.7	27.6	27.6	28.0
2003	27.5	27.6	27.7	27.5	27.9	30.2	30.4	30.1	28.2	28.1	28.1	28.2	28.5
2004	27.9	28.1	28.2	28.1	28.4	30.7	30.9	30.6	28.5	28.4	28.3	28.3	28.9
2005	28.0	28.3	28.3	28.4	28.6	31.0	31.1	30.9	28.8	28.4	28.5	28.6	29.1
2006	27.9	28.4	28.6	28.7	29.0	31.4	31.4	31.0	29.2	29.0	29.0	28.7	29.4
2007	28.3	28.7	28.9	28.7	29.1	31.4	31.5	30.9	29.2	29.0	29.0	28.7	29.5
Government													
2000	178.7	183.9	186.6	186.5	188.0	179.3	177.2	177.5	184.1	184.7	184.7	185.6	183.0
2001	179.3	185.6	187.4	187.6	188.1	184.1	178.5	180.0	189.3	188.3	188.5	188.8	185.5
2002	185.1	190.7	192.1	192.1	193.1	190.3	184.5	185.8	193.8	193.9	194.7	195.2	190.9
2003	190.5	195.3	196.5	197.3	196.6	193.7	188.3	189.3	196.8	199.2	199.0	199.1	195.1
2004	193.0	199.5	200.7	200.8	200.3	196.6	190.7	192.0	199.4	202.2	202.8	202.4	198.4
2005	196.2	202.1	203.4	203.7	204.1	199.5	193.8	194.8	203.4	204.6	205.0	204.4	201.3
2006	198.8	205.6	206.3	205.4	205.9	191.6	185.5	186.9	195.5	196.7	197.0	196.9	197.7
2007	190.6	196.0	197.7	196.8	196.7	192.7	186.9	188.5	196.1	198.2	198.8	198.8	194.8

Average Weekly Hours by Selected Industry: New Mexico, 2001–2007

(Not seasonally adjusted.)

Industry and year	January	February	March	April	May	June	July	August	September	October	November	December	Annual Average
Construction													
2001	38.7	39.2	39.1	37.9	39.0	39.1	38.5	39.5	39.0	39.5	38.1	38.0	38.8
2002	39.2	39.0	38.1	39.8	39.4	39.3	39.1	39.9	39.0	39.5	39.7	39.4	39.3
2003	39.8	38.9	39.7	39.5	39.1	39.6	39.8	39.7	39.8	39.8	40.0	39.9	40.0	39.7
2004	40.0	39.8	39.8	39.7	39.8	39.8	39.8	39.8	39.9	39.8	39.8	39.7	39.8
2005	39.7	39.7	39.6	39.6	39.6	39.6	39.7	39.7	39.8	39.8	39.8	39.7	39.7
2006	39.7	39.8	39.8	39.8	39.9	39.8	39.8	39.9	40.1	40.3	40.5	40.6	40.0
2007	40.5	40.4	40.3	40.4	40.4	40.3	40.1	40.0	39.9	40.1	40.0	40.2	40.2
Manufacturing													
2001	37.8	38.8	38.6	38.2	38.8	39.1	38.6	39.6	39.6	39.4	39.9	40.2	39.0
2002	38.8	39.7	39.3	39.9	40.1	41.0	39.8	40.1	40.3	39.7	40.2	39.7	39.9
2003	38.5	39.1	39.3	39.2	40.0	39.8	39.7	39.6	39.5	39.5	39.4	39.2	39.4
2004	39.4	39.7	39.7	39.7	39.7	39.7	39.7	39.7	39.7	39.6	39.5	39.4	39.6
2005	39.3	39.2	39.2	39.2	39.2	39.1	39.0	39.0	39.0	39.0	39.0	38.9	39.1
2006	39.0	39.1	39.2	39.3	39.2	39.2	39.2	39.2	39.2	39.2	39.3	39.2	39.2
2007	39.1	39.2	39.2	39.2	39.2	39.1	39.1	39.0	38.9	38.8	38.6	38.9	39.0
Wholesale Trade													
2001	30.9	31.9	32.3	32.3	31.4	32.2	32.3	32.4	32.7	31.9	32.9	33.1	32.2
2002	32.4	33.2	32.6	32.4	33.4	33.9	34.1	35.0	34.9	34.4	35.1	35.0	33.9
2003	34.1	34.7	35.4	35.6	35.7	34.9	35.2	35.7	35.6	35.9	36.0	36.1	35.4
2004	35.9	35.8	35.8	35.8	35.7	35.7	35.8	35.8	35.7	35.6	35.5	35.4	35.7
2005	35.4	35.3	35.2	35.1	35.2	35.2	35.2	35.1	35.1	35.1	35.0	35.0	35.2
2006	34.9	34.8	34.8	34.9	35.0	35.1	35.2	35.3	35.2	35.0	35.0	35.1	35.0
2007	35.2	35.1	35.1	35.1	35.1	35.2	35.3	35.3	35.1	35.1	35.2	35.1	35.2
Retail Trade													
2001	32.0	31.8	31.8	32.1	31.6	32.1	32.6	32.7	31.9	32.1	31.7	32.6	32.1
2002	31.7	31.9	32.2	32.0	32.2	32.8	33.1	32.6	32.0	31.8	31.5	31.8	32.1
2003	31.6	31.7	31.8	31.6	32.0	32.4	33.0	33.1	32.3	32.0	31.8	32.2	32.1
2004	32.1	32.2	32.0	32.2	32.3	32.3	32.2	32.2	32.2	32.2	32.3	32.3	32.2
2005	32.2	32.2	32.0	31.9	32.0	32.0	32.1	32.1	32.1	32.1	32.2	32.1	32.1
2006	32.1	32.1	32.0	32.1	32.1	32.1	32.1	32.2	32.2	32.5	32.5	32.4	32.2
2007	32.5	32.4	32.4	32.4	32.4	32.5	32.5	32.5	32.6	32.5	32.5	32.4	32.5

Average Hourly Earnings by Selected Industry: New Mexico, 2001–2007

(Dollars, not seasonally adjusted.)

Industry and year	January	February	March	April	May	June	July	August	September	October	November	December	Annual Average
Construction													
2001	15.06	15.12	15.14	15.13	14.94	15.12	14.87	14.93	14.82	14.94	14.78	14.85	14.97
2002	14.49	14.66	14.56	14.43	14.40	14.58	14.44	14.56	14.52	14.74	14.73	15.03	14.59
2003	15.03	15.08	15.18	15.13	15.14	14.99	15.05	15.02	15.05	15.08	15.08	15.11	15.08
2004	15.11	15.11	15.11	15.12	15.14	15.16	15.19	15.21	15.23	15.27	15.30	15.32	15.19
2005	15.35	15.41	15.46	15.53	15.57	15.62	15.68	15.72	15.76	15.79	15.82	15.86	15.64
2006	15.90	15.93	15.97	16.03	16.08	16.10	16.14	16.17	16.20	16.22	16.27	16.30	16.11
2007	16.31	16.34	16.36	16.39	16.41	16.42	16.47	16.51	16.56	16.60	16.65	16.70	16.48
Manufacturing													
2001	12.85	13.16	13.29	13.54	13.28	13.49	13.15	13.09	13.09	13.03	13.63	13.62	13.27
2002	13.50	13.82	13.84	13.37	13.70	13.49	13.28	13.22	13.12	13.12	13.26	13.25	13.41
2003	13.14	13.33	13.49	13.31	13.40	13.25	13.19	13.11	13.03	12.99	13.02	13.05	13.19
2004	13.08	13.08	13.08	13.12	13.11	13.09	13.09	13.08	13.11	13.18	13.26	13.32	13.13
2005	13.38	13.47	13.50	13.55	13.59	13.70	13.72	13.73	13.76	13.80	13.86	13.88	13.66
2006	13.95	13.99	13.98	14.00	14.01	14.05	14.04	14.03	14.06	14.12	14.21	14.26	14.06
2007	14.25	14.28	14.30	14.33	14.37	14.40	14.42	14.43	14.46	14.47	14.51	14.53	14.40
Wholesale Trade													
2001	13.74	13.69	13.44	13.59	13.88	13.99	14.26	14.02	14.29	14.03	13.85	14.25	13.92
2002	14.08	14.08	14.45	14.42	14.62	14.87	14.49	14.21	14.34	14.38	14.52	14.28	14.40
2003	14.74	14.85	14.87	14.83	14.68	14.54	14.49	14.42	14.38	14.41	14.43	14.44	14.59
2004	14.46	14.48	14.51	14.53	14.56	14.57	14.59	14.62	14.68	14.72	14.76	14.79	14.61
2005	14.80	14.80	14.80	14.79	14.79	14.78	14.79	14.80	14.81	14.82	14.82	14.84	14.80
2006	14.90	14.96	15.00	15.03	15.07	15.10	15.12	15.16	15.18	15.18	15.18	15.19	15.09
2007	15.21	15.23	15.24	15.26	15.27	15.29	15.30	15.32	15.34	15.35	15.36	15.37	15.30
Retail Trade													
2001	9.49	9.60	9.59	9.67	9.65	9.62	9.64	9.74	9.86	9.78	9.74	9.63	9.67
2002	9.62	9.61	9.84	9.56	9.72	9.63	9.62	9.63	9.64	9.65	9.75	9.98	9.69
2003	10.14	10.11	10.21	10.26	10.32	10.41	10.35	10.36	10.44	10.37	10.39	10.41	10.32
2004	10.42	10.40	10.42	10.52	10.61	10.68	10.73	10.76	10.77	10.80	10.82	10.84	10.65
2005	10.86	10.90	10.86	10.92	10.94	10.95	10.97	10.99	11.00	11.02	11.00	11.01	10.95
2006	11.02	11.05	11.09	11.15	11.17	11.18	11.19	11.20	11.21	11.19	11.20	11.21	11.16
2007	11.23	11.24	11.25	11.26	11.26	11.27	11.28	11.30	11.34	11.35	11.36	11.38	11.29

Average Weekly Earnings by Selected Industry: New Mexico, 2001–2007

(Dollars, not seasonally adjusted.)

Industry and year	January	February	March	April	May	June	July	August	September	October	November	December	Annual Average
Construction													
2001	582.82	592.70	591.97	573.43	582.66	591.19	572.50	589.74	577.98	590.13	563.12	564.30	580.84
2002	568.01	571.74	554.74	574.31	567.36	572.99	564.60	580.94	566.28	582.23	584.78	592.18	573.39
2003	598.19	586.61	602.65	597.64	591.97	593.60	598.99	596.29	598.99	603.20	601.69	604.40	598.68
2004	604.40	601.38	601.38	600.26	602.57	603.37	604.56	605.36	607.68	607.75	608.94	608.20	604.56
2005	609.40	611.78	612.22	614.99	616.57	618.55	622.50	624.08	627.25	628.44	629.64	629.64	620.91
2006	631.23	634.01	635.61	637.99	641.59	640.78	642.37	645.18	649.62	653.67	658.94	661.78	644.40
2007	660.56	660.14	659.31	662.16	662.96	661.73	660.45	660.40	660.74	665.66	666.00	671.34	662.50
Manufacturing													
2001	485.73	510.61	512.99	517.23	515.26	527.46	507.59	518.36	518.36	513.38	543.84	547.52	517.53
2002	523.80	548.65	543.91	533.46	549.37	553.09	528.54	530.12	528.74	520.86	533.05	526.03	535.06
2003	505.89	521.20	530.16	521.75	536.00	527.35	523.64	519.16	514.69	513.11	512.99	511.56	519.69
2004	515.35	519.28	519.28	520.86	520.47	519.67	519.67	519.28	520.47	521.93	523.77	524.81	519.95
2005	525.83	528.02	529.20	531.16	532.73	535.67	535.08	535.47	536.64	538.20	540.54	539.93	534.11
2006	544.05	547.01	548.02	550.20	549.19	550.76	550.37	549.98	551.15	553.50	558.45	558.99	551.15
2007	557.18	559.78	560.56	561.74	563.30	563.04	563.82	562.77	562.49	561.44	560.09	565.22	561.60
Wholesale Trade													
2001	424.57	436.71	434.11	438.96	435.83	450.48	460.60	454.25	467.28	447.56	455.67	471.68	448.22
2002	456.19	467.46	471.07	467.21	488.31	504.09	494.11	497.35	500.47	494.67	509.65	499.80	488.16
2003	502.63	515.30	526.40	527.95	524.08	507.45	510.05	514.79	511.93	517.32	519.48	521.28	516.49
2004	519.11	518.38	519.46	520.17	519.79	520.15	522.32	523.40	524.08	524.03	523.98	523.57	521.58
2005	523.92	522.44	520.96	519.13	520.61	520.26	520.61	519.48	519.83	520.18	518.70	519.40	520.96
2006	520.01	520.61	522.00	524.55	527.45	530.01	532.22	535.15	534.34	531.30	531.30	533.17	528.15
2007	535.39	534.57	534.92	535.63	535.98	538.21	540.09	540.80	538.43	538.79	540.67	539.49	538.56
Retail Trade													
2001	303.68	305.28	304.96	310.41	304.94	308.80	314.26	318.50	314.53	313.94	308.76	313.94	310.41
2002	304.95	306.56	316.85	305.92	312.98	315.86	318.42	313.94	308.48	306.87	307.13	317.36	311.05
2003	320.42	320.49	324.68	324.22	330.24	337.28	341.55	342.92	337.21	331.84	330.40	335.20	331.27
2004	334.48	334.88	333.44	338.74	342.70	344.96	345.51	346.47	346.79	347.76	349.49	350.13	342.93
2005	349.69	350.98	347.52	348.35	350.08	350.40	352.14	352.78	353.10	353.74	354.20	353.42	351.50
2006	353.74	354.71	354.88	357.92	358.56	358.88	359.20	360.64	360.96	363.68	364.00	363.20	359.35
2007	364.98	364.18	364.50	364.82	364.82	366.28	366.60	367.25	369.68	368.88	369.20	368.71	366.93

Population
    2000 census: 18,976,457
    2007 estimate: 19,297,729
    Percent change, 2000–2007: 1.7%

Percent change in total nonfarm employment, 2000–2007: 1.2%

Industry with the largest growth in employment, 2000–2007 (thousands)
    Education and health services, 218.7

Industry with the largest decline in employment, 2000–2007 (thousands)
    Manufacturing, -197.3

Civilian labor force
    2000: 9,166,972
    2007: 9,519,301

Employment-population ratio
    2000: 60.2%
    2007: 59.9%

Unemployment rate and rank among states
    2000: 4.5%, 38th
    2007: 4.5%, 27th

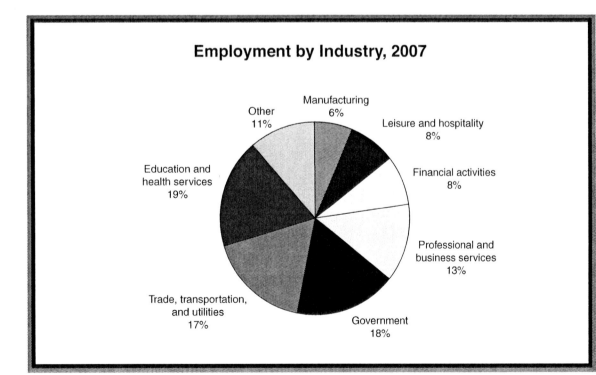

Employment by Industry, 2007

Employment by Industry: New York, 2000–2007

(Numbers in thousands, not seasonally adjusted.)

Industry and year	January	February	March	April	May	June	July	August	September	October	November	December	Annual Average
Total Nonfarm													
2000	8,394.2	8,445.8	8,520.4	8,590.7	8,676.0	8,719.3	8,648.0	8,606.0	8,666.4	8,754.0	8,800.8	8,834.2	8,638.0
2001	8,523.9	8,560.4	8,605.4	8,608.1	8,688.5	8,721.0	8,587.8	8,552.3	8,553.8	8,550.6	8,584.9	8,598.2	8,594.6
2002	8,294.4	8,342.2	8,395.4	8,430.6	8,510.7	8,540.2	8,459.2	8,444.1	8,446.3	8,528.7	8,563.4	8,585.9	8,461.8
2003	8,267.2	8,300.3	8,344.0	8,368.0	8,446.9	8,479.4	8,387.4	8,365.5	8,399.8	8,483.8	8,523.8	8,550.9	8,409.8
2004	8,235.7	8,292.2	8,365.7	8,401.1	8,499.6	8,543.8	8,480.9	8,453.2	8,485.1	8,572.2	8,607.0	8,642.3	8,464.9
2005	8,332.2	8,372.1	8,417.2	8,512.2	8,567.0	8,617.3	8,540.9	8,526.5	8,568.6	8,614.1	8,666.5	8,709.8	8,537.0
2006	8,405.3	8,446.7	8,511.7	8,568.6	8,647.4	8,704.7	8,608.4	8,584.9	8,634.2	8,715.0	8,771.8	8,821.9	8,618.4
2007	8,532.9	8,571.5	8,627.9	8,677.6	8,772.9	8,837.9	8,756.5	8,716.2	8,752.3	8,831.5	8,874.0	8,899.9	8,737.6
Total Private													
2000	6,949.1	6,981.6	7,041.7	7,098.9	7,162.7	7,239.5	7,194.3	7,195.3	7,239.9	7,277.2	7,315.5	7,353.6	7,170.8
2001	7,071.4	7,088.0	7,127.1	7,120.4	7,204.2	7,246.1	7,161.1	7,149.4	7,113.7	7,064.3	7,082.2	7,099.2	7,127.3
2002	6,817.8	6,840.5	6,885.5	6,929.5	7,001.3	7,034.8	6,989.0	6,996.0	6,993.0	7,031.5	7,049.3	7,067.7	6,969.7
2003	6,788.4	6,797.9	6,837.4	6,866.1	6,941.9	6,976.1	6,934.2	6,933.2	6,948.7	6,991.7	7,016.2	7,037.9	6,922.5
2004	6,764.8	6,799.2	6,865.8	6,904.8	6,991.3	7,040.2	7,026.6	7,020.8	7,036.6	7,081.0	7,103.3	7,137.6	6,981.0
2005	6,853.0	6,874.6	6,918.1	7,007.1	7,057.8	7,108.7	7,079.3	7,085.3	7,107.4	7,121.3	7,161.6	7,199.2	7,047.8
2006	6,930.0	6,953.5	7,016.1	7,069.8	7,143.4	7,203.6	7,156.5	7,154.5	7,176.6	7,220.2	7,265.4	7,307.4	7,133.1
2007	7,043.4	7,062.5	7,116.8	7,168.6	7,255.4	7,320.3	7,277.9	7,258.6	7,273.9	7,313.6	7,344.4	7,364.6	7,233.3
Goods-Producing													
2000	1,046.4	1,044.7	1,058.3	1,069.5	1,086.0	1,103.6	1,094.7	1,104.9	1,107.5	1,104.8	1,097.4	1,085.6	1,083.6
2001	1,035.6	1,033.8	1,039.8	1,046.4	1,061.8	1,073.9	1,056.6	1,057.8	1,047.3	1,037.8	1,026.2	1,011.9	1,044.1
2002	956.1	952.6	960.5	972.4	987.5	997.4	991.1	1,000.0	993.9	990.2	981.8	966.8	979.2
2003	918.8	911.8	921.1	928.1	945.1	955.6	948.2	955.6	953.2	947.3	941.4	928.3	937.9
2004	883.8	883.1	897.8	909.6	928.8	943.0	941.8	949.9	947.5	944.4	939.8	928.9	924.9
2005	881.3	875.2	882.8	901.6	916.3	929.7	928.0	935.7	932.6	925.0	924.3	912.1	912.1
2006	875.5	872.0	881.1	900.6	917.1	932.4	927.1	934.3	930.6	929.0	923.2	914.8	911.5
2007	878.6	869.3	879.0	897.0	918.8	934.6	931.3	935.6	931.2	924.8	917.9	904.5	910.2
Natural Resources and Mining													
2000	4.7	4.6	5.1	5.4	5.7	5.9	5.9	6.0	6.0	5.8	5.7	5.2	5.5
2001	4.6	4.7	5.0	5.2	5.6	5.6	5.7	5.7	5.5	5.7	5.5	5.2	5.3
2002	4.4	4.4	4.6	5.0	5.4	5.4	5.5	5.5	5.4	5.4	5.3	4.9	5.1
2003	4.4	4.4	4.6	5.0	5.5	5.6	5.7	5.8	5.8	5.7	5.6	5.4	5.3
2004	4.7	4.6	5.0	5.4	5.8	6.0	6.1	6.2	6.2	6.1	6.0	5.7	5.7
2005	4.9	4.8	5.0	5.7	6.0	6.3	6.4	6.5	6.4	6.4	6.2	5.9	5.9
2006	5.0	5.1	5.4	6.1	6.4	6.6	6.7	6.7	6.7	6.8	6.6	6.1	6.2
2007	5.2	5.3	5.5	5.9	6.4	6.8	6.8	6.8	6.8	6.8	6.5	6.1	6.2
Construction													
2000	289.5	286.9	299.6	312.3	327.4	338.5	343.3	348.1	349.3	349.0	346.3	337.6	327.3
2001	302.2	300.3	306.4	322.0	339.2	348.0	347.7	349.3	342.8	341.9	337.6	328.8	330.5
2002	293.8	291.5	297.1	311.3	323.9	332.0	338.4	342.7	338.5	337.4	332.7	323.2	321.9
2003	291.4	286.3	293.2	307.3	323.0	331.2	337.9	340.1	336.9	333.9	328.9	319.6	319.1
2004	285.6	283.7	293.6	309.8	325.3	334.6	341.6	344.5	342.4	340.4	336.9	327.9	322.2
2005	295.0	290.1	294.8	314.6	328.6	337.8	341.7	346.8	345.1	339.4	340.0	329.1	325.3
2006	303.3	300.3	308.0	326.3	340.6	350.8	353.1	358.6	356.2	356.0	351.1	344.9	337.4
2007	318.8	310.5	318.8	337.4	356.3	368.2	370.5	373.9	371.1	367.1	361.1	351.7	350.5
Manufacturing													
2000	752.2	753.2	753.6	751.8	752.9	759.2	745.5	750.8	752.2	750.0	745.4	742.8	750.8
2001	728.8	728.8	728.4	719.2	717.0	720.3	703.2	702.8	699.0	690.2	683.1	677.9	708.2
2002	657.9	656.7	658.8	656.1	658.2	660.0	647.2	651.8	650.0	647.4	643.8	638.7	652.2
2003	623.0	621.1	623.3	615.8	616.6	618.8	604.6	609.7	610.5	607.7	606.9	603.3	613.4
2004	593.5	594.8	599.2	594.4	597.7	602.4	594.1	599.2	598.9	597.9	596.9	595.3	597.0
2005	581.4	580.3	583.0	581.3	581.7	585.6	579.9	582.4	581.1	579.2	578.1	577.1	580.9
2006	567.2	566.6	567.7	568.2	570.1	575.0	567.3	569.0	567.7	566.2	565.5	563.8	567.9
2007	554.6	553.5	554.7	553.7	556.1	559.6	554.0	554.9	553.3	550.9	550.3	546.7	553.5
Service-Providing													
2000	7,347.8	7,401.1	7,462.1	7,521.2	7,590.0	7,615.7	7,553.3	7,501.1	7,558.9	7,649.2	7,703.4	7,748.6	7,554.4
2001	7,488.3	7,526.6	7,565.6	7,561.7	7,626.7	7,647.1	7,531.2	7,494.5	7,506.5	7,512.8	7,558.7	7,586.3	7,550.5
2002	7,338.3	7,389.6	7,434.9	7,458.2	7,523.2	7,542.8	7,468.1	7,444.1	7,452.4	7,538.5	7,581.6	7,619.1	7,482.6
2003	7,348.4	7,388.5	7,422.9	7,439.9	7,501.8	7,523.8	7,439.2	7,409.9	7,446.6	7,536.5	7,582.4	7,622.6	7,471.9
2004	7,351.9	7,409.1	7,467.9	7,491.5	7,570.8	7,600.8	7,539.1	7,503.3	7,537.6	7,627.8	7,667.2	7,713.4	7,540.0
2005	7,450.9	7,496.9	7,534.4	7,610.6	7,650.7	7,687.6	7,612.9	7,590.8	7,636.0	7,689.1	7,742.2	7,797.7	7,625.0
2006	7,529.8	7,574.7	7,630.6	7,668.0	7,730.3	7,772.3	7,681.3	7,650.6	7,703.6	7,786.0	7,848.6	7,907.1	7,706.9
2007	7,654.3	7,702.2	7,748.9	7,780.6	7,854.1	7,903.3	7,825.2	7,780.6	7,821.1	7,906.7	7,956.1	7,995.4	7,827.4
Trade, Transportation, and Utilities													
2000	1,524.8	1,508.2	1,514.6	1,515.2	1,528.8	1,548.6	1,527.7	1,534.8	1,547.9	1,559.1	1,588.7	1,618.7	1,543.1
2001	1,533.9	1,511.8	1,513.8	1,502.5	1,519.2	1,533.3	1,501.0	1,497.9	1,498.6	1,499.1	1,522.3	1,543.6	1,514.8
2002	1,467.3	1,447.0	1,455.7	1,457.0	1,471.9	1,489.0	1,466.1	1,467.2	1,481.0	1,491.1	1,514.8	1,541.6	1,479.1
2003	1,464.5	1,445.7	1,449.5	1,449.1	1,465.4	1,480.5	1,460.0	1,462.4	1,474.4	1,491.4	1,515.2	1,538.7	1,474.7
2004	1,457.1	1,443.2	1,451.3	1,453.1	1,476.2	1,494.2	1,481.3	1,481.5	1,493.2	1,512.2	1,536.1	1,562.0	1,486.8
2005	1,480.5	1,463.3	1,468.3	1,479.3	1,492.8	1,509.4	1,492.5	1,494.3	1,503.6	1,510.7	1,537.6	1,568.9	1,500.1
2006	1,493.2	1,469.8	1,477.9	1,483.4	1,499.0	1,519.9	1,498.1	1,496.5	1,506.6	1,524.1	1,556.5	1,583.2	1,509.0
2007	1,513.3	1,489.6	1,496.6	1,498.8	1,520.2	1,541.0	1,520.2	1,514.1	1,526.2	1,536.9	1,564.1	1,585.6	1,525.6
Wholesale Trade													
2000	369.7	370.9	373.4	370.5	372.3	375.3	372.8	374.0	374.7	375.0	375.3	377.3	373.4
2001	369.5	370.3	370.7	367.3	368.5	370.4	366.7	366.1	364.1	362.9	362.2	362.7	366.8
2002	352.8	353.0	354.0	353.5	355.2	356.7	353.6	355.4	354.9	357.2	357.9	358.8	355.3
2003	350.5	350.3	351.7	350.5	353.4	355.3	354.1	354.3	353.8	354.5	356.0	357.4	353.5
2004	347.8	348.2	350.3	351.2	353.4	355.8	355.9	355.4	354.2	356.6	357.2	359.0	353.8
2005	348.2	349.0	350.0	351.4	352.8	354.5	354.5	355.4	355.0	355.2	356.3	358.7	353.4
2006	348.9	348.8	350.9	352.2	354.0	357.0	355.5	356.2	355.1	356.2	356.6	359.9	354.3
2007	353.2	353.0	354.4	356.2	356.7	359.8	358.0	357.5	356.0	356.9	356.7	358.2	356.4

Employment by Industry: New York, 2000–2007—*Continued*

(Numbers in thousands, not seasonally adjusted.)

Industry and year	January	February	March	April	May	June	July	August	September	October	November	December	Annual Average
Retail Trade													
2000	877.9	860.3	863.1	866.3	875.6	890.2	881.2	887.6	887.5	894.6	924.5	950.7	888.3
2001	880.9	858.6	859.6	854.1	863.3	874.6	859.1	861.2	853.2	856.9	885.7	907.7	867.9
2002	850.1	830.7	837.7	837.8	847.9	862.1	854.2	856.8	857.1	862.0	886.5	912.0	857.9
2003	848.6	830.9	832.1	836.0	846.6	859.1	851.2	854.4	854.0	867.1	890.1	911.4	856.8
2004	849.0	835.3	840.0	841.0	856.8	870.7	867.6	869.1	870.1	881.6	905.6	928.9	868.0
2005	868.4	850.7	853.8	862.2	870.8	882.8	878.3	880.3	876.0	883.8	907.7	932.0	878.9
2006	875.6	853.2	857.8	862.4	871.5	886.0	881.3	880.5	875.8	891.8	922.1	940.4	883.2
2007	889.1	866.1	870.7	871.4	886.7	901.3	897.3	894.6	892.0	900.5	927.8	947.3	895.4
Transportation and Utilities													
2000	277.2	277.0	278.1	278.4	280.9	283.1	273.7	273.2	285.7	289.5	288.9	290.7	281.4
2001	283.5	282.9	283.5	281.1	287.4	288.3	275.2	270.6	281.3	279.3	274.4	273.2	280.1
2002	264.4	263.3	264.0	265.7	268.8	270.2	258.3	255.0	269.0	271.9	270.4	270.8	266.0
2003	265.4	264.5	265.7	262.6	265.4	266.1	254.7	253.7	266.6	269.8	269.1	269.9	264.5
2004	260.3	259.7	261.0	260.9	266.0	267.7	257.8	257.0	268.9	274.0	273.3	274.1	265.1
2005	263.9	263.6	264.5	265.7	269.2	272.1	259.7	258.6	272.6	271.7	273.6	278.2	267.8
2006	268.7	267.8	269.2	268.8	273.5	276.9	261.3	259.8	275.7	276.1	277.8	282.9	271.5
2007	271.0	270.5	271.5	271.2	276.8	279.9	264.9	262.0	278.2	279.5	279.6	280.1	273.8
Information													
2000	303.2	307.8	311.0	314.0	318.1	322.7	322.0	300.6	325.9	328.4	331.1	332.5	318.1
2001	325.6	328.5	329.0	326.4	329.2	329.3	325.1	322.9	317.2	315.4	318.5	316.3	323.6
2002	298.1	302.0	297.7	297.1	303.9	301.4	290.9	293.1	287.6	288.7	290.9	289.3	295.1
2003	275.7	279.7	276.8	273.8	279.1	275.4	270.9	274.7	271.1	273.5	277.4	276.1	275.4
2004	266.4	267.9	269.4	268.2	268.7	268.2	267.8	269.4	269.5	268.8	271.5	269.6	268.8
2005	263.2	265.4	266.2	266.5	268.3	272.4	269.7	270.6	270.3	271.1	272.3	275.5	269.3
2006	266.7	266.8	268.1	265.3	267.3	269.9	267.5	267.9	265.7	263.7	265.7	267.3	266.8
2007	260.4	261.9	262.3	262.6	265.1	267.7	265.4	266.3	265.2	267.3	268.7	269.2	265.2
Financial Activities													
2000	738.9	740.9	742.4	740.7	742.8	754.6	752.4	752.9	748.2	747.4	748.4	753.6	746.9
2001	739.9	740.2	742.4	737.7	738.0	747.2	745.4	742.4	733.3	704.1	701.7	707.8	731.7
2002	705.5	705.5	705.4	703.4	703.7	710.2	710.5	709.5	699.6	700.3	700.7	703.4	704.8
2003	692.2	690.1	689.7	689.9	693.5	701.6	704.7	704.0	696.7	695.6	696.8	702.8	696.5
2004	692.0	692.7	695.5	694.2	695.8	705.1	711.5	710.5	702.5	705.0	705.6	712.5	701.9
2005	701.0	701.2	703.4	707.1	707.2	717.6	723.6	723.6	716.3	716.4	718.2	723.8	713.3
2006	712.8	714.7	717.8	719.4	722.6	732.5	736.7	737.3	728.6	727.7	729.8	735.1	726.3
2007	723.0	724.4	726.4	727.5	728.2	740.0	743.3	739.9	731.2	729.6	730.7	732.9	731.4
Professional and Business Services													
2000	1,065.9	1,077.4	1,089.7	1,102.5	1,113.2	1,130.5	1,132.8	1,140.5	1,138.6	1,144.2	1,145.9	1,149.7	1,119.2
2001	1,101.4	1,105.5	1,108.8	1,103.7	1,109.6	1,117.4	1,109.9	1,107.4	1,096.6	1,077.1	1,075.3	1,076.0	1,099.1
2002	1,032.9	1,036.8	1,042.5	1,052.0	1,056.2	1,066.5	1,063.4	1,063.8	1,058.2	1,061.9	1,063.1	1,063.7	1,055.1
2003	1,019.9	1,019.6	1,029.2	1,039.3	1,042.3	1,053.5	1,049.9	1,049.9	1,047.2	1,053.3	1,055.8	1,060.4	1,043.4
2004	1,017.8	1,025.8	1,038.2	1,052.5	1,058.4	1,073.7	1,071.4	1,071.4	1,066.4	1,070.8	1,075.2	1,082.9	1,058.7
2005	1,045.4	1,047.0	1,053.1	1,076.4	1,077.6	1,092.5	1,095.6	1,098.0	1,096.9	1,096.4	1,103.4	1,110.2	1,082.7
2006	1,070.6	1,075.1	1,088.4	1,099.8	1,103.5	1,121.6	1,119.2	1,122.7	1,116.6	1,121.1	1,129.7	1,137.4	1,108.8
2007	1,099.4	1,104.8	1,116.4	1,126.8	1,133.4	1,152.6	1,152.9	1,153.5	1,141.9	1,150.9	1,152.7	1,154.9	1,136.7
Education and Health Services													
2000	1,359.7	1,379.7	1,390.4	1,398.8	1,390.2	1,368.7	1,348.5	1,342.0	1,373.6	1,402.3	1,420.3	1,426.4	1,383.4
2001	1,401.2	1,425.6	1,438.9	1,441.3	1,443.2	1,417.3	1,395.7	1,391.0	1,429.5	1,461.7	1,471.7	1,475.7	1,432.7
2002	1,433.3	1,461.4	1,474.8	1,477.4	1,475.8	1,446.1	1,434.8	1,428.9	1,470.0	1,503.2	1,511.4	1,512.9	1,469.2
2003	1,474.0	1,501.9	1,512.8	1,511.5	1,507.9	1,478.7	1,457.2	1,447.8	1,492.4	1,525.9	1,534.6	1,535.0	1,498.3
2004	1,494.0	1,526.4	1,539.2	1,536.0	1,536.0	1,501.5	1,483.5	1,472.7	1,514.7	1,553.6	1,561.2	1,564.1	1,523.6
2005	1,514.9	1,548.2	1,557.2	1,562.5	1,553.4	1,518.0	1,497.3	1,490.9	1,540.3	1,573.6	1,584.0	1,585.7	1,543.8
2006	1,541.0	1,576.0	1,586.8	1,589.2	1,584.4	1,549.0	1,521.4	1,513.0	1,571.2	1,608.1	1,618.2	1,623.9	1,573.5
2007	1,571.8	1,605.0	1,616.0	1,616.9	1,610.1	1,576.7	1,550.3	1,540.3	1,597.8	1,636.0	1,649.9	1,654.2	1,602.1
Leisure and Hospitality													
2000	581.7	591.1	600.2	621.4	644.5	670.4	676.6	680.4	658.0	647.6	639.7	641.5	637.8
2001	594.8	601.1	610.4	619.2	656.8	679.0	681.8	685.2	650.1	625.9	621.0	621.3	637.2
2002	584.3	592.8	603.8	624.0	653.4	674.0	683.3	686.0	656.9	646.2	635.2	638.0	639.8
2003	598.7	603.4	610.1	625.7	657.0	678.0	692.4	690.0	666.4	654.7	644.4	644.8	647.1
2004	608.7	613.3	624.3	640.0	672.5	697.8	714.6	712.7	690.3	670.5	657.8	659.5	663.5
2005	617.5	623.5	634.1	656.3	683.3	708.6	714.9	716.8	692.0	671.8	664.0	663.3	670.5
2006	620.7	628.4	641.7	656.6	690.7	717.5	728.6	727.1	700.3	686.7	681.6	682.4	680.2
2007	640.9	649.8	659.8	677.3	713.2	739.2	750.3	747.2	718.1	702.4	693.2	694.1	698.8
Other Services													
2000	328.5	331.8	335.1	336.8	339.1	340.4	339.6	339.2	340.2	343.4	344.0	345.6	338.6
2001	339.0	341.5	344.0	343.2	346.4	348.7	345.6	344.8	341.1	343.2	345.5	346.6	344.1
2002	340.3	342.4	345.1	346.2	348.9	350.2	348.9	347.5	345.8	349.9	351.4	352.0	347.4
2003	344.6	345.7	348.2	348.7	351.6	352.8	350.9	348.8	347.3	350.0	350.6	351.8	349.3
2004	345.0	346.8	350.1	351.2	354.9	356.7	354.7	352.7	352.5	355.7	356.1	358.1	352.9
2005	349.2	350.8	353.0	357.4	358.9	360.5	357.7	355.4	355.4	356.3	357.8	359.7	356.0
2006	349.5	350.7	354.3	355.5	358.8	360.8	357.9	355.7	357.0	359.8	360.7	363.3	357.0
2007	356.0	357.7	360.3	361.7	366.4	368.5	364.2	361.7	362.3	365.7	367.2	369.2	363.4
Government													
2000	1,445.1	1,464.2	1,478.7	1,491.8	1,513.3	1,479.8	1,453.7	1,410.7	1,426.5	1,476.8	1,485.3	1,480.6	1,467.2
2001	1,452.5	1,472.4	1,478.3	1,487.7	1,484.3	1,474.9	1,426.7	1,402.9	1,440.1	1,486.3	1,502.7	1,499.0	1,467.3
2002	1,476.6	1,501.7	1,509.9	1,501.1	1,509.4	1,505.4	1,470.2	1,448.1	1,453.3	1,497.2	1,514.1	1,518.2	1,492.1
2003	1,478.8	1,502.4	1,506.6	1,501.9	1,505.0	1,503.3	1,453.2	1,432.3	1,451.1	1,492.1	1,507.6	1,513.0	1,487.3
2004	1,470.9	1,493.0	1,499.9	1,496.3	1,508.3	1,503.6	1,454.3	1,432.4	1,448.5	1,490.2	1,503.7	1,504.7	1,483.8
2005	1,479.2	1,497.5	1,499.1	1,505.1	1,509.2	1,508.6	1,461.6	1,441.2	1,461.2	1,492.8	1,504.9	1,510.6	1,489.3
2006	1,475.3	1,493.2	1,495.6	1,498.8	1,504.0	1,501.1	1,451.9	1,430.4	1,457.6	1,494.8	1,506.4	1,514.5	1,485.3
2007	1,489.5	1,509.0	1,511.1	1,509.0	1,517.5	1,517.6	1,478.6	1,457.6	1,478.4	1,517.9	1,529.6	1,535.3	1,504.3

Average Weekly Hours by Selected Industry: New York, 2001–2007

(Not seasonally adjusted.)

Industry and year	January	February	March	April	May	June	July	August	September	October	November	December	Annual Average
Construction													
2001	38.4	38.0	37.6	37.9	39.2	38.7	38.4	38.5	37.0	40.0	39.4	39.3	38.6
2002	38.5	38.7	38.8	38.9	38.4	38.9	38.6	39.2	38.3	36.9	37.5	37.5	38.3
2003	37.4	35.5	37.2	37.6	39.0	39.4	38.5	39.3	38.6	37.3	37.6	36.2	37.9
2004	35.4	35.8	37.0	36.2	37.8	38.4	36.5	37.6	36.3	37.0	37.6	36.9	36.9
2005	35.9	36.3	36.5	37.5	37.4	37.6	37.2	37.9	37.2	36.2	37.4	36.4	37.0
2006	37.4	36.5	36.7	36.3	38.1	38.9	37.8	38.0	36.5	37.5	38.5	37.3	37.5
2007	37.1	35.9	38.0	37.6	39.4	39.2	38.9	38.5	38.6	38.5	38.5	38.5	38.3
Manufacturing													
2001	40.3	39.9	40.0	38.2	39.8	39.6	39.1	39.6	39.6	39.9	40.4	40.9	39.8
2002	39.8	40.3	40.6	40.2	40.5	40.3	39.6	40.0	40.6	40.4	40.6	41.1	40.3
2003	40.3	40.3	40.3	39.9	40.1	40.0	39.0	38.9	40.2	40.1	40.2	40.4	40.0
2004	39.6	39.6	39.7	39.1	39.9	39.6	38.9	39.7	39.5	39.7	40.2	40.5	39.7
2005	39.3	39.4	39.2	39.6	39.4	39.1	38.5	39.2	39.9	40.5	40.2	40.4	39.6
2006	40.7	41.3	41.7	40.0	41.2	41.5	40.3	41.0	41.5	40.8	41.1	41.8	41.1
2007	41.1	39.7	40.3	41.1	41.1	41.3	40.3	41.1	41.3	40.3	41.2	41.3	40.8

Average Hourly Earnings by Selected Industry: New York, 2001–2007

(Dollars, not seasonally adjusted.)

Industry and year	January	February	March	April	May	June	July	August	September	October	November	December	Annual Average
Construction													
2001	25.35	25.29	25.64	25.18	25.33	24.80	24.72	24.96	24.77	26.01	25.66	26.33	25.33
2002	25.72	26.64	26.44	26.43	26.46	26.18	26.06	25.55	26.37	25.64	26.05	26.36	26.15
2003	25.98	25.93	26.71	26.31	26.52	26.36	26.53	26.21	26.40	26.32	26.99	26.93	26.44
2004	27.07	27.60	27.50	27.22	26.90	26.44	26.45	26.18	26.54	26.43	26.54	26.35	26.73
2005	26.96	27.05	27.02	26.68	26.24	25.83	26.12	26.55	25.79	25.44	26.61	26.45	26.37
2006	26.73	26.64	26.49	25.90	25.73	26.10	26.30	26.67	26.49	26.49	26.25	27.32	26.42
2007	27.25	27.93	27.58	27.49	27.33	27.27	27.57	27.18	27.68	27.25	27.45	27.40	27.44
Manufacturing													
2001	15.89	15.88	15.86	16.03	16.00	15.98	16.14	16.42	16.60	16.52	16.72	16.93	16.24
2002	16.65	16.81	16.84	17.00	16.71	16.62	16.39	16.64	16.77	16.68	17.00	16.85	16.75
2003	16.79	16.70	16.74	16.69	16.70	16.60	16.56	16.88	16.89	16.71	16.91	17.20	16.78
2004	17.17	17.00	16.92	17.20	17.26	17.24	17.14	17.32	17.67	17.33	17.45	17.74	17.29
2005	17.76	17.74	17.56	17.77	17.72	17.83	17.55	17.86	17.89	17.62	17.95	17.93	17.77
2006	17.74	18.02	18.16	18.39	18.40	18.43	18.32	18.47	18.25	18.37	18.41	18.48	18.29
2007	18.33	18.43	18.59	18.68	18.48	18.75	18.57	18.78	18.64	18.24	18.18	18.17	18.49

Average Weekly Earnings by Selected Industry: New York, 2001–2007

(Dollars, not seasonally adjusted.)

Industry and year	January	February	March	April	May	June	July	August	September	October	November	December	Annual Average
Construction													
2001	973.44	961.02	964.06	954.32	992.94	959.76	949.25	960.96	916.49	1,040.40	1,011.00	1,034.77	977.74
2002	990.22	1,030.97	1,025.87	1,028.13	1,016.06	1,018.40	1,005.92	1,001.56	1,009.97	946.12	976.88	988.50	1,001.55
2003	971.65	920.52	993.61	989.26	1,034.28	1,038.58	1,021.41	1,030.05	1,019.04	981.74	1,014.82	974.87	1,002.08
2004	958.28	988.08	1,017.50	985.36	1,016.82	1,015.30	965.43	984.37	963.40	977.91	997.90	972.32	986.34
2005	967.86	981.92	986.23	1,000.50	981.38	971.21	971.66	1,006.25	959.39	920.93	995.21	962.78	975.69
2006	999.70	972.36	972.18	940.17	980.31	1,015.29	994.14	1,013.46	966.89	993.38	1,010.63	1,019.04	990.75
2007	1,010.98	1,002.69	1,048.04	1,033.62	1,076.80	1,068.98	1,072.47	1,046.43	1,068.45	1,049.13	1,056.83	1,054.90	1,050.95
Manufacturing													
2001	640.37	633.61	634.40	612.35	636.80	632.81	631.07	650.23	657.36	659.15	675.49	692.44	646.35
2002	662.67	677.44	683.70	683.40	676.76	669.79	649.04	665.60	680.86	673.87	690.20	692.54	675.03
2003	676.64	673.01	674.62	665.93	669.67	664.00	645.84	656.63	678.98	670.07	679.78	694.88	671.20
2004	679.93	673.20	671.72	672.52	688.67	682.70	666.75	687.60	697.97	688.00	701.49	718.47	686.41
2005	697.97	698.96	688.35	703.69	698.17	697.15	675.68	700.11	713.81	713.61	721.59	724.37	703.69
2006	722.02	744.23	757.27	735.60	758.08	764.85	738.30	757.27	757.38	749.50	756.65	772.46	751.72
2007	753.36	731.67	749.18	767.75	759.53	774.38	748.37	771.86	769.83	735.07	749.02	750.42	754.39

Population
    2000 census: 8,049,313
    2007 estimate: 9,061,032
    Percent change, 2000–2007: 12.6%

Percent change in total nonfarm employment, 2000–2007: 5.9%

Industry with the largest growth in employment, 2000–2007 (thousands)
    Education and health services, 136.7

Industry with the largest decline in employment, 2000–2007 (thousands)
    Manufacturing, -219.4

Civilian labor force
    2000: 4,123,812
    2007: 4,519,186

Employment-population ratio
    2000: 64.9%
    2007: 62.5%

Unemployment rate and rank among states
    2000: 3.7%, 22nd
    2007: 4.7%, 34th

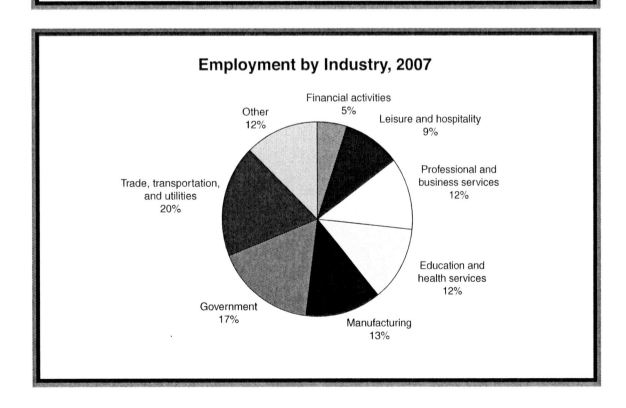

Employment by Industry, 2007

Financial activities 5%
Other 12%
Leisure and hospitality 9%
Professional and business services 12%
Trade, transportation, and utilities 20%
Education and health services 12%
Government 17%
Manufacturing 13%

Employment by Industry: North Carolina, 2000–2007

(Numbers in thousands, not seasonally adjusted.)

Industry and year	January	February	March	April	May	June	July	August	September	October	November	December	Annual Average
Total Nonfarm													
2000	3822.0	3842.8	3888.6	3911.2	3940.9	3960.0	3882.7	3932.6	3949.9	3945.2	3954.8	3950.5	3915.1
2001	3884.8	3896.7	3914.4	3917.5	3932.3	3924.0	3845.4	3887.5	3890.4	3885.6	3877.5	3866.7	3893.6
2002	3782.2	3798.7	3827.4	3852.0	3874.3	3857.2	3791.8	3842.1	3852.1	3857.4	3852.8	3845.7	3836.1
2003	3749.6	3752.5	3775.9	3796.5	3823.9	3808.3	3716.6	3776.6	3800.9	3821.9	3817.6	3821.9	3788.5
2004	3738.7	3748.9	3785.5	3818.6	3851.0	3844.3	3797.3	3858.6	3887.2	3891.3	3900.7	3910.1	3836.0
2005	3831.7	3848.0	3878.8	3905.3	3925.2	3909.4	3853.7	3925.5	3961.4	3968.8	3983.5	3986.1	3914.8
2006	3921.8	3936.6	3972.7	4019.5	4051.6	4048.6	3991.3	4063.7	4089.1	4111.2	4137.9	4143.3	4040.6
2007	4053.7	4076.8	4117.2	4126.3	4164.5	4167.5	4081.5	4159.4	4184.7	4198.1	4208.2	4210.9	4145.7
Total Private													
2000	3211.0	3224.6	3261.1	3281.2	3304.8	3338.3	3320.6	3324.5	3318.5	3306.1	3312.8	3311.3	3292.9
2001	3250.2	3255.3	3269.7	3276.8	3289.0	3306.6	3270.2	3272.3	3247.1	3227.2	3216.6	3210.2	3257.6
2002	3136.6	3146.1	3170.4	3197.2	3218.0	3233.9	3214.1	3225.9	3208.5	3197.1	3195.3	3192.7	3194.7
2003	3107.6	3105.1	3124.1	3146.4	3170.6	3185.5	3146.9	3162.4	3151.5	3150.8	3154.1	3160.7	3147.1
2004	3088.2	3093.4	3125.3	3159.4	3189.1	3214.1	3219.1	3229.1	3217.4	3217.3	3224.5	3234.9	3184.3
2005	3165.6	3175.5	3202.2	3229.2	3246.9	3267.8	3274.6	3287.8	3284.3	3287.4	3299.0	3303.6	3252.0
2006	3244.5	3253.0	3283.8	3328.2	3356.6	3383.0	3397.3	3410.0	3399.5	3413.1	3429.3	3436.5	3361.2
2007	3359.9	3376.3	3411.5	3420.8	3454.1	3486.1	3473.8	3488.7	3476.5	3480.6	3487.7	3492.9	3450.7
Goods-Producing													
2000	989.4	990.3	998.7	997.4	1001.2	1008.2	1002.1	998.8	1001.5	989.5	991.6	987.8	996.3
2001	972.9	968.5	965.4	959.8	953.4	953.0	938.3	934.8	927.3	916.2	905.6	898.4	941.1
2002	879.4	878.8	879.3	876.8	877.6	875.7	870.2	871.8	866.5	860.9	855.0	850.1	870.2
2003	834.6	829.2	830.0	829.1	828.9	827.9	810.4	810.5	808.0	806.2	802.4	799.9	818.1
2004	787.7	786.4	792.9	798.9	803.3	809.3	810.6	810.1	809.3	808.3	806.8	806.8	802.5
2005	794.6	795.6	798.5	800.7	803.8	807.7	805.9	807.7	808.2	802.8	802.6	800.8	802.4
2006	789.2	788.7	793.6	805.2	807.8	812.8	813.0	815.0	812.8	810.7	808.9	809.8	805.6
2007	797.6	797.8	801.5	795.9	798.6	806.4	801.4	803.7	802.0	800.2	799.7	799.3	800.3
Natural Resources and Mining													
2000	8.4	8.3	8.5	8.4	8.5	8.5	8.5	8.5	8.5	8.4	8.4	8.4	8.4
2001	8.2	8.1	8.1	8.2	8.2	8.2	8.1	8.1	8.1	8.0	8.0	8.0	8.1
2002	8.0	8.0	8.1	8.0	8.0	7.9	7.8	7.8	7.8	7.8	7.7	7.7	7.9
2003	7.6	7.5	7.6	7.6	7.6	7.6	7.1	7.2	7.1	7.2	7.0	7.0	7.3
2004	6.8	6.8	6.9	6.9	6.9	7.0	6.9	7.0	7.1	6.9	6.9	6.9	6.9
2005	6.8	6.8	6.8	6.7	6.6	6.7	6.6	6.6	6.6	6.7	6.7	6.6	6.7
2006	6.6	6.6	6.7	6.7	6.7	6.8	6.9	7.0	7.0	6.9	6.9	6.9	6.8
2007	6.9	6.9	7.0	7.1	7.1	7.1	7.1	7.1	7.1	7.0	7.0	7.0	7.0
Construction													
2000	220.0	219.3	227.4	228.1	231.2	235.2	233.8	235.2	235.0	232.4	232.0	230.7	230.0
2001	223.6	224.7	230.0	230.3	233.1	235.8	233.1	232.6	230.0	227.4	224.9	222.3	229.0
2002	214.4	214.4	216.9	221.0	223.3	224.1	222.7	223.3	220.1	217.2	214.5	213.7	218.8
2003	206.1	204.6	206.8	209.7	214.2	215.4	212.5	212.8	212.2	215.3	214.0	213.3	211.4
2004	206.0	205.0	210.1	214.9	218.2	221.0	223.7	223.9	222.9	224.3	223.9	224.6	218.2
2005	219.3	220.2	223.4	227.2	230.4	233.5	237.2	238.0	238.5	235.6	235.5	234.5	231.1
2006	230.2	231.2	236.4	242.1	244.7	248.7	251.5	253.5	252.5	251.9	252.5	252.7	245.7
2007	246.5	247.0	252.0	253.3	255.4	259.2	258.0	258.9	257.9	257.0	256.7	256.4	254.9
Manufacturing													
2000	761.0	762.7	762.8	760.9	761.5	764.5	759.8	755.1	758.0	748.7	751.2	748.7	757.9
2001	741.1	735.7	727.3	721.3	712.1	709.0	697.1	694.1	689.2	680.8	672.7	668.1	704.0
2002	657.0	656.4	654.3	647.8	646.3	643.7	639.7	640.7	638.6	635.9	632.8	628.7	643.5
2003	620.9	617.1	615.6	611.8	607.1	604.9	590.8	590.5	588.7	583.7	581.4	579.6	599.3
2004	574.9	574.6	575.9	577.1	578.2	581.3	580.0	579.2	579.3	577.1	576.0	575.3	577.4
2005	568.5	568.6	568.3	566.8	566.8	567.5	562.1	563.1	563.1	560.5	560.4	559.7	564.6
2006	552.4	550.9	550.5	556.4	556.4	557.3	554.6	554.5	553.3	551.9	549.5	550.2	553.2
2007	544.2	543.9	542.5	535.5	536.1	540.1	536.3	537.7	537.0	536.2	536.0	535.9	538.5
Service-Providing													
2000	2832.6	2852.5	2889.9	2913.8	2939.7	2951.8	2880.6	2933.8	2948.4	2955.7	2963.2	2962.7	2918.7
2001	2911.9	2928.2	2949.0	2957.7	2978.9	2971.0	2907.1	2952.7	2963.1	2969.4	2971.9	2968.3	2952.4
2002	2902.8	2919.9	2948.1	2975.2	2996.7	2981.5	2921.6	2970.3	2985.6	2996.5	2997.8	2995.6	2966.0
2003	2915.0	2923.3	2945.9	2967.4	2995.0	2980.4	2906.2	2966.1	2992.9	3015.7	3015.2	3022.0	2970.4
2004	2951.0	2962.5	2992.6	3019.7	3047.7	3035.0	2986.7	3048.5	3077.9	3083.0	3093.9	3103.3	3033.5
2005	3037.1	3052.4	3080.3	3104.6	3121.4	3101.7	3047.8	3117.8	3153.2	3166.0	3180.9	3185.3	3112.4
2006	3132.6	3147.9	3179.1	3214.3	3243.8	3235.8	3178.3	3248.7	3276.3	3300.5	3329.0	3333.5	3235.0
2007	3256.1	3279.0	3315.7	3330.4	3365.9	3361.1	3280.1	3355.7	3382.7	3397.9	3408.5	3411.6	3345.4
Trade, Transportation, and Utilities													
2000	735.4	734.6	741.8	746.9	753.2	759.2	751.1	753.8	752.6	755.6	765.1	772.7	751.8
2001	746.2	740.9	745.0	742.6	745.6	748.4	739.8	738.9	737.3	735.4	742.0	746.3	742.4
2002	715.3	710.2	716.6	720.1	723.8	728.4	725.0	727.4	724.9	725.2	738.2	745.0	725.0
2003	710.8	707.9	710.5	712.0	716.0	720.6	714.4	717.4	716.3	721.2	731.9	739.0	718.2
2004	710.2	706.9	712.6	718.7	724.7	728.4	727.7	729.9	728.5	731.5	743.2	751.9	726.2
2005	723.0	722.9	727.7	733.2	736.5	738.6	741.2	741.7	739.5	748.4	761.2	769.2	740.3
2006	739.5	734.4	740.4	749.8	755.0	756.1	761.6	763.4	761.4	767.9	784.5	791.4	758.8
2007	765.6	761.8	770.5	770.1	777.3	779.9	779.3	779.8	777.0	782.9	793.9	801.3	778.3
Wholesale Trade													
2000	160.7	161.6	162.9	163.9	164.6	165.7	165.2	165.8	165.6	166.1	165.3	166.1	164.4
2001	162.1	162.1	162.8	161.6	162.0	162.8	163.0	162.8	162.8	162.6	161.9	162.0	162.4
2002	160.1	160.1	160.7	162.3	162.7	163.6	163.4	163.4	163.6	164.0	164.2	164.2	162.7
2003	162.0	161.9	162.8	163.2	163.6	164.6	163.8	164.3	163.6	165.1	165.5	166.1	163.9
2004	164.5	164.2	165.3	165.6	166.2	167.0	167.0	167.6	167.7	167.9	168.0	168.8	166.7
2005	166.3	166.9	166.8	168.9	169.9	170.2	171.2	171.6	171.8	173.4	174.3	174.8	170.5
2006	171.7	172.1	172.9	175.5	176.3	176.7	176.7	177.7	177.7	177.7	178.6	179.1	176.1
2007	179.1	180.0	181.3	181.6	182.4	183.6	183.6	182.8	182.6	183.2	183.5	184.2	182.3

Employment by Industry: North Carolina, 2000–2007—*Continued*

(Numbers in thousands, not seasonally adjusted.)

Industry and year	January	February	March	April	May	June	July	August	September	October	November	December	Annual Average
Retail Trade													
2000	442.4	440.1	445.1	448.3	453.5	457.5	450.2	451.9	450.7	451.6	463.0	470.3	452.0
2001	448.9	442.8	446.1	444.5	447.1	449.4	442.5	443.0	442.3	441.5	451.0	455.6	446.2
2002	431.0	426.5	431.8	433.6	436.2	438.6	434.9	436.5	434.7	433.7	446.4	453.4	436.4
2003	424.7	421.2	423.6	425.0	428.2	431.5	427.0	428.7	427.0	430.6	441.5	446.9	429.7
2004	423.3	419.4	423.4	427.4	432.1	434.2	432.6	434.2	432.5	435.4	446.6	453.5	432.9
2005	430.7	429.7	434.0	437.0	438.9	439.9	442.6	442.3	439.5	445.6	456.5	462.9	441.6
2006	440.1	434.5	438.6	445.3	448.9	448.9	452.3	453.4	450.9	457.0	472.3	478.1	451.7
2007	456.3	452.3	458.7	458.3	463.9	465.1	465.1	465.7	463.1	468.0	479.3	485.2	465.1
Transportation and Utilities													
2000	132.3	132.9	133.8	134.7	135.1	136.0	135.7	136.1	136.3	137.9	136.8	136.3	135.3
2001	135.2	136.0	136.1	136.5	136.5	136.2	134.3	133.1	132.2	131.3	129.1	128.7	133.8
2002	124.2	123.6	124.1	124.2	124.9	126.2	126.7	127.5	126.6	127.5	127.6	127.4	125.9
2003	124.1	124.8	124.1	123.8	124.2	124.5	123.6	124.4	125.5	125.5	124.9	126.0	124.6
2004	122.4	123.3	123.9	125.7	126.4	127.2	128.1	128.1	128.3	128.2	128.6	129.6	126.7
2005	126.0	126.3	126.9	127.3	127.7	128.5	127.4	127.8	128.2	129.4	130.4	131.5	128.1
2006	127.7	127.8	128.9	129.0	129.8	130.5	131.6	132.3	132.8	133.2	133.6	134.2	131.0
2007	130.2	129.5	130.5	130.2	131.0	131.2	130.6	131.3	131.3	131.7	131.1	131.9	130.9
Information													
2000	72.3	72.7	73.5	75.0	75.4	76.6	77.1	77.6	77.6	78.0	78.6	78.5	76.1
2001	76.9	78.2	78.0	76.5	76.9	76.6	75.6	75.7	74.0	73.8	74.3	73.1	75.8
2002	73.8	73.6	73.8	73.5	73.7	73.6	72.8	72.4	71.7	71.9	71.9	72.1	72.9
2003	70.4	70.3	70.0	68.6	69.0	69.4	68.9	68.9	67.8	67.7	67.8	67.9	68.9
2004	67.2	66.7	67.0	66.4	66.3	67.1	67.1	67.2	66.7	68.1	69.3	69.7	67.4
2005	69.6	69.4	69.6	70.1	70.4	71.0	71.4	72.1	72.5	72.8	73.2	74.5	71.4
2006	74.1	74.0	73.9	72.7	72.9	73.5	72.6	72.7	72.3	72.5	72.5	72.9	73.1
2007	72.2	72.6	72.4	72.6	72.8	73.3	73.0	72.7	72.4	72.5	72.8	73.0	72.7
Financial Activities													
2000	181.8	182.6	183.8	183.8	185.2	187.6	187.8	188.1	187.0	187.7	187.0	188.4	185.9
2001	184.5	185.1	186.0	186.3	187.1	189.1	189.2	189.4	187.9	187.3	187.2	187.4	187.2
2002	185.3	185.9	187.1	186.5	187.2	189.5	190.5	191.0	190.1	190.4	189.6	190.1	188.6
2003	187.1	187.7	188.9	190.0	191.3	193.1	190.8	192.0	191.3	191.9	189.9	191.3	190.4
2004	189.4	189.8	190.5	191.7	192.0	194.2	195.9	196.2	195.5	195.4	193.6	193.2	193.0
2005	191.4	192.2	192.9	195.8	196.6	198.9	200.6	200.8	199.9	199.6	199.0	199.8	197.3
2006	196.6	198.0	199.4	203.5	204.7	206.9	210.6	211.0	209.2	209.4	208.8	209.1	205.6
2007	206.6	207.7	209.1	210.8	211.9	214.6	214.1	214.2	212.8	211.7	210.4	210.7	211.2
Professional and Business Services													
2000	406.2	410.8	417.7	421.7	421.9	426.7	425.0	428.3	427.4	427.8	426.9	422.2	421.9
2001	413.3	418.1	419.6	424.6	426.8	428.9	419.5	422.4	419.0	419.6	415.7	416.1	420.3
2002	405.6	411.9	416.4	421.7	425.6	428.8	422.9	429.6	429.5	427.1	424.4	423.8	422.3
2003	412.6	414.2	419.4	424.6	427.9	428.9	418.3	423.7	423.4	427.6	427.9	427.1	423.0
2004	417.8	421.7	426.5	429.6	432.8	435.8	437.0	441.3	440.0	444.7	442.6	442.7	434.4
2005	435.6	437.4	441.4	446.8	443.5	445.4	450.1	454.4	457.2	460.9	460.0	458.9	449.3
2006	455.4	458.7	463.4	470.3	473.7	479.8	483.4	488.7	489.8	493.9	493.9	492.6	478.6
2007	477.4	484.4	490.1	494.3	497.6	504.5	502.0	506.6	508.7	511.9	510.7	510.1	499.9
Education and Health Services													
2000	368.0	371.9	374.1	374.9	375.8	377.0	377.2	379.0	381.1	382.4	384.0	384.8	377.5
2001	387.5	391.1	394.0	396.6	398.1	398.8	398.7	402.3	403.9	406.1	408.1	409.5	399.6
2002	407.5	411.4	413.1	418.2	418.9	417.5	414.5	418.0	419.9	423.3	424.5	424.6	417.6
2003	420.3	423.4	425.4	426.9	428.0	427.2	426.8	431.2	433.7	435.3	436.5	438.3	429.4
2004	432.7	435.6	438.8	443.2	444.8	444.2	444.5	448.4	451.6	453.0	455.3	456.8	445.7
2005	453.1	456.6	460.2	461.3	462.8	461.3	462.8	467.7	472.0	472.7	475.5	475.3	465.1
2006	475.3	479.4	482.1	483.7	485.8	485.9	486.3	491.0	494.6	498.9	502.4	504.0	489.1
2007	499.0	505.3	509.1	512.3	514.8	514.2	510.5	516.3	518.6	521.6	523.8	524.5	514.2
Leisure and Hospitality													
2000	300.4	302.5	310.8	320.2	329.8	338.5	335.9	335.4	328.4	322.6	317.2	314.4	321.3
2001	306.6	309.9	317.1	326.1	335.0	343.2	340.1	340.6	330.5	322.0	316.5	312.3	325.0
2002	305.6	309.3	318.2	332.4	342.5	350.3	350.5	350.6	343.0	334.3	329.0	326.9	332.7
2003	313.2	313.5	320.8	333.2	345.5	352.1	350.7	352.7	345.0	339.1	336.4	334.8	336.4
2004	320.2	322.2	330.9	345.0	356.4	363.3	366.9	367.9	359.6	351.4	347.3	346.0	348.1
2005	332.1	334.0	343.6	353.1	362.9	371.6	371.9	372.6	365.5	359.3	356.2	353.5	356.4
2006	343.5	347.3	356.5	371.2	382.5	390.5	395.4	395.1	388.4	384.9	383.0	381.1	376.6
2007	367.0	370.8	381.0	388.7	402.5	411.2	409.3	411.3	402.7	397.1	393.3	390.8	393.8
Other Services													
2000	157.5	159.2	160.7	161.3	162.3	164.5	164.4	163.5	162.9	162.5	162.4	162.5	161.9
2001	162.3	163.5	164.6	164.3	166.1	168.6	169.0	168.2	167.2	166.8	167.2	167.1	166.2
2002	164.1	165.0	165.9	168.0	168.7	170.1	167.7	165.1	162.9	164.0	162.7	160.1	165.4
2003	158.6	158.9	159.1	162.0	164.0	166.3	166.6	166.0	166.0	161.8	161.3	162.4	162.8
2004	163.0	164.1	166.1	165.9	168.8	171.8	169.4	168.1	166.2	166.7	166.8	167.2	167.0
2005	166.2	167.4	168.3	168.2	170.4	173.3	170.7	170.8	169.5	170.9	171.3	171.6	169.9
2006	170.9	172.5	174.5	171.8	174.2	177.5	174.4	173.1	171.0	174.9	175.3	175.6	173.8
2007	174.5	175.9	177.8	176.1	178.6	182.0	184.2	184.1	182.3	182.7	183.1	183.2	180.4
Government													
2000	611.0	618.2	627.5	630.0	636.1	621.7	562.1	608.1	631.4	639.1	642.0	639.2	622.2
2001	634.6	641.4	644.7	640.7	643.3	617.4	575.2	615.2	643.3	658.4	660.9	656.5	636.0
2002	645.6	652.6	657.0	654.8	656.3	623.3	577.7	616.2	643.6	660.3	657.5	653.0	641.5
2003	642.0	647.4	651.8	650.1	653.3	622.8	569.7	614.2	649.4	671.1	663.5	661.2	641.4
2004	650.5	655.5	660.2	659.2	661.9	630.2	578.2	629.5	669.8	674.0	676.2	675.2	651.7
2005	666.1	672.5	676.6	676.1	678.3	641.6	579.1	637.7	677.1	681.4	684.5	682.5	662.8
2006	677.3	683.6	688.9	691.3	695.0	665.6	594.0	653.7	689.6	698.1	708.6	706.8	679.4
2007	693.8	700.5	705.7	705.5	710.4	681.4	607.7	670.7	708.2	717.5	720.5	718.0	695.0

Average Weekly Hours by Selected Industry: North Carolina, 2001–2007

(Not seasonally adjusted.)

Industry and year	January	February	March	April	May	June	July	August	September	October	November	December	Annual Average
Manufacturing													
2001	40.0	39.3	39.5	38.4	39.5	39.7	38.5	39.7	39.9	39.7	39.2	39.8	39.4
2002	39.8	39.7	40.1	40.5	40.2	40.8	39.0	41.3	40.8	39.6	39.7	41.1	40.2
2003	39.3	39.5	39.8	39.3	39.3	39.8	38.8	39.7	40.2	40.1	40.7	40.5	39.8
2004	40.0	40.1	40.5	40.1	40.8	40.4	39.7	40.9	40.2	40.4	40.4	40.7	40.3
2005	40.2	39.9	39.9	40.0	39.7	39.9	38.8	39.8	40.2	40.9	40.7	39.6	40.0
2006	39.8	39.2	39.6	39.0	39.8	39.8	38.9	39.9	40.5	41.0	41.2	41.6	40.0
2007	41.0	41.0	41.6	41.1	41.6	42.0	41.5	41.8	42.0	41.9	41.5	41.6	41.6

Average Hourly Earnings by Selected Industry: North Carolina, 2001–2007

(Dollars, not seasonally adjusted.)

Industry and year	January	February	March	April	May	June	July	August	September	October	November	December	Annual Average
Manufacturing													
2001	12.65	12.65	12.65	12.79	12.74	12.75	12.90	12.79	12.87	12.82	13.02	13.07	12.81
2002	13.08	13.08	13.11	13.13	13.22	13.26	13.31	13.10	13.11	13.17	13.17	13.38	13.18
2003	13.50	13.44	13.49	13.59	13.55	13.55	13.63	13.67	13.83	13.78	13.87	14.09	13.66
2004	13.96	13.98	14.03	14.23	14.21	14.41	14.44	14.27	14.49	14.31	14.27	14.38	14.25
2005	14.25	14.26	14.32	14.28	14.34	14.38	14.50	14.31	14.36	14.41	14.58	14.59	14.38
2006	14.46	14.33	14.30	14.47	14.44	14.49	14.53	14.53	14.72	14.73	14.85	14.96	14.57
2007	14.91	14.98	14.93	15.07	15.00	14.98	15.11	15.09	15.17	15.12	15.18	15.44	15.08

Average Weekly Earnings by Selected Industry: North Carolina, 2001–2007

(Dollars, not seasonally adjusted.)

Industry and year	January	February	March	April	May	June	July	August	September	October	November	December	Annual Average
Manufacturing													
2001	506.00	497.15	499.68	491.14	503.23	506.18	496.65	507.76	513.51	508.95	510.38	520.19	504.71
2002	520.58	519.28	525.71	531.77	531.44	541.01	519.09	541.03	534.89	521.53	522.85	549.92	529.84
2003	530.55	530.88	536.90	534.09	532.52	539.29	528.84	542.70	555.97	552.58	564.51	570.65	543.67
2004	558.40	560.60	568.22	570.62	579.77	582.16	573.27	583.64	582.50	578.12	576.51	585.27	574.28
2005	572.85	568.97	571.37	571.20	569.30	573.76	562.60	569.54	577.27	589.37	593.41	577.76	575.20
2006	575.51	561.74	566.28	564.33	574.71	576.70	565.22	579.75	596.16	603.93	611.82	622.34	582.80
2007	611.31	614.18	621.09	619.38	624.00	629.16	627.07	630.76	637.14	633.53	629.97	642.30	627.33

Population
  2000 census: 642,200
  2007 estimate: 639,715
  Percent change, 2000–2007: -0.4

Percent change in total nonfarm employment, 2000–2007: 9.2%

Industry with the largest growth in employment, 2000–2007 (thousands)
  Education and health services, 5.5

Industry with the largest decline in employment, 2000–2007 (thousands)
  Information, -0.8

Civilian labor force
  2000: 345,881
  2007: 365,598

Employment-population ratio
  2000: 69.2%
  2007: 71.2%

Unemployment rate and rank among states
  2000: 2.9%, 10th
  2007: 3.2%, 9th

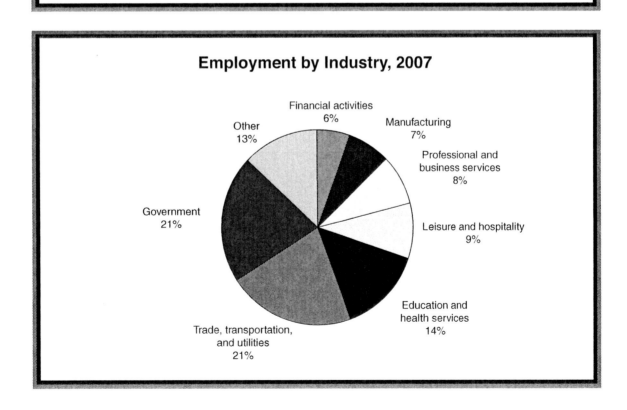

Employment by Industry, 2007

Financial activities 6%

Manufacturing 7%

Other 13%

Professional and business services 8%

Government 21%

Leisure and hospitality 9%

Education and health services 14%

Trade, transportation, and utilities 21%

Employment by Industry: North Dakota, 2000–2007

(Numbers in thousands, not seasonally adjusted.)

Industry and year	January	February	March	April	May	June	July	August	September	October	November	December	Annual Average
Total Nonfarm													
2000	319.2	320.4	323.2	327.1	332.8	329.0	327.6	327.2	331.5	332.9	330.9	330.9	327.7
2001	322.5	324.2	326.3	330.1	335.3	333.6	324.9	325.5	333.9	335.0	333.2	332.1	329.7
2002	322.6	323.9	323.9	328.6	333.8	333.4	325.1	327.0	334.2	335.5	334.5	334.5	329.8
2003	323.9	325.3	327.2	331.7	336.9	335.4	326.7	330.9	338.7	340.1	337.7	337.2	332.6
2004	326.5	328.2	330.6	337.1	342.0	341.2	334.9	336.2	343.7	346.1	344.8	343.9	337.9
2005	333.4	336.1	338.3	345.7	349.7	348.3	339.5	342.3	351.4	350.7	350.5	350.8	344.7
2006	341.1	343.7	347.0	352.2	357.0	356.2	345.6	349.1	358.6	358.8	358.3	359.0	352.2
2007	348.5	349.6	352.6	356.1	362.5	362.3	352.9	353.5	363.7	365.0	364.1	363.1	357.8
Total Private													
2000	246.4	246.0	248.3	252.5	257.4	260.1	261.1	260.8	258.5	258.5	256.7	256.1	255.2
2001	248.5	249.1	251.1	254.9	260.4	263.0	261.8	261.5	259.7	259.4	257.8	256.3	257.0
2002	247.5	247.8	247.9	252.3	257.3	261.3	260.7	261.0	258.6	258.3	257.2	256.2	255.5
2003	248.5	247.8	249.3	253.4	258.4	262.5	262.0	263.9	261.8	261.8	259.8	259.0	257.4
2004	251.0	251.6	253.8	259.9	265.0	268.9	270.6	270.2	267.5	268.3	267.2	266.0	263.3
2005	257.8	258.4	260.4	267.3	271.6	275.2	275.5	276.2	274.7	273.1	272.8	272.8	269.7
2006	264.9	266.0	268.8	273.7	278.6	282.5	281.4	282.8	281.7	280.3	279.8	280.1	276.7
2007	272.0	271.8	274.6	277.7	284.0	287.6	287.7	287.4	286.8	286.9	285.8	284.5	282.2
Goods-Producing													
2000	38.9	38.7	39.3	41.3	44.3	46.3	46.8	46.5	45.5	44.8	42.2	40.7	42.9
2001	38.9	38.5	39.6	41.0	43.7	45.4	46.3	46.1	46.2	45.2	43.1	41.1	42.9
2002	38.4	38.2	38.4	40.2	42.7	44.4	45.0	45.3	44.2	43.7	42.4	40.9	42.0
2003	38.5	38.0	38.4	40.2	43.2	45.4	45.9	46.7	46.2	45.7	43.6	42.1	42.8
2004	39.5	39.5	40.5	43.6	46.1	48.6	49.5	49.4	48.6	48.1	46.6	44.6	45.4
2005	42.0	42.3	43.2	45.8	48.2	50.1	51.1	51.2	50.4	49.6	48.8	47.3	47.5
2006	44.4	44.4	45.1	48.0	50.1	52.0	52.4	52.7	52.0	50.9	50.1	49.0	49.3
2007	45.9	45.3	46.4	48.1	50.7	52.8	53.6	53.4	53.0	52.6	50.8	49.3	50.2
Natural Resources and Mining													
2000	3.0	3.0	3.0	3.1	3.4	3.4	3.6	3.7	3.7	3.5	3.3	3.2	3.3
2001	3.1	3.1	3.3	3.3	3.5	3.7	3.8	3.7	3.7	3.7	3.5	3.3	3.5
2002	2.9	2.8	2.9	3.1	3.3	3.4	3.4	3.4	3.3	3.4	3.3	3.1	3.2
2003	2.9	2.9	3.0	3.2	3.5	3.6	3.6	3.6	3.5	3.6	3.4	3.3	3.3
2004	3.2	3.2	3.3	3.4	3.5	3.6	3.7	3.8	3.8	3.7	3.7	3.6	3.5
2005	3.6	3.7	3.7	3.9	4.1	4.2	4.3	4.5	4.4	4.3	4.4	4.4	4.1
2006	4.1	4.3	4.3	4.6	4.8	4.7	4.7	4.9	5.0	5.1	5.1	5.0	4.7
2007	4.8	4.7	4.8	4.9	5.1	5.2	5.2	5.2	5.2	5.2	5.2	5.2	5.1
Construction													
2000	13.2	12.9	13.3	14.9	17.1	18.5	18.9	18.6	17.3	16.9	14.8	13.5	15.8
2001	12.1	11.8	12.5	13.8	16.0	17.3	18.1	18.4	17.8	17.4	15.8	14.1	15.4
2002	12.4	12.2	12.2	13.6	15.7	16.9	17.6	17.8	17.1	16.4	15.3	14.2	15.1
2003	12.4	12.2	12.4	13.9	16.3	17.9	18.4	19.1	18.9	18.2	16.6	15.1	16.0
2004	13.1	13.0	13.7	16.3	18.2	19.8	20.4	20.1	19.5	19.0	17.6	15.9	17.2
2005	13.6	13.6	14.1	16.3	18.2	19.5	20.4	20.3	19.7	19.0	18.1	16.6	17.5
2006	14.8	14.7	15.2	17.6	19.4	20.9	21.0	21.2	20.6	20.2	18.8	17.6	18.5
2007	15.6	15.3	16.1	17.6	19.7	21.1	21.8	21.9	21.6	21.0	19.6	18.2	19.1
Manufacturing													
2000	22.7	22.8	23.0	23.3	23.8	24.4	24.3	24.2	24.5	24.4	24.1	24.0	23.8
2001	23.7	23.6	23.8	23.9	24.2	24.4	24.4	24.0	24.7	24.1	23.8	23.7	24.0
2002	23.1	23.2	23.3	23.5	23.7	24.1	24.0	24.1	23.8	23.9	23.8	23.6	23.7
2003	23.2	22.9	23.0	23.1	23.4	23.9	23.9	24.0	23.8	23.9	23.6	23.7	23.5
2004	23.2	23.3	23.5	23.9	24.4	25.2	25.4	25.5	25.3	25.4	25.3	25.1	24.6
2005	24.8	25.0	25.4	25.6	25.9	26.4	26.4	26.4	26.3	26.3	26.3	26.3	25.9
2006	25.5	25.4	25.6	25.8	25.9	26.4	26.7	26.6	26.4	25.6	26.2	26.4	26.0
2007	25.5	25.3	25.5	25.6	25.9	26.5	26.6	26.3	26.2	26.4	26.0	25.9	26.0
Service-Providing													
2000	280.3	281.7	283.9	285.8	288.5	282.7	280.8	280.7	286.0	288.1	288.7	290.2	284.8
2001	283.6	285.7	286.7	289.1	291.6	288.2	278.6	279.4	287.7	289.8	290.1	291.0	286.8
2002	284.2	285.7	285.5	288.4	291.1	289.0	280.1	281.7	290.0	291.8	292.1	293.6	287.8
2003	285.4	287.3	288.8	291.5	293.7	290.0	280.8	284.2	292.5	294.4	294.1	295.1	289.8
2004	287.0	288.7	290.1	293.5	295.9	292.6	285.4	286.8	295.1	298.0	298.2	299.3	292.6
2005	291.4	293.8	295.1	299.9	301.5	298.2	288.4	291.1	301.0	301.1	301.7	303.5	297.2
2006	296.7	299.3	301.9	304.2	306.9	304.2	293.2	296.4	306.6	307.9	308.2	310.0	303.0
2007	302.6	304.3	306.2	308.0	311.8	309.5	299.3	300.1	310.7	312.4	313.3	313.8	307.7
Trade, Transportation, and Utilities													
2000	71.5	70.7	70.8	71.9	72.6	72.2	71.9	72.1	71.8	72.7	73.6	74.3	72.2
2001	71.3	70.7	71.0	71.9	73.1	72.7	72.0	71.9	71.3	71.7	72.8	73.1	72.0
2002	71.0	70.3	70.3	70.9	72.2	72.4	71.7	71.5	71.2	71.8	72.9	73.6	71.7
2003	70.9	70.2	70.4	71.5	72.3	72.3	71.5	72.0	71.6	72.6	73.5	74.1	71.9
2004	71.3	71.0	71.3	72.4	73.5	73.4	73.0	72.9	72.5	73.5	74.8	75.6	72.9
2005	72.3	72.3	72.8	74.3	75.0	74.9	74.4	74.2	74.4	74.8	75.7	76.5	74.3
2006	74.0	73.9	74.6	76.0	76.9	76.9	76.1	76.3	76.2	76.4	77.4	78.0	76.1
2007	75.4	75.0	75.1	75.9	77.0	76.8	76.7	76.4	76.1	76.7	77.8	78.0	76.4
Wholesale Trade													
2000	18.1	17.9	18.0	18.5	18.7	18.6	18.3	18.3	18.1	18.2	18.2	18.2	18.3
2001	18.0	18.0	18.2	18.4	19.1	18.9	18.6	18.5	18.1	18.2	18.1	18.0	18.3
2002	17.8	17.7	17.7	18.0	18.4	18.6	18.2	18.1	17.8	18.0	17.9	17.8	18.0
2003	17.5	17.3	17.4	18.1	18.4	18.4	18.2	18.1	17.8	18.1	18.0	18.0	17.9
2004	17.8	17.8	18.0	18.6	18.8	18.8	18.7	18.6	18.2	18.4	18.5	18.6	18.4
2005	18.1	18.1	18.3	19.0	19.3	19.3	19.1	19.0	18.8	19.0	18.9	19.0	18.8
2006	18.6	18.6	18.8	19.3	19.6	19.6	19.2	19.2	19.0	19.1	19.0	19.0	19.1
2007	18.8	18.7	18.9	19.4	19.8	19.8	19.5	19.5	19.2	19.5	19.5	19.6	19.4

Employment by Industry: North Dakota, 2000–2007—*Continued*

(Numbers in thousands, not seasonally adjusted.)

Industry and year	January	February	March	April	May	June	July	August	September	October	November	December	Annual Average
Retail Trade													
2000	40.6	40.1	40.0	40.5	40.9	40.8	40.9	40.9	40.6	41.1	42.1	42.8	40.9
2001	40.3	39.8	40.0	40.4	41.0	40.7	40.4	40.4	40.2	40.5	41.6	42.0	40.6
2002	40.3	39.8	39.8	40.0	40.8	40.8	40.5	40.5	40.4	40.7	41.9	42.6	40.7
2003	40.3	39.9	39.9	40.3	40.9	41.0	40.5	41.0	40.7	41.2	42.2	42.8	40.9
2004	40.6	40.2	40.4	40.8	41.5	41.5	41.2	41.2	41.0	41.5	42.7	43.3	41.3
2005	41.1	41.0	41.2	41.9	42.3	42.3	42.1	42.0	42.1	42.3	43.3	43.8	42.1
2006	41.9	41.7	42.1	43.0	43.6	43.6	43.3	43.3	43.3	43.4	44.5	44.9	43.2
2007	42.9	42.5	42.4	42.6	43.1	43.1	43.2	42.9	42.7	43.0	43.9	44.3	43.1
Transportation and Utilities													
2000	12.8	12.7	12.8	12.9	13.0	12.8	12.7	12.9	13.1	13.4	13.3	13.3	13.0
2001	13.0	12.9	12.8	13.1	13.0	13.1	13.0	13.0	13.0	13.0	13.1	13.1	13.0
2002	12.9	12.8	12.8	12.9	13.0	13.0	13.0	12.9	13.0	13.1	13.1	13.2	13.0
2003	13.1	13.0	13.1	13.1	13.0	12.9	12.8	12.9	13.1	13.3	13.3	13.3	13.1
2004	12.9	13.0	12.9	13.0	13.2	13.1	13.1	13.1	13.3	13.6	13.6	13.7	13.2
2005	13.1	13.2	13.3	13.4	13.4	13.3	13.2	13.2	13.5	13.5	13.5	13.7	13.4
2006	13.5	13.6	13.7	13.7	13.7	13.7	13.6	13.8	13.9	13.9	13.9	14.1	13.8
2007	13.7	13.8	13.8	13.9	14.1	13.9	14.0	14.0	14.2	14.2	14.4	14.1	14.0
Information													
2000	8.4	8.4	8.5	8.5	8.5	8.5	8.5	8.3	8.4	8.4	8.4	8.5	8.4
2001	8.4	8.4	8.4	8.4	8.5	8.6	8.5	8.5	8.5	8.6	8.5	8.4	8.5
2002	8.0	8.0	7.9	7.9	8.0	8.0	8.0	7.9	7.8	7.8	7.8	7.9	7.9
2003	7.7	7.6	7.7	7.7	7.7	7.7	7.7	7.7	7.7	7.7	7.7	7.7	7.7
2004	7.6	7.6	7.6	7.6	7.7	7.7	7.8	7.8	7.7	7.8	7.8	7.7	7.7
2005	7.6	7.6	7.5	7.6	7.6	7.6	7.6	7.6	7.6	7.4	7.4	7.5	7.6
2006	7.4	7.4	7.4	7.4	7.4	7.5	7.5	7.6	7.5	7.5	7.6	7.6	7.5
2007	7.6	7.6	7.6	7.6	7.6	7.7	7.6	7.7	7.6	7.6	7.6	7.5	7.6
Financial Activities													
2000	16.9	16.9	16.9	16.7	17.0	17.0	17.1	17.2	17.2	17.2	17.3	17.5	17.1
2001	17.4	17.4	17.4	17.5	17.6	17.7	17.7	17.8	17.8	17.9	17.8	18.0	17.7
2002	17.7	17.8	17.8	17.8	17.9	18.1	18.1	18.3	18.1	18.3	18.3	18.4	18.1
2003	18.2	18.1	18.3	18.2	18.3	18.4	18.5	18.6	18.5	18.4	18.4	18.5	18.4
2004	18.5	18.6	18.7	18.5	18.6	18.7	18.7	18.6	18.6	18.6	18.7	18.8	18.6
2005	18.6	18.6	18.7	18.7	18.8	18.8	18.9	19.1	18.8	18.9	18.8	19.1	18.8
2006	18.9	19.0	19.1	19.0	19.1	19.3	19.4	19.4	19.3	19.2	19.3	19.6	19.2
2007	19.3	19.4	19.5	19.5	19.8	19.9	20.0	20.0	20.0	20.0	20.0	20.2	19.8
Professional and Business Services													
2000	23.2	23.7	24.2	24.5	24.7	25.2	25.6	25.3	25.0	25.2	25.1	25.2	24.7
2001	24.5	25.5	25.1	25.5	25.6	26.1	25.4	25.3	25.0	25.2	25.1	25.0	25.3
2002	23.1	23.5	23.6	24.1	24.1	25.0	24.6	24.7	24.7	24.4	24.0	23.8	24.1
2003	23.2	23.5	23.3	23.5	23.5	24.1	23.8	24.3	24.1	23.9	23.8	23.6	23.7
2004	22.9	23.3	23.4	24.2	24.5	25.0	25.0	25.1	24.7	25.6	25.1	25.2	24.5
2005	24.5	24.7	24.7	26.4	26.6	27.1	27.4	27.7	27.4	27.3	27.2	27.3	26.5
2006	26.8	27.1	27.5	27.8	28.4	29.1	28.9	28.9	29.1	29.0	28.7	28.6	28.3
2007	28.1	28.3	28.8	29.0	29.5	29.9	29.8	29.9	30.0	30.2	30.3	29.8	29.5
Education and Health Services													
2000	44.7	44.7	45.0	44.9	45.0	45.3	45.4	45.5	45.3	45.8	46.0	46.1	45.3
2001	45.5	45.8	45.9	45.8	46.0	46.2	46.3	46.2	45.8	46.1	46.4	46.6	46.1
2002	46.2	46.3	46.0	46.4	46.6	46.9	46.9	46.9	46.7	47.0	47.1	47.2	46.7
2003	46.9	47.0	47.1	47.4	47.5	48.1	48.1	47.9	47.7	47.8	48.0	48.3	47.7
2004	47.9	47.9	48.1	48.5	48.5	48.7	48.8	48.7	48.3	48.3	48.4	48.5	48.4
2005	48.2	48.2	48.2	48.5	48.4	49.1	48.9	49.0	49.0	49.0	49.1	49.4	48.8
2006	49.1	49.3	49.7	49.6	49.4	50.0	49.8	49.9	49.8	50.0	50.0	50.3	49.7
2007	50.0	50.1	50.3	50.3	50.6	51.0	51.0	51.0	51.2	51.2	51.2	51.4	50.8
Leisure and Hospitality													
2000	27.7	27.7	28.3	29.3	30.0	30.4	30.6	30.7	30.1	29.1	28.8	28.5	29.3
2001	27.5	27.7	28.5	29.4	30.5	31.0	30.5	30.5	29.8	29.4	28.8	28.7	29.4
2002	28.0	28.4	28.6	29.6	30.4	31.1	31.2	31.2	30.7	30.1	29.4	29.2	29.8
2003	28.1	28.2	28.9	29.6	30.6	31.3	31.4	31.5	30.6	30.4	29.6	29.4	30.0
2004	28.5	28.7	29.2	30.0	31.0	31.6	32.7	32.6	32.1	31.3	30.7	30.5	30.7
2005	29.7	29.7	30.1	30.8	31.8	32.5	32.3	32.5	32.2	31.2	30.9	30.7	31.2
2006	29.5	30.0	30.4	30.9	32.2	32.8	32.4	32.9	32.8	32.2	31.4	31.6	31.6
2007	30.7	31.1	31.7	32.1	33.5	34.4	33.9	34.0	33.8	33.4	32.7	32.8	32.8
Other Services													
2000	15.1	15.2	15.3	15.4	15.3	15.2	15.2	15.2	15.2	15.3	15.3	15.3	15.3
2001	15.0	15.1	15.2	15.4	15.4	15.3	15.1	15.2	15.3	15.3	15.3	15.4	15.3
2002	15.1	15.3	15.3	15.4	15.4	15.4	15.2	15.2	15.2	15.2	15.3	15.2	15.3
2003	15.0	15.2	15.2	15.3	15.3	15.2	15.1	15.2	15.4	15.3	15.2	15.3	15.2
2004	14.8	15.0	15.0	15.1	15.1	15.2	15.1	15.1	15.0	15.1	15.1	15.1	15.1
2005	14.9	15.0	15.2	15.2	15.2	15.1	14.9	14.9	14.9	14.9	14.9	15.0	15.0
2006	14.8	14.9	15.0	15.0	15.1	14.9	14.9	15.1	15.0	15.1	15.3	15.4	15.0
2007	15.0	15.0	15.2	15.2	15.2	15.2	15.1	15.0	15.1	15.2	15.4	15.5	15.2
Government													
2000	72.8	74.4	74.9	74.6	75.4	68.9	66.5	66.4	73.0	74.4	74.2	74.8	72.5
2001	74.0	75.1	75.2	75.2	74.9	70.6	63.1	64.0	74.2	75.6	75.4	75.8	72.8
2002	75.1	76.1	76.0	76.3	76.5	72.1	64.4	66.0	75.6	77.2	77.3	78.3	74.2
2003	75.4	77.5	77.9	78.3	78.5	72.9	64.7	67.0	76.9	78.3	77.9	78.2	75.3
2004	75.5	76.6	76.8	77.2	77.0	72.3	64.3	66.0	76.2	77.8	77.6	77.9	74.6
2005	75.6	77.7	77.9	78.4	78.1	73.1	64.0	66.1	76.7	77.6	77.7	78.0	75.1
2006	76.2	77.7	78.2	78.5	78.4	73.7	64.2	66.3	76.9	78.5	78.5	78.9	75.5
2007	76.5	77.8	78.0	78.4	78.5	74.7	65.2	66.1	76.9	78.1	78.3	78.6	75.6

Average Weekly Hours by Selected Industry: North Dakota, 2001–2007

(Not seasonally adjusted.)

Industry and year	January	February	March	April	May	June	July	August	September	October	November	December	Annual Average
Manufacturing													
2001	39.1	40.7	40.5	39.4	41.4	42.3	41.8	41.6	41.1	41.7	40.8	41.0	40.9
2002	39.1	39.3	38.9	39.8	40.5	41.9	39.5	40.8	40.8	41.4	39.5	41.3	40.2
2003	38.0	39.8	40.1	39.7	39.2	40.6	41.3	40.9	39.5	40.5	40.3	40.6	40.0
2004	39.6	40.6	39.5	39.0	39.5	39.2	38.5	39.7	39.3	39.3	38.5	39.0	39.3
2005	38.3	38.7	38.7	38.6	38.9	39.1	39.4	39.5	40.7	40.7	39.3	38.2	39.2
2006	38.3	38.7	38.4	38.8	39.1	40.0	38.2	39.1	38.7	39.7	38.9	40.6	39.0
2007	39.4	39.6	40.2	40.2	40.5	40.3	39.1	41.0	40.1	39.3	39.7	39.2	39.9

Average Hourly Earnings by Selected Industry: North Dakota, 2001–2007

(Dollars, not seasonally adjusted.)

Industry and year	January	February	March	April	May	June	July	August	September	October	November	December	Annual Average
Manufacturing													
2001	12.68	12.42	12.55	12.88	12.69	12.56	12.62	12.81	12.91	13.06	12.96	13.06	12.77
2002	13.36	13.25	13.32	13.43	12.98	12.91	13.19	13.04	13.05	12.90	13.16	13.52	13.17
2003	14.08	13.58	13.59	13.70	14.02	13.80	13.66	14.39	14.47	14.40	14.24	14.52	14.04
2004	14.09	13.91	14.18	14.26	14.30	14.20	14.10	14.46	14.65	14.73	14.67	14.58	14.35
2005	14.63	15.02	15.11	15.30	15.62	15.34	15.22	15.24	15.56	15.36	15.04	15.95	15.29
2006	15.19	15.22	15.17	15.09	15.29	14.87	14.82	14.76	14.86	15.08	14.87	14.52	14.98
2007	14.08	14.21	14.67	14.55	14.55	14.51	14.50	15.13	15.12	15.01	15.19	14.84	14.70

Average Weekly Earnings by Selected Industry: North Dakota, 2001–2007

(Dollars, not seasonally adjusted.)

Industry and year	January	February	March	April	May	June	July	August	September	October	November	December	Annual Average
Manufacturing													
2001	495.79	505.49	508.28	507.47	525.37	531.29	527.52	532.90	530.60	544.60	528.77	535.46	522.29
2002	522.38	520.73	518.15	534.51	525.69	540.93	521.01	532.03	532.44	534.06	519.82	558.38	529.43
2003	535.04	540.48	544.96	543.89	549.58	560.28	564.16	588.55	571.57	583.20	573.87	589.51	561.60
2004	557.96	564.75	560.11	556.14	564.85	556.64	542.85	574.06	575.75	578.89	564.80	568.62	563.96
2005	560.33	581.27	584.76	590.58	607.62	599.79	599.67	601.98	633.29	625.15	591.07	609.29	599.37
2006	581.78	589.01	582.53	585.49	597.84	594.80	566.12	577.12	575.08	598.68	578.44	589.51	584.22
2007	554.75	562.72	589.73	584.91	589.28	584.75	566.95	620.33	606.31	589.89	603.04	581.73	586.53

Population
 2000 census: 11,353,140
 2007 estimate: 11,466,917
 Percent change, 2000–2007: 1.0%

Percent change in total nonfarm employment, 2000–2007: -3.6%

Industry with the largest growth in employment, 2000–2007 (thousands)
 Education and health services, 109.9

Industry with the largest decline in employment, 2000–2007 (thousands)
 Manufacturing, -248.2

Civilian labor force
 2000: 5,807,036
 2007: 5,976,510

Employment-population ratio
 2000: 64.6%
 2007: 63.6%

Unemployment rate and rank among states
 2000: 4.0%, 28th
 2007: 5.6%, 46th

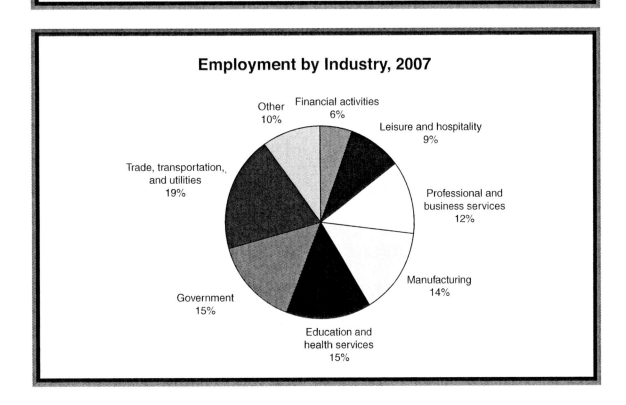

Employment by Industry, 2007

Other 10%
Financial activities 6%
Leisure and hospitality 9%
Professional and business services 12%
Manufacturing 14%
Education and health services 15%
Government 15%
Trade, transportation, and utilities 19%

Employment by Industry: Ohio, 2000–2007

(Numbers in thousands, not seasonally adjusted.)

Industry and year	January	February	March	April	May	June	July	August	September	October	November	December	Annual Average
Total Nonfarm													
2000	5,503.9	5,524.9	5,573.4	5,610.8	5,668.2	5,690.3	5,624.0	5,629.5	5,643.3	5,661.2	5,680.4	5,686.0	5,624.6
2001	5,488.3	5,501.1	5,532.2	5,560.1	5,596.3	5,612.1	5,529.5	5,533.5	5,530.6	5,539.3	5,546.9	5,541.5	5,542.6
2002	5,348.7	5,363.6	5,398.0	5,429.2	5,480.1	5,492.5	5,443.4	5,456.6	5,469.5	5,479.1	5,492.6	5,486.2	5,445.0
2003	5,309.8	5,307.0	5,338.5	5,390.0	5,439.9	5,440.2	5,389.2	5,405.0	5,414.5	5,441.1	5,446.5	5,450.7	5,397.7
2004	5,277.0	5,292.7	5,342.6	5,395.2	5,438.4	5,454.9	5,417.2	5,423.5	5,439.9	5,466.1	5,476.4	5,476.5	5,408.4
2005	5,287.2	5,313.9	5,354.0	5,424.3	5,465.4	5,472.4	5,431.2	5,440.1	5,469.1	5,476.8	5,494.6	5,491.3	5,426.7
2006	5,326.3	5,347.0	5,389.7	5,434.8	5,478.6	5,494.3	5,428.9	5,441.3	5,461.6	5,466.4	5,480.0	5,480.9	5,435.8
2007	5,324.2	5,321.0	5,369.0	5,414.3	5,469.4	5,487.2	5,421.3	5,435.8	5,449.6	5,456.6	5,473.1	5,471.3	5,424.4
Total Private													
2000	4,728.7	4,734.3	4,778.0	4,814.6	4,856.1	4,906.7	4,879.5	4,892.8	4,865.9	4,861.7	4,875.2	4,881.8	4,839.6
2001	4,702.0	4,697.6	4,724.2	4,754.3	4,788.2	4,822.7	4,781.2	4,788.2	4,742.2	4,728.3	4,729.7	4,724.3	4,748.6
2002	4,553.9	4,550.4	4,580.5	4,615.3	4,663.4	4,697.5	4,684.8	4,704.0	4,677.7	4,667.0	4,673.4	4,668.8	4,644.7
2003	4,511.5	4,493.9	4,520.9	4,573.2	4,619.6	4,642.1	4,625.4	4,648.1	4,621.8	4,627.1	4,627.3	4,630.3	4,595.1
2004	4,481.7	4,477.4	4,522.3	4,577.3	4,618.2	4,654.6	4,654.9	4,666.9	4,650.1	4,653.7	4,660.3	4,662.2	4,606.6
2005	4,494.9	4,501.5	4,539.6	4,611.7	4,646.7	4,677.6	4,672.1	4,683.9	4,677.7	4,664.1	4,676.8	4,678.1	4,627.1
2006	4,530.8	4,536.0	4,575.6	4,622.7	4,659.8	4,697.9	4,669.9	4,684.4	4,668.9	4,653.5	4,663.0	4,666.6	4,635.8
2007	4,530.4	4,513.3	4,557.7	4,605.1	4,658.1	4,693.2	4,664.2	4,679.6	4,659.7	4,645.3	4,656.8	4,657.8	4,626.8
Goods-Producing													
2000	1,258.9	1,259.4	1,273.0	1,281.2	1,292.7	1,307.1	1,290.3	1,294.2	1,285.7	1,280.7	1,276.0	1,261.8	1,280.0
2001	1,216.9	1,211.9	1,215.5	1,216.5	1,219.6	1,227.9	1,214.5	1,216.8	1,200.1	1,190.3	1,180.5	1,166.9	1,206.5
2002	1,117.8	1,113.3	1,118.0	1,125.1	1,137.5	1,150.8	1,143.4	1,155.9	1,147.0	1,138.8	1,131.9	1,119.6	1,133.3
2003	1,080.0	1,069.0	1,073.5	1,082.7	1,096.8	1,103.5	1,089.1	1,099.7	1,092.0	1,088.9	1,081.9	1,075.1	1,086.0
2004	1,037.2	1,034.8	1,047.9	1,063.5	1,074.5	1,086.1	1,083.6	1,089.1	1,083.2	1,079.8	1,073.5	1,066.3	1,068.3
2005	1,025.7	1,024.2	1,032.4	1,052.7	1,062.5	1,074.1	1,071.5	1,075.6	1,071.7	1,066.2	1,062.3	1,050.5	1,055.8
2006	1,018.1	1,016.0	1,024.1	1,039.4	1,046.3	1,059.4	1,049.0	1,054.1	1,048.8	1,039.3	1,032.4	1,024.5	1,037.6
2007	990.4	982.2	993.7	1,003.4	1,017.2	1,028.7	1,016.4	1,027.4	1,020.4	1,014.4	1,012.7	1,006.3	1,009.4
Natural Resources and Mining													
2000	12.5	12.5	12.8	12.9	13.1	13.3	13.0	13.0	13.0	13.0	13.0	12.8	12.9
2001	12.2	12.4	12.7	12.8	13.0	13.3	13.3	13.3	13.3	13.0	12.9	12.7	12.9
2002	12.0	12.0	12.1	12.4	12.0	12.3	12.2	12.3	12.2	12.2	12.0	11.9	12.1
2003	11.5	11.3	11.4	11.6	11.7	11.8	11.8	11.9	11.8	11.8	11.8	11.6	11.7
2004	11.3	11.3	11.5	11.6	11.8	11.9	11.9	11.9	11.9	11.7	11.6	11.6	11.7
2005	10.8	10.8	10.9	11.3	11.4	11.5	11.7	11.6	11.6	11.7	11.7	11.5	11.4
2006	11.0	11.0	11.2	11.6	11.6	11.8	11.8	11.9	11.7	11.7	11.7	11.6	11.6
2007	11.3	11.0	11.2	11.6	11.8	11.9	12.0	12.1	12.0	12.0	12.0	11.8	11.7
Construction													
2000	220.7	219.5	232.7	242.8	253.6	263.6	264.3	263.2	257.0	252.8	247.6	235.8	246.1
2001	212.5	213.1	221.4	232.6	243.1	252.8	258.7	260.3	253.8	252.3	247.8	238.1	240.5
2002	212.2	210.4	216.8	226.3	236.9	246.5	253.8	255.7	250.8	249.0	243.4	232.2	236.2
2003	207.5	200.8	207.5	224.0	234.2	242.6	246.0	248.7	245.2	245.5	240.1	232.8	231.2
2004	208.5	205.6	216.0	229.0	238.3	246.8	252.0	250.7	247.6	246.4	241.1	232.8	234.6
2005	204.9	203.9	209.5	228.3	237.6	246.0	250.4	250.3	247.3	244.9	241.4	230.0	232.9
2006	208.1	207.5	215.2	227.2	234.9	241.5	243.4	244.0	240.5	237.2	232.4	225.0	229.7
2007	204.3	195.6	206.1	219.0	230.9	238.1	239.5	239.7	236.7	234.8	230.6	223.3	224.9
Manufacturing													
2000	1,025.7	1,027.4	1,027.5	1,025.5	1,026.0	1,030.2	1,013.0	1,018.0	1,015.7	1,014.9	1,015.4	1,013.2	1,021.0
2001	992.2	986.4	981.4	971.1	963.5	961.8	942.5	943.2	933.0	925.0	919.8	916.1	953.0
2002	893.6	890.9	889.1	886.4	888.6	892.0	877.4	887.9	884.0	877.6	876.5	875.5	885.0
2003	861.0	856.9	854.6	847.1	850.9	849.1	831.3	839.1	835.0	831.6	830.0	830.7	843.1
2004	817.4	817.9	820.4	822.9	824.4	827.4	819.7	826.5	823.7	821.7	820.8	821.9	822.1
2005	810.0	809.5	812.0	813.1	813.5	816.6	809.4	813.7	812.8	809.6	809.2	809.0	811.5
2006	799.0	797.5	797.7	800.6	799.8	806.1	793.8	798.2	796.6	790.4	788.3	787.9	796.3
2007	774.8	775.6	776.4	772.8	774.5	778.7	764.9	775.6	771.7	767.6	770.1	771.2	772.8
Service-Providing													
2000	4,245.0	4,265.5	4,300.4	4,329.6	4,375.5	4,383.2	4,333.7	4,335.3	4,357.6	4,380.5	4,404.4	4,424.2	4,344.5
2001	4,271.4	4,289.2	4,316.7	4,343.6	4,376.7	4,384.2	4,315.0	4,316.7	4,330.5	4,349.0	4,366.4	4,374.6	4,336.2
2002	4,230.9	4,250.3	4,280.0	4,304.1	4,342.6	4,341.7	4,300.0	4,300.7	4,322.5	4,340.3	4,360.7	4,366.6	4,311.7
2003	4,229.8	4,238.0	4,265.0	4,307.3	4,343.1	4,336.7	4,300.1	4,305.3	4,322.5	4,352.2	4,364.6	4,375.6	4,311.7
2004	4,239.8	4,257.9	4,294.7	4,331.7	4,363.9	4,368.8	4,333.6	4,334.4	4,356.7	4,386.3	4,402.9	4,410.2	4,340.1
2005	4,261.5	4,289.7	4,321.6	4,371.6	4,402.9	4,398.3	4,359.7	4,364.5	4,397.4	4,410.6	4,432.3	4,440.8	4,370.9
2006	4,308.2	4,331.0	4,365.6	4,395.4	4,432.3	4,434.9	4,379.9	4,387.2	4,412.8	4,427.1	4,447.6	4,456.4	4,398.2
2007	4,333.8	4,338.8	4,375.3	4,410.9	4,452.2	4,458.5	4,404.9	4,408.4	4,429.2	4,442.2	4,460.4	4,465.0	4,415.0
Trade, Transportation, and Utilities													
2000	1,107.9	1,097.0	1,100.2	1,101.8	1,107.7	1,113.5	1,107.4	1,108.6	1,103.9	1,123.9	1,145.8	1,165.8	1,115.2
2001	1,105.8	1,089.5	1,091.8	1,094.0	1,098.7	1,102.3	1,088.2	1,086.3	1,081.2	1,087.4	1,107.2	1,117.0	1,095.8
2002	1,058.2	1,045.3	1,050.2	1,053.2	1,060.1	1,064.7	1,061.5	1,061.5	1,053.5	1,057.7	1,077.5	1,089.2	1,061.1
2003	1,034.7	1,023.7	1,026.8	1,035.9	1,042.4	1,044.6	1,040.2	1,042.7	1,039.2	1,051.1	1,067.2	1,078.6	1,043.9
2004	1,026.0	1,015.1	1,021.0	1,025.4	1,033.0	1,039.8	1,039.7	1,041.7	1,036.1	1,049.2	1,068.6	1,080.9	1,039.7
2005	1,028.2	1,020.4	1,027.2	1,035.0	1,041.3	1,043.1	1,042.8	1,042.2	1,038.5	1,044.5	1,066.3	1,082.4	1,042.7
2006	1,034.4	1,024.5	1,029.7	1,034.6	1,043.6	1,047.5	1,043.7	1,044.9	1,041.5	1,047.3	1,071.5	1,085.1	1,045.7
2007	1,038.6	1,024.8	1,033.8	1,039.1	1,050.9	1,055.2	1,053.0	1,051.3	1,047.8	1,052.3	1,073.5	1,086.1	1,050.5
Wholesale Trade													
2000	244.2	244.9	246.1	246.4	247.6	249.2	248.0	247.8	247.2	248.5	248.7	250.0	247.4
2001	247.6	247.6	248.4	248.2	248.8	249.3	247.9	247.1	244.6	243.8	242.8	243.1	246.6
2002	238.4	237.7	238.6	239.3	240.2	240.9	240.7	240.2	238.3	237.7	237.6	238.3	239.0
2003	233.7	233.5	234.1	234.4	235.1	235.3	235.1	234.7	232.5	232.9	232.4	232.4	233.8
2004	228.1	228.0	229.0	229.9	231.5	233.1	234.5	234.7	233.0	234.8	235.4	236.4	232.4
2005	232.0	232.1	232.9	234.9	235.7	237.0	238.1	237.6	236.2	235.9	236.6	237.4	235.5
2006	234.7	235.1	235.7	237.0	238.2	239.9	239.5	239.3	239.3	237.6	237.5	237.9	237.6
2007	236.5	236.1	237.1	237.9	239.5	240.9	241.1	240.7	238.9	238.9	239.2	240.1	238.9

Employment by Industry: Ohio, 2000–2007—*Continued*

(Numbers in thousands, not seasonally adjusted.)

Industry and year	January	February	March	April	May	June	July	August	September	October	November	December	Annual Average
Retail Trade													
2000	669.8	658.8	661.1	660.0	664.2	668.5	663.5	664.9	660.4	675.2	697.0	715.9	671.6
2001	665.9	651.0	652.6	652.8	656.8	660.4	648.7	647.5	645.4	651.5	673.3	684.4	657.5
2002	637.4	626.1	630.3	631.1	635.8	639.8	635.8	634.9	629.4	631.3	650.7	662.9	637.1
2003	618.8	609.4	612.3	619.4	623.8	626.1	622.5	624.4	622.5	629.8	646.2	657.5	626.1
2004	616.4	607.0	611.2	612.4	616.9	621.1	617.8	618.5	613.7	619.1	637.0	647.6	619.9
2005	607.0	598.8	603.4	608.7	613.0	613.0	609.7	608.7	604.3	607.2	624.6	637.6	611.3
2006	599.9	589.8	593.6	596.1	602.0	603.4	600.6	600.4	595.9	601.1	621.4	630.8	602.9
2007	594.7	583.3	590.4	593.3	601.6	603.4	602.6	600.0	596.8	600.4	619.7	629.9	601.3
Transportation and Utilities													
2000	193.9	193.3	193.0	195.4	195.9	195.8	195.9	195.9	196.3	200.2	200.1	199.9	196.3
2001	192.3	190.9	190.8	193.0	193.1	192.6	191.6	191.7	191.2	192.1	191.1	189.5	191.7
2002	182.4	181.5	181.3	182.8	184.1	184.0	185.0	186.4	185.8	188.7	189.2	188.0	184.9
2003	182.2	180.8	180.4	182.1	183.5	183.2	182.6	183.6	184.2	188.4	188.6	188.7	184.0
2004	181.5	180.1	180.8	183.1	184.6	185.6	187.4	188.5	189.4	195.3	196.2	196.9	187.5
2005	189.2	189.5	190.9	191.4	192.6	193.1	195.0	195.9	198.0	201.4	205.1	207.4	195.8
2006	199.8	199.6	200.4	201.5	203.4	204.2	203.6	205.2	208.0	208.7	212.2	215.5	205.2
2007	207.4	205.4	206.3	207.9	209.8	210.9	209.3	210.6	212.1	213.0	214.6	216.1	210.3
Information													
2000	106.7	106.8	107.6	106.4	106.6	107.7	107.1	107.6	106.8	107.2	107.8	108.5	107.2
2001	108.4	108.3	108.0	106.1	106.4	107.3	106.8	106.3	104.8	104.3	104.4	104.6	106.3
2002	103.5	102.5	102.2	101.9	101.7	101.9	101.3	100.8	99.5	98.4	99.1	99.2	101.0
2003	98.2	97.7	97.7	97.4	97.6	97.4	97.0	96.5	94.8	94.4	94.5	94.6	96.5
2004	93.4	93.0	92.9	92.4	92.6	92.6	93.3	92.9	92.3	90.8	90.5	91.5	92.2
2005	89.9	89.5	89.5	90.0	90.6	90.8	90.6	90.4	90.3	89.7	89.0	89.4	89.9
2006	88.8	88.6	88.7	88.3	88.6	88.9	88.8	88.9	88.6	87.8	87.5	88.0	88.4
2007	87.3	87.4	87.0	87.7	88.3	88.8	88.8	88.4	87.2	86.9	87.2	87.5	87.7
Financial Activities													
2000	304.2	304.1	304.5	304.7	305.2	307.4	305.9	305.9	304.6	303.2	305.3	307.7	305.2
2001	302.6	303.8	304.9	305.5	306.9	310.8	310.4	310.7	307.7	306.5	308.3	309.4	307.3
2002	305.6	306.9	307.5	306.4	307.5	309.6	310.7	310.3	307.9	308.0	309.6	311.1	308.4
2003	307.9	308.7	309.6	309.4	311.5	314.1	314.3	315.2	312.8	311.9	311.9	313.8	311.8
2004	309.8	310.5	311.3	310.4	311.1	313.5	313.5	313.5	311.3	309.6	308.8	309.9	310.9
2005	305.7	305.8	305.9	306.8	308.0	310.6	310.9	311.2	309.2	309.0	309.1	309.8	308.5
2006	305.6	305.5	306.3	306.1	306.5	307.9	307.3	306.1	304.2	304.5	304.1	303.5	305.6
2007	301.5	301.2	300.0	301.8	302.4	301.9	302.8	302.4	299.7	299.7	299.4	300.2	301.1
Professional and Business Services													
2000	618.5	622.4	630.9	642.7	645.4	655.2	653.3	657.6	656.0	654.1	653.0	649.5	644.9
2001	621.3	622.0	628.0	633.5	635.3	640.2	636.0	636.6	629.8	625.9	620.8	618.7	629.0
2002	596.8	597.0	603.2	610.5	613.8	618.9	621.4	626.3	625.4	627.1	625.2	621.5	615.6
2003	597.8	597.4	602.2	609.5	611.2	614.1	615.2	620.7	616.6	619.9	619.9	615.8	611.7
2004	600.5	601.1	608.6	620.0	622.0	631.1	634.0	639.7	640.2	641.9	640.4	638.8	626.5
2005	615.1	619.0	625.2	639.8	640.5	646.4	649.6	656.4	658.5	659.4	657.1	657.2	643.7
2006	633.4	636.0	644.2	653.4	654.9	663.6	661.2	668.9	666.4	666.0	664.3	664.4	656.4
2007	645.1	646.7	653.4	663.6	666.6	675.7	672.9	677.4	675.4	673.1	671.5	669.4	665.9
Education and Health Services													
2000	666.9	674.9	677.9	677.8	677.3	677.5	676.0	679.3	685.6	687.0	690.4	693.4	680.3
2001	680.1	690.2	691.7	696.2	693.5	688.6	680.3	683.6	695.4	706.7	710.5	711.2	694.0
2002	698.2	708.9	709.8	711.8	710.6	703.2	697.2	700.2	714.0	724.7	728.7	728.9	711.4
2003	719.1	725.2	727.2	730.1	726.9	719.6	717.7	719.9	734.4	743.8	746.9	747.2	729.8
2004	734.7	741.5	744.1	748.3	744.0	736.3	734.6	732.9	749.7	760.0	763.2	766.2	746.3
2005	748.6	757.1	760.2	763.3	759.8	753.3	748.7	750.2	768.6	775.8	780.0	781.4	762.3
2006	766.8	777.6	781.0	782.0	778.5	769.8	763.5	765.6	783.1	789.3	792.3	792.1	778.5
2007	779.9	785.2	789.5	791.2	789.9	781.7	775.8	778.5	796.9	803.1	806.1	804.4	790.2
Leisure and Hospitality													
2000	446.7	448.7	460.8	476.8	496.8	512.9	515.2	515.4	499.6	482.1	473.4	471.3	483.3
2001	443.8	447.6	458.5	474.7	498.0	514.6	515.4	516.6	495.2	478.5	469.0	467.3	481.6
2002	448.2	449.9	461.1	477.9	502.0	516.7	519.4	518.4	502.5	484.5	473.9	471.2	485.5
2003	449.1	447.1	456.7	480.5	504.2	519.3	523.1	524.7	506.0	490.3	479.5	479.3	488.3
2004	457.4	457.8	470.1	489.8	512.1	524.4	527.0	529.2	513.9	496.3	487.9	484.0	495.8
2005	460.6	463.2	475.1	498.4	517.5	531.8	531.7	532.0	517.8	496.6	488.7	483.7	499.8
2006	463.8	467.4	479.5	496.2	517.2	533.9	531.9	532.6	514.9	497.6	489.1	486.8	500.9
2007	468.3	466.4	478.4	496.0	519.2	535.2	530.4	530.7	511.6	494.8	486.0	483.2	500.0
Other Services													
2000	218.9	221.0	223.1	223.2	224.4	225.4	224.3	224.2	223.7	223.5	223.5	223.8	223.3
2001	223.1	224.3	225.8	227.8	229.8	231.0	229.6	231.3	228.0	228.7	229.0	229.2	228.1
2002	225.6	226.6	228.5	228.5	230.2	231.7	229.9	230.6	227.9	227.8	227.5	228.1	228.6
2003	224.7	225.1	227.2	227.7	229.0	229.5	228.8	228.7	226.0	226.8	225.5	225.9	227.1
2004	222.7	223.6	226.4	227.5	228.9	230.1	229.6	228.7	226.6	227.2	226.4	225.0	226.9
2005	221.1	222.3	224.1	225.7	226.5	227.5	226.3	226.0	223.7	223.6	223.9	223.3	224.5
2006	219.9	220.4	222.1	222.7	224.2	226.9	224.5	223.6	222.2	222.0	221.5	222.2	222.7
2007	219.3	219.4	221.9	222.3	223.6	226.0	224.1	223.5	220.7	221.0	220.4	220.7	221.9
Government													
2000	775.2	790.6	795.4	796.2	812.1	783.6	744.5	736.7	777.4	799.5	805.2	804.2	785.0
2001	786.3	803.5	808.0	805.8	808.1	789.4	748.3	745.3	788.4	811.0	817.2	817.2	794.0
2002	794.8	813.2	817.5	813.9	816.7	795.0	758.6	752.6	791.8	812.1	819.2	817.4	800.2
2003	798.3	813.1	817.6	816.8	820.3	798.1	763.8	756.9	792.7	814.0	819.2	820.4	802.6
2004	795.3	815.3	820.3	817.9	820.2	800.3	762.3	756.6	789.8	812.4	816.1	814.3	801.7
2005	792.3	812.4	814.4	812.6	818.7	794.8	759.1	756.2	791.4	812.7	817.8	813.2	799.6
2006	795.5	811.0	814.1	812.1	818.8	796.4	759.0	756.9	792.7	812.9	817.0	814.3	800.1
2007	793.8	807.7	811.3	809.2	811.3	794.0	757.1	756.2	789.9	811.3	816.3	813.5	797.6

Average Weekly Hours by Selected Industry: Ohio, 2001–2007

(Not seasonally adjusted.)

Industry and year	January	February	March	April	May	June	July	August	September	October	November	December	Annual Average
Construction													
2001	39.5	38.5	38.8	38.2	39.8	41.0	40.7	40.7	40.9	40.4	41.8	39.6	40.0
2002	39.4	39.0	39.9	39.2	39.6	40.1	40.3	40.1	40.0	40.3	39.5	38.2	39.7
2003	38.0	36.9	38.5	38.5	38.4	38.5	37.2	40.4	40.0	39.8	39.3	37.2	38.6
2004	37.4	38.6	37.9	37.5	39.5	38.1	39.9	40.8	38.5	39.1	39.9	38.0	38.8
2005	36.6	37.3	37.9	39.8	40.0	39.8	39.3	39.9	39.6	40.6	38.8	36.3	38.9
2006	37.5	37.1	36.8	38.5	36.4	41.1	38.8	40.0	38.0	38.7	37.1	38.4	38.3
2007	36.3	33.6	37.5	37.1	39.2	40.1	38.7	39.3	40.4	39.2	38.4	36.9	38.2
Manufacturing													
2001	41.3	40.9	40.9	40.2	41.2	41.1	40.7	41.2	41.6	40.9	41.6	42.4	41.2
2002	40.7	40.8	41.5	41.4	41.7	41.7	40.4	41.5	41.9	41.4	41.2	42.1	41.4
2003	41.5	41.1	41.4	40.8	41.1	40.6	39.4	40.1	41.3	41.4	41.3	41.7	41.0
2004	41.4	41.4	41.3	41.1	41.9	42.0	40.7	41.8	42.2	41.8	42.1	42.6	41.7
2005	41.8	42.0	41.4	41.0	41.4	41.5	40.0	41.6	42.1	41.8	41.4	41.4	41.4
2006	40.9	41.6	41.6	40.4	41.5	41.6	41.2	41.6	41.5	41.5	41.8	42.0	41.4
2007	41.6	39.2	41.4	41.2	41.7	42.2	41.3	42.5	42.2	42.1	42.5	41.8	41.7
Wholesale Trade													
2001	36.7	37.0	37.4	37.6	37.4	37.0	37.1	36.8	37.1	36.5	36.7	37.2	37.0
2002	36.6	35.8	35.8	35.9	36.1	36.9	37.6	37.6	38.0	37.0	37.3	38.1	36.9
2003	36.2	36.6	36.6	36.5	36.8	36.4	37.3	36.2	37.4	38.1	37.2	36.5	36.8
2004	37.2	37.1	37.2	37.3	36.8	36.3	36.6	37.1	37.4	37.1	36.9	36.1	36.9
2005	37.0	36.5	36.8	36.2	37.0	37.5	36.7	36.6	37.0	38.1	38.0	36.7	37.0
2006	37.0	37.3	38.6	39.6	38.5	38.6	39.3	38.9	37.9	38.0	37.1	37.0	38.2
2007	36.8	36.6	36.8	38.2	38.4	38.4	38.6	38.8	38.7	38.7	38.5	38.3	38.1
Retail Trade													
2001	28.2	28.1	28.3	28.9	28.9	29.1	29.5	29.2	29.0	28.7	28.6	29.7	28.9
2002	28.1	28.7	29.0	29.2	29.5	29.8	30.1	29.6	29.3	29.0	29.0	30.8	29.3
2003	28.7	29.1	29.4	29.7	30.1	30.4	30.3	30.4	30.1	29.8	29.8	30.3	29.8
2004	28.7	29.2	28.8	29.1	29.5	29.0	29.8	30.1	29.2	29.0	29.3	30.2	29.3
2005	28.3	29.0	28.5	29.0	29.5	30.2	29.9	30.1	29.2	29.1	29.6	30.5	29.4
2006	28.6	29.0	29.2	29.3	30.0	30.3	31.0	30.5	31.2	30.4	30.1	30.2	30.0
2007	28.5	28.3	29.5	29.7	29.3	29.8	29.6	29.7	30.5	30.9	31.6	31.7	29.9
Financial Activities													
2001	35.0	34.9	35.2	36.0	35.1	35.9	35.8	35.2	36.2	35.2	37.1	36.6	35.7
2002	35.3	35.6	35.4	35.2	35.9	36.5	35.7	35.6	36.3	35.2	35.4	36.0	35.7
2003	34.9	35.9	36.2	35.2	35.3	36.2	35.3	35.9	36.0	36.2	36.2	35.3	35.7
2004	35.6	36.1	35.2	35.2	36.6	35.5	36.6	35.8	35.7	35.8	35.5	35.9	35.8
2005	36.3	35.5	35.5	35.5	36.6	36.3	36.0	36.0	35.8	36.9	36.5	37.2	36.2
2006	37.4	36.7	36.4	36.9	36.6	37.3	37.5	36.7	36.4	37.0	36.4	36.4	36.8
2007	36.6	36.4	36.2	36.8	36.2	36.5	37.6	37.6	37.8	37.4	36.9	38.2	37.0

Average Hourly Earnings by Selected Industry: Ohio, 2001–2007

(Dollars, not seasonally adjusted.)

Industry and year	January	February	March	April	May	June	July	August	September	October	November	December	Annual Average
Construction													
2001	19.61	19.68	19.81	19.60	19.69	19.62	19.71	19.87	20.15	20.20	20.73	20.23	19.92
2002	20.44	20.81	20.65	20.64	20.60	20.36	20.59	20.47	20.64	20.62	20.03	20.27	20.51
2003	20.17	20.46	20.20	20.21	20.41	20.06	20.19	20.48	20.61	20.34	20.32	20.06	20.30
2004	20.34	20.67	20.76	20.56	20.59	20.48	20.82	20.92	20.72	21.16	20.92	20.70	20.73
2005	20.26	20.29	20.45	20.66	20.82	20.75	20.96	20.86	20.72	21.06	21.03	21.38	20.79
2006	21.47	21.49	21.22	21.87	21.26	21.72	21.59	21.91	21.92	21.89	21.82	21.74	21.68
2007	21.80	21.71	21.39	21.33	21.81	21.87	21.88	21.73	21.86	21.71	21.91	21.72	21.74
Manufacturing													
2001	16.45	16.44	16.50	16.57	16.77	16.85	16.68	16.87	16.97	16.92	17.07	17.41	16.79
2002	17.23	17.22	17.32	17.35	17.44	17.45	17.17	17.41	17.59	17.71	17.89	18.08	17.49
2003	18.00	17.96	18.01	17.74	17.72	17.83	17.97	18.27	18.33	17.99	17.90	18.16	17.99
2004	17.91	17.99	18.06	18.32	18.40	18.48	18.14	18.52	18.95	18.84	18.88	19.13	18.47
2005	19.14	19.07	18.99	18.89	18.86	18.93	18.75	19.13	19.28	19.22	19.27	19.28	19.07
2006	19.21	19.02	18.92	19.08	19.13	19.17	18.79	19.21	19.36	19.24	19.35	19.55	19.17
2007	19.26	19.29	19.48	19.50	19.58	19.53	19.37	19.44	19.18	19.22	19.28	18.89	19.34
Wholesale Trade													
2001	14.30	14.31	14.42	14.72	14.68	14.48	14.74	14.60	14.54	14.68	14.69	14.55	14.56
2002	14.77	15.04	14.99	14.89	14.86	15.00	14.98	14.75	15.13	15.11	15.20	15.33	15.00
2003	15.15	15.08	15.07	14.70	14.84	14.78	14.70	14.66	14.66	14.75	14.80	14.76	14.83
2004	14.83	14.96	14.71	14.77	15.42	15.60	15.68	16.02	16.34	16.52	16.35	16.58	15.65
2005	16.64	16.54	16.37	16.68	16.88	17.05	16.69	16.74	16.69	16.89	16.67	16.85	16.73
2006	17.30	17.89	17.55	17.58	17.43	17.41	17.96	17.31	17.48	17.76	17.81	17.75	17.60
2007	17.55	17.58	17.65	17.92	17.92	18.36	18.51	17.97	18.35	18.35	18.30	18.17	18.06
Retail Trade													
2001	10.61	10.88	11.02	11.04	10.96	11.03	11.19	10.96	10.94	10.77	10.85	10.96	10.93
2002	10.96	11.16	11.18	10.95	10.91	11.03	10.91	11.02	10.95	11.05	11.02	11.11	11.02
2003	11.23	11.25	11.40	11.23	11.21	11.21	11.16	11.28	11.33	11.20	11.19	11.22	11.24
2004	11.22	11.24	11.12	11.08	11.05	10.83	10.79	10.90	10.81	10.87	10.84	10.85	10.96
2005	11.07	11.07	11.04	11.33	11.01	10.99	10.92	11.07	10.92	10.99	10.88	11.11	11.03
2006	11.09	11.20	11.01	11.04	11.08	11.05	11.08	11.10	11.05	10.92	10.78	10.80	11.01
2007	11.02	11.15	11.09	11.04	11.09	11.09	11.02	11.22	11.32	11.19	11.11	11.16	11.13
Financial Activities													
2001	15.08	15.07	15.42	15.17	15.33	15.39	15.44	15.14	15.18	14.97	15.32	15.20	15.23
2002	15.22	15.26	15.16	15.33	15.27	15.42	15.40	15.39	15.15	15.32	15.24	15.25	15.29
2003	15.36	15.63	15.48	15.73	15.59	15.71	15.56	15.63	15.64	15.64	15.68	15.52	15.60
2004	15.57	15.52	15.40	15.41	15.54	15.41	15.34	15.80	15.99	15.75	15.61	15.72	15.59
2005	16.06	16.07	15.96	16.07	16.37	16.29	16.36	15.92	16.58	16.60	16.71	16.96	16.33
2006	17.24	17.00	16.94	17.07	16.93	16.91	16.83	16.90	17.39	17.39	17.59	17.48	17.14
2007	17.65	17.99	18.31	18.57	18.83	18.77	18.57	18.56	18.69	18.79	18.88	19.19	18.57

Average Weekly Earnings by Selected Industry: Ohio, 2001–2007

(Dollars, not seasonally adjusted.)

Industry and year	January	February	March	April	May	June	July	August	September	October	November	December	Annual Average
Construction													
2001	774.60	757.68	768.63	748.72	783.66	804.42	802.20	808.71	824.14	816.08	866.51	801.11	796.80
2002	805.34	811.59	823.94	809.09	815.76	816.44	829.78	820.85	825.60	830.99	791.19	774.31	814.25
2003	766.46	754.97	777.70	778.09	783.74	772.31	751.07	827.39	824.40	809.53	798.58	746.23	783.58
2004	760.72	797.86	786.80	771.00	813.31	780.29	830.72	853.54	797.72	827.36	834.71	786.60	804.32
2005	741.52	756.82	775.06	822.27	832.80	825.85	823.73	832.31	820.51	855.04	815.96	776.09	808.73
2006	805.13	797.28	780.90	842.00	773.86	892.69	837.69	876.40	832.96	847.14	809.52	834.82	830.34
2007	791.34	729.46	802.13	791.34	854.95	876.99	846.76	853.99	883.14	851.03	841.34	801.47	830.47
Manufacturing													
2001	679.39	672.40	674.85	666.11	690.92	692.54	678.88	695.04	705.95	692.03	710.11	738.18	691.75
2002	701.26	702.58	718.78	718.29	727.25	727.67	693.67	722.52	737.02	733.19	737.07	761.17	724.09
2003	747.00	738.16	745.61	723.79	728.29	723.90	708.02	732.63	757.03	744.79	739.27	757.27	737.59
2004	741.47	744.79	745.88	752.95	770.96	776.16	738.30	774.14	799.69	787.51	794.85	814.94	770.20
2005	800.05	800.94	786.19	774.49	780.80	785.60	750.00	795.81	811.69	803.40	797.78	798.19	789.50
2006	785.69	791.23	787.07	770.83	793.90	797.47	774.15	799.14	803.44	798.46	808.83	821.10	793.64
2007	801.22	756.17	806.47	803.40	816.49	824.17	799.98	826.20	809.40	809.16	819.40	789.60	806.48
Wholesale Trade													
2001	524.81	529.47	539.31	553.47	549.03	535.76	546.85	537.28	539.43	535.82	539.12	541.26	538.72
2002	540.58	538.43	536.64	534.55	536.45	553.50	563.25	554.60	574.94	559.07	566.96	584.07	553.50
2003	548.43	551.93	551.56	536.55	546.11	537.99	548.31	530.69	548.28	561.98	550.56	538.74	545.74
2004	551.68	555.02	547.21	550.92	567.46	566.28	573.89	594.34	611.12	612.89	603.32	598.54	577.49
2005	615.68	603.71	602.42	603.82	624.56	639.38	612.52	612.68	617.53	643.51	633.46	618.40	619.01
2006	640.10	667.30	677.43	696.17	671.06	672.03	705.83	673.36	662.49	674.88	660.75	656.75	672.32
2007	645.84	643.43	649.52	684.54	688.13	705.02	714.49	697.24	710.15	710.15	704.55	695.91	688.09
Retail Trade													
2001	299.20	305.73	311.87	319.06	316.74	320.97	330.11	320.03	317.26	309.10	310.31	325.51	315.88
2002	307.98	320.29	324.22	319.74	321.85	328.69	328.39	326.19	320.84	320.45	319.58	342.19	322.89
2003	322.30	327.38	335.16	333.53	337.42	340.78	338.15	342.91	341.03	333.76	333.46	339.97	334.95
2004	322.01	328.21	320.26	322.43	325.98	314.07	321.54	328.09	315.65	315.23	317.61	327.67	321.13
2005	313.28	321.03	314.64	328.57	324.80	331.90	326.51	333.21	318.86	319.81	322.05	338.86	324.28
2006	317.17	324.80	321.49	323.47	332.40	334.82	343.48	338.55	344.76	331.97	324.48	326.16	330.30
2007	314.07	315.55	327.16	327.89	324.94	330.48	326.19	333.23	345.26	345.77	351.08	353.77	332.79
Financial Activities													
2001	527.80	525.94	542.78	546.12	538.08	552.50	552.75	532.93	549.52	526.94	568.37	556.32	543.71
2002	537.27	543.26	536.66	539.62	548.19	562.83	549.78	547.88	549.95	539.26	539.50	549.00	545.85
2003	536.06	561.12	560.38	553.70	550.33	568.70	549.27	561.12	563.04	566.17	567.62	547.86	556.92
2004	554.29	560.27	542.08	542.43	568.76	547.06	561.44	565.64	570.84	563.85	554.16	564.35	558.12
2005	582.98	570.49	566.58	570.49	599.14	591.33	588.96	573.12	593.56	612.54	609.92	630.91	591.15
2006	644.78	623.90	616.62	629.88	619.64	630.74	631.13	620.23	633.00	643.43	640.28	636.27	630.75
2007	645.99	654.84	662.82	683.38	681.65	685.11	698.23	697.86	706.48	702.75	696.67	733.06	687.09

OKLAHOMA
At a Glance

Population
    2000 census: 3,450,654
    2007 estimate: 3,617,316
    Percent change, 2000–2007: 4.8%

Percent change in total nonfarm employment, 2000–2007: 5.8%

Industry with the largest growth in employment, 2000–2007 (thousands)
    Government, 33.2

Industry with the largest decline in employment, 2000–2007 (thousands)
    Manufacturing, -26.7

Civilian labor force
    2000: 1,661,045
    2007: 1,732,703

Employment-population ratio
    2000: 62.4%
    2007: 60.7%

Unemployment rate and rank among states
    2000: 3.1%, 12th
    2007: 4.3%, 23rd

Employment by Industry, 2007

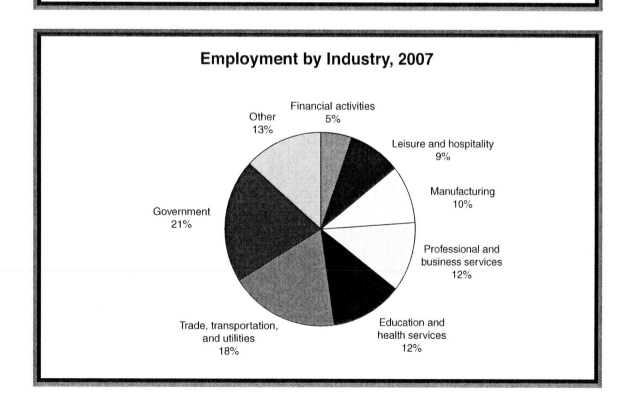

Other 13%

Financial activities 5%

Leisure and hospitality 9%

Manufacturing 10%

Professional and business services 12%

Government 21%

Education and health services 12%

Trade, transportation, and utilities 18%

171

Employment by Industry: Oklahoma, 2000–2007

(Numbers in thousands, not seasonally adjusted.)

Industry and year	January	February	March	April	May	June	July	August	September	October	November	December	Annual Average
Total Nonfarm													
2000	1,438.3	1,447.5	1,464.0	1,474.4	1,490.7	1,489.0	1,471.0	1,479.9	1,495.7	1,498.8	1,507.9	1,508.0	1,480.4
2001	1,467.5	1,480.1	1,493.8	1,503.2	1,512.3	1,507.0	1,481.0	1,488.9	1,499.2	1,492.9	1,501.9	1,498.5	1,493.9
2002	1,455.6	1,463.9	1,474.7	1,483.8	1,495.9	1,480.8	1,461.2	1,469.9	1,475.5	1,471.6	1,476.4	1,473.8	1,473.6
2003	1,435.2	1,439.2	1,442.6	1,448.2	1,457.5	1,440.4	1,429.2	1,435.7	1,448.0	1,453.3	1,456.4	1,457.7	1,445.3
2004	1,426.8	1,435.4	1,450.3	1,460.1	1,467.4	1,458.9	1,450.7	1,458.1	1,472.6	1,480.9	1,485.3	1,490.6	1,461.4
2005	1,452.6	1,467.0	1,483.9	1,497.8	1,506.5	1,500.3	1,486.3	1,497.6	1,514.3	1,520.0	1,531.1	1,536.5	1,499.5
2006	1,503.3	1,517.5	1,534.0	1,533.8	1,547.5	1,545.4	1,525.4	1,539.5	1,554.2	1,554.0	1,559.9	1,565.6	1,540.0
2007	1,528.8	1,543.8	1,565.2	1,561.0	1,572.1	1,570.8	1,550.8	1,565.7	1,579.3	1,582.6	1,586.0	1,584.3	1,565.9
Total Private													
2000	1,155.4	1,158.7	1,171.5	1,183.1	1,192.8	1,204.0	1,201.0	1,208.8	1,208.9	1,204.3	1,211.7	1,212.4	1,192.7
2001	1,175.5	1,181.6	1,193.4	1,203.1	1,209.4	1,217.4	1,203.2	1,208.3	1,201.3	1,188.5	1,194.8	1,192.6	1,197.4
2002	1,157.3	1,159.9	1,169.0	1,177.9	1,186.4	1,185.3	1,176.9	1,183.1	1,175.7	1,165.0	1,169.1	1,166.6	1,172.7
2003	1,140.1	1,138.1	1,141.8	1,148.0	1,155.3	1,151.3	1,150.7	1,156.1	1,152.4	1,151.7	1,153.9	1,154.5	1,149.5
2004	1,132.3	1,133.6	1,146.7	1,156.1	1,161.3	1,164.1	1,166.3	1,167.5	1,166.1	1,169.5	1,173.8	1,177.6	1,159.6
2005	1,147.4	1,154.5	1,169.3	1,181.6	1,187.9	1,194.0	1,194.0	1,199.6	1,200.6	1,198.9	1,208.7	1,214.2	1,187.6
2006	1,189.6	1,195.8	1,210.9	1,211.5	1,222.2	1,232.3	1,224.9	1,232.1	1,231.5	1,225.9	1,231.4	1,237.6	1,220.5
2007	1,209.0	1,217.4	1,237.0	1,234.3	1,243.5	1,254.1	1,251.6	1,261.1	1,257.4	1,255.6	1,260.0	1,258.9	1,245.0
Goods-Producing													
2000	260.4	260.7	263.2	262.6	264.7	267.6	267.7	269.1	267.9	266.0	266.7	268.5	265.4
2001	263.0	264.7	266.8	267.1	269.0	272.5	268.2	267.1	265.7	259.2	259.2	257.7	265.0
2002	246.6	246.3	246.7	245.8	248.1	248.7	247.1	246.8	243.7	241.2	240.1	239.6	245.1
2003	237.2	235.6	236.0	236.0	236.6	235.6	238.0	239.2	237.8	236.8	235.0	235.2	236.6
2004	231.8	230.9	233.9	234.8	236.9	237.5	241.0	240.8	240.2	241.3	240.5	242.2	237.7
2005	236.8	238.3	241.7	243.9	244.7	246.3	249.6	250.4	250.5	251.7	252.8	255.9	246.9
2006	253.8	255.4	258.7	256.7	259.7	263.8	263.3	265.6	265.0	264.5	264.4	266.0	261.4
2007	260.7	261.2	265.3	264.5	266.2	270.5	271.1	272.9	270.7	270.4	271.6	270.8	268.0
Natural Resources and Mining													
2000	26.5	26.6	26.6	25.5	26.0	26.3	27.2	27.4	27.5	27.3	27.6	28.6	26.9
2001	27.9	28.6	28.9	28.7	29.2	30.2	29.8	29.8	29.2	29.0	29.0	28.8	29.1
2002	28.1	28.1	28.1	28.2	28.7	29.0	28.9	28.9	28.3	27.9	27.8	27.9	28.3
2003	28.7	28.8	28.9	28.9	29.3	29.9	30.0	30.4	30.5	30.5	30.5	30.8	29.8
2004	30.8	30.9	31.3	31.6	32.1	32.8	32.9	33.0	32.9	33.5	33.9	34.4	32.5
2005	34.4	34.5	34.8	34.8	35.3	35.8	36.1	36.5	36.8	37.2	37.5	37.9	36.0
2006	38.4	39.2	40.0	40.7	41.3	42.4	42.5	43.5	43.6	43.4	43.9	44.5	42.0
2007	44.3	44.2	44.8	44.8	45.2	46.3	47.0	47.7	47.4	48.3	48.9	48.6	46.5
Construction													
2000	58.1	58.1	59.7	61.1	62.2	63.2	62.8	63.6	62.9	63.1	62.5	62.2	61.6
2001	60.6	62.5	65.0	66.3	67.6	69.4	68.9	69.5	67.6	66.3	65.1	64.4	66.1
2002	63.1	63.3	63.7	63.6	65.2	65.9	66.5	66.4	64.8	64.0	63.3	63.1	64.4
2003	62.0	61.3	61.8	63.7	64.6	65.9	65.9	65.7	64.3	63.6	62.1	62.3	63.6
2004	59.7	59.2	61.3	61.7	62.6	64.0	65.2	64.8	64.5	64.3	63.1	63.4	62.8
2005	61.1	61.4	63.6	65.5	65.3	66.9	68.1	68.1	68.0	68.1	68.0	68.8	66.1
2006	67.7	68.1	69.7	69.6	70.1	72.1	71.1	71.5	71.3	71.0	70.4	70.5	70.3
2007	67.5	67.7	70.2	70.1	70.8	73.2	72.7	73.8	72.8	72.5	72.7	72.1	71.3
Manufacturing													
2000	175.8	176.0	176.9	176.0	176.5	178.1	177.7	178.1	177.5	175.6	176.6	177.7	176.9
2001	174.5	173.6	172.9	172.1	172.2	172.9	169.5	167.8	168.9	163.9	165.1	164.5	169.8
2002	155.4	154.9	154.9	154.0	154.2	153.8	151.7	151.5	150.6	149.3	149.0	148.6	152.3
2003	146.5	145.5	145.3	143.4	142.7	139.8	142.1	143.1	143.0	142.7	142.4	142.1	143.2
2004	141.3	140.8	141.3	141.5	142.2	140.7	142.9	143.0	142.8	143.5	143.5	144.4	142.3
2005	141.3	142.4	143.3	143.6	144.1	143.6	145.4	145.8	145.7	146.4	147.3	149.2	144.8
2006	147.7	148.1	149.0	146.4	148.3	149.3	149.7	150.6	150.1	150.1	150.1	151.0	149.2
2007	148.9	149.3	150.3	149.6	150.2	151.0	151.4	151.4	150.5	149.6	150.0	150.1	150.2
Service-Providing													
2000	1,177.0	1,185.9	1,199.9	1,210.9	1,225.1	1,220.5	1,202.4	1,209.9	1,226.9	1,231.9	1,240.3	1,238.6	1,214.1
2001	1,204.5	1,215.4	1,227.0	1,236.1	1,243.3	1,234.5	1,212.8	1,221.8	1,233.5	1,233.7	1,242.7	1,240.8	1,228.8
2002	1,209.0	1,217.6	1,228.0	1,238.0	1,247.8	1,232.1	1,214.1	1,223.1	1,231.8	1,230.4	1,236.3	1,234.2	1,228.5
2003	1,198.0	1,203.6	1,206.6	1,212.2	1,220.9	1,204.8	1,191.2	1,196.5	1,210.2	1,216.5	1,221.4	1,222.5	1,208.7
2004	1,195.0	1,204.5	1,216.4	1,225.3	1,230.5	1,221.4	1,209.7	1,217.3	1,232.4	1,239.6	1,244.8	1,248.4	1,223.8
2005	1,215.8	1,228.7	1,242.2	1,253.9	1,261.8	1,254.0	1,236.7	1,247.2	1,263.8	1,268.3	1,278.3	1,280.6	1,252.6
2006	1,249.5	1,262.1	1,275.3	1,277.1	1,287.8	1,281.6	1,262.1	1,273.9	1,289.2	1,289.5	1,295.5	1,299.6	1,278.6
2007	1,268.1	1,282.6	1,299.9	1,296.5	1,305.9	1,300.3	1,279.7	1,292.8	1,308.6	1,312.2	1,314.4	1,313.5	1,297.9
Trade, Transportation, and Utilities													
2000	287.0	285.0	286.3	288.9	291.6	294.1	292.2	294.7	294.7	295.7	302.0	304.2	293.0
2001	290.7	287.7	289.2	289.8	291.1	292.2	287.9	288.5	286.5	286.7	291.2	293.0	289.5
2002	283.5	281.3	283.9	283.9	285.1	284.9	282.5	283.1	281.8	280.7	285.5	287.3	283.6
2003	275.9	273.8	274.9	275.4	277.0	276.1	274.6	276.0	275.2	277.0	281.5	284.5	276.8
2004	273.3	271.1	274.0	274.1	275.7	276.0	273.6	273.4	272.1	274.1	279.1	282.4	274.9
2005	272.1	271.8	274.3	276.7	278.1	278.5	279.0	280.3	280.5	282.3	287.6	290.6	279.3
2006	278.1	278.1	280.3	281.8	284.4	284.9	282.8	283.8	283.7	284.0	288.8	292.8	283.6
2007	282.8	282.6	288.3	285.0	287.3	288.3	287.3	289.3	288.6	288.5	294.1	295.8	288.2
Wholesale Trade													
2000	55.7	55.8	56.2	56.2	56.5	58.1	57.0	57.5	57.4	57.3	57.3	57.4	56.9
2001	56.0	55.9	56.4	56.6	56.9	57.7	57.0	57.1	56.9	56.8	56.7	57.0	56.7
2002	56.4	56.1	56.5	56.2	56.6	57.0	56.8	56.9	56.6	56.0	56.1	56.1	56.4
2003	54.9	54.5	54.9	54.6	55.0	55.3	54.6	54.5	54.6	54.9	54.6	54.7	54.8
2004	54.1	53.7	53.9	54.0	54.7	55.3	55.1	55.1	54.8	55.2	55.4	55.7	54.8
2005	54.9	55.1	55.5	56.0	56.3	56.9	57.1	57.2	57.0	57.3	57.4	57.7	56.5
2006	57.2	57.6	58.0	57.8	58.4	58.9	58.7	58.8	58.8	58.6	58.7	58.9	58.4
2007	58.4	58.6	59.4	59.4	59.7	60.5	59.9	60.2	60.0	59.8	60.2	60.1	59.7

Employment by Industry: Oklahoma, 2000–2007—*Continued*

(Numbers in thousands, not seasonally adjusted.)

Industry and year	January	February	March	April	May	June	July	August	September	October	November	December	Annual Average
Retail Trade													
2000	174.8	172.9	173.8	175.4	177.5	177.9	177.3	179.1	179.5	180.3	186.6	188.7	178.7
2001	176.2	173.6	174.5	174.6	175.5	175.9	172.8	173.4	172.5	173.2	177.9	179.8	174.9
2002	172.0	170.2	172.2	172.5	173.2	172.5	170.2	170.9	170.1	169.7	174.7	176.9	172.1
2003	167.6	165.8	166.6	167.9	169.1	168.5	167.8	169.1	168.7	170.0	174.8	177.6	169.5
2004	167.6	165.9	168.2	168.7	169.4	168.8	166.5	166.3	165.3	166.7	171.5	173.9	168.2
2005	165.5	164.9	166.7	168.1	169.0	168.5	168.6	169.5	170.0	171.6	176.4	178.5	169.8
2006	167.6	167.2	168.7	169.7	171.1	170.8	168.9	169.3	168.8	169.1	173.5	176.3	170.1
2007	167.8	167.1	171.7	169.0	170.6	170.3	169.6	171.3	171.0	171.0	176.0	177.3	171.1
Transportation and Utilities													
2000	56.5	56.3	56.3	57.3	57.6	58.1	57.9	58.1	57.8	58.1	58.1	58.1	57.5
2001	58.5	58.2	58.3	58.6	58.7	58.6	58.1	58.0	57.1	56.7	56.6	56.2	57.8
2002	55.1	55.0	55.2	55.2	55.3	55.4	55.5	55.3	55.1	55.0	54.7	54.3	55.1
2003	53.4	53.5	53.4	52.9	52.9	52.3	52.2	52.4	51.9	52.1	52.1	52.2	52.6
2004	51.6	51.5	51.9	51.4	51.6	51.9	52.0	52.0	52.0	52.2	52.2	52.8	51.9
2005	51.7	51.8	52.1	52.6	52.8	53.1	53.3	53.6	53.5	53.4	53.8	54.4	53.0
2006	53.3	53.3	53.6	54.3	54.9	55.2	55.2	55.7	56.1	56.3	56.6	57.6	55.2
2007	56.6	56.9	57.2	56.6	57.0	57.5	57.8	57.8	57.6	57.7	57.9	58.4	57.4
Information													
2000	33.9	34.4	34.5	34.8	35.0	35.6	36.0	36.2	36.6	36.1	36.5	36.7	35.5
2001	36.7	37.0	36.5	36.9	36.7	36.4	36.6	37.4	37.5	37.5	38.0	37.8	37.0
2002	36.8	36.9	36.4	35.6	35.4	35.1	35.0	34.9	34.5	34.3	34.4	34.0	35.3
2003	33.5	33.2	32.9	32.7	32.8	32.4	32.0	31.6	31.3	31.7	31.9	32.2	32.4
2004	31.6	31.6	31.4	31.2	31.1	31.4	31.4	30.9	30.1	30.5	30.4	30.5	31.0
2005	30.2	30.4	30.1	30.4	30.4	30.4	30.5	30.2	29.9	29.8	30.0	30.3	30.2
2006	30.0	30.0	30.0	29.7	29.8	29.8	29.9	29.8	29.6	29.3	29.3	30.2	29.8
2007	29.2	29.0	28.6	28.6	28.8	28.7	28.7	28.6	28.4	28.9	28.8	29.1	28.8
Financial Activities													
2000	80.1	80.3	80.4	81.0	81.6	82.7	81.8	82.2	81.9	81.6	81.5	82.0	81.4
2001	80.8	81.2	81.7	82.3	82.8	83.6	83.3	83.7	83.1	82.7	82.6	82.6	82.5
2002	82.9	82.6	82.6	82.7	83.3	84.0	83.8	83.8	82.9	82.4	82.5	82.5	83.0
2003	81.6	81.7	82.0	82.7	83.2	83.8	83.7	84.0	83.6	83.8	83.8	84.0	83.2
2004	83.1	83.3	83.9	84.1	84.1	84.7	84.2	84.2	83.6	83.7	83.7	84.0	83.9
2005	82.3	82.4	82.8	82.4	83.0	83.7	83.8	83.8	83.4	82.8	83.0	84.0	83.1
2006	83.5	83.5	84.0	83.0	83.5	84.0	83.4	83.5	83.1	82.9	82.9	83.0	83.4
2007	82.8	83.3	83.5	83.2	83.5	84.1	84.2	84.2	83.9	84.1	84.2	84.5	83.8
Professional and Business Services													
2000	154.9	156.0	159.6	162.8	164.3	166.3	167.0	168.7	168.3	168.2	168.3	167.1	164.3
2001	160.8	163.1	166.0	168.7	169.1	171.1	168.2	168.9	167.1	163.9	164.0	163.6	166.2
2002	156.5	158.3	160.7	163.9	165.6	165.1	162.2	164.2	163.5	161.4	160.7	160.5	161.9
2003	154.3	154.8	154.8	156.6	158.1	157.9	158.3	158.8	159.0	158.5	158.3	157.7	157.3
2004	154.2	155.8	157.0	161.3	161.3	162.5	165.0	165.8	166.3	167.9	168.4	168.1	162.8
2005	162.2	164.9	166.9	169.7	170.1	171.6	171.2	173.2	174.4	172.7	174.6	173.8	170.4
2006	170.1	172.1	174.8	174.7	175.8	178.0	176.5	178.4	178.9	176.5	177.3	176.6	175.8
2007	173.6	176.4	179.7	179.8	180.8	182.3	181.9	184.7	184.2	183.4	182.4	181.2	180.9
Education and Health Services													
2000	157.2	159.2	160.1	162.2	162.6	162.2	162.2	163.0	165.0	164.2	166.2	165.4	162.5
2001	163.2	164.8	165.9	167.1	166.9	165.4	164.8	167.2	169.1	169.1	171.1	170.9	167.1
2002	169.2	170.8	171.1	173.1	172.6	171.2	171.6	174.8	176.3	175.3	178.4	177.3	173.5
2003	175.2	175.9	175.7	176.3	175.9	173.6	173.3	174.7	176.4	175.8	177.4	175.7	175.5
2004	176.7	177.9	178.8	180.2	179.1	177.1	177.6	178.3	180.5	180.9	181.8	181.4	179.2
2005	178.6	179.4	181.1	183.0	183.5	183.4	182.6	184.2	186.0	185.7	187.4	187.7	183.6
2006	184.0	184.7	186.3	186.8	187.7	188.3	186.4	187.7	189.6	189.3	190.6	190.3	187.6
2007	186.8	188.6	190.0	191.3	191.9	192.6	192.0	193.6	195.1	195.9	196.8	196.6	192.6
Leisure and Hospitality													
2000	119.1	120.2	123.7	126.2	128.0	129.4	128.8	129.6	128.8	127.4	125.4	122.8	125.8
2001	119.2	121.4	124.6	129.3	131.3	132.6	131.0	132.0	129.3	126.5	125.9	124.3	127.2
2002	120.2	121.8	125.2	128.1	131.3	131.1	130.2	131.3	129.4	127.4	125.4	123.5	127.1
2003	120.9	121.4	123.8	127.6	130.5	130.1	129.4	130.6	128.3	127.6	125.7	124.5	126.7
2004	121.5	122.6	126.5	129.1	131.5	132.6	131.9	132.8	132.5	130.6	129.4	128.3	129.1
2005	124.9	126.6	131.1	134.5	136.9	138.5	135.6	136.2	134.8	132.9	132.3	130.9	132.9
2006	129.8	131.4	135.6	137.6	139.4	140.7	140.3	141.1	139.6	137.5	136.1	136.5	137.1
2007	131.6	134.2	138.9	139.3	142.0	143.5	143.0	144.4	143.2	141.3	139.2	138.1	139.9
Other Services													
2000	59.2	59.3	60.0	60.9	61.3	62.3	61.6	61.6	61.9	61.4	61.4	61.9	61.1
2001	61.1	61.7	62.7	61.9	62.5	63.6	63.2	63.5	63.0	62.9	62.8	62.7	62.6
2002	61.6	61.9	62.4	64.8	65.0	65.2	64.5	64.2	63.6	62.3	62.1	61.9	63.3
2003	61.5	61.7	61.7	60.7	61.2	61.8	61.4	61.3	60.8	60.5	60.3	60.7	61.1
2004	60.1	60.4	61.2	61.3	61.6	62.3	61.6	61.3	60.8	60.5	60.5	60.7	61.0
2005	60.3	60.7	61.3	61.0	61.2	61.6	61.7	61.3	61.1	61.0	61.0	61.0	61.1
2006	60.3	60.6	61.2	61.2	61.9	62.8	62.3	62.2	62.0	61.9	62.0	62.2	61.7
2007	61.5	62.1	62.7	62.6	63.0	64.1	63.4	63.4	63.3	63.1	62.9	62.8	62.9
Government													
2000	282.9	288.8	292.5	291.3	297.9	285.0	270.0	271.1	286.8	294.5	296.2	295.6	287.7
2001	292.0	298.5	300.4	300.1	302.9	289.6	277.8	280.6	297.9	304.4	307.1	305.9	296.4
2002	298.3	304.0	305.7	305.9	309.5	295.5	284.3	286.8	299.8	306.6	307.3	307.2	300.9
2003	295.1	301.1	300.8	300.2	302.2	289.1	278.5	279.6	295.6	301.6	302.5	303.2	295.8
2004	294.5	301.8	303.6	304.0	306.1	294.8	284.4	290.6	306.5	311.4	311.5	313.0	301.9
2005	305.2	312.5	314.6	316.2	318.6	306.3	292.3	298.0	313.7	321.1	322.4	322.3	311.9
2006	313.7	321.7	323.1	322.3	325.3	313.1	300.5	307.4	322.7	328.1	328.5	328.0	319.5
2007	319.8	326.4	328.2	326.7	328.6	316.7	299.2	304.6	321.9	327.0	326.0	325.4	320.9

Average Weekly Hours by Selected Industry: Oklahoma, 2001–2007

(Not seasonally adjusted.)

Industry and year	January	February	March	April	May	June	July	August	September	October	November	December	Annual Average
Natural Resources and Mining													
2001	43.0	44.3	46.3	47.4	47.4	48.4	46.3	44.1	44.7	42.7	41.5	42.0	44.8
2002	40.2	42.1	43.6	39.1	45.6	40.9	43.9	42.0	40.6	40.0	40.2	43.0	41.8
2003	43.9	43.9	44.2	41.0	42.2	44.1	44.8	43.1	42.6	43.5	41.9	42.9	43.2
2004	42.9	43.4	45.3	43.5	43.2	44.5	43.3	44.1	43.1	42.9	43.9	43.8	43.7
2005	45.1	40.9	44.5	45.0	42.2	42.2	40.3	38.8	42.0	42.2	42.5	45.6	42.6
2006	40.2	40.7	39.6	43.5	40.2	42.4	39.8	41.2	38.4	41.4	46.8	46.5	41.7
2007	42.0	43.9	42.0	42.5	42.6	43.5	43.6	43.8	43.5	44.4	43.1	43.9	43.3
Manufacturing													
2001	42.4	39.1	39.1	39.6	40.5	38.6	37.7	40.6	38.9	40.0	37.9	38.4	39.4
2002	39.1	39.2	39.3	39.2	39.4	39.3	39.0	39.1	39.4	39.1	39.0	39.1	39.2
2003	38.6	38.1	38.7	38.9	38.1	37.5	39.5	40.3	39.8	39.8	40.9	41.6	39.3
2004	40.3	39.7	40.6	41.0	40.4	41.0	40.1	41.0	39.8	40.9	40.6	40.2	40.5
2005	39.2	38.8	39.1	39.6	39.6	40.4	40.3	40.7	39.2	40.0	37.9	38.0	39.4
2006	38.7	40.8	41.6	41.2	41.9	42.1	40.2	38.6	38.0	39.8	39.1	37.6	39.9
2007	38.6	39.2	39.5	39.8	40.0	40.1	39.9	39.9	39.2	40.5	41.5	39.8	39.8
Trade, Transportation, and Utilities													
2001	34.1	33.7	33.1	33.8	33.8	34.5	35.2	33.6	33.7	33.2	33.4	33.3	33.8
2002	33.0	33.6	33.7	33.3	33.5	34.4	34.3	33.6	33.5	33.5	33.4	34.3	33.7
2003	33.1	33.8	34.1	33.3	34.0	35.1	34.2	34.6	34.1	33.5	33.6	33.7	33.9
2004	33.3	34.0	33.6	33.8	34.0	34.5	34.3	34.4	35.1	34.6	33.7	34.6	34.2
2005	34.2	34.5	34.5	34.8	34.9	34.5	34.8	34.4	34.5	34.1	35.2	35.0	34.6
2006	34.2	33.4	33.6	34.0	35.1	34.8	34.5	33.8	34.1	33.2	33.5	33.3	33.9
2007	31.6	32.2	32.4	31.9	31.2	32.6	32.8	32.6	33.5	32.5	33.4	32.2	32.4
Wholesale Trade													
2001	39.3	38.9	39.1	39.9	39.3	39.3	38.9	38.9	40.3	39.4	40.4	39.0	39.4
2002	40.2	39.9	39.0	38.8	38.3	40.2	37.6	38.4	38.2	40.4	40.4	40.9	39.3
2003	38.6	38.8	37.7	37.1	37.1	38.9	36.8	37.2	37.3	37.7	38.6	37.1	37.7
2004	37.7	38.0	38.0	38.1	38.7	39.8	37.8	38.3	38.1	38.0	37.9	37.2	38.1
2005	36.6	38.8	37.3	37.5	36.8	36.5	36.6	36.9	37.9	39.1	37.7	36.6	37.4
2006	39.8	38.0	41.8	40.1	43.4	42.5	40.8	38.9	38.7	38.4	36.6	36.4	39.6
2007	36.3	35.6	36.5	35.8	35.5	37.7	35.7	34.6	36.1	35.8	36.5	35.9	36.0

Average Hourly Earnings by Selected Industry: Oklahoma, 2001–2007

(Dollars, not seasonally adjusted.)

Industry and year	January	February	March	April	May	June	July	August	September	October	November	December	Annual Average
Natural Resources and Mining													
2001	16.56	16.35	16.97	16.00	15.65	16.48	16.70	15.45	16.73	16.86	16.30	17.05	16.42
2002	16.75	16.81	16.66	16.74	16.73	16.48	16.57	16.01	16.01	15.71	16.22	16.64	16.45
2003	16.16	15.86	16.19	15.79	15.71	15.37	15.55	15.53	15.73	16.65	15.85	15.82	15.82
2004	15.81	15.73	15.68	15.69	15.65	15.44	15.30	15.54	15.26	14.96	15.21	15.49	15.49
2005	15.53	15.38	15.53	15.39	16.00	15.35	15.98	16.41	15.70	14.83	14.74	14.48	15.43
2006	14.18	14.71	15.23	14.51	14.62	15.61	15.13	14.94	16.17	14.17	14.31	15.62	14.94
2007	16.74	16.49	16.77	17.17	16.78	16.37	17.33	17.87	17.74	17.62	17.97	18.02	17.26
Manufacturing													
2001	13.01	13.22	13.23	14.04	13.97	13.50	13.55	13.99	13.90	13.72	13.92	13.94	13.66
2002	13.81	14.01	14.12	14.18	14.16	14.13	14.11	14.14	14.17	14.14	14.23	14.17	14.11
2003	14.09	14.21	14.44	14.33	13.89	14.00	14.19	14.21	14.09	13.86	13.85	14.37	14.13
2004	14.12	14.63	14.62	14.69	14.62	13.70	13.90	13.95	14.28	14.05	14.05	14.26	14.24
2005	14.03	14.39	14.17	14.63	14.67	14.39	14.56	14.61	14.82	15.02	15.14	14.11	14.56
2006	14.83	14.45	14.51	14.56	14.61	14.47	14.54	15.28	15.14	15.07	14.72	14.98	14.77
2007	14.65	14.60	14.53	14.39	14.40	14.51	14.62	14.83	14.70	14.51	14.69	14.30	14.56
Trade, Transportation, and Utilities													
2001	10.36	10.68	10.72	10.78	10.78	10.59	10.54	11.05	10.95	11.12	10.91	10.83	10.77
2002	10.76	11.20	11.22	10.95	10.94	10.99	11.14	11.41	11.60	11.31	11.38	11.34	11.19
2003	11.82	11.95	12.06	12.25	12.27	12.03	12.14	12.38	12.76	12.63	12.64	12.48	12.28
2004	12.77	12.55	12.48	12.34	12.44	12.55	12.43	12.41	12.52	12.36	12.35	12.31	12.46
2005	12.78	12.54	12.74	12.59	12.86	12.85	12.78	13.06	13.22	13.60	13.00	13.12	12.93
2006	11.76	11.36	11.86	11.66	11.47	11.47	11.59	11.66	11.72	11.78	11.69	11.77	11.65
2007	12.01	11.99	12.62	12.51	12.52	12.58	12.74	12.52	12.66	12.70	12.60	12.89	12.53
Wholesale Trade													
2001	10.99	11.48	11.26	11.71	11.68	10.32	10.79	10.87	10.81	10.66	10.76	10.47	10.98
2002	10.54	10.70	10.80	10.40	10.61	10.52	11.27	12.28	12.38	11.11	11.55	11.36	11.12
2003	12.08	12.13	12.39	12.54	12.12	11.54	12.32	12.98	13.82	12.97	13.30	13.00	12.59
2004	13.84	13.87	13.49	13.26	13.79	13.89	13.78	13.67	14.16	13.56	13.78	14.01	13.76
2005	15.21	14.42	15.04	14.42	15.35	15.21	14.61	15.74	15.85	17.20	15.65	16.32	15.43
2006	15.65	14.48	14.36	13.86	13.11	13.49	13.62	13.67	14.17	14.27	14.53	14.65	14.13
2007	14.51	14.62	14.42	14.26	14.83	15.11	16.21	15.71	16.10	16.45	16.76	17.12	15.51

Average Weekly Earnings by Selected Industry: Oklahoma, 2001–2007

(Dollars, not seasonally adjusted.)

Industry and year	January	February	March	April	May	June	July	August	September	October	November	December	Annual Average
Natural Resources and Mining													
2001	712.08	724.31	785.71	758.40	741.81	797.63	773.21	681.35	747.83	719.92	676.45	716.10	735.62
2002	673.35	707.70	726.38	654.53	762.89	674.03	727.42	672.42	650.01	628.40	652.04	715.52	687.61
2003	709.42	696.25	715.60	647.39	662.96	677.82	696.64	669.34	670.10	675.56	697.64	679.97	683.42
2004	678.25	682.68	710.30	682.52	676.08	687.08	662.49	685.31	657.71	641.78	667.72	678.46	676.91
2005	700.40	629.04	691.09	692.55	675.20	647.77	643.99	636.71	659.40	625.83	626.45	660.29	657.32
2006	570.04	598.70	603.11	631.19	587.72	661.86	602.17	615.53	620.93	586.64	669.71	726.33	623.00
2007	703.08	723.91	704.34	729.73	714.83	712.10	755.59	782.71	771.69	782.33	774.51	791.08	747.36
Manufacturing													
2001	551.62	516.90	517.29	555.98	565.79	521.10	510.84	567.99	540.71	548.80	527.57	535.30	538.20
2002	539.97	549.19	554.92	555.86	557.90	555.31	550.29	552.87	558.30	552.87	554.97	554.05	553.11
2003	543.87	541.40	558.83	557.44	529.21	525.00	560.51	572.66	560.78	551.63	566.47	597.79	555.31
2004	569.04	580.81	593.57	602.29	590.65	561.70	557.39	571.95	568.34	574.65	570.43	536.18	576.72
2005	549.98	558.33	554.05	579.35	580.93	581.36	586.77	594.63	580.94	600.80	573.81	536.18	573.66
2006	573.92	589.56	603.62	599.87	612.16	609.19	584.51	589.81	575.32	599.79	575.55	563.25	589.32
2007	565.49	572.32	573.94	572.72	576.00	581.85	583.34	591.72	576.24	587.66	609.64	569.14	579.49
Trade, Transportation, and Utilities													
2001	353.28	359.92	354.83	364.36	364.36	365.36	371.01	371.28	369.02	369.18	364.39	360.64	364.03
2002	355.08	376.32	378.11	364.64	366.49	378.06	382.10	383.38	388.60	378.89	380.09	388.96	377.10
2003	391.24	403.91	411.25	407.93	417.18	422.25	415.19	428.35	435.12	423.11	424.70	420.58	416.29
2004	425.24	426.70	419.33	417.09	422.96	432.98	426.35	426.90	439.45	427.66	416.20	425.93	426.13
2005	437.08	432.63	439.53	438.13	448.81	443.33	444.74	449.26	456.09	463.76	457.60	459.20	447.38
2006	402.19	379.42	398.50	396.44	402.60	399.16	399.86	394.11	399.65	391.10	391.62	391.94	394.94
2007	379.52	386.08	408.89	399.07	390.62	410.11	417.87	408.15	424.11	412.75	420.84	415.06	405.97
Wholesale Trade													
2001	431.91	446.57	440.27	467.23	459.02	405.58	419.73	422.84	435.64	420.00	434.70	408.33	432.61
2002	423.71	426.93	421.20	403.52	406.36	422.90	423.75	471.55	472.92	448.84	466.62	464.62	437.02
2003	466.29	470.64	467.10	465.23	449.65	448.91	453.38	482.86	515.49	488.97	513.38	482.30	474.64
2004	521.77	527.06	512.62	505.21	533.67	552.82	520.88	523.56	539.50	515.28	522.26	521.17	524.26
2005	556.69	559.50	560.99	540.75	564.88	555.17	534.73	580.81	600.72	672.52	590.01	597.31	577.08
2006	622.87	550.24	600.25	555.79	568.97	573.33	555.70	531.76	548.38	547.97	531.80	533.26	559.55
2007	526.71	520.47	526.33	510.51	526.47	569.65	578.70	543.57	581.21	588.91	611.74	614.61	558.36

Population
    2000 census: 3,421,399
    2007 estimate: 3,747,455
    Percent change, 2000–2007: 9.5%

Percent change in total nonfarm employment, 2000–2007: 7.0%

Industry with the largest growth in employment, 2000–2007 (thousands)
    Education and health services, 39.3

Industry with the largest decline in employment, 2000–2007 (thousands)
    Manufacturing, -20.7

Civilian labor force
    2000: 1,810,150
    2007: 1,927,802

Employment-population ratio
    2000: 65.0%
    2007: 62.1%

Unemployment rate and rank among states
    2000: 5.1%, 47th
    2007: 5.2%, 42nd

Employment by Industry, 2007

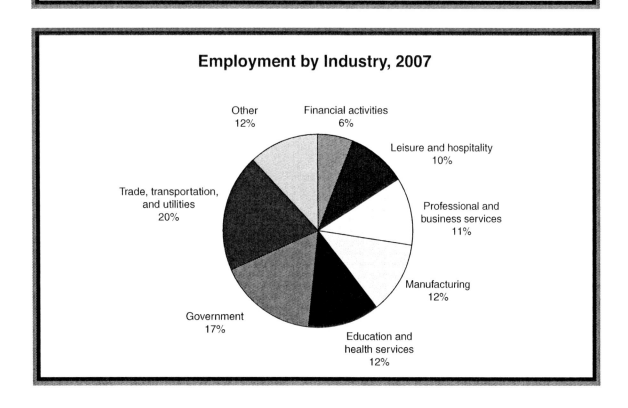

Other 12%

Financial activities 6%

Leisure and hospitality 10%

Professional and business services 11%

Manufacturing 12%

Education and health services 12%

Government 17%

Trade, transportation, and utilities 20%

Employment by Industry: Oregon, 2000–2007

(Numbers in thousands, not seasonally adjusted.)

Industry and year	January	February	March	April	May	June	July	August	September	October	November	December	Annual Average
Total Nonfarm													
2000	1,567.9	1,581.4	1,591.8	1,603.5	1,621.6	1,638.0	1,614.6	1,620.9	1,635.1	1,644.0	1,650.2	1,645.1	1,617.8
2001	1,593.1	1,600.9	1,606.0	1,607.5	1,616.3	1,629.4	1,597.3	1,600.1	1,606.0	1,610.0	1,603.1	1,596.3	1,605.5
2002	1,548.1	1,558.8	1,567.2	1,575.9	1,589.5	1,602.4	1,584.7	1,591.6	1,599.8	1,607.0	1,603.6	1,595.2	1,585.3
2003	1,552.9	1,557.7	1,561.6	1,561.2	1,572.4	1,582.6	1,561.4	1,570.9	1,582.1	1,597.8	1,595.8	1,595.5	1,574.3
2004	1,542.4	1,558.7	1,574.6	1,591.5	1,604.9	1,622.4	1,610.1	1,615.9	1,628.5	1,642.6	1,643.7	1,644.5	1,606.7
2005	1,598.9	1,613.8	1,628.4	1,640.2	1,651.2	1,668.0	1,651.3	1,658.6	1,673.0	1,683.6	1,691.7	1,694.7	1,654.5
2006	1,648.2	1,665.2	1,678.0	1,690.6	1,707.3	1,722.7	1,700.4	1,707.1	1,720.7	1,732.3	1,735.5	1,734.4	1,703.5
2007	1,688.3	1,704.5	1,717.7	1,721.0	1,736.3	1,749.3	1,728.1	1,733.7	1,742.4	1,753.9	1,755.6	1,748.7	1,731.6
Total Private													
2000	1,291.1	1,299.5	1,308.5	1,319.5	1,330.4	1,348.5	1,355.2	1,364.1	1,367.9	1,360.5	1,364.7	1,361.3	1,339.3
2001	1,314.7	1,315.9	1,318.7	1,320.8	1,325.7	1,338.2	1,336.8	1,340.7	1,333.7	1,320.2	1,311.6	1,307.1	1,323.7
2002	1,262.7	1,267.8	1,274.3	1,284.4	1,295.1	1,307.1	1,318.0	1,326.8	1,323.6	1,317.2	1,311.9	1,306.6	1,299.6
2003	1,267.3	1,269.3	1,273.4	1,274.6	1,284.0	1,295.4	1,305.3	1,314.2	1,314.7	1,313.8	1,309.9	1,312.0	1,294.5
2004	1,263.4	1,273.7	1,286.7	1,304.6	1,315.4	1,330.1	1,346.4	1,353.1	1,354.7	1,354.6	1,353.1	1,356.0	1,324.3
2005	1,312.8	1,323.4	1,337.0	1,348.3	1,357.7	1,372.6	1,387.1	1,394.9	1,398.7	1,395.1	1,399.5	1,405.5	1,369.4
2006	1,363.7	1,374.6	1,385.9	1,399.4	1,412.2	1,426.2	1,435.1	1,442.4	1,444.6	1,440.9	1,440.2	1,443.6	1,417.4
2007	1,401.7	1,412.4	1,423.5	1,426.8	1,437.3	1,449.0	1,457.3	1,464.0	1,463.3	1,457.4	1,455.7	1,451.1	1,441.6
Goods-Producing													
2000	306.6	308.0	309.7	311.1	314.5	323.1	327.4	329.5	329.9	323.1	320.3	317.3	318.4
2001	307.7	306.7	305.0	304.4	304.8	310.5	314.8	314.3	309.4	304.0	294.3	290.1	305.5
2002	280.5	280.5	281.6	283.7	287.0	292.7	299.6	301.3	298.3	294.0	287.7	283.5	289.2
2003	276.2	275.7	275.0	272.9	275.7	281.5	286.2	290.0	288.7	287.8	283.4	281.4	281.2
2004	272.1	275.4	278.4	284.2	288.3	295.0	304.0	306.2	304.9	303.4	298.4	296.3	292.2
2005	289.2	291.4	294.4	296.8	300.1	305.9	313.4	315.9	314.8	313.2	309.2	307.9	304.4
2006	302.3	305.4	308.0	311.1	315.0	321.4	328.6	330.2	328.3	325.1	319.5	316.8	317.6
2007	309.7	311.2	312.9	311.9	315.3	319.8	325.9	328.2	325.7	322.9	315.5	310.5	317.5
Natural Resources and Mining													
2000	9.2	9.3	9.1	9.3	9.7	10.2	10.3	10.4	10.3	10.4	10.0	9.7	9.8
2001	9.2	9.1	8.8	8.6	9.0	9.6	9.9	10.1	9.8	9.7	9.2	8.8	9.3
2002	8.7	8.7	8.7	8.6	9.0	9.5	9.9	9.9	9.8	9.8	9.7	9.5	9.3
2003	8.9	8.9	8.8	8.9	9.1	9.6	9.9	9.9	9.8	9.8	9.5	9.3	9.4
2004	8.8	9.0	9.2	9.4	9.6	10.0	10.2	10.2	10.1	10.0	9.7	9.7	9.7
2005	9.2	9.4	9.3	9.1	9.2	9.6	10.1	10.1	9.9	9.8	9.6	9.4	9.6
2006	8.8	9.0	8.9	9.0	9.3	9.7	9.9	10.0	9.9	9.8	9.4	9.2	9.4
2007	8.7	8.9	8.9	9.1	9.3	9.6	9.7	9.7	9.6	9.5	9.2	9.0	9.3
Construction													
2000	77.9	78.4	79.2	80.3	82.0	85.5	86.8	88.9	89.3	86.7	84.8	83.3	83.6
2001	78.6	78.4	78.9	78.6	79.7	82.2	83.6	85.0	83.2	81.7	78.8	76.8	80.5
2002	72.6	72.9	73.9	75.0	77.2	79.9	82.6	84.9	83.3	81.8	79.1	76.5	78.3
2003	72.1	72.0	72.1	72.6	74.6	76.9	79.9	82.4	81.7	81.6	79.5	78.1	77.0
2004	72.4	74.2	76.2	79.2	81.4	84.2	87.9	89.0	88.9	88.1	85.9	85.2	82.7
2005	80.8	82.0	84.0	86.1	88.5	91.4	95.2	97.3	98.0	96.9	95.3	95.1	90.9
2006	91.3	93.3	94.7	97.2	100.2	103.2	105.7	107.2	106.9	105.7	103.5	101.9	100.9
2007	97.4	98.9	100.5	101.4	104.2	105.8	109.5	110.7	109.2	107.4	102.4	99.0	103.9
Manufacturing													
2000	219.5	220.3	221.4	221.5	222.8	227.4	230.3	230.2	230.3	226.0	225.5	224.3	225.0
2001	219.9	219.2	217.3	217.2	216.1	218.7	221.3	219.2	216.4	212.6	206.3	204.5	215.7
2002	199.2	198.9	199.0	200.1	200.8	203.3	207.1	206.5	205.2	202.4	198.9	197.5	201.6
2003	195.2	194.8	194.1	191.4	192.0	195.0	196.4	197.7	197.2	196.4	194.4	194.0	194.9
2004	190.9	192.2	193.0	195.6	197.3	200.8	205.9	207.0	205.9	205.3	202.8	201.4	199.8
2005	199.2	200.0	201.1	201.6	202.4	204.9	208.1	208.5	206.9	206.5	204.3	203.4	203.9
2006	202.2	203.1	204.4	204.9	205.5	208.5	213.0	213.0	211.5	209.6	206.6	205.7	207.3
2007	203.6	203.4	203.5	201.4	201.8	204.4	206.7	207.8	206.9	206.0	203.9	202.5	204.3
Service-Providing													
2000	1,261.3	1,273.4	1,282.1	1,292.4	1,307.1	1,314.9	1,287.2	1,291.4	1,305.2	1,320.9	1,329.9	1,327.8	1,299.5
2001	1,285.4	1,294.2	1,301.0	1,303.1	1,311.5	1,318.9	1,282.5	1,285.8	1,296.6	1,306.0	1,308.8	1,306.2	1,300.0
2002	1,267.6	1,278.3	1,285.6	1,292.2	1,302.5	1,309.7	1,285.1	1,290.3	1,301.5	1,313.0	1,315.9	1,311.7	1,296.1
2003	1,276.7	1,282.0	1,286.6	1,288.3	1,296.7	1,301.1	1,275.2	1,280.9	1,293.4	1,310.0	1,312.4	1,314.1	1,293.1
2004	1,270.3	1,283.3	1,296.2	1,307.3	1,316.6	1,327.4	1,306.1	1,309.7	1,323.6	1,339.2	1,345.3	1,348.2	1,314.4
2005	1,309.7	1,322.4	1,334.0	1,343.4	1,351.1	1,362.1	1,337.9	1,342.7	1,358.2	1,370.4	1,382.5	1,386.8	1,350.1
2006	1,345.9	1,359.8	1,370.0	1,379.5	1,392.3	1,401.3	1,371.8	1,376.9	1,392.4	1,407.2	1,416.0	1,417.6	1,385.9
2007	1,378.6	1,393.3	1,404.8	1,409.1	1,421.0	1,429.5	1,402.2	1,405.5	1,416.7	1,431.0	1,440.1	1,438.2	1,414.2
Trade, Transportation, and Utilities													
2000	318.9	317.7	318.2	320.5	322.4	326.0	325.9	327.6	328.0	331.2	339.8	340.4	326.4
2001	320.7	316.9	317.6	317.6	318.9	321.4	321.2	321.7	321.0	320.5	325.4	326.7	320.8
2002	309.7	307.4	308.6	310.5	312.5	314.9	316.8	317.2	317.8	318.4	323.2	326.3	315.3
2003	310.4	308.3	308.4	308.6	310.9	312.9	314.8	315.9	316.5	319.4	324.7	326.5	314.8
2004	311.7	309.1	310.9	313.7	316.3	319.2	322.4	323.2	323.9	325.9	331.9	335.1	320.3
2005	319.1	317.8	320.5	321.6	323.1	327.0	329.2	331.3	332.9	334.1	341.2	345.5	328.6
2006	328.4	326.9	328.3	329.5	332.7	335.0	335.9	337.3	338.4	339.3	345.6	349.7	335.6
2007	334.4	332.3	333.8	334.3	336.3	339.3	341.2	341.7	343.4	343.4	349.8	351.2	340.1
Wholesale Trade													
2000	75.5	75.8	76.0	75.9	76.0	76.6	77.3	77.3	77.2	77.5	77.4	77.2	76.6
2001	74.7	74.8	75.2	75.0	74.8	75.3	75.7	75.4	75.2	74.1	73.6	73.2	74.8
2002	72.7	72.8	72.8	73.1	73.2	73.7	74.7	74.7	74.6	75.0	74.7	74.7	73.9
2003	73.7	74.0	74.0	74.0	74.2	74.4	75.6	75.1	75.4	75.2	75.1	74.9	74.6
2004	73.7	74.1	74.3	74.6	75.0	75.5	76.7	76.7	76.7	76.5	76.7	76.9	75.6
2005	76.1	76.6	76.9	77.1	76.9	77.7	78.5	78.6	79.1	78.7	78.9	78.9	77.8
2006	78.1	78.9	79.0	79.2	79.8	80.1	80.4	80.4	80.4	80.4	80.8	80.7	79.9
2007	80.1	80.6	80.5	80.4	80.6	81.0	81.7	81.7	80.1	80.3	79.7	80.2	80.5

Employment by Industry: Oregon, 2000–2007—*Continued*

(Numbers in thousands, not seasonally adjusted.)

Industry and year	January	February	March	April	May	June	July	August	September	October	November	December	Annual Average
Retail Trade													
2000	186.8	185.2	185.4	187.6	189.5	191.6	191.6	192.7	192.5	195.2	203.6	204.9	192.2
2001	189.5	185.7	186.2	186.6	187.4	189.5	189.2	189.0	188.4	188.5	194.3	196.2	189.2
2002	181.7	179.3	180.5	181.7	183.3	184.9	186.3	186.1	186.6	186.8	192.2	195.4	185.4
2003	181.2	179.0	179.4	179.7	181.6	183.1	184.1	184.8	184.7	187.3	192.9	195.0	184.4
2004	182.4	179.6	180.9	183.0	185.0	187.3	189.1	189.6	189.2	190.7	196.8	199.9	187.8
2005	186.8	184.8	186.7	187.9	189.6	192.3	194.2	195.7	195.7	197.5	204.3	207.4	193.6
2006	193.2	190.5	191.7	192.7	194.9	196.1	197.7	198.8	198.8	199.3	205.6	208.8	197.3
2007	196.6	193.9	195.3	195.8	197.4	199.2	201.7	203.2	203.5	204.2	210.0	210.8	201.0
Transportation and Utilities													
2000	56.7	56.8	56.8	57.1	57.3	57.8	56.9	57.6	58.6	58.5	58.9	58.3	57.6
2001	56.5	56.4	56.2	56.0	56.7	56.6	56.3	57.3	57.4	57.9	57.5	57.3	56.8
2002	55.3	55.3	55.3	55.7	56.0	56.3	55.8	56.4	56.6	56.6	56.3	56.2	56.0
2003	55.5	55.3	55.0	54.9	55.1	55.4	55.1	56.0	56.4	56.9	56.7	56.6	55.7
2004	55.6	55.4	55.7	56.1	56.3	56.4	56.6	56.9	58.0	58.7	58.4	58.3	56.9
2005	56.2	56.4	56.9	56.6	56.6	57.0	56.5	57.0	58.1	57.9	58.0	59.2	57.2
2006	57.1	57.5	57.6	57.6	58.0	58.8	57.8	58.1	59.2	59.2	59.2	60.2	58.4
2007	57.7	57.8	58.0	58.1	58.3	59.1	57.8	58.4	59.6	59.5	59.6	59.9	58.7
Information													
2000	38.1	38.2	38.6	38.6	39.2	39.6	40.4	40.4	40.5	41.1	41.2	41.8	39.8
2001	41.1	40.9	40.8	41.2	41.1	41.8	39.3	39.1	38.5	38.4	38.5	38.5	39.9
2002	38.1	38.2	37.5	36.0	36.0	35.9	35.7	35.7	35.4	35.4	35.3	36.0	36.3
2003	35.0	34.7	34.5	33.7	33.9	33.4	32.9	33.1	32.7	32.9	33.3	33.1	33.6
2004	32.7	32.8	32.6	32.8	33.1	33.2	33.1	33.2	32.9	32.8	33.2	33.1	33.0
2005	32.6	33.0	32.9	33.2	33.5	33.6	33.7	33.6	33.8	34.1	34.4	35.1	33.6
2006	34.1	34.5	34.5	34.2	34.5	34.8	35.0	35.1	35.1	35.3	35.3	35.9	34.9
2007	34.9	35.3	35.8	35.9	36.3	36.7	36.3	36.7	36.6	36.2	36.6	36.4	36.1
Financial Activities													
2000	94.2	94.1	94.4	95.3	95.9	96.4	96.4	96.5	95.8	94.8	94.7	95.4	95.3
2001	93.2	93.7	94.2	94.5	95.0	95.8	96.5	96.3	95.8	95.7	95.7	95.8	95.2
2002	93.7	94.1	93.9	93.6	94.1	94.5	96.5	96.9	96.5	96.4	96.3	97.1	95.3
2003	95.2	95.5	96.2	96.9	97.1	98.0	98.8	99.1	98.1	97.0	96.3	96.4	97.1
2004	94.1	94.4	94.9	95.9	96.9	98.0	98.7	99.2	98.8	99.1	99.1	99.9	97.4
2005	98.0	98.8	99.5	100.4	101.1	102.0	103.9	104.3	103.9	103.8	104.3	105.1	102.1
2006	103.2	103.8	104.3	105.1	105.8	106.8	107.4	107.9	107.6	107.0	106.9	107.6	106.1
2007	105.8	106.5	107.1	106.9	107.2	107.8	108.4	107.9	106.3	105.6	104.8	105.4	106.6
Professional and Business Services													
2000	172.9	175.4	178.1	180.8	182.0	185.0	187.2	189.4	190.1	188.6	187.9	186.2	183.6
2001	180.1	179.4	179.5	178.0	177.9	179.7	178.2	179.4	177.5	173.5	172.2	170.3	177.1
2002	164.6	166.7	168.4	170.4	171.7	174.0	176.1	179.4	177.5	176.4	174.1	171.0	172.5
2003	164.5	165.7	166.7	167.8	169.5	170.8	173.3	175.2	175.6	174.6	172.2	173.7	170.8
2004	165.5	168.1	171.0	173.9	174.5	177.0	179.8	181.2	180.5	181.2	180.4	181.7	176.2
2005	174.8	177.9	180.0	182.7	183.1	186.1	188.9	190.5	190.6	190.0	190.3	191.9	185.6
2006	184.2	187.0	188.8	191.6	193.0	196.2	197.8	199.5	199.7	199.5	198.0	197.4	194.4
Education and Health Services													
2000	167.9	171.4	172.2	172.6	172.4	169.5	166.8	168.5	173.9	176.8	177.8	177.9	172.3
2001	174.4	178.7	179.4	179.7	179.3	176.6	173.2	174.3	179.1	182.4	183.9	184.5	178.8
2002	180.5	184.0	185.1	186.6	186.4	183.4	180.4	180.9	185.2	189.5	190.7	190.1	185.2
2003	186.7	189.4	190.1	189.9	189.7	186.1	183.3	183.3	188.2	192.3	193.0	193.6	188.8
2004	187.0	191.8	193.1	193.8	193.0	190.2	187.5	187.7	193.9	197.5	199.9	199.1	192.8
2005	193.9	197.8	199.0	199.7	199.8	196.1	194.0	193.8	199.8	202.7	204.4	204.0	198.8
2006	200.1	204.1	205.5	206.8	206.7	202.7	198.5	199.0	205.2	208.9	210.9	211.0	205.0
2007	206.3	211.3	212.4	212.7	212.6	209.2	205.2	206.0	212.1	215.4	217.8	218.1	211.6
Leisure and Hospitality													
2000	138.8	140.2	142.2	145.3	148.3	153.2	156.2	156.8	153.7	148.9	147.1	146.7	148.1
2001	141.4	142.6	145.0	148.3	151.4	154.9	156.9	158.9	155.6	149.2	145.6	145.5	149.6
2002	140.8	141.6	143.6	147.4	150.8	155.1	156.6	159.0	156.3	150.5	148.1	146.4	149.7
2003	143.7	144.1	146.2	148.4	150.3	156.0	159.2	160.6	157.3	152.7	150.2	150.4	151.6
2004	144.9	145.9	148.8	153.1	156.0	159.5	162.9	164.6	161.6	156.0	154.0	154.0	155.1
2005	149.4	150.1	153.9	156.7	159.5	164.1	166.4	167.9	165.2	159.6	158.2	158.4	159.1
2006	154.6	155.5	158.4	162.5	165.2	169.4	172.6	173.9	170.8	166.2	164.6	165.6	164.9
2007	161.5	163.2	166.2	168.9	172.4	176.1	180.2	181.4	177.9	173.1	173.2	173.2	172.3
Other Services													
2000	53.7	54.5	55.1	55.3	55.7	55.7	54.9	55.4	56.0	56.0	55.9	55.6	55.3
2001	56.1	57.0	57.2	57.1	57.3	57.5	56.7	56.7	56.8	56.5	56.0	55.7	56.7
2002	54.8	55.3	55.6	56.2	56.6	56.6	56.3	56.4	56.6	56.6	56.5	56.2	56.1
2003	55.6	55.9	56.3	56.4	56.9	56.7	56.8	57.0	57.6	57.1	56.8	56.9	56.7
2004	55.4	56.2	57.0	57.2	57.3	58.0	58.0	57.8	58.2	58.7	57.2	56.8	57.3
2005	55.8	56.6	56.8	57.2	57.5	57.8	57.6	57.6	57.7	57.6	57.5	57.6	57.3
2006	56.8	57.4	58.1	58.6	59.3	59.9	59.3	59.5	59.5	59.6	59.4	59.6	58.9
2007	58.5	59.6	60.0	60.0	60.6	61.0	60.3	60.2	60.3	59.9	59.6	59.3	59.9
Government													
2000	276.8	281.9	283.3	284.0	291.2	289.5	259.4	256.8	267.2	283.5	285.5	283.8	278.6
2001	278.4	285.0	287.3	286.7	290.6	291.2	260.5	259.4	272.3	289.8	291.5	289.2	281.8
2002	285.4	291.0	292.9	291.5	294.4	295.3	266.7	264.8	276.2	289.8	291.7	288.6	285.7
2003	285.6	288.4	288.2	286.6	288.4	287.2	256.1	256.7	267.4	284.0	285.9	283.5	279.8
2004	279.0	285.0	287.9	286.9	289.5	292.3	263.7	262.8	273.8	286.0	290.6	288.5	282.3
2005	286.1	290.4	291.4	291.9	293.5	295.4	264.2	263.7	274.3	288.5	292.2	289.2	285.1
2006	284.5	290.6	292.1	291.2	295.1	296.5	265.3	264.7	276.1	291.4	295.3	290.8	286.1
2007	286.6	292.1	294.2	294.2	299.0	300.3	270.8	269.7	279.1	296.5	299.9	297.6	290.0

Average Weekly Hours by Selected Industry: Oregon, 2001–2007

(Not seasonally adjusted.)

Industry and year	January	February	March	April	May	June	July	August	September	October	November	December	Annual Average
Manufacturing													
2001	38.4	38.7	39.1	39.9	39.1	39.1	39.0	39.1	39.6	39.0	38.5	39.5	39.1
2002	37.9	38.5	39.0	39.1	38.9	39.9	38.3	40.0	39.9	39.4	38.8	39.3	39.1
2003	38.4	38.9	39.1	38.8	39.1	39.9	38.6	39.6	39.6	39.4	40.3	39.7	39.3
2004	37.2	39.7	38.9	38.9	40.2	39.3	38.5	39.3	39.0	39.0	39.5	39.6	39.1
2005	39.8	39.1	39.7	39.6	40.8	39.8	39.2	40.0	40.7	41.2	41.0	41.3	40.2
2006	40.6	40.2	40.6	40.1	40.2	40.5	41.6	40.2	40.3	41.3	39.9	40.2	40.5
2007	39.0	39.3	39.8	40.3	40.1	40.8	40.4	40.6	40.2	40.2	39.7	40.7	40.1

Average Hourly Earnings by Selected Industry: Oregon, 2001–2007

(Dollars, not seasonally adjusted.)

Industry and year	January	February	March	April	May	June	July	August	September	October	November	December	Annual Average
Manufacturing													
2001	14.50	14.49	14.51	14.81	14.60	14.76	15.03	14.68	14.80	14.72	14.95	15.02	14.74
2002	15.02	15.04	14.98	14.96	14.99	15.11	15.09	14.93	15.12	15.10	15.10	15.27	15.06
2003	15.30	15.24	15.21	15.22	15.26	15.22	15.24	15.01	15.07	14.97	15.31	15.41	15.20
2004	15.30	15.31	15.39	15.33	15.47	15.38	15.28	15.25	15.30	15.27	15.30	15.52	15.34
2005	15.43	15.36	15.36	15.44	15.44	15.48	15.54	15.65	15.37	15.58	15.59	15.62	15.49
2006	15.71	15.51	15.55	15.65	15.66	15.53	15.25	15.35	15.62	15.55	15.68	15.84	15.57
2007	16.05	16.01	16.32	16.28	16.19	16.36	16.63	16.37	16.73	16.71	16.88	16.85	16.45

Average Weekly Earnings by Selected Industry: Oregon, 2001–2007

(Dollars, not seasonally adjusted.)

Industry and year	January	February	March	April	May	June	July	August	September	October	November	December	Annual Average
Manufacturing													
2001	556.80	560.76	567.34	590.92	570.86	577.12	586.17	573.99	586.08	574.08	575.58	593.29	576.33
2002	569.26	579.04	584.22	584.94	583.11	602.89	577.95	597.20	603.29	594.94	585.88	600.11	588.85
2003	587.52	592.84	594.71	590.54	596.67	607.28	588.26	594.40	596.77	589.82	616.99	611.78	597.36
2004	569.16	607.81	598.67	596.34	621.89	604.43	588.28	599.33	596.70	595.53	604.35	614.59	599.79
2005	614.11	600.58	609.79	611.42	629.95	616.10	609.17	626.00	625.56	641.90	639.19	645.11	622.70
2006	637.83	623.50	631.33	627.57	629.53	628.97	634.40	617.07	629.49	642.22	625.63	636.77	630.59
2007	625.95	629.19	649.54	656.08	649.22	667.49	671.85	664.62	672.55	671.74	670.14	685.80	659.65

Population
  2000 census: 12,281,054
  2007 estimate: 12,432,792
  Percent change, 2000–2007: 1.2%

Percent change in total nonfarm employment, 2000–2007: 1.8%

Industry with the largest growth in employment, 2000–2007 (thousands)
  Education and health services, 155.8

Industry with the largest decline in employment, 2000–2007 (thousands)
  Manufacturing, -206.2

Civilian labor force
  2000: 6,085,833
  2007: 6,287,116

Employment-population ratio
  2000: 61.5%
  2007: 61.5%

Unemployment rate and rank among states
  2000: 4.2%, 33rd
  2007: 4.4%, 25th

Employment by Industry, 2007

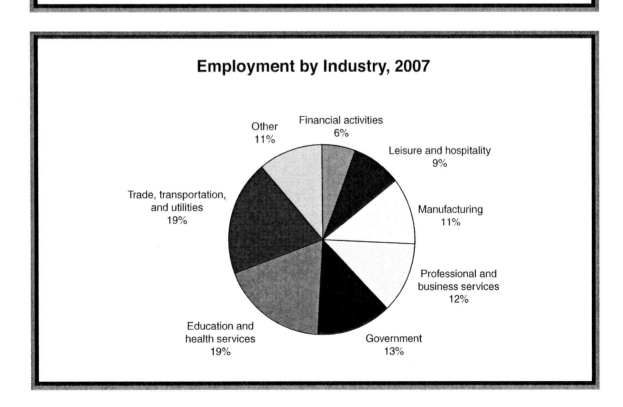

Other 11%
Financial activities 6%
Leisure and hospitality 9%
Manufacturing 11%
Professional and business services 12%
Government 13%
Education and health services 19%
Trade, transportation, and utilities 19%

Employment by Industry: Pennsylvania, 2000–2007

(Numbers in thousands, not seasonally adjusted.)

Industry and year	January	February	March	April	May	June	July	August	September	October	November	December	Annual Average
Total Nonfarm													
2000	5,547.2	5,577.0	5,635.7	5,690.1	5,730.3	5,740.2	5,688.3	5,673.7	5,734.4	5,744.8	5,766.6	5,767.1	5,691.3
2001	5,613.1	5,641.0	5,676.5	5,702.3	5,729.1	5,738.7	5,652.4	5,654.8	5,690.9	5,692.9	5,703.4	5,694.9	5,682.5
2002	5,549.6	5,575.0	5,613.8	5,647.0	5,680.8	5,692.4	5,614.3	5,614.2	5,661.8	5,681.0	5,689.2	5,670.0	5,640.8
2003	5,522.5	5,530.4	5,569.3	5,609.3	5,648.2	5,656.9	5,575.9	5,579.5	5,628.3	5,668.6	5,676.0	5,671.2	5,611.3
2004	5,507.1	5,530.4	5,582.2	5,633.9	5,674.8	5,691.9	5,628.4	5,622.1	5,679.2	5,719.0	5,732.4	5,728.7	5,644.2
2005	5,568.3	5,598.2	5,628.8	5,708.2	5,739.8	5,747.6	5,692.1	5,684.6	5,741.7	5,764.3	5,781.6	5,771.5	5,702.2
2006	5,621.9	5,656.0	5,700.7	5,760.2	5,795.2	5,800.3	5,731.5	5,729.6	5,787.3	5,821.1	5,835.1	5,834.2	5,756.1
2007	5,679.4	5,690.8	5,742.4	5,794.6	5,840.0	5,854.2	5,786.4	5,778.5	5,816.2	5,851.0	5,859.7	5,856.0	5,795.8
Total Private													
2000	4,828.7	4,840.6	4,891.3	4,943.4	4,973.9	5,020.4	5,010.1	5,005.5	5,014.5	5,009.2	5,025.2	5,031.7	4,966.2
2001	4,892.5	4,901.0	4,933.6	4,955.3	4,986.1	5,020.2	4,978.1	4,981.6	4,962.0	4,945.9	4,950.1	4,944.6	4,954.3
2002	4,814.1	4,819.6	4,856.6	4,887.4	4,926.4	4,960.3	4,932.1	4,938.9	4,925.2	4,924.7	4,925.0	4,912.3	4,901.9
2003	4,783.0	4,768.3	4,803.1	4,842.9	4,886.3	4,910.5	4,885.3	4,893.6	4,888.6	4,906.3	4,909.6	4,911.0	4,865.7
2004	4,766.0	4,770.3	4,817.1	4,866.1	4,911.1	4,947.5	4,942.8	4,942.1	4,938.5	4,959.5	4,965.8	4,970.5	4,899.8
2005	4,824.9	4,835.7	4,862.5	4,938.7	4,979.1	5,005.1	5,003.0	5,002.1	5,000.7	5,005.0	5,016.6	5,012.7	4,957.2
2006	4,882.1	4,894.6	4,936.4	4,994.2	5,031.1	5,058.0	5,044.2	5,044.1	5,043.9	5,060.1	5,066.3	5,071.5	5,010.5
2007	4,937.4	4,929.5	4,977.8	5,029.3	5,078.5	5,115.0	5,097.2	5,091.9	5,076.5	5,092.9	5,095.3	5,095.4	5,051.4
Goods-Producing													
2000	1,099.9	1,092.8	1,112.0	1,126.0	1,135.2	1,153.7	1,153.5	1,155.8	1,150.1	1,140.3	1,132.3	1,122.0	1,131.1
2001	1,096.3	1,090.4	1,095.9	1,101.6	1,105.7	1,114.7	1,105.2	1,105.1	1,093.7	1,077.5	1,063.6	1,051.0	1,091.7
2002	1,017.1	1,012.9	1,019.0	1,027.7	1,036.0	1,048.0	1,043.2	1,045.1	1,035.1	1,027.3	1,014.5	999.1	1,027.1
2003	972.6	959.4	965.5	975.1	985.1	992.8	989.3	989.0	982.4	977.7	969.0	957.8	976.3
2004	928.9	922.5	935.8	950.6	963.6	977.5	981.6	981.1	976.3	972.4	965.9	958.2	959.5
2005	928.9	921.9	928.3	948.9	961.6	973.7	975.6	976.2	969.3	964.4	961.4	947.7	954.8
2006	924.4	921.9	934.4	948.8	958.0	969.8	969.5	971.8	965.6	959.8	952.1	944.1	951.7
2007	921.6	906.3	922.4	936.5	949.1	963.0	962.6	962.2	955.3	950.3	942.5	931.4	941.9
Natural Resources and Mining													
2000	18.9	18.8	19.2	19.2	19.3	19.7	19.9	19.9	19.9	19.6	19.4	19.0	19.4
2001	18.6	18.6	18.9	19.2	19.7	20.0	20.1	20.2	20.0	19.9	19.7	19.3	19.5
2002	18.7	18.7	18.8	18.9	19.2	19.4	18.9	19.3	18.9	18.8	18.4	17.8	18.8
2003	17.2	17.1	17.3	17.5	17.8	18.1	18.3	18.3	18.4	18.4	18.3	17.9	17.9
2004	17.2	17.2	17.7	18.4	18.7	19.2	19.5	19.5	19.3	19.3	19.3	19.1	18.7
2005	18.6	18.6	18.6	19.6	19.8	20.3	20.5	20.4	20.4	20.2	20.1	19.6	19.7
2006	19.2	19.3	19.7	20.3	20.6	20.9	21.0	20.9	20.8	20.7	20.7	20.3	20.4
2007	19.9	19.8	20.2	20.9	21.3	21.8	22.0	22.1	21.8	21.7	21.5	21.0	21.2
Construction													
2000	220.5	215.9	230.3	245.0	254.5	261.7	263.9	265.3	262.3	258.6	252.8	241.6	247.7
2001	226.2	225.4	232.7	244.7	255.7	263.9	266.3	267.8	263.1	259.4	253.2	245.1	250.3
2002	225.3	224.8	231.9	243.9	253.4	260.8	264.0	265.8	260.4	258.6	252.2	240.7	248.5
2003	224.1	218.6	226.4	239.4	250.6	256.5	261.7	263.1	259.2	258.0	252.7	242.2	246.0
2004	223.8	219.9	231.3	243.7	254.1	262.0	266.7	266.5	264.9	262.4	257.1	249.5	250.2
2005	229.3	225.4	230.6	250.9	260.8	268.2	272.7	273.7	270.8	267.8	265.3	253.4	255.7
2006	237.2	236.4	245.3	258.1	265.9	272.3	274.8	276.6	274.2	270.4	263.7	256.6	261.0
2007	241.8	232.9	244.0	257.5	268.1	276.4	278.5	279.1	276.2	273.5	268.5	258.8	262.9
Manufacturing													
2000	860.5	858.1	862.5	861.8	861.4	872.3	869.7	870.6	867.9	862.1	860.1	861.4	864.0
2001	851.5	846.4	844.3	837.7	830.3	830.8	818.8	817.1	810.6	798.2	790.7	786.6	821.9
2002	773.1	769.4	768.3	764.9	763.4	767.8	760.3	760.0	755.8	749.9	743.9	740.6	759.8
2003	731.3	723.7	721.8	718.2	716.7	718.2	709.3	707.6	704.8	701.3	698.0	697.7	712.4
2004	687.9	685.4	686.8	688.5	690.8	696.3	695.4	695.1	692.1	690.7	689.5	689.6	690.7
2005	681.0	677.9	679.1	678.4	681.0	685.2	682.4	682.1	674.3	676.4	676.0	674.7	679.4
2006	668.0	666.2	669.4	670.4	671.5	676.6	673.7	674.5	670.6	668.7	667.7	667.2	670.4
2007	659.9	653.6	658.2	658.1	659.7	664.8	662.1	661.0	657.3	655.1	652.5	651.6	657.8
Service-Providing													
2000	4,447.3	4,484.2	4,523.7	4,564.1	4,595.1	4,586.5	4,534.8	4,517.9	4,584.3	4,604.5	4,634.3	4,645.1	4,560.2
2001	4,516.8	4,550.6	4,580.6	4,600.7	4,623.4	4,624.0	4,547.2	4,549.7	4,597.2	4,615.4	4,639.8	4,643.9	4,590.8
2002	4,532.5	4,562.1	4,594.8	4,619.3	4,644.8	4,644.4	4,571.1	4,569.1	4,626.7	4,653.7	4,674.7	4,670.9	4,613.7
2003	4,549.9	4,571.0	4,603.8	4,634.2	4,663.1	4,664.1	4,586.6	4,590.5	4,645.9	4,690.9	4,707.0	4,713.4	4,635.0
2004	4,578.2	4,607.9	4,646.4	4,683.3	4,711.2	4,714.4	4,646.8	4,641.0	4,702.9	4,746.6	4,766.5	4,770.5	4,684.6
2005	4,639.4	4,676.3	4,700.5	4,759.3	4,778.2	4,773.9	4,716.5	4,708.4	4,772.4	4,799.9	4,820.2	4,823.8	4,747.4
2006	4,697.5	4,734.1	4,766.3	4,811.4	4,837.2	4,830.5	4,762.0	4,757.8	4,821.7	4,861.3	4,883.0	4,890.1	4,804.4
2007	4,757.8	4,784.5	4,820.0	4,858.1	4,890.9	4,891.2	4,823.8	4,816.3	4,860.9	4,900.7	4,917.2	4,924.6	4,853.8
Trade, Transportation, and Utilities													
2000	1,112.0	1,101.1	1,106.2	1,119.0	1,125.0	1,131.0	1,119.1	1,123.4	1,131.5	1,142.5	1,164.7	1,179.3	1,129.6
2001	1,129.5	1,112.2	1,116.1	1,115.9	1,121.7	1,125.5	1,108.4	1,110.1	1,110.1	1,116.2	1,143.8	1,155.0	1,123.2
2002	1,111.4	1,094.5	1,101.1	1,101.7	1,111.9	1,115.5	1,102.3	1,104.8	1,109.1	1,117.9	1,135.7	1,148.5	1,112.9
2003	1,101.4	1,085.7	1,090.7	1,096.8	1,105.6	1,110.6	1,095.6	1,098.9	1,105.5	1,120.6	1,137.1	1,150.4	1,108.2
2004	1,102.3	1,091.8	1,097.7	1,101.9	1,111.3	1,115.4	1,104.6	1,105.2	1,110.1	1,123.9	1,142.2	1,157.3	1,113.6
2005	1,108.9	1,097.7	1,102.0	1,110.1	1,119.2	1,121.5	1,113.6	1,113.9	1,118.5	1,127.7	1,147.6	1,162.9	1,120.3
2006	1,119.6	1,103.2	1,110.5	1,115.2	1,122.7	1,123.7	1,113.6	1,115.2	1,122.2	1,135.0	1,156.5	1,172.3	1,125.8
2007	1,130.9	1,111.1	1,119.8	1,124.3	1,135.8	1,139.1	1,129.0	1,126.5	1,130.4	1,139.4	1,157.2	1,170.4	1,134.5
Wholesale Trade													
2000	221.0	221.3	223.0	227.6	227.6	229.4	228.5	228.7	227.7	228.4	228.6	228.9	226.7
2001	227.0	226.7	227.4	227.8	228.1	229.8	229.8	229.5	228.1	226.6	226.6	227.7	227.9
2002	225.4	224.3	225.2	225.3	226.8	228.3	227.9	227.3	225.9	226.5	226.8	228.6	226.4
2003	225.4	225.2	226.7	226.9	228.2	228.7	228.2	228.1	227.0	227.3	227.7	228.6	227.3
2004	225.7	225.4	227.1	227.9	229.0	231.1	231.8	231.8	230.5	231.1	231.3	232.4	229.6
2005	229.9	230.0	231.2	233.2	234.6	235.7	236.2	236.2	235.2	235.3	235.5	236.5	234.1
2006	233.3	233.8	235.0	236.7	238.2	239.9	239.7	239.9	238.6	239.0	239.0	239.3	237.7
2007	236.8	236.1	237.9	239.2	240.3	242.4	242.6	242.1	240.7	241.0	241.7	241.6	240.2

Employment by Industry: Pennsylvania, 2000–2007—*Continued*

(Numbers in thousands, not seasonally adjusted.)

Industry and year	January	February	March	April	May	June	July	August	September	October	November	December	Annual Average
Retail Trade													
2000	671.6	661.0	663.0	670.3	675.2	680.7	675.8	680.3	679.8	684.9	707.2	722.3	681.0
2001	679.7	663.3	666.5	663.8	668.0	672.5	664.3	667.3	664.7	668.9	689.9	701.6	672.5
2002	666.2	651.2	656.1	655.1	662.5	666.8	661.7	664.4	659.9	663.1	682.0	695.3	665.4
2003	657.1	642.8	646.4	650.7	656.7	662.4	657.3	660.4	657.8	667.2	683.7	697.0	661.6
2004	657.9	647.9	650.8	652.7	659.8	663.0	660.9	661.6	656.4	666.6	684.3	696.8	663.2
2005	658.2	647.0	648.6	652.9	658.7	661.2	661.3	660.9	653.5	661.0	678.4	690.0	661.0
2006	655.8	639.6	643.9	646.6	650.0	652.6	649.8	650.3	645.6	656.0	676.7	688.2	654.6
2007	655.7	637.7	642.8	645.0	653.7	656.2	656.0	654.1	647.6	653.9	671.1	681.9	654.6
Transportation and Utilities													
2000	219.4	218.8	220.2	221.1	222.2	220.9	214.8	214.4	224.0	229.2	228.9	228.1	221.8
2001	222.8	222.2	222.2	224.3	225.6	223.2	214.3	213.3	223.4	228.2	227.3	225.7	222.7
2002	219.8	219.0	219.8	221.3	222.6	220.4	212.7	213.1	223.3	228.3	226.9	225.7	221.1
2003	218.9	217.7	217.6	219.2	220.7	219.5	210.1	210.4	220.7	226.1	225.7	224.8	219.3
2004	218.7	218.5	219.8	221.3	222.5	221.3	211.9	211.8	223.2	226.2	226.6	228.1	220.8
2005	220.8	220.7	222.2	224.0	225.9	224.6	216.1	216.8	229.8	231.4	233.7	236.4	225.2
2006	230.5	229.8	231.6	231.9	234.5	231.2	224.1	225.0	238.0	240.0	240.8	244.8	233.5
2007	238.4	237.3	239.1	240.1	241.8	240.5	230.4	230.3	242.1	244.5	244.4	246.9	239.7
Information													
2000	132.5	133.2	133.8	133.3	134.7	136.8	138.6	129.4	138.9	138.6	140.2	141.3	135.9
2001	138.2	138.1	138.1	136.4	136.5	136.8	136.5	135.4	133.2	132.6	132.8	132.9	135.6
2002	130.6	130.2	130.9	129.3	129.9	129.6	128.3	127.9	126.3	125.7	126.0	125.9	128.4
2003	124.3	123.7	124.5	122.8	122.4	122.1	120.6	119.8	118.1	116.7	116.6	115.6	120.6
2004	114.1	113.4	113.4	112.7	112.8	113.2	113.1	112.2	110.8	110.4	110.3	110.2	112.2
2005	109.1	108.8	109.0	109.4	110.0	110.5	109.6	109.4	111.6	108.1	108.8	109.1	109.5
2006	107.6	108.0	107.7	108.1	108.7	108.9	108.6	108.4	108.3	108.0	107.5	108.3	108.2
2007	106.8	106.5	106.4	106.5	107.0	108.5	107.5	107.3	107.2	107.4	107.2	107.6	107.2
Financial Activities													
2000	335.9	335.4	335.9	337.0	338.0	342.2	342.1	341.4	338.4	337.8	338.8	341.1	338.7
2001	339.4	339.3	340.6	338.9	339.3	342.1	341.3	340.8	337.0	335.8	335.4	336.8	338.9
2002	334.7	334.5	335.5	335.1	336.3	339.7	340.1	340.6	337.4	335.4	335.7	337.1	336.8
2003	335.9	335.8	336.7	336.9	338.9	341.4	342.2	342.2	338.6	337.5	337.5	338.5	338.5
2004	336.5	335.4	336.4	335.4	337.0	339.0	339.8	338.6	334.3	333.4	333.2	335.2	336.2
2005	332.3	332.4	332.9	333.9	335.5	338.2	339.4	339.9	336.0	335.0	335.6	337.1	335.7
2006	333.9	333.7	334.1	334.9	335.9	339.3	338.9	337.4	333.6	332.7	332.6	333.2	335.0
2007	330.4	330.4	330.6	330.9	332.3	335.8	336.7	335.8	331.5	330.6	330.8	331.2	332.3
Professional and Business Services													
2000	589.1	592.4	603.4	611.1	611.4	619.9	623.4	625.3	621.9	616.9	616.9	616.4	612.3
2001	603.7	606.9	612.2	618.1	619.2	625.0	615.7	620.4	616.0	611.9	608.5	603.5	613.4
2002	589.0	589.9	596.7	604.8	607.0	613.3	611.6	615.5	611.1	610.6	610.4	608.4	605.7
2003	589.6	587.3	592.9	603.1	607.3	611.7	612.7	620.1	621.2	624.8	627.1	627.7	610.5
2004	610.1	611.8	620.1	631.1	634.9	644.3	645.4	649.1	647.9	654.0	654.3	653.6	638.1
2005	634.3	638.1	642.4	657.9	659.1	666.6	668.6	671.3	669.9	672.9	673.0	671.3	660.5
2006	653.8	658.9	666.9	679.1	682.6	692.3	693.0	697.3	696.1	701.4	701.8	700.4	685.3
2007	679.9	681.6	688.1	701.9	705.8	715.5	714.0	715.6	710.9	714.1	712.2	712.7	704.4
Education and Health Services													
2000	902.4	925.8	924.8	924.3	916.3	903.7	897.5	895.7	919.4	933.6	940.4	938.8	918.6
2001	917.5	941.2	946.0	944.9	937.2	928.4	923.7	922.6	944.2	956.0	963.8	962.7	940.7
2002	948.9	971.2	974.9	971.6	963.3	953.0	945.4	942.8	965.3	980.6	985.7	976.8	965.0
2003	965.6	985.5	989.7	988.8	979.6	967.6	957.9	954.2	977.9	998.2	1,002.1	998.7	980.5
2004	975.1	997.4	1,003.4	1,005.0	996.7	983.7	980.8	975.5	1,000.7	1,021.3	1,026.9	1,024.1	999.2
2005	1,005.1	1,029.6	1,030.2	1,037.9	1,027.7	1,010.3	1,010.4	1,006.5	1,034.4	1,055.3	1,058.7	1,054.4	1,030.0
2006	1,032.7	1,057.6	1,058.7	1,064.2	1,056.1	1,036.7	1,033.0	1,029.4	1,057.2	1,074.8	1,078.3	1,073.8	1,054.4
2007	1,052.3	1,076.0	1,081.2	1,082.5	1,074.1	1,056.4	1,052.8	1,050.4	1,074.3	1,096.4	1,100.5	1,095.7	1,074.4
Leisure and Hospitality													
2000	413.2	415.2	426.7	442.4	462.2	478.8	481.1	481.0	463.7	448.9	440.8	440.9	449.6
2001	420.3	424.2	431.7	445.8	470.1	487.9	488.1	488.7	466.5	452.7	445.6	444.9	455.5
2002	428.0	430.6	440.8	458.6	481.8	497.6	497.9	499.8	482.0	468.3	458.3	457.0	466.7
2003	437.4	435.1	444.7	460.4	486.3	500.4	502.9	506.4	485.2	470.9	460.7	461.8	471.0
2004	441.1	440.1	449.1	467.6	491.1	506.5	508.9	512.9	493.9	479.6	469.0	467.6	477.3
2005	446.1	446.5	455.6	477.9	502.4	518.3	519.6	521.4	501.6	483.0	473.1	472.5	484.8
2006	454.4	455.5	466.8	485.0	506.9	524.6	525.0	524.0	503.4	491.4	481.2	483.1	491.8
2007	463.0	464.8	474.9	490.7	516.5	535.7	532.8	534.1	510.0	497.8	487.9	488.5	499.7
Other Services													
2000	243.7	244.7	248.5	250.3	251.1	254.3	254.8	253.5	250.6	250.6	251.1	251.9	250.4
2001	247.6	248.7	253.0	253.7	256.4	259.8	259.2	258.5	255.2	255.7	256.6	257.8	255.2
2002	254.4	255.8	257.7	258.6	260.2	263.6	263.3	262.4	258.9	258.9	258.7	259.5	259.3
2003	256.2	255.8	258.4	259.0	261.1	263.9	264.1	263.0	259.7	259.9	259.5	260.5	260.1
2004	257.9	257.9	261.2	261.8	263.7	267.9	268.6	267.5	264.5	264.5	264.0	264.3	263.7
2005	260.2	260.7	262.1	262.7	263.6	266.0	266.2	263.5	259.4	258.4	258.4	257.7	261.6
2006	255.7	255.8	257.3	258.9	260.2	262.7	262.6	260.6	257.5	257.0	256.3	256.3	258.4
2007	252.5	252.8	254.4	256.0	257.9	261.0	261.8	260.0	256.9	256.9	257.0	257.9	257.1
Government													
2000	718.5	736.4	744.4	746.7	756.4	719.8	678.2	668.2	719.9	735.6	741.4	735.4	725.1
2001	720.6	740.0	742.9	747.0	743.0	718.5	674.3	673.2	728.9	747.0	753.3	750.3	728.3
2002	735.5	755.4	757.2	759.6	754.4	732.1	682.2	675.3	736.6	756.3	764.2	757.7	738.9
2003	739.5	762.1	766.2	766.4	761.9	746.4	690.6	685.9	739.7	762.3	766.4	760.2	745.6
2004	741.1	760.1	765.1	767.8	763.7	744.4	685.0	680.0	740.7	759.5	766.6	758.2	744.4
2005	743.4	762.5	766.3	769.5	760.7	742.5	689.1	682.5	741.0	759.3	765.0	758.8	745.1
2006	739.8	761.4	764.3	766.0	764.1	742.3	687.3	685.5	743.4	761.0	768.8	762.7	745.6
2007	742.0	761.3	764.6	765.3	761.5	739.2	689.2	686.6	739.7	758.1	764.4	760.6	744.4

Average Weekly Hours by Selected Industry: Pennsylvania, 2001–2007

(Not seasonally adjusted.)

Industry and year	January	February	March	April	May	June	July	August	September	October	November	December	Annual Average
Manufacturing													
2001	40.6	40.3	40.6	39.7	40.3	40.3	40.2	40.3	40.6	40.2	40.6	40.6	40.4
2002	39.6	39.9	40.5	40.3	40.5	40.6	40.4	40.7	40.7	40.5	40.4	39.8	40.3
2003	39.7	39.3	40.0	39.6	40.0	40.2	39.6	40.0	40.2	40.3	40.7	40.7	40.0
2004	40.3	40.2	40.4	40.0	40.3	40.4	40.4	40.6	40.2	40.4	40.4	40.2	40.3
2005	40.2	40.5	40.5	40.3	40.4	40.6	40.7	40.7	40.8	40.4	40.3	40.5	40.5
2006	40.6	40.5	40.7	40.8	41.1	41.0	40.9	40.9	40.9	40.9	40.9	40.8	40.8
2007	40.9	40.7	41.1	41.0	40.9	41.0	41.0	41.0	41.1	41.3	41.3	41.4	41.1

Average Hourly Earnings by Selected Industry: Pennsylvania, 2001–2007

(Dollars, not seasonally adjusted.)

Industry and year	January	February	March	April	May	June	July	August	September	October	November	December	Annual Average
Manufacturing													
2001	14.26	14.22	14.22	14.23	14.33	14.31	14.41	14.47	14.43	14.43	14.52	14.61	14.37
2002	14.58	14.61	14.62	14.65	14.63	14.66	14.80	14.79	14.91	14.89	14.87	14.99	14.75
2003	14.91	14.97	15.00	14.96	14.93	14.96	14.96	14.98	15.02	14.99	15.06	15.07	14.99
2004	15.04	15.10	15.08	15.06	15.15	15.12	15.14	15.17	15.24	15.25	15.25	15.24	15.16
2005	15.19	15.20	15.24	15.20	15.26	15.26	15.27	15.29	15.29	15.32	15.29	15.31	15.26
2006	15.32	15.34	15.38	15.36	15.39	15.35	15.36	15.35	15.40	15.43	15.41	15.45	15.38
2007	15.46	15.49	15.50	15.45	15.46	15.46	15.44	15.48	15.44	15.45	15.52	15.59	15.48

Average Weekly Earnings by Selected Industry: Pennsylvania, 2001–2007

(Dollars, not seasonally adjusted.)

Industry and year	January	February	March	April	May	June	July	August	September	October	November	December	Annual Average
Manufacturing													
2001	578.96	573.07	577.33	564.93	577.50	576.69	579.28	583.14	585.86	580.09	589.51	593.17	580.55
2002	577.37	582.94	592.11	590.40	592.52	595.20	597.92	601.95	606.84	603.05	600.75	596.60	594.43
2003	591.93	588.32	600.00	592.42	597.20	601.39	592.42	599.20	603.80	604.10	612.94	613.35	599.60
2004	606.11	607.02	609.23	602.40	610.55	610.85	611.66	615.90	612.65	616.10	616.10	612.65	610.95
2005	610.64	615.60	617.22	612.56	616.50	619.56	621.49	622.30	623.83	618.93	616.19	620.06	618.03
2006	621.99	621.27	625.97	626.69	632.53	629.35	628.22	627.82	629.86	631.09	630.27	630.36	627.50
2007	632.31	630.44	637.05	633.45	632.31	633.86	633.04	634.68	634.58	638.09	640.98	645.43	636.23

RHODE ISLAND
At a Glance

Population
    2000 census: 1,048,319
    2007 estimate: 1,057,832
    Percent change, 2000–2007: 0.9%

Percent change in total nonfarm employment, 2000–2007: 3.4%

Industry with the largest growth in employment, 2000–2007 (thousands)
    Education and health services, 16.2

Industry with the largest decline in employment, 2000–2007 (thousands)
    Manufacturing, -20.3

Civilian labor force
    2000: 543,404
    2007: 576,987

Employment-population ratio
    2000: 64.0%
    2007: 65.4%

Unemployment rate and rank among states
    2000: 4.2%, 33rd
    2007: 5.0%, 39th

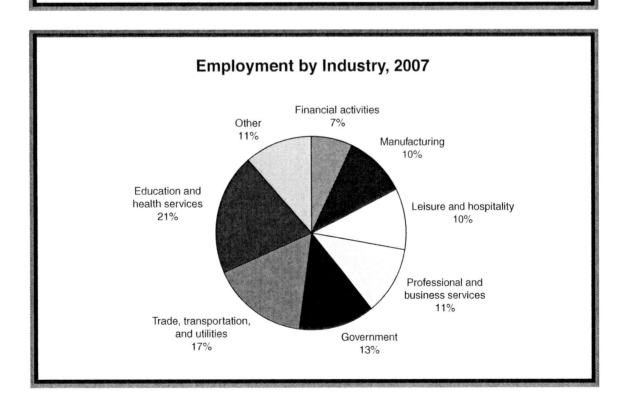

Employment by Industry, 2007

Financial activities 7%
Other 11%
Manufacturing 10%
Education and health services 21%
Leisure and hospitality 10%
Professional and business services 11%
Trade, transportation, and utilities 17%
Government 13%

Employment by Industry: Rhode Island, 2000–2007

(Numbers in thousands, not seasonally adjusted.)

Industry and year	January	February	March	April	May	June	July	August	September	October	November	December	Annual Average
Total Nonfarm													
2000	460.2	462.3	467.3	475.0	482.0	481.8	474.1	476.1	482.2	485.3	486.7	487.6	476.7
2001	468.4	471.0	472.8	479.1	483.2	484.2	474.1	478.5	481.8	482.6	482.1	483.1	478.4
2002	466.0	467.1	471.4	478.6	484.3	485.3	475.4	479.5	484.7	486.0	487.1	487.2	479.4
2003	469.9	469.9	473.5	482.0	489.4	490.7	482.7	485.1	490.5	492.1	492.8	492.4	484.3
2004	473.2	475.5	478.5	486.0	494.4	494.7	487.7	489.3	494.7	496.4	496.5	495.3	488.5
2005	475.8	478.6	481.0	491.0	495.7	498.1	491.2	492.8	497.5	496.7	497.8	496.1	491.0
2006	475.5	478.5	482.9	494.0	497.3	500.6	491.4	493.8	500.6	501.5	501.9	501.3	493.3
2007	481.9	483.5	485.9	493.2	499.4	501.4	493.1	492.6	496.0	497.1	496.1	495.2	493.0
Total Private													
2000	395.8	397.9	402.1	409.8	414.5	417.7	412.7	415.9	418.8	420.0	420.9	421.8	412.3
2001	403.0	405.4	407.0	413.2	416.8	418.6	412.4	417.3	417.3	416.4	415.1	415.9	413.2
2002	399.3	400.3	404.3	411.4	416.6	418.6	413.5	417.8	419.4	419.1	419.7	419.6	413.3
2003	402.8	402.8	406.1	414.8	421.7	422.9	420.7	423.0	424.8	425.4	426.0	425.5	418.0
2004	407.1	409.2	411.6	419.8	427.4	428.0	425.7	427.5	429.5	430.5	430.0	429.5	423.0
2005	410.3	412.8	415.1	425.2	429.6	432.2	429.7	432.1	433.4	430.9	431.7	430.2	426.1
2006	410.1	412.6	417.0	428.4	431.5	435.0	430.1	432.8	435.9	435.8	435.5	435.3	428.3
2007	416.7	418.1	420.6	427.9	433.4	436.5	431.6	431.4	432.1	431.7	430.4	429.6	428.3
Goods-Producing													
2000	87.1	87.2	88.2	88.6	90.0	91.5	86.6	90.8	91.3	91.6	91.1	90.7	89.5
2001	87.8	87.7	87.8	88.5	88.3	88.4	83.8	87.3	87.3	86.8	85.4	85.0	87.0
2002	81.1	81.0	81.9	82.1	83.0	83.6	79.4	82.8	82.7	82.2	82.0	80.9	81.9
2003	77.5	76.3	77.0	79.2	80.3	81.0	78.5	81.3	81.8	81.3	81.1	79.9	79.6
2004	75.5	75.0	75.4	77.5	78.5	79.5	77.8	79.8	79.9	80.3	79.9	79.1	78.2
2005	74.8	74.2	74.5	77.1	78.0	79.1	76.4	78.7	78.6	77.6	77.8	76.8	77.0
2006	73.1	72.8	73.4	76.0	76.7	77.8	75.5	77.5	77.3	76.9	76.4	76.0	75.8
2007	72.6	71.6	71.9	73.0	74.1	74.9	72.9	74.3	74.1	73.5	72.7	72.2	73.2
Natural Resources and Mining													
2000	0.2	0.2	0.2	0.2	0.2	0.2	0.2	0.2	0.2	0.3	0.3	0.2	0.2
2001	0.2	0.2	0.2	0.2	0.3	0.3	0.3	0.3	0.2	0.3	0.2	0.2	0.2
2002	0.2	0.2	0.2	0.2	0.2	0.2	0.3	0.2	0.2	0.2	0.2	0.2	0.2
2003	0.2	0.1	0.2	0.2	0.2	0.2	0.2	0.2	0.2	0.2	0.2	0.2	0.2
2004	0.2	0.2	0.2	0.2	0.2	0.2	0.2	0.2	0.3	0.3	0.3	0.3	0.2
2005	0.2	0.2	0.2	0.3	0.3	0.3	0.3	0.3	0.3	0.3	0.3	0.3	0.3
2006	0.2	0.2	0.2	0.3	0.3	0.3	0.3	0.3	0.3	0.3	0.3	0.3	0.3
2007	0.2	0.2	0.2	0.3	0.3	0.3	0.3	0.3	0.3	0.3	0.3	0.3	0.3
Construction													
2000	16.4	15.8	17.0	17.8	18.3	18.9	19.1	19.1	19.1	19.0	18.9	18.4	18.1
2001	16.6	16.5	16.9	18.6	19.2	19.8	20.3	20.5	20.3	20.0	19.8	19.5	19.0
2002	17.4	17.3	18.0	19.1	19.9	20.4	20.4	20.6	20.5	20.1	19.9	19.4	19.4
2003	17.2	16.6	17.3	19.6	21.1	21.8	22.8	23.0	23.0	22.7	22.4	21.5	20.8
2004	18.6	18.0	18.4	20.3	21.1	21.8	22.5	22.4	22.3	22.4	22.2	21.6	21.0
2005	18.8	18.3	18.6	21.3	22.3	23.4	23.5	23.6	23.5	22.8	23.1	22.2	21.8
2006	19.8	19.4	20.0	22.5	23.3	24.3	24.4	24.7	24.4	24.0	23.7	23.3	22.8
2007	21.0	19.9	20.4	21.6	22.7	23.4	23.5	23.3	22.8	22.4	22.1	21.7	22.1
Manufacturing													
2000	70.5	71.2	71.0	70.6	71.5	72.4	67.3	71.5	72.0	72.3	71.9	72.1	71.1
2001	71.0	71.0	70.7	69.7	68.8	68.3	63.2	66.5	66.8	66.5	65.4	65.3	67.8
2002	63.5	63.5	63.7	62.8	62.9	63.0	58.7	62.0	62.0	61.9	61.9	61.3	62.3
2003	60.1	59.6	59.5	59.4	59.0	59.0	55.5	58.1	58.6	58.4	58.5	58.2	58.7
2004	56.7	56.8	56.8	57.0	57.2	57.5	55.1	57.2	57.3	57.6	57.4	57.2	57.0
2005	55.8	55.7	55.7	55.5	55.4	55.4	52.6	54.8	54.8	54.5	54.4	54.3	54.9
2006	53.1	53.2	53.2	53.2	53.1	53.2	50.8	52.5	52.6	52.6	52.4	52.4	52.7
2007	51.4	51.5	51.3	51.1	51.1	51.2	49.1	50.7	51.0	50.8	50.3	50.2	50.8
Service-Providing													
2000	373.1	375.1	379.1	386.4	392.0	390.3	387.5	385.3	390.9	393.7	395.6	396.9	387.2
2001	380.6	383.3	385.0	390.6	394.9	395.8	390.3	391.2	394.5	395.8	396.7	398.1	391.4
2002	384.9	386.1	389.5	396.5	401.3	401.7	396.0	396.7	402.0	403.8	405.1	406.3	397.5
2003	392.4	393.6	396.5	402.8	409.1	409.7	404.2	403.8	408.7	410.8	411.7	412.5	404.7
2004	397.7	400.5	403.1	408.5	415.9	415.2	409.9	409.5	414.8	416.1	416.6	416.2	410.3
2005	401.0	404.4	406.5	413.9	417.7	419.0	414.8	414.1	418.9	419.1	420.0	419.3	414.1
2006	402.4	405.7	409.5	418.0	420.6	422.8	415.9	416.3	423.3	424.6	425.5	425.3	417.5
2007	409.3	411.9	414.0	420.2	425.3	426.5	420.2	418.3	421.9	423.6	423.4	423.0	419.8
Trade, Transportation, and Utilities													
2000	77.5	76.9	77.1	79.0	79.1	79.3	78.3	79.2	80.3	81.3	83.0	84.2	79.6
2001	78.9	77.9	77.7	78.5	78.6	79.7	78.7	78.8	79.2	79.8	81.4	82.4	79.3
2002	79.0	77.7	77.9	79.1	79.9	81.0	80.0	80.1	81.2	82.0	83.3	84.5	80.5
2003	79.6	78.5	78.6	79.3	80.4	81.3	80.2	80.4	81.3	81.9	83.4	84.3	80.8
2004	79.7	78.9	78.8	78.3	80.2	80.8	79.8	79.6	80.2	81.1	82.2	83.1	80.2
2005	78.9	78.3	78.3	79.3	79.9	80.7	79.8	80.0	80.1	80.7	82.1	83.1	80.1
2006	78.6	77.7	78.0	79.2	79.5	80.2	79.0	79.0	79.9	80.6	82.1	83.2	79.8
2007	79.1	78.0	78.2	78.9	79.7	80.6	79.8	79.4	79.7	80.2	81.5	82.2	79.8
Wholesale Trade													
2000	15.7	15.9	16.0	16.5	16.5	16.7	16.5	16.7	16.8	17.0	17.1	17.2	16.5
2001	16.0	16.2	16.3	16.5	16.5	16.6	16.6	16.7	16.6	16.7	16.7	16.8	16.5
2002	16.5	16.3	16.4	16.5	16.6	16.7	16.4	16.4	16.3	16.4	16.5	16.4	16.5
2003	16.4	16.2	16.3	16.4	16.6	16.7	16.5	16.4	16.4	16.4	16.4	16.3	16.4
2004	16.1	16.0	16.1	16.3	16.4	16.6	16.6	16.6	16.5	16.6	16.6	16.7	16.4
2005	16.3	16.4	16.5	16.8	16.9	17.0	16.9	17.0	16.9	16.9	16.9	17.0	16.8
2006	16.7	16.7	16.8	17.0	17.0	17.1	17.1	17.1	17.1	17.1	17.2	17.2	17.0
2007	17.0	16.9	16.9	17.2	17.3	17.3	17.3	17.2	17.0	17.1	17.0	17.0	17.1

Employment by Industry: Rhode Island, 2000–2007—*Continued*

(Numbers in thousands, not seasonally adjusted.)

Industry and year	January	February	March	April	May	June	July	August	September	October	November	December	Annual Average
Retail Trade													
2000	51.1	50.4	50.4	51.5	51.5	51.5	51.2	51.7	52.3	53.0	54.7	55.8	52.1
2001	52.0	50.7	50.4	50.7	50.9	51.8	51.3	51.4	51.3	51.7	53.3	54.4	51.7
2002	51.7	50.9	51.0	51.8	52.4	53.1	53.1	53.3	53.7	54.2	55.5	56.8	53.1
2003	52.4	51.5	51.3	51.8	52.4	53.1	52.9	53.3	53.3	54.0	55.5	56.5	53.2
2004	52.6	52.0	51.8	51.7	52.5	53.0	52.9	52.8	52.5	53.5	54.7	55.4	53.0
2005	52.1	51.4	51.3	51.7	52.0	52.5	52.2	52.2	51.9	52.6	54.0	54.8	52.4
2006	51.3	50.4	50.6	51.3	51.4	51.8	51.4	51.3	51.4	52.1	53.6	54.6	51.8
2007	51.3	50.5	50.7	50.7	51.3	51.9	51.8	51.5	51.2	51.7	53.2	54.0	51.7
Transportation and Utilities													
2000	10.7	10.6	10.7	11.0	11.1	11.1	10.6	10.8	11.2	11.3	11.2	11.2	10.9
2001	10.9	11.0	11.0	11.3	11.2	11.3	10.8	10.7	11.3	11.4	11.4	11.2	11.1
2002	10.8	10.5	10.5	10.8	10.9	11.2	10.5	10.4	11.2	11.4	11.3	11.3	10.9
2003	10.8	10.8	11.0	11.1	11.4	11.5	10.8	10.7	11.6	11.5	11.5	11.5	11.2
2004	11.0	10.9	10.9	10.3	11.3	11.2	10.3	10.2	11.2	11.0	10.9	11.0	10.9
2005	10.5	10.5	10.5	10.8	11.0	11.2	10.7	10.8	11.3	11.2	11.2	11.3	10.9
2006	10.6	10.6	10.6	10.9	11.1	11.3	10.5	10.6	11.4	11.3	11.3	11.4	11.0
2007	10.8	10.6	10.6	11.0	11.1	11.4	10.7	10.7	11.5	11.4	11.3	11.2	11.0
Information													
2000	10.8	10.9	10.8	10.9	11.0	11.2	11.2	10.0	11.1	11.1	11.1	11.1	10.9
2001	11.1	11.1	11.1	11.2	11.4	11.4	11.4	11.3	11.3	11.2	11.2	11.3	11.3
2002	11.3	11.2	11.3	11.2	11.2	11.3	11.3	11.2	11.2	10.9	11.1	11.2	11.2
2003	11.1	11.1	11.0	11.0	11.0	11.2	11.0	11.0	10.8	11.0	11.0	10.9	11.0
2004	11.1	11.0	11.1	11.1	11.0	10.9	10.7	10.7	10.6	10.6	10.6	10.6	10.8
2005	10.8	10.8	10.7	10.7	10.7	10.7	10.8	10.8	10.7	10.8	10.9	11.0	10.8
2006	11.0	10.9	11.0	11.3	11.3	11.4	10.8	10.7	10.7	10.6	10.8	10.9	11.0
2007	10.5	10.4	10.5	10.5	10.5	10.5	10.5	10.5	10.5	10.4	10.5	10.7	10.8	10.5
Financial Activities													
2000	30.0	30.0	30.2	30.7	30.5	31.4	32.0	31.7	31.6	31.5	31.7	32.0	31.1
2001	32.0	32.1	32.3	32.0	32.0	32.5	32.5	32.3	32.2	32.2	32.2	32.4	32.2
2002	32.3	32.3	32.2	32.6	32.6	32.9	33.3	33.2	33.1	33.2	33.3	33.6	32.9
2003	33.1	33.2	33.5	33.2	33.5	33.9	34.0	34.0	33.8	33.8	33.9	34.1	33.7
2004	33.8	33.8	33.8	33.9	34.2	34.3	34.2	34.2	34.0	34.1	34.1	34.1	34.0
2005	33.7	33.8	33.8	34.3	34.3	34.5	34.7	34.7	34.5	34.2	34.3	34.6	34.3
2006	34.2	34.1	34.4	34.5	34.8	34.9	35.2	35.6	35.7	35.6	35.7	36.1	35.1
2007	35.2	35.3	35.2	35.3	35.4	35.3	35.0	34.6	34.6	34.5	34.4	34.5	34.9
Professional and Business Services													
2000	48.2	48.4	49.5	50.9	51.5	52.2	51.0	51.4	51.8	51.9	51.7	51.9	50.8
2001	48.4	48.9	49.0	50.6	50.7	51.1	50.7	51.5	51.6	51.8	50.9	50.6	50.5
2002	47.2	47.0	47.7	49.4	49.4	50.1	48.9	49.3	49.7	49.7	49.4	48.8	48.9
2003	46.4	46.5	47.0	49.2	49.8	50.9	50.9	51.5	51.4	52.2	52.0	52.0	50.0
2004	49.9	50.3	50.9	53.2	53.7	54.5	54.3	55.0	55.4	55.6	55.2	54.7	53.6
2005	51.8	52.2	52.7	55.2	55.3	55.9	56.2	56.9	57.2	56.2	56.2	55.8	55.1
2006	52.6	53.0	53.6	56.6	56.8	57.9	56.9	57.8	58.7	58.4	57.8	57.3	56.5
2007	54.3	54.0	54.3	56.4	57.1	58.1	56.9	57.0	56.6	56.7	56.3	56.0	56.1
Education and Health Services													
2000	81.1	83.2	84.0	84.8	84.8	80.2	80.3	80.0	83.2	85.0	86.1	86.1	83.2
2001	83.0	85.4	86.2	86.1	86.3	82.0	81.2	82.1	84.8	86.5	87.5	88.0	84.9
2002	85.6	87.7	88.7	88.9	89.1	84.6	84.0	85.1	88.4	90.3	91.5	92.2	88.0
2003	89.6	91.6	92.6	93.0	93.2	88.0	87.1	86.6	90.3	92.6	93.4	93.7	91.0
2004	90.8	93.3	94.4	95.0	95.2	89.9	89.1	88.9	92.7	94.6	95.4	95.9	92.9
2005	92.7	95.2	96.2	96.7	96.6	92.5	92.0	91.7	96.0	97.9	98.5	97.8	95.3
2006	94.0	97.4	98.6	99.2	98.2	94.4	93.4	93.1	96.8	99.7	100.5	100.0	97.1
2007	96.9	100.1	101.0	101.3	100.9	96.9	95.7	95.5	99.3	101.4	101.8	101.4	99.4
Leisure and Hospitality													
2000	41.1	41.2	41.9	44.3	47.0	50.8	52.0	51.4	48.6	46.6	45.4	44.8	46.2
2001	41.1	41.7	42.2	45.4	48.4	51.8	52.4	52.2	49.8	47.0	45.2	44.8	46.8
2002	41.7	42.3	43.4	46.6	49.6	52.7	53.9	53.5	51.0	48.5	46.8	45.8	48.0
2003	43.3	43.4	44.0	47.1	50.4	53.1	55.2	54.6	52.3	49.6	47.9	47.2	49.0
2004	43.6	44.1	44.3	47.7	51.2	54.4	55.8	55.5	53.4	50.7	49.0	48.5	49.9
2005	44.7	45.4	45.8	48.8	51.4	55.1	55.8	55.3	53.2	50.5	48.8	48.1	50.2
2006	44.4	44.5	45.6	48.7	51.1	54.8	55.6	55.5	53.7	50.7	48.9	48.6	50.2
2007	45.5	46.0	46.7	49.5	52.4	56.3	56.9	56.5	54.4	51.8	49.9	49.4	51.3
Other Services													
2000	20.0	20.1	20.4	20.6	20.6	21.1	21.3	21.4	20.9	21.0	20.8	21.0	20.8
2001	20.7	20.6	20.7	20.9	21.1	21.7	21.7	21.8	21.1	21.1	21.3	21.4	21.2
2002	21.1	21.1	21.2	21.5	21.8	22.4	22.7	22.6	22.1	22.3	22.3	22.6	22.0
2003	22.2	22.2	22.4	22.8	23.1	23.5	23.8	23.6	23.1	23.0	23.3	23.4	23.0
2004	22.7	22.8	22.9	23.1	23.4	23.7	24.0	23.8	23.3	23.5	23.6	23.5	23.4
2005	22.9	22.9	23.1	23.1	23.4	23.7	24.0	24.0	23.1	23.0	23.1	23.0	23.3
2006	22.2	22.2	22.4	22.9	23.1	23.6	23.7	23.6	23.1	23.3	23.3	23.2	23.1
2007	22.6	22.7	22.8	23.0	23.3	23.9	23.9	23.6	23.0	23.1	23.1	23.1	23.2
Government													
2000	64.4	64.4	65.2	65.2	67.5	64.1	61.4	60.2	63.4	65.3	65.8	65.8	64.3
2001	65.4	65.6	65.8	65.9	66.4	65.6	61.7	61.2	64.5	66.2	67.0	67.2	65.2
2002	66.7	66.8	67.1	67.2	67.7	66.7	61.9	61.7	65.3	66.9	67.4	67.6	66.1
2003	67.1	67.1	67.4	67.2	67.7	67.8	62.0	62.1	65.7	66.7	66.8	66.9	66.2
2004	66.1	66.3	66.9	66.2	67.0	66.7	62.0	61.8	65.2	65.9	66.5	65.8	65.5
2005	65.5	65.8	65.9	65.8	66.1	65.9	61.5	60.7	64.1	65.8	66.1	65.9	64.9
2006	65.4	65.9	65.9	65.6	65.8	65.6	61.3	61.0	64.7	65.7	66.4	66.0	64.9
2007	65.2	65.4	65.3	65.3	66.0	64.9	61.5	61.2	63.9	65.4	65.7	65.6	64.6

Average Weekly Hours by Selected Industry: Rhode Island, 2001–2007

(Not seasonally adjusted.)

Industry and year	January	February	March	April	May	June	July	August	September	October	November	December	Annual Average
Manufacturing													
2001	39.2	39.3	39.8	38.2	39.9	40.2	38.5	38.8	40.0	38.7	39.6	40.4	39.4
2002	38.4	38.7	38.4	38.7	38.8	39.3	37.4	37.8	39.4	39.1	38.7	40.0	38.7
2003	38.3	38.4	39.3	38.5	39.6	39.5	38.3	39.1	39.7	39.2	40.1	40.9	39.3
2004	39.5	39.3	39.8	39.2	39.1	39.6	38.3	38.9	39.6	39.1	38.8	38.9	39.2
2005	37.9	37.9	37.9	38.4	38.7	38.9	38.6	38.3	39.3	38.7	38.5	37.9	38.4
2006	38.4	38.9	38.6	37.5	39.1	38.7	38.9	39.1	39.2	39.7	39.2	39.9	38.9
2007	39.3	39.3	39.0	38.2	39.6	39.4	38.6	39.5	39.3	39.3	39.5	39.4	39.2

Average Hourly Earnings by Selected Industry: Rhode Island, 2001–2007

(Dollars, not seasonally adjusted.)

Industry and year	January	February	March	April	May	June	July	August	September	October	November	December	Annual Average
Manufacturing													
2001	12.68	12.68	12.68	12.78	12.58	12.66	12.65	12.72	12.77	12.63	12.68	12.70	12.68
2002	12.63	12.76	12.64	12.74	12.72	12.74	12.70	12.79	12.84	12.80	12.81	12.84	12.75
2003	12.78	12.78	12.82	12.84	12.87	12.86	12.87	12.90	12.88	12.93	13.01	12.97	12.88
2004	12.95	12.97	12.99	13.00	13.06	13.04	13.08	13.04	12.99	13.03	13.08	13.12	13.03
2005	13.05	13.00	12.99	13.04	13.00	13.06	13.11	13.15	13.20	13.24	13.31	13.30	13.12
2006	13.31	13.34	13.46	13.51	13.42	13.49	13.38	13.43	13.45	13.44	13.43	13.39	13.42
2007	13.46	13.50	13.47	13.64	13.75	13.92	13.91	13.94	13.90	13.92	13.99	13.98	13.78

Average Weekly Earnings by Selected Industry: Rhode Island, 2001–2007

(Dollars, not seasonally adjusted.)

Industry and year	January	February	March	April	May	June	July	August	September	October	November	December	Annual Average
Manufacturing													
2001	497.06	498.32	504.66	488.20	501.94	508.93	487.03	493.54	510.80	488.78	502.13	513.08	499.59
2002	484.99	493.81	485.38	493.04	493.54	500.68	474.98	483.46	505.90	500.48	495.75	513.60	493.43
2003	489.47	490.75	503.83	494.34	509.65	507.97	492.92	504.39	511.34	506.86	521.70	530.47	506.18
2004	511.53	509.72	517.00	509.60	510.65	516.38	500.96	507.26	514.40	509.47	507.50	510.37	510.78
2005	494.60	492.70	492.32	500.74	503.10	508.03	506.05	503.65	518.76	512.39	512.44	504.07	503.81
2006	511.10	518.93	519.56	506.63	524.72	522.06	520.48	525.11	527.24	533.57	526.46	534.26	522.04
2007	528.98	530.55	525.33	521.05	544.50	548.45	536.93	550.63	546.27	547.06	552.61	550.81	540.18

Population
    2000 census: 4,012,012
    2007 estimate: 4,407,709
    Percent change, 2000–2007: 9.9%

Percent change in total nonfarm employment, 2000–2007: 4.9%

Industry with the largest growth in employment, 2000–2007 (thousands)
    Education and health services, 44.8

Industry with the largest decline in employment, 2000–2007 (thousands)
    Manufacturing, -86.1

Civilian labor force
    2000: 1,972,850
    2007: 2,136,516

Employment-population ratio
    2000: 62.8%
    2007: 59.7%

Unemployment rate and rank among states
    2000: 3.6%, 20th
    2007: 5.9%, 48th

Employment by Industry, 2007

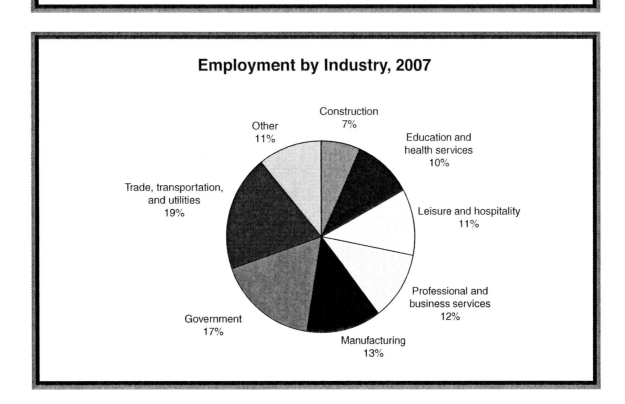

Other 11%

Construction 7%

Education and health services 10%

Leisure and hospitality 11%

Trade, transportation, and utilities 19%

Professional and business services 12%

Government 17%

Manufacturing 13%

Employment by Industry: South Carolina, 2000–2007

(Numbers in thousands, not seasonally adjusted.)

Industry and year	January	February	March	April	May	June	July	August	September	October	November	December	Annual Average
Total Nonfarm													
2000	1,824.0	1,836.7	1,862.4	1,868.4	1,887.1	1,900.5	1,834.5	1,851.9	1,851.5	1,861.2	1,864.4	1,866.3	1,859.1
2001	1,808.5	1,816.8	1,832.8	1,837.1	1,842.7	1,842.1	1,804.9	1,827.1	1,826.2	1,812.0	1,814.2	1,811.4	1,823.0
2002	1,761.6	1,773.0	1,794.3	1,812.5	1,823.8	1,829.5	1,784.5	1,813.9	1,813.9	1,814.3	1,813.8	1,813.7	1,804.1
2003	1,776.7	1,789.6	1,806.2	1,812.7	1,822.3	1,821.5	1,785.1	1,812.0	1,814.5	1,814.1	1,814.1	1,817.3	1,807.2
2004	1,781.0	1,790.7	1,815.8	1,835.6	1,848.0	1,851.3	1,816.7	1,842.7	1,846.2	1,852.5	1,857.7	1,857.4	1,833.0
2005	1,820.5	1,833.9	1,845.9	1,869.5	1,880.0	1,869.3	1,852.2	1,880.9	1,879.0	1,886.6	1,895.3	1,884.7	1,866.5
2006	1,859.4	1,877.8	1,898.7	1,916.0	1,925.1	1,905.7	1,875.8	1,902.7	1,910.1	1,931.8	1,935.7	1,943.0	1,906.8
2007	1,904.3	1,916.2	1,939.6	1,944.6	1,958.0	1,966.4	1,937.7	1,969.7	1,963.4	1,970.0	1,972.4	1,961.0	1,950.3
Total Private													
2000	1,502.4	1,512.1	1,533.9	1,541.3	1,554.1	1,570.4	1,539.7	1,540.0	1,530.6	1,535.2	1,536.6	1,538.1	1,536.2
2001	1,485.8	1,490.0	1,504.9	1,510.2	1,516.1	1,520.1	1,515.2	1,513.5	1,500.2	1,483.2	1,483.5	1,479.4	1,500.2
2002	1,436.2	1,444.2	1,464.3	1,482.4	1,493.2	1,505.1	1,493.5	1,494.7	1,485.4	1,483.4	1,480.4	1,480.1	1,478.6
2003	1,448.5	1,456.6	1,472.6	1,479.3	1,489.9	1,496.9	1,491.8	1,495.7	1,486.7	1,485.0	1,483.6	1,485.8	1,481.0
2004	1,454.6	1,462.6	1,486.0	1,505.0	1,517.7	1,528.2	1,527.2	1,526.7	1,518.9	1,522.2	1,526.0	1,525.5	1,508.4
2005	1,493.5	1,503.6	1,514.3	1,537.4	1,548.0	1,542.9	1,558.7	1,563.2	1,546.4	1,551.3	1,557.5	1,546.7	1,538.6
2006	1,528.5	1,542.6	1,559.6	1,577.2	1,586.2	1,579.3	1,581.2	1,584.3	1,578.5	1,593.5	1,596.8	1,602.9	1,575.9
2007	1,568.3	1,577.0	1,598.1	1,604.7	1,617.1	1,629.6	1,632.1	1,633.8	1,622.6	1,626.8	1,626.5	1,614.5	1,612.6
Goods-Producing													
2000	453.4	455.9	458.6	458.3	460.0	463.9	454.7	455.0	454.0	454.6	453.9	454.0	456.3
2001	444.1	442.5	442.6	440.4	439.3	436.8	431.3	428.5	425.0	419.2	418.6	415.9	432.0
2002	406.9	406.7	407.8	409.4	410.6	411.6	407.8	408.0	405.6	404.1	400.8	399.4	406.6
2003	397.4	397.9	398.6	396.3	395.1	393.7	392.5	391.7	391.0	390.4	388.0	387.2	393.3
2004	383.0	382.7	386.6	387.9	389.1	390.8	390.6	389.8	389.1	387.5	386.4	385.9	387.5
2005	382.6	383.2	384.3	384.6	385.3	383.3	383.1	383.5	380.6	381.2	381.2	378.2	382.6
2006	377.7	379.0	381.0	383.4	385.1	383.3	382.1	381.8	380.4	383.3	382.8	384.6	382.0
2007	378.9	379.8	382.8	380.9	381.7	384.3	385.3	383.9	383.4	383.7	382.5	380.4	382.3
Natural Resources and Mining													
2000	5.6	5.7	5.7	5.6	5.7	5.5	5.6	5.4	5.3	5.4	5.4	5.4	5.5
2001	5.2	5.2	5.2	5.2	5.2	5.2	5.2	5.2	5.2	5.2	5.2	5.2	5.1
2002	5.1	5.1	5.1	5.1	5.1	5.1	5.0	5.0	5.0	5.0	5.0	5.0	5.1
2003	5.1	5.1	5.1	5.0	5.0	5.0	5.0	5.0	5.0	5.0	5.0	5.0	5.0
2004	5.1	5.1	5.1	5.1	5.1	5.1	5.1	5.1	5.1	5.0	5.0	5.0	5.1
2005	4.9	4.9	4.9	4.9	4.9	4.9	4.8	4.8	4.7	4.7	4.7	4.7	4.8
2006	4.7	4.7	4.7	4.7	4.7	4.7	4.7	4.7	4.7	4.7	4.7	4.8	4.7
2007	4.7	4.7	4.7	4.6	4.6	4.6	4.6	4.6	4.6	4.5	4.5	4.6	4.6
Construction													
2000	112.7	113.4	116.1	115.4	116.7	118.9	113.3	113.3	112.4	114.4	114.0	114.1	114.5
2001	111.2	111.1	112.9	114.2	115.4	116.0	114.3	114.2	113.0	112.4	112.2	110.9	113.1
2002	107.5	108.8	110.4	112.0	113.4	114.2	113.9	113.8	112.8	112.5	111.8	111.0	111.8
2003	110.7	111.1	112.3	110.9	111.7	112.6	112.5	113.0	113.3	114.5	113.4	113.0	112.4
2004	110.8	110.9	113.2	114.4	115.3	115.7	116.4	116.0	115.6	115.5	114.7	113.8	114.4
2005	112.5	112.9	114.0	115.1	117.4	116.8	118.7	119.4	118.2	119.5	120.4	118.2	116.9
2006	119.3	120.8	122.5	123.8	125.4	123.9	125.7	126.2	125.8	128.1	127.7	127.6	124.7
2007	124.2	124.4	126.7	125.6	126.3	128.0	129.9	129.4	129.5	130.7	129.7	126.9	127.6
Manufacturing													
2000	335.1	336.8	336.8	337.3	337.6	339.5	335.8	336.3	336.3	334.8	334.5	334.5	336.2
2001	327.7	326.2	324.5	321.0	318.7	315.6	311.8	309.1	306.8	301.6	301.2	299.8	313.6
2002	294.3	292.8	292.3	292.3	292.1	292.3	288.9	289.2	287.8	286.6	284.0	283.4	289.7
2003	281.6	281.7	281.2	280.4	278.4	276.1	275.0	273.7	272.7	270.9	269.6	269.2	275.9
2004	267.1	266.7	268.3	268.4	268.7	270.0	269.1	268.7	268.4	267.0	266.7	267.1	268.0
2005	265.2	265.4	265.4	264.6	263.0	261.6	259.6	259.3	257.7	257.0	256.1	255.3	260.9
2006	253.7	253.5	253.8	254.9	255.0	254.7	251.7	250.9	249.9	250.5	250.4	252.2	252.6
2007	250.0	250.7	251.4	250.7	250.8	251.7	250.8	249.9	249.3	248.5	248.3	248.9	250.1
Service-Providing													
2000	1,370.6	1,380.8	1,403.8	1,410.1	1,427.1	1,436.6	1,379.8	1,396.9	1,397.5	1,406.6	1,410.5	1,412.3	1,402.7
2001	1,364.4	1,374.3	1,390.2	1,396.7	1,403.4	1,405.3	1,373.6	1,398.6	1,401.2	1,392.8	1,395.6	1,395.5	1,391.0
2002	1,354.7	1,366.3	1,386.5	1,403.1	1,413.2	1,417.9	1,376.7	1,405.9	1,408.3	1,410.2	1,413.0	1,414.3	1,397.5
2003	1,379.3	1,391.7	1,407.6	1,416.4	1,427.2	1,427.8	1,392.6	1,420.3	1,423.5	1,423.7	1,426.1	1,430.1	1,413.9
2004	1,398.0	1,408.0	1,429.2	1,447.7	1,458.9	1,460.5	1,426.1	1,452.9	1,457.1	1,465.0	1,471.3	1,471.5	1,445.5
2005	1,437.9	1,450.7	1,461.6	1,484.9	1,494.7	1,486.0	1,469.1	1,497.4	1,498.4	1,505.4	1,514.1	1,506.5	1,483.9
2006	1,481.7	1,498.8	1,517.7	1,532.6	1,540.0	1,522.4	1,493.7	1,520.9	1,529.7	1,548.5	1,552.9	1,558.4	1,524.8
2007	1,525.4	1,536.4	1,556.8	1,563.7	1,576.3	1,582.1	1,552.4	1,585.8	1,580.0	1,586.3	1,589.9	1,580.6	1,568.0
Trade, Transportation, and Utilities													
2000	359.1	359.0	363.7	362.3	365.7	368.2	362.2	363.0	361.6	363.9	370.1	372.7	364.3
2001	352.6	349.7	352.9	352.0	354.3	355.2	354.3	353.8	351.5	349.7	353.9	355.7	353.0
2002	339.9	339.0	343.3	345.8	347.6	349.5	346.8	346.5	345.3	346.1	351.5	355.1	346.4
2003	341.7	340.9	343.5	343.5	346.2	348.9	347.3	348.2	346.8	347.6	352.2	356.5	346.9
2004	345.1	344.4	348.8	350.0	353.2	353.8	356.0	356.2	354.7	357.2	363.0	366.7	354.1
2005	354.2	354.0	355.5	358.7	362.4	360.1	363.5	364.2	359.7	363.9	369.7	372.1	361.5
2006	360.4	363.7	367.7	367.8	367.9	366.5	366.5	368.0	367.6	373.1	381.0	384.0	369.5
2007	369.1	368.4	373.9	373.5	376.6	379.2	378.5	377.9	375.6	378.8	384.1	385.7	376.8
Wholesale Trade													
2000	61.9	62.1	63.0	62.6	63.0	63.3	62.6	62.5	62.6	62.9	63.0	63.3	62.7
2001	62.6	62.8	63.1	63.1	63.1	63.5	63.4	63.1	62.9	62.3	62.2	61.8	62.8
2002	60.8	61.5	62.2	62.4	62.4	63.1	62.6	62.2	61.9	62.6	62.7	62.5	62.2
2003	61.8	62.2	62.4	62.4	62.8	63.0	62.7	62.7	62.5	62.6	62.6	63.0	62.6
2004	62.6	62.8	63.5	63.9	64.4	64.7	65.3	65.6	65.5	65.7	66.1	66.1	64.7
2005	66.7	67.1	67.1	66.8	67.8	67.0	67.4	67.6	67.3	67.9	68.0	67.7	67.4
2006	68.1	68.6	68.8	69.7	69.8	69.6	68.5	68.9	69.3	70.5	70.7	70.8	69.4
2007	69.8	70.2	70.9	70.8	70.8	71.4	72.0	72.2	72.1	72.9	72.8	73.3	71.6

Employment by Industry: South Carolina, 2000–2007—*Continued*

(Numbers in thousands, not seasonally adjusted.)

Industry and year	January	February	March	April	May	June	July	August	September	October	November	December	Annual Average
Retail Trade													
2000	234.2	233.1	236.3	235.9	238.4	240.2	234.9	235.5	234.7	235.9	241.8	244.0	237.0
2001	229.2	226.2	228.7	228.3	230.0	230.7	229.4	228.9	227.1	225.9	230.3	232.9	228.9
2002	220.0	217.8	221.4	223.0	224.6	226.3	224.6	224.2	223.3	222.7	227.5	231.6	223.9
2003	219.8	218.3	220.5	221.0	222.9	225.2	224.3	224.9	223.8	224.0	228.4	232.0	223.8
2004	222.5	221.3	224.7	226.1	228.0	228.1	228.8	228.1	227.0	229.0	234.2	238.0	228.0
2005	226.7	225.9	227.2	230.0	231.8	230.7	232.9	233.1	229.0	232.6	238.0	240.2	231.5
2006	229.4	231.6	235.3	234.6	234.3	232.7	234.2	234.9	234.0	237.7	245.2	247.3	235.9
2007	235.4	233.7	238.2	237.7	240.3	241.6	240.0	238.9	236.7	238.8	244.0	244.7	239.2
Transportation and Utilities													
2000	63.0	63.8	64.4	63.8	64.3	64.7	64.7	65.0	64.3	65.1	65.3	65.4	64.4
2001	60.8	60.7	61.1	60.6	61.2	61.0	61.5	61.8	61.5	61.5	61.4	61.0	61.1
2002	59.1	59.7	59.7	60.4	60.6	60.1	59.6	60.1	60.1	60.8	61.3	61.0	60.2
2003	60.1	60.4	60.6	60.1	60.5	60.7	60.3	60.6	60.5	61.0	61.2	61.5	60.6
2004	60.0	60.3	60.6	60.0	60.8	61.0	61.9	62.5	62.2	62.5	62.7	62.6	61.4
2005	60.8	61.0	61.2	61.9	62.8	62.4	63.2	63.5	63.4	63.4	63.7	64.2	62.6
2006	62.9	63.5	63.6	63.5	63.8	64.2	63.8	64.2	64.3	64.9	65.1	65.9	64.1
2007	63.9	64.5	64.8	65.0	65.5	66.2	66.5	66.8	66.8	67.1	67.3	67.7	66.0
Information													
2000	30.0	30.0	30.4	29.9	30.2	31.0	30.5	30.8	30.7	30.6	30.8	31.2	30.5
2001	29.7	29.8	29.8	29.1	29.1	29.2	28.7	28.7	28.4	27.9	28.1	28.0	28.8
2002	27.7	27.6	27.8	27.5	28.0	28.1	27.8	27.9	27.4	27.9	28.3	28.3	27.9
2003	27.5	27.6	27.5	26.7	26.9	26.9	27.1	27.1	26.9	26.7	26.8	26.9	27.1
2004	26.8	26.5	26.5	26.5	26.9	27.0	27.0	26.9	26.6	26.8	26.7	27.2	26.8
2005	26.6	26.7	26.6	27.0	27.3	27.2	27.2	27.1	26.9	26.9	27.1	27.4	27.0
2006	27.2	27.6	27.4	27.5	27.6	27.7	27.5	27.4	27.1	27.3	27.8	27.9	27.5
2007	27.1	27.2	27.4	27.6	27.8	28.3	28.2	28.1	28.0	28.0	27.8	27.7	27.8
Financial Activities													
2000	85.9	86.4	87.0	87.6	88.3	89.7	87.9	88.1	86.7	87.4	87.1	87.3	87.4
2001	85.9	86.5	87.0	87.8	88.1	89.3	90.4	89.9	88.5	87.8	88.2	87.8	88.1
2002	86.4	86.7	87.5	88.9	89.7	90.8	90.4	90.0	89.3	89.2	89.2	89.6	89.0
2003	88.8	88.8	89.5	91.1	92.3	93.4	92.8	93.6	91.9	91.9	91.5	91.9	91.5
2004	90.3	91.0	92.0	93.1	93.8	95.4	95.0	95.2	94.9	95.2	95.3	95.9	93.9
2005	95.4	95.7	95.9	96.9	98.1	98.4	99.7	99.8	99.1	98.4	98.5	99.0	97.9
2006	99.4	100.0	100.3	102.0	102.6	103.2	104.0	104.5	104.0	104.5	104.3	104.8	102.8
2007	104.1	104.1	105.0	105.4	106.1	107.2	107.9	108.3	107.2	106.5	107.3	107.2	106.4
Professional and Business Services													
2000	186.9	188.2	192.1	195.9	197.8	200.9	197.1	198.1	197.8	197.2	195.9	195.7	195.3
2001	185.3	187.3	188.8	189.6	188.9	188.8	187.7	189.4	187.9	185.0	183.1	182.1	186.9
2002	174.4	176.7	179.4	183.7	184.4	186.6	184.3	187.2	186.5	187.8	185.9	185.4	183.5
2003	180.4	183.0	186.7	187.2	187.6	187.7	186.2	188.4	187.5	190.8	191.1	191.2	187.3
2004	185.1	187.4	191.8	195.5	195.3	197.8	197.9	199.3	198.2	200.9	200.8	199.4	195.8
2005	195.5	197.6	197.7	203.3	204.1	203.4	205.8	209.3	209.4	212.3	213.6	210.6	205.2
2006	211.6	213.6	215.1	217.9	219.2	217.0	216.3	218.3	219.7	222.7	220.7	223.3	218.0
2007	219.9	222.6	224.2	225.1	226.6	227.7	226.9	229.9	229.6	231.9	230.2	227.0	226.8
Education and Health Services													
2000	154.6	155.5	156.5	156.4	156.7	156.8	153.2	154.1	156.0	157.7	158.4	159.2	156.2
2001	158.7	160.1	161.3	161.4	162.4	163.3	163.7	165.3	167.9	168.0	169.4	170.4	164.3
2002	168.9	170.2	172.1	171.8	172.4	171.6	171.6	172.5	174.1	174.1	175.2	174.9	172.5
2003	173.2	174.5	175.4	176.4	176.9	176.2	175.6	177.4	179.6	179.0	179.2	179.6	176.9
2004	178.3	179.5	180.2	181.1	181.8	180.5	179.8	181.0	182.2	183.0	184.1	184.3	181.3
2005	182.6	184.3	184.7	187.5	187.8	184.7	187.2	187.8	189.2	190.5	191.0	189.9	187.3
2006	189.2	191.4	191.8	192.7	193.0	189.6	189.9	191.5	193.8	197.9	198.2	199.0	193.2
2007	196.0	198.1	199.1	199.3	199.9	199.6	200.5	202.4	203.7	204.6	204.0	205.3	201.0
Leisure and Hospitality													
2000	175.1	179.0	186.5	191.2	195.3	199.9	195.8	192.8	185.8	184.6	181.6	179.5	187.2
2001	169.1	173.2	180.4	187.6	191.3	194.8	196.7	195.2	188.4	183.0	179.2	176.5	184.6
2002	169.4	173.9	181.7	191.1	195.6	201.3	200.6	197.9	191.9	190.5	185.7	183.4	188.6
2003	176.1	180.0	186.7	194.0	200.1	204.8	205.4	204.1	197.7	193.3	189.2	186.5	193.2
2004	181.0	185.5	193.6	202.0	207.6	211.4	211.8	209.0	203.5	201.0	197.9	194.1	199.9
2005	185.5	189.7	196.5	206.7	209.7	212.9	217.3	215.9	206.1	202.7	200.7	194.6	203.2
2006	191.1	194.7	200.1	209.8	214.5	216.1	218.7	217.0	210.6	210.0	207.7	205.0	207.9
2007	199.8	203.0	211.3	219.6	224.1	228.5	230.9	229.7	221.3	219.4	216.8	208.2	217.7
Other Services													
2000	57.4	58.1	59.1	59.7	60.1	60.0	58.3	58.1	58.0	59.2	58.8	58.5	58.7
2001	60.4	60.9	62.1	62.3	62.7	62.7	62.4	62.7	62.6	62.6	63.0	63.0	62.2
2002	62.6	63.4	64.7	64.2	64.9	65.6	64.2	64.7	65.3	63.7	63.8	64.0	64.3
2003	63.4	63.9	64.7	64.1	64.8	65.3	64.9	65.2	65.3	65.3	65.6	66.0	64.9
2004	65.0	65.6	66.5	68.9	70.0	71.5	69.1	69.3	69.7	70.6	71.8	72.0	69.2
2005	71.1	72.4	73.1	72.7	73.3	72.9	74.9	75.6	75.4	75.4	75.7	74.9	74.0
2006	71.9	72.6	76.2	76.1	76.3	75.9	76.2	75.8	75.3	74.7	74.3	74.3	75.0
2007	73.4	73.8	74.4	73.3	74.3	74.8	73.9	73.6	73.8	73.9	73.8	73.0	73.8
Government													
2000	321.6	324.6	328.5	327.1	333.0	330.1	294.8	311.9	320.9	326.0	327.8	328.2	322.8
2001	322.7	326.8	327.9	326.9	326.6	322.0	289.7	313.6	326.0	328.8	330.7	332.0	322.8
2002	325.4	328.8	330.0	330.1	330.6	324.4	291.0	319.2	328.5	330.9	333.4	333.6	325.5
2003	328.2	333.0	333.6	333.4	332.4	324.6	293.3	316.3	327.8	329.1	330.5	331.5	326.1
2004	326.4	328.1	329.8	330.6	330.3	323.1	289.5	316.0	327.3	330.3	331.7	331.9	324.6
2005	327.0	330.3	331.6	332.1	332.0	326.4	293.5	317.7	332.6	335.3	337.8	338.0	327.9
2006	330.9	335.2	339.1	338.8	338.9	326.4	294.6	318.4	331.6	338.3	338.9	340.1	330.9
2007	336.0	339.2	341.5	339.9	340.9	336.8	305.6	335.9	340.8	343.2	345.9	346.5	337.7

Average Weekly Hours by Selected Industry: South Carolina, 2003–2007

(Not seasonally adjusted.)

Industry and year	January	February	March	April	May	June	July	August	September	October	November	December	Annual Average
Manufacturing													
2003	41.7	42.2	42.1	41.5	41.4	41.1	40.0	40.6	41.3	41.1	41.0	41.1	41.3
2004	40.4	39.7	39.5	39.3	39.3	39.8	39.0	39.1	39.5	38.6	39.7	40.5	39.5
2005	39.9	39.0	39.3	39.3	39.3	39.4	39.3	40.1	40.2	40.6	40.8	39.9	39.7
2006	40.0	40.0	40.4	40.4	40.2	41.1	41.0	41.5	41.5	41.3	42.3	42.4	41.0
2007	41.6	41.9	41.9	41.5	42.0	42.3	40.9	42.2	42.9	42.2	43.5	42.9	42.1

Average Hourly Earnings by Selected Industry: South Carolina, 2003–2007

(Dollars, not seasonally adjusted.)

Industry and year	January	February	March	April	May	June	July	August	September	October	November	December	Annual Average
Manufacturing													
2003	14.16	14.06	14.05	14.20	13.97	13.97	14.36	14.32	14.23	14.23	14.30	14.48	14.19
2004	14.43	14.33	14.43	14.56	14.47	14.56	14.89	14.30	14.99	15.45	15.08	15.33	14.73
2005	15.13	15.32	15.25	15.44	15.32	15.52	15.50	15.35	15.19	15.29	14.79	14.68	15.23
2006	14.70	14.69	14.95	14.92	14.96	14.94	15.14	15.01	15.05	15.15	15.08	15.72	15.03
2007	15.72	15.83	15.67	15.76	15.69	15.81	15.85	15.58	15.73	15.52	15.46	15.95	15.71

Average Weekly Earnings by Selected Industry: South Carolina, 2003–2007

(Dollars, not seasonally adjusted.)

Industry and year	January	February	March	April	May	June	July	August	September	October	November	December	Annual Average
Manufacturing													
2003	590.47	593.33	591.51	589.30	578.36	574.17	574.40	581.39	587.70	584.85	586.30	595.13	586.05
2004	582.97	568.90	569.99	572.21	568.67	579.49	580.71	559.13	592.11	596.37	598.68	620.87	581.84
2005	603.69	597.48	599.33	606.79	602.08	611.49	609.15	615.54	610.64	620.77	603.43	585.73	604.63
2006	588.00	587.60	603.98	602.77	601.39	614.03	620.74	622.92	624.58	625.70	637.88	666.53	616.23
2007	653.95	663.28	656.57	654.04	658.98	668.76	648.27	657.48	674.82	654.94	672.51	684.26	661.39

Population
    2000 census: 754,844
    2007 estimate: 796,214
    Percent change, 2000–2007: 5.5%

Percent change in total nonfarm employment, 2000–2007: 7.5%

Industry with the largest growth in employment, 2000–2007 (thousands)
    Education and health services, 8.7

Industry with the largest decline in employment, 2000–2007 (thousands)
    Manufacturing, -1.8

Civilian labor force
    2000: 408,685
    2007: 442,555

Employment-population ratio
    2000: 70.8%
    2007: 71.0%

Unemployment rate and rank among states
    2000: 2.7%, 3rd
    2007: 3.0%, 4th

Employment by Industry, 2007

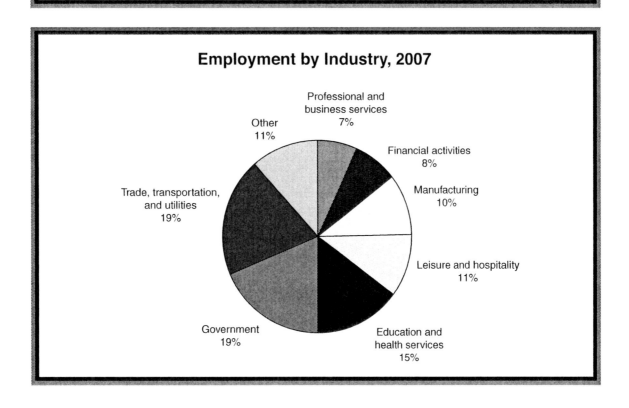

Professional and business services 7%

Other 11%

Financial activities 8%

Trade, transportation, and utilities 19%

Manufacturing 10%

Leisure and hospitality 11%

Government 19%

Education and health services 15%

Employment by Industry: South Dakota, 2000–2007

(Numbers in thousands, not seasonally adjusted.)

Industry and year	January	February	March	April	May	June	July	August	September	October	November	December	Annual Average
Total Nonfarm													
2000	367.1	367.7	371.8	376.7	383.5	388.3	381.8	382.2	380.3	379.9	377.6	377.3	377.9
2001	369.2	369.5	371.4	376.3	385.1	389.6	383.8	384.5	380.5	379.4	378.1	376.8	378.7
2002	365.7	365.7	367.3	373.6	382.9	388.1	383.2	384.7	381.1	380.9	378.7	378.6	377.5
2003	367.9	367.2	368.9	375.0	383.0	387.8	383.4	386.0	381.2	381.1	380.2	379.5	378.4
2004	369.7	370.0	372.1	381.0	388.9	394.1	388.4	391.2	388.9	388.0	386.3	385.4	383.7
2005	375.3	376.3	379.6	386.8	393.9	399.8	395.6	398.2	395.7	393.7	393.2	393.5	390.1
2006	384.0	385.0	388.1	393.3	402.7	408.8	404.0	407.4	403.4	402.6	401.8	401.9	398.6
2007	391.9	392.8	396.4	401.6	411.6	416.6	413.2	415.5	411.3	410.2	409.0	407.0	406.4
Total Private													
2000	296.8	296.5	299.3	304.1	309.6	315.4	314.6	314.7	309.5	308.1	305.8	305.2	306.6
2001	296.9	296.5	298.9	302.8	309.7	313.7	313.8	314.0	307.2	305.1	303.5	301.9	305.3
2002	292.4	291.6	293.1	299.3	306.8	311.8	312.0	313.2	307.1	305.9	303.5	303.0	303.3
2003	294.0	292.4	293.8	299.7	306.5	311.6	312.4	314.2	306.9	305.7	304.9	304.0	303.8
2004	295.4	295.1	297.0	304.9	311.7	317.3	317.2	320.1	313.8	312.1	310.1	309.1	308.7
2005	300.4	300.9	303.7	310.7	316.6	322.8	323.8	326.7	320.4	317.7	317.0	317.5	314.9
2006	309.6	309.5	312.3	317.4	325.2	331.5	332.1	335.4	328.5	326.5	325.4	325.8	323.3
2007	317.7	317.0	320.6	325.8	334.0	339.8	340.3	342.4	335.6	333.9	332.3	330.6	330.8
Goods-Producing													
2000	59.8	59.5	60.4	62.1	63.4	65.8	66.7	66.2	64.9	64.5	62.7	60.9	63.1
2001	59.1	58.3	58.5	60.1	61.6	63.7	63.7	63.3	61.4	60.7	59.3	57.7	60.6
2002	55.0	54.0	54.2	56.3	58.8	60.6	61.3	60.9	59.6	59.3	58.0	56.9	57.9
2003	54.3	53.6	54.2	56.7	59.1	60.6	61.0	61.0	59.5	59.3	58.4	56.9	57.9
2004	54.7	54.4	55.3	58.7	60.6	62.4	63.1	62.8	61.7	61.5	60.7	59.5	59.6
2005	56.9	56.8	57.7	60.5	62.3	64.3	64.9	64.7	63.7	63.7	63.0	61.5	61.7
2006	59.9	59.6	60.5	62.8	65.1	67.1	67.8	67.6	66.4	65.9	64.9	64.1	64.3
2007	61.5	60.6	61.9	63.6	65.9	67.8	68.1	67.8	66.8	66.4	66.0	64.2	65.1
Natural Resources, Mining, and Construction													
2000	16.1	15.8	16.7	18.6	20.1	21.7	22.3	22.1	21.2	20.5	18.8	17.7	19.3
2001	16.2	15.9	16.4	18.2	20.3	22.2	22.6	22.6	21.6	21.0	19.9	18.6	19.5
2002	16.4	16.1	16.3	18.1	20.5	21.9	22.2	22.1	21.2	20.9	19.9	19.0	19.6
2003	16.8	16.4	16.8	19.1	21.4	22.7	23.1	23.0	22.0	21.6	20.5	19.3	20.2
2004	17.1	16.7	17.4	20.0	21.7	22.9	23.5	23.4	22.4	22.2	21.4	20.5	20.7
2005	18.1	17.9	18.6	21.0	22.7	24.2	24.7	24.7	23.7	23.5	22.7	21.2	21.9
2006	19.5	19.3	19.8	21.8	23.7	25.1	25.7	25.5	24.4	23.7	22.7	21.8	22.8
2007	19.7	19.0	20.0	21.5	23.9	25.4	26.0	26.0	25.1	24.4	23.7	22.1	23.1
Manufacturing													
2000	43.7	43.7	43.7	43.5	43.3	44.1	44.4	44.1	43.7	44.0	43.9	43.2	43.8
2001	42.9	42.4	42.1	41.9	41.3	41.5	41.1	40.7	39.8	39.7	39.4	39.1	40.9
2002	38.6	37.9	37.9	38.2	38.3	38.7	39.1	38.8	38.4	38.4	38.1	37.9	38.4
2003	37.5	37.2	37.4	37.6	37.7	37.9	37.9	38.0	37.5	37.7	37.9	37.6	37.7
2004	37.6	37.7	37.9	38.7	38.9	39.5	39.6	39.4	39.3	39.3	39.3	39.0	38.9
2005	38.8	38.9	39.1	39.5	39.6	40.1	40.2	40.0	40.0	40.2	40.3	40.3	39.8
2006	40.4	40.3	40.7	41.0	41.4	42.0	42.1	42.1	42.0	42.2	42.2	42.3	41.6
2007	41.8	41.6	41.9	42.1	42.0	42.4	42.1	41.8	41.7	42.0	42.3	42.1	42.0
Service-Providing													
2000	307.3	308.2	311.4	314.6	320.1	322.5	315.1	316.0	315.4	315.4	314.9	316.4	314.8
2001	310.1	311.2	312.9	316.2	323.5	325.9	320.1	321.2	319.1	318.7	318.8	319.1	318.1
2002	310.7	311.7	313.1	317.3	324.1	327.5	321.9	323.8	321.5	321.6	320.7	321.7	319.6
2003	313.6	313.6	314.7	318.3	323.9	327.2	322.4	325.0	321.7	321.8	321.8	322.6	320.6
2004	315.0	315.6	316.8	322.3	328.3	331.7	325.3	328.4	327.2	326.5	325.6	325.9	324.1
2005	318.4	319.5	321.9	326.3	331.6	335.5	330.7	333.5	332.0	330.0	330.2	332.0	328.5
2006	324.1	325.4	327.6	330.5	337.6	341.7	336.2	339.8	337.0	336.7	336.9	337.8	334.3
2007	330.4	332.2	334.5	338.0	345.7	348.8	345.1	347.7	344.5	343.8	343.0	342.8	341.4
Trade, Transportation, and Utilities													
2000	75.1	74.7	75.0	76.9	77.7	78.0	77.3	77.4	76.5	77.2	78.1	78.4	76.9
2001	75.7	75.7	76.3	76.5	77.9	78.0	77.4	77.4	76.2	77.0	77.9	78.4	77.0
2002	75.0	74.3	74.3	75.9	77.2	77.8	77.0	77.4	76.4	77.1	77.7	78.2	76.5
2003	75.1	74.3	74.5	76.0	77.0	77.4	77.0	77.2	75.9	76.5	77.3	78.0	76.4
2004	75.2	74.4	74.7	76.2	77.7	78.2	77.8	78.7	77.1	77.8	78.7	79.3	77.2
2005	76.4	76.4	76.9	78.3	79.4	79.6	79.6	80.5	79.2	79.2	80.2	81.0	78.9
2006	78.3	77.7	78.3	79.0	80.4	81.2	80.7	81.6	80.1	80.5	81.4	82.2	80.1
2007	79.5	78.7	79.5	80.3	81.8	82.3	82.7	83.0	81.8	82.7	82.9	83.5	81.6
Wholesale Trade													
2000	16.3	16.4	16.5	16.7	16.7	16.7	16.5	16.5	16.4	16.5	16.5	16.5	16.5
2001	16.5	16.5	16.6	16.8	17.0	16.9	16.7	16.6	16.4	16.7	16.7	16.7	16.6
2002	16.6	16.6	16.6	16.9	16.9	17.0	16.7	16.6	16.3	16.6	16.6	16.6	16.7
2003	16.4	16.3	16.4	16.8	16.9	16.8	16.7	16.6	16.6	16.6	16.9	16.9	16.7
2004	16.6	16.6	16.9	17.2	17.3	17.3	17.1	17.1	16.9	17.4	17.3	17.4	17.1
2005	17.1	17.1	17.1	17.5	17.7	17.7	17.6	17.8	17.6	17.8	17.8	17.8	17.6
2006	18.0	18.0	18.1	18.3	18.6	18.6	18.3	18.3	18.0	18.2	18.1	18.1	18.2
2007	18.0	17.9	18.1	18.3	18.6	18.6	18.7	18.8	18.7	19.0	18.7	18.5	18.5
Retail Trade													
2000	46.9	46.5	46.8	48.3	48.9	49.4	49.0	49.0	47.9	48.4	49.3	49.6	48.3
2001	47.3	47.3	47.7	47.6	48.7	49.0	48.8	49.0	47.7	48.0	49.0	49.5	48.2
2002	46.8	46.1	46.1	47.2	48.3	48.9	48.7	49.1	48.2	48.7	49.4	49.8	48.1
2003	47.2	46.6	46.7	47.8	48.5	49.0	48.8	49.1	47.8	48.1	48.9	49.6	48.2
2004	47.4	46.7	46.7	47.7	48.9	49.3	49.2	50.0	48.4	48.5	49.5	50.1	48.5
2005	47.7	47.7	48.2	49.0	49.7	49.9	49.9	50.5	49.2	49.0	50.0	50.6	49.3
2006	48.0	47.4	47.8	48.2	49.0	49.8	49.7	50.3	49.1	49.3	50.4	51.0	49.2
2007	48.8	48.2	48.8	49.2	50.2	50.7	51.0	51.2	49.9	50.8	51.2	51.8	50.2

Employment by Industry: South Dakota, 2000–2007—*Continued*

(Numbers in thousands, not seasonally adjusted.)

Industry and year	January	February	March	April	May	June	July	August	September	October	November	December	Annual Average
Transportation and Utilities													
2000	11.9	11.8	11.7	11.9	12.1	11.9	11.8	11.9	12.2	12.3	12.3	12.3	12.0
2001	11.9	11.9	12.0	12.1	12.2	12.1	11.9	11.8	12.1	12.3	12.2	12.2	12.0
2002	11.6	11.6	11.6	11.8	12.0	11.9	11.6	11.7	11.9	11.8	11.7	11.8	11.8
2003	11.5	11.4	11.4	11.4	11.6	11.6	11.5	11.5	11.5	11.5	11.5	11.5	11.5
2004	11.2	11.1	11.1	11.3	11.5	11.6	11.5	11.6	11.8	11.9	11.9	11.8	11.5
2005	11.6	11.6	11.6	11.8	12.0	12.0	12.1	12.2	12.4	12.4	12.4	12.6	12.1
2006	12.3	12.3	12.4	12.5	12.8	12.8	12.7	13.0	13.0	13.0	12.9	13.1	12.7
2007	12.7	12.6	12.6	12.8	13.0	13.0	13.0	13.0	13.2	12.9	13.0	13.2	12.9
Information													
2000	6.8	6.7	6.8	6.9	7.0	7.0	7.0	6.9	6.9	6.8	6.9	6.9	6.9
2001	6.8	6.8	6.8	6.7	6.9	6.9	6.9	6.8	6.8	6.8	6.8	6.8	6.8
2002	6.8	6.7	6.8	6.7	6.8	6.9	6.9	6.8	6.7	6.9	6.9	6.9	6.8
2003	6.8	6.7	6.7	6.6	6.7	6.8	6.7	6.8	6.7	6.8	6.9	6.9	6.8
2004	6.8	6.8	6.8	6.7	6.8	6.7	6.8	6.8	6.7	6.6	6.6	6.6	6.7
2005	6.6	6.6	6.5	6.5	6.7	6.8	6.9	6.9	6.9	6.9	6.9	6.9	6.8
2006	6.8	6.9	6.9	6.8	6.9	7.0	7.1	7.1	7.0	6.9	6.9	7.0	6.9
2007	7.0	7.1	7.0	7.3	7.4	7.5	7.2	7.3	7.1	7.1	7.2	7.2	7.2
Financial Activities													
2000	25.6	25.6	25.7	25.9	26.0	26.4	26.5	26.4	26.3	26.5	26.7	27.2	26.2
2001	27.5	27.7	27.8	27.8	28.0	28.3	28.4	28.2	28.1	27.9	28.0	28.1	28.0
2002	28.0	28.0	27.9	27.9	27.9	28.1	28.0	28.0	27.7	27.6	27.7	28.0	27.9
2003	27.6	27.6	27.8	27.5	27.4	27.6	27.8	27.8	27.6	27.7	27.7	28.0	27.7
2004	27.7	27.6	27.8	27.5	27.7	28.0	27.9	28.0	27.9	27.8	27.8	28.1	27.8
2005	28.2	28.0	28.2	27.9	28.2	28.8	28.6	28.6	28.7	28.5	28.6	29.2	28.5
2006	29.0	29.0	29.1	29.0	29.2	29.5	29.7	29.9	29.8	29.8	29.9	30.2	29.5
2007	30.2	30.4	30.7	30.6	30.8	31.3	31.3	31.2	31.1	30.9	30.6	30.9	30.8
Professional and Business Services													
2000	26.8	27.1	27.2	27.4	27.4	28.0	27.9	27.7	27.3	27.3	26.7	27.0	27.3
2001	26.1	25.9	25.9	26.4	26.5	26.6	26.4	26.3	25.6	25.5	25.1	24.9	25.9
2002	24.2	24.6	24.7	25.1	25.1	25.5	25.1	25.4	24.7	24.9	25.0	24.9	24.9
2003	24.2	24.4	24.2	24.2	24.3	24.5	24.5	24.6	24.0	24.2	24.5	24.2	24.3
2004	23.2	23.8	23.4	24.3	24.5	24.5	24.5	25.2	24.7	24.5	24.1	24.0	24.2
2005	23.2	23.7	23.9	24.6	24.4	24.7	25.0	25.2	24.6	24.6	24.8	25.3	24.5
2006	24.6	25.0	25.0	25.5	25.7	26.0	26.1	26.1	25.8	26.1	26.1	26.4	25.7
2007	26.0	26.4	26.6	27.4	28.0	28.5	28.4	28.4	27.9	27.5	27.7	27.8	27.6
Education and Health Services													
2000	50.8	51.1	51.3	51.5	51.5	51.0	50.3	50.4	51.2	51.9	52.0	52.4	51.3
2001	51.7	52.3	52.7	52.8	52.9	52.1	51.9	52.0	52.5	53.1	53.7	53.6	52.6
2002	53.1	53.5	53.8	54.2	54.1	53.7	53.2	53.4	54.1	54.7	54.9	55.0	54.0
2003	54.9	54.8	54.9	55.2	55.3	54.9	55.0	55.2	55.4	56.2	56.4	56.5	55.4
2004	55.8	56.2	56.4	56.6	56.5	56.4	55.8	55.7	56.4	57.0	57.3	57.5	56.5
2005	56.8	57.0	57.3	57.5	57.3	57.2	56.6	57.0	57.6	57.9	58.2	58.4	57.4
2006	57.8	58.0	58.3	58.4	58.4	58.2	57.9	58.2	58.9	59.0	59.5	59.6	58.5
2007	58.9	59.1	59.5	59.8	60.1	59.7	59.4	59.9	60.5	60.7	61.1	61.0	60.0
Leisure and Hospitality													
2000	34.9	35.1	35.8	36.8	39.8	42.5	42.7	43.6	40.6	37.8	36.6	36.3	38.5
2001	34.5	34.3	35.3	36.9	40.1	42.2	43.1	44.0	40.8	38.2	36.9	36.6	38.6
2002	34.7	34.9	35.7	37.4	40.8	43.1	44.3	45.2	41.9	39.4	37.5	37.4	39.4
2003	35.6	35.5	36.0	37.8	40.9	43.9	44.5	45.7	42.0	39.3	38.0	37.7	39.7
2004	36.4	36.3	36.9	39.0	41.8	45.0	45.2	46.8	43.3	40.7	38.8	38.5	40.7
2005	37.0	37.0	37.8	39.9	42.7	45.7	46.5	48.1	44.1	41.5	39.8	39.7	41.7
2006	37.9	38.0	38.8	40.4	43.8	46.7	46.9	49.0	44.7	42.6	41.0	40.6	42.5
2007	39.0	39.1	39.7	41.1	44.1	46.7	47.1	48.7	44.5	42.7	41.0	40.2	42.8
Other Services													
2000	17.0	16.7	17.1	16.6	16.8	16.7	16.2	16.1	15.8	16.1	16.1	16.1	16.4
2001	15.5	15.5	15.6	15.6	15.8	15.9	16.0	16.0	15.8	15.9	15.8	15.8	15.8
2002	15.6	15.6	15.7	15.8	16.1	16.1	16.2	16.1	16.0	16.0	15.8	15.7	15.9
2003	15.5	15.5	15.5	15.7	15.8	15.9	15.9	15.9	15.8	15.7	15.7	15.8	15.7
2004	15.6	15.6	15.7	15.9	16.1	16.1	16.1	16.1	16.0	16.2	16.1	15.6	15.9
2005	15.3	15.4	15.4	15.5	15.6	15.7	15.7	15.7	15.6	15.4	15.5	15.5	15.5
2006	15.3	15.3	15.4	15.5	15.7	15.8	15.9	15.9	15.8	15.7	15.7	15.7	15.6
2007	15.6	15.6	15.7	15.7	15.9	16.0	16.1	16.1	15.9	15.9	15.8	15.8	15.8
Government													
2000	70.3	71.2	72.5	72.6	73.9	72.9	67.2	67.5	70.8	71.8	71.8	72.1	71.2
2001	72.3	73.0	72.5	73.5	75.4	75.9	70.0	70.5	73.3	74.3	74.6	74.9	73.4
2002	73.3	74.1	74.2	74.3	76.1	76.3	71.2	71.5	74.0	75.0	75.2	75.6	74.2
2003	73.9	74.8	75.1	75.3	76.5	76.2	71.0	71.8	74.3	75.4	75.3	75.5	74.6
2004	74.3	74.9	75.1	76.1	77.2	76.8	71.2	71.1	75.1	75.9	76.2	76.3	75.0
2005	74.9	75.4	75.9	76.1	77.3	77.0	71.8	71.5	75.3	76.0	76.2	76.0	75.3
2006	74.4	75.5	75.8	75.9	77.5	77.3	71.9	72.0	74.9	76.1	76.4	76.1	75.3
2007	74.2	75.8	75.8	75.8	77.6	76.8	72.9	73.1	75.7	76.3	76.7	76.4	75.6

Average Weekly Hours by Selected Industry: South Dakota, 2001–2007

(Not seasonally adjusted.)

Industry and year	January	February	March	April	May	June	July	August	September	October	November	December	Annual Average
Manufacturing													
2001	41.5	40.7	41.8	40.9	41.5	42.0	40.7	42.0	42.9	41.6	42.4	42.0	41.7
2002	40.5	41.0	41.6	42.8	42.4	42.7	41.7	42.5	43.1	43.8	42.3	43.3	42.3
2003	42.6	41.7	42.5	40.9	42.4	42.6	41.8	43.9	41.9	43.2	44.2	42.8	42.5
2004	40.8	40.4	40.5	41.3	42.1	41.5	42.3	41.7	42.5	43.8	43.5	43.6	42.0
2005	42.4	42.8	41.5	42.6	42.5	42.6	41.3	42.1	43.3	42.0	42.1	42.0	42.3
2006	41.4	42.3	41.1	40.5	42.2	41.4	41.9	42.5	43.7	43.1	42.3	42.5	42.1
2007	41.7	40.5	43.4	41.7	40.7	42.0	41.8	40.8	41.6	42.3	42.5	42.7	41.8

Average Hourly Earnings by Selected Industry: South Dakota, 2001–2007

(Dollars, not seasonally adjusted.)

Industry and year	January	February	March	April	May	June	July	August	September	October	November	December	Annual Average
Manufacturing													
2001	11.76	11.91	11.90	11.86	12.11	12.13	12.10	12.16	12.33	12.29	12.29	12.46	12.11
2002	12.45	12.48	12.50	12.58	12.57	12.44	12.41	12.43	12.64	12.93	12.77	13.01	12.60
2003	12.79	12.82	12.85	12.90	13.15	13.10	13.18	13.19	13.35	13.33	13.31	13.64	13.13
2004	13.49	13.37	13.25	13.24	13.40	13.20	13.24	13.29	13.65	13.35	13.28	13.61	13.37
2005	13.20	13.37	13.38	13.03	13.37	13.35	13.36	13.33	13.86	13.76	13.62	13.93	13.47
2006	13.65	13.88	13.64	13.52	13.72	13.66	13.61	13.80	13.78	13.99	13.94	13.84	13.75
2007	14.15	14.07	14.11	14.16	14.40	14.18	14.38	14.34	14.42	14.51	14.20	14.30	14.27

Average Weekly Earnings by Selected Industry: South Dakota, 2001–2007

(Dollars, not seasonally adjusted.)

Industry and year	January	February	March	April	May	June	July	August	September	October	November	December	Annual Average
Manufacturing													
2001	488.04	484.74	497.42	485.07	502.57	509.46	492.47	510.72	528.96	511.26	521.10	523.32	504.99
2002	504.23	511.68	520.00	538.42	532.97	531.19	517.50	528.28	544.78	566.33	540.17	563.33	532.98
2003	544.85	534.59	546.13	527.61	557.56	558.06	550.92	579.04	559.37	575.86	588.30	583.79	558.03
2004	550.39	540.15	536.63	546.81	564.14	547.80	560.05	554.19	580.13	584.73	577.68	593.40	561.54
2005	559.68	572.24	555.27	555.08	568.23	568.71	551.77	561.19	600.14	577.92	573.40	585.06	569.78
2006	565.11	587.12	560.60	547.56	578.98	565.52	570.26	586.50	602.19	602.97	589.66	588.20	578.88
2007	590.06	569.84	612.37	590.47	586.08	595.56	601.08	585.07	599.87	613.77	603.50	610.61	596.49

Population
    2000 census: 5,689,283
    2007 estimate: 6,156,719
    Percent change, 2000–2007: 8.2%

Percent change in total nonfarm employment, 2000–2007: 2.5%

Industry with the largest growth in employment, 2000–2007 (thousands)
    Education and health services, 68.6

Industry with the largest decline in employment, 2000–2007 (thousands)
    Manufacturing, -112.2

Civilian labor force
    2000: 2,871,539
    2007: 3,036,736

Employment-population ratio
    2000: 63.2%
    2007: 60.9%

Unemployment rate and rank among states
    2000: 4.0%, 28th
    2007: 4.7%, 34th

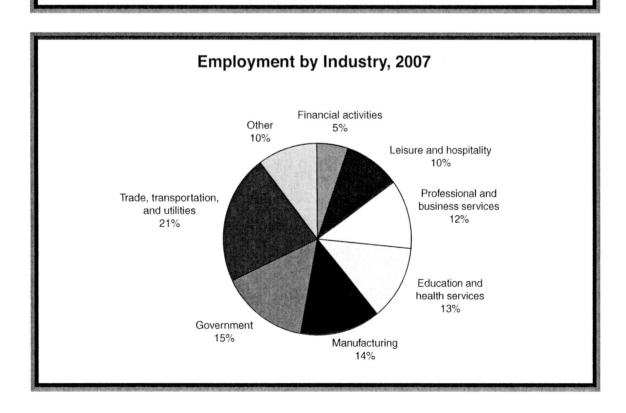

Employment by Industry, 2007

Other 10%
Financial activities 5%
Leisure and hospitality 10%
Professional and business services 12%
Trade, transportation, and utilities 21%
Education and health services 13%
Government 15%
Manufacturing 14%

Employment by Industry: Tennessee, 2000–2007

(Numbers in thousands, not seasonally adjusted.)

Industry and year	January	February	March	April	May	June	July	August	September	October	November	December	Annual Average
Total Nonfarm													
2000	2,665.1	2,683.9	2,727.5	2,725.7	2,740.8	2,745.2	2,719.4	2,737.3	2,748.5	2,745.9	2,753.1	2,754.7	2,728.9
2001	2,673.4	2,683.1	2,701.2	2,705.5	2,708.1	2,703.2	2,666.2	2,684.1	2,691.2	2,676.8	2,683.3	2,683.0	2,688.3
2002	2,611.9	2,622.8	2,643.7	2,660.0	2,670.2	2,672.0	2,657.2	2,674.7	2,684.2	2,684.6	2,693.5	2,698.1	2,664.4
2003	2,619.8	2,627.9	2,646.0	2,662.8	2,671.8	2,668.1	2,637.3	2,661.8	2,675.7	2,683.5	2,694.7	2,702.4	2,662.7
2004	2,637.4	2,668.4	2,678.9	2,700.4	2,706.7	2,710.6	2,693.6	2,716.3	2,725.5	2,732.6	2,746.2	2,756.2	2,706.1
2005	2,671.3	2,696.1	2,718.4	2,739.5	2,746.5	2,743.7	2,731.8	2,753.6	2,776.3	2,767.1	2,784.7	2,788.3	2,743.1
2006	2,727.1	2,734.8	2,765.3	2,781.4	2,791.6	2,791.4	2,769.8	2,796.8	2,810.2	2,793.8	2,811.4	2,818.6	2,782.7
2007	2,744.9	2,753.7	2,784.0	2,791.9	2,801.9	2,803.3	2,787.1	2,810.2	2,820.5	2,808.5	2,823.7	2,829.4	2,796.6
Total Private													
2000	2,275.0	2,285.7	2,308.6	2,322.4	2,332.8	2,352.7	2,341.2	2,349.3	2,352.3	2,342.3	2,347.8	2,348.9	2,329.9
2001	2,275.2	2,276.0	2,292.1	2,295.6	2,300.6	2,309.2	2,285.7	2,292.7	2,286.5	2,266.7	2,269.9	2,270.9	2,285.1
2002	2,205.5	2,208.0	2,226.9	2,240.8	2,255.1	2,266.4	2,271.0	2,278.9	2,275.1	2,268.9	2,274.5	2,278.7	2,254.2
2003	2,211.4	2,212.6	2,228.4	2,242.6	2,254.1	2,263.6	2,248.4	2,263.4	2,264.1	2,267.5	2,277.7	2,284.7	2,251.5
2004	2,226.3	2,235.3	2,257.8	2,279.7	2,289.2	2,303.1	2,301.8	2,313.8	2,310.2	2,313.6	2,325.0	2,334.3	2,290.8
2005	2,261.1	2,278.4	2,299.4	2,322.9	2,331.4	2,343.9	2,339.8	2,352.1	2,358.0	2,347.1	2,363.1	2,367.6	2,330.4
2006	2,315.1	2,317.2	2,345.0	2,359.3	2,371.0	2,387.0	2,371.8	2,386.7	2,387.4	2,370.0	2,385.1	2,393.4	2,365.8
2007	2,326.8	2,331.2	2,358.7	2,365.7	2,376.8	2,394.0	2,384.7	2,396.4	2,393.9	2,380.8	2,393.6	2,400.4	2,375.3
Goods-Producing													
2000	624.4	625.4	630.1	628.8	631.7	636.3	628.2	628.5	626.3	618.0	613.6	611.1	625.2
2001	593.0	588.5	591.4	588.8	586.8	587.6	579.3	578.8	574.3	565.2	561.8	558.5	579.5
2002	544.6	543.1	544.3	546.3	551.1	554.0	552.0	554.1	552.4	547.8	543.1	543.2	548.0
2003	530.3	528.2	530.3	532.4	534.7	537.0	532.0	534.9	534.5	533.6	532.3	533.5	532.8
2004	522.0	522.8	526.7	531.8	536.5	539.8	537.3	539.1	538.9	534.1	533.2	533.0	532.9
2005	526.0	527.4	531.2	532.4	535.0	538.4	534.3	538.1	539.7	535.6	536.5	533.3	534.0
2006	530.3	529.7	535.0	536.7	538.4	541.8	535.4	538.5	537.7	529.6	527.4	525.2	533.8
2007	517.8	517.4	522.1	519.5	518.1	521.6	517.7	521.3	520.6	516.8	515.0	513.7	518.5
Natural Resources, Mining, and Construction													
2000	125.6	126.6	131.2	130.5	133.1	135.1	133.1	133.6	133.9	130.7	129.1	127.6	130.8
2001	120.0	120.9	124.8	125.8	127.4	129.3	128.7	128.4	126.6	124.5	124.6	122.4	125.3
2002	114.5	114.3	115.9	117.9	120.5	122.5	122.4	122.7	122.3	121.1	119.9	120.1	119.5
2003	113.6	112.4	115.0	118.5	120.9	122.5	122.5	123.3	123.2	121.8	120.7	120.8	119.6
2004	115.3	115.2	117.8	120.2	122.8	124.8	124.8	124.4	123.8	122.0	121.8	120.9	121.2
2005	117.0	117.6	120.3	121.4	124.2	127.0	128.1	129.4	130.1	129.4	129.2	129.1	125.2
2006	126.4	126.9	131.6	133.3	135.2	138.3	137.4	138.4	138.6	136.5	135.5	134.8	134.4
2007	129.9	130.1	135.0	136.6	138.5	141.4	140.5	141.5	141.7	139.6	138.6	138.0	137.6
Manufacturing													
2000	497.7	497.6	497.7	497.1	497.3	499.8	493.8	493.5	491.0	485.9	483.1	482.1	493.1
2001	473.0	467.6	466.6	463.0	459.4	458.3	450.6	450.4	447.7	440.7	437.2	436.1	454.2
2002	430.1	428.8	428.4	428.4	430.6	431.5	429.6	431.4	430.1	426.7	423.2	423.1	428.5
2003	416.7	415.8	415.3	413.9	413.8	414.5	409.5	411.6	411.3	411.8	411.6	412.7	413.2
2004	406.7	407.6	408.9	411.6	413.7	415.0	412.5	414.7	415.1	412.1	411.4	412.1	411.8
2005	409.0	409.8	410.9	411.0	410.8	411.4	406.2	408.7	409.6	406.2	407.3	404.2	408.8
2006	403.9	402.8	403.4	403.4	403.2	403.5	398.0	400.1	399.1	393.1	391.9	390.4	399.4
2007	387.9	387.3	387.1	382.9	379.6	380.2	377.2	379.8	378.9	377.2	376.4	375.7	380.9
Service-Providing													
2000	2,040.7	2,058.5	2,097.4	2,096.9	2,109.1	2,108.9	2,091.2	2,108.8	2,122.2	2,127.9	2,139.5	2,143.6	2,103.7
2001	2,080.4	2,094.6	2,109.8	2,116.7	2,121.3	2,115.6	2,086.9	2,105.3	2,116.9	2,111.6	2,121.5	2,124.5	2,108.8
2002	2,067.3	2,079.7	2,099.4	2,113.7	2,119.1	2,118.0	2,105.2	2,120.6	2,131.8	2,136.8	2,150.4	2,154.9	2,116.4
2003	2,089.5	2,099.7	2,115.7	2,130.4	2,137.1	2,131.1	2,105.3	2,126.9	2,141.2	2,149.9	2,162.4	2,168.9	2,129.8
2004	2,115.4	2,145.6	2,152.2	2,168.6	2,170.2	2,170.8	2,156.3	2,177.2	2,186.6	2,198.5	2,213.0	2,223.2	2,173.1
2005	2,145.3	2,168.7	2,187.2	2,207.1	2,211.5	2,205.3	2,197.5	2,215.5	2,236.6	2,231.5	2,248.2	2,255.0	2,209.1
2006	2,196.8	2,205.1	2,230.3	2,244.7	2,253.2	2,249.6	2,234.4	2,258.3	2,272.5	2,264.2	2,284.0	2,293.4	2,248.9
2007	2,227.1	2,236.3	2,261.9	2,272.4	2,283.8	2,281.7	2,269.4	2,288.9	2,299.9	2,291.7	2,308.7	2,315.7	2,278.1
Trade, Transportation, and Utilities													
2000	580.5	582.0	586.8	590.1	590.8	596.0	593.9	592.1	592.7	596.4	604.9	608.2	592.9
2001	593.1	589.1	591.6	590.6	592.3	592.2	584.8	586.5	586.2	585.5	593.4	596.6	590.2
2002	569.4	566.1	570.1	570.3	572.3	573.6	576.6	576.6	577.5	581.3	590.2	597.1	576.8
2003	571.2	569.0	572.1	573.4	574.5	576.4	574.4	578.0	579.5	584.7	593.3	598.1	578.7
2004	575.9	574.8	580.0	582.0	583.1	586.0	584.9	587.3	587.6	594.5	604.9	613.0	587.8
2005	578.4	585.4	590.5	593.6	595.8	595.8	599.5	600.2	601.7	602.0	613.5	620.0	598.0
2006	598.3	596.2	602.2	603.5	606.1	607.0	604.2	607.7	608.6	607.4	619.4	626.6	607.3
2007	603.8	600.6	607.1	607.0	609.4	610.1	607.8	612.2	612.5	612.1	621.9	628.7	611.1
Wholesale Trade													
2000	133.3	134.0	134.9	133.7	133.2	133.4	132.8	132.5	132.4	131.5	131.4	131.5	132.9
2001	128.0	128.1	128.6	128.2	128.1	128.0	126.5	126.9	127.4	127.4	126.8	126.9	127.5
2002	124.7	125.0	125.2	125.4	125.8	126.1	126.1	127.0	127.2	127.0	127.8	128.1	126.5
2003	126.7	127.0	127.2	127.2	127.4	127.2	125.9	126.0	125.9	125.8	126.2	126.1	126.6
2004	124.9	125.4	126.6	127.2	127.5	128.4	128.7	129.1	129.0	129.5	129.9	130.2	128.0
2005	128.4	128.8	129.7	130.1	130.7	130.4	130.5	130.6	131.0	130.7	131.1	131.4	130.3
2006	130.0	130.6	131.4	131.7	132.3	132.5	132.6	132.9	133.0	132.4	132.5	132.5	132.0
2007	131.0	131.4	132.3	132.8	133.2	133.6	133.4	133.9	134.2	133.8	133.9	133.9	133.1
Retail Trade													
2000	311.1	310.6	313.3	315.8	316.7	320.5	319.4	319.6	320.6	323.6	332.2	335.8	319.9
2001	322.1	318.4	320.5	319.4	320.0	319.8	314.7	314.8	314.1	314.7	323.7	327.5	319.1
2002	307.8	304.8	307.5	307.7	309.0	310.0	311.2	310.6	312.4	313.9	322.3	328.9	312.2
2003	307.3	304.9	307.0	308.1	308.7	310.2	309.5	312.0	313.5	318.6	326.5	331.9	313.2
2004	313.7	312.2	314.8	315.5	316.3	317.9	316.3	317.4	317.5	322.7	332.4	337.0	319.5
2005	311.7	318.1	321.0	322.2	323.5	323.7	324.1	323.7	324.1	324.8	334.9	339.7	324.3
2006	323.2	320.8	324.7	325.9	327.0	327.4	325.7	327.1	326.7	327.6	338.6	343.7	328.2
2007	327.1	323.5	328.3	327.6	329.0	329.3	327.8	329.8	329.6	331.0	339.7	344.4	330.6

Employment by Industry: Tennessee, 2000–2007—*Continued*

(Numbers in thousands, not seasonally adjusted.)

Industry and year	January	February	March	April	May	June	July	August	September	October	November	December	Annual Average
Transportation and Utilities													
2000	136.1	137.4	138.6	140.6	140.9	142.1	141.7	140.0	139.7	141.3	141.3	140.9	140.1
2001	143.0	142.6	142.5	143.0	144.2	144.4	143.6	144.8	144.7	144.0	142.8	142.4	143.5
2002	136.9	136.3	137.4	137.2	137.5	137.5	138.4	138.8	138.1	139.6	139.8	139.3	138.1
2003	137.2	137.1	137.9	138.1	138.4	139.0	139.0	140.0	140.1	140.3	140.6	140.1	139.0
2004	137.3	137.2	138.6	139.3	139.3	139.7	139.9	140.8	141.1	142.3	142.6	145.8	140.3
2005	138.3	138.5	139.8	141.3	141.6	141.7	144.9	145.9	146.6	146.5	147.5	148.9	143.5
2006	145.1	144.8	146.1	145.9	146.8	147.1	145.9	147.7	148.9	147.4	148.3	150.4	147.0
2007	145.7	145.7	146.5	146.6	147.2	147.2	146.6	148.5	148.7	147.3	148.3	150.4	147.4
Information													
2000	55.1	55.2	55.6	54.6	54.7	55.2	54.6	54.9	55.0	55.2	56.4	56.8	55.3
2001	56.0	56.3	56.5	55.2	55.2	55.7	55.3	55.3	54.5	54.6	55.1	55.4	55.4
2002	54.1	53.9	54.4	53.6	53.8	53.3	52.9	53.0	52.4	52.7	53.1	52.9	53.3
2003	52.1	51.9	51.8	51.7	51.4	51.1	50.5	50.4	49.9	50.6	51.3	51.4	51.2
2004	50.1	49.9	49.7	49.7	49.4	49.6	49.5	49.5	48.3	49.0	49.3	50.0	49.5
2005	49.7	49.7	49.6	49.5	49.7	49.9	49.4	49.2	48.8	48.8	49.3	49.3	49.4
2006	49.1	49.2	49.4	49.9	50.1	50.2	49.3	49.2	49.4	49.4	49.8	50.0	49.6
2007	49.1	49.3	49.2	49.5	49.9	50.0	49.9	50.1	49.9	49.7	49.9	50.1	49.7
Financial Activities													
2000	140.2	140.2	140.4	140.3	140.8	141.9	141.3	141.0	140.7	139.9	140.0	140.7	140.6
2001	137.7	138.0	138.6	138.6	138.8	139.9	139.4	139.3	138.3	137.7	137.8	137.6	138.5
2002	137.2	137.6	137.9	137.7	138.2	138.9	138.2	138.5	137.6	138.0	138.8	139.1	138.1
2003	137.9	137.9	138.5	138.8	139.4	140.1	140.5	140.9	140.2	140.4	141.2	142.0	139.8
2004	140.6	140.4	140.8	141.0	141.5	142.0	142.3	142.5	142.1	142.8	143.1	144.0	141.9
2005	141.3	141.7	142.4	142.9	143.4	144.3	143.9	144.1	144.0	143.5	143.7	144.1	143.3
2006	142.5	142.8	143.5	143.1	143.6	144.3	143.7	144.2	143.7	143.2	143.5	144.2	143.5
2007	142.0	142.8	143.8	143.8	144.9	146.0	145.6	144.9	144.3	143.6	143.8	144.2	144.1
Professional and Business Services													
2000	295.4	298.7	302.7	302.2	302.5	304.8	304.2	308.4	310.4	307.2	305.7	305.6	304.0
2001	299.2	300.5	301.0	299.8	298.3	298.7	296.2	299.4	301.2	297.9	297.4	299.8	299.1
2002	292.3	293.4	297.3	297.4	297.4	297.6	297.8	300.4	298.6	296.2	295.8	293.4	296.5
2003	281.3	282.2	284.0	284.0	286.0	286.7	282.8	288.9	290.9	292.6	294.8	295.5	287.5
2004	288.5	291.8	294.5	299.2	298.9	301.7	301.5	306.5	307.4	312.4	313.6	314.4	302.5
2005	300.6	304.4	306.5	309.9	308.7	310.6	308.3	315.1	319.6	319.8	322.6	325.6	312.6
2006	310.9	311.3	314.9	316.2	316.0	319.6	315.4	321.6	324.3	321.9	327.2	329.1	319.0
2007	310.8	312.6	316.0	318.2	319.5	322.9	321.5	326.2	328.0	325.6	330.4	331.8	322.0
Education and Health Services													
2000	274.2	276.9	279.5	280.9	279.8	278.8	279.1	280.2	285.4	287.3	288.5	288.8	281.6
2001	278.0	281.7	283.6	284.7	285.0	284.0	284.4	286.0	289.5	289.9	291.0	291.9	285.8
2002	288.7	291.2	293.8	296.3	297.8	297.6	299.7	301.8	306.3	307.7	309.6	310.5	300.1
2003	307.2	310.5	311.3	312.7	312.3	311.3	310.1	311.6	314.8	316.9	316.9	317.5	312.8
2004	313.6	316.5	318.6	319.4	318.8	318.5	320.7	322.2	323.5	324.9	326.0	326.6	320.8
2005	323.1	325.2	325.9	329.6	329.5	329.1	330.0	331.7	334.0	334.3	335.2	335.8	330.3
2006	332.6	334.3	336.5	338.9	339.6	339.9	340.1	341.9	344.7	345.5	346.6	347.2	340.7
2007	342.7	345.7	347.4	347.5	348.7	349.0	350.3	351.0	354.0	354.5	355.8	356.3	350.2
Leisure and Hospitality													
2000	218.3	219.4	224.1	233.9	240.2	247.0	247.1	247.4	243.7	237.4	235.9	234.1	235.7
2001	219.0	220.8	228.0	236.5	242.1	247.6	245.4	246.3	240.9	235.4	232.9	231.3	235.5
2002	220.6	223.1	228.9	239.0	243.1	248.7	250.8	252.3	247.4	242.3	241.2	239.7	239.8
2003	229.9	231.6	238.2	247.0	252.6	257.6	255.6	256.6	252.2	247.0	246.2	245.0	246.6
2004	234.8	237.6	244.7	254.6	259.0	262.7	263.2	264.7	261.0	254.9	253.9	252.7	253.7
2005	243.0	244.8	252.0	263.6	268.0	273.4	272.9	272.9	269.3	263.1	261.8	259.6	262.0
2006	252.7	254.3	262.7	270.2	275.3	280.2	280.8	280.8	276.1	270.9	269.0	268.6	270.1
2007	258.9	260.5	268.9	276.2	281.1	288.0	286.6	288.0	281.8	276.5	274.7	273.2	276.2
Other Services													
2000	86.9	87.9	89.4	91.6	92.3	92.7	92.8	96.8	98.1	100.9	102.8	103.6	94.7
2001	99.2	101.1	101.4	101.4	102.1	103.5	100.9	101.1	101.6	100.5	100.5	99.8	101.1
2002	98.6	99.6	100.2	100.2	101.4	102.7	103.0	102.2	102.9	102.9	102.7	102.8	101.6
2003	101.5	101.3	102.2	102.6	103.2	103.4	102.5	102.1	102.1	101.7	101.7	101.7	102.2
2004	100.8	101.5	102.8	102.0	102.0	102.8	102.4	102.0	101.4	101.0	101.0	100.6	101.7
2005	99.0	99.8	101.3	101.4	101.3	102.4	101.5	100.8	100.9	100.0	100.5	99.9	100.7
2006	98.7	99.4	100.8	100.8	101.9	104.0	102.9	102.8	102.9	102.1	102.2	102.5	101.8
2007	101.7	102.3	104.2	104.0	105.2	106.4	105.3	102.7	102.8	102.0	102.1	102.4	103.4
Government													
2000	390.1	398.2	418.9	403.3	408.0	392.5	378.2	388.0	396.2	403.6	405.3	405.8	399.0
2001	398.2	407.1	409.1	409.9	407.5	394.0	380.5	391.4	404.7	410.1	413.4	412.1	403.2
2002	406.4	414.8	416.8	419.2	415.1	405.6	386.2	395.8	409.1	415.7	419.0	419.4	410.3
2003	408.4	415.3	417.6	420.2	417.7	404.5	388.9	398.4	411.6	416.0	417.0	417.7	411.1
2004	411.1	433.1	421.1	420.7	417.5	407.5	391.8	402.5	415.3	419.0	421.2	421.9	415.2
2005	410.2	417.7	419.0	416.6	415.1	399.8	392.0	401.5	418.3	420.0	421.6	420.7	412.7
2006	412.0	417.6	420.3	422.1	420.6	404.4	398.0	410.1	422.8	423.8	426.3	425.2	416.9
2007	418.1	422.5	425.3	426.2	425.1	409.3	402.4	413.8	426.6	427.7	430.1	429.0	421.3

Average Weekly Hours by Selected Industry: Tennessee, 2001–2007

(Not seasonally adjusted.)

Industry and year	January	February	March	April	May	June	July	August	September	October	November	December	Annual Average
Manufacturing													
2001	38.5	38.1	37.9	37.1	38.7	38.9	38.9	39.7	39.8	39.3	39.8	40.2	38.9
2002	39.8	39.7	40.1	39.6	39.5	40.1	39.9	40.5	40.7	40.3	40.1	40.7	40.1
2003	39.4	39.4	39.2	39.3	39.4	39.9	39.0	40.4	40.3	39.9	40.4	40.8	39.8
2004	40.4	40.6	40.6	39.7	40.7	40.5	39.0	40.1	39.4	39.3	39.1	40.2	40.0
2005	39.3	39.3	39.0	38.6	39.2	39.1	38.2	39.1	39.8	39.5	39.1	39.9	39.2
2006	39.3	39.3	39.2	38.9	39.6	39.8	37.8	39.5	39.6	39.6	40.2	39.4	39.4
2007	38.4	39.2	39.7	39.2	39.5	40.0	39.2	42.1	42.1	39.9	39.7	41.0	40.0

Average Hourly Earnings by Selected Industry: Tennessee, 2001–2007

(Dollars, not seasonally adjusted.)

Industry and year	January	February	March	April	May	June	July	August	September	October	November	December	Annual Average
Manufacturing													
2001	12.95	12.97	12.99	12.92	12.75	12.88	12.83	12.72	12.79	12.81	12.89	13.05	12.88
2002	13.09	13.01	13.13	13.00	13.07	13.18	13.11	13.13	13.16	13.19	13.28	13.47	13.15
2003	13.47	13.59	13.45	13.56	13.57	13.50	13.63	13.55	13.58	13.52	13.60	13.71	13.56
2004	13.70	13.75	13.72	13.89	13.81	13.78	13.92	13.78	13.93	13.86	14.01	13.96	13.84
2005	13.94	13.89	13.89	13.97	14.21	13.96	13.89	13.85	14.09	14.30	14.30	14.00	14.02
2006	14.07	14.07	14.02	14.07	14.06	13.95	14.04	14.01	14.07	14.04	14.09	13.95	14.04
2007	14.50	14.32	14.27	14.35	14.30	14.24	14.30	14.72	14.73	14.37	14.26	14.30	14.39

Average Weekly Earnings by Selected Industry: Tennessee, 2001–2007

(Dollars, not seasonally adjusted.)

Industry and year	January	February	March	April	May	June	July	August	September	October	November	December	Annual Average
Manufacturing													
2001	498.58	494.16	492.32	479.33	493.43	501.03	499.09	504.98	509.04	503.43	513.02	524.61	501.03
2002	520.98	516.50	526.51	514.80	516.27	528.52	523.09	531.77	535.61	531.56	532.53	548.23	527.32
2003	530.72	535.45	527.24	532.91	534.66	538.65	531.57	547.42	547.27	539.45	549.44	559.37	539.69
2004	553.48	558.25	557.03	551.43	562.07	558.09	542.88	552.58	548.84	544.70	547.79	561.19	553.60
2005	547.84	545.88	541.71	539.24	557.03	545.84	530.60	541.54	560.78	564.85	559.13	558.60	549.58
2006	552.95	552.95	549.58	547.32	556.78	555.21	530.71	553.40	557.17	555.98	566.42	549.63	553.18
2007	556.80	561.34	566.52	562.52	564.85	569.60	560.56	619.71	620.13	573.36	566.12	586.30	575.60

Population
    2000 census: 20,851,820
    2007 estimate: 23,904,380
    Percent change, 2000–2007: 14.6%

Percent change in total nonfarm employment, 2000–2007: 9.8%

Industry with the largest growth in employment, 2000–2007 (thousands)
    Education and health services, 251.7

Industry with the largest decline in employment, 2000–2007 (thousands)
    Manufacturing, -133.3

Civilian labor force
    2000: 10,347,847
    2007: 11,492,422

Employment-population ratio
    2000: 65.1%
    2007: 62.9%

Unemployment rate and rank among states
    2000: 4.4%, 37th
    2007: 4.3%, 23rd

Employment by Industry, 2007

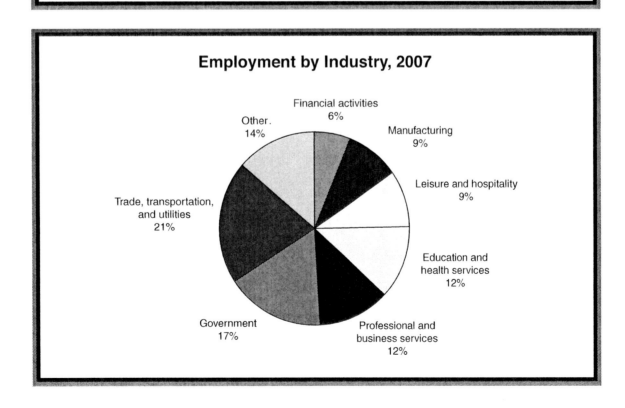

Employment by Industry: Texas, 2000–2007

(Numbers in thousands, not seasonally adjusted.)

Industry and year	January	February	March	April	May	June	July	August	September	October	November	December	Annual Average
Total Nonfarm													
2000	9,195.7	9,275.3	9,357.2	9,369.9	9,444.8	9,472.5	9,388.1	9,455.7	9,521.6	9,522.3	9,564.6	9,614.3	9,431.8
2001	9,423.5	9,493.3	9,550.1	9,547.6	9,574.7	9,583.5	9,460.9	9,511.3	9,532.2	9,488.8	9,498.6	9,502.8	9,513.9
2002	9,306.2	9,360.2	9,417.4	9,423.2	9,469.2	9,452.1	9,347.9	9,401.0	9,450.7	9,428.9	9,461.5	9,473.1	9,416.0
2003	9,280.8	9,327.0	9,361.1	9,374.5	9,402.3	9,380.0	9,281.4	9,337.0	9,394.7	9,404.0	9,432.4	9,465.3	9,370.0
2004	9,306.9	9,371.6	9,433.9	9,480.3	9,506.8	9,507.2	9,450.7	9,496.4	9,545.7	9,585.2	9,621.6	9,658.8	9,497.1
2005	9,493.0	9,563.8	9,634.0	9,700.8	9,730.9	9,736.6	9,697.9	9,751.5	9,834.1	9,847.1	9,926.9	9,968.8	9,740.5
2006	9,809.9	9,892.6	9,981.2	10,005.5	10,061.1	10,090.3	9,994.5	10,073.8	10,158.7	10,178.1	10,249.7	10,299.4	10,066.2
2007	10,106.1	10,206.6	10,301.8	10,303.8	10,365.1	10,405.7	10,311.9	10,369.5	10,419.6	10,470.4	10,511.5	10,538.0	10,359.0
Total Private													
2000	7,648.6	7,699.1	7,773.3	7,785.6	7,837.3	7,935.5	7,912.9	7,956.0	7,957.2	7,938.6	7,972.2	8,022.5	7,869.9
2001	7,857.8	7,898.6	7,950.1	7,946.4	7,972.7	8,023.8	7,966.7	7,988.5	7,929.1	7,864.7	7,862.3	7,872.0	7,927.7
2002	7,700.8	7,722.2	7,772.3	7,778.5	7,821.8	7,852.5	7,817.6	7,850.2	7,818.2	7,760.8	7,783.6	7,801.5	7,790.0
2003	7,638.0	7,649.2	7,685.0	7,697.1	7,725.1	7,747.9	7,726.0	7,766.5	7,752.5	7,739.9	7,759.1	7,801.6	7,724.0
2004	7,666.7	7,697.2	7,757.8	7,803.6	7,828.1	7,870.5	7,882.7	7,910.2	7,883.8	7,900.4	7,927.7	7,970.3	7,841.6
2005	7,826.5	7,863.1	7,930.9	7,995.6	8,023.9	8,076.2	8,100.4	8,133.1	8,143.8	8,131.2	8,199.1	8,253.4	8,056.4
2006	8,113.5	8,163.7	8,251.2	8,279.0	8,333.9	8,406.4	8,385.5	8,439.0	8,447.4	8,436.9	8,499.7	8,556.9	8,359.4
2007	8,389.8	8,458.5	8,547.3	8,552.4	8,609.6	8,688.2	8,666.8	8,714.5	8,695.7	8,720.5	8,749.5	8,783.6	8,631.2
Goods-Producing													
2000	1,738.4	1,754.4	1,772.6	1,764.6	1,775.3	1,798.1	1,791.1	1,795.2	1,795.8	1,786.2	1,783.2	1,786.4	1,778.4
2001	1,766.9	1,779.8	1,788.6	1,777.2	1,778.4	1,785.7	1,768.2	1,769.7	1,753.1	1,732.3	1,719.4	1,706.8	1,760.5
2002	1,673.5	1,674.2	1,680.7	1,669.9	1,674.5	1,681.5	1,668.5	1,671.2	1,659.0	1,640.4	1,631.1	1,622.6	1,662.3
2003	1,601.6	1,601.8	1,601.3	1,601.0	1,606.4	1,610.1	1,601.2	1,604.3	1,601.1	1,590.6	1,581.5	1,583.1	1,598.7
2004	1,566.5	1,569.7	1,578.3	1,581.6	1,584.1	1,594.7	1,597.5	1,599.8	1,597.1	1,598.9	1,597.6	1,600.7	1,588.9
2005	1,584.7	1,592.8	1,606.5	1,617.0	1,622.0	1,636.1	1,643.4	1,646.4	1,651.9	1,649.1	1,656.0	1,665.2	1,630.9
2006	1,655.1	1,671.3	1,691.4	1,691.8	1,707.9	1,732.3	1,727.0	1,736.4	1,743.8	1,740.7	1,746.7	1,753.0	1,716.5
2007	1,733.0	1,750.5	1,766.9	1,766.6	1,778.0	1,801.7	1,792.9	1,801.6	1,800.6	1,804.6	1,799.0	1,799.4	1,782.8
Natural Resources and Mining													
2000	140.7	140.6	141.6	139.6	140.7	142.3	143.4	144.2	144.7	146.2	146.4	149.5	143.3
2001	147.0	148.8	150.5	151.3	152.4	155.3	156.0	156.9	155.8	155.2	154.2	153.7	153.0
2002	147.8	146.9	146.1	144.6	145.4	146.3	145.0	145.6	145.6	143.8	143.9	144.2	145.4
2003	142.7	143.4	144.5	144.7	146.0	147.4	148.3	149.4	148.9	147.9	147.9	149.6	146.7
2004	149.3	149.4	150.7	150.3	151.3	153.0	153.9	154.7	154.7	155.7	156.4	157.6	153.1
2005	158.5	159.2	160.2	161.7	163.2	166.0	168.2	169.2	169.8	171.0	172.1	174.1	166.1
2006	173.3	175.7	177.6	179.4	181.5	186.0	188.1	190.4	192.6	194.4	195.6	197.2	186.0
2007	197.6	199.3	201.4	201.4	203.1	206.7	207.9	209.9	209.1	210.6	211.1	214.0	206.0
Construction													
2000	539.7	550.7	563.2	561.4	567.6	579.9	577.4	580.2	578.5	571.5	567.9	567.6	567.1
2001	564.5	575.8	584.7	581.7	586.8	591.8	586.5	590.7	584.0	576.8	574.4	568.8	580.5
2002	556.6	563.2	572.8	569.7	575.5	579.9	574.3	577.8	571.4	564.0	559.0	553.1	568.1
2003	545.8	547.4	550.0	551.3	558.3	559.8	555.9	558.9	556.7	552.3	543.8	543.7	552.0
2004	534.4	535.7	542.1	543.9	543.4	548.4	549.2	549.8	548.8	549.2	546.2	546.9	544.8
2005	540.4	545.8	555.6	565.0	566.3	571.0	573.9	575.1	579.6	576.9	578.2	581.4	567.4
2006	576.1	586.3	599.8	595.0	603.2	615.2	609.7	613.8	617.8	616.0	617.9	620.2	605.9
2007	609.2	622.2	635.2	633.7	640.9	653.6	647.2	653.1	654.0	656.6	651.8	649.3	642.1
Manufacturing													
2000	1,058.0	1,063.1	1,067.8	1,063.6	1,067.0	1,075.9	1,070.3	1,070.8	1,072.6	1,068.5	1,068.9	1,069.3	1,068.0
2001	1,055.4	1,055.2	1,053.4	1,044.2	1,039.2	1,038.6	1,025.7	1,022.1	1,013.3	1,000.3	990.8	984.3	1,026.8
2002	969.1	964.1	961.8	955.6	953.6	955.3	949.2	947.8	942.0	932.6	928.2	925.3	948.7
2003	913.1	911.0	906.8	905.0	902.1	902.9	897.0	896.0	895.5	890.4	889.8	889.8	900.0
2004	882.8	884.6	885.5	887.4	889.4	893.3	894.4	895.3	893.6	894.0	895.0	896.2	891.0
2005	885.8	887.8	890.7	890.3	892.5	899.1	901.3	902.1	902.5	901.2	905.7	909.7	897.4
2006	905.7	909.3	914.0	917.4	923.2	931.1	929.2	932.2	933.4	930.3	933.2	935.6	924.6
2007	926.2	929.0	930.3	931.5	934.0	941.4	937.8	938.6	937.5	937.4	936.1	936.1	934.7
Service-Providing													
2000	7,457.3	7,520.9	7,584.6	7,605.3	7,669.5	7,674.4	7,597.0	7,660.5	7,725.8	7,736.1	7,781.4	7,827.9	7,653.4
2001	7,656.6	7,713.5	7,761.5	7,770.4	7,796.3	7,797.8	7,692.7	7,741.6	7,779.1	7,756.5	7,779.2	7,796.0	7,753.4
2002	7,632.7	7,686.0	7,736.7	7,753.3	7,794.7	7,770.6	7,679.4	7,729.8	7,791.7	7,788.5	7,830.4	7,850.5	7,753.7
2003	7,679.2	7,725.2	7,759.8	7,773.5	7,795.9	7,769.9	7,680.2	7,732.7	7,793.6	7,813.4	7,850.9	7,882.2	7,771.4
2004	7,740.4	7,801.9	7,855.6	7,898.7	7,922.7	7,912.5	7,853.2	7,896.6	7,948.6	7,986.3	8,024.0	8,058.1	7,908.2
2005	7,908.3	7,971.0	8,027.5	8,083.8	8,108.9	8,100.5	8,054.5	8,105.1	8,182.2	8,198.0	8,270.9	8,303.6	8,109.5
2006	8,154.8	8,221.3	8,289.8	8,313.7	8,353.2	8,358.0	8,267.5	8,337.4	8,414.9	8,437.4	8,503.0	8,546.4	8,349.8
2007	8,373.1	8,456.1	8,534.9	8,537.2	8,587.1	8,604.0	8,519.0	8,567.9	8,619.0	8,665.8	8,712.5	8,738.6	8,576.3
Trade, Transportation, and Utilities													
2000	1,943.9	1,940.1	1,946.6	1,944.4	1,955.6	1,976.2	1,969.2	1,988.0	1,982.4	1,993.6	2,030.9	2,065.7	1,978.1
2001	1,987.5	1,975.6	1,982.6	1,978.9	1,984.0	1,992.5	1,983.7	1,991.5	1,980.4	1,977.1	1,994.5	2,015.4	1,987.0
2002	1,946.2	1,933.8	1,940.9	1,939.2	1,947.0	1,951.6	1,946.7	1,951.4	1,943.8	1,938.9	1,966.2	1,991.0	1,949.7
2003	1,912.0	1,897.3	1,900.1	1,898.2	1,899.0	1,904.7	1,902.1	1,917.1	1,915.4	1,923.9	1,952.8	1,980.0	1,916.9
2004	1,915.0	1,909.1	1,919.2	1,926.8	1,933.2	1,937.1	1,942.9	1,957.4	1,947.2	1,958.3	1,991.4	2,019.4	1,946.4
2005	1,955.5	1,944.1	1,955.8	1,966.0	1,974.7	1,984.8	1,994.1	2,008.5	2,005.7	2,007.9	2,056.4	2,087.5	1,995.1
2006	2,015.1	2,006.2	2,023.3	2,024.2	2,033.0	2,041.7	2,040.8	2,057.8	2,055.6	2,064.0	2,105.4	2,137.0	2,050.3
2007	2,072.1	2,064.6	2,085.0	2,075.5	2,086.6	2,100.1	2,098.9	2,111.7	2,108.7	2,118.8	2,151.0	2,174.4	2,104.0
Wholesale Trade													
2000	459.7	461.8	463.2	463.9	465.8	470.5	470.9	471.6	472.5	471.6	472.9	475.4	468.3
2001	472.9	474.5	476.7	475.8	475.8	477.1	476.0	475.6	472.9	470.0	467.5	468.1	473.5
2002	460.9	460.7	463.3	461.7	463.3	465.4	465.3	465.9	465.0	462.9	463.8	464.7	463.6
2003	457.2	456.8	458.0	457.2	458.2	460.4	459.3	459.8	459.7	458.3	458.8	460.5	458.7
2004	455.0	455.7	458.2	460.4	461.9	464.2	466.4	466.8	466.4	468.0	468.6	470.0	463.5
2005	465.4	466.4	469.0	473.0	475.2	478.0	481.2	482.1	484.1	483.2	485.4	489.1	477.7
2006	485.7	488.5	492.4	492.9	495.8	500.2	499.4	501.6	503.4	503.4	506.2	509.5	498.3
2007	504.7	508.1	511.4	505.1	508.1	513.7	513.2	515.5	515.5	514.8	513.2	516.5	511.7

Employment by Industry: Texas, 2000–2007—*Continued*

(Numbers in thousands, not seasonally adjusted.)

Industry and year	January	February	March	April	May	June	July	August	September	October	November	December	Annual Average
Retail Trade													
2000	1,087.1	1,079.3	1,084.3	1,081.5	1,089.0	1,101.0	1,094.3	1,109.0	1,101.6	1,112.1	1,146.1	1,172.8	1,104.8
2001	1,108.4	1,096.0	1,101.1	1,099.8	1,102.9	1,108.7	1,101.6	1,108.0	1,100.8	1,100.7	1,126.5	1,147.9	1,108.5
2002	1,094.6	1,083.6	1,088.5	1,088.8	1,092.9	1,094.4	1,088.2	1,090.2	1,085.7	1,081.0	1,108.2	1,131.5	1,094.0
2003	1,066.6	1,053.8	1,055.8	1,055.3	1,056.5	1,059.4	1,057.8	1,068.7	1,067.1	1,074.1	1,101.9	1,123.0	1,070.0
2004	1,069.5	1,061.2	1,067.9	1,071.4	1,075.2	1,076.3	1,076.9	1,090.4	1,080.7	1,087.8	1,118.8	1,139.9	1,084.7
2005	1,089.0	1,078.4	1,086.1	1,091.0	1,095.7	1,102.9	1,106.9	1,116.7	1,110.5	1,112.7	1,155.0	1,176.8	1,110.1
2006	1,119.4	1,107.3	1,117.9	1,117.6	1,121.3	1,123.3	1,123.3	1,134.9	1,128.7	1,136.1	1,172.8	1,191.8	1,132.9
2007	1,143.0	1,130.6	1,144.2	1,142.8	1,148.8	1,153.7	1,154.7	1,162.2	1,157.9	1,164.3	1,197.9	1,218.8	1,159.9
Transportation and Utilities													
2000	397.1	399.0	399.1	399.0	400.8	404.7	404.0	407.4	408.3	409.9	411.9	417.5	404.9
2001	406.2	405.1	404.8	403.3	405.3	406.7	406.1	407.9	406.7	406.4	400.5	399.4	404.8
2002	390.7	389.5	389.1	388.7	390.8	391.8	393.2	395.3	393.1	395.0	394.2	394.8	392.2
2003	388.2	386.7	386.3	385.7	384.3	384.9	385.0	388.6	388.6	391.5	392.1	396.5	388.2
2004	390.5	392.2	393.1	395.0	396.1	396.6	399.6	400.2	400.1	402.5	404.0	409.5	398.3
2005	401.1	399.3	400.7	402.0	403.8	403.9	406.0	409.7	411.1	412.0	416.0	421.6	407.3
2006	410.0	410.4	413.0	413.7	415.9	418.2	418.1	421.3	423.5	424.5	426.4	435.7	419.2
2007	424.4	425.9	429.4	427.6	429.7	432.7	431.0	434.0	435.3	439.7	439.9	439.1	432.4
Information													
2000	258.2	259.7	262.3	266.5	269.8	275.5	276.7	278.7	279.9	278.3	280.6	280.7	272.2
2001	273.4	274.6	274.9	273.7	273.3	273.6	269.7	268.7	266.5	264.8	264.1	261.9	269.9
2002	258.3	256.3	255.2	251.9	251.8	251.5	247.9	246.7	244.4	243.8	243.2	242.6	249.5
2003	238.6	237.9	237.5	235.4	235.3	235.3	234.3	233.1	230.5	229.4	229.8	229.4	233.9
2004	227.6	225.7	227.4	226.0	226.3	227.0	225.4	224.4	222.5	222.6	222.8	223.4	225.1
2005	222.0	222.3	222.7	223.0	223.3	224.8	224.3	224.1	224.1	222.2	223.3	223.9	223.3
2006	221.4	222.3	222.5	222.1	222.8	224.0	221.8	221.5	221.1	220.0	220.7	221.4	221.8
2007	219.4	220.7	220.7	219.1	220.8	221.4	221.3	221.7	219.8	220.8	222.4	223.0	220.9
Financial Activities													
2000	558.8	560.5	563.4	564.3	565.6	570.4	571.6	571.7	570.6	570.7	571.6	575.6	567.9
2001	569.5	572.5	574.9	576.1	577.9	582.7	582.6	582.6	579.5	578.3	577.4	580.3	577.8
2002	575.2	575.9	577.2	576.6	580.0	582.8	583.1	583.7	580.8	580.3	581.9	583.1	580.1
2003	577.8	579.8	581.2	582.6	585.2	587.9	589.4	591.3	588.2	588.2	588.0	590.6	585.9
2004	586.5	587.4	588.9	591.6	592.4	596.5	599.8	600.8	599.5	600.6	600.5	604.7	595.8
2005	597.4	599.1	600.6	602.8	604.1	608.6	614.3	616.5	617.2	617.5	619.1	622.0	609.9
2006	614.6	617.2	621.1	624.4	627.0	632.3	630.9	633.8	633.6	633.9	634.8	639.3	628.6
2007	633.7	636.8	639.8	639.4	643.2	647.7	647.9	649.0	645.4	647.2	647.5	651.1	644.1
Professional and Business Services													
2000	1,053.7	1,064.5	1,080.3	1,086.3	1,092.3	1,114.9	1,116.0	1,124.5	1,129.1	1,125.3	1,124.2	1,129.4	1,103.4
2001	1,102.4	1,108.2	1,114.2	1,110.6	1,108.4	1,115.7	1,105.1	1,107.8	1,096.3	1,079.9	1,076.1	1,074.6	1,099.9
2002	1,043.6	1,048.5	1,056.1	1,061.8	1,063.6	1,067.9	1,065.8	1,075.8	1,070.3	1,062.3	1,061.8	1,059.6	1,061.4
2003	1,034.4	1,038.7	1,045.0	1,050.7	1,051.1	1,052.1	1,051.2	1,060.0	1,060.6	1,062.3	1,065.4	1,074.0	1,053.8
2004	1,055.8	1,064.6	1,073.2	1,089.2	1,090.2	1,099.3	1,105.5	1,111.1	1,107.4	1,115.2	1,117.1	1,120.5	1,095.8
2005	1,103.6	1,117.4	1,126.8	1,145.7	1,143.2	1,152.9	1,158.2	1,168.0	1,178.7	1,188.2	1,195.4	1,203.6	1,156.8
2006	1,184.2	1,199.3	1,214.8	1,221.0	1,226.9	1,239.5	1,240.9	1,252.3	1,257.0	1,256.9	1,267.4	1,274.8	1,236.3
2007	1,245.1	1,263.1	1,276.9	1,274.6	1,279.9	1,294.0	1,293.8	1,306.6	1,306.2	1,317.1	1,316.5	1,320.3	1,291.2
Education and Health Services													
2000	981.0	989.1	994.6	996.1	1,000.1	999.7	996.8	1,006.1	1,018.8	1,016.4	1,019.9	1,022.2	1,003.4
2001	1,013.8	1,024.5	1,030.3	1,032.0	1,037.0	1,041.5	1,039.1	1,048.1	1,054.4	1,056.4	1,060.7	1,063.3	1,041.7
2002	1,054.8	1,066.2	1,071.0	1,074.5	1,080.4	1,077.1	1,077.6	1,090.1	1,101.2	1,097.0	1,103.0	1,105.7	1,083.2
2003	1,098.8	1,107.8	1,112.4	1,113.9	1,117.1	1,109.5	1,111.3	1,121.6	1,133.7	1,135.6	1,137.2	1,137.0	1,119.7
2004	1,124.8	1,135.8	1,141.1	1,144.5	1,146.1	1,141.9	1,143.8	1,150.8	1,159.9	1,169.9	1,171.6	1,174.6	1,150.4
2005	1,157.6	1,167.9	1,174.2	1,177.4	1,179.6	1,176.7	1,181.1	1,189.3	1,200.8	1,199.1	1,204.1	1,207.1	1,184.6
2006	1,193.3	1,201.9	1,206.1	1,206.7	1,210.1	1,210.2	1,208.0	1,221.3	1,231.2	1,232.6	1,236.6	1,240.4	1,216.5
2007	1,221.9	1,237.0	1,245.2	1,244.6	1,250.5	1,250.4	1,248.3	1,260.6	1,270.0	1,274.6	1,278.6	1,279.2	1,255.1
Leisure and Hospitality													
2000	776.0	789.6	808.8	817.8	831.1	848.0	840.0	840.9	829.9	819.2	813.7	813.8	819.1
2001	793.7	810.3	827.8	840.8	854.7	868.3	861.3	863.2	845.4	826.3	820.2	820.0	836.0
2002	801.5	816.3	835.3	848.3	865.1	877.0	869.3	872.2	860.5	843.3	840.2	840.8	847.5
2003	821.9	831.9	848.8	858.5	873.2	886.0	877.9	881.3	867.9	859.2	853.8	855.4	859.7
2004	839.3	851.4	870.9	885.4	898.4	913.3	909.9	910.8	898.7	887.1	881.1	881.4	885.6
2005	862.4	875.1	894.7	913.2	926.0	937.6	931.8	929.6	917.1	903.1	900.7	899.7	907.6
2006	888.7	902.7	924.9	939.3	955.6	971.4	965.4	966.5	956.8	941.6	940.1	942.9	941.3
2007	919.8	937.3	960.9	979.7	995.7	1,012.3	1,006.1	1,006.2	990.5	983.8	981.3	982.4	979.7
Other Services													
2000	338.6	341.2	344.7	345.6	347.5	352.7	351.5	350.9	350.7	348.9	348.1	348.7	347.4
2001	350.6	353.0	356.8	357.0	359.0	363.7	357.0	356.9	353.5	349.6	349.9	349.7	354.7
2002	347.7	351.1	355.9	356.3	359.5	363.2	358.7	359.1	358.2	354.7	356.2	356.1	356.4
2003	352.9	354.0	358.7	356.8	357.8	362.3	358.6	357.8	355.1	350.7	350.6	352.1	355.6
2004	351.2	353.5	358.8	358.5	357.4	360.7	357.9	355.1	351.5	347.8	345.6	345.6	353.6
2005	343.3	344.4	349.6	350.5	351.0	354.7	353.2	350.7	348.3	344.1	344.1	344.4	348.2
2006	341.1	342.8	347.1	349.5	350.6	355.0	350.7	349.4	348.3	347.2	348.0	348.1	348.2
2007	344.8	348.5	351.9	352.9	354.9	360.6	357.6	357.1	354.5	353.6	353.2	353.8	353.6
Government													
2000	1,547.1	1,576.2	1,583.9	1,584.3	1,607.5	1,537.0	1,475.2	1,499.7	1,564.4	1,583.7	1,592.4	1,591.8	1,561.9
2001	1,565.7	1,594.7	1,600.0	1,601.2	1,602.0	1,559.7	1,494.2	1,522.8	1,603.1	1,624.1	1,636.3	1,630.8	1,586.2
2002	1,605.4	1,638.0	1,645.1	1,644.7	1,647.4	1,599.6	1,530.3	1,550.8	1,632.5	1,668.1	1,677.9	1,671.6	1,626.0
2003	1,642.8	1,677.8	1,676.1	1,677.4	1,677.2	1,632.1	1,555.4	1,570.5	1,642.2	1,664.1	1,673.3	1,663.7	1,646.1
2004	1,640.2	1,674.4	1,676.1	1,676.7	1,678.7	1,636.7	1,568.0	1,586.2	1,661.9	1,684.8	1,693.9	1,688.5	1,655.5
2005	1,666.5	1,700.7	1,703.1	1,705.2	1,707.0	1,660.4	1,597.5	1,618.4	1,690.3	1,715.9	1,727.8	1,715.4	1,684.0
2006	1,696.4	1,728.9	1,730.0	1,726.5	1,727.2	1,683.9	1,609.0	1,634.8	1,711.3	1,741.2	1,750.0	1,742.5	1,706.8
2007	1,716.3	1,748.1	1,754.5	1,751.4	1,755.5	1,717.5	1,645.1	1,655.0	1,723.9	1,749.9	1,762.0	1,754.4	1,727.8

Average Weekly Hours by Selected Industry: Texas, 2001–2007

(Not seasonally adjusted.)

Industry and year	January	February	March	April	May	June	July	August	September	October	November	December	Annual Average
Natural Resources and Mining													
2001	46.0	47.7	47.2	49.1	48.0	48.7	48.6	48.3	49.8	49.4	48.8	47.7	48.3
2002	46.0	45.9	46.1	45.4	46.5	47.5	46.1	47.5	45.3	45.7	43.8	45.1	45.9
2003	44.0	44.7	43.2	41.6	43.3	43.4	44.8	45.0	46.8	45.3	46.1	45.1	44.5
2004	44.2	43.5	42.6	43.6	43.3	44.6	44.3	44.4	45.9	43.9	44.4	44.9	44.1
2005	44.8	43.4	43.5	44.2	45.7	44.4	44.5	45.6	44.0	45.2	43.7	44.6	44.5
2006	44.5	43.0	44.2	44.2	44.0	44.7	44.1	44.6	44.3	44.3	45.4	43.5	44.2
2007	42.2	42.9	41.3	41.9	40.9	40.5	40.9	41.1	41.5	41.6	42.8	43.2	41.7
Manufacturing													
2001	42.4	41.7	41.8	40.4	41.6	41.5	41.6	41.7	41.7	41.3	41.7	41.9	41.6
2002	41.2	40.4	40.9	40.6	41.0	42.1	41.1	41.7	41.4	40.8	40.9	41.6	41.1
2003	41.6	41.3	41.7	41.1	41.3	41.5	41.0	41.7	41.5	41.2	41.4	41.5	41.4
2004	40.6	40.2	39.9	39.8	40.1	39.5	39.2	40.1	39.4	39.5	39.3	40.3	39.8
2005	39.7	39.3	40.4	40.0	40.7	40.1	39.3	39.6	40.0	40.2	40.8	39.8	40.0
2006	40.0	40.3	40.6	40.6	40.9	40.8	40.9	41.1	41.3	41.4	41.3	41.5	40.9
2007	41.2	41.7	41.7	41.7	41.9	41.8	41.7	41.0	41.2	41.4	40.8	41.4	41.5
Wholesale Trade													
2001	39.4	39.5	39.6	39.6	38.7	39.6	40.6	40.7	41.1	40.3	41.1	41.3	40.1
2002	39.5	39.5	38.5	39.1	38.4	39.2	38.3	38.0	37.1	36.8	36.8	37.6	38.2
2003	37.4	37.9	37.6	37.2	38.2	38.2	37.4	36.9	36.6	37.3	37.3	37.8	37.5
2004	37.2	38.0	37.0	37.6	37.6	37.4	37.5	38.2	37.9	38.2	38.5	38.1	37.8
2005	39.5	39.1	39.1	38.3	38.8	40.1	39.8	39.4	40.8	41.6	40.7	40.6	39.8
2006	42.3	40.3	41.4	41.2	41.8	41.8	40.9	40.1	39.6	40.2	40.2	40.6	40.9
2007	40.0	41.4	41.5	42.4	41.7	42.3	41.9	40.3	41.4	40.2	40.4	41.4	41.2

Average Hourly Earnings by Selected Industry: Texas, 2001–2007

(Dollars, not seasonally adjusted.)

Industry and year	January	February	March	April	May	June	July	August	September	October	November	December	Annual Average
Natural Resources and Mining													
2001	15.50	15.21	15.61	15.31	15.50	15.41	15.46	15.37	15.21	15.43	15.50	15.38	15.41
2002	15.42	15.39	15.46	15.42	15.45	15.56	15.66	15.53	15.37	15.46	15.41	15.56	15.47
2003	15.51	15.50	15.36	15.59	15.10	15.15	15.08	15.05	15.19	15.20	15.11	15.26	15.25
2004	15.38	15.46	15.45	15.35	15.44	15.49	15.49	15.38	15.32	15.34	15.35	15.34	15.40
2005	15.40	15.30	15.40	15.48	15.39	15.39	15.39	15.54	15.64	15.68	15.51	15.50	15.47
2006	15.54	15.57	15.57	15.56	15.65	15.57	15.58	15.58	15.59	15.59	15.58	15.58	15.58
2007	15.60	15.66	15.70	15.73	15.79	15.86	15.91	15.86	15.90	15.89	15.78	15.82	15.79
Manufacturing													
2001	14.07	14.02	14.14	14.02	13.98	14.03	14.07	14.03	14.04	13.97	14.00	14.05	14.04
2002	13.97	13.95	13.95	13.91	13.83	13.92	13.97	13.92	14.00	13.90	13.90	13.95	13.93
2003	13.95	13.87	13.91	13.97	13.95	13.91	13.97	13.94	13.93	13.92	14.01	13.97	13.94
2004	13.99	13.95	13.96	13.94	14.01	13.97	13.97	13.98	13.97	13.99	14.01	14.00	13.98
2005	13.98	13.93	14.01	14.03	14.08	14.05	14.08	14.04	14.07	14.01	14.03	14.03	14.03
2006	14.01	14.01	13.96	13.96	13.97	13.96	14.01	13.97	14.01	14.05	14.04	14.08	14.00
2007	14.08	14.00	14.06	14.09	14.09	14.09	14.13	14.14	14.09	14.05	14.02	14.06	14.07
Wholesale Trade													
2001	15.20	15.41	15.43	15.36	15.30	15.18	15.24	15.15	15.23	15.18	15.08	15.20	15.25
2002	15.31	15.33	15.25	15.35	15.25	15.31	15.40	15.44	15.49	15.50	15.58	15.61	15.40
2003	15.51	15.55	15.49	15.43	15.50	15.54	15.60	15.62	15.66	15.62	15.69	15.68	15.57
2004	15.74	15.65	15.70	15.68	15.60	15.54	15.62	15.56	15.58	15.63	15.53	15.62	15.62
2005	15.66	15.73	15.79	15.84	15.76	15.74	15.82	15.81	15.87	15.90	15.86	15.90	15.81
2006	15.85	15.87	15.83	15.84	15.89	15.64	15.74	15.75	15.86	15.76	15.88	15.92	15.82
2007	15.88	15.56	15.87	15.73	15.84	16.08	16.11	15.83	15.94	16.01	16.06	15.92	15.90

Average Weekly Earnings by Selected Industry: Texas, 2001–2007

(Dollars, not seasonally adjusted.)

Industry and year	January	February	March	April	May	June	July	August	September	October	November	December	Annual Average
Natural Resources and Mining													
2001	713.00	725.52	736.79	751.72	744.00	750.47	751.36	742.37	757.46	762.24	756.40	733.63	744.30
2002	709.32	706.40	712.71	700.07	718.43	739.10	721.93	737.68	696.26	706.52	674.96	701.76	710.07
2003	682.44	692.85	663.55	648.54	653.83	657.51	675.58	677.25	710.89	688.56	696.57	688.23	678.63
2004	679.80	672.51	658.17	669.26	668.55	690.85	686.21	682.87	703.19	673.43	681.54	688.77	679.14
2005	689.92	664.02	669.90	684.22	703.32	683.32	684.86	708.62	688.16	708.74	677.79	691.30	688.42
2006	691.53	669.51	688.19	687.75	688.60	695.98	687.08	694.87	690.64	690.64	707.33	677.73	688.64
2007	658.32	671.81	648.41	659.09	645.81	642.33	650.72	651.85	659.85	661.02	675.38	683.42	658.44
Manufacturing													
2001	596.57	584.63	591.05	566.41	581.57	582.25	585.31	585.05	585.47	576.96	583.80	588.70	584.06
2002	575.56	563.58	570.56	564.75	567.03	586.03	574.17	580.46	579.60	567.12	568.51	580.32	572.52
2003	580.32	572.83	580.05	574.17	576.14	577.27	572.77	581.30	578.10	573.50	580.01	579.76	577.12
2004	567.99	560.79	557.00	554.81	561.80	551.82	547.62	560.60	550.42	552.61	550.59	564.20	556.40
2005	555.01	547.45	566.00	561.20	573.06	563.41	553.34	555.98	562.80	563.20	572.42	558.39	561.20
2006	560.40	564.60	566.78	566.78	571.37	569.57	573.01	574.17	578.61	581.67	579.85	584.32	572.60
2007	580.10	583.80	586.30	587.55	590.37	588.96	589.22	579.74	580.51	581.67	572.02	582.08	583.91
Wholesale Trade													
2001	598.88	608.70	611.03	608.26	592.11	601.13	618.74	616.61	625.95	611.75	619.79	627.76	611.53
2002	604.75	605.54	587.13	600.19	585.60	600.15	589.82	586.72	574.68	570.40	573.34	586.94	588.28
2003	580.07	589.35	582.42	574.00	592.10	593.63	583.44	576.38	594.39	582.63	585.24	592.70	583.88
2004	585.53	594.70	580.90	589.57	586.56	581.20	585.75	590.48	597.07	597.91	592.70	595.12	590.44
2005	618.57	615.04	617.39	606.67	611.49	631.17	629.64	622.91	647.50	661.44	645.50	645.54	629.24
2006	670.46	639.56	655.36	652.61	664.20	653.75	643.77	631.58	628.06	633.55	638.38	646.35	629.24
2007	635.20	644.18	658.61	666.95	660.53	680.18	675.01	637.95	659.92	643.60	648.82	659.09	655.08

Population
   2000 census: 2,233,169
   2007 estimate: 2,645,330
   Percent change, 2000–2007: 18.5%

Percent change in total nonfarm employment, 2000–2007: 16.4%

Industry with the largest growth in employment, 2000–2007 (thousands)
   Education and health services, 36.0

Industry with the largest decline in employment, 2000–2007 (thousands)
   Information, -3.0

Civilian labor force
   2000: 1,136,036
   2007: 1,361,768

Employment-population ratio
   2000: 69.3%
   2007: 70.3%

Unemployment rate and rank among states
   2000: 3.4%, 17th
   2007: 2.7%, 2nd

Employment by Industry, 2007

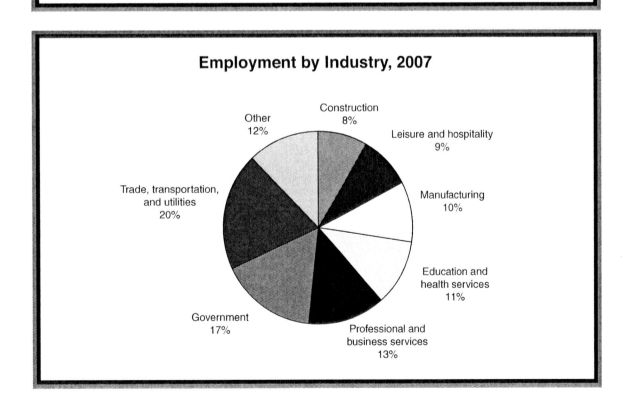

Construction 8%
Other 12%
Leisure and hospitality 9%
Trade, transportation, and utilities 20%
Manufacturing 10%
Education and health services 11%
Government 17%
Professional and business services 13%

Employment by Industry: Utah, 2000–2007

(Numbers in thousands, not seasonally adjusted.)

Industry and year	January	February	March	April	May	June	July	August	September	October	November	December	Annual Average
Total Nonfarm													
2000	1044.9	1053.3	1063.1	1071.1	1074.0	1083.5	1067.3	1073.8	1088.4	1089.0	1094.5	1101.7	1075.4
2001	1069.2	1072.9	1080.2	1083.5	1084.3	1091.3	1073.4	1078.4	1088.4	1083.5	1085.3	1085.7	1081.3
2002	1062.8	1069.6	1065.7	1073.4	1072.0	1077.1	1063.3	1066.5	1079.1	1080.3	1084.4	1087.1	1073.4
2003	1058.2	1059.0	1062.3	1069.2	1069.9	1076.0	1062.8	1070.0	1082.4	1087.8	1092.2	1099.2	1074.1
2004	1072.3	1077.7	1086.2	1098.8	1100.1	1109.8	1096.9	1102.9	1117.1	1123.1	1130.3	1136.4	1104.3
2005	1110.8	1118.0	1126.8	1138.4	1139.7	1149.0	1140.1	1152.1	1168.0	1170.0	1177.9	1185.3	1148.0
2006	1162.9	1171.5	1182.5	1192.9	1196.1	1211.1	1196.1	1208.2	1222.5	1222.8	1234.6	1243.3	1203.7
2007	1219.2	1226.7	1238.5	1247.6	1250.2	1261.0	1243.3	1254.2	1264.1	1262.6	1271.6	1278.7	1251.5
Total Private													
2000	863.7	866.4	874.6	880.7	882.2	895.7	894.7	901.7	902.7	900.5	905.2	912.1	890.0
2001	882.6	881.0	887.5	889.5	890.1	898.0	896.4	901.3	897.1	890.1	890.4	890.7	891.2
2002	868.5	874.6	867.7	874.5	874.4	879.3	878.9	883.6	883.3	882.5	885.9	888.7	878.5
2003	860.1	859.3	862.4	868.1	870.1	878.0	879.3	886.3	885.7	888.4	892.8	899.9	877.5
2004	873.9	877.7	885.1	895.8	898.6	909.4	911.4	915.8	916.8	920.1	926.9	933.5	905.4
2005	908.5	914.0	922.1	932.4	934.7	944.7	951.3	960.4	964.3	964.5	971.8	979.8	945.7
2006	958.9	965.3	975.6	985.2	989.5	1004.0	1004.8	1014.0	1016.5	1015.3	1026.2	1035.7	999.3
2007	1013.2	1018.7	1029.8	1037.6	1040.7	1051.4	1051.0	1058.2	1055.8	1052.7	1060.8	1068.7	1044.9
Goods-Producing													
2000	200.2	199.7	200.9	203.6	205.4	209.6	208.8	210.2	209.4	207.3	206.0	204.5	205.5
2001	198.4	197.1	198.5	198.5	201.3	204.2	204.9	206.5	204.1	202.0	199.6	194.7	200.8
2002	185.4	182.0	183.2	185.6	188.6	190.8	191.9	192.8	192.5	192.3	191.2	188.9	188.8
2003	181.3	179.8	180.4	182.8	186.2	188.7	189.4	191.0	190.2	191.2	190.1	189.0	186.7
2004	182.4	182.5	185.3	190.1	194.1	197.6	199.9	200.9	200.6	200.3	200.0	199.5	194.4
2005	194.0	195.4	196.9	202.8	206.4	210.4	213.3	215.6	216.4	215.3	216.4	216.0	208.2
2006	212.0	214.5	218.1	222.0	227.1	232.0	232.9	235.6	236.1	235.9	236.9	237.0	228.3
2007	231.6	232.8	236.7	239.6	243.5	248.2	248.1	249.8	247.5	246.1	245.7	245.0	242.9
Natural Resources and Mining													
2000	7.2	7.2	7.3	7.5	7.6	7.7	7.7	7.7	7.7	7.4	7.3	7.3	7.5
2001	7.2	7.2	7.3	7.3	7.5	7.5	7.4	7.5	7.3	7.1	7.1	7.0	7.3
2002	6.7	6.7	6.7	6.9	7.0	7.1	7.1	7.1	7.2	7.1	7.1	7.0	7.0
2003	6.6	6.5	6.6	6.7	6.8	6.9	6.9	6.8	6.8	6.9	6.8	6.8	6.8
2004	6.7	6.6	6.6	6.9	7.1	7.3	7.4	7.4	7.5	7.6	7.6	7.7	7.2
2005	7.6	7.8	7.8	8.2	8.4	8.6	8.8	8.9	9.0	9.0	9.2	9.2	8.5
2006	9.0	9.2	9.4	9.7	9.9	10.2	10.4	10.5	10.5	10.6	10.7	10.8	10.1
2007	10.6	10.6	10.8	10.9	11.1	11.2	11.3	11.4	11.1	11.2	11.3	11.3	11.1
Construction													
2000	68.0	67.9	68.9	71.0	72.8	75.8	75.5	76.5	75.4	74.1	72.7	71.3	72.5
2001	65.9	65.4	66.8	68.3	71.2	74.1	75.2	77.0	75.7	75.0	73.7	70.5	71.6
2002	63.9	61.5	62.9	65.1	67.6	69.5	70.8	71.6	71.4	71.3	70.4	68.3	67.9
2003	62.6	62.0	62.5	64.4	67.2	69.1	70.2	71.7	71.1	71.4	70.1	68.8	67.6
2004	63.9	63.8	66.1	69.8	72.5	75.2	77.1	77.9	77.6	77.1	76.1	75.2	72.7
2005	71.1	72.1	73.7	78.1	80.5	83.3	85.5	86.9	87.5	86.8	86.9	86.0	81.5
2006	83.0	84.5	87.3	90.4	94.6	98.4	99.1	101.1	101.5	100.8	100.8	100.2	95.1
2007	96.0	96.5	99.3	102.1	105.1	108.5	108.4	109.7	108.1	106.5	105.7	104.6	104.2
Manufacturing													
2000	125.0	124.6	124.7	125.1	125.0	126.1	125.6	126.0	126.3	125.8	126.0	125.9	125.5
2001	125.3	124.5	124.4	122.9	122.6	122.6	122.3	122.0	121.1	119.9	118.8	117.2	122.0
2002	114.8	113.8	113.6	113.6	114.0	114.2	114.0	114.1	113.9	113.9	113.7	113.6	113.9
2003	112.1	111.3	111.3	111.7	112.2	112.7	112.3	112.5	112.3	112.9	113.2	113.4	112.3
2004	111.8	112.1	112.6	113.4	114.5	115.1	115.4	115.6	115.5	115.6	116.3	116.6	114.5
2005	115.3	115.5	115.4	116.5	117.5	118.5	119.0	119.8	119.9	119.5	120.3	120.8	118.2
2006	120.0	120.8	121.4	121.9	122.6	123.4	123.4	124.0	124.1	124.5	125.4	126.0	123.1
2007	125.0	125.7	126.6	126.6	127.3	128.5	128.4	128.7	128.3	128.4	128.7	129.1	127.6
Service-Providing													
2000	844.7	853.6	862.2	867.5	868.6	873.9	858.5	863.6	879.0	881.7	888.5	897.2	869.9
2001	870.8	875.8	881.7	885.0	883.0	887.1	868.5	871.9	884.3	881.5	885.7	891.0	880.5
2002	877.4	887.6	882.5	887.8	883.4	886.3	871.4	873.7	886.6	888.0	893.2	898.2	884.7
2003	876.9	879.2	881.9	886.4	883.7	887.3	873.4	879.0	892.2	896.6	902.1	910.2	887.4
2004	889.9	895.2	900.9	908.7	906.0	912.2	897.0	902.0	916.5	922.8	930.3	936.9	909.9
2005	916.8	922.6	929.9	935.6	933.3	938.6	926.8	936.5	951.6	954.7	961.5	969.3	939.8
2006	950.9	957.0	964.4	970.9	969.0	979.1	963.2	972.6	986.4	986.9	997.7	1006.3	975.4
2007	987.6	993.9	1001.8	1008.0	1006.7	1012.8	995.2	1004.4	1016.6	1016.5	1025.9	1033.7	1008.6
Trade, Transportation, and Utilities													
2000	216.9	214.7	215.7	216.4	216.5	219.1	219.3	220.9	221.6	223.4	228.1	231.4	220.3
2001	219.8	218.1	218.6	219.0	218.7	218.9	218.4	218.8	217.6	217.1	220.7	222.4	219.0
2002	214.2	212.5	211.7	213.5	215.2	215.5	215.3	216.1	215.1	216.2	220.0	221.8	215.6
2003	211.1	209.6	210.0	210.6	212.1	212.8	212.9	214.5	213.9	215.8	220.5	223.4	213.9
2004	214.6	213.1	213.6	215.5	217.5	218.5	218.5	219.4	219.3	221.3	226.3	228.7	218.9
2005	219.7	218.8	221.2	221.8	223.0	223.8	225.1	227.5	227.6	229.7	234.2	237.3	225.8
2006	228.6	228.0	229.4	229.7	231.3	233.7	234.4	236.6	237.2	237.9	244.4	248.1	234.9
2007	240.4	239.9	241.8	241.8	243.3	244.2	245.4	247.1	247.2	248.2	254.7	258.1	246.0
Wholesale Trade													
2000	39.5	39.7	39.9	39.9	40.1	40.5	40.7	40.8	40.9	41.1	41.0	41.3	40.5
2001	40.9	41.1	41.3	41.2	41.4	41.5	41.5	41.4	41.1	40.9	40.9	40.9	41.2
2002	39.9	40.0	40.0	40.1	40.6	40.5	40.5	40.6	40.4	40.5	40.4	40.5	40.3
2003	39.8	39.8	39.9	40.1	40.4	40.5	40.2	40.3	40.2	40.3	40.4	40.5	40.2
2004	40.1	40.2	40.4	40.8	41.1	41.5	41.4	41.4	41.5	41.7	42.0	42.2	41.2
2005	41.8	42.0	42.2	42.4	42.9	43.1	43.1	43.3	43.3	43.5	43.7	43.8	42.9
2006	43.3	43.6	43.8	44.1	44.6	45.2	45.1	45.3	45.5	45.7	46.0	46.4	44.9
2007	46.2	46.4	46.6	46.6	47.1	47.4	47.5	47.8	47.7	47.7	48.0	48.3	47.3

Employment by Industry: Utah, 2000–2007—Continued

(Numbers in thousands, not seasonally adjusted.)

Industry and year	January	February	March	April	May	June	July	August	September	October	November	December	Annual Average
Retail Trade													
2000	129.3	127.0	127.5	128.2	128.6	130.1	129.7	130.9	131.3	132.7	137.1	139.5	131.0
2001	131.6	129.8	130.0	130.6	130.8	131.0	130.4	130.8	129.9	129.7	133.9	135.5	131.2
2002	129.6	127.5	127.5	129.0	130.1	130.6	130.3	131.0	130.5	130.9	135.0	137.1	130.8
2003	127.7	126.3	126.7	127.1	128.1	128.8	128.9	130.2	129.8	131.1	135.8	138.5	129.9
2004	130.1	128.5	128.8	130.2	131.7	132.2	132.3	133.1	132.9	134.2	138.7	140.6	132.8
2005	132.4	130.8	132.8	132.4	133.0	133.5	134.6	136.6	136.4	137.9	142.0	144.3	135.6
2006	137.0	135.8	136.9	136.8	137.9	139.4	140.1	141.7	141.8	142.5	148.2	150.7	140.7
2007	144.3	143.4	144.7	145.0	146.0	146.5	147.3	148.6	148.5	149.5	155.4	157.7	148.1
Transportation and Utilities													
2000	48.1	48.0	48.3	48.3	47.8	48.5	48.9	49.2	49.4	49.6	50.0	50.6	48.9
2001	47.3	47.2	47.3	47.2	46.5	46.4	46.5	46.6	46.6	46.5	45.9	46.0	46.7
2002	44.7	45.0	44.2	44.4	44.5	44.4	44.5	44.5	44.2	44.8	44.6	44.2	44.5
2003	43.6	43.5	43.4	43.4	43.6	43.5	43.8	44.0	43.9	44.4	44.3	44.4	43.8
2004	44.4	44.4	44.4	44.5	44.7	44.8	44.8	44.9	44.9	45.4	45.6	45.9	44.9
2005	45.5	46.0	46.2	47.0	47.1	47.2	47.4	47.6	47.9	48.3	48.5	49.2	47.3
2006	48.3	48.6	48.7	48.8	48.8	49.1	49.2	49.6	49.9	49.7	50.2	51.0	49.3
2007	49.9	50.1	50.5	50.2	50.2	50.3	50.6	50.7	51.0	51.0	51.3	52.1	50.7
Information													
2000	34.2	34.3	34.6	34.5	35.3	35.8	35.7	36.2	36.3	35.9	36.2	36.1	35.4
2001	34.5	33.9	33.8	33.8	34.1	34.2	33.7	33.4	33.0	32.5	32.9	32.5	33.5
2002	31.8	31.7	31.1	30.9	31.3	31.1	31.0	30.7	30.5	30.5	30.8	30.7	31.0
2003	30.1	30.0	29.9	29.4	30.1	30.2	29.8	30.0	29.8	30.2	30.1	30.6	30.0
2004	29.4	30.0	30.1	30.3	30.2	30.7	30.1	30.3	30.2	30.5	31.3	31.3	30.4
2005	31.0	31.5	31.8	31.6	31.7	31.7	32.4	33.0	32.7	32.2	32.5	32.3	32.0
2006	31.7	31.6	31.7	32.2	33.2	33.5	32.7	33.1	32.9	32.8	33.4	33.0	32.7
2007	32.0	32.0	32.2	32.3	32.6	32.6	32.6	32.9	32.4	32.2	32.7	32.4	32.4
Financial Activities													
2000	58.6	58.4	58.7	58.5	58.3	58.6	58.9	59.2	59.2	59.3	59.8	60.6	59.0
2001	61.2	61.5	61.8	61.6	61.7	62.2	62.6	63.1	63.0	62.7	63.3	63.9	62.4
2002	63.4	63.4	62.9	63.0	63.3	63.4	63.0	63.3	62.9	63.7	63.8	64.6	63.4
2003	64.1	64.8	64.4	64.6	64.9	64.6	65.1	65.2	64.6	64.4	64.3	64.9	64.7
2004	63.7	64.2	64.2	64.7	64.7	64.7	65.0	64.9	65.0	65.3	65.7	66.6	64.9
2005	65.5	66.0	65.5	66.8	66.7	67.2	67.9	68.1	68.1	68.7	69.0	70.3	67.5
2006	69.2	69.9	70.1	70.7	70.9	71.4	71.8	72.1	72.0	72.9	73.4	74.5	71.6
2007	73.7	74.4	74.6	74.8	75.0	75.2	75.0	75.0	74.4	74.4	74.4	75.2	74.7
Professional and Business Services													
2000	131.1	132.4	134.8	136.8	137.0	140.0	139.1	140.7	141.6	142.0	141.6	142.7	138.3
2001	136.8	135.9	137.0	137.3	137.9	138.1	137.4	138.3	136.3	134.7	132.9	131.8	136.2
2002	129.5	132.7	129.6	131.2	132.4	132.6	132.1	133.4	133.3	132.9	133.1	132.0	132.1
2003	126.5	126.4	127.0	129.3	131.0	132.0	132.8	134.6	134.2	135.7	136.1	136.4	131.8
2004	132.2	133.6	134.7	137.1	138.5	139.9	139.5	140.6	139.3	142.1	142.1	142.8	138.5
2005	138.2	139.5	140.9	143.4	145.3	146.1	147.4	149.0	149.1	150.1	150.5	151.1	145.9
2006	147.1	148.5	149.8	152.2	153.8	156.2	156.5	157.5	157.0	156.8	157.9	158.4	154.3
2007	153.5	154.5	156.4	159.6	162.2	163.5	162.4	163.6	162.4	162.1	163.2	163.4	160.6
Education and Health Services													
2000	99.9	102.6	103.1	103.8	103.4	102.5	101.7	102.4	105.1	106.2	107.4	108.2	103.9
2001	107.6	109.0	109.6	109.9	106.8	107.5	105.6	106.4	111.0	112.1	113.1	113.9	109.4
2002	111.7	112.9	113.4	114.5	110.8	110.7	110.0	111.6	116.3	117.6	118.1	119.2	113.9
2003	117.4	118.4	119.1	119.0	115.0	115.6	114.6	115.5	120.1	121.6	122.1	123.3	118.5
2004	121.4	122.9	123.8	123.7	120.2	121.0	120.0	120.9	125.5	126.8	127.8	128.3	123.5
2005	126.8	128.0	128.7	129.0	125.0	125.9	124.5	125.9	130.7	132.0	133.1	133.6	128.6
2006	132.6	133.5	134.6	134.8	131.2	131.6	130.2	131.9	136.5	137.6	138.6	139.1	134.4
2007	137.7	139.1	139.8	140.4	136.6	136.4	135.5	137.4	142.4	143.8	144.6	145.2	139.9
Leisure and Hospitality													
2000	92.5	94.2	96.7	96.8	95.9	99.2	100.0	100.9	98.8	96.4	95.9	98.4	97.1
2001	94.9	96.0	98.5	99.2	98.9	101.4	101.5	102.1	100.2	97.1	95.7	99.1	98.7
2002	100.5	106.3	103.3	103.1	100.0	102.1	102.1	102.2	99.9	96.8	96.1	99.0	101.0
2003	97.7	98.4	99.5	100.1	98.4	101.3	101.7	102.3	100.6	97.6	97.6	100.2	99.6
2004	98.4	99.4	100.9	101.8	100.5	103.9	104.4	104.9	103.9	101.0	100.9	103.5	102.0
2005	100.9	102.2	104.0	103.7	103.2	106.0	106.1	106.8	105.8	103.1	102.5	105.4	104.1
2006	104.5	105.8	107.8	109.5	107.4	110.4	110.8	111.6	109.6	106.8	107.0	110.6	108.5
2007	109.9	111.2	113.3	113.9	111.6	115.0	115.3	115.4	113.4	110.4	110.1	113.6	112.8
Other Services													
2000	30.3	30.1	30.1	30.3	30.4	30.9	31.2	31.2	30.7	30.0	30.2	30.2	30.5
2001	29.4	29.5	29.7	30.2	30.7	31.5	32.3	32.7	31.9	31.9	32.2	32.4	31.2
2002	32.0	33.1	32.5	32.7	32.8	33.1	33.5	33.5	32.8	32.5	32.8	32.5	32.8
2003	31.9	31.9	32.1	32.3	32.4	32.8	33.0	33.2	32.3	31.9	32.0	32.1	32.3
2004	31.8	32.0	32.5	32.6	32.9	33.1	34.0	33.9	33.0	32.8	32.8	32.8	32.9
2005	32.4	32.6	33.1	33.3	33.4	33.6	34.6	34.5	33.9	33.4	33.6	33.8	33.5
2006	33.2	33.5	34.1	34.1	34.6	35.2	35.5	35.6	35.2	34.6	34.6	35.0	34.6
2007	34.4	34.8	35.0	35.2	35.9	36.3	36.7	37.0	36.1	35.5	35.4	35.8	35.7
Government													
2000	181.2	186.9	188.5	190.4	191.8	187.8	172.6	172.1	185.7	188.5	189.3	189.6	185.4
2001	186.6	191.9	192.7	194.0	194.2	193.3	177.0	177.1	191.3	193.4	194.9	195.0	190.1
2002	194.3	195.0	198.0	198.9	197.6	197.8	184.4	182.9	195.8	197.8	198.5	198.4	195.0
2003	198.1	199.7	199.9	201.1	199.8	198.0	183.5	183.7	196.7	199.4	199.4	199.3	196.6
2004	198.4	200.0	201.1	203.0	201.5	200.4	185.5	187.1	200.3	203.0	203.4	202.9	198.9
2005	202.3	204.0	204.7	206.0	205.0	204.3	188.8	191.7	203.7	205.5	206.1	205.5	202.3
2006	204.0	206.2	206.9	207.7	206.6	207.1	191.3	194.2	206.0	207.5	208.4	207.6	204.5
2007	206.0	208.0	208.7	210.0	209.5	209.6	192.3	196.0	208.3	209.9	210.8	210.0	206.6

Average Weekly Hours by Selected Industry: Utah, 2001–2007

(Not seasonally adjusted.)

Industry and year	January	February	March	April	May	June	July	August	September	October	November	December	Annual Average
Construction													
2003	36.5	35.8	37.0	36.5	37.8	38.1	38.7	39.5	38.4	39.1	38.8	37.6	37.9
2004	36.9	36.9	36.6	37.5	40.0	39.9	39.4	40.1	38.3	38.7	38.5	38.0	38.5
2005	36.4	36.7	38.4	38.2	36.4	37.0	37.3	38.4	38.1	40.9	37.3	37.3	37.7
2006	36.8	37.0	37.5	38.9	39.5	40.4	39.9	41.1	39.5	40.0	38.7	38.8	39.1
2007	39.2	38.3	39.1	39.6	39.8	39.5	40.0	40.8	39.4	40.0	39.5	38.2	39.5
Manufacturing													
2001	38.6	39.2	38.8	38.1	38.2	38.4	38.1	38.7	38.5	37.7	38.3	38.3	38.4
2002	37.4	36.1	37.4	36.6	37.2	37.9	37.4	38.8	38.1	38.0	39.5	39.5	37.8
2003	38.5	40.1	39.8	40.4	40.1	39.8	38.6	40.5	39.8	40.0	38.8	39.9	39.7
2004	39.0	38.6	37.8	38.3	38.2	37.6	37.6	38.7	38.0	37.5	37.8	38.5	38.1
2005	38.1	38.2	38.1	38.4	38.8	39.4	38.2	38.6	38.9	39.8	41.9	42.2	39.2
2006	41.4	41.8	41.0	40.8	42.8	40.6	40.7	41.1	40.7	41.8	39.8	41.0	41.1
2007	40.0	40.0	41.5	40.8	41.7	41.4	41.6	41.6	41.1	41.0	40.1	41.9	41.1
Wholesale Trade													
2001	36.5	36.4	36.4	38.2	37.2	37.4	38.9	37.5	37.2	36.5	36.8	37.0	37.2
2002	35.9	36.6	36.6	36.0	37.3	38.2	38.3	38.6	39.0	38.5	38.5	38.3	37.7
2003	39.3	39.4	39.4	38.5	38.1	38.0	37.1	38.1	38.2	38.2	37.8	37.6	38.3
2004	37.6	37.7	38.0	36.8	36.3	35.1	37.1	38.0	39.2	37.5	39.2	37.6	37.5
2005	38.0	38.2	38.4	36.1	36.8	37.7	34.5	34.7	36.0	41.2	35.8	36.9	37.0
2006	39.2	37.6	38.3	38.0	35.7	38.7	39.5	40.5	41.1	38.4	40.5	40.4	39.0
2007	42.4	40.8	45.4	44.2	41.9	41.5	40.9	39.5	40.3	39.7	37.3	39.3	41.0
Retail Trade													
2001	27.9	28.0	28.2	28.9	28.7	29.2	29.7	29.1	29.0	28.7	28.1	28.9	28.7
2002	28.2	28.3	28.6	29.0	29.1	29.8	29.9	29.4	29.5	29.0	28.5	29.8	29.1
2003	27.9	28.5	29.1	29.0	29.2	30.1	29.8	29.6	29.6	29.2	28.4	29.3	29.1
2004	28.0	28.3	28.3	28.7	29.5	29.4	29.8	29.9	29.6	28.8	27.7	29.1	28.9
2005	28.2	28.9	28.9	29.4	29.7	29.7	29.9	29.8	30.2	28.9	29.7	30.2	29.5
2006	29.0	29.5	28.6	28.8	28.8	29.4	29.4	29.1	29.4	28.6	29.6	30.0	29.2
2007	28.5	28.8	28.7	29.2	28.6	29.8	29.5	29.0	29.6	28.9	29.8	29.8	29.2
Information													
2001	40.6	39.5	40.0	40.0	40.3	41.1	41.2	40.0	39.3	38.4	37.5	39.1	39.8
2002	37.0	38.5	37.3	35.2	35.2	37.2	36.3	35.9	35.9	36.3	35.5	37.5	36.5
2003	36.4	37.3	38.0	36.0	35.1	37.2	34.8	34.6	34.3	35.1	36.2	34.8	35.8
2004	34.0	36.8	34.7	35.2	36.0	35.3	34.9	36.5	34.4	34.7	34.5	34.9	35.2
2005	36.3	34.0	33.5	33.5	35.1	33.0	33.9	34.1	34.7	35.1	32.3	32.9	34.0
2006	34.2	32.6	33.3	33.7	33.3	35.0	36.9	35.0	34.6	35.6	33.7	27.8	33.8
2007	33.4	32.6	32.0	33.3	32.2	32.6	33.2	32.5	33.8	31.2	30.8	34.0	32.6

Average Hourly Earnings by Selected Industry: Utah, 2001–2007

(Dollars, not seasonally adjusted.)

Industry and year	January	February	March	April	May	June	July	August	September	October	November	December	Annual Average
Construction													
2003	17.91	17.88	17.52	17.20	16.93	16.48	16.44	16.38	16.72	16.81	16.58	16.69	16.92
2004	16.64	16.58	16.58	17.00	16.64	16.50	16.26	16.11	16.64	16.34	16.72	16.86	16.56
2005	17.04	17.02	16.93	16.95	16.59	16.62	16.99	17.10	16.86	16.81	16.93	17.36	16.93
2006	17.48	17.53	17.90	18.15	17.92	17.60	18.12	18.07	17.69	18.03	18.34	19.28	18.03
2007	18.76	19.02	19.17	19.15	19.16	18.86	19.53	19.54	16.70	16.98	17.38	19.76	18.63
Manufacturing													
2001	13.59	13.57	13.66	13.77	13.62	13.76	13.91	13.89	13.85	13.81	13.80	13.90	13.76
2002	13.75	14.08	14.09	14.19	13.80	14.27	14.28	14.17	14.39	14.17	13.80	14.45	14.12
2003	14.68	14.71	14.71	14.82	14.62	14.67	14.79	15.02	15.01	15.05	15.26	15.42	14.90
2004	15.39	15.27	15.55	15.35	15.35	15.61	15.52	15.40	15.36	15.27	15.38	15.11	15.38
2005	15.03	14.72	14.83	14.80	14.69	14.57	14.54	14.45	14.55	15.02	14.65	14.85	14.73
2006	14.76	14.66	15.03	15.50	14.72	15.73	15.58	15.32	15.47	15.11	15.39	15.67	15.25
2007	16.12	16.53	16.36	16.27	16.73	16.49	16.78	16.50	17.09	17.09	17.43	16.99	16.71
Wholesale Trade													
2001	14.54	14.35	14.29	14.45	14.18	14.70	14.61	14.17	14.73	14.42	14.37	14.94	14.48
2002	15.35	15.01	14.67	15.07	14.65	15.51	15.74	15.62	15.82	15.76	15.58	16.13	15.42
2003	16.01	16.26	16.08	16.60	16.30	16.66	17.06	16.87	17.55	17.01	16.80	16.34	16.63
2004	16.60	16.70	16.05	16.28	15.85	16.09	16.05	15.92	15.99	15.85	16.33	15.73	16.12
2005	16.01	15.69	15.58	15.57	15.08	15.18	15.13	14.33	15.95	14.38	15.23	16.66	15.40
2006	16.60	15.56	16.69	17.05	17.75	17.52	19.22	18.09	18.45	15.06	18.61	18.74	17.48
2007	20.17	19.27	19.49	18.46	18.41	19.25	19.87	19.54	18.30	18.73	23.78	24.10	19.93
Retail Trade													
2001	10.70	10.62	10.69	10.63	10.63	10.62	10.73	10.52	10.75	10.62	10.65	10.73	10.66
2002	11.01	10.81	11.09	10.79	10.96	11.24	11.17	11.06	11.58	11.18	10.87	11.13	11.08
2003	11.47	11.37	11.35	11.92	11.64	11.53	11.69	11.48	11.49	11.50	11.04	10.56	11.41
2004	10.79	11.04	11.05	11.06	10.97	11.07	11.03	10.99	11.05	11.03	11.03	10.82	10.99
2005	11.26	11.24	11.25	11.45	11.24	11.25	11.51	11.45	11.59	12.13	11.40	11.50	11.44
2006	11.97	11.51	11.67	11.95	11.91	12.09	12.32	12.13	12.11	12.05	11.82	11.50	11.92
2007	11.59	11.56	12.07	11.93	12.02	11.81	11.71	11.53	11.69	11.88	11.65	11.52	11.74
Information													
2001	17.08	17.08	17.03	17.46	17.41	17.46	16.96	16.83	17.50	17.62	17.71	17.52	17.30
2002	17.95	17.71	18.10	17.69	16.90	16.88	17.20	16.92	18.00	17.47	18.08	18.17	17.59
2003	17.92	19.36	19.34	19.47	20.12	21.22	22.55	22.13	22.91	23.04	23.13	23.77	21.26
2004	23.28	22.25	22.14	22.29	22.63	21.73	22.24	22.82	22.55	22.98	22.76	22.75	22.53
2005	23.15	22.75	23.03	23.47	23.48	23.24	23.26	23.35	23.64	25.03	24.70	25.14	23.69
2006	25.21	24.34	23.79	24.01	23.47	23.20	23.78	23.44	23.38	23.42	23.35	24.30	23.79
2007	24.43	25.53	23.97	23.90	23.60	24.15	24.26	23.42	24.59	24.17	24.29	24.96	24.27

Average Weekly Earnings by Selected Industry: Utah, 2001–2007

(Dollars, not seasonally adjusted.)

Industry and year	January	February	March	April	May	June	July	August	September	October	November	December	Annual Average
Construction													
2003	653.72	640.10	648.24	627.80	639.95	627.89	636.23	647.01	642.05	657.27	643.30	627.54	641.27
2004	614.02	611.80	606.83	637.50	665.60	658.35	640.64	646.01	637.31	632.36	643.72	640.68	637.56
2005	620.26	624.63	650.11	647.49	603.88	614.94	633.73	656.64	642.37	687.53	631.49	647.53	638.26
2006	643.26	648.61	671.25	706.04	707.84	711.04	722.99	742.68	698.76	721.20	709.76	748.06	704.97
2007	735.39	728.47	749.55	758.34	762.57	744.97	781.20	797.23	657.98	679.20	686.51	754.83	735.89
Manufacturing													
2001	524.57	531.94	530.01	524.64	520.28	528.38	529.97	537.54	533.23	520.64	528.54	532.37	528.38
2002	514.25	508.29	526.97	519.35	513.36	540.83	534.07	549.80	548.26	538.46	545.10	570.78	533.74
2003	565.18	589.87	585.46	598.73	586.26	583.87	570.89	608.31	597.40	602.00	592.09	615.26	591.53
2004	600.21	589.42	587.79	587.91	586.37	586.94	583.55	595.98	583.68	572.63	581.36	581.74	585.98
2005	572.64	562.30	565.02	568.32	569.97	574.06	555.43	557.77	566.00	597.80	613.84	626.67	577.42
2006	611.06	612.79	616.23	632.40	630.02	638.64	634.11	629.65	629.63	631.60	612.52	642.47	626.78
2007	644.80	661.20	678.94	663.82	697.64	682.69	698.05	686.40	702.40	700.69	698.94	711.88	686.78
Wholesale Trade													
2001	530.71	522.34	520.16	551.99	527.50	549.78	568.33	531.38	547.96	526.33	528.82	552.78	538.66
2002	551.07	549.37	536.92	542.52	546.45	592.48	602.84	602.93	616.98	606.76	599.83	617.78	581.33
2003	629.19	640.64	633.55	639.10	621.03	633.08	632.93	642.75	670.41	649.78	635.04	614.38	636.93
2004	624.16	629.59	609.90	599.10	575.36	564.76	595.46	604.96	626.81	594.38	640.14	591.45	604.50
2005	608.38	599.36	598.27	562.08	554.94	572.29	521.99	497.25	574.20	592.46	545.23	614.75	569.80
2006	650.72	585.06	639.23	647.90	633.68	678.02	759.19	732.65	758.30	578.30	753.71	757.10	681.72
2007	855.21	786.22	884.85	815.93	771.38	798.88	812.68	771.83	737.49	743.58	886.99	947.13	817.13
Retail Trade													
2001	298.53	297.36	301.46	307.21	305.08	310.10	318.68	306.13	311.75	304.79	299.27	310.10	305.94
2002	310.48	305.92	317.17	312.91	318.94	334.95	333.98	325.16	341.61	324.22	309.80	331.67	322.43
2003	320.01	324.05	330.29	345.68	339.89	347.05	348.36	339.81	340.10	335.80	313.54	309.41	332.03
2004	302.12	312.43	312.72	317.42	323.62	325.46	328.69	328.60	327.08	317.66	305.53	314.86	317.61
2005	317.53	324.84	325.13	336.63	333.83	334.13	344.15	341.21	350.02	350.56	338.58	347.30	337.48
2006	347.13	339.55	333.76	344.16	343.01	355.45	362.21	352.98	356.03	344.63	349.87	345.00	348.06
2007	330.32	332.93	346.41	348.36	343.77	351.94	345.45	334.37	346.02	343.33	347.17	343.30	342.81
Information													
2001	693.45	674.66	681.20	698.40	701.62	717.61	698.75	673.20	687.75	676.61	664.13	685.03	688.54
2002	664.15	681.84	675.13	622.69	594.88	627.94	624.36	607.43	646.20	634.16	641.84	681.38	642.04
2003	652.29	722.13	734.92	700.92	706.21	789.38	784.74	765.70	785.81	808.70	837.31	827.20	761.11
2004	791.52	818.80	768.26	784.61	814.68	767.07	776.18	832.93	775.72	797.41	785.22	793.98	793.06
2005	840.35	773.50	771.51	786.25	824.15	766.92	788.51	796.24	820.31	878.55	797.81	827.11	805.46
2006	862.18	793.48	792.21	809.14	781.55	812.00	877.48	820.40	808.95	833.75	786.90	675.54	804.10
2007	815.96	832.28	767.04	795.87	759.92	787.29	805.43	761.15	831.14	754.10	748.13	848.64	791.20

Population
    2000 census: 608,827
    2007 estimate: 621,254
    Percent change, 2000–2007: 2.0%

Percent change in total nonfarm employment, 2000–2007: 3.0%

Industry with the largest growth in employment, 2000–2007 (thousands)
    Education and health services, 10.8

Industry with the largest decline in employment, 2000–2007 (thousands)
    Manufacturing, -10.3

Civilian labor force
    2000: 335,798
    2007: 353,861

Employment-population ratio
    2000: 68.9%
    2007: 67.8%

Unemployment rate and rank among states
    2000: 2.7%, 3rd
    2007: 3.9%, 19th

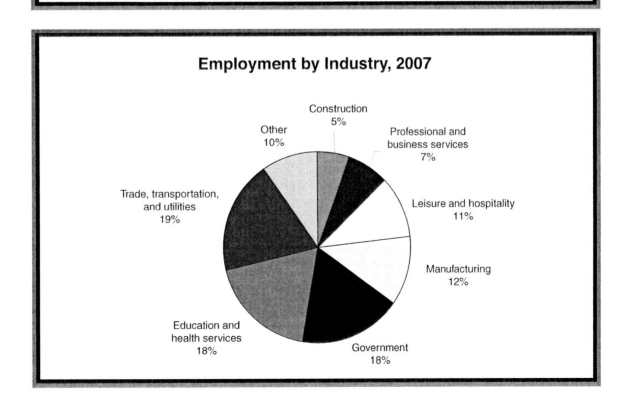

Employment by Industry, 2007

Construction 5%
Professional and business services 7%
Other 10%
Leisure and hospitality 11%
Trade, transportation, and utilities 19%
Manufacturing 12%
Education and health services 18%
Government 18%

Employment by Industry: Vermont, 2000–2007

(Numbers in thousands, not seasonally adjusted.)

Industry and year	January	February	March	April	May	June	July	August	September	October	November	December	Annual Average
Total Nonfarm													
2000	293.7	296.9	299.0	293.6	297.2	300.0	293.6	293.8	301.3	304.2	302.4	308.7	298.7
2001	301.7	302.6	302.0	299.6	301.2	304.6	297.8	297.5	303.7	305.3	303.1	306.0	302.1
2002	299.4	299.4	299.1	297.1	299.4	302.1	294.0	293.9	300.8	302.6	300.2	304.1	299.3
2003	297.2	297.8	296.9	293.6	298.0	301.1	294.2	294.9	301.7	304.4	302.5	307.9	299.2
2004	298.7	300.6	300.1	298.8	302.8	305.2	298.8	298.9	306.9	308.2	306.3	310.3	303.0
2005	302.9	304.0	303.5	302.4	305.1	307.1	300.7	301.1	308.4	309.5	308.1	313.6	305.5
2006	305.3	306.4	306.1	303.5	306.8	310.5	301.9	302.6	310.6	312.6	311.5	314.9	307.7
2007	305.8	306.8	306.4	302.7	308.3	310.8	302.6	302.3	310.0	312.1	310.5	314.8	307.8
Total Private													
2000	244.8	246.1	246.7	242.1	244.8	251.1	252.4	252.8	251.4	252.5	250.2	256.4	249.3
2001	251.6	251.0	250.3	247.9	249.4	254.7	256.1	255.8	252.6	251.9	249.6	252.4	251.9
2002	248.1	246.8	246.4	244.2	246.7	251.1	252.2	251.8	249.6	248.6	245.8	250.7	248.5
2003	245.1	243.9	243.1	239.7	244.1	249.2	250.9	252.0	248.9	249.5	247.3	252.8	247.2
2004	246.2	246.3	245.8	244.3	248.5	254.1	255.6	255.6	253.4	252.8	250.3	254.7	250.6
2005	249.5	248.9	248.3	247.3	250.1	255.2	257.3	256.9	254.3	253.3	251.6	257.3	252.5
2006	250.9	250.4	250.1	247.5	251.1	257.3	258.1	258.6	256.1	255.9	254.5	258.1	254.1
2007	251.0	250.4	250.0	246.4	251.3	256.8	258.4	258.1	255.4	255.5	253.7	257.9	253.7
Goods-Producing													
2000	58.8	58.6	59.2	60.7	62.1	64.1	64.2	64.5	63.8	64.0	63.6	63.0	62.2
2001	60.9	60.1	60.2	61.1	62.6	64.1	64.4	63.8	62.6	61.8	60.6	60.1	61.9
2002	56.5	55.3	55.1	56.2	57.6	58.4	58.1	57.0	56.4	56.2	55.3	54.0	56.3
2003	51.7	51.0	51.1	52.2	54.4	55.5	55.9	56.1	54.6	55.0	54.5	53.7	53.8
2004	51.1	51.1	51.0	53.1	55.2	56.6	57.0	57.0	56.3	56.0	55.3	54.5	54.5
2005	51.6	51.1	51.0	52.9	54.9	56.4	57.1	57.1	56.2	56.1	55.4	54.3	54.5
2006	51.7	51.1	51.1	53.3	54.9	56.2	56.8	56.8	56.0	55.9	55.4	54.6	54.5
2007	51.7	50.8	50.9	51.9	54.6	55.7	55.8	55.6	54.7	54.6	53.9	53.2	53.6
Natural Resources and Mining													
2000	1.0	0.9	1.0	1.1	1.1	1.1	1.1	1.2	1.1	1.1	1.1	1.1	1.1
2001	1.0	1.0	1.1	1.0	1.1	1.1	1.2	1.2	1.2	1.2	1.1	1.1	1.1
2002	0.9	0.9	0.9	1.0	1.0	1.1	1.1	1.1	1.1	1.0	1.0	0.9	1.0
2003	0.8	0.8	0.9	0.9	1.0	1.0	1.0	1.0	1.0	1.0	1.0	0.9	0.9
2004	0.8	0.8	0.8	0.9	1.0	1.0	0.9	0.9	0.9	0.9	0.9	0.9	0.9
2005	0.7	0.7	0.8	0.8	0.8	0.9	0.9	0.9	0.9	0.9	0.9	0.8	0.8
2006	0.8	0.7	0.8	0.9	0.9	0.9	0.9	0.9	0.9	0.9	0.9	0.9	0.9
2007	0.8	0.8	0.8	0.8	0.9	0.9	0.9	0.9	0.9	0.9	0.9	0.8	0.9
Construction													
2000	12.7	12.3	12.5	13.9	15.2	16.3	16.7	16.6	16.1	16.0	15.3	14.6	14.9
2001	13.2	12.7	12.8	13.8	15.5	16.6	17.2	17.2	16.5	16.1	15.6	15.1	15.2
2002	13.4	12.9	12.8	13.9	15.3	15.8	16.3	16.3	15.8	15.8	15.3	14.3	14.8
2003	13.0	12.4	12.5	13.7	15.6	16.6	17.2	17.4	16.9	17.0	16.5	15.8	15.4
2004	14.1	13.8	13.9	15.7	17.3	18.3	18.8	18.7	18.2	17.9	17.3	16.2	16.7
2005	14.4	13.8	13.8	15.4	17.3	18.3	19.2	19.1	18.5	18.3	17.6	16.6	16.9
2006	14.9	14.5	14.7	16.4	17.8	18.8	19.4	19.4	18.9	18.6	18.0	17.1	17.4
2007	15.1	14.2	14.4	15.3	17.7	18.5	18.7	18.6	18.0	17.8	17.1	16.3	16.8
Manufacturing													
2000	45.1	45.4	45.7	45.7	45.8	46.7	46.4	46.7	46.6	46.9	47.2	47.3	46.3
2001	46.7	46.4	46.3	46.3	46.0	46.4	46.0	45.4	44.9	44.5	43.9	43.9	45.6
2002	42.2	41.5	41.4	41.3	41.3	41.5	40.7	39.6	39.5	39.4	39.0	38.8	40.5
2003	37.9	37.8	37.7	37.6	37.8	37.9	37.7	37.7	36.7	37.0	37.0	37.0	37.5
2004	36.2	36.5	36.3	36.5	36.9	37.3	37.3	37.4	37.2	37.2	37.1	37.4	36.9
2005	36.5	36.6	36.4	36.7	36.8	37.2	37.0	37.1	36.8	36.9	36.9	36.9	36.8
2006	36.0	35.9	35.6	36.0	36.2	36.5	36.5	36.5	36.2	36.4	36.5	36.6	36.2
2007	35.8	35.8	35.7	35.8	36.0	36.3	36.2	36.1	35.8	35.9	35.9	36.1	36.0
Service-Providing													
2000	234.9	238.3	239.8	232.9	235.1	235.9	229.4	229.3	237.5	240.2	238.8	245.7	236.5
2001	240.8	242.5	241.8	238.5	238.6	240.5	233.4	233.7	241.1	243.5	242.5	245.9	240.2
2002	242.9	244.1	244.0	240.9	241.8	243.7	235.9	236.9	244.4	246.4	244.9	250.1	243.0
2003	245.5	246.8	245.8	241.4	243.6	245.6	238.3	238.8	247.1	249.4	248.0	254.2	245.4
2004	247.6	249.5	249.1	245.7	247.6	248.6	241.8	241.9	250.6	252.2	251.0	255.8	248.5
2005	251.3	252.9	252.5	249.5	250.2	250.7	243.6	244.0	252.2	253.4	252.7	259.3	251.0
2006	253.6	255.3	255.0	250.2	251.9	254.3	245.1	245.8	254.6	256.7	256.1	260.3	253.2
2007	254.1	256.0	255.5	250.8	253.7	255.1	246.8	246.7	255.3	257.5	256.6	261.6	254.1
Trade, Transportation, and Utilities													
2000	57.2	57.0	56.9	56.9	57.2	57.9	58.0	58.1	58.0	58.7	59.5	60.5	58.0
2001	58.1	57.6	57.5	57.7	58.4	58.9	58.4	58.5	58.3	59.2	60.1	61.1	58.7
2002	58.3	57.7	57.9	57.9	58.7	59.2	59.1	59.2	58.7	59.1	59.7	60.5	58.8
2003	57.9	57.4	56.8	57.0	57.6	58.4	57.9	58.1	57.8	59.1	59.9	61.1	58.3
2004	57.9	57.4	57.5	57.8	58.7	59.3	59.1	59.0	58.6	59.8	60.8	61.4	58.9
2005	59.0	58.6	58.1	58.6	59.1	59.7	59.4	59.4	59.2	59.8	60.6	61.6	59.4
2006	58.9	58.3	58.2	58.4	59.4	59.9	59.4	59.5	59.4	60.1	61.1	61.9	59.5
2007	59.2	58.4	58.0	57.7	58.7	59.4	59.1	58.7	58.6	59.4	60.5	61.4	59.1
Wholesale Trade													
2000	9.7	9.7	9.8	9.9	9.8	9.8	9.9	9.9	9.8	9.8	9.9	9.9	9.8
2001	9.9	10.0	10.0	10.1	10.0	10.1	10.1	10.1	10.1	10.1	10.1	10.3	10.1
2002	9.9	9.9	10.0	10.0	10.1	10.1	10.2	10.2	10.3	10.2	10.3	10.4	10.1
2003	10.1	10.1	10.1	10.1	10.2	10.3	10.3	10.3	10.3	10.5	10.4	10.4	10.3
2004	10.1	10.1	10.2	10.2	10.3	10.2	10.4	10.1	10.0	10.1	10.2	9.9	10.2
2005	9.9	9.9	9.8	10.0	10.0	10.1	10.2	10.3	10.2	10.2	10.3	10.3	10.1
2006	10.2	10.1	10.2	10.2	10.3	10.2	10.4	10.5	10.5	10.5	10.5	10.6	10.4
2007	10.4	10.3	10.3	10.3	10.3	10.3	10.3	10.2	10.2	10.3	10.3	10.5	10.3

Employment by Industry: Vermont, 2000–2007—*Continued*

(Numbers in thousands, not seasonally adjusted.)

Industry and year	January	February	March	April	May	June	July	August	September	October	November	December	Annual Average
Retail Trade													
2000	38.9	38.7	38.5	38.5	38.9	39.5	39.6	39.8	39.4	40.0	40.7	41.8	39.5
2001	39.6	39.0	39.0	39.0	39.8	40.0	39.9	40.0	39.4	40.2	41.1	41.9	39.9
2002	39.7	39.2	39.3	39.2	39.8	40.3	40.5	40.5	39.7	40.0	40.5	41.2	40.0
2003	39.2	38.8	38.3	38.4	38.9	39.4	39.6	39.7	39.0	39.9	40.9	42.0	39.5
2004	39.2	38.7	38.8	39.1	39.8	40.3	40.3	40.4	39.8	40.6	41.5	42.4	40.1
2005	40.1	39.8	39.4	39.8	40.3	40.7	40.8	40.7	40.2	40.6	41.2	42.1	40.5
2006	39.9	39.5	39.3	39.5	40.3	40.9	40.7	40.7	40.1	40.7	41.6	42.2	40.5
2007	40.0	39.4	39.1	39.0	39.7	40.3	40.4	40.2	39.6	40.2	41.2	41.8	40.1
Transportation and Utilities													
2000	8.6	8.6	8.6	8.5	8.5	8.6	8.5	8.4	8.8	8.9	8.9	8.8	8.6
2001	8.6	8.6	8.5	8.6	8.6	8.8	8.8	8.4	8.4	8.8	8.9	8.8	8.7
2002	8.7	8.6	8.6	8.7	8.8	8.8	8.8	8.4	8.5	8.7	8.9	8.9	8.7
2003	8.6	8.5	8.4	8.5	8.5	8.7	8.0	8.1	8.5	8.7	8.9	8.9	8.7
2004	8.6	8.6	8.5	8.5	8.6	8.8	8.4	8.5	8.8	8.7	8.6	8.7	8.5
2005	9.0	8.9	8.9	8.8	8.8	8.9	8.4	8.5	8.8	9.1	9.1	9.1	8.7
2006	8.8	8.7	8.7	8.7	8.8	8.9	8.4	8.4	8.8	9.0	9.1	9.2	8.9
2007	8.8	8.7	8.6	8.4	8.7	8.8	8.3	8.3	8.8	8.9	9.0	9.1	8.7
Information													
2000	6.7	6.8	6.8	6.8	6.8	6.9	6.9	6.3	6.9	6.9	7.0	7.0	6.8
2001	6.9	7.0	6.8	6.8	6.8	6.9	6.7	6.7	6.6	6.7	6.8	6.8	6.8
2002	6.7	6.7	6.7	6.8	6.7	6.7	6.7	6.7	6.6	6.6	6.6	6.6	6.7
2003	6.5	6.4	6.5	6.4	6.5	6.6	6.5	6.5	6.5	6.5	6.6	6.6	6.5
2004	6.4	6.4	6.4	6.4	6.4	6.4	6.4	6.4	6.2	6.5	6.5	6.5	6.4
2005	6.3	6.2	6.2	6.2	6.2	6.2	6.3	6.2	6.2	6.3	6.3	6.3	6.2
2006	6.1	6.1	6.2	6.0	6.0	6.0	6.0	6.2	6.2	6.2	6.2	6.3	6.2
2007	6.0	5.9	5.9	5.9	5.9	5.9	6.0	6.0	6.0	6.0	5.9	6.0	6.0
Financial Activities													
2000	13.0	12.9	13.0	12.8	13.0	13.1	12.9	13.0	12.7	13.0	12.9	13.2	13.0
2001	12.9	13.0	13.1	12.9	13.1	13.4	13.4	13.4	13.3	13.2	13.2	13.3	13.2
2002	13.0	13.0	13.0	12.9	13.1	13.3	13.5	13.5	13.2	13.2	13.2	13.3	13.2
2003	13.0	13.0	13.0	13.0	13.2	13.4	13.5	13.5	13.3	13.3	13.0	13.2	13.2
2004	13.3	13.1	13.1	13.1	13.3	13.4	13.5	13.5	13.3	13.3	13.2	13.5	13.3
2005	13.1	13.1	13.1	13.0	13.1	13.4	13.4	13.5	13.3	13.1	13.1	13.4	13.2
2006	13.2	13.2	13.2	13.1	13.2	13.4	13.4	13.4	13.2	13.2	13.1	13.3	13.2
2007	13.2	13.1	13.2	13.1	13.2	13.4	13.4	13.5	13.3	13.2	13.1	13.2	13.2
Professional and Business Services													
2000	19.5	19.8	20.3	20.7	21.0	21.5	21.4	21.3	20.9	21.0	20.7	20.9	20.8
2001	20.1	20.3	20.4	20.7	21.3	21.4	21.4	21.3	20.8	20.5	20.2	20.9	20.7
2002	19.2	19.2	19.3	20.0	20.5	20.6	20.7	20.9	21.0	20.9	20.4	20.0	20.3
2003	19.3	19.4	19.3	20.0	20.6	21.0	21.0	21.0	20.7	20.9	20.4	20.3	20.4
2004	20.0	20.0	20.3	21.4	21.2	21.7	21.8	21.9	21.8	21.8	21.6	21.8	21.3
2005	20.8	20.9	21.2	21.7	22.0	22.3	22.4	22.4	22.1	22.2	22.1	22.2	21.9
2006	21.5	21.5	21.6	22.0	22.3	22.8	22.8	22.9	22.5	22.4	22.1	22.2	22.2
2007	21.2	21.3	21.6	22.1	22.6	23.0	23.0	23.0	22.7	22.6	22.1	22.2	22.3
Education and Health Services													
2000	45.1	46.2	46.2	46.0	45.5	44.7	44.9	44.8	46.3	47.1	47.3	47.4	46.0
2001	46.8	47.5	47.7	47.7	47.7	47.2	47.1	46.8	48.6	49.0	49.2	49.7	47.9
2002	49.0	49.7	50.0	50.1	50.3	49.5	49.5	49.2	50.7	50.9	51.3	51.5	50.1
2003	50.9	51.4	51.8	52.0	52.2	51.7	51.8	51.7	53.0	53.0	52.9	53.3	52.1
2004	51.9	52.7	53.1	53.1	53.5	52.9	52.5	52.1	53.8	53.4	53.7	53.8	53.0
2005	53.3	53.9	54.2	54.5	54.6	53.7	53.5	53.2	54.7	54.3	54.6	55.2	54.1
2006	54.2	55.1	55.3	55.0	55.1	55.0	55.0	54.8	56.1	56.1	56.3	56.8	55.4
2007	55.3	56.3	56.4	56.6	56.5	56.5	56.5	56.3	57.7	57.6	57.7	58.3	56.8
Leisure and Hospitality													
2000	35.1	35.3	34.7	28.6	29.5	33.0	34.2	34.9	33.1	32.1	29.6	34.7	32.9
2001	36.1	35.8	34.9	31.2	29.6	32.6	34.3	35.1	32.5	31.5	29.6	34.7	32.9
2002	35.6	35.5	34.6	30.4	29.8	33.0	34.1	34.9	32.7	31.5	29.5	34.4	33.0
2003	35.9	35.4	34.6	29.1	29.5	32.2	34.0	34.8	32.7	31.7	29.5	34.4	33.0
2004	35.5	35.5	34.4	29.3	30.0	33.4	35.0	35.5	33.3	32.3	29.6	33.7	32.8
2005	35.6	35.3	34.7	30.4	30.1	33.2	35.0	35.1	32.8	31.7	29.8	34.5	33.1
2006	35.6	35.4	34.8	29.9	30.3	33.9	34.5	35.1	32.9	31.7	29.8	34.5	33.2
2007	34.6	34.8	34.2	29.4	29.9	32.9	34.5	35.2	32.9	32.4	30.8	33.7	32.9
Other Services													
2000	9.4	9.5	9.6	9.6	9.7	9.9	9.9	9.9	9.7	9.7	9.6	9.7	9.7
2001	9.8	9.7	9.7	9.8	9.9	10.2	10.4	10.2	9.9	10.0	10.0	10.0	10.0
2002	9.8	9.7	9.8	9.9	10.0	10.2	10.4	10.4	9.9	10.0	10.0	10.0	10.1
2003	9.9	9.9	10.0	10.0	10.1	10.4	10.5	10.4	10.3	10.1	10.0	10.2	10.1
2004	10.1	10.1	10.0	10.1	10.2	10.4	10.3	10.3	10.2	10.2	10.1	10.3	10.1
2005	9.8	9.8	9.8	10.0	10.1	10.3	10.2	10.1	10.1	10.1	9.9	10.0	10.1
2006	9.7	9.7	9.7	9.8	9.9	10.1	10.2	10.1	9.9	9.8	9.8	9.9	10.0
2007	9.8	9.8	9.8	9.7	9.9	10.0	10.1	10.1	10.0	10.0	9.8	9.9	9.9
Government													
2000	48.9	50.8	52.3	51.5	52.4	48.9	41.2	41.0	49.9	51.7	52.2	52.3	49.4
2001	50.1	51.6	51.7	51.7	51.8	49.9	41.7	41.7	51.1	53.4	53.5	53.6	50.2
2002	51.3	52.6	52.7	52.9	52.7	51.0	41.8	42.1	51.2	54.0	54.4	53.4	50.8
2003	52.1	53.9	53.8	53.9	53.9	51.9	43.3	42.9	52.8	54.9	55.2	55.1	52.0
2004	52.5	54.3	54.3	54.5	54.3	51.1	43.2	43.3	53.5	55.4	56.0	55.6	52.3
2005	53.4	55.1	55.2	55.1	55.0	51.9	43.4	44.2	54.1	56.2	56.5	56.3	53.0
2006	54.4	56.0	56.0	56.0	55.7	53.2	43.8	44.0	54.5	56.7	57.0	56.8	53.7
2007	54.8	56.4	56.4	56.3	57.0	54.0	44.2	44.2	54.6	56.6	56.8	56.9	54.0

Average Weekly Hours by Selected Industry: Vermont, 2001–2007

(Not seasonally adjusted.)

Industry and year	January	February	March	April	May	June	July	August	September	October	November	December	Annual Average
Construction													
2001	39.0	39.5	39.9	40.4	41.8	41.7	41.6	41.9	41.7	40.5	39.2	39.2	40.6
2002	38.5	39.5	39.2	39.8	40.4	41.6	41.5	41.7	41.8	40.3	39.1	38.7	40.3
2003	38.8	38.9	39.0	39.1	39.2	41.0	41.1	41.3	41.3	41.3	41.0	41.0	40.4
2004	41.0	41.0	41.1	41.0	41.1	41.2	41.2	41.2	41.2	41.2	41.3	41.3	41.2
2005	41.4	41.2	40.5	40.1	40.0	39.3	39.2	39.3	39.5	39.7	39.9	40.1	39.9
2006	39.4	39.5	39.3	39.1	39.3	39.5	39.7	39.9	40.1	40.2	40.3	40.1	39.7
2007	40.3	40.1	39.9	39.7	39.6	39.8	40.0	40.2	40.4	40.2	40.0	39.7	40.0
Manufacturing													
2001	39.9	39.3	39.7	39.8	39.3	39.4	39.6	39.8	39.5	40.1	39.5	40.2	39.6
2002	40.0	40.1	40.6	40.3	39.9	39.9	39.9	40.1	40.0	39.5	40.0	39.4	40.0
2003	39.8	39.9	40.0	40.1	40.1	40.2	39.9	40.0	40.1	40.1	40.2	40.0	40.0
2004	40.1	40.1	40.0	40.0	40.1	40.2	40.2	40.2	40.2	40.2	40.4	40.4	40.2
2005	40.4	40.3	39.5	39.3	38.7	38.6	38.3	38.7	38.8	38.9	39.2	39.4	39.2
2006	39.5	38.8	39.0	39.2	39.4	39.6	39.7	39.8	40.0	40.2	40.0	40.1	39.6
2007	40.1	40.0	39.8	39.6	39.4	39.2	39.1	39.0	38.9	39.2	39.2	39.1	39.4
Wholesale Trade													
2001	33.8	34.0	34.9	34.8	35.1	34.9	35.9	38.8	37.6	37.2	36.8	36.6	35.9
2002	34.1	35.0	34.9	35.5	35.7	36.0	36.4	36.5	36.6	36.4	36.3	35.9	35.8
2003	34.6	34.7	34.8	34.9	35.0	35.1	35.5	35.6	35.6	35.6	35.7	35.7	35.2
2004	35.6	35.7	35.8	35.7	35.8	35.9	35.9	35.9	35.9	35.9	35.9	36.0	35.8
2005	36.0	35.5	34.2	35.0	34.7	34.9	35.2	35.5	35.7	35.5	35.7	35.9	35.3
2006	36.2	36.5	36.3	36.1	36.3	36.1	35.9	36.1	35.9	36.0	36.2	36.4	36.2
2007	36.1	36.3	36.5	36.6	36.8	37.0	37.2	37.4	37.5	37.7	37.9	38.1	37.1
Retail Trade													
2001	30.4	28.8	29.2	29.6	29.0	29.7	30.9	30.0	29.9	29.8	29.6	30.2	29.8
2002	29.9	29.4	29.3	29.1	29.4	30.3	30.5	30.5	30.3	30.1	29.9	30.6	29.9
2003	30.3	30.4	30.4	30.6	30.5	30.7	30.8	30.9	30.9	30.9	30.9	30.8	30.7
2004	30.9	30.9	30.9	30.9	30.9	30.9	30.9	30.9	30.9	30.9	30.9	31.0	30.9
2005	31.0	30.9	31.3	31.2	30.8	30.5	31.1	30.5	30.2	30.0	30.3	30.5	30.7
2006	30.5	30.7	30.5	30.6	30.8	30.6	30.8	31.0	30.8	30.7	30.6	30.4	30.7
2007	30.3	30.1	29.9	29.7	29.5	29.2	29.4	29.6	29.7	29.9	30.1	30.1	29.8

Average Hourly Earnings by Selected Industry: Vermont, 2001–2007

(Dollars, not seasonally adjusted.)

Industry and year	January	February	March	April	May	June	July	August	September	October	November	December	Annual Average
Construction													
2001	15.23	15.21	15.25	15.27	15.36	15.41	15.45	15.49	15.50	15.42	15.38	15.30	15.37
2002	15.26	15.32	15.34	15.33	15.40	15.44	15.45	15.46	15.47	15.46	15.49	15.35	15.41
2003	15.33	15.35	15.37	15.39	15.41	15.46	15.47	15.49	15.49	15.49	15.50	15.50	15.44
2004	15.50	15.51	15.52	15.52	15.53	15.55	15.55	15.55	15.55	15.55	15.56	15.56	15.54
2005	15.57	15.70	15.75	15.80	15.92	16.00	16.07	16.15	16.23	16.30	16.38	16.48	16.05
2006	16.43	16.53	16.33	16.43	16.53	16.63	16.73	16.83	16.89	16.99	17.07	17.14	16.73
2007	17.22	17.38	17.47	17.56	17.64	17.72	17.80	17.89	17.97	17.89	17.82	17.75	17.69
Manufacturing													
2001	14.12	14.14	14.12	14.12	14.19	14.17	14.16	14.21	14.21	14.20	14.22	14.27	14.18
2002	14.29	14.30	14.31	14.35	14.32	14.31	14.31	14.30	14.31	14.40	14.38	14.44	14.33
2003	14.51	14.49	14.50	14.51	14.52	14.54	14.55	14.56	14.56	14.56	14.57	14.57	14.54
2004	14.58	14.58	14.57	14.59	14.65	14.60	14.60	14.60	14.60	14.60	14.61	14.62	14.60
2005	14.62	14.68	14.87	14.92	14.99	15.07	15.12	15.16	15.19	15.28	15.37	15.46	15.06
2006	15.56	15.62	15.53	15.63	15.68	15.73	15.78	15.87	15.88	15.98	16.05	16.15	15.79
2007	16.23	16.31	16.42	16.51	16.60	16.65	16.62	16.58	16.55	16.51	16.47	16.43	16.49
Wholesale Trade													
2001	17.70	17.75	17.80	17.74	17.84	17.81	17.77	17.75	17.77	17.71	17.79	17.72	17.76
2002	17.77	17.82	17.84	17.80	17.85	17.80	17.81	17.83	17.84	17.77	17.73	17.83	17.81
2003	17.89	17.90	17.89	17.90	17.91	17.93	17.94	17.97	17.97	17.97	17.97	17.98	17.94
2004	17.97	17.98	17.97	17.98	17.99	17.99	17.99	17.99	17.99	17.99	17.99	18.00	17.99
2005	18.00	17.50	17.35	17.40	17.27	17.17	17.07	17.03	16.97	16.89	16.79	16.89	17.19
2006	17.03	16.90	16.80	16.70	16.60	16.50	16.40	16.32	16.25	16.34	16.41	16.50	16.56
2007	16.59	16.68	16.60	16.67	16.75	16.84	16.77	16.68	16.75	16.80	16.87	16.95	16.75
Retail Trade													
2001	11.60	11.63	11.68	11.71	11.70	11.69	11.77	11.74	11.79	11.73	11.76	11.70	11.71
2002	11.62	11.67	11.71	11.76	11.81	11.75	11.82	11.85	11.87	11.88	11.94	11.88	11.80
2003	11.84	11.83	11.85	11.86	11.88	11.90	11.91	11.93	11.93	11.93	11.93	11.92	11.89
2004	11.93	11.92	11.93	11.93	11.94	11.94	11.94	11.94	11.94	11.94	11.94	11.95	11.94
2005	11.95	12.00	12.12	12.20	12.25	12.33	12.30	12.37	12.29	12.39	12.49	12.58	12.27
2006	12.51	12.61	12.71	12.80	12.90	12.85	12.78	12.70	12.62	12.70	12.80	12.89	12.74
2007	12.98	13.07	13.18	13.25	13.16	13.26	13.17	13.09	13.02	13.08	13.15	13.24	13.14

Average Weekly Earnings by Selected Industry: Vermont, 2001–2007

(Dollars, not seasonally adjusted.)

Industry and year	January	February	March	April	May	June	July	August	September	October	November	December	Annual Average
Construction													
2001	593.97	600.80	608.48	616.91	642.05	642.60	642.72	649.03	646.35	624.51	602.90	599.76	624.02
2002	587.51	605.14	601.33	610.13	622.16	642.30	641.18	644.68	646.65	623.04	605.66	594.05	621.02
2003	594.80	597.12	599.43	601.75	604.07	633.86	635.82	639.74	639.74	639.74	635.09	635.50	623.78
2004	635.50	635.91	637.87	636.32	638.28	640.66	640.66	640.66	640.66	640.66	642.63	642.63	640.25
2005	644.60	646.84	637.88	633.58	636.80	628.80	629.94	634.70	641.09	647.11	653.56	660.85	640.40
2006	647.34	652.94	641.77	642.41	649.63	656.89	664.18	671.52	677.29	683.00	687.92	687.31	664.18
2007	693.97	696.94	697.05	697.13	698.54	705.26	712.00	719.18	725.99	719.18	712.80	704.68	707.60
Manufacturing													
2001	563.39	555.70	560.56	561.98	557.67	558.30	560.74	565.56	561.30	569.42	561.69	573.65	561.53
2002	571.60	573.43	580.99	578.31	571.37	570.97	570.97	573.43	572.40	568.80	575.20	568.94	573.20
2003	577.50	578.15	580.00	581.85	582.25	584.51	580.55	582.40	583.86	583.86	585.71	582.80	581.60
2004	584.66	584.66	582.80	583.60	587.47	586.92	586.92	586.92	586.92	586.92	587.32	590.65	586.92
2005	590.65	591.60	587.37	586.36	580.11	581.70	579.10	586.69	589.37	594.39	602.50	609.12	590.35
2006	614.62	606.06	605.67	612.70	617.79	622.91	626.47	631.63	635.20	642.40	642.00	647.62	625.28
2007	650.82	652.40	653.52	653.80	654.04	652.68	649.84	646.62	643.80	647.19	645.62	642.41	649.71
Wholesale Trade													
2001	598.26	603.50	621.22	617.35	626.18	621.57	637.94	688.70	668.15	658.81	654.67	648.55	637.58
2002	605.96	623.70	622.62	631.90	637.25	640.80	648.28	650.80	652.94	646.83	643.60	640.10	637.60
2003	618.99	621.13	622.57	624.71	626.85	629.34	636.87	639.73	639.73	639.73	641.53	641.89	631.49
2004	639.73	641.89	643.33	641.89	645.84	645.84	645.84	645.84	645.84	645.84	645.84	648.00	644.04
2005	648.00	621.25	593.37	609.00	599.27	599.23	600.86	604.57	605.83	599.60	599.40	606.35	606.81
2006	616.49	616.85	609.84	602.87	602.58	595.65	588.76	589.15	583.38	588.24	594.04	600.60	599.47
2007	598.90	605.48	605.90	610.12	616.40	623.08	623.84	623.83	628.13	633.36	639.37	645.80	621.43
Retail Trade													
2001	352.64	334.94	341.06	346.62	339.30	347.19	363.69	352.20	352.52	349.55	348.10	353.34	348.96
2002	347.44	343.10	343.10	342.22	347.21	356.03	360.51	361.43	359.66	357.59	357.01	363.53	352.82
2003	358.75	359.63	360.24	362.92	362.34	365.33	366.83	368.64	368.64	368.64	368.64	367.14	365.02
2004	368.64	368.33	368.64	368.64	368.95	368.95	368.95	368.95	368.95	368.95	368.95	370.45	368.95
2005	370.45	370.80	379.36	380.64	377.30	376.07	382.53	377.29	371.16	371.70	378.45	383.69	376.69
2006	381.56	387.13	387.66	391.68	397.32	393.21	393.62	393.70	388.70	389.89	391.68	391.86	391.12
2007	393.29	393.41	394.08	393.53	388.22	387.19	387.20	387.46	386.69	391.09	395.82	398.52	391.57

Population
    2000 census: 7,078,515
    2007 estimate: 7,712,091
    Percent change, 2000–2007: 9.0%

Percent change in total nonfarm employment, 2000–2007: 6.9%

Industry with the largest growth in employment, 2000–2007 (thousands)
    Education and health services, 84.7

Industry with the largest decline in employment, 2000–2007 (thousands)
    Manufacturing, -84.9

Civilian labor force
    2000: 3,584,037
    2007: 4,054,199

Employment-population ratio
    2000: 66.0%
    2007: 66.9%

Unemployment rate and rank among states
    2000: 2.3%, 1st
    2007: 3.0%, 4th

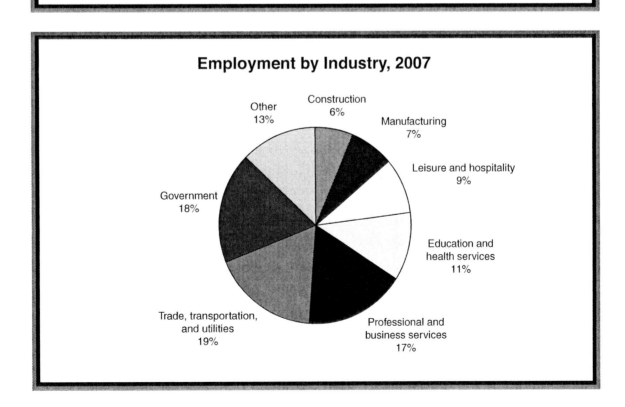

Employment by Industry, 2007

Other 13%
Construction 6%
Manufacturing 7%
Leisure and hospitality 9%
Government 18%
Education and health services 11%
Trade, transportation, and utilities 19%
Professional and business services 17%

Employment by Industry: Virginia, 2000–2007

(Numbers in thousands, not seasonally adjusted.)

Industry and year	January	February	March	April	May	June	July	August	September	October	November	December	Annual Average
Total Nonfarm													
2000	3,408.5	3,423.7	3,469.9	3,492.2	3,520.4	3,557.4	3,517.3	3,521.3	3,545.7	3,560.5	3,584.5	3,596.9	3,516.5
2001	3,472.6	3,484.7	3,514.3	3,519.6	3,537.9	3,568.1	3,516.5	3,515.6	3,520.7	3,507.4	3,522.0	3,524.9	3,517.0
2002	3,433.6	3,444.5	3,472.7	3,490.6	3,510.2	3,538.4	3,484.7	3,487.0	3,504.9	3,509.3	3,524.1	3,529.5	3,494.1
2003	3,439.0	3,435.7	3,460.8	3,476.6	3,502.5	3,529.0	3,485.9	3,492.6	3,512.8	3,527.5	3,548.8	3,558.4	3,497.5
2004	3,483.3	3,495.8	3,535.3	3,565.7	3,588.0	3,621.2	3,586.7	3,585.8	3,607.1	3,627.7	3,647.5	3,660.0	3,583.7
2005	3,573.4	3,588.8	3,614.4	3,651.0	3,671.6	3,701.3	3,667.3	3,668.2	3,698.5	3,695.0	3,717.0	3,725.8	3,664.4
2006	3,654.1	3,664.7	3,700.7	3,714.0	3,743.3	3,777.6	3,724.7	3,720.5	3,734.8	3,744.6	3,763.4	3,775.2	3,726.5
2007	3,699.8	3,705.7	3,737.1	3,751.3	3,777.6	3,809.4	3,758.0	3,752.3	3,770.0	3,777.6	3,791.5	3,797.5	3,760.7
Total Private													
2000	2,794.5	2,802.8	2,841.7	2,857.5	2,883.8	2,925.4	2,912.5	2,919.7	2,927.7	2,929.3	2,946.6	2,960.4	2,891.8
2001	2,847.3	2,849.4	2,877.9	2,882.5	2,904.7	2,933.8	2,907.0	2,911.7	2,898.9	2,874.6	2,880.4	2,885.6	2,887.8
2002	2,803.3	2,807.2	2,832.3	2,849.1	2,870.5	2,898.5	2,870.3	2,877.0	2,875.5	2,865.1	2,876.7	2,885.2	2,859.2
2003	2,805.1	2,795.6	2,819.1	2,833.5	2,861.3	2,886.6	2,870.6	2,881.3	2,876.4	2,884.0	2,896.8	2,909.2	2,860.0
2004	2,840.8	2,845.1	2,879.9	2,907.2	2,933.6	2,966.7	2,958.1	2,961.6	2,959.9	2,967.2	2,979.1	2,993.8	2,932.8
2005	2,919.5	2,927.5	2,950.3	2,980.6	3,003.4	3,033.8	3,027.1	3,033.1	3,037.2	3,025.3	3,040.1	3,052.1	3,002.5
2006	2,988.1	2,989.9	3,020.4	3,031.9	3,061.6	3,096.4	3,070.0	3,071.2	3,065.6	3,062.0	3,075.0	3,088.2	3,051.7
2007	3,020.7	3,017.9	3,047.8	3,058.0	3,086.0	3,118.3	3,094.2	3,092.7	3,086.6	3,082.2	3,091.1	3,099.2	3,074.6
Goods-Producing													
2000	574.0	573.8	581.4	582.2	585.7	591.0	585.6	589.4	591.8	588.7	589.1	588.9	585.1
2001	571.2	569.7	573.6	572.5	573.1	576.6	572.3	575.4	570.4	562.4	560.2	556.8	569.5
2002	539.1	538.5	542.5	544.4	547.9	551.4	546.9	550.1	547.5	545.6	543.4	541.2	544.9
2003	528.3	525.1	529.1	528.9	534.0	535.5	534.9	537.8	535.4	534.9	534.3	532.4	532.6
2004	522.6	522.4	529.6	536.0	539.8	545.8	546.4	547.5	546.9	547.5	546.9	547.0	539.9
2005	538.0	537.4	539.8	546.3	549.4	555.3	557.8	560.2	557.3	553.9	553.6	552.8	550.2
2006	543.1	543.0	547.4	549.9	553.7	558.6	554.9	554.9	548.8	543.6	540.4	539.2	548.1
2007	526.8	525.1	529.8	532.0	533.9	538.4	535.1	533.9	529.9	528.0	527.3	525.2	530.5
Natural Resources and Mining													
2000	11.4	11.3	11.4	11.4	11.4	11.5	11.5	11.5	11.5	11.5	11.5	11.6	11.4
2001	11.2	11.3	11.3	11.4	11.5	11.6	11.5	11.6	11.5	11.4	11.4	11.3	11.4
2002	11.0	10.9	11.0	10.7	10.8	10.7	10.5	10.4	10.4	10.2	10.2	10.2	10.6
2003	10.0	9.9	10.1	9.9	10.1	10.2	10.2	10.2	10.1	10.2	10.2	10.3	10.1
2004	10.0	10.1	10.2	10.2	10.3	10.4	10.3	10.3	10.3	10.3	10.4	10.4	10.3
2005	10.4	10.4	10.1	10.3	10.4	10.8	10.9	10.9	10.9	10.9	11.0	11.1	10.7
2006	11.0	11.0	11.2	11.0	11.2	11.5	11.5	11.5	11.3	11.2	11.3	11.3	11.3
2007	11.3	11.2	11.4	11.1	11.1	11.2	11.2	11.1	10.7	10.7	10.7	10.7	11.0
Construction													
2000	196.0	196.9	204.4	207.4	210.3	214.6	214.7	216.4	216.1	215.2	215.1	214.4	210.1
2001	205.9	207.7	213.1	215.9	219.8	223.4	223.3	224.3	221.5	217.7	216.1	214.5	216.9
2002	205.0	206.0	210.0	213.0	216.4	218.9	219.7	220.5	217.7	216.5	214.5	212.9	214.3
2003	204.4	202.6	208.1	211.6	218.3	220.2	224.2	225.7	223.7	225.0	223.5	222.8	217.5
2004	215.3	215.4	221.4	227.3	231.4	235.6	238.6	238.0	236.7	237.6	237.0	236.6	230.9
2005	230.5	230.1	232.9	239.6	242.7	247.5	252.5	253.1	250.9	248.5	248.2	247.1	243.6
2006	240.8	241.7	246.8	248.5	252.1	256.0	254.8	254.0	251.1	247.9	246.0	245.3	248.8
2007	236.1	233.3	237.6	240.7	243.1	245.8	244.8	244.6	241.9	241.4	240.7	239.3	240.8
Manufacturing													
2000	366.6	365.6	365.6	363.4	364.0	364.9	359.4	361.5	364.2	362.0	362.5	362.9	363.5
2001	354.1	350.7	349.2	345.2	341.8	341.6	337.5	339.5	337.4	333.3	332.7	331.0	341.2
2002	323.1	321.6	321.5	320.7	320.7	321.8	316.7	319.2	319.4	318.9	318.7	318.1	320.0
2003	313.9	312.6	310.9	307.4	305.6	305.1	300.5	301.9	301.6	299.7	300.6	299.3	304.9
2004	297.3	296.9	298.0	298.5	298.1	299.8	297.5	299.2	299.9	299.6	299.5	300.0	298.7
2005	297.1	296.9	296.8	296.4	296.3	297.0	294.4	296.2	295.5	294.5	294.4	294.6	295.8
2006	291.3	290.3	289.4	290.4	290.4	291.1	288.6	289.4	286.4	284.5	283.1	282.6	288.1
2007	279.4	280.6	280.8	280.2	279.7	281.4	279.1	278.2	277.3	275.9	275.9	275.2	278.6
Service-Providing													
2000	2,834.5	2,849.9	2,888.5	2,910.0	2,934.7	2,966.4	2,931.7	2,931.9	2,953.9	2,971.8	2,995.4	3,008.0	2,931.4
2001	2,901.4	2,915.0	2,940.7	2,947.1	2,964.8	2,991.5	2,944.2	2,940.2	2,950.3	2,945.0	2,961.8	2,968.1	2,947.5
2002	2,894.5	2,906.0	2,930.2	2,946.2	2,962.3	2,987.0	2,937.8	2,936.9	2,957.4	2,963.7	2,980.7	2,988.3	2,949.3
2003	2,910.7	2,910.6	2,931.7	2,947.7	2,968.5	2,993.5	2,951.0	2,954.8	2,977.4	2,992.6	3,014.5	3,026.0	2,964.9
2004	2,960.7	2,973.4	3,005.7	3,029.7	3,048.2	3,075.4	3,040.3	3,038.3	3,060.2	3,080.2	3,100.6	3,113.0	3,043.8
2005	3,035.4	3,051.4	3,074.6	3,104.7	3,122.2	3,146.0	3,109.5	3,108.0	3,141.2	3,141.1	3,163.4	3,173.0	3,114.2
2006	3,111.0	3,121.7	3,153.3	3,164.1	3,189.6	3,219.0	3,169.8	3,165.6	3,186.0	3,201.0	3,223.0	3,236.0	3,178.3
2007	3,173.0	3,180.6	3,207.3	3,219.3	3,243.7	3,271.0	3,222.9	3,218.4	3,240.1	3,249.6	3,264.2	3,272.3	3,230.2
Trade, Transportation, and Utilities													
2000	637.7	633.8	638.1	637.3	642.8	648.1	645.3	649.2	651.3	661.3	676.8	686.8	650.7
2001	644.0	634.8	638.3	635.0	640.7	645.2	642.9	643.8	641.6	646.0	658.7	664.9	644.7
2002	632.9	623.7	625.5	626.3	630.8	636.2	634.6	636.3	634.8	639.2	652.9	663.7	636.4
2003	625.3	618.4	621.0	622.9	628.5	632.7	632.8	636.0	634.0	643.7	657.8	669.2	635.2
2004	635.8	630.2	633.3	636.0	641.4	646.4	646.3	647.6	644.4	652.5	666.4	676.5	646.4
2005	646.9	640.6	643.6	648.1	651.6	655.1	656.1	657.2	655.6	662.7	678.4	689.4	657.1
2006	659.2	648.1	653.4	652.9	659.0	663.6	660.3	661.0	658.1	665.9	682.0	692.1	663.0
2007	663.5	654.2	658.5	657.5	664.2	668.3	668.4	667.2	665.6	668.4	682.9	691.3	667.5
Wholesale Trade													
2000	111.2	111.8	112.7	113.5	114.0	114.9	113.9	114.4	114.5	116.3	116.7	117.4	114.2
2001	113.9	114.1	115.1	115.2	115.1	115.9	115.2	115.0	114.4	114.1	114.3	114.4	114.7
2002	112.4	112.2	112.6	112.8	113.0	113.4	112.8	113.0	112.6	112.7	113.1	113.5	112.8
2003	112.3	112.3	112.6	112.5	113.3	113.5	113.5	113.5	113.7	113.1	113.6	113.8	113.2
2004	113.0	113.1	113.9	114.1	114.4	115.1	115.5	115.2	114.5	115.2	115.4	115.9	114.6
2005	114.7	115.0	115.6	116.8	117.2	117.4	117.9	118.2	117.8	118.1	118.7	119.1	117.2
2006	117.4	117.8	118.5	119.1	119.7	120.5	119.9	120.1	119.8	120.5	120.8	121.2	119.6
2007	120.0	120.4	121.1	120.7	121.2	121.9	121.6	121.7	121.2	121.2	121.0	121.1	121.1

Employment by Industry: Virginia, 2000–2007—*Continued*

(Numbers in thousands, not seasonally adjusted.)

Industry and year	January	February	March	April	May	June	July	August	September	October	November	December	Annual Average
Retail Trade													
2000	401.9	397.4	400.5	398.9	403.6	407.3	404.6	407.9	410.2	415.8	431.2	440.8	410.0
2001	405.2	395.9	398.2	395.6	400.6	404.0	402.3	404.0	402.9	407.9	421.9	429.1	405.6
2002	402.8	394.7	396.1	396.4	400.1	403.6	401.6	402.8	402.2	405.3	418.1	428.6	404.4
2003	395.8	389.6	391.3	392.8	397.1	400.4	398.9	402.1	401.6	409.4	424.2	434.5	403.1
2004	407.6	401.7	403.5	405.1	409.3	412.6	410.7	411.5	409.2	415.5	428.9	437.0	412.7
2005	412.3	405.9	407.3	410.4	413.3	416.1	416.8	417.7	417.1	422.6	436.5	445.5	418.5
2006	422.2	412.9	416.6	415.8	420.6	423.1	421.2	421.5	418.6	425.3	440.7	447.6	423.8
2007	425.5	416.2	419.2	418.5	424.1	426.2	426.3	425.2	424.3	426.0	440.3	446.9	426.6
Transportation and Utilities													
2000	124.6	124.6	124.9	124.9	125.2	125.9	126.8	126.9	126.6	129.2	128.9	128.6	126.4
2001	124.9	124.8	125.0	124.2	125.0	125.3	125.4	124.8	124.3	124.0	122.5	121.4	124.3
2002	117.7	116.8	116.8	117.1	117.7	119.2	120.2	120.5	120.0	121.2	121.7	121.6	119.2
2003	117.2	116.5	117.1	117.6	118.1	118.8	120.4	120.2	119.3	120.7	119.8	120.2	118.8
2004	115.2	115.4	115.9	116.8	117.7	118.7	120.1	120.9	120.7	121.8	122.1	123.6	119.1
2005	119.9	119.7	120.7	120.9	121.1	121.6	121.4	121.3	120.7	122.0	123.2	124.8	121.4
2006	119.6	117.4	118.3	118.0	118.7	120.0	119.2	119.4	119.7	120.1	120.5	123.3	119.5
2007	118.0	117.6	118.2	118.3	118.9	120.2	120.5	120.3	120.1	121.2	121.6	123.3	119.9
Information													
2000	112.6	113.5	114.7	115.5	117.7	120.0	121.2	116.4	123.3	123.4	124.3	125.3	118.9
2001	123.9	124.2	124.0	121.3	121.2	119.7	119.2	118.0	116.6	114.4	113.4	112.8	119.1
2002	109.9	109.4	108.8	107.4	107.5	107.3	104.9	104.4	102.6	102.2	102.9	102.6	105.8
2003	101.3	101.6	101.5	100.7	101.2	102.2	102.2	101.8	100.9	100.5	101.3	101.5	101.4
2004	101.1	100.7	101.2	99.4	99.1	99.1	98.8	97.7	96.2	95.4	95.5	95.0	98.3
2005	93.5	93.4	93.4	93.0	93.0	93.3	92.9	92.6	91.8	91.6	91.9	92.0	92.7
2006	91.3	91.7	91.8	91.1	93.4	91.8	92.9	91.8	91.3	90.4	90.8	90.8	91.6
2007	91.9	91.3	90.7	90.6	91.2	91.2	90.7	90.3	90.3	90.1	90.2	89.9	90.7
Financial Activities													
2000	173.8	174.3	175.3	176.4	178.0	180.7	180.1	181.0	180.4	181.3	181.8	183.4	178.8
2001	176.9	177.8	178.9	179.0	180.2	182.6	182.5	183.0	181.1	178.2	178.9	179.9	179.9
2002	179.0	179.7	180.4	180.3	181.6	184.0	183.9	183.9	182.6	182.4	183.4	184.4	182.1
2003	182.6	183.3	184.2	184.9	186.4	188.9	190.0	190.3	188.1	186.3	185.6	186.7	186.4
2004	184.8	185.0	186.0	188.2	189.0	191.1	191.9	191.9	190.0	189.5	189.8	190.8	189.0
2005	188.7	189.4	189.9	191.2	192.2	194.5	195.9	195.9	194.2	192.3	192.1	193.5	192.5
2006	191.9	192.6	193.6	193.6	195.0	197.6	197.0	197.1	194.8	194.4	194.3	195.5	194.8
2007	193.7	193.9	194.7	194.0	195.1	196.6	196.0	195.2	193.3	192.8	192.3	192.9	194.2
Professional and Business Services													
2000	542.0	548.4	558.0	563.1	564.1	575.2	572.9	575.6	576.1	578.1	579.3	583.4	568.0
2001	554.8	557.8	563.1	561.2	561.2	567.0	563.5	565.2	559.6	554.4	552.2	554.3	559.5
2002	537.1	541.5	547.3	548.4	548.5	552.0	550.3	551.7	548.1	545.7	546.1	546.9	547.0
2003	535.9	535.9	541.4	544.3	545.7	549.9	550.4	554.8	552.8	557.9	560.5	562.6	549.3
2004	551.7	556.7	563.7	570.0	573.5	581.0	586.0	590.5	587.7	592.1	592.9	596.4	578.5
2005	584.8	590.4	595.1	599.4	600.7	607.0	612.8	615.8	616.5	616.1	616.3	618.7	606.1
2006	610.5	615.0	621.1	622.3	625.4	632.4	633.2	636.0	634.3	636.1	637.2	639.0	628.5
2007	628.4	631.9	638.2	641.2	642.3	649.1	648.9	652.2	647.8	648.4	646.6	650.4	643.8
Education and Health Services													
2000	326.2	329.1	331.9	329.1	330.7	330.7	330.3	330.6	335.0	336.7	338.1	339.2	332.3
2001	339.5	342.8	344.6	345.2	346.5	346.7	331.6	332.0	350.1	353.7	355.1	356.5	345.4
2002	355.9	360.2	362.1	363.8	363.5	363.0	343.9	345.4	367.4	370.8	373.0	372.9	361.8
2003	370.2	370.3	370.0	372.7	372.3	371.7	352.9	354.5	373.5	375.6	377.5	378.5	370.0
2004	376.4	379.1	383.0	382.6	383.0	381.6	364.4	365.1	385.7	389.7	391.7	393.0	381.3
2005	387.3	391.3	393.0	395.3	396.9	395.4	377.0	377.9	401.7	400.6	402.8	403.1	393.5
2006	400.4	403.8	406.1	406.0	407.8	408.5	387.7	387.6	410.7	412.9	415.7	416.8	405.3
2007	412.0	414.9	417.7	417.2	420.4	420.9	401.3	401.8	422.4	423.5	425.7	426.4	417.0
Leisure and Hospitality													
2000	272.2	273.1	283.9	294.2	304.6	317.7	314.8	315.2	307.7	297.3	294.5	290.4	297.1
2001	275.1	279.5	289.9	299.8	311.9	324.4	324.0	323.2	309.9	296.9	291.1	289.1	301.2
2002	275.8	279.2	289.3	301.5	312.3	324.5	326.4	326.2	314.4	302.7	298.5	296.2	303.9
2003	283.5	282.7	292.0	303.2	316.9	328.4	330.4	329.7	316.7	310.2	304.8	303.0	308.5
2004	292.4	294.4	304.8	316.3	328.3	340.4	341.9	340.4	329.6	321.0	316.2	314.9	320.1
2005	302.3	305.9	315.6	326.2	337.6	349.9	350.8	350.6	338.4	328.1	324.9	322.2	329.4
2006	313.2	316.7	326.7	335.3	345.4	360.2	360.4	359.4	345.7	336.8	332.7	332.3	338.7
2007	322.3	323.9	333.7	340.7	353.0	366.5	366.9	365.6	352.2	346.6	341.4	338.1	345.9
Other Services													
2000	156.0	156.8	158.4	159.7	160.2	162.0	162.3	162.3	162.1	162.5	162.7	163.0	160.7
2001	161.9	162.8	165.5	168.5	169.9	171.6	171.0	171.1	169.6	168.6	170.8	171.3	168.6
2002	173.6	175.0	176.4	177.0	178.4	180.1	179.4	179.0	178.1	176.5	176.5	177.3	177.3
2003	178.0	178.3	179.9	175.9	176.3	177.3	177.0	176.4	175.0	174.9	175.0	175.3	176.6
2004	176.0	176.6	178.3	178.7	179.5	181.3	182.4	180.9	179.4	179.5	179.7	180.2	179.4
2005	178.0	179.1	179.9	181.1	182.0	183.3	183.8	182.9	181.7	180.0	180.1	180.4	181.0
2006	178.5	179.0	180.3	180.8	181.9	183.7	183.6	183.4	181.9	181.9	181.9	182.5	181.6
2007	182.1	182.7	184.5	184.8	185.9	187.3	186.9	186.5	185.1	184.4	184.7	185.0	185.0
Government													
2000	614.0	620.9	628.2	634.7	636.6	632.0	604.8	601.6	618.0	631.2	637.9	636.5	624.7
2001	625.3	635.3	636.4	637.1	633.2	634.3	609.5	603.9	621.8	632.8	641.6	639.3	629.2
2002	630.3	637.3	640.4	641.5	639.7	639.9	614.4	610.0	629.4	644.2	647.4	644.3	634.9
2003	633.9	640.1	641.7	643.1	641.2	642.4	615.3	611.3	636.4	643.5	652.0	649.2	637.5
2004	642.5	650.7	655.4	658.5	654.4	654.5	628.6	624.2	647.2	660.5	668.4	666.2	650.9
2005	653.9	661.3	664.1	670.4	668.2	667.5	640.2	635.1	661.3	669.7	676.9	673.7	661.9
2006	666.0	674.8	680.3	682.1	681.7	681.2	654.7	649.3	669.2	682.6	688.4	687.0	674.8
2007	679.1	687.8	689.3	693.3	691.6	691.1	663.8	659.6	683.4	695.4	700.4	698.3	686.1

Average Weekly Hours by Selected Industry: Virginia, 2001–2007

(Not seasonally adjusted.)

Industry and year	January	February	March	April	May	June	July	August	September	October	November	December	Annual Average
Manufacturing													
2001	40.1	39.7	40.0	38.9	40.0	40.7	40.1	39.9	40.7	40.1	40.3	40.8	40.1
2002	40.5	40.4	40.7	40.7	40.8	41.1	40.4	41.1	40.7	40.1	41.2	41.3	40.8
2003	40.3	40.2	41.0	40.0	40.9	41.2	40.0	40.9	40.6	41.1	41.7	41.6	40.8
2004	41.5	41.3	41.3	41.2	42.3	42.1	40.7	40.9	40.6	41.9	41.6	42.3	41.5
2005	41.6	41.7	40.8	41.5	41.3	41.3	40.3	40.4	42.3	41.8	41.3	42.1	41.4
2006	41.7	40.9	40.9	40.6	41.5	41.8	41.4	40.8	41.4	41.3	40.8	42.0	41.3
2007	41.3	41.1	41.5	41.1	41.5	42.6	41.8	42.2	41.8	41.8	43.6	43.7	42.0

Average Hourly Earnings by Selected Industry: Virginia, 2001–2007

(Dollars, not seasonally adjusted.)

Industry and year	January	February	March	April	May	June	July	August	September	October	November	December	Annual Average
Manufacturing													
2001	14.24	14.36	14.39	14.40	14.37	14.46	14.39	14.47	14.60	14.48	14.81	14.93	14.50
2002	14.99	14.88	14.93	14.97	15.21	15.09	15.17	15.37	15.47	15.49	15.57	15.81	15.20
2003	15.62	15.47	15.77	15.78	15.77	16.05	15.79	15.76	16.00	15.94	16.26	16.29	15.90
2004	16.13	15.91	15.97	16.26	16.15	16.22	16.04	15.96	16.12	16.12	16.10	16.35	16.11
2005	16.27	16.29	16.19	16.40	16.29	16.35	16.48	16.42	16.52	16.45	16.44	16.64	16.40
2006	16.51	16.71	16.75	16.70	16.63	16.81	16.62	16.70	16.74	16.90	16.90	16.97	16.75
2007	17.09	17.06	17.08	17.35	17.26	17.70	17.71	17.67	17.79	17.67	18.35	18.51	17.61

Average Weekly Earnings by Selected Industry: Virginia, 2001–2007

(Dollars, not seasonally adjusted.)

Industry and year	January	February	March	April	May	June	July	August	September	October	November	December	Annual Average
Manufacturing													
2001	571.02	570.09	575.60	560.16	574.80	588.52	577.04	577.35	594.22	580.65	596.84	609.14	581.30
2002	607.10	601.15	607.65	609.28	620.57	620.20	612.87	631.71	629.63	621.15	641.48	652.95	621.30
2003	629.49	621.89	646.57	631.20	644.99	661.26	631.60	644.58	649.60	655.13	678.04	677.66	647.70
2004	669.40	657.08	659.56	669.91	683.15	682.86	652.83	652.76	654.47	675.43	669.76	691.61	668.57
2005	676.83	679.29	660.55	680.60	672.78	675.26	664.14	663.37	698.80	687.61	678.97	700.54	678.96
2006	688.47	683.44	685.08	678.02	690.15	702.66	688.07	681.36	693.04	697.97	689.52	712.74	691.78
2007	705.82	701.17	708.82	713.09	716.29	754.02	740.28	745.67	743.62	738.61	800.06	808.89	739.62

Population
    2000 census: 5,894,121
    2007 estimate: 6,468,424
    Percent change, 2000–2007: 9.7%

Percent change in total nonfarm employment, 2000–2007: 8.1%

Industry with the largest growth in employment, 2000–2007 (thousands)
    Education and health services, 55.7

Industry with the largest decline in employment, 2000–2007 (thousands)
    Manufacturing, -38.6

Civilian labor force
    2000: 3,050,021
    2007: 3,408,191

Employment-population ratio
    2000: 64.9%
    2007: 64.8%

Unemployment rate and rank among states
    2000: 5.0%, 44th
    2007: 4.5%, 27th

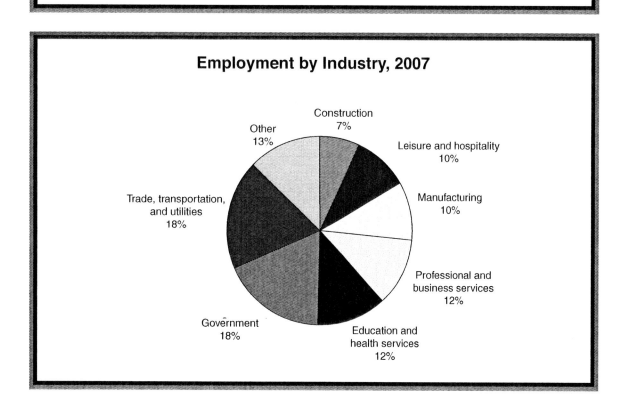

Employment by Industry, 2007

Construction 7%
Other 13%
Leisure and hospitality 10%
Trade, transportation, and utilities 18%
Manufacturing 10%
Professional and business services 12%
Government 18%
Education and health services 12%

Employment by Industry: Washington, 2000–2007

(Numbers in thousands, not seasonally adjusted.)

Industry and year	January	February	March	April	May	June	July	August	September	October	November	December	Annual Average
Total Nonfarm													
2000	2,638.8	2,645.3	2,688.2	2,687.0	2,721.2	2,744.6	2,709.3	2,721.1	2,739.6	2,741.7	2,749.6	2,749.0	2,711.3
2001	2,670.9	2,677.0	2,694.5	2,699.1	2,718.3	2,736.6	2,700.7	2,697.1	2,705.5	2,697.8	2,691.5	2,674.9	2,697.0
2002	2,606.2	2,611.2	2,623.0	2,637.6	2,663.7	2,679.4	2,661.3	2,660.3	2,674.8	2,678.5	2,683.4	2,669.4	2,654.1
2003	2,608.9	2,617.9	2,624.1	2,637.8	2,663.3	2,679.1	2,659.9	2,659.9	2,677.7	2,686.4	2,689.4	2,685.5	2,657.5
2004	2,613.8	2,633.5	2,659.6	2,682.5	2,705.0	2,727.5	2,710.8	2,705.9	2,725.9	2,744.6	2,753.6	2,749.6	2,701.0
2005	2,688.2	2,704.2	2,729.8	2,755.2	2,780.3	2,800.7	2,787.5	2,787.7	2,800.7	2,820.8	2,834.5	2,835.2	2,777.1
2006	2,775.7	2,796.2	2,816.9	2,832.6	2,862.7	2,893.8	2,863.5	2,867.7	2,894.5	2,897.4	2,906.6	2,903.0	2,859.2
2007	2,843.3	2,873.7	2,891.4	2,909.8	2,940.7	2,960.1	2,944.1	2,940.6	2,962.8	2,972.8	2,975.0	2,970.1	2,932.0
Total Private													
2000	2,159.5	2,158.1	2,198.6	2,198.9	2,221.6	2,249.7	2,245.5	2,266.0	2,268.7	2,255.1	2,255.9	2,258.0	2,228.0
2001	2,170.6	2,170.9	2,183.8	2,188.3	2,204.4	2,221.0	2,212.9	2,222.2	2,211.9	2,185.0	2,169.9	2,158.0	2,191.6
2002	2,093.9	2,092.1	2,102.0	2,115.9	2,139.2	2,154.7	2,163.1	2,175.3	2,170.7	2,154.9	2,150.5	2,142.8	2,137.9
2003	2,088.2	2,091.6	2,096.8	2,110.5	2,130.4	2,148.7	2,158.8	2,170.3	2,170.7	2,161.8	2,157.2	2,157.9	2,136.9
2004	2,092.1	2,105.9	2,129.3	2,152.2	2,172.8	2,193.8	2,204.4	2,213.4	2,214.1	2,215.9	2,216.0	2,218.7	2,177.4
2005	2,161.9	2,173.4	2,195.9	2,220.7	2,244.4	2,263.1	2,278.9	2,293.1	2,286.6	2,288.8	2,294.7	2,302.6	2,250.3
2006	2,246.1	2,259.7	2,278.7	2,295.8	2,323.6	2,351.9	2,354.2	2,370.9	2,376.6	2,362.3	2,364.0	2,366.7	2,329.2
2007	2,312.6	2,336.1	2,354.6	2,369.8	2,397.3	2,423.9	2,427.6	2,441.7	2,439.1	2,431.3	2,428.7	2,428.0	2,399.2
Goods-Producing													
2000	489.2	476.7	496.0	498.4	503.2	510.1	511.7	516.3	514.8	511.9	504.7	496.6	502.4
2001	483.6	480.5	483.5	483.9	488.4	493.6	494.7	498.3	494.1	484.1	471.6	459.7	484.7
2002	443.7	440.2	440.6	443.5	450.4	454.1	458.8	462.7	457.4	452.3	443.4	435.5	448.6
2003	422.4	421.7	421.3	424.8	430.2	436.0	440.5	444.2	442.8	439.0	432.1	427.7	431.9
2004	413.0	416.8	422.7	428.5	434.3	440.0	448.5	450.7	450.5	451.1	445.7	442.0	437.0
2005	431.1	435.0	442.1	448.8	455.7	462.6	472.4	476.2	464.1	477.3	472.0	470.2	459.0
2006	461.8	467.9	472.7	476.9	485.6	496.5	502.2	506.3	508.3	504.7	498.1	493.6	489.6
2007	484.5	490.4	494.5	499.2	507.4	517.8	522.0	526.1	525.2	521.6	513.3	506.8	509.1
Natural Resources and Mining													
2000	10.0	10.1	9.8	9.7	10.1	10.4	10.3	10.4	10.2	9.9	9.7	9.5	10.0
2001	9.9	9.7	9.2	9.0	9.5	9.9	10.4	10.4	10.3	10.1	9.8	9.4	9.8
2002	9.0	9.1	8.9	8.9	9.3	9.5	9.7	9.7	9.8	9.7	9.4	9.3	9.4
2003	8.7	8.7	8.5	8.3	8.5	8.7	8.8	8.8	8.7	8.7	8.5	8.6	8.6
2004	8.5	8.7	8.6	8.8	9.0	9.2	9.5	9.6	9.7	9.5	9.3	9.2	9.1
2005	8.8	8.9	8.8	8.8	9.1	9.2	9.2	9.1	9.1	8.9	8.8	8.8	9.0
2006	8.4	8.5	8.5	8.4	8.8	9.0	9.0	8.9	8.8	8.7	8.6	8.6	8.7
2007	8.4	7.9	7.6	7.9	8.3	8.5	8.5	8.4	8.3	8.3	8.0	8.0	8.2
Construction													
2000	146.7	149.2	153.1	155.8	159.3	163.8	166.6	169.7	170.1	168.1	164.7	159.7	160.5
2001	152.0	150.9	155.4	155.5	159.4	163.3	165.4	168.6	166.5	162.5	155.6	149.8	158.7
2002	143.2	143.5	144.6	148.4	153.6	156.6	161.3	166.0	163.9	161.2	156.5	151.6	154.2
2003	144.9	145.2	145.8	149.8	154.6	158.6	163.0	166.6	165.4	164.2	160.1	156.4	156.2
2004	147.3	151.0	155.5	158.8	163.1	166.5	172.0	174.0	172.7	172.9	170.2	166.6	164.2
2005	158.4	162.0	167.0	170.8	175.0	178.7	184.5	188.2	189.3	187.7	184.5	182.8	177.4
2006	175.6	179.5	184.2	187.7	193.8	200.1	203.3	206.9	207.1	204.6	200.0	196.4	194.9
2007	190.3	194.4	199.6	202.8	209.5	214.6	216.0	219.7	217.4	214.5	208.8	203.4	207.6
Manufacturing													
2000	332.5	317.4	333.1	332.9	333.8	335.9	334.8	336.2	334.5	333.9	330.3	327.4	331.9
2001	321.7	319.9	318.9	319.4	319.5	320.4	318.9	319.3	317.3	311.5	306.2	300.5	316.1
2002	291.5	287.6	287.1	286.2	287.5	288.0	287.8	287.0	283.7	281.4	277.5	274.6	285.0
2003	268.8	267.8	267.0	266.7	267.1	268.7	268.7	268.8	268.7	266.1	263.5	262.7	267.1
2004	257.2	257.1	258.6	260.9	262.2	264.3	267.0	267.1	268.1	268.7	266.2	266.2	263.6
2005	263.9	264.1	266.3	269.2	271.6	274.7	278.7	278.9	265.7	280.7	278.7	278.6	272.6
2006	277.8	279.9	280.0	280.8	283.0	287.4	289.9	290.5	292.4	291.4	289.5	288.6	285.9
2007	285.8	288.1	287.3	288.5	289.6	294.7	297.5	298.0	299.5	298.8	296.5	295.4	293.3
Service-Providing													
2000	2,149.6	2,168.6	2,192.2	2,188.6	2,218.0	2,234.5	2,197.6	2,204.8	2,224.8	2,229.8	2,244.9	2,252.4	2,208.8
2001	2,187.3	2,196.5	2,211.0	2,215.2	2,229.9	2,243.0	2,206.0	2,198.8	2,211.4	2,213.7	2,219.9	2,215.2	2,212.3
2002	2,162.5	2,171.0	2,182.4	2,194.1	2,213.3	2,225.3	2,202.5	2,197.6	2,217.4	2,226.2	2,240.0	2,233.9	2,205.5
2003	2,186.5	2,196.2	2,202.8	2,213.0	2,233.1	2,243.1	2,219.4	2,215.7	2,234.9	2,247.4	2,257.3	2,257.8	2,225.6
2004	2,200.8	2,216.7	2,236.9	2,254.0	2,270.7	2,287.5	2,262.3	2,255.2	2,275.4	2,293.5	2,307.9	2,307.6	2,264.0
2005	2,257.1	2,269.2	2,287.7	2,306.4	2,324.6	2,338.1	2,315.1	2,311.5	2,336.6	2,343.5	2,362.5	2,365.0	2,318.1
2006	2,313.9	2,328.3	2,344.2	2,355.7	2,377.1	2,397.3	2,361.3	2,361.4	2,386.2	2,392.7	2,408.5	2,409.4	2,369.7
2007	2,358.8	2,383.3	2,396.9	2,410.6	2,433.3	2,442.3	2,422.1	2,414.5	2,437.6	2,451.2	2,461.7	2,463.3	2,423.0
Trade, Transportation, and Utilities													
2000	520.6	518.8	523.6	522.5	527.1	533.5	530.2	533.0	533.3	539.2	548.2	552.5	531.8
2001	523.5	518.3	520.9	520.4	522.0	527.2	526.3	526.0	523.5	522.2	526.1	527.8	523.7
2002	505.1	498.9	500.1	501.3	505.7	509.9	512.5	512.0	512.8	512.6	518.3	522.2	509.3
2003	502.2	498.0	498.3	499.8	504.2	509.3	513.2	513.5	514.3	515.7	522.0	527.0	509.8
2004	501.9	500.9	504.1	509.1	513.7	519.4	521.1	524.0	523.7	527.4	535.4	540.6	518.4
2005	517.2	515.2	517.9	520.5	525.8	530.4	531.7	535.3	535.7	536.0	546.3	553.4	530.5
2006	530.4	527.2	530.4	531.4	537.4	543.5	543.0	546.0	546.0	546.2	556.2	561.5	541.6
2007	540.5	539.1	541.9	544.2	549.2	554.2	555.5	557.3	555.9	558.4	568.5	572.2	553.1
Wholesale Trade													
2000	118.0	118.8	120.2	120.0	120.6	123.3	121.7	122.4	122.0	123.2	122.6	122.1	121.2
2001	119.3	119.4	120.1	120.1	120.6	122.0	121.5	120.7	119.6	119.0	118.1	116.4	119.7
2002	114.8	115.0	115.3	115.0	115.8	116.3	116.4	116.5	116.4	116.2	115.6	114.5	115.7
2003	113.6	113.8	114.3	115.0	115.4	116.4	117.3	117.2	117.4	117.8	117.5	116.5	116.0
2004	114.9	115.7	116.9	118.7	118.9	119.8	120.8	120.8	120.9	121.7	121.4	121.1	119.3
2005	119.2	119.8	120.6	120.2	121.2	122.7	122.8	123.3	123.5	124.0	124.5	124.4	122.2
2006	123.7	124.2	125.0	124.8	126.0	127.9	128.1	128.1	127.8	127.9	128.3	128.1	126.6
2007	125.9	126.6	127.3	128.1	129.1	130.4	130.3	130.4	130.0	130.2	130.1	130.0	129.0

Employment by Industry: Washington, 2000–2007—*Continued*

(Numbers in thousands, not seasonally adjusted.)

Industry and year	January	February	March	April	May	June	July	August	September	October	November	December	Annual Average
Retail Trade													
2000	310.0	307.1	309.5	308.9	312.9	315.4	312.6	314.4	314.8	316.7	327.3	332.9	315.2
2001	312.3	307.4	308.9	307.9	308.7	311.1	311.6	312.4	310.9	309.6	317.1	321.2	311.6
2002	303.2	297.2	298.3	299.3	302.1	304.8	306.6	306.3	306.4	306.1	314.1	319.5	305.3
2003	301.7	297.8	298.0	298.7	302.1	305.2	307.4	307.7	307.0	308.0	316.1	321.1	305.9
2004	300.9	299.2	300.5	302.9	306.6	309.0	309.8	312.5	310.7	312.2	321.6	326.7	309.4
2005	308.7	305.5	307.1	309.1	312.4	314.6	316.5	319.2	318.3	319.1	328.6	334.2	316.1
2006	315.4	311.5	313.3	314.2	317.9	320.4	320.6	323.2	322.0	322.7	333.6	337.8	321.1
2007	321.2	318.9	320.3	321.2	324.4	326.7	328.7	329.6	328.2	330.0	339.7	344.1	327.8
Transportation and Utilities													
2000	92.6	92.9	93.9	93.6	93.6	94.8	95.9	96.2	96.5	99.3	98.3	97.5	95.4
2001	91.9	91.5	91.9	92.4	92.7	94.1	93.2	92.9	93.0	93.6	90.9	90.2	92.4
2002	87.1	86.7	86.5	87.0	87.8	88.8	89.5	89.2	90.0	90.3	88.6	88.2	88.3
2003	86.9	86.4	86.0	86.1	86.7	87.7	88.5	88.6	89.9	89.9	88.4	89.4	87.9
2004	86.1	86.0	86.7	87.5	88.2	90.6	90.5	90.7	92.1	93.5	92.4	92.8	89.8
2005	89.3	89.9	90.2	91.2	92.2	93.1	92.4	92.8	93.9	92.9	93.2	94.8	92.2
2006	91.3	91.5	92.1	92.4	93.5	95.2	94.3	95.0	96.1	95.2	94.5	96.6	94.0
2007	93.4	93.6	94.3	94.9	95.7	97.1	96.5	97.3	97.7	98.2	98.7	98.1	96.3
Information													
2000	90.5	92.0	93.5	94.1	95.9	98.7	99.9	101.0	102.0	100.9	101.6	101.9	97.6
2001	101.6	101.8	101.0	99.4	99.6	100.3	99.3	99.1	97.0	96.3	96.1	96.7	99.0
2002	94.2	93.9	93.5	93.2	93.3	93.8	93.9	94.0	93.1	93.3	93.4	93.3	93.6
2003	92.2	92.0	91.5	91.0	91.6	92.1	92.2	93.1	92.4	92.6	93.0	93.6	92.3
2004	91.7	91.7	92.1	92.1	92.8	93.2	93.4	93.7	93.7	92.7	93.0	94.2	92.9
2005	92.7	93.5	93.4	94.1	94.5	94.9	95.7	96.4	95.4	94.6	95.5	96.1	94.7
2006	94.8	95.2	95.9	96.2	96.9	99.5	100.0	100.7	100.6	99.7	100.6	101.1	98.4
2007	100.4	101.3	101.0	101.5	102.6	103.7	103.9	104.2	103.5	103.4	103.5	103.6	102.7
Financial Activities													
2000	141.9	142.6	142.5	141.7	142.2	142.6	142.6	143.0	142.9	141.3	141.6	142.7	142.3
2001	142.4	143.3	143.1	143.4	144.3	145.2	147.2	147.7	147.9	145.9	145.7	146.1	145.2
2002	143.0	143.6	144.0	144.7	145.6	146.2	147.1	148.1	147.8	147.1	148.1	148.7	146.2
2003	148.2	148.9	149.7	150.8	152.0	152.9	154.2	154.8	153.9	153.0	152.3	152.1	151.9
2004	149.9	150.2	151.4	151.0	151.6	152.3	152.8	153.0	152.3	152.2	151.9	153.3	151.8
2005	150.5	151.2	151.4	152.5	153.6	154.6	156.4	157.5	157.0	156.4	156.4	157.2	154.6
2006	155.2	155.4	155.8	156.0	156.7	157.5	157.7	157.5	156.6	155.6	155.1	155.5	156.2
2007	153.9	154.5	155.2	155.6	155.9	156.8	157.0	156.8	154.9	154.5	154.2	154.5	155.3
Professional and Business Services													
2000	290.3	293.1	298.3	298.6	300.7	305.2	305.9	311.6	312.8	309.8	309.0	310.6	303.8
2001	296.8	296.9	299.6	300.7	300.6	301.3	297.8	299.0	296.5	293.9	290.3	287.5	296.7
2002	279.8	282.3	284.6	287.1	288.6	291.5	293.2	297.2	297.1	295.3	294.9	291.3	290.2
2003	282.2	284.5	285.4	287.8	288.3	289.7	292.1	295.6	295.5	295.4	294.3	293.2	290.3
2004	286.0	289.8	294.2	298.8	299.9	303.0	306.2	308.6	308.1	309.6	309.3	307.4	301.7
2005	300.0	304.7	308.3	312.4	314.9	317.0	320.8	323.0	324.8	322.7	322.5	321.8	316.1
2006	313.6	317.4	320.6	325.6	328.5	333.3	335.1	338.8	339.2	338.3	338.6	338.0	330.6
2007	329.4	335.6	339.9	340.9	343.7	347.8	349.5	352.7	352.0	349.9	349.3	349.5	345.0
Education and Health Services													
2000	285.4	289.8	292.8	290.1	291.2	291.0	289.5	291.3	293.3	294.9	296.3	297.1	291.9
2001	292.4	296.8	298.0	298.6	299.7	298.1	291.6	292.9	299.2	302.5	305.1	305.0	298.3
2002	301.7	305.6	307.3	307.7	309.4	306.2	300.8	301.5	306.7	311.1	312.8	312.0	306.9
2003	307.8	311.4	312.6	314.0	314.7	312.1	308.1	307.8	312.6	316.8	318.3	318.3	312.9
2004	312.9	316.9	318.7	320.9	321.9	320.3	313.9	313.8	319.4	325.0	326.4	326.0	319.7
2005	322.1	325.5	328.2	331.1	332.1	328.3	322.9	323.7	331.2	334.8	336.3	335.5	329.3
2006	331.3	335.4	337.8	338.8	340.2	336.3	329.2	330.7	338.1	342.4	343.4	342.8	337.2
2007	338.9	344.7	346.9	347.6	350.3	347.0	340.8	342.2	349.0	354.1	355.5	354.5	347.6
Leisure and Hospitality													
2000	237.8	240.6	246.4	249.2	254.7	261.2	258.5	261.7	261.9	250.4	248.1	250.1	251.7
2001	235.0	237.7	241.2	245.4	252.4	256.7	257.6	260.6	256.6	243.7	238.9	239.1	247.1
2002	231.4	232.2	236.0	241.2	248.1	253.7	256.7	259.7	257.0	245.4	241.8	242.1	245.4
2003	235.7	237.2	239.6	243.7	249.9	256.2	258.4	261.3	259.8	250.7	247.1	247.6	248.9
2004	239.6	241.6	247.0	252.1	257.9	263.8	266.2	267.5	266.0	256.9	253.5	254.8	255.6
2005	248.1	247.2	252.4	259.2	265.1	271.2	274.7	276.7	274.9	264.4	263.1	265.4	263.5
2006	257.6	258.9	262.3	267.4	273.9	279.7	281.5	285.4	282.7	271.7	268.4	270.3	271.7
2007	262.9	266.7	270.5	276.0	282.6	289.8	292.0	295.1	292.4	284.1	279.6	281.9	281.1
Other Services													
2000	103.8	104.5	105.5	104.3	106.6	107.4	107.2	108.1	107.7	106.7	106.4	106.5	106.2
2001	95.3	95.6	96.5	96.5	97.4	98.6	98.4	98.6	97.1	96.4	96.1	96.1	96.9
2002	95.0	95.4	95.9	97.2	98.1	99.3	100.1	100.1	98.8	97.8	97.8	97.7	97.8
2003	97.5	97.9	98.4	98.6	99.5	100.4	100.4	100.1	100.0	99.4	98.6	98.1	98.9
2004	97.1	98.0	99.1	99.7	100.7	101.8	102.3	102.1	101.4	100.7	100.1	100.4	100.3
2005	100.2	101.1	102.2	102.1	102.7	104.1	104.3	104.3	103.5	102.6	102.6	103.0	102.7
2006	101.4	102.3	103.2	103.5	104.4	105.6	105.5	105.5	105.1	103.7	103.6	103.9	104.0
2007	102.1	103.8	104.7	104.8	105.6	106.8	106.9	107.3	106.2	105.3	104.8	105.0	105.3
Government													
2000	479.3	487.2	489.6	488.1	499.6	494.9	463.8	455.1	470.9	486.6	493.7	491.0	483.3
2001	500.3	506.1	510.7	510.8	513.9	515.6	487.8	474.9	493.6	512.8	521.6	516.9	505.4
2002	512.3	519.1	521.0	521.7	524.5	524.7	498.2	485.0	504.1	523.6	532.9	526.6	516.1
2003	520.7	526.3	527.3	527.3	532.9	530.4	501.1	489.6	507.0	524.6	532.2	527.6	520.6
2004	521.7	527.6	530.3	530.3	532.2	533.7	506.4	492.5	511.8	528.7	537.6	530.9	523.6
2005	526.3	530.8	533.9	534.5	535.9	537.6	508.6	494.6	514.1	532.0	539.8	532.6	526.7
2006	529.6	536.5	538.2	536.8	539.1	541.9	509.3	496.8	517.9	535.1	542.6	536.3	530.0
2007	530.7	537.6	536.8	540.0	543.4	536.2	516.5	498.9	523.7	541.5	546.3	542.1	532.8

Average Weekly Hours by Selected Industry: Washington, 2001–2007

(Not seasonally adjusted.)

Industry and year	January	February	March	April	May	June	July	August	September	October	November	December	Annual Average
Construction													
2001	36.3	35.0	35.9	36.0	36.8	36.1	37.0	37.3	37.4	36.3	35.1	35.3	36.2
2002	35.3	36.0	34.9	35.6	35.8	36.8	36.2	37.0	37.5	37.2	35.7	35.0	36.1
2003	35.4	36.1	35.7	36.1	36.9	37.3	36.5	37.4	37.4	36.2	37.0	35.8	36.5
2004	34.7	36.7	36.3	36.4	37.2	36.2	36.4	38.1	35.8	37.8	36.6	35.9	36.5
2005	34.5	35.8	36.2	36.0	37.1	37.1	37.3	38.3	38.5	38.7	36.5	36.6	36.9
2006	35.4	37.6	36.7	37.3	37.4	38.4	38.3	38.8	38.3	38.4	36.0	36.0	37.4
2007	32.7	35.5	35.9	37.2	37.1	37.3	38.5	38.1	38.7	38.3	36.4	36.6	36.9
Manufacturing													
2001	39.6	39.7	40.2	39.7	39.8	40.0	40.0	40.2	40.7	40.6	39.8	40.2	40.0
2002	39.8	40.2	40.3	39.9	40.0	40.7	39.5	40.1	40.6	40.7	40.0	39.7	40.1
2003	38.9	39.8	39.8	38.7	39.1	40.5	38.0	39.7	40.1	40.0	39.8	39.2	39.5
2004	38.8	40.2	39.9	39.9	40.3	40.2	40.0	40.9	40.4	40.5	40.1	39.2	40.0
2005	39.4	39.7	39.0	39.3	39.6	39.9	38.7	39.9	39.6	40.2	40.5	40.6	39.7
2006	40.5	40.8	40.8	40.1	39.4	40.0	40.5	40.7	41.0	41.6	40.9	41.1	40.6
2007	39.8	41.6	41.5	42.1	42.0	42.0	41.8	42.2	43.2	42.6	41.8	42.8	42.0
Trade, Transportation, and Utilities													
2001	32.8	33.4	33.5	34.0	33.4	33.8	34.2	33.8	33.8	33.2	32.9	34.1	33.6
2002	32.3	33.4	33.1	33.6	33.8	34.7	34.1	34.4	35.0	34.2	33.6	34.8	33.9
2003	32.8	34.4	34.2	34.1	34.2	35.1	34.4	34.8	34.5	34.2	34.4	33.8	34.2
2004	32.7	34.5	34.0	33.9	34.3	33.5	33.9	34.3	33.7	33.6	33.0	33.6	33.7
2005	33.5	33.7	33.4	33.7	34.4	34.0	33.9	34.4	34.4	34.6	33.8	34.2	34.0
2006	34.5	33.9	34.1	35.0	34.2	34.2	35.1	34.7	34.8	35.0	34.3	34.2	34.5
2007	33.1	33.1	33.5	34.4	33.8	34.0	34.8	34.8	35.3	33.9	33.7	34.2	34.1
Wholesale Trade													
2001	37.0	37.4	37.7	38.5	37.7	37.8	38.6	37.4	38.1	37.0	37.2	38.4	37.7
2002	36.3	36.5	36.6	37.2	37.0	38.2	37.2	37.4	38.3	37.5	37.4	38.7	37.4
2003	36.7	38.6	38.4	37.8	37.8	39.0	37.1	37.4	37.7	38.0	38.6	36.8	37.8
2004	36.5	39.3	38.1	38.0	38.0	36.8	37.1	38.4	36.6	37.3	37.1	37.1	37.5
2005	38.3	37.8	37.7	37.8	39.1	37.8	38.2	38.4	37.9	39.4	37.6	37.8	38.2
2006	37.8	37.3	37.7	39.7	37.9	37.9	38.4	38.7	38.7	41.3	39.1	38.7	38.6
2007	37.9	37.4	37.9	39.3	37.9	37.7	39.6	39.2	39.7	38.2	38.6	38.9	38.5
Retail Trade													
2001	30.6	31.1	31.2	31.9	31.2	31.5	32.1	31.6	31.6	31.0	30.6	31.8	31.4
2002	30.1	31.4	30.9	31.3	31.5	32.4	32.1	32.1	32.5	31.7	31.2	32.5	31.7
2003	30.7	32.3	32.0	32.0	32.0	32.8	32.6	33.0	32.4	31.9	32.0	32.0	32.1
2004	30.6	32.3	32.0	31.9	32.4	31.8	32.1	32.2	32.1	31.3	30.6	31.6	31.7
2005	31.3	31.5	31.1	31.6	31.8	31.5	31.6	31.9	31.8	31.6	31.3	31.7	31.6
2006	32.2	31.6	31.9	32.6	32.1	32.2	33.0	32.6	32.9	32.1	31.8	31.9	32.2
2007	30.8	31.3	31.5	32.2	31.9	32.3	32.7	32.6	33.0	31.9	31.7	32.3	32.0

Average Hourly Earnings by Selected Industry: Washington, 2001–2007

(Dollars, not seasonally adjusted.)

Industry and year	January	February	March	April	May	June	July	August	September	October	November	December	Annual Average
Construction													
2001	21.85	21.61	21.71	21.60	21.50	21.54	21.76	21.95	22.16	22.05	22.09	22.27	21.84
2002	22.53	22.44	22.23	22.28	22.21	22.23	22.54	22.93	22.76	22.70	22.66	23.08	22.56
2003	23.02	23.05	22.89	22.77	22.77	22.66	23.02	23.27	22.87	23.42	22.58	22.71	22.92
2004	23.08	22.57	22.71	22.24	22.48	22.41	22.22	22.46	22.38	22.65	22.59	22.42	22.51
2005	22.65	22.75	22.77	22.56	22.83	22.94	22.77	23.04	23.20	23.58	23.20	23.39	22.99
2006	23.00	22.86	22.80	22.90	22.99	23.30	23.38	23.47	23.54	23.72	23.54	26.37	23.50
2007	24.74	24.39	24.52	24.46	24.53	24.78	25.33	25.42	25.84	26.18	26.27	26.62	25.28
Manufacturing													
2001	17.75	17.65	17.94	17.72	17.65	17.74	17.93	17.82	18.17	18.10	18.52	18.59	17.96
2002	18.79	18.65	18.54	18.41	18.24	18.41	18.43	17.89	17.74	17.51	17.78	17.41	18.15
2003	18.12	18.00	18.01	18.05	17.88	17.66	17.97	17.85	18.00	18.05	18.28	18.39	18.02
2004	18.39	18.19	18.23	18.15	18.24	18.12	18.07	18.20	18.30	18.15	18.46	18.85	18.28
2005	18.85	18.71	18.80	18.79	18.75	18.88	18.80	18.72	17.00	19.40	19.23	19.85	18.83
2006	19.61	19.85	19.77	19.97	19.82	19.83	19.62	20.91	19.48	19.59	19.98	20.44	19.91
2007	20.52	20.26	20.36	20.55	20.35	20.54	20.58	20.40	20.40	20.42	20.74	20.95	20.51
Trade, Transportation, and Utilities													
2001	14.39	14.32	14.27	14.48	14.53	14.53	14.56	14.49	14.81	14.63	14.61	14.68	14.53
2002	14.89	14.98	14.93	15.01	14.93	15.15	14.96	15.02	15.25	15.13	14.91	14.89	15.01
2003	15.02	15.38	15.40	15.12	15.20	15.28	15.34	15.32	15.37	15.38	15.42	15.33	15.30
2004	15.75	15.82	15.98	16.12	16.37	16.43	16.37	16.31	16.44	16.36	16.24	16.10	16.20
2005	16.49	16.58	16.60	16.66	16.64	16.62	16.79	16.63	16.38	17.08	16.69	17.17	16.70
2006	16.90	16.93	17.28	17.04	16.92	17.31	17.73	17.11	17.17	17.22	17.47	17.74	17.24
2007	17.42	17.58	17.26	17.14	16.97	17.06	17.26	17.00	17.30	17.00	17.13	17.21	17.19
Wholesale Trade													
2001	16.20	16.24	15.95	16.23	16.48	16.48	16.48	16.36	16.65	16.39	16.40	16.68	16.38
2002	16.40	17.04	16.60	16.51	16.60	16.73	16.68	16.82	17.30	17.03	17.15	17.18	16.84
2003	17.17	17.48	17.52	17.34	17.56	17.66	17.98	17.67	17.83	18.01	18.53	18.86	17.81
2004	18.93	18.94	18.87	19.11	19.67	20.03	19.97	19.91	19.75	19.73	19.70	19.49	19.51
2005	19.50	19.85	19.57	20.07	19.86	20.22	20.40	19.97	19.05	20.68	20.25	20.34	19.98
2006	20.72	20.62	21.84	20.30	20.45	20.43	21.93	20.65	20.82	20.20	20.48	20.78	20.76
2007	20.58	21.38	20.85	19.58	19.64	20.10	20.26	19.59	20.15	19.90	20.96	20.28	20.26
Retail Trade													
2001	12.72	12.67	12.65	12.78	12.76	12.80	12.84	12.71	13.09	13.05	13.08	13.00	12.85
2002	13.35	13.19	13.35	13.40	13.36	13.64	13.38	13.39	13.56	13.31	13.05	13.03	13.33
2003	13.15	13.35	13.43	13.19	13.18	13.26	13.20	13.23	13.35	13.31	13.26	13.08	13.25
2004	13.61	13.67	13.63	13.78	13.91	13.91	13.77	13.80	14.08	13.91	13.78	13.68	13.80
2005	14.13	14.06	14.30	14.31	14.30	14.13	14.25	14.07	14.03	14.28	13.78	14.60	14.19
2006	14.20	13.95	13.99	14.37	14.17	14.63	14.73	14.20	14.22	14.52	14.37	15.25	14.39
2007	14.52	14.28	14.32	14.64	14.37	14.45	14.53	14.39	14.84	14.34	14.13	14.33	14.43

Average Weekly Earnings by Selected Industry: Washington, 2001–2007

(Dollars, not seasonally adjusted.)

Industry and year	January	February	March	April	May	June	July	August	September	October	November	December	Annual Average
Construction													
2001	793.16	756.35	779.39	777.60	791.20	777.59	805.12	818.74	828.78	800.42	775.36	786.13	790.61
2002	795.31	807.84	775.83	793.17	795.12	818.06	815.95	848.41	853.50	844.44	808.96	807.80	814.42
2003	814.91	832.11	817.17	822.00	840.21	845.22	840.23	870.30	855.34	847.80	835.46	813.02	836.58
2004	800.88	828.32	824.37	809.54	836.26	811.24	808.81	855.73	801.20	856.17	826.79	804.88	821.62
2005	781.43	814.45	824.27	812.16	846.99	851.07	849.32	882.43	893.20	912.55	846.80	856.07	848.33
2006	814.20	859.54	836.76	854.17	859.83	894.72	895.45	910.64	901.58	910.85	847.44	949.32	878.90
2007	809.00	865.85	880.27	909.91	910.06	924.29	975.21	968.50	1000.01	1002.69	956.23	974.29	932.83
Manufacturing													
2001	702.90	700.71	721.19	703.48	702.47	709.60	717.20	716.36	739.52	734.86	737.10	747.32	718.40
2002	747.84	749.73	747.16	734.56	729.60	749.29	727.99	717.39	720.24	712.66	711.20	691.18	727.82
2003	704.87	716.40	716.80	698.54	699.11	715.23	682.86	708.65	721.80	722.00	727.54	720.89	711.79
2004	713.53	731.24	727.38	724.19	735.07	728.42	722.80	744.38	739.32	735.08	740.25	738.92	731.20
2005	742.69	742.79	733.20	738.45	742.50	753.31	727.56	746.93	673.20	779.88	778.82	805.91	747.55
2006	794.21	809.88	806.62	800.80	780.91	793.20	794.61	851.04	798.68	814.94	817.18	840.08	808.35
2007	816.70	842.82	844.94	865.16	854.70	862.68	860.24	860.88	881.28	869.89	866.93	896.66	861.42
Trade, Transportation, and Utilities													
2001	471.99	478.29	478.05	492.32	485.30	491.11	497.95	489.76	500.58	485.72	480.67	500.59	488.21
2002	480.95	500.33	494.18	504.34	504.63	525.71	510.14	516.69	533.75	517.45	500.98	518.17	508.84
2003	492.66	529.07	526.68	515.59	519.84	536.33	527.70	533.14	530.27	526.00	530.45	518.15	523.26
2004	515.03	545.79	543.32	546.47	561.49	550.41	554.94	559.43	554.03	549.70	535.92	540.96	545.94
2005	552.42	558.75	554.44	561.44	572.42	565.08	569.18	572.07	563.47	590.97	564.12	587.21	567.80
2006	583.05	573.93	589.25	596.40	578.66	592.00	622.32	593.72	597.52	602.70	599.22	606.71	594.78
2007	576.60	581.90	578.21	589.62	573.59	580.04	600.65	591.60	610.69	576.30	577.28	588.58	586.18
Wholesale Trade													
2001	599.40	607.38	601.32	624.86	621.30	622.94	636.13	611.86	634.37	606.43	610.08	640.51	617.53
2002	595.32	621.96	607.56	614.17	614.20	639.09	620.50	629.07	662.59	638.63	641.41	664.87	629.82
2003	630.14	674.73	672.77	655.45	663.77	688.74	667.06	660.86	672.19	684.38	715.26	694.05	673.22
2004	690.95	744.34	718.95	726.18	747.46	737.10	740.89	764.54	722.85	735.93	730.87	723.08	731.63
2005	746.85	750.33	737.79	758.65	776.53	764.32	779.28	766.85	722.00	814.79	761.40	768.85	763.24
2006	783.22	769.13	823.37	805.91	775.06	774.30	842.11	799.16	805.73	834.26	800.77	804.19	801.34
2007	779.98	799.61	790.22	769.49	744.36	757.77	802.30	767.93	799.96	760.18	809.06	788.89	780.01
Retail Trade													
2001	389.23	394.04	394.68	407.68	398.11	403.20	412.16	401.64	413.64	404.55	400.25	413.40	403.49
2002	401.84	414.17	412.52	419.42	420.84	441.94	429.50	429.82	440.70	421.93	407.16	423.48	422.56
2003	403.71	431.21	429.76	422.08	421.76	434.93	430.32	436.59	432.54	424.59	424.32	418.56	425.33
2004	416.47	441.54	436.16	439.58	450.68	442.34	442.02	444.36	451.97	435.38	421.67	432.29	437.46
2005	442.27	442.89	444.73	452.20	454.74	445.10	450.30	448.83	446.15	451.25	431.31	462.82	448.40
2006	457.24	440.82	446.28	468.46	454.86	471.09	486.09	462.92	467.84	466.09	456.97	486.48	463.36
2007	447.22	446.96	451.08	471.41	458.40	466.74	475.13	469.11	489.72	457.45	447.92	462.86	461.76

Population
    2000 census: 1,808,344
    2007 estimate: 1,812,035
    Percent change, 2000–2007: 0.2%

Percent change in total nonfarm employment, 2000–2007: 2.9%

Industry with the largest growth in employment, 2000–2007 (thousands)
    Education and health services, 14.1

Industry with the largest decline in employment, 2000–2007 (thousands)
    Manufacturing, -16.9

Civilian labor force
    2000: 808,861
    2007: 808,840

Employment-population ratio
    2000: 53.4%
    2007: 53.4%

Unemployment rate and rank among states
    2000: 5.5%, 48th
    2007: 4.6%, 31st

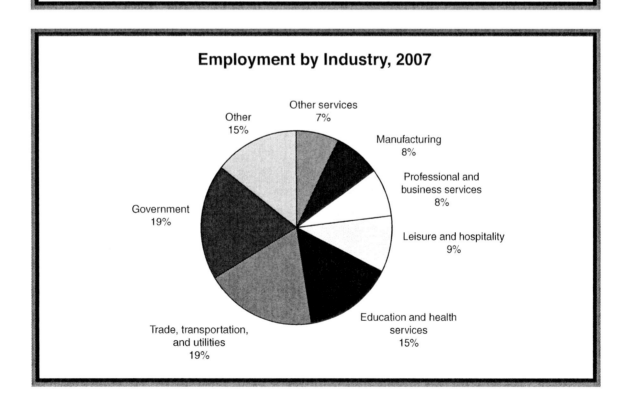

Employment by Industry, 2007

Other services 7%
Other 15%
Manufacturing 8%
Professional and business services 8%
Government 19%
Leisure and hospitality 9%
Trade, transportation, and utilities 19%
Education and health services 15%

Employment by Industry: West Virginia, 2000–2007

(Numbers in thousands, not seasonally adjusted.)

Industry and year	January	February	March	April	May	June	July	August	September	October	November	December	Annual Average
Total Nonfarm													
2000	714.1	714.1	728.6	733.1	751.5	741.1	742.1	733.8	739.8	741.7	744.9	744.8	735.8
2001	719.0	721.9	730.5	735.2	739.6	742.1	734.8	737.8	737.8	740.3	742.2	741.9	735.2
2002	717.2	719.9	727.5	731.5	747.3	737.1	733.8	735.4	735.6	735.9	738.2	737.2	733.1
2003	714.4	711.1	719.6	726.9	731.8	732.7	728.5	730.1	730.5	734.7	733.2	737.3	727.6
2004	716.2	717.4	728.0	736.8	742.1	741.2	739.3	739.9	742.1	746.2	745.9	747.3	736.9
2005	727.1	728.5	734.9	745.1	751.4	752.7	748.5	750.5	753.7	751.0	756.2	758.4	746.5
2006	738.2	741.3	750.4	754.3	759.3	762.5	752.8	756.8	761.6	762.1	766.4	766.1	756.0
2007	740.5	741.5	752.0	756.6	761.6	764.4	754.2	758.0	761.2	763.8	765.9	763.5	756.9
Total Private													
2000	574.9	574.0	583.7	589.6	594.1	599.1	597.1	595.6	600.7	599.9	601.7	601.7	592.7
2001	581.0	581.3	587.7	592.6	597.3	601.2	596.6	599.4	598.8	597.9	598.5	598.2	594.2
2002	578.1	578.9	583.8	588.1	592.8	594.9	596.0	597.0	595.0	592.6	593.1	592.3	590.2
2003	573.6	568.8	575.6	581.9	586.7	590.5	589.7	591.0	590.8	591.2	588.5	592.5	585.1
2004	575.8	575.4	583.3	591.6	597.1	597.9	599.3	600.0	600.3	600.4	600.5	602.2	593.7
2005	584.6	584.9	589.7	599.5	605.6	609.4	609.0	611.0	611.1	607.5	609.9	611.8	602.8
2006	596.9	596.5	603.9	607.9	612.8	618.9	613.6	615.8	617.5	617.2	618.5	618.1	611.3
2007	598.1	595.7	604.6	609.0	613.4	619.4	614.9	617.9	617.9	617.2	618.1	616.1	611.9
Goods-Producing													
2000	127.2	125.6	129.1	130.9	132.2	132.9	133.0	132.5	134.0	133.8	133.3	130.4	131.2
2001	125.0	125.1	127.6	129.9	131.2	132.4	132.0	132.9	133.2	133.8	133.0	131.1	130.6
2002	123.8	123.5	123.9	126.0	126.2	127.0	126.7	127.2	127.0	125.6	124.4	121.3	125.2
2003	116.0	113.6	116.3	118.4	119.8	121.1	121.5	121.1	121.4	121.3	120.6	118.9	119.2
2004	114.5	114.2	117.0	121.6	123.7	123.3	124.1	124.3	124.2	124.2	123.3	122.3	121.4
2005	118.3	118.8	119.9	123.4	125.6	127.3	127.1	127.1	127.9	129.0	128.7	128.1	125.1
2006	122.7	122.7	125.5	128.1	129.9	131.6	130.1	130.5	130.5	130.2	130.0	129.2	128.4
2007	123.4	121.0	124.3	125.9	127.3	129.3	128.4	128.5	127.7	127.7	127.0	124.3	126.2
Natural Resources and Mining													
2000	21.4	21.0	21.0	21.1	21.3	21.0	21.2	21.4	21.7	21.8	21.8	21.8	21.4
2001	21.8	21.8	22.1	22.6	23.0	23.8	24.2	24.2	24.3	24.6	24.8	24.9	23.5
2002	24.4	24.1	23.6	23.3	22.9	22.9	22.6	22.8	22.8	22.7	22.9	22.5	23.1
2003	22.1	21.6	22.1	22.1	22.0	22.1	22.1	21.7	21.8	21.8	22.0	22.2	22.0
2004	22.4	22.1	22.5	23.4	23.9	24.1	24.2	24.2	24.5	24.6	24.6	24.7	23.8
2005	24.4	24.7	25.0	25.4	25.4	26.0	26.2	26.4	26.7	26.8	27.2	27.4	26.0
2006	27.2	27.4	27.7	27.8	27.9	28.3	28.3	28.2	28.3	28.0	28.3	28.4	28.0
2007	28.1	27.9	27.9	28.2	28.2	28.9	28.9	29.2	28.9	28.8	28.9	28.9	28.6
Construction													
2000	28.9	28.1	31.6	33.9	35.2	35.5	35.7	35.5	36.8	36.8	36.4	33.7	34.0
2001	29.3	29.7	32.1	34.1	35.1	35.6	35.6	37.0	37.8	38.7	37.9	35.8	34.8
2002	29.7	30.0	31.0	33.4	34.0	34.9	35.4	35.8	35.7	35.2	34.3	31.8	33.4
2003	28.4	27.1	29.3	31.3	32.9	34.1	34.6	34.9	35.3	35.5	34.9	33.6	32.7
2004	29.1	29.2	31.7	34.7	36.0	36.2	36.8	37.0	36.6	36.9	36.2	34.9	34.6
2005	31.9	32.2	33.0	35.9	37.2	38.3	38.3	38.9	39.6	39.8	39.1	37.5	36.8
2006	34.3	34.0	36.2	39.1	40.8	42.0	40.8	41.3	41.2	41.8	41.3	40.3	39.4
2007	36.2	34.2	37.2	38.7	39.9	40.7	40.1	40.2	40.0	40.3	39.5	37.0	38.7
Manufacturing													
2000	76.9	76.5	76.5	75.9	75.7	76.4	76.1	75.6	75.5	75.2	75.1	74.9	75.9
2001	73.9	73.6	73.4	73.2	73.1	73.0	72.2	71.7	71.1	70.5	70.3	70.4	72.2
2002	69.7	69.4	69.3	69.3	69.3	69.2	68.7	68.6	68.5	67.7	67.2	67.0	68.7
2003	65.5	64.9	64.9	65.0	64.9	64.9	64.8	64.5	64.3	64.0	63.7	63.1	64.5
2004	63.0	62.9	62.8	63.5	63.8	63.0	63.1	63.1	63.1	62.7	62.5	62.7	63.0
2005	62.0	61.9	61.9	62.1	62.4	62.8	62.6	62.6	62.7	62.1	61.8	61.9	62.2
2006	61.2	61.3	61.6	61.2	61.2	61.3	61.0	61.0	61.0	60.4	60.4	60.5	61.0
2007	59.1	58.9	59.2	59.0	59.2	59.7	59.7	59.4	59.1	58.8	58.6	58.4	59.0
Service-Providing													
2000	586.9	588.5	599.5	602.2	619.3	608.2	609.1	601.3	605.8	607.9	611.6	614.4	604.6
2001	594.0	596.8	602.9	605.3	608.4	609.7	602.8	604.9	604.6	606.5	609.2	610.8	604.6
2002	593.4	596.4	603.6	605.5	621.1	610.1	607.1	608.2	608.6	610.3	613.8	615.9	607.8
2003	598.4	597.5	603.3	608.5	612.0	611.6	607.0	609.0	609.1	613.4	612.6	618.4	608.4
2004	601.7	603.2	611.0	615.2	618.4	617.9	615.2	615.6	617.9	622.0	622.6	625.0	615.5
2005	608.8	609.7	615.0	621.7	625.8	625.4	621.4	622.6	624.7	622.3	628.1	630.9	621.4
2006	615.5	618.6	624.9	626.2	629.4	630.9	622.7	626.3	631.1	631.9	636.4	636.9	627.6
2007	617.1	620.5	627.7	630.7	634.3	635.1	625.8	629.5	633.5	636.1	638.9	639.2	630.7
Trade, Transportation, and Utilities													
2000	142.6	141.3	142.6	142.9	144.3	145.5	144.9	145.4	145.1	145.0	147.9	148.8	144.7
2001	140.1	138.4	139.0	139.5	140.5	141.3	139.6	140.0	139.5	139.1	141.3	142.1	140.0
2002	136.1	134.9	134.9	135.9	136.2	137.4	137.7	137.1	136.9	136.2	136.6	138.6	136.9
2003	133.5	131.7	132.9	134.3	135.5	136.1	135.8	136.3	136.2	136.8	136.7	140.2	135.5
2004	134.7	133.3	134.2	135.3	136.5	137.0	137.4	137.9	138.0	139.0	141.4	142.3	137.3
2005	136.9	136.1	136.7	138.1	139.6	139.7	139.6	139.8	139.9	140.3	143.2	144.6	139.5
2006	139.0	138.1	139.6	140.3	141.1	142.1	141.2	141.6	142.2	143.2	146.5	147.2	141.8
2007	141.3	140.1	141.6	141.5	142.6	143.2	142.4	143.0	143.1	143.9	145.8	146.6	142.9
Wholesale Trade													
2000	23.7	23.8	24.0	24.0	24.1	24.1	24.1	24.2	24.3	24.0	24.2	24.1	24.1
2001	23.7	23.8	24.0	24.2	24.2	24.5	24.1	23.9	23.9	23.7	23.6	23.7	23.9
2002	23.0	23.2	23.4	23.5	23.5	23.4	23.3	23.2	23.1	23.0	23.0	23.0	23.2
2003	22.4	22.3	22.6	22.7	22.9	23.0	22.9	22.9	22.8	22.8	22.8	22.8	22.7
2004	22.7	22.8	23.0	23.2	23.2	23.2	23.2	23.1	23.3	23.5	23.6	23.7	23.2
2005	23.6	23.6	23.8	24.1	24.3	24.4	24.4	24.4	24.3	24.3	24.4	24.6	24.2
2006	24.3	24.3	24.5	24.7	24.8	25.3	24.9	25.0	25.0	25.1	25.2	25.5	24.9
2007	24.8	24.7	24.9	25.0	24.9	25.0	25.0	25.0	25.1	25.2	25.3	25.3	25.0

Employment by Industry: West Virginia, 2000–2007—*Continued*

(Numbers in thousands, not seasonally adjusted.)

Industry and year	January	February	March	April	May	June	July	August	September	October	November	December	Annual Average
Retail Trade													
2000	91.7	90.4	91.2	91.7	92.8	93.7	93.2	93.7	93.2	93.6	96.5	97.7	93.3
2001	90.3	88.4	88.8	88.9	89.7	90.0	89.0	89.6	89.2	89.0	91.4	92.1	89.7
2002	87.2	86.0	86.9	87.1	88.1	88.3	88.2	88.1	87.8	88.2	90.4	91.5	88.2
2003	86.0	84.5	85.3	86.6	87.4	87.9	87.8	88.2	88.2	89.0	89.0	92.5	87.7
2004	87.4	85.9	86.4	87.0	88.1	88.4	88.7	89.1	88.9	89.6	92.0	92.7	88.7
2005	88.0	87.0	87.3	88.3	89.4	89.2	89.2	89.3	89.3	89.7	92.5	93.5	89.4
2006	88.8	87.9	89.0	89.2	89.7	90.0	89.7	89.9	90.4	91.3	94.2	94.6	90.4
2007	90.0	89.0	90.2	89.9	90.8	91.2	90.6	91.1	91.1	91.7	93.7	94.6	91.2
Transportation and Utilities													
2000	27.2	27.1	27.4	27.2	27.4	27.7	27.6	27.5	27.6	27.4	27.2	27.0	27.4
2001	26.1	26.2	26.2	26.4	26.6	26.6	26.8	26.5	26.5	26.4	26.3	26.3	26.3
2002	25.9	25.7	25.6	25.6	25.8	26.0	25.6	26.5	26.4	26.4	26.3	26.3	26.3
2003	25.1	24.9	25.0	25.0	25.2	25.2	25.6	25.6	25.3	25.4	25.2	25.2	25.6
2004	24.6	24.6	24.8	25.1	25.2	25.4	25.1	25.2	25.2	25.0	24.9	24.9	25.1
2005	25.3	25.5	25.6	25.7	25.9	26.1	25.5	26.0	25.8	25.9	25.8	25.9	25.4
2006	25.9	25.9	26.1	26.4	26.6	26.8	26.1	26.2	26.3	26.3	26.3	26.5	26.0
2007	26.5	26.4	26.5	26.6	26.9	27.0	26.6	26.7	26.7	27.0	26.8	27.0	26.5
Information													
2000	14.0	14.1	14.1	14.2	14.2	14.3	14.4	11.7	14.3	14.3	14.5	14.7	14.1
2001	14.2	14.3	14.3	14.2	14.2	14.3	14.1	14.1	13.9	13.8	13.8	13.8	14.0
2002	13.4	13.4	13.4	13.2	13.3	13.3	13.3	13.3	13.2	13.2	13.4	13.4	13.3
2003	12.9	12.8	12.8	12.7	12.6	12.6	12.6	12.5	12.3	12.2	12.2	12.0	12.5
2004	11.8	11.7	12.0	11.9	11.9	12.0	12.0	12.0	11.8	11.7	11.8	11.8	11.9
2005	11.6	11.4	11.5	11.5	11.7	11.8	11.9	12.0	11.8	11.8	11.9	12.0	11.7
2006	11.7	11.5	11.5	11.4	11.5	11.6	11.5	11.6	11.5	11.5	11.4	11.4	11.5
2007	11.3	11.3	11.2	11.3	11.3	11.5	11.6	11.5	11.5	11.5	11.6	11.5	11.4
Financial Activities													
2000	30.7	30.8	31.2	31.1	31.3	31.6	31.3	31.4	31.1	31.1	31.2	31.6	31.2
2001	30.6	30.5	30.6	30.7	30.8	30.9	30.8	30.6	30.5	30.6	30.5	30.7	30.6
2002	30.2	30.4	30.7	30.8	31.0	31.3	31.5	31.7	31.5	31.6	31.6	31.8	31.2
2003	30.8	30.8	30.8	30.9	30.7	31.0	30.6	30.6	30.4	30.7	30.7	30.8	30.8
2004	30.3	30.1	30.4	30.5	30.5	30.7	30.7	30.7	30.1	30.1	29.9	30.0	30.3
2005	29.6	29.5	29.5	29.7	29.7	29.8	29.8	29.8	29.7	29.6	29.7	29.7	29.7
2006	29.9	29.9	30.0	30.1	30.3	30.7	30.1	30.1	30.0	30.0	29.9	30.0	30.1
2007	29.5	29.5	29.6	29.8	29.9	29.9	29.9	29.9	29.8	29.9	29.8	29.7	29.8
Professional and Business Services													
2000	52.9	53.6	54.8	56.5	56.1	57.2	56.6	56.5	56.8	56.3	56.6	57.0	55.9
2001	56.1	56.7	57.4	57.4	57.6	58.3	57.7	57.9	57.2	57.3	57.2	57.4	57.3
2002	54.5	54.8	55.6	56.5	56.6	57.4	57.8	58.4	57.7	56.8	57.0	57.5	56.7
2003	55.5	55.4	55.8	56.3	56.3	57.0	56.7	57.1	57.0	57.5	57.4	58.7	56.7
2004	57.3	57.2	57.6	57.7	57.6	58.4	59.0	59.2	59.0	59.1	58.5	60.1	58.4
2005	57.6	57.1	57.5	58.6	58.4	59.1	59.2	59.7	59.2	59.3	59.8	60.8	58.9
2006	59.4	59.5	59.7	60.0	59.5	60.6	60.2	60.3	60.2	59.4	59.8	60.8	59.9
2007	59.1	58.8	59.7	60.8	60.7	61.3	60.9	61.5	61.1	60.8	61.2	61.2	60.6
Education and Health Services													
2000	97.5	98.6	99.6	100.1	99.9	99.1	98.1	98.6	100.1	101.7	102.0	102.6	99.8
2001	100.8	101.8	102.7	102.8	102.9	102.4	101.5	102.3	103.9	105.1	105.9	106.7	103.2
2002	105.4	106.7	107.4	106.9	107.3	106.0	106.3	105.9	107.0	108.5	109.3	109.7	107.2
2003	108.4	108.2	108.7	108.6	109.0	107.9	107.0	107.6	108.6	110.3	110.5	110.8	108.8
2004	108.5	110.0	111.0	110.9	111.0	109.9	109.5	109.7	111.2	112.4	112.8	112.7	110.8
2005	110.9	112.1	112.6	113.0	113.1	113.1	112.8	113.2	114.1	113.3	113.9	114.3	113.0
2006	112.7	113.1	113.6	113.4	113.1	112.1	111.1	111.5	113.2	113.6	114.1	114.1	113.0
2007	111.3	112.7	113.5	113.1	113.4	113.3	112.3	113.1	115.0	116.0	116.5	116.4	113.9
Leisure and Hospitality													
2000	58.3	57.8	59.4	61.0	62.8	64.7	64.8	65.4	64.8	62.9	61.2	61.2	62.0
2001	59.2	59.4	60.8	62.6	64.4	65.8	65.6	66.4	65.3	63.1	61.8	61.2	62.9
2002	59.8	60.2	61.7	63.0	65.3	66.6	67.9	68.2	67.1	65.2	63.8	63.7	64.4
2003	61.8	61.7	63.3	65.4	67.6	69.3	70.0	70.4	68.9	66.9	65.4	66.0	66.4
2004	64.1	64.3	65.8	67.8	69.6	70.8	71.2	71.5	70.3	68.3	67.1	67.4	68.2
2005	65.1	65.3	66.6	68.5	70.6	72.0	72.7	73.0	71.7	69.2	68.1	68.3	69.3
2006	66.9	67.0	68.7	69.3	71.7	74.1	73.8	74.4	73.7	70.9	70.5	70.5	71.0
2007	67.0	66.9	69.0	70.8	72.5	74.7	73.9	75.1	74.1	71.9	70.7	70.7	71.4
Other Services													
2000	51.7	52.2	52.9	52.9	53.3	53.8	54.0	54.1	54.5	54.8	55.0	55.4	53.7
2001	55.0	55.1	55.3	55.5	55.7	55.8	55.3	55.2	55.3	55.1	55.0	55.2	55.2
2002	54.9	55.0	55.2	55.5	55.7	55.6	55.4	55.4	55.3	55.1	55.0	55.2	55.3
2003	54.7	54.6	55.0	55.3	55.2	55.5	55.5	55.4	55.7	55.5	55.0	55.1	55.2
2004	54.6	54.6	55.3	55.9	56.3	55.8	55.4	55.0	55.7	55.6	55.7	55.6	55.5
2005	54.6	54.6	55.4	56.7	56.9	56.6	55.9	55.6	55.7	55.3	55.7	55.3	55.7
2006	54.6	54.7	55.3	55.3	55.5	56.1	55.6	55.8	56.2	56.3	56.3	56.1	55.7
2007	55.2	55.4	55.7	55.8	55.7	56.2	55.5	55.3	55.6	55.5	55.5	55.7	55.6
Government													
2000	139.2	140.1	144.9	143.5	157.4	142.0	145.0	138.2	139.1	141.8	143.2	143.1	143.1
2001	138.0	140.6	142.8	142.6	142.3	140.9	138.2	138.4	139.0	142.4	143.7	143.7	141.0
2002	139.1	141.0	143.7	143.4	154.5	142.2	137.8	138.4	140.6	143.3	145.1	144.9	142.8
2003	140.8	142.3	144.0	145.0	145.1	142.2	138.8	139.1	139.7	143.5	144.7	144.8	142.5
2004	140.4	142.0	144.7	145.2	145.0	143.3	140.0	139.9	141.8	145.8	145.4	145.1	143.2
2005	142.5	143.6	145.2	145.6	145.8	143.3	139.5	139.5	142.6	143.5	146.3	143.7	143.7
2006	141.3	144.8	146.5	146.4	146.5	143.6	139.2	141.0	144.1	147.0	147.9	148.0	144.7
2007	142.4	145.8	147.4	147.6	148.2	145.0	139.3	140.1	143.3	146.6	147.8	147.4	145.1

Average Weekly Hours by Selected Industry: West Virginia, 2003–2007

(Not seasonally adjusted.)

Industry and year	January	February	March	April	May	June	July	August	September	October	November	December	Annual Average
Total Private													
2003	33.7	33.8	34.1	34.0	34.1	34.2	34.1	34.2	34.3	34.2	34.4	34.2	34.1
2004	33.9	34.0	34.1	34.0	34.4	34.3	34.4	34.4	34.4	34.4	34.4	34.3	34.3
2005	34.1	34.0	34.1	34.2	34.5	34.4	34.6	34.6	34.7	34.8	34.7	34.6	34.5
2006	34.3	34.1	34.3	34.6	34.6	34.8	34.3	34.3	34.3	34.4	34.3	34.3	34.4
2007	34.1	33.9	34.2	34.4	34.4	34.7	34.7	34.6	34.6	34.7	34.5	34.6	34.4
Goods-Producing													
2003	41.2	41.0	41.7	41.2	41.5	41.6	41.1	41.9	42.3	41.7	42.0	41.8	41.6
2004	41.9	41.4	41.3	41.2	41.9	42.0	41.8	42.1	42.2	41.9	42.0	41.9	41.8
2005	42.0	41.7	41.6	41.9	41.9	41.3	41.8	42.1	42.3	42.7	42.1	42.1	42.0
2006	41.8	42.0	41.8	42.0	42.1	42.0	41.1	41.2	41.1	41.6	41.3	41.5	41.7
2007	41.2	41.1	41.3	41.5	41.8	41.9	41.7	42.0	41.9	42.2	41.8	42.2	41.7
Natural Resources and Mining													
2003	46.6	46.9	46.5	46.2	46.3	46.1	44.4	46.9	46.9	46.9	46.3	46.6	46.4
2004	47.7	47.2	46.2	46.4	46.3	46.7	44.9	46.7	46.5	47.0	46.8	46.8	46.6
2005	47.2	47.1	47.7	47.5	46.4	46.0	45.0	46.4	46.8	47.2	46.9	46.5	46.7
2006	46.9	47.1	47.6	47.5	47.2	47.2	46.6	46.4	47.0	46.8	46.5	47.6	47.1
2007	46.9	47.1	47.6	47.5	47.6	46.8	44.7	46.6	47.4	46.9	46.5	47.5	46.9
Construction													
2003	37.8	37.0	38.4	37.5	39.3	39.3	39.5	40.3	40.5	39.0	38.5	38.7	38.9
2004	38.8	37.8	38.4	38.3	39.6	39.8	40.4	40.4	40.2	38.9	38.6	38.8	39.2
2005	39.1	38.3	38.3	38.8	39.6	40.0	40.5	40.2	40.3	40.0	38.6	38.7	39.4
2006	39.0	38.8	38.4	38.6	39.5	39.9	40.8	40.7	39.6	40.0	38.8	39.4	39.5
2007	39.0	38.0	38.5	38.7	39.5	40.4	40.8	40.5	39.4	40.0	38.8	39.5	39.5
Manufacturing													
2003	40.9	40.7	41.5	41.2	41.0	41.2	40.7	41.0	41.7	41.5	42.5	41.8	41.3
2004	41.1	40.9	41.0	40.9	41.4	41.4	41.3	41.2	41.7	41.6	42.1	41.7	41.4
2005	41.3	41.3	40.9	41.3	41.3	40.1	41.2	41.3	41.6	42.3	42.0	41.9	41.4
2006	40.9	41.2	41.0	41.4	41.4	41.2	41.2	41.2	41.5	41.9	41.9	41.5	41.3
2007	41.0	41.0	41.1	41.4	41.4	41.2	41.2	41.1	41.5	41.9	41.9	41.5	41.3
Trade, Transportation, and Utilities													
2003	34.3	34.6	35.0	35.4	35.7	35.7	35.9	35.6	35.3	35.5	35.7	35.6	35.4
2004	34.5	35.0	35.6	35.3	35.9	35.7	35.6	35.3	35.5	35.7	35.8	35.8	35.5
2005	34.8	35.0	35.6	35.5	35.8	36.0	35.6	35.6	35.7	35.6	35.8	36.0	35.6
2006	35.1	35.0	35.6	35.8	35.9	36.2	35.8	35.7	35.8	35.8	35.9	35.9	35.7
2007	35.2	35.1	35.6	35.8	35.8	36.2	35.8	35.7	35.8	35.8	35.8	35.9	35.7
Wholesale Trade													
2003	39.8	39.3	40.0	39.7	40.2	40.8	40.0	40.2	40.8	40.1	41.8	40.1	40.2
2004	39.8	39.6	40.0	39.9	40.0	40.6	40.4	40.5	40.3	40.5	41.7	40.3	40.3
2005	40.1	39.9	39.7	39.7	40.0	40.4	40.5	40.1	40.5	40.6	40.5	40.8	40.2
2006	40.2	39.8	39.7	40.0	40.1	40.4	40.5	40.1	39.7	40.5	40.3	40.1	40.1
2007	40.0	39.8	40.0	40.1	40.1	40.4	40.5	40.4	39.9	40.5	40.3	40.1	40.2
Retail Trade													
2003	30.9	31.5	32.0	32.4	32.8	32.8	33.1	32.6	32.0	32.4	32.4	32.9	32.3
2004	31.1	31.9	32.3	32.2	32.9	32.7	32.4	32.0	32.1	32.5	32.5	33.0	32.3
2005	31.4	31.7	32.3	32.3	32.7	33.0	32.4	32.3	32.4	32.2	32.7	33.0	32.4
2006	31.8	31.6	32.3	32.5	32.7	33.3	32.5	32.4	32.7	32.5	32.7	33.0	32.5
2007	31.8	31.6	32.3	32.6	32.7	33.3	32.5	32.4	32.7	32.5	32.7	33.0	32.5
Financial Activities													
2003	33.4	34.0	33.6	32.9	33.3	33.8	33.2	33.1	33.3	33.2	33.5	32.9	33.4
2004	32.7	32.9	33.6	32.9	32.8	33.2	32.8	33.1	33.4	33.2	33.1	33.4	33.1
2005	33.9	33.3	33.1	33.7	34.1	33.4	33.5	33.8	33.9	34.2	33.5	33.3	33.6
2006	33.5	33.0	33.2	33.2	33.6	33.8	34.0	33.4	33.8	34.2	33.7	33.4	33.6
2007	33.6	33.1	33.3	33.3	33.6	33.4	34.0	33.4	33.8	34.0	33.7	33.6	33.6
Professional and Business Services													
2003	35.2	35.3	36.1	35.2	35.0	34.9	35.0	35.1	35.4	35.4	34.8	34.3	35.1
2004	34.0	34.1	34.1	33.9	34.6	34.5	34.9	35.1	34.9	34.8	34.5	34.7	34.5
2005	34.4	34.4	34.1	34.0	34.3	34.6	34.9	34.7	34.6	34.8	34.8	34.9	34.6
2006	34.0	33.9	34.5	35.3	34.8	35.6	36.1	35.9	35.6	35.5	34.8	35.0	35.1
2007	34.0	33.6	34.7	35.3	34.8	35.6	36.0	35.7	35.7	35.1	34.9	35.0	35.0

Average Hourly Earnings by Selected Industry: West Virginia, 2003–2007

(Dollars, not seasonally adjusted.)

Industry and year	January	February	March	April	May	June	July	August	September	October	November	December	Annual Average
Total Private													
2003	12.36	12.36	12.37	12.40	12.37	12.43	12.46	12.51	12.66	12.62	12.71	12.68	12.50
2004	12.74	12.72	12.77	12.85	12.87	12.90	12.87	12.89	12.93	12.91	12.96	13.00	12.87
2005	13.17	13.20	13.29	13.35	13.27	13.39	13.43	13.47	13.72	13.77	13.70	13.81	13.47
2006	13.94	14.02	14.01	14.15	14.14	14.19	13.85	13.91	14.02	14.24	14.23	14.32	14.09
2007	14.46	14.43	14.54	14.61	14.55	14.65	14.78	14.74	14.77	14.88	14.91	14.95	14.69
Goods-Producing													
2003	16.49	16.38	16.46	16.54	16.45	16.53	16.55	16.61	16.60	16.52	16.61	16.74	16.54
2004	16.54	16.68	16.83	16.98	17.11	17.13	17.28	17.33	17.30	17.29	17.26	17.44	17.11
2005	17.37	17.54	17.72	17.77	17.69	17.83	17.80	17.98	18.20	18.14	18.16	18.31	17.89
2006	18.28	18.35	18.58	18.57	18.70	18.91	18.31	18.33	18.48	18.62	18.82	18.94	18.58
2007	19.01	19.16	19.40	19.46	19.38	19.48	19.61	19.52	19.52	19.59	19.83	19.94	19.50
Natural Resources and Mining													
2003	18.16	18.02	18.28	18.18	18.17	18.09	18.10	18.15	18.03	17.76	17.69	18.28	18.08
2004	18.01	18.13	18.26	18.54	18.32	18.21	18.46	18.64	18.31	18.47	18.59	18.76	18.40
2005	18.66	18.94	19.06	19.18	18.99	19.40	19.61	19.88	20.13	20.18	20.05	20.01	19.53
2006	20.28	20.05	20.43	20.24	20.54	20.86	20.66	20.46	20.42	20.82	20.57	20.58	20.44
2007	20.87	20.89	21.27	21.13	20.94	21.10	21.33	21.63	21.29	21.36	21.56	21.63	21.28
Construction													
2003	15.83	15.79	15.71	15.82	16.01	16.08	16.31	16.40	16.60	16.54	16.64	16.81	16.25
2004	16.52	16.73	16.94	16.82	17.08	17.00	17.12	16.95	17.08	17.11	16.99	17.24	16.98
2005	17.26	17.53	17.70	17.60	17.64	17.59	17.55	17.63	17.82	17.89	17.82	18.03	17.68
2006	17.90	17.98	18.21	18.36	18.48	18.61	18.44	18.66	18.77	18.94	19.13	19.32	18.60
2007	18.95	19.10	19.39	19.46	19.32	19.69	19.56	19.46	19.61	19.75	20.04	20.15	19.55
Manufacturing													
2003	16.07	15.93	16.02	16.19	15.96	16.12	16.06	16.08	16.02	15.99	16.14	16.04	16.05
2004	15.89	16.01	16.13	16.33	16.56	16.69	16.83	16.93	16.95	16.82	16.76	16.91	16.57
2005	16.78	16.83	17.02	17.13	17.04	17.17	17.05	17.20	17.40	17.21	17.31	17.52	17.14
2006	17.35	17.56	17.72	17.73	17.78	17.99	18.15	17.92	18.02	17.98	18.21	18.23	17.89
2007	18.47	18.60	18.72	18.80	18.77	18.64	18.91	18.58	18.59	18.61	18.83	18.94	18.71
Trade, Transportation, and Utilities													
2003	10.85	11.03	11.07	11.08	11.09	11.22	11.24	11.32	11.45	11.46	11.40	11.24	11.21
2004	11.43	11.46	11.52	11.54	11.58	11.73	11.75	11.64	11.75	11.72	11.72	11.76	11.64
2005	11.96	12.09	12.10	12.23	12.10	12.35	12.42	12.23	12.37	12.29	12.02	12.10	12.19
2006	12.23	12.35	12.27	12.44	12.49	12.51	12.60	12.63	12.69	12.85	12.56	12.54	12.52
2007	12.75	12.65	12.78	12.84	12.77	12.78	12.93	12.92	12.89	12.95	12.91	12.91	12.84
Wholesale Trade													
2003	13.89	14.04	14.09	14.12	14.27	14.39	14.50	14.70	14.92	14.80	14.78	14.92	14.46
2004	14.80	14.80	14.39	14.25	14.49	14.82	14.94	14.96	14.94	15.04	15.23	15.54	14.86
2005	15.65	15.87	15.51	15.86	15.63	15.73	15.70	15.70	15.82	15.74	15.96	15.92	15.76
2006	16.11	15.84	16.15	16.29	16.41	16.28	16.15	16.14	16.21	16.42	16.61	16.43	16.26
2007	16.43	16.51	16.23	16.61	16.48	16.50	16.66	16.26	16.50	16.51	16.73	16.55	16.50
Retail Trade													
2003	8.82	8.98	9.01	8.93	8.92	9.06	9.01	8.99	8.98	9.07	9.02	8.93	8.98
2004	9.02	9.04	9.15	9.18	9.30	9.48	9.47	9.35	9.47	9.43	9.44	9.44	9.32
2005	9.45	9.68	9.67	9.68	9.63	9.91	10.04	9.82	10.10	10.03	9.56	9.76	9.78
2006	9.76	9.90	9.75	10.01	10.06	10.12	10.25	10.34	10.37	10.51	10.18	10.25	10.13
2007	10.34	10.15	10.49	10.47	10.49	10.51	10.65	10.72	10.65	10.69	10.70	10.73	10.55
Financial Activities													
2003	10.59	10.62	10.42	10.61	10.63	10.49	10.66	10.75	10.83	11.01	11.17	11.02	10.70
2004	11.35	11.56	11.40	11.47	11.55	11.47	11.64	11.47	11.21	11.11	11.17	11.03	11.37
2005	11.55	11.10	11.25	11.47	11.08	10.94	10.87	10.75	10.94	11.11	11.31	11.77	11.17
2006	11.96	11.93	11.91	12.10	12.01	12.12	12.19	12.12	12.22	12.34	12.15	12.37	12.12
2007	12.28	12.50	12.47	12.47	12.53	12.70	12.77	12.68	12.61	12.67	12.65	12.62	12.58
Professional and Business Services													
2003	12.05	12.08	11.86	12.16	12.13	12.01	12.07	11.90	12.13	11.99	12.01	12.24	12.05
2004	12.42	12.40	12.34	12.44	12.25	12.20	12.03	12.33	12.24	12.21	12.07	12.14	12.25
2005	12.44	12.27	12.43	12.59	12.61	12.69	12.83	13.09	13.18	13.15	13.44	13.68	12.88
2006	13.94	14.02	13.52	14.10	13.52	13.67	14.20	14.34	14.30	14.49	14.77	14.77	14.14
2007	14.99	14.95	14.59	14.75	14.64	14.72	14.91	15.02	14.94	15.08	15.17	15.27	14.92

Average Weekly Earnings by Selected Industry: West Virginia, 2003–2007

(Dollars, not seasonally adjusted.)

Industry and year	January	February	March	April	May	June	July	August	September	October	November	December	Annual Average
Total Private													
2003	416.53	417.77	421.82	421.60	421.82	425.11	424.89	427.84	434.24	431.60	437.22	433.66	426.25
2004	431.89	432.48	435.46	436.90	442.73	442.47	442.73	443.42	444.79	444.10	445.82	445.90	441.44
2005	449.10	448.80	453.19	456.57	457.82	460.62	464.68	466.06	476.08	479.20	475.39	477.83	464.72
2006	478.14	478.08	480.54	489.59	489.24	493.81	475.06	477.11	480.89	489.86	488.09	491.18	484.70
2007	493.09	489.18	497.27	502.58	500.52	508.36	512.87	510.00	511.04	516.34	514.40	517.27	505.34
Goods-Producing													
2003	679.39	671.58	686.38	681.45	682.68	687.65	680.21	695.96	702.18	688.88	697.62	699.73	688.06
2004	693.03	690.55	695.08	699.58	716.91	719.46	722.30	729.59	730.06	724.45	724.92	730.74	715.20
2005	729.54	731.42	737.15	744.56	741.21	736.38	744.04	756.96	769.86	774.58	764.54	770.85	751.38
2006	764.10	770.70	776.64	779.94	787.27	794.22	752.54	755.20	759.53	774.59	777.27	786.01	774.79
2007	783.21	787.48	801.22	807.59	810.08	816.21	817.74	819.84	817.89	826.70	828.89	841.47	813.15
Natural Resources and Mining													
2003	846.26	845.14	850.02	839.92	841.27	833.95	803.64	851.24	845.61	832.94	819.05	851.85	838.91
2004	859.08	855.74	843.61	860.26	848.22	850.41	828.85	870.49	851.42	868.09	870.01	877.97	857.44
2005	880.75	892.07	909.16	911.05	881.14	892.40	882.45	922.43	942.08	952.50	940.35	930.47	912.05
2006	951.13	944.36	972.47	961.40	969.49	972.08	927.63	949.34	959.74	974.38	956.51	979.61	962.72
2007	978.80	983.92	1,012.45	1,003.68	996.74	987.48	953.45	1,007.96	1,009.15	1,001.78	1,002.54	1,027.43	998.03
Construction													
2003	598.37	584.23	603.26	593.25	629.19	631.94	644.25	660.92	672.30	645.06	640.64	650.55	632.13
2004	640.98	632.39	650.50	644.21	676.37	676.60	691.65	684.78	686.62	665.58	668.91	665.62	665.62
2005	674.87	671.40	677.91	682.88	698.54	703.60	710.78	708.73	718.15	715.60	687.85	697.76	696.59
2006	698.10	697.62	699.26	708.70	729.96	742.54	752.35	759.46	743.29	757.60	742.24	761.21	734.70
2007	739.05	725.80	746.52	753.10	763.14	795.48	798.05	788.13	772.63	790.00	777.55	795.93	772.23
Manufacturing													
2003	657.26	648.35	664.83	667.03	654.36	664.14	653.64	659.28	668.03	663.59	685.95	670.47	662.87
2004	653.08	654.81	661.33	667.90	685.58	690.97	695.08	697.52	706.82	699.71	705.60	705.15	686.00
2005	693.01	695.08	696.12	707.47	703.75	688.52	702.46	710.36	723.84	727.98	727.02	734.09	709.60
2006	709.62	723.47	726.52	734.02	736.09	741.19	747.78	738.30	747.83	753.36	763.00	756.55	738.86
2007	757.27	762.60	769.39	778.32	777.08	767.97	779.09	763.64	771.49	779.76	788.98	786.01	772.72
Trade, Transportation, and Utilities													
2003	372.16	381.64	387.45	392.23	395.91	400.55	403.52	402.99	404.19	406.83	406.98	400.14	396.83
2004	394.34	401.10	410.11	407.36	415.72	418.76	418.30	410.89	417.13	418.40	419.58	421.01	413.22
2005	416.21	423.15	430.76	434.17	433.18	444.60	442.15	435.39	441.61	437.52	430.32	435.60	433.96
2006	429.27	432.25	436.81	445.35	448.39	452.86	451.08	450.89	454.30	460.03	450.90	450.19	446.96
2007	448.80	444.02	454.97	459.67	457.17	462.64	462.89	461.24	461.46	463.61	462.18	463.47	458.39
Wholesale Trade													
2003	552.82	551.77	563.60	560.56	573.65	587.11	580.00	590.94	608.74	593.48	617.80	598.29	581.29
2004	589.04	586.08	575.60	568.58	579.60	601.69	603.58	605.88	602.08	609.12	635.09	626.26	598.86
2005	627.57	633.21	615.75	629.64	625.20	635.49	635.85	629.57	640.71	639.04	646.38	649.54	633.55
2006	647.62	630.43	641.16	651.60	658.04	657.71	654.08	647.21	643.54	665.01	669.38	658.84	652.03
2007	657.20	657.10	649.20	666.06	660.85	666.60	674.73	656.90	658.35	668.66	674.22	663.66	663.30
Retail Trade													
2003	272.54	282.87	288.32	289.33	292.58	297.17	298.23	293.07	287.36	293.87	292.25	293.80	290.05
2004	280.52	288.38	295.55	295.60	305.97	310.00	306.83	299.20	303.99	306.48	306.80	311.52	301.04
2005	296.73	306.86	312.34	312.66	314.90	327.03	325.30	317.19	327.24	322.97	312.61	322.08	316.87
2006	310.37	312.84	314.93	325.33	328.96	337.00	333.13	335.02	339.10	341.58	332.89	338.25	329.23
2007	328.81	320.74	338.83	341.32	343.02	349.98	346.13	347.33	348.26	347.43	349.89	354.09	342.88
Financial Activities													
2003	353.71	361.08	350.11	349.07	353.98	354.56	353.91	355.83	360.64	365.53	374.20	362.56	357.90
2004	371.15	380.32	383.04	377.36	378.84	380.80	381.79	379.66	374.41	368.85	369.73	368.40	376.35
2005	391.55	369.63	372.38	386.54	377.83	365.40	364.15	363.35	370.87	379.96	378.89	391.94	375.31
2006	400.66	393.69	395.41	401.72	403.54	409.66	414.46	404.81	413.04	422.03	409.46	413.16	407.23
2007	412.61	413.75	415.25	415.25	421.01	424.18	434.18	423.51	426.22	430.78	426.31	424.03	422.69
Professional and Business Services													
2003	424.16	426.42	428.15	428.03	424.55	419.15	422.45	417.69	429.40	424.45	417.95	419.83	422.96
2004	422.28	422.84	420.79	421.72	423.85	420.90	419.85	432.78	427.18	420.04	421.25	421.26	422.63
2005	427.94	422.09	423.86	428.06	432.52	439.07	447.77	454.22	456.03	457.62	467.71	477.43	445.65
2006	473.96	475.28	466.44	497.73	470.50	486.65	512.62	514.81	509.08	514.40	514.00	516.95	496.31
2007	509.66	502.32	506.27	520.68	509.47	524.03	536.76	536.21	533.36	529.31	529.43	534.45	522.20

Population
    2000 census: 5,363,675
    2007 estimate: 5,601,640
    Percent change, 2000–2007: 4.4%

Percent change in total nonfarm employment, 2000–2007: 1.7%

Industry with the largest growth in employment, 2000–2007 (thousands)
    Education and health services, 59.6

Industry with the largest decline in employment, 2000–2007 (thousands)
    Manufacturing, -93.5

Civilian labor force
    2000: 2,996,091
    2007: 3,089,321

Employment-population ratio
    2000: 70.8%
    2007: 67.4%

Unemployment rate and rank among states
    2000: 3.4%, 17th
    2007: 4.9%, 38th

Employment by Industry, 2007

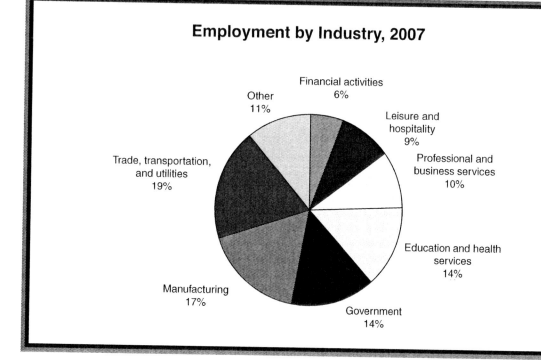

Financial activities 6%

Other 11%

Leisure and hospitality 9%

Trade, transportation, and utilities 19%

Professional and business services 10%

Education and health services 14%

Manufacturing 17%

Government 14%

Employment by Industry: Wisconsin, 2000–2007

(Numbers in thousands, not seasonally adjusted.)

Industry and year	January	February	March	April	May	June	July	August	September	October	November	December	Annual Average
Total Nonfarm													
2000	2,748.9	2,759.7	2,785.1	2,820.3	2,846.9	2,885.5	2,852.5	2,858.5	2,859.3	2,864.1	2,869.9	2,854.7	2,833.8
2001	2,770.7	2,776.5	2,788.9	2,813.6	2,840.1	2,861.6	2,829.3	2,829.1	2,825.0	2,820.8	2,812.6	2,798.4	2,813.9
2002	2,719.4	2,717.6	2,735.9	2,766.1	2,799.4	2,823.1	2,795.4	2,800.5	2,798.5	2,814.2	2,816.5	2,801.8	2,782.4
2003	2,710.5	2,718.4	2,726.6	2,761.5	2,795.8	2,818.2	2,781.8	2,783.9	2,793.0	2,810.3	2,803.4	2,800.1	2,775.3
2004	2,718.1	2,727.3	2,744.3	2,783.9	2,817.3	2,847.8	2,834.5	2,838.9	2,836.8	2,847.6	2,847.1	2,841.5	2,807.1
2005	2,757.2	2,768.8	2,783.5	2,830.7	2,854.9	2,880.4	2,861.8	2,864.1	2,877.0	2,874.1	2,876.0	2,876.3	2,842.1
2006	2,790.0	2,793.9	2,811.8	2,851.6	2,880.6	2,917.0	2,885.8	2,887.0	2,896.1	2,895.1	2,895.2	2,893.1	2,866.4
2007	2,814.4	2,810.0	2,830.0	2,862.0	2,904.0	2,942.3	2,901.0	2,904.0	2,902.7	2,909.8	2,904.4	2,896.0	2,881.7
Total Private													
2000	2,349.3	2,350.9	2,373.0	2,401.6	2,429.5	2,472.2	2,471.4	2,480.1	2,461.6	2,454.1	2,452.2	2,442.6	2,428.2
2001	2,368.4	2,358.8	2,367.9	2,388.5	2,415.6	2,445.5	2,441.9	2,445.1	2,413.4	2,396.8	2,386.0	2,374.1	2,400.2
2002	2,310.8	2,296.1	2,309.7	2,337.9	2,373.3	2,409.8	2,411.7	2,420.4	2,394.5	2,387.5	2,383.7	2,375.6	2,367.6
2003	2,306.2	2,293.5	2,300.4	2,332.6	2,370.8	2,397.9	2,398.8	2,404.0	2,393.8	2,389.9	2,381.1	2,379.9	2,362.4
2004	2,314.9	2,307.0	2,322.3	2,361.2	2,395.1	2,433.2	2,449.9	2,457.1	2,430.8	2,426.9	2,420.9	2,420.0	2,394.9
2005	2,346.3	2,344.2	2,359.7	2,403.5	2,428.9	2,466.1	2,476.1	2,482.6	2,462.7	2,451.0	2,450.6	2,449.3	2,426.8
2006	2,379.9	2,374.2	2,387.2	2,424.1	2,454.6	2,498.4	2,498.5	2,503.7	2,482.2	2,473.7	2,470.3	2,467.6	2,451.2
2007	2,404.2	2,393.2	2,407.5	2,435.0	2,477.0	2,520.4	2,515.5	2,520.6	2,491.6	2,483.0	2,473.1	2,466.8	2,465.7
Goods-Producing													
2000	701.3	700.7	708.0	716.5	724.4	742.7	741.7	742.5	734.2	729.5	722.6	711.8	723.0
2001	689.5	682.5	683.2	687.1	694.4	706.8	706.1	705.6	694.6	685.4	674.5	664.8	689.5
2002	643.5	634.9	638.6	646.8	658.0	671.8	673.1	675.7	667.4	662.4	657.0	645.7	656.2
2003	621.1	613.0	614.0	623.2	635.8	646.3	647.7	648.2	640.8	637.2	631.1	623.9	631.9
2004	607.0	603.4	608.7	623.3	634.0	646.1	654.6	655.8	648.5	644.1	640.0	634.3	633.3
2005	612.0	611.3	615.0	628.4	637.1	652.2	656.4	657.0	649.0	644.4	640.5	633.2	636.4
2006	618.8	613.9	617.2	629.7	638.8	656.0	656.7	656.9	648.4	642.9	636.5	630.2	637.2
2007	614.4	607.4	612.2	620.7	633.4	649.1	649.2	649.2	639.9	634.1	629.2	619.8	629.9
Natural Resources and Mining													
2000	3.5	3.6	3.7	3.9	4.3	4.4	4.4	4.4	4.3	4.2	4.1	3.6	4.0
2001	3.2	3.3	3.4	3.6	4.1	4.3	4.3	4.3	4.2	4.2	4.0	3.7	3.9
2002	3.2	3.2	3.3	3.6	4.1	4.2	4.2	4.2	4.2	4.1	3.9	3.6	3.8
2003	3.2	3.1	3.2	3.5	4.0	4.1	4.1	4.1	4.1	4.0	3.9	3.7	3.8
2004	3.1	3.2	3.3	3.7	4.0	4.1	4.2	4.2	4.1	4.2	4.1	3.9	3.8
2005	3.3	3.3	3.5	3.8	4.1	4.3	4.4	4.4	4.3	4.2	4.1	3.8	4.0
2006	3.4	3.4	3.5	3.8	4.2	4.3	4.3	4.3	4.2	4.1	3.9	3.7	3.9
2007	3.2	3.2	3.3	3.5	3.9	3.9	4.0	4.0	3.9	3.8	3.7	3.5	3.7
Construction													
2000	107.6	106.1	111.2	121.3	128.7	135.3	137.3	137.5	133.6	131.7	127.7	119.9	124.8
2001	109.3	108.0	110.1	118.1	128.0	134.6	138.1	138.8	134.8	133.3	129.0	122.3	125.4
2002	108.7	105.7	108.0	117.9	127.2	133.4	136.7	136.7	133.1	132.0	129.2	120.9	124.1
2003	108.6	105.0	106.6	116.2	127.8	133.6	136.0	136.5	133.3	132.8	129.1	123.4	124.1
2004	110.4	107.6	110.9	122.2	129.6	135.4	139.7	138.7	135.7	134.0	131.4	125.4	126.8
2005	112.1	109.5	111.8	123.2	130.5	136.5	139.5	138.9	136.2	134.6	132.2	125.2	127.5
2006	114.3	111.9	113.4	124.0	131.1	137.8	138.5	138.1	134.9	132.9	129.3	123.6	127.5
2007	112.5	107.9	113.0	120.0	130.2	135.9	136.8	136.7	133.6	132.0	128.3	120.3	125.6
Manufacturing													
2000	590.2	591.0	593.1	591.3	591.4	603.0	600.0	600.6	596.3	593.6	590.8	588.3	594.1
2001	577.0	571.2	569.7	565.4	562.3	567.9	563.7	562.5	555.6	547.9	541.5	538.8	560.3
2002	531.6	526.0	527.3	525.3	526.7	534.2	532.2	534.8	530.1	526.3	523.9	521.2	528.3
2003	509.3	504.9	504.2	503.5	504.0	508.6	507.6	507.6	503.4	500.4	498.1	496.8	504.0
2004	493.5	492.6	494.5	497.4	500.4	506.6	510.7	512.9	508.7	505.9	504.5	505.0	502.7
2005	496.6	498.5	499.7	501.4	502.5	511.4	512.5	513.7	508.5	505.6	504.2	504.2	504.9
2006	501.1	498.6	500.3	501.9	503.5	513.9	513.9	514.5	509.3	505.9	503.3	502.9	505.8
2007	498.7	496.3	495.9	497.2	499.3	509.3	508.4	508.5	502.4	498.3	497.2	496.0	500.6
Service-Providing													
2000	2,047.6	2,059.0	2,077.1	2,103.8	2,122.5	2,142.8	2,110.8	2,116.0	2,125.1	2,134.6	2,147.3	2,142.9	2,110.8
2001	2,081.2	2,094.0	2,105.7	2,126.5	2,145.7	2,154.8	2,123.2	2,123.5	2,130.4	2,135.4	2,138.1	2,133.6	2,124.3
2002	2,075.9	2,082.7	2,097.3	2,119.3	2,141.4	2,151.3	2,122.3	2,124.8	2,131.1	2,151.8	2,159.5	2,156.1	2,126.1
2003	2,089.4	2,105.4	2,112.6	2,138.3	2,160.0	2,171.9	2,134.1	2,135.7	2,152.2	2,173.1	2,172.3	2,176.2	2,143.4
2004	2,111.1	2,123.9	2,135.6	2,160.6	2,183.3	2,201.7	2,179.9	2,183.1	2,188.3	2,203.5	2,207.1	2,207.2	2,173.8
2005	2,145.2	2,157.5	2,168.5	2,202.3	2,217.8	2,228.2	2,205.4	2,207.1	2,228.0	2,229.7	2,235.5	2,243.1	2,205.7
2006	2,171.2	2,180.0	2,194.6	2,221.9	2,241.8	2,261.0	2,229.1	2,230.1	2,247.7	2,252.2	2,258.7	2,262.9	2,229.3
2007	2,200.0	2,202.6	2,217.8	2,241.3	2,270.6	2,293.2	2,251.8	2,254.8	2,262.8	2,275.7	2,275.2	2,276.2	2,251.8
Trade, Transportation, and Utilities													
2000	541.4	535.8	539.4	543.9	548.4	550.6	549.2	552.0	555.7	564.7	574.9	578.7	552.9
2001	549.2	540.0	541.7	544.1	549.2	549.8	543.5	546.2	544.2	548.0	557.2	558.8	547.7
2002	533.0	524.7	527.4	528.9	535.8	538.2	533.5	534.9	535.4	540.8	552.4	555.9	536.7
2003	528.3	521.9	521.8	528.4	535.8	540.1	533.3	535.6	537.7	543.7	551.8	557.7	536.3
2004	529.5	522.5	524.7	529.2	537.1	543.0	539.9	540.6	540.0	545.7	555.6	559.5	538.9
2005	532.0	526.7	529.0	535.4	541.3	543.8	542.1	543.9	544.1	551.7	561.4	566.8	543.2
2006	536.0	529.6	532.7	536.8	542.9	548.0	542.9	544.3	544.4	549.3	561.4	565.8	544.5
2007	541.3	533.5	536.3	538.4	547.9	552.4	548.2	547.7	547.1	550.7	560.3	564.0	547.3
Wholesale Trade													
2000	114.1	114.2	114.9	115.2	115.7	117.1	117.5	117.4	116.3	116.4	116.6	117.0	116.0
2001	115.4	115.2	115.5	115.4	116.4	117.5	117.2	116.8	115.4	115.3	114.8	114.9	115.8
2002	113.2	112.7	113.2	113.9	114.8	115.5	116.1	115.6	114.4	113.6	113.7	113.6	114.2
2003	111.3	111.1	111.3	112.5	113.2	114.4	114.1	114.1	113.2	113.7	113.2	113.9	113.0
2004	112.3	111.8	112.4	112.9	113.6	114.9	116.6	117.0	115.0	115.7	116.0	116.5	114.6
2005	115.0	114.7	114.9	116.9	117.8	119.3	119.8	119.6	118.4	118.9	119.1	119.8	117.9
2006	118.5	118.1	118.8	119.9	120.6	122.6	122.8	122.5	121.2	121.3	121.4	121.9	120.8
2007	120.0	119.7	120.0	121.0	122.1	123.9	124.1	123.3	122.1	122.2	122.4	122.3	121.9

Employment by Industry: Wisconsin, 2000–2007—*Continued*

(Numbers in thousands, not seasonally adjusted.)

Industry and year	January	February	March	April	May	June	July	August	September	October	November	December	Annual Average
Retail Trade													
2000	325.0	319.2	321.3	323.5	326.2	328.5	328.3	330.5	331.6	338.2	349.1	353.2	331.2
2001	326.4	317.7	318.8	319.6	322.4	323.6	320.4	323.0	319.6	323.1	333.6	336.3	323.7
2002	317.1	309.9	311.3	310.5	314.5	317.6	315.8	317.4	315.0	319.8	331.5	336.4	318.1
2003	314.2	308.0	307.2	310.7	315.6	318.3	315.9	318.3	316.7	321.2	330.6	336.6	317.8
2004	313.8	307.3	308.1	310.4	315.6	319.7	317.9	318.5	316.1	318.9	329.1	333.4	317.4
2005	311.7	306.2	307.4	310.2	314.0	315.4	315.7	317.7	315.1	321.9	331.5	336.1	316.9
2006	310.4	303.9	305.5	307.6	311.4	314.4	312.5	314.0	311.2	315.5	328.0	331.4	313.8
2007	313.5	305.6	307.6	308.1	314.4	316.6	316.0	315.2	312.2	315.0	325.2	329.0	314.9
Transportation and Utilities													
2000	102.3	102.4	103.2	105.2	106.5	105.0	103.4	104.1	107.8	110.1	109.2	108.5	105.6
2001	107.4	107.1	107.4	109.1	110.4	108.7	105.9	106.4	109.2	109.6	108.8	107.6	108.1
2002	102.7	102.1	102.9	104.5	106.5	105.1	101.6	101.9	106.0	107.4	107.2	105.9	104.5
2003	102.8	102.8	103.3	105.2	107.0	107.4	103.3	103.2	107.8	108.8	108.0	107.2	105.6
2004	103.4	103.4	104.2	105.9	107.9	108.4	105.4	105.1	108.9	111.1	110.5	109.6	107.0
2005	105.3	105.8	106.7	108.3	109.5	109.1	106.6	106.6	110.6	110.9	110.8	110.9	108.4
2006	107.1	107.6	108.4	109.3	110.9	111.0	107.6	107.8	112.0	112.5	112.0	112.5	109.9
2007	107.8	108.2	108.7	109.3	111.4	111.9	108.1	109.2	112.8	113.5	112.7	112.7	110.5
Information													
2000	52.5	52.4	52.5	52.6	52.9	53.4	53.8	53.9	53.8	54.6	55.6	55.6	53.6
2001	53.8	53.6	53.8	54.0	53.4	53.7	53.3	53.1	52.6	52.5	52.8	52.5	53.3
2002	51.8	51.3	51.2	51.1	51.0	51.1	51.1	51.2	50.6	50.8	51.2	51.4	51.2
2003	50.7	50.1	50.1	49.9	49.9	50.2	50.2	50.4	50.4	50.3	50.8	51.0	50.3
2004	50.2	49.8	49.9	49.6	49.6	49.7	50.2	50.3	49.7	49.6	50.0	50.1	49.9
2005	49.6	49.4	49.3	49.6	49.7	50.1	49.8	50.0	49.6	49.6	50.0	50.1	49.7
2006	49.6	49.3	49.1	48.9	48.9	49.1	49.2	49.2	49.4	48.9	49.3	50.0	49.3
2007	49.8	49.5	49.4	49.5	49.9	50.3	50.6	50.8	50.3	50.3	50.6	50.7	50.1
Financial Activities													
2000	146.7	146.6	146.8	148.1	148.6	150.6	151.0	150.8	149.8	149.7	150.0	150.9	149.1
2001	150.0	150.0	151.0	150.6	151.5	153.4	153.8	153.6	152.2	151.4	151.7	151.8	151.8
2002	151.4	151.7	151.7	152.4	153.1	154.8	155.6	156.0	154.5	154.2	154.8	155.5	153.8
2003	154.3	154.9	155.0	155.9	157.1	158.7	158.7	158.8	157.2	156.9	156.9	157.8	156.9
2004	156.7	156.5	156.7	157.7	158.3	159.9	160.8	161.0	158.9	159.1	159.1	160.4	158.8
2005	158.3	157.7	158.1	158.8	159.3	161.0	161.8	161.8	160.4	159.9	159.9	161.0	159.8
2006	159.5	159.2	159.2	160.6	161.7	163.2	164.2	163.9	162.6	162.3	162.3	163.3	161.8
2007	162.1	161.9	161.5	162.2	162.7	164.6	164.0	164.2	162.3	162.5	162.0	163.2	162.8
Professional and Business Services													
2000	236.5	238.7	242.0	245.5	248.8	252.4	250.0	253.0	252.1	250.4	249.4	245.0	247.0
2001	235.3	235.4	235.1	239.0	240.5	242.4	242.3	244.1	240.2	238.5	235.7	233.1	238.5
2002	228.8	229.5	233.1	239.8	241.5	244.2	245.1	247.1	244.6	244.5	240.8	238.7	239.8
2003	234.9	236.4	238.3	243.1	243.6	245.9	247.6	248.8	249.3	249.5	247.3	247.1	244.3
2004	240.0	241.0	243.3	249.5	250.8	256.3	258.4	262.6	258.7	260.7	257.8	257.2	253.0
2005	249.6	251.6	254.7	262.3	261.4	265.3	268.5	271.2	270.2	267.7	267.1	267.5	263.1
2006	257.2	260.2	261.6	270.1	270.7	275.4	275.1	277.5	276.6	276.9	275.4	273.6	270.9
2007	265.5	267.2	269.2	275.7	278.0	283.8	282.7	285.2	282.2	282.0	278.7	278.1	277.4
Education and Health Services													
2000	331.2	334.3	336.6	338.8	338.0	340.2	339.7	340.7	341.3	342.6	345.2	346.3	339.6
2001	341.9	347.6	349.0	349.5	349.3	349.0	347.9	347.9	350.0	352.6	355.2	355.3	349.6
2002	350.3	352.3	353.0	355.6	356.1	358.7	356.5	357.9	358.1	360.9	363.5	363.0	357.2
2003	359.8	361.6	361.9	363.9	363.9	359.5	360.3	360.6	368.0	371.9	372.0	371.5	364.6
2004	368.6	371.3	372.0	374.8	374.4	375.2	374.9	374.8	375.6	377.6	379.6	380.1	374.9
2005	377.1	379.1	380.3	382.7	382.4	384.0	382.5	382.9	385.1	386.4	388.6	388.7	383.3
2006	385.9	388.4	388.8	390.0	391.2	392.2	391.2	391.7	393.6	396.0	397.6	397.5	392.0
2007	393.1	395.4	396.4	396.9	398.7	399.5	398.3	399.6	400.7	403.0	404.2	404.1	399.2
Leisure and Hospitality													
2000	215.5	216.9	221.6	230.1	242.4	254.8	259.6	261.3	248.3	235.9	228.0	226.4	236.7
2001	219.4	220.1	223.0	233.9	246.7	257.7	263.0	262.4	247.8	236.8	227.6	224.7	238.6
2002	221.0	220.7	222.5	231.4	245.8	256.9	264.2	265.0	251.9	241.7	232.0	232.1	240.4
2003	225.6	224.0	226.6	235.8	252.2	262.6	267.5	268.2	257.5	248.3	239.5	237.9	245.5
2004	230.3	229.4	232.6	242.7	256.2	265.9	275.0	275.6	263.4	252.9	243.4	242.6	250.8
2005	233.8	233.9	237.7	250.3	261.5	271.9	278.0	278.8	267.7	255.2	247.7	245.6	255.2
2006	239.0	239.6	243.4	252.6	264.4	276.5	282.1	283.1	271.0	260.6	251.4	250.2	259.5
2007	242.9	242.8	246.0	254.3	268.5	281.0	283.7	285.7	271.3	262.4	250.8	249.1	261.5
Other Services													
2000	124.2	125.5	126.1	126.1	126.0	127.5	126.4	125.9	126.4	126.7	126.5	127.9	126.3
2001	129.3	129.6	131.1	130.3	130.6	132.7	132.0	132.2	131.8	131.6	131.3	133.1	131.3
2002	131.0	131.0	132.2	131.9	132.0	134.1	132.6	132.6	132.0	132.2	132.0	133.3	132.2
2003	131.5	131.6	132.7	132.4	132.5	134.6	133.5	133.4	132.9	132.1	131.7	133.0	132.7
2004	132.6	133.1	134.4	134.4	134.7	137.1	136.1	136.4	136.0	137.2	135.4	135.8	135.3
2005	133.9	134.5	135.6	136.0	136.2	137.8	137.0	137.0	136.6	136.1	135.4	136.4	136.0
2006	133.9	134.0	135.2	135.4	136.0	138.0	137.1	136.9	136.7	136.4	135.9	137.0	136.0
2007	135.1	135.5	136.5	137.3	137.9	139.7	138.8	138.2	137.8	138.0	137.3	137.8	137.5
Government													
2000	399.6	408.8	412.1	418.7	417.4	413.3	381.1	378.4	397.7	410.0	417.7	412.1	405.6
2001	402.3	417.7	421.0	425.1	424.5	416.1	387.4	384.0	411.6	424.0	426.6	424.3	413.7
2002	408.6	421.5	426.2	428.2	426.1	413.3	383.7	380.1	404.0	426.7	432.8	426.2	414.8
2003	404.3	424.9	426.2	428.9	425.0	420.3	383.0	379.9	399.2	420.4	422.3	420.2	412.9
2004	403.2	420.3	422.0	422.7	422.2	414.6	384.6	381.8	406.0	420.7	426.2	421.5	412.2
2005	410.9	424.6	423.8	427.2	426.0	414.3	385.7	381.5	414.3	423.1	425.4	427.0	415.3
2006	410.1	419.7	424.6	427.5	426.0	418.6	387.3	383.3	413.9	421.4	424.9	425.5	415.2
2007	410.2	416.8	422.5	427.0	**427.0**	**421.9**	**385.5**	**383.4**	**411.1**	**426.8**	**431.3**	**429.2**	**416.1**

Average Weekly Hours by Selected Industry: Wisconsin, 2001–2007

(Not seasonally adjusted.)

Industry and year	January	February	March	April	May	June	July	August	September	October	November	December	Annual Average
Manufacturing													
2001	40.5	39.7	40.5	39.1	40.3	39.9	40.2	40.4	40.9	39.8	39.6	41.1	40.2
2002	40.2	40.1	40.6	40.2	40.2	40.8	39.9	40.6	40.8	40.7	40.6	40.8	40.5
2003	40.2	40.3	40.3	40.3	40.0	40.7	39.2	40.0	40.5	40.1	40.9	40.9	40.3
2004	40.5	40.7	40.5	39.8	40.0	39.7	39.5	40.3	40.5	40.7	40.4	40.8	40.3
2005	40.7	40.1	40.1	39.8	40.0	40.0	39.7	40.6	41.4	40.4	40.8	41.3	40.4
2006	40.3	39.9	40.8	39.7	41.0	40.9	40.1	41.2	41.7	40.8	40.8	41.3	40.7
2007	40.1	40.1	40.1	39.9	40.3	39.9	39.7	40.8	40.9	40.4	40.0	40.1	40.2

Average Hourly Earnings by Selected Industry: Wisconsin, 2001–2007

(Dollars, not seasonally adjusted.)

Industry and year	January	February	March	April	May	June	July	August	September	October	November	December	Annual Average
Manufacturing													
2001	15.14	15.09	15.34	15.27	15.40	15.44	15.46	15.48	15.65	15.60	15.68	15.80	15.44
2002	15.82	15.85	15.96	15.82	15.87	15.80	15.71	15.69	15.85	15.90	15.94	16.13	15.86
2003	16.03	16.07	16.02	16.06	16.09	16.11	16.01	16.05	16.19	16.18	16.20	16.40	16.12
2004	16.18	16.17	16.18	16.37	16.16	16.18	16.09	16.08	16.25	16.06	16.19	16.42	16.19
2005	16.21	16.28	16.27	16.31	16.34	16.27	16.22	16.18	16.04	16.32	16.40	16.67	16.29
2006	16.60	16.57	16.39	16.46	16.67	16.42	16.28	16.34	16.51	16.64	16.65	16.97	16.54
2007	17.02	17.19	17.12	17.31	17.16	17.31	17.22	17.34	17.59	17.38	17.60	18.15	17.37

Average Weekly Earnings by Selected Industry: Wisconsin, 2001–2007

(Dollars, not seasonally adjusted.)

Industry and year	January	February	March	April	May	June	July	August	September	October	November	December	Annual Average
Manufacturing													
2001	613.17	599.07	621.27	597.06	620.62	616.06	621.49	625.39	640.09	620.88	620.93	649.38	620.69
2002	635.96	635.59	647.98	635.96	637.97	644.64	626.83	637.01	646.68	647.13	647.16	658.10	642.33
2003	644.41	647.62	645.61	647.22	643.60	655.68	627.59	642.00	655.70	648.82	662.58	670.76	649.64
2004	655.29	658.12	655.29	651.53	646.40	642.35	635.56	648.02	658.13	653.64	654.08	669.94	652.46
2005	659.75	652.83	652.43	649.14	653.60	650.80	643.93	656.91	664.06	659.33	669.12	688.47	658.12
2006	668.98	661.14	668.71	653.46	683.47	671.58	652.83	673.21	688.47	678.91	679.32	700.86	673.18
2007	682.50	689.32	686.51	690.67	691.55	690.67	683.63	707.47	719.43	702.15	704.00	727.82	698.27

WYOMING
At a Glance

Population
   2000 census: 493,782
   2007 estimate: 522,830
   Percent change, 2000–2007: 5.9%

Percent change in total nonfarm employment, 2000–2007: 20.4%

Industry with the largest growth in employment, 2000–2007 (thousands)
   Natural resources and mining, 11.0

Industry with the largest decline in employment, 2000–2007 (thousands)
   Manufacturing, -0.2

Civilian labor force
   2000: 266,882
   2007: 287,743

Employment-population ratio
   2000: 68.8%
   2007: 69.2%

Unemployment rate and rank among states
   2000: 3.8%, 25th
   2007: 3.0%, 4th

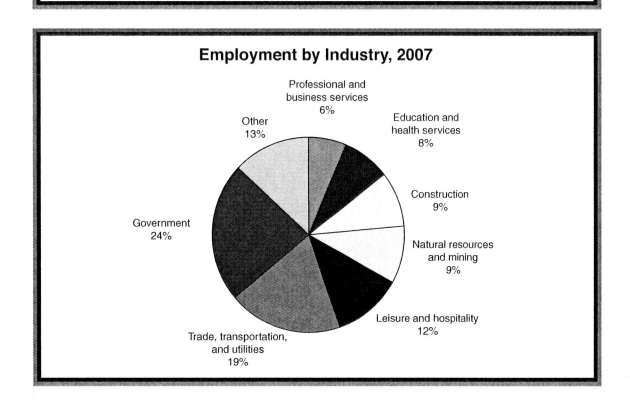

Employment by Industry, 2007

- Professional and business services 6%
- Education and health services 8%
- Construction 9%
- Natural resources and mining 9%
- Leisure and hospitality 12%
- Trade, transportation, and utilities 19%
- Government 24%
- Other 13%

239

Employment by Industry: Wyoming, 2000–2007

(Numbers in thousands, not seasonally adjusted.)

Industry and year	January	February	March	April	May	June	July	August	September	October	November	December	Annual Average
Total Nonfarm													
2000	227.8	228.5	232.2	234.1	241.7	248.8	246.4	247.1	245.0	242.9	238.2	239.3	239.3
2001	233.1	233.5	236.8	239.4	247.2	256.6	252.8	254.5	251.4	248.8	245.5	245.3	245.4
2002	237.9	237.7	240.2	242.4	250.2	258.2	255.7	255.4	254.2	250.5	246.5	246.1	247.9
2003	238.9	238.4	240.0	243.2	250.8	260.3	257.5	258.7	257.2	255.0	249.9	250.4	250.0
2004	243.9	244.3	246.9	250.8	256.4	266.0	263.2	262.8	260.1	258.4	255.4	256.0	255.4
2005	249.6	250.7	254.0	257.1	264.0	273.5	271.6	272.2	271.5	269.4	266.0	267.4	263.9
2006	262.4	264.3	267.5	269.8	277.8	288.7	284.3	284.6	284.7	281.9	279.3	281.9	277.3
2007	275.1	276.9	280.3	280.6	289.0	298.6	294.9	295.3	295.0	292.7	289.3	289.9	288.1
Total Private													
2000	167.7	167.9	169.9	172.1	178.1	187.5	190.1	190.6	184.8	180.8	176.2	177.3	178.5
2001	172.3	172.1	174.6	177.4	184.1	193.3	195.4	196.6	190.2	186.1	182.8	181.9	183.9
2002	176.0	175.4	176.8	179.4	186.1	194.1	197.2	197.0	191.5	186.3	182.2	181.0	185.3
2003	175.6	174.7	175.5	179.0	185.6	195.1	198.3	199.6	194.3	190.1	185.4	185.3	186.5
2004	179.7	179.7	181.6	185.3	189.9	199.6	202.4	202.4	196.4	192.8	189.9	190.3	190.8
2005	184.9	185.5	188.2	191.3	196.9	206.9	210.6	211.1	206.4	202.9	199.8	201.0	198.8
2006	197.6	198.7	201.3	203.7	210.7	221.3	223.0	223.7	219.2	215.0	212.8	214.9	211.8
2007	209.0	210.0	212.9	213.2	220.3	230.0	232.6	233.1	227.2	224.0	220.7	221.2	221.2
Goods-Producing													
2000	42.1	42.0	42.7	43.7	45.2	46.6	47.3	48.0	47.4	47.4	45.6	45.2	45.2
2001	43.0	43.0	43.9	45.6	47.7	49.9	50.6	51.3	50.4	51.2	50.3	48.1	47.9
2002	45.5	44.2	44.7	45.9	48.2	49.0	49.4	50.2	49.4	48.7	47.0	45.1	47.3
2003	42.9	42.3	42.6	44.5	46.8	48.3	49.4	50.9	50.5	50.4	48.8	47.6	47.1
2004	44.6	44.6	45.4	47.1	48.9	50.7	51.4	51.5	50.6	51.0	50.5	49.5	48.8
2005	47.6	47.8	49.0	50.8	52.6	54.4	55.6	56.2	56.0	56.5	56.1	55.3	53.2
2006	54.6	54.8	55.7	58.2	60.8	62.8	62.8	64.1	63.8	63.9	63.3	62.9	60.6
2007	59.7	59.4	60.6	61.8	63.8	65.7	66.1	66.9	65.7	66.4	65.2	64.1	63.8
Natural Resources and Mining													
2000	16.1	16.1	16.0	15.5	15.8	16.1	16.4	16.8	16.7	16.7	16.7	16.9	16.3
2001	16.6	16.8	17.3	17.4	18.0	18.8	19.0	19.3	19.3	19.5	19.3	19.1	18.4
2002	18.4	18.1	17.9	17.4	17.7	18.0	18.3	18.4	18.0	17.8	17.5	17.3	17.9
2003	17.1	17.2	17.2	17.4	17.8	18.3	18.9	19.1	18.9	19.1	19.0	19.2	18.3
2004	18.9	19.0	19.1	19.2	19.4	20.2	20.6	20.9	20.9	21.0	21.3	21.3	20.2
2005	21.0	21.3	21.6	21.8	22.1	22.9	23.2	23.4	23.5	23.6	23.9	24.3	22.7
2006	24.6	25.0	25.4	25.8	26.2	27.0	27.3	27.6	27.5	27.5	27.4	27.6	26.6
2007	27.0	26.9	26.8	26.8	27.2	27.7	27.6	27.7	27.5	27.8	27.3	27.5	27.3
Construction													
2000	15.9	15.8	16.7	18.0	19.1	20.0	20.3	20.7	20.3	19.8	18.1	17.5	18.5
2001	16.1	16.0	16.5	18.2	19.9	21.2	21.6	22.0	21.2	21.4	20.9	19.3	19.5
2002	17.6	17.0	17.5	19.2	21.1	21.5	21.6	22.2	21.9	21.2	19.8	18.2	19.9
2003	16.6	16.2	16.6	18.1	19.9	20.7	21.1	22.3	22.2	21.6	20.1	18.7	19.5
2004	16.5	16.6	17.2	18.7	20.3	20.9	21.2	21.0	20.2	20.2	19.5	18.5	19.2
2005	17.0	17.2	18.0	19.5	21.0	21.8	22.7	23.0	22.7	22.8	22.1	21.0	20.7
2006	20.2	20.1	20.6	22.6	24.6	25.5	25.1	26.2	26.0	25.9	25.4	24.8	23.9
2007	22.4	22.4	23.6	24.9	26.5	27.9	28.4	29.0	28.1	28.2	27.5	26.1	26.3
Manufacturing													
2000	10.1	10.1	10.0	10.2	10.3	10.5	10.6	10.5	10.4	10.9	10.8	10.8	10.4
2001	10.3	10.2	10.1	10.0	9.8	9.9	10.0	10.0	9.9	10.3	10.1	9.7	10.0
2002	9.5	9.1	9.3	9.3	9.4	9.5	9.5	9.6	9.5	9.7	9.7	9.7	9.5
2003	9.2	8.9	8.8	9.0	9.1	9.3	9.4	9.5	9.4	9.7	9.7	9.7	9.3
2004	9.2	9.0	9.1	9.2	9.2	9.6	9.6	9.6	9.5	9.8	9.7	9.7	9.4
2005	9.6	9.3	9.4	9.5	9.5	9.7	9.7	9.8	9.8	10.1	10.1	10.0	9.7
2006	9.8	9.7	9.7	9.8	10.0	10.3	10.4	10.3	10.3	10.5	10.5	10.5	10.2
2007	10.3	10.1	10.2	10.1	10.1	10.1	10.1	10.1	10.2	10.1	10.4	10.5	10.2
Service-Providing													
2000	185.7	186.5	189.5	190.4	196.5	202.2	199.1	199.1	197.6	195.5	192.6	194.1	194.0
2001	190.1	190.5	192.9	193.8	199.5	206.7	202.2	203.2	201.0	197.6	195.2	197.2	197.5
2002	192.4	193.5	195.5	196.5	202.0	209.2	206.3	205.2	204.8	201.8	199.5	201.0	200.6
2003	196.0	196.1	197.4	198.7	204.0	212.0	208.1	207.8	206.7	204.6	201.1	202.8	202.9
2004	199.3	199.7	201.5	203.7	207.5	215.3	211.8	211.3	209.5	207.4	204.9	206.5	206.5
2005	202.0	202.9	205.0	206.3	211.4	219.1	216.0	216.0	215.5	212.9	209.9	212.1	210.8
2006	207.8	209.5	211.8	211.6	217.0	225.9	221.5	220.5	220.9	218.0	216.0	219.0	216.6
2007	215.4	217.5	219.7	218.8	225.2	232.9	228.8	228.4	229.3	226.3	224.1	225.8	224.4
Trade, Transportation, and Utilities													
2000	46.3	46.0	45.9	46.6	47.7	48.9	49.7	50.0	49.1	48.7	49.1	49.4	48.1
2001	47.5	46.9	47.3	47.8	49.0	50.2	50.2	50.1	49.1	48.1	48.1	48.6	48.6
2002	47.0	46.4	46.7	47.2	48.5	49.7	50.0	50.0	49.1	48.7	49.0	49.2	48.5
2003	47.1	46.5	46.5	47.2	48.2	49.5	49.5	50.2	49.4	48.9	48.6	49.1	48.4
2004	47.5	47.4	47.6	48.3	49.1	50.5	51.0	50.8	49.9	49.4	49.5	50.0	49.3
2005	48.2	48.2	48.7	49.3	50.4	52.0	52.4	52.5	51.8	51.5	51.5	52.2	50.7
2006	50.7	50.6	51.1	51.0	52.1	53.9	54.2	54.0	53.3	52.8	53.4	54.0	52.6
2007	53.0	53.2	53.8	53.3	54.6	56.2	56.7	56.9	56.0	55.7	56.1	56.5	55.2
Wholesale Trade													
2000	6.1	6.2	6.2	6.3	6.3	6.5	6.5	6.5	6.5	6.4	6.4	6.5	6.3
2001	6.5	6.5	6.6	6.8	6.9	7.0	7.0	7.1	7.0	7.0	7.0	7.1	6.9
2002	7.0	7.0	7.0	7.0	7.0	7.1	7.1	7.1	7.0	7.0	7.0	7.1	7.0
2003	6.9	6.8	6.8	6.9	6.9	7.0	7.5	7.4	7.4	7.4	7.4	7.4	7.3
2004	7.1	7.2	7.2	7.3	7.4	7.4	7.5	7.9	7.9	7.9	7.9	8.0	7.8
2005	7.3	7.4	7.5	7.6	7.8	7.9	7.9	7.9	8.3	8.3	8.3	8.4	8.2
2006	7.8	7.9	8.0	8.0	8.2	8.4	8.3	8.3	8.3	8.3	8.4	8.4	8.8
2007	8.4	8.5	8.6	8.7	8.8	8.9	8.8	8.9	8.7	8.7	9.0	9.1	

Employment by Industry: Wyoming, 2000–2007—*Continued*

(Numbers in thousands, not seasonally adjusted.)

Industry and year	January	February	March	April	May	June	July	August	September	October	November	December	Annual Average
Retail Trade													
2000	28.7	28.4	28.3	28.8	29.9	30.7	31.5	31.7	31.0	30.5	30.8	31.0	30.1
2001	29.5	29.2	29.5	29.7	30.8	31.7	31.6	31.4	30.6	29.7	29.8	30.2	30.3
2002	28.9	28.4	28.7	29.1	30.3	31.2	31.5	31.4	30.7	30.1	30.4	30.6	30.1
2003	28.8	28.3	28.3	28.9	29.7	30.7	31.2	31.2	30.6	30.1	30.1	30.4	29.9
2004	28.8	28.6	28.8	29.2	29.9	31.0	31.3	31.2	30.4	30.0	30.1	30.4	30.0
2005	28.9	28.7	29.0	29.2	30.1	31.4	31.7	31.7	31.1	30.7	30.7	31.0	30.4
2006	29.8	29.5	29.8	29.7	30.5	31.8	32.2	32.0	31.3	30.9	31.4	31.7	30.9
2007	30.8	30.8	31.2	30.7	31.6	32.6	33.2	33.1	32.4	32.0	32.2	32.2	31.9
Transportation and Utilities													
2000	11.5	11.4	11.4	11.5	11.5	11.7	11.7	11.8	11.6	11.8	11.9	11.9	11.6
2001	11.5	11.2	11.2	11.3	11.3	11.5	11.6	11.6	11.5	11.4	11.3	11.3	11.4
2002	11.1	11.0	11.0	11.1	11.2	11.4	11.4	11.5	11.4	11.6	11.6	11.6	11.3
2003	11.4	11.4	11.4	11.4	11.6	11.8	11.8	11.9	11.8	11.8	11.5	11.6	11.6
2004	11.6	11.6	11.6	11.8	11.8	12.1	12.2	12.2	12.1	12.1	12.0	12.2	11.9
2005	12.0	12.1	12.2	12.5	12.5	12.7	12.8	12.9	12.8	12.9	12.9	13.2	12.6
2006	13.1	13.2	13.3	13.3	13.4	13.7	13.7	13.7	13.7	13.6	13.6	13.9	13.5
2007	13.8	13.9	14.0	13.9	14.2	14.7	14.7	14.9	14.9	15.0	14.9	15.2	14.5
Information													
2000	4.0	3.9	3.9	4.0	4.0	4.1	4.1	4.0	4.0	3.9	4.0	4.0	3.9
2001	4.0	3.9	3.9	3.9	4.0	4.1	4.1	4.2	4.2	4.1	4.2	4.2	4.1
2002	4.2	4.2	4.2	4.2	4.1	4.2	4.2	4.1	4.1	4.0	4.1	4.1	4.1
2003	4.1	4.1	4.2	4.1	4.2	4.3	4.3	4.3	4.2	4.3	4.3	4.3	4.2
2004	4.3	4.3	4.3	4.2	4.2	4.3	4.4	4.4	4.4	4.2	4.3	4.3	4.3
2005	4.3	4.3	4.3	4.3	4.3	4.4	4.3	4.3	4.3	4.2	4.3	4.3	4.3
2006	4.3	4.3	4.2	4.1	4.1	4.2	4.1	4.1	4.1	4.1	4.0	4.1	4.1
2007	4.0	4.0	4.0	4.0	4.0	4.1	4.1	4.1	4.1	4.0	4.0	4.0	4.0
Financial Activities													
2000	9.0	8.9	9.1	9.1	9.2	9.4	9.3	9.4	9.2	9.2	9.1	9.3	9.1
2001	9.0	9.0	9.1	9.3	9.4	9.7	9.7	9.9	9.7	9.6	9.6	9.6	9.5
2002	9.6	9.7	9.7	9.8	10.0	10.3	10.4	10.4	10.3	10.0	9.9	9.9	10.0
2003	9.8	9.8	10.0	10.0	10.1	10.4	10.3	10.4	10.3	10.3	10.2	10.2	10.2
2004	10.2	10.2	10.3	10.3	10.5	10.6	10.6	10.7	10.5	10.4	10.5	10.6	10.5
2005	10.5	10.4	10.6	10.6	10.8	11.0	11.0	11.0	10.9	10.8	10.8	11.0	10.8
2006	10.9	10.9	11.0	11.0	11.1	11.3	11.3	11.3	11.2	11.1	11.2	11.3	11.1
2007	11.0	11.0	11.1	11.2	11.3	11.6	11.6	11.7	11.6	11.5	11.5	11.6	11.4
Professional and Business Services													
2000	13.6	13.8	14.2	14.6	15.0	15.5	15.5	15.4	15.0	14.8	14.6	14.4	14.7
2001	14.9	15.0	15.3	15.8	16.0	16.3	16.4	16.5	15.9	15.6	15.4	15.1	15.7
2002	14.5	14.8	15.0	15.5	15.7	16.2	16.6	16.4	15.7	15.8	15.5	15.2	15.6
2003	14.3	14.5	14.5	15.3	15.7	16.5	16.7	16.8	16.0	16.1	15.2	14.9	15.5
2004	14.3	14.3	14.4	15.2	15.4	16.2	16.4	16.5	15.7	15.6	15.1	14.8	15.3
2005	14.5	14.6	14.9	15.5	15.8	16.6	16.8	17.0	16.4	16.3	15.9	15.6	15.8
2006	15.4	15.7	15.9	16.7	17.3	17.9	18.0	18.1	17.8	17.4	17.2	17.3	17.1
2007	16.8	17.1	17.5	17.9	18.8	19.6	19.6	19.7	19.2	18.9	18.2	17.8	18.4
Education and Health Services													
2000	17.6	17.9	18.1	18.0	18.2	18.3	18.2	18.4	18.3	18.7	18.5	18.7	18.2
2001	18.8	18.9	19.2	19.1	19.2	19.2	19.3	19.6	19.3	19.5	19.8	19.6	19.3
2002	19.3	19.7	19.8	19.7	19.9	20.0	20.0	20.1	20.0	19.9	20.1	20.2	19.9
2003	20.4	20.5	20.4	20.7	20.7	20.9	20.9	20.8	20.9	20.8	21.1	21.1	20.8
2004	21.2	21.1	21.2	21.3	21.2	21.5	21.5	21.7	21.6	21.5	22.0	22.0	21.5
2005	21.7	21.7	21.9	21.8	21.9	22.0	22.1	22.2	22.1	22.2	22.5	22.4	22.0
2006	22.1	22.2	22.5	22.3	22.6	22.8	22.7	22.8	22.7	22.7	23.0	22.8	22.6
2007	22.7	22.9	23.0	22.9	23.1	23.3	23.4	23.3	23.3	23.4	23.8	23.7	23.2
Leisure and Hospitality													
2000	26.2	26.4	26.9	27.0	29.6	35.4	36.7	36.1	32.7	29.0	26.2	27.2	29.9
2001	26.3	26.5	26.9	26.8	29.5	34.5	35.7	35.5	32.2	28.6	26.0	27.2	29.6
2002	26.6	27.0	27.2	27.5	29.9	34.9	36.7	35.9	33.2	29.6	27.1	27.7	30.3
2003	27.5	27.5	27.7	27.8	30.3	35.5	36.8	36.4	33.5	29.8	27.7	28.5	30.8
2004	28.1	28.2	28.8	29.2	30.8	36.0	37.1	36.8	34.0	31.1	28.4	29.4	31.5
2005	28.7	28.9	29.2	29.3	31.3	36.5	38.1	37.6	34.8	31.4	28.7	30.0	32.0
2006	29.3	29.8	30.2	29.6	31.6	37.0	38.4	37.8	35.0	31.8	29.4	31.0	32.6
2007	30.5	31.0	31.3	30.5	32.6	37.4	39.1	38.6	35.9	32.7	30.3	31.8	33.5
Other Services													
2000	8.9	9.0	9.1	9.1	9.2	9.3	9.3	9.3	9.1	9.1	9.1	9.1	9.1
2001	8.8	8.9	9.0	9.1	9.3	9.4	9.4	9.5	9.4	9.4	9.4	9.5	9.3
2002	9.3	9.4	9.5	9.6	9.8	9.8	9.9	9.9	9.7	9.6	9.5	9.6	9.6
2003	9.5	9.5	9.6	9.4	9.6	9.7	9.8	9.8	9.5	9.5	9.5	9.6	9.6
2004	9.5	9.6	9.6	9.7	9.8	9.8	10.0	10.0	9.7	9.6	9.6	9.7	9.7
2005	9.4	9.6	9.6	9.7	9.8	10.0	10.3	10.3	10.1	10.0	10.0	10.2	9.9
2006	10.3	10.4	10.7	10.8	11.1	11.4	11.5	11.5	11.3	11.3	11.3	11.5	11.1
2007	11.3	11.4	11.6	11.6	12.1	12.1	12.0	11.9	11.5	11.4	11.6	11.7	11.7
Government													
2000	60.1	60.6	62.3	62.0	63.6	61.3	56.3	56.5	60.2	62.1	62.0	62.0	60.7
2001	60.8	61.4	62.2	62.0	63.1	63.3	57.4	57.9	61.2	62.7	62.7	63.4	61.5
2002	61.9	62.3	63.4	63.0	64.1	64.1	58.5	58.4	62.7	64.2	64.3	65.1	62.7
2003	63.3	63.7	64.5	64.2	65.2	65.2	59.2	59.1	62.9	64.9	64.5	65.1	63.5
2004	64.2	64.6	65.3	65.5	66.5	66.4	60.8	60.4	63.7	65.6	65.5	65.7	64.5
2005	64.7	65.2	65.8	65.8	67.1	66.6	61.0	61.1	65.1	66.5	66.2	66.4	65.1
2006	64.8	65.6	66.2	66.1	67.1	67.4	61.3	60.9	65.5	66.9	66.5	67.0	65.4
2007	66.1	66.9	67.4	67.4	68.7	68.6	62.3	62.2	67.8	68.7	68.6	68.7	67.0

PART B

METROPOLITAN STATISTICAL AREA (MSA) DATA

MSA DATA NOTES

Employment data is provided for the 100 largest metropolitan statistical areas (MSAs) and New England city and town areas (NECTAs) in the United States from 2000 to 2007 in this part. As mentioned in the technical notes, all areas are MSAs unless otherwise noted. NECTAs are similar to MSAs but are defined by cities and towns rather than counties in the New England states.

According to the 2000 census, the largest MSAs included in this publication ranged in population from 18,323,002 in New York-Northern New Jersey-Long Island, NY-NJ-PA—a population greater than the populations of all but three states—to 443,343 in Deltona-Daytona Beach-Ormond Beach, FL.

Between the 1990 and 2000 decennial censuses, many areas in the west and the south experienced rapid growth. The population of Las Vegas-Paradise, NV, grew the most quickly, increasing by 85.5 percent followed by McAllen-Edingburg-Mission, TX, which grew at a rate of 48.5 percent and Austin-Round Rock, TX at 47.7 percent. Other MSAs that grew fast during this period include Raleigh-Cary, NC (47.3 percent); Boise City-Nampa, ID, (45.4 percent); Phoenix-Mesa-Scottsdale, AZ (45.3 percent); and Atlanta-Sandy Springs-Marietta, GA (38.4 percent). In contrast, Scranton–Wilkes-Barre, PA; Youngstown-Warren-Boardman, OH-PA; Buffalo-Niagra Falls, NY; Pittsburgh, PA; and Syracuse, NY, all experienced declines in their populations during this period. The population declined by 1.5 percent to 2.5 percent in each of these MSAs.

Employment trends were similar for the MSAs and the states from 2000 to 2007. Total nonfarm employ-ment declined in twenty of the MSAs during this period. New Orleans-Metairie-Kenner, LA experienced the sharpest decline in employment, decreasing 16.4 percent. Employment declined in every major industry that data is available for. Total nonfarm employment declined by 130,500 from August of 2005, when Hurricane Katrina made landfall, to September 2005. San Jose-Sunnyvale-Santa Clara, CA and Detroit-Warren-Livonia, MI also suffered from significant declines in employment from 2000 to 2007, dropping 13.0 percent and 11.0 percent respectively. Education and health services and leisure and hospitality were among the few industries that did not decline in employment in either of these MSAs.

While total nonfarm employment grew in the majority of the MSAs, manufacturing employment declined in all but six. The increase in employment was only significant in in Las Vegas-Paradise, NV, where manufacturing employment grew 32.7 percent and in Bakersfield, CA, which experienced a 23.1 percent increase. In the remaining four MSAs, manufacturing employment increased by less than 2.5 percent. Employment in education and health services, professional and business services, and leisure and hospitality grew rapidly in many MSAs from 2000 to 2007.

In 2007, unemployment rates ranged from a low of 2.5 percent in Honolulu, HI to a high of 8.8 percent in Modesto, CA. Washington-Arlington-Alexandria, DC-VA-MD-WV had the lowest unemployment rate at 3.0 percent among all MSAs with a population of one million or more according to the 2000 census. Detroit-Warren-Livonia, MI had the highest at 7.7 percent, followed by Riverside-San Bernardino-Ontario, CA and Cleveland-Elyria-Mentor, OH at 5.9 percent.

Employment by Industry: New York-Northern New Jersey-Long Island, NY-NJ-PA, 2000–2007

(Numbers in thousands, not seasonally adjusted.)

Industry and year	January	February	March	April	May	June	July	August	September	October	November	December	Annual Average
Total Nonfarm													
2000	8,165.3	8,197.9	8,279.1	8,357.8	8,417.7	8,491.0	8,403.0	8,353.9	8,404.8	8,485.3	8,545.4	8,604.6	8,392.2
2001	8,321.7	8,341.6	8,396.7	8,415.6	8,468.9	8,528.3	8,446.6	8,395.7	8,353.5	8,341.2	8,390.4	8,418.7	8,401.6
2002	8,134.3	8,165.3	8,223.3	8,252.4	8,311.8	8,356.4	8,268.0	8,232.9	8,239.2	8,316.4	8,373.5	8,407.8	8,273.4
2003	8,130.5	8,137.6	8,185.0	8,211.9	8,268.6	8,313.4	8,250.8	8,210.0	8,233.0	8,311.6	8,362.4	8,396.8	8,251.0
2004	8,092.7	8,122.4	8,201.5	8,239.8	8,312.0	8,376.6	8,323.8	8,280.1	8,294.3	8,366.1	8,413.8	8,462.5	8,290.5
2005	8,166.0	8,186.5	8,239.1	8,326.8	8,374.1	8,448.5	8,373.6	8,341.4	8,373.2	8,400.8	8,471.3	8,502.0	8,350.3
2006	8,260.0	8,281.3	8,358.3	8,400.6	8,474.7	8,551.1	8,465.2	8,428.3	8,464.1	8,531.4	8,600.3	8,662.1	8,456.5
2007	8,393.5	8,412.3	8,473.7	8,532.0	8,607.9	8,690.4	8,608.3	8,556.1	8,581.5	8,647.6	8,698.0	8,737.4	8,578.2
Total Private													
2000	6,948.0	6,977.0	7,045.9	7,111.3	7,157.8	7,244.5	7,166.1	7,156.5	7,207.1	7,248.6	7,302.3	7,358.6	7,160.3
2001	7,094.2	7,111.4	7,158.2	7,168.4	7,227.0	7,284.3	7,197.3	7,172.5	7,145.1	7,097.0	7,129.9	7,153.8	7,161.6
2002	6,882.4	6,905.0	6,955.1	6,987.3	7,040.6	7,083.8	7,018.0	7,009.3	7,013.0	7,057.8	7,098.5	7,128.3	7,014.9
2003	6,867.5	6,861.2	6,904.9	6,931.3	6,988.3	7,031.7	6,991.8	6,978.3	6,999.9	7,037.3	7,075.2	7,106.8	6,981.2
2004	6,831.1	6,846.9	6,918.6	6,958.2	7,027.0	7,087.1	7,059.3	7,042.5	7,054.8	7,089.0	7,124.4	7,172.9	7,017.7
2005	6,893.7	6,903.5	6,953.2	7,033.9	7,079.9	7,146.8	7,096.6	7,091.5	7,119.0	7,119.6	7,176.1	7,203.8	7,068.1
2006	6,981.7	6,993.1	7,066.0	7,107.1	7,178.8	7,252.9	7,195.1	7,185.1	7,208.5	7,244.0	7,300.4	7,355.6	7,172.4
2007	7,106.9	7,113.3	7,170.0	7,230.2	7,300.9	7,379.9	7,323.0	7,295.9	7,309.1	7,344.0	7,382.8	7,416.8	7,281.1
Goods-Producing													
2000	925.5	929.5	946.6	958.9	967.9	979.9	962.2	970.0	977.6	977.1	976.7	971.1	961.9
2001	912.7	917.5	926.2	933.8	942.5	951.2	931.7	935.4	930.1	926.5	919.9	910.9	928.2
2002	861.0	863.0	870.1	878.9	886.8	891.9	883.4	889.2	888.9	885.5	879.8	871.3	879.2
2003	828.8	824.8	832.5	842.1	852.5	858.6	851.8	855.0	856.8	851.9	849.2	843.1	845.6
2004	801.0	801.8	816.5	823.6	835.1	846.9	843.2	846.8	848.3	843.3	840.2	836.2	831.9
2005	791.4	788.7	796.5	810.4	819.5	828.6	822.7	829.3	831.7	822.9	825.4	821.3	815.7
2006	788.8	788.8	799.0	811.6	821.6	831.2	824.1	829.3	830.8	827.9	825.1	821.2	816.6
2007	790.0	783.6	792.3	808.3	820.1	830.5	825.2	827.7	826.8	823.1	819.5	813.0	813.3
Natural Resources, Mining, and Construction													
2000	292.0	290.4	303.6	314.3	322.1	329.0	328.0	331.7	335.2	336.0	337.5	335.1	321.2
2001	303.9	305.0	312.5	327.0	335.6	341.6	340.3	342.0	338.6	343.7	342.5	339.4	331.0
2002	309.6	310.0	315.3	326.7	332.3	337.3	340.7	343.7	342.6	342.2	339.8	334.9	331.3
2003	306.5	301.6	308.8	321.6	331.4	336.2	339.1	340.3	340.3	338.3	336.6	331.9	327.7
2004	303.5	301.9	313.3	324.8	333.9	342.0	345.2	347.7	347.6	345.0	343.2	340.1	332.4
2005	309.6	305.5	311.6	328.6	337.2	344.0	345.3	350.4	351.9	344.7	348.1	343.9	335.1
2006	320.4	320.2	329.2	342.8	351.1	358.7	359.7	364.6	365.3	363.3	361.6	359.9	349.7
2007	336.4	330.3	338.5	355.3	366.3	375.0	374.8	377.4	375.9	374.8	372.4	368.0	362.1
Manufacturing													
2000	633.5	639.1	643.0	644.6	645.8	650.9	634.2	638.3	642.4	641.1	639.2	636.0	640.7
2001	608.8	612.5	613.7	606.8	606.9	609.6	591.4	593.4	591.5	582.8	577.4	571.5	597.2
2002	551.4	553.0	554.8	552.2	554.5	554.6	542.7	545.5	546.3	543.3	540.0	536.4	547.9
2003	522.3	523.2	523.7	520.5	521.1	522.4	512.7	514.7	516.5	513.6	512.6	511.2	517.9
2004	497.5	499.9	503.2	498.8	501.2	504.9	498.0	499.1	500.7	498.3	497.0	496.1	499.6
2005	481.8	483.2	484.9	481.8	482.3	484.6	477.4	478.9	479.8	478.2	477.3	477.4	480.6
2006	468.4	468.6	469.8	468.8	470.5	472.5	464.4	464.7	465.5	464.6	463.5	461.3	466.9
2007	453.6	453.3	453.8	453.0	453.8	455.5	450.4	450.3	450.9	448.3	447.1	445.0	451.3
Service-Providing													
2000	7,239.8	7,268.4	7,332.5	7,398.9	7,449.8	7,511.1	7,440.8	7,383.9	7,427.2	7,508.2	7,568.7	7,633.5	7,430.2
2001	7,409.0	7,424.1	7,470.5	7,481.8	7,526.4	7,577.1	7,514.9	7,460.3	7,423.4	7,414.7	7,470.5	7,507.8	7,473.4
2002	7,273.3	7,302.3	7,352.2	7,373.5	7,425.0	7,464.5	7,384.6	7,343.7	7,350.3	7,430.9	7,493.7	7,536.5	7,394.2
2003	7,301.7	7,312.8	7,352.5	7,369.8	7,416.1	7,454.8	7,399.0	7,355.0	7,376.2	7,459.7	7,513.2	7,553.7	7,405.4
2004	7,291.7	7,320.6	7,385.0	7,416.2	7,476.9	7,529.7	7,480.6	7,433.3	7,446.0	7,522.8	7,573.6	7,626.3	7,458.6
2005	7,374.6	7,397.8	7,442.6	7,516.4	7,554.6	7,619.9	7,550.9	7,512.1	7,541.5	7,577.9	7,645.9	7,680.7	7,534.6
2006	7,471.2	7,492.5	7,559.3	7,589.0	7,653.1	7,719.9	7,641.1	7,599.0	7,633.3	7,703.5	7,775.2	7,840.9	7,639.8
2007	7,603.5	7,628.7	7,681.4	7,723.7	7,787.8	7,859.9	7,783.1	7,728.4	7,754.7	7,824.5	7,878.5	7,924.4	7,764.9
Trade, Transportation, and Utilities													
2000	1,609.5	1,595.1	1,603.6	1,610.0	1,616.6	1,634.0	1,605.6	1,607.4	1,625.8	1,643.8	1,678.2	1,713.3	1,628.6
2001	1,634.3	1,613.7	1,615.5	1,609.8	1,619.4	1,631.3	1,600.4	1,593.2	1,601.2	1,602.5	1,623.9	1,648.9	1,616.2
2002	1,573.2	1,557.0	1,567.6	1,562.8	1,570.9	1,586.7	1,561.1	1,557.3	1,577.6	1,590.1	1,618.0	1,648.7	1,580.9
2003	1,574.5	1,558.9	1,563.2	1,557.4	1,568.2	1,579.9	1,557.3	1,555.6	1,573.3	1,589.7	1,614.6	1,640.8	1,577.8
2004	1,561.8	1,549.0	1,558.4	1,555.2	1,572.2	1,588.6	1,570.1	1,567.7	1,582.7	1,600.1	1,625.2	1,653.7	1,582.1
2005	1,567.5	1,552.8	1,557.5	1,566.9	1,578.5	1,593.2	1,570.5	1,568.7	1,584.8	1,591.6	1,622.1	1,645.4	1,583.3
2006	1,582.5	1,561.3	1,569.9	1,572.4	1,586.6	1,603.5	1,580.8	1,576.4	1,592.8	1,610.9	1,646.0	1,677.2	1,596.7
2007	1,604.9	1,583.8	1,589.6	1,594.1	1,611.2	1,630.9	1,604.3	1,595.4	1,612.9	1,627.8	1,654.5	1,680.9	1,615.9
Wholesale Trade													
2000	440.0	441.5	444.1	443.7	444.6	448.2	443.9	445.2	446.6	447.6	448.6	451.6	445.5
2001	452.4	454.0	454.9	450.2	450.3	451.9	447.7	446.8	446.0	444.3	443.5	443.9	448.8
2002	434.5	435.1	437.5	432.3	432.6	433.5	429.3	430.3	431.1	432.8	433.5	435.0	433.1
2003	431.8	432.1	433.4	430.9	432.2	433.6	431.9	431.2	431.2	431.7	432.7	434.1	432.2
2004	425.4	426.4	428.9	427.9	429.3	432.2	432.1	431.8	431.5	432.9	433.2	435.1	430.6
2005	424.5	425.6	426.5	427.5	428.8	430.9	428.6	429.5	430.6	430.5	431.6	434.9	429.1
2006	425.3	425.6	427.5	429.4	431.7	434.5	432.9	432.6	432.4	434.4	435.4	438.4	431.7
2007	431.4	431.2	432.2	434.1	434.8	438.0	435.1	434.1	433.3	434.2	434.9	437.2	434.2
Retail Trade													
2000	833.7	817.9	822.9	828.1	833.2	845.1	830.7	834.5	837.0	847.1	879.6	910.0	843.3
2001	841.7	819.1	820.1	821.0	826.3	837.0	822.4	822.5	819.1	822.5	850.5	877.1	831.6
2002	819.5	802.6	810.3	810.2	816.8	830.6	820.2	820.3	823.9	830.6	859.0	887.9	827.7
2003	825.2	810.3	811.5	813.3	820.6	830.5	821.6	823.0	823.0	837.0	860.6	883.8	830.2
2004	823.2	810.9	815.5	816.1	827.5	839.5	834.6	834.7	835.6	847.2	872.0	897.6	837.9
2005	836.1	820.4	822.1	829.3	836.8	847.0	840.8	840.6	839.1	845.7	872.2	891.2	843.4
2006	843.8	822.7	828.0	829.3	836.7	848.4	843.6	842.0	839.6	854.6	886.1	907.7	848.5
2007	855.8	835.4	838.9	842.2	853.0	866.4	860.8	856.6	855.4	865.0	892.4	914.7	861.4

Employment by Industry: New York-Northern New Jersey-Long Island, NY-NJ-PA, 2000–2007—*Continued*

(Numbers in thousands, not seasonally adjusted.)

Industry and year	January	February	March	April	May	June	July	August	September	October	November	December	Annual Average
Transportation and Utilities													
2000	335.1	335.0	336.0	337.6	338.3	340.2	330.4	327.4	341.6	348.8	349.8	351.2	339.3
2001	340.6	341.0	340.9	338.9	343.1	342.7	330.6	324.2	336.5	336.0	330.2	328.2	336.1
2002	319.4	319.5	320.0	320.5	321.7	322.8	311.8	306.9	322.8	326.9	325.7	326.0	320.3
2003	317.5	316.5	318.3	313.2	315.4	315.8	303.8	301.4	317.1	321.0	321.3	322.9	315.4
2004	313.2	312.6	314.0	311.2	315.4	316.9	303.4	301.2	315.6	320.0	320.0	321.0	313.7
2005	306.9	306.8	308.9	310.1	312.9	315.3	301.1	298.6	315.1	315.4	318.3	319.3	310.7
2006	313.4	313.0	314.4	313.7	318.2	320.6	304.3	301.8	320.8	321.9	324.5	331.1	316.5
2007	317.7	317.2	318.5	317.8	323.4	326.5	308.4	304.7	324.2	328.6	327.2	329.0	320.3
Information													
2000	317.9	321.1	323.8	326.8	330.1	335.1	334.4	316.4	337.1	338.9	342.6	343.3	330.6
2001	348.3	351.4	352.0	349.6	351.8	351.9	348.0	345.0	341.0	338.2	342.2	339.4	346.6
2002	321.0	324.3	319.8	316.7	322.9	320.5	310.2	312.6	307.4	308.1	312.1	310.3	315.5
2003	296.3	299.3	296.3	293.2	297.8	295.0	292.3	296.2	292.6	294.4	298.4	296.7	295.7
2004	286.4	286.2	288.1	286.7	287.6	287.5	286.6	288.4	288.4	288.3	290.8	290.4	288.0
2005	282.4	284.1	284.9	284.1	286.2	291.0	288.6	289.7	289.7	290.1	292.1	292.5	288.0
2006	287.0	287.7	289.3	287.0	289.1	292.2	290.9	291.9	291.0	287.9	289.9	291.7	289.6
2007	284.9	287.0	287.2	287.0	289.1	291.5	289.5	290.4	290.0	291.3	292.9	294.1	289.6
Financial Activities													
2000	809.1	811.3	812.7	812.8	814.7	828.6	825.4	825.7	820.1	817.6	819.4	824.5	818.5
2001	807.3	807.0	808.3	804.7	805.0	815.1	815.0	811.0	801.1	773.0	774.4	777.8	800.0
2002	774.9	774.0	773.1	768.8	768.9	776.2	777.5	775.7	767.5	766.8	766.9	770.1	771.7
2003	764.8	762.8	762.4	760.4	762.7	770.0	773.8	772.6	765.7	764.0	765.4	770.2	766.2
2004	759.5	760.4	762.3	763.0	764.4	773.3	780.5	779.5	771.2	774.8	776.0	781.6	770.5
2005	768.0	767.7	770.3	774.4	774.1	784.3	791.0	791.3	784.1	783.2	785.2	786.7	780.0
2006	776.4	778.3	781.3	783.6	786.7	797.6	801.7	802.4	794.4	793.8	795.8	800.7	791.1
2007	788.5	789.9	791.6	793.8	794.4	805.9	808.7	804.8	796.8	795.9	796.4	798.2	797.1
Professional and Business Services													
2000	1,220.5	1,233.7	1,250.9	1,268.3	1,277.5	1,300.1	1,293.7	1,301.6	1,299.2	1,301.0	1,306.9	1,315.3	1,280.7
2001	1,283.0	1,290.5	1,300.1	1,298.4	1,300.8	1,313.4	1,302.0	1,297.8	1,288.6	1,263.5	1,262.3	1,258.6	1,288.3
2002	1,211.5	1,216.3	1,227.4	1,238.9	1,241.0	1,249.2	1,240.9	1,243.0	1,237.9	1,243.9	1,247.3	1,248.2	1,237.1
2003	1,194.3	1,191.5	1,204.1	1,213.6	1,217.2	1,228.7	1,226.5	1,229.7	1,229.6	1,234.4	1,237.7	1,242.6	1,220.8
2004	1,188.2	1,192.6	1,209.1	1,224.1	1,229.7	1,242.0	1,238.5	1,239.4	1,235.3	1,238.6	1,244.8	1,252.6	1,227.9
2005	1,204.6	1,205.7	1,215.0	1,239.0	1,240.6	1,257.6	1,254.2	1,257.7	1,256.7	1,255.1	1,262.4	1,263.0	1,242.6
2006	1,222.4	1,230.3	1,247.8	1,258.7	1,267.5	1,287.6	1,284.9	1,290.2	1,284.7	1,288.9	1,297.6	1,304.9	1,272.1
2007	1,256.3	1,260.8	1,276.3	1,291.7	1,300.2	1,320.5	1,319.9	1,321.8	1,311.4	1,316.7	1,320.3	1,321.7	1,301.5
Education and Health Services													
2000	1,225.4	1,238.1	1,246.4	1,249.9	1,247.8	1,236.3	1,218.1	1,212.4	1,238.4	1,265.3	1,272.9	1,281.5	1,244.4
2001	1,242.3	1,258.2	1,270.6	1,272.7	1,279.6	1,270.8	1,251.0	1,245.0	1,262.7	1,292.6	1,303.8	1,309.8	1,271.6
2002	1,278.1	1,298.8	1,310.4	1,314.1	1,319.6	1,306.0	1,291.9	1,283.6	1,305.2	1,334.8	1,345.1	1,347.0	1,311.2
2003	1,320.8	1,333.0	1,344.9	1,344.6	1,346.1	1,333.1	1,316.6	1,305.0	1,329.9	1,357.1	1,365.3	1,366.6	1,338.6
2004	1,333.9	1,350.9	1,364.3	1,362.1	1,367.5	1,351.8	1,335.4	1,324.3	1,344.2	1,376.7	1,383.9	1,389.3	1,357.0
2005	1,352.9	1,371.9	1,381.6	1,387.8	1,387.3	1,371.1	1,353.5	1,344.3	1,374.0	1,401.3	1,410.9	1,414.1	1,379.2
2006	1,387.5	1,405.6	1,417.3	1,420.1	1,423.1	1,408.0	1,383.0	1,373.7	1,406.3	1,438.3	1,447.9	1,456.6	1,414.0
2007	1,421.6	1,440.3	1,450.9	1,451.3	1,452.1	1,438.3	1,413.9	1,401.4	1,435.1	1,464.9	1,474.7	1,478.7	1,443.6
Leisure and Hospitality													
2000	515.5	521.4	532.0	552.3	568.9	593.1	590.5	589.6	575.6	569.9	569.4	571.7	562.5
2001	537.3	542.1	551.7	562.8	587.5	606.4	606.5	604.9	584.2	563.6	564.2	567.5	573.2
2002	527.5	534.5	547.0	567.1	587.0	607.2	607.9	605.6	588.8	584.4	583.1	585.3	577.1
2003	549.5	551.3	559.4	576.8	597.8	617.6	624.6	617.2	605.2	596.6	594.1	594.5	590.4
2004	560.2	563.1	574.8	592.4	615.5	638.4	646.2	639.3	627.5	611.1	606.3	609.5	607.0
2005	570.6	573.8	586.1	606.3	626.2	649.7	651.1	647.2	634.9	614.1	614.5	613.7	615.7
2006	580.6	583.2	599.7	613.9	640.3	664.2	667.6	661.6	647.3	636.0	635.6	637.5	630.6
2007	600.6	605.5	616.9	637.3	662.4	686.5	687.9	683.5	664.8	652.5	650.9	654.5	650.3
Other Services													
2000	324.6	326.8	329.9	332.3	334.3	337.4	336.2	333.4	333.3	335.0	336.2	337.9	333.1
2001	329.0	331.0	333.8	336.6	340.4	344.2	342.7	340.2	336.2	337.1	339.2	340.9	337.6
2002	335.2	337.1	339.7	340.0	343.5	346.1	345.1	342.3	339.7	344.2	346.2	347.4	342.2
2003	338.5	339.6	342.1	343.2	346.0	348.8	348.9	347.0	346.8	349.2	350.5	352.3	346.1
2004	340.1	342.0	345.1	351.1	355.0	358.6	358.8	357.1	357.2	356.1	357.2	359.6	353.2
2005	356.3	358.8	361.3	365.0	367.5	371.3	365.0	363.3	363.1	361.3	363.5	367.1	363.6
2006	356.5	357.9	361.7	359.8	363.9	368.6	362.1	359.6	361.2	360.3	362.5	365.8	361.7
2007	360.1	362.4	365.2	366.7	371.4	375.8	373.6	370.9	371.3	371.8	373.6	375.7	369.9
Government													
2000	1,217.3	1,220.9	1,233.2	1,246.5	1,259.9	1,246.5	1,236.9	1,197.4	1,197.7	1,236.7	1,243.1	1,246.0	1,231.8
2001	1,227.5	1,230.2	1,238.5	1,247.2	1,241.9	1,244.0	1,249.3	1,223.2	1,208.4	1,244.2	1,260.5	1,264.9	1,240.0
2002	1,251.9	1,260.3	1,267.2	1,265.1	1,271.2	1,272.6	1,250.0	1,223.6	1,226.2	1,258.6	1,275.0	1,279.5	1,258.4
2003	1,263.0	1,276.4	1,280.1	1,280.6	1,280.3	1,281.7	1,259.0	1,231.7	1,233.1	1,274.3	1,287.2	1,290.0	1,269.8
2004	1,261.6	1,275.5	1,282.9	1,281.6	1,285.0	1,289.5	1,264.5	1,237.6	1,239.5	1,277.1	1,289.4	1,289.6	1,272.8
2005	1,272.3	1,283.0	1,285.9	1,292.9	1,294.2	1,301.7	1,277.0	1,249.9	1,254.2	1,281.2	1,295.2	1,298.2	1,282.1
2006	1,278.3	1,288.2	1,292.3	1,293.5	1,295.9	1,298.2	1,270.1	1,243.2	1,255.6	1,287.4	1,299.9	1,306.5	1,284.1
2007	1,286.6	1,299.0	1,303.7	1,301.8	1,307.0	1,310.5	1,285.3	1,260.2	1,272.4	1,303.6	1,315.2	1,320.6	1,297.2

Employment by Industry: Los Angeles-Long Beach-Santa Ana, CA, 2000–2007

(Numbers in thousands, not seasonally adjusted.)

Industry and year	January	February	March	April	May	June	July	August	September	October	November	December	Annual Average
Total Nonfarm													
2000	5,343.5	5,395.6	5,437.4	5,446.6	5,475.9	5,477.2	5,425.2	5,440.1	5,490.0	5,499.1	5,534.6	5,566.3	5,461.0
2001	5,471.1	5,503.6	5,546.2	5,518.1	5,515.8	5,522.8	5,430.9	5,438.0	5,459.8	5,471.6	5,474.8	5,494.6	5,487.3
2002	5,364.4	5,393.5	5,442.0	5,436.3	5,453.6	5,456.5	5,374.3	5,389.1	5,427.0	5,455.5	5,481.4	5,492.1	5,430.5
2003	5,366.4	5,390.2	5,419.1	5,410.3	5,425.1	5,425.1	5,366.6	5,376.4	5,392.4	5,442.0	5,454.0	5,473.3	5,411.7
2004	5,378.2	5,408.8	5,443.7	5,447.4	5,469.7	5,467.5	5,429.9	5,415.9	5,439.9	5,493.3	5,522.7	5,528.8	5,453.8
2005	5,417.9	5,452.7	5,481.9	5,498.8	5,510.0	5,523.8	5,477.6	5,487.7	5,531.4	5,566.2	5,603.0	5,630.6	5,515.1
2006	5,519.6	5,566.8	5,597.4	5,597.5	5,613.8	5,635.0	5,576.8	5,581.3	5,619.9	5,652.9	5,675.2	5,700.9	5,611.4
2007	5,578.4	5,615.7	5,644.1	5,628.3	5,641.5	5,659.4	5,606.9	5,595.2	5,628.3	5,639.9	5,650.6	5,656.5	5,628.7
Total Private													
2000	4,625.3	4,667.5	4,700.9	4,707.1	4,716.9	4,743.3	4,727.4	4,751.7	4,772.4	4,767.8	4,792.4	4,824.8	4,733.1
2001	4,730.8	4,755.7	4,787.5	4,758.2	4,753.9	4,758.8	4,713.5	4,723.9	4,721.8	4,713.0	4,711.6	4,728.7	4,738.1
2002	4,605.3	4,630.1	4,667.9	4,662.9	4,677.1	4,682.9	4,644.1	4,667.4	4,677.5	4,687.5	4,708.3	4,720.6	4,669.3
2003	4,603.6	4,623.7	4,645.3	4,641.7	4,657.0	4,658.0	4,632.6	4,660.0	4,660.6	4,693.0	4,700.8	4,723.0	4,658.2
2004	4,631.2	4,660.5	4,688.9	4,693.8	4,714.9	4,714.8	4,711.8	4,715.1	4,716.0	4,752.0	4,775.6	4,785.2	4,713.3
2005	4,679.6	4,707.2	4,731.7	4,751.0	4,759.8	4,773.7	4,762.5	4,781.7	4,806.8	4,824.4	4,853.3	4,882.2	4,776.2
2006	4,778.2	4,818.1	4,842.7	4,843.5	4,857.3	4,878.7	4,852.1	4,869.3	4,886.5	4,899.9	4,914.9	4,942.4	4,865.3
2007	4,826.8	4,857.9	4,880.2	4,866.0	4,877.2	4,894.9	4,876.8	4,875.3	4,887.2	4,880.3	4,883.1	4,891.0	4,874.7
Goods-Producing													
2000	1,024.7	1,032.4	1,041.7	1,039.4	1,041.8	1,052.9	1,043.0	1,044.0	1,048.7	1,038.3	1,037.9	1,043.5	1,040.7
2001	1,023.2	1,025.1	1,030.5	1,023.7	1,022.0	1,022.6	1,007.6	1,007.5	1,001.1	988.0	977.5	971.3	1,008.3
2002	945.4	950.0	956.4	950.1	952.0	953.0	937.7	941.4	940.9	934.7	931.6	929.0	943.5
2003	910.7	909.9	913.4	907.6	910.0	912.6	901.8	905.3	904.2	900.5	899.7	901.9	906.4
2004	892.2	895.9	902.7	903.4	905.8	910.8	909.2	908.6	909.3	906.8	901.4	899.2	903.8
2005	884.9	893.2	898.1	904.2	908.0	912.4	913.9	916.4	918.2	915.1	913.9	913.2	907.6
2006	902.2	910.3	914.2	913.2	915.5	921.0	916.5	918.3	919.4	912.4	908.7	905.8	913.1
2007	890.0	895.7	900.0	896.1	897.4	903.2	899.3	895.8	892.4	886.4	884.0	879.3	893.3
Natural Resources and Mining													
2000	4.0	4.0	4.0	3.9	4.0	4.0	3.9	3.9	4.0	4.0	3.9	4.3	4.0
2001	4.5	4.4	4.4	4.4	4.4	4.4	4.4	4.4	4.4	4.4	4.4	4.4	4.4
2002	4.4	4.4	4.4	4.1	4.2	4.2	4.2	4.2	4.2	4.2	4.4	4.4	4.3
2003	4.3	4.4	4.4	4.3	4.3	4.3	4.3	4.4	4.2	4.4	4.4	4.4	4.3
2004	4.3	4.3	4.4	4.4	4.3	4.4	4.3	4.3	4.3	4.6	4.6	4.6	4.4
2005	4.5	4.5	4.5	4.3	4.3	4.3	4.4	4.4	4.4	4.3	4.4	4.4	4.4
2006	4.5	4.5	4.5	4.5	4.6	4.7	4.7	4.7	4.7	4.7	4.7	4.7	4.6
2007	4.9	5.0	5.0	4.9	5.0	5.0	5.0	5.0	5.0	5.0	5.1	5.1	5.0
Construction													
2000	198.3	199.1	202.1	203.3	206.6	211.6	208.8	212.9	215.2	214.4	215.0	216.5	208.7
2001	208.7	209.3	212.1	213.5	216.9	220.3	221.2	225.3	223.9	221.9	219.2	217.8	217.4
2002	208.8	209.5	211.8	209.7	211.7	213.2	212.5	217.9	218.2	217.3	216.6	216.5	213.7
2003	210.3	208.2	211.3	212.3	216.3	219.8	220.0	223.6	223.9	224.1	224.2	225.2	218.2
2004	221.9	222.1	224.7	228.2	230.4	234.1	236.6	239.2	240.5	238.7	236.2	235.3	232.3
2005	226.2	232.9	236.3	241.8	246.4	250.7	254.9	258.5	259.4	259.2	258.8	258.3	248.6
2006	253.9	257.0	259.1	260.0	263.5	267.3	267.9	271.0	272.0	267.9	265.6	264.2	264.1
2007	255.1	257.9	261.6	260.3	262.2	266.1	267.1	266.7	264.7	259.2	256.9	253.3	260.9
Manufacturing													
2000	822.4	829.3	835.6	832.2	831.2	837.3	830.3	827.2	829.5	819.9	819.0	822.7	828.1
2001	810.0	811.4	814.0	805.8	800.7	797.9	782.0	777.8	772.8	761.7	753.9	749.1	786.4
2002	732.2	736.1	740.2	736.3	736.1	735.6	721.0	719.3	718.5	713.2	710.6	708.1	725.6
2003	696.1	697.3	697.7	691.0	689.4	688.5	677.5	677.3	676.1	672.0	671.1	672.3	683.8
2004	666.0	669.5	673.6	670.8	671.1	672.3	668.3	665.1	664.5	663.5	660.6	659.3	667.1
2005	654.2	655.8	657.3	658.1	657.3	657.4	654.6	653.5	654.4	651.6	650.7	650.5	654.6
2006	643.8	648.8	650.6	648.7	647.4	649.0	643.9	642.6	642.7	639.8	638.4	636.9	644.4
2007	630.0	632.8	633.4	630.9	630.2	632.1	627.2	624.1	622.7	622.2	622.0	620.9	627.4
Service-Providing													
2000	4,318.8	4,363.2	4,395.7	4,407.2	4,434.1	4,424.3	4,382.2	4,396.1	4,441.3	4,460.8	4,496.7	4,522.8	4,420.3
2001	4,447.9	4,478.5	4,515.7	4,494.4	4,493.8	4,500.2	4,423.3	4,430.5	4,458.7	4,483.6	4,497.3	4,523.3	4,478.9
2002	4,419.0	4,443.5	4,485.6	4,486.2	4,501.6	4,503.5	4,436.6	4,447.7	4,486.1	4,520.8	4,549.8	4,563.1	4,487.0
2003	4,455.7	4,480.3	4,505.7	4,502.7	4,515.1	4,512.5	4,464.8	4,471.1	4,488.2	4,541.5	4,554.3	4,571.4	4,505.2
2004	4,486.0	4,512.9	4,541.0	4,544.0	4,563.9	4,556.7	4,520.7	4,507.3	4,530.6	4,586.5	4,621.3	4,629.6	4,550.0
2005	4,533.0	4,559.5	4,583.8	4,594.6	4,602.0	4,611.4	4,563.7	4,571.3	4,613.2	4,651.1	4,689.1	4,717.4	4,607.5
2006	4,617.4	4,656.5	4,683.2	4,684.3	4,698.3	4,714.0	4,660.3	4,663.0	4,700.5	4,740.5	4,766.5	4,795.1	4,698.3
2007	4,688.4	4,720.0	4,744.1	4,732.2	4,744.1	4,756.2	4,707.6	4,699.4	4,735.9	4,753.5	4,766.6	4,777.2	4,735.4
Trade, Transportation, and Utilities													
2000	1,032.7	1,030.6	1,032.3	1,028.6	1,030.7	1,037.3	1,036.0	1,040.6	1,044.5	1,052.7	1,070.3	1,089.7	1,043.8
2001	1,060.1	1,052.3	1,055.5	1,050.5	1,049.7	1,054.1	1,046.4	1,046.8	1,048.5	1,049.0	1,060.0	1,076.6	1,054.1
2002	1,035.6	1,030.0	1,032.4	1,034.2	1,038.3	1,041.1	1,039.1	1,042.4	1,046.3	1,047.8	1,065.6	1,086.5	1,045.2
2003	1,039.4	1,033.5	1,033.8	1,029.6	1,031.9	1,035.7	1,029.7	1,030.6	1,035.2	1,050.6	1,056.6	1,072.1	1,039.8
2004	1,030.3	1,026.3	1,031.6	1,034.5	1,039.2	1,045.2	1,042.1	1,043.2	1,044.9	1,055.4	1,076.3	1,088.3	1,046.4
2005	1,054.3	1,048.0	1,047.6	1,048.1	1,051.3	1,056.3	1,059.7	1,062.6	1,066.3	1,075.7	1,096.0	1,116.6	1,065.2
2006	1,074.5	1,069.6	1,073.4	1,070.9	1,073.9	1,079.3	1,080.1	1,084.5	1,088.6	1,095.7	1,117.4	1,134.8	1,086.9
2007	1,094.2	1,085.3	1,083.2	1,083.9	1,086.8	1,092.0	1,096.5	1,094.7	1,097.7	1,101.7	1,113.1	1,123.3	1,096.0
Wholesale Trade													
2000	298.3	299.7	300.4	298.3	298.3	299.5	299.9	300.5	300.8	300.9	301.1	302.0	300.0
2001	302.7	304.9	305.3	304.9	303.7	305.8	303.4	302.0	301.7	302.6	300.8	301.4	303.3
2002	296.1	297.5	299.5	299.2	299.5	300.5	300.0	300.5	301.1	300.1	300.7	302.0	299.7
2003	297.8	298.4	299.1	297.9	297.9	298.7	296.7	296.5	296.5	295.8	295.1	296.7	297.2
2004	294.3	295.3	297.1	297.0	297.7	299.5	298.0	297.1	296.7	299.0	299.3	299.2	297.5
2005	297.9	298.8	299.9	301.7	302.6	303.4	302.6	302.6	302.8	303.9	304.1	306.7	302.3
2006	303.5	305.7	307.0	307.5	308.5	309.9	310.3	310.3	311.4	311.9	312.2	314.5	309.4
2007	313.2	314.7	316.1	316.0	316.5	317.7	317.6	316.7	318.2	318.6	317.8	317.4	316.7

Employment by Industry: Los Angeles-Long Beach-Santa Ana, CA, 2000–2007—*Continued*

(Numbers in thousands, not seasonally adjusted.)

Industry and year	January	February	March	April	May	June	July	August	September	October	November	December	Annual Average
Retail Trade													
2000	532.9	528.6	529.5	526.4	528.2	533.3	533.0	536.1	539.0	543.4	560.5	578.3	539.1
2001	549.5	540.5	541.3	536.5	537.7	540.8	537.2	539.6	540.7	541.8	558.3	575.1	544.9
2002	545.3	536.9	540.0	539.1	541.9	546.5	543.5	545.1	548.6	551.4	569.0	587.4	549.6
2003	549.1	542.9	543.0	540.9	543.1	546.3	543.5	545.5	547.9	564.6	571.3	587.2	552.1
2004	548.9	544.2	546.2	548.6	552.3	556.1	554.0	556.1	556.4	561.7	581.9	596.7	558.6
2005	566.7	558.9	558.6	556.1	559.0	563.2	566.8	570.2	573.3	579.7	600.4	617.4	572.5
2006	580.6	572.7	574.5	571.9	573.5	576.6	576.6	580.8	581.9	588.2	608.6	622.7	584.1
2007	587.4	576.9	576.5	573.8	576.3	580.1	583.5	584.5	582.6	585.5	597.1	606.6	584.2
Transportation and Utilities													
2000	201.5	202.3	202.4	203.9	204.2	204.5	203.1	204.0	204.7	208.4	208.7	209.4	204.8
2001	207.9	206.9	208.9	209.1	208.3	207.5	205.8	205.2	206.1	204.6	200.9	200.1	205.9
2002	194.2	195.6	192.9	195.9	196.9	197.1	195.6	196.8	196.6	196.3	195.9	197.1	195.9
2003	192.5	192.2	191.7	190.8	190.9	190.7	189.5	188.6	190.8	190.2	190.2	188.2	190.5
2004	187.1	186.8	188.3	188.9	189.2	189.6	190.1	190.0	191.8	194.7	195.1	192.4	190.3
2005	189.7	190.3	189.1	190.3	189.7	189.7	190.3	189.8	190.2	192.1	191.5	192.5	190.4
2006	190.4	191.2	191.9	191.5	191.9	192.8	193.2	193.4	195.3	195.6	196.6	197.6	193.5
2007	193.6	193.7	190.6	194.1	194.0	194.2	195.4	193.5	196.9	197.6	198.2	199.3	195.1
Information													
2000	271.8	277.4	279.7	278.6	281.2	280.9	282.4	289.0	287.2	290.2	298.0	292.7	284.1
2001	282.1	285.8	287.3	277.0	265.3	264.8	256.9	256.3	257.3	253.3	255.4	255.9	266.5
2002	247.2	249.4	257.3	245.3	244.6	245.1	235.2	242.3	235.5	242.6	250.0	234.3	244.1
2003	237.1	241.5	239.6	233.7	237.1	229.3	230.1	241.8	230.9	241.9	246.8	240.9	237.5
2004	246.6	249.6	245.5	244.1	249.4	238.3	241.4	243.1	235.2	249.2	257.1	248.1	245.6
2005	238.6	240.3	245.0	237.9	236.7	236.7	234.5	240.5	240.8	241.0	247.8	244.3	240.3
2006	238.9	245.8	245.1	239.0	239.5	240.9	234.5	235.3	232.2	230.4	230.9	236.8	237.4
2007	234.7	241.2	243.6	237.6	241.9	244.1	239.6	245.5	248.2	236.9	235.7	236.4	240.5
Financial Activities													
2000	317.3	319.4	319.7	319.4	319.6	321.1	317.9	319.9	319.4	319.6	319.1	322.4	319.6
2001	329.6	332.5	334.9	333.0	333.3	335.2	332.8	335.8	335.4	337.3	337.8	340.6	334.9
2002	336.0	338.3	339.4	339.6	340.5	342.3	342.5	344.1	344.7	346.1	348.5	351.2	342.8
2003	350.3	352.5	354.9	358.4	360.8	362.8	364.0	366.7	366.6	367.4	367.6	369.7	361.8
2004	369.3	370.7	372.6	372.6	372.4	373.5	374.9	375.2	374.3	376.0	376.9	378.6	373.9
2005	374.9	376.5	378.3	380.0	380.9	381.7	382.6	384.0	384.7	386.9	387.5	390.3	382.4
2006	386.5	387.5	388.5	387.8	388.6	387.6	386.5	386.7	386.0	385.9	385.2	387.0	387.0
2007	382.2	383.3	383.6	379.7	377.3	375.0	374.0	371.6	367.0	365.6	362.7	360.4	373.5
Professional and Business Services													
2000	818.9	828.0	835.1	842.6	839.6	846.9	850.1	857.3	860.4	860.0	861.4	863.7	847.0
2001	836.5	841.7	848.1	835.6	841.1	838.5	833.6	839.5	835.8	830.7	826.9	829.1	836.4
2002	812.1	815.5	824.2	823.0	823.9	824.3	820.3	826.7	827.7	829.3	828.3	830.6	823.8
2003	806.4	808.9	816.0	812.7	811.7	812.2	808.7	815.7	813.0	813.8	813.8	817.1	812.5
2004	794.8	801.0	808.3	810.0	814.5	818.9	820.8	823.9	821.4	828.9	831.5	834.1	817.3
2005	820.8	827.2	829.6	835.1	834.9	838.7	838.4	845.0	849.0	852.5	855.4	859.0	840.5
2006	846.1	856.3	862.1	865.2	866.4	875.7	875.8	882.6	883.5	889.4	889.0	888.8	873.4
2007	866.5	875.9	881.5	873.6	874.5	882.2	877.8	881.6	879.8	880.7	879.8	881.7	878.0
Education and Health Services													
2000	517.3	527.9	532.6	535.1	533.0	525.9	518.2	519.7	531.2	534.3	535.5	538.1	529.1
2001	529.4	541.6	547.1	546.7	546.7	539.9	535.5	537.9	549.3	559.9	562.6	564.8	546.8
2002	552.8	563.2	567.1	572.4	572.0	564.3	556.8	558.2	571.3	580.3	583.3	584.5	568.9
2003	570.2	581.2	585.9	590.4	589.4	581.9	575.2	576.4	589.8	598.6	599.8	601.8	586.7
2004	588.4	599.7	604.1	604.7	602.0	592.7	584.2	585.0	597.9	604.8	605.5	606.7	598.0
2005	594.8	604.0	606.4	610.3	608.9	601.2	588.7	590.4	606.8	613.8	615.5	616.9	604.8
2006	603.8	615.7	618.7	620.5	619.0	611.4	599.7	601.8	618.8	627.6	629.1	630.4	616.4
2007	618.6	630.6	634.3	632.9	631.3	621.9	614.3	613.5	631.9	641.1	643.6	643.9	629.8
Leisure and Hospitality													
2000	463.3	471.1	476.6	479.8	486.5	491.3	494.9	496.6	495.3	488.5	486.1	490.2	485.0
2001	484.9	490.1	495.3	502.9	506.1	512.4	512.3	512.4	506.4	505.5	503.0	502.4	502.8
2002	490.7	495.7	501.5	507.9	513.4	516.5	519.9	520.1	517.7	513.0	508.2	511.2	509.7
2003	499.7	505.0	509.3	516.9	522.7	528.8	531.6	532.2	528.1	527.5	524.7	527.5	521.1
2004	520.5	526.8	531.7	531.9	538.0	541.1	546.6	544.9	540.3	539.0	535.4	538.2	536.2
2005	522.0	526.6	533.5	541.5	544.9	551.2	552.9	551.3	548.0	546.7	544.9	549.3	542.7
2006	536.4	541.3	547.8	554.7	560.5	567.3	567.0	568.1	563.8	564.8	560.8	565.1	558.1
2007	550.4	553.3	560.0	567.9	572.9	579.5	580.5	578.1	574.3	572.0	568.3	569.9	568.9
Other Services													
2000	179.3	180.7	183.2	183.6	184.5	187.0	184.9	184.6	185.7	184.2	184.1	184.5	183.9
2001	185.0	186.6	188.8	188.8	189.7	191.3	188.4	187.7	188.0	189.3	188.4	188.0	188.3
2002	185.5	188.0	189.6	190.4	192.4	193.3	192.6	192.2	193.4	193.7	192.8	193.3	191.4
2003	189.8	191.2	192.4	192.4	193.4	194.7	191.5	191.3	192.8	192.7	191.8	192.0	192.1
2004	189.1	190.5	192.4	192.6	193.6	194.3	192.6	191.2	192.7	191.9	191.5	192.0	192.0
2005	189.3	191.4	192.3	193.9	194.2	195.5	191.8	191.5	193.0	192.7	192.3	192.6	192.6
2006	189.8	191.6	192.9	192.2	193.9	195.5	192.0	192.0	194.2	193.7	193.8	193.7	192.9
2007	190.2	192.6	194.0	194.3	195.1	197.0	194.8	194.5	195.9	195.9	195.9	196.1	194.7
Government													
2000	718.2	728.1	736.5	739.5	759.0	733.9	697.8	688.4	717.6	731.3	742.2	741.5	727.8
2001	740.3	747.9	758.7	759.9	761.9	764.0	717.4	714.1	738.0	758.6	763.2	765.9	749.2
2002	759.1	763.4	774.1	773.4	776.5	773.6	730.2	721.7	749.5	768.0	773.1	771.5	761.2
2003	762.8	766.5	773.8	768.6	768.1	767.1	734.0	716.4	731.8	749.0	753.2	750.3	753.4
2004	747.0	748.3	754.8	753.6	754.8	752.7	718.1	700.8	723.9	741.3	747.1	743.6	740.5
2005	738.3	745.5	750.2	747.8	750.2	750.1	715.1	706.0	724.6	741.8	749.7	748.4	739.0
2006	741.4	748.7	754.7	754.0	756.5	756.3	724.7	712.0	733.4	753.0	760.3	758.5	746.1
2007	751.6	757.8	763.9	762.3	764.3	764.5	730.1	719.9	741.1	759.6	767.5	765.5	754.0

Employment by Industry: Chicago-Naperville-Joliet, IL-IN-WI, 2000–2007

(Numbers in thousands, not seasonally adjusted.)

Industry and year	January	February	March	April	May	June	July	August	September	October	November	December	Annual Average
Total Nonfarm													
2000	4,445.7	4,464.9	4,509.8	4,543.2	4,586.9	4,626.3	4,585.9	4,606.9	4,608.4	4,613.6	4,631.5	4,633.8	4,571.4
2001	4,491.0	4,498.8	4,529.9	4,552.3	4,590.7	4,625.9	4,568.8	4,571.4	4,555.9	4,528.8	4,527.6	4,529.0	4,547.5
2002	4,377.2	4,372.5	4,395.3	4,436.4	4,471.8	4,501.6	4,477.9	4,489.7	4,475.4	4,476.2	4,487.2	4,484.5	4,453.8
2003	4,341.1	4,337.1	4,358.1	4,391.0	4,432.2	4,461.2	4,446.9	4,451.3	4,436.4	4,428.2	4,426.7	4,436.6	4,412.2
2004	4,296.5	4,299.2	4,334.5	4,383.3	4,431.5	4,465.8	4,450.2	4,450.7	4,447.1	4,464.7	4,475.0	4,479.5	4,414.8
2005	4,339.5	4,347.2	4,372.8	4,440.5	4,474.7	4,496.9	4,498.1	4,497.4	4,505.1	4,510.7	4,526.5	4,527.0	4,461.4
2006	4,401.0	4,413.7	4,446.4	4,495.0	4,533.4	4,577.3	4,549.4	4,554.0	4,557.2	4,560.5	4,574.5	4,576.1	4,519.9
2007	4,451.7	4,450.3	4,489.7	4,532.6	4,580.2	4,615.7	4,591.3	4,593.6	4,587.8	4,588.5	4,595.6	4,596.7	4,556.2
Total Private													
2000	3,910.7	3,916.9	3,956.5	3,992.6	4,019.7	4,061.1	4,042.2	4,061.0	4,056.6	4,057.3	4,073.4	4,075.0	4,018.6
2001	3,946.8	3,940.8	3,969.6	3,994.9	4,025.3	4,062.5	4,018.4	4,024.7	4,002.3	3,965.2	3,962.3	3,961.7	3,989.5
2002	3,821.9	3,806.5	3,826.7	3,864.6	3,895.8	3,927.7	3,915.4	3,930.1	3,915.2	3,903.1	3,911.8	3,908.9	3,885.6
2003	3,778.6	3,764.2	3,782.7	3,818.5	3,855.5	3,886.2	3,875.1	3,888.1	3,875.0	3,862.7	3,861.2	3,873.6	3,843.5
2004	3,742.5	3,736.5	3,769.5	3,816.9	3,861.1	3,897.9	3,897.9	3,903.6	3,892.5	3,896.7	3,904.4	3,914.7	3,852.8
2005	3,783.2	3,780.6	3,802.0	3,868.9	3,900.1	3,927.7	3,941.2	3,947.2	3,943.9	3,943.4	3,956.0	3,961.3	3,896.3
2006	3,844.8	3,847.2	3,877.7	3,923.7	3,958.4	4,003.8	3,995.6	4,004.9	3,992.0	3,991.7	4,002.9	4,008.8	3,954.3
2007	3,893.9	3,881.7	3,918.6	3,961.6	4,007.1	4,045.4	4,033.4	4,037.9	4,018.3	4,016.0	4,022.0	4,024.4	3,988.4
Goods-Producing													
2000	827.6	828.9	841.2	851.5	856.4	862.3	858.0	863.7	862.0	861.1	859.1	847.8	851.6
2001	811.7	811.1	815.9	821.9	826.9	831.3	816.9	819.6	815.9	808.4	802.0	792.4	814.5
2002	754.9	750.8	755.5	765.6	771.1	778.3	773.0	777.0	775.8	772.5	768.7	758.9	766.8
2003	725.3	720.6	725.1	735.8	744.2	749.5	743.8	748.3	745.6	737.2	730.8	723.8	735.8
2004	691.4	687.1	696.5	709.1	719.0	726.5	727.3	728.8	728.6	727.3	724.5	718.0	715.3
2005	687.0	686.7	691.9	708.7	715.3	721.9	722.0	723.9	724.0	723.4	721.2	711.5	711.5
2006	688.9	688.9	692.8	709.3	715.3	724.7	720.3	722.1	721.2	720.1	715.8	709.0	710.7
2007	682.4	674.0	686.1	698.5	707.1	716.6	712.7	712.0	710.0	706.5	701.9	694.8	700.2
Natural Resources and Mining													
2000	2.2	2.1	2.2	2.4	2.4	2.5	2.5	2.6	2.5	2.7	2.6	2.5	2.4
2001	2.2	2.2	2.3	2.5	2.5	2.6	2.5	2.6	2.5	2.6	2.4	2.5	2.5
2002	2.2	2.2	2.4	2.4	2.4	2.6	2.5	2.6	2.5	2.5	2.4	2.5	2.4
2003	2.1	2.1	2.2	2.4	2.4	2.4	2.4	2.5	2.4	2.5	2.5	2.3	2.4
2004	2.0	2.1	2.3	2.4	2.4	2.4	2.4	2.5	2.5	2.4	2.5	2.4	2.4
2005	2.2	2.2	2.3	2.5	2.5	2.6	2.7	2.6	2.6	2.7	2.6	2.5	2.5
2006	2.2	2.2	2.3	2.6	2.7	2.8	2.8	2.8	2.8	2.7	2.8	2.6	2.6
2007	2.2	2.1	2.4	2.4	2.5	2.5	2.5	2.5	2.4	2.4	2.4	2.4	2.4
Construction													
2000	188.4	188.4	197.8	209.3	215.0	219.7	222.3	224.0	222.9	222.7	220.9	211.7	211.9
2001	189.6	191.5	198.1	211.5	220.3	225.4	226.9	228.9	227.1	226.7	226.2	220.5	216.1
2002	194.1	192.8	198.0	209.7	217.1	223.0	227.3	229.2	228.5	227.8	225.7	216.9	215.8
2003	196.0	192.7	198.0	210.4	220.9	226.5	229.6	232.6	231.0	225.6	220.6	214.4	216.5
2004	189.5	186.1	193.6	206.8	214.6	220.1	224.7	224.5	223.8	224.0	221.7	215.3	212.1
2005	189.4	188.9	193.0	209.1	215.3	220.4	224.4	225.6	226.1	226.3	223.9	214.2	213.1
2006	198.0	197.7	203.4	216.8	224.1	229.9	229.2	229.2	231.1	228.4	228.0	224.1	216.8	219.0
2007	196.5	188.5	199.5	212.2	220.8	227.0	226.8	226.5	224.7	222.1	218.2	210.0	214.4
Manufacturing													
2000	637.0	638.4	641.2	639.8	639.0	640.1	633.2	637.1	636.6	635.7	635.6	633.6	637.3
2001	619.9	617.4	615.6	607.9	604.1	603.3	587.5	588.1	586.3	579.1	573.4	569.4	596.0
2002	558.6	555.8	555.1	553.5	551.6	552.7	543.2	545.2	544.8	542.2	540.6	539.5	548.6
2003	527.2	525.8	524.9	523.0	520.9	520.6	511.8	513.2	512.2	509.1	507.7	507.1	517.0
2004	499.9	498.9	500.6	499.9	502.0	504.0	500.2	501.8	502.3	500.9	500.3	500.3	500.9
2005	495.4	495.6	496.6	497.1	497.5	498.9	494.9	495.7	495.3	494.4	494.7	494.8	495.9
2006	488.7	489.0	487.1	489.9	488.5	492.0	488.3	488.2	490.0	489.4	488.9	489.6	489.1
2007	483.6	483.3	484.0	483.9	483.7	487.1	483.3	483.0	482.8	481.9	481.2	482.4	483.4
Service-Providing													
2000	3,618.1	3,636.0	3,668.6	3,691.7	3,730.5	3,764.0	3,727.9	3,743.2	3,746.4	3,752.5	3,772.4	3,786.0	3,719.8
2001	3,679.3	3,687.7	3,714.0	3,730.4	3,763.8	3,794.6	3,751.9	3,751.8	3,740.0	3,720.4	3,725.6	3,736.6	3,733.0
2002	3,622.3	3,621.7	3,639.8	3,670.8	3,700.7	3,723.3	3,704.9	3,712.7	3,699.6	3,703.7	3,718.5	3,725.6	3,687.0
2003	3,615.8	3,616.5	3,633.0	3,655.2	3,688.0	3,711.7	3,703.1	3,703.0	3,690.8	3,691.0	3,695.9	3,712.8	3,676.4
2004	3,605.1	3,612.1	3,638.0	3,674.2	3,712.5	3,739.3	3,722.9	3,721.9	3,718.5	3,737.4	3,750.5	3,761.5	3,699.5
2005	3,652.5	3,660.5	3,680.9	3,731.8	3,759.4	3,775.0	3,776.1	3,773.5	3,781.1	3,787.3	3,805.3	3,815.5	3,749.9
2006	3,712.1	3,724.8	3,753.6	3,785.7	3,818.1	3,852.6	3,829.1	3,831.9	3,836.0	3,840.4	3,858.7	3,867.1	3,809.2
2007	3,769.3	3,776.2	3,803.6	3,834.0	3,873.1	3,899.1	3,878.5	3,881.5	3,877.8	3,881.9	3,893.7	3,901.9	3,855.9
Trade, Transportation, and Utilities													
2000	940.8	933.7	937.5	938.0	943.4	950.3	949.5	955.0	954.3	961.6	980.8	993.8	953.2
2001	957.5	944.4	947.0	950.5	954.7	961.2	950.2	949.2	947.1	939.4	952.7	963.6	951.5
2002	921.2	907.3	910.3	913.1	918.1	922.1	916.8	918.8	918.3	921.6	938.0	949.5	921.3
2003	904.0	895.2	897.0	897.0	903.4	907.8	899.9	902.2	903.8	907.6	921.5	935.1	906.2
2004	895.3	886.8	891.3	895.7	905.8	911.8	907.0	908.4	909.4	915.7	930.8	944.8	908.6
2005	902.6	892.9	896.2	902.3	909.3	913.9	911.6	913.8	915.0	918.9	934.5	949.5	913.4
2006	911.6	903.0	908.2	911.1	918.3	925.1	919.3	920.1	919.0	922.8	942.0	954.7	921.3
2007	923.8	911.9	918.2	916.2	926.6	933.9	928.5	928.9	927.8	931.6	949.6	961.0	929.8
Wholesale Trade													
2000	251.1	252.3	253.0	251.6	252.9	255.1	254.7	255.3	254.4	255.3	255.9	256.9	254.0
2001	255.5	255.1	255.2	258.2	259.6	261.5	261.4	260.9	260.1	255.9	254.7	255.5	257.8
2002	250.8	250.7	251.0	251.2	251.4	252.9	251.2	251.1	250.1	250.0	250.6	250.6	251.0
2003	248.5	248.4	248.9	247.4	247.9	248.6	247.1	246.2	245.1	243.2	243.9	244.6	246.7
2004	240.9	240.4	241.5	242.4	243.9	245.3	244.7	244.6	243.8	244.5	245.1	246.3	243.6
2005	241.1	240.9	241.7	243.4	244.5	246.2	246.4	245.9	246.0	246.3	247.5	249.1	244.9
2006	246.0	246.0	247.2	247.7	248.8	250.8	249.7	249.3	248.4	248.5	248.6	250.1	248.4
2007	247.7	247.6	248.7	249.1	250.6	252.7	252.0	251.4	250.6	250.1	250.1	250.7	250.1

Employment by Industry: Chicago-Naperville-Joliet, IL-IN-WI, 2000–2007—*Continued*

(Numbers in thousands, not seasonally adjusted.)

Industry and year	January	February	March	April	May	June	July	August	September	October	November	December	Annual Average
Retail Trade													
2000	475.2	467.3	470.4	470.3	473.3	477.8	477.5	481.1	479.8	484.5	501.9	512.9	481.0
2001	484.3	473.1	475.1	477.2	479.2	485.3	477.0	477.0	474.5	472.4	489.2	501.2	480.5
2002	469.7	457.6	461.1	461.3	466.1	470.6	466.9	467.9	466.8	469.2	485.8	497.6	470.1
2003	459.4	452.1	453.6	454.5	459.0	463.8	459.1	461.1	460.4	464.6	477.6	490.1	462.9
2004	458.7	451.4	454.1	455.5	462.2	468.5	463.9	465.0	463.6	467.3	481.8	494.2	465.5
2005	462.9	453.2	454.8	458.1	463.3	467.2	467.9	469.7	467.5	470.0	483.5	495.2	467.8
2006	466.8	457.6	460.1	461.7	466.0	471.6	469.2	469.9	465.1	469.8	487.8	496.6	470.2
2007	474.4	462.5	466.6	465.3	472.3	477.9	476.1	476.3	472.2	476.9	493.7	502.1	476.4
Transportation and Utilities													
2000	214.5	214.1	214.1	216.1	217.2	217.4	217.3	218.6	220.1	221.8	223.0	224.0	218.2
2001	217.7	216.2	216.7	215.1	215.9	214.4	211.8	211.3	212.5	211.1	208.8	206.9	213.2
2002	200.7	199.0	198.2	200.6	200.6	198.6	198.7	199.8	201.4	202.4	201.6	201.3	200.2
2003	196.2	194.7	194.6	195.2	196.5	195.5	193.7	194.9	198.4	199.9	200.1	200.5	196.7
2004	195.7	195.0	195.7	197.8	199.7	198.0	198.4	198.8	202.0	203.9	203.9	204.3	199.4
2005	198.6	198.8	199.7	200.8	201.5	200.5	197.3	198.2	201.5	202.6	203.5	205.2	200.7
2006	198.8	199.4	200.9	201.7	203.5	202.7	200.4	200.9	205.5	204.5	205.6	208.0	202.7
2007	201.6	201.6	202.7	201.6	203.7	203.2	200.3	201.1	204.8	204.5	205.6	208.2	203.2
Information													
2000	114.4	115.1	116.3	115.2	115.9	117.5	117.3	117.5	117.0	117.6	118.2	118.8	116.7
2001	117.9	118.1	118.4	117.4	118.0	119.1	117.7	117.7	116.1	114.0	114.0	114.1	116.9
2002	111.3	110.7	110.5	110.0	110.1	110.1	107.9	107.6	105.9	105.5	105.0	104.7	108.3
2003	102.1	102.2	101.2	100.3	100.2	100.4	99.8	98.9	97.8	97.5	97.1	96.9	99.6
2004	96.1	96.0	95.8	95.4	95.4	95.7	95.2	94.7	93.5	93.8	93.7	94.4	95.0
2005	93.3	93.0	93.0	93.3	93.0	93.3	93.5	92.7	91.9	91.7	91.6	91.6	92.7
2006	91.3	91.0	91.0	91.1	91.4	91.8	91.5	91.2	90.4	90.6	90.5	90.8	91.1
2007	90.2	90.5	90.2	90.6	90.8	91.6	91.6	91.7	91.2	91.1	91.0	91.2	91.0
Financial Activities													
2000	318.0	318.2	317.9	318.2	318.3	321.7	320.5	320.6	317.2	318.5	318.9	321.9	319.2
2001	321.6	322.3	324.6	325.0	326.1	329.4	328.6	328.0	324.2	322.8	323.7	325.4	325.1
2002	320.5	319.9	320.6	319.8	320.9	324.4	323.9	324.2	322.0	322.5	323.7	325.7	322.3
2003	323.8	323.6	324.6	325.2	326.6	330.4	330.6	330.9	328.2	324.9	325.1	326.6	326.7
2004	321.8	321.5	323.0	322.3	323.5	326.7	327.5	327.5	324.1	323.7	323.5	325.7	324.2
2005	323.1	322.8	323.4	325.2	326.2	329.1	331.4	331.4	329.6	329.7	330.0	332.1	327.8
2006	327.6	327.9	328.9	329.8	330.7	333.8	334.7	334.7	333.1	332.1	331.8	333.2	331.5
2007	329.8	329.4	329.3	329.7	330.6	333.3	332.5	331.2	327.5	327.4	327.9	328.5	329.8
Professional and Business Services													
2000	698.9	702.9	713.4	725.2	730.5	742.4	740.3	746.7	746.5	743.5	741.9	738.2	730.9
2001	704.4	701.8	705.5	709.0	714.2	721.9	711.1	714.1	708.6	703.1	694.3	690.9	706.6
2002	662.1	660.9	662.9	676.0	678.9	684.9	685.5	692.3	690.0	683.8	680.7	673.5	677.6
2003	647.0	644.9	646.9	659.1	663.4	668.0	667.7	673.2	675.7	676.4	671.0	671.8	663.8
2004	645.8	648.7	655.3	671.8	680.2	691.8	690.9	695.9	696.6	703.1	700.8	696.9	681.5
2005	672.0	675.2	680.8	698.7	702.5	711.7	714.5	719.5	721.8	728.2	727.7	723.5	706.3
2006	695.2	698.7	707.9	722.2	726.7	738.8	739.0	745.8	744.2	747.8	745.2	740.0	729.3
2007	711.3	713.9	721.0	740.2	746.0	754.3	752.2	757.8	753.7	755.8	752.0	750.1	742.4
Education and Health Services													
2000	486.9	491.1	493.1	496.0	497.0	496.1	486.9	487.2	495.6	500.5	503.9	504.9	494.9
2001	504.3	509.5	514.9	516.3	516.8	517.1	511.8	514.6	521.0	521.9	525.3	525.5	516.6
2002	518.9	524.0	526.9	528.3	530.3	527.1	521.5	523.0	529.9	533.9	537.0	537.4	528.2
2003	529.7	532.6	535.5	536.6	538.4	534.9	533.2	534.0	540.1	545.0	547.2	548.5	538.0
2004	539.9	543.7	545.9	549.5	549.6	545.1	542.4	542.2	548.6	554.1	556.9	560.1	548.2
2005	552.9	556.2	556.6	562.1	562.7	556.2	555.9	554.7	561.9	566.3	569.0	570.1	560.4
2006	563.0	569.8	572.3	573.1	574.8	571.7	568.6	569.9	578.1	581.9	585.3	585.3	574.5
2007	578.7	586.1	588.8	589.4	591.8	588.6	585.5	584.4	592.7	597.4	599.6	600.0	590.3
Leisure and Hospitality													
2000	340.9	342.9	351.5	361.8	371.3	380.7	379.5	380.1	374.2	367.0	363.0	361.6	364.5
2001	342.7	346.0	354.0	365.0	378.0	388.3	387.0	387.4	377.5	366.5	360.4	359.4	367.7
2002	345.8	345.7	351.6	363.0	376.9	387.9	389.8	389.9	382.4	373.0	367.9	367.8	370.1
2003	351.6	350.1	355.5	368.9	382.7	395.4	394.6	394.6	387.4	377.7	372.7	374.2	375.5
2004	358.1	357.8	365.3	377.3	390.8	400.8	403.3	402.8	395.3	382.9	378.1	377.1	382.5
2005	360.6	361.6	367.0	384.2	396.4	404.7	408.7	408.0	402.6	389.7	385.6	385.1	387.9
2006	370.8	372.6	379.4	392.3	405.1	418.9	419.7	418.5	409.6	399.9	395.6	397.1	398.3
2007	382.9	381.1	387.7	400.5	415.6	425.8	424.9	426.2	416.5	407.2	401.5	399.5	405.8
Other Services													
2000	183.2	184.1	185.6	186.7	186.9	190.1	190.2	190.2	189.8	187.5	187.6	188.0	187.5
2001	186.7	187.6	189.3	189.8	190.6	194.2	195.1	194.1	191.9	189.1	189.9	190.4	190.7
2002	187.2	187.2	188.4	188.8	189.5	192.9	197.0	197.3	190.9	190.3	190.8	191.4	191.0
2003	194.7	194.8	196.7	195.1	196.4	199.6	205.2	205.9	196.1	196.1	195.5	196.4	197.7
2004	194.1	194.9	196.4	195.8	196.8	199.3	204.3	203.3	196.4	196.1	196.1	197.7	197.6
2005	191.7	192.2	193.1	194.4	194.7	196.9	203.6	203.2	197.1	195.5	196.4	197.9	196.4
2006	196.4	195.3	197.2	194.8	196.1	199.0	202.5	202.6	196.4	196.5	196.7	198.7	197.7
2007	194.6	194.4	196.9	196.2	198.1	200.9	205.1	205.2	198.5	198.6	198.1	199.0	198.8
Government													
2000	535.0	548.0	553.3	550.6	567.2	565.2	543.7	545.9	551.8	556.3	558.1	558.8	552.8
2001	544.2	558.0	560.3	557.4	565.4	563.4	550.4	546.7	553.6	563.6	565.3	567.3	558.0
2002	555.3	566.0	568.6	571.8	576.0	573.9	562.5	559.6	560.2	573.1	575.4	575.6	568.2
2003	563.1	573.4	575.9	573.1	577.1	575.3	572.4	563.5	561.9	565.9	565.9	563.4	569.2
2004	554.0	562.7	565.0	566.4	570.4	568.1	552.3	547.1	554.6	568.0	570.6	564.8	562.0
2005	556.3	566.6	570.8	571.6	574.6	569.2	556.9	550.2	561.2	567.3	570.5	565.7	565.1
2006	556.2	566.5	568.7	571.3	575.0	573.5	553.8	549.1	565.2	568.8	571.6	567.3	565.6
2007	557.7	568.5	571.1	570.9	573.1	570.3	557.9	555.6	569.5	572.5	573.6	572.6	567.8

Employment by Industry: Philadelphia-Camden-Wilmington, PA-NJ-DE-MD, 2000–2007

(Numbers in thousands, not seasonally adjusted.)

Industry and year	January	February	March	April	May	June	July	August	September	October	November	December	Annual Average
Total Nonfarm													
2000	2,686.7	2,697.1	2,725.3	2,747.0	2,757.8	2,767.7	2,728.0	2,718.5	2,748.7	2,763.2	2,786.6	2,806.2	2,744.4
2001	2,717.3	2,728.8	2,746.4	2,759.1	2,768.3	2,778.7	2,733.1	2,728.3	2,743.1	2,754.8	2,772.9	2,781.2	2,751.0
2002	2,704.5	2,715.2	2,733.1	2,741.0	2,751.5	2,764.6	2,716.6	2,711.8	2,733.6	2,753.6	2,770.6	2,775.6	2,739.3
2003	2,692.1	2,694.4	2,714.5	2,732.3	2,743.9	2,751.6	2,715.0	2,705.6	2,727.2	2,749.4	2,763.4	2,768.4	2,729.8
2004	2,688.1	2,699.1	2,722.4	2,742.0	2,754.9	2,766.8	2,734.9	2,727.4	2,753.1	2,780.0	2,793.4	2,799.8	2,746.8
2005	2,717.5	2,730.0	2,742.8	2,778.8	2,791.4	2,791.7	2,767.7	2,757.0	2,783.1	2,801.7	2,818.3	2,821.0	2,775.1
2006	2,748.2	2,761.6	2,779.7	2,808.0	2,820.3	2,821.5	2,786.9	2,779.5	2,799.1	2,821.5	2,834.2	2,838.3	2,799.9
2007	2,765.6	2,771.8	2,791.2	2,812.3	2,826.9	2,837.1	2,807.1	2,797.6	2,810.8	2,835.6	2,851.4	2,856.4	2,813.7
Total Private													
2000	2,346.1	2,350.0	2,373.3	2,392.9	2,398.0	2,415.6	2,399.8	2,397.9	2,408.6	2,415.5	2,435.1	2,453.5	2,398.9
2001	2,370.0	2,374.6	2,390.7	2,402.1	2,414.0	2,428.2	2,405.6	2,406.2	2,400.9	2,402.5	2,416.1	2,422.0	2,402.7
2002	2,350.6	2,355.0	2,371.7	2,379.0	2,390.8	2,407.8	2,387.1	2,390.2	2,389.9	2,400.1	2,412.8	2,417.7	2,387.7
2003	2,341.3	2,336.8	2,354.7	2,372.1	2,384.7	2,395.3	2,383.8	2,381.0	2,381.2	2,391.9	2,402.8	2,407.8	2,377.8
2004	2,334.8	2,339.4	2,360.2	2,378.2	2,394.3	2,410.3	2,405.3	2,402.2	2,404.0	2,420.8	2,431.7	2,439.0	2,393.4
2005	2,362.6	2,368.9	2,379.2	2,414.9	2,429.9	2,434.8	2,431.9	2,426.1	2,434.2	2,443.1	2,458.2	2,461.8	2,420.5
2006	2,394.9	2,401.1	2,417.0	2,444.5	2,457.7	2,464.7	2,453.5	2,448.4	2,450.2	2,463.5	2,473.8	2,479.4	2,445.7
2007	2,415.2	2,413.6	2,430.8	2,452.2	2,467.7	2,481.0	2,474.6	2,468.7	2,463.6	2,478.8	2,491.7	2,496.3	2,461.2
Goods-Producing													
2000	400.7	397.5	405.2	411.5	413.4	418.1	414.9	416.6	415.5	414.2	412.7	411.7	411.0
2001	399.1	398.4	402.1	403.8	405.5	408.9	406.8	406.6	404.9	399.2	396.4	394.0	402.1
2002	381.6	380.9	382.3	382.6	385.7	388.0	386.1	387.3	385.1	382.5	380.3	377.3	383.3
2003	362.8	359.2	361.8	365.8	369.7	372.0	370.8	370.1	368.2	366.6	364.8	361.0	366.1
2004	351.2	350.1	355.1	357.8	362.0	366.0	366.9	367.0	365.7	364.3	363.3	360.6	360.8
2005	346.8	345.6	349.1	356.8	361.1	363.3	364.1	365.2	363.6	362.2	365.3	360.1	358.6
2006	352.7	351.4	355.2	360.3	363.4	365.1	363.0	362.9	360.1	358.3	354.7	352.7	358.3
2007	343.2	338.6	342.8	346.7	350.3	354.1	354.1	354.5	351.9	351.0	350.3	348.0	348.8
Natural Resources, Mining, and Construction													
2000	110.8	107.9	114.7	120.6	122.6	125.3	123.0	124.0	123.5	123.3	121.4	119.5	119.7
2001	112.3	112.3	116.1	119.9	122.9	125.8	126.9	127.8	127.0	125.7	124.7	122.0	122.0
2002	114.9	114.8	116.6	118.7	121.5	123.5	124.3	125.3	123.1	123.1	121.7	119.5	120.6
2003	113.0	109.8	112.3	118.9	123.0	124.9	127.3	127.4	125.6	125.3	124.6	121.5	121.1
2004	115.1	113.6	118.5	120.9	124.5	127.3	129.0	129.8	129.9	128.9	127.9	125.2	124.2
2005	116.6	114.7	117.6	125.3	129.1	131.5	133.4	133.4	132.7	133.0	134.3	130.1	127.6
2006	122.8	122.2	126.3	131.6	134.8	136.0	135.8	135.8	134.1	133.1	130.5	128.8	131.0
2007	121.7	117.9	121.7	126.2	129.1	131.6	132.7	133.5	132.6	132.2	130.7	128.4	128.2
Manufacturing													
2000	289.9	289.6	290.5	290.9	290.8	292.8	291.9	292.6	292.0	290.9	291.3	292.2	291.3
2001	286.8	286.1	286.0	283.9	282.6	283.1	279.9	278.8	277.9	273.5	271.7	272.0	280.2
2002	266.7	266.1	265.7	263.9	264.2	264.5	261.8	262.0	262.0	259.4	258.6	257.8	262.7
2003	249.8	249.4	249.5	246.9	246.7	247.1	243.5	242.7	242.6	241.3	240.2	239.5	244.9
2004	236.1	236.5	236.6	236.9	237.5	238.7	237.9	237.2	235.8	235.4	235.4	235.4	236.6
2005	230.2	230.9	231.5	231.5	232.0	231.8	230.7	231.8	230.9	229.2	231.0	230.0	231.0
2006	229.9	229.2	228.9	228.7	228.6	229.1	227.2	227.1	226.0	225.2	224.2	223.9	227.3
2007	221.5	220.7	221.1	220.5	221.2	222.5	221.4	221.0	219.3	218.8	219.6	219.6	220.6
Service-Providing													
2000	2,286.0	2,299.6	2,320.1	2,335.5	2,344.4	2,349.6	2,313.1	2,301.9	2,333.2	2,349.0	2,373.9	2,394.5	2,333.4
2001	2,318.2	2,330.4	2,344.3	2,355.3	2,362.8	2,369.8	2,326.3	2,321.7	2,338.2	2,355.6	2,376.5	2,387.2	2,348.9
2002	2,322.9	2,334.3	2,350.8	2,358.4	2,365.8	2,376.6	2,330.5	2,324.5	2,348.5	2,371.1	2,390.3	2,398.3	2,356.0
2003	2,329.3	2,335.2	2,352.7	2,366.5	2,374.2	2,379.6	2,344.2	2,335.5	2,359.0	2,382.8	2,398.6	2,407.4	2,363.8
2004	2,336.9	2,349.0	2,367.3	2,384.2	2,392.9	2,400.8	2,368.0	2,360.4	2,387.4	2,415.7	2,430.1	2,439.2	2,386.0
2005	2,370.7	2,384.4	2,393.7	2,422.0	2,430.3	2,428.4	2,403.6	2,391.8	2,419.5	2,439.5	2,453.0	2,460.9	2,416.5
2006	2,395.5	2,410.2	2,424.5	2,447.7	2,456.9	2,456.4	2,423.9	2,416.6	2,439.0	2,463.2	2,479.5	2,485.6	2,441.6
2007	2,422.4	2,433.2	2,448.4	2,465.6	2,476.6	2,483.0	2,453.0	2,443.1	2,458.9	2,484.6	2,501.1	2,508.4	2,464.9
Trade, Transportation, and Utilities													
2000	531.3	525.0	526.9	532.0	534.7	537.2	531.0	533.4	536.7	543.4	557.0	568.5	538.1
2001	542.4	533.2	534.8	532.0	533.6	536.0	527.6	527.9	529.4	533.9	546.5	554.7	536.0
2002	529.8	521.1	525.3	523.8	527.5	531.3	524.6	526.3	528.6	535.3	545.6	557.0	531.4
2003	528.4	520.6	523.4	525.7	528.7	532.2	525.5	525.5	528.4	534.9	545.0	553.4	531.0
2004	524.9	521.1	522.9	523.2	527.7	531.1	526.4	526.0	527.2	534.1	544.0	552.7	530.1
2005	529.0	523.3	525.0	527.4	531.1	532.1	529.8	528.9	529.8	534.3	544.8	554.6	532.5
2006	531.2	523.3	527.2	527.7	531.0	532.5	527.7	526.3	527.1	533.0	544.4	551.9	531.9
2007	530.8	521.3	523.3	524.6	529.7	533.3	531.0	529.0	529.3	535.3	546.6	555.2	532.5
Wholesale Trade													
2000	125.0	125.3	126.3	128.1	128.2	129.2	128.6	128.7	128.3	128.2	128.7	129.5	127.8
2001	130.0	130.2	130.7	131.1	131.0	131.3	131.2	130.7	130.4	130.0	130.2	130.9	130.6
2002	129.5	129.1	130.1	130.1	130.4	130.6	129.9	129.9	129.2	130.6	130.5	131.3	130.1
2003	129.1	129.0	129.9	129.8	130.0	130.3	129.5	129.5	129.4	129.4	130.0	130.5	129.7
2004	127.9	128.1	128.9	129.3	129.8	130.3	130.5	130.3	129.6	130.1	129.9	130.2	129.6
2005	128.9	129.1	129.7	130.1	130.4	130.6	130.5	130.5	129.8	129.9	130.1	130.7	130.1
2006	128.6	128.7	129.6	129.9	130.3	131.3	131.3	131.2	130.3	129.9	129.8	130.1	130.1
2007	128.7	128.2	129.0	130.1	130.3	131.5	132.2	131.7	130.8	130.8	131.0	131.2	130.5
Retail Trade													
2000	312.7	306.6	307.2	310.0	312.4	315.0	311.6	314.3	314.2	319.2	332.6	342.4	316.5
2001	317.8	308.9	310.3	305.7	307.4	310.0	304.7	306.9	305.6	308.6	321.5	329.4	311.4
2002	308.6	300.9	303.5	300.8	303.4	306.9	303.5	305.4	304.7	307.4	318.2	328.6	307.7
2003	304.4	297.0	299.2	300.7	303.6	307.3	304.6	305.7	305.2	310.3	320.2	328.2	307.2
2004	305.1	300.9	301.9	301.7	305.5	308.1	306.6	307.3	305.7	311.8	321.3	328.8	307.7
2005	308.4	303.4	304.0	305.5	308.5	309.0	309.0	308.7	306.6	310.6	319.7	327.5	310.1
2006	309.4	301.1	303.3	303.6	305.1	306.1	304.2	302.8	301.3	307.0	317.7	323.1	307.1
2007	307.5	299.0	299.8	300.4	304.4	306.4	306.0	305.3	303.0	308.4	318.9	325.9	307.1

Employment by Industry: Philadelphia-Camden-Wilmington, PA-NJ-DE-MD, 2000–2007—*Continued*

(Numbers in thousands, not seasonally adjusted.)

Industry and year	January	February	March	April	May	June	July	August	September	October	November	December	Annual Average
Transportation and Utilities													
2000	93.6	93.1	93.4	93.9	94.1	93.0	90.8	90.4	94.2	96.0	95.7	96.6	93.7
2001	94.6	94.1	93.8	95.2	95.2	94.7	91.7	90.3	93.4	95.3	94.8	94.4	94.0
2002	91.7	91.1	91.7	92.9	93.7	93.8	91.2	91.0	94.7	97.3	96.9	97.1	93.6
2003	94.9	94.6	94.3	95.2	95.1	94.6	91.4	90.3	93.8	95.2	94.8	94.7	94.1
2004	91.9	92.1	92.1	92.2	92.4	92.7	89.3	88.4	91.9	92.2	92.8	93.7	91.8
2005	90.8	90.8	91.3	91.8	92.2	92.5	90.3	89.7	93.4	93.8	95.0	96.4	92.3
2006	93.2	93.5	94.3	94.2	95.6	95.1	92.2	92.3	95.5	96.1	96.9	98.7	94.8
2007	94.6	94.1	94.5	94.1	95.0	95.4	92.8	92.0	95.5	96.1	96.7	98.1	94.9
Information													
2000	69.6	70.0	70.9	70.6	71.0	71.7	73.1	67.7	73.2	72.7	73.5	74.1	71.5
2001	72.4	72.4	72.3	71.4	71.8	72.4	71.8	70.8	70.0	69.5	70.0	70.2	71.3
2002	69.5	69.4	69.9	68.0	68.6	68.5	67.8	67.4	67.0	66.3	66.7	66.4	68.0
2003	65.2	64.9	65.3	64.1	63.6	63.0	62.0	61.1	60.1	58.9	58.6	57.6	62.0
2004	56.7	56.2	56.3	56.2	56.3	56.5	56.5	56.3	55.5	55.3	55.5	55.5	56.1
2005	54.7	54.7	54.9	55.4	55.5	56.1	55.7	55.7	58.6	55.7	56.0	56.3	55.8
2006	55.4	56.1	55.4	55.4	55.7	55.9	55.8	55.9	56.4	56.4	56.3	56.8	56.0
2007	56.4	56.4	56.5	57.0	57.2	58.0	57.5	57.9	58.6	57.9	58.0	58.0	57.5
Financial Activities													
2000	217.4	218.0	217.7	217.8	217.7	219.6	219.4	219.2	217.1	217.6	218.7	220.6	218.4
2001	218.2	218.5	219.2	220.1	220.3	221.4	220.9	221.0	217.8	217.6	217.4	218.6	219.3
2002	217.9	217.7	218.1	217.9	217.8	219.4	220.1	220.4	218.8	218.7	219.3	220.1	218.9
2003	219.0	219.2	219.7	220.1	220.7	222.2	223.1	222.9	220.5	219.2	219.2	219.5	220.4
2004	218.4	217.7	218.1	218.8	219.5	220.7	221.1	220.4	217.7	217.3	217.8	218.9	218.9
2005	217.9	218.0	218.1	218.4	219.3	221.1	221.9	222.1	220.2	219.8	220.3	221.3	219.9
2006	219.6	219.2	219.2	220.2	220.4	222.0	222.6	222.3	220.5	220.4	220.6	221.1	220.7
2007	219.6	219.6	219.6	219.9	219.8	221.6	222.5	221.4	218.9	218.5	218.5	219.2	219.9
Professional and Business Services													
2000	387.3	388.0	395.1	395.1	395.0	399.1	397.9	397.5	397.0	394.6	396.3	397.2	395.0
2001	386.1	387.2	391.6	394.3	395.7	397.2	392.0	394.3	392.4	391.2	390.9	388.9	391.8
2002	377.4	377.4	382.4	386.3	386.6	389.3	384.7	385.8	383.2	385.4	386.9	387.0	384.4
2003	378.6	377.0	381.3	387.3	388.6	390.4	390.2	391.0	392.6	394.7	396.5	398.3	388.9
2004	388.4	389.5	395.9	398.6	400.8	406.0	405.7	406.0	405.7	410.1	411.1	411.6	402.5
2005	395.7	396.8	399.1	410.7	410.8	413.2	414.7	413.2	413.0	415.3	416.4	417.2	409.7
2006	404.3	407.0	411.8	420.2	421.4	424.6	424.5	425.3	425.2	428.5	430.9	432.2	421.3
2007	417.6	418.3	422.6	430.3	432.5	435.4	433.6	433.8	430.7	434.0	435.5	435.7	430.0
Education and Health Services													
2000	448.9	460.0	458.6	460.4	455.5	452.3	446.2	447.5	457.2	462.7	466.3	470.3	457.2
2001	457.7	468.9	469.3	469.9	467.9	466.0	460.3	461.1	468.5	475.1	479.1	478.0	468.5
2002	471.1	482.8	483.0	480.8	476.8	475.3	470.3	470.2	479.4	486.2	489.5	486.4	479.3
2003	475.6	485.1	485.9	486.3	482.1	478.3	473.5	471.6	480.6	489.6	492.1	490.8	482.6
2004	479.5	490.0	491.8	493.5	490.2	484.2	482.3	480.2	491.5	501.2	503.5	502.1	490.8
2005	492.1	505.2	502.3	506.9	504.3	493.6	492.5	490.1	503.3	515.1	516.5	513.9	503.0
2006	503.8	516.0	513.5	518.6	516.5	507.3	505.4	502.3	514.7	523.8	525.9	523.3	514.3
2007	516.2	528.1	529.2	529.6	525.8	518.2	518.0	515.6	525.0	534.2	536.7	533.8	525.9
Leisure and Hospitality													
2000	182.2	182.0	187.8	194.3	199.0	204.8	204.3	203.4	200.1	197.0	196.7	196.9	195.7
2001	181.8	183.3	186.9	195.9	203.4	209.3	209.0	207.7	202.2	199.3	198.7	200.0	198.1
2002	186.5	188.0	192.3	200.3	206.4	212.6	210.9	210.1	206.3	204.9	203.9	202.8	202.1
2003	192.8	191.9	197.2	202.8	210.4	214.8	217.0	217.4	210.8	207.4	205.6	205.7	206.2
2004	196.2	195.0	198.9	207.8	214.6	221.1	221.1	221.0	216.0	214.4	212.3	213.1	211.0
2005	202.4	200.9	205.5	214.2	222.1	228.5	227.4	225.8	221.4	216.8	214.9	214.2	216.2
2006	205.0	205.0	210.5	218.1	224.6	231.5	229.7	229.5	223.6	220.4	218.5	218.9	219.6
2007	210.1	209.7	214.6	221.1	228.4	234.9	232.4	231.7	225.0	222.8	220.9	221.2	222.7
Other Services													
2000	108.7	109.5	111.1	111.2	111.7	112.8	113.0	112.6	111.8	113.3	113.9	114.2	112.0
2001	112.3	112.7	114.5	114.7	115.8	117.0	117.2	116.8	115.7	116.7	117.1	117.6	115.7
2002	116.8	117.7	118.4	119.3	121.4	123.4	122.6	122.7	121.5	120.8	120.6	120.7	120.5
2003	118.9	118.9	120.1	120.0	120.9	122.4	121.7	121.4	120.0	120.6	121.0	121.5	120.6
2004	119.5	119.8	121.2	122.3	123.2	124.7	125.3	125.3	124.7	124.1	124.2	124.5	123.2
2005	124.0	124.4	125.2	125.1	125.7	126.9	125.8	125.1	124.3	123.9	124.0	124.2	124.9
2006	122.9	123.1	124.2	124.0	124.7	125.8	124.8	123.9	122.6	122.7	122.5	122.5	123.6
2007	121.3	121.6	122.2	123.0	124.0	125.5	125.5	124.8	124.2	125.1	125.2	125.2	124.0
Government													
2000	340.6	347.1	352.0	354.1	359.8	352.1	328.2	320.6	340.1	347.7	351.5	352.7	345.5
2001	347.3	354.2	355.7	357.0	354.3	350.5	327.5	322.1	342.2	352.3	356.8	359.2	348.3
2002	353.9	360.2	361.4	362.0	360.7	356.8	329.5	321.6	343.7	353.5	357.8	357.9	351.6
2003	350.8	357.6	359.8	360.2	359.2	356.3	331.2	324.6	346.0	357.5	360.6	360.6	352.0
2004	353.3	359.7	362.2	363.8	360.6	356.5	329.6	325.2	349.1	359.2	361.7	360.8	353.5
2005	354.9	361.1	363.6	363.9	361.5	356.9	335.8	330.9	348.9	358.6	360.1	359.2	354.6
2006	353.3	360.5	362.7	363.5	362.6	356.8	333.4	331.1	348.9	358.0	360.4	358.9	354.2
2007	350.4	358.2	360.4	360.1	359.2	356.1	332.5	328.9	347.2	356.8	359.7	360.1	352.5

Employment by Industry: Dallas-Fort Worth-Arlington, TX, 2000–2007

(Numbers in thousands, not seasonally adjusted.)

Industry and year	January	February	March	April	May	June	July	August	September	October	November	December	Annual Average
Total Nonfarm													
2000	2,683.7	2,701.1	2,725.7	2,740.0	2,761.6	2,784.9	2,765.8	2,779.8	2,792.8	2,796.4	2,806.2	2,820.7	2,763.2
2001	2,764.0	2,777.0	2,792.7	2,795.1	2,797.4	2,805.5	2,770.3	2,780.5	2,773.2	2,752.8	2,747.1	2,744.1	2,775.0
2002	2,689.7	2,696.4	2,710.9	2,711.2	2,720.6	2,720.7	2,691.9	2,703.0	2,706.2	2,698.4	2,705.4	2,706.3	2,705.1
2003	2,646.6	2,654.2	2,660.1	2,665.3	2,670.4	2,668.6	2,646.7	2,658.3	2,668.6	2,676.1	2,684.1	2,687.9	2,665.6
2004	2,640.7	2,654.5	2,672.7	2,690.5	2,697.5	2,696.8	2,690.7	2,704.9	2,714.2	2,729.8	2,737.8	2,747.7	2,698.2
2005	2,689.1	2,707.0	2,725.5	2,751.0	2,760.1	2,765.7	2,763.9	2,779.3	2,796.9	2,804.7	2,824.2	2,830.1	2,766.5
2006	2,782.6	2,802.3	2,823.5	2,839.9	2,854.9	2,868.2	2,845.5	2,869.5	2,883.9	2,888.8	2,912.3	2,925.3	2,858.1
2007	2,861.8	2,889.5	2,917.2	2,925.9	2,942.8	2,959.0	2,932.6	2,954.5	2,964.1	2,976.5	2,984.1	2,991.8	2,941.7
Total Private													
2000	2,371.3	2,385.4	2,409.1	2,422.4	2,438.3	2,469.2	2,465.7	2,475.9	2,476.5	2,475.9	2,483.1	2,494.5	2,447.3
2001	2,443.4	2,451.1	2,466.4	2,470.1	2,472.2	2,484.2	2,465.5	2,470.4	2,449.2	2,421.7	2,413.1	2,410.9	2,451.5
2002	2,362.1	2,360.4	2,374.0	2,376.4	2,384.2	2,389.8	2,379.4	2,383.8	2,371.2	2,355.5	2,358.7	2,360.6	2,371.3
2003	2,309.7	2,308.0	2,314.7	2,319.3	2,323.0	2,326.4	2,324.3	2,334.9	2,326.5	2,330.1	2,335.3	2,342.2	2,324.5
2004	2,299.6	2,306.4	2,326.3	2,342.1	2,347.1	2,353.5	2,362.4	2,368.8	2,360.6	2,375.2	2,380.0	2,390.6	2,351.1
2005	2,337.2	2,347.8	2,367.2	2,391.7	2,399.7	2,414.1	2,428.2	2,435.1	2,436.5	2,440.7	2,456.9	2,468.9	2,410.3
2006	2,423.6	2,436.2	2,458.7	2,474.2	2,488.3	2,509.7	2,500.3	2,517.5	2,519.0	2,517.8	2,539.0	2,554.6	2,494.9
2007	2,495.1	2,516.0	2,542.9	2,554.4	2,569.2	2,591.7	2,581.8	2,600.8	2,594.2	2,599.8	2,604.5	2,611.7	2,571.8
Goods-Producing													
2000	507.1	511.2	516.5	516.2	519.6	526.1	524.5	524.0	523.1	520.3	518.0	516.4	518.6
2001	512.3	513.7	515.6	513.0	513.4	516.2	509.2	509.2	502.7	493.0	487.5	482.6	505.7
2002	473.5	472.4	474.0	472.7	474.0	477.3	475.0	474.0	469.4	461.9	459.7	456.2	470.0
2003	448.0	448.2	448.0	448.6	450.3	452.5	451.3	451.9	449.9	447.4	446.0	445.2	448.9
2004	441.2	442.6	446.0	448.7	449.9	452.2	455.1	454.6	453.3	451.4	449.4	449.4	449.5
2005	443.0	446.8	450.4	453.8	456.4	461.9	465.6	466.0	465.4	464.4	464.3	465.1	458.6
2006	459.2	463.4	468.0	469.5	474.2	480.7	477.7	480.5	482.1	478.8	480.5	480.9	474.6
2007	473.3	478.1	483.1	481.7	484.0	490.6	486.8	489.2	489.9	489.8	488.8	488.1	485.3
Natural Resources, Mining, and Construction													
2000	154.6	158.0	162.6	162.7	165.4	170.3	171.4	171.7	171.1	168.8	167.4	167.2	165.9
2001	164.8	166.4	169.0	169.7	171.9	174.7	172.6	173.5	170.1	166.1	163.8	162.0	168.7
2002	157.7	158.2	160.2	160.4	161.9	164.5	163.5	163.9	160.7	156.9	156.3	154.3	159.9
2003	150.0	150.2	151.0	152.2	154.2	156.2	157.4	157.8	156.4	154.8	153.9	153.2	153.9
2004	150.8	151.0	153.7	155.6	156.6	158.2	160.6	160.9	160.3	158.9	157.7	157.6	156.8
2005	155.8	157.4	160.1	163.1	165.0	168.4	169.6	169.9	170.5	169.6	168.8	169.0	165.6
2006	165.6	167.8	171.2	171.6	174.9	179.0	177.2	178.9	180.4	179.4	180.4	181.4	175.7
2007	176.9	179.9	184.3	184.6	186.3	190.8	188.6	191.5	192.4	193.2	191.6	190.4	187.5
Manufacturing													
2000	352.5	353.2	353.9	353.5	354.2	355.8	353.1	352.3	352.0	351.5	350.6	349.2	352.7
2001	347.5	347.3	346.6	343.3	341.5	341.5	336.6	335.7	332.6	326.9	323.7	320.6	337.0
2002	315.8	314.2	313.8	312.3	312.1	312.8	311.5	310.1	308.7	305.0	303.4	301.9	310.1
2003	298.0	298.0	297.0	296.4	296.1	296.3	293.9	294.1	293.5	292.6	292.1	292.0	295.0
2004	290.4	291.6	292.3	293.1	293.3	294.0	294.5	293.7	293.0	292.5	291.7	291.8	292.7
2005	287.2	289.4	290.3	290.7	291.4	293.5	296.0	296.1	294.9	294.8	295.5	296.1	293.0
2006	293.6	295.6	296.8	297.9	299.3	301.7	300.5	301.6	301.7	299.4	300.1	299.5	299.0
2007	296.4	298.2	298.8	297.1	297.7	299.8	298.2	297.7	297.5	296.6	297.2	297.7	297.7
Service-Providing													
2000	2,176.6	2,189.9	2,209.2	2,223.8	2,242.0	2,258.8	2,241.3	2,255.8	2,269.7	2,276.1	2,288.2	2,304.3	2,244.6
2001	2,251.7	2,263.3	2,277.1	2,282.1	2,284.0	2,289.3	2,261.1	2,271.3	2,270.5	2,259.8	2,259.6	2,261.5	2,269.3
2002	2,216.2	2,224.0	2,236.9	2,238.5	2,246.6	2,243.4	2,216.9	2,229.0	2,236.8	2,236.5	2,245.7	2,250.1	2,235.1
2003	2,198.6	2,206.0	2,212.1	2,216.7	2,220.1	2,216.1	2,195.4	2,206.4	2,218.7	2,228.7	2,238.1	2,242.7	2,216.6
2004	2,199.5	2,211.9	2,226.7	2,241.8	2,247.6	2,244.6	2,235.6	2,250.3	2,260.9	2,278.4	2,288.4	2,298.3	2,248.7
2005	2,246.1	2,260.2	2,275.1	2,297.2	2,303.7	2,303.8	2,298.3	2,313.3	2,331.5	2,340.3	2,359.9	2,365.0	2,307.9
2006	2,323.4	2,338.9	2,355.5	2,370.4	2,380.7	2,387.5	2,367.8	2,389.0	2,401.8	2,410.0	2,431.8	2,444.4	2,383.4
2007	2,388.5	2,411.4	2,434.1	2,444.2	2,458.8	2,468.4	2,445.8	2,465.3	2,474.2	2,486.7	2,495.3	2,503.7	2,456.4
Trade, Transportation, and Utilities													
2000	612.4	611.5	614.4	615.4	619.6	627.3	626.1	631.9	631.4	637.0	649.5	660.2	628.1
2001	637.6	634.0	636.7	634.2	634.0	636.8	634.5	634.8	631.2	633.2	637.7	635.2
2002	618.2	613.7	615.4	613.6	614.1	614.9	615.3	615.7	612.3	610.4	616.8	624.0	615.4
2003	598.5	592.7	592.3	588.8	587.0	585.8	583.2	588.1	586.0	588.8	596.1	601.2	590.7
2004	582.5	580.1	583.3	583.8	586.5	587.2	590.0	594.8	591.6	595.2	604.7	611.5	590.9
2005	591.7	586.6	590.7	591.6	593.8	596.9	600.1	604.3	604.1	605.0	618.8	626.6	600.9
2006	604.4	601.1	605.2	606.5	608.9	611.0	609.6	614.0	611.7	613.8	626.6	635.3	612.3
2007	614.5	612.1	617.3	616.8	619.4	623.6	621.0	624.3	623.8	628.4	635.7	643.9	623.4
Wholesale Trade													
2000	166.8	167.1	169.1	170.9	171.4	172.9	171.5	171.8	171.8	172.2	172.7	173.2	171.0
2001	173.3	174.2	175.0	173.9	173.2	173.9	172.8	172.6	171.2	170.2	168.9	168.6	172.3
2002	166.3	166.1	167.1	166.0	166.0	166.5	166.6	166.5	166.2	165.2	165.3	165.7	166.1
2003	162.6	162.1	162.6	161.9	161.3	161.5	160.9	160.6	159.9	159.6	159.1	159.3	161.0
2004	157.7	157.7	158.5	158.1	158.3	158.4	159.1	159.0	158.4	159.2	159.0	159.3	158.6
2005	157.2	157.5	158.2	159.3	159.7	160.2	161.6	162.0	162.4	161.8	162.4	163.5	160.5
2006	162.3	162.8	163.7	164.3	165.0	166.0	166.1	166.9	167.3	167.6	168.5	169.2	165.8
2007	166.9	168.0	168.9	168.9	169.7	171.3	171.0	171.9	171.9	172.2	172.1	173.0	170.5
Retail Trade													
2000	309.9	308.3	308.9	307.5	310.2	315.0	315.1	319.2	318.0	322.1	332.9	341.5	317.4
2001	323.6	319.3	321.1	319.9	319.7	321.1	319.8	321.5	321.2	320.6	327.0	332.2	322.3
2002	316.7	313.1	313.2	312.2	312.0	311.9	312.0	312.0	309.5	307.9	315.1	322.4	313.2
2003	302.2	297.6	296.9	294.3	293.7	293.3	292.2	296.3	295.1	297.1	304.7	309.5	297.7
2004	293.4	290.9	292.9	293.6	295.9	296.3	297.3	301.6	298.9	301.5	311.7	317.4	299.3
2005	300.8	297.1	299.0	300.1	301.3	303.8	304.8	307.4	306.0	307.5	319.7	325.7	306.1
2006	308.0	303.9	306.4	306.6	307.5	307.9	306.3	308.7	305.2	306.4	317.6	323.1	309.0
2007	307.8	303.9	307.4	307.1	308.2	309.9	308.6	310.2	309.1	312.5	320.9	328.1	311.1

Employment by Industry: Dallas-Fort Worth-Arlington, TX, 2000–2007—*Continued*

(Numbers in thousands, not seasonally adjusted.)

Industry and year	January	February	March	April	May	June	July	August	September	October	November	December	Annual Average
Transportation and Utilities													
2000	135.7	136.1	136.4	137.0	138.0	139.4	139.5	140.9	141.6	142.7	143.9	145.5	139.7
2001	141.0	140.5	140.6	140.4	141.1	141.8	141.9	143.1	142.4	140.4	137.3	136.9	140.6
2002	135.2	134.5	135.1	135.4	136.1	136.5	136.7	137.2	136.6	137.3	136.4	135.9	136.1
2003	133.7	133.0	132.8	132.6	132.0	131.0	130.1	131.2	131.0	132.1	132.3	132.4	132.0
2004	131.4	131.5	131.9	132.1	132.3	132.5	133.6	134.2	134.3	134.5	134.0	134.8	133.1
2005	133.7	132.0	133.5	132.2	132.8	132.9	133.7	134.9	135.7	135.7	136.7	137.4	134.3
2006	134.1	134.4	135.1	135.6	136.4	137.1	137.2	138.4	139.2	139.8	140.5	143.0	137.6
2007	139.8	140.2	141.0	140.8	141.5	142.4	141.4	142.2	142.8	143.7	142.7	142.8	141.8
Information													
2000	116.1	117.7	118.8	119.9	120.7	123.0	123.5	124.2	124.7	125.1	126.2	126.2	122.2
2001	122.8	122.9	124.0	123.1	122.6	122.2	120.4	119.8	118.3	117.5	116.7	115.5	120.5
2002	114.2	113.0	112.6	110.1	109.3	108.6	106.2	105.3	104.1	103.5	103.0	102.4	107.7
2003	100.6	100.4	100.1	98.9	98.5	98.2	98.0	97.5	96.4	96.7	96.3	96.3	98.2
2004	96.1	94.7	96.1	94.8	94.9	94.7	94.0	93.4	92.7	92.9	92.8	93.0	94.2
2005	92.5	92.5	92.7	92.4	92.2	92.5	92.8	92.5	92.7	92.2	92.4	92.2	92.5
2006	91.5	92.4	92.3	91.0	90.3	90.3	89.4	88.5	87.9	86.6	86.1	85.8	89.3
2007	87.8	88.4	88.5	88.0	88.7	88.7	89.6	90.2	89.5	89.9	90.0	89.2	89.0
Financial Activities													
2000	204.8	205.0	206.3	208.1	208.3	209.2	209.6	209.2	208.6	208.8	208.7	210.0	208.1
2001	207.2	208.3	209.0	209.7	210.3	212.4	212.3	212.8	211.9	212.4	212.9	213.9	211.1
2002	212.3	212.4	212.8	212.2	212.8	213.3	213.2	213.4	212.4	211.7	212.3	212.1	212.6
2003	210.4	211.2	210.7	211.1	211.9	212.7	213.4	214.2	213.4	213.0	212.9	213.7	212.4
2004	212.0	212.0	212.7	213.6	213.7	214.6	216.2	216.8	216.1	217.5	217.6	218.7	215.1
2005	216.5	217.0	217.3	218.3	218.8	220.4	222.5	223.6	224.2	224.3	225.2	226.4	221.2
2006	224.3	225.4	227.4	229.0	229.4	230.7	229.5	230.6	230.3	230.4	231.1	232.5	229.2
2007	229.3	230.3	231.6	232.1	233.0	235.2	234.6	235.8	233.9	233.9	233.7	234.5	233.2
Professional and Business Services													
2000	367.1	370.8	376.3	380.8	382.7	392.3	390.5	393.7	396.9	393.5	392.8	393.4	385.9
2001	380.3	381.2	382.6	384.0	382.8	383.5	379.4	379.8	375.4	366.5	364.0	362.3	376.8
2002	352.2	351.7	354.0	355.4	356.6	357.3	356.1	359.6	357.8	355.4	355.2	353.8	355.4
2003	344.0	343.5	345.4	349.3	349.8	351.5	353.7	356.6	357.3	358.5	361.0	364.5	352.9
2004	354.8	357.3	360.5	366.3	366.3	368.3	371.5	373.1	371.2	376.6	376.4	377.3	368.3
2005	366.4	370.4	373.7	383.0	382.2	385.1	389.7	392.3	395.5	400.1	402.9	405.3	387.2
2006	395.9	399.9	404.4	409.4	411.3	415.3	416.3	421.9	424.1	426.2	431.4	433.9	415.8
2007	422.3	428.3	433.2	436.7	437.7	442.8	442.5	448.5	448.4	446.1	445.6	444.4	439.7
Education and Health Services													
2000	239.0	240.1	242.0	242.3	243.5	242.7	243.2	244.5	246.9	246.5	246.9	247.5	243.8
2001	245.7	248.3	249.8	250.9	252.3	253.9	254.4	255.8	257.0	257.0	257.6	258.0	253.4
2002	256.0	258.5	259.3	260.7	262.2	260.8	260.9	263.7	265.4	265.1	266.5	266.8	262.2
2003	266.4	268.2	268.9	269.5	270.0	267.9	269.6	270.7	272.2	274.2	274.4	272.6	270.4
2004	268.5	272.2	273.1	274.4	274.4	271.5	274.0	274.9	277.3	283.0	283.2	284.1	275.9
2005	277.6	280.8	281.9	285.0	285.4	284.7	288.6	289.1	291.0	293.8	294.3	294.8	287.3
2006	293.0	295.2	295.8	296.7	297.3	298.3	298.1	302.4	305.0	306.6	307.9	310.3	300.6
2007	303.6	308.7	311.7	314.5	315.9	315.7	314.4	318.3	320.9	323.5	324.3	324.8	316.4
Leisure and Hospitality													
2000	225.0	228.4	232.7	236.9	240.8	244.3	244.5	244.8	242.0	241.9	238.5	238.3	238.2
2001	234.1	238.7	243.2	249.9	251.6	252.3	251.0	251.6	246.2	242.7	239.4	239.0	245.0
2002	234.7	236.8	241.9	246.8	250.0	251.5	248.2	247.8	245.8	244.1	241.4	241.5	244.2
2003	237.1	238.3	241.3	245.9	248.4	249.8	247.5	248.7	245.0	246.8	243.9	243.2	244.7
2004	239.3	241.2	245.6	252.8	254.5	257.2	255.7	256.4	254.9	256.3	253.7	253.7	251.8
2005	247.1	250.2	254.1	260.8	263.3	264.4	263.5	262.4	259.4	258.5	256.3	255.3	257.9
2006	252.6	255.3	259.6	264.7	269.4	274.2	270.9	271.1	269.4	267.9	267.0	267.2	265.8
2007	260.9	264.9	270.9	278.8	283.6	285.9	284.8	286.0	279.9	280.5	278.7	278.7	277.8
Other Services													
2000	99.8	100.7	102.1	102.8	103.1	104.3	103.8	103.6	102.9	102.8	102.5	102.5	102.6
2001	103.1	104.0	105.5	105.3	105.2	106.9	104.3	104.2	102.9	101.4	101.8	101.9	103.9
2002	101.0	101.9	104.0	104.9	105.2	106.1	104.5	104.3	104.0	103.4	103.8	103.8	103.9
2003	104.7	105.5	108.0	107.2	107.1	108.0	107.6	107.2	106.3	104.7	104.7	105.5	106.4
2004	105.2	106.3	109.0	107.7	106.9	107.8	105.9	104.8	103.5	102.3	102.2	102.9	105.4
2005	102.4	103.5	106.4	106.8	107.6	108.2	105.4	104.9	104.2	102.4	102.7	103.2	104.8
2006	102.7	103.5	106.0	107.4	107.5	109.2	108.8	108.5	108.5	107.5	108.4	108.7	107.2
2007	103.4	105.2	106.6	105.8	106.9	109.2	108.1	108.5	107.9	107.7	107.7	108.1	107.1
Government													
2000	312.4	315.7	316.6	317.6	323.3	315.7	300.1	303.9	316.3	320.5	323.1	326.2	316.0
2001	320.6	325.9	326.3	325.0	325.2	321.3	304.8	310.1	324.0	331.1	334.0	333.2	323.5
2002	327.6	336.0	336.9	334.8	336.4	330.9	312.5	319.2	335.0	342.9	346.7	345.7	333.7
2003	336.9	346.2	345.4	346.0	347.4	342.2	322.4	323.4	342.1	346.0	348.8	345.7	341.0
2004	341.1	348.1	346.4	348.4	350.4	343.3	328.3	336.1	353.6	354.6	357.8	357.1	347.1
2005	351.9	359.2	358.3	359.3	360.4	351.6	335.7	344.2	360.4	364.0	367.3	361.2	356.1
2006	359.0	366.1	364.8	365.7	366.6	358.5	345.2	352.0	364.9	371.0	373.3	370.7	363.2
2007	366.7	373.5	374.3	371.5	373.6	367.3	350.8	353.7	369.9	376.7	379.6	380.1	369.8

Employment by Industry: Miami-Fort Lauderdale-Pompano Beach, FL, 2000–2007

(Numbers in thousands, not seasonally adjusted.)

Industry and year	January	February	March	April	May	June	July	August	September	October	November	December	Annual Average
Total Nonfarm													
2000	2,121.1	2,134.4	2,153.1	2,153.5	2,165.3	2,164.5	2,131.3	2,146.3	2,180.0	2,186.1	2,220.1	2,248.6	2,167.0
2001	2,204.3	2,220.6	2,236.2	2,221.5	2,222.8	2,218.5	2,171.7	2,179.4	2,207.3	2,206.2	2,224.7	2,244.5	2,213.1
2002	2,202.8	2,211.7	2,230.6	2,216.6	2,219.8	2,210.0	2,164.1	2,172.2	2,201.4	2,208.9	2,231.4	2,252.9	2,210.2
2003	2,211.1	2,224.7	2,235.6	2,217.7	2,217.6	2,208.5	2,169.1	2,179.6	2,213.6	2,228.0	2,240.1	2,271.1	2,218.1
2004	2,242.4	2,260.8	2,277.4	2,280.3	2,282.5	2,275.1	2,246.1	2,257.9	2,275.1	2,310.6	2,342.0	2,371.5	2,285.1
2005	2,329.5	2,352.5	2,363.5	2,375.9	2,377.2	2,349.4	2,334.7	2,373.9	2,389.0	2,383.6	2,401.6	2,433.7	2,372.0
2006	2,390.4	2,413.3	2,434.2	2,419.0	2,428.3	2,403.7	2,371.9	2,410.0	2,418.6	2,420.9	2,451.4	2,476.1	2,419.8
2007	2,428.5	2,447.4	2,463.7	2,443.1	2,447.4	2,416.9	2,375.0	2,414.7	2,420.8	2,431.6	2,451.7	2,468.3	2,434.1
Total Private													
2000	1,834.4	1,846.6	1,863.0	1,857.5	1,863.4	1,873.3	1,859.5	1,873.5	1,886.4	1,888.7	1,920.8	1,947.8	1,876.2
2001	1,905.7	1,920.0	1,933.9	1,918.0	1,918.5	1,919.9	1,893.1	1,899.2	1,903.6	1,898.8	1,915.1	1,934.0	1,913.3
2002	1,894.9	1,902.6	1,918.4	1,906.0	1,907.2	1,905.2	1,879.8	1,885.8	1,890.2	1,896.7	1,916.6	1,936.4	1,903.3
2003	1,897.4	1,908.9	1,917.9	1,901.3	1,899.0	1,898.1	1,879.2	1,888.0	1,899.3	1,911.4	1,923.5	1,954.9	1,906.6
2004	1,927.1	1,944.1	1,959.9	1,961.8	1,963.2	1,963.0	1,954.1	1,963.4	1,957.5	1,989.2	2,020.4	2,049.5	1,971.1
2005	2,009.3	2,031.1	2,041.0	2,051.2	2,051.8	2,052.4	2,041.8	2,053.1	2,065.1	2,057.6	2,076.3	2,108.0	2,053.2
2006	2,066.1	2,087.8	2,107.2	2,093.6	2,102.4	2,106.0	2,078.4	2,087.9	2,092.8	2,093.7	2,121.1	2,146.5	2,098.6
2007	2,102.0	2,119.5	2,133.5	2,113.8	2,117.6	2,116.1	2,078.5	2,088.3	2,091.7	2,101.6	2,118.6	2,134.0	2,109.6
Goods-Producing													
2000	247.1	248.8	251.3	249.3	251.2	252.0	248.8	250.1	251.5	250.9	252.1	252.5	250.5
2001	246.8	247.5	247.6	244.1	244.1	244.5	240.2	241.3	240.9	239.6	239.2	239.3	242.9
2002	233.0	233.0	233.3	231.0	231.8	232.1	228.5	229.6	230.2	230.0	230.3	230.5	231.1
2003	225.0	225.2	225.4	222.2	222.7	223.0	220.6	222.7	224.2	224.3	223.2	225.1	223.6
2004	222.2	223.8	226.4	226.7	228.3	230.1	230.1	232.5	232.2	234.8	236.8	238.5	230.2
2005	235.6	237.6	239.3	241.3	243.7	246.3	247.4	249.7	252.7	252.9	254.2	256.6	246.4
2006	252.7	256.2	258.8	260.2	263.3	266.2	263.9	265.4	267.2	265.7	266.6	267.3	262.8
2007	261.6	262.9	264.0	258.9	258.2	259.8	253.1	253.7	252.6	250.9	249.1	248.6	256.1
Natural Resources and Mining													
2000	0.4	0.3	0.4	0.4	0.4	0.4	0.4	0.4	0.4	0.4	0.4	0.4	0.4
2001	0.5	0.4	0.5	0.5	0.5	0.5	0.5	0.5	0.5	0.5	0.5	0.5	0.5
2002	0.5	0.5	0.5	0.5	0.5	0.5	0.5	0.5	0.5	0.5	0.5	0.5	0.5
2003	0.5	0.4	0.4	0.4	0.4	0.4	0.4	0.4	0.4	0.4	0.4	0.4	0.4
2004	0.4	0.4	0.4	0.4	0.5	0.5	0.5	0.5	0.5	0.5	0.5	0.5	0.5
2005	0.6	0.6	0.6	0.6	0.7	0.7	0.7	0.7	0.6	0.6	0.6	0.5	0.6
2006	0.5	0.6	0.6	0.6	0.6	0.7	0.7	0.7	0.7	0.7	0.8	0.8	0.7
2007	0.8	0.8	0.8	0.8	0.7	0.8	0.7	0.7	0.7	0.7	0.7	0.7	0.7
Construction													
2000	111.1	112.0	113.8	114.2	115.6	116.9	116.6	118.0	119.2	119.6	120.3	121.1	116.5
2001	118.2	118.7	119.1	117.6	118.5	119.9	119.1	120.1	120.2	120.8	120.6	120.4	119.4
2002	116.9	116.8	117.4	116.8	117.8	118.5	117.0	118.4	118.9	119.9	119.7	119.7	118.2
2003	116.6	117.1	117.7	117.1	118.4	119.1	119.6	121.0	122.2	122.7	122.2	123.3	119.8
2004	121.7	122.6	124.4	124.9	125.8	128.2	129.4	131.3	131.5	133.9	135.6	136.8	128.8
2005	135.7	137.1	138.2	140.1	141.7	143.8	145.7	147.3	149.8	151.0	152.1	153.6	144.7
2006	151.2	154.2	157.0	159.2	161.9	164.3	163.4	164.5	165.8	165.5	165.9	165.6	161.5
2007	161.1	161.9	162.9	159.0	158.5	159.9	156.5	156.7	156.0	155.1	153.1	152.2	157.7
Manufacturing													
2000	135.5	136.4	137.0	134.6	135.1	134.6	131.7	131.6	131.8	130.8	131.3	130.9	133.4
2001	128.0	128.3	127.9	125.9	125.0	124.0	120.5	120.6	120.1	118.2	118.0	118.3	122.9
2002	115.5	115.6	115.3	113.6	113.4	113.0	110.9	110.6	110.7	109.5	110.0	110.2	112.4
2003	107.8	107.6	107.2	104.6	103.8	103.4	100.5	101.2	101.5	101.1	100.5	101.3	103.4
2004	100.0	100.7	101.5	101.3	101.9	101.3	100.1	100.6	100.1	100.3	100.6	101.1	100.8
2005	99.3	99.9	100.5	100.6	101.3	101.8	101.0	101.7	102.3	101.3	101.5	102.5	101.1
2006	101.0	101.4	101.2	100.4	100.8	101.2	99.8	100.2	100.7	99.5	99.9	100.9	100.6
2007	99.7	100.2	100.3	99.1	99.0	99.1	95.9	96.3	95.9	95.1	95.3	95.7	97.6
Service-Providing													
2000	1,874.0	1,885.6	1,901.8	1,904.2	1,914.1	1,912.5	1,882.5	1,896.2	1,928.5	1,935.2	1,968.0	1,996.1	1,916.6
2001	1,957.5	1,973.1	1,988.6	1,977.4	1,978.7	1,974.0	1,931.5	1,938.1	1,966.4	1,966.6	1,985.5	2,005.2	1,970.2
2002	1,969.8	1,978.7	1,997.3	1,985.6	1,988.0	1,977.9	1,935.6	1,942.6	1,971.2	1,978.9	2,001.1	2,022.4	1,979.1
2003	1,986.1	1,999.5	2,010.2	1,995.5	1,994.9	1,985.5	1,948.5	1,956.9	1,989.4	2,003.7	2,016.9	2,046.0	1,994.4
2004	2,020.2	2,037.0	2,051.0	2,053.6	2,054.2	2,045.0	2,016.0	2,025.4	2,042.9	2,075.8	2,105.2	2,133.0	2,054.9
2005	2,093.9	2,114.9	2,124.2	2,134.6	2,133.5	2,103.1	2,087.3	2,124.2	2,136.3	2,130.7	2,147.4	2,177.1	2,125.6
2006	2,137.7	2,157.1	2,175.4	2,158.8	2,165.0	2,137.5	2,108.0	2,144.6	2,151.4	2,155.2	2,184.8	2,208.8	2,157.0
2007	2,166.9	2,184.5	2,199.7	2,184.2	2,189.2	2,157.1	2,121.9	2,161.0	2,168.2	2,180.7	2,202.6	2,219.7	2,178.0
Trade, Transportation, and Utilities													
2000	517.3	515.8	516.5	517.0	518.2	520.4	514.9	518.2	518.8	520.6	533.6	545.0	521.4
2001	524.6	524.1	527.3	522.8	521.9	520.5	516.9	518.5	518.9	518.5	527.2	535.1	523.0
2002	517.8	514.0	517.3	512.4	512.8	512.3	508.3	510.7	512.1	512.5	521.2	530.7	515.2
2003	511.8	509.4	508.8	507.1	506.2	505.2	502.9	504.3	505.9	509.2	517.6	528.4	509.7
2004	512.7	511.8	513.0	513.2	513.0	512.3	511.2	512.9	510.4	516.7	528.9	538.8	516.2
2005	522.1	522.1	522.6	525.4	526.7	526.1	527.1	529.4	530.3	531.9	538.2	550.9	529.4
2006	537.2	537.8	540.5	538.9	541.0	541.4	536.7	538.9	539.1	542.1	553.8	564.1	542.6
2007	546.3	545.5	547.7	544.2	547.0	546.4	540.1	541.6	541.0	545.1	556.9	565.3	547.3
Wholesale Trade													
2000	119.4	120.0	120.9	123.0	123.7	124.5	124.1	124.6	125.6	125.3	126.2	127.8	123.8
2001	128.7	130.1	130.8	131.0	131.6	131.2	130.4	130.6	130.9	131.1	131.9	132.6	130.9
2002	131.2	131.9	132.7	131.4	131.9	131.6	131.1	131.7	131.6	132.1	132.9	133.8	132.0
2003	132.6	133.0	132.9	132.9	132.9	132.9	133.1	133.8	134.2	135.0	135.9	137.8	133.9
2004	136.5	137.4	138.4	138.5	138.9	138.6	137.5	137.6	137.2	138.4	139.7	140.3	138.3
2005	139.1	140.1	140.2	141.0	141.6	141.2	140.5	140.7	140.9	140.8	140.9	142.3	140.8
2006	141.1	142.5	143.2	143.1	143.7	144.3	143.8	144.7	144.9	145.3	146.3	147.8	144.2
2007	146.4	148.0	148.6	147.3	147.8	147.4	145.0	145.3	145.5	146.4	147.3	148.8	147.0

Employment by Industry: Miami-Fort Lauderdale-Pompano Beach, FL, 2000–2007—*Continued*

(Numbers in thousands, not seasonally adjusted.)

Industry and year	January	February	March	April	May	June	July	August	September	October	November	December	Annual Average
Retail Trade													
2000	295.4	293.9	293.9	292.6	293.6	295.6	290.6	293.7	293.2	295.9	307.0	315.1	296.7
2001	296.4	294.3	296.1	292.2	291.2	290.3	286.7	288.4	289.0	289.3	297.8	304.3	293.0
2002	290.1	285.7	286.7	284.3	284.1	283.9	280.3	282.0	283.5	283.6	290.6	298.2	286.1
2003	282.9	280.1	280.1	279.0	279.3	278.5	277.3	278.3	279.4	282.1	289.6	297.0	282.0
2004	283.4	281.3	281.6	281.7	282.3	281.9	281.5	282.9	280.9	284.8	294.2	301.6	284.8
2005	288.0	286.8	287.2	288.8	289.2	289.9	291.6	294.2	294.6	296.5	301.7	311.4	293.3
2006	300.0	299.0	300.7	299.8	301.9	301.4	298.7	299.2	299.1	302.1	311.9	318.3	302.7
2007	304.3	302.0	303.1	301.3	303.9	303.4	300.2	301.1	300.2	302.9	312.9	317.6	304.4
Transportation and Utilities													
2000	102.5	101.9	101.7	101.4	100.9	100.3	100.2	99.9	100.0	99.4	100.4	102.1	100.9
2001	99.5	99.7	100.4	99.6	99.1	99.0	99.8	99.5	99.0	98.1	97.5	98.2	99.1
2002	96.5	96.4	97.9	96.7	96.8	96.8	96.9	97.0	97.0	96.8	97.7	98.7	97.1
2003	96.3	96.3	95.8	95.2	94.0	93.8	92.5	92.2	92.3	92.1	92.1	93.6	93.9
2004	92.8	93.1	93.0	93.0	91.8	91.8	92.2	92.4	92.3	93.5	95.0	96.9	93.2
2005	95.0	95.2	95.2	95.6	95.9	95.0	95.0	94.5	94.8	94.6	95.6	97.2	95.3
2006	96.1	96.3	96.6	96.0	95.4	95.7	94.2	95.0	95.1	94.7	95.6	98.0	95.7
2007	95.6	95.5	96.0	95.6	95.3	95.6	94.9	95.2	95.3	95.8	96.7	98.9	95.9
Information													
2000	58.0	58.2	59.3	59.2	59.8	61.7	63.1	63.8	64.4	63.8	64.4	65.4	61.8
2001	65.9	66.5	67.2	66.7	67.1	67.0	65.6	65.7	64.9	64.4	64.2	64.7	65.8
2002	63.3	63.4	63.6	62.6	62.5	62.7	61.7	61.1	60.8	60.0	59.8	59.9	61.8
2003	58.1	57.8	58.2	57.1	57.2	57.4	57.4	57.4	57.0	57.3	57.4	57.8	57.5
2004	56.2	56.2	56.4	56.4	56.5	56.7	56.6	56.7	56.3	56.7	56.9	57.4	56.6
2005	56.5	56.9	57.0	56.5	56.4	56.5	55.9	55.7	55.6	54.5	54.8	54.9	55.9
2006	53.8	54.2	54.3	53.5	53.9	53.8	53.3	53.1	52.5	52.1	52.1	52.2	53.2
2007	51.5	51.9	52.2	52.1	52.4	52.6	52.0	52.0	51.6	51.7	52.0	52.3	52.0
Financial Activities													
2000	155.7	156.4	157.0	156.8	156.5	158.7	157.3	157.9	158.3	157.6	158.2	159.6	157.5
2001	156.8	158.1	159.4	159.0	159.3	160.2	159.6	160.2	159.8	159.9	160.3	160.8	159.5
2002	160.6	161.4	162.2	161.6	161.7	161.8	162.1	162.9	162.7	163.1	163.9	164.4	162.4
2003	162.2	162.8	163.1	162.8	163.1	163.5	163.7	164.4	164.6	165.2	165.0	166.7	163.9
2004	164.7	165.8	167.0	168.5	168.9	169.2	170.7	170.6	170.3	172.6	172.7	174.4	169.6
2005	172.8	174.3	175.0	176.3	176.8	177.9	178.3	179.4	179.6	179.8	180.8	182.8	177.8
2006	179.4	181.5	182.7	182.7	183.4	184.1	182.8	183.5	182.7	183.5	184.2	186.2	183.1
2007	181.8	182.8	182.9	180.8	180.4	180.9	180.0	179.4	178.5	180.0	179.7	180.9	180.7
Professional and Business Services													
2000	294.6	297.2	302.5	303.5	306.1	310.9	313.8	319.4	323.6	323.8	330.6	335.8	313.5
2001	333.7	336.5	338.3	338.1	337.6	341.2	337.6	338.0	340.2	340.6	341.1	343.7	338.9
2002	336.4	338.1	343.3	344.9	345.2	345.7	341.8	339.7	336.7	337.8	340.1	342.4	341.0
2003	337.7	342.5	345.3	341.0	340.0	341.3	341.0	343.5	344.9	348.4	348.9	355.6	344.2
2004	350.5	356.3	361.1	363.4	363.7	364.6	365.7	368.0	368.5	380.8	387.3	395.6	368.8
2005	387.7	394.6	397.6	398.7	397.4	397.4	394.9	396.7	400.8	395.9	400.2	405.5	397.3
2006	393.5	398.6	403.6	399.4	401.5	403.0	397.6	397.8	399.1	397.3	400.1	405.4	399.7
2007	395.6	401.0	403.8	399.7	400.2	400.8	393.9	396.8	397.9	397.7	398.2	399.4	398.8
Education and Health Services													
2000	253.0	256.1	257.6	255.0	255.8	256.7	253.2	254.5	257.3	258.1	259.7	261.9	256.6
2001	254.8	258.2	260.1	260.1	262.3	263.1	260.5	262.2	266.3	267.3	269.3	272.0	263.0
2002	267.9	271.1	273.8	272.4	273.4	273.8	269.0	271.9	276.1	277.4	279.0	281.0	273.9
2003	277.5	280.8	282.5	282.1	282.9	283.2	278.9	281.3	285.5	287.9	287.1	289.8	283.3
2004	286.6	290.1	291.0	292.6	293.7	292.7	289.3	291.3	292.3	295.9	297.6	298.6	292.6
2005	293.5	297.7	298.2	301.3	301.3	299.6	298.7	301.8	304.4	303.4	303.8	305.7	300.8
2006	300.0	303.0	305.4	305.3	307.2	306.6	303.8	307.2	309.7	310.6	312.6	314.9	307.2
2007	311.3	314.7	316.2	316.6	318.1	317.5	312.9	316.4	320.2	323.4	323.3	323.3	317.8
Leisure and Hospitality													
2000	214.4	219.3	223.4	221.3	219.7	216.4	213.0	214.2	216.3	217.4	225.2	230.4	219.3
2001	227.6	233.2	237.6	232.6	232.0	229.4	220.3	221.6	221.0	217.9	222.8	227.0	226.9
2002	224.0	228.6	231.3	228.5	227.0	224.0	215.8	217.0	218.1	221.4	226.5	230.8	224.4
2003	229.7	233.6	237.0	232.4	230.1	227.4	220.7	220.9	223.3	225.2	230.4	236.2	228.9
2004	238.9	243.6	247.5	244.7	242.2	239.4	233.5	233.6	229.7	234.7	241.7	247.6	239.8
2005	242.8	248.6	252.1	252.3	250.2	249.6	241.7	242.4	243.3	242.0	246.5	252.6	247.0
2006	250.4	256.1	260.2	254.8	253.1	251.2	242.9	244.4	244.7	245.0	253.4	257.2	251.1
2007	254.6	260.1	264.7	261.0	260.1	256.5	246.9	248.2	249.1	251.8	258.1	262.1	256.1
Other Services													
2000	94.3	94.8	95.4	95.4	96.1	96.5	95.4	95.4	96.2	96.5	97.0	97.2	95.9
2001	95.5	95.9	96.4	94.6	94.2	94.0	92.4	91.7	91.6	90.6	91.0	91.4	93.3
2002	91.9	93.0	93.6	92.6	92.8	92.8	92.6	92.9	93.5	94.5	95.8	96.7	93.6
2003	95.4	96.8	97.6	96.6	96.8	97.1	94.0	93.5	93.9	93.9	95.3	95.3	95.4
2004	95.3	96.5	97.5	96.3	96.9	98.0	97.0	97.8	97.8	97.0	98.5	98.6	97.3
2005	98.3	99.3	99.2	99.4	99.3	99.0	97.8	98.0	98.4	97.2	97.8	99.0	98.6
2006	99.1	100.4	101.7	98.8	99.0	99.7	97.4	97.6	97.8	97.4	98.3	99.2	98.9
2007	99.3	100.6	102.0	100.5	101.2	101.6	99.6	100.2	100.8	101.0	101.3	102.1	100.9
Government													
2000	286.7	287.8	290.1	296.0	301.9	291.2	271.8	272.8	293.6	297.4	299.3	300.8	290.8
2001	298.6	300.6	302.3	303.5	304.3	298.6	278.6	280.2	303.7	307.4	309.6	310.5	299.8
2002	307.9	309.1	312.2	310.6	312.6	304.8	284.3	286.4	311.2	312.2	314.8	316.5	306.9
2003	313.7	315.8	317.7	316.4	318.6	310.4	289.9	291.6	314.3	316.6	316.6	316.2	311.5
2004	315.3	316.7	317.5	318.5	319.3	312.1	292.0	294.5	317.6	321.4	321.6	322.0	314.0
2005	320.2	321.4	322.5	324.7	325.4	297.0	292.9	320.8	323.9	326.0	325.3	325.7	318.8
2006	324.3	325.5	327.0	325.4	325.9	297.7	293.5	322.1	325.8	327.2	330.3	329.6	321.2
2007	326.5	327.9	330.2	329.3	329.8	300.8	296.5	326.4	329.1	330.0	333.1	334.3	324.5

Employment by Industry: Washington-Arlington-Alexandria, DC-VA-MD-WV, 2000–2007

(Numbers in thousands, not seasonally adjusted.)

Industry and year	January	February	March	April	May	June	July	August	September	October	November	December	Annual Average
Total Nonfarm													
2000	2,583.6	2,594.1	2,629.4	2,656.5	2,677.5	2,711.9	2,691.0	2,694.1	2,702.8	2,714.7	2,733.1	2,752.5	2,678.4
2001	2,672.7	2,680.8	2,702.0	2,707.3	2,725.9	2,755.0	2,729.6	2,727.8	2,719.7	2,724.5	2,731.7	2,749.3	2,718.9
2002	2,680.9	2,688.7	2,709.6	2,715.4	2,733.1	2,754.7	2,730.5	2,730.8	2,735.7	2,741.1	2,752.9	2,761.9	2,727.9
2003	2,721.0	2,717.0	2,741.5	2,768.5	2,788.3	2,810.9	2,807.1	2,799.5	2,804.4	2,806.7	2,817.9	2,830.6	2,784.5
2004	2,772.6	2,784.5	2,819.3	2,830.8	2,854.3	2,875.5	2,869.7	2,866.6	2,872.3	2,892.7	2,905.1	2,915.7	2,854.9
2005	2,848.3	2,860.8	2,879.0	2,901.2	2,919.4	2,937.6	2,936.5	2,930.0	2,935.6	2,935.7	2,956.9	2,967.9	2,917.4
2006	2,908.6	2,919.7	2,946.7	2,953.7	2,971.7	2,996.1	2,979.6	2,972.5	2,973.9	2,980.7	2,992.6	3,006.9	2,966.9
2007	2,943.2	2,949.1	2,972.9	2,979.5	2,998.9	3,017.0	2,991.8	2,980.8	2,992.3	3,005.2	3,019.4	3,027.9	2,989.8
Total Private													
2000	2,010.8	2,020.3	2,050.7	2,075.0	2,089.5	2,124.8	2,128.3	2,132.7	2,126.7	2,136.6	2,150.8	2,166.6	2,101.1
2001	2,093.2	2,101.3	2,119.5	2,124.4	2,139.9	2,166.0	2,157.7	2,156.2	2,130.0	2,134.3	2,140.2	2,152.1	2,134.6
2002	2,086.0	2,090.9	2,108.5	2,116.6	2,130.8	2,150.6	2,146.0	2,144.8	2,131.7	2,132.4	2,143.1	2,149.4	2,127.6
2003	2,108.1	2,103.0	2,124.8	2,151.4	2,168.4	2,189.9	2,192.6	2,190.5	2,185.7	2,189.7	2,199.6	2,211.4	2,167.9
2004	2,156.8	2,164.7	2,195.0	2,209.6	2,228.7	2,254.3	2,257.4	2,255.9	2,250.8	2,259.9	2,269.0	2,280.1	2,231.9
2005	2,222.7	2,233.1	2,249.1	2,270.8	2,285.6	2,306.3	2,308.6	2,305.1	2,304.7	2,298.7	2,313.9	2,325.5	2,285.3
2006	2,275.8	2,281.6	2,305.1	2,313.5	2,328.0	2,356.4	2,345.4	2,341.9	2,334.8	2,333.8	2,344.3	2,356.6	2,326.4
2007	2,305.9	2,305.9	2,326.8	2,334.2	2,349.4	2,371.5	2,361.5	2,355.1	2,346.2	2,350.9	2,361.7	2,369.0	2,344.8
Goods-Producing													
2000	221.0	221.8	227.8	229.6	232.2	236.9	239.5	240.6	240.1	239.0	238.9	238.1	233.8
2001	231.2	232.4	236.0	238.0	241.4	244.4	244.1	244.9	242.7	240.2	239.2	237.1	239.3
2002	230.3	231.1	233.9	235.0	237.4	239.6	239.3	239.8	237.6	235.8	234.5	231.8	235.5
2003	226.5	225.7	228.7	231.9	235.5	237.8	240.5	241.4	240.2	239.4	238.6	237.3	235.3
2004	231.6	231.6	236.7	240.2	243.3	246.0	249.4	249.5	248.7	248.4	247.8	247.4	243.4
2005	240.7	240.6	242.9	249.1	251.9	256.0	257.9	259.0	258.7	255.4	256.3	255.6	252.0
2006	248.8	249.1	253.3	254.9	256.9	260.8	261.1	260.5	258.0	254.3	252.3	251.8	255.2
2007	244.2	241.0	245.0	247.3	249.4	252.6	251.8	251.9	249.3	246.9	245.8	244.3	247.5
Natural Resources, Mining, and Construction													
2000	141.4	141.8	147.4	149.6	151.9	155.5	158.0	159.0	158.8	157.9	158.2	157.4	153.1
2001	151.9	153.2	156.9	159.8	163.1	166.2	166.2	167.2	165.5	164.4	163.5	161.9	161.7
2002	156.6	157.8	160.2	161.9	164.5	166.9	167.1	168.0	166.1	165.4	164.6	162.1	163.4
2003	157.6	156.8	160.4	164.7	168.4	170.6	173.3	174.6	173.6	173.3	172.4	171.2	168.1
2004	165.9	166.0	170.7	174.4	177.5	179.8	182.6	182.9	182.3	182.5	181.9	181.4	177.3
2005	175.5	175.4	177.6	183.6	186.2	190.0	192.1	193.1	193.1	190.7	191.3	190.5	186.6
2006	185.4	185.7	189.7	191.1	193.2	196.5	196.4	196.1	194.2	191.3	189.6	188.7	191.5
2007	182.2	178.9	182.9	185.3	187.1	189.7	188.9	189.1	186.8	185.0	183.8	182.4	185.2
Manufacturing													
2000	79.6	80.0	80.4	80.0	80.3	81.4	81.5	81.6	81.3	81.1	80.7	80.7	80.7
2001	79.3	79.2	79.1	78.2	78.3	78.2	77.9	77.7	77.2	75.8	75.7	75.2	77.7
2002	73.7	73.3	73.7	73.1	72.9	72.7	72.2	71.8	71.5	70.4	69.9	69.7	72.1
2003	68.9	68.9	68.3	67.2	67.1	67.2	67.2	66.8	66.6	66.1	66.2	66.1	67.2
2004	65.7	65.6	66.0	65.8	65.8	66.2	66.8	66.6	66.4	65.9	65.9	66.0	66.1
2005	65.2	65.2	65.3	65.5	65.7	66.0	65.8	65.9	65.6	64.7	65.0	65.1	65.4
2006	63.4	63.4	63.6	63.8	63.7	64.3	64.7	64.4	63.8	63.0	62.7	63.1	63.7
2007	62.0	62.1	62.1	62.0	62.3	62.9	62.9	62.8	62.5	61.9	62.0	61.9	62.3
Service-Providing													
2000	2,362.6	2,372.3	2,401.6	2,426.9	2,445.3	2,475.0	2,451.5	2,453.5	2,462.7	2,475.7	2,494.2	2,514.4	2,444.6
2001	2,441.5	2,448.4	2,466.0	2,469.3	2,484.5	2,510.6	2,485.5	2,482.9	2,477.0	2,484.3	2,492.5	2,512.2	2,479.6
2002	2,450.6	2,457.6	2,475.7	2,480.4	2,495.7	2,515.1	2,491.2	2,491.0	2,498.1	2,505.3	2,518.4	2,530.1	2,492.4
2003	2,494.5	2,491.3	2,512.8	2,536.6	2,552.8	2,573.1	2,566.6	2,558.1	2,564.2	2,567.3	2,579.3	2,593.3	2,549.2
2004	2,541.0	2,552.9	2,582.6	2,590.6	2,611.0	2,629.5	2,620.3	2,617.1	2,623.6	2,644.3	2,657.3	2,668.3	2,611.5
2005	2,607.6	2,620.2	2,636.1	2,652.1	2,667.5	2,681.6	2,678.6	2,671.0	2,676.9	2,680.3	2,700.6	2,712.3	2,665.4
2006	2,659.8	2,670.6	2,693.4	2,698.8	2,714.8	2,735.3	2,718.5	2,712.0	2,715.9	2,726.4	2,740.3	2,755.1	2,711.7
2007	2,699.0	2,708.1	2,727.9	2,732.2	2,749.5	2,764.4	2,740.0	2,728.9	2,743.0	2,758.3	2,773.6	2,783.6	2,742.4
Trade, Transportation, and Utilities													
2000	386.3	382.6	385.5	385.1	388.3	393.5	391.8	393.2	392.5	397.1	408.6	418.7	393.6
2001	391.4	385.2	386.4	384.0	387.8	392.0	390.6	390.8	387.9	390.1	398.6	406.9	391.0
2002	384.7	379.7	381.1	381.5	384.6	388.7	386.9	386.7	386.2	389.2	397.1	405.4	387.7
2003	385.2	380.5	382.6	385.3	388.3	393.0	391.8	392.6	392.2	395.2	404.6	412.5	392.0
2004	391.8	388.1	391.5	390.6	395.0	402.1	398.8	399.2	397.6	404.9	413.8	422.0	399.6
2005	401.7	398.6	400.1	400.7	403.5	406.6	407.5	406.7	404.1	406.8	415.5	426.2	406.5
2006	405.3	396.7	398.7	397.4	401.8	405.8	403.6	403.3	402.1	404.5	414.4	422.8	404.7
2007	404.2	396.6	398.8	399.5	403.0	406.9	405.4	403.3	401.7	403.8	413.8	420.5	404.8
Wholesale Trade													
2000	66.8	67.3	67.7	67.6	68.0	68.6	68.3	68.3	68.1	68.1	68.5	68.8	68.0
2001	68.1	68.1	68.5	68.5	68.4	68.5	68.2	67.9	67.4	67.3	67.5	67.2	68.0
2002	66.5	66.3	66.4	66.4	66.5	66.6	66.4	66.3	65.7	66.3	66.5	66.8	66.4
2003	67.9	68.0	68.3	68.0	68.3	68.5	67.6	67.5	67.0	67.9	68.3	68.6	68.0
2004	68.6	68.8	69.2	68.3	68.3	68.8	69.0	68.8	68.7	69.8	70.3	70.5	69.1
2005	70.4	70.8	71.0	71.5	71.6	71.4	71.9	71.9	71.3	71.5	70.6	70.9	71.2
2006	69.4	69.6	70.0	70.0	70.5	70.7	70.4	70.3	69.9	70.1	70.1	70.5	70.1
2007	70.2	70.3	70.7	70.7	71.0	71.4	70.7	70.7	70.4	70.3	70.5	70.7	70.6
Retail Trade													
2000	251.2	247.1	249.2	249.2	251.8	255.5	254.3	255.8	256.0	258.6	269.9	279.6	256.5
2001	255.4	249.4	250.4	247.4	250.7	254.3	252.5	253.2	251.9	254.8	264.0	273.5	254.8
2002	253.7	249.0	250.4	250.4	252.9	256.0	254.0	253.8	254.6	256.0	263.4	271.7	255.5
2003	251.4	247.0	248.4	250.6	252.8	256.8	255.5	256.7	257.1	259.1	268.1	275.2	256.6
2004	257.3	253.5	255.7	256.4	260.1	265.6	262.8	263.2	261.5	267.4	275.6	283.2	263.5
2005	265.3	261.4	262.5	263.0	265.4	268.1	268.9	268.3	266.7	269.2	277.2	285.8	268.5
2006	270.5	263.7	264.8	263.8	267.1	270.1	269.0	269.1	267.8	270.5	280.1	285.5	270.2
2007	271.4	263.6	265.1	266.1	268.9	271.4	270.9	268.9	267.5	270.0	279.4	285.1	270.7

Employment by Industry: Washington-Arlington-Alexandria, DC-VA-MD-WV, 2000–2007—*Continued*

(Numbers in thousands, not seasonally adjusted.)

Industry and year	January	February	March	April	May	June	July	August	September	October	November	December	Annual Average
Transportation and Utilities													
2000	68.3	68.2	68.6	68.3	68.5	69.4	69.2	69.1	68.4	70.4	70.2	70.3	69.1
2001	67.9	67.7	67.5	68.1	68.7	69.2	69.9	69.7	68.6	68.0	67.1	66.2	68.2
2002	64.5	64.4	64.3	64.7	65.2	66.1	66.5	66.6	65.9	66.9	67.2	66.9	65.8
2003	65.9	65.5	65.9	66.7	67.2	67.7	68.7	68.4	68.1	68.2	68.2	68.7	67.4
2004	65.9	65.8	66.6	65.9	66.6	67.7	67.0	67.2	67.4	67.7	67.9	68.3	67.0
2005	66.0	66.4	66.6	66.2	66.5	67.1	66.7	66.5	66.1	67.1	67.7	69.5	66.9
2006	65.4	63.4	63.9	63.6	64.2	65.0	64.2	63.9	64.4	63.9	64.2	66.8	64.4
2007	62.6	62.7	63.0	62.7	63.1	64.1	63.8	63.7	63.8	63.5	63.9	64.7	63.5
Information													
2000	118.2	119.6	121.1	123.2	125.0	127.8	128.1	129.5	129.8	132.5	133.0	134.2	126.8
2001	134.9	135.4	135.4	133.8	133.5	132.2	131.4	130.3	128.5	126.6	125.3	124.9	131.0
2002	120.8	119.9	119.6	117.8	117.6	117.3	114.6	113.8	112.0	110.0	110.2	109.7	115.3
2003	109.7	109.9	110.0	109.2	109.9	110.4	110.2	110.1	109.2	108.3	109.0	109.1	109.6
2004	108.8	108.1	109.2	107.4	107.3	107.2	107.5	106.6	104.8	102.0	101.8	101.4	106.0
2005	100.0	100.4	100.3	99.6	99.7	100.2	100.4	99.7	99.5	99.4	99.3	99.4	99.8
2006	98.3	98.7	99.4	98.0	97.9	97.9	97.3	96.6	95.8	94.5	94.5	94.2	96.9
2007	94.5	94.6	94.4	93.4	93.8	94.3	94.2	94.0	93.1	92.4	92.6	92.9	93.7
Financial Activities													
2000	142.9	143.3	144.3	144.3	144.7	146.6	147.0	147.1	146.1	145.7	146.6	147.8	145.5
2001	145.0	145.5	146.3	146.9	147.7	149.2	149.6	149.6	147.9	148.1	148.4	149.6	147.8
2002	149.2	149.8	150.2	149.6	150.0	151.4	151.5	151.8	150.8	151.6	152.2	153.3	151.0
2003	152.9	153.0	153.4	155.3	156.2	157.7	159.2	158.8	157.2	155.9	155.3	155.6	155.9
2004	153.7	153.7	154.6	156.9	157.9	158.8	158.8	158.8	158.0	159.0	158.9	159.9	157.4
2005	158.3	158.8	158.6	160.3	161.0	161.9	162.1	161.6	161.0	160.2	159.9	160.8	160.4
2006	159.4	160.2	161.0	160.7	161.7	163.4	162.8	162.6	161.8	161.1	161.1	162.2	161.5
2007	160.2	160.6	160.8	159.8	160.1	160.9	160.3	159.2	157.8	157.0	156.9	157.2	159.2
Professional and Business Services													
2000	530.0	534.2	543.0	549.8	551.5	562.7	563.0	564.7	564.1	566.6	567.5	571.5	555.7
2001	561.4	566.0	570.6	571.1	571.6	578.6	573.4	572.7	564.5	568.3	567.2	569.8	569.6
2002	551.8	554.9	560.0	560.1	560.6	564.4	563.3	562.2	558.7	560.3	561.1	562.3	560.0
2003	565.8	565.7	571.1	583.6	586.5	592.2	594.2	594.9	592.8	596.3	598.0	602.1	586.9
2004	588.9	593.9	603.6	607.7	611.8	620.2	625.0	626.6	624.9	628.4	628.3	632.6	616.0
2005	623.4	629.1	634.9	641.5	643.5	650.6	655.6	655.7	656.3	654.0	655.3	656.6	646.4
2006	645.5	651.2	657.6	661.8	663.9	673.2	672.7	672.8	669.2	667.8	668.6	670.1	664.5
2007	659.9	664.9	670.3	674.7	677.8	685.6	683.9	684.4	678.3	681.3	681.5	683.6	677.2
Education and Health Services													
2000	264.6	269.5	271.9	276.3	274.6	275.1	276.8	276.6	277.9	281.3	284.1	283.8	276.0
2001	274.0	278.0	280.4	281.7	280.3	281.3	282.8	283.0	285.5	289.3	290.9	293.2	283.4
2002	289.1	291.5	292.7	293.4	294.4	293.6	292.9	293.5	295.9	299.9	302.0	301.9	295.1
2003	291.3	293.3	296.5	296.3	294.0	291.8	288.4	287.1	295.2	297.3	298.6	298.6	294.0
2004	296.7	302.3	305.2	305.2	303.4	300.2	296.8	294.7	303.1	308.2	309.8	308.9	302.9
2005	305.7	310.5	311.4	311.2	309.6	305.1	300.0	299.0	308.9	313.5	317.4	316.9	309.1
2006	311.5	317.0	319.3	319.7	317.0	313.7	307.9	307.0	317.3	323.7	327.5	328.1	317.5
2007	324.3	329.3	332.0	330.5	328.0	324.0	318.3	317.0	328.2	334.6	336.8	337.0	328.3
Leisure and Hospitality													
2000	202.7	203.6	209.9	217.7	223.7	231.8	231.1	230.5	225.4	221.5	218.8	218.3	219.6
2001	205.9	208.8	213.8	217.3	224.2	232.3	230.2	229.6	219.7	217.8	216.8	215.8	219.4
2002	207.1	209.7	215.5	222.7	229.4	237.0	237.6	236.9	232.0	227.4	227.6	225.7	225.7
2003	219.1	216.9	222.4	229.1	236.5	243.9	244.2	243.0	237.6	235.3	233.7	232.9	232.9
2004	224.5	225.5	231.3	236.7	244.1	252.2	252.4	252.5	246.8	243.1	242.0	241.8	241.1
2005	229.5	230.9	235.4	242.5	250.0	258.5	257.6	256.3	250.1	244.3	244.4	243.4	245.2
2006	234.8	235.9	241.8	245.8	252.7	263.2	261.1	260.9	253.7	248.8	247.0	247.3	249.4
2007	239.7	239.0	244.7	249.6	256.6	264.6	265.6	264.8	257.8	254.0	253.2	251.5	253.4
Other Services													
2000	145.1	145.7	147.2	149.0	149.5	150.4	151.0	150.5	150.8	152.9	153.3	154.2	150.0
2001	149.4	150.0	150.6	151.6	153.4	156.0	155.6	155.3	153.3	153.9	153.8	154.8	153.1
2002	153.0	154.3	155.5	156.5	158.8	158.6	159.9	160.1	158.5	158.2	158.4	159.3	157.4
2003	157.6	158.0	160.1	160.7	161.5	163.1	164.1	162.6	161.3	162.0	161.8	163.3	161.3
2004	160.8	161.5	162.9	164.9	165.9	167.6	168.7	168.0	166.9	165.9	166.6	166.1	165.5
2005	163.4	164.2	165.5	165.9	166.4	167.4	167.5	167.1	166.1	165.1	165.8	166.6	165.9
2006	172.2	172.8	174.0	175.2	176.1	178.4	178.9	178.2	176.9	179.1	178.9	180.1	176.7
2007	178.9	179.9	180.8	179.4	180.7	182.6	182.0	180.5	180.0	180.9	181.1	182.0	180.7
Government													
2000	572.8	573.8	578.7	581.5	588.0	587.4	565.7	562.5	576.1	578.1	582.3	585.9	577.7
2001	579.5	579.5	582.5	582.9	586.0	589.3	574.9	572.7	589.7	590.2	591.5	597.2	584.7
2002	594.9	597.8	601.1	598.8	602.3	604.5	587.7	587.2	604.0	608.7	609.8	612.5	600.8
2003	612.9	614.0	616.7	617.1	619.9	621.0	614.5	609.0	618.7	617.0	618.3	619.2	616.5
2004	615.8	619.8	624.3	621.2	625.6	621.2	612.3	610.7	621.5	632.8	636.1	635.6	623.1
2005	625.6	627.7	629.9	630.4	633.8	631.3	627.9	624.9	630.9	637.0	643.0	642.4	632.1
2006	632.8	638.1	641.6	640.2	643.7	639.7	634.2	630.6	639.1	646.9	648.3	650.3	640.5
2007	637.3	643.2	646.1	645.3	649.5	645.5	630.3	625.7	646.1	654.3	657.7	658.9	645.0

Employment by Industry: Houston-Sugar Land-Baytown, TX, 2000–2007

(Numbers in thousands, not seasonally adjusted.)

Industry and year	January	February	March	April	May	June	July	August	September	October	November	December	Annual Average
Total Nonfarm													
2000	2,198.2	2,218.6	2,235.6	2,237.5	2,253.9	2,262.7	2,247.0	2,258.4	2,276.4	2,277.2	2,286.6	2,302.5	2,254.6
2001	2,256.6	2,277.6	2,290.1	2,293.0	2,302.8	2,304.4	2,285.3	2,298.5	2,304.2	2,298.7	2,305.5	2,306.1	2,293.6
2002	2,263.3	2,278.7	2,288.6	2,286.1	2,295.5	2,298.4	2,276.8	2,287.0	2,294.0	2,291.1	2,296.6	2,302.9	2,288.5
2003	2,261.1	2,270.6	2,278.2	2,275.0	2,281.0	2,281.8	2,254.1	2,266.5	2,277.0	2,275.4	2,278.6	2,291.5	2,274.2
2004	2,256.9	2,268.4	2,279.6	2,283.7	2,287.5	2,293.2	2,279.8	2,287.2	2,294.8	2,303.8	2,314.1	2,329.0	2,289.8
2005	2,291.3	2,303.7	2,322.7	2,333.7	2,341.1	2,345.3	2,339.9	2,353.2	2,368.4	2,374.6	2,396.1	2,412.8	2,348.6
2006	2,373.6	2,394.5	2,418.8	2,418.7	2,436.3	2,448.0	2,437.9	2,455.1	2,472.8	2,479.5	2,499.9	2,518.6	2,446.1
2007	2,471.6	2,495.0	2,518.9	2,526.8	2,547.4	2,565.2	2,550.0	2,561.6	2,571.0	2,582.6	2,595.8	2,608.8	2,549.9
Total Private													
2000	1,892.2	1,906.6	1,922.8	1,923.8	1,934.1	1,957.9	1,954.6	1,965.2	1,962.7	1,963.3	1,972.9	1,988.9	1,945.4
2001	1,949.3	1,964.3	1,975.5	1,976.8	1,986.5	1,998.4	1,988.2	1,995.2	1,983.0	1,975.6	1,980.4	1,981.7	1,979.6
2002	1,943.0	1,951.2	1,960.0	1,957.6	1,969.0	1,977.7	1,967.4	1,974.7	1,964.1	1,953.6	1,958.9	1,965.6	1,961.9
2003	1,929.5	1,932.2	1,939.4	1,936.5	1,942.7	1,951.7	1,939.4	1,947.6	1,943.5	1,937.2	1,939.3	1,953.4	1,941.0
2004	1,921.7	1,928.4	1,939.2	1,944.3	1,948.4	1,960.8	1,962.0	1,966.8	1,958.6	1,964.4	1,973.9	1,988.8	1,954.8
2005	1,956.0	1,962.4	1,980.1	1,990.5	1,998.0	2,013.5	2,015.5	2,025.8	2,027.5	2,028.8	2,047.1	2,064.7	2,009.2
2006	2,030.2	2,045.0	2,068.6	2,071.3	2,088.5	2,110.0	2,112.2	2,124.3	2,126.1	2,127.0	2,145.6	2,165.6	2,101.2
2007	2,125.0	2,141.1	2,163.5	2,170.2	2,190.6	2,218.8	2,216.2	2,226.3	2,220.9	2,226.9	2,238.0	2,251.8	2,199.4
Goods-Producing													
2000	452.9	459.1	463.5	461.2	463.8	468.7	467.0	469.5	470.3	469.3	470.1	472.1	465.6
2001	469.5	476.5	479.3	480.5	482.0	481.5	477.9	480.0	478.4	477.0	476.7	472.8	477.7
2002	466.1	468.8	470.3	467.5	468.1	468.6	465.4	466.3	464.0	462.8	459.4	457.2	465.4
2003	453.0	452.9	452.1	450.1	450.8	452.0	446.9	447.4	448.3	445.8	441.4	442.0	448.5
2004	439.4	439.7	440.7	440.7	438.8	441.0	440.3	440.7	439.0	441.8	442.9	444.1	440.8
2005	441.1	443.4	447.5	448.3	447.7	451.8	452.8	454.6	456.8	457.0	459.8	462.9	452.0
2006	462.3	468.4	474.2	473.2	478.9	485.8	485.2	488.6	491.9	495.1	498.5	501.1	483.6
2007	497.3	503.1	507.1	506.8	512.5	520.0	517.7	517.7	517.3	520.1	521.4	523.8	514.1
Natural Resources and Mining													
2000	59.7	59.7	60.3	60.4	60.9	61.3	62.4	62.6	62.7	63.4	63.6	65.6	61.9
2001	63.0	63.8	64.3	64.4	64.8	65.5	66.2	66.5	66.0	66.1	66.5	66.2	65.3
2002	63.1	62.7	62.3	62.5	62.7	63.4	63.7	63.8	63.4	63.6	63.8	63.8	63.3
2003	63.5	63.5	63.8	64.0	64.4	64.9	65.7	65.9	65.5	65.4	65.3	66.4	64.8
2004	66.0	65.8	66.3	66.7	66.9	67.2	68.2	68.3	68.0	68.9	69.2	69.5	67.6
2005	69.5	69.9	70.2	69.3	69.7	71.0	71.6	71.8	72.0	72.7	72.9	72.9	71.1
2006	73.6	74.2	74.2	75.2	75.8	77.4	78.6	79.5	80.2	81.6	81.9	82.7	77.9
2007	82.6	83.0	83.3	83.2	84.0	85.4	85.5	85.7	85.1	86.0	86.4	87.3	84.8
Construction													
2000	166.0	170.3	173.0	170.8	172.3	175.2	172.4	173.9	174.6	173.1	172.3	171.6	172.1
2001	172.4	177.0	179.0	180.4	181.2	179.4	177.0	179.3	179.1	179.7	180.6	178.4	178.6
2002	177.6	180.8	183.4	181.8	182.9	182.2	180.2	181.1	180.7	180.9	178.4	176.4	180.5
2003	175.4	176.4	176.1	174.8	176.3	175.7	171.8	173.0	173.9	173.4	168.6	168.2	173.6
2004	166.0	166.5	166.7	166.9	164.8	165.3	163.3	163.5	163.6	165.8	165.2	165.7	165.3
2005	164.0	165.4	168.3	169.2	167.3	167.5	167.5	168.8	170.6	170.6	171.6	173.6	168.7
2006	172.8	177.6	181.9	177.7	180.4	183.2	181.6	182.9	185.6	187.1	188.4	188.9	182.3
2007	186.3	191.3	193.7	193.3	196.4	199.9	197.3	197.3	197.5	199.0	199.0	199.8	196.2
Manufacturing													
2000	227.2	229.1	230.2	230.0	230.6	232.2	232.2	233.0	233.0	232.8	234.2	234.9	231.6
2001	234.1	235.7	236.0	235.7	236.0	236.6	234.7	234.2	233.3	231.2	229.6	228.2	233.8
2002	225.4	225.3	224.6	223.2	222.5	223.0	221.5	221.4	219.9	218.3	217.2	217.0	221.6
2003	214.1	213.0	212.2	211.3	210.1	211.4	209.4	208.5	208.9	207.0	207.5	207.4	210.0
2004	207.4	207.4	207.7	207.1	207.1	208.5	208.8	208.9	207.4	207.1	208.5	208.9	207.9
2005	207.6	208.1	209.0	209.8	210.7	213.3	213.7	214.0	214.2	213.7	215.3	216.4	212.2
2006	215.9	216.6	218.1	220.3	222.7	225.2	225.0	226.2	226.1	226.4	228.2	229.5	223.4
2007	228.4	228.8	230.1	230.3	232.1	234.7	234.9	234.7	234.7	235.1	236.0	236.7	233.0
Service-Providing													
2000	1,745.3	1,759.5	1,772.1	1,776.3	1,790.1	1,794.0	1,780.0	1,788.9	1,806.1	1,807.9	1,816.5	1,830.4	1,788.9
2001	1,787.1	1,801.1	1,810.8	1,812.5	1,820.8	1,822.9	1,807.4	1,818.5	1,825.8	1,821.7	1,828.8	1,833.3	1,815.9
2002	1,797.2	1,809.9	1,818.3	1,818.6	1,830.4	1,829.8	1,811.4	1,820.7	1,830.0	1,828.3	1,837.2	1,845.7	1,823.1
2003	1,808.1	1,817.7	1,826.1	1,824.9	1,830.2	1,829.8	1,807.2	1,819.1	1,828.7	1,829.6	1,837.2	1,849.5	1,825.7
2004	1,817.5	1,828.7	1,838.9	1,843.0	1,848.7	1,852.2	1,839.5	1,846.5	1,855.8	1,862.0	1,871.2	1,884.9	1,849.1
2005	1,850.2	1,860.3	1,875.2	1,885.4	1,893.4	1,893.5	1,887.1	1,898.6	1,911.6	1,917.6	1,936.3	1,949.9	1,896.6
2006	1,911.3	1,926.1	1,944.6	1,945.5	1,957.4	1,962.2	1,952.7	1,966.5	1,980.9	1,984.4	2,001.4	2,017.5	1,962.5
2007	1,974.3	1,991.9	2,011.8	2,020.0	2,034.9	2,045.2	2,032.3	2,043.9	2,053.7	2,062.5	2,074.4	2,085.0	2,035.8
Trade, Transportation, and Utilities													
2000	480.7	479.2	481.0	479.8	481.7	486.0	485.1	488.9	485.5	489.5	497.4	507.6	486.9
2001	487.7	485.9	486.6	485.4	487.9	491.1	490.8	493.0	489.7	491.4	495.9	500.2	490.5
2002	484.0	482.3	483.4	481.2	482.9	484.2	482.3	483.5	481.0	480.2	487.2	494.7	483.9
2003	473.2	468.1	468.2	467.2	466.0	468.9	468.4	470.7	469.0	469.3	476.4	484.8	470.9
2004	466.6	464.5	467.0	469.9	469.9	472.1	472.5	475.2	471.6	474.1	482.5	491.8	473.1
2005	473.6	470.7	472.5	476.6	478.8	482.0	483.9	487.4	485.8	488.0	500.0	511.2	484.2
2006	491.0	489.2	493.5	493.5	495.0	498.4	499.1	502.5	501.9	504.1	513.0	522.8	500.3
2007	506.2	504.4	509.7	510.2	513.9	519.8	521.2	524.6	523.4	524.8	533.1	541.5	519.4
Wholesale Trade													
2000	116.8	117.3	117.8	118.0	118.1	118.9	118.9	118.9	118.9	117.9	118.0	118.6	118.2
2001	118.1	118.8	119.7	118.8	119.1	119.8	120.2	120.5	120.1	119.7	119.4	119.4	119.5
2002	117.6	118.0	118.6	117.8	118.2	118.4	118.2	118.5	118.5	118.1	118.5	118.4	118.2
2003	117.1	116.9	117.1	116.4	117.0	117.7	117.8	118.0	118.0	118.1	118.3	118.9	117.6
2004	116.8	117.0	117.8	118.2	118.6	119.4	119.4	119.4	119.6	120.0	120.2	120.8	118.9
2005	119.9	120.1	120.8	121.8	122.2	123.2	123.3	123.6	124.4	124.7	124.9	126.0	122.9
2006	125.3	126.5	127.8	127.5	128.1	129.3	129.3	129.8	129.8	130.5	130.7	131.0	131.6	129.0
2007	130.0	131.3	132.3	132.6	133.4	135.0	135.2	136.0	136.3	136.3	136.6	136.8	134.3

Employment by Industry: Houston-Sugar Land-Baytown, TX, 2000–2007—*Continued*

(Numbers in thousands, not seasonally adjusted.)

Industry and year	January	February	March	April	May	June	July	August	September	October	November	December	Annual Average
Retail Trade													
2000	247.0	243.4	245.0	243.0	244.4	246.6	245.6	248.4	245.4	249.3	256.7	263.8	248.2
2001	247.6	245.0	245.6	245.5	246.5	248.4	247.6	249.0	246.4	247.4	254.1	260.2	248.6
2002	247.4	245.7	247.5	246.4	247.4	247.8	245.3	245.9	244.4	244.0	250.9	257.2	247.5
2003	240.0	236.9	237.5	237.3	237.4	239.1	238.0	240.0	239.1	240.1	247.0	252.4	240.4
2004	239.7	236.8	238.6	241.3	240.1	241.2	240.4	243.6	240.9	241.9	248.7	254.8	242.3
2005	240.7	237.0	238.3	240.8	241.9	244.0	245.1	247.4	245.6	246.9	257.1	263.6	245.7
2006	248.8	245.8	247.9	248.4	248.6	249.9	250.6	252.8	251.2	252.4	260.8	265.6	251.9
2007	255.4	251.6	255.2	255.4	257.7	260.7	261.6	263.4	261.8	263.0	270.5	276.7	261.1
Transportation and Utilities													
2000	116.9	118.5	118.2	118.8	119.2	120.5	120.6	121.6	121.2	122.3	122.7	125.2	120.5
2001	122.0	122.1	121.3	121.1	122.3	122.9	123.0	123.5	123.2	124.3	122.4	120.6	122.4
2002	119.0	118.6	117.3	117.0	117.3	118.0	118.8	119.1	118.1	118.1	117.8	119.1	118.2
2003	116.1	114.3	113.6	113.5	111.6	112.1	112.6	112.7	111.4	111.1	111.1	113.5	112.8
2004	110.1	110.7	110.6	110.4	111.2	111.5	112.7	112.2	111.1	112.2	113.6	116.2	111.9
2005	113.0	113.6	113.4	114.0	114.7	114.8	115.5	116.4	115.8	116.4	118.0	121.6	115.6
2006	116.9	116.9	117.8	117.6	118.3	119.2	119.2	119.9	120.2	121.0	121.2	125.6	119.5
2007	120.8	121.5	122.2	122.2	122.8	124.1	124.4	125.2	125.3	125.5	126.0	128.0	124.0
Information													
2000	45.7	46.0	46.2	46.7	47.1	47.6	47.8	48.0	48.1	48.2	48.5	48.7	47.4
2001	47.8	48.1	48.2	48.0	47.5	47.4	45.8	45.6	44.7	44.4	44.3	43.8	46.3
2002	42.6	42.2	42.0	41.1	41.1	41.3	40.8	40.5	40.1	39.9	39.6	39.5	40.9
2003	39.3	39.2	39.2	38.9	38.8	38.8	38.9	38.6	38.2	37.8	37.8	37.8	38.6
2004	37.7	37.7	37.6	37.5	37.6	38.0	37.4	37.3	36.9	36.5	36.5	36.5	37.3
2005	36.9	36.9	37.1	36.2	36.2	36.5	36.1	36.2	35.8	35.4	35.6	35.7	36.2
2006	35.4	35.5	35.5	35.9	36.2	36.5	36.5	36.5	36.2	36.3	36.5	36.6	36.1
2007	36.6	36.8	36.7	36.7	37.0	37.2	36.9	37.0	36.7	36.8	37.0	37.2	36.9
Financial Activities													
2000	130.3	130.6	130.9	131.4	131.6	132.9	134.2	134.1	134.2	134.1	134.5	135.1	132.8
2001	133.7	134.3	134.7	134.6	134.8	135.4	135.3	135.0	134.2	133.2	132.7	132.9	134.2
2002	132.1	132.3	132.3	132.2	132.7	133.4	133.2	133.2	132.2	132.6	132.6	132.7	132.6
2003	131.0	131.4	132.0	132.9	133.7	134.4	134.5	135.4	134.6	135.7	135.5	135.9	133.9
2004	134.8	135.2	135.5	136.2	136.5	137.3	137.9	137.9	137.4	137.7	137.0	137.9	136.8
2005	136.3	136.7	137.1	137.3	137.4	138.4	139.8	140.4	140.3	139.5	139.9	139.9	138.6
2006	138.4	138.7	139.5	139.2	139.7	140.9	141.2	141.8	141.6	141.8	141.6	142.5	140.6
2007	141.4	142.3	143.0	143.4	144.2	145.7	145.9	146.3	145.7	145.9	145.6	146.5	144.7
Professional and Business Services													
2000	300.7	304.2	307.8	308.8	310.2	317.5	318.5	321.9	323.1	322.4	322.1	324.1	315.1
2001	316.2	319.1	320.6	320.8	320.3	323.3	321.4	321.4	318.8	316.1	316.5	315.9	319.2
2002	308.5	309.5	311.7	311.9	312.9	313.9	312.2	314.7	312.2	309.6	309.4	309.1	311.3
2003	305.2	306.4	307.3	307.9	306.5	306.9	304.8	306.7	306.8	306.0	306.0	309.2	306.6
2004	303.2	306.1	307.7	311.4	312.0	315.3	317.7	319.0	319.0	321.1	322.9	324.3	315.0
2005	321.1	324.9	328.4	330.8	331.3	333.8	335.7	337.8	341.0	345.1	346.7	348.2	335.4
2006	342.3	346.8	351.7	351.2	354.4	359.5	361.2	363.4	363.9	363.9	367.8	370.1	358.0
2007	362.6	366.6	370.7	374.7	377.8	383.5	385.9	387.5	387.0	388.8	389.4	390.0	380.4
Education and Health Services													
2000	219.0	220.5	222.3	222.9	223.3	222.8	222.5	223.4	225.3	224.6	225.3	226.2	223.2
2001	223.9	226.1	227.4	227.8	229.9	229.9	229.9	233.1	235.4	236.2	237.5	238.4	231.3
2002	237.1	239.4	240.2	241.0	241.9	242.2	241.7	244.3	245.4	243.8	245.3	245.5	242.3
2003	243.6	246.4	248.0	247.7	249.1	247.7	247.3	249.6	251.9	251.9	252.0	252.5	248.9
2004	250.2	252.1	252.8	251.8	252.7	251.8	251.8	254.1	256.0	258.4	258.8	259.9	254.2
2005	256.5	257.9	259.6	260.0	261.0	260.3	260.4	263.2	265.2	265.3	266.7	267.6	262.0
2006	264.6	266.6	267.8	269.0	270.2	269.8	269.4	271.7	273.6	273.8	274.4	276.1	270.6
2007	274.2	276.6	278.0	279.1	281.2	281.1	280.7	283.8	285.9	288.0	289.2	289.3	282.3
Leisure and Hospitality													
2000	174.2	177.5	181.2	183.0	186.2	190.8	187.7	188.0	184.7	183.6	183.1	182.9	183.6
2001	179.0	182.4	185.9	186.9	190.9	195.9	194.4	194.6	189.8	185.5	185.0	185.8	188.0
2002	181.4	184.7	187.5	190.5	196.1	199.8	198.0	198.5	195.8	191.7	192.1	193.3	192.5
2003	188.6	191.9	195.6	196.3	201.6	205.5	202.5	203.2	199.1	197.0	196.6	197.1	197.9
2004	195.5	198.1	201.5	202.3	206.3	209.7	210.0	209.5	206.0	203.7	202.4	203.0	204.0
2005	198.8	199.9	204.8	208.0	212.1	215.8	213.7	214.0	211.0	208.1	207.9	208.7	208.6
2006	206.4	209.3	215.1	216.6	220.7	223.7	224.8	225.2	222.6	217.9	219.3	221.2	218.6
2007	215.4	218.9	224.8	227.0	230.8	236.6	233.5	234.7	230.6	228.7	228.5	229.0	228.2
Other Services													
2000	88.7	89.5	89.9	90.0	90.2	91.6	91.8	91.4	91.5	91.6	91.9	92.2	90.9
2001	91.5	91.9	92.8	92.8	93.2	93.9	92.7	92.5	92.0	91.8	91.8	91.9	92.4
2002	91.2	92.0	92.6	92.2	93.3	94.3	93.8	93.7	93.4	93.0	93.3	93.6	93.0
2003	95.6	95.9	97.0	95.5	96.2	97.5	96.1	96.0	95.6	93.7	93.6	94.1	95.5
2004	94.3	95.0	96.4	94.5	94.6	95.5	94.4	93.1	92.7	91.1	90.9	91.3	93.7
2005	91.7	92.0	93.1	93.3	93.5	94.9	93.1	92.2	91.6	90.4	90.5	90.5	92.2
2006	89.8	90.5	91.3	92.7	93.4	95.4	95.4	94.8	94.6	94.4	94.1	95.2	93.4
2007	91.3	92.4	93.5	92.3	93.2	94.9	94.4	94.7	94.3	93.8	93.8	94.5	93.6
Government													
2000	306.0	312.0	312.8	313.7	319.8	304.8	292.4	293.2	313.7	313.9	313.7	313.6	309.1
2001	307.3	313.3	314.6	316.2	316.3	306.0	297.1	303.3	321.2	323.1	325.1	324.4	314.0
2002	320.3	327.5	328.6	328.5	329.5	320.7	309.4	312.3	329.9	337.5	337.7	337.3	326.6
2003	331.6	338.4	338.8	338.5	338.3	330.1	314.7	318.9	333.5	338.2	339.3	338.1	333.2
2004	335.2	340.0	340.4	339.4	339.1	332.4	317.8	320.4	336.2	339.4	340.2	340.2	335.1
2005	335.3	341.3	342.6	343.2	343.1	331.8	324.4	327.4	340.9	345.8	349.0	348.1	339.4
2006	343.4	349.5	350.2	347.4	347.8	338.0	325.7	330.8	346.7	352.5	354.3	353.0	344.9
2007	346.6	353.9	355.4	356.6	356.8	346.4	333.8	335.3	350.1	355.7	357.8	357.0	350.5

Employment by Industry: Boston-Cambridge-Quincy, MA-NH, NECTA, 2000–2007

(Numbers in thousands, not seasonally adjusted.)

Industry and year	January	February	March	April	May	June	July	August	September	October	November	December	Annual Average
Total Nonfarm													
2000	2,469.0	2,480.9	2,499.9	2,523.4	2,535.3	2,559.3	2,531.5	2,525.8	2,558.7	2,578.2	2,595.4	2,608.4	2,538.8
2001	2,531.3	2,535.2	2,539.7	2,553.7	2,557.2	2,565.7	2,523.3	2,515.2	2,521.8	2,524.1	2,524.7	2,526.4	2,534.9
2002	2,451.2	2,444.9	2,457.0	2,472.1	2,480.6	2,487.1	2,450.7	2,443.9	2,464.3	2,472.6	2,480.8	2,482.4	2,465.6
2003	2,394.3	2,384.3	2,392.5	2,413.6	2,423.7	2,430.4	2,401.9	2,391.6	2,414.1	2,419.9	2,429.6	2,426.5	2,410.2
2004	2,353.9	2,359.2	2,373.7	2,401.3	2,412.9	2,423.8	2,405.6	2,395.0	2,417.0	2,430.1	2,438.3	2,443.9	2,404.6
2005	2,370.7	2,379.7	2,385.6	2,421.4	2,431.1	2,443.3	2,422.7	2,415.8	2,439.2	2,447.9	2,462.1	2,468.4	2,424.0
2006	2,398.5	2,403.8	2,417.9	2,442.0	2,451.9	2,471.9	2,448.9	2,443.0	2,468.5	2,480.3	2,490.6	2,498.2	2,451.3
2007	2,435.2	2,436.4	2,446.3	2,474.8	2,493.4	2,510.2	2,482.3	2,475.7	2,494.2	2,504.7	2,514.3	2,517.4	2,482.1
Total Private													
2000	2,168.6	2,177.1	2,194.1	2,216.6	2,223.7	2,251.5	2,245.9	2,245.6	2,257.3	2,274.4	2,289.9	2,303.0	2,237.3
2001	2,227.2	2,228.2	2,232.6	2,245.9	2,248.9	2,259.6	2,236.9	2,231.0	2,217.0	2,218.3	2,217.9	2,218.8	2,231.9
2002	2,146.7	2,138.0	2,149.7	2,165.7	2,173.9	2,181.9	2,167.3	2,164.1	2,159.2	2,170.0	2,175.6	2,177.5	2,164.1
2003	2,093.5	2,081.1	2,089.6	2,110.3	2,120.8	2,128.9	2,119.1	2,115.3	2,114.4	2,122.0	2,130.6	2,128.1	2,112.8
2004	2,059.5	2,060.8	2,075.0	2,101.9	2,114.3	2,127.4	2,131.3	2,126.9	2,122.1	2,133.3	2,139.8	2,145.7	2,111.5
2005	2,075.3	2,079.5	2,085.5	2,120.6	2,130.1	2,145.9	2,146.7	2,145.7	2,143.2	2,148.3	2,160.4	2,167.9	2,129.1
2006	2,101.0	2,101.8	2,115.6	2,139.4	2,148.9	2,171.9	2,169.9	2,170.7	2,169.7	2,178.3	2,186.9	2,195.2	2,154.1
2007	2,134.7	2,132.5	2,141.9	2,169.5	2,187.1	2,207.9	2,203.7	2,203.3	2,193.8	2,201.0	2,208.3	2,211.6	2,182.9
Goods-Producing													
2000	380.9	379.9	384.4	390.4	394.0	401.6	397.6	401.2	401.1	401.8	402.8	402.2	394.8
2001	392.1	390.6	390.7	396.4	397.9	399.4	393.9	392.6	388.4	384.8	379.2	374.8	390.1
2002	362.4	356.6	357.9	362.0	365.7	367.2	362.6	363.0	360.5	360.1	358.0	352.8	360.7
2003	340.7	333.4	334.0	339.6	343.4	345.7	342.4	342.9	340.4	337.9	337.0	332.5	339.2
2004	319.9	318.2	322.2	329.7	335.3	340.0	339.7	340.9	338.3	335.2	334.1	331.6	332.1
2005	320.1	317.7	318.3	326.2	330.3	335.1	335.6	336.7	334.7	332.3	332.0	329.2	329.0
2006	318.9	316.5	317.8	324.2	327.3	331.7	332.1	333.4	331.6	329.6	327.2	325.1	326.3
2007	315.8	311.9	313.5	317.9	324.0	329.3	329.0	329.5	327.2	325.1	323.8	321.1	322.3
Natural Resources and Mining													
2000	0.8	0.7	0.8	1.0	1.0	1.1	0.9	1.0	1.0	1.0	1.0	0.9	0.9
2001	0.8	0.8	0.8	0.9	1.0	1.0	1.0	1.0	1.0	1.0	1.0	1.0	0.9
2002	0.8	0.8	0.9	1.0	1.1	1.1	1.1	1.1	1.1	1.1	1.1	1.1	1.0
2003	1.0	0.9	0.9	1.1	1.2	1.2	1.3	1.2	1.3	1.3	1.3	1.2	1.2
2004	1.0	1.0	1.0	1.2	1.3	1.3	1.3	1.3	1.3	1.3	1.3	1.3	1.2
2005	1.1	1.0	1.0	1.3	1.3	1.4	1.4	1.3	1.3	1.3	1.3	1.1	1.2
2006	1.0	1.0	1.0	1.1	1.2	1.2	1.3	1.2	1.2	1.2	1.2	1.1	1.1
2007	0.9	0.8	0.9	1.0	1.1	1.1	1.1	1.1	1.1	1.1	1.1	1.0	1.0
Construction													
2000	84.7	83.3	86.9	93.0	96.2	100.2	103.0	104.0	102.7	103.1	102.7	100.8	96.7
2001	93.7	92.6	94.0	100.7	104.7	107.6	109.7	109.7	107.4	107.8	106.3	103.5	103.1
2002	96.7	93.9	95.9	102.6	106.8	108.1	109.1	109.3	107.6	108.9	107.8	102.9	104.1
2003	95.0	90.5	91.6	98.6	103.0	104.8	105.8	106.0	104.5	103.2	102.4	98.9	100.4
2004	90.0	88.6	91.6	97.9	103.0	106.0	107.5	107.6	105.9	104.4	103.7	101.1	100.6
2005	91.5	89.2	90.3	98.5	102.4	105.7	108.2	108.6	107.7	105.5	105.4	102.5	101.3
2006	94.4	92.5	94.0	100.9	103.6	106.3	107.7	108.1	106.6	105.2	102.9	100.2	101.9
2007	92.4	88.9	90.5	95.5	100.7	104.2	105.6	105.7	104.5	102.9	101.8	99.0	99.3
Manufacturing													
2000	295.4	295.9	296.7	296.4	296.8	300.3	293.7	296.2	297.4	297.7	299.1	300.5	297.2
2001	297.6	297.2	295.9	294.8	292.2	290.8	283.2	281.9	280.0	276.0	271.9	270.3	286.0
2002	264.9	261.9	261.1	258.4	257.8	258.0	252.4	252.6	251.8	250.1	249.1	248.8	255.6
2003	244.7	242.0	241.5	239.9	239.2	239.7	235.3	235.7	234.6	233.4	233.3	232.4	237.6
2004	228.9	228.6	229.6	230.6	231.0	232.7	230.9	232.0	231.1	229.5	229.1	229.2	230.3
2005	227.5	227.5	227.0	226.4	226.6	228.0	226.0	226.8	225.7	225.5	225.3	225.6	226.5
2006	223.5	223.0	222.8	222.2	222.5	224.2	223.1	224.1	223.8	223.2	223.1	223.8	223.3
2007	222.5	222.2	222.1	221.4	222.2	224.0	222.3	222.7	221.6	221.1	220.9	221.1	222.0
Service-Providing													
2000	2,088.1	2,101.0	2,115.5	2,133.0	2,141.3	2,157.7	2,133.9	2,124.6	2,157.6	2,176.4	2,192.6	2,206.2	2,144.0
2001	2,139.2	2,144.6	2,149.0	2,157.3	2,159.3	2,166.3	2,129.4	2,122.6	2,133.4	2,139.3	2,145.5	2,151.6	2,144.8
2002	2,088.8	2,088.3	2,099.1	2,110.1	2,114.9	2,119.9	2,088.1	2,080.9	2,103.8	2,112.5	2,122.8	2,129.6	2,104.9
2003	2,053.6	2,050.9	2,058.5	2,074.0	2,080.3	2,084.7	2,059.5	2,048.7	2,073.7	2,082.0	2,092.6	2,094.0	2,071.0
2004	2,034.0	2,041.0	2,051.5	2,071.6	2,077.6	2,083.8	2,065.9	2,054.1	2,078.7	2,094.9	2,104.2	2,112.3	2,072.5
2005	2,050.6	2,062.0	2,067.3	2,095.2	2,100.8	2,108.2	2,087.1	2,079.1	2,104.5	2,115.6	2,130.1	2,139.2	2,095.0
2006	2,079.6	2,087.3	2,100.1	2,117.8	2,124.6	2,140.2	2,116.8	2,109.6	2,136.9	2,150.7	2,163.4	2,173.1	2,125.0
2007	2,119.4	2,124.5	2,132.8	2,156.9	2,169.4	2,180.9	2,153.3	2,146.2	2,167.0	2,179.6	2,190.5	2,196.3	2,159.7
Trade, Transportation, and Utilities													
2000	446.1	441.2	441.7	443.6	445.2	450.3	443.6	443.6	446.7	454.0	464.2	474.4	449.6
2001	450.4	442.5	442.2	442.4	443.5	448.4	440.4	439.2	438.8	441.7	449.9	455.9	444.6
2002	434.4	426.5	427.5	428.5	431.2	436.0	430.0	428.5	430.6	433.3	441.0	449.4	433.1
2003	426.0	419.3	420.7	421.5	423.9	428.5	422.7	422.2	424.3	428.5	436.7	442.0	426.4
2004	422.9	417.4	417.9	417.8	420.4	424.8	419.8	418.4	417.9	425.5	433.0	440.5	423.0
2005	420.1	415.8	414.8	417.6	420.2	423.8	418.8	418.5	417.7	420.9	428.5	437.5	421.2
2006	419.6	411.2	413.1	414.5	416.7	421.8	416.1	416.2	417.3	421.4	430.1	438.4	419.7
2007	419.3	411.1	411.9	412.4	417.6	423.2	417.7	417.0	417.1	419.4	427.3	434.7	419.1
Wholesale Trade													
2000	109.3	109.3	109.8	109.9	110.6	112.1	111.0	111.1	111.3	112.4	113.0	114.2	111.2
2001	111.9	112.0	112.1	111.8	111.4	111.8	111.5	110.8	109.5	109.2	108.7	108.7	110.8
2002	107.1	106.6	106.9	105.9	106.0	106.7	105.7	105.2	104.4	104.7	104.7	105.2	105.8
2003	104.7	104.2	104.1	103.7	103.9	104.4	104.5	104.4	103.6	103.8	104.2	104.7	104.2
2004	102.8	102.6	103.2	102.9	102.6	103.2	102.8	102.5	101.3	101.3	101.2	101.3	102.3
2005	100.8	100.6	100.2	100.9	101.5	102.1	102.8	102.8	102.3	103.1	103.4	104.1	102.1
2006	103.0	102.6	102.8	103.4	103.5	104.7	104.9	105.2	104.5	104.8	104.9	105.4	104.1
2007	104.3	103.9	104.2	104.0	104.4	105.5	105.5	105.4	104.6	104.8	105.0	105.8	104.8

Employment by Industry: Boston-Cambridge-Quincy, MA-NH, NECTA, 2000–2007—*Continued*

(Numbers in thousands, not seasonally adjusted.)

Industry and year	January	February	March	April	May	June	July	August	September	October	November	December	Annual Average
Retail Trade													
2000	263.7	258.7	259.0	259.1	260.0	262.8	259.5	259.4	260.1	265.3	275.5	284.9	264.0
2001	265.5	257.4	257.5	257.0	258.2	262.2	257.5	257.5	256.2	259.6	269.9	277.0	261.3
2002	259.7	252.6	253.5	255.1	257.0	260.6	258.3	257.8	257.8	259.5	267.5	276.0	259.6
2003	255.0	249.2	250.5	251.7	253.2	257.1	254.3	254.4	254.2	258.5	266.3	271.5	256.3
2004	256.6	251.8	251.7	251.1	253.4	257.1	254.9	254.5	253.2	259.6	267.5	275.3	257.2
2005	257.2	253.1	252.6	254.3	255.7	258.3	254.8	255.0	252.9	256.4	263.8	271.4	257.1
2006	256.7	248.8	250.2	250.7	252.0	254.8	251.0	251.3	249.5	253.8	262.5	269.3	254.2
2007	253.2	245.9	246.1	246.6	250.5	253.8	251.3	251.0	248.7	251.4	259.3	264.8	251.9
Transportation and Utilities													
2000	73.1	73.2	72.9	74.6	74.6	75.4	73.1	73.1	75.3	76.3	75.7	75.3	74.4
2001	73.0	73.1	72.6	73.6	73.9	74.4	71.4	70.9	73.1	72.9	71.3	70.2	72.5
2002	67.6	67.3	67.1	67.5	68.2	68.7	66.0	65.5	68.4	69.1	68.8	68.2	67.7
2003	66.3	65.9	66.1	66.1	66.8	67.0	63.9	63.4	66.5	66.2	66.2	65.8	65.9
2004	63.5	63.0	63.0	63.8	64.4	64.5	62.1	61.4	63.4	64.6	64.3	63.9	63.5
2005	62.1	62.1	62.0	62.4	63.0	63.4	61.2	60.7	62.5	61.4	61.3	62.0	62.0
2006	59.9	59.8	60.1	60.4	61.2	62.3	60.2	59.7	63.3	62.8	62.7	63.7	61.3
2007	61.8	61.3	61.6	61.8	62.7	63.9	60.9	60.6	63.8	63.2	63.0	64.1	62.4
Information													
2000	89.5	90.4	92.1	93.5	95.0	97.4	99.3	93.6	99.5	99.7	100.3	100.9	95.9
2001	99.8	99.7	99.0	99.4	98.0	97.9	96.2	95.2	93.3	91.3	90.5	89.8	95.8
2002	88.2	87.5	87.2	85.6	84.9	84.7	84.1	84.3	82.0	82.0	81.8	81.9	84.5
2003	79.5	79.1	79.0	78.0	77.6	78.0	76.9	76.5	75.7	75.4	75.2	75.2	77.2
2004	73.8	73.4	74.0	73.3	73.5	73.7	73.9	73.9	73.5	73.4	73.8	74.1	73.7
2005	73.4	73.6	73.6	73.7	73.8	74.4	74.6	74.3	73.7	73.8	74.0	74.3	73.9
2006	74.0	74.1	74.1	73.7	74.0	74.6	74.4	74.5	73.6	74.5	74.6	74.9	74.3
2007	73.6	73.8	74.0	74.1	74.4	75.2	75.3	75.2	74.6	75.2	75.4	75.8	74.7
Financial Activities													
2000	189.0	188.4	188.9	189.1	189.1	192.7	193.0	193.6	192.4	193.6	194.2	196.3	191.7
2001	195.9	196.0	197.1	194.2	193.9	196.4	197.4	197.4	194.7	193.8	194.3	195.3	195.5
2002	195.0	193.7	193.1	190.6	190.9	192.7	193.1	192.6	189.8	190.4	189.8	190.5	191.9
2003	188.5	187.3	187.2	187.1	187.3	188.4	188.3	188.2	184.9	183.7	184.0	184.4	186.6
2004	181.8	182.1	182.3	182.5	182.7	184.9	186.1	185.5	183.4	182.1	182.1	183.1	183.2
2005	182.5	182.4	182.6	183.2	184.1	186.9	189.7	189.9	188.6	187.0	187.8	189.4	186.2
2006	185.7	185.6	185.9	186.1	186.8	189.3	191.6	191.1	189.4	188.9	189.4	190.9	188.4
2007	188.5	188.5	188.5	188.6	189.1	191.3	191.6	191.5	188.6	188.7	188.7	189.7	189.4
Professional and Business Services													
2000	395.0	398.2	403.5	409.9	411.5	422.0	425.3	427.9	427.3	426.7	428.6	429.9	417.2
2001	416.7	414.9	415.6	417.6	416.7	418.7	410.8	409.2	403.3	399.6	396.3	395.2	409.6
2002	382.0	378.7	380.0	385.3	384.9	387.5	385.2	384.4	381.1	381.2	380.2	379.0	382.5
2003	363.4	359.4	359.7	367.0	367.7	370.5	371.8	371.6	369.9	371.2	372.4	371.9	368.0
2004	361.4	361.4	364.1	373.5	374.7	380.0	383.2	383.9	382.8	383.4	383.7	385.0	376.4
2005	372.6	373.1	374.8	384.2	384.9	390.2	391.4	392.2	390.9	390.9	393.3	393.4	386.0
2006	382.5	383.8	386.3	393.5	395.2	402.6	402.1	403.1	401.2	402.4	403.4	403.9	396.7
2007	393.5	395.3	397.6	406.8	409.5	415.0	414.6	416.3	411.8	413.3	414.0	412.4	408.3
Education and Health Services													
2000	404.1	413.1	414.2	412.9	406.2	395.9	393.3	392.9	403.9	413.2	417.3	417.7	407.1
2001	402.8	413.6	413.8	415.7	410.2	400.7	400.2	399.8	410.2	421.5	425.1	426.1	411.6
2002	413.5	423.2	426.2	427.2	421.0	410.3	408.9	407.8	420.1	430.0	435.1	434.9	421.5
2003	419.3	427.6	430.5	431.7	425.1	414.8	413.3	411.0	424.0	432.9	436.7	436.2	425.3
2004	423.9	433.3	435.5	437.1	430.6	420.3	420.8	418.0	429.0	439.0	442.1	441.7	430.9
2005	429.0	438.9	440.1	443.8	437.0	426.4	426.5	424.9	436.6	447.2	451.2	451.4	437.8
2006	439.2	449.7	453.0	453.8	448.3	440.4	438.5	437.1	450.2	458.9	462.6	462.8	449.5
2007	455.5	463.8	464.9	470.8	464.5	453.7	455.1	452.9	463.5	472.1	475.0	474.8	463.9
Leisure and Hospitality													
2000	181.8	183.2	186.1	193.6	198.5	206.0	207.7	207.0	202.4	200.6	197.4	196.1	196.7
2001	185.5	186.6	189.3	194.9	202.6	210.7	210.1	209.8	202.4	199.5	196.1	194.8	198.5
2002	185.9	186.4	191.4	200.0	207.9	215.2	214.7	215.0	208.7	206.1	202.6	201.6	203.0
2003	190.5	189.6	192.2	199.3	209.1	215.5	215.8	215.7	209.4	206.9	202.5	199.9	203.9
2004	190.8	190.2	193.3	202.3	210.8	217.3	220.5	219.3	212.2	209.7	205.6	203.9	206.3
2005	193.2	193.5	196.1	205.6	213.3	221.4	221.7	221.2	214.4	210.4	207.4	205.7	208.7
2006	195.4	195.7	199.1	207.0	213.7	223.2	226.0	226.1	219.3	215.4	212.5	211.7	212.1
2007	202.3	201.5	204.2	211.3	219.2	229.6	229.3	230.1	222.7	219.1	216.3	215.2	216.7
Other Services													
2000	82.2	82.7	83.2	83.6	84.2	85.6	86.1	85.8	84.0	84.8	85.1	85.5	84.4
2001	84.0	84.3	84.9	85.3	86.1	87.4	87.9	87.8	85.9	86.1	86.5	86.9	86.1
2002	85.3	85.4	86.4	86.5	87.4	88.3	88.7	88.5	86.4	86.9	87.1	87.4	87.0
2003	85.6	85.4	86.3	86.1	86.7	87.5	87.9	87.2	85.8	85.5	86.1	86.0	86.3
2004	85.0	84.8	85.7	85.7	86.3	86.4	87.3	87.0	85.0	85.0	85.4	85.8	85.8
2005	84.4	84.5	85.2	86.3	86.5	87.7	88.4	88.0	86.6	85.8	86.2	87.0	86.4
2006	85.7	85.2	86.3	86.6	86.9	88.3	89.1	89.2	87.1	87.2	87.1	87.5	87.2
2007	86.2	86.6	87.3	87.6	88.8	90.6	91.1	90.8	88.3	88.1	87.8	87.9	88.4
Government													
2000	300.4	303.8	305.8	306.8	311.6	307.8	285.6	280.2	301.4	303.8	305.5	305.4	301.5
2001	304.1	307.0	307.1	307.8	308.3	306.1	286.4	284.2	304.8	305.8	306.8	307.6	303.0
2002	304.5	306.9	307.3	306.4	306.7	305.2	283.4	279.8	305.1	302.6	305.2	304.9	301.5
2003	300.8	303.2	302.9	303.3	302.9	301.5	282.8	276.3	299.7	297.9	299.0	298.4	297.4
2004	294.4	298.4	298.7	299.4	298.6	296.4	274.3	268.1	294.9	296.8	298.5	298.2	293.1
2005	295.4	300.2	300.1	300.8	301.0	297.4	276.0	270.1	296.0	299.6	301.7	300.5	294.9
2006	297.5	302.0	302.3	302.6	303.0	300.0	279.0	272.3	298.8	302.0	303.7	303.0	297.2
2007	300.5	303.9	304.4	305.3	306.3	302.3	278.6	272.4	300.4	303.7	306.0	305.8	299.1

Employment by Industry: Detroit-Warren-Livonia, MI, 2000–2007

(Numbers in thousands, not seasonally adjusted.)

Industry and year	January	February	March	April	May	June	July	August	September	October	November	December	Annual Average
Total Nonfarm													
2000	2,160.7	2,163.0	2,177.3	2,210.9	2,238.2	2,250.0	2,171.6	2,192.4	2,203.1	2,225.4	2,234.4	2,235.9	2,205.2
2001	2,125.1	2,142.0	2,151.4	2,157.0	2,177.2	2,182.4	2,097.1	2,110.5	2,122.3	2,129.7	2,132.7	2,140.0	2,139.0
2002	2,049.4	2,059.2	2,071.3	2,088.7	2,114.3	2,121.6	2,060.5	2,080.8	2,094.0	2,105.6	2,114.4	2,117.1	2,089.7
2003	2,052.8	2,052.5	2,062.3	2,067.9	2,094.8	2,103.5	2,019.4	2,048.1	2,063.2	2,074.0	2,081.3	2,083.4	2,066.9
2004	2,011.7	2,012.9	2,025.1	2,048.7	2,072.1	2,075.0	1,993.7	2,036.2	2,061.3	2,072.5	2,083.1	2,081.7	2,047.8
2005	2,007.8	2,022.9	2,023.4	2,049.3	2,073.6	2,075.0	2,003.1	2,032.2	2,062.5	2,061.4	2,075.1	2,068.8	2,046.3
2006	1,990.5	1,993.8	2,001.9	2,014.1	2,032.5	2,037.9	1,956.1	1,984.6	2,003.7	1,997.5	2,012.5	2,009.5	2,002.9
2007	1,938.6	1,951.3	1,955.4	1,969.7	1,995.1	1,996.9	1,931.1	1,954.7	1,966.0	1,964.4	1,972.8	1,968.9	1,963.7
Total Private													
2000	1,926.4	1,926.6	1,938.2	1,970.4	1,994.9	2,011.9	1,970.0	1,995.2	1,978.3	1,985.4	1,992.2	1,994.5	1,973.7
2001	1,889.3	1,902.3	1,910.6	1,915.4	1,934.1	1,945.1	1,893.0	1,909.5	1,894.3	1,888.7	1,889.7	1,896.4	1,905.7
2002	1,815.2	1,820.1	1,830.5	1,849.2	1,872.7	1,884.5	1,855.0	1,878.5	1,865.9	1,863.1	1,871.0	1,874.3	1,856.7
2003	1,813.3	1,808.5	1,818.3	1,822.7	1,849.0	1,859.8	1,804.6	1,836.6	1,834.2	1,824.8	1,832.2	1,835.1	1,828.3
2004	1,772.4	1,769.6	1,780.5	1,805.2	1,827.1	1,834.9	1,782.9	1,828.5	1,826.9	1,830.5	1,838.8	1,840.1	1,811.5
2005	1,772.8	1,782.0	1,782.4	1,807.8	1,830.3	1,837.0	1,796.0	1,826.6	1,829.2	1,823.3	1,834.5	1,831.3	1,812.8
2006	1,759.2	1,756.9	1,763.8	1,776.5	1,793.8	1,803.6	1,748.7	1,780.9	1,776.9	1,763.8	1,777.0	1,776.8	1,773.2
2007	1,710.1	1,719.5	1,721.3	1,736.8	1,759.5	1,765.5	1,726.8	1,752.1	1,743.4	1,733.0	1,740.0	1,738.6	1,737.2
Goods-Producing													
2000	473.0	474.9	477.7	491.5	498.8	502.6	485.5	497.6	491.5	491.5	489.1	483.7	488.1
2001	446.5	457.9	457.7	459.1	462.5	464.4	445.1	452.5	452.3	448.0	443.9	444.3	452.9
2002	409.5	415.4	416.5	422.0	426.5	431.3	420.1	430.3	426.7	424.9	424.1	420.9	422.4
2003	400.0	396.1	398.2	395.2	403.9	409.2	378.9	403.4	402.5	395.9	397.9	395.3	398.0
2004	377.2	375.8	380.8	386.5	391.9	392.0	357.3	393.1	393.2	392.0	391.9	386.1	384.8
2005	363.8	369.9	365.1	369.1	379.9	381.7	353.8	375.5	379.5	377.0	379.5	371.7	372.2
2006	345.9	346.3	349.9	356.2	362.0	362.0	326.5	350.9	350.2	342.2	347.4	341.3	348.4
2007	316.6	328.1	328.3	330.5	335.8	338.2	316.1	334.9	332.4	320.9	324.5	322.3	327.4
Natural Resources, Mining, and Construction													
2000	85.5	85.2	88.5	95.5	99.6	102.5	103.9	102.8	101.8	100.5	98.4	93.7	96.5
2001	84.7	84.0	86.1	90.3	95.8	98.3	99.3	99.2	97.9	97.0	95.7	93.3	93.5
2002	83.5	81.8	82.7	87.0	92.3	94.9	95.8	95.4	93.1	92.0	89.9	86.2	89.6
2003	76.0	73.8	74.3	79.5	87.8	91.9	93.0	91.9	90.8	90.3	88.4	85.3	85.3
2004	75.2	74.0	75.8	82.0	87.2	90.8	93.2	92.3	91.0	90.7	89.5	85.7	85.6
2005	76.6	74.8	75.8	81.2	86.5	89.9	92.0	90.4	88.9	87.6	85.9	80.7	84.2
2006	71.6	70.2	70.9	74.6	80.0	82.6	82.8	81.8	79.8	78.5	76.8	72.8	76.9
2007	64.9	62.4	64.4	67.1	72.9	75.6	77.3	77.0	75.8	74.7	71.7	68.2	71.0
Manufacturing													
2000	387.5	389.7	389.2	396.0	399.2	400.1	381.6	394.8	389.7	391.0	390.7	390.0	391.6
2001	361.8	373.9	371.6	368.8	366.7	366.1	345.8	353.3	354.4	351.0	348.2	351.0	359.4
2002	326.0	333.6	333.8	335.0	334.2	336.4	324.3	334.9	333.6	332.9	334.2	334.7	332.8
2003	324.0	322.3	323.9	315.7	316.1	317.3	285.9	311.5	311.7	305.6	309.5	310.0	312.8
2004	302.0	301.8	305.0	304.5	304.7	301.2	264.1	300.8	302.2	301.3	302.4	300.4	299.2
2005	287.2	295.1	289.3	287.9	293.4	291.8	262.7	285.1	290.6	289.4	293.6	291.0	288.1
2006	274.3	276.1	279.0	281.6	282.0	279.4	243.7	269.1	270.4	263.7	270.6	268.5	271.5
2007	251.7	265.7	263.9	263.4	262.9	262.6	238.8	257.9	256.6	246.2	252.8	254.1	256.4
Service-Providing													
2000	1,687.7	1,688.1	1,699.6	1,719.4	1,739.4	1,747.4	1,686.1	1,694.8	1,711.6	1,733.9	1,745.3	1,752.2	1,717.1
2001	1,678.6	1,684.1	1,693.7	1,697.9	1,714.7	1,718.0	1,652.0	1,658.0	1,670.0	1,681.7	1,688.8	1,695.7	1,686.1
2002	1,639.9	1,643.8	1,654.8	1,666.7	1,687.8	1,690.3	1,640.4	1,650.5	1,667.3	1,680.7	1,690.3	1,696.2	1,667.4
2003	1,652.8	1,656.4	1,664.1	1,672.7	1,690.9	1,694.3	1,640.5	1,644.7	1,660.7	1,678.1	1,683.4	1,688.1	1,668.9
2004	1,634.5	1,637.1	1,644.3	1,662.2	1,680.2	1,683.0	1,636.4	1,643.1	1,668.1	1,680.5	1,691.2	1,695.6	1,663.0
2005	1,644.0	1,653.0	1,658.3	1,680.2	1,693.7	1,693.3	1,649.3	1,656.7	1,683.0	1,684.4	1,695.6	1,697.1	1,674.1
2006	1,644.6	1,647.5	1,652.0	1,657.9	1,670.5	1,675.9	1,629.6	1,633.7	1,653.5	1,655.3	1,665.1	1,668.2	1,654.5
2007	1,622.0	1,623.2	1,627.1	1,639.2	1,659.3	1,658.7	1,615.0	1,619.8	1,633.6	1,643.5	1,648.3	1,646.6	1,636.4
Trade, Transportation, and Utilities													
2000	412.2	408.3	409.3	411.9	415.8	419.7	410.2	413.8	412.7	421.1	431.2	440.5	417.2
2001	415.3	410.6	411.2	409.1	411.1	412.3	404.6	405.8	403.4	403.5	411.0	417.0	409.6
2002	394.2	389.0	391.6	390.5	395.9	397.2	392.5	394.3	394.8	393.7	402.1	407.7	395.3
2003	388.2	384.6	384.9	383.8	386.9	388.3	381.1	383.8	384.3	387.9	393.7	399.0	387.2
2004	379.4	376.3	376.4	378.4	383.2	384.6	378.3	380.3	378.2	382.7	390.9	396.4	382.1
2005	375.5	373.0	374.3	375.9	379.4	380.2	377.6	378.9	376.3	378.7	386.5	390.5	378.9
2006	371.2	367.0	368.1	369.1	372.2	373.8	368.2	370.3	368.8	370.9	379.0	383.5	371.8
2007	365.7	361.2	361.0	362.6	367.1	367.7	363.9	365.3	363.3	366.1	371.8	374.7	365.9
Wholesale Trade													
2000	101.0	101.2	101.4	102.6	103.4	104.2	102.9	102.8	102.1	102.7	102.5	103.3	102.5
2001	101.5	102.4	102.2	102.5	102.8	102.3	100.9	100.5	99.4	98.9	98.8	99.2	101.0
2002	97.7	98.1	98.2	98.1	98.7	99.2	98.0	98.3	97.9	96.9	97.2	97.8	98.0
2003	96.8	96.9	97.1	97.1	96.6	97.2	95.6	95.7	95.2	95.5	95.0	95.4	96.2
2004	93.0	93.0	93.4	93.8	94.2	94.5	94.2	93.9	93.2	93.4	93.4	93.6	93.6
2005	92.7	92.7	93.0	93.2	93.6	93.5	93.2	92.9	92.4	93.1	92.8	93.1	93.0
2006	91.8	91.9	92.1	92.4	92.7	93.2	92.4	92.1	91.3	91.2	91.1	91.3	92.0
2007	90.0	89.5	89.3	89.9	90.5	90.5	90.4	90.1	89.4	89.7	89.8	90.0	89.9
Retail Trade													
2000	240.9	237.0	237.9	237.9	241.1	243.8	238.5	241.0	240.9	246.6	256.9	265.6	244.0
2001	244.6	239.8	240.6	236.9	238.7	239.9	235.3	236.3	235.3	236.1	244.6	249.9	239.8
2002	230.8	225.3	226.9	225.9	229.9	231.0	228.0	228.5	229.4	228.9	237.2	242.9	230.4
2003	223.4	220.0	220.2	219.5	223.1	224.0	220.2	221.9	222.8	225.8	232.3	237.1	224.2
2004	221.9	218.6	218.7	219.9	224.3	225.1	220.3	221.6	220.1	223.1	231.3	236.3	223.4
2005	218.7	215.5	216.3	218.7	221.3	222.1	219.8	219.7	218.2	219.9	227.2	230.8	220.7
2006	215.1	210.9	211.5	212.3	214.7	215.7	213.8	214.4	213.5	216.2	223.8	226.6	215.7
2007	212.2	207.0	207.3	207.7	210.8	210.8	211.6	210.9	209.5	212.1	217.7	220.3	211.5

Employment by Industry: Detroit-Warren-Livonia, MI, 2000–2007—*Continued*

(Numbers in thousands, not seasonally adjusted.)

Industry and year	January	February	March	April	May	June	July	August	September	October	November	December	Annual Average
Transportation and Utilities													
2000	70.3	70.1	70.0	71.4	71.3	71.7	68.8	70.0	69.7	71.8	71.8	71.6	70.7
2001	69.2	68.4	68.4	69.7	69.6	70.1	68.4	69.0	68.7	68.5	67.6	67.9	68.8
2002	65.7	65.6	66.5	66.5	67.3	67.6	66.5	67.5	67.5	67.9	67.7	67.0	66.9
2003	68.0	67.7	67.6	67.2	67.2	67.1	65.3	66.2	66.3	66.6	66.4	66.5	66.8
2004	64.5	64.7	64.3	64.7	64.7	65.0	63.8	64.8	64.9	66.2	66.2	66.5	65.0
2005	64.1	64.8	65.0	64.0	64.5	64.6	64.6	66.3	65.7	65.7	66.5	66.6	65.2
2006	64.3	64.2	64.5	64.4	64.8	64.9	62.0	63.8	64.0	63.5	64.1	65.6	64.2
2007	63.5	64.7	64.4	65.0	65.8	66.4	61.9	64.3	64.4	64.3	64.3	64.4	64.5
Information													
2000	42.0	42.0	42.5	42.2	42.7	43.0	43.2	43.3	42.9	42.8	43.4	43.8	42.8
2001	42.6	42.7	42.8	42.6	42.8	42.9	42.9	41.9	41.2	40.3	40.8	40.2	42.0
2002	39.6	39.4	39.4	38.7	38.8	38.7	38.9	38.6	38.0	37.5	37.6	38.3	38.6
2003	38.0	38.1	38.2	37.5	37.7	38.0	37.4	37.2	36.8	36.9	37.2	37.1	37.5
2004	36.6	36.4	36.4	36.5	36.7	37.0	36.8	36.6	36.2	36.2	36.5	36.5	36.5
2005	36.1	35.7	35.7	35.6	35.8	35.9	35.7	35.5	35.1	34.6	34.9	35.0	35.5
2006	34.6	34.8	34.4	34.3	34.6	34.6	34.4	34.3	33.8	33.9	34.0	34.1	34.3
2007	34.3	34.2	34.1	34.1	34.4	34.3	34.3	34.2	33.7	33.6	33.7	33.6	34.0
Financial Activities													
2000	116.4	116.1	116.2	115.5	116.1	117.8	117.7	116.9	115.6	113.9	113.6	114.7	115.9
2001	113.6	115.0	115.5	114.8	116.2	117.3	116.6	116.6	114.9	113.8	114.0	116.4	115.4
2002	116.7	116.7	116.3	116.6	117.2	117.4	117.6	118.3	116.7	116.2	116.8	117.4	117.0
2003	117.8	117.8	117.8	119.8	120.9	121.8	121.4	121.3	119.3	118.1	117.5	118.1	119.3
2004	115.9	115.7	116.2	117.5	118.2	119.2	119.0	118.7	117.6	117.0	117.1	118.0	117.5
2005	117.4	117.5	117.5	118.0	118.2	119.4	118.7	118.7	117.4	117.0	117.0	117.0	117.8
2006	115.3	115.3	114.8	114.6	115.3	116.2	115.5	115.4	113.8	113.1	112.9	113.6	114.7
2007	112.4	112.2	111.9	112.2	112.5	113.2	113.2	112.3	110.1	109.5	109.6	110.0	111.6
Professional and Business Services													
2000	391.3	389.0	391.6	400.2	406.8	409.2	401.6	410.5	406.7	404.5	402.2	400.3	401.2
2001	378.8	379.9	381.2	381.3	383.1	385.0	371.8	379.5	374.6	372.5	369.2	367.9	377.1
2002	357.9	358.9	360.3	364.0	367.8	369.6	360.5	369.1	366.7	368.1	368.1	367.1	364.8
2003	358.2	356.8	357.9	362.5	366.8	368.7	358.5	364.8	363.6	357.0	358.6	358.4	361.0
2004	347.1	346.2	346.6	355.2	360.5	363.8	358.6	365.6	366.0	369.7	370.1	370.6	360.0
2005	360.4	360.9	360.2	368.4	370.9	372.9	367.4	373.0	374.7	371.2	371.7	371.0	368.6
2006	358.6	355.1	354.0	356.2	357.8	362.0	355.5	361.3	359.8	358.7	360.3	359.4	358.2
2007	346.1	346.2	343.6	350.4	352.0	354.0	347.4	354.4	351.3	351.1	349.6	347.8	349.5
Education and Health Services													
2000	233.0	235.6	236.8	238.4	238.1	239.1	236.4	236.7	237.7	239.3	242.1	240.9	237.8
2001	235.8	238.2	239.7	241.7	243.2	245.0	241.2	241.9	242.4	244.8	247.1	246.7	242.3
2002	243.9	245.9	246.8	250.5	251.0	252.7	248.4	248.7	248.2	251.7	253.4	252.9	249.5
2003	251.5	254.1	254.3	252.6	252.7	251.3	250.1	249.6	252.5	255.2	257.0	256.4	253.1
2004	253.3	255.7	256.5	258.7	258.8	256.6	257.2	256.7	259.6	262.4	264.1	264.5	258.7
2005	260.3	263.5	264.6	266.3	266.3	264.2	263.0	263.7	267.9	271.6	273.5	274.1	266.6
2006	269.8	271.8	273.7	271.6	272.9	271.9	269.1	268.8	274.0	273.8	275.4	276.3	272.4
2007	273.7	276.3	277.6	277.4	279.0	277.5	274.4	273.9	278.8	281.2	282.9	283.7	278.0
Leisure and Hospitality													
2000	169.6	170.8	172.5	177.6	183.2	186.1	182.0	182.4	178.3	179.9	177.6	177.3	178.1
2001	167.5	167.7	170.7	175.1	182.1	184.9	179.3	179.1	175.5	176.8	174.0	173.3	175.5
2002	165.5	166.3	169.6	175.3	182.3	182.9	183.5	184.7	181.3	180.4	178.5	178.4	177.4
2003	171.6	171.2	174.5	180.0	187.9	190.5	185.2	183.8	183.3	182.7	179.6	179.9	180.9
2004	172.7	172.9	175.8	181.3	187.5	189.9	187.6	188.6	186.1	182.2	178.9	178.5	181.8
2005	171.6	173.1	176.0	183.8	189.4	191.0	188.3	189.7	186.9	182.1	180.1	180.1	182.7
2006	174.3	176.9	178.7	184.3	188.3	191.8	189.5	189.8	186.8	182.3	179.0	179.4	183.4
2007	174.0	173.7	176.8	181.2	189.5	190.8	188.5	188.0	185.8	183.2	180.0	178.6	182.5
Other Services													
2000	88.9	89.9	91.6	93.1	93.4	94.4	93.4	94.0	92.9	92.4	93.0	93.3	92.5
2001	89.2	90.3	91.8	91.7	93.1	93.3	91.5	92.2	90.0	89.0	89.7	90.6	91.0
2002	87.9	88.5	90.0	91.6	93.2	94.1	93.5	94.5	93.5	90.6	90.4	91.6	91.6
2003	88.0	89.8	92.5	91.3	92.2	92.0	92.0	92.7	91.9	91.1	90.7	90.9	91.3
2004	90.2	90.6	91.8	91.1	90.3	91.8	88.1	88.9	90.0	88.3	89.3	89.5	90.0
2005	87.7	88.4	89.0	90.7	90.4	91.7	91.5	91.6	91.4	91.1	91.3	91.9	90.6
2006	89.5	89.7	90.2	90.2	90.7	91.3	90.0	90.1	89.7	88.9	89.0	89.2	89.9
2007	87.3	87.6	88.0	88.4	89.2	89.8	89.0	89.1	88.0	87.4	87.9	87.9	88.3
Government													
2000	234.3	236.4	239.1	240.5	243.3	238.1	201.6	197.2	224.8	240.0	242.2	241.4	231.6
2001	235.8	239.7	240.8	241.6	242.0	237.3	204.1	201.0	228.0	241.0	243.0	243.6	233.2
2002	234.2	239.1	240.8	239.5	241.6	237.1	205.5	202.3	228.1	242.5	243.4	242.8	233.1
2003	239.5	244.0	244.0	245.2	245.8	243.7	214.8	211.5	229.0	249.2	249.1	248.3	238.7
2004	239.3	243.3	244.6	243.5	245.0	240.1	210.8	207.7	234.4	242.0	244.3	241.6	236.4
2005	235.0	240.9	241.0	241.5	243.3	238.0	207.1	205.6	233.3	238.1	240.6	237.5	233.5
2006	231.3	236.9	238.1	237.6	238.7	234.3	207.4	203.7	226.8	233.7	235.5	232.7	229.7
2007	228.5	231.8	234.1	232.9	235.6	231.4	204.3	202.6	222.6	231.4	232.8	230.3	226.5

Employment by Industry: Atlanta-Sandy Springs-Marietta, GA, 2000–2007

(Numbers in thousands, not seasonally adjusted.)

Industry and year	January	February	March	April	May	June	July	August	September	October	November	December	Annual Average
Total Nonfarm													
2000	2,236.2	2,250.5	2,272.8	2,272.9	2,287.0	2,304.8	2,285.6	2,298.5	2,303.9	2,312.0	2,321.2	2,331.2	2,289.7
2001	2,276.0	2,285.2	2,301.8	2,307.7	2,310.4	2,314.0	2,300.1	2,312.9	2,311.1	2,298.2	2,299.8	2,299.5	2,301.4
2002	2,233.1	2,235.6	2,254.7	2,266.2	2,273.4	2,275.7	2,242.6	2,263.6	2,262.7	2,257.1	2,268.1	2,272.1	2,258.7
2003	2,207.4	2,217.6	2,231.1	2,227.8	2,235.2	2,231.1	2,219.7	2,244.1	2,246.9	2,246.6	2,259.5	2,267.8	2,236.2
2004	2,216.3	2,228.8	2,246.1	2,256.9	2,262.5	2,258.3	2,260.8	2,281.2	2,273.5	2,294.5	2,306.2	2,312.9	2,266.5
2005	2,277.9	2,289.7	2,296.7	2,327.0	2,338.9	2,329.2	2,327.7	2,352.3	2,353.9	2,367.2	2,384.8	2,389.6	2,336.2
2006	2,353.0	2,362.9	2,376.3	2,388.1	2,400.1	2,401.2	2,386.2	2,409.4	2,412.7	2,437.6	2,452.2	2,458.8	2,403.2
2007	2,419.9	2,432.8	2,444.8	2,443.7	2,455.8	2,450.1	2,445.7	2,469.9	2,466.9	2,479.5	2,489.8	2,494.6	2,457.8
Total Private													
2000	1,966.5	1,978.1	1,998.9	1,999.2	2,013.1	2,032.2	2,023.1	2,030.4	2,030.2	2,035.4	2,043.2	2,052.3	2,016.9
2001	1,996.8	2,002.5	2,017.7	2,024.8	2,026.0	2,032.6	2,027.6	2,028.0	2,022.0	2,006.8	2,006.3	2,007.2	2,016.5
2002	1,942.9	1,945.6	1,960.0	1,968.9	1,975.9	1,983.4	1,962.4	1,969.9	1,962.0	1,957.3	1,966.5	1,972.9	1,964.0
2003	1,908.2	1,916.7	1,928.5	1,926.2	1,935.6	1,940.9	1,938.9	1,952.3	1,947.5	1,945.7	1,958.3	1,967.1	1,938.8
2004	1,915.7	1,922.8	1,939.4	1,950.8	1,958.3	1,964.7	1,974.8	1,979.6	1,966.1	1,987.8	1,997.8	2,007.1	1,963.7
2005	1,972.6	1,980.0	1,986.3	2,016.0	2,028.2	2,029.2	2,036.1	2,043.7	2,042.0	2,052.2	2,068.8	2,074.3	2,027.5
2006	2,038.4	2,044.6	2,056.3	2,069.7	2,082.5	2,088.8	2,086.5	2,093.2	2,090.2	2,112.2	2,124.3	2,131.4	2,084.8
2007	2,094.5	2,103.1	2,113.8	2,113.7	2,126.3	2,128.9	2,130.6	2,140.6	2,132.4	2,142.9	2,151.5	2,156.6	2,127.9
Goods-Producing													
2000	331.8	333.8	337.4	336.9	338.4	342.1	340.8	341.0	341.1	340.2	338.5	338.1	338.3
2001	330.2	330.6	331.5	332.4	331.5	333.7	332.2	330.7	328.7	324.3	320.8	318.6	328.8
2002	311.5	311.5	313.9	314.8	314.5	315.9	314.9	315.0	312.9	309.2	308.2	305.8	312.3
2003	299.6	302.2	303.5	300.6	302.6	303.4	302.7	304.3	303.9	304.7	303.5	304.3	302.9
2004	298.1	301.2	302.8	303.7	303.9	306.5	308.6	309.1	307.6	308.7	309.0	309.2	305.7
2005	305.0	306.5	306.3	310.8	313.1	313.4	313.4	314.5	316.3	314.5	316.8	316.0	312.2
2006	312.8	314.6	315.0	315.2	317.4	320.0	319.8	322.6	321.7	323.0	319.8	318.3	318.4
2007	316.5	318.1	318.8	317.6	318.6	319.3	317.9	318.8	316.6	317.9	317.9	316.5	317.9
Natural Resources and Mining													
2000	2.6	2.7	2.7	2.6	2.6	2.6	2.6	2.7	2.6	2.8	2.8	2.7	2.7
2001	2.7	2.7	2.7	2.7	2.7	2.7	2.7	2.6	2.7	2.7	2.7	2.6	2.7
2002	2.7	2.6	2.6	2.6	2.6	2.6	2.6	2.7	2.7	2.6	2.6	2.5	2.6
2003	2.5	2.5	2.5	2.5	2.5	2.5	2.5	2.5	2.5	2.6	2.5	2.5	2.5
2004	2.5	2.5	2.5	2.5	2.5	2.6	2.6	2.6	2.6	2.5	2.6	2.6	2.6
2005	2.4	2.4	2.4	2.6	2.6	2.6	2.6	2.6	2.6	2.6	2.6	2.6	2.6
2006	2.7	2.6	2.6	2.6	2.6	2.6	2.6	2.6	2.5	2.6	2.6	2.6	2.6
2007	2.6	2.5	2.6	2.5	2.5	2.5	2.5	2.5	2.5	2.5	2.5	2.5	2.5
Construction													
2000	121.1	122.7	125.9	127.0	128.6	131.0	131.4	131.4	132.0	131.5	130.1	129.5	128.5
2001	124.9	126.3	127.3	129.6	130.2	131.8	132.5	131.7	130.5	129.2	127.8	126.0	129.0
2002	122.7	123.7	125.0	125.1	124.8	125.1	124.7	124.7	123.8	122.7	122.1	120.6	123.8
2003	117.4	118.0	119.3	119.1	120.1	121.2	122.1	123.2	123.6	123.6	123.4	123.8	121.2
2004	121.0	121.2	122.6	124.1	124.1	126.5	129.0	128.2	127.2	127.9	128.1	128.2	125.7
2005	125.9	127.1	127.0	130.1	132.1	132.5	133.3	134.1	135.0	134.5	135.0	133.8	131.7
2006	131.2	132.8	133.5	134.7	136.5	138.4	140.5	141.4	141.2	141.7	141.2	139.7	137.7
2007	137.0	138.7	139.6	139.1	139.9	140.4	139.9	140.5	139.2	140.1	139.3	138.5	139.4
Manufacturing													
2000	208.1	208.4	208.8	207.3	207.2	208.5	206.8	206.9	206.5	205.9	205.6	205.9	207.2
2001	202.6	201.6	201.5	200.1	198.6	199.2	197.0	196.4	195.5	192.4	190.3	190.0	197.1
2002	186.1	185.2	186.3	187.1	187.1	188.2	187.6	187.6	186.4	183.9	183.5	182.7	186.0
2003	179.7	181.7	181.7	179.0	180.0	179.7	178.1	178.6	177.8	178.5	177.6	178.0	179.2
2004	174.6	177.5	177.7	177.1	177.3	177.4	177.0	178.3	177.8	178.3	178.3	178.4	177.5
2005	176.7	177.0	176.9	178.1	178.4	178.3	177.5	177.8	178.7	177.4	179.2	179.6	178.0
2006	178.9	179.2	178.9	177.9	178.3	179.0	176.7	178.6	178.0	178.7	176.0	176.0	178.0
2007	176.9	176.9	176.6	176.0	176.2	176.4	175.5	175.8	174.9	175.3	176.1	175.5	176.0
Service-Providing													
2000	1,904.4	1,916.7	1,935.4	1,936.0	1,948.6	1,962.7	1,944.8	1,957.5	1,962.8	1,971.8	1,982.7	1,993.1	1,951.4
2001	1,945.8	1,954.6	1,970.3	1,975.3	1,978.9	1,980.3	1,967.9	1,982.2	1,982.4	1,973.9	1,979.0	1,980.9	1,972.6
2002	1,921.6	1,924.1	1,940.8	1,951.4	1,958.9	1,959.8	1,927.7	1,948.6	1,949.8	1,947.9	1,959.9	1,966.3	1,946.4
2003	1,907.8	1,915.4	1,927.6	1,927.2	1,932.6	1,927.7	1,917.0	1,939.8	1,943.0	1,941.9	1,956.0	1,963.5	1,933.3
2004	1,918.2	1,927.6	1,943.3	1,953.2	1,958.6	1,951.8	1,952.2	1,972.1	1,965.9	1,985.8	1,997.2	2,003.7	1,960.8
2005	1,972.9	1,983.2	1,990.4	2,016.2	2,025.8	2,015.8	2,014.3	2,037.8	2,037.6	2,052.7	2,068.0	2,073.6	2,024.0
2006	2,040.2	2,048.3	2,061.3	2,072.9	2,082.7	2,081.2	2,066.4	2,086.8	2,091.0	2,114.6	2,132.4	2,140.5	2,084.9
2007	2,103.4	2,114.7	2,126.0	2,126.1	2,137.2	2,130.8	2,127.8	2,151.1	2,150.3	2,161.6	2,171.9	2,178.1	2,139.9
Trade, Transportation, and Utilities													
2000	541.1	541.4	546.0	546.7	548.9	551.3	547.0	550.3	549.6	556.7	566.4	574.1	551.6
2001	551.9	548.9	552.2	547.7	547.9	549.3	547.5	546.5	546.3	546.1	552.0	557.1	549.5
2002	530.8	525.8	528.1	528.9	530.8	533.1	525.1	526.5	526.0	529.2	538.3	546.1	530.7
2003	516.7	513.6	514.9	511.7	514.0	514.1	514.2	516.8	516.1	518.2	528.2	533.5	517.7
2004	513.1	509.8	512.6	511.4	513.6	514.9	517.7	518.5	515.3	522.1	531.9	538.3	518.3
2005	522.1	521.0	522.7	529.7	532.3	532.6	538.3	537.0	535.1	541.2	553.0	559.8	535.4
2006	540.4	537.8	540.9	545.2	548.5	549.5	547.7	548.9	550.5	559.7	572.4	580.1	551.8
2007	560.4	556.4	557.1	557.7	561.3	561.8	562.4	562.5	562.8	566.1	575.1	581.2	563.7
Wholesale Trade													
2000	157.9	159.3	160.3	160.0	160.7	161.4	161.6	162.0	161.3	161.8	162.0	162.1	160.9
2001	161.0	161.2	161.8	162.3	162.1	163.3	163.0	161.8	160.8	159.2	158.2	158.2	161.1
2002	155.0	154.7	155.5	155.0	154.7	154.5	151.9	151.8	150.9	152.4	152.1	152.1	153.4
2003	151.1	151.4	151.9	150.9	151.3	151.3	151.3	151.1	150.5	150.1	151.0	151.7	151.1
2004	149.9	150.1	150.8	151.4	151.2	151.5	152.7	152.6	151.3	152.0	152.3	152.8	151.6
2005	153.2	154.0	154.4	155.3	155.2	155.2	155.8	156.2	155.9	155.4	155.5	156.1	155.2
2006	154.6	155.3	155.6	157.2	158.1	158.3	159.3	159.2	159.3	160.7	160.0	161.2	158.2
2007	159.2	159.6	159.6	160.3	160.3	160.2	161.3	161.5	161.2	161.3	160.6	161.1	160.5

Employment by Industry: Atlanta-Sandy Springs-Marietta, GA, 2000–2007—*Continued*

(Numbers in thousands, not seasonally adjusted.)

Industry and year	January	February	March	April	May	June	July	August	September	October	November	December	Annual Average
Retail Trade													
2000	258.5	257.6	260.6	260.0	261.6	263.2	258.5	260.7	260.3	264.8	274.0	281.4	263.4
2001	264.2	261.3	264.1	260.3	260.7	260.8	257.1	257.7	258.9	260.1	269.4	274.6	262.4
2002	256.8	252.7	254.3	253.9	255.4	256.3	252.8	253.5	254.3	254.8	263.7	271.6	256.7
2003	246.8	243.8	244.8	244.2	246.1	246.3	245.7	248.0	248.0	250.1	258.7	263.5	248.8
2004	245.9	242.6	244.0	241.6	243.5	244.7	245.2	245.9	244.7	250.0	259.0	264.7	247.7
2005	249.3	246.2	247.3	253.9	256.2	256.8	259.3	258.2	256.3	262.5	272.1	277.3	258.0
2006	263.2	259.8	261.7	263.7	265.3	265.6	262.2	263.0	263.3	271.2	283.8	288.0	267.6
2007	275.2	270.4	270.6	270.4	271.7	271.0	271.8	271.4	271.3	274.2	283.7	288.2	274.2
Transportation and Utilities													
2000	124.7	124.5	125.1	126.7	126.6	126.7	126.9	127.6	128.0	130.1	130.4	130.6	127.3
2001	126.7	126.4	126.3	125.1	125.1	125.2	127.4	127.0	126.6	126.8	124.4	124.3	125.9
2002	119.0	118.4	118.3	120.0	120.7	122.3	120.4	121.2	120.8	122.0	122.5	122.4	120.7
2003	118.8	118.4	118.2	116.6	116.6	116.5	117.2	117.7	117.6	118.0	118.5	118.3	117.7
2004	117.3	117.1	117.8	118.4	118.9	118.7	119.8	120.0	119.3	120.1	120.6	120.8	119.1
2005	119.6	120.8	121.0	120.5	120.9	120.6	123.2	122.6	122.9	123.3	125.4	126.4	122.3
2006	122.6	122.7	123.6	124.3	125.1	125.6	126.2	126.7	127.9	127.8	128.6	130.9	126.0
2007	126.0	126.4	126.9	127.0	129.3	130.6	129.3	129.6	130.3	130.6	130.8	131.9	129.1
Information													
2000	104.8	104.8	106.3	105.7	106.7	108.5	108.4	109.0	109.2	110.1	110.7	112.2	108.0
2001	110.1	110.3	110.9	110.3	110.0	110.1	108.5	107.8	107.0	106.3	105.9	106.0	108.6
2002	105.6	104.7	105.8	102.2	101.4	101.3	100.8	100.3	99.2	99.2	98.7	98.6	101.5
2003	93.7	93.9	94.1	92.5	92.0	92.4	91.8	92.4	91.4	91.6	92.6	92.6	92.6
2004	90.3	89.9	90.4	89.8	89.5	90.0	89.4	89.0	88.5	88.0	88.7	88.7	89.4
2005	86.9	86.9	87.4	87.4	86.4	87.9	87.4	86.1	86.7	87.1	87.9	88.3	87.2
2006	86.7	87.1	87.5	87.2	87.7	87.3	86.9	86.6	86.5	86.7	87.6	87.8	87.1
2007	88.2	88.0	88.1	87.3	87.8	87.9	87.4	87.7	87.8	88.0	87.8	88.1	87.8
Financial Activities													
2000	146.0	146.5	146.7	149.1	149.5	150.4	149.2	149.3	147.8	148.3	148.4	149.4	148.4
2001	147.4	147.6	148.4	150.9	150.8	151.4	152.5	152.6	152.2	152.1	152.5	152.5	150.9
2002	149.9	150.1	149.8	150.5	150.9	151.2	151.0	151.7	150.7	150.4	150.8	151.3	150.7
2003	149.1	149.7	150.3	150.4	151.5	152.3	152.6	153.3	152.9	150.1	150.4	150.8	151.1
2004	149.1	149.7	150.1	151.7	152.0	151.6	152.6	152.8	152.2	154.1	154.1	154.8	152.1
2005	155.0	155.4	155.4	156.1	157.0	157.3	156.7	157.7	157.7	159.9	160.1	161.4	157.5
2006	158.2	159.1	159.6	161.5	162.1	162.5	162.4	163.2	163.1	164.6	164.4	165.1	162.2
2007	162.1	163.6	163.9	163.3	163.2	163.3	163.4	163.2	162.1	161.8	161.2	161.1	162.7
Professional and Business Services													
2000	384.5	388.5	391.9	388.6	391.7	398.4	395.7	398.8	400.5	398.9	398.1	399.8	394.6
2001	384.3	386.1	388.9	391.5	389.1	388.3	388.3	390.6	387.4	381.5	378.1	377.9	386.0
2002	361.6	365.2	366.2	370.5	371.7	372.4	369.3	371.6	369.6	368.4	368.2	367.5	368.5
2003	356.4	360.0	360.6	362.3	360.1	361.3	361.2	364.6	363.7	365.4	366.3	367.4	362.4
2004	356.7	360.2	364.6	369.0	369.3	369.5	375.1	374.9	371.8	381.5	380.8	381.5	371.2
2005	376.2	379.7	380.4	384.0	384.6	385.1	389.7	393.0	394.4	396.2	397.3	395.7	388.0
2006	391.3	392.7	395.1	397.7	397.9	401.0	401.3	400.9	399.8	403.7	404.0	405.2	399.2
2007	399.4	402.9	406.5	403.2	405.3	406.6	410.5	413.6	412.8	414.3	413.9	414.9	408.7
Education and Health Services													
2000	186.9	188.8	189.6	191.0	191.5	191.2	188.3	189.1	191.7	195.1	196.0	195.2	191.2
2001	193.2	195.6	197.2	198.0	198.7	198.5	200.0	201.3	203.5	204.2	205.4	205.8	200.1
2002	201.5	204.5	206.9	206.6	207.2	207.0	206.1	209.2	210.4	211.5	213.3	213.2	208.1
2003	210.1	212.4	213.9	213.6	214.9	213.5	212.5	215.3	216.1	217.2	218.5	219.3	214.8
2004	217.6	219.1	220.0	221.1	222.0	220.3	221.1	223.6	223.7	227.5	228.4	228.9	222.8
2005	227.7	229.0	226.8	231.8	233.1	230.1	231.2	234.0	235.0	237.7	238.4	238.5	232.8
2006	239.1	240.7	240.8	241.1	241.8	238.8	239.4	241.8	243.9	249.2	249.8	249.7	243.0
2007	247.2	249.8	249.9	251.4	251.5	249.3	249.9	254.4	256.2	259.0	260.0	259.9	253.2
Leisure and Hospitality													
2000	184.9	187.1	193.0	193.2	197.6	200.7	203.7	203.2	200.9	198.4	197.5	195.6	196.3
2001	188.5	191.6	196.2	201.4	204.9	207.4	203.4	203.9	199.6	199.1	198.0	195.9	199.2
2002	189.7	191.7	196.8	203.1	207.2	209.6	203.4	203.8	201.7	199.5	199.4	201.0	200.6
2003	191.7	193.7	199.3	203.6	208.1	210.8	210.7	212.2	210.5	206.1	206.3	206.9	205.0
2004	199.3	201.5	206.1	211.6	215.1	218.4	216.6	218.0	214.5	213.9	212.8	213.7	211.8
2005	206.4	207.5	212.9	220.7	225.6	226.8	223.0	223.8	221.1	220.2	219.9	219.1	218.9
2006	214.6	217.1	221.8	224.8	229.4	231.7	230.6	231.4	228.1	228.7	229.7	229.1	226.4
2007	224.5	227.8	232.6	235.2	239.8	241.5	239.6	240.9	236.2	236.5	236.9	236.7	235.7
Other Services													
2000	86.5	87.2	88.0	88.0	88.8	89.6	90.0	89.7	89.4	87.7	87.6	87.9	88.4
2001	91.2	91.8	92.4	92.6	93.1	93.9	95.2	94.6	97.3	93.2	93.6	93.4	93.5
2002	92.3	92.1	92.5	92.3	92.2	92.9	91.8	91.8	91.5	89.9	89.6	89.4	91.5
2003	90.9	91.2	91.9	91.5	92.4	93.1	93.2	93.4	92.9	92.4	92.5	92.3	92.3
2004	91.5	91.4	92.8	92.5	92.9	93.5	93.7	93.7	92.5	92.0	92.1	92.0	92.6
2005	93.3	94.0	94.4	95.5	96.1	96.0	96.4	97.6	95.7	95.4	95.4	95.5	95.4
2006	95.3	95.5	95.6	97.0	97.7	98.0	98.4	97.8	96.6	96.6	96.6	96.1	96.8
2007	96.2	96.5	96.9	98.0	98.8	99.2	99.5	99.5	97.9	99.3	98.7	98.2	98.2
Government													
2000	269.7	272.4	273.9	273.7	273.9	272.6	262.5	268.1	273.7	276.6	278.0	278.9	272.8
2001	279.2	282.7	284.1	282.9	284.4	281.4	272.5	284.9	289.1	291.4	293.5	292.3	284.9
2002	290.2	290.0	294.7	297.3	297.5	292.3	280.2	293.7	300.7	299.8	301.6	299.2	294.8
2003	299.2	300.9	302.6	301.6	299.6	290.2	280.8	291.8	299.4	300.9	301.2	300.7	297.4
2004	300.6	306.0	306.7	306.1	304.2	293.6	286.0	301.6	307.4	306.7	308.4	305.8	302.8
2005	305.3	309.7	310.4	311.0	310.7	300.0	291.6	308.6	311.9	315.0	316.0	315.3	308.8
2006	314.6	318.3	320.0	318.4	317.6	312.4	299.7	316.2	322.5	325.4	327.9	327.4	318.4
2007	325.4	329.7	331.0	330.0	329.5	321.2	315.1	329.3	334.5	336.6	338.3	338.0	329.9

Employment by Industry: San Francisco-Oakland-Fremont, CA, 2000–2007

(Numbers in thousands, not seasonally adjusted.)

Industry and year	January	February	March	April	May	June	July	August	September	October	November	December	Annual Average
Total Nonfarm													
2000	2,053.8	2,074.5	2,095.8	2,106.0	2,123.4	2,143.0	2,129.4	2,139.0	2,150.5	2,151.1	2,169.4	2,184.4	2,126.7
2001	2,127.4	2,137.9	2,153.5	2,131.0	2,129.2	2,130.9	2,097.8	2,092.6	2,086.6	2,074.7	2,069.5	2,072.4	2,108.6
2002	2,013.3	2,020.4	2,033.0	2,026.8	2,034.4	2,038.5	2,014.4	2,017.8	2,022.5	2,027.4	2,036.8	2,037.7	2,026.9
2003	1,980.8	1,987.7	1,990.0	1,981.2	1,982.6	1,986.0	1,958.7	1,959.8	1,963.9	1,966.3	1,971.8	1,979.5	1,975.6
2004	1,933.8	1,943.9	1,954.6	1,957.7	1,965.9	1,972.0	1,956.5	1,951.4	1,957.4	1,957.3	1,978.0	1,988.9	1,960.8
2005	1,941.0	1,954.5	1,962.2	1,968.9	1,973.3	1,981.3	1,968.3	1,968.3	1,981.1	1,986.7	1,999.3	2,007.0	1,974.3
2006	1,968.5	1,984.9	1,993.5	1,994.6	2,012.0	2,022.4	2,005.7	2,009.5	2,019.5	2,027.6	2,038.2	2,041.2	2,009.8
2007	1,996.7	2,012.9	2,024.3	2,017.6	2,034.8	2,043.1	2,034.8	2,036.6	2,042.5	2,049.7	2,057.5	2,062.3	2,034.4
Total Private													
2000	1,753.8	1,771.1	1,789.0	1,793.0	1,804.7	1,826.5	1,830.8	1,838.7	1,847.9	1,842.5	1,857.1	1,873.2	1,819.0
2001	1,823.0	1,830.2	1,842.5	1,817.7	1,816.7	1,820.5	1,798.9	1,793.6	1,779.4	1,760.4	1,754.3	1,757.4	1,799.6
2002	1,699.6	1,703.4	1,711.8	1,704.3	1,711.5	1,718.0	1,710.0	1,714.2	1,708.7	1,705.5	1,713.5	1,716.0	1,709.7
2003	1,662.9	1,667.2	1,668.1	1,660.9	1,662.7	1,667.9	1,656.3	1,660.4	1,657.2	1,654.8	1,660.0	1,669.0	1,662.2
2004	1,625.4	1,632.8	1,641.6	1,645.1	1,653.3	1,660.2	1,657.0	1,657.3	1,656.3	1,660.4	1,666.9	1,679.3	1,653.0
2005	1,633.9	1,643.8	1,650.5	1,655.9	1,659.6	1,668.9	1,666.9	1,671.3	1,674.6	1,674.8	1,685.0	1,695.3	1,665.0
2006	1,654.2	1,667.2	1,673.5	1,675.2	1,691.9	1,703.9	1,696.5	1,702.6	1,704.6	1,705.9	1,713.5	1,720.1	1,692.4
2007	1,677.7	1,689.5	1,699.1	1,692.5	1,707.2	1,716.7	1,719.8	1,723.4	1,721.1	1,721.9	1,726.8	1,733.2	1,710.7
Goods-Producing													
2000	279.3	281.1	282.9	285.2	287.4	292.4	293.9	296.4	299.4	298.7	300.2	301.9	291.6
2001	293.7	294.3	297.3	293.5	292.3	293.1	289.6	289.4	285.4	280.3	276.1	273.6	288.2
2002	261.9	263.1	264.4	265.5	266.7	270.2	268.8	271.3	269.4	267.8	264.7	261.9	266.3
2003	254.2	253.8	253.9	252.7	252.8	254.4	254.7	257.0	256.9	257.6	256.6	255.2	254.9
2004	249.7	250.1	251.6	253.4	255.1	257.7	259.4	260.6	260.1	258.6	256.0	254.5	255.6
2005	246.4	248.2	250.0	250.5	251.0	254.5	256.7	258.0	258.1	257.7	257.2	255.5	253.7
2006	249.7	251.9	252.0	250.1	256.3	260.3	260.9	263.7	263.0	261.5	259.8	256.5	257.1
2007	251.0	251.6	254.1	253.2	255.0	257.8	260.2	262.2	260.8	259.9	259.2	257.0	256.8
Natural Resources and Mining													
2000	2.4	2.6	2.6	2.6	2.6	2.6	2.6	2.5	2.5	2.5	2.5	2.6	2.5
2001	2.0	2.0	2.0	1.9	1.9	1.8	1.8	1.7	1.7	1.7	1.6	1.6	1.8
2002	1.5	1.5	1.5	1.5	1.5	1.4	1.3	1.3	1.2	1.2	1.2	1.2	1.4
2003	1.0	1.0	1.0	1.0	1.0	1.0	1.0	1.0	1.0	1.4	1.4	1.4	1.1
2004	1.4	1.4	1.4	1.4	1.4	1.4	1.4	1.4	1.4	1.3	1.4	1.4	1.4
2005	1.3	1.4	1.3	1.3	1.3	1.3	1.4	1.3	1.3	1.3	1.3	1.3	1.3
2006	1.3	1.3	1.3	1.3	1.4	1.4	1.4	1.5	1.5	1.5	1.5	1.5	1.4
2007	1.4	1.5	1.4	1.4	1.4	1.4	1.5	1.5	1.5	1.5	1.5	1.5	1.5
Construction													
2000	103.0	102.9	105.1	106.3	108.3	111.6	114.3	116.2	117.6	116.4	115.8	115.6	111.0
2001	112.7	113.5	116.7	116.5	117.9	119.8	120.3	121.5	120.5	118.1	115.9	114.2	117.3
2002	106.5	107.7	108.7	110.1	111.2	114.0	113.8	116.4	115.4	114.7	112.7	110.8	111.8
2003	107.9	108.1	108.6	108.1	108.6	110.5	111.5	113.7	113.6	113.8	112.6	110.8	110.6
2004	106.2	106.1	107.2	109.5	111.1	113.3	115.0	116.3	116.8	116.0	113.4	112.2	111.9
2005	106.3	108.0	110.1	111.4	112.4	115.3	117.3	118.5	118.5	118.5	117.6	115.8	114.1
2006	110.1	112.0	111.0	109.7	115.5	118.4	120.0	122.3	122.1	121.2	118.8	116.2	116.4
2007	112.3	112.3	114.7	114.7	116.1	118.5	121.3	123.0	121.4	120.9	119.7	117.8	117.7
Manufacturing													
2000	173.9	175.6	175.2	176.3	176.5	178.2	177.0	177.7	179.3	179.8	181.9	183.7	177.9
2001	179.2	179.0	178.8	175.3	172.7	171.7	167.7	166.4	163.4	160.7	158.8	158.0	169.3
2002	153.9	153.9	154.2	153.9	154.0	154.8	153.7	153.6	152.8	151.9	150.8	149.9	153.1
2003	145.3	144.7	144.3	143.6	143.2	142.9	142.2	142.3	142.3	142.4	142.6	143.0	143.2
2004	142.1	142.6	143.0	142.5	142.6	143.0	143.0	142.9	141.9	141.3	141.2	140.9	142.3
2005	138.8	138.8	138.6	137.8	137.3	137.9	138.0	138.2	138.3	137.9	138.3	138.4	138.2
2006	138.3	138.6	139.7	139.1	139.4	140.5	139.5	139.9	139.4	138.8	139.5	138.8	139.3
2007	137.3	137.8	138.0	137.1	137.5	137.9	137.4	137.7	137.9	137.5	138.0	137.7	137.7
Service-Providing													
2000	1,774.5	1,793.4	1,812.9	1,820.8	1,836.0	1,850.6	1,835.5	1,842.6	1,851.1	1,852.4	1,869.2	1,882.5	1,835.1
2001	1,833.7	1,843.6	1,856.2	1,837.5	1,836.9	1,837.8	1,808.2	1,803.2	1,801.2	1,794.4	1,793.4	1,798.8	1,820.4
2002	1,751.4	1,757.3	1,768.6	1,761.3	1,767.7	1,768.3	1,745.6	1,746.5	1,753.1	1,759.6	1,772.1	1,775.8	1,760.6
2003	1,726.6	1,733.9	1,736.1	1,728.5	1,729.8	1,731.6	1,704.0	1,702.8	1,707.0	1,708.7	1,715.2	1,724.3	1,720.7
2004	1,684.1	1,693.8	1,703.0	1,704.3	1,710.8	1,714.3	1,697.1	1,690.8	1,697.3	1,698.7	1,722.0	1,734.4	1,705.2
2005	1,694.6	1,706.3	1,712.2	1,718.4	1,722.3	1,726.8	1,711.6	1,710.3	1,723.0	1,729.0	1,742.1	1,751.5	1,720.7
2006	1,718.8	1,733.0	1,741.5	1,744.5	1,755.7	1,762.1	1,744.8	1,745.8	1,756.5	1,766.1	1,778.4	1,784.7	1,752.7
2007	1,745.7	1,761.3	1,770.2	1,764.4	1,779.8	1,785.3	1,774.6	1,774.4	1,781.7	1,789.8	1,798.3	1,805.3	1,777.6
Trade, Transportation, and Utilities													
2000	391.5	389.0	391.1	392.7	395.4	398.5	399.8	399.8	400.2	399.0	408.6	417.4	398.6
2001	403.5	400.2	401.2	398.0	397.4	399.2	396.1	394.3	393.5	388.7	392.3	395.5	396.7
2002	381.6	378.5	379.0	374.7	376.2	378.1	377.4	376.3	377.1	378.5	385.5	390.3	379.4
2003	373.6	369.3	367.9	362.5	363.0	363.8	361.4	360.6	359.8	360.8	367.7	373.6	365.3
2004	355.7	353.1	353.5	354.2	356.5	358.0	356.6	356.1	355.6	360.1	368.0	375.1	358.5
2005	359.0	355.2	354.3	354.4	355.1	357.0	356.4	357.1	357.8	356.8	364.2	371.9	358.3
2006	358.8	355.3	355.6	354.1	356.2	358.6	357.6	358.2	358.5	359.7	367.4	373.8	359.5
2007	362.1	358.7	358.5	355.4	357.5	358.8	359.0	359.2	359.3	360.8	367.7	373.7	360.9
Wholesale Trade													
2000	83.1	83.6	84.7	85.1	85.5	86.0	86.7	86.7	87.0	86.6	86.8	87.8	85.8
2001	87.5	88.4	88.5	87.5	87.1	87.0	86.2	85.8	85.8	85.0	84.9	84.7	86.5
2002	83.0	83.4	83.6	82.0	82.3	82.3	81.9	81.8	81.6	81.2	81.1	81.2	82.1
2003	79.5	79.5	79.5	78.9	78.7	78.4	77.6	77.4	77.0	76.9	76.6	76.8	78.0
2004	74.3	74.4	74.8	75.7	75.7	76.2	76.0	75.8	76.0	76.1	76.4	76.6	75.7
2005	74.6	74.3	74.2	74.9	74.7	75.2	74.7	74.6	74.5	74.4	74.5	74.7	74.6
2006	74.1	74.5	74.9	75.2	75.6	76.0	75.4	75.6	75.8	76.1	76.1	76.6	75.5
2007	75.7	76.1	76.6	75.7	76.3	76.5	75.7	75.8	75.6	75.7	75.9	75.9	76.0

Employment by Industry: San Francisco-Oakland-Fremont, CA, 2000–2007—*Continued*

(Numbers in thousands, not seasonally adjusted.)

Industry and year	January	February	March	April	May	June	July	August	September	October	November	December	Annual Average
Retail Trade													
2000	210.1	207.2	207.6	208.4	210.4	212.5	212.8	212.7	212.6	213.9	222.4	229.1	213.3
2001	217.5	213.4	213.9	212.5	212.3	214.2	213.6	212.5	212.1	209.7	216.4	220.8	214.1
2002	209.2	205.7	206.5	205.4	206.3	207.6	207.5	206.8	208.0	209.3	216.8	221.4	209.2
2003	208.8	205.1	204.0	201.3	201.9	202.9	202.6	202.6	202.5	203.5	211.3	216.5	205.2
2004	202.5	200.0	199.9	199.8	201.5	202.2	202.2	202.5	201.6	204.0	211.4	218.0	203.8
2005	206.4	202.7	202.0	201.9	202.3	203.4	203.6	204.9	205.2	205.6	212.5	219.2	205.8
2006	208.2	203.8	203.6	202.5	203.5	204.8	205.5	206.1	205.2	206.5	214.0	218.7	206.9
2007	210.0	205.9	205.7	203.5	204.6	205.4	206.9	206.9	207.1	208.1	214.4	219.8	208.2
Transportation and Utilities													
2000	98.3	98.2	98.8	99.2	99.5	100.0	100.3	100.4	100.6	98.5	99.4	100.5	99.5
2001	98.5	98.4	98.8	98.0	98.0	98.0	96.3	96.0	95.6	94.0	91.0	90.0	96.1
2002	89.4	89.4	88.9	87.3	87.6	88.2	88.0	87.7	87.5	88.0	87.6	87.7	88.1
2003	85.3	84.7	84.4	82.3	82.4	82.5	81.2	80.6	80.3	80.4	79.8	80.3	82.0
2004	78.9	78.7	78.8	78.7	79.3	79.6	78.4	77.8	78.0	80.0	80.2	80.5	79.1
2005	78.0	78.2	78.1	77.6	78.1	78.4	78.1	77.6	78.1	76.8	77.2	78.0	77.9
2006	76.5	77.0	77.1	76.4	77.1	77.8	76.7	76.5	77.5	77.1	77.3	78.0	77.1
2007	76.4	76.7	76.2	76.2	76.6	76.9	76.4	76.5	76.6	77.0	77.4	78.0	76.7
Information													
2000	92.6	95.1	97.6	99.1	102.2	105.0	104.4	105.7	106.1	105.7	106.4	106.5	102.2
2001	109.7	108.6	107.9	102.3	99.9	98.3	95.3	93.6	91.3	89.9	88.6	87.7	97.8
2002	88.2	87.4	87.3	85.8	86.7	86.8	85.7	85.6	85.0	83.6	84.1	83.9	85.8
2003	81.7	82.1	80.6	79.5	79.5	79.2	78.4	78.0	77.2	76.4	76.9	76.6	78.8
2004	75.5	75.7	75.7	75.3	75.3	75.3	75.3	74.7	74.0	73.5	73.5	73.5	74.8
2005	73.1	73.5	72.5	71.8	71.7	71.7	71.3	71.3	70.6	70.1	70.2	69.9	71.5
2006	69.4	69.6	69.3	68.7	68.8	68.9	68.7	69.1	68.7	68.9	69.3	69.5	69.1
2007	68.2	68.4	68.4	68.2	68.6	68.6	69.1	69.1	68.6	68.2	68.2	68.3	68.5
Financial Activities													
2000	145.7	146.5	146.9	146.5	147.2	148.9	148.2	147.4	147.9	149.0	148.9	150.5	147.8
2001	158.7	159.9	161.9	161.5	161.0	161.9	160.9	160.4	159.9	159.8	159.9	160.1	160.5
2002	156.4	156.5	156.8	157.0	157.1	158.0	157.8	158.8	157.9	158.5	159.0	159.9	157.8
2003	158.3	159.1	159.7	158.9	159.2	159.2	157.4	157.2	156.6	155.4	155.0	155.5	157.6
2004	154.7	154.7	154.8	154.0	154.5	155.2	155.2	155.3	154.6	155.3	155.5	156.3	155.0
2005	155.9	156.3	156.7	156.7	157.4	158.4	158.0	157.9	157.6	157.0	157.1	157.7	157.2
2006	156.4	157.0	157.3	157.3	157.9	157.8	156.3	156.3	156.0	155.3	154.6	154.2	156.4
2007	152.4	153.0	153.2	152.2	152.9	153.0	152.3	152.4	151.2	150.5	149.3	149.2	151.8
Professional and Business Services													
2000	390.7	397.0	403.5	406.9	406.6	413.1	415.2	420.1	422.1	421.7	423.2	425.1	412.1
2001	394.7	396.2	397.0	386.2	383.7	383.7	375.6	372.7	367.2	362.2	359.2	360.6	378.3
2002	343.5	343.8	345.3	341.5	339.7	339.8	335.9	336.0	333.2	331.1	333.2	333.2	338.0
2003	321.8	323.1	324.0	322.3	320.2	321.4	319.9	321.0	319.5	319.1	320.0	322.6	321.2
2004	317.3	319.6	322.1	322.4	322.5	324.9	323.3	324.2	326.0	328.0	330.9	322.6	323.7
2005	325.6	328.9	331.0	331.2	330.2	332.6	333.3	335.2	335.4	336.7	339.6	342.7	333.5
2006	335.8	339.8	342.4	343.0	344.4	348.3	347.8	349.8	349.9	351.1	352.6	355.0	346.7
2007	346.2	349.8	351.9	350.5	352.9	356.2	358.3	360.6	359.4	360.7	361.3	363.0	355.9
Education and Health Services													
2000	205.3	209.8	210.8	205.2	205.3	204.0	202.8	202.1	204.7	205.5	207.6	208.9	206.0
2001	201.5	205.8	207.7	207.3	208.7	207.8	207.2	207.8	209.9	209.9	210.9	213.0	208.5
2002	209.9	213.5	215.2	211.0	211.6	208.7	209.4	209.3	211.3	213.5	213.0	213.9	212.0
2003	211.3	215.8	216.4	218.6	218.6	216.5	214.2	213.6	211.3	215.4	215.0	215.0	216.0
2004	214.0	218.4	219.4	219.6	219.2	217.3	214.0	213.3	215.5	216.1	217.4	218.0	217.2
2005	213.6	219.5	220.4	220.5	220.9	218.2	216.5	216.1	219.0	217.7	218.9	219.5	219.3
2006	218.1	223.2	224.5	226.5	227.2	225.3	222.1	221.9	225.3	221.3	222.4	223.0	225.0
2007	223.6	230.2	232.3	230.4	231.7	230.8	228.0	226.7	229.8	227.5	228.7	229.5	230.1
Leisure and Hospitality													
2000	179.0	181.9	184.8	185.5	188.3	191.6	193.2	194.3	195.2	190.3	189.3	189.6	188.6
2001	187.4	190.2	193.3	193.5	197.4	199.2	197.5	198.7	195.8	191.5	188.9	189.4	193.6
2002	182.8	184.4	187.2	192.1	196.4	198.8	197.3	199.6	197.5	196.0	194.9	195.0	193.5
2003	187.0	187.9	189.4	190.5	193.3	196.9	195.2	197.9	196.6	195.0	192.4	193.2	192.9
2004	186.2	188.2	190.6	192.1	195.8	197.4	198.9	199.6	199.7	196.3	194.6	196.5	194.7
2005	189.3	190.6	193.1	197.7	200.1	202.6	201.8	203.6	204.0	202.7	202.2	202.0	199.1
2006	195.1	198.6	200.0	202.6	207.1	210.0	209.0	209.9	209.5	208.5	207.9	208.0	205.5
2007	202.0	204.4	206.6	208.5	213.6	216.2	217.3	217.8	216.5	214.4	213.1	213.4	212.0
Other Services													
2000	69.7	70.7	71.4	71.9	72.3	73.0	73.3	72.9	72.3	72.6	72.9	73.3	72.2
2001	73.8	75.0	76.2	75.4	76.3	77.3	76.7	76.7	76.4	76.5	76.3	76.6	76.1
2002	75.3	76.2	76.6	76.7	77.1	77.6	77.7	77.3	77.3	76.5	76.7	76.8	76.8
2003	75.0	76.1	76.2	75.9	76.1	76.5	75.1	75.1	75.1	74.4	74.0	74.3	75.3
2004	72.3	73.0	73.9	74.1	74.4	74.4	74.3	73.5	73.7	72.9	72.4	73.0	73.5
2005	71.0	71.6	72.5	73.1	73.2	73.9	72.9	72.1	72.1	72.5	72.1	72.6	72.5
2006	70.9	71.8	72.4	72.9	74.0	74.7	74.1	73.7	73.7	73.4	73.2	73.6	73.2
2007	72.2	73.4	74.1	74.1	75.0	75.3	75.6	75.4	75.5	75.4	75.0	75.6	74.7
Government													
2000	300.0	303.4	306.8	313.0	318.7	316.5	298.6	300.3	302.6	308.6	312.3	311.2	307.7
2001	304.4	307.7	311.0	313.3	312.5	310.4	298.9	299.0	307.2	314.3	315.2	315.0	309.1
2002	313.7	317.0	321.2	322.5	322.9	320.5	304.4	303.6	313.8	321.9	323.3	321.7	317.2
2003	317.9	320.5	321.9	320.3	319.9	318.1	302.4	299.4	306.7	311.5	311.8	310.5	313.4
2004	308.4	311.1	313.0	312.6	312.6	311.8	299.5	294.1	301.1	308.8	311.1	309.6	307.8
2005	307.1	310.7	311.7	313.0	313.7	312.4	301.4	297.0	306.5	311.9	314.3	311.7	309.3
2006	314.3	317.7	320.0	319.4	320.1	318.5	309.2	306.9	314.9	321.7	324.7	321.1	317.4
2007	319.0	323.4	325.2	325.1	327.6	326.4	315.0	313.2	321.4	327.8	330.7	329.1	323.7

Employment by Industry: Riverside-San Bernardino-Ontario, CA, 2000–2007

(Numbers in thousands, not seasonally adjusted.)

Industry and year	January	February	March	April	May	June	July	August	September	October	November	December	Annual Average
Total Nonfarm													
2000	964.6	969.5	977.3	980.9	992.2	994.1	980.0	980.5	994.7	998.4	1,010.7	1,017.9	988.4
2001	1,010.1	1,011.4	1,022.8	1,023.1	1,029.2	1,034.6	1,026.4	1,023.9	1,034.5	1,039.8	1,049.4	1,051.7	1,029.7
2002	1,035.2	1,043.0	1,049.1	1,061.0	1,069.7	1,074.0	1,054.5	1,059.1	1,069.7	1,074.9	1,089.2	1,095.0	1,064.5
2003	1,075.5	1,078.6	1,088.1	1,090.9	1,096.8	1,101.3	1,089.9	1,088.3	1,102.5	1,117.8	1,126.9	1,133.7	1,099.2
2004	1,122.8	1,128.5	1,139.5	1,151.9	1,159.0	1,161.6	1,152.0	1,152.3	1,166.5	1,183.7	1,197.4	1,205.0	1,160.0
2005	1,184.4	1,195.8	1,207.7	1,220.1	1,221.0	1,221.8	1,210.0	1,213.6	1,230.1	1,240.6	1,254.3	1,264.4	1,222.0
2006	1,246.5	1,254.7	1,264.9	1,268.8	1,273.4	1,278.1	1,262.9	1,259.5	1,268.2	1,271.8	1,280.5	1,282.9	1,267.7
2007	1,262.7	1,267.4	1,275.0	1,271.9	1,278.2	1,278.0	1,263.3	1,254.8	1,262.0	1,266.4	1,272.5	1,272.8	1,268.8
Total Private													
2000	775.3	779.3	783.8	787.3	793.8	799.9	793.4	799.1	805.2	804.3	813.9	819.8	796.3
2001	811.9	814.2	821.8	823.8	828.6	832.9	831.7	835.3	835.0	835.9	840.1	842.9	829.5
2002	827.2	831.4	837.9	842.2	851.5	855.1	847.5	856.1	860.1	861.0	872.8	878.8	851.8
2003	860.3	863.4	870.8	874.3	881.9	887.2	884.3	888.9	895.6	907.8	914.7	922.4	887.6
2004	911.1	916.6	925.7	937.0	944.0	948.2	946.5	950.4	956.5	969.4	979.5	985.6	947.5
2005	964.4	974.3	984.5	995.6	996.5	1,001.6	999.2	1,003.0	1,012.6	1,018.1	1,030.0	1,038.9	1,001.6
2006	1,025.5	1,033.4	1,041.5	1,042.7	1,046.5	1,050.8	1,046.8	1,047.4	1,049.6	1,046.9	1,054.2	1,057.3	1,045.2
2007	1,038.0	1,042.2	1,047.4	1,043.3	1,048.6	1,048.5	1,045.1	1,043.2	1,041.6	1,037.1	1,041.1	1,040.3	1,043.0
Goods-Producing													
2000	191.1	192.7	193.8	197.4	199.5	202.9	203.2	205.6	206.6	205.7	206.0	205.9	200.9
2001	203.5	204.3	206.9	207.4	209.1	209.8	211.1	213.0	211.7	209.9	207.6	205.7	208.3
2002	199.8	201.4	203.1	204.0	206.0	207.8	208.2	212.4	212.1	212.2	212.5	210.8	207.5
2003	207.6	207.5	210.5	211.2	215.3	217.0	216.8	220.0	220.8	222.7	222.6	223.1	216.3
2004	221.3	223.2	224.2	229.0	231.5	234.4	237.0	238.4	240.2	240.8	239.1	238.2	233.1
2005	230.7	235.3	238.3	242.3	243.2	247.0	248.6	250.7	252.7	253.3	253.1	253.1	245.7
2006	250.4	253.4	254.4	253.7	256.5	259.4	257.1	256.7	255.3	247.7	242.2	240.3	252.3
2007	234.2	234.6	235.8	234.8	235.8	237.1	237.5	236.0	232.6	228.7	225.7	223.4	233.0
Natural Resources and Mining													
2000	1.3	1.3	1.3	1.3	1.2	1.2	1.3	1.3	1.2	1.2	1.2	1.2	1.2
2001	1.2	1.2	1.2	1.2	1.2	1.2	1.2	1.1	1.2	1.1	1.1	1.2	1.1
2002	1.1	1.1	1.1	1.2	1.2	1.2	1.3	1.3	1.3	1.2	1.3	1.3	1.2
2003	1.3	1.3	1.3	1.3	1.2	1.2	1.2	1.2	1.2	1.2	1.2	1.2	1.2
2004	1.2	1.2	1.2	1.2	1.2	1.2	1.2	1.2	1.2	1.2	1.3	1.3	1.2
2005	1.3	1.3	1.3	1.3	1.3	1.3	1.4	1.4	1.4	1.4	1.4	1.4	1.4
2006	1.4	1.4	1.4	1.4	1.4	1.4	1.5	1.4	1.4	1.4	1.4	1.4	1.4
2007	1.4	1.3	1.3	1.3	1.3	1.3	1.4	1.4	1.4	1.4	1.4	1.4	1.4
Construction													
2000	73.5	73.9	74.7	77.1	79.2	81.0	81.0	82.7	84.0	83.5	84.0	84.0	79.9
2001	81.6	82.2	84.5	86.5	88.6	89.7	90.9	93.0	92.3	92.1	90.9	89.6	88.5
2002	84.8	85.7	86.7	87.3	88.7	90.2	91.6	95.1	95.0	95.9	95.8	93.9	90.9
2003	92.7	91.9	94.2	94.6	98.6	99.8	99.7	102.2	102.7	104.0	103.7	104.4	99.0
2004	102.4	103.6	104.0	108.4	110.1	112.2	114.5	115.9	117.4	118.6	117.3	116.6	111.8
2005	109.9	113.8	116.1	120.5	121.7	124.9	125.7	127.6	129.3	130.2	130.2	129.9	123.3
2006	126.7	128.6	128.9	128.3	130.2	132.6	131.6	131.5	130.2	123.9	119.6	117.7	127.5
2007	112.2	112.9	114.2	114.2	114.8	115.9	116.6	115.6	113.0	110.0	107.6	106.5	112.8
Manufacturing													
2000	116.3	117.5	117.8	119.0	119.1	120.7	120.9	121.6	121.4	121.0	120.8	120.7	119.7
2001	120.7	120.9	121.2	119.7	119.3	118.9	119.0	118.9	118.2	116.7	115.6	114.9	118.7
2002	113.9	114.6	115.3	115.5	116.1	116.4	115.3	116.0	115.8	115.1	115.4	115.6	115.4
2003	113.6	114.3	115.0	115.3	115.5	116.0	115.9	116.6	116.9	117.5	117.7	118.5	116.1
2004	117.7	118.4	119.0	119.4	120.2	121.0	121.3	121.3	121.6	121.0	120.5	120.3	120.1
2005	119.5	120.2	120.9	120.5	120.2	120.8	121.5	121.7	122.0	121.7	121.5	121.8	121.0
2006	122.3	123.4	124.1	124.0	124.9	125.4	124.0	123.8	123.7	122.4	121.2	121.2	123.4
2007	120.6	120.4	120.3	119.3	119.7	119.9	119.5	119.0	118.2	117.3	116.7	115.5	118.9
Service-Providing													
2000	773.5	776.8	783.5	783.5	792.7	791.2	776.8	774.9	788.1	792.7	804.7	812.0	787.5
2001	806.6	807.1	815.9	815.7	820.1	824.8	815.3	810.9	822.8	829.9	841.8	846.0	821.4
2002	835.4	841.6	846.0	857.0	863.7	866.2	846.3	846.7	857.6	862.7	876.7	884.2	857.0
2003	867.9	871.1	877.6	879.7	881.5	884.3	873.1	868.3	881.7	895.1	904.3	910.6	882.9
2004	901.5	905.3	915.3	922.9	927.5	927.2	915.0	913.9	926.3	942.9	958.3	966.8	926.9
2005	953.7	960.5	969.4	977.8	977.8	974.8	961.4	962.9	977.4	987.3	1,001.2	1,011.3	976.3
2006	996.1	1,001.3	1,010.5	1,015.1	1,016.9	1,018.7	1,005.8	1,002.8	1,012.9	1,024.1	1,038.3	1,042.6	1,015.4
2007	1,028.5	1,032.8	1,039.2	1,037.1	1,042.4	1,040.9	1,025.8	1,018.8	1,029.4	1,037.7	1,046.8	1,049.4	1,035.7
Trade, Transportation, and Utilities													
2000	207.5	206.2	206.7	207.7	209.5	210.7	210.8	211.1	212.6	213.1	219.0	222.5	211.5
2001	218.6	215.9	217.4	217.2	217.9	218.9	219.3	219.2	219.6	221.0	225.0	227.7	219.8
2002	220.0	218.5	220.0	222.2	224.8	226.4	225.9	226.9	228.3	229.1	234.8	238.2	226.3
2003	231.0	229.8	230.6	231.8	233.3	234.5	234.2	235.1	236.5	243.0	245.5	249.9	236.3
2004	242.7	241.7	243.8	247.1	249.4	251.2	252.8	255.0	257.4	266.0	273.4	277.7	254.9
2005	268.8	267.0	268.4	270.0	271.3	272.7	273.7	275.3	278.4	280.2	288.8	295.7	275.9
2006	284.1	282.4	284.9	285.6	287.4	289.3	290.0	290.6	291.6	295.4	303.6	307.9	291.1
2007	297.6	295.2	296.4	295.6	297.3	297.6	297.8	297.9	298.6	298.9	303.6	305.4	298.5
Wholesale Trade													
2000	35.8	36.0	36.2	38.4	38.7	39.1	39.3	39.0	39.5	38.8	38.7	38.9	38.2
2001	41.7	41.9	42.7	42.6	42.3	42.0	42.2	41.6	41.2	40.8	40.3	40.1	41.6
2002	40.4	40.7	40.9	41.6	41.8	42.2	42.1	42.5	42.7	42.5	42.8	42.9	41.9
2003	42.9	43.3	43.5	44.0	44.1	44.0	43.4	43.4	43.4	43.4	43.0	43.1	43.5
2004	42.9	43.3	43.7	44.2	44.6	45.1	46.2	46.4	46.6	47.6	47.8	48.2	45.6
2005	47.9	48.0	48.5	49.3	49.6	49.9	50.2	50.4	50.8	51.1	51.4	52.1	49.9
2006	52.6	53.1	53.5	54.0	54.0	54.2	54.6	54.6	54.8	54.6	54.8	55.0	54.2
2007	55.3	55.9	56.2	56.1	56.3	56.5	56.9	57.0	57.0	56.6	56.6	56.5	56.4

Employment by Industry: Riverside-San Bernardino-Ontario, CA, 2000–2007—*Continued*

(Numbers in thousands, not seasonally adjusted.)

Industry and year	January	February	March	April	May	June	July	August	September	October	November	December	Annual Average
Retail Trade													
2000	125.0	123.5	123.6	123.1	124.4	125.1	125.3	126.2	126.7	128.8	134.3	137.4	127.0
2001	131.1	129.4	130.3	130.3	130.9	131.6	131.3	131.7	132.2	133.3	137.6	140.5	132.5
2002	134.3	132.4	133.9	134.8	136.6	137.3	137.1	137.4	138.0	138.6	143.9	146.0	137.5
2003	139.6	138.6	138.9	138.8	139.6	140.5	140.8	141.6	142.1	147.1	150.3	154.4	142.7
2004	147.9	146.0	147.5	149.1	150.7	151.3	151.5	152.9	154.1	159.0	166.1	169.8	153.8
2005	162.7	160.5	160.8	161.4	162.1	163.1	163.9	165.1	166.5	167.4	174.8	180.2	165.7
2006	169.4	167.4	168.7	169.2	170.3	171.6	172.1	172.4	172.4	175.7	182.9	185.8	173.2
2007	177.4	173.9	174.9	173.8	174.8	174.2	174.1	174.1	174.1	174.5	178.6	180.0	175.4
Transportation and Utilities													
2000	46.7	46.7	46.9	46.2	46.4	46.5	46.2	45.9	46.4	45.5	46.0	46.2	46.3
2001	45.8	44.6	44.4	44.3	44.7	45.3	45.8	45.9	46.2	46.9	47.1	47.1	45.7
2002	45.3	45.4	45.2	45.8	46.4	46.9	46.7	47.0	47.6	48.0	48.1	49.3	46.8
2003	48.5	47.9	48.2	49.0	49.6	50.0	50.0	50.1	51.0	52.5	52.2	52.4	50.1
2004	51.9	52.4	52.6	53.8	54.1	54.8	55.1	55.7	56.7	59.4	59.5	59.7	55.5
2005	58.2	58.5	59.1	59.3	59.6	59.7	59.6	59.8	61.1	61.7	62.6	63.4	60.2
2006	62.1	61.9	62.7	62.4	63.1	63.5	63.3	63.6	64.4	65.1	65.9	67.1	63.8
2007	64.9	65.4	65.3	65.7	66.2	66.9	66.8	66.8	67.5	67.8	68.4	68.9	66.7
Information													
2000	13.7	13.8	13.9	14.0	14.1	14.3	14.4	14.5	14.6	14.6	14.6	14.7	14.3
2001	14.7	14.6	14.3	14.3	14.5	14.7	14.8	14.7	14.5	14.4	14.5	14.7	14.6
2002	14.5	14.3	14.2	13.9	14.1	14.2	13.9	14.1	14.1	13.8	14.0	14.0	14.1
2003	13.9	13.9	13.8	13.6	13.7	13.8	14.1	14.0	13.9	13.8	14.0	13.9	13.9
2004	13.9	13.7	13.8	13.9	13.9	14.0	14.3	14.0	13.9	14.2	14.4	14.4	14.0
2005	14.3	14.5	14.5	14.6	14.7	14.6	14.5	14.2	14.4	14.4	14.6	14.7	14.5
2006	14.6	14.9	14.9	15.1	15.2	15.4	15.5	15.5	15.5	15.4	15.6	15.7	15.3
2007	15.7	15.6	15.3	15.2	15.3	15.3	15.2	15.2	15.0	14.9	14.8	14.8	15.2
Financial Activities													
2000	35.3	35.2	35.2	35.2	35.4	35.7	35.5	35.7	35.7	36.1	36.3	36.8	35.7
2001	35.9	36.4	36.7	36.8	37.0	37.3	37.3	37.3	37.4	38.3	38.5	38.8	37.3
2002	38.7	38.7	38.7	39.4	39.6	39.9	39.3	39.5	39.5	39.6	40.0	40.6	39.5
2003	40.3	40.7	40.9	41.9	42.3	42.9	43.0	43.5	43.8	43.7	44.1	44.4	42.6
2004	44.4	44.5	45.0	45.1	45.4	45.5	46.0	45.9	45.9	46.4	47.0	47.4	45.7
2005	47.6	47.9	48.1	48.5	48.5	48.5	49.0	49.3	49.6	49.9	50.2	50.4	49.0
2006	51.2	51.3	51.7	52.0	52.3	52.2	51.5	51.6	51.5	51.3	51.5	51.5	51.6
2007	51.4	51.6	51.7	50.7	50.5	50.1	49.7	49.3	49.1	48.8	48.9	48.8	50.1
Professional and Business Services													
2000	92.4	93.6	94.9	95.8	96.5	98.7	96.0	98.1	99.5	97.8	98.9	98.8	96.8
2001	97.3	98.3	99.2	99.7	100.9	103.5	103.8	104.7	105.7	103.0	102.6	102.5	101.8
2002	101.2	102.7	103.7	103.6	105.4	106.5	106.6	109.2	109.9	109.3	111.7	111.8	106.8
2003	109.4	109.6	111.0	111.1	112.6	113.9	117.0	117.8	119.9	120.3	121.1	121.6	115.4
2004	119.5	121.0	123.3	124.8	125.7	127.0	126.5	127.6	127.4	127.8	127.9	127.5	125.5
2005	125.4	128.4	130.3	132.7	131.4	132.7	133.7	135.1	136.4	137.1	137.8	137.0	133.2
2006	138.2	139.5	140.5	141.1	140.5	141.7	142.9	143.1	144.9	145.2	145.8	144.3	142.3
2007	142.3	144.2	145.7	144.1	145.4	145.4	146.1	146.8	147.6	146.5	146.9	145.2	145.5
Education and Health Services													
2000	101.1	101.9	102.1	101.7	102.4	101.5	100.1	100.6	101.4	103.1	102.9	103.4	101.9
2001	103.6	104.3	105.0	105.0	105.8	105.6	105.1	105.8	106.2	108.0	109.2	109.9	106.1
2002	109.7	110.9	111.5	111.1	112.6	112.6	110.1	111.0	113.3	114.2	115.3	116.0	112.4
2003	113.3	115.2	115.5	116.5	116.3	116.6	114.1	114.3	115.4	117.0	117.3	118.1	115.8
2004	116.6	118.2	118.8	119.7	119.4	119.3	117.2	116.7	117.3	118.7	119.1	119.5	118.4
2005	118.1	119.6	120.3	121.0	120.9	120.7	117.9	117.4	118.9	121.3	121.5	121.7	119.9
2006	120.5	122.7	123.1	122.9	122.5	121.7	119.9	120.3	121.2	122.9	123.5	123.6	122.1
2007	123.4	125.0	125.7	125.8	126.2	126.2	125.7	126.1	127.3	128.2	128.9	129.3	126.5
Leisure and Hospitality													
2000	100.3	101.6	102.4	101.1	101.8	101.0	98.5	98.3	99.1	99.0	101.2	102.4	100.6
2001	102.8	104.2	105.2	106.5	106.1	105.6	103.2	103.0	102.5	103.7	104.9	106.0	104.5
2002	106.2	107.3	108.7	109.5	110.1	108.8	105.3	104.8	105.0	104.9	106.6	109.5	107.2
2003	107.4	108.8	110.2	109.8	109.6	109.3	107.0	106.3	106.9	108.5	111.3	113.2	109.0
2004	114.1	115.4	117.1	118.2	119.4	117.6	113.4	113.6	115.0	115.8	119.1	121.3	116.7
2005	119.2	120.9	123.4	125.1	125.0	124.3	121.4	120.8	121.2	121.4	123.4	125.4	122.6
2006	125.3	127.2	129.4	130.0	129.4	128.4	127.0	126.6	126.4	126.4	129.5	131.5	128.1
2007	131.7	133.6	134.6	134.5	135.2	133.7	130.2	129.0	128.5	128.4	129.9	131.3	131.7
Other Services													
2000	33.9	34.3	34.8	34.4	34.6	35.1	34.9	35.2	35.6	34.9	35.0	35.3	34.8
2001	35.5	36.2	37.1	36.9	37.3	37.5	37.1	37.6	37.4	37.6	37.8	37.6	37.1
2002	37.1	37.6	38.0	38.5	38.9	38.9	38.2	38.2	38.2	37.7	37.9	37.9	38.1
2003	37.4	37.9	38.3	38.4	38.8	39.2	38.1	37.9	38.4	38.8	38.8	38.2	38.4
2004	38.6	38.9	39.7	39.2	39.3	39.2	39.3	39.2	39.4	39.7	39.5	39.6	39.3
2005	40.3	40.7	41.2	41.4	41.5	41.1	40.4	40.2	41.0	40.5	40.6	40.9	40.8
2006	41.2	42.0	42.6	42.3	42.7	42.7	42.9	43.0	43.2	42.6	42.5	42.5	42.5
2007	41.7	42.4	42.2	42.6	42.9	43.1	42.9	42.9	42.9	42.7	42.4	42.1	42.6
Government													
2000	189.3	190.2	193.5	193.6	198.4	194.2	186.6	181.4	189.5	194.1	196.8	198.1	192.1
2001	198.2	197.2	201.0	199.3	200.6	201.7	194.7	188.6	199.5	203.9	209.3	208.8	200.2
2002	208.0	211.6	211.2	218.8	218.2	218.9	207.0	203.0	209.6	213.9	216.4	216.2	212.7
2003	215.2	215.2	217.3	216.6	214.9	214.1	205.6	199.4	206.9	210.0	212.2	211.3	211.5
2004	211.7	211.9	213.8	214.9	215.0	213.4	205.5	201.9	210.0	214.3	217.9	219.4	212.5
2005	220.0	221.5	223.2	224.5	224.5	220.2	210.8	210.6	217.5	222.5	224.3	225.5	220.4
2006	221.0	221.3	223.4	226.1	226.9	227.3	216.1	212.1	218.6	224.9	226.3	225.6	222.5
2007	224.7	225.2	227.6	228.6	229.6	229.5	218.2	211.6	220.4	229.3	231.4	232.5	225.7

Employment by Industry: Phoenix-Mesa-Scottsdale, AZ, 2000–2007

(Numbers in thousands, not seasonally adjusted.)

Industry and year	January	February	March	April	May	June	July	August	September	October	November	December	Annual Average
Total Nonfarm													
2000	1,534.7	1,558.7	1,570.7	1,573.5	1,583.7	1,564.7	1,545.5	1,565.2	1,592.7	1,603.1	1,616.9	1,631.9	1,578.4
2001	1,582.2	1,606.8	1,617.8	1,611.9	1,607.7	1,589.3	1,566.4	1,583.9	1,597.4	1,600.4	1,602.3	1,606.0	1,597.7
2002	1,566.5	1,581.4	1,592.8	1,605.7	1,601.5	1,589.6	1,562.0	1,585.3	1,596.9	1,608.3	1,632.1	1,631.3	1,596.1
2003	1,587.2	1,606.3	1,614.7	1,621.0	1,623.1	1,604.8	1,582.5	1,609.3	1,621.9	1,642.6	1,656.6	1,667.8	1,619.8
2004	1,626.4	1,648.2	1,662.4	1,677.0	1,678.9	1,664.3	1,654.6	1,675.3	1,694.7	1,725.0	1,740.7	1,756.7	1,683.7
2005	1,714.5	1,742.5	1,758.4	1,783.1	1,785.2	1,768.3	1,761.7	1,787.9	1,816.5	1,825.6	1,848.1	1,860.5	1,787.7
2006	1,829.6	1,862.2	1,879.2	1,883.4	1,891.3	1,871.3	1,853.9	1,879.0	1,899.9	1,907.9	1,922.2	1,929.6	1,884.1
2007	1,881.9	1,908.3	1,921.2	1,914.6	1,919.3	1,897.5	1,872.0	1,903.5	1,911.2	1,917.6	1,927.3	1,928.0	1,908.5
Total Private													
2000	1,342.4	1,359.2	1,370.4	1,372.2	1,378.0	1,384.7	1,371.4	1,383.6	1,392.1	1,399.5	1,412.7	1,426.3	1,382.7
2001	1,387.3	1,400.4	1,410.8	1,404.4	1,401.2	1,402.9	1,383.8	1,389.2	1,387.4	1,385.8	1,386.8	1,391.1	1,394.3
2002	1,359.3	1,366.7	1,377.6	1,388.3	1,389.0	1,389.5	1,373.2	1,381.7	1,379.7	1,385.5	1,402.9	1,408.0	1,383.5
2003	1,375.4	1,384.3	1,392.7	1,398.9	1,401.7	1,399.1	1,390.3	1,400.6	1,403.9	1,418.7	1,432.1	1,442.5	1,403.4
2004	1,412.7	1,424.6	1,438.5	1,451.8	1,454.2	1,457.9	1,457.0	1,463.3	1,467.8	1,494.0	1,509.1	1,524.2	1,462.9
2005	1,493.4	1,510.7	1,528.3	1,552.1	1,555.9	1,559.3	1,560.3	1,571.1	1,584.7	1,592.0	1,612.9	1,625.6	1,562.2
2006	1,606.0	1,628.0	1,645.0	1,649.3	1,655.4	1,661.0	1,647.9	1,658.5	1,664.5	1,668.6	1,682.4	1,692.3	1,654.9
2007	1,651.1	1,667.8	1,679.3	1,673.0	1,676.9	1,678.0	1,654.8	1,664.3	1,663.6	1,666.8	1,674.1	1,675.3	1,668.8
Goods-Producing													
2000	278.8	281.3	283.0	282.9	284.8	288.9	288.4	290.1	290.8	290.8	290.6	291.5	286.8
2001	285.3	286.7	288.3	287.1	287.3	288.3	287.2	287.3	283.5	278.6	274.4	271.4	283.8
2002	265.8	265.5	266.3	266.6	267.1	268.6	268.3	268.7	266.1	263.6	262.5	260.8	265.8
2003	257.3	256.9	257.1	259.6	261.3	261.1	261.1	265.2	265.4	265.5	265.6	266.2	262.1
2004	262.2	264.3	266.6	269.1	271.4	275.0	277.4	279.6	281.1	285.0	286.3	288.6	275.6
2005	283.9	287.3	291.5	297.2	300.1	305.1	306.6	308.5	310.1	310.6	313.5	316.3	302.6
2006	312.8	317.9	321.9	324.1	326.3	329.5	328.3	327.9	325.8	321.6	318.9	317.0	322.7
2007	310.2	311.9	312.4	310.6	311.8	315.0	311.4	312.4	309.3	305.4	300.3	297.0	309.0
Natural Resources and Mining													
2000	2.4	2.4	2.4	2.4	2.4	2.4	2.4	2.4	2.4	2.4	2.4	2.4	2.4
2001	2.5	2.4	2.5	2.4	2.4	2.4	2.3	2.4	2.3	2.3	2.3	2.3	2.4
2002	2.3	2.3	2.3	2.3	2.3	2.3	2.2	2.3	2.1	2.1	2.0	2.0	2.2
2003	2.0	2.0	1.9	2.0	2.0	2.0	2.0	2.0	1.9	1.9	2.0	2.0	1.9
2004	1.9	1.9	1.9	2.0	2.0	2.1	2.1	2.1	2.1	2.2	2.2	2.2	2.1
2005	2.2	2.2	2.2	2.3	2.4	2.4	2.0	1.9	1.9	1.9	2.1	2.4	2.2
2006	2.5	2.4	2.5	2.6	2.6	2.8	2.8	2.9	2.9	2.8	2.9	2.9	2.7
2007	2.9	3.0	3.1	3.0	3.0	3.1	3.2	3.2	3.2	3.1	3.2	3.1	3.1
Construction													
2000	117.0	118.4	119.8	121.1	122.9	124.8	124.5	125.5	126.1	126.8	126.0	126.7	123.3
2001	122.8	124.9	127.1	127.6	128.9	131.3	131.8	133.4	131.3	128.8	126.7	124.5	128.3
2002	122.2	122.2	123.7	124.6	126.1	127.9	128.2	129.5	128.5	127.4	127.1	126.0	126.1
2003	123.7	124.0	124.6	125.8	127.9	129.7	130.4	132.2	132.9	133.4	133.5	133.8	129.3
2004	130.9	132.4	134.1	136.4	138.3	140.9	143.2	144.9	146.2	149.2	150.2	152.0	141.6
2005	149.0	151.8	155.4	159.7	161.4	165.1	166.8	168.4	170.2	170.7	173.2	174.7	163.9
2006	172.2	176.1	179.5	181.1	183.1	185.6	184.3	184.0	182.6	179.4	177.6	175.5	180.1
2007	169.8	171.0	171.4	170.2	171.1	174.1	170.6	171.5	169.5	166.0	161.1	158.2	168.7
Manufacturing													
2000	159.4	160.5	160.8	159.4	159.5	161.7	161.5	162.2	162.3	161.6	162.2	162.4	161.1
2001	160.0	159.4	158.7	157.1	156.0	154.6	153.1	151.5	149.9	147.5	145.4	144.6	153.2
2002	141.3	141.0	140.3	139.7	138.7	138.4	137.9	136.9	135.5	134.1	133.4	132.8	137.5
2003	131.6	130.9	130.6	131.8	131.4	131.4	130.7	131.0	130.6	130.2	130.1	130.4	130.8
2004	129.4	130.0	130.6	130.7	131.1	132.0	132.1	132.6	132.8	133.6	133.9	134.4	131.9
2005	132.7	133.3	133.9	135.2	136.3	137.6	137.8	138.2	138.0	138.0	138.2	139.2	136.5
2006	138.1	139.4	139.9	140.4	140.6	141.1	141.2	141.0	140.3	139.4	138.4	138.6	139.9
2007	137.5	137.9	137.9	137.4	137.7	137.8	137.6	137.7	136.6	136.3	136.0	135.7	137.2
Service-Providing													
2000	1,255.9	1,277.4	1,287.7	1,290.6	1,298.9	1,275.8	1,257.1	1,275.1	1,301.9	1,312.3	1,326.3	1,340.4	1,291.6
2001	1,296.9	1,320.1	1,329.5	1,324.8	1,320.4	1,301.0	1,279.2	1,296.6	1,313.9	1,321.8	1,327.9	1,334.6	1,313.9
2002	1,300.7	1,315.9	1,326.5	1,339.1	1,334.4	1,321.0	1,293.7	1,316.6	1,330.8	1,344.7	1,369.6	1,370.5	1,330.3
2003	1,329.9	1,349.4	1,357.6	1,361.4	1,361.8	1,341.7	1,319.4	1,344.1	1,356.5	1,377.1	1,391.0	1,401.6	1,357.6
2004	1,364.2	1,383.9	1,395.8	1,407.9	1,407.5	1,389.3	1,377.2	1,395.7	1,413.6	1,440.0	1,454.4	1,468.1	1,408.1
2005	1,430.6	1,455.2	1,466.9	1,485.9	1,485.1	1,463.2	1,455.1	1,479.4	1,506.4	1,515.0	1,534.6	1,544.2	1,485.1
2006	1,516.8	1,544.3	1,557.3	1,559.3	1,565.0	1,541.8	1,525.6	1,551.1	1,574.1	1,586.3	1,603.3	1,612.6	1,561.5
2007	1,571.7	1,596.4	1,608.8	1,604.0	1,607.5	1,582.5	1,560.6	1,591.1	1,601.9	1,612.2	1,627.0	1,631.0	1,599.6
Trade, Transportation, and Utilities													
2000	316.9	317.0	316.3	315.6	316.2	318.7	316.3	318.7	321.1	324.7	334.2	340.7	321.4
2001	326.1	324.3	323.4	323.2	322.7	323.0	320.5	320.8	320.7	324.6	330.0	333.0	324.4
2002	321.6	318.8	320.9	322.7	324.0	325.3	322.2	323.2	324.6	326.9	335.0	340.3	325.5
2003	326.5	325.4	325.5	325.2	325.5	324.8	324.4	325.8	325.9	332.2	340.2	345.0	328.8
2004	333.7	333.8	334.8	336.9	337.4	337.5	338.1	339.1	337.4	345.3	354.1	359.3	340.6
2005	352.1	353.3	354.9	357.4	358.0	358.0	361.0	362.0	364.1	366.7	376.3	381.4	362.1
2006	371.4	371.2	374.1	375.2	375.6	375.6	377.2	378.5	378.7	384.2	393.3	399.3	379.5
2007	386.5	385.9	386.9	387.3	388.2	388.5	385.1	386.2	386.4	389.9	396.6	398.5	388.8
Wholesale Trade													
2000	76.7	77.4	77.9	77.6	77.6	78.4	78.5	78.7	79.0	79.5	80.0	80.7	78.5
2001	80.3	80.9	80.9	80.4	80.4	79.9	79.4	79.3	78.6	78.4	78.2	78.1	79.6
2002	76.9	77.1	77.6	78.0	78.9	79.0	78.8	78.8	78.7	78.9	79.1	79.0	78.4
2003	77.9	78.0	77.8	77.7	78.0	77.8	77.0	77.1	76.9	76.8	77.1	77.5	77.4
2004	77.8	78.1	78.2	78.4	78.6	78.8	79.7	79.8	78.6	80.5	80.7	81.0	79.2
2005	80.4	81.3	81.8	82.5	82.6	82.7	83.3	83.3	83.5	83.9	84.7	85.3	82.9
2006	84.7	85.4	85.7	86.3	86.5	87.0	87.4	87.6	87.9	88.5	88.5	89.1	87.1
2007	88.0	88.5	88.9	89.2	89.4	90.1	89.5	89.5	89.3	89.6	89.8	89.7	89.3

Employment by Industry: Phoenix-Mesa-Scottsdale, AZ, 2000–2007—*Continued*

(Numbers in thousands, not seasonally adjusted.)

Industry and year	January	February	March	April	May	June	July	August	September	October	November	December	Annual Average
Retail Trade													
2000	182.8	182.5	182.2	181.8	182.3	183.6	181.1	182.7	184.3	187.0	195.2	200.5	185.5
2001	187.8	185.2	184.4	184.3	183.1	183.8	182.2	182.4	183.2	187.5	193.6	197.1	186.2
2002	187.2	184.3	185.3	186.4	186.5	186.8	184.1	184.8	186.3	187.7	195.5	201.0	188.0
2003	189.0	187.9	188.2	188.2	188.3	188.1	188.7	189.9	190.0	195.7	203.3	207.4	192.0
2004	196.4	196.2	196.6	198.2	198.6	198.5	197.9	198.8	198.7	203.0	211.7	216.8	201.0
2005	210.5	210.5	211.8	213.5	213.3	213.2	215.4	215.7	217.0	219.4	227.2	230.9	216.5
2006	223.2	222.3	224.7	224.6	224.6	224.3	225.0	225.4	224.8	229.8	238.5	242.6	227.5
2007	231.9	230.6	231.3	231.3	231.7	231.3	229.8	230.6	231.4	234.2	240.2	241.8	233.0
Transportation and Utilities													
2000	57.4	57.1	56.2	56.2	56.3	56.7	56.7	57.3	57.8	58.2	59.0	59.5	57.4
2001	58.0	58.2	58.1	58.5	59.2	59.3	58.9	59.1	58.9	58.7	58.2	57.8	58.6
2002	57.5	57.4	58.0	58.3	58.6	59.5	59.3	59.6	59.6	60.3	60.4	60.3	59.1
2003	59.6	59.5	59.5	59.3	59.2	58.9	58.7	58.8	59.0	59.7	59.8	60.1	59.3
2004	59.5	59.5	60.0	60.3	60.2	60.2	60.5	60.5	60.1	61.8	61.7	61.5	60.5
2005	61.2	61.5	61.3	61.4	62.1	62.1	62.3	63.0	63.6	63.4	64.4	65.2	62.6
2006	63.5	63.5	63.7	64.3	64.5	64.3	64.8	65.5	66.0	65.9	66.3	67.6	65.0
2007	66.6	66.8	66.7	66.8	67.1	67.1	65.8	66.1	65.7	66.1	66.6	67.0	66.5
Information													
2000	39.3	40.0	42.4	42.8	43.1	43.2	42.8	42.6	42.2	41.3	41.7	42.3	42.0
2001	41.3	42.4	42.1	42.4	41.6	42.1	41.6	41.5	41.1	41.0	41.4	40.8	41.6
2002	40.7	40.5	40.1	40.4	39.9	39.4	39.4	39.1	38.3	37.7	38.3	38.5	39.4
2003	37.5	37.7	38.0	38.1	37.8	37.9	37.2	37.0	36.5	36.5	37.1	36.9	37.3
2004	36.4	36.2	36.6	36.5	35.7	35.5	34.4	33.4	32.6	32.6	32.9	32.5	34.6
2005	32.2	32.9	33.2	34.0	34.1	33.7	33.3	33.0	32.6	32.9	33.5	34.0	33.3
2006	33.1	33.2	33.3	32.8	32.9	32.7	32.1	32.1	31.3	31.1	31.7	32.1	32.4
2007	30.1	31.0	30.9	31.3	32.0	32.0	32.1	31.5	31.1	31.1	31.4	31.5	31.3
Financial Activities													
2000	122.5	124.7	124.7	124.8	125.6	127.0	126.1	126.7	127.5	127.9	128.6	129.8	126.3
2001	125.9	127.4	128.6	128.2	128.9	129.4	130.1	130.7	131.4	130.9	131.3	132.4	129.6
2002	129.8	131.0	130.4	131.7	130.8	130.9	130.3	130.5	130.3	131.6	133.3	134.0	131.2
2003	132.2	132.8	134.0	133.8	134.5	134.8	135.2	136.0	135.1	134.8	135.3	136.0	134.5
2004	134.6	135.3	136.1	138.1	137.9	138.2	139.1	139.4	139.2	141.3	141.8	142.9	138.7
2005	141.7	143.1	143.3	145.5	145.7	146.1	147.3	148.4	149.1	150.5	151.0	152.0	147.0
2006	150.6	151.8	152.6	152.3	152.9	153.3	153.3	153.9	154.1	154.6	154.9	156.1	153.4
2007	154.0	155.2	155.7	155.7	155.5	154.9	153.1	152.3	151.8	151.7	151.6	152.1	153.6
Professional and Business Services													
2000	248.6	253.8	258.2	262.0	265.3	265.7	264.1	268.3	268.8	270.7	271.1	272.8	264.1
2001	260.1	264.2	267.8	265.4	263.7	263.8	257.3	257.7	257.4	253.9	250.1	251.4	259.4
2002	244.1	247.5	252.3	256.2	256.0	256.4	253.2	256.2	254.7	254.2	255.8	255.9	253.5
2003	248.3	252.8	256.2	258.3	259.4	259.3	256.2	258.6	259.8	263.3	264.1	266.6	258.6
2004	257.2	260.4	264.8	270.9	271.5	273.9	275.0	275.8	278.4	284.3	285.3	288.4	273.8
2005	279.9	284.3	288.5	294.4	294.0	296.7	298.0	300.9	304.6	304.3	307.3	308.6	296.8
2006	302.8	310.0	313.1	315.4	317.8	321.4	319.1	322.7	325.7	326.5	327.3	328.7	319.2
2007	317.9	322.3	326.3	324.7	325.4	327.7	323.2	325.4	323.9	323.3	325.3	325.5	324.2
Education and Health Services													
2000	134.5	136.5	137.6	136.8	137.1	136.9	135.3	137.0	138.5	138.9	139.6	141.1	137.5
2001	139.9	141.5	142.8	142.7	142.5	143.4	140.7	144.1	144.9	146.1	147.1	148.9	143.7
2002	148.5	149.9	151.0	150.8	152.0	152.3	149.5	152.7	154.0	156.9	158.7	159.4	153.0
2003	158.4	160.1	160.8	162.6	162.8	162.6	161.2	163.6	165.4	166.4	167.4	168.2	163.2
2004	167.9	169.6	170.4	172.5	172.8	173.0	171.2	173.6	175.0	178.0	179.0	180.5	173.6
2005	176.4	178.2	181.1	184.0	185.0	183.6	181.8	185.1	186.6	187.9	189.1	189.9	184.1
2006	189.3	192.1	194.0	194.9	195.4	194.7	193.7	197.5	198.8	200.1	201.4	203.5	196.3
2007	199.6	202.9	204.2	203.2	204.1	204.3	201.5	205.3	206.6	207.7	209.0	210.2	204.9
Leisure and Hospitality													
2000	147.8	150.9	152.7	152.8	151.0	148.9	143.7	145.6	148.6	150.3	151.8	152.7	149.7
2001	151.7	155.7	158.7	156.7	155.2	152.3	146.5	147.0	148.3	151.3	152.9	153.6	152.5
2002	148.9	153.1	155.5	158.0	157.1	153.8	148.9	149.6	149.8	152.7	157.3	157.0	153.5
2003	154.2	157.4	159.3	160.3	159.1	155.1	150.4	151.1	152.3	156.1	158.0	159.1	156.0
2004	157.5	160.8	164.7	164.2	163.9	160.9	157.6	158.1	159.8	162.9	165.1	167.0	161.9
2005	163.5	167.3	170.6	174.0	173.0	169.9	166.2	167.1	170.8	172.1	174.8	175.6	170.4
2006	175.5	179.6	182.6	183.5	182.4	180.3	175.1	176.2	179.4	181.2	184.7	185.1	180.5
2007	182.8	186.9	190.5	189.7	188.9	184.1	178.8	182.4	184.8	187.9	190.0	190.5	186.4
Other Services													
2000	54.0	55.0	55.5	54.5	54.9	55.4	54.7	54.6	54.6	54.9	55.1	55.4	54.9
2001	57.0	58.2	59.1	58.7	59.3	60.6	59.9	60.1	60.1	59.4	59.6	59.6	59.3
2002	59.9	60.4	61.1	61.9	62.1	62.8	61.4	61.7	61.9	61.9	62.0	62.1	61.6
2003	61.0	61.2	61.8	61.0	61.3	61.5	62.6	63.3	63.5	63.9	64.4	64.5	62.5
2004	63.2	64.2	64.5	63.6	63.6	63.9	64.2	64.3	64.3	64.6	64.6	65.0	64.2
2005	63.7	64.3	65.2	65.6	66.0	66.2	66.1	66.1	66.8	67.0	67.4	67.8	66.0
2006	70.5	72.2	73.4	71.1	72.1	73.5	69.1	69.7	70.7	69.3	70.2	70.5	71.0
2007	70.0	71.7	72.4	70.5	71.0	71.5	69.6	68.8	69.7	69.8	69.9	70.0	70.4
Government													
2000	192.3	199.5	200.3	201.3	205.7	180.0	174.1	181.6	200.6	203.6	204.2	205.6	195.7
2001	194.9	206.4	207.0	207.5	206.5	186.4	182.6	194.7	210.0	214.6	215.5	214.9	203.4
2002	207.2	214.7	215.2	217.4	212.5	200.1	188.8	203.6	217.2	222.8	229.2	223.3	212.7
2003	211.8	222.0	222.0	222.1	221.4	205.7	192.2	208.7	218.0	223.9	224.5	225.3	216.4
2004	213.7	223.6	223.9	225.2	224.7	206.4	197.6	212.0	226.9	231.0	231.6	232.5	220.8
2005	221.1	231.8	230.1	231.0	229.3	209.0	201.4	216.8	231.8	233.6	235.2	234.9	225.5
2006	223.6	234.2	234.2	234.1	235.9	210.3	206.0	220.5	235.4	239.3	239.8	237.3	229.2
2007	230.8	240.5	241.9	241.6	242.4	219.5	217.2	239.2	247.6	250.8	253.2	252.7	239.8

Employment by Industry: Seattle-Tacoma-Bellevue, WA, 2000–2007

(Numbers in thousands, not seasonally adjusted.)

Industry and year	January	February	March	April	May	June	July	August	September	October	November	December	Annual Average
Total Nonfarm													
2000	1,609.8	1,607.4	1,636.8	1,630.7	1,646.3	1,660.8	1,643.4	1,650.9	1,663.0	1,661.7	1,671.0	1,678.3	1,646.7
2001	1,629.0	1,631.1	1,636.9	1,632.4	1,640.2	1,646.3	1,629.6	1,625.5	1,629.2	1,615.9	1,615.8	1,610.2	1,628.5
2002	1,568.6	1,569.1	1,571.4	1,573.0	1,584.7	1,593.0	1,583.3	1,582.2	1,587.5	1,585.0	1,594.5	1,587.7	1,581.7
2003	1,552.9	1,556.7	1,557.6	1,559.2	1,572.0	1,577.0	1,568.8	1,568.6	1,577.6	1,579.2	1,586.8	1,588.6	1,570.4
2004	1,548.5	1,558.9	1,569.4	1,577.1	1,587.9	1,599.4	1,592.1	1,589.4	1,601.2	1,607.9	1,619.8	1,620.9	1,589.4
2005	1,586.3	1,593.9	1,605.6	1,616.2	1,630.9	1,642.1	1,640.2	1,641.0	1,643.1	1,656.9	1,671.7	1,676.7	1,633.7
2006	1,641.9	1,653.0	1,661.7	1,668.9	1,685.5	1,701.4	1,688.8	1,692.9	1,708.4	1,706.7	1,719.5	1,721.8	1,687.5
2007	1,689.1	1,709.1	1,716.8	1,722.5	1,739.5	1,754.4	1,745.8	1,744.1	1,752.8	1,761.6	1,768.6	1,767.8	1,739.3
Total Private													
2000	1,376.5	1,368.9	1,399.0	1,393.6	1,404.1	1,418.6	1,416.2	1,427.3	1,430.6	1,425.0	1,430.7	1,437.9	1,410.7
2001	1,388.1	1,387.8	1,391.8	1,387.6	1,394.1	1,398.6	1,392.5	1,396.4	1,388.7	1,370.6	1,363.7	1,360.8	1,385.1
2002	1,321.7	1,318.8	1,321.1	1,322.6	1,333.5	1,341.2	1,342.3	1,348.7	1,342.9	1,335.5	1,338.0	1,336.1	1,333.5
2003	1,302.4	1,302.8	1,304.2	1,306.1	1,314.6	1,322.2	1,326.9	1,332.2	1,331.7	1,328.5	1,330.6	1,333.6	1,319.7
2004	1,298.3	1,305.0	1,315.2	1,323.4	1,333.3	1,343.2	1,347.9	1,352.9	1,352.5	1,355.8	1,360.9	1,366.1	1,337.9
2005	1,334.5	1,340.1	1,350.6	1,361.5	1,375.3	1,385.6	1,395.4	1,404.0	1,394.0	1,403.9	1,412.6	1,422.2	1,381.6
2006	1,388.9	1,396.2	1,404.7	1,413.0	1,428.4	1,443.8	1,444.0	1,455.4	1,459.2	1,452.8	1,459.7	1,467.0	1,434.4
2007	1,436.0	1,452.1	1,459.7	1,465.7	1,481.6	1,495.5	1,498.0	1,506.7	1,505.3	1,504.7	1,508.7	1,509.0	1,485.3
Goods-Producing													
2000	312.1	298.2	315.9	315.1	315.9	318.2	317.8	319.4	318.9	317.3	315.2	313.4	314.8
2001	307.6	305.7	306.9	305.7	307.4	309.0	310.0	311.6	308.9	302.6	296.0	290.8	305.2
2002	282.2	280.0	278.9	277.9	280.2	281.2	281.0	282.5	278.8	275.9	272.0	268.2	278.2
2003	260.9	259.8	259.3	259.3	261.5	262.9	264.4	266.1	264.8	262.9	260.3	258.3	261.7
2004	252.9	254.1	256.4	257.5	259.8	261.8	266.0	267.4	266.6	268.1	266.9	266.3	262.0
2005	261.4	263.7	267.6	270.3	273.5	277.3	282.7	285.3	271.6	286.1	285.5	286.3	275.9
2006	283.1	286.9	288.5	290.5	294.3	299.0	301.5	303.9	305.3	304.5	303.1	302.4	296.9
2007	299.3	304.6	305.7	307.4	311.8	317.1	319.5	322.0	321.6	320.4	317.8	315.3	313.5
Natural Resources and Mining													
2000	2.4	2.5	2.6	2.6	2.6	2.7	2.6	2.7	2.7	2.7	2.5	2.4	2.6
2001	2.7	2.6	2.6	2.5	2.5	2.5	2.6	2.6	2.5	2.5	2.3	2.3	2.5
2002	2.1	2.2	2.3	2.2	2.2	2.2	2.2	2.2	2.2	2.2	2.1	2.1	2.2
2003	2.0	2.0	2.1	1.9	1.8	1.8	1.7	1.8	1.7	1.8	1.7	1.7	1.8
2004	1.6	1.6	1.6	1.6	1.7	1.7	1.6	1.6	1.6	1.6	1.6	1.6	1.6
2005	1.5	1.5	1.5	1.5	1.5	1.5	1.5	1.5	1.5	1.5	1.5	1.5	1.5
2006	1.4	1.5	1.5	1.5	1.5	1.5	1.5	1.5	1.5	1.5	1.5	1.5	1.5
2007	1.4	1.5	1.4	1.6	1.6	1.6	1.7	1.5	1.5	1.5	1.5	1.5	1.5
Construction													
2000	91.7	93.4	95.9	96.8	98.4	100.6	102.0	103.7	104.0	103.0	101.8	100.5	99.3
2001	96.7	95.9	97.3	96.2	97.9	99.5	101.1	102.5	101.3	97.9	94.2	91.2	97.6
2002	88.5	89.1	89.0	89.3	91.7	93.1	94.9	97.7	96.5	94.5	92.3	89.9	92.2
2003	86.2	86.4	86.6	88.3	90.9	92.8	94.9	97.0	96.6	95.7	94.0	92.4	91.8
2004	88.8	90.3	91.9	92.7	94.6	96.2	99.2	100.4	99.4	99.9	98.6	97.3	95.8
2005	93.1	94.9	97.1	98.9	101.1	103.2	106.5	108.7	109.9	108.9	107.9	107.9	103.2
2006	104.3	106.8	108.8	110.6	113.4	116.4	117.9	120.1	120.5	119.8	117.6	116.5	114.4
2007	114.4	117.5	119.7	121.4	124.7	127.9	128.7	131.1	130.0	128.5	125.7	123.4	124.4
Manufacturing													
2000	215.1	214.0	214.6	212.9	212.1	212.1	210.4	210.2	209.4	208.9	208.2	207.7	211.3
2001	205.4	204.4	204.3	204.3	204.1	204.2	203.6	203.8	202.4	199.4	196.9	194.6	202.3
2002	191.8	188.9	187.7	186.6	186.6	186.2	184.1	182.9	180.1	179.3	177.8	176.5	184.0
2003	172.7	171.4	170.6	169.1	168.8	168.3	167.8	167.3	166.5	165.4	164.6	164.2	168.1
2004	162.5	162.2	162.9	163.2	163.5	163.9	165.2	165.4	165.6	166.6	166.7	167.4	164.6
2005	166.8	167.3	169.0	169.9	170.9	172.6	174.7	175.1	160.2	175.7	176.1	176.9	171.3
2006	177.4	178.6	178.2	178.4	179.4	181.1	182.1	182.3	183.3	183.2	184.0	184.4	181.0
2007	183.5	185.6	184.6	184.4	185.5	187.6	189.1	189.4	190.1	190.4	190.6	190.4	187.6
Service-Providing													
2000	1,297.8	1,309.2	1,320.8	1,315.6	1,330.4	1,342.6	1,325.6	1,331.5	1,344.0	1,344.3	1,355.8	1,364.9	1,331.9
2001	1,321.4	1,325.4	1,329.9	1,326.7	1,332.8	1,337.3	1,319.6	1,313.9	1,320.3	1,313.4	1,319.8	1,319.4	1,323.3
2002	1,286.4	1,289.1	1,292.5	1,295.1	1,304.5	1,311.8	1,302.4	1,299.7	1,308.7	1,309.1	1,322.5	1,319.4	1,303.4
2003	1,292.0	1,296.9	1,298.3	1,299.9	1,310.5	1,314.1	1,304.4	1,302.5	1,312.8	1,316.3	1,326.5	1,330.3	1,308.7
2004	1,295.6	1,304.8	1,313.0	1,319.6	1,328.1	1,337.6	1,326.1	1,322.0	1,334.6	1,339.8	1,352.9	1,354.6	1,327.4
2005	1,324.9	1,330.2	1,338.0	1,345.9	1,357.4	1,364.8	1,357.5	1,355.7	1,371.5	1,370.8	1,386.2	1,390.4	1,357.8
2006	1,358.8	1,366.1	1,373.2	1,378.4	1,391.2	1,402.4	1,387.3	1,389.0	1,403.1	1,402.2	1,416.4	1,419.4	1,390.6
2007	1,389.8	1,404.5	1,411.1	1,415.1	1,427.7	1,437.3	1,426.3	1,422.1	1,431.2	1,441.2	1,450.8	1,452.5	1,425.8
Trade, Transportation, and Utilities													
2000	320.1	318.6	320.6	320.8	323.0	325.5	324.4	326.2	325.9	329.7	335.9	339.9	325.9
2001	324.3	320.6	320.9	319.4	319.2	320.8	320.6	320.3	318.5	316.5	319.5	322.2	320.2
2002	309.0	304.6	304.1	303.8	306.0	308.6	309.6	309.8	308.8	308.8	313.3	316.9	308.6
2003	304.5	301.3	300.9	300.3	302.0	304.0	306.5	306.1	305.2	305.8	311.1	316.1	305.3
2004	301.2	300.2	301.2	303.5	305.6	308.0	308.6	310.1	309.1	310.7	315.9	320.4	307.9
2005	307.0	305.6	306.6	307.1	310.4	312.3	313.6	315.3	315.0	315.7	322.0	327.7	313.2
2006	313.8	311.4	312.5	312.5	315.6	318.9	318.9	320.6	319.8	319.2	326.1	331.3	318.4
2007	319.5	319.0	319.5	320.2	322.9	325.4	326.7	327.5	325.8	327.2	334.9	338.1	325.6
Wholesale Trade													
2000	80.4	80.9	81.6	81.6	81.9	82.8	82.7	83.0	82.6	83.1	82.7	83.1	82.2
2001	81.3	81.6	81.7	81.7	81.6	82.0	81.7	81.8	81.3	80.1	79.6	79.5	81.2
2002	78.7	78.7	78.9	78.4	78.6	78.8	78.3	78.5	78.0	77.0	76.9	76.9	78.1
2003	76.8	76.9	77.1	76.9	77.0	77.0	77.4	77.3	77.0	76.9	76.8	77.1	77.0
2004	76.5	77.0	77.5	78.0	78.1	78.1	78.6	78.4	78.3	78.1	78.0	78.2	77.9
2005	77.5	77.9	78.3	77.6	78.0	78.4	78.9	79.3	79.4	79.4	79.6	80.2	78.7
2006	80.2	80.4	80.9	80.7	81.3	81.8	82.1	82.2	82.2	81.8	82.1	82.2	81.5
2007	81.6	82.0	82.3	82.5	83.1	83.6	83.6	83.8	83.6	83.8	84.2	84.4	83.2

Employment by Industry: Seattle-Tacoma-Bellevue, WA, 2000–2007—*Continued*

(Numbers in thousands, not seasonally adjusted.)

Industry and year	January	February	March	April	May	June	July	August	September	October	November	December	Annual Average
Retail Trade													
2000	34.3	34.3	34.2	33.9	34.4	34.4	34.5	34.3	34.1	34.8	35.1	35.2	34.5
2001	34.2	34.2	34.4	34.4	34.9	34.9	34.5	34.5	34.2	34.1	34.1	34.0	34.4
2002	33.1	32.8	32.8	32.6	32.8	32.8	32.6	32.2	32.0	32.0	31.8	31.4	32.4
2003	30.7	30.9	30.8	30.7	31.1	31.4	31.5	31.6	31.6	31.2	31.6	31.7	31.2
2004	30.8	31.0	31.1	31.0	31.7	31.8	32.0	32.3	32.3	32.1	32.3	32.5	31.7
2005	31.8	32.0	32.0	32.0	32.7	32.8	32.7	32.7	32.6	32.5	32.8	33.0	32.5
2006	30.7	30.8	30.8	30.7	31.1	31.5	31.3	31.6	31.6	31.3	31.8	32.0	31.3
2007	31.0	31.6	31.5	31.4	32.0	32.3	32.2	32.4	32.5	32.4	32.7	32.5	32.0
Transportation and Utilities													
2000	62.4	62.5	62.9	63.4	63.2	63.7	63.8	64.2	64.0	65.8	66.1	65.8	64.0
2001	64.0	63.8	63.5	63.3	63.3	63.4	62.9	62.6	62.1	61.7	60.7	60.5	62.7
2002	58.8	58.7	58.0	58.1	58.9	59.5	60.5	60.5	60.3	60.7	60.2	60.1	59.5
2003	59.0	58.3	58.1	58.0	58.4	58.9	59.6	59.5	59.5	59.3	59.1	59.7	59.0
2004	57.5	57.5	57.7	58.8	59.0	60.1	60.4	60.4	60.8	61.4	61.1	61.6	59.7
2005	59.2	59.7	60.0	60.4	61.1	61.6	61.3	61.2	61.7	61.2	61.6	62.7	61.0
2006	60.7	60.7	61.0	61.3	62.0	62.8	62.6	62.8	63.1	62.2	62.2	63.6	62.1
2007	61.7	61.9	62.2	62.8	63.2	64.0	63.8	64.1	63.7	63.7	64.9	65.2	63.4
Information													
2000	73.2	74.5	75.8	75.9	77.4	79.8	81.3	82.3	83.2	82.7	83.3	83.6	79.4
2001	82.4	82.7	82.1	80.6	80.8	81.3	80.4	80.3	78.6	78.4	78.4	78.8	80.4
2002	76.6	76.4	76.0	75.6	75.7	76.0	76.2	76.2	75.5	75.5	75.8	75.6	75.9
2003	74.6	74.5	74.0	73.6	74.1	74.3	74.7	75.4	75.0	75.1	75.4	75.8	74.7
2004	74.9	74.9	75.2	75.1	75.6	76.0	76.3	76.5	75.8	76.2	76.6	76.9	75.8
2005	76.2	76.8	76.6	76.8	77.1	77.3	78.1	78.8	78.1	77.6	78.4	78.9	77.6
2006	77.9	78.1	78.7	79.2	79.8	82.1	82.5	83.3	83.4	82.8	83.6	84.0	81.3
2007	83.3	84.3	83.9	84.3	85.1	86.0	86.1	86.6	86.0	85.8	85.8	85.7	85.2
Financial Activities													
2000	99.8	100.5	100.3	100.0	100.0	100.4	99.7	100.2	100.0	99.4	99.9	101.0	100.1
2001	100.2	100.9	100.8	100.7	101.0	101.4	102.8	102.9	103.2	101.8	101.8	102.3	101.7
2002	99.3	99.9	100.2	100.2	100.7	100.8	101.1	101.6	101.5	101.3	102.2	102.4	100.9
2003	101.9	102.4	102.6	102.9	103.7	104.0	104.9	105.4	104.9	104.7	104.4	104.1	103.8
2004	102.8	102.8	103.6	102.8	103.0	103.3	103.6	103.7	103.2	103.1	103.0	103.8	103.2
2005	101.7	102.1	102.2	102.5	103.1	103.6	105.0	105.7	105.4	105.6	105.8	106.2	104.1
2006	104.9	105.2	105.0	105.1	105.3	105.5	105.8	105.6	104.9	104.6	104.4	104.7	105.1
2007	103.5	103.8	104.2	104.3	104.2	104.5	104.7	104.7	103.5	103.1	102.9	103.1	103.9
Professional and Business Services													
2000	207.8	209.2	212.8	211.3	212.8	216.6	218.0	221.6	222.8	220.4	220.4	222.3	216.3
2001	214.5	214.0	215.4	214.1	214.3	213.9	210.0	210.3	208.3	206.1	203.8	201.7	210.5
2002	194.6	195.8	196.6	197.9	199.0	200.4	201.8	204.5	203.9	203.1	204.1	201.4	200.3
2003	192.8	194.1	194.3	195.1	195.1	195.8	197.1	199.2	199.0	199.5	199.1	198.1	196.6
2004	193.7	196.6	198.3	200.7	201.5	203.3	205.7	207.2	207.1	209.0	209.5	208.3	203.4
2005	203.6	206.2	207.4	210.1	212.0	213.8	216.8	218.9	220.6	220.4	221.3	221.2	214.4
2006	215.2	217.4	219.6	222.6	225.2	228.3	229.9	232.7	233.3	233.6	234.5	234.6	227.2
2007	228.0	232.3	234.7	235.3	237.4	240.1	241.1	243.5	243.7	243.1	243.6	242.7	238.8
Education and Health Services													
2000	158.7	160.9	162.8	162.7	163.1	162.5	161.0	161.5	164.0	165.3	166.3	166.0	162.9
2001	163.6	166.3	166.5	167.4	167.6	166.2	163.0	163.4	166.5	168.9	170.6	170.6	166.7
2002	169.2	171.4	172.1	171.9	172.6	171.3	167.9	168.2	170.3	173.7	175.0	174.5	171.5
2003	171.4	173.1	174.0	174.3	174.3	173.0	170.0	169.7	172.0	175.0	176.3	175.9	173.3
2004	173.4	175.4	176.4	177.0	177.8	176.5	172.5	172.8	175.8	179.2	180.7	180.1	176.5
2005	179.0	180.8	182.2	183.4	184.3	182.1	178.3	178.8	182.7	184.9	186.0	185.2	182.3
2006	183.7	185.7	186.9	187.1	188.2	185.9	181.1	182.1	185.8	188.8	189.6	189.0	186.2
2007	187.7	190.2	191.9	192.1	193.9	191.2	187.8	188.3	191.6	196.0	198.0	195.5	192.0
Leisure and Hospitality													
2000	139.1	140.7	143.7	143.9	146.1	149.3	146.6	148.4	149.2	144.2	143.7	145.8	145.1
2001	139.0	140.9	142.2	142.9	146.4	148.1	148.2	149.3	147.6	141.2	138.5	139.4	143.6
2002	135.5	135.3	137.3	139.1	142.4	145.8	146.9	148.2	147.4	141.3	139.9	141.2	141.7
2003	137.1	138.0	139.3	140.9	143.6	147.3	148.3	149.5	150.4	145.8	144.1	145.1	144.1
2004	140.3	141.4	144.0	146.3	148.9	152.5	153.0	153.0	153.3	148.5	147.3	149.1	148.1
2005	145.1	144.0	146.5	149.9	153.1	156.7	158.2	158.5	158.5	152.1	152.1	154.7	152.5
2006	149.3	150.0	151.6	154.0	157.5	160.8	161.3	164.0	163.7	157.5	156.5	158.7	157.1
2007	153.7	155.9	157.3	159.7	163.1	167.5	168.3	169.9	169.3	165.2	162.5	165.1	163.1
Other Services													
2000	56.8	57.3	57.9	58.0	59.0	59.6	59.8	60.1	59.9	59.2	59.1	59.3	58.8
2001	58.6	58.8	59.2	59.3	59.8	60.9	61.0	61.3	60.3	59.4	59.6	59.8	59.8
2002	58.3	58.5	58.9	59.6	60.2	61.1	61.6	61.9	61.1	60.2	60.4	60.8	60.2
2003	59.2	59.6	59.8	59.7	60.3	60.9	61.0	60.8	60.4	59.7	59.9	60.2	60.1
2004	59.1	59.6	60.1	60.5	61.1	61.8	62.2	62.2	61.6	61.0	61.0	61.2	61.0
2005	60.5	60.9	61.5	61.4	61.8	62.5	62.7	62.7	62.1	61.5	61.5	62.0	61.8
2006	61.0	61.5	61.9	62.0	62.5	63.3	63.0	63.2	63.0	61.8	61.9	62.3	62.3
2007	61.0	62.0	62.5	62.4	63.2	63.7	63.8	64.2	63.8	63.9	63.2	63.5	63.1
Government													
2000	233.4	238.6	237.8	237.1	242.2	242.2	227.2	223.6	232.3	236.7	240.4	240.4	236.0
2001	240.9	243.4	245.1	244.8	246.1	247.7	237.1	229.1	240.5	245.3	252.1	249.4	243.5
2002	247.0	250.4	250.3	250.5	251.3	251.8	241.0	233.5	244.6	249.6	256.5	251.6	248.2
2003	250.5	253.9	253.4	253.1	257.4	254.8	241.9	236.4	245.9	250.7	256.2	255.0	250.8
2004	250.2	253.9	254.2	253.7	254.6	256.2	244.2	236.5	248.7	252.1	258.9	254.8	251.5
2005	251.8	253.8	255.0	254.7	255.6	256.5	244.8	237.0	249.1	253.0	259.1	254.5	252.1
2006	253.0	256.8	257.0	255.9	257.1	257.6	244.8	237.5	249.2	253.9	259.8	254.8	253.1
2007	253.1	257.0	257.1	256.8	257.9	258.9	247.8	237.4	247.5	256.9	259.9	258.8	254.1

Employment by Industry: Minneapolis-St. Paul-Bloomington, MN-WI, 2000–2007

(Numbers in thousands, not seasonally adjusted.)

Industry and year	January	February	March	April	May	June	July	August	September	October	November	December	Annual Average
Total Nonfarm													
2000	1,698.8	1,705.1	1,717.7	1,736.4	1,753.8	1,769.8	1,747.2	1,754.7	1,763.2	1,771.4	1,778.2	1,779.5	1,748.0
2001	1,729.4	1,732.2	1,737.8	1,745.3	1,762.6	1,770.9	1,746.8	1,748.3	1,753.0	1,754.1	1,755.4	1,750.5	1,748.9
2002	1,695.9	1,694.5	1,697.2	1,708.2	1,729.0	1,737.9	1,720.9	1,719.7	1,733.3	1,736.2	1,742.9	1,737.2	1,721.1
2003	1,691.2	1,693.8	1,696.3	1,714.5	1,734.8	1,741.9	1,721.4	1,726.0	1,735.5	1,742.3	1,743.5	1,744.2	1,723.8
2004	1,692.9	1,694.9	1,700.0	1,732.0	1,751.3	1,765.1	1,738.3	1,738.3	1,750.8	1,764.0	1,767.9	1,767.9	1,738.3
2005	1,715.0	1,716.5	1,723.9	1,754.0	1,775.8	1,787.5	1,765.6	1,768.5	1,783.1	1,792.5	1,796.8	1,798.2	1,764.8
2006	1,754.2	1,751.1	1,760.2	1,777.9	1,797.9	1,815.8	1,787.0	1,787.2	1,794.5	1,801.1	1,809.6	1,808.1	1,787.1
2007	1,767.0	1,767.1	1,772.1	1,785.2	1,811.5	1,824.9	1,800.7	1,800.9	1,805.2	1,812.8	1,817.0	1,812.0	1,798.0
Total Private													
2000	1,464.8	1,467.3	1,477.9	1,494.8	1,509.4	1,530.9	1,530.0	1,538.1	1,532.9	1,536.3	1,539.9	1,542.0	1,513.7
2001	1,498.3	1,494.4	1,499.4	1,506.5	1,520.8	1,533.5	1,526.9	1,529.6	1,519.2	1,514.6	1,514.0	1,509.2	1,513.9
2002	1,459.0	1,452.5	1,454.7	1,465.7	1,484.4	1,498.7	1,497.5	1,504.2	1,495.4	1,494.1	1,492.7	1,482.9	1,482.9
2003	1,453.4	1,449.5	1,452.2	1,467.5	1,487.3	1,500.2	1,497.2	1,503.7	1,496.8	1,497.4	1,497.2	1,497.4	1,483.3
2004	1,452.1	1,448.5	1,454.3	1,485.9	1,503.0	1,521.3	1,517.8	1,521.5	1,513.2	1,520.2	1,518.5	1,521.6	1,498.2
2005	1,470.9	1,469.4	1,476.9	1,507.0	1,528.6	1,543.6	1,539.0	1,546.6	1,542.5	1,545.8	1,551.1	1,551.4	1,522.7
2006	1,511.1	1,506.1	1,514.9	1,532.8	1,551.8	1,572.8	1,560.5	1,566.0	1,553.6	1,554.8	1,561.9	1,560.0	1,545.5
2007	1,526.2	1,523.4	1,528.9	1,542.2	1,566.1	1,582.7	1,577.5	1,582.9	1,566.7	1,568.1	1,570.4	1,567.6	1,558.6
Goods-Producing													
2000	300.5	300.4	303.9	310.6	315.9	322.4	323.9	326.5	322.0	322.2	319.8	315.5	315.3
2001	305.1	303.4	303.7	305.7	310.2	314.0	315.2	315.3	313.8	308.7	304.3	298.7	308.2
2002	286.1	283.6	283.7	287.3	293.7	299.3	300.9	303.5	299.4	296.9	293.5	286.8	292.9
2003	277.5	274.2	274.4	279.5	286.5	292.8	292.9	295.1	291.7	289.4	287.1	282.5	285.3
2004	271.8	269.8	271.0	281.1	286.3	293.5	296.0	298.2	295.4	296.0	291.9	288.8	286.7
2005	277.1	275.7	277.3	285.5	293.1	299.8	299.2	301.0	297.8	293.9	292.2	286.5	289.9
2006	277.6	275.0	276.4	283.2	289.4	296.0	294.7	295.8	291.2	289.8	286.4	280.5	286.3
2007	272.0	269.1	269.9	272.7	280.9	286.8	286.1	287.4	282.5	280.5	277.4	272.2	278.1
Natural Resources, Mining, and Construction													
2000	66.4	66.2	68.7	74.6	79.6	84.1	85.6	86.5	84.8	84.0	81.2	77.3	78.3
2001	71.5	70.7	72.1	76.4	82.1	87.8	90.1	91.3	89.0	87.9	85.5	80.7	82.1
2002	72.3	70.9	71.0	75.8	82.6	86.6	89.6	90.7	88.8	87.3	84.6	79.3	81.6
2003	71.5	69.5	69.9	75.2	82.1	87.0	89.3	90.3	88.5	87.6	84.5	79.8	81.3
2004	71.5	70.3	71.9	79.7	85.0	89.0	92.0	92.6	91.1	90.9	88.8	84.3	83.9
2005	74.2	73.3	74.5	81.2	86.6	91.6	93.6	93.7	91.7	89.1	87.4	82.6	85.0
2006	75.0	74.1	74.8	79.7	85.1	89.1	89.4	89.1	87.7	85.3	82.1	77.0	82.4
2007	70.8	68.7	69.9	72.3	79.1	83.1	83.3	83.7	81.3	79.9	77.2	72.2	76.8
Manufacturing													
2000	234.1	234.2	235.2	236.0	236.3	238.3	238.3	240.0	237.2	238.2	238.6	238.2	237.1
2001	233.6	232.7	231.6	229.3	228.1	226.2	225.1	224.0	224.8	220.8	218.8	218.0	226.1
2002	213.8	212.7	212.7	211.5	211.1	212.7	211.3	212.8	210.6	209.6	208.9	207.5	211.3
2003	206.0	204.7	204.5	204.3	204.4	205.8	203.6	204.8	203.2	201.8	202.6	202.7	204.0
2004	200.3	199.5	199.1	201.4	201.3	204.5	204.0	205.6	204.3	205.1	203.1	204.5	202.7
2005	202.9	202.4	202.8	204.3	206.5	208.2	205.6	207.3	206.1	204.8	204.8	203.9	205.0
2006	202.6	200.9	201.6	203.5	204.3	206.9	205.3	206.7	203.5	204.5	204.3	203.5	204.0
2007	201.2	200.4	200.0	200.4	201.8	203.7	202.8	203.7	201.2	200.6	200.2	200.0	201.3
Service-Providing													
2000	1,398.3	1,404.7	1,413.8	1,425.8	1,437.9	1,447.4	1,423.3	1,428.2	1,441.2	1,449.2	1,458.4	1,464.0	1,432.7
2001	1,424.3	1,428.8	1,434.1	1,439.6	1,452.4	1,456.9	1,431.6	1,433.0	1,439.2	1,445.4	1,451.1	1,451.8	1,440.7
2002	1,409.8	1,410.9	1,413.5	1,420.9	1,435.3	1,438.6	1,420.0	1,416.2	1,433.9	1,439.3	1,449.4	1,450.4	1,428.2
2003	1,413.7	1,419.6	1,421.9	1,435.0	1,448.3	1,449.1	1,428.5	1,430.9	1,443.8	1,452.9	1,456.4	1,461.7	1,438.5
2004	1,421.1	1,425.1	1,429.0	1,450.9	1,465.0	1,471.6	1,442.3	1,440.1	1,455.4	1,468.0	1,472.1	1,479.1	1,451.6
2005	1,437.9	1,440.8	1,446.6	1,468.5	1,482.7	1,487.7	1,466.4	1,467.5	1,485.3	1,498.6	1,504.6	1,511.7	1,474.9
2006	1,476.6	1,476.1	1,483.8	1,494.7	1,508.5	1,519.8	1,492.3	1,491.4	1,503.3	1,511.3	1,523.2	1,527.6	1,500.7
2007	1,495.0	1,498.0	1,502.2	1,512.5	1,530.6	1,538.1	1,514.6	1,513.5	1,522.7	1,532.3	1,539.6	1,539.8	1,519.9
Trade, Transportation, and Utilities													
2000	345.6	342.0	341.7	341.9	343.9	347.4	346.7	347.9	347.4	352.1	359.3	364.4	348.4
2001	352.2	347.1	346.6	346.7	349.0	350.8	348.6	347.6	344.4	346.9	351.7	353.5	348.8
2002	339.5	332.6	332.6	333.9	336.7	338.2	334.9	335.0	333.4	335.3	346.1	347.0	336.9
2003	335.4	330.5	330.2	331.2	334.2	335.0	330.9	331.8	331.4	335.3	340.2	343.0	334.1
2004	329.6	326.0	326.0	331.4	335.5	338.7	338.2	338.2	336.3	340.8	347.0	350.6	336.5
2005	335.2	331.4	332.4	337.1	340.5	340.5	338.7	339.1	337.7	342.2	348.7	352.1	339.6
2006	338.7	333.8	334.0	335.7	338.7	341.4	337.4	337.5	336.5	338.8	346.9	349.3	339.1
2007	338.1	334.9	334.1	336.4	340.3	342.9	339.5	339.7	338.1	340.6	347.3	349.7	340.1
Wholesale Trade													
2000	84.0	84.0	84.4	84.6	85.2	87.0	85.9	86.0	85.2	85.5	85.7	86.1	85.3
2001	86.9	86.8	86.8	86.5	86.4	86.9	86.8	86.3	85.3	85.2	85.3	85.1	86.2
2002	83.8	83.8	83.6	83.6	83.7	84.2	84.4	84.3	83.3	83.6	83.4	83.4	83.8
2003	83.7	83.7	83.7	82.9	83.3	83.9	84.2	84.0	83.2	83.3	83.2	83.3	83.5
2004	82.4	82.4	82.5	84.1	84.5	85.4	86.2	86.0	84.9	84.9	84.8	84.9	84.4
2005	83.8	83.7	83.6	85.9	86.5	86.8	86.4	86.5	85.7	86.3	86.3	86.6	85.7
2006	85.8	85.9	86.4	86.6	87.1	88.1	88.1	88.2	87.2	87.3	87.2	87.3	87.1
2007	86.5	86.6	86.8	86.9	87.7	88.6	88.5	88.4	86.9	87.0	87.1	87.3	87.4
Retail Trade													
2000	187.2	183.6	183.0	182.3	183.6	185.5	186.1	187.1	186.3	190.2	197.2	202.0	187.8
2001	190.7	186.3	185.7	185.6	187.8	189.4	188.2	188.8	185.8	189.3	195.6	198.6	189.3
2002	187.5	181.7	181.9	182.6	184.9	186.5	185.3	185.6	183.4	185.2	192.7	196.8	186.2
2003	185.8	181.2	181.0	182.8	185.4	186.4	183.2	184.7	183.4	186.0	191.1	194.0	185.4
2004	183.0	179.4	179.2	181.9	185.1	187.4	186.1	186.2	183.7	186.3	192.4	195.9	185.6
2005	184.0	180.1	180.7	184.2	186.4	186.6	185.1	186.1	185.1	188.9	195.2	198.5	186.7
2006	187.2	182.8	182.5	184.3	186.3	188.4	186.0	186.2	183.8	186.1	193.0	195.8	186.9
2007	187.0	183.0	182.9	184.5	187.2	189.2	187.0	187.2	184.9	186.6	193.1	195.7	187.4

Employment by Industry: Minneapolis-St. Paul-Bloomington, MN-WI, 2000–2007—*Continued*

(Numbers in thousands, not seasonally adjusted.)

Industry and year	January	February	March	April	May	June	July	August	September	October	November	December	Annual Average
Transportation and Utilities													
2000	74.4	74.4	74.3	75.0	75.1	74.9	74.7	74.8	75.9	76.4	76.4	76.3	75.2
2001	74.6	74.0	74.1	74.6	74.8	74.5	73.6	72.5	73.3	72.4	70.8	69.8	73.3
2002	68.2	67.1	67.1	67.7	68.1	67.5	65.2	65.1	66.7	67.3	67.2	66.8	67.0
2003	65.9	65.6	65.5	65.5	65.5	64.7	63.5	63.1	64.8	66.0	65.9	65.7	65.1
2004	64.2	64.2	64.3	65.4	65.9	65.9	65.8	66.0	67.7	69.6	69.8	69.8	66.6
2005	67.4	67.6	68.1	67.0	67.6	67.1	67.2	66.5	66.9	67.0	67.2	67.0	67.2
2006	65.7	65.1	65.1	64.8	65.3	64.9	63.3	63.1	65.5	65.4	66.7	66.2	65.1
2007	64.6	65.3	64.4	65.0	65.4	65.1	64.0	64.1	66.3	67.0	67.1	66.7	65.4
Information													
2000	47.7	48.1	48.3	48.9	49.2	50.5	50.9	50.8	50.2	50.3	50.5	50.7	49.7
2001	50.5	50.4	50.7	50.1	50.1	50.8	50.5	49.7	49.1	49.4	49.5	49.3	50.0
2002	48.0	47.8	47.7	48.2	48.2	48.7	48.3	47.4	46.6	46.6	46.7	47.0	47.6
2003	45.6	45.4	45.3	45.9	45.8	45.4	44.9	44.5	43.9	43.7	43.9	44.3	44.9
2004	43.5	43.3	43.5	44.2	44.3	44.1	43.4	42.7	42.2	42.2	42.7	42.9	43.3
2005	42.1	42.1	41.9	43.6	43.6	43.8	43.0	42.5	42.2	42.0	42.2	42.2	42.6
2006	41.7	41.6	41.7	41.3	41.7	41.9	41.7	41.9	41.3	41.3	41.6	41.9	41.6
2007	42.1	42.2	42.4	42.1	42.5	42.7	42.5	42.7	42.4	42.3	42.4	42.6	42.4
Financial Activities													
2000	130.1	130.1	130.5	131.4	131.9	133.7	134.1	134.4	133.6	134.0	133.9	135.1	132.7
2001	133.1	133.8	134.3	134.8	135.1	136.5	136.9	136.9	135.4	135.0	135.3	135.9	135.3
2002	134.9	135.2	135.2	135.5	135.8	136.4	138.0	138.4	137.6	137.4	138.1	138.6	136.8
2003	135.6	136.2	137.0	138.7	139.4	141.0	142.1	142.4	141.4	140.2	140.1	140.5	139.6
2004	139.9	139.5	139.3	140.1	140.3	141.5	141.5	141.6	140.4	140.7	140.7	141.3	140.6
2005	139.2	139.3	139.6	140.8	141.4	143.6	143.4	143.9	142.9	142.4	142.6	143.3	141.9
2006	142.0	142.1	142.4	141.9	142.6	143.8	143.1	142.8	141.7	141.5	141.7	142.1	142.3
2007	141.2	141.7	141.7	140.9	141.1	142.3	142.5	142.6	141.1	140.6	140.7	141.5	141.5
Professional and Business Services													
2000	255.9	255.2	258.4	263.0	264.7	270.5	269.3	271.0	269.3	270.1	269.0	267.3	265.3
2001	260.5	258.3	258.4	261.8	261.7	263.5	260.6	260.5	257.6	255.8	253.0	251.8	258.6
2002	241.8	241.0	241.0	242.2	244.2	247.3	247.8	249.2	247.5	248.4	246.7	244.6	245.1
2003	237.2	237.5	237.7	238.8	240.0	242.2	243.1	244.2	244.5	246.2	245.0	245.5	241.8
2004	236.4	237.4	238.7	244.4	245.9	249.2	249.3	249.1	248.0	249.6	248.3	247.3	245.3
2005	238.0	238.4	240.6	247.3	249.4	252.6	251.8	254.0	255.4	259.2	259.2	259.0	250.4
2006	253.2	253.7	255.0	258.3	260.9	265.9	263.4	265.2	263.9	265.4	266.4	266.3	261.5
2007	259.1	259.9	261.5	262.7	265.5	268.9	269.6	271.4	268.1	269.6	268.4	267.3	266.0
Education and Health Services													
1999	172.3	174.7	176.6	178.4	178.8	176.2	175.7	176.2	180.2	184.4	185.5	186.1	178.8
2000	180.6	184.8	186.2	186.8	187.3	184.2	182.7	183.1	188.0	190.8	192.2	193.4	186.7
2001	185.9	189.0	190.9	191.0	192.3	189.2	187.9	188.5	193.2	197.0	198.7	199.1	191.9
2002	194.5	197.8	198.9	199.6	201.1	198.2	198.7	199.3	203.1	206.3	207.9	208.1	201.1
2003	205.7	210.0	210.9	211.4	212.5	210.5	208.8	208.7	210.5	213.5	214.7	214.3	211.0
2004	211.2	213.7	214.7	216.3	217.1	215.8	212.6	212.4	214.6	218.5	219.2	220.4	215.5
2005	216.7	220.5	221.5	222.6	224.0	222.0	221.8	223.0	225.9	228.7	230.3	231.9	224.1
2006	229.7	231.8	233.9	237.2	237.8	237.1	237.0	237.4	238.6	241.7	244.0	245.0	237.6
2007	244.7	246.6	248.1	250.7	252.1	250.4	249.4	250.3	251.1	254.8	257.1	257.0	251.0
Leisure and Hospitality													
2000	133.7	135.0	136.6	140.3	144.9	149.8	150.1	151.8	150.6	143.7	142.0	141.9	143.4
2001	138.2	139.5	141.0	143.2	148.7	154.4	153.6	157.3	153.0	147.3	144.9	145.5	147.2
2002	141.3	141.5	142.5	145.3	150.8	156.0	153.9	156.1	153.5	148.0	145.1	145.8	148.3
2003	143.1	142.3	142.8	148.2	154.6	158.1	157.1	159.5	156.6	152.6	149.4	150.5	151.2
2004	144.8	144.3	145.9	152.3	157.8	161.9	160.7	162.5	160.5	156.4	153.0	154.1	154.5
2005	148.3	147.7	149.0	153.7	159.1	164.5	164.4	165.9	163.8	160.8	159.4	159.2	158.0
2006	154.2	154.1	156.1	159.3	164.4	169.3	166.4	168.3	164.2	159.8	157.8	157.8	161.0
2007	154.5	154.6	155.5	160.8	167.4	171.6	170.7	171.6	167.8	163.6	161.0	160.9	163.3
Other Services													
2000	70.7	71.7	72.3	71.9	71.6	72.4	72.3	72.6	71.8	73.1	73.2	73.7	72.3
2001	72.8	72.9	73.8	73.2	73.7	74.3	73.6	73.8	72.7	74.5	76.6	75.4	73.9
2002	72.9	73.0	73.1	73.7	73.9	74.6	75.0	75.3	74.3	74.4	74.7	74.8	74.1
2003	73.3	73.4	73.9	73.8	74.3	75.2	77.4	77.5	76.8	76.5	76.8	76.8	75.5
2004	74.9	74.5	75.2	76.1	75.8	76.6	76.2	76.8	75.8	76.0	75.7	76.2	75.8
2005	74.3	74.3	74.6	76.4	77.5	76.8	76.7	77.2	76.8	76.6	76.5	77.2	76.2
2006	74.0	74.0	75.4	75.9	76.3	77.4	76.8	77.1	76.2	76.5	77.1	77.1	76.2
2007	74.5	74.4	75.7	75.9	76.3	77.1	77.2	77.2	75.6	76.1	76.1	76.4	76.0
Government													
2000	234.0	237.8	239.8	241.6	244.4	238.9	217.2	216.6	230.3	235.1	238.3	237.5	234.3
2001	231.1	237.8	238.4	238.8	241.8	237.4	219.9	218.7	233.8	239.5	241.4	241.3	235.0
2002	236.9	242.0	242.5	242.5	244.6	239.2	223.4	215.5	237.9	242.1	246.9	244.5	238.2
2003	237.8	244.3	244.1	247.0	247.5	241.7	224.2	222.3	238.7	244.9	246.3	246.8	240.5
2004	240.8	246.4	245.7	246.1	248.3	243.8	220.5	216.8	237.6	243.8	245.5	246.3	240.1
2005	244.1	247.1	247.0	247.0	247.2	243.9	226.6	221.9	240.6	246.7	245.7	246.8	242.1
2006	243.1	245.0	245.3	245.1	246.1	243.0	226.5	221.2	240.9	246.3	247.7	248.1	241.5
2007	240.8	243.7	243.2	243.0	245.4	242.2	223.2	218.0	238.5	244.7	246.6	244.4	239.5

Employment by Industry: San Diego-Carlsbad-San Marcos, CA, 2000–2007

(Numbers in thousands, not seasonally adjusted.)

Industry and year	January	February	March	April	May	June	July	August	September	October	November	December	Annual Average
Total Nonfarm													
2000	1,164.0	1,173.7	1,184.2	1,184.7	1,197.1	1,203.0	1,185.6	1,188.4	1,198.8	1,206.3	1,215.1	1,224.9	1,193.8
2001	1,196.9	1,205.6	1,214.0	1,217.7	1,225.6	1,229.6	1,211.1	1,213.2	1,216.6	1,225.4	1,231.0	1,234.5	1,218.4
2002	1,206.9	1,217.6	1,224.4	1,230.8	1,237.5	1,244.2	1,220.8	1,225.6	1,225.6	1,237.5	1,245.5	1,251.7	1,230.7
2003	1,221.4	1,226.7	1,231.8	1,236.6	1,240.9	1,246.5	1,234.0	1,240.3	1,240.5	1,249.9	1,252.5	1,260.5	1,240.1
2004	1,234.1	1,240.9	1,248.8	1,256.1	1,260.4	1,267.4	1,259.0	1,260.7	1,263.4	1,271.3	1,276.8	1,285.1	1,260.3
2005	1,256.1	1,264.3	1,271.3	1,280.8	1,285.5	1,290.9	1,279.3	1,282.4	1,287.3	1,287.0	1,296.2	1,303.9	1,282.1
2006	1,277.8	1,287.2	1,293.9	1,295.0	1,303.5	1,312.3	1,297.6	1,301.8	1,306.3	1,306.9	1,316.9	1,319.5	1,301.6
2007	1,288.7	1,297.1	1,305.1	1,302.5	1,310.7	1,318.7	1,307.4	1,310.1	1,308.3	1,313.1	1,316.9	1,319.8	1,308.2
Total Private													
2000	956.9	965.5	973.6	975.5	983.6	993.5	990.4	996.0	997.4	997.4	1,003.6	1,013.0	987.2
2001	986.9	993.0	999.3	1,000.8	1,006.3	1,011.6	1,008.7	1,011.9	1,006.9	1,006.9	1,009.9	1,013.8	1,004.7
2002	987.0	994.8	1,000.7	1,007.7	1,014.7	1,021.0	1,010.1	1,015.2	1,012.7	1,016.1	1,022.7	1,029.2	1,011.0
2003	1,000.5	1,005.2	1,009.6	1,014.9	1,019.9	1,025.5	1,025.0	1,032.0	1,028.8	1,033.0	1,035.8	1,044.0	1,022.8
2004	1,021.0	1,025.1	1,032.1	1,037.5	1,043.0	1,049.6	1,053.1	1,056.2	1,052.4	1,054.4	1,059.6	1,068.3	1,046.0
2005	1,041.1	1,047.5	1,053.7	1,062.8	1,066.8	1,071.8	1,071.4	1,077.1	1,075.8	1,071.0	1,078.3	1,086.4	1,067.0
2006	1,061.6	1,068.4	1,074.2	1,075.1	1,083.5	1,091.1	1,087.0	1,093.6	1,091.8	1,086.7	1,094.0	1,096.4	1,083.6
2007	1,067.3	1,073.6	1,080.3	1,077.4	1,085.5	1,092.7	1,093.3	1,097.8	1,089.9	1,089.3	1,092.0	1,093.7	1,086.1
Goods-Producing													
2000	186.6	187.4	187.8	188.8	190.2	192.8	191.5	192.4	192.3	192.6	193.2	194.7	190.9
2001	193.1	194.0	195.2	195.1	196.2	196.4	196.1	196.6	194.3	194.0	193.0	191.6	194.6
2002	188.2	188.5	189.5	189.5	191.1	191.8	189.3	189.9	188.9	188.0	187.7	186.9	189.1
2003	182.1	180.5	182.9	183.0	185.0	186.9	188.0	189.6	188.5	188.0	186.9	188.3	185.8
2004	185.9	187.0	189.0	190.1	191.6	193.2	195.1	195.8	195.7	195.6	195.0	195.0	192.4
2005	189.0	191.7	193.6	195.0	196.8	197.9	198.8	198.9	198.0	196.2	195.8	196.6	195.7
2006	194.2	196.1	197.4	196.6	198.8	200.3	198.4	198.8	198.1	196.0	195.6	194.6	197.1
2007	189.8	190.4	191.8	189.7	191.0	192.3	191.8	191.1	188.8	187.6	186.6	185.1	189.7
Natural Resources and Mining													
2000	0.3	0.3	0.3	0.3	0.3	0.3	0.3	0.3	0.3	0.3	0.3	0.3	0.3
2001	0.3	0.3	0.3	0.3	0.3	0.3	0.3	0.3	0.3	0.3	0.3	0.3	0.2
2002	0.3	0.3	0.3	0.3	0.3	0.3	0.3	0.3	0.3	0.3	0.3	0.3	0.3
2003	0.3	0.3	0.3	0.3	0.3	0.3	0.3	0.4	0.4	0.4	0.4	0.4	0.3
2004	0.4	0.4	0.4	0.4	0.4	0.4	0.4	0.4	0.4	0.4	0.4	0.4	0.4
2005	0.4	0.4	0.4	0.4	0.4	0.4	0.4	0.4	0.4	0.4	0.4	0.4	0.4
2006	0.5	0.4	0.4	0.4	0.5	0.5	0.5	0.5	0.5	0.5	0.5	0.5	0.5
2007	0.4	0.4	0.4	0.4	0.4	0.4	0.4	0.4	0.4	0.4	0.4	0.4	0.4
Construction													
2000	66.4	67.1	67.2	67.3	68.3	70.1	70.8	71.9	72.2	71.6	71.9	73.0	69.8
2001	72.3	72.5	73.1	73.9	75.5	75.9	76.2	77.4	76.4	77.0	76.4	75.8	75.2
2002	73.6	73.3	74.0	75.3	76.9	77.7	77.0	78.2	77.6	77.9	77.8	78.0	76.4
2003	75.9	74.5	76.2	76.5	78.9	80.7	82.8	84.3	83.5	83.4	82.3	83.2	80.2
2004	82.5	83.4	84.8	85.8	86.8	88.0	89.5	90.4	90.9	90.7	90.0	89.8	87.7
2005	84.1	86.6	88.5	89.9	91.5	92.7	93.4	93.7	93.5	91.9	91.6	92.4	90.8
2006	90.5	91.8	92.5	92.1	94.1	95.1	93.4	94.2	93.7	92.2	91.6	90.7	92.7
2007	86.8	87.6	88.7	87.9	89.0	89.9	88.8	88.6	86.8	85.4	84.1	82.4	87.2
Manufacturing													
2000	119.9	120.0	120.3	121.2	121.6	122.4	120.4	120.2	119.8	120.7	121.0	121.4	120.7
2001	120.5	121.2	121.8	120.9	120.4	120.2	119.6	118.9	117.6	116.7	116.3	115.5	119.1
2002	114.3	114.9	115.2	113.9	113.9	113.8	112.0	111.4	111.0	109.8	109.6	108.6	112.4
2003	105.9	105.7	106.4	106.2	105.8	105.9	104.9	104.9	104.6	104.2	104.2	104.7	105.3
2004	103.0	103.2	103.8	103.9	104.4	104.8	105.2	105.0	104.4	104.5	104.6	104.8	104.3
2005	104.5	104.7	104.7	104.7	104.9	104.8	105.0	104.8	104.1	103.9	103.8	103.8	104.5
2006	103.2	103.9	104.5	104.1	104.2	104.7	104.5	104.1	103.9	103.3	103.5	103.4	103.9
2007	102.6	102.4	102.7	101.4	101.6	102.0	102.6	102.1	101.6	101.8	102.1	102.3	102.1
Service-Providing													
2000	977.4	986.3	996.4	995.9	1,006.9	1,010.2	994.1	996.0	1,006.5	1,013.7	1,021.9	1,030.2	1,003.0
2001	1,003.8	1,011.6	1,018.8	1,022.6	1,029.4	1,033.2	1,015.0	1,016.6	1,022.3	1,031.4	1,038.0	1,042.9	1,023.8
2002	1,018.7	1,029.1	1,034.9	1,041.3	1,046.4	1,052.4	1,031.5	1,035.7	1,036.7	1,049.5	1,057.8	1,064.8	1,041.6
2003	1,039.3	1,046.2	1,048.9	1,053.6	1,055.9	1,059.6	1,046.0	1,050.7	1,052.0	1,061.9	1,065.6	1,072.2	1,054.3
2004	1,048.2	1,053.9	1,059.8	1,066.0	1,068.8	1,074.2	1,063.9	1,064.9	1,067.7	1,075.7	1,081.8	1,090.1	1,067.9
2005	1,067.1	1,072.6	1,077.7	1,085.8	1,088.7	1,093.0	1,080.5	1,083.5	1,089.3	1,090.8	1,100.4	1,107.3	1,086.4
2006	1,083.6	1,091.1	1,096.5	1,098.4	1,104.7	1,112.0	1,099.2	1,103.0	1,108.2	1,110.9	1,121.3	1,124.9	1,104.5
2007	1,098.9	1,106.7	1,113.3	1,112.8	1,119.7	1,126.4	1,115.6	1,119.0	1,119.5	1,125.5	1,130.3	1,134.7	1,118.5
Trade, Transportation, and Utilities													
2000	198.5	198.9	199.0	199.3	201.4	202.9	202.2	202.2	202.6	204.9	210.8	215.6	203.2
2001	207.6	206.1	206.0	206.0	207.1	208.4	207.9	207.9	207.1	209.3	212.6	215.7	208.5
2002	206.0	204.8	205.7	206.6	207.6	209.2	207.1	207.5	207.3	209.7	212.6	217.6	208.3
2003	205.7	204.7	205.0	205.3	206.5	207.2	208.2	209.4	209.9	215.6	217.1	221.7	209.7
2004	211.5	210.8	210.6	211.9	213.4	214.6	213.8	214.3	213.9	217.9	223.5	227.2	215.3
2005	217.6	216.1	215.6	215.4	216.5	216.7	217.7	218.8	220.0	220.3	226.2	231.3	219.4
2006	220.7	219.3	218.9	218.3	219.5	220.0	220.1	221.3	221.4	222.4	229.4	232.8	222.0
2007	222.3	220.4	219.9	218.8	220.3	220.8	221.9	223.5	222.6	224.0	229.0	232.0	223.0
Wholesale Trade													
2000	38.5	38.9	38.7	39.1	39.5	39.9	39.2	39.1	39.1	39.2	39.4	39.8	39.2
2001	40.5	41.0	41.1	41.2	42.3	42.8	41.3	41.4	41.2	41.5	41.5	41.7	41.5
2002	40.4	40.8	40.9	41.4	41.6	41.8	41.4	41.6	41.4	41.5	41.6	41.6	41.3
2003	40.9	41.2	41.4	41.5	41.8	41.9	41.6	41.7	41.6	41.6	41.9	41.9	41.6
2004	41.2	41.7	41.4	42.1	42.2	42.1	41.8	41.9	41.4	42.2	42.4	42.6	41.9
2005	42.3	42.8	42.7	43.3	43.6	43.7	43.8	43.9	44.2	44.2	44.5	44.5	43.6
2006	44.3	44.9	44.8	45.0	45.4	45.3	45.1	45.2	45.1	45.0	45.2	45.3	45.1
2007	44.7	45.2	45.3	45.1	45.5	45.4	45.6	45.5	45.5	45.8	46.0	46.1	45.5

Employment by Industry: San Diego-Carlsbad-San Marcos, CA, 2000–2007—*Continued*

(Numbers in thousands, not seasonally adjusted.)

Industry and year	January	February	March	April	May	June	July	August	September	October	November	December	Annual Average
Retail Trade													
2000	131.5	131.4	131.2	130.2	131.4	132.2	132.0	132.7	133.5	136.0	141.4	145.5	134.1
2001	136.9	134.8	134.2	133.7	133.9	134.6	134.8	135.4	135.5	136.2	140.3	143.6	136.2
2002	136.6	134.7	135.4	135.5	136.3	137.5	136.2	137.1	138.1	138.7	143.6	148.8	138.2
2003	138.6	137.3	137.0	136.9	137.6	138.0	139.0	139.9	140.4	145.8	147.2	151.7	140.8
2004	142.5	141.1	141.1	141.7	142.9	144.0	143.6	144.1	144.1	146.5	152.0	155.6	144.9
2005	146.8	144.8	144.4	143.9	144.5	144.8	145.5	146.6	147.4	148.1	153.6	158.1	147.4
2006	148.2	146.2	145.8	145.0	145.7	146.0	146.2	147.3	147.3	148.6	155.1	157.7	148.3
2007	149.5	146.9	146.6	145.9	146.7	146.8	147.3	148.8	148.0	148.9	153.3	155.9	148.7
Transportation and Utilities													
2000	28.5	28.6	29.1	30.0	30.5	30.8	31.0	30.4	30.0	29.7	30.0	30.3	29.9
2001	30.2	30.3	30.7	31.1	30.9	31.0	31.8	31.1	30.4	31.6	30.8	30.4	30.9
2002	29.0	29.3	29.4	29.7	29.7	29.9	29.5	28.8	27.8	27.6	27.4	27.2	28.8
2003	26.2	26.2	26.6	26.9	27.1	27.3	27.6	27.8	27.9	28.2	28.0	28.1	27.3
2004	27.8	28.0	28.1	28.1	28.3	28.5	28.4	28.3	28.4	29.2	29.1	29.0	28.4
2005	28.5	28.5	28.5	28.2	28.4	28.2	28.4	28.3	28.4	28.0	28.1	28.7	28.4
2006	28.2	28.2	28.3	28.3	28.4	28.7	28.8	28.8	29.0	28.8	29.1	29.8	28.7
2007	28.1	28.3	28.0	27.8	28.1	28.6	29.0	29.2	29.1	29.3	29.7	30.0	28.8
Information													
2000	37.2	37.9	38.9	39.5	40.4	41.1	39.7	39.7	39.8	38.9	39.1	39.1	39.3
2001	39.1	39.1	39.3	39.2	39.1	39.3	38.7	38.7	38.1	38.0	38.3	38.3	38.8
2002	38.0	38.0	38.2	38.1	38.0	37.8	37.0	36.7	36.3	38.3	38.3	38.0	37.7
2003	37.6	37.9	37.3	36.9	36.8	36.8	37.0	36.8	36.7	36.6	36.6	36.3	36.9
2004	36.3	36.3	36.2	35.9	36.1	36.5	36.7	36.7	36.5	37.0	37.1	37.4	36.6
2005	37.3	37.5	37.3	37.4	37.5	37.5	37.6	37.4	37.2	37.2	37.4	37.5	37.4
2006	37.2	37.1	36.9	36.7	36.8	37.2	37.7	37.7	37.2	37.6	37.6	37.9	37.3
2007	37.5	37.7	37.6	37.6	37.6	37.6	38.1	38.3	38.1	38.4	38.8	39.1	38.0
Financial Activities													
2000	70.2	70.7	71.0	71.1	71.3	71.7	71.4	71.5	71.3	71.7	72.0	72.2	71.3
2001	70.1	70.9	71.3	71.4	71.7	72.3	72.5	73.0	72.5	72.5	72.9	73.5	72.1
2002	72.2	73.1	73.5	74.0	74.6	75.1	75.0	75.7	75.7	76.3	77.3	77.9	75.0
2003	77.5	78.2	78.6	79.5	80.3	80.7	80.7	81.0	80.7	80.5	80.6	80.6	79.9
2004	80.6	80.9	81.4	81.7	81.8	81.8	82.4	82.4	82.2	82.6	82.5	83.0	81.9
2005	81.7	82.1	82.3	82.8	82.9	83.2	83.6	83.8	83.5	84.1	84.2	84.4	83.2
2006	83.9	84.4	84.4	84.2	84.7	84.5	83.5	83.6	83.2	82.8	82.6	82.6	83.7
2007	80.9	81.9	81.9	81.2	81.6	81.6	80.6	80.8	79.6	78.7	78.2	77.9	80.4
Professional and Business Services													
2000	187.3	189.4	192.8	191.7	192.3	194.6	196.1	199.0	200.5	200.2	200.6	202.2	195.6
2001	196.0	198.4	199.4	198.1	198.2	198.7	196.3	197.7	198.0	198.8	200.5	200.7	198.4
2002	197.7	200.7	201.9	200.8	200.9	202.1	200.7	202.5	202.0	203.0	204.0	204.9	201.8
2003	199.5	201.8	201.8	201.5	200.1	200.7	199.7	200.8	200.1	201.7	203.0	203.7	201.2
2004	200.6	201.9	203.5	203.5	202.7	204.0	205.9	205.5	205.5	206.0	206.6	208.8	204.5
2005	205.9	207.8	208.8	211.6	210.6	212.1	210.2	211.1	211.5	211.3	211.8	212.4	210.4
2006	209.0	211.6	212.7	212.8	213.5	215.3	214.3	215.8	216.1	214.2	214.3	213.9	213.6
2007	212.0	214.3	215.2	215.4	215.3	217.3	217.5	218.8	217.5	218.6	217.7	217.9	216.5
Education and Health Services													
2000	113.8	115.7	116.1	115.1	115.7	115.2	114.4	114.3	115.2	116.4	116.4	116.9	115.4
2001	111.4	112.8	114.4	115.0	116.2	116.1	115.6	115.7	117.4	118.8	119.1	119.4	116.0
2002	117.8	120.2	120.3	120.6	121.0	120.1	117.4	117.2	118.5	120.6	121.1	121.2	119.7
2003	119.8	120.5	121.2	123.0	123.2	122.7	119.9	120.5	121.6	122.2	123.1	124.0	121.8
2004	121.4	121.4	123.0	123.1	122.9	122.3	119.1	119.4	120.1	122.0	122.3	123.0	121.7
2005	121.1	121.5	122.5	123.9	123.6	122.8	120.1	120.3	122.5	122.8	124.5	124.6	122.5
2006	122.7	123.5	124.9	125.1	125.3	125.0	123.3	123.6	125.7	126.7	127.7	127.6	125.1
2007	125.4	126.9	128.7	128.6	129.4	128.3	127.0	128.0	129.7	131.2	131.4	131.5	128.8
Leisure and Hospitality													
2000	122.1	123.8	125.8	127.7	129.9	132.1	132.3	134.5	133.2	130.6	129.4	129.6	129.3
2001	126.8	128.4	129.7	131.7	132.8	134.1	135.6	136.5	133.2	130.6	128.7	129.5	131.5
2002	123.8	125.6	127.1	132.0	134.9	137.3	137.5	140.3	138.3	136.3	135.8	136.6	133.8
2003	132.9	135.9	136.8	138.7	140.5	142.2	144.4	146.7	144.0	142.0	142.1	142.6	140.7
2004	138.3	140.0	141.3	144.3	147.0	149.0	151.1	153.2	149.5	145.2	144.4	145.3	145.7
2005	141.0	142.5	144.9	147.7	149.7	152.2	154.2	157.5	154.4	150.5	149.7	150.7	149.6
2006	147.0	148.7	151.3	153.0	155.9	159.4	161.7	164.8	161.3	158.3	158.0	158.1	156.5
2007	152.1	154.2	157.0	158.3	161.7	165.4	167.1	168.1	164.4	161.5	160.8	160.7	160.9
Other Services													
2000	41.2	41.7	42.2	42.3	42.4	43.1	42.8	42.4	42.5	42.1	42.1	42.7	42.3
2001	42.8	43.3	44.0	44.3	45.0	46.3	46.0	45.8	46.3	44.9	44.8	45.1	44.9
2002	43.3	43.9	44.5	46.1	46.6	47.6	46.1	45.4	45.7	45.8	45.9	46.1	45.6
2003	45.4	45.7	46.0	47.0	47.5	48.3	47.1	47.2	47.3	46.4	46.4	46.8	46.8
2004	46.4	46.8	47.1	47.0	47.5	48.2	49.0	48.9	49.0	48.1	48.2	48.6	47.9
2005	47.5	48.3	48.7	49.0	49.2	49.4	49.2	49.3	48.7	48.6	48.7	48.9	48.8
2006	46.9	47.7	47.7	48.4	49.0	49.4	48.0	48.0	48.8	48.7	48.8	48.9	48.4
2007	47.3	47.8	48.2	47.8	48.6	49.4	49.3	49.2	49.2	49.3	49.5	49.5	48.8
Government													
2000	207.1	208.2	210.6	209.2	213.5	209.5	195.2	192.4	201.4	208.9	211.5	211.9	206.6
2001	210.0	212.6	214.7	216.9	219.3	218.0	202.4	201.3	209.7	218.5	221.1	220.7	213.8
2002	219.9	222.8	223.7	223.1	222.8	223.2	210.7	210.4	212.9	221.4	222.8	222.5	219.7
2003	220.9	221.5	222.2	221.7	221.0	221.0	209.0	208.3	211.7	216.9	216.7	216.5	217.2
2004	213.1	215.8	216.7	218.6	217.4	217.8	205.9	204.5	211.0	216.9	217.2	216.8	214.3
2005	215.0	216.8	217.6	218.0	218.7	219.1	207.9	205.3	211.5	216.0	217.9	217.5	215.1
2006	216.2	218.8	219.7	219.9	220.0	221.2	210.6	208.2	214.5	220.2	222.9	223.1	217.9
2007	221.4	223.5	224.8	225.1	225.2	226.0	214.1	212.3	218.4	223.8	224.9	226.1	222.1

Employment by Industry: St. Louis, MO-IL, 2000–2007

(Numbers in thousands, not seasonally adjusted.)

Industry and year	January	February	March	April	May	June	July	August	September	October	November	December	Annual Average
Total Nonfarm													
2000	1,311.1	1,310.8	1,324.1	1,340.8	1,349.3	1,362.1	1,331.6	1,332.0	1,348.6	1,350.4	1,351.6	1,347.4	1,338.3
2001	1,310.0	1,320.6	1,335.3	1,347.2	1,355.0	1,364.0	1,333.8	1,333.2	1,341.8	1,339.3	1,345.0	1,346.5	1,339.3
2002	1,309.0	1,311.8	1,320.8	1,333.2	1,341.0	1,351.0	1,324.7	1,329.8	1,340.4	1,340.3	1,342.0	1,345.1	1,332.4
2003	1,307.3	1,306.6	1,315.2	1,324.2	1,331.0	1,335.7	1,312.9	1,315.8	1,323.8	1,328.8	1,325.6	1,327.4	1,321.2
2004	1,293.9	1,292.4	1,307.9	1,321.5	1,328.8	1,333.6	1,311.4	1,318.1	1,329.6	1,336.1	1,336.9	1,339.0	1,320.8
2005	1,304.4	1,310.2	1,322.2	1,341.6	1,345.7	1,350.0	1,326.8	1,337.7	1,347.7	1,346.1	1,348.7	1,351.1	1,336.0
2006	1,319.5	1,324.3	1,335.7	1,351.4	1,358.4	1,366.0	1,343.0	1,345.7	1,360.6	1,362.3	1,362.2	1,367.3	1,349.7
2007	1,327.9	1,331.2	1,348.3	1,360.5	1,373.5	1,373.8	1,346.4	1,354.8	1,365.6	1,365.2	1,367.5	1,369.3	1,357.0
Total Private													
2000	1,146.2	1,143.6	1,155.2	1,171.7	1,179.4	1,192.8	1,185.8	1,184.3	1,179.8	1,181.6	1,181.2	1,176.5	1,173.2
2001	1,142.6	1,150.5	1,164.5	1,176.1	1,182.9	1,191.7	1,185.1	1,182.9	1,172.6	1,168.3	1,172.5	1,173.4	1,171.9
2002	1,138.8	1,140.3	1,148.8	1,161.2	1,167.2	1,180.7	1,176.7	1,178.6	1,171.4	1,168.5	1,169.0	1,172.3	1,164.5
2003	1,138.3	1,136.0	1,144.1	1,152.1	1,157.7	1,165.3	1,163.6	1,164.7	1,156.2	1,159.0	1,154.9	1,157.0	1,154.1
2004	1,125.9	1,123.0	1,138.0	1,151.0	1,157.1	1,166.3	1,162.8	1,166.1	1,161.4	1,166.2	1,166.0	1,168.1	1,154.3
2005	1,137.2	1,139.9	1,152.0	1,169.6	1,172.8	1,181.1	1,176.0	1,181.5	1,178.2	1,175.6	1,176.7	1,179.6	1,168.4
2006	1,151.6	1,153.5	1,164.6	1,179.1	1,185.0	1,198.5	1,192.0	1,190.9	1,190.1	1,190.0	1,188.8	1,193.8	1,181.5
2007	1,158.3	1,158.5	1,175.5	1,187.4	1,199.1	1,205.5	1,198.3	1,200.9	1,194.9	1,192.3	1,193.6	1,195.0	1,188.3
Goods-Producing													
2000	245.9	245.8	248.1	250.8	252.9	255.8	252.6	250.2	252.1	252.7	251.6	246.4	250.4
2001	237.4	243.1	246.6	248.8	249.7	251.0	250.8	249.1	247.3	241.2	243.7	241.2	245.8
2002	231.9	232.5	234.5	235.6	236.0	239.6	240.4	239.4	238.1	235.7	234.7	234.3	236.1
2003	224.4	222.4	225.3	226.6	228.4	231.2	229.4	231.7	228.6	228.0	226.4	225.0	227.3
2004	218.5	216.8	221.9	224.1	225.6	228.7	223.5	229.3	228.4	226.5	225.3	224.4	224.4
2005	216.6	217.0	220.4	223.1	224.7	226.7	221.7	226.9	226.3	225.6	224.6	223.0	223.1
2006	217.2	217.3	219.8	221.5	222.1	226.4	225.5	222.9	224.4	222.5	221.2	219.8	221.7
2007	210.9	210.6	216.1	217.5	220.6	221.8	218.9	220.4	219.6	218.7	218.0	215.8	217.4
Natural Resources, Mining, and Construction													
2000	71.3	71.1	73.8	76.3	78.0	80.1	79.9	80.5	80.5	79.8	78.1	75.7	77.1
2001	71.5	72.3	75.7	78.6	80.3	83.9	83.5	83.4	82.1	81.2	80.6	78.4	79.3
2002	73.8	73.5	75.3	77.1	78.0	81.0	82.8	82.3	81.2	80.1	78.8	77.9	78.5
2003	72.8	71.1	73.5	76.4	78.2	80.6	82.9	82.9	81.8	81.7	80.3	78.8	78.4
2004	74.0	72.2	77.0	79.8	81.1	83.1	84.8	84.3	83.6	82.1	81.1	80.0	80.3
2005	74.3	74.8	78.1	80.5	82.2	83.7	85.2	85.2	84.6	83.8	82.8	81.1	81.4
2006	78.2	78.0	79.8	82.4	83.0	86.0	86.1	86.0	85.1	83.8	82.5	80.8	82.6
2007	77.4	74.4	79.9	81.4	84.2	87.0	86.6	86.5	84.6	83.9	82.9	80.6	82.5
Manufacturing													
2000	174.6	174.7	174.3	174.5	174.9	175.7	172.7	169.7	171.6	172.9	173.5	170.7	173.3
2001	165.9	170.8	170.9	170.2	169.4	167.1	167.3	165.7	165.2	160.0	163.1	162.8	166.5
2002	158.1	159.0	159.2	158.5	158.0	158.6	157.6	157.1	156.9	155.6	155.9	156.4	157.6
2003	151.6	151.3	151.8	150.2	150.2	150.6	146.5	148.8	146.8	146.3	146.1	146.2	148.9
2004	144.5	144.6	144.9	144.3	144.5	145.6	138.7	145.0	144.8	144.4	144.2	144.4	144.2
2005	142.3	142.2	142.3	142.6	142.5	143.0	136.5	141.7	141.7	141.8	141.8	141.9	141.7
2006	139.0	139.3	140.0	139.1	139.1	140.4	139.4	136.9	139.3	138.7	138.7	139.0	139.1
2007	133.5	136.2	136.2	136.1	136.4	134.8	132.3	133.9	135.0	134.8	135.1	135.2	135.0
Service-Providing													
2000	1,065.2	1,065.0	1,076.0	1,090.0	1,096.4	1,106.3	1,079.0	1,081.8	1,096.5	1,097.7	1,100.0	1,101.0	1,087.9
2001	1,072.6	1,077.5	1,088.7	1,098.4	1,105.3	1,113.0	1,083.0	1,084.1	1,094.5	1,098.1	1,101.3	1,105.3	1,093.5
2002	1,077.1	1,079.3	1,086.3	1,097.6	1,105.0	1,111.4	1,084.3	1,090.4	1,102.3	1,104.6	1,107.3	1,110.8	1,096.4
2003	1,082.9	1,084.2	1,089.9	1,097.6	1,102.6	1,104.5	1,083.5	1,084.1	1,095.2	1,100.8	1,099.2	1,102.4	1,093.9
2004	1,075.4	1,075.6	1,086.0	1,097.4	1,103.2	1,104.9	1,087.9	1,088.8	1,101.2	1,109.6	1,111.6	1,114.6	1,096.4
2005	1,087.8	1,093.2	1,101.8	1,118.5	1,121.0	1,123.3	1,105.1	1,110.8	1,121.4	1,120.5	1,124.1	1,128.1	1,113.0
2006	1,102.3	1,107.0	1,115.9	1,129.9	1,136.3	1,139.6	1,117.5	1,122.8	1,136.2	1,139.8	1,141.0	1,147.5	1,128.0
2007	1,117.0	1,120.6	1,132.2	1,143.0	1,152.9	1,152.0	1,127.5	1,134.4	1,146.0	1,146.5	1,149.5	1,153.5	1,139.6
Trade, Transportation, and Utilities													
2000	259.0	255.0	256.8	257.9	259.1	259.4	258.7	258.1	259.3	261.2	265.4	269.3	259.9
2001	258.8	255.1	256.1	256.6	256.8	257.6	254.5	253.5	254.5	256.5	261.5	264.7	257.2
2002	256.1	252.2	253.4	254.4	256.1	258.9	256.9	257.5	258.7	258.5	263.5	267.1	257.8
2003	258.8	254.8	255.3	256.0	256.5	256.0	255.7	255.0	254.3	259.1	261.3	264.0	257.2
2004	251.7	248.2	249.8	250.7	252.7	253.3	253.6	252.1	252.1	254.8	259.9	263.2	253.5
2005	253.5	250.4	251.9	253.5	254.5	254.8	254.9	255.4	254.0	254.8	259.7	262.9	255.0
2006	252.9	249.8	251.2	252.4	254.1	255.5	254.3	255.0	254.9	256.6	261.3	265.1	255.3
2007	256.1	253.0	256.1	257.2	259.4	260.1	258.6	257.8	258.3	259.9	264.0	266.8	258.9
Wholesale Trade													
2000	57.7	57.8	58.1	58.5	58.6	59.2	59.1	59.1	59.0	59.0	59.1	59.3	58.7
2001	58.4	58.5	58.5	58.7	58.7	59.0	58.3	58.2	57.7	57.4	57.2	57.4	58.2
2002	56.6	56.5	56.7	56.7	56.9	57.2	56.8	56.8	56.5	56.2	56.0	55.9	56.6
2003	57.1	56.9	56.9	57.5	57.5	57.7	58.5	58.5	57.8	57.9	57.8	57.9	57.7
2004	58.2	58.2	58.6	58.6	58.7	59.1	60.4	59.7	59.5	58.9	58.9	59.1	59.0
2005	59.8	59.2	59.4	59.8	59.8	60.2	60.6	60.8	60.0	59.7	59.8	60.1	59.9
2006	59.5	59.4	59.7	60.5	60.8	61.5	61.6	61.7	61.5	61.5	61.5	62.0	60.9
2007	61.4	61.6	62.0	61.7	62.2	62.7	63.1	63.0	62.8	62.7	62.7	63.1	62.4
Retail Trade													
2000	147.1	143.3	144.6	144.4	145.3	146.1	145.7	145.2	145.1	146.4	151.0	155.0	146.6
2001	146.6	142.7	143.3	143.5	143.7	145.3	143.0	142.1	142.9	144.6	149.8	153.2	145.1
2002	146.1	142.8	143.5	143.9	145.0	146.8	146.0	146.4	147.1	146.6	152.0	156.3	146.9
2003	147.3	143.8	144.9	145.1	146.0	146.5	146.0	146.5	146.0	150.6	154.1	156.8	147.8
2004	145.4	141.9	142.7	143.7	145.2	146.2	145.8	144.6	144.0	147.1	152.1	154.6	146.1
2005	145.9	143.4	144.2	145.2	146.1	146.6	147.1	147.1	145.4	146.9	151.4	153.5	146.9
2006	145.4	142.4	143.4	144.2	145.2	146.2	145.6	145.6	145.5	144.7	146.7	151.4	153.9	146.2
2007	146.3	143.3	145.5	146.7	148.0	148.8	147.3	146.1	145.9	147.1	151.0	153.4	147.5

Employment by Industry: St. Louis, MO-IL, 2000–2007—*Continued*

(Numbers in thousands, not seasonally adjusted.)

Industry and year	January	February	March	April	May	June	July	August	September	October	November	December	Annual Average
Transportation and Utilities													
2000	54.2	53.9	54.1	55.0	55.2	54.1	53.9	53.8	55.2	55.8	55.3	55.0	54.6
2001	53.8	53.9	54.3	54.4	54.4	53.3	53.2	53.2	53.9	54.5	54.5	54.1	54.0
2002	53.4	52.9	53.2	53.8	54.2	54.9	54.1	54.3	55.1	55.7	55.5	54.9	54.3
2003	54.4	54.1	53.5	53.4	53.0	51.8	51.2	50.0	50.5	50.6	49.4	49.3	51.8
2004	48.1	48.1	48.5	48.4	48.8	48.0	47.4	47.8	48.6	48.8	48.9	49.5	48.4
2005	47.8	47.8	48.3	48.5	48.6	48.0	47.2	47.5	48.6	48.2	48.5	49.3	48.2
2006	48.0	48.0	48.1	47.7	48.1	47.8	47.1	47.8	48.7	48.4	48.4	49.2	48.1
2007	48.4	48.1	48.6	48.8	49.2	48.6	48.2	48.7	49.6	50.1	50.3	50.3	49.1
Information													
2000	31.2	31.2	31.5	31.5	31.7	32.1	32.1	32.1	32.1	32.5	32.9	32.4	31.9
2001	31.7	31.9	32.1	32.0	32.1	32.3	32.2	32.3	31.9	31.5	31.4	31.6	31.9
2002	30.8	30.7	30.5	30.4	30.6	30.5	29.8	29.9	29.4	29.3	29.3	29.4	30.1
2003	30.8	31.1	31.0	29.3	29.0	29.2	29.1	28.9	28.5	28.3	28.3	28.5	29.3
2004	29.5	29.5	29.5	29.5	29.5	29.6	29.5	28.8	28.8	29.4	29.4	29.3	29.4
2005	29.1	29.1	29.1	29.4	29.4	29.7	30.0	29.9	29.9	30.1	30.1	30.3	29.7
2006	30.1	29.9	29.9	29.9	30.0	30.2	30.4	30.3	30.1	30.5	30.5	30.7	30.2
2007	29.8	29.7	29.8	30.1	30.4	30.6	30.4	30.5	30.3	30.5	30.7	30.7	30.3
Financial Activities													
2000	74.4	74.3	74.1	74.8	75.0	76.0	76.0	75.8	75.0	74.8	74.7	75.1	75.0
2001	74.8	74.8	75.4	75.9	76.5	77.3	77.4	77.3	76.4	76.2	76.5	76.9	76.3
2002	76.6	76.7	77.2	77.4	77.9	78.5	78.7	79.0	78.4	78.8	79.2	80.0	78.2
2003	77.8	77.7	78.1	78.5	78.9	79.7	79.7	80.1	79.0	78.9	78.5	78.6	78.8
2004	76.7	76.5	76.7	76.9	77.2	78.0	78.9	78.7	77.9	78.3	78.1	78.5	77.7
2005	76.5	76.9	77.0	78.1	78.0	78.7	79.3	79.2	78.9	78.4	78.2	78.5	78.1
2006	77.5	77.7	77.9	78.6	79.2	79.7	79.6	79.7	79.2	79.0	79.1	79.3	78.9
2007	78.7	78.8	79.0	79.8	80.4	80.9	81.4	81.2	80.7	80.2	80.0	80.4	80.1
Professional and Business Services													
2000	182.4	182.4	185.2	189.7	188.6	192.6	192.2	192.9	189.6	189.4	189.8	189.6	188.7
2001	184.6	185.8	188.9	188.7	188.2	189.6	187.1	188.3	184.7	184.3	183.0	183.2	186.4
2002	177.7	178.6	179.6	180.1	179.2	180.3	179.1	179.8	178.3	178.4	178.7	178.6	179.0
2003	176.1	177.1	178.2	178.4	177.4	178.9	178.9	180.0	178.8	179.9	178.2	178.4	178.4
2004	174.7	175.0	178.7	180.1	179.2	181.5	180.8	181.8	181.0	181.6	181.5	182.0	179.8
2005	180.7	181.8	184.5	188.8	187.4	189.3	188.1	188.9	188.9	188.4	188.6	188.9	187.0
2006	185.7	186.6	189.3	192.4	192.1	195.3	193.5	194.7	194.8	195.7	194.5	196.0	192.6
2007	189.1	189.7	192.3	194.8	195.1	195.8	194.7	196.4	194.9	193.9	194.5	194.9	193.8
Education and Health Services													
2000	176.6	177.6	178.3	179.3	179.2	179.5	179.4	179.3	180.3	180.5	181.3	181.3	179.4
2001	178.8	181.1	181.9	183.8	184.0	184.6	184.7	185.1	185.9	187.0	188.2	188.9	184.5
2002	186.2	188.6	188.9	190.6	191.8	191.9	191.8	192.7	193.9	193.5	194.3	194.8	191.6
2003	190.1	191.5	192.1	191.4	191.0	190.6	191.0	190.9	192.3	192.8	192.9	193.8	191.7
2004	190.1	192.6	193.3	193.8	193.6	193.0	193.3	193.0	194.8	196.7	197.1	196.9	194.0
2005	194.7	197.3	197.6	198.2	197.5	197.0	196.8	196.4	199.2	200.3	201.0	201.6	198.1
2006	198.9	201.8	203.0	203.0	202.7	202.5	201.1	200.9	203.8	206.0	206.6	207.0	203.1
2007	203.3	206.0	207.1	207.6	207.6	207.0	206.4	206.2	208.5	209.7	210.2	210.1	207.5
Leisure and Hospitality													
2000	120.9	120.9	123.6	129.3	133.7	137.4	135.8	136.9	133.1	132.2	127.4	124.3	129.6
2001	119.9	121.0	124.1	130.8	135.3	138.2	138.6	137.3	132.7	132.8	128.6	127.1	130.5
2002	122.0	122.2	125.1	132.5	135.6	140.4	140.0	140.4	135.4	135.2	130.2	129.0	132.3
2003	123.1	123.4	125.6	132.9	137.0	139.7	140.9	139.6	137.0	134.2	131.8	130.9	133.0
2004	128.1	127.3	130.2	137.7	141.3	143.9	144.4	144.1	140.4	140.3	136.4	135.2	137.4
2005	129.1	129.9	133.5	140.6	143.6	146.5	147.3	147.1	144.1	140.6	137.4	137.0	139.7
2006	132.7	133.7	136.4	143.6	147.1	150.4	149.4	149.2	145.0	142.1	138.1	138.2	142.2
2007	133.7	133.8	137.7	142.8	147.7	151.0	149.9	150.3	145.2	142.5	138.9	138.5	142.7
Other Services													
2000	55.8	56.4	57.6	58.4	59.2	60.0	59.0	59.0	58.3	58.3	58.1	58.1	58.2
2001	56.6	57.7	59.4	59.5	60.3	61.1	59.8	60.0	59.2	58.8	59.6	59.8	59.3
2002	57.5	58.8	59.6	60.2	60.0	60.6	60.0	59.9	59.2	59.1	59.1	59.1	59.4
2003	57.2	58.0	58.5	59.0	59.5	60.0	58.9	58.5	57.7	57.8	57.5	57.8	58.4
2004	56.6	57.1	57.9	58.2	58.0	58.3	58.8	58.3	58.0	58.6	58.3	58.6	58.1
2005	57.0	57.5	58.0	57.9	57.9	57.7	58.4	57.9	56.9	57.4	57.1	57.4	57.6
2006	56.6	56.7	57.1	57.7	57.7	58.5	58.2	58.2	57.9	57.6	57.5	57.7	57.6
2007	56.7	56.9	57.4	57.6	57.9	58.3	58.0	58.1	57.4	56.9	57.3	57.8	57.5
Government													
2000	164.9	167.2	168.9	169.1	169.9	169.3	145.8	147.7	168.8	168.8	170.4	170.9	165.1
2001	167.4	170.1	170.8	171.1	172.1	172.3	148.7	150.3	169.2	171.0	172.5	173.1	167.4
2002	170.2	171.5	172.0	172.0	173.8	170.3	148.0	151.2	169.0	171.8	173.0	172.8	168.0
2003	169.0	170.6	171.1	172.1	173.3	170.4	149.3	151.1	167.6	169.8	170.7	170.4	167.1
2004	168.0	169.4	169.9	170.5	171.7	167.3	148.6	152.0	168.2	169.9	170.9	170.9	166.4
2005	167.2	170.3	170.2	172.0	172.9	168.9	150.8	156.2	169.5	170.5	172.0	171.5	167.7
2006	167.9	170.8	171.1	172.3	173.4	167.5	151.0	154.8	170.5	172.3	173.4	173.5	168.2
2007	169.6	172.7	172.8	173.1	174.4	168.3	148.1	153.9	170.7	172.9	173.9	174.3	168.7

Employment by Industry: Baltimore-Towson, MD, 2000–2007

(Numbers in thousands, not seasonally adjusted.)

Industry and year	January	February	March	April	May	June	July	August	September	October	November	December	Annual Average
Total Nonfarm													
2000	1,209.6	1,212.9	1,230.9	1,243.3	1,254.6	1,264.2	1,253.1	1,251.4	1,259.4	1,266.8	1,275.4	1,284.1	1,250.5
2001	1,231.6	1,238.3	1,249.6	1,255.3	1,262.8	1,271.9	1,260.7	1,257.4	1,257.6	1,260.1	1,268.0	1,271.2	1,257.0
2002	1,227.4	1,234.2	1,246.4	1,248.7	1,259.1	1,265.6	1,253.2	1,250.3	1,251.9	1,254.3	1,260.2	1,261.2	1,251.0
2003	1,225.9	1,223.0	1,235.3	1,247.4	1,256.9	1,252.5	1,241.7	1,253.1	1,255.8	1,260.2	1,266.1	1,269.4	1,248.9
2004	1,234.5	1,234.9	1,250.8	1,258.2	1,266.8	1,277.3	1,269.6	1,267.0	1,267.0	1,275.7	1,281.6	1,284.8	1,264.0
2005	1,248.8	1,255.2	1,263.3	1,278.5	1,287.6	1,294.7	1,292.7	1,288.1	1,300.3	1,300.3	1,306.5	1,311.1	1,285.6
2006	1,275.3	1,280.3	1,295.2	1,303.9	1,312.6	1,318.6	1,307.7	1,306.5	1,310.0	1,316.9	1,323.0	1,329.9	1,306.6
2007	1,292.7	1,293.0	1,309.0	1,315.4	1,325.6	1,330.5	1,321.0	1,321.4	1,322.0	1,328.4	1,334.9	1,338.1	1,319.3
Total Private													
2000	993.7	994.7	1,008.8	1,021.8	1,030.2	1,043.8	1,040.8	1,042.9	1,045.2	1,044.7	1,053.4	1,061.7	1,031.8
2001	1,014.3	1,016.9	1,026.7	1,032.3	1,040.9	1,053.1	1,047.2	1,046.8	1,040.2	1,038.1	1,044.2	1,047.8	1,037.4
2002	1,006.9	1,010.0	1,020.1	1,025.4	1,035.3	1,044.6	1,037.9	1,038.4	1,031.9	1,029.7	1,035.1	1,037.6	1,029.4
2003	1,007.5	1,000.8	1,011.2	1,024.0	1,034.3	1,037.1	1,031.9	1,036.4	1,038.4	1,039.5	1,044.7	1,049.3	1,029.6
2004	1,019.7	1,018.6	1,031.6	1,038.2	1,047.7	1,060.3	1,059.9	1,059.7	1,054.2	1,057.7	1,061.4	1,065.4	1,047.9
2005	1,035.2	1,037.1	1,045.2	1,058.6	1,066.8	1,076.6	1,082.6	1,082.3	1,083.2	1,078.3	1,082.5	1,087.7	1,068.0
2006	1,060.1	1,060.2	1,073.1	1,080.5	1,089.0	1,099.2	1,094.4	1,094.0	1,091.3	1,092.1	1,096.3	1,102.8	1,086.1
2007	1,073.6	1,069.1	1,082.6	1,089.2	1,098.8	1,108.2	1,105.4	1,105.9	1,101.7	1,103.2	1,108.6	1,112.2	1,096.5
Goods-Producing													
2000	163.6	162.2	165.9	166.9	168.4	170.8	170.4	171.3	171.6	170.4	170.6	170.4	168.5
2001	162.6	163.9	165.8	166.4	166.3	169.1	168.8	169.0	167.7	165.9	165.1	164.7	166.3
2002	156.2	157.2	158.4	159.6	160.4	162.1	160.3	160.8	159.3	157.8	157.5	156.4	158.8
2003	152.9	150.9	151.9	153.2	154.3	155.9	155.4	156.1	155.4	154.9	154.8	154.6	154.2
2004	150.0	149.0	152.0	154.1	155.4	157.4	158.5	159.1	158.2	158.1	158.1	158.6	155.7
2005	154.2	153.6	154.9	158.0	159.1	160.9	161.1	161.7	161.7	160.3	160.8	160.9	158.9
2006	157.0	156.5	158.6	159.3	159.9	161.9	161.8	161.8	161.8	160.9	159.1	158.1	159.4
2007	154.4	152.5	155.0	155.8	157.2	159.0	159.4	159.4	159.6	158.2	157.3	156.3	156.8
Natural Resources, Mining, and Construction													
2000	68.6	67.3	70.6	72.0	73.4	74.9	75.5	76.3	76.2	75.2	75.2	74.6	73.3
2001	70.4	71.2	73.3	74.2	75.1	76.9	76.5	77.0	76.0	75.0	74.6	74.1	74.5
2002	69.6	70.1	71.7	73.1	74.1	75.5	76.0	76.4	75.5	75.2	75.0	74.1	73.9
2003	71.3	69.6	70.6	72.2	73.9	75.4	76.6	77.5	77.3	77.3	77.4	77.4	74.7
2004	74.0	73.1	76.0	77.9	79.1	80.9	81.8	82.4	81.9	81.9	81.9	82.2	79.4
2005	78.9	78.1	79.4	82.3	83.6	85.3	85.9	86.3	86.3	85.6	86.0	85.9	83.6
2006	83.2	82.9	84.7	85.8	86.7	88.4	88.4	88.6	88.0	87.1	86.6	86.3	86.4
2007	83.2	81.5	83.9	84.9	86.2	87.7	88.1	88.4	87.5	86.9	86.3	85.9	85.9
Manufacturing													
2000	95.0	94.9	95.3	94.9	95.0	95.9	94.9	95.0	95.4	95.2	95.4	95.8	95.2
2001	92.2	92.7	92.5	92.2	91.2	92.2	92.3	92.0	91.7	90.9	90.5	90.6	91.8
2002	86.6	87.1	86.7	86.5	86.3	86.6	84.3	84.4	83.8	82.6	82.5	82.3	85.0
2003	81.6	81.3	81.3	81.0	80.4	80.5	78.8	78.6	78.1	77.6	77.4	77.2	79.5
2004	76.0	75.9	76.0	76.2	76.3	76.5	76.7	76.7	76.3	76.2	76.2	76.4	76.3
2005	75.3	75.5	75.5	75.7	75.5	75.6	75.2	75.4	75.4	74.7	74.8	75.0	75.3
2006	73.8	73.6	73.9	73.5	73.2	73.5	73.4	73.2	72.9	72.0	71.8	71.8	73.1
2007	71.2	71.0	71.1	70.9	71.0	71.3	71.3	71.2	70.7	70.4	70.4	70.4	70.9
Service-Providing													
2000	1,046.0	1,050.7	1,065.0	1,076.4	1,086.2	1,093.4	1,082.7	1,080.1	1,087.8	1,096.4	1,104.8	1,113.7	1,081.9
2001	1,069.0	1,074.4	1,083.8	1,088.9	1,096.5	1,102.8	1,091.9	1,088.2	1,089.9	1,094.2	1,102.9	1,106.5	1,090.8
2002	1,071.2	1,077.0	1,088.0	1,089.1	1,098.7	1,103.5	1,092.9	1,089.5	1,092.6	1,096.5	1,102.7	1,104.8	1,092.2
2003	1,073.0	1,072.1	1,083.4	1,094.2	1,102.6	1,096.6	1,086.3	1,097.0	1,100.4	1,105.3	1,111.3	1,114.8	1,094.8
2004	1,084.5	1,085.9	1,098.8	1,104.1	1,111.4	1,119.9	1,111.1	1,107.9	1,108.8	1,117.6	1,123.5	1,126.2	1,108.3
2005	1,094.6	1,101.6	1,108.4	1,120.5	1,128.5	1,133.8	1,131.6	1,126.4	1,138.6	1,140.0	1,145.7	1,150.2	1,126.7
2006	1,118.3	1,123.8	1,136.6	1,144.6	1,152.7	1,156.7	1,145.9	1,144.7	1,149.1	1,157.8	1,164.6	1,171.8	1,147.2
2007	1,138.3	1,140.5	1,154.0	1,159.6	1,168.4	1,171.5	1,161.6	1,161.8	1,163.8	1,171.1	1,178.2	1,181.8	1,162.6
Trade, Transportation, and Utilities													
2000	238.2	236.4	237.8	239.9	242.0	244.0	243.0	245.1	245.7	248.6	254.6	259.8	244.6
2001	243.6	240.2	241.1	240.7	242.3	243.6	239.9	240.1	240.8	241.7	245.9	249.5	242.5
2002	236.5	233.4	235.4	236.2	238.1	239.9	236.4	236.3	237.3	237.8	241.3	245.6	237.9
2003	234.2	231.2	233.0	234.0	236.5	238.3	236.1	237.8	238.9	241.1	246.2	250.1	238.1
2004	239.5	237.6	239.2	239.0	240.4	242.8	239.8	239.8	239.9	242.0	246.2	249.9	241.3
2005	239.1	237.1	238.1	239.2	240.9	242.7	242.8	242.2	243.4	244.4	248.4	253.1	242.6
2006	243.7	241.4	243.3	243.6	245.2	246.8	244.2	244.0	243.8	246.6	251.9	256.5	245.9
2007	246.3	242.3	244.4	243.5	246.5	247.9	246.5	245.6	245.4	246.4	251.3	255.0	246.8
Wholesale Trade													
2000	52.4	52.7	53.4	53.8	54.1	54.9	55.3	55.7	55.6	55.6	55.9	56.4	54.7
2001	55.4	55.6	56.1	56.4	56.5	56.5	56.2	56.1	56.0	55.7	55.5	55.7	56.0
2002	54.6	54.6	54.6	54.2	54.3	54.4	54.3	54.5	54.4	54.2	54.1	54.3	54.4
2003	53.3	52.9	53.3	53.2	53.4	53.6	53.3	53.3	53.3	53.1	53.1	53.2	53.3
2004	52.6	52.9	53.3	53.5	53.6	53.9	53.9	53.9	53.8	54.1	54.0	54.2	53.6
2005	54.3	54.4	54.5	54.8	55.1	55.6	55.9	55.7	55.8	56.0	56.1	56.5	55.4
2006	56.0	56.3	56.4	56.7	56.7	57.0	56.8	56.8	56.7	56.7	56.6	56.9	56.6
2007	55.9	56.0	56.0	56.3	56.4	56.7	56.6	56.5	56.4	56.6	56.8	57.0	56.4
Retail Trade													
2000	143.6	141.6	142.2	143.2	144.8	145.8	145.1	146.1	145.5	147.9	153.6	157.8	146.4
2001	144.9	141.5	141.9	140.8	142.1	143.3	142.0	142.4	142.0	142.9	147.7	150.9	143.5
2002	141.0	138.2	140.1	139.7	140.8	142.6	141.3	140.9	141.0	141.3	145.3	148.9	141.8
2003	140.1	137.7	138.4	139.8	141.2	142.8	142.2	143.7	143.5	144.8	149.9	153.3	143.1
2004	144.4	142.3	143.4	142.3	143.2	145.1	143.0	143.2	142.2	143.9	148.2	151.3	144.4
2005	140.7	138.7	139.3	140.6	141.6	142.5	143.2	143.2	142.9	143.7	147.7	151.2	142.9
2006	143.6	140.6	142.1	141.9	143.1	144.0	142.8	142.6	141.6	144.4	149.8	153.1	144.1
2007	145.1	141.2	142.8	142.1	144.4	145.0	144.9	144.6	143.7	144.4	149.0	152.3	145.0

Employment by Industry: Baltimore-Towson, MD, 2000–2007—*Continued*

(Numbers in thousands, not seasonally adjusted.)

Industry and year	January	February	March	April	May	June	July	August	September	October	November	December	Annual Average
Transportation and Utilities													
2000	42.2	42.1	42.2	42.9	43.1	43.3	42.6	43.3	44.6	45.1	45.1	45.6	43.5
2001	43.3	43.1	43.1	43.5	43.7	43.8	41.7	41.6	42.8	43.1	42.7	42.9	42.9
2002	40.9	40.6	40.7	42.3	43.0	42.9	40.8	40.9	41.9	42.3	41.9	42.4	41.7
2003	40.8	40.6	41.3	41.0	41.9	41.9	40.6	40.8	42.1	43.2	43.2	43.6	41.8
2004	42.5	42.4	42.5	43.2	43.6	43.8	42.9	42.7	43.9	44.0	44.0	44.4	43.3
2005	44.1	44.0	44.3	43.8	44.2	44.6	43.7	43.3	44.7	44.7	44.6	45.4	44.3
2006	44.1	44.5	44.8	45.0	45.4	45.8	44.6	44.6	45.5	45.5	45.5	46.5	45.2
2007	45.3	45.1	45.6	45.1	45.7	46.2	45.0	44.5	45.3	45.4	45.5	45.7	45.4
Information													
2000	24.5	24.3	24.5	24.1	24.4	25.0	25.0	22.5	25.3	25.3	25.8	26.5	24.8
2001	25.8	26.1	26.0	25.1	25.2	25.2	24.3	24.3	23.7	23.5	23.6	23.4	24.7
2002	22.5	22.5	22.4	22.3	22.3	22.2	21.7	21.8	21.2	20.6	21.1	20.8	21.8
2003	20.8	20.8	20.8	21.1	21.4	21.2	21.2	21.0	20.7	20.7	21.2	21.3	21.0
2004	21.2	20.8	21.1	21.0	21.2	21.5	21.0	21.3	21.0	21.0	21.2	21.0	21.1
2005	20.8	20.9	21.0	21.2	21.3	21.6	22.2	22.6	22.2	22.2	22.2	22.2	21.7
2006	21.6	21.8	21.9	21.9	22.1	22.3	22.1	22.2	22.3	22.2	22.7	22.9	22.2
2007	22.4	22.6	23.1	23.3	23.5	24.1	23.7	24.2	24.1	24.0	24.3	24.6	23.7
Financial Activities													
2000	76.7	77.1	77.6	77.0	77.5	78.7	79.0	79.1	78.7	78.7	79.2	79.9	78.3
2001	77.4	77.9	78.5	78.5	78.9	80.0	80.3	80.4	80.1	80.0	80.8	81.1	79.5
2002	79.0	79.1	79.3	79.5	79.8	80.6	80.6	80.7	80.8	80.5	81.0	81.3	80.2
2003	81.0	81.0	81.5	81.8	82.3	83.2	83.4	83.7	83.1	82.0	82.3	82.5	82.3
2004	81.4	81.6	82.1	82.1	82.2	82.4	82.2	82.3	81.7	82.0	81.9	82.0	82.0
2005	81.0	81.7	81.7	82.3	82.4	83.0	83.7	84.1	83.7	83.0	83.2	83.6	82.8
2006	82.8	82.9	83.2	82.9	82.7	83.3	83.1	82.8	82.4	82.0	81.8	82.4	82.7
2007	81.6	81.6	81.7	81.5	81.6	81.8	81.6	80.9	80.4	80.0	80.3	80.3	81.1
Professional and Business Services													
2000	161.0	162.1	166.1	173.0	174.0	176.6	175.8	177.3	175.7	176.5	176.1	175.9	172.5
2001	173.5	174.4	175.9	177.6	179.5	179.7	181.9	182.0	179.2	177.5	178.9	178.0	178.2
2002	171.2	171.8	174.0	174.4	176.5	177.5	177.2	178.7	176.1	175.1	175.3	175.0	175.2
2003	168.8	166.8	169.5	173.9	175.2	176.1	174.1	175.9	174.9	177.1	176.5	177.0	173.8
2004	171.4	172.0	174.9	175.8	178.3	180.4	181.8	181.9	180.0	181.8	181.8	181.7	178.5
2005	177.3	178.5	181.2	183.0	184.6	185.7	189.8	190.4	190.5	189.5	188.8	188.3	185.6
2006	182.0	183.5	186.6	188.9	190.1	191.5	191.6	192.0	191.4	191.3	190.8	191.3	189.3
2007	185.5	185.5	188.1	190.6	190.9	192.5	192.1	193.8	193.2	194.8	195.4	194.9	191.4
Education and Health Services													
2000	182.6	184.9	185.7	188.0	187.5	187.2	187.3	187.4	190.4	191.1	192.5	194.1	188.2
2001	185.6	188.2	189.2	190.3	191.0	191.9	189.8	189.1	190.4	193.1	194.9	195.9	190.8
2002	192.1	195.7	196.5	195.3	195.6	195.0	194.1	193.1	194.9	198.0	200.1	200.2	195.9
2003	196.0	197.7	198.8	199.4	199.8	193.0	192.8	193.0	200.1	201.8	202.9	203.5	198.2
2004	201.7	202.2	203.2	203.2	203.8	204.4	205.2	203.8	205.1	206.9	208.1	207.8	204.6
2005	204.6	206.8	207.0	208.4	209.0	208.2	208.6	208.1	211.0	213.5	214.9	215.8	209.7
2006	212.6	214.4	215.8	216.2	216.8	215.7	214.3	214.1	216.8	220.0	221.0	222.1	216.7
2007	218.6	220.6	222.1	222.7	223.1	222.3	221.7	221.2	223.6	225.6	227.2	228.0	223.1
Leisure and Hospitality													
2000	96.7	96.9	99.9	102.0	104.9	109.1	108.2	108.0	105.5	102.5	102.9	103.2	103.3
2001	94.2	94.3	97.2	100.9	104.1	109.0	107.7	107.5	105.1	103.0	101.5	101.4	102.2
2002	97.0	97.2	100.5	103.8	107.8	111.9	111.9	112.1	107.5	105.2	103.9	103.3	105.2
2003	99.7	98.2	100.7	106.1	109.9	113.7	113.7	114.4	111.2	107.9	106.9	106.3	107.4
2004	101.7	101.9	105.1	108.3	111.4	115.8	115.9	116.5	113.5	111.5	109.6	109.6	110.1
2005	104.4	104.3	106.6	111.4	114.2	118.6	118.9	117.9	115.8	110.8	109.5	108.8	111.8
2006	105.9	105.0	108.5	111.7	115.8	120.8	120.5	120.4	117.1	114.6	113.2	112.9	113.9
2007	108.7	108.0	111.5	115.4	119.2	123.1	122.9	123.6	120.1	118.5	116.7	116.3	117.0
Other Services													
2000	49.8	50.2	50.8	50.9	51.5	52.4	52.1	52.2	52.3	51.6	51.7	51.9	51.5
2001	51.9	52.5	53.2	52.8	53.6	54.6	54.5	54.4	53.4	53.5	53.6	53.9	53.5
2002	52.8	53.2	53.9	54.3	54.8	55.4	55.7	54.9	54.7	54.6	54.8	54.9	54.5
2003	53.8	53.9	54.8	54.5	54.9	55.7	55.2	54.5	54.0	54.0	53.9	54.0	54.4
2004	52.8	53.5	54.0	54.7	55.0	55.6	55.5	55.0	54.8	54.4	54.5	54.8	54.6
2005	53.8	54.2	54.7	55.1	55.3	55.9	55.5	55.3	54.9	54.6	54.7	55.0	54.9
2006	54.5	54.7	55.2	56.0	56.4	56.9	56.8	56.7	56.6	56.3	56.5	56.6	56.1
2007	56.1	56.0	56.7	56.4	56.8	57.5	57.5	57.0	56.7	56.6	56.7	56.8	56.7
Government													
2000	215.9	218.2	222.1	221.5	224.4	220.4	212.3	208.5	214.2	222.1	222.0	222.4	218.7
2001	217.3	221.4	222.9	223.0	221.9	218.8	213.5	210.6	217.4	222.0	223.8	223.4	219.7
2002	220.5	224.2	226.3	223.3	223.8	221.0	215.3	211.9	220.0	224.6	225.1	223.6	221.6
2003	218.4	222.2	224.1	223.4	222.6	215.4	209.8	216.7	217.4	220.7	221.4	220.1	219.4
2004	214.8	216.3	219.2	220.0	219.1	217.0	209.7	207.3	212.8	218.0	220.2	219.4	216.2
2005	213.6	218.1	218.1	219.9	220.8	218.1	210.1	205.8	217.1	220.0	224.0	223.4	217.6
2006	215.2	220.1	222.1	223.4	223.6	219.4	213.3	212.5	218.7	224.8	226.7	227.1	220.5
2007	219.1	223.9	226.4	226.2	226.8	222.3	215.6	215.5	220.3	225.2	226.3	225.9	222.8

Employment by Industry: Pittsburgh, PA, 2000–2007

(Numbers in thousands, not seasonally adjusted.)

Industry and year	January	February	March	April	May	June	July	August	September	October	November	December	Annual Average
Total Nonfarm													
2000	1,115.3	1,120.0	1,132.8	1,147.4	1,156.8	1,160.5	1,151.4	1,142.2	1,157.1	1,158.2	1,162.5	1,159.8	1,147.0
2001	1,137.9	1,142.6	1,149.7	1,158.1	1,164.1	1,172.1	1,154.2	1,150.2	1,154.2	1,154.1	1,156.8	1,152.8	1,153.9
2002	1,123.3	1,125.7	1,134.2	1,142.3	1,153.6	1,158.7	1,141.6	1,139.5	1,146.4	1,148.9	1,149.3	1,141.3	1,142.1
2003	1,117.8	1,113.2	1,121.5	1,134.2	1,141.8	1,147.6	1,130.0	1,128.2	1,137.8	1,145.6	1,146.4	1,143.9	1,134.0
2004	1,110.6	1,110.2	1,122.3	1,133.3	1,143.5	1,151.8	1,134.4	1,127.4	1,137.7	1,143.2	1,145.3	1,143.3	1,133.6
2005	1,110.9	1,110.8	1,118.2	1,134.7	1,142.6	1,147.7	1,133.6	1,129.6	1,138.9	1,141.0	1,144.3	1,141.2	1,132.8
2006	1,110.3	1,115.0	1,124.9	1,135.7	1,145.4	1,151.5	1,136.1	1,130.9	1,144.3	1,149.1	1,151.1	1,150.7	1,137.1
2007	1,120.1	1,119.4	1,131.5	1,141.8	1,156.4	1,164.4	1,145.9	1,144.4	1,152.4	1,156.5	1,157.5	1,155.9	1,145.5
Total Private													
2000	988.3	990.7	1,001.2	1,016.1	1,023.2	1,031.8	1,032.0	1,026.8	1,030.8	1,028.6	1,031.6	1,030.1	1,019.3
2001	1,009.4	1,012.4	1,018.8	1,026.9	1,033.3	1,044.3	1,036.4	1,034.7	1,026.5	1,023.1	1,024.5	1,022.1	1,026.0
2002	994.9	994.0	1,002.4	1,010.3	1,021.4	1,028.3	1,021.4	1,022.2	1,018.5	1,016.5	1,015.4	1,008.8	1,012.8
2003	987.8	980.5	987.9	1,001.2	1,009.6	1,016.7	1,011.6	1,012.4	1,009.3	1,012.8	1,012.8	1,011.7	1,004.5
2004	981.4	979.0	990.1	1,000.5	1,011.2	1,020.8	1,016.7	1,013.8	1,010.7	1,012.7	1,013.5	1,012.7	1,005.3
2005	983.1	980.8	987.3	1,003.7	1,012.3	1,018.3	1,017.6	1,017.6	1,013.2	1,011.7	1,013.1	1,011.1	1,005.8
2006	983.4	984.9	994.2	1,005.1	1,015.0	1,022.3	1,018.9	1,017.3	1,017.6	1,017.6	1,019.7	1,020.4	1,020.7	1,010.0
2007	993.4	989.9	1,001.2	1,011.9	1,027.7	1,037.8	1,030.2	1,029.5	1,027.1	1,028.1	1,027.8	1,027.0	1,019.3
Goods-Producing													
2000	183.6	183.0	187.5	191.3	194.1	196.4	198.5	198.0	199.2	195.4	193.8	190.3	192.6
2001	185.0	185.6	186.6	188.9	191.0	192.7	192.5	192.3	189.4	187.7	184.1	180.7	188.0
2002	172.5	173.1	174.9	178.3	181.1	182.6	181.3	182.7	180.8	180.0	176.7	172.2	178.0
2003	166.5	163.5	166.2	169.6	170.8	172.1	171.6	171.2	169.6	168.9	166.5	162.7	168.2
2004	154.4	153.1	156.8	160.8	164.2	166.8	167.0	165.9	164.6	164.0	162.0	159.0	161.6
2005	151.9	150.8	152.6	158.3	160.7	162.0	163.0	164.0	163.5	162.4	161.1	157.3	159.0
2006	152.1	152.5	155.8	159.5	161.5	163.0	164.2	164.9	164.8	163.7	162.7	160.5	160.4
2007	155.7	153.3	157.5	161.2	165.0	167.1	167.1	166.9	166.3	165.1	163.9	161.5	162.6
Natural Resources and Mining													
2005	5.1	5.1	4.7	5.1	5.0	5.0	5.0	5.0	5.0	4.9	5.0	5.0	5.0
2006	4.9	4.9	4.9	4.9	4.9	4.9	4.9	4.9	4.8	4.8	4.8	4.8	4.9
2007	4.8	4.7	4.7	4.7	4.8	4.9	4.9	5.0	4.9	4.9	4.9	4.8	4.8
Construction													
2005	46.0	45.3	47.0	52.3	54.8	55.6	57.0	57.9	57.9	57.3	56.0	52.1	53.3
2006	48.1	48.6	51.4	54.7	56.3	57.2	58.4	59.1	59.6	58.5	57.1	54.7	55.3
2007	50.6	48.7	52.5	55.8	59.3	60.6	60.7	60.8	60.9	60.5	59.1	56.7	57.2
Manufacturing													
2000	128.9	129.0	129.5	128.7	128.9	130.2	131.1	130.6	130.3	129.5	129.5	130.0	129.7
2001	127.9	127.4	126.6	125.8	124.5	124.7	123.7	123.1	121.8	120.6	119.5	119.0	123.7
2002	116.5	115.9	115.5	115.3	115.5	116.0	114.9	115.0	114.5	114.4	113.7	113.5	115.1
2003	112.4	110.2	110.0	110.4	109.7	109.6	108.3	107.3	106.3	105.5	104.7	104.5	108.2
2004	102.8	102.2	102.5	103.2	103.0	103.9	103.4	103.1	102.7	102.4	102.4	102.3	102.8
2005	100.8	100.4	100.9	100.9	100.9	101.4	101.0	101.1	100.6	100.2	100.1	100.2	100.7
2006	99.1	99.0	99.5	99.9	100.3	100.9	100.9	100.9	100.4	100.4	100.8	101.0	100.3
2007	100.3	99.9	100.3	100.7	100.9	101.6	101.5	101.1	100.5	99.7	99.9	100.0	100.5
Service-Providing													
2000	931.7	937.0	945.3	956.1	962.7	964.1	952.9	944.2	957.9	962.8	968.7	969.5	954.4
2001	952.9	957.0	963.1	969.2	973.1	979.4	961.7	957.9	964.8	966.4	972.7	972.1	965.9
2002	950.8	952.6	959.3	964.0	972.5	976.1	960.3	956.8	965.6	968.9	972.6	969.1	964.1
2003	951.3	949.7	955.3	964.6	971.0	975.5	958.4	957.0	968.2	976.7	979.9	981.2	965.7
2004	956.2	957.1	965.5	972.5	979.3	985.0	967.4	961.5	973.1	979.2	983.3	984.3	972.0
2005	959.0	960.0	965.6	976.4	981.9	985.7	970.6	965.6	975.4	978.6	983.2	983.9	973.8
2006	958.2	962.5	969.1	976.2	983.9	988.5	971.9	966.0	979.5	985.4	988.4	990.2	976.7
2007	964.4	966.1	974.0	980.6	991.4	997.3	978.8	977.5	986.1	991.4	993.6	994.4	983.0
Trade, Transportation, and Utilities													
2000	239.1	236.6	237.5	241.6	242.8	244.4	241.7	241.6	242.4	245.0	249.0	252.6	242.9
2001	243.9	240.6	241.4	242.0	243.5	244.7	239.9	239.8	240.3	241.0	245.4	246.3	242.4
2002	236.6	233.5	234.6	235.2	236.9	237.6	233.9	234.0	234.5	236.3	239.9	241.6	236.2
2003	231.2	227.9	228.2	230.0	231.9	232.7	229.6	230.6	231.7	235.0	238.5	241.4	232.3
2004	231.9	229.5	230.7	231.3	232.6	232.8	229.3	229.2	229.3	231.2	234.6	237.3	231.6
2005	226.6	224.0	224.8	225.9	227.6	227.9	225.5	225.9	225.7	227.8	231.9	235.3	227.4
2006	226.3	223.2	224.4	224.5	226.3	226.2	222.7	223.0	224.5	226.9	230.7	233.9	226.1
2007	225.9	221.5	223.3	223.6	226.5	227.1	223.4	223.1	223.8	225.1	228.9	231.4	225.3
Wholesale Trade													
2000	45.8	46.0	46.3	46.9	47.1	47.4	47.0	47.2	46.9	47.3	47.3	47.2	46.9
2001	46.7	46.8	46.9	47.2	47.2	47.4	47.3	47.2	46.6	46.2	46.1	45.9	46.8
2002	45.3	45.1	45.2	45.6	46.0	46.3	45.9	45.7	45.4	45.6	45.7	45.4	45.6
2003	45.2	45.1	45.2	45.6	45.8	45.9	46.0	45.9	45.9	46.3	46.4	46.6	45.8
2004	45.8	45.7	45.9	45.8	46.1	46.6	46.7	46.7	46.2	46.3	46.3	46.4	46.2
2005	46.4	46.6	46.7	47.0	47.4	47.7	47.7	47.8	47.6	47.8	48.0	48.1	47.4
2006	48.0	48.0	48.1	48.3	48.7	49.1	49.1	49.2	48.9	49.2	49.1	49.4	48.8
2007	49.1	48.9	49.2	49.2	49.4	49.8	49.5	49.7	49.2	49.3	49.2	49.4	49.3
Retail Trade													
2000	139.5	137.1	137.2	140.3	141.2	142.4	141.6	141.7	141.0	141.6	145.7	149.0	141.5
2001	141.9	138.6	139.2	139.2	140.2	141.5	139.3	139.4	138.2	138.5	143.2	145.6	140.4
2002	138.1	135.5	136.3	136.7	138.0	139.3	138.4	138.5	137.1	138.0	142.1	144.8	138.6
2003	136.6	133.8	134.3	135.7	137.0	138.2	137.5	137.5	136.9	138.8	142.2	145.1	137.8
2004	137.7	135.6	136.4	136.9	137.8	138.4	137.7	137.4	135.5	136.5	140.3	142.5	137.7
2005	133.9	131.5	132.0	132.8	134.0	134.7	135.0	135.0	132.0	133.8	137.5	140.3	134.4
2006	132.6	129.8	130.6	130.6	131.8	132.4	131.2	131.5	129.8	131.8	135.9	138.3	132.2
2007	131.6	127.7	129.0	129.1	131.4	132.1	131.6	131.1	129.0	130.1	134.2	136.5	131.1

Employment by Industry: Pittsburgh, PA, 2000–2007—*Continued*

(Numbers in thousands, not seasonally adjusted.)

Industry and year	January	February	March	April	May	June	July	August	September	October	November	December	Annual Average
Transportation and Utilities													
2000	53.8	53.5	54.0	54.4	54.5	54.6	53.1	52.7	54.5	56.1	56.0	56.4	54.5
2001	55.3	55.2	55.3	55.6	56.1	55.8	53.3	53.2	55.5	56.3	56.1	54.8	55.2
2002	53.2	52.9	53.1	52.9	52.9	52.0	49.6	49.8	52.0	52.7	52.1	51.4	52.1
2003	49.4	49.0	48.7	48.7	49.1	48.6	46.1	46.5	48.9	49.9	49.9	49.7	48.7
2004	48.4	48.2	48.4	48.6	48.7	47.8	44.9	45.1	47.6	48.4	48.0	48.4	47.7
2005	46.3	45.9	46.1	46.1	46.2	45.5	42.8	43.1	46.1	46.2	46.4	46.9	45.6
2006	45.7	45.4	45.7	45.6	45.8	44.7	42.4	42.3	45.8	45.9	45.7	46.2	45.1
2007	45.2	44.9	45.1	45.3	45.7	45.2	42.3	42.3	45.6	45.7	45.5	45.5	44.9
Information													
2000	25.8	25.9	25.9	25.1	25.4	25.7	26.3	23.6	26.3	26.7	26.9	27.1	25.9
2001	27.4	27.5	27.5	27.1	27.4	27.6	27.4	27.3	27.0	26.8	27.0	27.0	27.3
2002	26.7	26.4	26.4	26.1	26.3	26.1	25.9	25.8	25.4	25.2	25.5	25.5	25.9
2003	25.6	25.4	25.6	25.3	25.5	25.5	25.2	25.3	24.9	24.7	24.9	25.1	25.2
2004	24.8	24.5	24.5	24.2	24.3	24.3	24.1	23.8	23.5	23.3	23.2	23.1	24.0
2005	23.2	23.0	23.0	23.0	23.3	23.5	23.3	23.2	22.9	23.0	23.2	23.3	23.2
2006	22.9	22.9	23.0	23.0	23.0	23.1	23.0	22.9	22.6	22.6	22.4	22.7	22.8
2007	22.0	21.9	22.1	21.9	22.0	22.3	21.9	21.8	21.4	21.4	21.5	21.6	21.8
Financial Activities													
2000	67.0	66.9	66.8	67.4	67.5	68.0	67.8	67.5	66.9	66.8	67.1	67.3	67.3
2001	67.5	67.7	67.9	67.3	67.7	68.4	68.6	68.4	67.5	67.4	67.6	67.8	67.8
2002	67.7	68.0	68.3	68.0	68.6	69.1	69.1	69.1	68.5	68.2	68.3	68.6	68.5
2003	69.0	68.9	69.2	69.8	70.3	70.7	71.2	71.2	70.6	70.2	70.2	70.3	70.1
2004	70.0	69.7	69.9	69.5	69.8	70.2	70.3	70.0	69.1	69.0	68.9	69.1	69.6
2005	68.7	68.6	68.9	69.0	69.3	69.5	70.1	70.0	69.2	69.1	69.2	69.2	69.2
2006	68.1	68.3	68.4	68.7	69.0	69.6	69.0	69.0	68.8	67.9	67.7	67.9	68.4
2007	67.6	67.8	68.0	67.9	68.3	69.0	69.2	69.1	68.4	68.2	68.1	68.3	68.3
Professional and Business Services													
2000	134.8	135.4	136.4	140.3	139.9	142.1	142.3	141.9	140.4	139.1	139.2	138.5	139.2
2001	138.5	138.9	139.8	142.2	141.7	143.5	141.7	142.3	140.7	140.1	140.1	139.2	140.7
2002	134.6	134.0	134.6	136.3	137.2	138.5	138.8	139.0	137.1	136.5	136.6	136.6	136.7
2003	131.9	130.6	131.3	134.1	135.0	135.5	135.7	136.9	135.5	136.3	136.7	136.7	134.6
2004	133.7	133.8	135.3	138.4	139.6	141.8	142.5	143.7	143.1	144.7	145.2	145.7	140.6
2005	141.4	141.3	142.5	145.8	145.8	146.8	147.4	147.7	146.1	145.9	145.9	145.5	145.2
2006	141.5	142.5	144.2	146.4	147.4	149.7	151.1	151.2	150.7	151.4	151.6	150.8	148.2
2007	148.0	148.9	150.3	153.3	154.4	157.6	157.0	158.0	155.9	156.0	155.5	154.9	154.2
Education and Health Services													
2000	194.9	198.3	198.7	199.0	196.2	194.4	194.8	193.7	199.1	202.1	203.0	202.3	198.0
2001	199.2	202.3	203.6	202.9	199.1	200.1	199.5	197.7	202.4	203.3	204.6	204.9	201.6
2002	205.8	208.3	209.8	208.2	206.5	205.6	203.6	202.2	207.2	209.6	209.9	205.9	206.9
2003	211.2	212.9	213.6	212.4	210.1	209.6	207.5	205.2	210.1	214.0	214.7	214.3	211.3
2004	211.7	213.3	214.4	214.7	212.6	212.3	211.4	208.6	213.6	217.0	218.4	218.2	213.9
2005	217.0	218.8	219.3	219.9	217.2	217.1	217.2	215.4	220.1	222.9	224.1	224.6	219.5
2006	221.0	223.6	223.9	223.8	222.0	220.3	219.5	217.9	223.6	226.0	227.3	227.1	223.0
2007	222.6	225.4	226.5	226.4	225.3	224.0	223.2	221.6	226.7	230.0	230.7	230.8	226.1
Leisure and Hospitality													
2000	87.8	88.9	91.8	95.3	101.3	104.0	103.9	104.0	100.0	96.6	95.5	94.9	97.0
2001	90.8	92.1	94.1	98.5	104.5	108.3	107.9	108.5	101.7	99.2	98.0	98.6	100.2
2002	94.2	93.8	96.3	100.5	106.6	109.8	109.6	110.6	107.2	102.8	100.6	100.3	102.7
2003	95.3	94.3	96.4	101.8	107.5	111.5	111.0	112.3	108.3	104.8	102.5	102.3	104.0
2004	96.2	96.8	99.2	102.6	108.7	112.2	111.4	112.5	108.6	104.7	102.5	101.7	104.8
2005	96.3	96.3	98.0	103.7	110.4	113.4	113.4	114.7	110.9	106.2	103.7	102.7	105.8
2006	97.2	97.9	100.2	104.4	110.7	114.6	113.6	113.5	109.1	107.5	104.2	104.1	106.4
2007	98.7	98.4	100.2	104.2	112.4	116.3	113.9	115.0	111.1	109.4	106.1	105.7	107.6
Other Services													
2000	55.3	55.7	56.6	56.1	56.0	56.8	56.7	56.5	56.5	56.9	57.1	57.1	56.4
2001	57.1	57.7	57.9	58.0	58.4	59.0	58.9	58.4	57.5	57.6	57.7	57.6	58.0
2002	56.8	56.9	57.5	57.7	58.2	59.0	59.2	58.8	57.8	57.9	57.9	58.1	58.0
2003	57.1	57.0	57.4	58.2	58.5	59.1	59.8	59.7	58.6	58.9	58.8	58.9	58.5
2004	58.7	58.3	59.3	59.0	59.4	60.4	60.7	60.1	58.9	58.8	58.7	58.6	59.2
2005	58.0	58.0	58.2	58.1	58.0	58.1	57.7	56.7	54.8	54.4	54.0	53.2	56.6
2006	54.3	54.0	54.3	54.8	55.1	55.8	55.8	55.1	54.4	53.9	53.8	53.7	54.6
2007	52.9	52.7	53.3	53.4	53.8	54.4	54.5	54.0	53.5	52.9	53.1	52.8	53.4
Government													
2000	127.0	129.3	131.6	131.3	133.6	128.7	119.4	115.4	126.3	129.6	130.9	129.7	127.7
2001	128.5	130.2	130.9	131.2	130.8	127.8	117.8	115.5	127.7	131.0	132.3	130.7	127.9
2002	128.4	131.7	131.8	132.0	132.2	130.4	120.2	117.3	127.9	132.4	133.9	132.5	129.2
2003	130.0	132.7	133.6	133.0	132.2	130.9	118.4	115.8	128.5	132.8	133.6	132.2	129.4
2004	129.2	131.2	132.2	132.8	132.3	131.0	117.7	113.6	127.0	130.5	131.8	130.6	128.3
2005	127.8	130.0	130.9	131.0	130.3	129.4	116.0	112.0	125.7	129.3	131.2	130.1	127.0
2006	126.9	130.1	130.7	130.6	130.4	129.2	117.2	113.6	126.7	129.4	130.7	130.0	127.1
2007	126.7	129.5	130.3	129.9	128.7	126.6	115.7	114.9	125.3	128.4	129.7	128.9	126.2

Employment by Industry: Tampa-St. Petersburg-Clearwater, FL, 2000–2007

(Numbers in thousands, not seasonally adjusted.)

Industry and year	January	February	March	April	May	June	July	August	September	October	November	December	Annual Average
Total Nonfarm													
2000	1,155.5	1,170.9	1,190.2	1,188.0	1,193.3	1,181.5	1,168.5	1,183.8	1,189.5	1,189.4	1,201.5	1,209.8	1,185.2
2001	1,169.9	1,182.4	1,191.8	1,188.8	1,189.2	1,178.8	1,165.8	1,179.3	1,177.8	1,180.7	1,188.0	1,193.4	1,182.2
2002	1,165.9	1,178.7	1,185.9	1,185.6	1,185.7	1,168.6	1,157.7	1,169.9	1,169.5	1,172.2	1,184.3	1,189.2	1,176.1
2003	1,166.1	1,173.9	1,183.8	1,180.4	1,181.7	1,172.2	1,166.9	1,182.6	1,187.9	1,193.2	1,199.7	1,210.4	1,183.2
2004	1,201.0	1,214.2	1,226.3	1,234.3	1,237.3	1,229.3	1,223.5	1,236.8	1,239.4	1,252.6	1,265.0	1,275.0	1,236.2
2005	1,260.3	1,274.5	1,281.6	1,285.5	1,287.7	1,273.8	1,268.2	1,280.5	1,285.5	1,284.4	1,293.8	1,301.2	1,281.4
2006	1,285.4	1,295.3	1,312.0	1,309.7	1,312.0	1,300.9	1,289.4	1,306.0	1,308.4	1,304.9	1,312.3	1,320.4	1,304.7
2007	1,297.8	1,306.4	1,318.5	1,313.4	1,312.0	1,300.9	1,281.7	1,297.0	1,292.5	1,292.1	1,299.5	1,305.2	1,301.4
Total Private													
2000	1,013.7	1,028.5	1,047.0	1,043.1	1,046.0	1,048.3	1,036.7	1,042.5	1,045.4	1,043.4	1,053.7	1,061.9	1,042.5
2001	1,024.2	1,034.9	1,043.5	1,040.7	1,040.4	1,041.0	1,029.6	1,032.4	1,029.7	1,031.0	1,038.3	1,042.8	1,035.7
2002	1,018.9	1,029.9	1,036.8	1,036.5	1,037.6	1,032.1	1,022.5	1,023.6	1,021.5	1,022.6	1,033.7	1,037.5	1,029.4
2003	1,018.8	1,024.6	1,034.7	1,032.4	1,033.3	1,035.7	1,031.4	1,036.6	1,040.5	1,044.4	1,050.8	1,062.0	1,037.1
2004	1,054.8	1,065.0	1,077.5	1,085.3	1,087.9	1,091.8	1,086.7	1,089.5	1,090.7	1,102.3	1,114.1	1,124.1	1,089.1
2005	1,111.8	1,123.4	1,131.3	1,136.0	1,137.8	1,135.7	1,130.9	1,132.7	1,135.7	1,133.3	1,142.3	1,150.5	1,133.5
2006	1,135.8	1,144.9	1,161.7	1,158.9	1,161.7	1,162.4	1,152.0	1,156.8	1,156.3	1,151.1	1,158.8	1,167.5	1,155.7
2007	1,145.5	1,153.0	1,164.4	1,159.7	1,159.1	1,159.3	1,140.9	1,144.7	1,137.7	1,135.7	1,143.0	1,148.1	1,149.3
Goods-Producing													
2000	147.8	149.5	151.7	150.7	151.6	154.3	152.4	153.0	153.5	151.0	151.6	151.3	151.5
2001	146.1	146.3	146.7	146.0	146.3	146.9	146.3	146.6	145.7	144.9	145.4	145.3	146.0
2002	142.5	142.4	142.5	142.3	142.7	143.6	143.3	144.6	145.1	145.1	145.3	144.9	143.7
2003	141.2	142.1	142.0	141.5	142.2	142.8	141.5	142.4	142.3	142.1	142.0	143.2	142.1
2004	142.9	144.2	146.2	148.6	149.0	150.0	150.4	151.1	151.9	154.2	154.3	155.1	149.8
2005	153.4	154.9	156.0	157.0	158.2	159.4	161.1	161.8	162.7	163.0	164.3	164.8	159.7
2006	163.5	164.7	166.5	166.7	167.7	168.7	166.9	167.7	167.1	165.7	164.7	164.5	166.2
2007	162.2	162.4	163.1	159.4	159.1	159.1	156.2	155.6	154.6	153.8	153.7	153.4	157.7
Natural Resources and Mining													
2000	0.5	0.5	0.5	0.5	0.5	0.5	0.5	0.5	0.5	0.5	0.5	0.5	0.5
2001	0.5	0.5	0.5	0.5	0.5	0.5	0.5	0.5	0.5	0.5	0.5	0.5	0.5
2002	0.5	0.5	0.5	0.5	0.5	0.5	0.5	0.5	0.5	0.5	0.5	0.5	0.5
2003	0.5	0.5	0.5	0.5	0.5	0.5	0.5	0.5	0.5	0.5	0.6	0.6	0.5
2004	0.6	0.6	0.6	0.6	0.6	0.6	0.6	0.6	0.6	0.6	0.6	0.6	0.6
2005	0.6	0.6	0.6	0.6	0.7	0.7	0.7	0.8	0.8	0.8	0.8	0.8	0.7
2006	0.9	0.9	0.9	0.9	0.9	0.8	0.7	0.6	0.6	0.6	0.6	0.7	0.8
2007	0.6	0.6	0.6	0.6	0.6	0.6	0.6	0.6	0.6	0.6	0.6	0.6	0.6
Construction													
2000	60.5	61.5	62.8	62.9	63.5	65.3	64.0	64.4	64.8	63.9	64.5	64.4	63.5
2001	61.1	61.6	62.1	62.4	63.1	63.8	64.2	64.3	64.3	63.8	64.6	64.7	63.3
2002	63.1	63.5	63.5	63.7	64.5	64.8	64.9	66.0	66.6	67.1	67.5	67.3	65.2
2003	65.2	66.2	66.4	66.5	67.5	68.2	67.6	68.5	68.4	68.6	68.6	69.7	67.6
2004	69.3	70.4	71.9	73.3	73.7	74.2	75.0	75.4	76.3	78.4	78.5	79.2	74.6
2005	78.7	80.0	81.0	81.6	82.6	83.4	85.0	85.3	85.8	86.1	87.3	87.8	83.7
2006	86.6	87.7	88.9	89.6	90.3	90.9	90.1	90.6	90.2	89.3	88.5	88.3	89.3
2007	86.9	86.9	87.8	84.6	84.2	84.3	82.0	81.6	80.8	80.5	80.3	79.7	83.3
Manufacturing													
2000	86.8	87.5	88.4	87.3	87.6	88.5	87.9	88.1	88.2	86.6	86.6	86.4	87.5
2001	84.5	84.2	84.1	83.1	82.7	82.6	81.6	81.8	80.9	80.6	80.3	80.1	82.2
2002	78.9	78.4	78.5	78.1	77.7	78.3	77.9	78.1	78.0	77.5	77.3	77.1	78.0
2003	75.5	75.4	75.1	74.5	74.2	74.1	73.4	73.4	73.4	73.0	72.8	72.9	74.0
2004	73.0	73.2	73.7	74.7	74.7	75.2	74.8	75.1	75.0	75.2	75.3	75.3	74.6
2005	74.1	74.3	74.4	74.8	74.9	75.3	75.4	75.7	76.1	76.1	76.2	76.2	75.3
2006	76.0	76.1	76.7	76.2	76.5	77.0	76.1	76.5	76.3	75.8	75.6	75.5	76.2
2007	74.7	74.9	74.7	74.2	74.3	74.2	73.6	73.4	73.2	72.7	72.8	73.1	73.8
Service-Providing													
2000	1,007.7	1,021.4	1,038.5	1,037.3	1,041.7	1,027.2	1,016.1	1,030.8	1,036.0	1,038.4	1,049.9	1,058.5	1,033.6
2001	1,023.8	1,036.1	1,045.1	1,042.8	1,042.9	1,031.9	1,019.5	1,032.7	1,032.1	1,035.8	1,042.6	1,048.1	1,036.1
2002	1,023.4	1,036.3	1,043.4	1,043.3	1,043.0	1,025.0	1,014.4	1,025.3	1,024.4	1,027.1	1,039.0	1,044.3	1,032.4
2003	1,024.9	1,031.8	1,041.8	1,038.9	1,039.5	1,029.4	1,025.4	1,040.2	1,045.6	1,051.1	1,057.7	1,067.2	1,041.1
2004	1,058.1	1,070.0	1,080.1	1,085.7	1,088.3	1,079.3	1,073.1	1,085.7	1,087.5	1,098.4	1,110.7	1,119.9	1,086.4
2005	1,106.9	1,119.6	1,125.6	1,128.5	1,129.5	1,114.4	1,107.1	1,118.7	1,122.8	1,121.4	1,129.5	1,136.4	1,121.7
2006	1,121.9	1,130.6	1,145.5	1,143.0	1,144.3	1,132.2	1,122.5	1,138.3	1,141.3	1,139.2	1,147.6	1,155.9	1,138.5
2007	1,135.6	1,144.0	1,155.4	1,154.0	1,152.9	1,141.8	1,125.5	1,141.4	1,137.9	1,138.3	1,145.8	1,151.8	1,143.7
Trade, Transportation, and Utilities													
2000	235.4	236.4	239.3	236.6	237.9	239.2	236.0	238.0	238.1	238.7	245.0	248.5	239.1
2001	232.4	231.8	232.6	229.6	229.5	229.1	226.7	227.1	227.3	228.6	233.5	236.5	230.4
2002	229.8	228.1	228.2	226.8	227.0	224.7	222.7	224.2	222.6	223.8	226.6	230.3	226.2
2003	219.8	218.5	218.5	218.0	218.9	218.0	217.2	217.5	218.6	221.3	224.1	227.6	219.8
2004	223.1	222.7	223.1	223.1	223.9	223.8	222.5	222.3	222.2	225.5	230.9	234.7	224.8
2005	228.8	228.9	229.9	231.7	232.4	231.8	230.7	230.8	230.7	232.1	236.7	241.2	232.1
2006	234.7	234.1	236.1	233.9	234.3	233.4	231.8	232.1	231.9	232.1	237.0	241.1	234.4
2007	233.4	232.2	233.4	232.3	233.0	232.5	230.5	231.4	230.9	231.5	234.3	238.5	232.8
Wholesale Trade													
2000	54.4	54.6	55.3	55.5	56.0	56.7	55.5	55.7	56.1	56.4	57.0	57.4	55.9
2001	55.7	55.7	55.8	55.3	55.0	54.6	54.0	54.0	53.8	53.9	53.7	54.1	54.6
2002	54.1	54.1	54.1	53.6	53.9	53.4	52.9	52.9	52.7	52.6	52.6	52.7	53.3
2003	51.0	51.1	50.8	51.0	51.0	50.6	50.1	50.0	50.0	49.8	49.8	50.0	50.4
2004	50.4	50.9	50.7	50.6	50.8	51.1	50.7	50.8	50.8	51.0	51.5	51.8	50.9
2005	52.1	52.1	52.6	52.9	53.3	53.1	52.6	52.6	52.6	52.8	52.9	53.6	52.8
2006	53.3	53.5	53.8	53.8	54.2	54.0	53.7	54.0	54.0	54.1	54.6	55.0	54.0
2007	54.4	54.5	54.6	54.2	54.6	54.5	53.9	54.1	53.9	53.8	54.0	54.5	54.3

Employment by Industry: Tampa-St. Petersburg-Clearwater, FL, 2000–2007—*Continued*

(Numbers in thousands, not seasonally adjusted.)

Industry and year	January	February	March	April	May	June	July	August	September	October	November	December	Annual Average
Retail Trade													
2000	145.2	145.7	147.1	144.7	145.2	145.6	143.3	145.0	144.8	146.1	151.2	153.9	146.5
2001	142.5	141.8	142.5	140.2	140.3	140.3	138.9	139.4	140.0	141.5	146.6	148.6	141.9
2002	143.0	141.3	141.8	140.7	140.8	139.1	137.7	139.2	138.4	139.7	142.8	146.2	140.9
2003	138.6	137.3	137.5	136.8	137.5	137.2	136.5	136.8	137.6	140.3	143.1	145.6	138.7
2004	141.3	140.3	140.8	140.8	141.2	140.9	140.2	139.9	140.1	142.9	147.7	150.9	142.3
2005	145.2	145.1	145.5	146.9	147.4	147.3	147.0	147.2	147.2	148.5	152.8	155.7	148.0
2006	150.5	149.7	151.3	149.3	149.3	148.8	147.7	147.8	147.9	148.6	152.9	155.5	149.9
2007	150.0	149.0	149.9	149.4	149.8	149.3	147.9	148.4	148.2	148.9	151.2	153.8	149.7
Transportation and Utilities													
2000	35.8	36.1	36.9	36.4	36.7	36.9	37.2	37.3	37.2	36.2	36.8	37.2	36.7
2001	34.2	34.3	34.3	34.1	34.2	34.2	33.8	33.7	33.5	33.2	33.2	33.8	33.9
2002	32.7	32.7	32.3	32.5	32.3	32.2	32.1	32.1	31.5	31.5	31.2	31.4	32.0
2003	30.2	30.1	30.2	30.2	30.4	30.2	30.6	30.7	31.0	31.2	31.2	32.0	30.6
2004	31.4	31.5	31.6	31.7	31.9	31.8	31.6	31.6	31.3	31.6	31.7	32.0	31.6
2005	31.5	31.7	31.8	31.9	31.7	31.4	31.1	31.0	30.9	30.8	31.0	31.9	31.4
2006	30.9	30.9	31.0	30.8	30.8	30.6	30.4	30.3	30.0	29.4	29.5	30.6	30.4
2007	29.0	28.7	28.9	28.7	28.6	28.7	28.7	28.9	28.8	28.8	29.1	30.2	28.9
Information													
2000	38.1	38.4	39.1	38.4	38.7	39.7	39.5	39.8	40.3	41.0	41.5	41.7	39.7
2001	40.5	40.5	40.5	40.1	39.7	39.3	39.0	38.3	37.5	37.5	37.3	36.6	38.9
2002	36.7	36.3	36.5	36.1	36.0	35.6	35.4	35.3	35.4	35.2	35.7	35.6	35.8
2003	35.1	34.9	35.0	35.3	35.2	34.8	34.7	34.4	34.3	33.7	33.7	33.6	34.5
2004	33.4	33.1	33.7	32.8	32.9	33.0	32.4	32.6	32.6	32.6	32.7	32.8	32.9
2005	32.4	32.4	32.6	32.3	32.4	32.4	32.6	32.8	33.2	33.0	33.1	33.0	32.7
2006	32.9	33.0	32.8	32.6	32.7	32.8	32.6	32.5	32.4	32.3	32.4	32.5	32.6
2007	32.4	32.6	32.7	32.6	32.7	32.8	32.5	32.6	32.4	31.9	31.8	31.2	32.4
Financial Activities													
2000	88.9	89.4	90.3	91.1	91.2	91.1	91.0	91.1	91.3	91.2	91.8	92.1	90.9
2001	90.6	91.4	92.1	92.5	92.4	92.6	91.5	91.7	91.2	91.0	91.1	91.2	91.6
2002	90.6	91.6	91.6	91.2	91.3	91.7	92.0	92.2	91.8	92.1	92.7	93.2	91.8
2003	92.2	92.9	93.0	93.2	93.5	93.7	93.6	93.9	93.3	93.1	92.9	93.4	93.2
2004	93.0	93.5	93.9	95.1	95.2	94.9	94.7	94.8	94.6	95.5	95.9	96.4	94.8
2005	96.0	96.7	96.7	97.9	98.3	99.1	99.4	98.8	99.3	100.1	100.6	102.0	98.7
2006	101.0	101.8	102.4	102.6	102.8	102.7	101.9	101.9	101.5	101.6	101.4	102.1	102.0
2007	101.0	102.0	102.1	101.9	101.8	101.6	101.2	100.4	100.0	99.3	99.7	99.9	100.9
Professional and Business Services													
2000	221.3	226.7	232.9	232.1	233.6	232.3	230.1	233.7	235.1	235.1	235.5	238.9	232.3
2001	230.9	236.9	238.8	239.3	238.1	239.2	235.1	236.8	236.3	235.4	236.1	236.1	236.6
2002	229.2	236.4	237.7	239.5	238.9	235.8	233.2	228.8	227.2	226.4	231.8	229.9	232.9
2003	231.0	234.1	240.0	238.9	237.8	241.2	242.6	245.2	247.8	251.1	253.8	257.9	243.5
2004	257.2	261.3	265.4	270.6	271.2	275.2	275.2	276.4	276.2	280.3	283.7	287.9	273.4
2005	285.5	290.7	292.3	292.7	291.9	290.1	288.8	290.0	291.8	287.6	289.2	289.7	290.0
2006	288.3	291.1	298.1	298.0	298.5	299.3	298.4	300.3	299.2	295.4	296.5	297.7	296.7
2007	292.7	294.1	297.4	298.4	297.3	298.9	293.3	295.1	290.5	288.8	292.3	291.8	294.2
Education and Health Services													
2000	136.3	137.8	138.6	138.5	137.0	136.0	135.3	136.0	137.1	136.7	137.6	137.9	137.1
2001	134.3	135.3	136.4	136.7	136.9	137.4	135.7	137.0	138.1	138.7	139.5	140.7	137.2
2002	136.5	137.6	139.1	139.5	140.3	140.0	138.8	140.1	141.0	142.0	143.4	144.0	140.2
2003	140.8	142.1	143.4	144.2	144.8	144.4	143.8	145.7	146.9	146.4	147.2	147.8	144.8
2004	146.3	147.6	148.4	149.4	150.1	149.6	148.5	149.4	150.0	150.5	151.5	151.9	149.4
2005	150.1	151.0	151.6	152.7	152.3	151.7	150.7	151.6	151.8	152.5	153.0	153.8	151.9
2006	152.2	153.7	154.9	155.2	155.5	154.8	153.4	154.6	156.3	157.4	158.9	160.3	155.6
2007	158.4	160.2	162.1	162.1	162.4	162.1	159.6	161.7	162.6	164.6	165.0	165.3	162.2
Leisure and Hospitality													
2000	102.7	106.6	110.8	111.9	111.8	111.2	108.3	107.1	106.1	105.8	106.7	107.5	108.0
2001	106.5	109.7	112.8	112.7	113.0	111.1	110.6	110.2	108.9	110.1	110.1	110.7	110.5
2002	107.8	111.2	114.6	114.9	114.9	113.6	110.2	111.4	111.4	110.2	110.2	111.3	111.8
2003	110.6	112.0	115.0	114.3	113.9	113.5	111.3	111.3	111.0	110.8	111.1	112.1	112.2
2004	112.1	115.3	118.7	118.1	117.5	116.4	114.7	114.9	114.9	115.1	116.0	116.4	115.8
2005	116.5	119.2	122.4	122.1	122.6	121.5	119.1	119.1	118.6	118.2	118.8	119.6	119.8
2006	118.3	121.0	124.8	124.1	123.7	123.5	120.7	121.7	121.7	120.4	121.6	122.6	122.0
2007	119.5	122.7	126.1	126.2	125.3	124.1	120.9	121.2	120.2	119.7	119.5	120.5	122.2
Other Services													
2000	43.2	43.7	44.3	43.8	44.2	44.5	44.1	43.8	43.9	43.9	44.0	44.0	44.0
2001	42.9	43.0	43.6	43.8	44.5	45.4	44.7	44.7	44.7	44.8	45.3	45.7	44.4
2002	45.8	46.3	46.6	46.2	46.5	47.1	46.9	47.0	47.0	47.8	48.0	48.3	47.0
2003	48.1	48.0	47.8	47.0	47.0	47.3	46.7	46.2	46.3	45.9	46.0	46.4	46.8
2004	46.8	47.3	48.1	47.6	48.1	48.9	48.3	48.0	48.3	48.6	49.1	48.9	48.2
2005	49.1	49.6	49.8	49.6	49.7	49.7	48.5	47.8	47.6	46.8	46.6	46.4	48.4
2006	44.9	45.5	46.1	45.8	46.5	47.2	46.3	46.0	46.2	46.2	46.3	46.7	46.1
2007	45.9	46.8	47.5	46.8	47.5	48.2	46.7	46.7	46.5	46.1	46.7	47.5	46.9
Government													
2000	141.8	142.4	143.2	144.9	147.3	133.2	131.8	141.3	144.1	146.0	147.8	147.9	142.6
2001	145.7	147.5	148.3	148.1	148.8	137.8	136.2	146.9	148.1	149.7	149.7	150.6	146.5
2002	147.0	148.8	149.1	149.1	148.1	136.5	135.2	146.3	148.0	149.6	150.6	151.7	146.7
2003	147.3	149.3	149.1	148.0	148.4	136.5	135.5	146.0	147.4	148.8	148.9	148.4	146.1
2004	146.2	149.2	148.8	149.0	149.4	137.5	136.8	147.3	148.7	150.3	150.9	150.9	147.1
2005	148.5	151.1	150.3	149.5	149.9	138.1	137.3	147.8	149.8	151.1	151.5	150.7	148.0
2006	149.6	150.4	150.3	150.8	150.3	138.5	137.4	149.2	152.1	153.8	153.5	152.9	149.1
2007	152.3	153.4	154.1	153.7	152.9	141.6	140.8	152.3	154.8	156.4	156.5	157.1	152.2

Employment by Industry: Denver-Aurora, CO, 2000–2007

(Numbers in thousands, not seasonally adjusted.)

Industry and year	January	February	March	April	May	June	July	August	September	October	November	December	Annual Average
Total Nonfarm													
2000	1,168.0	1,177.6	1,188.3	1,196.6	1,210.5	1,223.8	1,221.1	1,225.8	1,227.2	1,224.1	1,231.3	1,239.7	1,211.2
2001	1,204.6	1,207.2	1,211.2	1,212.1	1,219.0	1,230.0	1,216.8	1,216.3	1,207.7	1,196.7	1,194.2	1,192.4	1,209.0
2002	1,152.5	1,155.8	1,159.9	1,170.2	1,181.1	1,188.8	1,177.7	1,182.1	1,175.0	1,172.1	1,175.3	1,177.4	1,172.3
2003	1,148.6	1,148.1	1,147.2	1,151.4	1,160.4	1,168.5	1,160.7	1,164.9	1,159.6	1,161.1	1,161.6	1,165.0	1,158.1
2004	1,135.2	1,138.3	1,148.1	1,162.3	1,170.2	1,180.8	1,175.3	1,177.3	1,176.0	1,177.6	1,180.8	1,186.1	1,167.3
2005	1,154.5	1,161.8	1,170.6	1,180.2	1,190.2	1,201.5	1,198.9	1,199.0	1,203.6	1,202.6	1,206.2	1,212.1	1,190.1
2006	1,182.1	1,187.7	1,196.4	1,204.2	1,217.1	1,231.8	1,222.3	1,225.8	1,225.3	1,225.3	1,229.6	1,234.1	1,215.1
2007	1,202.6	1,209.0	1,221.4	1,230.4	1,244.0	1,257.9	1,249.2	1,253.0	1,253.4	1,254.7	1,257.1	1,257.3	1,240.8
Total Private													
2000	1,018.4	1,024.1	1,033.2	1,040.8	1,051.5	1,067.8	1,071.3	1,074.9	1,070.3	1,067.5	1,073.5	1,081.0	1,056.2
2001	1,050.2	1,049.0	1,053.5	1,053.8	1,059.8	1,070.9	1,062.9	1,061.5	1,047.0	1,035.6	1,031.3	1,029.6	1,050.4
2002	993.0	993.1	995.8	1,005.8	1,015.4	1,024.2	1,018.8	1,021.7	1,010.7	1,006.0	1,008.4	1,010.9	1,008.7
2003	986.8	983.1	981.7	986.0	993.0	1,002.6	1,001.7	1,005.0	995.4	996.8	997.0	1,001.3	994.2
2004	976.1	975.7	984.2	997.0	1,004.3	1,016.0	1,017.4	1,019.1	1,011.8	1,012.1	1,014.6	1,020.1	1,004.0
2005	994.1	997.3	1,005.7	1,013.7	1,023.0	1,035.9	1,039.3	1,040.3	1,037.4	1,035.9	1,039.1	1,045.1	1,025.6
2006	1,019.5	1,021.2	1,028.8	1,037.1	1,048.4	1,063.5	1,061.2	1,063.9	1,057.5	1,057.3	1,060.7	1,064.9	1,048.7
2007	1,038.7	1,040.0	1,051.1	1,059.7	1,072.3	1,087.1	1,085.8	1,088.7	1,081.8	1,081.8	1,083.5	1,084.0	1,071.2
Goods-Producing													
2000	173.5	176.0	179.1	179.5	182.0	185.6	186.0	186.6	186.1	185.7	183.9	183.3	182.3
2001	178.6	178.8	180.2	180.0	181.5	183.3	181.9	181.6	179.4	175.9	172.3	169.0	178.5
2002	163.3	164.0	165.9	167.5	169.9	171.4	171.0	170.6	167.7	166.4	163.6	161.1	166.9
2003	157.9	156.7	156.1	156.5	158.4	160.6	160.0	159.5	157.5	157.4	155.7	154.1	157.5
2004	151.0	150.7	153.2	155.6	157.2	160.1	161.1	161.2	160.1	160.8	159.7	158.5	157.4
2005	154.3	155.7	158.1	158.9	160.8	164.6	166.8	167.3	166.8	166.2	165.6	164.3	162.5
2006	161.4	162.6	164.8	165.8	167.9	171.0	170.1	169.8	169.0	167.6	165.8	163.9	166.6
2007	157.3	158.0	161.1	162.5	164.8	167.9	168.4	168.8	167.1	166.6	164.2	161.6	164.0
Natural Resources, Mining, and Construction													
2000	86.4	88.7	91.5	92.9	95.5	98.5	98.9	99.6	99.4	99.1	97.6	96.9	95.4
2001	94.2	94.5	96.3	97.4	99.0	101.3	100.9	101.2	100.1	97.8	95.0	92.3	97.5
2002	88.3	89.2	91.1	93.2	95.5	96.9	96.8	96.6	94.1	92.9	90.8	88.5	92.8
2003	85.4	84.4	84.3	84.9	86.9	89.0	88.8	88.5	86.8	86.8	85.0	83.4	86.1
2004	80.6	80.1	82.3	84.3	85.8	88.1	88.7	88.5	87.9	88.4	87.3	86.2	85.7
2005	82.8	83.9	86.1	87.0	88.8	92.3	94.1	94.7	94.4	93.6	93.2	91.9	90.2
2006	89.7	90.8	92.7	93.7	95.7	98.4	97.4	97.1	96.5	95.3	93.6	92.0	94.4
2007	86.1	87.1	90.1	91.7	93.5	96.1	96.7	96.9	95.5	95.3	93.0	90.4	92.7
Manufacturing													
2000	87.1	87.3	87.6	86.6	86.5	87.1	87.1	87.0	86.7	86.6	86.3	86.4	86.9
2001	84.4	84.3	83.9	82.6	82.5	82.0	81.0	80.4	79.3	78.1	77.3	76.7	81.0
2002	75.0	74.8	74.8	74.3	74.4	74.5	74.2	74.0	73.6	73.5	72.8	72.6	74.0
2003	72.5	72.3	71.8	71.6	71.5	71.6	71.2	71.0	70.7	70.6	70.7	70.7	71.3
2004	70.4	70.6	70.9	71.3	71.4	72.0	72.4	72.7	72.2	72.4	72.4	72.3	71.8
2005	71.5	71.8	72.0	71.9	72.0	72.3	72.7	72.6	72.4	72.6	72.4	72.4	72.2
2006	71.7	71.8	72.1	72.1	72.2	72.6	72.7	72.7	72.5	72.3	72.2	71.9	72.2
2007	71.2	70.9	71.0	70.8	71.3	71.8	71.7	71.9	71.6	71.3	71.2	71.2	71.3
Service-Providing													
2000	994.5	1,001.6	1,009.2	1,017.1	1,028.5	1,038.2	1,035.1	1,039.2	1,041.1	1,038.4	1,047.4	1,056.4	1,028.9
2001	1,026.0	1,028.4	1,031.0	1,032.1	1,037.5	1,046.7	1,034.9	1,034.7	1,028.3	1,020.8	1,021.9	1,023.4	1,030.5
2002	989.2	991.8	994.0	1,002.7	1,011.2	1,017.4	1,006.7	1,011.5	1,007.3	1,005.7	1,011.7	1,016.3	1,005.5
2003	990.7	991.4	991.1	994.9	1,002.0	1,007.9	1,000.7	1,005.4	1,002.1	1,003.7	1,005.9	1,010.9	1,000.6
2004	984.2	987.6	994.9	1,006.7	1,013.0	1,020.7	1,014.2	1,016.1	1,015.9	1,016.8	1,021.1	1,027.6	1,009.9
2005	1,000.2	1,006.1	1,012.5	1,021.3	1,029.4	1,036.9	1,032.1	1,031.7	1,036.8	1,036.4	1,040.6	1,047.8	1,027.7
2006	1,020.7	1,025.1	1,031.6	1,038.4	1,049.2	1,060.8	1,052.2	1,056.0	1,056.3	1,057.7	1,063.8	1,070.2	1,048.5
2007	1,045.3	1,051.0	1,060.3	1,067.9	1,079.2	1,090.0	1,080.8	1,084.2	1,086.3	1,088.1	1,092.9	1,095.7	1,076.8
Trade, Transportation, and Utilities													
2000	240.3	240.4	239.2	241.2	243.4	245.3	245.9	246.7	246.1	248.1	256.2	261.1	246.2
2001	249.6	246.2	246.3	245.3	246.8	248.9	247.6	247.1	245.4	244.8	247.2	247.5	246.9
2002	233.5	231.1	230.7	232.5	235.5	237.6	236.7	236.8	235.0	235.7	241.6	245.2	236.0
2003	235.2	232.9	231.6	229.8	230.0	230.7	230.5	231.2	230.5	232.2	236.6	239.6	232.5
2004	229.6	227.3	228.3	229.7	231.3	232.7	233.0	233.2	231.8	233.8	238.6	242.4	232.6
2005	232.4	231.3	232.2	232.5	234.3	236.1	236.6	236.3	237.8	239.6	244.2	247.2	236.7
2006	236.6	233.5	234.3	235.3	236.8	238.8	238.4	239.0	238.6	241.4	246.8	250.8	239.2
2007	242.2	239.4	240.1	241.1	242.9	244.6	244.7	244.9	244.3	246.4	252.0	254.3	244.7
Wholesale Trade													
2000	65.4	66.8	67.3	68.1	68.6	69.0	68.4	67.8	67.6	68.3	68.6	69.0	67.9
2001	68.9	69.5	69.7	69.2	68.9	69.0	68.6	68.3	67.6	67.2	66.9	66.8	68.4
2002	65.4	65.3	65.3	65.1	65.2	65.2	64.9	64.5	64.0	63.9	63.7	63.8	64.7
2003	63.7	63.4	63.3	63.0	62.9	62.9	62.6	62.3	61.9	62.1	61.9	62.0	62.6
2004	61.3	61.5	61.9	62.0	62.1	62.4	62.2	62.2	61.9	62.0	62.1	62.3	62.0
2005	61.6	61.9	62.2	62.4	62.6	63.0	63.1	63.2	63.3	63.3	63.5	63.8	62.8
2006	63.3	63.6	64.0	64.3	64.7	65.4	65.3	65.5	65.3	65.6	65.9	66.4	64.9
2007	65.0	65.4	65.8	65.8	66.3	66.8	66.6	66.8	66.5	67.0	67.1	67.2	66.4
Retail Trade													
2000	123.3	121.9	121.2	120.9	122.2	123.7	123.6	125.1	124.4	125.7	130.9	135.2	124.8
2001	125.4	122.2	122.2	121.8	122.9	124.4	123.2	122.8	122.5	123.3	127.6	129.4	124.0
2002	121.1	118.5	118.7	119.9	121.5	123.2	122.4	122.5	121.3	121.8	127.0	129.8	122.3
2003	121.3	119.3	118.3	118.1	119.0	120.0	119.7	120.6	120.4	121.4	125.3	127.8	120.9
2004	119.8	117.3	117.7	118.5	119.7	120.5	120.7	121.2	120.3	122.3	126.9	129.7	121.2
2005	121.9	120.3	121.0	121.2	122.9	123.9	124.1	123.7	125.2	126.7	131.0	133.2	124.6
2006	124.4	121.1	121.3	122.3	123.2	123.9	123.9	124.3	124.0	126.4	131.3	133.4	125.0
2007	127.0	124.2	124.5	125.2	126.4	127.3	127.6	127.4	127.0	128.4	133.2	135.0	127.8

Employment by Industry: Denver-Aurora, CO, 2000–2007—*Continued*

(Numbers in thousands, not seasonally adjusted.)

Industry and year	January	February	March	April	May	June	July	August	September	October	November	December	Annual Average
Transportation and Utilities													
2000	51.6	51.7	50.7	52.2	52.6	52.6	53.9	53.8	54.1	54.1	56.7	56.9	53.4
2001	55.3	54.5	54.4	54.3	55.0	55.5	55.8	56.0	55.3	54.3	52.7	51.3	54.5
2002	47.0	47.3	46.7	47.5	48.8	49.2	49.4	49.8	49.7	50.0	50.9	51.6	49.0
2003	50.2	50.2	50.0	48.7	48.1	47.8	48.2	48.3	48.2	48.7	49.4	49.8	48.9
2004	48.5	48.5	48.7	49.2	49.5	49.8	50.1	49.8	49.6	49.5	49.6	50.4	49.4
2005	48.9	49.1	49.0	48.9	48.8	49.2	49.4	49.4	49.3	49.6	49.7	50.2	49.3
2006	48.9	48.8	49.0	48.7	48.9	49.5	49.2	49.2	49.3	49.4	49.6	51.0	49.3
2007	50.2	49.8	49.8	50.1	50.2	50.5	50.5	50.7	50.8	51.0	51.7	52.1	50.6
Information													
2000	68.6	69.3	70.1	70.9	71.1	71.9	72.8	73.0	72.9	72.9	72.8	73.2	71.6
2001	72.9	72.8	72.4	71.3	70.8	70.5	68.5	67.8	66.6	65.2	64.8	64.0	69.0
2002	62.3	62.0	61.3	60.6	59.6	59.3	58.2	57.9	57.2	56.9	56.9	56.6	59.1
2003	56.1	55.9	55.4	54.7	54.5	54.2	54.0	53.8	53.5	53.2	53.3	53.2	54.3
2004	52.5	52.6	52.3	51.9	52.0	51.9	51.3	51.1	50.4	50.1	50.2	50.0	51.4
2005	49.2	49.0	48.9	48.4	48.4	48.2	47.9	47.7	47.5	47.4	47.7	47.9	48.2
2006	47.7	47.8'	48.0	47.7	47.9	48.0	47.8	47.4	47.1	47.2	47.5	47.4	47.6
2007	47.0	47.2	47.2	47.9	48.1	48.5	48.3	48.2	47.9	48.3	48.8	48.5	48.0
Financial Activities													
2000	95.0	95.4	96.0	95.5	95.8	96.6	96.8	96.9	96.6	96.5	96.8	97.7	96.3
2001	96.1	96.3	96.2	96.1	96.1	96.6	95.8	95.4	94.6	94.6	94.6	95.0	95.6
2002	93.5	93.9	93.9	93.5	93.8	94.6	94.5	95.1	95.0	95.8	96.7	97.4	94.8
2003	96.5	96.8	96.9	97.5	98.0	98.7	99.1	99.5	98.9	98.5	98.1	98.6	98.0
2004	97.1	97.4	97.5	97.7	97.9	98.5	98.5	98.4	98.2	98.1	98.0	98.6	98.0
2005	97.3	97.9	98.5	98.8	99.2	99.7	100.3	100.5	100.7	100.6	101.0	101.8	99.7
2006	99.6	99.8	100.0	100.1	100.8	101.4	101.3	101.3	100.9	100.5	100.5	101.1	100.6
2007	99.4	99.9	99.9	100.0	100.2	100.5	100.5	100.2	99.3	98.9	98.4	98.4	99.6
Professional and Business Services													
2000	189.7	190.1	192.6	195.6	197.6	200.6	201.1	202.3	202.5	201.5	201.1	202.1	198.1
2001	193.9	194.9	195.6	197.3	197.2	198.4	197.4	196.8	192.9	189.6	187.0	187.5	194.0
2002	178.9	179.8	180.3	183.5	184.6	185.3	183.6	185.4	183.3	181.2	180.1	180.3	182.2
2003	175.3	175.2	175.5	177.6	178.8	181.1	181.1	182.8	180.7	181.6	180.2	182.1	179.3
2004	176.1	177.8	179.8	184.7	184.9	187.7	188.9	189.2	188.3	187.7	187.0	188.8	185.1
2005	184.3	184.8	186.7	191.1	191.8	194.5	195.9	196.5	195.8	195.1	194.8	196.9	192.4
2006	190.2	192.2	193.8	197.0	199.6	203.5	203.4	204.7	203.9	203.8	203.3	204.6	200.0
2007	201.6	202.7	205.5	208.1	211.0	215.2	215.0	216.3	216.3	216.1	215.0	215.1	211.5
Education and Health Services													
2000	99.8	100.5	100.6	101.4	101.7	102.7	102.4	103.1	103.7	103.7	104.5	105.2	102.4
2001	104.3	105.2	105.7	105.8	106.2	106.3	106.0	106.7	106.4	108.2	108.8	109.1	106.6
2002	108.0	108.6	109.0	109.8	110.0	109.7	109.6	110.2	110.4	111.0	111.4	111.8	110.0
2003	111.3	112.2	112.3	113.1	113.1	113.1	113.0	113.1	113.4	114.1	114.4	114.6	113.1
2004	114.2	115.2	115.7	115.9	116.2	116.1	115.6	116.2	117.0	117.9	118.3	118.5	116.4
2005	117.0	118.6	119.1	119.2	119.8	119.6	118.8	119.3	119.7	119.9	120.6	120.9	119.4
2006	120.3	121.7	122.0	122.7	123.1	123.0	122.3	122.9	123.5	124.7	125.1	125.5	123.1
2007	124.5	126.0	126.8	127.3	127.9	127.8	127.3	127.9	128.6	130.1	130.5	131.0	128.0
Leisure and Hospitality													
2000	108.1	109.3	112.0	113.8	116.7	120.9	121.9	122.0	118.6	115.5	114.6	114.5	115.7
2001	111.4	111.9	113.7	114.7	117.6	122.6	121.7	122.0	118.1	113.9	113.1	113.9	116.2
2002	109.8	110.0	110.8	114.3	117.8	121.6	120.4	120.9	118.0	115.2	114.2	114.6	115.6
2003	110.4	109.7	110.3	112.9	116.1	119.4	119.4	120.6	117.2	116.0	114.8	115.0	115.1
2004	111.4	110.8	113.2	117.1	120.0	123.5	123.4	124.0	120.5	118.2	117.5	117.9	118.1
2005	114.2	114.9	116.9	119.5	123.3	127.3	127.4	127.1	123.9	122.1	120.5	121.1	121.5
2006	118.0	118.1	120.0	122.4	126.0	130.7	131.2	132.0	128.1	125.9	125.5	125.2	125.3
2007	120.4	120.5	123.7	125.9	130.4	134.9	134.3	134.9	131.1	128.5	127.7	128.1	128.4
Other Services													
2000	43.4	43.1	43.6	42.9	43.2	44.2	44.4	44.3	43.8	43.6	43.6	43.9	43.7
2001	43.4	42.9	43.4	43.3	43.6	44.3	44.0	44.1	43.6	43.4	43.5	43.6	43.6
2002	43.7	43.7	43.9	44.1	44.2	44.7	44.8	44.8	44.1	43.8	43.9	43.9	44.1
2003	44.1	43.7	43.6	43.9	44.1	44.8	44.6	44.5	43.7	43.8	43.9	44.1	44.0
2004	44.2	43.9	44.2	44.4	44.8	45.5	45.6	45.8	45.5	45.5	45.3	45.4	45.0
2005	45.4	45.1	45.3	45.3	45.4	45.9	45.6	45.6	45.2	45.0	44.7	45.0	45.3
2006	45.7	45.5	45.9	46.1	46.3	47.1	46.7	46.8	46.4	46.2	46.2	46.4	46.3
2007	46.3	46.3	46.8	46.9	47.0	47.7	47.3	47.5	47.2	46.9	46.9	47.0	47.0
Government													
2000	149.6	153.5	155.1	155.8	159.0	156.0	149.8	150.9	156.9	156.6	157.8	158.7	155.0
2001	154.4	158.2	157.7	158.3	159.2	159.1	153.9	154.8	160.7	161.1	162.9	162.8	158.6
2002	159.5	162.7	164.1	164.4	165.7	164.6	158.9	160.4	164.3	166.1	166.9	166.5	163.7
2003	161.8	165.0	165.5	165.4	167.4	165.9	159.0	159.9	164.2	164.3	164.6	163.7	163.8
2004	159.1	162.6	163.9	165.3	165.9	164.8	157.9	158.2	164.2	165.5	166.2	166.0	163.3
2005	160.4	164.5	164.9	166.5	167.2	165.6	159.6	158.7	166.2	166.7	167.1	167.0	164.5
2006	162.6	166.5	167.6	167.1	168.7	168.3	161.1	161.9	167.8	168.0	168.9	169.2	166.5
2007	163.9	169.0	170.3	170.7	171.7	170.8	163.4	164.3	171.6	172.9	173.6	173.3	169.6

Employment by Industry: Cleveland-Elyria-Mentor, OH, 2000–2007

(Numbers in thousands, not seasonally adjusted.)

Industry and year	January	February	March	April	May	June	July	August	September	October	November	December	Annual Average
Total Nonfarm													
2000	1,113.8	1,118.2	1,126.4	1,132.1	1,144.5	1,149.7	1,138.4	1,139.9	1,140.5	1,140.0	1,143.4	1,145.2	1,136.0
2001	1,112.7	1,114.3	1,121.1	1,121.6	1,129.4	1,133.6	1,120.0	1,119.0	1,110.3	1,109.3	1,110.0	1,108.3	1,117.5
2002	1,069.6	1,072.2	1,078.5	1,078.7	1,087.5	1,091.2	1,081.7	1,084.1	1,084.5	1,087.0	1,086.8	1,085.9	1,082.3
2003	1,057.1	1,058.1	1,063.8	1,072.1	1,083.4	1,085.0	1,076.1	1,076.3	1,077.1	1,079.8	1,080.4	1,081.1	1,074.1
2004	1,047.3	1,050.5	1,059.9	1,067.7	1,076.8	1,082.6	1,076.2	1,076.4	1,077.1	1,082.0	1,084.8	1,084.0	1,072.1
2005	1,044.9	1,051.2	1,058.1	1,068.6	1,075.5	1,082.0	1,075.4	1,077.2	1,079.8	1,082.7	1,085.3	1,085.3	1,072.2
2006	1,053.6	1,057.6	1,065.4	1,074.8	1,082.1	1,088.9	1,076.9	1,078.4	1,079.1	1,080.2	1,081.1	1,081.3	1,075.0
2007	1,052.8	1,052.6	1,061.5	1,069.4	1,079.2	1,086.7	1,072.8	1,073.9	1,073.6	1,075.8	1,076.4	1,075.4	1,070.8
Total Private													
2000	975.4	977.3	984.4	990.9	999.0	1,008.5	1,002.9	1,003.7	999.5	996.8	999.5	1,000.7	994.9
2001	971.7	970.6	976.0	977.1	984.2	990.6	982.5	981.1	966.4	963.4	963.5	961.3	974.0
2002	927.5	926.0	931.4	932.8	940.4	946.4	945.3	946.6	940.7	940.6	940.0	939.6	938.1
2003	914.7	912.8	917.4	926.2	937.4	941.5	939.8	942.5	935.9	935.1	934.9	935.3	931.1
2004	906.0	905.8	914.1	922.0	930.4	938.6	941.0	942.6	937.7	939.0	940.9	940.6	929.9
2005	905.8	908.4	914.7	924.9	931.1	938.8	940.7	943.7	940.9	940.5	943.0	942.7	931.3
2006	914.8	915.8	922.3	931.7	938.1	946.6	943.0	945.3	940.3	938.2	937.9	938.2	934.4
2007	913.0	909.3	916.8	924.7	933.8	942.3	936.9	939.2	933.4	932.9	933.1	932.3	929.0
Goods-Producing													
2000	237.4	238.8	241.1	241.3	243.2	246.1	243.6	243.8	241.6	240.7	240.3	237.3	241.3
2001	229.6	228.1	228.2	226.4	227.3	227.8	225.3	224.7	219.6	217.0	216.4	213.8	223.7
2002	203.0	201.5	202.4	202.4	204.4	206.7	206.8	207.2	205.4	204.8	203.4	200.8	204.1
2003	195.1	194.0	195.0	195.8	199.5	200.5	198.5	199.0	197.4	197.5	196.7	194.5	196.9
2004	187.3	187.5	189.9	193.0	195.7	198.0	198.0	198.1	197.4	197.4	196.4	194.2	194.4
2005	185.8	185.4	187.1	191.6	193.4	195.9	195.3	195.8	195.4	194.7	194.1	191.2	192.1
2006	185.5	184.3	185.3	189.0	190.1	193.0	192.6	192.8	191.9	190.9	188.7	184.7	189.1
2007	180.8	178.8	181.1	182.7	186.3	188.3	184.4	186.7	185.5	184.6	183.8	180.9	183.7
Natural Resources, Mining, and Construction													
2000	40.5	40.3	42.6	44.4	46.7	49.0	49.3	49.3	47.6	47.0	46.3	43.7	45.6
2001	39.1	38.8	40.0	42.0	44.6	46.2	47.2	47.8	46.2	46.0	44.9	42.9	43.8
2002	37.8	37.2	38.3	40.3	42.6	44.5	45.9	46.3	45.5	45.5	44.3	42.0	42.5
2003	38.0	37.1	38.4	41.4	44.1	45.9	46.3	46.9	46.1	46.5	45.4	43.3	43.2
2004	38.3	38.4	40.1	42.4	44.8	46.4	47.3	47.0	46.6	46.7	45.6	43.5	43.9
2005	37.1	37.0	37.8	42.2	44.0	45.9	46.4	46.5	45.9	45.7	44.5	41.5	42.9
2006	37.0	36.5	37.5	40.7	42.5	43.7	44.7	44.8	44.3	44.0	43.0	40.7	41.6
2007	36.6	34.9	36.6	39.5	42.8	44.2	43.8	44.0	43.5	43.1	42.0	39.9	40.9
Manufacturing													
2000	196.9	198.5	198.5	196.9	196.5	197.1	194.3	194.5	194.0	193.7	194.0	193.6	195.7
2001	190.5	189.3	188.2	184.4	182.7	181.6	178.1	176.9	173.4	171.0	171.5	170.9	179.9
2002	165.2	164.3	164.1	162.1	161.8	162.2	160.9	160.9	159.9	159.3	159.1	158.8	161.6
2003	157.1	156.9	156.6	154.4	155.4	154.6	152.2	152.1	151.3	151.0	151.3	151.2	153.6
2004	149.0	149.1	149.8	150.6	150.9	151.6	150.7	151.1	150.8	150.7	150.8	150.7	150.5
2005	148.7	148.4	149.3	149.4	149.4	150.0	148.9	149.3	149.5	149.0	149.6	149.7	149.3
2006	148.5	147.8	147.8	148.3	147.6	149.3	147.9	148.0	147.6	146.9	145.7	144.0	147.5
2007	144.2	143.9	144.5	143.2	143.5	144.1	140.6	142.7	142.0	141.5	141.8	141.0	142.8
Service-Providing													
2000	876.4	879.4	885.3	890.8	901.3	903.6	894.8	896.1	898.9	899.3	903.1	907.9	894.7
2001	883.1	886.2	892.9	895.2	902.1	905.8	894.7	894.3	890.7	892.3	893.6	894.5	893.8
2002	866.6	870.7	876.1	876.3	883.1	884.5	874.9	876.9	879.1	882.2	883.4	885.1	878.2
2003	862.0	864.1	868.8	876.3	883.9	884.5	877.6	877.3	879.7	882.3	883.7	886.6	877.2
2004	860.0	863.0	870.0	874.7	881.1	884.6	878.2	878.3	879.7	884.6	888.4	889.8	877.7
2005	859.1	865.8	871.0	877.0	882.1	886.1	880.1	881.4	884.4	888.0	891.2	894.1	880.0
2006	868.1	873.3	880.1	885.8	892.0	895.9	884.3	885.6	887.2	889.3	892.4	896.6	885.9
2007	872.0	873.8	880.4	886.7	892.9	898.4	888.4	887.2	888.1	891.2	892.6	894.5	887.2
Trade, Transportation, and Utilities													
2000	219.1	216.7	217.2	217.5	219.0	220.3	219.0	219.2	218.5	221.3	225.3	229.1	220.2
2001	216.9	213.9	214.5	214.3	214.8	215.5	212.3	211.5	209.4	210.3	213.1	214.2	213.4
2002	204.6	201.3	202.6	200.9	202.5	203.3	202.9	202.9	200.9	202.6	204.9	207.5	203.1
2003	200.4	197.9	197.4	200.2	201.9	202.7	202.1	201.9	200.6	202.8	205.5	208.7	201.8
2004	199.3	197.2	198.0	197.8	199.0	200.4	199.6	199.6	197.5	199.8	203.7	206.1	199.8
2005	197.0	195.5	196.3	196.5	198.0	198.8	199.1	199.0	197.7	198.7	202.0	205.2	198.7
2006	197.6	196.0	197.1	198.5	199.6	200.4	198.9	199.3	198.2	199.3	203.1	206.5	199.5
2007	198.2	195.4	196.9	197.7	199.2	200.5	200.0	199.2	197.8	198.8	202.4	205.3	199.3
Wholesale Trade													
2000	56.8	56.9	57.0	57.2	57.5	57.7	57.8	57.9	58.2	58.5	58.7	58.9	57.8
2001	58.6	58.8	59.2	58.6	58.3	58.5	57.7	57.4	56.6	56.4	56.2	55.6	57.7
2002	55.5	55.1	55.4	54.9	54.9	54.6	54.6	54.3	53.6	53.5	53.2	53.5	54.4
2003	54.6	54.5	54.4	54.7	55.1	55.1	55.1	55.0	54.6	54.7	54.8	55.0	54.8
2004	54.1	54.1	54.3	54.2	54.5	54.9	54.9	54.9	54.3	54.9	55.1	55.4	54.6
2005	54.6	54.6	54.8	54.9	55.0	55.5	55.7	55.8	55.6	55.3	55.4	55.8	55.3
2006	55.5	55.6	55.9	56.2	56.3	56.6	56.5	56.3	56.1	55.8	55.9	56.2	56.1
2007	55.4	55.4	55.6	55.5	55.8	56.0	56.1	55.9	55.3	55.3	55.5	55.8	55.6
Retail Trade													
2000	124.5	122.3	122.6	121.9	123.0	124.1	122.8	123.1	122.1	123.9	127.8	131.5	124.1
2001	122.0	119.2	119.3	118.9	119.3	119.8	118.0	117.6	116.6	117.7	121.6	123.9	119.5
2002	115.9	112.9	114.0	112.4	113.6	114.5	114.1	114.2	113.0	114.0	116.8	119.5	114.6
2003	113.4	111.5	111.5	113.4	114.3	115.1	114.6	114.7	114.0	115.1	117.8	120.9	114.6
2004	113.5	111.5	111.9	111.8	112.6	113.3	112.4	112.2	110.6	111.6	115.1	117.4	112.8
2005	110.2	108.5	108.9	109.2	110.3	110.7	110.5	110.3	109.2	110.1	113.1	115.5	110.5
2006	109.0	107.4	108.0	108.7	109.6	109.9	108.9	109.1	107.8	109.3	112.8	115.4	109.7
2007	108.9	106.3	107.3	107.6	109.1	110.1	110.0	109.3	108.2	109.1	112.4	114.6	109.4

Employment by Industry: Cleveland-Elyria-Mentor, OH, 2000–2007—*Continued*

(Numbers in thousands, not seasonally adjusted.)

Industry and year	January	February	March	April	May	June	July	August	September	October	November	December	Annual Average
Transportation and Utilities													
2000	37.8	37.5	37.6	38.4	38.5	38.5	38.4	38.2	38.2	38.9	38.8	38.7	38.3
2001	36.3	35.9	36.0	36.8	37.2	37.2	36.6	36.5	36.2	36.2	35.3	34.7	36.2
2002	33.2	33.3	33.2	33.6	34.0	34.2	34.2	34.4	34.3	35.1	34.9	34.5	34.1
2003	32.4	31.9	31.5	32.1	32.5	32.5	32.4	32.2	32.0	33.0	32.9	32.8	32.3
2004	31.7	31.6	31.8	31.8	31.9	32.2	32.3	32.5	32.6	33.3	33.5	33.3	32.4
2005	32.2	32.4	32.6	32.4	32.7	32.6	32.9	32.9	32.9	33.3	33.5	33.9	32.9
2006	33.1	33.0	33.2	33.6	33.7	33.9	33.5	33.9	34.3	34.2	34.4	34.9	33.8
2007	33.9	33.7	34.0	34.6	34.3	34.4	33.9	34.0	34.3	34.4	34.5	34.9	34.2
Information													
2000	23.9	24.0	24.0	24.1	24.1	24.2	24.1	24.2	24.3	24.4	24.5	24.5	24.2
2001	24.5	24.5	24.6	24.3	24.2	24.3	24.2	23.9	23.5	23.3	23.3	23.3	24.0
2002	23.3	23.0	22.9	22.1	21.9	21.9	21.6	21.4	21.2	21.1	21.1	21.0	21.9
2003	21.3	21.2	21.2	21.0	21.0	20.9	20.7	20.5	20.2	20.2	20.2	20.4	20.7
2004	20.1	20.0	20.1	20.0	20.0	20.1	20.1	20.0	19.7	19.7	19.8	19.6	19.9
2005	19.5	19.5	19.4	19.7	19.7	19.6	19.5	19.5	19.2	19.2	19.3	19.2	19.4
2006	19.2	19.1	19.1	18.8	18.9	18.9	18.9	18.9	18.7	18.6	18.7	18.7	18.9
2007	18.4	18.5	18.3	18.5	18.6	18.6	18.8	18.6	18.5	18.5	18.5	18.4	18.5
Financial Activities													
2000	75.6	75.2	75.6	74.8	74.5	75.3	74.8	75.0	74.9	74.2	74.9	75.5	75.0
2001	75.5	75.9	76.1	76.1	76.0	77.1	77.1	77.1	76.0	75.8	76.5	76.9	76.3
2002	75.7	76.0	76.0	75.9	75.8	75.7	75.6	75.4	74.6	74.4	75.1	75.5	75.5
2003	75.8	75.9	76.2	76.0	76.5	77.5	77.7	77.9	77.2	76.6	76.9	77.6	76.8
2004	76.7	76.9	77.1	76.6	76.8	77.8	77.7	77.7	76.7	76.3	76.3	76.4	76.9
2005	75.5	75.4	75.2	74.4	74.3	75.3	75.1	75.0	74.2	74.9	74.7	74.6	74.9
2006	73.6	73.7	73.8	73.5	73.5	74.0	74.4	74.2	73.7	73.5	73.7	73.8	73.8
2007	73.1	73.0	72.9	72.9	73.2	73.2	73.4	73.1	72.2	72.2	72.1	72.3	72.8
Professional and Business Services													
2000	140.2	140.8	141.9	146.5	147.1	149.3	148.8	149.2	148.3	147.4	146.6	145.8	146.0
2001	143.6	143.7	145.2	145.4	145.9	146.7	145.6	145.1	141.3	140.3	138.6	137.4	143.2
2002	132.5	132.8	134.1	134.3	134.3	135.7	135.2	136.0	134.1	135.7	134.3	133.6	134.4
2003	131.5	131.6	132.9	134.5	135.3	136.6	137.1	138.7	136.5	135.5	134.6	133.1	134.8
2004	129.3	129.8	131.3	135.8	136.9	139.1	140.1	141.7	141.1	140.9	139.8	139.0	137.1
2005	133.2	134.9	136.2	139.4	139.5	141.3	143.0	144.3	144.2	144.6	144.3	143.1	140.7
2006	138.6	139.4	140.8	143.4	143.8	145.8	145.8	147.2	146.4	146.1	145.3	145.3	144.0
2007	140.2	140.4	140.9	143.2	143.9	145.9	145.9	146.7	145.7	145.9	144.9	144.5	144.0
Education and Health Services													
2000	147.4	149.5	150.2	149.9	150.0	149.4	147.7	147.9	150.7	150.8	151.4	152.0	149.7
2001	150.5	153.0	153.7	154.8	155.2	154.5	152.9	153.4	157.0	159.5	160.5	161.0	155.5
2002	158.8	162.2	162.5	162.6	162.4	161.1	160.3	160.7	164.3	165.9	166.8	167.1	162.9
2003	161.5	163.6	164.1	164.1	163.9	161.5	161.5	161.1	164.4	166.0	166.4	166.5	163.6
2004	163.0	165.1	165.7	164.2	163.5	161.5	162.9	161.8	166.0	168.2	168.7	169.3	165.0
2005	164.9	167.5	167.8	166.6	166.2	165.4	164.6	164.9	169.2	170.1	171.3	172.0	167.5
2006	168.5	171.7	172.2	171.3	170.7	169.9	168.0	167.7	170.8	172.5	173.4	173.3	170.8
2007	171.3	172.8	173.9	174.1	173.0	172.3	171.3	171.3	174.4	175.7	176.2	175.5	173.5
Leisure and Hospitality													
2000	86.9	87.1	88.9	91.7	95.7	98.4	99.5	99.1	95.8	92.6	91.1	90.9	93.1
2001	86.2	86.5	88.6	90.3	95.0	98.2	98.6	98.6	93.3	91.3	89.1	88.5	92.0
2002	84.1	83.6	85.0	88.8	93.0	95.4	96.4	96.7	94.2	90.7	89.1	88.8	90.5
2003	85.0	84.5	86.2	90.2	94.7	96.8	97.7	98.8	95.4	92.5	90.8	91.5	92.0
2004	86.6	85.6	87.6	90.1	93.8	96.6	97.5	98.9	94.9	92.3	91.8	91.7	92.3
2005	86.3	86.4	88.6	92.3	95.6	97.8	99.3	100.6	96.8	94.2	93.1	93.0	93.7
2006	88.1	87.9	90.2	93.5	97.4	99.7	99.8	101.0	96.7	93.5	91.3	91.8	94.2
2007	87.6	87.0	89.0	91.7	95.4	98.7	98.4	99.1	95.4	93.3	91.4	91.3	93.2
Other Services													
2000	44.9	45.2	45.5	45.1	45.4	45.5	45.4	45.3	45.4	45.4	45.4	45.6	45.3
2001	44.9	45.0	45.1	45.5	45.8	46.5	46.5	46.8	46.3	45.9	46.0	46.2	45.9
2002	45.5	45.6	45.6	45.8	46.1	46.6	46.5	46.3	46.0	45.4	45.3	45.3	45.9
2003	44.1	44.1	44.4	44.4	44.6	45.0	44.5	44.6	44.2	44.0	43.8	44.0	44.3
2004	43.7	43.7	44.4	44.5	44.7	45.1	45.1	44.8	44.4	44.4	44.4	44.3	44.5
2005	43.6	43.8	44.1	44.4	44.4	44.7	44.8	44.6	44.2	44.1	44.2	44.4	44.3
2006	43.7	43.7	43.8	43.7	44.1	44.9	44.6	44.2	43.9	43.8	43.7	44.1	44.0
2007	43.4	43.4	43.8	43.9	44.2	44.8	44.7	44.5	43.9	43.9	43.8	44.1	44.0
Government													
2000	138.4	140.9	142.0	141.2	145.5	141.2	135.5	136.2	141.0	143.2	143.9	144.5	141.1
2001	141.0	143.7	145.1	144.5	145.2	143.0	137.5	137.9	143.9	145.9	146.5	147.0	143.4
2002	142.1	146.2	147.1	145.9	147.1	144.8	136.4	137.5	143.8	146.4	146.8	146.3	144.2
2003	142.4	145.3	146.4	145.9	146.0	143.5	136.3	133.8	141.2	144.7	145.5	145.8	143.0
2004	141.3	144.7	145.8	145.7	146.4	144.0	135.2	133.8	139.4	143.0	143.9	143.4	142.2
2005	139.1	142.8	143.4	143.7	144.4	143.2	134.7	133.5	138.9	142.2	142.3	142.6	140.9
2006	138.8	141.8	143.1	143.1	144.0	142.3	133.9	133.1	138.8	142.0	143.2	143.1	140.6
2007	139.8	143.3	144.7	144.7	145.4	144.4	135.9	134.7	140.2	142.9	143.3	143.1	141.9

Employment by Industry: Cincinnati-Middletown, OH-KY-IN, 2000–2007

(Numbers in thousands, not seasonally adjusted.)

Industry and year	January	February	March	April	May	June	July	August	September	October	November	December	Annual Average
Total Nonfarm													
2000	995.4	1,001.6	1,011.7	1,015.2	1,025.2	1,027.4	1,016.7	1,017.9	1,020.3	1,022.1	1,025.2	1,029.9	1,017.4
2001	998.1	1,001.5	1,008.7	1,010.2	1,017.5	1,020.2	1,010.4	1,013.0	1,013.0	1,014.8	1,015.1	1,016.0	1,011.5
2002	988.2	991.4	998.7	1,004.3	1,013.3	1,014.3	1,009.0	1,012.8	1,014.4	1,015.6	1,019.8	1,021.9	1,008.6
2003	998.9	998.0	1,007.4	1,017.6	1,023.6	1,024.0	1,013.9	1,020.9	1,019.1	1,020.8	1,022.9	1,026.0	1,016.0
2004	997.8	999.8	1,012.1	1,022.3	1,029.9	1,034.2	1,029.4	1,033.7	1,033.1	1,034.4	1,037.7	1,039.4	1,025.3
2005	1,004.3	1,010.2	1,021.1	1,033.7	1,041.7	1,044.5	1,037.1	1,039.2	1,044.3	1,041.0	1,045.8	1,048.7	1,034.3
2006	1,017.3	1,020.9	1,028.1	1,036.5	1,043.9	1,046.8	1,036.4	1,041.7	1,043.1	1,040.5	1,044.4	1,047.1	1,037.2
2007	1,022.6	1,022.7	1,035.7	1,043.5	1,054.8	1,055.4	1,046.2	1,049.4	1,050.4	1,051.6	1,053.7	1,054.9	1,045.1
Total Private													
2000	872.1	873.8	882.8	885.7	893.4	901.1	898.7	900.6	896.5	895.0	897.0	901.4	891.5
2001	871.9	871.8	878.2	878.9	885.6	892.9	891.1	892.7	885.6	884.7	883.9	884.6	883.5
2002	858.9	858.6	864.7	870.5	878.8	885.6	886.9	888.7	885.2	882.9	886.5	889.2	878.0
2003	866.9	863.4	871.5	881.1	886.9	892.8	890.3	894.2	886.9	884.9	886.6	890.0	882.9
2004	865.7	864.4	875.3	885.2	892.4	901.6	905.9	907.9	901.5	899.2	902.0	904.6	892.1
2005	873.2	876.2	886.1	898.3	905.8	912.8	913.8	914.1	912.7	906.1	910.4	914.0	902.0
2006	886.0	886.4	892.3	900.5	907.1	915.4	913.4	916.6	911.1	905.5	909.1	912.0	904.6
2007	890.4	887.5	899.2	906.8	917.4	923.5	922.5	924.0	919.4	916.4	918.5	920.1	912.1
Goods-Producing													
2000	194.8	195.3	197.8	197.8	199.9	200.8	200.6	200.2	199.2	198.4	197.7	196.8	198.3
2001	190.6	190.7	192.0	191.3	192.4	193.3	191.9	192.6	190.5	188.8	186.8	185.2	190.5
2002	178.2	177.3	177.7	177.8	178.7	180.2	180.5	181.4	180.7	180.2	179.6	177.7	179.2
2003	174.2	172.8	174.9	177.4	178.4	179.3	178.0	178.8	177.5	176.6	175.8	175.5	176.6
2004	171.3	170.9	173.4	176.2	177.8	180.1	179.6	179.4	178.6	177.8	177.2	176.2	176.5
2005	169.7	170.1	172.3	174.6	176.8	178.0	178.5	178.6	178.5	177.4	177.1	175.7	175.6
2006	170.4	170.5	169.4	173.3	174.8	176.5	175.7	176.7	175.2	172.9	172.3	172.1	173.3
2007	167.8	166.8	170.0	172.0	173.9	174.9	174.5	175.1	174.1	172.9	171.7	171.2	172.1
Natural Resources, Mining, and Construction													
2000	47.5	47.3	49.4	49.9	51.4	52.8	53.0	52.9	51.8	51.2	50.6	49.6	50.6
2001	46.6	46.9	48.4	50.2	51.7	53.3	53.7	54.0	53.1	52.7	51.9	50.8	51.1
2002	46.1	46.0	46.8	47.7	48.9	50.6	51.2	51.6	51.0	50.8	50.4	48.7	49.2
2003	45.3	44.4	46.1	49.0	50.2	51.5	51.4	52.3	51.6	51.6	50.9	50.4	49.5
2004	48.3	48.0	49.9	51.7	53.0	54.8	55.2	55.1	54.4	53.6	52.9	51.8	52.4
2005	47.4	48.1	49.6	51.6	53.2	54.3	55.1	55.1	54.9	54.1	53.7	52.1	52.4
2006	48.5	48.8	49.9	52.0	53.0	54.1	54.2	54.8	53.6	52.1	51.4	50.5	51.9
2007	47.3	45.8	48.0	50.2	51.8	52.5	53.1	53.1	52.4	51.7	50.9	50.1	50.6
Manufacturing													
2000	147.3	148.0	148.4	147.9	148.5	148.0	147.6	147.3	147.4	147.2	147.1	147.2	147.7
2001	144.0	143.8	143.6	141.1	140.7	140.0	138.2	138.6	137.4	136.1	134.9	134.4	139.4
2002	132.1	131.3	130.9	130.1	129.8	129.6	129.3	129.8	129.7	129.4	129.2	129.0	130.0
2003	128.9	128.4	128.8	128.4	128.2	127.8	126.6	126.5	125.9	125.0	124.9	125.1	127.0
2004	123.0	122.9	123.5	124.5	124.8	125.3	124.4	124.3	124.2	124.2	124.3	124.4	124.2
2005	122.3	122.0	122.7	123.0	123.6	123.7	123.4	123.5	123.6	123.3	123.4	123.6	123.2
2006	121.9	121.7	119.5	121.3	121.8	122.4	121.5	121.9	121.6	120.8	120.9	121.6	121.4
2007	120.5	121.0	122.0	121.8	122.1	122.4	121.4	122.0	121.7	121.2	120.8	121.1	121.5
Service-Providing													
2000	800.6	806.3	813.9	817.4	825.3	826.6	816.1	817.7	821.1	823.7	827.5	833.1	819.1
2001	807.5	810.8	816.7	818.9	825.1	826.9	818.5	820.4	822.5	826.0	828.3	830.8	821.0
2002	810.0	814.1	821.0	826.5	834.6	834.1	828.5	831.4	833.7	835.4	840.2	844.2	829.5
2003	824.7	825.2	832.5	840.2	845.2	844.7	835.9	842.1	841.6	844.2	847.1	850.5	839.4
2004	826.5	828.9	838.7	846.1	852.1	854.1	849.8	854.3	854.5	856.6	860.5	863.2	848.8
2005	834.6	840.1	848.8	859.1	864.9	866.5	858.6	860.6	865.8	863.6	868.7	873.0	858.7
2006	846.9	850.4	858.7	863.2	869.1	870.3	860.7	865.0	867.9	867.6	872.1	875.0	863.9
2007	854.8	855.9	865.7	871.5	880.9	880.5	871.7	874.3	876.3	878.7	882.0	883.7	873.0
Trade, Transportation, and Utilities													
2000	216.8	215.3	216.5	215.9	217.3	217.5	215.6	215.9	215.7	219.6	223.4	227.4	218.1
2001	217.6	214.8	215.4	212.6	213.5	214.3	215.2	215.1	215.0	216.9	220.3	222.8	216.1
2002	212.5	210.9	211.7	212.1	213.1	213.6	213.0	212.9	213.0	212.5	217.3	221.2	213.7
2003	210.3	208.6	209.5	209.7	210.5	210.6	209.1	210.2	209.4	211.1	214.7	217.4	210.9
2004	207.3	205.3	206.5	207.2	208.3	209.4	210.5	212.2	210.5	211.9	216.1	218.8	210.3
2005	208.2	206.7	208.1	209.1	210.4	210.5	211.5	210.6	210.9	209.9	213.5	217.0	210.5
2006	208.6	206.3	207.0	207.2	209.0	209.5	208.7	209.2	209.6	210.5	214.9	217.5	209.8
2007	210.3	208.3	210.1	210.2	212.6	212.8	212.8	212.4	212.7	213.6	217.9	219.6	212.8
Wholesale Trade													
2000	58.6	58.9	59.1	59.4	59.6	59.4	59.3	59.2	59.4	59.6	59.6	59.8	59.3
2001	58.6	58.6	58.6	58.9	58.9	58.9	59.0	58.8	58.5	58.8	58.8	58.9	58.8
2002	57.6	57.7	57.7	57.9	58.0	58.2	58.7	58.4	58.5	58.7	58.8	59.0	58.3
2003	57.8	57.7	57.9	57.5	57.6	57.9	56.9	56.9	56.3	56.4	56.6	56.8	57.1
2004	55.6	55.5	55.6	55.6	55.8	56.2	57.8	57.9	57.7	57.1	57.4	57.9	56.7
2005	56.7	56.6	56.8	57.2	57.5	58.0	58.6	58.9	59.4	58.6	58.9	59.2	58.0
2006	58.9	58.9	59.0	59.1	59.3	59.8	59.6	59.8	59.5	59.4	59.5	59.9	59.4
2007	60.5	60.4	60.6	60.6	60.8	61.2	61.2	61.2	61.2	61.3	61.5	61.8	61.0
Retail Trade													
2000	114.6	113.2	113.9	113.7	114.5	115.3	114.0	114.2	113.5	116.4	120.1	123.9	115.6
2001	115.8	113.2	114.0	113.5	114.4	115.6	113.9	113.9	113.4	114.3	118.0	120.5	115.0
2002	111.9	110.5	111.2	111.4	112.2	113.2	112.1	112.1	111.7	111.1	115.3	118.6	112.6
2003	109.4	107.7	108.2	109.0	109.8	110.4	110.0	110.6	110.3	111.0	114.4	116.7	110.6
2004	109.5	107.9	108.9	109.3	109.9	110.9	110.9	110.3	111.3	109.7	111.0	114.6	116.7	110.8
2005	108.8	107.0	107.9	108.5	109.3	109.1	109.7	108.6	108.1	108.4	111.6	114.9	109.3
2006	108.1	106.2	106.9	107.4	108.7	108.7	108.8	108.6	108.8	108.4	109.2	112.8	114.4	109.0
2007	108.1	106.4	108.0	108.5	109.9	109.9	110.2	109.6	109.0	109.5	113.0	114.6	109.7

Employment by Industry: Cincinnati-Middletown, OH-KY-IN, 2000–2007—*Continued*

(Numbers in thousands, not seasonally adjusted.)

Industry and year	January	February	March	April	May	June	July	August	September	October	November	December	Annual Average
Transportation and Utilities													
2000	43.6	43.2	43.5	42.8	43.2	42.8	42.3	42.5	42.8	43.6	43.7	43.7	43.1
2001	43.2	43.0	42.8	40.2	40.2	39.8	42.3	42.4	43.1	43.8	43.5	43.4	42.3
2002	43.0	42.7	42.8	42.8	42.9	42.2	42.2	42.4	42.8	42.7	43.2	43.6	42.8
2003	43.1	43.2	43.4	43.2	43.1	42.3	42.2	42.7	42.8	43.7	43.7	43.9	43.1
2004	42.2	41.9	42.0	42.3	42.6	42.3	42.4	43.0	43.1	43.8	44.1	44.2	42.8
2005	42.7	43.1	43.4	43.4	43.6	43.4	43.2	43.1	43.4	42.9	43.0	42.9	43.2
2006	41.6	41.2	41.1	40.7	41.0	40.9	40.5	40.6	41.7	41.9	42.6	43.2	41.4
2007	41.7	41.5	41.5	41.1	41.9	41.7	41.4	41.6	42.5	42.8	43.4	43.2	42.0
Information													
2000	20.3	20.1	20.7	20.5	20.6	20.7	20.1	20.3	20.0	20.0	19.8	19.9	20.3
2001	20.1	19.9	20.0	19.5	19.6	19.7	19.4	19.3	18.9	18.8	18.6	18.5	19.4
2002	18.4	18.1	18.1	17.9	17.9	18.2	18.1	17.8	17.4	16.9	17.1	17.1	17.8
2003	16.4	16.2	16.3	16.3	16.5	16.4	16.5	16.3	16.0	15.7	15.9	16.0	16.2
2004	15.9	15.7	15.7	16.0	16.1	16.2	16.2	16.2	16.0	16.1	16.1	16.1	16.0
2005	15.9	15.9	15.9	15.8	16.0	15.9	15.9	15.8	15.7	15.8	15.9	16.1	15.9
2006	15.7	15.6	15.7	15.8	15.7	15.8	15.8	15.8	15.5	15.5	15.6	15.6	15.7
2007	15.3	15.4	15.3	15.5	15.6	15.7	16.0	15.9	15.6	15.6	15.7	15.5	15.6
Financial Activities													
2000	58.8	58.9	58.8	58.9	59.1	59.5	59.1	59.2	58.6	58.9	59.2	59.8	59.1
2001	59.5	59.8	59.6	60.4	60.6	61.3	61.2	61.6	61.3	61.5	61.7	62.3	60.9
2002	62.4	62.9	62.9	63.3	63.9	64.4	64.5	64.7	64.3	64.7	65.1	65.7	64.1
2003	65.6	65.9	65.9	65.6	65.9	66.2	66.3	66.6	66.1	65.9	65.8	66.0	65.9
2004	64.8	64.9	65.0	65.0	65.0	65.5	65.5	65.5	64.8	64.5	64.6	65.0	65.0
2005	64.7	64.8	64.8	65.0	65.2	65.8	65.6	65.6	65.0	64.9	65.0	65.5	65.2
2006	64.6	64.7	64.9	65.2	65.5	65.7	65.4	65.4	64.9	64.9	64.9	65.2	65.1
2007	65.0	65.2	65.3	65.1	65.4	65.7	66.4	66.2	65.8	65.6	65.5	65.6	65.6
Professional and Business Services													
2000	134.4	135.2	137.3	137.6	138.1	141.1	140.7	141.8	141.2	141.2	140.7	140.1	139.1
2001	136.1	136.6	137.8	139.4	139.4	140.5	138.9	139.5	139.6	141.3	139.9	137.9	138.9
2002	134.9	134.3	135.4	137.0	137.9	139.6	140.5	142.1	142.5	144.2	144.1	143.1	139.6
2003	141.7	141.3	142.7	144.3	144.0	144.7	143.8	144.8	144.5	146.3	145.6	145.2	144.0
2004	142.6	141.3	143.3	144.1	144.2	146.7	149.2	150.3	150.6	150.2	150.6	150.8	147.0
2005	145.0	146.3	148.3	150.5	150.9	153.5	153.9	155.7	157.2	156.8	157.3	158.0	152.8
2006	151.3	151.8	153.8	154.3	153.5	154.6	155.9	156.6	156.3	154.9	154.9	154.7	154.4
2007	150.6	150.6	153.2	154.3	154.1	156.0	155.9	157.0	157.0	156.6	156.3	156.1	154.8
Education and Health Services													
2000	116.9	118.2	118.5	119.3	119.9	119.3	119.6	119.9	121.1	120.1	120.9	121.3	119.6
2001	118.1	119.6	120.1	120.1	120.3	119.4	120.5	120.9	122.2	123.2	123.7	124.3	121.0
2002	121.4	122.6	122.8	123.9	124.4	123.5	123.4	124.4	126.0	127.2	127.8	128.4	124.7
2003	125.5	125.7	125.8	126.2	126.2	125.5	126.4	127.2	128.4	128.9	130.0	130.3	127.1
2004	128.8	129.7	130.3	131.0	130.9	130.4	130.8	130.6	131.6	132.5	133.4	133.6	131.1
2005	131.5	132.8	133.3	135.1	134.8	134.2	133.3	134.1	134.9	135.7	136.3	136.5	134.4
2006	135.1	136.2	137.0	138.1	138.1	137.7	136.6	137.6	138.9	140.1	140.8	141.0	138.1
2007	139.3	139.9	140.9	141.4	141.7	140.7	139.3	139.8	142.3	142.9	143.6	143.9	141.3
Leisure and Hospitality													
2000	88.9	89.5	91.8	94.2	96.8	100.7	101.7	102.2	99.7	96.0	94.6	95.5	96.0
2001	90.0	90.3	92.9	95.1	98.8	103.1	103.2	102.6	97.9	93.9	92.6	93.3	96.1
2002	90.7	91.8	95.1	97.4	101.5	104.2	105.3	104.0	100.7	96.8	95.1	95.6	98.2
2003	92.1	91.5	94.4	99.4	102.8	107.3	107.6	107.8	103.0	98.4	96.9	97.5	99.8
2004	93.4	94.7	98.6	102.7	106.8	109.7	110.7	110.2	106.1	103.2	101.2	101.2	103.2
2005	96.2	97.3	100.7	105.0	108.4	111.5	111.9	110.7	107.8	102.9	102.7	102.5	104.8
2006	98.5	99.5	102.3	104.3	107.8	112.5	112.1	112.1	107.7	104.0	103.1	103.1	105.6
2007	99.8	99.0	101.4	105.4	110.8	113.7	113.8	113.5	108.7	106.2	104.9	105.1	106.9
Other Services													
2000	41.2	41.3	41.4	41.5	41.7	41.5	41.3	41.1	41.0	40.8	40.7	40.6	41.2
2001	39.9	40.1	40.4	40.5	41.0	41.3	40.8	41.1	40.2	40.3	40.3	40.3	40.5
2002	40.4	40.7	41.0	41.1	41.4	41.9	41.6	41.4	40.6	40.4	40.4	40.4	40.9
2003	41.1	41.4	42.0	42.2	42.6	42.8	42.6	42.5	42.0	42.0	41.9	42.1	42.1
2004	41.6	41.9	42.5	43.0	43.3	43.6	43.4	43.5	43.3	43.0	42.8	42.9	42.9
2005	42.0	42.3	42.7	43.2	43.3	43.4	43.2	43.0	42.7	42.7	42.6	42.7	42.8
2006	41.8	41.8	42.2	42.3	42.7	43.1	43.2	43.2	43.0	42.7	42.6	42.8	42.6
2007	42.3	42.3	43.0	42.9	43.3	44.0	43.8	44.1	43.2	43.0	42.9	43.1	43.2
Government													
2000	123.3	127.8	128.9	129.5	131.8	126.3	118.0	117.3	123.8	127.1	128.2	128.5	125.9
2001	126.2	129.7	130.5	131.3	131.9	127.3	119.3	120.3	127.4	130.1	131.2	131.4	128.1
2002	129.3	132.8	134.0	133.8	134.5	128.7	122.1	124.1	129.2	132.7	133.3	132.7	130.6
2003	132.0	134.6	135.9	136.5	136.7	131.2	123.6	126.7	132.2	135.9	136.3	136.0	133.1
2004	132.1	135.4	136.8	137.1	137.5	132.6	123.5	125.8	131.6	135.2	135.7	134.8	133.2
2005	131.1	134.0	135.0	135.4	135.9	131.7	123.3	125.1	131.6	134.9	135.4	134.7	132.3
2006	131.3	134.5	135.8	136.0	136.8	131.4	123.0	125.1	132.0	135.0	135.3	135.1	132.6
2007	132.2	135.2	136.5	136.7	137.4	131.9	123.7	125.4	131.0	135.2	135.2	134.8	132.9

Employment by Industry: Portland-Vancouver-Beaverton, OR-WA, 2000–2007

(Numbers in thousands, not seasonally adjusted.)

Industry and year	January	February	March	April	May	June	July	August	September	October	November	December	Annual Average
Total Nonfarm													
2000	945.6	954.0	957.6	964.3	972.2	978.8	973.7	974.6	981.7	987.1	994.5	995.2	973.3
2001	970.6	973.2	974.0	973.4	974.5	975.9	957.1	954.3	962.2	960.8	960.0	956.6	966.1
2002	935.6	939.3	942.0	945.3	948.8	952.0	934.9	935.1	944.9	951.4	952.0	948.3	944.1
2003	926.7	927.4	928.9	930.8	933.5	934.3	926.6	929.3	936.5	943.8	946.8	947.1	934.3
2004	919.3	929.7	937.6	947.3	953.6	959.1	954.8	955.8	963.6	973.4	976.6	978.2	954.1
2005	954.3	962.8	969.0	975.6	981.0	985.9	980.1	983.7	990.8	1,000.6	1,007.8	1,012.1	983.6
2006	986.1	995.1	1,001.8	1,008.8	1,016.3	1,021.3	1,012.1	1,013.5	1,022.4	1,031.7	1,037.3	1,037.6	1,015.3
2007	1,013.3	1,022.8	1,029.6	1,030.5	1,038.0	1,039.4	1,033.3	1,033.9	1,040.6	1,050.2	1,054.9	1,056.1	1,036.9
Total Private													
2000	816.5	822.4	825.5	831.7	836.6	844.6	849.1	853.1	856.8	854.6	860.9	861.7	842.8
2001	838.7	839.8	839.8	839.4	838.8	840.8	837.9	838.1	833.4	824.8	822.8	819.8	834.5
2002	801.1	802.2	804.0	807.2	809.5	812.6	814.3	817.6	815.7	814.5	813.6	811.1	810.3
2003	792.6	792.1	793.2	794.5	796.4	798.4	801.9	806.2	806.3	808.1	809.6	810.4	800.8
2004	784.7	792.9	799.5	809.1	814.9	819.7	825.3	828.9	830.3	834.0	836.5	838.4	817.9
2005	816.0	822.5	828.4	835.3	839.9	844.5	851.2	856.4	858.9	861.3	866.4	871.4	846.0
2006	847.8	854.7	860.3	867.3	872.9	878.3	881.5	885.4	888.8	890.6	893.7	895.4	876.4
2007	872.2	879.9	885.6	886.3	891.4	892.9	897.8	901.8	903.9	904.9	907.7	909.0	894.5
Goods-Producing													
2000	191.0	192.3	193.3	194.1	196.1	200.0	202.5	203.0	204.9	201.1	201.7	200.7	198.4
2001	197.0	196.1	194.2	192.9	192.1	193.5	194.8	194.2	191.5	187.8	183.8	180.9	191.6
2002	176.0	175.7	175.6	175.6	176.0	178.1	180.4	182.5	180.0	177.7	175.0	172.4	177.1
2003	169.5	168.0	167.6	166.8	167.8	169.7	171.7	173.5	172.4	171.4	170.2	169.8	169.9
2004	164.5	166.9	169.1	171.8	174.0	176.9	180.8	182.1	182.1	181.7	179.3	179.1	175.7
2005	176.1	177.0	178.6	179.8	181.4	183.9	187.6	188.9	188.0	188.6	187.0	187.4	183.7
2006	184.0	185.4	186.7	188.1	189.8	193.3	196.0	197.2	196.9	195.3	193.0	192.3	191.5
2007	188.9	190.0	191.0	190.2	192.3	193.2	196.8	198.0	197.3	195.7	193.7	192.7	193.3
Natural Resources and Mining													
2000	1.8	1.9	1.8	1.8	1.8	2.0	1.9	2.0	1.9	1.9	1.9	1.8	1.9
2001	1.7	1.7	1.7	1.7	1.7	1.8	1.8	1.8	1.8	1.8	1.7	1.6	1.7
2002	1.5	1.5	1.5	1.6	1.6	1.7	1.8	1.8	1.8	1.8	1.7	1.6	1.7
2003	1.6	1.6	1.6	1.6	1.6	1.7	1.7	1.7	1.8	1.7	1.7	1.7	1.7
2004	1.5	1.5	1.6	1.6	1.7	1.7	1.8	1.8	1.8	1.8	1.7	1.7	1.7
2005	1.7	1.7	1.7	1.7	1.8	1.8	1.9	1.9	1.8	1.8	1.8	1.7	1.8
2006	1.6	1.6	1.6	1.6	1.7	1.8	1.8	1.8	1.8	1.7	1.6	1.6	1.7
2007	1.5	1.6	1.6	1.6	1.7	1.7	1.7	1.7	1.7	1.7	1.6	1.6	1.6
Construction													
2000	48.7	49.3	49.9	50.9	51.8	53.5	55.3	56.6	57.1	56.1	54.9	54.2	53.2
2001	53.5	53.4	53.6	52.8	53.3	54.6	55.8	56.7	55.7	54.3	52.6	51.4	54.0
2002	49.3	49.6	49.9	50.1	50.8	51.8	53.6	55.3	54.2	53.5	51.6	49.6	51.6
2003	48.2	47.6	47.6	47.4	48.6	49.6	51.3	53.2	52.8	52.7	51.4	50.7	50.1
2004	47.4	49.0	50.2	51.8	53.3	55.0	56.8	57.8	57.5	57.1	55.8	55.2	53.9
2005	53.3	53.8	55.1	55.8	57.1	58.4	60.8	62.2	62.2	61.8	60.6	60.8	58.5
2006	58.3	59.4	60.1	61.0	62.2	64.3	65.6	66.7	66.6	65.9	64.5	63.7	63.2
2007	61.4	62.2	63.1	63.4	65.4	65.5	68.4	69.6	69.1	68.2	66.6	65.2	65.7
Manufacturing													
2000	140.5	141.1	141.6	141.4	142.5	144.5	145.3	144.4	145.9	143.1	144.9	144.7	143.3
2001	141.8	141.0	138.9	138.4	137.1	137.1	137.2	135.7	134.0	131.7	129.5	127.9	135.9
2002	125.2	124.6	124.2	123.9	123.6	124.6	125.0	125.4	124.0	122.4	121.7	121.2	123.8
2003	119.7	118.8	118.4	117.8	117.6	118.4	118.7	118.6	117.8	117.0	117.1	117.4	118.1
2004	115.6	116.4	117.3	118.4	119.0	120.2	122.2	122.5	122.8	122.8	121.8	122.2	120.1
2005	121.1	121.5	121.8	122.3	122.5	123.7	124.9	124.8	124.0	125.0	124.6	124.9	123.4
2006	124.1	124.4	125.0	125.5	125.9	127.2	128.6	128.7	128.5	127.7	126.9	127.0	126.6
2007	126.0	126.2	126.3	125.2	125.2	126.0	126.7	126.7	126.5	125.8	125.5	125.9	126.0
Service-Providing													
2000	754.6	761.7	764.3	770.2	776.1	778.8	771.2	771.6	776.8	786.0	792.8	794.5	774.9
2001	773.6	777.1	779.8	780.5	782.4	782.4	762.3	760.1	770.7	773.0	776.2	775.7	774.5
2002	759.6	763.6	766.4	769.7	772.8	773.9	754.5	752.6	764.9	773.7	777.0	775.9	767.1
2003	757.2	759.4	761.3	764.0	765.7	764.6	754.9	755.8	764.1	772.4	776.6	777.3	764.4
2004	754.8	762.8	768.5	775.5	779.6	782.2	774.0	773.7	781.5	791.7	797.3	799.1	778.4
2005	778.2	785.8	790.4	795.8	799.6	802.0	792.5	794.8	802.8	812.0	820.8	824.7	800.0
2006	802.1	809.7	815.1	820.7	826.5	828.0	816.1	816.3	825.5	836.4	844.3	845.3	823.8
2007	824.4	832.8	838.6	840.3	845.7	846.2	836.5	835.9	843.3	854.5	861.2	863.4	843.6
Trade, Transportation, and Utilities													
2000	197.3	196.3	196.4	197.8	198.7	201.2	201.6	202.0	201.4	202.7	207.3	209.1	201.0
2001	199.6	198.0	197.9	197.7	197.9	199.6	198.5	198.4	196.6	195.5	198.0	199.3	198.1
2002	191.6	189.9	190.1	190.8	191.9	193.0	193.4	192.6	192.0	191.8	194.8	197.1	192.4
2003	189.8	188.0	187.8	187.9	189.0	190.3	190.7	191.3	190.6	192.3	195.8	197.3	190.9
2004	189.1	188.4	188.9	190.5	191.5	193.2	194.1	194.5	193.8	195.5	199.7	201.8	193.4
2005	193.9	193.0	193.6	194.3	195.2	196.9	198.3	199.1	199.1	199.3	204.7	207.9	198.0
2006	199.0	198.0	198.5	199.2	200.9	202.3	203.0	203.5	203.2	203.5	208.3	211.2	202.6
2007	203.1	201.9	202.4	202.7	204.1	205.6	206.9	207.9	208.0	208.7	213.4	215.0	206.6
Wholesale Trade													
2000	54.1	54.3	54.4	54.9	55.2	55.5	56.1	56.4	56.1	56.5	56.7	56.8	55.6
2001	56.6	56.8	56.9	56.8	56.7	57.0	56.7	56.7	56.0	55.2	55.2	54.9	56.3
2002	54.4	54.3	54.2	54.5	54.6	54.7	55.0	55.1	54.8	54.6	54.7	54.7	54.6
2003	54.7	54.7	54.7	54.7	54.7	55.0	55.2	55.2	54.9	54.6	54.6	54.5	54.8
2004	54.1	54.5	54.5	54.8	55.0	55.3	55.9	55.9	55.3	55.2	55.4	55.5	55.1
2005	55.2	55.7	55.8	55.8	56.0	56.4	56.8	56.7	56.8	56.6	56.7	57.0	56.3
2006	56.2	56.7	56.7	57.2	57.6	57.8	58.0	58.2	57.7	57.8	57.9	58.0	57.5
2007	57.7	58.0	58.1	58.2	58.6	58.8	59.0	58.9	58.6	58.3	58.3	58.4	58.4

Employment by Industry: Portland-Vancouver-Beaverton, OR-WA, 2000–2007—*Continued*

(Numbers in thousands, not seasonally adjusted.)

Industry and year	January	February	March	April	May	June	July	August	September	October	November	December	Annual Average
Retail Trade													
2000	105.1	104.1	104.1	104.3	105.1	106.7	107.1	107.0	106.3	107.2	111.1	113.2	106.8
2001	105.3	103.3	103.0	102.7	102.4	103.8	103.2	102.7	101.8	101.5	104.5	106.3	103.4
2002	100.0	98.4	98.6	98.8	99.7	100.6	101.0	100.2	99.9	100.0	103.3	105.5	100.5
2003	98.6	97.3	97.1	97.2	98.1	99.0	99.4	99.7	99.0	100.4	103.9	105.5	99.6
2004	98.4	97.3	97.8	98.9	99.8	101.1	101.6	101.9	101.3	102.3	106.5	108.4	101.3
2005	102.4	100.8	101.1	101.7	102.6	103.7	105.0	105.8	105.4	106.4	110.6	112.7	104.9
2006	105.9	104.1	104.5	105.0	106.1	106.8	107.8	108.1	107.8	107.9	112.4	114.6	107.6
2007	108.1	106.5	106.7	107.0	107.8	109.0	110.2	111.1	110.9	111.7	116.3	117.6	110.2
Transportation and Utilities													
2000	38.1	37.9	37.9	38.6	38.4	39.0	38.4	38.6	39.0	39.0	39.5	39.1	38.6
2001	37.7	37.9	38.0	38.2	38.8	38.8	38.6	39.0	38.8	38.8	38.3	38.1	38.4
2002	37.2	37.2	37.3	37.5	37.6	37.7	37.4	37.3	37.3	37.2	36.8	36.9	37.3
2003	36.5	36.0	36.0	36.0	36.2	36.3	36.1	36.4	36.7	37.3	37.3	37.3	36.5
2004	36.6	36.6	36.6	36.8	36.7	36.8	36.6	36.7	37.2	38.0	37.8	37.9	37.0
2005	36.3	36.5	36.7	36.8	36.6	36.8	36.5	36.6	37.1	37.1	37.4	38.2	36.9
2006	36.9	37.2	37.3	37.0	37.2	37.7	37.2	37.2	37.7	37.8	38.0	38.6	37.5
2007	37.3	37.4	37.6	37.5	37.7	37.8	37.7	37.9	38.5	38.7	38.8	39.0	38.0
Information													
2000	24.7	24.9	25.0	25.3	25.5	25.8	26.4	26.6	26.8	26.7	26.8	27.0	26.0
2001	27.0	27.0	26.8	26.5	26.3	26.1	25.8	25.5	25.3	25.0	24.8	24.8	25.9
2002	24.6	24.5	24.3	24.0	23.9	23.9	23.6	23.6	23.4	23.4	23.4	23.3	23.8
2003	23.0	22.7	22.5	22.3	22.5	22.5	22.4	22.3	22.3	22.4	22.6	22.7	22.5
2004	22.5	22.5	22.6	22.4	22.4	22.5	22.6	22.6	22.4	22.3	22.5	22.6	22.5
2005	22.5	22.6	22.6	22.8	23.0	23.2	23.3	23.3	23.3	23.3	23.5	23.7	23.1
2006	23.5	23.6	23.7	23.6	23.7	23.8	24.5	24.2	24.3	24.5	24.1	24.3	24.0
2007	24.2	24.4	24.6	24.7	24.9	24.9	25.0	25.0	24.8	24.8	24.8	24.8	24.7
Financial Activities													
2000	64.6	64.7	64.4	64.7	64.8	65.1	65.4	65.2	64.9	64.6	64.6	65.1	64.8
2001	64.3	64.6	65.0	65.0	65.1	65.3	65.5	65.3	65.1	64.9	65.1	65.3	65.0
2002	64.9	65.0	64.8	64.9	65.0	65.3	65.8	66.0	65.8	66.2	66.4	66.8	65.6
2003	66.8	66.9	67.3	67.4	67.1	67.0	66.6	66.7	66.0	65.5	65.0	64.9	66.4
2004	65.0	65.1	65.3	65.8	65.9	66.3	66.5	66.6	66.4	66.4	66.7	66.9	66.1
2005	66.4	66.6	66.7	67.2	67.7	68.2	68.8	69.1	69.1	69.3	69.7	70.0	68.2
2006	69.3	69.5	69.7	70.1	70.3	70.7	71.3	71.5	71.4	71.2	71.3	71.4	70.6
2007	70.9	71.3	71.6	71.6	71.8	72.1	72.2	71.9	71.4	71.1	70.9	71.0	71.5
Professional and Business Services													
2000	124.0	125.6	126.4	128.1	128.8	130.9	132.4	133.9	133.7	134.2	134.3	133.4	130.5
2001	129.8	130.2	130.9	130.5	129.4	129.3	127.7	127.5	126.3	124.8	123.9	122.4	127.7
2002	120.9	121.1	121.4	121.8	121.4	122.2	123.0	123.6	123.0	122.3	120.6	118.9	121.7
2003	115.4	116.2	116.2	116.8	116.7	117.0	118.9	119.5	120.1	119.9	119.2	119.0	117.9
2004	114.7	116.3	117.8	119.9	121.1	122.9	124.6	125.4	124.5	126.3	126.2	125.9	122.1
2005	121.6	123.4	124.8	126.9	127.1	128.8	130.4	131.6	131.7	131.9	132.0	132.2	128.5
2006	128.3	130.2	131.3	132.9	133.9	135.9	136.2	137.3	137.7	138.3	138.2	136.5	134.7
2007	132.5	133.8	135.5	135.7	135.6	136.6	136.7	138.0	138.2	138.1	137.0	137.6	136.3
Education and Health Services													
2000	101.0	103.1	103.3	103.5	102.9	100.2	98.7	99.4	103.5	106.1	106.7	106.7	102.9
2001	104.4	106.5	106.9	107.3	106.8	105.2	103.1	103.6	106.6	108.6	109.6	109.6	106.5
2002	108.1	110.3	111.2	112.0	111.6	109.2	107.4	107.7	110.8	114.1	114.9	114.4	111.0
2003	112.2	114.2	114.6	114.9	114.3	111.7	109.8	109.8	113.1	115.8	116.4	116.5	113.6
2004	112.5	115.7	116.5	116.9	116.2	113.4	111.7	111.6	116.2	118.6	119.3	119.2	115.7
2005	116.5	119.7	120.4	120.9	120.3	116.9	115.5	116.1	120.6	123.1	123.9	124.1	119.8
2006	120.1	123.5	124.3	124.9	124.1	120.6	118.0	118.5	122.9	126.6	127.6	127.8	123.2
2007	124.0	128.0	128.9	129.1	128.6	125.0	123.1	123.0	127.3	130.3	131.5	131.5	127.5
Leisure and Hospitality													
2000	81.7	82.8	83.5	85.0	86.2	87.8	88.7	89.4	87.7	85.5	85.5	85.8	85.8
2001	83.2	83.5	83.9	85.2	86.7	87.1	88.3	89.3	87.6	84.0	83.5	83.5	85.5
2002	81.3	81.7	82.5	84.0	85.6	87.0	87.0	88.0	87.0	85.0	84.4	84.5	84.8
2003	82.3	82.3	83.3	84.5	84.9	86.4	87.9	89.0	87.5	86.6	86.3	86.1	85.6
2004	82.9	83.8	84.6	87.0	88.8	89.3	89.9	91.1	89.7	88.2	88.0	88.5	87.7
2005	85.4	86.1	87.5	89.0	90.6	92.0	92.5	93.5	92.2	90.3	90.8	91.3	90.1
2006	89.3	89.7	91.0	93.1	94.3	95.5	96.4	97.3	96.5	95.2	95.2	95.7	94.1
2007	93.0	94.2	95.2	96.0	97.5	98.6	100.3	101.1	99.9	99.1	99.4	99.6	97.8
Other Services													
2000	32.2	32.7	33.2	33.2	33.6	33.6	33.4	33.6	33.9	33.7	34.0	33.9	33.4
2001	33.4	33.9	34.2	34.3	34.5	34.7	34.2	34.3	34.4	34.2	34.1	34.0	34.2
2002	33.7	34.0	34.1	34.1	34.1	33.9	33.7	33.6	33.7	34.0	34.1	33.7	33.9
2003	33.6	33.8	33.9	33.9	34.1	33.8	33.9	34.2	34.3	34.2	34.1	34.1	34.0
2004	33.5	34.2	34.7	34.8	35.0	35.2	35.1	35.0	35.2	35.0	34.8	34.4	34.7
2005	33.6	34.1	34.2	34.4	34.6	34.6	34.8	34.8	34.7	34.7	34.8	34.8	34.5
2006	34.3	34.8	35.1	35.4	35.9	36.2	36.1	35.9	35.9	36.0	36.0	36.2	35.7
2007	35.6	36.3	36.4	36.3	36.6	36.9	36.8	36.9	37.0	37.1	37.0	36.8	36.6
Government													
2000	129.1	131.6	132.1	132.6	135.6	134.2	124.6	121.5	124.9	132.5	133.6	133.5	130.5
2001	131.9	133.4	134.2	134.0	135.7	135.1	119.2	116.2	128.8	136.0	137.2	136.8	131.5
2002	134.5	137.1	138.0	138.1	139.3	139.4	120.6	117.5	129.2	136.9	138.4	137.2	133.9
2003	134.1	135.3	135.7	136.3	137.1	135.9	124.7	123.1	130.2	135.7	137.2	136.7	133.5
2004	134.6	136.8	138.1	138.2	138.7	139.4	129.5	126.9	133.3	139.4	140.1	139.8	136.2
2005	138.3	140.3	140.6	140.3	141.1	141.4	128.9	127.3	131.9	139.3	141.4	140.7	137.6
2006	138.3	140.4	141.5	141.5	143.4	143.0	130.6	128.1	133.6	141.1	143.6	142.2	138.9
2007	141.1	142.9	144.0	144.2	146.6	146.5	135.5	132.1	136.7	145.3	147.2	147.1	142.4

Employment by Industry: Kansas City, MO-KS, 2000–2007

(Numbers in thousands, not seasonally adjusted.)

Industry and year	January	February	March	April	May	June	July	August	September	October	November	December	Annual Average
Total Nonfarm													
2000	963.9	966.8	977.1	984.5	988.2	996.9	965.7	973.7	987.2	988.5	986.3	987.9	980.6
2001	970.0	971.6	980.8	983.1	987.2	992.7	960.2	967.1	976.5	975.7	973.0	973.5	976.0
2002	955.9	954.9	964.8	973.7	977.2	979.4	944.0	949.4	960.3	959.7	964.5	966.6	962.5
2003	945.9	946.0	951.4	959.3	963.6	969.4	948.7	953.4	963.7	966.3	967.3	968.3	958.6
2004	944.7	942.8	955.7	969.5	973.0	979.8	964.4	964.1	974.3	978.6	979.8	981.5	967.4
2005	955.0	960.8	972.6	983.0	986.0	990.7	972.9	974.1	984.1	986.1	990.2	992.3	979.0
2006	970.8	975.7	985.1	994.9	999.7	1,004.7	986.3	990.5	1,002.0	1,001.7	1,007.1	1,011.0	994.1
2007	988.3	991.6	1,007.1	1,013.4	1,019.6	1,024.7	1,015.8	1,018.4	1,022.3	1,022.4	1,026.7	1,024.3	1,014.6
Total Private													
2000	828.4	828.0	836.9	844.2	848.3	856.7	846.5	851.1	849.8	849.7	846.2	847.7	844.5
2001	829.3	828.7	836.9	839.5	843.3	850.3	837.8	842.2	837.5	834.4	830.8	830.1	836.7
2002	813.6	811.7	820.2	829.4	832.6	836.3	820.9	824.1	821.0	817.9	821.9	822.8	822.7
2003	803.4	801.0	805.3	812.5	816.9	824.0	816.7	823.4	821.3	822.3	823.1	824.0	816.2
2004	802.4	798.1	810.1	822.4	826.4	833.8	827.3	830.3	829.7	833.8	834.2	835.9	823.7
2005	811.8	814.7	824.9	834.0	838.7	845.3	837.7	841.6	839.7	840.8	843.8	845.9	834.9
2006	826.7	827.2	835.5	846.0	850.3	857.8	851.5	857.3	854.5	853.2	857.6	862.5	848.3
2007	841.0	840.6	854.6	859.4	866.3	872.8	871.2	874.7	871.8	871.3	874.3	872.4	864.2
Goods-Producing													
2000	142.4	142.1	143.2	145.0	146.0	148.7	143.2	147.1	145.9	145.4	143.8	142.3	144.6
2001	138.2	138.0	140.4	142.3	143.5	145.8	140.8	144.4	142.9	140.2	139.3	138.1	141.2
2002	133.0	131.9	133.5	135.2	135.9	137.7	133.6	137.5	135.6	134.6	133.7	133.0	134.6
2003	130.2	130.3	132.2	132.5	134.7	135.7	131.0	136.0	135.4	135.6	134.8	132.7	133.4
2004	129.5	126.9	131.3	134.6	135.3	138.0	134.5	137.7	137.4	137.5	136.9	136.2	134.7
2005	129.3	130.5	134.2	135.9	137.4	139.1	135.4	138.7	137.8	137.7	137.7	136.7	135.9
2006	133.4	133.8	136.7	137.9	138.8	141.8	137.4	140.7	137.7	136.8	138.3	138.2	137.6
2007	133.0	130.4	135.2	135.4	136.7	138.2	136.0	138.1	137.7	137.4	137.3	134.7	135.8
Natural Resources, Mining, and Construction													
2000	48.2	48.1	49.0	50.6	51.5	53.4	53.3	53.5	52.4	52.2	50.8	48.8	51.0
2001	46.4	45.9	48.2	50.6	51.8	53.6	53.8	53.4	52.1	50.8	50.6	49.8	50.6
2002	46.8	46.1	48.1	49.3	50.1	51.9	52.6	52.6	51.4	51.0	50.4	49.9	50.0
2003	47.6	47.5	48.8	50.9	51.6	52.6	52.9	52.9	52.3	52.5	51.5	49.3	50.9
2004	46.3	44.3	48.0	50.7	51.3	52.9	53.8	53.6	53.2	53.4	52.2	51.5	50.9
2005	46.1	47.2	50.3	52.0	53.6	55.1	55.9	55.7	55.1	54.8	54.2	53.0	52.8
2006	51.3	51.8	53.4	54.5	55.1	56.9	56.0	56.0	55.7	54.5	53.9	53.3	54.4
2007	50.3	47.8	51.9	52.6	53.9	55.0	55.8	55.4	55.2	55.3	54.6	52.4	53.4
Manufacturing													
2000	94.2	94.0	94.2	94.4	94.5	95.3	89.9	93.6	93.5	93.2	93.0	93.5	93.6
2001	91.8	92.1	92.2	91.7	91.7	92.2	87.0	91.0	90.8	89.4	88.7	88.3	90.6
2002	86.2	85.8	85.4	85.9	85.8	85.8	81.0	84.9	84.2	83.6	83.3	83.1	84.6
2003	82.6	82.8	83.4	81.6	83.1	83.1	78.1	83.1	83.1	83.1	83.3	83.4	82.6
2004	83.2	82.6	83.3	83.9	84.0	85.1	80.7	84.1	84.2	84.1	84.7	84.7	83.7
2005	83.2	83.3	83.9	83.9	83.8	84.0	79.5	83.0	82.7	82.9	83.5	83.7	83.1
2006	82.1	82.0	83.3	83.4	83.7	84.9	81.4	84.7	82.0	82.3	84.4	84.9	83.3
2007	82.7	82.6	83.3	82.8	82.8	83.2	80.2	82.7	82.5	82.1	82.7	82.3	82.5
Service-Providing													
2000	821.5	824.7	833.9	839.5	842.2	848.2	822.5	826.6	841.3	843.1	842.5	845.6	836.0
2001	831.8	833.6	840.4	840.8	843.7	846.9	819.4	822.7	833.6	835.5	833.7	835.4	834.8
2002	822.9	823.0	831.3	838.5	841.3	841.7	810.4	811.9	824.7	825.1	830.8	833.6	827.9
2003	815.7	815.7	819.2	826.8	828.9	833.6	817.6	817.4	828.3	830.7	832.5	835.6	825.1
2004	815.2	815.9	824.4	834.9	837.7	841.8	829.9	826.4	836.9	841.1	842.9	845.3	832.7
2005	825.7	830.3	838.4	847.1	848.6	851.6	837.5	835.4	846.3	848.4	852.5	855.6	843.1
2006	837.4	841.9	848.4	857.0	860.9	862.9	848.9	849.8	864.3	864.9	868.8	872.8	856.5
2007	855.3	861.2	871.9	878.0	882.9	886.5	879.8	880.3	884.6	885.0	889.4	889.6	878.7
Trade, Transportation, and Utilities													
2000	206.8	204.8	205.5	208.3	209.5	208.0	206.0	206.1	208.7	209.8	213.4	214.9	208.5
2001	207.7	205.3	205.4	205.8	207.2	206.2	204.8	205.3	206.5	207.1	209.2	210.0	206.7
2002	204.4	201.7	203.5	204.2	205.0	203.6	200.4	200.3	201.2	202.6	206.5	207.7	203.4
2003	200.4	198.8	199.1	199.0	199.1	199.9	199.3	201.1	201.9	203.9	207.4	209.2	201.6
2004	200.6	198.5	199.6	201.0	202.4	202.5	200.8	200.6	201.8	204.7	208.5	211.2	202.7
2005	202.5	201.1	202.2	202.5	203.6	203.6	201.5	201.8	202.2	204.3	208.3	210.5	203.7
2006	203.5	201.9	203.1	203.6	204.6	204.6	202.8	203.9	205.1	205.7	209.4	212.2	205.0
2007	204.9	204.0	206.0	206.4	207.4	207.6	207.3	207.7	208.3	208.9	212.1	213.6	207.9
Wholesale Trade													
2000	48.9	48.7	48.9	50.0	50.0	50.2	50.1	49.7	50.1	49.5	49.7	49.8	49.6
2001	49.5	49.3	49.3	49.5	49.4	49.5	49.0	48.5	48.6	48.7	48.2	48.2	49.0
2002	48.8	48.6	48.7	48.9	48.5	48.6	47.5	47.6	47.2	47.2	47.2	47.3	48.0
2003	47.3	47.5	47.4	47.2	47.1	47.3	47.0	47.0	46.5	46.6	46.5	46.5	47.0
2004	45.4	45.5	46.0	46.3	46.5	46.8	47.1	47.0	46.8	47.5	47.6	47.9	46.7
2005	48.1	48.2	48.5	49.3	49.4	49.6	49.3	49.4	49.2	49.0	49.3	49.4	49.1
2006	48.8	48.8	49.1	48.7	49.1	49.4	49.2	49.5	49.5	49.9	50.0	50.7	49.4
2007	50.2	50.4	51.1	50.6	50.8	51.2	51.5	51.6	51.6	51.8	51.9	52.1	51.2
Retail Trade													
2000	110.0	108.4	108.8	109.5	110.1	110.4	109.1	109.5	109.3	110.6	114.3	116.0	110.5
2001	110.5	108.8	108.7	108.7	109.6	110.2	109.7	110.4	109.9	110.7	113.5	114.9	110.5
2002	109.1	107.2	108.8	108.7	109.6	110.0	109.0	109.0	109.1	109.5	113.4	115.1	109.9
2003	108.2	106.5	107.0	106.8	107.2	107.9	108.3	109.4	110.0	111.5	115.0	116.6	109.6
2004	110.7	108.4	109.0	109.1	110.0	110.4	109.7	109.2	109.9	110.9	114.6	116.9	110.7
2005	110.2	108.5	109.0	108.8	109.3	109.4	108.9	108.2	107.9	109.5	113.0	114.6	109.8
2006	108.8	107.4	108.2	108.5	109.0	109.2	108.3	108.3	108.2	108.3	111.8	113.2	109.1
2007	107.4	106.5	107.6	108.0	108.5	108.8	108.5	108.0	107.4	107.5	110.7	112.0	108.4

Employment by Industry: Kansas City, MO-KS, 2000–2007—*Continued*

(Numbers in thousands, not seasonally adjusted.)

Industry and year	January	February	March	April	May	June	July	August	September	October	November	December	Annual Average
Transportation and Utilities													
2000	47.9	47.7	47.8	48.8	49.4	47.4	46.8	46.9	49.3	49.7	49.4	49.1	48.4
2001	47.7	47.2	47.4	47.6	48.2	46.5	46.1	46.4	48.0	47.7	47.5	46.9	47.3
2002	46.5	45.9	46.0	46.6	46.9	45.0	43.9	43.7	44.9	45.9	45.9	45.3	45.5
2003	44.9	44.8	44.7	45.0	44.8	44.7	44.0	44.7	45.4	45.8	45.9	46.1	45.0
2004	44.5	44.6	44.6	45.6	45.9	45.3	44.0	45.1	46.3	46.3	46.3	46.4	45.3
2005	44.2	44.4	44.7	44.4	44.9	44.6	43.3	44.2	45.1	45.8	46.0	46.5	44.8
2006	45.9	45.7	45.8	46.4	46.5	46.0	45.3	46.2	47.3	47.4	47.6	48.3	46.5
2007	47.3	47.1	47.3	47.8	48.1	47.6	47.3	48.1	49.3	49.6	49.5	49.5	48.2
Information													
2000	53.4	55.2	55.3	55.6	55.7	56.4	57.4	57.4	57.3	56.3	56.3	56.1	56.0
2001	55.1	54.6	54.1	54.0	53.3	55.0	53.9	54.0	53.6	52.6	52.9	51.5	53.7
2002	51.0	51.3	51.6	50.8	51.7	52.0	51.3	50.9	50.1	48.6	49.8	50.3	50.8
2003	49.1	48.5	48.3	48.5	48.2	48.5	47.7	47.6	46.9	46.8	46.6	46.7	47.8
2004	46.5	46.1	45.8	45.8	45.7	45.8	45.4	45.3	44.7	43.6	43.8	43.3	45.2
2005	43.2	43.1	43.1	43.0	42.9	43.1	43.1	42.8	42.3	42.0	41.1	40.9	42.4
2006	40.9	40.8	41.1	42.4	42.4	42.8	42.8	42.6	42.6	42.6	41.6	40.8	42.4
2007	42.2	42.1	42.0	42.0	42.1	42.2	42.2	42.6	42.4	42.0	41.8	42.2	42.2
Financial Activities													
2000	69.8	69.6	70.2	69.4	69.7	70.5	70.4	70.3	69.8	70.4	70.6	71.1	70.2
2001	70.4	70.6	71.1	71.0	71.3	71.7	71.7	71.7	71.1	71.2	71.2	71.6	71.2
2002	71.7	71.5	71.7	72.4	72.6	72.6	72.8	72.3	71.8	71.8	72.0	72.3	72.1
2003	70.9	70.9	70.9	71.1	71.0	71.3	71.3	71.5	70.8	70.5	70.2	70.3	70.9
2004	68.7	68.6	69.2	68.9	68.9	69.9	70.1	69.9	69.6	69.8	69.8	70.3	69.5
2005	70.0	70.1	70.3	70.8	71.0	71.4	71.8	71.6	71.4	71.6	71.7	72.2	71.2
2006	72.0	72.2	72.2	72.5	73.0	73.4	74.1	73.9	73.6	73.1	73.4	73.9	73.1
2007	73.5	73.8	74.5	73.9	74.0	74.7	76.2	76.0	75.6	75.4	75.6	75.4	74.9
Professional and Business Services													
2000	135.0	133.9	137.4	136.8	136.4	138.4	135.7	136.6	136.3	136.6	134.2	135.2	136.0
2001	133.5	134.2	136.2	133.2	133.1	133.4	129.6	130.1	130.0	128.8	126.6	127.2	131.3
2002	124.6	126.0	127.2	127.9	127.1	126.8	122.2	121.8	121.8	121.4	121.6	122.0	124.2
2003	119.9	119.5	119.5	122.0	122.0	124.3	123.2	123.6	123.5	124.2	126.5	126.5	122.6
2004	124.1	124.7	127.6	130.1	129.7	131.5	130.8	131.5	131.9	133.0	133.3	133.7	130.2
2005	131.1	132.9	135.2	137.3	137.0	138.8	138.8	139.6	139.8	139.8	140.8	142.0	137.8
2006	135.9	137.6	139.2	141.1	140.4	141.9	141.6	142.6	143.0	144.8	145.3	146.3	141.6
2007	142.7	143.7	145.7	146.2	147.4	149.3	149.0	150.1	150.6	150.5	150.5	150.9	148.1
Education and Health Services													
2000	98.7	99.7	99.6	100.2	100.1	100.2	100.7	100.2	101.1	101.2	101.5	101.7	100.4
2001	100.5	101.9	102.4	103.0	103.0	103.4	103.4	102.6	103.3	103.3	104.2	104.4	102.9
2002	103.5	104.1	104.5	105.8	106.2	106.4	105.7	106.1	106.7	107.2	107.6	107.7	106.0
2003	106.5	106.7	106.7	108.0	108.4	107.3	107.6	107.1	108.3	108.6	108.8	108.5	107.7
2004	107.0	107.8	108.0	109.0	109.1	108.6	109.1	108.8	109.8	111.2	111.1	110.7	109.2
2005	109.6	110.4	110.4	111.5	111.8	111.5	110.7	110.7	111.8	112.9	113.1	113.2	111.5
2006	111.6	112.7	112.7	114.0	114.3	114.1	114.1	114.1	114.2	115.8	116.4	116.8	114.5
2007	115.4	116.7	117.4	118.2	118.6	118.4	118.6	118.8	119.6	120.1	120.9	120.6	118.6
Leisure and Hospitality													
2000	84.3	84.5	86.4	89.6	91.6	93.7	92.7	93.2	91.4	90.7	87.6	86.6	89.4
2001	84.5	84.5	87.1	89.9	91.4	93.1	93.1	92.9	90.2	90.7	87.7	86.8	89.3
2002	85.1	85.0	87.3	91.2	92.3	93.7	92.4	93.3	91.3	90.1	89.0	87.6	89.8
2003	85.0	85.1	87.1	90.0	91.9	94.8	94.2	92.9	93.3	92.6	90.3	87.6	90.7
2004	86.1	85.7	88.5	92.6	95.0	96.7	95.9	96.1	94.4	93.7	90.8	89.4	92.2
2005	86.4	86.7	89.3	93.3	95.4	97.7	96.3	96.6	94.8	93.9	90.5	91.1	92.8
2006	88.7	88.7	91.0	94.8	96.9	98.9	98.6	99.2	96.9	95.2	91.9	92.8	94.6
2007	89.8	90.2	93.8	96.0	98.5	100.4	99.0	99.4	96.3	95.8	94.2	93.1	95.5
Other Services													
2000	38.0	38.2	39.3	39.3	39.3	40.8	40.4	40.2	39.3	39.3	38.8	39.8	39.4
2001	39.4	39.6	40.2	40.3	40.5	41.7	41.5	40.6	39.9	40.5	39.7	40.5	40.4
2002	40.3	40.2	40.9	41.9	41.8	43.5	42.5	42.3	42.5	41.6	41.7	42.2	41.8
2003	41.4	41.2	41.5	41.4	41.6	42.2	42.4	42.0	41.2	41.0	40.8	40.7	41.4
2004	39.9	39.8	40.1	40.4	40.3	40.8	40.7	40.4	40.1	40.3	40.0	40.0	40.2
2005	39.7	39.9	40.2	39.7	39.6	40.1	40.4	40.3	39.9	39.5	39.4	39.4	39.8
2006	40.7	39.5	39.5	39.7	39.9	40.3	40.3	40.2	39.8	39.6	39.6	39.6	39.9
2007	39.5	39.7	40.0	41.3	41.6	42.0	42.5	42.2	41.7	41.4	41.3	41.4	41.2
Government													
2000	135.5	138.8	140.2	140.3	139.9	140.2	119.2	122.6	137.4	138.8	140.1	140.2	136.1
2001	140.7	142.9	143.9	143.6	143.9	142.4	122.4	124.9	139.0	141.3	142.2	143.4	139.2
2002	142.3	143.2	144.6	144.3	144.6	143.1	123.1	125.3	139.3	141.8	142.6	143.8	139.8
2003	142.5	145.0	146.1	146.8	146.8	145.4	132.0	130.2	142.4	140.0	144.2	144.3	142.5
2004	142.3	144.7	145.6	147.1	146.6	146.0	137.1	133.8	144.6	144.8	145.6	145.6	143.7
2005	143.2	146.1	147.7	149.0	147.3	145.4	135.2	132.5	144.4	145.3	146.4	146.4	144.1
2006	144.1	148.5	149.6	148.9	149.4	146.9	134.8	133.2	147.5	148.5	149.5	148.5	145.8
2007	147.3	151.0	152.5	154.0	153.3	151.9	144.6	143.7	150.5	151.1	152.4	151.9	150.4

Employment by Industry: Sacramento–Arden-Arcade–Roseville, CA, 2000–2007

(Numbers in thousands, not seasonally adjusted.)

Industry and year	January	February	March	April	May	June	July	August	September	October	November	December	Annual Average
Total Nonfarm													
2000	773.3	778.7	786.0	789.5	795.9	805.6	795.2	803.6	804.5	804.0	811.8	818.2	797.2
2001	799.6	803.4	813.3	814.7	817.3	824.1	820.2	824.1	822.7	824.1	829.9	832.9	818.9
2002	814.8	817.1	827.6	826.9	833.6	837.7	832.1	834.6	836.7	839.0	842.7	843.5	832.2
2003	831.6	833.0	837.7	842.5	847.7	853.9	847.0	848.7	850.2	847.7	855.6	856.7	846.0
2004	843.3	845.5	850.3	856.4	859.5	866.0	861.1	858.8	864.0	865.2	868.0	870.7	859.1
2005	861.4	865.1	870.6	874.9	879.2	883.5	882.7	883.1	887.8	889.3	894.6	898.6	880.9
2006	888.0	891.7	893.3	890.1	899.8	907.6	900.6	901.5	903.9	901.5	904.3	905.9	899.0
2007	892.7	895.9	902.8	900.3	906.8	911.0	905.0	904.2	903.9	905.9	909.1	910.4	904.0
Total Private													
2000	567.0	569.5	574.1	577.7	580.6	589.8	590.8	596.5	596.1	592.0	598.9	605.5	586.5
2001	588.4	590.2	596.3	596.8	599.0	605.2	605.9	607.7	602.7	602.2	605.9	608.9	600.8
2002	592.8	593.3	598.4	597.6	603.0	608.0	608.5	610.2	610.6	611.4	614.7	616.0	605.4
2003	606.6	606.1	610.0	614.5	617.5	625.0	622.7	626.1	625.6	624.3	627.8	632.3	619.9
2004	620.8	622.4	627.3	632.8	635.1	641.1	643.5	643.6	644.7	643.8	645.3	649.6	637.5
2005	639.6	642.3	646.6	649.8	653.0	657.4	661.7	663.4	663.8	663.9	668.3	672.5	656.9
2006	662.9	664.4	664.7	661.1	670.1	676.8	675.0	678.4	676.7	671.8	672.6	673.2	670.6
2007	661.3	663.0	666.8	664.2	669.1	672.1	673.7	673.1	669.8	669.6	671.6	672.8	668.9
Goods-Producing													
2000	95.5	95.7	97.2	98.2	100.8	103.1	103.6	105.7	104.7	104.1	103.8	103.4	101.3
2001	99.4	99.7	101.9	103.6	106.2	108.5	109.0	109.5	108.5	107.5	105.6	103.5	105.2
2002	99.0	99.0	100.3	101.7	104.1	105.3	105.8	107.7	107.6	107.9	106.3	104.5	104.1
2003	100.8	101.8	103.7	105.3	107.7	111.0	110.8	113.5	113.9	113.5	111.5	109.9	108.6
2004	107.5	107.8	110.6	111.8	113.6	116.5	117.5	119.0	118.7	117.3	114.8	113.8	114.1
2005	110.8	112.0	113.7	114.5	116.1	118.0	119.8	121.7	122.0	121.0	119.1	117.4	117.2
2006	113.0	113.1	111.3	109.3	114.4	117.2	116.8	119.0	119.0	115.1	112.2	109.6	114.2
2007	107.2	107.4	108.5	108.1	110.8	112.1	111.2	111.6	109.9	108.2	106.2	104.6	108.8
Natural Resources and Mining													
2000	0.8	0.8	0.8	0.9	0.9	0.9	0.9	0.9	0.9	0.9	0.9	0.9	0.9
2001	0.8	0.8	0.8	0.9	0.9	0.9	0.9	0.9	0.9	0.9	0.8	0.8	0.9
2002	0.7	0.7	0.8	0.8	0.8	0.8	0.8	0.8	0.8	0.8	0.8	0.8	0.8
2003	0.6	0.6	0.6	0.6	0.6	0.7	0.7	0.7	0.7	0.7	0.7	0.7	0.6
2004	0.6	0.6	0.7	0.7	0.7	0.7	0.8	0.7	0.8	0.8	0.7	0.7	0.7
2005	0.7	0.7	0.7	0.7	0.7	0.7	0.8	0.8	0.7	0.7	0.7	0.7	0.7
2006	0.7	0.7	0.7	0.6	0.6	0.8	0.7	0.8	0.8	0.7	0.7	0.7	0.7
2007	0.6	0.6	0.6	0.6	0.7	0.7	0.8	0.8	0.8	0.8	0.8	0.8	0.7
Construction													
2000	47.7	47.3	48.5	50.9	52.9	55.2	55.1	56.2	56.3	55.7	55.6	55.2	53.1
2001	53.0	53.4	55.5	57.9	60.1	62.2	62.8	64.1	63.2	62.2	60.9	58.9	59.5
2002	55.8	56.5	57.6	58.8	61.0	62.3	63.1	64.9	64.9	64.6	64.1	62.3	61.3
2003	60.1	60.9	62.7	64.2	66.1	68.2	68.3	70.0	70.2	70.4	69.2	67.5	66.5
2004	65.3	65.8	68.5	69.6	70.9	73.2	73.5	74.2	73.5	73.2	71.3	70.3	70.8
2005	67.8	68.9	70.4	71.8	73.1	74.8	76.0	76.5	76.6	76.5	75.2	73.2	73.4
2006	69.5	69.6	67.9	66.1	71.1	73.3	73.4	74.6	74.3	71.4	69.7	67.1	70.7
2007	65.7	65.7	67.0	66.8	69.1	70.1	69.6	69.9	68.2	67.2	65.8	64.3	67.5
Manufacturing													
2000	47.0	47.6	47.9	46.4	47.0	47.0	47.6	48.6	47.5	47.5	47.3	47.3	47.4
2001	45.6	45.5	45.6	44.8	45.2	45.4	45.3	44.5	44.4	44.4	43.9	43.8	44.9
2002	42.5	41.8	41.9	42.1	42.3	42.2	41.9	42.0	41.9	42.5	41.4	41.4	42.0
2003	40.1	40.3	40.4	40.5	41.0	42.1	41.8	42.8	43.0	42.4	41.6	41.7	41.5
2004	41.6	41.4	41.4	41.5	42.0	42.6	43.2	44.1	44.4	43.3	42.8	42.8	42.6
2005	42.3	42.4	42.6	42.0	42.3	42.5	43.0	44.4	44.7	43.8	43.2	43.5	43.1
2006	42.8	42.8	42.7	42.6	42.7	43.1	42.7	43.6	43.9	43.0	41.8	41.8	42.8
2007	40.9	41.1	40.9	40.7	41.0	41.3	40.8	40.9	40.9	40.2	39.6	39.5	40.7
Service-Providing													
2000	677.8	683.0	688.8	691.3	695.1	702.5	691.6	697.9	699.8	699.9	708.0	714.8	695.9
2001	700.2	703.7	711.4	711.1	711.1	715.6	711.2	714.6	714.2	716.6	724.3	729.4	713.6
2002	715.8	718.1	727.3	725.2	729.5	732.4	726.3	726.9	729.1	731.1	736.4	739.0	728.1
2003	730.8	731.2	734.0	737.2	740.0	742.9	736.2	735.2	736.3	734.2	744.1	746.8	737.4
2004	735.8	737.7	739.7	744.6	745.9	749.5	743.6	739.8	745.3	747.9	753.2	756.9	745.0
2005	750.6	753.1	756.9	760.4	763.1	765.5	762.9	761.4	765.8	768.3	775.5	781.2	763.7
2006	775.0	778.6	782.0	780.8	785.4	790.4	783.8	782.5	784.9	786.4	792.1	796.3	784.9
2007	785.5	788.5	794.3	792.2	796.0	798.9	793.8	792.6	794.0	797.7	802.9	805.8	795.2
Trade, Transportation, and Utilities													
2000	136.7	135.2	135.3	135.9	135.9	137.0	137.6	139.4	139.8	139.6	144.6	147.3	138.7
2001	139.9	138.0	138.5	138.3	138.6	140.3	139.9	140.2	140.9	141.4	144.7	146.5	140.6
2002	138.5	137.4	138.5	138.6	139.0	140.2	140.3	140.5	140.7	141.8	145.0	146.8	140.6
2003	141.6	139.6	139.6	140.2	140.8	142.3	142.9	143.5	143.3	144.5	148.4	150.9	143.1
2004	144.1	143.1	143.0	143.9	144.8	145.9	145.8	145.7	145.8	147.5	151.0	152.3	146.1
2005	147.0	145.9	146.2	146.2	146.7	147.2	148.4	148.7	149.1	150.1	154.1	157.5	148.9
2006	151.2	149.9	150.8	150.4	151.8	153.1	154.3	155.1	154.4	154.6	157.8	159.9	153.6
2007	153.9	152.2	152.0	151.2	151.9	152.3	153.0	152.8	152.6	154.0	156.9	158.3	153.4
Wholesale Trade													
2000	24.4	24.6	24.8	25.2	25.2	25.5	25.2	25.3	25.3	25.5	25.4	25.2	25.1
2001	25.0	25.3	25.4	25.7	25.7	25.9	25.9	26.1	26.0	26.0	26.1	26.1	25.8
2002	25.3	25.5	25.7	25.5	25.6	25.5	25.5	25.6	25.5	25.7	25.8	25.7	25.6
2003	25.9	26.0	26.0	26.2	26.2	26.3	26.3	26.4	26.4	26.4	26.5	26.6	26.3
2004	26.3	26.4	26.4	26.3	26.4	26.6	26.7	26.8	26.7	26.6	26.5	26.6	26.5
2005	26.4	26.5	26.5	26.7	26.7	26.7	26.9	27.0	27.1	27.4	27.5	27.6	26.9
2006	27.7	28.0	28.3	28.1	28.5	28.7	28.8	28.8	28.6	28.7	28.6	28.4	28.4
2007	28.4	28.2	28.5	28.1	28.1	28.2	27.9	27.8	27.8	28.1	28.1	28.1	28.1

Employment by Industry: Sacramento–Arden-Arcade–Roseville, CA, 2000–2007—*Continued*

(Numbers in thousands, not seasonally adjusted.)

Industry and year	January	February	March	April	May	June	July	August	September	October	November	December	Annual Average
Retail Trade													
2000	88.6	86.9	86.9	87.1	87.3	88.1	88.9	90.2	90.6	90.9	95.5	98.0	89.9
2001	91.3	89.5	89.6	89.7	90.2	91.3	90.9	90.8	91.5	91.9	95.1	96.9	91.6
2002	91.3	89.9	90.7	90.6	90.8	92.0	92.1	92.3	92.8	93.8	96.9	99.0	92.7
2003	94.2	92.2	92.2	92.5	92.9	94.1	94.6	94.8	94.6	95.7	99.5	101.9	94.9
2004	95.2	94.3	94.3	95.1	95.9	96.6	96.4	96.0	95.9	97.3	101.1	102.3	96.7
2005	97.3	96.3	96.4	96.5	96.8	97.2	98.3	98.3	98.5	99.3	103.1	105.8	98.7
2006	100.1	98.7	99.1	98.9	99.7	100.3	100.9	101.0	100.3	100.6	103.7	105.2	100.7
2007	100.4	98.9	98.4	98.2	98.7	98.8	99.8	99.5	99.3	100.2	102.7	103.8	99.9
Transportation and Utilities													
2000	23.7	23.7	23.6	23.6	23.4	23.4	23.5	23.9	23.9	23.2	23.7	24.1	23.6
2001	23.6	23.2	23.5	22.9	22.7	23.1	23.1	23.3	23.4	23.5	23.5	23.5	23.3
2002	21.9	22.0	22.1	22.5	22.6	22.7	22.7	22.6	22.4	22.3	22.3	22.1	22.4
2003	21.5	21.4	21.4	21.5	21.7	21.9	22.0	22.3	22.3	22.4	22.4	22.4	21.9
2004	22.6	22.4	22.3	22.5	22.5	22.7	22.7	22.9	23.2	23.6	23.4	23.4	22.9
2005	23.3	23.1	23.3	23.0	23.2	23.3	23.2	23.4	23.5	23.4	23.5	24.1	23.4
2006	23.4	23.2	23.4	23.4	23.6	24.1	24.6	25.3	25.5	25.3	25.5	26.3	24.5
2007	25.1	25.1	25.1	24.9	25.1	25.3	25.3	25.5	25.5	25.7	26.1	26.4	25.4
Information													
2000	18.6	18.5	18.4	18.4	18.3	18.4	18.6	18.8	18.8	18.8	18.9	19.0	18.6
2001	20.7	20.8	21.2	22.0	22.0	21.9	22.7	23.0	22.9	23.6	23.6	23.7	22.3
2002	24.1	23.8	23.7	23.5	23.7	23.6	23.3	22.7	22.4	22.3	21.9	21.6	23.1
2003	21.8	22.0	21.7	22.2	22.6	22.8	21.7	21.6	21.3	21.4	21.5	21.6	21.9
2004	21.3	21.5	21.3	21.1	21.1	21.1	21.0	20.8	20.5	20.4	20.5	20.6	20.9
2005	20.5	20.6	20.2	20.3	20.1	19.9	19.8	19.8	19.5	19.2	19.4	19.5	19.9
2006	19.6	19.8	19.7	19.9	19.9	19.8	20.4	20.3	20.1	20.0	20.1	20.4	20.0
2007	20.4	20.7	20.4	20.1	20.3	20.1	20.3	20.3	20.1	20.1	20.1	20.2	20.3
Financial Activities													
2000	52.3	52.7	53.0	52.6	52.6	52.8	52.1	52.5	52.3	50.8	51.1	52.2	52.3
2001	51.6	52.1	52.5	51.9	52.0	52.5	52.4	52.8	52.4	52.9	53.1	53.5	52.5
2002	53.1	53.4	53.5	54.1	54.0	54.3	55.1	55.6	56.4	57.3	57.8	58.3	55.2
2003	57.9	58.5	58.6	59.5	59.7	59.8	59.9	60.2	59.8	59.4	59.3	59.6	59.3
2004	58.7	59.1	59.1	59.8	60.0	60.2	60.8	61.1	61.1	61.5	61.5	62.0	60.4
2005	61.9	62.2	62.6	62.9	63.4	63.4	63.8	64.0	64.1	64.2	64.4	64.7	63.5
2006	65.2	65.3	65.3	65.1	65.0	65.2	64.8	64.6	64.4	63.5	63.7	63.5	64.6
2007	63.0	63.2	62.8	62.9	62.6	62.6	62.9	62.8	62.1	61.9	61.7	61.9	62.5
Professional and Business Services													
2000	102.7	104.3	106.1	107.4	107.6	110.0	109.4	110.4	110.1	108.8	109.5	110.0	108.0
2001	104.6	105.5	106.3	104.9	105.0	105.3	105.7	105.1	103.3	101.6	101.5	101.7	104.2
2002	98.3	99.4	101.7	100.5	100.4	102.1	102.6	102.5	103.0	100.5	100.7	100.8	101.0
2003	99.5	100.0	100.2	100.3	100.3	101.2	100.5	100.9	101.4	100.2	101.5	101.5	100.6
2004	100.1	100.8	101.6	103.2	103.0	103.6	104.0	104.2	104.0	104.4	104.0	104.4	103.1
2005	103.6	105.0	106.3	107.7	107.9	109.7	109.7	109.7	109.7	110.5	111.3	112.0	108.6
2006	111.0	112.0	112.3	111.7	112.4	113.5	112.9	113.3	112.7	113.1	113.0	112.6	112.5
2007	108.6	110.0	110.8	111.3	111.1	112.0	112.1	112.2	111.8	112.0	112.2	112.3	111.4
Education and Health Services													
2000	68.5	68.9	68.9	69.2	69.0	69.4	70.4	70.5	71.4	73.1	73.3	74.2	70.6
2001	73.5	74.1	74.9	75.8	76.8	76.4	75.6	75.9	76.5	76.8	77.9	76.9	75.9
2002	78.3	77.3	77.6	76.6	78.6	77.4	77.1	76.6	77.7	79.0	80.2	79.2	78.0
2003	80.8	79.2	80.1	81.2	81.3	81.0	80.9	79.7	81.3	81.6	82.2	82.3	81.0
2004	83.1	83.1	83.4	84.4	85.0	84.6	84.8	82.9	85.9	85.5	85.7	86.2	84.6
2005	86.9	86.7	87.2	88.1	88.7	88.1	88.0	87.2	88.6	89.4	89.9	89.7	88.2
2006	91.2	90.7	91.3	91.3	92.4	92.4	91.4	91.0	92.4	94.0	93.6	93.5	92.1
2007	94.9	95.1	96.6	96.4	97.5	96.5	96.7	96.0	97.4	98.2	99.0	98.8	96.9
Leisure and Hospitality													
2000	66.9	67.8	68.5	69.4	69.4	71.8	72.2	72.4	71.7	70.0	71.0	72.5	70.3
2001	72.1	72.9	73.6	72.7	70.5	72.0	72.6	73.3	70.3	70.2	71.5	75.1	72.2
2002	73.9	74.8	75.3	74.9	74.5	76.6	76.0	76.6	74.8	74.2	74.5	76.4	75.2
2003	76.9	77.4	78.5	77.5	76.5	78.1	77.7	78.4	76.6	75.9	75.7	78.7	77.3
2004	78.3	79.1	80.1	80.1	78.8	80.6	80.8	81.2	79.8	78.4	79.3	81.7	79.9
2005	80.6	81.3	81.4	81.0	81.1	82.3	83.7	83.9	82.4	81.4	82.2	84.0	82.1
2006	83.8	85.2	85.5	85.2	85.5	86.9	86.5	87.0	85.2	83.2	83.9	85.6	85.3
2007	85.5	86.2	87.2	85.8	86.0	87.5	88.6	88.2	86.6	86.0	86.5	87.9	86.8
Other Services													
2000	25.8	26.4	26.7	26.6	27.0	27.3	26.9	26.8	27.3	26.8	26.7	26.9	26.8
2001	26.6	27.1	27.4	27.6	27.9	28.3	28.0	27.9	27.9	28.2	28.0	28.0	27.7
2002	27.6	28.2	27.8	27.7	28.7	28.5	28.3	28.0	28.0	28.4	28.3	28.4	28.2
2003	27.3	27.6	27.6	28.3	28.6	28.8	28.3	28.3	28.0	27.8	27.7	27.8	28.0
2004	27.7	27.9	28.2	28.5	28.8	28.6	28.8	28.7	28.9	28.8	28.5	28.6	28.5
2005	28.3	28.6	29.0	29.1	29.0	28.8	28.5	28.4	28.4	28.1	27.9	27.7	28.5
2006	27.9	28.4	28.5	28.2	28.7	28.7	27.9	28.1	28.5	28.3	28.3	28.1	28.3
2007	27.8	28.2	28.5	28.4	28.9	29.0	28.9	29.2	29.3	29.2	29.0	28.8	28.8
Government													
2000	206.3	209.2	211.9	211.8	215.3	215.8	204.4	207.1	208.4	212.0	212.9	212.7	210.7
2001	211.2	213.2	217.0	217.9	218.3	218.9	214.3	216.4	220.0	221.9	224.0	224.0	218.1
2002	222.0	223.8	229.2	229.3	230.6	229.7	223.6	224.4	226.1	227.6	228.0	227.5	226.8
2003	225.0	226.9	227.7	228.0	230.2	228.9	224.3	222.6	224.6	223.4	227.8	224.4	226.1
2004	222.5	223.1	223.0	223.6	224.4	224.9	217.6	215.2	219.3	221.4	222.7	221.1	221.6
2005	221.8	222.8	224.0	225.1	226.2	226.1	221.0	219.7	224.0	225.4	226.3	226.1	224.0
2006	225.1	227.3	228.6	229.0	229.7	230.8	225.6	223.1	227.2	229.7	231.7	232.7	228.4
2007	231.4	232.9	236.0	236.1	237.7	238.9	231.3	231.1	234.1	236.3	237.5	237.6	235.1

Employment by Industry: San Jose-Sunnyvale-Santa Clara, CA, 2000–2007

(Numbers in thousands, not seasonally adjusted.)

Industry and year	January	February	March	April	May	June	July	August	September	October	November	December	Annual Average
Total Nonfarm													
2000	999.6	1,008.5	1,023.2	1,023.4	1,036.7	1,051.9	1,056.7	1,058.4	1,060.9	1,061.9	1,070.3	1,080.3	1,044.3
2001	1,054.7	1,057.9	1,062.7	1,044.8	1,040.3	1,037.1	1,014.5	1,003.4	987.1	976.6	969.0	967.0	1,017.9
2002	933.1	933.7	938.9	929.2	927.8	926.2	915.2	908.9	901.1	900.6	897.2	894.1	917.2
2003	874.0	872.8	874.0	875.6	875.8	877.0	866.7	864.1	862.8	865.2	866.1	869.0	870.3
2004	849.5	854.1	859.3	859.0	864.0	868.6	861.1	860.7	859.4	866.8	869.3	872.1	862.0
2005	855.9	859.4	862.9	863.4	867.1	872.8	870.1	871.6	871.1	877.4	880.6	887.0	869.9
2006	872.2	880.0	883.4	883.6	890.8	896.3	893.3	895.2	895.2	896.9	900.5	906.4	891.2
2007	892.3	898.6	904.6	901.3	909.2	915.4	912.2	909.8	908.1	913.2	915.4	916.8	908.1
Total Private													
2000	901.5	910.7	923.3	923.8	936.0	948.2	957.3	964.2	967.1	963.0	971.0	981.3	945.6
2001	957.3	959.9	963.8	945.6	939.7	937.4	917.5	908.8	890.4	876.2	867.3	865.5	919.1
2002	831.9	831.5	835.5	824.6	823.1	821.8	813.9	810.3	801.4	797.4	793.6	791.0	814.7
2003	771.8	771.8	772.3	773.8	774.4	776.2	769.8	769.5	767.5	766.6	767.6	772.0	771.1
2004	753.6	757.3	761.4	761.1	765.9	771.0	766.3	767.8	765.9	770.6	771.9	776.1	765.7
2005	760.4	763.2	766.0	766.4	769.7	775.8	775.8	775.8	777.9	777.3	781.2	784.0	790.8	774.0
2006	776.5	783.5	786.7	786.3	793.0	798.9	798.2	801.5	800.9	799.2	802.9	808.9	794.7
2007	794.6	801.6	806.3	803.2	810.9	817.6	817.2	816.0	813.2	814.8	816.7	818.3	810.9
Goods-Producing													
2000	283.8	286.1	290.3	291.7	295.1	300.8	305.7	309.0	312.0	311.7	313.5	315.8	301.3
2001	307.9	307.9	306.7	301.8	298.4	296.6	289.7	286.4	279.9	273.8	267.7	265.6	290.2
2002	256.9	253.3	254.2	249.8	249.4	249.2	247.3	245.5	241.3	237.4	232.5	228.9	245.5
2003	223.9	221.6	221.0	219.2	217.5	217.9	217.2	216.7	215.6	213.1	211.7	211.6	217.3
2004	206.8	207.6	208.5	208.8	209.9	212.0	212.8	213.5	212.6	211.6	210.2	209.7	210.3
2005	206.3	206.0	206.0	208.3	208.4	210.7	212.4	212.8	212.0	211.7	210.2	210.7	209.6
2006	208.5	209.3	209.1	208.2	210.6	211.6	211.6	213.5	214.3	213.4	211.7	209.6	209.8	210.8
2007	208.1	209.8	210.6	210.1	212.0	214.7	216.7	217.1	216.2	215.2	214.6	214.7	213.3
Natural Resources and Mining													
2000	0.4	0.4	0.3	0.3	0.3	0.3	0.4	0.4	0.4	0.4	0.4	0.5	0.4
2001	0.2	0.2	0.2	0.2	0.2	0.2	0.2	0.2	0.2	0.2	0.2	0.2	0.2
2002	0.3	0.3	0.3	0.2	0.2	0.2	0.2	0.2	0.2	0.2	0.2	0.2	0.2
2003	0.2	0.2	0.2	0.2	0.2	0.2	0.2	0.2	0.2	0.2	0.2	0.1	0.1
2004	0.1	0.1	0.1	0.1	0.1	0.2	0.1	0.2	0.2	0.2	0.1	0.1	0.1
2005	0.1	0.1	0.1	0.2	0.2	0.2	0.2	0.2	0.2	0.3	0.3	0.2	0.2
2006	0.3	0.3	0.2	0.2	0.2	0.3	0.3	0.3	0.3	0.3	0.3	0.3	0.3
2007	0.3	0.3	0.3	0.3	0.3	0.3	0.3	0.3	0.3	0.3	0.3	0.3	0.3
Construction													
2000	45.4	45.4	46.7	47.3	48.3	49.7	50.7	51.5	52.5	52.0	52.2	52.0	49.5
2001	51.1	50.9	51.5	51.1	51.0	51.2	50.4	50.7	49.3	48.3	47.4	46.4	49.9
2002	43.7	43.3	44.1	43.6	44.4	45.3	45.6	46.7	45.6	44.5	43.8	42.2	44.4
2003	40.0	39.9	40.2	40.1	40.4	41.2	41.9	43.3	43.5	43.2	42.7	42.3	41.6
2004	40.3	40.8	41.2	41.7	42.4	43.7	44.2	44.6	44.5	44.8	44.2	43.9	43.0
2005	41.6	41.7	42.3	43.0	43.6	45.0	45.7	46.4	46.7	46.3	46.0	45.9	44.5
2006	44.9	45.4	45.1	44.3	46.2	47.4	47.9	48.7	48.9	48.2	47.6	46.9	46.8
2007	45.0	45.5	46.3	46.0	46.9	47.8	48.1	48.5	48.4	47.9	47.0	46.4	47.0
Manufacturing													
2000	238.0	240.3	243.3	244.1	246.5	250.8	254.6	257.1	259.1	259.3	260.9	263.3	251.4
2001	256.6	256.8	255.0	250.5	247.2	245.2	239.1	235.5	230.4	225.3	220.1	219.0	240.1
2002	212.9	209.7	209.8	206.0	204.8	203.7	201.5	198.6	195.5	192.7	188.5	186.5	200.9
2003	183.7	181.5	180.6	178.9	176.9	176.5	175.1	173.2	171.9	169.7	168.8	169.2	175.5
2004	166.4	166.7	167.2	167.0	167.4	168.1	168.5	168.7	167.9	166.6	165.9	165.7	167.2
2005	164.6	164.2	163.6	165.1	164.6	165.5	166.5	166.2	165.1	165.1	163.9	164.6	164.9
2006	163.3	163.6	163.8	163.7	164.2	163.9	165.3	165.3	164.2	163.2	161.7	162.6	163.7
2007	162.8	164.0	164.0	163.8	164.8	166.6	168.3	168.3	167.5	167.0	167.3	168.0	166.0
Service-Providing													
2000	715.8	722.4	732.9	731.7	741.6	751.1	751.0	749.4	748.9	750.2	756.8	764.5	743.0
2001	746.8	750.0	756.0	743.0	741.9	740.5	724.8	717.0	707.2	702.8	701.3	701.4	727.7
2002	676.2	680.4	684.7	679.4	678.4	677.0	667.9	663.4	659.8	663.2	664.7	665.2	671.7
2003	650.1	651.2	653.0	656.4	658.3	659.1	649.5	647.4	647.2	652.1	654.4	657.4	653.0
2004	642.7	646.5	650.8	650.2	654.1	656.6	648.3	647.2	646.8	655.2	659.1	662.4	651.7
2005	649.6	653.4	656.9	655.1	658.7	662.1	657.7	658.8	659.1	665.7	670.4	676.3	660.3
2006	663.7	670.7	674.3	675.4	680.2	684.7	679.8	680.9	681.8	685.2	690.9	696.6	680.4
2007	684.2	688.8	694.0	691.2	697.2	700.7	695.5	692.7	691.9	698.0	700.8	702.1	694.8
Trade, Transportation, and Utilities													
2000	152.3	151.3	152.1	151.7	152.5	153.3	154.2	154.7	154.6	153.5	156.8	159.8	153.9
2001	153.5	151.5	152.5	149.8	149.4	149.7	148.4	146.8	145.6	143.9	146.2	147.7	148.8
2002	139.8	138.3	138.8	137.0	137.0	136.8	136.4	136.0	135.5	135.5	137.6	139.5	137.4
2003	133.1	131.2	130.9	131.0	131.0	131.3	130.8	131.1	130.8	131.7	134.3	136.6	132.0
2004	130.7	129.6	129.2	128.8	129.8	130.1	129.8	130.1	129.9	131.4	134.2	136.6	130.9
2005	131.3	130.2	130.3	130.2	130.7	131.2	132.1	132.8	133.5	134.2	137.1	140.0	132.8
2006	135.3	133.8	133.8	133.7	134.4	135.2	136.4	137.6	138.1	138.6	142.6	145.1	137.1
2007	139.3	137.6	137.8	137.2	138.0	138.9	139.6	139.8	139.9	141.1	143.8	145.9	139.9
Wholesale Trade													
2000	42.9	43.1	43.2	43.0	43.1	43.0	42.9	42.8	42.5	42.4	42.1	41.9	42.7
2001	42.7	42.8	43.1	41.8	41.4	41.2	41.3	41.1	40.4	39.8	39.3	39.2	41.2
2002	38.6	38.1	38.2	37.2	37.0	36.5	35.9	35.5	34.9	34.6	34.0	33.6	36.2
2003	33.6	33.6	33.8	34.1	34.2	34.2	34.3	34.5	34.3	34.3	34.2	34.3	34.1
2004	34.0	33.9	33.9	34.3	34.4	34.6	34.5	34.6	34.5	34.9	34.9	34.9	34.5
2005	34.8	35.1	35.1	35.2	35.5	35.8	36.1	36.3	36.5	36.5	36.4	36.7	35.8
2006	37.0	37.3	37.4	37.8	37.9	38.2	38.7	38.8	39.0	39.0	39.1	39.3	38.3
2007	38.9	39.3	39.3	39.0	39.2	39.8	39.7	39.8	39.9	40.4	40.3	40.4	39.7

Employment by Industry: San Jose-Sunnyvale-Santa Clara, CA, 2000–2007—*Continued*

(Numbers in thousands, not seasonally adjusted.)

Industry and year	January	February	March	April	May	June	July	August	September	October	November	December	Annual Average
Retail Trade													
2000	92.2	91.0	91.6	90.8	91.7	92.4	93.4	93.8	94.1	93.1	96.6	99.6	93.4
2001	93.4	91.3	91.9	90.8	90.8	91.3	90.3	89.1	88.9	88.5	91.7	93.4	91.0
2002	86.5	85.4	85.8	84.8	84.6	84.9	85.1	85.2	85.6	85.5	88.3	90.6	86.0
2003	84.9	83.2	82.8	82.3	82.4	82.6	82.3	82.4	82.5	83.3	86.1	88.4	83.6
2004	82.9	81.9	81.5	81.1	81.9	81.9	82.0	82.3	82.0	83.0	85.8	88.2	82.9
2005	83.4	82.0	82.1	81.9	82.1	82.3	82.9	83.5	83.9	84.8	87.8	90.3	83.9
2006	85.8	83.9	83.8	83.4	83.7	84.0	84.8	85.6	85.8	86.5	90.1	92.3	85.8
2007	87.5	85.3	85.4	84.9	85.3	85.4	86.3	86.4	86.2	87.0	89.6	91.4	86.7
Transportation and Utilities													
2000	17.2	17.2	17.3	17.9	17.7	17.9	17.9	18.1	18.0	18.0	18.1	18.3	17.8
2001	17.4	17.4	17.5	17.2	17.2	17.2	16.8	16.6	16.3	15.6	15.2	15.1	16.6
2002	14.7	14.8	14.8	15.0	15.4	15.4	15.4	15.3	15.3	15.4	15.3	15.3	15.2
2003	14.6	14.4	14.3	14.6	14.4	14.5	14.2	14.2	14.0	14.1	14.0	13.9	14.3
2004	13.8	13.8	13.8	13.4	13.5	13.6	13.3	13.2	13.4	13.5	13.5	13.5	13.5
2005	13.1	13.1	13.1	13.1	13.1	13.1	13.1	13.0	13.1	12.9	12.9	13.0	13.1
2006	12.5	12.6	12.6	12.5	12.8	13.0	12.9	13.2	13.3	13.1	13.4	13.5	13.0
2007	12.9	13.0	13.1	13.3	13.5	13.7	13.6	13.6	13.8	13.7	13.9	14.1	13.5
Information													
2000	36.9	37.7	39.2	40.1	41.5	43.1	44.2	45.0	45.6	46.1	46.6	47.1	42.8
2001	46.5	46.2	46.1	43.8	43.4	42.8	41.4	40.7	39.6	38.3	37.6	37.3	42.0
2002	37.0	36.9	36.7	35.7	34.9	34.2	33.5	33.2	32.8	32.4	32.6	32.2	34.3
2003	31.8	32.0	31.6	31.1	31.1	31.2	31.2	31.1	31.0	31.3	31.5	31.7	31.4
2004	31.7	32.0	32.2	32.1	32.2	32.5	32.6	32.6	32.8	33.2	33.7	34.0	32.6
2005	33.8	34.1	34.4	34.0	34.4	35.0	35.5	35.8	35.7	36.2	36.9	37.3	35.3
2006	37.1	37.3	37.4	37.3	37.5	37.6	37.9	37.9	37.5	37.1	37.3	37.6	37.5
2007	37.8	38.2	38.5	38.6	39.3	40.0	40.2	40.4	40.2	40.1	40.2	39.9	39.5
Financial Activities													
2000	33.7	34.1	34.3	34.2	34.2	34.6	34.7	34.6	34.5	34.5	34.7	34.9	34.4
2001	34.5	34.8	35.2	35.4	35.6	36.0	35.9	36.3	36.1	35.8	36.0	36.3	35.7
2002	35.6	35.8	35.8	35.3	35.7	35.6	35.6	35.6	35.8	35.4	35.4	35.3	35.6
2003	34.9	34.9	35.1	35.1	35.2	35.1	35.3	35.4	35.2	35.0	34.9	35.1	35.1
2004	34.7	34.8	35.0	35.1	35.4	35.4	35.5	35.5	35.5	36.0	35.9	36.1	35.4
2005	35.9	35.8	36.0	35.9	36.0	36.2	36.3	36.6	36.4	36.7	36.7	37.0	36.3
2006	36.7	36.8	37.0	37.1	37.5	37.2	37.3	37.2	37.1	37.1	37.1	37.1	37.1
2007	37.3	37.4	37.4	37.2	37.4	37.4	37.3	37.1	36.8	36.8	36.6	36.5	37.1
Professional and Business Services													
2000	213.5	217.7	221.2	219.7	224.6	230.1	231.1	234.4	234.4	231.9	234.3	237.4	227.5
2001	229.7	230.8	231.7	223.8	219.6	218.0	210.3	206.1	199.9	195.1	191.1	189.0	212.1
2002	180.6	180.7	180.8	177.6	175.7	175.5	174.1	173.0	171.2	171.0	170.1	169.8	175.0
2003	166.4	166.7	166.9	168.1	168.6	169.3	166.1	167.8	168.4	166.9	167.0	168.4	167.6
2004	164.7	165.8	166.0	165.3	165.1	166.6	163.8	165.0	164.9	166.2	166.4	167.5	165.6
2005	164.3	166.0	166.8	164.9	165.1	166.0	164.4	165.2	165.7	166.2	166.5	168.4	165.8
2006	166.2	168.6	169.3	169.5	169.8	171.6	172.6	173.9	174.8	174.3	175.1	177.8	172.0
2007	176.2	177.7	177.8	177.1	177.7	178.2	178.8	177.9	177.4	177.5	177.8	177.7	177.7
Education and Health Services													
2000	87.0	87.5	87.6	86.5	87.2	84.4	84.0	83.0	83.3	86.1	86.8	87.4	85.9
2001	87.7	89.2	90.4	89.8	90.8	90.7	88.5	89.5	89.4	92.2	93.0	93.8	90.4
2002	89.4	92.1	93.1	93.1	93.1	92.6	89.5	89.7	89.4	91.9	93.0	93.0	91.7
2003	91.4	93.4	94.0	94.8	95.2	94.5	92.8	91.4	91.2	93.8	94.7	95.1	93.5
2004	93.8	94.7	95.7	95.0	95.9	95.9	93.4	93.2	93.2	95.9	96.8	96.9	95.0
2005	95.9	96.7	96.7	96.2	96.4	96.5	95.2	95.2	95.1	98.4	99.7	100.0	96.8
2006	98.2	100.8	101.6	101.0	101.7	102.0	98.8	98.3	98.4	100.5	101.7	101.5	100.4
2007	99.4	102.3	103.5	101.6	103.3	103.8	101.5	100.8	101.0	102.7	103.5	103.4	102.2
Leisure and Hospitality													
2000	68.2	69.8	71.7	72.7	73.7	74.3	75.7	75.8	75.5	72.7	71.8	71.8	72.8
2001	71.0	72.9	74.6	74.8	75.9	76.6	76.4	76.0	73.2	70.5	69.0	69.1	73.3
2002	66.3	67.7	69.2	69.4	70.6	71.2	70.8	70.5	69.3	68.1	66.5	66.5	68.8
2003	65.5	66.9	67.7	68.8	70.1	71.1	70.9	70.9	70.2	69.5	68.1	68.2	69.0
2004	66.9	68.0	69.9	70.8	72.2	73.1	73.2	72.9	72.0	71.3	69.7	70.2	70.9
2005	68.4	69.5	70.9	72.1	73.7	74.8	75.2	75.3	74.5	73.5	72.7	73.1	72.8
2006	70.5	72.4	73.8	74.7	76.2	77.9	76.9	77.4	76.6	75.4	74.9	75.3	75.2
2007	72.6	74.0	75.9	76.6	77.9	79.0	78.0	77.8	76.4	75.9	74.7	74.8	76.1
Other Services													
2000	26.1	26.5	26.9	27.2	27.2	27.6	27.7	27.7	27.2	26.5	26.5	27.1	27.0
2001	26.5	26.6	26.6	26.4	26.6	27.0	26.9	27.0	26.7	26.6	26.7	26.7	26.7
2002	26.3	26.7	26.9	26.7	26.7	26.7	26.7	26.6	26.2	25.7	26.0	25.8	26.4
2003	24.8	25.1	25.1	25.7	25.7	25.8	25.5	25.1	25.1	25.3	25.4	25.3	25.3
2004	24.3	24.8	24.9	25.2	25.4	25.4	25.2	25.0	25.0	25.0	25.0	25.1	25.0
2005	24.5	24.9	24.9	24.8	25.0	25.4	24.7	24.2	24.4	24.3	24.2	24.3	24.6
2006	24.0	24.5	24.7	24.8	25.3	25.8	24.8	24.9	25.0	24.5	24.6	24.7	24.8
2007	23.9	24.6	24.8	24.8	25.3	25.6	25.1	25.1	25.3	25.5	25.5	25.4	25.1
Government													
2000	98.1	97.8	99.9	99.6	100.7	103.7	99.4	94.2	93.8	98.9	99.3	99.0	98.7
2001	97.4	98.0	98.9	99.2	100.6	99.7	97.0	94.6	96.7	100.4	101.7	101.5	98.8
2002	101.2	102.2	103.4	104.6	104.7	104.4	101.3	98.6	99.7	103.2	103.6	103.1	102.5
2003	102.2	101.0	101.7	101.8	101.4	100.8	96.9	94.6	95.3	98.6	98.5	97.0	99.2
2004	95.9	96.8	97.9	97.9	98.1	97.6	94.8	92.9	93.5	96.2	97.4	96.0	96.3
2005	95.5	96.2	96.9	97.0	97.4	97.0	94.3	93.7	93.8	96.2	96.6	96.2	95.9
2006	95.7	96.5	96.7	97.3	97.8	97.4	95.1	93.7	94.3	97.7	97.6	97.5	96.4
2007	97.7	97.0	98.3	98.1	98.3	97.8	95.0	93.8	94.9	98.4	98.7	98.5	97.2

Employment by Industry: San Antonio, TX, 2000–2007

(Numbers in thousands, not seasonally adjusted.)

Industry and year	January	February	March	April	May	June	July	August	September	October	November	December	Annual Average
Total Nonfarm													
2000	727.4	734.8	738.4	744.0	751.2	751.2	744.2	746.3	752.1	748.1	750.3	754.5	745.2
2001	737.7	746.7	753.3	754.3	760.4	764.3	753.5	758.6	757.2	750.5	750.7	752.3	753.3
2002	737.2	745.0	751.6	755.2	760.8	759.5	750.6	756.1	760.0	756.5	758.0	758.2	754.1
2003	739.0	745.3	751.3	752.1	755.0	755.2	747.1	751.0	751.9	754.2	756.9	757.4	751.3
2004	742.0	749.8	756.5	759.8	763.3	765.4	759.5	764.0	764.1	763.8	765.7	766.2	760.0
2005	756.7	765.9	771.9	778.3	783.1	785.5	780.7	784.9	789.9	791.2	796.0	799.3	782.0
2006	786.9	795.0	803.7	809.6	814.4	817.5	809.7	814.1	818.7	819.8	823.2	825.8	811.5
2007	809.2	820.1	826.4	829.2	836.4	838.7	830.3	834.4	838.0	839.1	842.5	844.6	832.4
Total Private													
2000	588.6	593.6	596.8	602.2	607.0	614.0	612.4	613.7	614.0	608.4	610.1	614.5	606.3
2001	598.7	606.2	612.5	613.3	619.2	626.2	622.0	624.0	617.8	610.0	608.7	610.4	614.1
2002	597.0	601.7	607.9	611.9	616.6	620.2	617.6	621.2	618.4	612.3	613.2	613.6	612.6
2003	596.6	600.5	606.6	606.8	609.5	614.1	611.3	613.8	610.7	611.1	612.4	613.4	608.9
2004	600.8	605.3	612.3	615.4	618.4	624.6	623.6	625.5	621.0	619.7	621.3	621.9	617.5
2005	614.2	620.6	626.7	632.7	637.5	642.5	643.6	646.1	646.2	645.3	649.1	652.4	638.1
2006	641.5	647.2	656.1	660.2	665.3	670.7	670.3	673.5	672.4	670.4	672.9	675.8	664.7
2007	660.5	669.0	674.9	678.0	685.1	690.3	688.2	690.4	688.5	687.4	689.2	691.3	682.7
Goods-Producing													
2000	97.2	98.1	98.3	98.4	99.7	101.5	100.7	100.5	100.8	99.9	99.4	100.3	99.6
2001	98.0	98.7	99.8	99.7	100.4	101.6	101.6	101.5	101.3	99.2	97.9	98.0	99.8
2002	95.6	95.4	96.3	96.1	96.4	97.3	96.5	96.0	94.7	93.2	92.9	92.9	95.3
2003	91.0	91.5	91.4	91.8	92.1	92.5	91.9	91.8	91.4	91.1	90.6	90.6	91.4
2004	88.8	89.0	89.4	90.0	90.1	91.0	91.7	91.4	91.4	91.8	91.8	91.8	90.7
2005	90.6	91.2	92.4	93.8	94.0	94.7	95.1	94.9	95.6	95.4	95.7	96.7	94.2
2006	96.0	97.4	98.8	98.2	99.0	100.5	100.2	100.3	100.8	100.0	100.2	100.4	99.3
2007	98.9	100.3	100.7	100.8	102.1	103.8	103.3	103.7	103.4	103.6	103.1	103.3	102.3
Natural Resources and Mining													
2000	2.6	2.8	2.8	2.7	2.7	2.7	2.6	2.5	2.7	2.7	2.6	2.7	2.7
2001	2.7	2.7	2.8	3.0	3.0	3.1	3.1	3.2	3.3	3.5	3.6	3.6	3.1
2002	3.1	3.0	3.1	2.8	2.8	2.7	3.2	3.2	3.1	3.1	3.2	3.1	3.1
2003	2.5	2.7	2.7	2.8	2.7	2.8	2.8	2.8	2.9	2.9	2.9	3.0	2.8
2004	2.9	2.9	2.9	2.8	2.8	2.8	2.7	2.7	2.5	2.4	2.4	2.3	2.7
2005	2.3	2.4	2.4	2.4	2.4	2.5	2.6	2.6	2.6	2.8	2.8	2.8	2.5
2006	2.9	3.0	3.0	3.0	3.1	3.1	3.1	3.1	3.2	3.1	3.2	3.2	3.1
2007	3.1	3.2	3.2	3.2	3.3	3.4	3.4	3.5	3.5	3.6	3.6	3.6	3.4
Construction													
2000	39.7	39.9	40.2	40.0	40.6	41.7	41.7	42.2	42.0	41.3	41.4	41.5	41.0
2001	40.9	41.6	42.5	42.4	43.2	44.6	45.1	45.6	45.1	43.4	43.3	43.1	43.4
2002	42.2	42.5	43.0	43.4	43.9	44.6	43.7	43.9	43.0	42.0	41.6	41.4	42.9
2003	41.3	41.1	41.3	41.5	42.1	42.5	42.4	42.6	42.0	41.9	41.6	41.6	41.8
2004	40.6	40.5	40.8	41.1	41.5	42.4	42.8	43.1	43.1	43.4	43.6	43.8	42.2
2005	43.0	43.3	44.4	45.6	45.9	46.4	46.3	46.3	46.7	46.1	46.1	46.5	45.5
2006	45.9	46.7	47.6	47.4	47.7	48.7	48.3	48.3	48.2	47.6	47.5	47.4	47.6
2007	46.6	47.8	48.7	48.6	49.5	50.8	50.6	51.0	50.8	50.9	50.7	50.8	49.7
Manufacturing													
2000	54.9	55.4	55.3	55.7	56.4	57.1	56.4	55.8	56.1	55.9	55.4	56.1	55.9
2001	54.4	54.4	54.5	54.3	54.2	53.9	53.4	52.7	52.9	52.3	51.0	51.3	53.3
2002	50.3	49.9	50.2	49.9	49.7	50.0	49.6	48.9	48.6	48.1	48.1	48.4	49.3
2003	47.2	47.7	47.4	47.5	47.3	47.2	46.7	46.4	46.5	46.3	46.1	46.0	46.8
2004	45.3	45.6	45.7	46.1	45.8	45.8	46.2	45.6	45.8	46.0	45.8	45.7	45.8
2005	45.3	45.5	45.6	45.8	45.7	45.8	46.2	46.0	46.3	46.5	46.8	47.4	46.1
2006	47.2	47.7	48.2	47.8	48.2	48.7	48.8	48.8	49.4	49.3	49.5	49.8	48.6
2007	49.2	49.3	48.8	49.0	49.3	49.6	49.3	49.2	49.1	49.1	48.8	48.9	49.1
Service-Providing													
2000	630.2	636.7	640.1	645.6	651.5	649.7	643.5	645.8	651.3	648.2	650.9	654.2	645.6
2001	639.7	648.0	653.5	654.6	660.0	662.7	651.9	657.1	655.9	651.3	652.8	654.3	653.5
2002	641.6	649.6	655.3	659.1	664.4	662.2	654.1	660.1	665.3	663.3	665.1	665.3	658.8
2003	648.0	653.8	659.9	660.3	662.9	662.7	655.2	659.2	660.5	663.1	666.3	666.8	659.8
2004	653.2	660.8	667.1	669.8	673.2	674.4	667.8	672.6	672.7	672.0	673.9	674.4	669.3
2005	666.1	674.7	679.5	684.5	689.1	690.8	685.6	690.0	694.3	695.8	700.3	702.6	687.8
2006	690.9	697.6	704.9	711.4	715.4	717.0	709.5	713.8	717.9	719.8	723.0	725.4	712.2
2007	710.3	719.8	725.7	728.4	734.3	734.9	727.0	730.7	734.6	735.5	739.4	741.3	730.2
Trade, Transportation, and Utilities													
2000	135.2	134.7	134.6	135.5	136.0	137.6	138.0	139.4	139.2	140.5	143.4	145.6	138.3
2001	139.3	139.2	140.3	139.8	140.3	140.4	139.4	140.0	139.1	138.7	140.8	142.1	140.0
2002	136.7	135.3	136.4	137.2	137.8	137.9	137.7	138.3	138.5	137.8	140.2	141.2	137.9
2003	134.0	133.2	134.3	133.6	133.5	133.9	134.0	134.4	134.7	136.7	138.3	139.9	135.0
2004	134.4	133.9	135.0	135.6	135.8	135.9	136.2	137.5	136.9	137.4	139.6	141.2	136.6
2005	136.5	136.1	137.1	137.8	138.3	138.8	139.7	140.5	140.0	140.8	143.9	145.5	139.6
2006	141.0	140.4	142.0	142.0	142.5	142.8	143.1	144.5	144.7	146.8	150.7	152.7	144.4
2007	147.7	146.5	147.5	147.7	148.2	148.6	149.6	150.7	149.9	151.0	153.3	155.1	149.7
Wholesale Trade													
2000	26.2	26.4	26.6	26.5	26.6	26.9	27.2	27.2	27.4	27.4	27.2	27.4	26.9
2001	27.1	27.2	27.3	27.5	27.7	27.8	27.8	27.9	27.8	27.6	27.6	27.8	27.6
2002	27.0	26.9	27.1	27.1	27.2	27.4	27.4	27.4	27.3	27.2	27.3	27.3	27.2
2003	26.6	26.7	26.9	26.9	27.0	27.2	27.4	27.3	27.4	27.5	27.3	27.2	27.1
2004	27.0	27.0	27.0	27.1	27.1	27.1	27.2	27.1	26.8	26.7	26.3	26.2	26.9
2005	26.3	26.4	26.5	26.7	26.9	27.1	27.2	27.3	27.3	27.1	27.4	27.5	27.0
2006	27.5	27.6	27.7	27.8	28.0	28.4	28.4	28.5	28.6	28.7	29.1	29.1	28.3
2007	28.9	29.0	29.2	29.4	29.5	29.7	29.7	29.8	29.8	29.8	29.9	29.9	29.6

Employment by Industry: San Antonio, TX, 2000–2007—*Continued*

(Numbers in thousands, not seasonally adjusted.)

Industry and year	January	February	March	April	May	June	July	August	September	October	November	December	Annual Average
Retail Trade													
2000	88.8	88.3	88.2	89.0	89.3	90.4	90.6	91.7	91.3	92.2	95.0	96.8	91.0
2001	91.3	91.3	92.1	91.5	91.7	91.9	91.2	91.7	91.0	91.6	94.0	95.3	92.1
2002	90.9	89.5	90.0	90.7	90.9	90.6	90.5	90.9	91.4	90.7	92.8	93.9	91.1
2003	87.6	86.7	87.4	87.2	86.9	86.9	86.8	87.3	87.3	89.0	90.8	92.3	88.0
2004	87.4	86.7	87.6	88.2	88.2	88.3	88.6	90.0	89.7	90.4	92.9	94.4	89.4
2005	90.0	89.4	90.2	90.6	90.6	90.7	91.3	91.8	91.1	92.2	94.6	95.9	91.5
2006	92.0	91.2	92.4	92.3	92.5	92.3	92.7	93.9	93.9	95.9	99.2	100.8	94.1
2007	96.6	95.1	95.7	95.5	96.0	96.0	97.0	97.8	97.1	98.1	100.3	101.9	97.3
Transportation and Utilities													
2000	20.2	20.0	19.8	20.0	20.1	20.3	20.2	20.5	20.5	20.9	21.2	21.4	20.4
2001	20.9	20.7	20.9	20.8	20.9	20.7	20.4	20.4	20.3	19.5	19.2	19.0	20.3
2002	18.8	18.9	19.3	19.4	19.7	19.9	19.8	20.0	19.8	19.9	20.1	20.0	19.6
2003	19.8	19.8	20.0	19.5	19.6	19.8	19.8	19.8	20.0	20.2	20.2	20.4	19.9
2004	20.0	20.2	20.4	20.3	20.5	20.5	20.4	20.4	20.4	20.3	20.4	20.6	20.4
2005	20.2	20.3	20.4	20.5	20.8	21.0	21.2	21.4	21.6	21.5	21.9	22.1	21.1
2006	21.5	21.6	21.9	21.9	22.0	22.1	22.0	22.1	22.2	22.2	22.4	22.8	22.1
2007	22.2	22.4	22.6	22.8	22.7	22.9	22.9	23.1	23.0	23.1	23.1	23.3	22.8
Information													
2000	22.9	23.1	23.0	24.1	24.6	24.9	25.3	25.5	25.8	25.5	25.6	25.3	24.6
2001	24.4	24.5	24.5	24.7	24.6	25.0	25.0	25.1	24.7	24.9	24.8	24.9	24.8
2002	24.5	24.4	24.1	23.9	23.9	23.8	22.9	22.9	22.5	22.7	22.8	22.4	23.4
2003	22.2	22.0	22.2	22.2	22.3	22.4	22.6	22.5	22.4	22.4	22.7	22.5	22.3
2004	22.0	21.8	21.8	22.2	22.2	22.0	21.9	21.7	21.3	21.4	21.3	21.0	21.7
2005	20.6	20.7	20.5	20.2	20.4	20.8	20.7	20.8	20.7	20.8	21.1	21.1	20.7
2006	20.7	20.5	20.6	20.6	21.0	21.3	21.2	21.3	21.1	21.4	21.7	21.9	21.1
2007	21.7	21.9	21.7	21.6	21.9	21.9	21.8	21.7	21.5	21.5	21.6	21.5	21.7
Financial Activities													
2000	55.7	56.1	56.2	56.8	56.8	57.3	57.1	56.7	56.7	56.9	57.1	57.6	56.8
2001	57.1	57.7	58.2	58.3	58.9	59.5	59.5	59.8	59.6	58.7	58.9	59.3	58.8
2002	58.7	58.8	59.1	59.4	59.9	60.1	60.1	60.4	60.3	60.6	60.8	61.2	60.0
2003	60.2	60.4	60.7	60.5	60.5	61.0	60.9	61.1	60.7	60.6	60.7	61.1	60.7
2004	60.6	60.7	60.8	61.5	61.6	62.0	62.3	62.3	62.2	61.5	61.7	61.8	61.6
2005	61.2	61.4	61.3	61.5	61.8	62.3	63.3	63.4	63.3	63.4	63.4	63.7	62.5
2006	63.0	63.1	63.2	63.6	63.9	64.2	64.4	64.3	64.4	64.5	64.6	64.9	64.0
2007	64.3	64.9	64.7	64.9	65.6	65.4	65.3	65.0	64.7	64.9	65.0	65.2	65.0
Professional and Business Services													
2000	85.3	85.9	86.3	88.6	90.0	92.0	92.4	92.4	91.5	90.5	89.7	90.3	89.6
2001	88.2	89.0	89.4	89.8	90.2	92.2	90.7	90.7	88.5	85.9	84.7	85.5	88.7
2002	83.3	84.6	85.2	86.7	87.1	88.0	88.7	90.1	90.1	89.0	88.1	87.8	87.4
2003	84.6	85.6	87.0	86.8	87.7	88.2	87.7	89.0	88.1	88.6	89.0	88.4	87.5
2004	87.0	87.6	88.7	88.9	89.2	90.5	89.5	90.4	89.5	89.4	89.3	89.4	89.1
2005	92.2	93.7	94.1	96.7	97.4	97.9	96.7	97.8	99.4	99.9	100.0	101.1	97.2
2006	98.9	100.3	101.9	103.7	104.5	104.8	105.0	105.7	105.6	103.8	103.3	104.0	103.5
2007	101.4	102.6	103.3	104.7	105.5	106.0	105.1	105.7	105.7	105.2	105.0	104.6	104.6
Education and Health Services													
2000	89.7	91.3	91.0	90.4	90.5	89.1	88.6	89.4	92.1	90.7	91.0	90.9	90.4
2001	89.8	92.0	92.6	92.1	92.8	92.3	91.8	93.4	94.5	95.3	95.8	95.7	93.2
2002	94.5	96.1	96.4	96.7	97.0	95.8	95.0	96.7	98.6	98.9	99.4	99.5	97.1
2003	97.9	99.0	99.2	99.5	99.4	99.1	97.9	99.5	101.1	101.6	101.9	101.8	99.8
2004	101.4	102.1	102.9	102.7	102.5	103.1	101.9	103.2	103.7	105.2	105.5	105.6	103.3
2005	103.8	105.6	106.1	105.5	105.6	105.3	105.4	106.7	108.7	109.1	109.7	110.2	106.8
2006	108.4	109.6	110.3	109.4	109.8	109.4	108.4	110.2	112.1	112.0	112.1	112.1	110.3
2007	110.0	112.4	113.1	112.6	113.1	112.6	111.7	113.3	115.2	115.9	116.2	116.5	113.6
Leisure and Hospitality													
2000	75.5	77.1	79.9	80.6	81.4	83.0	81.8	81.4	79.6	76.9	76.3	76.6	79.2
2001	74.5	77.4	79.6	81.0	83.8	86.4	85.4	84.9	81.9	79.6	77.8	77.2	80.8
2002	76.2	79.2	82.3	83.5	85.8	88.1	88.0	88.0	84.9	81.7	80.1	80.0	83.2
2003	78.5	80.5	83.1	84.0	85.6	88.1	88.0	87.2	84.3	82.6	81.3	81.4	83.7
2004	79.2	82.5	85.8	86.8	89.2	91.9	92.5	91.4	88.6	86.2	85.0	84.2	86.9
2005	82.8	85.4	88.4	90.0	92.8	95.1	95.1	94.5	91.0	89.0	88.3	87.2	90.0
2006	86.8	88.9	92.0	94.6	96.2	98.9	99.3	98.5	94.9	93.4	91.5	91.3	93.9
2007	89.0	92.4	95.7	97.4	100.2	103.0	102.6	101.4	99.0	96.5	96.0	95.7	97.4
Other Services													
2000	27.1	27.3	27.5	27.8	28.0	28.6	28.5	28.4	28.3	27.5	27.6	27.9	27.9
2001	27.4	27.7	28.1	27.9	28.2	28.8	28.6	28.6	28.2	27.7	28.0	27.7	28.1
2002	27.5	27.9	28.1	28.4	28.7	29.2	28.7	28.8	28.8	28.4	28.9	28.6	28.5
2003	28.2	28.3	28.7	28.4	28.4	28.9	28.3	28.3	28.0	27.5	27.9	27.7	28.2
2004	27.4	27.7	27.9	27.7	27.8	28.2	27.6	27.6	27.4	26.8	27.1	26.9	27.5
2005	26.5	26.5	26.8	27.2	27.2	27.6	27.6	27.5	27.5	26.9	27.0	26.9	27.1
2006	26.7	27.0	27.3	28.1	28.4	28.8	28.7	28.7	28.8	28.5	28.8	28.5	28.2
2007	27.5	28.0	28.2	28.3	28.5	29.0	28.8	28.9	29.1	28.8	29.0	29.4	28.6
Government													
2000	138.8	141.2	141.6	141.8	144.2	137.2	131.8	132.6	138.1	139.7	140.2	140.0	138.9
2001	139.0	140.5	140.8	141.0	141.2	138.1	131.5	134.6	139.4	140.5	142.0	141.9	139.2
2002	140.2	143.3	143.7	143.3	144.2	139.3	133.0	134.9	141.6	144.2	144.8	144.6	141.4
2003	142.4	144.8	144.7	145.3	145.5	141.1	135.8	137.2	141.2	143.1	144.5	144.0	142.4
2004	141.2	144.5	144.2	144.4	144.9	140.8	135.9	138.5	143.1	144.1	144.4	144.3	142.5
2005	142.5	145.3	145.2	145.6	145.6	143.0	137.1	138.8	143.7	145.9	146.9	146.9	143.9
2006	145.4	147.8	147.6	149.4	149.1	146.8	139.4	140.6	146.3	149.4	150.3	150.0	146.8
2007	148.7	151.1	151.5	151.2	151.3	148.4	142.1	144.0	149.5	151.7	153.3	153.3	149.7

Employment by Industry: Orlando-Kissimmee, FL, 2000–2007

(Numbers in thousands, not seasonally adjusted.)

Industry and year	January	February	March	April	May	June	July	August	September	October	November	December	Annual Average
Total Nonfarm													
2000	890.6	901.1	908.6	907.5	912.7	909.8	900.4	912.4	918.3	918.2	925.6	932.5	911.5
2001	911.6	920.0	927.3	923.1	925.2	915.6	906.9	917.9	917.7	908.3	907.7	909.1	915.9
2002	892.0	901.8	908.8	906.3	909.6	901.2	895.5	908.2	909.4	914.1	922.3	929.0	908.2
2003	913.5	917.6	921.6	921.7	924.8	918.6	916.1	932.8	934.7	941.2	949.3	956.9	929.1
2004	949.8	957.2	963.2	971.3	975.6	969.6	969.7	982.2	983.0	996.6	1,008.7	1,017.4	978.7
2005	1,009.8	1,017.2	1,024.9	1,030.6	1,036.9	1,026.5	1,025.7	1,040.6	1,045.6	1,048.0	1,058.6	1,065.2	1,035.8
2006	1,055.5	1,062.3	1,071.2	1,075.8	1,079.7	1,069.8	1,060.3	1,077.6	1,082.1	1,082.1	1,093.7	1,100.7	1,075.9
2007	1,088.8	1,098.8	1,104.4	1,106.0	1,107.1	1,093.5	1,084.1	1,097.3	1,096.1	1,101.6	1,105.6	1,109.6	1,099.4
Total Private													
2000	799.0	807.8	814.8	813.9	816.9	825.4	817.9	820.7	825.6	824.6	831.5	837.8	819.7
2001	818.0	824.3	829.9	825.5	827.8	827.9	821.3	822.2	820.6	809.2	807.7	808.8	820.3
2002	791.9	800.7	807.6	804.5	807.1	809.5	805.7	806.8	806.4	809.6	817.2	823.5	807.5
2003	809.1	812.5	816.4	816.1	818.7	823.8	823.3	829.1	829.6	834.4	841.9	849.3	825.4
2004	843.1	849.2	855.0	863.2	867.3	872.8	874.9	876.1	874.3	885.9	897.1	905.9	872.1
2005	899.0	905.4	912.7	918.4	923.7	925.6	926.9	930.1	932.4	934.1	944.1	950.9	925.3
2006	941.6	947.0	956.0	959.6	963.7	964.7	957.5	962.3	965.3	964.7	975.6	983.4	961.8
2007	971.0	979.5	984.7	985.5	986.9	984.5	977.5	977.4	975.5	981.2	984.5	989.4	981.5
Goods-Producing													
2000	105.6	106.5	106.7	106.8	107.3	108.0	106.9	107.1	107.3	105.5	106.0	106.4	106.7
2001	104.9	104.7	105.2	104.7	104.1	104.6	103.9	104.2	103.6	102.7	102.0	101.4	103.8
2002	100.6	101.1	101.5	100.6	100.8	100.5	100.1	101.0	101.2	102.1	102.4	103.0	101.2
2003	100.8	101.6	102.2	101.7	102.4	103.3	103.0	104.2	104.9	105.7	105.8	107.1	103.5
2004	106.8	107.9	109.3	110.8	111.5	113.0	114.1	114.4	114.3	115.8	117.1	118.2	112.8
2005	118.3	119.4	120.7	122.4	123.5	124.6	125.8	126.3	126.9	126.5	127.4	128.0	124.2
2006	126.9	128.1	129.9	130.2	131.3	132.0	131.0	131.1	130.8	130.3	129.4	129.5	130.0
2007	126.1	125.8	126.3	124.8	124.6	124.7	123.3	123.9	123.1	120.9	120.0	119.1	123.6
Natural Resources and Mining													
2000	0.5	0.5	0.5	0.5	0.5	0.5	0.5	0.4	0.5	0.5	0.5	0.4	0.5
2001	0.4	0.5	0.5	0.5	0.5	0.5	0.5	0.5	0.5	0.5	0.4	0.5	0.5
2002	0.4	0.5	0.5	0.5	0.5	0.5	0.5	0.5	0.5	0.5	0.5	0.5	0.5
2003	0.5	0.5	0.5	0.5	0.5	0.5	0.5	0.5	0.5	0.4	0.4	0.4	0.4
2004	0.4	0.4	0.4	0.4	0.4	0.4	0.4	0.4	0.4	0.4	0.3	0.4	0.4
2005	0.3	0.3	0.3	0.4	0.4	0.4	0.3	0.3	0.3	0.3	0.3	0.3	0.3
2006	0.3	0.3	0.3	0.3	0.3	0.3	0.3	0.3	0.3	0.3	0.3	0.4	0.3
2007	0.3	0.4	0.4	0.4	0.4	0.4	0.3	0.3	0.3	0.3	0.3	0.3	0.3
Construction													
2000	53.6	54.5	54.5	55.5	55.6	56.4	55.5	55.6	55.9	54.7	54.8	55.1	55.1
2001	54.5	54.4	54.9	54.6	54.5	55.3	55.6	56.1	56.0	55.8	55.7	55.4	55.2
2002	54.6	54.9	55.3	55.0	55.4	55.5	55.8	56.8	57.1	58.0	58.5	59.0	56.3
2003	57.4	58.2	58.7	59.0	59.7	60.6	60.7	61.9	62.5	63.5	63.7	64.8	60.8
2004	64.6	65.5	66.6	67.6	68.1	69.3	70.3	70.7	70.6	71.5	72.6	73.3	69.2
2005	73.8	74.8	75.9	77.1	78.4	79.4	80.8	81.6	82.4	82.3	83.3	84.2	79.5
2006	83.5	84.7	86.0	86.5	87.4	87.8	87.1	87.3	87.1	86.5	85.7	85.6	86.3
2007	82.8	82.3	82.6	81.1	81.0	81.1	80.2	80.7	80.2	78.1	77.3	76.3	80.3
Manufacturing													
2000	51.5	51.5	51.7	50.8	51.2	51.1	50.9	51.1	50.9	50.3	50.7	50.9	51.1
2001	50.0	49.8	49.8	49.6	49.1	48.8	47.8	47.6	47.1	46.4	45.9	45.5	48.1
2002	45.6	45.7	45.7	45.1	44.9	44.5	43.8	43.7	43.6	43.6	43.4	43.5	44.4
2003	42.9	42.9	43.0	42.2	42.2	42.2	41.8	41.8	41.9	41.8	41.7	41.9	42.1
2004	41.8	42.0	42.3	42.8	43.0	43.3	43.4	43.4	43.3	43.9	44.2	44.5	43.2
2005	44.2	44.3	44.5	44.9	44.7	44.8	44.7	44.4	44.2	43.9	43.8	43.5	44.3
2006	43.1	43.1	43.6	43.4	43.6	43.9	43.6	43.5	43.4	43.5	43.4	43.5	43.5
2007	43.0	43.1	43.3	43.3	43.2	43.2	42.8	42.9	42.6	42.5	42.4	42.5	42.9
Service-Providing													
2000	785.0	794.6	801.9	800.7	805.4	801.8	793.5	805.3	811.0	812.7	819.6	826.1	804.8
2001	806.7	815.3	822.1	818.4	821.1	811.0	803.0	813.7	814.1	805.6	805.7	807.7	812.0
2002	791.4	800.7	807.3	805.7	808.8	800.7	795.4	807.2	808.2	812.0	819.9	826.0	806.9
2003	812.7	816.0	819.4	820.0	822.4	815.3	813.1	828.6	829.8	835.5	843.5	849.8	825.5
2004	843.0	849.3	853.9	860.5	864.1	856.6	855.6	867.8	868.7	880.8	891.6	899.2	865.9
2005	891.5	897.8	904.2	908.2	913.4	901.9	899.9	914.3	918.7	921.5	931.2	937.2	911.7
2006	928.6	934.2	941.3	945.6	948.4	937.8	929.3	946.5	951.3	951.8	964.3	971.2	945.9
2007	962.7	973.0	978.1	981.2	982.5	968.8	960.8	973.4	973.0	980.7	985.6	990.5	975.9
Trade, Transportation, and Utilities													
2000	176.7	176.7	177.7	178.0	178.3	179.6	177.9	179.3	179.9	180.1	184.4	187.4	179.7
2001	179.1	178.1	178.8	178.6	178.6	178.2	177.8	178.0	177.7	175.8	177.7	179.4	178.2
2002	171.9	170.6	171.0	170.6	170.9	170.3	169.2	170.1	170.6	170.9	174.8	178.2	171.6
2003	172.1	171.0	171.2	170.8	170.6	170.5	171.6	172.8	173.6	175.0	178.8	182.4	173.4
2004	176.9	175.7	176.6	179.0	179.9	180.5	181.3	181.8	181.2	184.5	189.4	193.1	181.7
2005	187.7	187.9	189.2	190.8	191.7	191.8	192.8	193.3	193.2	194.4	198.4	201.8	192.8
2006	196.8	196.3	196.7	197.3	198.3	198.1	197.4	198.0	197.8	198.4	203.5	207.1	198.8
2007	200.7	201.2	200.9	200.7	202.4	201.9	201.4	202.3	202.2	203.1	206.4	210.8	202.8
Wholesale Trade													
2000	38.0	38.4	38.7	40.3	40.6	41.1	41.3	41.5	41.7	41.5	41.6	41.9	40.6
2001	42.0	42.2	42.4	42.2	42.2	42.2	41.9	41.9	42.0	41.7	41.4	40.9	41.9
2002	39.9	39.9	40.0	39.7	39.7	39.4	39.2	39.2	39.3	39.4	39.5	39.4	39.6
2003	39.6	39.6	39.8	39.7	39.8	39.9	40.1	40.2	40.4	40.2	40.4	40.6	40.0
2004	40.8	41.0	41.2	41.9	42.0	42.2	42.3	42.2	42.1	42.3	42.5	42.8	41.9
2005	43.3	43.7	43.7	44.3	44.6	44.8	45.0	45.1	45.3	45.2	45.5	45.9	44.7
2006	45.7	46.1	46.2	46.2	46.8	46.5	46.4	46.0	46.2	46.1	46.1	46.3	46.2
2007	46.6	47.2	47.1	47.0	47.2	47.1	47.3	47.3	47.5	47.5	47.4	47.6	47.2

Employment by Industry: Orlando-Kissimmee, FL, 2000–2007—*Continued*

(Numbers in thousands, not seasonally adjusted.)

Industry and year	January	February	March	April	May	June	July	August	September	October	November	December	Annual Average
Retail Trade													
2000	109.9	109.3	109.9	108.1	108.3	109.4	107.3	108.3	108.5	108.9	112.5	114.5	109.6
2001	106.8	105.9	106.4	106.0	106.2	106.2	106.3	106.6	106.3	105.7	108.1	109.7	106.7
2002	104.9	103.7	104.0	103.4	103.8	103.6	102.7	103.6	104.0	104.5	108.1	110.7	104.8
2003	105.8	105.1	105.2	105.0	105.0	105.2	105.8	106.8	107.5	109.3	112.8	115.5	107.4
2004	110.8	109.2	109.8	111.0	111.7	112.2	113.0	113.3	112.9	115.6	119.9	122.3	113.5
2005	117.5	117.4	118.3	119.0	119.2	119.2	120.0	120.1	119.5	120.7	124.0	126.3	120.1
2006	122.1	121.2	121.3	121.6	121.6	121.6	121.0	121.3	120.6	121.3	126.1	128.4	122.3
2007	122.6	121.8	121.7	121.3	122.8	122.9	122.5	123.1	122.5	123.3	126.5	129.6	123.4
Transportation and Utilities													
2000	28.8	29.0	29.1	29.6	29.4	29.1	29.3	29.5	29.7	29.7	30.3	31.0	29.5
2001	30.3	30.0	30.0	30.4	30.2	29.8	29.6	29.5	29.4	28.4	28.2	28.8	29.6
2002	27.1	27.0	27.0	27.5	27.4	27.3	27.3	27.3	27.3	27.0	27.2	28.1	27.3
2003	26.7	26.3	26.2	26.1	25.8	25.4	25.7	25.8	25.7	25.5	25.6	26.3	25.9
2004	25.3	25.5	25.6	26.1	26.2	26.1	26.0	26.3	26.2	26.6	27.0	28.0	26.2
2005	26.9	26.8	27.2	27.5	27.9	27.8	27.8	28.1	28.4	28.5	28.9	29.6	28.0
2006	29.0	29.0	29.2	29.5	29.9	30.0	30.0	30.7	31.0	31.0	31.3	32.4	30.3
2007	31.5	32.2	32.1	32.4	32.4	31.9	31.6	31.9	32.2	32.3	32.5	33.6	32.2
Information													
2000	23.5	23.3	23.6	23.1	23.3	23.5	23.5	23.6	23.9	23.3	23.4	23.6	23.5
2001	23.2	23.3	23.1	22.9	23.1	23.1	23.0	22.9	22.8	22.6	22.8	23.0	23.0
2002	22.6	22.6	22.5	22.2	22.6	22.5	22.4	22.7	22.4	22.4	22.6	22.7	22.5
2003	22.4	22.9	22.8	22.6	23.2	23.3	23.0	23.4	23.1	23.1	23.5	23.6	23.1
2004	23.2	23.4	23.4	23.6	23.9	23.8	24.0	24.0	23.7	23.8	24.3	24.2	23.8
2005	23.8	24.2	24.1	24.2	25.1	24.9	24.8	24.9	24.9	24.9	25.2	25.4	24.7
2006	25.3	25.5	25.8	25.9	26.0	26.0	25.9	25.7	25.9	25.9	26.0	26.0	25.8
2007	26.2	26.4	26.9	27.2	27.5	27.5	27.1	26.9	26.7	26.7	27.1	27.0	26.9
Financial Activities													
2000	54.1	54.5	55.0	54.0	54.4	54.9	54.4	54.5	54.5	54.1	54.3	54.7	54.5
2001	53.3	53.4	53.7	54.4	54.4	54.9	54.7	54.9	54.6	53.9	54.0	54.3	54.2
2002	53.6	53.8	54.3	53.8	54.2	54.6	54.9	55.0	55.2	55.4	55.8	56.4	54.8
2003	56.0	56.4	56.7	56.6	56.7	57.4	57.5	57.9	57.9	58.2	58.4	58.9	57.4
2004	57.4	58.0	58.1	58.7	59.0	59.5	59.9	60.3	59.9	60.6	60.8	61.7	59.5
2005	60.7	61.5	61.9	62.6	63.0	63.4	64.5	64.8	64.9	65.3	65.6	66.2	63.7
2006	65.6	66.1	66.4	66.7	66.9	67.1	66.8	67.2	67.1	67.6	68.1	68.5	67.0
2007	67.3	67.9	68.1	67.7	67.9	68.4	67.7	67.4	67.1	67.6	67.4	67.5	67.7
Professional and Business Services													
2000	142.1	145.5	148.0	147.7	149.9	152.8	152.7	154.8	158.6	160.9	162.6	163.4	153.3
2001	160.7	163.3	165.2	162.5	163.3	161.0	160.3	160.6	160.1	159.3	158.3	158.0	161.1
2002	155.6	158.6	160.5	159.0	158.2	156.8	157.1	156.0	155.9	157.6	158.7	159.0	157.8
2003	156.7	156.3	156.2	157.3	157.0	158.0	157.4	159.3	159.9	162.5	162.9	162.5	158.8
2004	163.0	164.8	165.6	167.5	168.3	169.6	169.0	170.6	171.4	175.8	177.6	179.1	170.2
2005	180.5	181.6	182.7	183.8	184.3	184.3	183.2	184.4	185.3	186.1	188.0	188.2	184.4
2006	187.8	187.7	190.4	192.6	193.1	193.3	190.1	192.0	194.4	193.4	196.1	197.4	192.4
2007	196.7	199.3	199.9	200.8	200.7	197.2	196.9	196.4	196.7	201.0	201.4	201.1	199.0
Education and Health Services													
2000	84.1	84.4	84.9	85.8	86.4	86.0	85.1	85.8	86.4	85.9	85.7	86.1	85.6
2001	84.2	85.0	85.6	86.3	86.7	86.8	86.4	87.6	88.3	88.8	89.1	89.2	87.0
2002	86.9	87.8	88.1	88.9	89.3	88.8	88.6	89.9	90.5	90.9	91.3	91.4	89.4
2003	91.5	92.0	92.1	92.7	93.4	93.3	93.1	94.1	94.9	94.8	95.3	95.5	93.5
2004	95.2	96.1	96.5	96.7	97.3	97.1	97.1	97.4	97.7	98.4	99.1	99.3	97.3
2005	99.6	100.1	100.6	100.8	101.7	100.9	101.3	102.8	103.6	104.2	105.0	105.3	102.2
2006	104.8	105.8	106.3	106.4	107.0	106.8	106.3	107.9	108.9	109.3	109.9	110.3	107.5
2007	109.5	110.6	111.0	111.5	112.2	111.8	110.4	111.5	112.4	112.5	112.1	112.1	111.5
Leisure and Hospitality													
2000	173.6	177.4	179.4	178.6	177.3	180.5	178.0	176.4	175.6	174.8	175.4	176.4	177.0
2001	172.7	175.9	177.1	174.6	175.4	176.6	172.4	171.0	170.0	162.6	159.9	159.2	170.6
2002	156.2	161.3	164.6	164.7	166.0	170.7	168.0	166.4	164.7	164.4	165.5	166.9	165.0
2003	163.9	166.3	169.1	169.0	169.8	172.3	172.2	172.0	169.6	169.5	171.6	173.5	169.9
2004	174.1	176.6	178.4	179.9	180.0	181.3	181.7	180.3	178.4	179.1	180.5	181.8	179.3
2005	180.0	182.1	184.8	184.7	184.7	185.8	184.4	183.4	182.8	182.0	183.6	184.8	183.6
2006	183.0	185.5	188.4	188.5	188.5	188.3	187.0	186.8	185.9	184.7	187.0	188.6	186.9
2007	188.0	191.1	193.9	195.5	193.9	195.1	193.3	191.7	189.5	191.4	192.1	193.5	192.4
Other Services													
2000	39.3	39.5	39.5	39.9	40.0	40.1	39.4	39.2	39.4	40.0	39.7	39.8	39.7
2001	39.9	40.6	41.2	41.5	42.2	42.7	42.8	43.0	43.5	43.5	43.9	44.3	42.4
2002	44.5	44.9	45.1	44.7	45.1	45.3	45.4	45.7	45.9	45.9	46.1	45.9	45.4
2003	45.7	46.0	46.1	45.4	45.6	45.7	45.5	45.4	45.7	45.6	45.6	45.8	45.6
2004	46.5	46.7	47.1	47.0	47.4	48.0	47.8	47.3	47.7	47.9	48.3	48.5	47.5
2005	48.4	48.6	48.7	49.1	49.7	49.9	50.1	50.2	50.8	50.7	50.9	51.2	49.9
2006	51.4	52.0	52.1	52.0	52.6	53.1	53.0	53.6	54.5	55.1	55.6	56.0	53.4
2007	56.5	57.2	57.7	57.3	57.7	57.9	57.4	57.3	57.8	58.0	58.0	58.3	57.6
Government													
2000	91.6	93.3	93.8	93.6	95.8	84.4	82.5	91.7	92.7	93.6	94.1	94.7	91.8
2001	93.6	95.7	97.4	97.6	97.4	87.7	85.6	95.7	97.1	99.1	100.0	100.3	95.6
2002	100.1	101.1	101.2	101.8	102.5	91.7	89.8	101.4	103.0	104.5	105.1	105.5	100.6
2003	104.4	105.1	105.2	105.6	106.1	94.8	92.8	103.7	105.1	106.8	107.4	107.6	103.7
2004	106.7	108.0	108.2	108.1	108.3	96.8	94.8	106.1	108.7	110.7	111.6	111.5	106.6
2005	110.8	111.8	112.2	112.2	113.2	100.9	98.8	110.5	113.2	113.9	114.5	114.3	110.5
2006	113.9	115.3	115.2	116.2	116.0	105.1	102.8	115.3	116.8	117.4	118.1	117.3	114.1
2007	117.8	119.3	119.7	120.5	120.2	109.0	106.6	119.9	120.6	120.4	121.1	120.2	117.9

Employment by Industry: Columbus, OH, 2000–2007

(Numbers in thousands, not seasonally adjusted.)

Industry and year	January	February	March	April	May	June	July	August	September	October	November	December	Annual Average
Total Nonfarm													
2000	892.8	896.5	902.1	908.6	914.2	922.2	919.0	920.3	916.4	924.7	931.9	935.6	915.4
2001	912.4	914.3	918.3	921.1	924.3	927.6	919.2	917.7	912.6	919.7	924.6	926.6	919.9
2002	903.9	904.7	909.3	911.3	916.3	919.8	913.4	913.4	911.7	917.0	921.5	921.1	913.6
2003	901.3	898.8	902.2	907.5	912.0	914.3	910.8	911.8	908.0	916.8	921.8	922.6	910.6
2004	894.5	895.1	902.8	909.5	916.8	921.5	917.4	920.0	917.0	928.8	934.2	934.8	916.0
2005	902.7	903.7	909.3	917.7	923.4	926.9	923.2	925.2	925.8	933.9	939.8	940.5	922.7
2006	911.9	915.2	921.8	927.8	934.0	937.8	931.5	933.1	932.5	940.5	946.9	949.5	931.9
2007	926.1	922.5	929.5	938.7	947.0	950.7	945.4	947.9	945.0	951.8	957.8	960.6	943.6
Total Private													
2000	749.7	752.3	757.4	763.7	769.0	775.4	776.0	778.1	772.4	777.9	784.1	786.7	770.2
2001	766.8	766.8	770.0	773.1	775.4	778.3	773.2	773.0	765.7	769.3	773.1	774.5	771.6
2002	753.4	753.6	758.1	760.6	765.2	767.7	766.1	767.0	763.7	766.2	768.9	768.1	763.2
2003	749.3	746.2	749.6	755.2	759.0	760.9	761.2	763.6	759.1	764.7	768.5	768.8	758.8
2004	741.9	741.8	749.0	756.3	762.6	766.3	766.2	768.9	765.6	773.4	777.6	778.4	762.3
2005	748.2	747.5	752.8	761.4	766.4	769.1	769.4	771.4	772.8	776.6	781.8	782.8	766.7
2006	755.8	757.7	763.9	770.5	775.6	780.3	777.9	779.2	779.2	782.9	788.5	791.0	775.2
2007	769.1	765.0	771.6	781.5	788.8	792.5	791.3	793.3	791.3	793.9	798.5	801.2	786.5
Goods-Producing													
2000	138.7	138.7	141.1	142.2	143.9	146.2	146.2	146.1	144.8	144.2	143.3	141.9	143.1
2001	136.6	136.4	137.2	138.3	138.7	139.8	139.9	139.7	137.4	136.2	134.8	133.0	137.3
2002	128.2	127.8	128.5	129.2	130.9	132.6	131.9	133.1	132.5	131.2	129.7	127.9	130.3
2003	123.1	121.5	122.0	124.2	125.1	126.2	126.4	126.8	126.1	125.9	125.0	124.2	124.7
2004	118.6	118.0	119.2	121.8	123.5	123.8	123.7	123.8	123.1	122.1	121.5	120.7	121.7
2005	114.5	114.0	114.8	117.7	119.3	121.0	121.8	121.9	121.7	120.8	120.6	119.3	119.0
2006	114.2	114.3	115.3	117.4	118.3	119.9	119.6	119.9	119.6	118.5	117.2	116.6	117.6
2007	113.0	111.1	112.5	114.2	115.9	117.5	117.4	117.7	116.9	115.8	115.2	114.3	115.1
Natural Resources, Mining, and Construction													
2000	37.8	37.7	39.7	41.9	43.3	44.8	45.0	44.9	44.1	43.0	42.3	40.8	42.1
2001	37.8	38.2	39.5	41.6	42.7	44.4	45.2	45.5	44.4	43.2	42.6	41.3	42.2
2002	37.7	37.4	38.4	39.8	41.2	42.4	43.3	43.5	43.0	42.5	41.9	40.5	41.0
2003	37.1	36.1	36.8	39.6	40.8	42.0	42.7	43.0	42.6	42.5	41.9	41.1	40.5
2004	37.1	36.5	37.5	40.1	41.7	42.4	43.1	42.9	42.5	41.8	41.3	40.3	40.6
2005	35.7	35.3	36.2	39.1	40.7	41.8	42.9	43.0	42.6	41.8	41.5	40.1	40.1
2006	36.6	36.5	37.4	39.3	40.3	41.2	41.6	41.6	41.3	40.7	39.8	38.9	39.6
2007	35.9	34.4	35.8	37.2	38.8	40.2	40.4	40.4	39.7	39.1	38.5	37.7	38.2
Manufacturing													
2000	100.9	101.0	101.4	100.3	100.6	101.4	101.2	101.2	100.7	101.2	101.0	101.1	101.0
2001	98.8	98.2	97.7	96.7	96.0	95.4	94.7	94.2	93.0	93.0	92.2	91.7	95.1
2002	90.5	90.4	90.1	89.4	89.7	90.2	88.6	89.6	89.5	88.7	87.8	87.4	89.3
2003	86.0	85.4	85.2	84.6	84.3	84.2	83.7	83.8	83.5	83.4	83.1	83.1	84.1
2004	81.5	81.5	81.7	81.7	81.8	81.4	80.6	80.9	80.6	80.3	80.2	80.4	81.1
2005	78.8	78.7	78.6	78.6	78.6	79.2	78.9	78.9	79.1	79.0	79.1	79.2	78.9
2006	77.6	77.8	77.9	78.1	78.0	78.7	78.0	78.3	78.3	77.8	77.4	77.7	78.0
2007	77.1	76.7	76.7	77.0	77.1	77.3	77.0	77.3	77.2	76.7	76.7	76.6	77.0
Service-Providing													
2000	754.1	757.8	761.0	766.4	770.3	776.0	772.8	774.2	771.6	780.5	788.6	793.7	772.3
2001	775.8	777.9	781.1	782.8	785.6	787.8	779.3	778.0	775.2	783.5	789.8	793.6	782.5
2002	775.7	776.9	780.8	782.1	785.4	787.2	781.5	780.3	779.2	785.8	791.8	793.2	783.3
2003	778.2	777.3	780.2	783.3	786.9	788.1	784.4	785.0	781.9	790.9	796.8	798.4	785.9
2004	775.9	777.1	783.6	787.7	793.3	797.7	793.7	796.2	793.9	806.7	812.7	814.1	794.4
2005	788.2	789.7	794.5	800.0	804.1	805.9	801.4	803.3	804.1	813.1	819.2	821.2	803.7
2006	797.7	800.9	806.5	810.4	815.7	817.9	811.9	813.2	812.9	822.0	829.7	832.9	814.3
2007	813.1	811.4	817.0	824.5	831.1	833.2	828.0	830.2	828.1	836.0	842.6	846.3	828.5
Trade, Transportation, and Utilities													
2000	193.3	191.7	191.5	193.4	193.8	194.5	194.8	195.1	193.9	199.1	206.3	210.9	196.5
2001	198.6	194.5	194.5	194.6	194.5	194.3	191.7	191.2	191.2	194.6	199.9	203.4	195.3
2002	191.0	189.0	189.9	189.5	190.0	189.5	189.2	188.9	188.0	189.2	192.1	194.4	190.1
2003	185.1	182.8	183.4	184.2	184.6	184.6	184.3	185.2	184.5	187.1	191.1	193.6	185.8
2004	182.4	179.9	181.4	180.4	181.7	183.6	184.2	184.6	184.2	188.6	193.9	197.3	185.2
2005	185.8	183.2	184.1	184.2	184.8	184.3	184.1	184.2	184.7	187.8	193.3	197.2	186.5
2006	185.8	183.8	184.1	184.4	186.1	186.0	185.9	185.7	185.8	189.1	196.1	199.3	187.7
2007	189.2	185.9	187.1	188.1	190.3	190.4	191.3	191.6	192.0	194.6	200.0	202.1	191.9
Wholesale Trade													
2000	38.1	38.5	38.6	39.1	39.2	39.7	39.7	39.9	40.0	39.7	39.8	39.8	39.3
2001	39.4	39.5	39.8	40.0	40.0	40.0	39.8	39.7	39.3	39.5	39.2	39.7	39.7
2002	39.1	39.1	39.3	38.8	38.8	38.7	38.8	38.8	38.6	38.6	38.6	38.7	38.8
2003	38.1	38.1	38.3	38.2	38.1	37.8	37.8	37.8	37.8	37.2	37.4	37.3	37.7
2004	36.8	36.6	36.4	36.5	36.8	36.9	37.3	37.5	37.2	37.4	37.5	37.4	37.0
2005	37.0	37.0	37.0	37.3	37.3	37.2	37.7	37.5	37.5	37.4	37.7	37.7	37.4
2006	37.4	37.6	37.5	37.6	37.8	37.8	37.8	37.7	37.6	37.7	38.1	38.1	37.7
2007	37.8	37.8	38.0	38.2	38.8	38.9	39.1	39.2	39.0	39.2	39.5	39.5	38.8
Retail Trade													
2000	120.8	118.9	119.0	119.5	120.0	120.4	120.2	120.4	119.2	123.3	130.4	135.2	122.3
2001	123.5	119.6	119.8	119.1	119.2	119.3	116.4	116.0	116.6	119.0	124.6	127.9	120.1
2002	116.5	114.8	115.6	115.8	116.3	115.7	114.4	113.7	113.2	113.8	116.5	118.8	115.4
2003	110.7	108.4	108.9	109.4	109.7	109.9	109.4	109.9	109.5	111.2	115.0	117.4	110.7
2004	108.0	106.1	107.3	105.9	106.7	108.0	107.6	107.8	107.6	109.6	114.3	117.6	108.9
2005	108.4	106.1	106.8	106.6	107.0	106.5	105.4	105.4	105.4	106.7	110.5	114.3	107.4
2006	104.7	102.7	103.0	102.8	103.9	103.5	103.1	102.6	101.8	103.4	108.3	110.7	104.2
2007	102.2	99.9	100.9	101.4	102.4	102.1	102.8	102.7	102.4	104.1	107.9	109.9	103.2

Employment by Industry: Columbus, OH, 2000–2007—*Continued*

(Numbers in thousands, not seasonally adjusted.)

Industry and year	January	February	March	April	May	June	July	August	September	October	November	December	Annual Average
Transportation and Utilities													
2000	34.4	34.3	33.9	34.8	34.6	34.4	34.9	34.8	34.7	36.1	36.1	35.9	34.9
2001	35.7	35.4	34.9	35.5	35.3	35.0	35.5	35.5	35.3	36.1	36.1	35.8	35.5
2002	35.4	35.1	35.0	34.9	34.9	35.1	36.0	36.4	36.2	36.8	37.0	36.9	35.8
2003	36.3	36.3	36.2	36.6	36.8	36.9	37.1	37.5	37.8	38.5	38.8	38.9	37.3
2004	37.6	37.2	37.7	38.0	38.2	38.7	39.3	39.3	39.4	41.6	42.1	42.3	39.3
2005	40.4	40.1	40.3	40.3	40.5	40.6	41.0	41.3	41.8	43.7	45.1	45.2	41.7
2006	43.7	43.5	43.6	44.0	44.4	44.7	45.0	45.4	46.4	48.0	49.7	50.5	45.7
2007	49.2	48.2	48.2	48.5	49.1	49.4	49.4	49.7	50.6	51.3	52.6	52.7	49.9
Information													
2000	22.0	22.2	22.3	22.0	22.2	22.4	22.5	22.7	22.6	23.1	23.1	23.1	22.5
2001	23.4	23.3	23.0	22.7	22.8	22.9	22.5	22.5	22.0	21.7	21.7	21.5	22.5
2002	21.8	21.5	21.5	21.1	21.1	21.2	21.3	21.4	21.3	21.1	21.2	21.2	21.3
2003	21.1	21.1	20.8	20.7	20.6	20.6	20.4	20.4	20.1	20.2	20.2	20.1	20.5
2004	19.8	19.8	19.6	19.5	19.6	19.8	19.9	19.7	19.7	19.6	19.6	19.5	19.7
2005	19.4	19.2	19.3	19.3	19.4	19.4	19.4	19.5	19.6	19.2	19.2	19.2	19.3
2006	19.1	19.0	19.0	18.8	18.9	18.9	18.8	18.7	18.5	18.4	18.5	18.5	18.8
2007	18.7	18.8	18.7	18.8	18.9	18.9	18.9	18.8	18.5	18.5	18.6	18.6	18.7
Financial Activities													
2000	75.8	75.9	75.6	75.3	75.5	75.9	75.8	75.6	75.5	75.6	76.1	76.7	75.8
2001	76.0	76.4	77.0	77.1	77.2	77.9	77.4	77.3	77.1	76.4	76.8	77.2	77.0
2002	76.7	77.1	77.3	77.3	77.1	76.9	77.0	77.0	76.8	77.4	77.9	78.1	77.2
2003	76.1	76.6	76.6	75.9	75.9	76.1	75.8	75.9	75.4	74.9	75.0	75.1	75.7
2004	74.3	74.4	74.4	74.3	74.1	74.3	74.1	73.9	73.2	73.3	73.2	73.1	73.9
2005	72.3	72.3	72.3	72.3	72.5	72.8	73.1	73.2	73.3	73.3	73.5	73.8	72.9
2006	73.1	73.0	73.1	73.2	73.3	73.8	74.3	73.9	74.0	74.6	74.7	74.5	73.8
2007	74.1	74.0	73.4	74.4	74.0	73.5	74.0	74.1	73.7	73.7	74.0	74.1	73.9
Professional and Business Services													
2000	125.2	126.4	127.7	128.4	128.8	130.1	130.8	131.2	131.1	131.6	131.4	131.1	129.5
2001	133.0	133.4	133.8	133.8	132.6	132.3	132.3	132.0	130.5	131.3	130.5	130.5	132.2
2002	129.1	129.2	129.5	129.4	128.4	128.8	128.8	129.0	128.5	129.5	130.1	129.6	129.2
2003	131.4	130.6	131.3	130.9	130.4	129.7	130.5	131.1	130.3	132.2	133.1	132.0	131.1
2004	129.1	129.9	131.4	133.5	133.6	134.5	134.2	136.3	136.2	139.1	138.9	139.1	134.7
2005	134.3	135.0	136.0	136.9	137.0	137.4	137.8	139.6	140.4	142.0	141.7	141.9	138.3
2006	137.5	138.4	140.0	142.2	142.2	144.1	143.7	145.2	145.1	146.1	146.6	147.7	143.2
2007	143.9	144.1	145.9	148.4	148.8	150.7	150.4	151.4	151.0	152.2	152.6	153.8	149.4
Education and Health Services													
2000	86.6	87.7	87.7	88.1	88.0	87.6	87.3	88.4	88.4	89.2	89.4	89.9	88.2
2001	87.9	89.8	90.4	90.4	90.7	90.7	89.5	89.8	90.0	92.6	93.5	93.7	90.8
2002	92.4	93.7	94.1	94.3	94.5	93.7	93.2	93.2	94.4	96.7	97.2	97.3	94.6
2003	95.6	96.7	97.0	97.9	98.0	96.9	96.5	96.7	98.1	100.2	101.0	100.9	97.9
2004	98.4	100.0	100.7	102.1	102.2	100.8	100.6	100.4	101.9	104.0	104.4	104.5	101.7
2005	102.0	103.4	103.9	105.4	104.8	103.5	103.5	103.5	105.5	107.2	107.9	107.7	104.9
2006	105.7	107.6	108.4	108.8	108.1	106.4	105.4	105.6	108.4	109.6	110.1	109.8	107.8
2007	108.5	109.4	110.2	111.3	111.0	109.2	108.6	108.8	111.4	112.5	112.9	113.0	110.6
Leisure and Hospitality													
2000	74.8	76.0	77.6	80.0	82.3	84.0	83.9	84.2	81.7	80.8	80.2	78.9	80.4
2001	77.3	78.5	79.4	80.9	83.3	84.6	84.2	84.6	82.1	81.0	80.0	79.4	81.3
2002	78.8	79.4	81.2	83.2	86.1	87.6	87.4	87.0	85.1	84.1	83.5	82.3	83.8
2003	79.7	79.5	80.9	83.7	86.5	88.5	89.1	89.3	86.9	86.5	85.4	85.0	85.0
2004	81.6	81.8	83.7	86.1	89.3	90.6	90.5	91.3	88.9	88.0	87.0	86.5	87.1
2005	82.8	83.0	84.7	88.0	90.8	92.8	92.2	91.8	90.4	88.7	87.5	86.5	88.3
2006	83.4	84.4	86.5	88.1	91.0	92.9	92.3	92.3	90.3	89.0	87.8	87.3	88.8
2007	84.7	84.6	86.5	89.1	92.2	94.4	93.1	93.3	90.8	89.5	88.2	88.3	89.6
Other Services													
2000	33.3	33.7	33.9	34.3	34.5	34.7	34.7	34.8	34.4	34.3	34.3	34.2	34.3
2001	34.0	34.5	34.7	35.3	35.6	35.8	35.7	35.9	35.4	35.5	35.9	35.8	35.3
2002	35.4	35.9	36.1	36.6	37.1	37.4	37.3	37.4	37.1	37.0	37.2	37.3	36.8
2003	37.2	37.4	37.6	37.7	37.9	38.3	38.2	38.2	37.7	37.7	37.7	37.9	37.7
2004	37.7	38.0	38.6	38.6	38.6	38.9	39.0	38.9	38.4	38.7	39.1	37.7	38.5
2005	37.1	37.4	37.7	37.6	37.8	37.9	37.5	37.7	37.2	37.6	38.1	37.2	37.6
2006	37.0	37.2	37.5	37.6	37.7	38.3	37.9	37.9	37.5	37.6	37.5	37.3	37.6
2007	37.0	37.1	37.3	37.2	37.7	37.9	37.6	37.6	37.0	37.1	37.0	37.0	37.3
Government													
2000	143.1	144.2	144.7	144.9	145.2	146.8	143.0	142.2	144.0	146.8	147.8	148.9	145.1
2001	145.6	147.5	148.3	148.0	148.9	149.3	146.0	144.7	146.9	150.4	151.5	152.1	148.3
2002	150.5	151.1	151.2	150.7	151.1	152.1	147.3	146.4	148.0	150.8	152.6	153.0	150.4
2003	152.0	152.6	152.6	152.3	153.0	153.4	149.6	148.2	148.9	152.1	153.3	153.8	151.8
2004	152.6	153.3	153.8	153.2	154.2	155.2	151.2	151.1	151.4	155.4	156.6	156.4	153.7
2005	154.5	156.2	156.5	156.3	157.0	157.8	153.8	153.8	153.0	157.3	158.0	157.7	156.0
2006	156.1	157.5	157.9	157.3	158.4	157.5	153.6	153.9	153.3	157.6	158.4	158.5	156.7
2007	157.0	157.5	157.9	157.2	158.2	158.2	154.1	154.6	153.7	157.9	159.3	159.4	157.1

Employment by Industry: Virginia Beach-Norfolk-Newport News, VA-NC, 2000–2007

(Numbers in thousands, not seasonally adjusted.)

Industry and year	January	February	March	April	May	June	July	August	September	October	November	December	Annual Average
Total Nonfarm													
2000	699.7	703.7	713.1	714.4	720.6	731.1	722.4	726.0	726.6	726.0	730.6	730.5	720.4
2001	707.3	710.5	718.9	726.4	733.7	743.5	736.4	739.0	737.9	734.9	739.7	739.1	730.6
2002	714.4	719.2	725.6	730.4	737.5	746.5	734.7	738.5	736.1	739.2	742.3	744.2	734.1
2003	721.9	723.9	730.6	731.4	739.6	747.1	740.0	742.0	739.8	741.7	746.8	746.9	737.6
2004	729.4	730.3	738.3	746.1	752.9	761.2	754.6	756.7	755.7	754.4	758.1	759.8	749.8
2005	738.2	741.3	749.2	759.3	766.2	775.9	767.6	770.6	771.0	760.5	764.7	765.0	760.8
2006	747.8	750.0	759.2	766.1	772.7	782.7	772.1	772.4	768.0	768.7	773.2	774.8	767.3
2007	758.1	759.3	767.6	773.4	780.5	789.4	778.0	777.1	775.5	777.3	781.1	781.0	774.9
Total Private													
2000	554.5	557.8	566.1	567.9	573.7	584.6	580.1	584.0	581.3	578.9	582.2	583.4	574.5
2001	561.4	562.9	571.1	578.5	585.9	594.4	591.5	594.6	590.8	586.2	589.6	589.8	583.1
2002	566.7	569.9	575.3	580.3	586.5	595.0	589.5	593.0	587.1	588.1	590.9	593.1	584.6
2003	572.6	573.6	579.6	582.4	590.0	596.5	592.9	595.5	590.7	592.9	596.2	596.3	588.3
2004	579.6	579.2	586.5	594.5	600.7	608.2	606.8	607.8	604.9	602.7	604.6	606.8	598.5
2005	588.6	590.3	597.7	606.9	613.3	621.8	618.3	620.9	619.7	609.3	611.8	613.1	609.3
2006	597.2	598.3	606.9	612.0	618.5	627.6	620.9	621.6	617.0	614.9	617.7	619.7	614.4
2007	604.4	604.2	612.0	617.8	624.9	633.0	626.8	626.2	622.9	622.5	625.8	625.9	620.5
Goods-Producing													
2000	106.6	107.1	108.4	108.4	109.0	110.4	109.9	109.7	109.6	110.0	110.1	110.1	109.1
2001	106.4	106.8	108.1	108.4	109.0	109.6	108.6	110.3	109.4	108.4	108.2	108.2	108.5
2002	104.2	104.1	104.5	104.0	104.7	105.4	104.0	105.7	104.7	105.1	105.1	105.4	104.7
2003	103.9	104.4	105.5	105.0	106.3	107.1	106.4	107.3	106.2	108.5	110.0	108.9	106.5
2004	106.2	105.2	106.4	107.6	108.5	109.7	108.6	110.0	109.7	110.3	110.3	110.0	108.5
2005	108.3	108.3	109.0	110.4	110.6	111.4	110.0	112.0	111.2	109.2	109.0	109.2	109.9
2006	107.2	107.2	108.6	109.0	109.5	110.3	107.9	109.8	107.2	106.7	106.7	108.1	108.2
2007	105.9	104.8	105.7	106.8	106.8	107.5	106.3	106.2	105.4	106.5	106.8	106.8	106.3
Natural Resources, Mining, and Construction													
2000	41.8	42.1	43.2	43.6	44.0	45.0	44.8	44.8	44.6	44.5	44.8	44.8	44.0
2001	43.9	44.3	45.3	45.8	46.5	47.2	47.3	47.5	46.8	45.9	45.6	45.4	46.0
2002	43.6	44.0	44.6	44.3	44.8	45.3	45.7	45.5	44.6	44.7	44.4	44.5	44.7
2003	43.9	44.5	45.2	45.6	47.0	47.5	48.1	48.1	47.1	49.3	50.2	49.5	47.2
2004	46.9	46.3	47.2	48.3	48.9	49.8	50.4	49.9	49.3	49.6	49.2	49.3	48.8
2005	48.1	48.1	48.7	50.0	50.3	50.8	51.5	51.4	51.2	49.7	49.8	50.1	50.0
2006	48.6	48.6	49.8	50.4	50.6	51.1	50.6	50.3	49.8	49.3	49.3	49.3	49.8
2007	48.0	47.9	48.6	48.7	48.7	49.2	49.0	49.0	48.5	49.6	49.7	49.7	48.9
Manufacturing													
2000	64.9	65.0	65.2	64.8	65.1	65.4	65.1	64.8	64.9	65.5	65.2	65.2	65.1
2001	62.5	62.5	62.8	62.6	62.5	62.6	61.2	62.8	62.5	62.4	62.6	62.7	62.5
2002	60.6	60.3	60.0	59.9	60.0	60.1	58.3	60.2	60.3	60.4	60.7	60.8	60.1
2003	60.0	59.9	60.3	59.4	59.3	59.6	56.5	59.2	59.1	59.2	59.8	59.4	59.3
2004	59.3	58.9	59.2	59.3	59.6	59.9	58.2	60.1	60.4	60.7	61.1	60.7	59.8
2005	60.2	60.2	60.3	60.4	60.3	60.6	58.5	60.6	60.0	59.5	59.2	59.1	59.9
2006	58.6	58.6	58.8	58.6	58.9	59.2	57.3	59.5	57.4	57.4	57.4	58.8	58.4
2007	57.9	56.9	57.1	58.1	58.1	58.3	57.3	57.2	56.9	56.9	57.1	57.1	57.4
Service-Providing													
2000	593.1	596.6	604.7	606.0	611.6	620.8	612.5	616.3	617.0	615.9	620.6	620.4	611.3
2001	600.9	603.8	610.9	617.9	624.7	633.7	627.8	628.6	628.5	626.5	631.5	630.9	622.1
2002	610.2	614.9	621.1	626.4	632.8	641.2	630.8	632.9	631.3	634.1	637.3	638.8	629.3
2003	618.0	619.5	625.1	626.4	633.3	640.0	635.4	634.7	633.6	633.2	636.8	638.0	631.2
2004	623.2	625.1	631.9	638.5	644.4	651.5	646.0	646.7	646.0	644.1	647.8	649.8	641.3
2005	629.9	633.0	640.2	648.9	655.6	664.5	657.6	658.6	659.8	651.3	655.7	655.8	650.9
2006	640.6	642.8	650.6	657.1	663.2	672.4	664.2	662.6	660.8	662.0	666.5	666.7	659.1
2007	652.2	654.5	661.9	666.6	673.7	681.9	671.7	670.9	670.1	670.8	674.3	674.2	668.6
Trade, Transportation, and Utilities													
2000	134.6	134.4	134.8	134.6	135.9	137.2	136.4	138.0	138.5	141.4	144.9	146.6	138.1
2001	138.0	135.8	136.4	136.7	138.3	139.3	138.3	139.2	139.9	141.2	144.4	145.8	139.4
2002	138.1	136.4	135.5	136.6	138.2	140.1	138.7	139.2	138.9	141.3	145.0	147.3	139.6
2003	138.1	135.9	135.5	133.0	133.6	134.1	134.3	135.2	134.9	137.3	141.8	144.5	136.5
2004	136.8	135.8	135.4	136.8	138.1	139.2	139.6	140.1	139.5	141.2	144.7	146.1	139.4
2005	138.0	136.6	137.6	139.4	140.2	141.0	142.1	142.3	142.2	142.4	146.3	146.9	141.3
2006	139.9	138.3	139.7	140.4	141.6	142.6	142.4	141.9	140.8	143.2	147.9	148.4	142.3
2007	142.3	140.5	141.3	141.0	142.5	143.8	143.6	143.3	142.8	145.4	149.9	150.3	143.9
Wholesale Trade													
2000	23.6	23.9	24.0	24.0	24.1	24.2	24.1	24.3	24.2	24.4	24.5	24.6	24.2
2001	24.7	24.9	25.2	25.0	25.1	25.3	25.3	25.2	25.2	25.1	25.3	25.3	25.1
2002	25.2	25.2	25.2	25.5	25.6	25.7	25.3	25.3	25.2	25.3	25.5	25.5	25.4
2003	25.1	24.8	24.5	24.6	24.3	23.9	23.5	22.9	22.8	23.1	23.1	23.2	23.8
2004	22.8	22.9	23.0	23.1	23.2	23.4	23.6	23.6	23.4	23.5	23.6	23.7	23.3
2005	23.5	23.6	23.6	23.9	24.0	24.1	24.1	24.2	24.1	24.0	24.1	24.3	24.0
2006	23.9	23.9	24.0	24.1	24.1	24.2	24.3	24.1	24.1	24.1	24.2	24.2	24.1
2007	24.1	24.2	24.3	24.3	24.4	24.5	24.6	24.7	24.6	24.6	24.7	24.8	24.5
Retail Trade													
2000	85.6	85.1	85.2	84.8	85.9	87.0	86.0	87.2	88.1	89.8	93.6	95.0	87.8
2001	87.4	85.0	85.0	85.8	87.0	87.5	86.8	88.1	88.6	89.7	93.1	94.3	88.2
2002	87.7	85.8	84.7	85.7	86.9	88.1	87.1	87.8	87.7	89.5	93.0	95.0	88.3
2003	87.9	86.3	85.8	83.7	84.7	85.4	85.3	86.6	86.5	87.8	92.2	94.7	87.2
2004	88.7	87.5	86.9	88.1	89.2	89.9	90.1	90.4	90.2	91.3	94.7	95.8	90.2
2005	88.7	87.2	87.4	89.1	89.8	90.4	91.5	91.7	91.9	92.1	95.4	95.9	90.9
2006	90.6	88.9	89.9	90.5	91.5	92.2	92.1	91.7	90.7	92.8	97.1	97.8	92.2
2007	93.0	91.1	91.6	91.3	92.4	93.2	92.8	92.9	92.7	94.6	98.6	98.8	93.6

Employment by Industry: Virginia Beach-Norfolk-Newport News, VA-NC, 2000–2007—*Continued*

(Numbers in thousands, not seasonally adjusted.)

Industry and year	January	February	March	April	May	June	July	August	September	October	November	December	Annual Average
Transportation and Utilities													
2000	25.5	25.6	25.7	25.9	26.0	26.1	26.3	26.5	26.2	27.2	26.9	26.9	26.2
2001	26.0	25.9	26.2	26.0	26.3	26.5	26.2	26.0	26.2	26.5	26.2	26.2	26.2
2002	25.2	25.4	25.4	25.4	25.8	26.4	26.3	26.1	26.0	26.5	26.6	26.8	26.0
2003	25.1	24.8	25.2	24.7	24.6	24.8	25.5	25.7	25.6	26.4	26.5	26.6	25.4
2004	25.3	25.4	25.5	25.6	25.7	25.9	25.9	26.1	25.9	26.4	26.4	26.6	25.9
2005	25.8	25.8	26.6	26.4	26.4	26.5	26.5	26.4	26.2	26.3	26.8	26.7	26.4
2006	25.4	25.5	25.8	25.8	26.0	26.2	26.0	26.1	26.0	26.3	26.6	26.4	26.0
2007	25.2	25.2	25.4	25.4	25.7	26.1	26.2	25.7	25.5	26.2	26.6	26.7	25.8
Information													
2000	16.4	16.3	16.3	16.3	16.7	16.8	17.0	17.0	17.0	16.7	16.6	16.7	16.7
2001	15.6	15.5	15.6	15.6	15.8	16.1	16.4	16.5	16.5	16.6	16.9	17.0	16.2
2002	16.4	16.4	16.4	16.4	16.6	16.6	16.4	16.5	16.3	16.3	16.6	16.7	16.5
2003	16.1	16.1	16.1	16.0	16.0	16.3	16.3	15.9	15.9	15.8	15.9	15.9	16.0
2004	15.8	15.8	15.8	15.5	15.6	15.7	15.7	15.6	15.4	15.1	15.1	15.0	15.5
2005	15.0	14.8	14.7	14.9	15.0	15.1	15.3	15.4	15.3	15.2	15.3	15.5	15.1
2006	15.5	15.5	15.5	15.4	15.5	15.6	15.6	15.5	15.3	15.2	15.3	15.4	15.4
2007	15.5	15.6	15.6	15.7	15.8	15.9	15.7	15.7	15.5	15.4	15.5	15.6	15.6
Financial Activities													
2000	35.0	35.3	35.4	36.0	36.3	37.6	37.1	37.4	37.1	36.7	36.6	36.9	36.5
2001	35.5	35.8	36.0	36.5	36.8	37.7	37.7	37.7	37.1	36.3	36.3	36.2	36.6
2002	35.4	35.7	35.9	36.2	36.7	37.9	37.0	37.3	36.6	37.1	37.2	37.5	36.7
2003	36.2	36.5	36.7	36.9	37.5	38.2	38.7	38.7	38.3	37.6	37.5	37.8	37.5
2004	38.3	38.4	38.7	39.4	39.7	40.4	41.1	41.0	40.2	39.5	39.5	39.6	39.7
2005	38.4	38.6	38.7	39.9	40.2	41.4	41.5	41.4	40.7	39.3	39.3	39.8	39.9
2006	39.1	39.3	39.5	40.2	40.6	41.7	41.9	41.9	41.2	40.9	40.9	41.1	40.7
2007	40.9	41.1	41.3	41.7	41.9	42.4	42.3	42.2	41.5	41.2	41.2	41.3	41.6
Professional and Business Services													
2000	95.9	98.3	100.2	99.1	97.8	100.6	99.1	100.1	99.0	98.4	99.1	99.3	98.9
2001	97.8	98.9	100.3	102.8	102.9	104.3	103.3	104.9	105.3	105.0	105.7	105.9	103.1
2002	101.7	104.0	105.8	105.6	104.8	105.8	104.2	105.9	104.8	104.5	104.8	104.6	104.7
2003	101.8	102.4	104.3	106.2	104.2	105.0	104.6	105.0	104.6	105.9	105.0	103.2	104.4
2004	98.4	98.0	99.3	100.2	99.6	100.8	101.2	101.7	101.1	100.4	101.2	101.6	100.3
2005	99.2	100.2	101.3	101.4	101.7	102.6	102.3	102.6	102.8	101.0	101.2	101.3	101.5
2006	99.7	100.4	101.5	101.6	102.4	102.6	102.0	102.2	102.5	102.7	102.8	103.0	102.0
2007	100.0	100.4	101.7	101.8	102.1	102.5	102.3	103.3	103.0	103.0	103.4	103.4	102.2
Education and Health Services													
2000	71.2	71.9	72.2	71.8	73.1	72.9	72.7	72.7	73.5	73.6	73.9	74.1	72.8
2001	72.8	73.3	73.6	73.3	73.9	74.2	73.4	73.4	75.1	75.2	75.9	76.2	74.2
2002	75.0	75.9	76.6	76.1	76.8	77.0	75.9	76.0	77.5	78.4	78.9	79.2	76.9
2003	76.6	77.0	77.5	78.1	78.7	78.8	76.4	76.4	79.3	79.1	79.7	79.8	78.1
2004	81.2	81.7	82.5	82.4	82.7	81.8	78.7	78.6	82.7	83.4	83.7	84.3	82.0
2005	83.6	83.9	84.2	84.3	85.0	85.3	81.0	81.6	86.6	86.5	86.9	87.4	84.7
2006	86.0	86.7	87.1	86.9	87.6	88.2	84.1	83.7	88.6	88.9	89.1	89.7	87.2
2007	88.5	88.9	89.5	89.8	90.3	90.6	86.4	86.4	90.3	90.4	90.7	90.8	89.4
Leisure and Hospitality													
2000	67.0	66.4	70.4	73.5	76.7	80.6	79.5	80.4	78.0	73.7	72.6	71.3	74.2
2001	67.3	68.7	72.4	76.6	80.1	83.9	84.6	83.2	78.4	74.4	73.3	71.9	76.2
2002	67.7	68.8	71.7	76.6	79.8	83.2	84.0	83.4	79.1	76.2	74.3	73.5	76.5
2003	69.6	70.2	72.5	74.8	79.9	83.0	84.2	83.6	78.6	75.9	72.9	72.4	76.4
2004	69.3	70.6	74.3	78.6	82.4	86.2	87.5	86.4	81.9	78.6	76.0	76.0	79.0
2005	72.1	73.6	77.7	81.7	85.4	89.7	90.8	90.2	85.3	80.5	78.6	77.8	82.0
2006	75.8	76.7	80.4	84.6	87.2	92.3	92.9	92.4	87.2	83.4	81.0	79.8	84.5
2007	77.2	78.5	82.3	85.2	88.6	93.4	93.6	92.3	87.5	83.9	81.6	81.0	85.4
Other Services													
2000	27.5	27.8	28.1	28.1	28.3	28.5	28.5	28.6	28.6	28.5	28.5	28.3	28.3
2001	28.0	28.2	28.7	28.8	29.1	29.4	29.4	29.4	29.2	28.9	28.8	28.5	28.9
2002	28.1	28.4	28.9	28.8	28.9	29.2	29.2	29.0	29.1	29.2	29.0	29.0	28.9
2003	30.3	31.1	31.5	32.4	33.8	34.0	33.8	33.4	32.9	32.8	33.4	33.8	32.8
2004	33.6	33.7	34.1	34.0	34.1	34.4	34.4	34.4	34.4	34.2	34.1	34.2	34.1
2005	34.0	34.3	34.5	34.9	35.2	35.3	35.3	35.4	35.6	35.2	35.2	35.2	35.0
2006	34.0	34.2	34.6	33.9	34.1	34.3	34.1	34.2	34.2	33.9	34.0	34.2	34.1
2007	34.1	34.4	34.6	35.8	36.9	36.9	36.6	36.8	36.9	36.7	36.7	36.7	36.1
Government													
2000	145.3	145.9	147.1	146.5	147.0	146.5	142.2	142.0	145.3	147.0	148.4	147.2	145.9
2001	145.9	147.6	147.9	147.8	147.8	149.0	144.8	144.4	147.1	148.8	150.1	149.3	147.5
2002	147.6	149.2	150.3	150.1	151.0	151.6	145.3	145.5	149.0	151.1	151.4	151.1	149.4
2003	149.3	150.3	151.0	149.0	149.6	150.6	147.1	146.5	149.1	148.8	150.6	150.6	149.3
2004	149.8	151.1	151.8	151.6	152.2	153.0	147.8	148.9	150.8	151.7	153.5	153.0	151.3
2005	149.6	151.0	151.5	152.4	152.9	154.1	149.3	149.7	151.3	151.2	152.9	151.9	151.5
2006	150.6	151.7	152.3	154.1	154.2	155.1	151.2	150.8	151.0	153.8	155.5	155.1	153.0
2007	153.7	155.1	155.6	155.6	155.6	156.4	151.2	150.9	152.6	154.8	155.3	155.1	154.3

Employment by Industry: Indianapolis-Carmel, IN, 2000–2007

(Numbers in thousands, not seasonally adjusted.)

Industry and year	January	February	March	April	May	June	July	August	September	October	November	December	Annual Average
Total Nonfarm													
2000	832.9	839.3	849.3	850.3	860.2	862.7	848.9	857.1	861.6	861.1	858.3	859.4	853.4
2001	842.7	845.1	854.1	861.6	869.7	870.7	857.0	868.0	867.1	865.6	864.9	864.6	860.9
2002	838.6	841.4	847.1	854.1	865.0	864.9	852.6	861.9	863.1	865.8	868.3	868.0	857.6
2003	845.0	843.9	849.2	863.8	873.4	869.4	860.5	869.2	871.5	879.7	881.3	878.9	865.5
2004	851.5	851.2	862.3	874.5	883.7	882.2	879.0	882.4	887.2	891.6	894.2	892.7	877.7
2005	862.8	868.2	875.5	886.2	896.6	892.9	886.9	891.3	899.6	896.7	901.0	897.3	887.9
2006	875.1	881.0	890.2	898.8	911.6	908.2	896.6	903.9	911.7	914.5	919.1	918.2	902.4
2007	891.6	890.3	905.0	913.3	925.6	924.8	912.9	923.9	925.5	927.0	930.3	927.7	916.5
Total Private													
2000	725.3	728.4	737.6	739.9	748.9	756.7	750.9	753.8	749.3	749.6	746.1	747.1	744.5
2001	734.0	734.1	742.3	750.1	757.1	763.4	757.8	764.0	754.5	752.9	752.3	752.0	751.2
2002	729.5	728.4	733.8	740.7	750.6	756.1	751.7	756.1	749.1	750.0	751.7	751.4	745.8
2003	731.4	728.3	733.0	748.1	757.2	759.2	755.6	759.4	756.2	763.7	765.6	763.2	751.7
2004	736.9	735.0	745.7	758.7	767.4	772.6	777.1	776.2	771.0	774.1	776.7	775.2	763.9
2005	747.1	749.5	757.4	769.6	779.7	784.5	784.8	785.2	783.0	780.6	784.6	781.1	773.9
2006	759.9	762.2	771.0	779.6	791.3	797.9	792.4	795.0	792.8	793.7	798.0	796.6	785.9
2007	774.0	769.2	783.0	792.0	803.0	809.2	802.6	804.9	802.5	802.9	805.9	803.3	796.0
Goods-Producing													
2000	155.9	156.4	158.2	159.5	161.2	163.6	163.2	163.8	162.6	160.5	158.8	157.5	160.1
2001	154.8	154.7	156.1	157.9	159.5	161.4	160.4	161.9	159.9	158.1	156.6	155.3	158.1
2002	150.5	149.6	150.6	151.9	154.1	156.3	156.6	157.4	155.9	154.1	153.4	152.0	153.5
2003	148.0	146.9	147.6	150.0	152.0	153.6	153.3	153.7	152.6	153.5	153.1	151.6	151.3
2004	147.1	146.4	148.7	151.6	154.8	156.6	155.4	156.3	155.5	155.4	154.3	153.2	152.9
2005	148.1	147.7	149.4	151.9	153.1	155.3	154.4	155.7	155.0	154.4	154.5	152.8	152.7
2006	148.7	148.8	150.5	153.5	154.7	157.6	155.6	157.1	155.6	154.9	154.3	152.6	153.7
2007	147.6	144.7	148.0	150.5	152.4	154.2	153.5	154.3	153.4	152.8	151.6	150.6	151.1
Natural Resources and Mining													
2005	0.8	0.8	0.8	0.8	0.8	0.8	0.8	0.8	0.8	0.8	0.8	0.8	0.8
2006	0.8	0.8	0.8	0.8	0.8	0.8	0.8	0.8	0.8	0.8	0.8	0.8	0.8
2007	0.8	0.7	0.8	0.8	0.8	0.8	0.8	0.8	0.8	0.8	0.8	0.8	0.8
Construction													
2005	46.3	46.1	47.7	50.1	51.0	52.5	53.2	53.3	53.1	53.2	52.9	51.4	50.9
2006	47.7	48.0	49.4	52.0	53.2	54.9	54.8	55.0	54.5	54.2	53.5	52.5	52.5
2007	48.6	46.5	49.4	51.9	53.9	55.2	55.2	55.6	54.9	54.3	53.2	52.2	52.6
Manufacturing													
2000	111.1	111.5	111.3	111.1	111.8	113.2	112.8	113.6	113.1	112.6	111.8	112.0	112.2
2001	111.1	110.3	110.0	109.6	109.9	110.2	108.6	109.6	108.4	107.6	106.6	106.3	109.0
2002	104.5	104.0	104.2	103.5	104.2	105.4	104.6	105.4	104.8	103.9	103.8	103.5	104.3
2003	102.5	102.4	102.2	102.0	102.4	102.8	101.7	101.8	101.0	101.5	101.4	101.1	101.9
2004	100.1	100.0	100.3	100.3	101.2	102.2	101.2	102.4	102.0	101.9	102.0	102.1	101.3
2005	101.0	100.8	100.9	101.0	101.3	102.0	100.4	101.6	101.1	100.4	100.8	100.6	101.0
2006	100.2	100.0	100.3	100.7	100.7	101.9	100.0	101.3	100.3	99.9	100.0	99.3	100.4
2007	98.2	97.5	97.8	97.8	97.7	98.2	97.5	97.9	97.7	97.7	97.6	97.6	97.8
Service-Providing													
2000	677.0	682.9	691.1	690.8	699.0	699.1	685.7	693.3	699.0	700.6	699.5	701.9	693.3
2001	687.9	690.4	698.0	703.7	710.2	709.3	696.6	706.1	707.2	707.5	708.3	709.3	702.9
2002	688.1	691.8	696.5	702.2	710.9	708.6	696.0	704.5	707.2	711.7	714.9	716.0	704.0
2003	697.0	697.0	701.6	713.8	721.4	715.8	707.2	715.5	718.9	726.2	728.2	727.3	714.2
2004	704.4	704.8	713.6	722.9	728.9	725.6	723.6	726.1	731.7	736.2	739.9	739.5	724.8
2005	714.7	720.5	726.1	734.3	743.5	737.6	732.5	735.6	744.6	742.3	746.5	744.5	735.2
2006	726.4	732.2	739.7	745.3	756.9	750.6	741.0	746.8	756.1	759.6	764.8	765.6	748.8
2007	744.0	745.6	757.0	762.8	773.2	770.6	759.4	769.6	772.1	774.2	778.7	777.1	765.4
Trade, Transportation, and Utilities													
2000	188.9	188.4	190.0	188.3	189.6	190.6	191.6	191.1	190.3	193.3	195.8	199.4	191.4
2001	194.7	191.6	192.3	194.0	194.1	194.3	194.7	195.0	193.8	195.2	198.2	200.8	194.9
2002	191.4	189.5	190.0	190.5	191.7	192.4	191.1	191.6	190.6	190.7	194.7	196.9	191.8
2003	189.6	186.6	188.1	189.2	189.3	189.5	188.6	189.1	188.4	190.1	193.9	195.4	189.8
2004	185.7	183.7	185.2	186.7	188.3	189.4	190.4	190.9	188.9	192.3	196.2	198.2	189.7
2005	189.1	189.0	190.4	192.3	193.6	193.9	194.6	195.2	194.6	196.3	199.9	201.0	194.2
2006	192.8	191.4	193.0	192.7	194.3	195.2	195.0	194.8	194.3	195.7	200.2	202.1	195.1
2007	193.5	190.9	193.9	193.9	196.4	197.9	197.1	196.4	196.1	197.8	202.7	204.3	196.7
Wholesale Trade													
2000	47.6	47.9	48.3	48.1	48.4	48.8	48.8	48.8	48.6	48.8	48.6	48.7	48.5
2001	49.0	49.0	49.0	49.0	49.0	49.1	49.0	48.9	48.6	48.5	48.3	48.4	48.8
2002	47.4	47.7	47.5	47.4	47.7	47.7	47.3	47.2	46.8	46.8	46.7	46.8	47.3
2003	46.3	46.2	46.2	45.8	45.9	46.0	45.7	45.6	45.4	45.6	45.7	45.8	45.9
2004	45.4	45.6	46.0	46.0	46.2	46.6	46.9	46.7	46.3	46.6	46.6	46.5	46.3
2005	46.2	46.4	46.6	46.8	46.8	47.0	47.2	47.2	47.0	47.1	47.1	47.3	46.9
2006	46.9	46.9	47.0	47.1	47.4	47.7	47.5	47.3	47.2	47.5	47.4	47.6	47.3
2007	47.2	47.2	47.6	47.5	47.7	48.1	48.6	48.1	48.0	48.1	48.2	48.3	47.9
Retail Trade													
2000	96.0	94.9	95.8	94.9	96.0	96.8	96.0	96.1	95.6	98.0	101.0	103.4	97.0
2001	99.7	97.4	97.5	97.7	98.2	98.7	97.8	97.6	97.3	98.2	101.9	103.2	98.8
2002	97.8	96.2	96.9	96.4	97.4	98.1	96.8	96.8	96.4	96.0	99.3	101.4	97.5
2003	96.1	94.2	95.4	95.5	96.6	97.0	95.8	96.4	95.8	96.6	100.2	101.8	96.8
2004	95.2	93.0	93.6	94.2	95.4	96.0	95.9	96.2	95.0	97.1	100.9	102.5	96.3
2005	95.2	94.5	95.4	96.4	97.6	97.4	97.5	97.4	96.8	98.1	101.0	102.4	97.5
2006	96.1	94.7	95.8	95.4	96.2	96.5	96.6	96.3	95.6	96.4	100.1	101.6	96.8
2007	95.3	93.1	94.7	94.6	96.4	97.1	96.6	96.1	95.5	96.5	101.2	102.7	96.7

Employment by Industry: Indianapolis-Carmel, IN, 2000–2007—*Continued*

(Numbers in thousands, not seasonally adjusted.)

Industry and year	January	February	March	April	May	June	July	August	September	October	November	December	Annual Average
Transportation and Utilities													
2000	45.3	45.6	45.9	45.3	45.2	45.0	46.8	46.2	46.1	46.5	46.2	47.3	46.0
2001	46.0	45.2	45.8	47.3	46.9	46.5	47.9	48.5	47.9	48.5	48.0	49.2	47.3
2002	46.2	45.6	45.6	46.7	46.6	46.6	47.0	47.6	47.4	47.9	48.7	48.7	47.1
2003	47.2	46.2	46.5	47.9	46.8	46.5	47.1	47.1	47.2	47.9	48.0	47.8	47.2
2004	45.1	45.1	45.6	46.5	46.7	46.8	47.6	48.0	47.6	48.6	48.7	49.2	47.1
2005	47.7	48.1	48.4	49.1	49.2	49.5	49.9	50.6	50.8	51.1	51.8	51.3	49.8
2006	49.8	49.8	50.2	50.2	50.7	51.0	50.9	51.2	51.5	51.8	52.7	52.9	51.1
2007	51.0	50.6	51.6	51.8	52.3	52.7	51.9	52.2	52.6	53.2	53.3	53.3	52.2
Information													
2000	17.0	17.1	17.4	16.9	17.0	17.4	17.5	17.7	17.4	17.5	17.6	17.7	17.4
2001	17.6	17.4	17.6	17.0	17.2	17.4	17.2	17.0	16.8	16.7	16.7	16.7	17.1
2002	16.5	16.4	16.6	16.4	16.6	16.7	16.6	16.6	16.4	16.3	16.2	16.2	16.5
2003	16.0	15.9	16.1	15.9	16.2	16.6	16.6	16.8	16.5	16.3	16.4	16.4	16.3
2004	16.3	16.3	16.3	16.2	16.5	16.8	16.8	16.8	16.4	16.6	16.5	16.6	16.5
2005	16.1	16.3	16.3	16.3	16.5	16.7	16.6	16.6	16.2	16.1	16.2	16.4	16.4
2006	15.8	16.0	16.0	16.2	16.3	16.4	16.4	16.3	16.1	16.0	16.1	16.1	16.1
2007	16.1	16.2	16.1	16.2	16.4	16.6	16.8	16.8	16.7	16.6	16.7	16.7	16.5
Financial Activities													
2000	63.1	63.1	62.9	63.0	63.5	64.1	63.5	63.2	62.7	62.6	62.2	62.4	63.0
2001	61.9	62.1	62.3	62.9	63.2	63.9	63.2	62.9	62.2	61.2	61.5	61.8	62.4
2002	62.0	62.0	61.8	61.9	62.2	62.8	62.5	62.6	62.2	62.6	62.8	62.9	62.4
2003	62.7	62.8	62.9	63.2	63.6	64.2	64.2	64.2	63.9	63.9	63.7	63.7	63.6
2004	62.9	63.2	63.2	63.1	63.5	63.9	63.8	63.8	63.1	63.1	63.0	63.4	63.3
2005	62.4	62.5	62.4	62.8	62.8	63.3	63.8	63.8	63.4	63.3	63.2	63.4	63.1
2006	62.5	62.6	62.6	62.7	63.1	63.5	63.4	63.5	62.9	62.7	62.5	62.7	62.9
2007	61.5	61.9	62.0	62.3	62.4	63.0	63.4	63.2	62.7	62.7	62.6	62.7	62.5
Professional and Business Services													
2000	104.1	104.7	106.9	108.0	110.0	111.4	109.0	109.5	109.8	108.5	107.6	106.5	108.0
2001	103.4	104.1	106.3	108.3	108.5	109.3	108.6	109.8	107.3	106.9	106.1	104.6	106.9
2002	104.1	104.4	105.4	107.3	108.2	108.8	108.9	109.2	108.2	109.3	108.5	107.6	107.5
2003	105.0	105.1	105.2	107.8	110.2	110.7	111.2	111.9	111.5	113.7	114.6	113.1	110.0
2004	106.9	107.3	110.4	115.2	116.4	117.5	122.3	121.5	120.5	119.8	120.5	119.3	116.5
2005	115.4	115.8	117.2	118.9	119.5	120.1	121.8	121.2	121.1	122.2	122.2	120.3	119.6
2006	116.8	117.6	119.5	122.1	124.1	125.0	124.7	127.0	126.4	126.6	127.5	126.0	123.6
2007	123.9	123.3	126.5	129.4	131.1	130.8	130.0	131.5	131.5	131.8	131.7	129.2	129.2
Education and Health Services													
2000	90.5	91.8	92.6	91.4	91.3	90.8	90.7	91.1	92.3	92.4	92.3	92.6	91.7
2001	92.3	93.4	93.8	94.2	94.6	93.7	93.5	94.8	97.3	97.0	97.9	98.3	95.1
2002	96.4	96.9	97.5	97.5	97.8	96.8	96.0	96.8	98.8	100.0	100.8	101.0	98.0
2003	99.5	100.1	100.4	105.7	104.8	101.5	101.0	100.8	105.0	107.5	107.5	107.4	103.4
2004	107.1	107.1	107.9	107.6	105.6	103.9	104.6	102.0	105.5	107.3	107.3	106.4	106.0
2005	102.8	104.1	104.9	105.8	108.7	107.2	106.8	104.3	109.1	106.5	107.0	106.2	106.1
2006	106.1	107.6	108.6	108.3	111.1	110.2	109.3	107.0	111.6	113.5	113.7	113.5	110.0
2007	112.2	113.3	114.2	115.4	115.2	115.2	113.5	112.2	116.2	117.1	117.4	117.2	114.9
Leisure and Hospitality													
2000	73.5	74.3	76.6	79.9	83.2	85.3	82.2	84.2	81.7	82.0	79.2	78.4	80.0
2001	76.9	78.1	80.7	82.7	86.4	89.1	86.0	88.6	84.3	84.9	82.3	81.5	83.5
2002	76.2	76.9	78.8	81.6	85.7	87.4	85.3	87.4	83.4	83.4	81.6	81.2	82.4
2003	77.4	77.4	79.0	82.5	86.9	88.4	86.1	88.5	84.6	85.0	82.8	82.2	83.4
2004	77.6	77.5	80.1	84.0	87.6	89.5	88.6	89.7	86.5	85.2	84.7	84.0	84.6
2005	79.3	79.9	82.2	86.8	90.3	92.5	91.2	92.7	88.7	86.9	86.8	86.2	87.0
2006	82.8	83.5	85.8	88.7	92.0	93.6	92.0	93.3	90.4	89.0	88.4	88.3	89.0
2007	84.2	83.8	86.8	88.5	92.8	94.6	91.4	94.2	90.0	88.4	87.6	87.0	89.1
Other Services													
2000	32.3	32.6	33.0	32.9	33.1	33.5	33.2	33.2	32.5	32.8	32.6	32.6	32.9
2001	32.4	32.7	33.2	33.1	33.6	34.3	34.2	34.0	32.9	32.9	33.0	33.0	33.3
2002	32.4	32.7	33.1	33.6	34.3	34.9	34.7	34.5	33.6	33.6	33.7	33.6	33.7
2003	33.2	33.5	33.7	33.8	34.2	34.7	34.6	34.4	33.7	33.7	33.6	33.4	33.9
2004	33.3	33.5	33.9	34.3	34.7	35.0	35.2	35.2	34.6	34.4	34.2	34.1	34.4
2005	33.9	34.2	34.6	34.8	35.2	35.5	35.6	35.7	34.9	34.9	34.8	34.8	34.9
2006	34.4	34.7	35.0	35.4	35.7	36.4	36.0	36.0	35.5	35.3	35.3	35.3	35.4
2007	35.0	35.1	35.5	35.8	36.3	36.9	36.9	36.3	35.9	35.7	35.6	35.6	35.9
Government													
2000	107.6	110.9	111.7	110.4	111.3	106.0	98.0	103.3	112.3	111.5	112.2	112.3	109.0
2001	108.7	111.0	111.8	111.5	112.6	107.3	99.2	104.0	112.6	112.7	112.6	112.6	109.7
2002	109.1	113.0	113.3	113.4	114.4	108.8	100.9	105.8	114.0	115.8	116.6	116.6	111.8
2003	113.6	115.6	116.2	115.7	116.2	110.2	104.9	109.8	115.3	116.0	115.7	115.7	113.7
2004	114.6	116.2	116.6	115.8	116.3	109.6	101.9	106.2	116.2	117.5	117.5	117.5	113.8
2005	115.7	118.7	118.1	116.6	116.9	108.4	102.1	106.1	116.6	116.1	116.4	116.2	114.0
2006	115.2	118.8	119.2	119.2	120.3	110.3	104.2	108.9	118.9	120.8	121.1	121.6	116.5
2007	117.6	121.1	122.0	121.3	122.6	115.6	110.3	119.0	123.0	124.1	124.4	124.4	120.5

Employment by Industry: Milwaukee-Waukesha-West Allis, WI, 2000–2007

(Numbers in thousands, not seasonally adjusted.)

Industry and year	January	February	March	April	May	June	July	August	September	October	November	December	Annual Average
Total Nonfarm													
2000	850.2	852.8	857.8	865.8	869.4	879.4	869.1	871.7	871.5	874.3	878.0	874.9	867.9
2001	856.5	856.4	858.7	863.1	864.3	866.0	856.1	855.0	853.6	853.7	850.0	849.2	856.9
2002	829.0	828.2	832.4	839.3	843.8	848.7	840.3	840.5	839.0	844.7	845.0	843.6	839.5
2003	820.0	822.8	824.9	830.9	834.0	839.6	826.8	828.8	828.4	837.1	834.8	837.0	830.4
2004	815.1	817.9	822.8	827.1	833.1	842.0	833.9	836.4	834.8	841.0	841.0	840.5	832.1
2005	822.9	825.2	827.8	839.2	842.1	849.0	843.6	844.8	847.5	847.1	849.0	850.4	840.7
2006	830.0	832.5	836.1	845.8	850.7	859.2	851.7	855.1	858.3	861.4	863.0	863.2	850.6
2007	843.3	843.0	846.0	853.3	861.9	871.2	857.8	861.6	860.0	863.3	862.5	861.2	857.1
Total Private													
2000	759.5	760.8	765.3	771.1	775.6	782.5	781.8	784.0	780.9	780.5	783.3	782.2	775.6
2001	763.6	761.0	763.4	766.7	768.9	771.7	770.0	768.5	760.7	757.8	754.4	752.8	763.3
2002	734.8	731.1	734.9	742.6	747.8	752.4	753.0	753.2	747.6	746.6	746.5	745.3	744.7
2003	726.6	725.5	728.1	733.7	739.1	744.1	742.2	743.6	740.3	745.0	740.5	742.3	737.3
2004	725.3	723.0	727.5	733.5	739.5	748.5	750.0	751.5	745.0	748.8	747.5	747.6	740.6
2005	731.3	730.4	734.2	745.5	748.7	755.5	758.5	759.4	755.2	754.1	755.5	757.6	748.8
2006	739.8	739.6	742.7	752.1	757.2	765.3	766.2	769.2	766.1	767.8	769.4	770.0	758.8
2007	753.2	751.3	754.0	760.7	769.1	777.8	773.7	776.9	769.3	769.6	768.2	766.5	765.9
Goods-Producing													
2000	195.5	195.6	196.6	199.0	200.2	202.8	202.1	202.4	200.7	199.5	199.0	197.1	199.2
2001	192.3	190.8	190.8	189.9	189.9	191.6	190.7	190.8	188.8	187.1	184.6	183.2	189.2
2002	176.5	174.9	175.4	176.8	178.1	179.8	178.4	179.4	178.0	177.5	176.7	174.6	177.2
2003	169.1	167.9	167.9	169.5	170.7	172.1	171.2	172.8	171.1	170.7	169.9	168.7	170.1
2004	163.7	163.0	163.9	166.1	167.6	170.2	171.1	171.5	170.2	169.5	169.1	168.2	167.8
2005	164.1	163.8	164.4	166.9	168.3	170.7	171.1	170.9	169.4	168.2	167.7	166.7	167.7
2006	164.1	163.0	163.5	166.3	168.1	171.1	170.9	171.8	170.3	170.3	169.7	169.1	168.2
2007	165.8	163.7	164.8	167.2	169.8	172.4	171.8	172.2	170.2	169.8	169.1	166.6	168.6
Natural Resources and Mining													
2000	0.4	0.4	0.4	0.4	0.5	0.5	0.5	0.5	0.5	0.5	0.5	0.4	0.5
2001	0.4	0.4	0.4	0.4	0.5	0.5	0.5	0.5	0.5	0.5	0.4	0.4	0.4
2002	0.4	0.4	0.4	0.4	0.4	0.4	0.5	0.5	0.5	0.4	0.4	0.5	0.4
2003	0.4	0.4	0.4	0.4	0.5	0.5	0.5	0.5	0.5	0.5	0.5	0.5	0.5
2004	0.4	0.4	0.4	0.4	0.5	0.5	0.5	0.5	0.5	0.5	0.5	0.5	0.5
2005	0.4	0.4	0.4	0.5	0.5	0.5	0.5	0.5	0.5	0.5	0.5	0.5	0.5
2006	0.5	0.5	0.5	0.5	0.5	0.5	0.5	0.5	0.5	0.5	0.5	0.5	0.5
2007	0.5	0.4	0.5	0.5	0.5	0.5	0.5	0.5					
Construction													
2000	30.3	30.0	31.0	33.2	34.7	36.1	36.3	36.5	35.7	35.1	34.4	32.7	33.8
2001	30.9	30.9	31.4	32.8	34.6	35.9	36.8	36.9	36.0	35.5	34.7	33.6	34.2
2002	29.7	28.9	29.5	32.2	34.0	35.1	35.9	36.1	35.6	35.7	34.9	33.0	33.4
2003	29.9	29.2	29.4	31.5	33.6	34.7	35.7	36.1	35.5	35.4	34.5	33.1	33.2
2004	29.7	29.2	29.9	32.0	33.3	34.7	36.0	36.0	35.4	35.1	34.7	33.5	33.3
2005	30.3	29.9	30.4	32.7	34.4	35.6	36.1	36.0	35.5	35.1	34.8	33.4	33.7
2006	31.2	30.5	31.0	33.5	35.0	36.4	36.7	36.7	36.7	36.3	36.1	35.5	34.4
2007	31.9	30.6	32.3	33.8	36.1	37.5	37.8	37.8	37.0	36.9	36.5	33.9	35.2
Manufacturing													
2000	164.8	165.2	165.2	165.4	165.0	166.2	165.3	165.4	164.5	163.9	164.1	164.0	164.9
2001	161.0	159.5	159.0	156.6	154.8	155.2	153.4	153.4	152.3	151.1	149.5	149.2	154.6
2002	146.4	145.6	145.5	144.2	143.7	144.2	142.0	142.8	141.9	141.4	141.4	141.1	143.4
2003	138.8	138.3	138.1	137.6	136.7	136.9	135.0	136.2	135.1	134.9	135.0	135.1	136.5
2004	133.6	133.4	133.6	133.7	133.8	135.0	134.6	135.0	134.3	133.9	133.9	134.2	134.1
2005	133.4	133.5	133.6	133.7	133.4	134.6	134.5	134.4	133.4	132.6	132.4	132.8	133.5
2006	132.4	132.0	132.0	132.3	132.6	134.2	133.7	134.6	133.1	133.5	133.1	133.1	133.2
2007	133.4	132.7	132.0	132.9	133.2	134.4	133.5	133.9	132.7	132.4	132.1	132.2	133.0
Service-Providing													
2000	654.7	657.2	661.2	666.8	669.2	676.6	667.0	669.3	670.8	674.8	679.0	677.8	668.7
2001	664.2	665.6	667.9	673.2	674.4	674.4	665.4	664.2	664.8	666.6	665.4	666.0	667.7
2002	652.5	653.3	657.0	662.5	665.7	668.9	661.9	661.1	661.0	667.2	668.3	669.0	662.4
2003	650.9	654.9	657.0	661.4	663.3	667.5	655.6	656.0	657.3	666.4	664.9	668.3	660.2
2004	651.4	654.9	658.9	661.0	665.5	671.8	662.8	664.9	664.6	671.5	671.9	672.3	664.3
2005	658.8	661.4	663.4	672.3	673.8	678.3	672.5	673.9	678.1	678.9	681.3	683.7	673.0
2006	665.9	669.5	672.6	679.5	682.6	688.1	680.8	683.3	688.0	691.1	693.3	694.1	682.4
2007	677.5	679.3	681.2	686.1	692.1	698.8	686.0	689.4	689.8	693.5	693.4	694.6	688.5
Trade, Transportation, and Utilities													
2000	159.9	158.0	158.3	158.9	159.5	159.3	160.0	160.8	161.6	162.8	165.2	167.1	161.0
2001	163.5	160.9	161.2	161.0	161.3	160.3	158.0	158.3	157.3	157.9	159.9	160.4	160.0
2002	155.6	152.9	153.7	153.5	154.8	154.6	153.0	152.7	153.4	153.9	157.2	159.1	154.5
2003	152.3	150.4	150.6	151.1	152.3	152.9	149.8	150.7	151.9	153.8	155.6	157.5	152.4
2004	151.4	149.8	150.6	149.7	151.6	153.2	151.3	151.7	152.1	154.1	156.5	157.6	152.5
2005	152.2	150.8	151.3	151.9	153.0	153.6	153.1	153.9	154.2	154.9	157.5	158.9	153.8
2006	153.3	151.5	152.4	152.9	154.2	155.0	153.1	153.6	154.1	155.2	158.2	159.7	154.4
2007	154.2	152.1	152.1	152.0	153.9	154.5	152.7	152.6	152.2	152.9	154.8	156.2	153.4
Wholesale Trade													
2000	42.7	42.9	42.9	43.0	43.2	43.5	43.3	43.3	42.9	42.9	43.0	43.2	43.1
2001	42.9	43.0	43.1	42.7	42.7	42.9	42.5	42.5	41.9	41.7	41.5	41.6	42.4
2002	41.1	41.0	41.0	40.8	40.9	41.0	41.1	40.9	40.5	40.2	40.2	40.2	40.7
2003	40.0	40.0	40.0	39.9	39.9	40.1	40.1	40.0	39.7	39.5	39.3	39.4	39.8
2004	38.9	38.7	38.9	38.9	38.9	39.3	39.7	39.8	39.5	39.9	40.0	40.1	39.4
2005	39.9	39.9	39.8	40.4	40.5	40.9	41.2	41.0	40.7	40.8	40.9	41.0	40.6
2006	40.4	40.5	40.6	40.8	40.9	41.4	41.6	41.5	41.3	41.4	41.4	41.6	41.1
2007	40.9	41.0	41.0	41.0	41.1	41.7	41.8	41.6	41.3	41.2	41.1	41.1	41.2

Employment by Industry: Milwaukee-Waukesha-West Allis, WI, 2000–2007—*Continued*

(Numbers in thousands, not seasonally adjusted.)

Industry and year	January	February	March	April	May	June	July	August	September	October	November	December	Annual Average
Retail Trade													
2000	84.1	82.2	82.5	82.4	82.9	83.4	84.2	84.9	84.9	85.1	87.8	89.5	84.5
2001	86.8	84.5	84.9	84.7	85.1	85.0	83.9	84.0	82.7	83.3	85.9	86.8	84.8
2002	84.3	81.9	82.5	82.5	83.5	84.2	83.0	83.0	82.5	82.9	86.3	88.2	83.7
2003	82.3	80.3	80.5	80.6	81.7	82.2	81.2	81.8	81.4	83.2	85.3	87.1	82.3
2004	82.5	81.0	81.4	81.1	82.4	83.3	82.4	82.8	82.1	82.9	85.3	86.8	82.8
2005	82.0	80.6	81.1	81.6	82.3	82.8	82.6	83.5	82.7	83.3	85.4	86.6	82.9
2006	82.5	80.6	81.1	81.4	82.4	83.0	82.1	82.7	81.9	82.9	85.9	86.9	82.8
2007	83.3	81.1	81.1	80.7	82.2	82.2	82.0	81.7	80.3	81.0	83.2	84.6	82.0
Transportation and Utilities													
2000	33.1	32.9	32.9	33.5	33.4	32.4	32.5	32.6	33.8	34.8	34.4	34.4	33.4
2001	33.8	33.4	33.2	33.6	33.5	32.4	31.6	31.8	32.7	32.9	32.5	32.0	32.8
2002	30.2	30.0	30.2	30.2	30.4	29.4	28.9	28.8	30.4	30.8	30.7	30.7	30.1
2003	30.0	30.1	30.1	30.6	30.7	30.6	28.5	28.9	30.8	31.1	31.0	31.0	30.3
2004	30.0	30.1	30.3	29.7	30.3	30.6	29.2	29.1	30.5	31.3	31.2	30.7	30.3
2005	30.3	30.3	30.4	29.9	30.2	29.9	29.3	29.4	30.8	30.8	31.2	30.7	30.3
2006	30.4	30.4	30.7	30.7	30.9	30.6	29.4	29.4	30.9	30.9	31.3	31.3	30.3
2007	30.0	30.0	30.0	30.3	30.6	30.6	28.9	29.3	30.6	30.7	30.5	30.5	30.2
Information													
2000	19.9	20.1	20.2	20.2	20.3	20.4	20.4	20.5	20.6	20.8	20.9	21.0	20.4
2001	19.7	19.7	19.9	20.1	19.9	20.0	20.0	19.9	19.8	20.0	20.0	20.0	19.9
2002	19.7	19.5	19.6	19.5	19.3	19.3	19.2	19.2	18.9	18.8	18.8	18.8	19.2
2003	18.8	18.6	18.6	18.6	18.5	18.3	18.4	18.4	18.3	18.3	18.3	18.3	18.4
2004	18.5	18.5	18.5	18.6	18.5	18.4	18.6	18.6	18.3	18.2	18.3	18.3	18.4
2005	18.2	18.1	18.1	18.2	18.2	18.3	18.1	18.2	18.1	18.1	18.2	18.3	18.2
2006	18.0	18.1	18.0	17.9	17.9	17.7	17.7	17.7	17.7	17.5	17.5	17.5	17.8
2007	17.5	17.5	17.5	17.6	17.6	17.7	17.7	17.7	17.5	17.5	17.5	17.6	17.6
Financial Activities													
2000	56.6	56.7	56.6	57.0	57.2	58.0	58.2	58.1	57.8	58.3	58.8	59.2	57.7
2001	58.5	58.2	58.3	58.4	58.5	59.1	58.8	58.5	57.9	57.4	57.5	57.2	58.2
2002	57.1	57.1	57.0	57.3	57.4	57.9	58.6	58.6	57.9	57.8	58.1	58.1	57.7
2003	57.8	58.0	58.0	58.1	58.3	58.7	58.7	58.4	57.6	57.5	57.2	57.3	57.9
2004	57.4	57.2	57.4	57.6	57.6	58.1	58.5	58.6	57.5	57.9	58.1	58.1	57.8
2005	57.1	56.8	57.1	57.2	57.2	57.4	57.9	57.7	57.1	56.9	57.1	57.3	57.2
2006	57.0	56.8	56.7	57.3	57.5	57.9	58.4	58.3	58.0	58.0	58.1	58.2	57.7
2007	57.8	57.9	57.6	57.9	58.1	58.6	58.3	58.7	57.9	58.1	57.6	57.7	58.0
Professional and Business Services													
2000	108.5	109.7	110.6	110.8	112.0	113.2	111.7	112.2	113.0	111.8	112.3	109.8	111.3
2001	106.2	105.2	105.2	107.0	106.9	106.9	107.1	107.6	105.9	104.0	102.6	102.0	105.6
2002	100.1	100.1	101.6	105.3	105.6	105.7	106.3	106.9	106.0	105.6	103.5	102.8	104.1
2003	100.9	101.3	102.5	103.7	103.2	103.6	104.2	104.0	104.5	105.4	104.4	105.4	103.5
2004	102.0	101.6	103.0	104.4	104.0	106.5	107.0	107.6	106.9	105.9	105.6	105.6	105.1
2005	103.5	103.9	104.8	107.9	107.0	108.8	110.6	110.9	111.2	110.8	110.8	111.6	108.5
2006	106.4	107.3	107.9	110.7	110.3	111.9	112.7	113.7	113.9	114.4	114.1	113.6	111.4
2007	110.4	111.0	111.8	113.3	113.7	116.3	115.4	116.6	115.1	114.8	114.1	112.9	113.8
Education and Health Services													
2000	119.8	120.9	122.0	122.5	122.4	122.1	121.8	122.6	122.7	124.5	125.2	125.9	122.7
2001	121.5	124.2	125.0	124.6	124.7	123.9	124.0	124.1	124.9	126.4	126.6	126.6	124.7
2002	124.4	125.3	125.7	125.9	126.2	125.9	126.0	126.4	126.5	127.9	128.6	128.0	126.4
2003	125.8	128.0	128.1	128.5	128.4	128.0	127.7	127.7	128.1	129.2	129.6	129.4	128.2
2004	129.2	130.0	130.3	130.9	131.2	130.5	130.3	130.5	130.9	132.5	132.8	133.0	131.0
2005	131.1	132.0	132.3	133.2	133.2	132.7	131.7	132.1	133.2	134.8	135.0	135.5	133.1
2006	134.2	135.7	135.6	136.2	136.5	136.1	135.8	136.4	138.2	140.0	140.0	139.9	137.1
2007	137.5	138.9	139.1	139.5	139.8	139.2	138.1	138.9	140.2	141.3	141.4	141.6	139.6
Leisure and Hospitality													
2000	60.1	60.2	61.0	62.5	63.7	66.1	67.3	67.3	64.3	62.4	61.4	61.3	63.1
2001	60.6	60.8	61.5	65.1	66.9	68.5	70.0	68.1	64.9	63.9	62.1	61.8	64.5
2002	60.4	60.3	60.7	63.0	65.2	67.3	70.0	68.6	65.8	63.8	62.5	62.4	64.2
2003	60.9	60.5	61.3	63.2	67.0	68.8	71.0	70.3	68.0	66.3	64.9	64.8	65.5
2004	62.3	61.9	62.7	64.8	67.7	69.5	71.1	70.9	67.7	67.0	65.3	65.2	66.3
2005	63.8	63.6	64.7	68.4	70.1	71.8	73.9	73.6	70.7	69.2	68.2	68.2	68.9
2006	66.2	66.5	67.8	69.6	71.4	73.7	75.6	75.9	72.5	70.9	70.3	70.2	70.9
2007	68.9	68.9	69.7	71.1	74.2	76.3	77.2	77.7	74.1	73.2	71.9	71.7	72.9
Other Services													
2000	39.2	39.6	40.0	40.2	40.3	40.6	40.3	40.1	40.2	40.4	40.5	40.8	40.2
2001	41.3	41.2	41.5	40.7	40.8	41.4	41.4	41.2	41.2	41.1	41.1	41.6	41.2
2002	41.0	41.0	41.2	41.3	41.2	41.9	41.5	41.4	41.1	41.3	41.1	41.5	41.3
2003	41.0	40.8	41.1	41.1	40.9	41.7	41.2	41.3	40.8	40.8	40.6	40.9	41.0
2004	40.8	41.0	41.1	41.4	41.3	42.1	42.1	42.1	41.8	42.7	41.7	41.7	41.7
2005	41.3	41.4	41.5	41.8	41.7	42.2	42.1	42.1	41.3	41.2	41.0	41.1	41.6
2006	40.6	40.7	40.8	41.2	41.3	41.9	42.0	41.8	41.6	41.5	41.5	41.8	41.4
2007	41.1	41.3	41.4	42.1	42.0	42.8	42.5	42.5	42.1	42.0	41.8	42.2	42.0
Government													
2000	90.7	92.0	92.5	94.7	93.8	96.9	87.3	87.7	90.6	93.8	94.7	92.7	92.3
2001	92.9	95.4	95.3	96.4	95.4	94.3	86.1	86.5	92.9	95.9	95.6	96.4	93.6
2002	94.2	97.1	97.5	96.7	96.0	96.3	87.3	87.3	91.4	98.1	98.5	98.3	94.9
2003	93.4	97.3	96.8	97.2	94.9	95.5	84.6	85.2	88.1	95.1	94.3	94.7	93.0
2004	89.8	94.9	95.3	93.6	93.6	93.5	83.9	84.9	89.8	92.2	93.5	92.9	91.5
2005	91.6	94.8	93.6	93.7	93.4	93.5	85.1	85.4	92.3	93.0	93.5	92.8	91.9
2006	90.2	92.9	93.4	93.7	93.5	93.9	85.5	85.9	92.2	93.6	93.6	93.2	91.8
2007	90.1	91.7	92.0	92.6	92.8	93.4	84.1	84.7	90.7	93.7	94.3	94.7	91.2

Employment by Industry: Las Vegas-Paradise, NV, 2000–2007

(Numbers in thousands, not seasonally adjusted.)

Industry and year	January	February	March	April	May	June	July	August	September	October	November	December	Annual Average
Total Nonfarm													
2000	675.1	678.0	685.1	688.8	698.4	694.9	692.5	705.3	708.1	711.4	717.0	716.8	697.6
2001	716.5	723.5	728.8	728.8	732.6	731.9	725.3	731.1	735.5	722.3	722.9	720.9	726.7
2002	709.9	714.3	722.6	727.9	734.2	730.4	726.8	731.6	736.8	743.4	746.0	746.6	730.9
2003	738.2	743.4	749.5	750.0	756.4	754.2	754.0	761.8	770.3	778.8	780.9	785.0	760.2
2004	777.9	781.8	790.7	803.5	808.2	810.4	811.2	815.2	827.4	840.5	841.3	843.9	812.7
2005	832.4	840.6	850.5	867.3	869.9	872.4	870.3	873.4	887.4	892.6	899.2	903.3	871.6
2006	891.4	900.9	910.7	916.0	922.3	923.8	915.7	917.5	925.3	926.7	929.3	927.9	917.3
2007	913.2	923.9	927.9	930.3	936.5	933.2	920.4	920.4	923.4	927.1	932.2	932.9	926.8
Total Private													
2000	606.5	608.5	614.5	617.9	624.1	628.6	626.6	635.6	637.6	638.3	642.9	642.6	627.0
2001	644.8	649.6	654.6	653.0	658.2	659.6	656.7	662.2	659.7	645.8	646.1	644.1	652.9
2002	635.8	637.2	645.0	650.7	656.5	655.1	655.1	659.7	659.8	662.3	664.2	664.7	653.8
2003	659.9	662.2	667.9	668.5	674.5	675.5	678.9	687.1	689.8	695.9	697.6	701.4	679.9
2004	697.7	699.2	706.6	719.4	723.4	729.4	733.8	738.5	742.8	753.3	753.7	756.2	729.5
2005	748.4	753.5	761.9	778.5	780.8	786.9	788.5	792.6	799.9	801.3	806.9	810.7	784.2
2006	802.8	809.0	818.4	822.5	828.6	833.8	829.8	832.1	833.1	830.2	831.8	830.4	825.2
2007	819.4	826.1	829.6	830.4	836.5	837.3	828.9	830.5	826.5	826.1	830.6	830.8	829.4
Goods-Producing													
2000	83.6	84.0	86.1	86.5	87.4	89.2	88.9	89.3	88.1	87.3	87.7	87.8	87.2
2001	86.2	87.1	88.1	88.5	89.9	91.7	91.9	93.3	92.5	91.6	90.3	88.4	90.0
2002	85.4	85.8	87.5	89.5	91.0	91.1	92.2	93.6	92.9	93.1	92.4	91.8	90.5
2003	90.8	91.3	93.0	94.0	95.6	97.0	98.1	100.0	100.5	102.3	101.8	102.2	97.2
2004	100.5	102.6	104.1	108.4	109.7	112.1	115.1	116.6	118.5	120.8	119.7	120.5	112.4
2005	117.7	120.5	122.3	124.6	124.6	126.0	128.4	129.9	131.9	131.6	131.8	132.9	126.9
2006	130.8	133.6	135.8	137.3	138.5	139.9	138.8	139.3	138.2	135.6	133.7	132.3	136.2
2007	128.1	129.6	131.9	130.9	132.6	132.0	131.3	131.9	129.4	127.8	126.3	125.1	129.7
Natural Resources and Mining													
2000	0.5	0.5	0.6	0.6	0.6	0.6	0.6	0.6	0.6	0.6	0.5	0.5	0.6
2001	0.6	0.5	0.5	0.5	0.5	0.5	0.5	0.5	0.5	0.4	0.3	0.3	0.5
2002	0.4	0.3	0.4	0.3	0.3	0.3	0.3	0.3	0.3	0.3	0.3	0.3	0.3
2003	0.3	0.3	0.3	0.3	0.4	0.4	0.4	0.4	0.4	0.4	0.4	0.4	0.4
2004	0.4	0.4	0.4	0.4	0.4	0.4	0.4	0.4	0.4	0.4	0.4	0.4	0.4
2005	0.4	0.4	0.4	0.4	0.4	0.4	0.4	0.4	0.5	0.5	0.5	0.5	0.4
2006	0.4	0.4	0.4	0.4	0.4	0.5	0.5	0.5	0.5	0.5	0.5	0.5	0.5
2007	0.5	0.5	0.5	0.5	0.5	0.5	0.5	0.5	0.5	0.5	0.5	0.5	0.5
Construction													
2000	63.3	63.6	65.3	65.9	66.7	68.4	68.2	68.6	67.3	66.3	66.8	66.7	66.4
2001	65.0	65.8	66.9	67.2	68.4	70.0	70.3	71.5	70.8	70.2	69.0	67.2	68.5
2002	64.5	64.9	66.5	68.5	69.8	69.7	70.6	71.9	71.3	71.0	70.3	69.6	69.1
2003	69.1	69.6	71.3	72.2	73.6	74.8	75.7	77.4	77.9	79.4	78.7	79.1	74.9
2004	77.8	79.7	80.9	85.1	86.1	88.3	91.1	92.4	94.3	96.4	95.2	96.1	88.6
2005	93.2	96.0	97.5	99.5	99.4	100.6	102.9	104.3	105.9	105.6	105.7	106.8	101.5
2006	104.6	107.1	108.9	110.0	110.9	112.0	110.8	111.3	110.0	107.7	105.9	104.4	108.6
2007	100.9	102.4	104.5	103.5	105.2	104.3	103.8	104.5	102.2	100.6	99.1	97.9	102.4
Manufacturing													
2000	19.8	19.9	20.2	20.0	20.1	20.2	20.1	20.1	20.2	20.4	20.4	20.6	20.2
2001	20.6	20.8	20.7	20.8	21.0	21.2	21.1	21.3	21.2	21.0	21.0	20.9	21.0
2002	20.5	20.6	20.6	20.7	20.9	21.1	21.3	21.4	21.3	21.8	21.8	21.9	21.2
2003	21.4	21.4	21.4	21.5	21.6	21.8	22.0	22.2	22.2	22.5	22.7	22.7	21.9
2004	22.3	22.5	22.8	22.9	23.2	23.4	23.6	23.8	23.8	24.0	24.1	24.0	23.4
2005	24.1	24.1	24.4	24.7	24.8	25.0	25.1	25.2	25.6	25.6	25.7	25.7	25.0
2006	25.8	26.1	26.5	26.9	27.2	27.4	27.5	27.5	27.7	27.4	27.3	27.4	27.1
2007	26.7	26.7	26.9	26.9	26.9	27.2	27.0	26.9	26.7	26.7	26.7	26.7	26.8
Service-Providing													
2000	591.5	594.0	599.0	602.3	611.0	605.7	603.6	616.0	620.0	624.1	629.3	629.0	610.5
2001	630.3	636.4	640.7	640.3	642.7	640.2	633.4	637.8	643.0	630.7	632.6	632.5	636.7
2002	624.5	628.5	635.1	638.4	643.2	639.3	634.6	638.0	643.9	650.3	653.6	654.8	640.4
2003	647.4	652.1	656.5	656.0	660.8	657.2	655.9	661.8	669.8	676.5	679.1	682.8	662.9
2004	677.4	679.2	686.6	695.1	698.5	698.3	696.1	698.6	708.9	719.7	721.6	723.4	700.3
2005	714.7	720.1	728.2	742.7	745.3	746.4	741.9	743.5	755.5	761.0	767.4	770.4	744.8
2006	760.6	767.3	774.9	778.7	783.8	783.9	776.9	778.2	787.1	791.1	795.6	795.6	781.1
2007	785.1	794.3	796.0	799.4	803.9	801.2	789.1	788.5	794.0	799.3	805.9	807.8	797.0
Trade, Transportation, and Utilities													
2000	117.1	116.6	116.2	117.2	118.1	118.7	118.9	121.1	122.2	123.8	126.4	128.9	120.4
2001	126.0	125.0	125.2	126.3	127.1	128.0	128.1	128.3	128.1	128.0	129.9	130.9	127.6
2002	126.4	125.3	125.9	128.0	128.2	128.4	128.5	128.6	129.3	131.4	133.1	135.2	129.0
2003	129.3	129.1	130.3	129.4	130.0	130.6	130.9	132.7	134.0	136.9	139.8	142.2	132.9
2004	135.2	135.0	136.4	137.1	137.9	139.6	139.8	140.5	141.1	143.7	146.8	149.0	140.2
2005	143.7	143.2	144.0	145.6	146.2	147.3	148.2	149.0	150.6	151.8	155.2	157.2	148.5
2006	152.6	152.1	153.7	153.8	154.8	155.3	155.3	155.9	156.8	158.0	161.4	163.3	156.1
2007	158.4	157.7	158.4	158.7	159.9	160.6	159.8	160.6	160.7	162.1	166.2	167.8	160.9
Wholesale Trade													
2000	17.1	17.1	17.3	17.7	17.8	17.9	17.8	18.0	18.0	17.9	18.1	18.2	17.7
2001	19.0	19.1	19.3	19.6	19.7	20.0	19.8	19.9	19.9	19.8	19.8	19.9	19.7
2002	19.5	19.7	19.9	20.0	20.0	20.1	19.9	20.0	20.0	20.0	20.1	20.2	20.0
2003	19.7	19.8	19.8	19.7	19.7	19.8	19.9	19.8	19.8	20.0	20.1	20.2	19.8
2004	19.9	20.0	20.1	20.2	20.2	20.4	20.7	20.7	20.8	21.1	21.1	21.2	20.5
2005	21.2	21.4	21.6	21.9	22.0	22.2	22.4	22.5	22.7	22.6	22.7	22.9	22.2
2006	22.8	23.0	23.2	23.4	23.6	23.6	23.7	23.8	24.0	23.9	23.9	24.1	23.6
2007	23.8	23.9	24.0	24.0	24.2	24.3	24.2	24.3	24.3	24.4	24.4	24.5	24.2

Employment by Industry: Las Vegas-Paradise, NV, 2000–2007—*Continued*

(Numbers in thousands, not seasonally adjusted.)

Industry and year	January	February	March	April	May	June	July	August	September	October	November	December	Annual Average
Retail Trade													
2000	73.0	72.4	71.5	72.4	73.2	73.5	73.5	75.3	76.0	77.2	79.3	81.7	74.9
2001	78.5	77.3	77.2	77.8	78.2	78.9	79.1	79.3	79.5	79.6	81.7	82.8	79.2
2002	79.0	77.9	78.3	79.4	79.8	80.2	80.0	79.9	80.4	82.1	85.0	87.3	80.8
2003	81.9	81.3	82.3	81.6	82.3	82.7	83.0	84.6	85.5	87.8	90.4	92.4	84.6
2004	85.9	85.4	86.3	87.2	87.9	89.1	88.7	89.3	89.7	91.3	94.5	96.7	89.3
2005	91.6	90.7	91.1	91.7	91.9	92.6	93.5	93.9	94.9	96.1	99.0	100.5	94.0
2006	96.1	95.4	96.3	96.1	96.6	97.0	96.7	97.1	97.4	98.7	101.6	103.1	97.7
2007	98.7	97.8	98.1	98.4	99.2	99.4	99.3	99.7	99.4	100.6	104.4	105.7	100.1
Transportation and Utilities													
2000	27.0	27.1	27.4	27.2	27.1	27.3	27.6	27.9	28.3	28.8	29.1	29.0	27.8
2001	28.4	28.6	28.7	28.9	29.1	29.1	29.2	29.1	28.9	28.6	28.3	28.1	28.8
2002	27.8	27.6	27.7	28.6	28.4	28.2	28.6	28.7	28.9	29.2	28.1	27.8	28.3
2003	27.7	28.0	28.2	28.1	28.0	28.1	28.0	28.3	28.7	29.1	29.3	29.6	28.4
2004	29.4	29.6	30.0	29.7	29.8	30.1	30.4	30.5	30.6	31.3	31.2	31.1	30.3
2005	30.9	31.1	31.3	32.0	32.3	32.5	32.3	32.6	33.0	33.1	33.5	33.8	32.4
2006	33.7	33.7	34.2	34.3	34.6	34.7	34.9	35.0	35.4	35.4	35.9	36.1	34.8
2007	35.9	36.0	36.3	36.3	36.5	36.9	36.3	36.6	37.0	37.1	37.4	37.6	36.7
Information													
2000	13.1	12.7	13.1	12.9	13.7	13.4	13.1	13.4	13.2	13.6	13.8	13.1	13.3
2001	14.0	15.6	15.4	14.1	14.0	13.3	12.4	12.2	11.8	12.2	12.6	12.1	13.3
2002	12.1	11.9	11.6	11.7	11.8	11.4	11.2	11.2	11.2	11.0	11.1	11.0	11.4
2003	10.6	10.4	10.3	10.4	10.6	10.5	10.2	10.0	10.0	10.1	10.2	10.3	10.3
2004	10.2	10.0	10.0	11.1	10.5	10.4	10.4	10.2	10.1	10.5	10.4	10.1	10.3
2005	10.5	10.1	10.1	10.6	11.0	10.4	10.1	10.2	10.2	10.6	10.5	10.3	10.4
2006	10.8	10.8	10.5	10.9	10.9	11.0	11.5	11.5	11.1	11.1	11.0	10.8	11.0
2007	11.3	11.7	11.5	11.6	11.9	11.8	11.2	11.7	11.4	11.1	11.3	11.1	11.5
Financial Activities													
2000	36.9	37.0	37.4	37.4	37.5	37.9	38.3	38.5	38.6	38.3	38.9	39.2	38.0
2001	40.0	40.2	40.7	40.5	40.7	41.0	41.1	41.7	41.8	41.3	41.0	41.6	41.0
2002	40.5	41.0	41.2	41.3	41.3	41.5	41.6	41.5	41.4	41.8	42.3	42.3	41.5
2003	42.1	42.3	42.5	42.8	43.5	43.5	43.9	44.1	44.3	44.4	44.3	44.5	43.5
2004	44.6	44.8	44.9	45.3	45.4	45.8	46.5	46.6	46.7	47.6	47.7	48.4	46.2
2005	47.7	47.6	48.3	48.2	48.4	48.9	48.9	49.1	49.7	49.4	49.6	49.9	48.8
2006	49.0	49.0	49.6	49.6	50.0	50.4	50.5	50.6	50.9	50.6	50.8	51.3	50.2
2007	50.4	50.4	50.7	50.2	50.5	50.7	50.1	50.0	49.9	49.7	49.6	50.0	50.2
Professional and Business Services													
2000	70.9	71.9	72.5	73.7	74.8	74.9	72.5	75.1	77.9	77.1	78.1	76.0	74.6
2001	80.8	82.4	82.6	80.6	81.6	80.5	78.3	80.6	79.9	78.3	78.7	76.8	80.1
2002	80.0	79.7	81.2	80.5	81.3	80.0	79.7	82.3	82.9	82.4	83.2	81.9	81.3
2003	85.4	85.7	85.4	84.8	85.1	83.5	85.1	87.8	88.0	89.5	88.7	88.3	86.4
2004	93.6	92.2	92.6	94.4	95.1	95.0	95.2	97.0	97.6	101.5	99.3	97.8	95.9
2005	101.5	102.4	103.6	104.9	104.6	105.0	104.4	106.3	107.0	109.7	112.2	112.1	106.1
2006	113.0	114.2	115.3	115.5	116.3	116.6	114.4	115.6	115.2	115.6	116.2	114.0	115.2
2007	116.9	119.4	117.3	117.5	117.5	116.5	113.3	114.9	113.0	113.8	114.1	112.0	115.5
Education and Health Services													
2000	39.1	39.5	39.9	39.9	40.2	40.4	40.6	40.8	41.5	42.1	42.5	43.0	40.8
2001	43.3	43.8	44.2	44.5	44.9	45.2	45.0	45.8	46.0	46.0	46.2	46.6	45.1
2002	46.0	46.6	47.1	47.4	48.0	47.8	47.8	48.0	48.2	48.8	49.1	49.2	47.8
2003	48.7	49.5	49.7	50.0	50.4	50.3	50.1	50.6	51.2	51.4	52.0	52.2	50.5
2004	51.9	52.6	53.2	53.6	53.5	53.6	54.0	54.3	55.2	55.6	55.7	56.0	54.1
2005	55.8	56.4	57.0	57.7	57.9	58.1	57.6	57.7	58.1	58.0	58.4	59.0	57.6
2006	58.5	59.1	59.8	59.4	59.6	60.2	59.3	59.8	60.7	61.2	61.7	62.1	60.1
2007	61.5	62.4	62.7	62.7	63.2	63.5	63.3	63.6	64.1	64.6	65.0	65.4	63.5
Leisure and Hospitality													
2000	228.1	228.8	230.9	232.0	233.8	235.2	235.5	238.5	237.2	237.2	236.6	235.7	234.1
2001	235.7	236.4	238.9	238.7	239.8	239.3	239.8	239.8	239.1	228.5	227.8	228.1	236.0
2002	225.6	226.8	230.0	232.0	234.3	234.2	233.7	234.0	233.6	233.6	233.0	233.3	232.0
2003	233.3	234.0	236.5	237.2	239.2	239.6	240.1	241.3	241.2	240.9	240.2	240.9	238.7
2004	240.8	240.5	243.2	247.1	248.4	249.4	249.9	250.4	250.5	250.1	250.8	251.0	247.7
2005	249.2	250.7	253.7	263.9	264.8	267.5	267.2	266.6	268.3	266.2	265.0	264.8	262.3
2006	264.4	266.3	269.4	271.7	273.8	275.3	274.9	274.1	274.7	272.8	271.8	271.5	271.7
2007	268.3	270.4	272.1	273.4	275.2	276.1	273.9	271.7	271.8	271.1	272.2	273.7	272.5
Other Services													
2000	17.7	18.0	18.4	18.3	18.6	18.9	18.8	18.9	18.9	18.9	18.9	18.9	18.6
2001	18.8	19.1	19.5	19.8	20.2	20.6	20.1	20.5	20.5	19.9	19.6	19.6	19.9
2002	19.8	20.1	20.5	20.3	20.6	20.7	20.4	20.5	20.3	20.2	20.0	20.0	20.3
2003	19.7	19.9	20.2	19.9	20.1	20.5	20.5	20.6	20.6	20.4	20.6	20.8	20.3
2004	20.9	21.5	22.2	22.4	22.9	23.5	22.9	22.9	23.1	23.5	23.3	23.4	22.7
2005	22.3	22.6	22.9	23.0	23.3	23.7	23.7	23.8	24.1	24.0	24.2	24.5	23.5
2006	23.7	23.9	24.3	24.3	24.7	25.1	25.1	25.3	25.5	25.3	25.2	25.1	24.8
2007	24.5	24.5	25.0	25.4	25.7	26.1	26.0	26.1	26.2	25.9	25.9	25.7	25.6
Government													
2000	68.6	69.5	70.6	70.9	74.3	66.3	65.9	69.7	70.5	73.1	74.1	74.2	70.6
2001	71.7	73.9	74.2	75.8	74.4	72.3	68.6	68.9	75.8	76.5	76.8	76.8	73.8
2002	74.1	77.1	77.6	77.2	77.7	75.3	71.7	71.9	77.0	81.1	81.8	81.9	77.0
2003	78.3	81.2	81.6	81.5	81.9	78.7	75.1	74.7	80.5	82.9	83.3	83.6	80.2
2004	80.2	82.6	84.1	84.1	84.8	81.0	77.4	76.7	84.6	87.2	87.6	87.7	83.2
2005	84.0	87.1	88.6	88.8	89.1	85.5	81.8	80.8	87.5	91.3	92.3	92.6	87.5
2006	88.6	91.9	92.3	93.5	93.7	90.0	85.9	85.4	92.2	96.5	97.5	97.5	92.1
2007	93.8	97.8	98.3	99.9	100.0	95.9	91.5	89.9	96.9	101.0	101.6	102.1	97.4

Employment by Industry: Charlotte-Gastonia-Concord, NC-SC, 2000–2007

(Numbers in thousands, not seasonally adjusted.)

Industry and year	January	February	March	April	May	June	July	August	September	October	November	December	Annual Average
Total Nonfarm													
2000	748.5	750.3	758.7	766.0	769.8	774.6	759.9	767.2	771.4	778.5	778.0	779.0	766.8
2001	763.0	766.7	771.5	775.7	777.7	777.4	761.1	769.4	771.3	774.6	773.8	771.5	771.1
2002	757.4	761.1	767.3	768.2	771.5	773.8	761.3	770.8	775.2	777.0	777.9	776.3	769.8
2003	758.7	759.2	765.5	767.3	773.6	771.0	744.2	756.3	766.4	772.6	773.7	774.2	765.2
2004	756.0	757.9	764.1	766.2	772.6	771.7	755.6	770.1	778.8	786.4	788.1	787.4	771.2
2005	772.5	776.5	782.5	787.1	791.6	788.4	773.8	790.8	799.9	808.9	810.7	811.1	791.2
2006	801.7	805.1	813.1	821.3	827.0	822.0	808.8	828.8	837.7	844.0	850.2	851.2	825.9
2007	838.8	844.1	853.3	856.8	864.9	859.3	840.6	861.0	864.7	871.5	873.4	872.7	858.4
Total Private													
2000	660.1	661.6	668.8	676.1	680.2	687.2	681.8	683.8	683.3	686.3	686.4	687.5	678.6
2001	673.2	675.4	679.9	683.5	685.6	688.4	681.3	683.0	679.5	679.5	676.5	675.6	680.1
2002	663.4	665.6	671.0	672.7	676.1	681.2	678.5	682.3	680.7	678.5	679.0	678.9	675.7
2003	663.0	662.6	668.2	670.1	675.8	677.2	667.3	670.5	670.1	670.4	671.9	673.5	670.1
2004	657.2	658.1	664.2	666.2	672.4	675.6	677.5	681.9	678.8	683.2	684.4	684.9	673.7
2005	671.9	675.0	680.5	684.3	689.1	690.6	694.4	696.9	697.0	703.3	705.0	705.9	691.2
2006	697.4	700.2	707.8	715.7	721.3	724.9	728.8	732.5	731.5	736.5	740.9	741.9	723.3
2007	730.6	734.4	743.5	747.8	754.4	759.1	757.5	760.5	758.4	763.7	765.1	765.1	753.3
Goods-Producing													
2000	157.5	157.1	158.3	159.7	160.3	161.6	160.0	160.2	160.8	159.1	158.9	158.4	159.3
2001	155.4	155.8	156.4	156.3	156.3	156.6	154.8	154.7	154.5	152.7	150.9	150.1	154.5
2002	149.5	149.1	149.5	148.9	149.7	150.5	149.4	149.7	148.9	147.6	146.6	144.6	148.7
2003	142.5	141.8	142.5	140.7	140.8	140.6	136.3	135.9	135.4	135.6	135.0	134.5	138.5
2004	131.7	131.8	132.9	133.8	135.0	135.9	136.3	136.8	136.3	136.4	135.9	135.5	134.9
2005	133.9	134.6	135.3	134.8	135.7	136.5	136.9	137.1	137.0	136.8	136.8	136.6	136.0
2006	135.4	135.6	137.1	138.7	139.3	140.2	140.9	141.9	141.3	141.5	141.1	141.7	139.6
2007	139.9	140.3	140.7	141.1	141.2	141.9	141.9	142.1	141.6	141.7	141.3	140.8	141.2
Natural Resources, Mining, and Construction													
2000	48.3	48.3	49.6	50.3	51.0	51.7	51.6	51.8	51.8	51.5	51.4	51.2	50.7
2001	49.5	49.8	50.9	51.2	51.7	52.3	52.4	52.4	52.4	51.3	50.5	49.9	51.2
2002	50.0	49.8	50.7	50.9	51.6	51.9	52.1	52.2	51.2	50.2	49.7	49.4	50.8
2003	47.8	47.5	47.9	47.1	47.9	48.3	48.4	48.6	48.6	49.1	49.1	49.0	48.3
2004	47.4	47.3	48.1	48.9	49.8	50.3	50.7	51.0	50.5	51.4	51.3	51.3	49.8
2005	50.5	50.7	51.3	51.1	51.7	52.6	54.0	54.4	54.5	53.9	54.1	54.0	52.7
2006	53.3	53.6	54.8	56.0	56.5	57.4	58.1	58.8	58.5	58.7	58.5	58.7	56.9
2007	57.6	58.1	58.9	59.4	59.5	60.5	60.6	60.8	60.4	60.4	60.3	60.0	59.7
Manufacturing													
2000	109.2	108.8	108.7	109.4	109.3	109.9	108.4	108.4	109.0	107.6	107.5	107.2	108.6
2001	105.9	106.0	105.5	105.1	104.6	104.3	102.4	102.3	102.1	101.4	100.4	100.2	103.4
2002	99.5	99.3	98.8	98.0	98.1	98.6	97.3	97.5	97.7	97.4	96.9	95.2	97.9
2003	94.7	94.3	94.6	93.6	92.9	92.3	87.9	87.3	86.8	86.5	85.9	85.5	90.2
2004	84.3	84.5	84.8	84.9	85.2	85.6	85.6	85.8	85.8	85.0	84.6	84.2	85.0
2005	83.4	83.9	84.0	83.7	84.0	83.9	82.9	82.7	82.5	82.9	82.7	82.6	83.3
2006	82.1	82.0	82.3	82.7	82.8	82.8	82.8	83.1	82.8	82.8	82.6	83.0	82.7
2007	82.3	82.2	81.8	81.7	81.7	81.4	81.3	81.3	81.2	81.3	81.0	80.8	81.5
Service-Providing													
2000	591.0	593.2	600.4	606.3	609.5	613.0	599.9	607.0	610.6	619.4	619.1	620.6	607.5
2001	607.6	610.9	615.1	619.4	621.4	620.8	606.3	614.7	616.8	621.9	622.9	621.4	616.6
2002	607.9	612.0	617.8	619.3	621.8	623.3	611.9	621.1	626.3	629.4	631.3	631.7	621.2
2003	616.2	617.4	623.0	626.6	632.8	630.4	607.9	620.4	631.0	637.0	638.7	639.7	626.8
2004	624.3	626.1	631.2	632.4	637.6	635.8	619.3	633.3	642.5	650.0	652.2	651.9	636.4
2005	638.6	641.9	647.2	652.3	655.9	651.9	636.9	653.7	662.9	672.1	673.9	674.5	655.2
2006	666.3	669.5	676.0	682.6	687.7	681.8	667.9	686.9	696.4	702.5	709.1	709.5	686.4
2007	698.9	703.8	712.6	715.7	723.7	717.4	698.7	718.9	723.1	729.8	732.1	731.9	717.2
Trade, Transportation, and Utilities													
2000	163.0	163.0	164.3	165.3	166.3	167.9	166.2	166.5	166.5	167.7	170.2	171.7	166.6
2001	167.5	166.7	167.3	169.0	169.3	169.9	167.8	167.8	167.7	168.4	169.7	170.6	168.5
2002	164.4	163.2	164.3	163.3	163.3	164.0	163.6	164.4	163.8	163.8	167.1	168.8	164.5
2003	161.2	160.8	160.9	161.1	161.4	162.1	160.5	161.3	161.8	163.0	165.9	167.7	162.3
2004	162.0	161.8	161.9	163.6	165.0	165.0	164.7	166.0	165.4	166.2	168.6	170.4	165.1
2005	165.5	166.0	167.0	167.4	167.4	166.8	166.7	166.8	166.1	169.5	172.2	174.5	168.0
2006	168.8	167.7	168.8	171.1	172.2	172.1	172.4	172.8	172.5	175.1	179.5	180.9	172.8
2007	176.2	175.4	177.5	177.9	179.2	179.3	180.0	180.2	180.1	181.4	184.3	186.2	179.8
Wholesale Trade													
2000	46.2	46.4	46.8	47.1	47.4	47.8	47.6	47.7	47.8	47.8	48.0	48.1	47.4
2001	48.6	48.6	48.9	49.2	48.9	49.0	48.8	48.6	48.5	48.1	47.9	47.6	48.6
2002	46.8	46.7	46.9	46.8	46.5	46.4	46.5	46.5	46.5	46.4	46.5	46.4	46.6
2003	46.0	46.0	45.9	46.2	46.1	46.1	45.8	45.7	45.6	46.5	46.6	46.7	46.1
2004	47.3	47.4	47.5	46.9	46.9	46.8	47.1	47.1	46.9	46.0	45.7	45.6	46.8
2005	46.0	46.0	46.1	46.7	46.8	46.4	46.5	46.5	46.4	47.0	47.3	47.3	46.6
2006	47.5	47.6	47.8	48.2	48.3	48.2	47.5	47.5	47.3	47.3	47.4	47.5	47.7
2007	47.7	48.0	48.5	49.0	48.9	49.1	49.5	49.4	49.4	49.3	49.4	49.4	49.0
Retail Trade													
2000	83.7	83.3	83.7	84.2	84.9	86.0	84.2	84.1	83.9	84.3	86.9	88.4	84.8
2001	84.2	82.8	83.5	83.7	84.2	84.8	82.9	83.0	83.0	83.3	85.4	86.7	84.0
2002	82.1	81.2	82.1	81.7	81.8	82.2	81.4	81.8	81.5	81.8	85.0	86.6	82.4
2003	80.5	79.8	80.5	80.7	80.9	81.5	80.7	81.2	81.2	81.8	84.6	85.7	81.6
2004	81.0	80.3	80.7	81.7	82.8	82.9	81.8	82.8	82.6	84.3	86.8	88.4	83.0
2005	83.8	84.2	85.0	84.8	84.6	84.1	84.6	84.7	84.3	86.7	89.0	90.7	85.5
2006	85.9	84.7	85.4	87.2	88.1	87.9	88.7	88.9	89.0	91.5	95.7	96.8	89.2
2007	92.8	91.8	93.1	93.1	94.3	94.2	94.4	94.9	94.7	95.9	98.6	100.2	94.8

Employment by Industry: Charlotte-Gastonia-Concord, NC-SC, 2000–2007—*Continued*

(Numbers in thousands, not seasonally adjusted.)

Industry and year	January	February	March	April	May	June	July	August	September	October	November	December	Annual Average
Transportation and Utilities													
2000	33.1	33.3	33.8	34.0	34.0	34.1	34.4	34.7	34.8	35.6	35.3	35.2	34.4
2001	34.7	35.3	34.9	36.1	36.2	36.1	36.1	36.2	36.2	37.0	36.4	36.3	36.0
2002	35.5	35.3	35.3	34.8	35.0	35.4	35.7	36.1	35.8	35.6	35.6	35.8	35.5
2003	34.7	35.0	34.5	34.2	34.4	34.5	34.0	34.4	35.0	34.7	34.7	35.3	34.6
2004	33.7	34.1	33.7	35.0	35.3	35.3	35.8	36.1	35.9	35.9	36.1	36.4	35.3
2005	35.7	35.8	35.9	35.9	36.0	36.3	35.6	35.6	35.4	35.8	35.9	36.5	35.9
2006	35.4	35.4	35.6	35.7	35.8	36.0	36.2	36.4	36.2	36.3	36.4	36.6	36.0
2007	35.7	35.6	35.9	35.8	36.0	36.0	36.1	35.9	36.0	36.2	36.3	36.6	36.0
Information													
2000	23.8	23.9	24.0	24.1	23.8	24.0	24.0	24.1	24.2	24.3	24.7	24.4	24.1
2001	24.0	24.1	24.2	23.4	23.3	23.5	23.5	23.2	22.6	23.2	23.2	22.9	23.4
2002	23.1	23.0	23.2	22.8	22.8	23.0	22.9	22.8	22.7	23.0	23.0	23.2	23.0
2003	22.5	22.3	22.4	22.1	22.0	22.3	22.0	21.9	21.8	21.9	21.9	22.0	22.1
2004	22.0	21.9	22.0	21.8	21.6	21.8	21.1	20.9	20.6	21.0	21.1	20.8	21.4
2005	20.5	20.4	20.5	20.8	21.0	21.1	21.2	21.2	21.2	21.3	21.7	22.1	21.1
2006	22.2	22.2	22.2	21.9	22.0	22.1	21.7	22.1	22.0	21.9	22.1	22.3	22.1
2007	22.0	22.0	21.9	21.9	22.1	22.5	22.4	22.4	22.4	22.4	22.5	22.2	22.2
Financial Activities													
2000	54.5	54.8	54.8	56.1	56.6	57.5	57.2	57.4	57.2	57.4	57.5	57.8	56.6
2001	57.7	58.1	58.4	58.8	59.0	59.3	59.9	60.3	60.3	60.2	60.8	61.0	59.5
2002	61.5	61.8	62.3	62.8	63.1	63.8	64.7	65.2	65.1	65.8	66.2	66.4	64.1
2003	66.4	66.7	66.9	67.0	67.1	67.6	66.3	66.7	66.7	66.7	66.6	67.0	66.8
2004	66.8	67.0	67.1	67.1	67.1	67.5	68.7	69.0	68.9	69.1	69.3	69.3	68.1
2005	69.4	69.8	69.8	70.3	70.8	71.5	72.6	72.4	72.3	72.7	73.0	73.7	71.5
2006	73.8	74.7	75.2	76.1	76.2	76.6	78.2	78.1	77.7	77.2	77.1	77.2	76.5
2007	76.7	77.3	77.5	77.9	78.3	78.8	78.2	78.2	78.0	77.8	78.0	77.9	77.9
Professional and Business Services													
2000	113.5	114.2	116.5	120.4	120.4	121.1	121.3	122.2	122.3	123.6	122.2	122.2	120.0
2001	119.4	119.7	120.7	119.5	119.1	117.9	116.3	116.4	115.2	115.3	113.1	113.4	117.2
2002	110.2	112.2	112.9	113.3	114.4	114.9	114.0	116.1	116.2	114.9	113.7	112.8	113.8
2003	111.9	111.5	113.0	114.0	114.9	114.4	113.9	115.9	116.2	115.4	114.9	114.1	114.2
2004	110.1	111.9	113.5	111.3	111.5	113.1	113.8	115.3	115.1	117.5	117.1	115.2	113.8
2005	112.9	113.5	114.2	115.7	116.3	115.8	117.8	118.5	120.4	121.9	121.0	119.3	117.3
2006	117.5	118.7	120.1	122.5	123.9	124.5	125.9	127.3	128.4	129.8	130.2	128.1	124.7
2007	125.5	127.2	129.9	131.7	133.1	134.1	133.2	134.8	135.4	137.5	136.9	135.3	132.9
Education and Health Services													
2000	53.1	53.7	53.9	53.7	53.6	53.6	53.2	53.5	54.4	55.4	55.7	55.8	54.1
2001	54.4	55.2	55.9	55.5	55.8	56.6	55.8	56.6	57.1	57.7	58.2	58.2	56.4
2002	57.2	58.1	58.2	57.8	58.4	58.9	59.2	60.1	60.8	61.4	61.8	62.8	59.6
2003	62.0	62.7	63.2	63.3	63.8	63.9	63.4	64.2	64.2	65.0	65.2	65.9	63.9
2004	64.6	63.0	63.3	64.0	64.1	63.7	64.4	64.9	65.0	65.7	66.0	67.1	64.7
2005	65.7	65.8	66.5	67.0	67.0	66.8	67.2	67.9	68.3	69.1	69.3	69.3	67.5
2006	70.6	71.2	71.5	70.9	70.9	71.6	71.8	72.5	73.1	74.4	74.8	75.4	72.4
2007	74.7	75.7	76.1	76.7	76.9	77.1	76.9	77.9	77.6	78.3	78.6	79.5	77.2
Leisure and Hospitality													
2000	62.7	62.6	64.4	64.1	66.5	68.3	66.7	66.9	64.9	65.2	63.6	63.4	64.9
2001	61.4	61.9	62.6	66.3	67.4	68.7	67.2	67.7	65.6	65.3	63.6	62.1	65.0
2002	60.0	60.6	62.7	65.9	66.9	68.3	67.8	67.6	66.8	65.6	64.3	64.7	65.1
2003	61.9	62.4	64.8	66.8	70.4	70.9	69.4	69.3	68.4	68.3	67.9	67.8	67.4
2004	65.1	65.8	68.1	69.6	72.6	72.7	72.8	73.5	72.3	71.4	70.5	70.4	70.4
2005	68.2	69.0	71.0	72.4	74.4	75.3	75.3	76.4	75.1	75.3	74.4	73.8	73.4
2006	72.4	72.9	75.4	77.7	79.4	79.8	80.8	80.7	79.6	79.5	79.0	79.0	78.0
2007	78.4	79.0	81.8	83.2	85.8	87.1	86.1	86.1	84.6	85.3	84.3	83.8	83.8
Other Services													
2000	32.0	32.3	32.6	32.7	32.7	33.2	33.2	33.0	33.0	33.6	33.6	33.8	33.0
2001	33.4	33.9	34.4	34.7	35.4	35.9	36.0	36.3	36.5	36.7	37.0	37.3	35.6
2002	37.5	37.6	37.9	37.9	37.5	37.8	36.9	36.4	36.4	36.4	36.3	35.6	37.0
2003	34.6	34.4	34.5	35.1	35.4	35.4	35.5	35.3	35.6	34.5	34.5	34.5	34.9
2004	34.9	34.9	35.4	35.0	35.5	35.9	35.7	35.5	35.2	35.9	35.9	36.2	35.5
2005	35.8	35.9	36.2	35.9	36.5	36.8	36.7	36.6	36.6	36.7	36.6	36.6	36.4
2006	36.7	37.2	37.5	36.8	37.4	38.0	37.1	37.1	36.9	37.1	37.1	37.3	37.2
2007	37.2	37.5	38.1	37.4	37.8	38.3	38.8	38.8	38.7	39.3	39.2	39.4	38.4
Government													
2000	88.4	88.7	89.9	89.9	89.6	87.4	78.1	83.4	88.1	92.2	91.6	91.5	88.2
2001	89.8	91.3	91.6	92.2	92.1	89.0	79.8	86.4	91.8	95.1	97.3	95.9	91.0
2002	94.0	95.5	96.3	95.5	95.4	92.6	82.8	88.5	94.5	98.5	98.9	97.4	94.2
2003	95.7	96.6	97.3	97.2	97.8	93.8	76.9	85.8	96.3	102.2	101.8	100.7	95.2
2004	98.8	99.8	99.9	100.0	100.2	96.1	78.1	88.2	100.0	103.2	103.7	102.5	97.5
2005	100.6	101.5	102.0	102.8	102.5	97.8	79.4	93.9	102.9	105.6	105.7	105.2	100.0
2006	104.3	104.9	105.3	105.6	105.7	97.1	80.0	96.3	106.2	107.5	109.3	109.3	102.6
2007	108.2	109.7	109.8	109.0	110.5	100.2	83.1	100.5	106.3	107.8	108.3	107.6	105.1

Employment by Industry: New Orleans-Metairie-Kenner, LA, 2000–2007

(Numbers in thousands, not seasonally adjusted.)

Industry and year	January	February	March	April	May	June	July	August	September	October	November	December	Annual Average
Total Nonfarm													
2000	614.3	616.8	619.6	619.6	622.8	619.7	610.7	611.8	616.9	617.0	619.0	624.5	617.7
2001	616.1	621.0	625.2	622.8	623.9	623.1	611.6	612.5	617.7	614.5	617.1	618.2	618.6
2002	603.3	605.6	608.9	613.1	611.0	614.1	601.5	602.9	607.6	606.4	612.3	612.7	608.3
2003	604.2	607.4	608.8	615.5	614.2	615.5	607.0	604.2	610.1	611.1	616.5	617.6	611.0
2004	608.0	610.2	614.5	620.6	619.7	618.4	610.0	612.0	610.1	613.9	618.1	616.0	614.3
2005	606.5	607.2	613.1	613.0	612.4	616.3	604.5	603.7	473.2	425.8	438.9	450.9	555.5
2006	446.4	456.3	469.0	472.0	477.6	484.7	480.8	485.0	489.3	496.0	503.0	507.5	480.6
2007	503.8	508.5	515.2	515.4	517.2	519.8	511.6	516.3	517.5	521.4	523.5	525.4	516.3
Total Private													
2000	510.8	512.9	515.2	515.3	518.8	516.0	511.5	512.0	513.9	514.2	516.3	520.7	514.8
2001	512.6	516.8	521.1	518.1	519.6	518.9	512.4	511.8	514.8	511.7	514.6	515.0	515.6
2002	500.4	501.6	504.8	509.2	507.5	509.2	502.0	502.1	504.9	503.2	508.0	508.2	505.1
2003	500.4	502.6	503.6	510.7	509.8	510.3	503.8	504.0	505.6	508.0	512.5	513.7	507.1
2004	504.8	506.2	510.0	513.7	512.8	512.5	506.3	509.3	504.3	509.6	513.1	510.8	509.5
2005	501.3	500.9	506.2	507.9	507.8	511.4	503.1	501.5	371.3	345.5	358.9	371.3	457.3
2006	373.7	383.5	395.5	398.6	403.8	411.3	408.8	412.4	413.4	419.9	425.8	429.5	406.4
2007	427.5	431.1	437.1	436.9	438.1	440.6	434.6	438.2	436.5	440.3	441.8	443.5	437.2
Goods-Producing													
2000	88.6	88.4	88.8	87.7	88.8	89.1	88.6	89.2	87.8	86.9	85.9	85.7	88.0
2001	85.3	86.3	88.1	85.9	86.5	86.8	86.1	85.5	85.0	83.8	82.7	81.9	85.3
2002	80.4	79.9	80.6	80.6	81.1	81.3	80.2	80.7	80.4	80.2	80.1	79.9	80.5
2003	79.4	79.4	79.4	80.5	81.2	81.5	80.3	79.9	79.3	79.4	78.5	78.7	79.8
2004	77.8	77.5	78.2	78.8	78.2	78.4	77.7	77.5	76.9	77.2	76.9	76.9	77.7
2005	75.1	75.8	76.6	76.5	76.9	77.6	77.1	77.2	60.5	65.7	68.8	71.2	73.3
2006	71.5	72.5	73.9	74.5	74.8	74.8	76.5	74.8	75.9	75.9	76.6	76.9	75.0
2007	75.1	75.5	75.8	75.8	76.8	77.4	76.7	77.4	77.7	78.3	78.7	79.6	77.1
Natural Resources and Mining													
2005	8.3	8.4	8.6	8.3	8.4	8.6	8.4	8.5	8.1	8.3	8.3	8.4	8.4
2006	7.9	8.0	8.1	8.0	8.0	8.1	8.4	8.5	8.7	8.7	8.5	8.3	8.3
2007	7.8	8.0	8.1	8.2	8.4	8.4	8.5	8.5	8.6	8.7	8.6	8.6	8.4
Construction													
2005	29.2	29.0	29.6	29.8	30.0	30.0	29.8	29.7	21.8	25.8	28.4	29.4	28.5
2006	30.6	31.1	32.2	32.7	32.9	33.7	31.4	32.0	31.8	32.5	32.3	32.3	32.1
2007	31.6	31.6	31.9	31.9	32.2	32.4	31.9	32.5	32.6	32.9	33.3	34.1	32.4
Manufacturing													
2000	46.2	45.8	45.7	44.7	45.3	45.3	45.4	45.4	44.7	44.2	44.1	44.0	45.1
2001	44.2	44.1	44.2	43.7	44.0	44.3	43.4	43.1	43.2	42.3	42.2	42.1	43.4
2002	41.3	41.2	41.2	41.4	41.5	41.7	41.1	41.3	40.6	40.3	40.4	40.4	41.0
2003	39.5	39.4	39.3	39.1	39.3	39.4	39.3	39.3	39.1	39.3	39.0	39.4	39.3
2004	38.5	38.5	38.4	38.9	38.9	39.2	38.9	38.9	39.1	38.8	38.4	38.1	38.4	38.7
2005	37.6	38.4	38.4	38.4	38.5	39.0	38.9	39.0	30.6	31.6	32.1	33.4	36.3
2006	33.0	33.4	33.6	33.8	33.9	34.7	35.0	35.4	35.4	35.4	35.9	36.3	34.7
2007	35.7	35.9	35.8	35.7	36.2	36.6	36.3	36.4	36.5	36.7	36.8	36.9	36.3
Service-Providing													
2000	525.6	528.4	530.8	532.0	534.0	530.6	522.0	522.6	529.1	530.1	533.1	538.8	529.8
2001	530.9	534.6	537.0	536.9	537.4	536.3	525.5	527.0	532.8	530.6	534.4	536.3	533.3
2002	522.8	525.7	528.4	532.5	529.9	532.8	521.3	522.2	527.2	526.2	532.2	532.8	527.8
2003	524.8	528.0	529.4	535.0	533.0	534.0	526.7	524.3	530.8	531.7	538.0	538.9	531.2
2004	530.2	532.7	536.3	541.8	541.5	540.0	532.3	534.5	533.2	536.4	541.2	539.1	536.6
2005	531.4	531.4	536.5	536.5	535.5	538.7	527.4	526.5	412.7	360.1	370.1	379.7	482.2
2006	374.9	383.8	395.1	397.5	402.8	408.2	406.0	409.1	413.4	419.4	426.3	430.6	405.6
2007	428.7	433.0	439.4	439.6	440.4	442.4	434.9	438.9	439.8	443.1	444.8	445.8	439.2
Trade, Transportation, and Utilities													
2000	127.5	127.8	128.3	127.3	128.4	129.3	127.0	127.0	126.5	126.6	128.5	131.5	128.0
2001	127.1	127.2	127.8	127.4	127.3	127.8	126.3	126.8	126.5	125.7	127.3	128.8	127.2
2002	123.1	122.3	123.9	123.9	123.9	125.6	123.5	123.4	123.1	122.5	124.1	126.4	123.8
2003	121.0	120.9	121.3	121.0	120.9	121.4	121.4	121.8	121.1	121.9	124.2	125.6	121.9
2004	121.4	121.3	122.3	123.0	123.3	123.2	122.1	122.4	121.1	122.8	124.2	126.4	122.8
2005	121.5	120.7	121.7	121.3	121.6	122.0	121.1	120.6	88.6	84.1	89.9	94.3	110.6
2006	94.7	96.7	99.3	101.0	102.2	104.0	103.9	104.4	104.2	106.0	107.8	110.1	102.9
2007	107.6	107.2	108.4	108.0	108.2	108.5	107.3	107.5	107.4	107.1	108.7	109.2	107.9
Wholesale Trade													
2000	28.0	28.2	28.5	28.6	28.8	29.0	28.8	28.7	28.6	28.3	28.2	28.5	28.5
2001	28.4	28.5	28.6	28.5	28.6	28.8	28.2	28.2	28.1	28.1	27.9	27.9	28.3
2002	27.1	27.1	27.3	27.4	27.5	27.6	27.1	27.2	27.0	26.9	26.8	26.8	27.2
2003	27.0	27.1	27.1	26.6	26.6	26.6	26.6	26.6	26.3	26.8	26.7	26.6	26.7
2004	26.3	26.3	26.4	26.4	26.5	26.5	26.3	26.3	26.2	25.8	25.8	25.8	26.2
2005	25.3	25.3	25.4	25.8	25.9	26.0	26.2	26.1	21.8	21.9	22.2	22.5	24.5
2006	21.8	22.2	22.4	22.6	22.8	23.0	23.0	23.1	23.1	23.1	23.2	23.4	22.8
2007	23.6	23.7	24.0	24.0	24.1	24.2	23.6	23.7	23.8	23.7	23.9	24.0	23.9
Retail Trade													
2000	70.5	70.2	70.4	69.9	70.6	71.1	69.4	69.8	69.3	69.3	71.5	73.6	70.5
2001	69.4	68.8	69.2	68.6	68.6	68.8	68.3	68.7	68.6	68.1	70.3	71.5	69.1
2002	67.5	66.8	68.1	67.4	67.3	68.6	67.0	66.8	66.5	65.7	67.5	69.4	67.4
2003	66.1	65.9	66.5	66.3	66.5	67.0	66.7	67.3	67.0	67.3	69.5	71.0	67.3
2004	67.8	67.4	67.9	68.7	68.7	68.7	67.9	67.6	66.6	68.0	69.5	71.0	68.3
2005	67.6	66.8	67.4	67.5	67.8	68.0	67.2	66.9	44.1	41.0	45.7	48.8	59.9
2006	50.3	51.6	53.2	54.3	55.1	56.2	56.7	56.8	56.8	56.8	58.7	61.3	55.9
2007	59.4	58.9	59.7	59.1	59.4	59.5	59.2	58.9	59.0	58.8	60.1	60.5	59.4

Employment by Industry: New Orleans-Metairie-Kenner, LA, 2000–2007—*Continued*

(Numbers in thousands, not seasonally adjusted.)

Industry and year	January	February	March	April	May	June	July	August	September	October	November	December	Annual Average
Transportation and Utilities													
2000	28.9	29.3	29.3	28.8	28.9	29.2	28.8	28.5	28.6	29.0	28.8	29.4	29.0
2001	29.3	29.9	30.0	30.2	30.1	30.2	29.7	29.9	29.8	29.5	29.1	29.4	29.8
2002	28.5	28.4	28.5	29.1	29.1	29.5	29.4	29.5	29.6	30.0	29.8	30.3	29.3
2003	27.9	27.9	27.7	28.1	27.8	27.8	28.1	27.9	27.8	27.8	28.0	28.0	27.9
2004	27.3	27.6	28.0	27.9	28.1	28.0	27.9	28.5	28.3	29.0	28.9	29.6	28.3
2005	28.6	28.6	28.9	28.0	27.9	28.0	27.7	27.6	22.7	21.2	22.0	23.0	26.2
2006	22.6	22.9	23.7	24.1	24.3	24.8	24.2	24.5	24.3	24.2	24.5	25.4	24.1
2007	24.6	24.6	24.7	24.9	24.7	24.8	24.5	24.9	24.6	24.6	24.7	24.7	24.7
Information													
2000	10.3	10.3	10.4	10.4	10.5	10.8	11.3	11.3	11.0	10.8	10.9	11.2	10.8
2001	11.0	11.1	11.2	10.7	10.8	10.8	10.6	10.5	10.3	10.3	10.4	10.2	10.7
2002	10.0	10.0	10.0	9.6	9.5	9.7	9.6	9.6	9.5	9.3	9.3	9.4	9.6
2003	9.8	9.7	9.9	10.0	10.4	10.7	9.2	9.5	9.4	9.1	9.2	9.2	9.7
2004	9.4	9.8	9.8	10.7	10.4	10.7	9.7	11.2	10.1	11.0	12.7	10.8	10.5
2005	10.8	10.6	10.5	9.5	9.6	9.8	10.1	10.5	9.0	7.3	7.4	7.7	9.4
2006	7.1	7.3	8.8	8.1	8.4	7.5	6.7	6.8	6.9	6.9	7.4	7.5	7.5
2007	7.4	8.2	10.1	9.5	9.3	9.9	8.4	7.8	7.0	7.3	7.0	7.2	8.3
Financial Activities													
2000	33.5	33.7	33.8	33.8	33.7	33.5	34.0	34.0	33.7	33.4	33.4	33.6	33.7
2001	33.7	33.9	33.7	33.9	34.0	34.0	34.3	34.2	34.0	34.1	34.2	34.1	34.0
2002	33.7	33.9	34.1	34.5	34.6	34.9	34.7	35.2	35.0	35.5	35.6	35.5	34.8
2003	35.1	34.7	34.6	34.4	34.4	34.5	34.6	34.9	34.6	34.6	34.5	34.5	34.6
2004	33.9	33.8	33.8	34.2	34.1	34.2	34.7	34.7	34.3	34.3	34.1	34.2	34.2
2005	33.2	33.2	33.2	32.8	32.7	32.8	32.9	33.0	27.6	26.2	26.1	25.9	30.8
2006	25.7	25.8	26.1	25.7	26.0	26.3	26.4	26.4	26.4	26.6	26.7	26.8	26.2
2007	27.4	27.5	27.3	27.2	27.3	27.5	27.4	27.5	27.3	27.4	27.4	27.4	27.4
Professional and Business Services													
2000	72.8	72.7	73.3	74.9	74.7	74.2	73.9	74.5	75.0	74.3	75.4	75.6	74.3
2001	74.9	75.5	75.9	74.3	75.2	75.0	73.8	73.8	74.1	73.9	74.1	74.8	74.6
2002	72.8	72.9	73.2	73.5	72.1	72.2	71.5	71.9	71.3	70.4	70.4	70.9	71.9
2003	70.7	71.6	72.3	73.9	72.0	72.5	71.8	71.9	71.6	73.7	74.5	75.1	72.6
2004	72.8	73.4	73.8	75.0	74.6	74.7	71.5	71.7	71.0	73.1	73.7	73.6	73.2
2005	73.2	73.4	74.3	76.9	75.8	75.2	74.1	73.8	54.0	55.6	59.1	61.1	68.9
2006	60.7	62.8	64.4	64.5	65.1	66.3	65.6	66.6	66.2	66.7	67.0	67.4	65.3
2007	67.3	68.4	69.0	68.5	68.9	68.6	67.4	68.3	67.5	68.4	68.4	68.2	68.2
Education and Health Services													
2000	76.9	77.8	77.9	78.1	77.7	73.5	73.1	73.0	78.5	79.5	79.4	79.5	77.1
2001	78.8	79.3	79.2	81.1	80.3	78.3	76.8	76.3	81.3	81.5	83.7	82.9	80.0
2002	79.9	81.2	80.8	82.9	81.2	79.8	78.2	77.9	83.2	83.6	85.6	83.7	81.5
2003	83.0	83.4	82.5	84.0	83.5	81.6	80.9	80.5	85.3	85.3	87.5	85.9	83.6
2004	85.5	85.1	85.2	85.7	84.8	82.3	82.9	83.9	84.3	84.5	84.3	81.2	84.1
2005	81.9	81.5	82.1	82.3	81.5	82.9	79.4	78.4	64.4	51.1	50.2	50.9	72.2
2006	53.0	52.9	54.2	55.4	55.9	55.5	55.4	55.6	57.7	58.9	60.9	60.0	56.3
2007	61.5	62.2	62.8	63.1	61.8	61.6	61.4	63.1	64.1	65.1	65.4	64.6	63.1
Leisure and Hospitality													
2000	79.0	79.9	80.2	80.8	82.7	83.0	81.1	80.6	79.2	80.5	80.8	81.6	80.8
2001	80.0	81.6	82.9	82.8	83.1	83.6	82.3	82.2	81.1	79.8	79.7	79.7	81.6
2002	78.4	79.2	79.9	81.7	82.5	82.9	81.6	80.6	79.7	78.6	79.8	79.1	80.3
2003	78.5	79.8	80.5	83.2	83.5	84.9	83.1	83.0	81.9	81.0	81.1	81.7	81.9
2004	81.3	82.5	83.9	83.7	84.8	86.5	85.1	85.3	84.2	84.3	84.9	85.3	84.3
2005	83.6	83.6	85.5	86.2	87.2	88.6	85.8	85.6	51.7	42.2	44.1	46.3	72.5
2006	47.3	51.2	54.1	54.4	56.1	59.6	60.2	60.7	59.9	61.6	62.7	64.1	57.7
2007	63.5	64.0	65.4	65.5	66.3	67.4	66.9	67.2	66.1	67.1	66.6	67.7	66.1
Other Services													
2000	22.1	22.3	22.5	22.3	22.3	22.6	22.5	22.5	22.2	22.2	22.0	22.0	22.3
2001	21.7	21.9	22.1	22.1	22.3	22.6	22.3	22.3	22.4	22.5	22.6	22.6	22.3
2002	22.0	22.1	22.4	22.4	22.7	22.8	22.8	22.8	22.7	23.0	23.1	23.3	22.7
2003	22.9	23.1	23.1	23.7	23.9	23.2	22.5	22.5	22.4	23.0	23.0	23.0	23.0
2004	22.7	22.8	23.0	22.6	22.6	22.5	22.6	22.6	22.4	22.4	22.3	22.4	22.6
2005	22.0	22.1	22.3	22.4	22.5	22.5	22.6	22.4	15.5	13.3	13.3	13.9	19.6
2006	13.7	14.3	14.7	15.0	15.3	15.6	15.8	16.0	16.2	16.6	16.6	16.7	15.5
2007	17.7	18.1	18.3	19.3	19.5	19.7	19.1	19.4	19.4	19.6	19.6	19.6	19.1
Government													
2000	103.5	103.9	104.4	104.3	104.0	103.8	99.2	99.8	103.0	102.8	102.7	103.8	102.9
2001	103.5	104.1	104.1	104.7	104.3	104.2	99.2	100.7	103.0	102.8	102.5	103.2	103.0
2002	102.9	104.0	104.1	103.9	103.5	104.9	99.4	100.8	102.7	103.2	104.2	104.5	103.2
2003	103.8	104.8	105.2	104.8	104.4	105.2	103.2	100.2	104.5	103.1	104.0	103.9	103.9
2004	103.2	104.0	104.5	106.9	106.9	105.9	103.7	102.7	105.8	104.3	105.0	105.2	104.8
2005	105.2	106.3	106.9	105.1	104.6	104.9	101.4	102.2	101.9	80.3	80.0	79.6	98.2
2006	72.7	72.8	73.5	73.4	73.8	73.4	72.0	72.6	75.9	76.1	77.2	78.0	74.3
2007	76.3	77.4	78.1	78.5	79.1	79.2	77.0	78.1	81.0	81.1	81.7	81.9	79.1

Employment by Industry: Nashville-Davidson-Murfreesboro-Franklin, TN, 2000–2007

(Numbers in thousands, not seasonally adjusted.)

Industry and year	January	February	March	April	May	June	July	August	September	October	November	December	Annual Average
Total Nonfarm													
2000	683.7	687.8	699.1	696.5	700.0	700.7	693.3	698.0	701.3	703.5	705.7	706.2	698.0
2001	687.2	689.4	693.8	697.1	696.9	695.9	691.1	692.5	696.2	692.6	695.1	694.4	693.5
2002	674.2	677.7	682.5	685.1	688.1	685.6	688.4	692.7	697.1	698.0	701.7	703.0	689.5
2003	687.4	688.6	691.5	696.9	699.2	695.2	691.8	698.5	701.7	703.4	707.0	710.2	697.6
2004	695.8	701.3	705.5	711.1	711.8	709.5	712.4	719.6	721.6	727.9	732.0	735.5	715.3
2005	713.7	719.2	724.5	732.7	734.1	731.1	733.1	740.6	744.8	746.0	751.3	753.2	735.4
2006	736.9	739.4	746.9	748.8	750.0	750.3	749.6	757.5	760.0	756.1	761.7	764.2	751.8
2007	744.2	747.8	755.6	754.8	758.4	759.7	759.7	768.9	769.5	767.4	772.6	774.8	761.1
Total Private													
2000	594.5	597.2	604.5	605.2	607.5	613.0	609.2	610.0	612.4	612.2	613.8	614.4	607.8
2001	596.9	597.1	601.4	603.6	604.2	607.8	603.2	604.7	603.8	599.2	600.9	600.5	601.9
2002	582.0	583.8	587.7	591.0	594.5	597.3	602.2	604.6	604.5	604.3	607.9	608.7	597.4
2003	593.5	593.3	595.7	600.4	603.8	606.1	603.1	606.2	606.1	607.6	611.6	613.9	603.4
2004	599.8	601.2	607.0	613.0	615.2	619.9	623.0	626.5	625.8	630.8	634.6	636.9	619.5
2005	617.4	621.0	626.3	634.1	636.5	639.5	641.5	644.8	646.2	647.5	652.7	654.4	638.5
2006	638.7	639.5	646.7	648.7	651.0	657.7	656.2	660.1	659.8	655.8	660.7	662.8	653.1
2007	644.4	646.7	654.4	655.4	660.6	667.2	666.4	670.1	669.0	666.8	671.5	673.5	662.2
Goods-Producing													
2000	129.9	130.3	131.5	130.6	130.4	131.5	129.5	128.9	127.7	126.4	125.0	124.8	128.9
2001	124.7	123.5	124.0	122.9	123.1	124.1	122.7	122.8	122.2	120.6	119.7	119.5	122.5
2002	115.4	114.7	114.5	115.7	116.9	117.6	117.6	117.9	117.7	116.9	116.5	117.1	116.5
2003	114.9	114.7	114.9	115.4	116.4	117.0	116.8	117.0	117.2	117.0	116.6	116.7	116.2
2004	115.0	115.0	115.8	117.6	118.4	119.3	119.5	119.3	119.2	118.7	118.9	119.2	118.0
2005	116.5	117.3	118.2	120.1	120.7	121.7	120.7	121.9	121.8	122.0	122.2	122.5	120.5
2006	121.4	121.3	122.4	123.0	123.0	124.9	124.1	124.8	124.5	123.1	123.4	123.4	123.3
2007	120.7	120.3	121.4	121.1	121.6	122.7	122.0	122.1	122.2	121.2	120.9	120.7	121.4
Natural Resources, Mining, and Construction													
2000	34.5	34.5	35.6	36.1	37.0	37.5	36.9	36.8	36.1	35.6	34.9	34.7	35.9
2001	32.3	32.5	33.2	33.4	33.9	34.8	34.9	35.0	34.2	33.6	33.4	33.3	33.7
2002	31.1	31.0	31.2	31.5	32.5	33.0	33.6	34.1	34.0	33.6	33.8	33.8	32.8
2003	32.7	32.6	33.2	33.9	34.7	35.4	35.7	35.6	35.5	34.9	34.5	34.6	34.4
2004	33.1	32.9	33.4	34.0	34.6	35.4	35.5	35.3	35.1	34.6	34.5	34.5	34.4
2005	32.8	33.1	34.0	35.2	36.1	37.1	37.2	37.5	37.5	37.3	37.2	37.2	36.0
2006	37.0	37.3	38.3	38.7	39.2	40.3	40.1	40.3	40.2	39.6	39.5	39.6	39.2
2007	38.8	39.3	40.8	41.2	41.7	42.9	43.0	43.3	43.3	42.9	42.7	42.7	41.9
Manufacturing													
2000	95.4	95.8	95.9	94.6	93.4	94.1	92.6	92.1	91.6	90.8	90.0	90.1	93.0
2001	92.4	91.0	90.8	89.5	89.2	89.3	87.8	87.8	88.0	87.0	86.3	86.2	88.8
2002	84.3	83.7	83.3	84.2	84.4	84.5	83.9	83.9	83.7	83.3	82.7	83.3	83.8
2003	82.2	82.1	81.7	81.5	81.7	81.6	81.1	81.4	81.7	82.1	82.1	82.1	81.8
2004	81.9	82.1	82.4	83.6	83.8	83.9	84.0	84.0	84.1	84.1	84.4	84.7	83.6
2005	83.7	84.2	84.2	84.9	84.6	84.6	83.5	84.4	84.3	84.7	85.0	85.3	84.5
2006	84.4	84.0	84.1	84.3	83.8	84.6	84.0	84.5	84.3	83.5	83.9	83.8	84.1
2007	81.9	81.0	80.6	79.9	79.9	79.8	79.0	78.8	78.9	78.3	78.2	78.0	79.5
Service-Providing													
2000	553.8	557.5	567.6	565.8	569.7	569.2	563.8	569.1	573.6	577.2	580.8	581.4	569.1
2001	562.5	565.9	569.8	574.2	573.8	571.9	568.4	569.7	574.0	572.0	575.4	574.9	571.0
2002	558.8	563.0	568.0	569.3	571.2	568.1	570.8	574.7	579.4	581.1	585.2	585.9	573.0
2003	572.5	573.9	576.6	581.5	582.8	578.2	575.0	581.5	584.5	586.4	590.4	593.5	581.4
2004	580.8	586.3	589.7	593.5	593.4	590.2	592.9	600.3	602.4	609.2	613.1	616.3	597.3
2005	597.2	601.9	606.3	612.6	613.4	609.4	612.4	618.7	623.0	624.0	629.1	630.7	614.9
2006	615.5	618.1	624.5	625.8	627.0	625.4	625.5	632.7	635.5	633.0	638.3	640.8	628.5
2007	623.5	627.5	634.2	633.7	636.8	637.0	637.7	646.8	647.3	646.2	651.7	654.1	639.7
Trade, Transportation, and Utilities													
2000	139.6	139.5	140.2	140.4	140.2	141.0	142.0	142.6	143.9	146.3	148.4	149.3	142.8
2001	142.4	141.5	142.0	142.5	142.5	142.5	140.8	140.7	140.5	140.5	142.9	143.4	141.9
2002	135.8	134.7	136.0	134.5	135.2	136.0	137.2	137.6	138.3	140.7	143.1	145.4	137.9
2003	139.3	139.0	139.3	139.7	140.0	141.3	140.6	142.0	141.9	143.9	146.5	148.3	141.8
2004	142.5	141.8	142.9	143.0	143.7	144.8	144.9	146.1	146.6	149.2	152.2	153.7	146.0
2005	146.4	146.1	147.3	148.5	149.1	149.1	150.5	150.9	152.1	153.3	156.8	158.5	150.7
2006	151.9	151.4	152.9	152.5	153.0	153.7	152.7	153.6	153.9	153.3	156.4	158.6	153.7
2007	152.6	152.0	153.6	152.9	153.5	153.9	153.7	154.8	155.0	155.5	158.9	161.0	154.8
Wholesale Trade													
2000	35.5	35.4	35.6	35.7	35.6	35.8	36.1	36.2	36.6	37.2	37.7	37.9	36.3
2001	36.2	35.9	36.1	36.2	36.2	36.2	35.8	35.7	35.7	35.7	36.3	36.4	36.0
2002	34.5	34.2	34.6	34.2	34.3	34.5	34.8	35.0	35.1	35.7	36.3	36.9	35.0
2003	34.8	34.8	34.7	34.7	34.9	34.8	34.5	34.5	34.5	34.2	34.0	33.9	34.5
2004	33.7	33.9	34.1	34.2	34.3	34.6	34.6	35.0	35.1	35.5	35.4	35.5	34.7
2005	35.4	35.7	35.7	36.1	36.3	36.1	36.2	36.3	36.6	36.7	37.0	36.8	36.2
2006	36.4	36.5	36.5	36.4	36.5	36.6	36.5	36.7	36.9	36.3	36.2	36.3	36.5
2007	35.8	36.0	36.3	36.4	36.5	36.8	36.6	37.0	37.2	37.3	37.4	37.4	36.7
Retail Trade													
2000	77.9	77.8	78.2	78.3	78.2	78.7	79.2	79.6	80.3	81.6	82.8	83.3	79.7
2001	79.5	79.0	79.2	79.5	79.5	79.5	78.6	78.5	78.4	78.4	79.8	80.0	79.2
2002	75.8	75.2	75.9	75.0	75.5	75.9	76.6	76.8	77.2	78.5	79.8	81.1	76.9
2003	78.0	77.5	77.7	78.0	78.0	79.1	78.6	79.8	80.3	82.5	85.1	86.8	80.1
2004	81.9	80.9	81.3	81.2	81.5	82.1	81.9	82.4	82.5	84.3	87.0	88.0	82.9
2005	83.2	82.6	83.6	83.9	84.2	84.1	84.3	84.3	84.9	85.5	88.4	89.7	84.9
2006	84.8	84.3	85.3	85.5	85.8	86.0	85.3	85.8	85.6	85.8	89.1	90.6	86.2
2007	86.4	85.6	86.8	86.2	86.8	86.7	86.6	87.1	87.2	87.8	90.9	92.3	87.5

Employment by Industry: Nashville-Davidson-Murfreesboro-Franklin, TN, 2000–2007—*Continued*

(Numbers in thousands, not seasonally adjusted.)

Industry and year	January	February	March	April	May	June	July	August	September	October	November	December	Annual Average
Transportation and Utilities													
2000	26.4	26.4	26.5	26.5	26.5	26.6	26.8	27.0	27.2	27.7	28.1	28.2	27.0
2001	26.9	26.7	26.8	26.9	26.9	26.9	26.6	26.6	26.6	26.5	27.0	27.1	26.8
2002	25.7	25.5	25.7	25.4	25.6	25.7	25.9	26.0	26.1	26.6	27.0	27.5	26.1
2003	26.5	26.7	26.9	27.0	27.1	27.4	27.5	27.7	27.1	27.2	27.4	27.6	27.2
2004	26.9	27.0	27.5	27.6	27.9	28.1	28.4	28.7	29.0	29.4	29.8	30.2	28.4
2005	27.8	27.8	28.0	28.5	28.6	28.9	30.0	30.3	30.6	31.1	31.4	32.0	29.6
2006	30.7	30.6	31.1	30.6	30.7	31.1	30.9	31.1	31.4	31.2	31.1	31.7	31.0
2007	30.4	30.4	30.5	30.3	30.2	30.4	30.5	30.7	30.6	30.4	30.6	31.3	30.5
Information													
2000	21.1	21.0	21.3	21.2	21.2	21.4	21.7	21.7	21.7	21.8	22.3	22.5	21.6
2001	23.9	24.1	24.1	23.4	23.4	23.4	23.0	22.7	22.5	22.8	22.9	22.9	23.3
2002	22.3	22.2	22.4	21.9	21.8	21.5	21.5	21.3	21.0	21.3	21.1	20.9	21.6
2003	20.2	20.1	20.1	19.9	20.0	19.8	19.8	19.8	19.6	19.6	19.8	19.8	19.9
2004	19.5	19.4	19.3	19.3	19.3	19.5	19.5	19.5	18.8	19.1	19.2	19.9	19.4
2005	19.8	19.9	19.8	19.5	19.5	19.7	19.7	19.6	19.6	19.7	19.8	19.8	19.7
2006	19.6	19.6	19.7	19.6	19.7	19.7	19.0	18.9	19.0	19.0	19.1	19.2	19.3
2007	19.0	19.0	19.0	19.1	19.3	19.4	19.3	19.4	19.5	19.6	19.6	19.7	19.3
Financial Activities													
2000	47.2	47.3	47.3	47.0	47.0	47.3	47.2	46.8	46.5	46.1	46.3	46.3	46.9
2001	43.9	44.2	44.4	44.6	44.6	44.8	44.8	44.6	44.1	43.7	43.5	43.2	44.2
2002	42.7	42.8	42.7	43.1	43.3	43.9	43.8	44.0	43.8	44.1	44.3	44.4	43.6
2003	44.4	44.5	44.7	44.8	44.8	45.1	44.8	44.8	44.6	44.5	44.5	44.7	44.7
2004	44.0	44.0	44.2	44.5	44.4	44.4	44.5	44.6	44.5	44.9	45.1	45.2	44.5
2005	44.4	44.5	44.7	45.1	45.3	45.4	45.5	45.6	45.6	45.4	45.6	45.7	45.2
2006	45.3	45.2	45.5	45.7	45.9	45.9	46.0	45.9	45.7	45.8	45.7	45.9	45.7
2007	45.3	45.6	45.8	46.2	46.7	46.9	46.9	46.9	46.7	46.7	46.7	46.6	46.4
Professional and Business Services													
2000	85.0	86.4	88.1	88.0	88.7	89.0	88.0	88.9	90.1	90.3	90.2	90.2	88.6
2001	84.9	84.8	85.5	86.4	85.8	86.0	86.8	88.0	88.4	87.1	87.3	87.6	86.6
2002	84.3	85.7	86.8	87.2	87.5	87.2	87.9	88.7	88.0	86.7	87.5	86.3	87.0
2003	82.4	82.2	82.2	82.8	83.6	84.0	83.0	84.0	84.5	85.4	87.1	87.7	84.1
2004	85.7	86.6	87.7	89.4	89.7	91.0	91.5	93.0	94.0	96.5	96.6	96.5	91.5
2005	92.3	93.4	93.9	95.3	95.2	95.7	96.1	97.8	99.3	99.7	100.5	101.0	96.7
2006	95.4	95.4	96.3	96.6	96.9	99.3	98.7	101.1	102.4	100.8	102.1	102.1	98.9
2007	96.5	97.3	98.9	98.9	99.8	102.3	102.6	103.9	103.3	101.8	103.2	103.6	101.0
Education and Health Services													
2000	80.5	81.2	82.0	83.0	82.4	82.4	82.6	82.6	83.5	83.9	84.4	84.3	82.7
2001	83.3	84.3	84.7	86.1	86.0	86.5	86.7	86.7	87.0	86.7	87.1	87.7	86.1
2002	87.2	88.0	88.4	89.5	90.0	90.0	92.0	92.0	92.3	92.6	92.8	92.8	90.6
2003	93.0	93.4	93.7	94.9	94.9	94.9	95.5	95.5	95.5	95.6	95.6	95.8	94.9
2004	96.3	96.6	97.2	98.3	97.9	97.9	99.3	99.2	99.0	99.6	99.7	99.8	98.4
2005	98.7	99.4	99.5	101.2	101.7	101.6	102.5	102.5	102.3	102.2	102.3	102.5	101.4
2006	102.2	102.8	103.5	104.1	104.2	104.5	104.8	105.0	105.1	105.2	105.7	105.6	104.4
2007	104.9	105.8	106.2	106.8	107.3	107.6	108.7	109.3	109.9	110.2	110.6	110.6	108.2
Leisure and Hospitality													
2000	64.6	64.7	66.6	67.6	69.9	72.1	70.9	71.0	71.0	69.7	69.4	69.7	68.9
2001	66.4	66.8	68.4	68.9	69.7	71.0	69.5	70.2	69.4	68.0	67.9	67.4	68.6
2002	65.6	66.3	67.7	69.3	69.5	70.6	71.3	72.4	71.9	70.0	71.0	70.7	69.7
2003	68.1	68.8	70.1	71.9	73.1	73.8	73.0	73.7	73.1	71.8	71.9	71.6	71.7
2004	67.4	68.0	69.5	71.2	72.5	73.5	74.0	74.8	74.2	73.0	72.9	73.3	72.0
2005	70.4	71.3	72.7	74.6	75.4	76.3	76.7	76.8	75.6	75.4	75.4	74.7	74.6
2006	73.2	73.9	75.8	77.1	77.9	78.9	80.4	80.4	78.9	78.2	78.1	78.1	77.6
2007	75.9	76.8	79.0	80.1	81.8	83.7	82.8	83.2	81.9	81.3	81.2	81.2	80.7
Other Services													
2000	26.5	26.9	27.5	27.4	27.7	28.4	27.5	27.7	28.1	27.9	27.9	27.2	27.6
2001	27.4	28.0	28.4	28.9	29.1	29.6	29.0	29.1	29.8	29.9	29.6	28.7	29.0
2002	28.8	29.3	29.3	29.7	30.3	30.6	30.9	30.7	31.4	32.1	31.6	31.3	30.5
2003	31.2	30.6	30.7	31.0	31.0	30.2	29.6	29.4	29.7	29.8	29.6	29.3	30.2
2004	29.4	29.8	30.4	29.7	29.3	29.5	29.8	30.0	29.5	29.8	30.0	29.3	29.7
2005	28.9	29.1	30.2	29.8	29.6	30.0	29.8	29.7	29.9	29.8	30.1	29.7	29.7
2006	29.7	29.9	30.6	30.1	30.4	30.8	30.5	30.4	30.3	30.4	30.2	29.9	30.3
2007	29.5	29.9	30.5	30.3	30.6	30.7	30.4	30.5	30.5	30.5	30.4	30.1	30.3
Government													
2000	89.2	90.6	94.6	91.3	92.6	87.7	84.2	88.0	89.0	91.3	91.9	91.8	90.2
2001	90.3	92.3	92.4	93.6	92.8	88.2	87.9	87.8	92.4	93.4	94.2	93.9	91.6
2002	92.2	93.9	94.7	94.1	93.6	88.3	86.2	88.1	92.6	93.7	93.8	94.2	92.1
2003	93.9	95.3	95.8	96.5	95.4	89.1	88.7	92.3	95.6	95.8	95.4	96.3	94.2
2004	96.0	100.1	98.5	98.1	96.6	89.6	89.4	93.1	95.8	97.1	97.4	98.6	95.9
2005	96.3	98.2	98.2	98.6	97.6	91.6	91.6	95.8	98.6	98.5	98.6	98.8	96.9
2006	98.2	99.9	100.2	100.1	99.0	92.6	93.4	97.4	100.2	100.3	101.0	101.4	98.6
2007	99.8	101.1	101.2	99.4	97.8	92.5	93.3	98.8	100.5	100.6	101.1	101.3	99.0

Employment by Industry: Providence-Fall River-Warwick, RI-MA, NECTA, 2000–2007

(Numbers in thousands, not seasonally adjusted.)

Industry and year	January	February	March	April	May	June	July	August	September	October	November	December	Annual Average
Total Nonfarm													
2000	559.3	559.9	564.2	573.9	580.7	583.1	571.6	573.6	583.6	585.3	588.3	590.4	576.2
2001	565.2	566.5	568.5	574.9	579.0	580.4	566.0	571.7	577.8	576.0	576.1	577.6	573.3
2002	560.5	561.5	566.7	574.2	580.0	580.9	568.7	574.2	581.1	579.6	582.2	580.9	574.2
2003	564.5	563.3	566.8	575.4	583.3	585.3	572.2	574.9	583.5	585.8	587.9	587.5	577.5
2004	566.2	567.6	571.5	580.1	589.4	590.2	577.3	579.0	587.5	589.7	591.0	590.0	581.6
2005	568.3	570.1	571.7	583.8	588.3	591.2	579.9	581.6	588.9	588.6	590.9	589.2	582.7
2006	565.8	568.5	573.1	586.0	589.8	592.9	579.9	582.9	591.3	593.4	595.0	593.9	584.4
2007	571.9	572.4	575.1	583.1	590.1	592.1	580.4	580.8	585.0	587.5	587.3	586.2	582.7
Total Private													
2000	484.7	485.1	488.5	497.8	502.4	508.0	501.1	504.4	508.3	509.1	511.5	513.8	501.2
2001	489.2	490.4	491.8	498.8	502.6	504.5	494.8	501.3	502.3	501.3	500.6	501.8	498.3
2002	483.1	483.7	488.4	496.2	501.9	503.5	496.4	502.5	504.3	503.3	504.8	504.0	497.7
2003	487.4	486.1	489.5	498.3	505.7	507.7	502.2	505.5	508.3	509.5	511.4	510.9	501.9
2004	490.5	491.7	495.0	504.4	512.7	513.7	508.8	510.8	513.1	514.4	515.0	514.7	507.1
2005	493.3	494.9	496.7	508.6	512.6	515.7	511.0	513.4	515.7	513.5	515.4	513.8	508.7
2006	491.1	493.3	498.0	511.1	514.6	517.9	510.8	514.2	517.3	518.3	518.9	518.1	510.3
2007	497.0	497.4	500.0	508.1	514.5	517.3	510.6	511.4	511.9	512.7	512.1	511.1	508.7
Goods-Producing													
2000	114.7	114.9	115.3	117.4	118.6	119.6	115.0	118.7	119.8	120.2	119.6	119.3	117.8
2001	114.2	114.1	113.9	115.5	115.2	115.2	108.6	113.2	113.4	113.0	111.0	110.5	113.2
2002	105.3	105.2	106.2	106.9	108.2	108.4	103.3	108.2	108.3	107.4	107.0	105.8	106.7
2003	101.4	100.1	100.6	103.4	105.0	105.7	101.7	105.3	105.9	105.2	105.1	103.7	103.6
2004	98.4	97.6	98.5	101.0	102.6	104.0	101.9	104.2	104.1	103.9	103.6	102.5	101.9
2005	97.3	96.5	96.3	99.4	100.6	102.1	98.7	101.1	100.9	99.7	100.0	98.6	99.3
2006	93.8	93.7	94.3	97.5	98.3	99.7	96.6	99.0	98.5	98.0	96.9	96.2	96.9
2007	92.3	90.9	91.3	92.5	94.2	95.1	92.7	94.8	94.5	93.9	92.9	92.2	93.1
Natural Resources and Mining													
2000	0.3	0.3	0.3	0.3	0.3	0.3	0.3	0.3	0.3	0.3	0.3	0.3	0.3
2001	0.3	0.3	0.3	0.3	0.3	0.4	0.4	0.4	0.4	0.4	0.4	0.4	0.4
2002	0.3	0.3	0.3	0.3	0.3	0.3	0.3	0.3	0.3	0.3	0.3	0.3	0.3
2003	0.2	0.2	0.2	0.3	0.3	0.3	0.3	0.3	0.3	0.3	0.3	0.3	0.3
2004	0.3	0.2	0.2	0.3	0.3	0.3	0.3	0.3	0.3	0.3	0.3	0.3	0.3
2005	0.3	0.2	0.2	0.3	0.3	0.3	0.3	0.3	0.3	0.3	0.3	0.3	0.3
2006	0.2	0.2	0.2	0.3	0.3	0.3	0.3	0.3	0.3	0.3	0.3	0.3	0.3
2007	0.3	0.2	0.2	0.3	0.3	0.3	0.3	0.3	0.3	0.3	0.3	0.3	0.3
Construction													
2000	19.6	19.0	19.4	21.4	22.1	23.2	23.3	23.5	23.4	23.4	23.3	22.7	22.0
2001	20.2	20.1	20.7	23.0	23.8	24.4	24.5	24.7	24.4	24.5	24.1	23.8	23.2
2002	21.3	21.1	22.0	23.2	24.3	24.8	24.9	25.2	25.1	24.7	24.5	23.7	23.7
2003	21.2	20.3	21.1	23.9	25.8	26.6	27.6	27.9	27.9	27.6	27.3	26.2	25.3
2004	22.6	21.9	22.6	24.9	26.1	27.0	27.7	27.7	27.6	27.7	27.4	26.8	25.8
2005	23.2	22.6	23.0	26.4	27.6	28.8	29.0	29.2	29.0	28.4	28.9	27.7	27.0
2006	24.7	24.2	25.1	28.2	29.1	30.3	30.3	30.6	30.3	29.9	29.3	28.7	28.4
2007	25.9	24.5	25.1	26.6	28.2	29.0	29.3	29.2	28.6	28.2	27.8	27.2	27.5
Manufacturing													
2000	94.8	95.6	95.6	95.7	96.2	96.1	91.4	94.9	96.1	96.5	96.0	96.3	95.4
2001	93.7	93.7	92.9	92.2	91.1	90.4	83.7	88.1	88.6	88.1	86.5	86.3	89.6
2002	83.7	83.8	83.9	83.4	83.6	83.3	78.1	82.7	82.9	82.4	82.2	81.8	82.7
2003	80.0	79.6	79.3	79.2	78.9	78.8	73.8	77.1	77.7	77.3	77.5	77.2	78.0
2004	75.5	75.5	75.7	75.8	76.2	76.7	73.9	76.2	76.2	75.9	75.9	75.4	75.7
2005	73.8	73.7	73.1	72.7	72.7	73.0	69.4	71.6	71.6	71.0	70.8	70.6	72.0
2006	68.9	69.3	69.0	69.0	68.9	69.1	66.0	68.1	67.9	67.8	67.3	67.2	68.2
2007	66.1	66.2	66.0	65.6	65.7	65.8	63.1	65.3	65.6	65.4	64.8	64.7	65.4
Service-Providing													
2000	444.6	445.0	448.9	456.5	462.1	463.5	456.6	454.9	463.8	465.1	468.7	471.1	458.4
2001	451.0	452.4	454.6	459.4	463.8	465.2	457.4	458.5	464.4	463.0	465.1	467.1	460.2
2002	455.2	456.3	460.5	467.3	471.8	472.5	465.4	466.0	472.8	472.2	475.2	475.1	467.5
2003	463.1	463.2	466.2	472.0	478.3	479.6	470.5	469.6	477.6	480.6	482.8	483.8	473.9
2004	467.8	470.0	473.0	479.1	486.8	486.2	475.4	474.8	483.4	485.8	487.4	487.5	479.8
2005	471.0	473.6	475.4	484.4	487.7	489.1	481.2	480.5	488.0	488.9	490.9	490.6	483.4
2006	472.0	474.8	478.8	488.5	491.5	493.2	483.3	483.9	492.8	495.4	498.1	497.7	487.5
2007	479.6	481.5	483.8	490.6	495.9	497.0	487.7	486.0	490.5	493.6	494.4	494.0	489.6
Trade, Transportation, and Utilities													
2000	99.9	98.3	98.7	100.3	100.2	101.1	99.8	100.6	101.7	103.1	105.7	107.9	101.4
2001	101.4	99.6	99.2	100.1	100.3	101.8	100.6	100.7	101.8	102.2	104.9	106.9	101.6
2002	101.6	100.0	100.6	101.7	102.7	104.0	102.5	102.7	103.2	103.7	106.2	108.0	103.1
2003	102.2	100.7	100.8	101.6	102.8	103.8	102.2	102.5	103.7	104.8	107.1	108.3	103.4
2004	102.3	101.3	101.5	101.3	103.3	103.6	102.0	101.8	102.6	104.0	105.9	107.1	103.1
2005	101.7	100.8	100.7	102.0	102.6	103.5	102.1	102.5	102.9	103.9	106.0	107.8	103.0
2006	102.0	100.3	100.8	102.2	102.6	103.4	101.5	101.7	101.7	102.6	103.6	105.9	107.5
2007	102.2	100.4	100.7	101.4	102.3	103.3	101.7	101.3	101.7	102.3	104.3	105.2	102.2
Wholesale Trade													
2000	18.7	18.8	19.1	19.3	19.4	19.5	19.4	19.5	19.6	19.8	19.9	20.1	19.4
2001	19.6	19.8	19.9	20.2	20.1	20.2	20.5	20.5	20.4	20.2	20.3	20.5	20.2
2002	20.3	20.2	20.4	20.5	20.6	20.7	20.4	20.5	20.4	20.4	20.7	20.6	20.5
2003	20.5	20.3	20.4	20.5	20.8	20.9	20.7	20.6	20.5	20.6	20.8	20.6	20.6
2004	20.2	20.2	20.4	20.7	20.7	20.8	20.7	20.7	20.7	20.8	20.9	20.9	20.6
2005	20.5	20.5	20.6	21.0	21.0	21.2	21.1	21.2	21.1	21.1	21.2	21.5	21.0
2006	21.0	21.0	21.1	21.3	21.4	21.5	21.4	21.4	21.4	21.5	21.4	21.4	21.3
2007	21.3	21.1	21.1	21.4	21.5	21.6	21.5	21.4	21.2	21.3	21.2	21.2	21.3

Employment by Industry: Providence-Fall River-Warwick, RI-MA, NECTA, 2000–2007—*Continued*

(Numbers in thousands, not seasonally adjusted.)

Industry and year	January	February	March	April	May	June	July	August	September	October	November	December	Annual Average
Retail Trade													
2000	68.6	66.9	67.0	68.0	67.7	68.5	68.1	68.5	68.9	70.0	72.6	74.6	69.1
2001	69.0	67.1	66.6	66.8	67.1	68.4	67.6	67.8	68.1	68.9	71.5	73.4	68.5
2002	68.6	67.3	67.6	68.4	69.0	69.9	69.4	69.4	69.8	70.1	72.4	74.3	69.7
2003	68.9	67.6	67.5	68.1	68.7	69.5	69.0	69.4	69.6	70.7	72.8	74.2	69.7
2004	69.1	68.2	68.2	68.3	69.2	69.6	69.2	69.0	68.6	70.0	71.9	73.1	69.5
2005	68.7	67.8	67.7	68.2	68.6	69.1	68.6	68.8	68.6	69.6	71.6	73.0	69.2
2006	68.4	66.8	67.1	68.0	68.1	68.6	67.9	67.9	67.8	68.7	71.1	72.6	68.6
2007	68.1	66.8	67.0	67.1	67.7	68.3	67.8	67.5	67.1	67.6	69.8	70.8	68.0
Transportation and Utilities													
2000	12.6	12.6	12.6	13.0	13.1	13.1	12.3	12.6	13.2	13.3	13.2	13.2	12.9
2001	12.8	12.7	12.7	13.1	13.1	13.2	12.5	12.4	13.3	13.1	13.1	13.0	12.9
2002	12.7	12.5	12.6	12.8	13.1	13.4	12.7	12.8	13.0	13.2	13.1	13.1	12.9
2003	12.8	12.8	12.9	13.0	13.3	13.4	12.5	12.5	13.6	13.5	13.5	13.5	13.1
2004	13.0	12.9	12.9	12.3	13.4	13.2	12.1	12.1	13.3	13.2	13.1	13.1	12.9
2005	12.5	12.5	12.4	12.8	13.0	13.2	12.4	12.5	13.2	13.2	13.2	13.3	12.9
2006	12.6	12.5	12.6	12.9	13.1	13.3	12.2	12.4	13.4	13.4	13.4	13.5	12.9
2007	12.8	12.5	12.6	12.9	13.1	13.4	12.4	12.4	13.4	13.4	13.3	13.2	13.0
Information													
2000	11.6	11.7	11.5	11.6	11.7	12.0	12.1	10.6	11.9	11.7	11.8	11.8	11.7
2001	11.8	11.8	11.9	11.9	12.0	12.0	11.8	11.7	11.7	11.4	11.4	11.4	11.7
2002	11.9	11.9	11.9	11.9	11.9	12.1	12.0	12.0	11.9	11.6	11.9	11.9	11.9
2003	12.0	12.0	11.9	11.9	11.9	12.1	11.9	11.9	11.7	11.9	11.9	11.8	11.9
2004	11.9	11.9	11.9	11.9	11.8	11.8	11.6	11.5	11.4	11.4	11.5	11.5	11.7
2005	11.7	11.7	11.6	11.6	11.5	11.6	11.6	11.6	11.5	11.6	11.8	11.8	11.6
2006	11.9	11.8	11.8	12.2	12.1	12.2	11.6	11.5	11.5	11.4	11.7	11.7	11.8
2007	11.3	11.2	11.2	11.2	11.3	11.3	11.3	11.3	11.3	11.2	11.3	11.5	11.3
Financial Activities													
2000	32.7	32.8	32.9	33.3	33.2	34.1	34.6	34.3	34.1	34.0	34.2	34.5	33.7
2001	34.7	34.8	34.9	34.5	34.4	34.9	35.0	34.8	34.6	34.8	34.8	35.1	34.8
2002	35.1	35.0	35.0	35.4	35.3	35.9	36.0	36.0	36.0	36.2	36.4	36.6	35.7
2003	36.4	36.4	36.7	36.3	36.6	37.1	37.1	37.1	37.0	37.0	37.1	37.3	36.8
2004	37.0	37.0	37.0	37.1	37.4	37.4	37.3	37.3	37.1	37.3	37.3	37.3	37.2
2005	36.9	37.1	37.1	37.6	37.5	37.8	37.9	37.9	37.7	37.4	37.5	37.8	37.5
2006	37.3	37.3	37.5	37.7	37.9	38.1	38.3	38.7	38.8	38.7	38.9	39.3	38.2
2007	38.4	38.5	38.4	38.5	38.6	38.4	38.1	37.7	37.6	37.5	37.4	37.5	38.1
Professional and Business Services													
2000	56.7	56.7	57.9	59.2	59.7	60.7	58.6	59.6	59.9	59.9	59.8	60.0	59.1
2001	56.5	56.6	56.8	58.1	58.5	58.9	57.8	59.0	58.7	58.9	57.9	57.2	57.9
2002	55.1	54.6	55.2	56.8	57.1	57.6	56.5	57.0	57.4	57.7	57.2	56.3	56.5
2003	54.6	54.3	54.7	56.6	57.2	58.5	58.3	59.0	58.9	59.4	59.3	59.3	57.5
2004	57.8	57.9	58.4	60.7	61.4	62.2	61.3	62.1	62.5	62.4	62.0	61.5	60.9
2005	59.0	59.0	59.5	62.3	62.2	62.9	62.8	63.5	63.7	62.6	62.5	61.9	61.8
2006	58.8	59.1	59.8	63.0	63.0	64.2	63.1	64.3	65.0	65.0	64.4	63.7	62.8
2007	60.5	60.2	60.6	62.9	63.5	64.6	63.3	63.4	63.2	64.3	63.9	63.6	62.8
Education and Health Services													
2000	96.2	97.6	97.8	98.7	99.0	96.5	96.4	96.3	99.5	100.6	101.7	102.2	98.5
2001	96.6	98.8	99.8	100.4	100.6	96.0	95.3	96.3	99.2	100.7	101.8	102.2	99.0
2002	99.0	101.2	102.5	102.9	102.9	98.4	97.8	98.9	102.4	103.7	104.7	105.1	101.6
2003	102.8	104.7	106.0	106.3	106.2	101.8	100.5	99.9	103.7	106.3	107.1	107.4	104.4
2004	104.6	107.0	108.2	108.9	108.8	104.1	103.2	102.9	106.7	109.0	109.7	110.1	106.9
2005	106.8	109.4	110.4	110.9	110.6	106.7	106.0	105.6	110.1	112.3	112.9	112.0	109.5
2006	108.2	111.8	113.1	113.7	112.8	109.1	107.9	107.6	111.5	114.6	115.7	114.8	111.7
2007	111.5	115.0	115.6	116.0	115.8	111.6	110.3	110.2	113.8	116.1	116.6	116.1	114.1
Leisure and Hospitality													
2000	49.1	49.3	50.3	52.9	55.5	58.9	59.3	58.9	56.8	54.8	54.0	53.2	54.4
2001	49.4	50.1	50.6	53.3	56.5	60.0	59.8	59.6	57.8	55.2	53.5	53.2	54.9
2002	49.8	50.4	51.6	55.1	58.1	60.8	61.6	61.3	59.4	57.0	55.5	54.3	56.2
2003	52.0	51.9	52.6	56.2	59.6	61.9	63.3	62.9	61.1	58.6	57.2	56.5	57.8
2004	52.6	53.1	53.4	57.2	60.8	63.7	64.2	63.9	62.2	59.7	58.2	58.0	58.9
2005	53.8	54.3	54.8	58.4	61.0	64.1	64.6	63.9	62.5	59.7	58.3	57.5	59.4
2006	53.6	53.7	54.9	58.5	61.3	64.0	64.5	64.3	63.0	60.3	58.8	58.3	59.6
2007	54.8	55.2	56.0	59.3	62.2	65.6	65.8	65.6	63.7	61.0	59.3	58.7	60.6
Other Services													
2000	23.8	23.8	24.1	24.4	24.5	25.1	25.3	25.4	24.6	24.8	24.7	24.9	24.6
2001	24.6	24.6	24.7	25.0	25.1	25.7	25.9	26.0	25.1	25.1	25.3	25.3	25.2
2002	25.3	25.4	25.4	25.5	25.7	26.3	26.7	26.4	25.7	26.0	25.9	26.0	25.9
2003	26.0	26.0	26.2	26.0	26.4	26.8	27.2	26.9	26.3	26.3	26.6	26.6	26.4
2004	25.9	25.9	26.1	26.3	26.6	26.9	27.3	27.1	26.5	26.7	26.8	26.7	26.6
2005	26.1	26.1	26.3	26.4	26.6	27.0	27.3	27.3	26.4	26.3	26.4	26.4	26.6
2006	25.5	25.6	25.8	26.3	26.6	27.2	27.3	27.1	26.4	26.7	26.6	26.6	26.5
2007	26.0	26.0	26.2	26.3	26.6	27.4	27.4	27.1	26.2	26.3	26.2	26.2	26.5
Government													
2000	74.6	74.8	75.7	76.1	78.3	75.1	70.5	69.2	75.3	76.2	76.8	76.6	74.9
2001	76.0	76.1	76.7	76.1	76.4	75.9	71.2	70.4	75.5	74.7	75.5	75.8	75.0
2002	77.4	77.8	78.3	78.0	78.1	77.4	72.3	71.7	76.8	76.3	77.4	76.9	76.5
2003	77.1	77.2	77.3	77.1	77.6	77.6	70.0	69.4	75.2	76.3	76.5	76.6	75.7
2004	75.7	75.9	76.5	75.7	76.7	76.5	68.5	68.2	74.4	75.3	76.0	75.3	74.6
2005	75.0	75.2	75.0	75.2	75.7	75.5	68.9	68.2	73.2	75.1	75.5	75.4	74.0
2006	74.7	75.2	75.1	74.9	75.2	75.0	69.1	68.7	74.0	75.1	76.1	75.8	74.1
2007	74.9	75.0	75.1	75.0	75.6	74.8	69.8	69.4	73.1	74.8	75.2	75.1	74.0

Employment by Industry: Austin-Round Rock, TX, 2000–2007

(Numbers in thousands, not seasonally adjusted.)

Industry and year	January	February	March	April	May	June	July	August	September	October	November	December	Annual Average
Total Nonfarm													
2000	646.2	655.5	662.7	663.8	670.4	674.8	670.2	679.9	682.3	685.9	690.3	690.1	672.7
2001	675.2	679.8	682.8	679.2	678.3	677.7	666.7	672.6	671.5	669.6	669.2	666.2	674.1
2002	652.4	656.5	659.8	661.0	662.5	656.9	652.2	658.1	659.1	658.9	662.7	660.4	658.4
2003	646.5	648.7	649.4	653.6	654.8	653.2	649.3	652.8	654.3	656.3	658.0	659.1	653.0
2004	648.5	655.5	661.0	665.5	667.1	666.9	664.2	669.3	671.5	676.9	680.8	681.8	667.4
2005	672.2	679.2	684.4	690.3	692.8	693.4	690.1	693.7	698.4	699.1	705.7	706.9	692.2
2006	696.4	704.2	710.8	717.0	720.8	723.5	715.9	724.1	734.8	737.7	744.6	748.6	723.2
2007	731.7	743.5	751.5	755.5	759.5	762.0	753.8	758.8	763.6	766.3	769.7	771.3	757.3
Total Private													
2000	511.2	517.0	523.6	525.1	531.0	540.4	540.5	544.9	545.2	547.2	550.5	553.4	535.8
2001	538.6	540.0	541.9	538.4	537.9	540.5	533.8	533.8	528.2	525.1	522.8	523.1	533.7
2002	509.7	510.9	513.0	513.9	516.4	517.8	514.4	516.7	514.1	510.7	512.9	512.8	513.6
2003	499.9	499.6	500.8	503.8	506.2	508.5	508.2	510.7	510.4	511.7	513.1	515.6	507.3
2004	504.8	508.5	512.9	516.7	519.0	523.1	525.8	528.0	526.8	528.6	531.1	534.5	521.7
2005	525.3	528.5	533.5	538.6	541.1	545.8	546.9	549.3	550.6	548.6	553.5	557.2	543.2
2006	547.0	551.1	557.1	562.6	566.9	573.3	573.9	578.2	580.2	581.6	588.6	594.2	571.2
2007	577.7	586.1	592.9	596.6	600.8	606.6	604.7	607.9	607.5	607.5	609.7	614.1	601.0
Goods-Producing													
2000	117.6	119.2	121.8	121.9	122.9	125.9	126.1	126.8	126.7	126.6	126.8	126.8	124.1
2001	125.0	124.8	124.5	120.9	120.0	120.4	117.6	116.6	113.7	111.9	109.8	108.8	117.8
2002	105.4	104.7	104.7	103.0	103.0	103.7	102.1	101.4	99.5	98.6	97.5	96.8	101.7
2003	96.0	95.2	95.2	95.2	95.4	96.0	95.7	95.4	94.8	94.5	94.1	94.0	95.1
2004	92.4	92.6	93.2	94.1	94.4	95.6	96.6	96.7	96.3	96.7	96.4	96.1	95.1
2005	95.1	95.4	96.0	96.4	96.7	98.0	98.7	98.6	98.4	98.1	98.5	99.0	97.4
2006	98.5	99.5	101.0	101.5	102.4	104.5	105.2	105.5	105.3	105.3	105.9	106.9	103.5
2007	104.9	106.2	107.2	108.2	109.0	110.4	110.1	110.3	109.4	109.5	109.2	109.8	108.7
Natural Resources, Mining, and Construction													
2000	38.3	39.2	40.5	40.9	41.4	42.6	42.3	42.6	42.7	42.1	41.7	41.5	41.3
2001	40.4	41.4	42.0	42.0	42.6	43.3	42.7	42.6	41.8	40.8	39.7	39.2	41.5
2002	37.6	38.0	38.7	38.5	38.8	39.4	39.2	39.0	37.9	37.6	37.1	36.5	38.2
2003	36.6	36.5	36.6	37.3	37.8	38.3	38.3	38.3	37.9	37.5	37.1	36.9	37.4
2004	35.9	36.1	36.4	37.2	37.2	37.9	38.8	38.7	38.5	38.9	38.5	38.2	37.7
2005	37.8	38.2	38.8	39.3	39.8	40.5	41.2	41.1	41.3	41.0	41.3	41.5	40.2
2006	41.2	41.9	42.9	43.5	44.1	45.3	45.7	45.9	46.0	45.7	46.1	46.8	44.6
2007	45.7	46.7	47.5	48.2	48.8	49.8	49.6	50.0	49.6	49.3	49.2	49.3	48.6
Manufacturing													
2000	79.3	80.0	81.3	81.0	81.5	83.3	83.8	84.2	84.0	84.5	85.1	85.3	82.8
2001	84.6	83.4	82.5	78.9	77.4	77.1	74.9	74.0	71.9	71.1	70.1	69.6	76.3
2002	67.8	66.7	66.0	64.5	64.2	64.3	62.9	62.4	61.6	61.0	60.4	60.3	63.5
2003	59.4	58.7	58.6	57.9	57.6	57.7	57.4	57.1	56.9	57.0	57.0	57.1	57.7
2004	56.5	56.5	56.8	56.9	57.2	57.7	57.8	58.0	57.8	57.8	57.9	57.9	57.4
2005	57.3	57.2	57.2	57.1	56.9	57.5	57.5	57.5	57.1	57.1	57.2	57.5	57.3
2006	57.3	57.6	58.1	58.0	58.3	59.2	59.5	59.6	59.3	59.6	59.8	60.1	58.9
2007	59.2	59.5	59.7	60.0	60.2	60.6	60.5	60.3	59.8	60.2	60.0	60.5	60.0
Service-Providing													
2000	528.6	536.3	540.9	541.9	547.5	548.9	544.1	553.1	555.6	559.3	563.5	563.3	548.6
2001	550.2	555.0	558.3	558.3	558.3	557.3	549.1	556.0	557.8	557.7	559.4	557.4	556.2
2002	547.0	551.8	555.1	558.0	559.5	553.2	550.1	556.7	559.6	560.3	565.2	563.6	556.7
2003	550.5	553.5	554.2	558.4	559.4	557.2	553.6	557.4	559.5	561.8	563.9	565.1	557.8
2004	556.1	562.9	567.8	571.4	572.7	571.3	567.6	572.6	575.2	580.2	584.4	585.7	572.3
2005	577.1	583.8	588.4	593.9	596.1	595.4	591.4	595.1	600.0	601.0	607.2	607.9	594.8
2006	597.9	604.7	609.8	615.5	618.4	619.0	610.7	618.6	629.5	632.4	638.7	641.7	619.7
2007	626.8	637.3	644.3	647.3	650.5	651.6	643.7	648.5	654.2	656.8	660.5	661.5	648.6
Trade, Transportation, and Utilities													
2000	111.4	111.6	111.9	111.9	112.8	114.0	114.6	116.2	116.0	117.6	120.5	122.5	115.1
2001	118.6	116.8	116.4	116.6	116.7	116.2	115.5	115.7	115.3	115.9	116.9	118.6	116.6
2002	113.8	112.7	112.7	112.9	113.0	113.1	112.6	113.0	112.2	112.4	114.7	116.6	113.3
2003	110.9	109.7	109.6	109.7	109.9	110.4	111.6	112.7	112.8	113.8	116.1	117.9	112.0
2004	113.5	113.1	113.5	113.0	113.3	113.8	115.1	116.1	116.1	117.0	119.6	121.9	115.5
2005	117.8	117.7	118.6	119.1	120.2	121.4	122.4	123.4	123.1	123.0	126.1	128.3	121.8
2006	123.2	122.7	123.4	124.4	125.2	126.5	127.3	128.4	128.2	129.4	133.4	136.5	127.4
2007	131.9	132.2	133.3	134.0	134.4	136.0	136.2	136.8	136.5	136.7	137.7	141.0	135.6
Wholesale Trade													
2000	33.0	33.5	33.5	33.8	34.1	35.0	35.1	35.4	35.7	36.2	36.6	36.9	34.9
2001	37.0	36.5	36.1	36.5	36.3	35.4	35.5	35.1	34.6	34.5	34.3	34.5	35.5
2002	33.9	33.9	34.0	33.9	33.9	34.2	34.2	34.1	34.0	33.8	33.7	33.7	33.9
2003	33.4	33.4	33.3	33.3	33.5	33.7	33.9	33.9	33.8	33.8	34.1	34.5	33.7
2004	34.4	34.7	34.8	34.8	34.9	35.3	35.7	35.8	35.8	35.9	36.1	36.5	35.4
2005	36.5	36.8	36.8	37.0	37.3	37.5	38.0	38.1	38.0	37.5	37.4	37.4	37.4
2006	37.1	37.3	37.5	37.6	37.8	38.3	38.6	38.7	38.8	39.1	40.0	40.8	38.5
2007	40.4	40.7	40.9	41.0	41.3	42.3	42.0	41.9	41.6	41.0	39.6	41.1	41.2
Retail Trade													
2000	67.6	67.3	67.6	67.7	68.2	68.7	69.0	70.0	69.4	70.5	72.9	74.4	69.4
2001	70.3	69.1	69.1	68.9	69.1	69.6	68.8	69.3	69.3	69.9	71.2	72.7	69.8
2002	68.7	67.7	67.6	67.9	68.0	67.9	67.3	67.7	67.2	67.5	69.9	71.8	68.3
2003	67.0	65.9	65.9	66.0	66.0	66.3	67.2	68.2	68.4	69.2	71.2	72.6	67.8
2004	68.6	67.8	68.1	67.5	67.7	67.8	68.4	69.1	68.8	69.7	72.0	73.7	69.1
2005	69.9	69.5	70.2	70.6	71.3	72.3	72.9	73.6	73.2	73.7	76.7	78.5	72.7
2006	74.2	73.4	73.7	74.5	74.9	75.8	76.2	77.0	76.5	77.3	80.3	82.2	76.3
2007	78.6	78.5	79.1	79.9	79.9	80.5	81.0	81.4	81.3	82.0	84.4	86.1	81.1

Employment by Industry: Austin-Round Rock, TX, 2000–2007—*Continued*

(Numbers in thousands, not seasonally adjusted.)

Industry and year	January	February	March	April	May	June	July	August	September	October	November	December	Annual Average
Transportation and Utilities													
2000	10.8	10.8	10.8	10.4	10.5	10.3	10.5	10.8	10.9	10.9	11.0	11.2	10.7
2001	11.3	11.2	11.2	11.2	11.3	11.2	11.2	11.3	11.4	11.5	11.4	11.4	11.3
2002	11.2	11.1	11.1	11.1	11.1	11.0	11.1	11.2	11.0	11.1	11.1	11.1	11.1
2003	10.5	10.4	10.4	10.4	10.4	10.4	10.5	10.6	10.6	10.8	10.8	10.8	10.5
2004	10.5	10.6	10.6	10.7	10.7	10.7	11.0	11.2	11.3	11.4	11.5	11.7	11.0
2005	11.4	11.4	11.6	11.5	11.6	11.6	11.5	11.7	11.9	11.8	12.0	12.4	11.7
2006	11.9	12.0	12.2	12.3	12.5	12.4	12.5	12.7	12.9	13.0	13.1	13.5	12.6
2007	12.9	13.0	13.3	13.1	13.2	13.2	13.2	13.5	13.6	13.7	13.7	13.8	13.4
Information													
2000	21.9	22.3	22.7	23.5	24.1	25.0	25.5	25.7	25.5	25.0	25.1	25.3	24.3
2001	24.1	23.8	23.2	23.0	23.0	23.0	23.0	23.3	23.3	23.2	23.1	23.0	23.3
2002	23.0	22.9	23.0	22.9	22.8	23.0	22.7	22.5	22.3	22.1	22.0	21.8	22.6
2003	21.5	21.4	21.3	20.9	20.9	21.1	20.8	20.7	20.5	20.4	20.2	20.2	20.8
2004	20.1	20.1	20.3	20.2	20.4	20.7	20.6	20.7	20.6	20.6	20.9	21.0	20.5
2005	21.0	21.1	21.3	21.2	21.4	21.6	21.6	21.7	22.1	21.5	21.7	21.9	21.5
2006	21.8	21.8	21.8	21.8	21.7	21.7	21.5	21.5	21.6	21.6	21.8	22.1	21.8
2007	21.9	22.1	22.1	22.1	22.2	22.3	21.8	21.7	21.7	21.7	21.9	21.8	21.9
Financial Activities													
2000	34.6	34.9	34.9	35.0	35.0	35.4	35.4	35.6	35.4	35.6	35.5	35.8	35.3
2001	35.5	35.9	36.1	36.3	36.5	36.9	37.0	36.8	36.4	36.6	36.4	36.9	36.4
2002	36.7	36.9	37.0	37.4	37.7	38.1	38.2	38.4	38.5	38.7	38.9	39.1	38.0
2003	38.5	38.6	38.7	39.1	39.4	39.6	39.8	40.0	40.0	40.1	40.2	40.2	39.4
2004	39.3	39.4	39.5	39.7	39.7	40.0	40.0	40.1	40.1	40.4	40.5	40.8	40.0
2005	40.0	40.3	40.5	40.6	40.8	41.1	41.4	41.7	41.7	41.9	41.9	42.4	41.2
2006	41.9	42.2	42.5	42.6	42.9	43.3	43.4	43.7	43.9	44.1	44.1	44.6	43.3
2007	43.8	44.1	44.5	44.6	45.1	45.3	45.2	45.3	45.1	45.4	45.4	45.6	45.0
Professional and Business Services													
2000	86.5	87.0	88.6	88.9	90.3	92.7	93.5	94.2	94.4	95.0	95.4	95.8	91.9
2001	92.7	93.0	93.7	92.6	91.8	91.5	91.4	91.6	90.3	89.6	89.1	88.8	91.3
2002	86.3	86.4	86.7	87.0	87.4	88.0	87.6	88.8	87.7	86.9	87.1	86.6	87.2
2003	84.6	84.6	84.8	85.4	86.0	86.1	86.1	86.0	86.0	86.2	85.6	86.0	85.6
2004	84.9	86.1	87.1	88.0	88.5	89.4	90.4	91.2	90.9	90.9	90.8	91.4	89.1
2005	90.3	91.2	92.1	93.1	93.2	94.4	95.2	95.8	95.8	95.4	96.2	96.6	94.1
2006	94.7	95.6	96.9	97.5	98.6	99.7	100.2	101.1	101.4	102.1	103.5	103.7	99.6
2007	100.8	102.9	104.4	104.9	105.9	107.4	107.7	109.0	109.1	109.0	109.6	109.9	106.7
Education and Health Services													
2000	60.3	61.2	61.5	61.8	62.6	62.6	61.4	62.3	63.5	63.6	63.5	63.5	62.3
2001	61.5	62.7	63.3	63.5	63.3	64.5	62.5	62.8	63.7	63.8	63.8	63.7	63.3
2002	62.7	63.9	64.0	64.7	64.9	64.1	64.0	64.7	65.7	65.7	66.1	65.8	64.7
2003	64.6	65.4	65.1	65.9	65.9	65.2	65.0	65.8	66.9	67.3	67.3	67.2	65.9
2004	66.2	67.3	67.5	68.5	68.4	67.9	67.7	68.0	68.8	70.0	70.4	70.3	68.4
2005	69.4	70.3	70.8	71.2	71.3	70.5	69.9	70.4	72.1	72.1	72.2	72.5	71.1
2006	71.5	72.5	72.8	73.3	73.4	73.0	72.8	73.8	75.0	75.8	75.7	75.6	73.8
2007	73.6	75.5	76.3	76.0	76.6	75.9	75.8	76.5	77.9	78.0	78.6	78.6	76.6
Leisure and Hospitality													
2000	57.1	58.9	60.1	59.9	60.9	62.1	61.5	61.7	61.3	61.4	61.3	61.1	60.6
2001	58.6	60.2	61.7	62.1	63.0	64.0	63.0	63.5	62.5	61.3	60.7	60.4	61.8
2002	58.8	60.1	61.4	62.4	63.5	63.6	63.1	63.6	63.6	62.3	62.4	62.3	62.3
2003	60.3	61.0	62.2	63.7	64.6	65.4	64.7	65.3	64.8	64.3	64.3	64.6	63.7
2004	62.8	63.9	65.4	67.1	68.2	69.4	69.4	69.1	68.4	67.5	66.8	67.1	67.1
2005	65.8	66.5	68.0	70.3	70.9	71.7	70.9	71.1	70.6	70.4	70.6	70.1	69.7
2006	69.3	70.4	72.0	74.0	74.9	76.4	75.3	75.9	76.4	75.1	75.7	76.3	74.3
2007	73.7	75.3	77.0	78.6	79.2	80.5	79.6	80.0	79.5	79.1	79.1	79.1	78.4
Other Services													
2000	21.8	21.9	22.1	22.2	22.4	22.7	22.5	22.4	22.4	22.4	22.4	22.6	22.3
2001	22.6	22.8	23.0	23.4	23.6	24.0	23.5	23.5	23.1	23.0	23.0	22.9	23.2
2002	23.0	23.3	23.5	23.6	24.1	24.2	24.1	24.3	24.6	24.0	24.2	23.8	23.9
2003	23.5	23.7	23.9	23.9	24.1	24.7	24.5	24.8	24.7	25.2	25.4	25.5	24.4
2004	25.6	26.0	26.4	26.1	26.1	26.3	26.0	26.1	25.8	25.5	25.7	25.9	26.0
2005	25.9	26.0	26.2	26.7	26.6	27.1	26.7	26.8	26.8	26.2	26.3	26.4	26.5
2006	26.1	26.4	26.7	27.5	27.8	28.2	28.2	28.2	28.4	28.0	28.2	28.4	27.7
2007	27.1	27.8	28.1	28.2	28.4	28.8	28.3	28.3	28.3	28.1	28.2	28.3	28.2
Government													
2000	135.0	138.5	139.1	138.7	139.4	134.4	129.7	135.0	137.1	138.7	139.8	136.7	136.8
2001	136.6	139.8	140.9	140.8	140.4	137.2	132.9	138.8	143.3	144.5	146.4	143.1	140.4
2002	142.7	145.6	146.8	147.1	146.1	139.1	137.8	141.4	145.0	148.2	149.8	147.6	144.8
2003	146.6	149.1	148.6	149.8	148.6	144.7	141.1	142.1	143.9	144.6	144.9	143.5	145.6
2004	143.7	147.0	148.1	148.8	148.1	143.8	138.4	141.3	144.7	148.3	149.7	147.3	145.8
2005	146.9	150.7	150.9	151.7	151.7	147.6	143.2	144.4	147.8	150.5	152.2	149.7	148.9
2006	149.4	153.1	153.7	154.4	153.9	150.2	142.0	145.9	154.6	156.1	156.0	154.4	152.0
2007	154.0	157.4	158.6	158.9	158.7	155.4	149.1	150.9	156.1	158.8	160.0	157.2	156.3

Employment by Industry: Memphis, TN-MS-AR, 2000–2007

(Numbers in thousands, not seasonally adjusted.)

Industry and year	January	February	March	April	May	June	July	August	September	October	November	December	Annual Average
Total Nonfarm													
2000	610.6	614.7	623.3	623.5	626.1	627.3	622.3	629.4	628.3	628.7	629.4	629.5	624.4
2001	613.4	615.4	618.7	625.7	623.4	622.7	618.3	621.9	620.0	617.5	616.2	615.2	619.0
2002	603.4	606.9	609.7	613.0	612.6	611.7	610.0	614.2	614.1	618.9	621.5	621.1	613.1
2003	613.0	615.0	618.3	619.6	618.9	614.8	609.0	614.2	616.2	619.9	620.7	620.2	616.7
2004	605.4	610.4	611.5	616.6	614.1	613.3	614.7	620.1	620.9	622.4	624.5	625.3	616.6
2005	610.8	614.7	618.6	625.0	625.6	622.5	626.3	630.9	636.5	632.5	638.0	639.0	626.7
2006	627.8	627.5	632.3	634.2	634.9	633.6	635.5	640.6	643.8	641.2	648.4	649.3	637.4
2007	631.1	632.1	638.1	640.7	642.5	641.3	639.3	644.8	647.7	647.5	652.8	654.7	642.7
Total Private													
2000	528.1	529.8	534.2	537.4	540.6	544.6	543.1	546.3	544.4	542.3	542.8	542.8	539.7
2001	528.7	527.9	530.9	537.4	537.6	540.6	537.1	537.5	533.9	528.6	527.3	527.2	532.9
2002	516.4	516.9	519.4	522.2	523.9	526.9	527.9	528.3	525.6	527.8	529.3	529.6	524.6
2003	522.1	522.0	524.6	527.0	528.7	530.5	526.2	527.8	527.0	528.9	529.6	529.6	527.0
2004	515.3	516.6	519.7	525.4	525.4	528.4	531.7	532.9	543.9	547.2	547.4	549.2	537.9
2005	521.6	524.2	527.9	534.0	536.4	537.8	542.9	554.7	554.4	550.2	557.9	558.9	549.4
2006	539.3	538.4	542.9	545.2	548.0	550.5	552.7	554.7	554.4	556.4	562.1	564.0	553.9
2007	541.3	541.8	548.1	550.9	553.9	557.6	556.0	557.6	557.6	557.1			
Goods-Producing													
2000	90.1	90.3	91.2	91.0	91.8	92.4	91.6	91.8	91.2	89.6	88.8	88.2	90.7
2001	85.6	85.4	86.0	86.6	87.0	88.1	86.8	86.7	85.5	83.3	82.5	81.8	85.4
2002	79.0	78.8	79.5	79.9	80.6	81.5	82.0	81.9	81.8	81.0	80.0	79.6	80.5
2003	77.9	78.2	78.5	79.1	79.6	79.9	79.7	79.5	79.5	79.4	78.8	78.4	79.0
2004	76.7	77.1	78.1	78.9	79.3	80.7	80.9	81.0	80.6	79.2	78.9	77.4	79.1
2005	76.5	77.5	78.5	79.6	79.6	80.5	81.4	81.8	80.4	82.6	81.6	81.6	80.1
2006	79.9	80.4	81.3	81.4	82.0	83.0	82.7	82.6	82.5	80.5	79.9	77.5	81.1
2007	77.5	77.9	79.6	79.5	79.9	80.7	80.4						79.2
Natural Resources, Mining, and Construction													
2000	26.1	26.4	27.5	27.2	28.0	28.6	27.9	28.1	28.2	27.2	26.8	26.4	27.4
2001	25.6	25.8	26.8	27.0	27.3	27.7	27.6	27.5	27.0	26.6	25.7	25.5	26.6
2002	24.5	24.1	24.6	25.0	25.7	26.2	26.5	26.3	26.2	26.0	25.8	25.8	25.5
2003	24.3	24.2	24.6	25.2	25.7	25.9	26.0	26.1	26.2	25.7	25.6	25.1	25.5
2004	24.9	25.0	25.7	25.9	26.0	26.8	26.7	26.9	27.2	27.6	26.9	26.8	26.0
2005	23.7	24.1	24.7	25.3	25.3	26.0	26.7	28.3	28.2	28.0	27.0	26.5	26.1
2006	25.8	26.0	26.7	27.1	27.7	28.2	28.2	28.2	27.1	27.1	26.6	26.5	27.2
2007	25.5	25.5	26.0	26.4	26.8	27.3	27.1						26.6
Manufacturing													
2000	64.0	63.9	63.7	63.8	63.8	63.8	63.7	63.7	63.0	62.4	62.0	61.8	63.3
2001	60.0	59.6	59.2	59.6	59.7	60.4	59.2	59.2	58.5	57.7	56.8	56.4	58.9
2002	54.5	54.7	54.9	54.9	54.9	55.3	55.5	55.6	55.2	55.1	54.4	54.1	54.9
2003	53.6	54.0	53.9	53.9	53.9	54.0	53.7	53.4	53.3	53.4	53.0	52.6	53.6
2004	51.8	52.1	52.4	53.0	53.3	53.9	53.7	53.9	53.6	53.5	53.3	52.3	53.1
2005	52.8	53.4	53.8	54.3	54.5	54.7	54.9	54.4	54.4	54.5	53.5	51.2	54.1
2006	54.1	54.4	54.6	54.3	54.3	54.8	54.4	54.4	54.4	54.5	52.2	51.1	54.0
2007	52.0	52.4	53.6	53.1	53.1	53.4	53.3						52.7
Service-Providing													
2000	520.5	524.4	532.1	532.5	534.3	534.9	530.7	537.6	537.1	539.1	540.6	541.3	533.8
2001	527.8	530.0	532.7	539.1	536.4	534.6	531.5	535.2	534.5	534.2	533.7	533.4	533.6
2002	524.4	528.1	530.2	533.1	532.0	530.2	528.0	532.3	532.3	537.9	541.5	541.5	532.6
2003	535.1	536.8	539.8	540.5	539.3	534.9	529.3	534.7	536.7	540.5	541.9	541.8	537.6
2004	528.7	533.3	533.4	537.7	534.8	532.6	533.8	539.1	540.3	543.2	545.6	547.9	537.5
2005	534.3	537.2	540.1	545.4	545.1	541.1	544.5	550.5	553.9	550.9	556.4	559.8	546.6
2006	547.9	547.1	551.0	552.8	552.9	550.6	552.8	558.0	561.3	560.7	568.5	571.8	556.3
2007	553.6	554.2	558.5	561.2	562.6	560.6	558.9	564.9	568.1	568.0	574.0	577.1	563.5
Trade, Transportation, and Utilities													
2000	174.3	174.2	175.1	177.2	177.4	178.9	174.8	175.6	175.1	176.9	179.0	180.3	176.6
2001	176.9	174.3	173.9	175.5	175.2	175.3	174.0	174.7	173.9	173.4	174.4	174.7	174.7
2002	169.1	166.8	167.5	168.0	168.3	168.7	169.7	169.5	169.5	170.7	173.8	175.4	169.8
2003	171.4	170.2	170.8	170.9	170.7	170.8	169.8	170.0	170.3	170.1	172.7	175.3	171.1
2004	167.7	167.4	167.8	168.0	168.0	168.5	170.3	170.3	170.0	168.9	172.7	176.2	169.6
2005	169.8	168.7	169.7	170.0	170.5	170.5	173.5	173.2	175.1	174.9	178.2	179.9	172.2
2006	173.6	172.4	173.0	173.3	174.0	173.7	175.7	175.9	176.0	175.9	179.1	180.5	175.8
2007	173.3	172.5	173.8	174.8	175.7	175.9	175.7						
Wholesale Trade													
2000	38.2	38.4	38.2	38.1	38.0	38.2	38.2	38.4	38.4	38.3	38.4	38.5	38.3
2001	36.5	36.4	36.5	37.2	37.0	36.9	36.5	36.8	36.7	36.6	36.6	36.1	36.7
2002	36.1	36.0	36.1	36.1	36.2	36.4	36.3	36.2	36.2	36.2	36.4	36.3	36.4
2003	37.9	38.1	38.0	37.7	37.5	37.6	36.7	36.6	37.1	36.8	36.8	36.8	37.1
2004	35.8	35.9	36.2	36.5	36.6	36.9	37.3	37.3	38.0	37.7	37.6	37.7	36.7
2005	36.7	36.8	37.1	37.3	37.4	37.5	37.9	37.9	37.7	37.7	37.3	37.4	37.4
2006	37.3	37.4	37.5	37.5	37.7	37.8	37.8	37.9	37.9	37.7	37.5	37.6	37.6
2007	37.0	37.2	37.3	37.5	37.6	37.7	37.6						37.5
Retail Trade													
2000	69.6	68.9	69.6	70.2	70.6	70.8	69.9	69.9	69.6	70.8	72.9	74.2	70.6
2001	73.2	71.7	72.2	72.0	72.0	72.0	71.3	70.5	69.5	70.0	71.8	72.7	71.6
2002	70.4	69.0	69.4	69.6	69.8	70.1	70.4	70.1	70.4	70.4	73.1	74.8	70.6
2003	70.3	69.3	69.8	69.9	69.9	69.8	69.5	69.4	69.9	71.1	73.0	74.3	70.5
2004	69.4	69.3	69.4	69.3	69.4	69.6	70.8	70.3	69.7	70.8	73.0	74.5	70.5
2005	70.5	69.6	69.8	69.8	70.0	70.1	71.5	71.0	71.4	71.4	74.2	75.8	71.3
2006	72.4	71.2	71.8	71.6	71.9	71.8	72.9	72.7	72.6	72.5	75.3	76.3	72.8
2007	72.0	71.0	71.9	72.4	72.7	73.1	72.9						72.9

Employment by Industry: Memphis, TN-MS-AR, 2000–2007—*Continued*

(Numbers in thousands, not seasonally adjusted.)

Industry and year	January	February	March	April	May	June	July	August	September	October	November	December	Annual Average
Transportation and Utilities													
2000	66.5	66.9	67.3	68.9	68.8	69.9	66.7	67.3	67.1	67.8	67.7	67.6	67.7
2001	67.2	66.2	65.2	66.3	66.2	66.4	66.2	67.4	67.7	66.8	66.0	65.9	66.5
2002	62.6	61.8	62.0	62.3	62.3	62.2	63.0	63.2	62.9	63.4	63.6	63.3	62.7
2003	63.2	62.8	63.0	63.3	63.3	63.4	63.6	64.0	64.0	63.8	63.9	63.5	63.5
2004	62.5	62.2	62.2	62.2	62.0	62.0	62.2	62.4	62.1	62.5	62.9	64.0	62.4
2005	62.6	62.3	62.8	62.9	63.1	62.9	64.1	64.2	64.4	63.9	64.4	64.9	63.5
2006	63.9	63.8	63.7	64.2	64.4	64.1	64.0	64.5	64.6	64.9	65.4	66.2	64.5
2007	64.3	64.3	64.6	64.9	65.4	65.1	65.2	65.6	65.7	65.9	66.4	66.9	65.4
Information													
2000	10.1	10.1	10.2	10.2	10.3	10.4	10.1	10.4	10.3	10.3	10.5	10.6	10.3
2001	9.4	9.3	9.4	9.6	9.6	9.9	9.6	9.9	9.8	9.9	9.9	9.9	9.7
2002	10.2	10.1	10.2	10.1	10.1	10.0	9.6	10.0	9.8	10.0	10.1	10.0	10.0
2003	9.9	9.8	9.8	9.9	9.7	9.6	9.5	9.5	9.2	9.4	9.3	9.4	9.6
2004	9.0	8.9	8.8	8.8	8.6	8.6	8.5	8.6	8.6	8.6	8.6	8.4	8.7
2005	8.2	8.1	8.2	8.2	8.2	8.0	7.8	7.7	7.6	7.7	7.6	7.4	7.9
2006	7.3	7.3	7.3	7.4	7.5	7.5	7.5	7.5	7.8	7.7	7.8	7.9	7.5
2007	7.4	7.4	7.3	7.4	7.4	7.4	7.5	7.4	7.3	7.3	7.4	7.5	7.4
Financial Activities													
2000	32.6	32.4	32.5	32.8	33.0	33.2	33.7	33.5	33.3	32.6	32.5	32.7	32.9
2001	32.3	32.2	32.2	32.4	32.4	32.5	32.4	32.6	32.5	32.7	32.7	32.4	32.4
2002	32.3	32.4	32.6	32.5	32.6	32.6	32.2	32.3	31.9	32.1	32.3	32.3	32.3
2003	32.5	32.5	32.6	32.7	32.8	32.8	33.0	33.0	32.8	32.8	33.1	33.1	32.8
2004	32.8	32.7	32.6	33.1	33.2	33.2	33.6	33.6	33.4	33.4	33.4	33.5	33.2
2005	32.8	32.7	32.9	32.9	32.9	32.9	32.9	33.0	32.9	32.7	32.8	32.8	32.9
2006	32.7	32.8	32.9	32.7	32.8	33.2	33.1	33.1	33.0	32.5	33.0	33.1	32.9
2007	32.4	32.8	33.0	33.0	33.2	33.5	33.2	33.4	33.2	33.4	33.4	33.5	33.2
Professional and Business Services													
2000	70.8	71.2	72.4	70.9	71.8	72.8	76.9	78.5	79.3	78.5	77.6	77.4	74.8
2001	75.3	76.5	77.2	78.5	77.7	77.8	78.4	77.8	78.0	76.4	75.9	76.7	77.2
2002	75.5	77.0	75.8	75.6	74.5	74.9	74.6	74.0	73.6	74.2	74.0	74.2	74.8
2003	72.4	72.3	72.3	73.0	73.6	73.5	71.8	72.9	73.8	74.2	73.8	73.2	73.1
2004	70.2	70.6	70.7	71.9	71.6	72.1	72.9	73.9	73.9	76.1	76.7	77.6	73.2
2005	73.8	75.5	75.2	77.1	77.3	77.2	78.3	80.2	81.3	80.3	81.2	83.8	78.4
2006	79.2	78.9	79.3	79.6	80.0	80.2	81.9	83.5	84.1	83.4	87.2	88.8	82.2
2007	80.4	80.5	81.3	82.2	82.5	82.8	82.8	84.2	85.5	85.0	88.2	89.7	83.8
Education and Health Services													
2000	61.7	62.1	62.4	63.0	63.0	63.1	63.2	63.3	64.0	64.6	65.0	64.8	63.4
2001	63.9	64.4	64.5	64.9	65.1	64.8	65.0	65.4	66.1	65.5	65.6	65.9	65.1
2002	65.8	66.3	66.9	67.3	67.4	66.8	67.2	67.9	68.9	69.5	69.9	69.9	67.8
2003	69.9	70.5	70.6	70.2	70.4	69.9	69.1	69.9	70.4	71.3	71.0	71.2	70.4
2004	70.0	70.8	71.0	71.6	71.5	71.3	71.3	71.6	72.2	72.7	72.6	72.7	71.6
2005	72.4	73.1	73.3	73.7	73.9	73.4	73.4	74.5	75.1	74.5	75.0	74.7	73.9
2006	75.0	74.7	75.4	75.4	75.2	75.2	75.2	75.6	76.1	76.2	76.1	76.2	75.5
2007	76.1	76.3	77.1	77.0	77.5	77.3	77.3	78.0	78.2	78.2	78.1	78.1	77.4
Leisure and Hospitality													
2000	62.2	62.7	63.9	65.4	66.4	68.8	68.8	68.6	66.9	65.3	64.9	64.3	65.7
2001	61.4	61.8	63.4	65.8	66.4	67.8	66.9	66.5	64.4	63.9	62.8	62.3	64.5
2002	61.6	62.6	63.9	65.6	67.0	68.7	68.5	68.8	66.3	66.5	65.4	64.9	65.8
2003	64.2	64.5	65.7	66.8	67.6	69.3	68.8	68.4	66.7	66.5	66.1	66.0	66.7
2004	64.9	65.0	66.3	68.8	68.8	69.1	69.4	69.5	68.1	66.6	65.5	65.3	67.3
2005	63.9	64.2	65.5	67.8	68.4	69.4	70.4	70.3	69.6	68.1	68.6	68.6	67.9
2006	67.5	67.7	69.3	71.0	72.1	72.8	72.9	72.7	71.5	71.2	71.7	71.6	71.0
2007	70.5	70.7	71.9	72.7	73.1	75.0	74.3	74.2	73.0	72.7	72.7	72.4	72.8
Other Services													
2000	26.3	26.8	26.5	26.9	26.9	25.0	24.0	24.6	24.3	24.5	24.5	24.5	25.4
2001	23.9	24.0	24.3	24.1	24.2	24.4	24.0	23.9	23.7	23.5	23.5	23.5	23.9
2002	22.9	22.9	23.0	23.2	23.4	23.7	24.1	23.9	23.8	23.8	24.0	23.5
2003	23.9	24.0	24.3	24.4	24.3	24.7	24.5	24.6	24.3	24.2	24.2	24.2	24.3
2004	24.0	24.1	24.4	24.3	24.4	24.9	24.8	24.7	24.8	24.6	24.7	24.8	24.5
2005	24.2	24.4	24.6	24.7	24.7	25.0	24.8	24.6	24.6	24.4	24.4	24.3	24.6
2006	24.1	24.2	24.4	24.4	24.4	24.9	24.7	24.6	24.5	24.0	24.0	23.9	24.3
2007	23.7	23.7	24.1	24.3	24.6	25.0	24.8	24.6	24.3	24.4	24.4	24.7	24.4
Government													
2000	82.5	84.9	89.1	86.1	85.5	82.7	79.2	83.1	83.9	86.4	86.6	86.7	84.7
2001	84.7	87.5	87.8	88.3	85.8	82.1	81.2	84.4	86.1	88.9	88.9	88.0	86.1
2002	87.0	90.0	90.3	90.8	88.7	84.8	82.1	85.9	88.5	91.1	92.2	90.8	88.5
2003	90.9	93.0	93.7	92.6	90.2	84.3	82.8	86.4	89.2	91.0	91.1	90.6	89.7
2004	90.1	93.8	91.8	91.2	88.7	84.9	83.0	87.2	90.4	91.1	91.4	90.3	89.5
2005	89.2	90.5	90.7	91.0	89.2	84.7	83.4	87.0	89.3	90.3	90.6	89.8	88.8
2006	88.5	89.1	89.4	89.0	86.9	83.1	82.8	85.9	89.4	91.0	90.5	90.4	88.0
2007	89.8	90.3	90.0	89.8	88.6	83.7	83.3	87.2	90.6	91.1	90.7	90.7	88.8

Employment by Industry: Buffalo-Niagara Falls, NY, 2000–2007

(Numbers in thousands, not seasonally adjusted.)

Industry and year	January	February	March	April	May	June	July	August	September	October	November	December	Annual Average
Total Nonfarm													
2000	545.9	548.9	551.4	555.6	562.1	563.9	558.1	559.1	561.7	567.6	568.7	565.9	559.1
2001	546.9	548.3	550.0	546.6	556.3	558.8	546.6	546.6	547.4	551.1	551.7	550.2	550.0
2002	537.2	539.2	541.2	543.1	550.9	553.4	546.2	548.1	549.2	554.5	554.8	555.7	547.8
2003	535.7	537.5	540.2	542.1	547.6	550.3	541.0	541.8	548.0	551.7	555.1	555.4	545.5
2004	535.2	539.1	543.8	542.6	551.7	551.9	543.6	545.4	551.5	556.4	557.1	558.4	548.1
2005	535.0	538.0	538.9	545.2	550.1	551.0	540.7	543.9	552.0	555.5	556.1	555.4	546.8
2006	534.2	537.4	540.2	544.7	550.9	552.1	541.5	544.7	548.0	548.6	554.8	556.3	546.1
2007	534.6	537.5	541.2	541.0	550.7	552.1	544.0	544.6	550.6	554.7	556.5	555.9	547.0
Total Private													
2000	456.7	457.8	459.5	463.5	469.0	473.5	471.0	472.7	473.3	474.2	475.1	474.6	468.4
2001	456.5	455.7	457.3	454.2	463.1	467.2	459.9	460.1	457.4	458.0	458.1	457.3	458.7
2002	445.4	445.2	446.7	450.3	457.0	460.8	457.0	458.8	458.8	460.2	460.3	461.0	455.1
2003	442.6	441.9	443.2	446.2	451.4	454.9	450.7	451.9	455.0	456.8	457.0	457.2	450.7
2004	439.6	441.2	445.2	446.8	453.9	457.3	454.0	456.0	459.1	460.5	459.8	461.7	452.9
2005	440.4	441.3	443.5	449.9	454.4	457.7	452.7	456.1	459.4	460.2	460.4	459.9	453.0
2006	441.6	442.9	445.8	450.1	455.9	458.1	452.7	456.1	455.8	453.8	459.4	460.7	452.7
2007	441.0	442.3	445.7	446.1	455.1	457.3	453.9	455.2	457.6	458.3	459.6	459.1	452.6
Goods-Producing													
2000	101.2	100.7	101.3	103.2	105.1	106.6	106.2	107.2	106.6	106.4	105.6	103.7	104.5
2001	99.0	98.0	98.0	98.7	99.3	101.4	101.2	100.3	99.8	98.9	97.8	96.3	99.1
2002	89.9	89.4	89.9	92.1	94.1	95.1	95.1	94.9	94.0	94.3	93.8	91.5	92.8
2003	87.7	86.3	87.1	86.9	88.7	89.9	89.0	89.7	89.9	89.4	88.4	87.0	88.3
2004	83.2	82.9	84.4	85.6	87.5	88.7	88.1	89.3	89.2	88.6	88.1	87.0	86.9
2005	82.5	81.6	81.7	83.0	84.6	85.5	84.5	86.1	85.5	85.2	85.0	83.0	84.0
2006	80.5	79.7	80.2	82.2	83.8	85.0	84.0	85.0	84.2	82.8	82.9	81.5	82.7
2007	78.4	77.2	78.0	79.0	81.7	83.1	82.5	83.1	82.5	82.3	81.1	79.0	80.7
Natural Resources, Mining, and Construction													
2000	17.7	17.2	17.9	19.7	21.4	22.2	23.0	23.4	22.9	22.4	21.7	19.6	20.8
2001	17.6	17.3	17.8	19.5	21.5	22.5	23.2	23.3	22.7	22.3	21.6	20.6	20.8
2002	17.1	16.7	17.4	19.4	21.2	22.0	22.9	23.1	22.4	22.4	21.7	20.2	20.5
2003	17.3	16.6	16.9	18.2	20.1	20.9	21.9	22.5	22.0	22.0	20.8	19.8	19.9
2004	16.7	16.6	17.4	19.1	21.0	21.9	22.7	22.9	22.6	22.8	22.1	20.6	20.5
2005	17.4	17.0	16.7	18.7	20.2	21.2	21.7	22.3	21.7	21.6	21.3	19.6	20.0
2006	17.2	16.7	17.1	19.2	20.8	21.8	21.9	22.3	21.7	21.3	21.1	19.9	20.1
2007	17.6	16.3	17.2	18.3	20.8	21.9	22.1	22.3	21.7	21.7	20.5	18.5	19.9
Manufacturing													
2000	83.5	83.5	83.4	83.5	83.7	84.4	83.2	83.8	83.7	84.0	83.9	84.1	83.7
2001	81.4	80.7	80.2	79.2	77.8	78.9	78.0	77.0	77.1	76.6	76.2	75.7	78.2
2002	72.8	72.7	72.5	72.7	72.9	73.1	72.2	71.8	71.6	71.9	72.1	71.3	72.3
2003	70.4	69.7	70.2	68.7	68.6	69.0	67.1	67.2	67.9	67.4	67.6	67.2	68.4
2004	66.5	66.3	67.0	66.5	66.5	66.8	65.4	66.4	66.6	65.8	66.0	66.4	66.4
2005	65.1	64.6	65.0	64.3	64.4	64.3	62.8	63.8	63.8	63.6	63.7	63.4	64.1
2006	63.3	63.0	63.1	63.0	63.0	63.2	62.1	62.7	62.5	61.5	61.8	61.6	62.6
2007	60.8	60.9	60.8	60.7	60.9	61.2	60.4	60.8	60.8	60.6	60.6	60.5	60.8
Service-Providing													
2000	444.7	448.2	450.1	452.4	457.0	457.3	451.9	451.9	455.1	461.2	463.1	462.2	454.6
2001	447.9	450.3	452.0	447.9	457.0	457.4	445.4	446.3	447.6	452.2	453.9	453.9	451.0
2002	447.3	449.8	451.3	451.0	456.8	458.3	451.1	453.2	455.2	460.2	461.0	464.2	455.0
2003	448.0	451.2	453.1	455.2	458.9	460.4	452.0	452.1	458.1	462.3	466.7	468.4	457.2
2004	452.0	456.2	459.4	457.0	464.2	463.2	455.5	456.1	462.3	467.8	469.0	471.4	461.2
2005	452.5	456.4	457.2	462.2	465.5	465.5	456.2	457.8	466.5	470.3	471.1	472.4	462.8
2006	453.7	457.7	460.0	462.5	467.1	467.1	457.5	459.7	463.8	465.8	471.9	474.8	463.5
2007	456.2	460.3	463.2	462.0	469.0	469.0	461.5	461.5	468.1	472.4	475.4	476.9	466.3
Trade, Transportation, and Utilities													
2000	108.6	107.4	107.4	106.7	108.1	109.7	108.2	109.3	109.5	109.9	112.6	114.2	109.3
2001	110.1	108.1	108.2	105.9	107.7	108.6	106.0	105.8	105.6	106.2	108.2	109.5	107.5
2002	105.2	103.1	103.2	103.1	104.3	105.9	103.9	104.0	104.4	105.2	106.6	108.0	104.7
2003	102.4	100.4	100.5	100.7	102.1	103.2	102.1	102.3	102.9	103.7	105.4	106.7	102.7
2004	100.8	99.4	99.7	99.9	102.0	102.9	101.9	102.5	103.1	103.9	105.8	107.5	102.5
2005	102.0	100.7	101.8	102.4	103.3	104.3	103.1	103.3	103.6	103.9	105.2	107.1	103.4
2006	102.1	99.5	100.0	100.9	102.2	103.7	102.2	102.7	102.8	103.7	106.1	107.5	102.8
2007	102.7	100.9	101.2	100.9	102.9	104.2	103.0	103.1	104.4	104.6	107.1	108.5	103.6
Wholesale Trade													
2000	24.1	24.3	24.1	23.6	23.7	23.9	23.9	24.0	23.7	23.7	23.9	23.9	23.9
2001	24.0	24.0	24.0	23.8	23.9	24.1	23.9	23.7	23.5	23.6	23.5	23.5	23.8
2002	23.2	23.2	23.1	23.0	23.1	23.3	23.2	23.1	23.1	23.3	23.3	23.3	23.2
2003	22.5	22.4	22.5	22.4	22.8	22.7	23.0	23.0	22.9	22.9	23.0	23.1	22.8
2004	22.8	22.7	22.8	22.9	23.1	23.2	23.3	23.4	23.2	23.4	23.6	23.8	23.2
2005	23.4	23.4	23.5	23.6	23.6	23.7	23.8	23.6	23.5	23.3	23.5	23.5	23.5
2006	23.3	23.2	23.3	23.3	23.4	23.6	23.3	23.3	23.1	23.3	23.4	23.6	23.3
2007	23.6	23.5	23.5	23.6	23.6	24.0	24.0	23.9	23.9	24.0	24.0	23.9	23.8
Retail Trade													
2000	65.3	64.0	64.2	63.8	64.7	65.8	65.4	66.2	65.9	65.9	68.5	70.1	65.8
2001	65.8	64.1	64.1	62.7	63.8	64.4	63.1	63.2	62.5	63.0	65.2	66.5	64.0
2002	62.9	61.2	61.6	61.3	62.0	63.1	62.2	62.3	61.9	62.5	64.0	65.4	62.5
2003	61.2	59.6	59.6	60.0	60.8	61.9	61.4	61.7	61.5	62.3	64.1	65.5	61.6
2004	60.8	59.5	59.7	59.6	61.1	62.0	61.6	62.1	61.9	62.6	64.4	65.8	61.8
2005	61.4	60.2	61.1	61.5	62.0	62.7	62.3	62.6	62.4	62.8	64.2	65.8	62.4
2006	61.8	59.6	59.8	60.5	61.2	62.1	61.6	61.9	61.9	61.2	64.3	65.2	61.8
2007	61.2	59.6	59.8	59.3	60.8	61.5	61.3	61.7	61.7	61.8	64.3	65.8	61.6

Employment by Industry: Buffalo-Niagara Falls, NY, 2000–2007—*Continued*

(Numbers in thousands, not seasonally adjusted.)

Industry and year	January	February	March	April	May	June	July	August	September	October	November	December	Annual Average
Transportation and Utilities													
2000	19.2	19.1	19.1	19.3	19.7	20.0	18.9	19.1	19.9	20.3	20.2	20.2	19.6
2001	20.3	20.0	20.1	19.4	20.0	20.1	19.0	18.9	19.6	19.6	19.5	19.5	19.7
2002	19.1	18.7	18.5	18.8	19.2	19.5	18.5	18.6	19.4	19.4	19.3	19.3	19.0
2003	18.7	18.4	18.4	18.3	18.5	18.6	17.7	17.6	18.5	18.5	18.3	18.1	18.3
2004	17.2	17.2	17.2	17.4	17.8	17.7	17.0	17.0	18.0	17.9	17.8	17.9	17.5
2005	17.2	17.1	17.2	17.3	17.7	17.9	17.0	17.1	17.7	17.8	17.5	17.8	17.4
2006	17.0	16.7	16.9	17.1	17.6	18.0	17.3	17.5	18.5	18.4	18.4	18.7	17.7
2007	17.9	17.8	17.9	18.0	18.5	18.7	17.7	17.5	18.8	18.8	18.8	18.8	18.3
Information													
2000	9.7	9.8	9.7	10.0	10.1	10.1	10.2	9.0	10.3	10.1	10.1	10.2	9.9
2001	11.0	11.0	11.1	11.0	11.2	11.3	11.0	10.8	10.7	10.4	10.4	10.5	10.9
2002	10.4	10.5	10.6	10.6	10.9	10.9	10.7	10.9	10.9	10.8	10.2	10.3	10.6
2003	9.8	9.9	9.9	9.9	9.9	9.9	9.8	9.8	10.1	9.8	9.9	9.9	9.8
2004	9.8	9.8	9.9	9.9	9.9	9.9	9.8	9.9	9.7	9.7	9.6	9.6	9.8
2005	9.5	9.4	9.4	9.5	9.5	9.5	9.7	9.7	9.6	9.6	9.6	9.7	9.6
2006	9.4	9.3	9.3	9.2	9.3	9.3	9.2	9.1	8.9	8.6	8.6	8.6	9.1
2007	8.5	8.5	8.5	8.5	8.6	8.6	8.7	8.6	8.4	8.4	8.5	8.4	8.5
Financial Activities													
2000	29.3	29.3	29.5	29.4	29.8	30.3	30.3	30.3	30.1	30.0	30.2	30.3	29.9
2001	30.2	30.2	30.5	30.3	30.8	30.9	31.5	31.6	31.6	32.1	31.9	32.5	31.2
2002	33.1	33.1	32.9	32.8	32.9	33.3	33.4	33.3	32.9	33.4	33.7	33.8	33.2
2003	33.2	32.8	32.4	33.7	33.8	34.2	34.2	34.4	34.3	34.4	34.5	34.6	33.8
2004	34.4	34.4	34.7	34.1	34.1	34.2	34.5	34.3	34.0	34.0	34.0	34.1	34.2
2005	33.4	33.3	33.3	34.0	34.1	34.7	34.8	34.9	34.8	34.8	35.0	35.2	34.4
2006	35.0	35.1	35.2	34.9	35.1	35.2	35.1	35.0	34.5	34.0	34.0	34.3	34.8
2007	33.3	33.4	33.6	33.0	33.1	33.6	33.6	33.6	33.1	33.1	32.9	33.0	33.3
Professional and Business Services													
2000	59.5	60.1	60.2	60.8	61.6	62.2	62.9	63.0	62.3	62.3	61.7	60.8	61.5
2001	59.6	59.8	60.0	60.6	62.0	62.2	62.0	62.5	61.4	61.0	60.2	59.4	60.9
2002	59.6	59.7	59.6	60.2	61.2	62.3	62.7	63.5	63.6	63.3	63.2	63.0	61.8
2003	60.6	61.3	61.2	62.2	62.3	63.3	63.9	63.7	63.7	63.7	63.5	63.5	62.7
2004	61.3	61.8	62.4	63.6	64.3	65.9	65.7	65.9	65.5	65.6	65.3	65.2	64.4
2005	62.7	63.0	63.1	65.0	65.3	67.0	66.7	67.4	68.1	68.0	67.3	67.0	65.9
2006	64.9	65.3	65.6	67.1	67.4	68.6	68.0	69.1	68.1	68.3	69.7	69.6	67.6
2007	66.3	66.8	67.5	68.1	68.7	70.1	70.1	70.6	70.2	70.3	70.6	70.2	69.1
Education and Health Services													
2000	82.7	83.3	83.4	83.9	83.8	82.7	81.7	81.3	83.5	85.6	85.1	85.4	83.5
2001	80.3	80.7	80.4	80.3	80.8	79.7	78.1	78.0	80.2	81.4	81.8	81.5	80.3
2002	80.5	81.7	82.0	81.9	81.8	80.5	79.0	79.0	82.1	83.4	83.7	83.9	81.6
2003	81.5	83.2	83.8	83.5	83.2	81.8	79.9	79.8	83.7	85.2	85.6	85.7	83.0
2004	83.0	84.9	85.2	84.8	84.5	83.3	82.2	81.4	85.0	87.3	87.4	87.6	84.7
2005	83.4	86.2	86.1	86.6	86.1	83.9	81.6	81.2	85.4	86.8	87.2	86.8	85.1
2006	82.9	86.0	86.5	86.2	86.1	83.7	82.2	82.3	85.8	86.8	87.4	87.5	85.3
2007	83.6	86.1	86.9	86.4	86.4	83.8	81.9	81.7	85.7	87.0	87.3	87.0	85.3
Leisure and Hospitality													
2000	43.4	44.5	44.9	46.2	47.3	48.7	48.1	49.1	48.0	46.8	46.8	46.7	46.7
2001	43.0	44.4	45.3	43.9	47.5	48.9	46.9	47.8	45.1	44.7	44.4	43.9	45.5
2002	43.9	44.6	45.1	46.3	48.5	49.5	49.1	50.1	48.2	47.1	46.2	47.5	47.2
2003	44.7	45.1	45.2	45.9	48.0	49.2	48.5	49.0	47.8	47.6	46.8	46.7	47.0
2004	44.7	45.2	45.7	45.8	48.1	49.3	49.0	49.8	49.5	48.3	46.4	47.3	47.4
2005	44.2	44.4	44.8	46.4	48.3	49.7	49.5	50.7	49.6	49.0	48.2	48.0	47.7
2006	44.5	45.6	46.1	46.8	48.9	49.6	49.2	49.9	48.6	46.6	47.6	48.3	47.6
2007	45.6	46.5	46.8	47.1	50.4	50.5	50.8	51.1	50.1	49.3	48.7	49.4	48.9
Other Services													
2000	22.3	22.7	23.1	23.3	23.2	23.2	23.4	23.5	23.0	23.1	23.0	23.3	23.1
2001	23.3	23.5	23.8	23.5	23.8	24.2	23.2	23.3	23.0	23.3	23.4	23.7	23.5
2002	22.8	23.1	23.4	23.3	23.3	23.3	23.1	23.1	22.7	22.7	22.9	23.0	23.1
2003	22.7	22.9	23.1	23.4	23.4	23.5	23.3	22.9	22.9	22.9	22.9	23.0	23.0
2004	22.4	22.8	23.2	23.1	23.5	23.1	22.8	22.9	23.1	23.1	23.2	23.4	23.1
2005	22.7	22.7	23.3	23.0	23.2	23.1	22.8	22.8	22.8	22.9	22.9	23.1	22.9
2006	22.3	22.4	22.9	22.8	23.1	23.0	22.8	23.0	22.9	23.0	23.1	23.4	22.9
2007	22.6	22.9	23.2	23.1	23.3	23.4	23.3	23.4	23.2	23.3	23.4	23.6	23.2
Government													
2000	89.2	91.1	91.9	92.1	93.1	90.4	87.1	86.4	88.4	93.4	93.6	91.3	90.7
2001	90.4	92.6	92.7	92.4	93.2	91.3	86.7	86.5	90.0	93.1	93.6	92.9	91.3
2002	91.8	94.0	94.5	92.8	93.9	92.6	89.2	89.3	90.4	94.3	94.5	94.7	92.7
2003	93.1	95.6	97.0	95.9	96.2	95.4	90.3	89.9	93.0	94.9	98.1	98.2	94.8
2004	95.6	97.9	98.6	95.8	97.8	94.6	89.6	89.4	92.4	95.9	97.3	96.7	95.1
2005	94.6	96.7	95.4	95.3	95.7	93.3	88.0	87.8	92.6	95.3	95.7	95.5	93.8
2006	92.6	94.5	94.4	94.6	95.0	94.0	88.8	88.6	92.2	94.8	95.4	95.6	93.4
2007	93.6	95.2	95.5	94.9	95.6	94.8	90.1	89.4	93.0	96.4	96.9	96.8	94.4

Employment by Industry: Louisville-Jefferson County, KY-IN, 2000–2007

(Numbers in thousands, not seasonally adjusted.)

Industry and year	January	February	March	April	May	June	July	August	September	October	November	December	Annual Average
Total Nonfarm													
2000	609.9	612.0	617.4	619.6	624.7	629.6	620.7	623.6	622.3	621.1	622.3	621.7	620.4
2001	605.0	606.0	608.3	611.5	615.9	615.1	606.3	609.6	607.0	605.5	605.7	602.4	608.2
2002	586.1	587.1	591.2	596.0	601.4	601.9	594.6	600.6	599.9	600.6	602.5	602.7	597.1
2003	585.5	585.5	590.9	594.2	599.0	601.7	591.3	596.9	598.1	599.3	601.4	603.5	595.6
2004	586.4	587.7	593.2	597.5	599.5	602.9	593.2	603.1	604.2	606.2	609.6	609.3	599.4
2005	591.4	594.4	598.1	604.2	608.2	613.2	601.9	609.7	612.5	613.6	617.2	615.9	606.7
2006	600.9	603.3	611.4	615.7	621.8	625.3	611.1	620.3	622.7	616.5	619.5	626.4	616.2
2007	611.6	611.7	615.0	623.9	632.4	636.5	623.9	627.4	631.3	632.8	634.6	633.3	626.2
Total Private													
2000	534.7	534.9	539.6	540.6	543.9	549.0	547.0	547.6	545.7	544.3	545.5	545.1	543.2
2001	528.9	528.9	530.9	533.4	537.5	538.4	533.9	534.1	529.0	527.8	527.3	524.8	531.2
2002	510.3	510.1	514.1	518.3	524.1	525.8	523.6	526.5	523.6	523.6	525.4	525.7	520.9
2003	509.9	509.0	513.8	515.6	520.4	523.3	520.1	522.8	521.4	522.1	523.9	526.7	519.1
2004	511.1	510.9	516.0	519.8	522.1	525.7	520.6	528.4	526.7	528.9	531.9	532.4	522.9
2005	514.8	517.0	520.3	526.1	529.7	535.1	527.8	533.6	533.9	534.9	538.2	537.2	529.1
2006	523.1	524.5	532.3	536.2	541.9	546.0	535.6	542.1	541.6	536.5	539.3	546.6	537.1
2007	533.2	532.5	535.4	543.0	551.2	555.6	547.3	548.5	549.7	550.8	552.2	551.2	545.9
Goods-Producing													
2000	126.9	126.7	128.2	128.3	128.6	129.6	130.4	130.0	129.9	129.9	129.7	129.6	129.0
2001	124.9	125.2	125.5	126.4	126.7	126.9	125.0	124.3	123.1	122.8	121.3	119.8	124.3
2002	115.8	115.5	115.8	116.9	116.8	117.9	117.9	118.9	118.7	118.1	117.4	117.1	117.2
2003	112.6	112.0	112.6	112.7	113.1	113.8	113.6	114.1	114.0	115.0	114.0	114.8	113.5
2004	112.2	111.0	112.0	113.9	114.2	114.9	108.9	115.5	115.6	115.1	115.3	114.5	113.6
2005	111.1	111.2	112.0	113.2	113.5	115.2	109.6	114.3	113.8	113.7	114.0	112.8	112.9
2006	110.4	110.1	110.8	111.6	112.6	113.9	107.7	113.5	113.0	107.9	107.6	111.6	110.9
2007	108.5	107.7	106.1	110.4	111.9	113.4	107.8	108.9	112.0	111.8	111.0	110.2	110.0
Natural Resources, Mining, and Construction													
2000	31.8	31.9	33.4	34.0	34.5	35.1	35.5	35.0	34.9	34.4	34.0	33.8	34.0
2001	31.0	31.6	32.2	33.9	34.7	35.5	35.5	35.0	34.1	33.8	33.1	32.2	33.6
2002	30.4	30.7	31.1	31.9	32.6	33.6	33.9	34.2	34.3	33.8	33.6	33.1	32.8
2003	30.8	30.3	31.2	32.1	32.4	32.9	33.4	33.4	33.2	34.2	33.6	33.6	32.6
2004	31.6	31.0	32.1	33.7	34.1	35.0	36.0	35.6	35.7	35.3	35.0	34.4	34.1
2005	31.5	32.1	32.8	34.1	34.7	36.2	37.1	36.2	35.8	35.9	35.5	34.8	34.7
2006	32.5	32.2	32.9	33.4	34.1	34.6	34.7	34.4	34.1	33.6	33.2	33.0	33.6
2007	30.7	30.2	31.8	33.2	34.2	35.1	35.8	35.7	35.5	35.6	35.1	34.6	34.0
Manufacturing													
2000	95.1	94.8	94.8	94.3	94.1	94.5	94.9	95.0	95.0	95.5	95.7	95.8	95.0
2001	93.9	93.6	93.3	92.5	92.0	91.4	89.5	89.3	89.0	89.0	88.2	87.6	90.8
2002	85.4	84.8	84.7	85.0	84.2	84.3	84.0	84.7	84.4	84.3	83.8	84.0	84.5
2003	81.8	81.7	81.4	80.6	80.7	80.9	80.2	80.7	80.8	80.8	80.4	81.2	80.9
2004	80.6	80.0	79.9	80.2	80.1	79.9	72.9	79.9	79.9	79.8	80.3	80.1	79.5
2005	79.6	79.1	79.2	79.1	78.8	79.0	72.5	78.1	78.0	77.8	78.5	78.0	78.1
2006	77.9	77.9	77.9	78.2	78.5	79.3	73.0	79.1	78.9	74.3	74.4	78.6	77.3
2007	77.8	77.5	74.3	77.2	77.7	78.3	72.0	73.2	76.5	76.2	75.9	75.6	76.0
Service-Providing													
2000	483.0	485.3	489.2	491.3	496.1	500.0	490.3	493.6	492.4	491.2	492.6	492.1	491.4
2001	480.1	480.8	482.8	485.1	489.2	488.2	481.3	485.3	483.9	482.7	484.4	482.6	483.9
2002	470.3	471.6	475.4	479.1	484.6	484.0	476.7	481.7	481.2	482.5	485.1	485.6	479.8
2003	472.9	473.5	478.3	481.5	485.9	487.9	477.7	482.8	484.1	484.3	487.4	488.7	482.1
2004	474.2	476.7	481.2	483.6	485.3	488.0	484.3	487.6	488.6	491.1	494.3	494.8	485.8
2005	480.3	483.2	486.1	491.0	494.7	498.0	492.3	495.4	498.7	499.9	503.2	503.1	493.8
2006	490.5	493.2	500.6	504.1	509.2	511.4	503.4	506.8	509.7	508.6	511.9	514.8	505.4
2007	503.1	504.0	508.9	513.5	520.5	523.1	516.1	518.5	519.3	521.0	523.6	523.1	516.2
Trade, Transportation, and Utilities													
2000	143.1	141.6	142.1	142.4	143.0	143.8	143.7	143.9	142.7	143.1	145.2	146.3	143.4
2001	142.3	140.6	139.9	139.3	139.7	139.3	139.1	139.1	138.0	139.2	140.4	140.7	139.8
2002	135.1	133.8	134.6	134.6	135.4	136.0	135.5	135.9	135.1	134.9	137.3	138.4	135.6
2003	131.2	130.3	130.7	130.1	131.0	131.1	130.5	131.4	131.3	132.3	134.3	136.1	131.7
2004	130.5	129.5	130.2	129.6	130.4	131.2	131.3	131.7	131.4	132.6	134.2	135.4	131.5
2005	130.9	130.0	130.9	131.6	132.4	132.8	132.8	133.0	133.5	134.7	137.8	139.4	133.3
2006	133.9	133.0	135.0	135.5	137.1	138.0	136.4	136.9	137.0	137.5	140.6	142.9	137.0
2007	138.1	136.9	137.8	137.9	139.5	141.0	139.6	140.0	140.2	141.2	143.7	144.5	140.0
Wholesale Trade													
2000	31.4	31.5	31.6	31.4	31.5	31.5	31.2	31.3	31.2	31.4	31.4	31.3	31.4
2001	31.1	31.1	31.0	30.7	30.8	30.6	30.6	30.4	30.3	30.3	29.6	29.5	30.5
2002	29.3	29.3	29.2	29.2	29.3	29.1	29.1	29.6	28.9	29.0	28.9	28.9	29.2
2003	28.5	28.7	28.7	28.5	28.7	28.8	28.7	28.8	29.0	28.9	29.1	29.5	28.8
2004	29.1	29.1	29.2	29.2	29.2	29.3	29.5	29.5	29.3	29.4	29.4	29.5	29.3
2005	29.3	29.4	29.5	29.4	29.5	29.6	29.7	29.6	29.6	29.6	29.7	29.8	29.6
2006	29.9	29.9	30.1	30.0	30.2	30.4	30.1	30.2	30.1	30.2	30.3	30.4	30.2
2007	30.3	30.4	30.5	30.4	30.6	30.7	30.6	30.6	30.7	30.7	30.7	30.8	30.6
Retail Trade													
2000	70.5	69.5	70.0	69.3	70.1	71.2	69.8	70.2	69.7	68.8	71.3	72.8	70.3
2001	69.0	67.8	67.8	67.6	68.4	68.7	67.8	68.1	67.6	68.4	70.3	71.2	68.6
2002	66.7	65.8	66.7	66.7	67.4	68.2	67.5	67.3	67.1	66.7	69.4	70.7	67.5
2003	65.4	64.4	64.8	64.7	65.5	65.7	65.2	65.6	65.4	65.9	68.0	69.3	65.8
2004	64.9	64.0	64.5	64.2	64.8	65.3	65.2	65.4	65.3	65.7	67.5	68.7	65.5
2005	65.0	63.9	64.4	64.8	65.3	65.5	65.2	65.0	64.9	65.7	67.9	69.2	65.6
2006	65.2	64.3	65.2	65.3	65.7	65.4	64.7	64.3	63.8	64.4	66.7	67.7	65.2
2007	64.7	63.7	64.4	64.3	65.2	65.8	65.6	65.4	65.1	65.7	67.5	67.8	65.4

Employment by Industry: Louisville-Jefferson County, KY-IN, 2000–2007—*Continued*

(Numbers in thousands, not seasonally adjusted.)

Industry and year	January	February	March	April	May	June	July	August	September	October	November	December	Annual Average
Transportation and Utilities													
2000	41.2	40.6	40.5	41.7	41.4	41.1	42.7	42.4	41.8	42.9	42.5	42.2	41.8
2001	42.2	41.7	41.1	41.0	40.5	40.0	40.7	40.6	40.1	40.5	40.5	40.0	40.7
2002	39.1	38.7	38.7	38.7	38.7	38.7	38.9	39.0	39.1	39.2	39.0	38.8	38.9
2003	37.3	37.2	37.2	36.9	36.8	36.6	36.6	37.0	36.9	37.5	37.2	37.3	37.0
2004	36.5	36.4	36.5	36.2	36.4	36.6	36.6	36.8	36.8	37.5	37.3	37.2	36.7
2005	36.6	36.7	37.0	37.4	37.6	37.7	37.9	38.4	39.0	39.4	40.2	40.4	38.2
2006	38.8	38.8	39.7	40.2	41.2	42.2	41.6	42.4	43.1	42.9	43.6	44.8	41.6
2007	43.1	42.8	42.9	43.2	43.7	44.5	43.4	44.0	44.4	44.8	45.5	45.9	44.0
Information													
2000	12.1	12.0	12.0	12.0	12.0	12.1	12.0	12.0	12.0	12.0	12.0	12.0	12.0
2001	11.9	11.9	12.0	11.9	11.9	11.9	11.9	11.9	11.9	11.9	11.9	11.9	11.9
2002	11.9	11.9	12.0	11.5	11.3	11.4	11.4	11.2	11.2	11.1	11.2	11.3	11.5
2003	11.2	11.2	11.4	10.9	11.0	11.0	11.0	10.8	10.6	10.6	10.5	10.6	10.9
2004	10.4	10.4	10.3	10.2	10.2	10.3	10.3	10.2	10.1	10.0	10.1	10.2	10.2
2005	9.8	9.8	9.8	9.9	10.0	10.1	10.2	10.2	10.1	10.0	10.1	10.2	10.0
2006	9.9	10.0	10.0	10.0	10.1	10.2	10.2	10.2	10.1	10.3	10.3	10.5	10.2
2007	10.5	10.5	10.5	10.5	10.7	10.7	10.7	10.6	10.5	10.5	10.5	10.4	10.6
Financial Activities													
2000	38.0	38.2	37.8	37.8	37.8	38.8	37.3	37.5	37.2	36.9	37.0	37.0	37.6
2001	37.1	37.0	37.3	37.4	37.6	38.0	37.9	38.0	37.7	37.7	37.7	37.9	37.6
2002	38.0	38.2	38.2	38.4	38.6	38.6	37.8	37.9	38.3	38.1	38.2	38.3	38.2
2003	37.7	37.7	38.0	38.2	38.6	39.1	39.2	39.2	39.4	39.5	39.3	39.5	38.8
2004	39.2	39.2	39.3	39.1	39.0	39.1	39.3	39.2	38.8	38.7	39.0	39.4	39.1
2005	39.1	39.1	39.0	39.2	39.2	39.9	39.7	40.1	40.1	40.3	40.4	40.6	39.7
2006	40.8	41.1	41.4	41.5	41.8	42.2	41.9	42.0	42.2	42.1	42.5	43.1	41.9
2007	43.0	43.0	43.1	43.3	43.3	43.6	43.7	43.6	43.5	43.6	43.5	43.4	43.4
Professional and Business Services													
2000	64.3	64.9	66.5	65.2	65.6	66.2	67.2	67.7	68.1	68.5	68.4	68.0	66.7
2001	64.1	64.3	64.9	64.3	64.4	64.5	63.9	65.2	64.6	64.5	64.6	63.5	64.4
2002	62.1	62.2	63.1	63.5	65.1	64.8	64.2	65.6	64.7	65.2	65.5	65.0	64.3
2003	64.3	64.3	65.3	65.5	66.6	66.2	64.9	66.2	66.4	66.4	67.2	67.1	65.9
2004	62.9	63.7	64.9	64.9	65.5	65.5	66.6	68.1	68.6	69.9	71.0	70.6	66.9
2005	67.0	67.6	68.4	69.4	69.7	70.5	69.9	70.7	71.7	72.5	73.5	72.9	70.3
2006	69.7	70.4	73.3	72.9	73.2	74.0	73.2	73.9	74.8	74.7	74.7	74.9	73.3
2007	72.2	72.9	74.3	74.6	76.3	76.6	75.9	76.4	76.1	76.5	76.6	75.9	75.4
Education and Health Services													
2000	65.9	66.4	66.2	65.7	65.8	65.8	66.2	66.7	67.0	66.6	66.5	66.5	66.3
2001	66.9	67.1	67.5	67.4	67.4	67.6	67.2	67.2	67.4	68.1	68.1	68.3	67.5
2002	68.3	68.7	68.8	69.6	69.6	69.9	70.6	70.9	71.0	72.1	72.5	72.7	70.4
2003	72.6	72.9	73.4	73.5	73.3	73.3	73.0	73.3	73.8	73.8	73.9	74.2	73.4
2004	74.1	74.3	74.5	74.6	74.5	74.8	75.1	75.0	75.2	76.5	76.6	77.0	75.2
2005	75.5	76.9	76.3	76.4	76.7	76.7	76.7	76.7	76.8	77.0	76.6	76.6	76.6
2006	75.9	76.2	76.5	77.1	76.9	77.0	76.8	76.6	76.8	77.0	76.9	77.4	76.8
2007	76.7	77.1	77.4	77.7	78.3	78.6	79.2	78.8	78.9	78.9	78.7	79.3	78.3
Leisure and Hospitality													
2000	55.1	55.4	57.0	59.7	61.6	62.7	61.3	60.9	60.0	58.2	57.5	56.4	58.8
2001	52.8	53.8	54.6	57.6	60.6	60.6	59.4	59.1	57.2	55.1	54.8	53.7	56.6
2002	50.7	51.3	52.9	54.8	58.2	57.5	56.9	56.9	55.6	55.0	54.2	53.6	54.8
2003	51.6	51.9	53.4	55.7	57.6	58.9	58.5	58.3	56.9	55.8	55.9	55.3	55.8
2004	53.3	54.0	55.6	58.1	58.8	60.0	59.8	59.4	58.2	57.5	57.3	56.6	57.4
2005	53.2	54.0	55.3	58.2	59.6	61.1	60.6	60.3	59.7	58.4	57.5	56.3	57.9
2006	54.6	55.6	56.9	59.4	61.9	61.9	61.1	60.9	59.9	59.2	59.0	58.2	59.1
2007	56.5	56.7	58.3	60.4	62.7	62.9	62.2	62.0	60.4	60.1	60.0	59.0	60.1
Other Services													
2000	29.3	29.7	29.8	29.5	29.5	30.0	28.9	28.9	28.8	29.1	29.2	29.3	29.3
2001	28.9	29.0	29.2	29.1	29.2	29.6	29.5	29.3	29.1	28.5	28.5	29.0	29.1
2002	28.4	28.5	28.7	29.0	29.1	29.7	29.3	29.2	29.0	29.1	29.1	29.3	29.0
2003	28.7	28.7	29.0	29.0	29.2	29.9	29.4	29.3	28.9	28.9	28.8	29.1	29.1
2004	28.5	28.8	29.2	29.4	29.5	29.9	29.3	29.3	28.8	28.6	28.4	28.7	29.0
2005	28.2	28.4	28.6	28.2	28.6	28.8	28.3	28.3	28.2	28.3	28.3	28.4	28.4
2006	27.9	28.1	28.4	28.2	28.3	28.8	28.3	28.1	27.8	27.8	27.7	28.0	28.1
2007	27.7	27.7	27.9	28.2	28.5	28.8	28.2	28.2	28.1	28.2	28.2	28.5	28.2
Government													
2000	75.2	77.1	77.8	79.0	80.8	80.6	73.7	76.0	76.6	76.8	76.8	76.6	77.3
2001	76.1	77.1	77.4	78.1	78.4	76.7	72.4	75.5	78.0	77.7	78.4	77.6	77.0
2002	75.8	77.0	77.1	77.7	77.3	76.1	71.0	74.1	76.3	77.0	77.1	77.0	76.1
2003	75.6	76.5	77.1	78.6	78.6	78.4	71.2	74.1	76.7	77.2	77.5	76.8	76.5
2004	75.3	76.8	77.2	77.7	77.4	77.2	72.6	74.7	77.5	77.3	77.7	76.9	76.5
2005	76.6	77.4	77.8	78.1	78.5	78.1	74.1	76.1	78.6	78.7	79.0	78.7	77.6
2006	77.8	78.8	79.1	79.5	79.9	79.3	75.5	78.2	81.1	80.0	80.2	79.8	79.1
2007	78.4	79.2	79.6	80.9	81.2	80.9	76.6	78.9	81.6	82.0	82.4	82.1	80.3

Employment by Industry: Jacksonville, FL, 2000–2007

(Numbers in thousands, not seasonally adjusted.)

Industry and year	January	February	March	April	May	June	July	August	September	October	November	December	Annual Average
Total Nonfarm													
2000	553.0	555.9	560.9	564.1	568.3	565.5	561.2	568.8	568.7	571.3	572.5	576.3	565.5
2001	555.5	561.8	568.1	569.6	570.4	567.2	562.0	572.9	571.2	567.3	568.3	569.5	567.0
2002	557.5	559.5	564.9	565.2	566.8	560.7	553.5	561.4	558.8	559.9	563.3	565.5	561.4
2003	556.0	558.2	564.3	563.5	566.7	561.7	557.6	566.0	565.5	567.8	571.0	575.7	564.5
2004	567.5	570.1	575.7	579.5	581.6	579.4	576.9	583.9	583.4	587.5	595.4	602.4	581.9
2005	592.4	597.2	600.4	601.4	603.6	599.8	599.2	608.9	610.9	610.0	616.9	620.6	605.1
2006	612.2	617.8	623.7	621.2	625.0	620.0	616.9	624.8	625.6	627.8	634.9	636.6	623.9
2007	625.9	629.4	635.2	634.9	637.1	631.8	625.1	631.7	630.7	633.3	636.7	636.9	632.4
Total Private													
2000	484.3	486.3	490.9	493.8	496.2	499.8	496.7	498.9	499.0	500.8	502.1	505.6	496.2
2001	486.3	491.2	497.2	498.3	498.9	500.9	497.0	501.4	499.9	496.1	496.6	497.4	496.8
2002	487.3	488.6	494.0	493.7	495.1	494.2	488.5	490.0	487.6	488.2	491.0	492.8	490.9
2003	484.2	486.4	492.3	491.2	493.7	493.4	490.7	494.1	493.5	494.9	497.7	502.2	492.8
2004	494.9	496.9	502.2	505.8	507.7	510.0	508.9	510.5	509.6	512.6	519.9	526.2	508.8
2005	517.4	521.3	524.3	526.0	527.8	528.8	530.1	534.2	535.8	535.1	541.8	545.4	530.7
2006	537.8	542.6	548.4	546.8	550.8	550.2	548.6	551.2	551.3	552.4	558.5	560.1	549.9
2007	550.3	552.7	558.4	557.9	560.0	558.9	554.5	555.3	553.8	555.3	557.8	558.3	556.1
Goods-Producing													
2000	70.3	70.9	71.8	71.7	72.1	72.9	73.0	72.9	72.9	72.5	71.7	72.2	72.1
2001	68.6	69.3	69.4	69.3	69.0	69.7	69.8	69.4	68.8	68.8	68.7	68.5	69.1
2002	67.7	67.7	68.3	67.6	68.4	68.9	68.3	68.5	68.3	69.0	69.7	69.8	68.5
2003	69.5	70.1	70.9	69.3	69.9	70.7	69.5	69.7	69.7	69.7	70.2	70.8	70.0
2004	70.4	71.4	72.5	72.9	73.4	74.4	74.9	75.1	75.3	75.7	76.5	77.4	74.2
2005	76.2	76.5	77.3	77.7	78.0	79.0	79.5	80.0	80.6	80.0	80.9	81.5	78.9
2006	80.7	81.9	82.8	83.1	83.9	84.9	84.1	84.5	84.3	83.4	83.4	83.2	83.4
2007	81.6	81.5	82.4	81.5	82.1	82.6	81.2	81.2	80.1	79.8	79.6	79.7	81.1
Natural Resources and Mining													
2000	0.4	0.4	0.4	0.4	0.4	0.5	0.5	0.5	0.5	0.5	0.5	0.5	0.5
2001	0.4	0.5	0.5	0.4	0.4	0.5	0.5	0.5	0.5	0.5	0.5	0.5	0.5
2002	0.5	0.5	0.5	0.4	0.5	0.5	0.5	0.5	0.5	0.5	0.5	0.5	0.5
2003	0.5	0.5	0.5	0.5	0.5	0.5	0.5	0.5	0.5	0.5	0.5	0.5	0.5
2004	0.5	0.4	0.4	0.4	0.4	0.4	0.4	0.4	0.4	0.4	0.4	0.4	0.4
2005	0.4	0.4	0.4	0.4	0.4	0.4	0.4	0.4	0.4	0.4	0.4	0.4	0.4
2006	0.4	0.4	0.4	0.4	0.4	0.4	0.4	0.4	0.4	0.4	0.4	0.4	0.4
2007	0.4	0.4	0.4	0.4	0.4	0.4	0.4	0.4	0.4	0.4	0.4	0.4	0.4
Construction													
2000	30.9	31.2	31.9	31.7	32.0	32.4	32.5	32.6	32.8	32.7	32.5	32.8	32.2
2001	31.6	32.0	31.9	31.9	31.9	32.5	32.8	32.9	32.8	33.1	33.1	33.0	32.5
2002	32.3	32.2	32.9	32.8	33.6	34.0	33.5	33.8	33.8	34.4	35.0	35.2	33.6
2003	35.0	35.4	36.2	35.7	36.0	36.5	36.0	36.4	36.3	36.3	36.8	37.2	36.1
2004	37.3	38.2	39.1	39.4	39.7	40.4	41.0	41.3	41.6	41.9	42.6	43.3	40.5
2005	42.5	42.5	43.2	43.8	44.2	45.0	45.4	46.0	46.5	46.2	47.0	47.5	45.0
2006	46.9	48.1	48.9	49.5	50.1	50.9	50.3	50.8	50.6	50.0	50.1	49.9	49.7
2007	48.4	48.2	49.1	48.7	49.3	49.7	48.9	48.9	47.8	47.7	47.5	47.5	48.5
Manufacturing													
2000	39.0	39.3	39.5	39.6	39.7	40.0	40.0	39.8	39.6	39.3	38.7	38.9	39.5
2001	36.6	36.8	37.0	37.0	36.7	36.7	36.5	36.0	35.5	35.2	35.1	35.0	36.2
2002	34.9	35.0	34.9	34.4	34.3	34.4	34.3	34.2	34.0	34.1	34.2	34.1	34.4
2003	34.0	34.2	34.2	33.1	33.4	33.7	33.0	32.8	32.9	32.9	32.9	33.1	33.3
2004	32.6	32.8	33.0	33.1	33.3	33.6	33.5	33.4	33.3	33.4	33.5	33.7	33.3
2005	33.3	33.6	33.7	33.5	33.4	33.6	33.7	33.6	33.7	33.4	33.5	33.6	33.6
2006	33.4	33.4	33.5	33.2	33.4	33.6	33.4	33.3	33.3	33.0	32.9	32.9	33.3
2007	32.8	32.9	32.9	32.4	32.4	32.5	31.9	31.9	31.9	31.7	31.7	31.8	32.2
Service-Providing													
2000	482.7	485.0	489.1	492.4	496.2	492.6	488.2	495.9	495.8	498.8	500.8	504.1	493.5
2001	486.9	492.5	498.7	500.3	501.4	497.5	492.2	503.5	502.4	498.5	499.6	501.0	497.9
2002	489.8	491.8	496.6	497.6	498.4	491.8	485.2	492.9	490.5	490.9	493.6	495.7	492.9
2003	486.5	488.1	493.4	494.2	496.8	491.0	488.1	496.3	495.8	498.1	500.8	504.9	494.5
2004	497.1	498.7	503.2	506.6	508.2	505.0	502.0	508.8	508.1	511.8	518.9	525.0	507.8
2005	516.2	520.7	523.1	523.7	525.6	520.8	519.7	528.9	530.3	530.0	536.0	539.1	526.2
2006	531.5	535.9	540.9	538.1	541.1	535.1	532.8	540.3	541.3	544.4	551.5	553.4	540.5
2007	544.3	547.9	552.8	553.4	555.0	549.2	543.9	550.5	550.6	553.5	557.1	557.2	551.3
Trade, Transportation, and Utilities													
2000	128.4	128.6	130.2	129.7	130.1	131.6	127.7	129.0	129.1	129.1	131.1	131.8	129.7
2001	125.9	124.9	126.1	125.3	125.3	125.3	124.3	125.5	125.3	124.5	126.0	128.0	125.5
2002	122.9	122.7	124.1	124.0	124.2	124.0	123.2	124.1	124.1	124.3	126.5	128.9	124.4
2003	124.7	123.9	124.7	124.1	124.2	123.1	123.4	124.4	124.1	125.4	127.8	129.9	124.9
2004	125.5	125.5	126.4	127.5	127.4	126.7	127.0	127.9	127.3	128.9	132.3	134.5	128.1
2005	130.0	130.6	131.5	131.8	132.3	131.8	132.0	132.8	132.9	133.0	135.9	138.0	132.7
2006	133.8	133.6	135.1	135.1	135.8	135.8	135.8	137.1	137.4	138.7	141.2	143.1	136.9
2007	138.0	137.6	139.1	138.9	139.5	138.8	138.3	138.6	138.0	138.0	140.3	142.1	138.9
Wholesale Trade													
2000	26.1	26.3	26.7	26.2	26.3	26.3	26.4	26.3	26.1	26.3	26.5	26.6	26.3
2001	26.1	26.2	26.4	26.1	26.1	26.3	26.4	26.5	26.5	26.1	26.0	25.9	26.2
2002	25.1	25.3	25.4	25.5	25.6	25.9	25.9	26.1	26.2	26.3	26.6	26.9	25.9
2003	27.1	27.1	27.1	26.8	26.7	26.7	26.7	26.7	26.6	26.6	26.7	26.8	26.8
2004	26.4	26.7	26.8	26.7	26.7	26.9	27.0	26.9	26.7	27.1	27.2	27.2	26.9
2005	27.0	27.3	27.2	27.3	27.5	27.7	27.9	28.0	28.1	28.3	28.4	28.7	27.8
2006	29.0	29.1	29.3	29.4	29.6	29.9	29.8	30.1	30.3	30.6	30.7	30.9	29.9
2007	30.2	30.4	30.6	30.5	30.6	30.8	30.9	30.9	30.9	30.9	30.9	31.1	30.7

Employment by Industry: Jacksonville, FL, 2000–2007—*Continued*

(Numbers in thousands, not seasonally adjusted.)

Industry and year	January	February	March	April	May	June	July	August	September	October	November	December	Annual Average
Retail Trade													
2000	69.3	69.4	70.6	70.3	70.6	71.4	68.7	69.8	69.8	70.1	72.0	73.3	70.4
2001	68.0	67.2	67.9	67.2	67.5	67.4	66.8	67.2	67.0	66.9	68.6	69.7	67.6
2002	67.0	66.5	67.4	67.5	68.0	68.2	67.6	68.0	67.9	68.0	69.7	71.2	68.1
2003	68.6	67.9	68.2	67.8	68.2	68.3	68.2	68.4	68.3	68.9	70.8	72.2	68.8
2004	69.4	69.0	69.7	70.5	70.8	70.7	70.9	70.8	70.3	71.5	74.5	75.8	71.2
2005	72.2	72.4	73.3	73.4	73.6	73.8	73.9	73.9	73.7	73.6	75.8	77.0	73.9
2006	72.9	72.8	73.7	73.7	74.0	74.6	74.7	74.9	74.7	75.5	77.7	78.6	74.8
2007	75.5	75.0	76.2	75.6	76.0	75.6	75.5	75.7	75.2	74.9	76.8	77.6	75.8
Transportation and Utilities													
2000	33.0	32.9	32.9	33.2	33.2	33.9	32.6	32.9	33.2	32.7	32.6	31.9	32.9
2001	31.8	31.5	31.8	32.0	31.7	31.6	31.1	31.8	31.8	31.5	31.4	32.4	31.7
2002	30.8	30.9	31.3	31.0	30.6	29.9	29.7	30.0	30.0	30.0	30.2	30.8	30.4
2003	29.0	28.9	29.4	29.5	29.3	28.1	28.5	29.3	29.2	29.9	30.3	30.9	29.3
2004	29.7	29.8	29.9	30.3	29.9	29.1	29.1	30.2	30.3	30.3	30.6	31.5	30.1
2005	30.8	30.9	31.0	31.1	31.2	30.3	30.2	30.9	31.1	31.1	31.7	32.3	31.1
2006	31.9	31.7	32.1	32.0	32.2	31.3	31.3	32.1	32.4	32.6	32.8	33.6	32.2
2007	32.3	32.2	32.3	32.8	32.9	32.4	31.9	32.0	31.9	32.2	32.6	33.4	32.4
Information													
2000	15.3	15.3	15.3	15.0	15.2	15.2	15.3	15.2	15.3	15.0	15.3	15.6	15.3
2001	15.0	15.0	15.0	14.9	14.7	14.6	14.5	14.2	14.1	13.7	13.6	13.5	14.4
2002	13.8	13.6	13.7	13.6	13.4	13.2	13.2	13.0	12.9	12.9	12.8	12.8	13.2
2003	12.7	12.8	12.8	12.5	12.8	12.3	12.4	12.3	12.2	12.1	12.1	12.2	12.4
2004	12.0	11.5	11.5	11.3	11.4	11.6	11.5	11.6	11.5	11.7	11.9	12.1	11.6
2005	12.0	12.0	11.9	11.8	12.0	12.0	12.1	12.2	12.0	11.7	11.8	11.4	11.9
2006	11.5	11.5	11.5	11.4	11.3	11.4	11.4	11.1	10.6	10.5	10.4	10.5	11.1
2007	10.1	10.1	10.2	10.2	10.2	10.4	10.2	10.3	10.3	10.3	10.3	10.3	10.2
Financial Activities													
2000	55.8	55.8	55.9	56.5	56.8	57.1	57.1	56.7	56.4	56.4	56.6	57.0	56.5
2001	56.3	56.6	57.0	57.2	57.4	57.9	58.3	58.4	58.5	58.7	58.9	59.1	57.9
2002	58.6	58.0	57.9	57.9	57.8	57.7	57.6	57.5	57.2	57.3	57.4	57.4	57.7
2003	57.1	56.7	56.9	57.1	57.4	57.6	57.9	58.2	58.2	58.0	58.0	58.4	57.6
2004	57.9	57.8	57.8	58.4	58.5	58.6	58.5	58.7	58.6	58.5	58.7	59.1	58.4
2005	58.8	58.9	59.2	59.1	59.0	59.0	58.9	59.0	58.9	59.5	60.1	60.9	59.3
2006	59.7	60.1	60.3	60.4	60.4	60.2	59.9	59.6	59.4	59.1	59.3	59.6	59.8
2007	58.9	59.1	59.4	59.3	59.5	59.7	59.9	60.1	59.9	60.0	60.0	60.3	59.7
Professional and Business Services													
2000	83.3	83.6	84.5	86.5	86.5	87.2	90.5	91.4	91.7	95.0	94.2	94.9	89.1
2001	90.9	93.9	96.0	96.5	96.3	95.4	93.4	95.2	95.0	92.7	91.2	89.6	93.8
2002	87.8	89.1	90.3	90.1	89.4	87.6	85.2	84.6	83.7	83.0	81.8	80.7	86.1
2003	81.1	82.7	84.9	85.6	85.4	84.8	83.8	84.5	84.2	84.2	83.9	84.0	84.0
2004	83.4	84.0	85.6	85.8	86.2	87.6	86.5	85.9	85.8	85.5	86.8	88.2	85.9
2005	86.3	87.8	87.4	87.4	87.5	88.0	89.1	90.5	91.2	91.8	92.9	93.3	89.4
2006	92.6	94.3	95.6	93.9	94.9	93.3	93.2	93.6	93.9	95.1	97.2	96.7	94.5
2007	95.2	95.4	96.0	96.3	95.7	94.5	93.7	93.3	93.6	95.1	95.0	94.3	94.8
Education and Health Services													
2000	59.9	60.1	60.3	59.8	60.1	60.2	58.8	59.2	59.5	59.0	59.2	59.6	59.6
2001	59.0	59.6	60.1	60.1	60.5	61.1	60.8	61.4	61.9	62.6	62.8	63.1	61.1
2002	62.6	62.9	63.3	63.3	63.6	63.7	63.2	63.6	63.7	63.9	64.1	64.3	63.5
2003	63.5	64.0	64.4	64.0	64.4	64.3	64.2	64.6	65.2	66.0	65.9	66.2	64.7
2004	65.8	66.4	66.5	67.4	67.8	67.8	67.5	68.0	68.5	69.3	69.9	70.4	67.9
2005	70.1	70.4	70.6	70.7	71.2	70.8	70.8	71.3	72.3	72.1	72.3	72.7	71.3
2006	72.9	73.5	73.9	73.8	74.0	73.6	73.6	74.5	75.1	76.0	76.4	76.4	74.5
2007	76.2	77.1	77.5	77.3	77.3	77.0	76.5	77.0	77.9	78.1	78.9	78.9	77.5
Leisure and Hospitality													
2000	48.7	49.1	49.8	50.4	51.3	51.2	50.0	50.3	50.2	50.1	50.2	50.6	50.2
2001	47.7	48.6	50.1	51.5	52.2	52.7	51.6	52.8	52.1	50.9	51.2	51.6	51.1
2002	49.8	50.4	51.7	52.7	53.6	54.1	52.5	53.1	52.5	52.6	53.3	53.5	52.5
2003	50.7	51.1	52.4	53.1	53.9	54.4	53.6	54.6	54.1	53.6	53.9	54.5	53.3
2004	53.6	54.1	55.4	56.1	56.5	56.5	56.4	56.7	56.4	57.0	57.8	58.3	56.2
2005	57.8	58.7	59.9	60.7	60.9	61.0	60.5	61.4	60.8	60.4	61.2	61.0	60.4
2006	60.0	60.7	61.9	61.9	63.0	63.2	62.7	63.0	62.7	61.7	62.5	62.3	62.1
2007	62.0	63.4	64.9	65.7	66.8	66.5	65.7	66.0	65.3	65.5	65.2	64.0	65.1
Other Services													
2000	22.6	22.9	23.1	24.2	24.1	24.4	24.3	24.2	23.9	23.7	23.8	23.9	23.8
2001	22.9	23.3	23.5	23.5	23.5	24.2	24.3	24.5	24.2	24.2	24.2	24.0	23.9
2002	24.1	24.2	24.7	24.5	24.7	25.0	25.3	25.6	25.2	25.2	25.4	25.4	24.9
2003	24.9	25.1	25.3	25.5	25.7	26.2	25.9	25.8	25.8	25.9	25.9	26.2	25.6
2004	26.3	26.2	26.5	26.4	26.5	26.8	26.6	26.6	26.2	26.0	26.0	26.2	26.4
2005	26.2	26.4	26.5	26.8	26.9	27.2	27.2	27.0	27.1	26.6	26.7	26.6	26.8
2006	26.6	27.0	27.3	27.2	27.5	27.8	27.9	27.8	27.9	27.9	28.1	28.3	27.6
2007	28.3	28.5	28.9	28.7	28.9	29.4	29.0	28.8	28.7	28.5	28.5	28.7	28.7
Government													
2000	68.7	69.6	70.0	70.3	72.1	65.7	64.5	69.9	69.7	70.5	70.4	70.7	69.3
2001	69.2	70.6	70.9	71.3	71.5	66.3	65.0	71.5	71.3	71.2	71.7	72.1	70.2
2002	70.2	70.9	70.9	71.5	71.7	66.5	65.0	71.4	71.2	71.7	72.3	72.7	70.5
2003	71.8	71.8	72.0	72.3	73.0	68.3	66.9	71.9	72.0	72.9	73.3	73.5	71.6
2004	72.6	73.2	73.5	73.7	73.9	69.4	68.0	73.4	73.8	74.9	75.5	76.2	73.2
2005	75.0	75.9	76.1	75.4	75.8	71.0	69.1	74.7	75.1	74.9	75.1	75.2	74.4
2006	74.4	75.2	75.3	74.4	74.2	69.8	68.3	73.6	74.3	75.4	76.4	76.5	74.0
2007	75.6	76.7	76.8	77.0	77.1	72.9	70.6	76.4	76.9	78.0	78.9	78.6	76.3

Employment by Industry: Richmond, VA, 2000–2007

(Numbers in thousands, not seasonally adjusted.)

Industry and year	January	February	March	April	May	June	July	August	September	October	November	December	Annual Average
Total Nonfarm													
2000	574.3	576.3	582.3	585.5	589.8	595.2	587.4	587.9	590.5	589.3	593.2	596.2	587.3
2001	584.2	585.1	590.1	589.5	592.4	596.9	589.4	589.0	587.6	585.1	587.8	590.0	588.9
2002	578.5	581.3	586.7	587.3	591.4	594.7	586.2	586.8	586.3	585.6	588.1	589.1	586.8
2003	575.4	575.3	580.1	588.6	592.1	594.4	586.9	587.2	588.3	592.3	595.8	598.8	587.9
2004	589.7	592.1	598.3	601.7	605.8	609.4	601.7	597.7	605.1	610.6	613.4	615.0	603.4
2005	603.1	605.8	609.8	617.8	620.3	623.8	614.5	611.1	617.8	619.1	622.7	623.1	615.7
2006	612.3	612.7	620.7	622.0	627.5	629.9	626.5	625.0	623.8	631.5	635.6	636.5	625.3
2007	624.3	627.8	630.2	630.7	634.5	641.0	631.7	632.6	633.1	636.9	638.3	639.9	633.4
Total Private													
2000	467.8	469.6	474.8	477.7	481.6	486.0	482.5	483.2	483.7	481.4	483.8	486.4	479.9
2001	475.1	475.5	480.2	480.3	483.2	487.1	483.2	482.8	480.1	476.1	477.1	478.9	480.0
2002	468.3	470.2	475.2	476.0	480.1	483.0	478.7	479.2	478.1	475.3	476.9	477.8	476.6
2003	463.5	462.2	467.6	474.7	479.1	481.9	478.6	480.6	479.3	481.6	482.9	485.5	476.5
2004	478.2	478.8	484.1	488.2	492.5	496.8	493.5	493.0	493.3	495.5	497.6	500.0	491.0
2005	489.4	490.2	493.7	500.7	504.1	508.0	504.4	503.9	505.6	507.2	509.5	509.8	502.2
2006	498.5	497.9	505.7	507.6	513.0	515.6	516.5	515.5	512.6	517.5	520.3	521.0	511.8
2007	509.0	511.3	514.7	514.7	519.7	525.8	521.5	522.1	520.1	521.4	521.6	522.9	518.7
Goods-Producing													
2000	94.6	94.9	96.0	96.9	97.1	97.3	97.1	97.5	97.6	96.9	97.1	97.7	96.7
2001	95.3	95.6	96.2	96.1	95.9	96.1	95.1	94.8	94.5	93.2	93.1	92.7	94.9
2002	90.1	90.4	91.4	91.7	92.1	92.5	91.6	92.3	92.3	91.8	91.6	91.3	91.6
2003	88.0	87.5	88.7	89.8	90.3	89.7	89.6	89.8	89.3	88.6	88.2	87.9	88.9
2004	86.3	86.1	87.2	87.5	87.7	88.6	89.3	89.1	90.0	89.7	90.2	90.4	88.5
2005	89.3	88.6	88.6	89.3	89.5	90.2	91.1	91.1	90.5	90.0	90.3	90.2	89.9
2006	88.3	88.7	89.4	89.3	89.7	90.5	90.1	90.1	89.3	88.9	88.5	88.5	89.3
2007	87.4	87.1	87.8	88.5	89.3	90.3	89.9	90.1	89.6	89.5	89.2	89.2	89.0
Natural Resources, Mining, and Construction													
2000	37.5	37.7	39.0	40.3	40.5	40.9	40.7	41.2	41.1	40.9	40.9	40.7	40.1
2001	39.1	39.5	40.7	40.8	41.2	41.5	41.3	41.2	41.1	40.2	40.3	39.8	40.6
2002	38.5	38.7	39.9	40.5	41.0	41.0	40.7	41.3	41.3	41.1	40.9	40.6	40.5
2003	38.3	38.0	39.5	40.6	41.4	41.2	41.7	41.9	41.6	41.0	40.5	40.2	40.4
2004	39.2	39.2	40.3	41.2	41.9	42.6	43.3	43.0	43.7	43.8	44.1	44.1	42.2
2005	43.2	42.9	43.3	44.0	44.3	44.9	46.2	46.0	45.4	45.1	45.2	44.9	44.6
2006	43.7	44.2	45.1	45.0	45.7	46.5	46.6	46.5	46.0	46.0	45.8	45.7	45.6
2007	44.8	44.7	45.3	46.1	46.9	47.6	47.5	47.8	47.6	47.8	47.4	47.3	46.7
Manufacturing													
2000	57.1	57.2	57.0	56.6	56.6	56.4	56.4	56.3	56.5	56.0	56.2	57.0	56.6
2001	56.2	56.1	55.5	55.3	54.7	54.6	53.8	53.6	53.4	53.0	52.8	52.9	54.3
2002	51.6	51.7	51.5	51.2	51.1	51.5	50.9	51.0	51.0	50.7	50.7	50.7	51.1
2003	49.7	49.5	49.2	49.2	48.9	48.5	47.9	47.9	47.7	47.6	47.7	47.7	48.4
2004	47.1	46.9	46.9	46.3	45.8	46.0	46.0	46.1	46.3	45.9	46.1	46.3	46.3
2005	46.1	45.7	45.3	45.3	45.2	45.3	44.9	45.1	45.1	44.9	45.1	45.3	45.3
2006	44.6	44.5	44.3	44.3	44.0	44.0	43.5	43.6	43.3	42.9	42.7	42.8	43.7
2007	42.6	42.4	42.5	42.4	42.4	42.7	42.4	42.3	42.0	41.7	41.8	41.9	42.3
Service-Providing													
2000	479.7	481.4	486.3	488.6	492.7	497.9	490.3	490.4	492.9	492.4	496.1	498.5	490.6
2001	488.9	489.5	493.9	493.4	496.5	500.8	494.3	494.2	493.1	491.9	494.7	497.3	494.0
2002	488.4	490.9	495.3	495.6	499.3	502.2	494.6	494.5	494.0	493.8	496.5	497.8	495.2
2003	487.4	487.8	491.4	498.8	501.8	504.7	497.3	497.4	499.0	503.7	507.6	510.9	499.0
2004	503.4	506.0	511.1	514.2	518.1	520.8	512.4	508.6	515.1	520.9	523.2	524.6	514.9
2005	513.8	517.2	521.2	528.5	530.8	533.6	523.5	520.0	527.3	529.1	532.4	532.9	525.9
2006	524.0	524.0	531.3	532.7	537.8	539.4	536.4	534.9	534.5	542.6	547.1	548.0	536.1
2007	536.9	540.7	542.4	542.2	545.2	550.7	541.8	542.5	543.5	547.4	549.1	550.7	544.4
Trade, Transportation, and Utilities													
2000	111.2	110.7	111.4	111.4	112.1	112.3	112.4	113.0	112.8	113.6	115.8	117.5	112.9
2001	112.6	111.5	112.0	110.9	111.5	111.7	111.4	111.6	111.4	112.1	114.1	115.5	112.2
2002	111.1	109.9	110.7	110.6	111.3	111.8	111.6	112.2	111.9	112.6	114.4	116.2	112.0
2003	110.8	109.8	109.9	110.8	111.8	112.1	111.7	112.1	111.7	113.7	115.6	117.2	112.3
2004	112.8	111.9	112.4	112.7	113.2	113.5	113.0	112.7	111.9	113.2	114.8	116.1	113.2
2005	111.4	110.5	111.3	111.9	112.4	112.9	113.1	113.5	113.2	113.9	116.5	118.5	113.3
2006	114.5	113.2	114.2	113.9	115.0	115.3	115.1	115.5	114.8	116.6	119.0	121.1	115.7
2007	117.0	116.0	116.8	116.3	117.6	118.4	118.3	118.4	118.3	119.9	121.2	122.5	118.4
Wholesale Trade													
2000	23.7	23.7	24.0	24.1	24.1	24.3	24.3	24.4	24.4	24.5	24.6	24.7	24.2
2001	24.3	24.3	24.4	24.2	24.0	24.1	24.1	24.0	24.1	24.2	24.3	24.6	24.2
2002	24.3	24.4	24.8	24.7	24.9	25.1	25.3	25.5	25.6	25.6	25.7	25.9	25.2
2003	26.0	26.0	26.1	25.9	26.2	26.2	26.2	26.2	25.9	26.0	26.0	26.1	26.1
2004	25.7	25.8	25.9	26.1	26.2	26.3	26.4	26.2	26.0	26.2	26.1	26.1	26.1
2005	25.8	25.8	25.9	26.2	26.2	26.3	26.5	26.7	26.6	26.6	26.7	26.8	26.3
2006	26.9	27.0	27.1	27.2	27.4	27.6	27.8	27.9	27.8	28.0	28.1	28.1	27.6
2007	28.1	28.3	28.5	28.5	28.7	28.9	29.0	29.1	28.9	29.0	28.9	28.9	28.7
Retail Trade													
2000	66.3	65.7	66.2	66.0	66.8	66.9	66.5	67.1	67.0	67.5	69.6	71.2	67.2
2001	67.3	66.2	66.6	65.7	66.4	66.5	66.4	66.5	66.2	67.0	69.2	70.5	67.0
2002	66.9	65.8	66.3	65.9	66.4	66.8	66.1	66.4	66.1	66.7	68.3	70.0	66.8
2003	65.1	64.1	64.1	64.8	65.5	65.7	65.2	65.6	65.7	67.2	69.2	70.7	66.0
2004	67.2	66.2	66.6	66.3	66.7	66.9	65.9	65.8	65.4	66.6	68.2	69.2	66.8
2005	65.9	65.0	65.4	65.7	66.2	66.5	66.3	66.5	66.2	66.7	69.0	70.6	66.7
2006	67.3	66.1	66.8	66.6	67.4	67.4	67.0	67.0	66.3	67.7	69.9	71.4	67.6
2007	68.1	67.0	67.4	67.0	68.1	68.5	68.4	68.2	68.2	69.7	71.1	72.3	68.7

Employment by Industry: Richmond, VA, 2000–2007—*Continued*

(Numbers in thousands, not seasonally adjusted.)

Industry and year	January	February	March	April	May	June	July	August	September	October	November	December	Annual Average
Transportation and Utilities													
2000	21.2	21.3	21.2	21.3	21.2	21.1	21.6	21.5	21.4	21.6	21.6	21.6	21.4
2001	21.0	21.0	21.0	21.0	21.1	21.1	20.9	21.1	21.1	20.9	20.6	20.4	20.9
2002	19.9	19.7	19.6	20.0	20.0	19.9	20.2	20.3	20.2	20.3	20.4	20.3	20.1
2003	19.7	19.7	19.7	20.1	20.1	20.2	20.3	20.3	20.1	20.5	20.4	20.4	20.1
2004	19.9	19.9	19.9	20.3	20.3	20.3	20.7	20.7	20.5	20.4	20.5	20.8	20.4
2005	19.7	19.7	20.0	20.0	20.0	20.1	20.3	20.3	20.4	20.6	20.8	21.1	20.3
2006	20.3	20.1	20.3	20.1	20.2	20.3	20.3	20.6	20.7	20.9	21.0	21.6	20.5
2007	20.8	20.7	20.9	20.8	20.8	21.0	20.9	21.1	21.2	21.2	21.2	21.3	21.0
Information													
2000	12.5	12.4	12.6	12.6	12.8	13.1	13.2	13.3	13.4	13.1	13.2	13.3	13.0
2001	13.1	13.1	13.1	12.6	12.6	12.5	12.5	12.6	12.4	12.3	12.2	12.3	12.6
2002	12.6	12.6	12.6	12.5	12.6	12.5	12.3	12.4	12.2	11.9	12.2	12.2	12.4
2003	11.7	12.0	12.0	11.9	11.9	12.0	11.9	11.9	11.7	11.5	11.6	11.5	11.8
2004	11.5	11.4	11.5	11.2	11.2	11.2	11.1	11.0	10.9	10.9	11.0	11.0	11.2
2005	11.0	11.0	11.1	11.1	11.1	11.1	11.1	11.1	11.1	11.0	11.1	11.1	11.1
2006	11.0	11.0	11.0	10.8	12.9	10.8	11.8	11.2	11.1	11.1	11.2	11.2	11.3
2007	11.6	11.6	11.5	11.7	11.9	11.8	11.4	11.3	11.2	11.0	11.0	11.1	11.4
Financial Activities													
2000	44.3	44.3	44.5	44.4	44.8	45.1	45.3	45.5	45.3	45.4	45.8	46.5	45.1
2001	46.0	46.3	46.6	46.7	46.8	47.3	47.3	47.6	47.4	47.3	47.5	47.7	47.0
2002	47.0	47.2	47.3	47.2	47.0	47.1	46.8	46.3	46.4	46.1	45.9	45.7	46.7
2003	45.2	45.4	45.6	46.2	46.5	46.7	47.0	47.2	46.9	46.3	46.5	47.0	46.3
2004	46.6	46.9	46.8	47.1	47.0	47.3	47.1	47.2	46.7	46.5	46.6	46.8	46.9
2005	46.6	46.7	46.8	46.5	46.6	46.7	47.3	47.2	46.7	46.4	46.3	46.5	46.7
2006	46.4	46.5	46.8	46.5	46.7	46.9	47.0	47.0	46.4	46.4	46.0	46.1	46.5
2007	45.7	45.6	45.9	45.8	45.9	46.3	46.2	46.1	45.6	45.7	45.7	45.8	45.9
Professional and Business Services													
2000	88.3	90.0	91.0	92.2	92.9	93.8	92.8	92.3	93.0	92.2	92.2	92.5	91.9
2001	90.0	90.0	90.6	90.4	90.9	91.6	90.5	90.3	88.7	87.5	87.6	88.1	89.7
2002	86.5	87.6	88.3	88.6	88.9	89.0	88.3	88.0	87.9	86.4	86.8	86.6	87.7
2003	81.7	81.1	82.3	83.8	84.3	84.9	84.5	84.6	84.3	85.0	85.1	85.7	83.9
2004	84.5	84.6	85.0	86.4	87.4	88.4	88.8	89.4	89.1	90.9	91.1	92.3	88.2
2005	89.7	90.3	90.8	92.3	92.7	93.4	93.8	93.5	93.6	95.2	94.9	95.1	92.9
2006	93.2	93.4	94.3	93.7	94.6	95.4	95.3	95.9	96.4	98.5	98.8	99.3	95.7
2007	97.0	97.7	98.8	98.6	98.1	99.4	98.8	99.3	99.0	99.7	99.3	99.8	98.8
Education and Health Services													
2000	52.4	52.4	52.7	51.5	51.6	51.5	49.3	49.5	51.8	52.2	52.5	52.7	51.7
2001	53.0	53.2	53.4	53.5	53.8	54.2	52.5	52.6	54.7	55.2	55.2	55.4	53.9
2002	55.5	55.9	56.0	56.1	57.1	57.3	55.3	55.7	57.3	57.8	58.2	58.2	56.7
2003	59.8	59.9	60.0	60.7	60.5	60.2	57.7	59.4	61.6	62.1	62.4	62.8	60.5
2004	63.7	64.2	64.7	65.1	65.8	65.7	62.1	62.3	65.6	66.7	67.4	67.5	65.1
2005	67.2	68.0	68.0	68.6	69.0	68.5	64.8	64.7	69.6	71.2	71.7	70.9	68.5
2006	69.3	68.6	71.1	73.2	71.6	71.3	70.9	70.0	71.2	73.1	73.5	72.3	71.3
2007	71.9	74.3	72.9	72.0	71.9	71.8	68.9	68.9	72.1	72.9	73.8	73.3	72.1
Leisure and Hospitality													
2000	40.8	41.0	42.3	44.4	45.9	48.2	47.6	47.4	45.4	43.6	42.9	41.8	44.3
2001	41.4	41.8	44.1	45.8	47.0	49.0	49.1	48.7	46.6	44.2	42.9	42.8	45.3
2002	41.1	41.9	44.0	44.4	46.0	47.6	47.7	47.2	45.2	43.9	42.8	42.7	44.5
2003	41.7	41.7	44.1	46.0	47.8	49.6	49.3	48.7	46.7	46.9	45.5	45.2	46.1
2004	44.3	44.5	46.6	48.4	50.2	52.0	52.2	51.4	49.7	48.1	47.0	46.4	48.4
2005	44.8	45.3	47.4	49.3	50.9	52.9	52.9	52.4	50.9	49.4	48.7	47.8	49.4
2006	46.8	47.4	49.6	50.9	52.8	55.4	54.9	54.5	51.8	52.4	51.1	50.9	51.5
2007	48.6	49.1	50.7	51.6	53.8	56.3	55.9	55.4	53.1	51.9	50.6	50.5	52.3
Other Services													
2000	23.7	23.9	24.3	24.3	24.4	24.7	24.8	24.7	24.4	24.4	24.3	24.4	24.4
2001	23.7	24.0	24.2	24.3	24.7	24.7	24.8	24.6	24.4	24.3	24.5	24.4	24.4
2002	24.4	24.7	24.9	24.9	25.1	25.2	25.1	25.1	24.9	24.8	25.0	24.9	24.9
2003	24.6	24.8	25.0	25.5	26.0	26.7	26.9	26.9	27.1	27.5	28.0	28.2	26.4
2004	28.5	29.2	29.9	29.8	30.0	30.1	29.9	29.9	29.4	29.5	29.5	29.5	29.6
2005	29.4	29.8	29.7	31.7	31.9	32.3	30.4	30.4	29.9	30.1	30.0	29.7	30.4
2006	29.0	29.1	29.3	29.3	29.7	30.0	31.4	31.3	31.6	30.7	32.2	31.6	30.4
2007	29.8	29.9	30.3	31.2	31.2	31.5	32.1	32.6	31.2	30.8	30.8	30.7	31.0
Government													
2000	106.5	106.7	107.5	107.8	108.2	109.2	104.9	104.7	106.8	107.9	109.4	109.8	107.5
2001	109.1	109.6	109.9	109.2	109.2	109.8	106.2	106.2	107.5	109.0	110.7	111.1	109.0
2002	110.2	111.1	111.5	111.3	111.3	111.7	107.5	107.6	108.2	110.3	111.2	111.3	110.3
2003	111.9	113.1	112.5	113.9	113.0	112.5	108.3	106.6	109.0	110.7	112.9	113.3	111.4
2004	111.5	113.3	114.2	113.5	113.3	112.6	108.2	104.7	111.8	115.1	115.8	115.0	112.4
2005	113.7	115.6	116.1	117.1	116.2	115.8	110.1	107.2	112.2	111.9	113.2	113.3	113.5
2006	113.8	114.8	115.0	114.4	114.5	114.3	110.0	109.5	111.2	114.0	115.3	115.5	113.5
2007	115.3	116.5	115.5	116.0	114.8	115.2	110.2	110.5	113.0	115.5	116.7	117.0	114.7

Employment by Industry: Oklahoma City, OK, 2000–2007

(Numbers in thousands, not seasonally adjusted.)

Industry and year	January	February	March	April	May	June	July	August	September	October	November	December	Annual Average
Total Nonfarm													
2000	522.3	525.3	530.2	533.6	538.3	537.1	529.0	534.5	543.7	543.2	546.7	546.1	535.8
2001	532.9	535.5	540.7	544.6	547.7	548.4	534.9	539.0	546.8	544.0	547.8	547.4	542.5
2002	527.4	533.0	537.8	539.9	543.9	541.2	530.9	535.9	542.7	541.0	543.1	542.9	538.3
2003	523.1	526.0	527.3	529.5	532.3	526.2	520.9	525.1	532.7	534.9	535.7	537.2	529.2
2004	524.5	528.7	534.2	538.6	540.5	536.8	532.3	536.8	545.3	546.2	547.6	550.6	538.5
2005	532.6	539.3	545.1	551.3	552.8	550.2	545.3	549.5	557.8	557.6	562.2	564.4	550.7
2006	549.3	554.6	560.0	560.9	563.5	562.5	552.6	557.6	565.2	564.1	565.7	568.5	560.4
2007	554.8	560.4	567.7	566.0	568.6	568.6	559.0	564.3	570.6	572.6	575.4	575.1	566.9
Total Private													
2000	416.6	418.1	421.7	425.3	428.5	431.1	431.6	434.4	435.7	434.0	436.1	436.6	429.1
2001	424.9	425.9	430.3	434.6	437.0	440.7	435.3	436.2	436.0	431.3	433.8	434.0	433.3
2002	417.2	420.8	424.8	427.1	430.9	432.0	430.6	432.8	431.2	427.4	429.2	429.1	427.8
2003	414.3	414.3	416.3	418.7	421.6	419.0	421.2	423.7	423.1	423.8	424.2	425.5	420.5
2004	416.7	417.4	422.5	427.0	428.7	428.4	431.2	431.5	432.0	432.8	433.8	436.2	428.2
2005	421.7	426.1	431.5	437.1	438.2	439.8	441.8	443.8	444.5	442.4	446.3	448.7	438.5
2006	436.8	439.2	444.3	445.1	447.4	450.6	448.1	450.3	451.3	446.9	448.2	451.3	446.6
2007	440.0	443.4	450.0	448.5	450.8	454.3	452.3	456.6	456.6	457.1	459.7	460.6	452.5
Goods-Producing													
2000	79.7	80.0	80.6	80.1	80.6	81.5	81.5	82.2	82.0	81.4	81.8	82.0	81.1
2001	79.4	79.3	80.0	80.0	81.1	81.6	80.3	78.6	79.6	77.0	77.8	77.2	79.3
2002	70.6	71.7	71.9	70.9	72.2	72.4	72.4	72.2	71.5	70.4	70.1	69.9	71.4
2003	68.8	68.6	68.8	69.1	69.4	67.3	70.5	70.7	70.2	70.2	69.7	70.0	69.4
2004	69.3	69.0	69.7	70.8	71.6	70.3	73.1	73.3	73.1	72.9	72.2	73.2	71.5
2005	70.5	72.0	73.2	73.5	73.7	73.1	75.4	75.6	75.5	76.0	76.3	77.3	74.3
2006	76.3	76.7	77.5	77.1	77.5	78.4	77.5	77.9	77.7	77.7	77.3	77.9	77.5
2007	75.4	75.5	76.9	77.1	77.4	78.9	78.4	79.1	78.7	79.3	79.5	79.9	78.0
Natural Resources and Mining													
2000	6.0	6.2	6.2	6.3	6.3	6.5	6.7	6.9	6.9	7.1	7.2	7.5	6.7
2001	7.1	7.3	7.5	7.4	7.5	7.7	7.7	7.7	7.5	7.5	7.4	7.4	7.5
2002	7.4	7.5	7.5	7.3	7.5	7.5	7.6	7.6	7.5	7.4	7.4	7.4	7.5
2003	7.5	7.5	7.5	7.7	7.7	7.8	8.1	8.2	8.2	8.3	8.3	8.4	7.9
2004	8.5	8.5	8.6	8.8	8.9	9.1	9.2	9.2	9.3	9.4	9.5	9.6	9.1
2005	9.7	9.8	10.0	10.1	10.2	10.3	10.6	10.7	10.9	11.0	11.3	11.7	10.5
2006	11.7	12.0	12.2	12.4	12.6	12.8	12.7	13.0	13.1	13.3	13.5	13.8	12.8
2007	13.7	13.7	13.7	13.9	14.0	14.3	14.4	14.6	14.7	14.9	15.0	15.0	14.3
Construction													
2000	21.5	21.4	21.9	22.2	22.7	23.2	23.0	23.3	23.0	23.1	22.8	22.5	22.6
2001	21.7	22.2	22.8	23.4	24.0	24.6	24.3	24.5	23.9	23.2	22.6	22.3	23.3
2002	21.6	21.4	21.7	21.6	22.1	22.5	22.7	22.6	22.2	22.0	21.8	21.8	22.0
2003	21.5	21.4	21.6	22.0	22.8	23.6	23.6	23.7	23.3	23.2	22.8	22.9	22.7
2004	22.3	22.1	22.7	23.1	23.4	24.0	24.5	24.5	24.3	23.9	23.4	23.9	23.5
2005	23.1	23.2	24.1	24.6	24.9	25.7	26.0	26.1	26.0	26.1	26.2	26.4	25.2
2006	25.8	25.9	26.6	26.2	26.5	27.2	26.7	26.9	26.7	26.3	26.1	26.2	26.4
2007	25.3	25.2	26.2	26.3	26.4	27.4	27.1	27.5	27.3	27.9	27.9	28.2	26.9
Manufacturing													
2000	52.2	52.4	52.5	51.6	51.6	51.8	51.8	52.0	52.1	51.2	51.8	52.0	51.9
2001	50.6	49.8	49.7	49.2	49.6	49.3	48.3	46.4	48.2	46.3	47.8	47.5	48.6
2002	41.6	42.8	42.7	42.0	42.6	42.4	42.1	42.0	41.8	41.0	40.9	40.7	41.9
2003	39.8	39.7	39.7	39.4	38.9	35.9	38.8	38.8	38.7	38.7	38.6	38.7	38.8
2004	38.5	38.4	38.4	38.9	39.3	37.2	39.4	39.6	39.5	39.6	39.3	39.7	39.0
2005	37.7	39.0	39.1	38.8	38.6	37.1	38.8	38.8	38.6	38.9	38.8	39.2	38.6
2006	38.8	38.8	38.7	38.5	38.4	38.4	38.1	38.0	37.9	38.1	37.7	37.9	38.3
2007	36.4	36.6	37.0	36.9	37.0	37.2	36.9	37.0	36.7	36.5	36.6	36.7	36.8
Service-Providing													
2000	442.6	445.3	449.6	453.5	457.7	455.6	447.5	452.3	461.7	461.8	464.9	464.1	454.7
2001	453.5	456.2	460.7	464.6	466.6	466.8	454.6	460.4	467.2	467.0	470.0	470.2	463.2
2002	456.8	461.3	465.9	469.0	471.7	468.8	458.5	463.7	471.2	470.6	473.0	473.0	467.0
2003	454.3	457.4	458.5	460.4	462.9	458.9	450.4	454.4	462.5	464.7	466.0	467.2	459.8
2004	455.2	459.7	464.5	467.8	468.9	466.5	459.2	463.5	472.2	473.3	475.4	477.4	467.0
2005	462.1	467.3	471.9	477.8	479.1	477.1	469.9	473.9	482.3	481.6	485.9	487.1	476.3
2006	473.0	477.9	482.5	483.8	486.0	484.1	475.1	479.7	487.5	486.4	488.4	490.6	482.9
2007	479.4	484.9	490.8	488.9	491.2	489.7	480.6	485.2	491.9	493.3	495.9	495.2	488.9
Trade, Transportation, and Utilities													
2000	101.3	99.9	99.8	100.6	101.2	101.1	101.2	102.1	102.0	102.6	105.1	106.6	102.0
2001	101.7	100.0	100.1	100.8	100.8	100.9	99.8	99.8	99.5	100.1	101.9	103.0	100.7
2002	99.0	98.3	99.3	98.7	98.9	98.9	98.7	99.1	98.8	98.0	100.3	101.2	99.1
2003	96.6	95.5	95.9	96.0	96.4	96.4	95.8	96.5	96.5	97.5	99.5	101.0	96.9
2004	96.3	95.7	96.3	96.1	96.3	96.5	96.0	95.8	95.7	96.8	99.3	100.9	96.8
2005	96.4	96.4	97.1	97.8	98.0	98.0	98.6	99.3	99.5	100.0	102.6	104.2	99.0
2006	99.1	99.0	99.5	99.3	99.7	100.1	99.4	100.1	100.4	100.4	102.5	104.0	100.3
2007	100.3	100.3	102.0	100.5	101.1	101.1	101.2	102.5	102.2	102.1	105.1	106.2	102.1
Wholesale Trade													
2000	21.9	21.8	21.8	22.0	22.0	22.1	22.1	22.4	22.3	22.0	22.1	22.2	22.1
2001	21.3	21.4	21.5	21.5	21.6	22.0	21.9	22.0	21.9	21.8	21.8	22.0	21.7
2002	21.4	21.3	21.4	21.2	21.4	21.5	21.7	21.6	21.6	21.3	21.3	21.3	21.4
2003	21.2	21.1	21.2	21.0	21.0	21.0	20.9	20.9	21.0	21.0	20.9	21.1	21.0
2004	20.8	20.7	20.6	20.6	20.8	21.2	21.2	21.1	21.0	21.2	21.3	21.4	21.0
2005	21.1	21.2	21.3	21.4	21.4	21.6	22.0	22.0	21.9	22.0	22.2	22.4	21.7
2006	22.2	22.4	22.5	22.4	22.6	22.8	22.8	22.9	23.0	23.0	23.0	23.2	22.7
2007	22.8	22.9	23.0	23.0	23.1	23.2	23.1	23.5	23.5	23.5	23.8	23.8	23.3

Employment by Industry: Oklahoma City, OK, 2000–2007—*Continued*

(Numbers in thousands, not seasonally adjusted.)

Industry and year	January	February	March	April	May	June	July	August	September	October	November	December	Annual Average
Retail Trade													
2000	62.2	61.0	61.0	61.3	61.7	61.7	61.8	62.4	62.4	63.2	65.6	67.0	62.6
2001	62.9	61.4	61.4	61.4	61.5	61.5	60.4	60.3	60.3	61.2	63.1	64.2	61.6
2002	61.4	60.8	61.7	61.2	61.2	61.1	60.5	61.0	60.9	60.6	63.1	64.3	61.5
2003	60.0	59.0	59.2	59.7	60.1	60.2	59.6	60.3	60.3	61.1	63.3	64.7	60.6
2004	60.2	59.8	60.3	60.2	60.2	60.0	59.5	59.4	59.2	59.9	62.3	63.6	60.4
2005	60.0	59.8	60.3	60.7	60.8	60.7	60.6	61.2	61.4	61.9	64.2	65.4	61.4
2006	61.1	60.8	61.1	61.1	61.2	61.4	60.8	61.3	61.3	61.1	63.1	64.2	61.5
2007	61.1	60.9	62.2	60.8	61.2	61.1	61.3	62.0	61.8	61.6	64.2	65.3	62.0
Transportation and Utilities													
2000	17.2	17.1	17.0	17.3	17.5	17.3	17.3	17.3	17.3	17.4	17.4	17.4	17.3
2001	17.5	17.2	17.2	17.9	17.7	17.4	17.5	17.5	17.3	17.1	17.0	16.8	17.3
2002	16.2	16.2	16.2	16.3	16.3	16.3	16.5	16.5	16.3	16.1	15.9	15.6	16.2
2003	15.4	15.4	15.5	15.3	15.3	15.2	15.3	15.3	15.3	15.2	15.4	15.3	15.3
2004	15.3	15.2	15.4	15.3	15.3	15.3	15.3	15.3	15.5	15.7	15.7	15.9	15.4
2005	15.3	15.4	15.5	15.7	15.8	15.7	16.0	16.1	16.2	16.1	16.2	16.4	15.9
2006	15.8	15.8	15.9	15.8	15.9	15.9	15.8	15.9	16.1	16.3	16.4	16.6	16.0
2007	16.4	16.5	16.8	16.7	16.8	16.8	16.8	17.0	16.9	17.0	17.1	17.1	16.8
Information													
2000	12.8	13.2	13.3	13.9	13.8	14.0	14.2	14.2	14.4	14.4	14.4	14.4	13.9
2001	14.6	14.8	14.8	14.5	14.5	14.6	14.4	14.1	14.2	14.4	14.3	14.3	14.5
2002	14.3	14.4	14.2	14.1	14.2	14.1	14.0	14.0	13.8	13.7	13.9	13.8	14.0
2003	13.6	13.5	13.5	13.4	13.5	13.4	13.4	13.4	13.3	13.3	13.5	13.7	13.4
2004	13.5	13.4	13.3	13.5	13.5	13.8	14.0	13.8	13.5	13.8	13.7	13.7	13.6
2005	13.6	13.7	13.6	13.7	13.7	13.5	13.6	13.3	13.0	12.9	13.0	13.0	13.4
2006	12.4	12.5	12.6	13.5	13.4	13.3	13.5	13.5	13.4	13.2	13.2	13.7	13.2
2007	13.1	12.7	12.4	12.3	12.4	12.5	12.4	12.4	12.3	12.3	12.2	12.3	12.4
Financial Activities													
2000	33.5	33.7	33.6	33.5	33.6	33.7	33.7	33.9	33.8	33.8	33.9	34.0	33.7
2001	33.4	33.6	33.8	34.1	34.3	34.6	34.6	34.9	34.7	34.8	34.8	34.8	34.4
2002	34.8	34.8	34.9	34.9	35.1	35.6	35.6	35.8	35.6	35.5	35.6	35.8	35.3
2003	34.3	34.4	34.5	34.7	34.8	35.0	35.0	35.3	35.2	35.2	35.0	35.1	34.8
2004	34.8	34.9	35.1	35.8	35.7	35.9	35.6	35.5	35.3	35.3	35.2	35.3	35.4
2005	34.1	34.1	34.3	34.3	34.5	34.8	34.9	34.8	34.7	34.2	34.3	35.0	34.5
2006	34.6	34.5	34.6	34.2	34.4	34.4	34.5	34.6	34.5	34.5	34.4	34.4	34.5
2007	34.7	35.1	34.9	34.8	34.8	34.9	34.8	34.8	34.4	34.4	34.5	34.6	34.7
Professional and Business Services													
2000	62.8	63.5	64.8	65.8	66.5	67.7	68.4	68.3	69.0	67.7	67.4	68.0	66.7
2001	65.7	66.4	67.7	69.1	68.9	70.3	68.7	70.3	70.8	68.3	68.0	68.5	68.6
2002	65.6	67.0	68.1	69.4	69.4	69.5	67.8	68.5	68.5	67.0	66.7	66.8	67.9
2003	63.3	63.5	63.7	64.5	65.2	65.0	65.0	65.5	65.7	65.6	65.3	65.1	64.7
2004	63.1	63.3	64.6	66.5	66.4	66.7	67.6	68.0	67.9	68.0	68.1	68.0	66.5
2005	65.3	66.5	67.5	70.0	69.9	71.2	71.1	72.2	72.2	70.9	71.6	71.0	70.0
2006	69.6	70.1	71.3	71.4	72.1	73.4	73.0	73.6	74.3	72.1	72.5	72.8	72.2
2007	71.3	72.6	73.7	73.6	74.0	75.0	74.1	75.1	75.6	75.5	75.6	75.4	74.3
Education and Health Services													
2000	56.7	57.2	57.5	58.5	59.1	58.6	58.4	58.9	59.8	59.3	59.6	59.3	58.6
2001	58.9	59.5	60.1	59.9	60.6	60.7	60.5	61.3	61.6	62.2	62.1	62.3	60.8
2002	61.2	62.1	62.6	63.8	64.5	64.3	64.6	65.4	65.5	65.7	66.4	66.4	64.4
2003	64.5	65.3	65.8	65.4	65.4	64.9	64.8	65.5	66.3	65.8	66.1	65.9	65.4
2004	66.8	67.4	68.1	67.9	67.7	67.1	66.6	67.1	68.0	68.5	68.5	68.6	67.7
2005	66.6	67.3	67.9	68.8	68.5	68.3	68.7	69.6	70.6	70.5	70.7	71.1	69.1
2006	68.5	69.3	69.6	70.0	70.2	70.7	70.1	70.6	71.2	70.9	70.7	70.9	70.2
2007	70.5	71.2	71.8	71.9	72.2	72.2	71.7	72.3	73.3	73.8	73.8	73.8	72.4
Leisure and Hospitality													
2000	46.3	47.1	48.4	48.9	49.6	50.1	50.0	50.5	50.3	50.6	49.7	48.0	49.1
2001	47.5	48.5	49.6	52.1	52.5	53.1	52.4	52.6	51.3	50.4	50.8	49.9	50.9
2002	48.6	49.3	50.4	51.3	52.5	52.9	53.1	53.4	53.1	53.0	52.2	51.1	51.7
2003	49.7	50.0	50.6	52.2	53.3	53.1	53.0	53.3	52.6	52.9	51.9	51.4	52.0
2004	49.9	50.6	52.0	53.0	54.0	54.4	54.8	54.8	55.4	54.7	54.0	53.6	53.4
2005	52.3	53.1	54.8	55.9	56.8	57.6	56.0	55.7	55.7	54.7	54.6	53.9	55.1
2006	53.5	54.2	56.0	56.7	56.9	56.8	56.9	57.0	56.8	55.3	54.9	54.8	55.8
2007	52.1	53.3	55.4	55.4	55.9	56.3	56.6	57.4	57.2	57.0	56.4	55.8	55.7
Other Services													
2000	23.5	23.5	23.7	24.0	24.1	24.4	24.2	24.3	24.4	24.2	24.2	24.3	24.1
2001	23.7	23.8	24.2	24.1	24.3	24.9	24.6	24.6	24.3	24.1	24.1	24.0	24.2
2002	23.1	23.2	23.4	24.0	24.1	24.3	24.4	24.4	24.4	24.1	24.0	24.1	24.0
2003	23.5	23.5	23.5	23.4	23.6	23.9	23.7	23.5	23.3	23.2	23.2	23.3	23.5
2004	23.0	23.1	23.4	23.4	23.5	23.7	23.5	23.2	23.1	22.8	22.8	22.9	23.2
2005	22.9	23.0	23.1	23.1	23.1	23.3	23.5	23.3	23.3	23.2	23.2	23.2	23.2
2006	22.8	22.9	23.2	22.9	23.2	23.5	23.2	23.0	23.0	22.8	22.7	22.8	23.0
2007	22.6	22.7	22.9	22.9	23.0	23.4	23.1	23.0	22.9	22.7	22.6	22.6	22.9
Government													
2000	105.7	107.2	108.5	108.3	109.8	106.0	97.4	100.1	108.0	109.2	110.6	109.5	106.7
2001	108.0	109.6	110.4	110.0	110.7	107.7	99.6	102.8	110.8	112.7	114.0	113.4	109.1
2002	110.2	112.2	113.0	112.8	113.0	109.2	100.3	103.1	111.5	113.6	113.9	113.8	110.6
2003	108.8	111.7	111.0	110.8	110.7	107.2	99.7	101.4	109.6	111.1	111.5	111.7	108.7
2004	107.8	111.3	111.7	111.6	111.8	108.4	101.1	105.3	113.3	113.4	113.8	114.4	110.3
2005	110.9	113.2	113.6	114.2	114.6	110.4	103.5	105.7	113.3	115.2	115.9	115.7	112.2
2006	112.5	115.4	115.7	115.8	116.1	111.9	104.5	107.3	113.9	117.2	117.5	117.2	113.8
2007	114.8	117.0	117.7	117.5	117.8	114.3	106.7	107.7	114.0	115.5	115.7	114.5	114.4

Employment by Industry: Hartford-West Hartford-East Hartford, CT, NECTA, 2000–2007

(Numbers in thousands, not seasonally adjusted.)

Industry and year	January	February	March	April	May	June	July	August	September	October	November	December	Annual Average
Total Nonfarm													
2000	547.6	550.9	554.5	555.4	557.4	559.5	554.4	548.8	558.0	561.6	564.5	568.2	556.7
2001	552.4	552.5	554.1	554.9	555.8	557.7	550.2	547.5	552.4	554.2	556.4	557.5	553.8
2002	542.7	544.0	545.8	546.3	549.3	549.6	539.2	536.3	543.2	544.3	546.9	547.9	544.6
2003	534.3	533.2	533.3	536.5	539.0	538.1	529.2	526.4	533.5	539.0	540.9	541.3	535.4
2004	528.3	529.2	531.3	537.5	540.0	541.0	534.0	531.0	539.8	543.3	546.4	548.6	537.5
2005	535.0	536.2	537.3	545.0	546.6	548.8	539.9	538.0	546.8	547.7	552.4	553.2	543.9
2006	541.2	541.8	543.7	549.7	551.8	553.0	547.5	545.4	552.6	557.2	559.5	560.4	550.3
2007	547.0	548.7	550.2	554.9	558.5	561.8	553.5	551.2	558.5	562.6	565.3	565.6	556.5
Total Private													
2000	461.5	461.5	464.6	465.5	467.5	472.9	474.3	470.6	471.7	473.2	475.2	479.5	469.8
2001	465.8	462.9	464.4	465.1	466.7	471.6	469.4	467.3	465.0	464.3	465.0	466.4	466.2
2002	454.8	452.8	454.4	455.5	458.9	462.0	458.2	455.4	454.7	454.6	456.0	457.2	456.2
2003	447.3	443.2	443.8	447.5	451.1	452.7	450.6	448.6	449.9	452.2	453.7	454.2	449.6
2004	444.5	442.2	444.2	449.7	453.4	456.8	455.9	453.8	455.7	456.3	458.4	461.0	452.7
2005	450.6	449.0	450.5	456.8	459.3	464.0	460.4	459.4	460.0	459.3	462.1	464.6	458.0
2006	455.8	454.0	456.0	460.5	463.3	467.6	466.7	465.5	464.9	466.7	467.8	470.2	463.3
2007	459.6	458.6	460.2	464.4	470.6	476.2	472.7	471.3	471.0	472.2	473.7	475.6	468.8
Goods-Producing													
2000	93.7	93.3	94.5	96.0	96.5	97.7	98.6	98.4	99.1	99.2	99.2	99.3	97.1
2001	96.1	95.0	95.2	95.9	96.2	96.6	95.3	95.2	94.5	93.4	92.5	92.3	94.9
2002	89.6	88.7	89.2	90.2	90.8	91.2	90.0	89.7	89.4	88.8	88.1	87.3	89.4
2003	84.5	83.0	83.2	84.5	85.1	85.6	85.6	85.6	85.6	85.5	85.6	85.1	84.9
2004	82.4	81.8	82.6	84.5	85.4	86.6	86.9	86.8	86.9	86.6	86.7	86.3	85.3
2005	83.8	83.1	83.5	85.4	86.2	87.7	87.1	86.9	86.6	86.3	86.4	85.9	85.7
2006	84.1	83.8	84.2	86.1	86.8	88.1	88.6	88.6	88.1	88.0	87.8	87.6	86.8
2007	85.2	84.5	84.9	86.6	88.0	89.0	89.0	89.1	88.4	88.2	88.1	87.5	87.4
Natural Resources, Mining, and Construction													
2000	19.3	19.0	19.9	21.0	21.6	22.3	22.8	23.0	22.8	22.5	22.5	22.2	21.6
2001	20.1	19.8	20.2	21.5	22.4	22.9	22.8	22.9	22.4	21.8	21.2	20.7	21.6
2002	19.6	19.3	19.7	20.9	21.6	21.9	21.8	21.8	21.4	21.2	20.9	20.1	20.9
2003	18.5	17.7	17.9	19.2	20.1	20.6	21.5	21.6	21.4	21.3	21.4	20.7	20.2
2004	18.5	18.1	18.6	20.5	21.3	22.0	22.6	23.0	22.8	22.7	22.6	22.1	21.2
2005	20.1	19.5	19.8	21.3	22.0	23.0	23.1	23.2	22.8	22.4	22.4	21.7	21.8
2006	20.3	19.9	20.2	21.6	22.3	22.9	23.5	23.8	23.3	23.2	23.0	22.5	22.2
2007	20.8	20.1	20.5	22.1	23.4	23.9	24.1	24.2	23.9	23.6	23.4	22.6	22.7
Manufacturing													
2000	74.4	74.3	74.6	75.0	74.9	75.4	75.8	75.4	76.3	76.7	76.7	77.1	75.6
2001	76.0	75.2	75.0	74.4	73.8	73.7	72.5	72.3	72.1	71.6	71.3	71.6	73.3
2002	70.0	69.4	69.5	69.3	69.2	69.3	68.2	67.9	68.0	67.6	67.2	67.2	68.6
2003	66.0	65.3	65.3	65.3	65.0	65.0	64.1	64.0	64.2	64.2	64.2	64.4	64.8
2004	63.9	63.7	64.0	64.0	64.1	64.6	64.3	63.8	64.1	63.9	64.1	64.2	64.1
2005	63.7	63.6	63.7	64.1	64.2	64.7	64.0	63.7	63.8	63.9	64.0	64.2	64.0
2006	63.8	63.9	64.0	64.5	64.5	65.2	65.1	64.8	64.8	64.8	64.8	65.1	64.6
2007	64.4	64.4	64.4	64.5	64.6	65.1	64.9	64.9	64.5	64.6	64.7	64.9	64.7
Service-Providing													
2000	453.9	457.6	460.0	459.4	460.9	461.8	455.8	450.4	458.9	462.4	465.3	468.9	459.6
2001	456.3	457.5	458.9	459.0	459.6	461.1	454.9	452.3	457.9	460.8	463.9	465.2	459.0
2002	453.1	455.3	456.6	456.1	458.5	458.4	449.2	446.6	453.8	455.5	458.8	460.6	455.2
2003	449.8	450.2	450.1	452.0	453.9	452.5	443.6	440.8	447.9	453.5	455.3	456.2	450.5
2004	445.9	447.4	448.7	453.0	454.6	454.4	447.1	444.2	452.9	456.7	459.7	462.3	452.2
2005	451.2	453.1	453.8	459.6	460.4	461.1	452.8	451.1	460.2	461.4	466.0	467.3	458.2
2006	457.1	458.0	459.5	463.6	465.0	464.9	458.9	456.8	464.5	469.2	471.7	472.8	463.5
2007	461.8	464.2	465.3	468.3	470.5	472.8	464.5	462.1	470.1	474.4	477.2	478.1	469.1
Trade, Transportation, and Utilities													
2000	93.7	92.5	92.9	91.7	92.0	92.5	91.2	90.6	92.0	92.7	94.8	96.2	92.7
2001	91.8	89.9	90.3	91.1	91.5	91.9	90.6	90.0	91.1	91.7	93.4	94.3	91.5
2002	91.0	89.6	89.8	89.1	89.4	90.6	88.2	87.7	88.6	88.3	89.8	91.3	89.5
2003	88.1	86.7	87.0	86.8	87.3	87.7	86.3	86.0	87.5	88.7	90.0	90.8	87.7
2004	88.0	87.1	87.3	88.0	88.6	89.2	88.0	87.5	89.1	90.0	92.3	94.0	89.1
2005	90.2	89.1	89.3	90.1	90.2	90.8	88.4	88.2	89.8	89.7	92.0	93.6	90.1
2006	90.1	88.1	88.6	89.4	89.7	89.9	87.8	87.6	89.0	89.6	91.4	93.0	89.5
2007	89.1	87.6	88.1	88.0	89.6	90.5	88.9	88.5	89.8	90.5	92.5	94.1	89.8
Wholesale Trade													
2000	20.3	20.2	20.3	20.1	20.1	20.1	20.2	20.1	20.1	20.0	20.2	20.3	20.2
2001	20.1	20.1	20.1	20.2	20.1	20.2	20.2	20.1	19.9	20.1	19.9	20.0	20.1
2002	19.7	19.6	19.6	19.4	19.3	19.3	19.4	19.3	19.2	19.1	19.1	19.1	19.3
2003	19.5	19.4	19.6	19.5	19.5	19.6	19.4	19.4	19.4	19.3	19.2	18.9	19.4
2004	18.7	18.6	18.7	18.9	18.9	19.1	19.2	19.2	19.1	19.0	19.1	19.2	19.0
2005	19.1	19.0	19.1	19.4	19.5	19.7	19.5	19.5	19.6	19.5	19.6	19.6	19.4
2006	19.6	19.5	19.6	19.8	19.7	19.9	19.7	19.7	19.6	19.6	19.5	19.5	19.6
2007	19.5	19.5	19.6	19.6	19.7	19.8	20.0	19.9	19.8	19.9	19.8	19.8	19.7
Retail Trade													
2000	57.3	56.2	56.5	55.5	55.8	56.3	55.4	55.3	55.3	55.8	57.7	59.2	56.4
2001	55.7	54.3	54.7	55.5	56.1	56.5	56.0	56.0	55.9	56.1	58.0	58.9	56.1
2002	56.4	55.2	55.6	55.5	55.8	57.0	55.7	55.7	55.4	54.8	56.4	57.8	55.9
2003	54.6	53.4	53.5	53.6	54.0	54.3	53.9	54.0	54.2	55.0	56.2	57.4	54.5
2004	55.2	54.4	54.5	54.7	55.2	55.5	55.2	55.0	55.3	55.7	57.8	59.4	55.7
2005	56.2	55.4	55.4	55.8	55.8	56.0	55.0	55.1	55.3	55.3	57.2	58.5	55.9
2006	55.8	54.0	54.5	55.1	55.3	55.3	54.5	54.4	54.6	55.1	56.9	58.1	55.3
2007	54.9	53.5	53.9	54.0	55.4	56.0	55.2	55.3	55.2	55.7	57.5	58.8	55.5

Employment by Industry: Hartford-West Hartford-East Hartford, CT, NECTA, 2000–2007—*Continued*
(Numbers in thousands, not seasonally adjusted.)

Industry and year	January	February	March	April	May	June	July	August	September	October	November	December	Annual Average
Transportation and Utilities													
2000	16.1	16.1	16.1	16.1	16.1	16.1	15.6	15.2	16.6	16.9	16.9	16.7	16.2
2001	16.0	15.5	15.5	15.4	15.3	15.2	14.4	13.9	15.3	15.5	15.5	15.4	15.2
2002	14.9	14.8	14.6	14.2	14.3	14.3	13.1	12.7	14.0	14.4	14.4	14.4	14.2
2003	14.0	13.9	13.9	13.7	13.8	13.8	13.0	12.6	14.0	14.5	14.6	14.5	13.9
2004	14.1	14.1	14.1	14.4	14.5	14.6	13.6	13.3	14.7	15.3	15.4	15.4	14.5
2005	14.9	14.7	14.8	14.9	14.9	15.1	13.9	13.6	14.9	14.9	15.2	15.5	14.8
2006	14.7	14.6	14.5	14.5	14.7	14.7	13.6	13.5	14.8	14.9	15.0	15.4	14.6
2007	14.7	14.6	14.6	14.4	14.5	14.7	13.7	13.3	14.8	14.9	15.2	15.5	14.6
Information													
2000	12.5	12.6	12.7	12.8	12.9	13.0	13.2	13.2	13.2	13.3	13.4	13.4	13.0
2001	13.0	13.1	12.8	11.9	11.8	11.7	12.2	12.2	12.0	11.9	12.0	11.8	12.2
2002	11.4	11.3	11.3	11.4	11.4	11.5	11.4	11.3	11.2	11.2	11.2	11.2	11.3
2003	11.3	11.3	11.3	11.1	11.1	11.3	11.2	11.2	11.0	11.0	11.0	11.0	11.2
2004	11.3	11.2	11.3	11.3	11.3	11.4	11.4	11.4	11.3	11.3	11.4	11.4	11.3
2005	11.5	11.4	11.4	11.4	11.5	11.6	11.6	11.6	11.5	11.6	11.7	11.8	11.6
2006	12.0	12.0	12.0	11.9	11.9	12.1	12.1	12.0	11.8	11.9	11.9	11.9	12.0
2007	11.9	12.0	12.0	12.0	12.1	12.2	12.3	12.2	12.1	12.1	12.1	12.2	12.1
Financial Activities													
2000	69.3	69.2	69.6	69.1	69.2	70.2	70.5	70.5	69.8	69.7	69.8	70.2	69.8
2001	70.0	69.7	69.9	70.1	70.4	71.4	71.5	71.4	70.7	70.2	70.2	70.5	70.5
2002	70.2	69.7	69.7	69.3	69.6	70.3	70.6	70.5	69.9	69.5	69.7	69.7	69.9
2003	69.4	68.9	68.6	69.7	69.9	70.6	70.1	69.7	69.1	68.7	68.7	68.8	69.4
2004	68.2	67.6	67.4	67.4	67.3	68.2	68.8	68.7	68.2	67.8	68.0	68.2	68.0
2005	68.1	67.8	67.0	67.9	67.6	68.4	68.4	68.4	67.8	67.5	67.4	67.7	67.8
2006	67.8	67.6	67.5	67.1	67.2	67.9	68.2	68.0	67.4	67.3	67.4	67.6	67.6
2007	67.6	67.1	66.9	66.6	66.7	67.4	67.2	67.1	66.4	66.1	66.2	66.4	66.8
Professional and Business Services													
2000	58.7	58.7	59.0	59.9	59.6	61.0	61.2	61.1	60.6	60.7	60.7	61.1	60.2
2001	59.2	59.0	59.5	60.0	59.6	60.3	59.3	59.0	58.4	58.4	57.9	57.4	59.0
2002	56.5	56.6	57.5	57.7	57.6	57.9	57.1	57.0	56.7	56.9	57.0	56.8	57.1
2003	55.5	55.1	55.2	56.0	55.9	56.1	55.9	56.0	56.2	56.3	56.7	56.3	55.9
2004	55.7	55.4	55.8	57.1	56.9	57.5	57.5	57.7	57.8	57.8	58.0	58.1	57.1
2005	56.8	56.8	57.5	58.2	58.1	59.3	59.5	59.5	59.6	59.0	59.3	59.6	58.6
2006	58.3	58.6	58.9	60.0	59.8	60.7	60.7	60.8	60.6	60.7	60.5	60.6	60.0
2007	58.8	59.1	59.4	61.0	61.2	62.3	61.6	61.8	61.2	61.0	61.2	61.3	60.8
Education and Health Services													
2000	77.6	78.8	79.2	78.1	77.8	77.7	78.6	77.0	78.1	79.0	79.4	80.5	78.5
2001	79.3	80.0	79.9	79.5	78.4	79.8	80.4	79.9	80.4	81.4	82.4	83.1	80.4
2002	81.3	82.0	82.0	81.6	82.2	81.5	81.1	80.4	81.7	82.8	83.6	83.9	82.0
2003	82.6	82.7	82.5	82.5	82.7	81.7	81.5	80.5	82.3	83.7	84.2	84.3	82.6
2004	82.9	83.2	83.5	83.6	84.3	83.2	82.4	81.6	83.4	84.4	84.7	85.0	83.5
2005	83.6	84.1	84.2	84.6	84.8	83.9	83.3	83.0	84.4	85.9	86.1	86.3	84.5
2006	85.3	85.8	85.8	86.2	86.4	85.7	86.1	85.7	86.7	88.1	88.6	88.7	86.6
2007	88.2	89.2	89.6	89.8	89.9	89.7	89.0	88.2	90.3	91.7	91.9	92.0	90.0
Leisure and Hospitality													
2000	34.7	35.1	35.2	36.3	37.8	38.9	39.0	38.1	37.3	36.8	36.2	37.0	36.9
2001	35.1	34.9	35.3	35.0	37.2	38.0	38.1	37.8	36.5	35.6	34.8	35.1	36.1
2002	33.5	33.6	33.4	34.7	36.3	37.3	38.1	37.5	36.2	35.9	35.3	35.6	35.6
2003	35.2	34.8	35.1	36.0	38.1	38.5	38.8	38.7	37.5	37.6	36.9	37.2	37.0
2004	35.5	35.4	35.7	37.1	38.9	39.7	39.9	39.3	38.4	37.7	36.6	37.3	37.6
2005	36.2	36.3	37.1	38.4	40.2	41.2	41.2	41.1	39.8	38.7	38.6	39.0	39.0
2006	37.7	37.6	38.4	39.0	40.6	42.1	42.1	41.9	40.5	40.2	39.4	40.0	40.0
2007	38.1	38.4	38.6	39.5	42.1	43.7	43.6	43.4	41.9	41.6	40.8	41.2	41.1
Other Services													
2000	21.3	21.3	21.5	21.6	21.7	21.9	22.0	21.7	21.6	21.8	21.7	21.8	21.7
2001	21.3	21.3	21.5	21.6	21.6	21.9	22.0	21.8	21.4	21.7	21.8	21.9	21.7
2002	21.3	21.3	21.5	21.5	21.6	21.7	21.7	21.3	21.0	21.2	21.3	21.4	21.4
2003	20.7	20.7	20.9	20.9	21.0	21.2	21.2	20.9	20.7	20.7	20.6	20.7	20.9
2004	20.5	20.5	20.6	20.7	20.7	21.0	21.0	20.8	20.6	20.7	20.7	20.7	20.7
2005	20.4	20.4	20.5	20.8	20.7	21.1	20.9	20.7	20.5	20.6	20.6	20.7	20.7
2006	20.5	20.5	20.6	20.8	20.9	21.1	21.1	20.9	20.8	20.9	20.8	20.8	20.8
2007	20.7	20.7	20.7	20.9	21.0	21.4	21.1	21.0	20.9	21.0	20.9	20.9	20.9
Government													
2000	86.1	89.4	89.9	89.9	89.9	86.6	80.1	78.2	86.3	88.4	89.3	88.7	86.9
2001	86.6	89.6	89.7	89.8	89.1	86.1	80.8	80.2	87.4	89.9	91.4	91.1	87.6
2002	87.9	91.2	91.4	90.8	90.4	87.6	81.0	80.9	88.5	89.7	90.9	90.7	88.4
2003	87.0	90.0	89.5	89.0	87.9	85.4	78.6	77.8	83.6	86.8	87.2	87.1	85.8
2004	83.8	87.0	87.1	87.8	86.6	84.2	78.1	77.2	84.1	87.0	88.0	87.6	84.9
2005	84.4	87.2	86.8	88.2	87.3	84.8	79.5	78.6	86.8	88.4	90.3	88.6	85.9
2006	85.4	87.8	87.7	89.2	88.5	85.4	80.8	79.9	87.7	90.5	91.7	90.2	87.1
2007	87.4	90.1	90.0	90.5	87.9	85.6	80.8	79.9	87.5	90.4	91.6	90.0	87.6

Employment by Industry: Birmingham-Hoover, AL, 2000–2007

(Numbers in thousands, not seasonally adjusted.)

Industry and year	January	February	March	April	May	June	July	August	September	October	November	December	Annual Average
Total Nonfarm													
2000	509.4	511.3	514.8	514.8	518.3	518.3	516.3	515.4	519.6	520.2	522.0	522.7	516.9
2001	513.4	514.1	517.4	517.6	518.8	520.2	513.8	513.0	513.2	514.5	516.1	517.2	515.8
2002	506.5	507.1	510.2	509.7	510.2	509.4	507.5	506.4	508.1	508.6	511.5	511.1	508.9
2003	498.9	501.0	503.5	504.5	505.3	504.8	503.4	504.8	506.0	508.3	511.1	513.1	505.4
2004	503.5	505.4	508.2	509.9	510.6	511.6	510.2	509.8	510.3	513.2	516.5	517.7	510.6
2005	509.4	511.6	514.5	518.1	518.6	519.4	518.0	518.6	520.7	521.8	524.7	525.6	518.4
2006	518.1	520.5	523.6	525.9	527.8	532.0	527.0	528.4	530.4	530.2	533.3	534.1	527.6
2007	526.7	529.4	532.7	531.1	533.1	535.8	529.7	531.4	532.9	534.4	535.6	536.7	532.5
Total Private													
2000	434.3	436.0	438.9	438.9	440.9	444.3	443.4	444.0	444.5	444.0	446.0	446.5	441.8
2001	437.6	437.8	441.1	441.5	442.4	444.9	440.7	440.3	437.9	437.9	439.4	440.6	440.2
2002	430.5	430.8	433.6	433.0	433.1	433.5	434.2	433.5	431.7	430.9	433.3	432.9	432.6
2003	421.4	422.9	425.1	425.5	426.2	427.6	428.0	429.3	427.7	429.5	432.0	433.7	427.4
2004	424.5	426.3	429.3	430.4	431.5	433.3	433.7	433.3	431.6	434.1	436.9	438.2	431.9
2005	430.6	432.3	435.0	438.3	438.7	440.0	441.1	441.1	441.0	441.1	443.8	444.9	439.0
2006	436.7	438.9	441.9	443.7	445.4	449.7	447.9	448.8	448.1	447.2	450.1	450.8	445.8
2007	443.8	446.1	449.2	447.5	449.3	452.2	450.4	451.5	450.3	450.7	451.9	452.9	449.7
Goods-Producing													
2000	86.5	86.9	87.6	88.6	89.1	90.1	89.6	89.6	89.7	89.2	89.0	88.5	88.7
2001	87.2	86.4	87.2	86.8	86.6	86.6	84.8	84.5	83.9	83.5	82.9	82.8	85.3
2002	80.1	79.4	80.1	80.7	80.4	80.4	80.2	80.3	79.9	80.4	80.0	79.2	80.1
2003	77.7	77.7	78.4	78.4	78.3	78.2	78.2	78.7	78.5	79.9	80.1	80.0	78.7
2004	78.4	79.0	79.5	79.3	79.1	78.9	79.0	78.9	79.0	80.0	80.0	79.8	79.2
2005	78.7	78.9	79.2	80.1	79.7	79.6	80.4	80.8	80.9	81.2	81.4	80.9	80.2
2006	80.0	80.4	81.1	81.6	82.2	83.1	82.9	82.6	83.0	82.5	82.3	81.8	82.0
2007	81.4	82.2	82.7	82.0	81.9	82.7	81.9	82.2	82.7	82.8	82.6	82.3	82.3
Natural Resources and Mining													
2000	3.0	3.0	3.1	3.2	3.2	3.4	3.3	3.3	3.4	3.3	3.3	3.2	3.2
2001	3.1	3.2	3.2	3.3	3.3	3.3	3.3	3.3	3.3	3.3	3.2	3.2	3.3
2002	3.0	3.0	3.1	3.2	3.2	3.2	3.1	3.2	3.2	3.4	3.4	3.2	3.2
2003	3.1	3.0	3.0	3.0	3.0	3.0	2.9	2.8	2.8	2.8	2.8	2.8	2.9
2004	2.7	2.7	2.7	2.8	2.8	2.9	2.9	3.0	3.0	3.0	3.0	3.1	2.9
2005	3.0	3.0	3.1	3.1	3.2	3.2	3.3	3.3	3.3	3.3	3.3	3.3	3.2
2006	3.1	3.1	3.1	3.0	3.1	3.1	3.2	3.1	3.2	3.1	3.1	3.2	3.1
2007	3.1	3.1	3.1	3.0	3.0	2.9	3.0	3.0	3.1	3.0	3.0	3.0	3.0
Construction													
2000	31.0	31.2	31.6	31.9	32.2	32.9	33.0	33.0	33.1	32.6	32.6	32.5	32.3
2001	31.9	31.9	32.5	32.6	32.8	33.0	32.4	32.3	32.1	32.0	31.8	31.9	32.3
2002	30.3	30.6	31.0	31.7	31.6	31.4	31.8	31.8	31.7	32.2	32.0	31.5	31.5
2003	31.1	31.3	32.0	32.1	31.9	31.9	32.6	33.3	33.3	34.8	34.8	34.5	32.8
2004	34.0	34.5	34.9	34.3	33.8	33.3	33.3	33.1	33.2	33.9	33.6	33.1	33.8
2005	32.7	33.1	33.1	34.0	33.2	33.0	33.6	33.7	33.7	34.4	34.3	33.7	33.5
2006	33.3	33.5	34.2	34.6	34.8	35.4	34.9	35.0	35.1	34.9	34.9	34.2	34.6
2007	34.1	34.8	35.3	34.7	34.6	35.0	34.7	35.2	35.9	36.2	36.0	35.6	35.2
Manufacturing													
2000	52.5	52.7	52.9	53.5	53.7	53.8	53.3	53.3	53.2	53.3	53.1	52.8	53.2
2001	52.3	51.3	51.5	50.8	50.4	50.3	49.2	48.9	48.5	48.2	47.8	47.7	49.7
2002	46.8	45.8	46.0	45.8	45.6	45.8	45.2	45.3	45.0	44.7	44.7	44.5	45.4
2003	43.5	43.4	43.4	43.3	43.4	43.3	42.7	42.6	42.4	42.3	42.5	42.7	43.0
2004	41.7	41.8	41.9	42.2	42.5	42.7	42.8	42.8	42.8	43.1	43.4	43.6	42.6
2005	43.0	42.8	43.0	43.0	43.3	43.4	43.5	43.8	43.9	43.5	43.8	43.9	43.4
2006	43.6	43.8	43.8	44.0	44.3	44.6	44.8	44.5	44.7	44.5	44.3	44.4	44.3
2007	44.2	44.3	44.3	44.3	44.3	44.8	44.2	44.0	43.7	43.6	43.6	43.7	44.1
Service-Providing													
2000	422.9	424.4	427.2	426.2	429.2	428.2	426.7	425.8	429.9	431.0	433.0	434.2	428.2
2001	426.2	427.7	430.2	430.8	432.2	433.6	429.0	428.5	429.3	431.0	433.2	434.4	430.5
2002	426.4	427.7	430.1	429.0	429.8	429.0	427.3	426.1	428.2	428.2	431.5	431.9	428.8
2003	421.2	423.3	425.1	426.1	427.0	426.6	425.2	426.1	427.5	428.4	431.0	433.1	426.7
2004	425.1	426.4	428.7	430.6	431.5	432.7	431.2	430.9	431.3	433.2	436.5	437.9	431.3
2005	430.7	432.7	435.3	438.0	438.9	439.8	437.6	437.8	439.8	440.6	443.3	444.7	438.3
2006	438.1	440.1	442.5	444.3	445.6	448.9	444.1	445.8	447.4	447.7	451.0	452.3	445.7
2007	445.3	447.2	450.0	449.1	451.2	453.1	447.8	449.2	450.2	451.6	453.0	454.4	450.2
Trade, Transportation, and Utilities													
2000	114.1	113.3	113.6	112.4	113.3	113.4	112.9	112.9	114.0	114.4	116.4	117.4	114.0
2001	113.6	112.4	113.0	112.0	112.7	113.2	112.0	111.8	111.1	111.5	113.6	114.9	112.7
2002	110.9	110.2	110.7	109.3	109.7	109.6	109.9	109.8	108.9	109.6	112.0	113.5	110.3
2003	108.9	108.5	109.0	108.8	109.2	109.8	110.4	110.5	110.3	111.0	112.9	114.4	110.3
2004	110.9	110.8	111.5	111.3	111.6	111.6	111.2	111.1	110.7	111.3	113.4	115.3	111.7
2005	110.5	110.2	110.6	111.0	111.3	111.7	111.4	111.8	111.6	112.2	114.0	115.7	111.8
2006	112.4	112.1	112.9	112.9	113.3	114.0	113.5	114.0	113.8	115.0	117.2	118.7	114.2
2007	114.7	114.4	115.5	114.9	115.7	116.7	116.0	115.6	115.7	116.2	117.8	119.1	116.0
Wholesale Trade													
2000	31.1	31.2	31.3	30.6	30.7	30.8	30.8	30.8	31.0	30.9	31.0	31.0	30.9
2001	31.0	31.1	31.2	30.9	30.9	30.9	30.6	30.4	30.4	30.1	30.0	29.9	30.6
2002	29.9	29.8	29.8	29.6	29.5	29.5	29.5	29.6	29.3	29.2	29.3	29.3	29.5
2003	29.0	29.0	29.0	29.0	29.1	29.2	29.4	29.3	29.4	29.6	29.8	30.0	29.3
2004	29.7	29.8	29.9	29.9	30.1	30.1	30.2	30.3	30.1	30.2	30.3	30.4	30.1
2005	30.1	30.2	30.2	30.3	30.2	30.3	30.4	30.5	30.6	30.4	30.4	30.6	30.4
2006	30.6	30.8	31.0	31.1	31.2	31.5	31.5	31.6	31.5	31.5	31.6	31.7	31.3
2007	31.4	31.6	31.8	31.7	31.8	32.1	31.8	31.9	32.0	31.9	31.9	32.0	31.8

Employment by Industry: Birmingham-Hoover, AL, 2000–2007—*Continued*

(Numbers in thousands, not seasonally adjusted.)

Industry and year	January	February	March	April	May	June	July	August	September	October	November	December	Annual Average
Retail Trade													
2000	61.5	60.8	61.0	60.9	61.4	61.7	61.0	61.2	62.0	62.5	64.3	65.4	62.0
2001	61.6	60.3	60.8	60.2	60.8	61.3	60.5	60.5	60.0	60.6	62.9	64.1	61.1
2002	61.1	60.6	61.0	60.1	60.3	60.3	60.6	60.3	59.8	60.7	62.9	64.3	61.0
2003	60.4	60.0	60.5	60.5	60.7	61.1	61.5	61.9	61.8	62.1	63.8	65.1	61.6
2004	62.0	61.8	62.3	62.1	62.2	62.1	61.5	61.3	61.2	61.7	63.7	65.3	62.3
2005	61.5	61.0	61.2	61.5	61.8	62.0	61.7	62.0	61.6	62.2	64.1	65.5	62.2
2006	62.3	61.8	62.3	62.0	62.2	62.3	61.7	62.0	61.8	62.7	64.8	66.0	62.7
2007	62.8	62.2	62.9	62.5	63.2	63.6	63.1	62.6	62.6	63.0	64.6	65.8	63.2
Transportation and Utilities													
2000	21.0	20.8	20.8	20.4	20.7	20.4	20.6	20.4	20.5	20.5	20.6	20.5	20.6
2001	20.5	20.5	20.5	20.4	20.5	20.5	20.4	20.4	20.2	20.3	20.2	20.4	20.4
2002	19.4	19.3	19.4	19.1	19.4	19.3	19.3	19.4	19.3	19.2	19.3	19.4	19.3
2003	19.0	19.0	19.0	18.8	18.9	19.0	19.0	18.8	18.6	18.8	18.8	18.8	18.8
2004	18.7	18.7	18.8	18.8	18.8	18.9	19.0	19.0	18.9	18.9	18.9	19.1	18.9
2005	18.9	19.0	19.2	19.2	19.3	19.4	19.3	19.3	19.4	19.6	19.5	19.6	19.3
2006	19.5	19.5	19.6	19.8	19.9	20.2	20.3	20.4	20.5	20.8	20.8	21.0	20.2
2007	20.5	20.6	20.8	20.7	20.7	21.0	21.1	21.1	21.1	21.3	21.3	21.3	21.0
Information													
2000	14.3	14.3	14.4	14.1	14.1	14.3	14.7	14.8	14.7	15.0	15.1	15.2	14.6
2001	15.1	15.2	15.4	15.3	15.4	15.4	15.3	15.3	15.1	15.2	15.2	15.1	15.3
2002	15.1	15.0	15.2	15.0	14.9	14.9	15.0	14.8	14.6	14.8	14.7	14.5	14.9
2003	14.1	14.1	14.0	13.2	13.1	13.2	13.2	13.1	13.1	13.1	13.2	13.2	13.4
2004	13.2	13.0	13.1	13.1	13.1	13.2	13.2	13.0	12.8	12.9	13.0	12.9	13.0
2005	12.9	12.8	12.8	12.8	12.7	12.7	12.7	12.6	12.7	12.6	12.5	12.5	12.7
2006	12.2	12.1	12.2	12.0	12.0	12.0	11.9	11.8	11.7	11.7	11.7	11.7	11.9
2007	11.6	11.6	11.6	11.5	11.5	11.5	11.5	11.4	11.4	11.3	11.4	11.5	11.6	11.5
Financial Activities													
2000	40.3	40.4	40.5	40.7	40.7	40.9	41.4	41.4	41.2	40.9	40.9	41.0	40.9
2001	40.5	40.7	40.7	41.1	41.2	41.5	41.4	41.5	41.2	41.1	41.2	41.2	41.1
2002	41.0	40.8	40.7	40.8	41.0	41.0	41.0	41.0	40.8	40.9	41.0	41.2	40.9
2003	40.1	40.0	39.9	40.2	40.2	40.4	40.5	40.3	40.2	40.2	40.3	40.4	40.2
2004	40.0	40.1	40.1	40.1	40.2	40.4	40.3	40.3	40.1	40.4	40.4	40.5	40.2
2005	39.9	40.1	40.3	40.4	40.3	40.4	40.4	40.2	40.2	40.4	40.5	40.7	40.3
2006	39.9	40.0	40.0	40.0	40.0	40.1	40.1	40.0	39.8	40.0	40.2	40.4	40.0
2007	40.1	40.2	40.4	40.0	39.5	39.8	39.8	39.8	40.0	40.0	39.9	40.1	40.0
Professional and Business Services													
2000	61.6	62.1	62.6	62.9	62.7	63.6	63.3	63.8	64.0	63.5	63.5	63.2	63.1
2001	62.4	62.7	63.4	63.9	64.0	64.8	64.5	64.6	64.2	64.2	64.0	64.0	63.9
2002	62.8	63.0	63.8	63.6	63.2	63.4	62.4	62.6	62.1	61.5	61.3	61.0	62.6
2003	59.6	60.2	60.5	60.3	60.4	60.7	60.8	61.3	60.8	61.0	60.8	61.0	60.6
2004	59.7	59.9	60.1	60.8	61.2	61.8	62.7	62.8	62.6	63.4	63.5	63.6	61.8
2005	63.7	64.5	64.8	65.2	65.2	65.4	66.4	66.2	66.7	67.1	67.5	67.5	65.9
2006	66.8	67.2	67.7	67.9	67.7	69.0	68.6	69.1	69.2	68.9	69.0	69.1	68.4
2007	68.1	68.8	68.7	68.2	68.5	68.7	67.8	68.5	68.1	68.4	68.2	68.0	68.3
Education and Health Services													
2000	54.5	55.1	55.2	55.4	55.4	55.3	56.1	56.2	56.4	56.6	56.8	56.6	55.8
2001	55.6	56.5	56.6	57.0	56.8	56.6	56.5	56.3	57.0	57.5	58.1	58.0	56.9
2002	57.1	58.3	58.5	58.7	58.4	58.2	59.6	59.1	60.2	59.9	60.2	59.7	59.0
2003	59.0	59.8	60.1	60.1	59.8	59.4	59.4	59.5	59.7	60.1	60.7	60.5	59.8
2004	59.8	60.4	60.7	60.8	60.6	60.5	60.5	60.6	61.0	61.1	61.5	61.4	60.7
2005	60.9	61.4	61.7	62.0	62.1	61.9	62.2	62.1	62.1	62.4	62.5	62.5	62.0
2006	61.2	61.9	61.9	62.2	62.2	62.1	62.1	62.3	62.5	62.8	63.5	63.0	62.3
2007	62.2	62.7	62.8	63.3	63.6	63.7	64.3	64.6	64.4	64.4	64.5	64.4	63.7
Leisure and Hospitality													
2000	38.2	38.9	39.6	39.5	40.4	41.0	39.7	39.8	39.3	39.1	39.1	39.2	39.5
2001	38.2	38.9	39.8	40.2	40.6	41.5	40.7	40.8	40.0	39.4	39.2	39.3	39.9
2002	38.0	38.4	38.9	39.4	39.9	40.3	40.2	40.1	39.7	38.5	38.7	38.6	39.2
2003	37.4	38.0	38.6	39.7	40.3	40.8	40.5	40.9	40.5	39.8	39.8	40.1	39.7
2004	38.7	39.2	40.3	41.1	41.8	42.7	42.5	42.4	41.6	41.3	41.3	40.9	41.2
2005	40.5	40.9	42.1	43.2	43.8	44.5	43.8	43.8	43.5	42.0	42.2	42.0	42.7
2006	41.2	42.1	42.9	43.8	44.7	45.5	45.1	45.4	44.7	43.2	42.9	42.8	43.7
2007	42.4	42.9	43.9	43.9	44.8	45.2	45.2	45.6	44.6	44.1	44.0	44.0	44.2
Other Services													
2000	24.8	25.0	25.4	25.3	25.2	25.7	25.7	25.5	25.2	25.3	25.2	25.4	25.3
2001	25.0	25.0	25.0	25.2	25.1	25.3	25.5	25.5	25.4	25.4	25.3	25.3	25.3
2002	25.5	25.7	25.7	25.5	25.6	25.7	25.9	25.8	25.5	25.3	25.4	25.2	25.6
2003	24.6	24.6	24.6	24.8	24.9	25.1	25.0	25.0	24.6	24.4	24.2	24.1	24.6
2004	23.8	23.9	24.0	23.9	23.9	24.2	24.3	24.2	23.8	23.7	23.8	23.8	23.9
2005	23.5	23.5	23.5	23.6	23.6	23.8	23.8	23.6	23.3	23.2	23.2	23.1	23.5
2006	23.0	23.1	23.2	23.3	23.3	23.9	23.7	23.6	23.4	23.1	23.3	23.3	23.4
2007	23.3	23.3	23.6	23.7	23.8	23.9	24.0	23.8	23.5	23.4	23.4	23.4	23.6
Government													
2000	75.1	75.3	75.9	75.9	77.4	74.0	72.9	71.4	75.1	76.2	76.0	76.2	75.1
2001	75.8	76.3	76.3	76.1	76.4	75.3	73.1	72.7	75.3	76.6	76.7	76.6	75.6
2002	76.0	76.3	76.6	76.7	77.1	75.9	73.3	72.9	76.4	77.7	78.2	78.2	76.3
2003	77.5	78.1	78.4	79.0	79.1	77.2	75.4	75.5	78.3	78.8	79.1	79.4	77.9
2004	79.0	79.1	78.9	79.5	79.1	78.3	76.5	76.5	78.7	79.1	79.6	79.5	78.7
2005	78.8	79.3	79.5	79.8	79.9	79.4	76.9	77.5	79.7	80.7	80.9	80.7	79.4
2006	81.4	81.6	81.7	82.2	82.4	82.3	79.1	79.6	82.3	83.0	83.2	83.3	81.8
2007	82.9	83.3	83.5	83.6	83.8	83.6	79.3	79.9	82.6	83.7	83.7	83.8	82.8

Employment by Industry: Rochester, NY, 2000–2007

(Numbers in thousands, not seasonally adjusted.)

Industry and year	January	February	March	April	May	June	July	August	September	October	November	December	Annual Average
Total Nonfarm													
2000	517.3	521.1	524.1	531.0	535.0	538.6	529.7	529.8	535.1	534.8	536.7	537.8	530.9
2001	521.4	523.6	524.8	526.8	532.7	535.3	522.7	521.5	525.2	526.2	528.0	526.4	526.2
2002	505.4	507.0	508.5	511.8	517.9	518.4	510.3	511.0	513.2	517.0	518.7	518.9	513.2
2003	501.5	502.9	505.0	505.2	514.5	514.8	507.1	507.6	511.7	515.2	515.2	517.1	509.8
2004	499.5	502.3	504.7	507.6	516.1	517.1	508.8	507.8	512.9	520.4	520.2	520.1	511.5
2005	503.9	507.3	509.5	515.9	520.3	520.6	511.7	511.5	514.9	520.5	522.1	523.4	515.1
2006	504.0	506.3	508.6	512.1	516.3	518.1	507.7	507.7	514.1	519.8	520.7	521.3	513.1
2007	505.7	508.1	509.5	511.8	519.8	521.5	514.0	513.3	515.3	520.4	522.1	522.5	515.3
Total Private													
2000	441.1	441.5	443.7	450.3	454.6	459.9	458.3	458.5	458.2	455.9	456.2	457.6	453.0
2001	443.5	442.1	443.1	445.3	451.6	455.4	449.6	448.3	446.2	443.9	444.3	442.3	446.3
2002	426.4	424.1	424.9	429.7	435.4	436.5	436.0	436.9	434.9	434.7	435.3	434.3	432.4
2003	420.9	419.4	421.0	422.5	430.9	432.3	432.6	433.5	433.0	434.0	433.0	433.4	428.9
2004	419.5	422.0	423.7	425.3	432.6	434.6	434.3	433.6	434.5	438.3	437.4	436.0	431.0
2005	423.7	424.2	426.1	432.4	436.5	437.7	436.5	436.6	435.8	438.3	438.9	439.3	433.8
2006	425.0	424.9	426.6	430.6	434.8	438.1	435.4	435.5	435.9	439.3	439.3	439.7	433.8
2007	426.8	427.0	428.2	430.3	437.8	440.2	437.9	437.9	436.7	438.6	439.2	439.0	435.0
Goods-Producing													
2000	120.5	119.2	119.4	119.8	120.9	123.3	123.7	124.2	123.2	122.2	121.5	120.3	121.5
2001	117.4	115.9	115.5	115.9	117.1	117.8	118.1	117.9	115.8	113.4	111.6	109.9	115.5
2002	107.5	105.1	104.7	105.4	106.2	106.7	107.4	108.1	105.9	105.4	104.7	102.8	105.8
2003	99.9	98.0	98.0	97.9	99.9	100.9	102.9	103.3	102.1	101.2	100.2	98.9	100.2
2004	96.0	95.0	95.3	96.3	97.8	98.8	100.4	100.0	98.9	99.0	97.9	96.4	97.7
2005	94.1	93.3	93.3	95.1	96.5	97.8	99.2	99.6	98.6	97.9	97.3	95.6	96.5
2006	93.2	92.4	92.2	93.8	95.3	97.2	97.3	97.6	96.3	95.9	95.2	94.0	95.0
2007	91.3	90.2	90.5	91.7	93.3	94.4	94.3	94.6	93.3	92.9	92.3	91.0	92.5
Natural Resources and Mining													
2003	0.4	0.4	0.4	0.5	0.5	0.6	0.6	0.6	0.6	0.6	0.5	0.6	0.5
2004	0.6	0.6	0.6	0.6	0.6	0.6	0.6	0.6	0.6	0.6	0.6	0.6	0.6
2005	0.5	0.5	0.5	0.6	0.6	0.7	0.7	0.7	0.7	0.6	0.6	0.6	0.6
2006	0.5	0.5	0.5	0.6	0.6	0.7	0.7	0.7	0.6	0.6	0.6	0.4	0.6
2007	0.4	0.5	0.5	0.6	0.6	0.6	0.6	0.6	0.6	0.6	0.6	0.5	0.6
Construction													
2003	14.8	14.3	14.5	15.3	17.0	17.9	19.3	19.6	19.2	18.5	17.8	16.9	17.0
2004	15.2	14.8	15.1	16.5	17.9	18.9	19.9	20.3	19.8	19.6	19.0	17.9	17.9
2005	16.0	15.5	15.4	17.0	18.7	19.2	19.7	20.1	19.6	19.2	18.8	17.5	18.1
2006	16.0	15.3	15.2	16.5	18.0	19.0	19.4	19.6	19.0	18.9	18.3	17.7	17.7
2007	16.2	15.2	15.7	17.0	18.7	19.7	20.0	20.2	19.7	19.5	19.1	18.4	18.3
Manufacturing													
2000	104.0	103.2	103.1	102.2	102.1	103.2	103.0	103.0	102.9	102.2	101.7	101.4	102.7
2001	99.8	98.8	98.1	97.4	96.8	96.6	96.3	96.1	95.0	93.5	92.6	92.0	96.1
2002	91.4	89.7	89.2	88.6	88.2	87.8	87.7	87.8	86.3	86.2	86.2	85.7	87.9
2003	84.7	83.3	83.1	82.1	82.4	82.4	83.0	83.1	82.3	82.1	81.9	81.4	82.6
2004	80.2	79.6	79.6	79.2	79.3	79.3	79.9	79.1	78.5	78.8	78.3	77.9	79.1
2005	77.6	77.3	77.4	77.5	77.2	77.9	78.8	78.8	78.3	78.1	77.9	77.5	77.9
2006	76.7	76.6	76.5	76.7	76.7	77.5	77.2	77.3	76.7	76.4	76.3	75.9	76.7
2007	74.7	74.5	74.3	74.1	74.0	74.1	73.7	73.8	73.0	72.8	72.6	72.1	73.6
Service-Providing													
2000	396.8	401.9	404.7	411.2	414.1	415.3	406.0	405.6	411.9	412.6	415.2	417.5	409.4
2001	404.0	407.7	409.3	410.9	415.6	417.5	404.6	403.6	409.4	412.8	416.4	416.5	410.7
2002	397.9	401.9	403.8	406.4	411.7	411.7	402.9	402.9	407.3	411.6	414.0	416.1	407.4
2003	401.6	404.9	407.0	407.3	414.6	413.9	404.2	404.3	409.6	414.0	415.0	418.2	409.6
2004	403.5	407.3	409.4	411.3	418.3	418.3	408.4	407.8	414.0	421.4	422.3	423.7	413.8
2005	409.8	414.0	416.2	420.8	423.8	422.8	412.5	411.9	416.3	422.6	424.8	427.8	418.6
2006	410.8	413.9	416.4	418.3	421.0	420.9	410.4	410.1	417.8	423.9	425.5	427.3	418.0
2007	414.4	417.9	419.0	420.1	426.5	427.1	419.7	418.7	422.0	427.5	429.8	431.5	422.9
Trade, Transportation, and Utilities													
2000	89.1	87.5	87.6	87.9	89.0	89.8	88.8	89.5	89.0	89.4	91.1	92.9	89.3
2001	89.7	87.3	87.3	88.0	89.1	90.3	88.2	88.2	87.3	88.1	89.9	90.7	88.7
2002	86.9	84.7	84.5	84.7	86.1	87.1	86.0	86.3	85.3	85.5	86.9	87.9	86.0
2003	85.2	83.2	83.3	83.1	84.8	85.6	84.1	84.5	84.3	84.8	86.0	87.1	84.7
2004	83.6	82.5	82.6	82.2	84.9	86.0	85.4	85.3	85.4	86.2	87.3	88.6	85.0
2005	85.2	83.6	83.7	84.3	85.4	86.8	86.0	86.4	85.2	86.0	87.2	89.1	85.7
2006	85.2	82.9	83.2	83.2	84.5	86.2	85.1	85.6	84.8	85.9	87.3	88.5	85.2
2007	85.6	83.4	83.9	83.3	86.2	87.3	86.4	86.1	85.4	86.0	87.5	89.0	85.8
Wholesale Trade													
2000	18.2	18.1	18.2	18.6	18.7	19.0	19.1	19.2	18.9	19.0	19.1	19.2	18.8
2001	19.2	19.1	19.1	19.2	19.4	19.7	19.4	19.2	18.8	18.8	18.8	18.7	19.1
2002	18.6	18.5	18.3	18.6	18.7	18.8	18.8	18.7	18.4	18.1	18.1	18.1	18.5
2003	17.9	17.7	17.8	17.8	18.0	18.1	18.1	18.0	17.7	17.5	17.6	17.7	17.8
2004	17.7	17.8	17.8	17.9	18.1	18.4	18.3	18.3	17.9	18.1	18.0	18.1	18.0
2005	18.2	18.2	18.2	18.2	18.3	18.5	18.6	18.6	18.2	17.9	18.2	18.2	18.3
2006	18.2	18.1	18.2	18.2	18.3	18.7	18.8	18.8	19.1	18.6	18.4	18.5	18.5
2007	18.6	18.6	18.7	18.6	18.8	19.0	19.1	19.0	18.7	18.7	18.7	18.8	18.8
Retail Trade													
2000	60.2	58.7	58.7	58.5	59.5	60.0	59.5	60.1	59.2	59.5	61.1	62.0	59.8
2001	60.2	58.1	58.0	58.6	59.2	60.1	58.8	59.1	58.1	58.6	60.5	61.5	59.2
2002	58.9	56.8	56.9	56.8	58.0	58.8	58.4	58.8	57.6	57.9	59.4	60.4	58.2
2003	57.8	56.2	56.2	55.9	57.4	58.2	57.4	57.8	57.2	57.7	58.8	59.7	57.5
2004	56.4	55.2	55.3	54.4	56.7	57.4	57.3	57.3	57.3	57.8	59.0	60.2	57.0
2005	57.0	55.4	55.4	55.9	56.8	57.9	57.6	57.9	56.5	57.4	58.3	60.0	57.2
2006	56.6	54.4	54.6	54.5	55.6	56.7	56.1	56.3	55.5	56.8	58.2	59.2	56.2
2007	56.6	54.5	54.9	54.5	56.9	57.8	57.4	57.2	56.2	56.8	58.3	59.7	56.7

Employment by Industry: Rochester, NY, 2000–2007—*Continued*

(Numbers in thousands, not seasonally adjusted.)

Industry and year	January	February	March	April	May	June	July	August	September	October	November	December	Annual Average
Transportation and Utilities													
2000	10.7	10.7	10.7	10.8	10.8	10.8	10.2	10.2	10.9	10.9	10.9	11.7	10.8
2001	10.3	10.1	10.2	10.2	10.5	10.5	10.0	9.9	10.4	10.7	10.6	10.5	10.3
2002	9.4	9.4	9.3	9.3	9.4	9.5	8.8	8.8	9.3	9.5	9.4	9.4	9.3
2003	9.5	9.3	9.3	9.4	9.4	9.3	8.6	8.7	9.4	9.6	9.6	9.7	9.3
2004	9.5	9.5	9.5	9.9	10.1	10.2	9.8	9.7	10.2	10.3	10.3	10.3	9.9
2005	10.0	10.0	10.1	10.2	10.3	10.4	9.8	9.9	10.5	10.7	10.7	10.9	10.3
2006	10.4	10.4	10.4	10.5	10.6	10.8	10.2	10.2	10.7	10.7	10.7	10.8	10.5
2007	10.4	10.3	10.3	10.2	10.5	10.5	9.9	9.9	10.5	10.5	10.5	10.5	10.3
Information													
2000	11.3	11.4	11.4	11.5	11.6	11.7	11.8	11.9	11.9	12.0	12.1	12.3	11.7
2001	12.9	13.0	13.1	12.9	13.1	13.2	13.1	13.0	12.9	13.2	13.3	13.4	13.1
2002	13.5	13.1	13.3	13.0	13.1	12.9	12.7	12.6	12.5	12.4	12.4	12.5	12.8
2003	12.3	12.3	12.2	12.2	12.5	12.4	12.3	12.3	12.2	12.3	12.3	12.3	12.3
2004	12.4	12.3	12.3	12.2	12.2	12.2	12.1	12.0	12.0	12.0	12.0	11.9	12.1
2005	11.8	11.6	11.6	11.6	11.7	11.7	11.6	11.6	11.6	11.8	11.7	11.8	11.7
2006	11.7	11.6	11.5	11.1	11.1	11.1	10.9	10.7	10.5	10.6	10.6	10.5	11.0
2007	10.6	10.5	10.5	10.6	10.7	10.7	10.7	10.7	10.6	10.6	10.6	10.6	10.6
Financial Activities													
2000	21.3	21.4	21.3	21.7	21.8	22.3	22.0	21.8	21.2	21.4	21.4	21.4	21.6
2001	21.3	21.5	21.4	21.4	21.6	22.2	22.0	22.0	21.4	21.3	21.4	21.3	21.6
2002	20.7	20.7	20.6	20.6	20.9	21.3	21.7	21.8	21.1	21.2	21.2	21.2	21.1
2003	21.0	20.9	20.9	21.1	21.7	22.0	22.3	22.3	21.8	21.9	21.9	22.2	21.6
2004	21.5	21.5	21.6	21.7	21.8	22.1	22.6	22.7	22.2	21.9	21.9	22.1	22.0
2005	21.7	21.5	21.6	21.5	21.8	22.0	22.2	22.2	21.7	21.7	21.9	22.0	21.8
2006	21.7	21.5	21.5	21.5	21.7	22.1	22.5	22.5	21.6	21.8	21.6	21.6	21.8
2007	21.6	21.5	21.5	21.5	21.6	22.1	22.3	22.3	21.5	21.5	21.5	21.6	21.7
Professional and Business Services													
2000	58.5	58.7	59.1	59.8	60.3	62.1	63.0	62.8	62.1	61.5	61.1	60.7	60.8
2001	60.1	59.7	60.4	59.0	59.7	61.0	60.7	60.5	59.7	58.8	58.3	57.6	59.6
2002	54.5	54.5	54.6	56.5	57.4	58.4	58.2	58.1	58.0	57.6	57.9	57.6	56.9
2003	55.2	55.2	55.5	56.7	57.5	58.4	57.7	58.0	57.7	58.3	57.7	57.8	57.1
2004	54.9	55.6	55.7	56.4	57.0	58.6	58.0	58.0	58.1	59.1	58.8	58.2	57.4
2005	56.3	56.5	57.2	59.3	59.6	60.2	60.7	60.2	59.9	60.3	60.6	60.7	59.3
2006	58.3	57.7	58.4	59.7	59.5	60.9	60.6	60.4	61.2	61.4	60.8	61.3	60.0
2007	59.6	60.0	59.9	60.2	60.7	61.9	61.5	61.7	60.8	60.9	60.4	60.2	60.7
Education and Health Services													
2000	87.0	89.3	90.4	93.2	92.0	89.4	88.7	88.0	92.8	92.1	92.6	93.2	90.7
2001	90.5	92.6	92.8	94.1	94.0	91.3	88.1	87.6	92.5	93.5	94.4	94.1	92.1
2002	90.9	93.2	93.9	93.8	93.2	90.5	89.9	89.9	94.3	96.0	96.4	96.6	93.2
2003	93.5	96.1	96.5	96.2	95.4	92.8	92.0	92.0	96.1	97.9	98.2	98.4	95.4
2004	96.9	100.5	101.1	100.0	99.3	95.7	94.1	93.9	98.6	101.5	101.9	101.3	98.7
2005	99.1	102.0	102.4	102.5	100.9	96.9	95.2	95.0	100.0	102.7	103.4	103.2	100.3
2006	100.5	103.8	103.9	104.0	103.1	99.1	96.9	96.9	102.3	105.1	105.8	105.6	102.3
2007	102.3	105.4	105.6	105.9	104.5	100.4	99.3	99.5	105.2	107.7	108.5	108.0	104.4
Leisure and Hospitality													
2000	36.2	36.8	37.2	38.9	41.3	43.3	42.7	42.6	40.7	39.8	38.9	39.2	39.8
2001	34.8	35.1	35.5	36.8	39.7	41.9	41.8	41.5	39.4	38.2	37.7	37.7	38.3
2002	34.8	35.1	35.6	37.6	40.3	41.3	41.7	41.5	39.4	38.1	37.2	37.1	38.3
2003	35.4	35.3	36.0	36.6	40.2	41.3	42.3	42.2	40.1	38.8	37.8	37.7	38.6
2004	35.7	35.9	36.3	37.5	40.4	42.0	42.7	42.8	40.6	39.6	38.7	38.5	39.2
2005	36.6	36.7	37.1	38.6	41.1	42.8	42.4	42.6	40.0	38.9	37.8	37.8	39.4
2006	35.5	36.0	36.8	38.2	40.4	42.5	43.0	43.0	40.5	39.7	38.9	38.8	39.4
2007	36.6	36.8	37.1	37.9	41.3	43.9	44.1	43.7	40.9	39.9	39.2	39.5	40.1
Other Services													
2000	17.2	17.2	17.3	17.5	17.7	18.0	17.6	17.7	17.3	17.5	17.5	17.6	17.5
2001	16.8	17.0	17.1	17.2	17.3	17.7	17.6	17.6	17.2	17.4	17.7	17.6	17.4
2002	17.6	17.7	17.7	18.1	18.2	18.3	18.4	18.6	18.4	18.5	18.6	18.6	18.2
2003	18.4	18.4	18.6	18.7	18.9	18.9	19.0	18.9	18.7	18.8	18.9	19.0	18.7
2004	18.5	18.7	18.8	19.0	19.2	19.2	19.0	18.9	18.7	19.0	18.9	19.0	18.9
2005	18.9	19.0	19.2	19.5	19.5	19.5	19.2	19.0	18.8	19.0	19.0	19.1	19.1
2006	18.9	19.0	19.1	19.1	19.2	19.0	19.1	18.8	18.7	18.9	19.1	19.4	19.0
2007	19.2	19.2	19.2	19.2	19.5	19.5	19.3	19.3	19.0	19.1	19.2	19.1	19.2
Government													
2000	76.2	79.6	80.4	80.7	80.4	78.7	71.4	71.3	76.9	78.9	80.5	80.2	77.9
2001	77.9	81.5	81.7	81.5	81.1	79.9	73.1	73.2	79.0	82.3	83.7	84.1	79.9
2002	79.0	82.9	83.6	82.1	82.5	81.9	74.3	74.1	78.3	82.3	83.4	84.6	80.8
2003	80.6	83.5	84.0	82.7	83.6	82.5	74.5	74.1	78.7	81.2	82.2	83.7	80.9
2004	80.0	80.3	81.0	82.3	83.5	82.5	74.5	74.2	78.4	82.1	82.8	84.1	80.5
2005	80.2	83.1	83.4	83.5	83.8	82.9	75.2	74.9	79.1	82.2	83.2	84.1	81.3
2006	79.0	81.4	82.0	81.5	81.5	80.0	72.3	72.2	78.2	80.5	81.4	81.6	79.3
2007	78.9	81.1	81.3	81.5	82.0	81.3	76.1	75.4	78.6	81.8	82.9	83.5	80.4

Employment by Industry: Salt Lake City, UT, 2000–2007

(Numbers in thousands, not seasonally adjusted.)

Industry and year	January	February	March	April	May	June	July	August	September	October	November	December	Annual Average
Total Nonfarm													
2000	552.5	555.9	559.6	561.2	563.0	565.7	560.7	564.7	569.5	571.6	577.1	585.1	565.6
2001	573.9	574.6	576.8	574.6	574.1	576.1	568.4	570.5	572.6	570.5	572.1	576.6	573.4
2002	567.5	572.3	564.2	562.7	560.1	561.9	557.2	558.7	560.6	560.8	565.0	568.0	563.3
2003	553.8	553.5	553.4	553.5	553.4	554.9	552.2	555.5	556.4	558.2	562.0	567.8	556.2
2004	554.2	556.1	558.7	560.9	560.0	564.4	563.3	565.9	567.6	570.3	575.9	583.1	565.0
2005	572.1	574.9	576.4	581.5	580.8	585.2	586.5	591.3	594.3	595.2	601.5	608.9	587.4
2006	597.5	601.4	605.6	608.2	608.4	614.8	612.3	617.9	620.2	620.6	628.5	636.2	614.3
2007	625.8	628.6	632.4	634.8	635.5	640.8	636.5	642.0	641.4	640.7	648.5	655.7	638.6
Total Private													
2000	470.8	472.3	475.9	476.3	476.3	481.8	481.9	486.3	485.3	486.8	492.0	500.1	482.2
2001	489.1	487.9	490.1	487.4	486.3	489.1	487.4	489.6	485.8	483.1	484.2	487.9	487.3
2002	479.5	485.8	475.7	474.0	472.0	473.2	471.8	474.6	472.0	472.1	475.9	478.7	475.4
2003	464.9	464.2	464.4	464.0	464.6	466.1	467.0	470.9	467.9	469.3	473.2	478.9	468.0
2004	465.4	467.1	469.7	470.8	470.6	474.8	476.8	479.1	477.5	480.0	485.6	492.3	475.8
2005	481.6	484.1	485.9	490.4	490.2	494.5	498.4	502.9	503.1	503.7	509.7	516.8	496.8
2006	506.1	509.4	513.7	516.1	516.8	522.5	523.1	528.6	528.1	528.1	535.9	543.2	522.6
2007	533.6	536.2	540.0	541.9	542.8	547.4	547.1	551.9	548.7	547.6	555.2	562.1	546.2
Goods-Producing													
2000	93.7	93.5	93.9	95.3	96.5	98.2	97.3	98.4	97.8	97.4	96.7	96.1	96.2
2001	93.2	92.5	93.2	92.6	93.9	95.4	95.5	96.1	95.4	94.8	93.2	91.0	93.9
2002	86.8	84.8	85.1	85.6	86.8	87.9	88.0	88.3	87.9	87.4	86.6	85.4	86.7
2003	82.3	81.9	82.0	83.1	84.9	85.5	85.8	86.4	86.1	86.3	85.6	84.8	84.6
2004	81.8	81.8	83.0	84.9	86.9	88.0	89.1	89.5	89.4	89.1	88.5	88.5	86.7
2005	86.2	86.5	87.1	89.6	91.2	93.0	94.3	95.4	95.5	94.7	94.9	94.7	91.9
2006	92.8	93.9	95.4	97.0	99.7	102.0	102.4	103.7	104.1	104.1	104.2	103.7	100.3
2007	101.5	101.8	103.4	104.7	107.0	109.1	109.4	110.4	109.3	108.3	108.3	107.6	106.7
Natural Resources, Mining, and Construction													
2000	37.3	37.2	37.5	38.8	39.8	41.2	40.7	41.4	41.0	40.5	39.7	39.0	39.5
2001	36.4	35.9	36.5	36.7	38.1	39.6	39.7	40.5	40.0	39.7	38.8	37.0	38.2
2002	33.7	32.1	32.5	33.4	34.5	35.7	36.1	36.3	36.1	35.8	35.1	34.1	34.6
2003	31.8	31.5	31.7	32.6	34.0	34.5	34.9	35.4	35.1	35.1	34.3	33.4	33.7
2004	31.0	31.1	32.0	33.5	34.8	35.7	36.6	37.0	37.0	36.7	36.0	35.9	34.8
2005	34.0	34.1	35.1	37.0	38.1	39.2	40.4	41.2	41.3	41.0	41.0	40.6	38.6
2006	39.0	39.7	41.0	42.4	44.5	46.2	46.6	47.5	47.8	47.8	47.5	47.0	44.8
2007	45.2	45.2	46.4	47.5	49.3	50.8	50.9	51.5	50.7	49.8	49.5	48.8	48.8
Manufacturing													
2000	56.4	56.3	56.4	56.5	56.7	57.0	56.6	57.0	56.8	56.9	57.0	57.1	56.7
2001	56.8	56.6	56.7	55.9	55.8	55.8	55.8	55.6	55.4	55.1	54.4	54.0	55.7
2002	53.1	52.7	52.6	52.2	52.3	52.2	51.9	52.0	51.8	51.6	51.5	51.3	52.1
2003	50.5	50.4	50.3	50.5	50.9	51.0	50.9	51.0	51.0	51.2	51.3	51.4	50.9
2004	50.8	50.7	51.0	51.4	52.1	52.3	52.5	52.5	52.4	52.4	52.5	52.6	51.9
2005	52.2	52.4	52.0	52.6	53.1	53.8	53.9	54.2	54.2	53.7	53.9	54.1	53.3
2006	53.8	54.2	54.4	54.6	55.2	55.8	55.8	56.2	56.3	56.3	56.7	56.7	55.5
2007	56.3	56.6	57.0	57.2	57.7	58.3	58.5	58.9	58.6	58.5	58.8	58.8	57.9
Service-Providing													
2000	458.8	462.4	465.7	465.9	466.5	467.5	463.4	466.3	471.7	474.2	480.4	489.0	469.3
2001	480.7	482.1	483.6	482.0	480.2	480.7	472.9	474.4	477.2	475.7	478.9	485.6	479.5
2002	480.7	487.5	479.1	477.1	473.3	474.0	469.2	470.4	472.7	473.4	478.4	482.6	476.5
2003	471.5	471.6	471.4	470.4	468.5	469.4	466.4	469.1	470.3	471.9	476.4	483.0	471.7
2004	472.4	474.3	475.7	476.0	473.1	476.4	474.2	476.4	478.2	481.2	487.4	494.6	478.3
2005	485.9	488.4	489.3	491.9	489.6	492.2	492.2	495.9	498.8	500.5	506.6	514.2	495.5
2006	504.7	507.5	510.2	511.2	508.7	512.8	509.9	514.2	516.1	516.5	524.3	532.5	514.1
2007	524.3	526.8	529.0	530.1	528.5	531.7	527.1	531.6	532.1	532.4	540.2	548.1	531.8
Trade, Transportation, and Utilities													
2000	120.7	119.6	120.2	120.0	120.5	121.8	122.3	122.9	122.9	124.3	127.0	129.3	122.6
2001	124.9	123.8	123.7	123.5	123.0	123.0	122.9	122.9	122.2	122.4	124.2	125.6	123.5
2002	120.9	120.1	118.6	119.0	119.5	119.6	119.7	119.9	119.3	120.4	122.6	123.7	120.3
2003	116.9	115.8	115.8	115.4	116.0	116.1	116.4	117.2	116.5	117.4	119.8	121.6	117.1
2004	117.0	116.2	116.3	116.5	117.0	118.1	118.4	118.6	118.2	119.4	122.1	123.8	118.5
2005	119.8	119.5	119.9	120.7	121.2	121.4	122.4	123.3	123.0	124.2	126.6	128.5	122.5
2006	124.2	123.8	124.1	124.0	124.4	125.5	125.7	127.1	127.2	127.5	131.1	133.7	126.5
2007	129.9	129.4	130.2	129.7	130.4	131.0	131.4	132.4	132.1	132.5	136.2	138.7	132.0
Wholesale Trade													
2000	27.5	27.6	27.8	27.8	28.0	28.2	28.5	28.5	28.5	28.5	28.6	28.9	28.2
2001	28.7	29.0	29.1	29.0	29.1	29.2	29.2	29.2	28.9	28.8	28.7	28.6	29.0
2002	28.2	28.2	28.1	28.3	28.6	28.5	28.6	28.7	28.6	28.6	28.6	28.5	28.5
2003	27.1	27.0	27.1	27.2	27.4	27.3	27.3	27.4	27.3	27.2	27.2	27.3	27.2
2004	27.0	27.1	27.3	27.5	27.7	28.0	27.9	27.9	27.9	28.1	28.3	28.3	27.8
2005	28.1	28.2	28.4	28.5	28.7	28.6	28.7	28.7	28.6	28.7	28.8	28.8	28.6
2006	28.5	28.8	28.9	29.0	29.3	29.6	29.6	29.7	29.7	29.8	29.9	30.2	29.4
2007	30.0	30.1	30.2	30.2	30.6	30.8	30.8	31.1	31.0	31.0	31.2	31.5	30.7
Retail Trade													
2000	64.0	62.8	62.9	62.7	63.3	64.0	63.9	64.2	64.1	65.3	67.7	69.3	64.5
2001	65.7	64.5	64.3	64.4	64.4	64.4	64.3	64.3	63.9	64.2	66.4	67.8	64.9
2002	64.3	63.3	62.8	62.9	63.3	63.5	63.3	63.5	63.2	63.7	66.0	67.3	63.9
2003	62.9	62.1	62.1	62.0	62.2	62.4	62.5	63.0	62.6	63.5	65.9	67.4	63.2
2004	63.2	62.4	62.3	62.6	62.9	63.4	63.9	64.1	63.8	64.7	66.9	68.3	64.0
2005	64.5	63.5	63.5	63.7	64.0	64.3	65.1	66.0	65.7	66.6	68.6	70.1	65.5
2006	66.4	65.7	65.9	65.8	65.9	66.5	66.7	67.5	67.5	67.8	70.9	72.4	67.4
2007	69.3	68.6	69.2	69.0	69.4	69.7	70.1	70.7	70.4	70.8	74.0	75.6	70.6

Employment by Industry: Salt Lake City, UT, 2000–2007—*Continued*

(Numbers in thousands, not seasonally adjusted.)

Industry and year	January	February	March	April	May	June	July	August	September	October	November	December	Annual Average
Transportation and Utilities													
2000	29.2	29.2	29.5	29.5	29.2	29.6	29.9	30.2	30.3	30.5	30.7	31.1	29.9
2001	30.5	30.3	30.3	30.1	29.5	29.4	29.4	29.4	29.4	29.4	29.1	29.2	29.7
2002	28.4	28.6	27.7	27.8	27.6	27.6	27.8	27.7	27.5	28.1	28.0	27.9	27.9
2003	26.9	26.7	26.6	26.2	26.4	26.4	26.6	26.8	26.6	26.7	26.7	26.9	26.6
2004	26.8	26.7	26.7	26.4	26.4	26.7	26.6	26.6	26.5	26.6	26.9	27.2	26.7
2005	27.2	27.8	28.0	28.5	28.5	28.5	28.6	28.6	28.7	28.9	29.2	29.6	28.5
2006	29.3	29.3	29.3	29.2	29.2	29.4	29.4	29.9	30.0	29.9	30.3	31.1	29.7
2007	30.6	30.7	30.8	30.5	30.4	30.5	30.5	30.6	30.7	30.7	31.0	31.6	30.7
Information													
2000	20.0	20.0	20.1	19.9	20.6	21.2	21.2	21.6	21.7	21.7	22.2	22.0	21.0
2001	21.3	20.7	20.7	20.9	21.3	21.5	21.1	21.0	20.8	20.4	20.8	20.5	20.9
2002	20.0	19.9	19.2	18.9	19.2	19.0	19.0	18.6	18.5	18.6	18.7	18.5	19.0
2003	17.9	17.7	17.6	17.4	18.0	18.1	17.9	18.2	18.0	18.3	18.1	18.4	18.0
2004	17.4	17.9	17.9	17.9	17.8	18.1	17.5	17.5	17.6	17.8	18.3	18.1	17.8
2005	17.9	18.3	18.7	18.2	18.2	18.1	18.6	19.0	18.8	18.4	18.7	18.6	18.5
2006	18.2	18.4	18.5	18.8	19.6	19.8	19.1	19.3	19.3	19.2	19.6	19.6	19.1
2007	18.7	18.6	18.8	18.9	19.1	19.0	19.0	19.3	19.0	18.8	19.1	19.1	19.0
Financial Activities													
2000	42.4	42.2	42.4	42.3	42.0	42.1	42.4	42.5	42.5	42.8	43.2	44.0	42.6
2001	44.9	45.0	45.2	44.7	44.6	45.0	45.2	45.3	45.2	44.9	45.2	45.6	45.1
2002	46.1	46.0	45.5	45.3	45.5	45.6	45.1	45.3	44.9	45.3	45.1	45.6	45.4
2003	45.7	46.1	45.6	45.9	45.9	45.4	45.5	45.6	45.1	44.9	44.8	45.2	45.5
2004	44.5	44.7	44.7	44.8	44.6	44.4	44.6	44.5	44.5	44.7	45.2	45.8	44.8
2005	45.1	45.5	44.9	45.9	45.7	46.0	46.5	46.6	46.7	46.9	47.3	48.1	46.3
2006	47.6	48.2	48.3	48.5	48.5	48.8	49.2	49.4	49.3	49.9	50.3	51.0	49.1
2007	51.0	51.7	51.8	51.9	51.9	52.0	51.9	51.8	51.4	51.9	52.1	52.7	51.8
Professional and Business Services													
2000	84.4	85.7	87.3	88.2	88.7	90.0	90.3	91.0	91.1	91.7	91.7	93.0	89.4
2001	89.6	89.4	89.8	89.6	90.0	90.1	89.1	89.8	88.0	87.0	85.6	85.4	88.6
2002	82.8	85.7	82.6	82.8	83.4	83.3	82.9	84.1	83.5	82.9	83.3	82.6	83.3
2003	79.9	79.9	80.7	81.7	82.5	82.7	83.2	84.1	83.3	83.8	84.0	84.7	82.5
2004	81.8	82.5	83.1	83.9	84.5	85.3	85.7	86.7	85.8	87.5	87.7	88.7	85.3
2005	86.0	86.4	87.0	89.3	90.2	91.3	91.9	93.2	93.5	94.2	95.0	95.6	91.1
2006	92.8	93.6	94.8	96.4	97.2	97.9	98.6	99.0	98.6	98.1	99.0	99.1	97.1
2007	96.5	97.3	97.8	99.7	101.3	101.7	101.0	101.9	101.1	100.8	101.7	101.9	100.2
Education and Health Services													
2000	43.0	43.6	43.8	43.8	44.1	44.1	43.5	44.1	44.4	44.3	44.7	45.5	44.1
2001	46.3	46.9	47.0	47.3	47.5	47.7	46.9	47.1	47.8	48.0	48.7	49.4	47.6
2002	48.0	48.5	48.4	48.8	48.8	48.8	48.4	49.2	50.1	50.3	50.5	50.9	49.2
2003	50.4	50.7	51.0	50.7	50.8	50.9	50.7	51.1	51.7	52.1	52.3	52.5	51.2
2004	51.7	52.3	52.7	52.7	52.8	52.9	52.6	52.8	53.5	53.9	54.3	54.4	53.1
2005	53.9	54.5	54.5	55.0	55.0	55.1	54.5	54.7	55.5	55.8	56.3	56.4	55.1
2006	55.4	55.9	56.3	56.2	56.5	56.7	55.7	56.7	57.3	58.0	58.3	58.2	56.8
2007	57.8	58.4	58.8	59.2	59.3	59.2	58.8	59.9	60.8	61.3	61.5	61.5	59.7
Leisure and Hospitality													
2000	49.4	50.4	50.9	49.4	46.3	46.8	47.1	47.9	47.2	47.1	48.9	52.5	48.7
2001	51.9	52.5	53.3	51.5	48.7	48.9	48.8	49.4	48.9	48.1	49.0	52.9	50.3
2002	56.6	61.5	57.7	55.0	50.1	50.3	49.7	50.2	49.2	48.8	50.4	53.6	52.8
2003	53.8	54.1	53.7	51.7	48.5	49.3	49.2	49.9	49.2	48.6	50.6	53.7	51.0
2004	53.5	53.9	54.0	51.9	48.7	49.7	50.0	50.6	50.1	49.5	51.3	54.7	51.5
2005	54.5	55.1	55.3	53.1	50.2	51.0	51.0	51.6	51.2	51.0	52.4	56.2	52.7
2006	56.7	57.1	57.5	56.3	51.8	52.4	52.9	53.9	52.9	52.3	54.4	58.6	54.7
2007	59.2	59.9	59.9	58.5	54.2	55.6	55.4	55.8	55.1	54.5	56.7	60.8	57.1
Other Services													
2000	17.2	17.3	17.3	17.4	17.6	17.6	17.8	17.9	17.7	17.5	17.6	17.7	17.6
2001	17.0	17.1	17.2	17.3	17.3	17.5	17.9	18.0	17.5	17.5	17.5	17.5	17.4
2002	18.3	19.3	18.6	18.6	18.7	18.7	19.0	19.0	18.6	18.4	18.7	18.4	18.7
2003	18.0	18.0	18.0	18.1	18.0	18.1	18.3	18.4	18.0	17.9	18.0	18.0	18.1
2004	17.7	17.8	18.0	18.2	18.3	18.3	18.9	18.9	18.4	18.1	18.2	18.3	18.3
2005	18.2	18.3	18.5	18.6	18.5	18.6	19.2	19.1	18.9	18.5	18.5	18.7	18.6
2006	18.4	18.5	18.8	18.9	19.1	19.4	19.5	19.5	19.4	19.0	19.0	19.3	19.1
2007	19.0	19.1	19.3	19.3	19.6	19.8	20.2	20.4	19.9	19.5	19.6	19.8	19.6
Government													
2000	81.7	83.6	83.7	84.9	86.7	83.9	78.8	78.4	84.2	84.8	85.1	85.0	83.4
2001	84.8	86.7	86.7	87.2	87.8	87.0	81.0	80.9	86.8	87.4	87.9	88.7	86.1
2002	88.0	86.5	88.5	88.7	88.1	88.7	85.4	84.1	88.6	88.7	89.1	89.3	87.8
2003	88.9	89.3	89.0	89.5	88.8	88.8	85.2	84.6	88.5	88.9	88.8	88.9	88.3
2004	88.8	89.0	89.0	90.1	89.4	89.6	86.5	86.8	90.1	90.3	90.3	90.8	89.2
2005	90.5	90.8	90.5	91.1	90.6	90.7	88.1	88.4	91.2	91.5	91.8	92.1	90.6
2006	91.4	92.0	91.9	92.1	91.6	92.3	89.2	89.3	92.1	92.5	92.6	93.0	91.7
2007	92.2	92.4	92.4	92.9	92.7	93.4	89.4	90.1	92.7	93.1	93.3	93.6	92.4

Employment by Industry: Bridgeport-Stamford-Norwalk, CT, NECTA, 2000–2007

(Numbers in thousands, not seasonally adjusted.)

Industry and year	January	February	March	April	May	June	July	August	September	October	November	December	Annual Average
Total Nonfarm													
2000	416.3	416.6	420.0	423.9	427.4	433.3	427.2	424.6	430.2	430.1	431.8	434.9	426.4
2001	420.2	418.8	420.2	422.4	426.0	429.4	420.8	417.4	420.3	422.5	424.4	423.8	422.2
2002	410.6	409.5	412.5	416.8	418.9	421.5	410.7	408.9	412.0	414.7	417.8	418.9	414.4
2003	406.0	404.8	407.1	409.8	413.0	415.5	411.6	406.7	409.7	412.5	413.6	414.1	410.4
2004	402.5	402.1	405.8	407.2	411.4	415.2	412.1	408.2	410.5	412.9	415.1	416.3	409.9
2005	402.0	402.9	404.7	411.0	413.8	417.2	414.2	410.1	411.8	413.1	415.8	418.4	411.3
2006	408.4	408.9	408.8	415.6	418.9	422.1	417.8	414.3	416.0	418.1	421.4	425.2	416.3
2007	412.2	412.1	413.8	417.9	423.1	427.0	425.6	421.5	421.7	422.9	426.1	428.9	421.1
Total Private													
2000	370.6	370.0	373.3	377.5	380.6	386.5	385.5	383.2	383.4	383.7	384.8	387.7	380.6
2001	373.6	371.8	373.4	375.3	378.6	382.2	378.9	376.3	372.0	374.2	375.3	374.8	375.5
2002	362.9	361.4	364.2	368.0	369.9	372.4	369.8	367.5	365.1	366.3	368.6	369.9	367.2
2003	357.9	356.5	358.6	361.8	364.7	367.1	366.5	364.1	363.5	365.4	365.9	366.6	363.2
2004	355.0	354.1	357.3	359.7	363.8	367.7	367.6	365.2	363.8	365.1	366.9	368.8	362.9
2005	355.4	355.9	357.6	363.0	365.5	368.8	368.7	366.1	364.9	365.7	368.3	370.6	364.2
2006	361.1	361.1	360.8	367.8	370.9	375.2	373.5	371.4	369.5	370.9	373.7	377.7	369.5
2007	365.3	364.5	366.2	370.4	374.6	379.7	379.4	376.8	374.9	375.6	378.4	381.1	373.9
Goods-Producing													
2000	64.1	63.8	64.6	65.0	65.6	66.5	65.9	65.9	66.1	65.4	65.3	65.1	65.3
2001	63.1	62.7	63.0	64.1	64.7	64.9	63.3	63.3	63.0	62.1	61.7	61.4	63.1
2002	59.6	59.2	59.5	60.4	60.5	60.9	59.9	60.0	59.7	59.2	58.9	58.3	59.7
2003	56.7	56.2	56.3	56.9	57.5	57.8	56.8	57.2	56.9	57.0	56.8	56.4	56.9
2004	54.8	54.4	55.0	56.2	56.6	57.2	56.8	56.8	56.9	57.2	56.9	56.8	56.3
2005	55.2	54.9	54.9	56.3	56.7	57.2	57.1	56.7	56.3	56.4	56.4	55.9	56.2
2006	54.9	55.1	52.3	56.4	56.6	57.2	57.2	57.1	57.1	56.8	56.7	56.5	56.1
2007	55.0	54.7	55.1	55.8	56.3	57.3	57.3	57.2	57.0	56.8	56.9	56.6	56.3
Natural Resources, Mining, and Construction													
2000	13.1	12.8	13.6	14.2	14.7	15.1	15.3	15.3	15.2	15.1	15.0	14.6	14.5
2001	13.1	12.8	13.2	14.7	15.3	15.6	15.7	15.7	15.3	15.0	14.8	14.6	14.7
2002	13.6	13.4	13.8	14.5	14.8	15.2	15.2	15.2	15.0	14.7	14.6	14.0	14.5
2003	13.0	12.7	12.9	13.9	14.6	14.7	15.0	15.1	14.9	14.9	14.7	14.2	14.2
2004	12.9	12.5	12.9	14.2	14.7	15.0	15.3	15.4	15.2	15.3	15.1	14.8	14.4
2005	13.6	13.4	13.5	15.1	15.5	15.7	16.0	15.9	15.6	15.6	15.6	15.0	15.0
2006	14.3	14.2	14.6	15.5	15.8	16.0	16.4	16.3	16.1	16.0	15.8	15.5	15.5
2007	14.6	14.1	14.4	15.6	16.0	16.4	16.6	16.6	16.3	16.1	16.1	15.7	15.7
Manufacturing													
2000	51.0	51.0	51.0	50.8	50.9	51.4	50.6	50.6	50.9	50.3	50.3	50.5	50.8
2001	50.0	49.9	49.8	49.4	49.4	49.3	47.6	47.6	47.7	47.1	46.9	46.8	48.5
2002	46.0	45.8	45.7	45.9	45.7	45.7	44.7	44.8	44.7	44.5	44.3	44.3	45.2
2003	43.7	43.5	43.4	43.0	42.9	43.1	41.8	42.1	42.0	42.1	42.1	42.2	42.7
2004	41.9	41.9	42.1	42.0	41.9	42.2	41.5	41.4	41.7	41.9	41.8	42.0	41.9
2005	41.6	41.5	41.4	41.2	41.2	41.5	41.1	40.8	40.7	40.8	40.8	40.9	41.1
2006	40.6	40.9	37.7	40.9	40.8	41.2	40.8	40.8	40.7	40.7	40.7	40.8	40.6
2007	40.4	40.6	40.7	40.2	40.3	40.9	40.7	40.6	40.7	40.7	40.8	40.9	40.6
Service-Providing													
2000	352.2	352.8	355.4	358.9	361.8	366.8	361.3	358.7	364.1	364.7	366.5	369.8	361.1
2001	357.1	356.1	357.2	358.3	361.3	364.5	357.5	354.1	357.3	360.4	362.7	362.4	359.1
2002	351.0	350.3	353.0	356.4	358.4	360.6	350.8	348.9	352.3	355.5	358.9	360.6	354.7
2003	349.3	348.6	350.8	352.9	355.5	357.7	354.8	349.5	352.8	355.5	356.8	357.7	353.5
2004	347.7	347.7	350.8	351.0	354.8	358.0	355.3	351.4	353.6	355.7	358.2	359.5	353.6
2005	346.8	348.0	349.8	354.7	357.1	360.0	357.1	353.4	355.5	356.7	359.4	362.5	355.1
2006	353.5	353.8	356.5	359.2	362.3	364.9	360.6	357.2	359.2	361.4	364.9	368.9	360.2
2007	357.2	357.4	358.7	362.1	366.8	369.7	368.3	364.3	364.7	366.1	369.2	372.3	364.7
Trade, Transportation, and Utilities													
2000	79.2	78.7	79.1	79.5	79.9	80.5	79.2	78.4	79.6	80.3	82.0	84.0	80.0
2001	80.2	77.8	77.6	77.9	78.4	79.2	77.9	77.2	77.2	78.4	78.9	80.6	78.4
2002	77.4	75.9	76.4	76.9	77.3	78.3	76.4	75.7	76.4	75.5	78.1	79.6	77.0
2003	75.5	74.1	74.5	74.1	74.7	75.3	74.2	73.4	74.4	75.1	76.5	78.0	75.0
2004	74.8	73.6	73.7	73.6	74.5	75.3	74.3	73.5	74.4	75.2	77.1	78.5	74.9
2005	75.3	74.1	74.2	74.2	74.7	75.3	74.1	73.8	74.7	75.5	77.4	79.5	75.2
2006	76.4	75.1	75.3	75.3	75.7	76.6	75.1	74.6	74.9	75.8	78.1	80.0	76.1
2007	76.1	74.3	74.6	74.6	75.9	76.9	75.5	75.2	75.7	76.5	78.4	80.1	76.2
Wholesale Trade													
2000	16.4	16.4	16.4	16.3	16.4	16.5	16.3	16.2	16.2	15.9	16.0	16.2	16.3
2001	15.7	15.7	15.8	15.9	15.9	15.9	15.9	15.8	15.7	15.8	15.9	15.9	15.8
2002	15.8	15.6	15.7	15.6	15.6	15.5	15.5	15.5	15.4	15.4	15.4	15.5	15.5
2003	15.1	15.0	15.0	14.9	14.9	15.0	15.0	14.9	14.9	14.8	14.9	15.0	15.0
2004	14.9	14.8	14.8	14.7	14.8	15.0	14.9	14.9	14.7	14.7	14.8	14.8	14.8
2005	14.7	14.7	14.7	14.6	14.7	14.8	14.7	14.7	14.6	14.7	14.6	14.8	14.7
2006	14.6	14.7	14.7	14.6	14.6	14.6	14.6	14.4	14.4	14.5	14.5	14.6	14.6
2007	14.4	14.4	14.5	14.4	14.4	14.5	14.5	14.5	14.5	14.6	14.6	14.7	14.5
Retail Trade													
2000	52.0	51.4	51.8	52.0	52.2	52.7	52.1	51.7	52.0	52.7	54.3	56.0	52.6
2001	53.0	50.7	50.5	50.6	51.0	51.8	51.1	50.9	50.4	51.2	51.8	53.4	51.4
2002	50.7	49.4	49.8	50.2	50.6	51.6	50.5	50.1	50.0	49.9	51.5	52.9	50.6
2003	49.6	48.3	48.6	48.8	49.3	49.7	49.4	49.0	49.0	49.6	50.9	52.3	49.5
2004	49.5	48.5	48.6	48.5	49.2	49.7	49.5	49.1	49.3	49.8	51.6	53.0	49.7
2005	50.1	49.0	49.0	49.1	49.5	50.0	49.6	49.6	49.6	50.1	52.0	53.7	50.1
2006	51.1	49.7	49.9	49.9	50.1	50.9	50.2	50.0	49.4	50.0	52.2	53.6	50.6
2007	50.3	48.6	48.8	48.8	49.9	50.7	50.3	50.1	49.7	50.3	52.1	53.5	50.3

Employment by Industry: Bridgeport-Stamford-Norwalk, CT, NECTA, 2000–2007—*Continued*

(Numbers in thousands, not seasonally adjusted.)

Industry and year	January	February	March	April	May	June	July	August	September	October	November	December	Annual Average
Transportation and Utilities													
2000	10.8	10.9	10.9	11.2	11.3	11.3	10.8	10.5	11.4	11.7	11.7	11.8	11.2
2001	11.5	11.4	11.3	11.4	11.5	11.5	10.9	10.5	11.1	11.4	11.2	11.3	11.3
2002	10.9	10.9	10.9	11.1	11.1	11.2	10.4	10.1	11.0	10.2	11.2	11.2	10.9
2003	10.8	10.8	10.9	10.4	10.5	10.6	9.8	9.5	10.5	10.7	10.7	10.7	10.5
2004	10.4	10.3	10.3	10.4	10.5	10.6	9.9	9.5	10.4	10.7	10.7	10.7	10.4
2005	10.5	10.4	10.5	10.5	10.5	10.5	9.8	9.5	10.5	10.7	10.8	11.0	10.4
2006	10.7	10.7	10.7	10.8	11.0	11.1	10.3	10.2	11.1	11.3	11.4	11.8	10.9
2007	11.4	11.3	11.3	11.4	11.6	11.7	10.7	10.6	11.5	11.6	11.7	11.9	11.4
Information													
2000	14.8	14.8	14.8	14.8	14.9	15.2	15.3	15.1	15.0	15.0	15.1	15.2	15.0
2001	14.8	14.8	14.8	14.7	14.5	14.5	13.9	13.9	13.6	13.5	13.4	13.4	14.2
2002	13.2	13.0	13.0	12.8	12.7	12.7	12.7	12.6	12.4	12.4	12.4	12.4	12.7
2003	12.3	12.2	12.3	12.2	12.2	12.2	12.2	12.2	12.0	12.0	12.1	12.1	12.2
2004	12.2	12.1	12.0	12.0	12.1	12.2	12.1	12.1	11.9	11.7	11.8	11.7	12.0
2005	11.6	11.6	11.6	11.6	11.6	11.6	11.5	11.5	11.3	11.4	11.4	11.4	11.5
2006	11.3	11.2	11.4	11.3	11.4	11.4	11.3	11.2	11.2	11.1	11.2	11.4	11.3
2007	11.3	11.4	11.5	11.4	11.5	11.5	11.9	11.8	12.1	12.1	12.2	12.3	11.8
Financial Activities													
2000	40.2	40.2	40.3	40.4	40.7	41.4	41.5	41.6	41.2	41.3	41.4	41.8	41.0
2001	40.6	40.7	40.7	40.8	40.9	41.3	41.1	41.1	40.5	40.5	40.5	40.6	40.8
2002	40.0	40.1	39.8	40.3	40.4	40.8	41.0	41.1	40.7	41.0	41.2	41.7	40.7
2003	41.1	41.1	41.3	41.3	41.5	41.8	42.0	41.9	41.3	41.2	41.2	41.4	41.4
2004	40.9	41.0	41.2	41.0	41.3	41.8	42.2	42.2	41.9	42.0	42.1	42.3	41.7
2005	42.1	42.3	42.6	42.7	42.7	43.1	43.4	43.3	42.8	42.9	43.0	43.2	42.8
2006	43.1	43.1	43.4	43.3	43.7	44.2	44.4	44.8	44.4	44.6	45.0	45.2	44.1
2007	45.0	45.0	45.1	45.0	45.3	45.9	46.2	46.1	45.4	45.4	45.6	45.8	45.5
Professional and Business Services													
2000	75.7	75.8	77.1	78.0	78.4	79.9	79.9	79.5	79.9	79.5	79.1	79.1	78.5
2001	76.2	76.0	76.6	75.8	77.0	77.6	76.8	76.4	75.3	75.5	74.3	73.3	75.9
2002	70.4	70.3	71.1	71.8	71.7	72.2	70.9	71.0	70.5	71.1	70.8	70.5	71.0
2003	68.8	68.8	68.9	70.7	70.6	71.0	70.6	71.0	71.4	71.2	70.8	70.5	70.4
2004	67.7	67.8	68.8	69.3	70.1	71.1	70.5	70.4	69.9	69.6	69.8	70.2	69.6
2005	66.6	67.1	67.9	69.4	69.6	70.4	70.2	70.3	71.0	70.7	71.2	71.4	69.7
2006	68.6	69.3	70.5	71.5	71.7	72.6	71.1	71.2	71.2	70.9	71.1	72.0	71.0
2007	68.7	68.9	69.2	71.2	71.8	72.8	71.6	71.6	71.4	71.1	71.6	71.8	71.0
Education and Health Services													
2000	53.1	53.5	53.5	53.8	53.8	53.6	53.6	53.2	54.1	55.0	55.3	55.5	54.0
2001	54.1	55.2	55.4	55.7	54.8	54.8	55.1	54.5	55.2	57.1	59.6	58.0	55.8
2002	56.6	57.6	58.3	58.3	58.3	57.2	57.2	56.4	57.4	59.4	59.8	59.7	58.0
2003	58.0	58.7	59.1	58.9	58.8	57.9	58.3	57.2	58.5	60.1	60.2	60.0	58.8
2004	58.4	59.1	59.8	59.4	59.2	58.5	58.7	58.2	58.9	60.2	60.5	60.1	59.3
2005	58.4	59.6	59.4	59.8	59.8	58.7	59.1	58.2	59.0	59.9	60.3	60.3	59.4
2006	59.6	60.3	60.2	60.6	60.8	59.9	60.0	59.1	60.0	61.2	61.8	62.2	60.5
2007	60.6	62.0	61.9	62.2	61.8	61.3	61.4	60.4	61.5	62.8	63.2	63.6	61.9
Leisure and Hospitality													
2000	27.5	27.3	27.9	29.6	30.8	32.6	32.8	32.4	30.9	30.4	29.9	30.1	30.2
2001	28.3	28.2	28.8	29.6	31.5	32.9	33.3	32.6	30.5	30.2	30.0	30.5	30.5
2002	28.8	28.4	29.2	30.5	31.8	33.0	34.2	33.4	31.3	30.9	30.5	30.7	31.1
2003	29.0	28.9	29.6	31.0	32.7	34.3	35.2	34.3	32.5	32.2	31.8	31.7	31.9
2004	29.8	29.7	30.3	31.6	33.3	34.7	35.6	34.8	33.3	32.6	32.1	32.5	32.5
2005	29.8	29.8	30.3	32.1	33.4	35.3	35.8	35.2	33.1	32.2	31.8	31.9	32.6
2006	30.4	30.3	30.9	32.5	34.0	36.1	36.6	36.0	34.1	33.5	32.9	33.4	33.4
2007	31.5	31.2	31.7	33.0	34.7	36.5	37.5	36.8	34.6	33.6	33.1	33.4	34.0
Other Services													
2000	16.0	15.9	16.0	16.4	16.5	16.8	17.3	17.1	16.6	16.8	16.7	16.9	16.6
2001	16.3	16.4	16.5	16.7	16.8	17.0	17.5	17.3	16.7	16.9	16.9	17.0	16.8
2002	16.9	16.9	16.9	17.0	17.2	17.3	17.5	17.3	16.7	16.8	16.9	17.0	17.0
2003	16.5	16.5	16.6	16.7	16.7	16.8	17.2	16.9	16.5	16.6	16.5	16.5	16.7
2004	16.4	16.4	16.5	16.6	16.7	16.9	17.4	17.2	16.6	16.6	16.6	16.7	16.7
2005	16.4	16.5	16.7	16.9	17.0	17.2	17.5	17.1	16.7	16.7	16.8	17.0	16.9
2006	16.8	16.7	16.8	16.9	17.0	17.2	17.8	17.4	16.9	17.1	17.1	17.2	17.1
2007	17.1	17.0	17.1	17.2	17.3	17.5	18.0	17.7	17.2	17.3	17.4	17.5	17.4
Government													
2000	45.7	46.6	46.7	46.4	46.8	46.8	41.7	41.4	46.8	46.4	47.0	47.2	45.8
2001	46.6	47.0	46.8	47.1	47.4	47.2	41.9	41.1	48.3	48.3	49.1	49.0	46.7
2002	47.7	48.1	48.3	48.8	49.0	49.1	40.9	41.4	46.9	48.4	49.2	49.0	47.2
2003	48.1	48.3	48.5	48.0	48.3	48.4	45.1	42.6	46.2	47.1	47.7	47.5	47.2
2004	47.5	48.0	48.5	47.5	47.6	47.5	44.5	43.0	46.7	47.8	48.2	47.5	47.0
2005	46.6	47.0	47.1	48.0	48.3	48.4	44.5	44.0	46.9	47.4	47.5	47.8	47.0
2006	47.3	47.8	48.0	47.8	48.0	46.9	44.3	42.9	46.5	47.2	47.7	47.5	46.8
2007	46.9	47.6	47.6	47.5	48.5	47.3	46.2	44.7	46.8	47.3	47.7	47.8	47.2

Employment by Industry: Honolulu, HI, 2000–2007

(Numbers in thousands, not seasonally adjusted.)

Industry and year	January	February	March	April	May	June	July	August	September	October	November	December	Annual Average
Total Nonfarm													
2000	404.5	406.5	407.6	409.8	410.6	413.4	412.9	413.1	416.6	415.5	416.2	416.5	411.7
2001	405.9	415.2	417.9	413.0	414.3	419.1	409.3	410.6	412.3	408.3	410.7	413.4	412.5
2002	401.8	408.3	411.0	405.0	414.7	419.6	408.0	409.0	413.0	416.5	421.3	426.2	412.9
2003	414.2	418.8	421.0	416.6	421.2	420.8	414.1	414.6	417.2	420.9	426.4	429.8	419.6
2004	419.0	423.2	425.9	426.3	429.8	430.3	424.7	425.9	429.3	435.2	442.5	444.1	429.7
2005	429.9	437.3	440.0	440.4	443.5	444.3	437.6	441.0	444.2	446.2	451.1	456.3	442.7
2006	440.0	449.6	452.7	448.9	453.5	454.9	445.5	448.7	453.9	451.8	460.1	461.4	451.8
2007	447.2	454.2	457.2	449.6	457.3	458.7	447.0	448.6	454.9	455.3	460.3	464.1	454.5
Total Private													
2000	310.5	313.6	315.6	315.5	317.0	321.6	320.1	322.1	324.6	323.7	326.4	329.3	320.0
2001	320.4	322.2	324.1	321.0	322.7	325.2	323.3	323.7	323.1	316.2	315.6	317.3	321.2
2002	310.7	313.0	314.5	314.6	317.4	319.9	319.9	320.3	322.2	321.6	324.8	328.2	318.9
2003	319.5	321.5	323.2	322.1	323.5	324.1	324.3	325.5	326.7	325.5	329.4	332.4	324.8
2004	324.7	326.6	327.9	329.0	331.1	333.5	334.5	335.4	336.4	339.2	343.4	346.0	334.0
2005	337.8	340.5	342.4	343.6	345.4	347.6	348.0	349.8	351.7	350.7	354.1	358.3	347.5
2006	348.8	352.5	354.7	351.8	354.6	357.5	355.7	357.6	358.7	354.6	358.7	361.7	355.6
2007	352.6	355.4	357.7	355.1	357.7	360.7	356.9	358.7	359.3	357.7	361.2	364.2	358.1
Goods-Producing													
2000	28.7	28.8	29.4	29.5	29.9	30.3	30.6	31.0	31.2	31.0	30.8	31.0	30.2
2001	30.1	30.1	30.0	29.8	29.9	30.1	30.0	30.1	29.9	29.2	29.1	29.2	29.8
2002	28.7	28.6	29.1	28.9	29.2	30.0	30.1	30.3	30.0	29.9	30.1	30.2	29.6
2003	29.6	29.7	30.2	30.3	30.7	30.9	31.2	31.4	31.4	31.7	31.8	31.7	30.9
2004	31.2	31.3	30.7	31.7	32.3	32.9	33.1	33.2	33.4	33.4	33.4	33.7	32.5
2005	33.1	33.5	34.0	34.4	34.8	35.2	35.4	35.9	36.3	36.1	36.2	36.5	35.1
2006	35.5	35.7	35.7	35.5	36.2	36.7	36.9	37.3	37.7	37.3	37.8	38.1	36.7
2007	37.0	37.3	37.4	37.3	37.9	38.5	38.6	38.7	39.2	38.8	39.1	39.3	38.3
Natural Resources, Mining, and Construction													
2000	16.4	16.5	16.8	17.0	17.3	17.6	17.9	18.1	18.2	18.0	17.9	18.1	17.5
2001	17.3	17.2	17.2	16.9	17.0	17.1	17.1	17.2	17.0	16.7	16.6	16.7	17.0
2002	16.5	16.5	16.9	17.1	17.4	18.1	18.4	18.7	18.5	18.5	18.7	18.7	17.8
2003	18.3	18.4	18.8	19.0	19.3	19.4	19.7	19.8	19.8	19.9	19.9	19.7	19.3
2004	19.3	19.4	18.9	19.7	20.3	20.7	21.1	21.2	21.4	21.5	21.5	21.8	20.6
2005	21.4	21.6	22.1	22.6	23.0	23.4	23.7	24.0	24.4	24.3	24.4	24.6	23.3
2006	23.9	24.0	24.0	23.9	24.5	24.8	25.0	25.3	25.7	25.5	25.8	26.1	24.9
2007	25.2	25.4	25.6	25.6	26.0	26.6	26.8	26.9	27.3	27.1	27.4	27.6	26.5
Manufacturing													
2000	12.3	12.3	12.6	12.5	12.6	12.7	12.7	12.9	13.0	13.0	12.9	12.9	12.7
2001	12.8	12.9	12.8	12.9	12.9	13.0	12.9	12.9	12.9	12.5	12.5	12.5	12.8
2002	12.2	12.1	12.2	11.8	11.8	11.9	11.7	11.6	11.5	11.4	11.4	11.5	11.8
2003	11.3	11.3	11.4	11.3	11.4	11.5	11.5	11.6	11.6	11.8	11.9	12.0	11.6
2004	11.9	11.9	11.8	12.0	12.0	12.2	12.0	12.0	12.0	11.9	11.9	11.9	12.0
2005	11.7	11.9	11.9	11.8	11.8	11.8	11.7	11.9	11.9	11.8	11.8	11.9	11.8
2006	11.6	11.7	11.7	11.6	11.7	11.9	11.9	12.0	12.0	11.8	12.0	12.0	11.8
2007	11.8	11.9	11.8	11.7	11.9	11.9	11.8	11.8	11.9	11.7	11.7	11.7	11.8
Service-Providing													
2000	370.1	377.3	380.1	379.9	382.7	385.6	376.4	377.6	381.6	384.0	389.1	393.2	381.5
2001	375.8	385.1	387.9	383.2	384.4	389.0	379.3	380.5	382.4	379.1	381.6	384.2	382.7
2002	373.1	379.7	381.9	376.1	385.5	389.6	377.9	378.7	383.0	386.6	391.2	396.0	383.3
2003	384.6	389.1	390.8	386.3	390.5	389.9	382.9	383.2	385.8	389.2	394.6	398.1	388.8
2004	387.8	391.9	395.2	394.6	397.5	397.4	391.6	392.7	395.9	401.8	409.1	410.4	397.2
2005	396.8	403.8	406.0	406.0	408.7	409.1	402.2	405.1	407.9	410.1	414.9	419.8	407.5
2006	404.5	413.9	417.0	413.4	417.3	418.2	408.6	411.4	416.2	414.5	422.3	423.3	415.1
2007	410.2	416.9	419.8	412.3	419.4	420.2	408.4	409.9	415.7	416.5	421.2	424.8	416.3
Trade, Transportation, and Utilities													
2000	80.5	80.4	80.1	79.7	79.9	81.0	81.1	81.6	81.8	81.8	84.1	85.0	81.4
2001	82.3	81.7	81.8	81.1	81.3	81.8	81.7	81.7	81.5	79.1	77.9	79.0	80.9
2002	75.9	75.3	75.1	75.3	75.8	76.3	76.6	76.8	76.7	76.9	78.2	79.6	76.5
2003	76.6	76.3	76.1	75.7	75.6	76.0	76.3	76.5	76.5	76.6	78.1	79.6	76.7
2004	77.2	76.7	76.9	77.7	78.2	79.0	79.2	79.6	80.0	81.5	83.3	84.3	79.5
2005	81.8	81.7	81.9	82.3	83.1	83.9	84.6	85.1	85.4	85.3	86.7	88.1	84.2
2006	85.3	85.0	85.7	85.2	85.5	86.4	86.0	86.7	86.7	85.7	87.7	88.9	86.2
2007	86.3	85.3	85.8	84.9	85.2	85.4	85.2	85.1	85.0	85.0	86.9	88.3	85.7
Wholesale Trade													
2000	13.1	13.2	13.2	13.2	13.2	13.4	13.5	13.6	13.5	13.5	13.6	13.6	13.4
2001	13.5	13.6	13.6	13.5	13.6	13.7	13.6	13.7	13.6	13.4	13.4	13.5	13.6
2002	13.3	13.3	13.3	13.3	13.5	13.5	13.5	13.5	13.6	13.6	13.7	13.8	13.5
2003	13.5	13.6	13.6	13.7	13.7	13.7	13.7	13.7	13.7	13.6	13.7	13.7	13.7
2004	13.6	13.6	13.7	13.7	13.8	13.9	13.9	13.8	13.8	13.9	14.0	14.0	13.8
2005	13.8	13.9	14.0	14.0	14.1	14.1	14.2	14.3	14.4	14.4	14.4	14.5	14.2
2006	14.2	14.2	14.2	14.3	14.3	14.5	14.4	14.6	14.5	14.6	14.7	14.9	14.5
2007	14.6	14.6	14.7	14.6	14.7	14.8	14.7	14.8	14.8	14.8	15.0	15.0	14.8
Retail Trade													
2000	46.2	45.8	45.4	45.1	45.3	45.8	46.0	46.3	46.4	46.4	48.3	49.0	46.3
2001	46.7	46.0	46.0	45.5	45.4	45.6	45.6	45.6	45.6	44.6	45.0	46.0	45.6
2002	43.7	43.0	42.7	42.7	42.9	43.2	43.6	43.6	43.5	43.6	44.6	46.0	43.6
2003	43.4	42.9	42.7	42.4	42.5	43.0	43.3	43.4	43.3	43.6	44.9	46.4	43.5
2004	44.2	43.7	43.7	43.5	43.8	44.3	44.5	44.9	45.1	46.1	47.6	48.8	45.0
2005	46.3	45.9	45.9	45.7	45.8	46.1	46.7	46.9	46.9	47.3	48.6	49.9	46.8
2006	47.5	47.1	47.2	46.6	46.5	46.9	46.6	46.7	46.5	46.5	48.2	49.0	47.1
2007	47.0	46.3	46.5	45.9	45.9	46.2	46.0	45.8	45.8	46.0	47.7	48.7	46.5

Employment by Industry: Honolulu, HI, 2000–2007—*Continued*

(Numbers in thousands, not seasonally adjusted.)

Industry and year	January	February	March	April	May	June	July	August	September	October	November	December	Annual Average
Transportation and Utilities													
2000	21.2	21.4	21.5	21.4	21.4	21.8	21.6	21.7	21.9	21.9	22.2	22.4	21.7
2001	22.1	22.1	22.2	22.1	22.3	22.5	22.5	22.4	22.3	21.1	19.5	19.5	21.7
2002	18.9	19.0	19.1	19.3	19.4	19.6	19.5	19.7	19.6	19.7	19.9	19.8	19.5
2003	19.7	19.8	19.8	19.6	19.4	19.3	19.3	19.4	19.5	19.4	19.5	19.5	19.5
2004	19.4	19.4	19.5	20.5	20.6	20.8	20.8	20.9	21.1	21.5	21.7	21.5	20.6
2005	21.7	21.9	22.0	22.6	23.2	23.7	23.7	23.9	24.1	23.6	23.7	23.7	23.2
2006	23.6	23.7	24.3	24.3	24.7	25.0	25.0	25.4	25.7	24.6	24.8	25.0	24.7
2007	24.7	24.4	24.6	24.4	24.6	24.4	24.5	24.5	24.4	24.2	24.2	24.6	24.5
Information													
2000	9.2	9.2	9.3	10.1	10.1	10.9	10.1	10.7	11.4	11.0	10.5	10.3	10.2
2001	10.2	10.2	10.4	9.8	10.2	10.0	9.8	10.0	9.7	9.7	9.8	9.7	10.0
2002	9.8	9.7	9.7	9.5	9.5	9.3	9.1	9.2	9.9	9.1	9.1	9.7	9.5
2003	8.9	9.0	9.0	8.8	9.4	9.2	8.3	8.2	8.2	8.1	8.3	8.2	8.6
2004	8.4	8.4	8.7	8.5	9.0	8.8	9.2	9.2	9.2	9.3	9.8	9.7	9.0
2005	8.6	8.8	8.6	8.9	9.0	8.7	8.7	9.1	9.1	9.1	9.3	9.8	9.0
2006	9.0	9.3	9.2	8.4	9.2	8.9	8.5	8.7	9.2	8.4	8.8	9.0	8.9
2007	8.4	8.9	8.9	8.6	9.3	9.2	8.5	9.1	8.7	8.7	8.8	8.8	8.8
Financial Activities													
2000	22.9	22.9	22.9	22.7	22.7	22.8	22.8	22.8	22.6	22.5	22.4	22.5	22.7
2001	22.0	22.1	22.2	22.0	22.0	22.1	21.8	21.8	21.7	21.6	21.5	21.6	21.9
2002	21.1	21.2	21.4	21.3	21.5	21.6	21.6	21.5	21.5	21.6	21.7	21.8	21.5
2003	21.3	21.5	21.6	21.5	21.7	21.9	22.0	22.1	22.1	22.1	22.1	22.2	21.8
2004	22.0	22.0	22.1	22.1	22.2	22.2	22.2	22.1	22.0	22.3	22.3	22.4	22.2
2005	22.1	22.3	22.3	22.2	22.4	22.5	22.5	22.6	22.7	22.6	22.8	22.9	22.5
2006	22.5	22.7	22.9	22.8	22.9	23.2	23.0	23.0	22.8	22.9	22.9	23.0	22.9
2007	22.8	22.7	23.0	22.7	22.9	23.1	23.0	22.9	22.7	22.7	22.8	22.9	22.9
Professional and Business Services													
2000	48.1	48.6	49.3	49.5	49.5	50.1	50.3	50.5	51.0	51.2	51.6	52.1	50.2
2001	51.3	51.8	52.5	51.9	52.2	52.8	52.8	53.0	53.0	52.1	52.8	52.8	52.4
2002	52.4	53.5	53.7	54.0	54.5	55.3	55.7	56.3	56.4	56.4	56.5	58.1	55.2
2003	56.6	56.5	56.8	56.5	56.4	56.8	56.9	57.6	57.9	56.5	57.4	58.0	57.0
2004	56.6	57.2	57.5	57.1	56.3	56.9	57.2	57.6	57.2	57.7	58.3	59.1	57.4
2005	58.0	58.5	59.0	59.2	58.7	59.4	59.9	60.4	60.3	60.9	61.7	62.5	59.9
2006	61.0	62.5	62.8	62.0	61.7	62.5	62.2	62.3	61.6	60.2	60.4	61.1	61.7
2007	59.3	59.8	60.2	59.3	59.4	60.9	60.1	60.5	60.7	60.5	60.9	61.9	60.3
Education and Health Services													
2000	46.8	47.9	48.4	47.9	48.1	48.2	47.7	47.5	48.3	48.2	48.9	49.4	48.1
2001	47.8	48.7	49.1	48.9	49.3	49.4	49.0	48.7	49.2	49.2	49.9	50.0	49.1
2002	48.6	49.7	49.8	50.0	50.4	50.2	50.1	49.6	50.6	50.9	52.0	51.2	50.3
2003	50.3	51.6	51.9	51.9	52.1	51.7	51.9	51.7	52.6	52.7	53.4	53.6	52.1
2004	52.0	52.8	53.2	53.2	53.9	53.7	53.3	53.1	54.0	54.3	55.1	55.4	53.7
2005	54.4	55.1	55.5	55.3	55.7	55.5	54.9	54.6	55.5	55.3	55.7	56.1	55.3
2006	54.4	55.2	55.7	55.7	56.3	56.6	55.8	55.9	56.7	56.7	57.2	57.6	56.2
2007	56.3	57.3	57.6	57.6	57.7	58.0	56.9	56.9	57.5	57.2	57.7	57.9	57.4
Leisure and Hospitality													
2000	57.3	58.1	58.4	58.2	58.9	60.0	59.7	59.9	60.0	59.5	59.5	60.4	59.2
2001	58.2	58.9	59.3	58.6	58.9	59.8	59.1	59.5	59.2	56.7	56.0	56.3	58.4
2002	55.7	56.4	56.9	56.8	57.6	58.3	57.8	57.8	58.1	57.9	58.1	58.5	57.5
2003	57.5	57.9	58.5	58.1	58.3	58.3	58.5	58.8	58.8	58.6	59.0	59.8	58.5
2004	58.6	59.3	59.6	59.7	60.0	60.7	61.2	61.5	61.7	61.4	61.9	62.1	60.6
2005	60.8	61.5	61.9	61.8	61.9	62.7	62.4	62.4	62.6	61.7	61.8	62.3	62.0
2006	61.2	62.0	62.4	62.0	62.4	62.8	63.0	63.2	63.5	62.9	63.2	63.4	62.7
2007	62.5	63.7	64.2	64.2	64.6	64.9	64.1	64.8	64.6	63.9	64.0	64.1	64.1
Other Services													
2000	17.3	17.9	18.1	18.1	18.2	18.5	18.4	18.5	18.6	18.8	19.0	18.9	18.4
2001	18.5	18.7	18.8	18.9	18.9	19.2	19.1	18.9	18.9	18.6	18.6	18.7	18.8
2002	18.5	18.6	18.8	18.8	18.9	18.9	18.9	18.8	19.0	18.9	19.1	19.1	18.9
2003	18.7	19.0	19.1	19.3	19.3	19.3	19.2	19.2	19.2	19.2	19.3	19.3	19.2
2004	18.7	18.9	19.2	19.0	19.2	19.3	19.1	19.1	18.9	19.3	19.3	19.3	19.1
2005	19.0	19.1	19.2	19.5	19.8	19.7	19.6	19.7	19.8	19.7	19.9	20.1	19.6
2006	19.9	20.1	20.3	20.2	20.4	20.4	20.3	20.5	20.5	20.5	20.7	20.6	20.4
2007	20.0	20.4	20.6	20.5	20.7	20.7	20.5	20.7	20.9	20.9	21.0	21.0	20.7
Government													
2000	88.3	92.5	93.9	93.9	95.6	94.3	86.9	86.5	88.2	91.3	93.5	94.9	91.7
2001	85.5	93.0	93.8	92.0	91.6	93.9	86.0	86.9	89.2	92.1	95.1	96.1	91.3
2002	91.1	95.3	96.5	90.4	97.3	99.7	88.1	88.7	90.8	94.9	96.5	98.0	93.9
2003	94.7	97.3	97.8	94.5	97.7	96.7	89.8	89.1	90.5	95.4	97.0	97.4	94.8
2004	94.3	96.6	98.0	97.3	98.7	96.8	90.2	90.5	92.9	96.0	99.1	98.1	95.7
2005	92.1	96.8	97.6	96.8	98.1	96.7	89.6	91.2	92.5	95.5	97.0	98.0	95.2
2006	91.2	97.1	98.0	97.1	98.9	97.4	89.8	91.1	95.2	97.2	101.4	99.7	96.2
2007	94.6	98.8	99.5	94.5	99.6	98.0	90.1	89.9	95.6	97.6	99.1	99.9	96.4

Employment by Industry: Tulsa, OK, 2000–2007

(Numbers in thousands, not seasonally adjusted.)

Industry and year	January	February	March	April	May	June	July	August	September	October	November	December	Annual Average
Total Nonfarm													
2000	395.8	396.9	401.7	405.6	409.2	411.3	407.3	410.3	412.5	412.7	414.3	415.3	407.7
2001	400.4	403.9	407.1	411.1	413.2	415.2	410.2	412.8	411.6	410.0	411.7	411.8	409.9
2002	403.1	403.0	404.8	407.2	409.6	405.8	399.0	401.0	400.2	398.5	399.2	399.8	402.6
2003	391.3	390.8	391.2	392.6	394.0	390.6	387.3	388.6	389.1	390.5	391.4	392.7	390.8
2004	387.2	389.2	392.0	392.2	392.6	393.4	391.6	393.1	394.6	395.9	396.1	398.0	393.0
2005	394.3	397.0	400.3	403.3	406.6	408.3	405.1	408.2	411.2	411.4	414.2	416.5	406.4
2006	410.6	412.9	417.5	416.9	421.7	422.9	415.7	418.6	421.3	422.8	424.2	426.4	419.3
2007	416.7	420.7	426.3	424.5	427.5	427.9	425.2	428.3	427.4	429.0	428.5	428.1	425.8
Total Private													
2000	348.7	349.2	353.1	357.2	360.2	363.5	362.9	365.0	365.2	363.6	365.3	365.7	360.0
2001	353.2	355.5	358.5	362.6	364.1	367.0	365.2	367.2	363.6	360.5	362.1	362.0	361.8
2002	354.6	353.6	355.1	357.2	358.7	357.0	353.1	354.4	352.0	348.7	349.5	349.9	353.7
2003	342.9	341.7	342.1	343.7	344.6	342.8	341.7	342.9	340.9	341.6	342.6	343.6	342.6
2004	339.2	340.1	342.7	342.9	343.2	344.9	344.2	345.1	344.2	344.8	345.8	347.3	343.7
2005	343.5	345.3	348.4	351.1	353.8	356.0	357.2	358.9	359.4	357.7	360.6	362.7	354.6
2006	357.5	359.0	363.2	363.5	367.5	370.5	368.2	370.4	369.2	368.9	370.7	373.0	366.8
2007	364.9	367.5	372.6	370.7	373.3	376.6	376.1	378.5	375.7	375.2	375.4	375.0	373.5
Goods-Producing													
2000	79.6	79.5	80.3	79.6	80.0	80.9	81.0	81.5	81.1	80.1	80.4	80.6	80.4
2001	78.4	79.1	79.9	80.3	80.9	82.1	81.4	81.8	80.7	79.7	79.7	79.6	80.3
2002	78.4	77.3	77.1	76.7	76.8	76.6	75.4	75.3	73.9	73.0	72.6	72.7	75.5
2003	71.7	71.0	71.1	71.3	71.4	71.8	72.2	72.1	71.6	70.8	70.5	70.8	71.4
2004	69.4	69.4	69.8	69.8	70.2	70.9	71.4	70.8	70.3	70.0	69.7	69.9	70.1
2005	68.9	69.0	69.9	70.6	71.2	72.0	72.7	73.1	73.3	73.2	73.7	75.0	71.9
2006	74.5	75.0	76.2	75.0	76.3	77.5	77.7	78.4	78.2	78.3	78.7	79.0	77.1
2007	77.8	77.8	79.1	78.7	79.2	80.4	81.3	81.8	81.0	81.4	81.5	81.3	80.1
Natural Resources and Mining													
2000	5.8	5.9	5.7	5.2	5.1	5.2	5.1	5.1	5.0	4.6	4.7	4.6	5.2
2001	4.1	4.2	4.3	4.1	4.2	4.4	4.4	4.4	4.4	4.5	4.5	4.5	4.3
2002	4.3	4.4	4.4	4.3	4.3	4.5	4.2	4.2	4.1	4.0	3.9	3.9	4.2
2003	4.0	3.9	3.9	3.8	3.8	3.8	3.9	3.9	4.0	4.0	4.0	4.0	3.9
2004	4.4	4.4	4.3	4.3	4.3	4.4	4.5	4.4	4.4	4.4	4.3	4.4	4.4
2005	4.8	4.8	4.8	4.9	5.0	5.1	5.3	5.3	5.4	5.3	5.4	5.5	5.1
2006	5.6	5.7	5.8	6.2	6.1	6.2	6.3	6.3	6.3	6.2	6.3	6.3	6.1
2007	6.4	6.4	6.5	6.4	6.5	6.7	6.9	6.9	6.8	6.8	6.9	6.8	6.7
Construction													
2000	18.7	18.7	19.3	19.5	19.6	19.9	20.0	20.1	19.8	19.8	19.8	19.6	19.6
2001	19.1	19.7	20.3	20.7	21.1	21.6	21.5	21.8	21.1	21.2	21.0	21.0	20.8
2002	20.8	20.7	20.6	20.3	20.6	20.7	20.8	21.1	20.4	20.2	19.9	20.0	20.5
2003	19.4	19.1	19.4	20.1	20.4	20.6	20.9	20.8	20.4	19.7	19.4	19.5	19.9
2004	18.6	18.5	18.8	18.9	19.2	19.6	20.3	20.1	19.9	19.6	19.3	19.2	19.3
2005	18.4	18.4	18.9	19.3	19.7	20.1	20.7	20.8	20.8	20.6	20.5	20.9	19.9
2006	20.7	20.7	21.2	21.1	21.3	21.9	21.8	21.9	21.9	22.1	22.0	22.1	21.6
2007	20.6	20.6	21.5	21.4	21.5	22.2	22.3	22.6	22.3	22.7	22.8	22.5	21.9
Manufacturing													
2000	55.1	54.9	55.3	54.9	55.3	55.8	55.9	56.3	56.3	55.7	55.9	56.4	55.7
2001	55.2	55.2	55.3	55.5	55.6	56.1	55.5	55.6	55.2	54.0	54.2	54.1	55.1
2002	53.3	52.2	52.1	52.1	51.9	51.4	50.4	50.0	49.4	48.8	48.8	48.8	50.8
2003	48.3	48.0	47.8	47.4	47.2	47.4	47.4	47.4	47.2	47.1	47.1	47.3	47.4
2004	46.4	46.5	46.7	46.6	46.7	46.9	46.6	46.3	46.0	46.0	46.1	46.3	46.4
2005	45.7	45.8	46.2	46.4	46.5	46.8	46.7	47.0	47.1	47.3	47.8	48.6	46.8
2006	48.2	48.6	49.2	47.7	48.9	49.4	49.6	50.2	50.0	50.0	50.4	50.6	49.4
2007	50.8	50.8	51.1	50.9	51.2	51.5	52.1	52.3	51.9	51.9	51.8	52.0	51.5
Service-Providing													
2000	316.2	317.4	321.4	326.0	329.2	330.4	326.3	328.8	331.4	332.6	333.9	334.7	327.4
2001	322.0	324.8	327.2	330.8	332.3	333.1	328.8	331.0	330.9	330.3	332.0	332.2	329.6
2002	324.7	325.7	327.7	330.5	332.8	329.2	323.6	325.7	326.3	325.5	326.6	327.1	327.1
2003	319.6	319.8	320.1	321.3	322.6	318.8	315.1	316.5	317.5	319.7	320.9	321.9	319.5
2004	317.8	319.8	322.2	322.4	322.4	322.5	320.2	322.3	324.3	325.9	326.4	328.1	322.9
2005	325.4	328.0	330.4	332.7	335.4	336.3	332.4	335.1	337.9	338.2	340.5	341.5	334.5
2006	336.1	337.9	341.3	341.9	345.4	345.4	338.0	340.2	343.1	344.5	345.5	347.4	342.2
2007	338.9	342.9	347.2	345.8	348.3	347.5	343.9	346.5	346.4	347.6	347.0	346.8	345.7
Trade, Transportation, and Utilities													
2000	86.8	86.3	86.9	87.8	88.8	89.7	89.5	90.1	90.6	90.6	92.4	93.1	89.4
2001	88.0	87.1	87.6	87.6	87.9	88.4	86.8	87.0	86.3	85.8	87.3	87.5	87.3
2002	85.0	84.1	84.9	86.1	86.3	85.8	85.1	85.1	85.0	84.4	85.9	86.7	85.4
2003	83.7	82.7	82.7	83.0	82.9	82.1	81.7	81.9	81.3	82.0	83.5	84.6	82.7
2004	80.9	79.8	80.8	80.8	81.2	81.2	79.8	79.7	79.2	79.6	80.8	81.5	80.4
2005	79.9	79.3	79.4	79.7	80.1	80.2	80.8	81.3	81.4	81.7	83.2	84.2	80.9
2006	81.2	80.8	81.7	83.2	84.0	83.9	83.4	83.5	83.6	83.8	85.5	86.7	83.4
2007	83.8	83.9	85.2	84.6	85.1	85.4	84.9	85.2	85.1	85.2	87.0	87.7	85.3
Wholesale Trade													
2000	17.1	17.2	17.4	17.5	17.4	17.7	17.7	17.9	17.9	17.9	17.9	17.9	17.6
2001	17.7	17.7	17.8	18.0	18.1	18.1	17.7	17.6	17.5	17.3	17.5	17.5	17.7
2002	17.6	17.4	17.6	17.7	17.7	17.7	17.7	17.8	17.7	17.4	17.5	17.5	17.6
2003	17.0	16.8	16.9	16.9	16.8	16.8	16.9	16.8	16.8	16.8	16.7	16.8	16.8
2004	16.3	16.0	16.0	16.0	16.2	16.3	16.3	16.3	16.4	16.3	16.4	16.6	16.3
2005	16.7	16.7	16.8	16.9	17.0	17.2	17.5	17.5	17.5	17.5	17.6	17.7	17.2
2006	17.2	17.3	17.4	17.7	17.8	17.9	17.7	17.7	17.7	17.7	17.7	17.7	17.6
2007	17.8	18.0	18.2	18.3	18.3	18.5	18.2	18.2	18.0	18.1	18.2	18.3	18.2

Employment by Industry: Tulsa, OK, 2000–2007—*Continued*

(Numbers in thousands, not seasonally adjusted.)

Industry and year	January	February	March	April	May	June	July	August	September	October	November	December	Annual Average
Retail Trade													
2000	47.6	47.1	47.5	48.0	48.8	49.2	48.7	49.1	49.6	49.6	51.5	51.9	49.1
2001	47.7	46.8	47.1	47.3	47.4	47.6	46.5	46.8	46.5	46.7	48.1	48.7	47.3
2002	46.8	46.2	46.6	46.9	47.1	46.6	45.7	45.7	45.5	45.5	46.9	47.6	46.4
2003	45.2	44.5	44.5	44.9	45.0	44.7	44.4	44.6	44.3	44.9	46.5	47.4	45.0
2004	44.7	43.8	44.7	44.8	44.9	44.7	43.4	43.2	42.7	43.5	44.7	45.2	44.2
2005	43.2	42.6	42.6	42.8	43.0	42.8	43.2	43.5	43.8	44.2	45.5	46.3	43.6
2006	43.0	43.4	43.9	44.4	44.9	44.6	44.4	44.2	44.2	44.6	46.1	47.0	44.6
2007	44.1	43.8	44.9	44.6	45.0	45.0	44.5	45.0	45.0	45.0	46.8	47.3	45.1
Transportation and Utilities													
2000	22.1	22.0	22.0	22.3	22.6	22.8	23.1	23.1	23.1	23.1	23.0	23.3	22.7
2001	22.6	22.6	22.7	22.3	22.4	22.7	22.6	22.6	22.3	21.8	21.7	21.3	22.3
2002	20.6	20.5	20.7	21.5	21.5	21.5	21.7	21.6	21.8	21.5	21.5	21.6	21.3
2003	21.5	21.4	21.3	21.2	21.1	20.6	20.4	20.5	20.2	20.3	20.3	20.4	20.8
2004	19.9	20.0	20.1	20.0	20.1	20.2	20.1	20.2	20.1	19.8	19.7	19.7	20.0
2005	20.0	20.0	20.0	20.0	20.1	20.2	20.1	20.3	20.1	20.0	20.1	20.2	20.1
2006	20.3	20.1	20.4	21.1	21.3	21.4	21.3	21.6	21.7	21.5	21.7	22.0	21.2
2007	21.9	22.1	22.1	21.7	21.8	21.9	22.2	22.0	22.1	22.1	22.0	22.1	22.0
Information													
2000	14.3	14.5	14.5	14.3	14.7	14.9	15.1	15.3	15.6	15.5	15.9	15.9	15.0
2001	14.5	14.6	14.3	15.0	14.8	14.4	15.0	16.1	16.1	16.1	15.8	15.6	15.2
2002	15.7	15.8	15.4	14.6	14.4	14.2	14.0	13.9	13.8	13.7	13.6	13.2	14.4
2003	12.9	12.8	12.5	12.6	12.6	12.4	12.0	11.7	11.6	11.8	11.8	12.0	12.2
2004	12.0	12.0	11.9	11.5	11.3	11.2	11.1	10.8	10.5	10.5	10.5	10.5	11.2
2005	10.8	10.7	10.5	10.6	10.6	10.7	10.7	10.7	10.8	10.8	11.0	11.0	10.7
2006	10.5	10.3	10.3	10.0	10.1	10.1	10.0	10.0	9.7	9.8	9.8	10.2	10.1
2007	9.9	10.1	10.0	9.9	9.9	9.8	9.8	9.8	9.7	10.5	10.4	10.5	10.0
Financial Activities													
2000	24.6	24.6	24.6	25.0	25.2	25.7	25.0	25.1	25.1	24.9	24.7	24.9	25.0
2001	24.5	24.8	24.9	25.0	25.2	25.4	25.2	25.4	25.3	25.4	25.4	25.3	25.2
2002	25.0	24.9	24.8	24.9	24.9	25.0	25.0	24.9	24.7	24.5	24.5	24.5	24.8
2003	24.4	24.4	24.4	24.6	24.7	24.7	24.6	24.5	24.4	24.4	24.3	24.2	24.4
2004	24.7	24.8	24.9	24.7	24.7	24.8	24.6	24.7	24.5	24.5	24.6	24.6	24.7
2005	25.1	25.2	25.2	24.9	24.9	25.1	25.2	25.2	25.0	24.9	25.1	25.1	25.1
2006	25.3	25.4	25.5	25.3	25.4	25.7	25.3	25.4	25.3	25.4	25.5	25.7	25.4
2007	24.9	25.1	25.3	25.3	25.4	25.5	25.7	25.7	25.5	25.5	25.3	25.5	25.4
Professional and Business Services													
2000	49.8	50.2	51.5	53.5	54.0	54.3	54.7	55.2	55.0	55.8	55.6	54.7	53.7
2001	53.6	54.7	55.5	56.9	57.1	57.6	57.4	56.3	54.9	54.0	53.9	53.7	55.5
2002	51.5	51.8	52.0	52.6	53.4	52.8	51.6	51.8	51.2	50.7	50.2	50.1	51.6
2003	48.6	48.8	48.7	48.8	49.0	48.6	48.7	49.5	49.5	50.2	50.3	50.0	49.2
2004	50.6	51.8	51.5	52.2	51.8	52.4	53.4	54.1	54.9	56.1	56.2	56.6	53.5
2005	56.2	57.7	58.3	59.3	59.8	59.8	59.9	60.3	61.2	60.5	61.1	61.0	59.6
2006	59.8	60.7	61.1	61.1	61.7	61.8	61.2	62.1	61.9	61.4	61.4	60.5	61.2
2007	60.2	61.0	61.7	62.2	62.8	62.7	62.5	63.7	62.9	61.5	60.5	59.7	61.8
Education and Health Services													
2000	46.6	47.0	47.3	47.9	48.1	47.6	47.5	47.9	48.8	48.0	48.4	48.5	47.8
2001	47.2	47.4	48.0	48.8	48.5	48.4	48.7	49.2	49.9	49.4	50.2	50.4	48.8
2002	50.5	50.9	51.1	51.0	50.7	50.0	50.7	51.8	52.6	52.1	53.0	53.0	51.5
2003	52.7	52.8	52.7	53.0	52.8	51.9	51.7	52.1	52.4	52.2	52.3	52.0	52.3
2004	52.1	52.4	52.7	52.8	52.5	52.0	52.1	52.7	53.4	53.1	53.1	53.3	52.7
2005	52.7	53.1	53.5	53.8	54.0	54.0	53.9	54.2	54.4	54.4	54.6	54.7	53.9
2006	54.3	54.7	54.9	55.0	55.4	56.0	55.5	55.8	56.5	56.7	56.8	57.1	55.7
2007	56.1	56.7	57.2	57.0	57.4	58.0	57.8	58.0	58.2	58.3	58.5	58.2	57.6
Leisure and Hospitality													
2000	33.0	33.2	33.8	34.6	34.8	35.4	35.1	35.1	34.4	34.2	33.5	33.4	34.2
2001	32.6	33.2	33.5	34.1	34.5	35.1	35.1	35.5	34.7	34.4	33.9	34.0	34.2
2002	32.8	33.1	33.9	34.7	35.6	35.6	34.4	35.0	34.3	34.1	33.5	33.5	34.2
2003	32.4	32.6	33.2	33.9	34.5	34.4	34.0	34.4	33.5	33.5	33.3	33.2	33.5
2004	32.7	33.1	34.0	34.2	34.6	35.1	34.8	35.3	34.6	34.2	34.1	34.0	34.2
2005	33.1	33.4	34.5	35.5	36.2	36.9	36.4	36.8	36.1	35.2	34.9	34.6	35.3
2006	34.8	35.0	36.2	36.5	37.2	37.6	37.4	37.6	36.5	36.2	35.6	36.3	36.4
2007	35.0	35.6	36.6	35.3	35.8	36.3	35.9	36.1	35.3	34.7	34.1	34.0	35.4
Other Services													
2000	14.0	13.9	14.2	14.5	14.6	15.0	15.0	14.8	14.6	14.5	14.4	14.6	14.5
2001	14.4	14.6	14.8	14.9	15.2	15.6	15.6	15.9	15.7	15.7	15.9	15.9	15.4
2002	15.7	15.7	15.9	16.6	16.6	17.0	16.9	16.6	16.5	16.2	16.2	16.2	16.3
2003	16.5	16.6	16.8	16.8	16.7	16.9	16.8	16.7	16.6	16.7	16.6	16.8	16.7
2004	16.8	16.8	17.1	16.9	16.9	17.3	17.0	17.0	16.8	16.8	16.8	16.9	16.9
2005	16.8	16.9	17.1	16.9	17.0	17.3	17.6	17.3	17.2	17.0	17.0	17.1	17.1
2006	17.1	17.1	17.3	17.4	17.4	17.9	17.7	17.6	17.5	17.3	17.4	17.5	17.4
2007	17.2	17.3	17.5	17.7	17.7	18.5	18.2	18.2	18.0	18.1	18.1	18.1	17.9
Government													
2000	47.1	47.7	48.6	48.4	49.0	47.8	44.4	45.3	47.3	49.1	49.0	49.6	47.8
2001	47.2	48.4	48.6	48.5	49.1	48.2	45.0	45.6	48.0	49.5	49.6	49.8	48.1
2002	48.5	49.4	49.7	50.0	50.9	48.8	45.9	46.6	48.2	49.8	49.7	49.9	49.0
2003	48.4	49.1	49.1	48.9	49.4	47.8	45.6	45.7	48.2	48.9	48.8	49.1	48.2
2004	48.0	49.1	49.3	49.3	49.4	48.5	47.4	48.0	50.4	51.1	50.3	50.7	49.3
2005	50.8	51.7	51.9	52.0	52.8	52.3	47.9	49.3	51.8	53.7	53.6	53.8	51.8
2006	53.1	53.9	54.3	53.4	54.2	52.4	47.5	48.2	52.1	53.9	53.5	53.4	52.5
2007	51.8	53.2	53.7	53.8	54.2	51.3	49.1	49.8	51.7	53.8	53.1	53.1	52.4

Employment by Industry: Dayton, OH, 2000–2007

(Numbers in thousands, not seasonally adjusted.)

Industry and year	January	February	March	April	May	June	July	August	September	October	November	December	Annual Average
Total Nonfarm													
2000	426.4	429.3	432.1	434.5	439.6	437.7	430.5	433.0	435.7	439.6	441.8	443.1	435.3
2001	426.6	429.6	431.9	432.9	433.1	432.3	424.2	425.1	426.0	427.6	428.4	427.4	428.8
2002	418.1	420.4	421.8	421.4	422.2	422.1	417.3	418.3	421.2	420.6	422.3	421.4	420.6
2003	411.5	410.6	413.2	416.8	417.2	418.0	412.8	414.1	416.1	418.1	418.8	418.9	415.5
2004	406.0	406.8	409.1	413.3	413.5	414.6	410.2	411.8	413.8	414.2	414.2	414.4	411.8
2005	404.1	405.6	408.0	412.1	412.3	411.5	407.0	408.9	412.7	412.3	413.0	413.0	410.0
2006	401.9	404.4	407.9	410.1	412.2	412.0	404.5	406.2	408.3	408.5	410.1	411.2	408.1
2007	396.6	399.2	402.4	403.7	406.5	407.0	400.6	402.4	404.8	405.1	406.4	406.4	403.4
Total Private													
2000	362.3	363.0	365.4	367.4	371.0	369.6	365.9	368.9	369.1	371.4	373.3	374.2	368.5
2001	360.5	361.8	363.7	365.1	364.5	364.0	359.8	361.3	359.5	359.6	360.1	358.9	361.6
2002	351.3	352.2	353.7	353.9	353.8	354.3	352.3	353.8	354.5	352.7	354.0	353.4	353.3
2003	346.3	344.3	347.1	350.9	350.5	351.7	349.6	351.5	351.7	352.2	352.8	352.8	350.1
2004	341.3	341.2	343.3	347.6	347.0	348.7	347.3	349.2	349.4	348.6	348.4	348.8	346.7
2005	339.8	339.9	342.5	346.6	346.1	346.8	344.4	346.6	348.1	347.1	347.7	348.4	345.3
2006	337.9	338.9	342.4	344.7	345.8	346.2	341.6	343.6	344.5	343.1	344.7	345.8	343.3
2007	332.5	334.4	337.4	338.8	340.6	341.7	338.2	340.1	340.8	339.9	341.1	341.1	338.9
Goods-Producing													
2000	95.6	94.7	95.5	96.1	97.0	97.3	95.3	96.8	96.9	96.9	96.5	95.9	96.2
2001	89.5	89.7	89.2	88.0	87.7	88.1	86.7	87.0	85.6	85.4	84.6	83.9	87.1
2002	82.5	82.7	82.2	82.8	83.0	83.8	82.7	83.4	82.5	81.9	81.4	81.0	82.5
2003	79.0	77.6	77.7	78.8	79.4	79.9	77.7	78.9	78.0	77.8	77.5	77.1	78.2
2004	74.8	74.3	74.7	75.3	75.7	76.5	75.9	76.6	76.0	75.6	74.9	74.9	75.4
2005	72.5	72.2	72.4	73.8	74.0	75.2	74.5	75.2	74.9	74.3	73.6	73.0	73.8
2006	70.5	70.8	71.6	72.2	72.5	73.4	71.2	72.1	71.5	70.8	70.3	70.4	71.4
2007	64.9	66.7	67.3	68.0	68.5	69.4	68.2	69.2	68.5	68.0	68.0	67.4	67.8
Natural Resources, Mining, and Construction													
2000	14.8	14.6	15.5	16.0	16.7	17.3	17.4	17.2	16.7	16.4	16.0	15.5	16.2
2001	13.8	13.7	14.2	14.6	15.0	15.7	16.0	16.1	15.7	15.8	15.7	15.3	15.1
2002	14.1	14.1	14.4	14.9	15.3	15.8	16.2	16.2	15.8	15.9	15.4	15.0	15.3
2003	13.8	13.3	13.7	14.7	15.3	15.8	16.1	16.3	15.9	16.1	15.9	15.6	15.2
2004	14.5	14.1	14.5	15.2	15.7	16.3	16.8	16.5	16.2	16.0	15.7	15.5	15.6
2005	14.0	13.7	14.2	15.2	15.7	16.3	16.6	16.3	16.1	15.7	15.6	15.0	15.4
2006	14.1	14.0	14.4	15.0	15.4	16.1	16.2	16.2	15.7	15.1	14.8	14.5	15.1
2007	13.4	12.8	13.5	14.5	15.2	15.9	16.0	15.7	15.3	15.1	14.8	14.4	14.7
Manufacturing													
2000	80.8	80.1	80.0	80.1	80.3	80.0	77.9	79.6	80.2	80.5	80.5	80.4	80.0
2001	75.7	76.0	75.0	73.4	72.7	72.4	70.7	70.9	69.9	69.6	68.9	68.6	72.0
2002	68.4	68.6	67.8	67.9	67.7	68.0	66.5	67.2	66.7	66.0	66.0	66.0	67.2
2003	65.2	64.3	64.0	64.1	64.1	64.1	61.6	62.6	62.1	61.7	61.6	61.5	63.0
2004	60.3	60.2	60.2	60.1	60.0	60.2	59.1	60.1	59.8	59.6	59.2	59.4	59.9
2005	58.5	58.5	58.2	58.6	58.3	58.9	57.9	58.9	58.8	58.6	58.0	58.0	58.4
2006	56.4	56.8	57.2	57.2	57.1	57.3	55.0	55.9	55.8	55.7	55.5	55.9	56.3
2007	51.5	53.9	53.8	53.5	53.3	53.5	52.2	53.5	53.2	52.9	53.2	53.0	53.1
Service-Providing													
2000	330.8	334.6	336.6	338.4	342.6	340.4	335.2	336.2	338.8	342.7	345.3	347.2	339.1
2001	337.1	339.9	342.7	344.9	345.4	344.2	337.5	338.1	340.4	342.2	343.8	343.5	341.6
2002	335.6	337.7	339.6	338.6	339.2	338.3	334.6	334.9	338.7	338.7	340.9	340.4	338.1
2003	332.5	333.0	335.5	338.0	337.8	338.1	335.1	335.2	338.1	340.3	341.3	341.8	337.2
2004	331.2	332.5	334.4	338.0	337.8	338.1	334.3	335.2	337.8	338.6	339.3	339.5	336.4
2005	331.6	333.4	335.6	338.3	338.3	336.3	332.5	333.7	337.8	338.0	339.4	340.0	336.2
2006	331.4	333.6	336.3	337.9	339.7	338.6	333.3	334.1	336.8	337.7	339.8	340.8	336.7
2007	331.7	332.5	335.1	335.7	338.0	337.6	332.4	333.2	336.3	337.1	338.4	339.0	335.6
Trade, Transportation, and Utilities													
2000	81.0	80.4	80.6	80.9	81.7	81.2	80.3	80.3	80.2	82.2	84.1	85.6	81.5
2001	80.6	79.5	79.4	79.9	79.6	79.4	78.2	77.8	77.3	77.7	79.4	79.6	79.0
2002	75.9	75.2	75.4	74.8	75.1	75.5	74.8	74.2	74.0	73.6	75.2	76.0	75.0
2003	72.7	71.5	71.9	72.6	72.8	72.4	72.0	72.1	72.2	72.7	74.1	74.7	72.6
2004	70.4	69.9	70.4	71.3	71.6	72.0	71.5	71.4	71.5	72.2	73.3	73.9	71.6
2005	70.3	70.2	70.8	71.5	71.5	71.5	71.0	70.9	70.7	70.8	72.2	73.1	71.2
2006	69.6	69.1	69.8	69.9	70.6	70.4	69.7	69.9	69.0	69.2	70.7	71.5	70.0
2007	68.1	67.3	68.1	68.7	68.9	69.1	68.9	68.6	68.4	68.7	69.6	70.3	68.7
Wholesale Trade													
2000	14.8	14.8	14.9	15.0	15.1	15.1	14.8	14.8	14.9	15.0	15.0	15.0	14.9
2001	15.2	15.0	15.0	15.3	15.3	15.0	15.0	15.1	15.2	15.3	15.3	15.3	15.2
2002	15.3	15.4	15.3	15.3	15.2	15.1	15.2	15.0	15.1	15.3	15.2	15.2	15.2
2003	14.8	14.7	14.7	14.6	14.6	14.6	14.6	14.5	14.4	14.5	14.5	14.4	14.5
2004	14.1	14.0	14.1	14.2	14.3	14.4	14.5	14.4	14.4	14.5	14.4	14.4	14.3
2005	14.0	14.1	14.1	14.2	14.2	14.3	14.3	14.4	14.1	14.1	14.0	14.1	14.1
2006	13.8	13.8	13.9	13.9	14.1	14.1	14.1	14.0	14.0	14.0	14.0	14.1	14.0
2007	13.9	13.9	14.0	14.0	14.0	14.2	14.3	14.2	14.0	14.0	14.0	14.1	14.1
Retail Trade													
2000	51.2	50.4	50.6	50.7	51.3	50.9	50.5	50.5	50.1	51.5	53.5	55.0	51.4
2001	50.2	49.3	49.3	49.5	49.5	49.6	48.4	48.0	47.8	48.2	50.0	50.4	49.2
2002	47.1	46.4	46.8	46.3	46.6	47.0	46.3	46.0	45.8	45.5	47.0	47.9	46.6
2003	45.4	44.4	45.0	45.7	45.8	45.5	45.2	45.4	45.6	45.8	47.1	47.7	45.7
2004	44.6	44.0	44.4	45.1	45.2	45.3	44.8	44.7	44.8	45.2	46.3	46.9	45.1
2005	44.1	43.8	44.3	45.0	44.9	44.7	44.0	43.9	43.8	44.0	45.3	46.0	44.5
2006	43.3	42.6	43.1	43.0	43.4	43.1	42.7	42.9	42.8	43.1	44.6	45.2	43.3
2007	42.6	41.8	42.4	43.0	43.2	43.0	42.8	42.5	42.6	42.9	43.9	44.3	42.9

Employment by Industry: Dayton, OH, 2000–2007—*Continued*

(Numbers in thousands, not seasonally adjusted.)

Industry and year	January	February	March	April	May	June	July	August	September	October	November	December	Annual Average
Transportation and Utilities													
2000	15.0	15.2	15.1	15.2	15.3	15.2	15.0	15.0	15.2	15.7	15.6	15.6	15.3
2001	15.2	15.2	15.1	15.1	14.8	14.8	14.8	14.7	14.3	14.2	14.1	13.9	14.7
2002	13.5	13.4	13.3	13.2	13.3	13.4	13.3	13.2	13.1	12.8	13.0	12.9	13.2
2003	12.5	12.4	12.2	12.3	12.4	12.3	12.2	12.2	12.2	12.4	12.5	12.6	12.3
2004	11.7	11.9	11.9	12.0	12.1	12.3	12.2	12.3	12.3	12.5	12.6	12.6	12.2
2005	12.2	12.3	12.4	12.3	12.4	12.5	12.7	12.8	12.8	12.7	12.9	13.0	12.6
2006	12.5	12.7	12.8	13.0	13.1	13.2	12.9	13.0	12.2	12.1	12.1	12.2	12.7
2007	11.6	11.6	11.7	11.7	11.7	11.9	11.8	11.9	11.8	11.8	11.7	11.9	11.8
Information													
2000	10.3	10.3	10.3	10.1	10.2	10.1	10.1	10.1	10.3	10.5	10.8	11.0	10.3
2001	11.4	11.5	11.6	11.4	11.4	11.6	11.7	11.5	11.4	11.4	11.4	11.6	11.5
2002	11.7	11.6	11.6	11.5	11.5	11.5	11.5	11.6	11.6	11.6	11.5	11.5	11.6
2003	11.7	11.6	11.6	11.5	11.4	11.5	11.5	11.4	11.2	11.3	11.3	11.3	11.4
2004	11.1	10.9	10.9	11.0	10.9	11.2	11.3	11.4	11.2	11.2	11.3	11.3	11.1
2005	11.2	11.1	11.1	11.1	11.1	11.2	11.1	10.9	10.7	10.6	10.6	10.7	11.0
2006	10.6	10.6	10.6	10.6	10.6	10.7	10.8	10.9	10.8	10.9	10.9	11.0	10.8
2007	11.0	10.9	10.9	10.9	11.1	11.1	11.0	10.9	10.8	10.8	10.9	10.9	10.9
Financial Activities													
2000	17.2	17.1	17.1	17.3	17.4	17.3	17.3	17.2	17.0	17.2	17.4	17.6	17.3
2001	17.4	17.5	17.8	17.9	18.1	18.1	18.2	18.2	18.2	18.3	18.2	18.2	18.0
2002	18.0	18.1	18.2	18.3	18.3	18.4	18.5	18.6	18.5	18.4	18.4	18.4	18.3
2003	18.4	18.5	18.6	18.7	18.9	19.1	19.1	19.1	18.9	18.8	18.8	18.8	18.8
2004	18.6	18.6	18.8	18.9	19.1	19.2	19.3	19.3	19.1	19.2	19.1	19.2	19.0
2005	18.8	18.9	18.8	19.1	19.2	19.4	19.5	19.6	19.6	19.7	19.7	19.8	19.3
2006	19.7	19.9	20.0	20.1	20.1	20.2	20.2	20.2	20.1	20.2	20.2	20.2	20.1
2007	19.9	20.0	20.0	20.2	20.3	20.2	20.2	20.2	19.9	20.0	19.9	19.9	20.1
Professional and Business Services													
2000	50.3	51.2	51.6	52.7	53.0	52.8	52.2	52.6	53.0	53.6	53.2	53.0	52.4
2001	54.2	54.7	55.7	55.8	55.7	55.6	54.6	55.1	54.7	54.4	53.9	53.4	54.8
2002	53.1	53.1	53.6	53.3	53.0	52.9	52.7	52.6	52.7	51.8	52.0	51.3	52.7
2003	52.7	52.3	52.9	54.0	53.9	54.2	54.6	54.8	54.3	54.7	54.4	54.3	53.9
2004	52.5	52.4	52.5	53.6	53.7	54.0	53.4	53.5	54.1	53.3	52.9	52.8	53.2
2005	52.0	51.6	52.0	52.2	52.1	52.0	51.8	52.4	52.4	53.0	52.7	52.9	52.3
2006	51.2	51.1	51.6	52.3	52.7	53.1	52.7	52.9	52.6	52.4	52.4	52.6	52.3
2007	51.6	51.8	52.0	52.2	52.1	52.7	52.3	52.6	52.5	52.4	52.3	52.4	52.2
Education and Health Services													
2000	57.7	58.6	58.5	58.1	58.1	57.4	57.5	58.1	58.5	58.8	59.3	59.4	58.3
2001	58.6	59.7	59.5	60.4	59.0	57.4	56.7	57.1	59.4	60.8	61.4	61.1	59.3
2002	60.2	61.2	61.4	61.3	59.9	58.6	58.3	58.8	61.9	63.0	63.4	63.2	60.9
2003	61.2	62.0	62.4	62.5	60.1	59.4	59.2	59.4	62.8	63.8	64.1	63.6	61.7
2004	62.3	63.1	63.0	63.7	61.1	60.7	60.5	60.9	62.6	64.0	63.9	64.0	62.5
2005	63.4	64.1	64.5	64.8	63.3	61.9	61.7	61.9	65.2	65.7	66.1	66.1	64.1
2006	64.7	65.5	65.8	65.7	64.5	62.7	61.9	62.5	65.8	66.6	67.1	66.9	65.0
2007	65.5	66.2	66.5	65.3	65.1	64.0	63.0	63.9	67.1	67.4	67.9	67.5	65.8
Leisure and Hospitality													
2000	34.4	34.6	35.5	35.8	37.1	37.3	37.1	37.3	36.8	35.9	35.6	35.5	36.1
2001	33.1	33.5	34.6	35.4	36.6	37.3	37.4	37.5	36.5	35.1	34.7	34.7	35.5
2002	33.7	33.8	34.6	35.4	36.4	37.0	37.0	37.2	36.6	35.8	35.4	35.3	35.7
2003	34.2	34.3	35.2	36.0	37.2	38.1	38.4	38.3	37.4	36.3	36.0	36.3	36.4
2004	35.3	35.5	36.3	37.0	38.0	38.2	38.5	38.8	38.1	36.5	36.4	36.2	37.1
2005	35.2	35.4	36.3	37.4	38.1	38.7	38.2	38.6	38.0	36.7	36.6	36.6	37.2
2006	35.6	35.8	36.8	37.4	38.3	39.0	38.7	38.8	38.3	36.9	37.0	37.1	37.5
2007	35.7	35.7	36.5	37.4	38.4	38.9	38.5	38.7	37.6	36.8	36.7	36.9	37.3
Other Services													
2000	15.8	16.1	16.3	16.4	16.5	16.2	16.1	16.5	16.4	16.3	16.4	16.2	16.3
2001	15.7	15.7	15.9	16.3	16.4	16.5	16.3	17.1	16.4	16.5	16.5	16.4	16.3
2002	16.2	16.5	16.7	16.5	16.6	16.6	16.8	17.4	16.7	16.6	16.7	16.7	16.7
2003	16.4	16.5	16.8	16.8	16.8	17.1	17.1	17.5	16.9	16.8	16.6	16.7	16.8
2004	16.3	16.5	16.7	16.8	16.9	16.9	16.9	17.3	16.8	16.6	16.6	16.5	16.7
2005	16.4	16.4	16.6	16.7	16.8	16.8	16.6	17.1	16.6	16.3	16.2	16.2	16.6
2006	16.0	16.1	16.2	16.5	16.5	16.7	16.4	16.3	16.4	16.1	16.1	16.1	16.3
2007	15.8	15.8	16.1	16.1	16.2	16.3	16.1	16.0	16.0	15.8	15.8	15.8	16.0
Government													
2000	64.1	66.3	66.7	67.1	68.6	68.1	64.6	64.1	66.6	68.2	68.5	68.9	66.8
2001	66.1	67.8	68.2	67.8	68.6	68.3	64.4	63.8	66.5	68.0	68.3	68.5	67.2
2002	66.8	68.2	68.1	67.5	68.4	67.8	65.0	64.5	66.7	67.9	68.3	68.0	67.3
2003	65.2	66.3	66.1	65.9	66.7	66.3	63.2	62.6	64.4	65.9	66.0	66.1	65.3
2004	64.7	65.6	65.8	65.7	66.5	65.9	62.9	62.6	64.4	65.6	65.8	65.6	65.1
2005	64.3	65.7	65.5	65.5	66.2	64.7	62.6	62.3	64.6	65.2	65.3	64.6	64.7
2006	64.0	65.5	65.5	65.4	66.4	65.8	62.9	62.6	63.8	65.4	65.4	65.4	64.8
2007	64.1	64.8	65.0	64.9	65.9	65.3	62.4	62.3	64.0	65.2	65.3	65.3	64.5

Employment by Industry: Tucson, AZ, 2000–2007

(Numbers in thousands, not seasonally adjusted.)

Industry and year	January	February	March	April	May	June	July	August	September	October	November	December	Annual Average
Total Nonfarm													
2000	342.0	347.0	349.9	348.3	349.0	345.0	336.8	340.3	346.0	349.9	353.6	355.5	346.9
2001	341.2	346.9	349.6	349.7	348.1	341.6	333.8	339.3	344.3	343.9	347.3	347.7	344.5
2002	341.1	344.4	345.3	347.0	346.2	338.6	329.2	335.9	341.9	345.7	349.3	350.0	342.9
2003	340.6	343.7	345.8	345.9	346.2	338.6	333.4	340.4	347.0	350.7	353.3	356.8	345.2
2004	350.0	354.0	354.8	359.0	358.8	351.8	345.5	352.0	358.0	363.8	367.6	369.4	357.1
2005	356.3	362.2	364.2	368.5	368.4	361.1	358.7	364.7	370.8	371.4	374.9	378.8	366.7
2006	371.4	378.3	379.0	380.2	380.0	373.5	369.4	375.9	381.6	386.0	388.2	391.8	379.6
2007	380.6	387.5	388.7	386.8	386.2	377.9	374.2	376.3	381.9	384.8	386.9	385.9	383.1
Total Private													
2000	270.2	273.0	274.7	272.8	272.3	273.3	270.2	272.5	273.5	274.7	277.5	279.5	273.7
2001	268.6	271.3	273.2	273.0	271.8	271.0	269.5	270.6	269.6	268.3	269.9	270.5	270.6
2002	266.4	267.5	268.4	268.8	268.8	267.2	264.4	266.4	267.0	268.3	270.9	271.8	268.0
2003	264.9	265.6	267.3	267.7	267.9	267.9	266.7	269.7	271.0	272.6	275.4	277.8	269.5
2004	273.5	275.1	275.9	279.9	279.8	278.2	279.0	280.9	280.1	283.9	287.1	288.6	280.2
2005	280.1	282.7	284.3	288.8	288.8	288.2	288.3	291.3	293.2	293.1	296.0	300.1	289.6
2006	295.7	299.9	300.8	301.6	302.1	302.2	300.9	303.5	305.9	306.8	308.6	311.9	303.3
2007	303.8	307.4	308.9	307.2	307.5	306.4	302.8	302.2	301.7	303.8	305.8	305.7	305.3
Goods-Producing													
2000	56.1	56.2	56.8	56.7	56.6	57.7	57.9	58.5	58.5	58.2	58.5	59.1	57.6
2001	56.9	57.1	57.7	57.5	57.7	58.2	58.4	58.7	58.1	57.3	56.7	56.0	57.5
2002	55.1	54.5	54.6	54.4	54.7	55.0	54.9	55.1	54.7	54.2	54.0	53.9	54.6
2003	53.0	52.3	52.7	52.2	52.6	53.0	52.9	53.1	52.5	53.1	52.9	53.2	52.7
2004	52.9	52.8	52.9	53.2	53.4	53.6	54.2	54.0	54.1	54.4	54.4	54.8	53.7
2005	53.1	53.8	54.2	54.8	55.1	55.8	55.8	56.4	56.5	56.0	56.3	56.9	55.4
2006	56.3	57.3	57.0	57.5	57.8	58.5	58.8	58.6	58.4	58.1	56.6	56.3	57.6
2007	54.9	56.4	56.0	55.4	55.7	56.3	56.0	55.8	55.1	55.5	55.3	55.5	55.7
Natural Resources and Mining													
2000	1.8	1.8	1.8	1.8	1.8	1.8	1.8	1.8	1.8	1.8	1.8	1.8	1.8
2001	1.8	1.8	1.8	1.8	1.8	1.8	1.8	1.8	1.7	1.7	1.7	1.7	1.8
2002	1.7	1.6	1.6	1.6	1.6	1.6	1.4	1.4	1.5	1.4	1.4	1.4	1.5
2003	1.3	1.1	1.2	1.1	1.2	1.2	1.2	1.2	1.2	1.2	1.2	1.2	1.1
2004	1.2	1.2	1.2	1.3	1.3	1.3	1.3	1.3	1.4	1.4	1.4	1.4	1.3
2005	1.4	1.4	1.5	1.5	1.5	1.5	1.2	1.2	1.2	1.2	1.4	1.5	1.4
2006	1.4	1.5	1.5	1.5	1.5	1.6	1.6	1.6	1.6	1.6	1.7	1.7	1.6
2007	1.7	1.7	1.7	1.7	1.8	1.8	1.9	1.9	1.9	2.1	1.9	2.0	1.8
Construction													
2000	22.3	22.3	22.6	22.5	22.5	23.0	23.1	23.5	23.4	23.1	23.0	23.3	22.9
2001	21.9	22.2	22.6	22.3	22.5	22.9	23.3	23.6	23.5	22.9	22.6	22.3	22.7
2002	21.9	21.8	22.0	21.8	22.2	22.6	22.9	23.3	23.0	23.0	23.0	23.0	22.5
2003	22.5	22.3	22.4	22.5	22.8	23.2	23.1	23.2	22.8	23.4	23.3	23.4	22.9
2004	23.3	23.3	23.3	23.6	23.8	23.9	24.3	24.2	24.2	24.6	24.6	24.9	24.0
2005	23.7	24.2	24.6	25.3	25.5	26.0	26.2	26.5	26.8	26.4	26.6	26.8	25.7
2006	26.3	26.7	26.9	27.5	27.9	28.4	28.7	28.7	28.7	28.7	28.5	28.3	27.9
2007	27.1	26.9	26.9	26.4	26.6	26.9	26.4	26.2	25.7	25.7	25.7	25.7	26.4
Manufacturing													
2000	32.0	32.1	32.4	32.4	32.3	32.9	33.0	33.2	33.3	33.3	33.7	34.0	32.9
2001	33.2	33.1	33.3	33.4	33.4	33.5	33.3	33.3	32.9	32.7	32.4	32.0	33.0
2002	31.5	31.1	31.0	31.0	30.9	30.8	30.6	30.4	30.2	29.8	29.6	29.5	30.5
2003	29.2	28.9	29.1	28.6	28.6	28.6	28.6	28.7	28.5	28.5	28.4	28.6	28.6
2004	28.4	28.3	28.4	28.3	28.3	28.4	28.6	28.5	28.5	28.4	28.4	28.5	28.4
2005	28.0	28.2	28.1	28.0	28.1	28.3	28.4	28.7	28.5	28.4	28.3	28.6	28.3
2006	28.6	29.1	28.6	28.5	28.4	28.5	28.5	28.3	28.1	27.8	26.4	26.3	28.1
2007	26.1	27.8	27.4	27.3	27.3	27.6	27.7	27.7	27.5	27.7	27.7	27.8	27.5
Service-Providing													
2000	285.9	290.8	293.1	291.6	292.4	287.3	278.9	281.8	287.5	291.7	295.1	296.4	289.4
2001	284.3	289.8	291.9	292.2	290.4	283.4	275.4	280.6	286.2	286.6	290.6	291.7	286.9
2002	286.0	289.9	290.7	292.6	291.5	283.6	274.3	280.8	287.2	291.5	295.3	296.1	288.3
2003	287.6	291.4	293.1	293.7	293.6	285.6	280.5	287.3	294.5	297.6	300.4	303.6	292.4
2004	297.1	301.2	301.9	305.8	305.4	298.2	291.3	298.0	303.9	309.4	313.2	314.6	303.3
2005	303.2	308.4	310.0	313.7	313.3	305.3	302.9	308.3	314.3	315.4	318.6	321.9	311.3
2006	315.1	321.0	322.0	322.7	322.2	315.0	310.6	317.3	323.2	327.9	331.6	335.5	322.0
2007	325.7	331.1	332.7	331.4	330.5	321.6	318.2	320.5	326.8	329.3	331.6	330.4	327.5
Trade, Transportation, and Utilities													
2000	54.2	54.0	53.8	53.5	53.7	53.8	54.1	54.7	54.9	56.0	57.9	58.9	55.0
2001	55.7	55.2	55.1	55.0	55.0	54.9	54.6	54.6	54.9	54.9	56.5	57.6	55.3
2002	54.1	53.8	53.8	54.0	54.4	54.2	53.5	53.6	53.5	54.4	55.9	57.0	54.4
2003	54.0	54.0	54.4	54.1	54.1	54.2	54.0	54.9	54.9	55.7	57.6	58.8	55.1
2004	56.2	56.1	56.4	57.1	57.8	57.9	57.9	58.0	57.7	58.5	60.3	61.0	57.9
2005	58.0	58.0	58.2	58.3	58.3	58.3	58.8	59.4	59.8	60.8	62.6	64.1	59.6
2006	61.1	61.0	61.2	61.3	61.7	61.5	61.9	62.7	63.1	63.8	65.5	67.0	62.7
2007	63.9	63.3	64.0	63.8	64.0	63.7	63.3	63.3	63.1	63.9	65.5	65.5	63.9
Wholesale Trade													
2000	7.6	7.6	7.6	7.2	7.3	7.4	7.4	7.4	7.4	7.4	7.5	7.6	7.5
2001	7.3	7.3	7.4	7.4	7.4	7.5	7.4	7.4	7.4	7.3	7.4	7.4	7.4
2002	7.5	7.4	7.4	7.2	7.3	7.3	7.2	7.3	7.3	7.4	7.4	7.4	7.3
2003	7.2	7.3	7.3	7.3	7.4	7.4	7.4	7.5	7.5	7.5	7.6	7.6	7.4
2004	7.5	7.5	7.6	8.1	8.4	8.4	8.3	8.2	8.2	8.0	8.1	8.2	8.0
2005	8.0	8.1	8.2	8.3	8.4	8.5	8.6	8.7	8.9	9.0	9.0	9.2	8.6
2006	9.0	9.1	9.2	9.2	9.3	9.4	9.5	9.7	9.8	9.7	9.8	9.9	9.5
2007	9.6	9.6	9.8	9.8	9.8	9.9	9.8	9.8	9.7	9.9	10.0	10.0	9.8

Employment by Industry: Tucson, AZ, 2000–2007—*Continued*

(Numbers in thousands, not seasonally adjusted.)

Industry and year	January	February	March	April	May	June	July	August	September	October	November	December	Annual Average
Retail Trade													
2000	38.0	37.9	37.7	37.8	37.9	37.9	37.7	38.3	38.6	39.6	41.3	42.1	38.7
2001	39.0	38.5	38.3	38.3	38.2	38.1	37.9	37.9	38.3	38.6	40.1	41.3	38.7
2002	39.1	38.8	38.8	39.1	39.4	39.2	38.6	38.6	38.7	39.2	40.7	41.8	39.3
2003	39.0	38.9	39.3	39.0	38.9	39.0	38.8	39.2	39.3	40.0	41.8	42.9	39.6
2004	40.6	40.5	40.7	40.8	41.1	41.2	41.3	41.4	41.1	41.7	43.4	43.9	41.5
2005	41.2	41.0	41.0	41.1	41.0	40.8	41.3	41.8	42.0	42.8	44.6	45.8	42.0
2006	43.1	42.9	43.0	43.0	43.2	42.9	43.1	43.7	43.9	44.7	46.2	47.3	43.9
2007	45.1	44.6	45.0	44.8	44.9	44.5	44.1	44.2	44.2	44.8	46.3	46.3	44.9
Transportation and Utilities													
2000	8.6	8.5	8.5	8.5	8.5	8.5	9.0	9.0	8.9	9.0	9.1	9.2	8.8
2001	9.4	9.4	9.4	9.3	9.4	9.3	9.3	9.3	9.2	9.0	9.0	8.9	9.2
2002	7.5	7.6	7.6	7.7	7.7	7.7	7.7	7.7	7.5	7.8	7.8	7.8	7.7
2003	7.8	7.8	7.8	7.8	7.8	7.8	7.8	8.2	8.1	8.2	8.2	8.3	7.9
2004	8.1	8.1	8.1	8.2	8.3	8.3	8.3	8.4	8.4	8.8	8.8	8.9	8.4
2005	8.8	8.9	9.0	8.9	8.9	9.0	8.9	8.9	8.9	9.0	9.0	9.1	8.9
2006	9.0	9.0	9.0	9.1	9.2	9.2	9.3	9.3	9.4	9.4	9.5	9.8	9.3
2007	9.2	9.1	9.2	9.2	9.3	9.3	9.3	9.4	9.3	9.2	9.2	9.2	9.2
Information													
2000	7.9	8.1	8.0	8.0	8.1	8.0	7.9	8.1	7.8	7.8	7.8	7.8	7.9
2001	7.8	7.8	7.8	7.7	7.7	7.6	7.6	7.7	7.7	7.6	7.8	7.9	7.7
2002	7.9	8.0	8.0	7.9	8.0	7.8	7.8	7.9	7.8	7.8	7.9	7.8	7.9
2003	7.6	7.7	7.5	7.5	7.6	7.5	7.5	7.6	7.3	7.4	7.7	7.7	7.5
2004	7.5	7.7	7.5	7.5	7.6	7.5	7.6	7.8	7.3	7.4	7.7	7.6	7.6
2005	7.3	7.2	7.2	7.2	7.2	7.2	7.2	7.2	7.2	7.2	7.2	7.3	7.2
2006	7.5	7.5	7.4	6.9	6.9	6.9	6.7	6.5	6.5	6.3	6.2	6.0	6.8
2007	6.3	6.2	6.2	6.1	6.1	5.9	5.9	5.9	5.8	5.8	5.7	5.7	6.0
Financial Activities													
2000	14.6	14.8	14.9	14.6	14.6	14.7	14.9	15.0	15.0	15.2	14.8	14.8	14.8
2001	14.2	14.4	14.5	14.8	14.7	14.7	14.8	14.5	14.1	14.2	14.3	14.3	14.5
2002	14.0	14.1	14.2	14.2	14.4	14.3	14.2	14.3	14.4	14.7	14.7	14.8	14.4
2003	14.8	14.9	15.1	15.0	15.2	15.2	15.5	15.7	16.2	16.3	16.1	16.2	15.5
2004	16.1	16.2	16.1	16.2	16.1	15.8	16.0	15.9	15.7	15.7	15.7	15.8	15.9
2005	15.5	15.7	15.7	16.0	16.2	16.4	16.6	17.0	17.1	17.1	17.2	17.5	16.5
2006	16.7	16.9	17.0	17.3	17.4	17.5	17.6	17.8	18.0	18.3	18.4	18.7	17.6
2007	18.4	18.5	18.6	18.6	18.7	18.7	18.6	17.1	16.7	16.7	16.7	16.8	17.8
Professional and Business Services													
2000	42.3	43.4	44.6	44.2	44.1	44.5	42.8	43.4	43.3	42.8	43.0	43.3	43.5
2001	41.0	42.2	42.4	42.3	41.5	41.6	41.4	41.4	40.5	40.6	40.5	40.3	41.3
2002	40.4	41.0	41.3	41.5	40.9	41.1	41.2	41.9	42.0	42.0	42.4	42.2	41.5
2003	40.6	40.6	40.7	41.0	40.8	41.5	41.2	41.6	42.1	41.7	41.5	41.5	41.2
2004	41.2	41.7	41.8	43.4	42.7	42.8	43.5	43.9	43.8	45.3	45.3	45.4	43.4
2005	44.1	44.5	44.5	45.8	45.5	45.5	46.3	47.0	47.0	46.5	46.6	47.6	45.9
2006	47.3	48.4	48.5	48.6	48.6	49.1	49.5	50.0	50.9	50.9	52.0	53.1	49.7
2007	51.5	52.1	52.3	52.0	51.7	52.1	52.3	52.8	52.8	52.9	52.9	52.6	52.3
Education and Health Services													
2000	42.4	42.5	42.3	41.8	41.6	41.4	41.0	41.6	42.1	42.2	42.4	42.4	42.0
2001	40.7	41.0	41.6	41.5	41.4	41.3	41.3	41.7	42.2	42.4	42.9	43.2	41.8
2002	42.9	43.4	43.4	43.4	43.7	43.4	42.7	43.5	43.9	44.0	44.3	44.3	43.6
2003	44.3	44.9	45.0	45.4	45.5	45.3	45.3	46.1	46.5	46.1	46.6	46.8	45.6
2004	46.7	46.7	46.9	47.1	47.5	47.2	47.2	48.2	48.5	48.9	49.1	49.2	47.8
2005	49.1	49.5	49.7	50.2	50.5	49.8	49.9	50.8	51.4	51.6	51.7	52.2	50.5
2006	51.6	52.1	52.5	52.0	52.3	52.0	51.7	52.6	53.0	53.3	53.6	54.2	52.6
2007	53.5	54.0	54.3	53.9	54.5	53.8	53.6	54.2	54.5	54.7	54.8	54.8	54.2
Leisure and Hospitality													
2000	39.8	40.9	41.3	41.0	40.6	39.9	38.5	38.4	39.0	39.6	40.1	40.0	39.9
2001	38.5	39.7	40.0	40.0	39.4	38.1	36.9	37.4	37.6	37.0	36.9	36.9	38.2
2002	37.8	38.4	38.8	38.7	37.9	36.7	35.5	35.6	36.2	36.8	37.3	37.4	37.3
2003	36.4	36.9	37.5	37.9	37.5	36.6	35.7	36.1	36.9	37.5	38.2	38.9	37.1
2004	38.6	39.4	39.7	40.5	39.8	38.6	37.7	38.3	38.4	38.8	39.7	40.0	39.1
2005	38.7	39.6	40.2	41.6	41.1	40.4	39.0	38.9	39.6	39.1	39.4	39.6	39.8
2006	39.7	40.9	41.2	41.9	41.1	40.2	39.3	39.9	40.8	40.5	40.7	40.9	40.6
2007	39.8	41.1	41.5	41.5	41.0	39.9	37.8	37.8	38.5	39.1	39.8	39.9	39.8
Other Services													
2000	12.9	13.1	13.0	13.0	13.0	13.3	13.1	12.8	12.9	12.9	13.0	13.2	13.0
2001	13.8	13.9	14.1	14.2	14.4	14.6	14.5	14.6	14.5	14.5	14.3	14.3	14.3
2002	14.2	14.3	14.3	14.7	14.8	14.7	14.6	14.6	14.5	14.5	14.4	14.4	14.5
2003	14.2	14.3	14.4	14.6	14.6	14.6	14.6	14.6	14.6	14.8	14.8	14.7	14.5
2004	14.3	14.5	14.6	14.9	14.9	14.8	14.9	14.8	14.6	14.9	14.9	14.8	14.7
2005	14.3	14.4	14.6	14.9	14.9	14.8	14.7	14.6	14.6	14.8	15.0	14.9	14.7
2006	15.5	15.8	16.0	16.1	16.3	16.5	15.4	15.4	15.2	15.6	15.6	15.7	15.8
2007	15.5	15.8	16.0	15.9	15.8	16.0	15.3	15.3	15.2	15.2	15.1	14.9	15.5
Government													
2000	71.8	74.0	75.2	75.5	76.7	71.7	66.6	67.8	72.5	75.2	76.1	76.0	73.3
2001	72.6	75.6	76.4	76.7	76.3	70.6	64.3	68.7	74.7	75.6	77.4	77.2	73.8
2002	74.7	76.9	76.9	78.2	77.4	71.4	64.8	69.5	74.9	77.4	78.4	78.2	74.9
2003	75.7	78.1	78.5	78.2	78.3	70.7	66.7	70.7	76.0	78.1	77.9	79.0	75.7
2004	76.5	78.9	78.9	79.1	79.0	73.6	66.5	71.1	77.9	79.9	80.5	80.8	76.9
2005	76.2	79.5	79.9	79.7	79.6	72.9	70.4	73.4	77.6	78.3	78.9	78.7	77.1
2006	75.7	78.4	78.2	78.6	77.9	71.3	68.5	72.4	75.7	79.2	79.6	79.9	76.3
2007	76.8	80.1	79.8	79.6	78.7	71.5	71.4	74.1	80.2	81.0	81.1	80.2	77.9

Employment by Industry: Albany-Schenectady-Troy, NY, 2000–2007

(Numbers in thousands, not seasonally adjusted.)

Industry and year	January	February	March	April	May	June	July	August	September	October	November	December	Annual Average
Total Nonfarm													
2000	425.3	428.5	430.9	436.1	439.8	443.1	434.7	435.0	439.4	443.7	446.9	448.0	437.6
2001	433.5	435.7	438.2	440.7	445.3	446.7	439.8	442.9	440.7	443.3	446.4	445.4	441.6
2002	428.6	433.3	436.8	440.7	442.8	443.8	437.1	439.8	442.0	444.3	445.7	444.7	440.0
2003	429.4	433.0	434.0	437.1	441.4	441.7	436.8	439.3	440.3	444.1	446.7	446.4	439.2
2004	432.2	435.7	438.5	441.7	448.8	447.7	442.7	443.2	448.0	449.5	450.5	450.4	443.6
2005	436.2	439.0	439.4	446.2	447.7	449.0	444.5	445.5	447.1	449.9	451.6	451.1	445.6
2006	436.0	440.4	443.5	447.6	449.8	450.7	443.9	444.5	446.7	451.6	453.7	454.8	446.9
2007	438.7	441.5	444.2	445.6	451.1	453.7	447.3	447.3	449.1	453.3	454.0	454.3	448.3
Total Private													
2000	320.2	321.0	323.4	327.9	330.9	334.6	332.2	333.3	333.1	336.0	338.1	340.1	330.9
2001	327.1	326.6	329.3	331.3	335.9	338.5	335.8	338.4	333.7	334.3	336.1	336.1	333.6
2002	321.4	323.0	326.5	330.0	332.2	333.9	333.3	336.6	333.4	334.4	335.2	334.4	331.2
2003	321.4	322.8	324.4	328.1	332.4	333.5	333.9	337.1	333.5	335.6	338.0	337.6	331.5
2004	326.1	327.4	330.1	332.6	339.3	338.4	339.2	340.5	338.5	339.8	340.9	342.0	336.2
2005	329.0	330.5	330.8	337.1	338.6	340.6	341.7	343.4	341.2	341.6	343.1	342.5	338.3
2006	329.9	332.3	335.4	339.0	341.3	343.1	341.6	343.2	341.8	343.7	345.2	345.6	340.2
2007	331.8	332.6	335.6	336.9	341.8	344.2	343.3	344.1	343.0	344.3	344.7	344.0	340.5
Goods-Producing													
2000	43.8	43.1	43.9	45.4	47.0	47.8	47.3	47.8	47.3	47.3	46.9	46.2	46.2
2001	43.8	43.4	43.6	44.9	46.4	47.3	47.0	47.2	46.4	45.9	45.0	43.4	45.4
2002	40.4	39.7	40.3	41.5	42.7	43.4	43.9	44.1	43.6	43.0	42.4	40.8	42.2
2003	38.6	37.8	37.9	38.9	40.5	41.4	41.8	42.4	41.9	42.0	41.3	40.2	40.3
2004	38.0	37.5	37.9	39.6	41.1	41.8	42.7	42.9	42.3	42.0	41.7	40.4	40.7
2005	38.8	38.1	38.3	40.5	41.8	42.6	43.3	43.4	42.8	42.4	42.3	40.9	41.3
2006	39.1	38.5	39.1	40.9	42.1	42.9	43.0	43.3	42.7	42.7	42.0	40.8	41.4
2007	38.8	37.8	38.6	39.8	41.8	42.7	43.2	43.3	42.7	42.8	41.7	39.9	41.1
Natural Resources, Mining, and Construction													
2000	15.4	14.9	15.5	16.7	18.1	18.8	19.1	19.4	19.0	18.7	18.5	17.4	17.6
2001	15.8	15.4	15.6	17.0	18.5	19.2	19.6	19.9	19.4	19.1	18.5	17.3	17.9
2002	15.3	14.8	15.3	16.7	17.9	18.4	19.1	19.3	18.9	18.5	18.3	17.1	17.5
2003	15.5	14.9	15.0	16.1	17.7	18.6	19.5	19.8	19.3	19.3	18.6	17.6	17.6
2004	15.8	15.4	15.7	17.1	18.5	19.0	19.6	19.5	19.2	19.0	18.6	17.4	17.9
2005	16.0	15.4	15.5	17.4	18.6	19.3	20.0	20.0	19.6	19.4	19.2	17.9	18.2
2006	16.1	15.6	16.1	17.6	18.7	19.4	19.6	19.8	19.4	19.4	18.6	17.6	18.2
2007	16.0	15.1	15.7	16.8	18.7	19.4	20.0	20.1	19.8	20.0	18.9	17.2	18.1
Manufacturing													
2000	28.4	28.2	28.4	28.7	28.9	29.0	28.2	28.4	28.3	28.6	28.4	28.8	28.5
2001	28.0	28.0	28.0	27.9	27.9	28.1	27.4	27.3	27.0	26.8	26.5	26.1	27.4
2002	25.1	24.9	25.0	24.8	24.8	25.0	24.8	24.8	24.7	24.5	24.1	23.7	24.7
2003	23.1	22.9	22.9	22.8	22.8	22.8	22.3	22.6	22.6	22.7	22.7	22.6	22.7
2004	22.2	22.1	22.2	22.5	22.6	22.8	23.1	23.4	23.1	23.0	23.1	23.0	22.8
2005	22.8	22.7	22.8	23.1	23.2	23.3	23.3	23.4	23.2	23.0	23.1	23.0	23.1
2006	23.0	22.9	23.0	23.3	23.4	23.5	23.4	23.5	23.3	23.3	23.4	23.2	23.3
2007	22.8	22.7	22.9	23.0	23.1	23.3	23.2	23.2	22.9	22.8	22.8	22.7	23.0
Service-Providing													
2000	381.5	385.4	387.0	390.7	392.8	395.3	387.4	387.2	392.1	396.4	400.0	401.8	391.5
2001	389.7	392.3	394.6	395.8	398.9	399.4	392.8	395.7	394.3	397.4	401.4	402.0	396.2
2002	388.2	393.6	396.5	399.2	400.1	400.4	393.2	395.7	398.4	401.3	403.3	403.9	397.8
2003	390.8	395.2	396.1	398.2	400.9	400.3	395.0	396.9	398.4	402.1	405.4	406.2	398.8
2004	394.2	398.2	400.6	402.1	407.7	405.9	400.0	400.3	402.4	406.0	407.8	410.1	402.9
2005	397.4	400.9	401.1	405.7	405.9	406.4	401.2	402.1	404.3	407.5	409.3	410.2	404.3
2006	396.9	401.9	404.4	406.7	407.7	407.8	400.9	401.2	404.0	408.9	411.7	414.0	405.5
2007	399.9	403.7	405.6	405.8	409.3	411.0	404.1	404.0	406.4	410.5	412.3	414.4	407.3
Trade, Transportation, and Utilities													
2000	77.3	76.3	76.6	76.8	77.7	78.5	78.3	79.4	79.3	80.6	82.8	84.6	79.0
2001	78.8	77.6	77.4	76.8	77.6	78.5	77.3	77.5	76.7	77.9	80.5	81.5	78.2
2002	76.8	75.6	76.0	76.4	76.8	77.7	77.1	77.2	77.0	77.4	79.3	80.9	77.4
2003	77.4	76.4	76.5	76.4	77.3	78.4	77.5	78.0	78.1	79.5	81.8	83.2	78.3
2004	78.7	78.0	78.2	77.8	79.0	79.8	79.8	78.8	79.0	79.0	80.4	82.3	83.7	79.6
2005	79.4	78.0	77.9	78.6	79.1	79.1	79.7	79.8	80.1	79.6	80.2	82.0	83.5	79.8
2006	78.8	77.4	77.7	78.0	79.0	79.6	78.4	78.5	77.8	78.9	81.1	82.4	79.0
2007	77.9	76.1	76.8	76.1	77.3	78.0	77.6	77.4	77.3	78.2	79.6	81.0	77.8
Wholesale Trade													
2000	16.2	16.2	16.4	16.5	16.5	16.5	16.5	16.6	16.5	16.5	16.6	16.7	16.5
2001	16.3	16.3	16.2	16.4	16.4	16.6	16.8	16.6	16.5	16.3	16.2	16.3	16.4
2002	16.3	16.2	16.2	16.2	16.3	16.3	16.4	16.3	16.2	16.1	16.2	16.2	16.2
2003	16.5	16.5	16.5	16.4	16.5	16.6	16.6	16.6	16.6	16.6	16.8	17.0	16.6
2004	16.7	16.9	16.9	16.9	16.8	16.7	16.4	16.4	16.3	16.2	16.2	16.2	16.6
2005	15.9	15.7	15.7	15.7	15.6	15.6	15.9	15.8	15.6	15.6	15.7	15.7	15.7
2006	15.3	15.2	15.2	14.9	14.9	15.0	14.9	14.9	14.7	14.7	14.6	14.8	14.9
2007	14.7	14.6	14.8	14.8	14.8	14.9	14.8	14.9	14.7	14.8	14.7	14.8	14.8
Retail Trade													
2000	49.2	48.1	48.1	48.1	48.5	49.2	49.2	50.0	49.9	50.9	52.9	54.5	49.9
2001	49.3	48.2	48.1	47.2	47.7	48.4	47.5	47.7	46.9	48.1	50.8	51.7	48.5
2002	47.8	46.8	47.2	47.5	47.7	48.5	48.2	48.3	47.9	48.2	50.0	51.6	48.3
2003	48.1	47.0	47.1	47.3	48.0	49.0	48.6	49.0	48.8	50.1	52.2	53.5	49.0
2004	49.9	48.8	48.9	48.5	49.4	50.2	49.8	50.1	49.8	51.0	52.9	54.3	50.3
2005	50.6	49.3	49.2	49.5	49.9	50.3	50.3	50.5	49.8	50.5	52.0	53.5	50.5
2006	49.8	48.5	48.7	49.4	50.2	50.7	50.1	50.0	49.2	50.2	52.6	53.6	50.3
2007	50.0	48.4	48.7	48.2	49.1	49.7	49.6	49.4	49.1	49.9	51.3	52.6	49.7

Employment by Industry: Albany-Schenectady-Troy, NY, 2000–2007—*Continued*

(Numbers in thousands, not seasonally adjusted.)

Industry and year	January	February	March	April	May	June	July	August	September	October	November	December	Annual Average
Transportation and Utilities													
2000	11.9	12.0	12.1	12.2	12.7	12.8	12.6	12.8	12.9	13.2	13.3	13.4	12.7
2001	13.2	13.1	13.1	13.2	13.5	13.5	13.0	13.2	13.3	13.5	13.5	13.5	13.3
2002	12.7	12.6	12.6	12.7	12.8	12.9	12.5	12.6	12.9	13.1	13.1	13.1	12.8
2003	12.8	12.9	12.9	12.7	12.8	12.8	12.3	12.4	12.7	12.8	12.8	12.7	12.7
2004	12.1	12.3	12.4	12.4	12.8	12.9	12.6	12.5	12.9	13.2	13.2	13.2	12.7
2005	12.9	13.0	13.0	13.4	13.6	13.8	13.6	13.8	14.2	14.1	14.3	14.3	13.7
2006	13.7	13.7	13.8	13.7	13.9	13.9	13.4	13.6	13.9	14.0	13.9	14.0	13.8
2007	13.2	13.1	13.3	13.1	13.4	13.4	13.2	13.1	13.5	13.5	13.6	13.6	13.3
Information													
2000	11.8	11.9	12.0	12.3	12.3	12.5	12.3	10.7	12.3	12.0	12.1	12.2	12.0
2001	12.2	12.1	12.2	12.2	12.3	12.4	12.1	12.1	12.1	12.0	12.0	12.0	12.1
2002	11.9	11.9	12.0	12.0	12.1	12.1	11.9	11.9	11.8	11.9	12.0	12.0	12.0
2003	11.6	11.7	12.0	12.0	11.8	11.5	11.2	11.1	10.8	10.6	10.4	10.2	11.2
2004	11.1	11.1	11.5	11.0	10.7	10.7	10.8	10.8	10.8	10.6	10.7	10.5	10.9
2005	10.5	10.6	10.8	11.1	11.0	11.1	11.0	11.1	10.9	10.9	10.8	10.9	10.9
2006	10.8	10.7	10.7	10.6	10.6	10.6	10.5	10.4	10.1	10.2	10.2	10.2	10.5
2007	10.1	10.0	10.0	10.0	10.0	9.9	10.0	9.9	9.7	9.8	9.8	9.8	9.9
Financial Activities													
2000	24.6	24.7	24.7	24.9	25.0	25.3	25.2	25.3	24.9	24.8	24.9	25.3	25.0
2001	24.5	24.6	24.7	24.4	24.6	25.1	25.0	25.0	24.7	24.8	24.8	24.9	24.8
2002	24.4	24.7	24.9	24.8	25.1	25.4	25.0	25.3	24.8	25.2	25.3	25.4	25.0
2003	25.3	25.3	25.4	25.5	25.8	26.3	26.3	26.3	25.9	26.0	26.1	26.1	25.8
2004	25.8	25.6	25.9	25.7	25.8	26.5	26.6	26.5	26.4	26.3	26.1	26.3	26.1
2005	25.9	25.9	26.0	26.1	26.2	26.6	26.8	26.8	26.5	26.5	26.4	26.6	26.4
2006	26.2	26.3	26.5	26.7	26.6	27.0	27.1	27.0	26.6	26.7	26.7	26.7	26.7
2007	26.3	26.0	26.0	26.1	26.2	26.7	26.5	26.3	25.9	25.7	25.7	25.9	26.1
Professional and Business Services													
2000	50.0	50.0	50.3	51.3	51.6	52.4	52.1	52.5	51.7	52.2	52.5	52.7	51.6
2001	51.9	52.2	52.1	52.7	53.4	53.8	53.5	53.7	52.4	51.8	51.5	51.9	52.6
2002	49.2	49.0	49.5	50.2	49.9	50.7	50.5	50.8	50.2	50.1	49.5	49.2	49.9
2003	47.5	47.4	47.7	48.8	49.5	50.3	50.5	50.8	50.0	50.0	50.4	50.7	49.5
2004	49.1	49.2	49.6	50.6	51.2	52.2	52.2	52.3	51.6	50.9	51.1	51.2	50.9
2005	50.7	50.9	50.8	51.8	51.7	52.9	53.4	53.1	53.1	52.5	52.7	52.1	52.1
2006	51.8	52.1	52.7	53.6	53.0	53.8	54.3	54.3	54.0	53.5	54.0	54.1	53.4
2007	52.4	52.9	53.4	53.8	53.8	55.2	55.4	55.4	54.6	54.6	54.8	54.8	54.3
Education and Health Services													
2000	68.7	70.5	70.8	70.7	70.1	69.3	68.7	68.8	70.1	72.7	72.9	73.0	70.5
2001	71.3	72.2	74.1	74.0	73.2	71.2	71.2	71.1	73.6	74.8	75.3	75.3	73.1
2002	72.9	75.8	76.5	76.7	75.4	73.5	73.7	73.7	76.2	77.4	77.6	77.6	75.6
2003	74.8	77.6	77.8	78.2	77.6	75.1	74.4	74.1	76.6	77.9	78.7	78.3	76.7
2004	75.9	78.4	78.5	79.0	80.3	75.3	75.5	74.9	77.8	79.4	79.5	80.2	77.9
2005	76.3	79.2	78.8	79.5	78.2	75.9	75.6	75.0	77.4	79.0	79.2	78.8	77.7
2006	76.3	79.4	79.5	79.9	79.0	76.7	75.9	75.6	79.4	80.8	81.1	81.2	78.7
2007	77.9	81.0	81.1	81.2	80.5	78.3	76.9	76.6	80.6	82.1	82.6	82.2	80.1
Leisure and Hospitality													
2000	27.3	27.7	28.2	29.3	30.0	31.4	31.1	31.5	30.4	29.0	28.4	28.4	29.4
2001	27.3	27.2	27.8	29.1	31.0	32.6	32.5	34.6	30.6	29.8	29.4	29.4	30.1
2002	28.5	28.8	29.6	30.5	32.3	33.2	33.4	35.8	32.0	31.3	30.7	30.2	31.4
2003	28.0	28.4	28.9	30.1	31.7	32.3	33.8	36.0	32.0	31.2	30.8	30.5	31.1
2004	29.2	29.2	30.0	30.4	32.6	33.7	34.2	35.8	32.5	31.6	30.9	31.2	31.8
2005	29.1	29.3	29.8	31.1	32.3	33.6	33.8	35.9	32.9	31.9	31.4	31.5	31.9
2006	29.2	29.9	30.9	31.1	32.7	34.2	34.2	36.0	33.1	32.5	31.7	31.7	32.3
2007	30.2	30.4	31.2	31.7	33.9	35.1	35.5	37.2	34.3	33.0	32.3	32.2	33.1
Other Services													
2000	16.7	16.8	16.9	17.2	17.2	17.4	17.2	17.3	17.1	17.4	17.6	17.7	17.2
2001	17.3	17.3	17.4	17.2	17.4	17.6	17.2	17.2	17.2	17.3	17.6	17.7	17.4
2002	17.3	17.5	17.7	17.9	17.9	17.9	17.8	17.8	17.8	18.1	18.4	18.3	17.9
2003	18.2	18.2	18.2	18.2	18.2	18.2	18.4	18.4	18.2	18.4	18.5	18.4	18.2
2004	18.3	18.4	18.5	18.5	18.6	18.4	18.4	18.3	18.1	18.6	18.6	18.5	18.4
2005	18.3	18.5	18.4	18.4	18.3	18.2	18.0	18.0	18.0	18.2	18.3	18.2	18.2
2006	17.7	18.0	18.3	18.2	18.3	18.3	18.2	18.1	18.1	18.4	18.4	18.5	18.2
2007	18.2	18.4	18.5	18.2	18.3	18.3	18.2	18.0	17.9	18.1	18.2	18.2	18.2
Government													
2000	105.1	107.5	107.5	108.2	108.9	108.5	102.5	101.7	106.3	107.7	108.8	107.9	106.7
2001	106.4	109.1	108.9	109.4	109.4	108.2	104.0	104.5	107.0	109.0	110.3	109.3	108.0
2002	107.2	110.3	110.3	110.7	110.6	109.9	103.8	103.2	108.6	109.9	110.5	110.3	108.8
2003	108.0	110.2	109.6	109.0	109.0	108.2	102.9	102.2	106.8	108.5	108.7	108.8	107.7
2004	106.1	108.3	108.4	109.1	109.5	109.3	103.5	102.7	106.2	108.2	108.6	108.5	107.4
2005	107.2	108.5	108.6	109.1	109.1	108.4	102.8	102.1	105.9	108.3	108.5	108.6	107.3
2006	106.1	108.1	108.1	108.6	108.5	107.6	102.3	101.3	104.9	107.9	108.5	109.2	106.8
2007	106.9	108.9	108.6	108.7	109.3	109.5	104.0	103.2	106.1	109.0	109.3	110.3	107.8

Employment by Industry: Fresno, CA, 2000–2007

(Numbers in thousands, not seasonally adjusted.)

Industry and year	January	February	March	April	May	June	July	August	September	October	November	December	Annual Average
Total Nonfarm													
2000	261.7	264.7	267.0	268.4	271.2	271.8	272.1	272.1	274.3	274.3	274.8	275.2	270.6
2001	268.0	270.4	273.1	274.3	276.0	277.3	277.5	279.7	278.1	278.3	279.2	278.9	275.9
2002	271.8	275.0	277.7	280.3	283.6	284.2	282.9	285.4	286.1	285.2	286.6	284.8	282.0
2003	276.3	277.6	280.2	280.5	284.4	286.9	282.5	283.3	285.1	285.7	285.2	284.1	282.6
2004	277.9	281.2	282.0	285.6	288.9	287.6	286.8	289.2	291.2	291.5	291.3	289.9	286.9
2005	284.3	287.5	289.6	294.1	295.2	295.3	293.2	295.5	296.5	299.2	299.8	301.6	294.3
2006	293.7	297.7	301.1	301.7	304.8	303.7	300.7	302.9	306.2	306.1	306.4	306.2	302.6
2007	299.4	302.8	306.0	308.0	308.5	307.4	305.0	307.0	306.5	306.9	307.1	307.1	306.0
Total Private													
2000	198.1	199.5	201.1	202.2	204.0	207.0	209.0	210.4	210.4	207.8	208.0	208.7	205.5
2001	201.6	203.3	205.0	205.7	207.9	208.9	211.7	214.5	212.2	210.1	210.0	210.3	208.4
2002	203.6	205.4	207.2	209.2	211.9	213.6	216.0	219.2	219.2	216.0	216.6	216.1	212.8
2003	208.0	208.3	210.7	210.6	214.7	217.1	216.6	219.9	220.6	218.5	217.9	217.9	215.0
2004	211.5	213.2	213.8	216.7	221.1	220.8	223.3	225.8	226.0	224.3	223.9	223.3	220.3
2005	217.8	219.5	220.5	224.7	225.9	227.0	229.3	232.0	231.5	232.1	232.5	234.9	227.3
2006	227.2	229.5	231.1	231.8	234.5	235.9	237.0	239.3	240.2	237.6	237.9	238.3	235.0
2007	231.8	233.0	234.8	236.0	237.4	238.4	240.0	241.7	240.0	237.9	237.9	238.5	237.3
Goods-Producing													
2000	40.7	40.6	40.8	41.2	41.7	43.0	46.2	46.5	45.8	44.0	43.6	43.0	43.1
2001	41.2	41.4	41.9	42.1	43.0	43.4	45.5	47.3	46.5	44.3	42.5	42.4	43.5
2002	40.9	41.2	41.8	42.0	43.5	44.1	45.5	48.0	48.2	45.2	44.3	43.4	44.0
2003	42.0	42.0	42.8	42.6	44.9	46.6	46.5	49.1	49.5	47.6	45.8	45.2	45.4
2004	43.7	43.9	44.2	45.8	48.4	47.4	50.5	52.0	51.5	49.2	48.0	47.3	47.7
2005	45.3	46.0	46.1	47.1	47.6	48.4	51.5	52.7	51.6	50.7	50.0	50.5	49.0
2006	48.7	49.3	49.3	49.3	50.6	51.2	52.6	53.8	53.6	51.6	50.4	49.8	50.9
2007	48.2	48.1	48.6	48.7	49.3	49.7	51.4	51.8	50.3	48.6	47.6	47.3	49.1
Natural Resources and Mining													
2000	0.3	0.3	0.3	0.3	0.4	0.4	0.4	0.4	0.4	0.4	0.4	0.3	0.4
2001	0.3	0.3	0.3	0.3	0.3	0.4	0.4	0.4	0.4	0.4	0.3	0.3	0.3
2002	0.3	0.3	0.2	0.3	0.3	0.3	0.2	0.3	0.3	0.2	0.3	0.2	0.3
2003	0.2	0.2	0.2	0.2	0.2	0.2	0.2	0.2	0.2	0.2	0.2	0.2	0.2
2004	0.2	0.2	0.2	0.2	0.2	0.2	0.2	0.2	0.2	0.2	0.2	0.2	0.2
2005	0.2	0.2	0.2	0.2	0.2	0.2	0.2	0.2	0.2	0.2	0.2	0.2	0.2
2006	0.2	0.2	0.2	0.2	0.2	0.2	0.2	0.2	0.2	0.2	0.2	0.1	0.2
2007	0.1	0.1	0.1	0.1	0.1	0.1	0.2	0.2	0.2	0.2	0.2	0.2	0.2
Construction													
2000	14.1	14.0	14.1	14.6	14.9	15.5	15.6	15.8	16.1	15.5	15.7	15.7	15.1
2001	14.6	14.8	15.1	15.5	16.0	16.6	16.4	16.8	16.5	16.6	16.2	16.2	15.9
2002	16.0	16.2	16.6	16.7	17.1	17.1	17.2	17.4	17.1	17.1	17.2	17.0	16.9
2003	16.5	16.5	17.2	17.6	18.1	18.8	18.6	18.8	18.8	18.8	18.5	18.4	18.1
2004	18.4	18.7	19.0	19.7	19.8	20.1	20.5	20.8	20.8	20.7	20.3	20.3	19.9
2005	19.3	19.8	20.2	20.7	20.9	21.6	22.4	22.7	22.7	22.7	22.9	23.1	21.6
2006	22.3	22.6	22.6	22.8	23.4	23.7	23.8	24.0	23.6	23.3	23.0	22.9	23.2
2007	21.7	21.5	21.9	21.8	21.6	21.8	21.6	21.4	20.6	20.5	20.3	20.1	21.2
Manufacturing													
2000	26.3	26.3	26.4	26.3	26.4	27.1	30.2	30.3	29.3	28.1	27.5	27.0	27.6
2001	26.3	26.3	26.5	26.3	26.7	26.4	28.7	30.1	29.6	27.3	26.0	25.9	27.2
2002	24.6	24.7	25.0	25.0	26.1	26.7	28.1	30.3	30.8	27.9	26.8	26.2	26.9
2003	25.3	25.3	25.4	24.8	26.6	27.6	27.7	30.1	30.5	28.6	27.1	26.6	27.1
2004	25.1	25.0	25.0	25.9	28.4	27.1	29.8	31.0	30.5	28.3	27.5	26.8	27.5
2005	25.8	26.0	25.7	26.2	26.5	26.6	28.9	29.8	28.7	27.8	26.9	27.2	27.2
2006	26.2	26.5	26.5	26.3	27.0	27.3	28.6	29.6	29.8	28.1	27.2	26.8	27.5
2007	26.4	26.5	26.6	26.8	27.6	27.8	29.6	30.2	29.5	27.9	27.1	27.0	27.8
Service-Providing													
2000	221.0	224.1	226.2	227.2	229.5	228.8	225.9	225.6	228.5	230.3	231.2	232.2	227.5
2001	226.8	229.0	231.2	232.2	233.0	233.9	232.0	232.4	231.6	234.0	236.7	236.5	232.4
2002	230.9	233.8	235.9	238.3	240.1	240.1	237.4	237.4	237.9	240.0	242.3	241.4	238.0
2003	234.3	235.6	237.4	237.9	239.5	240.3	236.0	234.2	235.6	238.1	239.4	238.9	237.3
2004	234.2	237.3	237.8	239.8	240.5	240.2	236.3	237.2	239.7	242.3	243.3	242.6	239.3
2005	239.0	241.5	243.5	247.0	247.6	246.9	241.7	242.8	244.9	248.5	249.8	251.1	245.4
2006	245.0	248.4	251.8	252.4	254.2	252.5	248.1	249.1	252.6	254.5	256.0	256.4	251.8
2007	251.2	254.7	257.4	259.3	259.2	257.7	253.6	255.2	256.2	258.3	259.5	259.8	256.8
Trade, Transportation, and Utilities													
2000	51.3	51.3	51.7	51.5	52.2	52.9	53.1	53.5	53.9	53.7	54.9	55.3	52.9
2001	52.3	52.2	52.6	53.1	53.5	53.9	54.2	54.6	54.5	54.6	55.6	55.7	53.9
2002	53.0	52.7	52.7	53.5	53.5	54.6	55.2	55.7	55.8	56.1	57.5	57.9	54.9
2003	54.3	53.9	54.3	55.1	55.6	56.5	56.4	56.5	56.5	56.5	57.3	57.9	55.9
2004	54.5	54.3	54.0	54.6	55.4	56.2	56.0	56.1	56.4	56.5	57.3	57.6	55.7
2005	55.7	55.1	55.3	55.8	56.2	56.9	57.3	57.9	58.0	58.4	59.1	60.0	57.1
2006	56.8	56.4	57.0	56.9	57.5	58.4	58.7	59.0	59.5	59.6	60.8	60.9	58.5
2007	58.7	58.2	58.8	59.0	59.9	60.4	61.2	61.5	61.2	61.3	62.2	62.5	60.4
Wholesale Trade													
2000	11.7	11.8	12.0	12.0	12.1	12.2	12.3	12.4	12.2	12.0	12.0	12.0	12.1
2001	11.6	11.7	11.8	12.0	12.0	12.1	12.4	12.6	12.3	12.1	12.0	11.8	12.0
2002	11.8	11.8	11.9	12.3	12.3	12.7	12.8	12.9	12.8	13.0	12.9	12.9	12.5
2003	12.2	12.2	12.3	12.6	12.7	12.9	12.7	12.7	12.6	12.6	12.3	12.2	12.5
2004	11.6	11.8	11.7	11.9	12.2	12.4	12.6	12.7	12.7	12.6	12.3	12.2	12.2
2005	12.0	12.0	12.1	12.3	12.4	12.8	13.0	13.1	13.2	13.1	13.0	12.9	12.7
2006	12.7	12.8	12.9	12.9	13.1	13.7	13.6	13.6	13.6	13.6	13.3	13.0	13.2
2007	12.9	13.0	13.3	13.3	13.6	14.0	14.0	14.0	13.8	13.8	13.6	13.5	13.6

Employment by Industry: Fresno, CA, 2000–2007—*Continued*

(Numbers in thousands, not seasonally adjusted.)

Industry and year	January	February	March	April	May	June	July	August	September	October	November	December	Annual Average
Retail Trade													
2000	31.0	30.9	31.1	30.8	31.2	31.7	31.5	31.6	32.1	32.3	33.6	34.1	31.8
2001	32.0	31.8	32.0	32.1	32.4	32.6	32.3	32.4	32.6	32.8	34.0	34.5	32.6
2002	32.4	32.1	32.0	32.1	32.2	32.7	32.7	32.9	33.0	33.2	34.6	35.2	32.9
2003	33.0	32.6	32.7	33.0	33.2	33.7	33.8	33.8	34.0	34.0	35.4	36.1	33.8
2004	33.6	33.2	32.9	33.2	33.6	34.0	33.7	33.7	34.0	34.2	35.4	35.8	33.9
2005	34.6	34.0	34.0	34.4	34.5	34.6	34.7	35.1	35.1	35.6	36.6	37.7	35.1
2006	35.0	34.5	34.8	34.6	34.7	34.7	34.8	35.1	35.2	35.5	36.7	37.3	35.2
2007	35.7	35.1	35.3	35.5	35.9	35.9	36.4	36.5	36.3	36.4	37.6	38.0	36.2
Transportation and Utilities													
2000	8.6	8.6	8.6	8.7	8.9	9.0	9.3	9.5	9.6	9.4	9.3	9.2	9.1
2001	8.7	8.7	8.8	9.0	9.1	9.2	9.5	9.6	9.6	9.7	9.6	9.4	9.2
2002	8.8	8.8	8.8	9.1	9.0	9.2	9.7	9.9	10.0	9.9	10.0	9.8	9.4
2003	9.1	9.1	9.3	9.5	9.7	9.9	9.9	10.0	9.9	9.9	9.6	9.6	9.6
2004	9.3	9.3	9.4	9.5	9.6	9.8	9.7	9.7	9.7	9.7	9.6	9.6	9.6
2005	9.1	9.1	9.2	9.1	9.3	9.5	9.6	9.7	9.7	9.7	9.5	9.4	9.4
2006	9.1	9.1	9.3	9.4	9.7	10.0	10.3	10.3	10.7	10.5	10.8	10.6	10.0
2007	10.1	10.1	10.2	10.2	10.4	10.5	10.8	11.0	11.1	11.1	11.0	11.0	10.6
Information													
2000	4.8	4.9	4.9	4.9	4.9	5.0	5.1	5.1	5.1	5.1	5.1	5.1	5.0
2001	5.5	5.4	5.4	5.1	5.1	5.0	5.1	5.0	4.9	4.7	4.8	4.8	5.1
2002	4.9	4.8	4.9	4.8	4.7	4.7	4.6	4.6	4.5	4.6	4.6	4.5	4.7
2003	4.0	4.1	4.0	4.0	4.0	4.1	4.2	4.3	4.2	4.4	4.5	4.6	4.2
2004	4.5	4.5	4.5	4.5	4.6	4.6	4.6	4.6	4.6	4.7	4.5	4.5	4.6
2005	4.4	4.5	4.4	4.4	4.4	4.4	4.3	4.3	4.3	4.2	4.3	4.2	4.3
2006	4.2	4.2	4.2	4.2	4.2	4.2	4.2	4.2	4.2	4.2	4.2	4.2	4.2
2007	4.1	4.2	4.1	4.1	4.2	4.2	4.2	4.2	4.2	4.2	4.2	4.2	4.2
Financial Activities													
2000	13.4	13.6	13.6	13.2	13.2	13.5	13.4	13.4	13.5	13.4	13.4	13.6	13.4
2001	13.8	14.0	14.1	14.1	14.2	14.3	14.4	14.3	14.2	13.9	13.9	14.0	14.1
2002	13.7	13.7	13.8	14.1	14.2	14.2	14.5	14.5	14.4	14.1	14.2	14.2	14.1
2003	13.7	13.7	13.8	13.8	13.9	13.9	13.7	13.7	13.6	13.6	13.5	13.5	13.7
2004	13.5	13.6	13.7	13.7	13.9	14.0	14.0	14.0	14.1	14.2	14.2	14.3	13.9
2005	14.3	14.2	14.3	14.5	14.5	14.6	14.8	14.8	15.0	15.1	15.2	15.3	14.7
2006	15.2	15.3	15.3	15.5	15.6	15.6	15.7	15.7	15.7	15.5	15.5	15.6	15.5
2007	15.3	15.4	15.4	15.4	15.4	15.6	15.3	15.2	15.2	15.2	15.2	15.3	15.3
Professional and Business Services													
2000	24.7	24.7	24.8	26.2	26.0	26.3	25.4	25.6	25.7	25.9	25.4	25.8	25.5
2001	23.4	23.5	23.4	23.4	23.5	24.0	23.2	23.4	23.1	23.7	23.8	24.0	23.5
2002	23.8	24.3	24.2	25.0	25.2	25.3	25.2	25.6	25.5	26.1	26.1	26.1	25.2
2003	26.2	26.0	26.3	25.8	26.2	26.0	26.2	26.6	26.8	26.6	26.9	26.8	26.4
2004	26.7	27.1	27.2	27.4	27.4	27.4	27.6	28.1	28.1	28.3	28.6	28.2	27.7
2005	27.7	28.4	28.6	29.2	29.3	29.0	28.6	28.9	28.6	29.0	29.0	29.3	28.8
2006	28.7	29.1	29.4	29.8	29.5	29.4	29.3	29.9	29.8	29.9	29.7	29.7	29.5
2007	29.3	29.6	29.9	30.0	29.8	29.9	30.2	30.2	30.4	30.4	30.4	30.2	30.0
Education and Health Services													
2000	30.2	30.8	31.0	30.7	30.8	30.9	30.4	30.6	31.0	31.2	31.3	31.5	30.9
2001	31.2	31.6	31.9	32.5	32.3	32.1	32.4	32.7	33.1	33.1	33.5	33.4	32.5
2002	32.6	33.2	33.7	33.9	33.9	33.8	34.0	33.7	34.3	34.2	34.6	34.6	33.9
2003	34.0	34.3	34.7	34.8	34.7	34.7	34.5	34.6	35.2	35.7	35.9	35.9	34.9
2004	35.2	35.8	35.9	35.9	35.6	35.2	35.2	35.3	35.7	36.4	36.4	36.5	35.8
2005	35.7	36.0	36.2	36.9	36.6	36.4	36.1	36.2	37.0	37.4	37.4	37.5	36.6
2006	36.7	37.3	37.4	37.3	37.3	37.2	37.0	37.0	37.7	37.9	38.4	38.6	37.5
2007	38.1	38.7	38.8	39.0	38.6	38.6	38.2	38.8	39.2	39.4	39.4	39.7	38.9
Leisure and Hospitality													
2000	23.2	23.4	23.8	24.0	24.7	25.1	25.3	25.3	24.7	24.1	23.9	23.9	24.3
2001	23.4	23.9	24.4	24.1	24.7	25.0	25.6	25.3	24.4	24.4	24.4	24.5	24.5
2002	23.7	23.9	24.3	23.8	24.6	25.0	25.0	24.7	24.2	23.9	23.6	23.5	24.2
2003	22.6	23.0	23.3	23.2	24.0	24.3	24.5	24.3	23.8	23.3	23.4	23.2	23.6
2004	23.0	23.3	23.5	23.8	24.7	25.2	24.9	24.9	24.7	24.6	24.6	24.5	24.3
2005	24.4	24.8	25.1	25.8	26.3	26.3	26.1	26.1	26.0	26.3	26.5	27.0	25.9
2006	26.5	27.1	27.5	27.8	28.5	28.9	28.7	28.7	28.7	28.1	28.2	28.6	28.1
2007	27.5	27.9	28.3	28.6	28.9	29.0	28.7	28.7	28.2	27.7	27.7	28.0	28.3
Other Services													
2000	9.8	10.2	10.5	10.5	10.5	10.3	10.1	10.4	10.7	10.4	10.4	10.5	10.4
2001	10.4	10.9	10.9	11.3	11.6	11.2	11.3	11.9	11.5	11.4	11.5	11.5	11.3
2002	11.0	11.6	11.8	12.1	12.3	11.9	12.0	12.4	12.3	11.8	11.7	11.9	11.9
2003	11.2	11.3	11.5	11.3	11.4	11.0	10.6	10.8	11.0	10.8	10.6	10.8	11.0
2004	10.4	10.7	10.8	11.0	11.1	10.8	10.5	10.8	10.9	10.4	10.3	10.4	10.7
2005	10.3	10.5	10.5	11.0	11.0	11.0	10.6	11.1	11.0	11.0	11.0	11.1	10.8
2006	10.4	10.8	11.0	11.0	11.3	11.0	10.8	11.0	11.0	10.8	10.7	10.9	10.9
2007	10.6	10.9	10.9	11.2	11.3	11.0	10.8	11.3	11.3	11.1	11.2	11.3	11.1
Government													
2000	63.6	65.2	65.9	66.2	67.2	64.8	63.1	61.7	63.9	66.5	66.8	66.5	65.1
2001	66.8	67.5	68.5	68.6	68.1	68.4	65.8	65.2	65.9	68.2	69.2	68.6	67.6
2002	68.2	69.6	70.5	71.1	71.7	70.6	66.9	66.2	66.9	69.2	70.0	68.7	69.1
2003	68.3	69.3	69.5	69.9	69.7	69.8	65.9	63.4	64.5	67.2	67.3	66.2	67.5
2004	66.4	68.0	68.2	68.9	67.8	66.8	63.5	63.4	65.2	67.2	67.4	66.6	66.6
2005	66.5	68.0	69.1	69.4	69.3	68.3	63.9	63.5	65.0	67.1	67.3	66.7	67.0
2006	66.5	68.2	70.0	69.9	70.3	67.8	63.7	63.6	66.0	68.5	68.5	67.9	67.6
2007	67.6	69.8	71.2	72.0	71.1	69.0	65.0	65.3	66.5	69.0	69.2	68.6	68.7

Employment by Industry: Raleigh-Cary, NC, 2000–2007

(Numbers in thousands, not seasonally adjusted.)

Industry and year	January	February	March	April	May	June	July	August	September	October	November	December	Annual Average
Total Nonfarm													
2000	424.3	426.5	431.1	434.4	436.8	441.0	432.5	435.3	441.3	441.8	444.7	445.4	436.3
2001	435.5	437.8	440.1	442.0	443.4	445.0	433.6	434.8	437.2	438.2	437.8	437.8	438.6
2002	424.0	425.4	426.5	430.5	433.7	434.5	428.8	432.0	436.8	437.9	439.2	439.9	432.4
2003	427.3	428.3	429.9	434.0	437.3	438.4	431.2	434.7	436.4	440.7	441.6	442.6	435.2
2004	435.0	436.1	439.9	441.4	445.8	447.2	446.4	449.6	452.6	454.9	456.8	459.2	447.1
2005	449.4	451.3	454.8	459.8	463.5	464.9	464.8	470.4	473.2	472.5	477.2	477.7	465.0
2006	470.2	472.1	475.9	483.7	488.1	491.0	488.4	494.7	496.6	500.3	505.8	507.3	489.5
2007	499.4	502.8	507.4	509.3	515.4	518.7	514.7	521.6	522.0	525.5	528.0	529.3	516.2
Total Private													
2000	347.3	348.8	353.2	356.4	358.4	362.6	360.2	361.3	361.4	362.5	364.7	365.6	358.5
2001	355.7	357.1	359.3	361.5	362.7	364.4	359.8	359.9	356.7	356.8	356.5	357.1	359.0
2002	344.2	344.7	346.6	350.6	353.5	354.6	355.4	357.0	355.8	356.3	357.5	358.6	352.9
2003	346.5	347.0	348.2	352.0	354.9	356.6	352.9	355.5	353.7	355.6	357.2	358.5	353.2
2004	351.7	352.4	355.6	357.0	361.0	363.0	365.6	366.7	365.0	367.1	369.3	372.0	362.2
2005	363.2	364.4	367.4	372.4	375.9	378.6	381.1	382.3	383.7	385.1	388.1	390.9	377.8
2006	382.2	383.2	386.4	392.9	396.7	400.4	401.2	403.2	404.0	406.9	411.8	413.8	398.6
2007	406.2	408.7	412.7	414.3	419.7	424.6	424.0	427.5	426.0	428.5	430.9	432.5	421.3
Goods-Producing													
2000	68.9	68.9	70.2	71.3	71.9	73.0	73.3	73.6	73.6	73.5	73.7	73.4	72.1
2001	70.8	71.1	71.9	72.2	72.7	73.0	72.4	72.0	71.3	70.7	69.8	68.6	71.4
2002	66.4	66.6	66.7	67.0	67.3	67.1	67.2	67.0	66.3	66.0	65.4	65.0	66.5
2003	62.4	62.3	62.4	62.2	63.1	63.4	63.2	63.5	63.0	63.6	63.5	63.5	63.0
2004	61.8	61.8	62.9	63.6	64.2	64.4	65.1	64.8	64.4	65.4	65.2	65.0	64.1
2005	63.4	63.8	64.4	65.7	66.5	67.6	68.1	68.1	68.4	68.3	68.5	68.5	66.8
2006	67.6	67.8	68.9	69.7	70.8	71.8	72.3	72.6	72.5	72.5	72.7	72.9	71.0
2007	71.8	72.0	72.8	72.5	73.1	73.9	74.1	74.7	74.3	74.5	74.3	74.0	73.5
Natural Resources, Mining, and Construction													
2000	31.0	30.9	31.9	32.9	33.4	34.2	34.1	34.4	34.5	34.1	34.3	34.0	33.3
2001	31.8	32.1	33.1	33.6	34.5	35.0	34.8	34.9	34.5	34.3	33.7	33.0	33.8
2002	31.5	32.0	32.2	32.6	33.3	33.1	33.3	33.5	33.0	32.9	32.4	32.0	32.7
2003	30.1	30.1	30.3	30.2	31.0	31.4	31.8	32.1	31.9	32.2	32.1	32.1	31.3
2004	30.8	30.9	31.7	32.5	33.1	33.2	33.9	33.8	33.5	34.0	33.8	33.6	32.9
2005	32.3	32.5	33.0	33.8	34.6	35.3	35.7	35.8	36.0	36.1	36.1	35.9	34.8
2006	35.2	35.4	36.1	37.2	38.0	38.8	39.5	39.7	39.6	39.5	39.6	39.7	38.2
2007	39.2	39.4	40.1	40.2	40.7	41.2	41.5	41.9	41.6	41.6	41.3	41.0	40.8
Manufacturing													
2000	37.9	38.0	38.3	38.4	38.5	38.8	39.2	39.2	39.1	39.4	39.4	39.4	38.8
2001	39.0	39.0	38.8	38.6	38.2	38.0	37.6	37.1	36.8	36.4	36.1	35.6	37.6
2002	34.9	34.6	34.5	34.4	34.0	34.0	33.9	33.5	33.3	33.1	33.0	33.0	33.9
2003	32.3	32.2	32.1	32.0	32.1	32.0	31.4	31.4	31.1	31.4	31.4	31.4	31.7
2004	31.0	30.9	31.2	31.1	31.1	31.2	31.2	31.0	30.9	31.4	31.4	31.4	31.2
2005	31.1	31.3	31.4	31.9	31.9	32.3	32.4	32.3	32.4	32.2	32.4	32.6	32.0
2006	32.4	32.4	32.8	32.5	32.8	33.0	32.8	32.9	32.9	33.0	33.1	33.2	32.8
2007	32.6	32.6	32.7	32.3	32.4	32.7	32.6	32.8	32.7	32.9	33.0	33.0	32.7
Service-Providing													
2000	355.4	357.6	360.9	363.1	364.9	368.0	359.2	361.7	367.7	368.3	371.0	372.0	364.2
2001	364.7	366.7	368.2	369.8	370.7	372.0	361.2	362.8	365.9	367.5	368.0	369.2	367.2
2002	357.6	358.8	359.8	363.5	366.4	367.4	361.6	365.0	370.5	371.9	373.8	374.9	365.9
2003	364.9	366.0	367.5	371.8	374.2	375.0	368.0	371.2	373.4	377.1	378.1	379.1	372.2
2004	373.2	374.3	377.0	377.8	381.6	382.8	381.3	384.8	388.2	389.5	391.6	394.2	383.0
2005	386.0	387.5	390.4	394.1	397.0	397.3	396.7	402.3	404.8	404.2	408.7	409.2	398.2
2006	402.6	404.3	407.0	414.0	417.3	419.2	416.1	422.1	424.1	427.8	433.1	434.4	418.5
2007	427.6	430.8	434.6	436.8	442.3	444.8	440.6	446.9	447.7	451.0	453.7	455.3	442.7
Trade, Transportation, and Utilities													
2000	84.8	84.3	85.2	85.6	86.1	86.8	85.1	85.4	85.5	87.0	88.0	89.1	86.1
2001	84.6	83.8	84.2	85.4	85.5	85.0	84.9	84.9	84.8	85.1	85.7	86.6	85.0
2002	81.2	80.6	81.1	81.3	81.6	81.6	81.5	82.0	82.2	82.6	84.2	85.2	82.1
2003	80.9	80.5	80.8	81.9	82.6	83.4	81.5	82.4	82.5	83.8	85.2	86.2	82.6
2004	82.8	82.4	82.5	82.4	82.8	82.9	83.0	83.6	83.8	84.6	86.1	87.2	83.7
2005	84.1	83.4	83.9	84.5	85.1	85.2	85.8	85.9	86.0	87.4	89.0	90.6	85.9
2006	86.7	85.9	86.1	86.8	87.2	87.6	88.7	89.6	89.5	90.7	93.7	95.0	89.0
2007	91.7	90.9	91.9	92.1	93.0	93.4	93.2	93.1	93.1	94.1	95.6	96.7	93.2
Wholesale Trade													
2000	21.6	21.6	21.7	21.6	21.6	21.9	21.8	21.9	21.8	22.1	21.8	21.8	21.8
2001	21.7	21.7	21.8	21.3	21.2	21.2	21.2	21.0	20.9	20.7	20.4	20.3	21.1
2002	20.0	20.0	19.9	19.7	19.9	19.9	20.4	20.4	20.4	20.7	20.6	20.5	20.2
2003	20.1	20.0	20.2	20.1	20.0	20.1	20.0	20.1	20.1	20.2	20.0	20.0	20.1
2004	19.5	19.5	19.7	19.6	19.7	19.8	20.1	20.1	20.1	20.4	20.3	20.4	19.9
2005	19.8	19.8	19.8	19.9	20.1	20.2	20.1	20.3	20.4	20.6	20.5	20.7	20.2
2006	20.4	20.4	20.4	20.5	20.6	20.9	21.1	21.3	21.5	21.4	21.6	21.7	21.0
2007	21.9	22.0	22.2	22.2	22.3	22.5	22.6	22.5	22.6	22.7	22.7	22.7	22.4
Retail Trade													
2000	51.6	51.1	51.8	52.8	53.3	53.6	52.3	52.6	52.8	53.8	55.3	56.4	53.1
2001	52.0	51.3	51.5	53.3	53.5	53.0	52.6	52.9	53.0	53.3	54.9	55.6	53.1
2002	50.6	50.2	50.7	50.8	50.9	50.9	50.1	50.9	51.2	51.3	53.2	54.3	51.3
2003	50.2	49.9	50.0	51.0	51.8	52.4	50.7	51.3	51.4	52.7	54.4	55.3	51.8
2004	52.6	52.1	52.0	51.8	52.2	52.2	52.2	52.7	53.0	53.5	55.1	56.0	53.0
2005	53.3	52.7	53.0	53.5	53.9	53.8	54.3	54.2	54.2	54.8	56.4	57.8	54.3
2006	54.4	53.6	53.7	54.2	54.5	54.5	55.1	55.7	55.4	56.8	59.3	60.4	55.6
2007	57.1	56.3	57.0	57.0	57.8	57.9	57.8	57.8	57.7	58.5	60.1	61.1	58.0

Employment by Industry: Raleigh-Cary, NC, 2000–2007—*Continued*

(Numbers in thousands, not seasonally adjusted.)

Industry and year	January	February	March	April	May	June	July	August	September	October	November	December	Annual Average
Transportation and Utilities													
2000	11.6	11.6	11.7	11.2	11.2	11.3	11.0	10.9	10.9	11.1	10.9	10.9	11.2
2001	10.9	10.8	10.9	10.8	10.8	10.8	11.1	11.0	10.9	11.1	10.4	10.7	10.9
2002	10.6	10.4	10.5	10.8	10.8	10.8	11.0	10.7	10.6	10.6	10.4	10.4	10.6
2003	10.6	10.6	10.6	10.8	10.8	10.9	10.8	11.0	11.0	10.9	10.8	10.9	10.8
2004	10.7	10.8	10.8	11.0	10.9	10.9	10.7	10.8	10.7	10.7	10.7	10.8	10.8
2005	11.0	10.9	11.1	11.1	11.1	11.2	11.4	11.4	11.4	12.0	12.1	12.1	11.4
2006	11.9	11.9	12.0	12.1	12.1	12.2	12.5	12.6	12.6	12.5	12.8	12.9	12.3
2007	12.7	12.6	12.7	12.9	12.9	13.0	12.8	12.8	12.8	12.9	12.8	12.9	12.8
Information													
2000	17.6	17.7	18.0	17.9	18.0	18.5	18.7	18.7	18.6	18.4	18.5	18.6	18.3
2001	18.8	18.8	18.8	18.5	18.5	18.4	18.0	18.0	18.0	17.8	17.8	18.0	18.3
2002	18.3	18.2	18.4	18.2	18.1	18.2	17.9	17.8	17.7	17.7	17.7	17.7	18.0
2003	17.6	17.7	17.7	17.7	17.8	17.9	17.9	17.8	17.5	17.3	17.3	17.4	17.6
2004	17.5	17.4	17.5	17.1	17.0	17.1	17.0	17.0	17.0	16.8	16.5	16.8	17.1
2005	16.7	16.7	16.9	17.1	17.2	17.3	17.3	17.4	17.2	17.0	17.1	17.2	17.1
2006	17.0	16.9	16.6	16.8	16.8	16.8	16.7	16.6	16.5	16.4	16.4	16.4	16.7
2007	16.3	16.6	16.5	16.5	16.6	16.9	16.9	16.8	16.7	16.6	16.6	16.6	16.6
Financial Activities													
2000	21.4	21.6	21.9	22.0	22.2	22.4	22.0	22.1	22.2	22.4	22.4	22.5	22.1
2001	22.2	22.2	22.3	21.8	21.9	22.2	21.8	21.8	21.7	21.8	21.9	22.0	22.0
2002	22.2	22.3	22.1	21.9	22.1	22.4	22.0	22.4	22.4	22.4	22.5	22.3	22.3
2003	22.1	22.1	22.2	22.3	22.5	22.6	22.3	22.4	22.5	23.1	23.0	23.1	22.5
2004	23.6	23.8	23.9	23.8	23.6	23.6	24.0	23.9	23.7	23.8	23.9	23.9	23.8
2005	23.7	23.7	23.7	23.7	23.8	23.9	24.1	24.3	24.4	24.7	24.8	25.1	24.2
2006	24.7	24.7	24.9	25.2	25.3	25.5	25.6	25.7	25.7	25.9	26.1	26.2	25.5
2007	25.9	26.0	26.1	26.4	26.5	26.7	26.9	26.8	26.5	26.7	26.7	26.8	26.5
Professional and Business Services													
2000	69.9	70.5	71.2	72.2	72.0	72.6	72.2	72.9	73.1	73.1	73.6	73.7	72.3
2001	71.4	71.8	71.8	72.4	71.6	71.9	69.7	70.1	69.3	69.4	69.3	69.6	70.7
2002	66.5	66.6	66.9	67.5	68.0	68.4	69.6	70.2	70.0	70.1	70.1	70.8	68.7
2003	68.1	68.2	68.3	69.8	69.4	69.6	68.8	69.1	68.2	68.7	68.7	68.8	68.8
2004	67.6	68.1	68.6	69.4	70.3	71.3	72.5	72.7	72.6	73.3	73.4	74.6	71.2
2005	72.9	73.4	73.9	76.0	75.5	76.0	77.7	78.0	78.4	78.1	78.4	78.7	76.4
2006	77.8	78.1	78.9	80.8	80.8	81.8	82.6	83.0	84.2	85.4	85.7	85.7	82.1
2007	84.2	85.2	85.9	86.5	86.9	89.1	89.7	90.9	91.4	92.1	92.6	93.0	89.0
Education and Health Services													
2000	32.0	32.4	32.6	32.8	32.8	33.0	32.3	32.6	32.7	33.2	33.2	33.3	32.7
2001	33.5	33.9	34.2	34.4	34.7	34.6	34.2	34.8	34.8	35.3	35.6	35.8	34.7
2002	35.4	35.9	36.1	37.3	37.4	37.3	36.9	37.5	38.1	38.5	39.0	38.8	37.4
2003	38.6	39.2	39.3	39.2	39.4	38.9	38.8	39.3	39.9	39.9	40.1	40.2	39.4
2004	39.9	40.2	40.7	40.4	40.9	40.7	40.8	41.4	41.9	42.3	42.7	42.7	41.2
2005	42.2	42.7	43.0	42.9	43.1	42.7	42.8	43.1	44.2	44.8	45.2	45.1	43.5
2006	44.4	45.0	45.4	46.2	46.7	46.3	45.9	46.2	46.9	47.7	48.5	48.6	46.5
2007	47.8	48.7	49.1	50.1	50.5	50.1	48.8	49.7	50.2	51.1	51.5	51.5	49.9
Leisure and Hospitality													
2000	35.0	35.5	36.2	36.4	37.1	37.6	37.9	37.6	37.4	36.4	36.8	36.6	36.7
2001	36.1	36.9	37.5	38.0	38.6	39.7	39.0	38.6	37.5	37.1	36.7	36.9	37.7
2002	34.8	35.1	36.0	37.7	38.9	39.5	40.1	40.1	39.4	39.2	38.8	39.1	38.2
2003	37.2	37.3	37.8	38.8	39.2	39.7	39.0	39.7	38.9	38.4	38.5	38.3	38.6
2004	37.2	37.2	38.0	38.6	40.0	40.6	41.2	41.5	40.3	39.6	39.5	40.0	39.5
2005	38.6	39.0	40.0	40.5	42.0	43.0	42.6	42.7	42.8	42.1	42.3	42.8	41.5
2006	41.3	41.8	42.6	44.0	45.4	46.2	45.6	45.9	45.9	45.1	45.2	45.3	44.5
2007	44.7	45.2	45.8	45.5	48.0	49.0	48.6	49.5	48.6	48.0	48.2	48.5	47.5
Other Services													
2000	17.7	17.9	17.9	18.2	18.3	18.7	18.7	18.4	18.3	18.5	18.5	18.4	18.3
2001	18.3	18.6	18.6	18.8	19.2	19.6	19.8	19.7	19.3	19.6	19.7	19.6	19.2
2002	19.4	19.4	19.3	19.7	20.1	20.1	20.2	20.0	19.7	19.8	19.8	19.7	19.8
2003	19.6	19.7	19.7	20.1	20.9	21.1	21.4	21.3	21.2	20.8	20.9	21.0	20.6
2004	21.3	21.5	21.5	21.7	22.2	22.4	22.0	21.8	21.5	21.6	21.7	21.7	21.7
2005	21.6	21.7	21.6	22.0	22.7	22.9	22.7	22.8	22.3	22.7	22.8	22.9	22.4
2006	22.7	23.0	23.0	23.4	23.7	24.4	23.8	23.6	22.8	23.2	23.5	23.7	23.4
2007	23.8	24.1	24.6	24.7	25.1	25.5	25.8	26.0	25.2	25.4	25.4	25.4	25.1
Government													
2000	77.0	77.7	77.9	78.0	78.4	78.4	72.3	74.0	79.9	79.3	80.0	79.8	77.7
2001	79.8	80.7	80.8	80.5	80.7	80.6	73.8	74.9	80.5	81.4	81.3	80.7	79.6
2002	79.8	80.7	79.9	79.9	80.2	79.9	73.4	75.0	81.0	81.6	81.7	81.3	79.5
2003	80.8	81.3	81.7	82.0	82.4	81.8	78.3	79.2	82.7	85.1	84.4	84.1	82.0
2004	83.3	83.7	84.3	84.4	84.8	84.2	80.8	82.9	87.6	87.8	87.5	87.2	84.9
2005	86.2	86.9	87.4	87.4	87.6	86.3	83.7	88.1	89.5	87.4	89.1	86.8	87.2
2006	88.0	88.9	89.5	90.8	91.4	90.6	87.2	91.5	92.6	93.4	94.0	93.5	91.0
2007	93.2	94.1	94.7	95.0	95.7	94.1	90.7	94.1	96.0	97.0	97.1	96.8	94.9

Employment by Industry: Omaha-Council Bluffs, NE-IA, 2000–2007

(Numbers in thousands, not seasonally adjusted.)

Industry and year	January	February	March	April	May	June	July	August	September	October	November	December	Annual Average
Total Nonfarm													
2000	431.5	432.4	434.9	441.0	444.9	451.7	447.8	448.8	449.0	448.1	449.7	450.9	444.2
2001	438.4	437.6	439.7	444.7	448.4	454.0	449.4	450.7	449.4	447.8	450.9	450.9	446.8
2002	436.5	437.3	439.2	442.8	446.2	449.2	443.7	444.1	443.4	442.2	444.7	443.5	442.7
2003	438.1	437.5	439.4	440.1	443.2	444.9	445.8	446.8	446.6	447.9	449.0	448.1	444.0
2004	438.3	435.8	439.8	441.4	446.7	449.3	446.2	446.7	446.1	446.2	448.6	449.2	444.5
2005	439.9	440.4	444.2	449.1	452.7	456.2	452.4	452.7	453.7	455.6	458.5	458.7	451.2
2006	447.5	449.4	453.2	456.6	461.6	464.9	459.9	460.4	462.8	463.7	465.9	466.1	459.3
2007	453.9	454.7	457.1	462.8	467.2	470.0	465.6	468.1	468.0	468.5	468.8	470.7	464.6
Total Private													
2000	376.6	377.4	380.1	385.4	389.1	395.7	394.1	395.4	394.0	392.0	393.3	394.4	389.0
2001	382.5	381.5	383.6	388.0	391.3	396.4	394.4	395.9	393.2	390.7	393.5	393.3	390.4
2002	379.5	379.7	381.8	385.4	388.5	391.4	388.9	389.5	387.0	384.2	386.6	385.7	385.7
2003	380.4	379.4	380.6	380.9	383.8	385.5	390.1	392.6	390.0	388.9	390.0	389.5	386.1
2004	379.6	376.9	380.6	382.1	386.9	389.7	389.2	389.9	387.4	386.4	388.7	389.5	385.6
2005	380.4	380.4	384.3	389.0	392.1	395.9	395.3	395.8	394.3	394.5	397.2	397.8	391.4
2006	386.9	388.5	392.2	395.0	399.7	403.4	402.5	402.9	402.2	402.0	404.0	404.8	398.7
2007	392.6	393.1	395.7	400.1	404.1	407.7	407.7	409.2	406.6	404.9	405.7	407.6	402.9
Goods-Producing													
2000	55.6	55.9	56.8	58.3	59.2	60.8	60.5	60.7	60.5	60.4	59.6	58.5	58.9
2001	56.2	55.8	56.2	58.2	59.0	60.1	60.4	60.0	59.6	58.9	58.4	57.6	58.4
2002	55.4	55.2	55.7	57.1	57.6	58.3	58.0	58.0	57.5	57.3	57.3	56.4	57.0
2003	55.9	55.3	55.6	56.7	58.1	59.2	60.7	60.9	60.2	60.1	59.6	58.8	58.4
2004	56.4	55.4	57.1	58.1	59.1	59.7	59.9	59.5	59.0	58.9	58.7	58.3	58.3
2005	56.0	55.6	57.1	58.5	58.7	60.0	60.3	60.1	59.6	59.4	59.2	58.2	58.6
2006	56.4	56.8	57.7	59.2	60.2	61.4	61.6	61.6	61.6	61.7	61.1	60.2	59.8
2007	56.6	55.7	56.2	57.6	58.5	59.6	59.6	59.9	59.9	59.3	59.7	59.4	58.9	58.4
Natural Resources, Mining, and Construction													
2000	20.7	20.7	21.5	22.9	23.6	24.5	24.6	24.8	24.6	24.4	23.4	22.3	23.2
2001	20.4	20.3	20.8	22.8	23.8	24.5	24.8	24.8	24.3	24.2	23.8	23.1	23.1
2002	20.9	20.8	21.7	23.3	23.9	24.7	25.1	25.1	24.7	24.7	24.7	23.8	23.6
2003	23.0	22.4	22.8	24.0	25.1	25.9	27.6	27.8	27.1	27.0	26.6	25.8	25.4
2004	23.6	22.8	24.3	25.4	26.2	26.6	26.7	26.5	26.0	25.9	25.8	25.1	25.4
2005	23.1	23.0	24.3	25.5	25.9	27.0	27.2	27.3	26.8	26.7	26.4	25.3	25.7
2006	24.1	24.4	25.2	26.4	27.3	28.3	28.4	28.5	28.7	27.8	26.8	25.8	26.8
2007	23.7	22.7	23.1	24.4	25.2	26.1	26.1	26.3	25.9	26.1	25.7	25.1	25.0
Manufacturing													
2000	34.9	35.2	35.3	35.4	35.6	36.3	35.9	35.9	35.9	36.0	36.2	36.2	35.7
2001	35.8	35.5	35.4	35.4	35.2	35.6	35.6	35.2	35.3	34.7	34.6	34.5	35.2
2002	34.5	34.4	34.0	33.8	33.7	33.6	32.9	32.9	32.8	32.6	32.6	32.6	33.4
2003	32.9	32.9	32.8	32.7	33.0	33.3	33.1	33.1	33.1	33.1	33.0	33.0	33.0
2004	32.8	32.6	32.8	32.7	32.9	33.1	33.2	33.0	33.0	33.0	32.9	33.2	32.9
2005	32.9	32.6	32.8	33.0	32.8	33.0	33.1	32.8	32.8	32.7	32.8	32.9	32.9
2006	32.3	32.4	32.5	32.8	32.9	33.1	33.2	33.1	33.0	33.3	33.4	33.4	33.0
2007	32.9	33.0	33.1	33.2	33.3	33.5	33.5	33.6	33.4	33.6	33.7	33.8	33.4
Service-Providing													
2000	375.9	376.5	378.1	382.7	385.7	390.9	387.3	388.1	388.5	387.7	390.1	392.4	385.3
2001	382.2	381.8	383.5	386.5	389.4	393.9	389.0	390.7	389.8	388.9	392.5	393.3	388.5
2002	381.1	382.1	383.5	385.7	388.6	390.9	385.7	386.1	385.9	384.9	387.4	387.1	385.8
2003	382.2	382.2	383.8	383.4	385.1	385.7	385.1	385.9	386.4	387.8	389.4	389.3	385.5
2004	381.9	380.4	382.7	383.3	387.6	389.6	386.3	387.2	387.1	387.3	389.9	390.9	386.2
2005	383.9	384.8	387.1	390.6	394.0	396.2	392.1	392.6	394.1	396.2	399.3	400.5	392.6
2006	391.1	392.6	395.5	397.4	401.4	403.5	398.3	398.8	401.1	402.6	405.7	406.9	399.6
2007	397.3	399.0	400.9	405.2	408.7	410.4	406.0	408.2	408.7	408.8	409.4	411.8	406.2
Trade, Transportation, and Utilities													
2000	105.6	104.9	104.7	106.4	107.4	108.5	107.4	107.6	107.3	108.1	110.0	111.5	107.5
2001	107.2	106.3	106.2	106.7	107.2	107.5	106.6	107.4	107.0	107.7	110.3	111.5	107.7
2002	105.6	104.2	103.9	103.6	103.9	103.7	103.0	102.7	102.9	102.3	103.9	104.4	103.7
2003	99.3	98.2	98.9	97.2	97.8	97.9	97.9	97.9	98.0	97.9	99.2	100.1	98.4
2004	96.3	94.9	94.6	95.6	97.0	97.8	97.3	98.5	98.9	98.2	100.7	102.0	97.7
2005	98.1	97.8	98.2	98.1	99.4	99.4	98.8	99.2	99.3	99.8	101.9	102.8	99.4
2006	97.0	96.6	97.4	97.4	98.5	98.7	98.6	98.9	99.1	100.0	102.7	103.7	99.1
2007	98.6	98.1	98.7	99.1	100.0	100.0	99.5	99.9	100.0	100.7	101.7	103.7	100.0
Wholesale Trade													
2000	22.1	22.2	22.1	22.3	22.2	22.4	22.3	22.3	22.3	22.2	22.1	22.1	22.2
2001	21.6	21.7	21.7	22.0	22.0	22.1	22.0	21.7	21.6	21.6	21.5	21.4	21.7
2002	21.0	21.0	21.1	21.0	21.1	21.2	21.2	21.3	21.2	21.0	21.0	21.0	21.1
2003	20.7	20.7	20.9	20.8	20.6	20.5	20.4	20.3	20.2	19.6	19.7	19.6	20.3
2004	19.2	19.0	19.1	19.1	19.0	19.2	19.2	19.3	19.2	19.2	19.1	19.1	19.1
2005	18.6	18.6	18.8	18.6	18.6	18.6	18.7	18.5	18.3	18.4	18.4	18.4	18.5
2006	18.1	18.2	18.3	18.2	18.3	18.3	18.4	18.2	18.1	18.1	18.1	18.2	18.2
2007	17.7	17.7	17.8	17.9	17.9	18.1	18.1	18.0	18.1	18.2	18.0	18.2	18.0
Retail Trade													
2000	54.0	53.2	53.0	54.0	55.1	56.2	55.0	55.0	55.0	56.3	58.4	59.6	55.4
2001	54.8	53.5	53.7	54.4	54.9	55.1	54.7	55.6	56.1	56.6	59.1	60.0	55.7
2002	54.4	53.2	53.1	53.4	54.0	54.1	53.8	53.9	54.6	54.6	56.6	57.6	54.4
2003	53.2	52.0	52.3	51.3	51.5	51.4	51.2	51.1	51.2	52.1	53.7	54.6	52.1
2004	51.4	50.2	50.0	50.1	50.8	51.1	50.7	50.6	50.5	51.1	53.1	54.3	51.2
2005	50.8	50.1	50.2	50.6	51.2	51.0	50.8	51.0	50.9	51.8	53.6	54.4	51.4
2006	50.5	49.6	50.1	50.3	50.8	50.8	50.9	50.7	50.7	50.7	51.7	54.0	54.8	51.2
2007	50.9	50.2	50.6	51.1	52.0	52.0	51.7	51.7	51.5	52.2	53.9	55.1	51.9

Employment by Industry: Omaha-Council Bluffs, NE-IA, 2000–2007—*Continued*

(Numbers in thousands, not seasonally adjusted.)

Industry and year	January	February	March	April	May	June	July	August	September	October	November	December	Annual Average
Transportation and Utilities													
2000	29.5	29.5	29.6	30.1	30.1	29.9	30.1	30.3	30.0	29.6	29.5	29.8	29.8
2001	30.8	31.1	30.8	30.3	30.3	30.3	29.9	30.1	30.1	29.5	29.7	30.1	30.3
2002	30.2	30.0	29.7	29.2	28.8	28.4	28.0	27.5	27.1	26.7	26.3	25.8	28.1
2003	25.4	25.5	25.7	25.1	25.7	26.0	26.3	26.5	26.6	26.2	25.8	25.9	25.9
2004	25.7	25.7	25.5	26.4	27.2	27.5	27.4	28.6	29.2	27.9	28.5	28.6	27.4
2005	28.7	29.1	29.2	28.9	29.6	29.8	29.3	29.7	30.1	29.6	29.9	30.0	29.5
2006	28.4	28.8	29.0	28.9	29.4	29.5	29.5	30.0	30.3	30.2	30.6	30.7	29.6
2007	30.0	30.2	30.3	30.1	30.1	29.9	29.7	30.2	30.4	30.3	29.8	30.4	30.1
Information													
2000	15.7	15.5	15.3	15.3	15.1	15.0	14.9	14.9	14.8	14.8	14.9	14.9	15.1
2001	14.8	14.7	14.7	14.9	15.0	15.1	14.9	14.9	14.6	14.7	14.7	14.6	14.8
2002	14.4	14.4	14.4	14.3	14.4	14.4	14.4	14.3	14.1	14.0	14.1	14.1	14.3
2003	14.0	14.0	13.9	13.7	13.7	13.7	13.8	13.9	13.8	13.7	13.8	13.9	13.8
2004	13.6	13.6	13.6	13.4	13.5	13.5	13.6	13.5	13.4	13.4	13.4	13.5	13.5
2005	13.3	13.3	13.3	13.2	13.1	13.3	13.3	13.4	13.2	13.3	13.4	13.4	13.3
2006	13.1	13.0	13.0	13.0	13.1	13.1	13.0	12.8	12.7	12.5	12.6	12.6	12.9
2007	12.3	12.4	12.4	12.6	12.6	12.8	12.8	12.8	12.7	12.6	12.5	12.6	12.6
Financial Activities													
2000	35.2	35.2	35.3	35.3	35.6	35.9	35.7	35.8	36.0	36.0	36.0	36.4	35.7
2001	36.0	36.0	36.0	35.9	36.1	36.5	36.5	36.3	36.1	36.3	36.3	36.3	36.2
2002	35.5	35.8	36.0	36.1	36.6	36.9	37.3	37.4	37.2	37.5	37.8	38.0	36.8
2003	38.0	38.0	38.0	37.0	37.0	37.2	37.9	37.9	37.7	37.5	37.5	37.7	37.6
2004	37.2	37.2	37.6	36.9	37.0	37.2	37.1	37.0	36.7	37.0	36.9	37.0	37.1
2005	36.8	36.8	36.8	36.8	37.0	37.1	37.1	37.2	37.1	37.0	37.1	37.4	37.0
2006	37.2	37.5	37.6	37.7	38.0	38.4	38.5	38.7	38.4	38.4	38.6	38.9	38.2
2007	38.6	38.8	39.0	39.0	39.5	39.7	39.9	39.7	39.5	39.5	39.5	39.3	39.3
Professional and Business Services													
2000	56.4	56.8	57.6	59.3	59.4	60.9	60.8	61.3	60.7	60.0	60.2	61.2	59.6
2001	59.7	59.5	59.7	60.0	60.5	61.5	61.0	61.6	60.5	60.0	60.3	60.5	60.4
2002	58.0	58.6	59.1	59.6	59.5	60.1	58.1	58.3	57.4	57.7	57.9	57.7	58.5
2003	58.0	58.6	59.2	59.0	59.6	59.5	61.3	62.6	62.6	63.0	62.9	62.9	60.8
2004	61.2	61.0	61.7	60.9	61.1	61.3	60.5	60.9	59.7	60.0	60.3	60.2	60.7
2005	59.4	59.7	60.4	61.5	61.7	62.1	61.7	61.9	62.1	62.6	62.9	63.6	61.6
2006	61.8	62.3	63.1	63.4	63.7	64.6	64.4	64.1	63.9	63.3	63.1	63.2	63.4
2007	62.0	62.7	63.2	64.0	64.4	65.2	65.3	65.2	65.3	64.7	64.7	64.7	64.3
Education and Health Services													
2000	55.8	56.5	56.9	56.2	55.9	56.7	56.7	57.2	58.2	57.9	58.4	58.1	57.0
2001	56.7	57.3	57.9	57.8	57.7	58.5	58.1	58.6	59.4	59.3	59.8	59.6	58.4
2002	59.1	59.8	60.1	60.0	60.6	60.7	60.3	60.8	61.5	61.0	61.6	61.4	60.6
2003	62.4	62.6	62.3	62.3	60.9	60.3	60.8	61.6	61.6	61.5	62.5	62.2	61.8
2004	61.6	61.7	62.0	61.7	62.0	61.7	62.4	62.2	62.4	62.5	62.5	62.5	62.1
2005	61.7	62.0	62.4	62.8	62.9	63.0	63.3	63.2	63.7	64.2	64.7	64.9	63.2
2006	64.3	64.9	65.2	64.6	65.0	65.0	64.8	65.4	66.1	66.1	66.6	66.7	65.4
2007	65.4	66.4	66.6	66.3	66.0	66.3	66.9	67.8	67.4	66.8	67.0	67.7	66.7
Leisure and Hospitality													
2000	38.3	38.5	39.3	40.6	42.2	43.5	43.4	43.3	42.3	40.8	40.2	39.8	41.0
2001	37.7	37.9	38.5	39.8	41.0	42.1	42.1	42.4	40.7	39.1	39.0	38.6	39.9
2002	37.2	37.2	38.0	39.6	40.8	42.1	42.4	43.0	41.7	39.7	39.3	39.0	40.0
2003	38.4	38.3	39.0	39.9	41.0	41.8	41.7	42.0	40.5	39.5	38.9	38.4	40.0
2004	37.8	37.6	38.3	39.9	41.5	42.5	42.3	42.3	41.4	40.4	40.2	39.9	40.3
2005	39.2	39.2	40.1	42.1	43.2	44.7	44.4	44.5	43.3	42.1	41.9	41.5	42.2
2006	40.9	41.2	42.0	43.3	44.7	45.6	45.0	44.9	43.9	44.0	43.7	43.9	43.6
2007	42.7	42.6	43.1	44.9	46.5	47.4	47.1	47.5	46.0	44.6	44.5	44.3	45.1
Other Services													
2000	14.0	14.1	14.2	14.0	14.3	14.4	14.7	14.6	14.2	14.0	14.0	14.0	14.2
2001	14.2	14.0	14.4	14.7	14.8	15.1	14.8	14.7	14.5	14.7	14.7	14.6	14.6
2002	14.3	14.5	14.6	15.1	15.1	15.2	15.4	15.0	14.7	14.7	14.7	14.7	14.8
2003	14.4	14.4	14.6	15.1	15.7	15.8	15.9	15.9	15.7	15.6	15.6	15.5	15.4
2004	15.5	15.5	15.7	15.6	15.7	16.0	16.1	16.0	15.9	16.0	16.0	16.1	15.8
2005	15.9	16.0	16.0	16.0	16.1	16.3	16.4	16.3	16.0	16.1	16.1	16.0	16.1
2006	16.2	16.2	16.2	16.4	16.5	16.6	16.6	16.5	16.4	16.6	16.5	16.6	16.4
2007	16.4	16.4	16.5	16.6	16.6	16.7	16.6	16.4	16.4	16.3	16.4	16.4	16.5
Government													
2000	54.9	55.0	54.8	55.6	55.8	56.0	53.7	53.4	55.0	56.1	56.4	56.5	55.3
2001	55.9	56.1	56.1	56.7	57.1	57.6	55.0	54.8	56.2	57.1	57.4	57.6	56.5
2002	57.0	57.6	57.4	57.4	57.7	57.8	54.8	54.6	56.4	58.0	58.1	57.8	57.1
2003	57.7	58.1	57.9	59.2	59.4	59.4	55.7	54.2	56.6	59.0	59.0	58.6	57.9
2004	58.7	58.9	59.2	59.3	59.8	59.6	57.0	56.8	58.7	59.8	59.9	59.7	59.0
2005	59.5	60.0	59.9	60.1	60.6	60.3	57.1	56.9	59.4	61.1	61.3	60.9	59.8
2006	60.6	60.9	61.0	61.6	61.9	61.5	57.4	57.5	60.6	61.7	61.9	61.3	60.7
2007	61.3	61.6	61.4	62.7	63.1	62.3	57.9	58.9	61.4	63.6	63.1	63.1	61.7

Employment by Industry: Oxnard-Thousand Oaks-Ventura, CA, 2000–2007

(Numbers in thousands, not seasonally adjusted.)

Industry and year	January	February	March	April	May	June	July	August	September	October	November	December	Annual Average
Total Nonfarm													
2000	267.4	267.9	270.3	273.3	275.2	277.2	275.5	274.3	277.4	278.4	279.9	283.1	275.0
2001	277.3	277.1	278.8	279.0	280.6	280.9	279.3	277.8	279.6	281.4	283.0	284.5	279.9
2002	277.7	279.6	280.4	280.2	281.7	283.8	281.1	278.3	282.4	282.9	286.9	286.9	281.8
2003	279.7	280.1	282.4	283.5	285.9	287.5	283.1	281.7	284.3	286.7	287.7	287.9	284.2
2004	280.8	283.3	285.9	286.5	286.9	288.7	285.0	284.1	285.0	288.0	289.3	291.1	286.2
2005	285.7	288.4	290.3	291.5	292.1	293.2	289.1	288.9	291.1	292.3	294.5	296.7	291.2
2006	292.2	294.9	296.5	297.5	300.0	301.1	296.6	296.4	298.2	298.2	300.0	301.3	297.7
2007	293.7	295.4	297.3	295.9	297.9	299.6	295.5	294.8	295.3	293.8	295.3	295.3	295.8
Total Private													
2000	223.3	223.3	225.3	228.0	229.5	232.2	232.3	233.0	234.5	233.8	234.8	237.8	230.7
2001	231.5	231.5	233.4	234.3	235.7	236.7	234.4	235.1	235.4	235.8	236.4	237.7	234.8
2002	231.8	233.1	234.4	234.5	236.1	237.7	237.3	236.6	238.0	237.8	240.2	241.3	236.6
2003	234.2	234.6	236.3	237.7	239.3	241.5	240.1	240.1	240.7	241.9	242.5	244.1	239.4
2004	237.7	239.9	242.2	242.8	243.5	244.9	244.4	244.4	244.2	245.7	246.7	248.4	243.7
2005	243.5	245.7	247.5	248.8	249.0	250.3	248.9	249.0	249.3	250.1	251.6	253.9	249.0
2006	249.7	252.1	253.5	254.5	257.1	257.9	255.7	256.0	255.6	255.7	256.8	258.2	255.2
2007	251.0	252.3	254.0	252.4	254.2	255.8	254.4	254.1	252.6	250.9	251.8	251.9	253.0
Goods-Producing													
2000	55.0	54.8	55.3	56.0	56.7	57.8	58.1	58.4	59.1	58.8	58.3	58.5	57.2
2001	57.1	57.1	57.6	57.5	57.7	58.0	57.3	57.6	57.5	57.1	56.2	55.5	57.2
2002	53.9	54.7	54.7	54.4	54.8	55.2	54.4	54.0	54.2	53.7	54.2	54.0	54.4
2003	52.9	52.7	53.2	53.8	54.4	55.1	55.3	55.2	55.1	54.8	54.7	54.3	54.3
2004	54.0	54.7	55.3	55.8	56.0	56.5	56.7	56.4	56.3	56.4	56.4	56.5	55.9
2005	55.6	56.6	57.3	57.4	57.4	58.1	57.6	57.5	57.5	57.5	57.2	57.5	57.3
2006	57.7	58.8	59.1	59.3	60.2	61.2	61.1	61.2	61.1	60.2	59.8	59.2	59.9
2007	58.0	58.2	58.6	58.0	58.7	59.0	58.2	58.1	57.4	56.0	55.5	54.7	57.5
Natural Resources and Mining													
2000	0.7	0.7	0.7	0.7	0.7	0.7	0.7	0.7	0.7	0.7	0.6	0.6	0.7
2001	0.6	0.6	0.6	0.6	0.6	0.6	0.6	0.6	0.6	0.6	0.6	0.6	0.6
2002	0.6	0.7	0.7	0.7	0.7	0.7	0.7	0.7	0.7	0.7	0.7	0.6	0.7
2003	0.6	0.6	0.6	0.6	0.6	0.6	0.6	0.6	0.6	0.6	0.6	0.6	0.6
2004	0.6	0.6	0.7	0.7	0.7	0.7	0.7	0.7	0.7	0.7	0.7	0.7	0.7
2005	0.7	0.6	0.7	0.7	0.7	0.8	0.8	0.8	0.8	0.9	0.9	0.9	0.8
2006	1.0	1.0	1.0	1.0	1.0	1.0	1.1	1.1	1.1	1.1	1.1	1.1	1.1
2007	1.1	1.1	1.1	1.1	1.1	1.1	1.0	1.0	1.0	1.0	1.0	1.0	1.1
Construction													
2000	14.2	14.0	14.2	14.7	15.2	15.9	16.0	16.2	16.6	16.1	15.8	15.9	15.4
2001	15.1	15.0	15.4	15.7	16.1	16.5	16.4	16.9	16.9	16.6	16.2	16.0	16.1
2002	15.3	15.8	15.5	15.3	15.4	15.6	15.8	15.8	15.9	16.0	16.0	15.9	15.7
2003	15.3	15.1	15.4	16.0	16.9	17.3	17.6	17.7	17.5	17.1	17.0	16.8	16.6
2004	16.4	16.4	16.5	16.5	16.5	16.9	17.3	17.1	17.2	17.4	17.3	17.5	16.9
2005	16.6	17.4	18.0	18.5	18.7	19.2	19.2	19.4	19.5	19.7	19.5	19.8	18.8
2006	19.8	20.4	20.4	20.4	21.0	21.4	21.2	21.2	21.0	20.2	19.6	19.2	20.5
2007	18.3	18.5	18.7	18.5	19.1	19.7	19.5	19.6	19.0	18.1	17.7	17.0	18.6
Manufacturing													
2000	40.1	40.1	40.4	40.6	40.8	41.2	41.4	41.5	41.8	42.0	41.9	42.0	41.2
2001	41.4	41.5	41.6	41.2	41.0	40.9	40.3	40.1	40.0	39.9	39.4	38.9	40.5
2002	38.0	38.2	38.5	38.4	38.7	38.9	37.9	37.5	37.6	37.0	37.5	37.5	38.0
2003	37.0	37.0	37.2	37.2	36.9	37.2	37.1	36.9	37.0	37.1	37.1	36.9	37.1
2004	37.0	37.7	38.1	38.6	38.8	38.9	38.7	38.6	38.4	38.3	38.4	38.3	38.3
2005	38.3	38.6	38.6	38.2	38.0	38.1	37.6	37.3	37.2	36.9	36.8	36.8	37.7
2006	36.9	37.4	37.7	37.9	38.2	38.8	38.8	38.9	39.0	38.9	39.1	38.9	38.4
2007	38.6	38.6	38.8	38.4	38.5	38.2	37.7	37.5	37.4	36.9	36.8	36.7	37.8
Service-Providing													
2000	212.4	213.1	215.0	217.3	218.5	219.4	217.4	215.9	218.3	219.6	221.6	224.6	217.8
2001	220.2	220.0	221.2	221.5	222.9	222.9	222.0	220.2	222.1	224.3	226.8	229.0	222.8
2002	223.8	224.9	225.7	225.8	226.9	228.6	226.7	224.3	228.2	229.2	232.7	232.9	227.5
2003	226.8	227.4	229.2	229.7	231.5	232.4	227.8	226.5	229.2	231.9	233.0	233.6	229.9
2004	226.8	228.6	230.6	230.7	230.9	232.2	228.3	227.7	228.7	231.6	232.9	234.6	230.3
2005	230.1	231.8	233.0	234.1	234.7	235.1	231.5	231.4	233.6	234.8	237.3	239.2	233.9
2006	234.5	236.1	237.4	238.2	239.8	239.9	235.5	235.2	237.1	238.0	240.2	242.1	237.8
2007	235.7	237.2	238.7	237.9	239.2	240.6	237.3	236.7	237.9	237.8	239.8	240.6	238.3
Trade, Transportation, and Utilities													
2000	48.4	48.1	48.2	48.6	48.7	49.1	49.1	49.3	49.5	49.8	51.7	53.2	49.5
2001	51.1	50.5	50.7	50.7	50.4	50.4	50.1	50.6	50.4	51.0	52.2	53.3	51.0
2002	51.9	51.5	51.5	50.6	50.9	51.4	50.8	51.0	51.1	51.7	53.0	54.2	51.6
2003	51.5	51.3	51.3	51.0	51.2	51.3	51.3	51.5	51.8	53.1	53.4	54.9	52.0
2004	52.5	52.6	53.0	52.5	52.8	53.0	52.8	52.8	52.9	53.4	54.7	55.6	53.2
2005	53.7	53.5	53.6	54.0	54.2	54.6	54.5	54.7	55.0	55.3	56.8	58.1	54.8
2006	55.4	55.1	55.2	55.8	56.3	56.5	56.4	56.4	56.1	56.6	58.1	59.1	56.4
2007	56.4	55.8	55.9	55.5	55.8	56.3	56.7	57.0	56.6	56.5	57.6	58.2	56.5
Wholesale Trade													
2000	9.6	9.8	9.9	10.2	10.3	10.4	10.5	10.5	10.6	10.6	10.8	10.8	10.3
2001	10.8	11.0	11.2	11.1	11.0	11.0	11.0	11.2	10.9	10.9	11.0	11.1	11.0
2002	11.6	11.9	11.8	11.6	11.7	11.7	11.5	11.6	11.5	11.6	11.8	11.8	11.7
2003	11.7	11.8	12.0	12.0	12.0	12.0	11.9	11.9	11.9	11.5	11.6	11.7	11.8
2004	11.6	12.0	12.2	12.1	12.1	12.3	12.5	12.5	12.5	12.4	12.3	12.3	12.2
2005	12.3	12.4	12.4	12.5	12.5	12.6	12.6	12.7	12.7	12.6	12.5	12.6	12.5
2006	12.4	12.6	12.7	12.7	12.8	12.9	12.9	12.8	12.6	12.5	12.4	12.5	12.6
2007	12.6	12.9	13.0	13.1	13.1	13.1	13.2	13.2	13.2	13.1	13.1	13.1	13.1

Employment by Industry: Oxnard-Thousand Oaks-Ventura, CA, 2000–2007—*Continued*

(Numbers in thousands, not seasonally adjusted.)

Industry and year	January	February	March	April	May	June	July	August	September	October	November	December	Annual Average
Retail Trade													
2000	33.3	32.8	32.8	32.7	32.8	33.1	33.3	33.5	33.5	33.7	35.1	36.3	33.6
2001	34.1	33.3	33.3	33.2	33.2	33.4	33.5	33.7	33.9	34.3	35.5	36.5	34.0
2002	34.4	33.6	33.7	33.3	33.5	33.9	33.6	33.7	34.0	34.4	35.3	36.5	34.2
2003	34.1	33.8	33.7	33.5	33.7	33.8	33.8	34.0	34.2	35.9	36.1	37.5	34.5
2004	35.3	35.0	35.1	34.6	34.9	34.9	34.8	34.8	34.8	35.3	36.6	37.4	35.3
2005	35.7	35.5	35.4	35.6	35.8	36.1	36.2	36.3	36.5	36.9	38.4	39.5	36.5
2006	37.1	36.5	36.5	36.9	37.2	37.3	37.5	37.6	37.4	37.9	39.5	40.3	37.6
2007	37.9	37.0	36.9	36.6	36.7	37.0	37.3	37.6	37.2	37.1	38.2	38.7	37.4
Transportation and Utilities													
2000	5.5	5.5	5.5	5.7	5.6	5.6	5.3	5.3	5.4	5.5	5.8	6.1	5.6
2001	6.2	6.2	6.2	6.4	6.2	6.0	5.6	5.7	5.6	5.8	5.7	5.7	5.9
2002	5.9	6.0	6.0	5.7	5.7	5.8	5.7	5.7	5.6	5.7	5.9	5.9	5.8
2003	5.7	5.7	5.6	5.5	5.5	5.5	5.5	5.6	5.6	5.7	5.7	5.7	5.6
2004	5.6	5.6	5.7	5.8	5.8	5.8	5.5	5.5	5.5	5.6	5.7	5.9	5.7
2005	5.7	5.6	5.8	5.9	5.9	5.9	5.7	5.7	5.8	5.8	5.9	6.0	5.8
2006	5.9	6.0	6.0	6.1	6.2	6.3	6.1	6.2	6.2	6.1	6.2	6.3	6.1
2007	5.9	5.9	6.0	5.8	6.0	6.2	6.2	6.2	6.2	6.3	6.3	6.4	6.1
Information													
2000	7.8	7.8	7.9	7.6	7.7	7.8	7.9	7.9	8.0	8.1	8.1	8.3	7.9
2001	8.3	8.3	8.5	8.3	8.5	8.6	8.5	8.4	8.3	8.2	8.2	8.2	8.4
2002	8.3	8.3	8.4	8.3	8.3	8.2	8.0	7.9	7.8	7.8	7.8	7.8	8.1
2003	7.5	7.4	7.4	7.1	7.1	7.1	7.3	7.2	7.1	7.0	7.0	7.0	7.1
2004	6.9	6.7	7.1	7.0	7.0	7.0	6.9	6.8	6.6	6.5	6.4	6.3	6.8
2005	6.1	6.2	6.1	6.2	6.2	6.2	6.1	6.2	6.2	6.1	6.1	6.2	6.2
2006	6.1	6.1	6.1	6.0	6.1	6.0	6.0	5.9	5.8	5.8	5.7	5.8	6.0
2007	5.7	5.9	5.9	5.9	6.0	6.0	5.9	5.9	5.9	5.9	5.9	5.8	5.9
Financial Activities													
2000	17.2	17.1	17.3	17.4	17.6	17.7	17.9	18.0	18.1	18.2	18.1	18.3	17.7
2001	18.5	18.7	19.0	19.1	19.2	19.6	19.7	20.0	20.1	20.5	20.6	20.9	19.7
2002	20.9	21.1	21.4	21.8	22.0	22.2	22.5	22.7	22.8	22.9	23.2	23.3	22.2
2003	22.5	22.7	23.1	23.2	23.5	23.8	23.6	23.9	23.7	23.7	23.7	23.7	23.4
2004	23.5	23.8	23.8	24.1	24.2	24.5	24.3	24.3	24.5	24.3	24.4	24.5	24.2
2005	24.1	24.2	24.3	24.1	24.3	24.5	24.4	24.6	24.6	24.7	24.8	25.1	24.5
2006	25.0	24.8	24.9	24.6	24.5	24.4	23.9	23.6	23.3	23.2	22.9	23.3	24.0
2007	22.7	22.7	22.8	22.8	22.8	23.1	23.1	22.9	22.6	22.5	22.3	22.4	22.7
Professional and Business Services													
2000	38.0	37.9	38.4	40.0	39.9	40.4	40.0	39.8	40.0	39.3	39.1	39.6	39.4
2001	37.1	36.9	37.2	37.3	37.6	37.8	37.2	36.8	37.0	36.8	36.9	37.3	37.2
2002	35.9	36.1	36.3	36.7	36.8	36.9	36.8	36.4	36.7	36.6	36.9	37.0	36.6
2003	35.9	35.9	36.4	36.5	36.7	37.3	37.2	37.1	37.0	37.2	37.4	37.8	36.9
2004	36.4	36.8	37.2	37.1	36.9	37.3	37.2	37.6	37.2	37.9	37.7	38.4	37.3
2005	37.6	38.1	38.3	39.0	38.7	38.7	38.4	38.4	38.0	38.1	38.3	38.4	38.3
2006	38.0	38.8	39.2	39.4	40.0	39.9	39.1	39.6	39.5	39.5	39.4	39.7	39.3
2007	38.8	39.1	39.4	38.7	38.6	38.8	38.3	38.4	38.0	37.5	37.6	37.7	38.4
Education and Health Services													
2000	23.7	24.0	24.2	23.9	24.0	24.1	23.9	24.1	24.4	24.2	24.3	24.4	24.1
2001	24.4	24.7	24.6	25.3	25.6	25.5	25.4	25.3	25.6	25.8	25.9	25.9	25.3
2002	25.4	25.5	25.7	25.9	26.0	25.9	26.3	26.3	27.0	27.3	27.2	27.1	26.3
2003	27.0	27.3	27.5	27.9	28.0	28.2	27.1	27.1	27.7	27.8	27.9	28.0	27.6
2004	27.1	27.4	27.6	27.7	27.7	27.7	27.1	27.0	27.3	27.9	27.8	27.8	27.5
2005	27.7	28.1	28.4	28.5	28.5	28.5	28.1	27.8	28.3	28.6	28.6	28.7	28.3
2006	28.2	28.7	28.7	28.9	29.0	28.9	28.3	28.3	28.8	29.6	29.7	29.9	28.9
2007	29.3	29.9	30.2	30.0	30.2	30.2	29.8	29.9	30.3	30.5	30.8	30.7	30.2
Leisure and Hospitality													
2000	23.7	24.1	24.4	24.7	25.1	25.4	25.6	25.7	25.6	25.7	25.5	25.6	25.1
2001	25.6	25.8	26.1	26.6	27.0	27.1	26.8	27.0	26.8	26.6	26.5	26.7	26.6
2002	25.8	26.1	26.5	26.8	27.2	27.6	28.1	28.0	28.0	27.6	27.5	27.5	27.2
2003	26.7	27.0	27.1	27.5	27.7	27.9	27.8	27.8	28.0	27.9	28.1	28.1	27.6
2004	27.1	27.6	27.8	28.1	28.5	28.6	29.0	29.2	29.2	28.9	29.0	29.0	28.5
2005	28.2	28.4	28.8	29.0	29.2	29.3	29.5	29.6	29.4	29.6	29.6	29.7	29.2
2006	29.2	29.6	30.0	30.2	30.6	30.6	30.9	31.0	30.9	30.8	31.1	31.2	30.5
2007	30.6	31.1	31.4	31.7	32.2	32.5	32.4	32.1	31.8	32.0	32.1	32.3	31.9
Other Services													
2000	9.5	9.5	9.6	9.8	9.8	9.9	9.8	9.8	9.8	9.7	9.7	9.9	9.7
2001	9.4	9.5	9.7	9.5	9.7	9.7	9.4	9.4	9.7	9.8	9.9	9.9	9.6
2002	9.7	9.8	9.9	10.0	10.1	10.3	10.4	10.3	10.4	10.2	10.4	10.4	10.2
2003	10.2	10.3	10.3	10.7	10.7	10.8	10.5	10.3	10.3	10.4	10.3	10.3	10.4
2004	10.2	10.3	10.4	10.5	10.4	10.3	10.4	10.3	10.2	10.4	10.3	10.3	10.3
2005	10.5	10.6	10.7	10.6	10.5	10.4	10.3	10.2	10.3	10.2	10.2	10.2	10.4
2006	10.1	10.2	10.3	10.3	10.4	10.4	10.0	10.0	10.1	10.0	10.1	10.0	10.2
2007	9.5	9.6	9.8	9.8	9.9	9.9	9.9	10.0	9.8	10.0	10.0	10.1	9.9
Government													
2000	44.1	44.6	45.0	45.3	45.7	45.0	43.2	41.3	42.9	44.6	45.1	45.3	44.3
2001	45.8	45.6	45.4	44.7	44.9	44.2	44.9	42.7	44.2	45.6	46.6	46.8	45.1
2002	45.9	46.5	46.0	45.7	45.6	46.1	43.8	41.7	44.4	45.1	46.7	45.6	45.3
2003	45.5	45.5	46.1	45.8	46.6	46.0	43.0	41.6	43.6	44.8	45.2	43.8	44.7
2004	43.1	43.4	43.7	43.7	43.4	43.8	40.6	39.7	40.8	42.3	42.6	42.7	42.5
2005	42.2	42.7	42.8	42.7	43.1	42.9	40.2	39.9	41.8	42.2	42.9	42.8	42.2
2006	42.5	42.8	43.0	43.0	42.9	43.2	40.9	40.4	42.6	42.5	43.2	43.1	42.5
2007	42.7	43.1	43.3	43.5	43.7	43.8	41.1	40.7	42.7	42.9	43.5	43.4	42.9

Employment by Industry: Grand Rapids-Wyoming, MI, 2000–2007

(Numbers in thousands, not seasonally adjusted.)

Industry and year	January	February	March	April	May	June	July	August	September	October	November	December	Annual Average
Total Nonfarm													
2000	400.4	404.5	407.7	404.9	408.7	408.3	401.2	402.4	409.9	413.8	414.3	415.0	407.6
2001	400.9	400.1	401.2	406.5	410.7	408.5	396.7	399.5	403.9	404.4	403.3	403.2	403.2
2002	389.6	390.6	392.7	395.8	401.6	400.5	391.8	394.6	400.0	402.1	402.9	402.7	397.1
2003	381.1	381.7	381.4	382.0	391.5	388.8	380.0	384.8	389.6	394.1	396.6	397.8	387.5
2004	383.6	384.2	384.9	391.4	396.1	393.6	384.8	388.0	393.7	395.9	397.5	396.9	390.9
2005	383.9	386.4	389.4	393.7	398.5	395.7	390.7	393.6	399.6	399.9	401.2	400.7	394.4
2006	385.6	387.7	390.1	394.8	400.1	397.8	387.2	390.9	397.1	396.5	398.1	398.3	393.7
2007	385.7	387.7	389.4	392.0	399.5	397.1	386.0	389.8	396.8	397.6	399.6	399.4	393.4
Total Private													
2000	363.4	365.9	368.9	366.5	369.1	371.0	368.9	370.9	372.3	374.8	375.3	376.2	370.3
2001	362.4	360.6	361.4	367.5	370.9	371.4	364.6	367.7	366.4	365.5	364.4	364.1	365.6
2002	351.2	351.5	353.4	357.4	362.3	363.9	360.1	363.1	362.7	362.3	362.7	362.3	359.4
2003	341.9	341.9	341.6	342.9	351.3	351.0	347.0	351.1	351.8	354.5	356.8	357.9	349.1
2004	344.4	344.7	345.1	352.1	356.1	357.1	353.0	355.8	356.2	356.7	358.2	357.5	353.1
2005	345.9	347.1	350.0	354.4	358.4	357.9	358.5	361.1	362.6	360.9	362.1	362.0	356.7
2006	347.8	348.6	350.9	355.8	360.3	360.3	355.2	358.5	360.8	358.3	360.1	360.3	356.4
2007	349.3	350.5	352.1	354.9	361.9	360.6	353.7	357.2	360.7	359.8	361.7	361.6	357.0
Goods-Producing													
2000	109.0	109.6	110.4	109.3	109.9	111.6	110.8	111.5	111.4	112.8	112.0	111.5	110.8
2001	108.0	106.6	106.1	106.6	107.3	108.0	106.8	108.0	107.5	105.5	104.3	103.6	106.5
2002	98.5	97.8	97.7	98.7	100.2	100.7	99.4	99.9	99.2	99.2	98.4	97.8	99.0
2003	93.7	92.8	92.5	91.3	94.9	95.0	92.9	95.0	94.5	94.4	94.2	94.2	93.8
2004	92.1	91.1	91.2	92.8	93.6	94.5	92.9	94.4	94.1	94.0	93.2	93.2	93.1
2005	91.2	90.5	91.5	91.6	92.5	93.4	92.6	93.7	93.3	93.4	93.1	92.7	92.5
2006	90.1	89.5	89.8	91.5	92.6	93.4	91.1	92.7	92.1	90.8	90.0	89.7	91.1
2007	86.8	86.5	86.5	87.7	88.7	89.8	88.2	89.7	89.3	88.9	88.2	87.8	88.2
Natural Resources, Mining, and Construction													
2000	18.6	18.4	19.2	20.4	21.1	22.1	21.7	21.7	21.5	21.3	20.8	20.2	20.6
2001	18.2	18.1	18.6	19.9	20.9	21.7	22.3	22.4	22.2	21.6	21.2	20.5	20.6
2002	19.0	18.8	19.1	20.0	21.2	21.5	21.8	21.7	21.1	20.9	20.3	19.6	20.4
2003	17.2	16.8	16.8	18.1	19.0	19.7	20.3	20.4	19.9	19.6	19.3	19.1	18.9
2004	17.4	16.9	17.2	19.0	19.6	20.2	20.4	20.2	19.9	19.5	19.0	18.7	19.0
2005	17.1	16.6	16.9	18.3	19.0	19.5	19.8	19.8	19.5	19.1	18.7	18.0	18.5
2006	16.5	16.2	16.5	17.9	18.8	19.5	19.3	19.3	18.9	18.4	17.9	17.4	18.1
2007	15.9	15.5	15.7	16.7	17.5	18.2	18.1	18.0	17.7	17.4	16.9	16.4	17.0
Manufacturing													
2000	90.4	91.2	91.2	88.9	88.8	89.5	89.1	89.8	89.9	91.5	91.2	91.3	90.2
2001	89.8	88.5	87.5	86.7	86.4	86.3	84.5	85.6	85.3	83.9	83.1	83.1	85.9
2002	79.5	79.0	78.6	78.7	79.0	79.2	77.6	78.2	78.1	78.3	78.1	78.2	78.5
2003	76.5	76.0	75.7	73.2	75.9	75.3	72.6	74.6	74.6	74.8	74.9	75.1	74.9
2004	74.7	74.2	74.0	73.8	74.0	74.3	72.5	74.2	74.2	74.5	74.2	74.5	74.1
2005	74.1	73.9	74.6	73.3	73.5	73.9	72.8	73.9	73.8	74.3	74.4	74.7	73.9
2006	73.6	73.3	73.3	73.6	73.8	73.9	71.8	73.4	73.2	72.4	72.1	72.3	73.1
2007	70.9	71.0	70.8	71.0	71.2	71.6	70.1	71.7	71.6	71.5	71.3	71.4	71.2
Service-Providing													
2000	291.4	294.9	297.3	295.6	298.8	296.7	290.4	290.9	298.5	301.0	302.3	303.5	296.8
2001	292.9	293.5	295.1	299.9	303.4	300.5	289.9	291.5	296.4	298.9	299.0	299.6	296.7
2002	291.1	292.8	295.0	297.1	301.4	299.8	292.4	294.7	300.8	302.9	304.5	304.9	298.1
2003	287.4	288.9	288.9	290.7	296.6	293.8	287.1	289.8	295.1	299.7	302.4	303.6	293.7
2004	291.5	293.1	293.7	298.6	302.5	299.1	291.9	293.6	299.6	301.9	304.3	303.7	297.8
2005	292.7	295.9	297.9	302.1	306.0	302.3	298.1	299.9	306.3	306.5	308.1	308.0	302.0
2006	295.5	298.2	300.3	303.3	307.5	304.4	296.1	298.2	305.0	305.7	308.1	308.6	302.6
2007	298.9	301.2	302.9	304.3	310.8	307.3	297.8	300.1	307.5	308.7	311.4	311.6	305.2
Trade, Transportation, and Utilities													
2000	81.4	81.4	82.0	81.8	82.1	81.5	80.0	80.3	81.1	82.5	83.7	84.9	81.9
2001	82.6	81.6	81.4	82.1	82.4	81.6	79.4	79.5	79.0	79.7	80.5	80.8	80.9
2002	77.5	76.9	77.0	77.1	77.7	78.1	77.6	78.1	77.9	78.1	78.9	80.0	77.9
2003	76.2	75.1	75.0	75.5	76.5	77.0	76.2	76.1	76.1	76.8	78.1	78.8	76.5
2004	75.1	74.1	73.9	75.4	75.9	76.1	75.7	75.7	75.4	76.0	77.4	77.8	75.7
2005	74.5	74.0	74.4	75.5	76.4	76.7	76.7	76.7	76.3	76.3	77.4	77.8	76.1
2006	74.1	73.5	73.6	74.1	74.8	74.9	74.6	74.4	74.3	74.7	76.1	76.7	74.7
2007	74.5	73.4	73.6	74.3	75.0	75.2	74.7	74.8	74.4	74.8	75.8	76.4	74.7
Wholesale Trade													
2000	23.7	24.0	23.9	24.1	24.0	24.1	24.0	23.8	24.0	24.0	23.8	24.2	24.0
2001	24.3	23.9	24.1	24.3	24.0	23.8	23.3	23.2	23.0	23.0	22.9	22.8	23.6
2002	23.2	22.9	22.9	22.9	23.1	23.2	23.0	23.0	22.7	22.9	22.8	22.9	23.0
2003	22.6	22.4	22.3	22.4	22.6	22.5	22.2	22.1	22.0	22.3	22.3	22.3	22.3
2004	21.7	21.7	21.6	22.1	22.2	22.4	22.3	22.1	22.1	22.1	22.2	22.2	22.1
2005	21.7	21.7	21.8	22.0	22.3	22.4	22.4	22.4	22.3	22.4	22.3	22.4	22.2
2006	22.0	22.0	22.0	22.2	22.4	22.5	22.5	22.4	22.4	22.5	22.4	22.4	22.3
2007	22.2	22.1	22.2	22.7	22.8	22.8	22.8	23.0	22.7	22.9	22.7	22.7	22.6
Retail Trade													
2000	46.6	46.3	47.1	46.5	47.0	46.1	44.7	45.1	45.7	46.8	48.2	49.0	46.6
2001	46.8	46.3	45.9	46.1	46.6	46.1	44.5	44.6	44.4	44.9	46.1	46.6	45.7
2002	43.1	42.8	42.8	43.0	43.4	43.7	43.5	43.9	44.1	43.9	44.9	45.9	43.8
2003	43.4	42.7	42.7	42.8	43.5	44.0	43.8	43.9	44.0	44.3	45.7	46.3	43.9
2004	43.4	42.5	42.3	42.8	43.2	43.2	43.0	43.1	42.6	42.9	44.3	44.8	43.2
2005	42.4	41.9	42.1	42.8	43.3	43.3	43.3	43.2	42.9	42.9	44.1	44.3	43.0
2006	41.4	40.9	41.0	41.3	41.7	41.6	41.3	41.3	41.1	41.1	41.4	43.4	41.6
2007	41.7	40.8	40.8	40.9	41.4	41.4	41.0	40.9	40.8	41.0	42.2	42.8	41.3

Employment by Industry: Grand Rapids-Wyoming, MI, 2000–2007—*Continued*

(Numbers in thousands, not seasonally adjusted.)

Industry and year	January	February	March	April	May	June	July	August	September	October	November	December	Annual Average
Transportation and Utilities													
2000	11.1	11.1	11.0	11.2	11.1	11.3	11.3	11.4	11.4	11.7	11.7	11.7	11.3
2001	11.5	11.4	11.4	11.7	11.8	11.7	11.6	11.7	11.6	11.8	11.5	11.4	11.6
2002	11.2	11.2	11.3	11.2	11.2	11.2	11.1	11.2	11.1	11.3	11.2	11.2	11.2
2003	10.2	10.0	10.0	10.3	10.4	10.5	10.2	10.1	10.1	10.2	10.1	10.2	10.2
2004	10.0	9.9	10.0	10.5	10.5	10.5	10.4	10.5	10.7	11.0	10.9	10.8	10.5
2005	10.4	10.4	10.5	10.7	10.8	11.0	11.0	11.1	11.1	11.0	11.0	11.1	10.8
2006	10.7	10.6	10.6	10.6	10.7	10.8	10.8	10.7	10.8	10.8	10.8	10.9	10.7
2007	10.6	10.5	10.6	10.7	10.8	11.0	10.9	10.9	10.9	10.9	10.9	10.9	10.8
Information													
2000	6.1	6.0	6.0	6.0	6.1	6.1	6.2	6.3	6.2	6.1	6.1	6.2	6.1
2001	5.8	5.9	5.9	6.1	6.1	6.3	6.1	6.0	6.0	6.2	6.5	6.5	6.1
2002	6.5	6.5	6.6	6.1	6.1	6.1	6.0	6.0	5.9	6.1	6.1	6.2	6.2
2003	6.1	6.0	6.0	5.9	6.0	5.9	5.9	5.5	5.5	5.4	5.5	5.5	5.7
2004	5.6	5.6	5.6	5.6	5.5	5.6	5.6	5.5	5.4	5.3	5.4	5.4	5.5
2005	5.5	5.6	5.6	5.7	5.6	5.7	5.6	5.6	5.5	5.7	5.9	5.9	5.7
2006	5.7	5.7	5.7	5.6	5.6	5.7	5.5	5.5	5.4	5.4	5.4	5.4	5.6
2007	5.3	5.3	5.2	5.2	5.3	5.4	5.4	5.3	5.4	5.4	5.4	5.4	5.3
Financial Activities													
2000	21.8	21.9	21.8	20.4	20.4	20.4	20.2	20.2	20.3	20.6	20.7	20.8	20.8
2001	20.2	20.2	20.3	20.2	20.5	20.5	20.4	20.4	20.3	21.0	20.8	21.0	20.5
2002	20.9	21.1	21.3	20.9	20.9	20.7	20.6	20.7	20.5	20.9	20.7	20.8	20.8
2003	20.8	20.8	20.8	21.0	21.0	21.0	21.1	21.1	21.1	21.3	21.2	21.4	21.1
2004	21.4	21.4	21.6	21.7	21.8	21.8	21.7	21.7	21.6	21.3	21.4	21.5	21.6
2005	21.5	21.8	21.6	21.8	21.9	22.0	22.1	22.1	22.0	22.1	22.1	22.2	21.9
2006	22.4	22.4	22.4	22.5	22.5	22.5	22.4	22.4	22.3	22.1	22.1	22.0	22.3
2007	21.8	21.8	21.7	22.2	22.2	22.1	22.1	22.2	22.1	21.9	21.9	21.9	22.0
Professional and Business Services													
2000	53.8	54.1	54.6	55.0	55.3	56.7	58.0	58.7	58.4	57.9	57.8	57.7	56.5
2001	53.2	52.5	52.5	55.2	56.4	57.1	55.2	56.6	56.0	54.4	53.7	52.9	54.6
2002	51.5	51.8	52.2	54.4	55.8	56.3	56.3	57.5	56.6	56.0	56.2	55.6	55.0
2003	48.4	48.1	47.7	49.3	50.8	51.1	52.2	53.9	53.2	53.9	54.7	54.6	51.5
2004	49.7	50.5	50.3	52.8	54.1	54.4	53.9	55.5	54.6	54.1	53.9	53.2	53.1
2005	50.1	50.2	50.9	52.9	54.0	54.5	56.7	57.7	57.8	56.4	56.5	55.7	54.5
2006	52.0	52.8	52.6	54.5	55.8	57.1	56.6	58.0	58.4	57.4	58.1	58.5	56.0
2007	55.2	56.4	57.2	56.7	60.4	59.2	56.8	58.1	60.2	59.7	60.2	60.6	58.4
Education and Health Services													
2000	44.5	45.4	46.1	46.3	46.3	45.4	44.6	45.0	46.1	46.7	47.1	47.3	45.9
2001	47.0	47.7	48.5	49.2	49.1	48.8	47.9	47.7	48.8	50.1	50.6	50.8	48.9
2002	50.1	51.0	51.7	51.9	52.0	51.8	50.3	50.6	51.6	52.1	53.0	52.4	51.5
2003	50.1	52.5	52.4	52.3	52.9	51.2	50.3	50.4	52.0	53.9	54.8	54.8	52.3
2004	53.5	54.7	54.8	55.5	55.4	54.5	53.1	53.2	55.6	56.8	57.9	57.5	55.2
2005	55.3	56.8	57.3	57.8	57.5	54.7	54.7	54.7	57.0	57.8	58.1	58.1	56.7
2006	56.2	56.8	58.2	58.4	58.3	56.0	54.8	55.2	58.1	58.6	59.6	59.5	57.5
2007	58.5	59.7	60.0	60.6	60.6	58.6	57.0	57.3	59.9	60.5	61.7	61.4	59.7
Leisure and Hospitality													
2000	30.8	31.5	31.8	31.6	32.9	33.1	32.8	32.7	32.8	32.0	31.7	31.5	32.1
2001	29.6	30.0	30.4	31.5	32.5	32.4	32.2	32.9	32.4	32.0	31.4	31.7	31.6
2002	29.9	30.0	30.4	31.6	32.8	33.2	32.7	33.2	33.8	32.7	32.3	32.3	32.1
2003	29.7	29.6	29.9	30.8	32.2	32.6	31.7	31.9	32.1	31.6	31.2	31.2	31.2
2004	30.0	30.1	30.3	31.3	32.7	33.0	32.8	32.7	32.5	32.1	32.0	31.9	31.8
2005	30.6	30.8	31.2	32.4	33.7	33.9	33.2	33.8	34.1	33.0	32.7	33.3	32.7
2006	31.2	31.6	32.2	32.4	33.8	33.6	33.4	33.6	33.7	32.8	32.4	32.0	32.7
2007	31.1	31.3	31.6	31.7	33.2	33.5	33.1	33.4	33.3	32.5	32.4	32.0	32.4
Other Services													
2000	16.0	16.0	16.2	16.1	16.1	16.2	16.3	16.2	16.0	16.2	16.2	16.3	16.2
2001	16.0	16.1	16.3	16.6	16.6	16.7	16.6	16.6	16.4	16.6	16.6	16.8	16.5
2002	16.3	16.4	16.5	16.4	16.8	17.0	17.2	17.1	17.2	17.2	17.1	17.2	16.9
2003	16.9	17.0	17.3	16.8	17.0	17.2	17.1	17.2	17.4	17.1	17.1	17.4	17.1
2004	17.0	17.2	17.4	17.0	17.1	17.2	17.3	17.1	17.0	17.1	17.0	17.0	17.1
2005	17.2	17.4	17.5	16.7	16.8	17.0	16.9	16.8	16.6	16.2	16.3	16.3	16.8
2006	16.1	16.3	16.4	16.8	16.9	17.1	16.8	16.7	16.5	16.5	16.4	16.5	16.6
2007	16.1	16.1	16.3	16.5	16.5	16.8	16.4	16.4	16.1	16.1	16.1	16.1	16.3
Government													
2000	37.0	38.6	38.8	38.4	39.6	37.3	32.3	31.5	37.6	39.0	39.0	38.8	37.3
2001	38.5	39.5	39.8	39.0	39.8	37.1	32.1	31.8	37.5	38.9	38.9	39.1	37.7
2002	38.4	39.1	39.3	38.4	39.3	36.6	31.7	31.5	37.3	39.8	40.2	40.4	37.7
2003	39.2	39.8	39.8	39.1	40.2	37.8	33.0	33.7	37.8	39.6	39.8	39.9	38.3
2004	39.2	39.5	39.8	39.3	40.0	36.5	31.8	32.2	37.5	39.2	39.3	39.4	37.8
2005	38.0	39.3	39.4	39.3	40.1	37.8	32.2	32.5	37.0	39.0	39.1	38.7	37.7
2006	37.8	39.1	39.2	39.0	39.8	37.5	32.0	32.4	36.3	38.2	38.0	38.0	37.3
2007	36.4	37.2	37.3	37.1	37.6	36.5	32.3	32.6	36.1	37.8	37.9	37.8	36.4

Employment by Industry: Allentown-Bethlehem-Easton, PA-NJ, 2000–2007

(Numbers in thousands, not seasonally adjusted.)

Industry and year	January	February	March	April	May	June	July	August	September	October	November	December	Annual Average
Total Nonfarm													
2000	314.4	315.7	319.2	321.1	325.4	328.6	324.2	324.1	324.3	326.2	328.3	329.8	323.4
2001	322.8	323.3	326.7	326.0	329.2	331.3	324.9	326.2	325.8	325.6	325.4	325.6	326.1
2002	318.9	319.2	323.1	322.7	326.4	327.4	323.0	324.1	327.1	327.4	327.1	327.4	324.5
2003	320.7	319.8	322.8	324.9	329.0	329.9	321.4	322.1	328.4	330.3	330.9	330.8	325.9
2004	321.6	323.1	327.2	329.6	333.1	334.9	326.5	326.5	331.1	335.0	334.9	334.2	329.8
2005	325.8	328.1	331.1	336.7	339.5	340.7	334.9	334.1	339.1	340.6	341.4	341.1	336.1
2006	332.7	334.4	339.3	341.6	344.2	346.0	338.4	340.2	344.9	347.0	346.4	346.7	341.8
2007	336.7	337.0	341.8	343.6	348.0	350.5	342.5	342.2	346.0	346.5	346.3	346.4	344.0
Total Private													
2000	276.7	277.3	280.3	282.2	285.3	288.9	287.4	287.5	287.5	287.3	289.1	290.4	285.0
2001	284.9	284.4	287.5	286.9	289.8	292.4	289.2	290.0	287.9	286.2	285.9	285.8	287.6
2002	280.2	279.7	283.3	283.0	286.3	288.2	287.4	288.9	288.6	287.6	287.2	287.4	285.7
2003	281.3	279.2	281.9	284.0	287.7	289.0	286.7	287.9	288.5	289.4	289.3	289.5	286.2
2004	281.6	281.8	285.6	288.1	291.0	293.2	290.9	291.2	290.9	293.4	293.2	292.6	289.5
2005	285.5	286.3	289.2	293.9	297.0	299.2	299.2	299.2	298.5	299.0	299.4	299.0	295.5
2006	291.5	292.3	296.9	299.2	301.5	304.1	302.6	304.1	303.8	304.8	303.5	303.9	300.7
2007	295.2	294.3	298.9	300.5	304.3	307.3	305.2	305.1	303.9	303.3	302.6	302.4	301.9
Goods-Producing													
2000	67.9	67.2	68.4	68.3	68.8	70.2	69.7	70.9	70.5	69.8	70.3	70.4	69.4
2001	69.4	69.2	69.6	70.2	70.3	70.8	69.3	69.8	68.7	67.1	66.0	65.5	68.8
2002	64.5	64.2	64.7	64.6	65.1	65.5	64.6	64.6	63.7	62.6	61.9	61.1	63.9
2003	59.2	58.2	58.4	58.7	59.2	59.7	58.8	58.8	58.3	58.2	57.7	57.1	58.5
2004	56.0	55.7	56.5	57.0	57.7	58.7	58.6	59.1	58.7	58.5	58.6	58.3	57.8
2005	56.8	56.4	56.8	58.1	58.7	59.6	59.2	59.3	59.0	58.6	58.4	57.8	58.2
2006	56.1	56.1	56.8	57.2	57.2	58.4	57.6	58.2	57.5	57.4	56.8	56.6	57.2
2007	55.5	54.9	55.7	56.2	57.0	57.8	57.4	57.4	57.2	56.8	56.4	56.0	56.5
Natural Resources, Mining, and Construction													
2000	13.5	12.9	13.6	14.0	14.4	14.9	15.4	15.5	15.3	15.0	15.0	14.6	14.5
2001	13.9	13.6	13.8	14.4	14.8	15.3	15.6	15.7	15.4	15.0	14.7	14.5	14.7
2002	13.5	13.5	14.0	14.9	15.3	15.8	16.0	15.7	15.3	15.0	15.0	14.6	14.9
2003	13.4	13.0	13.4	14.3	15.0	15.6	15.9	16.0	15.7	15.7	15.5	15.1	14.8
2004	14.5	14.3	15.0	15.5	16.2	16.7	16.9	17.0	16.8	16.6	16.5	16.4	16.0
2005	15.3	15.1	15.3	16.6	17.1	17.8	18.0	17.9	17.6	17.3	17.4	16.9	16.9
2006	15.8	15.8	16.2	16.9	17.1	17.7	17.7	17.9	17.5	17.3	16.9	16.7	17.0
2007	15.6	14.9	15.4	16.2	17.0	17.5	17.7	17.8	17.4	17.2	17.0	16.7	16.7
Manufacturing													
2000	54.4	54.3	54.8	54.3	54.4	55.3	54.3	55.4	55.2	54.8	55.3	55.8	54.9
2001	55.5	55.6	55.8	55.8	55.5	55.5	53.7	54.1	53.3	52.1	51.3	51.0	54.1
2002	51.0	50.7	50.7	49.7	49.8	49.7	48.6	48.9	48.4	47.6	46.9	46.5	49.0
2003	45.8	45.2	45.0	44.4	44.2	44.1	42.9	42.8	42.6	42.5	42.2	42.0	43.6
2004	41.5	41.4	41.5	41.5	41.5	42.0	41.7	42.1	41.9	41.9	42.1	41.9	41.8
2005	41.5	41.3	41.5	41.5	41.6	41.8	41.2	41.4	41.4	41.3	41.0	40.9	41.4
2006	40.3	40.3	40.6	40.3	40.1	40.7	39.9	40.3	40.0	40.1	39.9	39.9	40.2
2007	39.9	40.0	40.3	40.0	40.0	40.3	39.7	39.6	39.8	39.6	39.4	39.3	39.8
Service-Providing													
2000	246.5	248.5	250.8	252.8	256.6	258.4	254.5	253.2	253.8	256.4	258.0	259.4	254.1
2001	253.4	254.1	257.1	255.8	258.9	260.5	255.6	256.4	257.1	258.5	259.4	260.1	257.2
2002	254.4	255.0	258.4	258.1	261.3	261.9	258.4	259.5	263.4	264.8	265.2	266.3	260.6
2003	261.5	261.6	264.4	266.2	269.8	270.2	262.6	263.3	270.1	272.1	273.2	273.7	267.4
2004	265.6	267.4	270.7	272.6	275.4	276.2	267.9	267.4	272.4	276.5	276.3	275.9	272.0
2005	269.0	271.7	274.3	278.6	280.8	281.1	275.7	274.8	280.1	282.0	283.0	283.3	277.9
2006	276.6	278.3	282.5	284.4	287.0	287.6	280.8	282.0	287.4	289.6	289.6	290.1	284.7
2007	281.2	282.1	286.1	287.4	291.0	292.7	285.1	284.8	288.8	289.7	289.9	290.4	287.4
Trade, Transportation, and Utilities													
2000	60.5	60.1	60.7	60.8	61.0	61.5	60.8	61.1	61.4	62.5	63.9	64.8	61.6
2001	62.5	61.3	61.9	61.5	61.9	63.1	62.4	62.9	62.4	63.2	64.7	65.5	62.8
2002	63.2	62.2	62.9	62.2	63.0	63.1	63.3	63.9	64.8	64.9	66.3	67.4	63.9
2003	65.0	63.7	64.1	64.4	65.1	65.6	64.3	64.5	64.9	65.8	66.7	67.7	65.2
2004	64.5	63.6	64.5	64.6	64.9	65.2	64.1	64.2	64.4	65.2	66.5	68.1	65.0
2005	66.1	65.5	65.9	66.7	67.5	68.0	67.6	67.7	67.6	68.3	70.0	70.9	67.7
2006	68.9	68.0	68.5	69.3	69.7	70.3	69.9	70.3	70.5	71.1	72.4	73.2	70.2
2007	70.3	68.9	69.3	69.4	70.1	70.8	70.1	69.7	69.5	69.6	70.8	71.2	70.0
Wholesale Trade													
2000	10.7	10.8	11.0	11.2	11.1	11.1	11.3	11.3	11.2	11.6	11.6	11.6	11.2
2001	11.6	11.4	11.6	11.3	11.3	11.6	11.4	11.6	11.3	11.2	11.4	11.4	11.4
2002	11.3	11.1	11.2	11.1	11.2	11.3	11.3	11.2	11.1	11.0	11.1	11.2	11.2
2003	11.2	11.1	11.2	11.1	11.2	11.3	11.3	11.4	11.3	11.4	11.5	11.6	11.3
2004	11.3	11.2	11.4	11.6	11.6	11.8	11.7	11.6	11.7	11.8	11.9	12.1	11.6
2005	12.1	12.1	12.3	12.6	12.6	12.6	12.6	12.5	12.3	12.3	12.3	12.3	12.4
2006	12.5	12.7	12.9	13.3	13.5	13.7	13.7	13.8	13.7	13.8	13.8	13.9	13.4
2007	13.4	13.4	13.5	13.6	13.8	14.0	14.1	13.8	13.7	13.8	13.8	13.8	13.7
Retail Trade													
2000	37.9	37.4	37.6	37.6	37.8	38.2	38.1	38.3	38.0	38.6	40.0	41.0	38.4
2001	38.6	37.6	37.8	37.6	38.0	39.0	38.9	39.2	38.4	39.2	40.6	41.4	38.9
2002	39.6	38.8	39.1	38.7	39.3	39.5	40.0	40.5	40.4	40.4	41.7	42.7	40.1
2003	40.4	39.4	39.6	39.8	40.3	40.7	40.3	40.5	40.4	41.0	41.9	42.9	40.6
2004	40.4	39.6	40.1	40.1	40.8	41.0	40.3	40.5	40.0	40.7	41.8	43.1	40.7
2005	41.2	40.6	40.6	40.8	41.4	41.8	41.6	41.6	40.9	41.2	42.5	43.3	41.5
2006	41.3	40.1	40.4	40.5	40.8	41.3	41.3	41.5	41.2	41.7	43.0	43.7	41.4
2007	41.5	40.2	40.4	40.3	40.8	41.3	41.2	41.2	40.6	40.5	41.6	42.1	41.0

Employment by Industry: Allentown-Bethlehem-Easton, PA-NJ, 2000–2007—*Continued*

(Numbers in thousands, not seasonally adjusted.)

Industry and year	January	February	March	April	May	June	July	August	September	October	November	December	Annual Average
Transportation and Utilities													
2000	11.9	11.9	12.1	12.0	12.1	12.2	11.4	11.5	12.2	12.3	12.3	12.2	12.0
2001	12.3	12.3	12.5	12.6	12.6	12.5	12.1	12.1	12.7	12.8	12.7	12.7	12.5
2002	12.3	12.3	12.6	12.4	12.5	12.3	12.0	12.2	13.3	13.5	13.5	13.5	12.7
2003	13.4	13.2	13.3	13.5	13.6	13.6	12.7	12.6	13.2	13.4	13.3	13.2	13.3
2004	12.8	12.8	13.0	12.9	12.5	12.4	12.1	12.1	12.7	12.7	12.8	12.9	12.6
2005	12.8	12.8	13.0	13.3	13.5	13.6	13.4	13.6	14.4	14.8	15.2	15.3	13.8
2006	15.1	15.2	15.2	15.5	15.4	15.3	14.9	15.0	15.6	15.6	15.6	15.6	15.3
2007	15.4	15.3	15.4	15.5	15.5	15.5	14.8	14.7	15.2	15.3	15.4	15.3	15.3
Information													
2000	8.7	8.7	8.9	8.9	9.0	9.3	9.3	9.0	8.9	9.0	9.1	9.3	9.0
2001	9.4	9.3	9.2	9.1	9.1	9.0	9.0	8.7	8.4	8.4	8.2	8.2	8.8
2002	7.8	7.8	7.8	7.8	7.8	7.9	7.8	7.7	7.6	7.6	7.6	7.7	7.7
2003	7.6	7.7	7.8	7.8	7.8	7.9	7.7	7.7	7.6	7.6	7.7	7.8	7.7
2004	7.6	7.6	7.6	7.7	7.7	7.8	7.8	7.7	7.6	7.7	7.7	7.8	7.7
2005	7.6	7.6	7.6	7.6	7.6	7.6	7.6	7.6	7.4	7.4	7.4	7.4	7.5
2006	7.4	7.4	7.4	7.4	7.5	7.6	7.5	7.5	7.5	7.4	7.4	7.5	7.5
2007	7.4	7.3	7.3	7.3	7.4	7.5	7.4	7.4	7.3	7.3	7.3	7.3	7.4
Financial Activities													
2000	15.7	15.7	15.9	15.9	16.0	16.2	16.2	16.2	16.1	16.2	16.3	16.5	16.1
2001	16.9	16.8	17.0	16.5	16.4	16.8	16.9	17.0	16.9	16.8	16.8	16.9	16.8
2002	16.6	16.6	16.6	16.6	16.5	16.8	16.9	17.0	16.8	16.5	16.5	16.8	16.7
2003	16.7	16.7	16.7	16.6	16.7	16.8	16.8	16.8	16.5	16.5	16.5	16.6	16.6
2004	16.3	16.1	16.2	16.3	16.5	16.5	16.4	16.4	16.2	16.4	16.4	16.5	16.4
2005	16.3	16.3	16.3	16.5	16.6	16.7	16.7	16.8	16.6	16.5	16.6	16.6	16.5
2006	16.4	16.5	16.6	16.6	16.6	16.8	16.7	16.7	16.6	16.6	16.4	16.5	16.6
2007	16.3	16.4	16.4	16.3	16.3	16.5	16.5	16.5	16.4	16.4	16.4	16.3	16.4
Professional and Business Services													
2000	35.9	35.9	36.5	37.4	37.5	38.0	38.4	37.7	37.7	37.6	37.5	37.4	37.3
2001	36.8	36.7	37.1	37.7	37.9	38.1	37.2	37.0	36.8	37.0	36.8	36.8	37.2
2002	36.1	35.9	36.6	37.0	36.8	37.3	37.5	38.0	37.7	38.1	37.9	37.9	37.2
2003	36.7	36.6	37.1	38.0	38.6	39.1	39.4	40.4	40.9	41.0	41.3	41.5	39.2
2004	40.1	39.9	40.4	41.1	41.1	41.4	41.4	41.6	41.3	42.2	41.9	41.5	41.2
2005	40.0	40.4	40.4	41.3	41.4	42.0	42.5	42.7	42.6	43.3	43.5	43.1	41.9
2006	41.4	41.6	42.3	42.6	43.0	43.7	44.0	44.5	44.3	44.9	44.4	44.1	43.4
2007	42.7	42.6	43.1	43.6	43.7	44.4	44.1	43.7	43.9	43.8	43.5	43.4	43.5
Education and Health Services													
2000	48.8	50.3	50.6	51.1	51.4	50.3	49.7	49.7	51.6	52.1	52.8	52.3	50.9
2001	50.5	51.8	52.7	52.3	52.1	50.9	50.8	51.3	53.2	53.4	54.0	53.7	52.2
2002	51.9	52.8	53.7	53.4	53.5	52.1	52.2	52.2	54.5	55.6	56.1	55.0	53.6
2003	54.5	55.0	55.9	56.0	55.8	54.3	54.1	54.2	56.3	57.4	57.9	57.5	55.7
2004	55.6	57.3	58.3	58.0	57.9	56.7	56.2	56.0	57.6	59.3	59.4	58.1	57.5
2005	57.4	58.1	59.3	59.6	59.2	57.8	58.1	57.7	59.5	60.8	60.9	60.5	59.1
2006	59.2	60.2	61.8	61.5	60.9	59.2	59.2	59.3	61.4	62.9	62.6	62.3	60.9
2007	60.6	61.6	63.3	63.2	63.0	61.3	61.0	61.9	63.1	63.9	64.0	63.9	62.6
Leisure and Hospitality													
2000	24.9	24.9	24.9	25.5	27.2	28.7	28.7	28.3	27.0	25.8	24.7	25.2	26.3
2001	25.0	24.9	25.3	24.9	27.2	28.5	28.3	28.2	26.8	25.7	24.6	24.4	26.2
2002	25.4	25.5	26.2	26.5	28.6	30.3	29.8	30.3	28.7	27.6	26.2	26.6	27.6
2003	27.0	26.7	27.1	27.7	29.5	30.4	30.3	30.4	29.1	28.0	26.6	26.4	28.2
2004	26.8	26.8	27.2	28.3	30.0	31.4	30.9	30.9	30.0	28.9	27.5	27.0	28.8
2005	26.2	26.7	27.5	28.9	30.6	31.9	31.9	32.0	30.6	29.2	27.7	27.7	29.2
2006	27.4	27.7	28.6	29.5	31.3	32.7	32.3	32.3	30.9	29.8	28.6	28.6	30.0
2007	27.6	27.8	28.7	29.4	31.5	33.6	33.1	33.0	31.2	30.2	28.9	28.9	30.3
Other Services													
2000	14.3	14.5	14.4	14.3	14.4	14.7	14.6	14.6	14.3	14.3	14.5	14.5	14.5
2001	14.4	14.4	14.7	14.7	14.9	15.2	15.3	15.1	14.7	14.6	14.8	14.8	14.8
2002	14.7	14.7	14.8	14.9	15.0	15.2	15.3	15.2	14.8	14.7	14.7	14.9	14.9
2003	14.6	14.6	14.8	14.8	15.0	15.2	15.3	15.1	14.9	14.9	14.9	14.9	14.9
2004	14.7	14.8	14.9	15.1	15.2	15.5	15.5	15.3	15.1	15.2	15.2	15.3	15.2
2005	15.1	15.3	15.4	15.2	15.4	15.6	15.6	15.4	15.2	14.9	14.9	15.0	15.3
2006	14.7	14.8	14.9	15.1	15.3	15.4	15.4	15.3	15.1	14.9	14.9	15.1	15.1
2007	14.8	14.8	15.1	15.1	15.3	15.4	15.6	15.5	15.3	15.3	15.3	15.4	15.2
Government													
2000	37.7	38.4	38.9	38.9	40.1	39.7	36.8	36.6	36.8	38.9	39.2	39.4	38.5
2001	37.9	38.9	39.2	39.1	39.4	38.9	35.7	36.2	37.9	39.4	39.5	39.8	38.5
2002	38.7	39.5	39.8	39.7	40.1	39.2	35.6	35.2	38.5	39.8	39.9	40.0	38.8
2003	39.4	40.6	40.9	40.9	41.3	40.9	34.7	34.2	39.9	40.9	41.6	41.3	39.7
2004	40.0	41.3	41.6	41.5	42.1	41.7	35.6	35.3	40.2	41.6	41.7	41.6	40.4
2005	40.3	41.8	41.9	42.8	42.5	41.5	35.7	34.9	40.6	41.6	42.0	42.1	40.6
2006	41.2	42.1	42.4	42.4	42.7	41.9	35.8	36.1	41.1	42.2	42.9	42.8	41.1
2007	41.5	42.7	42.9	43.1	43.7	43.2	37.3	37.1	42.1	43.2	43.7	44.0	42.0

Employment by Industry: Albuquerque, NM, 2000–2007

(Numbers in thousands, not seasonally adjusted.)

Industry and year	January	February	March	April	May	June	July	August	September	October	November	December	Annual Average
Total Nonfarm													
2000	346.2	349.2	352.8	355.0	358.4	357.9	356.3	357.7	362.6	361.9	364.4	365.9	357.4
2001	356.5	359.8	362.3	363.3	365.0	365.7	361.0	361.3	361.7	361.6	363.2	364.4	362.2
2002	355.5	357.2	359.9	360.7	363.3	364.0	361.4	361.7	364.7	362.1	364.0	366.1	361.7
2003	356.6	359.5	362.0	362.5	364.0	364.4	361.9	363.5	365.0	364.5	365.6	368.0	363.1
2004	360.2	364.5	367.5	369.6	371.3	371.1	369.1	369.4	371.4	375.1	376.0	376.9	370.2
2005	367.5	370.5	373.0	376.4	377.9	378.4	376.5	378.4	381.6	382.2	385.0	387.0	377.9
2006	381.5	385.2	389.6	389.8	391.8	393.8	390.1	391.2	394.8	395.2	397.2	397.8	391.5
2007	388.0	391.6	395.9	395.3	397.6	397.8	394.1	396.0	396.9	396.4	399.0	398.4	395.6
Total Private													
2000	279.2	279.9	282.8	285.0	287.6	290.0	289.2	291.1	292.9	292.4	294.6	296.1	288.4
2001	289.4	289.9	292.0	292.6	294.1	295.4	292.8	293.4	290.7	290.5	291.5	291.7	292.0
2002	285.6	284.7	287.1	287.9	290.5	290.8	290.2	290.9	291.3	289.3	290.8	292.3	289.3
2003	285.8	286.1	288.1	288.7	290.4	290.9	290.0	291.6	291.0	290.5	291.3	292.9	289.8
2004	288.6	289.5	292.0	294.3	296.1	296.6	296.7	297.0	296.3	298.9	299.4	300.0	295.5
2005	293.7	294.1	296.4	300.0	301.7	302.7	302.8	304.4	304.8	304.4	307.1	308.5	301.7
2006	305.1	306.7	310.7	311.2	313.3	316.0	314.2	314.1	315.4	315.4	317.1	317.4	313.1
2007	310.6	312.1	315.4	315.6	318.0	319.1	317.4	318.3	316.7	315.7	317.7	317.1	316.1
Goods-Producing													
2000	47.5	48.0	48.7	49.2	50.5	51.3	52.4	53.1	53.4	53.1	53.2	53.3	51.1
2001	52.4	52.5	52.9	52.7	52.9	53.3	52.2	52.2	51.1	50.5	50.1	49.6	51.9
2002	48.4	47.9	48.2	48.2	48.3	48.8	49.1	49.1	48.4	47.7	47.2	47.3	48.2
2003	46.8	46.7	46.9	47.0	47.5	47.9	48.3	48.6	48.0	47.5	47.1	47.1	47.5
2004	46.2	46.4	46.9	47.5	48.1	49.1	50.1	50.0	49.6	49.8	49.6	49.6	48.6
2005	48.9	49.1	49.6	50.5	51.0	51.5	52.2	52.3	52.4	52.8	53.3	53.6	51.4
2006	53.5	54.3	55.0	54.9	55.5	56.4	56.4	56.4	56.2	56.2	55.4	55.5	55.5
2007	53.6	54.0	54.6	54.5	55.1	55.4	54.8	54.7	53.8	52.9	52.5	52.0	54.0
Natural Resources, Mining, and Construction													
2000	20.9	21.2	21.8	22.2	23.2	23.8	24.3	24.9	25.2	25.0	25.2	25.1	23.6
2001	24.3	24.3	24.6	24.8	25.1	25.7	25.3	25.4	24.7	24.4	24.5	24.1	24.8
2002	23.4	23.1	23.4	23.3	23.4	23.7	23.8	23.9	23.4	23.2	23.1	23.2	23.4
2003	23.1	23.0	23.2	23.5	24.1	24.5	24.8	25.0	24.6	24.4	24.4	24.5	24.1
2004	24.0	24.3	24.7	25.0	25.4	26.3	27.1	27.0	26.7	27.0	26.9	26.9	25.9
2005	26.3	26.6	27.1	27.8	28.2	28.8	29.5	29.5	29.5	29.6	30.0	30.2	28.6
2006	30.2	30.5	31.2	31.0	31.6	32.2	32.0	32.0	31.7	31.7	31.3	31.4	31.4
2007	29.8	29.9	30.6	30.8	31.2	31.4	30.8	30.7	30.2	29.6	29.4	29.0	30.3
Manufacturing													
2000	26.6	26.8	26.9	27.0	27.3	27.5	28.1	28.2	28.2	28.1	28.0	28.2	27.6
2001	28.1	28.2	28.3	27.9	27.8	27.6	26.9	26.8	26.4	26.1	25.6	25.5	27.1
2002	25.0	24.8	24.8	24.9	24.9	25.1	25.3	25.2	25.0	24.5	24.1	24.1	24.8
2003	23.7	23.7	23.7	23.5	23.4	23.4	23.5	23.6	23.4	23.1	22.7	22.6	23.4
2004	22.2	22.1	22.2	22.5	22.7	22.8	23.0	23.0	22.9	22.8	22.7	22.7	22.6
2005	22.6	22.5	22.5	22.7	22.8	22.7	22.7	22.8	22.9	23.2	23.3	23.4	22.8
2006	23.3	23.8	23.8	23.9	23.9	24.2	24.4	24.4	24.5	24.5	24.1	24.1	24.1
2007	23.8	24.1	24.0	23.7	23.9	24.0	24.0	24.0	23.6	23.3	23.1	23.0	23.7
Service-Providing													
2000	298.7	301.2	304.1	305.8	307.9	306.6	303.9	304.6	309.2	308.8	311.2	312.6	306.2
2001	304.1	307.3	309.4	310.6	312.1	312.4	308.8	309.1	310.6	311.1	313.1	314.8	310.3
2002	307.1	309.3	311.7	312.5	315.0	315.2	312.3	312.6	316.3	314.4	316.8	318.8	313.5
2003	309.8	312.8	315.1	315.5	316.5	316.5	313.6	314.9	317.0	317.0	318.5	320.9	315.7
2004	314.0	318.1	320.6	322.1	323.2	322.0	319.0	319.4	321.8	325.3	326.4	327.3	321.6
2005	318.6	321.4	323.4	325.9	326.9	326.9	324.3	326.1	329.2	329.4	331.7	333.4	326.4
2006	328.0	330.9	334.6	334.9	336.3	337.4	333.7	334.8	338.6	339.0	341.8	342.3	336.0
2007	334.4	337.6	341.3	340.8	342.5	342.4	339.3	341.3	343.1	343.5	346.5	346.4	341.6
Trade, Transportation, and Utilities													
2000	65.2	64.6	64.8	65.3	66.0	65.9	65.2	66.0	66.2	66.7	69.1	69.6	66.2
2001	66.7	65.9	65.8	65.4	65.8	65.6	65.2	65.8	65.4	65.5	67.1	67.9	66.0
2002	65.6	64.5	64.5	64.9	65.8	65.5	65.3	65.7	65.9	66.1	67.8	68.9	65.9
2003	65.6	64.8	65.4	65.2	65.4	65.0	64.7	65.3	65.2	65.7	67.2	68.3	65.7
2004	65.8	65.4	65.6	65.8	65.8	65.5	65.6	65.8	65.6	66.6	68.1	68.8	66.2
2005	66.2	65.9	65.9	66.0	66.6	66.0	66.4	67.1	66.9	67.4	68.8	69.7	66.9
2006	66.7	66.0	66.5	66.6	67.2	66.9	67.1	67.5	67.6	67.8	69.5	70.2	67.5
2007	68.2	67.7	67.9	67.7	68.5	68.5	68.4	68.9	68.7	68.9	71.0	71.6	68.8
Wholesale Trade													
2000	13.9	14.0	14.1	14.2	14.3	14.2	14.1	14.3	14.3	14.1	14.2	14.1	14.2
2001	14.0	14.0	14.0	13.9	14.0	13.9	13.8	13.8	13.8	13.6	13.6	13.6	13.8
2002	13.6	13.5	13.5	13.4	13.5	13.4	13.4	13.5	13.4	13.4	13.4	13.3	13.4
2003	13.0	12.9	13.3	13.2	13.0	13.0	13.0	12.9	13.0	13.0	12.8	12.8	13.0
2004	12.8	12.8	13.0	13.2	12.9	12.8	12.9	12.7	12.7	12.7	12.7	12.7	12.8
2005	12.7	12.9	12.9	12.9	13.0	12.9	13.0	13.0	13.0	13.0	13.1	13.1	13.0
2006	12.9	13.0	13.1	13.2	13.3	13.3	13.3	13.3	13.4	13.4	13.3	13.4	13.2
2007	13.3	13.2	13.2	13.2	13.2	13.3	13.4	13.4	13.3	13.3	13.3	13.3	13.3
Retail Trade													
2000	40.6	40.0	40.1	40.3	40.8	41.1	40.7	41.1	41.2	41.8	44.0	44.7	41.4
2001	42.1	41.2	41.2	40.9	41.2	41.5	41.2	41.3	40.9	41.1	42.8	43.6	41.6
2002	41.4	40.4	40.6	41.0	41.8	41.8	41.5	41.6	41.8	41.9	43.5	44.6	41.8
2003	42.0	41.4	41.6	41.5	41.9	41.7	41.6	41.8	41.7	42.3	43.8	44.8	42.2
2004	42.4	41.9	42.0	42.0	42.3	42.5	42.5	42.6	42.4	43.3	44.9	45.5	42.9
2005	43.1	42.6	42.6	42.8	43.2	43.2	43.4	43.7	43.4	43.9	45.3	45.9	43.6
2006	43.3	42.6	43.0	43.0	43.4	43.3	43.5	43.6	43.6	43.8	45.5	45.8	43.7
2007	44.1	43.6	43.9	43.7	44.4	44.6	44.6	44.6	44.4	44.5	46.6	47.0	44.7

Employment by Industry: Albuquerque, NM, 2000–2007—*Continued*

(Numbers in thousands, not seasonally adjusted.)

Industry and year	January	February	March	April	May	June	July	August	September	October	November	December	Annual Average
Transportation and Utilities													
2000	10.7	10.6	10.6	10.8	10.9	10.6	10.4	10.6	10.7	10.8	10.9	10.8	10.7
2001	10.6	10.7	10.6	10.6	10.6	10.2	10.2	10.7	10.7	10.8	10.7	10.7	10.6
2002	10.6	10.6	10.4	10.5	10.5	10.3	10.3	10.7	10.7	10.8	10.9	11.0	10.6
2003	10.6	10.5	10.5	10.5	10.5	10.3	10.2	10.5	10.5	10.6	10.6	10.6	10.5
2004	10.6	10.7	10.6	10.6	10.6	10.2	10.2	10.5	10.5	10.6	10.5	10.6	10.5
2005	10.4	10.4	10.4	10.3	10.4	9.9	10.0	10.4	10.5	10.5	10.4	10.7	10.4
2006	10.5	10.4	10.4	10.4	10.5	10.3	10.3	10.6	10.6	10.6	10.7	11.0	10.5
2007	10.8	10.9	10.8	10.8	10.9	10.6	10.4	10.9	11.0	11.1	11.1	11.3	10.9
Information													
2000	11.1	10.9	11.1	11.0	11.0	11.1	10.9	11.0	11.1	11.0	11.0	11.4	11.1
2001	11.5	11.7	11.6	11.2	11.2	11.2	11.4	11.5	11.6	11.4	11.5	11.5	11.4
2002	11.2	11.4	11.5	11.3	11.4	11.1	10.9	10.7	10.4	10.5	10.8	10.8	11.0
2003	10.5	10.5	10.5	10.3	10.3	10.3	10.2	10.0	10.1	9.9	9.9	10.0	10.2
2004	9.9	9.9	9.9	9.6	9.8	9.6	9.4	9.3	9.0	9.4	9.5	9.5	9.6
2005	8.5	8.5	8.6	8.7	8.8	8.7	8.7	8.7	8.5	8.7	8.8	9.0	8.7
2006	8.7	9.3	9.5	9.1	9.2	9.9	9.2	9.3	9.7	9.4	9.9	10.0	9.4
2007	8.7	8.9	9.2	9.1	9.3	9.8	9.1	9.0	9.0	9.0	9.4	9.3	9.2
Financial Activities													
2000	19.2	19.2	19.2	19.4	19.4	19.4	19.5	19.4	19.5	19.6	19.7	19.8	19.4
2001	19.5	19.5	19.7	19.8	19.7	19.8	19.7	19.7	19.4	19.4	19.3	19.5	19.6
2002	18.7	18.6	18.7	18.7	18.8	18.9	19.0	19.1	19.0	19.0	18.9	19.0	18.9
2003	18.5	18.6	18.7	18.7	18.8	18.9	19.0	19.2	19.0	18.8	18.8	18.9	18.8
2004	18.8	18.8	19.0	19.0	19.0	19.1	19.1	19.1	19.1	19.1	19.2	19.3	19.1
2005	19.1	19.1	19.2	19.2	19.3	19.5	19.5	19.4	19.3	19.4	19.4	19.6	19.3
2006	19.3	19.3	19.3	19.3	19.3	19.4	19.3	19.2	19.1	19.1	19.1	19.2	19.2
2007	19.0	19.1	19.2	19.2	19.2	19.3	19.3	19.3	19.3	19.2	19.2	19.3	19.2
Professional and Business Services													
2000	56.6	56.8	57.4	58.6	58.8	59.6	59.1	59.5	60.0	59.4	59.3	59.8	58.7
2001	57.6	58.2	58.7	58.8	59.0	59.6	59.0	59.0	57.7	58.5	58.4	58.1	58.6
2002	57.2	57.1	57.8	57.1	57.7	57.9	58.0	58.0	58.5	57.8	57.9	58.4	57.8
2003	56.8	57.3	57.6	57.0	57.1	57.5	57.4	57.7	57.6	57.8	57.8	57.9	57.5
2004	57.4	57.8	58.5	58.6	59.0	59.3	59.4	59.6	59.7	60.8	60.1	60.1	59.2
2005	59.3	59.3	59.5	60.6	60.3	61.2	61.1	61.4	61.6	60.8	61.5	61.4	60.7
2006	61.7	62.2	62.7	62.9	62.8	63.8	62.8	62.8	62.9	63.3	63.3	63.6	62.9
2007	62.8	63.6	64.0	63.8	64.1	64.7	64.8	65.4	64.5	64.4	64.1	63.9	64.2
Education and Health Services													
2000	37.5	37.8	38.0	37.5	37.4	36.7	36.2	36.0	37.3	37.6	37.8	37.9	37.3
2001	38.3	38.6	39.0	39.2	39.4	39.0	38.7	38.6	39.7	40.0	40.2	40.4	39.3
2002	40.8	41.1	41.4	41.4	41.6	40.8	40.2	40.5	41.8	41.8	42.1	41.9	41.3
2003	42.4	42.7	42.9	43.0	43.0	42.2	41.5	41.9	43.2	43.2	43.4	43.5	42.7
2004	44.2	44.4	44.7	45.3	45.3	44.5	43.9	44.4	45.4	45.7	46.1	45.9	45.0
2005	45.7	45.9	46.5	46.5	46.7	45.8	45.2	45.6	46.7	46.9	47.1	47.1	46.3
2006	47.2	47.2	48.4	48.0	48.3	47.6	47.2	47.0	48.5	48.3	48.5	48.4	47.9
2007	48.5	48.8	49.5	49.7	49.8	48.7	48.4	48.2	49.1	49.3	49.5	49.4	49.1
Leisure and Hospitality													
2000	31.4	31.8	32.8	33.3	33.7	34.8	34.7	35.0	34.6	34.1	33.5	33.3	33.6
2001	32.5	32.7	33.3	34.4	34.9	35.3	35.1	35.2	34.7	34.2	33.9	33.6	34.2
2002	32.8	33.0	33.8	34.9	35.5	36.0	35.9	36.0	35.7	34.9	34.6	34.5	34.8
2003	33.7	34.0	34.5	36.0	36.7	37.2	36.9	37.0	36.2	35.9	35.5	35.6	35.8
2004	34.7	35.2	35.8	36.9	37.3	37.4	37.0	36.7	36.1	35.8	35.1	35.2	36.1
2005	34.4	34.7	35.4	36.8	37.2	37.8	37.4	37.7	37.5	36.6	36.4	36.3	36.5
2006	36.3	36.6	37.4	38.3	38.9	39.5	39.7	39.6	39.3	39.0	39.2	38.6	38.5
2007	37.9	38.0	38.8	39.5	39.8	40.2	40.0	40.4	40.0	39.7	39.7	39.4	39.5
Other Services													
2000	10.7	10.8	10.8	10.7	10.8	11.2	11.2	11.1	10.8	10.9	11.0	11.0	10.9
2001	10.9	10.8	11.0	11.1	11.2	11.6	11.5	11.4	11.1	11.0	11.0	11.1	11.1
2002	10.9	11.1	11.2	11.4	11.4	11.8	11.8	11.8	11.6	11.5	11.5	11.5	11.5
2003	11.5	11.5	11.6	11.5	11.6	11.9	12.0	11.9	11.7	11.7	11.6	11.6	11.7
2004	11.6	11.6	11.6	11.6	11.8	12.1	12.2	12.1	11.8	11.7	11.7	11.6	11.8
2005	11.6	11.6	11.7	11.7	11.8	12.2	12.3	12.2	11.9	11.8	11.8	11.8	11.9
2006	11.7	11.8	11.9	12.1	12.1	12.5	12.5	12.3	12.1	12.3	12.2	11.9	12.1
2007	11.9	12.0	12.2	12.1	12.2	12.5	12.6	12.4	12.3	12.3	12.3	12.2	12.3
Government													
2000	67.0	69.3	70.0	70.0	70.8	67.9	67.1	66.6	69.7	69.5	69.8	69.8	69.0
2001	67.1	69.9	70.3	70.7	70.9	70.3	68.2	67.9	71.0	71.1	71.7	72.7	70.2
2002	69.9	72.5	72.8	72.8	72.8	73.2	71.2	70.8	73.4	72.8	73.2	73.8	72.4
2003	70.8	73.4	73.9	73.8	73.6	73.5	71.9	71.9	74.0	74.0	74.3	75.1	73.4
2004	71.6	75.0	75.5	75.3	75.2	74.5	72.4	72.4	75.1	76.2	76.6	76.9	74.7
2005	73.8	76.4	76.6	76.4	76.2	75.7	73.7	74.0	76.8	77.8	77.9	78.5	76.2
2006	76.4	78.5	78.9	78.6	78.5	77.8	75.9	77.1	79.4	79.8	80.1	80.4	78.5
2007	77.4	79.5	80.5	79.7	79.6	78.7	76.7	77.7	80.2	80.7	81.3	81.3	79.4

Employment by Industry: Baton Rouge, LA, 2000–2007

(Numbers in thousands, not seasonally adjusted.)

Industry and year	January	February	March	April	May	June	July	August	September	October	November	December	Annual Average
Total Nonfarm													
2000	335.0	337.6	339.9	344.0	344.5	346.6	332.9	334.6	339.8	337.3	338.6	339.3	339.2
2001	333.6	332.9	334.5	336.3	339.4	339.4	328.6	331.4	334.2	337.1	338.0	337.7	335.3
2002	332.4	333.4	334.3	336.3	337.9	337.0	329.5	331.8	336.4	338.5	339.3	338.2	335.4
2003	331.5	335.3	336.2	339.6	340.7	339.1	336.3	336.5	340.2	343.5	342.7	340.9	338.5
2004	336.6	340.6	344.5	344.9	342.4	343.6	339.9	338.8	341.1	342.3	345.7	344.5	342.1
2005	337.7	343.0	346.1	352.6	350.8	350.4	350.2	351.7	358.1	360.2	364.7	364.0	352.5
2006	356.1	361.5	364.7	363.1	363.2	358.9	349.9	356.5	361.4	362.2	363.9	366.2	360.6
2007	360.1	365.5	369.5	370.2	371.3	372.0	366.7	371.0	373.7	375.3	375.7	375.5	370.5
Total Private													
2000	268.6	271.1	273.5	276.6	277.1	278.7	272.2	274.1	274.1	270.8	272.2	273.1	273.5
2001	267.1	266.4	268.0	269.4	271.9	271.5	267.9	270.4	267.9	269.6	269.8	269.9	269.2
2002	264.0	263.9	264.5	266.5	267.5	266.9	266.8	268.5	267.5	268.5	268.4	267.7	266.7
2003	260.2	261.2	261.9	265.8	266.8	266.3	265.4	266.2	266.5	269.0	268.2	268.4	265.5
2004	265.5	266.5	270.2	270.2	268.9	270.1	267.3	266.5	266.2	266.6	269.9	270.3	268.2
2005	265.1	267.8	270.7	277.3	277.1	276.9	278.7	279.1	282.6	283.3	287.3	287.9	277.8
2006	283.6	286.3	289.3	289.2	289.8	290.5	283.2	284.8	287.4	288.0	289.3	292.6	287.8
2007	287.6	290.3	293.6	294.3	296.1	297.1	293.9	296.3	296.6	297.3	297.6	297.8	294.9
Goods-Producing													
2000	70.7	71.6	72.8	72.9	73.2	72.2	68.2	69.4	68.3	67.6	67.2	66.7	70.1
2001	65.1	65.1	65.9	66.9	68.6	67.2	66.6	67.5	65.0	67.0	66.7	65.9	66.5
2002	64.1	63.2	62.4	63.4	63.5	62.3	62.6	63.3	63.2	65.4	63.3	61.8	63.2
2003	61.0	61.4	61.2	61.8	62.8	62.1	62.0	61.9	62.4	63.4	61.6	61.0	61.9
2004	62.7	62.7	64.9	62.3	61.2	61.1	58.9	58.2	58.9	59.9	61.0	60.7	61.0
2005	58.4	60.5	61.5	65.1	65.1	64.3	63.7	63.8	64.2	63.5	64.8	64.5	63.3
2006	65.6	66.1	67.0	67.4	66.9	66.7	62.6	63.2	64.4	65.4	65.4	66.8	65.6
2007	65.5	66.7	67.5	68.4	69.2	69.3	68.3	69.1	69.0	69.8	69.7	69.4	68.5
Natural Resources and Mining													
2005	1.5	1.5	1.5	1.6	1.5	1.6	1.5	1.5	1.6	1.8	1.8	1.8	1.6
2006	1.6	1.6	1.6	1.5	1.5	1.5	1.5	1.4	1.5	1.4	1.4	1.4	1.5
2007	1.6	1.7	1.7	1.8	1.9	1.9	1.9	1.9	2.0	2.0	2.0	1.9	1.9
Construction													
2005	31.4	33.4	34.2	37.5	37.6	36.9	36.2	36.4	36.8	36.0	37.3	36.9	35.9
2006	38.5	39.0	39.7	40.4	39.9	39.5	36.0	36.6	37.5	38.5	38.4	39.7	38.6
2007	38.1	39.1	39.8	40.4	41.0	40.8	40.1	41.2	40.9	41.7	41.6	41.2	40.5
Manufacturing													
2000	29.4	29.5	29.4	29.7	29.8	29.8	29.6	29.7	29.7	30.2	30.3	30.4	29.8
2001	30.2	30.1	30.2	29.9	30.1	30.3	29.9	30.0	29.9	29.9	29.7	29.6	30.0
2002	28.5	28.1	28.2	27.9	27.9	28.1	27.8	27.9	27.8	28.0	27.8	27.7	28.0
2003	27.5	27.4	27.5	27.4	27.5	27.5	26.9	26.8	26.8	27.1	27.0	27.0	27.2
2004	26.8	26.8	26.8	26.6	26.5	26.6	26.2	26.1	26.1	26.0	26.0	26.1	26.4
2005	25.5	25.6	25.8	26.0	26.0	25.8	26.0	25.9	25.8	25.7	25.7	25.8	25.8
2006	25.5	25.5	25.7	25.5	25.5	25.7	25.1	25.2	25.4	25.5	25.6	25.7	25.5
2007	25.8	25.9	26.0	26.2	26.3	26.6	26.3	26.0	26.1	26.1	26.1	26.3	26.1
Service-Providing													
2000	264.3	266.0	267.1	271.1	271.3	274.4	264.7	265.2	271.5	269.7	271.4	272.6	269.1
2001	268.5	267.8	268.6	269.4	270.8	272.2	262.0	263.9	269.2	270.1	271.3	271.8	268.8
2002	268.3	270.2	271.9	272.9	274.4	274.7	266.9	268.5	273.2	273.1	276.0	276.4	272.2
2003	270.5	273.9	275.0	277.8	277.9	277.0	274.3	274.6	277.8	280.1	281.1	279.9	276.7
2004	273.9	277.9	279.6	282.6	281.2	282.5	281.0	280.6	282.2	282.4	284.7	283.8	281.0
2005	279.3	282.5	284.6	287.5	285.7	286.1	286.5	287.9	293.9	296.7	299.9	299.5	289.2
2006	290.5	295.4	297.7	295.7	296.3	292.2	287.3	293.3	297.0	296.8	298.5	299.4	295.0
2007	294.6	298.8	302.0	301.8	302.1	302.7	298.4	301.9	304.7	305.5	306.0	306.1	302.1
Trade, Transportation, and Utilities													
2000	65.1	65.2	65.7	66.0	66.1	66.9	66.7	66.8	67.2	66.7	68.3	69.1	66.7
2001	66.8	66.0	66.2	65.9	66.0	66.1	65.1	65.7	65.6	65.7	66.7	67.4	66.1
2002	65.1	65.1	65.3	65.8	65.9	66.0	65.5	65.9	65.8	65.4	67.1	67.9	65.9
2003	63.1	62.9	63.1	64.0	63.9	64.0	63.5	63.7	63.7	64.1	65.1	65.9	63.9
2004	63.3	63.2	63.5	63.6	63.7	64.0	63.3	63.4	63.2	63.2	64.3	64.9	63.6
2005	62.3	62.3	62.8	63.1	63.6	63.7	64.7	64.9	65.7	66.5	68.6	69.4	64.8
2006	66.4	66.2	67.0	66.1	66.5	66.3	65.6	65.6	65.8	65.9	67.2	68.2	66.4
2007	65.7	65.5	66.3	65.6	66.0	66.2	65.9	66.5	66.8	67.1	68.1	68.0	66.5
Wholesale Trade													
2000	13.9	13.9	14.0	14.2	14.2	14.4	14.2	14.2	14.1	14.0	14.0	14.1	14.1
2001	14.1	14.2	14.3	14.2	14.2	14.3	14.1	14.0	14.1	14.0	14.0	14.0	14.1
2002	13.7	13.7	13.7	13.6	13.7	13.8	13.7	13.7	13.7	13.5	13.6	13.6	13.7
2003	13.5	13.4	13.5	13.4	13.4	13.5	13.4	13.4	13.4	13.3	13.3	13.2	13.4
2004	13.2	13.2	13.3	13.3	13.2	13.2	12.9	13.0	12.9	12.6	12.7	12.8	13.0
2005	12.6	12.5	12.6	12.7	12.8	12.8	13.1	13.1	13.1	12.9	12.9	13.0	12.8
2006	12.7	12.7	12.8	12.8	12.9	13.0	12.9	12.8	12.9	12.9	13.0	13.0	12.9
2007	13.2	13.2	13.3	13.3	13.4	13.6	13.3	13.3	13.4	13.3	13.4	13.3	13.3
Retail Trade													
2000	39.4	39.4	40.0	39.8	39.9	40.2	40.0	40.2	40.7	40.2	41.7	42.4	40.3
2001	40.1	39.2	39.3	38.9	39.0	38.9	38.5	39.1	38.9	39.0	40.1	40.7	39.3
2002	38.7	38.4	38.4	38.5	38.4	38.3	38.0	38.2	38.2	38.0	39.5	40.3	38.6
2003	36.4	36.2	36.3	37.1	36.9	37.0	36.7	36.8	36.7	37.2	38.1	39.0	37.0
2004	37.0	36.8	37.0	37.2	37.4	37.8	37.5	37.5	37.5	37.8	38.9	39.5	37.7
2005	37.5	37.5	37.9	37.9	38.2	38.4	39.1	39.3	40.1	41.1	43.0	43.6	39.5
2006	41.5	41.2	41.9	41.1	41.2	40.9	40.2	40.3	40.3	40.5	41.6	42.4	41.1
2007	40.3	40.0	40.8	40.1	40.3	40.3	40.4	40.8	40.9	41.3	42.2	42.2	40.8

Employment by Industry: Baton Rouge, LA, 2000–2007—*Continued*

(Numbers in thousands, not seasonally adjusted.)

Industry and year	January	February	March	April	May	June	July	August	September	October	November	December	Annual Average
Transportation and Utilities													
2000	11.8	11.9	11.7	12.0	12.0	12.3	12.5	12.4	12.4	12.5	12.6	12.6	12.2
2001	12.6	12.6	12.6	12.8	12.8	12.9	12.5	12.6	12.6	12.7	12.6	12.7	12.7
2002	12.7	13.0	13.2	13.7	13.8	13.9	13.8	14.0	13.9	13.9	14.0	14.0	13.7
2003	13.2	13.3	13.3	13.5	13.6	13.5	13.4	13.5	13.6	13.6	13.7	13.7	13.5
2004	13.1	13.2	13.2	13.1	13.1	13.0	12.9	12.9	12.8	12.8	12.7	12.6	13.0
2005	12.2	12.3	12.3	12.5	12.6	12.5	12.5	12.5	12.5	12.5	12.7	12.8	12.5
2006	12.2	12.3	12.3	12.2	12.4	12.4	12.5	12.5	12.6	12.5	12.6	12.8	12.4
2007	12.2	12.3	12.2	12.2	12.3	12.3	12.2	12.4	12.5	12.5	12.5	12.5	12.3
Information													
2000	4.8	4.8	5.0	5.3	5.2	5.3	5.5	5.6	5.6	5.6	5.6	5.6	5.3
2001	5.2	5.2	5.3	5.7	5.7	5.7	5.5	5.5	5.4	5.3	5.2	5.2	5.4
2002	5.2	5.2	5.3	5.0	5.1	5.1	5.2	5.2	5.2	5.0	5.0	5.0	5.1
2003	4.9	4.9	5.0	5.2	5.3	5.3	5.4	5.6	5.6	5.6	5.6	5.7	5.3
2004	5.6	5.6	5.6	5.6	5.6	5.6	5.5	5.5	5.4	5.4	5.5	5.5	5.5
2005	5.8	5.7	5.7	5.9	5.6	5.5	5.6	5.5	5.4	5.4	5.6	5.5	5.6
2006	5.6	5.6	5.7	5.7	5.6	5.5	5.4	5.3	5.2	5.4	5.5	5.4	5.5
2007	5.5	5.5	5.5	5.7	5.8	5.7	5.9	5.8	5.7	5.7	5.6	5.7	5.7
Financial Activities													
2000	15.8	15.9	16.0	16.2	16.2	16.4	16.0	16.0	16.0	15.8	15.8	16.0	16.0
2001	16.0	16.1	16.1	16.4	16.3	16.5	16.4	16.5	16.4	16.3	16.5	16.5	16.3
2002	16.7	16.7	16.5	17.0	17.0	17.0	17.1	17.2	17.0	17.3	17.2	17.4	17.0
2003	16.7	16.8	16.8	17.4	17.3	17.4	17.5	17.6	17.6	17.9	17.9	18.0	17.4
2004	17.9	17.9	18.0	18.2	18.2	18.2	18.1	18.1	17.9	17.8	17.8	18.0	18.0
2005	17.9	18.0	18.0	18.1	18.2	18.2	18.5	18.5	18.5	18.5	18.6	18.7	18.3
2006	18.5	18.5	18.6	18.6	18.6	18.6	18.4	18.5	18.5	18.7	18.7	18.8	18.6
2007	19.1	19.2	18.9	18.9	18.8	18.8	18.6	18.6	18.6	18.5	18.5	18.6	18.8
Professional and Business Services													
2000	38.9	39.6	39.6	40.2	40.2	40.7	40.0	40.3	40.7	40.5	40.5	40.4	40.1
2001	40.3	39.6	39.5	39.1	39.0	39.6	38.8	39.2	39.0	39.3	39.1	39.6	39.3
2002	39.0	39.0	39.2	39.1	38.9	38.9	38.7	38.8	38.4	38.6	38.6	38.7	38.8
2003	37.6	37.2	37.6	38.3	37.9	37.9	37.2	37.3	36.7	36.8	36.9	37.0	37.4
2004	36.8	37.2	37.5	38.1	37.3	37.6	37.6	37.4	36.9	36.6	36.8	36.8	37.2
2005	37.6	37.7	38.1	39.7	38.5	38.4	38.8	39.1	40.5	41.3	42.0	42.4	39.5
2006	41.1	41.8	42.3	42.7	42.7	43.0	42.5	42.6	43.1	43.4	43.0	43.8	42.7
2007	43.8	44.2	44.9	45.1	44.4	44.9	44.5	44.8	44.8	44.5	44.1	44.4	44.5
Education and Health Services													
2000	34.9	35.0	35.0	35.6	35.4	35.6	34.9	35.1	35.5	35.2	35.2	35.4	35.2
2001	34.8	34.9	35.0	34.9	35.0	35.0	34.8	35.1	35.5	35.4	35.6	35.5	35.1
2002	34.9	35.1	35.5	35.2	35.4	35.6	35.5	36.0	36.4	36.0	36.3	36.4	35.7
2003	35.8	36.1	36.1	36.2	36.4	36.5	37.2	37.4	37.7	38.1	38.1	38.2	37.0
2004	37.7	38.0	38.0	38.5	38.5	38.5	38.9	39.0	39.2	39.4	39.5	39.5	38.7
2005	39.4	39.6	39.7	40.1	40.4	40.4	41.3	41.2	41.6	42.4	42.4	42.0	40.9
2006	41.7	42.1	42.4	42.8	43.0	43.2	42.8	43.3	43.7	43.9	43.8	43.7	43.0
2007	42.9	43.3	43.5	44.1	44.7	44.5	44.0	44.7	44.9	45.1	44.8	44.7	44.3
Leisure and Hospitality													
2000	26.8	27.3	27.6	28.5	28.7	29.5	28.8	28.8	28.7	27.7	27.9	28.2	28.2
2001	27.1	27.6	28.1	28.3	29.1	29.0	28.6	28.8	28.8	28.4	28.1	27.9	28.3
2002	26.8	27.3	27.9	28.3	28.8	29.0	29.0	29.1	28.6	27.9	28.0	27.7	28.2
2003	28.3	29.1	29.3	29.9	30.1	30.0	29.8	29.9	30.0	30.0	30.0	29.7	29.7
2004	28.9	29.2	29.9	30.2	30.2	31.1	30.9	30.9	30.7	30.6	31.2	31.2	30.5
2005	30.2	30.5	31.1	31.5	31.9	32.4	32.0	32.0	32.6	32.0	31.7	31.7	31.6
2006	31.3	32.4	32.7	32.3	32.8	33.2	32.1	32.5	32.7	31.7	32.0	32.1	32.3
2007	31.3	32.0	33.0	32.5	33.1	33.4	32.6	32.7	32.9	32.9	32.9	33.1	32.7
Other Services													
2000	11.6	11.7	11.8	11.9	12.1	12.1	12.1	12.1	12.1	11.7	11.7	11.7	11.9
2001	11.8	11.9	11.9	12.2	12.2	12.4	12.1	12.1	12.2	12.2	11.9	11.9	12.1
2002	12.2	12.3	12.4	12.7	12.9	13.0	13.2	13.0	12.9	12.9	12.9	12.8	12.8
2003	12.8	12.8	12.8	13.0	13.1	13.1	12.8	12.8	12.8	13.1	13.0	12.9	12.9
2004	12.6	12.7	12.8	13.7	13.7	14.0	14.1	14.0	14.0	13.7	13.8	13.7	13.6
2005	13.5	13.5	13.8	13.8	13.8	14.0	14.1	14.1	14.1	13.7	13.6	13.7	13.8
2006	13.4	13.6	13.6	13.6	13.7	14.0	13.8	13.8	14.0	13.6	13.7	13.8	13.7
2007	13.8	13.9	14.0	14.0	14.1	14.3	14.1	14.1	14.0	13.7	13.9	13.9	14.0
Government													
2000	66.4	66.5	66.4	67.4	67.4	67.9	60.7	60.5	65.7	66.5	66.4	66.2	65.7
2001	66.5	66.5	66.5	66.9	67.5	67.9	60.7	61.0	66.3	67.5	68.2	67.8	66.1
2002	68.4	69.5	69.8	69.8	70.4	70.1	62.7	63.3	68.9	70.0	70.9	70.5	68.7
2003	71.3	74.1	74.3	73.8	73.9	72.8	70.9	70.3	73.7	74.5	74.5	72.5	73.1
2004	71.1	74.1	74.3	74.7	73.5	73.5	72.6	72.3	74.9	75.7	75.8	74.2	73.9
2005	72.6	75.2	75.4	75.3	73.7	73.5	71.5	72.6	75.5	76.9	77.4	76.1	74.6
2006	72.5	75.2	75.4	73.9	73.4	68.4	66.7	71.7	74.0	74.2	74.6	73.6	72.8
2007	72.5	75.2	75.9	75.9	75.2	74.9	72.8	74.7	77.1	78.0	78.1	77.7	75.7

Employment by Industry: Akron, OH, 2000–2007

(Numbers in thousands, not seasonally adjusted.)

Industry and year	January	February	March	April	May	June	July	August	September	October	November	December	Annual Average
Total Nonfarm													
2000	322.2	325.8	328.8	331.8	335.8	332.4	330.1	328.5	331.9	334.0	334.6	333.2	330.8
2001	321.6	323.4	325.5	328.2	329.9	330.2	324.8	325.3	328.5	329.9	330.8	330.0	327.3
2002	316.4	317.4	320.0	320.5	321.7	323.2	321.7	321.2	326.1	326.9	326.0	325.6	322.2
2003	317.3	318.6	320.8	326.5	329.0	326.7	326.3	327.0	331.2	332.2	332.5	333.3	326.7
2004	320.8	323.2	326.2	330.5	332.4	331.6	330.9	331.0	335.2	337.1	338.1	338.5	331.3
2005	328.0	330.8	332.9	337.8	340.7	336.4	336.7	337.3	341.1	341.9	342.7	342.2	337.4
2006	330.4	332.4	334.6	338.6	342.4	338.8	338.1	339.3	342.9	342.1	343.3	342.7	338.8
2007	332.0	333.1	334.8	337.8	339.6	339.3	338.9	339.3	342.5	342.5	344.3	344.4	339.0
Total Private													
2000	275.7	275.4	278.4	281.2	284.1	288.3	287.1	287.1	284.3	284.2	284.5	284.8	282.9
2001	273.8	273.3	274.4	277.3	282.0	285.3	281.3	283.2	280.0	279.7	280.0	280.7	279.3
2002	268.7	267.4	269.1	269.7	273.8	277.4	278.1	279.0	276.9	275.8	274.4	274.8	273.8
2003	269.0	268.1	269.3	273.9	278.0	280.2	281.0	282.2	280.6	280.1	280.0	280.7	276.9
2004	271.2	270.9	273.6	278.1	282.0	285.6	285.8	286.8	285.2	285.2	285.8	286.4	281.4
2005	277.7	278.7	280.7	285.8	288.7	291.1	292.2	292.6	290.9	290.7	290.8	290.7	287.6
2006	280.8	280.9	283.1	287.3	290.7	294.4	294.3	295.4	292.6	291.0	292.1	292.6	289.6
2007	283.8	281.9	283.6	287.0	291.3	295.3	295.3	294.7	292.3	291.4	292.9	293.1	290.2
Goods-Producing													
2000	72.1	72.1	72.5	73.8	74.7	75.6	74.8	74.5	73.5	73.6	73.2	72.1	73.5
2001	68.5	68.1	68.2	68.7	69.1	69.6	67.8	68.7	67.5	66.9	66.2	65.9	67.9
2002	62.1	61.6	62.0	62.2	63.7	64.4	65.2	65.4	64.8	64.3	63.7	63.1	63.5
2003	61.5	61.4	61.8	63.4	64.0	64.3	64.5	64.8	64.4	64.5	63.8	63.4	63.4
2004	60.7	60.6	61.5	62.7	63.8	64.5	64.6	65.3	64.8	64.6	64.2	63.7	63.4
2005	60.9	61.4	61.8	63.2	64.0	64.4	64.5	64.5	64.1	63.6	63.7	62.7	63.2
2006	60.4	60.6	61.7	62.8	63.5	64.2	63.4	63.8	63.6	63.2	62.8	62.4	62.7
2007	60.1	59.1	59.6	60.6	61.5	62.3	62.7	62.2	61.8	61.7	61.8	61.1	61.2
Natural Resources, Mining, and Construction													
2000	13.1	13.1	13.9	14.9	15.7	16.2	16.1	16.0	15.9	15.7	15.2	14.3	15.0
2001	12.7	12.7	13.3	14.1	15.1	15.8	16.1	16.1	15.5	15.4	14.9	14.3	14.7
2002	12.3	12.1	12.5	12.7	13.9	14.6	15.2	15.4	15.0	14.6	14.2	13.5	13.8
2003	12.1	11.7	12.2	13.5	14.3	14.7	14.9	15.2	15.0	14.9	14.4	13.8	13.8
2004	11.8	11.6	12.3	13.3	14.2	14.8	15.4	15.4	15.1	15.0	14.5	13.8	13.9
2005	12.0	12.0	12.2	13.7	14.7	15.3	15.6	15.7	15.6	15.3	15.3	14.4	14.3
2006	12.7	12.6	13.5	14.7	15.5	16.0	16.0	16.1	16.0	15.8	15.3	14.7	14.9
2007	12.9	12.3	13.0	13.9	14.7	15.4	15.6	15.4	15.1	15.1	15.0	14.4	14.4
Manufacturing													
2000	59.0	59.0	58.6	58.9	59.0	59.4	58.7	58.5	57.6	57.9	58.0	57.8	58.5
2001	55.8	55.4	54.9	54.6	54.0	53.8	51.7	52.6	52.0	51.5	51.3	51.6	53.3
2002	49.8	49.5	49.5	49.5	49.8	49.8	50.0	50.0	49.8	49.7	49.5	49.6	49.7
2003	49.4	49.7	49.6	49.9	49.7	49.6	49.6	49.6	49.4	49.6	49.4	49.6	49.5
2004	48.9	49.0	49.2	49.4	49.6	49.7	49.2	49.9	49.7	49.6	49.7	49.9	49.5
2005	48.9	49.4	49.6	49.5	49.3	49.1	48.9	48.8	48.5	48.3	48.4	48.3	48.9
2006	47.7	48.0	48.2	48.1	48.0	48.2	47.4	47.7	47.6	47.4	47.5	47.7	47.8
2007	47.2	46.8	46.6	46.7	46.8	46.9	47.1	46.8	46.7	46.6	46.8	46.7	46.8
Service-Providing													
2000	250.1	253.7	256.3	258.0	261.1	256.8	255.3	254.0	258.4	260.4	261.4	261.1	257.2
2001	253.1	255.3	257.3	259.5	260.8	260.6	257.0	256.6	261.0	263.0	264.6	264.1	259.4
2002	254.3	255.8	258.0	258.3	258.0	258.8	256.5	255.8	261.3	262.6	262.3	262.5	258.7
2003	255.8	257.2	259.0	263.1	265.0	262.4	261.8	262.2	266.8	267.7	268.7	269.9	263.3
2004	260.1	262.6	264.7	267.8	268.6	267.1	266.3	265.7	270.4	272.5	273.9	274.8	267.9
2005	267.1	269.4	271.1	274.6	276.7	272.0	272.2	272.8	277.0	278.3	279.0	279.5	274.1
2006	270.0	271.8	272.9	275.8	278.9	274.6	274.7	275.5	279.3	278.9	280.5	280.3	276.1
2007	271.9	274.0	275.2	277.2	278.1	277.0	276.2	277.1	280.7	280.8	282.5	283.3	277.8
Trade, Transportation, and Utilities													
2000	65.5	65.0	65.4	65.7	66.0	66.5	66.1	66.4	66.4	67.3	68.8	69.7	66.6
2001	68.6	67.4	67.5	67.9	68.6	68.9	67.6	67.4	66.9	67.0	67.7	68.4	67.8
2002	65.5	64.5	64.7	64.7	65.0	65.3	64.9	65.1	64.6	64.9	65.9	66.4	65.1
2003	64.5	63.7	64.1	64.5	65.0	65.4	65.1	65.4	65.6	66.3	67.4	68.1	65.4
2004	64.8	64.5	64.7	65.3	65.8	66.1	66.0	66.4	66.6	67.6	68.7	69.4	66.3
2005	66.7	66.7	67.1	68.0	68.0	68.1	67.9	67.6	67.3	67.6	68.8	69.5	67.8
2006	67.0	66.3	66.3	66.4	66.8	67.6	67.5	67.8	67.4	68.1	69.7	70.4	67.6
2007	67.7	66.6	66.8	66.8	67.6	67.9	67.7	67.8	67.7	68.2	69.6	70.2	67.9
Wholesale Trade													
2000	16.6	16.6	16.7	16.7	16.8	16.9	16.9	16.9	16.8	16.8	16.8	16.8	16.8
2001	17.5	17.4	17.4	17.3	17.6	17.6	17.3	17.3	17.1	17.0	16.9	17.0	17.3
2002	16.5	16.3	16.4	16.3	16.1	16.0	15.9	15.8	15.7	15.6	15.5	15.6	16.0
2003	16.1	16.1	16.2	16.1	16.1	16.2	16.1	16.2	16.2	16.2	16.3	16.3	16.1
2004	15.9	16.0	16.1	16.1	16.2	16.3	16.4	16.5	16.6	16.7	16.8	17.0	16.4
2005	17.0	17.1	17.2	17.3	17.3	17.4	17.4	17.3	17.3	17.5	17.6	17.7	17.3
2006	17.6	17.7	17.7	17.7	17.8	18.1	18.0	18.2	18.1	18.3	18.4	18.4	18.0
2007	18.4	18.3	18.4	18.3	18.3	18.4	18.3	18.4	18.3	18.3	18.3	18.4	18.3
Retail Trade													
2000	40.5	39.9	40.0	39.8	40.3	40.7	40.1	40.5	40.4	40.7	42.1	43.0	40.7
2001	40.7	40.1	40.0	40.4	40.6	40.8	40.0	39.7	39.4	39.9	40.9	41.5	40.3
2002	38.5	37.9	38.0	38.0	38.3	38.6	38.3	38.5	38.3	38.8	39.9	40.5	38.6
2003	37.9	37.5	37.7	37.9	38.3	38.5	38.4	38.5	38.7	39.2	40.3	41.0	38.6
2004	38.6	38.2	38.3	38.5	38.7	38.8	38.5	38.6	38.7	39.3	40.2	40.7	38.9
2005	38.3	38.1	38.3	38.9	39.0	38.9	38.6	38.5	38.2	38.6	39.6	40.2	38.8
2006	38.3	37.6	37.7	37.7	37.9	38.3	38.3	38.4	38.1	38.5	40.0	40.6	38.5
2007	38.5	37.6	37.7	37.5	38.2	38.3	38.3	38.3	38.3	38.4	38.9	40.3	40.8	38.6

Employment by Industry: Akron, OH, 2000–2007—*Continued*

(Numbers in thousands, not seasonally adjusted.)

Industry and year	January	February	March	April	May	June	July	August	September	October	November	December	Annual Average
Transportation and Utilities													
2000	8.5	8.4	8.4	8.9	9.0	8.9	9.2	9.2	9.3	9.7	9.7	9.8	9.1
2001	10.3	10.0	10.1	10.3	10.3	10.4	10.2	10.2	10.2	10.1	10.0	10.0	10.2
2002	10.5	10.3	10.3	10.4	10.6	10.7	10.7	10.8	10.8	10.6	10.5	10.5	10.3	10.5
2003	10.5	10.1	10.2	10.5	10.6	10.7	10.6	10.7	10.7	10.9	10.8	10.8	10.5
2004	10.3	10.3	10.3	10.7	10.9	11.0	11.1	11.3	11.3	11.6	11.7	11.7	11.0
2005	11.4	11.5	11.6	11.8	11.7	11.8	11.9	11.8	11.8	11.5	11.6	11.6	11.7
2006	11.1	11.0	10.9	11.0	11.1	11.2	11.2	11.2	11.2	11.3	11.3	11.4	11.2
2007	10.8	10.7	10.7	11.0	11.1	11.2	11.1	11.1	11.0	11.0	11.0	11.0	11.0
Information													
2000	5.0	5.1	5.1	5.2	5.1	5.2	5.3	5.3	5.4	5.4	5.4	5.4	5.2
2001	5.1	5.2	5.1	5.0	5.0	5.0	5.0	5.1	5.0	5.1	5.1	5.1	5.1
2002	5.5	5.5	5.4	5.3	5.3	5.4	5.5	5.5	5.5	5.5	5.5	5.6	5.5
2003	5.5	5.5	5.5	5.5	5.5	5.4	5.2	5.2	5.0	4.8	4.8	4.7	5.2
2004	4.8	4.7	4.6	4.6	4.6	4.6	4.5	4.4	4.3	4.3	4.3	4.4	4.5
2005	4.4	4.4	4.4	4.4	4.5	4.5	4.5	4.5	4.5	4.5	4.5	4.5	4.5
2006	4.5	4.5	4.5	4.6	4.6	4.6	4.7	4.6	4.5	4.4	4.4	4.5	4.5
2007	4.5	4.5	4.5	4.6	4.6	4.7	4.6	4.6	4.5	4.5	4.5	4.5	4.6
Financial Activities													
2000	14.5	14.4	14.6	14.3	14.6	14.9	14.7	14.8	14.8	14.6	14.6	14.7	14.6
2001	14.1	14.5	14.5	14.4	14.5	14.8	14.7	14.8	14.7	14.6	14.6	14.6	14.6
2002	14.1	14.2	14.2	13.9	14.1	14.2	14.2	14.3	14.3	14.3	14.3	14.4	14.2
2003	14.2	14.2	14.3	14.6	14.7	14.7	14.7	14.7	14.6	14.5	14.5	14.6	14.5
2004	14.5	14.4	14.6	14.6	14.8	14.9	14.9	14.9	14.8	14.7	14.9	15.0	14.8
2005	14.9	14.9	14.9	14.8	14.8	14.8	14.8	14.8	14.8	14.6	14.6	14.5	14.8
2006	14.5	14.4	14.4	14.6	14.6	14.6	14.5	14.5	14.3	14.4	14.4	14.4	14.5
2007	14.2	14.2	14.0	14.0	14.1	14.0	13.9	13.9	13.8	13.8	13.8	13.9	14.0
Professional and Business Services													
2000	37.3	37.1	38.0	39.2	38.8	39.6	39.4	39.5	39.4	39.3	38.7	38.3	38.7
2001	36.2	36.1	36.5	37.4	38.7	39.4	38.9	39.5	39.9	40.8	41.4	41.3	38.8
2002	38.7	38.7	39.2	39.0	39.1	39.6	40.0	40.5	40.8	41.0	40.1	40.1	39.7
2003	40.1	40.5	40.2	40.9	41.7	42.0	42.5	43.0	43.0	42.7	43.0	43.0	41.8
2004	41.9	42.0	42.8	43.8	43.9	44.9	45.1	45.1	45.2	45.1	45.4	45.5	44.2
2005	44.4	44.8	44.9	46.3	46.8	47.3	48.1	48.6	48.5	49.5	49.1	49.2	47.3
2006	47.0	47.4	47.8	49.4	50.0	50.7	51.3	51.8	51.3	50.6	50.4	50.4	49.8
2007	48.4	48.6	48.6	50.5	51.1	51.8	51.8	51.8	51.9	51.5	51.3	51.3	50.7
Education and Health Services													
2000	38.3	38.6	38.9	38.1	38.3	38.2	38.4	38.6	38.9	39.3	39.5	39.7	38.7
2001	39.0	39.3	39.6	39.8	40.0	39.9	39.5	39.9	40.3	40.6	40.9	41.3	40.0
2002	40.3	40.6	40.8	40.6	40.7	40.5	40.5	40.6	41.0	41.2	41.5	41.6	40.8
2003	41.2	41.2	41.2	41.2	41.3	41.2	41.2	41.3	42.0	42.1	42.3	42.5	41.5
2004	41.8	42.1	42.3	42.8	43.0	43.0	42.8	43.0	43.1	43.6	43.8	44.0	42.9
2005	43.3	43.4	43.7	43.9	44.0	43.8	44.1	44.2	44.6	45.3	45.3	45.5	44.3
2006	44.6	44.7	44.9	45.2	45.4	45.3	44.8	44.9	45.4	45.9	46.1	46.2	45.3
2007	45.9	46.0	46.3	46.2	46.7	46.7	46.8	46.9	47.2	47.5	47.6	47.7	46.8
Leisure and Hospitality													
2000	29.3	29.3	30.0	31.3	32.9	34.3	34.5	34.3	32.2	31.1	30.7	31.1	31.8
2001	28.2	28.4	28.8	29.8	31.7	33.2	33.3	33.3	31.4	30.4	29.9	29.8	30.7
2002	28.6	28.4	28.8	29.9	31.7	33.6	33.6	33.5	31.9	30.6	29.5	29.6	30.8
2003	28.1	27.7	28.2	29.8	31.7	33.0	33.7	33.8	32.2	31.4	30.4	30.6	30.8
2004	29.1	29.0	29.4	30.6	32.3	33.6	34.0	33.9	32.6	31.4	30.6	30.3	31.4
2005	29.3	29.1	29.8	31.1	32.4	33.9	34.1	34.2	33.1	31.6	30.8	30.7	31.7
2006	29.2	29.3	29.7	30.6	32.1	33.4	34.3	34.1	32.3	30.7	30.5	30.5	31.4
2007	29.4	29.4	30.1	30.7	32.1	34.1	34.0	33.7	31.8	30.5	30.6	30.6	31.4
Other Services													
2000	13.7	13.8	13.9	13.6	13.7	14.0	13.9	13.7	13.7	13.6	13.6	13.8	13.8
2001	14.1	14.3	14.2	14.3	14.4	14.5	14.5	14.5	14.3	14.3	14.2	14.3	14.3
2002	13.9	13.9	14.0	14.1	14.2	14.4	14.2	14.1	14.0	14.0	13.9	14.0	14.1
2003	13.9	13.9	14.0	14.0	14.1	14.2	14.1	14.0	13.8	13.8	13.8	13.8	13.9
2004	13.6	13.6	13.6	13.7	13.7	13.8	14.0	13.9	13.8	13.8	13.9	13.9	14.1	13.8
2005	13.8	14.0	14.1	14.1	14.2	14.3	14.2	14.2	14.0	14.0	14.0	14.1	14.1
2006	13.6	13.7	13.8	13.7	13.8	14.0	13.8	13.9	13.8	13.7	13.8	13.8	13.8
2007	13.6	13.5	13.7	13.6	13.6	13.8	13.8	13.8	13.6	13.7	13.7	13.8	13.7
Government													
2000	46.5	50.4	50.4	50.6	51.7	44.1	43.0	41.4	47.6	49.8	50.1	48.4	47.8
2001	47.8	50.1	51.1	50.9	47.9	44.9	43.5	42.1	48.5	50.2	50.8	49.3	48.1
2002	47.7	50.0	50.9	50.8	47.9	45.8	43.6	42.2	49.2	51.1	51.6	50.8	48.5
2003	48.3	50.5	51.5	52.6	51.0	46.5	45.3	44.8	50.6	52.1	52.5	52.6	49.8
2004	49.6	52.3	52.6	52.4	50.4	46.0	45.1	44.2	50.0	51.9	52.3	52.1	49.9
2005	50.3	52.1	52.2	52.0	52.0	45.3	44.5	44.7	50.2	51.2	51.9	51.5	49.8
2006	49.6	51.5	51.5	51.3	51.7	44.4	43.8	43.9	50.3	51.1	51.2	50.1	49.2
2007	48.2	51.2	51.2	50.8	48.3	44.0	43.6	44.6	50.2	51.1	51.4	51.3	48.8

Employment by Industry: El Paso, TX, 2000–2007

(Numbers in thousands, not seasonally adjusted.)

Industry and year	January	February	March	April	May	June	July	August	September	October	November	December	Annual Average
Total Nonfarm													
2000	252.0	253.6	255.4	255.0	256.3	255.9	254.3	256.7	259.1	257.9	259.5	260.7	256.4
2001	254.9	255.6	257.6	255.1	256.3	255.5	251.4	254.7	257.0	253.9	254.8	254.7	255.1
2002	251.6	251.9	254.7	255.3	255.7	254.7	251.7	256.1	261.0	258.6	260.2	261.1	256.1
2003	254.3	255.1	255.4	255.7	254.8	251.2	249.9	253.4	257.4	257.0	258.0	258.3	255.0
2004	254.3	255.8	256.0	256.1	257.3	255.5	255.3	255.7	258.9	258.8	260.7	260.5	257.2
2005	255.2	256.6	258.3	260.1	260.9	260.5	257.3	259.5	264.2	264.2	265.4	266.0	260.7
2006	261.2	262.9	265.4	263.9	264.8	263.5	259.8	262.6	267.7	267.7	269.4	271.3	265.0
2007	265.5	267.0	269.0	270.7	272.1	269.9	266.3	268.3	274.1	275.1	275.6	277.4	270.9
Total Private													
2000	196.0	196.5	198.2	197.5	198.7	200.6	198.9	201.1	202.8	200.8	202.3	203.3	199.7
2001	197.4	197.2	199.1	196.5	197.6	198.4	197.0	198.8	198.3	195.3	195.7	196.5	197.3
2002	193.2	192.5	195.5	196.6	197.9	199.0	198.3	201.1	201.6	198.4	199.8	201.7	198.0
2003	195.0	194.4	194.8	195.2	195.3	194.6	194.4	196.4	196.9	196.6	197.4	198.8	195.8
2004	194.2	194.7	195.0	195.2	195.9	197.0	197.8	198.8	198.3	197.9	198.9	199.6	196.9
2005	194.0	194.6	196.3	198.3	199.0	201.2	200.8	202.5	203.6	202.5	203.9	205.3	200.2
2006	200.2	200.9	203.3	202.2	203.0	205.1	203.8	206.1	206.3	204.9	206.4	208.2	204.2
2007	202.4	203.3	205.2	205.9	207.0	208.2	207.2	209.0	209.3	209.5	209.7	211.3	207.3
Goods-Producing													
2000	51.5	51.5	51.4	50.2	50.5	50.7	49.4	50.7	51.0	49.6	49.5	49.2	50.4
2001	47.7	47.7	47.7	46.0	46.1	46.2	45.7	46.3	46.3	44.9	44.2	44.1	46.1
2002	42.9	41.6	42.4	42.1	41.7	42.0	41.6	43.1	43.2	41.5	40.9	40.8	42.0
2003	39.7	39.6	39.4	39.0	38.3	37.8	37.3	37.7	37.8	36.8	36.4	36.1	37.9
2004	35.3	35.5	35.4	35.4	35.6	35.7	35.6	36.0	36.1	36.3	36.0	35.3	35.7
2005	34.2	34.3	34.6	34.7	35.2	35.3	34.7	35.0	35.6	34.8	34.8	34.7	34.8
2006	34.3	34.2	34.4	34.4	34.7	35.5	34.8	34.8	34.7	34.3	34.1	34.4	34.6
2007	33.7	33.9	34.2	34.4	34.4	34.8	34.5	35.3	35.5	35.3	35.1	35.2	34.7
Natural Resources, Mining, and Construction													
2000	12.9	12.8	12.9	12.6	12.8	12.9	12.5	12.6	12.7	12.5	12.5	12.6	12.7
2001	12.5	12.5	12.7	11.6	11.8	11.8	11.9	12.0	12.3	11.9	11.8	11.8	12.1
2002	11.7	11.7	12.0	11.6	11.5	11.8	11.7	12.0	12.0	11.7	11.7	11.6	11.8
2003	11.9	11.9	11.9	11.8	11.8	11.8	11.6	11.7	11.7	11.6	11.5	11.5	11.7
2004	11.1	11.2	11.3	11.3	11.4	11.6	11.7	11.6	11.6	11.9	11.8	11.8	11.5
2005	11.5	11.6	11.6	11.7	12.0	12.1	12.0	12.1	12.5	12.3	12.3	12.2	12.0
2006	12.2	12.2	12.4	12.5	12.6	12.9	12.8	12.8	12.9	12.9	13.0	13.2	12.7
2007	13.3	13.6	14.0	14.2	14.3	14.6	14.5	15.0	15.1	15.2	15.1	15.2	14.5
Manufacturing													
2000	38.6	38.7	38.5	37.6	37.7	37.8	36.9	38.1	38.3	37.1	37.0	36.6	37.7
2001	35.2	35.2	35.0	34.4	34.3	34.4	33.8	34.3	34.0	33.0	32.4	32.3	34.0
2002	31.2	29.9	30.4	30.5	30.2	30.2	29.9	31.1	31.2	29.8	29.2	29.2	30.2
2003	27.8	27.7	27.5	27.2	26.5	26.0	25.7	26.0	26.1	25.2	24.9	24.6	26.2
2004	24.2	24.3	24.1	24.1	24.2	24.1	23.9	24.4	24.5	24.4	24.2	23.5	24.2
2005	22.7	22.7	23.0	23.0	23.2	23.2	22.7	22.9	23.1	22.5	22.5	22.5	22.8
2006	22.1	22.0	22.0	21.9	22.1	22.6	22.0	22.0	21.8	21.4	21.1	21.2	21.9
2007	20.4	20.3	20.2	20.2	20.1	20.2	20.0	20.3	20.4	20.1	20.0	20.0	20.2
Service-Providing													
2000	200.5	202.1	204.0	204.8	205.8	205.2	204.9	206.0	208.1	208.3	210.0	211.5	205.9
2001	207.2	207.9	209.9	209.1	210.2	209.3	205.7	208.4	210.7	209.0	210.6	210.6	209.1
2002	208.7	210.3	212.3	213.2	214.0	212.7	210.1	213.0	217.8	217.1	219.3	220.3	214.1
2003	214.6	215.5	216.0	216.7	216.5	213.4	212.6	215.7	219.6	220.2	221.6	222.2	217.0
2004	219.0	220.3	220.6	220.7	221.7	219.8	219.7	219.7	222.8	223.5	224.7	225.2	221.5
2005	221.0	222.3	223.7	225.4	225.7	225.2	222.6	224.5	228.6	229.4	230.6	231.3	225.9
2006	226.9	228.7	231.0	229.5	230.1	228.0	225.0	227.8	233.0	233.4	235.3	236.9	230.5
2007	231.8	233.1	234.8	236.3	237.7	235.1	231.8	233.0	238.6	239.8	240.5	242.2	236.2
Trade, Transportation, and Utilities													
2000	53.4	52.7	53.2	53.2	53.8	54.2	53.9	54.3	54.7	55.0	56.3	57.0	54.3
2001	54.6	53.6	54.2	53.7	53.8	53.7	53.7	53.8	53.1	52.9	54.1	54.8	53.8
2002	53.0	52.2	53.0	53.2	53.8	54.1	53.7	54.1	54.4	54.6	55.6	56.7	54.0
2003	54.3	53.4	53.9	54.5	54.6	54.6	54.8	55.6	55.6	56.0	57.3	58.1	55.2
2004	55.7	55.4	55.6	54.8	54.9	55.1	55.1	55.3	54.9	55.5	56.8	57.5	55.6
2005	54.9	54.5	54.9	55.3	55.4	55.8	56.1	56.7	56.9	57.0	58.7	59.2	56.3
2006	56.9	56.8	57.6	57.3	57.5	57.7	57.7	58.4	58.5	58.3	59.7	60.4	58.1
2007	58.0	57.6	58.2	58.4	58.6	58.7	58.3	58.7	59.1	59.7	60.4	61.2	58.9
Wholesale Trade													
2000	10.4	10.3	10.4	10.4	10.5	10.5	10.3	10.3	10.3	10.2	10.2	10.3	10.3
2001	10.1	10.1	10.2	10.1	10.1	10.1	10.1	10.1	10.1	9.9	9.9	9.9	10.1
2002	9.7	9.7	9.8	9.8	9.9	9.9	9.8	9.9	9.8	9.7	9.6	9.7	9.8
2003	9.6	9.5	9.6	9.7	9.8	9.8	9.9	10.0	10.0	10.1	10.2	10.3	9.8
2004	10.4	10.3	10.4	10.2	10.2	10.3	10.4	10.4	10.3	10.5	10.5	10.4	10.4
2005	10.1	10.1	10.2	10.2	10.3	10.3	10.3	10.4	10.5	10.4	10.5	10.6	10.3
2006	10.5	10.5	10.6	10.5	10.6	10.6	10.6	10.6	10.6	10.5	10.5	10.5	10.6
2007	10.5	10.5	10.6	10.8	10.8	10.9	10.8	10.9	10.9	10.9	10.9	11.0	10.8
Retail Trade													
2000	30.8	30.1	30.5	30.6	30.9	31.1	31.1	31.4	31.7	32.3	33.5	34.0	31.5
2001	32.3	31.5	32.0	31.6	31.6	31.5	31.7	32.0	31.2	31.3	32.5	33.1	31.9
2002	31.7	30.9	31.5	31.6	32.0	32.3	31.8	32.1	32.5	32.6	33.6	34.5	32.3
2003	32.6	31.9	32.2	32.6	32.6	32.6	32.7	33.4	33.3	33.6	34.8	35.5	33.1
2004	33.1	32.8	32.8	32.2	32.2	32.2	32.0	32.3	31.9	32.1	33.2	34.0	32.6
2005	31.9	31.4	31.6	31.9	31.9	32.2	32.4	32.8	32.8	33.2	34.6	35.1	32.7
2006	33.1	32.9	33.5	33.4	33.4	33.4	33.4	34.0	34.1	34.0	35.4	36.0	33.9
2007	34.0	33.5	34.0	33.9	34.1	34.1	33.8	34.2	34.6	35.1	35.8	36.4	34.5

Employment by Industry: El Paso, TX, 2000–2007—*Continued*

(Numbers in thousands, not seasonally adjusted.)

Industry and year	January	February	March	April	May	June	July	August	September	October	November	December	Annual Average
Transportation and Utilities													
2000	12.2	12.3	12.3	12.2	12.4	12.6	12.5	12.6	12.7	12.5	12.6	12.7	12.5
2001	12.2	12.0	12.0	12.0	12.1	12.1	11.9	11.7	11.8	11.7	11.7	11.8	11.9
2002	11.6	11.6	11.7	11.8	11.9	11.9	12.1	12.1	12.1	12.3	12.4	12.5	12.0
2003	12.1	12.0	12.1	12.2	12.2	12.2	12.2	12.2	12.3	12.3	12.3	12.3	12.2
2004	12.2	12.3	12.4	12.4	12.5	12.6	12.7	12.6	12.7	12.9	13.1	13.1	12.6
2005	12.9	13.0	13.1	13.2	13.2	13.3	13.4	13.5	13.6	13.4	13.6	13.5	13.3
2006	13.3	13.4	13.5	13.4	13.5	13.7	13.7	13.8	13.8	13.8	13.8	13.9	13.6
2007	13.5	13.6	13.6	13.7	13.7	13.7	13.7	13.6	13.6	13.7	13.7	13.8	13.7
Information													
2000	4.9	4.8	4.9	4.9	4.9	4.9	4.9	4.9	4.9	4.8	4.9	5.0	4.9
2001	4.8	4.8	4.8	4.9	5.0	5.1	4.9	4.9	5.0	4.9	5.0	4.9	4.9
2002	5.0	4.9	4.9	5.0	5.0	5.0	5.1	5.2	5.2	5.2	5.3	5.5	5.1
2003	5.5	5.5	5.4	5.5	5.5	5.4	5.4	5.4	5.3	5.5	5.6	5.3	5.4
2004	5.1	5.1	5.0	4.9	4.9	4.9	4.9	4.9	4.8	4.9	4.8	4.9	4.9
2005	4.7	4.7	4.7	4.8	4.8	4.9	4.8	4.8	4.7	4.7	4.8	4.7	4.8
2006	4.7	4.7	4.9	4.6	4.7	4.9	4.6	4.6	4.7	4.8	4.8	5.0	4.8
2007	4.9	5.0	5.0	5.0	5.0	5.1	5.3	5.3	5.2	5.2	5.2	5.1	5.1
Financial Activities													
2000	10.2	10.1	10.1	10.1	10.1	10.3	10.3	10.3	10.3	10.3	10.3	10.4	10.2
2001	10.9	10.9	11.2	11.0	11.1	11.3	11.6	11.7	11.7	11.7	11.7	11.8	11.4
2002	11.8	11.9	12.0	11.8	11.8	11.8	11.8	11.7	11.7	11.8	12.0	12.0	11.8
2003	12.0	12.0	12.1	11.9	11.9	11.9	12.0	11.9	11.8	11.7	11.7	11.6	11.8
2004	11.5	11.6	11.6	11.4	11.3	11.4	11.4	11.4	11.4	11.4	11.3	11.4	11.4
2005	11.2	11.2	11.3	11.4	11.4	11.4	11.5	11.5	11.5	11.5	11.4	11.5	11.4
2006	11.2	11.3	11.3	11.0	11.0	11.1	11.1	11.2	11.3	11.3	11.4	11.5	11.2
2007	11.3	11.3	11.4	11.4	11.5	11.6	11.5	11.5	11.5	11.6	11.5	11.6	11.5
Professional and Business Services													
2000	23.8	24.6	25.4	25.2	25.2	25.6	25.0	25.3	25.8	26.0	26.3	26.5	25.4
2001	25.3	25.5	25.7	25.3	25.1	25.2	24.4	24.9	24.9	25.1	24.6	24.7	25.1
2002	24.9	25.5	25.8	26.1	26.1	26.3	26.5	26.8	27.1	27.4	27.3	27.9	26.5
2003	25.6	25.5	24.8	25.0	25.0	24.5	24.8	25.3	26.0	26.6	26.5	27.4	25.5
2004	26.6	26.5	26.1	27.2	27.1	27.4	28.0	28.1	27.8	26.9	26.9	26.9	27.1
2005	25.6	25.8	25.9	26.2	25.8	26.4	26.8	27.3	27.8	27.9	28.1	28.7	26.9
2006	28.2	28.3	28.6	28.6	28.7	29.2	29.3	30.7	30.9	31.0	31.4	31.6	29.7
2007	30.5	30.9	30.8	31.1	31.0	30.8	30.5	31.3	31.1	31.3	31.2	31.7	31.0
Education and Health Services													
2000	23.6	24.0	24.0	23.8	24.0	24.1	24.4	24.7	25.1	25.1	25.3	25.5	24.5
2001	25.1	25.3	25.6	25.6	25.8	26.2	26.1	26.3	26.5	26.0	26.2	26.4	25.9
2002	26.3	26.6	26.8	27.2	27.6	27.7	28.1	28.5	28.5	27.6	27.8	28.0	27.6
2003	27.7	28.0	28.3	28.5	28.6	28.7	28.7	29.0	29.2	29.1	29.2	29.3	28.6
2004	28.8	29.1	29.4	29.6	29.9	30.0	30.4	30.6	31.0	31.5	31.7	32.0	30.3
2005	31.8	32.1	32.3	32.4	32.5	32.9	33.0	33.1	33.2	33.2	33.3	33.5	32.8
2006	33.3	33.5	33.6	32.9	32.4	32.2	32.0	32.4	32.0	31.3	31.5	31.4	32.4
2007	31.0	31.3	31.5	31.5	31.8	32.1	32.3	32.6	32.6	32.5	32.6	32.7	32.0
Leisure and Hospitality													
2000	21.3	21.4	21.7	22.6	22.8	23.2	23.3	23.2	23.3	22.3	22.1	22.2	22.5
2001	21.5	21.8	22.2	22.3	22.9	22.9	22.9	23.0	23.0	22.0	22.1	22.0	22.4
2002	21.6	22.0	22.6	23.2	23.8	24.0	23.6	23.8	23.7	22.6	23.1	23.1	23.1
2003	22.7	22.8	23.3	23.3	23.9	24.1	23.9	24.0	23.8	23.2	23.2	23.5	23.4
2004	23.6	23.7	24.0	24.6	24.8	25.0	25.0	25.0	24.9	24.0	24.0	24.1	24.4
2005	24.2	24.6	25.0	25.7	26.0	26.5	26.2	26.3	26.1	25.6	25.2	25.5	25.6
2006	24.5	24.9	25.6	25.8	26.3	26.7	26.4	26.2	26.4	25.9	25.6	26.0	25.9
2007	25.6	25.8	26.5	26.6	27.1	27.4	27.2	26.8	26.8	26.3	26.2	26.3	26.6
Other Services													
2000	7.3	7.4	7.5	7.5	7.4	7.6	7.7	7.7	7.7	7.7	7.6	7.5	7.6
2001	7.5	7.6	7.7	7.7	7.8	7.8	7.7	7.9	7.8	7.8	7.8	7.8	7.7
2002	7.7	7.8	8.0	8.0	8.1	8.1	7.9	7.9	7.8	7.7	7.8	7.7	7.9
2003	7.5	7.6	7.6	7.5	7.5	7.6	7.5	7.5	7.4	7.7	7.5	7.5	7.5
2004	7.6	7.8	7.9	7.3	7.4	7.5	7.4	7.5	7.4	7.4	7.4	7.5	7.5
2005	7.4	7.4	7.6	7.8	7.9	8.0	7.7	7.8	7.8	7.8	7.6	7.5	7.7
2006	7.1	7.2	7.3	7.6	7.7	7.8	7.9	7.8	7.8	8.0	7.9	7.9	7.7
2007	7.4	7.5	7.6	7.5	7.6	7.7	7.6	7.5	7.5	7.6	7.5	7.5	7.5
Government													
2000	56.0	57.1	57.2	57.5	57.6	55.3	55.4	55.6	56.3	57.1	57.2	57.4	56.6
2001	57.5	58.4	58.5	58.6	58.7	57.1	54.4	55.9	58.7	58.6	59.1	58.2	57.8
2002	58.4	59.4	59.2	58.7	57.8	55.7	53.4	55.0	59.4	60.2	60.4	59.4	58.1
2003	59.3	60.7	60.6	60.5	59.5	56.6	55.5	57.0	60.5	60.4	60.6	59.5	59.2
2004	60.1	61.1	61.0	60.9	61.4	58.5	57.5	56.9	60.6	61.9	61.8	60.9	60.2
2005	61.2	62.0	62.0	61.8	61.9	59.3	56.5	57.0	60.6	61.7	61.5	60.7	60.5
2006	61.0	62.0	62.1	61.7	61.8	58.4	56.0	56.5	61.4	62.8	63.0	63.1	60.8
2007	63.1	63.7	63.8	64.8	65.1	61.7	59.1	59.3	64.8	65.6	65.9	66.1	63.6

Employment by Industry: Springfield, MA-CT, NECTA, 2000–2007

(Numbers in thousands, not seasonally adjusted.)

Industry and year	January	February	March	April	May	June	July	August	September	October	November	December	Annual Average
Total Nonfarm													
2000	294.9	295.3	296.8	301.2	303.5	305.5	299.2	298.7	302.3	306.2	307.4	310.1	301.8
2001	300.3	300.0	301.0	303.1	305.5	307.2	299.8	299.9	304.1	304.4	304.8	305.1	302.9
2002	294.6	294.5	296.5	299.0	302.3	303.9	297.6	294.5	301.9	301.0	301.3	301.5	299.1
2003	290.4	289.6	290.8	295.0	297.8	298.9	292.4	292.6	296.4	296.4	296.9	297.4	294.6
2004	287.7	288.2	291.2	295.7	297.8	299.0	293.8	292.5	298.2	299.3	299.5	299.8	295.2
2005	289.2	290.9	292.0	297.2	299.0	299.5	293.6	293.0	299.4	299.7	300.5	300.9	296.2
2006	290.5	292.1	293.8	300.3	300.8	301.6	294.7	293.1	300.2	301.1	301.8	302.4	297.7
2007	292.5	293.1	294.2	298.6	301.7	302.6	295.6	293.4	298.9	299.9	300.4	300.4	297.6
Total Private													
2000	245.2	245.5	246.9	251.0	252.6	254.3	251.1	251.0	252.3	255.7	256.2	258.5	251.7
2001	249.8	249.3	250.2	251.9	254.2	255.1	251.6	252.4	252.8	253.2	253.1	252.9	252.2
2002	243.6	243.6	245.5	248.3	251.4	252.5	249.5	249.4	251.1	250.4	250.1	249.9	248.8
2003	239.5	238.8	240.0	244.7	247.4	247.8	245.7	246.2	246.8	247.4	247.6	247.5	245.0
2004	239.1	239.1	241.7	245.9	247.8	249.0	248.6	247.9	249.4	250.1	250.0	249.8	246.5
2005	240.5	241.2	242.2	247.4	249.1	250.0	248.9	249.0	250.8	250.2	250.8	250.8	247.6
2006	241.8	242.4	243.9	250.2	250.6	251.7	249.9	249.5	250.8	251.0	251.1	251.3	248.7
2007	243.2	242.8	243.8	248.1	251.1	252.5	250.3	249.4	249.1	249.5	249.2	248.8	248.2
Goods-Producing													
2000	56.8	56.3	57.0	57.8	58.1	58.8	58.5	59.1	58.9	59.2	59.2	58.8	58.2
2001	56.3	55.9	55.8	55.8	56.2	56.8	55.7	56.1	55.8	55.5	55.1	54.6	55.8
2002	52.3	51.5	51.8	52.2	52.9	53.4	52.7	53.2	52.8	52.7	52.4	51.8	52.5
2003	49.1	48.6	48.9	50.0	50.9	51.3	50.7	51.3	50.8	50.6	50.5	50.0	50.2
2004	47.8	47.6	48.0	48.9	49.6	50.1	50.0	50.5	50.3	50.2	50.1	49.5	49.4
2005	47.6	47.0	47.2	49.0	49.6	50.2	50.1	50.5	50.3	49.6	49.4	49.0	49.1
2006	47.0	46.8	47.1	48.4	48.7	49.3	49.0	49.2	48.9	48.6	48.4	48.3	48.3
2007	46.5	45.9	46.0	47.0	47.9	48.7	48.3	48.6	48.3	48.1	48.0	47.4	47.6
Natural Resources, Mining, and Construction													
2000	8.7	8.4	9.0	9.9	10.3	10.7	10.9	11.1	10.8	10.7	10.5	10.0	10.1
2001	8.7	8.6	8.9	9.8	10.6	11.1	11.3	11.4	11.1	11.2	11.1	10.7	10.4
2002	9.4	9.0	9.3	10.3	10.9	11.3	11.3	11.3	11.0	10.9	10.7	10.2	10.5
2003	8.9	8.6	8.9	9.9	10.8	11.1	11.5	11.6	11.2	11.0	10.9	10.3	10.4
2004	8.9	8.7	9.1	10.1	10.8	11.1	11.6	11.6	11.4	11.3	11.1	10.7	10.5
2005	9.4	8.9	9.1	10.6	11.3	11.6	12.1	12.2	12.1	11.7	11.6	11.1	11.0
2006	9.8	9.5	9.8	11.1	11.5	11.8	12.0	12.0	11.8	11.5	11.3	10.9	11.1
2007	9.5	9.0	9.1	10.2	11.1	11.5	11.7	11.6	11.4	11.1	10.9	10.4	10.6
Manufacturing													
2000	48.1	47.9	48.0	47.9	47.8	48.1	47.6	48.0	48.1	48.5	48.7	48.8	48.1
2001	47.6	47.3	46.9	46.0	45.6	45.7	44.4	44.7	44.7	44.3	44.0	43.9	45.4
2002	42.9	42.5	42.5	41.9	42.0	42.1	41.4	41.9	41.8	41.8	41.7	41.6	42.0
2003	40.2	40.0	40.0	40.1	40.1	40.2	39.2	39.7	39.6	39.6	39.6	39.7	39.8
2004	38.9	38.9	38.9	38.8	38.8	39.0	38.4	38.9	38.9	38.9	39.0	38.8	38.9
2005	38.2	38.1	38.1	38.4	38.3	38.6	38.0	38.3	38.2	37.9	37.8	37.9	38.2
2006	37.2	37.3	37.3	37.3	37.2	37.5	37.0	37.2	37.1	37.1	37.1	37.4	37.2
2007	37.0	36.9	36.9	36.8	36.8	37.2	36.6	37.0	36.9	37.0	37.1	37.0	36.9
Service-Providing													
2000	238.1	239.0	239.8	243.4	245.4	246.7	240.7	239.6	243.4	247.0	248.2	251.3	243.6
2001	244.0	244.1	245.2	247.3	249.3	250.4	244.1	243.8	248.3	248.9	249.7	250.5	247.1
2002	242.3	243.0	244.7	246.8	249.4	250.5	244.9	241.3	249.1	248.3	248.9	249.7	246.6
2003	241.3	241.0	241.9	245.0	246.9	247.6	241.7	241.3	245.6	245.8	246.4	247.4	244.3
2004	239.9	240.6	243.2	246.8	248.2	248.9	243.8	242.0	247.9	249.1	249.4	250.3	245.8
2005	241.6	243.9	244.8	248.2	249.4	249.3	243.5	242.5	249.1	250.1	251.1	251.9	247.1
2006	243.5	245.3	246.7	251.9	252.1	252.3	245.7	243.9	251.3	252.5	253.4	254.1	249.4
2007	246.0	247.2	248.2	251.6	253.8	253.9	247.3	244.8	250.6	251.8	252.4	253.0	250.1
Trade, Transportation, and Utilities													
1999	59.4	58.9	58.9	59.4	59.6	60.4	59.6	60.0	60.9	62.0	63.4	65.3	60.7
2000	61.8	61.3	61.2	61.8	62.1	62.5	61.3	61.5	62.5	63.5	65.1	67.2	62.7
2001	63.7	62.7	62.7	63.0	63.3	63.3	61.8	61.9	62.8	63.1	64.2	64.9	63.1
2002	61.3	60.4	60.6	61.8	62.0	62.7	61.4	61.3	62.4	61.9	62.5	63.3	61.8
2003	60.0	59.3	59.3	60.4	60.6	60.9	59.3	59.3	60.6	61.3	62.4	62.9	60.5
2004	60.4	59.7	60.1	60.0	60.8	61.3	60.6	60.5	61.7	62.3	63.2	64.1	61.2
2005	61.4	60.9	60.8	61.3	61.8	62.1	60.9	60.8	61.6	61.8	63.1	64.0	61.7
2006	61.3	60.0	60.2	61.2	61.5	61.6	60.3	60.3	61.3	61.6	63.1	63.8	61.4
2007	60.9	59.8	59.8	60.0	60.8	60.8	59.7	59.5	60.0	60.2	61.4	62.2	60.4
Wholesale Trade													
2000	12.0	12.1	12.1	12.0	12.0	12.1	12.1	12.1	12.0	12.1	12.2	12.4	12.1
2001	12.3	12.2	12.2	12.0	11.9	12.0	11.8	11.9	11.9	11.7	11.7	11.7	11.9
2002	11.2	11.2	11.2	11.3	11.2	11.3	11.1	11.1	11.1	10.8	10.9	11.0	11.1
2003	10.6	10.6	10.6	10.7	10.7	10.8	10.7	10.6	10.8	10.8	10.9	10.9	10.7
2004	10.6	10.7	10.9	10.8	10.9	11.1	11.5	11.5	11.4	11.6	11.6	11.6	11.2
2005	11.6	11.5	11.5	11.5	11.6	11.6	11.4	11.4	11.3	11.2	11.2	11.2	11.4
2006	11.3	11.1	11.1	11.5	11.5	11.6	11.7	11.7	11.8	11.8	11.9	11.9	11.6
2007	11.7	11.6	11.6	11.6	11.7	11.7	11.6	11.6	11.5	11.5	11.6	11.6	11.6
Retail Trade													
2000	37.3	36.7	36.6	36.7	37.0	37.2	36.9	37.1	37.4	37.9	39.3	40.2	37.5
2001	37.2	36.4	36.4	36.7	37.1	37.1	36.6	36.8	36.8	37.2	38.3	39.0	37.1
2002	36.3	35.5	35.7	36.0	36.3	36.8	36.5	36.6	36.8	36.6	37.4	38.2	36.6
2003	36.0	35.4	35.5	36.3	36.6	36.8	36.2	36.4	36.6	37.1	38.1	38.6	36.6
2004	36.6	35.9	36.1	35.9	36.5	36.7	36.5	36.6	36.9	37.1	38.0	38.8	36.8
2005	36.3	35.9	35.8	36.3	36.6	36.8	36.5	36.6	36.6	36.9	38.0	38.6	36.7
2006	36.1	35.1	35.2	35.8	36.0	36.0	35.6	35.7	35.8	36.2	37.5	37.9	36.1
2007	35.9	35.0	35.0	35.0	35.7	35.6	35.2	35.2	35.1	35.3	36.3	36.8	35.5

Employment by Industry: Springfield, MA-CT, NECTA, 2000–2007—*Continued*

(Numbers in thousands, not seasonally adjusted.)

Industry and year	January	February	March	April	May	June	July	August	September	October	November	December	Annual Average
Transportation and Utilities													
2000	12.5	12.5	12.5	13.1	13.1	13.2	12.3	12.3	13.1	13.5	13.6	14.6	13.0
2001	14.2	14.1	14.1	14.3	14.3	14.2	13.4	13.2	14.1	14.2	14.2	14.2	14.0
2002	13.8	13.7	13.7	14.5	14.5	14.6	13.8	13.6	14.5	14.5	14.2	14.1	14.1
2003	13.4	13.3	13.2	13.4	13.3	13.3	12.4	12.3	13.2	13.4	13.4	13.4	13.2
2004	13.2	13.1	13.1	13.3	13.4	13.5	12.6	12.4	13.4	13.6	13.6	13.7	13.2
2005	13.5	13.5	13.5	13.5	13.6	13.7	13.0	12.8	13.7	13.7	13.9	14.2	13.6
2006	13.9	13.8	13.9	13.9	14.0	14.0	13.0	12.9	13.7	13.6	13.7	14.0	13.7
2007	13.3	13.2	13.2	13.4	13.4	13.5	12.9	12.7	13.4	13.4	13.5	13.8	13.3
Information													
2000	5.7	5.8	5.7	5.9	5.9	5.9	5.9	5.3	5.9	5.9	6.0	6.1	5.8
2001	6.1	6.0	6.0	6.0	6.0	6.0	5.9	5.8	5.7	5.8	5.8	5.8	5.9
2002	5.7	5.7	5.7	5.5	5.6	5.6	5.5	5.5	5.4	5.4	5.5	5.5	5.6
2003	5.4	5.3	5.3	5.3	5.2	5.2	5.2	5.2	5.1	4.9	4.9	4.9	5.2
2004	4.8	4.8	4.8	4.7	4.7	4.8	4.8	4.7	4.6	4.6	4.7	4.7	4.7
2005	4.6	4.6	4.6	4.6	4.6	4.6	4.6	4.6	4.5	4.4	4.5	4.5	4.6
2006	4.5	4.5	4.4	4.4	4.4	4.4	4.6	4.6	4.6	4.5	4.5	4.5	4.5
2007	4.5	4.5	4.4	4.4	4.4	4.5	4.5	4.4	4.4	4.4	4.5	4.4	4.4
Financial Activities													
2000	16.2	16.2	16.2	16.2	16.2	16.4	16.4	16.5	16.5	16.5	16.6	16.8	16.4
2001	16.7	16.7	16.7	16.8	16.9	17.1	17.1	17.1	16.9	17.0	17.1	17.0	16.9
2002	16.8	16.8	16.8	16.6	16.7	16.8	16.8	16.9	16.7	16.5	16.6	16.7	16.7
2003	16.4	16.3	16.4	16.4	16.5	16.7	16.6	16.6	16.4	16.3	16.1	16.2	16.4
2004	16.3	16.2	16.3	16.3	16.3	16.4	16.3	16.2	16.1	15.8	15.8	15.9	16.2
2005	15.7	15.6	15.8	15.7	15.7	15.8	16.3	16.3	16.2	16.3	16.4	16.5	16.0
2006	16.7	16.7	16.7	17.2	17.2	17.3	17.3	17.1	17.1	17.0	17.0	17.0	17.0
2007	17.2	17.2	17.2	17.2	17.3	17.4	17.4	17.4	17.2	17.1	17.0	17.0	17.2
Professional and Business Services													
2000	24.0	24.0	24.3	24.7	24.7	25.0	24.8	25.0	25.0	24.8	24.4	24.4	24.6
2001	23.6	23.7	23.9	24.1	24.3	24.3	24.0	24.1	24.0	24.1	23.7	23.4	23.9
2002	22.6	23.0	23.5	23.8	23.8	24.1	23.9	23.8	24.0	23.3	23.1	22.8	23.5
2003	21.6	21.4	21.7	22.8	23.0	23.1	23.1	23.2	23.0	23.4	23.5	23.7	22.8
2004	22.4	22.2	22.7	24.4	24.4	24.7	24.6	24.5	24.9	24.6	24.6	24.5	24.0
2005	23.0	22.9	23.2	24.4	24.2	24.4	24.3	24.2	24.6	25.1	24.8	24.4	24.1
2006	23.6	23.8	23.8	25.1	24.0	24.6	24.1	24.1	24.2	23.9	23.6	23.4	24.0
2007	22.3	22.3	22.5	23.8	23.9	24.6	23.9	24.0	23.6	23.4	23.1	22.9	23.4
Education and Health Services													
2000	47.2	48.2	48.2	48.7	48.9	47.8	46.5	46.2	46.7	49.2	49.4	49.8	48.1
2001	49.0	49.9	49.9	50.1	50.2	49.6	48.8	49.0	49.9	50.9	51.4	51.5	50.0
2002	50.4	51.6	51.7	52.1	52.3	51.5	50.4	50.2	51.6	52.9	53.5	53.5	51.8
2003	52.4	53.2	53.2	53.3	53.0	51.8	51.6	51.6	52.7	53.3	53.6	53.4	52.8
2004	52.2	53.3	53.5	53.8	53.3	52.2	52.1	51.8	53.2	54.4	54.8	54.4	53.3
2005	52.9	54.5	54.6	54.3	54.2	53.0	52.7	52.7	54.5	55.1	55.6	55.4	54.1
2006	53.4	55.1	55.5	55.5	55.2	53.9	54.1	53.6	55.3	56.3	56.7	56.6	55.1
2007	55.5	56.7	56.9	57.1	56.8	55.7	55.4	55.0	56.2	57.4	57.7	57.7	56.5
Leisure and Hospitality													
2000	22.6	22.7	23.1	24.8	25.5	26.5	26.2	26.0	25.7	25.3	24.2	23.9	24.7
2001	23.1	23.1	23.8	24.8	25.8	26.4	26.5	26.6	26.4	25.4	24.4	24.1	25.0
2002	23.1	23.2	23.9	24.9	26.4	26.9	27.0	26.8	26.9	26.3	25.0	24.6	25.4
2003	23.5	23.6	24.1	25.3	26.8	27.5	27.6	27.5	27.2	26.4	25.4	25.1	25.8
2004	24.2	24.3	25.2	26.7	27.5	28.3	28.6	28.1	27.5	26.9	25.6	25.3	26.5
2005	24.2	24.5	24.7	26.5	27.5	28.2	28.1	28.1	27.7	26.4	25.5	25.2	26.4
2006	24.1	24.2	24.8	26.9	28.0	28.7	28.7	28.6	28.1	27.5	26.2	25.9	26.8
2007	24.9	24.9	25.4	27.0	28.3	29.0	29.0	28.6	28.0	27.4	26.0	25.5	27.0
Other Services													
2000	10.9	11.0	11.2	11.1	11.2	11.4	11.5	11.4	11.1	11.3	11.3	11.5	11.2
2001	11.3	11.3	11.4	11.3	11.5	11.6	11.8	11.8	11.3	11.4	11.4	11.6	11.5
2002	11.4	11.4	11.5	11.4	11.7	11.5	11.8	11.7	11.3	11.4	11.5	11.7	11.5
2003	11.1	11.1	11.1	11.2	11.4	11.3	11.6	11.5	11.0	11.2	11.2	11.3	11.3
2004	11.0	11.0	11.1	11.1	11.2	11.2	11.6	11.6	11.1	11.3	11.2	11.4	11.2
2005	11.1	11.2	11.3	11.6	11.5	11.7	11.9	11.8	11.4	11.5	11.5	11.8	11.5
2006	11.2	11.3	11.4	11.5	11.6	11.7	12.0	12.0	11.5	11.6	11.6	11.8	11.6
2007	11.4	11.5	11.6	11.6	11.7	11.8	12.1	11.9	11.4	11.5	11.5	11.7	11.6
Government													
2000	49.7	49.8	49.9	50.2	50.9	51.2	48.1	47.7	50.0	50.5	51.2	51.6	50.1
2001	50.5	50.7	50.8	51.2	51.3	52.1	48.2	47.5	51.3	51.2	51.7	52.2	50.7
2002	51.0	50.9	51.0	50.7	50.9	51.4	48.1	45.1	50.8	50.6	51.2	51.6	50.3
2003	50.9	50.8	50.8	50.3	50.4	51.1	46.7	46.4	49.6	49.0	49.3	49.9	49.6
2004	48.6	49.1	49.5	49.8	50.0	50.0	45.2	44.6	48.8	49.2	49.5	50.0	48.7
2005	48.7	49.7	49.8	49.8	49.9	49.5	44.7	44.0	48.6	49.5	49.7	50.1	48.7
2006	48.7	49.7	49.9	50.1	50.2	49.9	44.8	43.6	49.4	50.1	50.7	51.1	49.0
2007	49.3	50.3	50.4	50.5	50.6	50.1	45.3	44.0	49.8	50.4	51.2	51.6	49.5

Employment by Industry: Bakersfield, CA, 2000–2007

(Numbers in thousands, not seasonally adjusted.)

Industry and year	January	February	March	April	May	June	July	August	September	October	November	December	Annual Average
Total Nonfarm													
2000	189.8	190.8	192.7	193.0	195.1	196.0	191.3	191.0	195.0	196.9	198.4	199.2	194.1
2001	199.3	200.1	201.5	202.2	202.9	205.3	197.9	200.1	201.8	204.2	205.8	205.8	202.2
2002	202.2	202.8	205.3	205.8	206.7	208.2	201.8	202.4	203.2	206.2	208.0	208.5	205.1
2003	204.9	205.2	207.8	207.0	208.0	208.1	205.0	205.4	206.4	208.4	209.3	209.8	207.1
2004	205.1	206.2	208.3	211.7	212.5	215.9	210.3	210.2	212.0	215.0	216.6	217.2	211.8
2005	214.6	215.9	217.4	220.1	222.3	223.8	220.6	221.8	224.6	226.5	228.1	229.0	222.1
2006	227.1	228.6	229.9	230.9	233.6	235.1	230.8	233.1	235.5	237.8	238.7	238.9	233.3
2007	235.3	236.3	237.7	239.7	240.8	240.8	234.9	236.4	239.0	240.4	241.8	242.0	238.8
Total Private													
2000	137.9	138.9	139.9	140.3	141.8	143.0	144.6	145.0	144.4	143.7	144.5	145.7	142.5
2001	146.1	146.2	147.3	147.6	148.3	149.7	149.5	149.8	149.3	149.4	150.2	150.1	148.6
2002	147.1	147.5	148.8	149.2	150.4	151.1	150.0	150.7	150.3	150.5	151.1	151.7	149.9
2003	148.4	149.1	151.0	151.0	152.4	152.8	153.6	154.0	154.2	154.7	154.5	155.2	152.5
2004	151.4	152.2	154.0	157.0	157.9	158.9	159.0	159.9	159.6	160.2	161.1	161.7	157.7
2005	159.3	159.9	161.1	163.9	165.9	167.1	168.6	168.5	170.0	169.1	170.6	171.7	166.3
2006	169.6	170.9	172.0	172.9	175.8	177.0	176.9	178.0	178.5	178.1	178.9	179.3	175.7
2007	175.8	176.7	178.0	177.9	179.2	179.2	179.5	180.0	180.1	179.2	179.7	180.0	178.8
Goods-Producing													
2000	28.5	28.9	29.5	29.8	30.4	30.9	31.4	31.5	31.6	31.5	31.5	31.9	30.6
2001	31.6	31.8	32.2	32.6	32.8	33.1	33.2	33.5	33.3	32.9	32.6	32.3	32.7
2002	31.9	31.9	32.2	32.2	32.4	32.8	33.0	33.2	33.3	33.5	33.5	33.6	32.8
2003	33.5	33.7	33.8	33.6	33.8	33.9	34.5	34.7	34.9	34.7	34.3	34.6	34.1
2004	34.5	34.7	35.3	36.1	36.2	36.8	36.8	36.9	37.2	37.2	36.7	37.2	36.3
2005	36.6	37.0	37.4	38.1	38.5	39.2	40.0	39.7	40.7	40.5	40.6	40.7	39.1
2006	40.6	41.2	41.5	41.5	42.3	42.8	43.2	43.2	43.5	43.1	42.6	42.5	42.3
2007	41.0	41.3	41.6	40.9	41.2	41.3	42.2	42.4	42.2	41.9	41.5	41.4	41.6
Natural Resources and Mining													
2000	7.6	7.8	8.0	7.8	7.9	8.0	8.4	8.6	8.6	8.5	8.6	8.7	8.2
2001	8.5	8.5	8.6	8.6	8.6	8.7	8.7	8.8	8.7	8.7	8.6	8.5	8.6
2002	8.2	8.0	7.9	7.8	7.7	7.8	7.9	7.9	7.9	7.9	7.9	7.9	7.9
2003	7.8	7.9	7.9	7.9	8.0	7.9	8.1	8.1	8.0	8.1	8.0	8.2	7.9
2004	8.0	8.1	8.2	8.1	8.2	8.3	8.1	8.2	8.1	8.1	8.1	8.2	8.1
2005	8.1	8.2	8.3	8.4	8.4	8.4	8.5	8.6	8.7	8.7	8.7	8.8	8.5
2006	8.9	8.9	9.0	9.1	9.2	9.4	9.4	9.6	9.6	9.7	9.7	9.7	9.4
2007	9.5	9.6	9.6	9.6	9.6	9.6	9.9	10.0	9.9	9.9	9.9	10.0	9.8
Construction													
2000	10.6	10.7	10.8	11.1	11.5	11.8	12.0	12.0	12.1	12.1	12.1	12.3	11.5
2001	12.1	12.3	12.7	13.0	13.1	13.2	13.3	13.6	13.4	13.1	13.0	12.9	12.9
2002	12.9	13.1	13.4	13.3	13.4	13.5	13.4	13.5	13.3	13.3	13.5	13.4	13.3
2003	13.2	13.2	13.3	13.2	13.3	13.4	13.7	13.9	13.9	13.9	14.0	14.0	13.5
2004	14.0	14.1	14.6	15.2	15.2	15.8	15.9	16.0	15.8	16.1	16.0	16.3	15.4
2005	15.9	16.3	16.8	17.4	17.8	18.5	19.0	18.7	19.2	19.3	19.5	19.5	18.2
2006	19.0	19.5	19.7	19.8	20.4	20.7	20.8	20.4	20.4	20.0	19.8	19.7	20.0
2007	18.8	18.9	19.1	18.5	18.7	18.7	18.8	18.9	18.4	18.2	17.9	17.7	18.6
Manufacturing													
2000	10.3	10.4	10.7	10.9	11.0	11.1	11.0	10.9	10.9	10.9	10.8	10.9	10.8
2001	11.0	11.0	10.9	11.0	11.1	11.2	11.2	11.1	11.2	11.1	11.0	10.9	11.1
2002	10.8	10.8	10.9	11.1	11.3	11.5	11.7	11.8	12.1	12.3	12.1	12.3	11.6
2003	12.5	12.6	12.6	12.5	12.5	12.6	12.7	12.7	13.0	12.7	12.4	12.4	12.6
2004	12.5	12.5	12.5	12.8	12.8	12.7	12.8	12.7	13.3	13.0	12.6	12.7	12.7
2005	12.6	12.5	12.3	12.3	12.3	12.3	12.5	12.4	12.8	12.5	12.4	12.4	12.4
2006	12.7	12.8	12.8	12.6	12.7	12.7	13.0	13.2	13.5	13.4	13.1	13.1	13.0
2007	12.7	12.8	12.9	12.8	12.9	13.0	13.5	13.5	13.9	13.8	13.7	13.7	13.3
Service-Providing													
2000	161.3	161.9	163.2	163.2	164.7	165.1	159.9	159.5	163.4	165.4	166.9	167.3	163.5
2001	167.7	168.3	169.3	169.6	170.1	172.2	164.7	166.6	168.5	171.3	173.2	173.5	169.6
2002	170.3	170.9	173.1	173.6	174.3	175.4	168.8	169.2	169.9	172.7	174.5	174.9	172.3
2003	171.4	171.5	174.0	173.4	174.2	174.2	170.5	170.7	171.5	173.7	175.0	175.2	172.9
2004	170.6	171.5	173.0	175.6	176.3	179.1	173.5	173.3	174.8	177.8	179.9	180.0	175.5
2005	178.0	178.9	180.0	182.0	183.8	184.6	180.6	182.1	183.9	186.0	187.5	188.3	183.0
2006	186.5	187.4	188.4	189.4	191.3	192.3	187.6	189.9	192.0	194.7	196.1	196.4	191.0
2007	194.3	195.0	196.1	198.8	199.6	199.5	192.7	194.0	196.8	198.5	200.3	200.6	197.2
Trade, Transportation, and Utilities													
2000	36.2	36.2	36.3	36.5	36.9	37.0	37.6	37.8	37.6	37.6	38.3	38.8	37.2
2001	38.3	37.8	38.0	38.1	38.2	38.6	38.4	38.2	38.1	38.6	39.2	39.3	38.4
2002	38.0	37.8	38.1	38.5	38.8	39.1	39.3	39.3	39.4	39.3	39.9	40.4	39.0
2003	38.6	38.7	39.2	39.3	39.5	39.7	39.9	39.7	39.6	40.3	40.5	41.0	39.6
2004	39.2	38.9	39.4	40.4	40.8	41.2	41.6	42.0	41.6	42.1	42.8	42.7	41.1
2005	41.5	41.6	41.9	42.4	43.3	43.3	43.7	43.9	44.3	44.6	45.6	46.5	43.6
2006	45.1	44.8	45.1	45.0	46.2	46.3	46.3	46.6	46.7	46.6	47.8	48.2	46.2
2007	46.0	45.6	46.1	46.1	46.9	46.7	46.6	46.7	46.6	46.7	47.4	47.6	46.6
Wholesale Trade													
2000	5.5	5.5	5.5	5.6	5.7	5.7	5.8	5.8	5.7	5.8	5.8	5.8	5.7
2001	5.7	5.7	5.7	5.9	5.9	6.0	5.9	5.9	5.9	6.0	6.0	6.0	5.9
2002	6.0	6.0	6.0	6.0	6.0	6.1	6.3	6.3	6.3	6.2	6.0	6.1	6.1
2003	5.9	5.9	6.0	6.1	6.2	6.2	6.3	6.2	6.2	6.3	6.4	6.5	6.1
2004	6.2	6.2	6.2	6.3	6.4	6.5	6.7	6.7	6.6	6.6	6.6	6.6	6.5
2005	6.6	6.6	6.6	6.8	6.8	6.9	6.9	6.9	6.9	7.0	7.0	7.1	6.8
2006	7.2	7.3	7.4	7.4	7.6	7.7	7.7	7.7	7.8	7.8	7.9	7.9	7.6
2007	7.8	7.8	7.9	8.0	8.1	8.2	8.2	8.2	8.2	8.2	8.2	8.2	8.1

Employment by Industry: Bakersfield, CA, 2000–2007—*Continued*

(Numbers in thousands, not seasonally adjusted.)

Industry and year	January	February	March	April	May	June	July	August	September	October	November	December	Annual Average
Retail Trade													
2000	22.7	22.6	22.7	22.6	22.9	23.0	23.1	23.2	23.2	23.3	24.1	24.6	23.2
2001	24.3	23.9	24.0	24.0	24.0	24.3	24.0	23.8	23.8	24.2	24.8	25.1	24.2
2002	24.0	23.7	24.0	24.4	24.6	24.8	24.5	24.5	24.6	24.6	25.4	25.9	24.6
2003	24.4	24.4	24.5	24.3	24.5	24.6	24.6	24.5	24.5	25.2	25.5	26.0	24.7
2004	24.8	24.5	24.9	25.6	25.7	25.9	25.8	26.0	25.9	26.3	27.2	27.2	25.8
2005	26.3	26.2	26.5	26.8	27.0	27.2	27.5	27.7	28.0	28.1	29.3	30.1	27.6
2006	28.9	28.4	28.6	28.5	28.9	29.1	29.1	29.4	29.4	29.4	30.5	30.8	29.3
2007	29.1	28.6	28.8	28.8	29.0	28.9	28.7	28.9	28.7	28.8	29.5	29.8	29.0
Transportation and Utilities													
2000	8.0	8.1	8.1	8.3	8.3	8.3	8.7	8.8	8.7	8.5	8.4	8.4	8.4
2001	8.3	8.2	8.3	8.2	8.3	8.3	8.5	8.5	8.4	8.4	8.4	8.2	8.3
2002	8.0	8.1	8.1	8.1	8.2	8.2	8.5	8.5	8.4	8.4	8.4	8.4	8.3
2003	8.3	8.4	8.7	8.9	8.8	8.9	9.0	9.0	8.9	8.8	8.6	8.5	8.7
2004	8.2	8.2	8.3	8.5	8.7	8.8	9.1	9.3	9.1	9.2	9.0	8.9	8.8
2005	8.6	8.8	8.8	8.8	9.5	9.2	9.3	9.3	9.4	9.5	9.3	9.3	9.2
2006	9.0	9.1	9.1	9.1	9.7	9.5	9.5	9.5	9.5	9.4	9.4	9.5	9.4
2007	9.1	9.2	9.4	9.3	9.8	9.6	9.6	9.7	9.6	9.7	9.7	9.6	9.5
Information													
2000	2.5	2.5	2.5	2.5	2.5	2.5	2.6	2.5	2.5	2.5	2.5	2.5	2.5
2001	2.5	2.5	2.5	2.6	2.6	2.7	2.6	2.5	2.5	2.5	2.5	2.5	2.5
2002	2.6	2.6	2.6	2.6	2.6	2.6	2.5	2.4	2.4	2.5	2.5	2.5	2.5
2003	2.6	2.6	2.6	2.6	2.6	2.5	2.5	2.5	2.5	2.5	2.5	2.5	2.5
2004	2.5	2.5	2.5	2.5	2.5	2.5	2.6	2.5	2.5	2.5	2.5	2.5	2.5
2005	2.5	2.5	2.5	2.5	2.5	2.5	2.6	2.5	2.6	2.5	2.5	2.6	2.5
2006	2.6	2.7	2.6	2.6	2.7	2.7	2.7	2.7	2.7	2.5	2.6	2.6	2.7
2007	2.8	2.8	2.7	2.8	2.8	2.8	2.8	2.8	2.7	2.6	2.7	2.7	2.8
Financial Activities													
2000	7.6	7.7	7.7	7.5	7.6	7.5	7.6	7.5	7.5	7.5	7.5	7.6	7.6
2001	7.6	7.6	7.6	7.7	7.7	7.9	7.8	7.8	7.8	7.8	7.8	7.9	7.8
2002	7.7	7.8	7.9	8.0	8.0	8.0	8.0	8.0	8.0	8.0	8.1	8.2	8.0
2003	8.1	8.1	8.2	8.2	8.3	8.4	8.4	8.5	8.4	8.4	8.4	8.4	8.3
2004	8.4	8.4	8.5	8.7	8.6	8.6	8.7	8.7	8.6	8.6	8.6	8.6	8.6
2005	8.6	8.5	8.6	8.6	8.7	8.8	8.9	8.9	8.8	8.7	8.8	8.8	8.7
2006	8.9	8.9	8.9	8.9	9.1	9.1	9.0	9.0	8.9	9.0	9.0	9.0	9.0
2007	9.1	9.2	9.2	9.1	9.1	9.2	9.1	9.0	8.9	8.9	8.9	8.9	9.1
Professional and Business Services													
2000	22.1	22.1	22.1	21.9	21.9	22.2	22.2	22.5	22.2	22.0	22.4	22.5	22.2
2001	23.1	23.1	23.2	22.7	22.7	23.0	22.6	23.0	22.7	23.2	23.5	23.5	23.0
2002	23.2	23.3	23.4	22.8	22.6	22.6	21.9	22.3	21.9	21.6	21.4	21.3	22.4
2003	20.7	20.7	21.2	21.3	21.5	21.8	21.8	22.1	22.3	22.1	22.3	22.3	21.6
2004	21.1	21.5	21.6	21.8	21.8	21.7	21.5	21.9	21.6	21.9	22.2	22.2	21.7
2005	22.1	22.1	22.0	22.8	22.8	23.0	23.4	23.6	23.9	23.4	23.8	23.6	23.0
2006	23.7	24.0	24.1	24.3	24.8	25.0	25.3	25.6	25.9	26.0	25.8	25.7	25.0
2007	26.0	26.3	26.2	26.5	26.6	26.4	26.0	26.4	26.6	26.2	26.2	26.3	26.3
Education and Health Services													
2000	18.6	18.9	19.0	19.1	19.2	19.4	19.5	19.4	19.5	19.2	19.2	19.3	19.2
2001	20.1	20.3	20.3	19.9	19.9	20.0	20.3	20.3	20.3	20.3	20.4	20.5	20.2
2002	20.1	20.3	20.4	20.7	20.9	21.0	20.6	20.8	20.8	20.9	21.0	21.1	20.7
2003	20.9	21.1	21.2	21.2	21.4	21.3	21.3	21.4	21.4	21.4	21.4	21.5	21.2
2004	21.2	21.2	21.4	21.5	21.6	21.7	21.7	21.8	21.7	21.6	21.7	21.9	21.6
2005	21.7	21.9	22.0	22.2	22.3	22.2	22.4	22.4	22.2	22.3	22.3	22.4	22.2
2006	22.4	22.6	22.7	22.7	22.7	23.0	22.7	23.0	23.1	23.5	23.7	23.8	23.0
2007	23.9	24.3	24.3	24.3	24.2	24.3	24.5	24.6	24.6	24.5	24.6	24.7	24.4
Leisure and Hospitality													
2000	15.9	16.1	16.2	16.4	16.7	16.9	17.1	16.9	16.7	16.6	16.4	16.4	16.5
2001	16.4	16.5	16.9	17.2	17.5	17.6	17.7	17.6	17.5	17.2	17.3	17.3	17.2
2002	16.8	16.9	17.3	17.6	18.1	18.2	17.9	17.9	17.8	17.7	17.6	17.7	17.6
2003	17.3	17.4	17.9	17.9	18.3	18.3	18.4	18.3	18.1	18.3	18.2	18.0	18.0
2004	17.6	18.1	18.4	19.0	19.4	19.4	19.3	19.3	19.3	19.1	19.3	19.4	19.0
2005	19.3	19.3	19.6	20.1	20.5	20.9	20.6	20.5	20.3	20.0	20.1	20.3	20.1
2006	19.6	19.9	20.2	20.9	21.0	21.3	21.0	20.9	20.9	20.6	20.7	20.9	20.7
2007	20.5	20.7	21.2	21.6	21.8	22.0	21.4	21.2	21.3	21.1	21.1	21.2	21.3
Other Services													
2000	6.5	6.5	6.6	6.6	6.6	6.6	6.6	6.9	6.8	6.8	6.7	6.7	6.7
2001	6.5	6.6	6.6	6.8	6.9	6.8	6.9	6.9	7.1	6.9	6.9	6.8	6.8
2002	6.8	6.9	6.9	6.8	7.0	6.8	6.8	6.8	6.7	7.0	7.1	6.9	6.9
2003	6.7	6.8	6.9	6.9	7.0	6.9	6.8	6.8	6.7	7.0	6.9	6.9	6.8
2004	6.9	6.9	6.9	7.0	7.0	6.9	6.8	6.8	7.0	7.0	6.9	6.9	7.0
2005	7.0	7.0	7.1	7.2	7.3	7.2	7.0	7.0	7.2	7.2	7.4	7.1	7.1
2006	6.7	6.8	6.9	7.0	7.0	6.8	6.7	7.0	6.9	6.7	6.8	6.8	6.8
2007	6.5	6.5	6.7	6.6	6.6	6.5	6.9	6.9	7.2	7.2	7.3	7.2	6.8
Government													
2000	51.9	51.9	52.8	52.7	53.3	53.0	46.7	46.0	50.6	53.2	53.9	53.5	51.6
2001	53.2	53.9	54.2	54.6	54.6	55.6	48.4	50.3	52.5	54.8	55.6	55.7	53.6
2002	55.1	55.3	56.5	56.6	56.3	57.1	51.8	51.7	52.9	55.7	56.9	56.8	55.2
2003	56.5	56.1	56.8	56.0	55.6	55.3	51.4	51.4	52.2	53.7	54.8	54.6	54.5
2004	53.7	54.0	54.3	54.7	54.6	57.0	51.3	50.3	52.4	54.8	55.5	55.5	54.0
2005	55.3	56.0	56.3	56.2	56.4	56.7	52.0	53.3	54.6	57.4	57.5	57.3	55.8
2006	57.5	57.7	57.9	58.0	57.8	58.1	53.9	55.1	57.0	59.7	59.8	59.6	57.7
2007	59.5	59.6	59.7	61.8	61.6	61.6	55.4	56.4	58.9	61.2	62.1	62.0	60.0

Employment by Industry: Toledo, OH, 2000–2007

(Numbers in thousands, not seasonally adjusted.)

Industry and year	January	February	March	April	May	June	July	August	September	October	November	December	Annual Average
Total Nonfarm													
2000	340.3	341.5	344.5	347.0	349.8	348.6	339.9	345.2	350.9	351.8	353.4	352.9	347.1
2001	339.0	339.3	341.7	343.1	346.1	343.8	335.4	339.9	344.0	345.7	345.3	345.2	342.4
2002	330.1	331.7	334.3	335.2	338.3	335.0	327.5	331.5	336.4	336.2	336.8	337.1	334.2
2003	324.3	325.5	325.8	329.9	333.9	329.4	324.8	329.5	333.4	335.1	334.9	335.1	330.1
2004	321.3	324.2	326.4	330.6	332.9	330.8	328.3	329.4	335.0	336.1	335.0	334.2	330.4
2005	319.7	323.0	325.3	331.1	335.0	331.9	330.4	333.1	337.0	338.0	338.4	337.2	331.7
2006	326.7	326.9	330.7	332.7	334.9	333.9	329.1	331.7	336.1	334.9	335.2	334.6	332.3
2007	321.3	322.5	324.8	327.4	330.3	330.7	323.1	329.1	333.0	330.0	331.5	331.1	327.9
Total Private													
2000	289.5	289.3	291.7	294.3	297.1	301.6	296.5	301.8	300.7	299.9	300.8	300.4	296.9
2001	288.4	287.4	289.4	290.9	294.4	296.6	291.7	296.2	293.0	292.6	291.8	291.6	292.0
2002	278.4	278.7	280.7	282.1	285.5	287.4	283.6	287.9	285.2	283.2	283.5	283.5	283.3
2003	272.5	272.4	272.7	277.2	281.3	282.5	279.6	284.1	282.3	282.7	282.3	282.4	279.3
2004	273.0	272.1	273.9	278.4	281.6	283.9	282.9	284.5	284.2	284.0	283.1	282.3	280.3
2005	271.2	270.9	273.3	279.3	283.2	285.3	284.4	286.3	285.5	285.3	285.5	284.9	281.3
2006	275.5	274.8	278.4	280.7	283.2	286.7	283.3	285.0	284.6	282.1	282.2	282.2	281.6
2007	270.3	270.2	272.4	275.1	279.7	283.1	276.8	282.2	281.3	277.1	278.5	278.8	277.1
Goods-Producing													
2000	77.4	77.4	78.7	79.8	80.9	82.1	76.8	81.3	81.1	80.0	79.5	78.4	79.4
2001	75.8	75.3	75.6	75.6	76.4	77.4	72.7	76.3	75.6	75.5	74.8	73.7	75.4
2002	69.9	70.6	70.8	71.1	72.0	72.5	68.8	72.5	71.7	70.5	70.4	69.5	70.9
2003	66.7	66.8	66.9	67.9	69.0	69.6	66.1	69.5	68.9	68.6	67.8	67.5	67.9
2004	65.9	65.3	66.5	67.3	67.6	68.5	67.2	68.7	68.4	68.5	67.9	67.0	67.4
2005	64.7	64.6	65.3	66.6	67.4	67.9	66.9	68.6	68.1	67.9	67.5	66.4	66.8
2006	64.3	64.0	65.2	66.3	66.5	67.8	65.0	66.2	66.5	65.9	65.7	65.2	65.7
2007	62.0	61.9	62.4	63.2	64.2	64.9	61.0	64.9	64.7	61.6	62.6	62.5	63.0
Natural Resources, Mining, and Construction													
2000	15.0	14.9	16.0	17.3	18.0	18.6	18.7	18.7	18.1	17.2	16.8	16.0	17.1
2001	14.8	14.7	15.3	15.7	16.7	17.4	17.9	17.9	17.7	18.3	17.9	17.0	16.8
2002	14.8	14.8	15.2	15.5	15.9	16.3	16.6	16.7	16.1	16.1	15.4	14.5	15.7
2003	13.5	13.1	13.4	14.7	15.5	16.0	16.4	16.5	16.3	16.4	15.6	15.1	15.2
2004	13.9	13.4	14.4	15.4	15.7	16.3	16.6	16.6	16.4	16.6	16.1	15.4	15.6
2005	13.5	13.3	13.9	15.2	15.8	16.5	17.0	17.2	16.9	17.1	16.6	15.4	15.7
2006	14.0	13.9	14.7	15.1	15.6	16.2	16.6	16.4	16.0	15.9	15.9	15.2	15.5
2007	13.8	12.9	13.5	14.6	15.4	15.9	15.9	16.1	16.0	16.2	16.1	15.6	15.1
Manufacturing													
2000	62.4	62.5	62.7	62.5	62.9	63.5	58.1	62.6	63.0	62.8	62.7	62.4	62.3
2001	61.0	60.6	60.3	59.9	59.7	60.0	54.8	58.4	57.9	57.2	56.9	56.7	58.6
2002	55.1	55.8	55.6	55.6	56.1	56.2	52.2	55.8	55.6	54.4	55.0	55.0	55.2
2003	53.2	53.7	53.5	53.2	53.5	53.6	49.7	53.0	52.6	52.2	52.2	52.4	52.7
2004	52.0	51.9	52.1	51.9	51.9	52.2	50.6	52.1	52.0	51.9	51.8	51.6	51.8
2005	51.2	51.3	51.4	51.4	51.6	51.4	49.9	51.4	51.2	50.8	50.9	51.0	51.1
2006	50.3	50.1	50.5	51.2	50.9	51.6	48.4	49.8	50.5	50.0	49.8	50.0	50.3
2007	48.2	49.0	48.9	48.6	48.8	49.0	44.9	48.9	48.5	45.5	47.0	47.8	47.9
Service-Providing													
2000	262.9	264.1	265.8	267.2	268.9	266.5	263.1	263.9	269.8	271.8	273.9	274.5	267.7
2001	263.2	264.0	266.1	267.5	269.7	266.4	262.7	263.6	268.4	270.2	270.5	271.5	267.0
2002	260.2	261.1	263.5	264.1	266.3	262.5	258.7	259.0	264.7	265.7	266.4	267.6	263.3
2003	257.6	258.7	258.9	262.0	264.9	259.8	258.7	260.0	264.5	266.5	267.1	267.6	262.2
2004	255.4	258.9	259.9	263.3	265.3	262.3	261.1	260.7	266.6	267.6	267.1	267.2	263.0
2005	255.0	258.4	260.0	264.5	267.6	264.0	263.5	264.5	268.9	270.1	270.9	270.8	264.9
2006	262.4	262.9	265.5	266.4	268.4	266.1	264.1	265.5	269.6	269.0	269.5	269.4	266.6
2007	259.3	260.6	262.4	264.2	266.1	265.8	262.1	264.2	268.3	268.4	268.9	268.6	264.9
Trade, Transportation, and Utilities													
2000	71.3	70.3	70.2	70.7	70.8	71.4	71.8	72.0	71.6	73.1	74.5	75.2	71.9
2001	71.1	70.1	70.0	70.1	70.1	70.4	70.2	70.7	70.3	70.9	71.8	72.6	70.7
2002	67.8	66.4	66.7	66.5	66.7	67.2	67.5	67.6	67.0	67.1	67.8	68.7	67.3
2003	65.2	64.7	64.6	65.2	65.6	65.6	66.0	66.2	66.3	66.7	68.0	68.3	66.0
2004	64.3	63.7	63.2	64.0	64.2	64.7	64.7	65.2	65.3	65.2	66.4	66.7	64.9
2005	63.5	63.0	63.0	64.0	64.7	65.0	64.9	65.0	65.4	65.5	66.9	67.8	64.9
2006	64.3	63.4	63.8	64.0	64.5	65.1	65.1	65.8	65.9	65.7	65.6	66.8	67.7	65.2
2007	63.7	63.2	63.5	64.0	65.2	65.8	65.8	65.0	65.3	65.2	65.3	66.4	67.1	65.0
Wholesale Trade													
2000	15.3	15.3	15.3	15.6	15.7	15.8	15.7	15.7	15.5	15.6	15.6	15.5	15.6
2001	15.2	15.2	15.1	15.4	15.5	15.5	15.6	15.7	15.5	15.4	15.1	15.1	15.4
2002	14.8	14.7	14.7	14.9	15.0	15.0	14.9	14.9	14.6	14.5	14.1	14.0	14.7
2003	13.7	13.8	13.8	14.0	14.1	14.2	14.3	14.4	14.3	14.1	14.1	13.8	14.0
2004	13.5	13.6	13.5	13.9	14.1	14.2	14.5	14.6	14.4	14.5	14.3	14.1	14.1
2005	13.9	13.9	13.9	14.1	14.3	14.4	14.4	14.5	14.3	14.1	14.0	13.8	14.1
2006	13.7	13.6	13.7	13.8	13.9	14.0	14.2	14.3	14.0	14.0	13.6	13.7	13.9
2007	13.4	13.4	13.4	13.4	13.8	13.9	13.8	13.8	13.5	13.5	13.4	13.4	13.6
Retail Trade													
2000	42.4	41.5	41.7	41.4	41.4	41.7	41.5	42.0	41.8	42.8	44.5	45.2	42.3
2001	42.0	41.0	40.9	40.6	40.4	40.5	40.0	40.4	40.3	40.9	42.3	43.1	41.0
2002	39.4	38.2	38.5	38.3	38.4	38.8	38.8	38.8	38.8	38.6	38.4	39.7	40.7	38.9
2003	38.3	37.8	37.7	38.0	38.1	38.0	38.3	38.5	38.7	39.0	40.3	41.1	38.7
2004	37.8	37.2	36.8	37.2	37.0	37.2	37.0	36.8	36.7	36.6	37.5	38.0	37.2
2005	35.5	35.0	34.9	35.6	35.8	35.8	35.7	35.6	36.1	36.3	37.5	38.2	36.0
2006	35.8	35.1	35.2	35.4	35.6	35.9	35.9	35.9	35.7	35.7	35.8	37.1	37.6	35.9
2007	35.2	34.8	35.0	35.2	35.9	36.1	35.7	35.8	36.0	36.2	37.2	37.7	35.9

Employment by Industry: Toledo, OH, 2000–2007—*Continued*

(Numbers in thousands, not seasonally adjusted.)

Industry and year	January	February	March	April	May	June	July	August	September	October	November	December	Annual Average
Transportation and Utilities													
2000	13.6	13.5	13.2	13.7	13.7	13.9	14.6	14.3	14.3	14.7	14.4	14.5	14.0
2001	13.9	13.9	14.0	14.1	14.2	14.4	14.6	14.6	14.5	14.6	14.4	14.4	14.3
2002	13.6	13.5	13.5	13.3	13.3	13.4	13.8	13.9	13.8	14.2	14.0	14.0	13.7
2003	13.2	13.1	13.1	13.2	13.4	13.4	13.4	13.3	13.3	13.6	13.6	13.4	13.3
2004	13.0	12.9	12.9	12.9	13.1	13.3	13.7	13.9	14.1	14.7	14.6	14.6	13.6
2005	14.1	14.1	14.2	14.3	14.6	14.8	14.8	14.9	15.0	15.1	15.4	15.8	14.8
2006	14.8	14.7	14.9	14.8	15.0	15.2	15.7	15.9	16.0	15.8	16.1	16.4	15.4
2007	15.1	15.0	15.1	15.4	15.5	15.8	15.5	15.7	15.7	15.6	15.8	16.0	15.5
Information													
2000	4.9	4.9	5.0	5.0	5.0	5.0	5.1	5.1	5.0	5.0	5.0	5.1	5.0
2001	5.0	5.0	5.0	5.0	5.1	5.2	5.1	5.2	5.1	5.1	5.1	5.2	5.1
2002	4.9	5.0	5.0	4.9	4.8	4.8	4.7	4.7	4.6	4.5	4.5	4.5	4.7
2003	4.6	4.6	4.6	4.7	4.7	4.7	4.7	4.7	4.6	4.7	4.7	4.7	4.6
2004	4.6	4.6	4.6	4.6	4.6	4.6	4.5	4.4	4.3	4.2	4.2	4.1	4.4
2005	4.1	4.0	4.0	4.0	4.1	4.1	4.1	4.1	4.0	4.0	4.0	4.0	4.0
2006	4.1	4.1	4.0	4.0	4.0	4.0	4.0	4.0	3.9	3.9	3.9	3.9	4.0
2007	3.8	3.8	3.8	3.8	3.8	4.0	3.9	3.9	3.8	3.8	3.9	3.9	3.9
Financial Activities													
2000	12.1	12.2	12.3	12.4	12.6	12.7	12.5	12.6	12.5	12.6	12.5	12.5	12.5
2001	12.2	12.2	12.3	12.4	12.5	12.7	12.7	12.7	12.5	12.6	12.6	12.5	12.5
2002	12.4	12.5	12.5	12.6	12.7	12.9	12.9	12.9	12.8	12.9	12.9	13.0	12.8
2003	12.9	12.8	12.7	12.8	12.9	13.0	13.0	13.1	12.9	13.4	13.1	13.3	12.9
2004	13.1	13.2	13.3	13.0	13.2	13.3	13.4	13.4	13.2	13.3	13.3	13.4	13.3
2005	13.2	13.3	13.4	13.5	13.6	13.7	13.7	13.6	13.5	13.5	13.4	13.3	13.5
2006	13.1	13.1	13.2	13.1	13.2	13.3	13.1	13.0	13.0	12.9	12.8	12.8	13.1
2007	12.7	12.7	12.8	12.8	12.9	13.1	13.0	12.9	12.8	12.8	12.7	12.8	12.8
Professional and Business Services													
2000	37.3	36.9	36.5	36.8	36.5	37.2	37.0	37.3	37.5	37.4	37.9	37.9	37.2
2001	36.5	36.1	36.3	36.3	36.2	36.3	36.1	36.2	35.5	35.5	34.9	34.8	35.9
2002	33.2	33.0	33.6	33.9	33.9	33.8	33.5	33.7	33.4	33.3	33.4	33.3	33.5
2003	32.5	32.6	32.7	33.6	33.9	33.8	34.2	34.7	34.3	34.8	34.7	34.6	33.8
2004	33.8	33.8	33.8	34.6	34.9	35.0	34.7	34.8	35.1	35.3	35.4	35.3	34.7
2005	32.8	32.4	32.7	33.6	34.0	34.1	34.4	34.6	34.4	35.7	35.5	35.4	34.1
2006	33.5	33.4	33.9	34.1	34.1	34.7	34.4	34.8	35.0	34.7	34.7	34.2	34.3
2007	33.0	33.3	33.5	33.9	34.0	34.4	33.9	34.8	35.4	35.3	35.0	34.7	34.3
Education and Health Services													
2000	42.7	43.2	43.6	43.3	43.1	43.6	43.2	43.6	43.6	43.8	44.1	44.5	43.5
2001	43.5	43.8	44.2	44.3	44.7	44.9	44.9	45.1	45.4	45.5	45.8	46.0	44.8
2002	45.7	46.2	46.3	46.4	46.7	46.7	46.5	46.7	46.9	47.2	47.3	47.5	46.7
2003	46.0	46.1	46.0	46.1	46.4	46.2	46.0	46.1	46.4	46.6	46.6	47.0	46.2
2004	46.1	46.3	46.5	47.0	47.2	47.1	47.4	47.6	48.1	48.6	48.9	49.3	47.5
2005	48.4	48.8	49.1	49.8	50.1	50.1	49.8	50.0	50.6	50.8	50.9	51.3	50.0
2006	50.7	51.1	51.4	51.0	51.2	51.1	50.5	50.9	51.1	51.3	51.3	51.4	51.1
2007	49.9	50.0	50.3	50.2	50.6	50.8	50.8	51.2	51.2	51.4	51.6	51.6	50.8
Leisure and Hospitality													
2000	29.8	30.2	30.9	32.1	33.8	35.1	35.6	35.5	34.8	33.4	32.7	32.2	33.0
2001	29.8	30.2	31.0	32.2	34.2	34.8	35.0	34.9	33.6	32.3	31.5	31.4	32.6
2002	29.5	29.9	30.4	31.4	33.2	33.7	34.3	34.2	33.5	32.1	31.7	31.4	32.1
2003	29.5	29.7	30.0	31.7	33.5	34.5	34.7	34.8	34.0	32.7	32.3	32.0	32.4
2004	30.4	30.2	30.7	32.4	34.1	34.9	34.8	34.8	34.6	32.7	32.1	31.6	32.8
2005	30.1	30.1	30.9	32.9	34.2	35.3	35.4	35.3	34.5	32.9	32.2	31.5	32.9
2006	30.7	30.6	31.7	33.0	34.4	35.5	35.6	35.3	34.5	33.0	32.2	32.2	33.2
2007	30.7	30.7	31.3	32.4	34.1	35.1	34.7	34.6	33.6	32.2	31.5	31.4	32.7
Other Services													
2000	14.0	14.2	14.5	14.2	14.4	14.5	14.5	14.4	14.6	14.6	14.6	14.6	14.4
2001	14.5	14.7	15.0	15.0	15.2	14.9	15.0	15.1	15.0	15.2	15.3	15.4	15.0
2002	15.0	15.1	15.4	15.3	15.5	15.8	15.4	15.6	15.3	15.6	15.5	15.6	15.4
2003	15.1	15.1	15.2	15.2	15.3	15.1	14.9	15.0	14.9	15.2	15.1	15.0	15.1
2004	14.8	15.0	15.3	15.5	15.8	15.8	15.7	15.5	15.3	15.6	14.9	14.9	15.3
2005	14.4	14.7	14.9	14.9	15.1	15.1	15.2	15.1	15.0	15.0	15.1	15.2	15.0
2006	14.8	15.1	15.2	15.2	15.3	15.2	14.9	14.9	14.9	14.8	14.8	14.8	15.0
2007	14.5	14.6	14.8	14.8	14.9	15.0	14.5	14.6	14.6	14.7	14.8	14.8	14.7
Government													
2000	50.8	52.2	52.8	52.7	52.7	47.0	43.4	43.4	50.2	51.9	52.6	52.5	50.2
2001	50.6	51.9	52.3	52.2	51.7	47.2	43.7	43.7	51.0	53.1	53.5	53.6	50.4
2002	51.7	53.0	53.6	53.1	52.8	47.6	43.9	43.6	51.2	53.0	53.3	53.6	50.9
2003	51.8	53.1	53.1	52.7	52.6	46.9	45.2	45.4	51.1	52.4	52.6	52.7	50.8
2004	48.3	52.1	52.5	52.2	51.3	46.9	45.4	44.9	50.8	52.1	51.9	51.9	50.0
2005	48.5	52.1	52.0	51.8	51.8	46.6	46.0	46.8	51.5	52.7	52.9	52.3	50.4
2006	51.2	52.1	52.3	52.0	51.7	47.2	45.8	46.7	51.5	52.8	53.0	52.4	50.7
2007	51.0	52.3	52.4	52.3	50.6	47.6	46.3	46.9	51.7	52.9	53.0	52.3	50.8

Employment by Industry: Syracuse, NY, 2000–2007

(Numbers in thousands, not seasonally adjusted.)

Industry and year	January	February	March	April	May	June	July	August	September	October	November	December	Annual Average
Total Nonfarm													
2000	317.5	319.9	321.9	326.4	328.8	328.5	322.6	321.6	328.8	331.3	331.3	330.7	325.8
2001	318.1	321.8	322.3	325.9	329.8	329.3	321.3	319.3	322.5	326.1	326.0	324.7	323.9
2002	313.4	314.9	316.6	317.7	321.3	321.4	315.5	318.9	323.1	324.7	325.0	324.0	319.7
2003	312.6	314.8	315.9	317.1	320.9	320.3	314.0	316.5	320.1	322.7	323.1	322.2	318.4
2004	310.4	313.4	315.6	318.2	321.8	321.8	315.7	317.3	322.0	325.3	325.6	325.6	319.4
2005	312.4	315.4	315.5	320.4	323.7	324.1	319.7	320.7	324.1	325.3	325.9	325.9	321.1
2006	314.3	316.6	317.0	320.4	323.3	323.7	318.5	319.2	322.9	325.2	325.6	326.3	321.1
2007	316.1	316.7	318.1	320.5	325.2	327.2	322.8	323.6	326.0	328.7	329.3	328.8	323.6
Total Private													
2000	262.4	263.1	265.1	268.6	270.7	271.6	269.0	269.4	272.2	274.0	273.0	273.2	269.4
2001	262.9	264.3	265.2	268.2	271.7	271.7	267.2	266.2	267.4	268.3	267.8	267.1	267.3
2002	257.0	256.3	258.1	259.3	262.7	263.3	259.9	264.7	266.9	266.5	266.2	265.4	262.2
2003	256.7	256.7	257.7	258.9	262.5	262.0	259.4	262.3	264.0	264.6	264.6	263.7	261.1
2004	254.2	255.7	257.6	260.4	263.7	264.3	261.4	263.8	266.5	267.5	267.2	267.3	262.5
2005	255.9	257.3	257.5	262.0	265.4	265.9	264.7	266.4	267.6	267.4	267.7	267.6	263.8
2006	257.8	258.9	259.4	262.2	264.6	265.2	263.4	264.9	266.4	266.8	267.2	267.7	263.7
2007	259.0	258.2	259.8	261.9	266.3	268.2	266.8	268.3	269.2	269.7	270.0	269.3	265.6
Goods-Producing													
2000	55.2	54.8	55.2	56.8	58.1	59.2	58.8	59.2	58.5	58.3	57.3	56.5	57.3
2001	52.6	53.1	53.2	53.7	54.8	55.7	54.7	54.2	53.6	53.2	52.4	51.4	53.6
2002	49.4	49.1	49.4	49.6	50.5	51.3	49.2	51.4	50.8	50.0	49.4	48.4	49.9
2003	46.9	46.3	46.5	47.1	48.1	48.8	47.4	49.0	48.2	47.7	47.0	46.0	47.4
2004	44.1	43.7	44.0	44.9	46.2	47.0	45.1	48.1	47.6	47.4	46.9	46.1	45.9
2005	44.1	43.3	43.3	44.4	45.9	47.0	47.1	47.4	46.7	46.5	46.3	45.5	45.6
2006	43.9	43.4	43.5	44.9	46.1	47.3	47.2	47.6	46.6	46.5	46.3	45.6	45.7
2007	44.4	43.1	43.4	44.3	46.2	47.4	47.6	47.6	46.9	46.7	46.4	45.4	45.8
Natural Resources, Mining, and Construction													
2000	10.6	10.4	10.8	12.1	13.2	14.1	14.5	14.7	14.3	14.0	13.4	12.4	12.9
2001	11.3	10.9	10.9	11.9	13.4	14.1	14.7	14.7	14.4	13.8	13.4	12.4	13.0
2002	10.8	10.6	10.8	11.4	12.6	13.4	14.0	14.1	13.6	13.5	13.1	12.1	12.5
2003	10.8	10.5	10.6	11.7	12.8	13.4	14.1	14.2	13.6	13.4	13.1	12.1	12.5
2004	10.3	10.1	10.4	11.4	12.7	13.3	14.0	14.1	13.7	13.6	13.1	12.3	12.4
2005	10.8	10.3	10.3	11.5	12.6	13.3	13.7	13.9	13.6	13.4	13.2	12.2	12.4
2006	11.0	10.6	10.6	12.0	13.0	13.8	14.2	14.4	13.8	13.9	13.6	12.7	12.8
2007	11.7	10.7	10.9	11.9	13.5	14.2	14.6	14.7	14.3	14.1	13.9	13.0	13.1
Manufacturing													
2000	44.6	44.4	44.4	44.7	44.9	45.1	44.3	44.5	44.2	44.3	43.9	44.1	44.5
2001	41.3	42.2	42.3	41.8	41.4	41.6	40.0	39.5	39.2	39.4	39.0	39.0	40.6
2002	38.6	38.5	38.6	38.2	37.9	37.9	35.2	37.3	37.2	36.5	36.3	36.3	37.4
2003	36.1	35.8	35.9	35.4	35.3	35.4	33.3	34.8	34.6	34.3	33.9	33.9	34.9
2004	33.8	33.6	33.6	33.5	33.5	33.7	31.1	34.0	33.9	33.8	33.8	33.8	33.5
2005	33.3	33.0	33.0	32.9	33.3	33.7	33.4	33.5	33.1	33.1	33.1	33.3	33.2
2006	32.9	32.8	32.9	32.9	33.1	33.5	33.0	33.2	32.8	32.6	32.7	32.9	32.9
2007	32.7	32.4	32.5	32.4	32.7	33.2	33.0	32.9	32.6	32.6	32.5	32.4	32.7
Service-Providing													
2000	262.3	265.1	266.7	269.6	270.7	269.3	263.8	262.4	270.3	273.0	274.0	274.2	268.5
2001	265.5	268.7	269.1	272.2	275.0	273.6	266.6	265.1	268.9	272.9	273.6	273.3	270.4
2002	264.0	265.8	267.2	268.1	270.8	270.1	266.3	267.5	272.3	274.7	275.6	275.6	269.8
2003	265.7	268.5	269.4	270.0	272.8	271.5	266.6	267.5	271.9	275.0	276.1	276.2	270.9
2004	266.3	269.7	271.6	273.3	275.6	274.8	270.6	269.2	274.4	277.9	278.7	279.5	273.5
2005	268.3	272.1	272.2	276.0	277.8	277.1	272.6	273.3	277.4	278.8	279.6	280.4	275.5
2006	270.4	273.2	273.5	275.5	277.2	276.4	271.3	271.6	276.3	278.7	279.3	280.7	275.3
2007	271.7	273.6	274.7	276.2	279.0	279.8	275.2	276.0	279.1	282.0	282.9	283.4	277.8
Trade, Transportation, and Utilities													
2000	67.6	66.7	67.1	67.1	68.1	68.9	68.2	68.8	68.2	68.9	69.8	70.6	68.3
2001	69.0	67.3	67.7	68.4	68.9	69.9	67.9	67.9	67.4	67.5	68.4	69.1	68.3
2002	67.0	65.1	65.5	65.7	66.9	68.2	66.9	68.0	67.8	68.1	68.7	69.5	67.3
2003	65.9	64.4	64.4	64.6	65.3	66.6	66.0	66.2	65.7	66.0	66.9	67.7	65.8
2004	65.2	64.0	64.5	64.4	65.6	66.6	66.2	66.1	65.9	66.9	67.8	68.8	66.0
2005	65.7	64.4	64.4	65.2	65.8	67.2	66.6	66.8	66.2	66.6	67.5	68.4	66.2
2006	65.6	63.9	64.2	64.1	65.0	66.1	65.3	65.4	64.7	65.1	66.0	66.8	65.2
2007	64.7	62.8	63.2	63.0	64.4	65.8	65.9	66.1	64.9	65.6	66.2	66.9	65.0
Wholesale Trade													
2000	15.4	15.4	15.6	15.5	15.7	15.7	16.0	16.0	15.9	15.9	16.0	16.1	15.8
2001	16.8	16.8	16.7	16.8	16.8	16.9	16.7	16.6	16.4	16.3	16.2	16.2	16.6
2002	15.9	15.6	15.6	15.8	16.0	16.3	16.0	16.3	16.2	16.2	16.3	16.4	16.1
2003	15.7	15.5	15.5	15.6	15.7	15.9	15.7	15.6	15.4	15.5	15.6	15.6	15.6
2004	15.6	15.5	15.5	15.5	15.7	15.9	15.9	15.9	15.7	15.8	15.8	15.7	15.7
2005	15.2	15.2	15.2	15.5	15.6	15.9	15.9	15.9	15.7	15.7	15.8	15.8	15.6
2006	15.7	15.6	15.7	15.8	15.9	16.1	16.0	16.0	15.9	15.8	15.7	15.8	15.8
2007	15.5	15.4	15.4	15.5	15.6	15.9	15.9	15.9	15.7	15.8	15.8	15.8	15.7
Retail Trade													
2000	37.9	36.9	37.0	37.2	38.0	38.7	38.0	38.4	37.7	38.4	39.3	40.0	38.1
2001	37.3	35.8	36.1	36.2	36.6	37.4	36.2	36.5	35.8	36.1	37.2	38.0	36.6
2002	36.3	34.9	35.1	35.1	35.8	36.6	36.1	36.9	36.4	36.8	37.2	38.1	36.3
2003	35.9	34.7	34.8	35.0	35.5	36.3	36.3	36.5	35.8	35.9	36.8	37.6	35.9
2004	35.5	34.5	34.9	34.7	35.6	36.4	36.2	36.3	36.1	36.7	37.7	38.8	36.1
2005	36.5	35.3	35.2	35.7	36.2	37.2	37.1	37.4	36.5	36.8	37.5	38.3	36.6
2006	36.2	34.7	34.8	34.7	35.4	36.2	36.1	36.2	35.1	35.7	36.7	37.3	35.8
2007	35.9	34.2	34.6	34.5	35.4	36.2	36.4	36.5	35.8	36.3	37.0	37.6	35.9

Employment by Industry: Syracuse, NY, 2000–2007—*Continued*

(Numbers in thousands, not seasonally adjusted.)

Industry and year	January	February	March	April	May	June	July	August	September	October	November	December	Annual Average
Transportation and Utilities													
2000	14.3	14.4	14.5	14.4	14.4	14.5	14.2	14.4	14.6	14.6	14.5	14.5	14.4
2001	14.9	14.7	14.9	15.4	15.5	15.6	15.0	14.8	15.2	15.1	15.0	14.9	15.1
2002	14.8	14.6	14.8	14.8	15.1	15.3	14.8	14.8	15.2	15.1	15.2	15.0	15.0
2003	14.3	14.2	14.1	14.0	14.1	14.4	14.0	14.1	14.5	14.6	14.5	14.5	14.3
2004	14.1	14.0	14.1	14.2	14.3	14.3	14.1	13.9	14.1	14.4	14.3	14.3	14.2
2005	14.0	13.9	14.0	14.0	14.0	14.1	13.6	13.5	14.0	14.1	14.2	14.3	14.0
2006	13.7	13.6	13.7	13.6	13.7	13.8	13.2	13.2	13.7	13.6	13.6	13.7	13.6
2007	13.3	13.2	13.2	13.0	13.4	13.7	13.6	13.7	13.4	13.5	13.4	13.5	13.4
Information													
2000	7.3	7.3	7.5	7.6	7.6	7.7	7.9	7.2	8.0	8.0	8.1	8.2	7.7
2001	8.3	8.4	8.3	8.3	8.2	8.4	8.4	8.1	8.0	7.9	7.9	7.8	8.2
2002	7.0	7.0	7.0	7.1	7.1	7.2	7.2	7.2	7.1	7.1	7.1	7.2	7.1
2003	7.0	6.9	6.8	6.9	7.0	7.0	7.1	7.2	7.1	7.2	7.3	7.3	7.0
2004	7.2	7.1	7.1	7.0	7.0	7.1	7.0	6.9	6.9	6.9	6.9	6.9	7.0
2005	6.7	6.7	6.7	6.4	6.5	6.6	6.3	6.3	6.1	6.2	6.2	6.2	6.4
2006	6.0	6.1	6.0	5.9	6.0	6.0	5.9	6.0	5.8	5.8	5.8	5.8	5.9
2007	5.8	5.8	5.8	5.7	5.7	5.8	5.9	5.9	5.8	5.8	5.9	5.8	5.8
Financial Activities													
2000	17.8	17.6	17.8	17.7	17.8	17.9	17.9	17.9	17.7	17.4	17.4	17.6	17.7
2001	17.6	17.6	17.6	17.6	17.8	18.1	17.8	17.9	17.5	17.7	17.6	17.7	17.7
2002	17.3	17.2	17.3	17.4	17.3	17.5	17.8	17.9	17.5	17.3	17.2	17.2	17.4
2003	17.3	17.2	17.3	17.1	17.3	17.6	17.8	17.9	17.6	17.4	17.4	17.4	17.4
2004	16.8	16.7	16.9	16.9	17.2	17.5	17.7	17.6	17.4	17.2	17.2	17.4	17.2
2005	17.1	17.1	17.2	17.3	17.4	17.7	18.1	18.0	17.8	17.8	18.0	18.0	17.6
2006	18.2	18.1	18.2	18.0	18.1	18.3	18.2	18.2	17.9	18.1	18.1	18.2	18.1
2007	18.0	17.9	17.9	18.1	18.1	18.4	18.5	18.5	18.1	18.1	18.1	18.1	18.2
Professional and Business Services													
2000	29.5	29.6	29.8	29.9	30.2	30.6	30.1	30.5	30.0	31.0	30.9	30.4	30.2
2001	29.5	29.6	29.5	30.1	30.5	30.8	30.6	30.2	29.7	30.2	29.8	29.8	30.0
2002	28.6	28.5	28.7	29.3	29.7	30.6	31.1	31.4	30.9	30.8	31.0	30.6	30.1
2003	31.4	31.3	31.5	32.4	32.8	33.2	33.6	34.2	33.6	33.6	33.8	33.4	32.9
2004	32.2	32.4	32.5	33.4	33.9	34.3	34.6	34.5	34.2	33.8	33.8	33.6	33.6
2005	32.3	32.8	32.8	34.2	34.4	35.1	35.2	35.5	35.1	34.7	34.4	34.5	34.3
2006	33.2	33.3	33.1	33.7	33.8	34.4	34.7	35.3	34.6	34.6	34.5	34.8	34.2
2007	33.7	33.7	34.0	34.5	35.2	36.1	36.0	36.4	35.9	35.7	35.7	35.8	35.2
Education and Health Services													
2000	48.9	50.3	50.7	51.1	49.4	47.7	46.8	46.5	50.0	51.1	51.0	51.3	49.6
2001	50.0	51.4	51.8	52.1	51.8	48.8	48.4	48.3	51.6	52.8	53.2	53.2	51.1
2002	51.6	53.0	53.3	52.4	52.1	49.0	48.2	49.0	52.7	54.0	54.3	54.4	52.0
2003	51.7	53.7	53.8	53.2	52.5	49.2	47.7	48.1	52.3	53.5	54.0	53.7	51.9
2004	52.3	54.7	55.1	55.4	53.6	51.5	50.1	50.3	54.4	55.7	56.0	56.0	53.8
2005	53.4	55.3	55.4	55.5	55.2	51.8	51.5	52.6	55.5	56.1	56.5	56.5	54.6
2006	54.4	56.6	56.9	57.2	55.3	52.8	52.0	52.2	56.7	57.6	58.0	58.2	55.7
2007	55.8	57.7	58.0	57.8	56.0	53.7	52.7	53.4	57.8	58.8	59.2	59.0	56.7
Leisure and Hospitality													
2000	23.1	23.6	23.7	24.9	26.1	26.4	26.0	26.2	26.5	25.7	25.1	25.1	25.2
2001	23.1	23.9	24.1	25.3	27.1	27.3	26.7	27.1	27.0	26.0	25.5	25.1	25.7
2002	23.4	23.6	24.1	25.1	26.4	26.6	26.7	26.9	27.2	26.2	25.4	25.0	25.6
2003	23.5	23.9	24.3	24.7	26.5	26.7	27.1	27.1	26.9	26.4	25.4	25.5	25.6
2004	23.9	24.5	24.9	25.7	27.3	27.5	28.1	27.8	27.6	26.8	25.9	25.8	26.3
2005	24.3	25.2	25.2	26.4	27.5	27.9	27.5	27.5	27.8	27.0	26.2	26.1	26.6
2006	24.1	25.0	24.9	25.8	27.5	27.6	27.6	27.7	27.6	26.6	26.0	25.8	26.4
2007	24.1	24.8	25.0	25.8	27.9	28.3	27.7	27.9	27.3	26.4	25.9	25.7	26.4
Other Services													
2000	13.0	13.2	13.3	13.5	13.4	13.2	13.3	13.1	13.3	13.6	13.4	13.5	13.3
2001	12.8	13.0	13.0	12.7	12.6	12.7	12.7	12.5	12.6	13.0	13.0	13.0	12.8
2002	12.7	12.8	12.8	12.7	12.7	12.9	12.8	12.9	12.9	13.0	13.1	13.1	12.9
2003	13.0	13.0	13.1	12.9	13.0	12.9	12.7	12.6	12.6	12.8	12.8	12.7	12.8
2004	12.5	12.6	12.6	12.7	12.9	12.8	12.6	12.5	12.5	12.8	12.7	12.7	12.7
2005	12.3	12.5	12.5	12.6	12.7	12.6	12.4	12.3	12.4	12.5	12.6	12.4	12.5
2006	12.4	12.5	12.6	12.6	12.8	12.7	12.5	12.5	12.5	12.5	12.5	12.5	12.6
2007	12.5	12.4	12.5	12.7	12.8	12.7	12.5	12.5	12.5	12.6	12.6	12.6	12.6
Government													
2000	55.1	56.8	56.8	57.8	58.1	56.9	53.6	52.2	56.6	57.3	58.3	57.5	56.4
2001	55.2	57.5	57.1	57.7	58.1	57.6	54.1	53.1	55.1	57.8	58.2	57.6	56.6
2002	56.4	58.6	58.5	58.4	58.6	58.1	55.6	54.2	56.2	58.2	58.8	58.6	57.5
2003	55.9	58.1	58.2	58.2	58.4	58.3	54.6	54.2	56.1	58.1	58.5	58.5	57.2
2004	56.2	57.7	58.0	57.8	58.1	57.5	54.3	53.5	55.5	57.8	58.4	58.3	56.9
2005	56.5	58.1	58.0	58.4	58.3	58.2	55.0	54.3	56.5	57.9	58.2	58.3	57.3
2006	56.5	57.7	57.6	58.2	58.7	58.5	55.1	54.3	56.5	58.4	58.4	58.6	57.4
2007	57.1	58.5	58.3	58.6	58.9	59.0	56.0	55.3	56.8	59.0	59.3	59.5	58.0

Employment by Industry: Columbia, SC, 2000–2007

(Numbers in thousands, not seasonally adjusted.)

Industry and year	January	February	March	April	May	June	July	August	September	October	November	December	Annual Average
Total Nonfarm													
2000	335.3	337.1	341.3	342.4	344.3	345.2	336.2	340.1	343.2	345.8	346.9	348.1	342.2
2001	337.2	338.8	341.0	340.1	341.6	341.7	333.8	338.0	338.9	338.6	340.3	340.7	339.2
2002	331.1	332.7	335.3	337.1	338.8	338.4	333.1	338.1	339.5	342.1	342.4	343.8	337.7
2003	334.9	336.1	337.0	337.2	339.1	337.7	331.3	337.4	338.9	341.9	342.5	344.5	338.2
2004	337.7	338.3	341.2	344.5	345.9	346.2	342.6	345.8	347.9	350.3	350.3	352.3	345.3
2005	347.8	350.5	350.7	351.9	351.8	348.9	349.1	353.9	353.6	355.9	358.6	359.2	352.7
2006	354.9	357.0	358.5	360.0	361.8	358.0	354.2	358.8	360.6	361.5	364.0	366.4	359.6
2007	359.4	361.8	363.7	365.8	368.4	368.9	365.3	368.4	370.0	371.7	373.1	373.5	367.5
Total Private													
2000	259.9	260.5	263.8	265.3	266.8	269.4	264.6	264.4	265.6	267.6	268.6	269.6	265.5
2001	259.8	260.6	262.3	262.0	263.6	265.6	262.1	262.4	261.8	261.8	263.0	263.0	262.3
2002	254.4	255.6	257.9	260.3	261.8	263.7	262.6	263.3	262.8	265.2	265.0	266.2	261.6
2003	257.7	258.3	259.0	260.0	262.0	262.8	261.3	263.4	262.8	265.6	265.7	267.4	262.2
2004	260.7	261.6	264.0	267.4	268.7	270.9	270.0	271.0	271.2	273.8	273.6	275.3	269.0
2005	271.8	273.9	273.8	274.6	274.7	274.0	276.7	278.2	276.3	278.3	280.6	281.3	276.2
2006	277.6	279.0	280.0	282.3	284.2	282.6	281.4	283.6	283.8	284.6	286.5	288.8	282.9
2007	282.4	283.9	285.5	287.9	290.2	291.9	291.0	291.5	291.5	292.5	293.3	293.4	289.6
Goods-Producing													
2000	56.4	56.4	56.9	57.2	57.4	58.0	57.8	57.6	57.6	57.5	57.2	57.4	57.3
2001	56.1	56.3	56.4	56.0	56.3	56.3	55.7	55.3	55.3	54.6	54.7	54.1	55.6
2002	53.3	53.3	53.3	53.7	54.5	54.5	54.4	54.7	54.2	54.0	53.5	53.4	53.9
2003	53.0	52.7	53.1	52.7	53.1	53.1	52.9	52.9	52.4	52.5	52.1	51.9	52.7
2004	50.9	50.9	51.2	51.8	51.8	52.2	52.2	52.3	52.4	52.3	52.2	52.4	51.9
2005	52.0	52.1	52.0	52.2	52.8	52.1	52.1	52.1	51.6	51.7	51.9	51.6	52.0
2006	51.6	51.9	52.1	53.2	53.6	53.8	53.3	53.4	53.1	52.8	52.9	52.5	52.9
2007	52.0	52.3	52.5	52.8	53.2	53.6	53.8	53.6	53.3	53.1	53.2	53.3	53.1
Natural Resources, Mining, and Construction													
2000	19.2	19.1	19.5	19.7	19.9	20.3	20.4	20.4	20.3	20.1	19.9	20.1	19.9
2001	19.6	19.6	19.9	19.9	20.3	20.5	20.1	20.1	20.2	19.7	19.7	19.2	19.9
2002	18.8	18.9	19.1	19.5	19.8	20.0	19.8	19.9	19.7	19.6	19.7	19.7	19.5
2003	20.0	20.0	20.2	19.7	20.1	20.3	20.5	20.6	20.6	20.8	20.5	20.5	20.3
2004	20.1	20.1	20.3	20.6	20.8	21.0	20.7	20.7	20.9	20.8	20.7	20.7	20.6
2005	20.2	20.2	20.0	20.6	21.1	20.5	20.7	20.7	20.4	20.6	20.8	20.6	20.5
2006	20.7	20.9	21.1	22.1	22.4	22.4	22.4	22.5	22.3	22.1	22.2	21.7	21.9
2007	21.0	21.2	21.4	21.6	21.9	22.0	22.1	22.1	21.9	21.8	21.9	21.9	21.7
Manufacturing													
2000	37.2	37.3	37.4	37.5	37.5	37.7	37.4	37.2	37.3	37.4	37.3	37.3	37.4
2001	36.5	36.7	36.5	36.1	36.0	35.8	35.6	35.2	35.1	34.9	35.0	34.9	35.7
2002	34.5	34.4	34.2	34.2	34.7	34.5	34.6	34.8	34.5	34.4	33.8	33.7	34.4
2003	33.0	32.7	32.9	33.0	33.0	32.8	32.4	32.3	31.8	31.7	31.6	31.4	32.4
2004	30.8	30.8	30.9	31.2	31.0	31.2	31.5	31.6	31.5	31.5	31.5	31.7	31.3
2005	31.8	31.9	32.0	31.6	31.7	31.6	31.4	31.4	31.2	31.1	31.1	31.0	31.5
2006	30.9	31.0	31.0	31.1	31.2	31.4	30.9	30.9	30.8	30.7	30.7	30.8	31.0
2007	31.0	31.1	31.1	31.2	31.3	31.6	31.7	31.5	31.4	31.3	31.3	31.4	31.3
Service-Providing													
2000	278.9	280.7	284.4	285.2	286.9	287.2	278.4	282.5	285.6	288.3	289.7	290.7	284.9
2001	281.1	282.5	284.6	284.1	285.3	285.4	278.1	282.7	283.6	284.0	285.6	286.6	283.6
2002	277.8	279.4	282.0	283.4	284.3	283.9	278.7	283.4	285.3	288.1	288.9	290.4	283.8
2003	281.9	283.4	283.9	284.5	286.0	284.6	278.4	284.5	286.5	289.4	290.4	292.6	285.5
2004	286.8	287.4	290.0	292.7	294.1	294.0	290.4	293.5	295.5	298.0	298.1	299.9	293.4
2005	295.8	298.4	298.7	299.7	299.0	296.8	297.0	301.8	302.0	304.2	306.7	307.6	300.6
2006	303.3	305.1	306.4	306.8	308.2	304.2	300.9	305.4	307.5	308.7	311.1	313.9	306.8
2007	307.4	309.5	311.2	313.0	315.2	315.3	311.5	314.8	316.7	318.6	319.9	320.2	314.4
Trade, Transportation, and Utilities													
2000	65.7	65.5	66.2	66.5	66.8	67.2	65.6	66.1	66.1	67.3	68.5	69.2	66.7
2001	65.7	64.9	65.2	64.7	65.2	65.7	64.1	63.8	63.6	63.8	64.7	65.6	64.8
2002	61.6	61.8	62.3	63.1	63.5	64.1	63.5	63.3	63.4	63.7	65.1	66.1	63.5
2003	60.9	61.4	61.8	62.2	62.6	63.4	62.3	62.7	63.1	63.9	65.1	66.2	63.0
2004	63.3	62.9	63.3	63.3	64.0	63.9	64.6	64.8	64.4	65.0	66.0	67.3	64.4
2005	65.2	65.0	65.3	65.7	65.6	65.2	65.9	66.0	65.5	66.6	68.0	68.9	66.1
2006	66.6	66.6	67.2	66.9	67.3	66.9	66.6	67.0	67.4	68.0	69.6	71.0	67.6
2007	68.6	68.7	68.9	69.0	69.7	69.9	69.2	69.6	69.5	69.9	70.7	71.6	69.6
Wholesale Trade													
2000	14.7	14.8	14.9	15.0	15.1	15.1	14.9	15.0	15.0	15.0	15.0	15.0	15.0
2001	15.1	15.0	15.1	15.0	15.1	15.2	14.9	14.8	14.8	14.7	14.5	14.7	14.9
2002	14.3	14.7	14.8	15.0	15.0	15.1	14.9	14.8	14.7	14.5	14.5	14.5	14.7
2003	13.5	13.5	13.5	13.8	13.9	14.1	13.8	13.9	14.0	14.0	14.1	14.2	13.9
2004	14.3	14.3	14.4	14.4	14.6	14.6	14.9	15.0	14.8	14.8	14.9	15.0	14.7
2005	15.8	15.7	15.8	15.7	15.8	15.7	16.0	16.0	15.9	16.0	16.0	16.1	15.9
2006	16.3	16.4	16.6	16.7	16.7	16.6	16.7	16.7	16.9	16.8	16.8	16.9	16.7
2007	17.2	17.7	17.5	17.1	16.9	17.0	17.1	17.1	17.1	17.1	17.1	17.2	17.2
Retail Trade													
2000	39.3	39.0	39.5	39.6	39.8	40.0	38.9	39.2	39.3	40.3	41.5	42.2	39.9
2001	39.1	38.4	38.6	38.4	38.8	39.1	38.0	38.0	37.9	38.0	39.1	39.8	38.6
2002	37.2	36.9	37.2	37.7	38.1	38.4	37.8	37.8	38.0	38.3	39.7	40.7	38.2
2003	37.3	37.8	38.1	38.1	38.3	38.8	38.1	38.3	38.5	39.0	40.1	40.9	38.6
2004	38.3	37.8	38.1	38.2	38.5	38.2	38.4	38.4	38.2	38.9	39.6	40.6	38.6
2005	38.2	38.1	38.1	38.7	38.4	38.1	38.4	38.4	38.0	38.8	40.0	40.6	38.7
2006	38.7	38.5	38.8	38.5	38.8	38.5	38.2	38.4	38.5	39.5	40.8	41.7	39.1
2007	39.7	39.3	39.7	40.0	40.7	40.6	39.8	40.1	40.0	40.3	40.9	41.6	40.2

Employment by Industry: Columbia, SC, 2000–2007—*Continued*

(Numbers in thousands, not seasonally adjusted.)

Industry and year	January	February	March	April	May	June	July	August	September	October	November	December	Annual Average
Transportation and Utilities													
2000	11.7	11.7	11.8	11.9	11.9	12.1	11.8	11.9	11.8	12.0	12.0	12.0	11.9
2001	11.5	11.5	11.5	11.3	11.3	11.4	11.2	11.0	10.9	11.1	11.1	11.1	11.2
2002	10.1	10.2	10.3	10.4	10.4	10.6	10.8	10.7	10.7	10.9	10.9	10.9	10.6
2003	10.1	10.1	10.2	10.3	10.4	10.5	10.4	10.5	10.6	10.9	10.9	11.1	10.5
2004	10.7	10.8	10.8	10.7	10.9	11.1	11.3	11.4	11.4	11.3	11.5	11.7	11.1
2005	11.2	11.2	11.4	11.3	11.4	11.4	11.5	11.6	11.6	11.8	12.0	12.2	11.6
2006	11.6	11.7	11.8	11.7	11.8	11.8	11.7	11.9	12.0	11.7	12.0	12.4	11.8
2007	11.7	11.7	11.7	11.9	12.1	12.3	12.3	12.4	12.4	12.5	12.7	12.8	12.2
Information													
2000	7.6	7.6	7.6	7.6	7.5	7.7	7.4	7.4	7.4	7.2	7.2	7.2	7.5
2001	6.9	6.7	6.7	6.6	6.6	6.7	6.3	6.3	6.2	6.3	6.3	6.4	6.5
2002	6.4	6.3	6.4	6.3	6.4	6.5	6.4	6.5	6.3	6.5	6.6	6.6	6.4
2003	6.2	6.1	6.2	6.1	6.3	6.2	6.4	6.3	6.3	6.2	6.2	6.3	6.2
2004	6.1	6.1	6.1	6.0	6.0	6.0	6.1	6.0	6.0	6.0	5.9	6.0	6.0
2005	6.0	6.1	6.0	6.1	6.1	6.2	6.2	6.1	6.0	6.1	6.1	6.1	6.1
2006	6.2	6.2	6.2	6.2	6.2	6.2	6.2	6.1	6.1	6.1	6.3	6.4	6.2
2007	6.1	6.1	6.1	6.2	6.3	6.3	6.3	6.3	6.3	6.3	6.2	6.2	6.2
Financial Activities													
2000	23.6	23.8	23.9	23.6	23.9	24.2	24.4	24.5	24.4	25.0	25.2	25.3	24.3
2001	24.6	24.6	24.6	25.2	25.3	25.9	25.6	25.6	25.5	25.7	26.2	25.9	25.4
2002	25.4	25.6	25.7	25.2	25.3	25.5	25.8	25.8	26.0	26.6	26.7	26.7	25.9
2003	26.3	26.0	26.6	26.2	26.5	26.6	26.2	26.6	26.3	26.5	26.6	26.7	26.4
2004	26.3	26.5	26.6	26.7	26.8	27.1	26.9	27.0	27.3	27.8	27.8	28.1	27.1
2005	28.5	28.9	28.7	28.5	28.9	29.0	29.2	29.2	29.2	29.1	29.3	29.7	29.0
2006	29.4	29.5	29.5	29.3	29.6	29.6	29.7	29.7	29.8	29.9	30.0	30.5	29.7
2007	30.4	30.4	30.3	30.4	30.4	30.6	30.7	30.8	30.9	30.9	31.2	31.3	30.7
Professional and Business Services													
2000	36.1	36.2	36.8	38.5	38.8	39.5	38.3	38.3	38.7	38.6	38.2	38.1	38.0
2001	36.3	37.0	37.4	37.8	37.9	37.9	37.7	38.1	37.8	36.6	36.3	36.2	37.3
2002	34.3	34.3	35.0	36.3	36.0	36.5	36.1	36.6	36.3	36.5	36.0	36.1	35.8
2003	35.0	35.2	33.6	35.6	35.6	35.7	35.6	36.1	35.8	36.8	36.8	36.9	35.7
2004	35.9	36.4	37.0	39.3	39.1	40.7	39.8	40.1	40.2	40.5	40.0	39.7	39.1
2005	39.2	39.9	39.2	39.7	39.0	40.2	40.6	41.8	42.0	42.2	42.9	43.0	40.8
2006	42.3	42.1	41.9	43.1	43.6	42.5	42.6	43.9	43.5	42.6	42.6	43.0	42.8
2007	42.1	42.4	42.6	42.6	42.6	42.9	43.0	43.0	43.2	43.2	42.9	42.6	42.8
Education and Health Services													
2000	31.9	31.9	32.2	32.4	32.4	32.5	32.1	32.0	32.4	32.6	32.9	33.1	32.4
2001	32.5	32.9	33.1	32.5	32.6	33.0	33.1	33.2	33.8	34.5	34.7	34.9	33.4
2002	34.8	35.1	35.4	35.6	35.7	35.7	36.1	36.2	36.5	36.4	36.7	37.1	35.9
2003	37.1	37.2	37.5	37.2	37.2	37.2	37.2	37.5	37.9	38.1	38.2	38.5	37.6
2004	37.7	37.9	38.2	38.2	38.2	38.0	38.0	38.1	38.3	38.3	38.6	38.6	38.2
2005	39.0	39.3	39.6	38.8	38.8	37.9	38.7	38.7	38.6	39.3	39.4	39.3	39.0
2006	39.2	39.9	39.8	39.5	39.5	39.3	39.3	39.4	39.7	41.0	41.0	41.1	39.9
2007	40.4	40.8	41.0	42.0	42.3	42.6	42.1	42.4	42.4	43.0	43.1	42.9	42.1
Leisure and Hospitality													
2000	26.7	27.1	27.9	27.4	27.6	27.7	27.0	26.8	27.0	27.4	27.4	27.6	27.3
2001	26.0	26.5	27.0	27.2	27.6	27.8	27.6	28.0	27.5	28.2	27.8	27.6	27.4
2002	26.5	27.1	27.5	27.5	27.8	28.1	28.0	27.9	27.8	28.8	27.8	27.6	27.7
2003	27.0	27.5	27.8	27.7	28.2	28.1	28.4	28.9	28.6	29.1	28.3	28.4	28.2
2004	28.2	28.5	29.1	29.4	29.9	29.9	29.3	29.5	29.4	30.5	29.7	29.7	29.4
2005	28.8	29.2	29.4	30.1	30.0	29.8	30.2	30.3	29.6	30.0	29.6	29.3	29.7
2006	28.8	29.2	29.8	30.4	30.5	30.4	30.2	30.4	30.3	30.7	30.5	30.7	30.2
2007	29.3	29.7	30.3	31.0	31.5	31.9	31.9	31.8	31.9	32.0	31.9	31.4	31.2
Other Services													
2000	11.9	12.0	12.3	12.1	12.4	12.6	12.0	11.7	12.0	12.0	12.0	11.7	12.1
2001	11.7	11.7	11.9	12.0	12.1	12.3	12.0	12.1	12.1	12.1	12.3	12.3	12.1
2002	12.1	12.1	12.3	12.6	12.6	12.8	12.3	12.3	12.3	12.7	12.6	12.6	12.4
2003	12.2	12.2	12.4	12.3	12.5	12.5	12.3	12.4	12.4	12.5	12.4	12.5	12.4
2004	12.3	12.4	12.5	12.7	12.9	13.1	13.1	13.2	13.2	13.4	13.4	13.5	13.0
2005	13.1	13.4	13.6	13.5	13.5	13.6	13.8	14.0	13.8	13.3	13.4	13.4	13.5
2006	13.5	13.6	13.5	13.7	13.9	13.9	13.5	13.7	13.9	13.5	13.6	13.6	13.7
2007	13.5	13.5	13.8	13.9	14.2	14.1	14.0	14.0	14.0	14.1	14.1	14.1	13.9
Government													
2000	75.4	76.6	77.5	77.1	77.5	75.8	71.6	75.7	77.6	78.2	78.3	78.5	76.7
2001	77.4	78.2	78.7	78.1	78.0	76.1	71.7	75.6	77.1	76.8	77.3	77.7	76.9
2002	76.7	77.1	77.4	76.8	77.0	74.7	70.5	74.8	76.7	76.9	77.4	77.6	76.1
2003	77.2	77.8	78.0	77.2	77.1	74.9	70.0	74.0	76.1	76.3	76.8	77.1	76.0
2004	77.0	76.7	77.2	77.1	77.2	75.3	72.6	74.8	76.7	76.5	76.7	77.0	76.2
2005	76.0	76.6	76.9	77.3	77.1	74.9	72.4	75.7	77.3	77.6	78.0	77.9	76.5
2006	77.3	78.0	78.5	77.7	77.6	75.4	72.8	75.2	76.8	76.9	77.5	77.6	76.8
2007	77.0	77.9	78.2	77.9	78.2	77.0	74.3	76.9	78.5	79.2	79.8	80.1	77.9

Employment by Industry: Greensboro-High Point, NC, 2000–2007

(Numbers in thousands, not seasonally adjusted.)

Industry and year	January	February	March	April	May	June	July	August	September	October	November	December	Annual Average
Total Nonfarm													
2000	358.6	360.3	364.0	365.2	366.7	368.3	362.0	366.8	368.0	369.4	371.2	371.7	366.0
2001	362.4	363.7	363.9	364.9	365.6	365.5	356.3	359.6	360.0	359.6	360.0	359.4	361.7
2002	350.4	351.6	353.6	358.7	359.8	360.4	354.5	359.1	360.8	362.8	364.2	363.7	358.3
2003	355.4	355.9	357.9	357.8	357.2	356.2	345.5	349.1	351.2	354.3	353.4	352.8	353.9
2004	346.6	347.7	351.1	357.1	358.8	358.9	351.8	355.8	358.5	360.5	361.0	362.3	355.8
2005	356.0	358.6	361.3	363.5	363.4	362.8	356.5	361.7	362.9	364.3	365.2	365.8	361.8
2006	361.0	362.5	365.7	369.4	372.2	369.3	363.7	369.2	369.6	373.3	375.1	376.5	369.0
2007	366.8	368.0	371.6	372.5	374.8	373.5	366.4	372.7	373.8	375.3	376.9	377.6	372.5
Total Private													
2000	320.4	321.9	324.9	326.0	327.5	329.1	328.3	329.5	329.4	329.6	330.4	330.6	327.3
2001	322.7	323.7	323.7	324.7	325.1	325.5	322.6	322.6	321.1	319.2	318.4	318.4	322.3
2002	310.1	311.0	312.5	317.1	318.3	320.0	320.0	321.5	320.5	321.2	321.6	321.6	318.0
2003	314.4	314.4	316.2	315.7	314.8	315.6	310.4	311.2	310.3	311.2	311.1	310.5	313.0
2004	305.3	306.2	309.1	314.7	316.3	317.8	316.6	317.4	317.3	317.9	318.6	319.5	314.7
2005	314.0	316.2	318.6	320.6	320.3	321.5	320.8	321.7	320.7	320.4	321.8	322.2	319.9
2006	318.3	319.4	322.0	325.3	327.9	327.5	327.2	328.5	326.7	329.2	330.5	331.5	326.2
2007	323.2	324.2	327.3	328.0	330.1	331.2	329.2	331.3	330.2	330.0	331.5	331.9	329.0
Goods-Producing													
2000	99.6	99.7	100.1	99.4	100.1	100.1	100.8	100.8	100.6	99.5	99.2	98.8	99.9
2001	97.1	96.4	96.0	95.6	95.1	95.1	93.8	93.4	92.8	91.7	91.0	90.4	94.0
2002	89.4	88.9	89.2	89.9	90.2	90.8	91.0	91.5	91.2	90.4	89.6	89.0	90.1
2003	88.8	88.6	88.4	87.5	87.4	87.4	85.1	85.2	85.0	84.3	84.1	84.3	86.3
2004	83.0	82.7	83.3	84.1	84.6	85.4	84.9	85.4	85.7	85.2	85.4	85.5	84.6
2005	85.3	85.4	85.5	86.0	86.1	86.4	85.6	85.4	84.9	84.1	84.0	84.1	85.2
2006	82.8	83.0	83.3	83.9	84.0	83.8	83.1	83.6	83.2	83.3	83.2	83.4	83.4
2007	82.4	82.1	82.5	82.7	82.7	83.0	82.3	82.5	82.0	81.4	81.7	81.7	82.3
Natural Resources, Mining, and Construction													
2000	18.8	18.7	19.0	18.7	18.9	19.0	19.2	19.6	19.8	19.7	19.5	19.3	19.2
2001	18.7	18.6	18.9	19.0	19.1	19.4	19.5	19.3	19.2	18.9	18.6	18.4	19.0
2002	17.4	17.4	17.6	17.7	17.7	17.9	18.1	18.1	17.9	17.5	17.3	17.1	17.6
2003	17.3	17.3	17.5	17.7	18.0	18.1	17.9	18.0	18.2	18.4	18.4	18.6	18.0
2004	17.8	17.5	17.9	18.3	18.5	18.9	18.8	19.0	19.0	18.9	18.9	18.9	18.5
2005	18.6	18.5	18.6	19.1	19.3	19.5	19.5	19.5	19.5	19.2	19.2	19.1	19.1
2006	18.6	18.6	18.9	19.2	19.3	19.5	19.6	19.7	19.6	19.5	19.5	19.5	19.3
2007	19.0	18.9	19.3	19.4	19.5	19.7	19.7	19.7	19.5	19.3	19.3	19.2	19.4
Manufacturing													
2000	80.8	81.0	81.1	80.7	81.2	81.1	81.6	81.2	80.8	79.8	79.7	79.5	80.7
2001	78.4	77.8	77.1	76.6	76.0	75.7	74.3	74.1	73.6	72.8	72.4	72.0	75.1
2002	72.0	71.5	71.6	72.2	72.5	72.9	72.9	73.4	73.3	72.9	72.3	71.9	72.5
2003	71.5	71.3	70.9	69.8	69.4	69.3	67.2	67.2	66.8	65.9	65.7	65.7	68.4
2004	65.2	65.2	65.4	65.8	66.1	66.5	66.1	66.4	66.7	66.3	66.5	66.6	66.1
2005	66.7	66.9	66.9	66.9	66.8	66.9	66.1	65.9	65.4	64.9	64.8	65.0	66.1
2006	64.2	64.4	64.4	64.7	64.7	64.3	63.5	63.9	63.6	63.8	63.7	63.9	64.1
2007	63.4	63.2	63.2	63.3	63.2	63.3	62.6	62.8	62.5	62.1	62.4	62.5	62.9
Service-Providing													
2000	259.0	260.6	263.9	265.8	266.6	268.2	261.2	266.0	267.4	269.9	272.0	272.9	266.1
2001	265.3	267.3	267.9	269.3	270.5	270.4	262.5	266.2	267.2	267.9	269.0	269.0	267.7
2002	261.0	262.7	264.4	268.8	269.6	269.6	263.5	267.6	269.6	272.4	274.6	274.7	268.2
2003	266.6	267.3	269.5	270.3	269.8	268.8	260.4	263.9	266.2	270.0	269.3	268.5	267.6
2004	263.6	265.0	267.8	273.0	274.2	273.5	266.9	270.4	272.8	275.3	275.6	276.8	271.2
2005	270.7	273.2	275.8	277.5	277.3	276.4	270.9	276.3	278.0	280.2	281.2	281.7	276.6
2006	278.2	279.5	282.4	285.5	288.2	285.5	280.6	285.6	286.4	290.0	291.9	293.1	285.6
2007	284.4	285.9	289.1	289.8	292.1	290.5	284.1	290.2	291.8	293.9	295.2	295.9	290.2
Trade, Transportation, and Utilities													
2000	79.0	79.1	79.7	80.3	80.4	80.6	80.0	80.3	80.2	81.1	82.0	82.7	80.5
2001	79.6	79.1	79.1	80.2	80.3	80.1	79.2	78.9	78.4	78.3	78.5	78.9	79.2
2002	74.9	74.3	74.5	75.0	75.1	75.1	74.2	74.4	73.9	74.3	75.7	76.4	74.8
2003	73.5	73.3	73.7	73.5	73.0	73.4	72.1	72.1	72.0	72.4	73.5	73.8	73.0
2004	71.8	71.2	71.8	72.0	72.3	72.3	72.5	72.6	72.3	72.9	74.3	75.4	72.6
2005	72.1	72.2	72.6	73.0	73.1	73.2	73.5	73.7	73.3	74.8	76.1	76.9	73.7
2006	75.4	75.0	75.1	75.8	76.2	75.4	75.6	75.7	75.7	76.3	78.1	78.9	76.1
2007	76.1	75.7	76.5	75.9	76.5	76.5	76.8	77.2	77.3	77.9	79.0	79.5	77.1
Wholesale Trade													
2000	19.0	19.2	19.3	19.6	19.7	19.7	19.8	19.8	19.8	19.8	19.7	19.8	19.6
2001	19.6	19.8	19.8	19.7	19.6	19.6	19.5	19.5	19.2	19.2	19.0	19.0	19.5
2002	18.8	19.0	18.9	19.2	19.1	19.2	19.3	19.3	19.3	19.3	19.4	19.4	19.2
2003	18.9	19.0	19.1	19.0	18.8	18.9	18.5	18.5	18.4	18.5	18.5	18.5	18.7
2004	18.6	18.5	18.6	18.9	18.8	18.8	18.5	18.5	18.3	18.3	18.3	18.3	18.5
2005	18.5	18.5	18.5	18.5	18.6	18.5	18.8	18.9	18.8	18.8	18.8	18.8	18.7
2006	18.9	19.1	19.1	19.4	19.6	19.5	19.5	19.6	19.7	19.8	19.9	20.0	19.5
2007	20.1	20.1	20.3	20.0	20.1	20.2	20.5	20.4	20.5	20.5	20.5	20.5	20.3
Retail Trade													
2000	39.4	39.3	39.8	39.7	39.8	39.9	38.9	39.1	39.1	39.3	40.3	41.0	39.6
2001	39.2	38.7	38.8	38.9	39.2	39.2	39.0	39.0	39.0	39.1	39.8	40.3	39.2
2002	38.2	37.7	38.0	38.1	38.3	38.3	37.7	37.9	37.5	37.6	38.8	39.5	38.1
2003	37.3	36.8	37.0	36.8	36.7	36.6	36.1	36.1	35.9	36.3	37.4	37.7	36.7
2004	35.9	35.5	35.8	36.2	36.6	36.5	36.4	36.6	36.5	37.0	38.3	39.2	36.7
2005	36.6	36.7	37.0	37.3	37.2	37.3	37.4	37.3	36.9	38.4	39.5	40.4	37.7
2006	39.4	38.9	38.9	39.2	39.4	38.8	38.9	39.1	38.9	39.5	41.2	41.8	39.5
2007	39.6	39.3	39.7	39.5	40.0	39.9	39.9	40.1	40.0	40.6	41.7	42.1	40.2

Employment by Industry: Greensboro-High Point, NC, 2000–2007—*Continued*

(Numbers in thousands, not seasonally adjusted.)

Industry and year	January	February	March	April	May	June	July	August	September	October	November	December	Annual Average
Transportation and Utilities													
2000	20.6	20.6	20.6	21.0	20.9	21.0	21.3	21.4	21.3	22.0	22.0	21.9	21.2
2001	20.8	20.6	20.5	21.6	21.5	21.3	20.7	20.4	20.2	20.0	19.7	19.6	20.6
2002	17.9	17.6	17.6	17.7	17.7	17.6	17.2	17.2	17.1	17.4	17.5	17.5	17.5
2003	17.3	17.5	17.6	17.7	17.5	17.9	17.5	17.5	17.7	17.6	17.6	17.6	17.6
2004	17.3	17.2	17.4	16.9	16.9	17.0	17.6	17.5	17.5	17.6	17.7	17.9	17.4
2005	17.0	17.0	17.1	17.2	17.3	17.4	17.3	17.5	17.6	17.6	17.8	17.7	17.4
2006	17.1	17.0	17.1	17.2	17.2	17.1	17.2	17.0	17.1	17.0	17.0	17.1	17.1
2007	16.4	16.3	16.5	16.4	16.4	16.4	16.4	16.7	16.8	16.8	16.8	16.9	16.6
Information													
2000	7.6	7.6	7.6	7.8	7.9	8.0	8.3	8.3	8.3	8.3	8.3	8.3	8.0
2001	8.4	8.3	8.4	8.3	8.4	8.5	8.6	8.4	8.4	8.0	8.0	8.1	8.3
2002	7.8	7.7	7.6	7.7	7.9	7.8	7.8	7.7	7.6	7.6	7.7	7.7	7.7
2003	7.5	7.4	7.4	7.4	7.6	7.5	7.5	7.6	7.5	7.4	7.5	7.5	7.5
2004	7.1	6.9	6.9	6.8	6.8	6.7	6.7	6.6	6.5	6.5	6.5	6.5	6.7
2005	6.5	6.4	6.5	6.6	6.6	6.6	6.6	6.6	6.6	6.5	6.5	6.6	6.6
2006	6.6	6.5	6.5	6.3	6.4	6.3	6.3	6.3	6.3	6.4	6.4	6.5	6.4
2007	6.3	6.3	6.2	6.3	6.3	6.3	6.3	6.3	6.3	6.2	6.3	6.3	6.3
Financial Activities													
2000	20.6	20.7	20.9	20.9	20.9	21.1	21.0	20.9	20.9	21.0	20.9	21.1	20.9
2001	20.8	20.8	20.9	20.9	20.9	21.1	21.3	21.5	21.4	21.3	21.3	21.4	21.1
2002	21.0	21.0	20.9	21.0	20.9	21.0	21.2	21.2	21.1	21.4	21.1	21.2	21.1
2003	21.6	21.6	21.8	21.4	21.1	20.9	20.7	20.5	20.3	20.1	19.8	19.7	20.8
2004	19.8	19.9	19.9	20.9	20.7	20.8	21.2	21.1	21.1	21.2	21.2	21.3	20.8
2005	21.1	21.2	21.3	21.4	21.4	21.5	21.7	21.7	21.7	21.4	21.5	21.5	21.5
2006	21.5	21.6	21.8	21.8	22.0	22.1	22.3	22.4	22.4	22.5	22.5	22.6	22.1
2007	22.3	22.5	22.5	22.5	22.5	22.7	22.5	22.5	22.6	22.5	22.6	22.7	22.5
Professional and Business Services													
2000	43.5	44.4	45.2	45.4	45.2	45.3	44.4	44.9	45.0	44.9	44.8	44.5	44.8
2001	42.8	43.1	43.2	42.5	42.4	42.3	41.1	41.6	41.8	41.1	40.6	39.9	41.9
2002	38.2	39.2	39.4	40.1	40.3	40.2	40.0	40.8	41.0	41.0	41.1	41.0	40.2
2003	38.9	39.3	40.2	40.4	40.3	40.4	39.8	40.4	40.8	41.9	41.5	40.7	40.4
2004	40.3	41.0	41.6	42.9	43.2	43.1	43.1	43.4	43.8	44.0	43.6	43.5	42.8
2005	43.7	44.8	45.2	44.9	44.0	44.1	44.2	44.6	45.0	44.3	44.4	44.2	44.5
2006	43.2	43.5	44.6	46.4	47.2	46.9	47.1	47.5	46.8	48.0	47.7	47.3	46.4
2007	44.3	45.2	46.0	46.3	46.5	46.5	45.6	46.8	47.0	46.9	47.1	47.1	46.3
Education and Health Services													
2000	36.1	36.2	36.4	36.0	36.2	36.5	36.7	37.1	37.3	37.6	38.1	37.9	36.8
2001	37.5	38.1	38.1	38.4	38.4	38.6	38.4	38.6	38.8	39.8	40.1	40.5	38.8
2002	39.8	40.2	40.5	40.7	40.7	40.9	40.8	40.9	41.1	41.8	41.9	41.8	40.9
2003	41.2	41.6	41.7	41.5	41.4	41.3	41.1	41.3	41.5	42.0	41.9	41.8	41.5
2004	41.6	42.1	42.1	42.6	42.6	42.6	42.3	42.7	42.9	43.6	43.7	43.8	42.7
2005	43.3	43.8	44.2	44.4	44.4	44.3	44.5	44.8	45.1	45.3	45.5	45.4	44.6
2006	45.6	46.0	46.1	46.0	45.9	45.9	45.8	46.1	46.1	46.4	46.5	46.6	46.1
2007	46.6	47.0	47.1	47.0	47.3	47.2	46.9	47.1	47.0	47.3	47.5	47.6	47.1
Leisure and Hospitality													
2000	25.1	25.0	25.5	26.5	26.8	27.3	26.8	26.7	26.4	26.4	26.1	26.1	26.2
2001	25.2	26.3	26.1	26.8	27.3	27.4	27.5	27.5	26.7	26.1	25.8	25.8	26.5
2002	25.5	25.9	26.4	28.3	28.7	29.3	29.7	29.6	29.4	29.3	29.1	29.2	28.4
2003	27.8	27.5	28.0	28.8	29.0	29.6	29.1	29.4	28.5	28.6	28.3	28.2	28.6
2004	27.2	27.8	28.7	29.9	30.5	31.2	30.8	30.9	30.4	29.7	29.4	29.0	29.6
2005	27.7	27.9	28.8	29.7	30.2	30.8	30.2	30.5	29.8	29.6	29.4	29.0	29.5
2006	28.9	29.4	30.0	30.8	31.6	32.6	32.8	32.9	32.3	32.0	31.9	31.9	31.4
2007	31.0	31.2	32.1	32.6	33.5	34.0	33.7	33.9	33.2	32.9	32.5	32.3	32.7
Other Services													
2000	8.9	9.2	9.5	9.7	10.0	10.2	10.3	10.5	10.7	10.8	11.0	11.2	10.2
2001	11.3	11.6	11.9	12.0	12.3	12.4	12.7	12.7	12.8	12.9	13.1	13.4	12.4
2002	13.5	13.8	14.0	14.4	14.5	14.9	15.3	15.4	15.2	15.4	15.4	15.3	14.8
2003	15.1	15.1	15.0	15.2	15.0	15.1	15.0	14.7	14.7	14.5	14.5	14.5	14.9
2004	14.5	14.6	14.8	15.5	15.6	15.7	15.1	14.7	14.6	14.8	14.5	14.5	14.9
2005	14.3	14.5	14.5	14.6	14.5	14.6	14.5	14.4	14.3	14.4	14.4	14.5	14.5
2006	14.3	14.4	14.6	14.3	14.6	14.5	14.2	14.0	13.9	14.3	14.2	14.3	14.3
2007	14.2	14.2	14.4	14.7	14.8	15.0	15.1	15.0	14.8	14.9	14.8	14.7	14.7
Government													
2000	38.2	38.4	39.1	39.2	39.2	39.2	33.7	37.3	38.6	39.8	40.8	41.1	38.7
2001	39.7	40.0	40.2	40.2	40.5	40.0	33.7	37.0	38.9	40.4	41.6	41.0	39.4
2002	40.3	40.6	41.1	41.6	41.5	40.4	34.5	37.6	40.3	41.6	42.6	42.1	40.4
2003	41.0	41.5	41.7	42.1	42.4	40.6	35.1	37.9	40.9	43.1	42.3	42.3	40.9
2004	41.3	41.5	42.0	42.4	42.5	41.1	35.2	38.4	41.2	42.6	42.4	42.8	41.1
2005	42.0	42.4	42.7	42.9	43.1	41.3	35.7	40.0	42.2	43.9	43.4	43.6	41.9
2006	42.7	43.1	43.7	44.1	44.3	41.8	36.5	40.7	42.9	44.1	44.6	45.0	42.8
2007	43.6	43.8	44.3	44.5	44.7	42.3	37.2	41.4	43.6	45.3	45.4	45.7	43.5

Employment by Industry: Poughkeepsie-Newburgh-Middletown, NY, 2000–2007

(Numbers in thousands, not seasonally adjusted.)

Industry and year	January	February	March	April	May	June	July	August	September	October	November	December	Annual Average
Total Nonfarm													
2000	234.1	235.2	237.9	238.9	240.4	240.8	236.9	238.9	238.7	242.1	244.1	245.4	239.5
2001	239.2	239.6	241.6	241.7	244.6	247.2	242.5	241.8	241.5	245.2	246.3	247.2	243.2
2002	238.6	239.4	242.4	242.1	244.3	246.6	243.9	242.9	246.0	249.4	250.6	250.3	244.7
2003	241.2	243.2	244.5	246.5	248.4	251.0	246.4	246.1	247.4	252.1	252.9	253.2	247.7
2004	243.3	245.3	247.9	249.6	252.0	253.2	251.4	250.7	252.7	256.7	258.6	258.5	251.7
2005	246.7	248.4	250.0	254.2	255.3	256.8	254.1	253.1	254.4	258.1	258.1	257.8	253.9
2006	249.2	250.3	252.6	254.8	256.8	258.2	255.0	254.4	255.6	259.8	259.1	259.6	255.5
2007	249.8	250.5	251.8	253.8	256.7	258.6	255.4	254.4	254.6	257.8	258.2	257.8	255.0
Total Private													
2000	186.0	185.9	188.2	189.8	190.6	191.4	191.0	192.3	191.3	192.1	193.7	195.4	190.6
2001	190.2	189.6	191.3	191.4	194.6	196.4	196.1	195.7	193.0	194.4	195.0	196.4	193.7
2002	188.3	188.0	190.6	190.8	192.8	194.9	195.1	195.6	195.8	197.2	198.1	198.4	193.8
2003	190.8	191.3	192.5	194.9	196.9	199.2	197.8	198.0	197.8	200.3	200.9	201.7	196.8
2004	193.7	194.2	196.3	198.4	200.6	201.2	202.6	202.6	202.5	204.9	206.6	206.8	200.9
2005	195.8	196.4	197.8	202.2	203.2	204.2	204.6	204.1	203.6	205.9	205.9	206.4	202.5
2006	198.2	198.2	200.4	202.6	204.8	205.4	205.7	205.7	205.0	207.4	206.9	208.0	204.0
2007	198.4	198.2	199.6	201.6	204.7	205.6	204.4	204.1	203.1	204.5	205.1	205.2	202.9
Goods-Producing													
2000	40.0	39.8	41.2	40.8	40.2	39.6	38.7	39.1	39.0	38.9	39.1	39.3	39.6
2001	37.8	37.7	38.4	38.5	39.4	40.0	39.7	39.3	38.9	38.2	37.8	37.7	38.6
2002	36.3	35.9	36.5	36.3	36.6	37.1	37.0	37.3	37.1	36.7	36.5	36.5	36.7
2003	35.4	35.3	35.8	36.1	36.8	37.1	36.7	36.7	36.4	36.1	35.9	35.8	36.1
2004	34.2	34.1	34.7	34.9	35.5	35.7	35.9	36.0	35.7	35.8	36.0	35.9	35.4
2005	34.3	34.1	34.4	35.1	35.4	35.9	36.2	36.1	35.8	35.6	35.7	35.7	35.4
2006	34.3	34.1	34.5	34.9	35.4	35.7	35.7	35.6	35.2	35.3	34.8	34.9	35.0
2007	33.2	32.8	33.0	33.7	34.4	34.7	34.7	34.8	34.7	34.4	34.1	33.8	34.0
Natural Resources, Mining, and Construction													
2000	9.1	9.0	9.5	10.0	10.4	10.8	10.9	11.1	11.1	10.9	10.8	10.7	10.4
2001	9.9	9.8	10.2	10.8	11.5	11.8	11.9	11.7	11.6	11.4	11.3	11.3	11.1
2002	10.2	10.0	10.1	10.5	10.8	10.9	11.2	11.4	11.3	11.2	11.1	11.1	10.8
2003	10.2	10.1	10.2	10.8	11.5	11.7	11.8	11.7	11.5	11.5	11.3	11.2	11.1
2004	10.0	9.8	10.1	10.8	11.3	11.5	11.8	12.0	12.0	12.1	12.2	12.1	11.3
2005	10.8	10.7	11.0	11.8	12.1	12.4	12.8	12.8	12.6	12.5	12.6	12.3	12.0
2006	11.3	11.1	11.4	12.0	12.4	12.5	12.6	12.6	12.4	12.7	12.4	12.4	12.2
2007	11.2	10.9	11.0	11.8	12.4	12.7	12.8	12.9	12.8	12.7	12.5	12.3	12.2
Manufacturing													
2000	30.9	30.8	31.7	30.8	29.8	28.8	27.8	28.0	27.9	28.0	28.3	28.6	29.3
2001	27.9	27.9	28.2	27.7	27.9	28.2	27.8	27.6	27.3	26.8	26.5	26.4	27.5
2002	26.1	25.9	26.4	25.8	25.8	26.2	25.8	25.9	25.8	25.5	25.4	25.4	25.8
2003	25.2	25.2	25.6	25.3	25.3	25.4	24.9	25.0	24.9	24.6	24.6	24.6	25.0
2004	24.2	24.3	24.6	24.1	24.2	24.2	24.1	24.0	23.7	23.7	23.8	23.8	24.1
2005	23.5	23.4	23.4	23.3	23.3	23.5	23.4	23.3	23.2	23.1	23.1	23.4	23.3
2006	23.0	23.0	23.1	22.9	23.0	23.2	23.1	23.0	22.8	22.6	22.4	22.5	22.9
2007	22.0	21.9	22.0	21.9	22.0	22.0	21.9	21.9	21.9	21.7	21.6	21.5	21.9
Service-Providing													
2000	194.1	195.4	196.7	198.1	200.2	201.2	198.2	199.8	199.7	203.2	205.0	206.1	199.8
2001	201.4	201.9	203.2	203.2	205.2	207.2	202.8	202.5	202.6	207.0	208.5	209.5	204.6
2002	202.3	203.5	205.9	205.8	207.7	209.5	206.9	205.6	208.9	212.7	214.1	213.8	208.1
2003	205.8	207.9	208.7	210.4	211.6	213.9	209.7	209.4	211.0	216.0	217.0	217.4	211.6
2004	209.1	211.2	213.2	214.7	216.5	217.5	215.5	214.7	217.0	220.9	222.6	222.6	216.3
2005	212.4	214.3	215.6	219.1	219.9	220.9	217.9	217.0	218.6	222.5	222.4	222.1	218.6
2006	214.9	216.2	218.1	219.9	221.4	222.5	219.3	218.8	220.4	224.5	224.3	224.7	220.4
2007	216.6	217.7	218.8	220.1	222.3	223.9	220.7	219.6	219.9	223.4	224.1	224.0	220.9
Trade, Transportation, and Utilities													
2000	50.9	49.9	49.8	50.8	51.2	51.6	51.3	51.5	51.8	52.6	54.2	55.4	51.8
2001	53.4	52.1	52.4	51.4	52.2	52.7	51.9	51.9	51.9	52.7	53.8	54.9	52.6
2002	51.9	51.2	51.9	52.2	52.6	53.2	52.7	52.7	53.5	54.2	55.6	56.4	53.2
2003	53.0	52.1	52.0	52.4	52.8	53.5	52.9	53.0	53.4	54.8	55.8	57.0	53.6
2004	54.1	53.3	53.6	54.0	54.5	55.2	54.8	54.8	55.1	56.5	57.8	58.6	55.2
2005	55.0	54.2	54.1	54.3	54.9	55.7	55.1	55.1	55.1	56.6	57.2	58.1	55.5
2006	55.9	54.8	55.0	55.2	55.6	56.2	55.6	55.5	55.8	57.4	58.3	59.4	56.2
2007	56.5	55.0	55.1	55.2	55.9	56.7	56.0	56.0	55.8	56.9	58.0	58.8	56.3
Wholesale Trade													
2000	9.3	9.4	9.4	9.7	9.8	9.7	9.7	9.6	9.4	9.6	9.6	9.8	9.6
2001	10.0	10.0	10.1	10.0	10.1	10.2	10.1	10.2	10.1	10.0	10.0	10.1	10.1
2002	9.6	9.5	9.6	9.7	9.7	9.9	10.0	10.1	10.0	10.0	10.0	10.0	9.8
2003	9.8	9.8	9.8	9.8	10.0	10.0	10.3	10.3	10.2	10.2	10.3	10.4	10.1
2004	10.2	10.2	10.3	10.3	10.3	10.4	10.4	10.3	10.3	10.4	10.5	10.5	10.3
2005	10.3	10.3	10.2	10.2	10.2	10.3	10.3	10.3	10.1	10.3	10.2	10.1	10.2
2006	10.0	10.1	10.0	10.1	10.1	10.2	10.1	10.2	10.2	10.1	10.1	10.3	10.1
2007	10.1	10.1	10.1	10.2	10.2	10.3	10.2	10.2	10.1	10.1	10.1	10.1	10.2
Retail Trade													
2000	32.7	31.7	31.6	32.2	32.5	32.9	32.6	33.0	33.2	33.6	35.2	36.3	33.1
2001	34.0	32.8	33.0	32.3	32.8	33.2	32.9	33.0	32.8	33.7	35.0	36.0	33.5
2002	33.6	33.0	33.5	33.7	34.0	34.3	34.0	34.0	34.4	34.8	36.2	37.1	34.4
2003	34.4	33.5	33.3	33.8	34.1	34.7	34.1	34.3	34.4	35.5	36.4	37.5	34.6
2004	35.0	34.3	34.4	34.6	35.0	35.5	35.4	35.4	35.3	36.3	37.4	38.3	35.6
2005	35.3	34.5	34.5	34.7	35.2	35.8	35.7	35.8	35.4	36.6	37.2	37.9	35.7
2006	35.9	34.8	35.1	35.4	35.6	36.1	36.0	35.9	35.8	37.3	38.1	38.8	36.2
2007	36.6	35.2	35.2	35.3	35.8	36.5	36.3	36.3	35.9	36.9	38.1	38.9	36.4

Employment by Industry: Poughkeepsie-Newburgh-Middletown, NY, 2000–2007—*Continued*

(Numbers in thousands, not seasonally adjusted.)

Industry and year	January	February	March	April	May	June	July	August	September	October	November	December	Annual Average
Transportation and Utilities													
2000	8.9	8.8	8.8	8.9	8.9	9.0	9.0	8.9	9.2	9.4	9.4	9.3	9.0
2001	9.4	9.3	9.3	9.1	9.3	9.3	8.9	8.7	9.0	9.0	8.8	8.8	9.1
2002	8.7	8.7	8.8	8.8	8.9	9.0	8.7	8.6	9.1	9.4	9.4	9.3	9.0
2003	8.8	8.8	8.9	8.8	8.7	8.8	8.5	8.4	8.8	9.1	9.1	9.1	8.8
2004	8.9	8.8	8.9	9.1	9.2	9.3	9.0	9.1	9.5	9.8	9.9	9.8	9.3
2005	9.4	9.4	9.4	9.4	9.5	9.6	9.1	9.0	9.6	9.7	9.8	10.1	9.5
2006	10.0	9.9	9.9	9.7	9.9	9.9	9.5	9.4	9.8	10.0	10.1	10.3	9.9
2007	9.8	9.7	9.8	9.7	9.9	9.9	9.5	9.5	9.8	9.9	9.8	9.8	9.8
Information													
2000	5.1	5.1	5.2	5.2	5.2	5.3	5.3	5.0	5.1	5.1	5.1	5.2	5.2
2001	5.2	5.1	5.2	5.1	5.2	5.2	5.1	5.1	5.0	5.1	5.3	5.3	5.2
2002	4.7	4.7	4.7	4.6	4.7	4.8	4.7	4.7	5.1	4.6	4.6	4.6	4.7
2003	4.7	4.7	4.7	4.6	4.6	4.6	4.5	4.7	4.6	4.6	4.6	4.6	4.6
2004	4.8	4.7	4.6	4.5	4.6	4.6	4.6	4.6	4.7	4.5	4.7	4.8	4.6
2005	4.5	4.4	4.5	4.4	4.4	4.5	4.6	4.5	4.4	4.4	4.6	4.6	4.5
2006	4.6	4.5	4.6	4.6	4.6	4.7	4.8	4.6	4.5	4.4	4.5	4.6	4.5
2007	4.5	4.4	4.6	4.6	4.6	4.6	4.6	4.7	4.6	4.5	4.6	4.6	4.6
Financial Activities													
2000	10.3	10.2	10.3	10.1	10.1	10.4	10.4	10.4	10.1	9.9	9.9	10.0	10.2
2001	9.9	9.9	10.0	10.0	10.1	10.4	10.6	10.5	10.3	10.1	10.1	10.2	10.2
2002	9.7	9.7	9.8	9.8	9.9	10.1	10.3	10.3	10.0	9.9	9.9	10.0	10.0
2003	9.9	9.9	10.0	10.0	10.2	10.4	10.7	10.7	10.0	9.9	9.9	10.0	10.0
2004	10.1	9.9	10.1	10.1	10.3	10.5	10.6	10.6	10.4	10.4	10.5	10.5	10.3
2005	10.2	10.2	10.3	10.2	10.3	10.5	10.4	10.4	10.3	10.2	10.2	10.3	10.3
2006	10.0	10.0	10.0	10.1	10.3	10.5	10.5	10.5	10.3	10.3	10.2	10.3	10.3
2007	10.1	10.0	10.1	10.0	10.1	10.2	10.2	10.1	9.9	9.8	9.8	9.8	10.0
Professional and Business Services													
2000	16.6	16.5	16.9	17.2	17.4	17.5	17.8	17.8	17.7	18.0	18.1	18.3	17.5
2001	18.8	18.8	18.9	19.2	19.3	19.2	18.5	18.3	18.1	18.5	18.4	18.8	18.7
2002	17.5	17.6	17.9	18.2	18.3	18.6	18.5	18.7	18.7	19.6	19.6	19.6	18.6
2003	19.3	19.0	19.1	19.6	19.5	19.7	19.7	19.8	19.7	19.9	19.8	19.9	19.5
2004	19.4	19.5	19.7	19.9	20.2	20.7	20.9	21.0	20.9	21.1	21.3	21.3	20.5
2005	20.2	20.1	20.4	21.4	21.4	21.6	21.7	21.6	21.4	21.5	21.4	21.5	21.2
2006	20.6	20.5	20.6	21.1	21.1	21.5	21.5	21.6	21.4	21.2	21.7	21.1	21.2
2007	19.9	20.0	20.0	20.4	20.6	21.0	21.0	20.8	20.7	20.9	20.8	20.8	20.6
Education and Health Services													
2000	39.4	40.3	40.4	40.1	40.2	39.8	39.3	39.3	40.6	41.3	41.5	41.5	40.3
2001	40.8	41.5	41.7	41.6	41.6	41.3	41.0	40.7	41.9	42.9	42.9	43.0	41.7
2002	42.8	43.3	43.6	43.1	43.1	42.6	42.4	42.1	43.7	44.4	44.4	44.0	43.3
2003	42.4	43.9	44.2	44.5	44.1	43.8	42.5	42.1	43.8	45.2	45.5	45.3	43.9
2004	44.1	45.6	46.0	46.3	45.9	44.1	44.4	44.0	45.9	47.3	47.6	47.0	45.7
2005	44.2	45.7	46.0	47.1	46.6	44.9	44.5	44.1	46.1	47.9	47.9	47.3	46.0
2006	45.9	47.4	47.8	47.9	47.8	45.8	45.2	45.3	47.3	48.2	48.3	48.0	47.1
2007	46.0	47.8	48.1	48.1	48.2	46.5	45.3	45.2	46.7	47.9	48.2	48.0	47.2
Leisure and Hospitality													
2000	15.2	15.5	15.8	16.9	17.5	18.2	18.8	19.8	18.0	17.4	16.9	16.8	17.2
2001	15.5	15.7	15.9	16.8	17.9	18.5	19.8	20.5	18.0	18.0	17.7	17.5	17.7
2002	16.6	16.8	17.3	17.7	18.7	19.4	20.0	20.4	19.1	18.6	18.3	18.1	18.4
2003	17.1	17.4	17.6	18.6	19.7	20.6	21.1	21.3	20.1	19.9	19.3	18.9	19.3
2004	17.6	17.7	18.1	19.1	19.9	20.7	21.5	21.8	20.3	19.9	19.4	19.4	19.6
2005	18.0	18.2	18.6	19.9	20.5	21.3	22.1	22.3	20.7	19.9	19.4	19.1	20.0
2006	17.4	17.4	18.3	19.1	20.2	21.1	22.1	22.6	20.8	20.1	19.7	19.7	19.9
2007	18.5	18.5	18.9	19.7	20.9	21.7	22.4	22.4	20.7	20.0	19.5	19.4	20.2
Other Services													
2000	8.5	8.6	8.6	8.7	8.8	9.0	9.4	9.4	9.0	8.9	8.9	8.9	8.9
2001	8.8	8.8	8.8	8.8	8.9	9.1	9.5	9.4	8.9	8.9	9.0	9.0	9.0
2002	8.8	8.8	8.9	8.9	8.9	9.1	9.5	9.4	9.1	9.2	9.2	9.2	9.1
2003	9.0	9.0	9.1	9.1	9.2	9.5	9.7	9.7	9.4	9.4	9.4	9.5	9.3
2004	9.4	9.4	9.5	9.6	9.7	9.7	9.9	9.8	9.6	9.6	9.7	9.7	9.6
2005	9.4	9.5	9.5	9.8	9.7	9.8	10.0	10.0	9.7	9.7	9.7	9.8	9.7
2006	9.5	9.5	9.6	9.7	9.8	10.0	10.2	10.1	9.9	9.9	9.9	9.8	9.8
2007	9.7	9.7	9.8	9.9	10.0	10.2	10.2	10.1	10.0	10.1	10.1	10.0	10.0
Government													
2000	48.1	49.3	49.7	49.1	49.8	49.4	45.6	46.3	47.1	50.0	50.4	50.0	48.7
2001	49.0	50.0	50.3	50.3	50.0	50.8	46.4	46.1	48.5	50.8	51.3	50.8	49.5
2002	50.3	51.4	51.8	51.3	51.5	51.7	48.8	47.3	50.2	52.2	52.5	51.9	50.9
2003	50.4	51.9	52.0	51.6	51.5	51.8	48.6	48.1	49.6	51.8	52.0	51.5	50.9
2004	49.6	51.1	51.6	51.2	51.4	52.0	48.8	48.1	50.2	51.8	52.0	51.7	50.8
2005	50.9	52.0	52.2	52.0	52.1	52.6	49.5	49.0	50.8	52.2	52.2	51.4	51.4
2006	51.0	52.1	52.2	52.2	52.0	52.8	49.3	48.7	50.6	52.4	52.2	51.6	51.4
2007	51.4	52.3	52.2	52.2	52.0	53.0	51.0	50.3	51.5	53.3	53.1	52.6	52.1

Employment by Industry: Knoxville, TN 2000–2007

(Numbers in thousands, not seasonally adjusted.)

Industry and year	January	February	March	April	May	June	July	August	September	October	November	December	Annual Average
Total Nonfarm													
2000	294.9	296.9	300.7	302.3	305.2	306.5	301.7	302.7	305.7	304.9	305.8	307.0	302.9
2001	302.4	303.8	306.8	308.4	309.3	310.7	306.2	305.8	308.1	307.9	309.0	310.2	307.4
2002	303.5	304.2	307.2	312.0	313.9	315.7	312.8	314.0	315.8	318.8	319.2	321.5	313.2
2003	311.2	311.4	313.7	316.8	318.2	318.9	314.0	316.1	316.8	319.0	320.3	320.8	316.4
2004	315.1	317.9	319.8	321.8	322.8	322.8	323.1	324.3	325.2	325.2	327.6	327.5	322.8
2005	321.7	321.9	324.7	325.4	326.5	327.1	325.0	326.5	329.3	328.3	329.7	330.9	326.4
2006	325.3	326.9	329.9	331.4	332.3	332.0	331.1	334.5	337.6	335.3	336.4	338.2	332.6
2007	331.6	332.5	335.4	336.3	337.4	336.4	336.3	339.5	340.8	339.8	340.7	341.3	337.3
Total Private													
2000	244.2	245.4	248.9	249.9	252.0	254.4	252.1	252.4	253.5	252.6	253.5	254.5	251.1
2001	251.2	251.7	254.6	256.2	257.2	258.9	256.2	255.8	256.1	254.8	255.9	257.0	255.5
2002	251.4	251.8	254.7	258.0	259.8	262.0	262.0	263.0	263.4	265.2	265.6	267.4	260.4
2003	259.0	258.9	260.9	263.6	265.0	266.3	263.9	265.7	266.1	265.8	267.1	268.0	264.2
2004	262.1	262.9	265.9	269.0	270.6	270.8	272.1	272.9	273.0	271.5	273.8	274.1	269.9
2005	269.3	268.9	271.9	272.6	274.2	275.6	275.0	276.4	277.3	275.4	276.7	277.6	274.2
2006	273.4	274.1	277.3	278.9	280.2	281.8	280.8	283.5	284.5	281.7	282.9	284.2	280.3
2007	279.2	279.3	282.2	283.2	284.6	285.7	285.6	287.5	287.2	285.8	286.7	287.1	284.5
Goods-Producing													
2000	59.4	59.6	60.4	59.8	59.8	60.1	59.4	59.6	59.6	58.9	58.7	58.9	59.5
2001	58.1	57.7	58.3	57.7	57.4	57.7	56.5	56.4	56.1	55.5	55.4	55.4	56.9
2002	54.5	54.4	55.0	55.3	55.7	56.2	56.6	56.6	56.4	57.0	56.6	56.7	55.9
2003	55.7	55.3	55.9	56.0	56.1	55.7	55.1	55.1	55.0	55.1	55.0	54.9	55.4
2004	54.2	54.3	54.8	55.2	55.3	55.1	55.6	55.6	55.6	55.2	55.4	55.1	55.1
2005	55.2	54.7	55.1	54.9	55.0	55.2	55.5	55.7	55.7	55.4	55.3	55.5	55.3
2006	55.6	55.5	56.2	56.6	56.7	57.3	56.8	57.3	57.5	56.4	56.1	55.8	56.5
2007	55.5	55.2	55.8	55.9	56.0	56.4	56.0	56.2	56.2	56.2	56.1	55.6	55.9
Natural Resources, Mining, and Construction													
2000	15.0	15.2	15.9	15.5	15.4	15.6	15.6	15.7	15.8	15.4	15.3	15.4	15.5
2001	14.4	14.6	15.1	15.2	15.3	15.7	15.2	15.1	15.1	15.0	15.1	15.2	15.1
2002	14.0	14.1	14.5	14.8	15.1	15.3	15.6	15.6	15.5	16.0	15.6	15.6	15.1
2003	15.1	14.7	15.4	15.7	16.0	15.9	15.6	15.7	15.8	16.1	16.0	16.2	15.7
2004	15.6	15.6	16.0	16.4	16.6	16.4	16.7	16.8	16.9	16.9	17.0	16.6	16.5
2005	16.6	16.4	16.6	16.5	16.5	16.7	16.8	17.0	17.1	16.9	16.8	16.7	16.7
2006	16.7	16.8	17.5	17.8	18.0	18.6	18.5	18.9	19.3	19.0	18.8	18.4	18.2
2007	18.0	18.0	18.6	18.8	19.0	19.2	18.9	19.2	19.2	19.2	19.0	18.5	18.8
Manufacturing													
2000	44.4	44.4	44.5	44.3	44.4	44.5	43.8	43.9	43.8	43.5	43.4	43.5	44.0
2001	43.7	43.1	43.2	42.5	42.1	42.0	41.3	41.3	41.0	40.5	40.3	40.2	41.8
2002	40.5	40.3	40.5	40.5	40.6	40.9	41.0	41.0	40.9	41.0	41.0	41.1	40.8
2003	40.6	40.6	40.5	40.3	40.1	39.8	39.5	39.4	39.2	39.0	39.0	38.7	39.7
2004	38.6	38.7	38.8	38.8	38.7	38.7	38.9	38.8	38.7	38.3	38.4	38.5	38.7
2005	38.6	38.3	38.5	38.4	38.5	38.5	38.7	38.7	38.6	38.5	38.5	38.8	38.6
2006	38.9	38.7	38.7	38.8	38.7	38.7	38.3	38.4	38.2	37.4	37.3	37.4	38.3
2007	37.5	37.2	37.2	37.1	37.0	37.2	37.1	37.0	37.0	37.0	37.1	37.1	37.1
Service-Providing													
2000	235.5	237.3	240.3	242.5	245.4	246.4	242.3	243.1	246.1	246.0	247.1	248.1	243.3
2001	244.3	246.1	248.5	250.7	251.9	253.0	249.7	249.4	252.0	252.4	253.6	254.8	250.5
2002	249.0	249.8	252.2	256.7	258.2	259.5	256.2	257.4	259.4	261.8	262.6	264.8	257.3
2003	255.5	256.1	257.8	260.8	262.1	263.2	258.9	261.0	261.8	263.9	265.3	265.9	261.0
2004	260.9	263.6	265.0	266.6	267.5	267.7	267.5	268.7	269.6	270.0	272.2	272.4	267.6
2005	266.5	267.2	269.6	270.5	271.5	271.9	269.5	270.8	273.6	272.9	274.4	275.4	271.2
2006	269.7	271.4	273.7	274.8	275.6	274.7	274.3	277.2	280.1	278.9	280.3	282.4	276.1
2007	276.1	277.3	279.6	280.4	281.4	280.0	280.3	283.3	284.6	283.6	284.6	285.7	281.4
Trade, Transportation, and Utilities													
2000	61.6	61.8	62.3	63.2	63.3	63.8	63.9	63.7	64.1	64.4	65.3	66.3	63.6
2001	64.5	64.3	64.6	65.1	65.2	65.3	64.5	64.5	64.7	65.3	66.0	66.8	65.1
2002	64.7	64.5	65.3	65.4	65.2	65.2	65.7	65.9	66.0	66.9	67.7	68.9	66.0
2003	65.4	65.1	65.2	65.4	65.8	66.4	66.0	66.6	66.6	67.1	68.3	69.2	66.4
2004	66.8	66.9	67.7	67.6	68.1	68.0	68.0	68.4	68.5	69.0	70.3	70.9	68.4
2005	69.0	68.7	69.4	68.9	69.4	69.3	69.4	69.8	69.7	69.2	70.5	71.3	69.6
2006	69.5	69.4	70.2	70.2	70.6	70.8	70.6	71.5	72.0	71.5	72.8	74.2	71.1
2007	72.0	71.5	72.3	72.7	73.1	72.9	72.9	73.4	73.5	73.1	74.1	74.8	73.0
Wholesale Trade													
2000	13.3	13.4	13.5	13.6	13.6	13.9	13.8	13.6	13.8	13.8	13.7	13.9	13.7
2001	14.0	14.1	14.1	13.9	14.0	14.0	13.9	13.8	13.9	14.0	13.9	13.9	14.0
2002	13.8	13.9	14.0	14.0	14.1	14.2	14.6	14.7	14.7	15.0	15.1	15.3	14.5
2003	14.9	14.9	14.9	14.9	14.9	15.1	15.2	15.3	15.3	15.4	15.5	15.6	15.2
2004	15.4	15.5	15.8	15.8	15.9	15.8	16.2	16.2	16.0	16.1	16.2	16.2	15.9
2005	16.0	16.0	16.0	15.8	15.7	15.7	15.8	15.8	15.7	15.5	15.4	15.4	15.7
2006	15.5	15.6	15.7	15.8	15.9	15.9	16.0	16.0	16.1	16.1	16.0	16.2	15.9
2007	16.3	16.2	16.2	16.3	16.4	16.4	16.5	16.5	16.6	16.6	16.6	16.6	16.4
Retail Trade													
2000	38.9	38.9	39.1	39.5	39.7	40.0	40.4	40.3	40.4	40.8	41.8	42.7	40.2
2001	40.6	40.2	40.4	40.7	40.7	40.8	40.2	40.2	40.4	40.5	41.5	42.3	40.7
2002	40.6	40.3	40.9	40.9	40.8	40.7	40.6	40.6	40.8	41.1	41.9	42.9	41.0
2003	40.5	40.0	40.2	40.4	40.7	41.0	40.7	41.0	41.0	41.2	42.3	43.1	41.0
2004	41.2	41.2	41.6	41.5	41.8	41.8	41.6	41.8	42.0	42.4	43.6	44.0	42.0
2005	42.6	42.3	42.8	42.8	43.2	43.1	42.9	43.1	43.0	42.9	44.2	44.8	43.1
2006	43.2	43.0	43.4	43.5	43.6	43.8	43.7	44.3	44.6	44.3	45.6	46.5	44.1
2007	44.8	44.3	44.9	45.3	45.5	45.3	45.2	45.5	45.5	45.3	46.2	46.6	45.4

Employment by Industry: Knoxville, TN 2000–2007—*Continued*

(Numbers in thousands, not seasonally adjusted.)

Industry and year	January	February	March	April	May	June	July	August	September	October	November	December	Annual Average
Transportation and Utilities													
2000	9.4	9.5	9.7	10.1	10.0	9.9	9.7	9.8	9.9	9.8	9.8	9.7	9.8
2001	9.9	10.0	10.1	10.5	10.5	10.5	10.4	10.5	10.4	10.8	10.6	10.6	10.4
2002	10.3	10.3	10.4	10.5	10.3	10.3	10.5	10.6	10.5	10.8	10.7	10.7	10.5
2003	10.0	10.2	10.1	10.1	10.2	10.3	10.1	10.3	10.3	10.5	10.5	10.5	10.3
2004	10.2	10.2	10.3	10.3	10.4	10.4	10.2	10.4	10.5	10.5	10.5	10.7	10.4
2005	10.4	10.4	10.6	10.3	10.5	10.4	10.7	10.9	11.0	10.8	10.9	11.1	10.7
2006	10.8	10.8	11.1	10.9	11.1	11.1	10.9	11.2	11.3	11.1	11.2	11.5	11.1
2007	10.9	11.0	11.2	11.1	11.2	11.2	11.2	11.4	11.4	11.2	11.3	11.6	11.2
Information													
2000	6.1	6.1	6.2	6.0	6.0	6.0	6.0	5.9	5.9	5.9	5.9	5.9	6.0
2001	5.8	5.8	5.8	5.7	5.6	5.7	5.7	5.6	5.6	5.8	5.8	5.8	5.7
2002	5.8	5.8	5.8	5.9	5.9	5.8	5.9	5.9	5.8	6.0	6.0	6.1	5.9
2003	5.9	5.9	5.9	5.9	5.9	6.0	6.0	6.0	6.0	6.0	6.2	6.2	6.0
2004	6.2	6.1	6.2	6.2	6.2	6.1	6.2	6.0	5.9	5.9	5.9	5.8	6.1
2005	5.8	5.8	5.9	5.9	5.9	5.9	6.0	5.9	5.9	5.9	5.9	5.9	5.9
2006	6.0	6.1	6.1	6.1	6.0	6.0	6.0	5.9	5.8	5.8	5.9	5.8	6.0
2007	5.6	5.6	5.6	5.6	5.7	5.7	5.7	5.7	5.7	5.8	5.8	5.9	5.7
Financial Activities													
2000	13.9	13.9	14.0	13.9	14.0	14.1	13.9	13.9	13.8	13.9	14.0	14.1	14.0
2001	13.9	14.0	14.0	14.1	14.2	14.3	14.4	14.3	14.2	14.3	14.4	14.4	14.2
2002	14.3	14.4	14.4	14.5	14.7	14.9	14.9	14.9	15.1	15.3	15.6	15.8	14.9
2003	15.6	15.7	15.8	15.9	16.1	16.3	16.3	16.5	16.5	16.4	16.4	16.5	16.2
2004	16.4	16.4	16.5	16.6	16.7	16.7	16.8	16.8	16.8	16.8	16.9	17.0	16.7
2005	16.9	16.9	17.0	17.1	17.2	17.4	17.2	17.3	17.2	17.2	17.2	17.3	17.2
2006	17.2	17.2	17.3	17.2	17.3	17.3	17.4	17.6	17.5	17.4	17.5	17.5	17.4
2007	17.3	17.3	17.4	17.3	17.4	17.5	17.5	17.5	17.5	17.5	17.5	17.6	17.4
Professional and Business Services													
2000	35.1	35.7	36.8	36.7	37.0	37.9	36.8	37.3	37.6	37.1	37.1	37.0	36.8
2001	37.1	37.2	37.7	38.2	38.0	37.9	38.0	37.7	38.0	37.1	37.4	37.9	37.7
2002	37.4	37.2	37.9	38.2	38.3	38.5	38.5	38.8	38.8	38.6	37.9	37.8	38.2
2003	37.5	37.6	37.9	39.1	38.9	38.8	38.1	38.8	39.0	38.8	38.4	38.4	38.4
2004	37.3	37.4	38.0	39.2	39.0	39.4	39.4	39.8	39.9	39.4	39.4	39.6	39.0
2005	38.0	38.2	38.8	39.2	39.1	39.1	38.7	39.4	40.0	39.5	39.3	39.3	39.1
2006	38.5	38.8	39.3	39.8	40.0	39.8	39.6	40.3	40.8	40.5	40.5	40.6	39.9
2007	39.7	40.2	40.4	40.8	40.5	40.3	40.2	40.9	40.8	40.6	40.5	40.6	40.5
Education and Health Services													
2000	30.8	31.3	31.4	31.5	31.8	31.8	31.5	31.7	31.9	32.2	32.5	32.5	31.7
2001	32.0	32.4	32.8	33.1	33.3	33.6	33.1	33.3	33.4	33.7	34.0	34.1	33.2
2002	33.8	34.1	34.2	34.8	35.0	35.5	35.1	35.4	35.7	36.0	36.3	36.3	35.2
2003	35.5	35.6	35.8	36.0	36.2	36.5	36.5	36.6	37.2	37.4	37.6	37.7	36.6
2004	36.7	36.9	37.1	37.3	37.5	37.7	37.9	38.1	38.2	38.2	38.4	38.5	37.7
2005	38.2	38.1	38.5	38.7	39.0	39.3	39.3	39.5	39.7	40.1	40.2	40.3	39.2
2006	39.9	39.8	40.3	40.2	40.4	40.8	40.8	41.0	41.0	41.1	41.1	41.3	40.6
2007	40.9	40.9	41.1	41.1	41.2	41.5	41.8	42.0	42.0	42.0	42.1	42.2	41.6
Leisure and Hospitality													
2000	25.8	26.0	26.7	27.2	28.5	28.7	28.5	28.3	28.9	28.2	28.1	27.9	27.7
2001	27.8	28.2	28.8	30.2	31.3	31.9	31.4	31.5	31.5	30.8	30.5	30.2	30.3
2002	28.4	28.8	29.3	31.0	31.9	32.6	32.1	32.3	32.2	32.1	32.2	32.3	31.3
2003	29.8	30.0	30.7	31.6	32.2	32.5	31.8	32.2	31.9	31.2	31.4	31.2	31.4
2004	30.7	31.1	31.7	33.0	33.9	33.8	34.3	34.4	34.3	33.4	33.9	33.6	33.2
2005	32.7	33.0	33.6	34.2	34.9	35.5	35.0	35.0	35.3	34.4	34.6	34.2	34.4
2006	33.1	33.6	34.1	35.0	35.3	35.6	35.4	35.8	35.8	35.1	35.0	35.0	34.9
2007	34.1	34.4	35.3	35.7	36.4	36.9	36.9	37.2	37.0	36.2	36.2	36.0	36.0
Other Services													
2000	11.5	11.0	11.1	11.6	11.6	12.0	12.1	12.0	11.7	12.0	11.9	11.9	11.7
2001	12.0	12.1	12.6	12.1	12.2	12.5	12.6	12.5	12.6	12.3	12.4	12.4	12.4
2002	12.5	12.6	12.8	12.9	13.1	13.3	13.2	13.2	13.4	13.3	13.3	13.5	13.1
2003	13.6	13.7	13.7	13.7	13.8	14.1	14.1	13.9	13.9	13.8	13.8	13.9	13.8
2004	13.8	13.8	13.9	13.9	13.9	14.0	13.9	13.8	13.8	13.6	13.6	13.6	13.8
2005	13.5	13.5	13.6	13.7	13.7	13.9	13.9	13.8	13.8	13.7	13.7	13.8	13.7
2006	13.6	13.7	13.8	13.8	13.9	14.2	14.2	14.1	14.1	13.9	14.0	14.0	13.9
2007	14.1	14.2	14.3	14.1	14.3	14.5	14.6	14.6	14.5	14.4	14.4	14.4	14.4
Government													
2000	50.7	51.5	51.8	52.4	53.2	52.1	49.6	50.3	52.2	52.3	52.3	52.5	51.7
2001	51.2	52.1	52.2	52.2	52.1	51.8	50.0	50.0	52.0	53.1	53.1	53.2	51.9
2002	52.1	52.4	52.5	54.0	54.1	53.7	50.8	51.0	52.4	53.6	53.6	54.1	52.9
2003	52.2	52.5	52.8	53.2	53.2	52.6	50.1	50.4	50.7	53.2	53.2	52.8	52.2
2004	53.0	55.0	53.9	52.8	52.2	52.0	51.0	51.4	52.2	53.7	53.8	53.4	52.9
2005	52.4	53.0	52.8	52.8	52.3	51.5	50.0	50.1	52.0	52.9	53.0	53.3	52.2
2006	51.9	52.8	52.6	52.5	52.1	50.2	50.3	51.0	53.1	53.6	53.5	54.0	52.3
2007	52.4	53.2	53.2	53.1	52.8	50.7	50.7	52.0	53.6	54.0	54.0	54.2	52.8

Employment by Industry: Little Rock-North Little Rock-Conway, AR, 2000–2007

(Numbers in thousands, not seasonally adjusted.)

Industry and year	January	February	March	April	May	June	July	August	September	October	November	December	Annual Average
Total Nonfarm													
2000	318.6	318.8	321.1	321.4	321.7	323.4	319.1	320.9	323.2	323.5	323.7	323.2	321.6
2001	322.7	324.5	326.4	325.6	325.9	326.5	322.3	323.8	324.2	323.7	323.5	323.0	324.3
2002	316.5	317.5	319.8	320.1	322.4	322.4	318.6	319.7	322.5	322.3	322.9	324.3	320.8
2003	318.2	319.2	321.2	322.1	323.8	324.0	321.2	324.8	326.2	326.5	326.3	328.3	323.4
2004	322.1	323.4	325.6	326.3	327.7	329.0	327.6	329.8	330.8	330.5	331.8	333.2	328.2
2005	325.4	327.7	330.3	332.8	333.6	334.6	331.3	332.8	335.8	334.8	337.2	338.9	332.9
2006	333.9	336.3	339.9	341.0	341.6	342.8	338.8	340.7	343.6	343.1	343.9	345.6	340.9
2007	339.7	341.2	344.7	345.4	346.2	348.3	343.6	346.2	348.7	348.7	349.4	350.8	346.1
Total Private													
2000	256.9	256.9	259.0	259.0	259.7	261.9	261.3	262.0	261.2	261.1	260.9	260.4	260.0
2001	260.1	261.3	262.8	261.8	262.7	264.1	262.5	263.1	261.3	259.9	259.3	258.8	261.5
2002	252.9	253.2	255.2	255.6	257.9	259.0	258.2	258.6	258.8	257.9	258.0	259.2	257.0
2003	253.8	254.5	256.4	257.0	259.4	260.1	259.3	262.1	262.0	261.4	260.8	263.2	259.1
2004	257.7	258.3	260.3	261.9	263.4	265.1	265.0	266.3	265.7	265.0	266.0	267.5	263.5
2005	260.7	262.4	264.9	266.5	268.2	269.5	269.1	269.2	270.0	268.6	270.8	272.9	267.7
2006	268.0	269.3	272.7	273.5	274.8	276.4	274.3	275.0	275.7	275.3	276.4	278.2	274.1
2007	272.8	273.5	276.7	276.8	278.4	280.5	278.8	280.3	280.1	279.4	279.9	281.4	278.2
Goods-Producing													
2000	49.4	49.4	50.1	49.7	49.8	50.4	50.3	50.3	49.8	49.3	49.1	48.8	49.7
2001	48.4	48.5	49.0	48.1	48.2	48.3	47.5	47.7	47.2	46.7	45.4	45.1	47.5
2002	44.5	44.3	44.4	44.5	44.9	45.0	45.1	45.2	44.7	44.4	43.7	43.5	44.5
2003	42.8	42.9	43.3	43.4	43.8	44.1	43.8	43.8	43.3	42.7	41.6	42.2	43.1
2004	41.3	41.1	41.5	42.5	43.0	43.6	43.4	43.5	43.3	42.9	42.8	42.6	42.6
2005	42.0	42.1	42.5	42.7	43.0	43.4	43.5	43.7	43.6	43.2	43.2	43.2	43.0
2006	42.9	43.0	43.3	43.5	43.9	44.5	44.1	44.6	44.6	44.2	44.0	44.0	43.9
2007	43.3	43.4	44.3	44.2	44.4	45.1	44.9	45.0	44.8	44.3	43.9	43.8	44.3
Natural Resources, Mining, and Construction													
2000	16.1	16.2	16.4	16.3	16.5	16.9	16.9	16.9	16.7	16.6	16.6	16.5	16.6
2001	16.3	16.4	17.0	16.7	17.1	17.4	17.5	17.6	17.4	17.1	16.9	16.8	17.0
2002	16.3	16.3	16.5	16.7	17.1	17.5	17.7	17.6	17.4	17.3	16.9	16.8	17.0
2003	16.9	16.9	17.3	17.4	17.8	18.1	18.0	18.0	17.7	17.5	17.1	17.0	17.4
2004	16.5	16.3	16.7	17.5	17.8	18.2	18.0	18.0	18.0	17.5	17.3	17.2	17.4
2005	16.7	16.9	17.3	17.5	18.0	18.1	18.1	18.3	18.2	17.7	17.8	17.9	17.7
2006	17.6	17.7	18.1	18.3	18.7	19.1	18.8	19.2	19.3	18.9	18.7	18.8	18.6
2007	18.3	18.4	19.3	19.3	19.5	20.2	20.0	20.1	20.0	19.6	19.3	19.2	19.4
Manufacturing													
2000	33.3	33.2	33.7	33.4	33.3	33.5	33.4	33.4	33.1	32.7	32.5	32.3	33.2
2001	32.1	32.1	32.0	31.4	31.1	30.9	30.0	30.1	29.8	29.6	28.5	28.3	30.5
2002	28.2	28.0	27.9	27.8	27.8	27.5	27.4	27.6	27.3	27.1	26.8	26.7	27.5
2003	25.9	26.0	26.0	26.0	26.0	26.0	25.8	25.8	25.6	25.2	24.5	25.2	25.6
2004	24.8	24.8	24.8	25.0	25.2	25.4	25.4	25.5	25.3	25.4	25.5	25.4	25.2
2005	25.3	25.2	25.2	25.2	25.0	25.3	25.4	25.4	25.4	25.5	25.4	25.3	25.3
2006	25.3	25.3	25.2	25.2	25.2	25.4	25.3	25.4	25.3	25.3	25.3	25.2	25.3
2007	25.0	25.0	25.0	24.9	24.9	24.9	24.9	24.9	24.9	24.8	24.7	24.6	24.9
Service-Providing													
2000	269.2	269.4	271.0	271.7	271.9	273.0	268.8	270.6	273.4	274.2	274.6	274.4	271.9
2001	274.3	276.0	277.4	277.5	277.7	278.2	274.8	276.1	277.0	277.0	278.1	277.9	276.8
2002	272.0	273.2	275.4	275.6	277.5	277.4	273.5	274.5	277.8	277.9	279.2	280.8	276.2
2003	275.4	276.3	277.9	278.7	280.0	279.9	277.4	281.0	282.9	283.8	284.7	286.1	280.3
2004	280.8	282.3	284.1	283.8	284.7	285.4	284.2	286.3	287.5	287.6	289.0	290.6	285.5
2005	283.4	285.6	287.8	290.1	290.6	291.2	287.8	289.1	292.2	291.6	294.0	295.7	289.9
2006	291.0	293.3	296.6	297.5	297.7	298.3	294.7	296.1	299.0	298.9	299.9	301.6	297.1
2007	296.4	297.8	300.4	301.2	301.8	303.2	298.7	301.2	303.9	304.4	305.5	307.0	301.8
Trade, Transportation, and Utilities													
2000	70.3	69.8	69.6	69.8	69.7	70.0	70.0	70.2	70.1	70.8	71.4	72.3	70.3
2001	70.7	70.1	70.5	70.4	70.5	70.8	70.1	70.1	69.9	69.8	70.8	71.1	70.4
2002	68.6	68.2	68.7	68.8	69.0	69.0	68.2	68.1	68.2	68.0	69.1	69.9	68.7
2003	67.7	67.3	67.4	67.4	67.6	67.6	67.2	67.7	68.3	69.3	69.7	70.7	68.1
2004	68.0	67.9	68.1	68.0	68.3	68.6	68.7	69.3	69.2	69.3	70.2	71.3	68.9
2005	68.6	68.5	68.7	69.0	69.1	69.0	69.1	69.2	69.8	69.7	71.1	71.9	69.5
2006	69.5	69.3	69.9	70.1	70.5	70.2	69.9	70.3	70.5	70.7	71.8	72.7	70.5
2007	70.1	69.7	70.6	70.0	70.5	70.5	70.2	70.4	70.5	70.7	71.4	72.4	70.6
Wholesale Trade													
2000	15.5	15.6	15.8	15.9	16.0	16.2	16.3	16.4	16.5	16.5	16.3	16.4	16.1
2001	16.6	16.6	16.6	16.6	16.6	16.8	16.7	16.7	16.7	16.3	16.3	16.3	16.6
2002	16.2	16.2	16.3	16.3	16.3	16.3	16.2	16.2	16.1	16.0	15.9	16.0	16.2
2003	15.9	16.0	15.9	16.0	16.2	16.2	16.3	16.3	16.4	16.5	16.5	16.6	16.2
2004	16.3	16.4	16.5	16.7	16.7	16.9	16.9	16.9	16.9	16.8	16.7	16.9	16.7
2005	16.7	16.8	16.8	16.9	16.9	17.1	17.2	17.2	17.3	17.2	17.3	17.4	17.1
2006	17.3	17.3	17.3	17.5	17.6	17.7	17.6	17.6	17.6	17.4	17.5	17.6	17.5
2007	17.1	17.2	17.3	17.3	17.3	17.4	17.4	17.4	17.4	17.3	17.2	17.3	17.3
Retail Trade													
2000	36.2	35.6	35.2	35.2	35.3	35.5	35.1	35.3	35.1	35.8	36.6	37.4	35.7
2001	35.9	35.5	35.9	35.8	36.0	36.1	35.4	35.3	35.2	35.4	36.6	37.1	35.9
2002	35.0	34.7	35.1	35.1	35.4	35.5	35.0	34.8	34.9	34.8	36.0	36.7	35.3
2003	34.5	34.1	34.2	34.3	34.4	34.5	34.1	34.5	34.9	35.6	36.2	37.1	34.8
2004	35.0	34.9	35.3	35.3	35.4	35.6	35.5	35.9	35.7	36.0	36.9	37.6	35.8
2005	35.8	35.5	35.6	35.7	35.7	35.7	35.6	35.6	35.8	36.0	37.2	37.8	36.0
2006	35.8	35.5	36.0	35.9	36.0	35.8	35.7	36.1	36.0	36.4	37.5	38.1	36.2
2007	36.5	35.9	36.6	36.1	36.5	36.5	36.3	36.3	36.3	36.6	37.4	38.2	36.6

Employment by Industry: Little Rock-North Little Rock-Conway, AR, 2000–2007—*Continued*

(Numbers in thousands, not seasonally adjusted.)

Industry and year	January	February	March	April	May	June	July	August	September	October	November	December	Annual Average
Transportation and Utilities													
2000	18.6	18.6	18.6	18.7	18.4	18.3	18.6	18.5	18.5	18.5	18.5	18.5	18.5
2001	18.2	18.0	18.0	18.0	17.9	17.9	18.0	18.1	18.0	18.1	17.9	17.7	18.0
2002	17.4	17.3	17.3	17.4	17.3	17.2	17.0	17.1	17.2	17.2	17.2	17.2	17.2
2003	17.3	17.2	17.3	17.1	17.0	16.9	16.8	16.9	17.0	17.2	17.0	17.0	17.0
2004	16.7	16.6	16.3	16.0	16.1	16.1	16.3	16.5	16.6	16.5	16.6	16.8	16.4
2005	16.1	16.2	16.3	16.4	16.5	16.2	16.3	16.4	16.7	16.5	16.6	16.7	16.4
2006	16.4	16.5	16.6	16.7	16.9	16.7	16.6	16.6	16.9	16.9	16.8	17.0	16.7
2007	16.5	16.6	16.7	16.6	16.7	16.6	16.5	16.7	16.8	16.8	16.8	16.9	16.7
Information													
2000	8.8	8.9	8.9	8.9	9.0	9.2	9.2	9.4	9.4	9.5	9.6	9.5	9.2
2001	9.4	9.4	9.2	9.0	9.1	9.1	9.3	9.3	9.3	9.2	9.2	9.1	9.2
2002	9.2	9.2	9.1	9.1	9.1	9.2	9.1	9.1	9.1	9.3	9.3	9.3	9.2
2003	9.3	9.3	9.3	9.3	9.4	9.5	9.4	9.5	9.4	9.4	9.5	9.3	9.4
2004	9.6	9.4	9.5	9.5	9.5	9.5	9.5	9.5	9.5	9.4	9.5	9.5	9.5
2005	9.3	9.4	9.3	9.2	9.3	9.4	9.4	9.4	9.3	9.3	9.5	9.5	9.5
2006	9.3	9.3	9.3	9.3	9.3	9.4	9.4	9.3	9.3	9.3	9.3	9.4	9.3
2007	9.4	9.4	9.3	9.4	9.5	9.6	9.5	9.5	9.5	9.6	9.7	9.7	9.5
Financial Activities													
2000	18.9	18.9	18.9	18.7	18.7	18.8	18.9	18.9	18.7	18.5	18.4	18.6	18.7
2001	19.1	19.1	19.2	19.2	19.3	19.4	19.4	19.3	19.2	19.0	19.1	19.3	19.2
2002	19.1	19.1	19.2	19.1	19.1	19.2	19.3	19.3	19.3	19.2	19.2	19.4	19.2
2003	19.2	19.2	19.2	19.3	19.5	19.7	19.7	19.7	19.3	19.2	19.2	19.4	19.5
2004	19.6	19.7	19.7	19.7	19.7	19.7	19.7	19.7	19.7	19.6	19.6	19.9	19.5
2005	18.8	18.8	18.8	19.5	19.6	19.7	19.8	19.8	19.8	19.0	19.0	19.1	19.5
2006	19.7	19.8	19.8	19.9	20.0	20.0	20.1	20.2	20.1	20.1	20.2	20.0	20.0
2007	20.2	20.2	20.2	20.2	20.4	20.5	20.5	20.6	20.6	20.5	20.5	20.6	20.4
Professional and Business Services													
2000	38.1	38.3	39.0	38.4	38.8	39.1	39.4	40.1	40.1	40.1	40.0	39.0	39.2
2001	39.5	40.3	40.1	39.6	39.5	39.4	39.8	40.2	39.8	39.1	38.8	38.5	39.6
2002	37.3	37.2	37.8	37.8	38.3	38.9	39.0	39.4	39.7	39.9	39.3	39.8	38.7
2003	38.9	39.0	39.6	39.2	39.7	39.2	39.5	41.3	41.0	41.1	40.8	41.1	40.0
2004	40.4	40.4	40.9	40.3	40.5	40.5	41.0	41.5	41.2	42.1	42.1	42.4	41.1
2005	40.8	41.2	41.8	41.5	41.4	41.7	41.6	41.6	41.7	41.6	42.1	42.9	41.7
2006	41.7	42.5	43.6	43.1	43.2	43.2	43.1	42.8	43.5	43.1	43.2	43.8	43.1
2007	42.7	43.0	43.2	43.3	43.3	43.5	42.5	43.5	43.6	43.4	43.3	43.6	43.2
Education and Health Services													
2000	36.8	37.0	37.1	37.2	37.2	37.1	36.9	36.6	37.1	37.1	37.1	37.0	37.0
2001	37.6	38.1	38.3	38.5	38.5	38.7	38.6	38.8	39.0	39.5	39.6	39.5	38.7
2002	38.9	39.3	39.6	39.5	39.8	39.5	39.6	39.7	40.6	40.3	40.5	40.5	39.8
2003	40.0	40.5	40.8	40.9	41.0	41.0	40.8	41.0	41.8	41.8	41.9	42.9	41.1
2004	41.2	41.5	41.6	42.2	42.1	42.1	42.1	42.1	42.8	43.1	43.0	42.9	42.2
2005	42.4	42.9	43.1	43.6	43.6	43.6	43.5	43.5	44.1	44.4	44.4	44.3	43.6
2006	44.2	44.7	45.1	45.0	45.0	45.2	44.9	45.1	45.9	45.7	45.8	46.0	45.2
2007	45.6	46.1	46.5	46.8	46.8	47.0	47.1	47.3	47.9	48.1	48.2	48.2	47.1
Leisure and Hospitality													
2000	22.8	22.8	23.5	24.4	24.5	25.0	24.5	24.4	24.1	24.1	23.6	23.5	23.9
2001	23.5	23.9	24.3	24.9	25.4	25.8	25.4	25.3	24.6	24.5	24.3	24.1	24.7
2002	23.2	23.8	24.2	24.6	25.3	25.5	25.2	25.1	24.6	24.5	24.5	24.5	24.6
2003	23.7	24.0	24.3	24.9	25.6	25.9	25.8	25.9	25.3	24.3	24.4	24.3	24.8
2004	24.0	24.5	25.2	25.8	26.4	26.8	26.5	26.7	26.1	25.6	25.6	25.9	25.8
2005	25.1	25.7	26.7	26.9	28.0	28.3	27.8	27.7	27.4	26.8	26.9	27.1	27.0
2006	26.6	26.5	27.4	28.2	28.4	29.1	28.1	28.0	27.3	27.9	27.8	27.9	27.8
2007	27.3	27.5	28.3	28.6	29.2	29.6	29.5	29.5	28.9	28.8	28.8	28.9	28.7
Other Services													
2000	11.8	11.8	11.9	11.9	12.0	12.3	12.1	12.1	11.9	11.7	11.7	11.7	11.9
2001	11.9	11.9	12.2	12.1	12.2	12.6	12.4	12.4	12.3	12.1	12.1	12.1	12.2
2002	12.1	12.1	12.2	12.2	12.4	12.7	12.7	12.7	12.6	12.3	12.4	12.3	12.4
2003	12.2	12.3	12.5	12.6	12.8	13.1	13.1	13.2	13.2	13.2	13.4	13.6	12.9
2004	13.6	13.8	13.8	13.9	13.9	14.3	14.1	14.0	13.9	13.6	13.8	13.8	13.9
2005	13.7	13.8	14.0	14.1	14.2	14.4	14.4	14.3	14.3	13.9	14.0	14.1	14.1
2006	14.1	14.2	14.3	14.4	14.5	14.8	14.8	14.7	14.6	14.5	14.4	14.4	14.5
2007	14.2	14.2	14.3	14.3	14.3	14.7	14.6	14.5	14.3	14.0	14.1	14.2	14.3
Government													
2000	61.7	61.9	62.1	62.4	62.0	61.5	57.8	58.9	62.0	62.4	62.8	62.8	61.5
2001	62.6	63.2	63.6	63.8	63.2	62.4	59.8	60.7	62.9	63.8	64.2	64.2	62.9
2002	63.6	64.3	64.6	64.5	64.5	63.4	60.4	61.1	63.7	64.4	64.9	65.1	63.7
2003	64.4	64.7	64.8	65.1	64.4	63.9	61.9	62.7	64.2	65.1	65.5	65.1	64.3
2004	64.4	65.1	65.3	64.4	64.3	63.9	62.6	63.5	65.1	65.5	65.8	65.7	64.6
2005	64.7	65.3	65.4	66.3	65.4	65.1	62.2	63.6	65.8	66.2	66.4	66.0	65.2
2006	65.9	67.0	67.2	67.5	66.8	66.4	64.5	65.7	67.9	67.8	67.5	67.4	66.8
2007	66.9	67.7	68.0	68.6	67.8	67.8	64.8	65.9	68.6	69.3	69.5	69.4	67.9

Employment by Industry: Youngstown-Warren-Boardman, OH-PA, 2000–2007

(Numbers in thousands, not seasonally adjusted.)

Industry and year	January	February	March	April	May	June	July	August	September	October	November	December	Annual Average
Total Nonfarm													
2000	250.8	251.0	253.8	256.1	259.4	260.6	256.9	257.7	260.3	256.9	258.0	257.2	256.5
2001	245.7	245.8	247.9	250.8	252.5	253.8	247.1	248.2	249.8	247.8	249.0	249.3	249.0
2002	241.4	242.3	243.9	245.5	248.9	249.6	245.8	246.9	247.8	247.4	248.5	248.0	246.4
2003	240.3	240.7	242.1	239.4	246.1	246.4	241.1	244.1	245.2	246.0	246.0	245.6	243.5
2004	236.3	237.7	238.7	241.2	244.4	245.6	244.5	244.3	245.8	246.2	245.9	246.3	243.1
2005	237.1	238.9	240.8	244.6	247.0	247.6	245.3	244.6	247.4	246.0	247.4	246.7	244.5
2006	238.9	239.4	241.2	244.2	246.2	245.5	243.2	242.0	244.1	244.5	245.0	245.8	243.3
2007	235.9	235.7	237.5	239.8	243.3	242.9	240.2	239.0	240.4	240.7	242.0	242.6	240.0
Total Private													
2000	219.0	218.5	220.9	223.9	225.9	228.1	227.2	227.9	227.7	224.5	224.9	224.2	224.3
2001	213.5	212.6	214.3	217.4	218.7	221.0	217.0	218.3	217.0	214.9	215.6	216.0	216.4
2002	209.3	209.1	210.3	212.1	215.1	217.1	215.7	217.2	215.1	214.6	214.9	214.8	213.8
2003	208.0	207.2	208.1	206.2	212.3	214.2	210.8	214.0	212.6	213.2	212.4	212.2	210.9
2004	204.5	204.4	205.6	208.5	211.0	213.7	214.5	214.4	213.9	213.6	212.7	213.5	210.9
2005	205.8	206.2	208.1	212.5	214.5	216.5	215.9	215.4	216.1	214.2	214.7	214.1	212.8
2006	207.5	207.0	208.5	211.9	213.3	214.3	213.7	212.6	212.6	212.5	212.9	213.3	211.7
2007	204.7	203.6	205.3	207.9	210.8	212.0	210.9	209.8	209.2	209.1	209.7	210.4	208.6
Goods-Producing													
2000	63.3	63.0	63.5	64.2	64.8	65.9	64.9	65.2	64.2	63.3	62.6	61.5	63.8
2001	58.9	58.1	58.4	58.6	59.2	60.0	58.6	59.3	58.6	58.1	57.7	57.4	58.6
2002	55.0	54.8	54.7	55.2	55.9	56.6	55.1	57.0	56.1	55.1	55.1	54.6	55.5
2003	53.7	52.8	53.0	49.2	53.5	54.0	51.3	54.1	53.5	53.6	52.7	52.5	52.8
2004	49.7	49.9	49.9	51.0	52.0	52.9	53.5	53.8	52.9	52.9	51.7	51.7	51.8
2005	49.4	49.4	49.7	51.3	52.0	52.4	52.6	52.8	52.2	52.1	51.9	51.0	51.4
2006	49.7	49.4	49.8	51.0	51.2	51.8	52.0	51.1	50.2	50.0	49.3	49.2	50.4
2007	46.2	45.2	45.6	46.4	47.0	47.6	47.6	47.5	47.0	47.2	47.0	46.8	46.8
Natural Resources, Mining, and Construction													
2000	9.5	9.4	10.0	10.8	11.4	12.0	12.2	12.3	11.7	11.6	11.2	10.3	11.0
2001	9.2	9.1	9.5	10.4	11.0	11.4	11.6	11.6	11.4	11.4	11.2	10.5	10.7
2002	9.2	8.9	9.2	9.8	10.5	10.9	11.5	11.5	11.1	10.9	10.6	10.1	10.4
2003	9.2	8.6	8.9	9.9	10.4	10.8	11.2	11.2	11.0	11.2	10.9	10.2	10.3
2004	9.1	8.7	9.1	9.9	10.6	11.3	11.7	11.6	11.3	11.4	10.8	10.3	10.5
2005	8.9	8.7	8.9	10.1	10.8	11.2	11.5	11.6	11.2	11.1	10.8	10.0	10.4
2006	8.9	8.8	9.2	10.1	10.4	10.8	11.2	11.2	10.9	10.9	10.5	10.3	10.3
2007	9.2	8.7	9.2	10.0	10.6	11.0	11.2	11.2	11.0	11.0	10.6	10.2	10.3
Manufacturing													
2000	53.8	53.6	53.5	53.4	53.4	53.9	52.7	52.9	52.5	51.7	51.4	51.2	52.8
2001	49.7	49.0	48.9	48.2	48.2	48.6	47.0	47.7	47.2	46.7	46.5	46.9	47.9
2002	45.8	45.9	45.5	45.4	45.4	45.7	43.6	45.5	45.0	44.2	44.5	44.5	45.1
2003	44.5	44.2	44.1	39.3	43.1	43.2	40.1	42.9	42.5	42.4	41.8	42.3	42.5
2004	40.6	41.2	40.8	41.1	41.4	41.6	41.8	42.2	41.6	41.5	40.9	41.4	41.3
2005	40.5	40.7	40.8	41.2	41.2	41.2	41.1	41.2	41.0	41.0	41.1	41.0	41.0
2006	40.8	40.6	40.6	40.9	40.8	41.0	40.8	39.9	39.3	39.1	38.8	38.9	40.1
2007	37.0	36.5	36.4	36.4	36.4	36.6	36.4	36.3	36.0	36.2	36.4	36.6	36.4
Service-Providing													
2000	187.5	188.0	190.3	191.9	194.6	194.7	192.0	192.5	196.1	193.6	195.4	195.7	192.7
2001	186.8	187.7	189.5	192.2	193.3	193.8	188.5	188.9	191.2	189.7	191.3	191.9	190.4
2002	186.4	187.5	189.2	190.3	193.0	193.0	190.7	189.9	191.7	192.3	193.4	193.4	190.9
2003	186.6	187.9	189.1	190.2	192.6	192.4	189.8	190.0	191.7	192.4	193.3	193.1	190.7
2004	186.6	187.8	188.8	190.2	192.4	192.7	191.0	190.5	192.9	193.3	194.2	194.6	191.3
2005	187.7	189.5	191.1	193.3	195.0	195.2	192.7	191.8	195.2	193.9	195.5	195.7	193.1
2006	189.2	190.0	191.4	193.2	195.0	193.7	191.2	190.9	193.9	194.5	195.7	196.6	192.9
2007	189.7	190.5	191.9	193.4	196.3	195.3	192.6	191.5	193.4	193.5	195.0	195.8	193.2
Trade, Transportation, and Utilities													
2000	53.6	52.8	53.0	54.0	54.3	54.8	55.0	55.2	55.1	55.6	56.7	57.5	54.8
2001	53.7	53.0	53.2	53.4	53.7	53.9	52.4	52.3	52.1	52.1	52.9	53.6	53.0
2002	51.0	50.1	50.2	50.6	51.2	51.7	51.7	51.3	50.9	51.2	52.0	52.4	51.2
2003	49.8	49.7	50.1	50.9	51.1	51.4	51.2	50.9	50.9	51.4	52.2	52.6	51.0
2004	50.3	49.6	49.8	50.5	50.9	51.3	51.2	51.1	51.2	51.6	52.5	53.2	51.1
2005	51.0	50.2	50.8	51.2	51.6	51.9	51.5	51.1	51.1	51.5	52.4	53.0	51.4
2006	51.1	50.1	50.5	51.0	51.3	51.7	51.6	51.4	51.4	52.2	53.4	54.1	51.7
2007	51.7	50.8	51.2	51.3	52.1	52.5	52.3	51.9	51.7	52.3	53.5	54.2	52.1
Wholesale Trade													
2000	10.5	10.4	10.5	10.5	10.6	10.7	10.8	10.7	10.5	10.4	10.3	10.4	10.5
2001	10.1	10.1	10.1	10.1	10.1	10.2	9.9	9.8	9.6	9.6	9.3	9.4	9.9
2002	9.1	9.0	9.1	9.2	9.2	9.3	9.4	9.4	9.3	9.3	9.3	9.3	9.2
2003	9.1	9.1	9.1	9.3	9.3	9.4	9.4	9.3	9.3	9.2	9.2	9.1	9.2
2004	9.1	9.0	9.1	9.1	9.1	9.2	9.3	9.3	9.3	9.3	9.3	9.4	9.2
2005	9.4	9.2	9.3	9.4	9.4	9.4	9.4	9.2	9.1	9.1	9.1	9.1	9.3
2006	9.1	9.0	9.0	9.1	9.1	9.2	9.3	9.3	9.3	9.4	9.4	9.5	9.2
2007	9.5	9.4	9.5	9.5	9.6	9.6	9.6	9.6	9.7	9.6	9.7	9.7	9.6
Retail Trade													
2000	36.3	35.5	35.6	36.3	36.5	37.0	37.0	37.2	37.1	37.6	38.6	39.4	37.0
2001	36.2	35.5	35.7	35.5	35.8	36.0	35.1	35.0	34.9	34.7	35.8	36.4	35.6
2002	34.1	33.3	33.3	33.5	34.0	34.5	34.5	34.1	33.8	33.9	34.8	35.2	34.1
2003	33.1	33.0	33.3	33.9	34.0	34.2	34.2	34.0	33.9	34.2	35.0	35.5	34.0
2004	33.4	32.8	32.9	33.4	33.8	34.0	33.8	33.6	33.5	33.8	34.6	35.2	33.7
2005	33.3	32.6	32.9	33.1	33.4	33.7	33.6	33.3	33.2	33.5	34.3	34.8	33.5
2006	33.0	32.2	32.5	32.9	33.1	33.4	33.2	33.0	32.8	33.4	34.5	35.0	33.3
2007	32.9	32.0	32.2	32.3	32.9	33.4	33.3	32.9	32.5	33.2	34.3	34.9	33.1

Employment by Industry: Youngstown-Warren-Boardman, OH-PA, 2000–2007—*Continued*

(Numbers in thousands, not seasonally adjusted.)

Industry and year	January	February	March	April	May	June	July	August	September	October	November	December	Annual Average
Transportation and Utilities													
2000	6.8	6.9	6.9	7.2	7.2	7.1	7.2	7.3	7.5	7.6	7.8	7.7	7.3
2001	7.4	7.4	7.4	7.8	7.8	7.7	7.4	7.5	7.6	7.8	7.8	7.8	7.6
2002	7.8	7.8	7.8	7.9	8.0	7.9	7.8	7.8	7.8	8.0	7.9	7.9	7.9
2003	7.6	7.6	7.7	7.7	7.8	7.8	7.6	7.6	7.7	8.0	8.0	8.0	7.7
2004	7.8	7.8	7.8	8.0	8.0	8.1	8.1	8.2	8.4	8.5	8.6	8.6	8.2
2005	8.3	8.4	8.6	8.7	8.8	8.8	8.5	8.6	8.8	8.9	9.0	9.1	8.7
2006	9.0	8.9	9.0	9.0	9.1	9.1	9.1	9.1	9.3	9.4	9.5	9.6	9.2
2007	9.3	9.4	9.5	9.5	9.6	9.5	9.4	9.4	9.5	9.5	9.5	9.6	9.5
Information													
2000	3.5	3.5	3.5	3.5	3.6	3.6	3.6	3.5	3.5	3.5	3.5	3.5	3.5
2001	3.6	3.6	3.6	3.6	3.6	3.6	3.5	3.5	3.4	3.4	3.4	3.5	3.5
2002	3.5	3.4	3.4	3.4	3.5	3.6	3.6	3.6	3.6	3.6	3.6	3.7	3.5
2003	3.8	3.8	3.8	3.9	3.9	4.0	4.0	4.1	4.0	4.0	3.9	3.9	3.9
2004	3.9	3.9	3.8	3.4	3.3	3.2	3.0	2.8	2.8	2.8	2.9	2.9	3.2
2005	2.9	2.9	2.9	3.0	3.0	3.1	3.1	3.1	3.2	3.1	3.1	3.2	3.1
2006	3.2	3.2	3.2	3.2	3.2	3.3	3.3	3.3	3.4	3.4	3.5	3.4	3.3
2007	3.3	3.3	3.3	3.3	3.4	3.4	3.4	3.4	3.3	3.3	3.3	3.3	3.3
Financial Activities													
2000	9.5	9.5	9.5	9.5	9.6	9.7	9.6	9.6	9.5	9.3	9.4	9.3	9.5
2001	9.0	8.9	9.0	9.1	9.2	9.4	9.4	9.5	9.4	9.3	9.4	9.4	9.3
2002	9.3	9.3	9.4	9.3	9.5	9.6	9.7	9.6	9.5	9.6	9.6	9.6	9.5
2003	9.4	9.4	9.3	9.4	9.6	9.7	9.7	9.8	9.7	9.7	9.6	9.8	9.6
2004	9.6	9.7	9.7	9.7	9.7	9.9	9.7	9.7	9.6	9.6	9.6	9.7	9.7
2005	9.4	9.4	9.4	9.5	9.6	9.7	9.7	9.7	9.6	9.9	10.0	9.7	9.6
2006	9.6	9.5	9.6	9.6	9.6	9.5	9.5	9.5	9.5	9.6	9.7	9.6	9.6
2007	9.6	9.5	9.5	9.5	9.5	9.5	9.4	9.5	9.4	9.5	9.5	9.6	9.5
Professional and Business Services													
2000	19.5	19.5	19.9	20.6	20.7	21.0	20.9	21.4	21.1	21.3	21.3	21.1	20.7
2001	18.9	18.9	19.2	20.2	20.1	20.5	20.7	20.2	19.7	19.9	20.0	20.1	19.9
2002	19.8	19.9	20.3	20.4	20.5	20.6	20.7	20.8	20.5	20.6	20.5	20.4	20.4
2003	18.7	18.8	18.6	18.6	18.7	19.0	18.6	18.7	18.5	18.9	18.9	18.5	18.7
2004	18.1	18.2	18.5	18.6	18.8	19.2	19.5	19.6	19.6	19.8	19.5	19.5	19.1
2005	19.0	19.4	20.0	20.6	20.8	21.2	21.0	21.0	21.0	20.9	20.9	20.9	20.6
2006	20.6	20.6	20.8	20.9	21.0	21.4	21.0	21.0	20.9	20.8	20.9	20.9	20.9
2007	20.3	20.5	20.6	21.2	21.5	22.1	21.8	21.5	21.0	20.9	21.0	21.1	21.1
Education and Health Services													
2000	36.5	36.8	37.4	37.3	37.4	37.3	37.2	37.1	37.7	37.5	37.6	37.7	37.3
2001	37.5	37.9	38.0	38.4	37.8	37.9	37.9	38.4	38.8	38.6	39.0	39.1	38.3
2002	38.8	39.1	39.3	39.6	39.8	39.7	39.5	39.6	39.7	40.4	40.7	40.8	39.8
2003	40.6	40.7	40.7	40.8	40.8	40.9	40.8	41.0	41.1	41.3	41.3	41.3	40.9
2004	40.8	40.9	41.0	41.4	41.5	41.7	42.1	41.9	42.3	42.8	42.9	43.1	41.9
2005	42.0	42.5	42.5	42.8	42.6	42.7	42.7	42.6	43.4	43.1	43.1	43.2	42.8
2006	41.7	42.5	42.6	42.8	42.8	41.7	41.5	41.3	42.3	43.0	42.9	43.0	42.3
2007	41.8	42.6	42.8	43.0	43.0	42.3	41.7	41.5	42.6	42.7	42.6	42.8	42.5
Leisure and Hospitality													
2000	22.5	22.7	23.2	23.8	24.4	24.8	25.3	25.2	25.7	23.5	23.1	22.9	23.9
2001	21.2	21.5	22.0	23.1	24.0	24.6	24.0	24.4	24.2	22.8	22.4	22.1	23.0
2002	21.5	21.8	22.3	22.8	23.7	24.3	24.7	24.6	24.0	23.1	22.6	22.5	23.2
2003	21.5	21.5	22.0	22.7	23.8	24.4	24.4	24.6	24.1	23.4	22.9	22.8	23.2
2004	21.5	21.5	22.1	23.0	23.9	24.6	24.8	24.8	24.8	23.4	22.9	22.7	23.3
2005	21.7	21.9	22.2	23.3	24.1	24.6	24.6	24.5	24.9	23.2	22.8	22.6	23.4
2006	21.2	21.3	21.6	22.9	23.6	24.2	24.2	24.4	24.4	23.1	22.7	22.5	23.0
2007	21.5	21.4	21.8	22.7	23.7	24.0	24.1	24.0	23.8	22.7	22.3	22.0	22.8
Other Services													
2000	10.6	10.7	10.9	11.0	11.1	11.0	10.7	10.7	10.9	10.5	10.7	10.7	10.8
2001	10.7	10.7	10.9	11.0	11.1	11.1	10.5	10.7	10.8	10.7	10.8	10.8	10.8
2002	10.4	10.7	10.7	10.8	11.0	11.0	10.7	10.7	10.8	11.0	10.8	10.8	10.8
2003	10.5	10.5	10.6	10.7	10.9	10.8	10.8	10.8	10.8	10.9	10.9	10.8	10.8
2004	10.6	10.7	10.8	10.9	10.9	10.9	10.7	10.7	10.7	10.7	10.7	10.7	10.8
2005	10.4	10.5	10.6	10.8	10.8	10.9	10.7	10.6	10.7	10.4	10.5	10.5	10.6
2006	10.4	10.4	10.4	10.5	10.6	10.7	10.6	10.6	10.5	10.4	10.5	10.6	10.5
2007	10.3	10.3	10.5	10.5	10.6	10.6	10.6	10.5	10.4	10.5	10.5	10.6	10.5
Government													
2000	31.8	32.5	32.9	32.2	33.5	32.5	29.7	29.8	32.6	32.4	33.1	33.0	32.2
2001	32.2	33.2	33.6	33.4	33.8	32.8	30.1	29.9	32.8	32.9	33.4	33.3	32.6
2002	32.1	33.2	33.6	33.4	33.8	32.5	30.1	29.7	32.7	32.8	33.6	33.2	32.6
2003	32.3	33.5	34.0	33.2	33.8	32.2	30.3	30.1	32.6	32.8	33.6	33.4	32.6
2004	31.8	33.3	33.1	32.7	33.4	31.9	30.0	29.9	31.9	32.6	33.2	32.8	32.2
2005	31.3	32.7	32.7	32.1	32.5	31.1	29.4	29.2	31.3	31.8	32.7	32.6	31.6
2006	31.4	32.4	32.7	32.3	32.9	31.2	29.5	29.4	31.5	32.0	32.1	32.5	31.7
2007	31.2	32.1	32.2	31.9	32.5	30.9	29.3	29.2	31.2	31.6	32.3	32.2	31.4

Employment by Industry: Bradenton-Sarasota-Venice, FL, 2000–2007

(Numbers in thousands, not seasonally adjusted.)

Industry and year	January	February	March	April	May	June	July	August	September	October	November	December	Annual Average
Total Nonfarm													
2000	241.0	243.5	246.3	247.5	247.4	246.7	242.8	246.1	246.1	248.2	251.0	253.2	246.7
2001	242.4	246.0	248.3	247.4	248.3	245.5	242.6	246.4	246.3	251.1	255.6	258.8	248.2
2002	253.0	257.0	260.9	262.9	261.5	258.3	256.1	259.9	260.4	261.8	263.8	266.0	260.1
2003	261.7	263.6	265.4	263.9	265.1	265.8	259.7	264.7	265.7	268.3	272.9	277.1	266.2
2004	271.1	274.1	277.7	278.7	280.3	278.8	279.0	282.9	283.5	287.6	291.2	295.9	281.7
2005	290.4	294.2	296.5	296.0	297.2	294.4	293.0	296.7	297.6	298.8	302.2	306.0	296.9
2006	300.0	304.2	308.5	307.0	308.0	306.2	301.7	305.0	305.5	303.4	306.6	308.8	305.4
2007	301.5	303.7	306.0	301.2	300.3	296.4	290.9	294.7	293.6	292.2	294.7	296.2	297.6
Total Private													
2000	216.7	219.0	221.7	222.8	222.0	224.2	220.6	221.8	222.0	223.8	226.3	228.3	222.4
2001	218.0	221.3	223.4	222.7	223.4	223.0	220.3	221.8	221.6	225.9	230.0	233.0	223.7
2002	227.7	231.3	235.1	237.2	235.6	234.9	232.9	234.3	234.6	235.9	237.6	239.8	234.7
2003	235.5	237.2	238.9	237.5	238.4	241.7	235.8	238.2	239.1	241.6	245.8	249.8	240.0
2004	244.4	247.1	250.7	251.6	253.0	254.2	254.7	255.9	256.7	260.6	264.0	268.5	255.1
2005	263.5	267.1	269.4	268.7	269.8	269.9	268.6	269.7	270.4	271.0	274.2	278.1	270.0
2006	272.2	276.3	280.4	278.6	279.5	280.6	276.4	276.8	276.9	274.8	277.3	279.5	277.4
2007	272.7	274.6	276.8	272.0	271.2	270.3	265.0	265.9	264.4	262.9	264.8	266.3	268.9
Goods-Producing													
2000	40.9	41.1	41.5	42.3	41.9	41.8	41.2	40.7	40.7	40.4	40.3	40.4	41.1
2001	39.5	39.3	39.4	39.3	39.5	39.9	39.7	39.9	40.1	40.5	40.7	40.8	39.9
2002	40.5	40.8	40.7	40.5	40.7	40.7	40.6	41.1	40.8	40.7	40.7	40.9	40.7
2003	40.1	40.6	40.4	39.8	40.0	40.2	40.1	40.2	40.1	40.6	40.5	40.8	40.3
2004	41.0	41.3	41.8	42.1	42.5	42.7	43.2	43.3	43.5	44.1	44.3	44.8	42.9
2005	44.1	44.8	45.1	45.0	45.7	45.9	46.4	46.7	47.3	47.4	47.8	48.3	46.2
2006	48.0	48.6	49.0	48.8	49.3	49.6	49.2	49.2	49.0	48.4	47.9	47.8	48.7
2007	46.3	45.9	45.8	44.3	44.1	43.5	42.3	42.1	41.3	41.2	40.8	40.8	43.2
Natural Resources, Mining, and Construction													
2000	18.9	19.2	19.4	19.8	19.8	19.9	19.7	19.6	19.5	19.6	19.6	19.8	19.6
2001	18.9	19.0	19.1	19.0	19.2	19.5	19.5	19.8	19.9	20.5	20.7	20.6	19.6
2002	20.6	20.8	20.8	20.7	21.0	21.1	21.1	21.4	21.3	21.6	21.7	21.9	21.2
2003	21.4	21.9	21.9	21.6	21.8	21.9	21.8	21.9	21.9	22.3	22.3	22.5	21.9
2004	22.8	23.0	23.4	23.8	24.0	24.1	24.5	24.4	24.6	25.3	25.4	25.7	24.3
2005	25.4	26.0	26.3	26.3	26.8	26.9	27.3	27.5	28.0	28.1	28.5	28.9	27.2
2006	28.8	29.4	29.8	29.7	30.1	30.3	30.1	30.3	30.3	29.9	29.5	29.3	29.8
2007	28.1	27.9	27.8	26.5	26.3	25.9	24.9	24.8	24.1	24.1	23.8	23.8	25.7
Manufacturing													
2000	22.0	21.9	22.1	22.5	22.1	21.9	21.5	21.1	21.2	20.8	20.7	20.6	21.5
2001	20.6	20.3	20.3	20.3	20.3	20.4	20.2	20.1	20.2	20.0	20.0	20.2	20.2
2002	19.9	20.0	19.9	19.8	19.7	19.6	19.5	19.7	19.5	19.1	19.0	19.0	19.6
2003	18.7	18.7	18.5	18.2	18.2	18.3	18.3	18.3	18.2	18.3	18.2	18.3	18.3
2004	18.2	18.3	18.4	18.3	18.5	18.6	18.7	18.9	18.9	18.8	18.9	19.1	18.6
2005	18.7	18.8	18.8	18.7	18.9	19.0	19.1	19.2	19.3	19.3	19.3	19.4	19.0
2006	19.2	19.2	19.2	19.1	19.2	19.3	19.1	18.9	18.7	18.5	18.4	18.5	18.9
2007	18.2	18.0	18.0	17.8	17.8	17.6	17.4	17.3	17.2	17.1	17.0	17.0	17.5
Service-Providing													
2000	200.1	202.4	204.8	205.2	205.5	204.9	201.6	205.4	205.4	207.8	210.7	212.8	205.6
2001	202.9	206.7	208.9	208.1	208.8	205.6	202.9	206.5	206.2	210.6	214.9	218.0	208.3
2002	212.5	216.2	220.2	222.4	220.8	217.6	215.5	218.8	219.6	221.1	223.1	225.1	219.4
2003	221.6	223.0	225.0	224.1	225.1	225.6	219.6	224.5	225.6	227.7	232.4	236.3	225.9
2004	230.1	232.8	235.9	236.6	237.8	236.1	235.8	239.6	240.0	243.5	246.9	251.1	238.9
2005	246.3	249.4	251.4	251.0	251.5	248.5	246.6	250.0	250.3	251.4	254.4	257.7	250.7
2006	252.0	255.6	259.5	258.2	258.7	256.6	252.5	255.8	256.5	255.0	258.7	261.0	256.7
2007	255.2	257.8	260.2	256.9	256.2	252.9	248.6	252.6	252.3	251.0	253.9	255.4	254.4
Trade, Transportation, and Utilities													
2000	48.6	48.8	48.8	49.4	49.1	48.8	47.7	48.0	47.9	48.6	50.3	51.1	48.9
2001	47.7	47.8	48.2	48.1	47.7	47.2	46.5	46.5	46.4	47.5	48.9	49.9	47.7
2002	48.3	48.0	48.3	48.0	47.7	47.4	46.8	47.0	47.3	47.5	48.8	49.9	47.9
2003	48.0	47.6	48.0	47.9	47.7	47.3	46.6	47.0	47.2	47.8	49.1	50.7	47.9
2004	49.3	49.5	49.7	49.5	49.4	49.2	49.3	49.3	49.3	50.3	51.9	52.8	50.0
2005	50.8	51.2	51.5	51.6	51.5	51.1	50.6	50.5	50.5	50.6	51.7	52.5	51.2
2006	50.7	50.8	51.3	51.4	51.4	51.2	50.1	50.1	50.1	50.1	51.4	52.5	50.9
2007	51.7	51.3	51.6	50.7	50.6	50.3	49.7	49.6	49.1	48.8	50.0	50.7	50.3
Wholesale Trade													
2000	6.9	6.9	7.0	7.0	7.0	6.8	6.8	6.8	6.8	6.9	7.1	6.9	6.9
2001	6.6	6.6	6.7	7.0	7.0	6.9	6.8	6.9	6.8	7.1	7.2	7.2	6.9
2002	7.1	7.1	7.1	7.2	7.2	7.2	7.2	7.3	7.4	7.5	7.5	7.5	7.3
2003	7.2	7.2	7.4	7.4	7.4	7.3	7.2	7.3	7.4	7.3	7.4	7.5	7.3
2004	7.3	7.4	7.4	7.6	7.6	7.4	7.5	7.5	7.5	7.6	7.9	7.9	7.6
2005	7.8	8.0	8.0	8.2	8.3	8.2	8.1	8.2	8.3	8.3	8.4	8.6	8.2
2006	8.4	8.5	8.6	8.6	8.7	8.8	8.6	8.6	8.7	8.5	8.4	8.6	8.6
2007	8.7	8.7	8.7	8.7	8.8	8.8	8.6	8.6	8.5	8.5	8.6	8.7	8.7
Retail Trade													
2000	38.3	38.5	38.4	39.0	38.8	38.7	37.6	37.8	37.7	38.4	39.9	40.7	38.7
2001	37.9	37.8	38.1	37.7	37.4	37.0	36.4	36.4	36.3	37.1	38.4	39.3	37.5
2002	38.0	37.7	38.0	37.6	37.3	37.0	36.4	36.6	36.7	36.9	38.1	39.1	37.5
2003	37.6	37.3	37.5	37.3	37.1	36.8	36.1	36.4	36.5	37.2	38.3	39.5	37.3
2004	38.5	38.5	38.6	38.3	38.2	38.2	38.1	38.1	38.1	38.8	40.0	40.9	38.7
2005	39.3	39.5	39.7	39.6	39.4	39.1	38.7	38.5	38.4	38.5	39.2	39.7	39.1
2006	38.5	38.5	38.9	38.9	38.8	38.6	37.8	37.8	37.6	37.8	39.1	39.6	38.5
2007	39.1	38.9	39.1	38.3	38.2	37.9	37.5	37.4	37.0	36.7	37.7	38.2	38.0

Employment by Industry: Bradenton-Sarasota-Venice, FL, 2000–2007—*Continued*

(Numbers in thousands, not seasonally adjusted.)

Industry and year	January	February	March	April	May	June	July	August	September	October	November	December	Annual Average
Transportation and Utilities													
2000	3.4	3.4	3.4	3.4	3.3	3.3	3.3	3.4	3.4	3.3	3.3	3.5	3.4
2001	3.2	3.4	3.4	3.4	3.3	3.3	3.3	3.2	3.3	3.3	3.3	3.4	3.3
2002	3.2	3.2	3.2	3.2	3.2	3.2	3.2	3.1	3.2	3.1	3.2	3.3	3.2
2003	3.2	3.1	3.1	3.2	3.2	3.2	3.3	3.3	3.3	3.3	3.4	3.7	3.2
2004	3.5	3.6	3.7	3.6	3.6	3.6	3.7	3.7	3.7	3.9	4.0	4.0	3.7
2005	3.7	3.7	3.8	3.8	3.8	3.8	3.8	3.8	3.8	3.8	4.1	4.2	3.8
2006	3.8	3.8	3.8	3.9	3.9	3.8	3.7	3.7	3.8	3.8	3.9	4.3	3.9
2007	3.9	3.7	3.8	3.7	3.6	3.6	3.6	3.6	3.6	3.6	3.7	3.8	3.7
Information													
2000	4.3	4.2	4.3	4.4	4.3	4.4	4.6	4.6	4.5	4.5	4.5	4.5	4.4
2001	4.5	4.5	4.4	4.3	4.4	4.5	4.4	4.4	4.3	4.2	4.3	4.3	4.4
2002	4.3	4.3	4.3	4.3	4.3	4.3	4.3	4.2	4.2	4.3	4.3	4.3	4.3
2003	4.3	4.3	4.3	4.2	4.3	4.3	4.3	4.4	4.3	4.2	4.3	4.3	4.2
2004	4.2	4.2	4.2	4.1	4.3	4.3	4.2	4.1	4.1	4.1	4.2	4.2	4.2
2005	4.1	4.2	4.2	4.3	4.3	4.4	4.4	4.4	4.3	4.3	4.4	4.4	4.3
2006	4.2	4.3	4.3	4.3	4.3	4.3	4.4	4.5	4.4	4.6	4.6	4.6	4.4
2007	4.4	4.3	4.3	4.3	4.2	4.2	4.1	4.1	4.1	4.0	4.1	4.1	4.2
Financial Activities													
2000	12.9	12.9	13.0	13.3	13.5	13.6	13.2	13.0	12.9	13.0	13.0	13.0	13.1
2001	12.9	12.9	13.0	13.1	13.1	13.3	13.2	13.3	13.3	13.4	13.6	13.7	13.2
2002	13.7	13.7	13.7	13.6	13.5	13.7	13.7	13.8	13.7	13.7	13.8	14.0	13.7
2003	13.7	13.6	13.6	13.8	13.8	13.8	14.1	14.1	14.0	14.1	14.1	14.3	13.9
2004	14.1	14.3	14.4	14.5	14.5	14.7	15.0	15.0	15.1	15.4	15.7	15.8	14.9
2005	15.4	15.5	15.4	15.6	15.6	15.7	15.7	15.9	15.9	16.2	16.3	16.5	15.8
2006	16.1	16.2	16.3	16.2	16.2	16.3	16.3	16.2	16.1	16.1	16.3	16.3	16.5	16.2
2007	16.0	16.0	16.1	16.2	16.2	16.1	15.9	15.9	15.9	16.0	15.9	15.9	16.0
Professional and Business Services													
2000	37.2	38.2	39.2	37.1	37.6	39.7	40.8	42.4	42.5	42.5	42.6	43.1	40.2
2001	39.6	41.7	42.4	42.2	43.9	43.7	43.2	43.9	43.6	45.7	46.5	47.3	43.6
2002	45.1	48.0	50.6	54.1	53.1	52.3	52.0	52.0	52.2	52.3	50.7	50.0	51.0
2003	50.5	50.9	51.2	51.8	52.8	57.1	53.6	55.2	56.1	57.0	58.3	59.3	54.5
2004	55.5	57.2	58.3	59.4	60.6	62.3	62.7	63.8	64.5	65.6	65.5	67.4	61.9
2005	66.3	67.8	68.5	68.5	69.4	70.2	70.5	70.9	71.0	70.8	71.0	72.6	69.8
2006	70.2	72.0	73.8	72.5	73.1	74.3	73.2	73.2	73.7	71.6	71.6	71.4	72.6
2007	68.4	69.4	70.1	68.7	69.0	69.6	68.6	69.4	69.6	68.2	68.0	68.3	68.9
Education and Health Services													
2000	34.0	34.4	34.7	35.2	34.9	35.4	34.5	34.7	35.2	35.6	35.9	36.0	35.0
2001	34.1	34.5	34.7	34.4	34.3	34.6	33.9	34.1	34.5	34.4	34.6	35.0	34.4
2002	34.3	34.4	34.7	34.7	34.9	35.0	34.9	35.4	35.8	36.2	36.7	37.0	35.3
2003	36.3	36.7	37.0	36.7	37.0	36.9	36.3	36.6	37.0	37.2	37.5	37.5	36.8
2004	37.1	37.4	37.6	37.7	38.0	37.9	37.5	37.8	38.1	38.5	38.8	39.0	38.0
2005	38.0	38.3	38.5	38.2	38.4	38.3	38.0	38.2	38.4	38.5	38.8	39.2	38.4
2006	38.4	38.9	39.2	39.1	39.3	39.3	38.9	38.9	39.2	39.4	39.2	39.6	40.0	39.2
2007	39.7	40.5	40.4	40.0	40.0	40.0	39.7	40.0	40.3	40.4	40.6	40.3	40.2
Leisure and Hospitality													
2000	27.0	27.6	28.3	29.1	28.6	28.1	26.6	26.4	26.2	27.0	27.5	27.9	27.5
2001	27.7	28.4	29.1	29.1	28.3	27.5	27.1	27.3	27.0	27.8	28.9	29.4	28.1
2002	28.7	29.2	30.0	29.1	28.5	28.6	28.0	28.2	27.9	28.4	29.7	30.7	28.9
2003	29.7	30.4	31.3	30.6	30.1	29.5	28.4	28.4	28.0	28.3	29.6	30.4	29.6
2004	30.5	30.9	31.8	31.8	31.1	30.4	30.1	29.9	29.5	30.2	31.1	31.9	30.8
2005	32.0	32.5	33.3	32.9	32.3	31.7	30.6	30.7	30.4	30.7	31.7	32.0	31.7
2006	31.8	32.5	33.3	33.2	32.7	32.3	31.5	31.4	30.9	31.3	32.3	33.1	32.2
2007	32.9	33.9	35.0	34.4	33.8	33.1	31.8	31.8	31.1	31.3	32.3	33.1	32.9
Other Services													
2000	11.8	11.8	11.9	12.0	12.1	12.4	12.0	12.0	12.1	12.2	12.2	12.3	12.1
2001	12.0	12.2	12.2	12.2	12.2	12.3	12.3	12.4	12.4	12.4	12.5	12.6	12.3
2002	12.8	12.9	12.8	12.9	12.9	12.9	12.6	12.6	12.7	12.8	12.9	13.0	12.8
2003	12.9	13.1	13.1	12.7	12.7	12.6	12.4	12.3	12.4	12.4	12.4	12.5	12.6
2004	12.7	12.3	12.9	12.5	12.6	12.7	12.7	12.7	12.6	12.4	12.5	12.6	12.6
2005	12.8	12.8	12.9	12.6	12.6	12.6	12.4	12.4	12.6	12.5	12.5	12.6	12.6
2006	12.8	13.0	13.2	13.1	13.2	13.3	12.9	13.1	13.3	13.3	13.6	13.6	13.2
2007	13.3	13.3	13.5	13.4	13.3	13.5	12.9	13.0	13.0	13.0	13.1	13.1	13.2
Government													
2000	24.3	24.5	24.6	24.7	25.4	22.5	22.2	24.3	24.1	24.4	24.7	24.9	24.2
2001	24.4	24.7	24.9	24.7	24.9	22.5	22.3	24.6	24.7	25.2	25.6	25.8	24.5
2002	25.3	25.7	25.8	25.7	25.9	23.4	23.2	25.6	25.8	25.9	26.2	26.2	25.4
2003	26.2	26.4	26.5	26.4	26.7	24.1	23.9	26.5	26.6	26.7	27.1	27.3	26.2
2004	26.7	27.0	27.0	27.1	27.3	24.6	24.3	27.0	26.8	27.0	27.2	27.4	26.6
2005	26.9	27.1	27.1	27.3	27.4	24.5	24.4	27.0	27.2	27.8	28.0	27.9	26.9
2006	27.8	27.9	28.1	28.4	28.5	25.6	25.3	28.2	28.6	28.6	29.3	29.3	28.0
2007	28.8	29.1	29.2	29.2	29.1	26.1	25.9	28.8	29.2	29.3	29.9	29.9	28.7

Employment by Industry: New Haven, CT, NECTA, 2000–2007

(Numbers in thousands, not seasonally adjusted.)

Industry and year	January	February	March	April	May	June	July	August	September	October	November	December	Annual Average
Total Nonfarm													
2000	269.0	272.7	275.0	275.1	276.6	278.9	269.8	269.0	275.5	275.5	277.5	279.2	274.5
2001	268.1	270.3	271.4	273.8	275.7	279.0	269.2	269.4	275.1	275.1	276.8	278.1	273.5
2002	269.0	270.9	272.6	275.2	277.6	281.3	271.0	270.5	276.0	275.0	277.0	278.1	274.5
2003	267.5	269.0	269.0	270.6	271.6	271.7	265.8	265.1	267.7	271.4	274.6	275.5	270.0
2004	266.6	268.0	269.2	271.5	273.4	273.8	269.8	267.6	271.3	275.5	277.0	278.0	271.8
2005	268.2	270.7	269.3	275.1	275.6	277.6	270.2	268.0	274.5	274.8	277.7	278.8	273.4
2006	270.2	273.7	273.4	276.9	278.8	280.3	272.2	270.5	276.6	278.7	280.5	281.9	276.1
2007	272.3	275.0	273.8	277.8	279.7	281.9	273.9	272.6	277.9	280.2	281.7	282.5	277.4
Total Private													
2000	234.3	236.9	239.1	239.1	241.2	243.9	239.2	238.6	240.7	240.1	241.7	243.3	239.8
2001	233.0	234.6	235.8	238.0	240.0	243.7	238.4	238.2	240.9	239.5	240.1	241.5	238.6
2002	233.3	234.6	236.4	239.5	241.8	245.1	240.3	239.5	241.9	239.3	240.2	241.3	239.4
2003	231.7	232.9	232.7	234.4	235.5	237.5	234.6	234.3	233.7	236.1	238.2	239.5	235.1
2004	231.8	232.4	233.3	235.8	237.7	239.8	238.3	237.1	237.8	240.3	241.2	242.3	237.3
2005	233.9	235.5	234.2	239.4	240.2	241.8	239.8	238.2	240.8	240.1	242.3	243.3	239.1
2006	234.9	238.2	238.0	241.5	243.1	244.3	241.4	240.1	242.7	243.8	245.1	246.4	241.6
2007	237.3	239.7	238.5	242.6	244.3	245.7	243.3	242.3	243.9	245.7	246.6	247.6	243.1
Goods-Producing													
2000	50.3	50.3	50.8	50.6	51.0	51.8	51.3	51.3	51.4	51.1	50.9	50.7	51.0
2001	49.3	48.8	49.3	49.6	49.8	50.4	50.6	50.1	50.2	49.8	49.4	48.9	49.7
2002	47.5	46.9	47.2	47.4	47.7	48.1	47.7	47.5	47.3	46.8	46.5	46.1	47.2
2003	44.4	44.0	44.0	44.6	45.1	45.7	45.3	45.4	45.1	45.1	45.0	45.0	44.9
2004	43.9	43.5	44.3	45.1	45.7	46.3	46.4	46.4	46.1	45.7	45.6	45.3	45.4
2005	43.9	43.4	43.7	44.2	44.5	45.3	45.3	45.1	44.5	44.2	44.1	43.8	44.3
2006	43.3	43.1	43.3	44.0	44.4	45.0	44.9	44.7	44.1	44.0	43.9	43.7	44.0
2007	42.9	42.5	42.7	43.4	43.7	44.2	44.0	44.2	43.8	43.6	43.6	43.2	43.5
Natural Resources, Mining, and Construction													
2000	10.1	10.0	10.4	10.7	11.2	11.7	11.7	11.7	11.6	11.4	11.2	10.9	11.1
2001	9.8	9.7	10.1	11.3	11.7	12.0	12.0	12.0	11.8	11.5	11.5	11.1	11.2
2002	10.0	10.0	10.4	11.1	11.5	11.7	11.7	11.7	11.5	11.3	11.2	10.6	11.1
2003	9.6	9.4	9.6	10.2	10.8	11.1	11.3	11.4	11.1	11.1	11.0	10.8	10.6
2004	9.9	9.7	10.3	11.3	11.8	12.1	12.3	12.3	12.0	11.7	11.5	11.1	11.3
2005	10.0	9.7	9.9	10.6	11.0	11.4	11.7	11.8	11.4	11.3	11.2	10.9	10.9
2006	10.1	10.1	10.3	11.1	11.5	11.9	12.1	12.1	12.0	11.7	11.6	11.4	11.3
2007	10.7	10.4	10.7	11.3	11.7	12.1	12.3	12.4	12.1	12.0	11.9	11.5	11.6
Manufacturing													
2000	40.2	40.3	40.4	39.9	39.8	40.1	39.6	39.6	39.8	39.7	39.7	39.8	39.9
2001	39.5	39.1	39.2	38.3	38.1	38.4	38.6	38.1	38.4	38.3	37.9	37.8	38.5
2002	37.5	36.9	36.8	36.3	36.2	36.4	36.0	35.8	35.8	35.5	35.3	35.5	36.2
2003	34.8	34.6	34.4	34.4	34.3	34.6	34.0	34.0	34.0	34.0	34.1	34.2	34.3
2004	34.0	33.8	34.0	33.8	33.9	34.2	34.1	34.1	34.1	34.0	34.1	34.2	34.0
2005	33.9	33.7	33.8	33.6	33.5	33.9	33.6	33.3	33.1	32.9	32.9	32.9	33.4
2006	33.2	33.0	33.0	32.9	32.9	33.1	32.8	32.6	32.1	32.3	32.3	32.3	32.7
2007	32.2	32.1	32.0	32.1	32.0	32.1	31.7	31.8	31.7	31.6	31.7	31.7	31.9
Service-Providing													
2000	218.7	222.4	224.2	224.5	225.6	227.1	218.5	217.7	224.1	224.4	226.6	228.5	223.5
2001	218.8	221.5	222.1	224.2	225.9	228.6	218.6	219.3	224.9	225.3	227.4	229.2	223.8
2002	221.5	224.0	225.4	227.8	229.9	233.2	223.3	223.0	228.7	228.2	230.5	232.0	227.3
2003	223.1	225.0	225.0	226.0	226.5	226.0	220.5	219.7	222.6	226.3	229.5	230.5	225.1
2004	222.7	224.5	224.9	226.4	227.7	227.5	223.4	221.2	225.2	229.8	231.4	232.7	226.5
2005	224.3	227.3	225.6	230.9	231.1	232.3	224.9	222.9	230.0	230.6	233.6	235.0	229.0
2006	226.9	230.6	230.1	232.9	234.4	235.3	227.3	225.8	232.5	234.7	236.6	238.2	232.1
2007	229.4	232.5	231.1	234.4	236.0	237.7	229.9	228.4	234.1	236.6	238.1	239.3	234.0
Trade, Transportation, and Utilities													
2000	49.1	48.6	49.1	48.8	49.0	49.3	48.8	48.8	49.4	49.8	50.8	51.7	49.4
2001	48.8	47.9	47.9	48.2	48.8	49.3	48.8	48.8	49.1	49.7	50.5	51.3	49.1
2002	49.5	48.7	49.0	50.2	50.7	51.4	50.1	49.7	50.5	50.5	51.4	52.3	50.3
2003	49.7	48.8	49.2	48.8	49.4	49.8	48.4	48.4	49.0	50.1	51.0	51.7	49.5
2004	49.8	48.9	49.3	49.2	49.7	50.3	49.7	49.6	50.4	51.2	52.1	52.9	50.3
2005	51.0	50.3	50.2	50.8	51.3	51.6	50.6	50.4	51.1	51.3	52.4	53.1	51.2
2006	51.4	50.4	50.8	51.1	51.7	52.1	50.8	50.5	51.0	51.4	52.5	53.3	51.4
2007	51.6	51.0	51.0	50.9	51.8	52.4	51.2	50.9	51.1	51.7	52.9	53.5	51.7
Wholesale Trade													
2000	11.2	11.3	11.4	11.3	11.4	11.5	11.4	11.4	11.5	11.4	11.5	11.6	11.4
2001	11.3	11.4	11.3	11.4	11.4	11.4	11.5	11.4	11.3	11.3	11.2	11.2	11.3
2002	11.1	11.0	11.0	11.3	11.4	11.4	11.1	11.1	11.1	11.0	11.0	11.0	11.1
2003	10.8	10.7	10.8	10.8	11.0	11.1	11.1	11.2	11.2	11.5	11.6	11.7	11.1
2004	11.4	11.3	11.4	11.5	11.5	11.6	11.3	11.3	11.4	11.4	11.4	11.5	11.4
2005	11.4	11.3	11.3	11.4	11.4	11.4	11.4	11.4	11.4	11.5	11.6	11.6	11.4
2006	11.5	11.5	11.5	11.6	11.7	11.8	11.7	11.7	11.6	11.5	11.5	11.5	11.6
2007	11.6	11.6	11.5	11.4	11.5	11.6	11.6	11.6	11.5	11.6	11.6	11.6	11.6
Retail Trade													
2000	30.2	29.6	30.1	29.8	29.9	30.1	30.0	30.1	30.0	30.4	31.3	32.1	30.3
2001	29.9	29.0	29.2	29.2	29.7	30.1	29.9	30.2	30.2	30.7	31.6	32.4	30.2
2002	31.0	30.2	30.6	30.9	31.2	32.0	31.5	31.3	31.4	31.4	32.3	33.2	31.4
2003	31.2	30.4	30.6	30.3	30.6	30.8	30.0	30.0	29.9	30.4	31.2	31.8	30.6
2004	30.4	29.6	29.9	29.7	30.0	30.4	30.6	30.6	30.4	30.8	31.6	32.2	30.5
2005	30.4	29.7	29.5	29.9	30.2	30.5	30.2	30.1	30.1	30.4	31.3	32.0	30.4
2006	30.7	29.8	30.1	30.3	30.8	31.2	30.8	30.7	30.5	31.1	32.2	32.8	30.9
2007	31.2	30.6	30.7	30.7	31.4	31.8	31.2	31.1	30.7	31.1	32.3	32.8	31.3

Employment by Industry: New Haven, CT, NECTA, 2000–2007—*Continued*

(Numbers in thousands, not seasonally adjusted.)

Industry and year	January	February	March	April	May	June	July	August	September	October	November	December	Annual Average
Transportation and Utilities													
2000	7.7	7.7	7.6	7.7	7.7	7.7	7.4	7.3	7.9	8.0	8.0	8.0	7.7
2001	7.6	7.5	7.4	7.6	7.7	7.8	7.4	7.2	7.6	7.7	7.7	7.7	7.6
2002	7.4	7.5	7.4	8.0	8.1	8.0	7.5	7.3	8.0	8.1	8.1	8.1	7.8
2003	7.7	7.7	7.8	7.7	7.8	7.9	7.3	7.2	7.9	8.2	8.2	8.2	7.8
2004	8.0	8.0	8.0	8.0	8.2	8.3	7.8	7.7	8.6	9.0	9.1	9.2	8.3
2005	9.2	9.3	9.4	9.5	9.7	9.7	9.0	8.9	9.6	9.4	9.5	9.5	9.4
2006	9.2	9.1	9.2	9.2	9.2	9.1	8.3	8.1	8.9	8.8	8.8	9.0	8.9
2007	8.8	8.8	8.8	8.8	8.9	9.0	8.4	8.2	8.9	9.0	9.0	9.1	8.8
Information													
2000	9.7	9.7	9.8	9.6	9.6	9.8	10.1	10.2	10.2	10.5	10.5	10.4	10.0
2001	10.6	10.6	10.5	10.2	10.2	10.2	10.1	10.2	10.1	10.1	10.1	10.3	10.3
2002	10.0	10.0	10.0	9.8	9.8	9.8	9.7	9.6	9.6	9.5	9.4	9.5	9.7
2003	9.2	9.2	9.2	9.1	9.1	9.1	9.1	9.1	9.0	8.9	9.0	9.0	9.1
2004	8.7	8.6	8.6	8.6	8.6	8.7	8.7	8.7	8.6	8.7	8.7	8.7	8.7
2005	8.6	8.8	8.5	8.4	8.4	8.5	8.4	8.3	8.3	8.2	8.3	8.2	8.4
2006	8.3	8.3	8.2	8.2	8.2	8.2	8.1	8.1	8.0	8.1	8.1	8.2	8.2
2007	8.1	8.2	8.1	8.2	8.1	8.1	8.1	8.0	8.0	8.0	8.0	8.0	8.1
Financial Activities													
2000	13.8	13.7	13.7	13.7	13.7	13.9	14.0	13.9	13.7	13.7	13.7	13.9	13.8
2001	13.9	14.0	14.0	13.8	13.9	14.1	14.2	14.2	14.1	14.1	14.1	14.2	14.1
2002	14.0	13.8	13.9	14.1	14.2	14.3	14.6	14.6	14.3	14.2	14.2	14.3	14.2
2003	14.1	14.1	14.1	14.1	14.2	14.4	14.4	14.5	14.4	14.2	14.2	14.3	14.3
2004	14.1	14.1	14.2	14.2	14.2	14.4	14.2	14.1	14.0	14.0	14.0	14.0	14.1
2005	13.8	13.8	13.8	13.9	14.1	14.3	14.3	14.3	14.1	14.0	14.1	14.1	14.1
2006	14.0	14.0	13.9	14.0	14.0	14.1	14.1	14.1	13.9	13.9	14.0	14.0	14.0
2007	13.8	13.8	13.7	13.7	13.8	13.9	13.8	13.8	13.5	13.4	13.4	13.5	13.7
Professional and Business Services													
2000	28.5	29.2	29.6	29.1	29.9	30.6	29.7	29.9	29.7	28.9	29.3	29.8	29.5
2001	27.6	27.9	28.5	28.3	29.4	29.5	28.6	28.9	29.5	27.9	27.8	28.3	28.5
2002	27.4	27.4	28.0	27.6	27.9	28.9	28.1	28.8	29.0	27.7	27.9	27.9	28.1
2003	26.5	26.7	26.6	26.4	26.6	26.8	26.4	26.6	26.5	26.5	26.8	26.9	26.6
2004	25.2	25.6	25.5	25.7	25.9	26.3	26.0	26.0	25.8	25.1	25.2	25.6	25.7
2005	24.6	24.7	24.8	25.7	25.5	26.5	26.2	26.1	25.9	25.5	25.6	25.9	25.6
2006	25.0	25.6	25.8	26.1	26.4	27.2	25.9	26.1	26.2	26.0	26.2	26.4	26.1
2007	25.4	25.6	25.8	26.0	26.2	26.7	26.3	26.5	26.5	26.5	26.7	26.6	26.2
Education and Health Services													
2000	56.3	58.4	58.8	59.3	59.3	58.2	54.8	54.3	57.3	57.5	57.8	58.0	57.5
2001	55.9	58.3	58.2	59.9	58.4	59.8	56.0	55.9	59.5	59.8	60.1	60.3	58.5
2002	58.1	60.7	60.3	61.6	61.6	61.5	58.9	58.4	61.8	61.8	62.4	62.6	60.8
2003	60.6	62.6	61.6	62.5	61.5	60.3	59.1	58.7	59.4	61.4	62.4	62.8	61.1
2004	61.5	63.2	62.1	62.8	62.0	60.9	60.2	59.2	61.2	64.7	65.1	64.8	62.3
2005	62.8	65.0	63.5	65.4	64.4	62.3	61.7	60.8	64.8	65.5	66.6	66.8	64.1
2006	62.7	66.7	65.1	66.9	65.9	64.0	63.9	63.1	67.1	68.4	68.9	68.8	66.0
2007	64.9	68.3	66.5	68.7	67.8	66.3	65.8	65.0	68.3	70.1	69.8	70.2	67.6
Leisure and Hospitality													
2000	16.8	17.1	17.4	18.0	18.7	20.2	20.4	20.2	18.9	18.5	18.5	18.6	18.6
2001	17.1	17.3	17.5	18.1	19.3	20.1	19.9	19.9	18.4	18.1	17.9	18.0	18.5
2002	16.6	16.9	17.6	18.5	19.4	20.5	20.7	20.5	19.1	18.6	18.2	18.2	18.7
2003	17.1	17.5	17.8	18.9	19.5	20.9	21.5	21.3	20.2	19.7	19.3	19.3	19.4
2004	18.4	18.4	19.0	19.8	20.8	22.0	22.1	22.0	21.0	20.3	19.8	20.1	20.3
2005	18.5	18.8	18.9	20.2	21.1	22.1	22.2	22.2	21.3	20.6	20.3	20.3	20.5
2006	19.5	19.5	20.2	20.4	21.5	22.6	22.6	22.4	21.5	20.9	20.4	20.8	21.0
2007	19.7	19.6	20.0	20.8	22.0	22.9	23.0	22.8	21.8	21.4	21.1	21.3	21.4
Other Services													
2000	9.8	9.9	9.9	10.0	10.0	10.1	10.1	10.0	10.1	10.1	10.2	10.2	10.0
2001	9.8	9.8	9.9	9.9	10.2	10.3	10.2	10.2	10.0	10.0	10.2	10.2	10.1
2002	10.2	10.2	10.4	10.3	10.5	10.6	10.5	10.4	10.3	10.2	10.2	10.4	10.4
2003	10.1	10.0	10.2	10.0	10.1	10.5	10.4	10.3	10.1	10.2	10.4	10.5	10.2
2004	10.2	10.1	10.3	10.4	10.8	10.9	11.0	11.1	10.7	10.6	10.7	10.9	10.6
2005	10.7	10.7	10.8	10.8	10.9	11.2	11.1	11.0	10.8	10.8	10.9	11.1	10.9
2006	10.7	10.6	10.7	10.8	11.0	11.1	11.1	11.1	10.9	11.1	11.1	11.2	11.0
2007	10.9	10.7	10.7	10.9	10.9	11.2	11.1	11.1	10.9	11.0	11.1	11.3	11.0
Government													
2000	34.7	35.8	35.9	36.0	35.4	35.0	30.6	30.4	34.8	35.4	35.8	35.9	34.6
2001	35.1	35.7	35.6	35.8	35.7	35.3	30.8	31.2	34.2	35.6	36.7	36.6	34.9
2002	35.7	36.3	36.2	35.7	35.8	36.2	30.7	31.0	34.1	35.7	36.8	36.8	35.1
2003	35.8	36.1	35.9	36.2	36.1	34.2	31.2	30.8	34.0	35.3	36.4	36.0	34.9
2004	34.8	35.6	35.9	35.7	35.7	34.0	31.5	30.5	33.5	35.2	35.8	35.7	34.5
2005	34.3	35.2	35.1	35.7	35.4	35.8	30.4	29.8	33.7	34.7	35.4	35.5	34.3
2006	35.3	35.5	35.4	35.4	35.7	36.0	30.8	30.4	33.9	34.9	35.4	35.5	34.5
2007	35.0	35.3	35.3	35.2	35.4	36.2	30.6	30.3	34.0	34.5	35.1	34.9	34.3

Employment by Industry: Wichita, KS, 2000–2007

(Numbers in thousands, not seasonally adjusted.)

Industry and year	January	February	March	April	May	June	July	August	September	October	November	December	Annual Average
Total Nonfarm													
2000	291.2	291.2	293.1	295.9	297.1	299.2	290.3	290.8	296.7	297.8	299.1	299.4	295.2
2001	293.2	294.3	298.4	301.1	302.8	304.1	293.5	293.7	301.1	300.8	300.2	299.8	298.6
2002	294.1	292.2	295.1	296.1	296.1	295.8	285.5	285.9	291.8	291.5	292.8	293.2	292.5
2003	280.3	281.8	283.3	283.0	284.2	282.0	273.6	273.3	281.2	282.2	283.1	283.8	281.0
2004	276.7	277.2	279.7	284.1	284.5	284.1	279.7	279.2	286.1	287.5	288.4	290.1	283.1
2005	282.9	283.5	284.7	287.0	288.0	288.5	283.5	283.4	288.4	289.5	291.8	292.5	287.0
2006	285.3	288.3	290.2	292.7	294.6	295.7	290.2	291.8	297.2	299.3	300.4	302.5	294.0
2007	295.6	295.7	300.1	301.5	302.7	306.2	300.5	300.2	305.0	306.5	308.0	308.5	302.5
Total Private													
2000	254.6	254.0	255.3	258.2	259.2	261.7	259.4	259.7	259.7	259.7	260.4	260.9	258.6
2001	254.7	255.7	259.1	262.2	263.3	265.5	263.2	263.4	263.0	261.3	260.5	260.1	261.0
2002	254.9	253.2	255.5	256.6	256.2	256.6	255.4	254.8	253.5	252.2	253.0	253.1	254.6
2003	240.8	242.1	243.6	243.2	244.2	241.4	242.9	242.1	243.0	243.0	243.2	243.7	242.8
2004	237.5	237.9	240.3	244.4	245.5	245.5	247.7	247.4	247.8	248.3	248.8	250.4	245.1
2005	243.6	243.8	244.7	247.0	247.8	249.4	248.6	248.8	248.9	248.7	250.5	251.1	247.7
2006	245.2	247.2	248.9	252.0	252.8	256.0	254.6	255.7	256.9	258.2	259.1	261.1	254.0
2007	255.4	254.9	258.9	260.9	262.0	265.1	264.5	264.2	264.6	265.1	266.2	266.6	262.4
Goods-Producing													
2000	88.2	88.0	88.5	89.1	89.3	90.3	89.3	89.6	89.1	89.0	89.0	88.9	89.0
2001	86.7	87.0	88.4	90.0	90.1	91.4	91.4	91.1	90.7	88.9	88.2	87.1	89.3
2002	85.0	83.2	83.3	82.5	82.0	82.3	82.4	81.7	80.8	79.9	79.1	78.9	81.8
2003	75.0	76.2	75.8	75.2	75.2	72.8	74.5	73.9	74.0	74.2	73.7	73.5	74.5
2004	72.1	72.4	73.3	74.0	74.1	73.0	76.2	75.5	75.8	75.6	75.6	76.0	74.5
2005	74.3	74.5	75.1	75.9	76.4	77.3	77.7	77.4	76.5	77.4	77.4	77.4	76.4
2006	76.8	77.8	77.7	77.7	78.0	79.4	80.2	80.3	80.3	79.8	80.3	80.5	79.1
2007	80.1	79.7	81.0	80.7	81.3	82.8	82.9	83.2	83.2	83.2	83.1	83.0	82.0
Natural Resources, Mining, and Construction													
2000	15.3	15.1	15.3	16.1	16.2	16.8	16.6	16.7	16.3	16.2	15.6	15.1	15.9
2001	14.3	14.3	15.0	16.5	16.9	17.6	17.5	17.4	17.2	16.5	16.3	16.2	16.3
2002	15.2	15.1	15.9	15.9	15.9	16.4	16.6	16.6	16.2	16.4	16.3	16.1	16.1
2003	14.9	15.1	15.5	15.9	16.1	16.5	16.5	16.6	16.3	16.3	15.9	15.6	15.9
2004	15.2	14.6	15.4	16.2	16.3	16.7	17.0	16.8	16.5	16.2	16.0	15.9	16.1
2005	14.6	14.7	15.2	15.7	15.9	16.3	16.4	16.4	16.2	16.1	15.7	15.6	15.7
2006	15.3	15.4	15.7	15.9	15.9	16.5	16.8	16.8	16.6	15.9	15.9	16.1	16.1
2007	15.8	15.2	16.2	16.2	16.5	17.3	17.3	17.6	17.5	17.4	17.1	16.7	16.7
Manufacturing													
2000	72.9	72.9	73.2	73.0	73.1	73.5	72.7	72.9	72.8	72.8	73.4	73.8	73.1
2001	72.4	72.7	73.4	73.5	73.2	73.8	73.9	73.7	73.5	72.4	71.9	70.9	72.9
2002	69.8	68.1	67.4	66.6	66.1	65.9	65.8	65.1	64.6	63.5	62.8	62.8	65.7
2003	60.1	61.1	60.3	59.3	59.1	56.3	58.0	57.3	57.7	57.9	57.8	57.9	58.6
2004	56.9	57.8	57.9	57.8	57.8	56.3	59.2	58.7	59.3	59.4	59.6	60.1	58.4
2005	59.7	59.8	59.9	60.2	60.5	61.0	61.3	61.0	60.3	61.3	61.7	61.8	60.7
2006	61.5	62.4	62.0	61.8	62.1	62.9	63.4	63.5	63.7	63.9	64.4	64.4	63.0
2007	64.3	64.5	64.8	64.5	64.8	65.5	65.6	65.6	65.7	65.8	66.0	66.3	65.3
Service-Providing													
2000	203.0	203.2	204.6	206.8	207.8	208.9	201.0	201.2	207.6	208.8	210.1	210.5	206.1
2001	206.5	207.3	210.0	211.1	212.7	212.7	202.1	202.6	210.4	211.9	212.0	212.7	209.3
2002	209.1	209.0	211.8	213.6	214.1	213.5	203.1	204.2	211.0	211.6	213.7	214.3	210.8
2003	205.3	205.6	207.5	207.8	209.0	209.2	199.1	199.4	207.2	208.0	209.4	210.3	206.5
2004	204.6	204.8	206.4	210.1	210.4	211.1	203.5	203.7	210.3	211.9	212.8	214.1	208.6
2005	208.6	209.0	209.6	211.1	211.6	211.2	205.8	206.0	211.9	212.1	214.4	215.1	210.5
2006	208.5	210.5	212.5	215.0	216.6	216.3	210.0	211.5	216.9	219.5	220.1	222.0	215.0
2007	215.5	216.0	219.1	220.8	221.4	223.4	217.6	217.0	221.8	223.3	224.9	225.5	220.5
Trade, Transportation, and Utilities													
2000	50.4	49.6	49.7	51.0	51.2	51.0	50.2	50.5	50.7	50.9	52.1	52.7	50.8
2001	50.7	50.2	50.2	50.3	50.6	50.7	50.5	50.5	51.1	51.2	51.3	51.8	52.1
2002	49.8	49.0	49.3	50.2	50.3	50.1	49.8	49.8	49.9	50.0	49.9	50.9	51.3
2003	49.0	48.6	48.6	48.7	49.0	48.4	48.9	49.1	49.6	49.7	50.7	51.2	49.3
2004	49.0	48.7	48.9	49.5	49.8	49.6	49.2	49.9	50.0	50.4	51.4	51.5	49.8
2005	49.3	48.8	48.8	49.2	49.4	49.1	49.1	49.8	49.8	49.7	50.9	51.1	49.6
2006	48.8	48.4	48.8	50.1	50.3	50.4	49.5	50.4	50.4	51.0	51.8	52.4	50.2
2007	50.9	50.4	51.3	51.1	51.4	51.6	51.3	52.2	51.9	51.9	52.7	53.1	51.7
Wholesale Trade													
2000	11.9	11.7	11.7	12.2	12.2	12.2	12.0	12.0	12.0	11.8	11.9	11.9	12.0
2001	12.0	11.9	12.0	12.0	12.0	12.1	11.9	12.0	12.0	12.1	12.1	12.1	12.0
2002	11.9	11.8	11.7	12.1	12.0	12.0	12.1	12.1	12.1	11.7	11.7	11.9	11.9
2003	11.2	11.2	11.1	11.1	11.1	11.1	11.5	11.5	11.5	11.4	11.5	11.6	11.3
2004	11.4	11.4	11.4	11.4	11.3	11.4	11.4	11.3	11.1	10.9	11.0	10.9	11.2
2005	10.7	10.7	10.6	10.6	10.6	10.8	10.8	10.7	10.6	10.4	10.5	10.5	10.6
2006	10.8	10.9	10.9	10.8	10.8	11.0	10.9	10.9	10.9	10.8	10.8	10.8	10.9
2007	10.8	10.8	10.9	10.9	10.9	11.1	11.2	11.2	11.0	10.9	10.9	10.9	11.0
Retail Trade													
2000	31.2	30.6	30.7	31.1	31.3	31.3	30.9	31.2	31.1	31.3	32.4	33.0	31.3
2001	31.2	30.7	30.5	30.6	30.9	31.1	31.2	31.7	31.5	31.4	32.1	32.5	31.3
2002	30.5	30.0	30.4	30.7	30.9	30.9	30.6	30.7	30.5	30.7	31.7	32.0	30.8
2003	30.1	29.7	29.8	30.3	30.4	30.5	30.3	30.4	30.3	30.3	31.1	31.5	30.4
2004	29.8	29.5	29.7	30.1	30.5	30.7	30.4	30.3	30.7	31.1	32.0	32.1	30.6
2005	30.2	29.8	29.9	30.2	30.4	30.5	30.4	30.4	30.4	30.7	31.8	31.9	30.6
2006	29.5	29.1	29.5	31.1	31.3	31.4	31.1	31.2	31.1	31.8	32.6	33.0	31.1
2007	31.8	31.3	32.1	31.9	32.2	32.2	32.5	32.7	32.5	32.7	33.6	34.0	32.5

Employment by Industry: Wichita, KS, 2000–2007—*Continued*

(Numbers in thousands, not seasonally adjusted.)

Industry and year	January	February	March	April	May	June	July	August	September	October	November	December	Annual Average
Transportation and Utilities													
2000	7.3	7.3	7.3	7.7	7.7	7.5	7.3	7.3	7.6	7.8	7.8	7.8	7.5
2001	7.5	7.6	7.7	7.7	7.7	7.5	7.4	7.4	7.7	7.8	7.6	7.5	7.6
2002	7.4	7.2	7.2	7.4	7.4	7.2	7.1	7.1	7.4	7.5	7.5	7.4	7.3
2003	7.7	7.7	7.7	7.3	7.5	6.8	7.1	7.2	7.8	8.0	8.1	8.1	7.6
2004	7.8	7.8	7.8	8.0	8.0	7.5	7.4	8.3	8.2	8.4	8.4	8.5	8.0
2005	8.4	8.3	8.3	8.4	8.4	7.8	7.9	8.7	8.8	8.6	8.6	8.7	8.4
2006	8.5	8.4	8.4	8.2	8.2	8.0	7.5	8.3	8.4	8.4	8.4	8.6	8.3
2007	8.3	8.3	8.3	8.3	8.3	8.3	7.6	8.3	8.4	8.3	8.2	8.2	8.2
Information													
2000	6.1	6.5	6.8	6.6	6.6	6.7	6.9	6.9	6.9	6.8	6.9	6.9	6.7
2001	6.6	6.9	7.2	7.2	7.1	7.4	7.0	7.0	6.9	6.7	6.7	6.6	6.9
2002	6.3	6.7	6.9	7.2	7.2	7.3	7.3	7.3	7.0	6.9	7.2	7.2	7.0
2003	6.7	6.6	6.6	6.5	6.5	6.8	6.8	6.5	6.7	6.5	6.4	6.4	6.6
2004	6.4	6.5	6.4	6.3	6.4	6.5	6.4	6.3	6.0	5.9	5.9	6.0	6.3
2005	5.8	5.8	5.6	5.8	5.9	5.9	6.0	5.9	5.9	5.9	6.0	6.1	5.9
2006	5.6	5.6	5.7	5.7	5.7	5.7	5.9	5.8	5.8	6.3	6.3	6.3	5.9
2007	6.3	6.3	6.3	6.4	6.4	6.4	6.4	6.4	6.3	6.3	6.3	6.3	6.3
Financial Activities													
2000	12.2	12.1	12.1	12.0	12.1	12.4	12.4	12.5	12.5	12.6	12.5	12.7	12.3
2001	13.1	13.0	13.1	13.0	13.0	13.0	13.0	12.9	12.7	12.9	12.8	13.0	13.0
2002	13.1	13.1	13.0	13.0	13.0	12.9	13.0	13.0	12.8	12.8	12.8	12.8	12.9
2003	12.4	12.4	12.6	12.7	12.7	12.7	12.7	12.7	12.6	12.6	12.6	12.6	12.6
2004	12.1	12.1	12.1	12.3	12.2	12.2	12.3	12.2	12.0	11.9	11.8	11.8	12.1
2005	11.5	11.4	11.4	11.5	11.5	11.5	11.5	11.6	11.5	11.5	11.3	11.3	11.4
2006	11.1	11.1	11.1	11.1	11.1	11.2	11.3	11.3	11.4	11.4	11.4	11.6	11.3
2007	11.4	11.3	11.3	11.4	11.5	11.6	11.6	11.6	11.5	11.5	11.5	11.5	11.5
Professional and Business Services													
2000	27.2	26.7	27.8	27.7	27.6	27.7	27.3	27.4	27.2	27.8	27.3	27.5	27.4
2001	26.4	26.9	27.5	28.6	28.7	28.8	27.8	27.7	27.8	27.5	27.1	27.1	27.7
2002	26.7	26.7	27.3	27.9	27.5	27.4	27.6	27.3	27.2	27.2	27.3	27.4	27.3
2003	25.4	25.7	26.2	25.9	25.9	26.1	25.7	25.7	25.5	25.5	25.4	25.8	25.7
2004	24.8	24.8	25.1	26.1	26.3	26.7	27.2	27.1	27.1	27.8	27.8	28.1	26.6
2005	26.9	26.8	26.4	26.6	26.3	26.7	26.9	27.1	27.1	27.2	27.4	27.5	26.9
2006	26.9	27.6	28.1	28.0	27.8	28.6	28.5	28.4	28.6	28.8	28.9	29.4	28.3
2007	28.7	28.7	29.3	29.8	29.4	30.0	30.5	30.1	30.4	30.6	30.6	30.5	29.9
Education and Health Services													
2000	35.1	35.3	35.3	35.3	35.5	35.4	35.5	35.7	35.9	35.8	35.8	36.2	35.6
2001	35.6	36.2	36.4	36.4	36.6	36.3	35.9	36.3	36.9	36.9	37.3	37.6	36.5
2002	37.5	37.8	38.3	38.8	39.0	38.8	38.1	38.4	39.1	39.3	39.5	39.4	38.7
2003	37.7	37.9	37.9	38.0	38.0	37.2	37.3	37.1	37.8	37.8	37.9	38.0	37.7
2004	37.8	38.0	38.1	38.2	38.3	38.7	38.2	38.2	39.0	39.3	39.3	39.4	38.5
2005	39.0	39.3	39.4	39.7	39.8	39.8	39.1	39.0	40.0	40.1	40.4	40.6	39.7
2006	39.8	40.2	40.3	41.3	41.4	41.3	40.5	40.6	41.8	42.4	41.9	42.2	41.1
2007	41.5	41.8	42.1	42.1	42.2	42.2	41.4	41.4	42.5	42.9	43.0	43.0	42.2
Leisure and Hospitality													
2000	25.1	25.4	25.4	26.4	26.7	27.4	27.0	26.9	26.7	26.4	26.3	25.9	26.3
2001	25.2	25.2	25.8	26.0	26.5	27.0	26.7	26.6	26.1	26.0	25.7	25.4	26.0
2002	24.7	24.8	25.4	25.6	25.8	25.9	25.4	25.4	24.6	24.6	24.5	24.1	25.1
2003	23.2	23.3	24.2	24.9	25.3	25.6	25.4	25.5	25.1	24.8	24.6	24.2	24.7
2004	23.6	23.5	24.3	25.8	26.3	26.4	26.1	26.2	25.8	25.5	25.2	25.4	25.3
2005	24.8	25.1	25.6	26.2	26.5	26.9	26.6	26.7	26.5	25.9	26.0	26.0	26.1
2006	25.3	25.6	26.1	27.2	27.5	28.2	27.7	27.9	27.6	27.6	27.6	27.6	27.2
2007	25.5	25.7	26.5	28.4	28.8	29.4	29.3	28.2	27.9	27.8	28.0	28.1	27.8
Other Services													
2000	10.3	10.4	9.7	10.1	10.2	10.8	10.8	10.2	10.7	10.4	10.5	10.1	10.4
2001	10.4	10.3	10.5	10.7	10.7	10.9	10.9	10.7	10.7	11.1	10.9	11.2	10.8
2002	11.8	11.9	12.0	11.4	11.4	11.9	11.8	11.8	12.0	11.6	11.7	12.0	11.8
2003	11.4	11.4	11.7	11.3	11.6	11.8	11.6	11.6	11.7	11.9	11.9	12.0	11.7
2004	11.7	11.9	12.1	12.2	12.1	12.4	12.1	12.0	12.1	11.9	11.8	12.2	12.0
2005	12.0	12.1	12.4	12.1	12.0	12.2	11.6	11.4	11.6	11.2	11.1	11.1	11.7
2006	10.9	10.9	11.1	10.9	10.9	11.1	11.0	10.9	11.0	10.9	10.9	11.1	11.0
2007	11.0	11.0	11.1	11.0	11.0	11.1	11.1	11.1	10.9	10.9	11.0	11.1	11.0
Government													
2000	36.6	37.2	37.8	37.7	37.9	37.5	30.9	31.1	37.0	38.1	38.7	38.5	36.6
2001	38.5	38.6	39.3	38.9	39.5	38.6	30.3	30.3	38.1	39.5	39.7	39.7	37.6
2002	39.2	39.0	39.6	39.5	39.9	39.2	30.1	31.1	38.3	39.3	39.8	40.1	37.9
2003	39.5	39.7	39.7	39.8	40.0	40.6	30.7	31.2	38.2	39.2	39.9	40.1	38.2
2004	39.2	39.3	39.4	39.7	39.0	38.6	32.0	31.8	38.3	39.2	39.6	39.7	38.0
2005	39.3	39.7	40.0	40.0	40.2	39.1	34.9	34.6	39.5	40.8	41.3	41.4	39.2
2006	40.1	41.1	41.3	40.7	41.8	39.7	35.6	36.1	40.3	41.1	41.3	41.4	40.0
2007	40.2	40.8	41.2	40.6	40.7	41.1	36.0	36.0	40.4	41.4	41.8	41.9	40.2

Employment by Industry: McAllen-Edinburg-Mission, TX, 2000–2007

(Numbers in thousands, not seasonally adjusted.)

Industry and year	January	February	March	April	May	June	July	August	September	October	November	December	Annual Average
Total Nonfarm													
2000	153.1	155.4	157.5	157.3	157.7	157.4	153.2	154.7	157.4	158.4	160.9	162.6	157.1
2001	160.3	161.4	163.2	163.7	163.9	163.1	156.6	159.0	161.8	163.8	165.6	167.5	162.5
2002	165.3	166.3	168.3	168.3	168.3	168.2	161.5	165.8	168.6	170.4	173.1	173.9	168.2
2003	172.3	174.0	174.8	175.1	175.8	175.2	170.2	172.9	176.2	178.2	181.1	183.2	175.7
2004	181.6	182.8	184.2	185.1	186.3	184.9	179.5	183.2	185.4	188.2	191.2	192.8	185.4
2005	189.9	192.1	193.5	196.2	195.6	195.0	187.7	192.5	195.3	198.2	200.1	202.0	194.8
2006	201.0	201.9	202.9	202.4	201.8	201.8	193.0	198.4	201.7	205.6	208.6	210.0	202.4
2007	208.3	209.0	210.1	212.1	211.5	210.6	204.1	207.5	209.9	211.6	212.9	214.4	210.2
Total Private													
2000	113.3	114.7	115.6	116.0	116.5	117.1	115.7	116.3	116.8	116.7	118.6	120.1	116.5
2001	118.6	118.6	120.4	121.2	121.2	121.3	118.8	120.1	120.0	120.5	121.9	123.7	120.5
2002	122.2	122.6	124.2	124.4	124.3	124.7	123.9	125.9	125.8	125.6	127.7	128.6	125.0
2003	127.2	128.7	129.5	129.5	130.0	130.4	130.4	131.6	131.8	132.3	134.3	136.3	131.0
2004	135.1	135.8	137.0	137.8	138.7	138.5	138.2	139.3	139.0	140.5	142.9	144.7	139.0
2005	142.2	143.5	144.8	147.5	146.9	146.9	146.7	147.2	147.7	148.9	150.4	152.3	147.1
2006	151.0	151.2	152.3	152.7	152.2	152.1	151.9	152.6	153.7	155.1	157.6	159.1	153.5
2007	158.1	158.2	159.0	161.5	160.8	159.9	160.4	161.3	161.0	161.5	162.4	163.9	160.7
Goods-Producing													
2000	21.8	22.0	21.9	21.9	22.0	21.9	21.6	21.7	21.9	22.1	22.2	22.3	21.9
2001	22.4	22.6	22.5	22.2	22.2	22.2	21.2	21.1	20.9	21.3	21.4	21.5	21.8
2002	21.0	21.0	21.2	20.6	20.3	20.5	20.4	20.8	20.4	20.1	20.2	20.2	20.6
2003	20.2	20.3	20.3	20.5	20.6	20.4	20.3	20.3	20.5	19.9	20.2	20.3	20.3
2004	19.9	19.9	20.1	19.8	20.0	19.6	19.4	19.4	19.3	19.4	19.4	19.6	19.7
2005	18.8	18.9	19.0	18.8	18.9	19.0	18.6	18.6	18.8	18.9	19.0	19.1	18.9
2006	18.9	19.0	19.2	19.0	18.9	18.9	18.6	18.8	18.9	18.6	19.0	19.2	18.9
2007	19.0	18.9	19.0	19.2	19.2	19.0	18.9	19.5	19.6	19.5	19.5	19.6	19.2
Natural Resources, Mining, and Construction													
2000	9.3	9.4	9.6	9.9	9.9	9.9	9.9	9.9	9.9	9.9	9.9	10.0	9.8
2001	10.1	10.3	10.2	10.2	10.3	10.5	10.5	10.4	10.1	10.3	10.3	10.5	10.3
2002	10.2	10.2	10.4	10.4	10.5	10.8	10.8	11.0	11.0	10.8	10.9	11.0	10.7
2003	10.9	10.9	11.0	11.2	11.3	11.4	11.3	11.4	11.3	11.1	11.1	11.2	11.1
2004	10.8	10.8	11.0	10.9	10.9	10.8	10.8	10.8	10.9	10.7	10.5	10.6	10.8
2005	10.3	10.5	10.5	10.6	10.7	10.9	10.6	10.6	10.7	10.5	10.6	10.6	10.6
2006	10.4	10.6	10.9	10.7	10.8	10.9	11.0	11.1	11.0	10.9	10.9	11.0	10.9
2007	10.9	10.9	11.0	11.1	11.1	11.2	11.3	11.7	11.6	11.5	11.5	11.6	11.3
Manufacturing													
2000	12.5	12.6	12.3	12.0	12.1	12.0	11.7	11.8	12.0	12.2	12.3	12.3	12.2
2001	12.3	12.3	12.3	12.0	11.9	11.7	10.7	10.7	10.8	11.0	11.1	11.0	11.5
2002	10.8	10.8	10.8	10.2	9.8	9.7	9.6	9.8	9.4	9.3	9.3	9.2	9.9
2003	9.3	9.4	9.3	9.3	9.3	9.0	9.0	9.1	9.2	8.8	9.1	9.1	9.1
2004	9.1	9.1	9.1	8.9	9.1	8.8	8.6	8.6	8.4	8.7	8.9	9.0	8.9
2005	8.5	8.4	8.5	8.2	8.2	8.1	8.0	8.0	8.1	8.4	8.4	8.5	8.3
2006	8.5	8.4	8.3	8.3	8.1	8.0	7.6	7.7	7.9	7.7	8.1	8.2	8.1
2007	8.1	8.0	8.0	8.1	8.1	7.8	7.6	7.8	8.0	8.0	8.0	8.0	8.0
Service-Providing													
2000	131.3	133.4	135.6	135.4	135.7	135.5	131.6	133.0	135.5	136.3	138.7	140.3	135.2
2001	137.9	138.8	140.7	141.5	141.7	140.9	135.4	137.9	140.9	142.5	144.2	146.0	140.7
2002	144.3	145.3	147.1	147.7	148.0	147.7	141.1	145.0	148.2	150.3	152.9	153.7	147.6
2003	152.1	153.7	154.5	154.6	155.2	154.8	149.9	152.4	155.7	158.3	160.9	162.9	155.4
2004	161.7	162.9	164.1	165.3	166.3	165.3	160.1	163.8	166.1	168.8	171.8	173.2	165.8
2005	171.1	173.2	174.5	177.4	176.7	176.0	169.1	173.9	176.5	179.3	181.1	182.9	176.0
2006	182.1	182.9	183.7	183.4	182.9	182.9	174.4	179.6	182.8	187.0	189.6	190.8	183.5
2007	189.3	190.1	191.1	192.9	192.3	191.6	185.2	188.0	190.3	192.1	193.4	194.8	190.9
Trade, Transportation, and Utilities													
2000	34.9	34.9	35.4	35.2	35.2	34.9	34.4	34.8	34.8	34.8	35.9	37.0	35.2
2001	35.5	35.0	35.4	35.8	35.4	35.1	34.2	34.3	34.1	34.0	34.7	35.6	34.9
2002	34.5	34.2	34.7	34.8	34.9	34.9	34.7	35.1	35.1	35.0	36.2	37.0	35.1
2003	35.5	35.5	35.8	36.1	36.2	36.3	36.2	36.2	36.2	36.6	37.9	39.2	36.4
2004	38.4	38.3	38.5	39.1	39.1	38.7	38.4	38.7	38.2	38.5	39.7	40.7	38.9
2005	39.4	39.2	39.6	40.8	40.6	40.6	40.7	40.8	40.5	40.8	42.0	42.9	40.7
2006	41.8	41.4	41.9	42.4	42.3	42.1	42.3	42.7	43.2	43.8	45.3	46.0	42.9
2007	44.7	44.3	45.0	45.5	45.2	44.9	45.4	45.8	45.5	45.4	46.1	47.1	45.4
Wholesale Trade													
2000	5.7	5.9	6.1	6.2	6.0	5.8	5.5	5.4	5.4	5.6	5.8	6.0	5.8
2001	5.9	5.9	6.1	6.5	6.3	6.0	5.6	5.5	5.4	5.3	5.4	5.5	5.8
2002	5.6	5.6	5.8	5.8	5.7	5.7	5.6	5.6	5.6	5.6	5.6	5.8	5.7
2003	5.9	6.0	6.1	6.3	6.3	6.3	6.0	5.9	5.9	5.9	6.0	6.3	6.0
2004	6.2	6.2	6.3	6.8	6.9	6.7	6.5	6.5	6.5	6.4	6.6	6.9	6.5
2005	6.8	6.7	6.7	6.9	6.7	6.7	6.6	6.4	6.5	6.6	6.7	6.8	6.7
2006	6.8	6.9	7.0	7.0	6.9	6.8	6.7	6.6	6.6	6.4	6.4	6.5	6.7
2007	6.3	6.4	6.6	6.8	6.7	6.6	6.6	6.5	6.6	6.5	6.5	6.7	6.6
Retail Trade													
2000	24.7	24.4	24.5	24.3	24.3	24.4	24.2	24.7	24.6	24.7	25.6	26.3	24.7
2001	24.9	24.4	24.6	24.6	24.5	24.5	24.1	24.3	24.1	23.9	24.5	25.3	24.5
2002	24.3	24.1	24.3	24.4	24.6	24.6	24.5	24.8	24.9	24.8	25.9	26.5	24.8
2003	25.0	24.8	25.0	24.9	25.0	25.0	25.2	25.2	25.3	25.7	26.8	27.8	25.4
2004	27.0	26.9	26.9	27.0	26.9	26.7	26.5	26.8	26.3	26.7	27.7	28.3	27.0
2005	27.1	27.0	27.3	28.2	28.1	28.0	28.1	28.4	28.0	28.4	29.4	30.1	28.2
2006	28.8	28.3	28.5	29.0	28.9	28.6	29.0	29.4	29.9	30.6	32.0	32.5	29.6
2007	31.6	31.0	31.5	31.8	31.5	31.2	31.7	32.2	31.7	31.6	32.3	33.1	31.8

Employment by Industry: McAllen-Edinburg-Mission, TX, 2000–2007—*Continued*

(Numbers in thousands, not seasonally adjusted.)

Industry and year	January	February	March	April	May	June	July	August	September	October	November	December	Annual Average
Transportation and Utilities													
2000	4.5	4.6	4.8	4.7	4.9	4.7	4.7	4.7	4.8	4.5	4.5	4.7	4.7
2001	4.7	4.7	4.7	4.7	4.6	4.6	4.5	4.5	4.6	4.8	4.8	4.8	4.7
2002	4.6	4.5	4.6	4.6	4.6	4.6	4.6	4.7	4.6	4.6	4.7	4.7	4.6
2003	4.6	4.7	4.7	4.9	4.9	5.0	5.0	5.1	5.0	5.0	5.1	5.1	4.9
2004	5.2	5.2	5.3	5.3	5.3	5.3	5.4	5.4	5.4	5.4	5.4	5.5	5.3
2005	5.5	5.5	5.6	5.7	5.8	5.9	6.0	6.0	6.0	5.8	5.9	6.0	5.8
2006	6.2	6.2	6.4	6.4	6.5	6.7	6.6	6.7	6.7	6.8	6.9	7.0	6.6
2007	6.8	6.9	6.9	6.9	7.0	7.1	7.1	7.1	7.2	7.3	7.3	7.3	7.1
Information													
2000	2.0	2.0	1.9	2.0	2.0	2.1	2.1	2.1	2.1	2.0	2.0	2.0	2.0
2001	1.8	1.8	1.8	1.8	1.8	1.9	1.8	1.8	1.8	1.8	1.8	1.8	1.8
2002	1.8	1.8	1.8	1.7	1.8	1.8	1.7	1.7	1.7	1.6	1.7	1.7	1.7
2003	1.7	1.7	1.7	1.7	1.8	2.0	2.1	2.1	2.1	2.2	2.3	2.4	1.9
2004	2.6	2.5	2.5	2.6	2.6	2.7	2.7	2.7	2.7	2.8	2.8	2.8	2.7
2005	2.7	2.7	2.7	2.8	2.8	2.9	2.9	2.9	3.0	3.0	3.0	3.0	2.9
2006	2.9	2.9	3.0	2.9	2.9	2.9	2.8	2.8	2.8	3.0	3.0	2.9	2.9
2007	2.9	3.0	3.0	3.1	3.1	3.1	3.1	3.1	3.0	3.1	3.1	3.1	3.1
Financial Activities													
2000	6.0	5.9	6.0	6.2	6.1	6.1	6.1	6.1	6.1	6.1	6.1	6.2	6.1
2001	6.1	6.1	6.2	6.2	6.2	6.3	6.4	6.4	6.4	6.4	6.5	6.5	6.3
2002	6.5	6.5	6.5	6.6	6.7	6.7	6.7	6.7	6.7	6.8	6.9	7.0	6.7
2003	7.0	7.1	7.1	7.1	7.2	7.3	7.3	7.3	7.3	7.4	7.4	7.4	7.2
2004	7.5	7.5	7.6	7.6	7.5	7.7	7.8	7.7	7.7	7.8	7.9	7.9	7.7
2005	7.9	7.9	8.0	8.1	8.0	8.1	8.2	8.2	8.2	8.3	8.3	8.3	8.1
2006	8.3	8.3	8.4	8.2	8.2	8.3	8.4	8.4	8.4	8.6	8.6	8.7	8.4
2007	8.7	8.7	8.7	8.9	8.8	8.8	8.8	8.7	8.7	8.8	8.8	8.8	8.8
Professional and Business Services													
2000	7.8	8.2	8.4	8.5	8.7	9.1	8.7	8.8	8.7	8.6	8.6	8.4	8.5
2001	8.5	8.4	9.1	9.5	9.6	9.8	9.5	9.9	10.1	10.2	10.5	10.7	9.7
2002	10.6	10.6	10.8	10.8	10.5	10.5	10.2	10.4	10.4	10.8	10.9	10.7	10.6
2003	10.4	11.0	10.7	10.6	10.5	10.6	10.5	11.0	11.1	11.2	11.3	11.5	10.8
2004	10.9	11.0	10.9	11.1	11.3	11.5	11.5	11.8	11.6	11.7	11.9	12.0	11.4
2005	11.8	12.3	12.6	12.9	12.7	12.8	12.8	13.0	13.0	13.0	13.1	13.3	12.8
2006	13.3	13.6	13.8	13.5	13.4	13.6	13.3	13.3	13.4	13.5	13.7	14.1	13.5
2007	14.0	14.1	14.2	14.2	14.2	14.2	13.7	13.7	14.1	14.2	14.2	14.3	14.1
Education and Health Services													
2000	23.3	23.7	23.7	24.0	24.2	24.1	24.3	24.4	24.8	24.8	25.3	25.3	24.3
2001	25.5	25.8	26.1	26.1	26.3	26.4	26.5	27.1	27.4	27.7	27.7	28.0	26.7
2002	28.2	28.4	28.8	29.4	29.7	29.9	30.4	31.0	31.4	31.6	32.1	32.2	30.3
2003	32.4	32.7	33.0	32.9	32.9	32.7	33.1	33.7	34.0	34.3	34.6	34.8	33.4
2004	35.1	35.6	36.0	36.1	36.7	36.8	37.4	37.9	38.7	39.5	40.1	40.5	37.5
2005	40.4	41.0	41.2	41.6	41.7	41.6	41.9	42.3	42.9	43.3	43.5	44.0	42.1
2006	43.6	43.9	43.8	43.9	44.0	44.0	44.0	44.5	44.9	45.0	45.3	45.5	44.4
2007	46.0	46.3	46.3	47.1	47.2	47.0	46.8	47.2	47.5	47.8	48.0	48.2	47.1
Leisure and Hospitality													
2000	13.5	13.9	14.2	14.1	14.2	14.8	14.3	14.3	14.2	14.1	14.3	14.6	14.2
2001	14.5	14.6	15.0	15.1	15.2	15.1	14.8	15.0	14.9	14.8	14.9	15.2	14.9
2002	15.3	15.7	16.0	15.9	15.9	15.9	15.4	15.8	15.8	15.3	15.3	15.4	15.6
2003	15.5	15.9	16.3	16.1	16.2	16.6	16.5	16.4	16.2	16.3	16.2	16.3	16.2
2004	16.2	16.5	16.8	17.0	16.9	16.9	16.4	16.5	16.3	16.3	16.5	16.6	16.6
2005	16.6	16.9	17.0	17.6	17.3	17.0	16.9	16.7	16.6	16.8	16.7	17.0	16.9
2006	17.6	17.5	17.5	17.9	17.6	17.4	17.4	17.1	16.9	17.4	17.4	17.4	17.4
2007	17.9	17.9	17.7	18.3	18.0	17.9	18.6	18.3	17.7	17.8	17.8	17.9	18.0
Other Services													
2000	4.0	4.1	4.1	4.1	4.1	4.1	4.2	4.1	4.2	4.2	4.2	4.3	4.1
2001	4.3	4.3	4.3	4.5	4.5	4.5	4.4	4.5	4.4	4.3	4.4	4.4	4.4
2002	4.3	4.4	4.4	4.6	4.5	4.5	4.4	4.4	4.3	4.4	4.4	4.4	4.4
2003	4.5	4.5	4.6	4.5	4.6	4.5	4.4	4.4	4.4	4.4	4.4	4.4	4.4
2004	4.5	4.5	4.6	4.5	4.6	4.6	4.6	4.6	4.5	4.5	4.6	4.6	4.6
2005	4.6	4.6	4.7	4.9	4.9	4.9	4.7	4.7	4.7	4.8	4.8	4.7	4.8
2006	4.6	4.6	4.7	4.9	4.9	4.9	5.1	5.0	5.2	5.2	5.3	5.3	5.0
2007	4.9	5.0	5.1	5.2	5.1	5.0	5.1	5.0	4.9	4.9	4.9	4.9	5.0
Government													
2000	39.8	40.7	41.9	41.3	41.2	40.3	37.5	38.4	40.6	41.7	42.3	42.5	40.7
2001	41.7	42.8	42.8	42.5	42.7	41.8	37.8	38.9	41.8	43.3	43.7	43.8	42.0
2002	43.1	43.7	44.1	43.9	44.0	43.5	37.6	39.9	42.8	44.8	45.4	45.3	43.2
2003	45.1	45.3	45.3	45.6	45.8	44.8	39.8	41.3	44.4	45.9	46.8	46.9	44.7
2004	46.5	47.0	47.2	47.3	47.6	46.4	41.3	43.9	46.4	47.7	48.3	48.1	46.5
2005	47.7	48.6	48.7	48.7	48.7	48.1	41.0	45.3	47.6	49.3	49.7	49.7	47.8
2006	50.0	50.7	50.6	49.7	49.6	49.7	41.1	45.8	48.0	50.5	51.0	50.9	49.0
2007	50.2	50.8	51.1	50.6	50.7	50.7	43.7	46.2	48.9	50.1	50.5	50.5	49.5

Employment by Industry: Stockton, CA, 2000–2007

(Numbers in thousands, not seasonally adjusted.)

Industry and year	January	February	March	April	May	June	July	August	September	October	November	December	Annual Average
Total Nonfarm													
2000	178.2	178.8	180.4	182.5	184.0	187.1	188.5	191.5	191.5	189.7	188.5	189.3	185.8
2001	186.0	186.4	188.1	189.2	191.4	193.3	191.7	195.3	194.1	193.0	192.3	191.9	191.1
2002	187.3	188.5	190.2	190.1	193.2	194.4	193.7	196.5	198.4	198.6	198.6	198.9	194.0
2003	193.5	194.1	196.1	195.8	196.9	198.4	195.6	197.6	201.4	199.5	199.4	198.7	197.3
2004	195.0	196.2	197.9	198.8	200.5	202.1	201.1	201.5	203.3	203.6	204.6	203.8	200.7
2005	199.2	200.9	203.2	204.4	205.9	207.2	205.6	207.0	209.0	209.0	209.9	208.8	205.8
2006	203.9	205.2	206.6	205.9	208.4	209.1	208.7	211.0	212.3	213.4	212.8	211.5	209.1
2007	207.2	207.7	210.2	209.8	210.2	212.1	210.7	213.3	214.5	214.8	215.5	215.8	211.8
Total Private													
2000	141.8	142.3	143.6	145.5	146.3	150.1	152.1	154.7	154.7	152.3	151.0	151.8	148.9
2001	148.4	148.5	149.9	150.7	152.3	154.4	153.5	156.0	155.2	153.3	152.4	152.1	152.2
2002	147.4	148.3	149.6	149.6	152.1	153.9	156.2	158.0	158.6	158.1	157.7	157.8	153.9
2003	153.0	153.6	155.6	155.5	156.7	158.5	158.9	160.8	162.4	159.9	159.6	159.0	157.8
2004	155.4	156.4	157.6	158.9	160.8	162.7	163.5	163.7	164.1	163.9	164.4	163.8	161.3
2005	159.6	160.7	162.9	164.2	165.5	167.4	168.1	169.0	169.8	169.4	170.0	168.9	166.3
2006	164.4	165.4	166.4	166.0	168.3	169.3	171.5	173.1	172.7	172.8	172.2	171.1	169.4
2007	166.9	167.2	169.2	169.0	169.1	171.2	172.2	174.4	174.6	174.0	174.3	174.7	171.4
Goods-Producing													
2000	33.3	33.0	33.5	34.1	34.7	36.9	39.2	41.2	40.2	38.0	37.1	36.4	36.5
2001	34.7	34.7	34.9	35.2	36.0	37.1	36.6	38.5	37.5	36.3	35.2	34.4	35.9
2002	32.9	33.0	33.1	32.9	33.8	35.0	35.6	36.5	36.3	35.4	35.3	34.3	34.5
2003	32.4	32.7	33.5	33.6	34.3	35.1	36.5	38.0	37.7	36.3	35.3	34.7	35.0
2004	33.7	33.8	34.3	35.0	35.6	37.2	38.4	38.3	37.7	37.5	36.5	36.0	36.2
2005	34.5	34.8	35.4	36.6	37.2	38.9	40.0	39.9	39.7	39.6	39.3	37.9	37.8
2006	36.5	36.7	36.5	36.1	37.4	37.8	39.4	40.5	39.4	38.7	37.4	36.4	37.7
2007	34.8	34.4	35.0	35.2	35.3	37.1	37.7	38.7	38.3	37.9	37.1	36.8	36.5
Natural Resources and Mining													
2000	0.1	0.1	0.1	0.1	0.1	0.2	0.2	0.2	0.2	0.2	0.2	0.2	0.1
2001	0.2	0.2	0.2	0.2	0.2	0.2	0.2	0.2	0.2	0.2	0.2	0.2	0.1
2002	0.2	0.2	0.2	0.2	0.2	0.2	0.2	0.2	0.2	0.2	0.2	0.2	0.2
2003	0.2	0.2	0.2	0.2	0.2	0.2	0.2	0.2	0.2	0.2	0.2	0.2	0.2
2004	0.2	0.2	0.2	0.2	0.2	0.2	0.2	0.2	0.2	0.2	0.2	0.2	0.2
2005	0.2	0.2	0.2	0.2	0.2	0.2	0.2	0.2	0.2	0.2	0.2	0.2	0.2
2006	0.2	0.2	0.2	0.2	0.2	0.2	0.2	0.2	0.2	0.2	0.2	0.2	0.2
2007	0.2	0.2	0.2	0.2	0.2	0.2	0.2	0.2	0.2	0.2	0.2	0.2	0.2
Construction													
2000	10.5	10.2	10.4	10.9	11.2	12.0	12.4	12.5	12.4	12.4	12.4	12.4	11.6
2001	11.9	12.2	12.7	13.1	13.5	13.9	14.0	14.2	13.7	13.6	13.2	12.7	13.2
2002	11.9	12.1	12.4	12.9	13.5	13.9	14.1	14.3	14.2	14.3	14.3	14.0	13.5
2003	13.1	13.2	13.8	13.9	14.2	14.6	15.2	15.3	15.1	15.0	14.8	14.6	14.4
2004	13.8	14.0	14.3	15.1	15.3	15.8	16.0	16.0	15.9	16.0	15.5	15.4	15.3
2005	14.8	15.1	15.6	16.2	16.7	17.2	17.5	17.6	17.6	17.6	17.6	17.2	16.7
2006	16.0	16.2	15.9	15.4	16.4	16.5	16.6	16.4	16.0	15.5	15.0	14.3	15.9
2007	13.7	13.4	13.9	14.0	14.1	14.5	14.2	14.3	13.7	13.4	12.9	12.8	13.7
Manufacturing													
2000	22.7	22.7	23.0	23.1	23.4	24.7	26.6	28.5	27.6	25.4	24.5	23.8	24.7
2001	22.6	22.3	22.0	21.9	22.3	23.0	22.4	24.1	23.6	22.5	21.8	21.5	22.5
2002	20.8	20.7	20.5	19.8	20.1	20.9	21.3	22.0	21.9	20.9	20.8	20.1	20.8
2003	19.1	19.3	19.5	19.5	19.9	20.3	21.1	22.5	22.4	21.1	20.3	19.9	20.4
2004	19.7	19.6	19.8	19.7	20.1	21.2	22.2	22.1	21.6	21.3	20.8	20.4	20.7
2005	19.5	19.5	19.6	20.2	20.3	21.5	22.3	22.1	21.9	21.8	21.5	20.5	20.9
2006	20.3	20.3	20.4	20.5	20.8	21.1	22.6	23.9	23.2	23.0	22.2	21.9	21.7
2007	20.9	20.8	20.9	21.0	21.0	22.4	23.3	24.2	24.4	24.3	24.0	23.8	22.6
Service-Providing													
2000	144.9	145.8	146.9	148.4	149.3	150.2	149.3	150.3	151.3	151.7	151.4	152.9	149.4
2001	151.3	151.7	153.2	154.0	155.4	156.2	155.1	156.8	156.6	156.7	157.1	157.5	155.1
2002	154.4	155.5	157.1	157.2	159.4	159.4	158.1	160.0	162.1	163.2	163.3	164.6	159.5
2003	161.1	161.4	162.6	162.2	162.6	163.3	159.1	159.6	163.7	163.2	164.1	164.0	162.2
2004	161.3	162.4	163.6	163.8	164.9	164.9	162.7	163.2	165.6	166.1	168.1	167.8	164.5
2005	164.7	166.1	167.8	167.8	168.7	168.3	165.6	167.1	169.3	169.4	170.6	170.9	168.0
2006	167.4	168.5	170.1	169.8	171.0	171.3	169.3	170.5	172.9	174.7	175.4	175.1	171.3
2007	172.4	173.3	175.2	174.6	174.9	175.0	173.0	174.6	176.2	176.9	178.4	179.0	175.3
Trade, Transportation, and Utilities													
2000	40.5	40.1	40.1	40.5	40.8	41.4	42.5	42.5	42.6	42.6	43.2	43.8	41.7
2001	42.9	42.2	42.6	42.7	43.2	43.8	44.2	44.6	44.4	44.1	44.3	44.3	43.6
2002	42.8	42.5	42.7	43.3	43.8	44.5	45.3	45.8	46.0	46.6	46.7	47.0	44.8
2003	45.7	45.5	45.8	45.9	46.0	46.4	46.8	46.7	47.5	47.0	47.7	47.3	46.5
2004	45.4	45.3	45.8	46.6	46.9	47.5	47.5	47.7	48.0	48.4	49.5	49.2	47.3
2005	47.4	47.2	48.0	48.0	48.4	48.7	49.1	49.5	49.7	50.2	50.8	50.7	49.0
2006	48.8	48.7	49.3	49.2	49.9	50.2	51.2	51.4	51.8	51.4	52.0	52.0	50.5
2007	50.2	49.9	50.4	50.2	50.4	50.8	52.0	52.0	51.8	51.8	52.6	53.0	51.3
Wholesale Trade													
2000	6.2	6.2	6.3	6.3	6.3	6.5	6.7	6.7	6.7	6.6	6.5	6.3	6.4
2001	6.2	6.2	6.3	6.5	6.6	6.9	6.9	7.1	7.0	7.1	6.9	6.8	6.7
2002	6.5	6.6	6.6	6.8	6.9	7.2	7.5	7.6	7.7	7.8	7.6	7.5	7.2
2003	7.6	7.7	7.8	7.9	7.9	8.0	7.9	8.1	8.0	7.8	7.8	7.5	7.8
2004	7.5	7.6	7.8	8.0	8.0	8.2	8.3	8.4	8.5	8.6	8.7	8.5	8.2
2005	8.4	8.5	8.7	8.9	9.0	9.1	9.5	9.6	9.6	9.7	9.6	8.9	9.1
2006	8.9	9.0	9.2	9.4	9.6	9.7	10.2	10.3	10.6	10.6	10.5	10.0	9.8
2007	9.9	10.0	10.2	10.4	10.4	10.3	10.9	10.8	10.7	10.6	10.6	10.4	10.4

Employment by Industry: Stockton, CA, 2000–2007—*Continued*

(Numbers in thousands, not seasonally adjusted.)

Industry and year	January	February	March	April	May	June	July	August	September	October	November	December	Annual Average
Retail Trade													
2000	23.0	22.7	22.6	22.9	23.1	23.2	23.6	23.5	23.5	24.0	25.0	25.7	23.6
2001	24.4	23.9	24.1	24.1	24.4	24.6	24.6	24.5	24.7	24.5	25.3	25.6	24.6
2002	24.3	24.0	24.2	24.4	24.6	24.6	24.7	24.7	24.9	25.2	25.8	26.4	24.8
2003	25.1	24.9	25.1	24.8	24.7	24.8	25.0	25.1	25.2	25.3	26.4	26.6	25.2
2004	24.9	24.7	25.0	25.4	25.5	25.7	25.7	25.8	26.1	26.3	27.4	27.7	25.9
2005	26.5	26.2	26.7	26.4	26.5	26.6	26.4	26.5	26.7	27.1	28.1	28.7	26.9
2006	26.6	26.4	26.8	26.7	27.0	27.1	27.2	27.2	27.2	27.1	28.2	28.5	27.2
2007	27.0	26.5	26.7	26.6	26.6	26.8	27.0	26.9	26.8	26.8	27.6	28.1	27.0
Transportation and Utilities													
2000	11.3	11.2	11.2	11.3	11.4	11.7	12.2	12.3	12.4	12.0	11.7	11.8	11.7
2001	12.3	12.1	12.2	12.1	12.2	12.3	12.7	13.0	12.7	12.5	12.1	11.9	12.3
2002	12.0	11.9	11.9	12.1	12.3	12.7	13.1	13.5	13.4	13.6	13.3	13.1	12.7
2003	13.0	12.9	12.9	13.2	13.4	13.6	13.9	13.5	14.3	13.9	13.5	13.2	13.4
2004	13.0	13.0	13.0	13.2	13.4	13.6	13.5	13.5	13.4	13.5	13.4	13.0	13.3
2005	12.5	12.5	12.6	12.7	12.9	13.0	13.2	13.4	13.4	13.4	13.1	13.1	13.0
2006	13.3	13.3	13.3	13.1	13.3	13.4	13.8	13.9	14.0	13.7	13.3	13.5	13.5
2007	13.3	13.4	13.5	13.2	13.4	13.7	14.1	14.3	14.3	14.4	14.4	14.5	13.9
Information													
2000	2.9	3.0	2.9	2.9	3.0	3.0	3.0	3.1	3.0	3.1	3.1	3.1	3.0
2001	3.4	3.4	3.4	3.3	3.3	3.3	3.4	3.3	3.1	3.1	3.0	3.0	3.3
2002	3.2	3.2	3.2	3.1	3.1	3.1	3.1	3.0	3.0	3.0	3.0	3.1	3.1
2003	3.0	3.0	2.9	2.9	2.9	2.9	2.9	2.9	2.9	2.8	2.8	2.8	2.8
2004	2.8	2.8	2.8	2.8	2.8	2.8	2.8	2.8	2.8	2.8	2.8	2.8	2.8
2005	2.7	2.7	2.6	2.6	2.6	2.5	2.5	2.5	2.5	2.5	2.5	2.5	2.6
2006	2.6	2.6	2.5	2.5	2.5	2.5	2.5	2.5	2.5	2.5	2.5	2.5	2.5
2007	2.5	2.6	2.6	2.5	2.5	2.5	2.5	2.5	2.5	2.5	2.5	2.5	2.5
Financial Activities													
2000	8.4	8.5	8.5	8.4	8.4	8.4	8.4	8.4	8.5	8.5	8.5	8.6	8.5
2001	8.6	8.7	8.7	8.7	8.8	8.9	8.9	8.9	8.8	8.9	9.0	9.2	8.9
2002	9.0	9.1	9.0	9.2	9.3	9.3	9.5	9.6	9.6	9.7	9.7	9.8	9.4
2003	9.9	9.9	10.0	10.0	10.0	10.1	9.9	9.9	9.8	9.8	9.7	9.8	9.9
2004	9.5	9.5	9.5	9.6	9.7	9.7	9.7	9.6	9.5	9.6	9.6	9.6	9.6
2005	9.5	9.6	9.6	9.7	9.7	9.7	9.8	9.9	9.9	9.9	9.9	9.9	9.8
2006	9.8	9.8	10.1	9.8	9.9	10.0	10.1	10.1	10.0	10.0	9.9	9.8	9.9
2007	9.8	10.0	10.3	10.1	10.0	9.9	9.9	10.0	9.9	9.6	9.5	9.5	9.9
Professional and Business Services													
2000	16.1	16.2	16.6	16.8	16.5	16.8	16.7	17.2	17.4	17.5	16.9	17.3	16.8
2001	16.6	16.5	16.7	16.9	16.7	17.0	16.9	17.1	17.5	17.1	16.7	17.1	16.9
2002	16.4	16.4	16.8	16.5	16.5	16.6	16.9	17.1	17.2	17.1	16.9	17.5	16.8
2003	17.0	17.1	17.6	16.8	16.7	16.8	16.8	16.9	17.1	16.8	17.1	17.2	17.0
2004	17.3	17.9	17.8	17.3	17.5	17.6	17.8	18.0	18.2	18.2	18.5	18.5	17.9
2005	18.0	18.2	18.5	18.0	18.0	18.3	17.7	18.2	18.4	17.9	17.9	18.5	18.1
2006	18.2	18.4	18.5	18.6	18.2	18.2	18.3	18.4	18.4	19.3	18.9	18.8	18.5
2007	18.4	18.3	18.1	18.1	17.6	17.8	17.5	18.2	18.3	18.4	18.6	19.0	18.2
Education and Health Services													
2000	21.4	22.0	22.1	22.3	22.3	22.4	21.3	21.4	22.0	22.3	22.1	22.4	22.0
2001	21.7	22.4	22.5	22.5	22.5	22.3	21.9	21.6	22.2	22.6	22.9	22.9	22.3
2002	22.5	23.3	23.5	23.0	23.2	22.6	22.8	22.8	23.3	23.6	23.6	23.6	23.2
2003	23.5	23.7	23.8	23.9	24.0	23.8	23.2	23.1	24.0	24.2	24.4	24.6	23.8
2004	24.4	24.4	24.4	24.5	24.6	24.1	23.8	23.7	24.6	24.7	24.8	24.9	24.4
2005	25.0	25.4	25.6	25.7	25.9	25.4	25.0	25.1	25.8	25.9	26.0	26.0	25.6
2006	25.8	26.1	26.3	26.3	26.4	26.1	25.5	25.4	26.0	26.3	26.5	26.8	26.1
2007	27.0	27.5	27.7	27.6	27.7	27.2	26.8	26.9	27.6	27.9	28.2	28.1	27.5
Leisure and Hospitality													
2000	13.5	13.8	14.1	14.6	14.7	15.1	14.9	14.8	14.8	14.3	14.3	14.3	14.4
2001	14.6	14.7	15.1	15.1	15.6	15.7	15.6	15.8	15.6	15.2	15.3	15.3	15.3
2002	14.6	14.8	15.2	15.4	16.1	16.3	16.5	16.6	16.6	16.2	16.1	16.1	15.9
2003	15.3	15.5	15.8	16.2	16.5	16.9	16.8	16.9	17.0	16.5	16.4	16.4	16.3
2004	16.1	16.4	16.6	16.9	17.4	17.4	17.1	17.2	17.0	16.5	16.6	16.6	16.8
2005	16.3	16.5	16.8	17.2	17.4	17.5	17.5	17.4	17.3	17.0	17.2	17.1	17.1
2006	16.6	16.9	17.0	17.2	17.4	17.6	17.6	17.7	17.5	17.3	17.3	17.4	17.3
2007	16.9	17.1	17.6	17.8	17.9	18.1	18.2	18.2	18.5	18.3	18.2	18.2	17.9
Other Services													
2000	5.7	5.7	5.8	5.9	5.9	6.1	6.1	6.1	6.2	6.0	5.8	5.9	5.9
2001	5.9	5.9	6.0	6.1	6.2	6.3	6.0	6.2	6.1	6.0	6.0	5.9	6.1
2002	6.0	6.0	6.1	6.2	6.3	6.5	6.5	6.6	6.6	6.5	6.4	6.4	6.3
2003	6.2	6.2	6.2	6.2	6.3	6.5	6.0	6.4	6.4	6.5	6.2	6.2	6.2
2004	6.2	6.3	6.4	6.2	6.3	6.4	6.4	6.4	6.3	6.2	6.1	6.2	6.3
2005	6.2	6.3	6.4	6.4	6.3	6.4	6.5	6.5	6.5	6.4	6.4	6.3	6.4
2006	6.1	6.2	6.2	6.3	6.6	6.9	6.9	7.1	7.1	7.3	7.7	7.4	6.8
2007	7.3	7.4	7.5	7.5	7.7	7.8	7.6	7.9	7.7	7.6	7.6	7.6	7.6
Government													
2000	36.4	36.5	36.8	37.0	37.7	37.0	36.4	36.8	36.8	37.4	37.5	37.5	37.0
2001	37.6	37.9	38.2	38.5	39.1	38.9	38.2	39.3	38.9	39.7	39.9	39.8	38.8
2002	39.9	40.2	40.6	40.5	41.1	40.5	37.5	38.5	39.8	40.5	40.9	41.1	40.1
2003	40.5	40.5	40.5	40.3	40.2	39.9	36.7	36.8	39.0	39.6	39.8	39.7	39.4
2004	39.6	39.8	40.3	39.9	39.7	39.4	37.6	37.8	39.2	39.7	40.2	40.0	39.4
2005	39.6	40.2	40.3	40.2	40.4	39.8	37.5	38.0	39.2	39.6	39.9	39.9	39.6
2006	39.5	39.8	40.2	39.9	40.1	39.8	37.2	37.9	39.6	40.6	40.6	40.4	39.6
2007	40.3	40.5	41.0	40.8	41.1	40.9	38.5	38.9	39.9	40.8	41.2	41.1	40.4

Employment by Industry: Scranton–Wilkes-Barre, PA, 2000–2007

(Numbers in thousands, not seasonally adjusted.)

Industry and year	January	February	March	April	May	June	July	August	September	October	November	December	Annual Average
Total Nonfarm													
2000	253.5	254.9	259.2	261.8	263.8	264.0	260.8	261.2	263.7	262.9	263.8	263.8	261.1
2001	256.8	258.3	260.7	260.5	262.5	262.0	257.9	258.8	258.6	258.3	258.7	257.7	259.2
2002	249.3	251.1	253.8	254.3	256.3	256.1	252.7	253.6	255.4	257.1	257.5	257.1	254.5
2003	249.4	250.2	252.6	254.3	257.0	257.0	253.0	253.6	256.2	258.9	259.0	259.1	255.0
2004	249.3	250.2	252.5	255.1	256.9	258.1	256.3	256.3	257.5	260.0	260.7	260.9	256.2
2005	252.9	254.1	255.5	259.8	261.1	262.2	260.4	260.0	262.4	263.3	263.9	262.4	259.8
2006	255.3	257.2	259.5	261.0	261.9	262.7	258.2	258.9	262.5	264.0	265.4	265.2	261.0
2007	257.0	256.8	259.5	262.4	263.8	265.7	260.7	259.8	263.1	264.7	265.3	265.0	262.0
Total Private													
2000	222.8	223.3	227.3	229.9	231.4	232.7	230.4	231.4	233.0	232.0	232.6	232.5	229.9
2001	226.0	226.7	229.1	229.1	231.0	230.8	228.2	229.1	228.1	227.0	227.0	226.0	228.2
2002	218.0	219.0	221.9	222.6	224.4	224.4	222.1	223.1	223.7	225.1	225.5	224.4	222.9
2003	217.4	217.5	219.7	222.0	224.5	224.8	222.6	223.7	224.2	226.7	226.8	226.6	223.0
2004	217.5	218.0	220.5	223.2	224.8	226.1	225.8	226.4	226.3	228.0	228.6	229.1	224.5
2005	221.5	222.2	223.6	228.0	229.2	229.7	229.7	229.7	230.7	231.4	231.6	230.4	228.1
2006	223.8	225.3	227.1	229.0	229.8	230.6	228.0	228.9	230.9	232.0	232.9	232.7	229.3
2007	225.4	225.0	227.3	230.0	231.5	233.6	230.9	230.2	232.0	233.2	233.2	232.9	230.4
Goods-Producing													
2000	52.9	52.5	54.1	55.3	55.9	57.0	57.3	58.1	58.0	57.1	56.9	56.2	55.9
2001	54.1	53.9	54.1	53.9	54.5	54.8	53.9	54.4	52.8	51.8	51.4	50.2	53.3
2002	47.8	47.5	48.2	48.4	49.1	50.0	50.2	50.7	50.3	50.1	49.6	48.6	49.2
2003	46.7	46.2	46.1	46.8	47.8	48.4	48.4	48.4	48.2	48.0	47.5	46.7	47.4
2004	44.4	44.2	44.5	45.5	46.2	47.0	46.8	46.9	46.3	46.2	45.4	45.3	45.7
2005	43.5	43.2	43.3	44.7	45.6	46.4	46.9	47.0	46.7	46.5	46.2	44.9	45.4
2006	43.7	43.5	44.1	44.7	45.1	45.8	45.7	46.0	45.9	45.7	45.3	44.9	45.0
2007	43.3	42.5	42.9	43.7	44.4	45.4	45.1	45.3	45.2	45.1	44.8	44.1	44.3
Natural Resources, Mining, and Construction													
2000	9.1	8.7	9.5	10.4	10.9	11.3	11.8	11.9	11.6	11.2	11.0	10.4	10.7
2001	9.4	9.3	9.4	10.0	10.8	11.3	11.5	11.6	11.3	11.2	11.0	10.5	10.6
2002	9.1	8.9	9.4	10.1	10.9	11.2	11.8	11.9	11.6	11.4	11.0	10.2	10.6
2003	9.0	8.7	9.0	9.8	10.6	10.9	11.1	11.2	11.0	11.0	10.7	10.1	10.2
2004	9.0	8.8	9.2	10.1	10.7	11.1	11.3	11.3	11.2	11.0	10.7	10.4	10.4
2005	9.2	9.0	9.1	10.3	11.0	11.3	11.7	11.7	11.5	11.3	11.1	10.4	10.6
2006	9.6	9.5	10.0	10.7	11.1	11.5	11.5	11.7	11.6	11.5	11.3	11.2	10.9
2007	10.2	9.6	10.0	10.9	11.6	12.1	12.2	12.3	12.2	12.1	11.9	11.5	11.4
Manufacturing													
2000	43.8	43.8	44.6	44.9	45.0	45.7	45.5	46.2	46.4	45.9	45.9	45.8	45.3
2001	44.7	44.6	44.7	43.9	43.7	43.5	42.4	42.8	41.5	40.6	40.4	39.7	42.7
2002	38.7	38.6	38.8	38.3	38.2	38.8	38.4	38.8	38.7	38.7	38.6	38.4	38.6
2003	37.7	37.5	37.1	37.0	37.2	37.5	37.3	37.2	37.2	37.0	36.8	36.6	37.1
2004	35.4	35.4	35.3	35.4	35.5	35.9	35.5	35.6	35.1	35.2	34.7	34.9	35.3
2005	34.3	34.2	34.2	34.4	34.6	35.1	35.2	35.3	35.2	35.2	35.1	34.5	34.8
2006	34.1	34.0	34.1	34.0	34.0	34.3	34.2	34.3	34.3	34.2	34.0	33.7	34.1
2007	33.1	32.9	32.9	32.8	32.8	33.3	32.9	33.0	33.0	33.0	32.9	32.6	32.9
Service-Providing													
2000	200.6	202.4	205.1	206.5	207.9	207.0	203.5	203.1	205.7	205.8	206.9	207.6	205.2
2001	202.7	204.4	206.6	206.6	208.0	207.2	204.0	204.4	205.8	206.5	207.3	207.5	205.9
2002	201.5	203.6	205.6	205.9	207.2	206.1	202.5	202.9	205.1	207.0	207.9	208.5	205.3
2003	202.7	204.0	206.5	207.5	209.2	208.6	204.6	205.2	208.0	210.9	211.5	212.4	207.5
2004	204.9	206.0	208.0	209.6	210.7	211.1	209.5	209.4	211.2	213.8	215.3	215.6	210.4
2005	209.4	210.9	212.2	215.1	215.5	215.8	213.5	213.0	215.7	216.8	217.7	217.5	214.4
2006	211.6	213.7	215.4	216.3	216.8	216.9	212.5	212.9	216.6	218.3	220.1	220.3	216.0
2007	213.7	214.3	216.6	218.7	219.4	220.3	215.6	214.5	217.9	219.6	220.5	220.9	217.7
Trade, Transportation, and Utilities													
2000	55.0	54.2	54.8	55.5	55.9	56.4	55.3	55.5	56.0	56.5	57.4	58.3	55.9
2001	56.4	55.4	56.0	56.1	56.6	56.7	55.9	56.2	56.9	57.8	59.1	59.9	56.9
2002	57.2	56.5	57.0	56.6	56.8	56.8	55.7	56.3	56.7	57.1	58.3	59.1	57.0
2003	56.8	56.1	56.4	56.8	57.1	57.2	56.4	56.9	56.8	57.7	58.6	59.2	57.1
2004	56.5	56.0	56.5	56.7	57.1	57.5	57.3	57.5	57.4	58.1	59.3	60.3	57.5
2005	57.8	57.0	57.5	58.1	58.5	58.7	58.3	58.5	58.8	59.1	60.2	61.1	58.6
2006	58.7	58.1	58.4	58.5	58.5	58.7	58.3	58.6	58.8	59.6	60.9	61.9	59.1
2007	59.8	59.0	59.8	60.1	60.5	60.8	59.9	59.6	60.3	60.9	61.5	62.3	60.4
Wholesale Trade													
2000	8.8	8.8	8.9	8.8	8.8	8.9	8.9	8.9	9.0	9.1	9.1	9.3	8.9
2001	9.5	9.4	9.5	9.5	9.6	9.7	9.8	9.9	9.9	10.0	10.0	10.1	9.7
2002	10.1	10.0	10.1	10.0	10.0	10.2	10.1	10.2	10.2	10.2	10.3	10.5	10.2
2003	10.7	10.8	10.9	11.0	11.1	11.1	11.2	11.3	11.0	10.7	10.7	10.7	10.9
2004	10.4	10.3	10.4	10.5	10.6	10.7	10.9	10.9	10.9	10.9	10.9	11.0	10.7
2005	11.1	11.0	11.2	11.3	11.3	11.5	11.6	11.6	11.6	11.7	11.7	11.8	11.5
2006	11.6	11.7	11.8	11.8	11.9	12.0	12.1	12.1	12.1	12.2	12.2	12.2	12.0
2007	12.3	12.3	12.4	12.3	12.3	12.5	12.4	12.4	12.3	12.4	12.3	12.3	12.4
Retail Trade													
2000	33.3	32.7	33.0	33.5	33.9	34.2	33.6	33.8	33.7	33.8	34.7	35.4	33.8
2001	33.6	32.7	33.0	32.9	33.2	33.3	32.7	32.9	32.9	33.7	34.9	35.5	33.4
2002	33.5	32.9	33.1	33.0	33.3	33.4	32.8	33.3	33.2	33.6	34.9	35.5	33.5
2003	33.5	32.8	32.9	33.1	33.2	33.3	33.0	33.3	33.3	33.9	34.8	35.4	33.5
2004	33.5	33.0	33.1	33.3	33.5	33.8	33.7	33.9	33.5	34.1	35.1	35.9	33.9
2005	33.7	33.0	33.1	33.4	33.6	33.6	33.6	33.7	33.3	33.6	34.4	35.0	33.7
2006	33.2	32.4	32.5	32.8	32.7	32.8	32.6	32.8	32.5	32.9	34.1	34.9	33.0
2007	33.2	32.4	32.8	33.1	33.5	33.6	33.3	33.2	33.2	33.6	34.4	35.3	33.5

Employment by Industry: Scranton–Wilkes-Barre, PA, 2000–2007—*Continued*

(Numbers in thousands, not seasonally adjusted.)

Industry and year	January	February	March	April	May	June	July	August	September	October	November	December	Annual Average
Transportation and Utilities													
2000	12.9	12.7	12.9	13.2	13.2	13.3	12.8	12.8	13.3	13.6	13.6	13.6	13.2
2001	13.3	13.3	13.5	13.7	13.8	13.7	13.4	13.4	14.1	14.1	14.2	14.3	13.7
2002	13.6	13.6	13.8	13.6	13.5	13.2	12.8	12.8	13.3	13.3	13.1	13.1	13.3
2003	12.6	12.5	12.6	12.7	12.8	12.8	12.2	12.3	12.8	13.1	13.1	13.1	12.7
2004	12.6	12.7	13.0	12.9	13.0	13.0	12.7	12.7	13.0	13.1	13.3	13.4	13.0
2005	13.0	13.0	13.2	13.4	13.6	13.6	13.1	13.2	13.9	13.8	14.1	14.3	13.5
2006	13.9	14.0	14.1	13.9	13.9	13.9	13.6	13.7	14.2	14.5	14.6	14.8	14.1
2007	14.3	14.3	14.6	14.7	14.7	14.7	14.2	14.0	14.8	14.9	14.8	14.7	14.6
Information													
2000	6.8	7.0	7.0	6.9	7.0	7.1	7.0	6.6	7.1	7.0	7.1	7.2	7.0
2001	6.9	6.8	6.9	7.0	7.0	7.0	6.9	6.8	6.8	6.8	6.7	6.8	6.9
2002	6.6	6.6	6.6	6.5	6.7	6.6	6.6	6.6	6.4	6.3	6.3	6.2	6.5
2003	6.1	6.2	6.2	6.2	6.3	6.4	6.3	6.4	6.4	6.4	6.5	6.6	6.3
2004	6.4	6.3	6.3	6.3	6.3	6.3	6.4	6.4	6.4	6.4	6.4	6.4	6.4
2005	6.2	6.2	6.3	6.4	6.4	6.4	6.3	6.3	6.2	6.2	6.2	6.2	6.3
2006	6.1	6.0	6.0	6.2	6.2	6.3	6.4	6.4	6.3	6.4	6.3	6.4	6.3
2007	6.2	6.2	6.2	6.2	6.1	6.3	6.1	6.0	6.0	6.0	6.0	6.0	6.1
Financial Activities													
2000	13.5	13.4	13.5	13.6	13.7	13.8	13.9	14.0	13.8	13.7	13.8	13.8	13.7
2001	14.0	13.9	14.0	13.9	13.9	14.2	14.1	14.0	13.7	13.6	13.5	13.6	13.9
2002	13.5	13.5	13.5	13.5	13.5	13.7	13.6	13.5	13.4	13.1	13.1	13.2	13.4
2003	13.3	13.3	13.4	13.5	13.7	13.9	14.0	14.0	14.0	13.9	13.9	13.9	13.7
2004	13.8	13.8	13.9	14.0	14.0	14.1	14.1	14.0	13.9	13.7	13.6	13.7	13.9
2005	13.5	13.5	13.5	13.6	13.6	13.6	13.5	13.4	13.2	13.1	13.0	12.9	13.4
2006	12.9	12.9	12.8	12.8	12.9	13.1	13.1	13.0	12.7	12.6	12.6	12.7	12.8
2007	12.4	12.3	12.2	12.3	12.5	12.7	12.7	12.6	12.4	12.4	12.3	12.3	12.4
Professional and Business Services													
2000	21.9	22.3	22.8	23.6	23.6	23.8	23.1	23.3	23.3	22.9	22.9	22.8	23.0
2001	22.9	22.8	23.1	23.1	23.7	23.5	23.1	23.4	23.0	21.6	21.0	20.4	22.6
2002	19.6	19.8	20.4	20.7	20.7	20.7	20.2	20.1	20.0	20.6	20.4	20.1	20.3
2003	19.2	19.1	19.5	19.9	20.0	20.0	19.7	20.2	20.2	20.5	20.5	20.4	19.9
2004	19.9	19.9	20.1	20.5	20.7	21.4	21.3	21.6	21.6	22.1	22.3	22.1	21.1
2005	21.9	22.2	22.3	22.8	22.7	23.4	24.1	24.4	24.4	24.6	24.5	24.0	23.4
2006	23.4	23.4	23.8	24.3	24.4	25.1	24.1	24.7	25.0	25.3	24.8	24.5	24.4
2007	23.6	23.2	23.8	24.5	24.5	25.2	25.4	25.3	25.5	25.5	25.1	24.9	24.7
Education and Health Services													
2000	44.8	46.2	46.7	46.1	45.3	44.2	43.8	43.7	45.0	46.0	46.1	46.0	45.3
2001	43.8	45.6	46.0	45.7	44.9	44.0	43.8	43.9	44.8	46.2	46.4	46.0	45.1
2002	44.6	46.5	47.0	47.1	46.8	45.5	45.1	45.2	46.3	47.8	48.1	47.6	46.5
2003	46.7	48.1	49.0	48.7	48.3	47.1	46.2	46.1	47.4	49.0	49.1	49.0	47.8
2004	46.3	47.7	48.3	48.6	47.9	46.5	46.6	46.4	47.8	49.5	49.9	49.7	47.9
2005	48.0	49.5	49.8	50.2	49.2	47.7	47.7	47.5	49.0	50.3	50.2	50.0	49.1
2006	48.7	50.7	50.9	50.8	50.1	48.5	48.2	48.2	49.9	50.7	51.0	50.2	49.8
2007	48.8	50.5	50.7	51.0	50.2	49.0	48.6	48.2	49.7	51.0	51.3	51.0	50.0
Leisure and Hospitality													
2000	18.1	17.9	18.4	18.9	19.8	20.2	19.8	20.0	19.8	18.8	18.4	18.2	19.0
2001	18.1	18.4	19.0	19.3	20.2	20.4	20.3	20.2	20.1	19.2	18.9	19.1	19.4
2002	18.6	18.6	19.2	19.8	20.6	20.9	20.4	20.5	20.5	20.1	19.7	19.7	19.9
2003	18.8	18.6	19.2	20.2	21.2	21.7	21.5	21.6	21.3	21.3	20.9	20.9	20.6
2004	20.3	20.2	20.7	21.4	22.3	22.9	22.9	23.2	22.7	22.0	21.7	21.5	21.8
2005	20.6	20.8	21.0	22.2	23.1	23.3	22.7	22.5	22.5	21.8	21.5	21.5	22.0
2006	20.7	21.0	21.4	22.0	22.7	23.1	22.3	22.2	22.5	22.1	22.4	22.4	22.1
2007	21.7	21.7	22.1	22.6	23.5	24.2	23.1	23.4	23.2	22.7	22.6	22.6	22.8
Other Services													
2000	9.8	9.8	10.0	10.0	10.2	10.2	10.2	10.2	10.0	10.0	10.0	10.0	10.0
2001	9.8	9.9	10.0	10.1	10.2	10.2	10.2	10.2	10.0	10.0	10.0	10.0	10.1
2002	10.1	10.0	10.0	10.0	10.2	10.2	10.3	10.2	10.1	10.0	10.0	9.9	10.1
2003	9.8	9.9	9.9	9.9	10.1	10.1	10.1	10.1	9.9	9.9	9.8	9.9	9.9
2004	9.9	9.9	10.2	10.2	10.3	10.4	10.4	10.4	10.2	10.0	10.0	10.1	10.2
2005	10.0	9.8	9.9	10.0	10.1	10.2	10.2	10.1	9.9	9.8	9.8	9.8	10.0
2006	9.6	9.7	9.7	9.7	9.9	10.0	9.9	9.8	9.8	9.6	9.6	9.7	9.8
2007	9.6	9.6	9.6	9.6	9.8	10.0	10.0	9.8	9.7	9.6	9.6	9.7	9.7
Government													
2000	30.7	31.6	31.9	31.9	32.4	31.3	30.4	29.8	30.7	30.9	31.2	31.3	31.2
2001	30.8	31.6	31.6	31.4	31.5	31.2	29.7	29.7	30.5	31.3	31.7	31.7	31.1
2002	31.3	32.1	31.9	31.7	31.9	31.7	30.6	30.5	31.7	32.0	32.0	32.7	31.7
2003	32.0	32.7	32.9	32.3	32.5	32.2	30.4	29.9	32.0	32.2	32.2	32.5	31.9
2004	31.8	32.2	32.0	31.9	32.1	32.0	30.5	29.9	31.2	32.0	32.1	31.8	31.6
2005	31.4	31.9	31.9	31.8	31.9	32.5	30.7	30.3	31.7	31.9	32.3	32.0	31.7
2006	31.5	31.9	32.4	32.0	32.1	32.1	30.2	30.0	31.6	32.0	32.5	32.5	31.7
2007	31.6	31.8	32.2	32.4	32.3	32.1	29.8	29.6	31.1	31.5	32.1	32.1	31.6

Employment by Industry: Greenville-Mauldin-Easley, SC, 2000–2007

(Numbers in thousands, not seasonally adjusted.)

Industry and year	January	February	March	April	May	June	July	August	September	October	November	December	Annual Average
Total Nonfarm													
2000	298.9	300.6	304.0	306.8	308.7	311.0	308.5	310.6	311.2	311.1	313.2	313.7	308.2
2001	308.7	309.7	311.7	311.6	311.9	312.4	302.4	304.9	302.9	300.7	302.4	302.2	306.4
2002	291.3	292.8	295.6	293.8	295.6	296.9	295.7	300.4	301.1	300.6	302.1	302.7	296.1
2003	290.0	291.4	293.3	294.6	294.9	296.1	290.9	291.4	294.2	295.1	296.9	297.1	291.7
2004	291.1	290.7	293.8	296.2	297.3	298.6	295.7	295.9	297.6	299.2	302.1	301.8	293.7
2005	296.5	298.4	298.8	301.4	303.3	300.9	299.0	300.9	304.5	306.4	309.2	306.5	301.2
2006	303.2	305.5	306.7	308.2	309.7	308.5	303.6	305.6	309.3	313.4	314.5	315.1	308.6
2007	309.6	312.4	315.0	317.2	319.0	319.3	317.6	316.6	322.6	323.4	324.0	324.3	318.4
Total Private													
2000	262.3	263.3	266.4	269.3	271.5	274.1	273.6	274.2	273.7	273.2	274.6	275.6	271.0
2001	271.1	271.6	273.5	273.4	274.0	274.3	267.0	267.5	264.8	262.2	263.5	263.2	268.4
2002	252.9	253.9	256.5	254.3	256.4	258.2	259.6	262.1	261.8	261.0	261.8	262.6	257.2
2003	250.3	251.3	253.0	254.3	255.1	256.3	254.3	254.3	254.9	255.4	256.7	257.2	252.3
2004	251.5	250.9	253.8	255.8	257.3	258.9	258.5	259.0	258.4	258.9	261.7	261.4	254.2
2005	257.0	258.4	258.7	261.3	263.1	261.1	262.5	264.3	264.2	265.6	268.0	265.4	261.6
2006	262.8	264.2	265.4	267.0	268.5	267.7	266.2	268.0	268.3	270.9	272.4	272.8	267.9
2007	267.8	270.1	272.4	274.7	276.3	277.0	278.2	277.1	279.3	279.7	279.9	280.3	276.1
Goods-Producing													
2000	75.7	75.9	76.5	77.6	78.0	78.9	78.8	79.2	79.1	78.9	78.2	78.3	77.9
2001	77.3	77.0	76.8	77.2	77.1	77.0	74.4	73.9	72.0	71.3	70.5	69.9	74.5
2002	67.3	67.1	67.4	66.8	66.9	67.4	68.3	68.3	67.7	67.7	66.9	67.0	67.4
2003	64.6	64.7	64.7	65.3	65.0	65.2	65.5	64.8	65.2	64.8	64.2	64.0	64.8
2004	62.4	61.7	62.8	62.5	63.2	63.5	63.5	63.3	63.5	62.9	62.7	62.2	62.9
2005	61.4	61.8	62.0	62.2	62.2	61.6	61.3	61.2	60.5	60.9	60.7	60.0	61.3
2006	59.6	59.7	59.6	59.7	60.3	60.0	59.3	59.4	59.5	59.8	60.2	60.2	59.8
2007	59.7	60.1	60.6	61.0	61.1	61.4	61.3	61.0	60.9	60.5	60.1	60.4	60.7
Natural Resources, Mining, and Construction													
2000	18.4	18.4	18.7	18.8	18.9	19.4	18.7	18.8	18.7	19.2	19.0	19.0	18.8
2001	18.4	18.2	18.4	19.0	19.0	19.0	17.9	18.0	17.3	17.3	17.2	17.0	18.1
2002	16.1	16.3	16.3	16.6	16.8	17.1	17.2	17.2	17.1	17.5	17.3	17.2	16.9
2003	16.1	16.0	16.0	16.4	16.6	17.0	17.2	17.1	17.3	17.3	17.2	17.2	16.8
2004	16.5	16.4	16.8	16.6	17.1	17.4	17.5	17.5	17.4	17.3	17.2	17.1	17.1
2005	16.9	17.0	17.1	17.4	17.6	17.7	18.1	18.1	18.0	18.0	18.2	17.9	17.7
2006	17.7	17.5	17.4	17.6	17.8	17.7	17.9	18.1	18.3	18.1	18.5	18.4	17.9
2007	18.0	18.0	18.5	18.7	18.8	19.1	19.5	19.6	19.6	19.4	19.2	19.3	19.0
Manufacturing													
2000	57.3	57.5	57.8	58.8	59.1	59.5	60.1	60.4	60.4	59.7	59.2	59.3	59.1
2001	58.9	58.8	58.4	58.2	58.1	58.0	56.5	55.9	54.7	54.0	53.3	52.9	56.5
2002	51.2	50.8	51.1	50.2	50.1	50.3	51.1	51.1	50.6	50.2	49.6	49.8	50.5
2003	48.5	48.7	48.7	48.9	48.4	48.2	48.3	47.7	47.9	47.5	47.0	46.8	48.1
2004	45.9	45.3	46.0	45.9	46.1	46.1	46.0	45.8	46.1	45.6	45.5	45.1	45.8
2005	44.5	44.8	44.9	44.8	44.6	43.9	43.2	43.1	42.5	42.9	42.5	42.1	43.7
2006	41.9	42.2	42.2	42.1	42.5	42.3	41.4	41.3	41.2	41.7	41.7	41.8	41.9
2007	41.7	42.1	42.1	42.3	42.3	42.3	41.8	41.4	41.3	41.1	40.9	41.1	41.7
Service-Providing													
2000	223.2	224.7	227.5	229.2	230.7	232.1	229.7	231.4	232.1	232.2	235.0	235.4	230.3
2001	231.4	232.7	234.9	234.4	234.8	235.4	228.0	231.0	230.9	229.4	231.9	232.3	231.9
2002	224.0	225.7	228.2	227.0	228.7	229.5	227.4	232.1	233.4	232.9	235.2	235.7	228.7
2003	225.4	226.7	228.6	229.3	229.9	230.9	225.4	226.6	229.0	230.3	232.7	233.1	226.9
2004	228.7	229.0	231.0	233.7	234.1	235.1	232.2	232.6	234.1	236.3	239.4	239.6	230.8
2005	235.1	236.6	236.8	239.2	241.1	239.3	237.7	239.7	244.0	245.5	248.5	246.5	239.9
2006	243.6	245.8	247.1	248.5	249.4	248.5	244.3	246.2	249.8	253.6	254.3	254.9	248.8
2007	249.9	252.3	254.4	256.2	257.9	257.9	256.3	255.6	261.7	262.9	263.9	263.9	257.7
Trade, Transportation, and Utilities													
2000	67.3	67.2	67.9	67.7	68.5	68.8	68.8	69.2	69.2	69.4	71.2	71.7	68.9
2001	69.2	68.2	68.9	67.9	68.3	68.4	67.4	67.2	66.4	65.8	67.4	67.4	67.7
2002	63.9	63.5	63.8	63.5	63.7	64.0	62.7	63.0	62.1	61.7	63.2	63.9	63.3
2003	58.9	58.8	58.7	59.4	59.5	60.2	59.6	59.6	59.4	59.7	60.9	61.5	59.7
2004	59.0	58.7	59.5	59.5	59.9	60.5	60.9	61.3	61.1	62.3	63.9	64.8	61.0
2005	62.0	62.0	62.3	63.0	63.5	62.5	63.4	63.9	63.4	64.2	66.0	66.6	63.6
2006	64.6	64.5	64.9	64.9	64.9	65.0	64.7	65.1	64.9	65.8	67.1	67.6	65.3
2007	65.3	65.5	65.8	66.3	66.8	67.1	67.8	67.6	67.6	67.2	68.3	68.9	67.0
Wholesale Trade													
2000	13.3	13.3	13.7	13.6	13.8	13.8	13.8	13.7	13.8	13.7	13.7	13.8	13.7
2001	13.9	13.9	14.0	13.8	13.7	13.9	13.5	13.3	13.1	13.0	13.1	12.7	13.5
2002	12.6	12.7	12.6	12.7	12.7	13.1	12.7	12.6	12.3	12.2	12.2	12.3	12.6
2003	11.5	11.6	11.6	11.7	11.8	11.9	11.5	11.5	11.4	11.4	11.4	11.4	11.6
2004	10.8	10.9	10.9	11.0	11.2	11.5	11.8	11.9	12.0	12.4	12.5	12.7	11.6
2005	12.4	12.6	12.6	13.1	13.3	13.1	13.3	13.3	13.3	13.6	13.7	13.9	13.2
2006	13.8	13.8	13.8	14.1	14.0	14.0	13.8	13.8	13.8	14.2	14.3	14.4	14.0
2007	14.3	14.6	14.4	14.5	14.5	14.9	14.9	15.0	14.8	14.9	14.9	15.0	14.7
Retail Trade													
2000	41.1	40.8	41.1	41.0	41.5	41.8	41.6	42.0	42.0	42.0	43.8	44.3	41.9
2001	41.8	40.8	41.1	40.6	40.7	40.7	40.3	40.4	39.9	39.6	41.2	41.6	40.7
2002	38.3	37.7	38.1	37.4	37.5	37.6	37.0	37.3	36.7	36.0	37.3	37.9	37.4
2003	34.8	34.5	34.5	34.6	34.8	35.2	35.1	35.3	35.3	35.7	37.0	37.7	35.4
2004	36.3	35.9	36.7	36.6	36.8	37.0	37.1	37.4	37.3	38.0	39.5	40.2	37.4
2005	37.9	37.5	37.7	38.1	38.3	37.6	38.0	38.4	37.9	38.6	40.1	40.7	38.4
2006	38.7	38.5	38.9	38.5	38.6	38.6	38.6	38.8	38.5	39.2	40.5	41.0	39.0
2007	38.7	38.3	38.8	39.1	39.4	39.3	39.8	39.5	39.7	39.0	40.0	40.4	39.3

Employment by Industry: Greenville-Mauldin-Easley, SC, 2000–2007—*Continued*

(Numbers in thousands, not seasonally adjusted.)

Industry and year	January	February	March	April	May	June	July	August	September	October	November	December	Annual Average
Transportation and Utilities													
2000	12.9	13.1	13.1	13.1	13.2	13.2	13.4	13.5	13.4	13.7	13.7	13.6	13.3
2001	13.5	13.5	13.8	13.5	13.9	13.8	13.6	13.5	13.4	13.2	13.1	13.1	13.5
2002	13.0	13.1	13.1	13.4	13.5	13.3	13.0	13.1	13.1	13.5	13.7	13.7	13.3
2003	12.6	12.7	12.6	13.1	12.9	13.1	13.0	12.8	12.7	12.6	12.5	12.4	12.8
2004	11.9	11.9	11.9	11.9	11.9	12.0	12.0	12.0	11.8	11.9	11.9	11.9	11.9
2005	11.7	11.9	12.0	11.8	11.9	11.8	12.1	12.2	12.2	12.0	12.2	12.0	12.0
2006	12.1	12.2	12.2	12.3	12.3	12.4	12.3	12.5	12.6	12.4	12.3	12.2	12.3
2007	12.3	12.6	12.6	12.7	12.9	12.9	13.1	13.1	13.1	13.3	13.4	13.5	13.0
Information													
2000	7.5	7.6	7.6	7.4	7.7	7.9	7.8	7.9	7.9	7.9	8.0	8.2	7.8
2001	7.8	8.1	8.0	7.6	7.5	7.5	7.3	7.4	7.4	7.3	7.4	7.1	7.5
2002	7.0	7.0	7.0	6.5	6.6	6.6	6.8	6.9	6.9	7.4	7.4	7.4	7.0
2003	6.9	6.9	6.9	6.9	6.8	6.8	7.0	7.0	7.0	7.0	7.1	7.1	7.0
2004	7.2	7.1	7.0	7.0	7.0	7.0	6.9	6.9	6.7	6.8	6.8	6.8	6.9
2005	6.5	6.6	6.6	6.7	6.7	6.7	6.6	6.6	6.6	6.5	6.4	6.6	6.6
2006	6.5	6.7	6.6	6.7	6.7	6.6	6.6	6.6	6.4	6.4	6.4	6.4	6.6
2007	6.3	6.4	6.4	6.4	6.5	6.6	6.5	6.5	6.5	6.6	6.5	6.5	6.5
Financial Activities													
2000	13.5	13.6	13.6	14.1	14.2	14.2	14.5	14.1	13.9	14.1	14.1	14.1	14.0
2001	13.6	13.8	14.1	14.0	13.8	13.8	13.6	13.4	13.3	13.6	13.5	13.7	13.7
2002	13.5	13.5	13.5	13.5	13.6	13.8	14.0	14.2	14.2	14.0	14.1	14.1	13.5
2003	13.6	13.6	13.8	14.0	14.0	14.1	14.0	14.2	14.2	14.4	14.3	14.4	13.4
2004	14.2	14.3	14.3	14.4	14.4	14.6	14.6	14.6	14.6	14.8	14.9	15.0	13.7
2005	15.3	15.4	15.6	15.5	15.4	15.4	15.4	15.4	15.4	15.0	15.1	14.8	15.0
2006	14.7	14.6	14.8	14.7	14.6	14.5	14.5	14.5	14.4	13.8	13.7	13.5	14.4
2007	13.7	13.7	13.8	14.1	14.2	14.2	14.3	14.4	14.3	14.3	14.4	14.4	14.2
Professional and Business Services													
2000	42.5	42.7	43.6	44.7	45.2	45.6	45.2	45.6	45.4	45.0	45.4	45.4	44.7
2001	45.3	45.7	46.1	46.5	45.9	45.9	43.3	44.1	43.9	44.1	44.0	43.9	44.6
2002	40.8	41.7	42.5	42.0	42.5	42.8	43.7	44.5	45.0	45.8	45.7	45.7	42.7
2003	43.0	43.4	44.4	43.9	44.1	44.1	42.5	43.1	43.1	44.3	45.0	45.1	42.3
2004	43.8	43.9	44.4	44.7	44.7	44.6	44.4	45.1	44.8	44.6	44.5	44.8	42.4
2005	44.9	44.9	44.0	45.6	46.4	45.9	46.2	47.4	48.4	49.4	49.6	48.0	46.1
2006	48.0	48.7	49.4	50.1	50.4	50.7	49.6	50.6	51.3	52.3	52.1	51.9	50.4
2007	50.8	51.8	52.8	53.1	53.8	53.7	54.3	53.4	55.5	55.8	55.6	55.3	53.8
Education and Health Services													
2000	21.9	22.0	22.4	22.7	22.7	22.9	22.5	22.5	22.7	22.5	22.6	22.7	22.5
2001	23.6	23.8	23.9	23.9	24.4	24.7	24.9	25.0	25.3	24.7	25.0	25.3	24.5
2002	25.4	25.5	25.8	26.0	26.3	26.3	26.4	27.2	27.9	27.5	27.6	27.6	26.6
2003	27.3	27.5	27.6	28.0	28.4	28.3	28.0	28.1	28.5	28.2	28.1	28.2	28.0
2004	28.0	28.1	28.2	28.4	28.5	28.8	28.9	28.8	28.8	28.8	29.0	29.1	28.6
2005	29.0	29.2	29.3	29.2	29.4	29.5	29.5	29.5	29.7	29.7	29.9	29.7	29.5
2006	29.9	30.0	29.9	30.0	30.2	29.8	29.7	29.9	30.0	30.6	30.4	30.4	30.1
2007	30.1	30.3	30.3	30.3	30.6	30.8	31.0	31.1	31.1	31.3	31.3	31.4	30.8
Leisure and Hospitality													
2000	24.7	25.2	25.5	25.8	25.9	26.5	26.7	26.5	26.2	26.0	25.9	26.0	25.9
2001	25.2	25.8	26.3	26.8	27.2	27.2	26.6	27.1	26.7	25.6	25.7	25.9	26.3
2002	25.2	25.5	26.0	25.8	26.4	26.8	27.7	28.0	27.6	27.0	27.0	26.9	26.7
2003	26.2	26.6	27.0	26.9	27.3	27.7	27.8	27.7	27.4	26.8	26.9	26.6	27.1
2004	26.5	26.7	27.1	28.1	28.3	28.4	28.4	28.2	27.9	27.6	28.6	27.4	27.8
2005	26.7	27.1	27.4	27.9	28.2	28.2	28.6	28.7	28.4	28.7	29.0	28.4	28.1
2006	28.3	28.6	28.7	29.2	29.6	29.3	29.9	29.9	29.7	30.1	30.3	30.5	29.5
2007	29.5	29.8	30.0	31.1	31.0	30.8	30.7	30.9	31.1	31.6	31.3	31.1	30.7
Other Services													
2000	9.2	9.1	9.3	9.3	9.3	9.3	9.3	9.2	9.3	9.4	9.2	9.2	9.3
2001	9.1	9.2	9.4	9.5	9.8	9.8	9.5	9.4	9.8	9.8	10.0	10.0	9.6
2002	9.8	10.1	10.5	10.2	10.2	10.4	10.5	10.0	10.0	10.4	9.9	9.9	10.0	10.1
2003	9.8	9.8	9.9	9.9	10.0	9.9	9.9	9.8	10.1	10.2	10.2	10.3	10.0
2004	10.4	10.4	10.5	11.2	11.3	11.5	10.9	10.8	11.0	11.1	11.3	11.3	11.0
2005	11.2	11.4	11.5	11.2	11.3	11.3	11.5	11.6	11.8	11.2	11.3	11.3	11.4
2006	11.2	11.4	11.5	11.7	11.8	11.8	11.9	12.0	12.1	12.1	12.2	12.3	11.8
2007	12.4	12.5	12.7	12.4	12.3	12.4	12.3	12.2	12.3	12.4	12.4	12.3	12.4
Government													
2000	36.6	37.3	37.6	37.5	37.2	36.9	34.9	36.4	37.5	37.9	38.6	38.1	37.2
2001	37.6	38.1	38.2	38.2	37.9	38.1	35.4	37.4	38.1	38.5	38.9	39.0	38.0
2002	38.4	38.9	39.1	39.5	39.2	38.7	36.1	38.3	39.3	39.6	40.3	40.1	39.0
2003	39.7	40.1	40.3	40.3	39.8	39.8	36.6	37.1	39.3	39.7	40.2	39.9	39.4
2004	39.6	39.8	40.0	40.4	40.0	39.7	37.2	36.9	39.2	40.3	40.4	40.4	39.5
2005	39.5	40.0	40.1	40.1	40.2	39.8	36.5	36.6	40.3	40.8	41.2	41.1	39.7
2006	40.4	41.3	41.3	41.2	41.2	40.8	37.4	37.6	41.0	42.5	42.1	42.3	40.8
2007	41.8	42.3	42.6	42.5	42.7	42.3	39.4	39.5	43.3	43.7	44.1	44.0	42.4

Employment by Industry: Charleston-North Charleston-Summerville, SC, 2000–2007

(Numbers in thousands, not seasonally adjusted.)

Industry and year	January	February	March	April	May	June	July	August	September	October	November	December	Annual Average
Total Nonfarm													
2000	258.0	258.7	262.1	262.1	265.2	268.5	258.8	259.1	258.8	261.6	263.0	264.2	259.4
2001	254.6	255.8	258.7	259.5	260.6	261.0	259.5	258.6	259.2	258.5	258.2	258.5	255.8
2002	254.1	257.7	260.6	260.5	263.3	263.1	266.1	267.0	267.4	266.5	266.0	265.9	259.9
2003	256.8	259.7	261.4	265.1	266.6	265.9	263.6	266.1	265.4	265.4	266.2	267.4	264.1
2004	263.0	266.4	269.7	272.3	275.3	274.9	272.3	274.0	273.6	275.3	276.9	276.0	272.5
2005	271.3	274.0	275.6	279.5	281.9	280.1	280.0	281.8	281.6	282.6	284.2	281.9	279.5
2006	278.0	280.9	281.6	286.5	288.8	285.6	285.0	287.6	289.2	290.2	292.2	293.5	286.6
2007	289.3	291.7	295.4	299.2	301.5	301.8	300.3	301.5	300.3	300.6	301.1	300.0	298.6
Total Private													
2000	207.7	207.9	210.9	211.1	213.5	216.4	210.9	210.4	209.4	211.1	212.2	212.9	209.2
2001	205.5	206.0	208.4	209.2	210.4	211.9	210.9	210.9	209.2	207.4	207.1	207.3	206.7
2002	204.0	206.6	209.4	209.0	211.7	212.2	216.1	216.3	215.5	214.2	213.4	212.8	209.8
2003	205.0	206.4	208.3	211.7	213.2	214.3	213.5	214.3	212.2	212.0	212.6	213.5	211.4
2004	210.1	213.1	216.1	218.5	221.4	222.6	221.8	221.5	220.0	221.6	223.0	222.0	219.3
2005	218.4	220.3	221.7	225.5	227.7	226.5	228.7	228.9	227.3	227.9	229.2	226.8	225.7
2006	224.3	226.9	227.3	231.3	233.5	232.7	234.3	234.8	234.5	234.5	236.4	237.6	232.3
2007	234.2	236.3	239.9	243.3	245.6	246.2	246.3	245.9	243.8	244.1	244.3	243.3	242.8
Goods-Producing													
2000	42.8	42.6	43.1	42.7	43.2	43.1	42.0	42.0	41.7	42.7	42.8	43.0	42.6
2001	41.7	41.7	42.2	42.2	42.5	42.8	42.2	42.2	41.9	41.6	41.5	41.2	42.0
2002	40.9	41.3	41.9	40.5	40.8	40.8	42.2	42.0	41.7	41.3	40.5	40.3	41.2
2003	38.6	38.8	39.1	40.0	39.9	40.1	39.6	39.8	39.3	39.4	39.5	39.9	39.5
2004	39.8	40.2	40.6	41.8	42.1	42.4	42.0	41.6	41.5	41.3	41.4	41.2	41.3
2005	41.5	41.6	41.3	41.2	41.5	41.3	41.9	42.0	41.9	41.8	42.1	41.5	41.6
2006	41.6	41.7	41.6	42.5	42.9	42.7	43.2	43.2	43.1	43.6	43.5	43.5	42.8
2007	43.3	43.6	43.9	44.1	44.3	44.5	44.5	44.4	44.2	44.3	44.2	44.0	44.1
Natural Resources, Mining, and Construction													
2000	19.3	19.2	19.6	20.0	20.4	20.2	19.5	19.4	19.2	19.9	20.0	20.1	19.7
2001	19.5	19.5	20.0	20.0	20.3	20.7	20.5	20.4	20.2	20.5	20.5	20.2	20.2
2002	20.1	20.3	20.7	19.7	20.0	20.0	21.2	21.0	20.7	20.3	19.7	19.6	20.3
2003	17.7	17.9	18.0	18.9	18.9	19.2	18.9	19.1	19.0	19.2	19.1	19.4	18.8
2004	19.3	19.4	19.7	20.8	21.1	21.1	20.9	20.6	20.4	19.8	19.7	19.5	20.2
2005	20.0	20.2	19.9	20.0	20.2	20.1	20.7	20.7	20.5	20.7	20.9	20.3	20.4
2006	20.5	20.6	20.8	21.3	21.6	21.5	22.0	22.0	21.8	22.1	21.9	21.7	21.5
2007	21.6	21.8	21.8	21.7	21.9	22.0	21.9	21.9	21.8	21.9	21.9	21.6	21.8
Manufacturing													
2000	23.5	23.4	23.5	22.7	22.8	22.9	22.5	22.6	22.5	22.8	22.8	22.9	22.9
2001	22.2	22.2	22.2	22.2	22.2	22.1	21.7	21.8	21.7	21.1	21.0	21.0	21.8
2002	20.8	21.0	21.2	20.8	20.8	20.8	21.0	21.0	21.0	21.0	20.8	20.7	20.9
2003	20.9	20.9	21.1	21.1	21.0	20.9	20.7	20.7	20.3	20.2	20.4	20.5	20.7
2004	20.5	20.8	20.9	21.0	21.0	21.3	21.1	21.0	21.1	21.5	21.7	21.7	21.1
2005	21.5	21.4	21.4	21.2	21.3	21.2	21.2	21.3	21.4	21.1	21.2	21.2	21.3
2006	21.1	21.1	20.8	21.2	21.3	21.2	21.2	21.2	21.3	21.5	21.6	21.8	21.3
2007	21.7	21.8	22.1	22.4	22.4	22.5	22.6	22.5	22.4	22.4	22.3	22.4	22.3
Service-Providing													
2000	214.7	215.6	218.5	218.9	221.5	224.9	216.3	216.7	216.6	218.4	219.7	220.8	216.8
2001	212.5	213.7	216.1	216.9	217.7	217.8	216.9	216.0	216.9	216.5	216.3	216.9	213.9
2002	212.8	216.0	218.3	219.6	222.1	221.9	223.5	224.6	225.3	224.8	225.1	225.2	218.8
2003	218.2	220.9	222.3	225.1	226.7	225.8	224.0	226.3	226.1	226.0	226.7	227.5	224.6
2004	223.2	226.2	229.1	230.5	233.2	232.5	230.3	232.4	232.1	234.0	235.5	234.8	231.2
2005	229.8	232.4	234.3	238.3	240.4	238.8	238.1	239.8	239.7	240.8	242.1	240.4	237.9
2006	236.4	239.2	240.0	244.0	245.9	242.9	241.8	244.4	246.1	246.6	248.7	250.0	243.8
2007	246.0	248.1	251.5	255.1	257.2	257.3	255.8	257.1	256.1	256.3	256.9	256.0	254.5
Trade, Transportation, and Utilities													
2000	54.3	54.1	54.7	53.8	54.1	55.3	54.5	54.7	54.8	55.0	56.0	56.5	54.8
2001	53.8	53.5	53.8	53.6	53.8	54.0	53.7	54.1	53.8	53.7	54.1	54.6	53.9
2002	52.9	53.1	53.5	53.5	54.2	53.8	54.1	54.4	54.6	54.6	55.3	55.9	54.2
2003	52.8	53.2	53.5	53.4	53.7	54.0	53.5	53.8	53.5	53.7	54.2	55.0	53.7
2004	53.0	53.6	54.2	54.0	54.9	55.2	56.0	55.7	55.4	56.2	57.3	57.4	55.2
2005	55.5	55.4	55.6	55.8	56.7	56.3	57.6	57.7	57.4	58.0	58.6	59.0	57.0
2006	56.7	57.4	57.7	57.0	57.8	57.6	58.0	58.0	57.8	57.7	59.7	60.2	58.0
2007	57.4	57.8	58.6	58.6	59.3	59.6	59.7	59.3	59.1	59.7	60.2	60.7	59.2
Wholesale Trade													
2000	7.0	7.0	7.0	7.0	7.0	7.1	7.4	7.4	7.5	7.5	7.6	7.6	7.3
2001	7.5	7.5	7.7	7.6	7.6	7.6	7.7	7.7	7.7	7.6	7.5	7.6	7.6
2002	7.6	7.8	8.0	7.8	7.8	7.8	8.0	8.0	8.1	8.0	8.0	8.1	7.9
2003	7.6	7.6	7.7	7.7	7.7	7.6	7.6	7.6	7.6	7.6	7.6	7.7	7.6
2004	7.5	7.6	7.7	7.9	7.9	7.8	8.0	8.0	7.9	8.0	8.2	8.1	7.9
2005	8.1	8.2	8.3	8.2	8.3	8.1	8.3	8.3	8.2	8.4	8.4	8.3	8.3
2006	8.4	8.3	8.3	8.3	8.4	8.3	8.4	8.4	8.5	8.7	8.8	8.8	8.5
2007	8.8	9.0	9.0	8.9	8.9	8.9	9.0	8.9	8.9	8.9	8.9	8.9	8.9
Retail Trade													
2000	34.1	33.9	34.2	33.8	34.1	34.8	33.8	33.8	34.0	34.2	35.0	35.4	34.3
2001	33.7	33.4	33.6	33.4	33.7	34.1	33.5	33.6	33.5	33.6	34.1	34.5	33.7
2002	33.3	33.1	33.4	33.6	33.9	34.1	33.8	33.8	33.9	34.0	34.6	35.4	33.9
2003	33.5	33.4	33.6	33.6	34.0	34.4	34.4	34.4	34.3	34.4	34.8	35.5	34.2
2004	33.8	34.0	34.5	34.4	34.9	35.2	35.2	35.0	34.9	35.5	36.5	37.1	35.1
2005	35.6	35.6	35.9	35.7	36.4	36.5	37.7	37.8	37.8	38.0	38.8	39.0	37.1
2006	37.1	37.5	37.8	37.4	37.9	37.8	38.2	38.1	38.0	37.5	38.9	39.0	37.9
2007	37.2	37.1	37.7	37.4	37.9	38.2	38.2	37.8	37.6	38.1	38.5	38.9	37.9

Employment by Industry: Charleston-North Charleston-Summerville, SC, 2000–2007—*Continued*

(Numbers in thousands, not seasonally adjusted.)

Industry and year	January	February	March	April	May	June	July	August	September	October	November	December	Annual Average
Transportation and Utilities													
2000	13.2	13.2	13.5	13.0	13.0	13.4	13.3	13.5	13.3	13.3	13.4	13.5	13.3
2001	12.6	12.6	12.5	12.6	12.5	12.3	12.5	12.8	12.6	12.5	12.5	12.5	12.5
2002	12.0	12.2	12.1	12.1	12.5	11.9	12.3	12.6	12.6	12.6	12.7	12.4	12.3
2003	11.7	12.2	12.2	12.1	12.0	12.0	11.5	11.8	11.6	11.7	11.8	11.8	11.9
2004	11.7	12.0	12.0	11.7	12.1	12.2	12.8	12.7	12.6	12.7	12.6	12.2	12.3
2005	11.8	11.6	11.4	11.9	12.0	11.7	11.6	11.6	11.4	11.6	11.4	11.7	11.6
2006	11.2	11.6	11.6	11.3	11.5	11.5	11.4	11.5	11.3	11.5	12.0	12.4	11.6
2007	11.4	11.7	11.9	12.3	12.5	12.5	12.5	12.6	12.6	12.7	12.8	12.9	12.4
Information													
2000	4.0	4.0	4.1	4.3	4.3	4.3	4.2	4.2	4.2	4.3	4.4	4.4	4.2
2001	4.2	4.2	4.2	4.1	4.1	4.1	4.1	4.1	4.0	3.9	4.1	4.1	4.1
2002	4.1	4.0	4.0	3.8	3.9	3.8	4.1	4.1	4.2	4.6	4.5	4.6	4.1
2003	4.3	4.3	4.3	4.4	4.4	4.5	4.5	4.5	4.5	4.4	4.4	4.4	4.4
2004	4.4	4.4	4.5	4.5	4.5	4.5	4.6	4.6	4.5	4.5	4.5	4.6	4.5
2005	4.6	4.6	4.5	4.6	4.7	4.8	4.7	4.6	4.6	4.7	4.7	4.7	4.7
2006	4.9	5.0	5.0	5.0	5.0	5.0	5.0	5.0	5.0	5.0	5.1	5.1	5.0
2007	5.0	5.1	5.1	5.1	5.1	5.1	5.1	5.1	5.1	5.1	5.1	5.1	5.1
Financial Activities													
2000	11.3	11.3	11.3	11.3	11.4	11.6	11.5	11.5	11.3	11.5	11.4	11.5	11.4
2001	11.1	11.2	11.2	11.4	11.4	11.5	11.8	11.7	11.6	11.4	11.3	11.5	11.4
2002	11.0	11.0	11.1	10.7	10.8	11.1	11.3	11.2	11.0	10.8	10.7	10.7	11.0
2003	11.2	11.1	11.1	11.2	11.3	11.4	11.4	11.4	11.2	11.3	11.2	11.1	11.2
2004	11.2	11.2	11.4	11.6	11.6	11.9	11.8	11.9	11.8	12.0	12.0	12.1	11.7
2005	12.7	12.8	12.8	13.1	13.3	13.1	13.3	13.2	13.1	13.1	13.1	13.0	13.1
2006	13.2	13.3	13.0	13.5	13.6	13.7	13.4	13.4	13.3	13.5	13.1	13.4	13.4
2007	13.6	13.6	13.7	14.0	14.1	14.3	14.4	14.5	14.4	14.3	14.4	14.6	14.2
Professional and Business Services													
2000	30.5	30.5	31.1	31.7	32.3	33.2	32.3	32.5	32.8	32.3	32.3	32.3	32.0
2001	32.0	32.1	32.2	32.4	32.2	32.5	32.8	32.9	32.9	32.7	32.5	32.5	32.5
2002	31.8	32.6	32.8	32.9	33.0	33.4	33.3	33.8	33.9	32.4	31.9	31.4	32.8
2003	29.6	29.9	30.3	31.8	32.2	32.1	32.5	32.5	32.2	32.5	32.6	32.5	31.7
2004	32.4	33.0	33.6	33.8	34.1	34.1	33.9	34.5	34.1	34.3	34.2	34.3	33.9
2005	33.3	33.7	33.8	35.5	35.3	34.7	35.1	35.3	35.4	36.0	36.1	35.9	35.0
2006	35.2	35.5	35.6	36.3	36.1	36.6	37.4	38.0	38.4	39.1	39.7	40.4	37.4
2007	40.4	40.8	41.6	41.7	41.8	41.8	41.4	41.6	41.2	41.2	41.4	41.3	41.4
Education and Health Services													
2000	23.8	23.8	23.9	23.8	23.8	23.8	22.8	22.9	23.2	23.8	23.9	24.1	23.6
2001	23.4	23.6	23.8	23.8	23.8	23.8	23.7	23.9	24.1	24.0	24.1	24.3	23.9
2002	24.1	24.4	24.5	25.5	25.8	25.5	26.3	26.2	26.4	27.0	27.2	27.0	25.8
2003	28.0	28.1	28.2	28.4	28.3	28.0	28.1	28.6	28.7	28.6	28.6	28.5	28.3
2004	28.4	28.7	28.5	28.5	28.4	27.9	27.8	28.1	28.2	28.2	28.6	28.2	28.3
2005	28.0	28.7	28.8	28.8	28.7	27.9	27.7	28.0	28.4	28.7	28.8	28.5	28.4
2006	28.4	28.9	28.9	29.5	29.6	28.6	28.8	29.1	29.8	29.4	29.4	29.6	29.2
2007	29.3	29.7	30.0	30.7	30.6	30.0	29.9	30.1	30.4	30.5	30.6	30.6	30.2
Leisure and Hospitality													
2000	29.4	30.0	31.0	31.8	32.7	33.2	32.1	31.3	30.2	30.2	30.1	29.8	31.0
2001	28.5	28.9	29.9	30.6	31.4	31.9	31.7	30.9	30.0	29.2	28.7	28.2	30.0
2002	28.1	28.9	29.9	30.6	31.6	31.8	33.3	33.0	31.8	32.2	31.8	31.3	31.2
2003	30.9	31.4	32.2	32.9	33.7	34.3	34.1	33.8	33.0	32.3	32.3	32.1	32.8
2004	31.2	32.2	33.4	34.2	35.4	35.8	35.3	34.7	34.0	34.3	33.9	33.2	34.0
2005	31.7	32.0	33.4	35.0	35.9	36.7	36.4	35.9	34.5	34.1	34.2	32.7	34.4
2006	32.5	33.2	33.8	35.5	36.5	36.6	37.0	36.6	35.3	34.6	34.3	33.6	35.0
2007	33.5	33.7	34.8	37.1	38.3	38.7	39.1	38.7	37.3	37.0	36.5	35.2	36.7
Other Services													
2000	9.3	9.3	9.4	9.4	9.4	9.5	9.2	9.1	9.0	9.1	9.1	9.1	9.5
2001	8.7	8.7	8.9	8.9	9.0	9.1	8.8	8.9	8.8	8.8	8.7	8.8	9.0
2002	8.9	9.1	9.4	9.2	9.3	9.6	9.2	9.3	9.5	9.1	9.2	9.3	9.6
2003	9.6	9.6	9.6	9.6	9.7	9.9	9.8	9.9	9.8	9.8	9.8	10.0	9.8
2004	9.7	9.8	9.9	10.1	10.4	10.8	10.4	10.4	10.5	10.8	11.1	11.0	10.4
2005	11.1	11.5	11.5	11.5	11.6	11.7	12.0	12.2	12.0	11.5	11.6	11.5	11.6
2006	11.8	11.9	11.7	12.0	12.0	11.9	11.5	11.5	11.8	11.6	11.6	11.8	11.8
2007	11.7	12.0	12.2	12.0	12.1	12.2	12.2	12.2	12.1	12.0	11.9	11.8	12.0
Government													
2000	50.3	50.8	51.2	51.0	51.7	52.1	47.9	48.7	49.4	50.5	50.8	51.3	50.2
2001	49.1	49.8	50.3	50.3	50.2	49.1	48.6	47.7	50.0	51.1	51.1	51.2	49.1
2002	50.1	51.1	51.2	51.5	51.6	50.9	50.0	50.7	51.9	52.3	52.6	53.1	50.2
2003	51.8	53.3	53.1	53.4	53.4	51.6	50.1	51.8	53.2	53.4	53.6	53.9	52.7
2004	52.9	53.3	53.6	53.8	53.9	52.3	50.5	52.5	53.6	53.7	53.9	54.0	53.2
2005	52.9	53.7	53.9	54.0	54.2	53.6	51.3	52.9	54.3	54.7	55.0	55.1	53.8
2006	53.7	54.0	54.3	55.2	55.3	52.9	50.7	52.8	54.7	55.7	55.8	55.9	54.3
2007	55.1	55.4	55.5	55.9	55.9	55.6	54.0	55.6	56.5	56.5	56.8	56.7	55.8

Employment by Industry: Worcester, MA-CT, NECTA, 2000–2007

(Numbers in thousands, not seasonally adjusted.)

Industry and year	January	February	March	April	May	June	July	August	September	October	November	December	Annual Average
Total Nonfarm													
2000	241.1	241.9	243.3	245.2	246.1	247.2	242.5	242.2	246.4	247.5	247.6	250.2	245.1
2001	243.1	243.6	244.2	247.6	249.1	249.4	243.3	241.8	246.8	247.0	246.9	247.5	245.9
2002	240.4	240.2	240.9	244.2	246.2	246.0	240.8	240.6	245.3	246.0	246.7	247.3	243.7
2003	240.9	239.7	240.6	242.4	244.4	244.6	241.1	239.9	244.7	246.5	246.3	246.6	243.1
2004	239.2	239.5	241.1	244.1	245.8	247.0	242.3	242.5	245.8	246.4	246.9	247.5	244.0
2005	239.9	240.7	241.1	244.3	246.3	246.9	242.4	241.5	245.8	246.5	247.8	248.2	244.3
2006	242.7	242.2	243.8	246.9	248.5	249.7	245.6	246.1	249.3	251.1	250.9	251.3	247.3
2007	244.3	245.0	245.9	247.8	250.7	252.0	245.3	245.9	249.2	249.4	249.6	250.8	248.0
Total Private													
2000	206.9	207.4	208.3	210.2	210.3	211.8	209.1	209.6	211.6	211.8	211.8	214.3	210.3
2001	207.8	207.9	208.5	211.7	212.6	213.0	209.0	209.0	211.2	210.9	210.5	210.8	210.2
2002	204.4	203.8	204.6	207.7	209.3	209.5	207.3	207.8	209.4	209.9	210.2	210.8	207.9
2003	205.2	203.7	204.4	206.4	208.2	208.4	207.5	206.9	208.7	210.8	210.8	210.5	207.6
2004	204.1	204.0	205.2	208.0	209.7	211.3	209.0	209.5	209.8	210.0	210.2	210.6	208.5
2005	203.8	204.0	204.7	208.0	209.7	210.5	209.3	209.3	210.2	209.7	210.9	211.3	208.5
2006	206.1	205.6	207.0	209.8	211.1	212.9	212.1	212.6	212.7	213.7	213.1	213.6	210.9
2007	207.3	207.6	208.5	210.2	212.5	214.2	211.2	212.1	212.1	211.9	212.0	212.4	211.0
Goods-Producing													
2000	46.8	46.3	46.7	47.4	47.8	48.7	48.2	48.5	48.6	49.0	48.7	49.0	48.0
2001	47.6	47.2	47.1	47.8	47.8	47.9	46.5	46.3	46.3	45.7	45.4	45.3	46.7
2002	43.2	42.6	42.6	43.1	43.4	43.6	42.7	43.1	43.0	42.7	42.5	42.3	42.9
2003	41.3	40.3	40.1	40.6	40.9	41.2	40.9	40.9	40.9	41.0	40.8	40.4	40.8
2004	39.1	38.5	38.8	39.9	40.4	40.8	40.7	41.2	41.0	40.7	40.7	40.5	40.2
2005	38.7	38.2	38.2	39.2	39.8	40.2	40.0	40.0	39.9	39.7	39.8	39.8	39.5
2006	38.9	38.5	38.4	39.3	39.8	40.4	40.4	40.6	40.2	40.0	39.7	39.6	39.7
2007	38.2	37.6	37.7	38.1	38.7	39.5	39.2	39.4	39.2	38.9	38.8	38.6	38.7
Natural Resources, Mining, and Construction													
2000	8.2	7.8	8.1	8.8	9.1	9.6	10.0	10.0	10.0	9.9	9.8	9.6	9.2
2001	8.9	8.8	8.8	9.7	10.1	10.3	10.6	10.7	10.7	10.1	10.0	9.8	9.9
2002	9.0	8.7	8.8	9.5	9.9	10.1	10.2	10.3	10.1	10.0	10.0	9.7	9.7
2003	8.8	8.2	8.3	9.2	9.9	10.1	10.5	10.7	10.6	10.7	10.6	10.2	9.8
2004	9.1	8.8	9.1	10.0	10.5	10.8	11.2	11.3	11.1	10.9	10.8	10.4	10.3
2005	9.2	8.8	8.9	9.9	10.5	10.8	11.2	11.2	11.1	10.8	10.9	10.6	10.3
2006	9.8	9.5	9.6	10.4	10.8	11.1	11.4	11.5	11.2	11.0	10.6	10.2	10.6
2007	9.1	8.6	8.7	9.2	9.9	10.3	10.4	10.5	10.4	10.2	10.1	9.8	9.8
Manufacturing													
2000	38.6	38.5	38.6	38.6	38.7	39.1	38.2	38.5	38.6	39.1	38.9	39.4	38.7
2001	38.7	38.4	38.3	38.1	37.7	37.6	35.9	35.6	35.6	35.6	35.4	35.5	36.9
2002	34.2	33.9	33.8	33.6	33.5	33.5	32.5	32.8	32.9	32.7	32.5	32.6	33.2
2003	32.5	32.1	31.8	31.4	31.0	31.1	30.4	30.2	30.3	30.3	30.2	30.2	31.0
2004	30.0	29.7	29.7	29.9	29.9	30.0	29.5	29.9	29.9	29.8	29.9	30.1	29.9
2005	29.5	29.4	29.3	29.3	29.3	29.4	28.8	28.8	28.8	28.9	28.9	29.2	29.1
2006	29.1	29.0	28.8	28.9	29.0	29.3	29.0	29.1	29.0	29.0	29.1	29.4	29.1
2007	29.1	29.0	29.0	28.9	28.8	29.2	28.8	28.9	28.8	28.7	28.7	28.8	28.9
Service-Providing													
2000	194.3	195.6	196.6	197.8	198.3	198.5	194.3	193.7	197.8	198.5	198.9	201.2	197.1
2001	195.5	196.4	197.1	199.8	201.3	201.5	196.8	195.5	200.5	201.3	201.5	202.2	199.1
2002	197.2	197.6	198.3	201.1	202.8	202.4	198.1	197.5	202.3	203.3	204.2	205.0	200.8
2003	199.6	199.4	200.5	201.8	203.5	203.4	200.2	199.0	203.8	205.5	205.5	206.2	202.4
2004	200.1	201.0	202.3	204.2	205.4	206.2	201.6	201.3	204.8	205.7	206.2	207.0	203.8
2005	201.2	202.5	202.9	205.1	206.5	206.7	202.4	201.5	205.9	206.8	208.0	208.4	204.8
2006	203.8	203.7	205.4	207.6	208.7	209.3	205.2	205.5	209.1	211.1	211.2	211.7	207.7
2007	206.1	207.4	208.2	209.7	212.0	212.5	206.1	206.5	210.0	210.5	210.8	212.2	209.3
Trade, Transportation, and Utilities													
2000	47.1	46.4	46.4	46.7	46.4	46.5	45.4	45.5	45.8	46.2	47.0	48.1	46.5
2001	45.8	45.0	45.1	45.8	46.0	46.3	45.3	45.5	45.7	46.5	47.4	48.0	46.0
2002	45.2	44.5	44.9	45.2	45.2	45.6	44.6	44.3	45.0	45.6	46.2	46.8	45.3
2003	45.1	44.2	44.6	45.0	45.3	45.7	45.2	45.2	45.8	46.1	46.6	46.8	45.5
2004	45.0	44.5	44.7	45.0	45.2	45.7	44.5	44.5	44.8	45.5	46.2	46.6	45.2
2005	45.4	44.7	44.8	45.1	45.5	45.6	44.9	45.1	45.3	45.5	46.3	46.7	45.4
2006	45.3	44.6	45.0	45.2	45.3	45.6	45.3	45.7	46.2	46.5	47.0	47.4	45.8
2007	46.1	45.5	45.9	45.9	46.4	46.8	46.0	45.8	46.3	46.5	47.0	47.3	46.3
Wholesale Trade													
2000	10.4	10.4	10.4	10.7	10.5	10.3	10.1	10.2	10.2	10.2	10.2	10.3	10.3
2001	9.9	10.0	10.0	10.0	10.1	10.1	9.9	10.1	9.9	10.1	10.0	9.9	10.0
2002	9.7	9.6	9.6	9.8	9.7	9.9	9.8	9.8	9.8	10.0	10.0	10.0	9.8
2003	10.0	9.9	10.0	10.0	10.0	10.0	10.1	10.0	9.9	9.8	9.8	9.7	9.9
2004	9.5	9.5	9.6	9.7	9.7	9.8	9.5	9.5	9.4	9.4	9.5	9.4	9.5
2005	9.4	9.3	9.4	9.6	9.6	9.7	9.6	9.8	9.7	9.8	9.9	9.9	9.6
2006	9.7	9.8	9.9	9.9	9.9	9.9	10.0	10.1	10.1	10.1	10.1	10.1	10.0
2007	9.9	9.9	10.0	10.0	10.1	10.1	10.2	10.1	10.1	10.0	10.1	10.1	10.1
Retail Trade													
2000	29.2	28.5	28.5	28.1	28.1	28.7	28.2	28.3	28.1	28.2	29.2	30.2	28.6
2001	28.4	27.6	27.6	28.1	28.3	28.7	28.2	28.3	28.2	28.7	29.8	30.5	28.5
2002	27.9	27.4	27.8	27.7	27.8	28.0	27.8	27.6	27.7	27.9	28.5	29.0	27.9
2003	27.6	27.0	27.2	27.5	27.8	28.2	28.0	28.2	28.4	28.6	29.2	29.5	28.1
2004	28.3	27.8	27.9	28.0	28.2	28.5	28.1	28.2	28.1	28.6	29.3	29.8	28.4
2005	28.8	28.2	28.1	28.2	28.5	28.5	28.2	28.3	28.0	28.1	28.7	28.9	28.4
2006	28.1	27.4	27.6	27.7	27.7	27.9	27.9	28.2	28.1	28.3	28.8	29.1	28.1
2007	28.2	27.6	27.9	27.9	28.2	28.6	28.2	28.1	27.9	28.2	28.7	29.0	28.2

Employment by Industry: Worcester, MA-CT, NECTA, 2000–2007—*Continued*

(Numbers in thousands, not seasonally adjusted.)

Industry and year	January	February	March	April	May	June	July	August	September	October	November	December	Annual Average
Transportation and Utilities													
2000	7.5	7.5	7.5	7.9	7.8	7.5	7.1	7.0	7.5	7.8	7.6	7.6	7.5
2001	7.5	7.4	7.5	7.7	7.6	7.5	7.2	7.1	7.6	7.7	7.6	7.6	7.5
2002	7.6	7.5	7.5	7.7	7.7	7.7	7.0	6.9	7.5	7.7	7.7	7.8	7.5
2003	7.5	7.3	7.4	7.5	7.5	7.5	7.1	7.0	7.5	7.7	7.6	7.6	7.4
2004	7.2	7.2	7.2	7.3	7.3	7.4	6.9	6.8	7.3	7.5	7.4	7.4	7.2
2005	7.2	7.2	7.3	7.3	7.4	7.4	7.1	7.0	7.6	7.6	7.7	7.9	7.4
2006	7.5	7.4	7.5	7.6	7.7	7.8	7.4	7.4	8.0	8.1	8.1	8.2	7.7
2007	8.0	8.0	8.0	8.0	8.1	8.1	7.6	7.6	8.3	8.3	8.2	8.2	8.0
Information													
2000	3.7	3.8	3.8	3.8	3.9	4.0	4.1	3.7	4.2	4.2	4.3	4.4	4.0
2001	4.4	4.4	4.4	4.5	4.5	4.5	4.4	4.4	4.3	4.4	4.3	4.3	4.4
2002	4.5	4.4	4.4	4.3	4.4	4.4	4.4	4.3	4.2	4.2	4.2	4.2	4.3
2003	4.1	4.1	4.0	4.0	4.0	4.0	4.0	3.9	3.8	3.9	3.9	3.9	4.0
2004	3.9	3.9	3.9	3.9	4.0	4.2	4.2	4.1	3.9	3.9	3.9	3.9	4.0
2005	3.9	3.9	3.9	3.7	3.7	3.6	3.6	3.6	3.6	3.6	3.6	3.6	3.7
2006	3.6	3.6	3.6	3.6	3.6	3.7	3.7	3.7	3.7	3.7	3.7	3.7	3.7
2007	3.9	3.9	3.9	3.9	4.0	4.0	4.0	4.0	3.9	3.9	4.0	4.0	4.0
Financial Activities													
2000	14.1	14.0	14.0	13.8	13.8	13.8	13.6	13.5	13.4	13.4	13.5	13.5	13.7
2001	13.5	13.4	13.4	13.8	13.9	14.0	14.1	14.1	14.0	14.2	14.1	14.1	13.9
2002	14.0	14.0	14.0	14.2	14.2	14.2	14.2	14.3	14.1	14.3	14.3	14.3	14.2
2003	13.9	13.9	14.0	14.1	14.1	14.2	14.3	14.3	14.2	14.2	14.2	14.2	14.1
2004	14.2	14.1	14.1	14.1	14.2	14.2	14.3	14.3	14.1	14.0	13.9	14.0	14.1
2005	13.8	13.8	13.9	14.0	14.0	14.2	14.3	14.3	14.2	14.1	14.2	14.3	14.1
2006	14.2	14.2	14.2	14.3	14.3	14.4	14.3	14.2	14.0	14.1	14.0	14.0	14.2
2007	13.9	13.8	13.8	13.8	13.7	13.7	13.7	13.8	13.6	13.6	13.5	13.5	13.7
Professional and Business Services													
2000	29.0	29.2	29.4	30.1	29.6	30.0	30.1	30.5	30.3	29.5	29.6	29.9	29.8
2001	27.8	27.8	28.0	28.6	28.5	28.8	28.2	28.5	28.3	27.5	27.3	27.3	28.1
2002	26.6	26.6	26.7	27.2	27.3	27.2	28.1	28.1	28.4	27.3	27.6	27.1	27.4
2003	26.6	26.5	26.6	27.1	27.3	27.4	27.6	27.6	27.7	27.9	28.0	28.3	27.4
2004	27.3	27.6	27.8	28.6	28.8	29.2	29.3	29.5	29.5	29.2	29.3	29.4	28.8
2005	27.7	27.9	28.2	29.1	29.5	29.7	29.6	29.7	30.0	29.8	30.1	30.0	29.3
2006	28.7	28.5	29.0	29.4	29.9	30.2	30.5	30.6	30.1	30.2	29.8	29.7	29.7
2007	28.1	28.1	28.1	29.0	29.4	29.7	28.9	28.8	28.5	28.6	28.5	28.4	28.7
Education and Health Services													
2000	40.6	41.8	41.7	41.8	41.6	41.0	40.2	40.2	41.9	41.9	41.9	42.0	41.4
2001	42.1	43.5	43.7	44.1	44.1	42.8	41.8	41.7	44.5	44.4	44.2	44.3	43.4
2002	43.5	44.4	44.6	45.6	45.7	44.9	44.0	43.9	45.4	46.2	46.2	46.5	45.1
2003	45.5	46.3	46.5	46.8	46.2	45.4	44.1	43.8	45.8	46.7	46.8	46.4	45.9
2004	45.5	46.3	46.5	46.3	45.8	45.4	44.4	44.3	45.6	46.2	46.3	46.2	45.7
2005	45.2	46.4	46.4	46.6	46.3	45.9	45.3	45.3	46.5	47.0	47.3	47.0	46.3
2006	46.2	47.3	47.5	47.8	47.4	46.6	46.1	46.0	47.4	48.6	48.6	48.6	47.3
2007	47.3	48.8	48.9	49.1	48.9	48.1	47.5	48.0	49.6	49.8	50.0	50.1	48.8
Leisure and Hospitality													
2000	17.4	17.6	18.0	18.3	18.8	19.2	18.9	19.0	18.9	19.0	18.2	18.7	18.5
2001	18.0	17.9	18.2	18.6	19.2	19.9	19.7	19.6	19.4	19.4	19.0	18.7	19.0
2002	18.6	18.5	18.6	19.4	20.3	20.7	20.6	20.9	20.8	21.0	20.6	20.9	20.1
2003	20.0	19.7	19.9	20.1	21.6	21.5	22.0	21.9	21.7	22.1	21.5	21.5	21.1
2004	20.2	20.1	20.4	21.3	22.3	22.7	22.7	22.2	22.0	21.6	21.0	21.1	21.4
2005	20.2	20.1	20.3	21.2	21.9	22.2	22.1	21.9	21.5	20.9	20.5	20.7	21.1
2006	20.1	19.9	20.2	21.1	21.7	22.7	22.4	22.4	22.0	21.7	21.3	21.5	21.4
2007	20.8	20.9	21.2	21.4	22.3	23.0	22.4	22.8	21.9	21.6	21.2	21.4	21.7
Other Services													
2000	8.2	8.3	8.3	8.3	8.4	8.6	8.6	8.7	8.5	8.6	8.6	8.7	8.5
2001	8.6	8.7	8.6	8.5	8.6	8.8	9.0	8.9	8.7	8.8	8.8	8.8	8.7
2002	8.8	8.8	8.8	8.7	8.8	8.9	8.7	8.9	8.5	8.6	8.6	8.7	8.7
2003	8.7	8.7	8.7	8.7	8.8	9.0	9.4	9.3	8.8	8.9	9.0	9.0	8.9
2004	8.9	9.0	9.0	8.9	9.0	9.1	9.4	9.4	8.9	8.9	8.9	8.9	9.0
2005	8.9	9.0	9.0	9.1	9.0	9.1	9.5	9.4	9.2	9.1	9.1	9.2	9.1
2006	9.1	9.0	9.1	9.1	9.1	9.3	9.4	9.4	9.1	8.9	9.0	9.1	9.1
2007	9.0	9.0	9.0	9.0	9.1	9.4	9.5	9.5	9.1	9.0	9.0	9.1	9.1
Government													
2000	34.2	34.5	35.0	35.0	35.8	35.4	33.4	32.6	34.8	35.7	35.8	35.9	34.8
2001	35.3	35.7	35.7	35.9	36.5	36.4	34.3	32.8	35.6	36.1	36.4	36.7	35.6
2002	36.0	36.4	36.3	36.5	36.9	36.5	33.5	32.8	35.9	36.1	36.5	36.5	35.8
2003	35.7	36.0	36.2	36.0	36.2	36.2	33.6	33.0	36.0	35.7	35.5	36.1	35.5
2004	35.1	35.5	35.9	36.1	36.1	35.7	33.3	33.0	36.0	36.4	36.7	36.9	35.6
2005	36.1	36.7	36.4	36.3	36.6	36.4	33.1	32.2	35.6	36.8	36.9	36.9	35.8
2006	36.6	36.6	36.8	37.1	37.4	36.8	33.5	33.5	36.6	37.4	37.8	37.7	36.5
2007	37.0	37.4	37.4	37.6	38.2	37.8	34.1	33.8	37.1	37.5	37.6	38.4	37.0

Employment by Industry: Colorado Springs, CO, 2000–2007

(Numbers in thousands, not seasonally adjusted.)

Industry and year	January	February	March	April	May	June	July	August	September	October	November	December	Annual Average
Total Nonfarm													
2000	239.9	240.7	243.2	245.7	249.3	253.6	253.3	253.7	253.2	253.8	254.8	255.4	249.7
2001	251.0	250.7	251.8	252.3	254.7	257.7	254.5	253.9	251.3	250.1	249.9	250.2	252.3
2002	243.5	244.1	245.7	246.4	250.3	252.1	249.2	249.9	249.0	248.2	248.1	248.0	247.9
2003	240.0	240.2	240.9	242.9	245.4	247.5	245.4	246.5	246.5	245.8	245.8	246.3	244.4
2004	240.4	241.3	242.9	246.1	248.6	251.5	249.1	251.1	250.6	250.4	250.6	252.1	247.9
2005	245.4	246.5	248.0	250.2	252.8	255.7	254.4	255.3	255.6	256.1	257.1	257.9	252.9
2006	252.3	253.6	256.0	257.6	261.1	263.9	258.8	259.5	259.4	259.3	259.9	260.5	258.5
2007	253.6	254.8	257.6	258.9	262.1	264.8	262.3	263.6	263.6	262.7	263.7	263.7	261.0
Total Private													
2000	202.1	201.9	204.1	206.1	209.0	213.9	215.7	216.9	215.5	214.4	215.0	216.1	210.9
2001	211.9	210.8	211.8	212.5	214.6	217.6	216.6	215.4	211.5	209.3	208.6	208.8	212.5
2002	203.0	202.9	204.0	204.8	208.3	210.6	210.3	211.0	208.2	206.1	205.7	205.6	206.7
2003	198.2	197.7	198.2	200.7	202.7	205.4	205.8	207.0	205.0	203.8	203.6	204.0	202.6
2004	198.8	198.9	200.2	203.3	205.5	208.8	209.3	210.3	207.8	207.2	207.3	208.7	205.5
2005	203.3	203.3	204.5	206.8	209.0	212.2	213.5	214.2	212.4	211.8	212.7	213.4	209.8
2006	208.7	209.2	211.1	212.9	215.9	219.0	217.1	216.9	214.9	214.0	214.4	215.0	214.1
2007	208.9	209.0	211.5	212.7	215.4	218.2	218.2	218.4	216.9	215.1	215.7	215.8	214.7
Goods-Producing													
2000	38.9	39.2	39.5	39.9	40.8	41.5	42.6	43.1	43.1	43.3	43.3	43.8	41.6
2001	43.2	43.0	43.3	43.2	43.3	43.3	42.9	42.2	41.1	40.9	39.8	39.5	42.1
2002	38.1	37.8	37.9	38.3	38.8	39.3	39.3	39.1	38.4	38.0	37.3	37.3	38.3
2003	36.3	36.0	36.0	36.4	36.7	37.0	36.7	36.5	36.1	35.9	35.6	35.5	36.2
2004	34.9	34.7	35.0	35.3	35.4	36.0	36.4	36.2	36.1	36.0	35.7	35.5	35.6
2005	35.1	34.9	34.9	34.7	35.0	35.7	36.3	36.5	36.2	35.9	35.8	35.8	35.6
2006	35.4	35.6	35.9	36.0	36.3	36.8	36.4	36.5	35.9	35.5	35.3	35.3	35.9
2007	34.1	33.9	34.5	34.5	34.9	35.3	35.4	35.0	34.5	34.3	34.0	33.8	34.5
Natural Resources, Mining, and Construction													
2000	14.3	14.5	14.9	15.1	15.7	16.2	16.9	17.2	17.1	17.1	17.0	17.1	16.1
2001	16.5	16.5	16.7	16.6	17.0	17.3	17.1	17.0	16.4	16.4	16.0	15.8	16.6
2002	15.0	15.1	15.3	15.6	16.0	16.5	16.6	16.6	16.1	15.9	15.5	15.3	15.8
2003	15.0	14.8	15.0	15.3	15.7	16.0	16.0	15.9	15.8	15.8	15.5	15.4	15.5
2004	15.0	14.8	15.1	15.6	15.8	16.3	16.6	16.6	16.4	16.4	16.2	16.1	15.9
2005	15.8	15.8	16.1	16.3	16.6	17.3	17.7	18.0	17.9	17.7	17.6	17.5	17.0
2006	17.2	17.4	17.6	18.0	18.3	18.7	18.5	18.5	18.1	17.7	17.5	17.4	17.9
2007	16.6	16.5	17.0	17.2	17.7	18.1	18.4	18.3	17.8	17.7	17.4	17.3	17.5
Manufacturing													
2000	24.6	24.7	24.6	24.8	25.1	25.3	25.7	25.9	26.0	26.2	26.3	26.7	25.5
2001	26.7	26.5	26.6	26.6	26.3	26.0	25.8	25.2	24.7	24.5	23.8	23.7	25.5
2002	23.1	22.7	22.6	22.7	22.8	22.8	22.7	22.5	22.3	22.1	21.8	22.0	22.5
2003	21.3	21.2	21.0	21.1	21.0	21.0	20.7	20.6	20.3	20.1	20.1	20.1	20.7
2004	19.9	19.9	19.9	19.7	19.6	19.7	19.8	19.6	19.7	19.6	19.5	19.4	19.7
2005	19.3	19.1	18.8	18.4	18.4	18.4	18.6	18.5	18.3	18.2	18.2	18.3	18.5
2006	18.2	18.2	18.3	18.0	18.0	18.1	17.9	18.0	17.8	17.8	17.8	17.9	18.0
2007	17.5	17.4	17.5	17.3	17.2	17.2	17.0	16.7	16.7	16.6	16.6	16.5	17.0
Service-Providing													
2000	201.0	201.5	203.7	205.8	208.5	212.1	210.7	210.6	210.1	210.5	211.5	211.6	208.1
2001	207.8	207.7	208.5	209.1	211.4	214.4	211.6	211.7	210.2	209.2	210.1	210.7	210.2
2002	205.4	206.3	207.8	208.1	211.5	212.8	209.9	210.8	210.6	210.2	210.8	210.7	209.6
2003	203.7	204.2	204.9	206.5	208.7	210.5	208.7	210.0	210.4	209.9	210.2	210.8	208.2
2004	205.5	206.6	207.9	210.8	213.2	215.5	212.7	214.9	214.5	214.4	214.9	216.6	212.3
2005	210.3	211.6	213.1	215.5	217.8	220.0	218.1	218.8	219.4	220.2	221.3	222.1	217.4
2006	216.9	218.0	220.1	221.6	224.8	227.1	222.4	223.0	223.5	223.8	224.6	225.2	222.6
2007	219.5	220.9	223.1	224.4	227.2	229.5	226.9	228.6	229.1	228.4	229.7	229.9	226.4
Trade, Transportation, and Utilities													
2000	37.5	37.3	37.4	37.8	38.1	38.2	38.5	38.8	38.9	39.5	40.4	40.7	38.6
2001	39.1	38.4	38.5	38.5	38.8	39.4	39.5	39.4	38.9	38.9	40.0	40.4	39.2
2002	38.3	37.8	37.9	38.0	38.5	38.8	38.7	39.0	39.0	38.8	39.6	40.1	38.7
2003	38.0	37.5	37.5	38.0	38.1	38.2	38.2	38.6	38.6	39.0	39.9	40.4	38.5
2004	38.7	38.2	38.1	38.6	39.0	39.3	39.3	39.7	39.3	39.5	40.4	40.9	39.3
2005	38.7	38.3	38.5	38.8	39.3	40.0	40.2	40.1	40.0	40.2	41.4	42.1	39.8
2006	39.9	39.1	39.4	39.9	40.5	41.1	40.9	40.9	40.8	40.7	41.5	41.8	40.5
2007	40.5	39.7	40.0	40.1	40.6	41.0	41.3	41.3	41.3	41.4	42.6	42.9	41.1
Wholesale Trade													
2000	6.0	6.0	6.1	6.1	6.2	6.3	6.4	6.4	6.4	6.4	6.4	6.3	6.3
2001	6.3	6.4	6.4	6.3	6.3	6.4	6.4	6.3	6.3	6.3	6.4	6.4	6.4
2002	6.2	6.2	6.2	6.1	6.1	6.1	6.1	6.2	6.2	6.1	6.1	6.2	6.2
2003	6.0	5.9	5.9	6.0	6.0	6.0	6.0	5.9	5.9	5.9	5.9	6.0	5.9
2004	5.9	5.9	5.9	5.9	6.0	6.0	6.0	6.1	6.0	6.0	6.1	6.1	6.0
2005	6.0	6.1	6.1	6.1	6.1	6.1	6.1	6.0	6.0	5.9	5.8	5.8	6.0
2006	5.7	5.7	5.7	5.8	5.8	5.9	5.9	5.9	5.9	5.8	5.8	5.8	5.8
2007	5.9	5.9	5.9	6.0	6.0	6.0	6.0	6.0	5.9	5.9	6.0	5.9	6.0
Retail Trade													
2000	27.7	27.4	27.4	27.6	27.9	27.9	28.0	28.2	28.3	29.0	29.9	30.3	28.3
2001	28.6	27.9	28.0	28.1	28.3	28.7	28.6	28.6	28.3	28.3	29.3	29.7	28.5
2002	27.9	27.4	27.5	27.7	28.1	28.4	28.2	28.4	28.5	28.6	29.3	29.8	28.3
2003	27.9	27.5	27.5	27.8	28.0	28.0	28.0	28.5	28.5	28.9	29.8	30.2	28.3
2004	28.9	28.3	28.2	28.6	28.8	29.0	28.9	29.1	28.8	29.0	29.8	30.2	29.0
2005	28.3	27.8	28.0	28.3	28.7	29.2	29.2	29.2	29.1	29.4	30.5	31.0	29.1
2006	29.2	28.4	28.6	29.0	29.4	29.7	29.6	29.6	29.6	29.8	30.6	30.7	29.5
2007	29.4	28.7	29.0	28.9	29.3	29.7	30.0	30.0	30.1	30.2	30.3	31.4	31.7	29.9

Employment by Industry: Colorado Springs, CO, 2000–2007—*Continued*

(Numbers in thousands, not seasonally adjusted.)

Industry and year	January	February	March	April	May	June	July	August	September	October	November	December	Annual Average
Transportation and Utilities													
2000	3.8	3.9	3.9	4.1	4.0	4.0	4.1	4.2	4.2	4.1	4.1	4.1	4.0
2001	4.2	4.1	4.1	4.1	4.2	4.3	4.5	4.5	4.3	4.3	4.3	4.3	4.3
2002	4.2	4.2	4.2	4.2	4.3	4.3	4.4	4.4	4.3	4.1	4.2	4.1	4.2
2003	4.1	4.1	4.1	4.2	4.1	4.2	4.2	4.2	4.2	4.2	4.2	4.2	4.1
2004	3.9	4.0	4.0	4.1	4.2	4.3	4.4	4.5	4.5	4.5	4.5	4.6	4.3
2005	4.4	4.4	4.4	4.4	4.4	4.5	4.7	4.9	4.9	4.9	5.1	5.3	4.7
2006	5.0	5.0	5.1	5.1	5.3	5.5	5.4	5.4	5.3	5.1	5.1	5.3	5.2
2007	5.2	5.1	5.1	5.2	5.3	5.3	5.3	5.2	5.2	5.2	5.2	5.3	5.2
Information													
2000	12.7	12.5	12.7	12.8	13.0	13.5	13.5	13.6	13.8	13.9	14.2	14.2	13.4
2001	14.5	14.2	13.7	13.6	13.5	13.8	13.6	13.6	13.5	13.5	13.7	13.7	13.7
2002	13.6	13.1	13.0	12.8	12.8	12.6	11.9	11.7	11.6	11.5	11.7	11.1	12.3
2003	11.0	10.7	10.5	10.5	10.5	10.5	10.4	10.2	10.1	10.2	10.4	10.5	10.5
2004	10.3	10.2	10.2	9.9	9.8	9.7	9.6	9.4	9.0	9.1	9.1	9.1	9.6
2005	8.9	8.6	8.6	8.4	8.4	8.5	8.6	8.5	8.5	8.6	8.6	8.5	8.6
2006	8.4	8.1	8.1	8.0	8.0	8.1	8.0	7.9	7.9	8.0	8.1	8.0	8.1
2007	7.8	7.7	7.7	7.6	7.7	7.8	7.8	7.7	7.7	7.7	7.7	7.7	7.7
Financial Activities													
2000	15.2	15.2	15.1	15.1	15.3	15.3	15.2	15.1	15.1	15.2	15.2	15.5	15.2
2001	15.5	15.7	15.9	15.9	16.0	16.1	16.2	16.2	16.2	16.1	16.3	16.3	16.0
2002	16.4	16.5	16.6	16.4	16.6	16.7	16.7	16.8	16.8	16.7	16.9	17.0	16.7
2003	16.9	17.0	17.1	17.1	17.2	17.3	17.4	17.5	17.3	17.3	17.2	17.2	17.2
2004	16.9	16.9	17.0	17.1	17.1	17.3	17.4	17.4	17.5	17.6	17.6	17.8	17.3
2005	17.7	17.7	17.8	18.0	18.0	18.3	18.3	18.3	18.3	18.3	18.4	18.4	18.1
2006	18.1	18.2	18.3	18.2	18.2	18.2	18.1	18.0	17.9	17.9	17.9	18.1	18.1
2007	17.7	17.7	17.7	17.7	17.6	17.8	17.6	17.6	17.5	17.5	17.6	17.6	17.6
Professional and Business Services													
2000	38.2	37.7	38.2	38.3	38.5	39.0	39.4	39.5	39.6	39.0	38.8	38.7	38.7
2001	37.2	36.8	37.0	36.9	37.0	37.3	36.7	36.5	35.8	35.5	35.2	35.0	36.4
2002	34.3	34.6	35.1	34.7	34.9	34.9	35.2	35.7	35.2	35.0	35.0	34.9	35.0
2003	32.6	33.0	33.0	33.6	33.5	33.8	34.3	35.0	34.8	34.5	34.1	34.1	33.9
2004	33.6	34.0	34.7	35.6	35.8	36.5	36.6	36.8	36.6	37.0	36.8	37.3	35.9
2005	36.7	36.8	37.0	38.0	38.1	38.3	38.6	38.4	38.3	38.8	38.7	38.7	38.0
2006	38.6	39.0	39.3	40.2	40.2	40.6	40.0	39.8	39.9	40.4	40.1	40.3	39.9
2007	39.4	39.8	40.5	41.2	41.4	41.6	41.6	41.8	41.7	41.4	41.4	41.5	41.1
Education and Health Services													
2000	20.4	20.6	20.9	21.2	20.3	21.3	21.2	21.6	21.5	21.3	21.5	21.6	21.1
2001	21.5	21.8	21.7	21.8	22.0	21.9	22.1	22.4	22.3	22.4	22.5	22.6	22.1
2002	22.1	22.5	22.5	22.7	22.8	22.6	22.6	23.0	23.0	23.1	23.1	23.1	22.8
2003	22.7	22.9	23.0	23.1	23.3	23.3	23.3	23.5	23.5	23.4	23.4	23.6	23.2
2004	23.2	23.4	23.4	23.7	23.8	23.8	23.6	24.0	24.0	24.1	24.3	24.4	23.8
2005	24.2	24.5	24.5	24.9	25.0	24.8	24.7	25.0	25.2	25.2	25.3	25.5	24.9
2006	24.9	25.4	25.5	25.5	25.8	25.7	25.4	25.8	26.0	26.0	26.2	26.3	25.7
2007	25.7	26.1	26.3	26.3	26.5	26.3	26.1	26.6	26.7	26.7	26.8	26.9	26.4
Leisure and Hospitality													
2000	26.5	26.7	27.3	28.0	29.8	31.4	31.8	31.8	30.1	29.0	28.3	28.2	29.1
2001	27.4	27.4	28.0	28.7	30.1	31.5	31.3	31.1	29.8	28.3	27.5	27.6	29.1
2002	26.5	26.9	27.1	27.9	29.8	31.2	31.4	31.4	30.2	29.0	28.2	28.2	29.0
2003	26.8	26.7	27.1	28.0	29.3	30.8	31.1	31.5	30.7	29.6	29.1	28.7	29.1
2004	27.2	27.5	27.8	29.0	30.3	31.6	31.8	32.2	30.8	29.5	28.9	29.1	29.6
2005	27.6	28.0	28.6	29.4	30.5	31.7	31.9	32.5	31.3	30.4	30.0	29.9	30.2
2006	28.8	29.1	29.8	30.3	32.0	33.2	33.3	33.1	31.8	30.9	30.6	30.5	31.1
2007	28.9	29.2	29.7	30.4	31.6	33.0	33.0	33.1	32.2	31.0	30.4	30.1	31.1
Other Services													
2000	12.7	12.8	13.0	12.9	13.2	13.7	13.5	13.5	13.4	13.1	13.3	13.4	13.2
2001	13.5	13.6	13.7	13.8	13.9	14.3	14.3	14.1	13.9	13.6	13.6	13.7	13.8
2002	13.7	13.8	13.9	13.9	14.1	14.5	14.5	14.4	14.0	13.9	13.9	13.9	14.0
2003	13.9	13.9	14.0	14.0	14.1	14.5	14.4	14.2	13.9	13.9	13.9	14.0	14.0
2004	14.0	14.0	14.0	14.1	14.3	14.6	14.6	14.6	14.5	14.4	14.5	14.6	14.4
2005	14.4	14.5	14.6	14.6	14.7	14.9	14.9	14.9	14.6	14.4	14.5	14.5	14.6
2006	14.6	14.7	14.8	14.8	14.9	15.3	15.0	14.9	14.7	14.6	14.7	14.7	14.8
2007	14.8	14.9	15.1	14.9	15.1	15.4	15.4	15.3	15.3	15.1	15.2	15.3	15.2
Government													
2000	37.8	38.8	39.1	39.6	40.3	39.7	37.6	36.8	37.7	39.4	39.8	39.3	38.8
2001	39.1	39.9	40.0	39.8	40.1	40.1	37.9	38.5	39.8	40.8	41.3	41.4	39.9
2002	40.5	41.2	41.7	41.6	42.0	41.5	38.9	38.9	40.8	42.1	42.4	42.4	41.2
2003	41.8	42.5	42.7	42.2	42.7	42.1	39.6	39.5	41.5	42.0	42.2	42.3	41.7
2004	41.6	42.4	42.7	42.8	43.1	42.7	39.8	40.8	42.8	43.2	43.3	43.4	42.4
2005	42.1	43.2	43.5	43.4	43.8	43.5	40.9	41.1	43.2	44.3	44.4	44.5	43.2
2006	43.6	44.4	44.9	44.7	45.2	44.9	41.7	42.6	44.5	45.3	45.5	45.5	44.4
2007	44.7	45.8	46.1	46.2	46.7	46.6	44.1	45.2	46.7	47.6	48.0	47.9	46.3

Employment by Industry: Harrisburg-Carlisle, PA, 2000–2007

(Numbers in thousands, not seasonally adjusted.)

Industry and year	January	February	March	April	May	June	July	August	September	October	November	December	Annual Average
Total Nonfarm													
2000	312.8	313.9	318.1	319.5	323.2	324.8	322.8	323.2	322.4	321.5	322.0	322.5	320.6
2001	314.3	316.7	317.8	321.3	324.1	325.2	321.6	321.4	321.3	321.3	321.2	322.2	320.7
2002	313.9	316.3	318.9	322.1	323.6	326.7	325.5	325.6	324.8	325.0	325.9	325.6	322.8
2003	316.6	316.7	318.6	320.4	324.2	324.5	321.4	321.7	321.8	321.4	321.5	321.5	320.8
2004	313.3	314.8	318.7	321.9	325.2	325.3	323.6	323.4	323.5	323.7	323.9	323.6	321.7
2005	316.3	317.7	319.8	324.0	327.1	328.3	325.9	326.6	327.5	326.6	328.2	327.7	324.6
2006	321.4	322.6	326.3	329.0	332.4	332.9	329.8	331.0	332.2	332.0	332.8	333.0	329.6
2007	324.9	325.2	327.7	330.2	334.6	336.1	332.7	332.3	332.2	333.0	333.6	333.3	331.3
Total Private													
2000	251.8	251.9	255.7	257.4	261.0	263.1	262.8	263.9	261.4	260.1	260.2	261.2	259.2
2001	254.1	254.9	255.8	259.1	262.1	263.5	262.1	262.1	259.7	258.9	258.6	259.9	259.2
2002	252.6	253.5	255.6	258.5	259.6	263.0	264.2	264.7	262.3	261.5	261.7	261.6	259.9
2003	254.0	252.3	254.1	255.8	259.7	261.3	260.8	261.4	259.1	257.9	257.8	258.0	257.6
2004	251.3	251.4	254.8	257.7	261.4	262.5	263.4	263.1	260.5	260.4	260.3	260.6	259.0
2005	254.5	254.4	256.4	260.1	263.5	265.8	266.3	267.0	264.6	263.6	264.9	265.0	262.2
2006	259.1	259.3	262.7	265.1	268.7	270.2	269.5	270.6	269.1	268.5	269.1	269.9	266.8
2007	262.8	262.1	264.5	266.6	271.0	273.5	272.7	273.1	270.4	270.9	271.2	271.0	269.2
Goods-Producing													
2000	42.6	42.2	43.0	43.7	44.3	45.0	44.6	45.0	44.3	43.9	43.5	43.0	43.8
2001	42.0	41.8	41.8	42.0	42.1	42.5	42.2	42.2	41.6	41.3	40.9	41.0	41.8
2002	40.0	39.8	40.7	40.8	38.6	40.6	42.0	42.0	41.3	41.2	40.7	40.3	40.7
2003	39.4	38.2	38.2	38.2	39.0	39.5	39.6	39.6	39.1	38.5	38.2	37.6	38.7
2004	36.6	36.2	36.9	37.3	38.0	38.1	38.7	38.6	38.1	38.0	37.8	37.6	37.7
2005	37.1	36.4	36.6	37.2	37.7	38.1	38.4	38.3	37.9	37.7	37.4	36.8	37.5
2006	36.3	36.5	37.1	37.1	37.7	38.4	38.3	38.6	38.4	38.2	37.6	37.3	37.6
2007	36.6	36.2	36.5	36.6	37.2	37.9	37.8	37.8	37.6	37.6	37.2	36.8	37.2
Natural Resources, Mining, and Construction													
2000	11.6	11.3	12.0	12.8	13.1	13.4	13.1	13.2	12.8	12.6	12.2	11.7	12.5
2001	11.5	11.4	11.7	12.5	12.9	13.5	13.4	13.5	13.0	13.1	12.9	12.9	12.7
2002	12.2	12.2	12.7	13.4	13.5	13.9	14.1	14.1	13.6	13.7	13.4	12.8	13.3
2003	12.1	11.6	11.8	11.9	12.6	12.7	13.1	13.2	12.9	12.6	12.3	11.9	12.3
2004	11.2	10.9	11.6	12.1	12.5	12.6	12.8	12.9	12.7	12.6	12.4	12.2	12.2
2005	11.7	11.6	11.9	12.3	12.7	13.1	13.3	13.3	13.2	13.1	12.9	12.3	12.6
2006	11.9	11.9	12.4	12.6	12.9	13.4	13.2	13.5	13.6	13.4	13.0	12.8	12.9
2007	12.3	11.8	12.4	12.7	13.0	13.4	13.3	13.3	13.4	13.4	13.2	12.9	12.9
Manufacturing													
2000	31.0	30.9	31.0	30.9	31.2	31.6	31.5	31.8	31.5	31.3	31.3	31.3	31.3
2001	30.5	30.4	30.1	29.5	29.2	29.0	28.8	28.7	28.6	28.2	28.0	28.1	29.1
2002	27.8	27.6	28.0	27.4	25.1	26.7	27.9	27.9	27.7	27.5	27.3	27.5	27.4
2003	27.3	26.6	26.4	26.3	26.4	26.8	26.5	26.4	26.2	25.9	25.9	25.7	26.3
2004	25.4	25.3	25.3	25.2	25.5	25.5	25.9	25.7	25.4	25.4	25.4	25.4	25.5
2005	25.4	24.8	24.7	24.9	25.0	25.0	25.1	25.0	24.7	24.6	24.5	24.5	24.9
2006	24.4	24.6	24.7	24.5	24.8	25.0	25.1	25.1	24.8	24.8	24.6	24.5	24.7
2007	24.3	24.4	24.1	23.9	24.2	24.5	24.5	24.5	24.2	24.2	24.0	23.9	24.2
Service-Providing													
2000	270.2	271.7	275.1	275.8	278.9	279.8	278.2	278.2	278.1	277.6	278.5	279.5	276.8
2001	272.3	274.9	276.0	279.3	282.0	282.7	279.4	279.2	279.7	280.0	280.3	281.2	278.9
2002	273.9	276.5	278.2	281.3	285.0	286.1	283.5	283.6	283.5	283.8	285.2	285.3	282.2
2003	277.2	278.5	280.4	282.2	285.2	285.0	281.8	282.1	282.7	282.9	283.3	283.9	282.1
2004	276.7	278.6	281.8	284.6	287.2	287.2	284.9	284.8	285.4	285.7	286.1	286.0	284.1
2005	279.2	281.3	283.2	286.8	289.4	290.2	287.5	288.3	289.6	288.9	290.8	290.9	287.2
2006	285.1	286.1	289.2	291.9	294.7	294.5	291.5	292.4	293.8	293.8	295.2	295.7	292.0
2007	288.3	289.0	291.2	293.6	297.4	298.2	294.9	294.5	294.6	295.4	296.4	296.5	294.2
Trade, Transportation, and Utilities													
2000	69.3	69.1	69.8	69.3	69.9	70.1	69.7	70.2	69.9	70.2	71.5	72.5	70.1
2001	70.4	69.7	69.6	70.5	70.5	70.3	69.7	69.8	69.7	70.3	71.2	72.1	70.3
2002	69.8	68.7	68.4	68.9	69.3	69.5	68.6	68.8	68.9	69.6	70.5	71.2	69.4
2003	68.5	67.6	67.6	67.7	67.9	68.1	67.2	67.6	67.7	68.8	69.8	70.7	68.2
2004	68.5	67.9	68.4	68.4	68.8	68.7	67.7	67.6	68.0	69.1	70.3	71.0	68.7
2005	68.2	67.5	67.5	67.4	68.0	68.0	67.9	67.7	68.1	69.0	70.6	71.3	68.4
2006	68.9	67.8	68.2	68.5	68.8	68.7	68.5	68.7	69.3	69.8	71.5	72.5	69.3
2007	70.1	68.9	69.3	69.1	69.8	69.9	69.5	69.9	70.1	71.0	72.3	72.8	70.2
Wholesale Trade													
2000	14.9	14.7	14.9	14.5	14.6	14.6	14.5	14.6	14.4	14.5	14.5	14.5	14.6
2001	14.2	14.2	14.2	14.3	14.2	14.3	14.2	14.2	14.0	14.1	14.0	14.2	14.2
2002	14.0	13.9	13.8	13.8	13.9	13.9	14.0	14.0	13.9	13.9	13.8	13.9	13.9
2003	13.7	13.7	13.7	13.7	13.8	13.9	13.9	13.9	13.8	13.9	13.8	13.9	13.8
2004	13.9	13.9	14.0	14.0	13.8	13.9	14.0	14.0	13.9	13.9	13.9	13.9	13.9
2005	13.9	13.9	13.9	14.0	14.1	14.1	14.3	14.3	14.3	14.3	14.3	14.3	14.1
2006	14.2	14.2	14.2	14.3	14.3	14.3	14.3	14.3	14.2	14.1	14.1	14.0	14.2
2007	14.0	14.0	14.0	14.0	14.1	14.2	14.2	14.2	14.1	14.2	14.2	14.2	14.1
Retail Trade													
2000	32.5	32.1	32.4	32.6	32.9	33.0	32.8	33.0	32.7	32.6	33.9	35.0	33.0
2001	33.7	33.2	33.2	33.4	33.5	33.6	33.5	33.9	33.6	33.6	34.5	35.4	33.8
2002	33.9	33.0	33.0	33.2	33.5	33.5	33.2	33.4	33.2	33.5	34.6	35.4	33.6
2003	33.3	32.5	32.5	32.5	32.5	32.6	32.2	32.3	32.0	32.4	33.3	34.1	32.6
2004	32.4	31.9	32.1	32.2	32.8	32.7	32.4	32.3	32.0	32.9	34.2	34.8	32.7
2005	33.0	32.3	32.2	32.3	32.7	32.8	32.9	32.7	32.4	33.1	34.3	35.0	33.0
2006	33.3	32.4	32.6	32.7	32.7	32.5	32.6	32.6	32.5	33.2	34.6	35.3	33.1
2007	33.5	32.5	32.8	32.7	33.1	33.1	33.4	33.4	33.1	33.9	35.2	35.8	33.5

Employment by Industry: Harrisburg-Carlisle, PA, 2000–2007—*Continued*

(Numbers in thousands, not seasonally adjusted.)

Industry and year	January	February	March	April	May	June	July	August	September	October	November	December	Annual Average
Transportation and Utilities													
2000	21.9	22.3	22.5	22.2	22.4	22.5	22.4	22.6	22.8	23.1	23.1	23.0	22.6
2001	22.5	22.3	22.2	22.8	22.8	22.4	22.0	21.7	22.1	22.6	22.7	22.5	22.4
2002	21.9	21.8	21.6	21.9	21.9	22.1	21.4	21.4	21.8	22.2	22.1	21.9	21.8
2003	21.5	21.4	21.4	21.5	21.6	21.6	21.1	21.4	21.9	22.5	22.7	22.7	21.7
2004	22.2	22.1	22.3	22.2	22.2	22.1	21.3	21.3	22.1	22.3	22.2	22.3	22.1
2005	21.3	21.3	21.4	21.1	21.2	21.1	20.7	20.7	21.4	21.6	22.0	22.0	21.3
2006	21.4	21.2	21.4	21.5	21.8	21.9	21.6	21.8	22.6	22.5	22.8	23.2	22.0
2007	22.6	22.4	22.5	22.4	22.6	22.6	21.9	22.3	22.9	22.9	22.9	22.8	22.6
Information													
2000	7.2	7.3	7.3	7.5	7.6	7.7	7.7	7.3	7.8	7.8	7.9	8.0	7.6
2001	8.0	8.1	8.1	8.1	8.1	8.1	8.2	8.2	8.1	8.0	8.0	8.1	8.1
2002	8.0	8.0	8.0	8.0	7.9	7.8	7.8	7.8	7.7	7.5	7.5	7.3	7.8
2003	7.3	7.3	7.3	7.1	7.0	7.1	7.0	7.0	6.9	6.8	6.8	6.7	7.0
2004	6.7	6.7	6.7	6.3	6.4	6.4	6.4	6.3	6.3	6.2	6.3	6.3	6.4
2005	6.1	6.1	6.0	6.1	6.2	6.3	6.3	6.4	6.4	6.4	6.5	6.6	6.3
2006	6.4	6.4	6.5	6.5	6.5	6.6	6.7	6.7	6.6	6.6	6.6	6.6	6.6
2007	6.6	6.5	6.5	6.5	6.5	6.6	6.5	6.5	6.5	6.5	6.5	6.5	6.5
Financial Activities													
2000	24.3	24.2	24.2	24.0	24.2	24.3	24.1	24.1	23.9	23.7	23.7	23.8	24.0
2001	23.9	24.0	24.1	23.9	24.0	24.2	24.2	24.2	24.0	24.0	24.2	24.3	24.1
2002	24.3	24.4	24.5	24.5	24.7	25.0	25.2	25.3	25.1	25.0	25.2	25.4	24.9
2003	25.2	25.3	25.3	25.2	25.3	25.4	25.3	25.3	25.2	25.1	25.2	25.2	25.2
2004	24.9	24.8	24.9	24.7	24.7	24.8	24.8	24.8	24.5	24.5	24.6	24.7	24.7
2005	24.6	24.6	24.7	24.6	24.5	24.8	24.7	24.8	24.5	24.5	24.6	24.6	24.6
2006	24.6	24.7	24.8	24.6	24.7	24.8	24.8	24.7	24.6	24.5	24.5	24.5	24.7
2007	24.3	24.3	24.4	24.3	24.4	24.7	24.7	24.7	24.5	24.4	24.5	24.5	24.5
Professional and Business Services													
2000	32.7	32.5	33.1	32.4	32.5	33.2	33.6	33.8	33.3	33.3	32.9	32.7	33.0
2001	32.2	31.9	31.9	32.5	32.9	33.3	32.7	32.7	32.6	32.7	31.8	31.6	32.4
2002	30.9	31.3	31.2	31.9	32.3	32.8	32.9	33.1	33.1	32.8	32.7	32.4	32.3
2003	31.3	30.9	31.2	31.4	32.0	32.3	32.2	32.8	33.1	33.4	32.9	32.9	32.2
2004	33.0	33.3	33.8	34.7	35.3	35.5	35.9	36.0	35.7	36.0	35.6	35.3	35.0
2005	35.4	35.4	35.7	36.7	37.3	37.8	37.5	37.9	37.9	37.5	37.7	37.6	37.0
2006	36.9	37.2	37.6	38.5	39.0	39.1	38.7	39.3	39.3	39.4	39.3	39.3	38.6
2007	38.0	38.1	38.2	38.7	39.6	40.0	40.0	40.1	40.0	40.1	39.7	39.6	39.3
Education and Health Services													
2000	39.3	40.4	40.8	40.8	41.0	39.8	39.9	40.5	41.7	42.1	42.2	42.5	40.9
2001	40.6	42.4	42.3	42.4	42.6	41.4	41.4	41.5	42.6	42.7	42.9	43.1	42.2
2002	41.3	42.7	42.9	42.8	43.2	42.3	42.5	42.5	43.5	43.9	44.0	43.9	43.0
2003	42.3	43.3	43.7	43.5	43.4	42.5	43.0	42.8	42.7	42.5	42.6	42.6	42.9
2004	41.4	42.3	42.6	42.6	42.5	42.2	42.9	42.7	42.8	43.0	43.0	43.3	42.6
2005	42.3	43.5	43.7	43.6	43.5	43.2	43.8	43.7	44.2	44.3	44.3	44.3	43.7
2006	43.3	44.5	44.9	44.8	45.0	44.1	44.0	44.3	44.8	45.0	45.1	45.3	44.6
2007	44.3	45.5	45.6	45.8	46.2	45.0	44.8	45.1	45.9	46.3	46.4	46.3	45.6
Leisure and Hospitality													
2000	21.1	20.9	22.0	24.2	25.9	27.3	27.4	27.2	24.7	23.6	23.0	23.0	24.2
2001	21.6	21.6	22.6	24.2	26.2	27.8	27.9	27.8	25.5	24.2	23.9	24.0	24.8
2002	22.5	22.8	23.9	25.6	27.5	28.7	29.1	28.9	26.6	25.4	24.9	25.0	25.9
2003	23.7	23.4	24.4	26.1	28.3	29.5	29.6	29.4	27.5	25.9	25.5	25.3	26.5
2004	23.5	23.4	24.5	26.5	28.5	29.4	29.8	29.8	27.9	26.3	25.5	25.5	26.7
2005	24.1	24.1	25.3	27.5	29.4	30.6	30.7	31.2	28.7	27.4	27.0	27.0	27.8
2006	26.0	25.4	26.7	28.2	30.1	31.7	31.7	31.5	29.3	28.2	27.9	27.9	28.7
2007	26.6	26.2	27.6	29.1	30.8	32.8	32.7	32.4	29.3	28.5	28.1	28.0	29.3
Other Services													
2000	15.3	15.3	15.5	15.5	15.6	15.7	15.8	15.8	15.8	15.5	15.5	15.7	15.6
2001	15.4	15.4	15.4	15.5	15.7	15.9	15.8	15.7	15.6	15.7	15.7	15.7	15.6
2002	15.8	15.8	16.0	16.0	16.1	16.3	16.1	16.3	16.1	16.1	16.2	16.1	16.1
2003	16.3	16.3	16.4	16.6	16.8	16.9	16.9	16.9	16.9	16.9	16.9	17.0	16.7
2004	16.7	16.8	17.0	17.2	17.2	17.4	17.2	17.3	17.2	17.3	17.2	16.9	17.1
2005	16.7	16.8	16.9	17.0	16.9	17.0	17.0	17.0	16.9	16.8	16.8	16.8	16.9
2006	16.7	16.8	16.9	16.9	16.9	16.8	16.8	16.8	16.8	16.8	16.6	16.5	16.8
2007	16.3	16.4	16.4	16.5	16.5	16.6	16.7	16.6	16.5	16.5	16.5	16.5	16.5
Government													
2000	61.0	62.0	62.4	62.1	62.2	61.7	60.0	59.3	61.0	61.4	61.8	61.3	61.4
2001	60.2	61.8	62.0	62.2	62.0	61.7	59.5	59.3	61.6	62.4	62.6	62.3	61.5
2002	61.3	62.8	63.3	63.6	64.0	63.7	61.3	60.9	62.5	63.5	64.2	64.0	62.9
2003	62.6	64.4	64.5	64.6	64.5	63.2	60.6	60.3	62.7	63.5	63.7	63.5	63.1
2004	62.0	63.4	63.9	64.2	63.8	62.8	60.2	60.3	63.0	63.3	63.6	63.0	62.8
2005	61.8	63.3	63.4	63.9	63.6	62.5	59.6	59.6	62.9	63.0	63.3	62.7	62.5
2006	62.3	63.3	63.6	63.9	63.7	62.7	60.3	60.4	63.1	63.5	63.7	63.1	62.8
2007	62.1	63.1	63.2	63.6	63.6	62.6	60.0	59.2	61.8	62.1	62.4	62.3	62.2

Employment by Industry: Madison, WI, 2000–2007

(Numbers in thousands, not seasonally adjusted.)

Industry and year	January	February	March	April	May	June	July	August	September	October	November	December	Annual Average
Total Nonfarm													
2000	311.1	311.6	313.9	319.3	319.6	324.2	320.2	320.9	321.1	324.0	326.4	324.5	319.7
2001	316.1	319.2	321.5	326.5	327.4	330.9	326.4	326.8	329.3	329.8	331.1	328.6	326.1
2002	319.3	321.5	323.3	327.6	328.1	330.1	328.5	330.8	330.5	332.6	336.3	333.9	328.5
2003	319.4	321.9	322.7	327.9	328.7	333.5	327.9	330.6	329.6	332.0	334.3	334.0	328.5
2004	327.6	327.8	328.9	334.1	336.9	337.6	337.5	339.2	339.0	341.5	343.4	342.8	336.4
2005	335.1	336.5	337.5	342.5	345.2	345.3	343.0	345.7	347.1	352.3	354.1	355.3	345.0
2006	338.9	338.4	341.4	344.7	347.4	350.9	346.6	348.2	348.8	349.6	350.1	349.8	346.2
2007	340.5	340.8	342.3	345.3	349.0	351.2	348.1	349.2	349.8	350.7	352.6	351.8	347.6
Total Private													
2000	232.3	231.7	233.3	236.7	239.6	243.8	244.3	245.6	243.6	245.0	245.1	244.6	240.5
2001	237.0	237.3	238.3	241.3	244.0	248.2	248.3	249.5	246.8	246.9	247.1	246.7	244.3
2002	240.4	240.5	241.5	243.7	246.6	250.5	250.7	252.3	250.0	250.8	252.2	252.3	247.6
2003	242.6	241.6	241.8	244.9	247.6	251.6	251.8	253.5	251.4	251.8	253.2	253.8	248.8
2004	247.6	247.6	248.6	253.0	256.0	259.5	261.4	262.0	259.9	260.7	261.3	262.1	256.6
2005	255.2	255.0	256.0	260.4	262.6	266.1	266.4	268.2	266.1	270.3	271.7	272.8	264.2
2006	258.8	257.6	258.5	262.0	264.9	270.1	269.4	269.9	267.8	268.3	269.0	268.9	265.4
2007	260.5	259.4	260.6	263.5	267.1	271.5	271.6	271.7	269.1	268.6	268.9	269.5	266.8
Goods-Producing													
2000	49.9	49.6	50.3	51.3	52.3	54.1	54.2	54.1	53.0	52.8	52.1	51.4	52.1
2001	49.2	48.5	48.6	49.5	50.6	52.4	52.5	52.8	51.5	50.6	49.2	48.6	50.3
2002	46.7	46.7	46.9	48.0	48.8	50.4	50.6	51.1	49.9	49.7	49.5	48.6	48.9
2003	47.0	46.4	46.5	47.8	48.5	50.3	50.1	50.4	49.3	48.9	48.4	48.0	48.4
2004	46.5	46.2	46.7	48.4	49.0	50.2	50.7	50.4	49.5	48.8	48.5	48.6	48.6
2005	46.9	46.5	46.7	48.4	49.2	50.9	51.4	51.5	50.6	50.6	50.0	49.5	49.4
2006	48.0	47.4	47.8	49.3	50.3	52.3	52.6	52.7	51.9	51.0	50.3	49.8	50.3
2007	48.1	47.4	47.9	49.1	50.3	51.9	52.1	52.0	50.7	50.2	49.7	49.1	49.9
Natural Resources, Mining, and Construction													
2000	14.1	13.9	14.4	15.1	15.7	16.6	16.8	16.8	16.3	16.2	15.9	15.3	15.6
2001	14.2	14.2	14.3	15.5	16.2	17.2	17.6	17.7	16.9	16.7	16.3	15.9	16.1
2002	14.4	14.4	14.5	15.6	16.3	17.3	17.6	17.5	16.7	16.6	16.5	15.9	16.1
2003	14.7	14.3	14.4	15.4	16.5	17.6	17.7	17.8	17.1	17.1	16.7	16.3	16.3
2004	15.1	14.8	15.1	16.5	17.0	17.8	18.1	18.0	17.4	16.9	16.7	16.4	16.7
2005	15.2	14.9	15.1	16.6	17.4	18.4	18.6	18.7	18.1	18.1	18.0	17.3	17.2
2006	16.1	15.7	15.8	17.0	17.8	18.8	19.0	19.0	18.5	18.1	17.6	17.1	17.5
2007	16.0	15.3	15.6	16.7	17.8	18.4	18.4	18.2	17.7	17.5	17.2	16.6	17.1
Manufacturing													
2000	35.8	35.7	35.9	36.2	36.6	37.5	37.4	37.3	36.7	36.6	36.2	36.1	36.5
2001	35.0	34.3	34.3	34.0	34.4	35.2	34.9	35.1	34.6	33.9	32.9	32.7	34.3
2002	32.3	32.3	32.4	32.4	32.5	33.1	33.0	33.6	33.2	33.1	33.0	32.7	32.8
2003	32.3	32.1	32.1	32.4	32.0	32.7	32.4	32.6	32.2	31.8	31.7	31.7	32.1
2004	31.4	31.4	31.6	31.9	32.0	32.4	32.6	32.4	32.1	31.9	31.8	32.2	32.0
2005	31.7	31.6	31.6	31.8	31.8	32.5	32.8	32.8	32.5	32.5	32.0	32.2	32.2
2006	31.9	31.7	32.0	32.3	32.5	33.5	33.6	33.7	33.4	32.9	32.7	32.7	32.7
2007	32.1	32.1	32.3	32.4	32.5	33.5	33.7	33.8	33.0	32.7	32.5	32.5	32.8
Service-Providing													
2000	261.2	262.0	263.6	268.0	267.3	270.1	266.0	266.8	268.1	271.2	274.3	273.1	267.6
2001	266.9	270.7	272.9	277.0	276.8	278.5	273.9	274.0	277.8	279.2	281.9	280.0	275.8
2002	272.6	274.8	276.4	279.6	279.3	279.7	277.9	279.7	280.6	282.9	286.8	285.3	279.6
2003	272.4	275.5	276.2	280.1	280.2	283.2	277.8	280.2	280.3	283.1	285.9	286.0	280.0
2004	281.1	281.6	282.2	285.7	287.9	287.4	286.8	288.8	289.5	292.7	294.9	294.2	287.7
2005	288.2	290.0	290.8	294.1	296.0	294.4	291.6	294.2	296.5	301.7	304.1	305.8	295.6
2006	290.9	291.0	293.6	295.4	297.1	298.6	294.0	295.5	296.9	298.6	299.8	300.0	296.0
2007	292.4	293.4	294.4	296.2	298.7	299.3	296.0	297.2	299.1	300.5	302.9	302.7	297.7
Trade, Transportation, and Utilities													
2000	58.1	56.3	56.3	57.1	57.7	58.1	58.3	59.2	59.5	61.6	62.9	63.5	59.1
2001	59.8	58.8	58.9	59.1	59.4	59.5	59.4	60.3	60.2	61.1	62.8	63.2	60.2
2002	58.8	57.7	57.7	57.8	58.3	58.6	58.5	59.0	59.4	60.6	62.7	63.6	59.4
2003	58.9	57.9	57.6	58.2	58.9	59.6	59.1	59.7	59.8	60.8	63.0	64.1	59.8
2004	59.2	58.6	58.3	58.9	59.7	60.3	60.2	60.3	60.3	61.4	63.5	64.6	60.4
2005	60.1	59.1	59.3	59.3	59.6	59.5	59.9	60.5	60.4	66.3	68.8	70.7	62.0
2006	60.0	59.0	58.9	59.0	59.4	60.0	59.3	59.4	59.7	60.8	63.0	63.9	60.2
2007	59.7	58.4	58.7	59.0	60.0	60.4	59.9	60.0	60.5	61.1	62.6	63.3	60.3
Wholesale Trade													
2000	11.1	11.2	11.3	11.3	11.4	11.6	11.6	11.8	11.5	11.4	11.5	11.6	11.4
2001	11.4	11.5	11.5	11.5	11.5	11.6	11.6	11.6	11.4	11.3	11.2	11.1	11.4
2002	11.0	11.1	11.1	11.2	11.3	11.3	11.4	11.3	11.3	11.1	11.1	11.2	11.2
2003	11.1	11.2	11.1	11.3	11.3	11.5	11.5	11.5	11.3	11.3	11.3	11.4	11.3
2004	11.4	11.5	11.4	11.5	11.5	11.7	12.0	12.1	11.9	11.9	12.0	12.1	11.8
2005	12.0	11.9	11.9	12.0	12.2	12.3	12.3	12.4	12.2	12.4	12.5	12.6	12.2
2006	12.6	12.6	12.6	12.5	12.5	12.7	12.7	12.6	12.4	12.4	12.4	12.5	12.5
2007	12.4	12.4	12.4	12.5	12.6	12.7	12.8	12.7	12.6	12.6	12.6	12.7	12.6
Retail Trade													
2000	39.3	37.3	37.2	37.6	38.0	38.3	38.5	39.1	39.5	41.5	42.9	43.5	39.4
2001	40.1	39.0	39.0	39.2	39.4	39.4	39.3	40.0	40.0	41.2	43.1	43.6	40.3
2002	39.7	38.5	38.5	38.3	38.6	38.8	38.8	39.4	39.5	40.7	43.0	43.9	39.8
2003	39.5	38.5	38.3	38.7	39.4	39.6	39.4	39.9	39.9	40.9	43.1	44.1	40.1
2004	39.6	38.8	38.7	39.0	39.7	40.0	39.8	39.9	39.9	40.8	42.8	43.7	40.2
2005	39.7	38.9	39.0	38.8	38.9	38.7	39.1	39.6	39.5	45.3	47.7	49.4	41.2
2006	38.9	37.9	37.8	37.9	38.2	38.6	38.1	38.3	38.5	39.7	41.9	42.5	39.0
2007	38.8	37.5	37.7	37.8	38.5	38.7	38.6	38.7	39.1	39.7	41.2	41.8	39.0

Employment by Industry: Madison, WI, 2000–2007—*Continued*

(Numbers in thousands, not seasonally adjusted.)

Industry and year	January	February	March	April	May	June	July	August	September	October	November	December	Annual Average
Transportation and Utilities													
2000	7.7	7.8	7.8	8.2	8.3	8.2	8.2	8.3	8.5	8.7	8.5	8.4	8.2
2001	8.3	8.3	8.4	8.4	8.5	8.5	8.5	8.7	8.8	8.6	8.5	8.5	8.5
2002	8.1	8.1	8.1	8.3	8.4	8.5	8.3	8.3	8.6	8.8	8.6	8.5	8.4
2003	8.3	8.2	8.2	8.2	8.2	8.5	8.2	8.3	8.6	8.6	8.6	8.6	8.3
2004	8.2	8.3	8.2	8.4	8.5	8.6	8.4	8.3	8.5	8.7	8.7	8.8	8.5
2005	8.4	8.3	8.4	8.5	8.5	8.5	8.5	8.5	8.7	8.6	8.6	8.7	8.5
2006	8.5	8.5	8.5	8.6	8.7	8.7	8.5	8.5	8.8	8.7	8.7	8.9	8.6
2007	8.5	8.5	8.6	8.7	8.9	9.0	8.5	8.6	8.8	8.8	8.8	8.8	8.7
Information													
2000	7.1	7.1	7.0	7.0	7.2	7.2	7.2	7.3	7.2	7.4	7.5	7.5	7.2
2001	7.3	7.3	7.3	7.3	7.2	7.0	7.1	6.9	6.8	6.7	6.7	6.7	7.0
2002	6.7	6.8	6.7	6.7	6.7	6.7	6.8	6.8	6.7	6.8	6.8	6.8	6.8
2003	7.0	7.0	7.0	7.1	7.2	7.3	7.5	7.5	7.6	7.8	7.9	8.0	7.4
2004	7.9	8.0	8.0	8.0	8.1	8.1	8.3	8.3	8.3	8.4	8.4	8.4	8.2
2005	8.6	8.5	8.5	8.6	8.6	8.7	8.8	8.9	8.9	8.9	8.9	8.9	8.7
2006	8.9	8.8	8.9	8.9	8.8	8.8	8.8	8.8	8.8	9.0	9.1	9.1	8.9
2007	9.1	9.1	9.1	9.1	9.1	9.1	9.5	9.5	9.5	9.5	9.5	9.6	9.3
Financial Activities													
2000	22.5	22.5	22.6	23.0	23.0	23.3	23.3	23.3	23.2	23.2	23.0	23.2	23.0
2001	22.8	23.0	23.2	23.5	23.6	23.8	24.3	24.4	24.2	24.1	24.2	24.3	23.8
2002	24.8	25.0	25.0	25.0	25.2	25.5	25.6	25.7	25.4	25.4	25.4	25.5	25.3
2003	25.8	25.9	25.9	26.0	26.2	26.5	26.7	26.8	26.5	26.4	26.7	26.9	26.3
2004	27.0	27.1	27.2	27.6	27.8	28.0	28.3	28.4	28.2	28.5	28.6	29.0	28.0
2005	28.8	29.0	28.9	29.1	28.9	29.0	29.0	29.0	28.5	28.3	28.1	28.2	28.7
2006	28.0	28.0	27.8	27.9	27.9	28.0	28.0	27.9	27.4	27.4	27.3	27.3	27.7
2007	26.9	27.0	26.9	27.1	27.1	27.4	27.3	27.2	26.8	26.8	26.7	26.9	27.0
Professional and Business Services													
2000	28.7	29.0	29.2	29.0	29.6	30.0	30.2	30.6	30.0	30.1	29.8	29.7	29.7
2001	29.3	30.1	30.1	30.9	31.1	32.1	31.2	31.2	30.9	32.2	32.2	32.0	31.1
2002	31.6	31.6	32.2	32.4	32.4	32.9	33.2	33.1	32.8	32.8	32.6	32.2	32.5
2003	30.9	31.1	31.1	31.5	31.1	31.1	31.1	31.8	31.5	31.3	30.9	30.4	31.1
2004	30.6	31.0	31.0	31.9	32.0	32.4	32.9	33.2	32.7	33.0	32.4	32.0	32.1
2005	32.2	32.7	32.8	33.7	33.8	34.1	34.5	35.1	34.8	34.7	34.5	34.5	34.0
2006	34.0	34.3	34.4	35.5	35.8	36.2	36.3	36.6	36.3	36.5	36.3	35.7	35.7
2007	35.7	36.0	36.2	37.0	37.1	37.7	37.9	38.1	37.9	37.8	37.6	37.7	37.2
Education and Health Services													
2000	28.9	29.2	29.3	29.7	29.7	29.9	29.5	29.5	29.6	29.8	29.8	29.6	29.5
2001	29.4	29.7	30.0	30.2	30.5	30.6	30.6	30.8	30.6	30.8	31.0	31.2	30.5
2002	31.4	31.6	31.8	31.9	32.3	32.5	32.2	32.6	32.6	32.7	33.1	33.3	32.3
2003	31.9	32.1	32.2	32.3	32.5	32.7	32.6	32.7	32.4	32.7	32.9	33.1	32.5
2004	33.2	33.2	33.4	33.5	33.6	33.6	33.4	33.5	33.5	33.4	33.6	33.8	33.5
2005	33.7	33.7	33.9	34.3	34.4	34.7	34.4	34.7	34.9	34.8	35.0	35.0	34.5
2006	34.5	34.5	34.7	34.7	34.8	35.3	34.8	34.9	34.8	34.8	34.9	35.1	34.8
2007	34.8	35.0	35.0	35.0	35.2	35.4	35.6	35.5	35.5	35.5	35.6	35.7	35.3
Leisure and Hospitality													
2000	23.6	24.3	24.6	25.4	26.1	27.1	27.3	27.3	26.8	25.9	25.7	25.4	25.8
2001	24.9	25.4	25.6	26.1	27.0	27.9	28.2	28.2	27.7	26.5	26.0	25.6	26.6
2002	25.1	25.7	25.6	26.3	27.4	28.0	28.0	28.3	27.6	27.1	26.4	26.5	26.8
2003	25.6	25.6	25.8	26.4	27.6	28.2	28.8	28.7	28.4	27.9	27.4	27.2	27.3
2004	26.6	26.7	27.1	27.9	28.9	29.7	30.3	30.6	30.0	29.3	28.7	28.5	28.7
2005	27.9	28.3	28.6	29.5	30.6	31.6	30.8	30.9	30.4	29.0	28.8	28.4	29.6
2006	27.9	28.1	28.4	29.2	30.4	31.6	32.0	32.0	31.3	31.1	30.4	30.5	30.2
2007	28.8	28.9	29.2	29.6	30.7	31.8	31.5	31.7	30.7	30.1	29.6	29.6	30.2
Other Services													
2000	13.5	13.7	14.0	14.2	14.0	14.1	14.3	14.3	14.3	14.2	14.3	14.3	14.1
2001	14.3	14.5	14.6	14.7	14.6	14.9	15.0	14.9	14.9	14.9	15.0	15.1	14.8
2002	15.3	15.4	15.6	15.6	15.5	15.9	15.8	15.7	15.6	15.7	15.7	15.8	15.6
2003	15.5	15.6	15.7	15.6	15.6	15.9	15.9	15.9	15.9	16.0	16.0	16.1	15.8
2004	16.6	16.8	16.9	16.8	16.9	17.2	17.3	17.3	17.4	17.9	17.6	17.2	17.2
2005	17.0	17.2	17.3	17.5	17.5	17.6	17.6	17.6	17.6	17.7	17.6	17.6	17.5
2006	17.5	17.5	17.6	17.5	17.5	17.9	17.6	17.6	17.6	17.7	17.7	17.5	17.6
2007	17.4	17.6	17.6	17.6	17.6	17.8	17.8	17.7	17.5	17.6	17.6	17.6	17.6
Government													
2000	78.8	79.9	80.6	82.6	80.0	80.4	75.9	75.3	77.5	79.0	81.3	79.9	79.3
2001	79.1	81.9	83.2	85.2	83.4	82.7	78.1	77.3	82.5	82.9	84.0	81.9	81.9
2002	78.9	81.0	81.8	83.9	81.5	79.6	77.8	78.5	80.5	81.8	84.1	81.6	80.9
2003	76.8	80.3	80.9	83.0	81.1	81.9	76.1	77.1	78.2	80.2	81.1	80.2	79.7
2004	80.0	80.2	80.3	81.1	80.9	78.1	76.1	77.2	79.1	80.8	82.1	80.7	79.7
2005	79.9	81.5	81.5	82.1	82.6	79.2	76.6	77.5	81.0	82.0	82.4	82.5	80.7
2006	80.1	80.8	82.9	82.7	82.5	80.8	77.2	78.3	81.0	81.3	81.1	80.9	80.8
2007	80.0	81.4	81.7	81.8	81.9	79.7	76.5	77.5	80.7	82.1	83.7	82.3	80.8

Employment by Industry: Augusta-Richmond County, GA-SC, 2000–2007

(Numbers in thousands, not seasonally adjusted.)

Industry and year	January	February	March	April	May	June	July	August	September	October	November	December	Annual Average
Total Nonfarm													
2000	205.2	206.0	207.8	207.4	208.4	209.3	207.6	208.6	209.9	208.1	208.4	209.3	208.0
2001	204.7	204.5	205.4	207.9	208.0	206.2	204.8	205.8	205.3	206.2	205.6	206.8	205.9
2002	203.2	204.1	205.5	208.7	208.2	207.5	205.0	206.9	206.7	208.0	209.7	210.3	207.0
2003	206.4	206.8	207.5	208.8	208.6	208.4	207.8	210.0	210.6	209.3	210.3	211.1	208.8
2004	210.4	210.6	212.4	214.2	214.8	213.6	212.4	213.6	213.3	215.0	216.4	216.7	213.6
2005	212.3	213.3	213.8	217.4	216.1	215.2	212.2	213.4	213.9	214.7	217.3	217.2	214.7
2006	212.9	214.7	215.4	214.7	214.9	212.9	211.7	214.1	214.5	213.7	214.6	216.1	214.2
2007	213.7	214.2	215.9	219.3	218.7	217.8	213.9	215.6	217.0	217.0	217.9	218.8	216.7
Total Private													
2000	166.2	166.8	168.4	167.9	168.2	169.7	169.4	170.5	170.8	168.7	168.9	169.6	168.8
2001	165.0	164.9	165.7	167.8	168.0	166.0	166.2	166.9	165.8	166.0	165.5	166.6	166.2
2002	163.4	164.3	165.6	168.8	168.2	167.7	166.3	167.5	166.8	167.3	168.9	169.4	167.0
2003	165.8	165.9	166.7	167.6	168.0	167.9	168.5	170.0	170.2	168.7	169.5	170.4	168.3
2004	169.6	169.8	171.5	173.4	174.3	173.2	173.6	174.1	173.0	174.1	175.3	175.6	173.1
2005	170.9	171.5	171.9	175.5	174.7	173.4	172.0	173.0	172.1	173.0	175.0	174.9	173.2
2006	171.2	172.3	172.9	172.7	172.9	170.9	171.6	173.0	172.2	171.2	171.9	173.2	172.2
2007	171.1	171.4	173.0	176.7	176.1	175.3	173.8	174.5	175.0	174.9	175.5	176.2	174.5
Goods-Producing													
2000	43.1	43.2	43.4	42.8	43.0	43.3	43.6	43.8	43.9	43.2	43.1	43.3	43.3
2001	42.5	42.6	42.6	42.8	42.8	41.0	42.4	42.4	42.4	42.3	41.6	41.4	42.2
2002	40.3	40.3	40.4	40.6	40.6	40.6	39.9	40.4	40.4	40.3	40.2	39.9	40.3
2003	39.6	39.5	39.7	39.5	39.7	39.6	38.9	38.9	39.5	39.6	39.3	39.5	39.5
2004	38.9	38.3	38.5	38.8	38.7	38.8	38.9	39.1	38.8	39.1	38.9	39.0	38.8
2005	38.3	38.2	38.1	38.6	38.5	38.9	38.7	38.9	38.3	38.9	39.3	38.8	38.6
2006	38.9	39.1	39.4	38.6	39.3	39.1	39.2	39.2	39.0	38.4	38.2	38.8	38.9
2007	38.4	38.4	38.4	38.4	38.5	38.6	38.5	38.2	38.2	38.2	38.2	38.5	38.4
Natural Resources, Mining, and Construction													
2000	13.4	13.3	13.6	13.3	13.4	13.6	13.4	13.4	13.5	13.2	13.2	13.4	13.4
2001	13.1	13.2	13.3	13.4	13.5	13.6	13.5	13.6	13.4	13.6	13.2	13.1	13.4
2002	12.8	12.9	13.1	13.5	13.7	13.7	13.3	13.3	13.3	13.2	13.2	13.2	13.3
2003	12.9	12.9	13.1	13.1	13.2	13.3	13.2	13.3	13.3	13.5	13.9	13.7	13.3
2004	13.8	13.3	13.5	13.6	13.4	13.4	13.3	13.5	13.3	13.8	13.6	13.7	13.5
2005	13.3	13.2	13.3	13.6	13.5	13.8	13.6	13.7	13.5	14.0	14.5	14.1	13.7
2006	14.1	14.1	14.2	13.9	14.2	14.1	14.3	14.5	14.4	13.9	14.0	14.1	14.2
2007	13.9	13.9	13.9	14.4	14.5	14.5	14.2	14.2	14.2	14.3	14.3	14.4	14.2
Manufacturing													
2000	29.7	29.9	29.8	29.5	29.6	29.7	30.2	30.4	30.4	30.0	29.9	29.9	29.9
2001	29.4	29.4	29.3	29.4	29.3	27.4	28.9	28.8	29.0	28.7	28.4	28.3	28.9
2002	27.5	27.4	27.3	27.1	26.9	26.9	26.6	27.1	27.1	27.1	27.0	26.7	27.1
2003	26.7	26.6	26.6	26.4	26.5	26.3	25.7	26.2	26.1	25.7	25.6	25.9	26.2
2004	25.1	25.0	25.0	25.2	25.3	25.4	25.6	25.6	25.5	25.3	25.3	25.3	25.3
2005	25.0	25.0	24.8	25.0	25.0	25.1	25.1	25.2	24.8	24.9	24.8	24.7	25.0
2006	24.8	25.0	25.2	24.7	25.1	25.0	24.9	24.7	24.6	24.5	24.2	24.7	24.8
2007	24.5	24.5	24.5	24.0	24.0	24.1	24.3	24.0	24.0	23.9	23.9	24.1	24.2
Service-Providing													
2000	162.1	162.8	164.4	164.6	165.4	166.0	164.0	164.8	166.0	164.9	165.3	166.0	164.7
2001	162.2	161.9	162.8	165.1	165.2	165.2	162.4	163.4	162.9	163.9	164.0	165.4	163.7
2002	162.9	163.8	165.1	168.1	167.6	166.9	165.1	166.5	166.3	167.7	169.5	170.4	166.7
2003	166.8	167.3	167.8	169.3	168.9	168.8	168.9	170.5	171.0	169.7	171.0	171.6	169.3
2004	171.5	172.3	173.9	175.4	176.1	174.8	173.5	174.5	174.5	175.9	177.5	177.7	174.8
2005	174.0	175.1	175.7	178.8	177.6	176.3	173.5	174.5	175.6	175.8	178.0	178.4	176.1
2006	174.0	175.6	176.0	176.1	175.6	173.8	172.5	174.9	175.5	175.3	176.4	177.3	175.3
2007	175.3	175.8	177.5	180.9	180.2	179.2	175.4	177.4	178.8	178.8	179.7	180.3	178.3
Trade, Transportation, and Utilities													
2000	35.9	35.9	36.2	36.0	36.1	36.2	36.0	36.1	36.4	36.4	36.7	37.3	36.3
2001	35.3	35.0	35.1	35.5	35.6	35.4	35.2	35.3	35.0	34.4	35.0	35.4	35.2
2002	34.8	34.5	34.6	35.3	35.4	35.4	34.8	34.9	34.6	34.5	35.4	35.5	35.0
2003	34.7	34.4	34.6	34.4	34.7	34.8	35.5	35.7	35.7	35.3	35.9	36.6	35.2
2004	35.7	35.4	35.9	36.3	36.5	36.7	36.7	36.6	36.5	36.5	37.2	37.9	36.5
2005	36.6	36.7	36.6	36.8	37.0	36.8	36.9	36.7	36.8	37.2	38.1	38.5	37.1
2006	36.2	36.1	36.3	36.1	36.4	36.1	36.6	36.7	36.5	36.5	37.4	37.8	36.6
2007	36.4	36.0	36.3	36.7	37.0	36.9	37.0	36.8	37.2	37.5	37.8	38.0	37.0
Wholesale Trade													
2000	3.8	3.8	3.8	3.8	3.8	3.8	3.6	3.6	3.7	3.8	3.8	3.9	3.8
2001	4.0	4.0	4.0	4.1	4.1	4.1	4.1	4.1	4.1	4.2	4.2	4.2	4.1
2002	4.3	4.3	4.2	4.3	4.3	4.3	4.2	4.2	4.2	4.3	4.3	4.3	4.3
2003	4.5	4.5	4.5	4.5	4.5	4.6	4.7	4.7	4.8	4.8	4.8	4.8	4.6
2004	5.3	5.3	5.3	5.4	5.4	5.5	5.4	5.4	5.4	5.3	5.3	5.3	5.4
2005	5.5	5.6	5.5	5.5	5.5	5.5	5.5	5.4	5.4	5.2	5.1	5.1	5.4
2006	5.2	5.3	5.4	5.4	5.4	5.4	5.4	5.5	5.5	5.4	5.4	5.5	5.4
2007	5.3	5.3	5.3	5.3	5.3	5.2	5.3	5.3	5.4	5.3	5.3	5.4	5.3
Retail Trade													
2000	26.5	26.5	26.8	26.6	26.7	26.7	26.5	26.6	26.8	26.7	27.0	27.5	26.7
2001	25.6	25.4	25.3	25.5	25.7	25.5	25.4	25.5	25.2	24.3	25.0	25.3	25.3
2002	24.5	24.2	24.3	24.8	24.9	24.9	24.6	24.8	24.6	24.3	25.2	25.4	24.7
2003	24.5	24.3	24.5	24.4	24.6	24.6	25.0	25.2	25.1	24.9	25.5	26.2	24.9
2004	24.6	24.3	24.8	25.0	25.2	25.2	25.3	25.2	25.1	25.3	26.0	26.6	25.2
2005	25.1	25.0	25.1	25.2	25.3	25.1	25.1	25.0	25.0	25.7	26.5	26.8	25.4
2006	24.8	24.7	24.8	24.5	24.8	24.5	24.9	24.9	24.7	24.7	25.7	25.9	24.9
2007	24.8	24.4	24.6	24.8	25.1	25.0	25.0	24.9	25.1	25.4	25.8	25.9	25.1

Employment by Industry: Augusta-Richmond County, GA-SC, 2000–2007—*Continued*

(Numbers in thousands, not seasonally adjusted.)

Industry and year	January	February	March	April	May	June	July	August	September	October	November	December	Annual Average
Transportation and Utilities													
2000	5.6	5.6	5.6	5.6	5.6	5.7	5.9	5.9	5.9	5.9	5.9	5.9	5.8
2001	5.7	5.6	5.8	5.9	5.8	5.8	5.7	5.7	5.7	5.9	5.8	5.9	5.8
2002	6.0	6.0	6.1	6.2	6.2	6.2	6.0	5.9	5.8	5.9	5.9	5.8	6.0
2003	5.7	5.6	5.6	5.5	5.6	5.6	5.8	5.8	5.8	5.6	5.6	5.6	5.7
2004	5.8	5.8	5.8	5.9	5.9	6.0	6.0	6.0	6.0	6.0	5.9	6.0	5.9
2005	6.0	6.1	6.0	6.1	6.2	6.2	6.3	6.3	6.4	6.3	6.5	6.6	6.3
2006	6.2	6.1	6.1	6.2	6.2	6.2	6.3	6.3	6.3	6.4	6.3	6.4	6.3
2007	6.3	6.3	6.4	6.6	6.6	6.7	6.7	6.6	6.7	6.8	6.7	6.7	6.6
Information													
2000	3.5	3.5	3.5	3.3	3.3	3.4	3.5	3.6	3.5	3.5	3.6	3.6	3.5
2001	3.6	3.6	3.6	3.6	3.6	3.7	3.5	3.5	3.5	3.5	3.5	3.5	3.6
2002	3.4	3.4	3.5	3.4	3.4	3.4	3.4	3.4	3.3	3.3	3.4	3.5	3.4
2003	3.3	3.4	3.3	3.4	3.5	3.5	3.5	3.5	3.4	3.4	3.4	3.4	3.4
2004	3.4	3.4	3.3	3.4	3.4	3.3	3.3	3.2	3.2	3.3	3.3	3.4	3.3
2005	3.4	3.4	3.4	3.4	3.4	3.4	3.4	3.4	3.4	3.4	3.4	3.5	3.4
2006	3.5	3.5	3.5	3.5	3.5	3.5	3.5	3.5	3.4	3.5	3.6	3.6	3.5
2007	3.4	3.3	3.3	3.7	3.7	3.7	3.9	3.9	3.9	3.9	4.0	3.9	3.7
Financial Activities													
2000	7.2	7.1	7.1	7.3	7.3	7.3	7.2	7.3	7.4	7.2	7.2	7.3	7.2
2001	7.2	7.3	7.3	7.4	7.3	7.4	7.3	7.4	7.3	7.3	7.3	7.4	7.3
2002	7.2	7.2	7.2	7.3	7.3	7.4	7.4	7.4	7.3	7.3	7.4	7.4	7.3
2003	7.3	7.3	7.4	7.2	7.2	7.2	7.4	7.4	7.4	7.3	7.2	7.2	7.3
2004	7.2	7.3	7.3	7.2	7.2	7.2	7.4	7.4	7.3	7.5	7.5	7.5	7.3
2005	7.7	7.7	7.7	7.6	7.6	7.6	7.5	7.6	7.6	7.6	7.6	7.7	7.6
2006	7.6	7.6	7.7	7.6	7.6	7.5	7.6	7.6	7.6	7.6	7.5	7.6	7.6
2007	7.5	7.4	7.3	7.5	7.5	7.5	7.4	7.4	7.5	7.4	7.4	7.5	7.4
Professional and Business Services													
2000	28.0	28.0	28.7	28.8	29.1	30.1	29.6	29.5	29.9	29.4	29.0	28.9	29.1
2001	28.5	28.4	28.3	28.2	28.4	28.4	28.2	28.2	27.9	28.3	27.9	28.7	28.3
2002	28.6	29.2	29.6	30.4	29.8	29.5	29.9	29.9	29.6	29.8	30.1	30.4	29.7
2003	29.8	29.9	30.0	30.1	30.1	30.3	31.1	31.1	31.3	30.5	30.7	30.8	30.5
2004	31.9	32.4	32.8	32.6	32.8	32.2	33.1	33.1	32.8	33.1	33.5	32.8	32.8
2005	30.6	31.0	30.9	31.5	31.2	30.7	30.6	30.8	30.4	30.4	30.8	30.6	30.8
2006	29.6	29.9	29.7	29.0	28.8	28.6	28.2	28.8	28.6	28.8	28.6	28.8	29.0
2007	29.5	29.9	30.2	30.5	30.4	30.4	29.7	30.0	30.2	30.3	30.1	30.4	30.1
Education and Health Services													
2000	22.9	23.1	23.0	22.8	22.9	22.8	23.1	23.5	23.6	23.4	23.6	23.7	23.2
2001	23.3	23.4	23.6	23.7	23.9	23.8	23.9	24.5	24.6	24.6	24.7	24.7	24.1
2002	24.3	24.3	24.7	24.8	25.1	24.9	24.9	25.5	25.7	25.9	26.2	26.5	25.2
2003	25.1	25.3	25.3	25.2	25.4	25.2	24.9	25.3	25.5	25.8	25.9	25.9	25.4
2004	26.0	26.2	26.3	26.1	26.4	26.0	26.2	26.5	26.5	26.8	26.9	26.9	26.4
2005	26.7	26.6	26.8	26.9	27.1	26.6	26.7	27.1	27.1	27.2	27.2	27.4	27.0
2006	27.4	27.7	27.5	27.2	27.3	26.7	27.4	27.8	27.8	27.3	27.4	27.5	27.4
2007	27.2	27.4	27.4	27.7	27.9	27.7	27.6	28.2	28.2	28.1	28.3	28.4	27.8
Leisure and Hospitality													
2000	17.8	18.1	18.6	19.0	18.6	18.7	18.5	18.6	18.1	17.7	17.8	17.5	18.3
2001	16.9	16.9	17.5	18.5	18.3	18.1	17.7	17.6	17.2	17.7	17.7	17.7	17.7
2002	17.1	17.6	17.8	19.3	18.8	18.7	18.2	18.1	17.9	18.3	18.3	18.3	18.2
2003	18.1	18.2	18.5	19.8	19.2	19.1	19.1	19.2	19.1	18.8	19.0	19.0	18.9
2004	18.5	18.7	19.3	20.5	20.7	20.3	19.5	19.6	19.3	19.3	19.4	19.5	19.6
2005	18.9	19.2	19.7	22.0	21.2	20.7	19.5	19.7	19.5	19.7	19.9	19.7	20.0
2006	19.5	19.8	20.2	22.0	21.1	20.6	20.0	20.3	20.2	20.2	20.3	20.3	20.4
2007	20.1	20.3	21.3	23.2	22.1	21.6	20.9	21.2	21.0	20.8	21.0	20.9	21.2
Other Services													
2000	7.8	7.9	7.9	7.9	7.9	7.9	7.9	8.1	8.0	7.9	7.9	8.0	7.9
2001	7.7	7.7	7.7	8.1	8.1	8.2	8.0	8.0	7.9	7.9	7.8	7.8	7.9
2002	7.7	7.8	7.8	7.7	7.8	7.8	7.8	7.9	8.0	7.9	7.9	7.9	7.8
2003	7.9	7.9	7.9	8.0	8.2	8.2	8.1	8.3	8.2	8.0	8.1	8.0	8.1
2004	8.0	8.1	8.1	8.5	8.6	8.7	8.5	8.6	8.6	8.5	8.6	8.6	8.5
2005	8.7	8.7	8.7	8.7	8.7	8.7	8.7	8.8	9.0	8.6	8.7	8.7	8.7
2006	8.5	8.6	8.6	8.7	8.9	8.8	9.1	9.1	9.1	8.9	8.9	8.8	8.8
2007	8.6	8.7	8.8	9.0	9.0	8.9	8.8	8.8	8.8	8.7	8.7	8.6	8.8
Government													
2000	39.0	39.2	39.4	39.5	40.2	39.6	38.2	38.1	39.1	39.4	39.5	39.7	39.2
2001	39.7	39.6	39.7	40.1	40.0	40.2	38.6	38.9	39.5	40.2	40.1	40.2	39.7
2002	39.8	39.8	39.9	39.9	40.0	39.8	38.7	39.4	39.9	40.7	40.8	40.9	40.0
2003	40.6	40.9	40.8	41.2	40.6	40.5	39.3	40.0	40.4	40.6	40.8	40.7	40.5
2004	40.8	40.8	40.9	40.8	40.5	40.4	38.8	39.5	40.3	40.9	41.1	41.1	40.5
2005	41.4	41.8	41.9	41.9	41.4	41.8	40.2	40.4	41.8	41.7	42.3	42.3	41.6
2006	41.7	42.4	42.5	42.0	42.0	42.0	40.1	41.1	42.3	42.5	42.7	42.9	42.0
2007	42.6	42.8	42.9	42.6	42.6	42.5	40.1	41.1	42.0	42.1	42.4	42.6	42.2

Employment by Industry: Jackson, MS, 2000–2007

(Numbers in thousands, not seasonally adjusted.)

Industry and year	January	February	March	April	May	June	July	August	September	October	November	December	Annual Average
Total Nonfarm													
2000	238.8	240.1	241.9	243.4	244.8	246.3	243.4	245.3	246.0	245.7	247.0	248.2	244.2
2001	244.7	246.3	247.1	248.3	248.4	248.7	246.3	248.1	247.8	247.3	247.8	248.3	247.4
2002	243.3	245.0	246.3	247.1	247.8	248.3	245.3	246.8	246.8	245.9	246.6	246.8	246.3
2003	244.0	244.7	246.7	247.8	248.7	249.5	250.3	251.2	252.2	253.9	255.0	255.8	249.9
2004	251.1	252.7	255.0	256.7	257.0	257.3	255.1	256.2	257.3	256.7	257.3	258.1	255.9
2005	253.1	255.2	257.2	257.0	256.9	257.1	254.2	255.6	255.5	257.4	259.5	261.1	256.7
2006	256.9	259.0	261.5	261.4	261.9	262.7	258.5	260.6	261.3	260.8	262.2	263.2	260.8
2007	257.6	258.4	260.7	260.6	261.5	262.4	259.8	261.7	262.3	263.5	264.3	264.5	261.4
Total Private													
2000	187.4	188.0	189.2	190.6	191.5	194.0	192.4	193.7	193.3	192.4	193.8	194.9	191.8
2001	191.8	192.7	193.2	194.2	194.4	195.6	194.7	195.7	194.3	193.0	193.7	194.6	194.0
2002	190.0	191.0	191.8	192.9	193.9	195.3	193.5	194.1	193.2	191.8	192.6	193.3	192.8
2003	190.4	190.4	192.0	193.4	194.5	195.8	197.2	197.8	197.6	198.9	200.3	200.9	195.7
2004	197.2	198.2	199.7	201.4	201.5	202.0	201.3	201.8	201.7	200.9	201.4	202.5	200.8
2005	199.6	201.0	202.7	202.9	202.9	203.4	202.3	202.7	201.9	204.1	206.2	207.9	203.1
2006	203.8	205.2	207.4	208.0	208.3	209.2	207.1	207.4	206.9	206.8	208.1	209.1	207.3
2007	203.8	204.0	205.8	206.2	206.8	208.6	206.4	207.6	207.2	208.4	209.1	209.3	206.9
Goods-Producing													
2000	32.8	32.9	32.9	33.1	33.3	33.6	33.0	33.2	33.1	33.0	33.0	33.2	33.1
2001	32.7	32.7	32.8	33.0	33.0	33.7	33.7	33.6	33.7	33.7	33.7	33.4	33.3
2002	32.5	32.6	32.8	32.9	33.1	33.2	32.7	32.6	32.4	32.1	31.7	31.6	32.5
2003	31.1	31.2	31.7	32.3	33.1	33.6	34.2	34.6	35.1	35.2	35.5	35.5	33.5
2004	35.0	35.1	35.2	35.8	35.4	35.8	35.5	36.0	35.7	35.3	35.2	35.5	35.5
2005	35.3	35.0	35.4	35.4	35.3	35.5	35.4	35.4	35.3	35.3	35.3	35.6	35.4
2006	35.0	35.0	35.6	35.8	36.1	36.4	36.2	36.1	36.2	36.2	36.3	36.1	35.9
2007	34.8	34.6	34.8	34.5	34.7	35.2	34.8	34.7	34.8	35.0	35.0	35.0	34.8
Natural Resources and Mining													
2000	0.8	0.9	0.9	0.8	0.9	0.8	0.9	0.9	0.9	1.0	1.0	1.1	0.9
2001	1.2	1.2	1.3	1.2	1.2	1.1	1.1	1.1	1.1	1.1	1.2	1.1	1.2
2002	1.0	1.0	0.9	0.9	0.9	0.9	0.9	0.9	0.8	0.8	0.8	0.8	0.9
2003	0.7	0.7	0.8	0.8	0.9	0.9	0.9	0.8	0.8	0.9	0.9	0.9	0.8
2004	0.9	0.8	0.8	0.8	0.8	0.8	0.8	0.9	0.9	0.9	0.9	0.9	0.9
2005	0.9	0.9	0.8	0.8	0.8	0.8	0.8	0.8	0.8	0.8	0.8	0.8	0.8
2006	0.8	0.8	0.9	0.9	0.9	0.9	0.9	0.9	1.0	1.0	1.0	1.0	0.9
2007	1.0	1.0	1.0	1.0	1.0	1.0	1.0	1.0	1.0	1.0	1.0	1.0	1.0
Construction													
2000	10.9	11.0	11.1	11.3	11.4	11.6	11.3	11.3	11.2	11.3	11.3	11.3	11.3
2001	11.0	11.3	11.4	11.5	11.7	12.0	12.1	12.3	12.3	12.4	12.5	12.5	11.9
2002	12.0	12.1	12.3	12.3	12.4	12.4	12.2	12.0	11.8	11.5	11.5	11.5	12.0
2003	11.2	11.2	11.4	11.8	12.0	12.2	12.2	12.3	12.4	12.2	12.1	12.0	11.9
2004	11.7	11.6	11.8	11.8	11.8	12.1	12.0	12.1	12.1	11.9	11.8	11.9	11.9
2005	11.6	11.6	11.9	12.0	12.1	12.3	12.3	12.3	12.4	12.4	12.4	12.6	12.2
2006	12.1	12.3	12.6	12.9	13.1	13.4	13.1	13.2	13.2	13.2	13.2	13.1	13.0
2007	12.7	12.6	12.9	12.8	13.0	13.3	13.1	13.1	13.3	13.4	13.5	13.4	13.1
Manufacturing													
2000	21.1	20.9	20.9	21.0	21.0	21.2	20.8	21.1	20.9	20.8	20.8	20.8	20.9
2001	20.6	20.2	20.1	20.2	20.1	20.5	20.4	20.2	20.3	20.1	20.0	19.8	20.2
2002	19.5	19.6	19.6	19.7	19.7	19.9	19.6	19.8	19.8	19.8	19.4	19.3	19.6
2003	19.2	19.3	19.5	19.7	20.2	20.5	21.1	21.5	21.9	22.1	22.5	22.6	20.8
2004	22.4	22.7	22.6	23.2	22.8	22.9	22.7	23.0	22.7	22.5	22.5	22.7	22.7
2005	22.8	22.6	22.7	22.6	22.4	22.4	22.3	22.3	22.2	22.1	22.1	22.2	22.4
2006	22.1	21.9	22.1	22.0	22.1	22.1	22.2	22.0	22.0	22.0	22.1	22.0	22.1
2007	21.1	21.0	20.9	20.7	20.7	20.9	20.7	20.6	20.5	20.6	20.5	20.6	20.7
Service-Providing													
2000	206.0	207.2	208.9	210.3	211.5	212.7	210.4	212.0	213.0	212.6	214.0	215.1	211.1
2001	212.0	213.6	214.3	215.3	215.4	214.9	212.6	214.5	214.1	213.6	214.2	214.9	214.1
2002	210.8	212.4	213.4	214.1	214.7	215.1	212.7	214.2	214.4	213.7	214.9	215.2	213.8
2003	212.9	213.5	215.0	215.5	215.6	215.9	216.1	216.6	217.1	218.7	219.5	220.3	216.3
2004	216.1	217.6	219.8	220.9	221.6	221.5	219.6	220.2	221.6	221.4	222.1	222.6	220.4
2005	217.8	220.2	221.8	221.6	221.6	221.6	218.8	220.2	220.1	222.1	224.2	225.5	221.3
2006	221.9	224.0	225.9	225.6	225.8	226.3	222.3	224.5	225.1	224.6	225.9	227.1	224.9
2007	222.8	223.8	225.9	226.1	226.8	227.2	225.0	227.0	227.5	228.5	229.3	229.5	226.6
Trade, Transportation, and Utilities													
2000	51.5	51.3	51.5	51.8	52.2	52.4	52.1	52.3	52.4	52.4	53.3	54.1	52.3
2001	52.4	52.4	52.5	52.6	52.5	52.5	52.2	52.3	52.0	51.6	52.2	52.8	52.3
2002	49.9	49.8	50.0	50.2	50.4	51.1	50.8	50.9	51.0	50.7	51.5	52.4	50.7
2003	50.8	50.6	50.8	50.6	50.6	50.7	50.8	51.0	50.8	51.2	52.0	52.5	51.0
2004	50.6	50.5	50.9	51.0	51.3	51.4	50.9	50.9	51.4	52.0	52.8	53.6	51.4
2005	50.6	50.9	51.4	51.8	51.4	51.7	51.6	51.9	51.4	52.1	53.4	54.5	51.9
2006	52.6	52.6	53.0	52.9	53.2	53.2	52.6	52.9	52.9	52.7	53.3	54.2	53.0
2007	52.3	52.0	52.6	52.6	52.7	53.0	52.5	52.9	52.9	53.1	53.8	54.1	52.9
Wholesale Trade													
2000	12.7	12.7	12.7	12.7	12.7	12.8	12.8	12.8	12.8	12.6	12.5	12.5	12.7
2001	12.4	12.0	12.0	11.9	11.8	11.9	11.9	11.8	11.8	11.6	11.6	11.6	11.9
2002	11.4	11.5	11.4	11.4	11.5	11.6	11.6	11.6	11.6	11.6	11.5	11.5	11.5
2003	11.6	11.6	11.7	11.6	11.6	11.6	11.5	11.6	11.5	11.5	11.5	11.4	11.5
2004	11.2	11.3	11.3	11.5	11.4	11.4	11.4	11.3	11.4	11.4	11.4	11.4	11.4
2005	11.2	11.3	11.3	11.5	11.5	11.6	11.6	11.7	11.6	11.7	11.7	11.9	11.6
2006	11.9	12.0	12.0	12.1	12.2	12.2	12.2	12.2	12.2	12.2	12.2	12.2	12.1
2007	12.0	12.0	12.2	12.1	12.1	12.2	12.1	12.1	12.1	12.1	12.1	12.1	12.1

Employment by Industry: Jackson, MS, 2000–2007—*Continued*

(Numbers in thousands, not seasonally adjusted.)

Industry and year	January	February	March	April	May	June	July	August	September	October	November	December	Annual Average
Retail Trade													
2000	28.3	28.2	28.3	28.5	28.8	28.9	28.7	28.8	29.1	29.4	30.4	31.2	29.1
2001	29.5	29.9	30.0	29.8	29.8	29.7	29.4	29.5	29.4	29.1	29.8	30.4	29.7
2002	28.1	27.9	28.0	28.3	28.5	29.0	28.7	28.7	28.8	28.7	29.7	30.5	28.7
2003	28.6	28.4	28.6	28.3	28.4	28.5	28.7	28.8	28.7	29.0	29.8	30.4	28.9
2004	28.6	28.3	28.5	28.7	29.0	29.0	28.5	28.4	28.5	29.0	29.9	30.4	28.9
2005	28.4	28.4	28.6	28.8	28.7	28.8	28.8	29.0	28.7	28.9	30.1	31.0	29.0
2006	29.3	29.2	29.7	29.5	29.6	29.7	29.3	29.3	29.2	29.1	29.8	30.5	29.5
2007	29.0	28.8	29.1	29.1	29.2	29.4	29.0	29.1	29.1	29.2	30.0	30.3	29.3
Transportation and Utilities													
2000	10.4	10.4	10.4	10.6	10.6	10.7	10.6	10.6	10.6	10.4	10.4	10.4	10.5
2001	10.5	10.5	10.5	10.9	10.9	10.9	10.9	10.9	10.8	10.9	10.8	10.8	10.8
2002	10.4	10.5	10.5	10.5	10.5	10.6	10.5	10.6	10.5	10.4	10.4	10.4	10.5
2003	10.6	10.6	10.5	10.7	10.6	10.6	10.6	10.6	10.6	10.6	10.7	10.7	10.6
2004	10.8	10.9	11.1	10.8	10.9	11.0	11.0	11.2	11.5	11.6	11.5	11.8	11.2
2005	11.0	11.2	11.5	11.5	11.2	11.3	11.2	11.2	11.1	11.5	11.6	11.6	11.3
2006	11.4	11.4	11.3	11.3	11.4	11.3	11.1	11.4	11.5	11.4	11.3	11.5	11.4
2007	11.3	11.2	11.3	11.4	11.4	11.4	11.4	11.7	11.7	11.8	11.7	11.7	11.5
Information													
2000	7.7	7.7	7.7	7.5	7.6	7.9	7.9	7.9	7.9	8.0	8.1	8.1	7.8
2001	8.0	8.0	7.8	7.6	7.5	7.6	7.5	7.4	7.3	7.2	7.2	7.2	7.5
2002	6.9	6.9	6.8	6.7	6.7	6.5	6.4	6.3	6.2	6.2	6.1	6.0	6.5
2003	6.0	5.9	5.9	5.8	5.7	5.6	5.7	5.7	5.6	5.5	5.4	5.4	5.6
2004	5.3	5.3	5.2	5.1	5.1	5.1	5.2	5.1	5.0	4.9	5.0	4.9	5.1
2005	4.8	4.8	4.8	4.8	4.8	4.8	4.7	4.7	4.7	4.6	4.6	4.6	4.7
2006	4.6	4.5	4.5	4.5	4.5	4.4	4.3	4.3	4.2	4.2	4.2	4.2	4.4
2007	4.1	4.2	4.2	4.2	4.2	4.3	4.3	4.3	4.3	4.3	4.3	4.2	4.2
Financial Activities													
2000	15.8	16.0	16.1	16.1	16.2	16.4	16.5	16.5	16.6	16.5	16.6	16.7	16.3
2001	16.4	16.6	16.7	16.6	16.6	16.8	16.7	16.7	16.6	16.7	16.6	16.7	16.6
2002	16.2	16.2	16.2	16.2	16.3	16.4	16.2	16.2	16.3	16.4	16.6	16.5	16.3
2003	16.3	16.2	16.3	16.2	16.2	16.3	16.2	16.2	16.1	16.1	16.1	16.1	16.1
2004	15.9	16.0	16.1	16.1	16.1	16.1	16.2	16.3	16.2	16.1	16.2	16.3	16.1
2005	16.1	16.1	16.1	16.1	16.1	16.1	16.2	16.3	16.2	16.8	16.9	16.9	16.3
2006	16.4	16.8	16.7	16.7	16.6	16.7	16.7	16.8	16.7	16.6	16.6	16.9	16.7
2007	16.6	16.6	16.6	16.7	16.6	16.7	16.6	16.6	16.5	16.4	16.4	16.6	16.6
Professional and Business Services													
2000	25.2	25.2	25.3	25.5	25.4	26.0	25.9	26.3	26.4	25.8	25.9	25.9	25.7
2001	25.6	25.4	25.1	25.8	25.6	25.5	25.6	26.0	25.6	25.3	25.5	25.7	25.6
2002	25.6	26.1	25.7	26.0	26.1	26.3	25.9	26.3	26.1	25.9	25.7	25.8	26.0
2003	25.5	25.5	25.8	26.6	26.5	26.4	27.3	27.1	27.2	27.7	27.9	28.1	26.8
2004	27.6	27.8	28.3	28.6	28.6	28.6	28.6	28.6	29.0	28.8	28.5	28.7	28.5
2005	29.7	30.2	30.4	29.7	29.6	29.5	29.2	29.0	29.2	29.9	30.3	30.4	29.8
2006	30.0	30.4	31.0	31.1	30.7	30.8	30.6	30.5	30.5	31.0	31.4	31.5	30.8
2007	30.7	30.7	30.9	31.2	31.0	31.5	31.3	31.4	31.3	31.5	31.6	31.6	31.2
Education and Health Services													
2000	28.0	28.1	28.2	28.6	28.6	28.4	27.9	28.4	28.6	28.8	28.9	28.9	28.5
2001	28.6	28.9	29.1	29.3	29.4	29.3	29.1	29.5	29.8	30.0	30.1	30.1	29.4
2002	30.4	30.5	30.7	30.9	31.0	31.0	30.7	31.0	31.1	30.9	30.9	31.0	30.8
2003	30.8	31.0	31.1	31.4	31.5	31.8	31.5	31.7	31.7	32.2	32.5	32.4	31.6
2004	32.5	32.8	32.8	33.0	33.0	32.7	32.8	33.0	33.0	33.0	32.9	32.9	32.9
2005	32.8	33.0	33.0	33.1	33.1	33.2	32.8	33.0	33.0	33.1	33.1	33.4	33.1
2006	33.2	33.3	33.4	33.3	33.3	33.2	33.2	33.3	33.7	33.8	33.9	34.0	33.5
2007	33.6	33.8	34.0	34.1	34.1	34.2	34.0	34.5	34.5	35.1	35.0	34.8	34.3
Leisure and Hospitality													
2000	16.9	17.2	17.6	18.1	18.2	19.1	18.9	18.9	18.2	17.9	17.8	17.7	18.0
2001	17.9	18.5	18.9	19.0	19.3	19.7	19.7	19.8	19.1	18.4	18.5	18.5	18.9
2002	18.3	18.7	19.2	19.7	20.1	20.5	20.4	20.5	19.9	19.5	19.8	19.7	19.7
2003	19.5	19.6	20.0	20.2	20.5	21.0	20.9	21.0	20.7	20.7	20.7	20.6	20.4
2004	20.0	20.4	20.9	21.5	21.7	21.9	21.9	21.9	21.5	20.8	20.8	20.7	21.2
2005	20.4	20.9	21.5	21.9	22.4	22.3	22.1	22.1	21.7	22.0	22.1	22.0	21.8
2006	21.5	22.0	22.5	23.2	23.4	23.8	23.0	23.0	22.4	22.0	22.1	22.0	22.6
2007	21.5	21.8	22.4	22.7	23.2	23.4	22.7	23.0	22.8	22.9	22.9	22.8	22.7
Other Services													
2000	9.7	9.7	9.8	9.9	10.0	10.2	10.2	10.1	10.2	10.1	10.1	10.2	10.0
2001	10.2	10.2	10.3	10.2	10.4	10.5	10.3	10.3	10.2	10.1	10.0	10.1	10.2
2002	10.1	10.1	10.2	10.3	10.3	10.3	10.3	10.3	10.2	10.1	10.3	10.3	10.2
2003	10.4	10.4	10.4	10.3	10.4	10.4	10.6	10.5	10.4	10.3	10.2	10.3	10.3
2004	10.3	10.3	10.3	10.3	10.3	10.4	10.2	10.0	9.9	10.0	9.9	9.9	10.2
2005	9.9	10.1	10.1	10.1	10.2	10.3	10.3	10.3	10.3	10.3	10.5	10.5	10.2
2006	10.5	10.6	10.7	10.5	10.5	10.7	10.5	10.5	10.3	10.3	10.3	10.2	10.5
2007	10.2	10.3	10.3	10.2	10.3	10.3	10.2	10.2	10.1	10.1	10.1	10.2	10.2
Government													
2000	51.4	52.1	52.7	52.8	53.3	52.3	51.0	51.6	52.7	53.2	53.2	53.4	52.5
2001	52.9	53.6	53.9	54.2	54.0	53.1	51.5	52.4	53.5	54.2	54.1	53.7	53.4
2002	53.3	54.0	54.4	54.2	53.9	53.0	51.9	52.6	53.6	54.1	54.0	53.6	53.6
2003	53.6	54.3	54.7	54.4	54.2	53.7	53.1	53.4	54.6	55.0	54.7	54.9	54.2
2004	53.9	54.5	55.3	55.3	55.5	55.3	53.8	54.4	55.6	55.8	55.9	55.6	55.1
2005	53.5	54.2	54.5	54.1	54.0	53.7	51.9	52.9	53.6	53.3	53.3	53.2	53.5
2006	53.1	53.8	54.1	53.4	53.6	53.5	51.4	53.2	54.4	54.0	54.1	54.1	53.6
2007	53.8	54.4	54.9	54.4	54.7	53.8	53.4	54.1	55.1	55.1	55.2	55.2	54.5

Employment by Industry: Lakeland-Winter Haven, FL, 2000–2007

(Numbers in thousands, not seasonally adjusted.)

Industry and year	January	February	March	April	May	June	July	August	September	October	November	December	Annual Average
Total Nonfarm													
2000	179.8	180.3	182.5	184.3	185.3	182.9	180.6	183.9	185.4	185.2	187.3	189.2	183.9
2001	185.6	187.1	188.7	186.2	187.0	184.3	181.5	184.5	185.6	186.7	187.6	189.2	186.2
2002	184.8	185.7	187.3	186.0	186.8	183.1	181.0	184.6	185.5	185.5	188.2	189.2	185.6
2003	184.7	184.8	186.4	187.9	187.7	184.5	182.5	187.1	188.6	189.3	191.7	194.7	187.5
2004	194.7	195.9	198.1	198.4	198.8	195.6	193.7	196.4	197.3	200.1	203.9	207.4	198.4
2005	205.2	208.4	209.9	211.4	211.4	208.9	206.3	210.7	212.5	213.0	215.8	217.0	210.9
2006	214.2	216.6	219.1	217.2	217.2	214.3	209.8	213.7	215.2	213.8	216.4	217.3	215.4
2007	215.1	217.0	218.9	218.0	218.5	215.0	210.5	213.4	213.9	213.9	214.3	215.7	215.4
Total Private													
2000	152.9	153.5	155.2	157.2	156.9	157.5	155.9	157.0	158.2	157.6	159.8	161.4	156.9
2001	159.4	160.1	161.3	159.5	160.2	160.2	158.0	158.4	159.1	160.1	161.5	162.0	160.0
2002	158.9	159.1	160.5	159.4	159.8	158.8	157.2	158.3	158.8	158.9	160.9	162.1	159.4
2003	157.6	157.4	159.1	160.7	160.5	160.0	158.7	160.7	161.8	162.2	164.4	167.4	160.9
2004	167.5	168.6	170.8	171.0	171.4	171.0	169.6	169.6	170.0	172.5	176.4	179.8	171.5
2005	177.8	180.8	182.2	183.8	183.5	184.0	181.8	183.5	184.5	184.4	187.0	188.3	183.5
2006	185.8	187.8	190.3	188.5	188.4	188.5	184.5	185.6	186.4	185.4	187.8	188.8	187.3
2007	185.7	187.3	189.2	188.2	188.6	188.2	184.3	184.2	184.1	184.5	184.8	186.3	186.3
Goods-Producing													
2000	34.2	34.1	34.3	34.4	34.0	34.4	33.9	34.0	34.2	33.7	33.6	33.6	34.0
2001	32.9	33.0	33.3	32.9	33.1	33.1	32.5	32.7	32.7	32.7	32.8	32.6	32.9
2002	32.1	32.3	32.5	32.0	32.1	31.9	31.8	32.0	31.8	32.1	32.1	31.9	32.1
2003	31.1	30.9	31.2	31.1	31.3	31.1	30.8	30.8	30.8	30.7	31.1	31.1	31.0
2004	31.7	31.7	32.1	32.3	32.5	32.8	32.6	32.5	32.7	33.1	33.3	33.8	32.6
2005	33.5	34.1	34.3	34.8	34.9	35.0	34.4	34.6	34.4	34.5	34.6	34.6	34.5
2006	34.2	34.8	35.3	35.2	35.2	35.4	34.4	34.6	34.4	34.3	34.5	34.6	34.7
2007	34.3	34.1	34.1	33.7	33.8	33.5	32.7	32.4	32.3	32.1	31.9	31.9	33.1
Natural Resources, Mining, and Construction													
2000	13.4	13.5	13.6	13.9	13.7	14.1	13.7	13.9	14.2	13.9	13.9	14.0	13.8
2001	13.8	13.9	14.2	14.0	14.2	14.2	13.9	14.0	13.9	14.1	14.0	13.8	14.0
2002	13.7	14.0	14.0	13.6	13.7	13.4	13.3	13.5	13.5	13.6	13.6	13.4	13.6
2003	12.8	12.8	12.9	13.0	13.1	13.0	12.8	12.9	12.8	12.7	13.0	13.1	12.9
2004	13.5	13.5	13.8	14.0	14.2	14.4	14.4	14.4	14.6	15.1	15.2	15.5	14.4
2005	15.3	15.7	15.9	16.4	16.4	16.6	16.2	16.4	16.4	16.5	16.4	16.2	16.2
2006	15.9	16.4	16.9	16.9	17.0	17.3	16.9	17.1	16.9	16.9	17.1	17.1	16.9
2007	16.7	16.6	16.6	16.2	16.3	16.2	15.7	15.7	15.5	15.4	15.2	15.2	15.9
Manufacturing													
2000	20.8	20.6	20.7	20.5	20.3	20.3	20.2	20.1	20.0	19.8	19.7	19.6	20.2
2001	19.1	19.1	19.1	18.9	18.9	18.9	18.6	18.7	18.8	18.6	18.8	18.8	18.9
2002	18.4	18.3	18.5	18.4	18.4	18.5	18.5	18.5	18.3	18.5	18.5	18.5	18.4
2003	18.3	18.1	18.3	18.1	18.2	18.1	18.0	17.9	18.0	18.0	18.1	18.0	18.1
2004	18.2	18.2	18.3	18.3	18.3	18.4	18.2	18.1	18.1	18.0	18.1	18.3	18.2
2005	18.2	18.4	18.4	18.4	18.5	18.4	18.2	18.2	18.0	18.0	18.2	18.4	18.3
2006	18.3	18.4	18.4	18.3	18.2	18.1	17.5	17.5	17.5	17.4	17.4	17.5	17.9
2007	17.6	17.5	17.5	17.5	17.5	17.3	17.0	16.7	16.8	16.7	16.7	16.7	17.1
Service-Providing													
2000	145.6	146.2	148.2	149.9	151.3	148.5	146.7	149.9	151.2	151.5	153.7	155.6	149.9
2001	152.7	154.1	155.4	153.3	153.9	151.2	149.0	151.8	152.9	154.0	154.8	156.6	153.3
2002	152.7	153.4	154.8	154.0	154.7	151.2	149.2	152.6	153.7	153.4	156.1	157.3	153.6
2003	153.6	153.9	155.2	156.8	156.4	153.4	151.7	156.3	157.8	158.6	160.6	163.6	156.5
2004	163.0	164.2	166.0	166.1	166.3	162.8	161.1	163.9	164.6	167.0	170.6	173.6	165.8
2005	171.7	174.3	175.6	176.6	176.5	173.9	171.9	176.1	178.1	178.5	181.2	182.4	176.4
2006	180.0	181.8	183.8	182.0	182.0	178.9	175.4	179.1	180.8	179.5	181.9	182.7	180.7
2007	180.8	182.9	184.8	184.3	184.7	181.5	177.8	181.0	181.6	181.8	182.4	183.8	182.3
Trade, Transportation, and Utilities													
2000	44.5	44.4	44.8	45.0	45.2	45.0	44.6	44.8	44.8	44.9	45.9	46.9	45.1
2001	45.9	45.7	45.7	45.2	44.9	44.8	44.3	44.5	44.8	45.3	45.9	46.7	45.3
2002	45.2	44.7	44.9	44.2	44.1	43.7	43.1	43.3	43.2	43.0	43.8	44.4	44.0
2003	41.8	41.6	41.9	42.3	42.3	41.8	41.4	41.5	41.7	42.0	42.9	44.0	42.1
2004	43.3	43.2	43.6	43.6	44.0	43.9	43.6	43.2	43.1	43.9	45.1	46.4	43.9
2005	45.7	46.3	46.8	47.2	47.4	47.5	47.4	47.6	47.9	48.1	49.3	49.9	47.6
2006	48.8	49.0	49.6	49.0	49.2	48.6	48.2	48.1	48.2	48.5	49.5	50.4	48.9
2007	49.1	49.3	49.7	49.5	49.9	49.6	49.1	48.9	48.6	48.5	49.0	49.9	49.3
Wholesale Trade													
2000	8.0	8.1	8.2	8.1	8.2	8.2	8.1	8.1	8.1	8.1	8.1	8.2	8.1
2001	8.4	8.5	8.5	8.4	8.4	8.4	8.4	8.5	8.6	8.6	8.6	8.7	8.5
2002	8.4	8.4	8.3	8.3	8.4	8.5	8.4	8.4	8.5	8.8	9.0	9.0	8.5
2003	8.9	9.0	9.2	9.1	9.1	9.1	8.9	9.0	9.0	9.0	9.1	9.2	9.0
2004	9.3	9.4	9.4	9.5	9.5	9.5	9.4	9.4	9.3	9.3	9.4	9.5	9.4
2005	9.7	9.8	10.0	10.1	10.1	10.2	10.3	10.4	10.5	10.6	10.7	10.7	10.3
2006	10.5	10.5	10.6	10.5	10.5	10.3	10.3	10.2	10.2	10.2	10.2	10.3	10.4
2007	10.3	10.5	10.5	10.4	10.4	10.4	10.2	10.2	10.2	10.2	10.2	10.3	10.3
Retail Trade													
2000	27.1	26.9	27.1	27.3	27.5	27.1	26.8	27.0	26.9	26.9	27.9	28.6	27.3
2001	27.2	26.8	26.9	26.4	26.1	26.0	25.6	25.7	25.8	26.2	26.7	27.2	26.4
2002	26.2	25.9	26.1	25.6	25.4	25.0	24.4	24.5	24.2	23.9	24.4	24.8	25.0
2003	22.4	22.2	22.3	22.7	22.5	22.1	21.9	22.0	22.2	22.6	23.2	24.1	22.5
2004	23.3	23.2	23.4	23.5	23.6	23.5	23.1	22.8	22.8	23.4	24.2	25.2	23.5
2005	24.4	24.7	25.0	25.1	25.2	25.1	25.0	25.0	25.1	25.4	26.3	26.7	25.3
2006	26.0	26.1	26.5	26.2	26.2	25.9	25.7	25.7	25.7	25.7	26.5	27.0	26.1
2007	26.2	26.3	26.5	26.3	26.6	26.5	26.3	26.2	26.0	25.9	26.3	26.8	26.3

Employment by Industry: Lakeland-Winter Haven, FL, 2000–2007—*Continued*

(Numbers in thousands, not seasonally adjusted.)

Industry and year	January	February	March	April	May	June	July	August	September	October	November	December	Annual Average
Transportation and Utilities													
2000	9.4	9.4	9.5	9.6	9.5	9.7	9.7	9.7	9.8	9.9	9.9	10.1	9.7
2001	10.3	10.4	10.3	10.4	10.4	10.4	10.3	10.3	10.4	10.5	10.6	10.8	10.4
2002	10.6	10.4	10.5	10.3	10.3	10.2	10.3	10.4	10.5	10.3	10.4	10.6	10.4
2003	10.5	10.4	10.4	10.5	10.7	10.6	10.6	10.5	10.5	10.4	10.6	10.7	10.5
2004	10.7	10.6	10.8	10.6	10.9	10.9	11.1	11.0	11.0	11.2	11.5	11.7	11.0
2005	11.6	11.8	11.8	12.0	12.1	12.2	12.1	12.2	12.3	12.1	12.3	12.5	12.1
2006	12.3	12.4	12.5	12.3	12.5	12.4	12.2	12.2	12.3	12.6	12.8	13.1	12.5
2007	12.6	12.5	12.7	12.8	12.9	12.7	12.6	12.5	12.4	12.4	12.5	12.8	12.6
Information													
2000	2.1	2.1	2.2	2.4	2.4	2.4	2.4	2.4	2.4	2.4	2.4	2.5	2.3
2001	2.5	2.5	2.5	2.5	2.6	2.6	2.6	2.6	2.6	2.5	2.6	2.6	2.6
2002	2.6	2.6	2.6	2.5	2.5	2.4	2.3	2.4	2.4	2.3	2.3	2.3	2.4
2003	2.3	2.3	2.3	2.3	2.3	2.2	2.2	2.2	2.2	2.2	2.2	2.2	2.2
2004	2.2	2.2	2.2	2.1	2.1	2.2	2.3	2.3	2.2	2.2	2.3	2.3	2.2
2005	2.2	2.2	2.2	2.2	2.3	2.3	2.3	2.3	2.3	2.3	2.4	2.4	2.3
2006	2.4	2.4	2.4	2.4	2.4	2.4	2.4	2.3	2.3	2.2	2.3	2.3	2.4
2007	2.1	2.2	2.1	2.2	2.2	2.3	2.2	2.2	2.1	2.1	2.1	2.1	2.2
Financial Activities													
2000	9.2	9.3	9.4	9.5	9.5	9.8	9.6	9.8	9.8	9.7	9.8	9.8	9.6
2001	10.0	9.9	10.1	10.2	10.2	10.4	10.3	10.3	10.4	10.4	10.4	10.5	10.3
2002	10.6	10.7	10.7	10.8	10.8	11.0	10.8	10.8	10.7	10.8	10.9	11.0	10.8
2003	10.9	10.9	10.9	11.0	11.1	11.1	11.1	11.1	11.0	11.0	11.0	11.1	11.0
2004	11.0	11.0	11.1	11.2	11.2	11.2	10.8	10.6	10.6	10.7	10.7	10.8	10.9
2005	10.8	10.8	10.8	11.0	11.1	11.1	11.1	11.1	11.1	11.4	11.4	11.5	11.1
2006	11.4	11.4	11.5	11.5	11.5	11.6	11.5	11.5	11.6	11.6	11.7	11.9	11.6
2007	11.8	11.9	11.9	11.8	11.8	11.9	11.8	11.8	11.6	11.6	11.6	11.7	11.8
Professional and Business Services													
2000	20.0	20.1	20.6	21.2	21.2	21.4	21.3	21.6	22.1	22.0	22.4	22.9	21.4
2001	23.7	24.1	24.3	23.7	24.3	24.6	24.3	23.9	23.9	24.0	23.9	23.5	24.0
2002	23.4	23.5	23.6	23.9	24.7	24.5	24.2	24.3	24.8	24.7	25.2	25.9	24.4
2003	26.3	26.2	26.8	27.7	28.2	28.8	28.8	30.1	30.9	31.1	31.9	33.4	29.2
2004	33.3	33.6	34.4	34.7	34.5	34.2	33.8	33.9	34.1	34.3	35.7	37.0	34.5
2005	36.2	37.0	37.2	37.3	36.7	37.4	36.6	37.0	37.0	36.6	37.1	37.5	37.0
2006	36.3	36.9	37.5	36.7	37.0	37.4	36.0	36.0	36.5	36.9	35.9	36.6	36.5	36.7
2007	35.5	36.2	36.8	36.5	36.5	36.7	35.1	35.2	35.3	35.8	35.4	35.9	35.9
Education and Health Services													
2000	21.8	22.1	22.0	22.4	22.2	22.2	21.8	22.2	22.7	22.8	23.0	23.0	22.4
2001	23.0	23.1	23.1	23.0	23.0	22.7	22.1	22.4	22.7	23.0	22.9	22.8	22.8
2002	21.9	22.1	22.7	22.5	22.3	22.1	22.0	22.4	22.9	23.1	23.1	23.0	22.5
2003	22.3	22.3	22.4	22.8	22.7	22.5	22.2	22.9	23.3	23.6	23.8	23.8	22.8
2004	24.0	24.1	24.3	24.0	23.7	23.5	23.5	23.8	24.0	24.5	24.8	24.9	24.1
2005	25.0	25.4	25.5	25.8	25.5	25.1	24.9	25.5	26.0	26.0	26.0	26.0	25.6
2006	26.3	26.5	26.6	26.6	26.5	26.3	25.9	26.4	26.9	27.1	27.3	27.1	26.6
2007	27.2	27.5	27.6	28.0	27.7	27.6	27.0	27.2	27.7	28.0	28.0	28.0	27.6
Leisure and Hospitality													
2000	14.2	14.4	15.0	15.2	15.0	14.9	15.0	14.9	14.8	14.8	15.2	15.4	14.9
2001	14.5	14.8	15.3	15.0	15.0	14.9	14.9	14.9	14.9	15.2	15.9	16.2	15.1
2002	15.9	16.0	16.3	16.2	15.9	15.7	15.6	15.7	15.5	15.4	15.9	16.0	15.8
2003	15.4	15.7	16.1	16.0	15.3	15.1	14.8	14.7	14.4	14.1	14.0	14.2	14.9
2004	14.2	15.0	15.2	15.2	15.4	15.2	15.0	15.2	15.1	15.7	16.2	16.3	15.3
2005	16.0	16.6	17.0	17.0	16.8	16.6	16.1	16.2	16.4	16.0	16.6	16.7	16.5
2006	16.7	17.0	17.6	17.5	17.1	17.2	16.7	16.8	16.8	16.5	16.7	16.8	17.0
2007	16.7	17.1	17.8	17.4	17.4	17.3	17.1	17.2	17.2	17.2	17.5	17.5	17.3
Other Services													
2000	6.9	7.0	6.9	7.1	7.4	7.4	7.3	7.3	7.4	7.3	7.5	7.3	7.2
2001	6.9	7.0	7.0	7.0	7.1	7.1	7.0	7.1	7.1	7.0	7.1	7.1	7.0
2002	7.2	7.2	7.2	7.3	7.4	7.5	7.4	7.4	7.5	7.5	7.6	7.6	7.4
2003	7.5	7.5	7.5	7.5	7.3	7.4	7.4	7.4	7.5	7.5	7.5	7.6	7.4
2004	7.8	7.8	7.9	7.9	8.0	8.0	8.0	8.1	8.2	8.1	8.3	8.3	8.0
2005	8.4	8.4	8.4	8.5	8.8	9.0	9.0	9.2	9.4	9.5	9.6	9.7	9.0
2006	9.7	9.8	9.8	9.6	9.5	9.6	9.4	9.4	9.3	9.3	9.2	9.2	9.5
2007	9.0	9.0	9.2	9.1	9.3	9.3	9.3	9.3	9.3	9.2	9.3	9.3	9.2
Government													
2000	26.9	26.8	27.3	27.1	28.4	25.4	24.7	26.9	27.2	27.6	27.5	27.8	27.0
2001	26.2	27.0	27.4	26.7	26.8	24.1	23.5	26.1	26.5	26.6	26.1	27.2	26.2
2002	25.9	26.6	26.8	26.6	27.0	24.3	23.8	26.3	26.7	26.6	27.3	27.1	26.3
2003	27.1	27.4	27.3	27.2	27.2	24.5	23.8	26.4	26.8	27.1	27.3	27.3	26.6
2004	27.2	27.3	27.3	27.4	27.4	24.6	24.1	26.8	27.3	27.6	27.5	27.6	26.8
2005	27.4	27.6	27.7	27.6	27.9	24.9	24.5	27.2	28.0	28.6	28.8	28.7	27.4
2006	28.4	28.8	28.8	28.7	28.8	25.8	25.3	28.1	28.8	28.4	28.6	28.5	28.1
2007	29.4	29.7	29.7	29.8	29.9	26.8	26.2	29.2	29.8	29.4	29.5	29.4	29.1

Employment by Industry: Des Moines-West Des Moines, IA, 2000–2007

(Numbers in thousands, not seasonally adjusted.)

Industry and year	January	February	March	April	May	June	July	August	September	October	November	December	Annual Average
Total Nonfarm													
2000	284.2	284.2	287.2	287.9	291.2	295.2	292.6	293.1	291.5	292.9	294.8	294.1	290.7
2001	289.1	288.4	290.6	293.6	297.4	301.6	295.0	295.7	294.9	293.9	295.9	295.6	294.3
2002	287.9	286.9	288.5	293.0	295.8	298.8	294.5	295.1	294.0	293.8	295.8	295.1	293.3
2003	286.6	285.2	286.6	290.5	294.2	297.3	293.0	294.5	294.9	296.5	297.3	297.4	292.8
2004	289.5	289.2	292.0	297.7	300.1	303.4	301.5	303.1	302.2	303.5	305.3	305.5	299.4
2005	296.2	296.9	300.7	305.1	308.2	311.3	307.4	307.2	308.1	309.1	310.2	310.7	305.9
2006	305.2	305.9	308.5	313.1	316.3	320.0	314.6	315.7	316.2	319.4	320.3	321.2	314.7
2007	313.8	314.0	316.0	320.4	324.5	328.1	322.4	323.2	323.8	325.1	325.3	326.3	321.9
Total Private													
2000	247.1	246.7	249.3	250.3	252.9	256.9	256.3	257.1	254.7	255.1	256.7	255.6	253.2
2001	250.5	249.5	251.5	254.6	258.2	262.0	257.8	258.8	256.6	254.7	256.5	256.6	255.6
2002	249.1	247.9	249.5	253.8	256.5	259.5	258.0	258.8	256.5	255.3	257.3	256.2	254.9
2003	248.3	246.5	247.6	252.0	255.3	258.3	256.8	258.4	257.1	257.2	257.9	257.9	254.4
2004	251.1	250.1	252.8	258.8	261.0	264.2	265.4	267.3	264.9	264.9	266.4	266.7	261.1
2005	258.0	258.2	261.6	266.2	268.8	271.9	271.3	271.4	270.1	270.0	271.0	271.2	267.5
2006	266.2	266.3	268.9	273.2	276.2	279.2	277.7	278.9	277.3	279.4	280.1	280.7	275.3
2007	273.0	273.1	275.1	279.4	283.0	286.3	284.3	284.7	282.7	283.0	283.1	283.7	281.0
Goods-Producing													
2000	34.2	34.0	34.7	36.2	36.9	37.8	37.9	37.9	37.3	36.8	36.6	35.0	36.3
2001	34.1	33.8	34.2	35.3	36.3	37.3	37.3	37.3	36.8	36.3	35.9	35.1	35.8
2002	33.0	32.7	33.2	35.1	35.8	36.5	36.4	36.3	35.7	35.7	35.5	34.5	35.0
2003	32.3	31.8	32.2	33.9	34.8	35.4	35.6	36.0	35.8	35.8	35.7	35.1	34.5
2004	33.5	33.1	34.3	36.4	36.8	38.2	38.4	38.4	38.2	38.2	38.1	37.6	36.8
2005	35.2	34.8	36.0	37.4	38.1	39.0	39.1	39.1	38.9	38.6	38.6	37.4	37.7
2006	36.1	36.0	36.6	37.9	38.4	39.2	38.7	39.0	38.6	38.3	37.7	37.0	37.8
2007	34.7	33.9	34.8	36.2	37.0	37.9	37.9	38.1	38.0	37.9	37.8	37.3	36.8
Natural Resources, Mining, and Construction													
2000	12.5	12.4	12.9	14.3	14.9	15.6	15.9	15.8	15.5	15.2	15.0	13.7	14.5
2001	12.7	12.4	12.8	14.1	15.0	15.9	16.2	16.3	16.0	15.6	15.3	14.6	14.7
2002	13.0	12.9	13.6	15.0	15.6	16.3	16.2	16.2	15.6	15.8	15.7	14.8	15.1
2003	13.3	12.7	13.1	14.6	15.4	16.0	16.2	16.6	16.4	16.6	16.5	16.0	15.3
2004	14.5	14.1	15.1	16.8	17.1	18.3	18.5	18.5	18.3	18.3	18.2	17.7	17.1
2005	15.5	15.2	16.2	17.4	18.0	18.7	19.0	19.0	18.8	18.7	18.7	17.6	17.7
2006	16.4	16.3	16.8	17.9	18.4	19.0	19.0	18.9	18.7	18.4	18.0	17.3	17.9
2007	15.2	14.5	15.3	16.6	17.4	18.2	18.4	18.5	18.4	18.4	18.3	17.7	17.2
Manufacturing													
2000	21.7	21.6	21.8	21.9	22.0	22.2	22.0	22.1	21.8	21.6	21.6	21.3	21.8
2001	21.4	21.4	21.4	21.2	21.3	21.4	21.1	21.0	20.8	20.7	20.6	20.5	21.1
2002	20.0	19.8	19.6	20.1	20.2	20.2	20.2	20.1	20.1	19.9	19.8	19.7	20.0
2003	19.0	19.1	19.1	19.3	19.4	19.4	19.4	19.4	19.4	19.2	19.2	19.1	19.3
2004	19.0	19.0	19.2	19.6	19.7	19.9	19.9	19.9	19.9	19.9	19.9	19.9	19.7
2005	19.7	19.6	19.8	20.0	20.1	20.3	20.1	20.1	20.1	19.9	19.9	19.8	20.0
2006	19.7	19.7	19.8	20.0	20.0	20.2	19.7	20.1	19.9	19.9	19.7	19.7	19.9
2007	19.5	19.4	19.5	19.6	19.6	19.7	19.5	19.6	19.6	19.5	19.5	19.6	19.6
Service-Providing													
2000	250.0	250.2	252.5	251.7	254.3	257.4	254.7	255.2	254.2	256.1	258.2	259.1	254.5
2001	255.0	254.6	256.4	258.3	261.1	264.3	257.7	258.4	258.1	257.6	260.0	260.5	258.5
2002	254.9	254.2	255.3	257.9	260.0	262.3	258.1	258.8	258.3	258.1	260.3	260.6	258.2
2003	254.3	253.4	254.4	256.6	259.4	261.9	257.4	258.5	259.1	260.7	261.6	262.3	258.3
2004	256.0	256.1	257.7	261.3	263.3	265.2	263.1	264.7	264.0	265.3	267.2	267.9	262.7
2005	261.0	262.1	264.7	267.7	270.1	272.3	268.3	268.1	269.2	270.5	271.6	273.3	268.2
2006	269.1	269.9	271.9	275.2	277.9	280.8	275.9	276.7	277.6	281.1	282.6	284.2	276.9
2007	279.1	280.1	281.2	284.2	287.5	290.2	284.5	285.1	285.8	287.2	287.5	289.0	285.1
Trade, Transportation, and Utilities													
2000	63.3	63.3	63.3	63.2	63.4	64.0	64.4	64.6	64.3	65.6	66.7	67.2	64.4
2001	65.0	63.9	64.1	64.2	64.6	64.7	64.2	64.4	64.3	63.9	65.2	65.8	64.5
2002	63.0	62.0	62.0	62.5	62.7	63.3	63.6	63.5	63.2	63.5	64.8	65.0	63.3
2003	62.5	61.4	61.5	62.2	62.9	63.1	63.0	63.0	62.7	63.2	64.2	64.6	62.9
2004	62.4	61.9	62.0	62.6	63.1	63.5	64.3	64.9	64.1	64.5	66.0	66.7	63.8
2005	64.0	63.6	64.0	64.2	64.4	64.8	64.8	64.8	64.5	64.8	66.1	66.9	64.7
2006	64.3	63.7	64.0	64.7	65.2	65.4	65.2	65.0	64.6	65.2	66.5	67.3	65.1
2007	64.8	64.1	64.2	64.3	65.0	65.6	65.3	65.1	64.6	65.1	65.9	66.5	65.0
Wholesale Trade													
2000	18.1	18.1	18.1	18.1	18.2	18.3	18.4	18.1	18.0	18.2	18.1	18.1	18.2
2001	18.0	17.9	18.0	17.9	17.9	18.0	17.8	17.7	17.8	17.5	17.4	17.5	17.8
2002	17.2	17.1	17.1	16.9	16.8	17.0	17.1	17.0	16.8	16.8	16.8	16.7	16.9
2003	16.4	16.3	16.3	16.4	16.6	16.8	16.8	16.8	16.6	16.9	16.8	16.8	16.6
2004	16.6	16.7	16.7	16.9	17.1	17.3	17.4	17.4	17.2	17.3	17.4	17.5	17.1
2005	17.5	17.6	17.7	17.6	17.6	17.7	18.0	17.9	17.8	17.9	17.9	17.9	17.8
2006	17.8	17.8	17.8	17.8	17.9	17.9	17.8	17.7	17.5	17.5	17.5	17.5	17.7
2007	17.4	17.4	17.5	17.4	17.5	17.6	17.7	17.7	17.6	17.8	17.8	17.8	17.6
Retail Trade													
2000	34.6	34.6	34.7	34.4	34.6	35.0	35.2	35.7	35.5	36.2	37.4	38.0	35.5
2001	36.3	35.4	35.5	35.5	35.9	35.8	35.6	35.8	35.7	35.6	37.0	37.5	36.0
2002	35.4	34.7	34.7	35.2	35.5	35.8	35.8	35.8	35.8	36.0	37.3	37.7	35.8
2003	35.7	34.9	35.0	35.5	35.9	35.9	35.7	35.7	35.7	35.8	36.9	37.4	35.8
2004	35.5	34.9	35.0	35.3	35.7	35.8	36.5	37.2	36.8	37.1	38.6	39.4	36.5
2005	36.8	36.3	36.4	36.7	36.9	37.1	36.8	36.8	36.5	36.7	37.8	38.5	36.9
2006	36.4	35.8	36.0	36.5	36.9	37.0	36.9	36.7	36.5	37.1	38.3	39.0	36.9
2007	37.0	36.4	36.3	36.4	36.9	37.3	37.0	36.7	36.4	36.6	37.4	38.0	36.9

Employment by Industry: Des Moines-West Des Moines, IA, 2000–2007—*Continued*

(Numbers in thousands, not seasonally adjusted.)

Industry and year	January	February	March	April	May	June	July	August	September	October	November	December	Annual Average
Transportation and Utilities													
2000	10.6	10.6	10.5	10.7	10.6	10.7	10.8	10.8	10.8	11.2	11.2	11.1	10.8
2001	10.7	10.6	10.6	10.8	10.8	10.9	10.8	10.9	10.8	10.8	10.8	10.8	10.8
2002	10.4	10.2	10.2	10.4	10.4	10.5	10.7	10.7	10.6	10.7	10.7	10.6	10.5
2003	10.4	10.2	10.2	10.3	10.4	10.4	10.5	10.5	10.4	10.5	10.5	10.4	10.4
2004	10.3	10.3	10.3	10.4	10.3	10.4	10.4	10.3	10.1	10.1	10.0	9.8	10.2
2005	9.7	9.7	9.9	9.9	9.9	10.0	10.0	10.1	10.2	10.2	10.4	10.5	10.0
2006	10.1	10.1	10.2	10.4	10.4	10.5	10.5	10.6	10.6	10.6	10.7	10.8	10.5
2007	10.4	10.3	10.4	10.5	10.6	10.7	10.6	10.7	10.6	10.7	10.7	10.7	10.6
Information													
2000	10.4	10.3	10.4	10.3	10.4	10.5	10.5	10.4	10.5	10.6	10.6	10.7	10.5
2001	10.6	10.6	10.5	10.3	10.3	10.3	10.2	10.2	10.1	10.2	10.0	9.8	10.3
2002	9.9	9.8	9.7	9.5	9.5	9.6	9.5	9.5	9.5	9.5	9.6	9.5	9.6
2003	9.3	9.3	9.3	9.2	9.3	9.4	9.3	9.3	9.2	9.2	9.3	9.3	9.3
2004	9.2	9.2	9.2	9.2	9.1	9.2	9.2	9.2	9.3	9.1	9.1	9.1	9.2
2005	9.0	9.0	9.1	9.1	9.1	9.2	9.2	9.0	8.9	8.9	8.9	9.0	9.0
2006	8.9	8.9	8.9	8.9	9.0	9.1	9.2	9.3	9.2	9.3	9.4	9.5	9.1
2007	9.4	9.5	9.5	9.7	9.7	9.8	9.7	9.6	9.5	9.5	9.5	9.6	9.6
Financial Activities													
2000	41.4	41.3	41.4	41.4	41.5	41.9	41.9	41.8	41.7	41.6	41.7	42.0	41.6
2001	42.6	42.5	42.8	43.1	43.2	44.1	43.8	43.6	43.6	43.7	44.1	44.4	43.5
2002	44.3	44.5	44.5	44.7	44.5	44.9	45.1	44.9	44.5	44.4	44.2	44.2	44.6
2003	44.4	44.5	44.6	44.6	44.9	45.3	45.4	45.5	45.4	45.7	46.0	45.9	45.2
2004	45.8	46.0	46.0	46.6	46.7	47.0	47.5	47.5	47.1	47.1	47.0	47.2	46.8
2005	46.8	47.0	47.0	46.9	47.1	47.6	47.6	47.7	47.7	47.7	48.0	48.3	47.5
2006	48.3	48.4	48.8	49.0	49.1	49.7	49.7	49.6	49.7	49.8	49.7	50.1	49.3
2007	50.4	50.6	50.8	50.9	51.1	51.7	52.0	51.8	51.6	51.5	51.1	51.5	51.3
Professional and Business Services													
2000	29.1	29.1	29.7	29.5	29.7	30.1	30.5	30.4	30.3	31.4	31.4	31.1	30.2
2001	30.7	30.7	30.7	31.2	31.6	31.9	31.1	31.3	31.1	31.1	30.8	30.8	31.1
2002	29.8	29.5	29.9	30.4	30.4	30.8	30.7	31.0	31.0	30.7	30.8	30.6	30.5
2003	29.8	29.7	29.9	30.5	30.5	31.2	31.3	31.9	31.8	31.6	31.4	31.4	30.9
2004	29.9	29.9	30.4	31.2	31.1	31.8	32.3	32.1	32.1	32.8	33.2	33.1	31.7
2005	31.3	31.4	32.1	32.7	32.9	33.8	33.8	33.9	33.7	34.4	34.3	34.2	33.2
2006	33.3	33.4	33.8	34.5	34.8	35.6	35.7	36.1	36.0	36.7	36.9	36.5	35.3
2007	35.5	36.0	36.1	37.4	37.2	38.1	37.8	38.1	37.8	37.8	38.2	37.9	37.3
Education and Health Services													
2000	34.7	35.0	35.2	34.9	35.0	34.9	33.4	33.7	34.1	33.7	34.9	35.0	34.5
2001	33.8	34.3	34.8	35.1	35.1	35.2	33.3	33.5	34.1	34.1	35.4	35.5	34.5
2002	34.9	35.0	35.2	35.4	35.6	35.4	33.8	34.1	34.9	34.8	36.1	36.1	35.1
2003	35.0	34.8	34.8	35.0	35.0	34.9	33.2	33.1	34.0	34.8	34.9	34.9	34.5
2004	34.5	34.6	34.7	35.4	35.3	34.5	33.5	33.5	34.3	34.8	34.9	34.9	34.6
2005	34.6	34.9	35.2	36.4	36.6	35.9	35.0	35.0	35.9	36.0	36.1	36.4	35.7
2006	36.8	37.2	37.4	37.7	37.6	37.1	36.0	36.1	37.0	38.3	38.5	38.7	37.4
2007	38.1	38.6	38.7	38.8	38.8	38.3	37.1	37.3	38.0	38.6	38.7	38.9	38.3
Leisure and Hospitality													
2000	22.8	22.5	23.4	23.5	24.6	26.2	26.2	26.9	25.2	24.0	23.3	23.2	24.3
2001	22.5	22.5	23.1	24.0	25.7	26.8	26.4	27.1	25.2	24.0	23.6	23.6	24.5
2002	22.6	22.7	23.2	24.4	26.0	26.7	26.6	27.2	25.7	24.5	24.1	24.3	24.8
2003	23.5	23.4	23.6	24.9	26.1	27.1	27.1	27.7	26.3	25.1	24.5	24.7	25.3
2004	23.8	23.7	24.4	25.6	27.0	27.9	28.0	29.4	27.8	26.1	26.0	26.2	26.3
2005	25.3	25.6	26.3	27.5	28.6	29.4	29.6	29.8	28.4	27.6	27.0	27.0	27.7
2006	26.4	26.7	27.3	28.3	29.8	30.7	30.8	31.4	29.7	29.3	28.7	29.0	29.0
2007	27.6	27.9	28.4	29.4	31.3	31.9	31.6	31.9	30.4	29.8	29.1	29.2	29.9
Other Services													
2000	11.2	11.2	11.2	11.3	11.4	11.5	11.5	11.4	11.3	11.4	11.5	11.4	11.4
2001	11.2	11.2	11.3	11.4	11.4	11.7	11.5	11.4	11.4	11.4	11.5	11.6	11.4
2002	11.6	11.7	11.8	11.8	12.0	12.3	12.3	12.3	12.0	12.2	12.2	12.0	12.0
2003	11.5	11.6	11.7	11.7	11.8	11.9	11.9	11.9	11.9	11.8	11.9	12.0	11.8
2004	12.0	11.7	11.8	11.8	11.9	12.1	12.2	12.2	12.2	12.3	12.1	11.9	12.0
2005	11.8	11.9	11.9	12.0	12.0	12.2	12.2	12.1	12.1	12.0	12.0	12.0	12.0
2006	12.1	12.0	12.1	12.2	12.3	12.4	12.4	12.4	12.5	12.5	12.7	12.6	12.4
2007	12.5	12.5	12.6	12.7	12.9	13.0	12.9	12.8	12.8	12.8	12.8	12.8	12.8
Government													
2000	37.1	37.5	37.9	37.6	38.3	38.3	36.3	36.0	36.8	37.8	38.1	38.5	37.5
2001	38.6	38.9	39.1	39.0	39.2	39.6	37.2	36.9	38.3	39.2	39.4	39.0	38.7
2002	38.8	39.0	39.0	39.2	39.3	39.3	36.5	36.3	37.5	38.5	38.5	38.9	38.4
2003	38.3	38.7	39.0	38.5	38.9	39.0	36.2	36.1	37.8	39.3	39.4	39.5	38.4
2004	38.4	39.1	39.2	38.9	39.1	39.2	36.1	35.8	37.3	38.6	38.9	38.8	38.3
2005	38.2	38.7	39.1	38.9	39.4	39.4	36.1	35.8	38.0	39.1	39.2	39.5	38.5
2006	39.0	39.6	39.6	39.9	40.1	40.8	36.9	36.8	38.9	40.0	40.2	40.5	39.4
2007	40.8	40.9	40.9	41.0	41.5	41.8	38.1	38.5	41.1	42.1	42.2	42.6	41.0

Employment by Industry: Chattanooga, TN-GA, 2000–2007

(Numbers in thousands, not seasonally adjusted.)

Industry and year	January	February	March	April	May	June	July	August	September	October	November	December	Annual Average
Total Nonfarm													
2000	232.0	234.8	238.0	238.1	238.7	238.3	236.8	237.7	241.8	240.9	242.4	241.7	238.4
2001	235.2	235.8	236.9	238.1	238.5	235.6	233.6	233.7	236.0	236.5	237.4	237.1	236.2
2002	231.9	233.5	233.6	234.9	234.1	234.8	233.8	234.8	236.6	238.2	238.8	239.5	235.4
2003	234.2	234.8	235.7	235.6	234.9	232.7	232.0	234.8	236.6	237.1	238.9	239.6	235.6
2004	233.8	235.6	236.8	238.4	238.1	236.2	236.0	238.4	239.2	238.9	240.3	242.5	237.9
2005	236.1	237.4	239.6	241.2	240.9	239.1	238.4	241.8	243.2	242.5	244.2	245.3	240.8
2006	238.1	239.9	243.0	245.2	245.5	244.7	244.0	247.2	249.0	248.9	249.9	250.5	245.5
2007	243.8	245.1	247.1	247.2	247.4	247.0	246.6	247.9	248.9	249.8	250.4	250.4	247.6
Total Private													
2000	198.6	201.1	203.8	204.2	204.7	206.5	205.4	206.1	207.8	206.4	207.6	206.6	204.9
2001	200.8	200.9	201.9	203.4	204.1	203.0	201.2	200.9	200.5	200.9	201.3	201.3	201.7
2002	196.7	197.5	197.6	199.1	199.1	199.6	199.4	199.6	200.3	201.9	202.3	202.9	199.7
2003	198.4	198.7	199.6	199.1	199.2	200.2	199.9	200.9	200.6	201.6	202.9	203.2	200.4
2004	198.4	198.8	200.8	202.2	202.6	204.0	204.1	203.5	203.5	204.1	204.9	206.8	202.8
2005	202.0	202.5	204.2	206.2	206.3	207.5	206.6	207.8	208.3	208.3	209.6	210.4	206.6
2006	204.6	205.7	208.3	210.6	211.1	212.4	211.7	213.0	213.7	214.2	215.2	216.0	211.4
2007	210.3	210.4	211.9	212.2	212.6	213.4	213.0	213.2	213.4	214.4	215.2	215.3	212.9
Goods-Producing													
2000	53.7	54.0	54.8	54.4	54.8	55.6	55.5	55.6	56.1	55.0	55.0	54.2	54.9
2001	52.0	51.6	51.6	51.6	51.6	51.3	50.6	50.4	50.1	50.0	49.6	48.9	50.8
2002	48.0	48.0	47.4	47.4	47.4	47.6	46.9	47.0	46.9	46.9	46.2	46.1	47.2
2003	45.3	45.5	45.4	44.9	44.9	45.2	45.6	45.7	45.7	45.3	45.4	45.1	45.3
2004	43.7	43.6	44.1	44.3	44.3	44.8	45.2	44.8	44.7	44.9	44.9	45.0	44.5
2005	45.3	45.4	46.2	46.0	45.9	46.1	45.0	45.7	45.9	45.9	46.4	46.7	45.9
2006	45.9	46.0	46.5	47.0	47.1	47.3	47.0	47.2	47.4	47.2	47.2	47.3	46.9
2007	45.7	45.4	46.0	45.0	44.9	45.4	45.4	45.7	45.4	45.7	45.7	45.8	45.5
Natural Resources, Mining, and Construction													
2000	9.6	9.9	10.5	9.7	10.0	10.3	10.4	10.6	11.2	10.6	10.7	10.1	10.3
2001	9.4	9.3	9.5	9.6	9.8	9.9	9.9	9.7	9.5	9.9	10.0	9.4	9.7
2002	8.8	8.7	8.8	8.8	8.9	9.0	8.8	8.9	8.9	9.0	8.9	8.8	8.9
2003	8.8	8.7	8.9	8.7	8.7	9.0	9.4	9.5	9.5	9.4	9.4	9.3	9.1
2004	8.7	8.6	8.8	9.2	9.3	9.6	9.8	9.8	9.8	10.1	10.0	10.1	9.5
2005	10.4	10.3	10.4	10.6	10.8	10.9	10.1	10.4	10.4	10.9	11.2	11.4	10.7
2006	11.0	11.0	11.3	11.4	11.6	11.7	11.4	11.5	11.6	11.7	11.6	11.8	11.5
2007	10.6	10.3	10.7	10.6	10.6	11.1	10.9	11.0	11.1	11.2	11.1	11.1	10.9
Manufacturing													
2000	44.1	44.1	44.3	44.7	44.8	45.3	45.1	45.0	44.9	44.4	44.3	44.1	44.6
2001	42.6	42.3	42.1	42.0	41.8	41.4	40.7	40.7	40.6	40.1	39.6	39.5	41.1
2002	39.2	39.3	38.6	38.6	38.5	38.6	38.1	38.1	38.0	37.9	37.3	37.3	38.3
2003	36.5	36.8	36.5	36.2	36.2	36.2	36.2	36.2	36.2	35.9	36.0	35.8	36.2
2004	35.0	35.0	35.3	35.1	35.0	35.2	35.4	35.0	34.9	34.8	34.9	34.9	35.0
2005	34.9	35.1	35.8	35.4	35.1	35.2	34.9	35.3	35.5	35.0	35.2	35.3	35.2
2006	34.9	35.0	35.2	35.6	35.5	35.6	35.6	35.7	35.8	35.5	35.6	35.5	35.5
2007	35.1	35.1	35.3	34.4	34.3	34.3	34.5	34.7	34.3	34.5	34.6	34.7	34.7
Service-Providing													
2000	178.3	180.8	183.2	183.7	183.9	182.7	181.3	182.1	185.7	185.9	187.4	187.5	183.5
2001	183.2	184.2	185.3	186.5	186.9	184.3	183.0	183.3	185.9	186.5	187.8	188.2	185.4
2002	183.9	185.5	186.2	187.5	186.7	187.2	186.9	187.8	189.7	191.3	192.6	193.4	188.2
2003	188.9	189.3	190.3	190.7	190.0	187.5	186.4	189.1	190.9	191.8	193.5	194.5	190.2
2004	190.1	192.0	192.7	194.1	193.8	191.4	190.8	193.6	194.5	194.0	195.4	197.5	193.3
2005	190.8	192.0	193.4	195.2	195.0	193.0	193.4	196.1	197.3	196.6	197.8	198.6	194.9
2006	192.2	193.9	196.5	198.2	198.4	197.4	197.0	200.0	201.6	201.7	202.7	203.2	198.6
2007	198.1	199.7	201.1	202.2	202.5	201.6	201.2	202.2	203.5	204.1	204.7	204.6	202.1
Trade, Transportation, and Utilities													
2000	54.6	55.2	55.4	55.7	56.1	55.6	55.6	55.7	56.1	56.6	57.6	57.7	56.0
2001	54.9	54.4	54.9	55.5	56.0	55.8	54.9	54.9	54.7	55.7	56.2	56.6	55.4
2002	54.8	54.7	54.7	55.0	54.9	54.8	55.0	55.1	55.0	55.8	56.5	57.2	55.3
2003	54.3	54.1	54.3	54.6	54.6	54.5	54.3	54.6	54.5	55.1	55.5	55.7	54.7
2004	54.2	53.9	54.6	54.5	54.7	55.0	55.0	55.2	55.1	55.7	56.5	58.3	55.2
2005	54.7	54.7	55.0	56.0	55.9	56.0	56.7	56.7	56.1	56.6	57.5	58.0	56.2
2006	55.1	54.9	55.5	55.7	55.8	56.0	55.8	56.1	56.2	56.5	57.6	58.0	56.1
2007	56.4	55.9	56.0	56.6	56.4	56.3	56.1	55.9	55.8	56.5	57.5	57.9	56.4
Wholesale Trade													
2000	8.8	8.8	8.9	8.8	8.8	8.8	8.8	8.8	8.9	8.9	9.1	9.2	8.9
2001	8.4	8.4	8.3	8.3	8.2	8.3	8.2	8.3	8.3	8.4	8.4	8.4	8.3
2002	8.3	8.2	8.1	8.2	8.2	8.2	8.3	8.3	8.4	8.5	8.5	8.7	8.3
2003	9.0	9.1	9.0	8.9	9.0	9.0	9.0	9.0	8.9	9.0	9.0	9.0	9.0
2004	9.0	9.0	9.0	9.0	9.0	9.0	9.1	9.1	9.0	9.1	9.1	9.2	9.1
2005	8.9	8.8	8.8	8.8	8.8	8.8	8.8	8.8	8.8	8.7	8.8	8.8	8.8
2006	8.8	8.8	8.8	8.8	8.8	8.8	8.9	8.9	8.9	8.8	8.8	8.8	8.8
2007	8.5	8.6	8.6	8.7	8.7	8.7	8.7	8.6	8.6	8.7	8.8	8.8	8.7
Retail Trade													
2000	26.2	26.2	26.1	26.2	26.4	26.2	26.3	26.1	26.7	27.0	27.8	28.0	26.6
2001	26.8	26.4	26.6	26.7	26.8	26.8	26.4	26.4	26.5	27.0	27.8	28.2	26.9
2002	26.7	26.6	26.8	26.7	26.6	26.6	26.8	26.7	26.6	26.8	27.4	27.8	26.8
2003	25.3	25.2	25.3	25.6	25.5	25.5	25.5	25.7	25.8	25.9	26.4	26.8	25.7
2004	25.2	25.1	25.4	25.4	25.7	25.8	25.4	25.6	25.6	25.9	26.8	27.2	25.8
2005	25.8	25.8	25.9	26.5	26.5	26.7	27.0	27.0	26.7	27.1	28.0	28.6	26.8
2006	26.3	26.2	26.3	26.6	26.5	26.3	26.2	26.4	26.4	26.8	27.9	28.4	26.7
2007	27.2	26.8	26.8	27.0	26.8	26.6	26.5	26.5	26.3	26.8	27.8	28.3	27.0

Employment by Industry: Chattanooga, TN-GA, 2000–2007—*Continued*

(Numbers in thousands, not seasonally adjusted.)

Industry and year	January	February	March	April	May	June	July	August	September	October	November	December	Annual Average
Transportation and Utilities													
2000	19.6	20.2	20.4	20.7	20.9	20.6	20.5	20.8	20.5	20.7	20.7	20.5	20.5
2001	19.7	19.6	20.0	20.5	21.0	20.7	20.3	20.2	19.9	20.3	20.0	20.0	20.2
2002	19.8	19.9	19.8	20.1	20.1	20.0	19.9	20.1	20.0	20.5	20.6	20.7	20.1
2003	20.0	19.8	20.0	20.1	20.1	20.0	19.8	19.9	19.8	20.2	20.1	19.9	20.0
2004	20.0	19.8	20.2	20.1	20.0	20.2	20.5	20.5	20.5	20.7	20.6	21.9	20.4
2005	20.0	20.1	20.3	20.7	20.6	20.5	20.9	20.9	20.6	20.8	20.7	20.6	20.6
2006	20.0	19.9	20.4	20.3	20.5	20.9	20.7	20.8	20.9	20.9	20.9	20.8	20.6
2007	20.7	20.5	20.6	20.9	20.9	21.0	20.9	20.8	20.9	21.0	20.9	20.8	20.8
Information													
2000	3.0	3.0	3.0	3.0	3.0	3.1	3.0	3.0	3.0	2.9	3.0	3.1	3.0
2001	2.9	2.9	2.8	2.7	2.7	2.7	2.7	2.7	2.7	2.7	2.6	2.6	2.7
2002	2.6	2.6	2.6	2.6	2.6	2.7	2.7	2.7	2.7	2.7	2.8	2.8	2.7
2003	2.7	2.7	2.7	2.7	2.8	2.8	3.0	3.0	2.9	3.0	3.0	3.0	2.9
2004	2.8	2.8	2.8	2.8	2.8	2.8	2.7	2.6	2.6	2.6	2.6	2.7	2.7
2005	2.7	2.7	2.7	2.7	2.7	2.9	2.7	2.8	2.8	2.8	2.9	2.9	2.8
2006	2.8	2.9	2.9	3.2	3.3	3.3	3.3	3.4	3.5	3.7	3.6	3.6	3.3
2007	3.7	3.8	3.9	3.9	3.9	3.9	3.9	3.9	3.8	3.9	3.9	3.8	3.9
Financial Activities													
2000	17.2	17.4	17.5	17.4	17.4	17.6	17.0	17.0	17.1	17.1	17.2	17.4	17.3
2001	17.3	17.4	17.6	17.8	17.8	17.9	17.8	17.9	17.8	17.8	18.0	18.0	17.8
2002	18.0	18.1	18.2	18.3	18.3	18.3	18.1	18.1	18.2	18.3	18.5	18.6	18.3
2003	18.2	18.1	18.2	17.8	17.8	17.8	17.8	17.9	17.8	17.9	18.5	18.8	18.1
2004	18.7	18.7	18.8	18.6	18.6	18.7	18.7	18.6	18.7	18.8	18.7	18.8	18.7
2005	18.6	18.6	18.6	18.5	18.7	18.9	18.9	18.8	18.8	19.0	19.0	19.1	18.8
2006	18.8	18.8	18.9	18.5	18.5	18.5	18.5	18.6	18.5	18.6	18.6	18.6	18.6
2007	18.6	18.6	18.6	18.5	18.5	18.7	18.6	18.6	18.7	18.6	18.7	18.5	18.6
Professional and Business Services													
2000	22.2	22.8	23.1	23.1	23.0	23.3	22.5	23.1	23.3	23.1	22.8	22.0	22.9
2001	24.6	24.7	24.9	25.0	25.0	24.4	24.3	23.9	23.8	24.2	24.2	24.6	24.5
2002	23.4	23.7	24.1	24.3	24.3	24.3	24.9	24.9	25.2	25.7	25.7	25.7	24.7
2003	25.5	25.6	25.7	25.0	25.0	25.2	25.3	25.6	25.5	25.9	26.0	26.0	25.5
2004	25.0	25.2	25.4	25.8	25.9	26.0	26.1	26.0	25.5	25.7	25.8	25.6	25.7
2005	25.1	25.1	25.5	25.6	25.4	25.5	25.7	25.9	26.2	26.1	25.9	25.8	25.7
2006	25.7	25.8	26.1	26.2	25.9	26.2	25.9	26.2	26.4	26.5	26.5	26.2	26.1
2007	24.3	24.4	24.6	25.0	25.5	25.3	25.1	25.4	25.5	25.7	25.8	25.8	25.2
Education and Health Services													
2000	19.7	20.2	20.4	20.4	19.9	20.1	20.1	20.2	21.0	21.2	21.4	21.5	20.5
2001	21.3	21.8	21.6	21.5	21.4	21.2	20.9	21.2	21.8	21.9	22.0	21.9	21.5
2002	21.8	21.9	21.8	22.0	21.7	21.7	21.7	21.8	22.5	22.8	22.9	22.9	22.1
2003	23.0	23.3	23.3	23.5	23.2	23.1	22.7	22.8	23.4	23.8	23.9	24.0	23.3
2004	23.8	24.1	24.2	24.4	24.1	23.9	23.9	23.9	24.5	24.8	24.9	24.9	24.3
2005	24.5	24.7	24.5	24.8	24.3	24.2	24.4	24.6	25.4	25.4	25.6	25.6	24.8
2006	24.8	25.4	25.6	26.1	26.4	26.2	26.4	26.8	27.7	28.1	28.5	29.0	26.8
2007	28.9	29.2	29.1	29.1	28.6	28.5	28.7	28.8	29.6	29.8	29.6	29.6	29.1
Leisure and Hospitality													
2000	18.1	18.0	18.5	19.2	19.4	19.9	20.4	20.3	20.0	19.3	19.1	19.1	19.3
2001	17.3	17.6	17.9	18.7	19.0	19.0	19.1	19.1	18.9	18.0	18.1	18.1	18.4
2002	17.6	17.9	18.2	18.8	19.1	19.2	19.2	19.3	19.1	18.9	18.9	18.8	18.8
2003	18.8	18.8	19.4	20.0	20.2	20.7	20.3	20.4	20.0	19.9	19.9	19.9	19.9
2004	19.6	19.9	20.4	21.2	21.6	22.0	21.7	21.8	21.7	20.9	20.9	20.9	21.1
2005	20.6	20.7	21.1	21.9	22.7	23.1	22.4	22.5	22.4	21.8	21.6	21.6	21.9
2006	20.9	21.2	22.0	23.2	23.4	23.9	23.9	23.8	23.2	22.9	22.5	22.6	22.8
2007	22.1	22.3	22.7	23.2	23.8	24.1	24.1	24.0	23.5	23.3	23.1	23.1	23.3
Other Services													
2000	10.1	10.5	11.1	11.0	11.1	11.3	11.3	11.2	11.2	11.2	11.5	11.6	11.1
2001	10.5	10.5	10.6	10.6	10.6	10.7	10.9	10.8	10.7	10.6	10.6	10.6	10.6
2002	10.5	10.6	10.6	10.7	10.8	11.0	10.9	10.7	10.7	10.8	10.8	10.8	10.7
2003	10.6	10.6	10.6	10.6	10.7	10.9	10.9	10.9	10.8	10.7	10.7	10.7	10.7
2004	10.6	10.6	10.5	10.6	10.6	10.8	10.8	10.6	10.7	10.7	10.6	10.6	10.6
2005	10.5	10.6	10.6	10.7	10.7	10.8	10.8	10.8	10.7	10.7	10.7	10.7	10.7
2006	10.6	10.7	10.8	10.7	10.7	11.0	10.9	10.9	10.8	10.7	10.7	10.7	10.8
2007	10.6	10.8	11.0	10.9	11.0	11.2	11.1	11.0	11.0	10.9	10.9	10.8	10.9
Government													
2000	33.4	33.7	34.2	33.9	34.0	31.8	31.4	31.6	34.0	34.5	34.8	35.1	33.5
2001	34.4	34.9	35.0	34.7	34.4	32.6	32.4	32.8	35.5	35.6	36.1	35.8	34.5
2002	35.2	36.0	36.0	35.8	35.0	35.2	34.4	35.2	36.3	36.3	36.5	36.6	35.7
2003	35.8	36.1	36.1	36.5	35.7	32.5	32.1	33.9	36.0	35.5	36.0	36.4	35.2
2004	35.4	36.8	36.0	36.2	35.5	32.2	31.9	34.9	35.7	34.8	35.4	35.7	35.0
2005	34.1	34.9	35.4	35.0	34.6	31.6	31.8	34.0	34.9	34.2	34.6	34.9	34.2
2006	33.5	34.2	34.7	34.6	34.4	32.3	32.3	34.2	35.3	34.7	34.7	34.5	34.1
2007	33.5	34.7	35.2	35.0	34.8	33.6	33.6	34.7	35.5	35.4	35.2	35.1	34.7

Employment by Industry: Palm Bay-Melbourne-Titusville, FL, 2000–2007

(Numbers in thousands, not seasonally adjusted.)

Industry and year	January	February	March	April	May	June	July	August	September	October	November	December	Annual Average
Total Nonfarm													
2000	186.9	188.0	190.4	189.9	191.2	190.9	189.9	192.7	193.4	193.1	195.4	196.6	191.5
2001	191.6	193.0	194.4	193.8	194.7	192.9	191.5	194.2	192.7	192.6	193.5	194.3	193.3
2002	190.6	191.6	192.5	192.7	193.3	192.1	189.8	192.4	192.6	192.4	194.2	195.8	192.5
2003	193.2	193.9	194.5	194.8	195.4	194.1	195.3	197.7	198.3	198.6	200.3	202.8	196.6
2004	201.7	203.3	204.8	206.1	206.4	205.9	205.2	206.7	203.8	204.4	206.7	208.6	205.3
2005	207.9	209.1	210.1	211.5	211.7	211.4	211.5	213.6	214.7	214.6	215.7	217.5	212.4
2006	214.9	216.7	218.4	218.0	218.6	217.2	214.1	216.2	215.2	213.5	214.6	216.1	216.1
2007	212.5	213.1	214.1	213.7	213.3	211.8	210.2	212.1	210.9	211.3	212.8	213.4	212.4
Total Private													
2000	161.4	162.3	164.6	163.6	164.4	165.9	165.3	166.8	167.1	166.7	168.8	169.9	165.6
2001	165.1	166.2	167.5	167.0	167.6	167.1	166.2	167.4	165.6	165.6	166.3	167.1	166.6
2002	163.5	164.4	165.2	165.2	165.7	165.8	164.0	165.1	164.9	164.8	166.6	168.1	165.3
2003	165.7	166.4	166.9	166.9	167.3	167.4	168.8	169.6	170.0	170.1	171.6	173.9	168.7
2004	172.7	174.2	175.6	176.8	177.1	178.0	177.7	177.5	174.8	175.5	178.0	180.0	176.5
2005	179.5	180.6	181.7	183.0	183.2	184.2	184.7	185.4	186.0	185.9	187.0	188.8	184.2
2006	186.3	188.1	189.6	188.9	189.4	189.3	186.7	187.3	186.1	184.4	185.4	187.0	187.4
2007	183.4	184.0	184.8	184.2	183.8	183.6	182.4	182.8	181.4	181.8	183.2	183.8	183.3
Goods-Producing													
2000	36.7	37.0	37.3	36.6	37.0	37.7	37.7	37.5	37.7	37.5	37.6	37.7	37.3
2001	36.9	37.1	36.9	36.7	36.8	37.1	37.3	37.5	37.4	36.8	36.5	36.6	37.0
2002	35.8	36.2	36.2	36.1	35.9	35.8	35.3	35.4	35.3	35.1	35.2	35.3	35.6
2003	35.1	35.1	35.1	35.2	35.4	35.8	36.2	36.2	36.5	36.1	36.3	36.8	35.8
2004	36.8	37.3	37.7	38.0	38.2	38.9	39.2	39.2	38.9	38.6	39.1	39.5	38.5
2005	40.0	40.1	40.3	40.7	40.9	41.4	41.6	41.5	41.7	41.6	41.7	42.2	41.1
2006	42.1	42.9	43.0	43.2	43.5	43.7	43.2	43.1	42.7	41.8	41.2	41.3	42.6
2007	39.9	39.9	39.6	39.2	39.2	39.6	39.0	38.9	38.5	38.2	37.9	38.0	39.0
Natural Resources, Mining, and Construction													
2000	11.8	12.0	12.1	12.2	12.5	12.9	12.7	12.7	12.8	12.8	12.8	12.9	12.5
2001	12.6	12.9	13.0	12.8	12.9	13.1	13.3	13.6	13.5	13.4	13.3	13.4	13.2
2002	13.0	13.3	13.2	13.0	12.9	12.7	12.4	12.5	12.4	12.4	12.5	12.6	12.7
2003	12.5	12.5	12.5	12.6	12.7	13.0	13.2	13.3	13.5	13.4	13.5	13.8	13.0
2004	14.0	14.5	14.7	14.7	14.7	15.0	15.0	14.9	14.6	14.9	15.3	15.5	14.8
2005	16.0	16.1	16.3	16.7	16.9	17.3	17.7	17.8	18.0	17.7	17.9	18.2	17.2
2006	18.0	18.4	18.5	18.6	18.8	18.8	18.5	18.3	18.0	17.3	16.9	16.8	18.1
2007	15.9	15.9	15.8	15.4	15.4	15.6	15.1	15.0	14.8	14.7	14.5	14.5	15.2
Manufacturing													
2000	24.9	25.0	25.2	24.4	24.5	24.8	25.0	24.8	24.9	24.7	24.8	24.8	24.8
2001	24.3	24.2	23.9	23.9	23.9	24.0	24.0	23.9	23.9	23.4	23.2	23.2	23.8
2002	22.8	22.9	23.0	23.1	23.0	23.1	22.9	22.9	22.9	22.7	22.7	22.7	22.9
2003	22.6	22.6	22.6	22.6	22.7	22.8	23.0	22.9	23.0	22.7	22.8	23.0	22.7
2004	22.8	22.8	23.0	23.3	23.5	23.9	24.2	24.3	24.3	23.7	23.8	24.0	23.6
2005	24.0	24.0	24.0	24.0	24.0	24.1	23.9	23.7	23.7	23.9	23.8	24.0	23.9
2006	24.1	24.5	24.5	24.6	24.7	24.9	24.7	24.8	24.7	24.5	24.3	24.5	24.6
2007	24.0	24.0	23.8	23.8	23.8	24.0	23.9	23.9	23.7	23.5	23.4	23.5	23.8
Service-Providing													
2000	150.2	151.0	153.1	153.3	154.2	153.2	152.2	155.2	155.7	155.6	157.8	158.9	154.2
2001	154.7	155.9	157.5	157.1	157.9	155.8	154.2	156.7	155.3	155.8	157.0	157.7	156.3
2002	154.8	155.4	156.3	156.6	157.4	156.3	154.5	157.0	157.3	157.3	159.0	160.5	156.9
2003	158.1	158.8	159.4	159.6	160.0	158.3	159.1	161.5	161.8	162.5	164.0	166.0	160.8
2004	164.9	166.0	167.1	168.1	168.2	167.0	166.0	167.5	164.9	165.8	167.6	169.1	166.9
2005	167.9	169.0	169.8	170.8	170.8	170.0	169.9	172.1	173.0	173.0	174.0	175.3	171.3
2006	172.8	173.8	175.4	174.8	175.1	173.5	170.9	173.1	172.5	171.7	173.4	174.8	173.5
2007	172.6	173.2	174.5	174.5	174.1	172.2	171.2	173.2	172.4	173.1	174.9	175.4	173.4
Trade, Transportation, and Utilities													
2000	33.7	33.7	34.0	33.5	33.7	34.0	33.5	34.2	33.8	33.9	35.1	35.7	34.1
2001	34.3	34.1	34.5	34.5	34.6	34.4	34.5	34.9	34.5	35.1	35.7	36.2	34.8
2002	34.8	34.5	34.7	34.4	34.8	34.7	34.3	34.6	34.9	34.5	35.0	35.7	34.7
2003	34.1	33.8	33.8	33.8	33.9	33.7	33.7	34.1	34.0	34.6	35.0	35.7	34.1
2004	34.7	34.8	35.0	35.3	35.7	35.6	35.3	35.1	34.9	35.4	36.4	37.3	35.5
2005	36.4	36.4	36.5	36.6	36.8	36.8	37.3	37.3	37.2	37.3	37.8	38.4	37.1
2006	37.3	37.3	37.8	37.6	37.6	37.5	37.1	37.2	36.8	36.7	37.7	38.5	37.4
2007	36.9	36.6	36.9	36.9	36.9	36.8	36.5	36.6	36.2	36.5	37.5	37.8	36.8
Wholesale Trade													
2000	5.0	4.9	5.0	4.9	5.0	5.2	5.1	5.2	5.2	4.9	4.9	4.9	5.0
2001	4.9	4.9	5.0	4.9	4.9	5.0	5.0	5.0	5.0	5.0	5.0	5.0	5.0
2002	4.9	4.9	4.9	4.7	4.9	4.9	4.9	4.9	4.9	4.7	4.7	4.7	4.8
2003	4.6	4.5	4.5	4.5	4.5	4.5	4.5	4.6	4.7	4.6	4.6	4.6	4.5
2004	4.5	4.6	4.6	4.6	4.7	4.6	4.7	4.7	4.7	4.7	4.8	4.9	4.7
2005	5.1	5.1	5.1	5.2	5.2	5.3	5.2	5.2	5.2	5.2	5.2	5.2	5.2
2006	5.3	5.3	5.4	5.5	5.5	5.6	5.6	5.6	5.5	5.6	5.6	5.7	5.5
2007	5.5	5.6	5.5	5.6	5.6	5.6	5.6	5.6	5.5	5.5	5.6	5.6	5.6
Retail Trade													
2000	26.0	26.0	26.2	25.8	25.9	26.1	25.7	26.3	25.9	26.0	27.2	27.8	26.2
2001	26.6	26.4	26.6	26.6	26.7	26.4	26.5	26.9	26.5	26.8	27.4	27.8	26.8
2002	26.6	26.3	26.5	26.4	26.6	26.4	26.1	26.4	26.7	26.5	27.0	27.6	26.6
2003	26.3	26.1	26.1	26.0	26.1	26.0	25.9	26.2	26.0	26.6	27.1	27.7	26.3
2004	26.7	26.7	26.8	27.0	27.3	27.2	27.0	26.8	26.6	27.1	28.0	28.7	27.2
2005	27.6	27.5	27.6	27.5	27.6	27.6	28.2	28.3	28.2	28.3	28.8	29.3	28.0
2006	28.4	28.4	28.8	28.5	28.4	28.2	28.0	28.0	27.8	27.6	28.5	29.0	28.3
2007	28.1	27.7	28.1	28.0	28.1	27.9	27.7	27.7	27.4	27.7	28.6	28.7	28.0

Employment by Industry: Palm Bay-Melbourne-Titusville, FL, 2000–2007—*Continued*

(Numbers in thousands, not seasonally adjusted.)

Industry and year	January	February	March	April	May	June	July	August	September	October	November	December	Annual Average
Transportation and Utilities													
2000	2.7	2.8	2.8	2.8	2.8	2.7	2.7	2.7	2.7	3.0	3.0	3.0	2.8
2001	2.8	2.8	2.9	3.0	3.0	3.0	3.0	3.0	3.0	3.3	3.3	3.4	3.0
2002	3.3	3.3	3.3	3.3	3.3	3.4	3.3	3.3	3.3	3.3	3.3	3.4	3.3
2003	3.2	3.2	3.2	3.3	3.3	3.2	3.3	3.3	3.3	3.4	3.3	3.4	3.2
2004	3.5	3.5	3.6	3.7	3.7	3.8	3.6	3.6	3.6	3.6	3.6	3.7	3.6
2005	3.7	3.8	3.8	3.9	4.0	3.9	3.9	3.8	3.8	3.8	3.8	3.9	3.8
2006	3.6	3.6	3.6	3.6	3.7	3.7	3.5	3.6	3.5	3.5	3.6	3.8	3.6
2007	3.3	3.3	3.3	3.3	3.2	3.3	3.2	3.3	3.3	3.3	3.3	3.5	3.3
Information													
2000	2.9	2.9	3.0	3.1	3.1	3.1	3.1	3.1	3.1	3.2	3.2	3.2	3.1
2001	3.2	3.2	3.3	3.2	3.2	3.2	3.2	3.1	3.0	3.0	2.9	2.9	3.1
2002	2.7	2.7	2.7	2.7	2.9	2.9	2.8	2.8	2.8	2.8	2.8	2.8	2.8
2003	2.8	2.8	2.8	2.8	2.9	2.9	2.8	2.7	2.7	2.7	2.8	2.7	2.7
2004	2.8	2.8	2.8	2.8	2.8	2.8	2.8	2.8	2.6	2.7	2.7	2.7	2.8
2005	2.6	2.7	2.6	2.6	2.7	2.8	2.8	2.8	3.1	3.5	3.5	3.4	2.9
2006	3.0	3.0	3.0	3.0	3.0	3.0	2.9	2.9	2.9	2.8	2.8	2.8	2.9
2007	2.8	2.8	2.8	2.8	2.9	2.9	2.9	2.9	2.8	2.8	2.8	2.8	2.8
Financial Activities													
2000	6.5	6.6	6.7	6.6	6.6	6.9	6.7	6.7	6.7	6.7	6.7	6.7	6.7
2001	6.7	6.8	6.9	6.9	6.9	7.0	7.1	7.2	7.2	7.3	7.3	7.4	7.1
2002	7.2	7.3	7.3	7.4	7.4	7.5	7.3	7.3	7.3	7.2	7.2	7.2	7.3
2003	7.2	7.1	7.2	7.3	7.3	7.4	7.4	7.4	7.4	7.5	7.5	7.5	7.3
2004	7.4	7.4	7.5	7.7	7.7	7.7	7.8	7.9	7.8	8.1	8.1	8.2	7.8
2005	8.1	8.0	8.0	8.1	8.2	8.3	8.4	8.5	8.6	8.8	8.8	8.8	8.4
2006	8.6	8.7	8.6	8.5	8.6	8.5	8.5	8.6	8.6	8.6	8.6	8.6	8.6
2007	8.6	8.7	8.7	8.7	8.7	8.8	8.7	8.6	8.6	8.6	8.6	8.6	8.7
Professional and Business Services													
2000	32.9	33.0	33.5	33.9	34.0	34.4	35.0	35.5	35.8	35.6	36.0	36.3	34.7
2001	34.7	34.8	34.9	34.7	34.6	34.5	34.0	34.0	33.4	33.3	33.3	33.1	34.1
2002	32.8	32.8	32.7	33.0	32.9	33.2	33.2	33.3	33.3	34.0	34.3	34.7	33.4
2003	34.1	34.5	34.5	34.4	34.2	33.9	34.6	34.8	35.0	35.1	35.3	36.1	34.7
2004	36.3	36.5	36.5	36.9	36.9	37.2	37.4	37.5	37.0	37.2	37.5	37.9	37.1
2005	38.1	38.3	38.4	38.5	38.4	38.5	38.7	38.9	39.0	39.1	39.3	39.5	38.7
2006	38.9	39.2	39.3	39.0	38.7	38.7	38.1	38.0	37.9	37.2	37.6	37.6	38.4
2007	37.6	37.7	37.6	37.7	37.3	37.0	37.2	37.5	37.1	37.4	37.8	37.8	37.5
Education and Health Services													
2000	23.4	23.6	23.9	24.1	24.1	24.0	23.6	23.9	24.0	24.1	24.2	24.3	23.9
2001	23.8	24.1	24.3	24.3	24.3	24.3	24.2	24.6	24.5	24.9	24.9	25.1	24.4
2002	24.7	24.9	25.1	25.2	25.2	25.2	25.1	25.4	25.4	25.4	25.9	26.0	25.3
2003	26.1	26.5	26.5	26.4	26.6	26.7	26.8	26.9	27.1	26.9	27.0	27.2	26.7
2004	26.6	26.7	26.7	26.7	26.9	26.9	26.9	27.0	26.7	26.8	26.9	26.9	26.8
2005	26.6	26.8	27.0	27.2	27.2	27.3	27.3	27.6	27.6	27.5	27.6	27.8	27.3
2006	27.7	27.7	28.0	28.0	28.2	28.1	27.8	28.2	28.4	28.5	28.5	28.7	28.2
2007	28.2	28.6	28.6	28.8	28.6	28.6	28.4	28.6	28.9	29.0	29.1	29.2	28.7
Leisure and Hospitality													
2000	17.8	18.0	18.6	18.3	18.2	18.1	17.9	18.2	18.2	17.9	18.2	18.2	18.1
2001	18.0	18.7	19.1	19.1	19.6	19.0	18.4	18.6	18.1	17.7	18.2	18.3	18.6
2002	18.2	18.6	19.1	19.0	19.1	18.9	18.5	18.6	18.2	18.0	18.3	18.4	18.6
2003	18.2	18.5	18.8	18.9	18.8	18.8	19.1	19.2	18.9	18.9	19.3	19.5	18.9
2004	19.3	19.8	20.4	20.7	20.3	20.3	20.0	19.8	18.9	18.8	19.5	19.8	19.8
2005	19.7	20.2	20.8	21.0	20.8	20.8	20.4	20.6	20.5	20.1	20.3	20.7	20.5
2006	20.6	21.2	21.7	21.6	21.7	21.7	21.2	21.3	20.8	20.7	20.9	21.2	21.2
2007	21.2	21.5	22.3	22.0	22.0	21.8	21.6	21.6	21.1	21.1	21.3	21.4	21.6
Other Services													
2000	7.5	7.5	7.6	7.5	7.7	7.7	7.8	7.7	7.8	7.8	7.8	7.8	7.7
2001	7.5	7.4	7.6	7.6	7.6	7.6	7.5	7.5	7.5	7.5	7.5	7.5	7.5
2002	7.3	7.4	7.4	7.4	7.5	7.6	7.5	7.7	7.7	7.8	7.9	8.0	7.6
2003	8.1	8.1	8.2	8.1	8.2	8.2	8.2	8.3	8.4	8.3	8.4	8.4	8.2
2004	8.8	8.9	9.0	8.7	8.6	8.6	8.3	8.2	8.0	7.9	7.8	7.7	8.4
2005	8.0	8.1	8.1	8.3	8.2	8.3	8.2	8.2	8.3	8.0	8.0	8.0	8.1
2006	8.1	8.1	8.2	8.0	8.1	8.1	7.9	8.0	8.0	8.1	8.1	8.3	8.1
2007	8.2	8.2	8.3	8.1	8.2	8.1	8.1	8.1	8.2	8.2	8.2	8.2	8.2
Government													
2000	25.5	25.7	25.8	26.3	26.8	25.0	24.6	25.9	26.3	26.4	26.6	26.7	26.0
2001	26.5	26.8	26.9	26.8	27.1	25.8	25.3	26.8	27.1	27.0	27.2	27.2	26.7
2002	27.1	27.2	27.3	27.5	27.6	26.3	25.8	27.3	27.7	27.6	27.6	27.7	27.2
2003	27.5	27.5	27.6	27.9	28.1	26.7	26.5	28.1	28.3	28.5	28.7	28.9	27.8
2004	29.0	29.1	29.2	29.3	29.3	27.9	27.5	29.2	29.0	28.9	28.7	28.6	28.8
2005	28.4	28.5	28.4	28.5	28.5	27.2	26.8	28.2	28.7	28.7	28.7	28.7	28.3
2006	28.6	28.6	28.8	29.1	29.2	27.9	27.4	28.9	29.1	29.1	29.2	29.1	28.8
2007	29.1	29.1	29.3	29.5	29.5	28.2	27.8	29.3	29.5	29.5	29.6	29.6	29.0

Employment by Industry: Lancaster, PA, 2000–2007

(Numbers in thousands, not seasonally adjusted.)

Industry and year	January	February	March	April	May	June	July	August	September	October	November	December	Annual Average
Total Nonfarm													
2000	219.9	221.6	225.0	225.7	227.5	229.0	228.3	228.1	229.4	228.4	228.5	229.1	226.7
2001	221.1	223.2	225.6	226.6	228.1	229.3	227.1	227.3	229.2	228.8	228.8	229.4	227.0
2002	222.3	224.1	226.9	227.1	228.7	230.0	228.2	229.0	230.2	230.3	230.3	230.1	228.1
2003	222.4	222.8	225.5	226.6	229.6	231.4	229.5	229.7	230.8	232.0	232.1	231.8	228.6
2004	225.1	226.8	229.6	231.8	233.0	235.5	233.1	232.5	234.3	235.2	235.3	236.3	232.4
2005	229.6	231.0	232.6	236.1	236.3	237.3	235.0	235.1	237.2	236.6	236.8	236.1	235.0
2006	230.3	231.1	233.0	236.5	237.9	239.3	236.2	237.2	238.8	238.8	239.3	240.0	236.5
2007	232.4	232.6	235.1	237.3	238.8	240.0	238.1	238.6	239.8	240.2	240.7	241.1	237.9
Total Private													
2000	201.3	202.1	205.2	205.6	207.1	210.1	210.7	210.9	210.2	208.4	208.3	209.2	207.4
2001	202.1	202.9	205.2	206.2	207.8	210.1	209.4	209.6	209.2	208.3	208.1	208.6	207.3
2002	202.7	203.4	205.9	206.1	208.6	210.1	209.8	210.3	209.5	209.0	208.8	209.3	207.8
2003	202.2	201.5	204.0	205.1	208.5	210.6	210.5	210.6	210.1	210.9	210.7	210.9	207.9
2004	204.2	205.4	208.0	210.3	212.3	215.0	214.1	213.7	213.6	213.6	213.5	215.2	211.6
2005	208.4	209.4	210.9	214.4	215.1	216.9	216.0	216.2	216.1	215.6	215.5	215.4	214.2
2006	209.7	209.9	211.9	215.2	216.7	218.8	217.3	218.3	218.1	217.5	217.8	218.9	215.8
2007	211.6	211.1	213.5	215.8	217.4	219.4	220.0	220.2	218.7	218.6	218.9	219.5	217.1
Goods-Producing													
2000	69.8	69.4	70.3	70.5	70.9	72.1	72.0	71.8	71.3	70.3	70.1	70.2	70.7
2001	68.3	67.5	68.0	68.2	68.3	68.9	68.7	68.5	67.8	67.3	66.6	66.5	67.9
2002	65.6	65.6	65.8	66.0	66.0	66.4	66.1	65.8	65.3	64.9	64.6	64.1	65.5
2003	62.9	61.9	62.3	62.2	63.1	63.7	63.1	63.0	62.7	62.4	62.1	61.9	62.6
2004	60.9	60.5	61.2	62.0	62.5	63.5	63.4	62.7	62.5	62.5	62.2	62.5	62.2
2005	61.1	60.5	60.9	61.7	62.0	62.6	62.5	62.6	62.1	61.7	61.7	61.4	61.7
2006	60.6	60.4	61.0	61.4	61.4	62.4	62.1	62.1	61.7	61.3	60.9	60.9	61.4
2007	59.4	58.8	59.4	60.1	60.3	60.9	60.8	60.7	60.1	59.7	59.6	59.4	59.9
Natural Resources, Mining, and Construction													
2000	13.6	13.3	13.9	14.1	14.4	14.9	15.1	15.1	14.9	14.7	14.6	14.5	14.4
2001	14.0	13.9	14.2	14.7	15.1	15.4	15.4	15.5	15.1	15.1	14.9	14.8	14.8
2002	14.4	14.3	14.5	14.9	15.2	15.6	15.9	15.9	15.7	15.7	15.7	15.5	15.3
2003	14.9	14.5	14.9	15.3	15.7	16.0	16.3	16.3	16.1	16.0	15.8	15.6	15.6
2004	15.2	14.9	15.3	16.1	16.5	17.0	17.2	17.2	16.9	17.0	16.8	16.8	16.4
2005	16.1	15.8	16.0	16.9	17.2	17.7	18.0	18.0	17.8	17.6	17.6	17.2	17.2
2006	16.8	16.7	17.2	17.5	17.7	18.2	18.2	18.2	18.1	17.7	17.5	17.4	17.6
2007	16.6	16.1	16.5	17.2	17.6	18.0	18.2	18.1	17.9	17.7	17.6	17.4	17.4
Manufacturing													
2000	56.2	56.1	56.4	56.4	56.5	57.2	56.9	56.7	56.4	55.6	55.5	55.7	56.3
2001	54.3	53.6	53.8	53.5	53.2	53.5	53.3	53.0	52.7	52.2	51.7	51.7	53.0
2002	51.2	51.3	51.3	51.1	50.8	50.8	50.2	49.9	49.6	49.2	48.9	48.6	50.2
2003	48.0	47.4	47.4	46.9	47.4	47.7	46.8	46.7	46.6	46.4	46.3	46.3	46.9
2004	45.7	45.6	45.9	45.9	46.0	46.5	46.2	45.5	45.6	45.5	45.4	45.7	45.8
2005	45.0	44.7	44.9	44.8	44.8	44.9	44.5	44.6	44.3	44.1	44.1	44.2	44.6
2006	43.8	43.7	43.8	43.9	43.7	44.2	43.9	43.9	43.6	43.6	43.4	43.5	43.8
2007	42.8	42.7	42.9	42.9	42.7	42.9	42.6	42.6	42.2	42.0	42.0	42.0	42.5
Service-Providing													
2000	150.1	152.2	154.7	155.2	156.6	156.9	156.3	156.3	158.1	158.1	158.4	158.9	156.0
2001	152.8	155.7	157.6	158.4	159.8	160.4	158.4	158.8	161.4	161.5	162.2	162.9	159.2
2002	156.7	158.5	161.1	161.1	162.7	163.6	162.1	163.2	164.9	165.4	165.7	166.0	162.6
2003	159.5	160.9	163.2	164.4	166.5	167.7	166.4	166.7	168.1	169.6	170.0	169.9	166.0
2004	164.2	166.3	168.4	169.8	170.5	172.0	169.7	169.8	171.8	172.7	173.1	173.8	170.2
2005	168.5	170.5	171.7	174.4	174.3	174.7	172.5	172.5	175.1	174.9	175.1	174.7	173.2
2006	169.7	170.7	172.0	175.1	176.5	176.9	174.1	175.1	177.1	177.5	178.4	179.1	175.2
2007	173.0	173.8	175.7	177.2	178.5	179.1	177.3	177.9	179.7	180.5	181.1	181.7	178.0
Trade, Transportation, and Utilities													
2000	47.4	47.3	47.9	48.2	48.3	48.4	48.2	48.6	48.6	48.3	48.8	49.5	48.3
2001	48.1	47.4	47.7	47.9	48.1	48.4	48.2	48.1	48.3	48.5	49.3	50.4	48.4
2002	48.7	47.5	47.9	48.3	48.8	48.9	48.6	48.7	48.7	49.0	49.8	50.6	48.8
2003	48.9	48.2	48.8	49.4	50.0	50.3	50.3	50.3	50.3	51.0	51.4	52.4	50.1
2004	50.1	49.7	50.0	50.3	50.7	51.0	50.6	50.7	51.2	51.4	52.1	53.1	50.9
2005	51.3	50.6	51.2	51.6	51.9	52.0	51.8	51.8	52.3	52.7	53.5	54.2	52.1
2006	52.3	51.8	52.0	52.7	53.1	53.3	52.7	52.9	53.3	53.6	54.7	55.8	53.2
2007	53.7	52.7	53.1	53.8	54.1	54.0	54.1	54.1	54.0	54.5	55.3	56.1	54.1
Wholesale Trade													
2000	11.2	11.3	11.4	11.6	11.7	11.8	11.8	11.8	11.7	11.3	11.1	11.2	11.5
2001	11.0	11.1	11.2	11.1	11.2	11.3	11.4	11.3	11.2	10.8	10.9	11.0	11.1
2002	10.9	10.7	10.7	10.9	11.0	11.2	11.3	11.3	11.3	11.4	11.5	11.7	11.2
2003	11.5	11.7	11.9	12.1	12.3	12.4	12.5	12.5	12.4	12.4	12.4	12.7	12.2
2004	12.2	12.2	12.4	12.4	12.4	12.6	12.6	12.6	12.6	12.5	12.6	12.7	12.5
2005	12.5	12.5	12.7	12.8	12.9	13.0	13.0	13.0	13.0	13.0	13.0	13.1	12.9
2006	13.0	13.1	13.2	13.3	13.4	13.5	13.4	13.5	13.4	13.5	13.5	13.6	13.4
2007	13.6	13.4	13.6	13.7	13.7	13.8	13.9	13.9	13.7	13.8	13.8	13.9	13.7
Retail Trade													
2000	29.4	29.2	29.6	29.8	29.9	30.0	29.8	30.1	30.1	30.2	30.9	31.5	30.0
2001	30.3	29.5	29.7	29.8	29.8	30.0	29.7	29.7	29.5	29.9	30.5	31.3	30.0
2002	30.0	29.2	29.5	29.6	29.9	29.8	29.8	29.9	29.6	29.6	30.4	31.0	29.9
2003	29.6	28.8	29.1	29.4	29.6	29.6	29.7	29.6	29.2	29.6	29.9	30.5	29.5
2004	29.0	28.6	28.6	28.8	29.2	29.3	29.3	29.4	29.3	29.6	30.2	31.0	29.4
2005	29.6	28.9	29.1	29.3	29.5	29.5	29.6	29.6	29.5	29.8	30.5	31.0	29.7
2006	29.7	29.0	29.1	29.5	29.6	29.6	29.4	29.4	29.4	29.6	30.6	31.4	29.7
2007	29.7	28.9	28.9	29.3	29.5	29.4	29.6	29.6	29.6	29.7	30.5	31.2	29.6

Employment by Industry: Lancaster, PA, 2000–2007—*Continued*

(Numbers in thousands, not seasonally adjusted.)

Industry and year	January	February	March	April	May	June	July	August	September	October	November	December	Annual Average
Transportation and Utilities													
2000	6.8	6.8	6.9	6.8	6.7	6.6	6.6	6.7	6.8	6.8	6.8	6.8	6.8
2001	6.8	6.8	6.8	7.0	7.1	7.1	7.1	7.1	7.6	7.8	7.9	8.1	7.3
2002	7.8	7.6	7.7	7.8	7.9	7.9	7.5	7.5	7.8	8.0	7.9	7.9	7.8
2003	7.8	7.7	7.8	7.9	8.1	8.3	8.1	8.2	8.7	9.0	9.1	9.2	8.3
2004	8.9	8.9	9.0	9.1	9.1	9.1	8.7	8.7	9.3	9.3	9.3	9.4	9.1
2005	9.2	9.2	9.4	9.5	9.5	9.5	9.2	9.2	9.8	9.9	10.0	10.1	9.5
2006	9.6	9.7	9.7	9.9	10.1	10.2	9.9	10.0	10.5	10.5	10.6	10.8	10.1
2007	10.4	10.4	10.6	10.8	10.9	10.8	10.6	10.6	10.9	11.0	11.0	11.0	10.8
Information													
2000	4.3	4.3	4.3	4.3	4.3	4.3	4.4	4.2	4.3	4.3	4.3	4.4	4.3
2001	4.1	4.2	4.2	4.2	4.2	4.3	4.3	4.2	4.2	4.1	4.2	4.2	4.2
2002	4.1	4.0	4.1	4.1	4.1	4.1	4.1	4.1	4.0	4.0	4.0	4.0	4.1
2003	4.0	4.0	4.0	4.0	3.9	4.0	4.1	4.1	4.0	4.0	4.0	4.0	4.0
2004	4.0	4.0	4.0	4.0	4.0	4.0	4.0	4.1	4.0	4.0	4.0	4.1	4.0
2005	4.1	4.1	4.1	4.1	4.0	3.9	3.9	3.9	3.8	3.7	3.6	3.6	3.9
2006	3.6	3.6	3.7	3.7	3.7	3.8	3.8	3.8	3.8	3.8	3.8	3.8	3.7
2007	3.8	3.8	3.8	3.8	3.8	3.8	3.9	3.9	3.9	3.9	3.9	3.9	3.9
Financial Activities													
2000	10.3	10.3	10.3	10.4	10.5	10.7	10.7	10.7	10.6	10.5	10.5	10.6	10.5
2001	10.7	10.8	10.9	11.0	11.0	11.1	11.3	11.4	11.3	11.2	11.3	11.4	11.1
2002	11.6	11.5	11.5	11.3	11.1	11.0	11.0	10.9	10.6	10.3	10.2	10.1	10.9
2003	10.0	9.9	9.9	9.9	10.0	10.1	10.2	10.2	10.1	10.0	10.0	10.0	10.0
2004	9.9	9.9	9.9	10.0	9.9	10.0	10.0	9.9	9.7	9.5	9.4	9.4	9.8
2005	9.3	9.3	9.4	9.3	9.4	9.5	9.5	9.5	9.4	9.4	9.4	9.5	9.4
2006	9.5	9.4	9.5	9.5	9.7	9.8	9.8	9.8	9.7	9.6	9.6	9.6	9.6
2007	9.6	9.5	9.6	9.7	9.7	9.8	9.7	9.7	9.5	9.5	9.5	9.5	9.6
Professional and Business Services													
2000	17.4	17.1	17.6	17.0	17.1	17.9	18.4	18.6	18.3	18.0	18.0	18.2	17.8
2001	17.7	18.1	18.6	18.5	18.9	19.3	18.8	19.2	19.4	19.0	18.6	18.4	18.7
2002	17.2	17.6	18.3	18.0	18.5	19.5	19.3	20.2	20.3	20.0	19.8	20.2	19.1
2003	19.1	19.2	19.7	19.8	20.2	20.2	20.6	21.0	20.8	21.2	21.2	20.9	20.3
2004	20.1	20.4	20.8	21.4	21.9	22.1	22.0	22.2	22.2	22.4	22.4	22.5	21.7
2005	21.5	22.2	22.3	22.4	22.5	22.5	21.8	22.0	22.1	21.6	21.2	21.1	21.9
2006	20.0	20.3	20.4	20.8	20.8	20.9	20.4	20.8	21.0	21.1	21.0	20.9	20.7
2007	20.1	20.2	20.7	20.7	20.8	21.5	21.2	21.5	21.6	21.5	21.4	21.3	21.0
Education and Health Services													
2000	24.9	26.2	26.5	26.1	25.8	25.7	26.0	25.9	26.8	27.1	27.3	27.2	26.3
2001	26.1	27.5	27.6	27.4	27.1	27.1	27.0	27.1	28.0	28.2	28.6	28.6	27.5
2002	27.7	29.0	29.2	28.9	29.1	28.7	29.0	29.0	29.9	30.4	30.6	30.7	29.4
2003	29.6	30.9	31.1	30.6	30.8	30.9	30.6	30.4	31.4	32.2	32.5	32.4	31.1
2004	31.4	32.9	33.2	32.5	32.4	32.5	32.1	32.0	32.5	32.9	33.3	33.5	32.6
2005	32.7	34.0	33.9	34.4	33.6	33.7	33.6	33.5	34.4	35.4	35.6	35.4	34.2
2006	34.7	35.8	35.8	36.0	35.7	35.2	35.1	35.3	36.1	36.3	36.6	36.7	35.8
2007	35.4	36.6	36.7	36.7	36.4	35.9	36.2	36.0	36.7	37.1	37.2	37.3	36.5
Leisure and Hospitality													
2000	17.1	17.4	18.0	18.9	19.9	20.6	20.7	20.7	20.0	19.6	19.0	18.9	19.2
2001	17.0	17.2	17.9	18.7	19.8	20.5	20.7	20.8	20.0	19.7	19.2	18.8	19.2
2002	17.5	17.8	18.6	19.1	20.6	21.0	21.2	21.2	20.4	20.1	19.6	19.3	19.7
2003	17.5	17.3	18.0	19.0	20.3	21.1	21.3	21.4	20.7	20.0	19.4	19.2	19.6
2004	17.7	17.9	18.6	19.7	20.5	21.4	21.6	21.7	21.2	20.6	19.9	19.8	20.1
2005	18.2	18.4	18.8	20.7	21.5	22.3	22.5	22.6	21.8	20.8	20.3	19.9	20.7
2006	18.8	18.4	19.2	20.7	21.9	23.0	22.9	23.1	22.1	21.3	20.7	20.6	21.1
2007	19.1	18.9	19.6	20.4	21.7	22.8	23.2	23.5	22.2	21.7	21.3	21.3	21.3
Other Services													
2000	10.1	10.1	10.3	10.2	10.3	10.4	10.3	10.4	10.3	10.3	10.3	10.2	10.3
2001	10.1	10.2	10.3	10.3	10.4	10.5	10.4	10.3	10.2	10.3	10.3	10.3	10.3
2002	10.3	10.4	10.5	10.4	10.4	10.5	10.5	10.4	10.3	10.3	10.2	10.3	10.4
2003	10.2	10.1	10.2	10.2	10.2	10.3	10.3	10.2	10.1	10.1	10.1	10.1	10.1
2004	10.1	10.1	10.3	10.4	10.4	10.5	10.4	10.4	10.3	10.3	10.2	10.3	10.3
2005	10.2	10.3	10.3	10.2	10.2	10.4	10.4	10.4	10.3	10.3	10.2	10.3	10.3
2006	10.2	10.2	10.3	10.4	10.4	10.4	10.5	10.5	10.4	10.5	10.5	10.6	10.4
2007	10.5	10.6	10.6	10.6	10.6	10.7	10.9	10.8	10.7	10.7	10.7	10.7	10.7
Government													
2000	18.6	19.5	19.8	20.1	20.4	18.9	17.6	17.2	19.2	20.0	20.2	19.9	19.3
2001	19.0	20.3	20.4	20.4	20.3	19.2	17.7	17.7	20.0	20.5	20.7	20.8	19.8
2002	19.6	20.7	21.0	21.0	20.1	19.9	18.4	18.7	20.7	21.3	21.5	20.8	20.3
2003	20.2	21.3	21.5	21.5	21.1	20.8	19.0	19.1	20.7	21.1	21.4	20.9	20.7
2004	20.9	21.4	21.6	21.5	20.7	20.5	19.0	18.8	20.7	21.6	21.8	21.1	20.8
2005	21.2	21.6	21.7	21.7	21.2	20.4	19.0	18.9	21.1	21.0	21.3	20.7	20.8
2006	20.6	21.2	21.1	21.3	21.2	20.5	18.9	18.9	20.7	21.3	21.5	21.1	20.7
2007	20.8	21.5	21.6	21.5	21.4	20.6	18.1	18.4	21.1	21.6	21.8	21.6	20.8

Employment by Industry: Boise City-Nampa, ID, 2000–2007

(Numbers in thousands, not seasonally adjusted.)

Industry and year	January	February	March	April	May	June	July	August	September	October	November	December	Annual Average
Total Nonfarm													
2000	216.7	219.1	222.7	226.4	229.7	230.9	231.4	232.5	234.4	234.4	235.7	233.9	229.0
2001	228.5	230.4	233.5	233.5	234.5	235.7	236.1	237.8	237.4	236.2	235.0	233.9	234.4
2002	226.9	228.4	230.7	232.5	234.8	236.0	234.9	235.7	236.0	235.9	235.8	235.5	233.6
2003	229.6	230.5	231.9	233.2	235.1	236.4	233.8	234.9	237.2	237.2	237.3	238.1	234.6
2004	231.1	233.5	236.7	240.2	242.5	243.9	243.2	244.5	245.2	246.4	247.8	248.5	242.0
2005	243.4	246.1	248.7	251.5	253.7	255.3	256.4	257.6	260.4	260.0	261.4	262.8	254.8
2006	256.8	260.7	264.4	269.7	272.9	275.0	274.3	276.0	277.5	276.3	277.3	277.6	271.5
2007	270.0	273.5	276.3	275.4	277.9	279.6	277.7	278.5	278.1	279.0	279.3	278.6	277.0
Total Private													
2000	182.8	184.0	187.1	190.6	192.9	195.6	196.7	198.5	199.0	198.1	199.4	198.5	193.6
2001	193.3	193.8	196.7	196.5	197.2	198.9	200.4	202.4	200.3	198.1	197.0	196.1	197.6
2002	190.3	190.4	192.4	194.2	196.2	198.0	198.6	199.9	198.7	198.3	197.8	197.3	196.0
2003	192.4	192.4	193.6	195.0	196.3	198.2	197.7	199.1	199.4	198.4	198.7	199.6	196.7
2004	193.5	195.0	198.0	200.9	203.2	205.7	206.1	207.1	206.2	206.8	208.0	209.1	203.3
2005	204.5	206.6	209.1	211.7	213.7	216.3	218.8	220.0	220.6	219.6	221.1	222.6	215.4
2006	217.6	220.3	223.9	229.1	232.0	235.3	235.4	237.1	236.8	234.9	235.8	236.4	231.2
2007	229.9	232.4	235.2	234.0	236.1	239.1	237.8	238.0	235.6	235.3	235.8	235.1	235.4
Goods-Producing													
2000	50.1	50.3	50.9	51.6	52.2	53.2	53.4	53.9	53.8	54.0	54.3	54.0	52.6
2001	52.3	52.5	53.1	52.9	52.8	53.7	53.3	53.3	52.4	51.5	50.1	49.2	52.3
2002	47.3	46.6	47.1	47.7	48.7	49.6	49.8	50.0	49.5	49.3	48.7	48.1	48.5
2003	46.1	46.1	45.4	45.8	46.1	46.9	46.3	46.6	46.6	46.8	46.4	46.2	46.3
2004	44.5	44.9	46.0	47.0	47.5	48.3	48.4	48.9	48.4	48.6	48.7	48.6	47.5
2005	46.9	47.5	48.5	49.0	49.7	50.5	51.8	52.2	52.3	52.3	52.6	53.1	50.5
2006	52.0	53.0	54.1	55.5	56.6	58.0	58.2	58.3	57.7	57.2	56.7	56.2	56.1
2007	54.3	54.8	55.4	55.3	55.8	56.4	56.1	55.0	53.8	53.6	53.6	53.1	54.8
Natural Resources, Mining, and Construction													
2000	15.3	15.4	16.0	16.5	16.9	17.6	17.7	17.9	17.9	17.9	17.8	17.5	17.0
2001	16.2	16.2	16.9	17.1	17.4	17.9	18.0	18.2	17.9	17.7	17.2	16.5	17.3
2002	14.9	14.8	15.2	15.8	16.6	16.9	17.2	17.2	17.0	16.6	16.4	16.1	16.2
2003	14.6	14.7	15.1	15.5	15.9	16.6	16.8	17.1	17.1	16.8	16.6	16.5	16.1
2004	15.2	15.4	16.1	16.9	17.2	17.7	18.1	18.5	18.3	18.2	18.2	18.2	17.3
2005	17.3	17.7	18.5	19.2	19.6	20.5	21.4	21.8	21.8	21.8	22.1	22.0	20.3
2006	21.3	22.1	22.9	23.9	24.9	26.0	26.1	26.2	25.7	25.0	24.7	24.1	24.4
2007	22.6	22.8	23.4	23.7	24.1	24.5	24.3	24.3	23.5	23.3	23.3	22.9	23.6
Manufacturing													
2000	34.8	34.9	34.9	35.1	35.3	35.6	35.7	36.0	35.9	36.1	36.5	36.5	35.6
2001	36.1	36.3	36.2	35.8	35.4	35.8	35.3	35.1	34.5	33.8	32.9	32.7	35.0
2002	32.4	31.8	31.9	31.9	32.1	32.7	32.6	32.8	32.5	32.7	32.3	32.0	32.3
2003	31.5	31.4	30.3	30.3	30.2	30.3	29.5	29.5	29.5	30.0	29.8	29.7	30.2
2004	29.3	29.5	29.9	30.1	30.3	30.6	30.3	30.4	30.1	30.4	30.5	30.4	30.2
2005	29.6	29.8	30.0	29.8	30.1	30.0	30.4	30.4	30.5	30.5	30.5	31.1	30.2
2006	30.7	30.9	31.2	31.6	31.7	32.0	32.1	32.1	32.0	32.2	32.0	32.1	31.7
2007	31.7	32.0	32.0	31.6	31.7	31.9	31.8	30.7	30.3	30.3	30.3	30.2	31.2
Service-Providing													
2000	166.6	168.8	171.8	174.8	177.5	177.7	178.0	178.6	180.6	180.4	181.4	179.9	176.3
2001	176.2	177.9	180.4	180.6	181.7	182.0	182.8	184.5	185.0	184.7	184.9	184.7	182.1
2002	179.6	181.8	183.6	184.8	186.1	186.4	185.1	185.7	186.5	186.6	187.1	187.4	185.1
2003	183.5	184.4	186.5	187.4	189.0	189.5	187.5	188.3	190.6	190.4	190.9	191.9	188.3
2004	186.6	188.6	190.7	193.2	195.0	195.6	194.8	195.6	196.8	197.8	199.1	199.9	194.5
2005	196.5	198.6	200.2	202.5	204.0	204.8	204.6	205.4	208.1	207.7	208.8	209.7	204.2
2006	204.8	207.7	210.3	214.2	216.3	217.0	216.1	217.7	219.8	219.1	220.6	221.4	215.4
2007	215.7	218.7	220.9	220.1	222.1	223.2	221.6	223.5	224.3	225.4	225.7	225.5	222.2
Trade, Transportation, and Utilities													
2000	44.7	44.8	45.1	45.6	46.2	46.5	47.2	47.8	47.7	47.4	48.0	48.1	46.6
2001	45.8	45.6	46.0	46.0	46.0	46.3	45.0	45.3	45.5	45.4	46.0	46.0	45.7
2002	44.1	43.8	44.1	44.3	44.8	44.8	45.2	45.5	45.3	44.9	45.7	45.7	44.9
2003	44.0	43.6	44.0	44.3	44.5	44.7	44.7	45.1	45.5	45.1	45.9	46.2	44.8
2004	43.9	43.7	44.3	44.7	45.3	45.7	45.9	46.1	46.1	46.8	47.8	48.4	45.7
2005	46.5	46.4	47.0	47.6	48.3	48.6	49.1	49.5	49.7	49.7	50.7	51.3	48.7
2006	49.1	49.1	49.7	50.9	51.5	52.3	52.4	52.9	53.5	53.6	54.7	55.3	52.1
2007	53.2	53.4	54.1	53.5	53.5	54.5	54.1	54.5	54.4	54.4	55.8	55.9	54.3
Wholesale Trade													
2000	9.9	10.0	10.1	10.2	10.3	10.4	10.6	10.5	10.4	10.5	10.4	10.4	10.3
2001	10.1	10.1	10.1	10.1	10.1	10.1	9.8	9.8	9.8	9.7	9.7	9.6	9.9
2002	9.5	9.7	9.7	9.8	9.9	10.0	10.1	10.1	10.1	10.0	10.0	9.8	9.9
2003	9.7	9.7	9.6	9.9	10.0	10.0	10.2	10.2	10.3	9.8	9.7	9.8	9.9
2004	9.6	9.7	9.8	9.9	10.0	10.1	10.4	10.5	10.5	10.5	10.5	10.6	10.2
2005	11.0	11.0	11.2	11.2	11.3	11.2	11.3	11.3	11.4	11.3	11.3	11.3	11.2
2006	11.1	11.5	11.6	12.2	12.4	12.6	12.6	12.5	12.7	12.6	12.7	12.8	12.3
2007	12.5	12.7	12.8	12.4	12.4	12.6	12.7	12.7	12.8	12.7	12.6	12.6	12.6
Retail Trade													
2000	27.3	27.2	27.4	27.8	28.3	28.4	29.0	29.6	29.5	29.1	29.8	29.9	28.6
2001	28.0	27.8	28.1	27.9	27.9	28.1	27.8	28.0	28.1	28.1	28.8	28.9	28.1
2002	27.6	27.1	27.4	27.5	27.8	27.8	28.2	28.3	28.1	27.8	28.7	29.0	27.9
2003	27.2	26.8	27.3	27.3	27.4	27.6	27.5	27.9	28.0	28.2	29.1	29.3	27.8
2004	27.4	27.1	27.5	27.9	28.3	28.5	28.5	28.5	28.6	29.2	30.2	30.7	28.5
2005	28.6	28.4	28.8	29.3	29.9	30.2	30.4	30.8	30.9	31.0	32.1	32.6	30.3
2006	30.8	30.3	30.7	31.2	31.5	32.0	32.1	32.6	32.9	33.2	34.2	34.5	32.2
2007	33.0	32.9	33.5	33.2	33.2	33.9	33.6	33.7	33.7	33.5	34.9	34.9	33.7

Employment by Industry: Boise City-Nampa, ID, 2000–2007—*Continued*

(Numbers in thousands, not seasonally adjusted.)

Industry and year	January	February	March	April	May	June	July	August	September	October	November	December	Annual Average
Transportation and Utilities													
2000	7.5	7.6	7.6	7.6	7.6	7.7	7.6	7.7	7.8	7.8	7.8	7.8	7.7
2001	7.7	7.7	7.8	8.0	8.0	8.1	7.4	7.5	7.6	7.6	7.5	7.5	7.7
2002	7.0	7.0	7.0	7.0	7.1	7.0	6.9	7.1	7.1	7.1	7.0	6.9	7.0
2003	7.1	7.1	7.1	7.1	7.1	7.1	7.0	7.0	7.2	7.1	7.1	7.1	7.1
2004	6.9	6.9	7.0	6.9	7.0	7.1	7.0	7.1	7.0	7.1	7.1	7.1	7.0
2005	6.9	7.0	7.0	7.1	7.1	7.2	7.4	7.4	7.4	7.4	7.3	7.4	7.2
2006	7.2	7.3	7.4	7.5	7.6	7.7	7.7	7.8	7.9	7.8	7.8	8.0	7.6
2007	7.7	7.8	7.8	7.9	7.9	8.0	7.8	8.1	8.1	8.2	8.3	8.4	8.0
Information													
2000	4.1	4.1	4.2	4.2	4.3	4.5	4.4	4.4	4.4	4.3	4.3	4.4	4.3
2001	4.1	4.2	4.1	4.0	4.0	4.1	4.0	4.1	3.9	3.8	3.7	3.7	4.0
2002	3.7	3.7	3.7	3.8	3.7	3.7	3.7	3.7	3.7	3.7	3.8	3.8	3.7
2003	4.0	4.0	4.0	4.0	4.0	4.0	4.0	3.9	3.9	3.9	4.0	4.0	4.0
2004	4.0	4.0	4.1	4.1	4.1	4.1	4.1	4.1	4.1	4.2	4.2	4.2	4.1
2005	4.3	4.3	4.3	4.4	4.5	4.5	4.5	4.5	4.5	4.5	4.5	4.6	4.5
2006	4.5	4.5	4.5	4.6	4.6	4.7	4.7	4.7	4.7	4.6	4.6	4.7	4.6
2007	4.6	4.6	4.6	5.3	5.4	5.5	4.7	4.7	4.7	4.7	4.7	4.7	4.9
Financial Activities													
2000	12.1	12.1	12.2	12.2	12.2	12.3	12.2	12.2	12.3	12.2	12.3	12.2	12.2
2001	12.0	12.0	12.2	12.3	12.3	12.4	11.9	12.0	11.8	11.7	11.7	11.8	12.0
2002	12.0	12.0	12.0	12.0	12.1	12.1	12.3	12.3	12.2	12.3	12.4	12.5	12.2
2003	12.3	12.3	12.3	12.4	12.6	12.7	12.7	12.7	12.7	12.7	12.7	12.7	12.6
2004	12.6	12.6	12.6	13.0	13.0	13.1	13.2	13.2	13.2	13.3	13.3	13.4	13.0
2005	13.3	13.3	13.3	13.5	13.6	13.7	14.0	14.2	14.2	14.3	14.3	14.4	13.8
2006	14.4	14.5	14.6	15.0	15.1	15.3	15.3	15.3	15.3	15.1	15.1	15.2	15.0
2007	15.0	15.1	15.1	14.3	14.4	14.3	15.1	15.0	14.8	14.8	14.8	14.4	14.8
Professional and Business Services													
2000	24.4	24.8	26.0	26.6	27.1	27.6	27.8	28.2	28.7	29.0	29.1	28.3	27.3
2001	27.6	27.3	28.0	27.9	28.0	28.1	32.0	33.0	32.1	32.0	31.5	31.0	29.9
2002	30.1	30.5	31.1	31.8	31.7	32.2	32.0	32.7	32.3	32.8	32.1	32.0	31.8
2003	30.7	31.0	31.8	31.7	31.9	32.4	32.6	33.2	33.1	33.1	32.9	33.2	32.3
2004	32.2	32.8	33.6	34.6	34.9	35.3	35.6	35.8	35.4	35.6	35.5	35.6	34.7
2005	34.8	36.0	36.4	37.2	37.2	37.9	38.2	38.4	38.5	38.3	38.2	37.9	37.4
2006	37.3	38.1	39.1	40.8	41.2	41.7	41.5	41.9	41.5	41.1	41.1	40.7	40.5
2007	39.3	40.2	40.7	40.6	40.9	41.2	41.3	41.8	41.3	41.5	40.5	40.5	40.8
Education and Health Services													
2000	22.8	23.1	23.2	23.6	23.7	23.8	23.9	24.0	24.4	24.7	24.9	25.0	23.9
2001	25.2	25.4	25.7	25.9	26.0	25.9	25.9	26.3	26.6	26.7	26.9	27.1	26.1
2002	26.9	27.2	27.4	27.4	27.5	27.3	27.4	27.4	27.8	27.9	27.9	28.1	27.5
2003	28.4	28.5	28.6	29.0	29.1	28.9	28.9	28.9	29.3	29.2	29.4	29.6	29.0
2004	28.9	29.2	29.4	29.4	29.6	29.8	29.6	29.7	30.1	30.5	30.5	30.5	29.8
2005	30.6	30.8	30.8	31.2	31.2	31.1	30.8	30.9	31.4	31.5	31.8	31.6	31.1
2006	31.0	31.4	31.6	31.6	31.8	31.5	31.3	31.6	32.0	32.1	32.2	32.3	31.7
2007	32.0	32.3	32.5	32.3	32.5	32.9	32.5	32.9	33.2	33.6	34.0	34.2	32.9
Leisure and Hospitality													
2000	17.9	18.1	18.7	20.0	20.3	20.7	20.9	21.0	20.8	19.6	19.6	19.6	19.8
2001	19.4	19.8	20.4	20.4	20.9	21.4	21.4	21.5	21.2	20.2	20.3	20.5	20.6
2002	19.6	19.8	20.2	20.4	20.9	21.4	21.3	21.4	21.1	20.6	20.4	20.4	20.6
2003	20.3	20.2	20.7	21.0	21.3	21.7	21.6	21.8	21.5	20.8	20.6	20.9	21.0
2004	20.7	21.0	21.1	21.1	21.8	22.3	22.1	22.2	21.9	20.9	21.1	21.5	21.5
2005	21.2	21.3	21.8	21.7	22.1	22.8	23.1	23.0	22.8	21.8	21.8	22.5	22.2
2006	22.1	22.3	22.8	23.1	23.5	24.0	24.1	24.4	24.2	23.5	23.7	24.2	23.5
2007	23.7	24.1	24.8	24.8	25.6	26.2	25.8	25.9	25.4	24.7	24.4	24.2	25.0
Other Services													
2000	6.7	6.7	6.8	6.8	6.9	7.0	6.9	7.0	6.9	6.9	6.9	6.9	6.9
2001	6.9	7.0	7.2	7.1	7.2	7.0	6.9	6.9	6.8	6.8	6.8	6.8	7.0
2002	6.6	6.8	6.8	6.8	6.8	6.9	6.9	6.9	6.8	6.8	6.8	6.7	6.8
2003	6.6	6.7	6.8	6.8	6.8	6.9	6.9	6.9	6.8	6.8	6.8	6.8	6.8
2004	6.7	6.8	6.9	7.0	7.0	7.1	7.2	7.1	7.0	6.9	6.9	6.9	7.0
2005	6.9	7.0	7.0	7.1	7.1	7.2	7.3	7.3	7.2	7.2	7.2	7.2	7.1
2006	7.2	7.4	7.5	7.6	7.7	7.8	7.9	8.0	7.9	7.7	7.7	7.8	7.7
2007	7.8	7.9	8.0	7.9	8.0	8.1	8.2	8.2	8.0	8.0	8.0	8.1	8.0
Government													
2000	33.9	35.1	35.6	35.8	36.8	35.3	34.7	34.0	35.4	36.3	36.3	35.4	35.4
2001	35.2	36.6	36.8	37.0	37.3	36.8	35.7	35.4	37.1	38.1	38.0	37.8	36.8
2002	36.6	38.0	38.3	38.3	38.6	38.0	36.3	35.8	37.3	37.6	38.0	38.2	37.6
2003	37.2	38.1	38.3	38.2	38.8	38.2	36.1	35.8	37.8	38.8	38.6	38.5	37.9
2004	37.6	38.5	38.7	39.3	39.3	38.2	37.1	37.4	39.0	39.6	39.8	39.4	38.7
2005	38.9	39.5	39.6	39.8	40.0	39.0	37.6	37.6	39.8	40.4	40.3	40.2	39.4
2006	39.2	40.4	40.5	40.6	40.9	39.7	38.9	38.9	40.7	41.4	41.5	41.2	40.3
2007	40.1	41.1	41.1	41.4	41.8	40.5	39.9	40.5	42.5	43.7	43.5	43.5	41.6

Employment by Industry: Santa Rosa-Petaluma, CA, 2000–2007

(Numbers in thousands, not seasonally adjusted.)

Industry and year	January	February	March	April	May	June	July	August	September	October	November	December	Annual Average
Total Nonfarm													
2000	178.6	180.2	182.5	184.5	186.8	188.5	184.5	186.4	189.5	190.4	190.4	190.6	186.1
2001	185.7	187.9	189.7	190.4	191.7	191.7	188.0	189.0	191.0	191.8	190.1	190.0	189.8
2002	184.3	185.3	187.2	186.6	187.9	188.8	184.0	185.1	188.3	188.5	187.0	185.7	186.6
2003	180.9	181.2	181.5	183.1	183.6	184.8	179.9	180.6	184.5	186.4	186.1	186.2	183.2
2004	180.9	181.4	182.4	184.3	185.5	187.0	183.2	186.3	187.6	187.4	187.0	186.2	184.9
2005	181.5	182.4	183.3	185.7	187.0	188.6	184.2	187.7	189.0	190.7	189.2	188.0	186.4
2006	184.1	185.5	185.7	187.4	190.5	192.9	186.1	190.2	191.6	192.4	192.3	190.8	189.1
2007	186.7	187.2	188.7	190.5	192.3	193.2	187.6	188.7	191.8	192.7	193.0	192.2	190.4
Total Private													
2000	151.4	151.9	153.7	155.7	157.4	160.1	161.0	162.3	161.9	161.9	161.8	162.5	158.5
2001	158.2	159.1	160.6	161.4	162.2	163.4	163.7	164.6	163.6	162.7	160.7	161.0	161.8
2002	155.7	156.1	157.4	156.8	158.7	159.7	159.9	160.6	160.1	159.2	157.4	156.8	158.2
2003	152.2	152.3	152.2	153.4	154.1	156.0	155.5	156.2	156.6	156.5	155.9	156.1	154.7
2004	151.2	151.6	152.2	154.2	155.5	156.5	157.6	158.0	157.9	156.7	155.7	156.2	155.3
2005	151.0	151.8	152.3	154.3	155.8	157.1	158.0	158.9	158.6	159.3	157.7	157.8	156.1
2006	153.5	154.5	154.5	155.7	158.6	161.0	160.1	161.4	160.8	160.7	160.2	159.8	158.4
2007	155.0	155.6	156.2	158.3	159.9	161.4	160.9	161.0	160.9	160.9	161.0	161.0	159.3
Goods-Producing													
2000	40.7	40.7	41.4	42.3	42.9	43.9	44.9	45.4	46.1	45.8	45.2	44.9	43.7
2001	43.6	43.8	44.3	44.6	44.9	45.5	45.5	45.5	45.3	44.7	42.6	41.8	44.3
2002	40.0	40.1	40.3	40.1	40.8	41.4	41.7	41.8	42.3	42.0	40.3	39.7	40.9
2003	38.1	38.3	37.7	38.3	38.3	38.9	38.8	39.2	39.7	39.5	38.3	37.8	38.5
2004	36.7	36.6	36.9	37.5	38.1	38.5	39.1	39.7	40.0	38.8	37.9	37.8	38.1
2005	36.7	37.0	37.2	37.6	37.9	38.4	38.6	38.7	38.9	39.1	37.8	37.4	37.9
2006	36.1	36.2	36.1	36.3	37.9	38.9	38.6	38.9	39.2	39.3	38.2	37.3	37.8
2007	35.5	35.5	35.9	36.5	36.9	37.4	37.0	37.5	38.1	38.0	37.3	36.8	36.9
Natural Resources and Mining													
2000	0.4	0.3	0.4	0.4	0.4	0.4	0.4	0.4	0.4	0.4	0.3	0.3	0.3
2001	0.3	0.3	0.3	0.3	0.3	0.3	0.3	0.3	0.3	0.3	0.3	0.3	0.3
2002	0.3	0.3	0.3	0.3	0.3	0.3	0.3	0.3	0.3	0.3	0.3	0.3	0.3
2003	0.2	0.2	0.3	0.3	0.3	0.3	0.3	0.3	0.3	0.3	0.3	0.3	0.2
2004	0.2	0.2	0.2	0.3	0.3	0.3	0.3	0.3	0.3	0.2	0.2	0.2	0.3
2005	0.2	0.2	0.2	0.2	0.2	0.2	0.2	0.2	0.2	0.2	0.2	0.2	0.2
2006	0.2	0.2	0.2	0.2	0.2	0.2	0.2	0.2	0.2	0.2	0.2	0.2	0.2
2007	0.2	0.2	0.2	0.2	0.2	0.3	0.3	0.3	0.2	0.2	0.2	0.2	0.2
Construction													
2000	11.7	11.6	11.9	12.6	13.0	13.5	13.9	14.1	14.2	13.9	13.6	13.5	13.1
2001	12.8	12.8	13.3	13.3	13.6	14.0	14.4	14.5	14.3	14.2	13.6	13.3	13.6
2002	12.4	12.7	12.8	12.9	13.2	13.7	13.8	14.1	14.0	13.8	13.4	13.0	13.3
2003	11.8	11.9	11.9	12.5	12.8	13.3	13.6	13.8	13.7	13.7	13.5	13.2	12.9
2004	12.3	12.3	12.6	13.3	13.7	14.1	14.4	14.5	14.5	14.4	14.1	14.1	13.7
2005	12.9	13.2	13.4	13.8	14.1	14.5	14.7	14.8	14.9	15.1	14.8	14.6	14.2
2006	13.8	14.0	13.6	13.5	14.8	15.4	15.4	15.6	15.5	15.1	15.0	14.5	14.7
2007	13.8	13.7	13.9	14.3	14.5	14.8	14.9	14.8	14.7	14.6	14.4	14.2	14.4
Manufacturing													
2000	28.6	28.8	29.1	29.3	29.5	30.0	30.6	30.9	31.5	31.5	31.3	31.1	30.2
2001	30.5	30.7	30.7	31.0	31.0	31.2	30.8	30.7	30.7	30.2	28.7	28.2	30.4
2002	27.3	27.1	27.2	26.9	27.3	27.4	27.6	27.4	28.0	27.9	26.6	26.4	27.3
2003	26.1	26.2	25.5	25.5	25.2	25.3	24.9	25.1	25.7	25.5	24.5	24.3	25.3
2004	24.2	24.1	24.1	23.9	24.1	24.1	24.4	24.9	25.2	24.2	23.6	23.5	24.2
2005	23.6	23.6	23.6	23.6	23.6	23.7	23.7	23.7	23.8	23.8	22.8	22.6	23.5
2006	22.1	22.0	22.3	22.6	22.9	23.3	23.0	23.1	23.5	24.0	23.0	22.6	22.9
2007	21.5	21.6	21.8	22.0	22.2	22.3	21.8	22.4	23.2	23.2	22.7	22.4	22.3
Service-Providing													
2000	137.9	139.5	141.1	142.2	143.9	144.6	139.6	141.0	143.4	144.6	145.2	145.7	142.4
2001	142.1	144.1	145.4	145.8	146.8	146.2	142.5	143.5	145.7	147.1	147.5	148.2	145.4
2002	144.3	145.2	146.9	146.5	147.1	147.4	142.3	143.3	146.0	146.5	146.7	146.0	145.7
2003	142.8	142.9	143.8	144.8	145.3	145.9	141.1	141.4	144.8	146.9	147.8	148.4	144.6
2004	144.2	144.8	145.5	146.8	147.4	148.5	144.1	146.6	147.6	148.6	149.1	148.4	146.8
2005	144.8	145.4	146.1	148.1	149.1	150.2	145.6	149.0	150.1	151.6	151.4	150.6	148.5
2006	148.0	149.3	149.6	151.1	152.6	154.0	147.5	151.3	152.4	153.1	154.1	153.5	151.4
2007	151.2	151.7	152.8	154.0	155.4	155.8	150.6	151.2	153.7	154.7	155.7	155.4	153.5
Trade, Transportation, and Utilities													
2000	33.0	32.6	32.6	33.0	33.3	33.5	33.5	33.6	33.5	34.0	34.9	35.5	33.6
2001	33.6	33.4	33.5	33.6	33.7	34.1	34.2	34.2	34.5	34.2	34.8	35.3	34.1
2002	33.8	33.4	33.5	33.6	33.7	34.0	34.2	34.2	34.2	34.3	35.0	35.3	34.1
2003	33.7	33.3	33.3	33.3	33.3	33.6	33.7	33.8	34.0	34.0	34.9	35.4	33.8
2004	33.8	33.6	33.5	33.8	34.0	34.3	34.3	34.0	34.1	34.3	34.9	35.3	34.2
2005	34.0	33.9	33.9	34.2	34.5	34.7	34.8	34.9	35.4	35.4	35.9	36.4	34.8
2006	34.8	34.9	34.8	34.8	35.2	35.5	35.4	35.7	35.4	35.7	36.5	37.1	35.5
2007	36.1	35.7	35.7	35.4	36.0	36.1	36.3	36.2	36.2	36.6	37.5	37.9	36.3
Wholesale Trade													
2000	5.6	5.6	5.7	5.8	5.8	5.9	5.9	5.9	5.9	5.8	5.8	5.8	5.8
2001	5.7	5.7	5.7	5.9	5.9	6.0	6.2	6.2	6.1	6.0	6.0	6.0	6.0
2002	5.9	5.9	6.0	6.0	6.0	6.1	6.1	6.1	6.0	6.0	6.0	6.0	6.0
2003	6.0	6.0	6.1	6.2	6.2	6.3	6.3	6.4	6.4	6.4	6.4	6.5	6.2
2004	6.5	6.5	6.5	6.6	6.7	6.7	6.7	6.7	6.7	6.7	6.7	6.8	6.7
2005	7.0	7.0	7.1	7.2	7.3	7.4	7.5	7.6	7.6	7.5	7.5	7.4	7.3
2006	7.4	7.5	7.5	7.6	7.6	7.6	7.6	7.6	7.6	7.5	7.5	7.5	7.5
2007	7.5	7.6	7.6	7.7	7.8	7.8	7.8	7.8	7.8	7.8	7.8	7.8	7.7

Employment by Industry: Santa Rosa-Petaluma, CA, 2000–2007—*Continued*

(Numbers in thousands, not seasonally adjusted.)

Industry and year	January	February	March	April	May	June	July	August	September	October	November	December	Annual Average
Retail Trade													
2000	23.4	23.0	22.9	23.1	23.4	23.4	23.5	23.6	23.5	24.2	25.1	25.6	23.7
2001	23.9	23.7	23.7	23.7	23.8	24.1	24.0	23.9	24.3	24.1	24.8	25.2	24.1
2002	23.9	23.5	23.5	23.7	23.7	23.8	24.0	24.0	24.1	24.1	24.9	25.2	24.0
2003	23.8	23.4	23.3	23.3	23.4	23.5	23.5	23.6	23.7	23.9	24.7	25.1	23.7
2004	23.5	23.3	23.2	23.3	23.4	23.6	23.6	23.5	23.5	23.6	24.4	24.7	23.6
2005	23.5	23.3	23.2	23.4	23.5	23.6	23.5	23.6	23.9	24.0	24.5	25.1	23.8
2006	23.5	23.4	23.3	23.2	23.5	23.7	23.7	23.8	23.5	23.9	24.7	25.2	23.8
2007	24.1	23.6	23.6	23.3	23.7	23.8	24.0	23.9	23.8	24.2	25.2	25.6	24.1
Transportation and Utilities													
2000	4.0	4.0	4.0	4.1	4.1	4.2	4.1	4.1	4.1	4.0	4.0	4.1	4.1
2001	4.0	4.0	4.1	4.0	4.0	4.0	4.0	4.1	4.1	4.1	4.0	4.1	4.0
2002	4.0	4.0	4.0	3.9	4.0	4.1	4.1	4.1	4.1	4.2	4.1	4.1	4.1
2003	3.9	3.9	3.9	3.8	3.7	3.8	3.9	3.8	3.9	3.9	3.8	3.8	3.8
2004	3.8	3.8	3.8	3.9	3.9	4.0	4.0	3.8	3.9	4.0	3.8	3.8	3.9
2005	3.5	3.6	3.6	3.6	3.7	3.7	3.8	3.7	3.9	3.9	3.9	3.9	3.7
2006	3.9	4.0	4.0	4.0	4.1	4.2	4.1	4.3	4.3	4.3	4.3	4.4	4.2
2007	4.5	4.5	4.5	4.4	4.5	4.5	4.5	4.5	4.6	4.6	4.5	4.5	4.5
Information													
2000	3.7	3.8	3.9	3.9	4.0	4.1	4.0	4.1	4.2	4.3	4.3	4.4	4.1
2001	4.6	4.7	4.5	4.8	4.7	4.7	4.6	4.5	4.4	4.2	4.2	4.2	4.5
2002	4.2	4.2	4.2	4.2	4.3	4.2	4.2	4.2	4.2	4.2	4.1	4.1	4.2
2003	4.0	4.0	4.0	3.9	3.9	4.0	4.0	4.0	4.0	4.0	4.0	4.1	3.9
2004	4.2	4.2	4.2	4.3	4.2	4.2	4.3	4.3	4.3	4.3	4.3	4.3	4.3
2005	3.9	3.8	3.8	3.8	3.8	3.8	3.7	3.7	3.5	3.5	3.5	3.4	3.7
2006	3.4	3.5	3.4	3.3	3.2	3.2	3.1	3.1	3.0	3.0	3.0	3.0	3.2
2007	3.0	3.0	3.0	3.0	3.0	3.0	3.0	3.0	3.0	3.0	3.0	3.0	3.0
Financial Activities													
2000	10.1	10.0	10.0	10.0	10.0	10.2	10.3	10.4	10.3	10.2	10.2	10.3	10.2
2001	10.0	10.0	10.1	10.2	10.3	10.4	10.5	10.5	10.5	10.6	10.5	10.7	10.4
2002	10.3	10.3	10.3	10.3	10.4	10.4	10.4	10.5	10.4	10.2	10.2	10.2	10.3
2003	10.4	10.4	10.4	10.4	10.5	10.5	10.3	10.3	10.2	10.3	10.2	10.1	10.3
2004	10.1	10.0	10.1	10.2	10.1	10.0	10.0	10.0	9.8	9.7	9.8	9.7	10.0
2005	9.6	9.6	9.6	9.7	9.8	9.8	9.8	9.9	9.8	9.9	9.8	9.8	9.8
2006	9.7	9.7	9.7	9.8	9.8	9.9	9.8	9.8	9.7	9.7	9.6	9.6	9.7
2007	9.5	9.5	9.5	9.5	9.5	9.4	9.4	9.3	9.1	9.1	9.1	9.1	9.3
Professional and Business Services													
2000	19.6	19.9	20.4	20.6	20.6	21.1	20.8	21.0	21.0	20.8	20.7	21.1	20.6
2001	20.3	20.4	20.8	20.1	20.0	19.9	19.8	20.2	19.7	19.6	19.4	19.7	20.0
2002	19.0	19.1	19.4	18.9	18.9	19.2	18.6	19.1	18.9	19.0	18.7	18.7	19.0
2003	18.2	18.3	18.4	18.5	18.7	19.2	19.1	19.4	19.4	19.5	19.6	19.8	19.0
2004	19.1	19.4	19.5	19.5	19.5	19.8	19.6	19.9	20.0	19.8	19.5	19.7	19.6
2005	19.1	19.3	19.6	19.9	19.9	20.1	21.2	21.2	21.0	21.4	21.1	21.3	20.4
2006	21.4	21.4	21.4	21.8	22.2	22.6	22.4	22.7	22.7	22.4	22.2	22.3	22.1
2007	21.9	22.0	21.8	23.1	23.2	23.2	23.6	23.7	23.6	23.4	23.3	23.5	23.0
Education and Health Services													
2000	21.6	21.8	21.8	21.9	22.0	22.1	22.0	22.1	22.1	22.3	22.3	22.2	22.0
2001	22.4	22.7	22.8	23.0	22.8	22.5	22.7	22.9	23.0	23.5	23.5	23.5	22.9
2002	23.5	23.8	24.0	23.8	23.7	23.4	23.0	23.1	23.0	22.9	22.9	22.7	23.3
2003	22.7	22.9	22.9	23.1	22.9	22.8	22.2	22.2	22.4	22.5	22.6	22.7	22.6
2004	22.3	22.4	22.4	22.7	22.7	22.7	22.2	22.2	22.3	22.8	22.8	22.8	22.5
2005	22.5	22.7	22.6	22.9	23.0	23.0	22.4	22.7	22.7	22.9	22.9	22.9	22.8
2006	22.8	23.1	23.1	23.2	23.2	23.3	22.7	23.0	23.1	23.3	23.4	23.3	23.1
2007	23.3	23.6	23.7	23.8	23.8	23.8	23.2	23.5	23.5	23.7	23.9	23.9	23.6
Leisure and Hospitality													
2000	16.4	16.8	17.2	17.6	18.2	18.6	19.0	19.2	18.3	18.2	17.9	17.8	17.9
2001	17.2	17.4	17.9	18.3	18.9	19.3	19.4	19.7	19.3	19.2	19.0	19.0	18.7
2002	18.4	18.6	19.0	19.2	20.0	20.3	20.6	20.9	20.4	20.0	19.6	19.5	19.7
2003	18.7	18.7	19.1	19.4	20.0	20.4	20.8	21.0	20.6	20.2	20.0	19.9	19.9
2004	18.7	19.1	19.2	19.8	20.4	20.5	21.4	21.3	20.9	20.6	20.2	20.2	20.2
2005	19.0	19.3	19.4	20.0	20.7	21.1	21.2	21.6	21.1	21.0	20.6	20.5	20.5
2006	19.3	19.6	19.9	20.2	20.7	21.2	21.6	21.8	21.3	20.8	20.8	20.7	20.7
2007	19.5	20.1	20.3	20.7	21.2	21.7	21.5	21.5	21.1	20.9	20.7	20.6	20.8
Other Services													
2000	6.3	6.3	6.4	6.4	6.4	6.6	6.5	6.5	6.4	6.3	6.3	6.3	6.4
2001	6.5	6.7	6.7	6.8	6.9	7.0	7.0	7.1	6.9	6.7	6.7	6.8	6.8
2002	6.5	6.6	6.7	6.7	6.9	6.8	7.2	6.8	6.7	6.6	6.6	6.6	6.7
2003	6.4	6.4	6.4	6.5	6.5	6.6	6.6	6.3	6.3	6.3	6.3	6.3	6.4
2004	6.3	6.3	6.4	6.4	6.5	6.5	6.7	6.6	6.5	6.4	6.3	6.4	6.4
2005	6.2	6.2	6.2	6.2	6.2	6.2	6.3	6.2	6.2	6.1	6.1	6.1	6.2
2006	6.0	6.1	6.1	6.3	6.4	6.4	6.5	6.4	6.4	6.5	6.5	6.5	6.3
2007	6.2	6.2	6.3	6.3	6.3	6.8	6.9	6.3	6.3	6.3	6.2	6.2	6.4
Government													
2000	27.2	28.3	28.8	28.8	29.4	28.4	23.5	24.1	27.6	28.5	28.6	28.1	27.6
2001	27.5	28.8	29.1	29.0	29.5	28.3	24.3	24.4	27.4	29.1	29.4	29.0	28.0
2002	28.6	29.2	29.8	29.8	29.2	29.1	24.1	24.5	28.2	29.3	29.6	28.9	28.4
2003	28.7	28.9	29.3	29.7	29.5	28.8	24.4	24.4	27.9	29.9	30.2	30.1	28.4
2004	29.7	29.8	30.2	30.1	30.0	30.5	25.6	28.3	29.7	30.7	31.3	30.0	29.7
2005	30.5	30.6	31.0	31.4	31.2	31.5	26.2	28.8	30.4	31.4	31.5	30.2	30.4
2006	30.6	31.0	31.2	31.7	31.9	31.9	26.0	28.8	30.8	31.7	32.1	31.0	30.7
2007	31.7	31.6	32.5	32.2	32.4	31.8	26.7	27.7	30.9	31.8	32.0	31.2	31.0

Employment by Industry: Lansing-East Lansing, MI, 2000–2007

(Numbers in thousands, not seasonally adjusted.)

Industry and year	January	February	March	April	May	June	July	August	September	October	November	December	Annual Average
Total Nonfarm													
2000	228.3	235.2	237.0	239.9	239.1	235.3	232.0	231.6	240.0	242.7	243.2	242.0	237.2
2001	231.7	234.5	236.4	238.6	238.3	235.0	232.1	231.6	238.2	239.4	240.7	240.5	236.4
2002	232.4	234.3	235.9	238.1	239.3	235.5	231.7	233.1	240.6	240.1	239.1	238.6	236.6
2003	229.6	232.5	233.5	234.6	235.7	232.7	227.7	228.7	236.4	234.1	237.5	235.4	233.2
2004	228.9	229.1	229.8	233.7	231.1	228.4	224.1	224.6	231.6	231.9	231.5	233.5	229.9
2005	222.3	227.6	228.6	231.2	227.3	222.8	219.1	220.2	230.0	230.2	230.7	229.7	226.6
2006	225.2	226.8	228.2	229.8	226.4	226.1	218.9	221.0	229.8	230.3	230.8	228.9	226.9
2007	221.2	224.5	225.8	227.0	228.5	223.5	218.1	218.9	227.5	228.8	229.4	228.3	225.1
Total Private													
2000	166.6	166.6	168.2	171.1	171.7	172.8	171.1	172.4	172.9	173.2	173.2	172.7	171.0
2001	166.2	165.6	166.8	167.6	168.6	169.8	168.3	169.0	168.8	167.9	168.9	168.8	168.0
2002	163.6	163.4	164.9	166.5	168.8	170.6	168.4	170.2	170.7	169.1	169.3	169.0	167.9
2003	163.5	163.0	163.4	165.0	167.5	169.3	167.8	169.8	170.2	165.7	169.2	169.0	167.0
2004	163.1	162.1	163.0	166.3	167.3	167.1	164.9	166.1	166.3	163.9	163.4	166.3	165.0
2005	158.1	160.9	162.0	164.2	164.0	161.8	162.0	163.2	164.4	163.4	163.7	163.8	162.6
2006	159.9	160.5	161.7	163.7	164.7	166.1	162.4	163.6	164.5	163.3	163.5	163.3	163.1
2007	157.8	158.7	159.8	161.4	162.8	163.8	161.6	162.3	162.5	161.5	162.0	161.6	161.3
Goods-Producing													
2000	37.0	36.9	37.4	38.6	39.0	39.9	39.7	40.2	39.9	39.5	38.7	38.2	38.8
2001	36.1	35.7	36.0	36.0	36.2	36.5	36.5	36.0	36.1	35.2	34.7	34.4	35.8
2002	32.8	32.9	32.8	33.3	34.0	35.0	34.5	35.1	34.9	34.3	34.0	33.6	33.9
2003	32.3	32.0	32.0	32.3	33.7	34.6	34.3	35.1	34.4	30.5	33.8	33.6	33.2
2004	31.9	31.2	31.4	32.6	33.2	33.0	32.2	32.5	31.9	29.6	28.7	31.4	31.6
2005	27.6	30.1	30.6	31.1	30.3	28.7	30.2	30.7	30.8	30.7	30.2	30.1	30.1
2006	29.6	29.3	29.4	30.1	30.4	31.2	30.0	30.5	30.3	30.3	29.6	29.2	30.0
2007	27.5	28.7	28.9	29.1	29.7	30.1	29.4	29.7	29.5	29.1	29.0	28.5	29.1
Natural Resources, Mining, and Construction													
2000	8.5	8.4	8.8	9.7	10.3	10.7	10.9	11.1	10.9	10.8	10.3	9.9	10.0
2001	9.1	9.0	9.3	9.8	10.2	10.5	10.9	10.8	10.7	10.3	9.9	9.6	10.0
2002	8.8	8.7	8.7	9.4	10.1	10.4	10.4	10.5	10.3	10.0	9.5	8.9	9.6
2003	8.2	7.8	7.8	8.4	9.2	9.7	10.0	10.1	9.8	9.6	9.2	8.8	9.1
2004	8.0	7.9	8.0	8.9	9.4	9.7	9.7	9.8	9.5	9.5	9.2	8.8	9.0
2005	7.7	7.7	7.8	8.4	8.9	9.2	9.4	9.5	9.3	9.1	8.9	8.2	8.7
2006	7.7	7.5	7.5	8.0	8.5	9.0	9.0	9.1	8.8	8.7	8.1	7.6	8.3
2007	7.3	7.0	7.1	7.4	8.1	8.4	8.4	8.2	8.0	7.9	7.7	7.1	7.7
Manufacturing													
2000	28.5	28.5	28.6	28.9	28.7	29.2	28.8	29.1	29.0	28.7	28.4	28.3	28.7
2001	27.0	26.7	26.7	26.2	26.0	26.0	25.6	25.2	25.4	24.9	24.8	24.8	25.8
2002	24.0	24.2	24.1	23.9	23.9	24.6	24.1	24.6	24.6	24.3	24.5	24.7	24.3
2003	24.1	24.2	24.2	23.9	24.5	24.9	24.3	25.0	24.6	20.9	24.6	24.8	24.2
2004	23.9	23.3	23.4	23.7	23.8	23.3	22.5	22.7	22.4	20.1	19.5	22.6	22.6
2005	19.9	22.4	22.8	22.7	21.4	19.5	20.8	21.2	21.5	21.6	21.3	21.9	21.4
2006	21.9	21.8	21.9	22.1	21.9	22.2	21.0	21.4	21.5	21.6	21.5	21.6	21.7
2007	20.2	21.7	21.8	21.7	21.6	21.7	21.0	21.5	21.5	21.2	21.3	21.4	21.4
Service-Providing													
2000	191.3	198.3	199.6	201.3	200.1	195.4	192.3	191.4	200.1	203.2	204.5	203.8	198.4
2001	195.6	198.8	200.4	202.6	202.1	198.5	195.6	195.6	202.1	204.2	206.0	206.1	200.6
2002	199.6	201.4	203.1	204.8	205.3	200.5	197.2	198.0	205.7	205.8	205.1	205.0	202.6
2003	197.3	200.5	201.5	202.3	202.0	198.1	193.4	193.6	202.0	203.6	203.7	201.8	200.0
2004	197.0	197.9	198.4	201.1	197.9	195.4	191.9	192.1	199.7	202.3	202.8	202.1	198.2
2005	194.7	197.5	198.0	200.1	197.0	194.1	188.9	189.5	199.2	199.5	200.5	199.6	196.6
2006	195.6	197.5	198.8	199.7	196.0	194.9	188.9	190.5	199.5	200.0	201.2	199.7	196.9
2007	193.7	195.8	196.9	197.9	198.8	193.4	188.7	189.2	198.0	199.7	200.4	199.8	196.0
Trade, Transportation, and Utilities													
2000	37.9	37.6	37.8	38.4	38.5	38.5	38.3	38.7	39.0	40.0	41.0	41.6	38.9
2001	40.2	39.6	39.4	39.3	39.3	39.6	39.0	39.0	39.3	39.2	40.7	40.7	39.7
2002	38.7	38.0	38.6	38.4	38.6	39.0	38.3	38.5	38.9	38.7	39.5	39.9	38.8
2003	38.0	37.5	37.3	37.4	37.8	38.3	37.7	37.9	38.2	38.3	38.9	39.3	38.1
2004	37.2	36.6	36.6	37.1	37.2	36.9	36.8	37.1	37.2	37.5	37.8	38.2	37.2
2005	36.6	36.2	36.1	36.2	36.5	36.3	36.2	36.4	36.5	36.3	37.1	37.6	36.5
2006	36.0	35.6	35.9	36.3	36.3	36.5	36.1	36.0	36.2	35.9	36.7	37.0	36.2
2007	35.6	34.9	35.2	35.5	35.5	35.5	35.4	35.4	35.2	35.1	35.7	36.1	35.4
Wholesale Trade													
2000	5.5	5.6	5.7	5.8	5.9	5.8	5.9	5.8	5.8	5.7	5.7	5.8	5.8
2001	6.0	6.0	6.0	6.1	6.2	6.2	6.2	6.1	6.1	6.0	6.0	6.0	6.1
2002	5.8	5.8	5.8	5.9	5.9	6.0	5.9	5.9	5.8	5.8	5.8	5.8	5.9
2003	5.6	5.6	5.6	5.8	5.8	5.9	5.7	5.7	5.7	5.7	5.7	5.6	5.7
2004	5.4	5.4	5.5	5.6	5.7	5.7	5.6	5.6	5.6	5.6	5.5	5.5	5.6
2005	5.5	5.5	5.5	5.5	5.6	5.6	5.7	5.7	5.6	5.4	5.4	5.4	5.5
2006	5.3	5.3	5.4	5.4	5.5	5.7	5.9	5.6	5.5	5.4	5.4	5.5	5.5
2007	5.4	5.3	5.3	5.4	5.4	5.5	5.7	5.6	5.5	5.4	5.4	5.4	5.4
Retail Trade													
2000	26.6	26.2	26.3	26.8	26.8	26.8	26.3	26.6	26.9	27.8	28.8	29.3	27.1
2001	28.1	27.6	27.4	27.0	26.8	26.9	26.4	26.7	26.6	26.9	28.0	28.1	27.2
2002	26.5	25.9	26.5	26.2	26.3	26.5	25.8	26.0	26.6	26.4	27.2	27.6	26.5
2003	26.1	25.6	25.4	25.3	25.7	26.0	25.5	25.7	26.0	25.9	26.5	27.0	25.9
2004	25.3	24.8	24.7	25.1	25.1	24.9	24.9	25.1	25.4	25.5	26.0	26.3	25.3
2005	24.9	24.5	24.4	24.5	24.7	24.5	24.2	24.3	24.5	24.4	25.1	25.5	24.6
2006	24.2	23.9	24.1	24.4	24.4	24.3	23.9	23.9	24.2	24.1	24.8	24.9	24.3
2007	24.0	23.4	23.7	23.9	23.9	23.7	23.3	23.4	23.3	23.2	23.8	24.1	23.6

Employment by Industry: Lansing-East Lansing, MI, 2000–2007—*Continued*

(Numbers in thousands, not seasonally adjusted.)

Industry and year	January	February	March	April	May	June	July	August	September	October	November	December	Annual Average
Transportation and Utilities													
2000	5.8	5.8	5.8	5.8	5.8	5.9	6.1	6.3	6.3	6.5	6.5	6.5	6.1
2001	6.1	6.0	6.0	6.2	6.3	6.5	6.4	6.5	6.5	6.7	6.7	6.6	6.4
2002	6.4	6.3	6.3	6.3	6.4	6.5	6.6	6.6	6.5	6.5	6.5	6.5	6.5
2003	6.3	6.3	6.3	6.3	6.3	6.4	6.5	6.5	6.5	6.7	6.7	6.7	6.5
2004	6.5	6.4	6.4	6.4	6.4	6.3	6.3	6.4	6.2	6.4	6.3	6.4	6.4
2005	6.2	6.2	6.2	6.2	6.2	6.2	6.3	6.4	6.4	6.5	6.6	6.7	6.3
2006	6.5	6.4	6.4	6.5	6.4	6.5	6.3	6.5	6.5	6.4	6.5	6.6	6.5
2007	6.2	6.2	6.2	6.2	6.2	6.3	6.4	6.4	6.4	6.5	6.5	6.6	6.3
Information													
2000	3.9	3.9	3.9	3.9	3.9	3.9	4.0	3.9	3.8	3.7	3.7	3.8	3.9
2001	3.8	3.5	3.5	3.6	3.5	3.6	3.6	3.5	3.5	3.5	3.6	3.7	3.6
2002	3.5	3.5	3.5	3.6	3.7	3.8	3.7	3.8	3.8	3.7	3.8	3.9	3.7
2003	3.8	3.8	3.9	3.5	3.5	3.5	3.4	3.4	3.4	3.3	3.4	3.5	3.5
2004	3.2	3.1	3.2	3.2	3.2	3.2	3.4	3.4	3.4	3.4	3.3	3.4	3.3
2005	3.2	3.2	3.2	3.2	3.2	3.1	3.1	3.1	3.0	3.0	3.0	3.0	3.1
2006	3.0	2.9	2.9	2.9	2.9	3.0	2.9	2.8	2.9	2.9	2.9	2.9	2.9
2007	2.9	2.9	2.9	2.9	2.9	2.9	2.9	2.9	2.9	2.9	2.9	2.9	2.9
Financial Activities													
2000	13.2	13.1	13.1	13.2	13.2	13.4	13.6	13.5	13.4	13.5	13.6	13.6	13.4
2001	13.3	13.4	13.4	13.6	13.8	13.9	13.9	14.0	13.7	13.8	14.0	14.0	13.7
2002	13.8	13.7	13.7	13.9	14.2	14.4	14.7	14.8	14.6	14.7	14.8	14.9	14.4
2003	14.8	14.8	14.8	15.1	15.4	15.5	15.5	15.5	15.4	15.3	15.2	15.2	15.2
2004	14.8	14.9	15.0	15.2	15.4	15.4	15.4	15.4	15.2	15.0	15.1	15.1	15.2
2005	14.8	14.8	14.7	14.8	15.0	15.2	15.2	15.3	15.1	15.0	15.2	15.2	15.0
2006	15.1	15.1	15.1	15.0	15.2	15.4	15.4	15.5	15.3	15.3	15.3	15.3	15.3
2007	15.0	15.1	15.1	15.2	15.2	15.3	15.4	15.4	15.3	15.2	15.2	15.3	15.2
Professional and Business Services													
2000	23.1	23.0	23.5	23.6	23.5	23.8	23.3	23.6	23.6	23.2	23.0	22.8	23.3
2001	22.7	22.8	23.3	22.9	22.9	23.2	22.8	23.3	23.2	22.8	22.6	22.4	22.9
2002	22.1	22.2	22.7	22.9	22.9	23.2	22.3	22.8	22.6	22.7	22.5	22.5	22.6
2003	21.5	21.6	21.9	22.0	21.5	21.8	21.3	21.9	21.7	21.7	21.3	21.2	21.6
2004	20.8	20.7	20.9	21.5	21.4	21.6	21.0	21.2	21.2	21.1	21.1	21.0	21.1
2005	20.2	20.3	20.5	20.8	20.6	20.5	19.9	20.1	20.1	20.4	20.4	20.3	20.3
2006	19.9	20.0	20.4	20.7	20.7	20.8	20.2	20.7	20.7	20.4	20.6	20.6	20.5
2007	19.9	20.1	20.2	20.3	20.1	20.3	19.7	20.0	20.0	20.0	20.1	20.0	20.1
Education and Health Services													
2000	23.9	24.1	24.3	24.2	24.1	23.9	23.0	23.1	23.5	23.9	24.0	23.9	23.8
2001	22.1	22.3	22.6	22.7	22.9	22.8	22.7	22.9	23.0	23.2	23.2	23.4	22.8
2002	23.4	23.4	23.5	23.7	24.0	24.0	23.8	24.0	24.1	23.8	23.9	23.9	23.8
2003	24.3	24.1	24.1	24.6	24.7	24.5	25.0	25.1	25.8	25.7	26.0	25.8	25.0
2004	25.7	25.9	26.1	26.3	25.9	25.6	25.4	25.7	26.1	26.6	26.7	26.4	26.0
2005	26.5	26.9	27.2	27.6	27.4	27.1	27.0	26.9	27.7	27.8	28.0	27.9	27.3
2006	27.8	28.3	28.3	28.1	28.1	28.0	27.3	27.3	27.9	28.1	28.1	28.2	28.0
2007	27.7	27.9	28.1	27.9	28.0	27.9	27.7	27.7	28.1	28.3	28.4	28.3	28.0
Leisure and Hospitality													
2000	17.8	18.0	18.2	19.1	19.3	19.0	18.8	19.0	19.4	19.2	19.0	18.7	18.8
2001	17.2	17.4	17.6	18.4	18.8	18.8	18.7	19.0	19.2	18.9	19.1	19.2	18.5
2002	18.4	18.6	19.0	19.5	20.1	19.9	19.7	19.9	20.6	19.9	19.7	19.2	19.5
2003	18.0	18.3	18.4	19.2	19.9	20.0	19.4	19.8	20.2	19.8	19.5	19.2	19.3
2004	18.8	18.8	18.8	19.6	20.1	20.3	19.9	20.0	20.4	19.7	19.6	19.6	19.6
2005	18.2	18.3	18.6	19.5	19.9	19.8	19.3	19.7	20.2	19.0	18.8	18.7	19.2
2006	17.7	18.3	18.7	19.3	19.7	19.7	19.1	19.4	19.8	19.1	19.1	19.0	19.1
2007	18.3	18.2	18.5	19.2	20.0	20.0	19.4	19.5	19.9	19.2	19.0	18.8	19.2
Other Services													
2000	9.8	10.0	10.0	10.1	10.2	10.4	10.4	10.4	10.3	10.2	10.2	10.1	10.2
2001	10.8	10.9	11.0	11.1	11.2	11.4	11.1	11.0	10.9	10.9	11.0	11.0	11.0
2002	10.9	11.1	11.1	11.2	11.3	11.3	11.4	11.3	11.2	11.3	11.1	11.1	11.2
2003	10.8	10.9	11.0	10.9	11.0	11.1	11.2	11.1	11.1	11.1	11.1	11.2	11.0
2004	10.7	10.9	11.0	10.8	10.9	11.1	10.8	10.8	10.9	11.0	11.1	11.2	10.9
2005	11.0	11.1	11.1	11.0	11.1	11.1	11.1	11.0	11.0	11.2	11.0	11.0	11.1
2006	10.8	11.0	11.0	11.3	11.4	11.5	11.4	11.4	11.4	11.3	11.2	11.1	11.2
2007	10.9	10.9	10.9	11.3	11.4	11.8	11.7	11.7	11.6	11.7	11.7	11.7	11.4
Government													
2000	61.7	68.6	68.8	68.8	67.4	62.5	60.9	59.2	67.1	69.5	70.0	69.3	66.2
2001	65.5	68.9	69.6	71.0	69.7	65.2	63.8	62.6	69.4	71.5	71.8	71.7	68.4
2002	68.8	70.9	71.0	71.6	70.5	64.9	63.3	62.9	69.9	71.0	69.8	69.6	68.7
2003	66.1	69.5	70.1	69.6	68.2	63.4	59.9	58.9	66.2	68.4	68.3	66.4	66.3
2004	65.8	67.0	66.8	67.4	63.8	61.3	59.2	58.5	65.3	68.0	68.1	67.2	64.9
2005	64.2	66.7	66.6	67.0	63.3	61.0	57.1	57.0	65.6	66.8	67.0	65.9	64.0
2006	65.3	66.3	66.5	66.1	61.7	60.0	56.5	57.4	65.3	67.0	67.3	65.6	63.8
2007	63.4	65.8	66.0	65.6	65.7	59.7	56.5	56.6	65.0	67.3	67.4	66.7	63.8

Employment by Industry: Modesto, CA, 2000–2007

(Numbers in thousands, not seasonally adjusted.)

Industry and year	January	February	March	April	May	June	July	August	September	October	November	December	Annual Average
Total Nonfarm													
2000	139.1	139.7	140.7	141.9	142.3	145.8	146.1	149.5	148.2	145.2	145.3	146.3	144.2
2001	143.7	145.0	146.3	146.4	148.1	151.1	152.2	157.6	155.2	151.1	151.1	149.1	149.7
2002	145.7	145.7	147.6	148.2	148.1	150.5	153.2	157.6	157.4	151.9	150.6	151.3	150.7
2003	147.8	148.5	150.1	150.8	151.7	152.6	153.2	158.4	157.7	152.1	152.0	152.5	152.2
2004	147.9	148.7	150.2	151.4	152.7	155.1	160.7	162.1	158.0	155.9	156.3	156.6	154.6
2005	152.7	153.9	155.3	156.9	157.8	159.6	161.4	166.3	163.1	160.7	160.6	160.7	159.1
2006	156.0	156.7	157.8	158.0	159.5	160.3	160.7	164.3	163.9	160.6	160.0	160.0	159.8
2007	156.9	157.5	158.8	158.5	159.0	161.2	162.7	163.7	162.9	159.0	159.4	160.4	160.0
Total Private													
2000	115.5	116.0	116.5	117.4	117.5	121.3	122.9	126.0	125.1	121.5	121.3	122.1	120.3
2001	120.1	121.0	121.9	121.8	123.5	126.8	129.0	133.6	130.7	124.6	124.1	124.7	125.2
2002	120.4	120.7	122.2	122.6	122.7	124.8	128.6	133.6	132.4	126.2	124.8	125.6	125.4
2003	122.5	123.1	124.6	125.3	126.4	127.3	129.3	134.9	133.2	127.0	126.9	127.6	127.3
2004	122.9	123.4	124.8	126.2	127.6	130.0	136.4	137.9	133.4	130.4	130.7	131.0	129.6
2005	127.4	128.3	129.5	131.0	132.2	134.1	137.0	140.9	137.8	134.4	134.3	134.5	133.5
2006	130.1	130.5	131.4	131.5	133.5	134.0	134.9	138.4	137.7	134.0	133.2	133.1	133.5
2007	130.4	130.6	131.9	131.6	132.5	134.7	137.6	138.3	137.0	132.7	133.1	134.2	133.7
Goods-Producing													
2000	28.9	29.2	29.4	30.5	30.6	32.8	35.2	39.0	37.0	32.8	31.9	31.8	32.4
2001	31.5	32.2	32.5	31.6	32.4	34.1	37.4	41.5	38.8	33.4	31.6	31.4	34.0
2002	29.8	30.1	30.4	31.2	31.1	32.5	36.1	40.7	39.2	33.5	31.6	31.9	33.2
2003	31.5	32.0	32.5	32.4	33.1	33.6	36.1	41.8	40.0	34.1	33.5	33.2	34.5
2004	31.7	32.0	32.6	33.1	33.5	34.9	40.6	41.9	37.7	34.5	33.8	33.5	35.0
2005	32.5	32.9	33.4	34.3	34.4	36.0	38.6	42.7	39.8	36.3	35.6	35.1	36.0
2006	33.9	34.4	34.2	34.1	35.2	35.0	36.3	39.7	39.2	35.5	33.9	33.3	35.4
2007	32.1	32.3	33.0	33.0	33.5	35.1	38.1	38.5	37.3	32.6	31.7	32.3	34.1
Natural Resources, Mining, and Construction													
2000	8.7	8.8	9.0	9.5	9.8	10.2	10.2	10.2	10.5	10.3	10.3	10.4	9.8
2001	10.0	10.5	10.9	10.7	11.1	11.5	11.5	11.8	11.6	11.2	10.7	10.5	11.0
2002	9.7	9.8	10.0	10.5	10.6	10.8	11.3	11.3	11.2	11.3	11.3	10.9	10.7
2003	10.6	10.7	10.9	11.1	11.6	11.8	11.8	11.9	11.6	11.7	11.5	11.4	11.4
2004	11.1	11.2	11.6	12.0	12.1	12.4	13.1	13.0	12.9	12.8	12.6	12.5	12.3
2005	11.8	12.1	12.3	12.8	13.0	13.4	13.9	14.3	14.4	14.2	14.3	14.0	13.4
2006	13.1	13.3	13.1	13.0	13.8	13.6	13.5	13.6	13.5	13.2	12.8	12.4	13.2
2007	11.3	11.2	11.5	11.6	11.9	12.0	12.0	11.8	11.2	11.0	10.7	10.5	11.4
Manufacturing													
2000	20.2	20.4	20.4	21.0	20.8	22.6	25.0	28.8	26.5	22.5	21.6	21.4	22.6
2001	21.5	21.7	21.6	20.9	21.3	22.6	25.9	29.7	27.2	22.2	20.9	20.9	23.0
2002	20.1	20.3	20.4	20.7	20.5	21.7	24.8	29.4	28.0	22.2	20.3	21.0	22.5
2003	20.9	21.3	21.6	21.3	21.5	21.8	24.3	29.9	28.4	22.4	22.0	21.8	23.1
2004	20.6	20.8	21.0	21.1	21.4	22.5	27.5	28.9	24.8	21.7	21.2	21.0	22.7
2005	20.7	20.8	21.1	21.5	21.4	22.6	24.7	28.4	25.4	22.1	21.3	21.1	22.6
2006	20.8	21.1	21.1	21.1	21.4	21.4	22.8	26.1	25.7	22.3	21.1	20.9	22.2
2007	20.8	21.1	21.5	21.4	21.6	23.1	26.1	26.7	26.1	21.6	21.0	21.8	22.7
Service-Providing													
2000	110.2	110.5	111.3	111.4	111.7	113.0	110.9	110.5	111.2	112.4	113.4	114.5	111.8
2001	112.2	112.8	113.8	114.8	115.7	117.0	114.8	116.1	116.4	117.7	119.5	117.7	115.7
2002	115.9	115.6	117.2	117.0	117.0	118.0	117.1	116.9	118.2	118.4	119.0	119.4	117.5
2003	116.3	116.5	117.6	118.4	118.3	119.0	117.1	116.6	117.7	118.0	118.5	119.3	117.8
2004	116.2	116.7	117.6	118.3	119.2	120.2	120.1	120.2	120.3	121.4	122.5	123.1	119.7
2005	120.2	121.0	121.9	122.6	123.4	123.6	123.6	123.6	123.3	124.4	125.0	125.6	123.1
2006	122.1	122.3	123.6	123.9	124.3	125.3	124.4	124.6	124.7	125.1	126.1	126.7	124.4
2007	124.8	125.2	125.8	125.5	125.5	126.1	124.6	125.2	125.6	126.4	127.7	128.1	125.9
Trade, Transportation, and Utilities													
2000	29.4	28.9	28.9	28.8	29.0	29.5	29.1	29.0	29.3	29.5	30.1	30.4	29.3
2001	30.1	29.7	29.8	30.1	30.5	31.2	30.8	31.1	31.1	30.9	31.8	32.1	30.8
2002	30.8	30.4	30.9	31.1	31.2	31.6	31.8	32.1	32.3	32.4	32.9	33.3	31.7
2003	31.5	31.1	31.3	31.5	31.8	32.1	32.1	32.2	32.2	32.1	32.6	33.2	32.0
2004	31.1	30.9	31.0	31.2	31.9	32.5	32.5	32.6	32.4	32.7	33.5	34.0	32.2
2005	32.8	32.6	32.9	33.0	33.3	33.5	33.7	33.8	33.8	34.2	35.0	35.6	33.7
2006	33.4	32.9	33.3	32.9	33.3	33.6	33.6	33.6	33.5	33.6	34.5	34.8	33.6
2007	33.5	33.2	33.4	33.1	33.3	33.5	33.5	33.6	33.6	33.9	35.0	35.5	33.8
Wholesale Trade													
2000	5.5	5.4	5.4	5.3	5.3	5.4	5.5	5.5	5.4	5.4	5.5	5.3	5.4
2001	5.3	5.3	5.3	5.3	5.4	5.5	5.5	5.6	5.5	5.5	5.3	5.2	5.4
2002	5.3	5.3	5.4	5.6	5.6	5.7	5.7	5.8	5.8	5.8	5.8	5.7	5.6
2003	5.5	5.5	5.6	5.6	5.6	5.7	5.8	5.8	5.7	5.7	5.7	5.7	5.6
2004	5.9	5.9	5.9	5.9	6.0	6.1	6.2	6.3	6.1	6.1	6.1	6.0	6.0
2005	6.0	6.0	6.1	6.2	6.3	6.3	6.4	6.4	6.4	6.4	6.3	6.2	6.3
2006	5.8	5.8	5.9	5.7	5.8	5.8	6.0	6.0	6.0	6.0	5.9	5.8	5.9
2007	5.9	6.0	6.0	6.0	6.0	6.2	6.1	6.1					
Retail Trade													
2000	20.1	19.8	19.8	19.7	19.9	20.2	19.7	19.7	20.0	20.2	21.1	21.4	20.1
2001	20.7	20.3	20.4	20.6	20.8	21.3	20.9	21.0	21.2	21.3	22.3	22.7	21.1
2002	21.2	20.8	21.2	21.2	21.2	21.4	21.6	21.6	21.6	21.7	22.0	23.3	21.7
2003	21.6	21.2	21.2	21.3	21.4	21.6	21.7	21.6	21.7	21.8	22.5	23.1	21.8
2004	21.1	20.9	20.9	21.1	21.5	21.7	21.4	21.3	21.3	21.5	22.3	22.8	21.5
2005	21.9	21.6	21.7	21.7	21.9	22.0	22.0	22.1	22.1	22.6	23.5	24.2	22.3
2006	22.6	22.1	22.3	22.2	22.3	22.5	22.4	22.3	22.1	22.2	23.2	23.5	22.5
2007	22.2	21.8	21.9	21.7	21.9	21.8	21.9	22.0	21.9	22.2	23.3	23.8	22.2

Employment by Industry: Modesto, CA, 2000–2007—*Continued*

(Numbers in thousands, not seasonally adjusted.)

Industry and year	January	February	March	April	May	June	July	August	September	October	November	December	Annual Average
Transportation and Utilities													
2000	3.8	3.7	3.7	3.8	3.8	3.9	3.9	3.9	3.9	3.8	3.7	3.7	3.8
2001	4.1	4.1	4.1	4.2	4.3	4.4	4.4	4.5	4.4	4.3	4.3	4.2	4.3
2002	4.3	4.3	4.3	4.3	4.4	4.5	4.5	4.7	4.7	4.6	4.4	4.4	4.5
2003	4.4	4.4	4.4	4.5	4.6	4.7	4.7	4.8	4.8	4.6	4.4	4.4	4.5
2004	4.1	4.1	4.2	4.2	4.4	4.7	4.9	5.0	5.0	5.1	5.1	5.2	4.7
2005	4.9	5.0	5.1	5.1	5.1	5.2	5.3	5.3	5.3	5.2	5.2	5.2	5.2
2006	5.0	5.0	5.1	5.0	5.2	5.3	5.2	5.3	5.4	5.4	5.4	5.4	5.2
2007	5.4	5.4	5.5	5.4	5.4	5.5	5.5	5.6	5.6	5.7	5.8	5.9	5.6
Information													
2000	2.0	2.0	2.0	1.9	2.0	2.0	2.0	1.9	1.9	2.0	2.0	2.0	2.0
2001	2.2	2.3	2.2	2.3	2.3	2.3	2.2	2.2	2.2	2.2	2.2	2.2	2.2
2002	2.0	2.0	2.0	2.0	2.1	2.0	2.1	2.0	2.1	2.1	2.1	2.2	2.1
2003	2.1	2.1	2.2	2.1	2.1	2.0	2.0	2.0	2.0	2.5	2.6	2.6	2.1
2004	2.6	2.6	2.5	2.5	2.5	2.5	2.6	2.5	2.5	2.5	2.5	2.6	2.5
2005	2.6	2.6	2.6	2.6	2.6	2.5	2.5	2.5	2.4	2.4	2.4	2.5	2.5
2006	2.4	2.4	2.5	2.5	2.5	2.4	2.4	2.4	2.3	2.4	2.4	2.4	2.4
2007	2.3	2.4	2.3	2.3	2.4	2.3	2.4	2.4	2.3	2.3	2.3	2.3	2.3
Financial Activities													
2000	5.2	5.3	5.2	5.0	5.0	5.1	5.0	4.9	5.0	5.1	5.1	5.2	5.1
2001	5.4	5.4	5.5	5.4	5.4	5.5	5.4	5.4	5.4	5.4	5.5	5.5	5.4
2002	5.4	5.4	5.4	5.4	5.5	5.6	5.5	5.6	5.7	5.6	5.7	5.8	5.6
2003	5.7	5.7	5.9	6.0	6.1	6.1	6.2	6.1	6.1	6.2	6.1	6.2	6.0
2004	5.9	6.0	6.1	6.0	6.0	6.1	6.2	6.2	6.2	6.2	6.2	6.2	6.1
2005	6.1	6.1	6.1	6.1	6.1	6.1	6.2	6.2	6.2	6.3	6.3	6.4	6.2
2006	6.3	6.3	6.3	6.4	6.4	6.4	6.3	6.3	6.2	6.2	6.1	6.1	6.3
2007	6.2	6.3	6.3	6.2	6.2	6.2	6.2	6.2	6.1	6.0	6.0	5.9	6.2
Professional and Business Services													
2000	16.7	16.9	17.0	17.2	16.9	17.3	17.4	17.3	17.6	17.5	17.5	17.9	17.3
2001	16.6	16.8	16.9	16.9	16.9	17.4	16.7	16.8	16.6	16.4	16.4	16.7	16.8
2002	15.9	15.9	16.1	15.4	15.1	14.9	14.9	15.0	14.5	14.3	14.0	13.9	15.0
2003	13.5	13.5	13.8	14.0	13.9	14.1	14.1	14.1	14.2	13.5	13.6	13.7	13.8
2004	13.6	13.6	13.9	14.0	14.1	14.2	14.4	14.5	14.3	14.4	14.6	14.6	14.2
2005	14.5	14.8	14.8	14.6	15.0	15.0	15.4	15.1	14.9	14.8	14.7	14.6	14.9
2006	14.4	14.5	14.6	14.7	14.8	14.9	15.1	15.2	15.0	14.9	14.6	14.7	14.8
2007	14.9	15.0	14.9	14.6	14.5	14.8	14.7	15.0	15.0	15.0	14.9	15.0	14.9
Education and Health Services													
2000	15.9	16.1	16.1	16.3	16.3	16.4	16.4	16.3	16.6	16.7	16.8	16.9	16.4
2001	16.2	16.3	16.4	17.0	17.3	17.4	17.4	17.4	17.4	17.2	17.4	17.3	17.1
2002	17.2	17.5	17.6	17.8	17.9	18.0	18.2	18.3	18.5	18.7	18.8	18.9	18.1
2003	18.6	18.8	18.9	19.2	19.3	19.3	18.8	18.9	19.0	18.9	18.8	18.8	18.9
2004	18.5	18.7	18.8	19.3	19.3	19.4	19.2	19.3	19.4	19.6	19.6	19.6	19.2
2005	18.9	19.0	19.1	19.3	19.5	19.5	19.4	19.4	19.6	19.5	19.5	19.5	19.4
2006	19.2	19.4	19.4	19.5	19.7	19.9	19.7	19.8	20.1	20.3	20.5	20.7	19.9
2007	20.8	20.9	21.1	20.9	21.0	21.1	21.1	21.1	21.2	21.3	21.5	21.5	21.1
Leisure and Hospitality													
2000	11.9	12.0	12.2	12.1	12.1	12.4	12.1	12.0	12.0	12.2	12.2	12.2	12.1
2001	12.5	12.6	12.8	12.7	12.9	13.0	13.1	13.2	13.1	13.2	13.2	13.5	13.0
2002	13.3	13.4	13.6	13.6	13.7	13.9	13.8	13.7	13.8	13.4	13.5	13.5	13.6
2003	13.5	13.6	13.8	13.8	13.9	13.9	13.8	13.6	13.5	13.5	13.6	13.7	13.7
2004	13.4	13.5	13.7	13.9	14.1	14.2	14.7	14.7	14.7	14.3	14.4	14.4	14.2
2005	14.0	14.2	14.5	14.9	15.1	15.3	15.0	15.0	15.0	14.7	14.7	14.7	14.8
2006	14.8	14.9	15.3	15.6	15.7	15.8	15.5	15.4	15.3	15.0	15.1	15.1	15.3
2007	14.8	14.6	15.0	15.4	15.6	15.7	15.6	15.5	15.4	15.5	15.6	15.7	15.4
Other Services													
2000	5.5	5.6	5.7	5.6	5.6	5.8	5.7	5.6	5.7	5.7	5.7	5.7	5.7
2001	5.6	5.7	5.8	5.8	5.8	5.9	6.0	6.0	6.1	5.9	6.0	6.0	5.9
2002	6.0	6.0	6.2	6.1	6.1	6.3	6.2	6.2	6.3	6.2	6.2	6.1	6.2
2003	6.1	6.3	6.2	6.3	6.2	6.2	6.2	6.2	6.2	6.2	6.1	6.2	6.2
2004	6.1	6.1	6.2	6.2	6.2	6.2	6.2	6.2	6.2	6.2	6.1	6.1	6.2
2005	6.0	6.1	6.1	6.2	6.2	6.2	6.2	6.2	6.1	6.2	6.1	6.1	6.1
2006	5.7	5.7	5.8	5.8	5.9	6.0	6.0	6.0	6.1	6.1	6.1	6.0	5.9
2007	5.8	5.9	5.9	6.1	6.0	6.0	6.0	6.0	6.1	6.1	6.1	6.0	6.0
Government													
2000	23.6	23.7	24.2	24.5	24.8	24.5	23.2	23.5	23.1	23.7	24.0	24.2	23.9
2001	23.6	24.0	24.4	24.6	24.6	24.3	23.2	24.0	24.5	26.5	27.0	24.4	24.6
2002	25.3	25.0	25.4	25.6	25.4	25.7	24.6	24.0	25.0	25.7	25.8	25.7	25.3
2003	25.3	25.4	25.5	25.5	25.3	25.3	23.9	23.5	24.5	25.1	25.1	24.9	24.9
2004	25.0	25.3	25.4	25.2	25.1	25.1	24.3	24.2	24.6	25.5	25.6	25.6	25.1
2005	25.3	25.6	25.8	25.9	25.6	25.5	24.4	25.4	25.3	26.3	26.3	26.2	25.6
2006	25.9	26.2	26.4	26.5	26.0	26.3	25.8	25.9	26.2	26.6	26.8	26.9	26.3
2007	26.5	26.9	26.9	26.9	26.5	26.5	25.1	25.4	25.9	26.3	26.3	26.2	26.3

Employment by Industry: Deltona-Daytona Beach-Ormond Beach, FL, 2000–2007

(Numbers in thousands, not seasonally adjusted.)

Industry and year	January	February	March	April	May	June	July	August	September	October	November	December	Annual Average
Total Nonfarm													
2000	144.1	146.3	147.2	147.2	147.9	146.5	146.6	148.9	149.3	148.0	148.8	149.4	147.5
2001	147.2	149.8	150.0	150.5	150.1	149.0	148.1	150.0	151.0	151.9	152.9	153.2	150.3
2002	150.8	152.8	153.0	154.1	153.9	152.2	150.7	152.8	152.7	153.9	154.7	156.1	153.1
2003	154.4	156.9	157.7	157.9	157.7	155.9	156.7	158.2	159.3	159.4	160.4	160.9	157.9
2004	160.9	163.3	164.6	165.6	165.6	163.9	163.5	164.6	163.2	165.2	167.8	169.5	164.8
2005	167.7	170.1	171.0	172.0	171.6	169.7	169.5	171.1	172.2	172.1	173.7	174.2	171.2
2006	172.4	174.7	176.7	176.4	176.3	173.6	172.1	174.1	174.0	173.5	174.2	173.4	174.3
2007	170.3	174.2	176.2	174.8	174.1	170.8	170.1	171.4	171.6	172.0	172.9	172.7	172.6
Total Private													
2000	122.7	124.5	125.2	125.2	125.8	126.8	126.8	127.5	127.5	126.3	127.0	128.5	126.2
2001	125.7	127.9	128.0	128.4	128.3	128.9	128.1	128.2	128.5	129.8	130.5	130.9	128.6
2002	128.5	130.6	130.8	131.8	131.8	131.8	130.4	130.8	130.5	131.6	132.4	133.7	131.2
2003	132.2	134.6	135.4	135.4	135.3	135.3	136.1	135.9	136.9	137.1	138.0	138.5	135.8
2004	138.3	140.6	141.8	142.6	142.9	143.0	142.6	141.9	140.4	142.4	144.8	146.6	142.3
2005	144.5	146.9	147.8	148.5	148.3	148.2	148.0	147.8	148.4	148.0	149.5	150.0	148.0
2006	148.1	150.2	152.2	152.1	151.8	151.1	149.7	149.5	149.3	148.9	149.4	148.6	150.1
2007	145.4	149.0	151.0	150.0	149.1	147.9	147.4	146.6	146.7	147.0	147.8	147.7	148.0
Goods-Producing													
2000	18.8	19.0	19.0	19.2	19.0	19.0	19.4	19.5	19.4	19.4	19.5	19.9	19.3
2001	19.2	19.1	18.9	19.0	19.1	19.2	19.1	19.1	19.0	19.2	19.2	19.5	19.1
2002	18.8	18.7	18.6	18.8	19.1	19.2	19.0	19.5	19.4	19.6	19.8	19.8	19.2
2003	19.7	19.7	19.7	19.5	19.7	19.9	19.8	19.9	20.1	20.0	20.2	20.4	19.8
2004	20.6	20.7	21.0	21.3	21.6	21.9	22.1	22.1	21.9	22.0	22.4	23.0	21.7
2005	22.4	22.9	23.2	23.6	23.9	24.2	24.1	24.2	24.6	24.9	25.1	25.1	24.0
2006	24.9	25.2	25.7	25.6	25.6	25.8	25.4	25.5	25.6	25.8	25.9	24.9	25.5
2007	24.0	24.5	24.9	24.7	24.1	23.9	23.2	23.2	23.4	23.4	23.2	23.1	23.8
Natural Resources, Mining, and Construction													
2000	8.1	8.2	8.2	8.2	8.1	8.0	8.3	8.4	8.5	8.5	8.6	8.8	8.3
2001	8.6	8.5	8.4	8.6	8.6	8.8	8.9	8.9	9.0	9.0	9.1	9.3	8.8
2002	8.9	8.9	8.9	9.1	9.3	9.4	9.5	10.0	10.0	10.4	10.5	10.6	9.6
2003	10.3	10.3	10.4	10.1	10.3	10.5	10.4	10.5	10.6	10.6	10.7	10.8	10.4
2004	11.1	11.2	11.4	11.6	11.8	11.9	12.1	12.1	12.0	12.3	12.6	13.0	11.9
2005	12.6	13.0	13.3	13.5	13.6	13.9	13.8	13.8	14.2	14.5	14.7	14.7	13.8
2006	14.4	14.7	15.1	14.9	14.9	15.0	14.8	14.9	15.0	15.2	15.3	14.3	14.9
2007	13.6	14.0	14.4	14.2	13.6	13.6	13.0	13.0	13.2	13.2	13.0	12.9	13.5
Manufacturing													
2000	10.7	10.8	10.8	11.0	10.9	11.0	11.1	11.1	10.9	10.9	10.9	11.1	10.9
2001	10.6	10.6	10.5	10.4	10.5	10.4	10.2	10.2	10.0	10.2	10.1	10.2	10.3
2002	9.9	9.8	9.7	9.7	9.8	9.8	9.5	9.5	9.4	9.2	9.3	9.2	9.6
2003	9.4	9.4	9.3	9.4	9.4	9.4	9.4	9.4	9.5	9.4	9.5	9.6	9.4
2004	9.5	9.5	9.6	9.7	9.8	10.0	10.0	10.0	9.9	9.7	9.8	10.0	9.8
2005	9.8	9.9	9.9	10.1	10.3	10.3	10.3	10.4	10.4	10.4	10.4	10.4	10.2
2006	10.5	10.5	10.6	10.7	10.7	10.8	10.6	10.6	10.6	10.6	10.6	10.6	10.6
2007	10.4	10.5	10.5	10.5	10.5	10.3	10.2	10.2	10.2	10.2	10.2	10.2	10.3
Service-Providing													
2000	125.3	127.3	128.2	128.0	128.9	127.5	127.2	129.4	129.9	128.6	129.3	129.5	128.3
2001	128.0	130.7	131.1	131.5	131.0	129.8	129.0	130.9	132.0	132.7	133.7	133.7	131.2
2002	132.0	134.1	134.4	135.3	134.8	133.0	131.7	133.3	133.3	134.3	134.9	136.3	134.0
2003	134.7	137.2	138.0	138.4	138.0	136.0	136.9	138.3	139.2	139.4	140.2	140.5	138.0
2004	140.3	142.6	143.6	144.3	144.0	142.0	141.4	142.5	141.3	143.2	145.4	146.5	143.1
2005	145.3	147.2	147.8	148.4	147.7	145.5	145.4	146.9	147.6	147.2	148.6	149.1	147.2
2006	147.5	149.5	151.0	150.8	150.7	147.8	146.7	148.6	148.4	147.7	148.3	148.5	148.8
2007	146.3	149.7	151.3	150.1	150.0	146.9	146.9	148.2	148.2	148.6	149.7	149.6	148.8
Trade, Transportation, and Utilities													
2000	30.8	30.8	30.9	31.2	31.4	31.9	31.1	31.5	31.2	31.1	31.8	32.3	31.3
2001	30.7	30.9	31.4	31.3	31.2	31.1	30.7	30.6	30.7	30.8	31.3	31.6	31.0
2002	30.7	30.8	30.8	31.0	31.0	30.9	30.6	30.5	30.4	30.6	31.0	31.8	30.8
2003	31.0	30.9	31.1	31.0	31.0	31.0	31.1	31.2	31.5	31.8	32.2	32.4	31.3
2004	31.7	31.7	31.9	31.7	31.9	31.7	31.7	31.6	31.3	31.8	32.7	33.1	31.9
2005	32.3	32.4	32.6	33.1	33.3	33.4	33.2	33.2	33.2	32.9	33.5	34.0	33.1
2006	33.0	33.1	33.2	33.2	33.2	33.1	32.6	32.8	32.8	32.9	33.4	34.0	33.1
2007	33.1	33.2	33.8	33.6	33.6	33.2	33.3	33.2	33.3	33.1	33.8	34.0	33.4
Wholesale Trade													
2000	4.3	4.3	4.4	4.4	4.5	4.5	4.4	4.5	4.5	4.4	4.4	4.5	4.4
2001	4.3	4.3	4.3	4.4	4.4	4.4	4.4	4.4	4.5	4.5	4.5	4.5	4.4
2002	4.5	4.6	4.6	4.7	4.7	4.7	4.7	4.7	4.7	4.7	4.7	4.7	4.7
2003	4.7	4.7	4.8	4.7	4.6	4.6	4.6	4.6	4.6	4.5	4.5	4.5	4.6
2004	4.7	4.8	4.8	4.7	4.7	4.7	4.6	4.6	4.6	4.6	4.6	4.6	4.7
2005	4.6	4.6	4.6	4.8	4.8	4.9	4.9	4.9	5.0	4.9	4.9	5.0	4.8
2006	4.9	4.9	4.9	5.0	5.0	5.0	4.9	5.0	5.0	5.0	5.0	5.0	5.0
2007	5.3	5.3	5.3	5.3	5.4	5.3	5.4	5.3	5.4	5.4	5.4	5.4	5.4
Retail Trade													
2000	23.8	23.8	23.7	24.1	24.2	24.6	23.9	24.2	23.9	24.0	24.8	25.1	24.2
2001	23.8	23.9	24.4	24.2	24.1	24.0	23.6	23.6	23.5	23.6	24.1	24.3	23.9
2002	23.6	23.5	23.5	23.7	23.7	23.6	23.4	23.3	23.2	23.4	23.8	24.5	23.6
2003	23.8	23.6	23.7	23.8	23.9	23.9	24.0	24.2	24.5	24.9	25.4	25.6	24.2
2004	24.8	24.7	24.9	24.9	25.0	24.8	24.9	24.8	24.5	25.0	25.9	26.2	25.0
2005	25.5	25.5	25.7	26.0	26.2	26.2	26.0	26.0	25.9	25.7	26.3	26.6	26.0
2006	25.8	25.9	26.0	26.0	25.9	25.8	25.5	25.6	25.6	25.7	26.2	26.5	25.9
2007	25.5	25.6	26.2	26.0	25.9	25.6	25.6	25.6	25.6	25.5	26.1	26.3	25.8

Employment by Industry: Deltona-Daytona Beach-Ormond Beach, FL, 2000–2007—*Continued*

(Numbers in thousands, not seasonally adjusted.)

Industry and year	January	February	March	April	May	June	July	August	September	October	November	December	Annual Average
Transportation and Utilities													
2000	2.7	2.7	2.8	2.7	2.7	2.8	2.8	2.8	2.8	2.7	2.6	2.7	2.7
2001	2.6	2.7	2.7	2.7	2.7	2.7	2.7	2.6	2.7	2.7	2.7	2.8	2.7
2002	2.6	2.7	2.7	2.6	2.6	2.6	2.5	2.5	2.5	2.5	2.5	2.6	2.6
2003	2.5	2.6	2.6	2.5	2.5	2.5	2.5	2.4	2.4	2.4	2.3	2.6	2.4
2004	2.2	2.2	2.2	2.1	2.2	2.2	2.2	2.2	2.2	2.2	2.3	2.3	2.2
2005	2.2	2.3	2.3	2.3	2.3	2.3	2.2	2.3	2.3	2.3	2.2	2.3	2.2
2006	2.3	2.3	2.3	2.2	2.3	2.3	2.2	2.2	2.2	2.3	2.3	2.4	2.3
2007	2.3	2.3	2.3	2.3	2.3	2.3	2.3	2.3	2.2	2.2	2.2	2.5	2.3
Information													
2000	3.1	3.0	3.1	3.1	3.1	3.2	3.2	3.2	3.2	3.1	3.2	3.2	3.1
2001	3.7	3.6	3.6	3.5	3.4	3.3	3.3	3.3	3.3	3.1	3.2	3.2	3.4
2002	3.1	3.1	3.0	3.0	3.0	3.0	3.1	3.3	3.3	3.1	3.2	3.2	3.0
2003	2.9	2.9	2.8	2.9	2.9	2.9	3.1	3.0	2.9	2.9	3.0	3.1	2.8
2004	2.7	2.7	2.7	2.8	2.8	2.8	2.8	2.8	2.8	2.8	2.8	2.7	2.8
2005	2.7	2.7	2.7	2.7	2.8	2.8	2.8	2.8	2.8	2.8	2.8	2.8	2.7
2006	2.8	2.8	2.8	2.9	2.9	2.9	2.7	2.7	2.7	2.7	2.7	2.7	2.7
2007	2.9	2.9	2.9	3.0	3.0	3.0	3.1	3.0	3.0	3.0	3.0	3.0	3.0
Financial Activities													
2000	6.8	6.8	6.9	6.8	6.8	6.8	6.8	6.9	6.9	6.7	6.7	6.6	6.8
2001	6.5	6.6	6.6	6.6	6.6	6.6	6.5	6.5	6.5	6.6	6.6	6.5	6.6
2002	6.3	6.3	6.4	6.3	6.4	6.4	6.4	6.5	6.5	6.6	6.6	6.5	6.4
2003	6.4	6.4	6.5	6.5	6.5	6.5	6.5	6.5	6.5	6.4	6.5	6.5	6.4
2004	6.6	6.7	6.7	7.0	7.0	7.1	7.1	7.1	7.0	7.0	7.0	7.1	7.0
2005	6.9	7.0	6.9	7.2	7.3	7.4	7.4	7.5	7.5	7.6	7.6	7.7	7.3
2006	7.5	7.5	7.7	7.8	7.9	7.9	8.0	8.0	8.0	8.0	8.0	8.0	7.9
2007	7.8	7.9	7.9	8.0	8.0	8.1	8.0	8.1	8.0	8.1	8.0	8.0	8.0
Professional and Business Services													
2000	12.6	13.4	13.0	12.7	12.7	13.1	13.2	13.4	13.7	13.8	14.1	14.4	13.3
2001	14.8	15.8	15.2	15.5	15.3	15.6	15.9	16.0	16.1	16.3	16.2	16.4	15.8
2002	16.0	16.9	16.3	16.9	16.3	16.5	15.9	15.8	15.9	16.7	16.5	16.6	16.4
2003	16.3	17.2	17.2	17.4	17.0	17.2	17.5	17.5	17.7	17.8	17.9	18.0	17.3
2004	17.8	18.1	18.2	18.7	18.8	18.9	19.0	19.3	19.3	19.7	20.5	20.8	19.1
2005	21.0	21.2	21.0	20.9	20.4	20.5	20.4	20.3	20.3	20.0	20.3	20.4	20.6
2006	20.2	20.5	20.6	21.1	20.8	20.8	20.7	20.7	20.4	19.7	19.6	19.4	20.4
2007	18.9	19.5	19.7	19.6	19.4	19.2	19.8	19.4	19.1	19.1	19.1	19.0	19.3
Education and Health Services													
2000	25.6	25.8	26.0	25.9	26.1	25.9	25.8	26.0	26.5	25.8	25.6	25.8	25.9
2001	25.3	25.5	25.3	25.7	25.6	25.6	25.7	26.0	26.7	27.4	27.8	27.9	26.2
2002	27.5	27.8	27.8	27.8	28.0	27.7	27.6	28.0	28.5	29.0	29.3	29.6	28.2
2003	29.4	29.9	29.9	30.0	30.0	29.6	29.7	29.8	30.5	30.7	30.9	31.0	30.1
2004	30.7	31.7	31.5	31.5	31.0	30.6	29.7	29.6	29.8	30.4	30.7	30.8	30.7
2005	30.2	30.7	30.9	30.9	30.8	30.0	29.9	29.7	30.4	30.6	30.8	30.7	30.5
2006	30.4	31.0	31.3	31.1	31.0	30.0	29.8	29.8	30.3	30.5	30.5	30.4	30.5
2007	29.5	30.0	30.2	30.3	30.2	29.5	29.1	29.1	30.1	30.4	30.6	30.7	30.0
Leisure and Hospitality													
2000	18.2	18.8	19.2	19.2	19.5	19.6	19.9	19.7	19.4	19.3	19.0	19.0	19.2
2001	18.5	19.3	19.8	19.6	19.8	20.2	19.8	19.6	19.1	19.0	19.1	18.8	19.4
2002	18.7	19.6	20.4	20.5	20.3	20.3	20.1	19.9	19.3	19.2	19.1	18.5	19.6
2003	18.9	20.0	20.6	20.3	20.3	20.3	20.7	20.3	19.8	18.6	18.5	18.5	19.9
2004	20.2	20.9	21.5	21.3	21.4	21.6	21.7	21.2	20.3	19.6	19.5	19.5	21.0
2005	21.1	22.1	22.6	22.1	21.8	21.8	21.7	21.2	20.3	20.7	20.7	21.0	21.7
2006	21.0	21.7	22.4	22.1	22.0	22.1	22.1	21.9	21.3	21.0	21.0	21.0	21.6
2007	21.2	22.9	23.4	22.5	22.5	22.6	22.0	21.6	21.1	21.1	21.0	20.8	22.2
Other Services													
2000	6.8	6.9	7.1	7.1	7.2	7.3	7.4	7.3	7.2	7.1	7.1	7.3	7.2
2001	7.0	7.1	7.2	7.2	7.3	7.3	7.1	7.1	7.1	7.2	7.1	7.0	7.1
2002	7.4	7.4	7.5	7.5	7.7	7.7	7.7	7.6	7.6	7.8	7.8	7.8	7.6
2003	7.6	7.6	7.6	7.8	7.9	7.9	8.0	7.9	8.0	7.9	8.0	8.0	7.8
2004	8.0	8.1	8.3	8.3	8.4	8.4	8.3	8.2	8.0	8.0	8.0	8.0	8.2
2005	7.9	7.9	7.9	8.0	8.1	8.2	8.3	8.3	8.4	8.3	8.0	8.4	8.2
2006	8.3	8.4	8.5	8.3	8.4	8.4	8.3	8.3	8.4	8.3	8.4	8.4	8.3
2007	8.0	8.1	8.2	8.3	8.3	8.4	8.2	8.2	8.2	8.1	8.1	8.1	8.2
Government													
2000	21.4	21.8	22.0	22.0	22.1	19.7	19.8	21.4	21.8	21.7	21.8	20.9	21.4
2001	21.5	21.9	22.0	22.1	21.8	20.1	20.0	21.8	22.5	22.1	22.4	22.3	21.7
2002	22.3	22.2	22.2	22.3	22.1	20.4	20.3	22.0	22.2	22.3	22.3	22.4	21.9
2003	22.2	22.3	22.3	22.5	22.4	20.6	20.6	22.3	22.4	22.3	22.4	22.4	22.0
2004	22.6	22.7	22.8	23.0	22.7	20.9	20.9	22.7	22.8	22.8	23.0	22.9	22.5
2005	23.2	23.2	23.2	23.5	23.3	21.5	21.5	23.3	23.8	24.1	24.2	24.2	23.3
2006	24.3	24.5	24.5	24.3	24.5	22.5	22.4	24.6	24.7	24.6	24.8	24.8	24.2
2007	24.9	25.2	25.2	24.8	25.0	22.9	22.7	24.8	24.9	25.0	25.1	25.0	24.6

APPENDIX

METROPOLITAN STATISTICAL AREAS (MSAS) (MSAS) AND COMPONENTS

New York-Northern New Jersey-Long Island, NY-NJ-PA
Edison, NJ, Metropolitan Division
    Middlesex County, NJ
    Monmouth County, NJ
    Ocean County, NJ
    Somerset County, NJ
Nassau-Suffolk, NY, Metropolitan Division
    Nassau County, NY
    Suffolk County, NY
New York-White Plains-Wayne, NY-NJ,
Metropolitan Division
    Bergen County, NJ
    Hudson County, NJ
    Passaic County, NJ
    Bronx County, NY
    Kings County, NY
    New York County, NY
    Putnam County, NY
    Queens County, NY
    Richmond County, NY
    Rockland County, NY
    Westchester County, NY
Newark-Union, NJ-PA, Metropolitan Division
    Essex County, NJ
    Hunterdon County, NJ
    Morris County, NJ
    Sussex County, NJ
    Union County, NJ
    Pike County, PA

Los Angeles-Long Beach-Santa Ana, CA
Los Angeles-Long Beach-Glendale, CA,
Metropolitan Division
    Los Angeles County, CA
Santa Ana-Anaheim-Irvine, CA, Metropolitan Division
    Orange County, CA

Chicago-Naperville-Joliet, IL-IN-WI
Chicago-Naperville-Joliet, IL, Metropolitan Division
    Cook County, IL
    DeKalb County, IL
    DuPage County, IL
    Grundy County, IL
    Kane County, IL
    Kendall County, IL
    McHenry County, IL
    Will County, IL
Gary, IN, Metropolitan Division
    Jasper County, IN
    Lake County, IN
    Newton County, IN
    Porter County, IN
Lake County-Kenosha County, IL-WI,
Metropolitan Division
    Lake County, IL
    Kenosha County, WI

Philadelphia-Camden-Wilmington, PA-NJ-DE-MD
Camden, NJ, Metropolitan Division
    Burlington County, NJ
    Camden County, NJ
    Gloucester County, NJ
Philadelphia, PA, Metropolitan Division
    Bucks County, PA
    Chester County, PA
    Delaware County, PA
    Montgomery County, PA
    Philadelphia County, PA
Wilmington, DE-MD-NJ, Metropolitan Division
    New Castle County, DE
    Cecil County, MD
    Salem County, NJ

Dallas-Fort Worth-Arlington, TX
Dallas-Plano-Irving, TX, Metropolitan Division
    Collin County, TX
    Dallas County, TX
    Delta County, TX
    Denton County, TX
    Ellis County, TX
    Hunt County, TX
    Kaufman County, TX
    Rockwall County, TX
Fort Worth-Arlington, TX, Metropolitan Division
    Johnson County, TX
    Parker County, TX
    Tarrant County, TX
    Wise County, TX

Miami-Fort Lauderdale-Pompano Beach, FL
Fort Lauderdale-Pompano Beach-Deerfield Beach, FL,
Metropolitan Division
    Broward County, FL
Miami-Miami Beach-Kendall, FL, Metropolitan Division
    Miami-Dade County, FL
West Palm Beach-Boca Raton-Boynton Beach, FL,
Metropolitan Division
    Palm Beach County, FL

Washington-Arlington-Alexandria, DC-VA-MD-WV
Bethesda-Gaithersburg-Frederick, MD,
Metropolitan Division
    Frederick County, MD
    Montgomery County, MD
Washington-Arlington-Alexandria, DC-VA-MD-WV,
Metropolitan Division
    District of Columbia, DC
    Calvert County, MD
    Charles County, MD
    Prince George's County, MD
    Arlington County, VA
    Clarke County, VA
    Fairfax County, VA
    Fauquier County, VA
    Loudoun County, VA

Prince William County, VA
Spotsylvania County, VA
Stafford County, VA
Warren County, VA
Alexandria city, VA
Fairfax city, VA
Falls Church city, VA
Fredericksburg city, VA
Manassas city, VA
Manassas Park city, VA
Jefferson County, WV

Houston-Sugar Land-Baytown, TX
Austin County, TX
Brazoria County, TX
Chambers County, TX
Fort Bend County, TX
Galveston County, TX
Harris County, TX
Liberty County, TX
Montgomery County, TX
San Jacinto County, TX
Waller County, TX

Boston-Cambridge-Quincy, MA-NH, NECTA
Boston-Cambridge-Quincy, MA, NECTA Division
Acton town, MA
Andover town, MA
Arlington town, MA
Ayer town, MA
Bedford town, MA
Belmont town, MA
Beverly city, MA
Bolton town, MA
Boston city, MA
Boxborough town, MA
Boxford town, MA
Braintree town, MA
Brookline town, MA
Burlington town, MA
Cambridge city, MA
Canton town, MA
Carlisle town, MA
Carver town, MA
Chelsea city, MA
Cohasset town, MA
Concord town, MA
Dedham town, MA
Dover town, MA
Duxbury town, MA
Essex town, MA
Everett city, MA
Foxborough town, MA
Franklin city, MA
Gloucester city, MA
Groton town, MA
Hamilton town, MA
Hanover town, MA
Harvard town, MA
Hingham town, MA
Holbrook town, MA

Boston-Cambridge-Quincy, MA-NH—*Continued*
Hull town, MA
Ipswich town, MA
Kingston town, MA
Lexington town, MA
Lincoln town, MA
Littleton town, MA
Lynnfield town, MA
Malden city, MA
Manchester-by-the-Sea town, MA
Mansfield town, MA
Marshfield town, MA
Maynard town, MA
Medfield town, MA
Medford city, MA
Medway town, MA
Melrose city, MA
Middleton town, MA
Millis town, MA
Milton town, MA
Needham town, MA
Newbury town, MA
Newburyport city, MA
Newton city, MA
Norfolk town, MA
North Reading town, MA
Norwell town, MA
Norwood town, MA
Pembroke town, MA
Plymouth town, MA
Quincy city, MA
Randolph town, MA
Reading town, MA
Revere city, MA
Rockland town, MA
Rockport town, MA
Rowley town, MA
Saugus town, MA
Scituate town, MA
Sharon town, MA
Sherborn town, MA
Shirley town, MA
Somerville city, MA
Stoneham town, MA
Stoughton town, MA
Stow town, MA
Sudbury town, MA
Topsfield town, MA
Wakefield town, MA
Walpole town, MA
Waltham city, MA
Watertown city, MA
Wayland town, MA
Wellesley town, MA
Wenham town, MA
Weston town, MA
Westwood town, MA
Weymouth town, MA
Wilmington town, MA
Winchester town, MA
Winthrop town, MA
Woburn city, MA

Boston-Cambridge-Quincy, MA-NH—*Continued*
    Wrentham town, MA
Brockton-Bridgewater-Easton, MA, NECTA Division
    Abington town, MA
    Avon town, MA
    Bridgewater town, MA
    Brockton city, MA
    East Bridgewater town, MA
    Easton town, MA
    Halifax town, MA
    Hanson town, MA
    Middleborough town, MA
    Plympton town, MA
    West Bridgewater town, MA
    Whitman town, MA
Framingham, MA, NECTA Division
    Ashland town, MA
    Berlin town, MA
    Framingham town, MA
    Holliston town, MA
    Hopedale town, MA
    Hopkinton town, MA
    Hudson town, MA
    Marlborough city, MA
    Mendon town, MA
    Milford town, MA
    Natick town, MA
    Southborough town, MA
    Upton town, MA
Haverhill-North Andover-Amesbury, MA-NH, NECTA
Division
    Amesbury town, MA
    Georgetown town, MA
    Groveland town, MA
    Haverhill city, MA
    Merrimac town, MA
    North Andover town, MA
    Salisbury town, MA
    West Newbury town, MA
    Atkinson town, NH
    Brentwood town, NH
    Danville town, NH
    East Kingston town, NH
    Epping town, NH
    Exeter town, NH
    Fremont town, NH
    Hampstead town, NH
    Hampton Falls town, NH
    Kensington town, NH
    Kingston town, NH
    Newfields town, NH
    Newton town, NH
    Plaistow town, NH
    Sandown town, NH
    Seabrook town, NH
    South Hampton town, NH
Lawrence-Methuen-Salem, MA-NH, NECTA Division
    Lawrence city, MA
    Methuen city, MA
    Salem town, NH
Lowell-Billerica-Chelmsford, MA-NH, NECTA Division
    Billerica town, MA

    Chelmsford town, MA
    Dracut town, MA
    Dunstable town, MA
    Lowell city, MA
    Tewksbury town, MA
    Tyngsborough town, MA
    Westford town, MA
    Pelham town, NH
Nashua, NH-MA, NECTA Division
    Pepperell town, MA
    Townsend town, MA
    Amherst town, NH
    Brookline town, NH
    Chester town, NH
    Derry town, NH
    Greenfield town, NH
    Greenville town, NH
    Hollis town, NH
    Hudson town, NH
    Litchfield town, NH
    Londonderry town, NH
    Lyndeborough town, NH
    Mason town, NH
    Merrimack town, NH
    Milford town, NH
    Mont Vernon town, NH
    Nashua city, NH
    Raymond town, NH
    Wilton town, NH
    Windham town, NH
Peabody, MA, NECTA Division
    Danvers town, MA
    Lynn city, MA
    Marblehead town, MA
    Nahant town, MA
    Peabody city, MA
    Salem city, MA
    Swampscott town, MA
Taunton-Norton-Raynham, MA, NECTA Division
    Berkley town, MA
    Dighton town, MA
    Lakeville town, MA
    Norton town, MA
    Raynham town, MA
    Taunton city, MA

Detroit-Warren-Livonia, MI
Detroit-Livonia-Dearborn, MI, Metropolitan Division
    Wayne County, MI
Warren-Troy-Farmington Hills, MI,
Metropolitan Division
    Lapeer County, MI
    Livingston County, MI
    Macomb County, MI
    Oakland County, MI
    St. Clair County, MI

Atlanta-Sandy Springs-Marietta, GA
    Barrow County, GA
    Bartow County, GA
    Butts County, GA
    Carroll County, GA
    Cherokee County, GA

Atlanta-Sandy Springs-Marietta, GA—*Continued*
    Clayton County, GA
    Cobb County, GA
    Coweta County, GA
    Dawson County, GA
    DeKalb County, GA
    Douglas County, GA
    Fayette County, GA
    Forsyth County, GA
    Fulton County, GA
    Gwinnett County, GA
    Haralson County, GA
    Heard County, GA
    Henry County, GA
    Jasper County, GA
    Lamar County, GA
    Meriwether County, GA
    Newton County, GA
    Paulding County, GA
    Pickens County, GA
    Pike County, GA
    Rockdale County, GA
    Spalding County, GA
    Walton County, GA

San Francisco-Oakland-Fremont, CA
Oakland-Fremont-Hayward, CA, Metropolitan Division
    Alameda County, CA
    Contra Costa County, CA
San Francisco-San Mateo-Redwood City, CA,
Metropolitan Division
    Marin County, CA
    San Francisco County, CA
    San Mateo County, CA

Riverside-San Bernardino-Ontario, CA
    Riverside County, CA
    San Bernardino County, CA

Phoenix-Mesa-Scottsdale, AZ
    Maricopa County, AZ
    Pinal County, AZ

Seattle-Tacoma-Bellevue, WA
Seattle-Bellevue-Everett, WA, Metropolitan Division
    King County, WA
    Snohomish County, WA
Tacoma, WA, Metropolitan Division
    Pierce County, WA

Minneapolis-St. Paul-Bloomington, MN-WI
    Anoka County, MN
    Carver County, MN
    Chisago County, MN
    Dakota County, MN
    Hennepin County, MN
    Isanti County, MN
    Ramsey County, MN
    Scott County, MN
    Sherburne County, MN
    Washington County, MN

Minneapolis-St. Paul-Bloomington, MN-WI—*Continued*
    Wright County, MN
    Pierce County, WI
    St. Croix County, WI

San Diego-Carlsbad-San Marcos, CA
    San Diego County, CA

St. Louis, MO-IL
    Bond County, IL
    Calhoun County, IL
    Clinton County, IL
    Jersey County, IL
    Macoupin County, IL
    Madison County, IL
    Monroe County, IL
    St. Clair County, IL
    Crawford County, MO[1]
    Franklin County, MO
    Jefferson County, MO
    Lincoln County, MO
    St. Louis County, MO
    Warren County, MO
    Washington County, MO
    St. Louis city, MO

Baltimore-Towson, MD
    Anne Arundel County, MD
    Baltimore County, MD
    Carroll County, MD
    Harford County, MD
    Howard County, MD
    Queen Anne's County, MD
    Baltimore city, MD

Pittsburgh, PA
    Allegheny County, PA
    Armstrong County, PA
    Beaver County, PA
    Butler County, PA
    Fayette County, PA
    Washington County, PA
    Westmoreland County, PA

Tampa-St. Petersburg-Clearwater, FL
    Hernando County, FL
    Hillsborough County, FL
    Pasco County, FL
    Pinellas County, FL

Denver-Aurora, CO
    Adams County, CO
    Arapahoe County, CO
    Broomfield County, CO
    Clear Creek County, CO
    Denver County, CO
    Douglas County, CO
    Elbert County, CO
    Gilpin County, CO
    Jefferson County, CO
    Park County, CO

---

[1] The portion of Sullivan city in Crawford County, Missouri, is legally part of the St. Louis, MO-IL, MSA. Census 2000 tabulations and intercensal estimates for the St. Louis, MO-IL, MSA do not include this area.

Cleveland-Elyria-Mentor, OH
    Cuyahoga County, OH
    Geauga County, OH
    Lake County, OH
    Lorain County, OH
    Medina County, OH

Cincinnati-Middletown, OH-KY-IN
    Dearborn County, IN
    Franklin County, IN
    Ohio County, IN
    Boone County, KY
    Bracken County, KY
    Campbell County, KY
    Gallatin County, KY
    Grant County, KY
    Kenton County, KY
    Pendleton County, KY
    Brown County, OH
    Butler County, OH
    Clermont County, OH
    Hamilton County, OH
    Warren County, OH

Portland-Vancouver-Beaverton, OR-WA
    Clackamas County, OR
    Columbia County, OR
    Multnomah County, OR
    Washington County, OR
    Yamhill County, OR
    Clark County, WA
    Skamania County, WA

Kansas City, MO-KS
    Franklin County, KS
    Johnson County, KS
    Leavenworth County, KS
    Linn County, KS
    Miami County, KS
    Wyandotte County, KS
    Bates County, MO
    Caldwell County, MO
    Cass County, MO
    Clay County, MO
    Clinton County, MO
    Jackson County, MO
    Lafayette County, MO
    Platte County, MO
    Ray County, MO

Sacramento–Arden-Arcade–Roseville, CA
    El Dorado County, CA
    Placer County, CA
    Sacramento County, CA
    Yolo County, CA

San Jose-Sunnyvale-Santa Clara, CA
    San Benito County, CA
    Santa Clara County, CA

San Antonio, TX
    Atascosa County, TX
    Bandera County, TX
    Bexar County, TX

San Antonio, TX—*Continued*
    Comal County, TX
    Guadalupe County, TX
    Kendall County, TX
    Medina County, TX
    Wilson County, TX

Orlando-Kissimmee, FL
    Lake County, FL
    Orange County, FL
    Osceola County, FL
    Seminole County, FL

Columbus, OH
    Delaware County, OH
    Fairfield County, OH
    Franklin County, OH
    Licking County, OH
    Madison County, OH
    Morrow County, OH
    Pickaway County, OH
    Union County, OH

Virginia Beach-Norfolk-Newport News, VA-NC
    Currituck County, NC
    Gloucester County, VA
    Isle of Wight County, VA
    James City County, VA
    Mathews County, VA
    Surry County, VA
    York County, VA
    Chesapeake city, VA
    Hampton city, VA
    Newport News city, VA
    Norfolk city, VA
    Poquoson city, VA
    Portsmouth city, VA
    Suffolk city, VA
    Virginia Beach city, VA
    Williamsburg city, VA

Indianapolis-Carmel, IN
    Boone County, IN
    Brown County, IN
    Hamilton County, IN
    Hancock County, IN
    Hendricks County, IN
    Johnson County, IN
    Marion County, IN
    Morgan County, IN
    Putnam County, IN
    Shelby County, IN

Milwaukee-Waukesha-West Allis, WI
    Milwaukee County, WI
    Ozaukee County, WI
    Washington County, WI
    Waukesha County, WI

Las Vegas-Paradise, NV
    Clark County, NV

Charlotte-Gastonia-Concord, NC-SC
    Anson County, NC
    Cabarrus County, NC

Charlotte-Gastonia-Concord, NC-SC—*Continued*
Gaston County, NC
Mecklenburg County, NC
Union County, NC
York County, SC

New Orleans-Metairie-Kenner, LA
Jefferson Parish, LA
Orleans Parish, LA
Plaquemines Parish, LA
St. Bernard Parish, LA
St. Charles Parish, LA
St. John the Baptist Parish, LA
St. Tammany Parish, LA

Nashville-Davidson–Murfreesboro–Franklin, TN
Cannon County, TN
Cheatham County, TN
Davidson County, TN
Dickson County, TN
Hickman County, TN
Macon County, TN
Robertson County, TN
Rutherford County, TN
Smith County, TN
Sumner County, TN
Trousdale County, TN
Williamson County, TN
Wilson County, TN

Providence-Fall River-Warwick, RI-MA, NECTA
Attleboro city, MA
Bellingham town, MA
Blackstone town, MA
Fall River city, MA
Millville town, MA
North Attleborough town, MA
Plainville town, MA
Rehoboth town, MA
Seekonk town, MA
Somerset town, MA
Swansea town, MA
Westport town, MA
Barrington town, RI
Bristol town, RI
Burrillville town, RI
Central Falls city, RI
Charlestown town, RI
Coventry town, RI
Cranston city, RI
Cumberland town, RI
East Greenwich town, RI
East Providence city, RI
Exeter town, RI
Foster town, RI
Glocester town, RI
Hopkinton town, RI
Jamestown town, RI
Johnston town, RI
Lincoln town, RI
Little Compton town, RI
Middletown town, RI
Narragansett town, RI

Providence-Fall River-Warwick, RI-MA—*Continued*
Newport city, RI
North Kingstown town, RI
North Providence town, RI
North Smithfield town, RI
Pawtucket city, RI
Portsmouth town, RI
Providence city, RI
Richmond town, RI
Scituate town, RI
Smithfield town, RI
South Kingstown town, RI
Tiverton town, RI
Warren town, RI
Warwick city, RI
West Greenwich town, RI
West Warwick town, RI
Woonsocket city, RI

Austin-Round Rock, TX
Bastrop County, TX
Caldwell County, TX
Hays County, TX
Travis County, TX
Williamson County, TX

Memphis, TN-MS-AR
Crittenden County, AR
DeSoto County, MS
Marshall County, MS
Tate County, MS
Tunica County, MS
Fayette County, TN
Shelby County, TN
Tipton County, TN

Buffalo-Niagara Falls, NY
Erie County, NY
Niagara County, NY

Louisville-Jefferson County, KY-IN
Clark County, IN
Floyd County, IN
Harrison County, IN
Washington County, IN
Bullitt County, KY
Henry County, KY
Jefferson County, KY
Meade County, KY
Nelson County, KY
Oldham County, KY
Shelby County, KY
Spencer County, KY
Trimble County, KY

Jacksonville, FL
Baker County, FL
Clay County, FL
Duval County, FL
Nassau County, FL
St. Johns County, FL

Richmond, VA
Amelia County, VA
Caroline County, VA

Richmond, VA—*Continued*
　　Charles City County, VA
　　Chesterfield County, VA
　　Cumberland County, VA
　　Dinwiddie County, VA
　　Goochland County, VA
　　Hanover County, VA
　　Henrico County, VA
　　King and Queen County, VA
　　King William County, VA
　　Louisa County, VA
　　New Kent County, VA
　　Powhatan County, VA
　　Prince George County, VA
　　Sussex County, VA
　　Colonial Heights city, VA
　　Hopewell city, VA
　　Petersburg city, VA
　　Richmond city, VA

Oklahoma City, OK
　　Canadian County, OK
　　Cleveland County, OK
　　Grady County, OK
　　Lincoln County, OK
　　Logan County, OK
　　McClain County, OK
　　Oklahoma County, OK

Hartford-West Hartford-East Hartford, CT, NECTA
　　Andover town, CT
　　Ashford town, CT
　　Avon town, CT
　　Barkhamsted town, CT
　　Berlin town, CT
　　Bloomfield town, CT
　　Bolton town, CT
　　Bristol city and town, CT
　　Burlington town, CT
　　Canton town, CT
　　Colchester town, CT
　　Columbia town, CT
　　Coventry town, CT
　　Cromwell town, CT
　　East Granby town, CT
　　East Haddam town, CT
　　East Hampton town, CT
　　East Hartford town, CT
　　Ellington town, CT
　　Farmington town, CT
　　Glastonbury town, CT
　　Granby town, CT
　　Haddam town, CT
　　Hartford city and town, CT
　　Hartland town, CT
　　Harwinton town, CT
　　Hebron town, CT
　　Lebanon town, CT
　　Manchester town, CT
　　Mansfield town, CT
　　Marlborough town, CT
　　Middlefield town, CT
　　Middletown city and town, CT

Hartford-West Hartford-East Hartford, CT—*Continued*
　　New Britain city and town, CT
　　New Hartford town, CT
　　Newington town, CT
　　Plainville town, CT
　　Plymouth town, CT
　　Portland town, CT
　　Rocky Hill town, CT
　　Simsbury town, CT
　　South Windsor town, CT
　　Southington town, CT
　　Stafford town, CT
　　Thomaston town, CT
　　Tolland town, CT
　　Union town, CT
　　Vernon town, CT
　　West Hartford town, CT
　　Wethersfield town, CT
　　Willington town, CT
　　Windsor town, CT

Birmingham-Hoover, AL
　　Bibb County, AL
　　Blount County, AL
　　Chilton County, AL
　　Jefferson County, AL
　　St. Clair County, AL
　　Shelby County, AL
　　Walker County, AL

Rochester, NY
　　Livingston County, NY
　　Monroe County, NY
　　Ontario County, NY
　　Orleans County, NY
　　Wayne County, NY

Salt Lake City, UT
　　Salt Lake County, UT
　　Summit County, UT
　　Tooele County, UT

Bridgeport-Stamford-Norwalk, CT, NECTA
　　Ansonia city and town, CT
　　Bridgeport city and town, CT
　　Darien town, CT
　　Derby city and town, CT
　　Easton town, CT
　　Fairfield town, CT
　　Greenwich town, CT
　　Milford city and town, CT
　　Monroe town, CT
　　New Canaan town, CT
　　Newtown town, CT
　　Norwalk city and town, CT
　　Oxford town, CT
　　Redding town, CT
　　Ridgefield town, CT
　　Seymour town, CT
　　Shelton city and town, CT
　　Southbury town, CT
　　Stamford city and town, CT
　　Stratford town, CT

Bridgeport-Stamford-Norwalk, CT—*Continued*
Trumbull town, CT
Weston town, CT
Westport town, CT
Wilton town, CT
Woodbridge town, CT

Honolulu, HI
Honolulu County, HI

Tulsa, OK
Creek County, OK
Okmulgee County, OK
Osage County, OK
Pawnee County, OK
Rogers County, OK
Tulsa County, OK
Wagoner County, OK

Dayton, OH
Greene County, OH
Miami County, OH
Montgomery County, OH
Preble County, OH

Tucson, AZ
Pima County, AZ

Albany-Schenectady-Troy, NY
Albany County, NY
Rensselaer County, NY
Saratoga County, NY
Schenectady County, NY
Schoharie County, NY

Fresno, CA
Fresno County, CA

Raleigh-Cary, NC
Franklin County, NC
Johnston County, NC
Wake County, NC

Omaha-Council Bluffs, NE-IA
Harrison County, IA
Mills County, IA
Pottawattamie County, IA
Cass County, NE
Douglas County, NE
Sarpy County, NE
Saunders County, NE
Washington County, NE

Oxnard-Thousand Oaks-Ventura, CA
Ventura County, CA

Grand Rapids-Wyoming, MI
Barry County, MI
Ionia County, MI
Kent County, MI
Newaygo County, MI

Allentown-Bethlehem-Easton, PA-NJ
Warren County, NJ
Carbon County, PA
Lehigh County, PA
Northampton County, PA

Albuquerque, NM
Bernalillo County, NM
Sandoval County, NM
Torrance County, NM
Valencia County, NM

Baton Rouge, LA
Ascension Parish, LA
East Baton Rouge Parish, LA
East Feliciana Parish, LA
Iberville Parish, LA
Livingston Parish, LA
Pointe Coupee Parish, LA
St. Helena Parish, LA
West Baton Rouge Parish, LA
West Feliciana Parish, LA

Akron, OH
Portage County, OH
Summit County, OH

El Paso, TX
El Paso County, TX

Springfield, MA-CT, NECTA
Agawam city, MA
Ashfield town, MA
Belchertown town, MA
Blandford town, MA
Brimfield town, MA
Chester town, MA
Chesterfield town, MA
Chicopee city, MA
Cummington town, MA
Deerfield town, MA
East Longmeadow town, MA
Easthampton city, MA
Goshen town, MA
Granby town, MA
Granville town, MA
Hadley town, MA
Hampden town, MA
Hatfield town, MA
Holyoke city, MA
Huntington town, MA
Longmeadow town, MA
Ludlow town, MA
Middlefield town, MA
Monson town, MA
Montgomery town, MA
Northampton city, MA
Palmer town, MA
Plainfield town, MA
Russell town, MA
South Hadley town, MA
Southampton town, MA
Southwick town, MA
Springfield city, MA
Tolland town, MA
Wales town, MA
Ware town, MA
West Springfield town, MA
Westfield city, MA
Westhampton town, MA

Springfield, MA-CT—*Continued*
  Whately town, MA
  Wilbraham town, MA
  Williamsburg town, MA
  Worthington town, MA
  East Windsor town, CT
  Enfield town, CT
  Somers town, CT
  Suffield town, CT
  Windsor Locks town, CT

Bakersfield, CA
  Kern County, CA

Toledo, OH
  Fulton County, OH
  Lucas County, OH
  Ottawa County, OH
  Wood County, OH

Syracuse, NY
  Madison County, NY
  Onondaga County, NY
  Oswego County, NY

Columbia, SC
  Calhoun County, SC
  Fairfield County, SC
  Kershaw County, SC
  Lexington County, SC
  Richland County, SC
  Saluda County, SC

Greensboro-High Point, NC
  Guilford County, NC
  Randolph County, NC
  Rockingham County, NC

Poughkeepsie-Newburgh-Middletown, NY
  Dutchess County, NY
  Orange County, NY

Knoxville, TN
  Anderson County, TN
  Blount County, TN
  Knox County, TN
  Loudon County, TN
  Union County, TN

Little Rock-North Little Rock-Conway, AR
  Faulkner County, AR
  Grant County, AR
  Lonoke County, AR
  Perry County, AR
  Pulaski County, AR
  Saline County, AR

Youngstown-Warren-Boardman, OH-PA
  Mahoning County, OH
  Trumbull County, OH
  Mercer County, PA

Bradenton-Sarasota-Venice, FL
  Manatee County, FL
  Sarasota County, FL

New Haven, CT, NECTA
  Bethany town, CT
  Branford town, CT
  Cheshire town, CT
  Chester town, CT
  Clinton town, CT
  Deep River town, CT
  Durham town, CT
  East Haven town, CT
  Essex town, CT
  Guilford town, CT
  Hamden town, CT
  Killingworth town, CT
  Madison town, CT
  Meriden city and town, CT
  New Haven city and town, CT
  North Branford town, CT
  North Haven town, CT
  Old Saybrook town, CT
  Orange town, CT
  Wallingford town, CT
  West Haven city and town, CT
  Westbrook town, CT

Wichita, KS
  Butler County, KS
  Harvey County, KS
  Sedgwick County, KS
  Sumner County, KS

McAllen-Edinburg-Mission, TX
  Hidalgo County, TX

Stockton, CA
  San Joaquin County, CA

Scranton–Wilkes-Barre, PA
  Lackawanna County, PA
  Luzerne County, PA
  Wyoming County, PA

Greenville-Mauldin-Easley, SC
  Greenville County, SC
  Laurens County, SC
  Pickens County, SC

Charleston-North Charleston-Summerville, SC
  Berkeley County, SC
  Charleston County, SC
  Dorchester County, SC

Worcester, MA-CT, NECTA
  Auburn town, MA
  Barre town, MA
  Boylston town, MA
  Brookfield town, MA
  Charlton town, MA
  Clinton town, MA
  Douglas town, MA
  Dudley town, MA
  East Brookfield town, MA
  Grafton town, MA
  Holden town, MA
  Holland town, MA
  Hubbardston town, MA

Worcester, MA-CT—*Continued*
    Lancaster town, MA
    Leicester town, MA
    Millbury town, MA
    New Braintree town, MA
    North Brookfield town, MA
    Northborough town, MA
    Northbridge town, MA
    Oakham town, MA
    Oxford town, MA
    Paxton town, MA
    Princeton town, MA
    Putnam town, CT
    Rutland town, MA
    Shrewsbury town, MA
    Southbridge town, MA
    Spencer town, MA
    Sterling town, MA
    Sturbridge town, MA
    Sutton town, MA
    Thompson town, CT
    Uxbridge town, MA
    Webster town, MA
    West Boylston town, MA
    West Brookfield town, MA
    Westborough town, MA
    Woodstock town, CT
    Worcester city, MA

Colorado Springs, CO
    El Paso County, CO
    Teller County, CO

Harrisburg-Carlisle, PA
    Cumberland County, PA
    Dauphin County, PA
    Perry County, PA

Madison, WI
    Columbia County, WI
    Dane County, WI
    Iowa County, WI

Augusta-Richmond County, GA-SC
    Burke County, GA
    Columbia County, GA
    McDuffie County, GA
    Richmond County, GA
    Aiken County, SC
    Edgefield County, SC

Jackson, MS
    Copiah County, MS
    Hinds County, MS
    Madison County, MS
    Rankin County, MS
    Simpson County, MS

Lakeland-Winter Haven, FL
    Polk County, FL

Des Moines-West Des Moines, IA
    Dallas County, IA
    Guthrie County, IA
    Madison County, IA
    Polk County, IA
    Warren County, IA

Chattanooga, TN-GA
    Catoosa County, GA
    Dade County, GA
    Walker County, GA
    Hamilton County, TN
    Marion County, TN
    Sequatchie County, TN

Palm Bay-Melbourne-Titusville, FL
    Brevard County, FL

Lancaster, PA
    Lancaster County, PA

Boise City-Nampa, ID
    Ada County, ID
    Boise County, ID
    Canyon County, ID
    Gem County, ID
    Owyhee County, ID

Santa Rosa-Petaluma, CA
    Sonoma County, CA

Lansing-East Lansing, MI
    Clinton County, MI
    Eaton County, MI
    Ingham County, MI

Modesto, CA
    Stanislaus County, CA

Deltona-Daytona Beach-Ormond Beach, FL
    Volusia County, FL

EMPLOYMENT, HOURS, AND EARNINGS

STATES AND AREAS

Third Edition
2008

Edited by Mary Meghan Ryan